HANDBOOK OF
PSYCHOTHERAPY
AND
BEHAVIOR CHANGE

HANDBOOK OF PSYCHOTHERAPY AND BEHAVIOR CHANGE

FOURTH EDITION

EDITORS

ALLEN E. BERGIN
Department of Psychology
Brigham Young University

SOL L. GARFIELD
Department of Psychology
Washington University

JOHN WILEY & SONS, INC

New York ▪ Chichester ▪ Brisbane ▪ Toronto ▪ Singapore

ACQUISITIONS EDITOR   Karen Dubno
MARKETING MANAGER   Catherine Faduska
PRODUCTION EDITOR   Marcia Craig
DESIGNER   Madelyn Lesure
MANUFACTURING MANAGER   Inez Pettis
ILLUSTRATION   Jaime Perea

This book was set in Souvenir Light by Digitype and printed and bound by
Hamilton Printing. The cover was printed by New England Book Components.

Recognizing the importance of preserving what has been written, it is a
policy of John Wiley & Sons, Inc. to have books of enduring value published
in the United States printed on acid-free paper, and we exert our best
efforts to that end.

Library of Congress Cataloging in Publication Data:
Handbook of psychotherapy and behavior change / editors, Allen E. Bergin, Sol
    L. Garfield. — 4th ed.
        p.   cm.
    Includes index.
    ISBN 0-471-54513-9 (cloth : alk. paper)
    1. Psychotherapy.   2. Psychotherapy—Research.   I. Bergin, Allen E.,
1934–   .   II. Garfield, Sol L. (Sol Louis), 1918–   .
    [DNLM: 1. Psychotherapy.   2. Behavior Therapy.   WM 420 H2323
1994]
RC480.H286   1994
616.89'14—dc20
DNLM/DLC   93-23313
for Library of Congress   CIP

Printed in the United States of America

10   9   8   7   6   5   4   3   2   1

CONTRIBUTORS

James F. Alexander, Ph.D.
Professor of Psychology
University of Utah
Salt Lake City, Utah

Aaron T. Beck, M.D.
University Professor of Psychiatry
Center for Cognitive Therapy
University of Pennsylvania
Philadelphia, Pennsylvania

Richard L. Bednar, Ph.D.
Professor of Psychology
Brigham Young University
Provo, Utah

Allen E. Bergin, Ph.D.
Professor of Psychology
Brigham Young University
Provo, Utah

Larry E. Beutler, Ph.D.
Professor and Program Director
Counseling/Clinical/School Psychology
University of California
Santa Barbara, California

Edward B. Blanchard, Ph.D.
Distinguished Professor of Psychology
Center for Stress and Anxiety Disorders
The University at Albany
State University of New York
Albany, New York

Irene Elkin, Ph.D.
Professor, School of Social Service Administration
and Department of Psychiatry
University of Chicago
Chicago, Illinois

Robert K. Elliott, Ph.D.
Professor of Psychology
Director of Clinical Training
University of Toledo
Toledo, Ohio

Paul M. G. Emmelkamp, Ph.D.
Professor of Clinical Psychology and
Psychotherapy
Department of Clinical Psychology
Academic Hospital
Groningen
The Netherlands

Sol L. Garfield, Ph.D.
Professor Emeritus of Psychology
Department of Psychology
Washington University
St. Louis, Missouri

Louise Gaston, Ph.D.
Assistant Professor
Department of Psychiatry
McGill University Medical School
Montreal, Canada

Ira Glick, M.D.
Professor of Psychiatry
Stanford University School of Medicine
Stanford, California

Klaus Grawe, Ph.D.
Professor of Psychology
Universität Bern
Bern, Switzerland

Leslie S. Greenberg, Ph.D.
Professor of Psychology
York University
North York, Ontario, Canada

William P. Henry, Ph.D.
Research Assistant Professor of Psychology
Vanderbilt University
Nashville, Tennessee

Clara E. Hill, Ph.D.
Professor of Psychology
University of Maryland
College Park, Maryland

Steven D. Hollon, Ph.D.
Professor of Psychology
Vanderbilt University
Nashville, Tennessee

AMY HOLTZWORTH-MUNROE, Ph.D.
Assistant Professor of Psychology
Indiana University
Bloomington, Indiana

PENNY BROOKE JAMESON
Department of Psychology
University of Utah
Salt Lake City, Utah

THEODORE KAUL, Ph.D.
Associate Professor of Psychology
Ohio State University
Columbus, Ohio

ALAN E. KAZDIN, Ph.D.
Professor of Psychology
Director of Clinical Training
Yale University
New Haven, Connecticut

GERALD L. KLERMAN, M.D.*
Professor of Psychiatry and Associate Chairman
    for Research
Cornell University Medical College
New York, New York

MARY P. KOSS, Ph.D.
Professor
Family and Community Medicine
College of Medicine
University of Arizona
Tucson, Arizona

MICHAEL J. LAMBERT, Ph.D.
Professor of Psychology
Brigham Young University
Provo, Utah

GERMAIN LIETAER, Ph.D.
Professor of Psychology
Center of Client-Centered Therapy
University of Leuven
Leuven, Belgium

PAULO P. P. MACHADO
Counseling/Clinical/School Psychology
University of California
Santa Barbara, California

JOHN C. MARKOWITZ, M.D.
Professor of Psychiatry
Director, Psychopharmacology Clinic
Payne Whitney Clinic
Cornell University Medical College
New York, New York

BARBARA MASON, Ph.D.
Associate Professor of Psychiatry
Director, Division of Substance Abuse
Department of Psychiatry
University of Miami Medical School
Miami, Florida

SUSAN ALLSTETTER NEUFELDT, Ph.D.
Lecturer and Clinic Director
Counseling/Clinical/School Psychology
University of California
Santa Barbara, California

DAVID E. ORLINSKY, Ph.D.
Professor
Committee on Human Development
University of Chicago
Chicago, Illinois

BARBARA K. PARKS, M.B.A., M.A.
Committee on Human Development
University of Chicago
Chicago, Illinois

THOMAS E. SCHACHT, Psy.D.
Associate Professor
Department of Psychiatry
James Quillen College of Medicine
East Tennessee State University
Johnson City, Tennessee

M. KATHERINE SHEAR, M.D.
Associate Professor of Psychiatry
Director, Anxiety Disorders Clinic
University of Pittsburgh Medical School
Pittsburgh, Pennsylvania

JULIA SHIANG, Ed.D., Ph.D.
Assistant Professor of Psychology
Pacific Graduate School of Psychology,
Palo Alto, California
Lecturer, Department of Psychiatry and Behavioral
    Sciences
Stanford University School of Medicine
Stanford, California

HANS H. STRUPP, Ph.D.
Distinguished Professor of Psychology
Vanderbilt University
Nashville, Tennessee

STANLEY SUE, Ph.D.
Professor of Psychology and Director
National Research Center on Asian American
    Mental Health
University of California at Los Angeles
Los Angeles, California

*Please see editors' memorial footnote to Chapter 18.

MYRNA M. WEISSMAN, Ph.D.
Professor of Epidemiology in Psychiatry
College of Physicians and Surgeons, Columbia
  University
Director of Division of Clinical and Genetic
  Epidemiology
New York State Psychiatric Institute
New York, New York

PHILIP J. WILNER, M.D.
Assistant Professor of Psychiatry
Cornell University Medical College
New York, New York

KATHLEEN YOUNG
Clinical Psychology
University of California at Los Angeles
Los Angeles, California

NOLAN ZANE, Ph.D.
Assistant Professor of Psychology
Counseling/Clinical/School Psychology
University of California
Santa Barbara, California

This fourth edition is dedicated
to three distinguished pioneers
who taught us how to study therapeutic change

ALBERT BANDURA

JEROME D. FRANK

CARL R. ROGERS

PREFACE

We are pleased once again to publish a new edition of our *Handbook*. The response to the previous three editions has been most gratifying. The *Handbook* has become a standard reference throughout the world, wherever psychotherapy is an important subject, and it has served as a textbook for numerous graduate programs in the United States. One survey of psychologists ranked it first among books on psychotherapy, and a survey of psychology departments listed it as the second most frequently recommended book in departmental reading lists for graduate students. We could not have asked for a better reception and we are grateful for it. At the same time, we wish to thank publicly all of the past and present contributing authors, advisory editors, and consultants who have made this collaborative venture successful. It appears that there has been wide acceptance of the empirical and eclectic approach to this subject presented in these editions, which has not always been the case.

There is always some change in the content of each edition as we attempt to correlate the book with contemporary developments in the field. This time our decisions were also influenced by a survey we conducted of 23 leaders in the field, by citation counts of the chapters from all three previous editions, and by the publisher's evaluations gathered from professors who use the book in graduate courses.

As a result, we significantly modified the introductory set of four chapters by dropping the two chapters on developmental and social psychological perspectives on therapeutic change. This was a difficult decision because of our continuing belief that basic fields of psychological research should and do have significant implications for psychotherapy. Nevertheless, professional opinions prevailed, and we included two additional research methodology chapters in this section. One considers measuring and assessing change, and one illustrates the problems, potentialities and methodological issues of conducting major, multisite collaborative research studies, as exemplified by the NIMH Treatment of Depression Collaborative Research Program. Including the latter is unusual in that it concerns a single major study and correlated substudies; however, this was done to illustrate important points about collaborative research and to pro-

vide the basis for the numerous references to the study that arise elsewhere in the book.

Part II of the *Handbook* remains the same, with the same four chapters updated by the same four senior authors. This section forms the heart of the book and has been the most frequently cited, with its focus on outcomes and processes and client, therapist, and technique variables and their interactions.

In Part III, the cognitive and behavioral therapies continue in their important place, but this time we have added a new chapter devoted entirely to experiential therapies, for which research has expanded substantially, especially in Europe. We have also reintroduced here a chapter on psychodynamic studies, after a one-time absence from the third edition, due to an increase in process–outcome studies.

The remainder of the book stays essentially the same except that the chapters on educational counseling and the training of therapists were dropped, while that on therapy with the disadvantaged was substantially altered to take into account a major new spectrum of research on culturally diverse populations. Finally, a new concluding overview chapter was added.

This outline represents our best estimate of where the foci of research attention are today. Decisions to omit topics are difficult, but, as in previous editions, we have decided on the basis of where the significant research developments appear to be. We have been essentially uninfluenced by "popular" trends in therapy practices and their proliferations where there is little or no empirical research. Thus, some clinically important movements are regrettably omitted from this work because they are not buttressed by substantial efforts to document their processes and efficacy objectively.

We do not expect that everyone will agree with our decisions concerning the selection of the chapters in the current *Handbook*, but most should respond favorably to the topics included because so many of them are revised versions of those from the previous edition. As in the previous volumes, the emphasis in the present work is on a critical appraisal of existing empirical research findings with an evenhanded or eclectic attitude toward divergent orientations in the area of psychotherapy and behavior change along with their implications for research and practice.

A number of interesting developments have taken place since the appearance of the previous edition. Among them is a continuing increase of sophistication in the design of research and in statistical analysis and methods of measurement. There has also been a surge of process research in attempts to delineate the ingredients of the significant change processes that appear to be taking place. Although the proliferation of therapeutic approaches has seemingly not abated, a greater interest has also been evident in rapprochement and integration among a number of well-known psychotherapists, as well as a greater willingness to consider potential therapeutic variables common to most forms of psychotherapy.

As in the previous editions, the editors have found the preparation of the present volume a very demanding, but stimulating and rewarding experience. We find it necessary to immerse ourselves in an incredibly complex and broad effort to be aware of important issues and studies throughout the field and then to negotiate with each author the best possible summary and interpretation of developments in his or her special area. We have once again been fortunate in securing the collaboration of knowledgable experts who have performed admirably. We wish to express our gratitude to our contributing authors, the outside reviewers, and the editorial and production personnel of Wiley publishers, all of whom have helped immeasurably to make this edition of the *Handbook* a product worthy of our best efforts, particularly Marcia Craig

who contributed above and beyond the call of duty. We sincerely hope that the *Handbook* will continue to be of value to students, researchers, and practitioners in the area of psychotherapy and behavior change.

An important footnote to this edition is that it will likely be the last one edited by us. Dr. Garfield is now professor emeritus and, by the time another edition is due, Dr. Bergin will also be retired. Though we intend to be active in the field, we do not anticipate participating in a fifth edition.

We began our work together on this project in 1967, so the effort has spanned more than a quarter-century of collaboration during which we have observed many positive changes in this field. Those developments have benefited both the profession and the public. We have been pleased to recognize in these volumes significant contributions by a large number of dedicated researchers. At the same time, the most important reward for us, on a personal level, has been our relationship with so many outstanding colleagues and the deepening of the friendship and mutual regard between the two of us. The four editions of the *Handbook* stand as a testimony to our friendship and to our ability to work together in a harmonious manner. In keeping with our reference to values in Chapter 1, we have come to acknowledge that the value of relationships is equal to or greater than that of professional achievements. Perhaps, in communicating this perspective, we leave behind not only four volumes but a message of therapeutic value.

A.E.B.
S.L.G.

ALLEN E. BERGIN

SOL L. GARFIELD

ACKNOWLEDGMENTS

We are grateful to all of those who assisted the editors and contributors in completing this fourth edition of the *Handbook*. We specifically acknowledge the help of individuals whom we called upon to review specific chapters. They are

W. Stewart Agras, M.D.
Stanford University School of Medicine

Arthur Auerbach, M.D.
University of Pennsylvania Medical School

David H. Barlow, Ph.D.
State University of New York, Albany

Lorna S. Benjamin, Ph.D.
University of Utah

Larry E. Beutler, Ph.D.
University of California, Santa Barbara

Simon H. Budman, Ph.D.
Innovative Training Systems, Newton Centre, Massachusetts

David D. Burns, Ph.D.
Presbyterian Medical Center of Philadelphia

A. Dean Byrd, Ph.D.
LDS Social Services, Salt Lake City

Paul Crits-Christoph, Ph.D.
University of Pennsylvania

Marvin R. Goldfried, Ph.D.
State University of New York, Stony Brook

Alan S. Gurman, Ph.D.
University of Wisconsin Medical School

Janet Helms, Ph.D.
University of Maryland

Kenneth I. Howard, Ph.D.
Northwestern University

Peter Jensen, M.D.
National Institute of Mental Health

Teresa D. LaFromboise, Ph.D.
Stanford University

Michael J. Lambert, Ph.D.
Brigham Young University

Morton A. Lieberman, Ph.D.
University of California, San Francisco

Steven Lopez, Ph.D.
UCLA

Morris B. Parloff, Ph.D.
Georgetown University

William B. Stiles, Ph.D.
Miami University, Ohio

We are particularly grateful for the extra efforts of Dr. Michael J. Lambert who was a steady and valuable editorial advisor. We also appreciate the outstanding efforts of Lorraine Jeffery in helping us to produce the final manuscript, as well as the careful work of Scott Nebeker in preparing the indexes.

We are also grateful to the following for granting permission to reproduce previously published materials. Each reprinted item, its original reference, and the copyright are listed in the specific chapters where the materials appear.

American Psychological Association
Pergamon Press
American Medical Association

CONTENTS

PART

I

HISTORICAL, METHODOLOGICAL, ETHICAL, AND CONCEPTUAL FOUNDATIONS

1
INTRODUCTION AND HISTORICAL OVERVIEW

- **SOL L. GARFIELD**
  Washington University

- **ALLEN E. BERGIN**
  Brigham Young University

Psychotherapy has continued to be a field characterized by new developments, changing emphases, and controversial issues. It remains a popular field in which many professions and subprofessions are involved; it receives regular coverage in the newspapers and other media; and it is regarded as an accepted form of treatment for a variety of mental health problems. At the same time, as the field has developed, the means of providing psychotherapeutic services also have been changing and new problems have appeared. The procedures and emphases in research on psychotherapy also have undergone change with a greater emphasis on ascertaining the variables that actually lead to significant client change. However, before we discuss these recent developments, let us briefly note some of the important historical developments that have occurred in psychotherapy's past.

HISTORICAL BACKGROUND

For many years, approximately from the end of the nineteenth century to about the 1960s, the dominant influence in psychotherapy was psychoanalysis and its derivatives. Freud (1938), the father of psychoanalysis, guided its development until his death in 1939 and generally resisted attempts by others to offer significant modifications in psychoanalytic theory or procedures. However, a number of his earlier (and later) followers, such as Adler, Jung, Horney, and Sullivan, offered significant modifications of the Freudian scheme. Although certain features of traditional psychoanalytic theory and therapy, such as the importance of repressed conflicts, unconscious motivation, and early life experiences, tended to be retained in these variations, significant differences in emphases and procedures also occurred.

Besides the development of these offshoots of Freudian psychoanalysis, other important new schools or approaches to psychotherapy made their appearance over the years. One new approach that differed in important respects from the prevailing analytically oriented therapies was the client-centered approach developed by Carl Rogers (1942). Rogers was critical of the "expert" role played by the more traditional therapists with their emphasis on interpretations of clients' underlying conflicts. Instead, Rogers emphasized the client's potential for growth and the ability of the therapist to be empathically sensitive to the feelings of the client.

Another more radical development was the gradual growth of behavior therapy. Although learning theory–based approaches had been introduced relatively early (Jones, 1924; Mowrer & Mowrer, 1938), they had only a modest impact on practice until the publication of Joseph Wolpe's book *Psychotherapy by Reciprocal Inhibition* in 1958. Although Wolpe was a psychiatrist, behavior therapy was more directly linked to the field of psychology than were other forms of psychodynamic psychotherapy, and psychologists have played an important role in its development.

The primary contribution of behavior therapy was the obvious emphasis on behavior and performance as well as a more directive role for the therapist. Furthermore, both Rogers and the behavior therapists placed a greater emphasis on the importance of evaluating the results of their therapy than was true of the practitioners of other orientations. Another apparent difference between these two orientations and the more traditional forms of psychoanalysis and psychoanalytically oriented psychotherapy was the relative brevity of the former. Although there were controversies concerning the different goals and types of outcomes secured by means of the different therapeutic approaches, the fact was that the client-centered and behavior therapies lasted for a period of weeks or months whereas the psychoanalytically oriented therapies required a few years for completion.

Whether or not the length of the more traditional psychoanalytically oriented therapy contributed to its decline in popularity, there were other concurrent developments that also were of some significance. In the mid-1950s, a Joint Commission on Mental Illness and Health was appointed by the U.S. Congress to conduct a comprehensive study of mental illness and its treatment. The study, in which many mental health professional organizations took part, lasted five years and a multivolume report was published, including a summary report, *Action for Mental Health* (Joint Commission on Mental Illness and Health, 1961). In addition to citing deficiencies in our mental health system, the Joint Commission pointed out that long-term psychotherapy, and psychoanalysis in particular, was provided mainly for individuals in the middle and upper social classes who were not very seriously disturbed.

The report of the Joint Commission also contributed to the community mental health movement in the 1960s, which had a strong impact on psychotherapy and the provision of psychotherapeutic services. Among the new developments and emphases manifested during this period were provisions for the mental health needs of the underprivileged in their own communities, the emergence of briefer forms of therapy that would be available in times of emergency, and a broader concern with crisis intervention. There was also an important emphasis placed on the prevention and early detection of psychological problems.

The decade of the 1960s thus was an exciting and innovative period for the field of psychotherapy and for the mental health field in general. Although the funding for community mental health centers and the emphasis on prevention appear to have diminished, the relative decline of long-term psychotherapy and the popularity of briefer forms of therapy have continued, and we will say more about this later. The developments mentioned reflected a national concern about the quality and availability of mental health services for all segments of the population. However, the decisions made were not based on any meaningful research data for research on the efficacy of psychotherapy was rather limited.

In 1952, however, the British psychologist Hans Eysenck published a review of 24 studies and concluded that there was no research evidence to support the effectiveness of psychotherapy and that psychoanalysis, specifically, was less effective than no therapy. Needless to say, this provocative conclusion was strongly criticized by a number of

psychologists (Bergin, 1971; Garfield, 1981). Although Eysenck (1991, 1992), a proponent of behavior therapy, remains critical of other forms of psychotherapy, his 1952 article did appear to stimulate a greater awareness of the need for systematic research on psychotherapy. Since that time, there has been a gradual increase in both the quantity and quality of research on various aspects of change. Although research is an integral part of the present *Handbook*, and Chapters 2 and 3 specifically discuss and evaluate basic topics of research design and assessment, we can note here some of the past research on psychotherapy with particular reference to the evaluation of outcome.

Since the 1952 review by Eysenck, a number of reviews evaluating the efficacy of psychotherapy have been published. Meltzoff and Kornreich in 1970 and Bergin in the first edition of our *Handbook* in 1971 came to more positive conclusions than did Eysenck—and in general, most of the reviews that have followed since then have tended to report favorable results. This literature will be reported and evaluated in more detail in Chapter 5. However, the number of research publications and reviews that have appeared during the past 25 years or so clearly reflect the importance of research in evaluating the efficacy of psychotherapy (Bergin & Lambert, 1978; Garfield & Bergin, 1986; Luborsky, Crits-Christoph, Mintz, & Auerbach, 1988; Rachman & Wilson, 1980; Smith, Glass, & Miller, 1980; Williams & Spitzer, 1984).

Several other developments have also taken place as the field of psychotherapy has grown and expanded over time. The number of forms or theories of psychotherapy has increased noticeably; the practitioners of psychotherapy have grown in number and diversity; a variety of training programs now exist; insurance and third-party payments for psychotherapeutic services have emerged as important features of the current scene; and greater interest has been focused on issues of ethics and values. All of these topics merit further discussion and the rest of the chapter will be devoted to them.

THE PRACTITIONERS OF PSYCHOTHERAPY

Although we have made frequent reference to the *field* of psychotherapy and others have spoken of the *profession* of psychotherapy, psychotherapy is in some ways quite unique. Unlike the professions of law and medicine, where the practitioners are all lawyers or physicians respectively, many different professions or subprofessions are involved in the practice of psychotherapy. This has led to different programs of training as well as different professional or field loyalties.

In Freud's time and for some time afterward, the practitioners of psychotherapy were primarily physicians. Although Freud, himself, did not advocate medical training for psychotherapists, and some well-known analysts were referred to as "lay analysts" because they lacked medical training, most of the psychotherapy was conducted by psychiatric physicians. It is also well to remember that psychotherapy was in no way as popular as it is today. Furthermore, prior to the Second World War, clinical psychology was a relatively small and underdeveloped field with a major emphasis on the administration of psychological tests. After the war, however, the situation changed drastically. In the United States, there was a shortage of psychiatrists and a great need for trained personnel to care for the veterans who had developed psychiatric difficulties. With government support, graduate programs in clinical and counseling psychology were developed and psychotherapy became an important part of the training. Although there were subsequent conflicts with organized medical groups about the independent practice of psychotherapy by psychologists, these diminished and psychotherapy became the primary function of clinical psychologists (Garfield, 1983a).

The greater participation of clinical psychologists in psychotherapy has been paralleled by a similar pattern in other groups. As we noted previously:

Counseling psychologists, school psychologists, social workers, psychiatric nurses, pastoral counselors, and a number of other professional groups participate in some type of psychotherapy or counseling; indeed, these groups account for the largest portion of therapy hours conducted annually. Thus, it is evident that psychotherapy does not constitute a distinctive profession but rather is an activity that is performed by members of many different professions. Furthermore, there are some individuals referred to as paraprofessionals who also function in a psychotherapeutic role. (Garfield & Bergin, 1986, p. 5)

This expansion of providers of psychotherapeutic services was a direct response to the shortage of mental health personnel to meet the needs of individuals with various psychological problems. Thus, in addition to federal support for training programs for psychiatrists, psychologists, psychiatric social workers, and psychiatric nurses, the core mental health professions, there were experimental programs to provide training in psychotherapy for middle-aged college graduates (Rioch, 1971). There were also a variety of other programs to train individuals to perform specific therapeutic procedures with such diverse groups as emotionally disturbed children and adult alcoholics. So-called "indigenous nonprofessionals" were trained to work in different types of neighborhood centers. Such individuals were trained and supervised by professional mental health workers.

Needless to say, such attempts to meet the special needs of different groups in our society were not always well received by many professional therapists and the positive results reported in research reviews (Durlak, 1979; Hattie, Sharpley, & Rogers, 1984) have received some criticism (Nietzel & Fisher, 1981). However, this trend has continued in various ways. Many institutions and mental or behavioral health centers utilize psychologists with less than doctoral training and social workers and others with undergraduate degrees. Programs recently developed for chemical and alcohol dependent individuals utilize such individuals as important members of their therapeutic team.

On the basis of such developments, it is quite evident that no single profession has a monopoly on the field of psychotherapy nor can any group clearly demonstrate a consistent superiority in efficacy over all other groups. Furthermore, it would appear most likely that this situation will continue in the future and, with perhaps some local differences, is the situation in most other countries as well as in the United States. A single profession of psychotherapy was considered seriously some years ago, but the professions involved emphasized their particular value systems and no real agreement was reached (Holt, 1971). No more recent attempt has been made since that time, but cross-disciplinary interests have flourished in the Society for Psychotherapy Research and the Society for the Exploration of Psychotherapy Integration, both international organizations.

It should be evident that with such a diversity of therapists and counselors, the types of training provided also would vary considerably. Psychiatrists are trained first in medicine, whereas psychologists receive their training in academic departments of psychology, in freestanding professional schools of psychology, in doctoral psychology programs located in medical schools, or even in graduate schools of education. Whereas practically all psychiatrists have M.D. degrees, clinical psychologists can receive either the more traditional research-oriented Ph.D. degree or the more recent professionally oriented Doctor of Psychology or Psy.D. degree. Counseling psychologists can also obtain these degrees as well as a doctorate in education or Ed.D. degree. School psychologists, who may engage in psychotherapy, have similar choices in terms of degrees. Social workers may earn a doctoral degree, Ph.D. or D.S.W. (Doctor of Social Work), although this is not as typical of social work practitioners as it is of psychologists.

There are also a significant number of individuals performing psychotherapeutic services who have a master's degree or less. The traditional degree for professional social workers has been the M.S.W. (Master of Social Work), and many guidance counselors, marriage and family counselors, school psychologists, as well as clinical psychologists have received training at the master's level. The training for all of these professional groups is thus quite diverse. In addition, not only does the emphasis on psychotherapy vary from program to program, but the quality and extent of training vary as well. Furthermore, in the case of psychologists, since Ph.D. and Psy.D. degrees can be obtained from either graduate programs in universities or from freestanding professional schools, one cannot distinguish the training a particular psychologist has received by simply knowing the type of degree he or she has. Since the various programs may emphasize different theoretical orientations and different practicum experiences, the diversity in training can be quite marked.

Thus, would-be psychotherapists graduate from a variety of programs with different values, orientations, disciplinary allegiances, and amounts and types of therapeutic training. In addition, there are a number of postdoctoral training programs in psychotherapy, psychoanalytic institutes of various kinds, and a variety of workshops of varying lengths and topics that cater to workers in the psychotherapeutic field. For some of the professions involved, continuing education in the form of attending professional meetings or workshops may be required in order to keep one's license active.

A relatively large number of journals feature articles on psychotherapy and psychotherapy research. Some are identified with specific professions such as the *Archives of General Psychiatry*, *Journal of Consulting and Clinical Psychology*, *Journal of Counseling Psychology* and *Social Work*. However, other journals are specifically devoted to psychotherapy and are not identified with any single professional group. Examples of the latter are the *American Journal of Psychotherapy, Behavior Therapy, Cognitive Therapy and Research*, and the *Journal of Integrative and Eclectic Psychotherapy*. As is true of most things, the journals also vary in terms of quality and their respective emphases on research. With reference to the latter, psychologists with Ph.D. degrees from university programs receive the most training in research methods and are proportionately the most frequent contributors

to the research conducted on psychotherapy. This is an important contribution to the field of psychotherapy since demands for empirical demonstrations of the efficacy of psychotherapy have become more frequent.

PROLIFERATION, ECLECTICISM, AND INTEGRATION

Another interesting development has been the surprising increase in the number of different forms or orientations in psychotherapy. Around the mid-1960s one of us assembled a list of over 60 different forms of psychotherapy and considered this an amazing development (Garfield, 1982). However, this phenomenal growth has continued unabated. In 1975, it was estimated that there were over 125 different forms of psychotherapy (Research Task Force of the National Institute of Mental Health, 1975). Just five years later, Herink (1980) listed over 200 separate approaches to psychotherapy, and in 1986 Kazdin made reference to over 400 variants of psychotherapy. Clearly, this type of proliferation is a serious problem for the field. Apart from other considerations, most of these new forms of psychotherapy have not received any systematic research evaluation, and any attempt to evaluate 400 or so different techniques is not realistically within our capabilities. As Parloff pointed out earlier, "A systematic approach to dealing with a matrix of 250 psychosocial therapies and 150 classes of disorders would require approximately 47 million separate comparisons" (Parloff, 1982, p. 723).

Despite this trend for the expansive growth of the psychotherapies, a somewhat opposite trend has also been apparent. This is the popularity of *eclecticism* among psychotherapists and a related and slower developing movement for some type of integration among selected forms of psychotherapy. As we pointed out in the previous edition of this *Handbook*:

A decisive shift in opinion has quietly occurred; and it has created an irreversible change in professional attitudes about psychotherapy and behavior change. The new view is that the long-term dominance of the major theories is over and that an eclectic position has taken precedence. (Garfield & Bergin, 1986, p. 7)

The popularity of eclecticism and the trend of psychotherapists to utilize procedures and views from more than one theoretical orientation have been clearly manifested in a number of surveys over the past 15–20 years. Table 1.1 presents the

TABLE 1.1   Percentage of eclectics in various studies

Study	Percentage of Eclectics	N	Therapists
Jensen, Bergin, & Greaves (1990)	68	423	Psychiatrists, clinical psychologists, social workers, and marriage and family therapists
Larson (1980)	65	398	Psychotherapists
Garfield & Kurtz (1976)	55	855	Clinical psychologists
Jayaratne (1978)	55	489	Clinical social workers
Watkins, Lopez, Campbell, & Himmell (1986)	40	579	Counseling psychologists
Norcross, Kirtland, & Missar (1988)	38[a]	710	Psychologists, psychiatrists, and social workers
Norcross, Prochaska, & Gallagher (1989)	29	579	Clinical psychologists

results of representative studies. Most of these surveys have been of psychologists, but the study by Jensen, Bergin, and Greaves (1990) included samples of four professional groups involved in psychotherapy—psychiatrists, clinical psychologists, social workers, and marriage and family therapists. Although the precise percentages vary among the different studies due to limitations in samples and differences in the procedures used, the overall pattern is relatively clear. Therapists identify themselves as eclectics more frequently than any other orientation. This choice of eclecticism is also viewed as allowing therapists to select therapeutic procedures from any orientation that appear to be the best ones for a particular patient.

At the same time, the use of the term *eclectic* does not have any precise operational meaning beyond the general definition of selecting from diverse sources what is considered best for the individual case. The fact that two psychotherapists identify themselves as eclectics does not in any way indicate that they would treat a specific case in exactly the same way. In an earlier study of 154 eclectic clinical psychologists, 32 different combinations of theoretical orientations were used by this sample (Garfield & Kurtz, 1977). In the more recent survey by Jensen et al. (1990), comparable results were secured. Dynamic orientations were selected most frequently by eclectics among psychiatrists, social workers, and marriage and family therapists, whereas clinical psychologists identified cognitive therapy (63%) slightly more often than dynamic therapies. Whereas clinical psychologists and psychiatrists often put cognitive and behavioral strategies at or near the top, marriage and family therapists and social workers chose to use systems theory most often after psychodynamic theory. . . .

Of individuals endorsing an exclusively psychodynamic approach, 74% were either psychiatrists or social workers, whereas psychologists and marriage and family therapists accounted for only one fourth of the strictly psychodynamic therapists. (Jensen et al., 1990, p. 127)

Psychiatrists also had the relatively smallest percentage of eclectics, 58 percent compared to 68–72 percent for the other three groups.

Although the popularity of an eclectic approach to psychotherapy may indicate a reluctance on the part of many psychotherapists to adhere strictly to only one theoretical orientation, an eclectic approach also has some limitations. Eclecticism does not represent any truly systematic view, and thus research on this approach has been minimal and in fact is not really possible. It seems likely that eclecticism actually may be a stage in the development of a more refined and efficacious type of psychotherapy. One such potential development is the recent attempt on the part of a group of psychotherapists to foster some type of integration of approaches or procedures in a more systematic manner. Several psychoanalytically oriented therapists, for example, attempted to integrate behavioral procedures into their therapeutic approach (Birk & Brinkley-Birk, 1974; Marmor, 1971, 1973; Wachtel, 1977). Marmor (1971) specifically discussed the need for both dynamically oriented therapists and behaviorists to become more aware of the overlap and similarities between these two forms of psychotherapy.

Since these earlier developments, there has been

a slow but steady growth in the integrative movement. An important leader in this movement has been the behavioral psychologist Marvin Goldfried (1980, 1982, 1991). He and Paul Wachtel, a more dynamically oriented therapist, have been instrumental in forming the Society for the Exploration of Psychotherapy Integration (SEPI). Although the membership of this organization is small, it has a number of very distinguished psychologists and psychiatrists on its governing and advisory boards who represent a diversity of therapeutic orientations. Although U.S. therapists dominate the organization, its international membership has been growing. The 1991 annual meeting was held in London, and the first issue of its *Journal of Psychotherapy Integration* made its appearance in 1991.

There is also another international organization espousing interest in eclecticism and integration in psychotherapy—The International Academy of Eclectic Psychotherapists. The *Journal of Integrative and Eclectic Psychotherapy* is published by this group, who also sponsored the "First International Congress on Integrative and Eclectic Psychotherapy" in Mazatlan, Mexico, in the summer of 1992. The first *Handbook of Eclectic Psychotherapy* (Norcross, 1986) made its appearance and was followed a year later by the *Casebook of Eclectic Psychotherapy* (Norcross, 1987). In 1992, Norcross and Goldfried published a revised version of the handbook as the *Handbook of Integrative Psychotherapy*. All of these developments may reflect something of a trend or *zeitgeist* that is of importance for the field of psychotherapy.

Thus, this trend that was noted in the previous edition has continued to grow and develop. Furthermore, although the two designations, eclecticism and integration, have tended to be used together and sometimes interchangeably, integration has come to signify a more systematic attempt at combining elements of two or more forms of psychotherapy—although different individuals may have different ideas about how this integrative process takes place. Some beginning research attempts have been undertaken and some of the difficulties discussed. Wolfe and Goldfried (1988) have suggested that the common and unique change processes emphasized by the different psychotherapeutic orientations are more likely to be noted at a level of abstraction that exists between the level of theory and the actual observations that occur in the clinical interaction. Thus far, most of the attempts at integration appear to have focused mainly on combining aspects of psychodynamic theory and behavior therapy.

A brief mention can also be made of another emphasis that is related to eclecticism and integration, namely the recognition of common and spe-cific therapeutic factors or variables (Garfield, 1980, 1991). The past reviews of research have essentially revealed few important differences in outcome among the different forms of psychotherapy evaluated (Lambert, Shapiro, & Bergin, 1986; Smith et al., 1980). If two supposedly very different forms of psychotherapy secure outcomes that are quite comparable, one possible explanation is that there may be therapeutic factors operating that are common to both forms of psychotherapy (Frank, 1971; Garfield, 1980). Furthermore, these hypothesized common factors may account for a significant portion of the positive changes secured through psychotherapy. Among the common factors suggested have been the therapeutic relationship that develops in practically all forms of psychotherapy, the creation of hope, the opportunity for emotional release, explanations and interpretations of one's problems, support, advice, the trying out of new behaviors, and the modification of cognitions.

The analysis and appraisal of potential common therapeutic factors also provides us with an opportunity for integration that differs somewhat from the attempt at integrating two or more forms of psychotherapy mentioned earlier. In the former, the emphasis is on basic variables that are not tied to any specific theoretical system, and thus preconceived or long-held theoretical views are removed as barriers to integration. Although significant research remains to be performed, there has been an increasing awareness and acceptance of potential common factors as important variables in psychotherapy. Furthermore, although common factors are emphasized as important and as offering one means of integration in psychotherapy, it is not claimed that by themselves they explain all of the changes produced by means of psychotherapy. Rather, the possibility of specific factors or methods that are therapeutic for several specific disorders is also recognized and is seen as complementing the common factors (Garfield, 1980; Lambert et al., 1986).

At the present time, then, we have both a great abundance of types of psychotherapy and clear evidence of movements identified as eclectic and integrative. Although this may be somewhat confusing for newcomers to the field, there are some positive aspects as well. There is a less entrenched view on the part of a number of individuals who have been identified with particular orientations. Behavior therapists are now inclined to acknowledge the importance of the therapeutic relationship (Emmelkamp, 1986; O'Leary & Wilson, 1987), and analytically oriented therapists are willing to use behavioral procedures (Wachtel, 1991). Also, the positive response to the development of cognitive therapies has led to a greater acceptance and incorporation of cognitive emphases. In fact, cognitive therapies and behavioral therapies are each being increasingly referred to as cognitive-behavioral therapies, which is at least evidence of some integrative development in psychotherapy.

It is perhaps important also to point out, as we did in the previous edition, that this *Handbook* has been eclectic in orientation from the time the first edition (Bergin & Garfield, 1971) was conceived in 1967. As we mentioned then;

Empirical findings on all approaches were welcomed and each was highlighted within its own research domain. Being open to divergent approaches was important, but emphasizing empirical tests of efficacy has been an equally vital feature of the Handbook *and of the modern eclectic trend. Without an unyielding link to empirical research, eclecticism could deteriorate into another inflexible school dominated by the opinions of its leaders. (Garfield & Begin, 1986, p. 9)*

THE CONTINUED EMPHASIS ON BRIEF THERAPIES

The clear trend toward the practice of relatively brief forms of psychotherapy also has continued, and such therapy has become the modal form of treatment (Budman & Gurman, 1988; Garfield, 1989). Although for many years effective psychotherapy was considered to be a long-term process, and brief therapy was viewed essentially as superficial, viewpoints have changed considerably. For a variety of reasons, brief therapy has now become acceptable.

Psychoanalysis has generally been seen as the form of psychotherapy requiring the longest period of time. Although there have been few systematic surveys of the length of psychoanalysis, one report of a study of psychoanalysis gave the average number of sessions as 835 (Voth & Orth, 1973). It is rare to hear of an analysis taking less than four years and many apparently take longer. The cost of such therapy, obviously, is beyond the means of most people, and a significant number of those who undergo analyses are those who want to be psychoanalysts themselves or who are engaged in the mental health field (Kadushin, 1969).

As distinguished from psychoanalysis, analytically oriented psychotherapy was a less intensive form of therapy that perhaps required two to three years for completion. All of the "psychodynamic" forms of psychotherapy attempted to get at the underlying (unconscious) causes of the individual's problems and thus required at least a moderate length of time. In contrast, behavior therapies that focused on the modifications of behavior appeared to require much less time. Nevertheless, studies of the length of psychotherapy as practiced in most clinics have generally indicated that most of the therapy provided is surprisingly brief (see Chapter 6, this volume). Many individuals do not seem to want to spend a great deal of time and money on their personal psychotherapy but prefer to be helped as quickly as possible.

One earlier impetus for briefer forms of psychotherapy was related to the emphasis on community mental health that was manifested in the 1960s (Joint Commission on Mental Illness and Health, 1961). As mentioned previously, a survey of mental health activities in the United States revealed that such services were distributed unequally among our population, that there was a need for increased services, and that preventative efforts were also required. One of the outcomes was a greater sensitivity to the needs of the underprivileged members of our society and the provision of crisis intervention and emergency services in the local communities. As a result, innovative attempts at brief therapy programs organized in terms of crisis intervention were developed in a number of settings (Garfield, 1983a). Such programs tended to emphasize periods of brief therapy of 6 to 10 sessions and generally reported positive results. This did appear to stimulate a greater interest in briefer therapies. Obviously, if therapy lasts for 20 sessions or so, more patients or clients can be seen than if therapy lasts for 200 sessions. Most brief therapies now tend to be in the 15–30 session range.

Another important development in recent years that very definitely has made brief therapy the treatment of choice for most clients has been the growth of health maintenance organizations (HMOs) and managed health care generally. The growth of health insurance, including the coverage for mental health treatment, so-called third-party payments, has also played a role in the growth and prominence of brief therapy. Most health insurance plans place a limit on the number of therapy sessions they will reimburse, with many also requiring specified evaluations in order that the therapy not go beyond what is deemed as the basic necessary length. Because a large number of individuals cannot afford private treatment or long-term psychotherapy, the managed care programs determine the length of psychotherapy for a very large number of cases.

It can also be mentioned that the variety of brief psychotherapies has increased greatly in recent years. What is particularly interesting is the growth of different cognitive-behavioral and psychodynamic brief therapies. There are at least five different cognitive-behavioral therapies for depression, all of which have reported positive outcomes (Lewinsohn & Hoberman, 1982). Similarly, there are a number of brief psychodynamic therapies, all of which appear to have different theoretical emphases and, of course, all claiming to be effective therapies (Garfield, 1990). These and related developments in the area of brief psychotherapy will be discussed in more specific detail in Chapter 16.

PSYCHOTHERAPY RESEARCH

In the previous edition of the *Handbook*, we discussed the important issues of efficacy and accountability, which were particularly prominent then. In other words, increasing demands were made of psychotherapists to demonstrate that psychotherapy actually did produce positive outcomes. Although such issues have not fully disappeared, greater attention to appraisals of efficacy and the emphasis on brief psychotherapy have lessened earlier concerns. At the same time, there has been a greater sophistication in the research conducted on psychotherapy and more attention to the clinical significance of the research reported (Garfield, 1992; Jacobson & Revenstorf, 1988).

Because of the need to answer critics of psychotherapy and to demonstrate the efficacy of psychotherapeutic procedures, a major emphasis in psychotherapy research for the past 40 years has been on evaluating outcome. Although the issue of effectiveness has not been fully resolved as far as some critics are concerned (Eysenck, 1983, 1992; Prioleau, Murdock, & Brody, 1983; Rachman & Wilson, 1980), there has been at least some consensus that psychotherapy does have some positive effects (Elkin, et al., 1989; Garfield, 1983b; Lambert, 1991; Lambert, et al., 1986; McNeilly & Howard, 1991; Smith et al., 1980). The extent of the changes secured by means of psychotherapy, however, is an issue on which there is less agreement. Also, there would appear to be no agreement on which of the several hundred forms of psychotherapy secure the best results. Although most forms of psychotherapy have not been evaluated or compared in any systematic fashion, devoted followers of the different schools show strong feelings of affiliation and loyalty.

Nevertheless, on the basis of the existing research in which relatively small differences have been secured among the forms of psychotherapy evaluated, there appears to be a diminished need for comparative studies. What do appear to be important new trends are a greater emphasis on developing specific therapies for specific disorders

and a greater interest in improved research on the variables that actually account for the positive changes secured by psychotherapeutic interventions. We shall comment briefly on each of these potentially important developments.

Probably the most important influence on developing and using specific therapies for specific disorders has been the recently revised *Diagnostic and Statistical Manual of Mental Disorders* (DSM) of the American Psychiatric Association. The revised third edition of the DSM (American Psychiatric Association, 1987) has over 260 different mental disorders, a significant increase over the barely 100 disorders in the first edition published in 1952. Although this surprising increase undoubtedly does not indicate an epidemic of mental disorders in the United States, it does have an influence on practice, including the practice of psychotherapy. This is particularly true in relation to insurance reimbursement based on specific psychiatric diagnoses. This development also raises the issue of what form of therapy is most effective and most efficient. Thus, in recent years, we have seen more research organized around psychotherapy for specific disorders as contrasted with earlier research that dealt with psychotherapy administered to a sample that varied greatly in terms of psychiatric diagnosis.

The increased acceptance of behavioral approaches to psychotherapy has played a role in this development. Unlike the more traditional psychoanalytic views that regarded the treatment of symptoms as superficial, behavior therapists, with considerable success, focus on changing the disturbed symptomatic behavior. Although behavioral psychologists formerly were critical of psychiatric concepts of "mental illness," at present they tend to emphasize specific treatments for specific mental disorders. Although the idea of such specific treatments has an obvious attraction, it does raise some questions concerning how many forms of therapy a psychotherapist needs to learn or whether psychotherapists will become specialists for specific disorders. Even though there is somewhat of a trend toward the latter, it is too early for us to speculate about what the future pattern will be.

The final topic to be mentioned in this section concerns process research, or research devoted to discovering the actual therapeutic variables that account for the changes secured by psychotherapy. With the large number of therapeutic approaches, process research has tended to cover a wide spectrum of hypothesized therapeutic variables. Thus, this research area is even more complicated than the research on outcome (Garfield, 1990). The diversity of psychodynamic, experiential, and cognitive-behavioral approaches, let alone eclectic approaches, illustrates the potential range of variables for research appraisal. For some of us, therefore, it seems potentially more fruitful to explore the possibility of meaningful research on common factors that appear to operate in most forms of therapy.

ETHICS AND VALUES

Ethics

There is a continuing interest in ethics and values in the mental health disciplines that is manifested by an array of publications that emphasize these issues (Bergin, 1991; Carrol, Schneider, & Wesley, 1985; Lewis, 1990; May, 1991; Rosenbaum, 1982; Steininger, Newell, & Garcia, 1984; Thompson, 1990). In addition, there are new emphases on professional standards for the conduct of treatment and a growing array of intimidating legal issues that underscore the risks of practicing psychotherapy (Bednar, Bednar, Lambert, & Waite, 1991). All of these issues have become a focus of vital concern to practitioners, educators, administrators, and researchers; and the trend has had an impact upon research, especially in a new emphasis upon informed consent and protection from harm for participants in empirical studies (Stricker, 1982).

There is also a continuing concern that the use of no-treatment or placebo control groups may be unfair or harmful to clients (Garfield, 1987). In addition, there is a growing disillusionment with the value of such control groups, on substantive and conceptual grounds (see Chapter 5, this volume). Although there is an increasing trend to compare treatments with each other, which reduces the need for untreated or placebo controls, some authors continue to argue in favor of placebo baselines for comparative purposes (see Chapter 4, this volume). The trend away from placebos is one possible alternative in response to ethical concerns about withholding treatment, an issue that was raised early in the history of controlled therapy outcome studies (Rogers & Dymond, 1954).

The protection of subjects' rights and welfare has generally been a positive development. It has made researchers much more sensitive and responsible about their work. The use of elaborate consent forms and Human Subjects Review Committees has effectively prevented previous abuses of participants' welfare. Although taking this to extremes can inhibit creative inquiry and slow down progress unnecessarily, such developments have generally had a positive effect on research.

Other standards for the conduct of research studies have always been very clear and generally followed. These pertain to objectivity and honesty in recording, tabulating, analyzing, and reporting results of studies. Professional ethics are very specific on these points, and any violation should be promptly confessed or reported—without such basic integrity, no science can exist for very long. It is imperative that we avoid the slightest breach in such principles, let alone the fraudulent practices that have been exposed in some fields in recent years, which have included tampering with data or even the reporting of nonexistent data!

Thus far, psychotherapy research has been relatively free from such difficulties; however, there is an important historical incident that provides a lesson for us. This concerns a controversy that developed during a study of psychotherapy with schizophrenics conducted at the University of Wisconsin's Psychiatric Institute during the 1960s. The book reporting the results of that project mentions a crisis created by the mysterious disappearance of all of the data analyses and the excerpts of tape recordings of therapy sessions upon which the data were based (Rogers, Gendlin, Kiesler, & Truax, 1967). Apparently, this major project involving dozens of staff members nearly came to a halt without any results being published. Ultimately, new tape excerpts were extracted and an entirely new set of ratings on empathy and other therapeutic conditions was provided and analyzed. Carl Rogers's introduction to the book reporting the results refers to a "staff crisis, where for a time the whole project seems doomed. It is the frightful moment in which much of the rated data disappears" (p. xvi). Rogers also stated that

> Dr. Charles B. Truax organized the initial data collection and analysis. The ratings on which his studies were based mysteriously disappeared and have not been recovered. This unfortunate fact made Dr. Truax's preliminary reports unusable in this book. Dr. Donald J. Kiesler gave leadership to the re-rating and reanalysis of all of the data. (p. xviii)

It turns out that Truax published his own version of some of the Wisconsin project data (Truax & Carkhuff, 1967) at about the same time that the Rogers et al. book was published (1967). No one closely associated with the project has ever produced a convincing explanation for the disappearance of the first set of data, although they acknowledge that this event occurred in the midst of a period when there were intense conflicts among members of the research staff. There are some discrepancies between the reported results on the same cases in the two books and in subsequent publications by Truax (Truax & Mitchell, 1971). These have never been fully explained. Both Rogers and Truax are now deceased. Since 1967, scholars have appeared to treat with caution any of the published reports by Truax (but not his coauthors) concerning the Wisconsin Schizophrenia Project data. No one was ever convicted of illegal or unethical conduct in the episode.

The difficulties associated with that project serve as a warning to all of us that the mishandling of data can have serious negative consequences both for the status of scientific information and for one's career. Given the heightened sensitivity we have today regarding ethical misconduct, intentional mishandling of data has to be perceived as simply intolerable.

There is a related ethical standard that is not adhered to rigidly enough in our field — the *interpretation* of one's own or other hypotheses or theories. There have been, perhaps, too many instances of setting up double standards for interpreting findings: a severe standard for evaluating the validity of data contradicting one's position and a flexible standard for evaluating results that support one's views. Given the difficulties of doing precise research in this field and the ambiguities attending measurements of outcome, it is possible to stretch one's interpretive criteria so as to keep one's prejudices intact regardless of the weight of contrary evidence. Significant controversies in the history of psychotherapy and its evaluation may have been affected by the problem of bias and consequent misinterpretations of findings (Eysenck, 1993a,b; Lambert, 1992, 1993a, b; McNeilly & Howard, 1991).

All of us are subject to bias, which may be an inevitable aspect of being human. However, it seems that a reasonable degree of humility would assist progress toward increased knowledge to a considerable extent. As Carl Rogers was fond of saying, "The facts are friendly." However, the "facts" often contradict our prejudices, so we become defensive and distort their meaning. A more flexible attitude is likely to facilitate the pursuit of truth and a more cooperative approach by scholars.

We can recall comparing our evaluations of studies with the assessments of other reviewers and sometimes wondering whether we had read the same studies (Bergin, 1971; Bergin & Lambert, 1978; Rachman, 1971; Rachman & Wilson, 1980). Although reviewers, including ourselves, do make mistakes in reviewing studies, we are generally willing to correct such miscues. Thus, the chapters in the four editions of this book have continually improved as a result of critical feedback that has been incorporated into subsequent revisions. It is quite a different matter to cling to a biased interpretation for the sake of defending one's prior position. The motives for such behavior soon become all too apparent, and the defensive reviewer loses credibility while trying to win debating points.

To a degree, it is a matter of being able to learn from our mistakes versus becoming entrenched in our own narcissism, a dilemma most of us face. The three people to whom this book is dedicated all manifested significant maturation in this area, and all were able to alter their views at times. Their determination to continue to grow is a positive example for us.

From an ethical point of view, we have to recognize that having prejudices is not necessarily unethical; rather, it is when the prejudice grossly distorts the interpretation of data that one may become systematically unfair, and thus dishonest, in reporting or evaluating. An ingenious corrective for this tendency was the development of meta-analysis (Glass, McGaw, & Smith, 1981). Although meta-analysis can be used in the service of personal distortions of evidence, its procedures are public and exacting; consequently, the specific instances of bias can be identified and other reviewers can reliably repeat the review process with a precision and objectivity not heretofore possible. Although meta-analytic procedures are not entirely free from biasing choices, the decision rules are public and thus provide a powerful means for exposing deliberately distorted reviewing practices, which improves the likelihood of ethical reporting (see Chapter 2, this volume).

Values

The issue of values in psychotherapy has been marked by new developments in recent years and by some surprising turns. In contrast to views expressed in previous decades, the decade of the 1980s marked a substantial change in that the vast majority of therapists were found to believe that values are embedded in psychotherapy and are a natural part of the change process (Jensen & Bergin, 1988). Evidence of this shifting perspective has occurred in both professional and popular literature. Clinical research indicates that a variety of value issues come to the fore in the psychotherapy process (Bergin, 1991; see also Chapter 7, this volume); but more conceptual perspectives such as those of Rollo May (1991) show the broader cultural and historical significance of such themes in treatment. They are not merely individual expressions but are manifestations of deep trends in human history. Hunter Lewis's (1990) critical analysis of human values further makes the point in a sweeping essay. Paul Vitz (1990) specifically addresses psychologists in his analysis of narrative meanings in the study of moral development, a perspective that may have particular implications for psychotherapy research. In addition, it is hard to ignore the visibility of serious popular literature on values and spiritual issues in psychotherapy, such as that by the psychiatrist M. Scott Peck (1978), whose book has been on the best-seller lists for more than 15 years. There is also some measure of external validation of the significance of these trends when they are featured in a review essay in the science section of the *New York Times* (Goleman, 1991).

The renewed emphasis on values has been somewhat obscured by a secular focus upon new and more effective techniques of psychotherapy and their evaluation in standard research paradigms, as exemplified in the chapters throughout this book. The growing literature on values, hermeneutics, and qualitative research remind us, however, that our quest for a technology of change actually reflects changes that are deeply human and are not merely the result of technical processes or "mechanisms" of change. Therapeutic changes affect the ways in which people view themselves and life, and these changes in turn influence families, social structures, and lifestyles as well.

Understanding these issues is not so difficult when there is widespread agreement about values and the goals of treatment, but difficulties do arise when there are differences in perspective as to what constitutes desirable change. Psychotherapy outcome evaluations often ignore long-term and social implications of therapeutic change in favor of clinical criteria that are focused on narrowly individual and temporally immediate measurements.

As Strupp and Hadley (1977) showed, the ideals that guide the setting of standards for evaluating outcome should be set by multiple criteria from diverse value perspectives. By examining the treatment of individual symptoms in different problem areas, one can observe the role of value decisions in assessing treatment outcomes and their social consequences (Bergin, 1983, 1985). Many approaches to psychotherapy can produce changes in specific behaviors and feelings, but the value of those changes has been debated by persons observing the change phenomena from different perspectives. An example of this problem exists in the area of assertiveness training that assists people in overcoming anxiety and depressive symptoms. Such persons may suffer from inhibitions, feelings of inadequacy, and a failure to master effective social skills. Many techniques have been developed to approach these problems therapeutically, but often they are applied with a primary emphasis upon immediate relief for the client with insufficient reference to the situational context and the other persons involved.

While assertiveness methods are appropriately designed to aid people in overcoming extremely dependent and exploitive situations, wise therapists attempt to help clients achieve a balanced style of self-expressiveness that lies between humiliating passivity and intimidating aggression. Appropriate assertiveness, particularly for women and children, can in many cases be seen as a positive therapeutic result; however, the way this is done sometimes has disastrous effects and needs to be considered within a more systemic framework of the kind that Strupp and Hadley advocated. Liberating a woman by providing her with the tools of emotional combat and counting her as "cured" when she is able to achieve "emotional victories" do meet the narrow criterion of relieving certain kinds of symptomatic stress; but we also have to evaluate the effects on her social network that could be nurturing for her in the broader sense if change is properly managed.

There also continues to be considerable debate over how best to counsel people who are considering abortions, are in gay or lesbian relationships, or are approaching marriage and family life from divergent perspectives (see Chapter 14, this volume). The implication of all of this for psychotherapy research is that there is often a meaning component associated with the symptom change dimensions that are usually targeted in research. The meaning dimensions are rarely measured and monitored in a way that would enhance our understanding of the potential links between symptomatic change and changes in values and lifestyles. Harmonizing technique with value orientations may have synergistic effects that have not yet been assessed in research studies.

It is interesting that attempts to monitor values changes have shown that there is a domain of values that seems to be particularly relevant to psychotherapy change that is somewhat different from the general domain of moral values. The Jensen and Bergin study (1988), for instance, showed that there are values that therapists believe to be specifically embedded in standard theories of change, such as the importance of developing autonomy and responsibility, emotional sensitivity, self-control, and so on. On the other hand, there are broader social and religious values that seem to be less intrinsic to psychotherapy. Research evidence suggests that the former change substantially during therapy while the latter may remain unchanged (see Chapter 7, this volume). Of course, the reports that reflect this information are based on psychotherapy that has been evaluated in research programs, so we cannot generalize to the broad array of treatment done by practitioners in general that could show a different pattern.

Another relevant trend is the development of a diverse array of spiritual approaches to psychotherapy, some of which have now been subjected to empirical evaluation (Payne, Bergin, & Loftus,

1992). The work by Rebecca Propst in which religious imagery is used in the place of standard cognitions in cognitive-behavioral therapy for depression is a particularly good case in point. Propst's research report (Propst, Ostrom, Watkins, Dean, & Masburn, 1992) is the first major outcome study showing a positive effect of psychotherapy with specifically religious content, and the results suggest that this approach works better than standard cognitive therapy for religious clients. Other reports, such as Thoreson's (1987) and Martin and Carlson's (1988), suggest that spiritual themes have been shown to have specific and significant effects in health psychology interventions. In their work with Type A precoronary patients, Martin and Carlson have stated the following:

> We proceed systematically to program into their daily lives the prayer, meditation, worship time, rest, and loving time with family that are clearly prescribed by their religion. . . . belief-mediated behavior . . . is tapped to . . . enhance the effectiveness of the primary behavioral contingency-management therapy deemed necessary to change their health and disease risk behaviors. Not only is this dual approach well received by the patient as being highly consistent with their spiritual belief systems, but it also tends to result in significant social, emotional, and spiritual support from . . . wives and significant others who share the same faith. (1988, p. 88)

So, the growth of values awareness in psychotherapy practice and research is not geared so much to separating values from the therapy process or attempting to constrain the influence of values so much as it is to utilizing values to enhance the efficacy of change.

It appears, therefore, that the evaluation of techniques needs to take this dimension into consideration and that this is beginning to happen on a more systematic basis than previously. It appears, also, that specific techniques that can be powerful aids to symptom relief need to be considered within a multidimensional approach to therapy and its evaluation. This takes into account the fabric of social life and keeps the techniques within the context of the social consequences that are valued by the patient and those who count most in their lives, as well as the society in a broader sense. Ultimately, the welfare of the individual will be enhanced more by such an orientation than by a simple devotion to technical methods for obtaining self-focused improvements that may reinforce narcissism (Lasch, 1978; Vitz, 1977).

If we restrict ourselves to standard outcome criteria, such as inventory scales or behavioral indices, we might observe immediate positive results from most of the major therapies in terms of symptom relief. However, we conceivably would have fulfilled a clinically pragmatic value and not necessarily a moral one that assesses the individual's *lifestyle* and the ultimate consequences of that lifestyle for the person and the social system (Bergin, 1983, 1985; Worthington, 1989). This is clearly a more complex evaluative problem, but one of potentially great importance.

QUALITATIVE APPROACHES TO RESEARCH

In this volume, there are sporadic references to descriptive, qualitative, small sample, and case study approaches to research. It is important to acknowledge that this represents a significant trend in the field of social science inquiry that is reflected in a growing number of publications and in changing attitudes toward the nature of science as it is applied to human beings, particularly those in complex personal or social situations, including psychotherapy (Marshall & Rossman, 1989; Patton, 1990; Strauss & Corbin, 1990).

Qualitative and descriptive methods have had a place in psychotherapy for a long time, but there has been a traditional bifurcation between this "tender-minded" approach and the more exact approach that tends to dominate in the field and in the studies that have been reviewed in this book. Traditional quantitative and experimental thinking continues to be the dominant influence in the field, and it is supported by most journal editors and granting agencies. The dominance of this traditional thought is particularly reflected in Chapter 2, (Kazdin), Chapter 4 (Elkin), and Chapter 18 (Klerman et al.).

There is still something to be said for the richer and more meaningful accounts of therapeutic change advocated by several of the writers cited by Alexander et al. in Chapter 14. These authors assert that the majority of practitioners are turned off and uninfluenced by psychotherapy research because it does not capture the essential phenomena that the clinician perceives. Various attempts have been made to bridge this gap, such as the research on the therapeutic alliance as framed within the psychodynamic orientation described in Chapter 11 (Henry et al.) and in the experiential research on change that flows from the influence of Rogers, Perls, and others reviewed in Chapter 12 (Greenberg et al.). These latter trends still attempt to bring quantification into the descriptive accounts of the phenomena, much as is done in content analysis of psychotherapy (see Chapter 3 by Lambert & Hill).

It remains to be seen whether less quantitative, more narrative approaches that may be influenced by hermeneutic or social constructionist perspectives will have an influence upon the field. As Alexander et al. have proposed, it may be valuable to consider an eclectic approach to research methodology much as we have seen the evolution of an eclectic approach to psychotherapy. In such a case, there would be less of a value hierarchy regarding different approaches to inquiry and more of a harmony among the different approaches. Divergent ways of understanding and knowing might complement each other and bring us to a point where clinicians will feel more comfortable with our conclusions because they are closer to the clinical phenomena that are being evaluated.

OVERVIEW OF THE BOOK

The *Handbook* is divided into five main sections, although the last section is a brief summation of the previous four larger sections. As has been true of the previous three editions, each chapter in the various sections will include a review and appraisal of the existing research in the topical area covered. As mentioned earlier in this chapter, the importance of empirical research on psychotherapy has received greater recognition in recent years. This is a positive development both for increasing our knowledge of the psychotherapeutic process and the effectiveness of our procedures.

The first part of the book consists of four chapters, two of which were not included in the previous edition. Following the present introductory chapter is a chapter on research designs and statistical methods that should help the reader understand what is involved in psychotherapy research and help also to evaluate the existing research. The chapter that follows reviews and discusses the various measurement and assessment devices that have been developed for conducting research on both process and outcome in psychotherapy. The fourth and final chapter in this section is devoted to a description and evaluation of what is undoubtedly the most carefully planned and conducted study of psychotherapy to date: the NIMH Treatment of Depression Collaborative Research Program.

The second part, a very important one, deals with evaluating the ingredients of therapeutic efficacy. The first chapter reviews the research conducted on psychotherapeutic outcomes, in many ways the basic issue concerning both research and practice. This is followed by appraisals of the research that has attempted to evaluate the importance of client or patient variables and therapist

variables on outcome. In other words, what are the client or therapist characteristics that appear to play an important positive or negative role on the process and outcome of psychotherapy? The final chapter in this section attempts to evaluate what therapeutic process variables actually are related to outcome in psychotherapy. Thus, at the end of this section, the reader should have become acquainted with the main variables postulated to contribute to positive outcome and the status of outcome research in general.

The third part reviews the research on four major approaches to psychotherapy. A chapter is devoted to each of the approaches evaluated. Included are "Behavior Therapy with Adults," "Cognitive and Cognitive-Behavioral Therapies," "Psychodynamic Approaches," and "Research on Experiential Psychotherapies." Although not every single form of psychotherapy is included because most have not received much in the way of research evaluations, many of the well-known approaches are included.

The fourth part, "Research on Applications in Special Groups and Settings," is the longest section with seven separate chapters. Included here are chapters on child and adolescent therapies, marriage and family therapies, and group psychotherapies. To a certain extent, these represent specializations in psychotherapy. This is particularly true with regard to the practice of psychotherapy with children. Most psychotherapists work either with children or adults, and adolescents may be seen by psychotherapists of either group depending on preference and experience. Work with families also tends to be somewhat of a specialty, although many therapists work with married couples.

The fourth chapter in this part reviews the area of brief psychotherapy, which we discussed earlier. This is followed by a chapter on behavioral medicine and health psychology. This area of research and practice is a relatively new one in which psychological procedures have been applied to more general health problems, whereas traditionally counseling and psychotherapy have been associated more with "mental health" problems. The sixth chapter reviews the research on the use of medications and psychotherapy, both comparatively and when used together. This is also an area of increasing interest to many investigators. In contrast to this emphasis, the last chapter in this part deals with "Research on Psychotherapy with Culturally Diverse Populations." In recent years, a greater awareness of the diverse cultural groups that exist in the United States and the potential problems this can present in terms of providing psychotherapeutic services has become evident. The problems presented are quite different from those that Sigmund Freud encountered in Vienna early in the present century.

The final part of the book, Chapter 20, is entitled "Overview, Trends, and Future Issues." It is intended to be a brief summation of the preceding 19 chapters, an attempt to highlight what appear to be important or promising trends, and with the aid of our crystal ball, our attempt to delineate future issues in the field of psychotherapy. We sincerely hope that the *Handbook* will give the reader a comprehensive picture of the empirical status of psychotherapy and a sound basis for evaluating the field both at present and as it develops in the future.

REFERENCES

American Psychiatric Association Mental Hospital Service. (1952). *Diagnostic and statistical manual. Mental disorders.* Washington, DC: Author.

American Psychiatric Association. (1987). *Diagnostic and statistical manual of mental disorders* (rev. 3rd ed.). Washington, DC: Author.

Bednar, R. L., Bednar, S. C., Lambert, M. J., & Waite, D. R. (1991). *Psychotherapy with high-risk clients.* Pacific Grove, CA: Brooks/Cole.

Bergin, A. E. (1971). The evaluation of therapeutic outcomes. In A. E. Bergin & S. L. Garfield (Eds.), *Handbook of psychotherapy and behavior change: An empirical analysis* (pp. 217–270). New York: Wiley.

Bergin, A. E. (1983). Values and evaluating therapeutic change. In J. Helm & A. E. Bergin (Eds.), *Therapeutic behavior modification* (pp. 9–14). Berlin: VEB Deutscher Verlag der Wissenschaften.

Bergin, A. E. (1985). Proposed values for guiding and evaluating counseling and psychotherapy. *Counseling and Values, 29,* 99–116.

Bergin, A. E. (1991). Values and religious issues in psychotherapy and mental health. *American Psychologist, 46,* 394–403.

Bergin, A. E. & Garfield, S. L. (Eds.) (1971) *Handbook of psychotherapy and behavior change.* New York: Wiley.

Bergin, A. E., & Lambert, M. J. (1978). The evaluation of therapeutic outcomes. In S. L. Garfield & A. E. Bergin (Eds.), *Handbook of psychotherapy and behavior change* (2nd ed., pp. 139–189). New York: Wiley.

Birk, L. & Brinkley-Birk, A., (1974). Psychoanalysis and behavior therapy. *American Journal of Psychiatry 131,* 499–510.

Budman, S. H., & Gurman, A. S. (1988). *Theory and practice of brief therapy.* New York: Guilford.

Carroll, M. A., Schneider, H. B., & Wesley, G. R. (1985). *Ethics in the practice of psychology.* Englewood Cliffs, NJ: Prentice Hall.

Durlak, J. A. (1979). Comparative effectiveness of paraprofessional and professional helpers. *Psychological Bulletin, 86,* 80–92.

Elkin, I., Shea, T., Watkins, J. T., Imber, S. D., Stotsky, S. M., Collins, J. F., Glass, D. R., Pilkonis, P. A., Leber, W. R., Docherty, J. P., Fiester, S. J., & Parloff, M. B. (1989). National Institute of Mental Health Treatment of Depression Collaborative Research Program. General effectiveness of treatments. *Archives of General Psychiatry, 46,* 971–982.

Emmelkamp, P. M. G. (1986). Behavior therapy with adults.

In S. L. Garfield & A. E. Bergin (Eds.), *Handbook of psychotherapy and behavior change* (3rd ed., pp. 385–442). New York: Wiley.

Eysenck, H. J. (1952). The effects of psychotherapy: An evaluation. *Journal of Consulting Psychology, 16,* 319–324.

Eysenck, H. J. (1983). The effectiveness of psychotherapy: The specter at the feast. Commentary. *The Behavioral and Brain Sciences, 6,* 290.

Eysenck, H. J. (1991). Maverick psychologist. In C. E. Walker (Ed.), *The history of clinical psychology in autobiography* (Vol. I, pp. 39–86). Pacific Grove, CA: Brooks/Cole.

Eysenck, H. J. (1992). The outcome problem in psychotherapy. In W. Dryden & U. C. Feltham (Eds.), *Psychotherapy and its discontents.* London: Open University Press.

Eysenck, H. J. (1993a). Eysenck, Freud, and Lambert: A question of bias. *Contemporary Psychology, 38,* 658–659.

Eysenck, H. J. (1993b). Biased is as biased does. *Contemporary Psychology, 38,* 659.

Frank, J. D. (1971). Therapeutic factors in psychotherapy. *American Journal of Psychotherapy, 25,* 350–361.

Freud, S. (1938). *The history of the psychoanalytic movement.* In *The basic writings of Sigmund Freud.* New York: Modern Library, Random House.

Garfield, S. L. (1980). *Psychotherapy: An eclectic approach.* New York: Wiley.

Garfield, S. L. (1981). Psychotherapy. A 40-year appraisal. *American Psychologist, 36,* 174–183.

Garfield, S. L. (1982). Eclecticism and integration in psychotherapy. *Behavior Therapy, 13,* 610–623.

Garfield, S. L. (1983a). *Clinical psychology. The study of personality and behavior* (2nd ed.). New York: Aldine.

Garfield, S. L. (1983b). Effectiveness of psychotherapy: The perennial controversy. *Professional Psychology: Research and Practice, 14,* 35–43.

Garfield, S. L. (1987). Ethical issues in research on psychotherapy. *Counseling and Values, 31,* 115–125.

Garfield, S. L. (1989). *The practice of brief psychotherapy.* Elmsford, NY: Pergamon.

Garfield, S. L. (1990). Issues and methods in psychotherapy process research. *Journal of Consulting and Clinical Psychology, 58,* 273–280.

Garfield, S. L. (1991). Common and specific factors in psychotherapy. *Journal of Integrative and Eclective Psychotherapy, 10,* 5–13.

Garfield, S. L. (1992). Major issues in psychotherapy research. In D. K. Freedheim (Ed.), *History of psychotherapy: A century of change* (pp. 335–359). Washington, DC: American Psychological Association.

Garfield, S. L. & Bergin, A. E. (Eds.). (1986). *Handbook of psychotherapy and behavior change* (3rd ed.). New York: Wiley.

Garfield, S. L., & Kurtz, R. (1976). Clinical psychologists in the 1970's. *American Psychologist, 31,* 1–9.

Garfield, S. L., & Kurtz, R. (1977). A study of eclectic views. *Journal of Consulting and Clinical Psychology, 45,* 78–83.

Glass, G. V., McGaw, B., & Smith, M. L. (1981). *Meta-analysis in social research.* Beverly Hills: Sage Publications.

Goldfried, M. R. (1980). Toward a delineation of therapeutic change principles. *American Psychologist, 35,* 991–999.

Goldfried, M. R. (1982). *Converging themes in psychotherapy.* New York: Springer-Verlag.

Goldfried, M. R. (1991). Research issues in psychotherapy integration. *Journal of Psychotherapy Integration, 1,* 5–25.

Goleman, D. (1991, September 10). Therapists see religion as an aid, not an illusion. *New York Times,* pp. B5, B7.

Hattie, J. A., Sharpley, C. F., & Rogers, H. J. (1984). Comparative effectiveness of professional and paraprofessional helpers. *Psychological Bulletin, 95*, 534–541.

Herink, R. (Ed.). (1980). *The psychotherapy handbook: The A to Z guide to more than 250 different therapies in use today*. New York: A Meridan Book, New American Library.

Holt, R. R. (Ed.). (1971). *New horizon for psychotherapy*. New York: International Universities Press.

Jacobson, N. S., & Revenstorf, D. (1988). Statistics for assessing the clinical significance of psychotherapy techniques: Issues, problems, and new developments. *Behavioral Assessment, 10*, 133–145.

Jayaratne, S. (1978). A study of clinical eclecticism. *Social Service Review, 52*, 621–631.

Jensen, J. P., & Bergin, A. E. (1988). Mental health values of professional therapists: A national interdisciplinary survey. *Professional Psychology: Research and Practice, 19*, 290–297.

Jensen, J. P., Bergin, A. E., & Greaves, D. W. (1990). The meaning of eclecticism: New survey and analysis of components. *Professional Psychology: Research and Practice, 21*, 124–130.

Joint Commission on Mental Illness and Health. (1961). *Action for mental health*. New York: Basic Books.

Jones, M. C. (1924). The elimination of children's fears. *Journal of Experimental Psychology, 7*, 383–390.

Kadushin, C. (1969). *Why people go to psychiatrists*. New York: Atherton.

Kazdin, A. E. (1986). Comparative outcome studies of psychotherapy: Methodological issues and strategies. *Journal of Consulting and Clinical Psychology, 54*, 95–105.

Lambert, M. J. (1991). Introduction to psychotherapy research. In L. E. Beutler & M. Crago (Eds.), *Psychotherapy research. An international review of programmatic studies* (pp. 1–11). Washington, DC: American Psychological Association.

Lambert, M. J. (1992). Eysenck on Freud: An objective scientific analysis? [Review of *Decline and fall of the Freudian empire*.] *Contemporary Psychology, 37*, 786–787.

Lambert, M. J. (1993a). Lambert on Eysenck: When is an objective appraisal biased? *Contemporary Psychology, 38*, 659.

Lambert, M. J. (1993b). If the bias fits, wear it. *Contemporary Psychology, 38*, 659.

Lambert, M. J., Shapiro, D. A., & Bergin, A. E. (1986). The effectiveness of psychotherapy. In S. L. Garfield & A. E. Bergin (Eds.), *Handbook of psychotherapy and behavior change* (3rd ed., pp. 157–211). New York: Wiley.

Larson, D. (1980). Therapeutic schools, styles, and schoolism: A national survey. *Journal of Humanistic Psychology, 20*, 3–20.

Lasch, C. (1978). *The culture of narcissism*. New York: W. W. Norton.

Lewinsohn, P. M., & Hoberman, H. M. (1982). Behavioral and cognitive approaches. In E. S. Paykel (Ed.), *Handbook of affective disorders* (pp. 338–345). Edinburgh: Churchill Livingstone.

Lewis, H. (1990). *A question of values*. New York: Harper & Row.

Luborsky, L., Crits-Christoph, P., Mintz, J., & Auerbach, A. (1988). *Who will benefit from psychotherapy?* New York: Basic Books.

Marmor, J. (1971). Dynamic psychotherapy and behavior therapy—Are they irreconcilable? *Archives of General Psychiatry, 24*, 22–28.

Marmor, J. (1973). The future of psychoanalytic therapy. *American Journal of Psychiatry, 130*, 1197–1202.

Marshall, C., & Rossman, G. B. (1989). *Designing qualitative research*. Newbury Park, CA: Sage Publications.

Martin, J. E., & Carlson, C. R. (1988). Spiritual dimensions of health psychology. In W. R. Miller and J. E. Martin (Eds.), *Behavior therapy and religion: Integrating spiritual and behavioral approaches to change* (pp. 57–110). Newbury Park, CA: Sage Publications.

May, R. (1991). *The cry for myth*. New York: W. W. Norton.

McNeilly, C. L., & Howard, K. I. (1991). The effects of psychotherapy: A reevaluation based on dosage. *Psychotherapy Research, 1*, 74–78.

Meltzoff, J., & Kornreich, M. (1970). *Research in psychotherapy*. New York: Atherton Press.

Mowrer, O. H., & Mowrer, W. (1938). Enuresis: A method of its study and treatment. *American Journal of Orthopsychiatry, 8*, 436–459.

Nietzel, N. T., & Fisher, S. G. (1981). Effectiveness of professional and paraprofessional helpers: A comment on Durlak. *Psychological Bulletin, 89*, 555–565.

Norcross, J. D. (Ed.). (1986). *Handbook of eclectic psychotherapy*. New York: Brunner/Mazel.

Norcross, J. C. (1987). *Casebook of eclectic psychotherapy*. New York: Brunner/Mazel.

Norcross, J. C. & Goldfried, M. R. (Eds.) (1992) *Handbook of psychotherapy integration*. New York: Basic Books.

Norcross, J. C., Kirtland, D. S. & Missar, C. D. (1988). The processes and outcomes of psychotherapist's personal treatment experiences. *Psychotherapy, 25*, 36–43.

Norcross, J. C., Prochaska, J. O., & Gallagher, K. (1989). Clinical psychologists in the 1980's: II. Theory, research and practice. *The Clinical Psychologist, 42*(3), 45–53.

O'Leary, K. D., & Wilson, G. T. (1987). *Behavior therapy: Application and outcome* (2nd ed.). Englewood Cliffs, NJ: Prentice-Hall.

Parloff, M. B. (1982). Psychotherapy research evidence and reimbursement decisions: Bambi meets Godzilla. *American Journal of Psychiatry, 139*, 718–727.

Patton, M. Q. (1990). *Qualitative evaluation and research methods* (2nd ed.). Newbury Park, CA: Sage Publications.

Payne, I. R., Bergin, A. E., & Loftus, P. E. (1992). A review of attempts to integrate spiritual and standard psychotherapy techniques. *Journal of Psychotherapy Integration, 2*, 171–192.

Peck, M. S. (1978). *The road less traveled: A new psychology of love, traditional values and spiritual growth*. New York: Simon & Schuster.

Propst, L. R., Ostrom, R., Watkins, P., Dean, T., & Mashburn, D. (1992). Comparative efficacy of religious and nonreligious cognitive-behavioral therapy for the treatment of clinical depression in religious individuals. *Journal of Consulting and Clinical Psychology, 60*, 94–103.

Prioleau, L., Murdock, M., & Brody, N. (1983). An analysis of psychotherapy versus placebo studies. *The Behavioral and Brain Sciences, 6*, 275–285.

Rachman, S. J. (1971). *The effects of psychotherapy*. Oxford: Pergamon Press.

Rachman, S. J., & Wilson, G. T. (1980). *The effects of psychological therapy* (2nd ed.). New York: Pergamon.

Report of the Research Task Force of the National Institute of Mental Health. (1975). *Research in the service of mental health* (DHEW Publication No. ADM 75-236). Rockville, MD.

Rioch, M. J. (1971). Two pilot projects in training mental health counselors. In R. R. Holt (Ed.), *New horizon for psychotherapy* (pp. 294–311). New York: International Universities Press.

Rogers, C. R. (1942). *Counseling and psychotherapy*. Boston: Houghton Mifflin.

Rogers, C. R., & Dymond, R. F. (Eds.). (1954). *Psychotherapy and personality change.* Chicago: University of Chicago Press.

Rogers, C. R., Gendlin, E. T., Kiesler, D. J., & Truax, C. B. (1967). *The therapeutic relationship and its impact.* Madison: University of Wisconsin Press.

Rosenbaum, M. (Ed.). (1982). *Ethics and values in psychotherapy: A guidebook.* New York: Free Press.

Smith, M. L., Glass, G. V., & Miller, T. L. (1980). *The benefits of psychotherapy.* Baltimore: The Johns Hopkins University Press.

Steininger, M., Newell, J. D., & Garcia, L. T. (1984). *Ethical issues in psychology.* Homewood, IL: Dorsey.

Strauss, A., & Corbin, J. (1990). *Basics of qualitative research.* Newbury Park, CA: Sage Publications.

Stricker, G. (1982). Ethical issues in psychotherapy research. In M. Rosenbaum (Ed.), *Ethics and values in psychotherapy: A guidebook* (pp. 402–424). New York: Free Press.

Strupp, H. H., & Hadley, S. M. (1977). A tripartite model of mental health and therapeutic outcomes. *American Psychologist, 32,* 187–196.

Thompson, A. (1990). *Guide to ethical practice in psychotherapy.* New York: Wiley.

Thoresen, K. (1987, June). *Development and modification of Type A behavior patterns.* Paper presented at San Diego State University Summer Symposium. "Type A Coronary Prone Behavior Pattern: A Comprehensive Look," San Diego, CA.

Truax, C. B., & Carkhuff, R. R. (1967). *Toward effective counseling and psychotherapy.* Chicago: Aldine.

Truax, C. B., & Mitchell, K. M. (1971). Research on certain therapist interpersonal skills in relation to process and outcome. In A. E. Bergin & S. L. Garfield (Eds.), *Handbook of psychotherapy and behavior change* (pp. 299–344). New York: Wiley.

Vitz, P. (1977). *Psychology as religion: The cult of self-worship.* Grand Rapids, MI: Eerdmans.

Vitz, P. (1990). The use of stories in moral development: New psychological reasons for an old education method. *American Psychologist, 45,* 709–720.

Voth, H. M., & Orth, M. H. (1973). *Psychotherapy and the role of the environment.* New York: Behavioral Press.

Wachtel, P. L. (1977). *Psychoanalysis and behavior therapy.* New York: Basic Books.

Wachtel, P. L. (1991). From eclecticism to synthesis: Toward a more seamless psychotherapeutic integration. *Journal of Psychotherapy Integration, 1,* 43–54.

Watkins, C. E., Jr., Lopez, F. G., Campbell, V. L., & Himmell, C. D. (1986). Contemporary counseling psychology: Results of a national survey. *Journal of Counseling Psychology, 33,* 301–309.

Williams, J. B. W., & Spitzer, R. L. (1984). *Psychotherapy research: Where are we and where should we go?* New York: Guilford.

Wolfe, B., & Goldfried, M. R. (1988). Research on psychotherapy integration: Recommendation and conclusions from an NIMH workshop. *Journal of Consulting and Clinical Psychology, 56,* 448–451.

Wolpe, J. (1958). *Psychotherapy by reciprocal inhibition.* Stanford: Stanford University Press.

Worthington, E. L. (Ed.). (1989). Religious faith across the lifespan: Implications for counseling and research [Special Issue]. *The Counseling Psychologist, 17*(4).

2

METHODOLOGY, DESIGN, AND EVALUATION IN PSYCHOTHERAPY RESEARCH

- **ALAN E. KAZDIN**

Yale University

Psychotherapy focuses on broad fundamental questions about the nature and organization of personality, interpersonal processes and their interplay, the course of development over the life span, and the full range of factors that can have an impact on adjustment, maladjustment, and psychopathology. The research methods used to address the many issues of psychotherapy are critically important to understand because answers to the substantive questions that guide psychotherapy research are inextricably bound to the methods employed to answer them. Consider examples of the intertwining of substantive questions and research methods. First, there is general consensus that many forms of psychotherapy are effective; that is, treatments lead to markedly greater change than no-treatment. This is a statement about the impact of treatment (e.g., Smith, Glass, & Miller, 1980). Yet, this statement cannot be divorced from the methods used to evaluate treatment impact. The methods used to calculate the effects of treatment vary and can lead to diverse conclusions from the same data base (e.g., Matt, 1989). Second, comparative studies often show that two different forms of psychotherapy are similar in the outcomes they produce (e.g., Stiles, Shapiro, & Elliott, 1986). This finding raises important questions about whether common mechanisms underlie treatment. Yet, methods of evaluation are critical to the conclusion. It is possible that the manner in which treatment is studied may lead to a no-differences finding. The vast majority of therapy studies, by virtue of their design, may not be able to detect differences among alternative treatments even if differences exist (Kazdin & Bass, 1989). The point is not to oversimplify the complex

issues and questions of psychotherapy, but rather to highlight the interdependence of the substantive questions of therapy with the methods used to answer them.

The present chapter discusses methodology, research design, and data evaluation. The chapter begins with a discussion of the goals of psychotherapy research, how these goals relate to research methods, and alternative method and design options. Several research designs are illustrated to convey the range of methods on which therapy research relies. Methodological issues in relation to clients, therapists, treatment and implementation, data evaluation, and data interpretation are presented. The chapter ends with a discussion of questions to guide the researcher in the design of research on psychotherapy.

INTERFACE OF GOALS AND METHODS OF RESEARCH IN PSYCHOTHERAPY

Goals of Psychotherapy Research

The overarching goal of psychotherapy research is to understand alternative forms of treatment, the mechanisms and processes through which these treatments operate, and the impact of treatment and moderating influences on maladaptive and adaptive functioning. In the context of research, psychotherapy serves as a laboratory for studying human interaction and individual differences in relation to specific types of interventions, processes, and outcomes. The task of understanding treatment and the manifold conditions that may affect processes and outcomes is daunting when one considers what therapy is, how and to whom it is applied, and methods of evaluating its impact.

The scope of treatments, client conditions to which they can be applied, and methods of evaluating their impact is vast. First, over 400 psychother-

*Completion of this paper was facilitated by a Research Scientist Award (MH00353) and a grant (MH35408) from the National Institute of Mental Health.

apy techniques are in use for adults, over 200 for children and adolescents (T. B. Karasu, personal communication, March 1, 1985; Kazdin, 1988). The range of investigations the alternative treatments could generate to establish their effectiveness and to examine the relative impact of viable treatments for a given problem is enormous. Second, almost 300 different forms of psychological syndromes or symptom patterns are currently recognized in diagnostic systems to which psychotherapy can be applied (e.g., *Diagnostic and Statistical Manual of Mental Disorders* [DSM-III-R]; American Psychiatric Association, 1987). This count omits the many problems of living (e.g., life crises, stress) that do not necessarily meet criteria for recognizable disorders but often serve as the focus of psychotherapy. Finally, the methods of assessing treatment outcome are vast and include measures obtained from different informants (e.g, clients, clinicians, significant others in everyday contact with the client), assessment formats (e.g., paper-and-pencil measures, direct observations of behavior), and domains of functioning (e.g., affect, cognition, behavior) (Lambert, Christensen, & DeJulio, 1983). Different measures of outcome do not necessarily intercorrelate highly so that conclusions about treatment can vary as a function of the type of assessment. The possible interactions of techniques, disorders, and assessments are virtually infinite. Selection of the methods requires conceptualization of the treatment focus, techniques, relevant domains of process and outcome, and assessment devices to represent these.

The effort to understand psychotherapy has been represented in different ways that emphasize treatment and other influences (e.g., patients, therapists, in-session processes) that may contribute to change (Goldfried, Greenberg, & Marmar, 1990; Kiesler, 1971; Lambert, Shapiro, & Bergin, 1986; Paul, 1967). Thus, as researchers we are interested in the impact of alternative treatments, on alternative clinical problems, with clients of varying characteristics, and other manifold conditions that may mediate outcome. At the concrete level of individual investigations, understanding how treatment operates and the factors that contribute to change can be translated into several specific treatment evaluation strategies that guide individual studies (Kazdin, 1992a). Table 2.1 presents major strategies and the empirical questions they are designed to address. Individual strategies can be employed in a given study to evaluate some facet of treatment. Diverse strategies across multiple studies elaborate the range of factors that may contribute to treatment and represent a progression of research. For example, an initial study might examine treatment relative to a no-treatment control group (treatment package) to see the overall effects

of the intervention; further studies may examine a particular characteristic of the cases or those who administer treatment (client–therapist variation) in relation to outcome or critical emergent processes, interactions and relationship factors (process strategy) within the session. The manner in which treatments operate can be revealed within the context of a broad portfolio of research that represents increasingly sophisticated questions about treatment.

The different strategies emphasize the importance of treatment *techniques* or procedures and their variations. The focus on techniques is represented by varying some aspect of a given treatment (parametric strategy), by deleting a component of treatment (dismantling strategy) or adding new ingredients (constructive strategy), or by contrasting two or more different treatments (comparative strategy). The emphasis on treatment technique as a main effect in producing treatment outcome guides much of research (e.g., Kazdin, Bass, Ayers, & Rodgers, 1990). At the same time, the goals of therapy research also entail understanding how treatment operates, the factors with which treatment interacts, and the mechanisms of change within the therapy process. Two strategies listed in the table carry much of the burden of this goal. Psychotherapy is concerned with individual differences, that is, how different people respond to different conditions, as well as a variety of potential moderator variables. The client–therapist variation strategy focuses on the broad range of characteristics (e.g. client history, personality, family characteristics, cognitive processes, therapist experience and personality) that influence treatment process and outcome. Understanding the many factors that contribute to outcome and theoretically driven investigations to evaluate them are high priorities in contemporary psychotherapy research (Beutler, 1991; Smith & Sechrest, 1991). The purpose of identifying factors is not merely to describe or to catalogue them, but to explore how client and treatment characteristics combine to produce changes and what mechanisms account for their manifestation (Smith & Sechrest, 1991).

The mechanisms of change are also approached by the process evaluation strategy. This strategy includes studies devoted to understanding the unfolding of treatment, the experience of therapy by clients, and therapists, relationship issues, and how these relate to change. Processes of therapy can reflect the dynamic features at a microscopic level. Processes are central both to describe the structure and function of events as well as to predict changes that appear at the end of treatment (see Beutler, 1990).

The research strategies obviously can be used to understand individual treatment techniques and

TABLE 2.1   Alternative treatment evaluation strategies to develop and identify effective interventions

Treatment Strategy	Question Asked	Basic Requirements
Treatment Package	Does treatment produce therapeutic change?	Treatment vs. no-treatment or waiting-list control
Dismantling Strategy	What components are necessary, sufficient, and facilitative of therapeutic change?	Two or more treatment groups that vary in the components of treatment that are provided
Constructive Strategy	What components or other treatments can be added to enhance therapeutic change?	Two or more treatment groups that vary in components that are provided
Parametric Strategy	What changes can be made in the specific treatment to increase its effectiveness?	Two or more treatment groups that differ in one or more facets of the treatment
Comparative Outcome Strategy	Which treatment is the more or most effective for a particular population?	Two or more different treatments for a given problem
Client and Therapist Variation Strategy	Upon what patient, family, or therapist characteristic does treatment depend for it to be effective?	Treatment as applied separately to different types of cases, therapists, and so on
Process Strategy	What processes occur in treatment that affect within-session performance and may contribute to treatment outcome?	Treatment groups in which patient and therapist interactions are evaluated within the sessions

how they operate. At the same time, the nature and scope of the research agenda across different treatments, disorders, and problems of living draw our attention to a broader focus. The overriding goal is to understand fundamental processes related to the development, change, and alteration of affect, cognition, and behavior. Many processes central to therapy such as patient–therapist interaction may have generality across alternative treatments and clinical problems. We expect and seek to identify in research those processes that might be similar across the manifold treatments and the circumstances to which they can be applied. Thus, research in psychotherapy is not only designed to evaluate the impact and moderating influences of specific treatments, but also to reveal fundamental processes and mechanisms of change that may transcend individual techniques.

Another important goal of therapy research is to develop and evaluate treatments that can be used in clinical practice (i.e., to place clinical practice on firm empirical grounds). Although this latter goal is served by understanding treatments and how they operate, the extension, generality, and applicability of research findings to clinical practice cannot be assumed. Thus, therapy research also is conducted that is designed to extend treatments developed in research to the circumstances and conditions that resemble or reflect clinical practice.

The Role of Methodology and Research Design

A general statement of the goals of therapy research is critical to place into context the role of methodology and research design. *Methodology* refers to diverse principles, practices, and procedures that govern research. These principles and practices are of interest as a means of addressing substantive questions about the phenomena of interest. Practices that constitute research methodology are used to uncover relations between variables that otherwise could not be readily detected and to verify relations that have been hypothesized. Without controlled research, potential relations between variables must be viewed in their full complexity as they appear in nature and are often difficult to decipher.

Research design refers to a way of arranging the situation so that inferences about the variables of interest can be drawn. The design helps to simplify the situation in which the influence of many variables, often operating simultaneously, can be separated from the variable(s) of interest to the investigator. Experimental designs are often used in which conditions are carefully controlled and varied by the investigator to maximize clarity. Alternatively, in many cases, conditions cannot be completely controlled by the investigator or he or she is not interested in manipulating or controlling them. In such cases, special arrangements and control procedures (e.g., statistical controls) are deployed to separate and to evaluate the variables of interest. Without such simplification and isolation of variables, many if not an unlimited number of interpretations could explain a particular phenomenon. Research is designed to help rule out or make implausible different factors that might explain a particular phenomenon. A study does not necessarily rule out all possible explanations. The extent to which it is successful in doing so is a matter of degree. From a methodological standpoint, the better the design of a study the more implausible it makes competing explanations of the results. Not all psychotherapy research is designed to test hypotheses about treatment. Research also is designed to generate hypotheses. Even so, the methodological desiderata are similar, namely, to design the study in such a way as to maximize interpretability of the findings.

The purpose of research is to reach well-founded (i.e., valid) conclusions about the effects of a given intervention and the conditions under which it operates (see Kazdin, 1992a). There are several domains of influences that can interfere with draw-

ing valid inferences. The main influences have been codified as types of experimental validity. Four types of experimental validity have been identified: *internal, external, construct,* and *statistical conclusion validity* (Cook & Campbell, 1979). Table 2.2 lists each type of validity, the issue to which each is addressed, and the major threats to validity. The threats to validity refer to those factors of the study that affect interpretation of the findings. Methodology, research design, and statistical evaluation are deployed to address, rule out, or make plausible these alternative threats.

Threats to validity vary in their subtlety and ease of control in research in general. For example, internal validity threats refer to a variety of influences that might explain those differences the investigator attributes to the intervention. Historical events, maturational processes, repeated testing (where there is a pre- and posttreatment assessment), regression toward the mean, and related factors lead to changes over time and possibly group differences. These factors generally can be controlled experimentally by assigning subjects randomly to groups, assessing subjects in the same

TABLE 2.2   Types of experimental validity, questions they address, and their threats to drawing valid inferences

Type of Validity	Questions Addressed	Threats to Validity
Internal Validity	To what extent can the intervention, rather than extraneous influences, be considered to account for the results, changes, or group differences?	Changes due to influences other than the experimental conditions such as events (history) or processes (maturation) within the individual, repeated testing, statistical regression, and differential loss of subjects
External Validity	To what extent can the results be generalized or extended to persons, settings, times, measures, and characteristics other than those in this particular experimental arrangement?	Possible limitations on the generality of the findings because of characteristics of the sample; therapists; or conditions, context, or setting of the study
Construct Validity	Given that the intervention was responsible for change, what specific aspects of the intervention or arrangement were the causal agents; that is, what is the conceptual basis (construct) underlying the effect?	Alternative interpretations that could explain the effects of the intervention, that is, the conceptual basis of the findings, such as attention and contact with the subject, expectancies of subjects or experimenters, cues of the experiment
Statistical Conclusion Validity	To what extent is a relation shown, demonstrated, or evident, and how well can the investigation detect effects if they exist?	Any factor related to the quantitative evaluation that could affect interpretation of the findings, such as low statistical power, variability in the procedures, unreliability of the measurement, inappropriate statistical tests

Note: For further discussion of individual threats to validity in research in general or clinical and psychotherapy research more specifically, see Cook and Campbell (1979) and Kazdin (1992a), respectively.

way, and including a group that does not have the intervention so that influences occurring over time and experiences can be separated from the intervention. These are rather basic requirements and are met in most studies. More subtle influences are raised by other types of validity. For example, statistical conclusion validity refers to those factors related to evaluation of the data. Many such issues such as selection of measures, sample size, and selection of statistical tests also can influence conclusions. These issues are somewhat more subtle, not easily pointed to as flagrant flaws in evaluating a single study, and, as discussed later, not well attended to in large numbers of studies (see Kazdin, 1992a, for a further discussion).

Each type of validity raises critical points; not all potential threats to validity can be addressed in a given study because attention to one often has direct implications for another. For example, efforts to control and hold constant variables in the study are very important to minimize variability within the design. Selection of homogeneous subjects (rather than all who volunteer to receive treatment), delivering and monitoring treatment carefully, and using therapists who are trained in a similar way and whose treatment is rigorously monitored may provide an excellent test of the treatment. As rigor, control, and monitoring procedures increase, the generality of the results (external validity) may be raised as an issue. Can the results be obtained when certain constraints, controls, and rigor are relaxed? The answer may or may not be important depending on the purpose and research questions underlying the original study. In any given study of therapy, the priority accorded a particular type of validity and threat to validity may vary. For this reason methodology requires appreciation of the underlying concepts rather than application of design prescriptions and practices.

Types of experimental validity also illustrate the critical interplay between methodological and substantive issues in psychotherapy research. Consider the notion of construct validity, as highlighted in Table 2.2. An investigator may propose that cognitive therapy is effective for depression and complete a study comparing this treatment with a no-treatment control. At the end of the study, assume that the treatment group is significantly (statistically) different from the no-treatment group. The investigator may wish to discuss the impact of cognitive therapy and perhaps even how cognitive changes lead to changes in depression. With the usual procedures and controls (e.g., random assignment, group equivalence prior to treatment), the threats to internal validity are largely controlled. Given the design, issues of construct validity (interpretation of the basis for the differences) emerge.

The treatment group may have changed for a variety of reasons (e.g., relationship with the therapist, catharsis, behavioral assignments) that have little to do with cognitions. Other groups added to the design (e.g., that include these other components so their impact can be separately evaluated) and various assessment procedures (e.g., the study of cognitive changes over the course of treatment and their relation to outcome) could clarify construct validity. In short, the substantive questions and conclusions about treatment very much depend on the control conditions and assessment procedures of the study.

OVERVIEW OF ALTERNATIVE METHOD AND DESIGN OPTIONS

Research design broadly refers to the alternative arrangements or plans used in research to draw valid inferences. Research in psychotherapy is unusually rich in terms of the range of designs and evaluative practices that are in use. A consideration of the major distinctions and design methods in use follows.

Types of Investigations

Research on psychotherapy actively draws upon three major types of studies: true experiments, quasi-experiments, and passive-observational or naturalistic designs. *True experiments* consist of investigations that permit maximum control over the independent variable or manipulation of interest. The investigator is able to assign subjects to different conditions on a random basis, to vary alternative conditions (e.g., treatment and control conditions) as required by the design, and to control possible sources of bias within the study in order to permit the comparisons of interest. From the standpoint of demonstrating the impact of a particular variable of interest, true experiments permit the strongest basis for drawing inferences.

Occasionally, the investigator cannot control all features that characterize true experiments. Some facet of the study, such as the assignment of subjects to conditions or variations of treatments among subjects, cannot be controlled. *Quasi-experiments* refer to those designs in which the conditions of true experiments are approximated (Cook & Campbell, 1979). For example, an investigator may evaluate alternative treatments as conducted in a clinic or psychiatric hospital setting. The investigator wishes to use a waiting-list control group because the passage of time and course of development (e.g., history, maturation, testing, and other internal validity threats) can lead to change. Ethical and practical concerns may preclude withholding treatment. To evaluate the impact of a particular treatment, patients from other clinics receiving different treatments or who are part of a waiting list normally used at these clinics may be used to provide a comparison group of similar patients assessed without intervention. These comparison patients may be matched on a variety of characteristics to those included in treatment. Random assignment of cases to conditions is not part of the design. Even so, valid inferences can still be drawn to the extent that potential sources of bias may be made implausible within the design.

True and quasi-experiments refer primarily to studies where an independent variable is manipulated in some way, as illustrated by providing treatment or an experimental condition to some persons but not to others. In contrast, *passive-observational* investigations refer to studies where the relations among variables are observed but not manipulated (Cook & Campbell, 1979).[1] The term *passive* emphasizes the fact that the experimenter does not intervene, manipulate, and control the intervention of interest. Rather, the investigator observes variables of interest that have been allowed to vary. For example, in the context of therapy, the investigator may examine treatment delivered by different therapists. The goal may be to identify different interaction patterns that emerge and then to explain antecedent factors or client/therapist characteristics that might contribute to or predict these interaction patterns. In this example, the variables of interest (interaction patterns, client and therapist characteristics) are not manipulated by the investigator.

For didactic purposes, it is useful to delineate different types of investigation. In practice, combinations are used to address the goals of therapy research. Investigations that combine true experiments and passive-observational studies are represented by the manipulation of experimental conditions (e.g., alternative treatments) in a randomized controlled trial and the identification of cases who vary in a characteristic of interest (client – therapist variation strategy). For example, alternative treat-

ments may be evaluated among patients who differ in levels of stress or in some personality characteristic considered to relate to treatment. The impact of alternative conditions as applied to varied types of cases can yield conclusions about the separate and combined effects of these factors in therapeutic change.

Design Strategies

The ways in which the conditions are arranged in the investigation vary widely in psychotherapy research. Group designs, single-group studies, and single-case research designs illustrate the diversity of design strategies. In *group designs*, several subjects are recruited for the investigation and assigned to various groups or conditions (e.g., treatment vs. no-treatment). Clients in each group usually receive one of the treatment or control conditions. The effects of different experimental and control conditions among groups are evaluated statistically by comparing groups on the dependent measures. Preliminary assignment of subjects to groups usually is determined randomly to produce groups equivalent on factors possibly related to the independent variable (intervention) or that might also account for group differences on the measures (dependent variables). If groups are equivalent on such factors *before* the experimental manipulation or treatment, any differences among groups *after* the manipulation are assumed to result from the effects of different experimental conditions.

Psychotherapy research is also conducted with designs that do not rely on several cases or group comparisons. This is illustrated most clearly by investigation of a given individual, a few individuals, or one group over time. For example, in single-case research, one or a few subjects are studied. The dependent measures of interest are assessed on multiple occasions before, during, and after treatment. The manner in which the independent variable is implemented is examined in relation to the data pattern for the subject or group of subjects over time. Single-case designs can be used to address diverse research questions. These designs play a special role in the field because in clinical work a central concern is the treatment of individual clients. Single-case designs can be used to experimentally evaluate the impact of a given intervention or alternative interventions.

Conditions of Experimentation

The conditions under which the investigation is conducted can vary widely. To convey the diversity, consider research conducted in varied circumstances of the laboratory compared with clinical settings. *Laboratory research* often focuses on evaluation of treatment under conditions that are highly

---

[1]Historically, these designs have been referred to as correlational designs to emphasize that the studies explore relations among variables as they exist rather than as experimentally manipulated by the investigator. The term has been replaced to disentangle the design (nonmanipulation of independent variables and arrangement of selecting conditions or groups) from the methods of data analyses (e.g., correlation) (see Cook & Campbell, 1979). Passive designs can be evaluated in a variety of ways beyond correlations. Also, true experiments can be evaluated with correlation techniques, which is another reason to avoid characterizing the design by a type of statistical analysis.

controlled and often contrived for research purposes. An example might be evaluation of the performance of college students who receive instructions designed to alter their mood or engage in a discussion with an experimenter. The experimental arrangement may be posed as an analogue of processes that emerge in ongoing psychotherapy. In contrast, *clinical research* may be conducted at a treatment facility (e.g., outpatient clinic, hospital) where patients are seen for treatment. The research may evaluate the impact of different types of treatment or therapeutic processes that emerge over the course of a given treatment. In laboratory- and clinic-based research, the differences encompass more than merely the settings. Characteristics of the subjects, the nature of the dependent variable, and the research problems that emerge can vary greatly as well.

The complexities of psychotherapy often make research in the clinical setting impractical or prohibitive. Examining isolated variables or analyzing the impact of components of a treatment is often difficult, unfeasible, or ill-advised in clinical settings because of the diverse ethical responsibilities to the client and emergent practical obstacles of the setting. Consequently, treatment research is often conducted under conditions analogous to those available in the clinic or other applied setting. Research that evaluates treatment under conditions that only resemble or approximate the clinical situation has been referred to as *analogue research*. An analogue study usually focuses on a carefully defined research question under well-controlled conditions. The purpose of the research is to illuminate a particular process or to study treatment that may be important in clinical applications.

Analogue research can refer to a wide range of studies. For example, one might conduct animal laboratory research to study the development or elimination of fears. Animal analogues are critical to clinical research and have served as the basis for studying the underpinnings of treatments for various clinical problems (e.g., anxiety). Also, analogue research has consisted of interpersonal interactions in laboratory studies where interviews or personal exchanges resemble in varying degrees the interactions of a therapist and patient in psychotherapy. The analogue conditions most widely discussed have been in relation to laboratory versus clinic study of alternative treatments. In this context, an analogue study has come to mean a study in which the conditions depart from those of clinical work (see Kazdin, 1978a).

Laboratory analogue and clinical research represent end points on a continuum. Several conditions of an investigation (e.g., who is recruited for treatment, who serves as therapist, the nature and dura-

tion of the treatment) vary in the extent to which they resemble those conditions ordinarily evident in clinical work. Laboratory analogues are critically important to the goals of therapy research because they allow careful experimental control and isolation of specific processes. At the same time, a goal of therapy is to place clinical practice on firm clinical footing. To that end, it is important to ensure that treatments and mechanisms elaborated in research exert similar influences when applied. Research in clinical settings, with persons who are usually seen in treatment and are treated by professional therapists, is critical to the process.

MAJOR DESIGN STRATEGIES: SELECTIONS AND ILLUSTRATIONS

Different types of research, categories of design, and conditions of experimentation, previously highlighted, yield a vast array of design options and methods of evaluation that are used in psychotherapy research. The present section considers major design strategies and examples from contemporary research.

Group Comparison Designs

The vast majority of studies of psychotherapy consist of group designs in which alternative treatment and control conditions are compared. In group research, the basis for drawing valid inferences stems from comparing groups that receive different conditions. Typically, the study begins with selection of a number of cases, assignment of cases to different groups or conditions (e.g., treatment vs. no-treatment), and evaluation of group differences at the end of treatment. Several group designs are used in therapy research (see Kazdin, 1992a; Rosenthal & Rosnow, 1991). Two variations are considered to illustrate central strategies.

Pretest–posttest control group design. One of the most commonly used group designs in psychotherapy research is the *pretest–posttest control group design*. The design consists of a minimum of two groups. The essential feature of the design is that subjects are tested before and after the intervention. Thus, the effect of the intervention is reflected in the amount of change from pre- to posttreatment assessment. In the true experimental version of this design, subjects are assigned randomly to groups either prior to or after completion of the pretest.

As an illustration, consider the Collaborative Study for the Treatment of Depression (Elkin et al., 1989; Chapter 4, this volume). This study represents a major collaborative investigation of several researchers. The investigation was designed to evaluate three viable and well-researched treatments (cognitive therapy, interpersonal psychotherapy, and pharmacotherapy [imipramine]) compared to a placebo (pill) control condition. Among the many unique features of the study was its execution across three research sites. Approximately 160 patients (of the 250 that were randomly assigned) completed treatment and served as the basis for evaluating alternative conditions. Prior to treatment, cases completed an extensive assessment battery involving diagnostic, self-report, and clinician-report measures. Several of the measures were readministered at posttreatment and at follow-up. The design is a pretest–posttest true experimental design given the assessment and random assignment of cases to conditions. The main results of the study are described in Chapter 4 of this volume. Further reports of outcome effects, processes associated with improvement, the relation of outcome to severity of dysfunction, and related findings continue to emanate from the project.

The pretest–posttest control group design enjoys widespread use in psychotherapy research because of the many advantages that derive from the use of a pretest (see Kazdin, 1992a). First, the data obtained from the pretest allow the investigator to match cases on different variables and to assign matched sets of cases randomly to groups. Matching permits the investigator to equalize groups on pretest performance. Second and related, the pretest data permit evaluation of the effect of different levels of pretest performance. Within each group, different levels of performance (e.g., moderate vs. severe anxiety) on the pretest can be used as a separate variable in the design. Thus, the investigator can examine whether the intervention varied in impact as a function of the initial standing on the pretested measure. Third, the use of a pretest affords statistical advantages for the data analysis. By using a pretest, within-group (error) variability is reduced and more powerful statistical tests of the intervention, such as analyses of covariance or repeated measures analyses of variance, can be applied than if no pretest were used. Fourth, the pretest allows the researcher to make specific statements about change. For example, an investigator can assess how many clients improved, as determined by a certain amount of change from pre- to posttreatment for each individual. Thus, in clinical research where individual performance is very important, the pretest affords information beyond mere group differences at posttreatment. Finally, by using a pretest, the investigator can evaluate loss of subjects (attrition) in a more analytic fashion than would be the

case without a pretest. If subjects are lost over the course of the study, a comparison can be made of pretest data between those who dropped out and those who completed treatment. The analysis can test and raise hypotheses about who drops out of treatment and for what reasons.

There are considerations and potential obstacles of the design. To begin, if the pretest assessment is costly, invasive, or otherwise objectionable, ethical and practical considerations may preclude its use. This usually does not emerge in psychotherapy studies. At worst, a partial or abbreviated pretest battery could be used if the full battery of measures must be confined to the posttreatment assessment. The use of a few central measures of functioning at pretest still preserves several of the advantages of the pretest–posttest design. In psychotherapy and psychotherapy research, the use of a pretest battery is often advisable for both clinical and methodological purposes. Pretest data serve as a basis to understand client functioning, to identify the scope of domains that might warrant treatment, and to invoke inclusion and exclusion criteria for providing a particular treatment or for considering cases for an investigation.

A second consideration in using the design pertains to the possible influence of administering a pretest. It is possible that administration of a pretest battery may sensitize participants to the intervention. The effect, referred to as *pretest sensitization*, means that the intervention may have shown its effect in part because the pretest made subjects more responsive to the intervention. In treatment research, a sensitization effect is not usually viewed as an obstacle in using the design because pretest information is important clinically, because sensitization had not been shown to be a pervasive influence on results, and because its effect may be equal across conditions (see Kazdin, 1992a).

Factorial design. The evaluation of alternative treatment and control conditions in group research usually consists of investigation of a single variable (e.g., the effect of the treatment approach or some variation of a parameter of treatment). Investigation of a single variable in a study has its limitations. The main limitation is that it often raises relatively simply questions about treatment. The simplicity of the question should not demean its importance. In relatively new areas of research, the simple questions are the bedrock of subsequent research. However, more complex and refined questions can be raised to unravel the interrelations of multiple variables that can operate simultaneously to produce particular outcomes. A more intricate question might be raised by including more than one variable and asking whether certain treatments are more effective with certain types of therapists or clients. The later type of question is somewhat more specific, entails evaluation of the separate and combined effects of two or more variables, and can yield a deeper level of understanding how treatment operates.

Factorial designs allow the simultaneous investigation of two or more variables (factors) in a single investigation. Within each variable, two or more conditions are administered. In the simplest factorial design, two variables (e.g., therapist experience and type of treatment) would each consist of two different levels (e.g., experienced vs. inexperienced therapists and Treatment A vs. Treatment B). In this 2×2 design, there are four groups that represent each possible combination of the levels of the two factors.

The factorial design is not a single design but rather a family of designs that vary in the number and types of variables and the number of levels within each variable. The variation of factorial designs also is influenced by whether or not a pretest is used. If a pretest is used, testing can become one of the variables or factors (time of assessment) with two (pretest vs. posttest) or more levels. The data can be analyzed to assess whether subjects changed with repeated assessment, independently of a particular intervention.

A major reason for completing a factorial experiment is that the combined effect, that is, the interaction, of two or more variables may be of interest. Many different interaction patterns are possible in therapy research even in the simplest version of the factorial design (two variables each with two levels) (Smith & Sechrest, 1991). Generally, the interaction means that the effect of one of the variables (e.g., treatment A or B) depends on the level of one of the other variables (e.g, experience level of the therapist). Stated another way, treatment may have different effects as a function of other conditions. The importance of interactions has been repeatedly underscored in the context of psychotherapy research to assess the extent to which the impact of a given treatment may depend on a host of other factors such as who administers treatment, type of client problem, conditions of administration, duration, and so on (e.g., Beutler, 1991; Kiesler, 1971; Smith & Sechrest, 1991). These qualifiers refer to variables with which treatment is likely to interact. Finding that the effects of treatment do or do not interact with the levels of another variable may have important theoretical value by establishing how variables operate in conjunction and may have important clinical value by identifying the conditions in which favorable outcomes are and are not obtained.

As an example, Beutler and his colleagues

(1991) evaluated the impact of alternative treatments for adults with major depressive disorder. The authors predicted that treatment outcome would be influenced by patient coping styles as well as by treatment technique. Two patient characteristics were studied, namely, internalizing/externalizing style (e.g., self-punishing vs. acting out styles) and resistance potential (defensiveness). Three treatments (cognitive therapy, experiential therapy, and supportive self-directed treatment) were compared. Generally, few overall differences (main effects) were found at posttreatment. As the authors point out, this finding could lead to the conclusions that treatments are equally effective. However, interactions were found indicating that the impact of alternative treatments varied considerably as a function of client characteristics. Among the salient patterns, cognitive therapy was more effective for persons with an externalizing coping style; the same type of patient did poorly with supportive therapy. In relation to defensiveness, supportive therapy was more effective with defensive persons; cognitive therapy was more effective with less defensive persons. The type of research illustrated by this example is more sophisticated than a study of treatment technique alone in the sense of the type of predictions that are made. Different types of variables (treatment, subject) are combined. Although the usual control conditions might be used, the question focuses on comparison groups that are comprised of combinations of treatment and subject characteristics.

The strength of a factorial design is that it can assess the effects of separate variables in a single study. This feature is economical because different variables can be studied with fewer subjects and observations in a factorial design than in a series of single-variable studies of the individual variables. In addition, the factorial design provides unique information about the combined effects of the independent variables.

The concerns about using the factorial designs are both practical and interpretive. On the practical side, the number of groups in the investigation multiplies quickly as new factors or new levels of a given factor are added. A 2×2 design with 4 groups quickly extends to a large-scale study of 8 groups if another factor with even the minimum number of levels (2) is added. As a general point, the number of groups in a study may quickly become prohibitive as factors and levels are increased. In practice, there are constraints in the number of subjects that can be run in a given study and the number of factors (variables) that can be easily studied.

A related issue is interpreting the results of multiple-factor experiments. Factorial designs are optimally informative when an investigator predicts interactions among two or more variables. Simple interactions involving two or three variables often are relatively straightforward to interpret. Yet, when multiple variables interact, the investigator may be at a loss to describe the complex relation in a coherent fashion, let alone offer an informed or theoretically plausible explanation. A factorial design is useful for evaluating the separate and combined effects of variables of interest when these variables are conceptually related and predicted to generate interactive effects. The inclusion of factors in the design is dictated by conceptual considerations of those variables and the interpretability of the predicted relations.

General comments.   Among group designs, the pretest – posttest control designs characterize the bulk of research. Factorial designs, less commonly used, reflect the type of question that research strives to answer, namely, the combined influences of different variables. The critical feature of all group designs in the use of two or more groups. The specific groups, of course, depend on the question of interest. Among the groups commonly included are no-treatment and waiting-list control groups. These groups are included to control for the many threats to internal validity mentioned previously. These groups permit us to ask whether the impact of treatment surpasses the changes that are otherwise made due to other influences in time and indeed within the investigation (e.g., repeated testing on the assessment battery). As the questions increase in sophistication, the nature of the control or comparison groups varies. Efforts to control for contact with the therapist (so called "attention-placebo" control groups) or to compare alternative treatments with each other (e.g., alternative variations of a given treatment) often address matters of construct validity (i.e., they attempt to elaborate the basis for group treatment effects). The prior discussion of treatment evaluation strategies and the questions they pose illustrates the comparisons that are made to address specific questions. The nature of the question dictates the type of comparison group or condition essential to the design (see Kazdin, 1992a).

Single-Group and Small Sample Designs

Group designs dominate psychotherapy research. Nevertheless, a number of design options are available that do not depend primarily on group comparisons as the basis of drawing valid inferences. In a single-group study, each subject in the group receives the same experimental condition (treatment); no control or comparison is included in the usual fashion. Differences that emerge within the group serve as the basis of study. In this sense, subgroups that naturally emerge are delineated to examine variation within the group.

As an illustration, Rounsaville et al. (1986) examined the relation of alternative therapy processes in predicting outcome for the treatment of depression. Patients ($N = 35$) received interpersonal psychotherapy for depression. Therapists ($N = 11$) who provided treatment were evaluated by their supervisors after observing tapes of several therapy sessions. Processes rated by the supervisors included therapist (exploration, warmth, and friendliness, and negative attitude) and patient factors (participation, exploration, hostility, psychic distress). This was a passive-observational (naturalistic) study in the sense that therapist and patient variables were not manipulated in the design. Treatment outcome was assessed with measures of psychiatric symptoms, social functioning, and patient-evaluated change.

The results indicated that one patient factor (hostility) was related to outcome on a measure of change completed by the patients. In contrast, a number of therapist factors were strongly related to outcome. Therapist exploration was significantly and positively related to reductions in clinician evaluations of depression and patient-rated improvements. Therapist warmth and friendliness correlated significantly with improved social functioning and patient-rated improvements. These results convey the importance of specific therapist characteristics as a contributor to treatment outcome. In this study, no control or comparison was used. The purpose was to correlate specific processes with specific outcomes within a particular technique. The correlational nature of the study means that some other constructs that might have varied with therapist processes (e.g., experience of the therapist) could account for the results. As is invariably the case, further research can help to establish the plausibility of alternative interpretations.

Studies of small samples are particularly important in psychotherapy research to examine complex interaction sequences between therapists and patients. The focus is on detailed and fine-gained elaboration of such facets of treatment as moment-to-moment changes in therapists, patients, and their combination; emergent treatment processes within or over the course of sessions; and sequences or patterns of events (e.g., language changes over time). A small number of subjects studied intensively are extremely useful to address these issues.

As an illustration, Henry, Schacht, and Strupp (1986) described the problematic interaction sequences between therapists and patients. The authors evaluated complementarity (in which communication of one participant is considered to "pull" for a complementary communication from the other) and multiple communications (communicating more than one message). Four therapists were studied; for each therapist a case with a "good" or "poor" outcome was selected. Outcome was defined by changes in symptom scores and target complaints (e.g., MMPI changes). The authors used the structural analysis of social behavior (SASB) method to evaluate therapist–patient interactions. Specifically, therapy transcripts from one treatment session (third session) were coded to evaluate interaction. The analyses indicated that cases with "good" treatment outcomes had greater complementarity; cases with "poorer" outcomes had greater levels of multiple communications. The design utilized a very small number of cases (four therapists, eight patients). The intensive and detailed measurement served as a microscope to make complex interaction sequences visible and sensitive to analysis.

Single-Case Designs

In single-case experimental designs, inferences can be drawn about intervention effects by utilizing the subject as his or her own control (see Barlow & Hersen, 1984; Kazdin, 1982). The underlying rationale of single-case experimental designs is similar to that of the more familiar group designs. Virtually all experiments compare the effects of different conditions (independent variables) on performance. In group experimentation, the comparison is made between groups of subjects who are treated differently. In single-case research, inferences usually are made about the effects of the intervention by comparing different conditions presented to the same subject over time.

Experimentation with the single case has special requirements that must be met if inferences are to be drawn about the effects of the intervention. First, client performance is assessed in some way (e.g., self-report, direct observation) on several occasions, usually before the intervention is applied and continuously over the period while the intervention is in effect. Typically, observations are conducted on a daily basis or at least a few times each week. Continuous assessment allows the investigator to examine the pattern and stability of performance (e.g., frequency or severity of anxiety symptoms) before treatment is initiated. This initial period of observation, referred to as the *baseline phase*, provides information about the level of behavior before the intervention begins. The baseline phase is intended to describe the existing level of performance and to predict the level of performance for the immediate future if the intervention were not provided. To evaluate the impact of an intervention in single-case research, it is important to have an idea of what performance would be like in the future without the intervention. When the intervention is presented or altered over the course of treatment, performance is evaluated against the level of baseline performance.

A second requirement of the designs is the delineation of separate phases or periods in which alternative conditions (e.g., baseline, treatment, alternative treatments) are in effect. Typically, the designs begin with baseline observations to describe the existing level of functioning and to predict tentatively how performance would be if current conditions (no-treatment) continued. Treatment is implemented and observations continue to be made to identify if the level of functioning departs from the baseline level and the level tentatively predicted from baseline. A number of experimental and quasi-experimental single-case designs are available to evaluate treatment (see Barlow & Hersen, 1984; Kazdin, 1982).

As an example, Ronen (1991) treated a four-year-old girl who had been suffering sleep problems. The child would not fall asleep in her bed, awoke when placed in her bed, and engaged in tantrums throughout the night. A behavioral intervention was implemented to manage her sleep routine. The intervention was developed in consultation with a therapist but carried out by the child's parents at home. The intervention consisted of reinforcement (e.g., praise, attention, candy) for more appropriate sleep behaviors and extinction of tantrums, and time out for inappropriate behaviors. Observations by the parents were obtained daily for several behaviors. After baseline information was obtained, the intervention was applied to the separate behaviors in sequence, an arrangement referred to as a multiple-baseline design. Figure 2.1 conveys the behaviors, observations, and points in time when the intervention was introduced. The figure shows child performance during baseline before the intervention was implemented (Phase I). The intervention (Phase II) was introduced to each behavior at different points in time. The pattern of change suggests that the intervention was responsible for change; the reason is that each behavior changed when the intervention was introduced. The most plausible interpretation of this pattern is that the intervention rather than some other event occurring in time led to change. Assessment continued over a period of weeks to evaluate follow-up (Phase III). The follow-up assessment suggests that the gains were maintained.

Single-case designs have been utilized in several studies in which treatment effects have been successfully documented with diverse clinical problems (Kazdin, 1989). The use of one or a few subjects

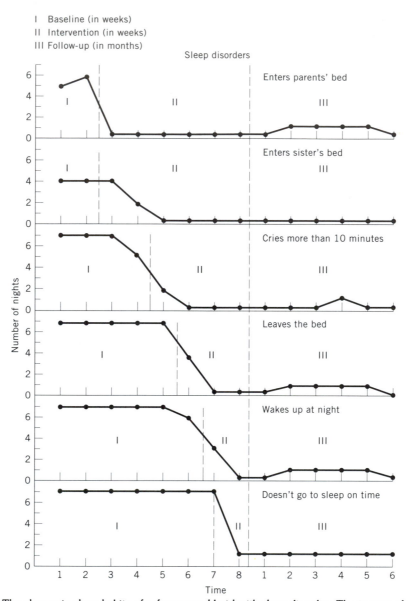

I Baseline (in weeks)
II Intervention (in weeks)
III Follow-up (in months)

Sleep disorders

Enters parents' bed

Enters sister's bed

Cries more than 10 minutes

Leaves the bed

Wakes up at night

Doesn't go to sleep on time

Number of nights

Time

FIGURE 2.1   The change in sleep habits of a four-year-old girl with sleep disorder. The impact of the intervention is demonstrated in a multiple-baseline design. After baseline data were obtained on each behavior (Phase I), the intervention was introduced (Phase II) separately across each of the different behaviors. Each behavior changed when the intervention was introduced; with some exceptions behavior change closely followed the application of the intervention to that behavior. Consequently, the pattern of change suggests that the intervention, rather than more general extraneous influences, accounts for the changes. In the final phase (III), follow-up data were gathered. Reprinted with permission from Ronen (1991), Pergamon Press Ltd.

often evokes concern with the generality (external validity) of the results among cases. However, this is not necessarily an inherent problem with the designs or necessarily even reasonable as a threat to external validity unless specific hypotheses can be offered making the lack of generality plausible.

There are a number of considerations that warrant mention. First, the designs often impose special requirements about implementing treatment

that are not always feasible in clinical settings. A few design options, for example, require withdrawing treatment to demonstrate experimental control. There are a variety of design options that do not make this requirement (see Kazdin, 1982). The designs as a rule include a number of conditions (e.g., evaluation of ongoing treatment, feedback to both therapist and client regarding progress on the treatment goals) that make them quite feasible for clinical work. Second, in the context of treatment evaluation, single-case designs have been restricted largely to evaluation of behavioral and cognitive-behavioral treatments (see Kazdin, 1978b). Yet, the designs are quite suitable for more general treatment evaluation that is independent of the conceptual origin of that technique. Application of the designs to evaluate other types of interventions such as psychoanalysis and paradoxical intention attests to their broader utility (Fonagy & Moran, 1990; Kolko & Milan, 1983).

A final consideration regarding the designs is the type of question they address. By and large, most of the questions that guide treatment, as reflected in the treatment evaluation strategies, can be addressed in the context of single-case designs. A critical but important exception is the evaluation of interactions of client and therapist factors in relation to treatment. The use of one or a few cases does not provide an immediate method of evaluating client $\times$ treatment interactions. Also, if two or three persons are treated and respond differently, there is no clear way to analyze the probable basis for this difference. In group designs, subanalyses and post hoc statistical analyses often provide useful guides to evaluate subject differences as a factor in the design to generate hypotheses about differential responsiveness to treatment. In single-case designs with a few subjects, exploratory statistical analyses to evaluate various subject characteristics (e.g., age, sex, type of dysfunction) are not feasible because of the very small number of cases.

Meta-Analysis

The prior discussion of alternative designs considered individual investigations where conclusions are drawn on the basis of data subjects provide across various conditions within an investigation. Alternative ways of arranging conditions among subjects is the way one usually conceives of testing hypotheses about therapy and evaluating intervention effects. Within the last 15–20 years, meta-analysis has emerged as a method and design strategy to test hypotheses and to evaluate alternative conditions of interest (see Bangert-Drowns, 1986; Rosenthal, 1984; Smith et al., 1980).

Meta-analysis is a procedure that summarizes a large number of studies. The basic unit of analysis is effect size from individual investigations. Effect size provides a common metric across a variety of investigations. Typically, effect size is calculated as the difference between means of an experimental (e.g., psychotherapy) and control (e.g., no-treatment) group divided by the standard deviation (either of the control group or the pooled sample of both groups). Symbolically this is represented by:

$$ES = \frac{m_1 - m_2}{s}$$

where

m_1 = the mean of the treatment group
m_2 = the mean of the control group
s = the pooled standard deviation.

Effect size can be computed from the means and standard deviations provided for the groups included in the study or derived from other statistics reported within the study (e.g., χ^2, t, F, r). The terms m_1 and m_2 can stand for the means of any two groups of interest such as two different types of therapy conditions; in the usual case, treatment versus no-treatment have been the two groups.

The utility of the statistic is that it can convert any measure to a common metric. Thus, within a given study, separate outcome measures can be converted to effect sizes. Across a large set of studies, these effect sizes can be combined and compared to address specific questions about treatment. To translate the effect sizes into more meaningful terms, consider the differences in means that the effect represents and the impact of treatment on the average client. Effect size refers to group differences in standard deviation units on the "normal" distribution. For example, comparison of treatment versus no-treatment across a large number of studies might yield an overall effect size of .70, the magnitude very similar to that found in meta-analyes of adult and child psychotherapy. Two hypothetical distributions of scores might be drawn to reflect performance of clients who do not receive treatment (controls) and those who do. The distributions reflect hypothetical scores on some measure of treatment outcome (e.g., symptom ratings). Assume for the moment that a bell-shaped (normal) curve reflects the performance of clients on the measures at posttreatment assessment within the individual groups. The bell-shaped curve not only provides a reasonable assumption about the likely distribution of scores but also facilitates evaluation of the impact of treatment on the average client.

Figure 2.2 shows two hypothetical distributions with the mean difference in outcome separated by .70 standard deviation units (i.e., mean effect size). This difference or degree of separation in standard deviation units can be converted into differences in percentages of clients at a given point or level of improvement on the measure. One can compare how persons in the treatment group are likely to fare relative to persons in the no-treatment group. Given the effect size, the average client who is treated is better off at the end of therapy than 76

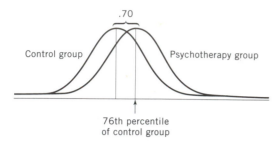

.70

Control group   Psychotherapy group

76th percentile
of control group

FIGURE 2.2 Representation of the effect of psychotherapy across outcome measures based on meta-analysis. The illustration is hypothetical to show how an effect size of a given magnitude, in this case .70, translates to differences in the distributions of treatment and no-treatment control clients.

percent of the persons who did not receive treatment. Therapy is clearly effective on the average in improving clients.

Of course, few researchers, least of all those involved in psychotherapy, are concerned with treatment for the average client. The goal of identifying effect size is to conduct an evaluation of psychotherapy research. In a meta-analysis, effect size is used as the dependent variable. Characteristics of the investigations included in the analyses become the independent variables. These characteristics may encompass the full range of variables that distinguish studies, including different treatment techniques, types of clinical problems, assessment devices, settings in which treatment is applied, and so on.

The initial meta-analysis of psychotherapy (Smith & Glass, 1977) and its subsequent expansion (Smith et al., 1980) encompassed hundreds of outcome studies. Since those analyses, scores of meta-analyses have been completed. Many of these address broad literatures encompassing, for example, a range of psychotherapies for adults, children, and adolescents (e.g., Brown, 1987; Casey & Berman, 1983; Shapiro & Shapiro, 1982; Weisz, Weiss, Alicke, & Klotz, 1987). Other meta-analyses have focused on specific treatment approaches such as short-term psychodynamic therapy (Svartberg & Stiles, 1991), family therapy (Hazelrigg, Cooper, & Borduin, 1987), and paradoxical interventions (Shoham-Salomon & Rosenthal, 1987) and on specific treatments as applied to specific types of dysfunction such as cognitive therapy for depression (Dobson, 1989), social skills training for schizophrenia (Benton & Schroeder, 1990), and behavioral treatment for marital distress (Hahlweg & Markman, 1988), to mention a few.

Meta-analyses have served several interrelated uses in relation to psychotherapy research. First, the analyses have been used as a means of sum-

marizing a body of literature. In this use, meta-analysis is referred to as a quantitative review of a literature and is distinguished from a qualitative or more narrative review of the literature. An advantage of the quantitative procedure for reviewing is that decisions, rules, and judgments about the literature and how studies are to be considered, counted, and weighed are made explicit.

Second, and more critical for purposes of illustrating alternative designs in psychotherapy research, is the use of meta-analysis to test, evaluate, and generate hypotheses. Consider two general types of hypotheses that can be evaluated by meta-analysis. To begin, many variables can be studied within the context of a single investigation. Questions about the impact of alternative treatments, the interaction of treatment and client variables, and parametric variations of treatment usually serve as the basis of individual psychotherapy studies. These studies then, of course, can be combined in a summary fashion to be studied in meta-analyses.

In addition, meta-analysis can examine variables and questions that are not readily addressed in a single study, including many questions of interest that span several studies, such as the impact of different approaches to treatment (e.g., family therapies vs. cognitive therapies), selected methodological features (e.g., random assignment), and type of measurement strategy (e.g., clinician vs. self-report). The impact of these variables on outcome (effect size) is addressed by classifying studies on the characteristics (variables) of interest and analyzing the impact of these characteristics on effect size. Individual studies that were not designed or capable of addressing various hypotheses can be utilized in a meta-analysis to address these hypotheses. This use of individual studies as a unit of analysis is particularly noteworthy in an area of research such as psychotherapy where completion of investigations may require protracted periods and tests of some variables within a single investigation (e.g., therapist characteristics, type of patient dysfunction) that are difficult to address (e.g., Crits-Christoph et al., 1991). Utilizing a large number of studies as a way to test novel hypotheses that cannot be addressed in any single study is an efficient use of the research base.

A third use and methodological benefit of meta-analysis has been the identification of deficiencies in the reporting of psychotherapy research. Meta-analysis relies upon classifying studies on a variety of characteristics of interest to the investigator. Efforts to code studies on alternative characteristics have made salient several deficiencies in the conduct or reporting of psychotherapy research. For example, Shapiro and Shapiro (1983) noted significant inadequacies in the reporting of research revealed in their meta-analytic review of psychotherapy research. Only 60 percent of the studies they reviewed included means and standard deviations. Other critical information was missing, including the number of therapists (from 26% of the studies), experience of the therapists (from 37% of the studies), information about subject attrition (from 19% of the studies), and whether persons who completed assessments were "blind" to subject conditions (from 45% of the studies). The information omitted from individual reports often is pertinent to design and hence to the conclusions that can be drawn.

Additional meta-analyses have identified methodological issues in relation to therapy research, including the frequent use of small sample sizes and insufficient power to detect differences when two or more treatments are compared, the paucity of studies that evaluate treatment integrity, the absence of follow-up information, and the brevity of follow-up among studies that do obtain such information (Kazdin & Bass, 1989; Kazdin et al., 1990; Weiss & Weisz, 1990). In many cases, the information about deficiencies in research is not new. Meta-analyses have made the prevalence of selected deficiencies more salient. The effect has been to sensitize researchers to the need for further information in the reporting of research to permit evaluation of individual investigations and the further use and integration through quantitative reviews.

As a related influence, meta-analysis has sensitized researchers to the notion of effect size in general and to consideration of the impact of treatment, a point to which we shall return. Here again, a concern with the magnitude of impact that an intervention produces is not new (see Mullen, 1989). Meta-analysis has contributed by emphasizing the question of impact directly through its translation of tests of statistical significance into a measure of magnitude of effect. Recommendations have been made for incorporating effect size estimates routinely into research (e.g., Rosenthal, 1984) to improve the yield from individual studies as well as to more readily permit integration of the studies in subsequent analyses.

Meta-analysis has carved a significant role in the methodological approaches to evaluation in general. The method is mentioned here as a type of design strategy because it can be used to test and to generate hypotheses about psychotherapy. The impact of meta-analysis on psychotherapy evaluation has been remarkable, as well as controversial. Salient methodological points of contention include how to compute effect sizes, whether studies of varying degrees of methodological rigor ought to be included, whether combinations of techniques into broad classes (e.g., behavior therapy, family therapy) can be meaningfully interpreted, how alternative outcome measures ought to be weighted (in computing effects size) and analyzed, the coding of nonsignificant findings within individual studies, whether studies should be weighted differently based on their sample size or number of outcome measures, whether and how inferential statistical techniques are to be used to evaluate effect sizes, and others (see Garfield, 1983a; Michelson, 1985; Mullen, 1989). The quantitative nature of meta-analyses has led to unrealistic expectations that the method provides a degree of objectivity that is not captured by other forms of review and analyses. However, there are many assumptions and subjective decisions that underlie quantitative rules on which a given meta-analysis and its conclusions depend (e.g., Matt, 1989; Wanous, Sullivan, & Malinak, 1989). In general, there needs to be broad recognition that many forms of "analysis," whether meta-, psycho-, regression, factor, or cluster, include assumptions and presuppositions that can be challenged. In the case of meta-analysis, the ability to make several of these explicit and to deploy the method to address fundamental questions about treatment have been major advantages.

General Comments
Group, small sample, and single-subject designs reflect primary level studies insofar as each is drawn upon data generated by subjects. Meta-analysis represents a secondary level study insofar as investigations, rather than data from subjects, serve as the source of data. The diversity of approaches in psychotherapy research is underscored by the scope of design approaches from the focus on the single-case to scores of investigations via meta-analysis. The breadth of designs is vital to the field and contributes to the advances. The reason is that each particular design strategy alone has its weaknesses. The use of different designs expands upon the range of questions that can be addressed about therapy and the individuals to whom it is applied and provides opportunities of convergence when different designs can be used to evaluate similar questions.

The availability of design options does not itself improve the yield of psychotherapy research. An essential requirement is to utilize the designs to address conceptually important questions and to test and to generate hypotheses that will deepen our understanding. Sophisticated methods alone will not accomplish that. Consider, for example, the use of meta-analysis. The majority of analyses have focused on overall effects of therapy, particularly broad classes of treatment (e.g., psychodynamic, behavioral). The impact is evaluated to seek main effects of a given treatment and possible interactions with somewhat straightforward descriptive variables (e.g., client sex and age, therapist experience) that may mediate treatment outcome. The tests and variables under investigation are rarely based on conceptualization of therapy, the process of therapeutic change, or underlying theory about treatment. Consequently, the yield often is difficult to interpret. For example, client sex and age and therapist experience are broad labels that are not informative without specifying the processes of these variables that might affect outcome. What processes, factors, or mechanisms underlie these and other variables? Elaboration of the processes would lead to different ways to operationalize and to measure the variables and potentially augment our understanding of treatment (e.g., Shadish & Sweeney, 1991).

The concerns raised here are not unique to meta-analysis. There has been a broader concern that theory and conceptualization of therapy have a diminished role in psychotherapy research (Omer & Dar, 1992). Alternative designs can be of use in exploring data and in generating hypotheses. However, their primary value stems from serving as aids to understanding. Testing informed and conceptually driven views of therapy and therapeutic change is a prerequisite.

METHODOLOGICAL ISSUES AND PRACTICES

Alternative designs reviewed previously denote the ways in which the intervention and other conditions of the investigation are arranged to evaluate hypotheses about treatment. Methodological practices and decision points in the execution of the study are critical to varied design options. How the study is conducted affects the extent to which clear inferences can be drawn and the extent to which a given study can be integrated with other studies into a broader knowledge base. Several practices and issues related to how psychotherapy research is conducted are discussed next.

Identification and Specification of Clinical Dysfunction

Among the goals of treatment research is the understanding of the persons for whom and clinical problems for which alternative treatments are effective. Critical to the goal is the careful delineation of the cases or subjects and their dysfunction. The domains that are relevant to characterize the cases may be broad and include various subject and demographic variables (e.g., age, sex, race, ethnicity, socioeconomic status). Mention of the need for

basic descriptive information would seem to be obvious. Surprisingly perhaps, evaluation of the reporting practices of psychotherapy research indicates that the majority of studies do not include information regarding economic status, race, and education of the participants (Francis & Aronson, 1990). Sex, age, and type of dysfunction are not invariably reported either. Basic descriptive information is critically important because the variables may contribute to the generality (external validity) of the findings and be relevant to further efforts to replicate treatment effects.

The scope, type, severity, and breadth of symptoms are particularly central. These characteristics reflect facets of dysfunction presumably underlying the rationale for treatment. Performance on diagnostic interviews and multidimensional scales that are relatively standardized or commonly used (e.g., Symptom Checklist 90, Minnesota Multiphasic Personality Inventory) provides data that are likely to permit comparisons across studies. The absence of such information increases the difficulty in determining the persons for whom treatment in a given study was effective.

In general, there is no standardized or agreed upon method of describing clinical dysfunctions that is in widespread use in psychotherapy research. Psychiatric diagnosis as a means of classifying clinical dysfunction might be a prima facie candidate. The focus of treatment often is directed toward clinical dysfunction. Moreover, diagnostic systems such as the DSM enjoy international use (Maser, Kaelber, & Weise, 1991). Diagnostic classification, however, is not necessarily the method of choice upon which to delineate cases for psychotherapy research for a variety of reasons. To begin with, diagnosis is not based on any particular theory of dysfunction. In contrast, alternative treatments as applied to alternative dysfunctions often draw upon conceptual models to characterize patients in more specific and molecular ways than diagnosis allows. Thus, there is no strong a priori conceptual reason to utilize diagnosis to predict treatment $\times$ diagnosis interactions in general (Beutler, 1991). Moreover, for the vast majority of diagnoses, the empirical base for recommending which treatments for which disorders is very weak (Karasu, 1990). Second, diagnostic categories themselves are tentative hypotheses about how to organize symptom patterns. The patterns currently recognized vary in the extent to which they can be reliably assessed and validly delineated; this is not a criticism of diagnosis but rather a statement of the empirical status of delineating dysfunction. The point, in relation to psychotherapy research, is that diagnostic categories themselves are developing based on theory and research. Diagnosis can be a useful way of describing patients to facilitate communication and in some cases data analyses, but it is only one way of delineating dysfunction.

In a few areas of treatment research, commonly used diagnostic and assessment practices have emerged to permit accumulation of information. For example, in the treatment of depression, studies routinely specify that the persons included in treatment met diagnostic criteria (e.g., DSM-III-R, Research Diagnostic Criteria) for Major Depressive Disorder or have met specific cutoff scores on standardized and widely used measures (e.g., Beck Depression Inventory, Hamilton Rating Scale for Depression). Studies are by no means uniform in how they invoke these criteria. Yet from the standpoint of methodological practices, specification of level of severity on a standardized measure and the use of diagnostic criteria are exemplary because the criteria are explicit.

Diagnostic assessment and the use of standardized assessments within a given domain of clinical dysfunction can facilitate accretion of the knowledge base. Without agreed upon systems or assessments, it is important to advocate the general principle — to wit, scope, type, severity, and breadth of clinical dysfunction should be carefully assessed in treatment research. As part of the explicit description, it is useful to specify exclusion and inclusion criteria for case selection (see Garfield, 1983b). Inclusion and exclusion criteria clarify the boundaries of the sample and the presence or absence of other (comorbid) conditions besides the primary condition of interest that might influence the findings. Explicit and thorough specification of the problem permits replication of findings of other investigators and optimizes the possibility of analyzing and re-evaluating client characteristics across several studies as in meta-analyses.

Subject Assignment and Group Formation

In psychotherapy research involving group designs, the manner of assignment of subjects to groups is pivotal. The relative impact of alternative treatments or the impact of treatment versus no-treatment is usually determined on the basis of group differences on various dependent measures. A rudimentary axiom of design is that there must be some assurance that groups would not have differed without the experimental manipulation or interventions. The manner in which subjects are assigned to groups influences the confidence that one can place in the initial group equivalence and consequently the likelihood that subsequent group differences reflect the effects of the manipulation.

Once a sample of subjects has been specified, individual members can be assigned to groups in an unbiased fashion. Random assignment consists of allocating subjects to groups in such a way that the probability of each subject's appearing in any of the groups is equal. Usually this is accomplished by determining the group to which each subject is assigned by a table of random numbers. For power (sensitivity) of statistical tests and convenience in conducting several statistical analyses, it is better to have equal rather than unequal group sizes. Ensuring that groups are equal in size and similar on selected characteristics (e.g., sex, age) can be accomplished without violating random assignment. Subjects are grouped into sets or blocks that are similar in the characteristic(s) of interest. The number of subjects within a set or block is equal to the number of groups or conditions within the study. Subjects within each set or block of subjects are assigned randomly to conditions.

Random assignment is important as a means of distributing characteristics of the sample among groups. There are several subject characteristics (e.g., age, sex, motivation for participation), circumstances of participation (e.g., how referred, order of appearance or entry into the study), and other factors that might, if uncontrolled, interfere with interpretation of group differences. In some studies, evaluating the impact of these variables may be the central purpose. In other studies, they might be regarded as "nuisance" variables that, if uncontrolled, may obscure interpretation. Random assignment is an effort to distribute nuisance variables unsystematically across groups. An advantage of random assignment is that it does not require the investigator to be aware of all of the important variables that might be related to the outcome of the investigation. Over an infinite number of subjects, the many different nuisance variables can be assumed to be distributed evenly among groups.

In a given study, random assignment does not necessarily produce equivalent groups. With random assignment, the likelihood that groups are equivalent increases as a function of the size of the sample. This means that with small samples, equivalence of the groups may not be assumed. This is especially relevant to studies of psychotherapy where sample sizes typically are relatively small (e.g., 10 – 20 subjects per group) (see Kazdin & Bass, 1989; Shapiro & Shapiro, 1983). When the total sample is relatively small (e.g., 24 subjects total in a 2-group study), the likelihood that groups are *not* equivalent across a number of nuisance variables can be high (Hsu, 1989). The net effect is that at the end of the study, the difference between groups due to the intervention may be obscured or misrepresented because of the nonequivalence of groups (see Hsu, 1989; Strube, 1991).

Investigators wish to establish that the groups are equivalent by comparing groups after their random assignment on such variables as age, sex, IQ, years of institutionalization, pretest performance on the measure of interest, and so on. The absence of differences (nonsignificant t tests or analyses of variance) may provide false comfort that the groups are equivalent. When the samples are relatively small, statistical tests are not sufficiently powerful to reveal group differences on variables that might well influence the results. Thus, the situation in which random assignment is least likely to obtain equivalence (small samples) is also one in which such differences may be the most difficult to detect. With larger samples, the absence of differences between groups on alternative subject variables and pretreatment measures provides greater assurance of group equivalence.

In general, random assignment remains vitally important as a concept and procedure. Interestingly, there is a belief that the procedure guarantees group equivalence in situations when this is not likely, that is, when the sample size is relatively small (Hsu, 1989; Tversky & Kahneman, 1971). Use of larger than usual sample sizes (e.g., > 40 subjects in each group) or more precise preassignment blocking can increase the confidence in the equivalence of groups.

Treatment Administration

Representativeness of treatment. A pivotal issue in designing a treatment outcome study is ensuring that the treatment will be fairly and faithfully represented. This warrants consideration before the study begins to ensure that the test is not a unique or idiosyncratic application that has little relation to the treatment as usually conceived, practiced, or researched. The need to address this issue *before* carrying out the treatments has become especially clear in comparative outcome studies (e.g., DiLoreto, 1971; Paul, 1966; Sloane, Staples, Cristol, Yorkston, & Whipple, 1975). The results of such studies are often discounted by critics after the fact because the specific treatments, as tested, did not represent their usual application in practice (e.g., Boy, 1971; Ellis, 1971; Heimberg & Becker, 1984; Rachman & Wilson, 1980; Roback, 1971).

As a more recent example, Snyder and his colleagues (1991; Snyder & Wills, 1989) reported a study that compared behavioral marital therapy and insight-oriented therapy for the treatment of marital discord. The results indicated no differences at posttreatment and at six-month follow-up on several standardized and commonly used measures of marital adjustment. At a four-year follow-up, a significantly greater percentage of couples in the behavior condition had been divorced. An issue that has emerged is the representativeness of treatment (behavioral, insight-oriented) and the implications for interpretation of the findings (Collins &

Thompson, 1988; Jacobson, 1991). Scrutiny of the treatment manuals for each intervention has raised ambiguities about treatments and the conclusions to be drawn from the study. Specifically, Jacobson (1991) noted that the insight-oriented treatment resembled behavioral marital training used in contemporary research and practice more than the behavioral treatment used in the study. The challenge raises questions about the extent to which the insight-oriented therapy represented that modality of treatment. Both treatments in the study could be considered variations of behavioral management training rather than competing treatments. The more effective version, Jacobson maintained, is consistent with existing results from other studies on the impact of behavioral treatment.

As a general statement, efforts to evaluate treatment can profit from assurances that the treatments are representative of the approach or versions the study is designed to test. In many cases, it may be difficult to select and evaluate treatments that are known or established as faithful renditions of the treatments. Perhaps the main issue is that rarely is there a single, agreed upon, or standardized method that can be gleaned from prior research or clinical practice. Thus, investigators usually develop treatment guidelines and manuals to make explicit those procedures that are poorly specified or highly variable in clinical work. Also, in clinical work the therapist has the luxury and obligation to vary critical dimensions of treatment (e.g., number of sessions, focus of content) in response to changes or lack of changes in the patient. Some of the departures in research are intentional to help standardize treatment or to evaluate treatment by itself without the addition of many accoutrements or other interventions that clinicians are wont to introduce.

Prior to the investigation, those features of treatment that might depart from standard practice to permit experimental investigation should be specified. Even more important, it is essential to ensure that treatment reflects or represents a reasonable variation or approximation of the treatment of interest. Currently there are no standard ways to evaluate at the inception of a study whether the treatment faithfully represents the intervention(s) of interest. One alternative is to develop the treatment in manual form and to submit the manual to proponents and practitioners of the technique (Sechrest, West, Phillips, Redner, & Yeaton, 1979). The experts can examine whether specific procedures are faithfully represented and whether the strength and dose of treatment (e.g., duration, number of sessions) are reasonable. The information so gained might be useful to revise the manual to represent treatment better. Another alternative is to rely on existing manuals of treatment for the techniques of interest, as discussed next.

Treatment manuals. Treatment manuals consist of written materials to guide the therapist in procedures, techniques, themes, therapeutic maneuvers, and actions. Over the past $10-15$ years in particular, a large number of treatment manuals have emerged; they encompass psychodynamic, psychoanalytic, behavioral, cognitive, family, interpersonal, experiential, and other therapies (see Lambert & Ogles, 1988; Luborsky & DeRubeis, 1984). The manuals represent an effort to operationalize to the extent possible the practices that constitute "doing therapy" according to a particular approach. Clinical researchers recognize that manuals do not mirror or reflect all that transpires within treatment or the sessions any more than a "map is the terrain."

There are obvious methodological advantages of the development and use of treatment manuals. First, the codification of treatment in manual form permits therapist training in light of prespecified procedures and monitoring of adherence to these procedures. Both of these are likely to minimize variability in treatment delivery and to increase the sensitivity of a test that compares different treatment conditions. Variability between therapists who apply treatment appears to be reduced when treatment manuals are used (Crits-Christoph et al., 1991). From a methodological standpoint, reduction of such variability is desirable unless therapist differences are the substantive focus of the study. Second, the prospect of replication research is enhanced when manuals are available. Manuals provide explicit statements about how treatment is implemented, often on a session-by-session basis, which is extraordinarily helpful to researchers who wish to replicate treatment. Third, interpretation of treatment outcomes is enhanced when manuals are available. An example was noted previously in which the outcome results of two treatments were reinterpreted based on scrutiny of the manuals (Jacobson, 1991). Reinterpretation can raise hypotheses about potentially critical but neglected features of treatment within the manuals that would not otherwise be retrieved without codification of the intervention.

Beyond methodological advantages, it is worth noting other advances that the development of treatment manuals provide. Manuals permit extension of treatments to clinical practice.[2] The use of

manuals allows persons involved in clinical practice to explore the impact of treatments investigated in research. This feature can help narrow the hiatus between research and clinical practice. In addition, within a given research program, manualized treatments can be revised. The accumulation of experience and research findings can be codified in manual revisions so that the gains of an investigative team are not lost.

Although treatment manuals represent a methodological advance, they have raised concerns as well. In clinical research, one concern is that manuals may lead to rigid application of treatment without responding to the "needs of the individual client," that complex processes of therapy cannot be adequately captured in manualized form, and that technique variables are emphasized and specified at the expense of other variables (see Crits-Christoph et al., 1991; Dobson & Shaw, 1988). Manuals represent an effort to operationalize treatment. As with any operationalization effort, the result is not necessarily complete or reflective of all dimensions of interest. Concerns over manualized treatment also pertain to the potential absence of flexibility once a manual is written and implemented. Perhaps as manuals evolve, efforts will be made to make explicit how novel situations and circumstances are to be handled. Many departures from the manuals can be specified to permit more flexible practice.

Treatment integrity. The specification of treatment has broad advantages for the field at large. Yet, within an investigation there is a more immediate and methodologically critical purpose. An essential prerequisite of outcome research is to ensure the integrity of treatment, that is, that the procedures are carried out as intended (Yeaton & Sechrest, 1981). A number of interrelated concepts are encompassed by treatment integrity, including adherence, differentiation, and competence. *Treatment adherence*, the most central to the definition of integrity, refers to whether the therapists carried out treatment as intended. *Differentiation* refers to whether two or more treatments differed from each other along critical dimensions that are central to their execution. For example, certain types of comments should vary between cognitive therapy and psychodynamic treatment; a study comparing these two treatments might assess whether treatments differed in several such dimensions that on a priori grounds ought to distinguish them. Treatments may be differentiated from one another along critical dimensions (e.g., Luborsky, Woody, McLellan, O'Brien, & Rosenzweig, 1982), but this does not necessarily mean that each was adhered to or met some absolute criterion used to define

---

[2] A number of commercial publishers have devised book series designed to publish treatment manuals or books that approximate treatment manuals. Consequently, manuals for many treatments are available for clinical use.

adherence. *Competence* refers to delivery of treatment as intended but with special skill. The notion entails quality of delivery over and above the criteria for adherence (Hill, O'Grady, & Elkin, 1992). The special skills can refer to those components that are consistent with but not encompassed fully by the treatment manual (e.g., timing of the therapeutic strategies, ability to invoke critical processes).

The most common concern is with treatment adherence. Treatment can depart from the intended procedures in many ways. In perhaps the most dramatic examples where integrity has been sacrificed, none of the intended treatment sessions was actually held with the clients (see Sechrest, White, & Brown, 1979). More subtle departures from delivering the treatment as intended are as, if not more, problematic because they are not readily detectable and cannot serve to qualify a pattern of results. Indeed, the breakdown of treatment integrity is one of the greatest dangers in outcome research. Interpretation of outcome assumes that the treatments were well tested and carried out as intended. A number of outcome studies have shown no differences between treatment conditions when individual interventions were not administered as intended, treated patients in one condition received interventions from another condition, or patients in a control condition received interventions they were not supposed to receive (e.g., Feldman, Caplinger, & Wodarski, 1983; Liberman & Eckman, 1981). The exemplary feature of these studies is that they provided data to permit evaluation of treatment integrity.

In psychotherapy outcome studies comparing two or more treatments, it is often the case that there are no statistically significant differences between these treatments (see Kazdin & Bass, 1989). There are many interpretations of this finding related to theories about critical and common factors that transcend alternative models of therapy (Stiles et al., 1986). A number of methodological interpretations are viable as well. One interpretation has been the weak power of such comparisons. Two other interpretations pertain to treatment integrity. It is possible that there is an unintended diffusion of treatments, that is, an overlap in conditions that were intended to be delivered to the separate groups. Also, it is possible that variability in implementing treatment within a condition was sufficiently great as to obscure group differences. Large variation in how individual treatments are carried out across patients within a given condition and failure to implement critical portions of treatments may also lead to no differences between two or more treatment conditions. In general, it is difficult to identify the role of lapses in treatment integrity

in accounting for results in many studies because the assessment of treatment integrity in psychotherapy research is the exception rather than the rule (Kazdin et al., 1990; Moncher & Prinz, 1991).

Even when two treatments differ in the outcomes they produce, it is important to rule out the possibility that the differences are due to variations of integrity with which each was conducted. One treatment, perhaps because of its complexity or novelty, may be more subject to procedural degradation and appear less effective because it was less faithfully rendered. Thus, integrity of treatment is relevant in any outcome study independent of the specific pattern of results.

There are several steps that can be performed to address treatment integrity. To begin with, the specific criteria, procedures, tasks, and therapist and patient characteristics that define the treatment can be well specified. Second, therapists can be trained to carry out the techniques. Usually training is defined by the number of cases the therapist has seen or amount of time (years of experience) in using the techniques, rather than proficiency in the constituent skills (see Kazdin, Kratochwill, & VandenBos, 1986). The training experience, however defined, obviously has important implications for how faithfully treatment is likely to be rendered. Third, and related, when treatment has begun, it may be valuable to provide continued case supervision. Listening to or viewing tapes of selected sessions, meeting regularly with therapists to provide feedback, and similar monitoring procedures may reduce therapist drift (departure) from the desired practices.

Whether treatment has been carried out as intended can only be evaluated definitively after the treatment has been completed. This evaluation requires measuring the implementation of treatment. Audio- or videotapes of selected treatment sessions from each condition can be examined. Codes for therapist and/or patient behaviors or other specific facets of the sessions can operationalize important features of treatment and help decide whether treatment was conducted as intended (e.g., DeRubeis, Hollon, Evans, & Bemis, 1982; Wills, Faitler, & Snyder, 1987). An alternative might be to utilize information obtained from clients to identify differences among varied treatment conditions. For example, clients can report on the therapist's behavior after individual treatment sessions, and this information can be used to reflect the extent to which intended variations across conditions were achieved (Iberg, 1991).

Treatment integrity is not an all-or-none matter. Hence, it is useful to identify what a faithful rendition of each treatment is and what departures fall within an acceptable range. On some variables, decisions may be difficult to defend but making them explicit facilitates interpretation of the results. For example, to consider a relatively simple characteristic, treatment may consist of 20 sessions of individual therapy. The investigator may specify that treatment is administered adequately (i.e., is reasonably tested) only if a client receives 15 (75%) or more of the sessions. For other variables, particularly those within-session procedures that distinguish alternative treatments, specification of criteria that define an acceptable range may be more difficult. In some cases, the presence of select processes (e.g., discarding irrational beliefs, improving one's self-concept) might be sufficient; in other cases, a particular level of various processes (e.g., exploration, transference) might be required to denote that treatment has been adequately provided.

Therapist Issues

Therapists and the design of the study. Treatment usually is administered by a therapist, trainer, or counselor. Although many substantive questions about therapist influences can be studied, there are manifold methodological considerations to address. In the general case, it is important to make implausible the possibility that treatment outcome differences or the absence of differences can be attributed to therapist characteristics, competence, or execution of treatment, unless evaluation of these features is of interest in the design of the study.

Different methodological issues emerge depending upon the characteristics of the study. If one treatment is being tested (e.g., treatment vs. no-treatment or waiting-list control condition), the major issue is ensuring that more than one therapist provides treatment in the study. With only one therapist, any intervention effects might really reflect an effect unique to that therapist (see Maher, 1978). This amounts to a therapist effect or a treatment × therapist interaction that cannot be detected by the design. If two or more therapists are utilized, then the effect of the therapist can be evaluated as part of the results.

In a study with two or more treatments, other issues emerge. Depending on many practical issues as well as the specific treatments that are studied, a decision needs to be made whether therapists as a factor should be crossed with or nested within treatment. When therapists are *crossed with* treatment, each therapist administers each of the treatment conditions in the investigation. Therapists can then be evaluated as a "factor" in the data analysis. Such analyses permit evaluation of the impact of therapists alone (as a main effect) and in combination (interaction) with treatment.

If therapists are *nested within* treatments, separate sets of therapists are used to administer the separate treatments. Thus, therapists administer only one of the treatments rather than all of the different treatments. The impact of therapists as a group cannot be separated from treatment effects. Any treatment difference can be reinterpreted as a difference in the therapists who provided the respective treatments. The alternative hypothesis of therapist effects cannot be treated lightly because different sorts of therapists might be attracted to different treatments. It is important to try to rule out the alternative hypothesis that therapist variables accounted for the results. To that end, such characteristics as age, gender, and professional experience should be similar across the sets of therapists administering alternative conditions. It may be difficult to match on other characteristics that in a given case might differentiate groups of therapists because the number of such therapists in any single outcome study typically is small (e.g., two or three therapists for each treatment condition). The small contingent of therapists may also preclude meaningful statistical evaluation of therapist attributes in relation to outcome.

Purely from the standpoint of experimental design, crossing therapists with treatment is preferable because, theoretically, that portion of patient change attributed to therapists (therapist variance) can be separated from the portion due to treatment technique (treatment variance) and other variables included in the design. Yet in outcome studies, overriding reasons may dictate the nesting of therapists within treatments. An obvious advantage of nesting therapists is that therapists of a given technique can be selected for their background, skill level, commitment to, and enthusiasm for that technique. The alternative of having all therapists administer all techniques raises other problems, such as the differential skill level and background for the different techniques for a given therapist and among therapists. Also, each therapy technique may require considerable training and experience. Consequently, it may be unreasonable to attempt to train novices to master each technique. Furthermore, it may not be feasible to conduct such training because professional therapists, unlike graduate student therapists, may have less time available or be less willing to learn multiple treatments for a research project. Even when therapists are selected for their expertise or proficiency within a given technique, the multiple considerations related to treatment integrity should be addressed. Therapist training in the specific version that is to be tested should be provided; supervision should be ongoing to avoid drift from the treatment guidelines or manual; and selected sessions should be assessed to evaluate treatment integrity.

Therapist characteristics. It seems obvious that there will be differences among persons who administer treatment and that some of these differences will influence therapeutic change. Indeed, characteristics of therapists have been studied rather extensively (Beutler, Crago, & Arizmendi, 1986; see also Chapter 7, this volume). A variety of therapist characteristics can play an important role in treatment outcome, such as level of empathic understanding, amount of experience, and degree of openness and directiveness, to mention a few.

Of interest here are the methodological conditions raised by the study of therapist characteristics. First, many different types of characteristics can be studied, and these may raise different sorts of problems. Subject and demographic characteristics (e.g., age, experience, treatment orientation) may be of interest. Alternatively, characteristics that emerge over the course of treatment (e.g., expressions of warmth, self-disclosure) can be evaluated as well. Selection of characteristics for study ideally relies upon theory about the treatment, clinical problem, and clients to whom treatment is applied. Second, the study of therapist characteristics requires a sufficient number of therapists to evaluate different levels or degrees of the characteristic of interest. For example, evaluation of the impact of therapist warmth (high vs. low) is not well studied by utilizing two therapists to administer treatment. Several therapists are required, and they may need to be carefully selected for their initial characteristics.

Many considerations that might be raised in studying patients are somewhat neglected when therapists become the subjects. For example, the importance of sampling and sample size to provide statistically sensitive tests are obviously important. Typically, procuring therapists as subjects is much more difficult than procuring patients. The exception is analogue research for which students are placed in quasi-therapist roles as part of a laboratory study designed to resemble a segment of treatment. The difficulties in obtaining large numbers of cases for the study of therapist characteristics has implications for the types of designs and tests that can be provided and the generality of effects beyond the specific characteristics of the sample that might be conveniently available. Also, with a relatively small number of therapists as subjects, analyses of the data to partial out potential influences (e.g., sex, race, experience, orientation) are extremely difficult. One possibility is to evaluate the effects of therapists with more lenient alpha levels (e.g., $p \leq .20$ rather than $p \leq .05$) so that therapist effects would not be overlooked due to low power (Crits-Christoph & Mintz, 1991). If spe-

cific predictions are made in advance of the study and the differences are likely to be small, adjustments in alpha levels may be reasonable (see Kazdin, 1992a).

Therapist characteristics are not directly of interest or readily assessed in most treatment studies. Rather, the investigator wishes to ensure that the influences of such characteristics is minimal and can be separated from effects of the other variables of primary interest. A recent review has suggested that differences among therapists within a study, that is, the impact of therapists on treatment outcome (as measured by effect size), are less in studies that utilize treatment manuals and relatively experienced psychotherapists (Crits-Christoph et al., 1991). Presumably, treatment manuals also permit training of therapists in ways that increase homogeneity of practices within the study.

Assessment Issues

Assessment issues in the context of therapy research are intricate. Major advances in process and outcome research have been associated with and in part due to advances in measurement (see Elliott & James, 1989; Hill, 1990; Lambert et al., 1983; see also Chapter 3, this volume). The purpose here is not to trace these but rather to highlight methodological issues and practices more broadly.

Selection of outcome measures. There is general consensus that outcome assessment needs to be multifaceted, involving different perspectives (e.g., patients, significant others, mental health practitioners), characteristics of the individual (e.g., affect, cognitions, and behavior), domains of functioning (e.g., work, social, marital adjustment), and methods of assessment (e.g., self-report, direct observation) (see Kazdin & Wilson, 1978; Lambert et al., 1983; Strupp & Hadley, 1977). The diversity of measures relevant to evaluate outcome leads to multifaceted assessment batteries in individual outcome studies. The inevitable result often is the ambiguity in comparisons of treatments. Professionals and laypersons alike often wish to know whether treatment "worked," which treatment was "more successful," or how many persons "got better." Although one can sympathize with these questions, the answers depend on the specific outcome measure. Different conclusions are quite possible, if not likely, as a function of different outcome measures (e.g., Szapocznik et al., 1989; Webster-Stratton, Hollinsworth, & Kolpacoff, 1989).

The differences in measures are not inherently problematic. However, from the standpoint of the design of a study, it is useful to identify in advance the goals of treatment and the primacy of alternative outcome measures in relation to these goals. Specification of the goals and relations to specific measures will not reduce the ambiguity that different outcome measures produce. Yet, these strategies will permit stronger conclusions about the extent to which well-specified goals are achieved by a given technique.

Reducing symptoms and increasing prosocial functioning. The impetus for seeking treatment usually is the presence of various symptoms; reactions to stress; or maladaptive, disturbing, or disruptive behaviors. Naturally, the effects of treatment would be measured by the extent to which the problems identified at the outset are reduced when treatment is completed. Often assessment includes other symptom areas to see if treatment reduced dysfunction in domains other than those initially identified as problematic. The reduction of symptoms that impair performance is obviously central to the evaluation of outcome.

In addition to symptom reduction, it is important to assess prosocial functioning. Prosocial functioning refers to the presence of positive adaptive behaviors and experiences such as participation in social activities, social interaction, and making friends. Reducing symptoms no doubt can improve a person's functioning. Yet, the overlap of symptom reduction and positive prosocial functioning may not be great. As might be expected, symptoms and prosocial behavior tend to be inversely related (e.g., Kazdin, Siegel, & Bass, in press). Even so, the magnitude of the correlations tends to be in the low-to-moderate range and hence represents little shared variance. These findings suggest that prosocial functioning and symptom reduction are not equivalent.

Prosocial functioning may be an important indicator for treatment evaluation in separate ways. It is possible that treatments that appear equally effective in reducing symptoms vary in the extent to which they promote and develop prosocial behaviors. In addition, for clients whose symptom reduction is similar, the prognosis may vary as a function of prosocial behaviors evident at treatment outcome. For these reasons, assessment of prosocial behavior is worth incorporating into treatment outcome.

Other types of measures. The emphasis of outcome measures overlooks many other types of measures that may contribute as much or more information about the relative utility and value of alternative treatments. One type of measure worth including pertains to the *processes* that are considered to be critical to treatment and therapeutic change. Considerable advances have been made in

psychodynamic therapy relating various processes to outcome (e.g., Luborsky, Crits-Christoph, Mintz, & Auerbach, 1988). The development of measures of therapeutic processes and constructs that emerge in treatment (e.g., therapeutic alliance, interpretation accuracy) can serve to derive and test theoretical propositions about alternative models of treatment (see Hill, 1990; Mahrer, 1988). In general, it is valuable to show changes in various processes (e.g., cognitive, familial) that occur during treatment when such processes are assumed to mediate change. Findings that critical processes have changed and that these changes correlate with outcome can greatly enhance the interpretation (construct validity) of the study.

Another type of measure that is important to include in outcome studies might be referred to generally as *client reactions to treatment*. These measures may reflect dimensions that do not necessarily refer to the adjustment or dysfunction of the clients but still may distinguish alternative treatments. For example, attrition, untoward side effects, adherence to prescribed regimens, attendance, and satisfaction with and acceptability of treatment might vary among treatments. Even if the outcomes of alternative treatments are identical, the treatment of choice might be determined by one or more of these other criteria. Indeed, these other criteria may be of such significance that one treatment slightly less effective than another might still be preferred because the loss in effectiveness is much less than the gain in other benefits. For example, a treatment that clients find quite acceptable and easy to comply with might be the treatment of choice over an alternative that is slightly more effective but does not have these characteristics.

Finally, and related to the previous discussion, measures concerning the *administration of treatment* can elaborate the yield from outcome studies. Such measures as cost of the treatments, requirements for training therapists, ease of application of procedures by paraprofessionals, and resistance of treatment to violations of integrity are quite relevant. Again, treatments similar in outcome may differ on these measures. In general, the extent to which treatment leads to improvements on outcome measures is obviously of central importance. Yet, the exclusive focus on outcome neglects many other significant measures that professionals and consumers consider as important distinctions among alternative treatments.

Timing of follow-up assessment. Assessment immediately after treatment is referred to as *posttreatment* assessment; any point beyond that ranging from weeks to years typically is referred to as *follow-up* assessment. Follow-up raises important issues for psychotherapy outcome research, such as whether gains are maintained and whether conclusions can be reached at all given patient attrition. In addition, conclusions about the efficacy of a treatment or relative effectiveness of alternative treatments may vary greatly depending on when assessments are conducted. In one study, two of the interventions (group therapy, behavior modification) provided to maladjusted children showed different outcome effects depending on the point in time that assessment was completed (Kolvin et al., 1981). Immediately after treatment, relatively few improvements were evident in the areas of neuroticism, antisocial behavior, and total symptom scores. These areas improved markedly over the course of follow-up approximately 18 months after treatment ended. The authors discussed a "sleeper effect," that is, improvements that are not evident immediately after treatment but emerged and/or increased over time. Other studies comparing alternative forms of treatment for children, adolescents, or adults point to the significance of the timing of outcome assessments (for reviews, see Kazdin, 1988; Wright, Moelis, & Pollack, 1976). In these studies, conclusions about the effectiveness of a given treatment relative to a control condition or another treatment differed at posttreatment and follow-up. Thus, the treatment that appeared more or most effective at posttreatment did not retain this status at follow-up.

Not all studies find that the pattern of results and conclusions about a given treatment relative to another treatment or control condition vary from posttreatment to follow-up assessment (Nicholson & Berman, 1983). Yet, the number of clear exceptions suggests that the conclusions about a given treatment in any particular study might well depend on when the assessment is conducted. The occasional finding that treatment effects are delayed and that changes at follow-up are often greater than those immediately after treatment underscores the possibility that a given treatment may vary in outcomes at different assessment points. In current therapy research, evidence indicates that the inclusion of follow-up assessment in the study is the exception rather than the rule (Kazdin et al., 1990).

Attrition

Discussion of the timing of assessment and follow-up raises the topic of attrition or loss of subjects over the course of the study. Clients in a psychotherapy investigation traverse several stages, which typically include pretreatment assessment, the course of treatment, posttreatment assessment, and then perhaps a period of follow-up. Over the time course, the loss of subjects is virtually inevitable. Indeed, one can expect a "decay curve" in which the number of persons who drop out of the study increases as a function of time (Phillips, 1985). The loss of subjects during an investigation has special significance as a topic in therapy research. The topic is a substantive area of research in which researchers attempt to develop conceptual models of who drops out of treatment and to study the manifold client, therapist, and treatment factors that may contribute to dropping out. At the same time, attrition raises several methodological issues. This latter facet concerns us here.

As noted previously, the reasons for conducting psychotherapy research are to draw valid inferences about treatment. Methodology and research design are intended to address the alternative types of validity (see Table 2.2). The loss of clients during the course of an investigation can affect each type of validity by altering random composition of the groups and group equivalence (internal validity), limiting the generality of findings to a special group such as those subjects who are sufficiently persistent to complete treatment (external validity), raising the prospect that the intervention combined with special subject characteristics accounts for conclusions the investigator would like to attribute to the intervention (external and construct validity), and reducing sample size and power (statistical conclusion validity).

Consider the methodological issues raised by attrition in psychotherapy research. First and most obvious, subjects who drop out of an investigation are likely to differ from those who remain in the study. Dropouts may differ on a range of variables (e.g., type, severity, or chronicity of dysfunction; family history; past treatment experiences) that could interact with (moderate) the intervention in the outcomes that are produced. Conclusions about the effects of treatment may be restricted to a highly select group, depending on the proportion of subjects lost and their characteristics.

Second, it is possible that characteristics of persons who drop out of separate groups or conditions within a study are not the same. For example, if five subjects drop out of a psychotherapy condition and five other subjects in the study drop out of a medication condition, it is not necessarily the case that these persons are similar. There may be systematic differences in the conditions leading to attrition in ways that affect different types of people. Perhaps those psychotherapy subjects who did not wish to chat about their past and never considered their therapists to be like a father (transference) tired of psychotherapy and left; those medication subjects who were discomforted by a dry mouth and heart palpitations (side effects) may have quit their treatment. The subjects remaining in each of the groups and included in statistical comparisons may be different kinds of subjects in terms of subject, demographic, and personality characteristics; this cannot be easily tested given the small sample sizes and absence of available information on a vast range of possible differences in these characteristics. The number of attrition cases is usually too small to compare groups in a statistically sensitive way. Indeed, investigators may show no statistically significant differences in the subject characteristics between dropouts from two or more groups. This could provide illusory comfort that attrition did not lead to any selection biases that would favor one group.

Third, the number of subjects who drop out may vary significantly between or among groups. For example, in a classic study of cognitive therapy, this form of treatment was shown to be superior in reducing depression in adults when compared to medication (imipramine) (Rush, Beck, Kovacs, & Hollon, 1977). Interestingly, medication led to a significantly larger number of subjects leaving treatment before posttreatment assessment. Differential attrition across groups itself is an interesting outcome and may say something important about treatment conditions. Treatments that generate relatively high attrition rates may be relatively aversive, place special demands on the clients, have untoward side effects, or perhaps simply not work. In the case of this study, differential attrition between the two treatment groups clearly raises questions for all comparisons at posttreatment. Were the two treatments differentially effective on measures of depression or were group differences due to differential selection? The question is not easily resolved.

Finally, it is possible that so many cases drop out that valid conclusions about treatment cannot be made. For example, in one large-scale investigation, youth ($N = 450$, ages 8–17) received one of three treatment or control conditions designed to reduce antisocial behavior (Feldman et al., 1983). The design evaluated several factors (therapist experience, type of treatment, type of group) in a factorial design ($2 \times 3 \times 3$ or 18 groups). At a one-year follow-up, almost 90 percent of the cases (396/450) who completed treatment were lost from the study. The small sample for whom follow-up data were available ($n = 54$) divided among the set of experimental conditions precluded evaluation of the effects of treatment. The loss of a large number of subjects in intervention research is not at all rare. Upwards of 50 percent of cases who begin treatment may drop out (e.g., Petarik & Stephenson, 1988; Vaile-Val, Rosenthal, Curtiss, & Marohn, 1984). In such cases, selection biases are

readily plausible. Also, the large number of lost cases has dire consequences for sample sizes and hence statistical conclusion validity. Studies of treatment in clinical research usually begin with samples that are relatively small (see Kazdin & Bass, 1989; Rossi, 1990). Attrition further weakens the sensitivity of statistical tests.

The problem of subjects dropping out or terminating their participation may be exacerbated greatly by investigators. Investigators may use subjects who drop out in such a way as to obfuscate further the conclusions that might be drawn by reassigning subjects to conditions in the investigation on the basis of whether they have dropped out. For example, in one study cases who dropped out of treatment (approximately 28%) were used as the no-treatment control group (Beneke & Harris, 1972). Of course, the superiority of treatment to no-treatment on outcome might well have been due to differences related to attrition status rather than to treatment. In general, attrition can create many different problems for an investigator. However, the conclusions that can be drawn tend to be restricted even further if those subjects who are lost are reassigned to some conditions within the investigation. The assumption that lost subjects are no different from those who continue along important subject variables can be easily challenged (see Flick, 1988; Chapter 6, this volume). Threats to internal validity become plausible as rival hypotheses in explaining group differences or the absence of differences.

There are several options available to address the problems of attrition. A variety of procedures and interventions have been explored to reduce subject loss (see Baekeland & Lundwall, 1975; Flick, 1988; Stark, 1992). Examples include special orientation (pretreatment) interviews, various mailings during the course of treatment, reminders and novel methods of scheduling appointments, and monetary incentives or penalties. Development of interventions to combat attrition is likely to derive from efforts to understand factors that place clients at risk for premature termination from treatment (e.g., Kazdin, 1990) and from models of the critical factors that will help engage cases in treatment (e.g., Szapocznik et al., 1988). From a methodological perspective, statistical approaches to attrition have been developed and provide useful strategies to complement active efforts to minimize attrition. Statistical approaches utilize existing data (e.g., the last available data point) from cases who drop out and utilize other data in the study to estimate what the lost data might reflect. These methods allow researchers to identify the likely bias that attrition introduces into the data and the conclusions that would be warranted if the lost subjects had improved, remained the same, or become worse (see Flick, 1988; Howard, Krause, & Orlinsky, 1986; Little & Rubin, 1987).

STATISTICAL EVALUATION: SELECTED ISSUES AND METHODS

Psychotherapy research, like psychological research more generally, relies primarily on statistical evaluation to determine whether groups receiving different conditions are reliably different on the dependent measure(s). Statistical evaluation consists of applying tests to assess whether the difference obtained on the dependent measure is likely to have occurred by "chance." Typically, a level of confidence (such as .05 or .01) is selected as the criterion for determining whether the results are statistically significant. A statistically significant difference indicates that the probability level is equal to or below the level of confidence selected, for example, $p < .05$. If the probability obtained in the study is lower than .05, most researchers would concede that group differences probably were *not* the result of chance but reflected a genuine relation between the independent and dependent variables.

To state that a relation in a study is statistically significant does not mean that there is necessarily a genuine relation between the variables studied. Chance is the one rival hypothesis that can never be completely ruled out. There may be no relation between the variables in fact, but a statistically significant difference exists because of a special or biased sampling of subjects, as well as other factors. Nevertheless, by tradition, researchers have agreed that when the probability yielded by a statistical test is as low as .05 or .01, that is a sufficiently conservative level of confidence to permit one to conclude that the differences between groups or conditions are veridical (see Cowles & Davis, 1982).

Essentially, statistical evaluation provides a criterion to separate probably veridical from possibly change effects. Subjectivity and bias enter into the process of statistical evaluation, for example, in terms of the tests that are applied and the criteria for statistical significance (e.g., Berger & Berry, 1988; Cowles & Davis, 1982). Yet the goal of statistics is to provide a relatively bias-free and consistent method of interpreting results. The prevalent use of statistics does not imply that agreement on their value is universal. Diverse facets of statistical evaluation have been challenged, including the arbitrary criterion that a particular confidence level such as $p < .05$ represents the all-or-none decision making based on that criterion, the absence of information regarding the practical value of the relation whether or not statistical sig-

nificance is attained, and the likelihood that the null hypothesis upon which tests are based is never really true (Chow, 1988; Kupfersmid, 1988; Meehl, 1978). Statistical significance is a function of many different features of an investigation, only *one* of which is whether or not there is a relation between the independent and dependent variables. Several issues related to a statistical evaluation influence the conclusions that are drawn (see Kazdin, 1992a, 1992b).

Significance Level (Alpha)
Obviously, a decision about whether a difference between alternative forms of psychotherapy is veridical varies as a function of alpha. Although tradition has fixed $p < .05$ and .01 as the criteria, there are separate circumstances in which we may wish to reconsider the alpha level we select. In some situations, the investigator may decide to relax the alpha level (reduce the probability of Type I error) based on substantive or design issues that are decided in advance of data collection. Several circumstances may lead to such a decision. For some of these, the investigator may anticipate specific constraints that will attenuate the likely effect.

First, in some situations in which treatment trials are to be conducted, the available sample may be small. Power will be weak unless sampling is extended across different research sites or is continued over a protracted period to accumulate cases. If there are inherent constraints in sample size, it might be reasonable to increase the alpha level for deciding the reliability of treatment effects between groups. Second and related, the specific comparison of interest may be expected to generate a very small difference (effect size) between groups. The difference may be one that is important to detect. For example, if the difference is important to detect for theoretical reasons and sample size cannot reasonably be increased, we might consider an increase in alpha to, say, $p < .10$. Finally, we might alter our criterion for alpha based on consideration of the consequences of our decisions. Consequences here may refer to cost, patient treatment (benefit, suffering), policy issues (e.g., ease of dissemination, providing the greatest care to the greatest number), and other instances where the weight of accepting or rejecting the null hypothesis has greatly different implications and value. For example, if we are studying whether a particular therapy has side effects, we might want to alter alpha to, say, $p < .20$. In such a study, we may wish to err on the side of stating the side effects exist if there is any reasonable suggestion in the data that they might.

In a given study, alpha is one of many decision points. The fact that a particular alpha level is deeply ingrained in tradition does not exonerate the investigator from considering thoughtful departures based on circumstances of the particular study. There are circumstances when the investigator may plan on using different levels of alpha within an investigation. A salient example in psychotherapy outcome research would be a situation in which two or more active treatments and a control condition are studied: (1) Treatment A, (2) Treatment A with an added ingredient to enhance outcome, and (3) no-treatment control. Suppose we sample 75 persons who meet various criteria (e.g., diagnosis, age, physical health) and then assign subjects randomly to conditions with the restriction that an equal number will appear in each group. What shall we use for our alpha level?

We could use an alpha of .05 for all comparisons in the usual way. Alternatively, *in advance* of the study we might consider the comparisons of interest and their likely effect sizes. The difference between treatments versus no-treatment is likely to be large. This we already know from several meta-analyses of psychotherapy (Brown, 1987). The usual alpha level ($p < .05$) to detect a difference might well be reasonable here. In contrast, the differences between Treatment A with and without a special ingredient is likely to be smaller. A sample of 75 subjects with 25 cases per group in our hypothetical study is larger than the sample size for groups ($n = 12$) that psychotherapy studies average (Kazdin & Bass, 1989; Kazdin et al., 1990). Yet, the sample size is not very large for detecting group differences between two active treatments. With constraints of time and clinic resources, it may be unreasonable to increase the sample size. It might be reasonable to use a more lenient alpha level (e.g., $p < .20$) for comparisons of the two active treatments.

The suggestion to consider more lenient alpha levels is proposed as a decision to be made well in advance of the study. No doubt evidence in many data sets would reveal that several findings would be significant if alpha had been set at $p < .10$. The adoption of a less stringent alpha may be convenient to support a hypothesis. The danger to be avoided is the situation in which alpha level is altered in light of peeking at the results. Investigators could not be faulted for the temptation because few believe that a finding supported at $p < .05$ is unsupported at a p level above that (e.g., $p = .06$). The issue for statistical evaluation has been the selection of some generally agreed-upon criterion. Whatever that is, there would always be instances that "just miss" and in which the investigator, but not many others of the scientific community, would say that the effect is close enough to be regarded as reliable.

In general, in a given instance it may be useful to reconsider alpha level in advance of the study and for some of the tests or comparisons within that study. If on a priori grounds special conditions within the design can be expected to attenuate sensitivity of an effect, a more lenient alpha may be justified. Both theoretical and applied concerns might lead to reconsidering alpha. Altering alpha level might be guided by evaluating the nature of the consequences of different decisions (i.e., concluding that there is or is not a reliable difference between conditions).

Power to Detect Group Differences

A critical research issue is the extent to which an investigation can detect differences between groups when differences exist within the population. This notion is referred to as *statistical power* and reflects the probability that the test will lead to rejection of the null hypothesis.[3] Power is a function of the criterion for statistical significance (alpha), sample size (N), and the difference that exists between groups (effect size).

Although power is an issue in virtually all research, it raises special questions in studies in which two or more conditions (groups) are not significantly different. The absence of significant differences can contribute to knowledge under a variety of circumstances (Kazdin, 1992a). An essential precondition is that the investigation was sufficiently powerful to detect meaningful differences. In the vast majority of psychotherapy outcome studies that contrast two or more treatments, the power may be relatively weak due to small sample sizes.

There are many reasons to suspect that outcome studies as a general rule provide weak tests. Analyses of research in clinical psychology have repeatedly revealed relatively weak power in detecting group differences. In the seminal review that sensitized researchers to the issue, Cohen (1962) evaluated published clinical research to examine the power to detect differences of varying magnitudes. Cohen examined differences between alternative groups and distinguished three levels of effect sizes (small = .25; medium = .50; and large = 1.00). He evaluated the power of published studies to detect differences at these levels, assuming alpha = .05 and nondirectional (two-tailed) tests. The results, now well known, revealed that power was generally weak for detecting differences equivalent to small and medium effect sizes. For example, studies had slightly less than a 1 in 5 chance to detect small effect sizes and less than a 1 in 2

---

[3]Power (1—beta) is the probability of rejecting the null hypothesis when it is false. Stated differently, power is the likelihood of finding differences between the treatments when in fact the treatments are truly different in their outcomes.

chance to detect medium effect sizes. These levels are considerably below the recommended level of power = .80 (4 in 5 chance).[4] Cohen concluded that the power of the studies was weak and that sample sizes in future studies routinely should be increased (see also Cohen, 1977). Subsequent reviews of clinical research (Rossi, 1990) and psychological research in general (Sedlmeier & Girgerenzer, 1989) have revealed that the vast majority of studies continue to be quite weak with regard to detecting small and medium effects.

In psychotherapy research, issues of power might emerge as a function of the different types of comparisons that are made and the different effect sizes the comparisons are likely to yield. The comparison of treatment versus no-treatment is likely to produce relatively large effect sizes. In contrast, comparisons of two or more active treatments or treatment variations (e.g., dismantling, parametric, comparative outcome strategies) are likely to produce smaller effect sizes. Thus, the power of a study to detect differences with a given sample size may vary with the type of comparison of interest.

An evaluation of psychotherapy outcome research suggests that studies comparing treatment versus no-treatment generally are sufficiently powerful to detect such differences (Kazdin & Bass, 1989). Given the effect sizes usually reported in such comparisons (median effect size = .78), sample sizes need not be large to detect group differences (e.g., sample size of 27 cases per group for this effect size with power = .80). However, in studies in which the investigator wishes to detect differences between alternative treatments or variations of treatments, effect sizes tend to be much smaller (median effect size = .47). A much larger sample would be needed to detect differences (e.g., sample size of approximately 70 cases per group for this effect size with power = .80). In fact, approximately 55 percent of treatment outcome studies examined over a two-year period failed to meet power of ≥ .80 in their comparisons of groups at posttreatment; approximately 70 percent failed to meet the power criterion for comparisons at follow-up (see Kazdin & Bass, 1989).

The claim that the power of most studies is likely

to be inadequate is too general to convey its impact on the interpretation of individual studies. Consider an example that is rather typical in the types of comparisons and conclusions that are drawn in studies of psychotherapy. Alexander, Nermeyer, Follette, Moore, & Harter (1989) compared two treatments and a waiting-list control condition on the adjustment of women who as children had been victims of sexual abuse. One treatment (interpersonal transaction) focused on discussion of experiences and feelings associated with abuse in the context of the group. The other treatment (process group format) focused primarily on processes within the group and styles of relating to others in the group. At posttreatment the results indicated treatments were no different from each other but were superior to the wait-list condition in measures of fearfulness, depression, and social adjustment. Are the treatments different in their outcomes? We really do not know given the likelihood of weak power. With a sample size of 65 (minus 7 lost to attrition) divided among three groups, weak power to detect between-treatment differences remains plausible as an explanation of the pattern of results.

The weak power of therapy research is not a minor methodological annoyance. Rather, the neglect of power has major implications for interpreting research. Psychotherapy research is an area where the absence of differences (i.e., support for the null hypothesis) is often taken to be quite significant from conceptual and clinical perspectives (see Frank & Frank, 1991; Luborsky, Singer, & Luborsky, 1975; Stiles et al., 1986). It may well be the case that treatments are similar in the outcomes they produce and "no difference" reflects the actual state of affairs. Yet, a plausible alternative is that the power of studies comparing alternative treatments is relatively weak.

Selecting the size of the sample. Four interrelated concepts of statistical inference are relevant in designing an investigation: alpha, power, effect size, and sample size. These concepts are interrelated in the sense that when three of them are known, the remaining one can be determined. Their interrelations are critical in that they permit consideration of all sorts of options in a study, such as what power is needed (given a specific level of alpha, effect size, and N), what effect size is needed (if alpha, power, and sample size are predetermined), and so on.

The most frequent consideration is how many subjects to include in a study. Thus, to identify our sample size, we need to make decisions to fix the other three parameters—alpha, power, and effect size. At this point, let us adopt alpha of .05 to adhere slavishly to tradition. As for level of power,

---

[4]The level of power that is "adequate" is not easily specified nor justified mathematically. As with the level of confidence (alpha), the decision is based on convention about the margin of protection one should have against falsely accepting the null hypothesis (beta). Cohen (1977) recommended adoption of the convention that beta = .20 and hence power (1−beta) = .80 when alpha = .05. Although power ≥ .80 has become a reference point for research, higher levels (.90, .95) are often encouraged (e.g., Friedman, Furberg, & DeMets, 1985).

we also might follow convention and accept power of .80. Now we must estimate effect size [ES = $(m_1 - m_2)/s$]. In psychotherapy research, estimates can be obtained from published research, including individual studies or more conveniently meta-analysis. Effect sizes vary across measures so there is no one effect size for psychotherapy. These variations are of lesser importance at this point. One is advised to err on the side of conservative estimates of effect size by choosing a lower bound estimate with the idea that one's own investigation may not generate as potent effects.

A second way to estimate effect size is on rational grounds, especially if there is no clear precedent in previous work to serve as a guide. The investigator may estimate whether the effect size is likely to be small, medium, or large. Cohen (1988) has provided us with admittedly arbitrary but quite useful guidelines in this regard by noting small, medium, and large effect sizes to reflect approximately .20, .50, and .80, respectively.[5] It is helpful again to select a conservative estimate.

In any case, assume that by one of these methods we consider the likely effect size to be about .40. Thus, we have alpha = .05, power = .80, and effect size estimated at .40. At this point, we can enter tables or various books provided to us (e.g., Cohen, 1988; Kraemer & Thiemann, 1987) or can enter the information on a computer program designed to provide power analyses (Borenstein & Cohen, 1988). Entering the tables requires selection of three values (in our case alpha, power, and effect size) to decide the remaining value (sample size). The tables tell us the size of the groups (n) we need (e.g., 40 Ss/group) to detect an effect size estimated at .40. We might learn that to detect such an effect size, we need a much larger N than we can obtain. This is excellent to identify before the study. We can then decide to vary alpha (e.g., $p < .10$), to reduce power slightly (e.g., power = .75), or to select alternative conditions in which effect size is likely to be larger than .40. The use of power tables helps one to experiment intelligently with possible options regarding alpha, power, effect size, and N.

One further point about sample size and power is worth noting. Power pertains to the statistical comparisons the investigator will make, including subanalyses that may divide groups into various subgroups. For example, the investigator may have $N = 100$ subjects in two groups. The main comparison of interest may contrast group 1 ($n = 50$) with group 2 ($n = 50$). The investigator may plan several analyses that further divide the sample, for example, by sex (males vs. females), age (younger vs. older), intelligence (median IQ split), or some other variable. Such comparisons divide the groups into smaller units (or subgroups). Instead of groups $ns = 50$, the subgroups are much smaller. Power is commensurately reduced as the comparisons entail subgroups with smaller group ns. A central reason to consider power in advance of the study is to ensure that comparisons of primary interest will be sufficiently sensitive.

Variability in the data. Power is also a function of variability in an investigation. The investigator can inadvertently increase variability in ways that will reduce the obtained effect size. Obviously, for a constant mean difference between groups, effect size in the investigation will increase or decrease depending on the size of the standard deviation by which that difference is divided. For example, the more heterogeneous the subjects (e.g., in age, background, sex, socioeconomic class, and other variables), the more variable the effects of the independent variable are likely to be. The heterogeneity of the subjects is reflected in a larger within-group variability. This variability (error variance) is directly related to effect size and statistical significance. For a given difference between groups on the dependent measure, the larger the error variance, the lower the effect size.

Other sources of variability are pivotal for the investigator to consider. The assessment instruments play an important role in the variability of the results. Measures vary in their reliability in assessing the construct of interest. To the extent that the measures assess true scores of the subjects on the construct, error variance in the study will be reduced. In developing and designing a study, the quality of the measures, as reflected in various psychometric characteristics, is quite important. Although there is no substitute for well-developed measures whose reliabilities and validities have been well established, such measures are not always available for the constructs of interest. The unreliability of these latter measures can introduce rather large variability and diminish power. One option is to increase the measurement occasions; instead of pre- and posttreatment assessment, the measures can be administered more frequently (e.g., weekly). The increased assessment occasions provide improved estimates of client performance and operate to increase effect size if sample differences exist (see Kraemer & Thiemann, 1989).

[5]The level of small, medium, and large effect sizes is different here from that noted previously in the chapter. In an early paper by Cohen (1962), small, medium, and large effect sizes were specified as .25, .50, and 1.00. More recent references (e.g., Cohen, 1977) utilize effect sizes of .20, .50. and .80, respectively.

Error variance is also a function of variation in the procedures. If experimenters administer conditions slightly differently from each other, or if a single experimenter administers conditions differently over time, error variability will increase. Hence, the magnitude of group differences will need to be greater to achieve a given level of statistical significance. If the procedures are unvarying across subjects, this eliminates a source of error variance. Prior discussions noted the importance of treatment integrity. The careful execution of the study can minimize unnecessary variability.

Statistical Tests to Augment Power

The discussion of efforts to minimize error variability in an investigation as a means toward increasing power points to additional alternatives. The design and statistical evaluation of the study can greatly affect power. Research designs that use pretests provide several advantages, as noted previously. The statistical advantage is central. The use of a pretest increases power because the error term in evaluating effect size is reduced. With repeated assessment of the subjects (pre- and posttest), the within group (subject) variance can be taken into account to reduce the error term. Consider the impact on the effect size formula.

We have noted previously that the formula for effect size is $ES = (m_1 - m_2)/s$. When there is a pretest measure or another measure that has been assessed and is related to performance at posttreatment (e.g., covariate) the effect size error term is altered. The formula is represented by $ES = (m_1 - m_2)/s\sqrt{1 - r^2}$, where r equals the correlation between the pretest (or other variable) and posttest. As the correlation between the pre- and posttest increases, the error term and hence the power of the analysis increase. Several statistical analyses can be used to take advantage of the use of a pretest. Prominent among these are analyses of covariance, repeated measures analyses of variance, and gain scores (see Lipsey, 1990).

Another issue related to power is the controversial matter of one- versus two-tailed tests. In significance testing, alpha is used to decide whether a difference between groups is reliable. Consider a two-group study and a t test to evaluate group differences. The null hypothesis is that the groups do not differ (ES = 0). A two-tailed test evaluates the obtained difference in light of departures from 0 in either direction, that is, whether one group is better or worse than another. The alpha of .05 refers to both "tails" or ends of the normal distribution, which are used as the critical region for rejection. In much research, the investigator may have a view about the direction of the differences.

He or she may not wish to test if the effect size is different from zero but rather whether the treatment is better than the control condition or whether Treatment A is better than Treatment B. The hypothesis to reject is not bidirectional but unidirectional. At such, the investigator may wish to use a one-tailed test. A lower t value is required for the rejection of the null hypothesis if a one-tailed directional test is provided.

Most hypotheses in research are directional in the sense that investigators have an idea and interest in differences in a particular direction. For this reason, some authors have suggested that most significance testing should be based on one-tailed tests (e.g., Mohr, 1990). Clearly, there is no agreement on this matter. On the other side of the issue is the likelihood that investigators even with directional hypotheses are interested in detecting differences that might occur in the opposite direction. That is, investigators would want to report and have a statistical basis for saying that the treatment hypothesized to be better in fact was reliably worse on a particular measure. Interest in effects in both directions requires the use of two-tailed tests. Nevertheless, one-tailed tests may be of use in a number of situations. As a caution, there is often an implicit assumption that investigators who use one-tailed tests may have done so because the results would not be statistically significant otherwise. It is unclear that the use of one-tailed tests was decided in advance of seeing the results. The implicit assumption does not give the benefit of doubt to the investigator. At the same time, relatively few studies in clinical psychology and related areas utilize one-tailed tests. One rarely sees such tests or sees them in situations where the results would be significant whether the tests were completed as one- or two-tailed tests.

The rationale for utilizing one-tailed tests can be detailed at the outset of the study based on theoretical or other issues that lobby for interest in unidirectional differences. Perhaps as well, the investigation might wish to note in passing those tests that would or would not have been significant with two-tailed tests. Comments on both types of test within a study do not reflect concerns of the statistician who might lobby for a rational evaluation of using one or the other form of tests (but not both). Yet, comments about the conclusions drawn from statistical tests raise broader issues. Among these is the importance of informing colleagues about the dependence of conclusions on assumptions and methods of analyses.

Statistical Significance and Magnitude of Effect

Statistical evaluation of the data usually consists of

testing to see if differences between groups are statistically significant. In addition to the presence of group differences, it would be useful to know how strong the effect was or how strong the relation was between the independent variable and performance on the dependent measures. The strength refers to the magnitude of the contribution of the independent variable to performance on the dependent variable. In psychotherapy research, the notion of the strength of the relation is obviously important. Among the many variables that contribute to outcome (e.g., client expectancies, treatment technique, therapeutic alliance), we would like to know the strength of these connections and their relative contribution.

Magnitude of effect or strength of the relation can be expressed in many different terms including omega^2 (ω^2), eta (η), epsilon^2 (ϵ^2), and correlation squared (r^2) (e.g., Haase, Ellis, & Ladany, 1989; Rosenthal, 1984). One measure of strength of association we have already discussed is effect size, and it illustrates nicely the informational yield provided beyond statistical significance. As mentioned already, in the simple case of two groups, effect size represents the magnitude of the differences between groups in terms of standard deviation units. It is important to note that magnitude of effect, and in our illustration effect size, is *not* the same as noting that a finding is or is not statistically significant. There is a relation between measures of statistical significance and measures of magnitude of effect. The relation varies as a function of the specific statistical test and measure of strength of effect. This relation is worth highlighting because of the implications for drawing conclusions from research.

Consider for a moment that we have completed a study and obtained an effect size of .70. This magnitude of effect is one that is about the level of effect size demonstrated when psychotherapy is compared with no-treatment. An effect size of this magnitude indicates a fairly strong relation and would be considered as a moderate-to-large effect size. Would an effect size of this magnitude also be reflected in statistically significant group differences? The answer depends on the sample size.

Consider two studies with an effect size of .70. In one case, we have a 2-group study with 10 cases in each group ($N = 20$). In another study, suppose we have 2 groups with 30 cases in each group ($N = 60$). We complete each study and are ready to analyze the data. In each study, we have 2 groups, so we decide to evaluate group differences using a t test. The test formula can be expressed in many ways. The relation between statistical significance and effect size for our 2-group study can be seen in the formula:

$$t = \text{ES} \times \frac{1}{\sqrt{1/n_1 + 1/n_2}}$$

where

$\text{ES} = (m_1 - m_2)/s$
n = sample size for individual groups.

When $\text{ES} = .70$, and there are 10 cases in each of the 2 groups, this formula yields a $t = 1.57$ with degrees of freedom (df) of 18 ($n_1 + n_2 - 2$). If we consult a table for the Student's t distribution, we note that a t of 2.10 is required for $p = .05$. Our t does not meet the $p < .05$ level, and we conclude that Groups 1 and 2 are *not* different. In contrast, when $\text{ES} = .70$ and there are 30 cases in each of the two groups, the formula yields a $t = 2.71$, with a df of 58. If we consult Student's t distribution, we note that it is higher than the t of 2.00 required for this df at $p < .05$. Thus, we conclude that Groups 1 and 2 *are* different.

Separate points are worth noting from this example. First, the strength of an effect can be distinguished from statistical significance. Second, sample size can be a critical determinant of statistical significance. Finally and related, the conclusions reached from the two studies would be very different based on whether one examined statistical significance or effect size. In both hypothetical studies, the effect size was identical. If these effect sizes were obtained in two studies, the results of course would be replicated and the conclusions about treatment impact would be similar. On the other hand, if statistical significance were the criterion used to evaluate the studies, the results would appear to be quite different.

Investigations that utilize statistical tests could increase their informational yield by also including measures of strength of relations between variables. The difficulty is deciding among many contenders how to best measure strength of the relation. Among the available options, no single measure has been adopted. Effect size has been discussed here as an example because of its widespread use in meta-analyses of psychotherapy. Effect size, the methods of its computation, and virtues of alternative methods are topics of discussion and debate (e.g., Haase et al., 1989; Murray & Dosser, 1987; O'Grady, 1982; Rosenthal, 1984). The main point to emphasize is the importance of including measures of strength of the relation such as effect size or one of the many correlational measures.

Multiple Comparisons

In a study, the investigator is likely to include multiple groups and to compare some or all of them with each other. For example, the study may include four groups, say, three treatment and one control group. The investigator may conduct an overall test (analysis of variance) to see if there are differences. If the test is significant, several individual comparisons may be made to identify which groups differ from each other. Alternatively, the investigator may forgo the overall test and proceed to the individual comparisons. In each case, several two-group (pair-wise) comparisons usually are completed as each treatment is compared to each other treatment and to the control group. Alpha might be set at $p = .05$ to protect against the risk of a Type I error (rejecting the null hypothesis when that hypothesis is false). This alpha refers to the risk for a given comparison, sometimes referred to as a *per comparison error rate*. However, there are multiple comparisons. With multiple tests, the overall error rate or risk of a Type I error can be much higher. This increase is sometimes referred to as *probability pyramiding* to note the accumulation of the actual probability of a Type I error increases with the number of tests. How much higher the p level increases depends on the number of different comparisons. In fact, with a number of comparisons, each held at the per comparison rate of .05, the probability of concluding that some significant effect has been obtained can be very high.

In our hypothetical example with four groups, the investigator may make all possible (six) pair-wise comparisons of the groups. The alpha selected must account for the number of pair-wise comparisons. Although the pair-wise error rate is .05, the risk of a Type I error for the study is higher because of the number of tests. This overall rate is referred to as the *experiment-wise error rate*. We must control for the probability of a Type I error for all of the comparisons or for the experiment-wise error rate.

There are alternative multiple-comparison tests that are available to address the problem of experiment-wise error rate and to control the increased Type I risk (see Hochberg & Tamhane, 1987). A relatively simple alternative is referred to as the Bonferroni procedure and consists of a way to adjust alpha in light of the number of comparisons that are made. There are several variations; consider the most commonly used version to adjust alpha levels.

In a set of comparisons, the upper boundary of the probability of rejecting the null hypothesis is the number of comparisons (k) times alpha (α) (e.g., $p = .05$). Obviously, if there are 10 comparisons to be made, then the overall error rate could be as high as .50. As a protection against a Type I error, $p = .50$ would clearly be unacceptable. To control the overall error rate, alpha can be adjusted

for the number of comparisons. The Bonferroni adjustment is based on dividing alpha ($p = .05$) by the number of comparisons. In our four-group study, there are six possible pair-wise comparisons. If we set alpha at .05, we know our risk is actually much higher given the number of comparisons. To make an adjustment, we divide alpha by the number of tests. In our example, we divide .05/6, which yields $p = .0083$. For each of the individual pair-wise comparisons we complete (Treatment 1 vs. Treatment 2, Treatment 1 vs. control group, etc.), we use $p < .0083$ as the criterion for significance. If we use this criterion, then our overall experiment-wise error rate is controlled at $p < .05$.[6]

The adjustment of alpha as noted previously arises when several pair-wise comparisons are made on a given measure. A similar concern (i.e., elevated alpha) emerges when there are multiple outcome measures and several tests comparing the same groups are made across each measure. For example, if two groups of patients (anxious vs. nonanxious) are compared on several different measures, the chance of finding a significant difference, when there is none in the population, is higher than $p = .05$ for a given comparison. Here too, the Bonferroni adjustment can be used for the number of comparisons where k refers still to the number of comparisons or tests. As before, for each test, the adjusted level is used to decide whether the effects are statistically significant.

There is general agreement that multiple comparisons require some adjustment. Failure to consider the multiplicity of the comparisons has direct implications for statistical conclusion validity, in this case, often concluding that there are significant differences when, by the usual criteria for alpha, there are none. Beyond these general points, and at the point investigators need to make data analytic decisions, agreement diminishes. For example, which multiple comparison tests are appropriate and whether a given test is too conservative or stringent are two areas where reasonable statisticians can disagree.

Use of an adjustment such as the Bonferroni procedure is fairly common. Although the adjusted alpha is reasonable, the consequence can be sober-

---

[6]The Bonferroni adjustment controls the overall (experiment-wise) error rate, for example, at $p = .05$. The error rates for the individual comparisons (per comparison) need not be equal (e.g., all at $p = .0083$ in the prior example). Individual comparisons can vary in their per comparison alpha level, if the investigator wishes greater power for some tests rather than others, as long as the overall per comparison alpha levels do not exceed the experiment-wise error rate of .05 when summed for all comparisons.

ing in a given study. In practice, the number of significant effects is likely to decrease when an adjusted level is used. Stated differently, as the alpha for individual pair-wise comparisons becomes more stringent, power decreases, and the probability of accepting the null hypothesis when that hypothesis is false increases.

Investigators are reluctant to adjust for the large number of tests that are often completed. There are alternatives for the investigator who believes central findings are supported by the statistical comparisons but sees them disappear when alpha is adjusted to control the experiment-wise error rate. First, the investigator can present the results for both adjusted and nonadjusted alpha levels. Presentation of the findings can note those tests that remain significant under both circumstances and those that are significant only when the overall rate is uncontrolled. Second, the investigator can select an experiment-wise alpha that is slightly more lenient than $p < .05$, such as $p < .10$, prior to making the adjustment. The Bonferroni adjustment will divide this alpha by the number of comparisons. The per comparison alpha is still below .05 depending on the number of comparisons. Adopting a experiment-wise rate of .10 is usually less of a concern to other researchers than adopting this rate for individual comparisons (per comparison rate). Finally, the investigator may not be interested in all possible comparisons, but rather in only a preplanned subset that relates specifically to one or two primary hypotheses. Adjusting alpha for this smaller number of comparisons means that the per comparison rate (of alpha) is not as restrictive.

The alternatives do not exhaust the range of possibilities. For example, among the options is the use of less conservative variations of the Bonferroni adjustment (Simes, 1986) or a variety of other procedures to control Type I error (Hochberg & Tamhane, 1987). The central point is not to argue for any one solution but rather to underscore the importance of addressing the issue in the data analyses. Any data analytic issue that can be anticipated also requires consideration at the design stage before the study is completed. Identifying the major comparisons of interest in the study, the statistical tests that will be used, the number of tests, and so on may have implications for sample size and power. All such matters directly affect the conclusions to which the investigator is entitled and hence are critical.

Multiple Outcomes: Multivariate and Univariate Analyses

In most psychotherapy outcome studies, multiple measures are used to evaluate the impact of an intervention. For example, several measures may be obtained to assess the different perspectives (e.g., clients, relatives, therapists) and domains of functioning (e.g., depression, self-esteem, adjustment at home and at work). As noted in the previous discussion, the data analyses may include a number of individual tests. Each group can be compared to every other group in the design on each of the outcome measures. Although the per comparison rate might be .05, we already noted that the actual likelihood of a chance finding multiples quickly as the number of comparisons increases. The number of comparisons can increase when there are many groups compared to each other and/or a few groups that are compared when there are multiple measures. The Bonferroni adjustment is an alternative to address the issue of Type I error when such comparisons are made.

When there are multiple outcome measures, another issue emerges, namely, the interrelations of the measures. Performance on several outcome measures may be conceptually related, because they reflect a domain the investigator views as a unit, or empirically related, because the measures correlate highly with each other. If we have, say, 10 dependent measures, we could analyze these separately with t or F tests. We could avoid the problem of an inflated Type I error with an alpha adjustment, as noted previously. However, the other issue pertains to the fact that the measures may be interrelated.

Univariate tests (i.e., separate tests for each measure) do not take into account the possible redundancy of the measures and their relation to each other. It is possible, for example, that two outcome measures show significant effects due to treatment. The two measures may be interpreted by the investigator separately as two constructs. A high correlation of these measures (e.g., $r > .9$) may mean that they can be accounted for by a single construct. In a different vein, it is possible as well that none of the measures when subjected to separate univariate tests would show a difference but would show an effect when viewed and analyzed as a conceptual whole.

When there are multiple outcome measures, we can consider the data to be *multivariate*. It may be desirable to conduct multivariate analyses (e.g., such as multivariate analyses of variance). Multivariate analyses include several measures in a single data analysis, whereas univariate analyses examine one measure at a time. We do not use multivariate analyses merely because we have several dependent measures. Rather, the primary basis is when the investigator is interested in understanding the relations among the dependent measures. The multivariate analyses consider these relations by providing a linear combination of the measures and evaluating if that combination provides evidence for significant differences. If an overall multivariate analysis indicates a significant effect, this suggests that some combination of variables has shown the effect of the intervention or independent variable of interest. In many studies, multivariate analyses are used when there are several measures and then univariate analyses are completed if the overall multivariate analysis is statistically significant. Whether multivariate analyses are appropriate is based on several considerations. The mere presence of several measures is not sufficient to proceed to conducting multivariate analyses. It may be quite appropriate to analyze the multiple outcome measures with multivariate analysis, with several univariate tests, or by other means (see Haase & Ellis, 1987; Huberty & Morris, 1989).

Multivariate analyses are particularly appropriate if the investigator views the measures as conceptually interrelated and is interested in various groupings of the measures separate from or in addition to the individual measures themselves. For example, there may be several measures of patient adjustment and family functioning. Within the study, the investigator may group all of the measures of patient adjustment and conduct a multivariate analysis to identify a combination for this overall conceptual domain and do the same for the measures of family functioning. Separate analyses may also be conducted for the individual scales within each conceptual domain, if they are of interest as well. Multivariate analyses evaluate the composite variables based on their interrelations. This is a unique feature and is not addressed by performing several separate univariate tests. Separate univariate tests might be appropriate under a variety of conditions if the investigator does not view the measures as conceptually related, if the measures in fact are uncorrelated, or if the primary or exclusive interest is in the individual measures themselves rather than how they combine or relate to each other.[7]

Investigators occasionally use the multivariate analysis as an overall test. If significant, they then proceed with several univariate tests. Objections are occasionally raised for this procedure. First, the univariate tests still do not control for the number of comparisons and hence the increased risk of a Type I error unless some other adjustment is made. Second, interpretation of the univariate tests is

unclear if the measures analyzed separately are in fact highly related. Alternative follow-up analyses after multivariate tests that consider the contribution of several variables to the overall multivariate effect are available (see Bernstein, 1988; Haase & Ellis, 1987).

General Comments

Statistical evaluation is the mainstay of contemporary research. Application of statistical tests is not that straightforward. The complexities and options as well as their implications for experimental validity lobby for careful consideration of the methods of statistical evaluation at the design stage. Issues related to alpha, power, and error rates, to mention a few, are critical to address as the study is being planned. These are not esoteric issues nor merely quantitative ones. Rather, they will squarely affect the conclusions the investigator wishes to draw and the strength and quality of the design that tests the investigator's hypotheses or predictions.

CLINICAL SIGNIFICANCE OF THERAPEUTIC CHANGE

In therapy and therapy research, we wish to produce an effect that makes a difference to the person who has received treatment. Statistical significance does not really assess the practical or applied importance of treatment for individual patients. Measures of magnitude of effect such as effect size are valuable complements to statistical significance. Although "magnitude of effect" sounds close to clinical importance, the measures also are statistical concepts about such notions as shared variance or how much of an effect was obtained in standard deviation units (e.g., r^2, effect size) rather than whether treatment produced clinically important changes. In treatment research, clinical significance has emerged as a way to evaluate the magnitude of change from the standpoint of impact on the client. *Clinical significance* refers to the practical value or importance of the effect of an intervention, that is, whether it makes any "real" difference to the clients or to others. Evaluation of the clinical or applied importance of the change usually is used as a supplement to statistical methods of determining whether group differences or changes overtime are reliable. Once reliable changes are evident, further efforts are made to quantify whether treatment has moved the client appreciably closer to adequate functioning, that is, whether the change is important.

Clinical significance is important for separate reasons. Perhaps most obviously, the persons included in treatment research often are recruited

---

[7]Whether one should use multivariate tests when this option is available is based on several considerations beyond the scope of the present chapter. For further discussion, the reader is referred elsewhere (e.g., Bernstein, 1988).

because of their dysfunction and are keenly interested in relief or improvement. Clinical significance includes measures to evaluate that improvement in terms more closely aligned with clinical ends. In addition, clinical significance provides an important criterion for examining accomplishments and limitations of a given treatment. Statistically significant changes and differences, however potent, do not convey to us as researchers the extent to which we can have marked impact on the problem, dysfunction, or source of stress. Measures of clinical significance include outcome criteria designed to address impact in this way. Several methods of evaluating the clinical significance of treatment effects have emerged. Three general strategies can be delineated: comparison with other groups, subjective evaluation, and social impact (Jacobson & Revenstorf, 1988; Kazdin, 1977; Wolf, 1978).

Comparison Methods

Normative samples. Comparison methods, as the name suggests, involve direct comparison of clients with others. The initial comparison method involves comparing clients who complete treatment with other persons similar to them (e.g., in age, sex, socioeconomic status) who are functioning well in their everyday life. Prior to treatment, presumably the patient sample would depart considerably from their well-functioning peers in the area identified for treatment (e.g., anxiety, depression, social withdrawal, aggression, tics). One measure of clinical significance is the extent to which the patient sample is, at the end of psychotherapy, indistinguishable from or well within the range of a normative, well-functioning sample on the measures of interest. To invoke this criterion, a comparison is made between treated patents and peers who are functioning well or without significant problems in everyday life or a normative sample.

As a typical example, in a recent study we evaluated alternative interventions for aggressive and antisocial children ages 7 – 13 (Kazdin et al., 1992). The effectiveness of three conditions was examined including problem-solving skills training (PSST), parent management training (PMT), and PSST + PMT combined. Treatment was provided to children (PSST) and/or their parents (PMT) individually for a period of six to eight months. Among the outcome measures were standardized scales (Child Behavior Checklist) completed by parents and teachers. The scales reflect a broad range of emotional and behavioral problems. Original development of the scales included normative data of children delineated separately by age and sex (Achenbach & Edelbrock, 1983, 1986). From this original work, analyses indicated that among the normative sample, the 90th percentile is the cutoff

point that best delineated clinic from community (nonreferred) samples. In the treatment study, scores at this percentile were used to define the upper limit of the range of deviance. Change was considered to be clinically significant if children's scores were reduced to fall below this cutoff.

Figure 2.3 shows the means at pretreatment, posttreatment, and a one-year follow-up for antisocial children. Both parent (Figure 2.3a) and teacher (Figure 2.3b) evaluations are presented and show some movement of groups within the normative range. The results in Figure 2.3 are presented on the basis of means. However, clinically significant change is of equal if not greater interest in relation to individuals. One can compute how many individuals fall within the normative range at the end of treatment. In the present example, in the parent-based measure referred to in the figure, results at posttreatment indicated that 33 percent, 39 percent, and 64 percent of youth from PSST, PMT, and combined treatment, respectively, fell within the normal range. The results are interesting in the sense that statistical evaluation of changes was marked across a variety of measures. The percentage of youth returned to "normative" levels of functioning suggested more modest accomplishments.

Many other studies might be cited that use the normative range (see Kazdin, 1977; Kendall & Grove, 1988). In each case, the study depends on identifying nondeviant peers who can serve as a basis for comparison. The performance of these peers is assessed to identify normative functioning. The mean and some interval about that mean are used to provide a window of functioning that is considered to represent persons in the normal range. This range is noted for each of the measures of interest in a study or for a smaller number of measures that are considered by the investigator as particularly important.

Dysfunctional samples. A related method is a comparison of clients after treatment with a dysfunctional sample that has not been treated (Jacobson & Revenstorf, 1988; Jacobson & Truax, 1991). Rather than compare treated clients with a normative (nonreferred) sample, this method compares scores of the treated sample with scores of the untreated sample who were similar to them prior to treatment. The notion is that at posttreatment clients who have made a clinically significant change will depart markedly from the original sample of dysfunctional cases.

Different criteria can be used to determine whether the departure of the treated from the untreated sample is marked. One proposed criterion is 1.96 standard deviation units from the mean of

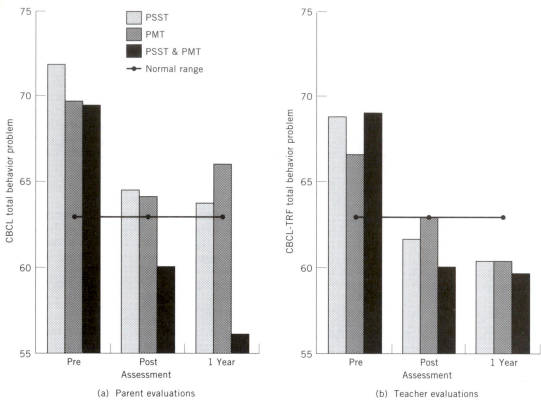

FIGURE 2.3 Mean scores for problem-solving skills training (PSST), parent management training (PMT), and PSST + PMT combined for the total behavior problem scales of the (a) parent-completed Child Behavior Checklist (CBCL, a) and (b) teacher-completed CBCL (b). The horizontal line reflects the *upper* limit of the nonclinical ("normal") range of children of the same age and sex. Scores *below* this line fall within the normal range. Reprinted by permission from Kazdin, Siegel, & Bass. Copyright 1992 American Psychological Association.

the dysfunctional sample to delineate that magnitude of change that reflects a clinically significant change. Thus, at posttreatment, individuals whose scores depart 1.96 standard deviations or more from the mean of the dysfunctional group (untreated cases with demonstrated dysfunction) would be regarded as having made an important change. The criterion of 1.96 standard deviations has been suggested to be consistent with the criterion used for statistical significance when groups are compared (e.g., 1.96 standard deviations for a two-tailed t test that compares groups for the $p < .05$ level of significance). With a similar rationale, if an individual's score is ≥ 1.96 standard deviations units away from the mean of the original group, this suggests that his or her score is not represented by the original distribution and mean of that (dysfunctional) group.

At first blush, the criterion seems identical to the one used for ordinary statistical significance, namely, a comparison of two groups with the same clinical dysfunction; one group is treated, the other

is not. However, this criterion is invoked in relation to the performance of individual clients. Clinically significant change is evaluated in relation to whether the score of a given client departs from the mean of the dysfunctional sample by at least 1.96 standard deviations. To be considered as clinically significant, the changes of course must reflect a departure from the deviant sample in the direction of a decrease of symptoms or increase in prosocial functioning.

As an illustration, Nezu and Perri (1989) compared two variations of problem solving to treat depression. In evaluating the clinical significance of change, the investigators examined the proportion of cases in each group whose score on measures of depression fell two or more standard deviations below (i.e., less depressed) the mean of the untreated sample. For example, on one measure (the Beck Depression Inventory), 85.7 percent of the cases who received the full problem-solving condition achieved this level of change. In contrast, 50 percent of the cases who received the abbreviated problem-solving condition attained this level of change. The comparisons add important information about the impact of treatment.

Within-Individual Change

These comparisons usually are based on between-subject or between-group comparisons. The extent of change is also examined by comparing an individual's performance at pre and post as a basis for deciding clinically significant effects. Here too a statistical criterion ($t \geq 1.96$) has been suggested for making this judgment following the usual criteria for statistical significance (Jacobson & Truax, 1991). In this instance, the formula is:

$$t = \frac{m_{pre} - m_{post}}{s_{diff}}$$

where

m = obtained means for the client

s_{diff} = the standard error of differences between pre- and posttest scores based on the distribution of change scores for all clients.

The measure reflects the amount of change. The rationale is that this level of change represents a marked departure from the original distribution represented by the individual's initial (pretreatment score).

Use of a statistical criterion to determine if the amount of change is important is not the only within-individual comparison method. Occasionally studies have used diagnostic criteria to identify whether the changes with treatment have had clinically important impact. For example, Hoberman, Lewinsohn, and Tilson (1988) recruited patients who met Research Diagnostic Criteria for depression (current episode, nonbipolar). At the end of treatment and at a one-year follow-up, 85 percent of the individuals no longer met the diagnostic criteria for depressive disorder. The change in diagnostic status is useful supplementary information for comparing various treatment and control conditions.

Issues and considerations. The comparative methods for evaluating clinical significance raise diverse issues. The use of a normative group for comparison is a valuable frame of reference for evaluating the end state functioning of individual clients after treatment. Obstacles for using the method include the absence of normative data for many outcome measures of interest in therapy, the unclear criteria to invoke for defining the specific range of scores that define normative functioning, and the unclear applicability of the criterion in evaluating various patient groups (e.g., persons whose symptom constellations are diagnosed as schizophrenia or pervasive developmental disorder) (see Kazdin, 1992a).

Departure of clients from a dysfunctional sample, the second comparison method, does not require normative data. Departure from the mean of a dysfunctional sample in standard deviation units can reflect marked changed. However, whether change does or does not meet this criterion does not speak to the matter of one's level of functioning at the end of treatment. A marked change by this criterion could still leave one well outside the range of adaptive functioning. The criterion says little about the experience of change on the part of the client, whether the change at that point is perceived as adaptive or has in fact actually altered his or her life. There is also the problem with a criterion based on a statistical threshold where a clinically important or significant change would be evident at one point (a change of standard deviation 1.96 units) but not at another (a change of 1.95 units). In general, statistical criteria for deciding statistical significance are recognized as arbitrary. Extending these criteria to deciding critical levels that mean a clinically important change is difficult to defend. The point at which there is a clinically important change for individual clients may need to rely on more concrete evidence that the individual's life has improved in some way. Standard deviation units applied to any particular measure do not necessarily assess that.

A critical issue for each comparison method is that the measure(s) used to reflect clinical significance usually is based on performance of some psychological test. Paper-and-pencil measures, questionnaires, interviews, and other frequently used measures may not reflect adaptive functioning for a given individual. Even for measures with high levels of established validity, performance of a given individual does not mean that he or she is happy, doing well, or adjusting in different spheres of life. The concerns and limitations noted here argue for cautions in interpreting comparison methods to assess clinical significance rather than against their use. The alternative methods provide information that extends the usual statistical evaluation and comparison of means.

Subjective Evaluation

The subjective evaluation method refers to determining the importance of behavior change in the client by assessing the opinions of the client, individuals who are likely to have contact with the client, or others who are in a position of expertise. The question addressed by this method of evaluation is whether behavior changes have led to differences in how the client views himself or herself or is viewed by others. The views of others are relevant because people in everyday life often have a critical role in identifying, defining, and responding to persons they may regard as dysfunctional or deviant (Strupp & Hadley, 1977). Subjective evaluations permit assessment of the extent to which the effects of an intervention, whether or not statistically significant on primary outcome measures, can be readily noticed by others.

As an example of the role of subjective evaluation as a measure of clinical significance, consider the case of Steven, a college student who wished treatment to eliminate two muscle tics (uncontrolled head and eyebrow movements) (Wright & Miltenberger, 1987). Treatment (self-monitoring and awareness training) was evaluated in a multiple-baseline design in which each tic was altered in sequence. The demonstration showed that each tic declined in frequency when treatment was applied.

A central question is whether the reduction was very important or made a difference either to Steven or to others. At the end of treatment, Steven's responses to a questionnaire indicated that he no longer was distressed by the tics and that he felt they were no longer very noticeable to others. In addition, before and after treatment videotapes of Steven were made to provide direct observations of his tics. Four observers rated randomly selected tapes without knowing which ones were from pre- and posttreatment. Observers rated the tics from the posttreatment tapes as not at all distracting, normal to very normal in appearance, and small to very small in magnitude. In contrast, they rated tics on the pretreatment tapes as much more severe on these dimensions. Observers were then informed which were the posttreatment tapes and asked to report how satisfied they would be if they had achieved the same results as Steven had. All observers reported they would have been satisfied with the treatment results. The evaluations from Steven and independent observers help attest to the importance of the changes that were achieved and provide information that cannot readily be discerned from the reductions of overt behavior alone.

Subjective evaluation of treatment effects may be especially relevant when persons other than the client (e.g., spouses, parents, teachers) have some role in identifying and referring the case and making other decisions based on their evaluations of the problem. The opinions of others in contact with the client are important as a criterion in their own right because they often serve as a basis for seeking treatment in the first place and also reflect the evaluations the client will encounter after leaving treatment. Subjective ratings can reflect important information regarding how the problem is viewed.

Issues and considerations. Perhaps the most significant concern with the subjective evaluation method is relying on the opinions of others for determining whether treatment effects were important. Subjective evaluations and the global ratings on which they often depend may be readily susceptible to biases on the part of raters (see Kazdin, 1992a). Thus, one must treat subjective evaluations cautiously; it is possible that subjective evaluations will reflect change when other measures of change do not. Also, it is usually the case that measures of subjective evaluation are global ratings and are less psychometrically sound than standardized outcome measures used in the study. The absence of reliability and validity data requires caution in their interpretation beyond tentative statements about the constructs they putatively assess.

In addition, the fact that persons associated with a client claim to notice a qualitative difference in behavior as a function of the client's treatment does not mean that the extent of the client's change is clinically significant. Persons in contact with the client may perceive a small change and report this in their ratings. But this says nothing about whether treatment has accomplished enough to alleviate the problem for which treatment was sought or to bring the client within normative levels of behaving. A related factor is that if persons associated with a client do not see a difference in client functioning after treatment, this too does not necessarily mean that clients did not change in significant and important ways. In a given instance, the perceptions of others may be less amenable to change because they see the "same old pattern" of functioning. The adage that "seeing is believing" is complemented by the equally pertinent adage that "believing is seeing." Perceptions by others and their views of how much impact has been achieved are important; their interpretation also raises cautions.

Social Impact Measures

Another type of measure to evaluate the clinical or applied importance of treatment outcome is to see if measures of social impact are altered. *Social impact measures* refer to outcomes assessed in everyday life that are of importance to society at large. These measures often are gross indices of change to which a broad audience can relate because they extend beyond the seemingly esoteric nature of psychological tests. For example, measures for interventions designed to decrease alcohol consumption and to prevent coronary illness might include days absent from work and mortality rate, respectively.

Studies of treatment occasionally include such measures. As one example, Paul and Lentz (1977) evaluated an extensive social learning–based program for chronic hospitalized psychiatric patients. Among the many outcome measures and criteria, discharge and rehospitalization are examples that might be considered to reflect social impact. As another example, Lovaas (1987) evaluated treatment for autistic children. Among the outcome measures were the effects of treatment on youth entering and remaining in "normal" classrooms at school. Apart from other measures, this clearly suggests a criterion of broad social interest. Finally, and more closely aligned with adult psychotherapy, an extensive literature has been devoted to marital therapy. One potential impact measure is the extent to which treatments avert separation and divorce (Snyder et al., 1991).

Issues and considerations. Measures of social impact have a number of liabilities that prompt interpretive caution. Measures (e.g., hospital visits, recidivism, grades, crime rates, fatalities) often are relatively insensitive as measures of intervention effects. They are gross measures and subject to a variety of influences other than those associated with the intervention. Error in the measures can be relatively high. Random error may come from variations in how consistently the measures are recorded, as in the case of many archival records (e.g., attendance in school, records in city hall). We take for granted that most psychological measures have a standardized method of administration. Social impact measures are more likely to be recorded and scored somewhat haphazardly over time, which introduces "noise" (error variability) into the results. Also, systematic error may be introduced by systematic changes in how the measure is scored (instrumentation) over time. Changes in policy, procedures, persons responsible for recording, formulae for scoring, budget cuts, and so on all may influence the measurement procedures. Both random and systematic error can introduce variability into the measure and make the measure insensitive as an outcome measure.

Social impact measures are often seized upon by nonresearchers as reflecting the critical tests to evaluate the value and effectiveness of a program. Thus, if the intervention has not shown social impact, this is often considered in the media or by nonresearchers as evidence that the intervention makes no difference, is not important, and perhaps has failed. In a given case, it is quite possible that this interpretation is accurate. Yet, social impact measures need to be thoughtfully evaluated and

interpreted. The absence of change on such a measure, given the very nature of many of these measures, may not be an adequate, reasonable, or interpretable index of the program's effect.

The danger of social impact measures comes from their two most salient characteristics, namely, their high believability coupled with their often poor psychometric properties (e.g., alternative types of reliability and validity). Notwithstanding these caveats, social impact data can be quite useful to see if the improvements identified on specific psychological measures are reflected directly on measures of primary interest to consumers of treatment and to society at large. When such measures show a change, they convey important evidence that the impact of the intervention was socially important.

General Comments

The use of comparative data, subjective evaluations of client functioning, and social impact measures represents an important step toward quantifying the extent to which outcomes produced with treatment have made a difference in the clients' everyday lives. The methods address somewhat different questions about the importance of change and hence are by no means mutually exclusive. Methods of evaluating clinical significance are used increasingly in outcome studies of therapy. As yet, there is no standard or uniformly adopted procedure or measurement strategy in widespread use. Also, several critical issues that affect use and interpretation of alternative methods remain to be resolved (see Jacobson & Revenstorf, 1988; Kazdin, 1992a). These issues do not detract from the significant step such measures represent in examining treatment outcome.

In many areas of interest in clinical psychology and where psychotherapies are applied, standards of clinically significant change are readily available. For example, in health psychology there are consensually agreed-upon standards for normative and "healthy" levels of weight, hypertension, and blood cholesterol. Many of the standards are data based; they are derived from epidemiological studies and predictions of mortality. The standards often change as new data, better measurement of outcomes, interactions among variables, and related factors come to light. Nevertheless, for many health-related domains, interventions can be evaluated in relation to the extent to which they return individuals to a "normative" range.

For many psychological tests, extensive normative data also exist. Examples would include standardized intelligence tests (e.g., Weschler Intelligence Scales) and measures of personality and psychopathology (e.g., Minnesota Multiphasic Personality Inventory-2). From such measures, means and standard deviations can be used to identify ranges of performance associated with adaptive levels of functioning. Normative ranges on standardized psychological measures as well as indices of optimal health are prone to change over time as a function of new knowledge and data. Thus, standards and criteria for evaluating functioning are not immutable. Nevertheless, the levels provide useful targets toward which interventions can aim.

The methods developed to date are significant insofar as they reflect efforts to quantify clinically significant change. Individual measures are subject to criticisms, as already noted. Further discussion of the methods; alternative ways to compute, apply, and interpret existing measures; and new measures are likely to continue (e.g., Bagne & Lewis, 1992; Speer, 1992). Novel methods might be explored as well that focus on what is assessed rather than amount of change. For example, in most of psychotherapy the goal is to improve the individual client's quality of life. In fact, there may be many clinical samples seen in treatment (e.g., persons with severe forms of mental retardation, patients with a diagnosis of schizophrenia or antisocial personality disorder) for whom the criteria for clinical significance noted previously might not be appropriate. Improvements in the quality of life of such individuals and those with whom they are in contact could be readily defended as a measure of clinical significance. There are few constructs as global but also perhaps as clinically important as quality of life. Despite its breadth, the construct is by no means illusive. Advances have been made in developing assessment devices for quality of life that might be integrated with the evaluation of clinical improvement (see Frisch, Cornell, Villaneuva, & Retzlaff, 1992; Keith & Schalock, 1992).

In general, a critical issue that applies to most of the methods of defining clinical significance in current psychotherapy research is the inattention to the measures and constructs they assess. Degrees of change across measures are not equally important. Clinical significance usually focuses on evaluation of change on symptom measures. However, the goals and accomplishments of treatment may require a focus on broader constructs such as quality of life, values, and quality of relationships (e.g., Kelly & Strupp, 1992).

The message for evaluation is not to endorse one specific measure to reflect clinical or applied significance of change. Any individual measure will possess its own problems. Rather, the issue is to incorporate some measures of clinical significance within intervention research. The measures expand upon statistical methods noted previously by addressing the extent to which an intervention has genuine impact on client functioning. The methods enable one to test in a quantifiable way whether treatment produced change for individual cases. From the standpoint of evaluation, the conclusions regarding the effectiveness of treatment may depend on whether the literature is analyzed in relation to statistical significance (e.g., Dobson, 1989) or clinical significance of the change (e.g., Nietzel, Russell, Hemmings, & Gretter, 1987). As a general rule, it is useful to invoke multiple criteria to evaluate client change in research. Among the broad methods mentioned, statistical significance, magnitude of effects, and clinical significance were discussed. Exemplary psychotherapy investigations that incorporate each of the methods (e.g, Piper, Azim, McCallum, & Joyce, 1990) provide a model for outcome evaluation.

INTERPRETATION OF THE DATA: SELECTED TOPICS

Interpretation of the data refers to the conclusions that are drawn by the investigator. How the study was planned, executed, and analyzed directly affect the substantive statements that the investigator is entitled to make as the study is interpreted. The absence of differences among conditions within a study and the replication of research findings are two broad issues that convey the role of methodology in data interpretation.

Negative Results or No-Difference Findings
In most investigations, the impact of variables of interest are evaluated by statistical criteria. The presence of an effect is decided if the null hypothesis (H_0) is rejected. Advances in research usually are conceived as a result of rejecting the null hypothesis and showing that groups or conditions within the study differ statistically. Yet, as researchers know all too well, many investigations do not yield statistically significant findings or any other evidence that the independent variable influenced the subjects. The frequently discussed notion of *negative results* is used to refer to such a research outcome.

Actually, the value of a study can be measured by its conceptualization and methodological adequacy, rather than by the presence of statistically significant differences. The conceptualization and design of an investigation bear no necessary relation to the outcome. Group differences might occur at the sacrifice of methodological rigor. Poor methodology and sources of experimental bias are more likely to be overlooked when a predicted or plausible finding of significant differences is obtained. The implicit view is that group differences demonstrate that whatever the failings of the study, they were not sufficient to cancel the effects of the independent variable. In contrast, so-called negative results often imply that the independent variable was weak or that the dependent variable was a poor test of the treatment. As investigators, we wish to proceed with the best or strongest available design and greatest methodological care so that the results, whatever their pattern, will be interpretable. The difficulty in judging the value of any study is that neither the importance of a finding nor methodological adequacy is invariably agreed upon by those who do the judging. Statistical criteria may be overly relied on because they present relatively simple bases for evaluating research.

Ambiguity of negative results.   The reason for "no-difference" findings usually cannot be identified in the study. The most straightforward reason for accepting the null hypothesis is that there is in fact no relation between the independent and dependent variables. Also, it is possible that no-difference is a chance finding, based on sampling theory and statistical evaluation. However, assume for a moment that there is a relation; many explanations might account for a no-difference finding.

To begin, any spurious influence within the study that operates to keep the means (on the dependent measures) near each other can lead to no-difference. The intervention may not have been manipulated adequately because individual treatments were not delivered as intended or conditions were not kept distinct. In one therapy study with antisocial youth, the control group inadvertently received some treatment and the treatment groups did not receive their respective interventions consistently (Feldman et al., 1983). The outcome results yielded no consistent mean differences between treatment and control conditions, an effect that would be expected given diffusion of treatments and lapses in treatment integrity.

The absence of group differences may also result from the particular levels of the independent variable selected for the study. Group differences might result from comparing other levels of the same variable. For example, there appears to be a duration or dose-response effect of psychotherapy (Howard, Kopta, Krause, & Orlinsky, 1986). Across a large number of patients and studies, more sessions were associated with greater patient improvements. However, the relation is not linear. As shown in Figure 2.4, 38 percent of the patients are markedly improved by Session 8 (solid line) and 75 percent markedly improved by Session 26. Assume we did not know of this relation and conducted a study to evaluate treatment duration. We may compare a group that receives 20 sessions

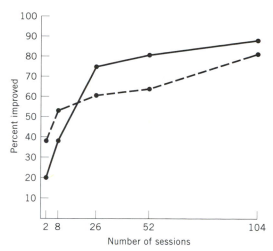

FIGURE 2.4   The relation between the number of sessions of psychotherapy for adult patients and the percentage of patients improved. The solid line reflects ratings at the end of treatment completed by researchers based on chart review. The broken line reflects patient self-report ratings during the course of treatment. Reprinted by permission from Howard, Kopta, Krause, & Orlinsky. Copyright 1986 by the American Psychological Association.

with another group that receives 30 sessions. The difference in outcome between these groups may be too small to produce a statistically significant difference. On the other hand, if the levels of the independent variable were more discrepant and at different stages of treatment (e.g., 10 vs. 30 sessions), group differences might be more likely.

In a given study, there are no simple rules to identify how to select optimal conditions or groups to test the hypotheses. Conceptualization of the relations between the condition (independent variable) and outcome dictates the conditions that are selected; rigorous methodology then follows to provide a strong test. The absence of group differences may be due to the specific levels or conditions that were included. Possibly, different conditions to test the same hypotheses might yield different findings.

The discussion of group differences or the absence of differences usually draws attention to the means between groups. Features of a study that operate to increase within-group variability also may increase the likelihood of a no-difference finding. The sensitivity of a study in detecting a difference can be reduced by allowing uncontrolled sources of variation or noise into the study. As discussed earlier, inadequate training or supervision of therapists, lapses in treatment integrity, and the use of assessment devices with low reliability and validity can increase variability and help to produce no-differences between groups, when such differences exist.

When negative results are interpretable and important. There are several situations in which negative results are very informative and interpretable. Negative results in the context of a series of studies (research program) by an investigator or group of investigators can be illuminating. In a program of research, presumably several of the studies would have produced group differences. Such a demonstration in some of the studies means that the experimental procedures are sensitive to at least some interventions. Thus, one can usually rule out the problem that the studies are conducted poorly or that the methodology is too insensitive to detect group differences. In any given instance, these explanations may be true. However, if the program of research has established itself in terms of demonstrating group differences, research showing no-differences for a related variable can be viewed with greater confidence than would be the case in an isolated study.

A second situation in which negative results are informative occurs when these results are replicated (repeated) across several different investigations. A problem in the psychological literature, and perhaps in other areas as well, is that once a relation is reported, it is extremely difficult to qualify or refute with subsequent research. If negative results accumulate across several studies, however, they strongly suggest that the original study resulted either from very special circumstances or possibly through various artifacts (see Kazdin, 1992a).

Under a variety of circumstances, finding no-differences may be very important (Julnes & Mohr, 1989; Yeaton & Sechrest, 1986). Many questions of interest are important in relation to demonstrating no difference. Does consumption of a particular fruit laced with pesticide increase risk for cancer? Is a less painful, expensive, or invasive treatment as effective as the usual treatment alternative? Do children who spend time in day care differ in psychological dysfunction from those who spend that time at home with a parent? No-difference between the appropriate comparison groups in well-conducted studies of these questions would be quite informative and socially important.

Alternative forms of psychotherapy can vary widely in their cost to the patient as well as to society (training and educating therapists) and are not available to large numbers of persons who might profit from treatment. Comparisons of treatments that differ in the extent to which they can be applied with minimal cost or on a large scale would be important. No-difference findings may also be of importance because of the potential questions they raise. Treatments that omit ingredients that are seemingly essential on conceptual grounds but generate therapeutic change in a well-designed study can raise important theoretical as well as applied questions.

In the general case, negative results may be important based on substantive *and* methodological considerations. The substantive considerations refer to the significance of the experimental or clinical questions that guide the investigation. The methodological considerations refer to the care with which the study is planned, implemented, and evaluated. In particular, given documented weaknesses of research, the power of the study to have demonstrated differences if they exist is pivotal. No-difference findings in a well-conceived and controlled study with adequate power (e.g., $> .80$) ought to be taken as seriously as any other finding.

Replication

Evaluation of the results of a study, whether or not a significant difference is demonstrated, entails more than scrutiny of that study alone. The reliability of a finding across studies greatly enhances evaluation of any particular investigation. Replication is a pivotal topic that relates to evaluation of findings and accumulation of knowledge (see Neuliep, 1991).

Types of replication. *Replication* refers to repetition of an investigation. Replication can vary along a variety of characteristics (e.g., subject characteristics, setting, type of investigation). Different points on a continuum of replication efforts are worth noting to convey the range of research opportunities (see Hendrick, 1991). *Direct or exact replication* refers to an attempt to repeat an investigation exactly as it was conducted originally. Ideally, the conditions and procedures across the replication and original study are identical. *Systematic replication* refers to repetition of the study by purposely allowing features to vary. The conditions and procedures of the replication are deliberately designed only to approximate those of the original study. Finally, a *conceptual replication* consists of an effort to test the relation, theory, or principle in a very different context. Replication focuses on the constructs and the processes they reflect. For example, replication of a specific process from a psychotherapy study might be tested in a laboratory experiment with college students or in laboratory animal research. In psychotherapy, conceptual replication and extensions have traversed both directions from research to practice. That is, processes revealed in therapy have been explored in laboratory research and processes revealed in animal laboratory research have been extended to develop alternative forms of psychotherapy (see Kazdin, 1978b).

All replications are departures from the original study. An exact replication is not possible since repetition of the study involves new subjects tested at a different point in time and by different experimenters, all of which conceivably could lead to different results. Thus, all replications necessarily allow some factors to vary; the issue is the extent to which the replication study departs from the original investigation.

Importance of replication. The importance of replication in scientific research in general cannot be overemphasized (see Amir & Sharon, 1991). Unfortunately, the importance is not commensurate with the number of replications that seem to be attempted or at least reported. It is often stated that there are few professional rewards for replication attempts, particularly direct replication attempts. The major reason that replications are not usually viewed with great excitement is that, by definition, they are partly *repetitions* of investigations. Repetition of the study at first blush seems undramatic and certainly lacking in originality. Rather, replications can be better conceptualized either as tests of robustness and generality of the original finding or more careful evaluations of the original hypotheses. Replication studies ask whether the relation holds across changes in the conditions of the study. If the results of a replication do not support the original research, they do not necessarily impugn the original finding. Rather, they may suggest that the relation holds only for a narrow set of conditions or relates to a specific circumscribed set of factors, perhaps some even unspecified in the original report. The original finding may be veridical and not the result of experimental biases or artifacts, but still insufficiently robust to have wide generality.

Replications as tests of generality are particularly important in psychotherapy research. To begin, some evidence has suggested that the investigator's preference for or allegiance to a particular treatment is related to outcome. For example, research comparing cognitive therapy and systematic desensitization has indicated that the direction of the differences between the two treatments and the magnitude of effect sizes are in line with the allegiance of the investigator (Berman, Miller, & Massman, 1985). The reasons for this effect and the generality of the effect are not clear and do not necessarily imply bias. At the same time, the findings alert us to the importance of replication among different investigators and research teams. Indeed, replication of an effect by others is a broad scientific goal toward which research is to strive in general.

Replication and tests of generality are also important in psychotherapy research to address the applied value of many findings and have implications for decisions about treatment. Researchers and practitioners alike wish to know how widely the results of a given treatment can be applied or, indeed, whether the results can be applied at all beyond a very narrow set of experimental conditions. Replications add to knowledge in different ways. Replications that closely approximate the conditions of the original study increase one's confidence that the original finding is reliable and not likely to result from a particular artifact. Replications that deviate from the original conditions suggest that the findings hold across a wider range of conditions. Essentially, the greater the divergence of the replication from the conditions of the original investigation, the greater the generality of the relation that was demonstrated.

From the standpoint of a prospective investigator, replication work is important to consider as a research strategy, particularly at the inception of one's work in an area, when it is important to ensure that the phenomena can be reproduced. After a phenomenon has been reproduced, it can be analyzed and elaborated in subsequent research. Although replication research is advocated here, it would be naive to neglect professional contingencies that currently exist. The rewards are for "original experimentation" or for something that has not been done before. An excellent strategy is to include in one's investigation a partial replication of previous research; for example, an experimenter could include conditions that closely resemble those in a previous study. In addition, conditions can be included that conceptually extend the study and the experimental conditions. The results of such research, assuming that the study meets methodological desiderata at least equal to the original investigation, not only allows one to comment on the reliability of the phenomenon but its generality all within the same study.

PLANNING, IMPLEMENTING, AND EVALUATING AN OUTCOME STUDY

Questions to Guide Research

The previous comments are directed to several issues that relate to methodology of psychotherapy research. Alternative designs, methodological practices, and methods of data evaluation raise many options and decision points for the investigator. Although a discussion of the manifold issues is useful, it is also important to go beyond a general discussion to help guide research. To that end, salient points raised in prior sections are translated into a set of questions the investigator might wish

TABLE 2.3   Selected questions to raise in planning a study of psychotherapy

Sample Characteristics

1. Who are the subjects and how many of them are there in this study?

2. Why was this sample selected in light of the research goals?

3. How was this sample obtained, recruited, and selected?

4. What are the subject and demographic characteristics of the sample (e.g., sex, age, ethnicity, race, socioeconomic status)?

5. What, if any, inclusion and exclusion criteria were invoked (i.e., selection rules to obtain participants)?

6. How many of those subjects eligible or recruited actually were selected and participated in the study?

7. With regard to clinical dysfunction or subject and demographic characteristics, is this a relatively homogeneous or heterogeneous sample?

Design

1. How were subjects assigned to groups or conditions?

2. How many groups were included in the design?

3. How are the groups similar and different in how they are treated in the study?

4. Why are these groups critical to address the questions of interest?

Procedures

1. Where was the study conducted (setting)?

2. What measures, materials, equipment, and/or apparatus were used in the study?

3. What is the chronological sequence of events to which subjects were exposed?

4. What intervals elapsed between different aspects of the study (assessment, treatment, follow-up)?

5. What variation in administration of conditions emerged over the course of the study that may introduce variation within and between conditions?

6. What procedural checks were completed to avert potential sources of bias in implementation of the manipulation and assessment of dependent measures?

7. What checks were made to ensure that the conditions were carried out as intended?

8. What other information does the reader need to know to understand how subjects were treated and what conditions were provided?

Therapists

1. Who are the therapists, and why are these individuals selected?

2. Can the influence of the therapist be evaluated in the design either as a "factor" (as in a factorial design) or can therapist effects be evaluated within a condition?

3. Are the therapists adequately trained? By what criteria?

4. Can the quantity and quality of their training and implementation of treatment be measured?

Treatment

1. What characteristics of the clinical problem or cases make this particular treatment a reasonable approach?

2. Does the version of treatment represent the treatment as it is usually carried out?

3. Does the investigation provide a strong test of treatment? On what basis has one decided this is a strong test?

4. Has treatment been specified in manual form or have explicit guidelines been provided?

5. Has the treatment been carried out as intended? (Integrity is examined during but evaluated after the study is completed.)

6. Can the degree of adherence of therapists to the treatment manual be codified?

7. What defines a completed case (e.g., completion of so many sessions)?

Assessment

1. If specific processes in the clients or their interpersonal environment are hypothesized to change with treatment, are these to be assessed?

2. If therapy is having the intended effect on these processes, how would performance be evident on the measure? How would groups differ on this measure?

TABLE 2.3 *continued*

3. Are there additional processes in therapy that are essential or facilitative to this treatment and are these being assessed?

4. Does the outcome assessment battery include a diverse range of measures to reflect different perspectives, methods, and domains of functioning?

5. What data can be brought to bear regarding pertinent types of reliability and validity for these measures?

6. Are treatment effects evident in measures of daily functioning (e.g., work, social activities)?

7. Are outcomes being assessed at different points in time after treatment?

Data Evaluation

1. What are the primary measures and data upon which the predictions depend?

2. What statistical analyses are to be used and how specifically do these address the original hypotheses and purposes?

3. Are the assumptions of the data analyses met?

4. What is the likely effect size that will be found based on other treatment studies or meta-analyses?

5. Given the likely effect size, how large a sample is needed to provide a strong (powerful) test of treatment (e.g., power $\geq .80$)?

6. Are there subdivisions of the sample that will be made to reduce the power of tests of interest to the investigator?

7. What is the likely rate of attrition over the course of treatment and posttreatment and follow-up assessments?

8. With the anticipated loss of cases, is the test likely to be sufficiently powerful to demonstrate differences between groups if all cases complete treatment?

9. If multiple tests are used, what means are provided to control error rates?

10. Prior to the experimental conditions, were groups similar on variables that might otherwise explain the results (e.g., diagnosis, age)?

11. Are data missing due to incomplete measures (not filled out completely by the subjects) or loss of subjects? If so, how are these handled in the data analyses?

12. Will the clinical significance of client improvement be evaluated and if so by what method(s)?

13. Are there ancillary analyses that might further inform the primary analyses or exploratory analyses that might stimulate further work?

---

to consider in the design and execution of a study of psychotherapy. Table 2.3 presents salient questions that can directly affect the quality of the study, its contribution, and integration in the body of scientific evidence. The questions are discussed briefly here.

Sample characteristics. Questions in Table 2.3 raise multiple issues regarding the sample and clarification of their characteristics. In general, investigations could be improved by specifying the criteria of clinical dysfunction that served as the basis for selection of the sample. Investigators frequently allude to the fact that patients were referred for treatment. This is of little use in terms of understanding the problems the patients present. Progress can be enhanced by specifying the inclusion and exclusion criteria for patient selection. Use of a specific diagnostic system such as DSM-III-R or scores on a dimensional scale to describe or to

select patients would be helpful as well. It is unreasonable to expect different investigators to adopt the same criteria to delineate a given clinical problem. Yet, in any study it is reasonable to demand that the criteria be specified and operationalized.

Specification of the sample involves more than a clarification of the clinical dysfunction and criteria for selection. Subject and demographic variables, including of course age, sex, socioeconomic status, intelligence, and achievement are prime candidates. These characteristics are often related to clinical dysfunction and adaptive functioning and may influence treatment efficacy. Race, ethnicity, and geographical locale (e.g., country; urban vs. rural within a country) may be important to specify as well to describe the sample and to permit others to evaluate the potential role in generality of the results. The full range of subject and demographic variables that might be relevant in a given study or to future generations of meta-analysts who include the study in a larger data base cannot be elaborated a priori. As a general rule, it is useful to err on the side of careful description so that it is clear to others who was treated. Although the point seems obvious, very basic descriptors are routinely omitted from studies of psychotherapy, as reviewed earlier.

Design.   There are many different ways in which the conditions of the investigation can be arranged. In the usual study of psychotherapy, conditions and variables of interest are evaluated in a group design. In such designs, methods for obtaining subjects; allocating subjects to conditions; and selecting conditions, treatments, or groups in relation to the hypotheses of interest need to be made explicit. As a broader guide, how threats to experimental validity (internal, external, construct, and statistical conclusion validity) are addressed in the design warrant consideration. The issues specific to the area of research may demand special attention in the study, such as why a particular group was or was not included if there is evidence that such a group is relevant for interpretation of the findings.

Although group designs dominate research, the consideration of alternative design options is critical. From the standpoint of the investigator, the question might be addressed by focusing on fewer subjects and more measures rather than more subjects with fewer measures. The range of designs that have helped elaborate the characteristics of therapy provides multiple options for the researcher to consider.

Procedures.   The procedures encompass what is to be done in relation to the subjects, therapists, treatment delivery, and related factors. Careful description of the procedures and means to ensure the procedures are executed as intended is critically important. Studies conducted within clinical settings and with patient samples are as a matter of course subject to all sorts of procedural departures that can add variability to the study. Patients coming late (and receiving only one-half of a session), incomplete questionnaires at pretreatment that are not detected until data entry, therapists omitting a procedure that is central, and a variety of other departures from the intended procedures are critical to monitor. Little checks on procedures can mean a lot because they reflect on the quality of the study and the variability introduced into the design.

Therapists.   It is valuable to specify characteristics of the therapists in a similar way to those that are identified for the patients. The relevant dimensions may vary but presumably include experience

and level of training, age, sex, race, and ethnicity, to mention a few. In the usual study, therapists are described by referring to therapist experience, orientation, and professional degree. This is fine, but further information on skills in using the technique(s) in the study would be helpful. The likelihood of replicating the findings of the study may be influenced greatly by knowing the characteristics of the therapists and the details of their training.

The reason(s) why a particular set of therapists is to be used may also be important. It is possible that the therapists were selected because of convenience or their availability to work on a project or because of a special therapeutic orientation. The selection for convenience (e.g., graduate student therapists) is not inherently undesirable. However, persons available to serve as therapists might have special skills, orientations, or status that could influence the generality of the results. It is important to specify the characteristics that might be unique to those who were selected to serve as therapists because selection usually cannot be assumed to reflect a representative or random sample from the population of persons who are therapists.

An evaluation of the influence of therapists on outcome is worthwhile planning in the design if at all feasible. If each therapist administers each of the conditions, then the effects can be examined in a factorial design. A therapist × condition analysis at posttreatment will examine if therapists differed (main effect of therapist) or if some therapists were more (or less) effective with one or more of the treatments compared to other therapists (therapist × condition interaction). It is often the case that different therapists administer the different treatment conditions. In this case, for a given treatment, the investigator could evaluate the effects of therapists (A vs. B vs. C for Treatment 1). An evaluation of therapists is important to present even when a factorial design does not isolate the effects independently (i.e., statistically) of treatments.

Treatment.   The treatment implicitly embraces a particular conceptual view about processes related to the specific clinical dysfunction and the way in which these are to be addressed in treatment. The connections between means, ends, and intervening processes of treatment and the connection of the clinical problem and this particular treatment need to be explicitly stated. It is quite likely that the investigator will not be able to trace fully the connections between conceptualization of the clinical problem, treatment techniques, intervening processes that produce change, and improvements on the outcome measures. The importance of the process of specifying the connections stems from revealing those areas that are not clear. The gaps in the conceptual process generate thoughts and hypotheses about what may be needed in treatment and can accelerate the development of techniques.

Several questions about the specific version of treatment are important to raise, including whether the version represents the treatment the investigator wishes to study, whether the version is a strong test, and whether the treatment could be followed and replicated by others. The use of treatment manuals facilitates training of therapists, replication of treatment by others, and evaluation of treatment integrity. Within the investigation, methods to ensure treatment integrity and evaluation of the extent to which treatments were faithfully rendered are critically important.

Assessment. It is very helpful to specify and then to assess processes within treatment that are assumed to mediate therapeutic change. Assessment of such processes as attributions, beliefs, or self-esteem, if these are central to the technique of interest, can provide extremely valuable information. Apart from the evaluation of treatment outcome, the investigator can correlate changes in processes with changes in outcome. In effect, the study can become a test of the model of therapeutic change as well as treatment outcome.

Assessment of processes or mechanisms of change in treatment are important for methodological reasons, even among researchers who consider themselves primarily or exclusively interested in treatment outcome. The reason has to do with construct validity, mentioned earlier, to wit, the extent to which the constructs of interest to the investigator can be considered to be the basis of outcome results. Group differences (e.g., treatment vs. controls) do not automatically provide insights into the reason for these differences. Data on intervening process or constructs to which change is attributed can bolster the strength of the conclusions.

Central assessment questions pertain to the outcome assessment battery and the administration of this battery over time. A great deal has been written about the assessment of therapeutic change (e.g., Lambert et al., 1983). There is incomplete agreement on measures but general consensus that multiple domains of functioning need to be selected that directly reflect the basis for clinical referral. Usually this refers to reductions of symptoms in specific areas of functioning. In addition, it is important to examine prosocial functioning. The ultimate adjustment of the case may not only derive from the reduction of symptoms but also from increases in prosocial functioning in everyday life.

The timing of assessment is important too. Administration of the assessment battery prior to treatment usually is desirable on clinical and methodological grounds. Pretreatment data identify the initial level and scope of dysfunction. Also, such data increase the power of the statistical analyses to evaluate treatment differences. Posttreatment assessment obviously is provided to evaluate the change after treatment. Follow-up assessment permits examination of the extent to which treatment effects are stable and/or change in relation to other treatment and control conditions within the study. Studies of diverse techniques cited earlier have shown that the conclusions drawn about the effects of a treatment or relative effectiveness of alternative treatments may vary greatly over time. Different assessment occasions (e.g., posttreatment, one-year and two-year follow-up assessments) are difficult to obtain but very important to seek. As a field, we have only sparse data on the long-term (e.g., $\geq$ five-year) impact of any treatment for any well-defined clinical dysfunction.

Data evaluation. The manner in which data are to be evaluated is important to consider well in advance of data collection. No doubt completion of data collection will lead to novel analyses that may not have been considered at the outset of the study. The primary analyses and how they relate to the hypotheses warrant identification at the outset and the design stage. Table 2.3 raises questions designed to draw attention to those data analytic questions (e.g., anticipated effect size, power) that may influence the design itself. In addition to the statistical questions, the clinical significance of change warrants consideration.

A Perspective on Methodology in Planning Research

The questions highlighted previously alert the investigator to major considerations in the design of psychotherapy research. The questions and considerations they reflect are not intended to be complete, nor could they be in principle and practice, given the scope of psychotherapy research and the diversity of designs and variables. Underlying the questions are more general considerations that are useful guides as well.

First, it is important to be as explicit as possible about all facets of the study related to assessment, procedures, and data analyses. Usually, explicitness of one's procedures is advocated as a basis to permit subsequent replication of research. Yet, there is a more immediate basis for specification of procedures in concrete terms. Making details of the study explicit helps the investigator identify potential and actual departures in integrity of procedures. The quality of executing the study is critically important; explicitness in procedures facilitates checking to detect and to prevent such departures. Replication of a study is a more distant goal; the initial task is to execute a high-quality investigation whose results are clear. As mentioned in the discussion of sample characteristics, explicitness of characteristics of the study is also useful because of the increased evaluation of research via meta-analyses. Characteristics of the study, as well as characteristics of the sample, are often evaluated as factors that may have impact on effect size (e.g., Shadish & Sweeney, 1991). Details of procedures and analyses are important for secondary analyses, as well as for interpretation of the individual studies.

Second, the rationale for methodological decisions is useful to elaborate at the design stage. Why were these treatment conditions selected, why these constructs, and for these constructs why these particular measures, why this data analytic method as opposed to other available options, and so on? These questions are less concrete but no less important. They become obviously important in the preparation of written reports of the study once the study is completed (see Kazdin, 1992a). At the design stage, it is useful to self-challenge on each of the decision points to ensure that the rationale for the proposed design is well based. Occasionally, the rationale for using a particular procedure, method, design, or data analytic procedure is based on the fact that the practice has appeared in the literature previously, perhaps even in one of the allegedly better journals. There is some merit in this point insofar as the use of common procedures and measures permits one to compare and combine separate studies in the knowledge base. At the same time, tradition can also transmit and perpetuate weak measures, methods, and data analytic strategies.

FINAL COMMENTS

The goals of psychotherapy research are to understand alternative forms of treatment, the mechanisms and processes through which these treatments operate, and the impact of treatment and moderating influences on client functioning. Methodology, research design, and statistical analyses are deployed in the service of these goals. The manifold practices that are used to study psychotherapy are not mere practices or accouterments of the research enterprise. The quality of the yield from individual studies and the verdict reached about critical substantive questions rely heavily on research methodology.

Designing experimental research often is presented as a straightforward enterprise. At the most rudimentary level, the design includes an experimental and a control group. The experimental group receives some form of the experimental condition or intervention; the control group does not receive the intervention. Differences between groups are considered to reflect the effect of the experimental manipulation. Although the basic comparison is well intentioned in principle, it greatly oversimplifies the bulk of contemporary research and the type of control procedures used in most psychotherapy studies. Methodology of psychotherapy research is a fascinating topic because of the many different ways in which studies can be completed, the advantages and disadvantages associated with the available design options, and the contribution of different designs to the results.

Methodology is directed at planning an investigation in such a way as to rule out competing explanations of the results. The better an investigation is designed, the fewer the alternative plausible explanations that can be advanced to account for the findings. Ideally, only the effects of the independent variable could be advanced as the basis for the results. Psychotherapy trials are very difficult to mount and usually costly in both time and money. A given investigator is not likely to conduct very many research projects involving clinical treatments and samples given the complexity of individual projects and current life expectancies. All the more is methodology critical. The cost of such studies lobbies for ensuring that the knowledge yield of individual projects is maximized.

This chapter has sampled the diversity of methods and methodological issues of psychotherapy research. Methodological diversity and pluralism are to be encouraged because different types and levels of analyses provide different insights about the phenomena of interest. The methods discussed fall within the quantitative and positivistic research paradigm that dominates contemporary psychotherapy research. Familiar concepts within this approach are operational definitions, standardized assessment, hypotheses testing, and quantitative methods of evaluation. Another paradigm derives from a phenomenological and hermeneutic approach to the subject matter of therapy. Concepts within this approach focus on experiences of the individual patient, meaning, intentionality, and qualitative and descriptive methods (e.g., Howard, 1991; Toukmanian & Rennie, 1992). Different methods often focus on difference problems, issues, and concerns. The present chapter elaborates the methodological practices of quantitative research and the effort to understand and elaborate psychotherapy and the mechanisms of change. The richness of theories of psychotherapy and the treatments these theories generate is complemented by the richness of the methods of evaluating treatment.

REFERENCES

Achenbach, T. M., & Edelbrock, C. S. (1983). *Manual for the Child Behavior Checklist and Revised Child Behavior Profile*. Burlington, VT: University Associates in Psychiatry.

Achenbach, T. M., & Edelbrock, C. S. (1986). *Manual for the Teacher's Report Form and teacher version of the Child Behavior Profile*. Burlington, VT: University of Vermont.

Alexander, P. C., Neimeyer, R. A., Follette, V. M., Moore, M. K., & Harter, S. (1989). A comparison of group treatments of women sexually abused as children. *Journal of Consulting and Clinical Psychology, 57*, 479–483.

American Psychiatric Association. (1987). *Diagnostic and statistical manual of mental disorders* (3rd ed., rev.). Washington, DC: Author.

Amir, Y., & Sharon, I. (1991). Replications research: A "must" for the scientific advancement of psychology. In J. W. Neuliep (Ed.), *Replication research in the social sciences* (pp. 51–69). Newbury Park, CA: Sage Publications.

Baekeland, F., & Lundwall, L. (1975). Dropping out of treatment: A critical review. *Psychological Bulletin, 82*, 738–783.

Bagne, C. A., & Lewis, R. F. (1992). Evaluating the effects of drugs on behavior and quality of life: An alternative strategy for clinical trials. *Journal of Consulting and Clinical Psychology, 60*, 225–239.

Bangert-Drowns, R. L. (1986). Review of developments in meta-analytic method. *Psychological Bulletin, 99*, 388–399.

Barlow, D. H., & Hersen, M. (1984). *Single-case experimental designs: Strategies for studying behavior change* (2nd ed.). Elmsford, NY: Pergamon.

Beneke, W. N., & Harris, M. B. (1972). Teaching self-control of study behavior. *Behaviour Research and Therapy, 10*, 35–41.

Benton, M. K., & Schroeder, H. E. (1990). Social skills training with schizophrenics. *Journal of Consulting and Clinical Psychology, 58*, 741–747.

Berger, J. O., & Berry, D. A. (1988). Statistical analysis and the illusion of objectivity. *American Scientist, 76*, 159–165.

Berman, J. S., Miller, R. C., & Massman, P. J. (1985). Cognitive therapy versus systematic desensitization: Is one treatment superior? *Psychological Bulletin, 97*, 451–461.

Bernstein, I. H. (1988). *Applied multivariate analysis*. New York: Springer-Verlag.

Beutler, L. E. (1990). Special series: Advances in psychotherapy process research. *Journal of Consulting and Clinical Psychology, 58*, 263–264.

Beutler, L. E. (1991). Have all won and must all have prizes? Revising Luborsky et al.'s verdict. *Journal of Consulting and Clinical Psychology, 59*, 226–232.

Beutler, L. E., Crago, M., & Arizmendi, T. G. (1986). Therapist variables in psychotherapy process and outcome. In S. L. Garfield & A. E. Bergin (Eds.), *Handbook of psychotherapy and behavior change* (3rd ed., pp. 257–310). New York: Wiley.

Beutler, L. E., Engle, D., Mohr, D., Daldrup, R. J., Bergan, J., Meredity, K., & Merry, W. (1991). Predictors of differ-

ential response to cognitive, experiential, and self-directed psychotherapeutic procedures. *Journal of Consulting and Clinical Psychology, 59*, 333–340.

Borenstein, M., & Cohen, J. (1988). *Statistical power analysis: A computer program*. Hillsdale, NJ: Lawrence Erlbaum.

Boy, A. V. (1971). A critique by Angelo V. Boy. In A. O. DiLoreto (Ed.), *Comparative psychotherapy: An experimental analysis* (pp. 233–245). Chicago: Aldine-Atherton.

Brown, J. (1987). A review of meta-analyses conducted on psychotherapy outcome research. *Clinical Psychology Review, 7*, 1–23.

Casey, R. J., & Berman, J. S. (1985). The outcome of psychotherapy with children. *Psychological Bulletin, 98*, 388–400.

Chow, S. L. (1988). Significance test or effect size? *Psychological Bulletin, 103*, 105–110.

Cohen, J. (1962). The statistical power of abnormal–social psychological research: A review. *Journal of Abnormal and Social Psychology, 65*, 145–153.

Cohen, J. (1977). *Statistical power analysis for the behavioral sciences* (2nd ed.). New York: Academic Press.

Cohen, J. (1988). *Statistical power analysis in the behavioral sciences* (2nd ed.). Hillsdale, NJ: Lawrence Erlbaum.

Collins, F. L., Jr., & Thompson, J. K. (1988). On the use of symbolic labels in psychotherapy outcome research: Comment on Wills, Faitler, and Synder. *Journal of Consulting and Clinical Psychology, 56*, 932–933.

Cook, T. D., & Campbell, D. T. (Eds.). (1979). *Quasi-experimentation: Design and analysis issues for field settings*. Chicago: Rand McNally.

Cowles, M., & Davis, C. (1982). On the origins of the .05 level of statistical significance. *American Psychologist, 37*, 553–558.

Crits-Christoph, P., Baranackie, K., Kurcias, J. S., Beck, A. T., Carroll, K., Perry, K., Luborsky, L., McLellan, A. T., Woody, G. E., Thompson, L., Gallagher, D., & Zitrin, C. (1991). Meta-analysis of therapist effects in psychotherapy outcome studies. *Psychotherapy Research, 1*, 81–91.

Crits-Christoph, P., & Mintz, J. (1991). Implications of therapist effects for the design and analysis of comparative studies of psychotherapies. *Journal of Consulting and Clinical Psychology, 59*, 20–26.

DeRubeis, R. J., Hollon, S. E., Evans, M. D., & Bemis, K. M. (1982). Can psychotherapies for depression be discriminated? A systematic investigation of cognitive therapy and interpersonal therapy. *Journal of Consulting and Clinical Psychology, 50*, 744–756.

DiLoreto, A. O. (1971). *Comparative psychotherapy: An experimental analysis*. Chicago: Aldine-Atherton.

Dobson, K. (1989). A meta-analysis of the efficacy of cognitive therapy for depression. *Journal of Consulting and Clinical Psychology, 57*, 414–419.

Dobson, K., & Shaw, B. F. (1988). The use of treatment manuals in cognitive therapy: Experience and issues. *Journal of Consulting and Clinical Psychology, 56*, 673–680.

Elkin, I., Shea, M. T., Watkins, J. T., Imber, S. D., Sotsky, S. M., Collins, J. F., Glass, D. R., Pilkonis, P. A., Leber, W. R., Docherty, J. P., Fiester, S. J., & Parloff, M. B. (1989). NIMH Treatment of Depression Collaborative Research Program: 1. General effectiveness of treatments. *Archives of General Psychiatry, 46*, 971–982.

Elliott, R., & James, E. (1989). Varieties of client experiences in psychotherapy: An analysis of the literature. *Clinical Psychology Review, 9*, 443–467.

Ellis, A. (1971). A critique by Albert Ellis. In A. O. DiLoreto (Ed.), *Comparative psychotherapy: An experimental analysis* (pp. 213–221). Chicago: Aldine-Atherton.

Feldman, R. A., Caplinger, T. E., & Wodarski, J. S. (1983).

The St. Louis conundrum: The effective treatment of anti-social youths. Englewood Cliffs, NJ: Prentice Hall.

Flick, S. N. (1988). Managing attrition in clinical research. *Clinical Psychology Review, 8,* 499–515.

Fonagy, P., & Moran, G. S. (1990). Studies on the efficacy of child psychoanalysis. *Journal of Consulting and Clinical Psychology, 58,* 684–695.

Francis, J. R., & Aronson, H. (1990). Communicative efficacy of psychotherapy research. *Journal of Consulting and Clinical Psychology, 58,* 368–370.

Frank, J. D., & Frank, J. B. (1991). *Persuasion and healing* (3rd ed.). Baltimore: The Johns Hopkins University Press.

Friedman, L. M., Furberg, C. D., & DeMets, D. L. (1985). *Fundamentals of clinical trials* (2nd ed.). Littleton, MA: PSG Publishing Company.

Frisch, M. B., Cornell, J., Villanueva, M., & Retzlaff, P. J. (1992). Clinical validation of the Quality of Life Inventory: A measure of life satisfaction for use in treatment planning and outcome assessment. *Psychological Assessment, 4,* 92–101.

Garfield, S. L. (1983a). Meta-analysis and psychotherapy: Introduction to special section. *Journal of Consulting and Clinical Psychology, 51,* 3.

Garfield, S. L. (1983b). Editorial: Suggested recommendations for publication in the area of depression. *Journal of Consulting and Clinical Psychology, 51,* 807–808.

Goldfried, M. R., Greenberg, L. S., & Marmar, C. (1990). Individual psychotherapy: Process and outcome. *Annual Review of Psychology, 41,* 659–688.

Haase, R. F., & Ellis, M. V. (1987). Multivariate analysis of variance. *Journal of Counseling Psychology, 34,* 404–413.

Haase, R. F., Ellis, M. V., & Ladany, N. (1989). Multiple criteria for evaluating the magnitude of experimental effects. *Journal of Counseling Psychology, 4,* 511–516.

Hahlweg, K., & Markman, H. J. (1988). Effectiveness of behavioral marital therapy: Empirical status of behavioral techniques in preventing and alleviating marital distress. *Journal of Consulting and Clinical Psychology, 56,* 440–447.

Hazelrigg, M. D., Cooper, H. M., & Borduin, C. M. (1987). Evaluating the effectiveness of family therapies: An integrative review and analysis. *Psychological Bulletin, 101,* 428–442.

Heimberg, R. G., & Becker, R. E. (1984). Comparative outcome research. In M. Hersen, L. Michelson, & A. S. Bellack (Eds.), *Issues in psychotherapy research* (pp. 251–283). New York: Plenum.

Hendrick, C. (1991). Replications, strict replications, and conceptual replications: Are they important? In J. W. Neuliep (Ed.), *Replication research in the social sciences* (pp. 41–49). Newbury Park, CA: Sage Publications.

Henry, W. P., Schacht, T. E., & Strupp, H. H. (1986). Structural analysis of social behavior: Application to a study of interpersonal process in differential psychotherapeutic outcome. *Journal of Consulting and Clinical Psychology, 54,* 27–31.

Hill, C. (1990). Exploratory in-session process research in individual psychotherapy: A review. *Journal of Consulting and Clinical Psychology, 58,* 288–294.

Hill, C. E., O'Grady, K. E., & Elkin, I. (1992). Applying the Collaborative Study Psychotherapy Rating Scale to rate therapist adherence in cognitive-behavior therapy, interpersonal therapy, and clinical management. *Journal of Consulting and Clinical Psychology, 60,* 73–79.

Hoberman, H. M., Lewinsohn, P. M., & Tilson, M. (1988). Group treatment of depression: Individual predictors of outcome. *Journal of Consulting and Clinical Psychology, 56,* 393–398.

Hochberg, Y., & Tamhane, A. C. (1987). *Multiple comparison procedures.* New York: Wiley.

Howard, G. S. (1991). Culture tales: A narrative approach to thinking, cross-cultural psychology, and psychotherapy. *American Psychologist, 46,* 187–197.

Howard, K. I., Kopta, S. M., Krause, M. S., & Orlinsky, D. E. (1986). The dose-effect relationship in psychotherapy. *American Psychologist, 41,* 159–164.

Howard, K. I., Krause, M. S., & Orlinsky, D. E. (1986). The attrition dilemma: Toward a new strategy for psychotherapy research. *Journal of Consulting and Clinical Psychology, 54,* 106–110.

Hsu, L. M. (1989). Random sampling, randomization, and equivalence of contrasted groups in psychotherapy outcome research. *Journal of Consulting and Clinical Psychology, 57,* 131–137.

Huberty, C. J., & Morris, J. D. (1989). Multivariate analysis versus multiple univariate analyses. *Psychological Bulletin, 105,* 302–308.

Iberg, J. R. (1991). Applying statistical control theory to bring together clinical supervision and psychotherapy research. *Journal of Consulting and Clinical Psychology, 59,* 575–586.

Jacobson, N. S. (1991). Behavioral versus insight-oriented marital therapy: Labels can be misleading. *Journal of Consulting and Clinical Psychology, 59,* 142–145.

Jacobson, N. S. & Revenstorf, D. (1988). Statistics for assessing the clinical significance of psychotherapy techniques: Issues, problems, and new developments. *Behavioral Assessment, 10,* 133–145.

Jacobson, N. S., & Truax, P. (1991). Clinical significance: A statistical approach to defining meaningful change in psychotherapy research. *Journal of Consulting and Clinical Psychology, 59,* 12–19.

Julnes, G., & Mohr, L. B. (1989). Analysis of no-difference findings in evaluation research. *Evaluation Review, 13,* 628–655.

Karasu, T. B. (Ed.). (1990). *Treatment of psychiatric disorders: A task force report of the American Psychiatric Association* (Vols. 1–4). Washington, DC: American Psychiatric Association.

Kazdin, A. E. (1977). Assessing the clinical or applied importance of behavior change through social validation. *Behavior Modification, 1,* 427–452.

Kazdin, A. E. (1978a). Evaluating the generality of findings in analogue therapy research. *Journal of Consulting and Clinical Psychology, 46,* 673–686.

Kazdin, A. E. (1978b). *History of behavior modification: Experimental foundations of contemporary research.* Baltimore: University Park Press.

Kazdin, A. E. (1982). *Single-case research designs: Methods for clinical and applied settings.* New York: Oxford University Press.

Kazdin, A. E. (1988). *Child psychotherapy: Developing and identifying effective treatments.* Elmsford, NY: Pergamon.

Kazdin, A. E. (1989). *Behavior modification in applied settings* (4th ed.). Pacific Grove, CA: Brooks/Cole.

Kazdin, A. E. (1990). Premature termination from treatment among children referred for antisocial behavior. *Journal of Child Psychology and Psychiatry, 31,* 415–425.

Kazdin, A. E. (1992a). *Research design in clinical psychology* (2nd ed.). Needham Heights, MA: Allyn & Bacon.

Kazdin, A. E. (Ed.). (1992b). *Methodological issues and strategies in clinical research.* Washington, DC: American Psychological Association.

Kazdin, A. E., & Bass, D. (1989). Power to detect differences between alternative treatments in comparative psychotherapy outcome research. *Journal of Consulting and Clinical Psychology, 57,* 138–147.

Kazdin, A. E., Bass, D., Ayers, W. A., & Rodgers, A. (1990). Empirical and clinical focus of child and adolescent psychotherapy research. *Journal of Consulting and Clinical Psychology, 58,* 729–740.

Kazdin, A. E., Kratochwill, T. M., & VandenBos, G. R. (1986). Beyond clinical trials: Generalizing from research to practice. *Professional Psychology: Research and Practice, 17,* 391–398.

Kazdin, A. E., Siegel, T., & Bass, D. (1992). Cognitive problem-solving skills training and parent management training in the treatment of antisocial behavior in children. *Journal of Consulting and Clinical Psychology, 60,* 733–747.

Kazdin, A. E., & Wilson, G. T. (1978). *Evaluation of behavior therapy: Issues, evidence, and research strategies.* Cambridge, MA: Ballinger.

Keith, K. D., & Schalock, R. L. (1992). The Quality of Life Questionnaire. *The Behavior Therapist, 15,* 106–107.

Kelly, T. A., & Strupp, H. H. (1992). Patient and therapist values in psychotherapy: Perceived changes, assimilation, similarity, and outcome. *Journal of Consulting and Clinical Psychology, 60,* 34–40.

Kendall, P. C., & Grove, W. M. (1988). Normative comparisons in therapy outcome. *Behavioral Assessment, 10,* 147–158.

Kiesler, D. J. (1971). Experimental designs in psychotherapy research. In A. E. Bergin & S. L. Garfield (Eds.), *Handbook of psychotherapy and behavior change: An empirical analysis* (pp. 36–74). New York: Wiley.

Kolko, D. J., & Milan, M. A. (1983). Reframing and paradoxical instruction to overcome "resistance" in the treatment of delinquent youths: A multiple-baseline analysis. *Journal of Consulting and Clinical Psychology, 51,* 655–660.

Kolvin, I., Garside, R. F., Nicol, A. R., MacMillan, A., Wolstenholme, F., & Leitch, I. M. (1981). *Help starts here: The maladjusted child in the ordinary school.* London: Tavistock.

Kraemer, H. C., & Thiemann, S. (1987). *How many subjects? Statistical power analysis in research.* Newbury Park, CA: Sage Publications.

Kraemer, H. C., & Thiemann, S. (1989). A strategy to use soft data effectively in randomized controlled clinical trials. *Journal of Consulting and Clinical Psychology, 57,* 148–154.

Kupfersmid, J. (1988). Improving what is published: A model in search of an editor. *American Psychologist, 43,* 635–642.

Lambert, M. J., Christensen, E. R., & DeJulio, S. S. (Eds.). (1983). *The assessment of psychotherapy outcome.* New York: Wiley.

Lambert, M. J., & Ogles, B. M. (1988). Treatment manuals: Problems and promise. *Journal of Integrative and Eclectic Psychotherapy, 7,* 187–204.

Lambert, M. J., Shapiro, D. A., & Bergin, A. E. (1986). The effectiveness of psychotherapy. In S. L. Garfield & A. E. Bergin (Eds.), *Handbook of psychotherapy and behavior change* (3rd ed., pp. 157–211). New York: Wiley.

Liberman, R. L., & Eckman, T. (1981). Behavior therapy vs. insight-oriented therapy for repeated suicide attempters. *Archives of General Psychiatry, 38,* 1126–1130.

Lipsey, M. W. (1990). *Design sensitivity: Statistical power for experimental research.* Newbury Park, CA: Sage Publications.

Little, R. J. A., & Rubin, D. B. (1987). *Statistical analysis with missing data.* New York: Wiley.

Lovaas, O. I. (1987). Behavioral treatment and normal educational/intellectual functioning in young autistic children. *Journal of Consulting and Clinical Psychology, 55,* 3–9.

Luborsky, L., Crits-Cristoph P., Mintz, & Auerbach, A. (1988). *Who will benefit from psychotherapy? Predicting therapeutic outcomes.* New York: Basic Books.

Luborsky, L., & DeRubeis, R. J. (1984). The use of psychotherapy treatment manuals: A small revolution in psychotherapy research style. *Clinical Psychology Review, 4,* 5–14.

Luborsky, L., Singer, B., & Luborsky, L. (1975). Comparative studies of psychotherapies: Is it true that "everyone has won and all must have prizes"? *Archives of General Psychiatry, 32,* 995–1008.

Luborsky, L., Woody, G. E., McLellan, A. T., O'Brien, C. P., & Rosenzweig, J. (1982). Can independent judges recognize different psychotherapies? An experience with manual-guided therapies. *Journal of Consulting and Clinical Psychology, 50,* 49–62.

Maher, B. A. (1978). Stimulus sampling in clinical research: Representative design reviewed. *Journal of Consulting and Clinical Psychology, 46,* 643–647.

Mahrer, A. R. (1988). Discovery-oriented psychotherapy research: Rationale, aims, and methods. *American Psychologist., 43,* 694–702.

Maser, J. D., Kaelber, C., & Weise, R. E. (1991). International use and attitudes toward DSM-III and DSM-III-R: Growing consensus in psychiatric classification. *Journal of Abnormal Psychology, 100,* 271–279.

Matt, G. E. (1989). Decision rules for selecting effect sizes in meta-analysis: A review and reanalysis of psychotherapy outcome studies. *Psychological Bulletin, 105,* 106–115.

Meehl, P. (1978). Theoretical risks and tabular asterisks: Sir Karl, Sir Ronald, and the slow progress of soft psychology. *Journal of Consulting and Clinical Psychology, 46,* 806–834.

Michelson, L. (1985). Editorial: Introduction and commentary. *Clinical Psychological Review, 5,* 1–2.

Mohr, L. B. (1990). *Understanding significance testing.* Newbury Park, CA: Sage Publications.

Moncher, F. J., & Prinz, R. J. (1991). Treatment fidelity in outcome studies. *Clinical Psychology Review, 11,* 247–266.

Mullen, B. (1989). *Advanced BASIC meta-analysis.* Hillsdale, NJ: Lawrence Erlbaum.

Murray, L. W., & Dosser, D. A., Jr. (1987). How significant is a significant difference? Problems with the measurement of magnitude of effect. *Journal of Counseling Psychology, 34,* 68–72.

Neuliep, J. W. (Ed.). (1991). *Replication research in the social sciences.* Newbury Park, CA: Sage Publications.

Nezu, A. M., & Perri, M. G. (1989). Social problem-solving therapy for unipolar depression: An initial dismantling investigation. *Journal of Consulting and Clinical Psychology, 57,* 408–413.

Nicholson, R. A., & Berman, J. S. (1983). Is follow-up necessary in evaluating psychotherapy? *Psychological Bulletin, 93,* 555–565.

Nietzel, M. T., Russell, R. L., Hemmings, K. A., & Gretter, M. L. (1987). Clinical significance of psychotherapy for unipolar depression: A meta-analytic approach to social comparison. *Journal of Consulting and Clinical Psychology, 55,* 156–161.

O'Grady, K. E. (1982). Measures of explained variance. *Psychological Bulletin, 92,* 766–777.

Omer, H., & Dar, R. (1992). Changing trends in three decades of psychotherapy research: The flight from theory into pragmatics. *Journal of Consulting and Clinical Psychology, 60,* 88–93.

Paul, G. L. (1966). *Insight versus desensitization in psychotherapy: An experiment in anxiety reduction.* Stanford, CA: Stanford University Press.

Paul, G. L. (1967). Outcome research in psychotherapy. *Journal of Consulting Psychology, 31,* 109–118.

Paul, G. L., & Lentz, R. J. (1977). *Psychosocial treatment of chronic mental patients: Milieu versus social learning program.* Cambridge, MA: Harvard University Press.

Pekarik, G., & Stephenson, L. A. (1988). Adult and child client differences in therapy dropout research. *Journal of Clinical Child Psychology, 17,* 316–321.

Phillips, E. L. (1985). *Psychotherapy revisited: New frontiers in research and practice.* Hillsdale, NJ: Lawrence Erlbaum.

Piper, W. E., Azim, H. F. A., McCallum, M., & Joyce, A. S. (1990). Patient suitability and outcome in short-term individual psychotherapy. *Journal of Consulting and Clinical Psychology, 58,* 475–481.

Rachman, S. J., & Wilson, G. T. (1980). *The effects of psychological therapy* (2nd ed.). Oxford: Pergamon.

Roback, H. B. (1971). The comparative influence of insight and non-insight psychotherapies on therapeutic outcome: A review of experimental literature. *Psychotherapy: Theory, Research and Practice, 8,* 23–25.

Ronen, T. (1991). Intervention package for treating sleep disorders in a four-year-old girl. *Journal of Behavior Therapy and Experimental Psychiatry, 22,* 141–148.

Rosenthal, R. (1984). *Meta-analytic procedures for social research.* Beverly Hills, CA: Sage Publications.

Rosenthal, R., & Rosnow, R. L. (1991). *Essentials of behavioral research: Methods and data analysis* (2nd ed.). New York: McGraw-Hill.

Rossi, J. S. (1990). Statistical power of psychological research: What have we gained in 20 years? *Journal of Consulting and Clinical Psychology, 58,* 646–656.

Rounsaville, B. J., Chevron, E. S., Prusoff, B. A., Elkin, I., Imber, S., Sotsky, S., & Watkins, J. (1986). The relation between specific and general dimensions of the psychotherapy process in Interpersonal Psychotherapy of depression. *Journal of Consulting and Clinical Psychology, 55,* 379–384.

Rush, A. J., Beck, A. T., Kovacs, M., & Hollon, S. (1977). Comparative efficacy of cognitive therapy and pharmacotherapy in the treatment of depressed outpatients. *Cognitive Therapy and Research, 1,* 17–37.

Sechrest, L., West, S. G., Phillips, M. A., Redner, R., Yeaton, W. (1979). Some neglected problems in evaluation research: Strength and integrity of treatments. In L. Sechrest, S. G. West, M. A. Phillips, R. Redner, & W. Yeaton (Eds.), *Evaluation studies: Review annual* (Vol. 4, pp. 15–35). Beverly Hills: Sage Publications.

Sechrest, L., White, S. O., & Brown, E. D. (Eds.). (1979). *The rehabilitation of criminal offenders: Problems and prospects.* Washington, DC: National Academy of Sciences.

Sedlmeier, P. & Gigerenzer, G. (1989). Do studies of statistical power have an effect on the power of studies? *Psychological Bulletin, 105,* 309–316.

Shadish, W. R., Jr. & Sweeney, R. B. (1991). Mediators and moderators in meta-analysis: There's a reason we don't let dodo birds tell us which psychotherapies should have prizes. *Journal of Consulting and Clinical Psychology, 59,* 883–893.

Shapiro, D. A., & Shapiro, D. (1982). Meta-analysis of comparative therapy outcome research: A replication and refinement. *Psychological Bulletin, 92,* 581–604.

Shapiro, D. A., & Shapiro, D. (1983). Comparative therapy outcome research: Methodological implications of meta-analysis. *Journal of Consulting and Clinical Psychology, 51,* 42–53.

Shoham-Salomon, V., & Rosenthal, R. (1987). Paradoxical interventions: A meta-analysis. *Journal of Consulting and Clinical Psychology, 55,* 22–28.

Simes, R. J. (1986). An improved Bonferroni procedure for multiple tests of significance. *Biometrika, 74,* 751–754.

Sloane, R. B., Staples, F. R., Cristol, A. H., Yorkston, N. J., & Whipple, K. (1975). *Psychotherapy versus behavior therapy.* Cambridge, MA: Harvard University Press.

Smith, B., & Sechrest, L. (1991). Treatment of aptitude X treatment interactions. *Journal of Consulting and Clinical Psychology, 59,* 233–244.

Smith, M. L., & Glass, G. V. (1977). Meta-analysis of psychotherapy outcome studies. *American Psychologist, 32,* 752–760.

Smith, M. L., Glass, G. V., & Miller, T. I. (1980). *The benefits of psychotherapy.* Baltimore: The Johns Hopkins University Press.

Snyder, D. K., & Wills, R. M. (1989). Behavioral versus oriented marital therapy: Effects on individual and interspousal functioning. *Journal of Consulting and Clinical Psychology, 57,* 39–46.

Snyder, D. K., Wills, R. M., Grady-Fletcher, A. (1991). Long-term effectiveness of behavioral versus insight-oriented marital therapy: A 4-year follow-up study. *Journal of Consulting and Clinical Psychology, 59,* 138–141.

Speer, D. C. (1992). Clinically significant change: Jacobson and Truax (1991) revisited. *Journal of Consulting and Clinical Psychology, 60,* 402–408.

Stark, M. J. (1992). Dropping out of substance abuse treatment: A clinically oriented review. *Clinical Psychology Review, 12,* 93–116.

Stiles, W. B., Shapiro, D. A., & Elliott, R. (1986). "Are all psychotherapies equivalent?" *American Psychologist, 41,* 165–180.

Strube, M. J. (1991). Small sample failure of random assignment: A further examination. *Journal of Consulting and Clinical Psychology, 59,* 346–350.

Strupp, H. H., & Hadley, S. W. (1977). A tripartite model of mental health and therapeutic outcomes. *American Psychologist, 32,* 187–196.

Svartberg, M., & Stiles, T. C. (1991). Comparative effects of short-term psychodynamic psychotherapy: A meta-analysis. *Journal of Consulting and Clinical Psychology, 59,* 704–714.

Szapocznik, J., Perez-Vidal, A., Brickman, A., Foote, F. H., Santisteban, D., Hervis, O., & Kurtines, W. H. (1988). Engaging adolescent drug abusers and their families into treatment: A strategic structural systems approach. *Journal of Consulting and Clinical Psychology, 56,* 552–557.

Szapocznik, J., Rio, A., Murray, E., Cohen, R., Scopetta, M., Rivas-Vazquez, A., Hervis, O., Posada, V., & Kurtines, W. (1989). Structural family versus psychodynamic child therapy for problematic Hispanic boys. *Journal of Consulting and Clinical Psychology, 57,* 571–578.

Toukmanian, S. G., & Rennie, D. L. (Eds.). (1992). *Psychotherapy process research: Paradigmatic and narrative approaches.* Newbury Park, CA: Sage Publications.

Tversky, A., & Kahneman, D. (1971). Belief in the law of small numbers. *Psychological Bulletin, 76,* 105–110.

Vaile-Val, G., Rosenthal, R. H., Curtiss, G., & Marohn, R. C. (1984). Dropout from adolescent psychotherapy: A preliminary study. *Journal of the American Academy of Child Psychiatry, 23,* 562–568.

Wanous, J. P., Sullivan, S. E., & Malinak, J. (1989). The role of judgment calls in meta-analysis. *Journal of Applied Psychology, 74,* 259–264.

Webster-Stratton, C., Hollinsworth, T., & Kolpacoff, M. (1989). The long-term effectiveness and clinical significance of three cost-effective training programs for families with conduct-problem children. *Journal of Consulting and Clinical Psychology, 57,* 550–553.

Weiss, B., & Weisz, J. R. (1990). The impact of methodological factors on child psychotherapy outcome research: A meta-analysis for researchers. *Journal of Abnormal Child Psychology, 18,* 639–670.

Weisz, J. R., Weiss, B., Alicke, M. D., & Klotz, M. L. (1987). Effectiveness of psychotherapy with children and adolescents: Meta-analytic findings for clinicians. *Journal of Consulting and Clinical Psychology, 55,* 542–549.

Wills, R. M., Faitler, S. L., & Snyder, D. K. (1987). Distinctiveness of behavioral versus insight-oriented marital therapy: An empirical analysis. *Journal of Consulting and Clinical Psychology, 55,* 685–690.

Wolf, M. M. (1978). Social validity: The case of subjective measurement or how applied behavior analysis is finding its heart. *Journal of Applied Behavior Analysis, 11,* 203–214.

Wright, K. M., & Miltenberger, R. G. (1987). Awareness training in the treatment of head and facial tics. *Journal of Behavior Therapy and Experimental Psychiatry, 18,* 269–274.

Wright, D. M., Moelis, I., & Pollack, L. J. (1976). The outcome of individual child psychotherapy: Increments at follow-up. *Journal of Child Psychology and Psychiatry, 17,* 275–285.

Yeaton, W. H., & Sechrest, L. (1981). Critical dimensions in the choice and maintenance of successful treatments: Strength, integrity, and effectiveness. *Journal of Consulting and Clinical Psychology, 49,* 156–167.

Yeaton, W. H., & Sechrest, L. (1986). Use and misuse of no-difference findings in eliminating threats to validity. *Evaluation Review, 10,* 836–852.

3

ASSESSING PSYCHOTHERAPY OUTCOMES AND PROCESSES

■ **MICHAEL J. LAMBERT**

Brigham Young University

■ **CLARA E. HILL**

University of Maryland

A central task of psychotherapy is to assist patients in making changes in their lives. A central task of psychotherapy research is to examine empirically both the process of the therapeutic encounter and the changes that result from participation in this process. The expected consequence of both process and outcome research is for therapists to become more effective in assisting clients. This chapter provides the reader with a methodological resource to be used in understanding and conducting psychotherapy research with particular regard to measuring the processes and outcomes of therapy. Process research typically addresses what happens *in* psychotherapy sessions, examining variables such as therapist behaviors, client behaviors, and interactions between therapists and clients during treatment (Hill, 1982, 1990). In contrast, outcome research investigates the presence and magnitude of both immediate and long-term changes that result from the processes of psychotherapy. In reality, process and outcome overlap, in that changes in process can be early indications of positive or negative outcome (Greenberg & Pinsof, 1986).

In the first part of this chapter, we focus on methodological issues in measuring therapeutic outcome. A conceptual scheme is offered that could serve as a guide for selecting outcome measures. The possibility of tailoring change measures to each client is discussed. In addition, the development of standards for defining clinically meaningful change is elaborated upon. Some suggestions for data collection and statistical analyses are made. Next the reader is introduced to methodological issues in measuring therapeutic process, types of

process measures, their psychometric properties, the implications of decisions regarding when and how to assess process, tips for using nonparticipant judges, and issues in data collection.

ASSESSING PSYCHOTHERAPY OUTCOMES

A central issue in outcome research is how to measure the changes that occur in patients as a result of their participation in therapy. A great deal of effort has been spent on defining change and selecting measures. Yet, the lack of agreement in what constitutes adequate outcome measurement has created many problems. These problems are apparent when scholars attempt to reconcile conclusions drawn from psychotherapy research literature based on different or ambiguous criteria of success. For a classic example, the reader may be amused by the different conclusions drawn by Eysenck and Bergin regarding the effectiveness of psychoanalysis, in which Eysenck was shown to have drawn very negative conclusions about the effects of psychoanalysis based upon a selective use of change criteria (Bergin, 1971; Eysenck, 1952). The curious reader can find further examples across a variety of studies. For example, although it is widely believed that the success rates for patients with a circumscribed sexual dysfunction, such as premature ejaculation, range somewhere between 75 and 90 percent (Carson & Butcher, 1992), one can find substantial differences between individual studies and their reported outcomes. On careful examination of these studies, the differences between rates of successful outcome appear to be not so much a function of the techniques or therapists who offer the treatments, as they are the result of applying different definitions of success.

This conclusion was dramatized in a report by Levine and Agle (1978), who studied the treatment outcome of 16 male patients who were diagnosed with "chronic secondary psychological impotence." The authors noted that this dysfunction could be viewed as a performance problem only, but that it was more realistic to consider the sexual life of patients more broadly. As a result, they not only collected outcome data on changes in performance, but also on sexual desire and emotional satisfaction with sexual relations. Functioning in these three broad areas was evaluated prior to therapy, at termination, and at 3, 6, 9, and 12 months following treatment. These later data added a fourth dimension to those already discussed: How stable were the observed changes?

The authors noted that the outcome data collected could be summarized to show conservative and liberal views of improvement. Thus, if one were to consider the criterion of success to be "better erectile functioning at one-year follow-up than at initial evaluation—regardless of any interim relapses," then 69 percent of the men could be considered improved. This figure is identical to the rate of 69 percent reported by Masters and Johnson (1970), suggesting perhaps that their results had been replicated. This figure is misleading, however, in that a substantial portion of these patients continued to have "profound" disturbances in their sexual lives.

When a more conservative estimate of improvement was used, namely, "improvement in sexual functioning and satisfaction plus stability over time," only one couple (6.3%) of the 16 cases was improved. This couple had achieved good sexual functioning and was able to maintain this comprehensive and substantial improvement. Since the criterion of improvement used by Masters and Johnson (1970) was never clearly defined, it is impossible to replicate their findings. The 69 percent improvement rate found by Levine and Agle is no more a confirmation of the Masters and Johnson figure than is the 6.3 percent improvement figure a refutation of it. Within a single study, a variety of success rates can be offered and defended. This example illustrates (1) the need to provide operation definitions of success, (2) the varied definitions of success that can be used, (3) the possibility of drawing misleading conclusions by using only sim-

ple indices of change, and (4) the value of standardizing practices across studies so that comparisons between these studies can be made. Some uniformity in outcome measures, coupled with comparable measurement techniques, research design, and sample population, will result in more rapid advances in our knowledge about effective treatments.

Figure 3.1 suggests several dimensions upon which assessments have varied during the relatively short history of studying outcome. The field has gradually moved from primary reliance on therapist ratings of gross general improvement to the use of outcome indices of specific symptoms that are quantified from a variety of viewpoints, including the patient, trained observers, relatives, physiological indices, and environmental data such as employment records. The data generated from these viewpoints are always subject to the limitations inherent in the methodology relied upon; none is "objective" or most authoritative, but all represent an improvement from previous measurement methods, which were difficult to replicate because they were seldom based on scales with explicit instructions.

In the past, attempts at measuring change have reflected the fashionable theoretical positions of the day. Early studies relied on devices developed out of Freudian dynamic psychology. These devices (e.g., the Rorschach and TAT) have largely been discarded because of their poor psychometric qualities, reliance on inference, and their reflection of orientations that emphasize unconscious processes. Even if scoring systems, such as Exner's (1986) for the Rorschach, have overcome some of these problems, these devices are not preferred for outcome studies because they take so much time and are so costly in relation to the information they provide.

The use of these dynamic measures was followed by the use of devices consistent with client-centered theory (e.g., the Q-sort technique) and behavioral and cognitive theories (e.g., Irrational Beliefs Inventory). Theoretical interests have led to marked changes in the types of measures employed.

The most important developments in assessing

Change rated by therapist	→ Multiple sources
Ratings of gross change	→ Specific change/multiple technology
Theory bound	→ Emphasis on practical
Unidirectional change	→ Change can be for better or worse
Unidimensional change	→ Multidimensional Change
Stable changes	→ Unstable Changes

Figure 3.1 Developmental history of outcome assessment

outcome have been the tendencies to (1) clearly specify what is being measured, so that replication is possible; (2) measure change from multiple perspectives, with several types of rating scales and methods; (3) employ symptom-based, atheoretical measures; and (4) examine, to some extent, patterns of change over time. These practices are an improvement over the past and they will be further highlighted in the sections that follow (see also, Sobell, Brochu, Sobell, Roy, & Stevens, 1987).

REVIEW OF MEASURES USED IN ASSESSING OUTCOME: DIVERSITY OR CHAOS?

It is startling to discover the seemingly endless number of measures used to objectify outcome. Froyd and Lambert (1989) reviewed 348 outcome studies published in 20 selected journals from 1983 through 1988. These journals were selected to represent therapy as practiced and reported in contemporary professional literature. A total of 1,430 outcome measures were identified for a wide variety of patient diagnoses, treatment modalities, and therapy types. Of this rather large number, *840 different measures were used just once!* A second review of a more homogeneous set of studies of agoraphobia outcome published during the 1980s located 106 studies that used *98* different outcome measures (Ogles, Lambert, Weight, & Payne, 1990). This occurred with a well-defined, limited disorder, treated with an equally narrow range of interventions, mainly behavioral and cognitive-behavioral therapies. The proliferation of outcome measures (a sizable portion of which were unstandardized scales) is overwhelming if not disheartening.

It is rare to find consensus about using a specific measure within a limited disorder even when a particular measure has been recommended at professional meetings (Ogles et al., 1990). Wells, Hawkins, and Catalano (1988), for example, reviewed how researchers studied "drug use" in outcome studies. Ignoring the many other types of outcomes that could be and were assessed (such as employment or arrest records) and focusing only on *drug usage*, the authors identified five categories of use. The five categories, together, produced more than 25 distinct procedures and measures to assess drug use.

The seeming disarray of instruments and procedures being used to assess outcome is partly a function of the complex and multifaceted nature of psychotherapy as reflected in the diversity of clients and their problems, treatments and their underlying assumptions and techniques, as well as

the multidimensionality of the change process itself. But it also represents the dismal failure of researchers in this field to create a coherent applied science!

In terms of self-report measures, Lambert (1983) noted that the following self-report scales were the most commonly used outcome measures in the *Journal of Consulting and Clinical Psychology* from 1976 through 1980: State-Trait Anxiety Inventory (STAI), Minnesota Multiphasic Personality Inventory (MMPI), Rotter Internal-External Locus of Control (I-E), S-R Inventory of Anxiousness, and the Beck Depression Inventory (BDI). Froyd and Lambert (1989), in their previously cited review, indicated that the most frequently used self-report scales were the BDI, STAI, Symptom Checklist-90 (SCL-90), Locke-Wallace Marital Adjustment Inventory, and the MMPI. In a more recent review of the *Journal of Consulting and Clinical Psychology* for 1986–1991, Lambert and McRoberts (1993) reviewed 116 studies of psychotherapy with adults. The frequency of outcome measures categorized by source is presented in Table 3.1. As can be seen, the BDI, STAI, SCL-90, and MMPI remain the most popular self-report measures used across a broad sampling of disorders. If the survey had concerned itself with a homogeneous disorder, the list of measures could be expected to change. The popularity of the BDI and STAI is probably due to the fact that problems of anxiety and depression are frequently studied and that symptoms of anxiety and depression frequently occur across a wide variety of disorders.

Beyond self-report methodology, there is less consensus within categories of usage. The Hamilton Rating Scale for Depression (HRSD) was frequently used in the studies reviewed by Lambert (1983) and Froyd and Lambert (1989). In the more recent survey, the HRSD remains relatively popular, either used by the therapist or expert raters. The Locke-Wallace Marital Adjustment Inventory (Locke & Wallace, 1959) was the most frequently used specific scale employed with significant others. Beyond these measures, reviews of the research literature fail to show many patterns of measurement popularity, although there is some consensus within certain specialty areas.

Researchers should give serious consideration to employing measures that are commonly used to facilitate comparisons across studies. This is especially true within "homogeneous" patient samples.

ISSUES IN MEASURING CHANGE

Monotrait Versus Multitrait Scales
A question of concern for the researcher is whether

TABLE 3.1   Commonly used inventories and methods of assessments

SELF-REPORT (N = 384)	No. of Times Used	% of Total
Beck Depression Inventory	40	10.4
Experimenter-created scales or questionnaires	37	9.6
Diary-behavior and/or thoughts	27	7.0
State-Trait Anxiety Inventory	14	3.6
Symptom Checklist 90-R	12	3.1
Minnesota Multiphasic Personality Inventory	6	1.6
Dysfunctional Attitude Scale	6	1.6
Hassles Scale	5	1.3
Schedule for Affective Disorders and Schizophrenia	5	1.3

INSTRUMENTAL (N = 50)	No.	%
Heart rate	9	18
Blood pressure	7	14
Weight	5	10
Saliva composition	5	10
CO level	3	6
Respiration rate	2	4

SIGNIFICANT OTHERS (N = 15)	No.	%
Information on specific behavior	5	33
Problem check list — informant	6	40
Single use of measures of family functioning (e.g., Family Life Questionnaire, Family Environment Scale, Family Adjustment)	3	20

TRAINED THERAPIST (N = 66)	No.	%
Interview — Global or level of functioning ratings	35	53
Hamilton Rating Scale for Depression	14	21

OBSERVER (N = 67)	No.	%
Frequency of specific behavior	13	19.0
Rating of client behavior or characteristics	27	40.3
Interview of subject	12	17.9

Note: N = the total number of times a scale appeared within a source category.
[a]This scale was also counted as a Trained Observer measure when it was administered by someone other than the therapist. Based on a poster presented at the annual meetings of the Western Psychological Association, Lambert, M.J. & McRoberts, C. (1993, April) Phoenix, Arizona by permission of authors.

to select a scale that purportedly taps a single trait, such as the BDI, or one that assesses multiple symptoms, such as the MMPI-2 (Butcher, Dahlstrom, Graham, Tellegen, & Kaemmer, 1989). Multitrait scales have the seeming advantage of assessing a wide variety of symptoms and thus capturing elements of psychopathology that may not be readily apparent or identifiable prior to commencement of the study. It is especially beneficial when the patients under investigation are not presumed to be homogeneous or to have a specific limited disorder. Since scales such as the MMPI-2 are commonly and extensively used for diagnostic purposes, their selection for use as outcome measures might seem highly desirable. Nevertheless, there are some disadvantages that argue against using multitrait personality scales.

Let us consider the MMPI as an example. The major advantage of using the MMPI is the massive amount of research available on it and its widespread clinical use (Piotrowski & Keller, 1989). Consequently, for many clinicians, incorporating an MMPI-2 in a pretreatment assessment is already common practice and would not require any major adjustments in their work. Additionally, since most clinicians understand how to interpret the MMPI, they would not have to learn about a new instrument and would feel comfortable using the results to guide treatment. Although the MMPI has been used relatively frequently in outcome studies, many believe that the scales are not sensitive enough to detect short-term changes (Beutler & Crago, 1983). On the other hand, Kolotkin and Johnson (1983) strongly support the use of the MMPI for outcome assessment in brief and crisis therapies based on research conducted by Butcher and Herzog (1982).

However, there are also serious drawbacks to using the MMPI as a measure of outcome. Many patients find the task of completing the test to be aversive. Some of the questions are well beyond their normal range of experience and are consequently viewed as odd and discomforting (although this has been corrected somewhat in the MMPI-2). The most significant deterrent to using the MMPI is its length. The test is simply too long to be administered repeatedly, and shortened versions have not performed adequately. Of course, there are instruments that have been derived from the MMPI that could be used as specific measures. However, to get a general or global measure from the MMPI, the entire test needs to be administered, which is often difficult in actual clinical settings where samples may be small and repeated measurement may be vitally important (Kazdin, 1980).

A further disadvantage of the MMPI and similar multitrait measures is their limited value with regard to statistical analysis. Unless research samples are very large, using each of the MMPI's clinical scales (not to mention special population research scales) can inflate the chances of making a Type I error because many statistical comparisons are required. In addition, the presence of so many scores increases the temptation to look for statistically significant change after the data are in, rather than formulating specific hypotheses prior to making statistical comparisons. Furthermore, all patients are not likely to show elevations on all MMPI scales. The chances of finding group differences are diminished whenever individuals are already within the normal range on a particular scale. Thus, researchers handicap themselves by mixing in scale scores from such individuals with the scale scores of individuals who show psychopathology on such traits unless a composite score is used for analysis.

A solution to these problems is to consider only a limited set of scores on the MMPI or to use a single composite score such as the sum of clinical scales. Certain MMPI scales (e.g., D, Pt, and Sc) are useful measures of change in psychotherapy research (Garfield, Prager, & Bergin, 1971) and appear to be sensitive enough to measure short-term changes. The sum of clinical scales also has been shown to be a useful index of overall distress that is sensitive to change (Kolotkin & Johnson, 1983).

Nevertheless, given the time investment needed to take the MMPI twice (or even up to four times if follow-ups are called for in the design) as well as its other limitations, *the MMPI cannot be recommended as an efficient outcome measure.*

Criticisms have also been leveled at briefer multitrait scales, such as the Symptom Checklist-90-Revised (SCL-90-R); however, they do provide some advantages. The SCL-90-R (Derogatis & Meliseratos, 1983) is a 90-item self-report symptom inventory designed to reflect the psychological symptom patterns of patients. There are nine primary symptom dimensions and three global indices of distress for which the Global Severity Index (GSI) is the best single indicator of the current level of depth of disturbance. The GSI is often used as a single summary measure because it combines information on the number of symptoms a patient has and the intensity of the patient's perceived distress. The GSI is also used because of high intercorrelations between scales (Parloff, Waskow & Wolfe, 1978) and because construct validity for the primary symptom dimension scales is not convincing.

We recommend the SCL-90-R if the research involves a relatively nonhomogeneous patient sample in which the researcher wants a brief measurement of a variety of psychological and relevant physical symptoms and a measure that is sensitive to change. Because of its brevity, the interested researcher can concurrently use several other measures of outcome without unduly burdening clients. Additionally, cutoff points to denote significant changes have been established and will be discussed later in this chapter.

In contrast to multitrait measures are scales designed to measure a single trait or disorder that can be used with homogeneous patient samples. The most important advantage of these scales is that they are brief (typically containing 20–30 items), usually taking 5 to 10 minutes to complete. These inventories are typically easy to administer and score. Thus, they can be repeated several times without discomfort or even taken on a weekly basis. They also provide fairly extensive coverage of the single dimension they are intended to measure. Many monodimensional scales measure symptoms (anxiety, depression, self-esteem) that are generally important across all kinds of pathological conditions and have a substantial research base with which to compare results. Many have adequate, if not outstanding, reliability.

However, a disadvantage of many of these single-trait scales is the difficulty of establishing their validity. The single-trait self-report scales have precise names that provide the illusion that they precisely measure the construct of interest. Often they do not, or the constructs themselves (e.g., anxiety, depression) are not as distinct as has been assumed. Unfortunately, they are often highly correlated with scales presumed to measure a different construct. Most researchers, nevertheless, have an interest in specifying beforehand the dimensions of interest in their study. The use of multiple monotrait scales allows one to at least try to tailor outcome measures to the disorder of interest and the treatment of choice.

Do Individualized Measures of Change Provide a Solution to Diagnostic and Outcome Complexity?

Even though current research studies focus on seemingly homogeneous samples of patients (e.g., unipolar depression, agoraphobia), it is clear that each patient is unique and brings unique problems to treatment. For example, while the major complaint of a person may be summed up as "depression" and the person may meet diagnostic criteria for major depression (Axis I), this same patient can have serious interpersonal problems (e.g., Axis II disorders), somatic concerns, evidence of anxiety, financial difficulties, problems at work, problems parenting children, substance abuse, and so on. These diverse problems are often addressed in therapy, such that proper assessment of outcome requires that changes in all these areas be measured to obtain a complete picture of change. This is obviously a demanding task, one that cannot be fully accomplished in any particular study. The complexity of human behavior and the complexity of theories and conceptions of human behavior invite incredible difficulty in operationalizing the changes that occur as a result of psychotherapy.

Williams (1985) has documented considerable evidence that even within the seemingly limited diagnosis of agoraphobia, there is considerable diversity among patients and in the situations that provoke panic across patients, including numerous phobias that often appear as simple phobias (e.g., fear of flying, heights). The most frequent panic-provoking situation (driving on freeways) was rated as "no problem" by nearly 30 percent of agoraphobics. The typical agoraphobic will usually be severely handicapped in some situations, moderately handicapped in others, and not at all restricted in still others. Williams concludes: "The configuration of fears in agoraphobics is so highly idiosyncratic that it is substantially true that no two agoraphobics have exactly the same pattern of phobias, and that two people with virtually no overlapping areas of phobia disability can both be called agoraphobic" (1985, p. 112).

Furthermore, agoraphobics have many fears that are common to social phobia as well as many somatic complaints for which they often and persistently seek medical consultation even after agoraphobia is diagnosed. They are also inclined toward associated problems, such as generalized anxiety disorder, depression, obsessions, compulsions, and depersonalization. Given the multitude of symptoms that any specific patient could present, assessment of outcome may need to be individualized.

The earliest studies of psychotherapy usually produced gross ratings of improvement drawn from clinical records. A clinician, usually the therapist, viewed the progress of an individual patient and noted improvement in relation to initial status. This was a highly individualized approach; but because the formulation of problems and symptoms was never clearly operationalized, they could not be reliably measured. This procedure gave way to more formal assessments, including the use of standardized scales. During the last 20 to 30 years, researchers have relied more heavily on standardized research scales applied to all clients than on careful formulation of the goals and outcomes of individual clients. These different procedures for assessing change reflect the long-standing conflict in general and personality psychology between the nomothetic and the idiographic approaches.

The possibility of tailoring change criteria to each individual in therapy was mentioned frequently in the 1970s and seemed to offer a possible solution to resolving several recalcitrant problems in measuring change (e.g., Bergin, 1971). In the 1980s and early 1990s, there has been a new surge of interest in making change measures more idiographic. This interest has been bolstered by the flux of general articles on qualitative research methods (e.g., Polkinghorne, 1991).

Numerous procedures for individualizing patient treatment goals have been proposed over the years. The Target Complaints measure (Battle et al., 1966) was selected for inclusion in the NIMH core battery proposed by Waskow and Parloff (1975). Unfortunately, the Target Complaints Method has not generated a great deal of research in the ensuing years. Typical of these approaches is the "case-formulation" method advocated by Persons (1991). Her suggestions for improving psychotherapy research call for individualization of outcome: Each patient will have a different set of problems assessed with a different set of measures. Similarly, Strupp, Schacht, and Henry (1988) have argued for the principle of problem–treatment–outcome congruence. The conceptualizations and suggestions have not gone unchallenged (Garfield, 1991; Herbert & Mueser, 1991; Messer, 1991; Schacht, 1991; Silverman, 1991). These proposals have yet to face the foreboding task of empirical application.

One method that has received widespread attention and use is Goal Attainment Scaling (GAS) (Kiresuk & Sherman, 1968). Goal Attainment Scaling requires that a number of mental health goals be formulated prior to treatment by an individual or a combination of clinicians, client, and/or a committee assigned to the task. For each goal specified, a scale with a graded series of likely outcomes, ranging from least to most favorable, is devised. An attempt is made to formulate and specify goals with sufficient precision to allow an independent observer to determine how well a patient is functioning at a given time. Each goal is weighted to give those with high priority in therapy more weight than less important goals. The procedure also allows for transformation of the overall attainment of specific goals into a standard score.

In using the GAS method for the treatment of obesity, for example, one goal could be the specification and measurement of weight loss. A second goal could be reduction of depressive symptoms as measured by a single symptom scale such as the Beck Depression Inventory. Or, marital satisfaction could be assessed if the patient has serious marital problems. Each of these therapy goals is assigned a weight consistent with its importance. The particular scales and behaviors examined are varied from patient to patient, and, of course, one may include other specific types of diverse measures from additional points of view.

GAS has been applied within a variety of settings with varied success. Woodward, Santa-Barbara, Levin, and Epstein (1978) examined the role of GAS in studying family therapy outcome. Their study focused on termination and six-month follow-up goals for 270 families and resulted in an analysis of 1,005 goals. The authors, who seem to be advocates of GAS, reported reliable ratings that reflected diverse changes in the families studied. This interesting, although somewhat uncritical, report is a good demonstration of the flexibility and wealth of information resulting from the use of these idiographic procedures and their applicability with individuals as well as larger systems. Thus, the GAS has been recommended for use in marital and family therapy (Russell, Olson, Sprenkle, & Atilano, 1983) and continues to be applied with families as a way of expressing changes in the family as a whole, rather than limiting assessment to the identified patient (Fleuridas, Rosenthal, Leigh, & Leigh, 1990). GAS has been applied in a variety of settings, such as inpatient and school (e.g., Maher & Barbrack, 1984); with a variety of patient groups and treatment methods, such as group therapy (e.g., Flowers & Booaren, 1990); and with the intellectually handicapped (e.g., Bailey & Simeonson, 1988).

Many methodological issues need to be attended to while using GAS or similar methodology (Cytrynbaum, Ginath, Birdwell, & Brandt, 1979). For example, research use may require that treatment goals be set by someone other than the therapist in order to separate therapist treatment effects from therapist goal-setting biases. In addition, randomization should occur *following* goal setting and, ideally, some follow-up raters would be independent of goal setters and therapists.

Critical analyses show that GAS suffers from many of the same difficulties as other goal-setting procedures. The correlations between goals often seem to be fairly high, raising questions of independence. Goals judged either too easy or too hard to obtain are often included for analysis, but most important, goal attainment is judged on a relative rather than an absolute basis so that behavior change is inevitably confounded with expectations. The choice of goals and the attainment of goals are related to client as well as therapist characteristics that affect goal setting. Despite a manual of instructions and ample discussion, setting realistic, useful goals is not an easy task (Baily & Simeonson, 1988).

Calsyn and Davidson (1978) reviewed and assessed GAS as an evaluative procedure. These authors suggest that GAS occasionally has poor interrater agreement for goal attainment, indicating too much variability among those making ratings (e.g., therapist, client, expert judge). In general, most studies that have correlated GAS improvement ratings with other ratings of improvement, such as MMPI scores, client satisfaction, and therapist improvement ratings, have failed to show concurrent validity. Coefficients have been below .30 (e.g., Fleuridas et al., 1990). In addition, Calsyn and Davidson (1978) point out that the use of GAS also frequently eliminates the use of statistical procedures, such as covariance, that could otherwise correct for sampling errors.

Suggestions for the use of GAS in psychotherapy research have been made by Mintz and Kiesler (1982). Since their review, Lewis, Spencer, Haas, and DiVittis (1987) have described specific procedures for goal creation and later evaluation that increase reliability and validity without reducing the advantages of individualized goals. Lewis et al. suggest using GAS ratings only after follow-up data are collected, with evaluations of the *pattern of adjustment* built into goal expectations and evaluations.

Examination of studies using GAS reveals widespread modification in its use by numerous researchers, so that it is misleading to consider it a single method: *GAS is itself a variety of different methods for recording and evaluating client goal attainment.* It is not possible to compare accurately the goal attainment scores from one study to the next.

Similar procedures used in the evaluation of mental health services include the Problem-Oriented System (POS) (Klonoff & Cox, 1975; Weed, 1969), the Monthly Behavioral Progress Report and Projection Line System (Lloyds, 1983), and the Progress Evaluation Scales (Ihilevich & Glesser, 1979). These procedures suffer from many of the same deficiencies; they remain only frameworks for structuring the statement of goals and do not assure that the individualized goals that are specified will be much more than poorly defined subjective decisions by patient or clinician. This subjectivity leads to problems with setting up goals, which are often not only difficult to state but are written at various levels of abstraction.

Given these problems, the likelihood that units of change derived from individually tailored goals are unequal and therefore hardly comparable, the fact that different goals are differentially susceptible to psychotherapy influence, and the tendency for goals to change early in therapy (which requires revision of the goals), the status of individualized measures of change is tenuous. Effective individualization of goals for the purpose of assessing patient change remains an ideal rather than a reality. The intention to individualize goals is very appealing but the gap between intention and effective application appears to be rather large.

Conceptualizing Measures and Methods

Content. Figure 3.2 presents a conceptual scheme that organizes several important issues in measuring outcome. The first concept is "Content." Content areas covered by outcome measures can be divided into intrapersonal, interpersonal, and social role performance. Thus, content can be seen as a dimension that reflects the need to assess changes that occur within the client, in the client's intimate relationships, and more broadly, in the client's participation in community and social roles. This dimension could be considered a continuum that represents the degree to which an instrument measures intrapsychic attributes and bodily experiences versus characteristics of the client's participation in the interpersonal world. It is a matter of intellectual curiosity and values, if not empirical importance, to know about the kinds of changes that are targeted in treatment efforts. Empirically, the results of outcome studies are more impressive when content is broadly measured because interventions can have indirect effects as well as more and less extensive direct effects.

Temporality. Temporality reflects the fact that outcome, like process, is a dynamic state. Researchers have relied on single assessments of outcome posttherapy, on repeated measures of outcome pre- and posttherapy, and occasionally on trying to capture the pattern of behavior during and

Content	Temporality	Source	Technology
Intrapersonal	Single measure	Self-report	Global ratings
1		1	1
2		2	2
3		*	*
*	Repeated measure	Trained	Specific symptom index
*		Observers	1
*		1	2
Interpersonal		2	*
1		*	*
2		*	Observer ratings
*	Pattern measure	Relevant other	1
*		1	2
Social role		2	*
performance		*	*
1		*	Physiological measures
2		Therapist rating	1
*		1	2
		2	*
		*	*
		*	Life records
	Institutional	1
		1	2
		2	*
		*	
		*	

Figure 3.2 Scheme for organizing and selecting outcome measures

following treatment. This latter method is most common in the study of addictions where outcome must be assessed over a long period of time and in relation to patterns of behavior such as lapses, relapses, and increased abuse of other chemicals.

When outcome assessment includes attempts to study the persistence of change and especially the persistence of behaviors over substantial periods of time in a variety of settings and in the presence of normal life stresses and opportunities, as well as the vagaries of life, a more conservative appraisal of outcome usually results. When the durability of change is considered as part of the outcome question, estimates of the effectiveness of therapy are invariably reduced. This is true whether one considers addictions, depression, marital dysfunction, or a host of other disorders (cf. Chapter 5, this volume). Studies that attempt to assess the temporal stability of change may use a variety of methods. It often is important to select measures of change that are suitable for repeated measures. This is the advantage of brief single-symptom–oriented scales.

Source. In the ideal study of change, all the parties involved who have information about change can be represented, including the client, therapist, relevant (significant) others, trained judges (or observers), and societal agencies that store information such as employment and educational records (Strupp & Hadley, 1977). Unlike the physical sciences, measurement in psychotherapy is highly affected by the politics, values, and biases of those providing the data. Seldom are we able to merely observe phenomena of interest to us.

In a study examining recent trends in outcome assessment, Lambert and McRoberts (1992) reviewed 123 outcome studies from 1986 through 1991 published in the *Journal of Consulting and Clinical Psychology*. Specific outcome measures were classified into one of five "source" categories: *self-report, trained observer, significant other, therapist,* or *instrumental* (a category that included societal records or instruments such as physiological recording devices). Frequency data were then computed on the usage of specific instruments and on the usage of instrument sources across studies (see Table 1). As might be expected, the most popular source for outcome data was client self-report. In fact, 25 percent of the studies used client self-report data as the sole source for evaluation. Of the studies that relied solely on client self-report scales, 75 percent used more than one self-report scale. The next most frequent procedure employed both client self-report and observer ratings (20%), followed by client self-report and therapist ratings (15%), and self-report and instrumental sources

(8%). Significant other ratings were utilized alone or in combination with all other sources in only about 9 percent of the studies reported. The therapist-rated outcome was used alone or in combination with other measures in about 25 percent of the studies. Impressively, 30 percent of the studies used 6 or more instruments to reflect changes in patients. The most ambitious effort had a combination of 12 distinct measures from 3 sources to assess changes following psychotherapy.

The now necessary and, to some degree, common practice of applying multiple criterion measures in research studies (Lambert, 1983) has made it obvious that multiple measures from different sources do not yield unitary results (Farrell, Curran, Zwick, & Monti, 1983; Monti, Wallander, Ahern, Abrams, & Munroe, 1983). For example, we find that a specific treatment used to reduce seemingly simple fears may result in a decrease in behavioral avoidance of the feared object according to observers but no change in the self-reported level of discomfort associated with the feared object (Mylar & Clement, 1972; Ross & Proctor, 1973; Wilson & Thomas, 1973). Likewise, a physiological indicator of fear may show no change in response to a feared object as a result of treatment, whereas improvement in subjective self-report may be marked (Ogles et al., 1990).

The lack of agreement between sources is further supported by factor analytic studies that have combined a variety of outcome measures. The main factors derived from such studies tend to be associated closely with the measurement method or the source of observation used in collecting data rather than being identified by some theoretical or conceptual variable that would be expected to cut across techniques of measurement (Beutler & Hamblin, 1986; Cartwright, Kirtner, & Fiske, 1963; Forsyth & Fairweather, 1961; Gibson, Snyder, & Ray, 1955; Nichols & Beck, 1960; Pilkonis, Imber, Lewis, & Rubinsky, 1984; Shore, Massimo, & Ricks, 1965). For example, Pilkonis et al. (1984) factor analyzed 15 scales representing a variety of traits and symptoms from the client, therapist, expert judges, and significant others. These scales were reduced to three factors that most clearly represented the source of data rather than the content of the scale.

The fact that differences in outcomes have been found to be a function of source rather than content has been replicated across a variety of scales and patient populations and across three or four decades suggests that this finding is very robust. The consistency of these findings highlights the need to pay careful attention to the complexity of changes that follow psychological interventions and the way information from different perspectives is analyzed and reported. Few studies recognize or deal adequately with the complexities that result from divergence between sources, although creative efforts and some progress have been made (e.g., Berzins, Bednar, & Severy, 1975; Mintz, Luborsky, & Christoph, 1979).

The lack of consensus across sources of outcome evaluation, especially when each source is presumably assessing the same phenomena, has been viewed as a threat to the validity of data. Indeed, outcome data not only provide evidence about changes made by the individual, but also information about the differing value orientations and motivations of the individuals providing the data. This issue has been dealt with in several ways, ranging from discussion of "biasing motivations" and ways to minimize bias, to discussions of the value orientation of those involved (e.g., Strupp & Hadley, 1977). Clearly, there are times when we want measures to converge in providing identical estimates of change, as well as times when we collect data from different sources with the hope that the sources will make a unique contribution with little or no overlap. Researchers clearly need to collect outcome data from a variety of sources. Finding ways to combine or compare these data in estimating overall change (when it is appropriate) remains a vital task in the continuing development of sophisticated outcome assessment.

Technology of change measures. In addition to selecting different sources to reflect change, the technology or procedures used in devising scales and collecting data can have an impact on the final index of change. Smith, Glass, and Miller (1980) suggested that several factors associated with rating scales affect estimates of psychotherapy outcome. These factors, collectively called *reactivity*, were (1) the degree to which a measure could be influenced by either the client or therapist; (2) the similarity between therapy goals and the measure itself; and (3) the degree of "rater awareness" in the assessment process. Relatively nonreactive measures were presumably not so easily influenced in any direction by the parties involved. Using this definition of reactivity, a five-point scale was created, with low reactive measures including the Palmer Sweat Index, Galvanic Skin Response, and grade point average, and high reactive measures including therapist ratings of improvement and the Behavioral Approach Test. Smith et al. (1980) found the correlation between reactivity ratings and effect size to be .18.

Figure 3.2 lists several different technologies that have been employed in outcome measurement, including global ratings, specific symptom indexes, observer ratings (behavioral counts), phys-

iological measures, and life records. One broad dimension on which these procedures (or technologies) vary appears to be a direct–indirect dimension. Here the data are seen as possibly reflecting a bias determined by the propensity of subjects to produce effects consciously. Thus, global ratings of outcome either implicitly or explicitly call for raters to evaluate outcome directly. Their attention is drawn to the question, "Did I (the patient) get better in therapy?" In contrast, specific symptom indices focus the rater's attention (before and after treatment) on the status of specific symptoms and signs at the time the rating is made without explicit references to the outcome of therapy. Whereas the patient may realize at the time of posttesting that the therapy (or even the therapist) is being directly evaluated, the tendency to enter into the politics of this state of affairs is diminished if specific symptom indices are used.

Green, Gleser, Stone, and Siefert (1975) compared final status scores, pretreatment to posttreatment difference scores, and direct ratings of global improvement in 50 patients seen in brief crisis-oriented psychotherapy. They concluded that the percentage of patients considered improved has more to do with the type of rating scale employed than improvement per se! Global improvement ratings by therapists and patients showed very high rates of improvement with no patients claiming they were worse. When patients had to rate their symptoms more specifically, however, as with the Hopkins Symptom Checklist, they were likely to indicate actual intensification of some symptoms and to provide more conservative data than gross estimates of change (see also, Garfield et al., 1971).

Observer ratings in the form of behavioral counts can supply information that is subject to minimal rater distortion if enough attention is devoted to the procedures that are used. Ideally, these observer ratings call for counting behaviors in real-life circumstances in which the patients do not know they are being observed or have enough to focus on besides the impression they are making on the observer. However, Smith et al. (1980) rated some observer ratings as highly reactive because observer data are collected in circumstances that sometimes exaggerate the effectiveness of treatment. For example, the Behavioral Approach Test, often used after desensitization of phobias, calls for the client to approach a feared object. In most cases, the experimenter, evaluator, or even the therapist may be in the room with the patient. All know the desired outcome for control and treated patients and can provide subtle cues to elicit and discourage behavior. The client may want to please the evaluator and the therapist and acts in his or her behalf. Certain patients may also intend to distort in the direction of denying improvement (e.g., those with personality disorders).

Physiological monitoring is not usually under the conscious control of the patient, or at the very least presents a real and serious challenge to conscious distortion. Life records, such as grade point average and employment records, usually reflect a host of complex behaviors influenced by a wide variety of factors. Because such life records are produced without reference to the research project, they are potentially the least reactive data that can be collected.

Rather than making unqualified prejudgments about the reactivity of specific procedures for collecting data, future research needs to continue exploring the implications of technology in outcome research. This promises to be an area of continuing controversy. Smith et al. (1980) found that when they took reactivity of measures into account, the superiority of behavioral treatments over other treatments disappeared. Ogles et al. (1990), on the other hand, found no relation between reactivity and outcome within the narrow domain of agoraphobia. Other meta-analytic reviews have even found an inverse relationship between reactivity and effect size. Future research may clarify how data collection procedures consistently over- or underestimate treatment gains, thereby making estimates of change across measures easier to compare.

PSYCHOMETRICS OF CHANGE MEASUREMENT

Researchers have to consider certain other qualities of assessment devices that can have a dramatic impact on research studies. Among these qualities are those that are traditionally considered relevant in psychological testing generally — reliability and validity.

Reliability

Reliability is of particular importance in measuring outcome because the most common procedure for measuring change involves administering the assessment device before and after treatment. Some kind of change score is then calculated. Unfortunately, the reliability of change scores is not equal to the reliability of the measure (Cronbach, 1990). Changes in test scores from one occasion to another are due not only to true differences in whatever is being measured but also to "error" — other factors that affect the score (such as item sampling, the test taker's physical and mental state, the test environment, and administrative instructions). The standard error of the difference between two scores

is larger than the standard error of measurement for either score alone. Thus, reliability in outcome assessment is especially critical because low reliability of a measure is compounded with computation of a change score. The problems associated with unreliability are not solved by ignoring reliability or by using experimental scales with unknown reliability. The use of unstandardized scales makes it difficult, at best, to estimate the amount of change necessary to conclude that the difference between two scores is not due to chance fluctuations in the scores.

Validity

Validity is the ability of a measure to estimate or describe the dimension, phenomenon, or construct it purports to measure. Validity is an essential ingredient of outcome measures and one that is at the core of most discussions of outcome measurement. The limited validity of any specific measure necessitates the use of multiple measures from multiple perspectives. The development of valid measures of important constructs should continue to be a high-priority topic in psychotherapy research.

Sensitivity to Change

A central issue in outcome assessment is the degree to which a measure is likely to reflect changes that actually occur following participation in therapy. For example, if the Beck Depression Inventory is chosen as an outcome measure, will it reflect the same degree of change as the Hamilton Rating Scale for Depression? Will gross ratings of overall change provided by the patient show larger or smaller amounts of improvement than a scale that measures change on specific symptoms? To what extent are the conclusions drawn in comparative outcome studies determined by the specific measures selected by researchers? Do the techniques of meta-analysis actually allow us to summarize across the different outcome measures that are employed in different studies (essentially combining them) and thereby facilitate accurate conclusions about differential treatment effects?

There is a growing body of evidence to suggest that there are reliable differences in the "sensitivity" of instruments to change. In fact, the differences between measures is not trivial but large enough to raise questions about the interpretation of research studies. Two examples of such differences will make the importance of instrument selection clear.

Table 3.2 presents data from a review of agoraphobia outcome studies published in the 1980s. The effect sizes presented (based on pretest/posttest differences) show remarkable disparity in estimates of improvement as a function of the outcome instrument or method of measurement selected for

TABLE 3.2 Overall effect size (ES) means and standard deviations by scale

Scale	N[a]	MES	SDES
Phobic anxiety & avoidance	65	2.66	1.83
Global Assessment Scale	31	2.30	1.14
Self-Rating Severity	52	2.12	1.55
Fear Questionnaire	56	1.93	1.30
Anxiety during Behavioral Approach Test	48	1.36	0.85
Behavioral Approach Test	54	1.15	1.07
Depression measures	60	1.11	0.72
Fear Survey Schedule	26	0.99	0.47
Heart rate	21	0.44	0.56

[a]N equals the number of treatments whose effects were measured by each scale.
Source: Adapted by permission from Ogles, Lambert, Weight, and Payne (1990, Table 3). Copyright 1990 by the American Psychological Association.

study. The average patient taking the Fear Survey Schedule moved from the mean (50th percentile) of the pretest group to the 16th percentile of the pretest group after treatment. In contrast, the average patient being assessed with measures of phobic anxiety and avoidance moved from the 50th percentile of the pretest group to the .00 percentile of the pretest group following treatment.

Comparisons between the measures depicted in Table 3.2 are confounded somewhat by the fact that the data were aggregated across all studies that used either measure. But similar results can be found when only studies that give both measures to a patient sample are aggregated.

Table 3.3 presents data from a comparison of three frequently employed measures of depression: the Beck Depression Inventory (BDI) and the Zung Self-Rating Scale for Depression (ZSRS), both self-report inventories, and the Hamilton Rating Scale

TABLE 3.3 Matched pairs of mean effect size (ES) values

Scale pair	N[a]	MES[b]	SDES	t
HRSD/ZSRS	17	0.94*/0.62*	0.61/0.30	1.88
BDI/HRSD	49	1.16**/1.57**	0.86/1.08	2.11
ZSRS/BDI	13	0.70/1.03	0.46/0.52	1.65

Note: HRSD = Hamilton Rating Scale for Depression: ZSRS = Zung Self-Rating Scale; BDI = Beck Depression Inventory
[a]N = the number of treatments whose effects were measured by each pair of depression scales.
[b]Values derived from studies in which subjects' depression was measured on two scales at a time. Effect size represents within-study comparisons.
*P < .05
**P < .025
Source: Reprinted by permission from Lambert, Hatch, Kingston, and Edwards (1986). Copyright 1986 by the American Psychological Association.

for Depression (HRSD), an expert judge rating. Meta-analytic results suggest that the most popular dependent measures used to assess depression following treatment provide reliably different pictures of change. The HRSD as employed by trained professional interviewers provides a significantly larger index of change than the BDI and ZSRS, two brief patient self-report measures. Because the amount of actual improvement patients experience after treatment is never known, these findings are subject to several different interpretations. The HRSD may overestimate patient improvement, but it could just as easily be argued that the HRSD accurately reflects improvement and that the BDI and ZSRS underestimate the amount of actual improvement. Both over- and underestimation may also be suggested with true change falling somewhere in between the HRSD estimate and those provided by the BDI and ZSRS.

It does appear, however, that there are reliable differences between measures and that these differences need to be explored and understood. Additional meta-analytic data suggest further differences between the size of treatment effects produced by different outcome measures (cf. Christensen, Hadzi-Pavlovic, Andrews, & Mattick, 1987; Jacobson, Wilson, & Tupper, 1988; Miller & Berman, 1983; Ogles et al., 1990; Robinson, Berman, & Neimeyer, 1990; Shapiro & Shapiro, 1982; Smith et al., 1980). Abstracting from these and related studies (e.g., Horowitz, Marmar, Weiss, Kaltrider, & Wilner, 1986), the following conclusions can be tentatively drawn:

1. Therapist and expert judge–based data in which judges are aware of the treatment status of clients produce larger effect sizes than self-report data, data produced by significant/relevant others, institutional data, and instrumental data.

2. Gross ratings of change produce larger estimates of change than ratings on specific dimensions or symptoms.

3. Change measures based on the specific targets of therapy (such as individualized goals or anxiety-based measures taken in specific situations) produce larger effect sizes than more distal measures, *including a wide variety of personality tests.*

4. Life adjustment measures that tap social role performance in the natural setting (e.g., grade point average) produce smaller effect sizes than analogue or laboratory-based measures.

5. Measures collected soon after therapy show larger effect sizes than measures collected at a later date.

6. Physiological measures such as heart rate usually show relatively small treatment effects com-

pared to other measures across a variety of contexts even when they are specifically targeted in treatment.

Many measures are very susceptible to the instructional set given to those who are providing the data. Further research is needed to clarify the various factors that inflate and deflate estimates of change. *For now, however, it is clear that dependent measures are not equivalent in their tendencies to reflect change and that meta-analysis, as it is typically used to combine different measures, cannot overcome the differences between measures.*

CLINICAL VERSUS STATISTICAL SIGNIFICANCE

Most psychotherapy research is aimed at questions of theoretical and practical interest. Is dynamic therapy more effective than cognitive therapy? Is exposure in vivo necessary for fear reduction? These and a host of similar questions give rise to the research designs that have been used in outcome research. The data acquired in such studies are submitted to statistical tests of significance. Group means are compared; within-group and between-group variabilities are considered; and the resulting numerical figure is compared with a preset critical value. When the magnitude of the distance between groups is sufficiently large, it is agreed that the results are *not* likely to be the result of chance fluctuations in sampling, thus demonstrating statistical significance. This procedure is the standard for most research and is an important part of the scientific process.

A common criticism of outcome research, however, is that the results of studies, as they are typically reported in terms of statistical significance, obscure both the clinical relevance of the findings and the impact of the treatment on specific individuals. Unfortunately, statistically significant improvements do not necessarily equal practically important improvements for the individual client. Statistically significant findings may, therefore, be of limited practical value. This fact raises questions about the real contributions of empirical studies for the practice of psychotherapy and begs for practical solutions.

The troubling fact is that in a well-designed study, small differences after treatment between large groups could produce findings that reach statistical significance, while the real-life difference is trivial in terms of the reduction of symptoms. For example, a behavioral method of treatment for obesity may create a statistically significant difference between treated and untreated groups if all treated

subjects lost 10 pounds and all untreated subjects lost 5 pounds. However, the clinical utility of an extra 5-pound weight loss is debatable, especially in the clinically obese patient. This dilemma goes right to the core of the problems with outcome measurement—adequate definitions and quantification of improvement.

Numerous attempts have been aimed at translating reports of treatment effects into metrics that reflect the importance of the changes that are made. In the earliest studies of therapy outcome, patients were categorized posttherapy with gross ratings of "improved," "cured," and the like, implying meaningful change. The lack of precision in such ratings, however, resulted in their waning use (Lambert, 1983). Those interested in operant conditioning and single-subject designs developed concepts such as *social validity* to describe practically important improvement (Kazdin, 1977; Wolf, 1978). Some disorders easily lend themselves to analysis of important changes because improvement can be defined as the absence of a behavior, for example, cessation of drinking, smoking, or drug use. But most symptoms targeted in psychotherapy cannot be so easily defined and measured.

Clinical Significance
Jacobson, Follette, and Revenstorf (1984) brought clinical significance into prominence by proposing statistical methods that would illuminate the degree to which individual clients recover at the end of therapy. Recovery was proposed to be a posttest score that was more likely to belong to the functional than the dysfunctional population of interest. Estimating clinical significance requires that norms for the functional sample have been established and that certain assumptions about the test scores have been met. For change to be clinically significant, a patient must also change enough so that one can be confident that the change exceeds measurement error (calculated by a statistic titled the *reliable change index*). When a patient moves from one distribution (dysfunctional) into another (functional) and the change reliably exceeds measurement error (calculated by dividing the absolute magnitude of change by the standard error of measurement), then change is viewed as clinically significant and the patient is more likely functional than dysfunctional. A growing number of studies have employed these techniques with various treatment samples (e.g., Jacobson et al., 1984b; Lacks & Powlista, 1989; Mavissakalian, 1986; Perry, Shapiro, & Firth, 1986; Schmaling & Jacobson, 1987). Tingey, Burlingame, Lambert, and Barlow (1989) demonstrate how cutoff scores on the GSI of the SCL-90-R can be used to define clinically significant change (see Figure 3.3).

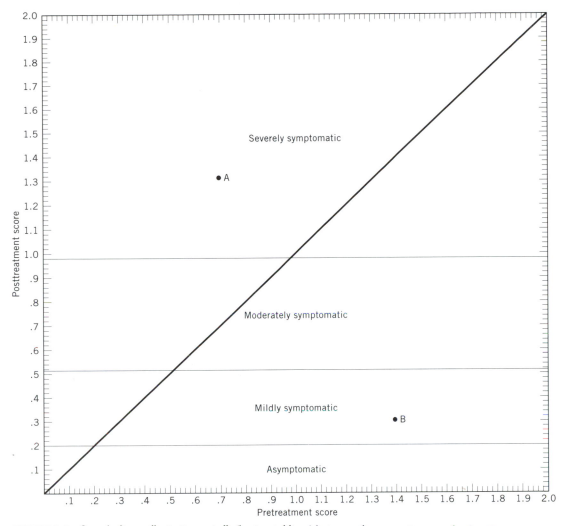

FIGURE 3.3 Sample figure illustrating cutoffs (horizontal lines) between the normative samples (continuous diagonal line indicates points of no change between pre- and post-treatemnt scores). *Source:* From Tingey et al. (1989), used by permission of the authors.

Plotted points ("A" and "B") on Figure 3.3 would indicate Subject A's and Subject B's pre- and posttreatment GSI score, prettreatment along the horizontal axis and posttreatment along the vertical. The continuous diagonal line signifies no change between pre- and posttreatment scores; a subject receiving identical pre- and posttreatment scores would fall on this line. The area above this line denotes an increase in the GSI score from pretreatment, indicating greater symptomatology (Subject A), while the area below denotes a decrease and less symptomatology (Subject B).

The three horizontal lines signify the cutoff points between two adjacent samples' distributions and are used in determining the clinical significance of pre- to posttreatment change. The areas they separate indicate the four normative samples: asymptomatic and mildly, moderately, and severely

symptomatic. A plotted point on the graph indicates a subject's placement (in reference to the normative samples) at posttreatment. Unless there is no change pre- to posttreatment, this point will fall some place other than the diagonal line. By drawing an imaginary vertical line from this point to the no-change diagonal line, the subject's placement at prettreatment can be determined. For example, Subject A's posttreatment plotted point places him or her in the severely symptomatic sample, and the vertical line drawn down from this point places him or her at prettreatment in the moderately symptomatic sample (the line intersects the no-change line within this sample's area). This indicates, according to GSI scores, that during the course of therapy this subject deteriorated and moved from the moderately symptomatic to the severely symptomatic sample. Subject B, however, improved and moved from the severely symptomatic sample to the mildly symptomatic sample.

To produce Figure 3.3, it was necessary to find normative data. The normative data for the severely symptomatic sample were found in existing literature on the SCL-90-R as applied to inpatients (Derogatis, 1983), outpatients (Burlingame & Barlow, in press), and the original normative standardization sample (general population) collected by Derogatis (1983). The asymptomatic sample was collected for the purpose of identifying a group of subjects who were nominated and carefully screened to exclude persons who were not well adjusted (in contrast to the typical normative sample that is based on a random sample of persons, some of whom may evidence psychopathology).

Through these procedures, the patient's status in relation to patients and nonpatients was carefully defined and could be observed along the dimension of mental health, with severe pathology at one end and ideal mental health (being asymptomatic) at the other end. Efforts such as this need to be carried out with other standardized measures.

Normative Comparison

Another method of estimating clinically significant change, advanced by Kendall and Grove (1988) and Nietzel, Russell, Hemmings, and Gretter (1987), is normative comparison. Examples include the use of social drinking behaviors as criteria for outcome in the treatment of problem drinking or the use of definitions of adequate sexual performance (e.g., ratio of orgasms to attempts at sex; or time to orgasm following penetration; Sabalis, 1983). These criteria are based on data about the normative functioning of individuals and can be easily and meaningfully applied with a number of disorders for which normal or ideal functioning is readily apparent and easily measured (e.g., obesity). But normative comparison can also be used as a method of quantifying clinical significance. This strategy involves comparing the behavior of clients before and after treatment to that of a sample of nondisturbed "normal" peers. An advantage of this method is that comparisons can be directly based on the psychological tests that are commonly used to measure therapy outcome, if a standardization sample of nonpatients is also available. Usually the procedure involves comparing the posttest scores of treated clients to those of various control groups. Thus, standards of clinical improvement can be based on normative data and posttreatment status gathered through meta-analysis of multiple samples of patients, instead of the magnitude of change of specific individual patients.

Trull, Nietzel, and Main (1988), for example, reported a meta-analytical review of 19 studies of agoraphobia that used the Fear Questionnaire. Self-reported posttreatment adjustment of agoraphobics was compared with that of two normative samples. The normative samples were based on college students (at two universities) or a community sample drawn randomly from the phone directory. Both samples included only subjects who had never received treatment for a phobic condition. As might be expected, the community sample was more disturbed than the college sample, probably because agoraphobia prohibits or inhibits attendance in college classes. As a consequence, estimates of clinically significant change via normative comparison turned out to be a function of the normative groups used for comparison. Agoraphobics, treated mainly with exposure, improved during treatment. However, the average agoraphobic started at the 99th percentile of the *college norms* and improved only to the 98.7th percentile of this normative sample at the end of treatment. The average agoraphobic also started at the 97th percentile of the *community norm* and progressed to the 68th percentile at posttreatment and to the 65.5th percentile at follow-up.

Using similar methodology, Nietzel et al. (1987) studied the clinical significance of psychotherapy for unipolar depression. They compared the posttherapy adjustment of depressed and nondepressed adults who took the Beck Depression Inventory. In all, 28 published studies were used to calculate composite BDI norms; these were compared with results from 31 outcome studies that yielded 60 effect sizes. Three normative groups could be identified: a nondistressed group, a general population group (consisting mostly of college subjects), and a situationally distressed group (pregnant women) who were very similar to the general population samples. Comparisons contrasting the depressed patients with the normative samples suggested that the various treatments (all of which appeared similar in their effectiveness) produced clinically significant changes. In fact, the average depressed patient moved from the 99th percentile of the general population norms to the 76th percentile of this reference sample. These gains were maintained at follow-up. The average patient moved from the 99th percentile to only the 95th percentile on the norms for the nondistressed group. The authors concluded that clinically significant improvement depends on the nature of the normative sample.

A more recent study combining various methods of calculating clinical significance illustrates the potential of using more than one procedure. Scott and Stradling (1990) studied and contrasted the effects of cognitive therapy offered in either an individual or group format to patients who were depressed.

Besides the usual group comparisons based on inferential statistics, the authors reported clinically significant improvements as well. Using Kendall, Hollon, Beck, Hammen, and Ingram's (1987) criteria for nondepressed, mild depression, moderate depression, and severe depression on the BDI, the authors showed obvious differences between wait-list and psychotherapy outcome over the 12 weeks of treatment and for one-year follow-up. Using the criteria developed by Nietzel et al. (1987), they estimated that after treatment the average treated patient had moved from the 99th plus percentile to the 94th percentile of the nondistressed comparison group and the 74th percentile of the general population comparison group.

They also applied the Reliable Change Index (Jacobson et al. 1984a), showing that patient change was of a great enough magnitude so that the patients could reasonably be considered to have left the ranks of the dysfunctional. In fact, they estimated that 100 percent of those in the group treatment and 84 percent of those in individual treatment manifested clinically significant improvement, while 53 percent on the wait-list showed similar improvement. In addition, 5 percent of the wait-list subjects deteriorated while none of the treatment subjects did.

High End-State Functioning

Another method of calculating clinically significant change is through a priori derivation of "high end-state functioning" based on multiple measures. Jacobson et al. (1988) proposed three methods for defining high end-state functioning and compared them with their normative methods. High end-state functioning defines clinical improvement as reaching normality by setting a cutoff score on each outcome measure prior to completion of therapy. These cutoffs are based on clinical judgments about normality. The advantage of this method is that it allows theoretical considerations to enter into definitions of improvement while taking into account multiple measures. High end-state functioning has the disadvantage of being based upon consensus among investigators rather than being purely norm-based. In their comparison of these methods with those from statistical estimates based on norm groups, Jacobson et al. (1988) found end-state analysis depended upon the reliability of the measures that were used to calculate cutoff scores. When reliability was high, the statistically based technique was more conservative.

Despite the advantages of defining clinically significant change, problems include the complexities that are created by the fact that researchers use multiple outcome measures, each one possibly providing different information regarding both the indi-

vidual as well as the group as a whole. What shall we do with the lack of congruence between clinically significant improvement on one dependent measure, but not on others? Should a patient be required to change on more than one measure to be declared improved to the degree that clinical significance implies? Although high end-state functioning deals with this problem to some degree, so far no study has really addressed these issues in any substantial way.

Other problems include the use of discrete cutoff points and their derivation (how should these points be set?); the problems that result from score distributions that are not normal (how serious are violations of this assumption of normality?); and the limitations of floor and ceiling effects in many of the most frequently used tests. The problem of floor and ceiling effects is especially serious as many tests are heavily weighted toward pathology and not developed for use with people who represent the actualized end of the functioning continuum. In some instances, it is this actualized end of the continuum that represents the patients' nondisturbed peers. There is also considerable controversy about procedural and statistical analyses (cf. Jacobson & Truax, 1991; Lacks & Powlista, 1989; Chapter 2, this volume) that have substantial impact on estimates of clinical significance. Finally, we are reminded by a special issue of *Behavioral Assessment* edited by Jacobson (1988) that despite the precision that may be used to define improvement, definitions of improvement are somewhat arbitrary and culturally ascribed.

Despite these problems, clinical significance in its various forms appears to us to be an important topic of future research. Advances in operationalizing clinical significance promise to make psychotherapy outcome assessment richer and more relevant to clinical practice, an improvement that is long overdue. Already, however, there is evidence that these methods will provide more conservative estimates of treatment effects and more modest conclusions about the efficacy of psychotherapy (Jacobson & Truax, 1991).

ISSUES IN DATA COLLECTION AND ANALYSIS

Influence of Assessor

The responses of clients may well be affected by characteristics and communications of the assessor (Rosenthal, 1969). This is an especially important problem in outcome research where judges, clinical experts, significant others, and therapists are involved in the assessment. Here, some of the same procedures used in process research (to be discussed shortly) can be employed to increase the veracity of outcome data. Several authors have offered suggestions for enhancing the validity of therapist ratings (Newman, 1983), expert observer ratings (Auerbach, 1983), ratings by significant others (Davidson & Davidson, 1983), client self-report (Beutler & Crago, 1983; Cameron & Evers, 1990; Sobell & Sobell, 1990), and institutional measures (Maisto & Maisto, 1983).

The general principle in all these efforts is to try to measure the actual state, beliefs, or behavior of clients. Thus, the instructions from researchers to assessors, including the client, encourage candor through some means (Rankin, 1990). Assessors are typically offered a degree of anonymity, especially with regard to telling clients that their responses will not be shared with the therapist or used to evaluate the therapist. The confidentiality offered clients not only encourages more honest responses from them, but ethical responsibility as well.

Guidelines are available in many areas of research. For example, Babor, Brown, and Del Boca (1990) summarized reviews of methodological studies pertinent to the accuracy of verbal reports of persons with addictive disorders. Although generally reliable, the accuracy of self-reports depends on (1) sensitivity of information sought (e.g., demographics vs. arrest record); (2) specificity of validation criteria (e.g., archival data vs. urine tests); (3) personal characteristics of informant (e.g., sober vs. intoxicated); (4) reference to time (e.g., immediate past vs. early life); and (5) demand characteristics of the situation surrounding the research (e.g., intake interview vs. program evaluation). Babor et al. suggest a model and an interview format that enhances the accuracy of verbal reports based on interviews.

Psychotherapy research is usually so complex and cumbersome that the details regarding administration of instruments are very vague or absent in the methodology section of most published research. This often stands in contrast to basic research in other areas of psychology where more attention is given to this topic. One can only hope that researchers take the precautions normally assumed to be taken in the field (cf. Kazdin, 1980) or that they report deviations from accepted standards. For example, given that researchers normally inform clients that their posttherapy outcome ratings will not be shared with their therapist, deviations from this standard should be reported. The reader of these studies can then safely assume that treatment effects may be exaggerated when contrasted with anonymous ratings (e.g., Shadish & Sweeney, 1991; Smith et al. 1980).

Posttherapy Improvement Ratings Versus Pre – Post Outcome Ratings

Many researchers have employed posttherapy improvement ratings as a means of judging the effects of psychotherapy (Beutler & Crago, 1983). These measures, although popular, seem to be inordinately influenced by the client's status at the termination of treatment and are thus not the most accurate measures of actual change in therapy. There is good reason to argue that these "improvement ratings" are actually measures of current status. Because they do not reflect the degree of actual change in therapy, they are not likely to be sensitive to psychotherapy effects (Garfield, 1986). Beutler and Crago (1983) have suggested methods for converting posttherapy ratings into actual measures of change. These methods seem promising but are infrequently applied. Therefore, those who carry out or evaluate outcome research need to keep in mind that posttherapy improvement ratings are not necessarily measures of improvement.

The Use of Difference Scores

Just as improvement ratings are inordinately affected by posttherapy status, change scores (or difference scores) may be inordinately influenced by pretreatment status. Patients who have the highest level of pathology pretherapy have the greatest opportunity to show positive changes (Mintz & Kiesler, 1982). This also suggests that some of the change reflected in pre- minus postdifference scores may be the result of regression to the mean.

How should the researcher analyze the possible changes in status consequent to some intervention? This is a common problem in psychological and educational research. Probably the most commonly used procedure has been the analysis of variance of raw gain (or difference) scores (Ashcroft, 1971). Because of problems of unreliability of difference scores, some researchers have proposed calculation of a true gain score or residual gain score (Cronbach & Furby, 1970). Hummel-Rossi and Weinberg (1975) have recommended either the true residualized gain score (a score that is independent of pretest status) or partial correlation (multiple regression with posttest as the criterion and pretest as the covariate). The true residual gain score is used when the focus is on the change of an individual (with respect to the group), and partial correlation is used when the interest is in relating group change to other variables.

Tucker, Damarin, and Messick (1966) have recommended a base-free measure of change, but it has not been frequently used. Beutler and Crago (1983) have recommended use of Cronbach and

Gleser's (1953) D^2 transformation. The use of this statistic is based on the assumption that the reliability of raw change scores may, in fact, be higher than either pre or post measures alone. D^2 requires that pre–post status be measured in several areas. It is a method for combining several scores and reducing error variance. Beutler and Crago (1983) suggest that both methods of deriving unbiased change scores should be used because they correct for different problems. Both procedures are attempts to reflect actual change accurately, and any discrepancy between the results of using either method could be explored. There is not yet a standard procedure in outcome research, although one is needed (see Beutler & Hamblin, 1986, for further discussion of this issue). The most common procedure is analysis of covariance or multiple analysis of covariance with pretreatment performance being the covariate (cf. Kazdin, Bass, Siegel, & Thomas, 1989).

Statistical Power

As Beutler and Hill (1992) pointed out, investigators often ignore the fact that the power of univariate comparisons to detect a difference is limited by the size of the smallest sample, the number of comparison groups, and the nature of the dependent measures. When a large number of measures are used, methods should be employed to correct for data redundancy. Rather than exploring all possibilities and thereby reducing statistical power, planned comparisons should first be employed with the theoretically important measures. Multivariate procedures should be used wherever possible, thus reducing the number of analyses and study-wise error rates. Planned comparisons allow one to examine only the specific hypotheses and thereby limit the effects of multiple analyses on error rates, while preserving power. (See Chapter 2, this volume, for additional discussions of clinical significance, statistical power, etc.)

SUMMARY

Many advances have been made in outcome assessment over the years; yet, outcome issues are, as Luborsky (1971) has suggested, hardy perennials in the field of psychotherapy research. At present, there is enough evidence of such divergence, and even chaos, that the time is ripe for fundamental change. No new paradigm shift is on the horizon, however; and until such a shift occurs, we will have to be content with the gradual improvements that have characterized the last five decades.

We turn our attention now to methodological issues that are important in measuring therapeutic process. In contrast to the outcome section, the process section of this chapter deals almost exclusively with methods that reflect contemporary wisdom for collecting process data rather than commentary on specific process measures.

METHODOLOGICAL ISSUES IN PROCESS RESEARCH

Our emphasis here is upon methods and procedures (the conditions) that impact process research rather than the process of therapy itself. We want the reader to understand some of the choices available in process research and to grasp the strengths and limitations of such choices.

MEASURES IN PROCESS RESEARCH

Types of Measures

Process measures can be categorized according to several different dimensions that illuminate their important characteristics: direct versus indirect measurement, perspective, focus, aspect of process, use of a classical or pragmatic coding strategy, type of scaling, and theoretical orientation. A number of attempts have been made to classify process systems according to a few of these dimensions (Hill, 1991; Russell, 1988; Russell & Stiles, 1979), but no classification system encompasses all the permutations of the dimensions listed. Such a classification scheme would be unwieldy and would yield many cells where no measures have been developed. *Researchers need to be sure that the measure they select assesses the dimensions they want and meets the necessary assumptions.*

Direct versus indirect measurement. Kiesler (1973) defined direct measures as those that code or rate behaviors in live therapy sessions or from transcripts, audiotapes, or videotapes of the sessions. Direct measures tend to be used primarily by nonparticipant[1] judges to rate some excerpt from a therapy session, although some more recent mea-

---

[1]The term *raters* usually refers to persons who rate behaviors on interval rating scales, whereas the terms *judges* and *observers* usually refer to persons who classify behaviors into categories. For this chapter, we will use the more generic term *judges* to refer to persons who do either type of judgment task.

sures have been developed to examine therapist or client perspectives of specific in-session events based on reviews of tapes of the session (Elliott, 1986).

Kiesler (1973) defined indirect measures as those that use a questionnaire format to tap therapist and/or client global (rather than moment-by-moment) experiences in sessions. These questionnaires are usually completed immediately after particular therapy sessions and ask participants about their states (rather than traits) during the session.

Perspective.   Another major way to categorize process measures is by the perspective from which therapy is described: therapist, client, or nonparticipant judge, the latter being the most typical perspective relied upon in process research (Elliott, 1991). In the past, judges were thought to be objective about the process because they were not involved personally. Now we are more aware that judges have as many biases as do therapists and clients, but that these biases differ based on the level of involvement in the therapy. Therapists and clients have to participate in the therapy session; nonparticipant judges do not.

Most empirical research has found minimal correlations among the three perspectives on various measures (e.g., Caracena & Vicory, 1969; Fish, 1970; Hansen, Moore, & Carkhuff, 1968; Hill, 1974; Hill, Helms, Tichenor et al., 1988; Kurtz & Grummon, 1972; Tichenor & Hill, 1989; Truax, 1966). For example, Lambert, DeJulio and Stein (1978) concluded that there is minimal relationship among measures of facilitative conditions for therapists, clients, and judges. Further, reviews by both Luborsky, Chandler, Auerbach, Cohen, and Bachrach (1971) and Gurman (1977) have suggested that client perceptions of facilitative conditions are more strongly related to outcome than are ratings by judges.

Focus.   Elliott (1991) pointed out three foci for process measures: client(s), therapist(s), or dyad/system. Most current process measures focus on the client or therapist, although there has been increased interest in a dyadic or systemic focus (e.g., Benjamin, 1974; Budman et al., 1987).

Aspect of process.   Elliott (1991) indicated four kinds of communication variables that could be studied: *content* (what is said or meant, e.g., discussion of loss, vocational concerns), *action* (what is done, e.g., question, disclosure), *style/state* (how it is said or done, e.g., empathically, judgmentally), and *quality* (how well it is done or said, e.g., competence). Of these four communication variables,

action has been studied most often and content least often.

Coding strategies.   The classical and pragmatic methods are two major coding strategies that have been identified (Marsden, 1965, 1971; Russell, 1988; Russell & Stiles, 1979). In a classical strategy, judgments are based on observable behaviors, with minimal inference about intentions or states (e.g., head nods; Hill & Stephany, 1990). In the pragmatic strategy, coders make inferences about the speaker's intention or internal state based on observable behavior (e.g., dynamic motive states such as dependency, or hostility; Dollard & Auld, 1959). With pragmatic coding, the judges make inferences on the basis of their observation of behavior; whereas with classical coding, judges stick very close to the observable data and the researcher makes inferences about what the data mean. A classical strategy tends to result in higher interjudge reliability than a pragmatic strategy because variables are operationally defined and rely on observation rather than inference.

Type of scaling.   Although many types of scales have been developed, rating scales and nominal category systems have been used most extensively in process research. Additionally, Q-sorts have been used sporadically.

Rating scales typically use five-, seven-, or nine-point Likert-type scales, although some researchers use even-numbered scales to force a decision toward one extreme of the scale or the other. Rating scales are advantageous from a data analytic viewpoint because the interval scale allows combination of data across raters and data points. For example, an average score of "depth" can be calculated across all interpretations (Harway, Dittman, Raush, Bordin, & Rigler, 1955). Unfortunately, many of our process variables do not fit the assumptions necessary for interval data, in that there is neither an equal distance between scale points nor a hierarchical difference between points such that some points are "better than" other points. Further, Coombs (1951) and Bordin et al. (1954) noted that rating scales often force data into unidimensional continua even when a single dimension does not exist. For example, the Experiencing Scale (Klein, Mathieu, Gendlin, & Kiesler, 1970) seems to involve more than a single dimension, making it difficult to determine whether a high score on that scale reflects high client involvement or insight. Researchers should be cautious about using rating scales for constructs that do not meet the assumptions of interval data; however, pragmatic considerations often preclude meeting such criteria and researchers proceed, knowing that there is a risk of obtaining ambiguous findings.

With a nominal strategy, data are classified into categories. Use of categories assumes that observations of behaviors can be segmented into chunks, ignoring the gray areas between categories. A judgment is made about the presence or absence of behaviors without regard to their manner or quality. Because categories cannot readily be summed, however, nominal data are harder to use.

Items or categories can be developed to be either mutually exclusive or nonmutually exclusive. In a mutually exclusive system, only one category can apply for any given behavior or observation. For example, with the Counselor Verbal Response Modes Category System (Hill, 1986), judges assign each therapist response unit (sentence) to only one response mode because each unit usually fits only one grammatical speech structure. In a nonmutually exclusive system, more than one category or item can apply for a given behavior or observation. In using the Intentions List (Hill & O'Grady, 1985), judges assign up to three intentions to each therapist speaking turn (during a videotape-assisted review of the session) because therapists often have more than one intention when delivering interventions. With nonmutually exclusive categories, definitions need to be as distinct as possible, so that truly separate behaviors are occurring rather than there simply being two categories that cannot be distinguished. Lack of separateness can be determined by noting whether judges always assign the same categories together.

Another type of scaling is the Q-sort method, in which judges sort items about the therapy process into a number of categories distributed across a rating scale. For example, with Jones, Cummings, and Horowitz's (1988) Psychotherapy Process Q-Set, judges sort items in a normal distribution of nine categories with the middle categories including progressively more items. Thus, items are rated relative to one another in their salience. Jones et al. (1988) indicated that this method can capture the uniqueness of each therapy case as well as the similarities or dissimilarities of one case to another. The advantage of the Q-sort method is that it forces a distribution across a scale, compared to rating scales that generally elicit only positive ratings. The disadvantage is that Q-sorts impose a particular distribution on the items.

Theoretical orientation. Some measures have been developed specifically to measure constructs from a particular theory. For example, the Experiencing Scale (Klein et al., 1970) was developed to measure constructs from client-centered theory related in client involvement. Because it was devel-

oped to measure client-centered therapy, the Experiencing Scale would not be as appropriate for measuring process in cognitive-behavioral therapy. Other measures have been developed to be pantheoretical or to assess behaviors valued across therapies, for example, the Psychotherapy Process Q-Set (Jones et al., 1988).

Summary of types of measures. Researchers can use the preceding dimensions to provide a description of their measure. These dimensions can help researchers to be clear about whether the intent of their study, theory of change, and assumptions about process are consistent with their methodological choices. In general, a measure should represent only single aspects of each dimension. Thus, a measure could use only interval data, could assess only client behavior, and could use the perspective of nonparticipant judges. By recognizing the type of measure that is being employed, the researcher and reader of research can immediately see the limitations of the research.

Validity of Process Measures

As with outcome measures, researchers need to provide evidence for validity and reliability of all measures used in process research. However, researchers also need to strike a balance between validity and reliability. Researchers often present evidence of interjudge reliability, but ignore validity, which is equally important. We must have evidence both that our instruments measure what we want them to measure and that they can do so reliably.

Face and content validity. Preliminary face and content validity can be obtained by developing items similar to those used in past measures of the same construct, assuming that these items measure the appropriate content of interest. Face and content validity can also be obtained from experts from a range of orientations, who give feedback about the clarity and completeness of the measure after examining or using the instrument. Both face and content validity are very important to establish in the preliminary phases of measure development.

Construct validity. Construct validity cannot be established directly; it can only be inferred when the measure operates in expected ways. Hence, construct validity can be established by demonstrating that the measure is sensitive to predictable differences between groups. For example, therapists have been found to use response modes in ways that fit their stated theoretical orientations (Elliott et al., 1987; Hill, Thames, & Rardin, 1979;

Stiles, 1979; Stiles, Shapiro, & Firth-Cozens, 1988; Strupp, 1955, 1957).

Convergent validity. Convergent validity means that a measure is related to other similar measures of the same construct. Although this step is rarely done, it aids tremendously in the evaluation of measures of supposedly similar constructs. For example, Elliott et al. (1987) found high agreement among judges for six specific response modes (question, information, advisement, reflection, interpretation, and self-disclosure) across six different measures of therapist response modes. Thus, results for the six response modes across these measures can be compared across studies. Tichenor and Hill (1989) found that three of four measures of judge-rated working alliance were highly related, although none was related to client or therapist ratings of working alliance. Thus, the three measures seem to be measuring a similar construct, but we cannot be sure that the other measures are measuring the same construct.

Discriminant validity. Discriminant validity means that a measure is not highly related to measures of dissimilar constructs. Of particular importance is that a process measure adds new information above and beyond what we could obtain with measures of intelligence, social desirability, and other variables that are conceptually distinct. Unfortunately, developers of process instruments typically do not demonstrate discriminant validity of their measures. For example, although therapist response modes and therapist empathy theoretically should not be related given that a therapist could give any of the response modes with any degree of empathy, we do not know if they are correlated. We encourage researchers to use multitrait, multimethod analyses (Campbell & Fiske, 1959) to demonstrate the convergent and discriminant validity of their measures.

Reliability

Most process researchers are interested more in the behavior being studied than in the variation among the judges who make observations about the behavior. Heyns and Zander (1966) indicated that the consistency of target behavior is a substantive problem but that the consistency of observers is a methodological problem. Only after the consistency of the judges has been established can the consistency of the target behavior be determined. Thus, consistency (or reliability) across judges is very important. Before one can study the data generated by the judges, mean differences between judges must be removed (by averaging across judges for consensus judgments).

Different statistics are involved in assessing the reliability of interval and nominal data. Additionally, the issues for determining the reliability among judges and the reliability of the measure require separate attention. We touch only briefly on many of these issues in this chapter and encourage readers to seek out the references for more complete discussion.

Interval rating scales. Reliability between raters often is determined through some form of intraclass correlation (Shrout & Fleiss, 1979) for either a fixed-effects or a random-effects model. A fixed-effects model yields an estimate of the reliability of a single or mean rating of a particular sample of raters and reflects the degree of consistency in a specific set of ratings. A random-effects model provides an estimate of the reliability of a single or mean rating that might be obtained with an independent sample of raters and represents the generalizability of the mean rating. If raters have been chosen nonrandomly because of certain characteristics, a fixed-effects model should be used. If raters have been chosen at random out of a larger population (even a population with specified characteristics) and the researcher wishes to generalize the results to the larger population of raters, a random-effects model should be chosen. Researchers should be aware, however, that random-effects models tend to yield lower estimates of reliability because higher order interactions are included in the error term and larger error terms yield less significance.

In using intraclass correlation, variance due to unrelated factors needs to be partialed out, so that the result obtained is a reflection of interrater agreement rather than an inflation due to other effects (Finn, 1974). For example, when applying an intraclass correlation to determine interrater reliability for the Collaborative Study Psychotherapy Rating Scale for the NIMH Treatment of Depression Collaborative Research Program, Hill, O'Grady, and Elkin (1992) partialed out modality of treatment, therapist, client, session, site, and all possible two-way interactions between these variables, yielding an estimate of interrater reliability somewhat unconfounded by these extraneous variables. For intraclass correlations, .70 is generally considered a standard cutoff for high reliability (with higher estimates expected for judgments requiring low inference).

As an alternative to intraclass correlations, Cronbach, Gleser, Nanda, and Rajaratnam (1972), Gottman and Markman (1978), and Mitchell (1979) suggest that reliability and validity can be combined within the concept of generalizability. The idea of generalizability theory is to partition the total variance in a study into those facets across which one wants to generalize. As an example, in assessing reliability across judges, researchers would obtain the rating of a particular item by independent judges across clients and therapists. Good reliability would mean that the total variance in this repeated measures model is mostly attributable to variation across clients and therapists rather than across judges or the interaction between judges and clients or therapists. In this method, reliability is an assessment of the work one wants the system to do (e.g., discriminate among therapists and clients), rather than a claim of no differences between judges.

In addition to interrater reliability, the reliability of the measure also needs to be established for rating scales. In general, more than one item per scale should be used to enable a stable measurement of the construct. Internal consistency estimates can be used to determine the stability of the items within scales. Principal components analyses can also be conducted to determine the subscale structure of measures. To determine stability of the variable, test–retest reliability is necessary (Nunnally, 1978).

Nominal category systems. In the past, percent agreement has been used generally to assess interjudge agreement. The use of percent agreement, however, is problematic because it does not correct for chance agreement. To correct for chance in the calculation, the kappa statistic has become a standard in the field (Cohen, 1960; Tinsley & Weiss, 1975). Kappas can be computed for all the categories in a measure together, using a weighted kappa (Cohen, 1968) if some disagreements are more serious than others (e.g., disagreements outside a cluster of categories might be considered more serious than disagreements within a cluster). A caution is that kappa assumes an approximately equal distribution of data across categories. Thus, if all the data fall into one or two out of several categories, the kappas can be artificially low. In this case, percentage agreement can be reported along with kappa. Further, kappa cannot distinguish differential agreement levels among categories, such as when one category may result in high agreement whereas another does not. To obtain agreement levels for individual categories, kappa or a Pearson correlation coefficient can be calculated by comparing judges' use of each category with all other categories.

In general, kappas are lower than intraclass correlations, so the two figures are not directly comparable. Fleiss (1981) indicates that $< .40$ is poor agreement; between .40 and .75 is fair-to-good agreement; and $> .75$ is strong agreement. When researchers expect to obtain kappas less than .75, they should use more than two judges, so that the data across judges can be pooled and an approximation of the "true" categorization can be obtained.

In addition to reliability between judges, reliability of the category system itself needs to be established. Methods to assess the reliability of categorical measures are not as well known. Two methods that can be useful are cluster analyses (Borgen & Barnett, 1987) and examinations of the overlaps between judges using a confusion matrix (e.g., when two of three judges agreed on a therapist response mode category, Hill et al., 1979, charted the category assigned by the third judge to determine which categories overlapped). Using either of these methods, researchers can determine categories that are difficult for judges to distinguish. Researchers might collapse categories that have high overlap and place categories that have moderate overlap in clusters (to keep conceptually similar categories together).

Bakeman (personal communication, June 1990) noted another problem with reliability estimates. For categorical data that cannot be averaged across judges, most process researchers estimate the interjudge agreement of the independent codings but often use a consensus judgment for subsequent data analyses. Bakeman argues that because the reliability of this consensus judgment is unknown, researchers should do separate analyses on the data from each of the judges to determine the replicability of results across judges. Replicating analyses across all judges, however, would become very complicated in research that uses several measures and could result in more statistical tests on the data, which could inflate the Type I error rate. We suggest that a consensus judgment be used but that researchers take great care so that the process of reaching consensus is monitored carefully to avoid undue influence of particular judges (see section on "Rater Training"). Test–retest reliability could also be done on consensus judgments to determine their stability across time.

Issues about reliability for both interval and nominal data. Although interjudge reliability is the most important estimate of reliability given that data analyses use the averaged ratings of judges, intrajudge reliability also needs to be assessed (Kiesler, 1973). Having an estimate of judges' consistency in scoring data across times is helpful as an estimate of stability and can act as an index of judge drift or the need for recalibration.

Researchers can report consistency of the target behavior in addition to agreement across judges about the behavior (Mitchell, 1979). Consistency of the behavior can be determined by examining random subdivisions of the data, such as odd- and even-numbered minutes or units, in a manner analogous to split-half reliability of a standardized test. Testing consistency by comparing larger units such as odd- and even-numbered sessions, however, would not be appropriate because of the expected fluctuation in process across time in therapy.

Kiesler (1973) and Mitchell (1979) noted that interjudge agreement should be presented for the "summarizing unit" used for the data analysis. Thus, if the scoring unit is the sentence but the figure used in analyzing the data is the session, they suggest that the reliability presented should be for the session rather than the sentence. Although we concur that agreement levels ultimately are only needed for the summarizing unit used in the analyses, we also would like to see researchers report reliability for the scoring unit so that future researchers would know exactly where the problems are with the measure.

Before ending this section on reliability, we must note that we should not assume that high reliability (>.70) is always necessary. Cartwright (1966) stated that too many studies have been guided by a sheer fascination with counting and that it is an error to equate "scientific" with "reliable and quantitative." Many variables of interest to nonbehavioral psychotherapy researchers require some inference, often resulting in lower interjudge reliability. Once again, of course, researchers need to balance validity with reliability. Researchers also need to struggle to define their variables as completely as possible to ensure both validity and reliability.

Choice of Measures
The most widely used process measures are reviewed in three volumes (Greenberg & Pinsof, 1986; Kiesler, 1973; Russell, 1987). We briefly review measures in three areas: therapist techniques, client behaviors, and therapeutic interaction, recognizing that we are precluding many other important process measures.

Therapist techniques. Therapist techniques can be defined as the tools or methods that are employed by therapists to facilitate effective therapy or positive behavioral change in clients (Harper & Bruce-Sanford, 1981). Three major ways that therapist techniques have been measured are (1) judgments of response modes in the session, (2) global judgments of the presence of specific therapist techniques, and (3) therapist report of techniques used.

Therapist response modes refer to the grammatical structure of therapist speech, independent of the topic or content of the speech (e.g., direct guidance, paraphrase, or interpretation). Well over 30 nominal category systems have been developed to measure response modes based on judging each sentence or speaking turn in a session. Two measures that have been used most often and have demonstrated validity and reliability are by Hill (1978, 1986, 1992a, b) and Stiles (1979, 1986, 1992). Similarly, the Hill Interaction Matrix (Hill, 1965) has been a standard for examining therapist interventions in groups, and the Family Therapy Coding System (Pinsof, 1986) has been used with families.

Therapist techniques have also been measured more globally by examining how much a given technique (e.g., setting an agenda, interpreting transference) occurs within an entire session. Perhaps the best measures of this type are the Psychotherapy Process Q-Set (Jones, 1985; Jones et al., 1988; Jones, Krupnick, & Kerig, 1987) and the Therapist Action Scale (Hoyt, Marmar, Horowitz, & Alvarez, 1981). Other measures, such as the Collaborative Study Psychotherapy Rating Scale (Hill et al., 1992; Hollon et al., 1988) have been developed to examine therapist behaviors expected within specific theoretical modalities such as cognitive-behavioral therapy, interpersonal therapy, and clinical management.

Therapist reports have also been used. For example, using a videotape-cued recall procedure after sessions, therapists have been asked to report about intentions they had for using specific interventions (e.g., Hill & O'Grady, 1985). More globally, therapists have been asked to report after sessions about what techniques they used during a specific session (e.g., the Therapeutic Procedures Inventory-Revised; McNeilly & Howard, 1991). Other measures (e.g., McNair & Lorr, 1964) use checklists of therapist techniques to ask therapists to report about their characteristic techniques. Most of the measures within this category have been pantheoretical and can be used across a variety of orientations.

Client behaviors. Client behavior has been measured from the perspective of judges rating actual behavior in sessions, judges globally rating behavior as it occurred across entire sessions, and clients rating their own behavior. Perhaps the most widely used and best-researched observer-rated measures of client involvement in the therapy process are the Experiencing Scale (Klein et al., 1970; Klein, Mathieu-Coughlan, & Kiesler, 1986) and the Client Vocal Quality measure (Rice & Kerr, 1986). Both the Experiencing and Vocal Quality scales were developed within the client-centered therapy tradition and so emphasize emotional expressiveness rather than cognitive expression. From a more pantheoretical perspective, client behavior has been measured using response modes (e.g., recounting and insight; Hill et al., 1992; McCollough, 1990).

Client behavior also has been judged more globally by trained observers using pantheoretical measures such as the Psychotherapy Process Q-Set (Jones et al., 1988) and the Patient Action Scale (Hoyt et al., 1981). Additionally, clients have been asked to report on their own in-session reactions or impacts using videotape-cued recall procedures (Elliott, 1985; Hill et al., 1988).

Therapeutic interaction. On the basis of Rogers's (1957) theory, the therapeutic relationship has been measured through judges' ratings of therapist-offered empathy (e.g., Carkhuff, 1969) or therapist and client perceptions of therapist-offered facilitative conditions by using measures such as the Barrett-Lennard Relationship Inventory (Barrett-Lennard, 1962). Given the identified problems with the research on the facilitative conditions (see Lambert et al., 1978; Parloff et al., 1978) and recent theoretical insights (e.g., Bordin, 1979; Gelso & Carter, 1985), research emphasis has shifted away from the facilitative conditions and toward measuring the therapeutic or working alliance.

The therapeutic alliance has been measured by examining the client contribution, the therapist contribution, and the interaction (e.g., the California Psychotherapy Alliance Scales; Gaston & Marmar, 1990). However, we feel that including the client and therapist contributions muddies the concept of the therapeutic or working alliance. We prefer the Working Alliance Inventory (Horvath & Greenberg, 1989) because it measures just the interaction between therapist and client in terms of the bond and agreement on tasks and goals. However, we should note that recent research (Salvio, Beutler, Wood, & Engle, 1992) has indicated high intercorrelations among the subscales of the Working Alliance Inventory and the Barrett-Lennard Relationship Inventory, indicating that although they may be theoretically distinct they have not been teased apart empirically.

In groups, the parallel of the therapeutic alliance is cohesion. Measures have been developed for ratings by judges (Budman et al., 1987) as well as for ratings by therapists and clients (MacKenzie, 1981).

A measure that has been widely used for measuring interactions between therapists and clients in both individual and family therapy is the Structural Analysis of Social Behavior (SASB; Benjamin, 1974; Benjamin, Foster, Roberto, & Estroff,

1986). The SASB allows researchers to examine complementary interactions between therapists and clients on the dimensions of dominance and affiliation.

Recommendations. *We recommend that researchers use measures that are theoretically appropriate to answer their questions. Further, when possible, researchers should use measures that have already been developed, if they have adequate validity and reliability.* Kiesler (1973), Garfield (1990), and others have noted that many researchers develop a measure and then never use it again, resulting in little accumulation of knowledge across studies. In many ways, this situation parallels that found in outcome research. Using the same measure allows researchers to replicate findings across different samples.

DATA COLLECTION ISSUES

When properly addressed, several procedural issues can strengthen the results of process research, regardless of the type of process measure that is used in a study. We turn our attention now to these important methodological considerations.

Control. Researchers need to have control over data collection to ensure that their data are accurate. Well-trained researchers turn on tape recorders, monitor sessions to ensure that participants adhere to instructions, and distribute and collect measures. Additionally, if participant-rated process measures that require training are used, participants need to be trained with a simulation of the therapy process prior to participation. Otherwise, there may be a "break-in" period before participants really understand how to use the measures, resulting in a loss of data or the use of inaccurate data. Finally, all data should be checked periodically during completion of tasks for missing data or inaccuracy in completion.

Cooperation. Participants should not be burdened with having to complete too many measures and procedures. Although participants often learn from research procedures, they may quit if testing requires too much time. Furthermore, the more research time required, the less generalizable to naturally occurring therapy the study becomes.

Additionally, researchers are most likely to gain cooperation by treating therapists and clients as collaborators. If one believes and communicates to participants that they are the best informants about their experiences of the process, a research alliance can be formed that will result in richer, more complete information. Such collaboration also increases the probability that participants will become invested in the research. Further, asking clients and therapists about their experiences of the treatment and research often provides rich sources of data. On the other hand, researchers need to guard against becoming too involved in the therapy and intruding on the therapeutic relationship, which could bias the data in such a way as to make it less generalizable to actual therapy.

Intrusiveness. Collecting process data from therapists and clients needs to be done carefully to minimize intruding on the treatment. For example, some studies have had participants push buttons under their seats to indicate their feelings at particular moments in the session, which is quite intrusive. *As much as possible, the therapy process should be allowed to proceed unencumbered by the research.*

Effects of taping sessions. Kiesler (1973) noted that several early studies from the 1940s and 1950s indicated no adverse effects of audiotaping on clients. More recent evidence indicates that taping does have some effect on the process of therapy (Gelso, 1973, 1974). Roberts and Renzaglia (1965) found that when taping was introduced, Rogerian therapists behaved in less client-centered ways and clients made more favorable self-reference statements. Despite the fact that there may be some negative effects, Kielser (1973) recommends using tapes over therapist report because tapes can be reviewed at any time and are accurate representations of the original observable events.

Carmichael (1966) noted that although most clients have no problems with being recorded, therapists are often resistant and reluctant to have others observe them, perhaps fearing damage to their self-esteem. In our research, both therapists and clients often report nervousness in anticipating the taping but generally forget the taping once they get involved in the session.

Effects of reviewing sessions. A relatively new method of doing process research involves having therapists and/or clients review the audio- or videotape of sessions, usually within 24 hours of the session (e.g., Elliott, 1984; Hill, 1989). During such reviews, researchers ask participants to remember what they were feeling during the session. This method resolves some of the problems of intrusiveness given that the session itself is not interrupted (except for the effects of recording). Use of such reviews, however, raises issues about whether anticipation of the review changes sessions, whether participants can report accurately what they were

feeling and thinking during the time of the session itself, and whether the review itself intrudes on or facilitates the subsequent therapy process. Unfortunately, no research that we know of has addressed these methodological issues. Anecdotally, Hill (1989) reported that some clients indicated that reviews were more helpful than therapy sessions, although other clients reported difficulty watching themselves on videotape. More research needs to be done on these review methods, given their promise for capturing participants' phenomenological experiences.

JUDGMENT DECISIONS

Several issues involved in how to present data to judges or participants, such as units of measurement, context, and stimulus materials, are addressed in this section.

Choosing the Appropriate Unit

After choosing a variable and a measure for assessing this variable, investigators need to determine the unit of behavior to be rated or categorized with the measure. Units used in past research have been single words, phrases, sentences, thought units (separate and coherent ideas), speaking turns, topics, events, narratives, relationship episodes, specific time intervals such as five-minute segments, whole sessions, or whole treatments.

Several reviewers have expressed concern about arbitrary units. Bordin et al. (1954) suggested that use of time intervals may undermine the meaning of the interview, giving the example that assessing transference in a small unit would destroy the essence of a construct that occurs over long and variable periods of time. On the other hand, they point out that for some variables that fluctuate greatly over time, such as level of involvement, smaller units may be needed. Ekman and Friesen (1968) noted that although nonverbal behaviors are usually measured in predetermined time units (e.g., five seconds), they do not necessarily fall into these units. Marmar (1990) suggested that predetermined standard units have yielded little clinical information because context is ignored. In this regard, Knapp (1974) recommended demarcation according to change in some overall pattern. Bordin et al. (1954) warned, however, that reliability of identifying the unit is often quite low when units are defined based on meaning. Fiske (1977) noted that judgments of behavior are often less reliable with longer units because of fluctuation in behavior across units.

The unit will influence what data are collected and how they are interpreted. For example, in judging therapist intentions, Hill and O'Grady (1985) used a unit of a therapist speaking turn (all therapist speech between two client speeches), which occurs approximately once a minute. Horvath, Marx, and Kamann (1990), in contrast, allowed therapists to choose their own unit by indicating during a postsession videotape review whenever their intentions changed, which averaged about six to eight minutes. When the tape was stopped every six to eight minutes, participants combine a lot of information into their judgments, losing information about specific interventions.

We found only a few empirical studies on the effects of different units of analysis. Kiesler, Mathieu, and Klein (1967) found that longer segments received higher ratings on the Experiencing Scale, but that reliabilities were equal across 2-, 4-, 8-, and 16-minute segments. Using the Therapist and Patient Action Checklists, Weiss, Marmar, and Horowitz (1988) found no differences between ratings of the first half of sessions compared to ratings of entire sessions. Using several process measures and data sets, Friedlander, Ellis, Siegel, Raymond, and Haase (1988) tested whether different lengths of excerpts and different starting points within sessions affected the ratings of judges. Results indicated that starting points made no difference, but that generalizing from any size segment to a whole session could not be done when interviews were examined individually. When interviews were aggregated across several cases, however, even small segments were representative of whole sessions. Variability across participants in particular segments probably overwhelmed differences between segment sizes given that therapists and clients vary tremendously in their behavior.

We recommend that researchers choose units that match their constructs, balancing issues of reliability in judging the unit and clinical meaningfulness. When using multiple measures that employ different units, researchers may have to aggregate across units. Researchers should also present separate reliability data for the unitization and scoring processes. Reliability of unitization becomes an issue when the scoring unit is not automatic (such as five-minute segments) but requires some inference by raters. Rules for determining sentences have been presented by Auld and White (1956) and modified by Hill (1985). Rules for segmenting narratives (stories) were presented by Angus (1992). Although words, phrases, and sentences are relatively easy to determine, longer units such as thought units and events are more difficult to determine reliably. Lower reliability should not necessarily discourage researchers from using thought units, however, because they are often more clinically meaningful divisions.

Context

Greenberg (1986) notes that units can be arranged in a hierarchy. Speech acts are embedded within therapeutic episodes, which in turn are embedded within the therapeutic relationship. Shoham-Salomon (1990) adds that these three levels are embedded within the client's life outside of treatment.

Kiesler (1973) makes a distinction between the scoring unit and the contextual unit. The scoring unit is the entity that is actually rated or coded. The contextual unit consists of the portion of the interview that is considered when one judges the scoring unit. The contextual unit could be the same as the scoring unit (e.g., the Experiencing Scale often is used with five-minute excerpts) or it could be considerably larger than the scoring unit (e.g., when categorizing therapist response modes, judges read the entire transcript leading up to the unit).

Heatherington (1989) has noted that some measures need context for raters to make accurate judgments. In her measure of relational control, for example, context is necessary to judge whether a question reflects dominant behavior. Similarly, raters need to know what has transpired between the therapist and client up until the point where a rating is required to judge the depth of an interpretation (Harway et al., 1955). Messer, Tishby and Spillman (1992) have demonstrated the use of context in ratings of patient progress as well as treatment plan compatibility and quality of therapist interventions.

In contrast, raters may be prone to bias on some types of measures if they have knowledge of context. When coding the occurrence of nonverbal behaviors (e.g., Hill, Siegelman, Gronsky, Sturniolo, & Fretz, 1981; Hill & Stephany, 1990), the sound is often deleted so that raters are not influenced by the verbal content of the session. Similarly, in judging therapist empathy (at least as defined by Carkhuff, 1969), raters need to hear what the client has said prior to the therapist intervention to know what the therapist is responding to, but they might be unduly influenced if they hear how the client responds afterwards. To have separate indices of therapist empathy and client response, separate sets of raters would be needed.

In contrast, Schoeninger, Klein, and Mathieu (1967) found no differences for client experiencing ratings when therapist speech was or was not included. In a study that Bordin et al. (1954) discussed, they examined the effects on context of judgments on whether the therapist stayed within the client's frame of reference. Judges were presented with either the entire transcript or just the therapist responses (in either the correct sequence or random sequence). They reported the "embarrassing results" (p. 81) that different contexts were a negligible source of variance in the agreement among raters. They suggested that ratings were independent of client verbalization or that raters may have relied on stylized phrases such as "You feel" to determine whether therapists stayed within the client's frame of reference. *These findings emphasize the need to examine the context of judgments for each measure.*

Sampling from the Whole of Therapy

A related topic concerns how much and what part of the therapy needs to be rated or categorized to generalize to the entire treatment. Examining the whole course of therapy would be ideal but is often financially and practically unfeasible. Thus, the question becomes how much one needs to sample to obtain a representative portion of the treatment.

Kiesler (1973) indicated that sampling within particular sessions and sampling sessions across the course of therapy are separate issues. Regarding the former, Kiesler, Klein, and Mathieu (1965) found that neurotic clients showed a consistently upward trend of experiencing during a therapy hour, schizophrenics showed a saw-tooth pattern, and normals an inverted U-shaped trend of experiencing. Thus, sampling decisions would affect the data for different diagnostic groups in different ways.

Regarding the issue of sampling sessions across the course of treatment, Rogers, Gendlin, Kiesler, and Truax (1967) and Kiesler (1971) showed that for schizophrenics experiencing is U-shaped until about Session 20 and then drops. Given this fluctuation, one could misrepresent the trend across therapy if only a few points were analyzed. Kiesler (1973) concluded that for the Experiencing Scale, researchers need to sample many points both within and across sessions.

Beutler, Johnson, Neville, and Workman (1973), Gurman (1973), and Karl and Abeles (1969) found that therapists differed in their behaviors across segments of sessions. Mintz and Luborsky (1971) found that judgments of empathy obtained from brief segments of sessions had low correlations with judgments of whole sessions. Hill, Carter, and O'Farrell (1983), Hill and O'Grady (1985), and O'Farrell, Hill, and Patton (1986) found that therapist and client behavior changed from the first third to the final part of sessions. Because of the fluctuation of process, researchers need to be careful to sample enough of each case to provide a representative sample of the phenomenon.

An example of an oft-cited study that used inadequate sampling to compare psychoanalytic and behavioral therapists was that by Sloan, Staples, Cristol, Yorkston, and Whipple (1975). They used ratings of four 4-minute segments from the fifth session to represent the process of therapy that lasted about four months. Further, the sampling procedure was peculiar in that behavioral therapists were not sampled randomly from within the hour but were studied when they acted like psychotherapists as opposed to times when they were using behavioral techniques. Not surprisingly, Sloan et al. found few differences between psychoanalytic and behavioral therapists.

The sampling issue, as with the unit issue, needs to be considered within the context of the theoretical framework and design of the particular study (Kiesler, 1973). Thus, the amount that should be sampled depends on the question that one is asking. If one has empirical evidence that a variable occurs consistently across therapy, then only a small portion needs to be sampled. But if one suspects that the variable fluctuates across therapy given the stage of therapy and the problem being discussed, then larger portions need to be sampled. Further, researchers need to determine that the samples they have taken are representative of the portion of the therapy to which they wish to generalize. *On the basis of our experience, we recommend that if researchers wish to generalize to stages of treatment across entire cases, they should sample at least two complete adjacent sessions from the beginning, middle, and end of treatment.*

Studying Infrequently Occurring Events

Infrequently occurring events, such as confrontation, self-disclosure, touching, crying, or laughter, are often of interest to researchers because of the importance of critical events in therapy. Because these events occur infrequently in general but more frequently for some dyads, separating the confounding variables of therapist and/or client characteristics from the actual event is difficult. Researchers need to deal with issues about selecting equivalent numbers of events from all cases so that confounding variables can be reduced. *In general, when studying infrequently occurring events, researchers need to begin with a large number of cases from which to choose so that they can select a smaller number of cases in which the event occurs relatively often (of course documenting how the selected cases differ from the larger body of cases).* For example, Gervaize, Mahrer, and Markow (1985) previewed 280 hours of therapy to extract 60 instances of strong laughter. Unless doing case studies, researchers need to be careful to include more than one or two cases with such events, however, or results will be confounded.

Medium of Stimulus Materials

If using archival data, researchers need to decide how to present the stimuli to raters: transcript, audiotape, videotape, or some combination. Bordin et al. (1954) noted that using either audiotape or videotape is necessary for variables that depend on nonlinguistic factors such as tone of voice or emphasis on different words. Lambert et al. (1978) advocated videotapes, however, because they noted that audiotapes are insensitive to nonverbal and behavioral cues.

A further issue is whether transcripts are needed in addition to audio- or videotapes. Use of tapes is quite appropriate for measures in which there are clearly defined units (e.g., five-minute time spans or speaking turns). When data need to be broken into more arbitrary units, such as thought units, using tapes without transcripts is problematic because raters have to unitize data at the same time as they categorize it. Doing both tasks concurrently usually results in lowered reliability. Transcripts are expensive to obtain, but they are invaluable for increasing reliability. Further, accurate transcripts ensure that judges are responding to similar verbal data, given that it is sometimes difficult to understand what is spoken. When you type transcripts, you realize that you often need to listen to the tape several times to hear accurately. Raters listening through just one time are quite likely to fill in the spaces when they do not hear completely, resulting in their hearing different things.

Several studies have examined the effects of different forms of stimulus materials. Shapiro (1968) found that audio-only and video-only ratings of facilitative conditions were correlated with the audio-video ratings but not with each other. Weiss (1979) found that judges' descriptions of personality traits were less differentiated when made from written materials than from personal contact. Waxer (1981) found that judgments of anxiety depended on nonverbal cues present in audio and video materials. McDaniel, Stiles, and McGaughey (1981) obtained higher reliability for verbal response modes using transcripts rather than audiotapes. Tracey and Guinee (1990) found that a transcript-only mode resulted in lower reliability than videotape, audiotape, videotape plus transcript, and audiotape plus transcript on the Interpersonal Communications Rating Scale. Weiss et al. (1988) reported that more reliable ratings were made with audio/visual cues than with only audio cues on the Therapist and Patient Action Checklists. They speculated that video holds raters' attention better and concluded that having more channels of information leads to higher reliability because raters make fewer inferences about intention, affect, and interaction.

We recommend using a combination of videotape and transcript whenever possible, so that raters have access to as much information as possible in making their ratings. We also encourage researchers to use the standards for transcriptions developed by Mergenthaler and Stinson (1992). They provide common symbols for spelling, pauses, paraverbal and nonverbal utterances, incomplete utterances, and punctuation.

USE OF NONPARTICIPANT JUDGES

Many process measures rely on nonparticipant observers to judge the presence, intensity, and frequency of certain events. Judges are "two-legged meters" who interpret process based on their own reactions to the material. Fiske (1977) noted that the use of human judges introduces noise and undependability in the data. Similarly, Mercer and Loesch (1979) suggested that judges, rather than measures, are the actual measuring instruments. Hence, the measures cannot be considered independently of the judges who use them. Researchers must be aware of how the judgment process influences the data with observer-rated measures.

Number of Judges

The number of judges that should be used for any given measure is directly linked to issues of reliability and validity. If high reliability is expected, fewer judges can be used. But if low reliability is expected, researchers should use more judges because pooling data from several judges increases reliability and heightens the probability of approximating the "true" score. In our opinion, researchers should not necessarily base their choice of measures on how high the reliability is between raters. Many measures that assess clinically meaningful variables result in low reliability because these phenomena are difficult to assess. Using more judges (or training judges more thoroughly) on a clinically meaningful measure is preferable to not attempting to measure the construct.

Many researchers demonstrate minimally adequate reliability on a portion of the data and then proceed with having one judge rate the remainder of the data. This procedure is problematic from a methodological standpoint, because this minimal level of reliability indicates that judges are often disagreeing with one another. The use of just one judge could thus yield biased data. In general, it is better to err on the side of too many judges rather than too few. In the extreme, Mahrer, Paterson, Theriault, Roessler, and Quenneville (1986) advocate using 8–10 judges of varying orientations to provide higher validity of judgments. Unless researchers reach incredibly high reliability (e.g., above .95, which is possible only for highly operationalized constructs), we recommend using *at least two raters for interval or ordinal scales and three judges for nominal scales,* with more judges for measures that require high inference.

Tsujimoto, Hamilton, and Berger (1990) provide a formula to estimate the gain in validity that is produced when different numbers of judges are used. In general, they note that increasing the number of judges is similar to increasing the number of items on a self-report measure. They suggest that there is an inherent trade-off in deciding how many judges to use. Using more judges increases the cost of doing the study but also increases the expected validity of measurement. Additionally, they point out that using more judges sometimes decreases the number of therapy dyads needed to attain a given level of statistical power because composite ratings decrease random error of measurement.

Many researchers complain that using multiple judges is expensive or impractical. However true this may be, it is often necessary to employ multiple judges to generate credible data. Methodological shortcuts will, in the long run, be even more expensive because of the confusion that inevitably results in sorting out conflicting data when such shortcuts are taken.

Rater Selection

The capabilities and qualities of judges can have a profound effect on the validity of ratings and the ultimate expense of process research. Moras and Hill (1991), in a review of the rater selection procedures for process measures, concluded that minimal research has been conducted on the qualities needed for using different instruments. Most researchers simply indicate what type of judges they have used, but they provide no empirical evidence about the effects of their selection criteria. Kiesler (1973) and Moras and Hill (1991) indicate that the level of clinical experience and/or theoretical sophistication needed by judges is directly related to the amount of inference required by the judging task. Trained undergraduates can rate highly operationalized variables, such as nonverbal behaviors, and are often desirable as judges because they attend to what they have been taught as opposed to clinical intuition (Arnhoff, 1954; Cronbach, 1960). Experienced clinicians are generally required for more abstract constructs that require clinical experience, such as transference or working alliance. However, experienced clinicians are sometimes difficult to train if they are set in their beliefs about definitions of constructs and rely on theoretical biases to judge behavior. Mercer and Loesch (1979) remind us that determining who the best judges are is somewhat circular because there is a problem of deciding who is qualified to determine whether judges are accurate. Determining accuracy is a problem because we have no criteria for the validity of our judgments.

Nevertheless, specific selection criteria for judges for particular measures can go a long way toward increasing reliable if not valid judgments. Mercer and Loesch (1979) note that intelligence and unimpaired interpersonal skills are helpful in the development of valid rating skills. Further, most process researchers value judges who are attentive to detail, yet not so compulsive that they cannot make decisions about gray areas. Judges who ask questions are also valued because questions help to clarify the concepts involved. The judges must be able, however, to "buy" into the system that is being used even though it may not match their thinking style. Thus, someone who can point out the imperfections thoughtfully but can still work within the system is a desirable judge. Other desired characteristics of judges are dependability, trustworthiness, and a sense of ethics. *We recommend that researchers not only specify the criteria they have used to select judges and provide detailed descriptions of the judges they end up with, but also do the empirical research to determine whether the criteria are valid.*

Mercer and Loesch (1979) also suggest that judges should be sampled at random from the potential population of judges. Random selection allows researchers to consider judges to be a random factor (see section on "Reliability") and increases the generalizability of findings. Such random selection is often hard to do because there is a limited pool of raters, but *researchers need to be careful to choose randomly from within those who are eligible; otherwise, unknown selection factors could contaminate the rating process.*

Rater Bias

Rater bias occurs whenever raters are unable to make totally objective judgments. Fiske (1977) suggested that judgments are affected by judges' interpretation of the words used in rating scales, reactions to the task of rating therapists and clients, past experiences, and mental processes as they recall past experiences and relate them to the present judgment task. Additionally, variables such as mood, attitude, and personality characteristics might interfere with the ability to be objective, particularly with measures that involve inference.

Hill, O'Grady, and Price (1988) found no evidence of rater bias on highly operationalized indices of therapist adherence to treatment manuals. They found, however, that when assessing the facilitative skills of therapists, raters were influenced by how similar they judged themselves to be to the participants they were rating. Similarly, Mahalik, Hill, Thompson, and O'Grady (1989) found that perceived similarity as well as rater personality characteristics (dominance, sociability) influenced ratings of therapist and client affiliation. Thus, preliminary evidence exists that perceived similarity and personality characteristics influence some global judgments.

Defining bias is a difficult issue because, as mentioned earlier, we often have no criteria for accuracy or validity of data. After struggling with these issues in our own research, we defined bias using interval data as a deviation from the mean score of several raters, given the assumption that the mean score approximated the "true score" (Hill et al., 1988; Mahalik et al., 1989). For examining bias of judges using categorical systems, Mahrer et al. (1986) examined the number of times a particular judge selected a category when the majority did not and the number of times a particular judge did not select a category when the majority of judges did.

Reliability estimates could be improved by selecting raters who are homogeneous on the personality dimensions that affect ratings on a given scale. Unfortunately, however, we usually do not know the relevant personality dimensions that influence ratings on different measures. Moreover, if homogeneous groups of raters were selected, the validity of the data would be compromised because of confounding with the variable on which raters were selected.

One solution to the bias problem is to select a large group of raters at random and thereby obtain a range on the "problematic" personality characteristics. Researchers could then statistically remove variance due to rater characteristics when conducting the analysis (cf. Mahalik et al., 1989), although removing all of the bias is probably never possible. This solution also presents many practical problems, especially in terms of cost of judges. *We recommend that researchers at the very least randomly select a number of diverse judges to spread out the bias.*

Rater Errors

In performance appraisal ratings within the industrial psychology area, a fair amount of research has been done on other types of rater errors (Latham & Wexley, 1981; Saal, Downey, & Lahey, 1980). In addition to the perceived similarity error (discussed under "Rater Bias"), these authors mention (1) halo, a rater's failure to discriminate among conceptually distinct and potentially independent aspects of a ratee's behavior; (2) leniency, a tendency to rate higher than the midpoint; (3) severity, a tendency to rate lower than the midpoint; (4) central tendency, a tendency to rate at the midpoint with a consequent restriction in range; (5) contrast effect, a tendency for a rater to evaluate a ratee relative to last person rated rather than relative to the universe of possibilities; and (6) first-

impression rating, the tendency to make an initial judgment and then not change based on subsequent information. Latham and Wexley (1981) and Saal et al. (1980) provide ways to analyze whether these rater errors exist and to train raters not to commit them. *We encourage psychotherapy researchers to study how different types of errors influence process judgments.*

Rater Training

Training can reduce both the influence of contaminating rater characteristics and the influence of idiosyncratic interpretations of items. Training is necessary to draw valid conclusions given that researchers never know how untrained judges have interpreted definitions of items (Bachrach, Mintz, & Luborsky, 1971; Caracena & Vicory, 1969; Klein & Cleary, 1967; Mercer & Loesch, 1979).

Researchers need to be careful, however, to use training to sensitize judges to the phenomena and not just to catch phrases (Bordin et al., 1954). For example, raters using the Carkhuff (1969) empathy scale were sometimes told that open questions should be rated as a 2.5 and reflections of feelings a 3.0. Such practices increase reliability but may reduce the validity of the judgment process.

Mercer and Loesch (1979) described two types of training: informal and formal. In both methods, judges are given copies of the measure, definitions of scales or categories, and tape segments to practice on. In the informal method, they practice making independent judgments and discuss discrepancies until they reach consensus among themselves. In contrast, the goal of the formal method is to train judges to high agreement with a standard (calibrated) set of judgments of expert judges. The advantage of the formal method is that judges are trained to some standard within the field and are more likely to produce replicable judgments across trainers and sites. Unfortunately, most process measures are not accompanied by such standard sets of judgments. *We encourage developers of process measures to develop standard sets of judgments that can be distributed to other researchers who want to use their measure.*

Further, in both the informal and formal training methods, trainers need to be experts in the system. They should preferably be trained by the developer or people with demonstrated proficiency in using the measure to ensure that they train judges to use the measure as it was intended to be used. The use of expert trainers, along with using calibration sets of ratings against which to test judges, could help in establishing standard process measures.

Trainees should be exposed to a wide range of levels of the dimension on which they are being trained (Mercer & Loesch, 1979). Introducing trainees to the whole range enables them to see how behaviors to be judged fit into the universe of possibilities. Use of "flat data" (segments representing a narrow range of levels) may lead judges to make discriminations where none should be made. Training with a wide range is particularly important if segments in the final study show minimal variation.

Trainers also need to be aware of social influence processes at work among raters. One rater sometimes dominates the process and persuades other raters to adopt his or her opinion, a problem that is exacerbated if there are different levels of power within the rating team or if one person is dogmatic in his or her opinions. To handle this problem, initial ratings should be made independently without interaction among the judges. In subsequent discussions, the order of reporting and defending ratings should be alternated to reduce the input of particularly dominant individuals. Every judge needs to feel that his or her opinions are important. Thorough discussion helps judges sort through their thinking processes, solidify their rationales, and increase their understanding of the measure.

Kiesler (1973) notes that the amount of training required of judges varies directly with how clearly the variables are defined and how much inference is required in the judgment task. The more abstract the judgments, the longer the training will need to be to achieve desired levels of reliability.

Marmar (1990) makes the following recommendations for training raters: (1) use of detailed manuals with clear examples of all items or categories, (2) use of calibrated master ratings on extensive examples, (3) discussion of items or categories to clarify subtleties, (4) training to a preestablished criterion of reliability before beginning the actual rating task, and (5) frequent recalibration sessions during the rating process to maintain fidelity to the original measure.

Lambert et al. (1978) noted that the training procedures have frequently gone undescribed. Given that many measures have items or categories that are not clearly defined, parts of definitions are often communicated during training rather than being written and are thus not standardized across trainers. *We recommend that training be described in detail.*

Assigning Judges to Data

If not all judges will be rating every piece of data, members of teams should be rotated so that the error associated with each judge gets spread around. A randomized incomplete block design (Fleiss, 1981) is a useful way to rotate judges so that each person judges the same number of tapes of each type (e.g., each therapist, client, agency, etc.).

Different teams of judges should be used to judge each construct to avoid confounding between the construct and the judges. When the same judges evaluate different dimensions, the validities of the ratings on any one dimension are contingent upon the abilities of the raters to differentiate among the dimensions (Mercer & Loesch, 1979). For example, Muehlberg, Pierce, and Drasgow (1969) found that raters were not able to distinguish between different facilitative conditions.

Judgment Task

Some controversy has arisen over whether to present segments to judges randomly or sequentially as they occur within the therapy. Bozarth and Krauft (1972) found that random presentation of segments produced greater independence between ratings than sequential presentation. We agree with this position when variables require no knowledge of context (e.g., nonverbal behavior) but note that (as discussed earlier under "Context") some variables require knowledge of what has occurred previously in the therapy (e.g., transference).

All data should be judged independently by judges prior to discussion, with judges being given as much time as necessary to make their judgments (Rogers et al., 1967). *Reliability should be calculated on the independent judgments, although data analyses usually require consensus judgments. Reliability for the independent judgments of actual data needs to be reported in addition to the reliability obtained during training.* Mercer and Loesch (1979) noted that some studies have failed to report interrater reliability and others have reported reliability as established by other researchers in other studies. Both procedures are clearly inadequate for determining the agreement levels for the set of judges used for a particular study.

In cases where judgments cover a long span of time (e.g., 15 minutes or an entire session), an issue arises of how to make the judgments. In one method, judges make global, relatively subjective judgments based on listening or watching the entire segment. In a second method, they make tallies of each occurrence of each item and then use their judgment to decide how many tallies are needed to make a particular rating. Weiss et al. (1988) found that the tally method was superior to the global rating method for ratings on the Therapist and Patient Action Checklists, yielding a small effect size of .10. They concluded that the less inference needed, the better the judgments. Further, keeping tallies or writing notes is a useful means to keep judges alert and involved with the task.

Maintaining Morale Among Judges

Judges need to feel that what they are doing is important and that their contribution is valued. *To* obtain cooperation, researchers need to make the task as meaningful as possible. Assigning readings (as long as they do not reveal the hypotheses of the study) and talking about therapy can be useful ways to involve the judges in the scientific endeavor. Researchers should also spend time with the judges talking about their reactions to the task, so that they know when judges are bored or unhappy. Mahrer and Gagnon (1991) present one account of how a research team deals with these issues.

Drift of Judgments

Judges are typically very conscientious initially. As familiarity increases and routines become established, judgments frequently become less reliable. Judges may make assumptions about the data, become less attuned to nuances, or make snap judgments after listening to small segments. Moreover, once a judgment is made, judges may listen only for evidence that confirms their viewpoint rather than assessing disconfirming evidence. Additionally, judges may be more accurate when they think their behavior is being checked or monitored (Mitchell, 1979; Reid, 1970; Romanczyk, Kent, Diament, & O'Leary, 1973; Taplin & Reid, 1973). *We recommend that researchers continue meeting with raters after training to maintain group morale, reduce drift, and prevent judges from developing idiosyncratic ways of interpreting items.*

Debriefing Judges

While being trained and doing ratings, judges should be unaware of the hypotheses being studied. Judges will be very aware of what variable they are attending to but should not be aware of the hypotheses regarding how that variable relates to other variables. For example, in the Hill and Stephany (1990) study, judges coded nonverbal behavior but were not informed that the researchers were relating nonverbal behavior to client reactions. *After a study is completed, however, judges should be informed about the hypotheses of the study.* This debriefing also provides a good opportunity to discuss problems with measures and to explore different ways of conducting the judgment process. Results of the debriefings can be reported along with the data analyses.

Data Aggregation

For interval data, ratings can be averaged or "pooled" across raters to yield a master rating. For nominal data, a master judgment needs to be determined. One way of determining master or consensus judgments when using three judges is to consider the master judgment to be the one in which two of three judges agree in their independent judgments. When all three judges disagree, they can discuss the judgment until they arrive at a consensus. Alternatively, Mahrer, Markow, Gervaize, and Boulet (1987) used a procedure in which 8 out of 11 judges had to agree. If this level of agreement is not reached, the piece of data is thrown back, mixed with other data, and rerated at a later time. If consensus is still not reached, the data are not used.

In aggregating nominal data across sessions, Marsden, Kalter, and Ericson (1974) suggest that the proportion of each behavior to the total number of behaviors is more appropriate than the raw frequencies. Proportions correct for the amount of activity in the session. Thus, therapists who use the same amount of an intervention but differ in their overall activity would have different proportions of that intervention in relation to total utterances. Prior to analyses, proportions often need to be transformed using an arc sine transformation because proportions tend to be skewed.

Fiske (1977) raises the issue of which aggregate of data is most representative of the process. One could use the proportion (of nominal data), the average (of interval data), the highest value (for interval data), the predominant judgment (for nominal data), or the value at critical moments. Given that a lot of noise may occur in sessions, the highest value or the value at critical moments may be the best estimate for some measures. Klein et al. (1986) use peak experiencing ratings in segments to describe the highest level attained. Rice and Kerr (1986) give preference to a focused voice quality when it occurs in segments. Hill et al. (1992) used the predominant client behavior in speaking turns. To reduce the amount of noise, *we recommend using the peak rating or predominant judgment rather than simply presenting frequencies or proportions of all the data (which can lead to problems in data analyses).*

LINKING PROCESS TO OUTCOME

Perhaps the biggest challenge in psychotherapy research is linking process to outcome. Because of the complexity of variables (pretherapy characteristics, therapist techniques, client behavior, the therapeutic relationship, and events that occur outside of therapy) that influence change as well as the nonlinear growth curve of change, simple equations often are not adequate. In this section, we cover several approaches that have been attempted: correlational approaches, sequential analyses, and analyses of patterns.

CORRELATIONAL APPROACHES TO LINKING PROCESS AND OUTCOME

Most process researchers have used a correlational strategy, in which they relate the frequency or proportion of occurrence of a process variable to some outcome measure. For example, Sloan et al. (1975) correlated the occurrence of process variables in the fifth session with outcome. These correlational designs are inadequate because they do not take into account the timing, appropriateness, quality, or context of the process variable (Gottman & Markman, 1978; Hill, 1982; Hill, Helms, Tichenor et al., 1988; Russell & Trull, 1986; Stiles, 1988). Thus, one moderately deep interpretation given to an introspective client who is pondering why she or he behaves in a particular way may be more helpful than 10 poorly timed interpretations (see Spiegel & Hill, 1989). Further, Stiles (1988) noted that correlational designs fail to account for client needs. He suggested that more disturbed clients may need more of certain interventions but still may end up with poorer outcome, not because the interventions were not effective but because the client could not use the intervention effectively. Hence, client disturbance level may moderate process–outcome links.

We would note that the problem is not so much the correlational design, per se, as the fact that frequency (or proportion) data are used in the design. As a demonstration of this, McCullough et al. (1991) found that when they added the client response to the therapist intervention, they were able to demonstrate a meaningful relationship between therapist interpretation and outcome. Although their findings need to be replicated, they suggest that it is not just the specific therapist intervention that makes a difference, but whether the client is able to use the therapist intervention. Further exploration of correlational designs with modifications for client responsiveness or therapist competence seem warranted.

SEQUENTIAL ANALYSES

Rather than test process in relation to outcome at the end of treatment, as in the traditional correlational approach, several writers have recommended using sequential analyses to study the immediate effects of process events (Bakeman, 1978; Bakeman & Gottman, 1986; Russell & Trull, 1986). Sequential analyses allow researchers to establish the temporal contiguity of the effect in interactive data (e.g., to determine which therapist intentions lead to which client reactions). Examples of sequential analyses include Benjamin's (1979) Markov chain analysis on interactional data, Gottman's (1979) examination of mutually criticizing cycles in married couples, and Lichtenberg and Hummel's (1976) analysis of stochastic process in counseling sessions. Russell and Trull (1986) noted advances in sequential analyses, such as testing for differences in sequences, cyclicity, and latent structures.

Marmar (1990) advocates use of sequential analyses because he feels that researchers need to account for context and temporal sequencing. He notes that several researchers have studied shifts in functioning: The effectiveness of therapist interventions was studied by examining short-term shifts in depth of experiencing, boldness, and in-session anxiety (Sampson & Weiss, 1986) and in shifts in alliance (Foreman & Marmar, 1985; Gaston, Marmar, & Ring, 1989). He cautions, however, that because immediate negative effects can be followed by productive shifts, sequential analyses need to be able to account for these clinically relevant phenomena.

Sequential analysis is an approach to analyzing interactional data, rather than a specific statistical technique (Bakeman & Gottman, 1986). Researchers can use various statistical techniques, such as analysis of variance or loglinear analyses, to test whether different process variables co-occur at a level greater than chance. Although intuitively appealing for process research, sequential analysis has limitations: (1) Only stable, immediate effects can be determined, although researchers have some latitude in determining the window of those effects (e.g., the number of lags that they expect the effects to appear in), and (2) it does not provide us with links to outcome after treatment. Despite the limitations, we believe that sequential analysis is applicable to a variety of contexts and may prove to be one of the best methods for studying process.

ANALYSES OF PATTERNS

An extension of sequential analysis is to consider longer sequences or patterns. Sequences of interactions might be studied in general or more narrowly for well-defined events. For example, Rice and Sapiera (1984) postulated that clients undergo a certain sequence of steps when therapists use a technique called *systematic evocative unfolding*, which is intended to enable clients to resolve problematic reaction points (points at which clients recognize that their reactions to particular situations are puzzling or unexpected). Similarly, Greenberg proposed that experiential therapists go through specific steps when helping clients resolve conflict (e.g., Greenberg & Webster, 1982).

Methods for analyzing prolonged sequences are

relatively new and have been much discussed and advocated (e.g., task analysis; Greenberg, 1984, 1986, 1991). Examples of actual studies are just beginning to emerge (see Toukmanian & Rennie, 1992). Methodological issues around identifying steps, transitions between steps, the relationship between resolution and outcome, and whether resolution patterns are similar across therapeutic approaches need to be addressed.

beyond measuring which process variables occur and study the context in which particular process variables occur. Potentially relevant context variables are stage of treatment, quality of the relationship, client readiness, transference and counter-transference issues, and content of what has transpired in treatment (i.e., topic, problem area discussed).

SUMMARY

Despite the advances made with sequential analyses and pattern analyses, we still do not have good methods for linking process variables at a given point in time in therapy with long-term outcome. For example, we can know through sequential analyses that accurate interpretations are particularly helpful, and we can use task analyses to study the steps of a successful interpretive sequence; but we do not have methods for determining how a particular interpretation or interpretive segment leads to change. Perhaps clients have to be in a certain amount of pain before lasting change can occur. Perhaps the change has to be salient enough to become incorporated into the client's sense of self. Perhaps the change has to be supported by significant others. Perhaps the interpretive sequence needs to be repeated numerous times in therapy with slightly different problems to lead to longer term change. Perhaps clients have to do something different in their lives after experiencing the significant event in therapy to set the snowball of change rolling. All these and more possibilities need to be pursued if we are to understand how therapy process leads to meaningful changes in a person's life.

Many of our process analyses have been focused on understanding the relationship of a process variable with either immediate or longer-term outcome. Our energy now needs to turn to understanding more about how different individuals respond to different process events (Marmar, 1990; Shoham-Salomon, 1990; Stiles et al., 1990). For example, we need to study client pretherapy characteristics by process interactions to determine how clients react differently to different interventions. Marmar (1990) noted that high-functioning patients did best with exploratory interventions, whereas poorly functioning patients did best with supportive interventions. One caution here is that Beutler (1991) lists a myriad of client and therapist pretherapy characteristics that could influence the relationship of process and outcome.

Another area that we need to attend to in understanding process variables is context (Greenberg, 1986; Hill, 1990; Marmar, 1990). We need to go

CONCLUSION

In our review of measures and methods that apply to process and outcome research, we were struck by the different issues confronting these related but largely independent domains of inquiry. This chapter reflects many of these differences. A primary difference is that outcome researchers can agree on many of the general targets of measurement as well as the procedures to be used in assessment. They cannot agree upon the specific measures to be employed. Process researchers, perhaps because their work is more often driven by a complex theory, cannot agree upon what process should be measured, let alone what measures to employ in studying these processes. Nevertheless, one of the achievements of psychotherapy research is the increased sophistication in methods and methodology in both process and outcome research documented by this chapter. We have come a long way since the initial studies were undertaken. It is our hope that future research on psychotherapy and its effects will build on the foundation laid by this past research. We are optimistic that proper outcome and process assessment can build a stronger bridge between research and practice. Process research is clearly making strides toward developing procedures to ensure reliable, valid, and useful measurements of the changes that take place within therapy sessions. While the search goes on for the most important theoretical and pragmatic aspects of the therapeutic process, the methodology necessary to measure these processes is becoming more obvious.

The measurement of change following therapy is in a state of chaos, with little agreement among researchers about the specific measures to be used. We look forward to the day when researchers can agree on a minimal core outcome battery for measuring changes in patients with specific disorders. We are convinced that most of the necessary measures to be included in such batteries already exist. It remains a task for researchers in their specialty areas to agree upon a few measures while continuing to explore the possibilities of newly created measures. Certainly the field of process and outcome assessment is still in its infancy, offering abundant opportunities to the curious and dedicated student. We invite such students to join in the search for effective ways of helping people change.

REFERENCES

Angus, L. (1992, June). *Narrative processes in psychotherapy.* Paper presented at the annual meeting of the Society for Psychotherapy Research, Berkeley, CA.

Arnhoff, F. N. (1954). Some factors influencing the unreliability of clinical judgments. *Journal of Clinical Psychology, 10,* 272–275.

Ashcroft, C. (1971). The latest school achievement of treated and untreated emotionally handicapped children. *Journal of School Psychology, 9,* 338–342.

Auerbach, A. H. (1983). Assessment of psychotherapy outcome from the viewpoint of expert observer. In M. J. Lambert, E. R. Christensen, & S. S. DeJulio (Eds.), *The assessment of psychotherapy outcome* (pp. 537–568). New York: Wiley.

Auld, F. Jr., & White, A. (1956). Rules for dividing interviews into sentences. *Journal of Psychology, 42,* 273–281.

Babor, T. F., Brown, J., & Del Boca, F. K. (1990). Validity of self-reports in applied research on addictive behaviors: Fact or fiction? *Behavioral Assessment, 12,* 5–31.

Bachrach, H., Mintz, J., & Luborsky, L. (1971). On rating empathy and other psychotherapy variables: An experience with the effects of training. *Journal of Consulting and Clinical Psychology, 36,* 445.

Bailey, D. B., & Simeonson, R. J. (1988). Investigation of use of goal attainment scaling to evaluate individual progress of clients with severe and profound mental retardation. *Mental Retardation, 26,* 289–295.

Bakeman, R. (1978). Untangling streams of behavior: Sequential analysis of observation data. In G. P. Sackett (Ed.), *Observing behavior: Vol 2. Data collection and analysis methods* (pp. 63–78). Baltimore: University Park Press.

Bakeman, R., & Gottman, J. M. (1986). *Observing interaction: An introduction to sequential analysis.* New York: Cambridge University Press.

Barrett-Lennard, G. T. (1962). Dimensions of therapist response as causal factors in therapeutic change. *Psychological Monographs, 76* (43, Whole No. 562).

Battle, C. C., Imber, S. D., Hoehn-Saric, R., Stone, A. R., Nash, C., & Frank, J. D. (1966). Target complaints as criteria of improvement. *American Journal of Psychotherapy, 20,* 184–192.

Benjamin, L. S. (1974). Structural analysis of social behavior. *Psychological Review, 81,* 392–425.

Benjamin, L. S. (1979). Use of structural analysis of social behavior (SASB) and Markov chains to study dyadic interactions. *Journal of Abnormal Psychology, 88,* 303–319.

Benjamin, L. S., Foster, S. W., Roberto, L. G., & Estroff, S. E. (1986). Breaking the family code: Analysis of videotapes of family interactions by Structured Analysis of Social Behavior (SASB). In L. S. Greenberg & W. M. Pinsof (Eds.), *The psychotherapeutic process: A research handbook* (pp. 391–438). New York: Guilford.

Bergin, A. E. (1971). The evaluation of therapeutic outcomes. In A. E. Bergin & S. L. Garfield (Eds.), *Handbook*

of psychotherapy and behavior change (pp. 217–270). New York: Wiley.

Berzins, J. I., Bednar, R. L., & Severy, L. J. (1975). The problem of intersource consensus in measuring therapeutic outcomes: New data and multivariate perspectives. *Journal of Abnormal Psychology, 84,* 10–19.

Beutler, L. E. (1991). Have all won and must all have prizes? Revisiting Luborsky et al.'s verdict. *Journal of Consulting and Clinical Psychology, 59,* 226–232.

Beutler, L. E., & Crago, M. (1983). Self-report measures of psychotherapy outcome. In M. J. Lambert, E. R. Christensen, & Steven S. DeJulio (Eds.), *The assessment of psychotherapy outcome* (pp. 453–497). New York: Wiley.

Beutler, L. E., & Hamblin, D. L. (1986). Individualized outcome measures of internal change: Methodlological considerations. *Journal of Consulting and Clinical Psychology, 54,* 48–53.

Beutler, L. E., & Hill, C. E. (1992). Process and outcome research in the treatment of adult victims of childhood sexual abuse: Methodological issues. *Journal of Consulting and Clinical Psychology, 60,* 204–212.

Beutler, L. E., Johnson, D. T., Neville, C. W., & Workman, S. N. (1973). Some sources of variance in "accurate empathy" ratings. *Journal of Consulting and Clinical Psychology, 40,* 17–19.

Bordin, E. S. (1979). The generalizability of the psychoanalytic concept of the working alliance. *Psychotherapy: Theory, Research, and Practice, 16,* 252–260.

Bordin, E. S., Cutler, R. I., Dittmann, A. T., Harway, N. I., Rausch, H. L., & Rigler, D. (1954). Measurement problems in process research on psychotherapy. *Journal of Consulting Psychology, 18,* 79–82.

Borgen, F. H., & Barnett, D. C. (1987). Applying cluster analysis in counseling psychology research. *Journal of Counseling Psychology, 34,* 456–468.

Bozarth, J. D., & Krauft, C. J. (1972). Accurate empathy ratings: Some methodological considerations. *Journal of Clinical Psychology, 23,* 408–411.

Budman, S. H., Demby, A., Feldstein, M., Redondo, J., Scherz, B., Bennett, M. J., Koppenaal, G., Daley, B. S., Hunter, M., & Ellis, J. (1987). Preliminary findings on a new instrument to measure cohesion in group psychotherapy. *International Journal of Group Psychotherapy, 37,* 75–94.

Burlingame, G., & Barlow, S. H. (1991, July). *The outcome of group therapy conducted by professional therapists or college professors.* Paper presented at the annual meetings of the Society for Psychotherapy Research, Lyon, France.

Butcher, J. N., Dahlstrom, W. G., Graham, J. R., Tellegen, A., & Kaemmer, B. (1989). *Minnesota Multiphasic Personality Inventory (MMPI-2). Manual for administration and scoring.* Minneapolis: University of Minnesota Press.

Butcher, J. N., & Herzog, J. G. (1982). Individual assessment in crisis intervention: Observation, life history, and personality approaches. In C. D. Spielberger & J. N. Butcher (Eds.), *Advances in personality assessment* (Vol. 1). Hillsdale, NJ: Lawrence Erlbaum.

Calsyn, R. J., & Davidson, W. S. (1978). Do we really want a program evaluation strategy based on individualized goals? A critique of goal attainment scaling. *Evaluation Studies: Review Annual, 1,* 700–713.

Cameron, R., & Evers, S. E. (1990). Self-report issues in obesity and weight management: State of the art and future directions. *Behavioral Assessment, 12,* 91–106.

Campbell, D. T., & Fiske, D. W. (1959). Convergent and discriminant validation by the multitrait-multimethod matrix. *Psychological Bulletin, 56,* 81–105.

Caracena, P. F., & Vicory, J. R. (1969). Correlates of phenomenological and judged empathy. *Journal of Counseling Psychology, 16*, 510–515.

Carkhuff, R. R. (1969). *Human and helping relations* (Vols. 1 & 2). New York: Holt, Rinehart and Winston.

Carmichael, H. T. (1966). Sound-film recording of psychoanalytic therapy: A therapist's experience and reactions. In L. A. Gottschalk & A. H. Auerbach (Eds.), *Methods of research in psychotherapy* (pp. 50–59). New York: Appleton-Century-Crofts.

Carson, R. C., & Butcher, J. N. (1992). *Abnormal psychology and modern life* (9th ed.). Glenview, IL: Scott, Foresman.

Cartwright, R. (1966). Analysis of qualitative material. In L. Festinger & D. Katz (Eds.), *Research methods in the behavioral sciences* (pp. 421–470). New York: Holt, Rinehart and Winston.

Cartwright, D. S., Kirtner, W. L., & Fiske, D. W. (1963). Method factors in changes associated with psychotherapy. *Journal of Abnormal and Social Psychology, 66*, 164–175.

Christensen, H., Hadzi-Pavlovic, D., Andrews, G., & Mattick, R. (1987). Behavior therapy and tricyclic medication in the treatment of obsessive-compulsive disorder: A quantitative review. *Journal of Consulting and Clinical Psychology, 55*, 701–711.

Cohen, J. (1960). A coefficient of agreement for nominal scales. *Educational and Psychological Measurement, 20*, 37–46.

Cohen, J. (1968). Weighted kappa: Nominal scale agreement with provision for scaled disagreement or partial credit. *Psychological Bulletin, 70*, 213–220.

Coombs (1951). Mathematical models in psychological scaling. *Journal of the American Statistical Association, 46*, 480–489.

Cronbach, L. J. (1960). *Essentials of psychological testing.* New York: Harper & Row.

Cronbach, L. J. (1990). *Essentials of psychological testing* (3rd ed.) New York: Harper & Row.

Cronbach, L. J., & Furby, L. (1970). How we should measure "change"—or should we? *Psychological Bulletin, 74*, 68–80.

Cronbach, L. J., & Gleser, G. C. (1953). Assessing similarity between profiles. *Psychological Bulletin, 50*, 456–473.

Cronbach, L. J., Gleser, G. C., Nanda, H., & Rajaratnam, N. (1972). *The dependability of behavioral measurements.* New York: Wiley.

Cytrynbaum, S., Ginath, Y., Birdwell, T., & Brandt, L. (1979). Goal attainment scaling: A critical review. *Evaluation Quarterly, 3*, 5–40.

Davidson, C. V., & Davidson, R. H. (1983). The significant other as data source and data problem in psychotherapy outcome research. In M. J. Lambert, E. R. Christensen, & S. S. DeJulio (Eds.), *The assessment of psychotherapy outcome* (pp. 569–602). New York: Wiley.

Derogatis, L. R. (1983). *SCL-90: Administration, Scoring and Procedures Manual for the Revised Version.* Baltimore: Clinical Psychometric Research.

Derogatis, L. R., & Melisaratos, N. (1983). The brief symptom inventory: An introductory report. *Psychological Medicine, 13*, 595–605.

Dollard, J., & Auld, F., Jr. (1959). *Scoring human motives: A manual.* New Haven, CT: Yale University Press.

Ekman, P., & Friesen, W. V. (1968). Nonverbal behavior in psychotherapy research. In J. M. Sclien et al. (Eds.), *Research in psychotherapy* (Vol. 3, pp. 179–216). Washington DC: American Psychological Association.

Elliott, R. (1984). A discovery-oriented approach to significant events in psychotherapy: Interpersonal process recall and comprehensive process analysis. In L. Rice & L.

Greenberg (Eds.), *Patterns of change* (pp. 249–286). New York: Guilford.

Elliott, R. (1985). Helpful and unhelpful events in brief counseling interviews: An empirical taxonomy. *Journal of Counseling Psychology, 32*, 307–322.

Elliott, R. (1986). Interpersonal Process Recall as a psychotherapy process recall method. In L. S. Greenberg & W. M. Pinsof (Eds.), *The psychotherapeutic process: A research handbook* (pp. 503–528). New York: Guilford.

Elliott, R. (1991). Five dimensions of therapy process. *Psychotherapy Research, 1*, 92–103.

Elliott, R., Hill, C. E., Stiles, W. B., Friedlander, M. L., Mahrer, A. R., & Margison, F. R. (1987). Primary therapist response modes: Comparison of six rating systems. *Journal of Consulting and Clinical Psychology, 55*, 218–223.

Eysenck, H. J. (1952). The effects of psychotherapy: An evaluation. *Journal of Consulting Psychology, 16*, 319–324.

Exner, J. E., Jr. (1986). *The Rorschach: A comprehensive system: Vol. 1. Basic foundation* (2nd ed.). New York: Wiley.

Farrell, A. D., Curran, J. P., Zwick, W. R., & Monti, P. M. (1983). Generalizability and discriminant validity of anxiety and social skills ratings in two populations. *Behavioral Assessment, 6*, 1–14.

Finn, J. D. (1974). *A general model for multivariate analysis.* New York: Holt, Rinehart and Winston.

Fish, J. M. (1970). Empathy and the reported emotional experiences of beginning psychotherapists. *Journal of Consulting and Clinical Psychology, 35*, 64–69.

Fiske, D. W. (1977). Methodological issues in research on the psychotherapist. In A. S. Gurman & A. M. Razin (Eds.), *Effective psychotherapy* (pp. 23–43). New York: Pergamon Press.

Fleiss, J. L. (1981). Balanced incomplete block designs for interrater reliability studies. *Applied Psychological Measurement, 5*, 105–112.

Fleuridas, C., Rosenthal, D. M., Leigh, G. K., & Leigh, T. E. (1990). Family goal recording: An adaption of goal attainment scaling for enhancing family therapy and assessment. *Journal of Marital and Family Therapy, 16*(4), 389–406.

Flowers, J. V., & Booaren, C. D. (1990). Four studies toward an empirical foundation for group therapy. *Journal of Social Service Research, 13*(2), 105–121.

Foreman, S., & Marmar, C. R. (1985). Therapist actions that address initially poor therapeutic alliances in psychotherapy. *American Journal of Psychiatry, 142*, 922–926.

Forsyth, R. P., & Fairweather, G. W. (1961). Psychotherapeutic and other hospital treatment criteria: The dilemma. *Journal of Abnormal and Social Psychology, 62*, 598–604.

Friedlander, M. L., Ellis, M. V., Siegel, S. M., Raymond, L., & Haase, R. F. (1988). Generalizing from segments to sessions: Should it be done? *Journal of Counseling Psychology, 35*, 243–250.

Friedlander, M. L., & Heatherington, L. (1989). Analyzing relational control in family therapy interviews. *Journal of Counseling Psychology, 36*, 139–148.

Froyd, J., & Lambert, M. J. (1989, May). A survey of outcome research measures in psychotherapy research. Paper presented at the meeting of the Western Psychological Association, Reno, NV.

Garfield, S. L. (1986). Research on client variables in psychotherapy. In S. L. Garfield & A. E. Bergin (Eds.), *Handbook of psychotherapy and behavior change* (pp. 213–256). New York: Wiley.

Garfield, S. L. (1990). Issues and methods in psychotherapy

process research. *Journal of Consulting and Clinical Psychology, 58,* 273–280.

Garfield, S. L. (1991). Psychotherapy models and outcome research. *American Psychologist, 46,* 1350–1351.

Garfield, S. L., Prager, R. A., & Bergin, A. E. (1971). Evaluation of outcome in psychotherapy. *Journal of Consulting and Clinical Psychology, 37,* 307–313.

Gaston, L., & Marmar, C. R. (1990). *Manual for the California Psychotherapy Alliance Scales.* Unpublished manuscript.

Gaston, L., & Marmar, C. R., & Ring, J. M. (1989, June). *Engaging the difficult patient in cognitive therapy: Actions developing the therapeutic alliance.* Paper presented at the annual meeting of the Society for Psychotherapy Research, Toronto, Ontario, Canada.

Gelso, C. J. (1973). The effects of audiorecording and videorecording on client satisfaction and self-exploration. *Journal of Consulting and Clinical Psychology, 40,* 455–461.

Gelso, C. J. (1974). Effects of recording on counselors and clients. *Counselor Education and Supervision, 14,* 5–12.

Gelso, C. J., & Carter, J. A. (1985). The relationship in counseling and psychotherapy. *Counseling Psychologist, 13,* 155–243.

Gervaize, P. A., Mahrer, A. R., & Markow, R. (1985). Therapeutic laughter: What therapists do to promote strong laughter in patients. *Psychotherapy in Private Practice, 3,* 65–74.

Gibson, R. L., Snyder, W. U., & Ray, W. S. (1955). A factors analysis of measures of change following client-centered psychotherapy. *Journal of Counseling Psychology, 2,* 83–90.

Gottman, J. M. (1979). Detecting cyclicity in social interaction. *Psychological Bulletin, 86,* 338–348.

Gottman, J. M., & Markman, H. J. (1978). Experimental designs in psychotherapy research. In S. L. Garfield & A. E. Bergin (Eds.), *Handbook of psychotherapy and behavior change* (2nd ed., pp. 23–62). New York: Wiley.

Green, B. C., Gleser, G. C., Stone, W. N., & Siefert, R. F. (1975). Relationships among diverse measures of psychotherapy outcome. *Journal of Consulting and Clinical Psychiatry, 43,* 689–699.

Greenberg, L. S. (1984). Task analysis of interpersonal conflict. In L. N. Rice & L. S. Greenberg (Eds.), *Patterns of change: Intensive analysis of psychotherapeutic process.* New York: Guilford.

Greenberg, L. S. (1986). Change process research. *Journal of Consulting and Clinical Psychology, 54,* 4–9.

Greenberg, L. S. (1991). Research on the process of change. *Psychotherapy Research, 1,* 3–16.

Greenberg, L. S., & Pinsof, W. (Eds.). (1986). *The psychotherapeutic process: A research handbook.* New York: Guilford.

Greenberg, L. S., & Webster, M. C. (1982). Resolving decisional conflict by gestalt two-chair dialogue: Relating process to outcome. *Journal of Counseling Psychology, 29,* 468–477.

Gurman, A. S. (1973). Effects of therapist and patient mood on the therapeutic functioning of high- and low-facilitative therapists. *Journal of Consulting and Clinical Psychology, 40,* 48–58.

Gurman, A. S. (1977). The patient's perception of the therapeutic relationship. In A. S. Gurman & A. M. Razin (Eds.), *Effective psychotherapy: A handbook of research* (pp. 503–543). New York: Pergamon.

Hansen, J. C., Moore, G. D., & Carkhuff, R. R. (1968). The differential relationships of objective and client perceptions of counseling. *Journal of Clinical Psychology, 24,* 244–246.

Harper, F. D., & Bruce-Sanford, G. C. (1981). *Counseling techniques: An outline and overview.* Alexandria, VA: Douglass Press.

Harway, N., Dittman, A., Raush, H., Bordin, E., & Rigler, D. (1955). The measurement of depth of interpretation. *Journal of Consulting Psychology, 19,* 247–253.

Heatherington, L. (1989). Toward more meaningful clinical research: Taking context into account in coding psychotherapy interaction. *Psychotherapy, 26,* 436–447.

Herbert, J. D., & Mueser, K. T. (1991). Proof is in the pudding: A commentary on Persons. *American Psychologist, 46,* 1347–1348.

Heyns, R. W., & Zander, A. F. (1966). Observation of group behavior. In L. Festinger & D. Katz (Eds.), *Research methods in the behavioral sciences* (pp. 381–417). New York: Holt, Rinehart and Winston.

Hill, C. E. (1974). A comparison of the perceptions of a therapy session by clients, therapists, and objective judges. *Journal Supplements Abstract Service, 4*(564).

Hill, C. E. (1978). Development of a counselor verbal response category system. *Journal of Counseling Psychology, 25,* 461–468.

Hill, C. E. (1982). Counseling process research: Philosophical and methodological dilemmas. *The Counseling Psychologist, 10*(4), 7–19.

Hill, C. E. (1985). *Manual for the Hill counselor verbal response modes category system* (ref. ed.). Unpublished manuscript. University of Maryland, College Park.

Hill, C. E. (1986). An overview of the Hill counselor and client verbal response modes category systems. In L. S. Greenberg & W. M. Pinsof (Eds.), *The psychotherapeutic process: A research handbook* (pp. 131–160). New York: Guilford.

Hill, C. E. (1989). *Therapist techniques and client outcomes: Eight cases of brief psychotherapy.* Newbury Park, CA: Sage Publications.

Hill, C. E. (1990). A review of exploratory in-session process research. *Journal of Consulting and Clinical Psychology, 58,* 288–294.

Hill, C. E. (1991). Almost everything you ever wanted to know about how to do process research on counseling and psychotherapy but didn't know who to ask. In C. E. Watkins & L. J. Schneider (Eds.), *Research in counseling* (pp. 85–118). Hillsdale, NJ: Lawrence Erlbaum.

Hill, C. E. (1992). An overview of four measures developed to test the Hill process model: Therapist intentions, therapist response modes, client reactions, and client behaviors. *Journal of Counseling and Development, 70,* 728–739.

Hill, C. E. (1992b). Research on therapist techniques in brief individual therapy: Implications for practitioners. *The Counseling Psychologist, 20,* 689–711.

Hill, C. E., Carter, J. A., & O'Farrell, M. K. (1983). A case study of the process and outcome of time-limited counseling. *Journal of Counseling Psychology, 30,* 3–18.

Hill, C. E., Helms, J., Spiegel, S. B., & Tichenor, V. (1988). Development of a system for categorizing client reactions to therapist interventions. *Journal of Counseling Psychology, 35,* 27–36.

Hill, C. E., Helms, J. E., Tichenor, V., Spiegel, S. B., O'Grady, K. E., & Perry, E. (1988). The effects of therapist response modes in brief psychotherapy. *Journal of Counseling Psychology, 35,* 222–233.

Hill, C. E., & O'Grady, K. E. (1985). List of therapist intentions illustrated in a case study and with therapists of varying theoretical orientations. *Journal of Counseling Psychology, 32,* 3–22.

Hill, C. E., O'Grady, K. E., & Elkin, I. E. (1992). Applying the Collaborative Study Psychotherapy Rating Scale to rate therapist adherence in cognitive-behavior therapy, interpersonal therapy, and clinical management. *Journal of Consulting and Clinical Psychology, 60,* 73–79.

Hill, C. E., O'Grady, K. E., & Price, P. (1988). A method for investigating sources of rater bias. *Journal of Counseling Psychology, 35,* 346–350.

Hill, C. E., Siegelman, L., Gronsky, B., Sturniolo, F., & Fretz, B. R. (1981). Nonverbal communication and counseling outcome. *Journal of Counseling Psychology, 28,* 203–212.

Hill, C. E., & Stephany, A. (1990). The relationship of nonverbal behaviors to client reactions. *Journal of Counseling Psychology, 37,* 22–26.

Hill, C. E., Thames, T. B., & Rardin, D. (1979). A comparison of Rogers, Perls, and Ellis on the Hill Counselor Verbal Response Category System. *Journal of Counseling Psychology, 26,* 198–203.

Hill, W. F. (1965). *Hill Interaction Matrix.* Los Angeles: University of California Youth Study Center.

Hollon, S. D., Evans, M. D., Auerbach, A., DeRubeis, R. J., Elkin, I., Lowery, A., Kriss, M., Grove, W., Tuason, V. B., & Piasecki, J. (1988). *Development of a system for rating therapies for depression: Differentiating cognitive therapy, interpersonal psychotherapy, and clinical management pharmacotherapy.* Unpublished manuscript.

Horowitz, M. J., Marmar, C. R., Weiss, D. S., Kaltrider, N. B., & Wilner, N. R. (1986). Comprehensive analysis of change after brief psychotherapy. *American Journal of Psychiatry, 143,* 582–589.

Horvath, A. O., & Greenberg, L. S. (1989). Development and validation of the Working Alliance Inventory. *Journal of Counseling Psychology, 36,* 223–233.

Horvath, A. O., Marx, R. W., & Kamann, A. M. (1990). Thinking about thinking in therapy: An examination of clients' understanding of their therapists' intentions. *Journal of Consulting and Clinical Psychology, 58,* 614–621.

Hoyt, M. F., Marmar, C. R., Horowitz, M. J., & Alvarez, W. F. (1981). The Therapist Action Scale and the Patient Action Scale: Instruments for the assessment of activities during dynamic psychotherapy. *Psychotherapy: Theory, Research, and Practice, 18,* 109–116.

Hummel-Rossi, B., & Weinberg, S. L. (1975). Practical guidelines in applying current theories to the measurement of change. Part I: Problems in measuring change and recommended procedures. *Journal Supplement Abstract Service,* MS No. 916.

Ihilevich, D., & Glesser, G. C. (1979). *A manual for the progress evaluation scales.* Shiawassee, MI: Community Mental Health Services Board.

Jacobson, N. S. (1988). Defining clinically significant change: An introduction. *Behavioral Assessment, 10,* 131–132.

Jacobson, N. S., Follette, W. C., & Revenstorf, D. (1984a). Psychotherapy outcome research: Methods for reporting variability and evaluating clinical significance. *Behavior Therapy, 15,* 336–352.

Jacobson, N. S., Follette, W. C., Revenstorf, D., Baucom, D. H., Hahlwey, K., & Margolin, G. (1984b). Variability in outcome and clinical significance of behavioral marital therapy: A reanalysis of outcome data. *Journal of Consulting and Clinical Psychology, 52,* 497–504.

Jacobson, N. S., & Truax, P. (1991). Clinical significance: A statistical approach to defining meaningful change in psychotherapy research. *Journal of Consulting and Clinical Psychology, 59,* 12–19.

Jacobson, N. S., Wilson, L., & Tupper, C. (1988). The clinical significance of treatment gains resulting from exposure-based interventions for agoraphobia: A re-analysis of outcome data. *Behavior Therapy, 19,* 539–554.

Jones, E. E. (1985). *Manual for the psychotherapy process Q-set.* Unpublished manuscript.

Jones, E. E., Cummings, J. D., & Horowitz, M. J. (1988). Another look at the nonspecific hypothesis of therapeutic effectiveness. *Journal of Consulting and Clinical Psychology, 56,* 48–55.

Jones, E. E., Krupnick, J. H., & Kerig, P. K. (1987). Some gender effects in brief psychotherapy. *Psychotherapy, 24,* 336–352.

Karl, N. J., & Abeles, N. (1969). Psychotherapy process as a function of the time segment sampled. *Journal of Consulting and Clinical Psychology, 33,* 207–212.

Kazdin, A. E. (1977). Assessing the clinical or applied importance of behavior change through social validation. *Behavior Modification, 1,* 427–452.

Kazdin, A. E. (1980). *Research design in clinical psychology.* New York: Harper & Row.

Kazdin, A. E., Bass, D., Siegel, T., & Thomas C. (1989). Cognitive-behavioral therapy and relationship therapy in treatment of children referred for anti-social behavior. *Journal of Consulting and Clinical Psychology, 57,* 522–535.

Kendall, P. C., & Grove, W. M. (1988). Normative comparisons in therapy outcome. *Behavioral Assessment, 10,* 147–158.

Kendall, P. C., Hollon, S., Beck, A. T., Hammen, C., & Ingram, R. E. (1987). Issues and recommendations regarding use of the Beck Depression Inventory. *Cognitive Therapy and Research, 11,* 289–300.

Kiesler, D. J. (1971). Patient experiencing and successful outcome in individual psychotherapy of schizophrenics and psychoneurotics. *Journal of Consulting and Clinical Psychology, 37,* 370–385.

Kiesler, D. J. (1973). *The process of psychotherapy.* Chicago: Aldine.

Kiesler, D. J., Klein, M. H., & Mathieu, P. L. (1965). Sampling from the recorder therapy interview: The problem of segment location. *Journal of Consulting Psychology, 29,* 337–344.

Kiesler, D. J., Mathieu, P. L., & Klein, M. H. (1967). Patient experiencing level and interaction chronograph variables in therapy interview segments. *Journal of Consulting Psychology, 31,* 224.

Kiresuk, T. J., & Sherman, R. E. (1968). Goal attainment scaling: A general method for evaluating comprehensive community mental health programs. *Community Mental Health Journal, 4,* 443–453.

Klein, D. F., & Cleary, T. A. (1967). Platonic true scores and error in psychiatric rating scales. *Psychological Bulletin, 68,* 77–80.

Klein, M. H., Mathieu, P. L., Gendlin, E. T., & Kiesler, D. J. (1970). *The experiencing scale: A research and training manual.* Madison: Bureau of Audio-Visual Instruction, University of Wisconsin.

Klein, M. H., Mathieu-Coughlan, P., & Kiesler, D. J. (1986). The experiencing scales. In L. Greenberg and W. Pinsof (Eds.), *The psychotherapeutic process: A research handbook* (pp. 21–72). New York: Guilford.

Klonoff, H., & Cox, B. A. (1975). Problem-oriented approach to analysis of treatment outcome. *American Journal of Psychiatry, 132,* 836–841.

Knapp, P. H. (1974). Segmentation and structure in psychoanalysis. *Journal of the American Psychoanalytic Association, 22,* 14–36.

Kolotkin, R. L., & Johnson M. (1983). Crisis intervention and measurement of treatment outcome. In M. J. Lambert, E. R. Christensen, & S. S. DeJulio (Eds.), *The assessment of psychotherapy outcome* (pp. 132–159). New York: Wiley.

Kurtz, R. R., & Grummon, D. L. (1972). Different approaches to the measurement of therapist empathy and their relationship to therapy outcome. *Journal of Consulting and Clinical Psychology, 39,* 106–115.

Lacks, P., & Powlista, K. (1989). Improvement following behavioral treatment for insomnia: Clinical significance, long-term maintenance, and predictions of outcome. *Behavior Therapy, 20,* 117–134.

Lambert, M. J. (1983). Introduction to assessment of psychotherapy outcome: Historical perspective and current issues. In M. J. Lambert, E. R. Christensen, & S. S. DeJulio (Eds.), *The assessment of psychotherapy outcome* (pp. 3–32). New York: Wiley-Interscience.

Lambert, M. J., DeJulio, S. S., & Stein, D. M. (1978). Therapist interpersonal skills: Process, outcome, methodological considerations, and recommendations for future research. *Psychological Bulletin, 85,* 467–489.

Lambert, M. J., Hatch, D. R., Kingston, M. D., & Edwards, B. C. (1986). Zung, Beck, and Hamilton rating scales as measures of treatment outcome: A meta-analytic comparison. *Journal of Consulting and Clinical Psychology, 54,* 54–59.

Lambert, M. J., & McRoberts, C. (1993, April). *Survey of outcome measures used in JCCP: 1986–1991.* Poster presented at the annual meetings of the Western Psychological Association, Phoenix, AZ.

Latham, G. P., & Wexley, K. N. (1981). *Increasing productivity through performance appraisal.* Reading, MA: Addison-Wesley.

Levine, S. B., & Agle, D. (1978). The effectiveness of sex therapy for chronic secondary psychological impotence. *Journal of Sex and Marital Therapy, 4,* 235–258.

Lewis, A. B., Spencer, J. H., Haas, G. L., & DiVittis, A. (1987). Goal attainment scaling: Relevance and replicability in follow-up of inpatients. *The Journal of Nervous and Mental Diseases, 175,* 408–418.

Lichtenberg, J. W., & Hummel, T. J. (1976). Counseling as a stochastic process: Fitting a Markov chain model to initial counseling interviews. *Journal of Counseling Psychology, 23,* 310–315.

Lloyds, M. E. (1983). Selecting systems to measure client outcome in human service agencies. *Behavioral Assessment, 5,* 55–70.

Locke, H. J., & Wallace, K. M. (1959). Short marital-adjustment and prediction test: Their reliability and validity. *Marriage and Family Living, 21,* 251–255.

Luborsky, L. (1971). Perennial mystery of poor agreement among criteria for psychotherapy outcome. *Journal of Consulting and Clinical Psychology, 37,* 316–319.

Luborsky, L., Chandler, M., Auerbach, A. H., Cohen, J., & Bachrach, H. M. (1971). Factors influencing the outcome of psychotherapy: A review of quantitative research. *Psychological Bulletin, 75,* 145–185.

MacKenzie, K. R. (1981). Measurement of group climate. *International Journal of Group Psychotherapy, 31,* 287–295.

Mahalik, J., Hill, C. E., Thompson, B., & O'Grady, K. E. (1989, June). *Rater bias in the Checklist of Psychotherapy Transactions measure.* Paper presented at the Society for Psychotherapy Research, Toronto, Ontario, Canada.

Maher, C. A., & Barbrack, C. R. (1984). Evaluating the individual counseling of conduct problem adolescents: The goal attainment scaling method. *Journal of School Psychology, 22,* 285–297.

Mahrer, A. R., & Gagnon, R. (1991). The care and feeding of a psychotherapy research team. *Journal of Psychiatry and Neuroscience, 16,* 188–192.

Mahrer, A. R., Markow, R., Gervaize, P. A., & Boulet, D. B. (1987). Strong laughter in psychotherapy: Concomitant patient verbal behavior and implications for therapeutic use. *Voices, 23,* 80–88.

Mahrer, A. R., Paterson, W. E., Theriault, A. T., Roessler, C., & Quenneville, A. (1986). How and why to use a large number of clinically sophisticated judges in psychotherapy research. *Voices: The Art and Science of Psychotherapy, 22,* 57–66.

Maisto, S. A., & Maisto, C. A. (1983). Institutional measures of treatment outcome. In M. J. Lambert, E. R. Christensen, & S. S. DeJulio (Eds.), *The assessment of psychotherapy outcome* (pp. 603–625). New York: Wiley.

Marmar, C. R. (1990). Psychotherapy process research: Progress, dilemmas, and future directions. *Journal of Consulting and Clinical Psychology, 58,* 265–272.

Marsden, G. (1965). Content analysis studies of therapeutic interviews: 1954–1964. *Psychological Bulletin, 63,* 298–321.

Marsden, G. (1971). Content analysis studies of psychotherapy: 1954 to 1968. In A. E. Bergin & S. L. Garfield (Eds.), *Handbook of psychotherapy and behavior change* (pp. 345–407). New York: Wiley.

Marsden, G., Kalter, N., & Ericson, W. A. (1974). Response productivity: A methodological problem in content analysis studies in psychotherapy. *Journal of Consulting and Clinical Psychology, 42,* 224–230.

Masters, W. H., & Johnson, V. E. (1970). *Human sexual inadequacy.* Boston: Little, Brown.

Mavissakalian, M. (1986). Clinically significant improvement in agoraphobia research. *Behaviour Research and Therapy, 24,* 369–370.

McCollough, L. (1990). *Psychotherapy Interaction Coding System Manual.* Unpublished manuscript. Beth Israel Hospital, New York.

McCullough, L., Winston, A., Farber, B. A., Porter, F., Pollack, J., Laikin, M., Vingiano, W., & Trujillo, M. (1991). The relationship of patient–therapist interaction to outcome in brief psychotherapy. *Psychotherapy, 28,* 525–533.

McDaniel, S. H., Stiles, W. B., & McGaughey, K. J. (1981). Correlations of male college students' verbal response mode use with measures of psychological disturbance and psychotherapy outcome. *Journal of Consulting and Clinical Psychology, 49,* 571–582.

McNair, D. M., & Lorr, M. (1964). An analysis of professed psychotherapeutic techniques. *Journal of Consulting Psychology, 28,* 265–271.

McNeilly, C. L., & Howard, K. I. (1991). The Therapeutic Procedures Inventory: Psychometric properties and relationship to phase of treatment. *Journal of Psychotherapy Integration, 1,* 223–234.

Mercer, R. C., & Loesch, L. C. (1979). Audio tape ratings: Comments and guidelines. *Psychotherapy: Theory, Research and Practice, 16,* 79–85.

Mergenthaler, E., & Stinson, C. H. (1992). Psychotherapy transcription standards. *Psychotherapy Research, 2,* 125–142.

Messer, S. B. (1991). The case formulation approach: Issues of reliability and validity. *American Psychologist, 46,* 1348–1350.

Messer, S. B., Tishby, O., & Spillman, A. (1992). Taking context seriously in psychotherapy research: Relating therapist interventions to patient progress in brief psychodynamic therapy. *Journal of Consulting and Clinical Psychology, 60,* 678–688.

Miller, R. C., & Berman, J. S. (1983). The efficacy of cognitive behavior therapies: A quantitative review of the research evidence. *Psychological Bulletin, 94,* 39–53.

Mintz, J., & Kiesler, D. J. (1982). Individualized measures of psychotherapy outcome. In P. C. Kendall & J. N. Butcher

(Eds.) *Handbook of research methods in clinical psychology* (pp. 491–534). New York: Wiley.

Mintz, J., & Luborsky, L. (1971). Segments vs. whole sessions: Which is the better unit for psychotherapy research? *Journal of Abnormal Psychology, 78,* 180–191.

Mintz, J., Luborsky, L., & Christoph, P. (1979). Measuring the outcomes of psychotherapy: Findings of the Penn. Psychotherapy Project. *Journal of Consulting and Clinical Psychology, 47,* 319–334.

Mitchell, S. K. (1979). Inter-observer agreement, reliability, and generalizability of data collected in observational studies. *Psychological Bulletin, 86,* 376–390.

Monti, P. M., Wallander, J. L., Ahern, D. K., Abrams, D. B., & Monroe, S. M. (1983). Multi-modal measurement of anxiety and social skills in a behavioral role-play test: Generalizability and discriminant validity. *Behavioral Assessment, 6,* 15–25.

Moras, K., & Hill, C. E. (1991). Rater selection in psychotherapy process research: Observations on the state-of-the-art. *Psychotherapy Research, 1,* 113–123.

Muehlberg, G. N., Pierce, R., & Drasgow, J. (1969). A factor analysis of therapeutically facilitative conditions. *Journal of Clinical Psychology, 25,* 93–95.

Mylar, J. L., & Clement, P. W. (1972). Prediction and comparison of outcome in systematic desensitization and implosion. *Behavior Research and Therapy, 10,* 235–246.

Newman, F. L. (1983). Therapist's evaluation of psychotherapy. In M. J. Lambert, E. R. Christensen, & S. S. DeJulio (Eds.), *The Assessment of Psychotherapy Outcome* (pp. 498–536). New York: Wiley.

Nichols, R. C. & Beck, K. W. (1960). Factors in psychotherapy change. *Journal of Consulting Psychology, 24,* 388–399.

Nietzel, M. T., Russell, R. L., Hemmings, K. A., & Gretter, M. L. (1987). Clinical significance of psychotherapy for unipolar depression: A meta-analytic approach to social comparison. *Journal of Consulting and Clinical Psychology, 55,* 156–161.

Nunnally, J. C. (1978). *Psychometric theory.* New York: McGraw-Hill.

O'Farrell, M. K., Hill, C. E., & Patton, S. (1986). Comparison of two cases of counseling with the same counselor. *Journal of Counseling and Development, 65,* 141–145.

Ogles, B. M., Lambert, M. J., Weight, D. G., & Payne, I. R. (1990). Agoraphobia outcome measurement: A review and meta-analysis. *Psychological Assessment: A Journal of Consulting and Clinical Psychology, 2,* 317–325.

Parloff, M. B., Waskow, I. E., & Wolfe, B. E. (1978). Research on therapist variables in relation to process and outcome. In S. L. Garfield & A. E. Bergin (Eds.), *Handbook of psychotherapy and behavior change* (2nd ed., pp. 233–283). New York: Wiley.

Perry, G., Shapiro, D. A., & Firth, J. (1986). The case of the anxious executive: A study from the research clinic. *British Journal of Medical Psychology, 59,* 221–233.

Persons, J. B. (1991). Psychotherapy outcome studies do not accurately represent current models of psychotherapy: A proposed remedy. *American Psychologist, 46,* 99–106.

Pilkonis, P. A., Imber, S. D., Lewis, P., & Rubinsky, P. (1984). A comparative outcome study of individual, group, and conjoint psychotherapy. *Archives of General Psychiatry, 41,* 431–437.

Pinsof, W. M. (1986). The process of family therapy: The development of the Family Therapist Coding System. In L. S. Greenberg & W. M. Pinsof (Eds.), *The psychotherapeutic process: A research handbook* (pp. 201–284). New York: Guilford.

Piotrowski, C., & Keller, W. (1989). Psychological testing in outpatient mental health facilities: A national study. *Professional Psychology: Research and Practice, 20,* 423–425.

Polkinghorne, D. E. (1991). Two conflicting calls for methodological reform. *The Counseling Psychologist, 19,* 103–114.

Rankin, H. (1990). Validity of self-reports in clinical settings. *Behavioral Assessment, 12,* 107–116.

Reid, J. B. (1970). Reliability assessment of observation data: A possible methodological problem. *Child Development, 41,* 1143–1150.

Rice, L. N., & Kerr, G. P. (1986). Measures of client and therapist vocal quality. In L. S. Greenberg & W. M. Pinsof (Eds.), *The psychotherapeutic process: A research handbook* (pp. 73–105). New York: Guilford.

Rice, L. N., & Sapiera, E. P. (1984). Task analysis of the resolution of problematic reactions. In L. N. Rice & L. S. Greenberg (Eds.), *Patterns of change: Intensive analysis of psychotherapeutic process* (pp. 29–66). New York: Guilford.

Roberts, R. R., & Renzaglia, G. A. (1965). The influence of tape recording on counseling. *Journal of Counseling Psychology, 12,* 10–16.

Robinson, L. A., Berman, J. S., & Neimeyer, R. A. (1990). Psychotherapy for the treatment of depression: A comprehensive review of controlled outcome research. *Psychological Bulletin, 108,* 39–40.

Rogers, C. (1957). The necessary and sufficient conditions of therapeutic personal change. *Journal of Counseling Psychology, 21,* 93–103.

Rogers, C. R., Gendlin, E. T., Kiesler, D. J., & Truax, C. B. (1967). *The therapeutic relationship and its impact: A study of psychotherapy with schizophrenics.* Madison: University of Wisconsin Press.

Romanczyk, R. G., Kent, R. N., Diament, C., & O'Leary, K. D. (1973). Measuring the reliability of observational data: A reactive process. *Journal of Applied Behavior Analysis, 6,* 175–184.

Rosenthal, R. (1969). Interpersonal expectation. In R. Rosenthal and R. L. Rosnow (Eds.), *Artifact in Behavioral Research* (pp. 181–277). New York: Academic Press.

Ross, S. M., & Proctor, S. (1973). Frequency and duration of hierarchy item exposure in a systematic desensitization analogue. *Behavior Research and Therapy, 11,* 303–312.

Russell, C. S., Olson, D. H., Sprenkle, D. H., & Atilano, R. B. (1983). From family system to family system: Review of family therapy research. *The American Journal of Family Therapy, 11,* 3–14.

Russell, R. L. (1987). *Language in psychotherapy: Strategies of discovery.* New York: Plenum.

Russell, R. L. (1988). A new classification scheme for studies of verbal behavior in psychotherapy. *Psychotherapy, 25,* 51–58.

Russell, R. L., & Stiles, W. B. (1979). Categories for classifying language in psychotherapy. *Psychological Bulletin, 86,* 404–419.

Russell, R. L., & Trull, T. J. (1986). Sequential analysis of language variables in psychotherapy process research. *Journal of Consulting and Clinical Psychology, 54,* 16–21.

Saal, F. R., Downey, R. G., & Lahey, M. A. (1980). Rating the ratings: Assessing the psychometric properties of rating data. *Psychological Bulletin, 88,* 413–428.

Sabalis, R. F. (1983). Assessing outcome in patients with sexual dysfunctions and sexual deviations. In M. J. Lambert, E. R. Christensen, & S. S. DeJulio (Eds.), *The assessment of psychotherapy outcome* (pp. 205–262). New York: Wiley.

Salvio, M., Beutler, L. E., Wood, J. M., & Engle, D. (1992).

The strength of the therapeutic alliance in three treatments for depression. *Psychotherapy Research, 2,* 31–36.

Sampson, H., & Weiss, J. (1986). Testing hypotheses: The approach of the Mount Zion Psychotherapy Research Group. In L. S. Greenberg & W. M. Pinsof (Eds.), *The psychotherapeutic process: A research handbook* (pp. 519–613). New York: Guilford.

Schact, T. E. (1991). Formulation based psychotherapy research: Some further considerations. *American Psychologist, 46,* 1346–1347.

Schmaling, K. B., & Jacobson, N. S. (1987, November). *The clinical significance of treatment gains resulting from parent-training interventions for children with conduct problems: A reanalysis of outcome data.* Paper presented at the annual meeting of the Association for the Advancement of Behavior Therapy, Boston.

Schoeninger, D. W., Klein, M. H., & Mathieu, P. L. (1967). Sampling from the recorded therapy interview: Patient experiencing ratings made with and without therapist speech cues. *Psychological Reports, 20,* 250.

Scott, M. J., & Stradling, S. G. (1990). Group cognitive therapy for depression produces clinically significant reliable change in community-based settings. *Behavioral Psychotherapy, 18,* 1–19.

Shadish, W. R., Jr., & Sweeney, R. B. (1991). Mediators and moderators in meta-analysis: There's a reason we don't let dodo birds tell us which psychotherapies should have prizes. *Journal of Consulting and Clinical Psychology, 59,* 883–893.

Shapiro, D. A., & Shapiro, D. (1982). Meta-analysis of comparative therapy outcome studies: A replication and refinement. *Psychological Bulletin, 92,* 581–604.

Shapiro, J. G. (1968). Relationships between visual and auditory cues of therapeutic effectiveness. *Journal of Clinical Psychology, 34,* 236–239.

Shoham-Salomon, V. (1990). Interrelating research processes of process research. *Journal of Consulting and Clinical Psychology, 58,* 295–303.

Shore, M. F., Massimo, J. L., & Ricks, D. F. (1965). A factor analytic study of psychotherapeutic change in delinquent boys. *Journal of Clinical Psychology, 21,* 208–212.

Shrout, P. E., & Fleiss, J. L. (1979). Intraclass correlations: Uses in assessing rater reliability. *Psychological Bulletin, 86,* 420–428.

Silverman, W. K. (1991). Person's description of psychotherapy outcome studies does not accurately represent psychotherapy outcome studies. *American Psychologist, 46,* 1351–1352.

Sloan, R. B., Staples, F. R., Cristol, A. H., Yorkston, N. J., & Whipple, K. (1975). *Psychotherapy vs. behavior therapy.* Cambridge, MA: Harvard University Press.

Smith, M. L., Glass, G. V., & Miller, T. I. (1980). *The benefits of psychotherapy.* Baltimore: The Johns Hopkins University Press.

Sobell, M. B., Brochu, S., Sobell, L. C., Roy, J., & Stevens, J. A. (1987). Alcohol treatment outcome evaluation methodology: State of the art 1980–1984. *Addictive Behaviors, 12,* 113–128.

Sobell, L. C., & Sobell, M. B. (1990). Self-reports across addictive behaviors: Issues and future directions in clinical and research settings. *Behavioral Assessment, 12,* 1–4.

Spiegel, S. B., & Hill, C. E. (1989). Guidelines for research on therapist interpretation: Toward greater methodological rigor and relevance to practice. *Journal of Counseling Psychology, 36,* 121–129.

Stiles, W. B. (1979). Verbal response modes and psychotherapeutic technique. *Psychiatry, 42,* 49–62.

Stiles, W. B. (1986). Development of a taxonomy of verbal response modes. In L. S. Greenberg & W. M. Pinsof (Eds.), *The psychotherapeutic process: A research handbook* (pp. 161–200). New York: Guilford.

Stiles, W. B. (1988). Psychotherapy process-outcome correlations may be misleading. *Psychotherapy, 25,* 27–35.

Stiles, W. B. (1991, June). Reliability and validity in quantitative studies. Paper presented at the North American meeting of the Society for Psychotherapy Research, Panama City, FL.

Stiles, W. B. (1992). *Describing talk.* Newbury Park, CA: Sage Publications.

Stiles, W. B., Elliott, R., Llewelyn, S. P., Firth-Cozens, J. A., Margison, F. R., Shapiro, D. A., & Hardy, G. (1990). Assimilation of problematic experiences by clients in psychotherapy. *Psychotherapy, 27,* 411–420.

Stiles, W. B., Shapiro, D. A., & Firth-Cozens, J. (1988). Verbal response mode use in contrasting psychotherapies: A within-subjects comparison. *Journal of Consulting and Clinical Psychology, 56,* 727–733.

Strupp, H. H. (1955). An objective comparison of Rogerian and psychoanalytic techniques. *Journal of Consulting Psychology, 19,* 1–7.

Strupp, H. H. (1957). A multidimensional analysis of therapist activity in analytic and client-centered therapy. *Journal of Consulting Psychology, 21,* 301–308.

Strupp, H. H., & Hadley, S. W. (1977). A tripartite model of mental health and therapeutic outcomes: With special reference to negative effects in psychotherapy. *American Psychologist, 32,* 187–196.

Strupp, H. H., Schacht, T. E., & Henry, W. P. (1988). Problem–treatment–outcome congruence: A principle whose time has come. In H. Dahl, H. Kaechele, & H. Thoma (Eds.), *Psychoanalytic process research strategies* (pp. 1–14). Berlin: Springer-Verlag.

Taplin, P. S., & Reid, J. B. (1973). Effects of instructional set and experimenter influence on observer reliability. *Child Development, 44,* 547–554.

Tichenor, V., & Hill, C. E. (1989). A comparison of six measures of working alliance. *Psychotherapy, 26,* 195–199.

Tingey, R., Burlingame, G., Lambert, M. J., & Barlow, S. H. (1989, June). *Assessing clinical significance: Extensions and applications.* Paper presented at the Society for Psychotherapy Research, Wintergreen, VA.

Tinsley, H. E. A., & Weiss, D. J. (1975). Interrater reliability and agreement of subjective judgments. *Journal of Counseling Psychology, 22,* 358–376.

Toukmanian, S. G., & Rennie, D. L. (Eds.). (1992). *Psychotherapy process research: Paradigmatic and narrative approaches.* Newbury Park, CA: Sage Publications.

Tracey, T. J., & Guinee, J. P. (1990). Generalizability of interpersonal communications rating scale ratings across presentation modes. *Journal of Counseling Psychology, 37,* 330–336.

Truax, C. B. (1966). Therapist empathy, warmth, and genuineness and patient personality change in group psychotherapy: A comparison between interaction unit measures, time sample measures, and patient perception measures. *Journal of Clinical Psychology, 22,* 225–229.

Trull, T. J., Nietzel, M. T., & Main, A. (1988). The use of meta-analysis to assess the clinical significance of behavior therapy for agoraphobia. *Behavior Therapy, 19,* 527–538.

Tsujimoto, R. N., Hamilton, M., & Berger, D. E. (1990). Averaging multiple judges to improve validity: Aid to planning cost-effective clinical research. *Psychological Assessment, 2,* 432–437.

Tucker, L. R., Damarin, F., & Messick, S. (1966). A base free measure of change. *Psychometrika, 31,* 432–437, 457–473.

Waskow, I. E., & Parloff, M. B. (1975). *Psychotherapy change measures* (DEW, No. 74–120). Washington, DC: U.S. Government Printing Office.

Waxer, P. H. (1981). Channel contribution in anxiety displays. *Journal of Research in Personality, 15,* 44–56.

Weed, L. L. (1969). *Medical records, medical education and patient care: The problem oriented record as a basic tool.* Cleveland: Case Western Reserve University Press.

Weiss, D. S. (1979). The effects of systematic variations in information on judges' descriptions of personality. *Journal of Personality and Social Psychology, 37,* 2121–2136.

Weiss, D. S., Marmar, C. R., & Horowitz, M. J. (1988). Do the ways in which psychotherapy process ratings are made make a difference? The effects of mode of presentation, segment, and rating format on interrater reliability. *Psychotherapy, 25,* 44–50.

Wells, E. A., Hawkins, J. D., & Catalano, R. F. (1988). Choosing drug use measures for treatment outcome studies. 1. The influence of measurement approach on treatment results. *International Journal of Addictions, 23,* 851–873.

Williams, S. L. (1985). On the nature and measurement of agoraphobia. *Progress in Behavior Modification, 19,* 109–144.

Wilson, G. T., & Thomas, M. G. (1973). Self versus drug-produced relaxation and the effects of instructional set in standardized systematic desensitization. *Behavior Research and Therapy, 11,* 279–288.

Wolf, M. M. (1978). Social validity: The case for subjective measurement or how applied behavior analysis is finding its heart. *Journal of Applied Behavior Analysis, 11,* 203–214.

Woodward, C. A., Santa-Barbara, J., Levin, S., & Epstein, N. B. (1978). The roles of goal attainment scaling in evaluating family therapy outcome. *American Journal of Orthopsychiatry, 48,* 464–475.

4

THE NIMH TREATMENT OF DEPRESSION COLLABORATIVE RESEARCH PROGRAM: WHERE WE BEGAN AND WHERE WE ARE

- **IRENE ELKIN**

University of Chicago

BACKGROUND, DESIGN, AND IMPLEMENTATION

There were two major goals of the NIMH Treatment of Depression Collaborative Research Program (TDCRP): (1) to test the feasibility and usefulness of the collaborative clinical trial model in the area of psychotherapy research and (2) within the context of this model, to test the effectiveness of two brief psychotherapies for the treatment of outpatient depression. Since there have been some misunderstandings about the origins and purposes of this program, these will be described briefly here. (For fuller descriptions, the reader may refer to Elkin, Parloff, Hadley, & Autry, 1985; Elkin et al., 1989; and Parloff & Elkin, 1992.)

The major motivation behind this program was the perceived need by the National Institute of Mental Health (NIMH) staff for the facilitation of research on the effectiveness of various forms of psychotherapy. The impetus for developing the program came both from the field of psychotherapy research, where collaborative studies had been suggested for some time as a means to accumulate more "definitive" knowledge about the effectiveness of various forms of psychotherapy for particular types of patients, and from the Alcohol, Drug Abuse, and Mental Health Administration (ADAMHA), in response to increasing demands for "accountability" from consumers, third-party payers, and policymakers. Although there are some differences in the emphasis given to these different factors by the initiators of the TDCRP (see Parloff & Elkin, 1992), there is no doubt that the program was an attempt to address some of the needs in the field of psychotherapy research and that it was more likely to be funded due to the interest in accountability.

Since the late 1960s, psychotherapy researchers had been pointing out the need to study the effectiveness of *specific* forms of therapy for *specific* types of patients (e.g., Kiesler, 1966; Paul, 1967).[1] Yet, despite a large number of studies investigating the outcome of psychotherapy, in 1977, when the TDCRP was initiated, there were very few definitive answers to these "specificity" questions. This was largely due to the difficulty of cumulating findings from diverse studies. One proposed approach for addressing these problems was the use of collaborative clinical trials, similar to those that had proved very productive in the field of psychopharmacology (e.g., NIMH-PSC, 1964). A collaborative clinical trial is, essentially, a well-controlled outcome study that uses a common research protocol at two or more participating sites. Ideally, the replication of the study in different settings provides more evidence of the consistency and generalizability of the findings. In the late 1960s, Allen Bergin and Hans Strupp had been commissioned by the NIMH to study the feasibility of carrying out collaborative research in the field of psychotherapy. Their conclusion (Bergin & Strupp, 1972) was that investigators in the field of psychotherapy re-

---

[1]It is of historical interest that Edwards and Cronbach (1952) made this same point in 1952.

search were generally unwilling to participate in such a study and that it was unlikely that it could be launched and implemented.

In 1977, however, the NIMH initiators of the TDCRP (Parloff and Waskow [now Elkin]) determined, on the basis of formal position papers and informal discussions with researchers, that the field had become more receptive to a collaborative venture, and that the area of outpatient depression was particularly ready for such a study. We decided to launch the Collaborative study, with the major aim of testing the feasibility and usefulness of this model in psychotherapy research. The implicit expectation was that, should the program prove feasible and productive, independent researchers would launch similar programs, and this would lead to an advance in the state of psychotherapy research. A secondary, and more substantive, aim was to test the relative efficacy of two brief psychotherapeutic approaches for treating outpatient depression. The choice of the specific therapies, cognitive behavior therapy (Beck, Rush, Shaw, & Emery, 1979) and interpersonal psychotherapy (Klerman, Weissman, Rounsaville, & Chevron, 1984) was based on several criteria: Each method had been developed to treat depressed outpatients; there was already some demonstration of their effectiveness; and the approaches were sufficiently standardized (e.g., in the form of a manual) so that others could reliably carry out the treatment. Finally, the hope was that the focus of the NIMH research staff, their expert consultants, and the TDCRP collaborators on various design and methodological issues posed by the study would prove generally useful for researchers in the field.

Following a good deal of consultation with individual experts in the areas of psychotherapy research, psychopharmacology, and depression, a preliminary research plan was presented to a group of consultants, a revised plan was developed, and a permanent Advisory Group was established (consisting of Paul Chodoff, Sol Garfield, Martin Katz, Donald Klein, Perry London, Morris Parloff, Jeanne Phillips, Hans Strupp, and Eberhard Uhlenhuth). An announcement was made to the field, soliciting first letters of intent and then applications for participation as research sites in the program. Following peer review of the research plan and the site applications, three research sites (University of Pittsburgh, Stanley Imber, P.I.; George Washington University, Stuart Sotsky, P.I.; and University of Oklahoma, John Watkins, P.I.) were funded, as were three sites for training therapists (Yale University, Myrna Weissman, P.I., for interpersonal psychotherapy; Clarke University, Brian Shaw, P.I., for cognitive behavior therapy; and Rush Presbyterian–St. Luke's Medical Center, Jan Faw-

cett, P.I., for pharmacotherapy [see later discussion of standard reference condition]). In addition, an intergovernmental agreement provided for data management and analysis to be carried out by the Perry Point, M.D., V.A. Cooperative Studies Program (Joseph Collins, biostatistician, and C. James Klett, statistical consultant).

The final design for the study was a 3 (research sites) $\times$ 4 (treatment conditions) factorial design, with 250 patients randomly assigned to 4 treatment conditions: cognitive behavior therapy (CBT), interpersonal psychotherapy (IPT), imipramine plus clinical management (IMI-CM), and pill-placebo plus clinical management (PLA-CM). The *relative* effectiveness of CBT and IPT could be studied by comparing the outcome of these two treatment conditions. Although we were interested in possible differences between the two psychotherapies in speed and extent of reduction of depressive symptomatology and improvement in functioning, we were even more interested in addressing the specificity question, that is, the possible differential effects that might be related to particular patient characteristics or that might be specific to domains of functioning targeted by each of the approaches.

How were we to establish, however, that either or both of the psychotherapies were actually effective, and that changes from pre- to posttreatment were not due to factors that were not specific to these therapeutic approaches? We faced the age-old problem in psychotherapy research of choosing appropriate control and/or comparison groups that would allow us to answer those questions. Our first approach was to compare CBT and IPT with a treatment condition for which efficacy in treating depressed patients had already been clearly established. Since there was no psychotherapy that met this criterion, we decided to utilize the most frequently studied antidepressant drug (imipramine-hydrochloride) as a standard reference condition. This was the approach that had also been used in the classic study of CBT by Rush, Beck, Kovacs, and Hollon (1977) and later by Murphy, Simons, Wetzel, and Lustman (1984).

In contrast to those studies, however, we also considered it important to include a control condition that would allow for the evaluation of whether changes in the psychotherapies might be due to such factors as the passage of time, attention of the therapist, and the raising of hope and expectation of improvement. Ideally, what was needed was a "psychotherapy-placebo" condition that would contain all of these factors but not the "active ingredients" of the two psychotherapies. Despite a great deal of time and attention given to the pursuit of such a condition, it was not possible to find one that met ethical concerns yet did not constitute a credible treatment in its own right. We decided, as a compromise, to use the pill-placebo plus clinical management condition (PLA-CM) as a control or comparison group for the psychotherapies. The placebo condition had been introduced into the study as a control for the medication condition, to ensure that imipramine was an adequate standard reference treatment in this study with these patients. To handle ethical concerns about using a placebo with some of the more severely depressed patients, a clinical management (CM) component was introduced (Fawcett, Epstein, Fiester, Elkin, & Autry, 1987). Guidelines for CM included not only management of the medication and side effects, but also the provision of general support and encouragement; PLA-CM was thus essentially a pill-placebo plus minimal supportive therapy condition. (Since the two pharmacotherapy conditions were administered double-blind, the imipramine condition [IMI-CM] also contained the minimal supportive therapy.)

The PLA-CM condition was, of course, not an ideal control condition for the psychotherapies. It was a double-faceted control, including not only this minimal supportive therapy, but also the actual administration of a pill. Nonetheless, if the two psychotherapies were actually effective in the manner postulated, one would expect them to demonstrate superiority to this admittedly stringent control condition, particularly in those areas targeted by each of them.

Thus the study consisted of four treatment conditions[2]: the two psychotherapies of major interest (CBT and IPT); an antidepressant drug that provided a standard reference condition (IMI-CM); and a placebo condition (PLA-CM), primarily introduced as a control for IMI-CM and secondarily used as an admittedly imperfect control condition against which to compare the psychotherapies. It should be clear from this description of the genesis of the design of the TDCRP that the study was not meant to be a "horse race" between the psychotherapies and an antidepressant drug, despite this impression in some quarters; by considering the drug a reference treatment, we clearly *expected* it to be effective. Our question was whether the psychotherapies would be significantly less effective than this standard in reducing depressive symptomatology and whether they might be significantly superior in outcome in areas targeted by each therapy or in preventing or delaying relapse. We were

also interested, of course, in whether there were significant differences between the two psychotherapies, especially in areas targeted by each, and whether either or both were significantly superior to the placebo "control" condition.

An important focus in the TDCRP was the clear specification of the treatment conditions. In order to be able to answer the question of which specific treatment was effective for a particular sample of patients, we sought both to define the treatments carefully and to assure that they had been carried out as described. To this end, we had stimulated work by the originators and/or previous investigators of the two psychotherapies (Aaron T. Beck and Myrna Weissman) to develop systematic training programs, to put the finishing touches on treatment manuals, and to develop instruments to measure therapist competence in carrying out the treatments. A leading pharmacotherapy researcher (Jan Fawcett) was also commissioned to complete a parallel manual and plan a training program for pharmacotherapists.

The treatments were carried out by experienced therapists (10 each in IPT and pharmacotherapy, 8 in CBT), who had been carefully selected to take part in the program and received further training in their respective treatment approaches. Only therapists who met specified competence criteria following training took part in the actual outcome study. Although therapists received weekly supervision on training cases, in general only monthly consultation was provided by the trainers during the outcome study. (For further details regarding therapist training programs and other information regarding therapists and treatments, see Elkin et al., 1985, 1989; Rounsaville, Chevron, & Weissman, 1984; Shaw, 1984; Waskow, 1984.) As a final check on whether the treatments were carried out as intended, audiotapes of treatment sessions were rated on a measure of adherence, the Collaborative Study Psychotherapy Rating Scale (CSPRS), developed for the TDCRP by Hollon and associates (see Hollon, Waskow, Evans, and Lowery 1984).

Specifying the treatment intervention allows one to answer questions about "what specific treatment . . ." We also wished to be able to say "for what specific patients." The patient population of interest consisted of nonbipolar, nonpsychotic depressed outpatients, similar to those treated in the major previous studies of CBT and IPT. Uniform inclusion criteria (e.g., Research Diagnostic Criteria [Spitzer, Endicott, & Robins, 1978] diagnosis of Major Depressive Disorder and a score of 14 or greater on a modified 17-item Hamilton Rating Scale for Depression [Hamilton, 1960, 1967]) and uniform exclusion criteria were used across sites. We also obtained information on a number of pa-

---

[2]In addition to the four treatment conditions in the study, we also considered a number of others, including treatment-as-usual and combinations of drug and psychotherapy. These were not added to the design largely for practical, as well as some conceptual, reasons.

tient clinical, demographic, and personality variables, to serve as possible predictors of outcome in later analyses.

One final component of the specificity question was addressed in the choice of instruments to evaluate treatment outcome. In addition to measures of depressive symptomatology, overall symptomatology, and general functioning, measures were included to tap areas targeted by each of the treatments. These included measures of social adjustment (targeted by IPT), dysfunctional attitudes (CBT), and endogenous symptoms (IMI-CM). (For a complete list of outcome measures and timing of evaluations, see Elkin et al., 1985.)

Although the major focus of the TDCRP was on treatment outcome, we were also interested in studying mechanisms of change, both those that might be common to the different treatments and those that might be unique to one or another. For that reason, a few relevant instruments were included in the battery, such as the Barrett-Lennard Relationship Inventory (Barrett-Lennard, 1962, 1969) and an Attitudes and Expectations form developed for the study. All treatment sessions were videotaped, to enable collaborators and other researchers to conduct studies focused on processes of change.

FEASIBILITY

The TDCRP did prove to be feasible. It was possible to launch and to implement the study and to maintain the collaboration of all of the sites throughout the life of the project. The major challenge for the Collaborative group was to carry out the treatments and the entire research protocol in a standard fashion across the three research sites. NIMH staff (primarily myself as coordinator and M. Tracie Shea as associate coordinator) coordinated the efforts to maintain standard procedures at all sites. These efforts were for the most part successful. A detailed procedural manual was developed,[3] and procedural updates were periodically added, especially during the training/pilot phase, in response to problems encountered and questions raised by individual sites. In addition to procedures for screening and evaluating patients throughout the study, specific guidelines were also provided for such procedures as withdrawal of patients for clinical reasons and referral (or nonreferral) of patients at termination of treatment. Clinical evaluators were trained in a standard fashion by experts

on various instruments used in the study; they were able to attain adequate reliability levels on diagnostic and outcome measures (both within and across research sites). Research assistants were also trained in a standard fashion on those instruments they administered.

As noted earlier, three sites, one for each of the treatments, were funded to carry out uniform training of therapists across sites. In addition to initial institutes attended by all therapists in a particular approach,[4] this training included monitoring of videotapes and telephone supervision. All therapists had to meet and then maintain criterion levels of competence in carrying out their respective treatments. Ratings of therapist adherence on audiotapes of treatment sessions indicated that the interventions of therapists in all three conditions (CBT, IPT, and pharmacotherapy) were quite specific to their own treatment, and the three treatments could be discriminated almost perfectly using scores on the Collaborative Study Psychotherapy Rating Scale (Hill, O'Grady, & Elkin, 1992).

Thus, it was possible to carry out this large-scale psychotherapy outcome study in a quite consistent fashion across three research sites. The fact that it was possible to launch the study and to carry it to its conclusion does not mean, however, that it was without its problems. The need for collaborative decision making sometimes delayed the work at individual sites; the process of establishing standard training programs and attaining cross-site reliabilities was costly and time-consuming; the coordinating functions at NIMH were often arduous, especially at times when we were understaffed; and collaborative decisions regarding publication rights and responsibilities sometimes required lengthy negotiations.

At the same time, there were also clear positives due to the collaborative nature of the study, over and above the benefits of simultaneous replication and the large N, which made possible more sensitive statistical tests and predictor analyses. The need to maintain consistent procedures and the process of collaborative decision making resulted in careful consideration of many important methodological issues, issues that can be resolved more easily in single-site studies. These included the need for specific definitions and consistent application of criteria for patient inclusion and exclusion; clear delineation and categorization of various types of attrition; questions such as whether pharmacotherapists should be allowed to change medications or whether advertisements should be used for recruiting patients (see Krupnick, Shea, &

---

[3]Here we are appreciative of the contributions of early participants in the TDCRP, especially Reginald Schoonover and Suzanne Hadley.

[4]The initial institute for CBT was conducted by Dr. Aaron T. Beck and his staff.

Elkin, 1986); and the development of consistent guidelines for clinical withdrawal during the study and for referrals at termination. The group deliberations regarding these and many other issues were enriched by drawing on the varying backgrounds, interests, and expertise of the collaborators in the TDCRP.

SUBSTANTIVE FINDINGS

There was a large amount of data collected in the TDCRP, and it was clearly impossible to carry out all of the analyses that we were interested in before publishing initial outcome findings. There was also some pressure to report on and publish findings at an early date, because of the interest that had been generated by this large, federally initiated and supported study. The collaborators felt, however, that it was important that the first report of findings address at least the four major questions listed here, in order to provide a comprehensive picture of the findings, with adequate attention paid to the specificity questions of such concern in the field.[5]

Initial outcome analyses focused, then, on the following four questions:

1. Were there differences among the four conditions (at termination of treatment) in the reduction of depressive symptomatology and in improvement of general functioning? Specifically, were there significant differences between the two psychotherapies and between each of them and the standard reference and placebo control conditions? Also of interest, of course, was the comparison of imipramine to the placebo control condition in order to establish the adequacy of imipramine as a standard reference condition.

2. Were the psychotherapies more effective than the other treatments in bringing about change in those areas targeted by each (i.e., in the area of social functioning for IPT and dysfunctional attitudes for CBT)? Similarly, was IMI-CM differentially effective in reducing endogenous symptomatology?

3. Were there differences in the temporal course of symptom reduction (both depressive symptoms and targeted areas) over the 16-week treatment period?

4. What pretreatment patient characteristics might predict outcome, both across conditions and differentially for the different treatments?

Four papers, each reporting on analyses addressing one of these four questions, were submitted as a "package" to the *Archives of General Psychiatry* in December 1987. This journal was chosen in order to reach a readership that included psychiatrists as well as psychologists. Unfortunately, the journal did not accept the papers as a package; they published only the first article, which focused on general effectiveness of the treatments (Elkin et al., 1989). The publication of this paper by itself, together with earlier press reports following a presentation at the American Psychiatric Association meeting in 1986, unfortunately put undue emphasis on the "horse race question," especially the comparison of psychotherapy and an antidepressant medication.

The articles reporting on mode-specific effects (Imber et al., 1990) and patient predictors of outcome (Sotsky et al., 1991) have now been published, and the paper on temporal effects (Watkins et al., in press) is forthcoming. The following discussion will integrate the findings reported in all four of these papers, as well as three additional publications reporting on outcome and follow-up findings. (It will not include presentations or articles not yet in press.)

General Effectiveness of Treatments

In order to evaluate the relative effectiveness of the treatments in reducing depressive and overall symptomatology and in improving functioning, we focused on four measures: the modified version of the Hamilton Rating Scale for Depression (HRSD) (Hamilton, 1960, 1967), the Beck Depression Inventory (BDI) (Beck & Beamesderfer, 1974; Beck, Ward, Mendelsohn, Mock, & Erbaugh, 1961), the Hopkins Symptom Checklist-90 (HSCL-90) (Lipman, Covi, & Shapiro, 1979), and the Global Assessment Scale (GAS) of the Schedule for Affective Disorders and Schizophrenia — Change Version (SADS-C) (Endicott, Cohen, Nee, Fleiss, & Sarantakos, 1981). The choice of these instruments was based on their previous performance in studies of treatment for depression, including studies of IPT and CBT (especially the HRSD and BDI), their psychometric characteristics, and their reflection of two different rater perspectives, those of the patient (BDI and HSCL-90) and the independent clinical evaluator (HRSD and GAS). (For further general discussion of outcome evaluation, see Elkin et al., 1985, 1989.)

Analyses were carried out on three overlapping samples of patients: a "completer" sample of 155

---

[5]The presentation of four papers also allowed for first authorship by each of the major collaborators, the principal investigator at each of the three research sites, and the NIMH coordinator. In a collaborative venture of this type, it is extremely important for participating investigators both to share responsibilities and to receive adequate credit for their contributions.

patients who had received at least 12 sessions and at least 15 weeks of treatment; an "endpoint 204" sample of patients who had received at least a minimal exposure of 3.5 weeks (usually at least 4 sessions) of treatment, and an "endpoint 239" sample of all patients who had entered treatment. By presenting the results of analyses on all three samples, alternatively including or excluding early terminators, we hoped to provide the most complete and accurate representation of the findings. Results of a more recent random regression analysis of HRSD data, utilizing all available data for the 239 sample, will also be discussed.

As shown in Table 4.1, the general direction of results was similar on all measures and in all samples, with IMI-CM (and, in one instance, IPT) having the least symptomatic scores, PLA-CM the most symptomatic, and the psychotherapies in between, usually closer to IMI-CM. The magnitude of these differences was, however, not large. The results of 12 covariance analyses (4 measures $\times$ 3 samples) were presented in the first publication of outcome findings (Elkin et al., 1989). Statistically significant differences were found in only 4 of the 12 covariance analyses. Follow-up comparisons between pairs of treatment conditions revealed no differences between the two psychotherapies or between either of them and IMI-CM. There were two instances in which IMI-CM had significantly lower (less symptomatic) scores as compared to PLA-CM and two in which IMI-CM showed a trend toward lower scores. There was one trend toward lower scores for IPT as compared to PLA-CM, but no significant or trend difference for CBT.

In addition to the statistical significance of differences between mean scores, we were interested in the clinical significance of the findings. We looked, therefore, at the percentage of patients who reached two stringent "recovery" criteria: a score of six or less on the HRSD and nine or less on the BDI. As shown in Table 4.2, significant differences were found on the HRSD criterion across the treatment conditions in all three samples. Pair-wise comparisons revealed that IPT as well as IMI-CM had a significantly higher percentage of recovered patients than did the PLA-CM condition in the endpoint 239 sample, with trends toward significance in the other two samples. The favorable results for IPT in the endpoint 239 sample seemed to be due, at least in part, to the lower rate of attrition in this condition (23% compared to 40% for PLA-CM and 32% and 33% for CBT and IMI-CM, respectively). Thus, more IPT than PLA-CM patients seemed to have stayed in treatment long enough to attain clinically significant improvement. There were, again, no statistically significant differences between the two psychotherapies or between either

of them and IMI-CM. No significant differences were found on the BDI, at least in part because the PLA-CM group did so well on this criterion.

What do the findings, described thus far, indicate? First of all, there is some evidence of the adequacy of IMI-CM as a standard reference treatment in the study. There is no evidence of any differences between the two psychotherapies in their ability to reduce depressive and general symptomatology or to improve functioning, nor is there evidence of their inferiority to the standard reference condition. IPT does show some specific effectiveness when compared to the PLA-CM control condition, especially when a criterion of clinical significance is used. The favorable findings for IPT are limited, however, to different measures based on one instrument, the HRSD. For CBT, there is no evidence of *specific* effectiveness over and above what is provided by PLA-CM.

It is important to note that significant improvement ($p < .001$) from pre- to posttreatment was found for all groups, including PLA-CM, on all four measures in all three samples. Thus, as we have suggested elsewhere (Elkin et al., 1989), the general lack of significant findings seems to be due not to a lack of improvement for the psychotherapies, but rather to the relatively good performance of the PLA-CM condition. Outcome for the patients in CBT and IPT is in the same general ballpark as that found in previous studies of IPT and CBT (e.g., DiMascio et al., 1979; Hollon et al., 1992; Murphy et al., 1984; Weissman et al., 1979), with the exception of the Rush et al. (1977) study for CBT. Although comparisons are difficult to make, the PLA-CM condition seems to have done better than other control conditions used in earlier studies of CBT (usually waiting-list or delayed treatment conditions) and IPT (nonscheduled treatment), as well as drug study placebos.

Mode-Specific Effects

The findings summarized thus far deal only with improvement in terms of depressive symptoms and general symptomatology and functioning. But what about the areas targeted by each of the psychotherapies—might they not provide more evidence of the specific effectiveness of these treatments? Imber et al. (1990) report on outcome at termination of treatment on "mode-specific" measures. These measures included a modified version of the Social Adjustment Scale (SAS) (Weissman & Paykel, 1974) for IPT, the Dysfunctional Attitude Scale (DAS) (Weissman & Beck, 1978) for CBT, and the Endogenous Scale of the SADS-C (Endicott et al., 1981) for IMI-CM. I will focus here, as did Imber et al., on results for the completer sample, those patients who had exposure to a complete

TABLE 4.1   Mean pretreatment and adjusted termination scores for the four primary outcome measures*

		CBT		IPT		IMI-CM		PLA-CM	Significance
	N	Mean ± SD	N	Mean ± SD	N	Mean ± SD	N	Mean ± SD	Level†

COMPLETER PATIENTS

	N	Mean ± SD	N	Mean ± SD	N	Mean ± SD	N	Mean ± SD	Sig. Level†
HRSD									
Prestudy	37	19.2 ± 3.6	47	18.9 ± 3.9	37	19.2 ± 5.0	34	19.1 ± 3.7	.984
Termination	37	7.6 ± 5.8	47	6.9 ± 5.8	37	7.0 ± 5.7	34	8.8 ± 5.7	.458
GAS									
Prestudy	37	52.8 ± 7.2	47	52.6 ± 6.6	37	51.6 ± 7.1	34	53.1 ± 7.3	.813
Termination	37	69.4 ± 11.0	47	70.7 ± 11.0	37	72.5 ± 10.8	34	67.6 ± 10.7	.271
BDI									
Prestudy	37	26.8 ± 8.4	47	25.5 ± 7.7	36	27.1 ± 8.8	35	28.1 ± 6.7	.538
Termination	37	10.2 ± 8.7	47	7.7 ± 8.6	36	6.5 ± 8.6	35	11.0 ± 8.5	.081
HSCL-90 T									
Prestudy	37	1.38 ± 0.55	47	1.35 ± 0.45	36	1.43 ± 0.46	35	1.58 ± 0.49	.159
Termination	37	0.47 ± 0.43	47	0.48 ± 0.43	36	0.38 ± 0.42‡	35	0.67 ± 0.43	.046

END POINT 204 PATIENTS

	N	Mean ± SD	N	Mean ± SD	N	Mean ± SD	N	Mean ± SD	Sig. Level†
HRSD									
Prestudy	50	19.6 ± 3.7	55	19.2 ± 4.4	49	19.1 ± 4.7	50	19.0 ± 4.2	.914
Termination	50	9.0 ± 7.0	55	9.1 ± 7.0	49	8.3 ± 6.9	50	11.3 ± 6.9	.161
GAS									
Prestudy	50	52.1 ± 7.9	55	52.1 ± 7.3	49	52.1 ± 6.7	50	52.2 ± 7.2	1.000
Termination§	50	66.5 ± 12.6	55	67.2 ± 12.6	49	69.7 ± 12.4‖	50	63.9 ± 12.4	.137
BDI									
Prestudy	50	27.5 ± 8.1	55	25.5 ± 7.6	49	25.8 ± 8.6	50	27.4 ± 6.8	.427
Termination	50	11.5 ± 9.7	55	10.6 ± 9.7	49	8.6 ± 9.6	50	12.5 ± 9.6	.214
HSCL-90 T									
Prestudy	50	1.44 ± 0.55	55	1.33 ± 0.44	48	1.40 ± 0.48	50	1.53 ± 0.47	.200
Termination	50	0.60 ± 0.49	55	0.60 ± 0.50	48	0.51 ± 0.49	50	0.70 ± 0.49	.289

END POINT 239 PATIENTS

	N	Mean ± SD	N	Mean ± SD	N	Mean ± SD	N	Mean ± SD	Sig. Level†
HRSD									
Prestudy	59	19.6 ± 3.9	61	19.6 ± 4.6	57	19.5 ± 4.6	62	19.5 ± 4.6	.999
Termination§	59	10.7 ± 7.9	61	9.8 ± 7.9‖	57	9.8 ± 7.8‖	62	13.2 ± 7.8	.053
GAS									
Prestudy	59	52.4 ± 7.9	61	52.0 ± 7.1	57	52.2 ± 6.7	62	52.5 ± 7.1	.985
Termination	59	64.4 ± 12.4	61	66.3 ± 12.4	57	67.4 ± 12.3‡	62	61.6 ± 12.3	.053
BDI									
Prestudy	59	27.0 ± 7.9	61	26.0 ± 7.8	57	26.8 ± 8.7	62	27.1 ± 6.9	.871
Termination	59	13.4 ± 10.6	61	12.0 ± 10.6	57	11.6 ± 10.5	62	15.0 ± 10.5	.290¶
HSCL-90 T									
Prestudy	59	1.42 ± 0.54	61	1.41 ± 0.51	56	1.43 ± 0.48	62	1.49 ± 0.49	.819
Termination	59	0.73 ± 0.57	61	0.71 ± 0.57	56	0.66 ± 0.57	62	0.83 ± 0.57	.413

Source: Elkin et al (1989) — see References page 137

*Prestudy scores are means from a one-way analysis of variance. Adjusted termination scores are treatment main effect least-square mean scores from a treatment by site analysis of covariance with prestudy scores and marital status used as covariates. Completer patients indicates patients with at least 12 sessions and 15 weeks of treatment; end point 204 patients, patients with at least 3.5 weeks of treatment; end point 239 patients, all patients entering treatment; CBT, cognitive behavior therapy; IPT, interpersonal psychotherapy; IMI-CM, imipramine hydrochloride plus clinical management; PLA-CM, placebo plus clinical management; HRSD, Hamilton Rating Scale for Depression; GAS, Global Assessment Scale; BDI, Beck Depression Inventory; and HSCL-90 T, Hopkins Symptom Checklist-90 Total Score. Higher scores on GAS indicate better functioning.

†Probability level for F test comparing the four treatment groups.
‡Significantly different from PLA-CM (observed $P < .017$; with Bonferroni correction, $P < .10$).
§Only marital status was used as covariate because of the lack of equality of slopes between prestudy and termination scores.
‖Trend for difference from PLA-CM (observed $P < .025$; with Bonferroni correction, $P < .15$).
¶Significant ($P < .10$) treatment by site interaction.

TABLE 4.2   Patients recovered at termination*

	CBT	IPT	IMI-CM	PLA-CM	Significance Level†
		No. (%)			
	COMPLETER PATIENTS				
N	37	47	37	34	
HRSD≤6	19 (51)	26 (55)‡	21 (57)‡	10 (29)	.074
BDI≤9	24 (65)	33 (70)	25 (69)	18 (51)	.299
			(N = 36)	(N = 35)	
	END POINT 204 PATIENTS				
N	50	55	49	50	
HRSD≤6	20 (40)	26 (47)‡	24 (49)‡	13 (26)	.076
BDI≤9	29 (58)	33 (60)	30 (61)	25 (50)	.668
		END POINT 239 PATIENTS			
N	59	61	57	62	
HRSD≤6	21 (36)	26 (43)§	24 (42)§	13 (21)	.042
BDI≤9	29 (49)	34 (56)	30 (53)	25 (40)	.353

Source: Elkin et al (1989) — see References page 137.
*See Table 4.1 for explanation of abbreviations.
†Probability level for χ^2 test comparing the four treatment groups.
‡Trend for difference from PLA-CM (observed $P<.025$; with Brunden correction, $P<.15$).
§Significantly different from PLA-CM (observed $P<.017$; with Brunden correction, $P<.10$).

treatment trial, where one might expect more evidence of treatment-specific effects.

For IPT, there was no evidence of differential effectiveness on any of three primary measures, the global, social and leisure, and work scores of the SAS. For CBT, there was evidence for differential effectiveness on one of the three primary measures, the Need for Social Approval factor on the DAS; differences were not significant for either the DAS total score or the Perfectionism factor. On the Need for Social Approval factor, multiple comparisons revealed, as predicted, significantly lower scores for CBT as compared to IPT and IMI-CM. (The difference between CBT and PLA-CM, although of comparable magnitude, did not reach significance because of the greater variability in the PLA-CM condition.) The results on the Endogenous Scale did not indicate differential effectiveness for IMI-CM in the completer sample, although all three active treatments had lower scores than PLA-CM.

Imber et al. (1990) concluded that "The support for the specificity hypothesis in the study seems quite limited" (p. 356) and that "None of the therapies produced consistent effects on measures related to its theoretical origins" (p. 352). Only one measure, in fact, provided clear evidence of differential effectiveness as predicted by the specificity hypothesis. It is interesting to look more closely, however, at this measure, the Need for Social Approval factor of the DAS. This factor (as well as the Perfectionism factor) was derived from a factor analysis conducted on data from the TDCRP and

thus may be specifically relevant to patients in this study. In addition, Brian Shaw, the primary CBT trainer and therapist supervisor in the TDCRP, notes (personal communication, 1986) that it was the types of beliefs measured by the Need for Social Approval factor that were a major focus in the treatment of many of the patients in this program. As suggested elsewhere (Elkin, 1990), it seems likely that one can find more specific effects with measures that are both relevant to the particular treatment *and* to the particular patient sample. It will be important, of course, to see if this finding can be replicated in studies of CBT using similar patient populations. To date, such studies have generally looked only at the DAS total score (DeRubeis et al., 1990; Simons, Garfield, & Murphy, 1984).

It will be of interest to derive factors based on TDCRP data from the SAS, as well, to see if measures more specific to this population might be differentially sensitive to IPT effects. We must also note that a previous study of IPT found differential effectiveness in the area of social adjustment only at follow-up, rather than at termination of treatment (Weissman, Klerman, Prusoff, Sholomskas, & Padian, 1981). Analyses of TDCRP follow-up data on mode-specific measures are currently being conducted.

Temporal Course of Change

We were also interested in the temporal course of change, both in terms of whether one of the treatments might have a more rapid effect in reducing depressive symptoms and whether there might be earlier changes in areas targeted by a specific treatment. Watkins et al. (in press) have reported on findings based on evaluations at 4, 8, and 12 weeks. Analyses included both repeated measures analyses of variance for patients in the completer sample and separate cohort analyses for all patients in treatment at 4 weeks, at 8 weeks, and at 12 weeks. On measures of depressive symptoms (HRSD and BDI), IMI-CM clearly had more rapid effects, with consistently significant differences from the other conditions by the 12th week of treatment. On mode-specific measures, the Endogenous scale scores paralleled those on the HRSD, with more rapid change for IMI-CM. There was no evidence of differential rates of response, however, on the two psychotherapy mode-specific measures, the total DAS and global SAS score. (The DAS factor of Need for Social Approval was not included in these analyses.)

Random Regression Model Analysis

A more recent analysis of the HRSD data utilized a random regression model (Gibbons et al., in press). Among the many advantages of this method is the inclusion, in one analysis, of all data points for all patients entering treatment (allowing us to avoid the interpretive problems due to multiple statistical tests in our previous analyses). The use of this model resulted in findings largely in agreement with those already presented in the articles by Elkin et al. and Watkins et al. The new analysis does, however, allow for even clearer statements of some of the findings and for greater confidence in them. In the results based on the random regression analysis, there is again the lack of significant differences between CBT and IPT; the adequacy of IMI-CM as a standard reference condition (with clearer differences from PLA-CM in this analysis at 16 weeks than in the previous analyses); the faster rate of improvement for IMI-CM as compared to the two psychotherapies through the 12-week evaluation, with this difference no longer significant at 16 weeks; and considerable improvement across the 16-week treatment period for all conditions, including PLA-CM.

We conclude then that, although the two psychotherapies are not significantly inferior to the standard reference treatment in reducing depressive symptoms across the 16 weeks of treatment, they are somewhat slower in their rate of response. We also conclude that, except for some limited findings for IPT as compared to PLA-CM (particularly in recovery rates) and the one differential effect for CBT at termination of treatment, there is not much

support thus far for specificity of the two psychotherapies.

Patient Characteristics and Outcome

We come then to another aspect of the specificity question: Are certain patient characteristics differentially related to outcome in the different treatment conditions? The first patient variable addressed was pretreatment severity of depression. The patient sample had included, by design, a fairly large range in terms of severity of depression. This variable had been of interest from the beginning, and plans for statistical analysis included initial scores as covariates. As we continued to think about the analyses during the course of the study and as we talked to our colleagues and advisory group members, we began to focus even more on the question of whether severity might differentially predict outcome in the different treatment conditions. Pharmacotherapy researchers, in particular, stressed that the antidepressant medication might be differentially effective, as compared to the psychotherapies, for the more severely depressed patients. Secondary analyses were therefore planned to address this question, and their results were reported in Elkin et al. (1989). These were considered exploratory analyses, since the design had not included stratification on severity.

Two definitions of severity were used: a score on the pretreatment HRSD of 20 or greater (a level that would generally be considered quite severely depressed in an outpatient sample) and a score of 50 or less on the GAS (which reflected both depressed symptomatology and functional impairment). The latter criterion had been used in a previous NIMH study (Prien et al., 1984). For each of these criteria, analyses of covariance (2 levels of severity $\times$ 4 treatment conditions) were carried out for the four measures of symptomatology and functioning and the three samples described earlier. For the HRSD breakdown, these yielded two significant treatment by severity interactions (and one near significant); for the GAS breakdown, there were seven significant interactions. Examples of these interactions are given in Figure 4.1. Subsequent covariance analyses carried out for the more and less severe subsamples revealed *no* significant differences among treatments in the less severe groups, but consistently significant differences among treatments in the more severe subsample in every instance in which there had been a significant treatment by severity interaction. Pair-wise comparisons revealed consistently lower scores (significant in 8 of 10 comparisons) for IMI-CM as compared to PLA-CM, and three instances of significantly lower scores for IPT compared to PLA-CM, all on the HRSD.

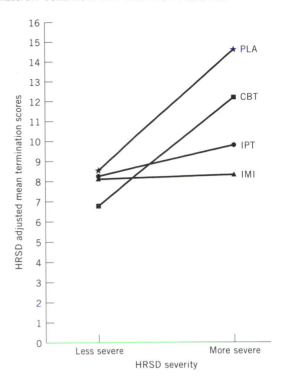

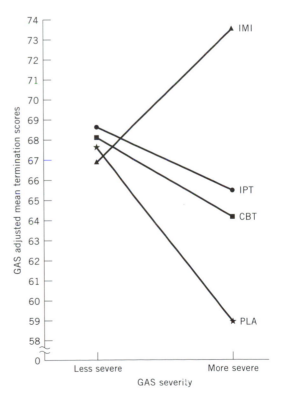

FIGURE 4.1 Treatment ✕ severity interactions. Hamilton Rating Scale for Depression (HRSD) scores are least-square mean termination scores from a two-way analysis of covariance with marital status used as a covariate; less severe indicates a prestudy total score of less than 20, and more severe, a prestudy total score of 20 or more. Global Assessment Scale (GAS) scores are least-square mean termination scores from a two-way analysis of covariance with marital status used as a covariate; less severe indicates a prestudy score of greater than 50, and more severe, a prestudy score of 50 or less. Data are for end point 204 sample. PLA indicates placebo plus clinical management; CBT, cognitive behavior therapy; IPT, interpersonal psychotherapy; and IMI, imipramine hydrochloride plus clinical management.

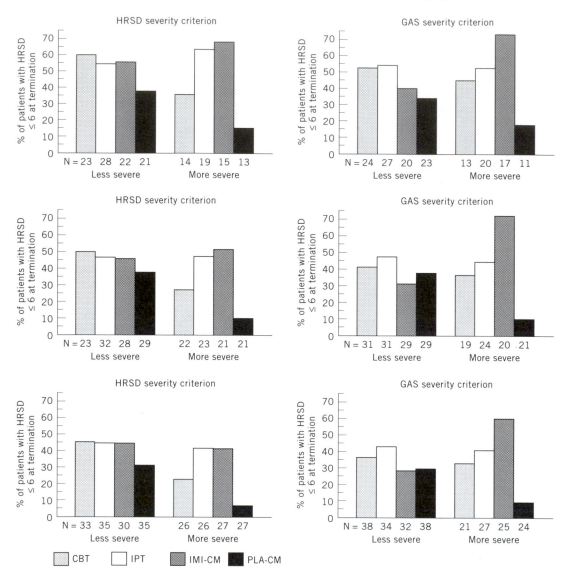

FIGURE 4.2 Percentage of patients in more and less severely depressed groups "recovered" at termination, by treatment condition. Top, Completer patients; middle, end point 204 patients; and bottom, end point 239 patients. For the Hamilton Rating Scale for Depression (HRSD), less severe indicates a prestudy total score of less than 20, and more severe, a prestudy total score of 20 or more. For the Global Assessment Scale (GAS), less severe indicates a prestudy score of greater than 50, and more severe, a prestudy score of 50 or less. CBT indicates cognitive behavior therapy; IPT, interpersonal psychotherapy; IMI-CM, imipramine hydrochloride plus clinical management; and PLA-CM, placebo plus clinical management.

significantly higher percentage of patients reaching the recovery criterion in five of six tests, and IMI-CM had a significantly higher percentage than PLA-CM in all six tests.

Additional analyses, using the recovery criterion of six or less on the HRSD, yielded similar but more striking findings (see Figure 4.2). Again, there were no significant differences among treatments for the less severe subgroups, while there were very consistent differences among the more severe groups: As compared to PLA-CM, IPT had a

There were again, in all of these analyses, *no*

significant differences between the two psychotherapies and only one instance in which IMI-CM was superior to one of the psychotherapies (CBT in the endpoint 204 sample on the recovery criterion for the GAS-defined severe subgroup). For the HRSD breakdown, IMI-CM and IPT had very similar results and were about equally effective for the more and less severely depressed patients, while CBT and PLA-CM did somewhat better for the less, than for the more, depressed patients. For the GAS breakdown, the interaction was due largely to the marked difference between IMI-CM and the other groups, particularly PLA-CM. All treatments did about the same for the less severely depressed and functionally impaired patients but IMI-CM did much better, and PLA-CM much worse, for the more severely depressed and impaired, while IPT and CBT were similar to each other and were in between IMI-CM and PLA-CM.

Thus, while keeping in mind the exploratory nature of these analyses, the evidence here strongly suggests that severity is an important variable to consider, and that it is especially in the more severely depressed and functionally impaired patients that antidepressant medication — and, to a more limited degree, IPT — might be particularly effective. The other side of the coin is that for the *less* severely depressed patients, there was no indication of differential effectiveness among the four treatment conditions, including PLA-CM. It is important to remember here that PLA-CM is *not* a no-treatment condition, but that patients receive a fair amount of support and encouragement in addition to a pill. The findings suggest, however, that for less severely depressed patients, such minimal supportive therapy in the hands of an experienced therapist may be sufficient to bring about a significant reduction of depressive symptomatology.

Additional analyses were carried out within the more and less severe subsamples, focusing on the possible interaction of treatment with research site. (The one significant treatment by site interaction found in the primary analyses did not affect our conclusions.) Analyses based on the two sites with a sufficient number of patients with a GAS score of 50 or less revealed quite consistently significant treatment by site interactions. Although IMI-CM did quite well with this subsample at both sites, CBT did considerably better at one site than another and IPT did the reverse. Of interest here is the recent report by Hollon and colleagues (1992) of numerically very similar scores for the more severely depressed patients in their CBT and imipramine treatment conditions. These findings are quite similar to those at one of the research sites in the TDCRP. Thus, for the more severely depressed patients, there seems to be some variability in CBT results, both between studies and between different research sites within our study. Further explorations of the interaction found in the TDCRP are now being pursued, in an effort to learn more about the conditions under which each of the psychotherapies may be effective in treating severely depressed and functionally impaired outpatients. We are looking at the possible role played by therapist variables (e.g., previous experience, trainer-rated competence), patient variables (including demographic, clinical, and expectation variables), and therapist – patient interactions as they are manifest in the videotaped therapy sessions.

In addition to severity, a number of other patient characteristics have been explored as possible differential predictors of outcome. Sotsky et al. (1991) reported on analyses investigating the predictive capacities of variables in three categories: (1) sociodemographic characteristics, (2) diagnostic and course variables, and (3) function, personality, and symptom variables. The two dependent measures of depression outcome at termination of treatment were "complete response" (an HRSD score equal to or less than 6 *and* a BDI score equal to or less than 9) and depression severity (23-item HRSD, including cognitive and atypical vegetative symptoms). Analyses were conducted on both the completer and endpoint-239 samples. Following preliminary regression analyses to reduce the number of predictors, 13 variables were selected for analysis, using either analyses of covariance or log linear analyses, with treatment as one factor and 2 or more levels of a predictor variable as the other. The 13 variables were age, sex, marital status, endogenous depression, double depression, family history of affective disorder, duration of current episode, acuteness of onset, cognitive dysfunction, social dysfunction, work dysfunction, anxiety, and patient expectation of improvement. Only 3 of the variables (cognitive dysfunction, social dysfunction, and work dysfunction) demonstrated any significant differential treatment effects. Although these are not much more than might be expected by chance, the pattern of these findings is of some interest.

For Social Dysfunction (SAS social and leisure activities score), significant differences among treatments were found only for the patients with lower social dysfunction; here, IPT patients had the lowest mean depression severity scores at termination, significantly lower than those for PLA-CM. Similarly, differences were found for those patients initially lower on cognitive dysfunction (DAS total score); both CBT and IMI-CM patients had significantly lower depression scores at termination than did PLA-CM patients. There was also some indication that IMI-CM was particularly effective for those patients initially higher on work dysfunction (SAS work score). The results on cognitive and social dysfunction may seem counterintuitive as one might expect patients *high* on these variables to respond differentially to the treatments targeting these areas. Yet these results are quite consistent with others reported in the literature (Rude & Rehm, 1991).

Sotsky et al. (1991) suggest that

One possible explanation for these results is that each psychotherapy relies on specific and different learning techniques to alleviate depression, and thus each may depend on an adequate capac-

ity in the corresponding sphere of patient function to produce recovery with the use of that approach. Therefore, patients with good social function may be better able to take advantage of interpersonal strategies to recover from depression, while patients without severe dysfunctional attitudes may better utilize cognitive techniques to restore mood and behavior. (p. 1006)

Patients with more impairment in these areas may require longer term treatment or alternative approaches. It is also possible that it may be counterproductive to focus too directly in early stages of therapy on issues that may reflect major underlying problems. (It is of interest to note that patients with lower cognitive dysfunction also did well in the IMI-CM condition. In fact, the difference between initially high vs. low scores on the DAS was even more marked for IMI-CM than for CBT.)

In addition to these few differential effects, a number of variables were related to improvement *across* treatments. The most consistent of these were lower cognitive dysfunction and higher patient expectation of improvement, while less consistent effects were found for shorter duration of the current episode, endogenous depression, absence of double depression (i.e., chronic minor or intermittent depression, as well as major depressive disorder), lower social dysfunction, and younger age.

Separate analyses were conducted investigating the relationship between the presence of personality disorders and treatment outcome in the TDCRP (Shea et al., 1990). Although there were no significant differences in mean scores on the HRSD for patients with and without personality disorders (as measured by the Personality Assessment Form [Shea, Glass, Pilkonis, Watkins, & Docherty, 1987]), there were differences on the recovery criterion. Significantly fewer patients with personality disorders reached a score of six or less on the HRSD. Thus, although these patients improved, they were more likely to retain residual symptoms of depression. In addition, they had poorer outcome in terms of social adjustment (SAS social and leisure scale). There were, however, no significant personality disorder by treatment interactions in these analyses; contrary to expectations, there was, then, no evidence of a superiority of the psychotherapies over pharmacotherapy in the treatment of patients with personality disorders. In retrospect, however, it might not be reasonable to expect such differences with *short-term* psychotherapies.

Although there were no differential effects for different treatments related to the presence of personality disorders, the findings across treatments

remind us once again of the value of more targeted questions. It seems quite reasonable that the presence of personality disorders would have more of an effect on social functioning and on residual symptomatology than on average level of depressive symptomatology per se.

Summing up the outcome findings to date for the two psychotherapies, we must conclude that aside from the superiority of CBT at termination of treatment on one factor of the DAS, there is no evidence of differential effects for the two psychotherapies. The major difference between the two therapies and the standard reference condition of IMI-CM lies in the more rapid reduction of symptomatology for patients in the IMI-CM condition. There is some evidence (restricted to scores on the HRSD) for specific effectiveness of IPT as compared with PLA-CM, particularly for the more severely depressed patients, but none for CBT. As we have suggested, this relative lack of differences seems, at least in part, due to the good outcome for PLA-CM, especially with the less severely depressed patients.

Follow-up Findings

Thus far, all of the results that have been discussed deal with short-term outcome, outcome during and at termination of treatment. But what about long-term outcome? Do CBT and IPT have any prophylactic effects? Can they reduce or delay relapse in patients who have recovered? Do they result in a lower level of symptomatology for patients in the period following termination of treatment? These are questions that we hoped to address by the analysis of our follow-up data at 6, 12, and 18 months. The follow-up findings for the TDCRP have recently been reported by Shea et al. (1992).

The major analysis of follow-up findings focused on the percentage of patients who both met a stringent criterion of recovery (at least eight consecutive weeks following completion of treatment with little or no symptomatology) and did not relapse (at least two weeks of MDD*-level symptoms) over the 18-month follow-up period. Twenty-four percent of the patients with follow-up data met these criteria for getting well and staying well: 30 percent in CBT, 26 percent in IPT, 19 percent in IMI-CM, and 20 percent in PLA-CM (see Table 4.3). Although the psychotherapies seem to do a little better (more so in the subsample of patients who are less severely depressed and functionally impaired), these differences are not statistically significant. The main conclusion drawn from the follow-up findings concerned the relatively small percentage of patients who were both fully recovered

*Major Depressive Disorder

TABLE 4.3   Proportion of patients from original sample recovering following short-term treatment and remaining well over follow-up*

	CBT	IPT	Imipramine-Hydrochloride +CM	Placebo +CM	Total
Treatment					
Entered	59	61	57	62	239
Completed					
N	40	47	38	37	162
Recovered†					
N	23	21	18	16	78
(%)‡	(39)	(34)	(32)	(26)	(33)
(%)§	(49)	(40)	(38)	(31)	(39)
Recovered and no relapse					
MDD					
N	14	14	9	10	47
(%)‡	(24)	(23)	(16)	(16)	(20)
(%)‖	(30)	(26)	(19)	(20)	(24)
MDD or treatment					
N	13	9	7	9	38
(%)‡	(22)	(15)	(12)	(15)	(16)
(%)‖	(28)	(17)	(15)	(18)	(19)

Source: Shea et al. (1992) — see References page 138
*CBT indicates cognitive behavior therapy; IPT, interpersonal therapy; CM, clinical management; and MDD, Major Depressive Disorder.
†Psychiatric status ratings of 1 or 2 (minimal or no symptoms) for a minimum of 8 consecutive weeks following termination.
‡Percentage of all patients entering treatment.
§Percentage of all patients entering treatment and with 6-month follow-up data.
‖Percentage of all patients with complete follow-up data (6, 12, and 18 months).

following treatment and remained well throughout the 18-month follow-up. Although most patients did improve with these short-term treatments and recovered patients were generally asymptomatic over most of the follow-up period, questions are raised by the findings about whether these short-term treatments are sufficient for helping the majority of patients to reach full recovery and attain lasting remission. This will be discussed further in the "Discussion and Conclusions" section.

Shea et al. (1992) also looked at the recovered sample in terms of the percentage who relapsed, time to relapse, number of weeks asymptomatic, and percentage of patients who received at least three weeks of treatment during the 18-month follow-up. On most of these indicators, CBT seemed to do somewhat better, especially as compared to the IMI-CM condition (see Table 4.4). This is consistent with findings in other studies (Evans et al., 1992; Kovacs, Rush, Beck, & Hollon, 1981; Simons, Murphy, Levine, & Wetzel, 1986) that have reported better outcomes during follow-up for CBT-treated patients than for patients treated with tricyclic antidepressants. It is important to note, however, that on some of these measures, outcome for patients in PLA-CM was similar to that for CBT. Statistical tests were not conducted on any of the

data for the recovered sample in the TDCRP, due to the loss of randomization and the possibility of selectivity in the recovered samples for the different treatment conditions. As Shea et al. (1992) point out,

While statistical significance levels may serve as an indicator of the likelihood that any differences among treatment conditions in this sample are due to chance vs other factors, no conclusions can be reached regarding the "other factors" (ie, selection or treatment effects). Thus, any potential "significant" differences in outcome would be difficult to interpret. (p. 784)

This is obviously true for other naturalistic follow-up studies as well. Thus, here as elsewhere, it was not possible to report conclusions in as clear-cut a fashion as we and others might have wished (e.g., were there "significantly more relapses" in one or another of the treatment conditions?). It is hoped, however, that the consideration of methodological and interpretive problems in the area of treatment research will ultimately prove of greater benefit to the field than would forcing statements of "definitive" findings.

TABLE 4.4   Outcome for recovered sample*

	CBT (N = 22)‡	IPT (N = 21)	Imipramine-Hydrochloride +CM (N = 18)	Placebo +CM (N = 15)‡
Treatment during follow-up†				
Any treatment 1–18 mo, No. (%)	3 (14)	9 (43)	8 (44)	4 (27)
Psychotherapy 1–18 mo, No. (%)	2 (9)	7 (33)	7 (39)	3 (20)
Antidepressants 1–18 mo, No. (%)	2 (9)	3 (14)	6 (33)	2 (13)
Weeks in any treatment§ 1–18 mo, mean ± SD	4.2 ± 14.2	11.0 ± 19.7	20.3 ± 29.6	7.8 ± 16.4
Rates of relapse				
1–18 mo				
MDD, No. (%)	8 (36)	7 (33)	9 (50)	5 (33)
MDD or treatment, No. (%)	9 (41)	12 (57)	11 (61)	6 (40)
Weeks with minimal or no symptoms‖				
1–18 mo				
Mean ± SD	67.0 ± 12.9	63.0 ± 18.2	53.2 ± 26.8	67.0 ± 17.4

Source: Shea et al. (1992) — see References page 138.
*CBT indicates cognitive behavior therapy; IPT, interpersonal therapy; CM, clinical management; and MDD, Major Depressive Disorder.
†Treatment for depression for at least 3 consecutive weeks.
‡N differs due to missing data.
§Mean weeks in any treatment for depression for all those in the sample.
‖Psychiatric status ratings of 1 or 2 on all affective disorder scales.

DISCUSSION AND CONCLUSIONS

Feasibility and Value of Collaborative Studies

The primary purpose of the TDCRP was to test the feasibility and value of carrying out multisite collaborative outcome studies in the area of psychotherapy. As discussed in detail in an earlier section of this chapter, the study was feasible; it was possible for three research sites, with the cooperation of three sites training therapists and with central coordination by NIMH staff, to carry out the same research protocol in a relatively standard fashion and to complete the study. But what does the experience of carrying out this study tell us in general about the usefulness of this model of research in the area of psychotherapy? We probably cannot answer that question adequately until all of the findings are in, including analyses that are still in process. Of particular interest, from the vantage point of a multisite study, will be our attempt to understand the differential outcome (in the more severely depressed and functionally impaired subsample) for the two psychotherapies, where CBT did very well at one research site for these patients, but not at another, and vice versa for IPT. Perhaps it is here, in the context of a study that *did* try to standardize the treatment approaches and evaluation methods and to control for many "extraneous" factors, that the lack of consistent findings across sites will allow us to learn more about how these treatments actually function.

This suggestion would seem to turn on its head one of the major purposes of a collaborative study: to gain more confidence in, and generalizability of, findings through replication at more than one site. Such replication has often been the case in studies in the area of psychopharmacology. And, to a certain extent, for the entire sample in this study, we do have some consistent findings. But the absence of such consistency across sites (in general or in a particular subsample, as in this study), can also be very instructive. Since so many factors that could be responsible for these differences have been controlled, we should be able to get a better handle on what factors in the patient, the therapist, and their interaction allow a particular treatment to be effective in one setting and not another. Thus, whether the findings are or are not consistent across sites, the use of the collaborative model can provide us with important information about the effectiveness of the treatments and important leads for understanding more about the circumstances in which they are effective and the relevant mechanisms of change.

The multisite, collaborative nature of the TDCRP may thus be especially helpful in advancing knowledge about some of the ever-present specificity questions in our field. Perhaps the greatest contribution that the TDCRP as a collaborative venture has made, and will continue to make, however, is in the areas of conceptual, methodological, and ethical issues in psychotherapy research. We feel that we learned a great deal from our collaborative efforts and wish to share this learning with the field. To this end, we have already published a number of articles exploring issues in the specification of treatment conditions (Rounsaville et al., 1984; Shaw, 1984; Waskow, 1984); ethical issues in psychotherapy research (Imber et al., 1986); conceptual and methodological issues in comparing drugs and psychotherapy (Elkin, Pilkonis, Docherty & Sotsky, 1988a, 1988b); issues of randomization in clinical trials (Collins & Elkin, 1985); and a general consideration of advantages and disadvantages of collaborative multisite studies (Elkin, 1992). The sites responsible for training therapists in the TDCRP have contributed a number of articles on selection and training of therapists and evaluation of therapist competence (Chevron & Rounsaville, 1983; Chevron, Rounsaville, Rothblum, & Weissman, 1983; Dobson, Shaw, & Vallis, 1985; Foley, O'Malley, Rounsaville, Prusoff, & Weissman, 1987; O'Malley et al., 1988; Rounsaville, Chevron, Weissman, Prusoff, & Frank, 1986; Rounsaville et al., 1987; Shaw & Dobson, 1988; Vallis, Shaw, & Dobson, 1986; Weissman, Rounsaville, & Chevron, 1982). A significant contribution to the psychopharmacology literature was also made through the development of a manual for the pharmacotherapy conditions (Fawcett et al., 1987).

Other investigators in the area of psychosocial treatments are now independently conducting similar collaborative studies (e.g., the Multicenter Collaborative Comparative Treatment Study of Panic Disorder, being conducted by Barlow, Gorman, Shear, Woods, and colleagues; see Sholomskas et al., 1990). Since the experience of the TDCRP was of value to these investigators, part of its purpose has been realized. There may be some marked advantages in the independent initiation of collaborative studies as compared to those initiated by the NIMH, at least in the area of psychosocial treatments. Some of the problems that we encountered seem to have been related to the fact that the TDCRP was a large government-initiated study. Two factors were especially important here: the reliance on NIMH administrative support for the central coordination of the study and the visibility of the study.

The NIMH administrative support for its staff coordinating the TDCRP varied greatly over the life of the project, particularly in regard to the provision of staff positions. This variation may have been partly due to NIMH budget realities and to the shift over time toward a greater focus on biological factors in etiology and treatment of psychiatric disorders. But more important, in my opinion, were the particular individuals in the administrative hierarchy at different times over the years and the value that they placed on studying psychosocial

interventions. The unevenness of support increased the difficulty of carrying out the necessary coordination tasks, and much time was lost in trying to get additional support.

In regard to the visibility of the program, a great deal of attention was focused on the study from its inception. Interested parties included not only psychotherapy and pharmacotherapy researchers, but also a broad range of mental health professionals, present and potential consumers, and the press. Particular concern was voiced about the possible implications of the findings (even before any outcome data had been collected), including effects on third-party payment for psychotherapy. The initial presentation, press reports, and later publication of our findings were accompanied by considerable controversy (see, e.g., Letters to the Editor, *Archives of General Psychiatry*, July 1990). Proponents of the different treatments in the TDCRP (particularly those favoring pharmacotherapy) were disappointed that we had not drawn conclusions that clearly supported the superiority of their approaches. As a result, a great deal of NIMH staff time had to be devoted to responding to questions, from both professional colleagues and the press.

In regard to the ultimate "value" of the collaborative model in this area, it is too early to tell. Only the total yield from such studies, in terms of advances in our knowledge regarding the effectiveness of psychosocial treatments, will eventually provide an answer. In the meantime, we are hopeful that the contributions of the TDCRP, especially in our discussions of the various methodological, analytic, and ethical issues that have been addressed in the study, will be of value to the field. There has already been some influence, it seems (see, e.g., Luborsky & DeRubeis, 1984), in terms of more careful definitions and descriptions of treatment interventions.

In discussing the contribution of the TDCRP, it is important to point out that the collaborative model, and indeed clinical trials in general, represent only one of a number of routes to knowledge about psychotherapy, and different approaches may complement each other. Just as particular findings in a clinical trial may lead us to more specific questions about processes of change, so, too, may intensive study of change processes lead to the development of improved treatments to be studied in clinical trials.

Substantive Findings

The second aim of the TDCRP was to provide substantive information regarding the effectiveness of two specific forms of psychotherapy, CBT and IPT, in treating depressed outpatients. In the following section, I will try, as best as I can, to summarize the findings that we have at the present time.

The findings in which we can have most confidence are those based on preplanned analyses of the data in the original design of the study (i.e., three sites by four treatment conditions). Although there was significant improvement from pre- to posttreatment for all treatment conditions, there were surprisingly few significant differences among the treatments at termination. There was some evidence in the initial analyses (more clearly seen in the random regression analyses) for the effectiveness of IMI-CM as compared to PLA-CM, justifying the use of IMI-CM as a standard reference condition. We also found some limited evidence for the effectiveness of IPT in its higher rate of recovery as compared to PLA-CM.

Except for one instance in which CBT patients achieved significantly lower scores on the Need for Social Approval factor of the Dysfunctional Attitude Scale, there were *no* differences between IPT and CBT on measures of depressive symptoms, overall functioning, or mode-specific measures. Similarly, there were no significant differences at termination of treatment between the two psychotherapies and the IMI-CM standard reference condition. We would not, however, be justified in interpreting this lack of differences as evidence of the "equivalence" of psychotherapy and drug therapy, particularly in light of the fairly consistent, if small, numerical superiority of IMI-CM. One should note, however, that the imipramine condition also included the clinical management component, rendering it in some ways a "combination" treatment (i.e., a combination of drug and minimal supportive therapy). Thus, it was a very stringent standard reference condition, rendering the lack of significant differences more meaningful. This is especially true in light of the fact that comparisons were made on instruments traditionally used in psychopharmacology research (the HRSD and HSCL-90) and that the N provided adequate statistical power to find medium-to-large effect size differences if they did exist.

In terms of the temporal pattern of effects, IMI-CM was more rapid, with significant differences in symptom reduction clearly apparent by 12 weeks of treatment (although one doesn't find the early — e.g., at 4 weeks — differential response that one might expect for a pharmacotherapy condition). Thus, in a situation in which a more rapid response is considered critical, these findings suggest that one might want to try an antidepressant drug. Again, it is important to keep in mind, however, that the medication was not provided in a vacuum but was accompanied by the clinical management component.

As we have indicated previously, the general lack of significant differences (in mean scores) between either of the psychotherapies and PLA-CM did not seem due to poor performance of the psychotherapies, but rather to quite good outcome for the patients in PLA-CM, at least in the less severely depressed subsample. Even while recognizing the stringent nature of this control condition (including both a minimal supportive therapy plus a pill), these results must raise some questions about the specificity of the effects of the psychotherapies, particularly CBT.

Furthermore, despite the conceptual problems in using a "placebo" condition as a control for psychotherapy (see, e.g., Basham, 1986; O'Leary & Borkovec, 1978; Parloff, 1986), these findings do suggest the importance of including in an outcome study some type of active control condition if one wants to draw conclusions about the *specificity* of a treatment's effects (see, also, Critelli & Neumann, 1984). The question of credible, ethical, and feasible placebo or other control conditions in psychotherapy research has clearly not yet been resolved and remains one of the thorniest and most controversial issues in the outcome study arena. The suggestion of using alternative treatments as controls for each other (Basham, 1986; Parloff, 1986) does not resolve this issue adequately, at least on a practical level, because of the large N needed to attain sufficient statistical power to detect differences among active treatments (see, e.g., Kazdin & Bass, 1989).

When secondary analyses were conducted, looking at the role played by initial severity of the depressive illness, a more detailed picture emerged in regard to the effectiveness of the treatments.[6] Here, IMI-CM appeared particularly effective for the more severe group (and PLA-CM did very poorly), especially when using the GAS severity criterion. Although IMI-CM did consistently better than PLA-CM for these patients, it did *not*, with only one exception for CBT, do significantly better than either of the psychotherapies (although it is important to remember that statistical power was lower here than in the overall analyses). Nonetheless, the strikingly consistent findings for IMI-CM with the more severely depressed and functionally impaired patients do suggest that one would want to consider the use of antidepressant medication with these patients, perhaps combined with psychotherapy or at least with a minimal supportive therapy, as used in this study.

There is also some evidence, on the HRSD, for

---

[6]In all discussions of severity, it must be borne in mind that we are talking about severity in the context of a nonpsychotic, nonbipolar depressed outpatient sample.

the effectiveness of IPT with the more severely ill patients, especially in terms of recovery rates. Finally, as mentioned earlier, the results of Hollon et al. (1992) (as well as our own findings at one of the research sites) suggest that, at least in some settings, CBT (as well as IPT) may result in improvement similar to that found for imipramine with these patients. There were no significant differences in outcome in the less severe groups (although there was a hint in the follow-up analyses that the psychotherapies may do a bit better in the long term). This includes a lack of significant differences between IMI-CM and PLA-CM. A question may be raised, then, about the need for antidepressant medication or highly specified forms of psychotherapy for the resolution of the depressive episode in these patients.

One of the important questions in studying the effectiveness of psychotherapies in the treatment of depression is whether they have long-term or prophylactic effects as compared to antidepressant drugs, particularly whether, by providing patients with coping skills, they can help to prevent or delay relapse. Unfortunately, as we have indicated, this is an extremely difficult question to address, because of the possible differential selection of recovered patients in the different treatment conditions. Although CBT patients did seem to do somewhat better during the follow-up, particularly as compared to the IMI-CM condition, it is not completely clear whether this represents a prophylactic effect.

What is most striking in the follow-up findings is the relatively small percentage of patients who remain in treatment, fully recover, and remain completely well throughout the 18-month follow-up period. Although it is difficult to make direct comparisons, this percentage seems fairly similar to that in other studies (e.g., Evans et al., 1992; Kovacs et al., 1981; Simons et al., 1986; Weissman et al., 1981) and raises questions about whether the potency of the short-term treatments for depression has been "oversold." While recognizing the fact that these treatments are helpful to many patients, more serious consideration must also be given to their limitations and to the investigation of alternatives, such as longer periods of initial treatment, maintenance treatments, "booster sessions," and other forms of treatment, including integrated combinations of some of our present approaches.

As mentioned earlier, a great deal of attention has been paid to the TDCRP. Hopes were high that we would report definitive findings in regard to the effectiveness of the psychotherapies, although one study, even a multisite study, cannot by itself fulfill this wish. There has been disappointment that our results were not more clear-cut. The fact of the matter is that sometimes results are *not* clear-cut. For example, there is no way around the fact that although CBT in this study was not significantly inferior to the standard reference medication condition in reducing depressive symptomatology, it was also not significantly superior to the control condition of placebo with minimal supportive therapy. Thus, the findings are somewhat equivocal in terms of the *specific* effectiveness of CBT as carried out in this study. (There was some evidence, however, of the specificity of its effects in reducing certain types of dysfunctional attitudes.)

Since many questions have been raised about the differences between results of the TDCRP and other studies, particularly in terms of CBT's effectiveness in reducing depressive symptoms and its relative effectiveness in comparison to tricyclic medication, these questions will be addressed here. First, it is important to repeat that, as in a number of other studies, there were virtually no *significant* differences in the TDCRP between CBT and the medication condition. Also, the numerical scores on the HRSD and BDI and, especially, the recovery rates were in the same general range as in some of these other studies (e.g., Hollon et al., 1992; Murphy et al., 1984). Yet, CBT was not significantly superior to a control condition, as it has often been reported to be in the literature (see Dobson, 1989; Jarrett & Rush, 1985; Shea, Elkin & Hirschfeld, 1988); it did not seem to do as well as in the study by Rush et al. (1977), where it was significantly superior to medication; and it did not seem to do as well for the more severely depressed patients as in the study recently reported by Hollon et al. (1992). What might be the reasons for any differences that seem to be present?

1. Most studies comparing CBT to a control condition used wait-list and other "inactive" control conditions (Shea et al., 1988). Patients in the TDCRP, especially those who were less severely depressed, fared quite well in the PLA-CM condition, in which therapists provided both a pill and support and encouragement. Thus, as we have suggested, this condition constituted a more stringent control for the active treatments. The improvement found for CBT patients (and there was considerable improvement for many of them) may not, in fact, have been due to the more specific factors postulated for this approach.

2. Therapists in the TDCRP received intensive training and supervision during the pilot/training phase of the study. This was decreased at the beginning of the outcome study to monthly individual consultation calls, occasional group calls with therapists at each site, and additional calls if videotape monitoring revealed departures from the

treatment protocol or performance below competence standards. Other studies of CBT had much more frequent supervision during the actual outcome study (e.g., weekly supervision in the study by Rush et al. [1977] and twice-weekly group sessions, later tapered to once a week, in the study by Hollon et al. [1992]). As we have suggested previously (Elkin et al., 1989), any differences in CBT results that are present (and perhaps particularly for the more severe patients) may have been due to these differences in the intensity of supervision.

The rationale, however, for the decreased frequency of supervision was to allow for the evaluation of treatment effectiveness in a more "real-world" context, where therapists, following training in a new approach, generally carry out treatment relatively independently. Hollon, Shelton, and Loosen (1991), also focusing on differences in intensity of supervision, question the "adequacy of the execution of cognitive therapy" in the TDCRP. They state that "it is not clear that recently trained cognitive therapists can be expected to maintain high levels of competence in the absence of ongoing supervision." It should be noted, however, that therapists met competence criteria, applied not only by the trainers but also by outside CBT experts, both before and during the outcome study. Analyses now being carried out by Brian Shaw and colleagues should help to answer questions regarding the relationship of CBT therapist competence to outcome in the TDCRP. Hollon et al.'s statement raises a broader question, however, for psychotherapy outcome researchers: Are we interested in assessing treatment effectiveness in ideal settings, which may include very intensive supervision, or in settings more similar to actual practice? (I recognize, of course, that the treatment conditions in the TDCRP, including the use of manuals, may have departed in other ways from real-world practice.)

3. The treatment by site interaction in the subsample of more severely depressed and functionally impaired patients highlights the variability of effects for CBT (and, to a somewhat lesser extent, for IPT) in this group of patients. The pursuit of the possible determinants of this variability should generate hypotheses for further study.

4. In regard to follow-up findings, CBT did appear to do somewhat better than the medication condition, a finding similar to others reported in the literature. The difficulty of disentangling prophylactic factors from differential selection of "recoverers" in the different treatments and the fact that the PLA-CM patients also did quite well in the follow-up contribute to our caution in interpreting these findings.

Findings for IPT were less equivocal. As with

CBT, there were no significant differences from IMI-CM, but there were some significant findings on the HRSD, with IPT doing better than PLA-CM, especially on the recovery criterion and for the more severely depressed patients. It is important to remember, however, that IPT did *not* do significantly better than CBT on any measures, so one cannot conclude that IPT is more effective than CBT. In terms of the specificity of IPT effects, since an earlier study (Weissman et al., 1981) suggested that effects on measures of social functioning may not be present until sometime after treatment, it is important that we wait for the follow-up findings on mode-specific effects (analyses being conducted by Sotsky and colleagues) before drawing final conclusions.

Questions have also been raised (largely by psychopharmacological researchers) about the absence of significant superiority of medication over the psychotherapy conditions. Suggestions have been made attributing our conclusions to such factors as the probability levels stipulated for accepting differences as statistically significant (Klein, 1990). Although we considered our initial preplanned analyses and interpretations adequate, we did address this criticism, as we have previously reported (Elkin et al., 1989, 1990), by also applying alternative statistical criteria. This did not result in any major changes in our interpretations, except for a slight increase in evidence for the effectiveness of IPT. Moreover, as we had originally observed (Elkin et al., 1989), the IMI-CM condition was extremely effective in this study, with, for example, 76 percent of the completers in the GAS-defined severe subgroup reaching the recovery criterion (compared with only 18% of the patients in PLA-CM). Given these findings, it is difficult to justify criticisms of the adequacy of our drug condition. What our findings do suggest is that imipramine may *not* be specifically effective for the *less* severely depressed patients in our sample, where recovery rates were not significantly higher for the IMI-CM than for the PLA-CM condition. We should also point out that although IMI-CM is not significantly superior to the psychotherapies, even for the more severe patients, its results for these patients (especially using the GAS-criterion) are more consistent across sites, while the psychotherapies are quite variable, probably depending more on the particular patient, therapist, and therapist – patient interaction.

In discussing findings in the TDCRP relative to those in other studies, one important point has generally been overlooked. Unlike most of the comparative studies to date, inclusion criteria in the TDCRP included "stability" of the depression (i.e., the maintenance of diagnosis and severity level at a rescreening one to two weeks after patients met the original inclusion criteria). This requirement led to the exclusion of 21 percent of the sample that had passed original screening, undoubtedly resulting in a reduced number of very early responders who may have been present in other studies.

Additional Analysis of TDCRP Data

In the foregoing discussion, I have tried to summarize the substantive findings of the Collaborative as best I can at the present time. It is important to recognize that the findings are not all in. Although we have conducted our major preplanned outcome analyses and have reported on their results, there are many questions in which we were originally interested that have not yet been addressed and others that have been stimulated by the findings thus far. So, together with colleagues, I am continuing to pursue a more detailed understanding of the severity findings, including the treatment by site interaction for the more severe patients, and I am also relating adherence ratings to outcome; Sotsky and colleagues are looking at the role played by the therapeutic alliance and the predictive utility of different diagnostic categories; Leber and colleagues are studying predictors of relapse; Shea and colleagues are looking at a more detailed picture of attrition and its determinants; Pilkonis and colleagues are studying the role of life events, social supports, and various personality factors. We will also pursue a number of methodological issues, including differences in recovery rates depending on rater perspective (especially between therapists and independent clinical evaluators) and depending on the definition of recovery (status at termination vs. stability for eight weeks following termination). In addition, we will continue to do psychometric work on some new instruments, such as the General Life Functioning Scale and the Attitudes and Expectations forms, and will study their role as predictors and measures of outcome. Thus, although many of our analyses will be exploratory, we hope that they will help us to arrive at a more detailed understanding of our results and will generate hypotheses for other investigators to pursue.

As so many of our colleagues have discovered, it is difficult to continue to conduct data analyses and process studies when funding has ended and investigators have other full-time commitments. In addition to our own work, we have therefore made data available to other investigators, and several published meta-analyses have already included our data (e.g., Crits-Christoph et al., 1991; Mintz, Imber, Arruda, & Hwang, 1992). Others have made use of a Public Use Data Tape, and the video- and audiotapes are being deposited for use by qualified process researchers in an archive at the University of Pennsylvania Psychotherapy Research Center.

Design and Methodological Issues

As I have indicated, the Collaborative group confronted many design and methodological issues during the course of this study; some are quite specific to a collaborative study, but others are relevant to any psychotherapy research. Many of these issues have already been touched on in this chapter; some are discussed at greater length in cited publications. I will now summarize a few specific methodological learnings from the TDCRP, especially as they might lead to decisions other than those that are made in this study. I will conclude by focusing on two major issues: the use of a drug condition as a "standard reference treatment" against which to compare a psychotherapy and the role of placebo and/or control conditions.

Methodological learnings

Definition of the intervention.   We paid a great deal of attention to the careful definition of the treatment interventions in the TDCRP. Yet, we now recognize one additional component that should be included in the definition and in the interpretation of the effects of an intervention: the nature and intensity of supervision received by therapists during the outcome phase of a study. Since the psychotherapy intervention in a clinical trial such as the TDCRP (and in other psychotherapy outcome studies) is, in fact, a "package" of the treatment and the therapists who carry it out (and the conditions under which they carry it out), it is difficult to draw conclusions about the effectiveness of the treatment per se. Although practical questions will probably continue to be addressed by studying such packages, it is hoped that there will also be more studies of components or dimensions of psychotherapy, which may cut across different treatment approaches.

Patient population.   Although we tried by our patient inclusion and exclusion criteria to reduce heterogeneity, we are well aware that we did not have a homogeneous sample in the TDCRP. In designing the study, we chose not to stratify our sample on the basis of any patient characteristics, but rather to examine the contribution of a number of variables in predictor analyses. Since, as investigators in this field have increasingly stressed, one tends to find interactions, rather than main effects, in psychotherapy outcome studies, it might have been preferable to specify in advance variables that might differentially affect outcome for the different treatments, and to build one or more into a stratified design.

It is important, in any event, to ensure relatively equivalent distributions of major variables in the different treatment conditions. Even with as large a sample as that in the TDCRP, however, randomization does not ensure such equivalence (although it does ensure a lack of systematic bias). It was necessary, as we have reported elsewhere (Collins & Elkin, 1985), to revise our randomization procedure part way through the study in order to correct for an imbalance in the distribution in terms of gender and race. Fortunately, adaptive randomization procedures (e.g., Efron, 1980; Pocock & Simon, 1975) are now available that simultaneously achieve treatment balance across a number of specified patient variables.

I mentioned earlier the implications, for comparison with other studies, of our having excluded from the study sample the 21 percent of the screened patients who did not meet criteria for stability of symptomatology and diagnosis at rescreening. This points to the broader issue of the difficulty of comparing results of different studies that, although studying the same disorder, vary in their inclusion and exclusion criteria as well as in the final sample of patients on whom their analyses are based (especially since some may exclude patients on various grounds, after the fact).

Evaluation of outcome. To the extent that we focused on specificity issues, we might have been wise to include more measures aimed at tapping mode-specific effects. The finding of a "specific" effect of CBT on a measure derived from a factor analysis of data from the TDCRP also pointed to the importance of looking for differential effects on measures that are not only specific to particular therapy approaches but also to the specific patient population being studied. In addition, for those of us interested in mechanisms of change, it would have been helpful to have measures of patients' and therapists' perceptions of the therapy process (in addition to the twice-administered Barrett-Lennard Relationship Inventory). Here, of course, we were faced with the perennial difficulty of balancing the various aims of the study with the burden placed on patients and other study participants.

Several issues arose in regard to the timing of evaluations. Previous studies had pointed to the importance of measuring the effects of a drug treatment *before* the patient is tapered off the drug, and this is the procedure that we followed. In retrospect, it might have been instructive to measure outcome again after the patient was completely off the drug, especially since psychotherapy patients are "off" psychotherapy at the time of a termination evaluation. Patients in the IMI-CM condition also received one or two brief sessions after termination in order to complete the tapering-off process. Discussions with some psychotherapists, particularly in the IPT condition, revealed that they would have also preferred to have one or two scheduled meetings with patients in the month following therapy, rather than have what to them felt like an abrupt termination. This might usefully be considered in future short-term treatment studies.

Timing of the termination evaluation also needs careful consideration. There is some suggestion in our data (particularly for the IPT condition, where scores dropped sharply between the 12th week and termination evaluations) that patients may have responded to demand characteristics of a termination evaluation. Some investigators, therefore, have suggested that outcome evaluations actually be held some time after termination. There are, of course, both pros and cons to these alternatives. Finally, in terms of timing of evaluations, if one wants to test hypotheses regarding the course of change and particularly regarding the sequencing of different effects, consideration should be given to the inclusion of at least one or two weekly measures.

In order to address the question of clinical significance, we analyzed our findings in terms of a recovery criterion (a score of six or less on the HRSD) that reflected little or no remaining depressive symptomatology. In addition to the extent of symptomatology, however, it may also be important to consider the stability of the recovery. The criterion of recovery used in our follow-up analyses, which did include a stability component (eight weeks with little or no symptomatology), produced somewhat different percentages of recovered patients from those found using our HRSD recovery criterion at termination. We intend to look into the implications of these different definitions in more detail.

Statistical analyses. One of the issues we grappled with at length involved the sample of patients on which our major analyses would be based. Some psychotherapy researchers prefer to focus on a sample of completers, in order to study only those patients who received a full exposure to the treatment. Many pharmacotherapy researchers, on the other hand, focus on patients who have had at least a minimum exposure to the treatment (the definition of "minimum exposure" may of course differ for a psychotherapy and a drug treatment) or to all patients who entered treatment. The latter definition is also generally preferred in the clinical trials literature, since it maintains the originally randomized sample. To provide a comprehensive picture of our findings, we originally presented results for all three samples. In addition, temporal course of symptom reduction was studied by a repeated measures analysis of completers and cohort analyses of all patients completing 4, 8, and 12 weeks of treatment. In our more recent random regression analysis, we included, in one analysis, all available data (on the

HRSD) for the total sample of patients who entered treatment. This approach was helpful in minimizing Type I errors, as well as in addressing other statistical problems. One aspect of this analysis that must be kept in mind, however, is that it does give weight to the rapidity of change; one may be interested, in addition, in simply how patients do at the termination of their treatment.

We have addressed some of the problems confronted in interpreting follow-up data, particularly since patients who improve in one treatment may differ from those who improve in another. (Evans, Hollon, and colleagues [1992] also addressed this issue in their recent article.) In the article reporting on TDCRP follow-up findings, this issue was resolved by carrying out statistical tests only on the original randomized sample, focusing on the percentage of patients who both recovered and remained well throughout the follow-up. This article also reported, more descriptively, on the course during follow-up of the subsample of recovered patients. It is hoped that investigators will continue to address this difficult problem and will develop new approaches for dealing with it.

Drug as standard reference treatment. In the absence of a psychotherapy that had already been accepted as a standard treatment for outpatient depression, we decided (following the lead of Rush et al. [1977]) to use an antidepressant medication that had a good track record in this area. We hoped that by comparing the psychotherapies to imipramine-hydrochloride, we might establish whether the psychotherapies did significantly worse than the drug in reducing depressive symptomatology and whether they might do better than the drug in areas targeted by each of the psychotherapies. During the course of designing and implementing the TDCRP, we became aware of the many conceptual and methodological problems in comparing psychotherapy and pharmacotherapy treatment conditions. These include differences in the active ingredients and hypothesized mechanisms of change, related issues regarding the standardization and adequate delivery of treatments, and the difficulty of establishing controls for factors other than the active ingredients of each treatment; differences in the nature of treatment effects and related goals for treatment; and differences in the time course of treatment effects. We have already written about these at some length (Elkin et al., 1988a, 1988b).

Aside from the interpretive problems due to intrinsic differences between drug treatment and psychotherapy, there are difficulties in comparing any standard reference treatment to another active treatment condition. As in any comparative study, large Ns are needed to provide adequate statistical power to detect significant differences, and there are problems in drawing conclusions when differences are not significant. Even with adequate power, one still cannot legitimately conclude that treatments that are not significantly different are equivalent, particularly when there is a fairly consistent directional difference in scores. Interpretive problems are also increased when the drug is accompanied by any psychological intervention (such as our CM component), thus creating what might be viewed as a combination of drug and minimal supportive therapy. We became more acutely aware of these problems than we had been previously during data analysis and write-up of our findings.

Given the conceptual, methodological, and interpretive problems in comparing a psychotherapy to a drug condition, one must ask the question of whether this is a reasonable thing to do. It depends, it seems to me, on the question that is being addressed in a study. If there is an intrinsic interest in the comparative effectiveness of a particular psychotherapy and a particular drug in treating a specific disorder, then there is no other way to answer the question than to directly compare the two treatments and deal with the problems in doing so as carefully and explicitly as possible. If, on the other hand, one is primarily interested in the effectiveness of the psychotherapy in treating the disorder, I am not sure that much is gained by the comparison with the "standard" drug treatment, given all of the problems that this poses. It may be preferable to focus on control conditions that will allow one to answer this question more clearly.

Control conditions. This brings us to the ever-present problem in psychotherapy research of the choice of control conditions against which to compare the treatment of interest. As mentioned earlier, we attempted to find a psychotherapy-placebo condition that would control for factors other than the active ingredients in the therapies we were studying. Failing to identify such a condition that did not itself constitute a treatment (with the need for manuals, training, etc.), we compromised by using PLA-CM as a control condition against which to compare the psychotherapies as well as the drug. As we have indicated, this was a double-faceted control condition, due to the administration of a pill along with what could be considered minimal supportive therapy. The fact that the less severely ill patients did quite well in this condition created some interpretive problems and has raised the question of whether this was too stringent a control condition. Based on our experience in the study, I would now suggest the possibility of building the CM (clinical management) aspects of the intervention into a control condition, without the administration of a pill. One recent investigator (Arkowitz, 1992) has, in fact, drawn on the CM component of the TDCRP pharmacotherapy condition, combined with a client-centered therapy approach, to propose a "common factors" therapy against which to compare more specific treatments for depression.

A number of authors have in recent years questioned the viability of the placebo concept in psychotherapy research, and they have put forth some fairly convincing arguments regarding the ethical, conceptual, and practical problems with this concept. I do not propose to go into these arguments here, although I am in agreement with many of them. (I am sure that they will be covered well in other chapters in this volume.) Regardless of the problems with this concept, however, it seems to me that we cannot dispense with the use of control conditions in psychotherapy research if we are to be able to answer questions about the specific effectiveness of certain "active ingredients" in a treatment approach. Perhaps the field would be best served were we to stop using the term "*placebo*" and instead focus on the specific "extraneous" or "irrelevant" factors that we wish to control in order to isolate, as best we can, the influence of the variables in which we are most interested. The difficult task would still remain, of course, of defining the "active ingredients" of a particular intervention as well as the "extraneous factors," given the important and intertwined role of relationship and technique factors in psychotherapy.

I was asked to write this chapter because I am the only person who was involved in the TDCRP from its inception until the present time, first as one of the NIMH initiators and designers of the program, as coordinator throughout the years of its planning and implementation, and now as one of the continuing collaborators in analysis and publication of findings. Not all of the views expressed here are necessarily shared by all of my colleagues in the TDCRP. But the credit for various aspects of the initiation, implementation, and analysis and interpretation of the findings is shared by the collaborating investigators and the other individuals listed in the acknowledgments that follow.

Health. The program was funded by cooperative agreements to six participating sites (George Washington University [MH 33762]; University of Pittsburgh [MH 33753]; University of Oklahoma [MH 33760]; Yale University [MH 33827]; Clarke Institute of Psychiatry [MH 38231]; and Rush Presbyterian–St. Luke's Medical Center [MH 35017]). The principal NIMH collaborators were Irene Elkin, PhD, Coordinator (now at the University of Chicago); M. Tracie Shea, PhD, Associate Coordinator (now at Brown University); Morris B. Parloff, PhD (now at Georgetown University); and John P. Docherty, MD (now at Nashua Brookside Hospital). The principal investigators and project coordinators at the three participating research sites were George Washington University — Stuart M. Sotsky, MD, and David R. Glass, PhD; University of Pittsburgh — Stanley D. Imber, PhD, and Paul A. Pilkonis, PhD; and the University of Oklahoma — John T. Watkins, PhD, and William R. Leber, PhD. The principal investigators and project coordinators at the three sites responsible for training therapists were Yale University — Myrna M. Weissman, PhD (now at Columbia University); Eve S. Chevron, MS, and Bruce J. Rounsaville, MD; Clarke Institute of Psychiatry — Brian F. Shaw, PhD, and T. Michael Vallis, PhD; and Rush Presbyterian–St. Luke's Medical Center — Jan A. Fawcett, MD, and Phillip Epstein, MD. Collaborators in the data management and data analysis aspects of the program were C. James Klett, PhD; Joseph F. Collins, ScD; and Roderic Gillis of the Veterans Administration Cooperative Studies Program, Perry Point, MD.

A number of additional individuals made important contributions to the TDCRP: Suzanne W. Hadley, Joseph H. Autry, Susan J. Fiester, H. Alice Lowery, James Perel, Anne Horney, members of the Advisory Group, clinical evaluators and therapists at the research sites, research assistants and secretaries at all the sites and NIMH, and, of course, the patients, who gave generously of their time.

I would like to express especially warm appreciation to my colleagues Morris B. Parloff and M. Tracie Shea, not only for their helpful comments on this chapter, but also for their extraordinary collegiality throughout the years of our joint work on this project.

ACKNOWLEDGMENTS

The NIMH Treatment of Depression Collaborative Research Program is a multisite program initiated and sponsored by the National Institute of Mental

REFERENCES

Arkowitz, H. (1992). A common factors therapy for depression. In J. C. Norcross & M. R. Goldfried (Eds.), *Handbook of psychotherapy integration*. New York: Basic Books.

Barrett-Lennard, G. T. (1962). Dimensions of therapist response as causal factors in therapeutic change. *Psychological Monographs, 76*(43), 1–36.

Barrett-Lennard, G. T. (1969). *Technical note on the 64-item revision of the Relationship Inventory.* Unpublished manuscript. University of Waterloo, Waterloo, Ontario.

Basham, R. B. (1986). Scientific and practical advantages of comparative design in psychotherapy outcome research. *Journal of Consulting and Clinical Psychology, 54*, 88–94.

Beck, A. T., & Beamesderfer, A. (1974). Assessment of depression: The Depression Inventory. In P. Pichot (Ed.), *Modern problems of pharmacopsychiatry: Psychological measurements in pharmacology* (pp. 151–169). Basil, Switzerland: Karger.

Beck, A. T., Rush, A. J., Shaw, B. F., & Emery, G. (1979). *Cognitive therapy of depression.* New York: Guilford.

Beck, A. T., Ward, C. H., Mendelsohn, M., Mock, J., & Erbauch, J. (1961). An inventory for measuring depression. *Archives of General Psychiatry, 4*, 561–571.

Bergin, A. E., & Strupp, H. H. (1972). *Changing frontiers in the science of psychotherapy.* Chicago: Aldine-Atherton.

Chevron, E. S., & Rounsaville, B. J. (1983). Evaluating the clinical skills of psychotherapists: A comparison of techniques. *Archives of General Psychiatry, 40*, 1129–1132.

Chevron, E. S., Rounsaville, B. J., Rothblum, E. D., & Weissman, M. M. (1983). Selecting psychotherapists to participate in psychotherapy outcome studies: Relationship between psychotherapist characteristics and assessment of clinical skills. *The Journal of Nervous and Mental Disease, 171*(6), 348–353.

Collins, J. F., & Elkin, I. (1985). Randomization in the NIMH Treatment of Depression Collaborative Research Program. In R. F. Boruch & W. Wothke (Eds.), *New directions for program evaluation, no. 28: Randomization and field experimentation* (pp. 27–37). San Francisco: Jossey-Bass.

Critelli, J. W., & Neumann, K. F. (1984). The placebo: Conceptual analysis of a construct in transition. *American Psychologist, 39*, 32–39.

Crits-Christoph, P., Baranackie, K., Kurcios, J. S., Beck, A. T., Carroll, K., Perry, K., Luborsky, L., McLellan, A. T., Woody, G. E., Thompson, L., Gallagher, D., & Zitrin, C. (1991). Meta-analysis of therapist effects in psychotherapy outcome studies. *Psychotherapy Research, 1*, 81–91.

DeRubeis, R. J., Evans, M. D., Hollon, S. D., Garvey, M. J., Grove, W. M., & Tuason, V. B. (1990). How does cognitive therapy work? Cognitive change and symptom change in cognitive therapy and pharmacotherapy for depression. *Journal of Consulting and Clinical Psychology, 58*, 862–869.

DiMascio, A., Weissman, M. M., Prusoff, B. A., Neu, C., Zwilling, M., & Klerman, G. L. (1979). Differential symptom reduction by drugs and psychotherapy in acute depression. *Archives of General Psychiatry, 36*, 1450–1456.

Dobson, K. S. (1989). A meta-analysis of the efficacy of cognitive therapy for depression. *Journal of Consulting and Clinical Psychology, 57*, 414–419.

Dobson, K. S., Shaw, B. F., & Vallis, T. M. (1985). Reliability of a measure of the quality of cognitive therapy. *British Journal of Clinical Psychology, 24*, 295–300.

Edwards, A. L., & Cronbach, L. J. (1952). Experimental design for research in psychotherapy. Reprinted in G. E. Stollak, B. G. Guerney, Jr., & M. Rothberg (Eds.). (1966). *Psychotherapy research: Selected readings* (pp. 56–66). Chicago: Rand McNally.

Efron, B. (1980). Randomizing and balancing a complicated sequential experiment. In R. G. Miller, Jr., B. Efron, D. W. Brown, Jr., & L. E. Moses (Eds.), *Biostatistics casebook.* New York: Wiley.

Elkin, I. (1990, June). *The middle generation: The seventies.* Paper presented in Panel on Lessons in History: Three Generations of Therapy Research at the 21st annual meeting of the Society for Psychotherapy Research, Wintergreen, VA.

Elkin, I. (1992). Études multicentriques: Advantges et inconvénients. In P. Gerin & A. Dazord (Eds.), *Recherches cliniques "planifées" sur les psychothérapies: Méthodologie.* Paris: INSERM. (Available in English from the author.)

Elkin, I., Parloff, M. B., Hadley, S. W., & Autry, J. H. (1985). NIMH Treatment of Depression Collaborative Research Program: Background and research plan. *Archives of General Psychiatry, 42*, 305–316.

Elkin, I., Pilkonis, P. A., Docherty, J. P., & Sotsky, S. M. (1988a). Conceptual and methodological issues in comparative studies of psychotherapy and pharmacotherapy, I: Active ingredients and mechanisms of change. *American Journal of Psychiatry, 145*, 909–917.

Elkin, I., Pilkonis, P. A., Docherty, J. P., & Sotsky, S. M. (1988b). Conceptual and methodological issues in comparative studies of psychotherapy and pharmacotherapy, II: Nature and timing of treatment effects. *American Journal of Psychiatry, 145*, 1070–1076.

Elkin, I., Shea, M. T., Collins, J. F., Klett, C. J., Imber, S. D., Sotsky, S. M., Watkins, J. T., & Parloff, M. B. (1990) NIMH Collaborative Research on Treatment of Depression [Letter to the Editor]. *Archives of General Psychiatry, 47*, 684–685.

Elkin, I., Shea, M. T., Watkins, J. T., Imber, S. D., Sotsky, S. M., Collins, J. F., Glass, D. R., Pilkonis, P. A., Leber, W. R., Docherty, J. P., Fiester, S. J., & Parloff, M. B. (1989). National Institute of Mental Health Treatment of Depression Collaborative Research Program: General effectiveness of treatments. *Archives of General Psychiatry, 46*, 971–982.

Endicott, J., Cohen, J., Nee, J., Fleiss, J. L., & Sarantakos, S. (1981). Hamilton Depression Rating Scale: Extracted from regular and change versions of the Schedule for Affective Disorders and Schizophrenia. *Archives of General Psychiatry, 38*, 98–103.

Evans, M. D., Hollon, S. D., DeRubeis, R. J., Piasecki, J. M., Grove, W. M., Garvey, M. J., & Tuason, V. B. (1992). Differential relapse following cognitive therapy and pharmacotherapy for depression. *Archives of General Psychiatry, 49*, 802–808.

Fawcett, J., Epstein, P., Fiester, S. J., Elkin, I., & Autry, J. H. (1987). Clinical Management-Imipramine/Placebo Administration Manual: NIMH Treatment of Depression Collaborative Research Program. *Psychopharmacology Bulletin, 23*, 309–324.

Foley, S. H., O'Malley, S., Rounsaville, B., Prusoff, B. A., & Weissman, M. M. (1987). The relationship of patient difficulty to therapist performance in interpersonal psychotherapy of depression. *Journal of Affective Disorders, 12*, 207–217.

Gibbons, R. D., Hedeker, D., Elkin, I., Waternaux, C., Kraemer, H. C., Greenhouse, J. B., Shea, M. T., Imber, S. D., Sotsky, S. M., & Watkins, J. T. (in press). Some conceptual and statistical issues in analysis of longitudinal psychiatric data. *Archives of General Psychiatry.*

Hamilton, M. A. (1960). A rating scale for depression. *Journal of Neurology, Neurosurgery, and Psychiatry, 23*, 56–62.

Hamilton, M. A. (1967). Development of a rating scale for primary depressive illness. *British Journal of Social and Clinical Psychology, 6*, 278–296.

Hill, C. E., O'Grady, K. E., & Elkin, I. (1992). Applying the Collaborative Study Psychotherapy Rating Scale to rate therapist adherence in cognitive-behavior therapy, interpersonal therapy, and clinical management. *Journal of Consulting and Clinical Psychology, 60,* 73–79.

Hollon, S. D., DeRubeis, R. J., Evans, M. D., Wiemer, M. J., Garvey, M. J., Grove, W. M., & Tuason, V. B. (1992). Cognitive therapy and pharmacotherapy for depression: Singly or in combination. *Archives of General Psychiatry, 49,* 774–781.

Hollon, S. D., Shelton, R. C., & Loosen, P. T. (1991). Cognitive therapy and pharmacotherapy for depression. *Journal of Consulting and Clinical Psychology, 59,* 88–99.

Hollon, S. D., Waskow, I. E., Evans, M., & Lowery, H. A. (1984, May). *System for rating therapies for depression.* Paper presented at the annual meeting of the American Psychiatric Association, Los Angeles, CA. For copies of the Collaborative Study Psychotherapy Rating Scale and related materials prepared under NIMH contract 278-81-003 (ER), order "System for Rating Psychotherapy Audiotapes" from U.S. Department of Commerce, National Technical Information Service, Springfield, VA 22161.

Imber, S. D., Glanz, L. M., Elkin, I., Sotsky, S. M., Boyer, J. L., & Leber, W. R. (1986). Ethical issues in psychotherapy research: Problems in a collaborative clinical trials study. *American Psychologist, 41,* 137–146.

Imber, S. D., Pilkonis, P. A., Sotsky, S. M., Elkin, I., Watkins, J. T., Collins, J. F., Shea, M. T., Leber, W. R., & Glass, D. R. (1990). Mode-specific effects among three treatments for depression. *Journal of Consulting and Clinical Psychology, 58,* 352–359.

Jarrett, R. B., & Rush, J. A. (1985). Psychotherapeutic approaches for depression. In J. O. Cavenar (Ed.), *Psychiatry* (pp. 1–35). Philadelphia: J. P. Lippincott.

Kazdin, A. E., & Bass, D. (1989). Power to detect differences between alternative treatments in comparative psychotherapy outcome research. *Journal of Consulting and Clinical Psychology, 57,* 138–147.

Kiesler, D. J. (1966) Some myths of psychotherapy research and the search for a paradigm. *Psychological Bulletin, 65,* 110–136.

Klein, D. F. (1990). NIMH Collaborative Research on Treatment of Depression [Letter to the Editor]. *Archives of General Psychiatry, 47,* 682–684.

Klerman, G. L., Weissman, M. M., Rounsaville, B. J., & Chevron, E. S. (1984). *Interpersonal psychotherapy of depression.* New York: Basic Books.

Kovacs, M., Rush, A. J., Beck, A. T., & Hollon, S. D. (1981). Depressed outpatients treated with cognitive therapy or pharmacotherapy: A one-year follow-up. *Archives of General Psychiatry, 38,* 34–39.

Krupnick, J., Shea, T., & Elkin, I. (1986). Generalizability of treatment studies utilizing solicited patients. *Journal of Consulting and Clinical Psychology, 54,* 68–78.

Letters to the Editor. (1990). *Archives of General Psychiatry, 47,* 682–688.

Lipman, R. S., Covi, L., & Shapiro, A. K. (1979). The Hopkins Symptom Checklist: Factors derived from the HSCL-90. *Journal of Affective Disorders, 1,* 9–24.

Luborsky, L., & DeRubeis, R. J. (1984). The use of psychotherapy treatment manuals: A small revolution in psychotherapy research style. *Clinical Psychology Review, 4,* 5–14.

Mintz, J., Imber, L. I., Arruda, M. J., & Hwang, S. S. (1992). Treatment of depression and the functional capacity to work. *Archives of General Psychiatry, 49,* 761–768.

Murphy, G. E., Simons, A. D., Wetzel, R. D., & Lustman, P. J. (1984). Cognitive therapy and pharmacotherapy: Singly and together in the treatment of depression. *Archives of General Psychiatry, 41,* 33–41.

NIMH-PSC. (1964). Phenothiazine treatment in acute schizophrenia. *Archives of General Psychiatry, 10,* 246–261.

O'Leary, K. D., & Borkovec, T. D. (1978). Conceptual, methodological, and ethical problems of placebo groups in psychotherapy research. *American Psychologist, 33,* 821–830.

O'Malley, S. S., Foley, S. H., Rounsaville, B. J., Watkins, J. T., Sotsky, S. M., Imber, S. D., & Elkin, I. (1988). Therapist competence and patient outcome in interpersonal psychotherapy of depression. *Journal of Consulting and Clinical Psychology, 56,* 496–501.

Parloff, M. B. (1986). Placebo controls in psychotherapy research: A sine qua non or a placebo for research problems? *Journal of Consulting and Clinical Psychology, 54,* 79–87.

Parloff, M. B., & Elkin, I. (1992). Historical development in research centers: NIMH Treatment of Depression Collaborative Research Program. In D. K. Freedheim (Ed.), *A history of psychotherapy* (pp. 442–449). Washington, DC: American Psychological Association.

Paul, G. L. (1967). Strategy of outcome research in psychotherapy. *Journal of Consulting Psychology, 31,* 109–118.

Pocock, J. J., & Simon, R. (1975). Sequential treatment assignments with balancing for prognostic factors in the controlled clinical trial. *Biometrics, 31,* 103–117.

Prien, R. F., Kupfer, D. J., Mansky, P. A., Small, J. G., Tuason, V. B., Voss, C. B., & Johnson, W. E. (1984). Drug therapy in the prevention of recurrences in unipolar and bipolar affective disorder. Report of the NIMH Collaborative Study Group comparing lithium carbonate, imipramine, and a lithium carbonate-imipramine combination. *Archives of General Psychiatry, 41,* 1096–1104.

Rounsaville, B. J., Chevron, E. S., Prusoff, B. A., Elkin, I., Imber, S., Sotsky, S., & Watkins, J. (1987). The relation between specific and general dimensions of the psychotherapy process in interpersonal psychotherapy of depression. *Journal of Consulting and Clinical Psychology, 55,* 379–384.

Rounsaville, B. J., Chevron, E. S., & Weissman, M. M. (1984). Specification of techniques in interpersonal psychotherapy. In J. B. W. Williams & R. L. Spitzer (Eds.), *Psychotherapy research: Where are we and where should we go?* (pp. 160–172). New York: Guilford.

Rounsaville, B. J., Chevron, E. S., Weissman, M. M., Prusoff, B. A., & Frank, E. (1986). Training therapists to perform interpersonal psychotherapy in clinical trials. *Comprehensive Psychiatry, 27,* 364–371.

Rude, S. S., & Rehm, L. P. (1991). Response to treatments for depression: The role of initial status on targeted cognitive and behavioral skills. *Clinical Psychology Review, 11,* 493–514.

Rush, A. J., Beck, A. T., Kovacs, M., & Hollon, S. (1977). Comparative efficacy of cognitive therapy and pharmacotherapy in the treatment of depressed patients. *Cognitive Therapy Research, 1,* 17–37.

Shaw, B. F. (1984). Specification of the training and evaluation of cognitive therapists for outcome studies. In J. B. W. Williams & R. L. Spitzer (Eds.), *Psychotherapy research: Where are we and where should we go?* (pp. 173–189). New York: Guilford.

Shaw, B. F., & Dobson, K. S. (1988). Competency judgements in the training and evaluation of psychotherapists. *Journal of Consulting and Clinical Psychology, 56,* 666–672.

Shea, M. T., Elkin, I., & Hirschfeld, R. M. A. (1988). Psychotherapeutic treatment of depression. In R. E. Hales & A. J. Frances (Eds.), *American Psychiatric Press Review of Psychiatry,* Vol. 7 (pp. 235–255). Washington, DC: American Psychiatric Press.

Shea, M. T., Elkin, I., Imber, S. D., Sotsky, S. M., Watkins, J. T., Collins, J. F., Pilkonis, P. A., Beckham, E., Glass,

D. R., Dolan, R. T., & Parloff, M. B. (1992). Course of depressive symptoms over follow-up: Findings from the National Institute of Mental Health Treatment of Depression Collaborative Research Program. *Archives of General Psychiatry, 49,* 782–787.

Shea, M. T., Glass, D., Pilkonis, P. A., Watkins, J., & Docherty, J. (1987). Frequency and implications of personality disorders in a sample of depressed outpatients. *Journal of Personality Disorders, 1,* 27–42.

Shea, M. T., Pilkonis, P. A., Beckham, E., Collins, J. F., Elkin, I., Sotsky, S. M., & Docherty, J. P. (1990). Personality disorders and treatment outcome in the NIMH Treatment of Depression Collaborative Research Program. *American Journal of Psychiatry, 147,* 711–718.

Sholomskas, D. E., Barlow, D. H., Cohen, J., Gorman, J., Moras, K., Papp, L., Shear, M. K., & Woods, S. W. (1990, May). *Drug/behavior treatment of panic: Study design.* Paper presented at the annual meeting of the American Psychiatric Association, New York.

Simons, A. D., Garfield, S. L., & Murphy, G. E. (1984). The process of change in cognitive therapy and pharmacotherapy for depression. *Archives of General Psychiatry, 41,* 45–51.

Simons, A. D., Murphy, G. E., Levine, J. L., & Wetzel, R. D. (1986). Cognitive therapy and pharmacotherapy for depression: Sustained improvement over one year. *Archives of General Psychiatry, 43,* 43–48.

Sotsky, S. M., Glass, D. R., Shea, M. T., Pilkonis, P. A., Collins, J. F., Elkin, I., Watkins, J. T., Imber, S. D., Leber, W. R., Moyer, J., & Oliveri, M. E. (1991). Patient predictors of response to psychotherapy and pharmacotherapy: Findings in the NIMH Treatment of Depression Collaborative Research Program. *American Journal of Psychiatry, 148,* 997–1008.

Spitzer, R. L., Endicott, J., & Robins, E. (1978). Research Diagnostic Criteria: Rationale and reliability. *Archives of General Psychiatry, 35,* 773–782.

Vallis, T. M., Shaw, B. F., & Dobson, K. S. (1986). The Cognitive Therapy Scale: Psychometric properties. *Journal of Consulting and Clinical Psychology, 54,* 381–385.

Waskow, I. E. (1984). Specification of the technique variable in the NIMH Treatment of Depression Collaborative Research Program. In J. B. W. Williams & R. L. Spitzer (Eds.), *Psychotherapy research: Where are we and where should we go?* (pp. 150–159). New York: Guilford.

Watkins, J. T., Leber, W. R., Imber, S. D., Collins, J. F., Elkin, I., Pilkonis, P. A., Sotsky, S. M., Shea, M. T., & Glass, D. R. (in press). NIMH Treatment of Depression Collaborative Research Program: Temporal course of symptomatic change. *Journal of Consulting and Clinical Psychology.*

Weissman, A. N., & Beck, A. T. (1978, December). *Development and validation of the Dysfunctional Attitude Scale.* Paper presented at the 12th annual meeting of the Association for the Advancement of Behavior Therapy, Chicago, IL.

Weissman, M. M., Klerman, G. L., Prusoff, B. A., Sholomskas, D., Padian, N. (1981). Depressed outpatients: Results one year after treatment with drugs and/or interpersonal psychotherapy. *Archives of General Psychiatry, 38,* 51–55.

Weissman, M. M., & Paykel, E. S. (1974). *The depressed woman: A study of social relationships.* Chicago: University of Chicago Press.

Weissman, M. M., Prusoff, B. A., DiMascio, A., Neu, C., Goklaney, M., & Klerman, G. L. (1979). The efficacy of drugs and psychotherapy in the treatment of acute depressive episodes. *American Journal of Psychiatry, 136,* 555–558.

Weissman, M. M., Rounsaville, B. J., & Chevron, E. (1982). Training psychotherapists to participate in psychotherapy outcome studies. *American Journal of Psychiatry, 139,* 1442–1446.

PART

II

EVALUATING THE INGREDIENTS OF THERAPEUTIC EFFICACY

5

THE EFFECTIVENESS OF PSYCHOTHERAPY

■ **MICHAEL J. LAMBERT**
Brigham Young University

■ **ALLEN E. BERGIN**
Brigham Young University

In this chapter, we review the status of empirical evidence on the efficacy of psychotherapy, mainly with adult outpatients. We also discuss related issues, such as (1) change without treatment, (2) negative effects of treatment, (3) comparative outcomes across techniques, (4) causal factors in outcome, and (5) the permanence of change. As in the previous editions of this *Handbook*, we consider mainly the practice of individual therapies, such as the many variations of psychoanalytically oriented psychotherapy, various humanistic and relationship therapies, cognitive and behavioral therapies, as well as eclectic mixtures of these and similar types of interventions. Full accounts of these approaches are reserved for other chapters, but here we focus on an integration and comparison of results along with issues of central importance to the effectiveness of all therapies.

Research on therapy outcome from the 1930s through the mid-1980s was summarized in the three previous editions of this chapter (Bergin, 1971; Bergin & Lambert, 1978; Lambert, Shapiro, & Bergin, 1986). Our review of this literature and the related controversies is well documented in these earlier editions. Research and reviews since those editions have confirmed our original conclusion — psychotherapies, in general, have positive effects — but have also added considerable information and raised numerous other issues. The interested reader is invited to review earlier editions of this chapter in order to gain an appreciation of the historical context of the current chapter, the nature and quality of prior research, and the controversies that have attended analyses of therapeutic outcomes.

Before introducing specific studies and results,

however, it is important to note that significant changes have occurred in recent years that alter the complexion of this review in comparison with that in previous editions because the field is maturing in many respects.

As noted in Chapter 1, there is a major trend toward eclecticism or integration of diverse techniques and concepts into a broad, comprehensive, and pragmatic approach to treatment that avoids strong allegiances to narrow theories or schools of thought. While there are some exceptions to this trend — and there continue to exist rigid adherents to specific orientations — the field as a whole has moved to a new position of cooperative endeavor. This trend toward integration is well documented in a recent *Handbook* (Norcross & Goldfried, 1992) and in surveys of practicing clinicians. Smith's (1982) survey of the clinical and counseling divisions of the American Psychological Association showed that a startling 98 percent of his 415 respondents identified some form of eclectic system as representing the future trend in psychotherapy. Later surveys have confirmed that this trend of thought is affecting the practices of a large population of clinicians (Norcross & Newman, 1992). All of these studies suggest that there are many kinds of eclectic combinations and that there is great diversity in the techniques selected as "most beneficial" by eclectic practitioners. Jensen, Bergin, and Greaves (1990), for example, conducted a study that attempted to discover how many therapists claim to be eclectic therapists and, of those, which forms of therapy they most often used. In order to accomplish these goals, the authors sent questionnaires about theoretical orientation to 800 therapists in the United States from within the fields of clinical psychology, marriage and family therapy, social work, and psychiatry. They found that 68 percent of the therapists who responded claimed to be eclectic in orientation. They further discovered that eclectic therapists most often claimed their theoretical orientation to be primarily dynamic, cognitive, or behavioral. The authors determined that within the sample, the modal eclectic therapist used about four different approaches in clinical practice. The most common combination of orientations included psychodynamic, cognitive-behavioral, humanistic, and systems techniques.

Despite the widespread use of integrative and eclectic approaches, few studies have been conducted on the efficacy of these combination therapies (Lambert, 1992). For this reason, it is not possible to directly analyze and compare the outcome of therapies as they are often practiced in contemporary clinical consulting rooms. By and large, we are limited to integrating the findings coming from studies of specific treatments with patients who have a particular disorder or problem. The results of these outcome studies are rich with implications for the practice of school-based as well as integration-based interventions.

We have tried, therefore, to highlight the contributions of diverse therapies, unencumbered by an allegiance to theory and school, with the intent of informing the clinician about the most significant and robust findings that have been published, while being open to evidence, positive and negative, concerning any and all approaches. It is difficult to provide a review that is perceived as evenhanded by a variety of therapeutic orientations, but we have tried to avoid taking sides and we believe the vast majority of research-oriented therapists have moved beyond defensive posturing as the field has matured. Although advocates of specific orientations have made important and lasting contributions to the field, even these advocates have become more broad-minded and flexible in assessing the meaning of outcome data.

Given these orienting remarks, we now turn to our assessment of the results of studies and the implications of these studies for the practice of psychotherapy.

THE GENERAL EFFECT OF PSYCHOTHERAPY

The present summary has benefited from numerous controlled studies that have appeared in the literature since our last review (Lambert et al., 1986). Many new treatments and variations on the old ones have evolved over the course of studying psychotherapy so that improvements in research methodology have gone hand in hand with changes in the phenomenon under investigation. There is now little doubt that psychological treatments are, overall and in general, beneficial, although it remains equally true that not everyone benefits to a satisfactory degree. The evidence for this conclusion is demonstrated in part by quantitative surveys of the literature that have used the technique of meta-analysis to summarize large collections of empirical data.

Psychotherapy outcome research is but one of several domains of the social and behavioral sciences with a history of controversy and dispute concerning the interpretation of the evidence at hand (e.g., Bergin & Lambert, 1978; Rachman & Wilson, 1980). To meet the need for efficient and maximally objective integrative summaries of such data sets, the technique, or family of techniques, known as meta-analysis was developed (cf. Cohen, 1988; Glass, McGaw, & Smith, 1981; Hedges & Olkin, 1985; Michelson, 1985; Rosenthal, 1983; Strube & Hartman, 1982, 1983).

Meta-analysis applies the methods and principles of empirical research to the process of reviewing literature. It begins with a systematic search of the literature to locate studies meeting predefined inclusion criteria. The findings of individual studies are then quantified on some common metric (such as an effect size expressing differences between group means in standard deviation units or a statistical probability level). Salient features of each study (such as the nature of the client population, type of treatment, and methodological strengths and weaknesses of the study) are recorded systematically, and statistical techniques are then used to arrive at summary statements of the size or statistical significance of the effects accumulated across studies. Further statistical analyses are used to identify quantitative relationships between study features and the results obtained (see Chapter 2, this volume, for a more complete review of meta-analysis as a method).

Early applications of meta-analysis to psychotherapy outcomes (Smith & Glass, 1977; Smith, Glass, & Miller, 1980) addressed the overall question of the extent of benefit associated with psychotherapy as evidenced in the literature as a whole, compared the outcomes of different treatments, and examined the impact of methodological features of studies upon the reported effectiveness of treatments. For example, Smith et al. (1980) found an average effect size of 0.85 standard deviation units over 475 studies comparing treated and untreated groups. This indicates that, at the end of treatment, the average treated person is better off than 80 percent of the untreated sample.

Subsequent meta-analytic reviews, including both critical replications using the same data base as Smith et al. (Andrews & Harvey, 1981; Landman & Dawes, 1982) and independent analyses of other large samples of studies, have yielded comparable effects (Shapiro & Shapiro, 1982a). A listing of meta-analytic summaries of outcome research is presented in Tables 5.1 to 5.3. Table 5.1 summarizes meta-analytic reviews that quantify the outcomes of treating patients with a variety of depressive disorders, mainly unipolar depression. Results

TABLE 5.1 Meta-analytic reviews of outcome with depression

Researchers	Patient Diagnosis/Treatment	Number of Studies	Effect Size
Dobson (1989)	Depression/Cognitive therapy	10	2.15
Nietzel, Russell, Hemmings, & Gretter (1987)	Unipolar depression	28	.71
Quality Assurance Project (1983)	Depression	10	.65
Robinson, Berman, & Neimeyer (1990)	Depression	29	.84
Steinbrueck, Maxwell, & Howard (1983)	Depression	56	1.22

in treating depression appear rather consistent. In all five reviews patients undergoing psychotherapy surpassed no-treatment and wait-list control patients. For example, in the Dobson (1989) report, the average client treated with Beck's cognitive therapy surpassed 98 percent of the control patients. Similar but less dramatic results are found in the other reviews listed in Table 5.1. Robinson, Berman, and Neimeyer (1990), for example, found that behavioral, cognitive-behavioral, and, to a lesser extent, general verbal therapies all had positive effects on outcome compared to no-treatment or wait-list controls.

Of even more interest to practicing clinicians was the finding that the effects of psychotherapy were equal to or surpassed a variety of antidepressant medications. Since antidepressant medication is often considered the treatment of choice for depression, psychotherapies that produce comparable effects are significant (Robinson et al., 1990; Steinbrueck, Maxwell, & Howard, 1983). It would appear that antidepressant medications sometimes surpass psychotherapy in the short term and in the treatment of endogenous depression (Andrews, 1983; see also Chapters 10 and 18, this volume). Robinson et al.'s (1990) review, the most well-controlled and exhaustive of the reviews of depression, suggests that future research on depression should focus on questions dealing with *how* psychotherapy works rather than *whether* it works.

Table 5.2 summarizes meta-analytic reviews of a variety of treatments for anxiety-based disorders. It summarizes data on a more diverse sample of disorders than Table 5.1, ranging from those that might be expected to show high improvement rates (e.g., public speaking anxiety) to those where improvement is more difficult to attain (e.g., obsessive compulsive disorder). But the general conclusions are the same: Psychotherapies clearly show effectiveness compared to wait-list and no-treatment control comparison groups. For example, the four reviews that summarize results on agoraphobia, a complicated anxiety disorder with biological as well as psychological components, show rather substantial gains for patients who received cognitive-behavioral interventions. Typical of outcome on this dis-

TABLE 5.2 Meta-analytic reviews of outcome in anxiety disorders

Researchers	Patient Diagnosis/Treatment	Number of Studies	Effect Size
Allen, Hunter, & Donohue (1989)	Public speaking anxiety	97	.51
Christensen, Hadzi-Pavlovic, Andrews, & Mattick (1987)	Obsessive compulsive disorder/Exposure treatment	5	1.37
Clum (1989)	Panic, agoraphobia/Behavior therapy	283	70%[a]
	No therapy	46	30%[a]
Hyman, Feldman, Harris, Levin, & Malloy (1989)	Relaxation training	48	.58
Jorm (1989)	Trait anxiety and neuroticism	63	.53
Mattick, Andrews, Hadzi-Pavlovic, & Christensen	Agoraphobia	51	1.62[bc]
	Wait-list controls		.02[ac]
Quality Assurance Project (1982)	Agoraphobia	25	1.2[c]
Quality Assurance Project (1985a)	Anxiety	81	.98
Quality Assurance Project (1985b)	Obsessive compulsive/Exposure therapy	38	1.34
Trull, Neitzel, & Main (1988)	Agoraphobia	19	2.10[c]

[a]Percent improved.
[b]Weighted average.
[c]Pretest/posttest measurement.

order, Mattick, Andrews, Hadzi-Pavlovic, and Christensen (1990) found no gains (mean effect size = − 0.02) in wait-list subjects while the average gain in treated patients on measures of phobia averaged 1.62 standard deviation units. This occurred despite the fact that the typical patient had suffered from agoraphobic symptoms an average of nine years prior to the initiation of treatment.

Similarly, Trull, Nietzel, and Main (1988) were able to show that the average treated patient started out at the 97th percentile of a "normative community sample on a measure of agoraphobia and progressed (toward being less fearful) to the 68th percentile of the normative sample by the end of treatment.

Reviews of the treatment of agoraphobia and panic disorder have produced results similar to those on depression. The psychotherapies that have been tested with these disorders are, in general, equal to or more effective than pharmacotherapeutic interventions, especially when follow-up data are considered because relapse rates are typically higher for treatment with medication only.

Table 5.3 presents reviews of a much broader

TABLE 5.3 Meta-analytic reviews of outcome on a variety of disorders and techniques

Researchers	Diagnosis/Treatment	Number of Studies	Effect Size
Andrews & Harvey (1981)	Neurotic	81	.72
Andrews, Guitar, & Howie (1980)	Stuttering	29	1.30
Asay, Lambert, Christensen, & Beutler (1984)	Mixed mental health centers	9[a]	.82[b]
Balestrieri, Williams, & Wilkinson (1988)	Mixed	11	.22
Barker, Funk, & Houston (1988)	Mixed	17	1.05
Benton & Schroeder (1990)	Schizophrenia	23	.76[b]
Blanchard, Andrasik, Ahles, Teders, & O'Keefe (1980)	Headache	35	40–80%[c]
Bowers & Clum (1988)	Behavior therapy	69	.76
Christensen, Hadzi-Pavlovic, Andrews, & Mattick (1987)	Behavior treatment	10	1.16
	Control	4	.04
Crits-Christoph (1992)	Short-term dynamic therapy	11	86%[c]
			50%[c]
Dush, Hirt, & Schroeder (1983)	Self-statement modification	69	.74
Giblin, Sprenkle, & Sheehan (1985)	Family therapy	85	.44
Hahlweg & Markman (1988)	Behavioral marital therapy	17	.95
	Premarital intervention	7	.79
Hazelrigg, Cooper, & Borduin (1987)	Family therapy/Family interaction	7	.45
	Self-rating	6	.50
Hill (1987)	Paradoxical treatment	15	.99
Holroyd (1990)	Migraine headache/Biofeedback	22	47.3%[c]
	No treatment	15	.2%[c]
Laessle, Zoettle, & Pirke (1987)	Bulimia	9	1.14[b]
Landman & Dawes (1982)	Mixed	42	.90
Lyons & Woods (1991)	Rational emotive therapy	70	.98
Markus, Lange, & Pettigrew (1990)	Family therapy	10	.70[d]
Miller & Berman (1983)	Cognitive-behavioral therapy	38	.83
Nicholson & Berman (1983)	Neurotic	47[e]	.70
Prout & De Martino (1986)	School-based therapy	33	.58
Quality Assurance Project (1984)	Schizophrenia	5	.00
Shapiro & Shapiro (1982a)	Mixed	143	1.03
Shoham-Salomon & Rosenthal (1987)	Paradoxical treatment	10	.42
Smith, Glass, & Miller (1980)	Mixed	475	.85
Svartberg & Stiles (1991)	Short-term dynamic therapy	7	55%[c]
	No treatment	7	45%[c]
Wampler (1982)	Marital communication	20	.43
Weisz, Weiss, Alicke, & Klotz (1987)	Mixed adolescent	108	.79

[a]Number of mental health centers.
[b]Pretest/posttest measurement.
[c]Percent improved.
[d]Control included alternative treatment and nontreatment.
[e]Number of comparison groups.

range of client disorders and treatment methods. While Tables 5.1 and 5.2 dealt with the most frequently occurring clinical problems in outpatient practice (depressed and anxious patients), Table 5.3 summarizes patients ranging from schizophrenic (Quality Assurance Project, 1984) and the chronically mentally ill (Asay, Lambert, Christensen, & Beutler, 1984) to clients undergoing preventative measures (e.g., Hahlweg & Markman, 1988). Most of these studies provide evidence on a combination of disorders and treatments. The data in Table 5.3 are similar to the other reports in suggesting significant treatment effects compared to a variety of control conditions.

The studies in these tables provide data that are far more complex than can be conveyed here, but these meta-analytic reviews provide the reader with a general picture of the results measuring the general effectiveness of psychotherapy. They represent summary figures on thousands of patients and hundreds of therapists from across the Western world. They represent data from mildly disturbed persons with specific limited symptoms as well as severely impaired patients whose disorders are both personally intolerable and socially dysfunctional. The changes made by these patients are reflected in diverse and comprehensive measures of improvement that include a variety of perspectives, including those of patients, patients' families, therapists, and various measures of social role functioning.

Tables 5.1 to 5.3 show that the average effect associated with psychological treatment approaches one standard deviation unit. By the standards developed by Cohen (1977) for the quantitative evaluation of empirical relations in behavioral science, the effects shown are statistically large. The results of meta-analyses suggest that the assignment to treatment versus control conditions accounts for some 10 percent of the variation in outcome among individuals assessed in a typical study. Smith et al. (1980) illustrated the clinical meaning of this effect size by contrasting effect sizes derived from therapy outcome studies to those achieved in other situations. For example, in elementary schools the effect of nine months of instruction in reading is about 0.67 standard deviation units. The increment in mathematics achievement resulting from the use of computer-based instruction is 0.40 standard deviation units.

The effect sizes produced in psychotherapy can also be compared to those that are derived from the use of psychoactive medication. For example, Andrews found that treatments for agoraphobics involving graded exposure produced a median effect size of 1.30 while antidepressant medication produced an average effect size of 1.10 (Quality

Assurance Project, 1983). With depression, the effect sizes produced for antidepressants ranged from 0.81 to 0.40 depending upon the type of antidepressant and patient population. Thus, the effect sizes produced through the application of psychotherapies are typically as large as or larger than those produced by a variety of methods typically employed in medical and educational interventions.

While the aforementioned data provide one way of examining the effects of therapy and the strength of psychosocial treatments on symptoms and adjustments, effect sizes are an abstraction. There is a need to move from that abstraction back to the clinical significance of changes summarized in the effect size statistic. Rosenthal (1983) recognized the need to make effect sizes more intuitively appealing and suggested that an effect size could be reexpressed as a comparison of the percentage of cases considered improved versus the percentage of cases considered unimproved (binomial effect size display). The expression of the 10 percent figure mentioned by Smith et al. (1980) and previously noted here can be transformed into percentage of persons improved (see Table 5.4, adapted from Rosenthal [1983]). This table shows that the proportion of variance accounted for by being in treatment is equivalent to increasing the success rate from 34 to 66 percent.

The use of the binomial effect size display to index the practical value of research results has been called into question by some researchers (Crow, 1991; McGraw, 1991; Strahan, 1991) but has been defended by Rosenthal (1990, 1991) as effective at clarifying treatment results under most circumstances.

Another method of converting effect size data into more clinically meaningful statistics was reported by Asay et al. (1984) in their study of community mental health center clients. In this study, the average effect size for the 2,405 clients

TABLE 5.4   The binomial effect size display for a correlation between assignment to treatment and therapeutic outcome of 0.32.*

Condition	TREATMENT OUTCOME Percentage Improved	Percentage Not Improved	Sum
Treatment	66	34	100
Control	34	66	100
Sum	100	100	200

*That is, when 10% of the variance is accounted for.
Source: Adapted by permission from Rosenthal (1983). Copyright 1983 by the American Psychological Association.

(seen at nine different locations and exposed to a wide variety of treatments) was 0.92. When one sets a somewhat arbitrary cutoff score of 0.50 standard deviation units as the defining point for considering people improved, then 66 percent of the cases would be considered improved, 26 percent unchanged, and 8 percent worse. Thus, the effect size can be used to estimate improvement rates.

It is important to reiterate that the changes occurring in patients as a result of therapy are neither trivial nor just cold statistics but are instead substantial. A considerable number of people who might be classified as "cases" before treatment would be considered sufficiently enough improved that they would no longer be so classified following treatment. Although the exact proportion who are improved is subject to considerable interpretation (Jacobson, 1988), clinically meaningful changes are taking place whether the goals of treatment are narrowly defined and specific (symptoms of anxiety, depressed affect, sleep disturbance, grade point average, etc.) or are more global in nature (social adjustment, work adjustment, marital adjustment, etc.). A discussion of the clinical significance of outcomes is further elaborated upon in Chapters 2 and 3 in this volume. Suffice it to say here that even more stringent criteria can be applied to change indexes that greatly reduce the percentage of patterns considered improved. Nevertheless, even that percentage substantially exceeds improvement rates in untreated groups.

The use of meta-analysis in psychotherapy outcome research has provoked controversy, despite its claims to objectivity. Detailed consideration of such issues is beyond our present scope; but Kazdin (Chapter 2, this volume) provides a more complete analysis of these issues.

Is improvement related to amount of therapy received? Data relevant to the general effects of therapy have been published that examine improvement rates in treated groups over time. Howard, Kopta, Krause, and Orlinsky (1986) reported a meta-analysis on 2,431 patients from published research covering a 30-year period. Their analysis showed a stable pattern across studies reflecting the relationship of amount of therapy and improvement. An illustration of their results displaying the dose-response relationship is reproduced in Figure 5.1.

Their analysis of these data indicates that by the eighth session approximately 50 percent of patients are measurably improved and that 75 percent of patients have shown measurable improvement by the end of six months of once-a-week psychotherapy (26 sessions), thus indicating a substantial therapeutic effect that occurs in a relatively

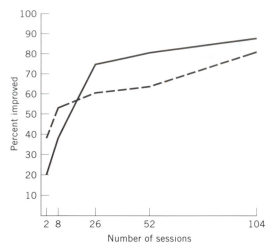

FIGURE 5.1 Relation of number of sessions of psychotherapy and percent of patients improved: objective ratings at termination (solid line); subjective ratings during therapy (broken line). (Reproduced by permission from H. I. Howard, S. M. Kopta, M. S. Krause, & D. E. Orlinsky [1986]. Copyright 1986 by the American Psychological Association.)

short period of time. This is an important observation because of arguments that positive change may occur due to "spontaneous remission" over time in untreated cases (Eysenck, 1952). Howard et al. (1986) have demonstrated that the amount of change and the rate of change in untreated groups are substantially less than those occurring among treated cases, and McNeilly and Howard (1991) have recently shown this even more dramatically. The more rapid effect of psychotherapy versus no-treatment is important because suffering is relieved faster, just as in many medical treatments where rapid relief is judged valuable even though symptoms may eventually improve with time without treatment.

This improvement takes place even with symptoms that suggest characterological problems and serious psychopathology. Kopta, Howard, Lowry, and Beutler (1992) also attempted to analyze the dose-effect relationship by examining differential dose-effect curves in relation to types of symptoms: acute distress, chronic distress, and characterological symptoms. As expected, differential response rates were associated with dose and type of symptom. For example, chronic distress was alleviated to clinically significant levels in 74 to 89 percent of the patients by the 52nd session. In contrast, characterological symptoms responded substantially but slowly with less than 60 percent of patients improved by the 52nd session.

The positive overall results of psychotherapy by no means suggest, however, that every participant gains from treatment to a clinically meaningful extent; results are also compatible with the suggestion, discussed elsewhere in this chapter, that some clients do not change and some may even deteriorate during therapy.

Despite some residual difficulties in interpreting results, the overall finding that psychological treatments are in general effective cannot be "explained away" by reference to methodological weaknesses in the data reviewed or to the reviewing methods. An overwhelming number of controlled studies reveal a positive therapeutic effect when compared with no-treatment; and very few reviewers disagree with this basic overall observation. Much of this chapter, and much of the rest of this book, is therefore devoted to analyzing other specific questions that take us beyond the issue of whether an average positive change occurs in treated cases.

Do the Effects of Therapies Exceed Those Resulting from Placebo Controls?

It has been adequately demonstrated that a variety of psychotherapies have effects that are greater than those of spontaneous remission and of a variety of no-treatment controls. This is no small achievement. However, psychotherapy's effect in relation to placebo effects remains somewhat controversial. Debates about this issue (cf. Prioleau, Murdock, & Brody, 1983, and responses in the same journal issue; see also Bloch & Lambert, 1985; Shepherd, 1984, for early discussions; and Bowers & Clum, 1988; Brody, 1990; Clum & Bowers, 1990, for more contemporary discussions) are reminiscent of the previous debates about spontaneous remission documented in earlier editions of this *Handbook* chapter. While the data are not altogether clear and sufficient to resolve all of the issues surrounding the degree to which psychotherapies surpass placebos, there is considerable disillusionment with the placebo concept in psychotherapy research.

Psychology borrowed the idea of placebo controls from medicine. In medical research, the effects of an active pharmacological agent are contrasted with the effects of a pharmacologically inert or nontherapeutic substance, called a *placebo*. This contrast makes good sense with respect to drug therapies. It allows for the attribution of success to the pharmacological agent rather than any improvement due to the psychological effects of being treated or taking "medicine."

Placebo controls make less sense, however, when extended to psychotherapy research where the effects of both formal treatments *and* placebos depend upon psychological mechanisms. Many authors entirely reject the placebo concept in psychotherapy research because it is not conceptually consistent with testing the efficacy of psychological

procedures (e.g., Dush, 1986; Senger, 1987; Horvath, 1988; Wilkins, 1984).

In psychology, the placebo construct has taken on a variety of meanings. For example, Rosenthal and Frank (1956) defined a placebo as being theoretically inert. It is inert, however, only from the standpoint of the *theory* of the therapy studied. As Critelli and Neumann (1984) have pointed out, a problem with this definition is that "virtually every currently established psychotherapy would be considered inert, and therefore a placebo, from the viewpoint of other established theories of cure" (p. 33). This definition of a psychological placebo is highly questionable.

Placebos have also been labeled as *nonspecific* factors. This conceptualization, however, raises serious questions about the definition of that term. For example, once a nonspecific factor is labeled, does it then become a specific factor and fall outside the domain of a placebo effect? Similarly, if an influence such as "therapist warmth" is considered to be a placebo because it is not a specific technique, how can it also be a substantial factor in client change, as some theories postulate and many studies show?

Others have suggested the term *common factors* in recognition that many therapies have ingredients that are not unique. Thus, research on placebo effects would be better conceptualized as research on common factors versus the specific effects of a particular technique. Common factors are those dimensions of the treatment setting (therapist, therapy, client) that are not specific to any particular technique. Research on the broader concept of common factors will be discussed later in this chapter; here it is important to note that those factors that are common to most therapies (such as expectation for improvement, persuasion, warmth and attention, understanding, and encouragement) should not be viewed as theoretically inert or as trivial. Indeed, these factors are central to psychological interventions in both theory and practice. They play an active role in patient improvement (cf. Butler & Strupp, 1986; Critelli & Neumann, 1984; Omer, 1989; Parloff, 1986). This role will be spelled out later in this chapter.

It shouldn't matter whether therapy effects are the result of common factors or unique techniques. But psychotherapy research is often designed to find effects that are incremental to common factors. In interpreting this research, it is important to keep in mind that failure to find incremental effects (effects beyond those attributable to common factors) for a specific therapy does not mean that psychotherapy is ineffective. Rather it means that no effect has been demonstrated beyond the effects of the common factors. This is a critical point because research that is aimed at discovering the incremental effects of therapy has been misinterpreted as suggesting that therapies are ineffective (e.g., Prioleau et al., 1983; Shepherd, 1984).

The most controversial article on this subject was published by Prioleau et al. (1983), who reanalyzed data from the Smith et al. (1980) meta-analysis. Prioleau et al. interpreted these data as suggesting that formal psychotherapy was not more effective than placebo therapies designed to emphasize attention and support, but the validity of the conclusions of this review were seriously questioned in the majority of commentaries accompanying the article. Prioleau et al.'s conclusions cannot be accepted at face value.

In fact, a number of additional analyses have now been conducted comparing the outcome of patients in so-called "placebo" or "nonspecific" comparison groups[1] with patients who were either treated or in wait-list control groups. Table 5.5 summarizes studies and reviews of research on this topic. The reviews in this table overlap to various degrees so that each does not contain totally independent in-

formation. The number of studies contained in each review is listed, but the mean effect size presented is often based on a smaller number of studies. The n presented by each mean effect size represents the number of effects calculated (i.e., the number of treatment groups used in its calculation). These reviews consider a wide variety of disorders with an overrepresentation of anxiety-based problems and behavioral interventions. Verbal therapies are seldom tested in placebo comparison research designs.

The reader will note that the effect sizes for the psychotherapy versus no-treatment group are consistently larger than those of the placebo versus no-treatment comparison. In addition, when psychotherapy effect sizes are calculated in relation to placebo controls (the last column in Table 5.5), they still show psychotherapy to surpass placebo comparison treatments.

These data are displayed graphically in Figure 5.2 and can be expressed in percentage improvement rates. The average patient undergoing a placebo treatment appears to be better off than 66 percent of the no-treatment controls. The average patient undergoing psychotherapy appears to be better off than 79 percent of the no-treatment controls. These data are similar to those presented by Schroeder and Dush (1987) based upon two meta-

[1]We use the term *comparison* group rather than *control* group because so-called placebo therapies are, in fact, forms of therapeutic psychological influence that are being compared with another form of therapeutic influence.

TABLE 5.5   Comparisons of no-treatment, placebo control, and psychotherapy

Study	n^a	Psychotherapy vs. No-treatment ES(n^b, σ_{ES^c})	Placebo vs. No-treatment ES(n^b, σ_{ES^c})	Psychotherapy vs. Placebo ES(n^b, σ_{ES^c})
Andrews & Harvey (1981)	81	.72 (292, .03)*	—	.55 (28, .06)
Barker, Funk, & Houston (1988)	17	1.06 (20, .136)*	.47 (20, .071)	.55 (31, .11)
Bowers & Clum (1988)	69	.76 (n = 40)	.55 (n = 69)	—
Dush, Hirt, & Shroeder (1983)	31	—	.21 (219, .03)	—
Dush, Hirt, & Schroeder (1989)	48	.51 (n = 60)	—	.41 (n = 142)
Eppley, Abrams, & Sheer (1989)	70	.43 (100, .076)*	.23 (14, .14)	—
Hill (1987)	15	.99 (39, .123)*	.56 (60, .062)	—
Hyman, Feldman, Harris, Levin, & Malloy (1989)	48/8[e]	.58 (55, .115)	—	.66 (14, .142)
Jorm (1989)	63	.53 (100, .048)	—	.46 (10, .146)
Laessle, Zoettle, & Pirke (1987)	23	1.12[d] (n = 37)	—	.10[d] (n = 8)
Landman & Dawes (1982)	42	.80 (5, . 30)	.58 (4, .31)	.51 (5, .32)
Miller & Berman (1983)	48	.78	.38	—
Prioleau, Murdock, & Brody (1983)	32	—	.32	—
Quality Assurance Project (1983)	10	1.72[d]	.65[d] (10, .17)	1.07[d]
Smith, Glass, & Miller (1980)	475	.85 (1761, .03)*	.56 (200, .05)	—
Total[f]	1,080	.82 (n = 2,309)	.42 (n = 596)	.48 (n = 250)

Source: Reprinted by permission of the authors, Lambert, Weber & Sykes (1993).

[a]Number of studies.

[b]Number of effects.

[c]Standard error of the mean.

[d]Effect sizes based on pre/post changes rather than control/treatment comparison.

[e]Two separate meta-analyses were done.

[f]Totals do not represent independent information because some reviews include studies also reviewed by other researchers.

*p<.005.

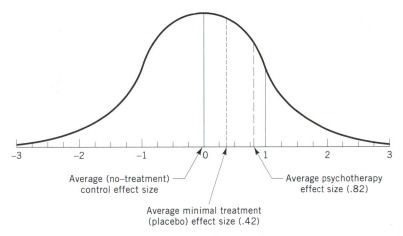

FIGURE 5.2   Comparison of placebo and psychotherapy effects in relation to no-treatment control. (Reprinted by permission of the authors, Lambert, Weber, & Sykes [1993].)

analytic reviews (Dush, Hirt, & Shroeder, 1983; Smith et al., 1980).

Data from these two meta-analytic reviews resulted in an average effect size of 0.93 (psychotherapy versus no-treatment) and 0.33 (placebo versus no-treatment). In terms of percentage improved, the average placebo patient moved to the 63rd percentile of no-treatment controls, while the average psychotherapy patient moved from the 50th percentile to the 82nd percentile of the no-treatment group. These estimates of treatment effects seem fairly consistent with the data presented in Tables 5.1 to 5.5 and provide a reasonable baseline for contrasting treatment effects with so-called placebo controls. We recommend their use to researchers as a substitute for the placebo control group because further experimentation with the placebo control is not as useful as a variety of alternative research strategies such as components analysis.

The results presented in Table 5.5 are as might be expected: Patients in so-called placebo control groups typically show greater improvement than patients who are assigned to a wait-list or no-treatment control group. Although the effects of these common factors placebo approaches are smaller than those of formal psychotherapy, they do seem to show that the common factors do have efficacy, and so yield substantial effect sizes.

This finding is also reported in a variety of traditional reviews. Clum (1989), for example, reviewed psychological and pharmacological interventions used to treat agoraphobia and panic. The psychological treatments employed in numerous studies resulted in a 70 percent improvement rate compared to 40 percent for placebo clients and 30 percent for no-treatment controls. Holroyd (1990) reported similar differences in his review of psychological versus pharmacological treatment of mi-

graine headache. He reported that 47 percent of those getting a psychological intervention (mostly relaxation-based) improved, while 12 percent of the placebo controls and less than 1 percent of the no-treatment subjects improved. His review considered approximately 35 to 50 clinical trials over two decades!

In one of the more interesting studies of this topic, Barker, Funk, and Houston (1988) used meta-analysis to compare the effectiveness of psychological treatments to nonspecific (placebo) control conditions and no-treatment controls. They limited their review to studies in which no significant differences were found in the subjects' expectancies for improvement (between the treatment and placebo groups). Seventeen studies that met the inclusion criteria were located. Barker et al. found that treatments and placebos were more effective than no-treatment and that the treatments were superior to the placebos, having about twice the effect that placebos had. Some potentially important study characteristics were found to be related to outcome. For example, greater treatment effects were noted in nonuniversity settings with nonstudent clients and when a mixture of professionals and graduate students provided therapy (rather than graduate students alone). These findings suggest that placebo comparison methods may have less impact on more severe disorders and when compared with the effectiveness of more experienced therapists.

The review by Barker et al. (1988) has the advantage of including a limited set of studies that employed carefully developed placebos, a rarity in this area. The placebo manipulations were examined and found to be successful because they produced expectations for improvement to the same degree as the bonafide treatments. This is a rigorous test of the strength of treatment effects. Despite the fact that some aspects of the placebo were genuinely seen as helpful by patients, the formal therapy resulted in greater change.

Unfortunately, these results are limited by the small number of studies that made up this review and also by the relatively brief therapy (mean = 6.9 contact hours). They are also limited by the types of active treatments and psychological conditions for which placebo controls were used. The studies reviewed had a narrow cross section of commonly employed psychotherapies and placebo control groups. To what extent do placebo control groups really encompass that which is embodied in psychotherapy as it is usually practiced? Here we may note that Horvath (1988) reviewed two decades of research on placebos and came to a conclusion different from many other writers by arguing that placebo therapies do not, in fact, have much in common with bonafide therapies. He suggests that placebo control groups are not adequate to control for the host of various nonspecific variables present in psychotherapy.

After reviewing a wide array of methodological designs and treatment outcomes, we have concluded that the typical placebo controls used in outcome studies are so conceptually and procedurally flawed that they have essentially failed in their purpose of helping to isolate the active therapeutic ingredients. It is time to discontinue placebo controls and design studies with more meaningful comparison groups.

Are Patients Who Improve in Therapy Able to Maintain Their Gains?

While outcome research has focused primarily upon the immediate posttreatment status of patients who have participated in therapy, there is considerable interest in the long-term effects of treatment. Several issues are important here: What kinds of changes persist? At what level? What factors influence the likelihood of maintenance and relapse? How can we maximize the likelihood that the resolution of current and past problems will also increase the patient's ability to cope with future events?

Although there is no reason to believe that a single course of psychotherapy should inoculate a person forever from psychological disturbance and the development of symptoms, many patients who undergo therapy achieve healthy adjustment for long periods of time. This is true despite the fact that they have had a long history of recurrent problems. At the same time, there is clear evidence that a portion of patients who are improved at termination do relapse and continue to seek help from a variety of mental health providers, including their former therapists. In fact, several problems such as drug addictions, alcohol abuse, smoking, obesity, and possibly depression are so likely to recur that they are not considered properly studied without data collection one year after treatment. Yet, even with alcohol problems, 30 percent stay sober and 30 percent and above return to a *reduced* level of drinking after treatment (Bellack & Hersen, 1990).

Nicholson and Berman (1983) used meta-analytic techniques to answer the question: Is follow-up necessary in evaluating psychotherapy? In their review of research in this area, they were primarily concerned with whether follow-up evaluations provided different evidence and conclusions than posttreatment evaluations. The review excluded psychotic disorders, organic disorders, antisocial personality disorders, and addictive problems such as obesity, smoking, and alcoholism. They included 67 studies (21% of which evaluated a verbal therapy) of a broad range of patients with neurotic disorders who were self-referred rather than recruited and that involved both posttesting and follow-up data. The analysis was approached in several ways: (1) Does posttreatment status correlate with follow-up status? (2) Were treatment differences apparent at the posttesting still apparent at follow-up? (3) Are any changes at follow-up testing due to deterioration or improvements in treated groups?

The results of this meta-analytic review are complicated by the divergence in the studies that were examined, but, in general, the findings suggest that treatment gains are maintained. Posttherapy status correlated with follow-up status; differences between treatments apparent at the end of therapy were virtually the same at follow-up. This finding held up whether the comparison was with no-treatment controls or another therapy. And the level of outcome was typically unchanged during the follow-up period. These findings held across a variety of treatment methods (79% were behavioral or an eclectic combination of cognitive-behavioral), patient populations, and sources for assessing outcome. The mean length of follow-up assessment was over eight months, but varied from one month to several years. The correlation between posttreatment and follow-up results was unrelated to the length of follow-up. The authors concluded:

Past reviews have revealed that psychotherapy produces considerable initial improvement, and our findings indicate that for a broad range of disorders this improvement stands the test of time. Thus, our evidence should be heartening both to practitioners, who are increasingly being asked to defend the efficacy of treatment, and to researchers, who have long struggled with the costs of follow-up designs. (Nicholson & Berman, 1983, p. 275)

The review by Nicholson and Berman (1983) is especially important because it stands in marked contrast to earlier reviews both in its conclusions and in its methodological sophistication. For example, Smith et al. (1980) as well as Shapiro and Shapiro (1982a), using meta-analysis, and Goldstein, Lopez, and Greenleaf (1979), using traditional reviewing methods, all found that differences between treated groups and controls were smaller at follow-up than at the end of therapy often because of gains in control subjects rather than relapse in those who were involved in treatment. In contrast, Landman and Dawes (1982), who, with a subset of Smith et al.'s data, examined only studies that had both posttreatment and follow-up assessment, reported results consistent with Nicholson and Berman (1983). Andrews and Harvey (1981) also found improvement to be stable over time. They concluded that improvement following treatment is stable for many months and then slowly declines at a rate of 0.2 effect size units per annum.

More recent reviews present findings that are consistent with the report by Nicholson and Berman (1983). Some even suggest a trend toward continuing improvement during the follow-up period for a number of subjects. These reviews looked at a broad spectrum of problems and at a full range of therapies (especially behavioral therapy).

Jorm (1989) reviewed the effects of various therapies on the modification of trait anxiety and neuroticism. This meta-analysis identified 12 studies that included follow-up evaluation at least 12 months following termination of treatment. The correlation between posttest and follow-up effect size was 0.43. The mean ES at posttest was 0.45 and at follow-up it was 0.58. This difference was not statistically significant. It suggests that the differences between treated and untreated subjects was not reduced even a year or more after treatment was terminated.

Typical of reviews in the area, Nietzel, Russell, Hemmings, and Gretter (1987) summarized the maintenance of gains in patients who underwent treatments for depression. This review involved 28 studies (70% of which provided follow-up data) that had relied on a self-report of depressive symptoms. The treatment involved a variety of therapies, almost two-thirds of which were provided in a group format. Treatment of the 1,040 clients lasted for an average of 16 hours and follow-up data were collected (on average) four months posttherapy. For the studies providing follow-up data, patients mean depression scores were slightly lower (improved) at

follow-up than at posttreatment. The length of follow-up was not related to the degree of depression at the end of the follow-up period.

Similar results were found in a broader review of the depression literature. Robinson et al. (1990) reported the meta-analysis of treatment outcomes for depression that was not limited to self-report data. Data from nine studies reporting both posttreatment and follow-up results provided almost identical effect sizes. The effect sizes present at posttreatment were highly predictive of follow-up effect size ($r = .98$, $p < .001$). This finding prompted the authors to suggest that researchers may want to invest time and energy on aspects of the research protocol other than follow-up. Unfortunately, the follow-up period ranged from 2 to 52 weeks with an average of only 13 weeks and no correlation between effect size and time was reported.

A few typical studies may help the reader grasp the nature and breadth of findings in this area, especially the variations in results that occur as a function of patient diagnosis. Gallagher-Thompson, Hanley-Peterson, and Thompson (1990) reported a 2-year follow-up study of 91 depressed older adults who had undergone brief cognitive, behavioral, or psychodynamic psychotherapy. Using research diagnostic criteria, 52, 58, and 70 percent of patients who underwent any of the treatments were improved at posttherapy, 12 months, and 24 months following therapy, respectively. The majority of patients who were not depressed at the end of therapy remained depression-free at follow-up (e.g., 83% of those free of depression posttherapy were depression-free at the 1-year follow-up, 77% at the 2-year follow-up).

Blanchard (1987) summarized effects of cognitive, behavioral, and relaxation treatments on the long-term outcome of chronic headache. Results from nine studies that followed patients from one to four years present a mixed picture. Headache relief appears to be fairly lasting over two to four years for the cognitive-behavioral treatments. Patients who undergo relaxation alone seem to show a gradual but steady increase in headache over the follow-up, although patients as a group do not return to pretreatment levels. Booster sessions do not seem to have a lasting effect, and there is evidence that many patients maintain their gains without continual practice of relaxation techniques.

Brownell and Jeffery (1987) criticize past behavioral work with obesity as insufficient. They note that the weight losses that are to be "maintained" are not large and that research needs to become more intensive, innovative, long term, and selective. Research in this area suggests that interventions are becoming longer or more intensive, resulting in greater initial weight loss. In addition, the length of follow-up periods is increasing so that a clearer picture of long-term group effects of treatment is emerging. Unfortunately, fluctuations in weight loss for specific individuals are rarely studied. Doing so would illuminate individual behavior patterns and identify the percentage of patients who are able to steadily maintain weight losses in the long run.

In contrast to the extensive work on obesity, other eating disorders show less intensive study. Oesterheld, McKenna, and Gould (1987) summarized and compared the key features of group treatment of bulimia in 18 reports and found outcome (usually a percentage reduction in binge/purge episodes) ranged from a *52 to a 97 percent* reduction in binging, purging, or binge/purge episodes. Most groups clustered around *70 percent reduction in symptoms* at the end of treatment. Although the overall results of the studies seemed impressive, they represented short-term gains with a notable lack of long-term follow-up data. In most of the reports, it was either unclear or unknown whether the posttreatment gains were sustained over time. Many reports presented no long-term follow-up or only impressionistic data, and only 4 (Dixon & Kiecolt-Glaser, 1984; Schnieder & Agras, 1985; Stevens & Salisbury, 1984; Wolchik, Weiss, & Katzman, 1986) presented comparable data on percentage reduction in symptoms posttreatment and at follow-up. At variable periods of follow-up, all less than a year, the patients in these four groups maintained good results. Unfortunately, outcome data in this area is often expressed as percentage reduction in symptoms, rather than complete abstinence, and many improved subjects continued to binge close to three times per week.

Jacobson (1989) reported a synopsis of research on the maintenance of treatment gains following social learning – based marital therapy. Of patients who received only behavioral exchange training, 80 percent relapsed during the six-month follow-up. Those who received communication/problem-solving training and behavioral exchange, or communication/problem-solving training alone reported higher levels of marital satisfaction at the end of the follow-up than they did at posttesting, with relapse rates close to 15 to 20 percent. During the second six months following termination, couples who received the combined treatments continued to do well while those who received just the communication/problem-solving treatment relapsed to the level of patients receiving only behavioral exchange. During the second follow-up year, the combined group showed more relapse but remained, as a group, significantly better off than they had been at the start of treatment. In fact, half the couples in

the combined treatment were functioning in the nondistressed range of marital satisfaction. Unfortunately, nearly 25 percent of the couples had deteriorated to levels below those of their initial consultation. In summarizing, Jacobson suggests that of those patients who are initially helped by therapy, 70 percent continue to maintain their gains and 30 percent return to baseline or are worse two years following treatment. Therefore, of those couples who come for therapy the probability is .5 that they will benefit to a clinically significant degree and maintain this improvement for two years.

Snyder, Wills, and Grady-Fletcher (1991) reported a four-year follow-up of behavioral versus insight-oriented marital therapy. While no differences were found between these two treatments at termination or six months following termination, some differences were present at the four-year follow-up. Of most interest was the fact that a significantly higher percentage of those who had received behavioral marital therapy were divorced during the follow-up period (38%), while only 3 percent of the couples receiving insight-oriented treatment had divorced. Snyder et al. (1991) suggest the high rate of deterioration in behavioral therapy is typical of rates found in long-term follow-up studies. What is unusual is the low rate found in couples who received the more affectively based insight-oriented treatment.

Results from studies and reviews of follow-up studies are encouraging, and therefore greater selection in the application of follow-up designs is recommended. For example, continuing use of follow-up studies on depression outcome is recommended, but only if the length of the follow-up time is extended to at least one year. *Short-term follow-up studies are no longer needed because treatment effects are usually maintained for at least several months.*

Behavioral psychologists have been very active in developing strategies that will enhance maintenance (e.g., Annis, 1990; Goldstein & Kanfer, 1979; Karoly & Steffan, 1980). Such tactics as "tapering off," "intervening treatments," "lifelong treatment," and "booster sessions" have some limited empirical support. The use of booster sessions is a well-researched area. For example, Whisman (1990) reviewed 30 studies of behavior therapy that employed booster maintenance sessions to enhance the permanence of behavioral change. The studies were published over an 18-year span and included 8 different problem areas, from addictions to physical health problems. Just over half the studies reviewed found some evidence for effectiveness for some subjects, but there was even more evidence for no effect and some evidence that boosters were effective only in delaying relapse. Thus, the status of booster treatments is unclear. Calls for eliminating maintenance sessions have been made, although Whisman (1990) suggests that even *delaying* relapse is a notable and important accomplishment with some disorders.

Dissatisfaction with the booster method has led in recent years to more emphasis on making sure that maintenance strategies focus more specifically and differentially on the needs of specific patients during the follow-up period. For instance, the types of situations that pose high risk for relapse appear to be similar across a variety of addictive behaviors. Unpleasant emotions, interpersonal conflict, and social pressure situations have been found to account for almost three-quarters of the relapses reported by alcoholics, smokers, and heroin addicts (Cummings, Gordon, & Marlatt, 1980).

A significant number of studies outside behavioral psychology have explored strategies to enhance the maintenance of treatment effects. A major factor in maintaining treatment gains seems to be the degree to which patients (as well as therapists) recognize that changes are partially the result of effective patient effort. For example, in a series of studies reported by the Johns Hopkins Psychotherapy Research Unit, patients who attributed their improvement to medication (actually a placebo) were not able to maintain improvement, while those who understood improvement to be a result of their own efforts did maintain their gains (Frank, 1976; Liberman, 1978).

In theory, when an individual enters a high-risk situation for relapse, a process of cognitive appraisal of past performances in the situation is triggered, resulting in an efficacy judgment that then determines whether or not a lapse will take place. Bandura's (1987) self-efficacy theory proposed that the most powerful methods of changing cognitions of self-efficacy are performance based. Thus, many relapse prevention models focus on having the client engage in homework assignments involving the performance of alternative coping responses in a high-risk situation for relapse. The expectation is that if an individual successfully implements alternative behaviors in the high-risk situations, appraisal of personal coping abilities will improve and increases in judgments of self-efficacy will result.

A distinction is clearly made between treatment strategies aimed at initiating a change in behavior and strategies aimed at actually maintaining a change in behavior. After the initial change in an addictive behavior, the second phase of treatment is the maintenance phase. During this phase of treatment, all external aids (such as drug treatment) are gradually withdrawn, and the focus shifts to promoting client self-inferences of personal efficacy. Empirical findings on a range of addictive behaviors support the relationship between self-efficacy ratings and treatment outcome. For example, the relation between self-efficacy and drinking behavior has been studied by various researchers, and they have found self-efficacy ratings to be significantly related to alcoholism treatment outcome (Annis, 1990). Research results regarding the cessation of drinking are consistent with findings on smoking behavior.

Imber, Pilkonis, Harway, Klein, and Rubinsky (1982) have provided a model that may be easily adopted in outpatient therapy with a broad spectrum of nonaddictive problems. As with some of the behavioral interventions, they stress termination and follow-up sessions. Within these sessions patients are encouraged to see *change* and its *maintenance* as a consequence of their own efforts. They are also helped to anticipate future life crises/stresses and their reactions to them. Patient attributional style and patient strengths are emphasized. Applications of these methods outside of problems with addiction have met with mixed success (Berlin, 1985).

A model for research in the area is an important study conducted on a subgroup of depressed patients who showed a clear history of repeated episodes of depression. What effects can maintenance strategies have on this difficult group of patients? Frank et al. (1990) studied 128 patients over a three-year period to determine the most effective strategy to reduce relapse in patients with recurrent depression. Based on past research, the authors decided to use a modified version of interpersonal psychotherapy in a maintenance format (IPT-m). They believed that despite limited empirical support, the improved social adjustment that results from this therapy would provide additional protection against future episodes. This therapy was contrasted with alternative treatments and a control group. In all, five treatment groups were employed: (1) a maintenance form of IPT (IPT-m), (2) IPT-m plus acute treatment doses of imipramine, (3) IPT-m with placebo, (4) imipramine alone, (5) placebo alone.

Only patients who were in their third or greater episode of unipolar depression were studied. And only those who manifested improvement following brief drug and IPT treatment were allowed into a 17-week continuation phase of the study. Maintenance treatment was then undertaken following random assignment to one of the conditions.

At the end of three years, only 20 percent of those on the medication placebo had not relapsed, a rate that is consistent with the natural course of this disorder. This outcome is in sharp contrast to patients who were maintained on treatment levels of medication, either alone or in combination with psychotherapy. At the end of the three-year maintenance period, nearly 80 percent of those on medication had not relapsed. Psychotherapy given at a rate of once a month seemed to result in a maintenance rate of 46 percent, a figure between the placebo and medication groups.

These results clearly suggest that psychotherapy at "low doses" can lengthen the time between depressive episodes in patients who are not receiving medication. This is especially important for patients who cannot or do not wish to continue receiving medication at therapeutic levels (e.g., 200 mg per day).

Research across a broad spectrum of disorders, including depression, suggests that there is no "magic pill" or simple insight that brings about ultimate recovery—recovery is most likely to result from continued efforts on the part of the patient. At the same time, many patients gain lasting improvements without using the techniques they have been taught. This is most evident in research on physiological disorders. As Blanchard (1987) states, "I suggest that maintenance of treatment effects endures in spite of almost universal cessation of regular home practice because the self-perpetuating cycle of chronic headache has been broken" (p. 381). It may be equally true in the treatment of depressive and anxiety-based disorders. Future research will help to determine which patients are in need of maintenance and which have somehow changed in some significant way, such that they will maintain a state of health, with or without additional treatment or strategies aimed at maintenance.

COMPARISONS AND CAUSATIVE FACTORS IN TREATMENT OUTCOMES: THE ROLE OF COMMON FACTORS AND SPECIFIC THERAPY INTERVENTIONS

In this section, we review research that further clarifies the factors associated with improvement during psychotherapy. This research, to a large extent, employs designs that are aimed at discovering the effects of specific therapeutic factors by contrasting an established treatment with a new treatment, an effective treatment with one or more of its component factors, or an effective treatment with a different effective treatment on a group of patients with special characteristics.

First, we explore evidence that deals with the differential effectiveness of different schools of therapy. Afterwards we return to the possibility that factors common across therapies may account for many of the therapeutic gains that are apparent in treatment groups.

Does the "Dodo Bird Verdict" Still Hold?

Historically, there has been a clear difference of approach between "schools" of therapy associated with psychodynamic and humanistic theories ("verbal" or "insight" therapies), on the one hand, and behavioral and cognitive theories ("action" therapies), on the other. Of course, it cannot be assumed that such global and philosophical divisions between treatment approaches are faithfully or functionally represented in the actual procedures implemented in the delivery of their respective therapies. There is a growing body of evidence, however, that the use of manuals to specify treatment techniques characteristic of the different schools results in objectively discriminable therapist behaviors (Luborsky & DeRubeis, 1984; Rounsaville, O'Malley, Foley, & Weissman, 1988). The use of therapy manuals and more experienced therapists also has been found to reduce the variability in outcome due to the therapist, allowing for more appropriate comparisons in comparative outcome studies (Crits-Christoph & Mintz, 1991). Whether these differences hold up in everyday routine clinical practice is an open question, however. The use of manuals is presumed to magnify the differences between therapies by reducing error that is introduced by specific therapists.

Many older reviews have analyzed studies comparing a wide range of psychotherapies (e.g., Bergin & Lambert, 1978; Bergin & Suinn, 1975; Beutler, 1979; Goldstein & Stein, 1976; Kellner, 1975; Lambert & Bergin, 1973; Meltzoff & Kornreich, 1970; Rachman & Wilson, 1980). The conclusion of most, but not all, of these reviews is like that drawn by Luborsky, Singer, and Luborsky (1975), who suggested a verdict similar to that of the Dodo bird in *Alice in Wonderland*: "Everyone has won and all must have prizes."

These reviews used traditional scholarly methods of reaching conclusions without reference to meta-analytic procedures. However, meta-analytic methods have now been extensively applied to large groups of comparative studies, and these reviews generally offer similar conclusions (i.e., little or no difference between therapies; see Table 5.3).

Some of the meta-analytic reviews show a small, but consistent, advantage for cognitive and behavioral methods over traditional verbal and relationship-oriented therapies (e.g., Dobson, 1989; Dush et al., 1983; Nicholson & Berman, 1983; Robinson et al., 1990; Shapiro & Shapiro, 1982a; Smith et al., 1980; Svartberg & Stiles, 1991). This is certainly not always the case (e.g., Shoham-Salomon & Rosenthal, 1987) but when differences are found they often favor cognitive or behavior approaches across a variety of patient diagnostic categories.

Such differences are, however, often explainable

in terms of methodological artifacts. Let us try to explain and clarify these issues, providing illustrations of the way they may impact evaluations of comparative outcomes.

Smith et al. (1980) reported some substantial differences between behavioral therapy and other approaches. However, the relatively large effect sizes reported for behavioral therapy were reduced when the analysis took into account the fact that behavioral studies used outcome measures that were judged to be more reactive to experimental demand. This resulted in Smith et al. (1980) concluding that the differences between therapies were minimal.

A problem in the Smith et al. review was that they had to rely on cross-study comparisons in which behavioral therapy in one study was compared with verbal therapy from another study. In this situation, many variables besides treatment modality also differ across studies. Comparisons like this, of which there are many in the Smith et al. (1980) report, cannot be as conclusive as comparisons in which the compared treatments are offered within a given study. These studies are much more likely to hold numerous variables constant while comparing one type of therapy with another.

To examine this issue more carefully, let us consider Shapiro and Shapiro's (1982b) extensive meta-analysis, which focused exclusively on studies comparing two or more active treatments with control conditions. Their data contained more replicated comparisons between treatment methods than found in the Smith et al. (1980) review and permitted more definitive statements concerning the comparative efficacy of treatments. Based on an examination of 143 studies, Shapiro and Shapiro (1982b) found that cognitive and various behavioral treatments yielded more favorable outcomes (1.00 and 1.06 ES, respectively) than dynamic and humanistic therapies, which yielded inferior outcomes (ES = 0.40).

As in the Smith et al. study, however, these authors also attributed the larger behavior therapy effect sizes to strong biases in the behavioral and cognitive literature toward analogue studies, mild cases, and highly reactive criteria. They stated that the treatments and cases studied were unrepresentative of clinical practice but very representative of the simple experiments on these techniques that are frequently conducted in university settings. While such criticisms must be taken into account, they are based upon post hoc analyses that may not do justice to cognitive and behavioral interventions.

Another issue of interest to practitioners and researchers is the relative effectiveness of cognitive versus behavioral methods. The Shapiro and Shapiro report showed a significantly larger effect size for cognitive therapy over systematic desensitization. This conclusion, however, has been challenged by yet another meta-analysis. Miller and Berman (1983) compared cognitive-behavioral therapy with various other therapies, mainly behavioral. The procedures followed were quite similar to those of Smith et al. (1980) except that the study rather than the individual measure of effect was used as the unit of analysis, and cognitive-behavioral therapies that differed in their emphasis upon behavioral techniques were accorded their own effect sizes within an analysis contrasting such treatments.

In comparisons with untreated groups, cognitive-behavorial therapies secured a mean effect size of 0.83 posttreatment (38 studies) and 0.63 at follow-up (18 studies). Comparisons with other therapies yielded a differential effect size of 0.21 at the end of treatment (36 studies) and 0.24 at follow-up (26 studies). Comparison with desensitization, the most frequent alternate treatment, yielded a nonsignificant effect size difference of 0.21 posttreatment (13 studies) and 0.23 at follow-up (9 studies).

A subsequent analysis (Berman, Miller, & Massman, 1985) using a larger sample of studies showed no difference between cognitive and desensitization therapies (ES difference 0.06). It also revealed that the larger effect sizes for cognitive therapy occurred in studies conducted by investigators having an allegiance to that method. Finally, the combination of desensitization with a cognitive method did not increase effects beyond those obtainable by either treatment alone.

In a more limited domain of inquiry, the treatment of depression, similar results were found. Dobson (1989) reviewed the effects of Beck's cognitive therapy for depression with a variety of other treatments including mostly behavioral therapy and pharmacotherapy as measured by changes in Beck Depression Inventory scores. In all, 28 studies were identified that met inclusion criteria. Of the 9 studies that compared cognitive and behavioral therapies, the average cognitive therapy client had an outcome that was superior to 67 percent of the behavioral therapy clients. Of the 8 studies comparing cognitive therapy with pharmacotherapy, the average cognitive therapy client surpassed 70 percent of those treated by medication. These results add to those already reported by Miller and Berman (1983) by including additional studies published since their review. This later review also has the advantage of examining a clearly defined type of cognitive therapy with a well-defined disorder.

Unfortunately, the analysis by Dobson is very brief and many of its details are left undefined. If taken at face value, it certainly suggests the specific superiority of cognitive therapy over a limited number of comparative treatments.

Robinson et al. (1990) have provided the most up-to-date, comprehensive review of comparative outcomes with depressive disorders. In their analysis of direct comparisons (i.e., within-study comparisons) of cognitive, behavioral, cognitive-behavioral, or general verbal therapies, they found equivalence between cognitive and cognitive-behavioral approaches, with the latter treatment showing some superiority to a strictly behavioral approach. Verbal therapies were less effective than all three alternative therapies with which they were compared.

When two independent raters judged investigator allegiance toward a treatment, and allegiance was then taken into account through regression, the differences between treatments vanished. Ratings were based on reading the introduction of the study. Some investigators had strong theoretical preferences for a particular treatment. In some cases preferences had to be inferred. Preferred therapies produced more improvement than their less favored counterparts; but when this bias was eliminated, therapies were equivalent. Similar results were reported for analysis of drug versus psychotherapy comparisons. The evidence that favored psychotherapies over medication disappeared when comparisons took into account experimenter allegiance.

Some meta-analytic reviews present evidence for the superiority of one treatment over another without identifying reasons for the difference. For example, Svartberg and Stiles (1991) examined the effects of short-term dynamic psychotherapy (STDP) in 19 studies published between 1978 and 1988. Their analysis showed that while STDP was superior to no-treatment, it was less effective than alternative therapies even at a one-year follow-up. In fact, the authors note that at the one-year follow-up, patients increased their chance of improvement from 33 percent in STDP to 67 percent in an alternative therapy. STDP seemed to be particularly inferior to cognitive-behavioral therapy with a subsample of patients with major depression. For every one depressed patient undergoing STDP, two depressed patients undergoing cognitive-behavioral therapy improved.

The foregoing meta-analyses reveal a mixed picture. There is a strong trend toward no difference between techniques in amount of change produced, which is counterbalanced by indications that, under some circumstances, cognitive and behavioral methods are superior even though they do not generally differ in efficacy between themselves. An examination of selected exemplary studies allows us to further explore this matter. Research carried out with the intent of contrasting two or more bonafide treatments shows surprisingly small differ-ences between the outcomes for patients who undergo a treatment that is fully intended to be therapeutic. Several studies illustrate this point.

Illustrative Comparative Studies

Among the most substantial studies comparing verbal and behavioral methods, the work of Sloane, Staples, Cristol, Yorkston, and Whipple (1975) established a standard of methodological sophistication that few subsequent studies have surpassed. Ninety predominantly neurotic outpatients were assigned at random to short-term analytically oriented psychotherapy, behavioral therapy, or a minimal-treatment wait-list group. The therapists were experienced and respected exponents of their respective approaches, who assented to a list of stipulated definitions of the techniques to be used. An independent assessment of therapist activities was based upon a single recorded session from each case. Four months after commencing treatment, all three groups had improved significantly on target symptoms, but the treated groups had improved significantly more than the wait-list group. There were no differences between behavioral therapy and psychotherapy on any of the target symptoms as rated by an independent assessor, kept as blind as possible to the assignment of patients to treatments. Ratings of global improvement and of social functioning based upon a structured interview slightly favored the behavioral therapy group — within-group differences were significant pre- to posttesting but between-group differences were not significant. There was some suggestion that behavioral therapy was helpful with a broader range of patients. The eight-month follow-up data, albeit compromised by further treatment received by patients in all three groups, showed no overall differences among the groups on any measure. Patients seemed to maintain treatment gains over time, while wait-list (minimal treatment) patients eventually reached the improvement levels attained by the patients who had undergone either of the active therapies.

This study has several merits, including the use of expert therapists, the recruitment of a large number of well-motivated clinic patients, random allocation to treatment or control groups, low attrition, and the inclusion of a wait-list control group. A number of criticisms of this study have been raised (Bergin & Lambert, 1978; Rachman & Wilson, 1980); but despite these problems, it represents one of the best this area has to offer. Wolpe (1975) referred to it as "unmatched — in the history of psychotherapy" (p. xix). It provides evidence for the notion that experts using their favorite method, whether behavioral or psychodynamic, can produce substantial therapeutic change.

Since the Sloane et al. study, additional well-designed comparative studies have been published. None is more important than the NIMH Collaborative Depression study, which is described in Chapter 4 of this book. This study has the advantage of the collaboration of investigators who were equally interested in each of the two psychotherapies that were investigated as well as the treatment of patients with medication. This study clearly marked a change in research strategies, from examining therapy as usually practiced to studying "ideal" therapy as guided by manuals and competency ratings.

Elkin et al. (1989) and Imber et al. (1990) reported on the comparative outcomes of this study, which compared a standard reference treatment (imipramine plus clinical management) with two psychotherapies (cognitive-behavioral therapy and interpersonal psychotherapy, a kind of dynamic and humanistic therapy). These three treatments were contrasted with a drug placebo plus clinical management control group. This study was the first head-to-head comparison of these two psychotherapies that had been shown in previous research to be specifically effective with depression (see Chapter 4, this volume).

The 250 patients seen in this study were randomly assigned to the four treatments that were offered in Pittsburgh, Oklahoma City, and Washington, DC. They met Research Diagnostic Criteria for a major depressive episode and a score of 14 or more on the 17-item Hamilton Rating Scale for Depression. A host of exclusion criteria were also applied so as to leave the sample who were treated as free from other disorders as possible.

The therapists were 28 psychiatrists and psychologists who were carefully selected, trained, and monitored in the specific treatment they offered. Each therapist saw between 1 and 11 patients. The treatments were carefully defined and followed manuals that spelled out theoretical issues, general strategies, major techniques, and methods of managing typical problems. Treatments were intended to last 16–20 weeks. In fact, the total sample averaged 13 sessions. Those who completed therapy averaged 16.2 sessions. The battery of outcome measures included symptomatic and adjustment ratings from multiple perspectives.

Numerous comparisons were made and the results of this study are very complex. Among the more interesting findings were comparisons of the two psychotherapies with the medication placebo plus clinical management (PLA-CM). This latter condition was intended to control for the effects of regular contact with an experienced and supportive therapist, the general support of the research setting, and the effects of receiving a "drug" that was thought to be helpful. Did the psychotherapies have any effects beyond what could be achieved through this rather extensive "placebo"?

There was limited evidence of the specific effectiveness of the interpersonal psychotherapy (IPT) and no evidence for the specific effectiveness of cognitive-behavioral therapy (CBT). Surprisingly, there was little evidence for superiority of the therapies in contrast to the placebo plus clinical management. The therapies were effective, but the patients who received the placebo plus clinical management also improved.

In head-to-head comparisons of IPT and CBT, no significant differences were found in any of the major analyses nor in comparisons with more and less severely disturbed patients. This similarity held up even on measures that were thought to be differentially sensitive to the two therapies. In some post hoc comparisons, modest evidence of specific effects could be found. While all patient groups improved by the end of treatment, superior recovery rates were found for both interpersonal psychotherapy and imipramine plus clinical management, when compared to the placebo plus clinical management. When patients were dichotomized on initial level of severity, the specific effects of treatment emerged. For those patients who were most severely depressed and functionally impaired, some evidence for the superiority of IPT over the placebo emerged. Imipramine plus clinical management showed even stronger evidence of effectiveness. Despite these differences, effect size comparison between the two psychotherapies remained small and little evidence could be found for differential effectiveness.

Another comparative outcome study illustrates many of the general findings already summarized.[2] The Second Sheffield Psychotherapy Project (SPP2; Shapiro, Barkham, Hardy, Morrison et al., 1990) compared the outcomes of psychodynamic-interpersonal and cognitive-behavioral therapies for depression. Therapist effects were controlled by having the same five therapists conduct both treatments; nonetheless, adherence to the treatment protocols (Shapiro & Startup, in press; Startup & Shapiro, in press) was strict, with 97 percent of sessions correctly classified in a discriminant function analysis (Startup & Shapiro, 1992). In addition, therapists' delivery of facilitative conditions, common factors that cut across treatment methods, was identical in the two treatments. The study built on the first Sheffield Psychotherapy Projection (SPP1; Shapiro & Firth, 1987), in which a crossover design had revealed a marginal superiority of the cognitive-behavioral method.

[2]We wish to thank David A. Shapiro for providing us with a prepublication summary of the Sheffield results.

The design of this study allowed for analysis not only of differences between therapy techniques, but also of the dose-effect relationship as well as the interaction between dose and severity of depression. SPP2, therefore, compared 4 treatment conditions: 8 versus 16 weekly sessions of the 2 methods, all 4 conditions involving the same therapists. Patients differing in severity of symptoms were randomly assigned to all 4 treatment conditions.

Preliminary findings from 117 clients completing treatment were reported by Shapiro, Barkham, Hardy, Reynolds et al. (in press). On the Beck Depressions Inventory (BDI), mean scores fell from about 25 at screening to about 10 posttreatment; the 16-session treatment yielded a marginally significant 2-point (0.3 of a standard deviation) advantage over the 8-session treatment when assessed at corresponding points in time; a similar marginal superiority was enjoyed by the cognitive-behavioral treatment over the psychodynamic-interpersonal treatment.

The most striking finding, however, was a significant interaction between severity of depression and duration of treatment: Clients with mild and moderate depression (BDI scores between 16 and 26) did as well with 8 as with 16 sessions, both during treatment and over a 3-month follow-up period; in contrast, clients with severe depression (BDI scores of 27 and above) improved more over 16 than over 8 sessions. This difference widened over the 3-month follow-up period, where severe depressives who had received 8 sessions deteriorated a mean 3 points while those assigned to 16 sessions improved a further mean 2 points. Some of this difference may reflect regression to the mean, since by chance the severe group assigned to 16 sessions were a mean 7 points more severe at intake than those assigned to 8 sessions. However, regression cannot entirely explain the finding, because the difference was reversed by the 3-month follow-up, with the 16-session group now 7 points below the 8-session group.

Further analyses considered the relationship between severity of depression and duration and method of treatment. Evidence emerged to suggest that the posttreatment *deterioration* of severe depressives assigned to 8 sessions of treatment may be confined to the cognitive-behavioral method, where mean rating of depression rose by nearly 7 points over the 3-month follow-up. However, the numbers involved were too small to permit firm conclusions at this level of detail.

A definitive account of this study awaits further analysis of the wide range of outcome measures employed, together with the extensive process measures included. These will aid interpretation of the outcome findings and throw light on the mechanisms of change (Shapiro, Barkham, Hardy, Morrison et al., 1990). The findings already available are important, however. They suggest a scientific basis for assigning clients to differing amounts of treatment according to the severity of their depression, with self-evident benefits to the cost-effectiveness of psychotherapy for depression. They confirm the marginal effect on outcome of depression treatments of the method employed (Robinson et al., 1990; Stiles, Shapiro, & Elliott, 1986) even when therapist effects are controlled. The differing effects of treatment duration with severely depressed as opposed to mildly or moderately depressed patients underscores the importance of studying "real" patients to advance our knowledge of the effects of psychotherapy. These results have clear implications for practice and policy decisions. Together with the other evidence on dose-effect, they suggest that mental health care cost-containment measures can be based on patient severity ratings rather than on *arbitrarily* set limits. Surely we should make enough treatment available so that patients derive a benefit.

Among the methodological advances that have special implications for the practice of psychotherapy is the use of "dismantling" studies to identify the active components of treatment procedures (Gottman & Markman, 1978). The dismantling strategy involves the controlled comparison of groups of participants undergoing the complete treatment with groups undergoing portions of the treatment. This strategy allows for the identification of elements of the treatment that are most essential in facilitating improvement. Since many treatments ordinarily combine several techniques, such a strategy may ultimately illuminate those techniques that are necessary and sufficient for improvement.

To date, this design has been effectively used with behavioral and cognitive procedures and eclectic combinations of these procedures in the treatment of obesity, smoking, alcohol abuse, nonassertiveness (social skills training), sleep disorders, headache, depression, a number of anxiety-based problems, and marital and sexual dysfunctions.

An illustrative study illuminates the possibilities of discovering differences between treatments based on the dismantling strategy. Since the revision of DSM-III-R made panic disorders a primary diagnosis, there has been increasing interest in treating panic and examining outcomes. Treatment development and research have both made impressive strides over the past several years. Much of this research has been summarized by Barlow (1988) and Michelson and Marchione (1991). Treatment strategies are based on a cognitive model of panic that posits that panic disorders are amenable to psychological interventions that modify catastrophic appraisals or misinterpretations of bodily sensations. Interoceptive conditioning is also posited as important; thus, the cognitive-based strategies attempt to remediate this conditioning as well. The treatment package for panic disorders with agoraphobia includes relaxation, breathing retraining, cognitive restructuring, simulation of the sensations of panic within the session to practice coping, and exposure. This treatment appears to nearly eliminate panic and to improve phobic avoidance.

Typical of comparative research in this area, Barlow, Craske, Cerny, and Klosko (1989) compared relaxation training (RT), imaginal exposure plus cognitive restructuring (E + C), and a combined modality (RT + E + C) versus a wait-list control condition (WL). Sixty patients who had a panic disorder (but no or mild agoraphobia) were treated for 15 weekly individual sessions. Results showed that 36 percent of the WL patients, 60 percent of RT, 85 percent of E + C, and 87 percent of the RT + E + C patients were panic free at posttreatment. When high end-state functioning (an a priori combination of criteria indicating improvement) was analyzed, the percentages of clients achieving high end-state functioning at posttreatment were WL = 0 percent, RT = 50 percent, E + C = 46 percent, and RT + E + C = 46 percent. Thus, while differential outcome was apparent only for panic attacks (with the exposure plus cognitive therapies showing superiority to relaxation and wait-list), all of the treatments were essentially equal to each other but superior to the wait-list in improving *residual anxiety and phobic symptomatology* as measured by the high end-state functioning index.

The results of six-month follow-up analysis showed either maintenance of treatment gains or further improvement. When the results from this study are combined with other published research (e.g., Clark, Salkovskis, & Chalkey, 1985; Michelson et al., 1990), the treatment of choice for panic seems to be the cognitive-behavioral therapy currently outlined by Barlow and Cerny (1988). A hypothetical description of outcomes based on this research has been presented by Michelson and Marchione (1991). Their outcome estimates are reproduced in Table 5.6.

Should these results hold up over the next few years, we will clearly see that there are instances where specific techniques have particular effects on a specific disorder. However, future research is needed to see if the results hold up when comparisons are made with a broader range of treatments and with clients who are not as carefully screened

to exclude other pathology such as personality disorders and depression. The presence of concomitant Axis I and II disorders may reduce the rather stunning results of these recent experimental studies.

To this point, our focus has been on research that examines the main effects comparisons of treatments, or the interaction of specific disorders with type of treatment. Another strategy for examining the "Dodo bird" question involves examining interactions between patient attributes other than diagnosis, such as coping styles and type of treatment. There have been many studies examining questions with this design. Unfortunately, the intuitive appeal of this line of research has never been matched by a consistently supportive body of findings, but some remain highly optimistic (e.g., Beutler, 1991) about the future of research in this area. Increased sophistication in theoretical conceptualizations and research strategies may yet produce a body of literature that allows us to understand and apply matching strategies based on patient characteristics (Shoham-Salomon, 1991). This view suggests that differential outcomes do and will occur when technique factors are matched with client dispositions (see Chapter 7, this volume).

COMMON FACTORS AND OUTCOME

Although there are a large number of therapies, each with its own rationale and specific techniques, there is only modest evidence to suggest the superiority of one school or technique over another. While there are exceptions, the equivalence among seemingly highly diverse therapies has numerous implications for practice. The general finding of no-difference in the outcome of therapy for clients who have participated in highly diverse therapies has a number of alternative explanations:

1. Different therapies can achieve similar goals through different processes.

2. Different outcomes do occur but are not detected by past research strategies.

3. Different therapies embody *common factors* that are curative although not emphasized by the theory of change central to a particular school.

At this time, any of these interpretations can be advocated and defended, as there is not enough evidence available to rule out any one of them.

Clearly, different therapies require the client to undergo different experiences and engage in differ-

TABLE 5.6 Hypothetical cohort of 100 PDA clients

Measure	Beta Blockers		Low-potency Benzodiazepines		High-potency Benzodiazepines		Monoamine Oxidase Inhibitors		Tricyclic Antidepressants		Programmed Practice		Relaxation Training		Graduated Exposure		Imipramine + Graduated Exposure		Cognitive therapy + Graduated Exposure		Cognitive-behavioral Treatment of Panic Disorder Without Agoraphobia	
	%	$n$rem	%	$n$rem	%	$n$rem	%	$n$rem	%	$n$rem	%	$n$rem	%	$n$rem	%	$n$rem	%	$n$rem	%	$n$rem	%	$n$rem
Attrition	20	80	15	85	15	85	35	65	25	75	15	85	15	85	15	85	25	75	15	85	5	95
Clinically significant improvement	10	8	15	13	60	51	45	29	60	45	25	21	55	47	65	55	70	53	87	74	90	86
Relapse	90	1	85	2	90	5	40	17	35	29	15	18	15	40	15	47	25	39	10	67	5	81
Long-term overall efficacy index	1		2		5		17		29		18		40		47		39		67		81	

Note. PDA = panic disorder with agoraphobia; $n$rem = number remaining. Because of the routine use of exposure instructions in many PDA pharmacotherapy studies, the unitary effectiveness of these medications awaits future research. However, the efficacy rates of these agents might be reduced if administered in the absence of behavioral counseling.

Source: Reproduced by permission from Michelson & Marchione (1991). Copyright 1991 by the American Psychological Association.

ent behaviors. Diverse therapies could be effective for different reasons. But we do not yet know enough about the boundaries of effectiveness for each therapy to discuss Alternative 1 and its merits. Alternative 2, the inadequacy of past research, will not be fully discussed here. Suffice it to say that there are many methodological reasons for failing to reject the null hypothesis. Kazdin and Bass (1989), for example, have questioned the value of the majority of past comparative studies on the basis of a lack of statistical power. There are also serious problems in accurately measuring change (see Chapter 3, this volume). In fact, any of a host of methodological problems could result in a failure to detect differences between therapies.

The third alternative, emphasizing common factors in different therapies, is the possibility that has received the most research attention and the one that has the clearest implications for practice. It was first hypothesized by Rosenzweig (1936). It is not only an interpretation of the comparative outcome literature, but it is also based on *other* research aimed at discovering the active ingredients of psychotherapy. Alternative 3 is also consistent with the results of the placebo literature to which we have already alluded.

There are a number of views represented in the literature about the possible role that common factors might have in the psychotherapeutic change process. Some consider them to be both necessary and sufficient (e.g., Patterson, 1984), whereas others view them as being an important component of change but do not rule out the possible role of more unique variables (e.g., Garfield, 1991). At this point it seems impossible to declare either of these contrasting positions as "truth" — their accuracy can only be determined through further empirical investigation. However, based on our review of the evidence, it appears that what can be firmly

stated is that factors common across treatments are accounting for a substantial amount of improvement found in psychotherapy patients. These so-called common factors may even account for most of the gains that result from psychological interventions. So, while we do not rule out the possibility of the additional contribution that variables specific to one school or technique might be found to have, at this point it is important to recognize that common factors are contributing a great deal to positive outcome. Therefore, it is crucial for therapists to intentionally incorporate them. The question then becomes, what are these common factors?

Common factors can be conceptualized in a variety of ways (see Grencavage & Norcross, 1990), and unfortunately, this term has been used to mean a variety of things. To organize and clarify this broad term, we have grouped common factors into the support, learning, and action categories in Table 5.7. These categories were chosen to represent a sequence that we presume operates in many psychotherapies. This developmental sequence is at least partially mediated through factors common across therapies. The developmental nature of this sequence presumes that the supportive functions precede changes in beliefs and attitudes, which precede attempts by the therapist to encourage patient action.

A variety of common factors attributable to the therapist, therapy procedures, and the client are listed in this table. As already mentioned, these factors would seem to operate most potently during the process of therapy. Together they provide for a cooperative working endeavor in which the patient's increased sense of trust, security, and safety, along with decreases in tension, threat, and anxiety, leads to changes in conceptualizing his or her problems and ultimately in acting differently by refacing fears, taking risks, and working through

TABLE 5.7   Sequential listing of factors common across therapies that are associated with positive outcomes

Support Factors	Learning Factors	Action Factors
Catharsis	Advice	Behavioral regulation
Identification with therapist	Affective experiencing	Cognitive mastery
Mitigation of isolation	Assimilation of problematic	Encouragement of facing fears
Positive relationship	experiences	Taking risks
Reassurance	Changing expectations for personal	Mastery efforts
Release of tension	effectiveness	Modeling
Structure	Cognitive learning	Practice
Therapeutic alliance	Corrective emotional experience	Reality testing
Therapist/client active participation	Exploration of internal frame of	Success experience
Therapist expertness	reference	Working through
Therapist warmth, respect, empathy,	Feedback	
acceptance, genuineness	Insight	
Trust	Rationale	

TABLE 5.8 **Relationship of specific techniques of different schools of psychotherapy to three nonspecific change agents shared by all schools**

AFFECTIVE EXPERIENCING		COGNITIVE MASTERY		BEHAVIORAL REGULATION	
Technique	School	Technique	School	Technique	School
Encounter	Existential analysis	Interpretation Clarification	Psychoanalysis Supportive therapy	Conditioning	Behavior therapy
Flooding	Implosion therapy	Attacking	Rational therapy	Teaching skills	Assertiveness training
Meditation	Arica	irrational ideas		Saying "hmmm"	Client-centered therapy
Shared dialogue	Gestalt therapy	Providing	Sex therapy	Direct feedback	Biofeedback
Body manipulation	Rolfing	information Thought	Behavior therapy	Giving rewards Direct example	Token economy Modeling
Group regression	Erhard seminars training	stopping Search for meaning	Logotherapy		therapy
Massage	Arica	Correcting false beliefs	Cognitive therapy	Identification	Psychoanalysis
Free association	Psychoanalysis	Analysis of transference	Psychoanalysis	Reassurance	Supportive therapy
Isolation	Primal scream	Paradoxical intention	Behavior therapy	Suggestion	Hypnotherapy
Role playing	Psychodrama	Analysis of body armor	Character analysis	Punishment	Aversiveness therapy
Intravenous drugs	Narcotherapy	Confronting decisions	Direct decision therapy	Relaxation	Systematic desensitization

Source: Reprinted by permission from Karasu (1986). Copyright 1986 by the American Psychological Association.

problems in interpersonal relationships. The variables and constructs organized in Table 5.7 were derived from our reading of empirical research. These are variables that have been operationally defined and correlated with outcome in research studies of therapy.

In one of many alternative conceptualizations, Karasu (1986) has examined common factors from a theoretical perspective, arguing that three patient factors can be identified: affective experiencing, cognitive mastery, and behavioral regulation. He suggests that these factors can be activated in diverse ways via the techniques central to particular treatment orientations. His conceptualization is reproduced in Table 5.8. From this table, it is clear that each therapy employs specific mechanisms to elicit similar goals or processes in patients. There are a limited number of important therapeutic goals or processes but an unlimited number of ways that these processes can be activated. Regardless of the conceptual scheme that is used to organize common factors, it is obvious that emphasizing the study of common factors in addition to specific techniques will encourage greater cooperation and harmony among competing approaches, ultimately increasing the effectiveness of psychotherapy. The

conceptual schemes offer a plausible explanation for the failure to find differences in outcome between different therapies. What kind of empirical support suggests the importance of common factors?

Client-centered Approach

Among the common factors most frequently studied have been those identified by the client-centered school as "necessary and sufficient conditions" for patient personality change: accurate empathy, positive regard, nonpossessive warmth, and congruence or genuineness. Virtually all schools of therapy accept the notion that these or related therapist relationship variables are important for significant progress in psychotherapy and, in fact, fundamental in the formation of a working alliance (Lambert, 1983).

Studies showing both positive and equivocal support for the hypothesized relationship among therapist, attitudes, and outcome have been reviewed elsewhere (cf. Gurman, 1977; Howard & Orlinsky, 1986; Lambert, DeJulio, & Stein, 1978; Levant & Shlien, 1984; Mitchell, Bozarth, & Krauft, 1977; Patterson, 1984; and Chapters 8 and 12, this volume). Reviewers are virtually unanimous in their opinion that the therapist–patient relationship is critical; however, they point out that research support for this position is more ambiguous than once thought. Studies using ratings of client-perceived relationship factors, rather than objective raters' perceptions of the relationship, obtain consistently more positive results, and the larger correlations with outcome are often between client process ratings and client self-reports of outcome.

For example, Miller, Taylor, and West (1980) investigated the comparative effectiveness of various behavioral approaches aimed at helping problem drinkers control their alcohol consumption. Although the focus of the study was on the comparative effects of focused versus broad-spectrum behavioral therapy, the authors also collected data on the contribution of therapist empathy to patient outcome. One finding — surprising to the authors and important for our discussion — was the discovery of a strong relationship between empathy and patient outcome obtained from the six-to-eight–month follow-up interviews used to assess drinking behavior. Therapist rank on empathy correlated ($r = 0.82$) with patient outcome, thus accounting for 67 percent of the variance in the criteria. These results argue for the importance of therapist communicative skills even with behavioral interventions. They were also presented in a context in which variations in specific techniques did not prove to have a similarly powerful effect on outcome.

More recently, Lafferty, Beutler, and Crago (1991) explored differences between more and less effective trainee psychotherapists, specifically examining which of several therapist variables most consistently distinguished between them. Therapist effectiveness was determined by comparing the level of symptomatic distress experienced by patients before and subsequent to treatment (as measured by the Symptom Checklist 90-Revised pre- to posttreatment differences). Those whose patients typically manifested more distress after than before treatment were assigned to the less effective group, whereas therapists whose patients experienced relatively less distress following treatment as compared to before were designated as being in the more effective group. One of the therapist variables considered was relationship skills, as measured by a revised version of the Barrett-Lennard Relationship Inventory. Of interest here is the finding that the less effective therapists were shown to have lower levels of empathic understanding. The authors state: "The present study supports the significance of the therapist's empathy in effective psychotherapy. Patients of less effective therapists felt less understood by their therapists than did patients of more effective therapists" (p. 79).

Therapeutic Alliance

The importance of the therapeutic relationship has been bolstered in recent years by investigations of the therapeutic alliance. While most of this work has been generated by psychodynamically oriented researchers, this construct is receiving increasing emphasis within other approaches as well. It has been conceptualized and defined differently by a host of interested investigators. And, like the client-centered dimensions, it has been measured by client ratings, therapist ratings, and judge ratings.

There is more disagreement about the therapeutic alliance construct than there was with the client-centered conditions. This may prove to be a hindrance in drawing conclusions in this area because there are now several popular methods for measuring this construct, rather than the limited number of scales evidenced in the client-centered literature. In addition, the alliance is seen as a necessary, but not sufficient, condition for personality change and so assumes a less important theoretical position in dynamic therapies (and certainly other therapies) than the facilitative conditions did in client-centered therapy. In contrast to ratings from the client-centered tradition, ratings of the therapeutic alliance contain a heavy emphasis on *patient* variables, mainly the client's ability to participate productively and collaboratively in therapy. Since alliance ratings go well beyond measuring therapist behaviors, they can be expected to correlate more highly with outcome than the client-centered measures. At the same time, alliance measures are less useful for training because they may not lead directly into modification of specific therapist attitudes and behaviors.

Gaston (1990), in trying to integrate the various constructs that have been offered to describe the therapeutic alliance, has suggested that some of the following components of the alliance are measured by some but not all current rating scales: (1) the patient's affective relationship to the therapist, (2) the patient's capacity to purposefully work in therapy, (3) the therapist's empathic understanding and involvement, and (4) patient–therapist agreement on the goals and tasks of therapy.

Research literature on the alliance has been reviewed elsewhere (Horvath & Symonds, 1991; Lambert, 1992; Chapters 7 and 11, this volume). So far it is not nearly as extensive as that coming from client-centered researchers. In our opinion, evidence on the alliance strengthens the view that outcome can be predicted from early ratings of the therapeutic relationship. These ratings produce data very similar to the client-centered data (Frank & Gunderson, 1991; Gaston, Marmar, Gallagher, & Thompson, 1991; Salvio, Beutler, Wood, &

Engle, 1992; Tichener & Hill, 1989) and suggest that the alliance not only reflects positive change but may produce it as well. The alliance is related to outcome, although there are instances when it fails to predict or produces associations that are quite small (see Lambert, 1992).

Other Approaches

Another approach to understanding the contribution of the therapist to effective outcome has involved the use of behavioral and adjective checklists filled out by clients following their therapeutic contacts. Lorr (1965), for example, had 523 psychotherapy patients describe their therapists on 65 different statements. A subsequent factor analysis identified five factors: understanding, accepting, authoritarian (directive), independence-encouraging, and critical-hostile. Scores on these descriptive factors were correlated with improvement ratings, with the result that client ratings of understanding and accepting correlated most highly with client- and therapist-rated improvement.

In a more recent study, Cooley and LaJoy (1980) attempted to replicate the Lorr study. In addition, they studied the relationship between therapist ratings of themselves and outcome, as well as the relationship of discrepancies between patient and therapist ratings and outcome ratings. The patients were 56 adult community mental health outpatients who had been treated by one of eight therapists at the clinic. As with the Lorr study, patient ratings of therapist understanding and acceptance correlated most highly with client-rated outcome. On the other hand, when self-ratings of therapists' attributes were compared to therapist-rated patient outcome, the correlations were insignificant, suggesting that therapists did not perceive their personal attributes as a factor influencing therapeutic outcome.

Similar findings have been reported in group treatment. Glass and Arnkoff (1988) examined common and specific factors in client descriptions and explanations of change. The clients were shy and consequently treated in one of three structured group therapies for shyness or in an unstructured therapy group. Each group was based on a different theory of change and differed in its content and focus. Nevertheless, content analysis revealed that in addition to specific treatment factors, all groups contained considerable emphasis on group process and common factors such as support. Glass and Arnkoff suggest that "the role of common group process factors appeared to be at least as important to subjects as the specific therapy program content" (1988, p. 437).

Murphy, Cramer, and Lillie (1984) studied common factors by having outpatients generate a list of curative factors that they believed to be associated with their cognitive-behavioral therapy. Those factors suggested by a significant portion of patients were advice (79%), talking to someone interested in my problems (75%), encouragement and reassurance (67%), talking to someone who understands (58%), and "installation" of hope (58%). The two factors that correlated most highly with outcome, as assessed by both therapist and patient, were talking to someone who understands and receiving advice. It is interesting to note that the patients in this study were predominantly from the lower socioeconomic class and past research has shown that these patients expect advice (Goin, Yamamoto, & Silverman, 1965).

Patients frequently attribute their success in treatment to personal qualities of the therapist. That these personal qualities bear a striking resemblance to each other across studies and methodologies is evidence that they are highly important in psychotherapy outcome. This notion was also emphasized by Lazarus (1971) in an uncontrolled follow-up study of 112 patients he had seen in therapy. These patients were asked to provide information about the effects of their treatment, the durability of improvement, and their perceptions of the therapeutic process and characteristics of the therapist. With regard to therapist characteristics, those adjectives used to describe Lazarus most often were sensitive, gentle, and honest. Patients clearly believed that the personal qualities of the therapist were more important than specific technical factors, about which there was little agreement.

In the NIMH Collaborative Depression study already summarized, the failure to find significant differences in head-to-head comparisons of CBT and IPT led the authors to conclude: "The general lack of differences between the two psychotherapies, together with the good results for the PLA-CM condition, suggests once again the importance of common factors in different types of psychologically mediated treatment" (Elkin et al., 1989, p. 979).

Similar conclusions were reached by Zeiss, Lewinsohn, and Munoz (1979). These authors compared interpersonal-skills training, a reinforcement-theory program to increase pleasant activities (and the enjoyment of potentially pleasant activities), and a cognitive approach to the modification of depressive thoughts. They found that all treatments were associated with reduction in depression, without any differential changes specific to aspects of the patients' problems targeted by the three treatments. Zeiss et al. (1979) note the improvements also recorded by the waiting-list group and cite Frank's (1974) demoralization hypothesis as the most parsimonious explanation for the results. These researchers suggest that the impact of treatment was due to the enhancement of self-efficacy via training in self-help skills, thus increasing expectations of mastery and perception of greater positive reinforcement as a function of the patient's greater skillfulness. Therefore, the common components of therapy for depression emerge as important.

Another study, conducted by Thompson, Gallagher, and Breckenridge (1987), examined the effectiveness of three brief psychotherapeutic modalities (behavioral, cognitive, and psychodynamic) in treating elderly patients with a clinically diagnosable major depressive disorder. The cognitive and behavioral therapies were guided by manuals, and those therapists using the psychodynamic format utilized a "prescribed outline with some variations depending on patient progress" (p. 385). A number of outcome measures were employed that supported the conclusion that all treatments were associated with improvement, but no differences were evident in their effectiveness. The investigators note that this finding of no-difference between these modalities essentially replicates their earlier research (Gallagher & Thompson, 1982) and is in accordance with the nonspecific improvement effects in depression discussed by Zeiss et al. (1979) and previously mentioned here.

Summary

Common factors loom large as mediators of treatment outcome. The research base for this conclusion is substantial and multidimensional, and we must attend to its import. While there is some resistance to acknowledging the importance that common factors have, possibly as Frank (1976) states because "little glory derives from showing that the particular method one has mastered with so much effort may be indistinguishable from other methods in its effects" (p. 74), it seems imperative that we continue moving toward an understanding of how change occurs in psychotherapy—whether through common or unique mechanisms. Clearly, the issue of differential effectiveness is not yet closed. Specific techniques at times may contribute to outcome, and possibly this depends on the patient population (e.g., Fariburn, Kirk, O'Conner & Cooper, 1986). However, this fact does not contradict the evidence regarding the significant role of common factors, but rather it suggests that more unique variables may be important at times as well.

Although we have dichotomized research on specific techniques and research on common factors to some degree, we realize that they are not necessarily in opposition as explanatory factors in treatment outcome. There is a growing sentiment among researchers and clinicians that techniques and atti-

tudes cannot be easily distinguished—that they are so interwoven, research cannot hope to separate their unique contributions to outcome. This is certainly a dominant view in Karasu's (1986) conceptualization and characterizes the recent *Handbook of Eclectic and Integrative Psychotherapy* (Norcross & Goldfried, 1992).

This position is clearly outlined by Butler and Strupp (1986), who question the value of separating specific techniques from common factors. They note that the term *active ingredient* does not describe psychotherapy. In their view, techniques can never be offered in a context free of interpersonal meaning. They write: "The complexity and subtlety of psychotherapeutic processes cannot be reduced to a set of disembodied techniques because techniques gain their meaning and, in turn, their effectiveness from the particular interaction of the individuals involved" (p. 33). As a simple example, they use the application of the "empty-chair" technique. One therapist applies it with confidence as a means to help the client experience an internalized representation of a significant other. Another therapist feels a bit silly in its use. One patient greets the suggestion with enthusiasm having read about it somewhere, while another, expecting therapy to be a bit gimmicky, reacts with cynicism or resentment.

For Butler and Strupp, psychotherapy is the "systematic use of a human relationship for therapeutic purposes" (p. 36). In this view, techniques cannot be separated from the human encounter; techniques are interpersonal events inevitably linked to expectations and beliefs.

COMMON AND SPECIFIC FACTORS AND THE USE OF TREATMENT MANUALS

A major limitation of the earliest therapy studies (most of which showed no differences between treatments) was that they did not clearly specify treatments and ensure that the treatments were offered to patients in the prescribed manner. An important development in psychotherapy (even a "minor revolution," Luborsky & DeRubeis, 1984) is the emergence and now common use of therapy treatment manuals. The use of therapy manuals can be traced back to the sixties (e.g., Lang & Lazovik, 1963) but became common with some treatment approaches in the seventies (Beck, Rush, Shaw, & Emery, 1979). Their initial use was in group workshops that emphasized training and teaching more than therapy (e.g., assertiveness training with shy college students, interpersonal skills training in both in- and outpatient populations, and behavioral therapy with overweight clients). Through the 1980s, there was an increased interest in using such manuals in individual psychosocial therapies. Manuals have now become so common in some forms of therapy that outcome studies that do not employ them are rare. For example, in Dobson's (1989) review of cognitive therapy outcome, every study cited the use of a treatment manual. Manuals have become commonplace in comparative research studies with a wide variety of patient problems, and with a variety of treatment approaches. Lambert and Ogles (1988), for example, identified 10 different manuals describing various behavioral, cognitive, and psychodynamic approaches to treating outpatients, and since that review, the number of available manuals has more than doubled, becoming even more specialized and including humanistic approaches as well (e.g., Gestalt experiential therapy, Greenberg & Goldman, 1988; focused expressive therapy, Daldrup, Beutler, Engle, & Greenberg, 1988).

One notable difference between the older behavioral therapy manuals and those developed out of humanistic, dynamic, and cognitive therapy traditions is the latter's greater emphasis on flexibility in application of techniques. These manuals take a middle ground between highly structured "activity-by-activity" guides and general, theoretically rich, full-length textbooks on conducting therapy. Typically, they not only provide techniques but specify the general process or stages of treatment. Techniques are then structured around this process and the movement of patients through the stages that are likely to occur (Dobson & Shaw, 1988).

There are remarkable differences among existing manuals—they vary from standard textbook length to 20–30 pages. The focus also varies from manuals aimed generally at outpatients to the more common variety that tailors a general treatment method to a specific population (e.g., behavioral therapy for borderline personality disorder, Linehan, 1987; supportive-expressive psychodynamic therapy for addictions, Luborsky, Woody, Hale, & Velleco, 1977).

The development and use of treatment manuals in the NIMH Depression Collaborative study (Elkin, Parloff, Hadley, & Autry, 1985) illustrate the possible role of manuals and associated rating scales in psychotherapy research. Cognitive therapy, interpersonal therapy, and clinical management manuals were used to (1) guide the selection of therapists, (2) train therapists, (3) develop various rating scales to assess the effects of training, (4) test the degree to which the therapy offered conformed to the manual, and (5) measure the degree to which therapies can be discriminated. Manuals facilitated the application of the research protocol across the three research sites and encouraged the identification and analysis of data on therapeutic operations that are unique to a given treatment as well as shared by treatments (DeRubeis, Hollon, Evans, & Bemis, 1982; Evans et al., 1983; Luborsky, Woody, McLellan, O'Brien, & Rosenzweig, 1982; Neu, Prusoff, & Klerman, 1978; Rounsaville et al., 1988).

There are several advantages offered by treatment manuals that have implications for therapy, research, training, and practice.

1. Manuals can enhance the internal validity of comparative outcome studies by standardizing and purifying the technical aspects of the treatment being offered. This is clearly illustrated in the NIMH Collaborative Depression project in which a pharmacotherapy manual was produced and could be used to ensure minimal overlap of drug intervention and psychotherapies.

2. Manuals provide a precise and organized way of training and supervising therapists. They provide clear-cut guidelines for training and the evaluation of the consequences of training in very concrete ways. As a result, training for practice can move toward more competency-based criteria. Indirectly, manuals have served as a valuable vehicle for transferring the innovative and effective interventions of researchers to practicing clinicians.

3. Manuals facilitate the development of rating scales for treatment integrity or therapist "conformance" by specifying both prescribed and proscribed aspects of treatment.

4. Manuals also facilitate the development of rating scales to assess competence. While the jury is still out on how strong the relationship between competence and outcome is, some evidence shows a significant relationship (Rounsaville et al., 1988).

5. The effective use of manuals can speed up the process of training. Rounsaville et al. (1988) report that carefully selected and highly experienced therapists can achieve a high level of competence with the first training case after review of the manual and participation in brief didactic training. Initial competence can be maintained over a long period of time with minimal supervision and possibly without supervision. Dobson and Shaw (1988), on the other hand, suggest the need for more extensive training and supervision in cognitive therapy, extending perhaps for six months to two years.

6. Manual-based training can result in treatments that are replicable across locations and time.

7. Manual-based therapies can help us sort out the active ingredients of psychotherapy by facilitating the comparison of the common components of treatments. This latter point is illustrated in an interchange between Snyder et al. (1991) and Jacobson (1991). Snyder and colleagues presented

data on a four-year follow-up comparative outcome study of behavioral versus insight-oriented marital therapy. Insight-oriented therapy was shown to be more effective than behavioral therapy in the long run (e.g., 3% vs. 38% divorce rate). Because the original marital therapies were guided by manuals and measures of conformance were taken, Jacobson, an advocate of behavioral therapy, was able to argue that the behavioral marital therapy offered was not representative of contemporary behavioral therapy.

In fact, Jacobson further indicated that the insight therapy manual used in the research protocol incorporated many techniques in common use in contemporary behavioral therapy: He asserted that of the 31 intervention strategies listed in the insight manual, 26 were now integral to the behavioral approach. Jacobson (1991) therefore argues that this follow-up study is not a fair comparison of behavioral and insight therapies as they are practiced today.

Important for our discussion is the degree to which manuals containing a clear specification of treatment procedures allow researchers and clinicians to analyze the commonalities and differences between treatments. If Jacobson's analysis is correct, there is really very little difference between these two types of therapies. If this is true, then, despite the different theoretical underpinnings and labels given to these two therapies, there is little reason to compare their effectiveness. The manuals used to guide these therapies provide an important base for an analysis of significant practical differences between these treatment approaches. Apparently insight and contemporary behavioral therapies may not only have equivalent effects but use equivalent techniques! Manuals not only guide therapy but may help us clarify the commonalities and differences between alternative approaches.

8. Therapy manuals reduce identification with a single therapeutic orientation. This final advantage is simultaneously viewed as a serious disadvantage by some psychotherapists. As Omer and London (1988) have pointed out, manuals mark a change in the profession's view of therapy. They make therapy easier to transfer and thus support the trend toward eclecticism. To those deeply involved in a school approach, this must seem like a betrayal of the school position because of the likely reliance on or superficial adherence to technique by the eclectic therapist. The school position calls for immersion of the novice therapist in theory and practice within the language system of adherents. The novice therapist might even develop a personal identification with the therapy. With manuals, following the rules rather than personal identification is required. Advocates of therapy manuals renounce

therapy training by total commitment and lengthy apprenticeship. The experienced therapist may borrow from numerous manuals and make treatment of patients specific to patient problems.

A comparative study of four treatment manuals comparing their characteristics, qualities, and usefulness has been done by Rosengard (1991). She asked a sample of American and German experienced and inexperienced therapists to rate the manuals on several dimensions. She also formed some guidelines for ideal manuals. In general, the four manuals reviewed (Luborsky's, Stupp's, Klerman's, and Beck's) were found to be useful in many ways across cultures and levels of experience. For those wishing to create a therapy manual, her guidelines would be most helpful.

In a series of studies Strupp and colleagues (Henry, Schacht, Strupp, Butler, & Binder, in press-b; Henry, Strupp, Schacht, Binder, & Butler, in press-c; Henry, Butler, Strupp, Schacht, & Binder, 1993-a) reported on the effects of manuals on training and outcome of time-limited dynamic psychotherapy. Among other conclusions, they caution that use of the manual successfully changed therapists' technical interventions but had unexpected negative effects on therapeutic behaviors. Among the unhelpful changes was a tendency for therapists to become less approving and supportive, less optimistic, and more authoritative and defensive. Henry et al. (1993-a) write: "One of the apparent paradoxical results of training was that at the same time therapists were becoming more intellectually sensitized to the importance of in-session dyadic process, they were actually delivering a higher 'toxic-dose' of disaffiliative and complex communications" (p. 20). Henry et al. (in press-a) also offer guidelines for the use of manuals in training.

THE COMPARATIVE EFFECTIVENESS OF PROFESSIONAL VERSUS PARAPROFESSIONAL, EXPERIENCED VERSUS INEXPERIENCED THERAPISTS

In addition to no-treatment and wait-list control groups, and in keeping with the previous description of placebo and common factors, the effects of psychotherapy offered by experienced clinicians have been contrasted with the effects of helping efforts on the part of lay therapists, paraprofessionals, and inexperienced clinicians. Many of the studies in this area have been aimed at sorting out the value of therapy beyond the contribution of warm and caring human encounters and wise advice. Other studies have investigated and helped to establish the boundaries of therapeutic procedures (e.g., the level of training and skill required to be effective with specified problems). Most typically, researchers have merely examined the relationship of amount of therapist experience to outcome in research that was designed to study other variables.

The available literature on such efforts has been reviewed and debated. Bergin and Lambert (1978), for example, suggested that more experienced clinicians obtain superior outcomes to less experienced therapists. Auerbach and Johnson (1977), on the other hand, found less support for this conclusion and suggested that the empirical base for differential outcomes as a function of level of experience was meager.

Some meta-analytic reviews (e.g., Lyons & Woods, 1991; Quality Assurance Project, 1982; Robinson et al., 1990; Shapiro & Shapiro, 1983; Smith et al., 1980) have analyzed the relationship of experience and outcome by correlating effect size data with experience level. Occasionally, these analyses turn up relationships that favor experience or formal training. For example, in their meta-analysis of the effectiveness of psychotherapy with children and adolescents, Weisz, Weiss, Alicke, and Klotz (1987) reported a significant interaction between client age and therapist training. Trained professionals (either master's or doctoral degree) were found to be equally effective with all age groups, while graduate students and paraprofessionals were more effective with younger than with older clients. In addition, it was reported that professionals differed from graduate students and paraprofessionals in their effectiveness with overcontrol problems (i.e., phobias and shyness); as amount of formal training increased, so did effectiveness.

In contrast, therapist level of training did not differentially impact effectiveness with undercontrol problems, such as aggression and impulsion. Despite the fact that training entered into two interactions, the authors report that the main effect of training was not significant. They note that while this failure to detect an overall difference between professionals, paraprofessionals, and graduate students might be unsettling, a more thoughtful consideration of the findings suggests otherwise: "First, it should be noted that the therapeutic work of the graduate students and paraprofessionals did not take place in a vacuum. In nearly every instance, these therapists were selected, trained, and supervised by professionals in techniques that professionals had designed" (p. 548).

Dush, Hirt, and Schroeder (1989) provide a meta-analysis of outcome studies that evaluates self-statement modification in the treatment of childhood behavioral disorders of clinically relevant severity. These authors found that treatment effi-

cacy varied considerably with length of follow-up, experience level of therapists, age of children, and outcome content area, among other things. In the results section pertaining specifically to therapist level of experience, the authors indicate that when experience level was reported or estimable, it showed a strong, positive, and rather linear relationship to outcome ($r = .31$). Furthermore, it is reported that "at the extremes, doctoral-level therapists were associated with outcomes over seven times larger than those of therapists without graduate training" (p. 102). The data suggest that while self-statement modification is a straightforward procedure and undergraduates and paraprofessionals were typically trained in the delivery of treatment, it is possible that "more skill, subtlety, and perhaps more sophistication in the therapeutic relationship may be needed to obtain acceptable treatment outcomes" (p. 105). These authors concluded that, collectively, self-statement modification outcomes were superior to no-treatment and placebo conditions by about a half of a standard deviation. In outlining their suggestions for further study, these authors note that until additional research is able to delineate the conditions under which paraprofessionals and inexperienced therapists may achieve acceptable results, caution should be exerted in employing such less trained individuals.

Overall, the meta-analytic reviews of psychotherapy that have provided correlational data have not suggested a substantial relationship between experience and outcome; however, experience levels were usually compared across studies rather than within studies, and comparisons within studies often were between inexperienced and slightly experienced clinicians. Differences in outcome between highly experienced and inexperienced therapists have generally not been tested. Some reviews have considered the body of research that directly studies professional status or experience level, and these reviews and studies are considered next.

The results of three meta-analytic reviews of studies bearing directly on this issue are presented in Table 5.9. Using meta-analytic methods, Hattie, Sharpley, and Rogers (1984) reanalyzed the studies reviewed by Durlak (1979). One hundred fifty-

TABLE 5.9 Effectiveness of professionals versus paraprofessionals in psychotherapy

Researchers	N	ES
Berman & Norton (1985)	32	−.02[a]
Hattie, Sharpley, & Rogers (1984)	39	−.34[a]
Stein & Lambert (1984)	40	.0

[a]Negative effect size indicates paraprofessionals were more effective.

four comparisons from 39 studies indicated that clients who seek help from paraprofessionals are more likely to achieve resolution of their problems than those who consult professionals (ES = 0.34)! Despite this overall conclusion, several subcomparisons suggested that the most effective therapists were those who were currently undergoing training or had just completed it (graduate students), and that experienced paraprofessionals were superior to less experienced paraprofessionals. There was also a positive relationship between amount of training received by paraprofessionals and outcome.

A major problem with the Hattie et al. review was its reliance on a questionable data base containing many studies with methodological flaws. These flaws have been noted by several reviewers (cf. Lambert, 1979; Nietzel & Fisher, 1981; Stein, 1980). Berman and Norton (1985) replicated this meta-analysis excluding some of the poorer studies. They also excluded studies that counted social workers as paraprofessionals. They reported, however, that there was no difference in effect size for the two classes of service providers but that professionals tended to have better results in brief treatments and with patients over 21 years of age.

In contrast to the preceding reviews, Stein (1980) and Stein and Lambert (1984) were more selective in their choice of research literature. For example, studies of vocational counseling and academic advising and analogue interviews were not included in their reviews. In addition, reliable ratings were made of the design characteristics of each study (random assignment of patients to therapists, etc.), and greater attention was directed toward operationally defining experience and training.

Despite improvements in the selection and inclusion of studies for review, Stein and Lambert (1984) reported results similar to those of Berman and Norton (1985). In general, there was no difference between the outcome of patients treated by trained and untrained persons. At the same time, Stein and Lambert (1984) found that differences in outcome were most likely to occur when there was a large discrepancy in experience between the therapists offering treatment within a study, and when the treatment modality involved more than simple counseling or specific behavioral techniques (e.g., psychodynamic therapy, marital therapy).

Over the past decade, there have been surprisingly few research studies in the area of level of experience and client outcome. This is especially true when one considers the small number of studies that have directly examined this question through the use of appropriate and relevant designs. As was the case with much early research,

even when this topic commanded considerable interest and controversy, most recent studies have failed to achieve acceptable levels of internal validity, external validity, and construct validity — thus limiting the interpretations and generalizations that can be made on the basis of reported findings. Designs have generally failed to adequately address the differential effects of professionals versus paraprofessionals, experienced versus less experienced therapists, trained versus untrained individuals, and so forth. Problems such as inadequate controls, the unclear influence of supervision, confounding of treatment technique with level of experience, and unclear definition of categories (professional, paraprofessional, trained, untrained, etc.) continue to jeopardize the quality of research findings. With the exception of results provided by a few higher quality studies, such as Burlingame, Fuhriman, Paul, and Ogles (1989), it would seem that little empirically solid data has been added to the debate over whether experience and professional training make a difference in client outcome.

Although the general failure of this literature to show unique therapeutic effectiveness for trained professionals is sobering, these studies are flawed in several respects. Many of the studies deal with cases that are not typical of those treated in the outcome studies reported elsewhere in this chapter. Controls, criteria, and follow-up are often not rigorous; and frequently we seem to be observing improvements in the morale of schizophrenics or mildly distressed persons due to attention and support. We are not observing substantial therapeutic effects in the usual kinds of cases. This is not to downgrade the importance of the effects observed, but to suggest that the noted design limitations may result in a failure of the findings to generalize to representative patient populations or less selective groups of paraprofessionals. On the other hand, studies in this area certainly suggest that common therapeutic factors as well as specific interventions are not the sole domain of formal therapy and that nonprofessional providers may be useful in many cases and settings.

Examples can still be found in the literature that document differences in outcome favoring highly trained therapists over less trained therapists (e.g., Barabasz, Baer, Sheehan, & Barabasz, 1986; Carey & Burish, 1987; Lyons & Woods, 1991), but frequently differences are not reported or analyzed or do not reach statistical significance. It would seem appropriate at this point to consider both why so few studies and reviews have been added to this literature in the past five or six years and why more debate and discussion have not ensued. A number of possibilities surface: First, considering the somewhat exhaustive debate and analysis of the research that took place in the early 1980s and ended equivocally, perhaps enough time simply has not passed for more studies to be conducted, published, and evaluated in a manner that would contribute meaningfully to the experience level and outcome issue.

A second possibility concerns whether this area of research lacks the conceptual clarity necessary to progress to a more sophisticated level of findings in regard to outcome. It appears that poor definition of the constructs under investigation has led to a state of disorganized, dissociated, and hard to decipher results and conclusions, which may in turn have discouraged researchers from continuing the inquiry into the relationship between experience level and outcome. Previous studies have operationalized the so-called "experience" construct in a variety of ways—categorically, such as qualified versus unqualified; ordinally, such as trainee, intern, experienced psychologist; and as a continuous variable, such as in number of years of experience. The difficulty this creates is that conclusions about the experience–outcome issue may be based on the assumption that homogeneity in construct definition exists between studies, when in fact studies may be investigating very different things. This general lack of clarity as to what the experience construct is really referring to may continue to interfere with the quality of future research. Further confusing this issue is the problem of where the construct or variable of training fits into the larger conceptual picture. One wonders if the more relevant question for investigation might be found in inquiry into the differential effects of *training* as it relates to outcome. There has clearly been overlap in the use of training and experience as dimensions for study; and until the definitional parameters of what is meant by these constructs become more precise, it is likely that confusion will continue to characterize this literature.

Although many of the psychotherapies that have been tested empirically have been shown to be generally effective, and we are arriving at a clearer picture of the causal factors in these positive changes, there are two additional important issues to consider: (1) How can we identify and promote larger effects? and (2) What is the extent of negative effects during therapy?

THE SEARCH FOR LARGER EFFECTS

Despite the fact that faith in treatment efficacy has increased over the years due to increasing positive evidence, concerns about therapeutic potency continue and engender hope that new knowledge will enhance the amount of change experienced as a result of treatment. There are several important themes that bear on this matter.

We have argued for many years (Bergin, 1966) that average psychotherapy and behavior change outcome indices mask a great deal of variability, and that this variability represents a diversity in therapeutic potency ranging from bad to excellent. Translating average outcomes into effect sizes does not change this fact; indeed, the meta-analyses based on effect sizes have abundantly documented this point. Although the average effect sizes discussed in this chapter are impressive by comparison with no-treatment or by comparison with other kinds of social interventions, it is a point of some concern that an average effect size of 0.85 implies that many of the treated samples attained effects smaller than 0.85, and many of these had to be near zero due to the large standard deviations of the average effect sizes reported. Indeed, Shapiro and Shapiro (1982a) reported that about 30 percent of their 1,828 ESs were near zero and 11 percent were negative!

While meta-analyses have been useful, we still have to be sobered by the average sizes of the effects; and we have to look closely at the tremendous variability in the changes reported. This variability is a likely key to discovering the means of improving therapeutic effects because hidden in the variation are some very large changes that tend to get washed out by averaging the data. The following sections deal with some of these problems.

The Therapist as a Variable Factor Influencing Comparisons of Techniques

Although an excellent chapter in this book (Chapter 7) reviews a massive number of studies on therapist characteristics in relation to outcome, these are essentially correlational data that do not address the question of differences in individual therapists' efficacy. The reason for this is that there is little literature that tests the outcome of each therapist. Such data are hidden in comparisons of techniques. If, however, we were to compare the outcomes of each therapist as we do each technique, we may find considerable variation in effectiveness. Of course, therapists are always using "techniques," so such comparisons inevitably confound personal and technical aspects of interventions (Henry, 1985).

The idea that the individual therapist plays an important role in therapy outcome is a phenomenon that has wide acceptance in clinical practice. Few clinicians refer patients to just any practitioner. It is assumed that some therapists (with their techniques) as opposed to techniques per se obtain large positive effects while many obtain modest effects, and a few often cause people to worsen in adjustment. What research evidence can be brought to bear on this issue?

Orlinsky and Howard (1980) have produced an interesting set of data on this question. Although this was a retrospective study based on case files, important hypotheses about therapist differences were generated. The outcome ratings of 143 female cases seen by 23 traditional verbal psychotherapists were listed therapist by therapist. Six of the 23 therapists were rated ✓ + , which means that at least 70 percent of their cases were improved, and none were rated worse. Overall, 84 percent of patients treated by these six therapists were improved at termination. Five of the 23 therapists, on the other hand, were x-rated, which means that 50 percent or less of their cases improved while more than 10 percent were worse. Overall, 44 percent of their 25 cases improved. The types of cases seen by the different therapists were generally similar, although the results have to be interpreted with some caution because there was neither random assignment of cases to therapists nor any attempt to equate caseloads for severity of disturbance. Further analyses showed that experienced therapists obtained better results and, rather dramatically, that the ambulatory female schizophrenics in the sample improved at an 89 percent rate with female therapists but only at a 43 percent rate with male therapists.

These findings reveal how much improvement rates may vary as a function of therapist factors and suggest how outcomes with other samples may improve when poorer therapists are dropped out, thus indicating the larger effects of the better therapists. It is possible that outcome statistics, especially from poorly controlled studies, are deflated by the use of practitioners who are conducting only a mere semblance of psychotherapy. The improvement rate for the better therapists in this study is comparable to the high rates reported during the early days of behavioral therapy by Wolpe (1958, 1964) and Lazarus (1963). It is also representative of the effectiveness shown by the six therapists in the Sloane study who were preselected for their expertise in dynamic and behavioral methods. Indeed, Wolpe and Lazarus were two of the therapists. Sloane et al. (1975) reported that there were no differences in improvement rates across the six therapists in that study.

Some outcome studies have actually studied therapist competence and used competence ratings to select therapists. For example, Rounsaville et al. (1988) reported results related to training therapists in interpersonal therapy for the NIMH Collaborative Depression project. The decisions concerning therapist inclusion in the treatment phase of the project were made by expert independent evalua-

tors who had not participated in the training or supervision of the original group of 11 carefully selected, experienced therapists. On the basis of ratings made from viewing two randomly selected, videotaped sessions, 2 of the 11 therapists were judged as not performing interpersonal therapy at an acceptable level. Later ratings resulted in dropping one therapist from the study. Unsatisfactory ratings resulted from either a failure to apply techniques consistently or a failure to refrain from using techniques incompatible with interpersonal therapy.

This finding suggests that a small number of therapists who received relatively intense training and were highly motivated to learn were not able to achieve competent performance. Most outcome studies have not provided such data on therapists, so it is impossible to estimate the breadth and depth of this phenomenon. Therapist variability can be found across a variety of treatment modalities and within very narrow treatments as well as treatments that focus on more general patient problems (e.g., Miller et al., 1980; Romney, 1988; Turner & Ascher, 1982).

A significant program of inquiry into the therapist's contribution has been conducted by the University of Pennsylvania psychotherapy research group. Luborsky, McClellan, Woody, O'Brien, and Auerbach (1985) reported the results of their analysis of the differential outcome of clients seen by nine different therapists. The patients were opiate-dependent males who underwent drug counseling alone or in combination with either supportive-expressive psychotherapy or cognitive-behavioral psychotherapy. One of the more important aspects of the methodology in this study was the use of treatment manuals to guide the delivery of services. Not only were therapists trained to offer the prescribed treatment, but their work was supervised and monitored. Thus, we have a situation (common in contemporary research) in which the individual differences between therapists within a treatment are intentionally minimized. In such an experimental design, one might reasonably expect that patient improvement would not be linked to the personal qualities of the therapist or at most would be linked in ways that would be small and hard to detect. The critical process of therapy would be technique bound, rather than person bound. Despite this, Luborsky et al. report that "profound differences were discovered in the therapists' success with the patients in their case load" (p. 602). Table 5.10 reproduces data from this study. It should be noted that all the treatments were effective but that the treatment involving either of the psychotherapies was more effective than drug counseling alone. In addition to and de-

TABLE 5.10 Percentage change from start of treatment to seven-month follow-up[a]

						Outcome Measures[b]			
			ASI						
Therapist	N	Drug Use	Employment Status	Legal Status	Psychiatric Status	Beck Depression Scale	SCL-90	Maudsley N Scale	Average Effect Size[c]
SE									
A	10	34	32	20	82	58	44	64	0.74
B	8	33	34	17	41	37	46	59	0.59
C	8	−14	12	7	−1	8	−2	13	0.19
CB									
D	11	61	19	17	36	36	39	44	0.53
E	10	70	22	13	17	17	30	30	0.44
F	9	48	10	11	14	14	21	33	0.46
DC									
G	9	51	8	13	7	4	9	−1	0.20
H	6	46	−4	6	10	−3	11	3	0.13
I	7	66	17	7	12	14	15	17	0.27

[a]Abbreviations are as follows: ASI, Addiction Severity Index; SCL-90, Hopkins Symptom Checklist-90: SE, supportive; CB, cognitive-behavioral; and DC, drug counseling.
[b]All criteria were measured during the 30 days before treatment start and before seven-month follow-up. Factor scores represent composites of several items indicative of patient status in that area. Percentage change was calculated against the treatment start baseline.
[c]Within-therapist effect size was averaged across all seven criteria. Effect size calculation for each criterion was pretreatment mean minus posttreatment mean, divided by pretreatment SD. Small change = 0.2; moderate change = 0.5; large change = 0.8.
Source: Reprinted by permission from Luborsky et al. (1985). Copyright 1985, American Medical Association.

spite a general psychotherapy effect, it is clear that substantial differences between therapists, within and between treatments, were apparent.

In their analysis of the therapy process, Luborsky et al. (1985) found that differences in outcome between therapists could be attributed to a number of interactional variables. Although there were minor differences between the patients seen by individual therapists, none of the differences found were typical of those that could be attributed to a "good" versus "poor" patient prognosis. No general patterns of favorable or unfavorable patient qualities were associated with a particular therapist. For example, each therapist saw about the same number of patients who met Research Diagnostic Criteria for antisocial personality and depression, and the patients had similar ratings of severity.

Although Luborsky et al. (1985) offer several important conclusions, two interpretations of their research will be emphasized here. The first is that despite careful selection, training, monitoring, and supervision, therapists offering the same treatments can have highly divergent results. Most notable were the differences between Therapists A and C who saw 10 and 8 patients respectively. While A's patients showed substantial improvement on a wide variety of outcomes, C's patients averaged

little improvement and on some criteria actually showed an average negative change!

The second conclusion is that the outcomes of individual therapists could be reanalyzed and summarized to draw general conclusions about therapist behaviors that were associated with positive and negative outcomes. Three therapist qualities were identified as discriminating more helpful from less helpful therapists: (1) the therapist's adjustment, skill, and interest in helping patients; (2) the purity of the treatment each offered; and (3) the quality of the therapist–patient relationship.

Crits-Christoph and Mintz (1991) have shown that the importance of the therapist (percentage of variance contributed to outcome) varies greatly across studies and possibility outcome measures. However, looking at selected studies published over a 20-year period, they report that the impact of the therapist has become smaller in more recent studies. This may be a result of the greater emphasis of contemporary studies on selecting, training, and monitoring therapist performance.

Crits-Christoph et al. (1991) have reported a meta-analytic study of therapist effects on outcome. Their meta-analysis of 15 studies and 27 treatment groups revealed an average therapist effect of 9 percent of the outcome variance, a figure equal to Cohen's (1977) definition of a medium effect size. One study showed therapist effects accounting for 49 percent of the outcome variance (!) while other studies showed no independent therapist effect. The highest partial correlations between independent variables and size of therapist effect were produced by *use of a treatment manual* and *therapist experience level*, where manuals and more experience were associated with smaller therapist differences. The authors argue further that "by ignoring the therapist factor, some investigators may have reported differences between treatments that were actually a function of therapist differences" (p. 89).

An example of this was obtained in the Sheffield Psychotherapy Project (Shapiro & Firth, 1987), where, it will be recalled, each client – therapist pair worked in both of two treatments. Shapiro, Firth-Cozens, and Stiles (1989) found that the advantage of prescriptive over exploratory therapy was largely confined to one of two principal project therapists. The therapist who was more effective in prescriptive therapy was less effective in the exploratory approach. Such an interaction effect may reflect differential skill, aptitude, or attitudinal compatibility with the two techniques.

Of course, the studies cited here constitute a mere beginning to the examination of the contribution of the individual therapist. We simply do not know enough yet about the therapist factor to specify when and how it makes a difference, nor when it matters more than technique. What we do know is that there are intriguing possibilities for new discoveries here and that this issue has been ignored to a surprising degree (Lambert, 1989). Researchers, influenced by mechanistic models, have placed their bets on technique factors as the more powerful agents in therapeutic change.

Control Group Data as Moderators of Therapeutic Effects

We have stated previously (Bergin, 1971) that true no-treatment control groups are impossible to set up as contrast groups for psychotherapy efficacy studies. Distressed human beings do not sit still like rats in cages waiting for an experiment to end. They act to relieve their distress, and we documented in the previous editions of this chapter how they may seek relief from their pain. A follow-up of a previous U.S. national study on this matter by Veroff, Kulka, and Douvan (1981), spanning the period from 1957 to 1976, revealed an amazing increase in resources and methods of self-help outside the formal mental health establishment. Past studies showed that as many as 50 percent of persons seeking formal therapeutic help had also sought help from other sources (cf. Bergin, 1971). Veroff et al. found in their 1976 sample that 20 to

38 percent of persons who felt they were "ready for professional help" also sought informal help.

Studies examining psychotherapy are confounded by a number of self-help methods that have been shown to be effective. For example, Morawetz (1989) examined the effectiveness of a commercial self-help manual and tapes (Bootzin, 1976) on a large group of adults suffering from insomnia. The self-help therapy significantly reduced sleep problems and was as effective as therapy in some cases. Of importance here is the fact that this material is easily obtained and offers technically sound therapy developed by a professional.

These results are comparable to similar research on a variety of other behavioral therapy manuals for fear reduction, weight reduction, study behavior, and the like (Glasgow & Rosen, 1978). Rosen (1988) suggests that there are more than 150 self-help programs based on behavioral principles alone. The most popular areas for self-help reading would seem to be parenting, personal growth, and relationship problems (Starker, 1988). Coleman and Ganong (1990) have suggested the benefits of self-help books in other contexts, namely, adjustment of step-family members to their new family.

Ogles, Lambert, and Craig (1991) examined the relative value of self-help books for dealing with the breakup of an intimate relationship. Surprisingly, people who read self-help books in this area seemed to show improvement in a variety of symptoms, including depression, especially if expectations were high and few previous books had been read.

Not only are hundreds of books with specific psychological techniques readily available, but a wide variety of other media-based approaches as well as a host of highly specific self-help groups are also available and popular (e.g., AA, Overeaters Anonymous).

The range and substance of life-changing events occurring in so-called control subjects are rarely monitored. One study that did so (Cross, Sheehan, & Khan, 1980) showed that a surprisingly large amount of outside advice and counsel seeking occurred in both treated and untreated groups. Even more surprising was the finding that the treated groups engaged in this behavior more frequently than controls and that behavioral therapy cases did so substantially more than the insight therapy cases! If this finding holds up, it would prove the opposite of our contention that control groups deflate effect sizes because they participate in quasi-therapy experiences during the control period. Even though controls are obtaining outside counsel, they may be doing less of it than the treated cases. If outside support and advice have positive effects, then some of the therapeutic effect in treated groups is due to extra therapy factors, especially in behavioral therapy. Of course, it may be that good therapy stimulates people to utilize outside resources more effectively, which is in itself an important therapeutic benefit.

In any event, it is evident that treated and untreated groups differ in several ways other than treatment versus no-treatment. Until such differences are eliminated or are systematically measured, correlated with outcomes, or held constant by analysis of covariance, and so on, ambiguity must continue in our interpretation of outcome. The true size of the therapeutic effect may be larger or smaller, depending on the results of such new observations.

We have already noted our conclusion that placebo control groups do not help with these problems because placebo groups are, in essence, therapy groups, and effective placebos include many of the very same ingredients as treatment groups. As things stand now, it appears that the various control group methods that have been designed are inadequate, that they do not provide fair tests of therapy effects, and that often effect sizes for therapy would be larger if they were not reduced in magnitude by subtracting or comparing them with the effect sizes of so-called control groups. A real test of treatment efficacy ought to be uncontaminated by control conditions that overlap with the treated conditions.

DETERIORATION, NEGATIVE EFFECTS, AND ESTIMATES OF THERAPEUTIC CHANGE

We suggested in the preceding commentary on the therapist factor in estimating outcomes that therapist variability has an effect on average estimates of change. Evidence was presented there of some rather large differences in outcome rates when they were estimated therapist by therapist. In that context, negative change appeared in some cases and was associated more with some therapists than with others. To the extent that negative changes occur, they obviously subtract from overall therapeutic effect sizes. To the extent that such events can be understood and reduced, improvement rates will be greater.

Although negative effects are difficult if not impossible to study in an experimentally controlled way, research more than suggests that some patients are worse as a result of psychotherapy. This does not mean that all worsening is therapy produced. Some cases may be on a progressive decline that no therapist effort can stop. The extent or rate of such negative change or of "spontaneous" deterioration in untreated groups has never been deter-

mined, so there is no baseline from which to judge deterioration rates observed in treated groups. The alternative is to observe negative change in experiments using treated versus control conditions and to study the specific connections between therapy processes and patient responses.

In prior work (Bergin & Lambert, 1978; Lambert, Bergin, & Collins, 1977) evidence from over 50 studies on the incidence, prevalence, and magnitude of negative change was described. That process involved piecing together obscure bits of evidence since there are few, if any, definitive studies. We concluded that the negative effects were sufficient to reduce estimates of the efficacy of therapy. In addition, it was concluded that the occurrence of therapy- or therapist-induced worsening was widespread, occurring across a variety of treatment modalities including group and family therapies. Further, we implied that there was a causal link between negative outcomes and therapeutic activities, particularly for some specific clients.

Many more recent studies continue to document rates of deterioration in patients, even in those who participate in carefully controlled research protocols (cf. Beutler, Frank, Schieber, Calvert, & Gaines, 1984; Doherty, Lester, & Leigh, 1986; Emmelkamp, DeHaan, & Hoogduin, 1990; Henry, Schacht, & Strupp, 1986; Holtzworth-Munroe, Jacobson, DeKlyen, & Whisman, 1989; Jacobson et al., 1984; Lafferty et al., 1991; McGlashan et al., 1990; Szapocznick et al., 1989). Those studies that use controls usually show that deterioration is lower in controls than in treated samples.

After reviewing the empirical literature and the critiques of the evidence accumulated (cf. Mays & Franks, 1980, 1985), it is our view that psychotherapy can and does harm a portion of those it is intended to help. The study of negative change has important implications for the selection of clients for treatment, the suitability of specific procedures for some clients, and the selection, training, and monitoring of therapists. We turn now to a discussion of these issues and a review of studies that further elucidate the nature of the problem.

What Causes Deterioration?

Client and technique interaction effects. Despite the lack of specificity in research reports, it is apparent that patient diagnosis and degree of disturbance are related variables that appear to be linked to deterioration, especially when they are combined with therapeutic techniques that are aimed at breaking down, challenging, or undermining habitual coping strategies or defenses. Indications are that more severely disturbed (psychotic) patients, as in Fairweather et al. (1960) and Feighner, Brown, and Oliver (1973); borderline patients, as in Horwitz (1974) and Weber, Elinson, and Moss (1965); or the initially most disturbed encounter group participants, as in Lieberman, Yalom, and Miles (1973) are the most likely to experience negative outcomes. Berzins, Bednar, and Severy (1975) also found that the patients who showed a consistent pattern of negative change were typified by a disproportionate number of schizophrenics and that other client characteristics were not significantly related to this pattern.

These findings are consistent with long-term follow-up data on borderline personality disorder (McGlashan, 1986; Stone, 1990; Stone, Stone, & Hurt, 1987). Although these patients have a more positive outcome if followed for 10 to 20 years into their thirties and forties, during the follow-up period nearly 10 percent die of suicide. Many also reenter therapy and remain in treatment despite the fact that they have had intensive inpatient treatment for two or more years.

Similar interaction between diagnosis and treatment strategies has also been reported in group treatment. In a widely quoted study reported by Lieberman et al. (1973), it was found that variables such as low involvement in the group, low levels of self-esteem, low positive self-concept, and greater anticipation or need for fulfillment were positively related to deterioration. Likewise, casualties were less effective at using interpersonal skills in their adaptation to the group experience.

Kernberg (1973) reported that low quality of interpersonal relationships was a prognostically poor sign, and that this, coupled with low initial anxiety tolerance and low motivation, yielded poor outcomes in psychoanalysis and purely supportive psychotherapies but better outcomes in supportive-expressive treatments. Strupp (1980a, 1980b, 1980c, 1980d) obtained a similar set of findings in his analyses of improvers and nonimprovers in the Vanderbilt study. Similar conclusions were reached by Stone (1985) in an analysis of his own private practice of dynamic therapy. Of those who were worse at the end of therapy, seven out of eight had been diagnosed as either borderline or psychotic at the inception of therapy.

Stone (1990) has further tried to specify patients with a borderline personality disorder who are not suitable candidates for exploratory psychotherapy. Among these he includes certain fragile, traumatized patients, those with pronounced psychopathic traits, or those who have some psychopathic traits combined with narcissism. He suggests that many should not undergo psychotherapy, while others are significantly helped by an eclectic combination of interventions, including medications. Crown (1983) has also offered some sound guidelines for practice.

Beutler et al. (1984) report an important study of group therapy in which significant amounts of deterioration were found. The study sought to measure the incremental effects of adding a behaviorally oriented group, a supportive-feedback–oriented group, or an expressive-experiential group to routine care offered to patients in an acute, short-term inpatient program. The most salient finding of the study was the nearly one standard deviation net deterioration in patients undergoing the expressive-experiential treatment. The authors could not determine if the negative effects were due to the inexperience and noncompliance of the therapists who offered this form of treatment or to the treatment itself. The experiential group emphasized emotional expression, breaking down defenses, and emotional release.

They state that "even with caution, expressive-experiential treatments are inappropriate in short-term, acute care centers" (p. 75). Beutler et al. (1984) are to be complimented for the publication of their results and their forthright intention to identify the causes of negative effects.

Therapist factors.   Few direct studies of therapist characteristics and negative outcome have been conducted. Lafferty et al. (1991) studied the relationship of therapist characteristics to therapy outcome. They divided 30 trainees into two groups based on the residual change scores (pre- to posttreatment) of patients they treated. Those whose patients had negative change scores that exceeded one-half standard deviation were assigned to the "ineffective" group. The therapy variables of interest were therapist emotional adjustment, relationship attitudes, patient involvement, directiveness/support, credibility, theoretical orientation, and values.

Discriminant function analysis indicated that therapist empathy was most predictive of being an effective or ineffective therapist. This was followed by therapist perception of greater patient involvement in therapy and greater directiveness and support by the therapist.

Value differences were also clear. Less effective therapists placed more emphasis on the terminal values of "have a comfortable (i.e., prosperous) and exciting (i.e., stimulating, active) life." More effective therapists placed significantly more emphasis on intellectual values (i.e., intelligence and reflection). An important examination of mechanisms through which negative effects are transmitted by therapists was described by Yalom and Lieberman (1971). Their main finding was that the style of the group leaders was most predictive of negative outcomes. These leaders were impatient and authoritarian in approach, and they insisted on immediate self-disclosure, emotional expression, and attitude change. There were five leaders of this type, and all produced casualties but one. The one exception stated that he realized there were fragile persons in his group, so that he deviated from his usual style and "pulled his punches."

Kaplan (1982), as well as Bentley, DeJulio, Lambert, and Dinan (1975), replicated the Lieberman, Yalom, and Miles study. Both replications found far less evidence for negative effects. Although these studies used a somewhat different methodology, the major difference seemed to be the power of the leaders. In both replications, the group leaders (who were graduate students) were not nearly as confrontational and aggressive as leaders in the original study.

Typical of the research in this area is that reported on the growing number of nonprofessional programs that seem to be led by charismatic leaders who foster an emotionally intense pressure for disclosure and conformity. For example, Doherty et al. (1986) examined essay and interview data for 50 married couples who had undergone a 44-hour "marriage encounter" weekend. The authors estimate that one in eight couples is strongly affected by the encounter. Of these, approximately 50 percent are helped and 50 percent are negatively affected (7%).

Interestingly, the rate of negative effects is similar to the nearly 10 percent proposed by Lieberman et al. (1973) for encounter groups as well as Gurman and Kniskern (1978) for marital and family therapy. The mechanisms for passing on negative effects seem similar as well. The group experience is intense; and some persons use the experience to be brutally honest. Unrealistic expectations for help by some participants are also commonly mentioned, as well as coercive group norms for openness and intimacy. The leaders strive for rapid *rebirth* rather than enrichment, so that the marriage encounter has a religious flare similar to that found in the Lieberman et al. report.

Certainly the professional clinician should not only avoid these techniques (see the ethical and practical guidelines offered by Jones, 1985; Korda & Pancrazio, 1989; Schwitzgebel & Schwitzgebel, 1980) but should also carefully consider the legal and ethical ramifications of referring clients to groups in which these techniques are employed.

Information on negative consequences of therapist maladjustment, exploitiveness, and immaturity can be gathered with ease from client self-reports. Striano (1982), in a consumer report study, examined the personal experiences of 25 selected cases who had been to more than one therapist, one of whom was reported as being helpful and one of whom was said be unhelpful or harmful. Through the reports of these clients, she documented a variety of "horror stories" of the type that are often shared privately among clients and professionals but are rarely published. A number of such reports are also recounted in previous editions of this chapter and in Lambert et al. (1977). Striano has also published popular preventive books (1987, 1988) to guide clients as they choose therapists and monitor the process of their own therapy. Grunebaum (1985) has added to this repertoire of reports via surveys of mental health professionals who described therapy they had undergone. Ten percent of these professionals reported being harmed by therapy. Such accounts lack documentation independent of client report, so they could be laden to an unknown degree with subjective biases; however, such complaints are of social and clinical importance, and they provide reasons to continue inquiries into therapist factors in negative change.

Another study more extensively and objectively examined the process of positive and negative change conducted by two contrasting therapists. Ricks (1974) studied the adult status of a group of disturbed adolescent boys who had been seen by either of two therapists in a major child guidance clinic. Although the long-term outcomes of these two therapists were not different for less disturbed clients, there were striking differences in their therapeutic styles and outcomes with the more disturbed boys. For all cases in the sample, 55 percent were judged to have become schizophrenic in adulthood. Only 27 percent of Therapist A's cases, however, had such an outcome, whereas 88 percent of Therapist B's cases deteriorated to such a state. The caseloads of the two therapists were equal in degree of disturbance and other characteristics at the beginning of therapy.

In analyzing differences in therapist styles, it was found that Therapist A devoted more time to those who were most disturbed while the less successful therapist (B) did the opposite. Therapist A also made more use of resources outside the immediate therapy situation, was firm and direct with patients, supported movement toward autonomy, and facilitated problem solving in everyday life, all in the context of a strong therapeutic relationship.

Therapist B seemed to be frightened by severe pathology and emotionally withdrew from the more difficult cases. He frequently commented on the difficulties of cases and seemed to become depressed when confronted with a particularly unpromising one. He became caught up in the boys' depressed and hopeless feelings and thereby reinforced the client's sense of self-rejection and futility. Careful studies like this give strong support to traditional clinical beliefs regarding the effects of therapist personality and countertransference phenomena on outcomes.

Sachs (1983) conducted one of the most careful empirical investigations specifically aimed at illuminating the process that leads to negative effects. Most dramatic in identifying success and failure in psychotherapy were the Errors in Technique subscale ratings, which indicated that therapist competence and skill in applying verbal techniques led to positive or negative change. One error in technique that could be reliably rated, and proved all too frequent, involved the failure to structure or focus the session. Additionally, several other errors seemed important, including the failure of the therapist to address patient's negative attitudes toward either the therapist or therapy, the passive acceptance of problematic aspects of the patient's behavior such as resistance or evasiveness, and the use of harmful interventions such as poorly timed or inappropriate interpretations. In a related effort, Henry et al. (1986) examined the interpersonal interactions of high changers versus low changers for patterns of interaction. Good versus poor outcome was differentiated by greater levels of "helping and protecting" and "offering and understanding" and lower levels of "blaming and belittling." Poor outcome cases seemed to be more passive dependent and avoidant or defensive in their interactions.

Other factors. While negative effects have been widely observed across the spectrum of therapies, including group, marriage, and family therapy, there is presently no clear evidence on differential effects as a function of modality. It may be that dynamic treatments with seriously disturbed cases and aggressive group techniques yield more risk; while nondirective therapy and behavior therapies yield less risk, but, thus far, the data on these hypotheses are limited. Some behavioral methods involving aversion or environmental controls have been reported as producing negative consequences but the data are unsystematic (cf. Bergin & Lambert, 1978). Previous fears that "flooding" (intense

or prolonged exposure to anxiety-provoking stimuli) would produce harmful effects have not so far been supported (Shipley & Boudewyns, 1980).

Of considerable interest is a reanalysis of data from the NIMH Collaborative Depression study. Ogles, Sawyer, and Lambert (1993) presented rates of improvement based on an analysis of clinically significant change that shows some differences among theoretical orientations. The percentage of negative change by treatment group is presented in Table 5.11. Surprisingly, in this well-controlled study of a widely accepted treatment for depression, those receiving cognitive-behavioral therapy had a greater chance of having a negative outcome.

Two areas of investigation related to treatment modality have aroused considerable interest in the last decade. First is the issue of outcomes in conjoint marital therapy versus individual marital therapy. Since Gurman and Kniskern (1978) suggested high rates of deterioration in individual marital therapy compared to conjoint sessions, attempts to offer patients conjoint therapy have increased if not become codified. Wells and Giannetti (1986) have questioned the accuracy and basis of Gurman and Kniskern's (1981) suggestion that individual therapy for marital problems leads to greater deterioration than conjoint therapy for these problems. Gurman and Kniskern (1986) replied to this critique and reasserted their original position, but neither article presents new data that bear on the issue.

On a related topic, one can find clinicians and researchers cautioning practitioners to include family members besides the identified patient in treatment or either family members or the family as a unit may suffer a negative outcome (e.g., Phillips, 1983). Of course, these calls often come from family therapists. There is some, albeit limited, empirical support for this position. For example, Szapocznick et al. (1989) studied structural family therapy and psychodynamic child therapy for Hispanic boys having emotional and behavioral problems. Among the most important findings of this study was the relative equivalence of the treatments in reducing a

TABLE 5.11 Frequency and percent of reliable negative change by treatment group and measurement method for clients who completed treatment[a]

	CBT	IPT	Imipramine-CM	PLA-CM	Total
	n (%)	n (%)	n (%)	n (%)	n (%)
Beck Depression Inventory	4(10)	0(0)	2(5)	2(5)	8(5)
Hamilton Depression Rating	5(13)	0(0)	2(5)	3(8)	10(6)
Hopkins Symptom Checklist	4(10)	1(2)	2(5)	2(5)	9(6)

[a]CBT = cognitive-behavioral therapy; IPT = interpersonal psychotherapy; CM = clinical management; PLA-CM = medication placebo plus clinical management. Reprinted by permission of the authors: Ogles, Lambert, & Sawyer (1993).

variety of symptoms while the therapies had different impacts on families. The families of boys treated with dynamic therapy began to deteriorate after the boys in those families improved.

On the other hand, there is also evidence for negative effects related to spouse involvement in the therapy of individual pathology. Badenoch, Fisher, Hefner, and Swift (1984) report on the use of spouse-aided therapy for persistent psychiatric disorders. They identified patients and spouses who responded negatively to adjunctive marital therapy. The patients who got worse following therapy were those whose problems came to the surface more clearly during therapy. Negative effects seemed to be related to either an extrapunitive style in both partners or the repression and denial of marital dissatisfaction that became clear during the therapy.

A specific controversy of some interest in the literature has been the possible negative effects of treating some problems such as agoraphobia and obsessive compulsive disorder (OC) without involvement of the spouse. The clinical suggestion is that marital problems are more frequent in these disorders and that marital relationships may deteriorate if left untreated while pursuing individual therapy for the neurotic problem. A few studies have examined the effects on the neurotic problem of including the spouse in the treatment process (Barlow, O'Brien, & Last, 1984; Cobb, Mathews, Childs-Clark, & Blowers, 1984) with mixed results. Emmelkamp et al. (1990) investigated whether partner involvement would enhance the effectiveness of treatment of obsessive compulsive disorder (by in vivo self-exposure); whether outcome of treatment was affected by the quality of the marriage; and whether the treatment affected the marriage or the psychological problems of the partner. Although a substantial number of OCs were found to have marital problems, behavioral treatment directed at the OC disorder resulted in improvement irrespective of marital quality and partner involvement in the therapy. The effects of treatment led neither to a *deterioration* of the marriage nor to adjustment problems in the partner. This report suggests that while clinicians may observe occasional negative effects of individual therapy on a marital relationship, systematic support for this conclusion is lacking (see also Chapter 9, this volume).

One final issue that should be mentioned is that we have limited our discussion of negative effects to scientifically important dimensions of outcome —such as patient diagnosis and treatment techniques. We have not gone into aspects of the therapeutic encounter that are rarely observed in research settings. These neglected topics include violations of the contractual obligations of therapists, such as violation of patients' rights to confidentiality, failure to report child abuse, and other violations of ethical standards of practice such as sexual contact with the patient. The number of lawsuits aimed at such violations is rising markedly and these index a complete failure of the therapeutic encounter with its ensuing negative consequences.

Apfel and Simon (1985) elaborate on the negative aspects of sexual contact between therapist and client. Rates of such contact are difficult to establish, but estimates based on questionnaire data suggest that anywhere from 5 to 20 percent of male therapists and 2 percent of female therapists have had some erotic contact with patients. Given these relatively large figures and the likelihood of repeated contacts with multiple patients, the damage to patients is a significant event, so far untapped in research on the process and outcome of therapy. We are limited here to case study methodology. Using these procedures, Apfel and Simon (1985) outlined eight broad categories of harm to patients and provided case examples for support.

This has become such a widespread and serious problem that the Committee on Women in Psychology (1989) published consumer guidelines to help patients deal with sexual issues with therapists. The guidelines clarify appropriate and inappropriate touching and suggest steps to be taken to avoid sexual contact and deal with it if it occurs.

CONCLUSION

Research on psychotherapy outcomes has resulted in conclusions that have implications for theory, research, and clinical practice.

1. Many psychotherapies that have been subjected to empirical study have been shown to have demonstrable effects on a variety of clients. These effects are not only statistically significant but also clinically meaningful. Psychotherapy facilitates the remission of symptoms. It not only speeds up the natural healing process but also often provides additional coping strategies and methods for dealing with future problems. Psychologists, psychiatrists, social workers, and marriage and family therapists as well as patients can be assured that a broad range of therapies, when offered by skillful, wise, and stable therapists, are likely to result in appreciable gains for the client.

2. We now have better general estimates of the amount of therapy needed in order to bring about clinically meaningful change. Data support the use

of brief therapies for some problems and cast doubt on their value for other problems. The issue of dose-effect promises to be an important area of future study because of its practical, economic, and ethical consequences.

3. The effects of therapy tend to be lasting. While some problems, such as addictive disorders, tend to recur, the gains many patients make in therapy endure. This is probably due to the fact that most therapists are interested in enduring changes rather than symptomatic improvements. Research suggests that therapists should expend greater systematic efforts at helping patients solidify the gains made in therapy and focus attention near the end of treatment on the meaning of improvement to the patient and methods of coping with future problems. As difficult as it is to study the long-term effects of therapy, continued effort should be expended on long-term follow-up studies and upon strategies that are intended to increase the permanence of change.

4. Not only is there clear evidence for the effectiveness of therapy relative to untreated patients, but psychotherapy patients show gains that surpass those resulting from pseudotherapies and placebo controls. These types of control groups are aimed at discovering whether therapies add anything beyond what can be achieved through treatments that offer a supportive relationship and hope or expectancy of improvement. Again, psychotherapists are more than placebologists. Indeed, the placebo concept is not viable in psychotherapy research. Future research would do well to focus on dismantling studies, components analysis studies, and comparative outcome studies that use an accepted treatment in comparison to a new treatment in order to identify therapeutic factors rather than focusing on the outdated notion of placebo controls.

5. Although research continues to support the efficacy of those therapies that have been rigorously tested, differences in outcome between various forms of therapy are not as pronounced as might have been expected. Behavioral therapy, cognitive therapy, and eclectic mixtures of these have shown superior outcomes to traditional verbal therapies in several studies on specific disorders, but this is by no means the general case. When this superiority is in evidence, the results have been attributed to the bias of researchers and the selectivity in criteria of change; however, the critics can be biased and selective too. Although there is little evidence of clinically meaningful superiority of one form of psychotherapy over another with respect to moderate outpatient disorders, behavioral and cognitive methods appear to add a significant increment of

efficacy with respect to a number of difficult problems (e.g., panic, phobias, and compulsion) and to provide useful methods with a number of nonneurotic problems with which traditional therapies have shown little effectiveness (e.g., childhood aggression, psychotic behavior, and health-related behaviors).

6. Given the growing evidence that there are probably some specific technique effects, as well as large common effects across treatments, the vast majority of therapists have become eclectic in orientation. This appears to reflect a healthy response to empirical evidence and a rejection of previous trends toward rigid allegiances to schools of treatment. It also opens up the possibility of more carefully matching techniques to client dispositions, personality traits, and other diagnostic differences. Most outcome research has focused on main effects of techniques, but there is still the potential for delineating differential interaction effects between therapy method and client type.

7. Interpersonal, social, and affective factors common across therapies still loom large as stimulators of patient improvement. It should come as no surprise that helping people deal with depression, inadequacy, anxiety, and inner conflicts, as well as helping them form viable relationships and meaningful directions for their lives, can be greatly facilitated in a therapeutic relationship that is characterized by trust, warmth, acceptance, and human wisdom. These relationship factors are probably crucial even in the more technical therapies that generally ignore relationship factors and emphasize the importance of technique in their theory of change. This is not to say that techniques are irrelevant but that their power for change is limited when compared with personal influence. Common factors that are currently popular for explaining improvement in therapy also include exposure to anxiety-provoking stimuli, the encouragement to participate in other risk-taking behavior, and efforts at mastery. Research suggests not only that clients would be wise to pick therapists on the basis of their ability to relate, but also that training programs should emphasize the development of the therapist as a person in parity with the acquisition of therapeutic techniques.

The individual therapist can play a surprisingly large role in treatment outcome even when treatment is being offered within the stipulations of manual-guided therapy. Recognition of the important place held by a therapist's relationship skills, facilitative attitudes, wisdom based on experience, and related nontechnical skills in producing positive change in patients should in no way be construed as suggesting that technical proficiency has no unique contribution to make. Future research should focus not only on the important factors common across therapies but also on the specific effects of particular interventions. The current trend to provide therapy in a systematic way, as characterized by the use of treatment manuals, and further studies of the process of therapy may yet allow for more definitive conclusions regarding the contribution of technique factors.

8. Research on the effects of less experienced clinicians and paraprofessionals complements the conclusions drawn about schools of therapy and common factors. Paraprofessionals, who in many cases are selected, trained, and supervised by professional therapists, are sometimes able to be as helpful as practicing clinicians. These paraprofessionals should continue to play an important role in providing some mental health services. They are especially useful in providing social support and in offering structured treatment programs under supervision.

9. The development and use of meta-analytic procedures for integrating outcome research is a methodological advancement that has enabled scholars and clinicians to better understand research findings. As more and more meta-analytic reviews are published, it is becoming obvious that this group of techniques has not reduced the controversies surrounding the interpretation of research findings. Meta-analysis is not a panacea and cannot be used to create worthwhile information if it is based on poorly designed studies. An important task of future meta-analytic reviews will be to translate the abstract review into clinically meaningful terms.

10. Although the foregoing broad, positive statements about psychotherapy can be made with more confidence than ever before, it is still important to point out that average positive effects mask considerable variability in outcomes. Wide variations exist in therapists. The therapist factor, as a contributor to outcome, is looming large in the assessment of outcomes. Some therapists appear to be unusually effective. Nevertheless, we end this review on a cautionary note. It is apparent that not all are helped by therapy and that a portion of those whom it is intended to help are actually harmed by inept applications of treatments, negative therapist characteristics, or poor combinations of treatment technique and patient problem.

Much more research needs to be conducted before the exact relationship between the process of therapy and its outcome will be known. The public deserves treatments that are based not only on our best clinical judgment but also on systematic research conducted under controlled situations. It is

our duty to be sensitive to both the positive and negative effects of therapy and to base our treatment efforts on a broad empirical foundation.

REFERENCES

Allen, M., Hunter, J. E., & Donohue, W. A. (1989). Meta-analysis of self-report data on the effectiveness of public speaking anxiety treatment techniques. *Communication Education, 38,* 54–76.

Andrews, G. (1983). A treatment outline for depressive disorders. *Australian and New Zealand Journal of Psychiatry, 17,* 129–146.

Andrews, G., Guitar, B., & Howie, P. (1980). Meta-analysis of the effects of stuttering treatment. *Journal of Speech and Hearing Disorders, 45,* 287–307.

Andrews, G., & Harvey, R. (1981). Does psychotherapy benefit neurotic patients: A re-analysis of the Smith, Glass, & Miller data. *Archives of General Psychiatry, 38,* 1203–1208.

Annis, H. M. (1990). Relapse to substance abuse: Empirical findings within a cognitive-social learning approach? *Journal of Psychoactive Drugs, 22,* 117–124.

Apfel, R. J., & Simon, B. (1985). Patient–therapist sexual contact: I. Psychodynamic perspectives on the causes and results. *Psychotherapy and Psychosomatics, 43,* 57–62.

Asay, T. P., Lambert, M. J., Christensen, E. R., & Beutler, L. E. (1984). *A meta-analysis of mental health treatment outcome.* Unpublished manuscript, Brigham Young University, Department of Psychology.

Auerbach, A. H., & Johnson, M. (1977). Research on the therapist's level of experience. In A. S. Gurman & A. M. Razin (Eds.), *Effective psychotherapy: A handbook of research* (pp. 84–102). New York: Pergamon Press.

Badenoch, A., Fisher, J., Hefner, R. J., & Swift, H. (1984). Predicting the outcome of spouse-sided therapy for persisting psychiatric disorders. *American Journal of Family Therapy, 12,* 59–71.

Balestrieri, M., Williams, P., & Wilkinson, G. (1988). Special mental health treatment in general practice: A meta-analysis. *Psychological Medicine, 18,* 717.

Bandura, A. (1987). Self-efficacy: Towards a unifying theory of behavior change. *Psychological Review, 84,* 191–215.

Barabasz, A. F., Baer, L., Sheehan, D. V., & Barabasz, M. (1986) A three year follow-up of hypnosis and restricted environmental stimulation therapy for smoking. *The International Journal of Clinical and Experimental Hypnosis, 34,* 169–181.

Barker, S. L., Funk, S. C., & Houston, B. K. (1988). Psychological treatment versus nonspecific factors: A meta-analysis of conditions that engender comparable expectations for improvement. *Clinical Psychology Review, 8,* 579–594.

Barlow, D. H. (1988). *Anxiety and its disorders: The nature and treatment of anxiety and panic.* New York: Guilford.

Barlow, D. H., & Cerny, J. A. (1988). *Psychological treatment of panic.* New York: Guilford.

Barlow, D. H., Craske, M., Cerny, J. A., & Klosko, J. (1989). Behavioral treatment of panic disorder. *Behavior Therapy, 20,* 261–282.

Barlow, D. H., O'Brien, G. T., & Last, C. G. (1984). Couples treatment of agoraphobia. *Behavior Therapy, 15,* 41–58.

Beck, A. T., Rush, A. J., Shaw, F. B., & Emery, G. (1979). *The cognitive therapy of depression.* New York: Guilford.

Bellack, A. B., & Hersen, M. (1990). *Handbook of comparative treatments for adult disorders.* New York: Wiley.

Bently, J. L., DeJulio, S. S., Lambert, M. J., & Dinan, W. (1975). *The effects of traditional versus confrontive leadership styles in producing casualties in encounter group participants.* Unpublished manuscript, Brigham Young University, Provo, UT.

Benton, M. K., & Schroeder, H. E. (1990). Social skills training with schizophrenics: A meta-analytic evaluation. *Journal of Consulting and Clinical Psychology, 58,* 741–747.

Bergin, A. E. (1966). Some implications of psychotherapy research for therapeutic practice. *Journal of Abnormal Psychology, 71,* 235–246.

Bergin, A. E. (1971). The evaluation of therapeutic outcomes. In A. E. Bergin & S. L. Garfield (Eds.), *Handbook of psychotherapy and behavior change* (pp. 217–270). New York: Wiley.

Bergin, A. E., & Lambert, M. J. (1978). The evaluation of therapeutic outcomes. In S. L. Garfield & A. E. Bergin (Eds.), *Handbook of psychotherapy and behavior change: An empirical analysis* (2nd ed.). New York: Wiley.

Bergin, A. E., & Suinn, R. M. (1975). Individual psychotherapy and behavior therapy. *Annual Review of Psychology, 26,* 509–556.

Berlin, S. (1985). Maintaining reduced levels of self-criticism through relapse-prevention treatment. *Social Work Research and Abstracts, 21,* 21–33.

Berman, J. S., Miller, R. C., & Massman, P. J. (1985). Cognitive therapy versus systematic desensitization: Is our treatment superior? *Psychological Bulletin, 97,* 451–461.

Berman, J. S., & Norton, N. C. (1985). Does professional training make a therapist more effective? *Psychological Bulletin, 98,* 401–406.

Berzins, J. I., Bednar, R. L., & Severy, L. J. (1975). The problem of intersource consensus in measuring therapeutic outcomes: New data and multivariate perspectives. *Journal of Abnormal Psychology, 84,* 10–19.

Beutler, L. E., (1979). Toward specific psychological therapies for specific conditions. *Journal of Consulting and Clinical Psychology, 47,* 882–892.

Beutler, L. E. (1991). Have all won and must all have prizes? Revisiting Luborsky et al.'s verdict. *Journal of Consulting and Clinical Psychology, 59,* 226–232.

Beutler, L. E., Frank, M., Schieber, S. C., Calvert, S., & Gaines, J. (1984). Comparative effects of group psychotherapies in a short-term inpatient setting: An experience with deterioration effects. *Psychiatry, 47,* 66–76.

Blanchard, E. B. (1987). Long-term effects of behavioral treatment of chronic headache. *Behavior Therapy, 18,* 375–385.

Blanchard, E. B., Andrasik, F., Ahles, T. A., Teders, S. J., & O'Keefe, D. (1980). Migraine and tension headache: A meta-analytic review. *Behavior Therapy, 11,* 613–631.

Bloch, S., & Lambert, M. J. (1985). What price psychotherapy? A rejoinder. *British Journal of Psychiatry, 146,* 96–98.

Bootzin, R. R. (1976). Self-management techniques for controlling insomnia. In C. M. Franks (Ed.), *Behavior therapy: Techniques, principles and patient aids.* New York: Biomonitoring Applications, Inc. (audiotape).

Bowers, T., & Clum, G. (1988). Relative contributions of specific and nonspecific treatment effects: Meta-analysis of placebo-controlled behavior therapy research. *Psychological Bulletin, 103,* 315–323.

Brody, N. (1990). Behavior therapy versus placebo: Comment on Bowers and Clum's meta-analysis. *Psychological Bulletin, 107,* 106–109.

Brownell, K. D., & Jeffery, R. W. (1987). Improving long-term weight loss: Pushing the limits of treatment. *Behavior Therapy, 18,* 353–374.

Burlingame, G. M., Fuhriman, A. J., Paul, S., & Ogles, B. M. (1989). Implementing a time-limited therapy program: Differential effects of training and experience. *Psychotherapy, 26,* 303–313.

Butler, S. F., & Strupp, H. H. (1986). Specific and nonspecific factors in psychotherapy: A problematic paradigm for psychotherapy research. *Psychotherapy, 23,* 30–40.

Carey, M. P., & Burish, T. G. (1987). Providing relaxation training to cancer patients: A comparison of three delivery techniques. *Journal of Consulting and Clinical Psychology, 55,* 732–737.

Christensen, H., Hadzi-Pavlovic, D., Andrews, G., & Mattick, R. (1987). Behavior therapy and tricyclic medication in the treatment of obsessive-compulsive disorder: A quantitative review. *Journal of Consulting and Clincial Psychology, 55,* 701–711.

Clark, D. M., Salkovskis, P. M., & Chalkey, A. J. (1985). Respiratory control as a treatment for panic attacks. *Journal of Behavior Therapy and Experimental Psychiatry, 16,* 23–30.

Clum, G. A. (1989). Psychological interventions vs. drugs in the treatment of panic. *Behavior Therapy, 20,* 429–457.

Clum, G. A., & Bowers, T. G. (1990). Behavior therapy better than placebo treatments: Fact or artifact? *Psychological Bulletin, 107,* 110–113.

Cobb, J. P., Mathews, A. M., Childs-Clark, A., & Blowers, C. M. (1984). The spouse as co-therapist in the treatment of agoraphobia. *British Journal of Psychiatry, 144,* 282–287.

Cohen, J. (1977). *Statistical power analysis for the behavioral sciences.* New York: Academic Press.

Cohen, J. (1988). *Statistical power analysis for the behavioral sciences.* Hillsdale, NJ: Lawrence Erlbaum.

Coleman, M., & Ganong, L. H. (1990). The use of juvenile fiction and self-help books with stepfamilies. *Journal of Counseling and Development, 68,* 327–331.

Committee on Women in Psychology. (1989). If sex enters into the psychotherapy relationship. *Professional Psychology: Research and Practice, 20,* 112–115.

Cooley, E. F., & LaJoy, R. (1980). Therapeutic relationship and improvement as perceived by clients and therapists. *Journal of Clinical Psychology, 36,* 562–570.

Critelli, J. W., & Neumann, K. F. (1984). The placebo: Conceptual analysis of a construct in transition. *American Psychologist, 39,* 32–39.

Crits-Christoph, P. (1992). The efficacy of brief dynamic psycho-therapy: A meta-analysis. *The American Journal of Psychiatry, 149,* 151–158.

Crits-Christoph, P., et al. (1991). Meta-analysis of therapist effects in psychotherapy outcome studies. *Psychotherapy Research, 1,* 81–91.

Crits-Christoph, P., & Mintz, J. (1991). Implications of therapist effects for the design and analysis of comparative studies of psychotherapies. *Journal of Consulting and Clinical Psychology, 59,* 20–26.

Cross, D. G., Sheehan, P. W., & Khan, J. A. (1980). Alternative advice and counsel in psychotherapy. *Journal of Consulting and Clinical Psychology, 48,* 615–625.

Crow, E. L. (1991). Response to Rosenthal's comment "How are we doing in soft psychology?" *American Psychologist, 46,* 1083.

Crown, S. (1983). Contra indications and dangers of psychotherapy. *British Journal of Psychiatry, 143,* 436–441.

Cummings, C., Gordon, J., & Marlatt, G. A. (1980). Relapse: Prevention and prediction. In W. Miller (Ed.), *The addictive behaviors.* Oxford: Pergamon Press.

Daldrup, R., Beutler, L., Engle, D., & Greenberg, L. (1988). *Focused expressive psychotherapy.* New York: Guilford.

DeRubeis, R. J., Hollon, S. D., Evans, M. D., & Bemis, K. M. (1982). Can psychotherapies for depression be discriminated? A systematic investigation of cognitive therapy and interpersonal therapy. *Journal of Consulting and Clinical Psychology, 50,* 744–756.

Dixon, K., & Kiecolt-Glaser, J. (1984). Group therapy for bulimia. *Hillside Journal of Clinical Psychiatry, 6,* 165–170.

Dobson, K. S. (1989). A meta-analysis of the efficacy of cognitive therapy for depression. *Journal of Consulting and Clinical Psychology, 57,* 414–419.

Dobson, K. S., & Shaw, B. F. (1988). The use of treatment manuals in cognitive therapy: Experience and issues. *Journal of Consulting and Clinical Psychology, 56,* 673–680.

Doherty, W. J., Lester, M. E., & Leigh, G. K. (1986). Marriage encounter weekends: Couples who win and couples who lose. *Journal of Marital and Family Therapy, 12,* 49–61.

Durlak, J. A. (1979). Comparative effectiveness of paraprofessional and professional helpers. *Psychological Bulletin, 86,* 80–92.

Dush, D. M. (1986). The placebo in psychosocial outcome evaluations. *Evaluation & the Health Professions, 9,* 421–438.

Dush, D. M., Hirt, M. L., & Schroeder, H. E. (1983). Self-statement modification with adults: A meta-analysis. *Journal of Consulting and Clinical Psychology, 94,* 408–442.

Dush, D. M., Hirt, M. L., & Schroeder, H. E. (1989). Self-statement modification in the treatment of child behavior disorders: A meta-analysis. *Psychological Bulletin, 106,* 97–106.

Elkin, I., Parloff, M., Hadley, S., & Autry, J. (1985). NIMH Treatment of Depression Collaborative Research Program: Background and research plan. *Archives of General Psychiatry, 42,* 305–316.

Elkin, I., Shea, M. T., Watkins, J. T., Imber, S. D., Sotsky, S. M., Collins, J. F., Glass, D. R., Pilkonis, P. A., Weber, W. R., Docherty, J. P., Fiester, S. J., & Parloff, M. B. (1989). NIMH Treatment of Depression Collaborative Research Program: General effectiveness of treatments. *Archives of General Psychiatry, 46,* 971–983.

Emmelkamp, P. M., DeHaan, E., & Hoogduin, C. A. (1990). Marital adjustment and obsessive-compulsive disorder. *British Journal of Psychiatry, 156,* 55–60.

Eppley, K. R., Abrams, A. I., & Sheer, J. (1989). Differential effects of relaxation techniques on trait anxiety: A meta-analysis. *Journal of Clinical Psychology, 45,* 957–973.

Evans, M., Hollon, S., DeRubeis, R., Auerbach, A., Tuason, V. B., & Wiemer, M. (1983). *Development of a system of rating psychotherapies for depression.* Paper presented at the 14th annual meeting of the Society of Psychotherapy Research, Sheffield, England.

Eysenck, H. J. (1952). The effects of psychotherapy: An evaluation. *Journal of Consulting Psychology, 16,* 319–324.

Fairburn, C. G., Kirk, J., O'Connor, M. E., & Cooper, P. J. (1986). A comparison of two psychological treatments for bulimia nervosa. *Behavior Research and Therapy, 24,* 629–643.

Fairweather, G., Simon, R., Gebhard, M. E., Weingarten, E., Holland, J. L., Sanders, R., Stone, G. B., & Reahl, J. E. (1960). Relative effectiveness of psychotherapeutic programs: A multicriteria comparison of four programs for three different patient groups. *Psychological Monographs: General and Applied, 74* (5, Whole No. 492).

Feighner, J. P., Brown, S. L., & Oliver, J. E. (1973). Electrosleep therapy. *Journal of Nervous and Mental Disease, 157,* 121–128.

Frank, A. F., & Gunderson, J. G. (1991). The role of the therapeutic alliance in the treatment of schizophrenia: Relationship to course and outcome. *Archives of General Psychiatry, 47,* 228–236.

Frank, E., Kupfer, D. J., Perel, J. M., Cornes, C., Jarrett, D. B., Mallinger, A. G., Thase, M. E., McEachran, A. B., & Grochocinski, V. J. (1990). Three-year outcomes for maintenance therapies in recurrent depression. *Archives of General Psychiatry, 47,* 1093–1099.

Frank, J. D. (1974). *Persuasion and healing. A comparative study of psychotherapy.* Baltimore: The Johns Hopkins University Press.

Frank, J. D. (1976). Psychotherapy and the sense of mastery. In R. L. Spitzer & D. F. Klein (Eds.), *Evaluation of psychotherapies: Behavioral therapies, drug therapies and their interactions* (pp. 47–56). Baltimore: The Johns Hopkins University Press.

Gallagher, D. E., & Thompson, L. W. (1982). Treatment of major depressive disorder in older outpatients with brief psychotherapies. *Psychotherapy: Theory, Research and Practice, 19,* 482–490.

Gallagher-Thompson, D., Hanley-Peterson, P., & Thompson, L. W. (1990). Maintenance of gains versus relapse following brief psychotherapy for depression. *Journal of Consulting and Clinical Psychology, 58,* 371–374.

Garfield, S. L. (1991). Common and specific factors in psychotherapy. *Journal of Integrative and Eclectic Psychotherapy, 10,* 5–13.

Gaston, L. (1990). The concept of the alliance and its role in psychotherapy: Theoretical and empirical considerations. *Psychotherapy, 27,* 143–153.

Gaston, L., Marmar, C. R., Gallagher, D., & Thompson, L. W. (1991). Alliance prediction of outcome beyond in-treatment symptomatic change as psychotherapy progresses. *Psychotherapy Research, 1,* 104–112.

Giblin, P., Sprenkle, D. H., & Sheehan, R. (1985). Enrichment outcome research: A meta-analysis of premarital, marital and family interventions. *Journal of Marital and Family Therapy, 11,* 257–271.

Glasgow, R. E., & Rosen, G. M. (1978). Behavior bibliotherapy: A review of self-help behavioral therapy manuals. *Psychological Bulletin, 85,* 1–23.

Glass, G. V., McGaw, B., & Smith, M. L. (1981). *Meta-analysis in social response.* Beverly Hills: Sage Publications.

Glass, C., & Arnkoff, D. B. (1988). Common and specific factors in client descriptions of and explanations for change. *Journal of Integrative and Eclectic Psychotherapy, 7,* 427–440.

Goin, M. K., Yamamoto, J., & Silverman, J. (1965). Therapy congruent with class-linked expectations. *Archives of General Psychiatry, 38,* 335–339.

Goldstein, A. P., & Stein, N. (1976). *Prescriptive psychotherapies.* New York: Pergamon.

Goldstein, A. P., Lopez, M., & Greenleaf, D. O. (1979). Introduction. In A. P. Goldstein & F. H. Kanfer (Eds.), *Maximizing treatment gains: Transfer enhancement in psychotherapy* (pp. 1–22). New York: Academic Press.

Goldstein, A. P., & Kanfer, F. H. (Eds.). (1979). *Maximizing treatment gains: Transfer enhancement in psychotherapy.* New York: Academic Press.

Gottman, J., & Markman, H. J. (1978). Experimental designs in psychotherapy research. In S. L. Garfield & A. E. Bergin (Eds.), *Handbook of psychotherapy and behavior change* (2nd ed., pp. 23–62). New York: Wiley.

Greenberg, L. S., & Goldman, R. L. (1988). Training in experiential therapy. *Journal of Consulting and Clinical Psychology, 56,* 696–702.

Grencavage, L. M., & Norcross, J. C. (1990). Where are the common factors? *Professional Psychology: Research and Practice, 21,* 372–378.

Grunebaum, H. (1985). Helpful and harmful psychotherapy. *The Howard Medical School Mental Health Newsletter, 1,* 5–6.

Gurman, A. S. (1977). The patient's perception of the therapeutic relationship. In A. S. Gurman & A. M. Razin (Eds.), *Effective psychotherapy: A handbook of reserach* (pp. 503–543). New York: Pergamon.

Gurman, A. S., & Kniskern, D. P. (1978). Research on marital and family therapy: Progress, perspective, and prospect. In S. L. Garfield & A. E. Bergin (Eds.), *Handbook of psychotherapy and behavior change* (2nd ed.) pp. 817–902. New York: Wiley.

Gurman, A. S., & Kniskern, D. P. (1981). *Handbook of family therapy.* New York: Brunner/Mazel.

Gurman, A. S., & Kniskern, D. P. (1986). Commentary: Individual marital therapy—have the parts of your death been somewhat exaggerated? *Family Process, 25,* 51–62.

Hahlweg, K., & Markman, H. J. (1988). Effectiveness of behavioral marital therapy: Empirical status of behavioral techniques in preventing and alleviating marital distress. *Journal of Consulting and Clinical Psychology, 56,* 440–447.

Hattie, J. A., Sharpley, C. F., & Rogers, H. F. (1984). Comparative effectiveness of professional and paraprofessional helpers. *Psychological Bulletin, 95,* 534–541.

Hazelrigg, M. D., Cooper, H. M., & Borduin, C. M. (1987). Evaluating the effectiveness of family therapies: An integrative review and analysis. *Psychology Bulletin, 101,* 428–442.

Hedges, L. V., & Oklin, I. (1985). *Statistical methods for meta-analysis.* Orlando, FL: Academic Press.

Henry, W. P. (1985). The time released placebo: A reply to Critelli and Neumann. *American Psychologist, 40,* 239.

Henry, W. P., Schacht, T. E., & Strupp, H. H. (1986). Structural analysis of social behavior: Application to a study of interpersonal process of differential psychotherapeutic outcome. *Journal of Consulting and Clinical Psychology, 54,* 27–31.

Henry, W. P., Strupp, H. H., Schacht, T. E., Binder, J. L., & Butler, S. F. (1993a). The effects of training in time-limited dynamic psychotherapy: Changes in therapist behavior. *Journal Consulting and Clinical Psychology.*

Henry, W. P., Strupp, H. H., Schacht, T. E., Binder, J. L., & Butler, S. F. (1993b). The effects of training in time-limited, dynamic psychotherapy: Mediators of therapists' response to training. *Journal of Consulting and Clinical Psychology, 61.*

Henry, W. P., Strupp, H. H., Schacht, T. E., Binder, J. L., Butler, S. F. (in press). The effects of training in time-limited dynamic psychotherapy: Changes in therapeutic outcome. *Journal of Consulting and Clinical Psychology.*

Hill, K. A. (1987). Meta-analysis of paradoxical interventions. *Psychotherapy, 24,* 266–270.

Holroyd, K. A. (1990). Pharmacological versus non-pharmacological prophylaxis of recurrent migraine headache: A meta-analytic review of clinical trials. *Pain, 42,* 1–13.

Holtzworth-Munroe, A., Jacobson, N. S., DeKlyen, M., & Whisman, M. A. (1989). Relationship between behavioral marital therapy outcome and process variables. *Journal of Consulting and Clinical Psychology, 57,* 658–662.

Horvath, A. O., & Symonds, B. D. (1991). Relationship between working alliance and outcome in psychotherapy: A meta-analysis. *Journal of Counseling Psychology, 38,* 139–149.

Horvath, P. (1988). Placebos and common factors in two decades of psychotherapy research. *Psychological Bulletin, 104,* 214–225.

Horwitz, L. (1974). *Clinical prediction in psychotherapy.* New York: Jason Aronson.

Howard, K. I., Kopta, S. M., Krause, M. S., & Orlinsky, D. E. (1986). The dose-effect relationship in psychotherapy. *American Psychologist, 41,* 159–164.

Howard, K. I., & Orlinsky, P. E. (1986). Process and outcome. In S. L. Garfield and A. E. Bergin (Eds.), *Handbook of psychotherapy and behavior change* (3rd ed., pp. 311–381). New York: Wiley.

Hyman, R. B., Feldman, H. R., Harris, R. B., Levin, R. F., & Malloy, G. B. (1989). The effects of relaxation training on clinical symptoms: A meta-analysis. *Nursing Research, 38,* 216–220.

Imber, S. D., Pilkonis, P. A., Harway, N. I., Klein, R. H., & Rubinsky, P. A. (1982). Maintenance of change in the psychotherapies. *Journal of Psychiatric Treatment and Evaluation, 4,* 1–5.

Imber, S. D., Pilkonis, P. A., Sotsky, S. M., Elkin, I., Watkins, J. T., Collins, J. F., Shea, M. T., Leber, W. R., & Glass, D. R. (1990). Mode-specific effects among three treatments for depression. *Journal of Consulting and Clinical Psychology, 58,* 352–359.

Jacobson, N. S. (1988). Defining clinically significant change: An introduction. *Behavioral Assessment, 10,* 131–132.

Jacobson, N. S. (1989). The maintenance of treatment gains following social learning–based marital therapy. *Behavior Therapy, 20,* 325–326.

Jacobson, N. S. (1991). Behavioral versus insight-oriented marital therapy: Labels can be misleading. *Journal of Consulting and Clinical Psychology, 59,* 142–145.

Jacobson, N. S., Follette, W. C., Revenstorf, D., Baucom, D. H., Hahlweg, K., & Margolin, G. (1984). Variability in outcome and clinical significance of behavioral marital therapy: A re-analysis of outcome data. *Journal of Consulting and Clinical Psychology, 52,* 497–504.

Jensen, J. P., Bergin, A. E., & Greaves, D. W. (1990). The meaning of eclecticism: New survey and analysis of components. *Professional Psychology: Research and Practice, 21,* 124–130.

Jones, C. W. (1985). Strategic interventions within no-treatment frame. *Family Process, 24,* 583–595.

Jorm, A. F. (1989). Modifiability of trait anxiety and neuroticism: A meta-analysis of the literature. *Australian and New Zealand Journal of Psychiatry, 23,* 21–29.

Kaplan, R. E. (1982). The dynamics of injury in encounter groups: Power, splitting, and the mismanagement of resistance. *International Journal of Group Psychotherapy, 32,* 163–187.

Karasu, T. B. (1986). Specificity versus nonspecificity. *American Journal of Psychiatry, 143,* 687–695.

Karoly, P., & Steffen, J. (1980). *Improving the long-term effects of psychotherapy.* New York: Gardner.

Kazdin, A. E., & Bass, D. (1989). Power to detect differences between alternative treatments in comparative psychotherapy outcome research. *Journal of Consulting and Clinical Psychology, 57,* 138–147.

Kellner, R. (1975). Psychotherapy in psychosomatic disorders: A survey of controlled outcome studies. *Archives of General Psychiatry, 35,* 1021–1028.

Kernberg, O. F. (1973). Summary & conclusion of "Psychotherapy and Psychoanalysis: Final Report of the Menninger Foundation's Psychotherapy Research Project." *International Journal of Psychiatry, 11,* 62–77.

Kopta, S. M., Howard, K. I., Lowry, J. L., & Beutler, L. E. (1992, June). *The psychotherapy dosage model and clinical significance: Estimating how much is enough for psychological symptoms.* Paper presented at the Society for Psychotherapy, Berkeley, CA.

Korda, L. J., & Pancrazio, J. J. (1989). Limiting negative outcome in group practice. *Journal of Specialists in Group Work, 14,* 112–120.

Laessle, R. G., Zoettle, C., & Pirke, K. M. (1987). Meta-analysis of treatment studies for bulimia. *International Journal of Eating Disorders, 6,* 647–653.

Lafferty, P., Beutler, L. E., & Crago, M. (1991). Differences between more and less effective psychotherapists: A study of select therapist variables. *Journal of Consulting and Clinical Psychology, 57,* 76–80.

Lambert, M. J. (1979). *The effects of psychotherapy* (Vol. 1). New York: Eden Press.

Lambert, M. J. (1983). Introduction to assessment of psychotherapy outcome: Historical perspective and current issues. In M. J. Lambert, E. R. Christensen, & S. S. DeJulio (Eds.), *The assessment of psychotherapy outcome* (pp. 3–32). New York: Wiley-Interscience.

Lambert, M. J. (1989). The individual therapist's contribution to psychotherapy process and outcome. *Clinical Psychology Review, 9,* 469–485.

Lambert, M. J. (1992). Implications of outcome research for psychotherapy integration. In J. C. Norcross & M. R. Goldstein (Eds.), *Handbook of psychotherapy integration.* New York: Basic Books.

Lambert, M. J., & Bergin, A. E. (1973). Psychotherapeutic outcomes and issues related to behavioral and humanistic approaches. *Cornell Journal of Social Relations, 8,* 47–61.

Lambert, M. J., Bergin, A. E., & Collins, J. L. (1977). Therapist-induced deterioration in psychotherapy. In A. S. Gurman & A. M. Razin (Eds.), *Effective psychotherapy: A handbook of research* (pp. 452–481). New York: Pergamon.

Lambert, M. J., DeJulio, S. S., & Stein, D. M. (1978). Therapist interpersonal skills: Process, outcome, methodological considerations and recommendations for future research. *Psychological Bulletin, 85,* 467–489.

Lambert, M. J., & Ogles, B. M. (1988). Treatment manuals: Problems and promise. *Journal of Integrative and Eclectic Psychotherapy, 7,* 187–204.

Lambert, M. J., Shapiro, D. A., & Bergin, A. E. (1986). The effectiveness of psychotherapy. In S. L. Garfield & A. E. Bergin (Eds.), *Handbook of psychotherapy and behavior change* (3rd ed., pp. 157–211). New York: Wiley.

Lambert, M. J., Weber, F. D., & Sykes, J. D. (1993, April). *Psychotherapy versus placebo.* Poster presented at the annual meetings of the Western Psychological Association, Phoenix.

Landman, J. T., & Dawes, R. M. (1982). Smith and Glass' conclusions stand up under scrutiny. *American Psychologist, 37,* 504–516.

Lang, P. J., & Lazovik, A. D. (1963). Experimental desensitization of a phobia. *Journal of Abnormal and Social Psychology, 66,* 519–525.

Lazarus, A. A. (1963). An evaluation of behavior therapy. *Behavior Research and Therapy, 63,* 504–510.

Lazarus, A. A. (1971). *Behavior therapy and beyond.* New York: McGraw-Hill.

Levant, R. F., & Shlien, J. M. (Eds.). (1984). *Client-centered therapy and the person-centered approach: New directions in theory, research and practice.* New York: Praeger.

Liberman, B. L. (1978). The maintenance and persistence of change: Long-term follow-up investigations of psychotherapy. In J. D. Frank, R. Hoehn-Saric, S. D. Imber, B. L. Liberman, & A. R. Stone (Eds.), *Effective ingredients of successful psychotherapy.* New York: Brunner/Mazel.

Lieberman, M. A., Yalom, I. D., & Miles, M. B. (1973). *Encounter groups: First facts.* New York: Basic Books.

Linehan, M. M. (1987). Dialectical behavior therapy in groups: Treating borderline personality disorders and suicidal behavior. In C. M. Brody (Ed.), *Women's therapy groups: Paradigms of feminist treatment.* New York: Springer.

Lorr, M. (1965). Client perceptions of therapists. *Journal of Consulting Psychology, 29,* 146–149.

Luborsky, L., & DeRubeis, R. J. (1984). The use of psychotherapy treatment manuals—a small revolution in psychotherapy research style. *Clinical Psychology Review, 4,* 5–14.

Luborsky, L., McClellan, A. T., Woody, G. E., O'Brien, C. P., & Auerbach, A. (1985). Therapist success and its determinants. *Archives of General Psychiatry, 42,* 602–611.

Luborsky, L., Singer, B., & Luborsky, L. (1975). Comparative studies of psychotherapy. *Archives of General Psychiatry, 32,* 995–1008.

Luborsky, L., Woody, G., Hale, A. V., & Velleco, A. (1977). *Special manual for dynamic therapy of drug dependence—adaption of the general manual for supportive-expressive psychotherapy.* Unpublished manuscript. University of Pennsylvania.

Luborsky, L., Woody, G., McLellan, A. T., O'Brien, C. P., & Rosenzweig, J. (1982). Can independent judges recognize different psychotherapies? *Journal of Consulting and Clinical Psychology, 50,* 49–62.

Lyons, L. C., & Woods, P. J. (1991). The efficacy of rational-emotive therapy: A quantitative review of the outcome research. *Clinical Psychology Review, 11,* 357–369.

Markus, E., Lange, A., & Pettigrew, T. F. (1990). Effectiveness of family therapy: A meta-analysis. *Journal of Family Therapy, 12,* 205–221.

Mattick, R. P., Andrews, G., Hadzi-Pavlovic, D., & Christensen, H. (1990). Treatment of panic and agoraphobia. *The Journal of Nervous and Mental Disease, 178,* 567–573.

Mays, D. T., & Franks, C. M. (1980). Getting worse: Psychotherapy or no treatment. The jury should still be out. *Professional Psychology, 11,* 78–92.

Mays, D. T., & Franks, C. M. (1985). *Negative outcome in psychotherapy and what to do about it.* New York: Springer.

McGlashan, T. H. (1986). The chestnut lodge follow-up study. *Archives of General Psychiatry, 43,* 20–30.

McGlashan, T. H., Mohr, D. C., Beutler, L. E., Engle, D., Shoham-Salomon, V., Bergan, J., Kaszniak, A. W., & Yost, E. B. (1990). Identification of patients at risk for nonresponse and negative outcome in psychotherapy. *Journal of Consulting and Clinical Psychology, 58,* 622–628.

McGraw, K. O. (1991). Problems with the BESD: A comment on Rosenthal's "How are we doing in soft psychology?" *American Psychologist, 46,* 1084.

McNeilly, C. L., & Howard, K. I. (1991). The effects of psychotherapy: A reevaluation based on dosage. *Psychotherapy Research, 1,* 74–78.

Meltzoff, J., & Kornreich, M. (1970). *Research in psychotherapy.* New York: Atherton.

Michelson, L. (Ed.). (1985). Meta-analysis and clinical psychology. *Clinical Psychology Review, 5,* 1–89.

Michelson, L. K., & Marchione, K. (1991). Behavioral, cognitive and pharmacological treatment of panic disorder with agoraphobia: Critique and synthesis. *Journal of Consulting and Clinical Psychology, 59,* 100–114.

Michelson, L., Marchione, K., Greenwold, M., Glanz, L., Marchione, N., & Testa, S. (1990). Cognitive-behavioral treatment of panic disorder. *Behavioral Research and Therapy, 28,* 141–151.

Miller, R. C., & Berman, J. S. (1983). The efficacy of cognition behavior therapies: A quantitative review of the research evidence. *Psychological Bulletin, 94,* 39–53.

Miller, W. R., Taylor, C. A., & West, J. C. (1980). Focused versus broad-spectrum behavior therapy for problem drinkers. *Journal of Consulting and Clinical Psychology, 48,* 590–601.

Mitchell, K. M., Bozarth, J. D., & Krauft, C. C. (1977). A re-appraisal of the therapeutic effectiveness of accurate empathy, nonpossessive warmth, and genuiness. In A. S. Gurman & A. M. Razin (Eds.), *Effective psychotherapy: A handbook of research.* New York: Pergamon.

Morawetz, D. (1989). Behavioral self-help treatment for insomnia: A controlled evaluation. *Behavior Therapy, 20,* 365–379.

Murphy, P. M., Cramer, D., & Lillie, F. J. (1984). The relationship between curative factors perceived by patients in their psychotherapy and treatment outcome: An exploratory study. *British Journal of Medical Psychology, 57,* 187–192.

Neu, C., Prusoff, B., & Klerman, G. (1978). Measuring the interventions used in the short-term psychotherapy of depression. *American Journal of Orthopsychiatry, 48,* 629–636.

Nicholson, R. A., & Berman, J. S. (1983). Is follow-up necessary in evaluating psychotherapy? *Psychological Bulletin, 93,* 261–278.

Nietzel, M. T., & Fisher, S. G. (1981). Effectiveness of professional and paraprofessional helpers: A comment on Durlack. *Psychological Bulletin, 89,* 555–565.

Nietzel, M. T., Russell, R. L., Hemmings, K. A., & Gretter, M. L. (1987). Clinical significance of psychotherapy for unipolar depression: A meta-analytic approach to social comparison. *Journal of Consulting and Clinical Psychology, 55,* 156–161.

Norcross, J. C., & Goldfried, M. R. (Eds.). (1992). *Handbook of psychotherapy integration.* New York: Basic Books.

Norcross, J. C., & Newman, C. F. (1992). Psychotherapy integration: Setting the context. In J. C. Norcross & M. R. Goldfried (Eds.), *Handbook of psychotherapy integration.* New York: Basic Books.

Oesterheld, J. R., McKenna, M. S., & Gould, N. B. (1987). Group psychotherapy of bulimia: A critical review. *International Journal of Group Psychotherapy, 37,* 163–184.

Ogles, B. M., Lambert, M. J., & Sawyer, J. D. (1993, June). *The clinical significance of the NIMH Treatment of Depression Collaborative Research.* Paper presented at the Annual Meetings of the Society for Psychotherapy Research, Pittsburgh.

Ogles, B. M., Lambert, M. J., & Craig, D. (1991). A comparison of self-help books for coping with loss: Expectations and attributions. *Journal of Counseling Psychology, 38,* 387–393.

Ogles, B. M., Sawyer, J. D., & Lambert, M. J. (1993, June). *The clinical significance of the NIMH Treatment of Depression Collaborative Research Program data.* Paper presented at the annual meeting of the Society of Psychotherapy Research, Pittsburgh.

Omer, H. (1989). Specifics and nonspecifics in psychotherapy. *American Journal of Psychotherapy, 43,* 181–192.

Omer, H., & London, P. (1988). Meta-morphosis in psychotherapy: End of the systems era. *Psychology, 25,* 171–180.

Orlinsky, D. E., & Howard, K. I. (1980). Gender and psychotherapeutic outcome. In A. M. Brodsky & R. T. Hare-Mustin (Eds.), *Women and psychotherapy* (pp. 3–34). New York: Guilford.

Parloff, M. B. (1986). Placebo controls in psychotherapy research: A sine qua non or a placebo for research problems? *Journal of Consulting and Clinical Psychology, 54,* 79–87.

Patterson, C. H. (1984). Empathy, warmth, and genuineness in psychotherapy: A review of reviews. *Psychotherapy, 21,* 431–438.

Phillips, J. B. (1983). Some ethical concerns regarding the individual psychotherapy of the married client. *Canadian Psychology, 24,* 8–13.

Prioleau, L., Murdock, M., & Brody, N. (1983). An analysis of psychotherapy versus placebo studies. *The Behavioral and Brain Sciences, 6,* 275–310.

Prout, H. T., & De Martino, R. A. (1986). A meta-analysis of school-based studies of psychotherapy. *Journal of School Psychology, 24,* 285–292.

Quality Assurance Project. (1982). A treatment outline for agoraphobia. *Australian and New Zealand Journal of Psychiatry, 16,* 25–33.

Qualtiy Assurance Project. (1983). A treatment outline for depressive disorders. *Australian and New Zealand Journal of Psychiatry, 17,* 129–146.

Quality Assurance Project. (1984). Treatment outlines for the management of schizophrenia. *Australian and New Zealand Journal of Psychiatry, 18,* 19–38.

Quality Assurance Project. (1985a). Treatment outlines for the management of anxiety states. *Australian and New Zealand Journal of Psychiatry, 19,* 138–151.

Quality Assurance Project. (1985b). Treatment outlines for the management of obsessive-compulsive disorders. *Australian and New Zealand Journal of Psychiatry, 19,* 240–253.

Rachman, S. J., & Wilson, G. T. (1980). *The effects of psychological therapy* (2nd ed.). New York: Pergamon.

Ricks, D. F. (1974). Supershrink: Methods of a therapist judged successful on the basis of adult outcomes of adolescent patients. In D. F. Ricks, M. Roff, & A. Thomas (Eds.), *Life history research in psychopathology.* Minneapolis: University of Minnesota Press.

Robinson, L. A., Berman, J. S., & Neimeyer, R. A. (1990). Psychotherapy for the treatment of depression: A comprehensive review of controlled outcome research. *Psychological Bulletin, 100,* 30–49.

Romney, D. M. (1988, March). A retrospective study of dropout rates from a community mental health center and associated factors. *Canada's Mental Health,* pp. 2–4.

Rosen, G. M. (1988). Self-help treatment books and the commercialization of psychotherapy. *American Psychologist, 42,* 46–51.

Rosengard, P. (1991). *A comparative analysis of four psychotherapy manuals and a proposed model for psychotherapy manuals.* Frankfurt am Main: Peter Lang.

Rosenthal, D., & Frank, J. D. (1956). Psychotherapy and the placebo effect. *Psychological Bulletin, 53,* 294–302.

Rosenthal, R. (1983). Assessing the statistical and social importance of the effects of psychotherapy. *Journal of Consulting and Clinical Psychology, 51,* 4–13.

Rosenthal, R. (1990). How are we doing in soft psychology? *American Psychologist, 45,* 775–777.

Rosenthal, R. (1991). Effect sizes: Pearson's correlation, its display via the BESD, and alternative indices. *American Psychologist, 46,* 1086.

Rosenzweig, S. (1936). Some implicit common factors in diverse methods of psychotherapy. *American Journal of Orthopsychiatry, 6,* 422–425.

Rounsaville, B. J., O'Malley, S., Foley, S., & Weissman, M. W. (1988). Role of manual-guided training in the conduct and efficacy of interpersonal psychotherapy for depression. *Journal of Consulting and Clinical Psychology, 56,* 681–688.

Sachs, J. S. (1983). Negative factors in brief psychotherapy: An empirical assessment. *Journal of Consulting and Clinical Psychology, 51,* 557–564.

Salvio, M., Beutler, L. E., Wood, J. M., & Engle, D. (1992). The strength of the therapeutic alliance in three treatments for depression. *Psychotherapy Research, 2,* 31–36.

Schneider, J., & Agras, W. (1985). A cognitive behavioral group treatment of bulimia. *British Journal of Psychiatry, 146,* 66–69.

Schroeder, H. E., & Dush, D. M. (1987). Relinquishing the placebo: Alternatives for psychotherapy outcome research. *American Psychologist, 42,* 1129–1130.

Schwitzgebel, R. L., & Schwitzgebel, R. K. (1980). *Law and psychological practice.* New York: Wiley.

Senger, H. L. (1987). The "placebo" effect of psychotherapy: A moose in the rabbit stew. *American Journal of Psychotherapy, 41,* 68–95.

Shapiro, D. A., Barkham, M., Hardy, G. E., Morrison, L. A., Reynolds, S., Startup, M., & Harper, H. (1990). University of Sheffield Psychotherapy Research Program: Medical Research Council/Economic and Social Research Council Social and Applied Psychology Unit. In L. E. Beutler & M. Crago (Eds.), *Psychotherapy research programs* (pp. 234–242). Washington, DC: American Psychological Association.

Shapiro, D. A., Barkham, M., Hardy, G. E., Reynolds, S., Rees, A., & Startup, M. (in press). Effects of treatment duration and severity of depression on the effectiveness of Cognitive/Behavioral and Psychodynamic/Interpersonal Psychotherapy. *Journal of Consulting and Clinical Psychology.*

Shapiro, D. A., & Firth, J. A. (1987). Prescriptive vs. exploratory psychotherapy: Outcomes of the Sheffield Psychotherapy Project. *British Journal of Psychiatry, 151,* 790–799.

Shapiro, D. A., Firth-Cozens, J., & Stiles, W. B. (1989). The question of therapists' differential effectiveness: A Sheffield Psychotherapy Project addendum. *British Journal of Psychiatry, 154,* 383–385.

Shapiro, D. A., & Shapiro, D. (1982a). Meta-analysis of comparative therapy outcome studies: A replication and refinement. *Psychological Bulletin, 92,* 581–604.

Shapiro, D. A., & Shapiro, D. (1982b). Meta-analysis of comparative therapy outcome research: A critical appraisal. *Behavioral Psychotherapy, 10,* 4–25.

Shapiro, D. A., & Shapiro, D. (1983). Comparative therapy outcome research: Methodological implications of meta-analysis. *Journal of Consulting and Clinical Psychology, 51,* 42–53.

Shapiro, D. A., & Startup, M. J. (in press). Measuring therapist adherence in exploratory psychotherapy. *Psychotherapy Research.*

Shepherd, M. (1984). What price psychotherapy? *British Medical Journal, 288,* 809–810.

Shipley, R. H., & Boudewyns, P. A. (1980). Flooding and implosive therapy: Are they harmful? *Behavioral Therapy, 11,* 503–508.

Shoham-Salomon, V. (1991). Introduction to special section on client–therapy interaction research. *Journal of Consulting and Clinical Psychology, 59,* 203–204.

Shoham-Salomon, V., & Rosenthal, R. (1987). Paradoxical interventions: A meta-analysis. *Journal of Consulting and Clinical Psychology, 55,* 22–28.

Sloane, R. B., Staples, F. R., Cristol, A. H., Yorkston, N. J., & Whipple, K. (1975). *Short-term analytically oriented psychotherapy vs. behavior therapy.* Cambridge, MA: Harvard University Press.

Smith, D. (1982). Trends in counseling and psychotherapy. *American Psychologist, 37,* 802–809.

Smith, M. L., & Glass, G. V. (1977). Meta-analysis of psychotherapy outcome studies. *American Psychologist, 32,* 752–760.

Smith, M. L., Glass, G. V., & Miller, T. I. (1980). *The benefits of psychotherapy.* Baltimore: The Johns Hopkins University Press.

Snyder, D. K., Wills, R. M., & Grady-Fletcher, A. (1991). Long-term effectiveness of behavioral versus insight-oriented marital therapy: A four-year follow-up study. *Journal of Consulting and Clinical Psychology, 59,* 138–141.

Starker, S. (1988). Do-it-yourself therapy: The prescription of self-help books by psychologists. *Psychotherapy, 25,* 142–146.

Startup, M. J., Shapiro, D. A. (1992). *Therapist treatment fidelity in prescriptive vs. exploratory psychotherapy.* University of Sheffield: SAPU Memo 1263.

Startup, M. J., & Shapiro, D. A. (in press). Dimensions of cognitive therapy for depression: A confirmatory factor analysis. *Psychotherapy Research.*

Stein, D. M. (1980). *The comparative effectiveness of paraprofessional therapists.* M. J. Lambert (Chair). Society for Psychotherapy Research. Pacific Grove, CA.

Stein, D. M., & Lambert, M. J. (1984). On the relationship between therapist experience and psychotherapy outcome. *Clinical Psychology Review, 4,* 1–16.

Steinbrueck, S. M., Maxwell, S. E., & Howard, G. S. (1983). A meta-analysis of psychotherapy and drug therapy in the treatment of unipolar depression with adults. *Journal of Consulting and Clinical Psychology, 51,* 856–863.

Stevens, E., & Salisbury, J. (1984). Group therapy for bulimic adults. *American Journal of Orthopsychiatry, 54,* 156–161.

Stiles, W. B., Shapiro, D. A., & Elliott, R. K. (1986). "Are all psychotherapies equivalent?" *American Psychologist, 41,* 165–180.

Stone, M. H. (1985). Negative outcome in borderline states. In D. T. Mays & C. M. Franks (Eds.), *Negative outcome in psychotherapy and what to do about it.* New York: Springer.

Stone, M. H. (1990). Treatment of borderline patients: A pragmatic approach. *Psychiatric Clinics of North America, 13,* 265–285.

Stone, M. H., Stone, D. K., & Hurt, S. (1987). Natural history of borderline patients treated by intensive hospitalization. *Psychiatric Clinics of North America, 10,* 185–206.

Strahan, R. F. (1991). Remarks on the binomial effect size display. *American Psychologist, 46,* 1083.

Striano, J. (1982). Client perception of "helpful" and "not helpful" psychotherapeutic experiences. *Dissertation Abstracts International, 43,* 4303B. (University Microfilms No. 80-17, 382)

Striano, J. (1987). *How to find a good psychotherapist: A consumer guide.* Santa Barbara, CA: Professional Press.

Striano, J. (1988). *Can psychotherapists hurt you?* Santa Barbara, CA: Professional Press.

Strube, M. J., & Hartman, D. P. (1982). A critical appraisal of meta-analysis. *British Journal of Clinical Psychology, 21,* 129–139.

Strube, M. J., & Hartman, D. P. (1983). Meta-analysis: Techniques, applications, and function. *Journal of Consulting and Clinical Psychology, 51,* 14–27.

Strupp, H. H. (1980a). Success and failure in time-limited psychotherapy: A systematic comparison of two cases—comparison 1. *Archives of General Psychiatry, 37,* 595–603.

Strupp, H. H. (1980b). Success and failure in time-limited psychotherapy: A systematic comparison of two cases—comparison 2. *Archives of General Psychiatry, 37,* 708–716.

Strupp, H. H. (1980c). Success and failure in time-limited psychotherapy: A systematic comparison of two cases—comparison 4. *Archives of General Psychiatry, 37,* 947–954.

Strupp, H. H. (1980d). Success and failure in time-limited psychotherapy: With special reference to the performance of a lay counselor. *Archives of General Psychiatry, 37,* 831–841.

Svartberg, M., & Stiles, T. C. (1991). Comparative effects of short-term psychodynamic psychotherapy: A meta-analysis. *Journal of Consulting and Clinical Psychology, 59,* 704–714.

Szapocznik, J., Rio, A., Murray, E., Cohen, R., Scopetta, M., Rivas-Vazquez, A., Hervis, O., Posda, V., & Kurtines, W. (1989). Structural family versus psychodynamic child therapy for problematic Hispanic boys. *Journal of Consulting and Clinical Psychology, 57,* 571–578.

Thompson, L. W., Gallagher, D., & Brekenridge, J. S. (1987). Comparative effectiveness of psychotherapies for depressed elders. *Journal of Consulting and Clinical Psychology, 55,* 385–390.

Tichenor, V., & Hill, C. E. (1989). A comparison of six measures of working alliance. *Psychotherapy, 26,* 195–199.

Trull, T. J., Nietzel, M. T., & Main, A. (1988). The use of meta-analysis to assess the clinical significance of behavior therapy for agoraphobia. *Behavior Therapy, 19,* 527–538.

Turner, R. M., & Ascher, L. M. (1982). Therapist factor in the treatment of insomnia. *Behavior Research and Therapy, 20,* 33–40.

Veroff, J., Kulka, R. A., & Douvan, E. (1981). *Mental health in America.* New York: Basic Books.

Wampler, K. S. (1982). Bringing the review of literature into the age of quantification: Meta-analysis as a strategy for integrating research findings in family studies. *Journal of Marriage and the Family, 44,* 1009–1023.

Weber, J. J., Elinson, J., & Moss, L. M. (1965). The application of ego strength scales to psychoanalytic clinic records. In G. S. Goldman & D. Shapiro (Eds.), *Developments in psychoanalysis at Columbia University: Proceedings of the 20th anniversary conference.* New York: Columbia Psychoanalytic Clinic for Training and Research.

Weisz, J. R., Weiss, B., Alicke, M. D., & Klotz, M. L. (1987). Effectiveness of psychotherapy with children and adolescents: A meta-analysis for clinicians. *Journal of Consulting and Clinical Psychology, 55,* 542–549.

Wells, R. A., & Gianetti, V. J. (1986). Individual marital therapy: A critical reappraisal. *Family Process, 25,* 43–51.

Whisman, M. A. (1990). The efficacy of booster maintenance sessions in behavior therapy: Review and methodological critique. *Clinical Psychology Review, 10,* 155–170.

Wilkins, W. (1984). Psychotherapy: The powerful placebo. *Journal of Consulting and Clinical Psychology, 52,* 570–573.

Wolchick, S., Weiss, L., & Katzman, M. (1986). An empirically validated, short-term psycho-educational group treatment program for bulimia. *International Journal of Eating Disorders, 5,* 21–34.

Wolpe, J. (1958). *Psychotherapy by reciprocal inhibition.* Stanford, CA: Stanford University Press.

Wolpe, J. (1964). Behavior therapy in complex neurotic states. *British Journal of Psychiatry, 110,* 28–34.

Wolpe, J. (1975). Foreward. In B. Sloane, F. Staples, A. Cristol, N. Yorkston, & K. Whipple (Eds.), *Psychotherapy versus behavior therapy.* Cambridge, MA: Harvard University Press.

Yalom, I. D., & Lieberman, M. A. (1971). A study of encounter group casualties. *Archives of General Psychiatry, 25,* 16–30.

Zeiss, A. M., Lewinsohn, P. M., & Munoz, R. F. (1979). Nonspecific improvement effects in depression using interpersonal skills training, pleasant activity schedules, and cognitive training. *Journal of Consulting and Clinical Psychology, 47,* 427–439.

6

RESEARCH ON CLIENT VARIABLES IN PSYCHOTHERAPY

- **SOL L. GARFIELD**

  Washington University

As the preceding chapters have indicated, a number of variables need to be considered in evaluating the factors influencing outcome in psychotherapy. One of these important variables is the client or patient. Although the client's contribution to therapeutic outcomes is influenced by the type of therapist, the form of therapy, and daily life events, our focus in this chapter will be on the client.

A considerable amount of research has been reported on a variety of client attributes in relation to outcome and continuation in psychotherapy. Among these attributes are social class, personality, diagnosis, age, sex, intelligence, length of disturbance, and the like. As one surveys this body of research, some problems and limitations can be noted, particularly in the earlier research. First of all, we must keep in mind that although most of us refer to psychotherapy as if it were a unitary process, there are in actuality literally hundreds of supposedly different forms of psychotherapy (Herink, 1980; Kazdin, 1986). Furthermore, even when therapies have been designated as behavioral, psychodynamic, or humanistic, such designations are essentially overly gross designations and do not provide an adequate picture of the actual therapeutic operations. Another aspect is that the therapists used in the different studies also varied in terms of training, experience, and skill. In a similar fashion, a variety of evaluation or outcome measures have been used, which also limits the comparisons of studies and our ability to draw firm conclusions.

In light of these concerns, there have been several attempts to improve the quality of psychotherapy research. Specific training manuals were developed for cognitive therapy (Beck, Rush, Shaw, & Emery, 1979) and interpersonal therapy (Klerman, Weissman, Rounsaville, & Chevron, 1984) for the collaborative research study on the treatment of depression coordinated by the National Institute of Mental Health (Elkin, Parloff, Hadley, & Autry, 1985; also Chapter 4). Thus, therapists were trained to perform these specific forms of therapy, and their therapy was monitored to ensure conformity with the manuals. The therapists in this study also met minimum requirements of professional training (e.g., PhD or MD degree) and experience. The patients also met specific diagnostic criteria for unipolar depression, and several standard evaluation instruments were used to measure outcome. In this way, most of the limitations mentioned previously were avoided. However, only a very few studies have been conducted with such meticulous regard for basic design considerations in psychotherapy research. Consequently, the reader should not be surprised if some of the research on client variables produces conflicting or inconsistent results. In the pages that follow, representative samples of the research literature will be reviewed and evaluated and an attempt made to draw implications for both practice and research.

THE PSYCHOTHERAPY CLIENT

The individuals who may be considered as potential therapy clients vary in a number of ways. There are individuals who voluntarily seek out psychotherapeutic treatment, individuals who are referred for psychotherapy, those who eventually are selected for psychotherapy, and those who refuse psychotherapy.

Frank (1974a) has suggested the importance of demoralization as a possible factor that brings people to seek out personal psychotherapy. Several studies have found that those individuals who secured treatment exhibited more helplessness, social isolation, and a sense of failure or lack of worth than those who did not seek treatment (Galassi & Galassi, 1973; Kellner & Sheffield, 1973; Vaillant, 1972). In another study, a group of treated depressed patients was matched with an untreated group for degree of depression. The treated group was found to be more self-accusatory and helpless (Katz, 1971). Frank (1974a) also believes that the most frequent symptoms of patients in psychotherapy, anxiety and depression, are actually expressions of the patients' feelings of demoralization. Thus, clinical symptomatology, alone, does not appear to necessarily motivate individuals to seek out psychotherapy.

Research conducted in the past also has indicated that not all individuals who applied for treatment received psychotherapy and that social class status was positively related to acceptance for treatment (Garfield, 1986b). Comparable findings were reported in a study of a large urban mental health center (Lubin, Hornstra, Lewis, & Bechtel, 1973). Significant associations were found between such variables as education, occupation, age, race, and diagnosis and the type of treatment initially accorded the patient. Patients with less than 12 years of education and with lower occupational ratings were assigned disproportionately more frequently to inpatient treatment, and less frequently to individual psychotherapy. The converse was true for those with some college education and higher occupational ratings. Race and age were also related to type of assignment, with blacks and those over 39 years of age being overrepresented in the inpatient service and underrepresented in individual psychotherapy. A study of a walk-in clinical also found a significant relationship between low socioeconomic status and the likelihood of receiving drugs rather than psychotherapy (Shader, 1970).

There is another aspect of this problem. As pointed out by Hollingshead and Redlich (1958) in their classic study, different social classes receive different kinds of treatment, with long-term psychoanalytic treatment given mainly to middle- and upper-class clients. It is very likely that such individuals still make up the largest proportion of those in private therapy. The results of the mental health survey reported by Ryan (1969) for the City of Boston appears to support this view. According to Ryan, of those who are judged to be emotionally disturbed, less than 10 percent will apply for treatment at one of the outpatient psychiatric clinics in Boston—and of these, less than half may be accepted for treatment. Less than 1 percent of those judged to be disturbed were treated by psychiatrists in private practice, and these were a highly selected group. About two-thirds were females, four out of five had gone to college or were in college, "and occupations [were] generally consistent with education, reflecting a class level in the middle and upper ranges" (Ryan, 1969, p. 15).

In a study of different kinds of clinics in New York City, Kadushin (1969) concluded that social class was the most important factor distinguishing the applicants to the various clinics. Furthermore,

"the more closely affiliated a clinic is with the orthodox psychoanalytic movement, the higher the social class of its applicants will be" (Kadushin, 1969, p. 51).

A more recent report of 1,582 patients who were accepted and treated at the Columbia University Center for Psychoanalytic Training and Research is generally consistent with the earlier studies (Weber, Solomon, & Bachrach, 1985): "The patients are young, nearly all white, highly educated students, housewives and high vocational achievers" (p. 21). Although two different samples over time were studied and compared, the distribution of patients in terms of income, sex, age, and ethnic background did not change in any significant way. In fact, "The originally high educational level went even higher" (in the second sample) (Weber, Solomon, & Bachrach, 1985, p. 21). Furthermore, patients assigned to psychoanalysis were better educated and tended to be employed in more high-status jobs than was the case for patients assigned to psychotherapy. In fact nearly two-thirds of the patients in the second sample who received psychoanalysis had graduate school experience.

It is evident that many clinics in the past have been somewhat selective in whom they accept for treatment; that this varies for the type of clinic; that selection is frequently related to social class criteria; and that the more expert the therapeutic staff, the more stringent are the procedures used for selection and acceptance of clients. Psychoanalytic or psychoanalytically oriented clinics that are looking for suitable candidates for their particular variants of psychotherapy use some degree of selectivity in deciding which clients are best suited for treatment, and generally these are the better educated, intelligent, verbal, and "motivated" clients. On the other hand, such selectivity poses a problem for those who are seen as less desirable candidates, or who appear less interested in psychotherapy. It is also possible that with a reduction in government funding of clinics and the willingness of third-party payers to provide for treatment, many clinics (and practitioners) are less selective now than they had been in the past.

REFUSAL OF THERAPY

Not all individuals who are offered psychotherapy, however, actually accept it—a finding that is usually surprising to most graduate students. Nevertheless, several studies have documented this fact. In a study of a sample of 2,551 cases drawn from 17 community mental health facilities, it was found that 40.8 percent of the cases failed to return after the intake interview (Sue, McKinney, & Allen,

1976). A report of 2,922 students seen at a university counseling center over a period of 8 years indicated that almost 49 percent failed to come to the first therapy session (Phillips & Fagan, 1982). Marks (1978) reported that of several hundred patients offered behavioral treatment in his unit at the Maudsley Hospital, 23 percent refused the treatment. Comparable results were secured by Betz and Shullman (1979) with 24 percent of clients failing to show for the first interview.

In a report of therapy for sexual difficulties, 142 couples out of 339 who had requested therapy refused it when therapy was offered to them (Fordney-Settlage, 1975). This is approximately 42 percent of the group originally requesting therapy. Everaerd (1983) makes reference to a study by Arentewicz and Schmidt (1980) in which 27 percent of couples who had registered for sex therapy did not actually begin therapy. It is pointed out, too, that males less readily accept such treatment than do females. Similarly, one study reported that 6 of 18 men with agoraphobia refused treatment as compared with 4 of 49 women patients (Hafner, 1983).

Several studies have investigated the possible factors or variables related to this rejection of therapy. In one of the earliest studies, Rosenthal and Frank (1958) found a significant relationship between acceptance on the part of the client and the client's income, and between acceptance and rated level of motivation. Level of education was related to acceptance only at a suggestive level of significance ($p < .10$). Yamamoto and Goin (1966) also reported a significant correlation between lower socioeconomic status and the failure of a client to keep his or her initial appointment. Thus, there is a suggestion of some relationship between socioeconomic variables and the acceptance of psychotherapy on the part of patients. In one other study in which 64 self-referred patients who failed to keep their first therapy appointment were compared with a comparable number of those who did, no differences were secured in the terms of age, sex, or education (Noonan, 1973). However, a difference was noted between these groups of patients in the way they originally presented their problems. The group that did not show up tended to state their problems in a vague and evasive manner, whereas the others verbalized more specific problems.

Two reports based on two different samples of referrals to the Psychiatric Outpatient Department of Boston City Hospital also indicated a large percentage of nonattenders for the initial appointment. In one study of 267 referrals, 42 percent did not keep their appointment (Raynes & Warren, 1971a). In the first report, it was also found that

age and race were related to attendance. Blacks and those under 40 were significantly more likely to fail to keep their appointments. No such data were reported in the second study (Raynes & Warren, 1971b), but there appeared to be a relationship between time on the waiting list and nonattendance.

More recently, Weisz, Weiss, and Langmeyer (1987), in a study of child psychotherapy, found that those who failed to show up for any therapy sessions after the intake interview were virtually indistinguishable from those who continued in therapy for at least five sessions. Although those who failed to show up for the postintake sessions were categorized as dropouts from therapy, they were essentially refusers of therapy since therapy was never begun (Garfield, 1989a).

Although some relationship between selected social class variables and rejection of therapy has been secured, there is as yet no completely adequate explanation for this phenomenon. A number of possible hypotheses have been suggested, including the following: inadequate motivation to undergo therapy, fear of finding out that one is seriously disturbed, a reluctance to acknowledge that one needs help in resolving personal difficulties, the possible stigma of seeing a mental health professional, and a significant change in one's life situation. The possible causes, of course, may vary with different individuals. However, research investigation in this area has been limited.

RESEARCH PERTAINING TO CONTINUATION IN PSYCHOTHERAPY

Another problem encountered in clinical practice concerns those patients who begin psychotherapy but terminate their participation and drop out of therapy relatively early. Generally, such termination appears to be initiated by the client before there has been some mutual agreement that therapy has been completed. Such discontinuers, premature terminators, or dropouts constitute a sizable percentage of those who begin therapy, and they have been considered as problems by many therapists who believe the therapeutic process has not been completed. Before attempting to appraise this issue, however, let us review some representative findings on continuation in psychotherapy.

In Table 6.1, data are presented on the length of psychotherapy, expressed in terms of the number of interviews, for 560 patients seen at a VA Outpatient Clinic (Garfield & Kurz, 1952). This group of patients consisted of all of those who had been offered and had accepted treatment at the clinic, and whose cases were officially closed at the time

TABLE 6.1   Length of treatment

Number of Interviews	Number of Cases	Percentage of Cases
Less than 5	239	42.7
5–9	134	23.9
10–14	73	13.0
15–19	41	7.3
20–24	24	4.3
25 and over	49	8.8
Total	560	100.0

of the study. The clinic staff prided themselves on offering intensive psychodynamic therapy. However, the median length of treatment actually was around 6 interviews, with approximately two-thirds of the cases receiving less than 10 interviews. By contrast, less than 9 percent of the patients came for 25 or more interviews and only 7 cases received over 50 treatment interviews.

Although the data just presented were published in the early 1950s, they are typical of the kinds of results secured from other clinics over a period of many years. For example, in a more recent large-scale study by Sue et al. (1976), it can be noted

that 23 percent of the cases who actually started therapy dropped out after the first session. Furthermore, 69.6 percent terminated before the tenth session, which is quite comparable to the 66.6 percent indicated in Table 6.1. Comparable figures are reported in a study of psychiatrists and psychologists in private practice, with 65 and 63 percent of the patients respectively terminating before the tenth session (Taube, Burns, & Kessler, 1984). The respective medians were four and five sessions in this study. Most recently, a case review of 138 patients with prepaid mental health insurance and 283 with fee-for-service health insurance at an HMO revealed a mean of 6.1 treatment sessions. In fact, 78 percent completed treatment within 8 sessions (Blackwell, Gutmann, & Gutman, 1988).

Table 6.2 summarizes the findings of a representative number of investigations carried out over a period of many years in several types of clinical settings. As can be seen, a majority of the clinics have terminated or lost half of their therapy clients before the eighth interview. Although the median length of treatment varies from 3 to 13 interviews for the different clinics, there is a clustering around 6 interviews. It can be emphasized, also, that in those studies that excluded all the patients who

TABLE 6.2   Median number of psychotherapy interviews for outpatient clinics

Clinical Setting	Median Number of Interviews	Date	Source
VA Clinic, St. Louis	5	1948	Blackman
VA Clinic, Boston	10	1949	Adler, Valenstein, & Michaels
VA Clinic, Milwaukee	6	1952	Garfield & Kurz
VA Clinic, Baltimore	4	1956	Kurland
VA Clinic, Oakland	9	1958	Sullivan, Miller, & Smelser
VA Clinic, Chicago	3	1959	Affleck & Mednick
Psychiatric clinics—general hospitals, NYC	6	1949	NYC Commission on Mental Hygiene
Clinics in four states plus VA Clinic, Denver	5–7	1960	Rogers
Yale University Clinic	4	1954	Schaffer & Myers
Henry Phipps Clinic	6	1958	Rosenthal & Frank
Nebraska Psychiatric Institute	12	1959	Garfield & Affleck
Nebraska Psychiatric Institute	8	1961	Affleck & Garfield
University of Oregon Clinic	4	1964	Brown & Kosterlitz
Ohio State University Clinic	4	1970	Dodd
Private Psychology Practice – Ohio	8	1980	Koss
Washington University Psychological Service Center	8	1981	Berrigan & Garfield
Texas Tech Psychology Clinic	6	1982	Walters, Solomon, & Walden
Three outpatient clinics—San Francisco Bay Area	5	1984	Billings & Moos
Office-based practice	4 (psychiatrists) 5 (psychologists)	1984	Taube, Burus, & Kessler
Institute of Psychiatry, Northwestern Memorial Hospital	13	1989	Howard, Davidson, O'Mahoney, Orlinsky, & Brown

were offered therapy but refused it, and included only actual therapy patients, the median number of interviews was between 5 and 8 (Garfield, 1986b).

Additional studies in 3 urban mental health centers reported that 37 to 45 percent of adult outpatients terminated psychotherapy after the first or second session (Fiester & Rudestam, 1975), a finding that was also secured in another study (Pekarik, 1983a). A report from an inner-city mental health clinic indicated that only 57 percent of patients admitted to the clinic remained for 4 or more interviews (Craig & Huffine, 1976).

The problem of continuation was even more apparent in a study of length of treatment in a barrio-neighborhood mental health service (Kahn & Heiman, 1978). In this setting, where the clinic population was composed largely of lower socioeconomic Mexican Americans, *75 percent of the cases came for only 1 interview, 15 percent for 2 interviews, and only 10 percent for 3 or more interviews.*

A report of outpatient statistics on over 350,000 children and youths seen in selected outpatient facilities indicated that 69 percent had 5 visits or fewer and 12.5 percent had more than 10 visits (National Institute of Mental Health, 1981).

Other more recent large-scale studies also report similar findings. Howard, Davidson, O'Mahoney, Orlinsky, and Brown (1989) mention that a national survey of the utilization of mental health services indicated that 44 percent of the persons who visited office-based psychologists or psychiatrists "made fewer than four visits and accounted for only 6.7 percent of the total expenditures. By contrast 16.2 percent made more than 24 visits and accounted for 57.4 percent of the total expenditures" (p. 775). These authors also evaluated the length of treatment for the Greater Baltimore Epidemiologic Catchment Area Program site and secured a median length of treatment of about four sessions.

A rather comprehensive review of the literature on attrition and its significance for the field of psychotherapy was prepared by Phillips (1985). All of the studies reviewed revealed the same pattern—over a relatively short period of time, there is a negatively accelerating, declining, attritional curve. Depending on the sample studied, between the fourth and tenth interview, most of the clients terminated or were terminated from psychotherapy. Phillips believes that these data raise a question about the research on psychotherapy outcome because the groups evaluated tend to be selected ones and the mental health delivery system needs to be the focus of study. Howard, Kopta, Krause, and Orlinsky (1986) have also presented an analysis of 15 studies, only one of which is included in

Table 6.2. The median sessions reported for these studies range from 4 to 33 with a median of 12 for the sample of medians.

It is interesting to note that this pattern has occurred over time in a variety of clinical settings with different types of patients or disorders, and with varied forms of therapy. For example, in the 10-year report of the Berlin Psychoanalytic Institute published in 1930, 241 out of 721 cases, or 33 percent of the cases, were considered to have terminated prematurely (Bergin, 1971). A later report of a committee of the American Psychoanalytic Association stated that of 1,269 patients in psychoanalysis, 43 percent did not complete treatment (Hamburg et al., 1967). In a private outpatient psychotherapy clinic, 718 long-term psychotherapy cases were reviewed to determine whether termination had been premature (Greenspan & Kulish, 1985). Thirty-eight percent were judged to be premature terminators. An interesting study of the effect of time-limited psychotherapy (12 sessions) on patient dropout rates secured a 32 percent dropout rate for time-limited therapy as compared with dropout rates of over 60 percent for brief therapy (3–4 months) and open-ended therapy (Sledge, Moras, Hartley, & Levine, 1990). In a university psychological service center, 26 percent of the 91 cases studied dropped out of treatment (Berrigan & Garfield, 1981). A study of depressed patients in a psychiatric setting by McLean and Hackstian (1979) reported dropout rates that ranged from 5 percent for behavioral therapy to 30 percent for dynamic psychotherapy and 34 percent for drug therapy. Dropouts were defined as clients "who chose to terminate treatment prematurely" (p. 823). A report on the psychological group treatment of 107 obese essential hypertensives also indicated that 26 percent attended 6 or fewer sessions (Basler, Brinkmeier, Buser, Hoehn, & Mölders-Kober, 1982).

One additional study of a rather selected sample of clients seen in a private practice setting emphasizing long-term psychodynamic therapy is also worth discussing here. These clients were viewed as representing "a unique population, generally underrepresented in research in psychotherapy, who have made a choice to enter long-term treatment in the private-practice sector . . . and made a decision to commit a sizable amount of time and money to their treatment" (DuBrin & Zastowny, 1988, p. 393). Thirty-four percent of the clients had college degrees and 35 percent possessed either a graduate or professional degree. In this select group, 13 percent failed to return after the intake session and 28 percent dropped out by the eighth session.

It is apparent, therefore, that contrary to many

traditional expectations concerning length of therapy, *most clients remain in therapy for a relatively few interviews.* In most of the clinical settings studied, this pattern was viewed as a problem and was not the result of a deliberately planned brief therapy, even in clinics that rely on brief therapy. Rather, in most instances, the patient failed to return for a scheduled appointment. As Sledge et al. (1990, p. 1341) emphasized, "Patient dropout results in inefficient use of treatment personnel, particularly in the public sector and other managed health care settings. Furthermore, unexplained patient dropout can be demoralizing to therapists." This occurrence can be particularly upsetting for beginning therapists who need to be prepared for it and to receive supervisory support when it occurs.

The unanticipated withdrawal from psychotherapy by a number of those who seemed to be in need of it has been a perplexing and troublesome finding that has received increased attention and research in recent years (Howard, Krause, & Orlinsky, 1986; Phillips, 1985). For example, in the NIMH Treatment of Depression Collaborative Research Program, 32 percent and 23 percent respectively of the two psychotherapy groups studied dropped out before the brief therapy trials (16 sessions) were completed (Elkin et al., 1989). Thus, premature termination is a problem for researchers and practitioners alike.

A number of studies have attempted to discover correlates and potential predictors of premature termination and continuation in psychotherapy. However, there are a number of problems in this area. A major problem is the definition of dropout or premature terminator. The definition that I have followed in my own research is "A dropout from psychotherapy is one who has been accepted for psychotherapy, who actually has at least one session of therapy, and who discontinues treatment on his or her own initiative by failing to come for any future arranged visits with the therapist." There is no mutual agreement between patient and therapist to terminate therapy and therapy is viewed by the therapist as just begun, in process, or noncompleted. Individuals who never show up for their first appointment would be viewed as rejectors of therapy rather than premature terminators since therapy had not yet been instituted.

Although the preceding definition seems both clear and logical, it has not been followed with any consistency in the published literature (Garfield, 1987, 1989a; Phillips, 1985, 1987; Weisz, Weiss, & Langmeyer, 1987, 1989). It is important to emphasize, also, that not all early terminators should be viewed as treatment failures. Some who depart early may be regarded rightly as dropouts who have shown little change. Others, however, may actually have received sufficient help or their problems may have diminished during their brief stay in psychotherapy. Thus, length of therapy per se is not necessarily a clear or accurate indication of premature termination.

A similar problem is encountered in the operational designation of "remainers" or "continuers" in psychotherapy. In some studies, arbitrary designations have been used that seriously limit the comparability and meaningfulness of the studies conducted. Thus, in some studies four sessions have been the dividing line between continuers and dropouts (Beck et al., 1987; Vail, 1978), whereas in others 20 sessions or more may be used to designate continuers in therapy (Hiler, 1959). In some studies, attending just one session differentiates remainers from dropouts, whereas in others the number is much larger. As a result, one must ascertain operational definitions of the categories used and be cautious in offering generalizations, particularly as we focus on possible correlates of length of stay in psychotherapy.

Demographic Variables

One set of variables that has been studied in relation to length of stay in psychotherapy concerns social class. Some investigations have used an index of social class such as that of Hollingshead, while others have studied specific components such as education, income, or occupation. Those who have used the former have generally found some relationship between length of stay and social class index. Dodd (1970) reported that patients from the upper three social classes on the Hollingshead Index remained in treatment longer than those in the lower two classes, but the finding was not replicated on a smaller sample of 57 patients. Fiester and Rudestam (1975) also found a relationship between social class status on the Hollingshead Index and premature termination in one clinic but not in a hospital-based community health center.

More recently, using more rigorously defined criteria, two studies secured significant correlations between social class and continuation in psychotherapy. In one, patients from the lower social classes were reported to be significantly less likely to remain in treatment after the sixth session ($p <$ .005) (Pilkonis, Imber, Lewis, & Rubinsky, 1984). Berrigan and Garfield (1981) also found a significant relationship between socioeconomic status (Hollingshead Index) and premature termination. In fact, there was a clear linear relationship between social class and continuation in psychotherapy, with increasing proportions of dropouts as social class level decreased. The range was from zero in Class I to 50 percent in Class V. It should also be mentioned that several studies have indicated significant differences between individuals in social classes IV and V (Lorion, 1978; Schubert & Miller, 1980). The largest dropout rates are noted for those in Class V, the lowest social class designation.

A study in Great Britain also secured comparable results. Termination of attendance in outpatient clinics was significantly related to lower social class (Weighill, Hodge, & Peck, 1983). Furthermore, in this study as well as the one by Berrigan and Garfield (1981), lower-class patients missed more scheduled appointments. On the basis of the latter study in particular, missed appointments, as contrasted with canceled appointments, were related to discontinuation of therapy. This is an important point that therapists should keep in mind. The difference between session cancellations and "no shows" and the importance of the latter in predicting premature termination have also been emphasized in a study by Tracey (1986), thus providing some confirmation for the results secured by Berrigan and Garfield (1981).

Education, which is one of the factors in the Hollingshead two-factor index and is highly correlated with social class, has also been evaluated separately. As indicated in the previous review (Garfield, 1986b), most studies have reported a positive relationship between education and length of stay, but some have not. In more recent studies, the findings have been somewhat mixed. In the study by DuBrin and Zastowny (1988), occupation and education were correlated significantly with dropping out of therapy. A study of 147 depressed women also indicated that those of higher socioeconomic status and those who endorsed expectancies congruent with the offered treatment rationale were most likely to continue in treatment (Rabin, Kaslow, & Rehm, 1985). On the other hand, two other investigations failed to secure clear differences between remainers and discontinuers in terms of education or occupational status (Beck et al., 1987; Sledge et al., 1990). In the latter study, only type of psychotherapy appeared to be related to continuation. Two studies of children in therapy also found few differences between remainers and dropouts (Gould, Shaffer, & Kaplan, 1985; Weisz et al., 1987).

Part of the differences in the findings reported may be due to differences in the samples used, the type of screening employed in selecting patients for psychotherapy, and other variables. Where there are more rigorous standards for acceptance into treatment, the dropout rate tends to be less and the sample biased in favor of better educated clients. Other factors may also play a role. In a study by Weissman, Geanakapolis, and Prusoff (1973), for example, 40 depressed patients received both casework and drugs. The low attrition rate and lack of difference between socioeconomic groups secured may have been influenced by the administration of medication, since it appears that medication may facilitate treatment continuation (Craig & Huffine, 1976; Dodd, 1970). In any event, it appears that educational level does show some relationship to continuation in psychotherapy, but it is not a marked one.

It is also possible that studies based on regular samples of clinic patients may secure results that are different from those secured with research samples selected to meet specified diagnostic criteria. For example, there have been several studies conducted with depressed patients in which different forms of therapy have been compared. As noted previously, the problem of premature termination is a serious one for such researchers, since it can reduce sample size and result in unequal groups. However, not all investigators report adequate data on this matter. In one report in which seven studies were compared, two studies provided no information on dropouts, whereas different types of information were provided by the other studies (Simons, Levine, Lustman, & Murphy, 1984). Furthermore, since there may be more efforts made to keep research subjects in a study than in normal clinical practice, the results on continuation may not be completely comparable with studies of clinic samples.

Besides education and social class, the most frequently studied actuarial variables examined in relation to length of stay have been sex, age, and diagnosis. Although income and occupation have also been evaluated, these have frequently been combined with education in estimates of social class.

The variable of sex has been investigated in a number of studies over a period of many years with most of the results showing no significant differences between males and females in terms of premature termination (Affleck & Garfield, 1961; Berrigan & Garfield, 1981; Craig & Huffine, 1976; Frank, Gliedman, Imber, Nash, & Stone, 1957; Garfield & Affleck, 1959; Grotjahn, 1972; Heisler, Beck, Fraps, & McReynolds, 1982; Koran & Costell, 1973; Koss, 1980; Rodolfa, Rapaport, & Lee, 1983; Weighill et al., 1983). Males were found to be continuers in psychotherapy more frequently in a much smaller number of studies (Brown & Kosterlitz, 1964; Carpenter & Range, 1983; Cartwright, 1955; Rosenthal & Frank, 1958; Weiss & Schaie, 1958). Several more recent studies also have reported no significant sex differences between continuers and premature terminators (DuBrin & Zastowny, 1988; Greenspan & Kulish, 1985; Sledge et al., 1990). On the whole, it does not appear that sex is an important predictor of continuation in psychotherapy (Garfield, 1977).

Age also does not appear to be an important variable as far as continuation in psychotherapy is concerned (Affleck & Garfield, 1961; Berrigan & Garfield, 1981; Cartwright, 1955; Frank et al., 1957; Garfield & Affleck, 1959; Heisler et al., 1982; Rosenthal & Frank, 1958; Rubinstein & Lorr, 1956). In two studies where statistically significant results were secured, the actual findings had little clinical value (Sue et al., 1976; Sullivan, Miller, & Smelser, 1958). In four more recent studies, one found age to be significantly correlated with continuation (Greenspan & Kulish, 1985), but the other three did not find age to differentiate continuers from early terminators (DuBrin & Zastowny, 1988; Gunderson et al., 1989; Sledge et al., 1990). For practical purposes, therefore, age also is not a significant variable in terms of continuation in therapy, even though the age range of the patients in the published studies varied widely.

Psychiatric diagnosis has also been evaluated in relation to length of stay in outpatient psychotherapy. By and large, such diagnostic classification did not bear any clear relationship to continuation in outpatient psychotherapy in an earlier appraisal of six studies (Garfield, 1986b). In one other study, patients diagnosed as having anxiety or depressive reactions remained in treatment significantly longer than all others (Frank et al., 1957). In another study (Dodd, 1970), patients diagnosed as having either a psychotic or psychoneurotic reaction remained in treatment longer than those with other diagnoses. However, this finding was not replicated with a new sample of 57 patients, and Sue et al. (1976) reported that patients diagnosed as psychotic were more likely to drop out of treatment than patients with other diagnoses. In contrast to this, in a study of 287 clients in a private nonprofit community mental health center, Hoffman (1985) reported that psychotic patients and patients with a presenting problem of thought disorder were more likely than other diagnostic groups to remain in therapy. These results were statistically significant at the .05 or .01 level, but data on the practical clinical significance of these results were not provided.

Craig and Huffine (1976) also reported that patients with a psychosis or personality disorder remained in therapy longer than did patients diagnosed as having a neurosis or transient situational disorder. However, they also found a relationship between length of stay and prescription of medication. Since psychotic patients usually received medication, the results may be questionable.

Gunderson et al. (1989) conducted a study of the dropout rate among so-called borderline patients.

Sixty patients with a mean age of 25 were treated by very experienced therapists in long-term psychodynamic therapy. Over 50 percent of the patients discontinued therapy within the first six months. The remainers tended to have more psychopathology and to have seen more psychotherapists previously. No other differences were secured on a variety of demographic and personal variables.

It is possible that patients with certain diagnoses may reject psychotherapy or be excluded from it more than others, and thus they have less opportunity to drop out of therapy. However, premature termination has been reported for all groups of patients receiving therapy for specifically targeted syndromes or disorders and thus psychiatric diagnosis at present does not appear to be a significant correlate of premature termination.

Another variable that has been investigated in relation to continuation in psychotherapy is race. Although racial identity has tended to be correlated with social class status, it has also been evaluated separately. Krebs (1971) studied all cases opened during a nine-month period in an adult outpatient service and analyzed the type of therapy assignment and number of appointments kept in terms of race and sex. He found that a disproportionate number of black females were assigned to crisis-oriented brief therapy as compared with whites and black males. Black females also were reported to have missed a significantly larger number of appointments than white males or females or black males. Although the black females had a higher rate of hourly employment than their white counterparts, a factor of possible importance, those who missed a majority of their appointments did not differ on this variable from the black women who kept a majority of their appointments.

A study of the differential attitudes of black and white families toward treatment in a child guidance clinic, however, did not secure any significant differences between the black and white patients, and the length of therapy also was not significantly longer for white patients (Warren, Jackson, Nugaris, & Farley, 1973).

In a large-scale study of 17 community mental health clinics, black patients were found to attend significantly fewer sessions than whites and also to terminate therapy more frequently after the intake session (Sue, McKinney, Allen, & Hall, 1974). In two other studies there was a greater tendency for black patients to see their therapists only briefly (Salzman, Shader, Scott, & Binstock, 1970; Yamamoto, James, & Palley, 1968). Rosenthal and Frank (1958) also reported that almost twice as many white patients as black patients remained for six therapy interviews. On the other hand, Weiss and Dlugokinski (1974) did not find race related to length of treatment for children, and at the Stanford University Mental Health Clinic, the termination rates of black students did not differ from those of other students (Gibbs, 1975).

In a study of lower-class black patients in an inner-city community mental health clinic, 43 patients who came for 3 sessions or fewer were considered dropouts and compared with 44 patients who continued after the third session (Vail, 1978). The patients were assigned randomly to therapists who were black or white, male or female. The only significant result secured was a sex of therapist × sex of patient interaction with most of this interaction related to male therapists' securing less continuation from black males. Various measures of attitudes toward whites were unrelated to continuation.

In the study by Billings and Moos (1984), patients' sociodemographic characteristics generally showed little relationship to their actual treatment experiences in the settings evaluated. Among their results was the finding that ethnic minority (nonwhite) patients did not receive less intensive treatment than whites. It is possible that the more recent studies reflect a more positive view of psychotherapy on the part of minority patients, and that this, in turn, is responded to more positively by therapists. Some therapists may also be more sensitive to cultural differences among clients.

In two more recent studies, the findings on race differences and premature termination were mixed. In one, significant differences were obtained with black clients having a larger number of premature terminators (Greenspan & Kulish, 1985). In the other, no significant differences were secured (Sledge et al., 1990).

In another study, 25 Mexican Americans, 25 blacks, and 24 Anglo-Americans who had previously terminated treatment in a public psychiatric outpatient clinic were interviewed (Acosta, 1980). Most of them were low-income patients and all had left therapy within 6 sessions without notifying their therapists or receiving their therapists' consent to terminate treatment. The patients had received psychodynamic therapy for a wide range of symptomatic problems. Seven common reasons for termination were given by all groups and rank ordered in the same way. The four with the greatest frequency were negative attitudes toward the therapist, no benefit from therapy, environmental constraints, and self-perceived improvement. It is interesting that all groups of terminators appeared to give similar reasons for their early termination.

Some related investigations that did not deal directly with continuation also can be mentioned. In a study of precollege counseling, 3 experienced black counselors and 8 experienced white counselors each saw 13 black and 13 white students (Ewing, 1974). The racial similarity of client and counselor was not found to be an important factor in this situation. Cimbolic (1972) studied black clients paired with white and black counselors and did not find any significant racial preference. In Acosta and Sheehan's (1976) study of preferences toward Mexican-American and Anglo-American psychotherapists, two groups of college students selected from these ethnic classifications both indicated a clear preference for the Anglo-American professional.

Sattler (1977) also reviewed a number of studies pertaining to the possible effects of therapist–client racial similarity in psychotherapy. Most of these contained interview and questionnaire data concerning attitudes toward black or white therapists or counselors. In 10 of 19 studies, the black subjects revealed a preference for black therapists or indicated negative opinions toward white therapists. In the other nine studies, no preference was expressed for either a white or black therapist. Most of these studies, as indicated, evaluated attitudes and not premature termination.

A more recent study examined the preferences of 128 black college students, age 17–52 years, for salient counselor characteristics (Atkinson, Furlong, & Poston, 1986). According to the authors, these subjects "expressed preferences for counselors who, in comparison to themselves, were more educated, had similar attitudes and values, were older, and had similar personalities; these characteristics were more important to the Ss than the counselor's race or ethnicity" (p. 326).

Recently, also, a large-scale study of community mental health services for ethnic minority groups in Los Angeles County was conducted by Sue, Fujino, Hu, Takeuchi, and Zane (1991). Over 13,000 patients representing four ethnic groups were evaluated: Asian Americans, African Americans, Mexican Americans, and whites. Asian Americans and Mexican Americans were underrepresented in the utilization of services, whereas African Americans overutilized services. The latter group also secured less positive outcomes. The study also evaluated the effect of therapist–client matches in ethnicity and languages. Ethnic match was related to length of treatment for all groups and was also related to treatment outcomes for Mexican Americans. As might be expected, for those clients who did not speak English as a primary language, "ethnic and language match was a predictor of length and outcome of treatment" (Sue et al., 1991, p. 533).

The overall picture is thus far from conclusive. Although there appears to be a tendency for more black than white clients to terminate early from psychotherapy, this is by no means a consistent pattern. This problem is also compounded by social class factors that generally have not been partialed out in most investigations.

The research findings reviewed so far indicate a frequent but not invariant relationship between social class and length of stay; some relationship of educational level, particularly an inverse one at the lower educational levels; and no clear relationship between length of stay and such variables as age, sex, and psychiatric diagnosis. It is also likely that such variables as social class may be related to other variables that might influence continuation in psychotherapy.

In an early study in which acceptance for psychotherapy was positively related to social class status, an attempt was made to evaluate "psychological mindedness" in relation to social class (Brill & Storrow, 1960). Low social class was found to be significantly related to several other variables, including a desire for symptomatic relief, lack of understanding of the psychotherapeutic process, and lack of desire for psychotherapy. In addition, the intake interviewer had less positive feelings for lower-class patients and saw them as less treatable by means of psychotherapy. Such findings do suggest an interaction effect between attributes and expectations of lower-class clients and attitudes of middle-class therapists that may play a role in length of stay in psychotherapy.

Socioeconomic level also was found to be related to therapists' ratings of patient attractiveness and the ease of establishing rapport and prognosis, each of which in turn was related to continuation in psychotherapy (Nash et al., 1965). Another study investigated the relationship between values, social class, and duration of psychotherapy and found a relationship between the interaction of social class and the discrepancy between patient and therapist values and continuation (Pettit, Pettit, & Welkowitz, 1974). A related aspect, which was commented upon by Hollingshead and Redlich (1958) as well as others (Lerner & Fiske, 1973), is that therapists generally appear to prefer and be more comfortable with clients in the upper classes, that is, clients who talk their language and are more similar to them.

The relationship between social class variables and continuation in psychotherapy thus may be a function of several variables acting independently or in interaction with each other. The attributes and expectations of the patient clearly contribute one source of variance to this problem, while the personality, attitudes, and skill of the therapist contribute another. These, furthermore, may act singly or in combination. We clearly need to know much more about such interactions and their potential impact.

Pretherapy Training and Continuation

Since premature termination from psychotherapy has been viewed as a potential waste of mental health resources, one response to this problem was to advocate careful screening of applications for psychotherapy. Only those clients should be accepted for therapy who are viewed positively and "unsuitable clients" screened out. Such a view clearly favored the more educated, intelligent, psychologically sophisticated, and less disturbed clients. Although such a view might be received positively by some therapists, it would mean a rejection of a number of individuals in need of psychological help.

A second means of responding to the problem was to provide pretherapy training to help prepare the client for psychotherapy (Heitler, 1976), or to prepare the therapist to deal with anticipated problems. In some instances, this called for a more active and flexible role on the part of the therapist (Baum & Felzer, 1964). In one study, a "role induction interview," based on the anticipatory socialization interview of Orne and Wender (1968), was developed to give the patient appropriate expectations about certain aspects of psychotherapy in the hope that this would facilitate the process and outcome of therapy (Hoehn-Saric et al., 1964). The role induction interview stressed (1) a general exposition of psychotherapy, (2) the expected behavior of patient and therapist, (3) preparation for certain phenomena in therapy such as resistance, and (4) expectation for improvement within four months of treatment. The experimental group significantly exceeded the control group in this study on 6 of the 16 criterion measures used, including that of attendance at scheduled therapy sessions. Two other studies, however, did not secure any significant differences in premature termination as a result of therapy preparation (Sloane, Cristol, Pepernik, & Staples, 1970; Yalom, Houts, Newell, & Rand, 1967).

There also have been some specific attempts to prepare lower-class individuals for psychotherapy. Heitler (1973) utilized an "anticipatory socialization interview" with 48 inpatients in expressive group psychotherapy. Although no data on outcome or continuation are provided, the experimental group did exceed the control group on a number of process measures. Strupp and Bloxom (1973) developed a role-induction film for lower-class patients and compared its effectiveness with a role-induction interview and a control film with 122 patients with an average grade level of 10.8. Twelve weekly group therapy sessions were conducted. Those patients receiving the role-induction film and the induction interview showed significantly more gains on a number of attitudinal and in-therapy measures, as well as higher ratings of improvement. However, there were no differences between the groups on attendance, on therapists' ratings of improvement, and on a symptom checklist.

In another study (Jacobs, Charles, Jacobs, Weinstein, & Mann, 1972), lower-class patients (Classes IV and V, Hollingshead Index) in a walk-in clinic were assigned to one of four groups. In one, the patient was given a brief preparatory interview; in another, the resident psychiatrist was given brief instruction in working with lower-class patients; in a third, both patients and therapists were "prepared"; and the fourth was essentially a control group. Although the report is unclear, it appears that the dropout rate was not affected by the experimental treatment. However, more patients who were in the three preparation groups came for more than four sessions and were judged to be more improved than was true for the control group.

Still another attempt at pretherapy training or instruction was conducted with 55 "low-prognosis" clients receiving time-limited, client-centered psychotherapy (Warren & Rice, 1972). This training consisted of two parts and involved four half-hour sessions with someone other than the therapist. These sessions preceded the second, third, fifth, and eighth therapy sessions. The first part, labeled "stabilizing," was designed to encourage the client to discuss problems he or she might be having with therapy or the therapist and lasted from 5 to 10 minutes. The remaining time was spent in "structuring," which was an attempt to train the client to participate productively in the process of client-centered therapy. The experimental group had a significantly smaller amount of attrition than the control group.

Lambert and Lambert (1984) also conducted a small study on role preparation for psychotherapy on immigrants who were seeking mental health services in Hawaii. These were individuals who were receiving psychotherapy for the first time. Using six sessions as the point of comparison, the investigators reported that 13 percent of the role preparation group dropped out of treatment whereas 47 percent of a control group terminated prematurely. Thus, role preparation for psychotherapy did make a significant difference.

Lastly, mention can be made of a study by Holmes and Urie (1975) in which half of a group of 88 children were given a therapy preparation interview, while the controls were given a social history interview. The prepared children dropped out significantly less than did the control children, but outcome ratings were not affected. The type of pretherapy training conceivably might explain the varying results secured.

Other attempts also were made to modify or adapt conventional procedures to better meet the needs of those who are viewed as poor candidates for therapy (Lorion, 1978). Goldstein (1973), for example, developed a structured learning therapy specifically for the poor. However, although there were several such developments in the 1960s and 1970s, the interest in them has appeared to diminish in more recent years: "Over the past decade, only limited additions have been made to our scientific understanding of the nature and treatment of mental disorders and behavioral dysfunctions among the disadvantaged" (Lorion & Felner, 1986, p. 740). Perhaps, as another aspect of this issue, there is currently a greater interest in work with culturally diverse groups (see Chapter 19, this volume). All of these developments were attempts to be sensitive to the needs of certain groups of clients and to devise procedures that would enhance continuation and outcome in psychotherapy.

Psychological Test Variables and Continuation in Psychotherapy

A variety of psychological tests and procedures have been investigated as possible correlates or predictors of continuation in psychotherapy. However, this research is difficult to integrate or use as a basis for drawing reliable generalizations. Besides variations in psychotherapy, there are also sample differences, varying criteria for designating dropouts from therapy, different statistical analyses and treatment of the data, different uses of the same test, and variations in therapists and therapeutic settings. Such differences clearly complicate the problem, make replications difficult, and must be kept in mind in evaluating existing research.

A number of early studies investigated the use of the Rorschach Test in relation to continuation in psychotherapy. Overall, the past findings have been contradictory, and there is little need to review them here. Those who are interested in this earlier work are referred to a previous review (Garfield, 1978). Essentially, the findings were not definitive enough to warrant use of the Rorschach or related procedures as bases for selecting patients for psychotherapy. Very few studies of continuation have used the Rorschach in recent years.

Other tests and techniques also have been tried in relation to continuation in psychotherapy, but there is relatively little to be gained in a review of single studies that have not been replicated. However, a few studies can be mentioned for illustrative purposes. In fact, one older study with the MMPI can be used both as a model of desirable research and as an illustration of some of the problems mentioned earlier. This well-designed study by Sullivan et al. (1958) used three moderately large groups of subjects and attempted two cross-validations of the findings secured with the initial sample of subjects, an important but rare event in clinical research. In this investigation, significant differences between the "stay" and "nonstay" groups were found for several MMPI scales for each of the several groups of subjects studied. However, these scales were different for each of the groups studied, and not one single scale held up for even two of the groups. The authors emphasized the necessity for cross-validation in studies of this type, a conclusion that is clearly supported by much of the research in this area.

Generally, investigations utilizing the MMPI, or scales derived from it, have not reported any consistent results with regard to continuation in psychotherapy. Wolff (1967) secured significant modest correlations between continuation and three MMPI scales for 24 female patients, but no such relationship was secured for 33 male subjects. The small sample and lack of replication obviously limit these findings, and just the opposite findings were reported more recently by Walters, Solomon, and Walden (1982). In this study, the MMPI was found to have some predictive value for male outpatients, but not for females. However, the correct prediction for males was only 60 percent, slightly above chance. Males who continued in therapy tended to be less defensive while experiencing greater distress.

In the study and cross-validation by Dodd (1970), MMPI scores did not differentiate between continuers and dropouts. Similarly, scores on the Barron Ego Strength Scale, derived from the MMPI, were not significantly different for continuers and dropouts in group therapy, although the number of patients studied was small (Rosenzweig & Folman, 1974). Nacev (1980) also found no correlation between the Barron Ego Strength Scale and continuation. It does appear, therefore, "that use of the MMPI to make global predictions of persistence in psychotherapy is generally inadvisable" (Walters et al., 1982, p. 83).

The most comprehensive and replicated series of studies in this area were conducted with relatively large samples of subjects from VA outpatient clinics (Lorr, Katz, & Rubinstein, 1958; Rubinstein & Lorr, 1956). A battery of four or five brief tests and questionnaires was used after extensive preliminary work; and in terms of the patient samples used, those who stayed less than 7 weeks were compared with those who remained more than 26 weeks. A multiple correlation of .39 was secured in one cross-validation study and a multiple R of .44 with a new sample of 282 patients (McNair, Lorr, & Callahan, 1963). Remainers were found to be more anxious, more self-dissatisfied, more willing to explore problems, more persistent and depend-

able, and less likely to have a history of antisocial acts. In a later study, three of the previous tests were used and no significant relationship between predictions and continuation in therapy was found (Stern, Moore, & Gross, 1975). However, in this study patients were categorized as remainers "if they kept appointments for six consecutive sessions or if they missed only one of these sessions but had notified their therapist beforehand" (Stern et al., 1975, p. 342). Clearly, this definition of continuation differed considerably from that of the previous studies and highlights once again one important reason why reliable generalizations are difficult to secure. One investigator's continuers are another investigator's premature terminators.

In general, the use of psychological tests to predict continuation in psychotherapy have not been very successful. However, one interesting and somewhat serendipitous finding peripherally related to test materials has been noted in at least three studies. This is that patients who are asked to complete test questionnaires prior to therapy, and do in fact comply with this request, are more likely to continue in therapy than those who fail to complete the test. In one study, those patients completing the MMPI continued in therapy significantly more than those who failed to do so (Wirt, 1967). In another investigation, similar findings were secured with one sample of patients, but not with another smaller sample in an attempted replication (Dodd, 1970). In a third study, those patients who failed to complete a pretherapy packet of questionnaires dropped out of group therapy significantly more than those who completed the questionnaires (Koran & Costell, 1973). Compliance with requests to complete questionnaires may indicate a general pattern of compliance or a greater degree of motivation to cooperate in therapy.

Client Expectations in Relation to Continuation in Psychotherapy

Another area of investigation has been the relationship of the clients' expectancies concerning therapy to duration of stay. Clients may have various expectations about psychotherapy and if these are incongruent with what actually occurs, the client could become dissatisfied and withdraw from therapy.

In some of the early studies reviewed in the previous edition (Garfield, 1986b), it was reported that early terminators emphasized passive cooperation and expected specific advice or medical treatment. Furthermore, those patients whose expectations were generally least accurate in terms of therapist role were significantly less likely to return for treatment. Frank, Eisenthal, and Lazare (1978) used an 84-item questionnaire to evaluate the requests for help of 278 walk-in–clinic clients. They obtained no marked differences in terms of social class. Patients from Class I through Class IV showed no differences. However, Class V clients differed in terms of requests for social interventions, administrative help, and psychological expertise although the differences were not pronounced. The investigators concluded that social class differences in treatment disposition and outcome reflected the attitudes of middle-class therapists.

Garfield and Wolpin (1963) evaluated the expectations of 70 patients referred for outpatient psychiatric treatment. The median level of education was 12 years, and none of the patients had had previous psychiatric treatment. In general, these patients indicated psychotherapy as the treatment of choice (88 percent), and a majority of them saw emotional factors as important in their difficulties. However, despite such positive attitudes toward psychotherapy, over a third thought the therapy sessions would last 30 minutes or less, 73 percent anticipated some improvement by the fifth session, and 70 percent expected treatment to last 10 sessions or less. These expectations were clearly not congruent with those held by the therapists but are not too discrepant from the median length of treatment reported by most clinics. In fact, one can say that the clients were more accurate in their expectations than were the therapists!

Pekarik and Wierzbicki (1986) investigated the relationship between clients' expected and actual treatment duration in a sample of 148 outpatients. The clients both expected and attended a relatively small number of sessions. Comparable to other studies, 73.3 percent of the clients did not remain in therapy beyond the tenth session and approximately the same number expected that they would not remain in therapy beyond the tenth session. Although the correlation between the predicted number of sessions and the actual number was only .28, it was statistically significant and was the best predictor of the number of sessions attended. Whereas the therapists in the study preferred a longer duration of therapy, the opposite was clearly true of the clients.

In a study of 173 psychotherapists, it was also found that they overestimated actual treatment length and underestimated the actual dropout rates (Pekarik & Finney-Owen, 1987). The therapists also mentioned clients' dislike of therapy or the therapist less often than did clients as a reason for discontinuing therapy.

Somewhat comparable findings have been reported also in another study of therapy expectations (Kupst & Schulman, 1979). In comparing professional and lay expectations of psychotherapy, the largest difference was found on the following item: "If I saw a professional helper, I would expect it to take a long time before I solved my problems, maybe years." Whereas only 17 percent of the lay group agreed with this statement, 96 percent of the mental health professionals agreed.

It is true that many psychotherapists, particularly those with a psychodynamic orientation, favor long-term psychotherapy even though most of the therapy conducted is relatively short-term. For example, a descriptive report of the psychotherapy program developed by the Harvard Community Health Plan indicated that only 1 to 2 percent of patients require long-term psychotherapy (Bennet & Wisneski, 1979). In a study of clients seen in private practice, Koss (1979) also concluded that "The view that long-term psychotherapy is the treatment of choice for verbal, mild to moderately disturbed persons is questioned by the results. Long-term psychotherapy was rejected by a high proportion of clients who appeared to be appropriate candidates" (p. 211).

Although the patients today appear to be more sophisticated about psychotherapy than they were in the past, they do not necessarily expect or favor long-term psychotherapeutic treatment. There are, of course, individual differences among patients that influence their preferences and expectations and interact with therapist variables. At the same time, there has been a definite increase in the popularity of brief psychotherapy (Budman & Gurman, 1988; Garfield, 1989b).

Interactional Variables and Continuation in Psychotherapy

Although the focus in this chapter is on client variables or attributes, as indicated in the preceding section, how the therapist perceives and regards the client may also affect the progress of therapy. If the therapist regards the client as unmotivated, overly defensive, hostile, and difficult, it is conceivable that his or her attitudes may be communicated to the client and influence his or her participation and continuation in psychotherapy. Some studies that appear pertinent to this hypothesis can be alluded to briefly here, although therapist variables and related interactional aspects of psychotherapy will be reviewed in the following chapter.

In one study, therapists' ratings at the end of the second session of group therapy on three factors were related significantly to continuation in therapy (Rosenzweig & Folman, 1974). These were the therapist's estimate of his or her ability to empathize with the client, positive feelings toward the client, and judgment of the client's ability to form a therapeutic relationship. In another study, the therapists' positive feelings toward clients and their positive prognoses for treatment were related to continuation, whereas ratings of psychopathology were not so related (Shapiro, 1974).

The skill or experience of the therapist and how he or she is perceived by the client also may play a role in continuation. Dodd (1970) found that medical students had a significantly higher rate of patients dropping out than did psychiatric residents, and this finding was cross-validated on a new sample. Baekland and Lundwall (1975) also reported a relationship between therapist experience and continuation in psychotherapy in their review article, and a relationship between judged therapists' level of skill and continuation was found by Garfield, Affleck, & Muffley (1963). It can also be noted that when very experienced and nationally recognized therapists were used in one study, there were no dropouts at the fourth interview, the point set for designating dropouts (Sloane, Staples, Cristol, Yorkston, & Whipple, 1975).

Some interesting findings also were reported in a study of the therapeutic relationship in relation to both continuation and outcome in psychotherapy (Saltzman, Leutgert, Roth, Creaser, & Howard, 1976). The subjects were 91 students who sought treatment at a university counseling center. Dropouts were defined as those who did not continue beyond the ninth interview. Both clients and therapists filled out forms pertaining to the treatment process after each of the first 10 interviews, and analyses were made of the responses to the first, third, and fifth interviews, the period during which most of the premature terminations occurred.

At the end of the first session, dropouts reported less anxiety than did the remainers. At the third and fifth sessions, dropouts gave significantly lower responses than remainers on a number of dimensions pertaining to the relationship, such as the therapist's respect, confidence in the therapist, and involvement in therapy. In a complementary fashion, dropouts were significantly lower than remainers on items completed by the therapists that pertained to the therapist's respect for the client and his or her own involvement in therapy. Thus, both clients' and therapists' views of the relationship early in therapy appeared to be related to continuation in therapy. However, therapist experience level and gender similarity of client–therapist pairs were not related to either continuation or outcome.

Fiester (1977) compared therapists with high client attrition rates versus therapists with low attrition rates on demographic and initial-session therapy-process variables. The two groups did not differ in such variables as age, sex, profession, experience, or personal therapy. However, several process variables did differentiate the groups and the author concluded that such variables have greater explanatory power for attrition than do client characteristics.

In another study, little relationship was found between continuation and therapists' sex, professional affiliation, and democratic values (Carpenter & Range, 1982). Mogul (1982), in reviewing studies dealing with the sex of the therapist in relation to duration of treatment and satisfaction with treatment, also concluded that there were "no clear, replicable results salient to decision making" (p. 1).

Duehn and Proctor (1977) compared 32 individuals who terminated after the first interview with a like number who continued for additional interviews. Stimulus–response congruence (whether the clinician's verbal responses acknowledged the content of the patient's preceding communication) and content congruence (the clinician's verbal statement's being consistent with the patient's expectations concerning what was to be discussed) were the variables appraised. The therapists were significantly more incongruent with terminators and their verbal content was also significantly more irrelevant to the content expectations of the terminators.

A related study of interactional correlates of premature termination focused on the relationship of topic determination to premature termination (Tracey, 1986). Topic determination was characterized as reaching agreement early in therapy regarding the goals and tasks of therapy. A main conclusion in this study was that "Whether a dyad continues past the first few sessions is related to how well participants establish mutually agreeable definitions of what each is to do" (Tracey, 1986, p. 787). However, there were no differences in this regard between continuing dyads who did well in therapy and those who did not.

Another potential source of information about factors influencing premature termination are the clients' own reasons for terminating their psychotherapy. One of the first studies of this kind was a follow-up study of 12 individuals who dropped out of psychotherapy before the seventh interview (Garfield, 1963). Eleven of the 12 cases were contacted by a social worker and, among other questions, were asked why they discontinued psychotherapy. Six of the terminators gave as their reason some external difficulty, such as lack of transportation, no babysitter, and inability to get away from work. Of the remaining five, three were dissatisfied with the results of therapy or with the therapist, and two stated that they had improved.

In a somewhat comparable study with 46 patients, 39 percent stated they had no need for services, 35 percent mentioned environmental constraints, and 26 percent indicated a dislike of the services received (Pekarik, 1983b). Silverman and Beech (1979) also questioned whether all dropouts should be viewed as failures. I would agree that not all dropouts automatically should be viewed as treatment failures. However, their study does not provide an adequate answer. The sample used was small and not clearly described, and only 25 percent of the group who failed to return for treatment after the first interview participated in the study.

Two studies of university students evaluated their perceptions of their counselors in relation to continuation in counseling. In one investigation where 30 of 134 students failed to return for scheduled appointments after intake, it was reported that client satisfaction and perceptions of trustworthiness and expertness were related to continuation (Kokotovic & Tracey, 1987). In the second study, the premature terminators were less satisfied with the counseling they received and viewed their counselors as less expert and less trustworthy than did the completers (McNeill, May, & Lee, 1987). What is of interest here is that both of these studies secured comparable findings in terms of the clients' perceptions of the attributes mentioned, although other therapist attributes were not as consistently perceived. It would appear that the client's perceptions of the therapist's competence and trustworthiness in the early therapy sessions play a role in continuation.

In a follow-up study of 71 self-terminated cases at a children's psychiatric center, 52 households agreed to be interviewed. The three main reasons for leaving treatment were that expectations about treatment were "somewhat or fully unfulfilled" (46%); the child did not progress (37%); and the family was dissatisfied with the services received (35%). More than one reason could be given by the participants (Farley, Peterson, & Spanos, 1975).

Also of interest is a recent study of 96 patients at the time of their initial screening interviews (Mohl, Martinez, Ticknor, Huong, & Cordell, 1991). Those patients who dropped out early liked the clinician less, felt less liked and respected, experienced a weaker helping alliance, and viewed the interviewer as more passive and psychotherapy as less potent than did the others. Also, one of the interviewers had a significantly higher dropout rate and was seen as more passive and offering less understanding than the others.

There are also a few reports where dropouts from group therapy were asked their reasons for terminating. Although group therapy has features that distinguish it from individual psychotherapy, the results of these studies are worth noting. Yalom (1966) was able to contact 26 of 35 dropouts and reported that there was rarely "a single cause for any patient's termination and often it was difficult to determine the major reason for the dropout" (p. 397). He grouped his responses into nine differ-

ent categories, some of which dealt specifically with the group process. However, seven patients did indicate that they had a mistaken notion of therapy. A smaller study of 9 of 15 dropouts also secured results that were similar to Yalom's in showing a diversity of reasons for termination (Koran & Costell, 1973).

In a study of patients who had been prepared for therapy, 29 percent dropped out of group therapy (Lothstein, 1978):

Although the patients' reasons for dropping out focused on such factors as no longer needing treatment and scheduling problems, the therapists focused on dynamic reasons for the dropouts. All of the therapists reported that they disliked the patients who dropped out, and many of those patients were seen as hostile toward the therapist. (p. 1494)

At the same time, the author also mentioned that some dropouts felt that the therapist and other patients were unsympathetic. However, he concluded that the dropout rate may not be preventable and is necessary for development of cohesiveness in the group. Whether this is true or not, it seems likely that variations in therapists, clients, and type of therapy, singly or in interaction, may influence the dropout rate.

We have now reviewed a number of variables in relation to duration of stay in psychotherapy and have commented upon some of the problems in securing reliable and generalizable results. Many findings are not confirmed when applied to new and different samples, and conditions from clinic to clinic and study to study vary. The variations in the definitions of premature terminators and continuers used in the published reports also limit our ability to draw definitive conclusions.

Of the variables studied, those pertaining to social class appear to have the most consistent supporting evidence. However, while this relationship does have some empirical support, it is not invariant and the explanations advanced are not definitive. Mutuality of expectations on the part of therapist and client is one hypothesis that seems plausible and has some supporting data, but it is not limited to social class differences between clients and therapists. The matter of differing value systems and orientations among middle-class therapists and lower-class clients also has been hypothesized as a possible explanation for the results secured, but systematic research on this has been limited (Lerner & Fiske, 1973).

Finally, it can be noted that premature termination and rejection of therapy occur with practically all forms of psychotherapy. The reasons for this undoubtedly vary, and one general explanation would not appear to be adequate. In some cases, the individual may terminate because his or her concerns have lessened, and the therapist apparently fails to recognize this. In such instances, was the brief opportunity to verbalize personal feelings of concern, demoralization, and the like sufficient for the individual to feel helped? Was the acceptance, support, or explanations of the therapist in the early interviews sufficiently helpful for some clients? We have few answers to such questions. In other instances, however, as indicated previously, a variety of factors may account for the termination.

In this chapter we have focused primarily on client variables, but investigators will have to go beyond single variables if more progress is to be made in understanding premature termination as well as outcome in psychotherapy. The interactions that occur between clients and therapists clearly are important and they are particularly important in the first few interviews. Some implications that seem plausible are as follows: (1) The therapist should ascertain the client's expectations concerning therapy. If these are very discrepant with those of the therapist, the latter should do some preparatory work with the client. (2) The client should be given a clear explanation of what to expect in therapy. (3) Since both the client's expectation of the length of therapy and the actual duration of most therapy are brief, the therapist, except in certain cases, should provide brief therapy (Pekarik, 1985).

Thus, although the variables that influence premature termination vary from study to study or show limited predictive value, therapists should be aware of the problem and strive to be as sensitive as possible to cues from the client and to respond appropriately.

RESEARCH ON CLIENT VARIABLES AND OUTCOME IN PSYCHOTHERAPY

Although the problem of premature termination in psychotherapy is of some importance, the most critical issue is the kind of outcome that is secured by means of psychotherapeutic intervention. As indicated earlier, not all dropouts from psychotherapy can be considered treatment failures. However, truly adequate appraisals of the outcome of early terminators are exceedingly rare. In one follow-up study of 12 terminators and 12 remainers, both groups stated that they were getting along quite well (Garfield, 1963). However, the follow-up was based on the self-reports of the clients and no pre- and posttherapy measures were used. In contrast to this report, Yalom (1966) indicated that all

but perhaps 3 of 35 dropouts from group therapy showed no improvement. Still other more positive results were secured on the basis of a telephone inquiry (Silverman & Beech, 1979).

In another investigation, clinic patients were divided into dropouts or appropriate terminators on the basis of their therapists' judgments (Pekarik, 1983a). A dropout was defined as a client in need of further treatment; an appropriate terminator required no further treatment. Over four-fifths of the clients had 4 or fewer visits, with the dropouts averaging 2.8 visits and the appropriate terminators averaging 3.8 visits. Sixty-four percent of the group were considered dropouts. Although the author concluded that the appropriate terminators had better outcomes than the dropouts, this finding was due mainly to the patients who attended one session. The brevity of the therapy as well as the criteria used seriously limit what conclusions can be drawn.

Problems in Evaluating Outcome

Although the importance of the client as a factor in securing positive outcome has been emphasized by a number of psychotherapists (Frank, 1974b; Garfield, 1989b; Strupp, 1973), and the various editions of the *Handbook of Psychotherapy and Behavior Change* have included a chapter on research on client variables in psychotherapy, it is interesting that two more recent reviews of individual psychotherapy in the *Annual Review of Psychology* reported little research on this topic (Goldfried, Greenberg, & Marmar, 1990; Parloff, London, & Wolfe, 1986). Whether this reflects a diminishing interest in such research or whether there are particular difficulties inherent in investigations of this sort is unclear. However, we shall explore this area and attempt to draw whatever conclusions seem plausible.

Any research in psychotherapy that involves the evaluation of outcome usually has to contend with a number of possible difficulties (see Chapters 2 and 5, this volume). One problem is the large number of variable and fallible criteria of outcomes. Among the frequently used criteria for appraising outcome are therapists' judgments, clients' evaluations, judges' ratings, a variety of tests and questionnaires, behavioral tasks, and the like. This variety of measures poses a number of difficulties in comparing the results of potential predictor variables among different studies. Several investigations, for example, have shown rather low agreement among different outcome criteria (Cartwright, Kirtner, & Fiske, 1963; Garfield, Prager, & Bergin, 1971; Horenstein, Houston, & Holmes, 1973; Keniston, Boltax, & Almond, 1971; Sloane et al., 1975). In some of these studies, it has also been shown that clients' and therapists' ratings of outcome tend to be more positive than other measures. In addition to these problems, there have also been methodological issues concerning whether only global ratings of outcome at termination are used, or whether difference scores, in terms of pre–post measures, or other procedures to take into account initial differences between clients have been used (Fiske et al., 1970; Luborsky, Singer, & Luborsky, 1975; Mintz, 1972). As a result, it is quite difficult and, at times, misleading to lump together studies that have utilized different measures of outcome.

In addition to the problems encountered with outcome criteria, there are also variations in the type of therapy offered, in the training and competence of the therapists studied, and in the kinds of client samples treated. Such problems not only place limitations on the value of any single study, but also seriously limit the generalizations to be drawn from the existing studies. Being forewarned, let us now look at some representative studies.

Social Class Variables and Outcome

Social class variables have not been studied as frequently with reference to outcome as they have with relation to the topics previously discussed. In the review by Luborsky, Chandler, Auerbach, Cohen, and Bachrach (1971), for example, only a relatively small number of such studies were mentioned. In general, other variables have received greater attention, and thus our discussion of social class variables will be brief.

In their review of five studies dealing with social class, Luborsky et al. (1971) reported essentially no relationship between this variable and outcome. Lorion (1973), in a general discussion of socioeconomic status and traditional treatment approaches, also concluded that "while socioeconomic status appears to be a significant correlate of acceptance for, and duration of, individual psychotherapy, it does not relate to treatment outcome" (p. 263). Thus, two previous reviews of this problem came to quite similar conclusions. Schmidt and Hancey (1979) also did not find any relationship between social class and outcome in their investigation. In addition, the findings on the relation of the client's educational status to outcome have been inconclusive (Garfield, 1986b).

It is also of interest to note that whereas the importance of socioeconomic status has been discussed a number of times with reference to so-called traditional or psychodynamic psychotherapy, it is rarely mentioned in reports of behavioral therapy. This is evident in a review of individual psychotherapy and behavioral therapy by Gomes-Schwartz, Hadley, and Strupp, (1978). The section

of the review that discusses psychotherapy has a subsection devoted to socioeconomic status, but there is no such subsection in the section that discusses behavioral therapy. These reviewers state initially that lower-class patients "are less likely to be accepted for traditional insight-orient therapy . . . and less likely to benefit from expressive psychotherapies" (Gomes-Schwartz et al., 1978, p. 439). However, shortly after making this statement, they also state that these views have begun to be challenged and that some of the more negative results may be related to the attitudes and expectations that many therapists may have toward such patients.

Several individuals have discussed the matter of differential therapists' attitudes toward lower-class patients and their potential importance for continuation in psychotherapy (Jones, 1974; Lerner, 1972; Lorion, 1973, 1974; Lorion & Felner, 1986). However, there have been few, if any, systematic studies that attempted to relate therapists' attitudes toward lower-class patients and outcome in psychotherapy. The existing data, however, do not indicate any strong relationship between social class and outcome.

In a related study of racial match, Jones (1982) compared four comparable groups of black and white clients who were seen by equal numbers of black and white therapists. All clients had to have been seen for at least eight sessions in individual dynamic therapy. Essentially similar results were secured for the four groups and the investigator concluded that "Therapist–patient racial match has little influence on outcome in longer term psychotherapy" (Jones, 1982, p. 730). A possible limitation of the study is that the criteria of outcome were therapists' ratings.

Some limited attention has been paid to the possible differential response to certain modes of psychotherapy by lower-class individuals and those with lower levels of education (Lorion & Felner, 1986). In general, as noted previously, patients accepted for psychoanalysis and for long-term psychodynamic therapy tend to be well-educated individuals in the upper social classes. It is difficult to state how lower-class individuals actually perform in such therapies because very few of them have sought or been accepted for such treatments, both clients and therapists have very different expectations about therapy, and lower-class individuals would not be able to afford such treatments. In the study by Sloane et al. (1975) comparing brief psychoanalytically oriented therapy and behavioral therapy, wider differences in outcome were found among the patients receiving the psychodynamic therapy than was the case for the behavioral therapy patients. Thus, patients with higher incomes and less pathology did better than their opposites in analytically oriented therapy, whereas such differences were not noted in the behavioral therapy group where there was less variance in outcome among the patients treated.

Age and Outcome

It has generally been assumed that older people tend to be more rigid and fixed in their ways. Their patterns of behavior have a longer reinforcement history and supposedly their defenses and character structure are relatively resistant to change. We do know from more systematic studies that older subjects show some decline in mental functioning (Matarazzo, 1972), and that they may not learn new skills as readily as younger individuals. Consequently, it could be presumed that they would be less favorable candidates for psychotherapy in terms of their potential for change. This, apparently, was Freud's view and it has been an influential view for a number of therapists. However, I do not believe that there are adequate research data to support the view that older clients are less desirable in terms of most psychotherapeutic approaches.

There is a problem pertaining to the research on age and outcome, however, that does not exist with regard to the variable of sex. By and large, in the latter instance, all studies use the same criteria and subjects are classified into the same two categories—male and female. Age, however, is a different matter. It is a continuous variable and not a dichotomous one. Consequently, one cannot generalize from a group of studies unless they have comparable samples of subjects. If one investigator has a group of patients ranging in age from 20 to 40 years, and another has a sample ranging in age from 40 to 60 years, the "older" patients in one sample become the younger patients in the other sample. This problem has limited the findings reported in this area.

In Luborsky et al.'s (1971) tally of 11 studies, 4 studies purportedly secured a positive relationship between age and outcome (favoring the younger age), 2 secured a negative relationship, and 5 secured no relationship. However, one of the "positive studies" actually did not deal with age and psychotherapy outcome, thus, reducing the "positive" studies to 3. Although the reviewers concluded that "older patients tend to have a slightly poorer prognosis" (p. 151), the data in support of this conclusion are weak. A more detailed analysis of the individual studies is contained in an earlier review by the present writer (Garfield, 1978).

A study of short-term interpersonal therapy for depressed patients also reported no relationship of age to outcome (Rounsaville, Weissman, & Prusoff,

1981). In another study of early recurrence in unipolar depression, age was not found to be significantly related to a reoccurrence of a depressive episode (Frank, Kupfer, & Perel, 1989).

Although there has been an increased interest recently in work with the elderly, there has not been much systematic research on psychotherapy with the aged (Mintz, Steuer, & Jarvik, 1981; Storandt, 1983). It does seem, however, that the negative views toward the elderly associated with long-term analytically oriented psychotherapy may have diminished greatly as the modal therapy today is distinctly brief therapy. For example, in a study of 412 patients who entered treatment for unipolar depression in six different treatment centers, there was "little evidence of clinician bias against providing treatment to less 'desirable' patients, such as those who were older or of lower social status" (Billings & Moos, 1984, p. 119). It can also be noted that Smith, Glass, and Miller (1980) secured an overall correlation of .00 between age and outcome in their large-scale meta-analysis of outcome in psychotherapy.

Several more recent studies comparing cognitive, behavioral, and brief psychodynamic therapies with depressed individuals 60 years of age or over have been conducted by Gallagher, Thompson, Breckenridge, and colleagues (Breckenridge, Zeiss, Breckenridge, Gallagher, & Thompson, 1985; Thompson, Gallagher, & Breckenridge, 1987). The results have been quite impressive, with 52 percent of the patients judged to be in remission at the end of treatment. Furthermore, there were no differences among the results secured with the three different therapies. These findings are quite comparable to those secured in the NIMH collaborative study (Elkin et al., 1989).

Sex and Outcome in Psychotherapy

Most of the studies of the relationship of the sex of the client to outcome in psychotherapy have not indicated any significant relationship. However, it is conceivable that there are possible interaction effects between the sex of the therapist and that of the client. If this is so, then focusing solely on one part of the equation may not provide meaningful answers. However, we can discuss some of those studies briefly.

Several older studies reported no relationship between sex and outcome (Gaylin, 1966; Hamburg et al., 1967; Knapp, Levin, McCarter, Wermer, & Zetzel, 1960), and two reported positive findings for women (Mintz, Luborsky, & Auerbach, 1971; Seeman, 1954). However, in the latter two studies, 11 and 12 women respectively were studied and we need not place much emphasis on the findings. More recently, a comparison and reanalysis of two well-known studies also indicated inconclusive findings as regards sex and outcome in psychotherapy (Luborsky, Mintz, & Christoph, 1979). Although in the University of Chicago Counseling Center Project (Fiske, Cartwright, & Kirtner, 1964) there were low but significant correlations (.26, .33) between sex of client and two measures of outcome, the comparable correlations secured in the Penn Psychotherapy Project were not significant (Luborsky et al., 1979). In a Temple University study comparing psychotherapy and behavioral therapy, the "amount of improvement shown appeared to be independent of the sex of the patient" (Sloane et al., 1975). Similar findings were also reported in a study of psychoanalytically oriented psychotherapy conducted at the Michael Reese Medical Center in Chicago (Siegel, Rootes, & Taub, 1977). An educational approach to depression based on social learning theory also found no relationship between sex and outcome (Steinmetz, Lewinsohn, & Antonucio, 1983). The review by Gomes-Schwartz et al. (1978), although referring to only a few studies, also refers to null or conflicting results when discussing the relation of sex to outcome.

One recent study did attempt to evaluate the impact of client and therapist gender on psychotherapy process and outcome (Jones & Zoppel, 1982). Former therapy clients were interviewed about their experiences in treatment and assessments of their therapy were secured. In general, women therapists appeared to form more effective therapeutic alliances with clients of both sexes, but both male and female clients of the male therapists reported significant improvement in therapy. The authors concluded that "gender was not an overriding influence in psychotherapy" (p. 271).

Perhaps because of the results reviewed here, there have been very few studies of the relationship of sex of client to outcome in psychotherapy since the 1986 edition of this *Handbook*. On the basis of these results, one cannot make much of a case for sex of client as a significant variable related to outcome in psychotherapy. Others factors would appear to be of greater importance. However, the sex or gender of the therapist has been considered an important issue in the treatment of rape victims, although research data on this matter are still very limited at present (Calhoun & Atkeson, 1991). In a study by Dye and Roth (1990), female therapists displayed more knowledge about problems of rape and had more positive attitudes toward rape victims than did male therapists. Younger therapists also had more positive attitudes toward such victims than did older therapists. Silverman (1977) identified a number of potential problems that male therapists may have in treating rape victims.

Personality and Test Variables Related to Outcome

A number of studies carried out in the search for variables related to outcome in psychotherapy have dealt with the personality and test patterns of clients. Numerous prognostic and personality variables have been investigated and include the following: level or degree of disturbance, life situation, support systems, expectancies for improvement, type of symptoms, duration of symptoms, likeability, motivation for treatment, ego strength, developmental level, ability to form therapeutic relationships, cognitive structures, neuroticism, and the like. No attempt will be made here to review all of the individual and frequently unreplicated studies that exist in the published literature. Instead, we will focus on studies that have appeared promising or that illustrate research problems in this area.

In the late 1940s and 1950s particularly, when psychologists were identified to a large extent with psychological tests, a variety of investigations were conducted in which test findings were related to outcome in psychotherapy. One of the serious problems with much of this early research (and even with more recent research) was the failure in the attempted replication of the results secured. Roberts (1954) compared 11 Rorschach indices alleged to have prognostic significance for outcome with judges ratings of outcome. None of the measures were related significantly to the outcome criteria. In another comparable study, 95 Rorschach signs and three types of clinical judgments failed to differentiate patients judged to be improved (Rogers & Hammond, 1953). Whereas Harris and Christiansen (1946) found positive results with the Rorschach Prognostic Index and no relationship between improvement and intelligence test scores, Barron (1953a) secured just the opposite result. The subjects in the latter study had much higher IQs than subjects in the former study.

Another early study using a battery of psychological tests found high IQs to be related positively to outcome but also mentioned a number of other positive attributes (Rosenberg, 1954). Besides superior intelligence, these included the ability to produce associations easily; a lack of rigidity; a wide range of interests; sensitivity to the environment; and the ability to feel deeply, to have a high energy level, and to be free from bodily concerns. How many patients with these fine attributes actually seek psychotherapy is not completely known!

The number of studies of this type has diminished noticeably in more recent years. For example, in a brief summary of 18 studies that evaluated various Rorschach scores in relation to outcome in psychotherapy, the most recent study cited was published in 1967 and the findings were mixed (Luborsky, Crits-Christoph, Mintz, & Auerbach, 1988).

Degree of Disturbance and Related Variables

Probably the most frequent client variable evaluated in relation to outcome has been some variant of degree of personality disturbance, integration, or psychopathology. Most of the studies to be reviewed in this section will make some reference to such variables.

A five-year follow-up study by Stone, Frank, Nash, and Imber (1961) utilized a self-report scale tapping five areas of symptomatology as a measure of initial disturbance and reported a significant association between greater initial disturbance and more positive outcome. Truax, Tunnell, Fine, and Wargo (1966) secured somewhat comparable results for group psychotherapy clients on four scales of the MMPI. However, Barron (1953a) found that the least "sick" patients at the beginning of therapy were most likely to get well. The report of the Wisconsin Project on a hospitalized group of psychotic patients also indicated that high mental health ratings and generally low level of manifest psychotic disturbance were positively related to outcome (Rogers, Gendlin, Kiesler, & Truax, 1967).

Conflicting results were also reported in two studies of VA outpatients. Katz, Lorr, and Rubinstein (1958) found no relationship between degree of disturbance and outcome in an investigation of 232 outpatients. Degree of disturbance was based on four categories of diagnosis—psychoneurosis, psychosomatic disorders, character disorder, and psychosis. *Both* diagnoses and ratings of improvement were provided by the therapists. However, another study of 83 patients in a VA clinic using the MMPI found significant differences on a majority of the clinical scales, indicating "that those persons who are least equipped to meet life challenges are the ones who stand to gain least from psychotherapy" (Sullivan et al., 1958, p. 7). To complicate matters further, essentially null results were reported in three other earlier studies (Cartwright & Roth, 1957; Muench, 1965; Seeman, 1954). It would be rather foolhardy to attempt to draw any reliable conclusions from this collection of studies that used different samples and different measures of disturbed functioning and outcome.

Sloane et al. (1975) found that the less disturbed patients, as measured by the MMPI, secured more positive outcome with analytically oriented psychotherapy. On the other hand, "behavior therapy was equally successful whether the patient had a high or low degree of pathology" (p. 176). In this instance, at least, the type of therapy appeared to be an important variable. They also reported that those patients in both groups who spoke in longer utterances showed more improvement than those who spoke in shorter units.

In a study of psychoanalytically oriented therapy (Siegel et al., 1977), no differences were obtained when patients were dichotomized into two broad groupings of diagnostic categories in terms of severity. However, when the patients were viewed in terms of the focus of symptomatology or distress, patients with a "neurotic focus" tended to secure good outcomes, whereas those whose complaints focused on a "behavioral" area ordinarily under voluntary control did not.

In a study of time-limited counseling, degree of client disturbance as rated by therapists after the initial session did not correlate with therapists' ratings of outcome after treatment or with clients' ratings of outcome one month or 18 months after treatment (Gelso, Mills, & Spiegel, 1983). Although adequacy of client functioning is mentioned as one of the relatively better predictors of outcome in the Penn Psychotherapy Project, the overall correlations reported are low (Luborsky et al., 1980, 1988).

In the past dozen years or so, there has been considerable interest in the treatment of depression and a number of brief therapies for depression have been developed. Several studies have also investigated potential prognostic indicators of outcome. In one investigation of 75 depressed clients who received a group psychoeducational treatment for unipolar depression, a clear relationship was evident between degree of depression at the start of therapy and at termination (Steinmetz et al., 1983): "Participants at all levels of depression severity improved markedly, but those who were initially more depressed tended to maintain their relative ranking in posttreatment" (p. 331). The pretreatment scores of the Beck Depression Inventory accounted for 27 percent of the variance in posttreatment scores and were clearly the best predictor of outcome. A study of interpersonal therapy with depressed patients also found that the best predictor of outcome was the general emotional health of the patient at the beginning of therapy (Rounsaville et al., 1981).

In another study of 40 diagnosed depressed patients receiving the Coping with Depression Course, essentially similar findings were secured (Hoberman, Lewinsohn, & Tilson, 1988). Client predictive variables that were replicated were pretreatment depression level, perceived mastery, social adjustment, social support, and outcome expectancies. Comparable results were also reported in a study that attempted to identify variables that would predict rapid responders to treatment: "The best predictor of response at session 6 was level of depression at the beginning of the first treatment session. On the average, patients who were severely depressed at the beginning of treatment . . . did not improve at all by session 6" (Beckham, 1989, p. 949).

In a study of cognitive therapy of depression, pretreatment symptom severity was associated with negative outcome at the end of treatment, but the investigators secured the best predictions with a measure of learned resourcefulness (Simons, Lustman, Wetzel, & Murphy, 1985). Interestingly, in contrast to this latter finding, in the previously cited study by Hoberman et al. (1988), clients who scored higher on the Learned Resourcefulness Inventory (or Self-Control Scale, Rosenbaum, 1980) were more likely to be depressed after treatment. Since two different approaches to psychotherapy were used in these two investigations, it is conceivable that the different therapies could have different predictors of outcome, and although the data are to be viewed only as suggestive, some differential predictors were secured for cognitive therapy and interpersonal therapy in the NIMH collaborative study of depression (Stotsky et al., 1991). Low social dysfunction predicted a superior response to interpersonal therapy, whereas low cognitive dysfunction predicted superior response for the cognitive-behavioral therapy. It can also be mentioned that in the latter study, depressed patients who also had personality disorders had significantly poorer outcomes in social functioning and were more likely to have residual symptoms of depression than were depressed patients without personality disorders (Shea et al., 1990).

Finally, in a study of coping styles and homework compliance of patients who received cognitive-behavioral therapy for affective disorders, Burns and Nolen-Hoeksema (1991) reported that patients who were the most depressed initially were also the most depressed 12 weeks later. However, even though the initial severity of depression accounted for the largest share of the variance in the 12-week depression ratings, patient willingness to learn new coping strategies at intake also was correlated with improved depression scores.

The research findings reviewed in this section do not allow one to reach conclusions with any marked degree of confidence. Positive, negative, and inconclusive findings have all been reported. However, there appears to be greater consistency among the more recent findings indicating that individuals with more serious levels of disturbance have poorer outcomes. Other personality variables, however, may

also be involved as well as possible methodological factors that will be discussed later.

It is also worth mentioning here that with the most recent revision of the Diagnostic and Statistical Manual (DSM) of the American Psychiatric Association, greater attention has been given to psychiatric diagnosis. Problems of reliability and validity of clinical diagnosis have been important issues in past research, and the large increase in the number of official diagnoses provided in DSM-III and DSM-III Revised Edition (American Psychiatric Association, 1980, 1987) would not appear to improve the situation (Garfield, 1986a, 1993). However, a task force of the American Psychiatric Association has recently published three large volumes that examine the current use of various treatments for the disorders listed in the current manual (American Psychiatric Association, T. B. Karasu, Chairperson, 1989). The report includes other treatments besides psychotherapeutic ones, but it does make reference to specific psychotherapeutic approaches such as cognitive therapy, behavioral therapy, and family therapy. The amount of research varies considerably for both therapeutic modalities and type of disorder, and a simple matching of diagnosis and preferred treatment does not yet seem feasible. An excellent review of this work is provided by Kazdin (1990).

Ego Strength and Outcome

Another personality variable or construct that has been mentioned frequently by psychoanalytically oriented therapists as a correlate of positive outcome is "ego strength." In the long-term Menninger Foundation study of psychoanalysis and psychoanalytic psychotherapy, clinical appraisals of ego strength did show a small positive correlation with a measure of global improvement ($r = .35$) (Kernberg et al., 1972). However, these investigators did emphasize that the appraisals were relative to the patients studied, basically patients included within the broad categories of neurosis and "borderline" conditions. In the Columbia Psychoanalytic Center Project, the correlations between clinical appraisals of ego strength and outcome were not significant (Weber, Bachrach, & Solomon, 1985).

Two specific measures of ego strength have been evaluated in a number of studies of psychotherapy outcome. The ES Scale, consisting of items selected from the MMPI, was developed by Barron, who reported a positive relationship between the scale and outcome (Barron, 1953b). However, investigators during the next 20 years generally failed to replicate these positive results (Fiske et al. 1964; Gallagher, 1954; Getter & Sundland, 1962;

Gottschalk, Fox, & Bates, 1973; Newmark, Finkelstein, & Frerking, 1974; Sullivan et al., 1958; Taulbee, 1958). There have been very few studies with the scale in recent years.

More positive results have been reported with the use of another index of ego strength derived from six components of the Rorschach Test, the Rorschach Prognostic Rating Scale (RPRS) (Klopfer, Kirkner, Wisham, & Baker, 1951). In a previous review (Garfield, 1978), eight studies reported positive results and three secured negative results, although some of the subject samples were quite small and varied. The Penn Psychotherapy Project, which used this measure among others, also failed to secure any positive findings between ego strength and outcome (Luborsky et al., 1980). In the review by Luborsky et al. (1988), six studies were noted as securing positive results and three as securing nonsignificant results. These authors also emphasized the fact that the RPRS is a time-consuming measure and this may be one reason for its diminished use in more recent years.

Although positive findings have been reported more frequently than negative findings for the RPRS, it is difficult to draw definite conclusions. The mean scores for various groups of subjects (judged to be improved or unimproved) show considerable variability; there is a noticeable overlap in scores between improved and unimproved clients; and the predictive norms provided by Kopfer et al. (1951) do not always appear applicable. The criteria for judging improvement also vary considerably among the studies just cited and, consequently, there is a question of what is actually being predicted (Garfield, 1978).

Finally, as Frank (1967) has emphasized, the use of the RPRS in predicting outcome leads to a correct prediction in about two-thirds of the cases, which, on the basis of some reported success rates in psychotherapy, might be predicted without utilizing any measures. Here, we have the old problem of base rates, which is frequently overlooked in this area of research. An effective predictor, however, should exceed the base rates. The overall impression, therefore, is that whereas those with adequate ego strength or personality integration, as measured by the RPRS, appear to do better in psychotherapy than those with poor ego strength, prediction on this basis may not exceed the base rates for this problem, and considerable extra effort and time would be required.

Additional Appraisals of Personality Attributes

Other studies also have made reference to personality attributes in relation to psychotherapy outcome. Frank (1974b), in a review of 25 years of research, concluded "that the most important determinants of long-term improvement lie in the patient" (p. 339). He found that symptoms of anxiety and depression improved the most, whereas poorer results were secured with somatic complaints. The presence of anxiety at the initiation of therapy has also been noted as a positive prognostic sign in other studies (Kernberg et al., 1972; Luborsky et al., 1975), although inconclusive studies have also been reported. The type and severity of anxiety must also be considered, as well as the stimuli that influence it. As Frank (1974b) emphasized, "long-term prognosis largely depends on the strength of the person's coping capacities and the modifiability of the stress which leads him to seek help" (p. 339). In other words, as indicated in another study also (Smith, Sjoholm, & Nielzen, 1975), patients who manifest anxiety in relation to their current situation or stress appear to secure better outcome.

Since the previously mentioned studies were conducted, an increased focus on the development of specific therapies for specific disorders has been evident. This was noted in the previous section with reference to several predictive studies in the area of depression. At the same time, there are still recent studies that place the focus on a specific form of psychotherapy, such as brief psychodynamic therapy or psychoanalysis, and evaluate prognosis in terms of the therapy instead of a specific disorder (Piper, Azim, McCallum, & Joyce, 1990; Weber, Bachrach, & Solomon, 1985). We shall discuss later some of the implications of these different types of studies for research on prognostic factors for outcome in psychotherapy.

Studies of behavioral therapy also have dealt with correlates of behavioral change or outcome. In one study of participant modeling with snake phobics, "Neither initial attitudes toward snakes, severity of phobic-behavior, performance aroused fears, nor fear proneness correlated with degree of behavior change" (Bandura, Jeffery, & Wright, 1974, p. 62). However, some measures of fear reduction taken after the initiation of therapy were predictive of subsequent behavioral change. The greater the fear decrements on the initially failed task and the less fear aroused by this task, the greater the degree of improvement.

In another study of 36 phobic patients, attempts were made to evaluate several predictor variables in relation to outcome with desensitization, flooding, and a control treatment (Mathews, Johnston, Shaw, & Gelder, 1974). Only two measures were significantly related to outcome at both termination and follow-up, and both pertained to extroversion and traits related to it. However, severity of symptoms, high anxiety and neuroticism, low expectancy, and low-rated motivation for treatment were not related to outcome. In general, "There was no evidence that by using the measures examined, patients could be individually allocated in advance to the treatment most likely to help them" (Mathews et al., 1974, p. 264). However, as in the previous study (Bandura et al., 1974), there was a greater reduction in measures of rated anxiety early in therapy by those who subsequently improved. Thus, it appears that one can predict outcome more accurately during an early stage of therapy than at the very beginning, a hypothesis that also receives support from some studies of psychotherapy process to which we shall refer later.

Somewhat comparable results have also been reported in an appraisal of research on agoraphobia (Mathews, Gelder, & Johnston, 1981): "Nearly all published reports of behavioral treatment have included a section on prognostic factors that describes efforts to improve patient selection. The results have been almost uniformly disappointing" (p. 143). Emmelkamp and Kuipers (1979), in a four-year follow-up study of agoraphobic clients, also did not secure positive findings between selected client variables and outcome: "No clear relationship was found between external control, social anxiety, depression and duration of the complaint at the beginning of treatment on the one hand and the results at follow-up on the other" (p. 352).

An essentially similar conclusion was reached by Rachman and Hodgson (1980) in their work on obsessions and compulsions. However, a recent report of research on behavioral treatments of obsessive compulsives contains some positive findings (Foa et al., 1983). Low initial anxiety was positively related to successful outcome, whereas high levels of depression were correlated with failure. Earlier age of onset of symptoms was also related to successful outcome at follow-up. At the same time, it can be noted that in the Sloane et al. (1975) study, the more disturbed patients did as well as the other patients when they received behavioral therapy.

A number of other personality attributes have been investigated in relation to outcome in psychotherapy. Many reflect the specific interests of particular investigators and few have received any wide application or replication. We can note some of them briefly.

Filak, Abeles, and Norquist (1986) investigated whether clients' pretherapy interpersonal attitudes related to an affiliation–hostility dimension would have a significant impact on therapy outcome. Seventy-two percent of those with an affiliative stance had a highly successful outcome whereas only 38 percent of those with a pretherapy hostile interpersonal stance had a successful outcome. These results differ from those reported by Moras and Strupp (1982). Although psychodynamic therapy was evaluated in both instances, different measures for appraising interpersonal attributes were used. In another small study, both negative and positive responders to therapy were judged to have high levels of interpersonal difficulty (Mohr et al., 1990). However, whereas negative responders also showed low levels of subjective distress, the opposite was true for the positive responders. Nevertheless, the actual differences between groups was quite small. In all of these studies, it is difficult to know if the same or similar variables are being appraised.

Piper and his colleagues have conducted several studies investigating patient correlates of positive outcome in short-term dynamically oriented individual psychotherapy. Using a psychoanalytic framework, Piper, de Carufel, and Szkrumelak (1985) secured two pretherapy predictors — defensive style of the patient and object choice of the patient. Following up on this exploratory study, a rather large-scale investigation of 144 outpatients with experienced therapists was conducted (Piper et al., 1990). In this investigation, the focus was on object choice, which was evaluated in two 1-hour sessions. Although the level of object choice only approached significance, the investigators felt the results suggested a good match between type of patient and type of therapy. A high level of object relations was positively correlated with outcome in brief psychodynamic therapy, whereas low levels were not.

The report of the large Columbia Psychoanalytic Center Research Project is also of interest (Weber, Bachrach, & Solomon, 1985). In this investigation of 119 patients who had undergone psychoanalysis and a similar number who had received psychoanalytically oriented psychotherapy, initial clinical evaluations had little predictive value in terms of outcome. According to the authors, "the prudent conclusion from these findings is *not* that therapeutic benefit or analysability are *per se* unpredictable, but that once a case has been carefully selected as suitable for an analysis by a candidate, its eventual fate remains relatively indeterminate" (Weber, Bachrach, & Solomon, 1985, p. 135). This is a rather pessimistic conclusion, and although there are other variables besides client variables that are involved in therapeutic success, it is conceivable that more objective and valid assessment procedures might produce somewhat better predictions of eventual outcome.

Motivation for treatment is another client attribute that has been emphasized both in terms of continuation and outcome. However, despite its apparent importance, it has not received strong research support. In some of the research, the selection of subjects was not random, motivation was not appraised the same way, and ratings were not infrequently made by the investigators or therapists (Butcher & Koss, 1978; Keithly, Samples, & Strupp, 1980; Malan, 1963; Malan, 1976; Sifneos, 1972). In one study conducted with a sample of 18 clients (Keithly et al., 1980), the results of multiple regression analyses showed significant relationships between ratings of motivation and therapists' and clinicians' ratings of outcome ($p < 0.05$), but not with two sets of patients' rating of change. However, in another study, no significant relationship between motivation and outcome as evaluated by independent clinical judges was secured (Horowitz, Marmar, Weiss, DeWitt, & Rosenbaum, 1984).

Some psychotherapists have also emphasized the importance of the clients' payment for services as another index of motivation. Thus, clients who paid for their treatment were considered to have a higher level of motivation than those who did not or who paid a nominal fee. However, in a more recent study of clients who sought psychotherapy from a low-cost treatment center, no reliable differences were secured between a group who paid the usual fees and a group whose fees were paid by a grant (Yoken & Berman, 1987). Thus, although clinicians have tended to emphasize the importance of the client's motivation for positive therapeutic outcome, the research findings are as yet far from definitive.

Another variable that has received some attention is *intelligence*. Although most therapists would probably prefer reasonably intelligent clients who also possess other virtues (Schofield, 1964), no clear-cut minimum requirement has been established for successful performance in psychotherapy. However, certain types of therapy may require more highly intelligent or selected clients than others. In psychoanalysis, where candidates apparently are rigorously screened, the majority are college graduates or better, and presumably of above average or superior intelligence (Hamburg et al., 1967; Reder & Tyson, 1980; Weber, Solomon, & Bachrach, 1985). On the other hand, behavioral therapists have apparently not been concerned with this matter. It is interesting, too, that two earlier reviews of research on this topic reached somewhat different conclusions.

In the review by Luborsky et al. (1975), 10 of 13 studies were listed as showing a positive relationship between intelligence and outcome in psychotherapy. Some studies merely indicated that a significant difference was obtained between improved and unimproved subjects, but others listed correla-

tions ranging from .24 to .46. In the study reporting the correlation of .46, the total group of patients had a relatively high mean IQ (117), with the unimproved group alone having a mean IQ of 112 (Barron, 1953a). If we applied these results strictly, we would conclude that over 75 percent of the population would not be helped by psychotherapy!

Meltzoff and Kornreich (1970), in their review, presented a different summary. Seven studies secured a positive relationship between IQ and outcome, and eight studies found no relationship. One of the studies listed as positive by Luborsky et al. (1975) is listed otherwise by Meltzoff and Kornreich because two different criteria are referred to by the different authors. Since Meltzoff and Kornreich's tally differs from that of Luborsky et al., they reach a different conclusion and state that high intelligence is not a necessary condition for successful psychotherapy, even though it may be more important in some therapies than others.

What then might we conclude? If psychotherapy is a learning process or involves learning, as many believe, then some minimum amount of intelligence would seem to be required. As yet, no precise estimate of this has been clearly agreed upon, nor is such a minimum level likely. Most psychotherapists, I believe, would agree that other aspects of the individual besides sheer intellect are also of importance, and perhaps of greater significance. If we were to take a correlation of around .30 as indicating the possible relationship of intelligence to outcome, intelligence would still account for less than 10 percent of the variance. Clearly, we should maintain a flexible posture on this matter and try to adjust our therapeutic communications and procedures to the individual client.

Methodological Issues

There are additional studies of client attributes and outcome that have reported both positive and negative findings with a variety of evaluative techniques. However, there is little point in reviewing these studies. A number have used idiosyncratic procedures, small subject samples, and questionable outcome criteria and have not been replicated. It is preferable, instead, to discuss and evaluate some of the methodological problems evident in this area of research. This is particularly important in appraising the research on client personality variables, especially degree of disturbance, in relation to outcome in psychotherapy.

Some of the measurement problems may be illustrated by reference to an earlier study in which the author participated (Prager & Garfield, 1972). A number of indices of client disturbance were used, as well as six measures of outcome. In general, ratings of disturbance made at the beginning of therapy by clients, therapists, and supervisors were unrelated to the six measures of outcome used. However, initial disturbance as measured by the mean scale elevation of the MMPI, elevation of the neurotic triad of the MMPI, and a disturbance scale completed by the client were *significantly* and *negatively* correlated with various ratings of outcome provided by clients, therapists, and supervisors at the completion of therapy. At the same time, these latter measures of initial disturbance were not significantly related to three outcome measures based on differences in scores obtained at the beginning and termination of therapy. Thus, the finding that degree of initial or felt disturbance was negatively related to outcome was true *only* for *certain* indices of disturbance *and* certain criteria of outcome.

Two other important observations were made by Prager and Garfield (1972). First, those studies that found that patients with higher levels of disturbance secured more positive results than those with less disturbance generally used the same instrument to measure both initial level of disturbance and outcome. Studies that reported a negative relationship between initial level of disturbance and outcome used an independent outcome measure such as therapists' or judges' ratings. The second point was that initial level of disturbance was found to be inversely related to outcome primarily when global ratings of improvement made at the termination of therapy were used as the criteria of outcome. In these instances, the judgment of change involves the rater's *perception of change*, whereas actual difference scores require information relevant to the symptoms and feelings of the client at a particular time. It has also been reported that judgments of outcome, particularly by therapists, tend to be more favorable than other types of measures or ratings (Garfield, 1980; Garfield et al., 1971; Horenstein et al., 1973).

The points just discussed should help explain the discrepant findings mentioned earlier concerning the relationship of the degree of adjustment or level of disturbance to outcome in psychotherapy. How outcome is evaluated is one important consideration. As Mintz (1972) has emphasized, global ratings of improvement made at the *end* of treatment tend to be very much influenced by the actual condition of the client at that time, irrespective of how the individual was at the beginning of therapy. Consequently, the person who functions at a relatively high level at the start and shows only slight change, is still rated as greatly improved as compared with someone who begins at a much lower level and, while progressing more, does not function terminally at the high level of the other client. It may well be that part of this apparent confusion is due to *what* is being evaluated as well as to *how* it

is being evaluated. Clients who begin therapy at a *high level of functioning* terminate therapy at higher levels than those who begin at relatively low levels. However, those patients with the *greatest symptom distress* generally will tend to show the greatest reduction in symptom distress. Thus, evaluating the amount of therapeutic change is more complicated than it may appear.

Another important issue concerns how personality functioning or psychopathology is defined or appraised. Severity of disturbance, for example, can be viewed in terms of clinical diagnosis ("psychosis" vs. "neurosis"), intensity of discomfort or symptoms, duration of disturbance or chronicity, adjustment to current life situation, or degree of social or occupational impairment or in terms of scores on tests or rating scales. If a hypothetical personality construct such as ego strength, presumably reflecting personality integration and adjustment, is assessed by different techniques that show little relationship to each other, conflicting or confusing results are very likely to occur, as we have noted earlier.

What also appears to be an important factor in accounting for the conflicting findings on the relationship of degree of disturbance to outcome is the type of subject sample evaluated. As previously noted, many of the samples used in the earlier investigations included a wide range of diagnoses and psychopathology. Depending on the measures used, the results obtained could vary widely. However, the more recent trend to conduct research on specific diagnostic groups and the greater attention paid to the reliability of diagnoses as noted in our previous discussion of research with depressed patients have produced more consistent findings. Those patients who are most depressed at the start of therapy end therapy with higher scores on scales of depression than those who are less depressed at the beginning of therapy.

It is also important to evaluate the actual predictive value of the positive findings reported. In many instances where statistically significant results are secured, the correlations tend to be low and to account for a limited portion of the variance. In one of the earlier comprehensive attempts to ascertain if psychotherapeutic changes were predictable, the investigators reported that their results were "distinctly unpromising" (Fiske et al., 1964). A more recent report of the findings of the Penn Psychotherapy Project also indicated very limited ability to predict the outcomes of psychotherapy: "The success of the predictive measures were generally insignificant, and the best of them were in the .2 to .3 range, meaning that only 5% to 10% of the outcome variance was predicted" (Luborsky et al., 1979, p. 471).

It appears then, that although a number of investigators have reported some positive findings, most of the relationships secured between personality variables and outcome have been of limited strength and have varied from one investigation to another, depending on methods of appraisal, criteria, subject samples, and the like. It would appear that client variables centering on pretherapy adjustment and personality may not be as highly predictive of outcome as some have believed. These conclusions are based on appraisals made prior to the beginning of therapy. As will be noted later, more positive predictions may be made after the first three or four therapy sessions have occurred.

Client Expectations and Other Variables in Relation to Outcome in Psychotherapy

Frank and his colleagues were among the earliest to call attention to client expectancies and their relation to symptom change (Frank, 1959; Frank, Gliedman, Imber, Stone, & Nash, 1959; Rosenthal & Frank, 1956). Among other things, they asserted that the beliefs or expectancies about therapy that the patient brings to therapy may influence the results of therapy, and that the greater the distress or need for relief, the greater the expectancy or likelihood of such relief. Significant correlations between expectancies of improvement in patients and perceived improvement also were secured in other studies (Goldstein, 1960; Lennard & Bernstein, 1960). Friedman (1963) observed a direct relationship between expectancy and symptom reduction after an initial evaluation interview, although Goldstein and Shipman (1961) secured a curvilinear relationship in a similar study — in the latter instance those patients with very high or low expectancies for improvement showed the smallest symptom reduction.

Since these earlier reports were published, there have been additional studies conducted and several critical reviews of the research in this area also have appeared (Lick & Bootzin, 1975; Morgan, 1973; Wilkins, 1971, 1973, 1979). Tollinton (1973), utilizing a variety of measures, found that initial expectations were significantly related to outcome in the early stages of treatment but were "dissipated over time by the effects of neuroticism" (p. 256). In another study, Uhlenhuth and Duncan (1968) used symptom checklists, the MMPI, and subjects' ratings and reported that more favorable expectations were associated with improvement. Piper and Wogan (1970), however, did not find a relationship between prognostic expectancies and reported improvement. Negative results were also secured in another study where attempts were made to induce a positive expectancy for

improvement within a treatment period of four weeks (Imber et al., 1970).

Expectancy was reported to be a significant predictor of outcome in a study of 36 agoraphobics (Mathews et al., 1976). In this study, expectancy was appraised by having the patients estimate prior to treatment how likely they believed they would achieve each of 15 phobic situations in the behavioral hierarchy. In this instance, the patients who were most confident about possible improvement were the most likely to improve. However, a simpler rating of expectations did not predict outcome. Thus, the method of securing expectations may be important, and an overly gross measure may not be effective.

Although several of the studies have shown a positive association between client expectancies and outcome, these investigations also have been criticized (Perotti & Hopewell, 1980; Wilkins, 1973). Among the deficiencies noted have been the fact that expectancies have been inferred rather than actually measured or appraised, and that most studies have relied on self-reports for measures of expectancies and outcome. How the effects of expectancies are appraised also appears to be a problem of some importance. Wilson and Thomas (1973), for example, secured significant correlations between high expectancy ratings and self-report measures of outcome but found no relationship between expectancy ratings and a behavioral measure of outcome.

Perhaps, because of the earlier criticism, attempts have been made to manipulate the expectancies of the client. In contrast to the studies mentioned previously, which have been characterized as studies of "expectancy traits," the more recent investigations have focused on experimentally created "expectancy states" and have tended largely to be studies of behaviorally oriented therapy.

In his review of expectancy states and their effect on outcome, Wilkins (1973) listed 6 studies that showed positive results, 8 that did not show such effects, and 1 that showed both effects. In a brief summary of 10 studies, Luborsky et al. (1988) listed 6 as having positive results and 4 without such results. Here again, the picture is one of mixed results.

A number of conceptual and methodological issues also were discussed by Wilkins (1973), including how the expectancy instructions are given, whether or not the therapists were blind to the experimental conditions, confounding of measures of outcome with those of expectancy, and confounding of expectancy and feedback effects. Accordingly, he concluded that there was insufficient evidence to support the construct of expectancy of therapeutic gain.

Another review of expectancy factors in the treatment of fears by Lick and Bootzin (1975) came to a somewhat different conclusion and highlighted some additional problems. They noted that most of the subjects used in the studies of systematic desensitization (SD) were students who manifested relatively mild fears of small animals and who became subjects in order to meet course requirements. They also emphasized the importance of the way in which expectancies were created and assessed and stated that although methodological problems in previous research "preclude firm empirical conclusions about the importance of therapeutic instruction in SD . . . , the available data do suggest that these influences are sizable" (Lick & Bootzin, 1975, p. 925).

Reviewing many of the same studies, Perotti and Hopewell (1980) also concluded that expectancy effects are important in SD, but they differentiated two kinds of expectancies. Initial expectancy, which the client has at the beginning of therapy about the probable success of treatment, has been the focus in most studies, and they believe it has little effect. However, the second type, which deals with beliefs the subject has *during the treatment process* about improvement as well as an increased ability to handle fear-provoking stimuli, is considered to be of some importance. A somewhat similar point was made by Lick and Bootzin (1975), who hypothesized that expectancy manipulation may motivate subjects to more readily test reality conditions that could increase fear extinction and provide further reinforcement for improved behavior. This appears to be a reasonable hypothesis and at least is congruent with studies that indicate better predictions of outcome after a few early therapy sessions than at pretreatment assessment (Bandura et al., 1974; Mathews et al., 1974).

It has also been suggested that "it may be more correct to assume that client motivation, desire for therapy, and expectations of change may have more to do with prompting the patient to *initially* become involved in therapy than with directly influencing the therapeutic process or its outcome" (Thurer & Hursh, 1981, p. 71). This suggestion appears to be a reasonable one since the pretherapy expectations of the client will be very much influenced by the client's early experiences in therapy and perceptions of the therapist. Positive expectations can be reinforced or extinguished by the actual experience of therapy and the same would appear likely for negative expectations.

The possible importance of client expectancies for research on evaluating the effectiveness of SD and psychotherapy generally has been stressed also by Kazdin and Wilcoxon (1976). Particular emphasis was placed on the importance of creating control conditions that are as potent in creating positive client expectancies for improvement as the experimental therapy being evaluated. Thus, expectancies for therapeutic success are viewed by these authors as having some significance.

In addition to the distinction made between expectancy traits and states, there is also the issue of what different individuals mean when they employ the general term, *expectancy*. In some instances, it has been used to designate the expectation a client has with regard to positive outcome or the therapeutic effectiveness of a particular therapist. In other instances, some of us have discussed the expectations clients have about the procedures in psychotherapy, the role of the therapist, the length of therapy, and the like (Bent, Putnam, Kiesler, & Nowicki, 1975; Garfield, 1989b; Garfield & Wolpin, 1963). Future research will have to specify more precisely the types of expectancies under investigation, and also consider the possible interaction of different kinds of expectancies and the interaction of expectancies with other variables. One study, for example, besides validating an expectancy manipulation on one group of subjects and then testing its effectiveness for behavioral effects with another group, also compared the effects of initial expectations concerning the helpfulness of psychotherapy, as well as those of an experimental manipulation (Lott & Murray, 1975). The results showed a positive effect for the expectancy manipulation but not for the initial expectancy. It would appear, however, that research interest in expectancies has peaked and investigations of this type have diminished.

Client – Therapy Interaction and Choice of Therapy

Another area of research has been concerned with the frame of reference of the client in relation to type of therapy and outcome. In one study, two groups of clients were exposed to different forms of therapy designated as "relatively directive" and "relatively nondirective" (Abramowitz, Abramowitz, Roback, & Jackson, 1974). Locus of control was measured by nine items from the Rotter I-E Scale (1966) and several scales were utilized to appraise outcome. Although the number of cases was small, the findings suggested that "externals" did better in the directive therapy, while "internals" did better with the nondirective therapy. In another investigation, patients were rated on the basis of their symptoms or complaints as predominantly "externalizers" or "internalizers" (Stein & Beall, 1971). In this study female externalizers showed significant negative association with various therapist ratings of change, but this was not true for male externalizers.

In a study of the differential effectiveness of muscular and cognitive relaxation as a function of locus of control, Ollendick and Murphy (1977) reported that internally controlled subjects showed a greater decrement in heart rate and subjective distress with cognitive relaxation. Externally controlled subjects, on the other hand, secured better results with muscular relaxation. In another investigation, internally controlled patients secured better results than externally controlled patients when they were led to believe that their improvement was due to their own efforts and not to a placebo (Liberman, 1978). The opposite results were secured when therapeutic progress was believed to be due to a placebo. On the other hand, an examination of studies that have claimed that internals are more successful in nondirective therapy and externals in directive therapy noted a number of deficiencies in these studies, including research design, statistical analysis, and outcome measures (Messer & Meinster, 1980).

A related study on choice of therapy also was conducted in which 32 subjects with a fear of snakes viewed a videotape of four therapists who described and illustrated their particular methods of treatment (Devine & Fernald, 1973). The four treatments were systematic desensitization, an encounter approach, rational-emotive therapy, and a combination of modeling and behavioral rehearsal. The subjects then rated their preferences for the various therapies and were assigned to a preferred, nonpreferred, or random therapy. Although there was no significant difference in outcome between therapies, the difference between the preference conditions was significant. Subjects receiving a preferred treatment exhibited less fear of the snakes than those receiving a nonpreferred or random therapy. Studies of this type with regular clinical patients would have more direct relevance for practice, but as far as this writer is aware, such studies have not been done.

Recently, a study of depressed patients was conducted to evaluate patient predictors of differential response to three types of psychotherapy—cognitive therapy, a form of so-called experiential therapy, and a supportive self-directed therapy (Beutler et al., 1991). Specifically, coping style (externalization) and resistance potential were the two patient characteristics appraised. Externalizing depressed patients were found to improve more than nonexternalizing depressed patients in cognitive therapy, whereas the latter group improved most in the supportive self-directed therapy. Conversely, resistant (defensive) patients improved more in the self-directed therapy than in the other two therapies, and low-resistant patients improved more in cognitive therapy than in the self-directed therapy.

Although these results are interesting, considerably more research will have to be done before results can be applied practically since clients can be categorized in many different ways and possible combinations of traits and characteristics would also have to be considered.

Client Attractiveness and Outcome

Client attractiveness was found to be positively related to outcome in one study (Nash et al., 1965), but this relationship was not evident in a five-year follow-up study (Liberman et al., 1972). In another study, therapists' ratings of patient attractiveness were not related to two measures of outcome (Luborsky et al., 1980).

Several studies also attempted to appraise the importance of patient likability for therapy process and outcome. Stoler (1963) reported that successful clients received significantly higher likability ratings based on taped therapy segments than did the less successful clients, and the level of likability remained fairly constant from early to late interviews. A subsequent study, however, carried out with schizophrenic patients instead of neurotics secured different findings (Tomlinson & Stoler, 1967). The less successful patients were better liked than the more successful ones.

In a study of psychiatric residents, Ehrlich and Bauer (1967) found that inexperienced therapists liked their patients less than did the relatively more experienced therapists; patients who were rated either extremely anxious or nonanxious were less well liked by their therapists; and patient prognosis was positively related to patient likability. Furthermore, patients who received low ratings in terms of likability were three times more likely to be placed on multiple drug regimes than were those who received high ratings. In addition, the therapists' ratings of change were positively correlated with such ratings.

There appears to be some indication that the likability of the client may be related to outcome. However, because of the variation in patients, therapists, and outcome criteria, the available findings are far from clear. There is an obvious problem of potential contamination when therapists provide the ratings of outcome as well as likability. Also, likability may be influenced by such factors as intelligence, education, and attitudes toward therapy and the therapist. Patients who demonstrate progress in therapy are likely to be viewed more favorably by their therapists.

Client–Therapist Similarity

The matter of client–therapist similarity or complementarity has received some research attention in the past, although with rather conflicting results.

Carson and Heine (1962) used the MMPI to compare therapists and clients and reported that a curvilinear relationship existed between therapist–client similarity and rated improvement. Lichtenstein (1966), and Carson and Llewellyn (1966), however, failed to replicate these findings. Some partial support for the importance of client–therapist complementarity was offered by Swenson (1967) for one personality dimension (dominance–submission), but not for another (love–hate).

More recently, Beutler, Jobe, and Elkins (1974) reported that initial patient–therapist similarity and acceptability of attitudes were related more to patients' ratings of improvement than was attitude dissimilarity. On the other hand, Melnick (1972) found that greater patient identification with the therapist during therapy was moderately related to successful outcome. In a study of group therapy patients, McLachlan (1972) found that when patients and therapist were matched for conceptual level, there was significant improvement on patients' ratings, but not on staff ratings of improvement. The conceptual levels of patients and therapists separately were not related to outcome. Berzins (1977) also published a comprehensive and critical review of the area of therapist–patient matching in psychotherapy. As he pointed out, although the idea of matching patients and therapists for the best therapeutic outcome is responded to favorably by clinicians and researchers alike, "there is at present no organized body of knowledge that could serve as an effective guide for implementing matching strategies" (p. 222). (See also Chapter 7, this volume.)

Using the Interpersonal Discrimination Test as a measure of cognitive match, 63 cognitively matched or unmatched therapist–client pairs were evaluated in a double-blind study. Although there was greater premature termination among the unmatched pairs, for those who remained in therapy, the outcomes were similar for matched and unmatched pairs (Hunt, Carr, Dagadakis, & Walker, 1985). It does appear as if the research literature on therapist–client matching still provides too limited a basis from which to draw firm conclusions.

In-Therapy Process Variables and Outcome

More recently, process aspects of psychotherapy have been investigated with particular attention devoted to what has been referred to as the helping or therapeutic alliance. Essentially, this refers to the relationship established in therapy between therapist and client. This, of course, involves the therapist as well as the client and cannot be viewed solely from the standpoint of client variables. However, certain client features have been emphasized in these studies, and we shall discuss them here.

In a study of process variables as potential predictors of outcome in psychotherapy, Gomes-Schwartz (1978) secured the most consistent results between a variable labeled "patient involvement" and outcome. This variable represented both patient participation in therapy and manifestations of patient hostility and was measured by scales derived from the Vanderbilt Psychotherapy Process Scale. The results of this investigation, based on data from the Vanderbilt research project, were particularly interesting in that psychoanalytically oriented therapists, experiential therapists, and nontherapeutically trained college professors were evaluated and compared. All three groups of therapists secured comparable outcomes and for all three, patient involvement appeared as the best predictor of outcome.

Another process study focused on negative factors in psychotherapy and used the Vanderbilt Negative Indicators Scale (VNIS) (Sachs, 1983). A subscale of four items, the Patient Qualities subscale, did show a statistically significant correlation with outcome when it was based on the third interview, but not on the first or second interview. Patient qualities on this scale referred to such characteristics as negative attitudes and passivity. In general, the variable tapped by the VNIS showed some relationship to outcome in psychodynamic therapy, but not to experiential therapy.

An additional study investigated pretherapy interpersonal relations, the patients' therapeutic alliance, and outcome (Moras & Strupp, 1982). Although there was a small significant correlation between pretherapy interpersonal relations and the therapeutic alliance, most correlations between interpersonal relations and outcome were low. Thus, they were not considered good predictors of outcome.

In yet another study reported on the Vanderbilt Psychotherapy Process Scale using some of the same subjects as in the previously mentioned studies, client involvement was found to have the highest relationship to outcome of the variables studied (O'Malley, Suh, & Strupp, 1983). However, as noted in some of the other studies, this relationship was not evident in the first therapy session but emerged clearly during the third session. This pattern, as mentioned earlier, was also noted in some behavioral studies, although with different variables, mainly measures of early progress.

Using therapist ratings, Kolb, Beutler, Davis, Crago, and Shanfield (1985) also reported that patient involvement in the therapy process was the best single predictor of symptomatic change. They also stated that process variables rather than patient traits were the best predictors of outcome, although their appraisal of patient variables was limited to two scales. In a study of behavioral marital therapy, client involvement also was emphasized as important for positive outcome: "The results suggest that success in social learning–based marital therapy depends on the clients' involvement and compliance in therapy" (Holtzworth-Munroe, Jacobson, DeKlyen, & Whisman, 1989).

Somewhat related to these findings are the results summarized by Orlinsky and Howard (1986) pertaining to the importance of what they categorize as "patient self-relatedness." In particular, they found the dimension of the patient's openness versus defensiveness in psychotherapy to be related to outcome. Better outcomes were significantly associated with the patient's openness during therapy.

Because of the low predictive power found for most of the pretherapy variables appraised, Luborsky and his colleagues at the University of Pennsylvania explored aspects of patient–therapist interaction and developed two methods for evaluating the helping alliance. One of these methods is a global rating method, whereas the other is based on counting specific instances in which the patient experiences the therapist as providing the help needed or "in which the patient experiences treatment as a process of working together with the therapist toward the goals of the treatment" (Luborsky, Crits-Cristoph, Alexander, Margolis, & Cohen, 1983, p. 481). Both procedures, when applied to the 10 most improved and 10 least improved cases in the Penn Psychotherapy Project, showed modest to moderate correlations with some composite measures of outcome. However, when comparable comparisons are made with the pretreatment measures used in the Penn study for these two extreme groups of clients, the two types of predictions are quite similar (Morgan, Luborsky, Crits-Christoph, Curtis, & Solomon, 1982). Analyses of extreme groups selected post hoc generally produce better results than analyses based on the total distribution of clients. However, in a later report with an additional sample of subjects, a measure of the helping alliance was the best correlate of outcome (Luborsky et al., 1988).

Although a number of psychodynamically oriented researchers tend to emphasize the importance of the therapeutic alliance as a significant factor in therapeutic outcome as well as a potential early predictor of outcome, the issue is a complex one. As indicated by Luborsky et al. (1983), the most frequently positive helping alliance signs "were those in which the patients felt helped" (p. 482). The one category of "feels changed" was rated positively almost twice as frequently as all other categories combined for the "more improved patients" and was rated over six times as fre-

quently for these patients as all positive categories combined for the "less improved patients." Thus, it does appear as if the patients' subjective feeling of change may really be the essential variable. If one can view this as the patient's feeling better or seeing himself or herself as improving early in therapy, then this early state of improvement may be indicative of positive outcome at termination. This view would also be congruent with the findings mentioned earlier by Bandura et al. (1974) and Mathews et al. (1974). The construct, patient involvement, might also be related to the patient's feeling of being changed positively. The latter can act as a reinforcement for greater involvement in therapy. The fact that all of these related variables are not linked to outcome until the third interview also would appear congruent with this general hypothesis.

At present there does appear to be considerable interest in the relationship of process variables to outcome in psychotherapy and Chapter 8 deals in considerable detail with this area of research. As noted, the somewhat limited or modest predictions based on client variables exclusively has led to a greater focus on interactional variables in early therapy sessions (Henry et al., 1986). However, as some investigators have emphasized, we need to consider the interplay of techniques, patient variables, the type of disorder, and therapist characteristics (Horowitz, et al., 1984). One recent study, for example, reported that practically all of the significant correlations secured between in-therapy ratings and outcome were interaction effects with patient pretreatment disturbance level and that *healthier patients* secured better outcomes (Jones, Cumming, & Horowitz, 1988).

CONCLUSIONS AND IMPLICATIONS

As should be evident after our review of representative research on client variables in psychotherapy, the problems are complex and one should be cautious in offering generalizations. The diversity of the variables investigated, the varying methods of appraisal, the heterogeneity of the clients and patients studied, the differences in the training and skill of the therapists used, and the variations in the clinical settings sampled all contribute to the difficulties involved in attempting valid generalizations.

In the previous edition of this *Handbook*, I concluded that "A host of idiosyncratic studies of poorly defined populations with vaguely described therapies and exceedingly variable outcome criteria will not produce findings of any substance" (Garfield, 1986b, p. 246). Although this statement is true, there has been an increased recognition of such problems in recent years and more adequate and sophisticated research investigations have been evident in the area of psychotherapy. This was noted earlier in our discussion of recent research on the treatment of depression. The NIMH collaborative study of depression is one clear example of a very well-planned and rigorously conducted study of psychotherapy: The patients were selected in terms of specifically defined criteria; three large medical centers were used in order to provide adequate samples of patients; manuals were available for each of the forms of psychotherapy being evaluated; the therapists were experienced clinical psychologists and psychiatrists who received specialized training in one of the psychotherapies being evaluated; a variety of well-known standardized evaluative procedures were used; and competent statistical consultants participated in the project. Although not every clinical or research center can carry out such a project, the model provided should have a positive impact on future research.

Nevertheless, it is also apparent that making predictions prior to therapy about continuation or outcome that are based *solely* on client variables are not as successful as we would like. As emphasized in this chapter, predictions that pay attention to the type of client *and* to the therapy process early in therapy are relatively more successful. It should be apparent that psychotherapy involves a therapist and a particular approach to therapy as well as a client or patient. Predictions based on only one of the variables involved is bound to be less successful than predictions or appraisals based on the totality of the therapeutic interaction.

Nevertheless, the research on client variables has produced data that are of some real practical value. For example, it was always assumed in the past that psychotherapy was a long-term process and that patients remained in therapy for relatively long periods. Clearly, as research over a period of 40 years has consistently shown, the reverse is true. This is important information and today clinical practice and the popularity of brief therapy acknowledge this fact. Increased attention also has been paid to the problem of premature termination and various attempts have been made to reduce or overcome this problem. On the basis of the existing research results, it would appear worthwhile for each clinical setting to evaluate its own pattern of continuation and outcome. Since settings differ, such relatively direct and uncomplicated investigations may provide findings that are meaningful and can help improve the quality of professional service at the particular clinical center. Also, since some research findings indicate that improved predictions of outcome are possible by the third or fourth therapy session, therapists should be particularly attentive and sensitive to what takes place during these early sessions. The early perceptions and reactions of the client appear to be of great importance for both continuation and outcome in psychotherapy.

REFERENCES

Abramowitz, C. V., Abramowitz, S. I., Roback, H. B., & Jackson, C. (1974). Differential effectiveness of directive and nondirective group therapies as a function of client internal-external control. *Journal of Consulting and Clinical Psychology, 42,* 849–853.

Acosta, F. X. (1980). Self-described reasons for premature termination of psychotherapy by Mexican-American, Black-American, and Anglo-American patients. *Psychological Reports, 47,* 435–443.

Acosta, F. X., & Sheehan, J. G. (1976). Preferences toward Mexican-American and Anglo-American psychotherapists. *Journal of Consulting and Clinical Psychology, 44,* 272–279.

Adler, M. H., Valenstein, A. F., & Michaels, J. J. (1949). A mental hygiene clinic. Its organization and operation. *Journal of Nervous and Mental Disease, 110,* 518–533.

Affleck, D. C., & Garfield, S. L. (1961). Predictive judgments of therapists and duration of stay in psychotherapy. *Journal of Clinical Psychology, 17,* 134–137.

Affleck, D. C., & Mednick, S. A. (1959). The use of the Rorschach Test in the prediction of the abrupt terminator in individual psychotherapy. *Journal of Consulting Psychology, 23,* 125–128.

American Psychiatric Association. (1980). *Diagnostic and statistical manual of mental disorders.* (3rd. ed.) Washington, DC: Author.

American Psychiatric Association. (1987). *Diagnostic and statistical manual of mental disorders* (3rd. ed., Revised). Washington, DC: Author.

American Psychiatric Association (T. B. Karasu, Chairperson). (1989). *Treatments of psychiatric disorders: A task force report of the American Psychiatric Association, Vol. 1–3 and index.* Washington, DC: Author.

Arentewicz, G., & Schmidt, G. (1980). *Sexuell gestorte Beziehungen.* Berlin: Springer Verlag.

Atkinson, D. R., Furlong, M. J., & Poston, W. C. (1986). Afro-American preferences for counselor characteristics. *Journal of Counseling Psychology, 33,* 326–330.

Baekeland, F., & Lundwall, L. (1975). Dropping out of treatment: A critical review. *Psychological Bulletin, 82,* 738–783.

Bandura, A., Jeffery, R. W., & Wright, C. L. (1974). Efficacy of participant modeling as a function of response induction aids. *Journal of Abnormal Psychology, 83,* 56–64.

Barron, F. (1953a). Some test correlates of response to psychotherapy. *Journal of Consulting Psychology, 17,* 235–241.

Barron, F. (1953b). An ego-strength scale which predicts response to psychotherapy. *Journal of Consulting Psychology, 17,* 327–333.

Basler, H. D., Brinkmeier, U., Buser, K., Hoehn, K. D., & Mölders-Kober, R. (1982). Psychological group treatment of essential hypertension in general practice. *British Journal of Clinical Psychology, 21,* 295–302.

Baum, O. E., & Felzer, S. B. (1964). Activity in initial interviews with lower class patients. *Archives of General Psychiatry, 10,* 345–353.

Beck, A. T., Rush, A. J., Shaw, B. F., & Emery, G. (1979).

Cognitive therapy of depression. A treatment manual. New York: Guilford.

Beck, N. C., Lamberti, J., Gamache, M., Lake, E. A., Fraps, C. L., McReynolds, W. T., Reaven, N., Heisler, G. H., & Dunn, J. (1987). Situational factors and behavioral self-predictions in the identification of clients at high risk to drop out of psychotherapy. *Journal of Clinical Psychology, 43,* 511–520.

Beckham, E. E. (1989). Improvement after evaluation in psychotherapy of depression: Evidence of a placebo effect? *Journal of Clinical Psychology, 45,* 945–950.

Bennett, M. J., & Wisneski, M. J. (1979). Continuous psychotherapy within an HMO. *American Journal of Psychiatry, 136,* 1283–1287.

Bent, R. J., Putnam, D. G., Kiesler, D. J., & Nowicki, S., Jr. (1975). Expectancies and characteristics of outpatient clients applying for services at a community mental health facility. *Journal of Consulting and Clinical Psychology, 43,* 280.

Bergin, A. E. (1971). The evaluation of therapeutic outcomes. In A. E. Bergin & S. L. Garfield (Eds.), *Handbook of psychotherapy and behavior change: An empirical analysis* (pp. 217–270). New York: Wiley.

Berrigan, L. P., & Garfield, S. L. (1981). Relationship of missed psychotherapy appointments to premature termination and social class. *The British Journal of Clinical Psychology, 20,* 239–242.

Berzins, J. I. (1977). Therapist–patient matching. In A. S. Gurman & A. M. Razin (Eds.), *Effective psychotherapy. A handbook of research* (pp. 222–251). Oxford: Pergamon.

Betz, N., & Shullman, S. (1979). Factors related to client return following intake. *Journal of Counseling Psychology, 26,* 542–545.

Beutler, L. E., Engle, D., Mohr, D., Doldrup, R. J., Bergan, J., Meredith, K., & Merry, W. (1991). Predictors of differential response to cognitive, experiential, and self-directed psychotherapeutic procedures. *Journal of Consulting and Clinical Psychology, 59,* 333–340.

Beutler, L. E., Jobe, A. M., & Elkins, D. (1974). Outcomes in group psychotherapy: Using persuasion theory to increase treatment efficiency. *Journal of Consulting and Clinical Psychology, 42,* 547–553.

Billings, A. G., & Moos, R. H. (1984). Treatment experiences of adults with unipolar depression: The influence of patient and life context factors. *Journal of Consulting and Clinical Psychology, 52,* 119–131.

Blackman, N. (1984). Psychotherapy in a Veterans Administration mental hygiene clinic. *Psychiatric Quarterly, 22,* 89–102.

Blackwell, B., Gutmann, M., & Gutman, L. (1988). Case review and quantity of outpatient care. *American Journal of Psychiatry, 145,* 1003–1006.

Breckenridge, J. S., Zeiss, A. M., Breckenridge, J. N., Gallagher, D., & Thompson, L. W. (1985). Solicitation of elderly depressives for treatment outcome research: A comparison of referral sources. *Journal of Consulting and Clinical Psychology, 53,* 552–554.

Brill, N. Q., & Storrow, H. A. (1960). Social class and psychiatric treatment. *Archives of General Psychiatry, 3,* 340–344.

Brown, J. S., & Kosterlitz, N. (1964). Selection and treatment of psychiatric outpatients. *Archives of General Psychiatry, 11,* 425–438.

Budman, S. H., & Gurman, A. S. (1988). *Theory and practice of brief therapy.* New York: Guilford.

Burns, D. D., & Nolen-Hoeksema, S. (1991). Coping styles, homework compliance, and the effectiveness of cognitive-behavioral therapy. *Journal of Consulting and Clinical Psychology, 59,* 305–311.

Butcher, J. N., & Koss, M. P. (1978). Research on brief and crisis-oriented psychotherapies. In S. L. Garfield & A. E. Bergin (Eds.), *Handbook of psychotherapy and behavior change* (2nd ed., pp. 725–768). New York: Wiley.

Calhoun, K. S., & Atkeson, B. M. (1991). *Treatment of rape victims. Facilitating psychosocial adjustment.* Elmsford, NY: Pergamon.

Carpenter, P. J., & Range, L. M. (1982). Predicting psychotherapy duration from therapists' sex, professional affiliation, democratic values, and community mental health ideology. *Journal of Clinical Psychology, 38,* 90–91.

Carpenter, P. J., & Range, L. M. (1983). The effects of patients' fee payments source on the duration of outpatient psychotherapy. *Journal of Clinical Psychology, 39,* 304–306.

Carson, R. C., & Heine, R. W. (1962). Similarity and success in therapeutic dyads. *Journal of Consulting Psychology, 26,* 38–43.

Carson, R. C., & Llewellyn, C. E. (1966). Similarity in therapeutic dyads: A re-evaluation. *Journal of Consulting Psychology, 30,* 458.

Cartwright, D. S. (1955). Success in psychotherapy as a function of certain actuarial variables. *Journal of Consulting Psychology, 19,* 357–363.

Cartwright, D. S., Kirtner, W. L., & Fiske, D. W. (1963). *Journal of Abnormal and Social Psychology, 66,* 164–175.

Cartwright, D. S., & Roth, I. (1957). Success and satisfaction in psychotherapy. *Journal of Clinical Psychology, 13,* 20–26.

Cimbolic, P. (1972). Counselor race and experience effects on black clients. *Journal of Consulting and Clinical Psychology, 39,* 328–332.

Craig, T., & Huffine, C. (1976). Correlates of patient attendance in an inner-city mental health clinic. *The American Journal of Psychiatry, 133,* 61–64.

Devine, D. A., & Fernald, P. S. (1973). Outcome effects of receiving a preferred, randomly assigned, or non-preferred therapy. *Journal of Consulting and Clinical Psychology, 41,* 104–107.

Dodd, J. A. (1970). A retrospective analysis of variables related to duration of treatment in a university psychiatric clinic. *Journal of Nervous and Mental Disease, 151,* 75–85.

DuBrin, J. R., & Zastowny, T. R. (1988). Predicting early attrition from psychotherapy: An analysis of a large private practice cohort. *Psychotherapy, 25,* 393–408.

Duehn, W. D., & Proctor, E. K. (1977). Initial clinical interaction and premature discontinuance in treatment. *American Journal of Orthopsychiatry, 47,* 284–290.

Dye, E., & Roth, S. (1990). Psychotherapists' knowledge about and attitudes toward sexual assault victim clients. *Psychology of Women Quarterly, 14,* 191–212.

Ehrlich, H. J., & Bauer, M. L. (1967). Therapists' feelings toward patients and patient treatment outcome. *Social Science and Medicine, 1,* 283–292.

Elkin, I., Parloff, M. B., Hadley, S. W., & Autry, J. H. (1985). NIMH. Treatment of Depression Collaborative Research Program. *Archives of General Psychiatry, 42,* 305–316.

Elkin, I., Shea, T., Watkins, J. T., Imber, S. D., Sotsky, S. M., Collins, J. H. F., Glass, D. R., Pilkonis, P. A., Leber, W. R., Docherty, J. P., Fiester, S. J., & Parloff, M. B. (1989). National Institute of Mental Health Treatment of Depression Collaborative Research Program. *Archives of General Psychiatry, 46,* 971–982.

Emmelkamp, P. M. G., & Kuipers, A. C. M. (1979). Agoraphobia: A follow-up study four years after treatment. *British Journal of Psychiatry, 134,* 352–355.

Everaerd, W. T. A. M. (1983). Failures in treating sexual dysfunctions. In E. B. Foa & P. M. G. Emmelkamp (Eds.), *Failures in behavior therapy* (pp. 392–405). New York: Wiley.

Ewing, T. N. (1974). Racial similarity of client and counselor and client satisfaction with counseling. *Journal of Consulting Psychology, 21,* 446–469.

Farley, W. O., Peterson, K. D., & Spanos, G. (1975). Self-termination from a child guidance center. *Community Mental Health Journal, 11,* 325–334.

Fiester, A. R. (1977). Clients' perceptions of therapists with high attrition rates. *Journal of Consulting and Clinical Psychology, 45,* 954–955.

Fiester, A. R., & Rudestam, K. E. (1975). A multivariate analysis of the early dropout process. *Journal of Consulting and Clinical Psychology, 43,* 528–535.

Filak, J., Abeles, N., & Norquist, S. (1986). Clients' pretherapy interpersonal attitudes and psychotherapy outcome. *Professional Psychology: Research and Practice, 17,* 217–222.

Fiske, D. W., Cartwright, D. S., & Kirtner, W. L. (1964). Are psychotherapeutic changes predictable? *Journal of Abnormal and Social Psychology, 69,* 418–426.

Fiske, D. W., Hunt, H. F., Luborsky, L., Orne, M. T., Parloff, M. B., Reiser, M. F., & Tuma, A. H. (1970). Planning of research on effectiveness of psychotherapy. *Archives of General Psychiatry, 22,* 22–32.

Foa, E. B., Grayson, J. B., Steketee, G. S., Doppelt, H. G., Turner, R. M., & Latimer, P. R. (1983). Success and failure in the behavioral treatment of obsessive-compulsives. *Journal of Consulting and Clinical Psychology, 51,* 287–297.

Fordney-Settlage, D. S. (1975). Heterosexual dysfunction: Evaluation of treatment procedures. *Archives of Sexual Behavior, 4,* 367–387.

Frank, A., Eisenthal, S., & Lazare, A. (1978). Are there social class differences in patients' treatment conceptions? *Archives of General Psychiatry, 35,* 61–69.

Frank, E., Kupfer, D. J., & Perel, J. M. (1989). Early recurrence in unipolar depression. *Archives of General Psychiatry, 46,* 397–400.

Frank, G. H. (1967). A review of research with measures of ego strength derived from the MMPI and the Rorschach. *Journal of General Psychology, 77,* 183–206.

Frank, J. D. (1959). The dynamics of the psychotherapeutic relationship. *Psychiatry, 22,* 17–39.

Frank, J. D. (1974a). Psychotherapy: The restoration of morale. *American Journal of Psychiatry, 131,* 271–274.

Frank, J. D. (1974b). Therapeutic components of psychotherapy. A 25-year progress report of research. *The Journal of Nervous and Mental Disease, 159,* 325–342.

Frank, J. D., Gliedman, L. H., Imber, S. D., Nash, E. H., Jr., & Stone, A. R. (1957). Why patients leave psychotherapy. *Archives of Neurology and Psychiatry, 77,* 283–299.

Frank, J. D., Gliedman, L. H., Imber, S. D., Stone, A. R., & Nash, E. H. (1959). Patients' expectancies and relearning as factors determining improvement in psychotherapy. *American Journal of Psychiatry, 115,* 961–968.

Friedman, H. J. (1963). Patient-expectancy and symptom reduction. *Archives of General Psychiatry, 8,* 61–67.

Galassi, J. P., & Galassi, M. D. (1973). Alienation of college students: A comparison of counseling seekers and non-seekers. *Journal of Counseling Psychology, 20,* 44–49.

Garfield, S. L. (1963). A note on patients' reasons for terminating therapy. *Psychological Reports, 13,* 38.

Garfield, S. L. (1977). Further comments on "dropping out of treatment": Reply to Baekeland and Lundwall. *Psychological Bulletin, 84,* 306–308.

Garfield, S. L. (1978). Research on client variables in psychotherapy. In S. L. Garfield & A. E. Bergin (Eds.), *Handbook of psychotherapy and behavior change* (2nd ed., pp. 191–232). New York: Wiley.

Garfield, S. L. (1980). *Psychotherapy. An eclectic approach.* New York: Wiley.

Garfield, S. L. (1986a). Problems in diagnostic classification. In T. Millon & G. L. Klerman (Eds.), *Contemporary directions in psychopathology* (pp. 99–114). New York: Guilford.

Garfield, S. L. (1986b). Research on client variables in psychotherapy. In S. L. Garfield & A. E. Bergin (Eds.), *Handbook of psychotherapy and behavior change* (3rd ed., pp. 213–256). New York: Wiley.

Garfield, S. L. (1987). Premature termination: A difference of definition. *Contemporary Psychology, 32,* 680.

Garfield, S. L. (1989a). Giving up on child psychotherapy: Who drops out? Comment on Weisz, Weiss, and Langmeyer. *Journal of Consulting and Clinical Psychology, 57,* 168–169.

Garfield, S. L. (1989b). *The practice of brief psychotherapy.* Elmsford, NY: Pergamon.

Garfield, S. L. (1993). Methodological problems in clinical diagnosis. In P. B. Sutker & H. E. Adams (Eds.), *Comprehensive handbook of psychopathology* (2nd ed., pp. 27–46). New York: Plenum.

Garfield, S. L., & Affleck, D. C. (1959). An appraisal of duration of stay in outpatient psychotherapy. *Journal of Nervous and Mental Disease, 129,* 492–498.

Garfield, S. L., Affleck, D. C., & Muffley, R. A. (1963). A study of psychotherapy interaction and continuation in psychotherapy. *Journal of Clinical Psychology, 19,* 473–478.

Garfield, S. L., & Kurz, M. (1952). Evaluation of treatment and related procedures in 1216 cases referred to a mental hygiene clinic. *Psychiatric Quarterly, 26,* 414–424.

Garfield, S. L., Prager, R. A., & Bergin, A. E. (1971). Evaluation of outcome in psychotherapy. *Journal of Consulting and Clinical Psychology, 37,* 307–313.

Garfield, S. L., & Wolpin, M. (1963). Expectations regarding psychotherapy. *Journal of Nervous and Mental Disease, 137,* 353–362.

Gaylin, N. (1966). Psychotherapy and psychological health: A Rorschach function and structure analysis. *Journal of Consulting Psychology, 30,* 494–500.

Gelso, C. J., Mills, D. H., & Spiegel, S. B. (1983). Client and therapist factors influencing the outcomes of time-limited counseling one month and eighteen months after treatment. In C. J. Gelso & D. H. Johnson (Eds.), *Explorations in time-limited counseling and psychotherapy* (pp. 87–114). New York: Teachers College Press.

Getter, H., & Sundland, D. M. (1962). The Barron ego-strength scale and psychotherapy outcome. *Journal of Consulting Psychology, 26,* 195.

Gibbs, J. T. (1975). Use of mental health services by black students at a predominantly white university: A three-year study. *American Journal of Orthopsychiatry, 45,* 430–445.

Goldfried, M. R., Greenberg, L. S., & Marmar, C. (1990). Individual psychotherapy: Process and outcome. *Annual Review of Psychology, 41,* 659–688.

Goldstein, A. P. (1960). Patients' expectancies and nonspecific therapy as a basis for (un)spontaneous remission. *Journal of Clinical Psychology, 16,* 399–403.

Goldstein, A. P. (1973). *Structured learning therapy: Toward a psychotherapy for the poor.* New York: Academic Press.

Goldstein, A. P., & Shipman, W. G. (1961). Patient expectancies, symptom reduction and aspects of initial psychotherapeutic interview. *Journal of Clinical Psychology, 17,* 129–133.

Gomes-Schwartz, B. (1978). Effective ingredients in psychotherapy: Predictions of outcome from process variables. *Journal of Consulting and Clinical Psychology, 46,* 1023–1035.

Gomes-Schwartz, B., Hadley, W. W., & Strupp, H. H. (1978). Individual psychotherapy and behavior therapy. *Annual Review of Psychology, 29,* 435–471.

Gottschalk, L. A., Fox, R. A., & Bates, D. E. (1973). A study of prediction and outcome of a mental health crisis clinic. *American Journal of Psychiatry, 130,* 1107–1111.

Gould, M. S., Shaffer, D., & Kaplan, D. (1985). The characteristics of dropouts from a child psychiatry clinic. *Journal of the American Academy of Child Psychiatry, 24,* 316–328.

Greenspan, M., & Kulish, N. M. (1985). Factors in premature termination in long term psychotherapy. *Psychotherapy, 22,* 75–82.

Grotjahn, M. (1972). Learning from dropout patients: A clinical view of patients who discontinued group psychotherapy. *International Journal of Group Psychotherapy, 22,* 306–319.

Gunderson, J. G., Frank, A. F., Ronningstam, E. F., Wachter, S., Lynch, V. J., & Wolf, P. J. (1989). Early discontinuance of borderline patients from psychotherapy. *Journal of Nervous and Mental Disease, 177,* 38–42.

Hafner, R. J. (1983). Behavior therapy for agoraphobic men. *Behavior Research & Therapy, 21,* 51–56.

Hamburg, D. A., Bibring, G. L., Fisher, C., Stanton, A. H., Wallerstein, R. S., Weinstock, H. I., & Haggard, E. (1967). Report of Ad Hoc Committee on central fact-gathering data of the American Psychoanalytic Association. *Journal of the American Psychoanalytic Association, 15,* 841–861.

Harris, R. E., & Christiansen, C. (1946). Prediction of response to brief psychotherapy. *Journal of Psychology, 21,* 269–284.

Heisler, G. H., Beck, N. C., Fraps, C., & McReynolds, W. T. (1982). Therapist ratings as predictors of therapy attendance. *Journal of Clinical Psychology, 38,* 754–758.

Heitler, J. B. (1973). Preparation of lower-class patients for expressive group psychotherapy. *Journal of Consulting and Clinical Psychology, 41,* 251–260.

Heitler, J. B. (1976). Preparatory techniques in initiating expressive psychotherapy with lower-class, unsophisticated patients. *Psychological Bulletin, 83,* 339–352.

Henry, W. P., Schact, T. E., & Strupp, H. H. (1986). Structural analysis of social behavior: Application to a study of interpersonal process in differential psychotherapeutic outcome. *Journal of Consulting and Clinical Psychology, 54,* 27–31.

Herink, R. (Ed.). (1980). *The psychotherapy handbook. The A to Z guide to more than 250 different therapies in use today.* New York: New American Library.

Hiler, E. W. (1959). The sentence completion test as a predictor of continuation in psychotherapy. *Journal of Consulting Psychology, 23,* 544–549.

Hoberman, H. M., Lewinsohn, P. M., & Tilson, M. (1988). Group treatment of depression: Individual predictors of outcome. *Journal of Consulting and Clinical Psychology, 56,* 393–398.

Hoehn-Saric, R., Frank, J. D., Imber, S. D., Nash, E. H., Stone, A. R., & Battle, C. C. (1964). Systematic preparation of patients for psychotherapy. I. Effects on therapy behavior and outcome. *Journal of Psychiatric Research, 2,* 267–281.

Hoffman, J. J. (1985). Client factors related to premature termination of psychotherapy. *Psychotherapy, 22,* 83–85.

Hollingshead, A. B., & Redlich, F. C. (1958). *Social class and mental illness.* New York: Wiley.

Holmes, D. S., & Urie, R. G. (1975). Effects of preparing children for psychotherapy. *Journal of Consulting and Clinical Psychology, 43,* 311–318.

Holtzworth-Munroe, A., Jacobson, N. S., DeKlyen, M., & Whisman, M. A. (1989). Relationship between behavioral marital therapy outcome and process variables. *Journal of Consulting and Clinical Psychology, 57,* 658–662.

Horenstein, D., Houston, B. K., & Holmes, D. S. (1973). Clients', therapists', and judges' evaluations of psychotherapy. *Counseling Psychology, 20,* 149–158.

Horowitz, M. J., Marmar, C., Weiss, D. S., DeWitt, K. N., & Rosenbaum, R. (1984). Brief psychotherapy of bereavement reactions: The relationship of process to outcome. *Archives of General Psychiatry, 41,* 438–448.

Howard, K. I., Davidson, C. V., O'Mahoney, M. T., Orlinsky, D. E., & Brown, K. P. (1989). Patterns of psychotherapy utilization. *American Journal of Psychiatry, 146,* 775–778.

Howard, K. I., Kopta, S. M., Krause, M. S., & Orlinsky, D. E. (1986). The dose-effect relationship in psychotherapy. *American Psychologist, 41,* 159–164.

Howard, K. I., Krause, M. S., & Orlinsky, D. E. (1986). The attrition dilemma: Toward a new strategy for psychotherapy research. *Journal of Consulting and Clinical Psychology, 54,* 106–110.

Hunt, D. D., Carr, J. E., Dagadakis, C. S., & Walker, E. A. (1985). Cognitive match as a predictor of psychotherapy outcome. *Psychotherapy, 22,* 718–721.

Imber, S. D., Pande, S. K., Frank, J. D., Hoehn-Saric, R., Stone, A. R., & Wargo, D. G. (1970). Time-focused role induction. *Journal of Nervous and Mental Disease, 150,* 27–30.

Jacobs, D., Charles, E., Jacobs, T., Weinstein, H., & Mann, D. (1972). Preparation for treatment of the disadvantaged patient: Effects on disposition and outcome. *American Journal of Orthopsychiatry, 42,* 666–674.

Jones, E. E. (1974). Social class and psychotherapy. A critical review of research. *Psychiatry, 37,* 307–320.

Jones, E. E. (1982). Psychotherapists' impression of treatment outcome as a function of race. *Journal of Clinical Psychology, 38,* 722–731.

Jones, E. E., Cumming, J. D., & Horowitz, M. J. (1988). Another look at the nonspecific hypothesis of therapeutic effectiveness. *Journal of Consulting and Clinical Psychology, 56,* 48–55.

Jones, E. E., & Zoppel, C. L. (1982). Impact of client and therapist gender on psychotherapy process and outcome. *Journal of Consulting and Clinical Psychology, 50,* 259–272.

Kadushin, C. (1969). *Why people go to psychiatrists.* New York: Atherton.

Kahn, M. W., & Heiman, E. (1978). Factors associated with length of treatment in a barrio-neighborhood mental health service. *International Journal of Social Psychiatry, 24,* 259–262.

Katz, M. M. (1971). The classification of depression. In R. R. Fieve (Ed.), *Depression in the 1970's* (pp. 31–40). Amsterdam: Excerpta Medica.

Katz, M. M., Lorr, M., & Rubinstein, E. A. (1958). Remainer patients' attributes and their relation to subsequent improvement in psychotherapy. *Journal of Consulting Psychology, 22,* 411–413.

Kazdin, A. E. (1986). Comparative outcome studies of psychotherapy: Methodological issues and strategies. *Journal of Consulting and Clinical Psychology, 54,* 95–105.

Kazdin, A. E. (1990). Review of American Psychiatric Association (T. B. Karasu, Chairperson) (1989). *Treatments of psychiatric disorders: A task force report of the American Psychiatric Association, Vols. 1–3 and index.* Washington, DC: American Psychiatric Association.

Kazdin, A. E., & Wilcoxon, L. A. (1976). Systematic desensitization and nonspecific treatment effects: A methodological evaluation. *Psychological Bulletin, 83*, 729–758.

Keithly, L. J., Samples, S. J., & Strupp, H. H. (1980). Patient motivation as a predictor of process and outcome in psychotherapy. *Psychotherapy and Psychosomatics, 33*, 87–97.

Kellner, R., & Sheffield, B. F. (1973). The one-week prevalence of symptoms in neurotic patients and normals. *American Journal of Psychiatry, 130*, 102–105.

Keniston, K., Boltax, S., & Almond, R. (1971). Multiple criteria of treatment outcome. *Journal of Psychiatry, 8*, 107–118.

Kernberg, O. F., Burstein, E. D., Coyne, L., Appelbaum, A., Horwitz, L., & Voth, H. (1972). Psychotherapy and psychoanalysis: Final Report of the Menninger Foundation's Psychotherapy Research Project. *Bulletin of the Menninger Clinic, 36* (Nos. 1/2), 1–276.

Klerman, G. L., Weissman, M. M., Rounsaville, B. J., & Chevron, E. S. (1984). *Interpersonal therapy of depression (I.P.T.).* New York: Basic Books.

Klopfer, B., Kirkner, F., Wisham, W., & Baker, G. (1951). Rorschach prognostic rating scale. *Journal of Projective Techniques, 15*, 425–428.

Knapp, P. H., Levin, S., McCarter, R. H., Wermer, H., & Zetzel, E. (1960). Suitability for psychoanalysis: A review of 100 supervised analytic cases. *Psychoanalytic Quarterly, 29*, 459–477.

Kokotovic, A. M., & Tracey, T. J. (1987). Premature termination in a university counseling center. *Journal of Counseling Psychology, 34*, 80–82.

Kolb, D. L., Beutler, L. E., Davis, C. S., Crago, M., & Shanfield, S. B. (1985). Patient and therapy process variables relating to dropout and change in psychotherapy. *Psychotherapy, 22*, 702–710.

Koran, L., & Costell, R. (1973). Early termination from group psychotherapy. *International Journal of Group Psychotherapy, 23*, 346–359.

Koss, M. P. (1979). Length of psychotherapy for clients seen in private practice. *Journal of Consulting and Clinical Psychology, 47*, 210–212.

Koss, M. P. (1980). Descriptive characteristics and length of psychotherapy of child and adult clients seen in private psychological practice. *Psychotherapy: Theory, Research, and Practice, 17*, 268–271.

Krebs, R. L. (1971). Some effects of a white institution on black psychiatric outpatients. *American Journal of Orthopsychiatry, 41*, 589–597.

Kupst, M. J., & Schulman, J. L. (1979). Comparing professional and lay expectations of psychotherapy. *Psychotherapy: Theory, Research, and Practice, 16*, 237–243.

Kurland, S. H. (1956). Length of treatment in a mental hygiene clinic. *Psychiatric Quarterly Supplement, 30*, 83–90.

Lambert, R. G., & Lambert, M. J. (1984). The effects of role preparation for psychotherapy on immigrant clients seeking mental health services in Hawaii. *Journal of Community Psychology, 12*, 263–275.

Lennard, H. L., & Berstein, A. (1960). *Tha anatomy of psychotherapy: Systems of communication and expectation.* New York: Columbia University Press.

Lerner, B. (1972). *Therapy in the ghetto.* Baltimore: The Johns Hopkins University Press.

Lerner, B., & Fiske, D. W. (1973). Client attributes and the eye of the beholder. *Journal of Consulting and Clinical Psychology, 40*, 272–277.

Liberman, B. L. (1978). The role of mastery in psychotherapy: Maintenance of improvement and prescriptive change. In J. D. Frank, R. Hoehn-Saric, S. D. Imber, B. L.

Liberman, & A. R. Stone (Eds.), *Effective ingredients of successful psychotherapy.* New York: Brunner/Mazel.

Liberman, B. L., Frank, J. D., Hoehn-Saric, R., Stone, A. R., Imber, S. D., & Pande, S. K. (1972). Patterns of change in treated psychoneurotic patients: A five-year follow-up investigation of the systematic preparation of patients for psychotherapy. *Journal of Consulting and Clinical Psychology, 38*, 36–41.

Lichtenstein, E. (1966). Personality similarity and therapeutic success: A failure to replicate. *Journal of Consulting Psychology, 30*, 282.

Lick, J., & Bootzin, R. (1975). Expectancy factors in the treatment of fear: Methodological and theoretical issues. *Psychological Bulletin, 82*, 917–931.

Lorion, R. P. (1973). Socioeconomic status and traditional treatment approaches reconsidered. *Psychological Bulletin, 79*, 263–270.

Lorion, R. P. (1974). Patient and therapist variables in the treatment of low-income patients. *Psychological Bulletin, 81*, 344–354.

Lorion, R. P. (1978). Research on psychotherapy and behavior change with the disadvantged. In S. L. Garfield & A. E. Bergin (Eds.), *Handbook of psychotherapy and behavior change* (2nd ed., pp. 903–938). New York: Wiley,

Lorion, R. P., & Felner, R. D. (1986). Research on psychotherapy with the disadvantaged. In S. L. Garfield & A. E. Bergin (Eds.), *Handbook of psychotherapy and behavior change* (3rd ed., pp. 739–775). New York: Wiley.

Lorr, M., Katz, M. M., & Rubinstein, E. A. (1958). The prediction of length of stay in psychotherapy. *Journal of Consulting Psychology, 22*, 321–327.

Lothstein, L. M. (1978). The group psychotherapy dropout phenomenon revisited. *American Journal of Psychiatry, 135*, 1492–1495.

Lott, D. R., & Murray, E. J. (1975). The effect of expectancy manipulation on outcome in systematic desensitization. *Psychotherapy: Theory, Research, and Practice, 12*, 28–32.

Lubin, B., Hornstra, R. K., Lewis, R. V., & Bechtel, B. S. (1973). Correlates of initial treatment assignment in a community mental health center. *Archives of General Psychiatry, 29*, 497–504.

Luborsky, L., Chandler, M., Auerbach, A. H., Cohen, J., & Bachrach, H. M. (1971). Factors influencing the outcome of psychotherapy: A review of quantitative research. *Psychological Bulletin, 75*, 145–185.

Luborsky, L., Crits-Christoph, P., Alexander, L., Margolis, M., & Cohen, J. (1983). Two helping alliance methods of predicting outcomes of psychotherapy. *Journal of Nervous and Mental Disease, 171*, 480–491.

Luborsky, L., Crits-Christoph, P., Mintz, J., & Auerbach, A. (1988). *Who will benefit from psychotherapy? Predicting therapeutic outcomes.* New York: Basic Books.

Luborsky, L., Mintz, J., Auerbach, A., Christoph, P., Bachrach, H., Todd, T., Johnson, M., Cohen, M., & O'Brien, C. (1980). Predicting the outcome of psychotherapy. *Archives of General Psychiatry, 37*, 471–481.

Luborsky, L., Mintz, J., & Christoph, P. (1979). Are psychotherapeutic changes predictable? Comparison of a Chicago Counseling Center project with a Penn Psychotherapy Project. *Journal of Consulting and Clinical Psychology, 47*, 469–473.

Luborsky, L., Singer, B., & Luborsky, L. (1975). Comparative studies of psychotherapies. Is it true that "Everyone has won and all must have prizes"? *Archives of General Psychiatry, 32*, 995–1007.

Malan, D. H. (1963). *A study of brief psychotherapy.* London: Tavistock.

Malan, D. H. (1976). *The frontier of brief psychotherapy: An example of the convergence of research and clinical practice.* New York: Plenum.

Marks, I. (1978). Behavioral psychotherapy of adult neurosis. In S. L. Garfield & A. E. Bergin (Eds.), *Handbook of psychotherapy and behavior change* (2nd ed., pp. 493–547). New York: Wiley.

Matarazzo, J. D. (1972). *Wechsler's measurement and appraisal of adult intelligence* (5th and enl. ed.). Baltimore: Williams & Wilkins.

Mathews, A. M., Gelder, M. G., & Johnston, D. W. (1981). *Agoraphobia. Nature and treatment.* London: Tavistock.

Mathews, A. M., Johnston, D. W., Lancashire, M., Munby, M., Shaw, P. M., & Gelder, M. G. (1976). Imaginal flooding and exposure to real phobic situations: Treatment outcome with agoraphobic patients. *British Journal of Psychiatry, 129,* 362–371.

Mathews, A. M., Johnston, D. W., Shaw, P. M., & Gelder, M. G. (1974). Process variables and the prediction of outcome in behaviour therapy. *The British Journal of Psychiatry, 125,* 256–264.

McLachlan, J. C. (1972). Benefit from group therapy as a function of patient–therapist match on conceptual level. *Psychotherapy: Theory, Research, and Practice, 9,* 317–323.

McLean, P. D., & Hakstian, A. R. (1979). Clinical depression: Comparative efficacy of outpatient treatments. *Journal of Consulting and Clinical Psychology, 47,* 818–836.

McNair, D. M., Lorr, M., & Callahan, D. M. (1963). Patient and therapist influences on quitting psychotherapy. *Journal of Consulting Psychology, 27,* 10–17.

McNeill, B. W., May, R. J., & Lee, V. E. (1987). Perceptions of counselor source characteristics by premature and successful terminators. *Journal of Counseling Psychology, 34,* 86–89.

Melnick, B. (1972). Patient–therapist identification in relation to both patient and therapist variables and therapy outcome. *Journal of Consulting and Clinical Psychology, 38,* 97–104.

Meltzoff, J., & Kornreich, M. (1970). *Research in psychotherapy.* New York: Atherton.

Messer, S. B., & Meinster, M. O. (1980). Interaction effects of internal vs. external locus of control and directive vs. non-directive therapy: Fact or fiction? *Journal of Clinical Psychology, 36,* 283–288.

Mintz, J. (1972). What is "success" in psychotherapy? *Journal of Abnormal Psychology, 80,* 11–19.

Mintz, J., Luborsky, L., & Auerbach, A. H. (1971). Dimensions of psychotherapy: A factor-analytic study of ratings of psychotherapy sessions. *Journal of Consulting and Clinical Psychology, 36,* 106–120.

Mintz, J., Steuer, J., & Jarvik, L. (1981). Psychotherapy with depressed elderly patients: Research considerations. *Journal of Consulting and Clinical Psychology, 49,* 542–548.

Mogul, K. M. (1982). Overview: The sex of the therapist. *American Journal of Psychiatry, 139,* 1–11.

Mohl, P. C., Martinez, D., Ticknor, C., Huang, M., & Cordell, M. D. (1991). Early dropouts from psychotherapy. *Journal of Nervous and Mental Disease, 179,* 478–481.

Mohr, D. C., Beutler, L. E., Engle, D., Shoham-Salomon, V., Bergan, J., Kaszniak, A. W., & Yost, E. B. (1990). Identification of patients at risk for nonresponse and negative outcome in psychotherapy. *Journal of Consulting and Clinical Psychology, 58,* 622–628.

Moras, K., & Strupp, H. H. (1982). Pretherapy interpersonal relations, patients' alliance, and outcome in brief therapy. *Archives of General Psychiatry, 39,* 405–409.

Morgan, R., Luborsky, L., Crits-Christoph, P., Curtis, H., & Solomon, J. (1982). Predicting the outcomes of psycho-therapy by the Penn Helping Alliance Rating Method. *Archives of General Psychiatry, 39,* 397–402.

Morgan, W. G. (1973). Nonnecessary conditions or useful procedures in desensitization: A reply to Wilkins. *Psychological Bulletin, 79,* 373–375.

Muench, G. A. (1965). An investigation of the efficacy of time-limited psychotherapy. *Journal of Counseling Psychology, 12,* 294–298.

Nacev, V. (1980). Dependency and ego-strength as indicators of patient attendance in psychotherapy. *Journal of Clinical Psychology, 36,* 691–695.

Nash, E. H., Hoehn-Saric, R., Battle, C. C., Stone, A. R., Imber, S. D., & Frank, J. D. (1965). Systematic preparation of patients for short-term psychotherapy. II. Relations to characteristics of patient, therapist, and the psychotherapeutic process. *Journal of Nervous and Mental Disease, 140,* 374–383.

National Institute of Mental Health. (1981). *Use of psychiatric facilities by children and youth. United States 1975* (DHHS Publication No. ADM 81-1142). Washington, DC: U.S. Government Printing Office.

Newmark, C. S., Finkelstein, M., & Frerking, R. A. (1974). Comparison of the predictive validity of two measures of psychotherapy prognosis. *Journal of Personality Assessment, 38,* 144–148.

New York City Committee on Mental Hygiene of the State Charities Aid Association (1949). *The functioning of psychiatric clinics in New York City.* New York: Author.

Noonan, J. R. (1973). A follow-up of pretherapy dropouts. *Journal of Community Psychology, 1,* 43–45.

Ollendick, T. H., & Murphy, M. J. (1977). Differential effectiveness of muscular and cognitive relaxation as a function of locus of control. *Journal of Behavioral Therapy and Experimental Psychiatry, 8,* 223–228.

O'Malley, S. S., Suh, C. S., & Strupp, H. H. (1983). The Vanderbilt Psychotherapy Process Scale: A report on the scale development and a process–outcome study. *Journal of Consulting and Clinical Psychology, 51,* 581–586.

Orlinksy, D. E., & Howard, K. I. (1986). Process and outcome in psychotherapy. In S. L. Garfield & A. E. Bergin (Eds.), *Handbook of psychotherapy and behavior change* (3rd ed., pp. 311–384). New York: Wiley.

Orne, M. T., & Wender, P. H. (1968). Anticipatory socialization for psychotherapy: Method and rationale. *American Journal of Psychiatry, 124,* 1202–1212.

Parloff, M. B., London, P., & Wolfe, B. (1986). Individual psychotherapy and behavior change. *Annual Review of Psychology, 37,* 321–349.

Pekarik, G. (1983a). Follow-up adjustment of outpatient dropouts. *American Journal of Orthopsychiatry, 53,* 501–511.

Pekarik, G. (1983b). Improvement in clients who have given different reasons for dropping out of treatment. *Journal of Clinical Psychology, 39,* 909–913.

Pekarik, G. (1985). Coping with dropouts. *Professional Psychology: Research and Practice, 16,* 114–123.

Pekarik, G., & Finney-Owen, K. (1987). Outpatient clinic therapist attitudes and beliefs relevant to client drop out. *Community Mental Health Journal, 23,* 120–130.

Pekarik, G., & Wierzbicki, M. (1986). The relationship between clients' expected and actual treatment duration. *Psychotherapy, 23,* 532–534.

Perotti, L. P., & Hopewell, C. A. (1980). Expectancy effects in psychotherapy and systematic desensitization: A review. *JSAS: Catalog of Selected Documents in Psychology, 10* (Ms. No. 2052).

Pettit, I., Pettit, T., & Welkowitz, J. (1974). Relationship between values, social class, and duration of psychotherapy. *Journal of Consulting and Clinical Psychology, 42,* 482–490.

Phillips, E. L. (1985). *Psychotherapy revised. New frontiers in research and practice.* Hillsdale, NJ: Lawrence Erlbaum.

Phillips, E. L. (1987). Reply to Garfield's review of *Psychotherapy revised. Contemporary Psychology, 32,* 680.

Phillips, E. L., & Fagan, P. J. (1982, August). *Attrition: Focus on the intake and first therapy interviews.* Paper presented at the 90th annual convention of the American Psychological Association, Washington, DC.

Pilkonis, P. A., Imber, S. D., Lewis, P., & Rubinsky, P. (1984). A comparative outcome study of individual, group, and conjoint psychotherapy. *Archives of General Psychiatry, 41,* 431–437.

Piper, W. E., Azim, H. F. A., McCallum, M., & Joyce, A. S. (1990). Patient suitability and outcome in short-term individual psychotherapy. *Journal of Consulting and Clinical Psychology, 58,* 475–481.

Piper, W. E., de Carufel, F. L., & Szkrumelak, N. (1985). Patient predictors of process and outcome in short-term individual psychotherapy. *The Journal of Nervous and Mental Disease, 173,* 726–733.

Piper, W. E., & Wogan, M. (1970). Placebo effect in psychotherapy: An extension of earlier findings. *Journal of Consulting and Clinical Psychology, 34,* 447.

Prager, R. A., & Garfield, S. L. (1972). Client initial disturbance and outcome in psychotherapy. *Journal of Consulting and Clinical Psychology, 38,* 112–117.

Rabin, A. S., Kaslow, N. J., & Rehm, L. P. (1985). Factors influencing continuation in a behavioral therapy. *Behaviour Research and Therapy, 23,* 695–698.

Rachman, S., & Hodgson, R. (1980). *Obsessions and compulsions.* Englewood Cliffs, NJ: Prentice Hall.

Raynes, A. E., & Warren, G. (1971a). Some distinguishing features of patients failing to attend a psychiatric clinic after referral. *American Journal of Orthopsychiatry, 41,* 581–588.

Raynes, A. E., & Warren, G. (1971b). Some characteristics of "drop-outs" at first contact with a psychiatric clinic. *Community Mental Health Journal, 7,* 144–151.

Reder, P., & Tyson, R. L. (1980). Patient dropout from psychotherapy. A review and discussion. *Bulletin of the Menninger Clinic, 44,* 229–251.

Roberts, L. K. (1954). The failure of some Rorschach indices to predict the outcome of psychotherapy. *Journal of Consulting Psychology, 18,* 96–98.

Rodolfa, E. R., Rapaport, R., & Lee, V. E. (1983). Variables related to premature terminations in a university counseling service. *Journal of Counseling Psychology, 30,* 87–90.

Rogers, C. R., Gendlin, E. T., Kiesler, D. J., & Truax, C. B. (Eds.). (1967). *The therapeutic relationship and its impact.* Madison: University of Wisconsin Press.

Rogers, L. S. (1960). Drop-out rates and results of psychotherapy in government-aided mental hygiene clinics. *Journal of Clinical Psychology, 16,* 89–92.

Rogers, L. S., & Hammond, K. R. (1953). Prediction of the results of therapy by means of the Rorschach test. *Journal of Consulting Psychology, 17,* 8–15.

Rosenbaum, M. (1980). A schedule for assessing self-control behavior: Preliminary findings. *Behavior Therapy, 11,* 109–121.

Rosenberg, S. (1954). The relationship of certain personality factors to prognosis in psychotherapy. *Journal of Clinical Psychology, 10,* 341–345.

Rosenthal, D., & Frank, J. D. (1956). Psychotherapy and the placebo effect. *Psychological Bulletin, 53,* 294–302.

Rosenthal, D., & Frank, J. D. (1958). The fate of psychiatric clinic outpatients assigned to psychotherapy. *Journal of Nervous and Mental Disorders, 127,* 330–343.

Rosenzweig S. P., & Folman, R. (1974). Patient and therapist variables affecting premature termination in group psychotherapy. *Psychotherapy: Theory, Research, and Practice, 11,* 76–79.

Rounsaville, B. J., Weissman, M. M., & Prusoff, B. A. (1981). Psychotherapy with depressed outpatients. Patient and process variables as predictors of outcome. *British Journal of Psychiatry, 138,* 67–74.

Rubinstein, E. A., & Lorr, M. (1956). A comparison of terminators and remainers in outpatient psychotherapy. *Journal of Clinical Psychology, 12,* 345–349.

Ryan, W. (Ed.). (1969). *Distress in the city: Essays on the design and administration of urban mental health services.* Cleveland: Case Western Reserve University Press.

Sachs, J. S. (1983). Negative factors in brief psychotherapy: An empirical assessment. *Journal of Consulting and Clinical Psychology, 51,* 557–564.

Saltzman, C., Luetgert, M. J., Roth, C. H., Creaser, J., & Howard, L. (1976). Formation of a therapeutic relationship: Experiences during the initial phase of psychotherapy as predictors of treatment duration and outcome. *Journal of Consulting and Clinical Psychology, 44,* 546–555.

Salzman, C., Shader, R. I., Scott, D. A., & Binstock, W. (1970). Interviewer anger and patient dropout in walk-in clinic. *Comprehensive Psychiatry, 11,* 267–273.

Sattler, J. M. (1977). The effects of therapist–client racial similarity. In A. S. Gurman & A. M. Razin (Eds.), *Effective psychotherapy: A handbook of research* (pp. 250–288). Elmsford, NY: Pergamon.

Schaffer, L. & Myers, J. K. (1954). Psychotherapy and social stratification: An empirical study of practices in a psychiatric outpatient clinic. *Psychiatry, 17,* 83–93.

Schmidt, J. P., & Hansey, R. (1979). Social class and psychiatric treatment: Application of a decision-making model to use patterns in a cost-free clinic. *Journal of Consulting and Clinical Psychology, 47,* 771–772.

Schofield, W. (1964). *Psychotherapy: The purchase of friendship.* Englewood Cliffs, NJ: Prentice Hall.

Schubert, D. S. P., & Miller, S. I. (1980). Differences between the lower social classes. *American Journal of Orthopsychiatry, 50,* 712–717.

Seeman, J. (1954). Counselor judgments of therapeutic process and outcome. In C. Rogers & R. F. Dymond (Eds.), *Psychotherapy and personality change.* Chicago: University of Chicago Press.

Shader, R. I. (1970). The walk-in service: An experience in community care. In T. Rothman (Ed.), *Changing patterns in psychiatric care.* New York: Crown.

Shapiro, R. J. (1974). Therapist attitudes and premature termination in family and individual therapy. *The Journal of Nervous and Mental Disease, 159,* 101–107.

Shea, M. T., Pilkonis, P. A., Beckham, E., Collins, J. F., Elkin, I., Sotsky, S. M., & Docherty, J. P. (1990). Personality disorders and treatment outcome in the NIMH Treatment of Depression Collaborative Research Program. *American Journal of Psychiatry, 14   711–718.*

Siegel, S. M., Rootes, M. D., & Traub   (1977). Symptom change and prognosis in clinic psychotherapy. *Archives of General Psychiatry, 34,* 321–331.

Sifneos, P. E. (1972). *Short-term psychotherapy and emotional crisis.* Cambridge, MA: Harvard University Press.

Silverman, D. (1977). First do no more harm: Female rape victims and the male counselor. *American Journal of Orthopsychiatry, 47,* 91–96.

Silverman, W. H., & Beech, R. P. (1979). Are dropouts, dropouts? *Journal of Community Psychology, 7,* 236–242.

Simons, A. D., Levine, J. L., Lustman, P. J., & Murphy, G. E. (1984). Patient attrition in a comparative outcome study of depression. A follow-up report. *Journal of Affective Disorders, 6,* 163–173.

Simons, A. D., Lustman, P. J., Wetzel, R. D., & Murphy, G. E. (1985). Predicting response to cognitive therapy of depression: The role of learned resourcefulness. *Cognitive Therapy and Research, 9,* 79–89.

Sledge, W. H., Moras, K., Hartley, D., & Levine, M. (1990). Effect of time-limited psychotherapy on patient dropout rates. *American Journal of Psychiatry, 147,* 1341–1347.

Sloane, R. B., Cristol, A. H., Pepernik, M. C., & Staples, F. R. (1970). Role preparation and expectation of improvement in psychotherapy. *Journal of Nervous and Mental Disease, 150,* 18–26.

Sloane, R. B., Staples, F. R., Cristol, A. H., Yorkston, N. J., & Whipple, K. (1975). *Psychotherapy versus behavior therapy.* Cambridge, MA: Harvard University Press.

Smith, G. J. W., Sjoholm, L., & Nielzen, S. (1975). Individual factors affecting the improvement of anxiety during a therapeutic period of 1½ to 2 years. *Acta Psychiatrica Scandinavica, 52,* 7–22.

Smith, M. L., Glass, G. V., & Miller, T. I. (1980). *The benefits of psychotherapy.* Baltimore: The Johns Hopkins University Press.

Stein, K. B., & Beall, L. (1971). Externalizing-internalizing symptoms and psychotherapeutic outcome. *Psychotherapy: Theory, Research, and Practice, 8,* 269–272.

Steinmetz, J. L., Lewinsohn, P. M., & Antonuccio, D. O. (1983). Prediction of individual outcome in a group intervention for depression. *Journal of Consulting and Clinical Psychology, 51,* 331–337.

Stern, S. L., Moore, S. F., & Gross, S. J. (1975). Confounding of personality and social class characteristics in research on premature termination. *Journal of Consulting and Clinical Psychology, 43,* 341–344.

Stoler, N. (1963). Client likeability: A variable in the study of psychotherapy. *Journal of Consulting Psychology, 27,* 175–178.

Stone, A., Frank, J. D., Nash, E., & Imber, S. (1961). An intensive five-year follow-up study of treated psychiatric outpatients. *Journal of Nervous and Mental Disease, 133,* 410–422.

Storandt, M. (1983). *Counseling and therapy with older adults.* Boston: Little, Brown.

Stotsky, S. M., Glass, D. R., Shea, M. T., Pilkonis, P. A., Collins, J. F., Elkin, I., Watkins, J. T., Imber, S. D., Leber, W. R., Moyer, J., & Oliveri, M. E. (1991). NIMH Treatment of Depression Collaborative Research Program: Patient predictors of response to psychotherapy and pharmacotherapy. *American Journal of Psychiatry, 148,* 997–1008.

Strupp, H. H. (1973). On the basic ingredients of psychotherapy. *Journal of Consulting and Clinical Psychology, 41,* 1–8.

Strupp, H. H., & Bloxom, A. L. (1973). Preparing lower-class patients for group psychotherapy: Development and evaluation of a role-induction film. *Journal of Consulting and Clinical Psychology, 41,* 373–384.

Sue, S., Fujino, D. C., Hu, L., Takeuchi, D. T., & Zane, N. W. S. (1991). Community mental health services for ethnic minority groups: A test of the cultural responsiveness hypothesis. *Journal of Consulting and Clinical Psychology, 59,* 533–540.

Sue, S., McKinney, H. L., & Allen, D. B. (1976). Predictors of the duration of therapy for clients in the community mental health system. *Community Mental Health Journal, 12,* 365–375.

Sue, S., McKinney, H., Allen, D., & Hall, J. (1974). Delivery of community mental health services to black and white clients. *Journal of Consulting and Clinical Psychology, 42,* 794–801.

Sullivan, P. L., Miller, C., & Smelzer, W. (1958). Factors in length of stay and progress in psychotherapy. *Journal of Consulting Psychology, 1,* 1–9.

Swenson, C. H. (1967). Psychotherapy as a special case of dyadic interaction: Some suggestions for theory and research. *Psychotherapy: Theory, Research, and Practice, 4,* 7–13.

Taube, C. A., Burns, B. J., & Kessler, L. (1984). Patients of psychiatrists and psychologists in office-based practice: 1980. *American Psychologist, 39,* 1435–1447.

Taulbee, E. S. (1958). Relationship between certain personality variables and continuation in psychotherapy. *Journal of Consulting Psychology, 22,* 83–89.

Thompson, L. W., Gallagher, D., & Breckenridge, J. S. (1987). Comparative effectiveness of psychotherapies for depressed elders. *Journal of Consulting and Clinical Psychology, 55,* 385–390.

Thurer, S., & Hursh, N. (1981). Characteristics of the therapeutic relationship. In C. E. Walker (Ed.), *Clinical practice of psychology* (pp. 62–82). Elmsford, NY: Pergamon.

Tollinton, H. J. (1973). Initial expectations and outcome. *British Journal of Medical Psychology, 46,* 251–257.

Tomlinson, T. M., & Stoler, N. (1967). The relationship between affective evaluation and ratings of therapy process and outcome with schizophrenics. *Psychotherapy: Theory, Research, and Practice, 4,* 14–18.

Tracey, T. J. (1986). Interactional correlates of premature termination. *Journal of Consulting and Clinical Psychology, 54,* 784–788.

Truax, C. B., Tunnell, B. T., Jr., Fine, H. L., & Wargo, D. G. (1966). *The prediction of client outcome during group psychotherapy from measures of initial status.* Unpublished manuscript. University of Arkansas, Arkansas Rehabilitation Research and Training Center, Fayetteville.

Uhlenhuth, E. H., & Duncan, D. B. (1968). *Subjective change in psychoneurotic outpatients with medical students. II. The kind, amount, and course of change.* Unpublished manuscript, The Johns Hopkins University, Baltimore.

Vail, A. (1978). Factors influencing lower class black patients remaining in treatment. *Journal of Consulting and Clinical Psychology, 46,* 341.

Vaillant, G. E. (1972). Why men seek psychotherapy. I: Results of a survey of college graduates. *American Journal of Psychiatry, 129,* 645–651.

Walters, G. C., Solomon, G. S., & Walden, V. R. (1982). Use of the MMPI in predicting persistence in groups of male and female outpatients. *Journal of Clinical Psychology, 38,* 80–83.

Warren, N. C., & Rice, L. N. (1972). Structuring and stabilizing of psychotherapy for low-prognosis clients. *Journal of Consulting and Clinical Psychology, 39,* 173–181.

Warren, R. C., Jackson, A. M., Nugaris, J., & Farley, G. K. (1973). Differential attitudes of black and white patients toward treatment in a child guidance clinic. *American Journal of Orthopsychiatry, 43,* 384–393.

Weber, J. J., Bachrach, H. M., & Solomon, M. (1985). Factors associated with the outcome of psychoanalysis: Report of the Columbia Psychoanalytic Center Research Project (II). *International Review of Psychoanalysis, 12,* 127–141.

Weber, J. J., Solomon, M., & Bachrach, H. M. (1985). Characteristics of psychoanalytic clinic patients: Report of the Columbia Psychoanalytic Center Research Project (I). *International Review of Psychoanalysis, 12,* 13–26.

Weighill, V. E., Hodge, J., & Peck, D. F. (1983). Keeping appointments with clinical psychologists. *The British Journal of Clinical Psychology, 22,* 143–144.

Weiss, S. L., & Dlugokinski, E. L. (1974). Parental expectations of psychotherapy. *Journal of Psychology, 86,* 71–80.

Weiss, J., & Schaie, K. W. (1958). Factors in patient failure to return to clinic. *Diseases of the Nervous System, 19,* 429–430.

Weissman, M. M., Geanakapolas, E., & Prusoff, B. (1973). Social class and attrition in depressed outpatients. *Social Casework, 54,* 162–170.

Weisz, J. R., Weiss, B., & Langmeyer, D. B. (1987). Giving up on child psychotherapy: Who drops out? *Journal of Consulting and Clinical Psychology, 55,* 916–918.

Weisz, J. R., Weiss, B., & Langmeyer, D. B. (1989). On dropouts and refusers in child psychotherapy: Reply to Garfield. *Journal of Consulting and Clinical Psychology, 57,* 170–171.

Wilkins, W. (1971). Desensitization: Social and cognitive factors underlying the effectiveness of Wolpe's procedure. *Psychological Bulletin, 76,* 311–317.

Wilkins, W. (1973). Expectancy of therapeutic gain: An empirical and conceptual critique. *Journal of Consulting and Clinical Psychology, 40,* 69–77.

Wilkins, W. (1979). Expectancies in therapy research: Discriminating among heterogeneous nonspecifics. *Journal of Consulting and Clinical Psychology, 47,* 837–845.

Wilson, G. T., & Thomas, M. G. W. (1973). Self- versus drug-produced relaxation and the effects of instructional set in standardized systematic sensitization. *Behavior Research & Therapy, 11,* 279–288.

Wolff, W. M. (1967). Psychotherapeutic persistence. *Journal of Consulting Psychology, 31,* 429.

Yalom, I. D. (1966). A study of group therapy dropouts. *Archives of General Psychiatry, 14,* 393–414.

Yalom, I. D., Houts, P. S., Newell, G., & Rand, K. H. (1967). Preparation of patients for group therapy. *Archives of General Psychiatry, 17,* 416–427.

Yamamoto, J., & Goin, M. K. (1966). Social class factors relevant for psychiatric treatment. *Journal of Nervous and Mental Disease, 142,* 332–339.

Yamamota, J., James, Q. C., & Palley, N. (1968). Cultural problems in psychiatric therapy. *Archives of General Psychiatry, 19,* 45–49.

Yoken, C., & Berman, J. S. (1987). Third-party payment and the outcome of psychotherapy. *Journal of Consulting and Clinical Psychology, 55,* 571–576.

7

THERAPIST VARIABLES

- **LARRY E. BEUTLER**
  University of California, Santa Barbara

- **PAULO P. P. MACHADO**
  University of California, Santa Barbara

- **SUSAN ALLSTETTER NEUFELDT**
  University of California, Santa Barbara

Therapist qualities are among the most frequently studied contributors to psychotherapeutic change. Researchers and clinicians alike have been unyielding in their belief that characteristics of therapists are associated with or predictive of psychotherapy outcome. On one hand, these views are supported by three related observations: (1) In statistical analyses, magnitude of benefit is more closely associated with the identity of the therapist than with the type of psychotherapy that the therapist practices (Crits-Christoph & Mintz, 1991; Luborsky et al., 1986); (2) some therapists in all therapeutic approaches produce consistently more positive effects than others (Lambert, 1989; Luborsky et al., 1986; Luborsky, Woody, McLellan, O'Brien, & Rosenzweig, 1982; Orlinsky & Howard, 1980); and (3) some therapists produce consistently negative effects (Lafferty, Beutler, & Crago, 1989; Orlinsky & Howard, 1980).

On the other hand, efforts to identify the therapist attributes that account for these systematic variations have often been unproductive. This is probably because therapist characteristics interact in complex ways with characteristics of the client, the situation, and the type of therapy practiced (see Lyons & Howard, 1991, for a review of the statistical implications of these complexities). As we discover more about the contributors to effective psychotherapy, it becomes increasingly difficult, and more than a little impractical, to separate therapist

Partial support for writing this chapter was provided by NIAAA grant No. AA 08970, awarded to the first author. The authors also wish to thank Maria Guiterrez for her assistance in preparing this chapter.

variables from other contributors to psychotherapy outcome. Yet, in the service of clarity, it is both conventional and convenient to distinguish among these contributors when evaluating the current state of knowledge. While the material presented in this chapter necessarily overlaps with the chapters in this book on client and process variables, our specific objectives are to

1. Define the major dimensions that affect therapeutic outcome and on which therapists differ.

2. Identify some of the major conceptual and methodological issues that affect the translation of research to clinical practice.

3. Summarize the status of therapist contributors to therapeutic efficacy, including data on how these factors interact with patient or client qualities.

OVERVIEW

The body of literature on therapist characteristics is too extensive to allow comprehensive and exhaustive coverage in a single chapter. Moreover, doing so would be unlikely to yield clear conclusions both because the time period covered by this literature has seen dramatic changes in therapist roles and theories and because there are tremendous variations in the outcomes addressed, the nature of the treatments utilized, and the sophistication of the research designs employed. Hence, we have imposed certain limitations on the current review in order to ensure that the best available research is represented and that the conclusions reached reflect the most current findings.

First, we have chosen to concentrate on research accumulating since 1985, with a more limited review extending to 1980 and before. We include landmark studies from previous decades, especially when it is apparent that more recent research has introduced substantial changes in the conclusions reached in earlier editions of the *Handbook*. We believe that this decision best serves our intentions of both providing a contemporary view of the field and giving due consideration to the historical development of research methods and results.

Second, we emphasize studies that address clinical outcomes, usually symptoms that are measured either at the end of treatment or at the end of a posttreatment follow-up. Only in those areas where outcome studies are limited or unavailable will we include studies that have used, as dependent variables, within-session and end-of-session changes, variables that are relevant only to certain theories, and constructs whose relationship to clinical functioning is uncertain.

Third, we devote little space to reviews of subject or procedural analogue studies. That is, for the most part, we do not give in-depth consideration to studies of nonclinical samples of therapists and clients, or to those that do not assess actual clinical procedures. When nonanalogue studies are not available, however, we seek to find a pattern of results among studies in which nonclinical groups are used to represent "clients," where naive students or paraprofessionals are used to represent therapists, and where enactments of psychotherapy are used to represent therapeutic procedures.

Finally, we give preference in our review to studies that have employed either experimental or quasi-experimental designs (Kazdin, 1991) on clinical samples of therapists and clients. As in earlier editions of the *Handbook*, we include in our review naturalistic studies (those that did not employ systematic comparisons and controlled assignment of subjects) that we judge to represent unusually important and/or consistent findings. Such studies also are included when (1) those based upon experimental and quasi-experimental methods are not available and (2) the designs used are especially appropriate and sound. We do this because naturalistic studies allow the most direct generalization of findings to clinical practice and because they frequently include larger samples of clients and therapists than do more controlled studies.

Studies representing a fourth set of methodologies will also be incorporated into the current review in order to ensure that our conclusions are sensitive to the history of research in each area. Over the past decade, meta-analysis has evolved as a set of statistical procedures for extracting meaning from collections of separately conducted studies. In meta-analysis, the magnitude of the relationship existing between variables is reported as an effect size (ES). Effect sizes are typically reported in terms of one of two statistical metrics. The more conventional, or Cohen's *d* statistic, expresses the difference between groups as a proportion of a standard deviation. The *d* method is easily understood when two discrete groups (e.g., two types of psychotherapy) are being compared. However, it makes less sense when the therapist variable, whose effect on psychotherapy outcome is being assessed, is not a categorical one. If one assesses

the relationship between years of experience and effectiveness of psychotherapy using only one group of therapists, for example, it makes more sense to express the findings as a correlation (r) than as a proportion of a standard deviation. Hence, a correlation is the second statistical metric that is conventionally used to report an ES.

The *d* and *r* statistics that are used in reporting ESs are not equivalent to one another. For example, *d* can range to 4.0 or more while *r* ranges only between -1.0 and $+1.0$. Likewise, *r*s can be added and subtracted under some circumstances while *d*s cannot. Since most therapist variables are studied as continuous qualities of therapists, in the current chapter we will use *r* as the standard metric for reporting effect size.[1] Where appropriate and in order to maintain consistency, when other authors report ESs in the form of Cohen's *d*, we will convert these results to *r*s before we report them, using the following formula:

$$r = \frac{\sqrt{d^2}}{\sqrt{d^2 + (1/n_1 + 1/n_2)\,(n_1 + n_2) - 2}}$$

where

n_1 = the mean sample size for the treatment group

n_2 = the mean sample size for the control or comparison group

d^2 = the square of Cohen's *d*.

We begin our discussion of each therapist variable considered in this chapter by summarizing the conclusions that have been published in one or more comprehensive literature reviews on the topic. We then summarize the results from the most rigorously conducted contemporary research and illustrate some of these studies. Through a selective analysis of individual studies that meet the limiting criteria of inclusion described in the foregoing paragraphs, we attempt to distill an understanding of therapist effects.

In our initial review of each variable, we give priority to literature reviews that have been based on meta-analytic procedures and include empirically derived estimates of effect size. This will allow

[1]The use of *r* as an effect size has several advantages over other statistics. Most notably, it can be used for the direct comparison of variables. It can be added and subtracted, and through translation to Fisher's *z* to be averaged, tested for differences, and so on (Rosenthal, 1984). The authors wish to thank Dr. Jeffrey Berman for his assistance in selecting and defining the appropriate statistic to use in the current context. His consultation throughout is appreciated.

us to compare the strength of the different therapist variables as we summarize our findings at the end of the chapter.

A TAXONOMY OF THERAPIST VARIABLES

Most of the major therapist characteristics that have been studied fall along two dimensions (Beutler, Crago, & Arizmendi, 1986). The first dimension represents a dichotomy of externally observed versus inferred qualities and the second represents a bifurcated separation of general or cross-situational qualities and qualities that are specific to the therapy setting. This categorization scheme is presented in Figure 7.1. "Objective" qualities are those that can be observed by an external rater without benefit of therapist self-report. In contrast, "subjective" qualities cannot be assessed meaningfully without benefit of self-report. These represent internal qualities of the therapist, and their presence can only be inferred.

The second dimension differentiates therapist "cross-situational traits" from "therapy-specific states." Cross-situational therapist traits are enduring qualities that supersede the therapy relationship and are not subject to rapid, volitional change by the therapist. On the other hand, therapy-specific states are systematically developed through training for the purpose of enhancing psychotherapy outcomes. Traits endure, while states may change. However, some states are more enduring than others. Theoretical preferences, for example, are quite complex and are likely to be closely interwoven with life attitudes generally. Nonetheless, these beliefs are considered to be states in the current context because they are acquired intentionally during training and their relevance is specific to the domain of psychotherapy.

OBJECTIVE, CROSS-SITUATIONAL TRAITS

Objective, cross-situational traits consist of the demographic qualities that therapists bring to the treatment setting. Historically, these were some of the first therapist variables to which researchers looked in their quest for predictors and correlates of treatment outcome. Among the variables of age, sex, and ethnicity, therapist age has consistently received the least study and therapist sex has received the greatest amount of empirical support. Even though these variables have been widely studied historically, a search for recent empirical reports suggests that there has been less and less effort directed to the study of therapist demographics in recent years. This may well be because their study has historically yielded so little benefit in so far as treatment outcome is concerned and because interest in them has given way to a study

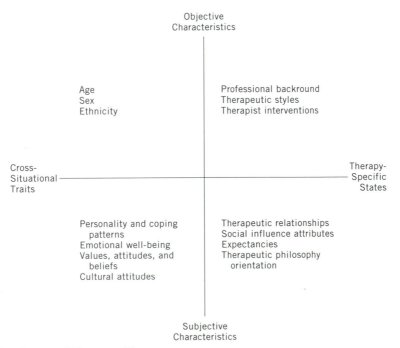

FIGURE 7.1 Classification of Therapist Characteristics.

of more complex variables of which demographics are only a part.

Age

Most research on therapist age has either employed naturalistic designs or focused on aspects of treatment process qualities, rather than outcomes, as the dependent variables. This places such research outside the priorities defined for the current review. Perhaps the weak relationships that characterize the findings from research in this area can partially be attributed to the inevitable confounding of variables that is inherent to this type of research methodology. Under the best of circumstances, for example, therapist age is at least partially confounded with both level of experience and theoretical orientation, at least to the degree that one's orientation is reflected in the theories that are in vogue at the time one is trained. To complicate this problem, age has seldom been the a priori focus of study and has become the topic of focus only after analysis of the variables that are of most interest to the investigators has been exhausted. Such concerns have not deterred researchers from studying other, equally confounded variables, such as experience and training levels, however, and one wonders why therapist age has been so neglected as a primary topic of investigation in an aging society.

Since meta-analytic studies of age are notably absent from the body of research, a historical perspective on the role of therapist age is available only through general literature reviews that have included this variable as one of several that are given attention. These reviews almost uniformly conclude that therapist age bears little relationship to outcome (e.g., Sexton & Whiston, 1991).

Unfortunately, the strength of empirically based conclusions regarding the relationship between therapist age and effectiveness rests with uncontrolled, naturalistic studies. Ordinarily, such methods are too weak to detect small but meaningful relationships. Hence, it is not surprising that most studies of this type have failed to find therapist age, by itself, to be significantly related either to the efficacy of psychotherapy or to early treatment dropout (Beck, 1988; Greenspan & Kulish, 1985).

Likewise, studies that have sought to determine if therapist age interacts with client age to jointly affect outcome have often been inconclusive. In an extensive review of research on therapist–client similarities, Atkinson and Schein (1986), for example, found no studies that reported a positive relationship between the degree of age similarity and outcome. On the other hand, there are several studies that were not included in this review that do suggest the presence of a modest relationship between age similarity and treatment benefit (e.g., Luborsky, et al., 1980; Morgan, Luborsky, Crits-Christoph, Curtis, & Solomon, 1982). In one of the more carefully controlled investigations of this type, Dembo, Ikle, and Ciarlo (1983) found that clients aged 18 to 30 whose therapists' ages were within the same age range experienced less distress and social isolation after treatment than did clients whose therapists were 10 or more years either older or younger than they.

A slightly different conclusion was reached by Beck (1988) from a correlational analysis of 17 branches of the Family Service Agencies of America. Therapists who were more than 10 years *younger* than their clients obtained the poorest outcomes when compared to those whose age was either similar or older than their clients'. This latter study investigated nearly 250 therapists and over 1,500 clients, and unlike many studies of demographic qualities, therapists within the middle-age groups were well represented (mean age = 40 years). With samples of this size and type, small differences should have been detectable. With the exception of termination status, however, the outcome data were solely client self-report. Moreover, most therapists (97%) held subdoctoral degrees. These methodological constraints limit the comparability to other studies that have utilized a broader range of outcome data and therapists with more advanced levels of training.

Indirect evidence that the amount of difference between therapist and client ages is a weak predictor of outcome also arises from clinical trials studies of aging adults, children, and adolescents. While this research does not typically report actual therapist–client age differences, ordinarily one can safely assume that therapists are significantly younger than their clients in samples of post–age 65 adults, and older than those who are pubescent or younger. Research on manualized therapies within these populations suggests that therapists can be quite successful when treating clients who are older than they (e.g., Beutler et al., 1987; Thompson and Gallagher, 1984; Thompson, Gallagher, & Breckenridge, 1987) and when treating clients who are younger than they (e.g., Weisz, Weiss, Alicke, & Klotz, 1987).

Notably, the promising relationships between age similarity and various therapeutic processes that have been found in some studies (e.g., Luborsky, Crits-Christoph, Alexander, Margolis, & Cohen, 1983; see review by Beutler et al., 1986) have not been pursued in recent years. Given the increasing attention that must be given to client age in aging Western societies in the next decade, more research on these relationships is needed.

Sex

The seminal work of Billingsley (1977) stimulated concerns that a male-oriented bias dominated the attitudes of psychotherapists and that this bias tended to victimize and disempower female clients (Cooke & Kipnis, 1986; Kaplan, 1985). In spite of the extensive attention that this suggestion has received in popular and clinical literature, few studies have incorporated the methodological controls that are necessary to determine if therapist sex is as important as this sociopolitical literature suggests. Research on the topic has been largely confined to naturalistic studies in which the relationship between therapist sex and outcome has been studied as one of several variables that supplement discussion of topics that are of greater interest to the investigators.

Most reviews of research on the topic (e.g., Atkinson & Schein, 1986) have failed to support the concern that male therapists may inhibit the progress of female clients. Extrapolating from both process research and naturalistic studies of outcome, for example, Beutler et al. (1986) found only very limited support for the possibility that, among female clients, some benefits accrue in favor of female therapists. However, only 5 of the 19 studies reviewed included a direct measure of outcome. None of these latter studies revealed direct evidence of female therapists' superiority. Unfortunately, the naturalistic methods that were utilized in these studies failed to control for the possibility that male and female therapists draw from different referral sources and utilize different methods of treatment.

In a study that is marked by its contrast to the naturalistic methods used by most investigations of therapist sex, Jones, Krupnick, and Kerig (1987) compared posttreatment outcome and satisfaction levels of 60 women who were assigned to one of 11 male or 14 female therapists. This quasi-experimental study included the use of a manualized brief treatment, equivalently trained and experienced therapists, monitoring of therapist procedures, random assignment of clients to therapists, equivalent distribution of client severity, and the use of carefully selected outcome measures. These features reduced the possibility of confounding effects associated with referral patterns, skill levels, experience, and intervention methods.

The results indicated that greater symptomatic improvement, both at treatment's end and several months later, occurred among those clients whose therapists were female. Unfortunately, the absence of a male client sample prevented a determination of whether this result reflected a general superiority of female therapists. Nonetheless, these results are similar to those reached in a tightly controlled naturalistic study of female patients by Orlinsky and Howard (1980) and parallel the self-rated success rates of male and female therapists reported by Jones and Zoppel (1982).

However, Jones and Zoppel failed to replicate their findings when they used patient reports of outcome instead of therapist reports. This finding emphasizes the value of the efforts made by Jones et al. (1987) to obtain a variety of standard and reliable outcome measures. Indeed, as a general rule, naturalistic studies have not yielded findings that are as clear-cut as those reported by Jones and his group. For example, in her naturalistic study of over 1,500 clients and 244 therapists, representing both sexes, Beck (1988) failed to find significant differences in reported benefits that were attributable to therapist sex. Likewise, neither a post hoc comparison of archival data by Sexton and Whiston (1991), two studies of changes in self-esteem in short-term counseling (Berry & Sipps, 1991; Wiggins & Giles, 1984), nor a naturalistic comparison of 63 psychiatric outpatients (Hunt, Carr, Dagodakis, & Walker, 1985) found differences in outcome when including analyses of both therapist and client sex.

While none of these latter studies provide support for either sex of therapist or therapist–client matching effects on treatment outcomes, Beck (1988) found a significant tendency for both the most effective male and the least effective female therapists to leave the public agencies studied. Hence, the nonsignificant effects of therapist sex reported in naturalistic studies that do not control for therapist skill levels may reflect a differential "skill drain" of males and females from institutional environments. Beyond this, Beck's findings have implications for the maintenance of competency within service delivery institutions.

In spite of the weak and largely negative conclusions that come from these studies, more research on therapy outcome as a function of therapist–client sex matching should be encouraged for two reasons. First, the contrasting nature of the quasi-experimental findings of Jones et al. (1987) and the naturalistic findings of others emphasizes the possibility that therapist skill, client factors, unequal distribution of cases, and selective assignment in naturalistic studies may have masked important results. There is a need to replicate Jones et al.'s findings in order to clarify these issues and to extend the methodology to include male client groups.

Second, the social importance ascribed to the power differential that is thought to exist between male therapists and female clients demands that the effects of therapist sex be clearly understood. The importance of these sociopolitical concerns is increased all the more because there is accumulating survey evidence that male therapists receive more training in and report greater preferences for the use of directive and controlling procedures than do female therapists (Nelson & Holloway, 1990; Norcross & Wogan, 1983; Wogan & Norcross, 1985). The emphasis upon directive control by the supervisors of male therapists may parallel those socialization processes of children that provide greater power of abuse to men than to women (see Lytton & Romney, 1991).

Ethnicity

Research on therapist ethnicity parallels that on therapist sex. It is a topic that has many sociopolitical implications, and yet, outcome studies are still conspicuously absent in psychotherapy research literature. Most research in this area addresses the role of ethnicity on clinician attractiveness (e.g., Atkinson & Matsushita, 1991) or on clinical judgment (e.g., Lopez & Hernandez, 1987; Malgady, Rogler, & Costantino, 1987; Pavkov, Lewis, & Lyons, 1989). Nonetheless, the opinion has abounded that both ethnic similarity (e.g., Hall & Malony, 1983) and, more generally, ethnic sensitivity of the therapist (e.g., Leong, 1986; Ridley, 1984; Sue, 1990; Turner & Armstrong, 1981) enhance the efficacy of psychotherapy. This opinion has received only limited support from psychotherapy research, however.

For example, four overlapping reviews (Atkinson, 1983, 1985; Atkinson & Schein, 1986; Sexton & Whiston, 1991) have all concluded that the effect of client–therapist ethnic similarity on outcome is equivocal. Noting that research in this area is comprised of an amalgamation of analogue studies, investigations of therapist preferences, and assessments of single-session outcomes, Atkinson (1985) reanalyzed the studies previously reviewed by Sattler (1977), Harrison (1975), and Atkinson (1983). He grouped studies according to which of seven dependent variables were used: patterns of service usage, client preferences for therapists, stereotyping clients, diagnostic bias, psychotherapy process variables, selection of therapeutic procedures, and client outcomes. Atkinson (1985; also see Atkinson & Schein, 1986) concluded that even the preferences that African-American clients have for ethnically similar therapists is not evident among other minority groups. The studies, which addressed qualitative aspects of outcome, were equally divided between those that demonstrated no effect of ethnic matching and those that favored ethnic similarity.

Controlled assignment (quasi-experimental) studies are curiously missing in the literature on therapist ethnicity. Most studies continue to reflect supplementary analyses of larger projects, employing archival and other naturalistic designs and mixed groups of ethnic samples. Such studies either fail to differentiate among African-American, Hispanic, Asian, and other groups (e.g., Neimeyer & Gonzales, 1983) or fail to include an adequate number of ethnically identified therapists (e.g., Proctor & Rosen, 1981) to allow a full comparison of the permutations of matching dimensions.

In the absence of more rigorously controlled investigations, the results of two large-sample, naturalistic studies are notable. In a carefully conceived retrospective study, Jones (1982) provided data on 164 clients, equally representing African-American and white ethnic groups, and 136 (less evenly distributed) ethnically diverse therapists. Utilizing empirical measures of symptomatic change and satisfaction, Jones concluded that psychotherapy outcome was not significantly affected by either therapist ethnicity or client–therapist ethnic similarity.

Beck (1988) studied both African-American, white, and Hispanic client–counselor pairs in her study of nearly 1,500 clients and 244 subdoctoral counselors. Among Hispanic pairs, she found that ethnically similar dyads were associated with higher client satisfaction rates than ethnically dissimilar pairs. On the other hand, among African Americans, client–counselor ethnic similarity was not related to client satisfaction. However, Beck notes that relatively few African-American therapists were represented in these latter samples.

Among the naturalistic studies of therapy outcome, only dropout rate appears to be consistently and negatively affected when the therapist and client come from different backgrounds. Several studies (e.g., Krebs, 1971; Terrell & Terrell, 1984; Yamamoto, James, Bloombaum, & Hattem, 1967) have suggested that dropout rates increase among ethnic minority clients whose therapists are white. Atkinson (1983; Atkinson & Schein, 1986) also observed this pattern among the studies that he reviewed.

Any interpretation of data on therapist–client ethnic similarity must keep in mind that minority clients do not tend to seek out or use traditional mental health services (Atkinson, 1983; Hough et al., 1987; Taube, Goldman, Burns, & Kessler, 1988). Those who do use conventional services may be uncharacteristically susceptible to the views of the majority culture, including those of middle-class therapists. Even further and to reiterate a caution expressed by Abramowitz and Murray (1983), conclusions based on historical reviews of the literature regarding the role of ethnic similarity in treatment outcome may be dependent on the ethnic identity of the reviewer. A systematic compilation of research in this area using the statistical procedures of meta-analysis might reduce some of the sources of potential bias in these reports and clarify this picture.

SUBJECTIVE, CROSS-SITUATIONAL TRAITS

Enduring, subjective therapist traits include personality and coping patterns, emotional well-being, values and beliefs, and cultural attitudes. Because these factors are both internal to the therapist and dependent upon client perceptions for effect, it is conceptually possible to implement true experimental designs in order to study them. This could be done by adjusting the ways in which therapists are described to potential clients. Indeed, while still the exception to the norm, some excellent research is emerging in this area that developed creative ways to implement experimental studies of therapist variables. These studies have yielded some very promising and interesting findings.

Personality and Coping Patterns

Theorists have posed the existence of a very wide array of "personality" dimensions, but these are frequently overlapping. Many are of uncertain interest to psychotherapy. Others have been proposed as client, not as therapist, qualities; and still others are too abstract to be testable or are discounted by psychotherapy researchers because there is no psychometrically sound method for measuring them. As a result, the large number of personality descriptors that one finds in the theoretical literature on psychopathology and psychotherapy contrasts sharply with the small number of variables that have been applied to research on psychotherapists. Very few subjective therapist traits have accumulated a sufficient body of research data to assess their importance adequately.

Research on therapist personality traits is of two major types: (1) empirically driven studies that correlate a loosely related set of personality measures to indices of change, and (2) theory-driven studies that correlate theoretically derived concepts with change. Empirically driven studies focus on specific measurement procedures, are driven by prior empirical findings, and seek patterns of correlations between multidimensional personality variables and outcomes. In contrast, theory-driven studies focus on theoretically derived constructs and seek to test a priori hypotheses.

Early attempts to apply empirical methods to psychotherapy yielded some initially promising results, from time to time, but subsequent research efforts to cross-validate these dimensions were often quite disappointing (e.g., Carson & Heine, 1962; Carson & Llewellyn, 1966). The task of selecting valuable therapist personality dimensions

from among the thousands that are potentially available has proven to be too great to be addressed adequately with shotgun methodologies and post hoc analyses (Beutler, 1991).

The demise of purely empirically driven efforts to find therapist correlates of outcome has been speeded by the accumulation of a large body of nonsignificant findings, many of them from well-designed quasi-experimental studies. For example, Antonuccio, Lewinsohn, and Steinmetz (1982) correlated a variety of therapist characteristics to outcomes, through post hoc analyses, in a study of over 100 depressed subjects. Patients were randomly assigned to a homogeneous type of therapy and both the experience and skill levels of the therapists were carefully controlled. Yet, none of the therapist personality traits were found to be significantly related to treatment efficacy.

The history of the A–B therapist typology exemplifies the fate of research that is purely empirically driven. The initial, serendipitous finding by Whitehorn and Betz (1960) that a pattern of therapist responses on the Strong Vocational Interest Blank predicted differential response among schizotypal and neurotic client subgroups stimulated considerable research for over 20 years. While predictions were reliable and often robust, a theory to account for the effects never evolved. As medications became more widely used for schizophrenic disorders, interest in the A–B therapist dimension has waned and research on this topic has passed into history.[2]

In contrast, if concepts have roots in theoretical descriptions of change, they tend to survive both the passage of time and the absence of consistent research support. For example, in what has been a very widely cited report of an initial study and a prospective cross-validation, Berzins (1977) demonstrated that contrasting patterns of interpersonal dependency and autonomy[3] enhanced treatment efficacy. Dependent subjects were more likely to improve if treated by autonomy-oriented therapists, while independent clients responded best to attachment-oriented therapists. The autonomy–dependency dimension noted by Berzins was quickly incorporated within a larger body of Jungian theoretical literature on interpersonal compati-

---

[2]This literature has been reviewed in previous editions of the *Handbook*. The absence of significant new research precludes detailed presentation here.

[3]It is of interest to note that while therapists and clients in this series of studies were assessed on different measures, the dimensions that proved to be of significance in predicting benefits were conceptually similar in the two groups.

bility.[4] This process demonstrates that theory-driven research allows for a more efficient selection of dimensions than purely empirical approaches and results in findings that are more believable and generalizable.

Theory-driven research has the added advantage of not being tied to specific instruments and retaining viability even when research methods change or go out of vogue. For example, over the course of years, a large number of matching studies found the Myers-Briggs Type Indicator (MBTI), based on the *circumplex*—an analysis of interpersonal interactions derived initially from Jungian theory, to be promising for predicting efficacious client–therapist matches (Mendlesohn & Geller, 1963). The MBTI has fallen out of favor among psychotherapy researchers, however. A review of the literature on the MBTI revealed relatively few systematic investigations on actual therapy populations during the previous 10 years (Carlson, 1985). In a study that is representative of the diminishing body of research in this area, Berry and Sipps (1991) explored therapist–client match on the MBTI as a predictor of termination status among counseling center students. Using a naturalistic design, these authors assessed the relative match of 9 therapists and their 55 clients on the MBTI and correlated these matching dimensions with termination status and number of sessions attended. The results generally failed to support the hypotheses that differences in personality traits associated with the MBTI circumplex (e.g., sensing vs. intuition, thinking vs. feeling, introversion vs. extraversion, judging vs. perceiving) were predictive of the type of termination or magnitude of change experienced. A global therapist factor that the authors refer to as "unconditional positive regard" (p. 121), coupled with client self-esteem, accounted for most of the observed differences in termination rate.

Although a modified and extended circumplex theory originally arising from the work of Leary (1957) continues to be viable and visible in contemporary literature, the efficacy of the MBTI for predicting outcome or accounting for therapeutic changes has not lived up to its initial billing. Contemporary researchers on the circumplex model have refined the dimensions associated with interpersonal relationships and are studying them as observable states, rather than as personality traits. Research on these qualities will be considered in later sections of this chapter.

[4]Berzins himself laid the foundation for this incorporation by interpreting the results as being supportive of Jungian theories of interpersonal compatibility.

Contemporary research on therapist personality traits is coming to focus on a few, well-defined variables. Among these, the greatest amount of attention has been paid to a cluster of traits variously identified as therapist dominance, dogmatism, locus of perceived control, and conceptual level.

Dominance and related constructs.   Dominance and dogmatism are considered, ordinarily, to be traits that inhibit therapist flexibility and bode poorly for outcome. Henry, Schacht, and Strupp (1990) supported this view in a post hoc analysis of 14 therapist–client dyads. Poor outcomes in short-term psychodynamic therapy were associated with therapists who had internalized dogmatic and controlling introjects. In view of their potentially negative effects, therefore, it may be disconcerting to note that there is evidence that graduate training programs may systematically (and successfully) encourage the development of these potentially negative qualities among graduate therapists (Zook & Sipps, 1987). On the other hand, several research studies have found the opposite results, suggesting that factors such as the nature of treatment may be a mediating variable.

McWhirter and Frey (1987) found that, contrary to their expectations, field independent (a measure of dominance) group leaders were rated more positively than field dependent leaders by participants in career counseling groups. Using a similarly indirect measure of "dominance," Tracey (1985) demonstrated that the most successful among 15 clients in a university counseling center had therapists who were relatively dominant. Likewise, Zimpfer and Waltman (1982) found that a direct measure of therapist dogmatism was also positively correlated with the expressions of warmth among adolescents in group therapy.

In a review of literature on therapist dominance as a variable in the treatment of minority clients, moreover, Hall and Malony (1983) concluded that dominant therapists are likely to function more effectively with culturally similar clients than with culturally dissimilar ones. Specifically, the authors suggest that clinicians who have low dominance needs are more effective than those with high dominance needs among clients who are ethnically different from them, but not with those who are similar to themselves.

Dimensions that are assumed to be inversely related to dominance and dogmatism, such as therapist open-mindedness and flexibility, have been found to be either unrelated (Zimpfer & Waltman, 1982) or positively related (Weinstock-Savoy, 1986) to subsequent psychotherapy processes and outcomes. Such findings suggest that therapist dogmatism, dominance, flexibility, and openness are complex, interrelated but not isomorphic concepts that may interact with yet undisclosed variables such as the type of therapy offered by the therapist.

Locus of perceived control. Therapist locus of perceived control is another variable that has received wide attention in the literature and may be related to dominance and openness (see Harvey & Weary, 1985). While the theoretical and conceptual literature abounds as applied to clinical practice (e.g., Forsterling, 1988; Snyder & Forsyth, 1991), applications of perceived control have not been widely made to efforts to understand psychotherapists. When such research has been done, it has typically involved naturalistic designs and post hoc analyses, without benefit of prospectively driven hypotheses.

For example, locus of perceived control was one of the several therapist variables studied by Antonuccio, Davis, Lewinson, and Breckenridge (1987). Their results suggested that group cohesiveness, but not outcomes, was facilitated in group treatments for depression when leaders had an external locus of perceived control. In another study, Deysach, Rooss, and Hiers (1977) found a positive relationship between internal locus of control and peer and supervisor ratings of effectiveness among nonprofessional counselors in two therapeutic camps for emotionally disturbed children.

In contrast, and also based on a naturalistic design, Foon (1985, 1986) reported that among 78 adult outpatients and 21 therapists,[5] relationships between outcomes and either initial therapist locus of control or initial similarity of client and therapist locus of perceived control were nonsignificant. However, end-of-therapy similarity of locus of control was positively associated with improvement, implying that convergence of client–therapist perceptions is a factor in achieving benefit. More research on this promising possibility as well as on the influence of initial client–therapist similarity is still warranted in view of the increasing significance of perceived control to various theories of interpersonal behavior (Bandura, 1986).

Conceptual level. Finally, therapist conceptual level (CL) has been the focus of both theoretical and empirical work over several years. A meta-analysis by Holloway and Wampold (1986) reviewed 24 studies of counseling and psychotherapy that were published since 1967. Most of these studies were both subject and situational analogue designs in which trained or untrained subjects were asked to engage in tasks that were designed to be similar to those required of a therapist in psychotherapy. Nonetheless, several interesting findings emerged. Subjects ("therapists") who had more abstract and complex cognitive processing styles were found to be more effective in learning and performing therapy-like tasks than those whose cognitive structures were relatively concrete and nondiscriminating.

A review of the specific studies reviewed by Holloway and Wampold suggests that a variety of psychotherapy processes may be enhanced by client–therapist CL similarity (e.g., Lamb, 1977; McLachlan, 1972; Stein & Stone, 1978). However, when only studies that included both therapy dyads (i.e., clients and therapists or analogue therapists and clients) and an outcome measure were analyzed, the overall effect size disappeared altogether ($r = .05$).

More recently, Hunt et al. (1985) explored the effects of cognitive style match on the Interpersonal Discrimination Test among consecutive admissions to the University of Washington Psychiatric Outpatient Clinic. They found that 60 percent of the premature terminations occurred in mismatched or dissimilar dyads while only 24 percent occurred in dyads with similar cognitive styles. Among clients who continued therapy, at the end of 12 weeks of treatment, similar dyads were associated with more symptomatic changes than dissimilar dyads. The groups were not distinguished by the end of 24 weeks of therapy, however, largely because the mismatched or dissimilar group had caught up to the similar group. These findings suggest that similarity of cognitive style and level may facilitate retention in therapy and speedier improvement in the early sessions of therapy.

Emotional Well-Being

Research on therapist well-being has largely been of two types: (1) studies of therapist level of disturbance, and (2) studies of therapists who have and have not received personal psychotherapy. Both of these lines of research have relied heavily on naturalistic comparisons, but they warrant separate consideration because they have different implications for the role of therapist mental health.

Disturbance/distress. Levels of personal distress, aspects of self-concept, severity of symptomatology, and strength of self-confidence have all

---

[5]Foon does not cross-cite these two articles. An inspection of sampling methods, nature of subjects, and therapist samples, however, suggests that the two articles were based on the same data pool. Hence, they are reported here as duplicate findings from a single study rather than as findings from two separate and independent studies.

served as indices of therapist well-being and adjustment in studies of therapist efficacy. Reviews of this literature have been consistent in concluding that therapist level of adjustment is related to good treatment outcomes. For example, Beutler et al. (1986) reviewed 10 empirical studies of process and outcome, all but one of which indicated the value of therapist well-being. Likewise, Lambert and Bergin (1983) concluded that therapist emotional health facilitates treatment outcome and, conversely, that therapists who lack emotional well-being inhibit client progress.

The specific studies that comprise these reviews have pointed to the presence of inconsistent and disrupted skill that occurs when the therapist's own conflicts are activated while he or she is conducting psychotherapy (Bergin & Jasper, 1969; Cutler, 1958; Donner & Schonfield, 1975). Unfortunately, these reviews have included only a limited number of studies that have actually assessed the effect of therapist distress on therapy outcome (e.g., Garfield & Bergin, 1971; VandenBos & Karon, 1971). However, recent quasi-experimental studies have further supported these naturalistic findings. Luborsky, McLellan, Woody, O'Brien, and Auerbach (1985) found that a composite index of therapist personal adjustment correlated positively with overall effectiveness. Using a similar methodology, Williams and Chambless (1990) found that clients who judged their therapist to have high levels of self-confidence, a variable that is probably associated with the subjective sense of well-being, were among the most likely to improve.

Of particular interest, recent studies have suggested that high therapist distress or disturbance levels may not only prevent client growth, but actually induce negative changes. Using a naturalistic design, Wiggins and Giles (1984), for example, found that even adolescent clients who had relatively healthy levels of self-esteem initially lost self-confidence when treated by low self-esteem therapists.

While it is tempting to conclude that therapist adjustment should be a factor in the selection of trainees and a focus of training in psychotherapy, it should be pointed out that not all studies have reached equally consistent conclusions. Using naturalistic designs, several studies have found nonsignificant relationships between client outcomes and such indicators of therapist well-being levels as neuroticism (Antonuccio et al., 1982; Lafferty et al., 1989), therapist self-esteem (Wiggins & Giles, 1984), stressful life events (Greenspan & Kulish, 1985), and burnout (Beck, 1988). One study (Luborsky et al., 1980) even observed that a measure of discrepancy between perceived self- and ideal self-concepts (an indication that therapists were not

self-actualized from the viewpoint of client-centered theory) was *positively* related to composite measures of benefit in long-term psychotherapy—conflicted therapists do better than consistent ones. While nonsignificant findings in studies may reflect low statistical power to detect actual differences, these latter findings are harder to understand.

As a side note, research suggests that one advantage to manualizing psychotherapies may be that imposing this type of structure attenuates the deleterious effects of therapist distress levels. When therapists follow treatment manuals, they obtain more consistent results and fewer negative effects than when they do not (Henry, Schacht, Strupp, Butler, & Binder, 1993; Piper, Azim, McCallum, & Joyce, 1990). This finding suggests that manualizing psychotherapies may provide some protection against the negative effects of therapist inconsistency induced by therapist distress.

While one can currently conclude only that therapist mental health may be an important but not necessary condition for improvement in high-functioning clients, the possibility that emotional problems on the part of the therapist may negatively affect even relatively well-functioning clients should be given considerably more attention. This type of finding has significant implications for the next topic, the role of psychotherapy for therapists.

Personal therapy. Therapists have long held the belief that personal psychotherapy facilitates their clinical effectiveness (e.g., Buckley, Karasu, & Charles, 1981; Prochaska & Norcross, 1983) and inhibits burnout (Farber, 1983). These beliefs have supported the incorporation of personal psychotherapy as part of training activities, a point of view that is strongly endorsed by psychodynamic theories. However, direct comparisons of outcome rates among therapists with differing amounts of personal therapy do not yield results that can be comfortably interpreted either as support for or evidence against its importance for therapist efficacy.

The absence of a clear relationship between personal therapy and therapist efficacy can be attributed to a variety of factors. For example, there is reasonably good reason to believe that therapists who enter personal therapy are not representative of psychotherapists in general. A survey of nearly 750 practicing psychotherapists revealed, for example, that those who were likely to seek therapy either during their training experience or subsequent to it were dominantly psychoanalytic in orientation (Guy, Stark, & Poelstra, 1988). Another survey (Norcross & Prochaska, 1986), moreover, indicated that these therapists were also more inclined to self-inspection and self-blame than those who did not seek personal therapy.

Likewise, therapists who do enter personal therapy do so for many different reasons, some in order to correct problems or cope with stressful life events (Norcross & Prochaska, 1986) and others for purposes of self-discovery or for the prevention of burnout. Functioning in the role of therapist induces stress and even serious disturbance among many psychotherapists (Guy & Liaboe, 1986), and psychotherapy may be helpful in ameliorating these effects. Thus, Guy et al. (1988) found that the decision to enter personal therapy was a positive function of how many hours per week one spent in the role of therapist. While psychotherapy may be especially encouraged as a preventive measure, it should be noted that some special consideration must be given to the possibility that while one is engaged in intensive self-exploration, therapeutic skills and effectiveness may suffer (e.g., Buckley et al., 1981).

Given the many reasons and factors that enter into the decision to enter psychotherapy, it is not surprising that the two overlapping reviews of literature published to date on the relationship between effectiveness and personal therapy for psychotherapists (Clark, 1986; Greenberg & Staller, 1981) are inconclusive. Of all the studies reviewed (11 in both reviews), only two (Guild, 1969; Kernberg, 1973) supported the proposition that therapy efficacy was better among therapists who had received previous therapy. Unfortunately, one of these studies (Kernberg, 1973) did not factor out the effects of therapist experience. In this study, experienced therapists who had completed personal analysis were compared with inexperienced therapists who were still undergoing analysis. The other study (Guild, 1969) found that experienced, analyzed therapists had a more effective therapeutic relationship with patients than did experienced nonanalyzed therapists. However, no relationship with therapy outcome was assessed. A third study found some trends that were considered interesting, but no significant differences (Holt & Luborsky, 1958).

Seven studies in these reviews failed to show any relationship between therapy outcome and whether the therapists had or had not experienced personal therapy. And one study (Garfield & Bergin, 1971) suggested that trainee therapists who had or were receiving therapy may evoke deleterious effects among their clients. Due to the small sample size, no tests of statistical significance were performed in this latter study, thus limiting the interpretation of these findings.

Collectively, the research on therapist personal therapy suggests that one cannot equate receiving

previous psychotherapy either with initially having poor mental health or with subsequent good mental health. Like those who seek to improve themselves through continuing education programs (Brown, Leichtman, Blass, & Fleisher, 1982), those therapists who utilize psychotherapy are not necessarily the ones who need it the most. Thus, one must consider the act of receiving personal psychotherapy as an index of a correlated group of features, including personal openness, desire to avoid professional burnout, motivation, distress, life stress, sensitivity, and faith in treatment. Because the reasons for entering therapy are so diverse and the effects so varied, the role of personal therapy on efficacy remains varied, and future research on this topic may be advised to consider the reasons for entering therapy as an important variable in assessing its impact on therapeutic efficacy.

Values, Attitudes, and Beliefs
Because a psychotherapist is identified as an agent of change, and because the objects of these change efforts are, by agreement, the attitudes, beliefs, and lifestyles of clients, most of whom are distraught and potentially victimized, society has always expressed great concern with the possibility that the therapist will exert unwarranted or unwanted influence on them.

Researchers, as well, have frequently regarded psychotherapy as a process in which therapist values were a central ingredient. Reflecting on 20 years of research, for example, Frank and Frank (1991) maintain that the evidence does little to refute the early opinion of Frank (1973) that psychotherapy is a process of interpersonal persuasion in which therapist values, beliefs, and optimism serve to overcome demoralization, instill hope, and provide a believable meaning of life for clients. While most psychotherapists would agree that psychotherapy is a value-laden process, the nature of the values inherent in this process are not well understood. Worthington (1988) has thoughtfully argued that a useful distinction can be made between those values of the therapist that are inherent to the form of therapy used (what we will call *therapy values*) and the personal or idiosyncratic values of the therapist him- or herself (what we will call *therapist values*[6]). Yet, personal beliefs arising from developmental experience provide the cognitive elements that underwrite one's professional

[6]Worthington refers to these two types of values as *therapeutic* and *therapy* values, respectively. However, we have adopted the terms *therapy* and *therapist* values to differentiate between those that are embedded in the theoretical form of therapy used and those that are idiosyncratic to the particular therapist.

striving. Hence, many authors (e.g., Bergin, 1980; Beutler, Clarkin, Crago, & Bergan, 1991; Khan & Cross, 1983; Seymour, 1982) have pointed out that in practice, one's professional and personal values become so intertwined that it is virtually impossible to differentiate among them.

Bolter, Levenson, and Alvarez (1990) have demonstrated the symphonic confounding that often exists between personal and professional beliefs by the finding that therapists who prefer short-term psychotherapy over long-term therapy on theoretical grounds also have correspondingly distinctive personal values. Likewise, Seymour (1982) has illustrated how therapists' personal views about such widely diverse issues as women's roles, sexual freedom, dual careers, abortion, minority relationships and rights, religion, death, and disability may all be challenged and conveyed in the process of conducting family therapy. If one attempts to maintain a distinction between therapy and therapist values, one may be called to answer the imponderable question of which came first — the theoretical values or the personal viewpoints.

While one may question whether therapists have the extensive power implied by the many fears and the number of laws that have been devised to protect clients from therapist influence, several large-scale surveys have confirmed that psychotherapists' values do, in fact, differ in some substantial ways from those of the average citizen (Bergin & Jensen, 1989; Jensen & Bergin, 1988; Khan & Cross, 1983; Shafranske & Malony, 1990). Therapists are more permissive of sexual expression (Khan & Cross, 1983) and value autonomy, expression of feelings, and personal growth more than their clients, while they devalue submission to authority and God (Bergin & Jensen, 1989). These differences, coupled with the potential power that therapists have over clients, underline the need to evaluate the roles of therapist values on therapy outcome.

Religious beliefs.   While many, if not most, psychotherapists were raised in a religious tradition and believe that client problems frequently reflect religious conflicts or concepts, few therapists believe that religious themes are within the province of psychotherapeutic work (Bergin & Jensen, 1989; Shafranske & Malony, 1990). Religious values, from the broad perspective ordinarily studied in psychotherapy, bear an uncertain relationship either to the topics actually discussed in psychotherapy or to treatment outcome. Two studies published by Propst and her colleagues represent, by far, the most systematic research conducted to date on the topic of religious values. The unique aspects of these studies include the use of well-controlled and carefully monitored psychotherapy, homogeneous client samples, and separate analyses of therapist religiousness and the religiously based therapy.

In the first of these studies, Propst (1980) randomly assigned depressed, religious females to one of two variations of cognitive therapy, both of which were conducted by religiously oriented therapists. One manualized therapy encouraged clients to practice religiously oriented, corrective cognitions, while the other applied traditional and secular cognitive interventions. The results indicated that the religious clients in religiously oriented psychotherapy experience more symptom change than those in nonreligiously oriented psychotherapy.

Since all therapists in the foregoing study had a similar religious orientation, the results could not be attributed to therapist personal values. In order to separate the role of therapist personal values from those values inherent to the therapy, as suggested by Worthington (1988), Propst, Ostrom, Watkins, Dean, and Mashburn (1992) replicated the earlier study using nonreligious as well as religious therapists. In this study, moreover, the authors added two treatment conditions: a pastoral counseling condition to control for the common variables in therapeutic relationships, and a waiting-list control group to allow for the evaluation of clinical efficacy of the therapies.

The results indicated that religiously congruent cognitive therapy conducted by nonreligious therapists was even more effective than religiously oriented cognitive therapy conducted by religious therapists. These findings suggest that both similarity and dissimilarity of client–therapist religious values may be facilitative of therapeutic progress.

General values and attitudes.   There is little agreement on what constitutes a "value." The Rokeach Value Survey (Rokeach, 1973) embodies the definition of values and provides the measurement procedure that is most often used in research on the influence of therapist values. For example, using this instrument in a retrospective, naturalistic study of more and less effective therapy trainees, Lafferty et al. (1989) suggest that therapists who value intellectual pursuits and hard work tend to be more effective than those who place relatively more value on social and economic status. It is interesting to note that these productive values may be more characteristic of academic teachers than they are of most therapy practitioners, however (Conway, 1988).

Most of the literature on therapist values and attitudes has attended to issues of similarity with the client, rather than to the problem of identifying specific therapist values that are associated with various treatment outcomes. Concern with this topic arises from research that suggests that treatment benefit is linearly associated with the degree to which clients acquire the beliefs and values of their therapists (e.g., Hamblin, Beutler, Scogin, & Corbishley, 1988; Kelly & Strupp, 1992).

For example, six critical qualitative reviews have been conducted on this issue of value convergence (Atkinson & Schein, 1986; Beutler, 1981; Beutler & Bergan, 1991; Beutler, Clarkin et al., 1991; Kelly, 1990; Tjelveit, 1986), and all have concluded that clients tend to adopt the personal values of their therapists during the course of successful psychotherapy.

Additionally, three of the six reviews (Beutler, 1981; Kelly, 1990; Tjelveit, 1986) inspected the relationship between initial therapist–client similarity and subsequent improvement, noting that initial *dissimilarity* of client and therapist values was associated with the subsequent adoption of the therapists' values and beliefs. On the other hand, none of the six qualitative reviews reached a clear determination as to whether initial value similarity or dissimilarity is more conducive to client improvement. In his review, for example, Beutler (1981) concluded that of 21 outcome studies, 12 favored the presence of initial value similarity. The remaining studies found results that were distributed quite equally among nonsignificant, negative, and curvilinear relationships between dissimilarity and outcome.

These findings indicate that psychotherapy improvement may be enhanced by a complex pattern of similarity and dissimilarity between client and therapist belief and value systems (e.g., Beutler, Jobe, & Elkins, 1974; Cheloha, 1986). However, the specific beliefs that contribute to this value conversion process remain open to question (Tjelveit, 1986). Likewise, a review of the six most methodologically sound studies on this topic (Kelly, 1990) suggests that value conversion may be related most closely to therapist ratings of improvement. The effect is less strong for independent raters and for client ratings.

A large number of mostly naturalistic studies have now been devoted to determining if similarity in some types of values is more closely related to psychotherapy outcome than others. This research has noted that both similarities and differences in client–therapist value patterns are related to outcome. Treatment success has been found to be enhanced when clients and therapists are similar in the relative value placed upon such qualities as wisdom, honesty, intellectual pursuits, and knowledge (e.g., Arizmendi, Beutler, Shanfield, Crago, & Hagaman, 1985). A relatively larger variety of values have been found to be associated with treatment benefit if client and therapist are dissimilar, however. Client–therapist discrepancies in the value placed on personal safety (Beutler, Pollack, & Jobe, 1978), interpersonal goals of treatment (Charone, 1981), social status and friendships (Arizmendi et al., 1985; Beutler, Arizmendi, Crago, Shanfield, & Hagaman, 1983; Beutler et al., 1974) have all been found to facilitate improvement.

Observing these findings, Beutler and Clarkin (1990) have suggested that the preponderance of similarities associated with improvement reflects humanistic values that are important for maintaining social order. In contrast, the values on which differences are associated with improvement are more frequently associated with maintaining intimate involvement and may thus be more closely related to the issues that precipitate one's seeking psychotherapy. They suggest that philosophical similarities may enhance engagement in therapy while value dissimilarity around issues of social attachment and intimacy may facilitate both therapeutic movement and value "convergence." This observation is consistent with recent efforts to incorporate cultural differences into theories of client–therapist matching (Beutler & Bergan, 1991; Reid, 1989).

The observation that converging beliefs and values are associated with improvement may trouble therapists whose own values emphasize free will and self-selection. Certainly there are many weaknesses in the current array of studies that may lead one to disregard the significance of suggestions to match therapist and client values to obtain a good "fit." The methodological weaknesses in current studies include the failure to control for regression toward the mean (the tendency for extreme value scores to move toward more "normal" values), the absence of prospective research on the topic, and the fact that both the meaning and measurement of values lack consensual agreement. While it is true that conclusions from studies such as these must be made cautiously, there is a good deal of consistency to the finding of a relationship between improvement and value convergence, and this argues for researchers and clinicians alike giving careful consideration to the role that therapist values may play in the process of psychotherapy.

To clinicians who are uncomfortable with the possible unintended influence that their values may exert over clients, some comfort may be found in the observations that therapists' values are more similar than they are different from those of their clients (Beutler et al., 1978), and that religious attitudes, those on which clients and therapists are most likely to differ (Bergin, 1980), are seldom found among those that either change during treatment or contribute to improvement (Chesner & Baumeister, 1985; Houts & Graham, 1986; Hill, Howard, & Orlinsky, 1970; Howard & Orlinsky, 1972; Lewis, 1983). Even more important, evidence suggests that it is the therapist's ability to communicate within the client's value framework more than the particular values held by the therapist that contribute to client improvement (Propst, 1980; Propst et al., 1992).

Cultural Attitudes

Gender and lifestyle. The concern that therapist attitudes, both toward the roles of women and toward those who have adopted gay and lesbian lifestyles, may have negative consequences is larger than the question of whether or not client−therapist similarity is conducive to psychotherapeutic improvement. Implicit in much of the written work in this area is a suggestion that the attitudes that are conveyed by the therapist about these topics may not be beneficial for the society, even if they may not directly impede symptomatic improvement. This point is illustrated in a recent survey of practicing psychologists that concluded that many therapists who routinely provide what they assume to be effective service to gay and lesbian clients hold attitudes that may be unfavorable to these client's self-esteem (Garnets, Hancock, Cochran, Goodchilds, & Peplau, 1991).

Out of a fear that the attitudes held by Western societies are damaging to women, gays, and lesbians, some authors have proposed that it may be irresponsible for therapists who do not share the gender and/or lifestyles of their clients to serve as their therapists (see Brown, 1991; Cammaert & Larsen, 1988; Kaplan, 1985). These proposals assume that sharing the client's gender identity and lifestyle is necessary to facilitate healthy change, even though the client may be indifferent to lifestyle patterns as issues in psychotherapy. Unfortunately, while therapist lifestyle may be a cue to the presence of some shared experiences, it is likely to be an inaccurate indicator of the ability to understand the client's background. There are many differences that can exist among people within any cultural group, and the importance, to psychotherapy outcome, of shared cultural attitudes or sexual lifestyles may be overshadowed by differences in educational attitudes, religious views, attitudes toward intimate relationships, and level of general conservatism. These latter attitudes cannot be divorced from one's cultural characteristics, but neither are they isomorphic with them.

In view of the central place that cultural attitudes play in establishing standards of sociopolitical behavior, it is unfortunate that so little outcome research on shared cultural beliefs has been conducted to date. To address this issue, Smith, Glass,

and Miller (1980) assigned an index of cultural similarity to each of the 475 studies in their meta-analysis of psychotherapy outcome, based on the degree to which client and therapist samples shared a common educational, economic, and upwardly mobile history. An effect size of only .10 was obtained using this variable, suggesting that little variance in outcomes could be attributed to similarity of culturally derived attitudes. The method used by Smith et al. is only a very indirect and crude index of shared cultural and personal values, however, partially because it reflected only current status and not formative background experiences.

If the cultural attitudes of therapists, rather than the objective demographic similarities of clients and therapists, account for some portion of outcomes, one would expect that the strength of the demographic similarity effect on treatment outcome would change over time as attitudes within a culture change. To inspect this possibility, Fisher and Howard (1984) explored the changes in patterns of relationship between client and therapist sex matches and outcomes over the course of two decades, using a long-term data base from a metropolitan outpatient clinic. They determined that during the 1960s client−therapist sexual similarity was linearly and moderately related to therapeutic outcome (also see Orlinsky & Howard, 1980), but that this effect became more complex and weaker with the ensuing decade, during which time sexual attitudes were undergoing considerable change within the culture.

These findings are complemented by research on lifestyle similarities. In a selective review of literature on the treatment of lesbian clients and mixed therapists, Cantor (1991) determined that feminist therapists may be more likely to relate effectively than traditional therapists to the concerns of their clients. In one of the few studies on this topic that actually attended to psychotherapy benefit, Brooks (1981) found that a large percentage of lesbian clients who reported having achieved poor effects in therapy indicated that they had received psychotherapy from heterosexual males. While such retrospective results as these latter ones are subject to a host of biases and distortions, there have been a number of more carefully controlled naturalistic studies that have indicated that, regardless of gender orientation or biological sex, therapists who hold nontraditional views of female roles promote more beneficial change and satisfaction among female clients than those who hold traditional gender views (e.g., Banikiotes & Merluzzi, 1981; Hart, 1981).

These latter findings have led some to consider the role of androgyny (e.g., Merluzzi & Merluzzi, 1981; Petry & Thomas, 1986) as a potentially beneficial quality of psychotherapists. Unfortunately, controlled research has yet to be conducted on this variable, and many authors have raised arguments against it on methodological grounds (e.g., Gilbert, 1981; Taylor & Hall, 1982; Zeldow, 1982).

Socioeconomic background. In addition to gender attitudes, therapist socioeconomic (SES) background is another but more remote index of cultural attitudes. The significance of this factor is illustrated by Cline (1984), who observed the therapy interactions of middle- and lower-class couples and their therapists. He found that among distressed couples, social class similarity to therapists may be a more important determiner of therapy-relevant behaviors and outcomes than client sex. In explaining such findings, Zimpfer and Waltman (1982) suggest that therapists from low SES backgrounds may have developed more accepting attitudes toward deviance than those from middle- and upper-SES families. However, based on an overview of the few studies available in this area, Sexton and Whiston (1991) reported that the mixed results and lack of equivalence among dependent variables preclude a conclusion regarding the relationship between therapist SES background and treatment benefits.

Most studies on therapist SES background either utilize very broad and indirect measures of this construct (e.g., Luborsky et al., 1980) or fail to evaluate outcomes (e.g., Mitchell & Atkinson, 1983; Mitchell & Namenek, 1970). Collectively, these studies suggest some promising directions for future research, but they presently are both too reliant on weak measures of outcome or attitudes and too confounded by political and research biases to serve as the basis for meaningful conclusions.

SUBJECTIVE, THERAPY-SPECIFIC STATES

Therapeutic Relationships

Rogers's (1957) conceptualizations of the "necessary and sufficient" conditions for effective psychotherapy formed the foundation for the preponderance of research on the psychotherapy relationship over three decades. Most contemporary investigators would probably agree that these facilitative qualities play a central role in therapeutic change. In clinical practice, they are equally well accepted and have been assimilated into much of contemporary theory. These variables are the ones most often considered when the topic of "common" or "shared" psychotherapy characteristics comes up. These are the qualities of the therapy relationship to which much of the therapeutic change is attributed.

Over the course of time, however, it has become apparent that the "therapist facilitative conditions" that Rogers described as qualities of the therapist are, in fact, qualities of both the client and the relationship, as well (Gurman, 1977). Considered as qualities of the relationship, rather than of the therapist, however, Rogers's facilitative conditions are very similar to contemporary, psychodynamic conceptualizations of the "working," "helping," or "therapeutic" alliance.

In the mid-1980s, Beutler et al. (1986) observed that the study of the therapeutic alliance was still in its infancy. Since then, research in this area has virtually exploded. This research has (1) developed the conceptual and operational underpinnings of the therapy relationship (e.g., Bordin, 1976; Frieswyk et al., 1986; Tichenor & Hill, 1989); (2) revealed that different methods of assessing the therapeutic relationship embody a common, reliably measured quality (Safran & Wallner, 1991; Salvio, Beutler, Engle, & Wood, 1992); (3) demonstrated that both clients and therapists are able to observe this quality, although they are differentially sensitive to aspects of it (Weiss, Marmar, & Horowitz, 1988); and (4) determined that the relationship quality remains stable over time and continues to be predictive of outcome throughout therapy (Horvath & Symonds, 1991).

Methodologically, the feature that has distinguished between various conceptualizations of the alliance and therapist facilitative skill has been the point in time at which the measurements were taken. Measurements of the therapeutic alliance are typically taken early in therapy or periodically throughout treatment. On the other hand, assessments of therapist facilitative conditions are typically derived at the termination of treatment. However, evidence is accumulating to indicate that measures of facilitative therapist skills and those of therapeutic alliance reflect the same change-enhancing processes (Salvio et al., 1992). Although other chapters in this volume are more directly devoted to relationship processes, the similarity of various conceptualizations of the alliance to Rogers's concepts of therapist facilitative skill requires that they be given some attention here as well. In the current review, the related constructs that comprise alliance and common process qualities will be considered collectively under the general heading, *therapeutic relationship*.

In a review of the conclusions reached by nine major review articles on relationship variables, Patterson (1983) concludes that "there are few things in the field of psychology for which the evidence is so strong" as that supporting the "necessity if not sufficiency, of the therapist conditions of accurate empathy, respect, or warmth, and therapeutic genuineness" (p. 437). This conclusion has been reiterated in numerous reviews of this literature (Beutler et al., 1986; Lambert & Bergin, 1983; Orlinsky & Howard, 1986).

In a meta-analysis of 24 studies that related measures of the therapeutic alliance, as a relationship measure, to subsequent assessments of outcome, Horvath and Symonds (1991) found an overall ES (r) of .26 favoring the value of the therapeutic relationship as a predictor of subsequently derived outcome. While only moderate in size, this ES masks a large degree of variability both across studies, the nature of the rater, and the types of therapies. Effect sizes based on relationship ratings by therapists were especially variable, with an average ES (r) of only .17, while client ratings earned an average ES (r) of .21. The largest ES was observed when the client rated both the outcome and the quality of the therapeutic relationship (.31), suggesting the importance of client faith in the therapist for achieving subsequent relief.

Several studies have been conducted on highly trained therapists using a variety of manualized therapies and employing random assignment to therapist procedures. These studies have consistently shown that a positive association exists between quality of the therapeutic relationship and subsequent treatment benefit. For example, well-controlled, quasi-experimental studies have demonstrated relationships between therapeutic relationship quality and outcomes in short-term psychodynamic psychotherapy (Piper, Azim, Joyce, & McCallum, 1991a) and interpersonal psychotherapy (Rounsaville et al., 1987). Similarly, Luborsky et al. (1985) evaluated relationship quality among 9 counselors and their 110 clients who were treated in a time-limited manualized drug therapy regime. Measures of the quality of the therapeutic relationship after the fifth treatment session were strongly predictive of longer term outcomes representing a variety of dimensions.

Findings of this nature generalize to nonpsychodynamic therapies as well, even though the relationship qualities themselves often derive from a psychodynamic framework. For example, Safran and Wallner (1991) related two measures of the early (Session 3) therapeutic relationship to treatment outcomes in manualized cognitive therapy. The length of treatment was controlled; patients were randomly assigned to one of nine therapists; and internal integrity of the therapy was monitored. The results indicated that there was a consistent pattern of moderately high correlations between relationship measures and diverse outcomes.

Williams and Chambless (1990) considered relationship quality as a predictor of success among agoraphobic clients. Ratings of therapist warmth, respect, interest, encouragement, and so on indicated that clients who evaluated their therapists in a positive light showed higher levels of improvement on a behavioral avoidance test than those whose ratings reflected a poorer quality relationship.

Comparisons among behavioral and dynamic treatments suggest that the contributors to the alliance are similar in different psychotherapies (e.g., Gaston, Marmar, Thompson, & Gallagher, 1988), but that qualities of the relationship interact differently with different therapeutic procedures to produce success (Rounsaville et al., 1987). Apparently, different psychotherapies work through similar but not identical types of relationships.

Additionally, the power of the therapeutic alliance seems to transverse many cultural differences. For example, Rudolf (1991) correlated three temporal measurements of a therapeutic relationship measurement and various indices of outcome among a sample of over 200 clients in various German mental health facilities. He observed moderately strong relationships with improvement at each of the three time periods. Likewise, in a naturalistic approach to the issue of therapeutic relationship quality in the Netherlands, Dormaar, Kijkman, and de Vries (1989) developed an interesting variation on the concept of *therapeutic relationship*. This concept appears similar to that of *therapeutic resonance* suggested independently by Orlinsky and Howard (1987) and Larson (1987). In the case of Dormaar et al., however, "consensus" represented an agreement among several dimensions of therapist–client verbal behaviors over time, along with a self-rating of "atunement" after the second session. These consensus ratings were correlated against self-reported symptoms and target complaints. The results again demonstrated a positive and moderate relationship between relationship quality and therapeutic gains.

Collectively, the quality of the therapeutic relationship, by its various terms, has consistently been found to be a central contributor to therapeutic progress. Its significance traverses theoretical schools, theory-specific concepts, and a diversity of measurement procedures. Current literature, however, clearly indicates that the therapeutic relationship is not a therapist quality but is a set of processes that are dependent on both therapist and client. Contemporary research is needed in order to clarify the different ways that these common relationship qualities exert their effects in different therapies and among different therapists.

Social Influence Attributes

In an effort to understand psychotherapy outcomes within a general theory of change, a number of theorists (Frank & Frank, 1991; Goldstein, 1971) have described therapist characteristics as variables that enhance the power of social influence. In one of the early efforts to operationalize therapist qualities from this point of view, Strong (1968) proposed a two-stage model for explaining the influence in counseling and psychotherapy. In the first stage, therapists establish themselves as *attractive*, *trustworthy*, and *expert*. These three qualities are considered to establish the therapist's persuasive power, and thereby, in the second stage of influence, the therapist works to use this persuasive power to employ procedures that encourage and facilitate therapeutic change.

Applications of concepts in social persuasion to clinical practice have ranged from investigations of isolated concepts to comprehensive theories of social persuasion (cf. Brehm, 1976; Maddux, Stoltenberg, & Rosenwein, 1987; Snyder & Forsyth, 1991). Many of the client variables studied (e.g., locus of perceived control, reactance, etc.) have been well incorporated into the clinical literature and are discussed elsewhere in this *Handbook*. Given both their salience to our discussion of therapist characteristics and the large body of research generated by them, the qualities originally defined by Strong (1968) will form the basis of our discussion in this section.

The roles of perceived expertness, attractiveness, and trustworthiness have been the focus of three major, but overlapping reviews of literature (Corrigan, Dell, Lewis, & Schmidt, 1980; Heppner & Claiborn, 1989; Heppner & Dixon, 1981). These reviews reveal that most of the contemporary research has focused on how therapist influence qualities are developed or enhanced, rather than on their effects on outcome. All three studies, for example, conclude that therapist expertness and attractiveness are affected by training, consistency of performance, and a variety of nonverbal (e.g., smiles gestures, eye contact) and verbal (e.g., self-disclosure) behaviors. Responsive nonverbal behavior, interpretative sentences, and the maintenance of confidentiality, on the other hand, are apparently related to perceived trustworthiness. Heppner and Claiborn conclude that nonverbal therapist responses exert a more powerful and consistent effect on clients' perceptions of therapist persuasive skills than verbal behaviors or therapy content.

In spite of the consistency of these conclusions among the three reviews, research on the impact of global therapist traits (e.g., training, prestige, etc.) on perceptions of therapist expertness, attractiveness, and trustworthiness is still inconclusive, in our judgment because most of the research in this area has relied upon nonclinical samples. For example, in the most comprehensive review of this literature (Heppner & Claiborn, 1989), only four of the studies reviewed were conducted with actual psychotherapy clients in clinical settings. Studies that address treatment outcome, even in situational analogue designs, are even more scarce. Heppner and Claiborn (1989) report that only 20 percent of contemporary studies address some aspect of end-of-treatment outcome, and these are either analogue in nature or naturalistic in design.

In spite of their scarcity, clinical studies of the effect of therapist persuasive qualities on outcome are both consistent and promising. Three clinical studies (Heppner & Heesacker, 1983; McNeil, May, & Lee, 1987; Zamosttny, Corrigan, & Eggert, 1981) found a moderate-to-strong relationship between perceived expertness, attractiveness, and trustworthiness and satisfaction with therapy. Dorn and Day (1985) found a relationship between perception of therapist's social attributes and client's changes in self-concept. LaCrosse (1980) found that perceived expertness, attractiveness, and trustworthiness at intake and end of therapy were strongly correlated with the achievement of pretherapy goals. In the latter study, the three therapist influence variables together accounted for over 30 percent of the variability in outcomes.

Other studies have found that premature therapy terminators viewed their therapists as less expert, attractive, and trustworthy than did successful terminators (McNeil et al., 1987); and clients' satisfaction with therapy and perceptions of therapist expertness, attractiveness, and trustworthiness were more positive for continuers than for premature terminators. In a particularly well-designed prospective study, Grimes and Murdock (1989) assessed the impact of initial (after first session) perceptions of therapist's level of expertness, attractiveness, and trustworthiness on both symptomatic change and premature termination in an outpatient client sample. Fifty-one clients rated both their own symptoms and the therapist's persuasive qualities after the first therapy session and again after the fourth session. A significant and moderately strong (rs of approximately .40) relationship was obtained between both symptom change and retention, on one hand, and each of the therapist qualities, on the other.

However, a few studies have failed to find significant effects. Zamosttny et al. (1981) reported that clients' perceptions of therapists' social attributes were not related to number of visits after intake. Likewise, Heppner and Heesacker (1982) found that perceptions of therapist's attributes were not related to therapists' subsequent ratings of client behaviors. However, in the latter study, those therapists who were rated as increasing (vs. decreasing) in perceived social influence attributes over time reported having more impact on clients.

Clinical outcome research on therapist influence variables suffers from methodological weaknesses beyond the use of naturalistic designs. For example, the correlational nature of the data does not allow a determination of whether a social influence process can account for the magnitude of treatment outcome. Moreover, the use of outcomes based either on therapists' early impressions or on global outcome ratings, as is true of much of this literature (cf. Heppner & Heesacker, 1982), provides a limited view of both how these attributes might change and the specific influences that they might have on different indices of change. Clearly more systematic empirical field research is needed on the second stage of influence, as initially defined by Strong (1968) — the actual influence process. It is questionable whether more can be learned about psychotherapy from further efforts to identify, within analogue situations, therapists' behaviors or characteristics that influence the perception of social influence attributes.

Expectancies

Direct research on therapist expectations has not been advanced in the past decade, perhaps because the concept is very broad and the types of clients studied have varied widely. Therapists hold expectations toward such diverse aspects of therapy as length and type of treatment, the type of client behaviors that will be exhibited, and the consequences of implementing interventions. This variety of expectations and the diverse samples on which they have been studied may account for why some studies (e.g., Bonner & Everett, 1986) fail to find significant effects of therapist outcome expectations, while others (e.g., Jenkins, Fuqua, & Blum, 1986) find that duration expectations are related to actual length of treatment. Such inconsistency is reflected in qualitative reviews of the literature (e.g., Beutler et al., 1986; Lambert & Bergin, 1983), most of which conclude that the effects of therapist expectations on treatment outcomes are negligible.

In spite of such conclusions, and in view of two persistent findings, one may have cause to wonder if therapist effects are not stronger than is currently apparent: (1) The theoretical leanings of investigators, who have no direct contact with clients in their studies, exert an influence on the results of treatment comparisons (e.g., Berman, 1989; Berman, Miller, & Massman, 1985; Robinson, Berman, & Neimeyer, 1990), and (2) preparatory procedures, which bring client expectations into conformity with therapy demands, facilitate both treatment outcomes and retention rates (e.g., Mayerson, 1984; Meichenbaum & Turk, 1987; Tryon, 1989). Perhaps the naturalistic and analogue nature of most of the studies that evaluate therapist expectations directly are simply too confounded with other factors to allow relationships to be observed.

Moreover, most research on therapist expectations has failed to account for the observation that therapists' expectations change over the course of therapy (Heppner & Heesaker, 1983). This failure may have also precluded the emergence of consistent findings. This latter possibility has received some support in the form of a series of well-designed, naturalistic studies by Martin and colleagues (Martin & Sterne, 1975; Martin, Moore, & Sterne, 1977; Martin, Sterne, & Hunter, 1976) in which prognostic expectations were assessed repeatedly during the course of therapy. The results indicated that improvement was related to the degree to which therapist expectations were met, especially if therapist expectations came to coincide with client expectations over time.

An emerging but related area of study, "therapist intentions," has attracted the interest of some investigators (e.g., Hill & O'Grady, 1985; Horvath, Marx, & Kamann, 1990; O'Donohue, Fisher, Plaud, & Curtis, 1990). Therapist intentions evolved from research on therapist expectations, and the two concepts are conceptually similar. Comparatively, however, therapist intentions are more specifically definable and more easily measured. Although they are usually considered to be process rather than therapist variables, they bear brief mention in this chapter because the methods for studying them are still evolving.

Several promising studies of therapist intentions have emerged. For example, Taylor, Adelman, and Kaser-Boyd (1986) determined that therapists who intended (i.e., expected) their verbal responses to encourage autonomy among adolescent clients were among the most effective at eliciting client satisfaction. In a study that is more illustrative of research in this area, Hill et al. (1988) used a standard list of therapist intentions to examine their relationship to the outcomes of eight brief psychotherapy client–therapist dyads. They found that therapist intentions accounted for more of the therapeutic changes observed than the specific interventions selected to achieve these intentions.

In a carefully constructed naturalistic investigation on this topic, Joyce and Piper (1990) employed a manualized, short-term (12-session) psychodynamic psychotherapy to control for therapy-specific intentions. They developed a list of 5 general expectations from an initial list of 19 specific intentions and compared the clustering of these variables among the therapists of 14 outpatient clients who were judged to have either "good" or "poor" outcomes on each of 5 outcome indices. The authors found that clients who experienced good results tended to have therapists who expected that their own personal experiences would be helpful.

Collectively, therapist expectations appear to have earned an uneven record of effects in psychotherapy outcome research. The best evidence available suggests that while expectations may be predictive of therapy benefit, this relationship is enhanced when the correspondence between therapist and client expectations is also considered. Likewise, research on related variables, such as pretherapy preparation, also suggests that correspondent expectations between therapist and client may enhance benefit. Other concepts, such as therapist intentions, are emerging and promising areas for research, but their effects on outcome are as yet largely unstudied.

Therapeutic Philosophy/Orientation

Disagreement about the effectiveness of therapeutic treatment models forms the basis for much controversy among clinical practitioners. Theorists have disagreed about the nature of the problems to be treated, the objectives of treatment, and the means by which change might be initiated. Resolving these controversies has been complicated because of the large number of theoretical formulations available, by the failure to distinguish between theories and techniques, and by the absence of research on specific procedures.

While both qualitative (e.g., Luborsky, Singer, & Luborsky, 1975; Stein & Lambert, 1984) and meta-analytic (e.g., Smith et al., 1980; Shapiro, & Shapiro, 1982) reviews of literature have sought to compare different psychotherapy models, the research published prior to 1980 almost entirely consisted of studies in which different psychotherapies were identified on the basis of therapist reference group identification. Thus, these studies were really evaluations of therapist philosophies, rather than of therapist interventions. It has been primarily since the advent of therapy-guided manuals that it has been feasible to differentiate empirically between studies of therapist orientation and studies of therapist interventions. Making a distinction between therapist orientation and interventions (see Lambert & Bergin, 1983) is especially important from an empirical perspective because of the observation that very different interventions are used by different therapists whose theoretical allegiances are similar (cf. Lambert, 1989; Luborsky et al., 1985; Luborsky et al., 1986; Sloane, Staples, Cristol, Yorkston, & Whipple, 1975). Because of this variability, it should not be surprising that few differences have been noted in the effect sizes associated with different theoretical orientations. Even reviews that have been restricted to a consideration of one disorder (e.g., Nietzel, Russell, Hemmings, & Gretter, 1987) or to one type of subject (e.g., Durlak, Fuhrman, & Lampman, 1991) have failed

to find reliable differences in outcomes that can be attributed to therapist orientations.

Interestingly, however, nonstatistical reviews of therapist orientation literature, particularly those that focus on behavioral therapy, often reach conclusions that are at variance with quantitative reviews of this literature. This contradiction reveals the ease with which the views of the reviewer might affect the conclusions without the protection of systematic observational and analytic methods. Contrast, for example, the nonstatistically derived conclusion (Giles, 1983) favoring behavioral therapy over other therapeutic philosophies with meta-analytic reviews of the same or overlapping literature, all of which conclude that the mean effect size differences are negligible (e.g., Brown, 1987; Lyons & Woods, 1991; Miller & Berman, 1983).

The small effect sizes that are observed when the main effects attributable to different therapist philosophies contrast with the moderate effect sizes that characterize comparisons of samples treated by therapists of almost any given therapeutic philosophy and those in a no-treatment control condition. This latter literature has been reviewed elsewhere in this volume and the results do not bear detailed inspection here. Table 7.1 summarizes the effect sizes (expressed as both *d* and *r* values) attributable to different orientations of the therapist compared to a no-treatment condition in three of the six reviews reported by Brown (1987). These meta-analytic reviews (Smith & Glass, 1977; Smith et al., 1980; Shapiro & Shapiro, 1982) were selected for this summary because each was conducted on studies that were completed prior to the advent of therapy manuals. Hence, these reviews represent relatively pure indications of the effects of therapist philosophy. The other reviews (Landman & Dawes, 1982; Miller & Berman, 1983; Prioleau, Murdock, & Brody, 1983) did not provide effects sizes for different therapy orientations.

While differences among therapy orientations of therapists are not statistically significant, the effect sizes attributable to each orientation are relatively large. However, there are notable inconsistencies reported for the ES magnitudes for certain orientations from review to review, sometimes even when these reviews are conducted on similar data sets (cf. Gestalt therapy as reported by Smith & Glass, 1977, vs. Smith et al., 1980). These inconsistencies confirm the observation that therapist effects vary widely within theoretical orientations (e.g., Luborsky et al., 1985).

With the advent of manualized therapies and controlled clinical comparisons of different treatment models, research that bears on the theoretical affiliations of therapists is declining (Moncher &

TABLE 7.1   Summary of effect sizes associated with different therapist orientations

Reference (No. of Studies)	Therapist Orientation	Effect Size d	r
Smith & Glass, 1977 (375)	Psychodynamic	.59	.29
	Adlerian	.71	.34
	Transactional analysis	.58	.29
	Rational-emotive	.77	.37
	Gestalt	.26	.13
	Client-centered	.63	.31
	Systematic desensitization	.91	.42
	Implosive therapy	.64	.31
	Behavior modification	.76	.36
Smith, Glass, & Miller, 1980 (475)	Psychodynamic	.69	.33
	Dynamic eclectic	.89	.41
	Adlerian	.62	.30
	Hypnotherapy	1.82	.68
	Client-centered	.62	.30
	Gestalt	.64	.31
	Rational-emotive	.68	.33
	Transactional analysis	.67	.33
	Reality therapy	.14	.07
	Systematic desensitization	1.05	.47
	Implosive	.68	.33
	Behavior modification	.73	.35
	Cognitive-behavioral	1.13	.50
	Eclectic behavioral	.89	.42
	Vocational-personal	.65	.32
Shapiro & Shapiro, 1982 (214)	Behavioral	1.06	.48
	Self-control	1.01	.46
	Biofeedback	.91	.42
	Covert behavioral	1.52	.61
	Flooding	1.12	.50
	Relaxation	.90	.42
	Systematic desensitization	.97	.45
	Reinforcement	.97	.45
	Modeling	1.43	.59
	Cognitive	1.00	.46
	Dynamic/Humanistic	.40	.20

tions may be differentially effective with clients representing certain coping styles.

Beutler and Mitchell (1981) compared the outcomes of therapists representing different theoretical philosophies among outpatients who represented either internal/intropunitive or external/impulsive coping styles. They found analytically oriented trainee therapists exerted their strongest effects on clients with internalizing coping styles and were less effective in working with clients whose coping styles were characterized by acting out patterns. This finding was cross-validated by Calvert, Beutler, and Crago (1988) using a larger sample of trainee therapists who represented either insight or behavioral orientations. Moreover, this latter study also determined that behaviorally oriented trainee therapists obtained the most positive effects on outpatient clients who were identified as relying on externalizing, compared to those with internalizing, coping styles.

Given the findings reviewed here, we can conclude that therapist theoretical orientation is not strongly related to treatment outcome. Yet, suggestive evidence is available to indicate that therapist preferences for different theoretical orientations may predispose differential outcome rates among client groups representing external and internal coping styles. However, the relationship between theoretical orientation and actual therapy procedures is still sufficiently uncertain as to make it difficult to extract the effects of therapist orientation from therapeutic intervention. Thus, drawing firm conclusions regarding the effects of therapist theoretical orientations is still premature.

OBJECTIVE, THERAPY-SPECIFIC STATES

Professional Background

Therapist values, skills, and behaviors change during the course of formal training (Thompson, 1986) and with clinical experience (e.g., Guest & Beutler, 1988; Tracey, Hays, Malone, & Herman, 1988). Research on the effects of these changes has addressed three interrelated variables that are assumed to affect the skill and effectiveness with which the therapist implements therapeutic interventions—level of professional training, amount of experience, and professional discipline (see Beutler et al., 1986; Parloff, Waskow, & Wolfe, 1978). These variables are often confounded in research, both with each other and with the nature of the therapeutic interventions studied. For example, studies that have compared experienced therapists with therapists who are still in training as a means of assessing the effects of therapist experience levels often confound variables

Prinz, 1991). This trend is reflected in the fact that the studies that have explored therapist theoretical preferences over the past decade (e.g., Bolter et al., 1990; Mahoney, Norcross, Prochaska, & Missar, 1989) infrequently assess clinical outcomes. Two exceptions to this rule are worth noting because they have specifically tested the hypothesis that therapists with different theoretical orienta-

such as the amount of training, the therapists' ages, and the amount of pre- and postgraduate experience achieved. At the same time, efforts to control for the confounding of age and level of training may result in therapist samples that are significantly constricted in the range of experience represented. Similarly, comparisons of therapists who represent different training traditions (e.g., psychologists and psychiatrists) fail to disentangle type of training from either amount or type of experience.

These confounded variables make it difficult to tease apart the effects of different aspects of professional background. As a result, research on therapist background characteristics has yielded equivocal and contradictory results. Literature reviews have suggested that there is little effect of either experience or level of training (e.g., Auerbach & Johnson, 1977; Beutler et al., 1986; Stein & Lambert, 1984); others have concluded that outcomes favor experienced therapists (e.g., Baekeland & Lundwall, 1975; Luborsky, Chandler, Auerbach, Cohen, & Bachrach, 1971); and still others have argued that inexperienced and paraprofessional therapists may have advantages over professional therapists (Durlak, 1979, 1981; Hattie, Sharpley, & Rogers, 1984). Unfortunately, meta-analytic reviews of this literature do not help a great deal.

In a meta-analytic review of studies that addressed level of training, Berman and Norton (1985) concluded that professionally trained therapists had no systematic advantage over nonprofessional therapists in evoking treatment gains (ES [r] of .01). This review was notable because it imposed relatively strict standards of adequacy on the studies included in the analysis. In fact, the authors extracted the 32 studies reviewed from a total of 43 cited by Hattie et al. (1984) after a careful review suggested that 11 of the original studies failed to meet criteria of adequacy.

Similar conclusions were reached by Weisz et al. (1987) in a meta-analysis of 108 studies of children and adolescents. In this review, the presence or absence of professional training was analyzed as one of a large variety of potential contributors, and unlike the previous review that specifically focused on training level, studies were not excluded if comparison groups were not available. In spite of this lack of specificity, the effect size attributable to professional training was not significant (ES [r] <.15).

However, both of these reviews indicated that the effects of therapist training level may vary significantly as a function of certain characteristics of the therapy and the clients being treated. For example, among their studies of adult clients, Berman and Norton (1985) found that professionally trained therapists were more effective than nonpro-

fessional therapists when treatment was either shorter than 12 sessions (ES [r] = .43) or the clients were over the age of 21 (ES [r] = .19). In their studies of children, Weisz et al. (1987) also found a client age by therapist training level interaction effect. In contrast to the adult studies, however, these latter authors concluded that professionals were more effective than nonprofessionals among younger children (ES [r] = .15) and among those children who overcontrolled their feelings and impulses (ES [r] = .20).

When research attention turns from level of professional training to length of experience, the results are equally mixed. Most meta-analytic reviews suggest that length of therapist experience by itself is neither a strong nor a significant predictor of amount of improvement (e.g., Stein & Lambert, 1984; Nietzel et al., 1987). However, Crits-Christoph et al. (1991) demonstrated that moderately high outcome differences favored experienced therapists (ES [r] = .41) when only the most rigorously controlled studies were included in the meta-analysis.

Moreover, length of therapist experience has been found to be related to the quality of the therapeutic alliance (e.g., Mallinckrodt & Nelson, 1991) and to the likelihood (as opposed to the magnitude) of improvement. In a study of the latter outcome variable, for example, Orlinsky and Howard (1980) found that therapists who had more than six years of experience had a disproportionately high percentage of clients who improved and a disproportionately low percentage of clients who deteriorated during open-ended, relationship-oriented psychotherapy.

Therapist experience level may also exert a differential effect on magnitude of improvement among different types of clients. In a meta-analysis of 25 studies, for example, Stein and Lambert (1984) found that differences between experienced and inexperienced therapists emerged only when either the nature of outcomes or the severity of client disturbance was considered. Experienced therapists were significantly more effective than less experienced therapists at retaining clients in treatment and also produced larger outcomes among more disturbed clients.[7]

An analysis of 19 studies by Svartberg and Stiles (1991) further suggests that the type of therapy orientation represented by the therapist may moderate the effects of therapist experience level. When compared to therapists with other therapeutic orientations, those with psychodynamic philoso-

[7]Unfortunately, the effect sizes for these findings were not reported and could not be extracted from the data given.

phies tended to become less effective with experience (ES $[r] = -.47$). Even the modest effects that favored time-limited, psychodynamic psychotherapy over a no-treatment group (ES $[r] = .10$) approached 0.0 when adjusted for therapist experience levels.

Studies of therapists who come from different professional disciplines also present mixed results. In a meta-analytic review that included therapist discipline, Smith et al. (1980) reported an overall effect size for psychologists (ES $[r] = .43$) that was somewhat higher than that for psychiatrists (ES $[r] = .30$). When differences between effect sizes for therapists of various disciplines have been compared through meta-analyses, they range from moderate in favor of psychologists (ES $[r] = .28$; Smith et al., 1980) to negligible (ES $[r] = 0.0$; Prioleau et al., 1983). These variations among findings of meta-analyses based on overlapping samples of studies suggest that any effects that can be attributable to discipline may interact with other variables that distinguish various study samples, Indeed, some research supports this conclusion. For example, Schindler, Berren, Hannah, Beigel, and Santiago (1987) surveyed attitudes toward mental health professionals among 119 mental health clients and 114 demographically similar nonclients drawn from civic groups in a major metropolitan area. The groups rated the effectiveness of psychiatrists, psychologists, nonpsychiatric physicians, and clergy in treating 10 types of clients (alcoholics, sexual abuse victims, martially distressed individuals, depressed women, drug-abusing teenagers, etc.).

Client and nonclient samples rated psychiatrists and psychologists as more competent than other help providers and rated the attitudinal qualities of psychologists as more positive than those of psychiatrists. Psychiatrists and psychologists were judged to have different areas of competency, however. Both client and nonclient samples perceived psychologists as being more effective than psychiatrists in treating marital difficulties, drug-abuse among teenagers, abusive marriages, and problems of loneliness and social isolation. In contrast, psychiatrists were judged to be more effective than psychologists in treating alcoholism, sexual abuse, and severe mental illness. Differences in the training experiences required of psychiatrists and psychologists may account for these differences in perceived competencies (see Kingsbury, 1987).

The confusing results of studies on therapist professional background characteristics reflect a variety of uncontrolled variables in addition to the confounded effects of therapist age, experience, level, and type of training. Experienced therapists, for example, may have access to more interesting and difficult clients than less experienced ones (e.g., Knapp, Levin, McCarter, Wermer, & Zetzel, 1960) and referral patterns to psychologists and psychiatrists are also likely to differ. A related concern is the still uncertain relationship that exists between amount of training and the acquisition of expertise. The assumption that exposure and practice alone, in the absence of specifically targeted skills and systematic methods of instruction, result in the acquisition of skill has been criticized (Guest & Beutler, 1988). Certainly, in the development of clinical judgment, the relationship between amount of training and skill acquisition may be less direct and lower than commonly thought (e.g., Garb, 1989). Likewise, in the practice of psychotherapy, prior experience and supervision alone have little relationship to the level of skill achieved by a therapist (Shaw & Dobson, 1988; Strupp, 1981). Skill acquisition in psychotherapy derives more from the use of targeted goals, specific feedback, and guided practice than from simple exposure and unstructured supervision (Luborsky, 1990).

These latter considerations emphasize the need for research to place more emphasis on the therapeutic skill level achieved, rather than on experience level, amount of training, and discipline, when exploring therapist effectiveness. Direct assessment of therapist skill level may circumvent some of the confounding of variables that exists among experience level, training level, and discipline. Moreover, assessment of skill possesses considerable face validity as a potential contributor to treatment efficacy.

Therapeutic Styles

Therapeutic styles reflect those behavioral predilections that are used to communicate with another person and that are independent of the constructs espoused to be important change agents by different theoretical models. Yet, these stylistic qualities cannot be considered to be traits. While stylistic qualities such as therapist posture and activity are correlated with traitlike personality and interest patterns (Smith, 1972), they also vary as a function of the nature of the client being seen (Fairbanks, McGuire, & Harris, 1982) and of the type of therapy being practiced (e.g., Hardy & Shapiro, 1985). There are limits to this variability, however, and even therapists who are following highly structured, manual-guided procedures have distinctive styles (Stiles, Shapiro, & Firth-Cozens, 1988).

Therapist "styles" contrast with therapist "interventions"—the latter are the discrete procedures or techniques that are touted by various schools of psychotherapy (Lambert & Bergin, 1983). But the stylistic qualities of therapists are difficult either to dissect into component parts or to separate from interventions for the purposes of research. Therapist styles and interventions are dynamic, multidimensional, and interactive and change with the nature of the interpersonal contexts of different psychotherapy sessions. Further, specific lexical qualities of language (e.g., open vs. closed questions) are closely related both to the nature of the therapist's moment-to-moment intentions and to theoretically conceived objectives of therapy (Elliott, 1985).

Because of their complexity, it may be argued that both therapist styles and interventions should legitimately be considered to lie outside the purview of a chapter on therapist characteristics. However, both styles and interventions are considered briefly in this chapter for the sake of continuity. Traditionally, both of these classes of variables have been considered to be qualities of the therapist more than of the therapy (Lambert & Bergin, 1983; Beutler et al., 1986; Parloff et al., 1978). Nonetheless, the reader will find additional reviews of the roles that are played by many of these variables in psychotherapy in other chapters of this *Handbook*. In this section, we will first explore research on therapist interpersonal styles. Thereafter, we will extract for special consideration some of the more easily defined and more specific therapist styles. Following conventional wisdom, these will include verbal and nonverbal therapist styles, but in addition, they will include two combination patterns of verbal and nonverbal behaviors — verbal–nonverbal congruence and therapist formality.

Interpersonal styles. A number of frameworks have been proposed for assessing the interpersonal styles of psychotherapists. By far the most well developed from a theoretical perspective are frameworks that emanate either directly or indirectly from what are called "circumplex models" of interactions. Largely, this work is rooted in the early efforts of Leary (1957) to describe interpersonal compatibility as the interplay of two orthogonally defined and dimensional motives: friendly to unfriendly and dominant to submissive. In applications to psychotherapy, contemporary models (e.g., Benjamin, 1974; Kiesler, 1988) propose that when either member of a therapist–client dyad engages in behaviors toward one end of the dominance–submission dimension, the other member responds with behaviors that are toward the other end of the same dimension (i.e., dominance elicits submission). On the other hand, if one member of the dyad emits behaviors that are toward one end of the friendly–unfriendly dimension, the other member of the dyad responds in kind (i.e.,

friendliness begets friendliness). The interdependence of these two dimensions is the circumplex.

Response dispositions as predicted from the circumplex have been applied to patient diagnosis (McLemore & Benjamin, 1979), to predicting the development of good therapeutic relationships (Kiesler & Watkins, 1989; Kivlighan, McGovern, & Corazzini, 1984; Reandeau & Wampold, 1991), to evaluating theory-relevant changes during psychotherapy (Henry et al., 1990), and to assessing therapist–client compatibility (Henry & Strupp, 1991; Rudy, McLemore, & Gorsuch, 1985). Generally, at least moderate levels of complementarity (i.e., similar levels of friendliness and contrasting levels of dominance) in therapeutic communications have been found to be associated with positive outcomes (Dietzel & Abeles, 1975; Kiesler & Watkins, 1989; Rudy et al., 1985; Tracey & Hays, 1989).

To date, relatively little research has been done to relate these interpersonal styles to treatment outcomes. In an exception to this rule, Andrews (1990) followed three groups of client–therapist dyads using a quasi-experimental design. One dyad was characterized by complementary patterns of communication (i.e., reciprocity on the control axis and correspondence on the friendly axis); another was characterized by a complementarity (i.e., complementarity on only one of the two axes); and still another was characterized by anticomplementarity (i.e., correspondence on the dominance axis and reciprocity on the friendly axis). As expected, clients in those dyads that were characterized by anticomplementarity were less likely to improve than those with more complementary stylistic behaviors.

In another, quasi-experimental study in which therapeutic procedures were controlled and manualized, Henry et al. (1990) found that poor outcome client–therapist dyads were distinguished from good outcome dyads by a pattern of therapist hostility and reciprocal client self-criticism (a dominance–submission pattern). Such findings suggest that interpersonally compatible styles among therapists and clients may be indicative of whether or not psychotherapy will proceed in a positive direction.

Verbal styles. Verbal styles include both noncontent (e.g., the number of words and sentences used) and content (i.e., topical) aspects of speech. For three decades, noncontent aspects of speech generated a relatively large body of analogue and naturalistic research on therapy process variables. The results of this research indicated that (1) therapist verbal responses change as a function of training, and (2) client patterns of verbal behaviors parallel those used by the therapists (see Kivlighan, 1989).

While few of the verbal patterns that have been identified in process research have successfully been applied to investigations of psychotherapy outcome, Bennun and Schindler (1988) found that among 35 adult phobic subjects undergoing cognitive-behavioral therapy, therapist verbal activity level was positively associated with treatment benefit. Naturalistic studies have confirmed and extended this finding in the demonstration that both therapist–client speech activity levels (e.g., Horn-George & Anchor, 1982; Pope, 1979) and topics (Horvath & Greenberg, 1986) converge in effective therapy.

In a particularly interesting extension of these observations, Tracey and his colleagues explored psychotherapy process and outcome as a function of the proportion of time that a topic initiated by the client or therapist is pursued by the other member of the dyad (Tracey, 1987; Tracey & Dundon, 1988; Tracey & Ray, 1984). In a well-designed naturalistic study, for example, Tracey (1986) compared two matched pairs of continuing and prematurely terminated client–therapist dyads in a planned, short-term therapy format. He determined that high proportions of client–therapist topic agreement, regardless of who initiated the topic, were associated with both continuance in therapy and the amount of benefit achieved. These findings were then cross-validated on a larger sample of therapist–client dyads and in a different setting.

Overall, verbal activity and patterns suggest that verbal styles of therapists and clients converge over time. The strength of this relationship appears to be related to client improvement and retention. Further confirmation of these findings is needed, however, utilizing experimental and quasi-experimental research designs in order to determine if these patterns are predictive or simply correlates of beneficial change.

Nonverbal styles. Researchers estimate that from 65 to 85 percent of the communication in groups takes place through nonverbal behaviors (Burgoon & Ruffner, 1978; Harper, Wiens, & Matarazzo, 1978; Kleinke, 1986) and may play an especially important role in communicating reactions that are not consciously controlled or monitored (Brown, Warner, & Williams, 1985). Because of this, nonverbal behaviors are thought to afford a practical, direct, and unobtrusive means of assessing the role of emotional intensity and quality in human interactions (Burgoon, Kelley, Newton, & Keeley-Dyreson, 1989) and promise to be highly potent sources of information in psychotherapy (Robbins & Haase, 1985).

An accumulating body of theory (e.g., Goodman

& Teicher, 1988) and naturalistic research (e.g., Davis & Hadiks, 1991; Hermansson, Webster, & McFarland, 1988; Hill & Stephany, 1990; Patterson, 1984) has suggested that nonverbal behaviors, such as touch and the selective use of interpersonal proximity, can enhance the therapeutic alliance, facilitate the experience of support, and diminish negative countertransference. However, clinical judgment suggests that many such nonverbal behaviors should be used judiciously because they carry potentially negative consequences as well. Moreover, at this point in time, outcome literature is lacking. One can only conclude that while nonverbal communication appears to be a powerful source of influence in most interpersonal relationships and tends to create a therapeutic climate in psychotherapy, its effect on therapeutic outcomes is still to be determined.

Combined verbal and nonverbal patterns. It has been suggested that when people are attempting to conceal emotional states, they exhibit discrepant verbal and nonverbal cues and their nonverbal behaviors tend to belie their verbal reticence. Voice tone, body posture, and proxemic presentations tend to "leak" the undisclosed information (Babad, Bernieri, & Rosenthal, 1989; Ekman & Friesen, 1969). If such discrepancies between nonverbal and verbal communication channels can be reliably measured, they may be used by therapists to identify client emotional states. Indeed, it appears that both noncontent qualities of speech samples (content-filtered speech) and nonprosaic laden speech contents (written therapy transcripts) provide reliable, independent, and frequently contradictory information about the presence of emotional states (Mohr, Shoham-Salomon, Engle, & Beutler, 1991). When applied to psychotherapists and their clients, content-filtered speech samples and written transcripts may offer different views of clients, as well as a methodology by which to study channel incongruence. This methodology has been used successfully to investigate therapy process variables. Bernieri, Blanck, Rosenthal, Vannicelli, and Yerrell (1991) compared audiorecorded speech samples of therapists speaking *to* and subsequently *about* former clients of a drug and alcohol treatment program and found that correspondence between content and prosaic channels of speech was higher when speaking *about* clients than when speaking *to* them. In corresponding fashion, therapists were rated as less helpful and more dishonest when speaking *to* rather than *about* clients.

A related area of research, in which multichannel communication has been assessed, is the "formality" of the therapeutic communication (see Beutler, 1983). One method of studying communication formality has been to compare interventions that differ in the use of verbal patterns or styles. For example, Burton, Parker, and Wollner (1991) compared verbal "chats" with client-centered interventions among presurgical breast cancer patients. While differences in verbal behavior distinguished the two treatments, few differences were noted in subsequent patient reports of helpfulness and benefit.

Another method of studying formality relies on nonverbal patterns, such as variations in office decor and therapist attire (e.g., Amira & Abramowitz, 1979; Tessler, 1975). Studies that use this method have related formality to ratings of therapeutic attachment, therapist credibility, and other process dimensions (see review by Beutler et al., 1986).

The few naturalistic studies conducted on the issue of formality yielded ambiguous results. For example, Childress and Gillis (1977) found a positive association between therapist formality as expressed in variations of office decor and attire and therapy outcome among clinic outpatients, but Beutler and Mitchell (1981) found a modest but negative relationship between supervisors' ratings of therapist formality of approach and treatment benefit among subgroups of both impulsive and depressive clinic outpatients. Dissimilarity of measures and the uncertain meaning attached to the term *formality* have precluded the emergence of stable conclusions.

Therapist Interventions

Therapist interventions are the technical procedures that are designed to initiate therapeutic change. The use of such procedures reflects both the theoretical philosophy held by the therapist and the therapist's personal preferences and styles. Interventions bridge the gap between therapist qualities and therapy processes. With the advent of treatment manuals, it is increasingly difficult to distinguish between interventions that are employed because they are prescribed by the model of therapy used by the therapist and those that are reflective of more general qualities of the therapist.

Our inclusion of interventions under the topic of therapist characteristics unavoidably introduces some overlap with other chapters in this volume. In an effort to avoid undue repetition while, at the same time, maintaining continuity with prior listings of therapist variables (e.g., Lambert & Bergin, 1983; Beutler et al., 1986; Parloff et al., 1978), we will restrict our consideration of therapist interventions to (1) research that bears implications for therapist training and skill and (2) a sampling of the effects of some specific interventions that are likely to vary among therapists, both within and across therapeutic schools.

In adhering to these two considerations, the reader may note that the current review excludes some interventions on which a significant body of research exists (e.g., paradoxical interventions, see Shoham-Salomon & Rosenthal, 1987). At the same time, this review will be found to include a discussion of the implications of psychotherapy manuals for therapist efficacy and skill, topics that have not traditionally been considered in reviews of therapist characteristics. These departures from other reviews on therapist characteristics reflect contemporary developments in manualizing treatments. These developments have resulted in some interventions being so specific and well defined that they no longer reflect qualities that are unique to a given therapist and have raised new issues of therapist training with which the psychotherapy community must contend.

The use of therapy manuals. The advent of treatment manuals not only opened a new era in psychotherapy research methodology (Luborsky & DeRubeis, 1984), but also had an unforseen impact on training and clinical practice as well (e.g., Dobson & Shaw, 1988; Rounsaville, O'Malley, Foley, & Weissman, 1988; Strupp, Butler, & Rosser, 1988). Since the initiation of the now well-known NIMH Collaborative Study of Depression (Elkin, Parloff, Hadley, & Autry, 1985; Elkin et al., 1989), manual-guided therapies have become standard in research on therapeutic efficacy. Because manual-guided therapies can be empirically distinguished by what therapists actually do (e.g., Hill, O'Grady, & Elkin, 1992; Luborsky et al., 1982), manuals make it possible to apply standardized interventions independently of therapist philosophy.

The effect of using therapy manuals on the therapist is illustrated in a meta-analysis by Crits-Christoph et al. (1991) who found a substantial decrease in the variability of outcomes attributable to therapist effects when treatments were manual-driven (ES $[r] = .45$). Another effect of manuals on therapist efficacy is illustrated by the observation that while outcomes are quite similar when different manual-driven therapies are compared, a significant, positive relationship exists between the degree to which a therapist complies with a treatment manual and the outcome of treatment (Luborsky et al., 1985; Shaw, 1983). From such observations, it appears that the structure imposed on therapists by the use of manuals facilitates the development of technical proficiency and enhances outcomes. Indeed, the efficacy of training appears to depend less on what specific techniques are being used than on the structure, explicitness, and organization imposed on their use by the manual.

The foregoing conclusion must be tempered by recent experience with time-limited psychodynamic psychotherapy, however. Henry et al. (1993), in a pre–post study of manualized training, found that while technical proficiency is increased following training, therapists' relationship skills and supportiveness may decline. Moreover, they (Henry, Schacht, Strupp, Butler, & Binder, 1993) suggest that therapists who have self-reported introjects that are hostile and controlling are the most likely to develop technical proficiency with the use of a dynamic therapy manual. Such findings may account for why Svartberg and Stiles (1992) found that degree of therapist compliance with manual-guided psychodynamic therapy did not increase therapeutic effectiveness.

A direct test of the degree to which using manuals increases therapist efficacy in treating major depression also sheds some light on the issue of manual-guided therapies. Robinson et al. (1990) compared the effect sizes attributable to therapy in 14 studies in which therapists employed manual-guided therapies and 17 studies in which manuals were not used. They found equivalent effect sizes (rs = .51) for manual-guided and non–manual-guided therapies. They concluded that there is little evidence that manual-guided interventions improve therapist efficacy. These meta-analytic results are consistent with termination outcomes for the clients of therapists who were treated either before or after therapists were trained in time-limited dynamic psychotherapy (Henry, Strupp, Schacht, Binder, & Butler, 1992). However, Henry et al. found that a year later, clients who had been treated after the therapists had been trained were experiencing fewer symptoms and problems than those treated before therapist training.

Such negative and equivocal findings as these have led several authors to propose that therapist efficacy when using manual-guided interventions may be masked by the possibility that most interventions are only effective on some types of clients (Beutler, 1991; Mahalik, 1990; Norcross & Prochaska, 1988; Shoham-Salomon & Hannah, 1991). Accordingly, research using manuals to guide therapist interventions has begun to look more specifically at the efficacy of using certain specific interventions among various client types (e.g., Beutler, Engle, et al. 1991; Cooney, Kadden, Litt, & Getter, 1991; Kadden, Cooney, Getter, & Litt, 1990). The results suggest that this approach is promising and parallels the findings reported earlier of matching therapist orientation to therapist coping style. These findings lend credence to arguments that therapy efficacy may be enhanced by training therapists to use different treatment models or techniques with different clients (e.g., Horvath & Goheen, 1990; Shoham-Salomon, 1991) and is enhanced by the demonstration that therapists can be taught to use different, manual-

ized models of therapy with equivalent levels of proficiency (Hardy & Shapiro, 1985).

Therapist skill. The assumption that therapist skill or competence at applying interventions is associated with treatment effectiveness underlies the extensive effort garnered by professional training programs to provide intensive supervision to fledgling psychotherapists. The supervision of psychotherapy has generated a considerable body of literature, most of which is theoretical in nature (see Robiner & Schofield, 1990). In view of these facts, it is surprising that so little has been done to assess therapist skill or competence as variables in psychotherapy outcome. Moncher and Prinz (1991), for example, reviewed 359 treatment outcome studies and concluded that most ignored or failed to adequately assess therapist competence or skill as a variable in treatment efficacy.

Moreover, empirical literature is far from consistent in providing support for the importance of supervision on skill development. In their review of training studies, Alberts and Edelstein (1990) concluded that there was some support for instruction, modeling, and feedback as training methods for enhancing interviewing skills. But they criticized the absence of training studies that focused on complex integration, application, and evaluation of skills on a theoretical and empirical basis and pointed out the dearth of evidence that the skills trained were implicated in actual client change. Pursuing this latter point, in a naturalistic study of outcome, Sandell (1985) found that if anything, supervision impeded the efficacy of therapists who conducted short-term psychodynamic psychotherapy. Similarly, in a study of supervised and unsupervised trainees, Wiley and Ray (1985) observed that supervised trainees increased their ability to understand their impact on clients and incorporated a theoretical framework for their work, but they did not demonstrate that specific therapy skills resulted from supervision. Holloway (1992) and Dobson and Shaw (1988) summarized some of the issues in this area by observing that competence and compliance with supervisor recommendations are independent phenomena and that the effectiveness of supervision for producing therapist competency can only be assessed when necessary skills and criteria for the professional competence of therapists have been specified.

In contrast to this gloomy picture, there are a variety of studies, usually naturalistic in design, that have found therapist competence and skill to be related both to facilitative therapeutic qualities of the therapist and to positive outcome (e.g., Bennun & Schindler, 1988). Likewise, research on the application of specific interventions (e.g., Crits-

Christoph, Cooper, & Luborsky, 1988) suggests that therapist skill or accuracy enhances end-of-treatment outcomes. The consistency of these latter findings suggests the need for more rigorous and specific training methods than current supervision models and course work provide. Competency-based training using therapy manuals may provide such an alternative.

Based on the studies of therapist skill utilizing manual-guided therapies and competency-based criteria, some tentative conclusions can be reached regarding therapist skill and therapy outcome. Specifically, this research suggests that (1) common or nonspecific skills of therapists are manifested differently in different therapies (Rounsaville et al., 1987); (2) skillfulness generally is associated with effectiveness in different treatment models (Shaw & Dobson, 1988); (3) therapist skill is relatively distinct from both experience level and compliance with a therapy model (Shaw & Dobson, 1988; Strupp, 1981); and (4) criteria-based training in specific procedures tends to increase levels of compliance and skill (Bootzin & Ruggill, 1988; Davis et al., 1985; Henry et al., in press-a).

To advance this area, research on instrument development is needed. Contemporary methods of assessing therapist skill have varied greatly, usually as a function of the therapy model being taught. These measures have ranged from global ratings to assessments of specific procedures. Cross-cutting assessments of both general and specific skills are needed in order to disentangle skill from the rationales by which effects are explained.

Specific therapeutic procedures. A number of authors have proposed taxonomies of therapist interventions. Some of these systems have been developed to reflect theory-defined behaviors (e.g., Goldberg et al., 1984), while others have specifically attempted to be free of single theories (e.g., Elliott, 1985; Hill, 1978; Stiles, 1979). Some of the methods have been found to be sensitive to global differences among therapists representing different theories (e.g., Hill, 1990; Hill, Thames, & Rardin, 1979; Stiles et al., 1988) and a comparison of them within psychotherapy sessions suggests that they measure common, but largely verbal behaviors (Elliott et al., 1987).

While response taxonomic categories are associated in predictable ways with both different therapeutic approaches (cf. Hardy & Shapiro, 1985; Hill, 1990) and therapeutic process dimensions (e.g., Barkham & Shapiro, 1986), their reliance on verbal behavior may render them insensitive to interventions that rely on nonverbal activities like behavioral rehearsal and imagery induction. Hence, it is still uncertain if various interventions can be

most advantageously studied on their own or if there are underlying dimensions and relationships among similar and dissimilar techniques which potentiate, synergize, or attenuate the effects of one another. Moreover, research is scarce regarding the relationship of these interventions to outcomes.

Some evidence on the role of various verbal interventions on therapist efficacy is available from client reports of what they found helpful and not helpful. Elliott (1985), for example, found that therapist actions designed to introduce new perspectives, facilitate problem resolution, clarify issues, focus awareness, convey understanding, enhance client involvement, provide reassurance, and maintain personal contact were considered to be helpful. In contrast, therapist responses that raise unwanted thoughts, introduce unrelated topics, assign responsibility for feelings to the client, distance therapists from the client's problems, or provide unacceptable interpretations were all seen as not being helpful.

In an interesting approach to the study of therapeutic procedures, Gaston and Ring (1992) studied the behaviors of therapists who had been assigned to treat depressed, older adult clients after these clients had initially failed to benefit from treatment within a research study of cognitive therapy. The authors found that therapists who were subsequently successful with these clients differed from unsuccessful ones by their focus on the internal experiences of the clients, their encouragement of the client's expression of negative feelings toward others, their articulation of explicit treatment goals, and their ability to direct the client's attention to issues that seemed central to the presenting problems.

More explicit information about the efficacy of therapist interventions can be best understood by considering more specific and isolated types of interventions. Three types of interventions will be reviewed to illustrate some of the more important aspects of current knowledge: therapist directiveness, therapist self-disclosure, and therapist interpretation.

Therapist directiveness Psychotherapists have consistently been found to differ in the emphasis placed upon providing directions to clients (see Beutler, 1983; Hardy & Shapiro, 1985; Sundland, 1977). Those who adopt behavioral, cognitive, and other "action-oriented" philosophies tend to emphasize interventions that place the therapist in the role of teacher and guide, while those who select "insight-oriented" philosophies adopt more passive, evocative, and supportive roles (London, 1986). Yet, individual therapists within any theoretical orientation vary in how directive or evocative they may be. This interplay between therapy and therapist argues for a consideration of therapist directiveness as a psychotherapist intervention to be considered in this chapter.

In their meta-analytic review of short-term psychodynamic psychotherapy in comparison to alternative treatments, Svartberg and Stiles (1991) incorporated a composite dimension of therapist directiveness. Their assessment of 19 studies suggested that the mean effect size attributable to this dimension was $(r =) - .45$. Thus, therapist directiveness was generally counterproductive to therapeutic outcomes in psychodynamic therapy. There is some evidence to indicate that this result can be generalized to other therapies as well. For example, in two interrelated studies of compliance among mothers of adolescent clients in behavioral family therapy, Patterson and Forgatch (1985) found that directiveness interfered with client compliance. Similarly, in a comparison of the most and least effective therapists within a multidisciplinary training clinic, Lafferty et al. (1989) found that after the quality of the relationship (i.e., facilitative skills of the therapist) was partialed out, therapist directiveness was negatively related with symptom reduction.

On the other hand, a relatively large number of naturalistic and post hoc studies of therapist directiveness (e.g., Beutler, Dunbar, & Baer, 1980; Elliott, Barker, Caskey, & Pistrang, 1982; Hill, Carter, & O'Farrell, 1983; Luborsky et al., 1980; McLellan, Woody, Luborsky, & Goehl, 1988) noted a preponderance of positive relationships between therapist directiveness and beneficial outcomes. For example, in a summary of the Penn Psychotherapy Project, Luborsky et al. (1980) reported that therapist directiveness was positively associated with benefit by four of six psychotherapy raters. Similarly, the frequency of direct advisement by therapists was found to be modestly but positively associated with ratings of helpfulness in both an analogue and a clinical sample by Elliott et al. (1982).

It is possible that these contradictory findings result from the fact that the therapists in these various studies may actually have differed in how directive they were. Perhaps moderate levels of directiveness facilitate outcomes while high levels do not. The absence of standard and comparable measures of therapist directiveness prevent an analysis of this possibility. Another possibility is that different types of clients react differently to therapists who are and are not highly directive. In this case, client sample differences among the studies may account for the contradictions. These possibilities have led several investigators to look for qualities of clients that portend the differential use of directive and evocative interventions (e.g., Beutler, 1983, 1991; Shoham-Salomon, Avner, &

Neeman, 1989; Shoham-Salomon & Hannah, 1991).

A prospective test of the hypothesis that clients who varied on resistance potential would also vary in response to directive and nondirective therapies was undertaken by Beutler, Engle et al. (1991). This study employed an experimental design; manualized therapies; random assignment; and homogeneous, clinical samples of depressed patients. The authors demonstrated that therapists who were trained to use two different manualized therapies, both of which utilized similar amounts of therapist directiveness, were more effective at reducing depressive symptoms than those who were trained to use a nondirective intervention among subjects who were predetermined to be resistance prone. Conversely, among low resistance-prone depressed subjects, the nondirective therapists surpassed the directive ones in effecting change in depressive symptoms. This result was later cross-validated on one-year follow-up data in which relapse rates were studied (Beutler, Machado, Engle, & Mohr, 1993). The results also were independently replicated in a quasi-experimental, cross-validation study on a sample from the Bern Psychotherapy Research Program (Beutler, Mohr, Grawe, Engle, & MacDonald, 1991).

Overall, these results represent some of the strongest evidence available for the differential effects of directive and nondirective treatments, both because they tested prospective hypotheses and because these hypotheses were well founded in soical persuasion theory (Brehm & Brehm, 1981).

Therapist self-disclosure. The salience of therapist self-disclosure in psychotherapy was best captured by Jourard (1971), who proposed that disclosing therapists precipitated client self-disclosure. Early reviews seemed to support Jourard's proposal (e.g., Cozby, 1973), but the data were sparse and based upon poorly controlled studies. While the concept has continued to be discussed as a theoretical one that is applicable to psychotherapy in the social psychological literature, research on clinical populations and/or outcome effects is still virtually nonexistent.

At least part of the dearth of research may be attributable to the complexity of disclosure. There are many ways that a therapist may disclose information, ranging from subtle (e.g., displaying pictures of one's family) to obvious (e.g., discussing one's own experience). There are also variations in what information may be disclosed. Disclosures may be of either positive or negative feelings; they may range from very personal to impersonal (e.g., information about one's professional qualifications); they may describe ways in which the therapist and client are similar or ways in which they are different; or they may be directed at either in-therapy or out-of-therapy experiences.

Watkins (1990) suggests that the most obvious dimensions of self-disclosure include its positive versus negative quality, whether it is personal or demographic, whether it expresses similarity or dissimilarity to the client, whether it addresses present or past experience, and whether it is currently self-involving or temporally remote. After an intensive search of the literature, Watkins identified over 200 studies on self-disclosure, but only 35 of these addressed actual psychotherapy relationships. All of these latter studies, moreover, were either with nonclients, nontherapists, or nontherapy (e.g., portrayed therapy or vignettes of treatment). Although the conclusions may lack ecological validity, Watkins summarizes the findings as indicating that (1) self-involving disclosures are more helpful than temporally remote and uninvolving disclosures; (2) intimate disclosures are both favorably viewed and reciprocated more than nonintimate disclosures; and (3) different ethnic groups may respond differently to therapist disclosure, partly as a function of therapist–client ethnic similarity.

In one of the few nonanalogue studies available, Hill, Mahalik, and Thompson (1989) evaluated the effect of therapist self-disclosure on ratings of helpfulness. Both therapists and clients reviewed videotapes of sessions and rated each therapist intervention. Independent raters evaluated both the type and the level of each therapist's self-disclosure. Disclosures that were rated as supporting and reassuring were rated as more helpful than more confronting and challenging disclosures, by both clients and therapists, and they led to higher levels of client emotional experiencing.

Only three studies to our knowledge have assessed outcome directly as a function of therapist disclosure. Two of these studies employed naturalistic designs. One of these (Beutler & Mitchell, 1981) found a positive relationship between therapist self-disclosure and treatment benefit while the other (Alexander, Barton, Schiavo, & Parsons, 1976) found a nonsignificant relationship. The third study (Barrett & Berman, 1991) used a rigorous, experimental design. Fifteen therapists were pretrained and then instructed to increase the number of self-disclosures made to one randomly selected client and to refrain from self-disclosure to another similarly selected client. Symptomatic changes were evaluated after four sessions. The results indicated that when therapists disclosed personal information, their clients experienced greater symptomatic improvement than when they did not disclose.

While the latter study was rigorously conducted, the absence of a critical mass of outcome studies in this area renders the conclusions tentative. One can conclude only that therapist disclosure is a promising variable and may be of some importance to early symptomatic change.

Therapist interpretation.   The therapist's interpretations of client transference, motives, and resistance are central processes in psychodynamic psychotherapy. However, their use and usefulness undoubtedly extend beyond the confines of psychoanalytic viewpoints. For example, several studies have found that frequency of interpretations are correlated with perceived helpfulness and benefit among mixed clinical samples of clients and theoretically diverse therapists (Elliott et al., 1982; Gomez, 1982; Jacobs & Warner, 1981).

Accumulating evidence suggests that the efficacy of therapist interpretations may vary as a function of several variables. For example, in a retrospective study of 43 clients and 28 therapists in moderately intensive psychodynamic psychotherapy, Crits-Christoph, Cooper, and Luborsky (1988) found that the degree to which therapists' interpretations corresponded with independently derived clinical formulations was positively related to composite ratings of end-of-treatment benefit. Using a similar design, Piper et al. (1991, a, b) observed that an observed correspondence between the frequency of therapist transference interpretations and perceived benefits held only among clients who had histories of poor object relationships. Interestingly, those clients who had a history of good object relationships tended to do poorly when therapists made transference interpretations.

The meager amount of research on this topic and particularly the reliance on naturalistic designs speak of the need for more rigorous research designs. However, the promising results regarding the accuracy of therapist interpretations (i.e., their correspondence with independent formulations) have led to efforts to refine and standardize patient formulations so that they might be applicable to clinical practice (Crits-Christoph, Luborsky et al., 1988). (See also Chapter 11, this volume, for a more extended treatment of this topic.)

CONCLUSIONS

Psychotherapy research has undergone considerable change in the past decade. The advent of psychotherapy manuals, the introduction of meta-analysis, and the emphasis given to randomized clinical trials have led research consistently toward more pragmatic and clinician-ready questions (Omer & Dar, 1992; Piper, 1988). As a result of these changes, the answers that are emerging from contemporary literature regarding the role of therapist variables are becoming clearer.

TABLE 7.2   Summary of effect sizes associated with classes of therapist variables

Variable	ES (r)	Reference
Objective, Cross-Situational Traits		
Age	N/A	
Sex	N/A	
Ethnicity	N/A	
Subjective, Cross-Situational Traits		
Personality and coping patterns		
Cognitive level – lab	.38	Holloway & Wampold, 1986
Cognitive level – clinic	.05	Holloway & Wampold, 1986
Emotional well-being	N/A	
Values, attitudes, and beliefs	N/A	
Cultural attitudes	.10	Smith, Glass, & Miller, 1980
Subjective, Therapy-Specific States		
Therapeutic relationships		
Overall mean	.26	Horvath & Symonds, 1991
Therapist ratings	.17	Horvath & Symonds, 1991
Client ratings	.21	Horvath & Symonds, 1991
Social influence attitudes	N/A	
Expectancies	N/A	
Therapeutic philosophy/orientation		
Behavior therapy vs. other	.10	Miller & Berman, 1983
Behavior therapy vs. treatment	.51	Miller & Berman, 1983
Rational-emotive therapy vs. other	.15	Lyons & Woods, 1991
Rational-emotive therapy vs. no treatment	.63	Lyons & Woods, 1991
Range for all treatment	.13 – .68	Brown, 1987
Objective, Therapy-Specific States		
Professional background		
Level of training	.01	Berman & Norton, 1985
Treatment × age	.19	Berman & Norton, 1985
Short-term therapy	.43	Berman & Norton, 1985
Children	.15	Weisz, Weiss, Alicke, & Klotz, 1987
Treatment × problem	.20	Weisz, Weiss, Alicke, & Klotz, 1987
Profession	.00	Prioleau, Murdock & Brody, 1983
	.28	Smith, Glass & Miller, 1980
Experience	.01	Stein & Lambert, 1984
Therapist style	N/A	
Therapist Interventions		
Manuals	.38	Robinson, Berman, & Neimeyer, 1990
Skillfulness	N/A	
Directiveness	−.45	Svartberg & Stiles, 1991
Self disclosure	N/A	
Interpretation	N/A	

Table 7.2 provides a recapitulation of various therapist variables in the form of associated effect sizes extracted from various meta-analytic reviews. This table reports effect sizes (r) separately for each therapy quality presented in Figure 7.1. It will be noted that effect sizes based on meta-analytic reviews are not available, to our knowledge, for any of the three variables (age, sex, ethnicity) comprising objective, cross-situational traits. From our review, a tentative rule of thumb can be applied, however, suggesting that similarity on these dimensions facilitates retention in therapy. Even a more

tentative suggestion may be offered that sexual similarity may enhance therapeutic change, especially among female clients. Overall, however, available literature suggests that neither age, sex, nor ethnicity plays a major role in therapy outcome.

We conclude that future research on therapist objective, cross-situational traits must begin to address more complex issues than it has in the past. Instead of simply assessing the efficacy associated with therapist and client groups who are defined by demographic status, researchers may do well to evaluate differential impacts of therapist demographics with clients who vary in cultural attitudes and socialization processes.

With respect to the other three classes of variables, Table 7.2 suggests that, as judged by the relative strength of effect sizes, variables within the class of objective, therapy-specific states exert the most powerful effects on psychotherapeutic outcome. These effects are variable, however, depending on both the nature of the specific variable studied and the therapy and client qualities with which it interacts. Therapists who use psychotherapy manuals to guide their interventions, for example, appear to enhance therapeutic benefit over those who do not use such structured intervention packages. One may also compare the moderate effect size obtained by therapists who use manuals with the low effect size attributable to therapist theoretical orientation. However, there is considerable variation in the effects attributable to the use of different manuals. While the differences in these effects are seldom statistically significant, their variability raises the suspicion that not all manualized interventions are equally effective under all conditions. To the degree that various interventions within the different manuals can be extracted and applied selectively to the client group for which they are most effective, one may find credence in the contemporary movement toward integrating the use of techniques and treatment models (cf. Mahalik, 1990; Norcross & Prochaska, 1988).

Indeed, research that has studied specific types of interventions has observed that differential effects frequently emerge for different types of clients. For example, therapist directiveness has been found to inhibit treatment outcome, on the average (ES [r] = −.45), but the evidence reviewed in this chapter suggests that certain types of clients may actually benefit from directive therapists but not nondirective ones.

Research on the therapeutic efficacy of other therapist interventions is also promising. Specifically, further research is warranted on the possibility that differential efficacy rates accrue for different client groups when the therapist provides psychodynamic interpretations or self-discloses personal information. The stability of client object relationships, receptivity to therapy, and coping style may be especially promising variables that are associated with differential levels of efficacy.

Likewise, research seems to hold promise in other areas of therapist–client matching, specifically research that seeks to find differential indicators for varying the therapist's use of different verbal interventions and for the assignment of therapists with different therapeutic training backgrounds. Included among the particularly promising domains in which client–therapist matches may

produce differential effects are qualities associated with various circumplex models of social interaction and therapist experience levels. Some of this research is likely to reach fruition only if expanded or extended in new directions, however. Research on therapist experience, for example, would benefit from employing carefully controlled, quasi-experimental designs that explore different matches or client–therapist "fits." An experienced therapist may facilitate improvement among some clients, but not among others. The nature of the client variables that portend positive responses is currently unclear, however.

Among the therapist subjective traits and states, consistent evidence exists to support the assertion (now nearly a "truism") that a warm and supportive therapeutic relationship facilitates therapeutic success (ES [r] = .26). Research in this area continues to be strong but is now poised to move toward developing methods for enhancing the therapeutic relationship among groups who do not typically respond to psychotherapy. Indeed, we have noted several investigations that have begun to move in this direction.

There are a number of other promising subjective therapist variables as well. Research on patterns of therapist–client value and attitudinal similarity and differences continues to suggest predictive power for matching clients and therapists in these dimensions. Likewise, assessment of similarities in cultural attitudes holds promise as a means for facilitating retention in and commitment to the psychotherapy experience.

Finally, there are areas of research within the domains of subjective traits and states that have born little fruit and may well be abandoned in favor of new and more specific directions. Efforts to match therapists and clients on global personality dimensions or to predict therapeutic effects from global therapist personality measures appear to be fruitless. We have noted the decline of interest in the A–B therapist typology and in the use of the Myers-Briggs typology. We have also noted the lack of consistent progress in the effort to define therapist cognitive styles that are predictive of treatment benefit. This is observable in the failure of analogue findings on therapist conceptual level to be cross-validated in clinical settings and with clinical populations (note the contrast between the effect sizes in laboratory [.38] and clinical [.05] studies in Table 7.2).

Overall, we observe that research methodologies are improving and there are some interesting new variables being introduced as replacements for some that have yielded unproductive results. This is a different picture than the one reported in the last edition of the Handbook. At that time, it was lamented that research methods had changed but had added little new information (Beutler et al., 1986). Treatment manuals and effect size analyses have added an avenue for experimental control not previously used and have provided an empirical basis for summarizing data. In turn, these advances have allowed researchers to begin disentangling complex concepts from one another, such as therapist theoretical orientations, therapy interventions, and therapy models. Concomitantly, some areas of research continue to receive a dearth of attention and others have even been abandoned. Some of this neglect may be attributed to the fact that available research did not support continuing work in these areas. Less positively, however, the lack of attention given to certain areas of research may reflect a premature abandonment of topics of investigation simply because they are difficult to research and the methodologies required are inconsistent with the quick, pragmatic approaches demanded in the current *zeitgeist*. This is lamentable.

On a positive note, we find some reason to disagree with Piper (1988) and with Omer and Dar (1992) in suggesting that theory-driven research is no longer in vogue. While pragmatic rather than theory-driven research is the norm, it is also notable that there are several areas in which theory-driven research continues and the list of these areas may be expanding. Although only time will tell, we think we perceive an indication that contemporary theory-driven research is more sophisticated than previous work and attends more closely to the needs of clinicians for finding applications. For example, complex theory-driven analyses of social interaction have largely replaced shotgun approaches to exploring differential efficacy associated both with client–therapist and client–therapy pairings.

Similarly, we note a reliance on theory-driven investigations in the emerging evidence of the efficacy of specific therapeutic techniques such as interpretations, as well as in the promising findings suggesting that different client qualities may serve as indicators and even contraindicators for various interventions. These are promising directions. Perhaps the next edition of this *Handbook* will see more amalgamation of theory with the pragmatics of application. Our optimism for the peaceful coexistence of research and practice dies hard.

REFERENCES

Abramowitz, S. I., & Murray, J. (1983). Race effects in psychotherapy. In J. Murray & P. R. Abramson (Eds.), *Bias in psychotherapy* (pp. 215–255). New York: Praeger.

Alberts, G., & Edelstein, B. (1990). Therapist training: A critical review of skill training studies. *Clinical Psychology Review, 10,* 497–511.

Alexander, J. F., Barton, C., Schiavo, R. S., & Parsons, B. V. (1976). Systems-behavioral interventions with families of delinquents: Therapist characteristics, family behavior, and outcome. *Journal of Consulting and Clinical Psychology, 17,* 656–664.

Amira, S., & Abramowitz, S. I. (1979). Therapeutic attraction as a function of therapist attire and office furnishing. *Journal of Consulting and Clinical Psychology, 47,* 198–200.

Andrews, J. D. W. (1990). Interpersonal self-confirmation and challenge in psychotherapy. *Psychotherapy, 27,* 485–504.

Antonuccio, D. O., Davis, C., Lewinsohn, P. M., & Breckenridge, J. S. (1987). Therapist variables related to cohesiveness in a group treatment for depression. *Small Group Behavior, 18,* 557–564.

Antonuccio, D. O., Lewinsohn, P. M., & Steinmetz, J. L. (1982). Identification of therapist differences in group treatment for depression. *Journal of Consulting and Clinical Psychology, 50,* 433–435.

Arizmendi, T. G., Beutler, L. E., Shanfield, S., Crago, M., & Hagaman, R. (1985). Client–therapist value similarity and psychotherapy outcome: A microscopic approach. *Psychotherapy: Theory, Research, and Practice, 22,* 16–21.

Atkinson, D. R. (1983). Ethnic similarity and counseling psychology. *The Counseling Psychologist, 11,* 79–92.

Atkinson, D. R. (1985). A meta-review of research on cross-cultural counseling and psychotherapy. *Journal of Multicultural Counseling and Development, 13,* 138–153.

Atkinson, D. R., & Matsushita, Y. J. (1991). Japanese-American acculturation, counseling style, counselor ethnicity, and perceived counselor credibility. *Journal of Counseling Psychology, 38,* 473–478.

Atkinson, D., & Schein, S. (1986). Similarity in counseling. *The Counseling Psychologist, 14,* 319–354.

Auerbach, A. H., & Johnson, M. (1977). Research on the therapist's level of experience. In A. S. Gurman & A. M. Razin (Eds.), *Effective psychotherapy: A handbook of research* (pp. 84–102). Elmsford, NY: Pergamon.

Babad, E. Y., Bernieri, F., & Rosenthal, R. (1989). Nonverbal communication and leakage in the behavior of biased and unbiased teachers. *Journal of Personality and Social Psychology, 56,* 89–94.

Baekeland, F., & Lundwall, M. A. (1975). Dropping out of treatment: A critical review. *Psychological Bulletin, 82,* 738–783.

Bandura, A. (1986). *Social foundations of thought and action.* Englewood Cliffs, NJ: Prentice Hall.

Banikiotes, P. G., & Merluzzi, T. V. (1981). Impact of counselor gender and counselor sex role orientation on perceived counselor characteristics. *Journal of Counseling Psychology, 28,* 342–348.

Barkham, M., & Shapiro, D. A. (1986). Counselor verbal response modes and experienced empathy. *Journal of Counseling Psychology, 33,* 3–10.

Barrett, M. S., & Berman, J. S. (1991, October). *Is psychotherapy more effective when therapists disclose information about themselves?* Paper presented at the North American Society for Psychotherapy Research, Panama City, FL.

Beck, D. F. (1988). *Counselor characteristics: How they affect outcomes.* Milwaukee, WI: Family Service America.

Benjamin, L. S. (1974). Structural analysis of social behavior. *Psychological Review, 81,* 392–445.

Bennun, I., & Schindler, L. (1988). Therapist and patient factors in the behavioural treatment of phobic patients. *British Journal of Clinical Psychology, 27,* 145–150.

Bergin, A. E. (1980). Psychotherapy and religious values. *Journal of Consulting and Clinical Psychology*, *48*, 95–105.

Bergin, A. E., & Jasper, L. G. (1969). Correlates of empathy in psychotherapy: A replication. *Journal of Abnormal Psychology*, *74*, 477–481.

Bergin, A. E., & Jensen, J. P. (1989). Religiosity of psychotherapists: A national survey. *Psychotherapy*, *27*, 3–7.

Berman, J. S. (1989, June). *Investigator allegiance and the findings from comparative outcome studies*. Paper presented at the annual meeting of the Society for Psychotherapy Research, Toronto.

Berman, J. S., Miller, R. C., & Massman, P. J. (1985). Cognitive therapy versus systematic desensitization: Is one treatment superior? *Psychological Bulletin*, *97*, 451–461.

Berman, J. S., & Norton, N. C. (1985). Does professional training make a therapist more effective? *Psychological Bulletin*, *98*, 401–407.

Bernieri, F., Blanck, P. D., Rosenthal, R., Vannicelli, M., & Yerrell, P. H. (1991). *Verbal–nonverbal congruency and affect in therapists' speech in speaking to and about patients*. Unpublished manuscript. Oregon State University, Corvallis.

Berry, G. W., & Sipps, G. J. (1991). Interactive effects of counselor–client similarity and client self-esteem on termination type and number of sessions. *Journal of Counseling Psychology*, *38*, 120–125.

Berzins, J. I. (1977). Therapist–patient matching. In A. S. Gurman & A. M. Razin (Eds.), *Effective psychotherapy: A handbook of research* (pp. 222–251). Elmsford, NY: Pergamon.

Beutler, L. E. (1981). Convergence in counseling and psychotherapy: A current look. *Clinical Psychology Review*, *1*, 79–101.

Beutler, L. E. (1983). *Eclectic psychotherapy: A systematic approach*. Elmsford, NY: Pergamon.

Beutler, L. E. (1991). Have all won and must all have prizes? Revisiting Luborsky et al.'s verdict. *Journal of Consulting and Clinical Psychology*, *59*, 226–232.

Beutler, L. E., Arizmendi, T. G., Crago, M., Shanfield, S., & Hagaman, R. (1983). The effects of value similarity and clients' persuadability on value convergence and psychotherapy improvement. *Journal of Social and Clinical Psychology*, *1*, 231–245.

Beutler, L. E., & Bergan, J. (1991). Value change in counseling and psychotherapy: A search for scientific credibility. *Journal of Counseling Psychology*, *38*, 16–24.

Beutler, L. E., & Clarkin, J. (1990). *Systematic treatment selection: Toward targeted therapeutic interventions*. New York: Brunner/Mazel.

Beutler, L. E., Clarkin, J., Crago, M., & Bergan, J. (1991). Client–therapist matching. In C. R. Snyder & D. R. Forsyth (Eds.), *Handbook of social and clinical psychology: The health perspective* (pp. 699–716). Elmsford, NY: Pergamon.

Beutler, L. E., Crago, M., & Arizmendi, T. G. (1986). Therapist variables in psychotherapy process and outcome. In S. L. Garfield & A. E. Bergin (Eds.), *Handbook of psychotherapy and behavior change* (3rd ed., pp. 257–310). New York: Wiley.

Beutler, L. E., Dunbar, P. W., & Baer, P. E. (1980). Individual variation among therapists' perceptions of patients, therapy process and outcome. *Psychiatry*, *43*, 205–210.

Beutler, L. E., Engle, D., Mohr, D., Daldrup, R. J., Bergan, J., Meredith, K., & Merry, W. (1991). Predictors of differential and self-directed psychotherapeutic procedures. *Journal of Consulting and Clinical Psychology*, *59*, 333–340.

Beutler, L. E., Jobe, A. M., & Elkins, D. (1974). Outcomes in group psychotherapy: Using persuasion theory to increase treatment efficiency. *Journal of Consulting and Clinical Psychology*, *42*, 547–553.

Beutler, L. E., Machado, P. P. P., Engle, D., & Mohr, D. (1993). Differential patient × treatment maintenance of treatment effects among cognitive, experiential, and self-directed psychotherapies. *Journal of Psychotherapy Integration*, *3*, 15–31.

Beutler, L. E., & Mitchell, R. (1981). Psychotherapy outcome in depressed and impulsive patients as a function of analytic and experiential treatment procedures. *Psychiatry*, *44*, 297–306.

Beutler, L. E., Mohr, D. C., Grawe, K., Engle, D., & MacDonald, R. (1991). Looking for differential effects: Cross-cultural predictors of differential psychotherapy efficacy. *Journal of Psychotherapy Integration*, *1*, 121–142.

Beutler, L. E., Pollack, S., & Jobe, A. M. (1978). "Acceptance," values and therapeutic change. *Journal of Consulting and Clinical Psychology*, *46*, 198–199.

Beutler, L. E., Scogin, F., Kirkish, P., Schretlen, D., Corbishley, M. A., Hamblin, D., Meredith, K., Potter, R., Bamford, C. R., & Levenson, A. I. (1987). Group cognitive therapy and alprazolam in the treatment of depression in older adults. *Journal of Consulting and Clinical Psychology*, *55*, 550–556.

Billingsley, D. (1977). Sex bias in psychotherapy: An examination of the effects of client sex, client pathology, and therapist sex on treatment planning. *Journal of Consulting and Clinical Psychology*, *45*, 250–256.

Bolter, K., Levenson, H., & Alvarez, W. (1990). Differences in values between short-term and long-term therapists. *Professional Psychology: Research and Practice*, *21*, 285–290.

Bonner, B. L., & Everett, F. L. (1986). Influence of client preparation and problem severity on attitudes and expectations in child psychotherapy. *Professional Psychology: Research and Practice*, *17*, 223–229.

Bootzin, R. R., & Ruggill, J. S. (1988). Training issues in behavior therapy. *Journal of Consulting and Clinical Psychology*, *56*, 703–709.

Bordin, E. S. (1976). The generalizability of the psychoanalytic concept of the working alliance. *Psychotherapy: Theory, Research, and Practice*, *16*, 252–260.

Brehm, S. S. (1976). *The application of social psychology to clinical practice*. New York: Wiley.

Brehm, S. S., & Brehm, J. W. (1981). *Psychological reactance: A theory of freedom and control*. New York: Academic Press.

Brooks, V. R. (1981). Sex and sexual orientation as variables in therapist's biases and therapy outcomes. *Clinical Social Work Journal*, *9*, 198–210.

Brown, B. L., Warner, C. A., & Williams, R. N. (1985). Vocal paralanguage without unconscious processes. In A. W. Siegman & S. Feldstein (Eds.), *Multichannel integrations of nonverbal behavior* (pp. 149–193). Hillsdale, NJ: Lawrence Erlbaum.

Brown, J. (1987). A review of meta-analyses conducted on psychotherapy outcome research. *Clinical Psychology Review*, *7*, 1–23.

Brown, L. S. (1991). What female therapists have in common. In D. W. Cantor (Ed.), *Women as therapists: A multitheoretical casebook* (pp. 227–242). New York: Springer.

Brown, R. A., Leichtman, S. R., Blass, T., & Fleisher, E. (1982). Mandated continuing education: Impact on Maryland psychologists. *Professional Psychology*, *13*, 404–411.

Buckley, P., Karasu, T. B., & Charles, E. (1981). Psychotherapists view their personal therapy. *Psychotherapy: Theory, Research, and Practice, 18,* 299–305.

Burgoon, J. K., Kelley, D. L., Newton, D. A., & Keeley-Dyreson, M. P. (1989). The nature of arousal and nonverbal indices. *Human Communication Research, 16,* 217–255.

Burgoon, M., & Ruffner, M. (1978). *Human communication.* New York: Holt, Rinehart and Winston.

Burton, M. V., Parker, R. W., & Wollner, J. M. (1991). The psychotherapeutic value of a "chat": A verbal response modes study of a placebo attention control with breast cancer patients. *Psychotherapy Research, 1,* 39–61.

Calvert, S. J., Beutler, L. E., & Crago, M. (1988). Psychotherapy outcome as a function of therapist–patient matching on selected variables. *Journal of Social and Clinical Psychology, 6,* 104–117.

Cammaert, L. P., & Larsen, C. C. (1988). Feminist frameworks of psychotherapy. In M. A. Dutton-Douglas & L. E. Walker (Eds.), *Feminist psychotherapies: Integration of therapeutic and feminist systems* (pp. 12–36). Norwood, NJ: Ablex.

Cantor, D. W. (1991). Women as therapists: What we already know. In D. W. Cantor (Ed.), *Women as therapists: A multitheoretical casebook* (pp. 3–19). New York: Springer.

Carlson, J. G. (1985). Recent assessments of the Myers-Briggs Type Indicator. *Journal of Personality Assessment, 49,* 356–365.

Carson, R. C., & Heine, R. W. (1962). Similarity and success in therapeutic dyads. *Journal of Consulting Psychology, 26,* 38–43.

Carson, R. C., & Llewellyn, C. E., Jr. (1966). Similarity in therapeutic dyads. *Journal of Consulting Psychology, 30,* 458.

Charone, J. K. (1981). Patient and therapist treatment goals related to psychotherapy outcome. *Dissertation Abstracts International, 42,* 365B.

Cheloha, R. S. (1986). The relationship between client–therapist mental health, value similarity, and psychotherapy outcome. *Dissertation Abstracts International, 47,* 1716B.

Chesner, S., & Baumeister, R. (1985). Effect of therapist's disclosure of religious beliefs on the intimacy of client self-disclosure. *Journal of Clinical Psychology, 3,* 97–105.

Childress, R., & Gillis, J. S. (1977). A study of pretherapy role induction as an influence process. *Journal of Clinical Psychology, 33,* 540–544.

Clark, M. M. (1986). Personal therapy: A review of empirical research. *Professional Psychology, 17,* 541–543.

Cline, V. B. (1984). The relationship between therapist behaviors and outcome for middle- and lower-class couples in marital therapy. *Journal of Clinical Psychology, 40,* 691–704.

Conway, J. B. (1988). Differences among clinical psychologists: Scientists, practitioners, and scientist-practitioners. *Professional Psychology: Research and Practice, 19,* 642–655.

Cooke, M., & Kipnis, D. (1986). Influence tactics in psychotherapy. *Journal of Consulting and Clinical Psychology, 54,* 22–26.

Cooney, N. L., Kadden, R. M., Litt, M. D., & Getter, H. (1991). Matching alcoholics to coping skills or interactional therapies: Two-year follow-up results. *Journal of Consulting and Clinical Psychology, 59,* 598–601.

Corrigan, C. D., Dell, D. M., Lewis, K. N., & Schmidt, L. D. (1980). Counseling as social influence process: A review. *Journal of Counseling Psychology, 27,* 395–441.

Cozby, P. C. (1973). Self-disclosure: A literature review. *Psychological Bulletin, 79,* 73–91.

Crits-Christoph, P., Baranackie, K., Kurcias, J. S., Beck, A. T., Carroll, K., Perry, K., Luborsky, L., McLellan, A. T., Woody, G. E., Thompson, L., Gallagher, D., & Zitrin, C. (1991). Meta-analysis of therapist effects in psychotherapy outcome studies. *Psychotherapy Research, 1,* 81–92.

Crits-Christoph, P., Cooper, A., & Luborsky, L. (1988). The accuracy of therapists' interpretations and the outcome of dynamic psychotherapy. *Journal of Consulting and Clinical Psychology, 56,* 490–495.

Crits-Christoph, P., & Mintz, J. (1991). Implications of therapist effects for the design and analysis of comparative studies of psychotherapies. *Journal of Consulting and Clinical Psychology, 59,* 20–26.

Crits-Christoph, P., Luborsky, L., Dahl, L., Popp, C., Mellon, J., & Mark, D. (1988). Clinicians can agree in assessing relationship patterns in psychotherapy. *Archives of General Psychiatry, 45,* 1001–1004.

Cutler, R. L. (1958). Countertransference effects in psychotherapy. *Journal of Consulting Psychology, 22,* 349–356.

Davis, K. L., Hector, M. A., Meara, N. M., King, J. W., Tracy, D. C., & Wycoff, J. P. (1985). Teaching counselor trainees to respond consistently to different aspects of anger. *Journal of Counseling Psychology, 32,* 580–588.

Davis, M., & Hadiks, D. (1991, October). *Nonverbal communication of therapist interventions.* Paper presented at the meeting of the North American Chapter of the Society for Psychotherapy Research, Panama City, FL.

Dembo, R., Ikle, D. N., & Ciarlo, J. A. (1983). The influence of client–clinician demographic match on client treatment outcomes. *Journal of Psychiatric Treatment and Evaluation, 5,* 45–53.

Deysach, R. E., Rooss, A. W., & Hiers, T. G. (1977). Locus of control in prediction of counselor effectiveness within a therapeutic camp setting. *Journal of Clinical Psychology, 33,* 273–278.

Dietzel, C. S., & Abeles, N. (1975). Client–therapist complementarity and therapeutic outcome. *Journal of Counseling Psychology, 22,* 264–272.

Dobson, K. S., & Shaw, B. F. (1988). The use of treatment manuals in cognitive therapy: Experience and issues. *Journal of Consulting and Clinical Psychology, 56,* 673–680.

Donner, L., & Schonfield, J. (1975). Affect contagion in beginning psychotherapists. *Journal of Clinical Psychology, 31,* 514–518.

Dormaar, M., Kijkman, S. I. M., & de Vries, M. W. (1989). Consensus in patient–therapist interactions: A measure of the therapeutic relationship related to outcome. *Psychotherapy Psychosomatica, 51,* 69–76.

Dorn, F. J., & Day, B. J. (1985). Assessing change in self-concept: A social psychology approach. *American Mental Health Counselors Association Journal, 7,* 180–186.

Durlak, J. A. (1979). Comparative effectiveness of paraprofessional and professional helpers. *Psychological Bulletin, 86,* 80–92.

Durlak, J. A. (1981). Evaluating comparative studies of paraprofessional and professional helpers: A reply to Nietzel and Fisher. *Psychological Bulletin, 89,* 566–569.

Durlak, J. A., Fuhrman, T., & Lampman, C. (1991). Effectiveness of cognitive-behavior therapy for maladapting children: A meta-analysis. *Psychological Bulletin, 110,* 204–214.

Ekman, P., & Friesen, W. V. (1969). Nonverbal leakage clues to deception. *Psychiatry, 32,* 88–106.

Elkin, I., Parloff, M. B., Hadley, S. W., & Autry, J. H. (1985). NIMH Treatment of Depression Collaborative Research Program. *Archives of General Psychiatry, 42,* 305–316.

Elkin, I., Shea, T., Watkins, J. T., Imber, S. D., Sotsky, S. M., Collins, J. F., Glass, D. R., Pilkonis, P. A., Leber, W.

R., Docherty, J. P., Feister, S. J., & Parloff, M. B. (1989). National Institute of Mental Health Treatment of Depression Collaborative Research Program. *Archives of General Psychiatry, 46,* 971–982.

Elliott, R. (1985). Helpful and nonhelpful events in brief counseling interviews: An empirical taxonomy. *Journal of Counseling Psychology, 32,* 307–322.

Elliott, R., Barker, C. B., Caskey, N., & Pistrang, N. (1982). Differential helpfulness of counselor verbal response modes. *Journal of Counseling Psychology, 29,* 354–361.

Elliott, R., Hill, C. E., Stiles, W. B., Friedlander, M. L., Mahrer, A. R., & Margison, F. R. (1987). Primary therapist response modes: A comparison of six rating systems. *Journal of Consulting and Clinical Psychology, 55,* 218–223.

Fairbanks, L. A., McGuire, M. T., & Harris, C. J. (1982). Nonverbal interaction of patients and therapists during psychiatric interviews. *Journal of Abnormal Psychology, 91,* 109–119.

Farber, B. A. (1983). The effects of psychotherapeutic practice upon psychotherapists. *Psychotherapy: Theory and Practice, 20,* 174–182.

Fisher, E. H., & Howard, K. I. (1984, June). *The process of outcome in psychotherapy as a function of gender pairing.* Paper presented at the Society for Psychotherapy Research, Lake Louise, Ontario, Canada.

Foon, A. E. (1985). Similarity between therapists' and clients' locus of control: Implications for therapeutic expectations and outcome. *Psychotherapy, 22,* 711–717.

Foon, A. E. (1986). Locus of control and clients' expectations of psychotherapeutic outcome. *British Journal of Clinical Psychology, 25,* 161–171.

Fosterling, F. (1988). *Attribution theory in clinical psychology.* New York: Wiley.

Francis, D. J., Fletcher, J. M., Stuebing, K. K., Davidson, K. C., & Thompson, N. M. (1991). Analysis of change: Modeling individual growth. *Journal of Consulting and Clinical Psychology, 59,* 27–37.

Frank, J. D. (1973). *Persuasion and healing: A comparative study of psychotherapy* (rev. ed.). Baltimore: The Johns Hopkins University Press.

Frank, J. D., & Frank, J. B. (1991). *Persuasion and healing* (3rd ed.). Baltimore: The Johns Hopkins University Press.

Frieswyk, S. H., Allen, J. G., Colson, D. B., Coyne, L., Gabbard, G. O., Horwitz, L., & Newsom, G. (1986). Therapeutic alliance: Its place as a process and outcome variable in dynamic psychotherapy research. *Journal of Consulting and Clinical Psychology, 54,* 32–38.

Garb, H. N. (1989). Clinical judgment, clinical training, and professional experience. *Psychological Bulletin, 105,* 387–396.

Garfield, S. L., & Bergin, A. E. (1971). Personal therapy, outcome, and some therapist variables. *Psychotherapy: Theory, Research, and Practice, 8,* 251–253.

Garnets, L., Hancock, K. A., Cochran, S. D., Goodchilds, J., & Peplau, L. A. (1991). Issues in psychotherapy with lesbians and gay men. *American Psychologist, 46,* 964–972.

Gaston, L. & Ring, J. M. (1992). Preliminary results on the inventory of therapeutic strategies. *Journal of Psychotherapy Practice and Research, 1,* 1–13.

Gaston, L., Marmar, C. R., Thompson, L. W., & Gallagher, D. (1988). Relation of patient pretreatment characteristics to the therapeutic alliance in diverse psychotherapies. *Journal of Consulting and Clinical Psychology, 56,* 483–489.

Gilbert, L. A. (1981). Toward mental health: The benefits of psychological androgyny. *Professional Psychology, 12,* 29–38.

Giles, T. R. (1983). Probable superiority of behavioral interventions. II: Empirical status of the equivalence of therapies hypothesis. *Journal of Behavior Therapy and Experimental Psychiatry, 14,* 189–196.

Goldberg, D. P., Hobson, R. F., Maguire, G. P., Margison, F. R., O'Dowd, T., Osborn, M., & Moss, S. (1984). The clarification and assessment of a method of psychotherapy. *British Journal of Psychiatry, 144,* 567–580.

Goldstein, A. P. (1971). *Psychotherapeutic attraction.* Elmsford, NY: Pergamon.

Gomez, E. A. (1982). The evaluation of psychosocial casework services to Chicanos: A study of process and outcome. *Dissertation Abstracts International, 43:3A,* 925.

Goodman, M., & Teicher, A. (1988). To touch or not to touch. *Psychotherapy, 25,* 492–500.

Greenberg, R. P., & Staller, J. (1981). Personal therapy for therapists. *American Journal of Psychiatry, 138,* 1467–1471.

Greenspan, M., & Kulish, N. M. (1985). Factors in premature termination in long-term psychotherapy. *Psychotherapy, 22,* 75–82.

Grimes, W. R., & Murdock, N. L. (1989). Social influence revisited: Effects of counselor influence on outcome variables. *Psychotherapy, 26,* 469–474.

Guest, P. D., & Beutler, L. E. (1988). The impact of psychotherapy supervision on therapist orientation and values. *Journal of Consulting and Clinical Psychology, 56,* 653–658.

Guild, M. (1969). *Therapeutic effectiveness of analyzed and unanalyzed therapists.* Unpublished doctoral dissertation. St. John's University, New York.

Gurman, A. S. (1977). Therapist and patient factors influencing the patient's perception of facilitative therapeutic conditions. *Psychiatry, 40,* 16–24.

Guy, J. D., & Liaboe, G. P. (1986). The impact of conducting psychotherapy on psychotherapists' interpersonal functioning. *Professional Psychology: Research and Practice, 17,* 111–114.

Guy, J. D., Stark, M. J., & Poelstra, P. L. (1988). Personal therapy for psychotherapists before and after entering professional practice. *Professional Psychology: Research and Practice, 19,* 474–476.

Hall, G. C. N., & Malony, H. N. (1983). Cultural control in psychotherapy with minority clients. *Psychotherapy: Theory, Research, and Practice, 20,* 131–142.

Hamblin, D. L., Beutler, L. E., Scogin, F. R., & Corbishley, A. (1988, June). *Patient responsiveness to therapist values and outcome in group cognitive therapy.* Paper presented at the annual meeting of the Society for Psychotherapy Research, Santa Fe, NM.

Hardy, G. E., & Shapiro, D. A. (1985). Therapist response modes in prescriptive vs. exploratory psychotherapy. *British Journal of Clinical Psychology, 24,* 235–245.

Harper, R. G., Wiens, A. N., & Matarazzo, J. D. (1978). *Non-verbal communications: The state of the art.* New York: Wiley.

Harrison, D. K. (1975). Race as a counselor–client variable in counseling and psychotherapy. *The Counseling Psychologist, 5,* 124–133.

Hart, L. E. (1981). An investigation of the effect of male therapists' views of women on the process and outcome of therapy with women. *Dissertation Abstracts International, 42,* 2529B.

Harvey, J. H., & Weary, G. (Eds.). (1985). *Attribution: Basic issues and applications.* Orlando, FL.: Academic Press.

Hattie, J. A., Sharpley, C. F., & Rogers, H. J. (1984). Comparative effectiveness of professional and paraprofessional helpers. *Psychological Bulletin, 95,* 534–541.

Henry, W. P., Schacht, T. E., & Strupp, H. H. (1990).

Patient and therapist introject, interpersonal process, and differential psychotherapy outcome. *Journal of Consulting and Clinical Psychology, 58,* 768–774.

Henry, W. P., Schacht, T. E., Strupp, H. H., Butler, S. F., & Binder, J. L. (1993a). The effects of training in time-limited dynamic psychotherapy. Changes in therapist behavior. *Journal of Consulting and Clinical Psychology, 61,* 434–440.

Henry, W. P., Schacht, T. E., Strupp, H. H., Butler, S. F., & Binder, J. L. (1993b). The effects of training in time-limited dynamic psychotherapy. Mediators of therapists' response to training. *Journal of Consulting and Clinical Psychology, 61,* 441–447.

Henry, W. P., & Strupp, H. H. (1991). Vanderbilt University: The Vanderbilt Center for Psychotherapy Research. In L. E. Beutler & M. Crago (Eds.), *Psychotherapy research: An international review of programmatic studies* (pp. 166–174). Washington, DC: American Psychological Association.

Henry, W. P., Strupp, H. H., Schacht, T. E., Binder, J. E., & Butler, S. F. (1992, June). *The effects of training in time-limited dynamic psychotherapy: Changes in therapeutic outcome.* Paper presented at the international meeting of the Society for Psychotherapy Research, Berkeley, CA.

Heppner, P. P., & Claiborn, C. D. (1989). Social influence research in counseling: A review and critique. *Journal of Counseling Psychology, 36,* 365–387.

Heppner, P. P., & Dixon, D. N. (1981). A review of the interpersonal influence process in counseling. *Personnel and Guidance Journal, 59,* 542–550.

Heppner, P. P., & Heesacker, M. (1982). Interpersonal influence process in real-life counseling: Investigating client perceptions, counselor experience level, and counselor power over time. *Journal of Counseling Psychology, 29,* 215–223.

Heppner, P. P., & Heesacker, M. (1983). Perceived counselor characteristics, client expectations, and client satisfaction with counseling. *Journal of Counseling Psychology, 30,* 31–39.

Hermansson, G. L., Webster, A. C., & McFarland, K. (1988). Counselor deliberate postural lean and communication of facilitative conditions. *Journal of Counseling Psychology, 35,* 149–153.

Hill, C. E. (1978). The development of a system for classifying counselor responses. *Journal of Counseling Psychology, 25,* 461–468.

Hill, C. E. (1990). A review of exploratory in-session process research in individual psychotherapy. *Journal of Consulting and Clinical Psychology, 58,* 288–294.

Hill, C. E., Carter, J. A., & O'Farrell, M. K. (1983). A case study of the process and outcome of time-limited counseling. *Journal of Counseling Psychology, 30,* 3–18.

Hill, C. E., Helms, J. E., Tichenor, V., Spiegel, S. B., O'Grady, K. E., & Perry, E. S. (1988). Effects of therapist response modes in brief psychotherapy. *Journal of Counseling Psychology, 33,* 222–233.

Hill, C. E., Mahalik, J. R., & Thompson, B. J. (1989). Therapist self-disclosure. *Psychotherapy, 26,* 290–295.

Hill, C. E., & O'Grady, K. E. (1985). A list of therapist intentions: Illustrated in a single case and with therapists of varying theoretical orientations. *Journal of Counseling Psychology, 32,* 3–22.

Hill, C. E., O'Grady, K. E., & Elkin, I. (1992). Applying the collaborative study psychotherapy rating scale to rate therapist adherence in cognitive-behavior therapy, interpersonal therapy, and clinical management. *Journal of Consulting and Clinical Psychology, 60,* 73–79.

Hill, C. E., & Stephany, A. (1990). Relation of nonverbal behavior to client reactions. *Journal of Counseling Psychology, 37,* 22–26.

Hill, C. E., Thames, T. B., & Rardin, D. (1979). A comparison of Rogers, Perls, and Ellis on the Hill Counselor Verbal Response Category system. *Journal of Counseling Psychology, 26,* 198–203.

Hill, J. A., Howard, K. I., & Orlinsky, D. E. (1970). The therapist's experience of psychotherapy: Some dimensions and determinants. *Multivariate Behavioral Research, 5,* 435–451.

Holloway, E. L. (1992). Supervision: A way of teaching and learning. In S. D. Brown & R. W. Lent (Eds.), *Handbook of counseling psychology* (2nd ed.). New York: Wiley.

Holloway, E. L., & Wampold, B. E. (1986). Relation between conceptual level and counseling-related tasks: A meta-analysis. *Journal of Counseling Psychology, 33,* 310–319.

Holt, R. R., & Luborsky, L. (1958). *Personality patterns of psychiatrists* (Vol. 1). New York: Basic Books.

Horn-George, J. B., & Anchor, K. N. (1982). Perceptions of the psychotherapy relationship in long- versus short-term therapy. *Professional Psychology, 13,* 483–491.

Horvath, A. O., & Goheen, M. D. (1990). Factors mediating the success of defiance- and compliance-based interventions. *Journal of Counseling Psychology, 37,* 363–371.

Horvath, A. O., & Greenberg, L. (1986). The development of the Working Alliance Inventory. In L. S. Greenberg & W. M. Pinsof (Eds.), *The psychotherapeutic process.* New York: Guilford.

Horvath, A. O., Marx, R. W., & Kamann, A. M. (1990). Thinking about thinking in therapy: An examination of clients' understanding of their therapists' intentions. *Journal of Consulting and Clinical Psychology, 58,* 614–621.

Horvath, A. O., & Symonds, B. D. (1991). Relation between working alliance and outcome in psychotherapy: A meta-analysis. *Journal of Counseling Psychology, 38,* 139–149.

Hough, R. L., Landsverk, J. A., Karno, M., Burnam, A., Timers, D. M., Escobar, J. I., & Reigier, D. A. (1987). Utilization of health and mental health services by Los Angeles Mexican Americans and non-Hispanic whites. *Archives of General Psychiatry, 44,* 702–709.

Houts, A. C., & Graham, K. (1986). Can religion make you crazy? Impact of client and therapist religious values on clinical judgments. *Journal of Consulting and Clinical Psychology, 54,* 267–271.

Howard, K. I., & Orlinsky, D. E. (1972). Psychotherapeutic processes. *Annual Review of Psychology, 23,* 615–668.

Hunt, D. D., Carr, J. E., Dagodakis, C. S., & Walker, E. A. (1985). Cognitive match as a predictor of psychotherapy outcome. *Psychotherapy, 22,* 718–721.

Jacobs, M. A., & Warner, B. L. (1981). Interaction of therapeutic attitudes with severity of clinical diagnosis. *Journal of Clinical Psychology, 37,* 75–82.

Jenkins, S. J., Fuqua, D. R., & Blum, C. R. (1986). Factors related to duration of counseling in a university counseling center. *Psychological Reports, 58,* 467–472.

Jensen, J. P., & Bergin, A. E. (1988). Mental health values of professional therapists: A national interdisciplinary survey. *Professional Psychology: Research and Practice, 19,* 290–297.

Jones, E. E. (1982). Psychotherapists' impressions of treatment outcome as a function of race. *Journal of Clinical Psychology, 38,* 722–731.

Jones, E. E., Krupnick, J. L., & Kerig, P. K. (1987). Some gender effects in brief psychotherapy. *Psychotherapy, 24,* 336–352.

Jones, E. E., & Zoppel, C. L. (1982). Impact of client and therapist gender on psychotherapy process and outcome. *Journal of Consulting and Clinical Psychology, 50,* 259–272.

Jourard, S. M. (1971). *The transparent self*. Princeton, NJ: Van Nostrand Rheinhold.

Joyce, A. S., & Piper, W. E. (1990). An examination of Mann's model of time-limited individual psychotherapy. *Canadian Journal of Psychiatry, 35*, 41–49.

Kadden, R. M., Cooney, N. L., Getter, H., & Litt, M. D. (1990). Matching alcoholics to coping skills or interactional therapies: Posttreatment results. *Journal of Consulting and Clinical Psychology, 57*, 698–704.

Kaplan, A. G. (1985). Female or male therapists for women patients: New formulations. *Psychiatry, 48*, 111–121.

Kazdin, A. E. (1991). *Research design in clinical psychology* (2nd ed.). Elmsford, NY: Pergamon.

Kelly, T. A. (1990). The role of values in psychotherapy: Review and methodological critique. *Clinical Psychology Review, 10*, 171–186.

Kelly, T. A., & Strupp, H. H. (1992). Patient and therapist values in psychotherapy: Perceived changes, conversion, similarity, and outcome. *Journal of Consulting and Clinical Psychology, 60*, 34–40.

Kernberg, O. (1973). Psychotherapy and psychoanalysis: Final report of the Menninger Foundation's psychotherapy research project. *International Journal of Psychiatric Medicine, 11*, 62–77.

Khan, J. A., & Cross, D. G. (1983). Mental health professional and client values: Similar or different? *Australian Journal of Sex, Marriage & Family, 4*, 71–78.

Kiesler, D. J. (1988). *Therapeutic metacommunication: Therapist impact disclosure as feedback in psychotherapy*. Palo Alto, CA: Consulting Psychologists Press.

Kiesler, D. J., & Watkins, L. M. (1989). Interpersonal complementarity and the therapeutic alliance: A study of relationship in psychotherapy. *Psychotherapy, 26*, 183–194.

Kingsbury, S. J. (1987). Cognitive differences between clinical psychologists and psychiatrists. *American Psychologist, 42*, 152–156.

Kivlighan, D. M., Jr. (1989). Changes in counselor intentions and response modes and in client reactions and session evaluation after training. *Journal of Counseling Psychology, 36*, 471–476.

Kivlighan, D. M., Jr., McGovern, T. V., & Corazzini, J. G. (1984). Effects of content and timing of structuring interventions on group therapy process and outcome. *Journal of Counseling Psychology, 31*, 363–370.

Kleinke, C. L. (1986). Gaze and eye contact: A research review. *Psychological Bulletin, 100*, 78–100.

Knapp, P. H., Levin, S., McCarter, R. H., Wermer, H., & Zetzel, E. (1960). Suitability for psychoanalysis: A review of one hundred supervised analytic cases. *Psychoanalytic Quarterly, 29*, 459–477.

Krebs, R. L. (1971). Some effects of a white institution on black psychiatric outpatients. *American Journal of Orthopsychiatry, 41*, 589–596.

LaCrosse, M. B. (1980). Perceived counselor social influence and counseling outcomes. *Journal of Counseling Psychology, 27*, 320–327.

Lafferty, P., Beutler, L. E., & Crago, M. (1989). Differences between more and less effective psychotherapists: A study of select therapist variables. *Journal of Consulting and Clinical Psychology, 57*, 76–80.

Lamb, K. L. (1977). Matching persons and counseling environments to foster self-control of test anxiety. *Dissertation Abstracts International, 38*, 3890B–3891B.

Lambert, M. J. (1989). The individual therapist's contribution to psychotherapy process and outcome. *Clinical Psychology Review, 9*, 469–485.

Lambert, M. J., & Bergin, A. E. (1983). Therapist characteristics and their contribution to psychotherapy outcome. In C. E. Walker (Ed.), *The handbook of clinical psychology*

(Vol. 1, pp. 205–241). Homewood, IL: Dow Jones-Irwin.

Landman, J. T., & Dawes, R. M. (1982). Psychotherapy outcome: Smith and Glass' conclusions stand up under scrutiny. *American Psychologist, 37*, 504–516.

Larson, V. A. (1987). An exploration of psychotherapeutic resonance. *Psychotherapy, 24*, 321–324.

Leary, T. (1957). *Interpersonal diagnosis in personality*. New York: Ronald Press.

Leong, F. T. (1986). Counseling and psychotherapy with Asian-Americans: Review of literature. *Journal of Counseling Psychology, 33*, 196–206.

Lewis, K. N. (1983, August). *The impact of religious affiliation on therapists' judgments of clients*. Paper presented at the American Psychological Association Convention, Anaheim, CA.

London, P. (1986). *The modes and morals of psychotherapy* (2nd ed.). Washington, DC: Hemisphere Publishing Co.

Lopez, S., & Hernandez, P. (1987). When culture is considered in the evaluation and treatment of Hispanic patients. *Psychotherapy, 24*, 120–126.

Luborsky, L. (1990). Theory and technique in dynamic psychotherapy—curative factors and training therapists to maximize them. *Psychotherapy and Psychosomatics, 53*, 50–57.

Luborsky, L., Chandler, M., Auerbach, A. H., Cohen, J., & Bachrach, H. M. (1971). Factors influencing the outcome of psychotherapy. *Psychological Bulletin, 75*, 145–185.

Luborsky, L., Crits-Christoph, P., Alexander, L., Margolis, M., & Cohen, M. (1983). Two helping alliance methods for predicting outcomes of psychotherapy: A counting signs vs. a global rating method. *Journal of Nervous and Mental Disease, 171*, 480–491.

Luborsky, L., Crits-Christoph, P., McLellan, A. T., Woody, G., Piper, W., Liberman, B., Imber, S., & Pilkonis, P. (1986). Do therapists vary much in their success? Findings from four outcome studies. *American Journal of Orthopsychiatry, 56*, 501–512.

Luborsky, L., & DeRubeis, R. J. (1984). The use of psychotherapy treatment manuals: A small revolution in psychotherapy research style. *Clinical Psychology Review, 4*, 5–14.

Luborsky, L., McLellan, A. T., Woody, G. E., O'Brien, C. P., & Auerbach, A. (1985). Therapist success and its determinants. *Archives of General Psychiatry, 42*, 602–611.

Luborsky, L., Mintz, J., Auerbach, A., Crits-Christoph, P., Bachrach, H., Todd, T., Johnson, M., Cohen, M., & O'Brien, C. P. (1980). Predicting the outcome of psychotherapy: Findings of the Penn Psychotherapy Project. *Archives of General Psychiatry, 37*, 471–481.

Luborsky, L., Singer, B., & Luborsky, L. (1975). Comparative studies of psychotherapies. *Archives of General Psychiatry, 32*, 995–1008.

Luborsky, L., Woody, G. E., McLellan, A. T., O'Brien, C. P., & Rosenzweig, J. (1982). Can independent judges recognize different psychotherapies? An experience with manual-guided therapies. *Journal of Consulting and Clinical Psychology, 50*, 49–62.

Lyons, J. S., & Howard, K. I. (1991). Main effects analysis in clinical research: Statistical guidelines for disaggregating treatment groups. *Journal of Consulting and Clinical Psychology, 59*, 745–748.

Lyons, L. C., & Woods, P. J. (1991). The efficacy of rational-emotive therapy: A quantitative review of the outcome research. *Clinical Psychology Review, 11*, 357–370.

Lytton, H., & Romney, D. M. (1991). Parents' differential socialization of boys and girls: A meta-analysis. *Psychological Bulletin, 109*, 267–296.

Maddux, J. E., Stoltenberg, C. D., & Rosenwein, R. (Eds.). (1987). *Social processes in clinical and counseling psychology*. New York: Springer-Verlag.

Mahalik, J. R. (1990). Systematic eclectic models. *The Counseling Psychologist, 18,* 655–679.

Mahoney, M. J., Norcross, J. C., Prochaska, J. O., & Missar, C. D. (1989). Psychological development and optimal psychotherapy: Converging perspectives among clinical psychologists. *Journal of Integrative and Eclectic Psychotherapy, 8,* 251–263.

Malgady, R. G., Rogler, L. H., & Costantino, G. (1987). Ethnocultural and linguistic bias in mental health evaluation of Hispanics. *American Psychologist, 42,* 228–234.

Mallinckrodt, B., & Nelson, M. L. (1991). Counselor training level and the formation of the psychotherapeutic working alliance. *Journal of Counseling Psychology, 38,* 135–138.

Martin, P. J., Moore, J. E., & Sterne, A. L. (1977). Therapists as prophets: Their expectancies and treatment outcome. *Psychotherapy: Theory, Research, and Practice, 14,* 188–195.

Martin, P. J., & Sterne, A. L. (1975). Prognostic expectations and treatment outcome. *Journal of Consulting and Clinical Psychology, 43,* 572–576.

Martin, P. J., Sterne, A. L., & Hunter, M. L. (1976). Share and share alike: Mutuality of expectations and satisfaction with therapy. *Journal of Clinical Psychology, 32,* 677–683.

Mayerson, N. H. (1984). Preparing clients for group therapy: A critical review and theoretical formulation. *Clinical Psychology Review, 4,* 191–213.

McLachlan, J. F. (1972). Benefit from group therapy as a function of patient–therapist match on conceptual level. *Psychotherapy: Theory, Research, and Practice, 9,* 317–323.

McLellan, A. T., Woody, G. E., Luborsky, L., & Goehl, L. (1988). Is the counselor an "active ingredient" in substance abuse rehabilitation? *The Journal of Nervous and Mental Disease, 176.*

McLemore, C., & Benjamin, L. S. (1979). Whatever happened to interpersonal diagnosis: A psychosocial alternative to DSM-III. *American Psychologist, 34,* 17–34.

McNeil, B. W., May, R. J., & Lee, V. E. (1987). Perceptions of counselor source characteristics by premature and successful terminators. *Journal of Counseling Psychology, 34,* 86–89.

McWhirter, J. F., & Frey, R. E. C. (1987). Group leader and member characteristics and attraction to initial and final group sessions and to the group and group leader. *Small Group Behavior, 18,* 533–547.

Meichenbaum, D. J., & Turk, D. C. (1987). *Facilitating treatment adherence: A practitioner's guidebook.* New York: Plenum.

Mendelsohn, G. A., & Geller, M. H. (1963). Effects of counselor–client similarity on the outcome of counseling. *Journal of Counseling Psychology, 10,* 71–77.

Merluzzi, T. V., & Merluzzi, B. (1981). Androgyny, stereotyping and the perception of female therapists. *Journal of Clinical Psychology, 37,* 280–284.

Miller, R. C., & Berman, J. S. (1983). The efficacy of cognitive behavior therapies: A quantitative review of the research evidence. *Psychological Bulletin, 94,* 39–53.

Mitchell, K. M., & Atkinson, B. (1983). The relationship between therapist and client social class and participation in therapy. *Professional Psychology, 14,* 310–316.

Mitchell, K. M., & Namenek, T. M. (1970). A comparison of therapist and client social class. *Professional Psychology, 1,* 225–230.

Mohr, D. C., Shoham-Salomon, V., Engle, D., & Beutler, L. E. (1991). The expression of anger in psychotherapy for depression: Its role and measurement. *Psychotherapy Research, 1,* 125–135.

Moncher, F. J., & Prinz, R. J. (1991). Treatment fidelity in outcome studies. *Clinical Psychology Review, 11,* 247–266.

Morgan, R., Luborsky, L., Crits-Christoph, P., Curtis, H., & Solomon, J. (1982). Predicting the outcomes of psychotherapy by the Penn Helping Alliance Rating Method. *Archives of General Psychiatry, 39,* 397–402.

Neimeyer, G. J., & Gonzales, M. (1983). Duration, satisfaction, and perceived effectiveness of cross-cultural counseling. *Journal of Counseling Psychology, 30,* 91–95.

Nelson, M. L., & Holloway, E. L. (1990). Relation of gender to power and involvement in supervision. *Journal of Counseling Psychology, 37,* 473–481.

Neitzel, M. T., Russell, R. L., Hemmings, K. A., & Gretter, M. L. (1987). Clinical significance of psychotherapy for unipolar depression: A meta-analytic approach to social comparison. *Journal of Consulting and Clinical Psychology, 55,* 156–161.

Norcross, J. C., & Prochaska, J. O. (1986). Psychotherapist heal thyself. II: The self-initiated and therapy-facilitated change of psychological distress. *Psychotherapy, 23,* 345–356.

Norcross, J. C., & Prochaska, J. O. (1988). A study of eclectic (and integrative) views revisited. *Professional Psychology: Research and Practice, 19,* 170–174.

Norcross, J. C., & Wogan, M. (1983). American psychotherapists of diverse persuasions: Characteristics, theories, practices and clients. *Professional Psychology: Research and Practice, 14,* 529–539.

O'Donohue, W., Fisher, J. E., Plaud, J. J., & Curtis, S. D. (1990). Treatment decisions: Their nature and their justification. *Psychotherapy, 27,* 421–427.

Omer, H., & Dar, R. (1992). Changing trends in three decades of psychotherapy research: The flight from theory into pragmatics. *Journal of Consulting and Clinical Psychology, 60,* 88–93.

Orlinsky, D. E., & Howard, K. I. (1980). Gender and psychotherapeutic outcome. In A. M. Brodsky & R. T. Hare-Mustin (Eds.), *Women and psychotherapy* (pp. 3–34). New York: Guilford.

Orlinsky, D. E., & Howard, K. I. (1986). Process and outcome in psychotherapy. In S. L. Garfield & A. E. Bergin (Eds.), *Handbook of psychotherapy and behavior change* (3rd ed., pp. 311–384). New York: Wiley.

Orlinsky, D. E., & Howard, K. I. (1987). A generic model of psychotherapy. *Journal of Integrative and Eclectic Psychotherapy, 6,* 6–28.

Parloff, M. B., Waskow, I. E., & Wolfe, B. E. (1978). Research on therapist variables in relation to process and outcome. In S. L. Garfield & A. E. Bergin (Eds.), *Handbook of psychotherapy and behavior change* (2nd ed., pp. 233–282). New York: Wiley.

Patterson, C. H. (1984). Empathy, warmth, and genuiness in psychotherapy: A review of reviews. *Psychotherapy, 21,* 431–438.

Patterson, G. R., & Forgatch, M. S. (1985). Therapist behavior as a determinant for client noncompliance: A paradox for the behavior modifier. *Journal of Consulting and Clinical Psychology, 53,* 846–851.

Patterson, M. L. (1983). *Nonverbal behavior: A functional perspective.* New York: Springer-Verlag.

Pavkov, T. W., Lewis, D. A., & Lyons, J. S. (1989). Psychiatric diagnoses and racial bias: An empirical investigation. *Professional Psychology: Research and Practice, 20,* 364–368.

Petry, R. A., & Thomas, J. R. (1986). The effect of androgyny on the quality of psychotherapeutic relationships. *Psychotherapy, 23,* 249–251.

Piper, W. E. (1988). Psychotherapy research in the 1980s: Defining areas of consensus and controversy. *Hospital and Community Psychiatry, 39,* 1055–1063.

Piper, W. E., Azim, H. F. A., Joyce, A. S., & McCallum, M. (1991b). Transference interpretation, therapeutic alliance, and outcome in short-term individual psychotherapy. *Archives of General Psychiatry, 48,* 946–953.

Piper, W. E., Azim, H. F. A., Joyce, A. S., & McCallum, M. (1991a). Quality of object relations vs. interpersonal functioning as predictors of therapeutic alliance and psychotherapy outcome. *Journal of Nervous and Mental Disease. 179,* 1–10.

Piper, W. E., Azim, H. F. A., McCallum, M., & Joyce, A. S. (1990). Patient suitability and outcome in short-term individual psychotherapy. *Journal of Consulting and Clinical Psychology, 58,* 475–481.

Pope, B. (1979). *The mental health interview: Research and application.* Elmsford, NY: Pergamon.

Prioleau, L., Murdock, M. & Brody, N. (1983). An analysis of psychotherapy versus placebo studies. *The Behavioral and Brain Sciences, 8,* 275–285.

Prochaska, J. O., & Norcross, J. N. (1983). Contemporary psychotherapists: A national survey of characteristics, practices, orientations, and attitudes. *Psychotherapy: Theory, Research, and Practice, 20,* 161–173.

Proctor, E. K., & Rosen, A. (1981). Expectations and preferences for counselor race and their relation to intermediate treatment outcomes. *Journal of Counseling Psychology, 28,* 40–46.

Propst, L. R. (1980). The comparative efficacy of religious and nonreligious imagery for the treatment of mild depression in religious individuals. *Cognitive Therapy and Research, 4,* 167–178.

Propst, L. R., Ostrom, R., Watkins, P., Dean, T., & Mashburn, D. (1992). Comparative efficacy of religious and nonreligious cognitive-behavioral therapy for the treatment of clinical depression in religious individuals. *Journal of Consulting and Clinical Psychology, 60,* 94–103.

Reandeau, S. G., & Wampold, B. E. (1991). Relationship of power and involvement of working alliance: A multiple-case sequential analysis of brief therapy. *Journal of Counseling Psychology, 38,* 107–114.

Reid, T. (1989, May). *Cultural differences.* Paper presented at the annual meeting of the Society for the Exploration of Psychotherapy Integration, Berkley, CA.

Ridley, C. R. (1984). Clinical treatment of the nondisclosing black client: A therapeutic paradox. *American Psychologist, 39,* 1234–1244.

Robbins, E. S., & Haase, R. F. (1985). Power of nonverbal cues in counseling interactions: Availability, vividness, or salience? *Journal of Counseling Psychology, 32,* 502–513.

Robiner, W. N., & Schofield, W. (1990). References on supervision in clinical and counseling psychology. *Professional Psychology: Research and Practice, 21,* 297–312.

Robinson, L. A., Berman, J. S., & Neimeyer, R. A. (1990). Psychotherapy for the treatment of depression: A comprehensive review of controlled outcome research. *Psychological Bulletin, 108,* 30–49.

Rogers, C. R. (1957). The necessary and sufficient conditions of therapeutic personality change. *Journal of Consulting Psychology, 21,* 95–103.

Rokeach, M. (1973). *The nature of human values.* New York: Free Press.

Rounsaville, B. J., Chevron, E. S., Prusoff, B. A., Elkin, I., Imber, S., Sotsky, S., & Watkins, J. (1987). The relation between specific and general dimensions of the psychotherapy process in interpersonal psychotherapy of depression. *Journal of Consulting and Clinical Psychology, 55,* 379–384.

Rounsaville, B. J., O'Malley, S., Foley, S., & Weissman, M. M. (1988). The role of manual guided training in the conduct and efficiency of interpersonal psychotherapy for depression. *Journal of Consulting and Clinical Psychology, 56,* 681–688.

Rudolf, L., (1991). *Die therapeutische Arbeitsbeziehung.* Berlin: Springer.

Rudy, J. P., McLemore, C. W., & Gorsuch, R. L. (1985). Interpersonal behavior and therapeutic progress: Therapists and clients rate themselves and each other. *Psychiatry, 48,* 264–281.

Safran, J. D., & Wallner, L. K. (1991). The relative predictive validity of two therapeutic alliance measures in cognitive therapy. *Psychological Assessment, 3,* 188–195.

Salvio, M., Beutler, L. E., Engle, D., & Wood, J. M. (1992). The strength of therapeutic alliance in three treatments for depression. *Psychotherapy Research, 1,* 31–36.

Sandell, R. (1985). Influence of supervision, therapist's competence, and patient's ego level on the effects of time-limited psychotherapy. *Psychotherapy and Psychosomatics, 44,* 103–109.

Sattler, J. M. (1977). The effects of therapist–client racial similarity. In A. S. Gurman & A. M. Razin (Eds.), *Effective psychotherapy: A handbook of research* (pp. 252–290). Elmsford, NY: Pergamon.

Schindler, F., Berren, M. R., Hannah, M. T., Beigel, A., & Santiago, J. (1987). How the public perceives psychiatrists, psychologists, nonpsychiatric physicians, and members of the clergy. *Professional Psychology: Research and Practice, 18,* 371–376.

Sexton, T. L., & Whiston, S. C. (1991). A review of the empirical basis for counseling: Implications for practice and training. *Counselor Education and Supervision, 30,* 330–354.

Seymour, W. R. (1982). *Values, ethics, legalities, and the family.* Rockville, MD: Aspen Systems Corp.

Shafranske, E. P., & Malony, H. N. (1990). Clinical psychologists' religious and spiritual orientations and their practice of psychotherapy. *Psychotherapy, 27,* 72–78.

Shapiro, D. A., & Shapiro, D. (1982). Meta-analysis of comparative therapy outcome studies: A replication and refinement. *Psychological Bulletin, 92,* 581–604.

Shaw, B. F. (1983, July). *Training therapists for the treatment of depression: Collaborative study.* Paper presented at the meeting of the Society for Psychotherapy Research, Sheffield, England.

Shaw, B. F., & Dobson, K. S. (1988). Competency judgments in the training and evaluation of psychotherapists. *Journal of Consulting and Clinical Psychology, 56,* 666–672.

Shoham-Salomon, V. (1991). Introduction to special section on client–therapy interaction research. *Journal of Consulting and Clinical Psychology, 59,* 203–204.

Shoham-Salomon, V., Avner, R., & Neeman, K. (1989). "You are changed if you do and changed if you don't:" Mechanisms underlying paradoxical interventions. *Journal of Consulting and Clinical Psychology, 57,* 590–598.

Shoham-Salomon, V., & Hannah, M. T. (1991). Client–treatment interactions in the study of differential change processes. *Journal of Consulting and Clinical Psychology, 59,* 217–225.

Shoham-Salomon, V., & Rosenthal, R. (1987). Paradoxical interventions: A meta-analysis. *Journal of Consulting and Clinical Psychology, 55,* 22–27.

Sloane, R. B., Staples, F. R., Cristol, A. H., Yorkston, N. J.,

& Whipple, K. (1975). *Psychotherapy versus behavior therapy*. Cambridge, MA: Harvard University Press.

Smith, E. W. (1972). Postural and gestural communication of A and B "therapist types" during dyad interviews. *Journal of Consulting and Clinical Psychology, 39,* 29–36.

Smith, M. L., & Glass, G. V. (1977). Meta-analysis of psychotherapy outcome studies. *American Psychologist, 32,* 752–760.

Smith, M. L., Glass, G. V., & Miller, T. I. (1980). *The benefits of psychotherapy*. Baltimore: The Johns Hopkins University Press.

Snyder, C. R., & Forsyth, D. R. (Eds.). (1991). *Handbook of social and clinical psychology: The health perspective.* Elmsford, NY: Pergamon.

Stein, D. M., & Lambert, M. J. (1984). On the relationship between therapist experience and psychotherapy outcome. *Clinical Psychology Review, 4,* 127–142.

Stein, M. L., & Stone, G. L. (1978). Effects of conceptual level and structure on initial interview behavior. *Journal of Counseling Psychology, 25,* 96–102.

Stiles, W. B. (1979). Verbal response modes and psychotherapeutic technique. *Psychiatry, 42,* 49–62.

Stiles, W. B., Shapiro, D. A., & Firth-Cozens, J. (1988). Verbal response mode use in contrasting psychotherapies: A within-subjects comparison. *Journal of Consulting and Clinical Psychology, 56,* 727–733.

Strong, S. R. (1968). Counseling: A social influence process. *Journal of Counseling Psychology, 15,* 215–224.

Strupp, H. H. (1981). Toward the refinement of time-limited dynamic psychotherapy. In S. H. Budman (Ed.), *Forms of brief therapy* (pp. 219–242). New York: Guilford.

Strupp, H. H., Butler, S. F., & Rosser, C. (1988). Training in psychodynamic therapy. *Journal of Consulting and Clinical Psychology, 56,* 689–695.

Sue, D. W. (1990). Culture-specific strategies in counseling: A conceptual framework. *Professional Psychology: Research and Practice, 21,* 424–433.

Sundland, D. M. (1977, June). *Theoretical orientation: A multiprofessional American sample.* Paper presented at the eight annual meeting of the Society for Psychotherapy Research, Madison, WI.

Svartberg, M., & Stiles, T. C. (1991). Comparative effects of short-term psychodynamic psychotherapy: A meta-analysis. *Journal of Consulting and Clinical Psychology, 59,* 704–714.

Svartberg, M., & Stiles, T. C. (1992). Predicting patient change from therapist competence and patient–therapist complementarity in short-term anxiety-provoking psychotherapy. *Journal of Consulting and Clinical Psychology, 60,* 304–307.

Taube, C. A., Goldman, H. H., Burns, B. J., & Kessler, L. G. (1988). High users of outpatient health service. I: Definition and characteristics. *American Journal of Psychiatry, 145,* 19–24.

Taylor, L., Adelman, H., & Kaser-Boyd, N. (1986). The Origin Climate Questionnaire as a tool for studying psychotherapeutic process. *Journal of Child and Adolescent Psychotherapy, 3,* 10–16.

Taylor, M. C., & Hall, J. A. (1982). Psychological androgyny: Theories, methods, and conclusions. *Psychological Bulletin, 92,* 347–366.

Terrell, R., & Terrell, S. (1984). Race of counselor, client sex, cultural mistrust level, and premature termination from counseling among black clients. *Journal of Counseling Psychology, 31,* 371–375.

Tessler, R. C. (1975). Clients' reactions to initial interviews: Determinants of relationship-centered and problem-centered satisfaction. *Journal of Counseling Psychology, 22,* 187–191.

Thompson, A. P. (1986). Changes in counseling skills during graduate and undergraduate study. *Journal of Counseling Psychology, 33,* 65–72.

Thompson, L. W., & Gallagher, D. (1984). Efficacy of psychotherapy in the treatment of late-life depression. *Advances in Behavioral Research and Therapy, 6,* 127.

Thompson, L., Gallagher, D., & Breckenridge, J. (1987). Comparative effectiveness of psychotherapies for depressed elders. *Journal of Consulting and Clinical Psychology, 55,* 385–390.

Tichenor, V., & Hill, C. E. (1989). A comparison of six measures of working alliance. *Psychotherapy: Research and Practice, 26,* 195–199.

Tjelveit, A. C. (1986). The ethics of value conversion in psychotherapy: Appropriate and inappropriate therapist influence on client values. *Clinical Psychology Review, 6,* 515–537.

Tracey, T. J. (1985). Dominance and outcome: A sequential examination. *Journal of Counseling Psychology, 32,* 119–122.

Tracey, T. J. (1986). Interactional correlates of premature termination. *Journal of Consulting and Clinical Psychology, 54,* 784–788.

Tracey, T. J. (1987). Stage differences in the dependencies of topic initiation and topic following behavior. *Journal of Counseling Psychology, 34,* 123–131.

Tracey, T. J., & Dundon, M. (1988). Role anticipations and preferences over the course of counseling. *Journal of Counseling Psychology, 35,* 3–14.

Tracey, T. J., & Hays, K. (1989). Therapist complementarity as a function of experience and client stimuli. *Psychotherapy, 26,* 462–468.

Tracey, T. J., Hays, K. A., Malone, J., & Herman, B. (1988). Changes in counselor response as a function of experience. *Journal of Counseling Psychology, 35,* 119–126.

Tracey, T. J., & Ray, P. B. (1984). The stages of successful time-limited counseling: An interactional examination. *Journal of Counseling Psychology, 31,* 13–27.

Tryon, G. S. (1989). Study of variables related to client engagement using practicum trainees and experienced clinicians. *Psychotherapy, 26,* 54–61.

Turner, S., & Armstrong, S. (1981). Cross-racial psychotherapy: What the therapists say. *Psychotherapy: Theory, Research, and Practice, 18,* 375–378.

VandenBos, G. R., & Karon, B. P. (1971). Pathogenesis: A new therapist personality dimension related to therapeutic effectiveness. *Journal of Personality Assessment, 35,* 252–260.

Watkins, C. E., Jr. (1990). The effects of counselor self-disclosure: A research review. *Counseling Psychologist, 18,* 477–500.

Weinstock-Savoy, D. E. (1986). *The relationship of therapist and patient interpersonal styles to outcome in brief dynamic psychotherapy.* Unpublished doctoral dissertation, Boston University.

Weiss, D. S., Marmar, C. R., & Horowitz, M. J. (1988). Do the ways in which psychotherapy process ratings are made make a difference? The effects of mode of presentation, segment, and rating format on interrater reliability. *Psychotherapy, 25,* 44–50.

Weisz, J. R., Weiss, B., Alicke, M. D., & Klotz, M. L. (1987). Effectiveness of psychotherapy with children and adolescents: A meta-analysis for clinicians. *Journal of Consulting and Clinical Psychology, 55,* 542–549.

Whitehorn, J. C., & Betz, B. (1960). Further studies of the doctor as a crucial variable in the outcome of treatment of schizophrenic patients. *American Journal of Psychiatry, 117,* 215–223.

Wiggins, J. D., & Giles, T. A. (1984). The relationship between counselors' and students' self-esteem as related to counseling outcomes. *The School Counselor, 32,* 18–22.

Wiley, M. O., & Ray, P. B. (1986). Counseling supervision by developmental level. *Journal of Counseling Psychology, 33,* 439–445.

Williams, K. E., & Chambless, D. L. (1990). The relationship between therapist characteristics and outcome of in vivo exposure treatment for agoraphobia. *Behavior Therapy, 21,* 111–116.

Wogan, M., & Norcross, J. C. (1985). Dimensions of therapeutic skills and techniques: Empirical identification, therapist correlates, and predictive utility. *Psychotherapy, 22,* 63–74.

Worthington, E. L., Jr. (1988). Understanding the values of religious clients: A model and its application to counseling. *Journal of Counseling Psychology, 35,* 166–174.

Yamamoto, J., James, Q., Bloombaum, M., & Hattem, J. (1967). Racial factors in patient selection. *American Journal of Psychiatry, 124,* 630–636.

Zamosttny, K. P., Corrigan, J. D., & Eggert, M. A. (1981). Replication and extension of social influence process in counseling: A field study. *Journal of Counseling Psychology, 28,* 481–489.

Zeldow, P. B. (1982). The androgynous vision: A critical examination. *Bulletin of the Menninger Clinic, 46,* 401–413.

Zimpfer, D., & Waltman, D. (1982). Correlates of effectiveness in group counseling. *Small Group Behavior, 13,* 275–290.

Zook, A., II, & Sipps, G. J. (1987). Machiavellianism and dominance: Are therapists in training manipulative? *Psychotherapy, 24,* 15–19.

8

PROCESS AND OUTCOME IN PSYCHOTHERAPY — NOCH EINMAL

- **DAVID E. ORLINSKY**
  University of Chicago

- **KLAUS GRAWE**
  Universität Bern

- **BARBARA K. PARKS**
  University of Chicago

The claim of process–outcome research to a special place in the study of psychotherapy arises from the fact that it represents an empirical strategy for determining which aspects and modes of therapeutic process are particularly helpful or harmful to patients. In doing so, these studies link the often separate domains of *process* and *outcome* research. The two domains may be compared to one another and also to the clinical literature by observing that whereas clinical theories and histories attempt to illustrate what psychotherapy *ought to be*, process research aims to determine what psychotherapy *is* and outcome studies seek to evaluate what therapy *does*. In these terms, process–outcome studies aim to identify the parts of what therapy is that, singly or in combination, bring

The contribution of the first author was partially supported by research grant R01 MH42901 from the National Institute of Mental Health. We are grateful to Professor Kenneth Howard (Northwestern University) for advice in planning the project; to Professor Dietmar Schulte, Dr. Johanna Hartung, and Dr. Ulrike Willutzki (Ruhr-Universität Bochum) and Professor Germain Lietaer (University of Leuven) for help in interpreting results of studies done by their research teams; to Professor Horst Kächele (Universität Ulm) for help with German language references; to Ms. Nathalie Baumann (Bern) for assistance abstracting and coding German language studies; and to Ms. Marcia Bourland (Chicago) for her unfailing patience and support.

about what therapy does. The master question guiding process–outcome research is, What is effectively therapeutic about psychotherapy?

This chapter reviews a large body of empirical studies that have examined measures of specific aspects of therapeutic process in relation to assessments of clinical outcome. Our aims are threefold: to identify relevant studies; to compare their findings by classifying them within a comprehensive conceptual framework; and, by this means, to synthesize the results into a cumulatively meaningful body of knowledge. By identifying areas of substantial consensus over numerous replications, we hope to extract at least a handful of established facts from a myriad of empirical findings. Facts thus identified invite the further development of scientific theory, to guide more incisive research and promote more effective practice.

This is the third in a series of reports on the relation of process to outcome in psychotherapy, and it builds on the foundation laid down by earlier reports (Orlinsky & Howard, 1978, 1986a). The 1986 report in particular constitutes an important bibliographic resource, since considerations of space require this report to concentrate on the addition and integration of new and previously uncovered findings to our overall knowledge. "Previously uncovered findings" refers to empirical work published in German prior to 1985 or overlooked in our past reviews;[1] "new research" refers to studies published in English from 1985 through 1992 and in German through 1991.

The inclusion criteria for this chapter are the same as in prior editions. First, studies had to concern actual treatments of "real" patients with

[1]To our sadness we have relearned the old truth that a complete bibliographic search is humanly impossible. We apologize to authors of relevant studies (of any date) that we did not find and ask them to send copies to David Orlinsky for future reference.

significant personal or emotional problems, by "real" therapists having at least minimal professional training, rather than experimental analogues of therapy using actors or experimental subjects as surrogate patients or therapists. In recent years these boundaries have been increasingly blurred by studies in which nonpatients with measurably real problems were recruited from the college classroom or the community to serve as clients and were subjected to experimental conditions that were reasonable facsimiles of real treatments. These might be called simulated therapy, as opposed to analogue studies. We included those simulated therapy studies that met our criteria, since to do otherwise would have been unrepresentative of work in the field and would have restricted this review largely to studies with naturalistic research designs.

As a second criterion of inclusion, studies had to measure specifically differentiated features of therapeutic process, either as they naturally occurred or as they were experimentally manipulated (confirmed, in the latter case, by process measures assessing the experimental conditions), and they had to quantitatively assess variations in process in relation to concomitant variations in treatment outcome. This criterion eliminated all comparative outcome studies that focused on whole treatment packages rather than on specifically differentiated treatment components. Another group of studies excluded by this criterion were those in which process and outcome variables were assessed, but were not analyzed in relation to each other. However, the greatest gap in coverage caused by this second criterion concerns numerous (and sometimes quite important) studies of process that did not also use outcome measures.

Furthermore, we applied our own definitions of process and outcome, which differ in some respects from those used by other researchers (Orlinsky & Howard, 1986a). Thus it sometimes happened that we viewed as process some variables that other researchers called outcome and viewed as outcome some variables that others called process. For example, although some researchers have used treatment duration or premature termination as outcome variables, in our view they are process variables; accordingly, we treated such studies as process–process rather than process–outcome studies. Similarly, some highly respected process researchers (e.g., Elliott, 1985; Elliott et al., 1985) have found it convenient to use in-session impacts (e.g., patients' attainment of insight, catharsis, or other helpful experiences) as outcomes, in the sense of immediate effects of therapist interventions. Since our definition of outcome requires that

impact be evaluated outside sessions, we had to view those in-session impacts as another aspect of process, and such studies as process–process rather than process–outcome. Some quite useful and frequently used instruments, such as Stiles's *Session Evaluation Questionnaire*, required particularly close attention, since by our criteria its depth and smoothness scales seem to describe session process, while its mood scales (patient positivity and arousal) describe postsession outcome (Stiles & Snow, 1984b).

The third criterion concerns the way we counted findings. We defined a *finding* as a methodologically independent observation of a relationship between process and outcome variables. We took findings, rather than whole studies, as our basic unit of analysis. Simple studies, and studies that focused on other topics in which process–outcome analyses were incidentally reported, often yielded only one or two findings; other, more complexly designed studies yielded up to a dozen or more process–outcome findings.

A further problem arose because researchers have typically compensated for over-specificity of focus and unreliability in measuring instruments by using multiple instruments to assess particular process and outcome variables. To cope with this intentional redundancy, we categorized process and outcome measures by their *data source*— patients, therapists, raters (that is, nonparticipant observers), and objective indexes or psychometric measures— on the grounds that measures of particular variables, made from different data sources, have often been found to be largely uncorrelated. Therefore, we treated the association of process measures from *one* data source (e.g., ratings by independent observers) with outcome measures from *one* data source (e.g., patients' judgments) as a *single* finding. Hypothetically, a particular process variable (e.g., therapist empathy) could be assessed using measures based on judgments by patients, therapists, independent observers, and objective indexes, and these could all be tested in relation to measures of clinical outcome as assessed by patients, therapists, independent observers, and psychometric tests. In this extreme case, 16 (4 times 4) methodologically independent findings could be counted. In the event that associations between some measures in a process-by-outcome cell were statistically significant and associations between other measures in the *same* cell were not, we counted it as a significant finding overall. We reasoned that false negatives are more likely than false positives, owing to common methodological problems, such as small samples, limited reliability of measures, and the inability of some frequently used statistical tests to detect significant but nonlinear patterns of association. This potential bias favoring significant findings over null findings was substantially offset by deemphasizing individual findings and drawing conclusions only about well-replicated findings based on multiple data sets. Findings were then categorized as indicating a significant or nonsignificant association and, in the former case, were further noted as significantly positive or negative. We have continued to use the conventional criterion of the .05 probability level to assess the statistical significance of findings. The limitations of reliance on this statistical convention have been offset to some extent by reporting or estimating, where possible, effect sizes associated with findings. (The mean ES is reported when there are multiple findings within process-by-outcome cells.)

The authors' interpretations clearly have influenced this review at many levels. First, we had to make judgments concerning which studies to include or exclude. Second, we had to make judgments with regard to the meaning of the variables investigated (whenever possible, we examined the content of research instruments and factorial dimensions to identify the variables, and sometimes disagreed in our interpretation with the researchers who used them). Third, we had to make judgments about the nature of the findings (researchers sometimes differ in their standards of statistical significance). Fourth, we had to make judgments in classifying and aggregating the findings from different studies (that is, fitting them into our conceptual framework). Fifth, we had to make judgments in assessing the overall import of the cumulative research record. In addition, of course, we tried to cope with the inevitable human errors that creep into every large-scale project dependent on complex judgments. We hope that the potential biases introduced by these factors will be minimized by our explicitness about them and by the reader's own critical vigilance.

Our search of the literature started with the abstracts found in *PsycSCAN: CLINICAL PSYCHOLOGY* from 1985 through 1992, inclusive. About half the 22 English journals listed there publish empirical research on psychotherapy. We also searched through several recently founded journals, the most relevant of which is *Psychotherapy Research: Journal of the Society for Psychotherapy Research.*[2] We did not use computer searches, which depend on key words provided by authors

rather than on our conceptual definitions of process and outcome. We obtained full copies of all promising titles and numerous additional titles from the references cited in those studies. As a further resource, we scanned the bibliographies of review articles and meta-analyses published between 1985 and 1992 (e.g., Goldfried, Greenberg, & Marmar, 1990; Parloff, London, & Wolfe, 1986). We also sought relevant references (and data) in an extraordinary series of important new books bearing on psychotherapy research. Since we cannot fully do them justice in this review, we urgently call them to our readers' attention. Listed alphabetically, they include: Beutler & Clarkin (1990); Beutler & Crago (1991); Dahl, Kächele, & Thomä (1988); Gelso & Johnson (1983); Greenberg & Pinsof (1986b); Hahlweg & Jacobson (1984); C. E. Hill (1989); Horowitz (1991); Huber (1987); Lietaer, Rombauts, & Van Balen (1990); Luborsky & Crits-Christoph (1990); Luborsky, Crits-Christoph, Mintz, & Auerbach (1988); Sachse (1992); Safran & Segal (1990); Toukmanian & Rennie (1992); Tscheulin (1992); Wallerstein (1986). We ended by citing new findings from studies published in 46 journals in three languages and over a dozen books.

This report has four main parts. The first seeks to clarify the fundamental concepts of therapeutic process and outcome that long and varied usage has rendered ambiguous. The second section creates a basis for examining new process–outcome findings by summarizing what was known when the last edition of this chapter was written. Using this conceptual structure and baseline knowledge, the third section presents new and previously uncovered research findings. The final section comments on the progress made in this area since the mid-1980s, which has taken two main forms. One is the accumulation of new knowledge through the application of new empirical and statistical methods and through the extension of established methods into new areas. The second is a change in understanding, coupled with a redirection in aims, that has occurred among leading researchers in the field as they have attempted to address their difficulties and dissatisfactions with earlier work. Both trends reflect the creative ferment that has characterized this field in recent years.

---

[2]Other relevant new journals include *Research in Social Work Practice*, *Psychotherapy Practice and Research*, and the *Journal of Psychotherapy Integration*.

BASIC CONCEPTS

Sigmund Freud is rarely cited as a philosopher of science, but he made at least one acute observation on that subject:

We have often heard it maintained that sciences should be built up on clear and sharply defined basic concepts. In actual fact no science, not even the most exact, begins with such definitions. The true beginning of scientific activity consists rather in describing phenomena and then in proceeding to group, classify and correlate them. Even at the stage of description it is not possible to avoid applying certain abstract ideas to the material in hand, ideas derived from somewhere or other but certainly not from the new observations alone. Such ideas — which will later become the basic concepts of the science — are still more indispensable as the material is further worked over. They must at first necessarily possess some degree of indefiniteness; there can be no question of any clear delimitation of their content. So long as they remain in this condition, we come to an understanding about their meaning by making repeated references to the material of observation from which they appear to have been derived, but upon which, in fact, they have been imposed. Strictly speaking, they are in the nature of conventions — although everything depends on their not being arbitrarily chosen but determined by their having significant relations to the empirical material, relations that we seem to sense before we can clearly recognize and demonstrate them. It is only after more thorough investigation of the field of observation that we are able to formulate its basic scientific concepts with increased precision, and progressively so to modify them that they become serviceable and consistent over a wide area. Then, indeed, the time may have come to confine them in definitions (Freud, 1915/1957, p. 117).

The basic concepts of our relatively new science are *process* and *outcome*. These concepts emerged as useful abstractions for organizing "the material of observation" during the 40-plus years since psychotherapy became the subject of systematic empirical research (e.g., Bordin, 1948; Butler, 1948; Covner, 1942; Fiedler, 1950; Raimy, 1948; Seeman, 1949; Snyder, 1945, 1946).

In earlier days the field was served well enough simply by reference to process variables or outcome variables, since everyone recognized that *process* referred to what happened during treatment, while *outcome* concerned its results. Process studies aimed to "group, classify, and correlate" measures delineating the events of treatment — hopefully, the important events, although perhaps too often just the measurable events. Outcome studies aimed to tell us whether psychotherapy worked, whether clients or patients got better.

Since the new field was wide open, researchers studied the psychotherapies that they liked and that allowed this sort of empirical scrutiny, and evaluated the outcomes of treatments whose efficacy they wished either to defend or attack (e.g., Eysenck, 1952; Knight, 1941).

An early definition of process and outcome research was provided by O. H. Mowrer:

With modern electronic devices it is now entirely feasible, at relatively small cost and trouble, to obtain a complete record of the verbal behavior of both patient and therapist during the course of treatment; and since psychotherapy is preeminently a matter of conversation, a relatively complete replica of therapy is thus obtained. . . . When therapy is concluded, the recordings can be subjected to the most minute and searching kinds of scientific analysis, with no sacrifice whatever of therapeutic considerations. And since, in the ordinary course of events, different therapists will employ different types of approach, comparisons become possible which are only a little less interesting and significant than would be the results of formal experimentation. . . . This strategy is now aptly known as **process research** and holds many promising possibilities. A step removed from process research but still closely related to it is **outcome research**. Here the emphasis is upon measuring significant aspects of personality before and after treatment and noting the nature and extent of the resulting changes (1953, p. 4, italics in original).

The field of psychotherapy research has naturally grown more complex over time, and it is no longer enough simply to talk about process and outcome. As the number of methods, measures, and findings have proliferated, the original referents of those terms have become much more finely differentiated (e.g., Elliott, 1991; Thommen, Ammann, & von Cranach, 1988). Ambiguities in the original terms arising from increased complexity have been further compounded by a largely unrecognized tendency of researchers to use these basic concepts in somewhat discrepant ways.

THE MEANING OF PROCESS

Several important variations have accrued to the meaning of *process*, which, unless clearly recognized, are likely to cause confusion. These reach beyond the usual distinctions among various specific aspects of process (techniques of intervention, states of relationship, etc.) with which we shall be concerned later. Four areas of variability deserve special attention: (1) the question of observational perspective; (2) the focus on treatment process versus change process; (3) the analysis of temporal sequences or causal sequences; and (4) the use of multiple levels of description.

Observational Perspectives

Therapeutic processes are naturally observed and also can be assessed for research purposes by the participants themselves, that is, by patients and therapists. The most common way of having patients and therapists generate research data is through the use of postsession questionnaires and rating scales, although techniques such as interpersonal process recall have been used as well (e.g., Elliott, 1986; C. E. Hill, 1989). Therapeutic processes may also be observed and assessed by nonparticipants (persons who do not directly interact with the patient and therapist) from recordings or other records made of therapy sessions. In their efforts to compare internally reliable assessments of the same substantive variable (e.g., therapist empathy) made by patients, therapists, and nonparticipant observers, process researchers have been forced to recognize that these are often not very highly correlated and often produce divergent findings in relation to other process or outcome variables (e.g., Gurman, 1977; Orlinsky & Howard, 1975).

It seems that the perspectives from which specific aspects of process are observed must be incorporated into the empirical and conceptual meaning of variables, since reliability and validity of assessments *within perspectives* can be established. This implies that the meaning of process from a patient's perspective, though not unrelated, is not the same as the meaning of process from a therapist's perspective, nor is each the same as what process means to external observers. As a result, we began to tabulate process–outcome findings separately by process and outcome perspectives in the third edition of this *Handbook* (Orlinsky & Howard, 1986a) and continue the practice in this report.

Treatment Process and Change Process[3]

Some investigators use the term *process* to refer to processes of change through which clients or patients are hypothesized to improve. These change processes tend to be viewed as occurring within the patient, often, but by no means exclusively or even mainly, during therapy sessions. For example, Carl

Rogers's (1961) "process conception of psychotherapy" focused on stages of change occurring in several aspects of the client's psychological functioning (e.g., manner of experiencing, construal of meaning, relationship to problems, manner of relating). The therapist's behavior during sessions was not viewed as part of this therapeutic process, but rather as "therapist-offered conditions" creating an interpersonal environment more or less "facilitative" of "the patient's process."

The influential change events paradigm of process research proposed by Rice and Greenberg (1984; Greenberg, 1991) follows this tradition to some extent, although with a broader clinical conception of client change events. It focuses specifically on therapy segments in which predefined change events can be scrutinized as an alternative to exhaustively describing or randomly sampling the ordinary flow of events during sessions. Yet another example of identifying the term *process* with change processes is found in the concept of therapeutic alliance formulated by researchers at the Menninger Foundation, who defined this concept "narrowly as the patient's active collaboration" (Frieswyk, Colson, & Allen, 1984, p. 460) and yet also stipulated that this should include "the extent to which the patient makes active use of the treatment as a resource for constructive change" (Frieswyk et al., 1986, p. 36)—the latter being usually reserved for the evaluation of outcome.

Other researchers use the term *process* primarily to refer to the events—any and all of the events—that may be observed and experienced during therapy sessions, without making prior distinctions between merely neutral events and specifically helpful (or hindering) events. Various well-known schemes of process assessment exemplify this approach (e.g., Bastine, Fiedler, & Kommer, 1989; Benjamin, Foster, & Estroff, 1986; Czogalik, 1991; Elliott, 1984; C. E. Hill, 1986; Kächele, 1992; Orlinsky & Howard, 1975, 1986b; Stiles, 1986). These focus on the actions, perceptions, intentions, thoughts, and feelings of the patient and therapist, as well as the relationship between them, which are generally viewed as occurring inside therapy sessions. This more pragmatic and descriptive approach to process analysis tends to be taken when investigators do not have strong a priori hypotheses about the sources of change in psychotherapy.

Drawing a potentially misleading metaphor (Stiles & Shapiro, 1989) from the field of pharmacology, treatment processes sometimes have been described as including both inert and active ingredients (e.g., Gomes-Schwartz, 1978). Active ingredients are conceived as having a demonstrable

---

[3]The first author thanks Professor Irene Elkin (University of Chicago) for sharing in discussions that clarified this distinction.

causal relation to change processes and, through these change processes, to outcome. Researchers who assess the relation of outcome to explicitly stipulated change processes are, in effect, attempting to validate clinically derived hypotheses. On the other hand, researchers who assess the relation of outcome to various treatment processes are taking a more empirical path to discovering the "effective ingredients" of psychotherapy. Both strategies seem legitimate, and researchers should of course be free to do what best suits them, but at least there will be less confusion if we use specifically qualified phrases such as *treatment process* and *change process* instead of the traditional, but more ambiguous, term *process*.

Temporal and Causal Sequences

Confusion can also arise from discrepancies in how researchers construe the sense of sequence implied by the idea of process. Sequence may be understood descriptively as temporal succession, or logically as causal consequence. The former is the more general meaning, since simple temporal succession does not imply cause and effect, whereas causal sequences do imply some passage of time. Both meanings may be used in considering either treatment processes or change processes.

Researchers face a dilemma in this regard. Although psychotherapy occurs in real time, temporal analyses of therapeutic processes require costly longitudinal research designs and typically demand herculean efforts involving vast amounts of data. Some notable attempts have been made by a few researchers (e.g., Labov & Fanshel, 1977; Pittenger, Hockett, & Danehy, 1960; Scheflen, 1973), but their studies generally have focused on fairly circumscribed segments of treatment (for an important exception, see Czogalik, 1991). On the other hand, although cross-sectional research designs may permit causal inferences and produce more manageable amounts of data, they promote a synchronic causal analysis of therapy process in which temporal sequences are left unspecified (e.g., Orlinsky & Howard, 1987). Consequently, those wishing to specify how the results of such research ought to be implemented in real-time practice typically have been forced to rely on clinical intuition rather than a solid research base.

Multiple Levels of Description

Finally, the venerable problem of units of measurement or levels of description in process research must be addressed. As Greenberg noted, "the unit chosen, be it word, phrase, utterance, problem area, initial period of therapy, and so on, will depend on the constructions of interest and on the questions being asked by a particular study" (1986, p. 715). Over the past 4 decades, process studies have focused on virtually all descriptive levels, although for reasons of economy and accessibility rather more on the microscopic end of the spectrum.

Wide variations in descriptive levels have stretched to the limit whatever meaning *process* retains as a simple, unqualified term. Comparing microanalyses of actions or utterances (e.g., Bänninger-Huber, 1992) to macroanalyses of treatment phases (e.g., Howard, Lueger, Maling, & Martinovich, 1992) is not so much like comparing apples to oranges as amoebas to elephants. Greenberg and Pinsof (1986a, p. 7) referred to the macro–micro distinction of scale in outcome variables made by researchers as "big O" versus "little o," but did not similarly dramatize distinctions of scale in process variables as "big P" versus "little p." In fact, this would be far too simple. Greenberg (1986) proposed distinguishing four levels of description —content (utterance), speech act, episode, and relationship—but even these cover only a portion of the spectrum of units studied by process researchers. Elliott (1991) recently proposed six unit levels. We have found it meaningful to distinguish as many as nine levels of process measurement (Orlinsky, 1988; see Table 8.1). As these are essentially heuristic distinctions, the number of levels actually used in any given case is largely a matter of practical convenience.

The point here is simply that the familiar term *process* signifies many different things in the psychotherapy research literature, and careful readers must therefore be attentive to subtle but important variations of meaning. In addition to noting the specific content aspect of process under study, it never hurts to ask the following questions: Is treatment process or change process the actual topic? Is process understood mainly in temporal or in causal terms? At what descriptive levels, from micro to mega, were process variables assessed? And, from whose perspective were the observations made?

THE MEANING OF OUTCOME

The concept of *outcome* has also been subject to an accumulation of divergent meanings. Two areas of variant usage have already been noted in the discussion of process: observational perspective and level of analysis. Regarding observational perspective, Strupp, Hadley, and Gomes-Schwartz (1977) established that definitions and criteria of outcome differ according to whether assessments are made by the patient, the therapist, an expert nonpartici-

TABLE 8.1   Levels of descriptive analysis for psychotherapeutic process and outcome

Level and Timeframe	Timescale	Process Focus	Outcome Focus
Level 1: Liminal	Split seconds	Micromomentary processes (gaze shifts; facial expressions)	
Level 2: Momentary	Large fractions to small multiples of minutes	Moment-by-moment processes (tactical moves, e.g., specific utterances; interactive turns)	In-session impacts (emergent helpful or hindering experiences, e.g., insight, catharsis)
Level 3: Situational	Large fractions to small multiples of hours	Session processes (strategic change events; rupture and repair of alliance; dynamics of whole sessions)	Postsession outcome (immediate improvements in mood, motivation, and cognition, e.g., resolution of "splitting")
Level 4: Daily	Large fractions to small multiples of days	Session-sequential processes (intersession experiences; use of homework assignments; very brief treatment episodes, e.g., emergency therapy)	Micro-outcome (enhancement of current functioning, e.g., boost in morale; communication skills; better handling of problem situations)
Level 5: Monthly	Large fractions to small multiples of months (weeks at a time)	Phase/short course processes (blocks of successive sessions; formation and evolution of a stable therapeutic alliance; short-term treatment episodes, e.g., 12–26 weeks)	Mini-outcome (upgrading of week-to-week psychological state, e.g., symptom reduction, reduction in irrational cognitions)
Level 6: Seasonal	Large fractions to small multiples of years (months at a time)	Medium course processes (work on recurrent interpersonal, cognitive and motivational conflicts; medium-term treatment episodes, e.g., 6–24 months)	Meso-outcome (change in personal adaptation, e.g., increase in self-ideal congruence, resolution of dysfunctional attitudes and cognitions)
Level 7: Perennial	Large fractions of decades (years at a time)	Long course processes (long-term treatment episodes, e.g., 2–7+ years)	Macro-outcome (personality change, e.g., modification of defenses; removal of neurotic blocks to growth)
Level 8: Developmental	Small multiples of decades	Multi-treatment processes (sequential treatment episodes)	Mega-outcome (character change, e.g., modification of axis-II personality disorder)
Level 9: Biographic	"3 score years plus 10"	Therapeutic career (total treatment history)	Meta-outcome (retrospective view of life course as influenced by treatment experience)

pant, or interested laypersons, such as the patient's family. Like process, outcome has a different yet valid meaning in each perspective, which can be shown by disaggregating perspectives for outcome as well as process in the tabulation of findings.

Level of analysis presents a more difficult problem, particularly at the microscopic end of the hierarchy. Some investigators tend to view the immediate consequences of a therapeutic intervention as outcome events despite the fact that they occur within the session; for example, patient insights following therapist interpretations, expressive behavior indicating softening of internal conflict following the use of a Gestalt two-chair technique, or increase in self-efficacy expectation toward a specific situation after behavioral rehearsal by roleplaying. Against this we have long argued that, as a practical matter, evidence of outcome ought to be observed *outside* the patient-therapist relationship (Orlinsky & Howard, 1972). Of what value is a treatment that proceeds well in itself but changes little in the patient's ongoing life or personality? We agree with Greenberg and Pinsof (1986a) that it is crucial to distinguish between little o's and big O's, but believe these distinctions only apply at level 3 and higher (see Table 8.1). Thus we view changes made by patients *inside* therapy as a distinct aspect of process, which we call in-session impacts (level 2) or therapeutic realizations. However, this does not mean that outcome cannot be evaluated until the termination of treatment or a specified follow-up period. In principle, immediate outcomes or micro-outcomes (levels 3 and 4) can be meaningfully assessed after any session—the 1st, 5th, or 15th—or intermittently over the course of treatment, as is often done in research on cognitive-behavioral therapy (e.g., DeRubeis & Feeley, 1990; Fennell & Teasdale, 1987).

Variations in a third area involve the use of either evaluative or descriptive assessments. Some researchers do not limit outcome to clinical improvement or deterioration, but refer instead to any type of serial dependency in treatment. From our point of view, outcome is a clinical concept signifying some degree of *improvement* or *deterioration* in the patient's condition, as judged from some observer's perspective by some value criterion (Orlinsky & Howard, 1980). For the sake of clarity, we proposed the term *output* to designate the whole spectrum of changes that may arise as a result of psychotherapy—whether in patients, therapists, their families and associates, or in the organizations, institutions, and value patterns of their social milieu (Orlinsky & Howard, 1986a).

As with in-session impacts, this confusion tends to arise particularly at the more microscopic levels

of analysis. For example, Czogalik (personal communication, 1992) remarked that time-series analyses of serial dependency between patient and therapist utterances in his data show that therapist self-disclosures do have significant effects on some patients, in contrast to our earlier report that therapist self-disclosure has little apparent effect on outcome (Orlinsky & Howard, 1986a). Our response (aside from the noting that the term *self-disclosure* has been variously defined) is that serially dependent responses to specific processes, even when they occur outside sessions, do not constitute clinical outcome unless they indicate some favorable or unfavorable change in the patient's condition. There are multiple value criteria by which such judgments can be made. Patients' behaviors can be assessed as more or less effective, authentic, or benevolent toward self and others; their products, as more or less beautiful or creative; their persons, as more or less normal, noble, or spiritually fulfilled (Orlinsky, 1989). Although there are many possible criteria and points of view on outcome, someone must take a stand.

A GENERIC SYSTEMS FRAMEWORK

Commentators on psychotherapy and reviewers of therapy research are often driven, with varying amounts of amusement or despair, to comment on the amazing number of *specific types of therapy* that are offered to the public. One prominent reviewer counted "well over 200 different kinds of psychotherapy in existence" and wondered if it were possible to "speak meaningfully of psychotherapy in general, even though there may be commonalities among the psychotherapies" (Herink, 1980, cited in Garfield, 1986, p. 214).

Taking only the insiders' (that is, therapists' or patients') view, only the *specific forms* of therapy being practiced will be seen: particular variants of therapeutic schools, or a particular integrative or eclectic combination of several. If the specific variants are counted, the number mounts quickly, as does the danger of missing a view of the forest by staring at individual trees. Yet, even allowing for some doubtfully marginal cases, clinicians, scientists, and laypersons still seem able to apply the general term *psychotherapy* with reasonable confidence to a broad range of professional psychosocial interventions.

In order to speak meaningfully of *psychotherapy in general*, however, an outsider's view is needed; not, perhaps, that of the proverbial Martian visitor, but one at least from neighboring social sciences. To gain an informed outsider's view of psychotherapy, we draw mainly on the perspectives of sociologist and anthropologist and, to a lesser extent, on those of mental health epidemiologists and medical economists. Like sociologists (e.g., McCall & Simmons, 1978; Turner, 1988) we view psychotherapy as a distinctively patterned "system of action" (Parsons, 1951) produced by persons engaged jointly in performing the socially recognized *roles* of therapist (or counselor, or analyst) and patient (or client, or analysand). Like anthropologists contemplating the variety of modern and indigenous modes of healing, we view psychotherapy as "the activation through the process of interpersonal communication of a powerful endogenous therapeutic system that is part of the psychophysiology of all individuals and the sociophysiology of relationships" (Kleinman, 1988, p. 112), noting that "the mode of clinical communication between healer and client may be somatic, psychological, moral, religious, or social idioms of distress and care; [that] their semiotic codes create a keyboard of nonverbal, verbal, and special signs through which these idioms are transmitted and received" (ibid., p. 118). Like epidemiologists and economists (e.g., Taube, Mechanic, & Hohmann, 1989) we also view psychotherapy generally as part of an organized mental health service delivery system operating in the context of, and responsive to, other social institutions.

The Generic Model of Psychotherapy

From these perspectives, we constructed the Generic Model of Psychotherapy to comprehend the genus to which the many species of psychotherapy belong (Orlinsky & Howard, 1987) — a model that emphasizes not only commonalities, but also points of systematic variation by which the species are differentiated. This generic model provides both a framework for systematically integrating the results of prior research (Orlinsky & Howard, 1986a) and an evolving set of hypotheses to be tested by new observations (e.g., Ambühl, 1989, 1993; Foppa-Drew, 1989; Grawe, 1989a; Kolden, 1991).

The model distinguishes, first, between psychotherapy as a "system of action" and the milieu in which it takes place. The psychotherapeutic system is defined as a set of reciprocal *roles*, and the actions and experiences of therapists and patients are viewed as attributes of the psychotherapeutic system insofar as they are performed and experienced with reference to those roles. However, the *persons* who perform those roles are viewed as part of the context in which therapy occurs, insofar as they have many other characteristics and involvements extending beyond their immediate roles as patient and therapist. This is illustrated simply by considering that a person may perform the role of therapist vis-à-vis patients in his or her professional life and, at other times, the roles of patient, or patient's parent or spouse, in his or her personal life. Only part of a therapist's or a patient's life is spent in therapy. What each one does and is the rest of the time forms a large part of the milieu in which therapeutic activities and experiences occur. This distinction is important because it allows the process – outcome to be formulated in terms of the effect that events experienced in one part of the patient's life (that is, in his or her role as a patient in therapy) have on events in other parts of the patient's life (e.g., his or her modes of action and experience in family relations, occupational activities, or other situations).

A second distinction can then be drawn between the varied influences that the milieu (including other aspects of the patient's and therapist's lives) may exert on the psychotherapeutic system, and the varied influences that the psychotherapeutic system may exert on the milieu. Influences of the milieu on the psychotherapeutic system may be called *inputs*. Input variables can be distinguished by the fact that they are studied prior to the beginning of treatment, or concurrently with treatment prior to the start of any particular session. Inputs include somatic and psychological influences from the internal milieus of the persons performing the roles of patient and therapist; and physical, social, and cultural influences from the external milieus comprising the local practice setting, the service delivery system, and the community at large. In psychotherapy research, the most commonly studied input variables are sociodemographic and psychological (e.g., education, age, gender, and cognitive styles or personality traits).

Looking at the same factors from the opposite angle, influences of the psychotherapeutic system on its internal and external milieus may be called *outputs*. These may occur at varied levels (Table 8.1) and in respect to varied sectors of the milieu. The psychological, somatic, physical, social, and cultural condition of persons in the patient role are the sectors of primary clinical interest. We believe the term *treatment outcome* should refer to changes in these conditions reflecting favorable or adverse effects on the patient's well-being. Of course, outputs of psychotherapy other than treatment outcome are worthy of study, for example, influences of the psychotherapeutic system on therapists (e.g., Farber, 1983) and the aggregate influences of psychotherapy on other institutions (e.g., Schlesinger, Mumford, Glass, Patrick, & Sharfstein, 1983) or on society at large (e.g., Bellah, Madsen, Sullivan, Swidler, & Tipton, 1985; MacIntyre, 1981; Newman & Howard, 1986).

In the generic model, the psychotherapeutic system itself, in all its aspects, is defined broadly as treatment process (in the sense indicated previously). The term includes all actions and experiences of patients and therapists *with each other* in therapy sessions and *with respect to each other* outside sessions. We leave the eventual definition of patient *change* processes to be determined by the empirical analysis of process–outcome relations.

Viewed in terms of inputs, processes, and outputs, we can appreciate that the field of psychotherapy research includes multiple modes of inquiry. Pure input research focuses on pretreatment characteristics of the persons who practice or undergo treatment and who may become each other's patient or therapist. Pure process research focuses on delineating the characteristics of actual treatments and their interrelations with one another. Pure output research for the most part focuses on treatment outcome, evaluating the effectiveness of treatments both in themselves vis-à-vis control groups and with respect to other treatments (comparative outcome research). Various combinations of input, process, and output are also commonly found. Analyses of the influence of pretreatment characteristics on the events and course of treatment may be classified as input–process studies, and analyses of their influence on the clinical effects of treatment on patients as input–outcome studies. Although all modes of research contribute to understanding psychotherapy, the focus in this chapter is limited to the flourishing field of *process–outcome* studies.

Aspects of Therapeutic Process

The inherent complexity of the psychotherapeutic system requires that it be observed from many aspects. Following the research literature, the Generic Model of Psychotherapy distinguishes six aspects of process that, in varied configurations, may be found in all forms of therapy: a formal aspect (*therapeutic contract*); a technical aspect (*therapeutic operations*); an interpersonal aspect (*therapeutic bond*); an intrapersonal aspect (*self-relatedness*); a clinical aspect (*in-session impacts*); and, finally, a temporal aspect (*sequential flow*).

The interactions of patients and therapists in therapy sessions are neither random nor determined solely by the participants' individual dispositions. "Patient" and "therapist" are social roles, and the actions and experiences of persons as patients and therapists are constrained by the normative expectations they have concerning these roles, the state of their consensus about their respective roles, and their faithful adherence to (or deviation

from) those roles. The *therapeutic contract* is their "understanding" about their goals and conditions for engaging each other as patient and therapist. This is at its simplest in the dyadic pairings of individual psychotherapy, and becomes progressively more complex in couple, group, and family therapy, which involve not only the relations of patients and therapists vis-à-vis one another but also the relations of patients vis-à-vis one another, sometimes also of therapists vis-à-vis one another, and the relations of each participant to the group as a whole. However the social unit of therapy is composed, the shape of therapeutic events is framed by the efforts that participants make to negotiate, implement, enforce, or alter the therapeutic contract.

Therapeutic operations are the specific technical procedures that patients and therapists commit themselves to perform under the therapeutic contract. Viewed generically, such operations always involve some forms of problem presentation, expert understanding, therapist intervention, and patient cooperation. A way has to be provided for persons in the patient role to present their complaints and otherwise make their problematic experiences available to the scrutiny and influence of the therapist (*problem presentation*). Persons in the therapist role have to apply their professional skills and knowledge to assess and evaluate what their patients present (*expert understanding*) and, however that may be construed, to present some course of action for dealing with the problematic situation (*therapist interventions*). Finally, participation in a course of therapeutic action typically requires patients to become actively involved in some fashion (*patient cooperation*).

While negotiating a therapeutic contract and performing their respective therapeutic operations, the persons involved invariably begin to generate some form of interpersonal relationship or *therapeutic bond*. This may be positive or negative in character, and can importantly support or interfere with the aims of therapy.[4] A strong therapeutic bond

---

[4]Readers familiar with the psychoanalytic approach to psychotherapy may miss the mention of transference under the concept of the therapeutic bond. The reason for this omission is that *transference* may refer to several things, unconscious and conscious. In the strict sense transference refers to the unconscious reenactment of core conflictual patterns of relationship that were repressed during early childhood. Unconscious transferences may be positive (erotic, dependent) or negative (hostile, competitive) and tend to appear in a person's life as recurrent patterns of emotionally charged interpersonal involvement (Freud, 1912/1958). In psychotherapy, unconscious transferences can be discerned in the persistent themes manifest in patient

Footnote continues on next page.

generally involves effective teamwork (personal role-investment and good interactive coordination) as well as personal rapport (expressive attunement and mutual affirmation). In therapy as elsewhere, little is likely to be accomplished by persons who can't work well together, and neither understand nor like each other. (If more than two participants are involved, the therapeutic bond takes the form of a group process in which effective teamwork and morale are important factors.)

Participants also respond to themselves while they interact with one another. *Self-relatedness* in therapy refers to the ways that patients and therapists experience and react to varying levels of internal arousal, perceive and construe their own desires and intentions, exercise self-control, experience self-efficacy or shame, and so forth. The observable behavioral aspect of self-relatedness is reflected in each person's bearing or social demeanor (Goffman, 1956). Clinically relevant aspects of negative self-relatedness in therapy are usually labeled defensiveness or constriction, while positive self-relatedness may be called openness or centeredness.

Participants in therapy also experience various *in-session impacts* as a result of specific therapeutic operations and states of the therapeutic bond, within limits imposed by the therapeutic contract and their states of personal self-relatedness. Favorable in-session impacts on patients include such events as insight, catharsis, softening of intrapersonal conflict, reinforcement of hope, and enhancement of self-efficacy (called "therapeutic realizations" in our last report). Patients may also

---

narratives about past and present life events (e.g., Luborsky & Crits-Christoph, 1988). These are considered under therapeutic operations as an aspect of the patient's *problem presentation* and as an aspect of the therapist's technical activity under *therapist interventions*. Transference patterns may also be discerned in the patient's behavior toward the therapist, for example, as unconscious "tests" of the therapist's ability to recognize and disconfirm the patient's core pathogenic beliefs or "plans" (Silberschatz, Curtis, Fretter, & Kelly, 1988), and in the patient's experience of relationship with the therapist (Hoffman & Gill, 1988). These latter forms can be considered aspects of the therapeutic bond. However, more confusion occurs when all aspects of the relationship with the therapist are referred to by the term *transference*, since only a portion of the patient's response to the therapist (or to other group participants and to the group as a whole) is attributable to unconscious transferences. Another portion is attributable to the actual relationship (or group process) that develops between patients and therapists as real individuals forming a history of new involvement with one another —however much transferences (in the strict sense) may have played a part in the formation of that new involvement.

experience negative in-session impacts, such as confusion, anxiety, or embarrassment. Therapists, too, experience positive and negative in-session impacts (Farber & Heifetz, 1981) which, although generally of secondary interest, may become clinically important if they interfere with effective performance of the therapist role (for example, through burnout).

Finally, in therapy as in other contractual relationships, time is of the essence. Little was made of this fact in the last edition of this *Handbook*, because there were few process–outcome studies to report beyond the accumulation of evidence linking treatment duration to outcome. Since then, considerable progress has been made in examining *sequential flow* both within and across therapy sessions. A number of investigators have begun to reveal the orderly nature of patterns of *session development* by applying sophisticated methods of statistical analysis. Similar techniques have been used to delineate sequential patterns of stages in the *therapeutic course*.

These six aspects of the psychotherapeutic process serve as categories for organizing the survey of process–outcome findings presented in this chapter. Although they are presented separately and serially, it is important to remember that they are conceived not as separate steps or pieces of process but as concurrent features of a complex human reality. In other words, all therapies involve some form of therapeutic contract, some type of therapeutic operations, some kind of therapeutic bond, some mode of participant self-relatedness, some degree of in-session impact, and occur in some temporal order. The six process aspects are functionally interrelated, and this unit as a whole defines the psychotherapeutic system.

Two consequences of this conception deserve brief comment. First, the model presents these process aspects at a level of abstraction one step removed from directly observable forms of treatment.[5] To distinguish among the various observable species of psychotherapy would require describing how each process aspect is configured and how the several process aspects are interrelated. The process aspects very likely are differentially configured, and also differently interrelated, in each

---

[5]Taken together, the six process aspects provide an approximate definition of the genus *psychotherapy*. This taxonomic conception of successive levels — specimen (particular therapy cases), species (specific types of therapy), and genus (psychotherapy per se) — may be extended another step by viewing the genus psychotherapy as one member of a broader family of care-giving or helping relationships, of which the generic categories of teaching, ministering, and parenting are others.

specific type of therapy. These specific types of treatment, in turn, very likely produce differential results for different types of patients and therapists (e.g., Beutler & Clarkin, 1990; Beutler, Mohr, Grawe, Engle, & MacDonald, 1991; Grawe, 1989b, 1991). A number of process-by-input interaction effects with outcome are cited in this chapter; even more may be expected in the next edition of this volume.

Second, the process aspects are understood to operate within determinate contexts. Their active interrelations define the psychotherapeutic system as a whole, and that specifically configured system constitutes an immediate context for the several aspects of therapeutic process. Further contextual connections may be discerned between aspects of the psychotherapeutic system and aspects of the social and cultural environment in which therapy takes place. These include: the immediate *treatment setting* (e.g., university counseling center, community mental health clinic, inpatient psychiatric ward, or private office practice) and personnel in the treatment setting who interact regularly with patients and therapists (e.g., receptionists, supervisors); the wider *service delivery system* in which the treatment setting is located; *other social institutions* located within or outside the service delivery system (e.g., welfare agencies, law courts, patients' and therapists' families); social, economic, and political *currents of change* affecting community life (e.g., holiday seasons, industrial recessions, protest movements); and, most broadly, the *cultural belief and value orientations* of the society at large.

PROCESS–OUTCOME FINDINGS

The findings reviewed in this chapter were systematically tabulated whenever a reasonable number had accumulated for a process variable. For each of the findings, tables show (1) the bibliographic reference, (2) the observational perspectives used in assessing process and outcome, (3) the statistical significance and the direction of association[6] if significant (≤ 05), and (4) a note about effect size.[7]

---

[6]Note that "+" and "−" refer to the direction of association between process and outcome variables rather than a positive therapeutic outcome. Generally, higher process levels associated with better outcomes or lower process levels associated with poorer outcomes are considered *positive* findings (e.g., the association of lack of therapist skill with negative outcome is +).

[7]Effect size is shown when it was easily calculable (e.g., $ES = r^2$); otherwise a note indicates whether data for calculating effect sizes were available, for readers who desire to conduct a formal meta-analysis of the variable.

The last information should help to correct overreliance on conventional significance levels, which are affected by uncontrolled methodological factors such as sample size and instrument reliability. Within each table findings for *macro* outcomes (termination or follow-up assessment) are given first, followed by findings for *micro* outcomes (immediate postsession evaluations). *Interaction effects* are listed separately from *main effects* within each category, and both are amplified by footnotes as needed to give the reader an idea of the study. If available, published meta-analyses of research are also listed. Variables for which few process–outcome findings have yet accumulated are cited in the text with bibliographic references for interested readers.

Continuity with findings reported in the last edition has been established in two ways. First, findings that were tabulated in the last edition are summarized separately in each table. Second, findings that were cited in the text but not tabulated in the last edition are included in the appropriate tables of this edition when warranted by the further accumulation of relevant research. A final tally of all findings for each variable is presented in the summary section, and interpretive comments are based primarily on the overall summaries.

THERAPEUTIC CONTRACT

Process–outcome findings concerning the therapeutic contract were divided among variables reflecting the *contractual provisions* that determine how therapy is organized and other variables describing the manner of *contractual implementation*. In the last edition, formal contractual provisions that had been studied showed little consistent relation to outcome. By contrast, certain aspects of contractual implementation seemed more important, such as pretreatment orientation for unsophisticated patients, active conversational input from patients, and therapist skillfulness. Recent studies continue to support these impressions.

Contractual Provisions
As Beutler and Clarkin (1990) noted, the basic framework of treatment is largely determined by decisions concerning its setting, format, frequency, and contractual duration. No process–outcome studies fairly comparing treatment settings are known to us, but the other factors have been studied.

Collectivity, or format, concerns the structure and size of the unit in which therapy takes place; for example, individual (dyadic) therapy, couple (triadic) therapy, family therapy, group therapy, and so on. Table 8.2 summarizes the research accumulated to date on this variable. Nearly 75% of the findings fail to show any consistent main effect indicating an advantage for either individual therapy or some other format, such as group or family therapy, although there are a few significant interaction effects. A meta-analysis by Russell, Greenwald, and Shirk (1991) marshaled evidence suggesting that individual therapy is the preferred treatment modality for children with language problems.

Schedule concerns the frequency of therapy sessions, and most of the relevant findings compare once-weekly sessions with more or less frequent alternatives. A potential problem discussed in the last edition of the *Handbook* is the confounding of frequency with overall treatment duration. Few additional studies have been done since then, and nearly 70% of the findings summarized in Table 8.3 indicate no differential main effects. Positive and negative findings are evenly balanced, although most of the negative findings (showing better outcome with once-monthly than with once-weekly sessions) derive from a single study of a behavioral program for treating orgasmic dysfunction in women.

Term concerns the open-ended or time-limited duration of the therapeutic contract. Although time-limited therapies have become very popular, few studies have compared their effectiveness with that of open-ended therapies, and the results are almost equally divided among positive, negative, and null findings (Table 8.4). However, it is worth remembering that much recent research has been done in the context of relatively brief time-limited treatment of, for example, 12–26 sessions — mainly because an adequate number of completed cases can be collected in a reasonable amount of time. Consequently, many of the process–outcome results reported in other tables may in fact represent hidden interaction effects with this contractual variable. A second point is that patients who agree to a specific time-limited term often end up having longer treatments in time-limited than in nominally unlimited therapy, because the median length of unlimited treatment is only 5 or 6 sessions (Garfield, 1986; Phillips, 1985). Given the fact that longer treatment durations tend to be associated with better outcomes, comparisons between time-limited and open-ended therapies need to control for this factor.

Fees are an issue in the United States and in other countries where therapy is not provided as a health care entitlement, but on a fee-for-service basis. The point in question is whether outcome is affected one way or another by fee reductions to the patient, either as a service provider policy (slid-

ing fee scale) or through third party (insurance) payment for all or a portion of the cost. The few studies of this matter summarized in Table 8.5 suggest that outcome is not affected, although in some circumstances having the client pay something apparently can be a positive influence.

A small number of studies have focused on two other contractual provisions: using patient self-monitoring assignment as a part of therapy (Gasman, 1992; Hisli, 1987; Neimeyer & Feixas, 1990) and using cotherapists versus one therapist in conducting sex therapy with couples (LoPiccolo, Heiman, Hogan, & Roberts, 1985; also see Libman, Fichten, & Brender, 1985).

For the variables that have been studied thus far, it seems that research still has not shown the various provisions of the therapeutic contract, in and of themselves, to be significant determinants of outcome. A contract of some sort is necessary if therapy is to proceed, but it is not clear that what sort of contract it is makes a great difference to the result.

Contractual Implementation

The first condition of contractual implementation is the achievement of a consensus between the parties as to what they may expect. Given requisite levels of therapist skill and patient suitability, other facets of implementation involve preparation, performance, and termination of treatment.

Research on the relation of *expectational clarity and goal consensus* to outcome has only recently begun, but a number of findings can already be cited. Most are a product of interest in therapeutic alliance measures that include a focus on goals and tasks. Table 8.6 summarizes 35 new findings indicating that clarity and consensus tend to be important factors when assessed from the patient's perspective or by means of an objective index, but curiously irrelevant from the therapist's process perspective.

Patient role preparation involves providing some type of formal instruction for prospective clients concerning what they should expect and how they can best participate in their own treatment. Three recent studies add a mixed report to the few previous studies, but overall the findings summarized in Table 8.7 indicate that role preparation produces better outcomes more often than not and does no harm. Thus, it seems particularly worth considering for patients who are new to therapy and do not have an educational background that would have familiarized them with psychotherapy.

Once in treatment, most of the activity required of patients and therapists involves conversation. A number of studies cited in the last edition as to the

Text continues on p. 291.

N.B. For Tables 8.2 through 8.5: *Outcome* refers to the observational perspective from which outcome was evaluated. P = patient ratings; T = therapist ratings; R = ratings by independent raters; S = psychometric test score or objective index; CI = combined perspectives index. *ES* = effect size. na = data not available; a/c = data available but not computed.

TABLE 8.2 Therapeutic collectivity: Dyad versus group

Reference	Outcome	Finding[a]	ES
Bennett (1986)	S	0	na
Pilkonis et al. (1984)	T	0	a/c
Lipman & Covi (1976)	S	0	na
Pilkonis et al. (1984)[b]	R	—	a/c
Pilkonis et al. (1984)	S	0	a/c
Szapocznik (1983)[c]	T	0	a/c
Szapocznik (1983)[c]	R	0	a/c
Szapocznik (1986)[c]	T	0	a/c
Szapocznik (1986)[c]	R	0	a/c
INTERACTION EFFECTS			
Gerin et al. (1987)[d]	R	+	.52
Pilkonis et al. (1984)	T	0	a/c
Pilkonis et al. (1984)	R	0	a/c
Pilkonis et al. (1984)[e]	S	—	a/c
Piper et al. (1984)[f]	P	+	a/c
Piper et al. (1984)[f]	T	+	a/c
Piper et al. (1984)	S	0	a/c
META-ANALYSIS [not tallied]			
Casey & Berman (1985)[g]	CI	0	a/c
Libman et al. (1985)[h]	CI	0	na
Neimeyer et al. (1989)[i]	CI	0	.01
Nietzel et al. (1987)[j]	S	+	a/c
Nietzel et al. (1987)[j]	S	0	a/c
Russell et al. (1991)[k]	S	+	1.31

SUMMARY A: TO 1985																OUTCOME			
	Patient			Therapist			Rater			Score			Combined			Total			
	−	0	+	−	0	+	−	0	+	−	0	+	−	0	+	−	0	+
Ind.> Grp.	0	2	1	0	0	0	0	1	0	0	8	2	0	0	0	0	11	3

SUMMARY B: TOTAL TO DATE																OUTCOME			
	Patient			Therapist			Rater			Score			Combined			Total			
	−	0	+	−	0	+	−	0	+	−	0	+	−	0	+	−	0	+
Ind.> Grp.	0	2	2	0	4	1	1	4	1	1	12	2	0	0	0	2	22	6

[a] + = outcome of individual therapy superior to group or other therapy modality; 0 = no significant difference; − = outcome of individual therapy inferior to group or other therapy modality.

[b] Patients in conjoint therapy had better outcomes, from the perspective of family members (R), than did patients in individual or group therapy.

[c] Brief strategic family therapy conducted with patient alone in contrast to patient plus family members.

[d] Improvement in nonpsychotic inpatients was associated with number of individual and group therapy sessions attended, whereas improvement in psychotic inpatients was associated with the number of family therapy sessions attended.

[e] Patients with longer standing problems had poorer outcomes in individual therapy than in other modalities; patients from lower social classes had better outcomes in individual therapy whereas those from higher social classes had better outcomes in group therapy.

continued

Footnote continued from Table 8.2

[f]Patients in contractually short-term (6 months) individual therapy and contractually long-term (24 months) group therapy had better outcomes than patients in contractually short-term (6 months) group therapy and contractually long-term (24 months) individual therapy. See De Carufel & Piper (1988) for interaction effects with patient characteristics.

[g]Child psychotherapies.

[h]Standard couple therapy, group therapy, and minimal therapist contact bibliotherapy were demonstrably but not differentially effective for delivery of behavioral sex therapy.

[i]Group therapies for depression.

[j]Depressed patients in individual cognitive, behavioral, and other types of therapy had better outcomes than patients in group therapy at termination but not at follow-up.

[k]Meta-analysis of studies of child therapy that included at least one language outcome measure indicated that effect size for individual therapies, across all types of outcome measures, was 10 times greater than that of group and/or parent-focused therapies.

TABLE 8.3   Schedule of sessions: Weekly versus other

Reference	Outcome	Finding[a]	ES
Beutler et al. (1984)[b]	R	0	.00
Beutler et al. (1984)[b]	S	0	.01
Calvert et al. (1988)[c]	S	−	.08
Morokoff & LoPiccolo (1986)[d]	P	0	a/c
Morokoff & LoPiccolo (1986)[d]	S	0	a/c
Morokoff & LoPiccolo (1986)[d]	S	−	a/c
INTERACTION EFFECT			
Morokoff & LoPiccolo (1986)[e]	P	−	a/c

SUMMARY A: TO 1985   *OUTCOME*

	Patient − 0 +	Therapist − 0 +	Rater − 0 +	Score − 0 +	Combined − 0 +	Total − 0 +
wk > other	1 2 2	0 2 1	0 1 0	0 8 1	0 0 0	1 13 4

SUMMARY B: TOTAL TO DATE   *OUTCOME*

	Patient − 0 +	Therapist − 0 +	Rater − 0 +	Score − 0 +	Combined − 0 +	Total − 0 +
wk > other	2 3 2	0 2 1	0 2 0	2 10 1	0 0 0	4 17 4

[a]+ = outcome for once-weekly sessions superior to other schedules; 0 = no significant difference; − = outcome for once-weekly sessions inferior to other schedules.

[b]For psychiatric inpatients, number of individual, group, or family sessions attended per day of hospitalization was unrelated to outcome.

[c]For psychiatric inpatients, number of group therapy sessions attended per day of hospitalization was associated with higher level of psychopathology at discharge.

[d]Comparison of once-monthly and once-weekly sessions in behavioral treatment of orgasmic dysfunction in women showed no significant differences in outcome between schedules, except for greater frequency of orgasm achieved by patients in minimal contact condition.

[e]Female partners of pairs in minimal contact condition in sex therapy made greater gains in marital happiness than male partners and couples in weekly sessions.

TABLE 8.4   Contractual term: Time-limited versus unlimited

Reference	Outcome	Finding[a]	ES
Keilson et al. (1983)	S	−	a/c
Gelso, Spiegel, & Mills (1983)[b]	P	+	a/c
Gelso, Spiegel, & Mills (1983)[b]	T	0	a/c
Gelso, Spiegel, & Mills (1983)[c]	P	0	a/c
Zola et al. (1987)	S	−	na

SUMMARY A: TO 1985   *OUTCOME*

	Patient − 0 +			Therapist − 0 +			Rater − 0 +			Score − 0 +			Combined − 0 +			Total − 0 +		
lim>unlim	0	0	1	0	0	0	0	0	0	1	3	2	0	0	0	1	3	3

SUMMARY B: TOTAL TO DATE   *OUTCOME*

	Patient − 0 +			Therapist − 0 +			Rater − 0 +			Score − 0 +			Combined − 0 +			Total − 0 +		
lim>unlim	0	1	2	0	1	0	0	0	0	3	3	2	0	0	0	3	5	4

[a] + = time-limited therapy superior to unlimited therapy; 0 = no significant difference; − = unlimited therapy superior to time-limited therapy.
[b] At termination (therapists) or 1 month posttermination (patients).
[c] Follow-up at 18 months.

TABLE 8.5   Fees: Normal versus reduced

Reference	Outcome	Finding[a]	ES
Bush et al. (1986)[b]	CI	0	a/c
Gully & Harris (1982)[d]	P	0	a/c
Gully & Harris (1982)[d]	T	0	a/c
Meinberg & Yager (1985)[d]	S	+	a/c
Stanton (1976)	S	+	a/c
Subich & Hardin (1985)	P	0	a/c
Wood (1982)[e]	P	0	a/c
Yoken & Berman (1987)	P	0	a/c
Yoken & Berman (1987)	T	0	a/c
Yoken & Berman (1987)	S	0	a/c
[cited but untabulated in 1986]			
Pope et al. (1975)	T	0	a/c
Rosenbaum et al. (1956)	T	+	an

SUMMARY: TOTAL TO DATE   *OUTCOME*

	Patient − 0 +			Therapist − 0 +			Rater − 0 +			Score − 0 +			Combined − 0 +			Total − 0 +		
Hi > Lo	0	4	0	0	3	1	0	0	0	0	1	2	0	1	0	0	9	3

[a] + = fee level positively associated with outcome; 0 = no significant difference; − = fee level negatively associated with outcome.
[b] Neither method of fee setting nor amount of fee was associated with outcome in therapies conducted at a community mental health center.
[c] Neither fee source nor fee amount was associated with improvement ratings of children or of families.
[d] Level of stress reduction greater for fee-paying than non-fee-paying participants in a stress-management-skills workshop.
[e] Fee level, source of payment (third party or self only), and actual amount paid, all unrelated to outcome.

N.B. For Tables 8.6 through 8.11: *Process* refers to the observational perspective from which process was assessed. P = patient ratings; T = therapist ratings; R = ratings by nonparticipant raters; I = objectively determined index of process, for example, assignment to a specified treatment condition. *Outcome* refers to the observational perspective from which outcome was evaluated. P = patient ratings; T = therapist ratings; R = ratings by independent raters; S = psychometric test score or objective index; CI = combined perspectives index. *ES* = effect size. na = data not available; a/c = data available but not computed.

TABLE 8.6 Expectational clarity/goal consensus

Reference	Process	Outcome	Finding[a]	ES
Dormaar et al. (1989)[b]	P	P	0	na
Dormaar et al. (1989)[b]	P	T	+	.03
Dormaar et al. (1989)[b]	P	S	+	a/c
Dormaar et al. (1989)[b]	T	P	0	na
Dormaar et al. (1989)[b]	T	T	0	na
Dormaar et al. (1989)[b]	T	S	0	na
Dormaar et al. (1989)[b]	I	P	0	na
Dormaar et al. (1989)[c]	I	T	+	a/c
Dormaar et al. (1989)[d]	I	S	+	.06
Gaston et al. (1991)[e]	P	S	0	.00
Goldstein et al. (1988)[f]	P	P	+	.15
Goldstein et al. (1988)[f]	T	T	0	.02
Hoge et al. (1988)[g]	P	P	+	na
Horowitz et al. (1984)[h]	T	S	0	na
Horowitz et al. (1984)[h]	R	R	0	na
Horowitz et al. (1984)[h]	R	S	0	na
Lansford (1986)[i]	R	R	0	na
Marmar, Gaston, et al. (1989)[j]	P	S	0	.01
Safran & Wallner (1991)[j]	P	S	+	.36
Tracey (1988)[k]	I	CI	+	a/c
Tracey (1988)[l]	I	CI	0	a/c
Tracey (1988)[k,m]	I	P	0	a/c
Tracey (1988)[k,m]	I	T	+	a/c
Tracey (1988)[k,m]	I	S	0	a/c
INTERACTION EFFECTS				
Horowitz et al. (1984)[n]	T	R	+	.10
Jones et al. (1988)[o]	R	S	+	.10
[postsession outcome]				
Eisenthal et al. (1983)[p]	R	P	+	.09
Eisenthal et al. (1983)[p]	R	T	+	.12
Hoyt (1980)[q]	R	R	0	.01
Hoyt et al. (1983)[q]	T	T	−	.06
Hoyt et al. (1983)[q]	R	R	+	.09
Kirk et al. (1988)[r]	I	T	+	a/c
Kirk et al. (1988)[r]	I	S	+	a/c
Tracey (1988)[k]	I	P	+	a/c
Tracey (1988)[k]	I	T	+	a/c

SUMMARY: TOTAL TO DATE — OUTCOME

Process	Patient −	Patient 0	Patient +	Therapist −	Therapist 0	Therapist +	Rater −	Rater 0	Rater +	Score −	Score 0	Score +	Combined −	Combined 0	Combined +	Total −	Total 0	Total +
Patient	0	1	2	0	0	1	0	0	0	0	2	2	0	0	0	0	3	5
Therapist	0	1	0	1	2	0	0	0	1	0	2	0	0	0	0	1	5	1
Rater	0	0	1	0	0	1	0	3	1	0	1	1	0	0	0	0	4	4
Index	0	2	1	0	0	4	0	0	0	0	1	2	0	1	1	0	4	8
Total	0	4	4	1	2	6	0	3	2	0	6	5	0	1	1	1	16	18

[a]+ = good contractual consensus positively associated with good outcome, or poor contractual consensus negatively associated with poor outcome; 0 = no significant difference; − = good contractual consensus negatively associated with good outcome, or poor contractual consensus positively associated with poor outcome.

[b]Experienced consensus unrelated to outcome, except that patients' experienced consensus was slightly but significantly correlated with therapist-rated outcome.

[c]Consensus index was associated with positive therapist-rated outcome.

[d]Curvilinear relationship indicating that the mid-range of a consensus index was most associated with positive scale-assessed outcome.

[e]CALPAS scale of goal/strategy disagreement.

[f]Clarity of role expectations in a partial hospital program.

[g]Structure (including elements of routine, direction, activity, and sense of purpose) was endorsed as an important therapeutic factor by 95% of participants in a partial hospital program.

[h]Therapist's effort to clarify focus of therapy in session 4 of time-limited dynamic psychotherapy unrelated to outcome, except as noted in footnote n.

[i]Discussion of task of therapy.

[j]Patient rating of goal disagreement on CALPAS-P.

[k]Congruence in problem source attributions.

[l]Congruence in problem-solving attributions.

[m]High patient-therapist consensus as to problem source, but not problem-solving responsibility, was significantly associated with first session postsession outcome, with continuation in treatment, and with therapist-rated but not patient-rated posttermination outcome.

[n]Therapist's effort to clarify focus of treatment early in therapy (but not at other times) as perceived by therapists (but not by judges) was associated with better outcome.

[o]For patients with low level of pretreatment disturbance, good outcome was positively associated with "T explains rationale behind treatment" and "P understands nature of therapy and what is expected."

[p]Patient-therapist mutuality in making treatment decisions and in communicating explanatory information during initial psychiatric interviews in a walk-in clinic.

[q]Discussion of therapy goals, focus, and process in time-limited dynamic psychotherapy.

[r]Match between patient and therapist perceptions of patient requests made during initial crisis-intervention interview was associated with decrease in patient stress.

TABLE 8.7 Role preparation for patient

Reference	Outcome	Finding[a]	ES
Coleman & Kaplan (1990)	P	0	a/c
Coleman & Kaplan (1990)	R	+	a/c
Deane et al. (1992)	P	0	a/c
Deane et al. (1992)	T	+	a/c
Deane et al. (1992)	S	0	a/c
Zwick & Attkisson (1985)	P	0	a/c
Zwick & Attkisson (1985)	T	0	a/c
Zwick & Attkisson (1985)	S	+	a/c

SUMMARY A: TO 1985   *OUTCOME*

	Patient − 0 +	Therapist − 0 +	Rater − 0 +	Score − 0 +	Combined − 0 +	Total − 0 +
Prep> No Prep	0 6 5	0 2 4	0 1 3	0 4 9	0 0 0	0 13 21

SUMMARY B: TOTAL TO DATE   *OUTCOME*

	Patient − 0 +	Therapist − 0 +	Rater − 0 +	Score − 0 +	Combined − 0 +	Total − 0 +
Prep> No Prep	0 9 5	0 3 5	0 1 4	0 5 10	0 0 0	0 18 24

[a]+ = role preparation positively related to outcome; 0 = no significant difference; − = role preparation negatively related to outcome.

TABLE 8.8   Therapist's verbal activity

Reference	Process	Outcome	Finding[a]	ES
Gabbard et al. (1986)	P	P	0	.00
Gabbard et al. (1986)	R	R	0	.02
Green & Herget (1991)[b]	R	P	0	.11
Green & Herget (1991)[b]	R	T	0	.07
Green & Herget (1991)[b]	R	R	0	.23
Green & Herget (1991)[c]	R	R	+	.42
McCullough et al. (1991)[d]	R	CI	0	na
Meyer (1981)/Meyer (1990)[e]	R	S	+	.54
Meyer (1981)/Meyer (1990)[e]	R	S	0	.13
Tracey (1987)[f]	R	CI	+	a/c
Westermann et al. (1983)[g1]	P	CI	+	na
Westermann et al. (1983)[g2]	P	CI	+	na
INTERACTION EFFECTS				
Jones et al. (1988)[h]	R	S	+	.07
Schulte (in press)[i]	I	CI	+	.09
[postsession outcome]				
Hoyt (1980)	R	R	0	.02
Hoyt et al. (1983)	T	T	0	.02
Hoyt et al. (1983)	R	R	+	.18
Orlinsky & Howard (1967, 1975)[j]	P	P	—	na
Orlinsky & Howard (1967, 1975)[j]	P	T	0	na
Orlinsky & Howard (1967, 1975)[j]	T	P	0	na
Orlinsky & Howard (1967, 1975)[j]	T	T	—	na

SUMMARY A: TO 1985   *OUTCOME*

Process	Patient − 0 +	Therapist − 0 +	Rater − 0 +	Score − 0 +	Combined − 0 +	Total − 0 +
Index	0 1 2	0 2 2	0 0 0	1 5 1	0 0 0	1 8 5

SUMMARY B: TOTAL TO DATE   *OUTCOME*

Process	Patient − 0 +	Therapist − 0 +	Rater − 0 +	Score − 0 +	Combined − 0 +	Total − 0 +
Patient	1 1 0	0 1 0	0 0 0	0 0 0	0 0 2	1 2 2
Therapist	0 1 0	1 1 0	0 0 0	0 0 0	0 0 0	1 2 0
Rater	0 1 0	0 1 0	0 3 2	0 1 2	0 1 1	0 7 5
Index	0 1 2	0 2 2	0 0 0	1 5 1	0 0 1	1 8 6
Total	1 4 2	1 5 2	0 3 2	1 6 3	0 1 4	3 19 13

[a] + = more talking positively related to outcome; 0 = no statistical difference; − = more talking negatively related to outcome.
[b] 1-month outcome.
[c] 3-year outcome.
[d] Frequency of therapist verbal intervention.
[e] Frequency of therapist intervention was associated with better outcome in short-term individual client-centered therapy, but not in short-term individual psychodynamic therapy.
[f] Therapist verbal responses more often followed patient initiated topics in successful as compared with unsuccessful cases of time-limited counseling, but were not different with respect to sequential (intrachain) consistency or interactive (interchain) patterns.
[g] Outcome in group therapy was positively associated with perceived activity of (1) senior therapist and (2) student cotherapist.
[h] For patients with low level of pretreatment disturbance, good outcome was associated with silences occurring during the session.
[i] Amount of topic initiation by therapy in early (but not middle or late) sessions was positively associated with outcome at termination (but not at 2-year follow-up).
[j] Activity without affectivity.

TABLE 8.9 Therapist's skillfulness

Reference	Process	Outcome	Finding[a]	ES
Ambühl & Grawe (1988)[b]	R	CI	+	a/c
Bennun et al. (1986)[c]	P	P	+	.08
Bennun et al. (1986)[c]	P	T	+	.05
Bennun et al. (1986)[d]	P	P	+	.20
Bennun et al. (1986)[d]	P	T	+	.32
Crits-Christoph et al. (1988)[e]	R	CI	0	.02
Gabbard et al. (1986)[f]	P	P	0	.00
Gabbard et al. (1986)[f]	R	R	0	.00
Glass et al. (1989)[g]	R	CI	+	.20
Green & Herget (1991)[h]	R	P	+	.42
Green & Herget (1991)[h]	R	T	+	.40
Green & Herget (1991)[h]	R	R	+	.52
Green & Herget (1991)[i]	R	R	+	.31
Grimes & Murdock (1989)	P	S	+	.19
Hagborg (1991)	P	P	+	.35
Hagborg (1991)	P	S	0	.01
Holtzworth-Munroe et al. (1989)[j]	P	P	+	.07
Holtzworth-Munroe et al. (1989)[k]	P	P	0	.07
Horvath (1981)	P	P	0	.02
McNeill et al. (1987)	P	P	+	.10
O'Malley et al. (1988)	R	P	+	.31
O'Malley et al. (1988)	R	R	0	.10
Sander et al. (1973)	P	S	+	.14
Schindler (1991)	P	S	0	.17
Svartberg & Stiles (1992)	R	R	0	.02
[cited but untabulated in 1986]				
Feifel & Eells (1963)	P	P	0	na
Feifel & Eells (1963)	T	T	+	na
Kaschak (1978)	P	P	0	na
Kaschak (1978)	T	T	+	na
Kernberg et al. (1972)	R	CI	+	.26
Sachs (1983)	R	P	0	.13
Sachs (1983)	R	T	+	.35
Sachs (1983)	R	R	+	.28
Shyne & Kogan (1957)	R	R	+	na
Sloane et al. (1975)[l]	P	P	+	na
[postsession outcome]				
Hoyt (1980)	R	R	+	.08

SUMMARY B: TOTAL TO DATE *OUTCOME*

Process	Patient − 0 +			Therapist − 0 +			Rater − 0 +			Score − 0 +			Combined − 0 +			Total − 0 +		
Patient	0	5	6	0	0	2	0	0	0	0	2	2	0	0	0	0	7	10
Therapist	0	0	0	0	0	2	0	0	0	0	0	0	0	0	0	0	0	2
Rater	0	1	2	0	0	2	0	3	5	0	0	0	0	1	3	0	5	12
Total	0	6	8	0	0	6	0	3	5	0	2	2	0	1	3	0	12	24

[a] + = skillfulness positively related to outcome; 0 = no significant association; − = skillfulness negatively related to outcome.
[b] Skillfulness at efforts to "further the therapeutic relationship" (also see Ambühl, 1991).
[c] German inpatient sample.
[d] U.K. outpatient sample.
[e] "Errors in technique" subscale of Vanderbilt Negative Indicators Scale.
[f] Therapist adaptability vis-à-vis client maturity level.
[g] Schizophrenic patients in individual exploratory and supportive dynamic psychotherapy.
[h] 1-month outcome.
[i] 3-year outcome.
[j] Husbands' ratings of process in behavioral marital therapy.
[k] Wives' ratings of process in behavioral marital therapy.
[l] Patient view of therapist skill associated retrospectively with outcome for psychotherapy but not behavior therapy.

TABLE 8.10   Patient's suitability for treatment

Reference	Process	Outcome	Finding[a]	ES
Colson et al. (1985)[b]	R	R	+	.24
Colson et al. (1991)[b]	R	R	+	.24
Crane et al. (1986)[c]	P	P	+	.34
Erle (1979)	R	T	+	na
Fennell & Teasdale (1987)	R	R	+	.58
Morrison & Shapiro (1987)[d]	P	CI	0	a/c
Neimeyer & Feixas (1990)[e]	R	R	0	a/c
Neimeyer & Feixas (1990)[e]	R	S	0	a/c
Neimeyer & Feixas (1990)[f]	R	S	+	.15
Rosenbaum et al. (1986)[g]	R	R	+	.15
Rosenbaum et al. (1986)[g]	R	S	0	.02
Weber et al. (1985a)[h]	T	R	+	.10–16
Weber et al. (1985b)[h]	T	R	+	na
Weber et al. (1985b)[h,i]	T	S	+	.64
INTERACTION EFFECT				
Gelso, Mills, & Spiegel (1983)[j,k]	T	P	+	.23
Gelso, Mills, & Spiegel (1983)[j,l]	T	P	0	.03
Gelso, Mills, & Spiegel (1983)[j,m]	T	P	0	.03
Gelso, Mills, & Spiegel (1983)[j,k]	T	T	+	.36
Gelso, Mills, & Spiegel (1983)[j,l]	T	T	+	.10
Gelso, Mills, & Spiegel (1983)[j,m]	T	T	+	.34

SUMMARY A: TO 1985   *OUTCOME*

	Patient − 0 +	Therapist − 0 +	Rater − 0 +	Score − 0 +	Combined − 0 +	Total − 0 +
Patient	0 0 0	0 0 1	0 0 1	0 0 0	0 0 0	0 0 2
Therapist	0 2 1	0 2 4	0 1 1	0 2 5	0 0 0	0 7 11
Total	0 2 1	0 2 5	0 1 2	0 2 5	0 0 0	0 7 13

SUMMARY B: TOTAL TO DATE   *OUTCOME*

Process	Patient − 0 +	Therapist − 0 +	Rater − 0 +	Score − 0 +	Combined − 0 +	Total − 0 +
Patient	0 0 1	0 0 1	0 0 1	0 0 0	0 1 0	0 1 3
Therapist	0 4 2	0 2 7	0 1 3	0 2 6	0 0 0	0 9 18
Rater	0 0 0	0 0 1	0 1 4	0 2 1	0 0 0	0 3 6
Total	0 4 3	0 2 9	0 2 8	0 4 7	0 1 0	0 13 27

[a] + = patient suitability positively related to outcome, or patient unsuitability negatively related to outcome; 0 = no significant association; − = patient suitability negatively related to outcome, or patient unsuitability positively related to outcome.
[b] Staff ratings of overall treatment difficulty of inpatients related to poor therapeutic progress.
[c] Patients' rating of "how well the treatment approach used seemed to fit [their own] specific needs."
[d] Patient's view of "treatment credibility," interpreted as the patient's judgment of suitability.
[e] Outcome at termination.
[f] Outcome at 6-month follow-up.
[g] "Patient difficulty" rated with regard to patient's interpersonal style.
[h] Terminal assessment of "analyzability," evaluating patient's contribution, in-treatment use, and adaptive application of psychological data and resources.
[i] Outcome as measured by ego-strength scales.
[j] Outcome related to therapist's "confidence patient will profit."
[k] 8-session time-limited treatment.
[l] 16-session time-limted treatment.
[m] Time-unlimited treatment; outcome assessed at termination.

TABLE 8.11   Termination procedures

Reference	Process	Outcome	Finding[a]	ES
Clementel-Jones et al. (1990)[b]	I	R	+	a/c
Horowitz et al. (1984)[c]	T	R	0	na
Horowitz et al. (1984)[c]	R	R	0	na
Horowitz et al. (1984)[c]	T	S	0	na
Horowitz et al. (1984)[c]	R	S	0	na
Kolb et al. (1985)[d]	I	P	0	a/c
Kolb et al. (1985)[d]	I	T	0	a/c
Kolb et al. (1985)[d]	I	S	0	a/c
McNeill et al. (1987)[e,f]	I	P	+	a/c
Persons et al. (1988)[f]	T	S	+	a/c
Quintana & Holahan (1992)[g]	T	T	+	.47
Sashin et al. (1975)[h]	T	T	+	a/c
INTERACTION EFFECTS				
Horowitz et al. (1984)[i]	T	R	0	na
Horowitz et al. (1984)[i]	R	R	0	na
Horowitz et al. (1984)[i]	T	S	+	.16
Horowitz et al. (1984)[i]	R	S	0	na
[postsession outcome]				
Hoyt (1980)	R	R	0	.01
Hoyt et al. (1983)	T	T	0	.00
Hoyt et al. (1983)	R	R	0	.02

SUMMARY: TOTAL TO DATE   *OUTCOME*

Process	Patient −	0	+	Therapist −	0	+	Rater −	0	+	Score −	0	+	Combined −	0	+	Total −	0	+
Therapist	0	0	0	0	1	2	0	2	0	0	1	2	0	0	0	0	4	4
Rater	0	0	0	0	0	0	0	4	0	0	2	0	0	0	0	0	6	0
Index	0	1	1	0	1	0	0	0	1	0	1	0	0	0	0	0	3	2
Total	0	1	1	0	2	2	0	6	1	0	4	2	0	0	0	0	13	6

[a] + = proper termination positively related to good outcome, or improper termination negatively related to poor outcome; 0 = no significant association; − = proper termination negatively related to good outcome, or improper termination positively related to poor outcome.

[b] Termination by mutual agreement appeared more characteristic of successful than of less successful cases.

[c] Therapist discussion of "termination reactions and feelings" in time-limited psychodynamic therapy was unrelated to outcome as a main effect.

[d] Premature terminators failed to attend two consecutively scheduled appointments and refused to continue treatment against therapist's advice.

[e] Premature terminators were clients who terminated without knowledge or against advice of their therapists.

[f] Patients who terminated against advice or without notification of therapist had significantly poorer outcomes than completers.

[g] In unsuccessful cases, counselors reported less frequent discussion of termination, less review of the course of counseling, less activity to gain closure on the relationship, and less discussion of clients' affective reactions to termination, but not less discussion of plans for the future.

[h] Outcomes of analyses terminated by mutual agreement ($M = 741$ sessions, $n = 90$) were significantly better than those terminated prematurely either by patient ($M = 414$ sessions, $n = 23$) or analyst ($M = 393$ sessions, $n = 12$), and those judged to be interminable analyses ($M = 1058$ sessions, $n = 5$).

[i] Therapist discussion of termination in time-limited psychodynamic therapy, in interaction with patients' level of self-concept development, was unrelated to outcome, except that discussion of termination was associated with better outcomes for patients low in initial motivation for treatment and with poorer outcomes for patients high in initial motivation for treatment.

relation of *patient conversational engagement (verbal activity)* to outcome suggested that patients who talk more tend to have better outcomes. Two of the three more recently reported findings lend additional support to that impression (Henry, Schacht, & Strupp, 1990; Schulte, in press; Tracey, 1987).

New findings about the relation of *therapist conversational engagement (verbal activity)* to outcome are presented in Table 8.8, suggesting a somewhat more complex situation. Null findings constitute about 55% of the total, but almost 40% of the total consist of significant findings (including two with substantial ES) indicating a positive association between the amount that therapists talk and outcome. However, a few significant negative findings also suggest that in some situations therapists can talk too much.

Researchers have made a number of qualitative as well as quantitative assessments of contractual implementation. For example, Table 8.9 summarizes 36 findings on the relation of *therapist skillfulness* to outcome, 68% of which are significantly positive (many with ES $\geq .20$). Patients and external raters in particular provided criterion valid ratings of therapist competence. Similarly, 68% of the 40 findings summarized in Table 8.10 indicate a significant positive association of outcome with judgments of *patient suitability* for the treatments in which they are placed. Researchers attempting to assess the relative efficacy of treatments or of other process variables should be mindful of the need to control these qualitative variables.[8]

The final stage of contractual implementation involves *procedures for termination*. Of the 19 process–outcome findings in this area, summarized in Table 8.11, only 32% show a positive association with outcome. Although this seems to indicate that what happens prior to termination may have more to do with outcome, it also suggests that proper handling of termination can be important.

Smaller numbers of studies have accumulated regarding other aspects of contractual implementation. Four new results from two studies (Collins et al., 1985; Gardner, Hurt, Maltman, Greenberg, & Holtzman, 1985), added to two mentioned in the last edition (Kaufman, Frank, Friend, Heims, & Weiss, 1962; Rosenbaum, Friedlander, & Kaplan, 1956), provide preliminary evidence on the importance of *stability in treatment arrangements* for outcome in both inpatient and outpatient settings. Similarly, *therapist adherence* to a specific treatment model and norms of the therapist's role was consistently related to outcome in three other studies (DeRubeis, & Feeley, 1990; Grunebaum, 1986; Luborsky, Crits-Christoph, Alexander, Margolis, & Cohen, 1983). The use of *supervision or case consultation* in relation to outcome was examined, with mixed results (Clementl-Jones, Malan, & Trauer, 1990; Green & Herget, 1991; Sandell, 1985; Steinhelber, Patterson, Cliffe, & LeGoullon, 1984). Finally, in the last edition, five of the six available findings indicated that *timeliness in starting treatment* (versus delay, e.g., by placement on a waiting list) was significantly associated with good outcome. Since then only one study (Budman & Springer, 1987) has contributed additional findings which call earlier results into question.

In sum, the findings on contractual implementation clearly indicate that therapist skill at, and patient suitability for, the treatment in question are important factors in outcome. The findings also suggest that patient suitability and expectational clarity probably can be enhanced by appropriate patient role-induction procedures. Adherence to the therapeutic model, active conversational engagement (especially on the patient's part), and stability of treatment arrangements are also positively associated with outcome. From the perspective of the grand clinical theories, these are relatively humble factors, but they should not be overlooked.

THERAPEUTIC OPERATIONS

The business of getting and giving professional help is conducted through a series of overlapping therapeutic operations. Patients must present and manifest to therapists the conditions and problems that led them to seek treatment. Therapists must construe the information they glean from their patients within a body of expert practical and theoretical knowledge in order to know how to proceed effectively. Therapists must then apply this specialized understanding of their patients in a program of intervention, and patients must cooperate in specified ways if the program is to succeed. The research available on therapeutic operations in the last edition left the impression that it was important for patients to focus on their problems in their conversation during sessions and for therapists to focus on patients' feelings and on transference issues, but that the use of specific therapeutic interventions (e.g., interpretation, exploration, support) was not consistently associated with outcome. This impression has been augmented and somewhat modified by more recent research.

Problem Presentation

Does what patients talk about make a difference? Process–outcome studies thus far have concentrated on three broad topic areas: patients' problems in living; the here-and-now of in-session behavior; and core personal relationships.

Table 8.12 summarizes 11 findings on the association between outcome and patients' *focusing on life problems*, of which 64% are significant and positive. Other studies provided initial evidence that patients' *focusing on core personal relation-*
Text continues on p. 296.

---

[8]Therapist skillfulness and patient suitability were reviewed under the heading "Therapeutic Interventions" in the last edition.

N.B.   For Tables 8.12 through 8.14: *Process* refers to the observational perspective from which process was assessed. P = patient ratings; T = therapist ratings; R = ratings by nonparticipant raters; I = objectively determined index of process, for example, assignment to a specified treatment condition. *Outcome* refers to the observational perspective from which outcome was evaluated. P = patient ratings; T = therapist ratings; R = ratings by independent raters; S = psychometric test score or objective index; CI = combined perspectives index. *ES* = effect size. na = data not available; a/c = data available but not computed.

TABLE 8.12   Patient's focusing on life problems

Reference	Process	Outcome	Finding[a]	ES
Jones et al. (1992)[b]	R	CI	+	.23
Lietaer et al. (1985)[c]	P	P	0	na
Lietaer et al. (1985)[c]	T	T	0	na
Munton & Antaki (1988)[d]	R	R	0	a/c
Sorenson et al. (1985)[e]	P	P	+	a/c
INTERACTION EFFECTS				
Jones et al. (1988)[f]	R	S	+	.09
[cited but untabulated in 1986]				
Feifel & Eells (1963)	P	P	+	na
Piper et al. (1979)	R	P	0	na
Piper et al. (1979)	R	S	+	.17
Rounsaville et al. (1981)	T	R	+	.14
[postsession outcome]				
Hoyt (1980)	R	R	+	.09

SUMMARY: TOTAL TO DATE   *OUTCOME*

Process	Patient − 0 +			Therapist − 0 +			Rater − 0 +			Score − 0 +			Combined − 0 +			Total − 0 +		
Patient	0	1	2	0	0	0	0	0	0	0	0	0	0	0	0	0	1	2
Therapist	0	0	0	0	1	0	0	0	1	0	0	0	0	0	0	0	1	1
Rater	0	1	0	0	0	0	0	1	1	0	0	2	0	0	1	0	2	4
Total	0	2	2	0	1	0	0	1	2	0	0	2	0	0	1	0	4	7

[a]+ = focus positively related to outcome; 0 = no significant association; − = focus negatively related to outcome.
[b]Focus on patients' aspirations and ambitions.
[c]Patients' discussion of various life domains in relation to session outcome.
[d]Changes in causal attributions regarding significant problems were unrelated to outcome in family therapy.
[e]Improvement in patients' presenting target problems was related to overall improvement at termination only if no additional problems were formulated, but only improvement in patients' additional problems was related to overall improvement at termination if an additional target problem was formulated.
[f]For patients with high level of pretreatment disturbance, good outcome was associated with patients' discussing physical symptoms.

TABLE 8.13   Patient's focusing on here-now involvement

Reference	Process	Outcome	Finding[a]	ES
INTERACTION EFFECTS				
Jones et al. (1988)[b]	R	S	+	.10
[cited but untabulated in 1986]				
Braaten (1961)	R	T	+	.15
Braaten (1961)	R	R	0	.01
Braaten (1961)	R	S	0	.01
Gendlin et al. (1960)	T	T	0	.04
Oclatis (1978)	R	P	0	na
Oclatis (1978)	R	R	0	na
Oclatis (1978)	R	S	0	na
Seeman (1954)	T	T	0	.04
Wogan et al. (1977)	R	S	+	na
Yalom et al. (1967)[c]	T	P	+	.11
Yalom et al. (1967)[c]	T	R	0	na
Yalom et al. (1967)[d]	T	P	0	na
Yalom et al. (1967)[d]	T	R	0	na
[postsession outcome]				
Hoyt (1980)	R	R	0	.00
Orlinsky & Howard (1967, 1975)	P	P	0	na
Orlinsky & Howard (1967, 1975)	P	T	+	na
Orlinsky & Howard (1967, 1975)	T	P	0	na
Orlinsky & Howard (1967, 1975)	T	T	0	na

SUMMARY: TOTAL TO DATE   *OUTCOME*

Process	Patient −	0	+	Therapist −	0	+	Rater −	0	+	Score −	0	+	Combined −	0	+	Total −	0	+
Patient	0	1	0	0	0	1	0	0	0	0	0	0	0	0	0	0	1	1
Therapist	0	2	1	0	3	0	0	2	0	0	0	0	0	0	0	0	7	1
Rater	0	1	0	0	0	1	0	3	0	0	2	2	0	0	0	0	6	3
Total	0	4	1	0	3	2	0	5	0	0	2	2	0	0	0	0	14	5

[a] + = focus positively related to outcome; 0 = no significant association; − = focus negatively related to outcome.
[b] For patients with high levels of pretreatment disturbance, good outcome was associated with the patients' concern about their therapists' view of them and with patients commenting on their therapists' personal characteristics.
[c] Patient revealing feelings about other members in group therapy.
[d] Patients' here-and-now communication in group therapy.

TABLE 8.14   Patient's cognitive and behavioral processing

Reference	Process	Outcome	Finding[a]	ES
Dziewas (1980)/Dziewas et al. (1979)[b]	P	CI	+	.19
Dziewas (1980)/Dziewas et al. (1979)[b]	R	CI	0	.23
Hartung (1990)/Hartung & Schulte (1991)[c]	R	CI	+	na
INTERACTION EFFECTS				
Brykczynska (1990)[d]	P	S	+	.09
Jones et al. (1988)[e]	R	S	+	.10
Neimeyer et al. (1991)[f]	I	R	+	.17
Neimeyer et al. (1991)[f]	I	S	+	.08
Neimeyer et al. (1991)[g]	I	R	+	.16
Neimeyer et al. (1991)[g]	I	S	+	.09
Schulte (in press)[h]	I	CI	−	.11
[cited but untabulated in 1986]				
INTERACTION EFFECTS				
Schauble & Pierce (1974)[i]	R	R	+	a/c
[postsession outcome]				
Orlinsky & Howard (1967, 1975)[j]	P	P	+	na
Orlinsky & Howard (1967, 1975)[j]	P	T	+	na
Orlinsky & Howard (1967, 1975)[j]	T	P	+	na
Orlinsky & Howard (1967, 1975)[j]	T	T	+	na

SUMMARY: TOTAL TO DATE   *OUTCOME*

Process	Patient −	Patient 0	Patient +	Therapist −	Therapist 0	Therapist +	Rater −	Rater 0	Rater +	Score −	Score 0	Score +	Combined −	Combined 0	Combined +	Total −	Total 0	Total +
Patient	0	0	1	0	0	1	0	0	0	0	0	1	0	0	1	0	0	4
Therapist	0	0	1	0	0	1	0	0	0	0	0	0	0	0	0	0	0	2
Rater	0	0	0	0	0	0	0	0	1	0	0	1	0	1	1	0	1	3
Index	0	0	0	0	0	0	0	0	2	0	0	2	1	0	0	1	0	4
Total	0	0	2	0	0	2	0	0	3	0	0	4	1	1	2	1	1	13

[a] + = appropriate cognitive or behavioral processes positively related to outcome, or inappropriate processes negatively related to outcome; 0 = no significant association; − = appropriate cognitive or behavioral negatively related to outcome, or inappropriate processes positively related to outcome.

[b] Patient social skills important for participation in behavioral group therapy.

[c] Successful phobic patients in cognitive-behavioral therapy more often expressed an "action-oriented" intentional disposition, whereas unsuccessful patients more often expressed a "state-oriented" intentional disposition.

[d] Reduction in polarization (extreme ratings) of patients' images of therapists was associated with better outcomes in individual but not group therapy.

[e] For patients with high levels of pretreatment disturbance, good outcome was associated with patients' maintenance of specific focus in dialogue.

[f] Tendency to "polarized construing" of other members (but not of group leaders) early in treatment was associated with negative outcome at termination (but not at 6-month follow-up) in group treatment of incest survivors.

[g] Tendency to "polarized construing" of group leaders (but not of other members) later in treatment was associated with negative outcome at termination (and both early and later in treatment at 6-month follow-up).

[h] Patient initiating or changing level of "processing" in early and middle (but not late) sessions was negatively associated with termination (but not follow-up) outcome in behavioral treatment of phobia.

[i] Internal (in contrast to external) view of relationship problems was associated with better outcomes in the final (but not the first) third of treatment in individual client-centered or psychoanalytically-oriented therapy.

[j] Patient ability to focus on issues of genuine concern.

ships (e.g., families of origin) is associated with improvement in individual psychodynamic therapy, particularly as judged from an external rater's process perspective (Jones, Cumming, & Horowitz, 1988; Luborsky, Crits-Christoph, & Mellon, 1986; Orlinsky & Howard, 1967, 1975). By contrast, findings from the 9 studies summarized in Table 8.13 suggest that patients' *focusing on here-and-now involvement* in therapeutic interaction makes little difference to outcome, with the possible exception of group psychotherapy.

More important than what patients talk about are the *cognitive and behavioral processes* they manifest while talking. Table 8.14 summarizes 8 varied studies, of which 87% of their 15 findings[9] indicate the importance of patients being able to perform in appropriate ways during therapy. This may be just another side of the issue brought forth under the heading of patient suitability, and of the finding in input–outcome research that psychologically stronger patients (e.g., those with greater ego strength) tend to benefit most from treatment.

Expert Understanding

Process–outcome studies of expert understanding have concentrated thus far on the topics that therapists select for investigation. Seven studies summarized in Table 8.15 yielded 19 findings, of which 53% indicate the importance of therapists' *focusing on patients' problems*—except in situations where a persistent problem focus is disruptive to the patient's defenses (as demonstrated by 2 negative findings). Similarly, 50% of the 18 findings summarized in Table 8.16 indicate that therapists' *focusing on patients' affect* is positively associated with outcome, but 2 negative findings show that focusing on feelings is contraindicated under some circumstances. Therapists should exercise even greater caution when *focusing on patients' here-and-now involvements* in sessions, as Table 8.17 indicates that this approach was negatively associated with outcome in 3 of 11 findings, and only once was it positively associated with outcome. The fact that a here-and-now focus is more frequently associated with negative than with positive outcomes might be due to an unwitting tendency on the therapist's part to make negative or ambivalent attributions about the patient (e.g., Henry, Schacht, & Strupp, 1990; Shoham-Salomon & Rosenthal, 1987). Alternatively, the negative association with outcome might be due to the therapist's attempt to confront the immediate behavioral situation when therapy is going poorly (e.g., by addressing transference issues), but in that event it does not seem to be a very successful strategy. This impression is reinforced by 7 reports from psychoanalytically oriented investigators on the association between outcome and therapists' directly *focusing on core personal relationships and transference issues*: 2 of the 27 findings are significantly negative and fewer than 40% indicate significant positive associations with outcome (see Table 8.18). On the other hand, 3 of the studies show that therapists' *focusing on patient self-understanding* is relatively safe (no negative findings), but only 3 of their 11 findings show a significant positive association with outcome (Horowitz, Marmar, Weiss, Dewitt, & Rosenbaum, 1984; Hoyt, 1980; Hoyt, Xenakis, Marmar, & Horowitz, 1983).

Therapist Interventions

Therapist interventions are defined both by their specific aims and by the means or methods through which those aims are pursued. The aims in question are not the ultimate outcome goals of treatment, such as the remission of a depressive disorder or the resolution of a serious marital conflict. Rather, they involve strategies to develop the psychological states and skills that can induce change (e.g., restoration of morale) or can help patients bring about desired changes in themselves and their life situations. These process strategies resemble the "change principles" discussed by Goldfried (1980) and have been described in greater detail by Ambühl and Grawe (1988) as "therapeutic heuristics." The latter distinguished four process heuristics, namely, strengthening the alliance, furthering reflective abstraction, deepening emotional processing, and enhancing adaptive skills.

Typically, a given heuristic goal may be approached by any one or a combination of several techniques; for example, reflective abstraction may conceivably be approached through interpretation, exploration, experiential confrontation, or therapist self-disclosure. A specific technique may also be used to approach various heuristic goals; for example, interpretation to further reflective abstraction, deepen emotional processing, or strengthen the therapeutic alliance. Achievement of the aims implicit in the various therapeutic heuristics during therapy may be hypothesized to result in a series of corresponding in-session impacts for patients; for example, a strengthened alliance should support the patient's morale, reflective abstraction should expand the patient's insight, enhanced adaptive skills should promote a sense of self-efficacy, and so on.

Table 8.19 lists 22 findings concerning *change*

Text continues on p. 306.

---

[9]On examination, the one apparently negative finding was clearly susceptible to an alternative interpretation.

N.B. For Tables 8.15 through 8.18: *Process* refers to the observational perspective from which process was assessed. P = patient ratings; T = therapist ratings; R = ratings by nonparticipant raters; I = objectively determined index of process, for example, assignment to a specified treatment condition. *Outcome* refers to the observational perspective from which outcome was evaluated. P = patient ratings; T = therapist ratings; R = ratings by independent raters; S = psychometric test score or objective index; CI = combined perspectives index. *ES* = effect size. na = data not available; a/c = data available but not computed.

TABLE 8.15 Therapist's focusing on patient problems

Reference	Process	Outcome	Finding[a]	ES
Goldstein et al. (1988)[b]	P	P	−	.03
Goldstein et al. (1988)[b]	T	T	+	.35
Horowitz et al. (1984)[c]	T	R	0	na
Horowitz et al. (1984)[c]	R	R	0	na
Horowitz et al. (1984)[c]	T	S	0	na
Horowitz et al. (1984)[c]	R	S	0	na
INTERACTION EFFECTS				
Horowitz et al. (1984)[c]	T	R	0	na
Horowitz et al. (1984)[c]	R	R	0	na
Horowitz et al. (1984)[d1]	T	S	+	.10
Horowitz et al. (1984)[d1]	R	S	+	.21
Horowitz et al. (1984)[d2]	T	S	+	.13
Horowitz et al. (1984)[d2]	R	S	+	.11
McCullough et al. (1991)[e]	R	CI	+	.36
[cited but untabulated in 1986]				
Feifel & Eells (1963)	P	P	+	na
Piper et al. (1979)	R	S	+	.17
Rounsaville et al. (1981)	T	R	0	na
[postsession outcome]				
Hoyt (1980)	R	R	+	.10
Hoyt et al. (1983)	T	T	−	.18
Hoyt et al. (1983)	R	R	+	.05

SUMMARY: TOTAL TO DATE — OUTCOME

Process	Patient − 0 +	Therapist − 0 +	Rater − 0 +	Score − 0 +	Combined − 0 +	Total − 0 +
Patient	1 0 1	0 0 0	0 0 0	0 0 0	0 0 0	1 0 1
Therapist	0 0 0	1 0 1	0 3 0	0 1 2	0 0 0	1 4 3
Rater	0 0 0	0 0 0	0 2 2	0 1 3	0 0 1	0 3 6
Total	1 0 1	1 0 1	0 5 2	0 2 5	0 0 1	2 7 10

[a] + = focusing on patient problems positively related to outcome; 0 = no significant association; − = focusing on patient problems negatively related to outcome.
[b] Staff "personal problem orientation" in partial hospital program positively associated with staff-rated outcome but negatively associated with patient-rated outcome.
[c] Therapists' discussion and differentiation of "real versus fantasized meanings of stress event" in time-limited psychodynamic therapy for posttraumatic stress.
[d] Therapists' discussion and differentiation of "real versus fantasized meanings of stress event" in time-limited psychodynamic therapy for posttraumatic stress was (1) positively associated with outcome for patients high in initial motivation for treatment and self-concept development, and (2) was negatively associated with outcome for patients low in motivation and self-concept development.
[e] Interpretive interventions focused on family of origin/transference patterns that elicited affective response were associated with better outcomes in brief dynamic psychotherapy.

TABLE 8.16   Therapist's focusing on patient affect

Reference	Process	Outcome	Finding[a]	ES
Braswell et al. (1985)[b]	R	T	—	.10
Braswell et al. (1985)[b]	R	R	—	.10
Braswell et al. (1985)[b]	R	S	0	na
Coady (1991b)	R	CI	0	a/c
Jones et al. (1992)	R	CI	+	.10
[postsession outcome]				
Hoyt (1980)	R	R	+	.16
Hoyt et al. (1983)	T	T	+	.11
Hoyt et al. (1983)	R	R	+	.22

SUMMARY A: TO 1985   OUTCOME

Process	Patient − 0 +	Therapist − 0 +	Rater − 0 +	Score − 0 +	Combined − 0 +	Total − 0 +
Rater	0 1 0	0 2 0	0 0 2	0 2 3	0 0 0	0 5 5

SUMMARY B: TOTAL TO DATE   OUTCOME

Process	Patient − 0 +	Therapist − 0 +	Rater − 0 +	Score − 0 +	Combined − 0 +	Total − 0 +
Therapist	0 0 0	0 0 1	0 0 0	0 0 0	0 0 0	0 0 1
Rater	0 1 0	1 2 0	1 0 4	0 3 3	0 1 1	2 7 8
Total	0 1 0	1 2 1	1 0 4	0 3 3	0 1 1	2 7 9

[a] + = focusing on patient affect positively related to outcome; 0 = no significant association; − = focusing on patient affect negatively related to outcome.
[b] Cognitive-behavioral treatment of children with classroom behavior problems.

TABLE 8.17   Therapist's focusing on here-now involvements

Reference	Process	Outcome	Finding[a]	ES
Coady (1991b)	R	CI	0	a/c
INTERACTION EFFECTS				
Jones et al. (1988)[b]	R	S	+	.10

SUMMARY A: TO 1985   OUTCOME

Process	Patient − 0 +	Therapist − 0 +	Rater − 0 +	Score − 0 +	Combined − 0 +	Total − 0 +
Rater	1 1 0	1 1 0	0 1 0	1 3 0	0 0 0	3 6 0

SUMMARY B: TOTAL TO DATE   OUTCOME

Process	Patient − 0 +	Therapist − 0 +	Rater − 0 +	Score − 0 +	Combined − 0 +	Total − 0 +
Rater	1 1 0	1 1 0	0 1 0	1 3 1	0 1 0	3 7 1

[a] + = therapist's focusing on here-now involvements positively related to outcome; 0 = no significant association; − = therapist's focusing on here-now involvements negatively related to outcome.
[b] For patients with low levels of pretreatment disturbance, good outcome was associated with therapists' drawing attention to patients' nonverbal behavior, remarking on patient-therapist interaction, and connecting therapeutic relationship with other significant patient relationships.

TABLE 8.18 Therapist's focusing on core personal relationships and transference issues

Reference	Process	Outcome	Finding[a]	ES
Crits-Christoph et al. (1988)[b]	R	CI	+	.18
Horowitz et al. (1984)[c]	T	R	0	na
Horowitz et al. (1984)[c]	R	R	0	na
Horowitz et al. (1984)[c]	T	S	0	na
Horowitz et al. (1984)[c]	R	S	0	na
McCullough et al. (1991)	R	CI	0	.00
Piper et al. (1991)	R	R	0	a/c
Piper et al. (1991)[d]	R	S	−	.12
Piper et al. (1991)	R	CI	0	a/c
Piper et al. (1986)[e]	R	P	+	.20
Piper et al. (1986)[f]	R	T	+	.24
Piper et al. (1986)[g]	R	R	−	.40
Piper et al. (1986)	R	S	0	na
INTERACTION EFFECT				
Horowitz et al. (1984)[h]	T	R	0	na
Horowitz et al. (1984)[h]	R	R	0	na
Horowitz et al. (1984)[h]	T	S	0	na
Horowitz et al. (1984)[h]	R	S	+	.18
McCullough et al. (1991)[i]	R	CI	+	.36
[postsession outcome]				
Hoyt (1980)	R	R	+	.07
Hoyt et al. (1983)	T	T	0	.00
Hoyt et al. (1983)	R	R	0	.00

SUMMARY A: TO 1985   *OUTCOME*

Process	Patient − 0 +	Therapist − 0 +	Rater − 0 +	Score − 0 +	Combined − 0 +	Total − 0 +
Rater	0 1 0	0 1 0	0 0 2	0 0 2	0 0 0	0 2 4

SUMMARY B: TOTAL TO DATE   *OUTCOME*

Process	Patient − 0 +	Therapist − 0 +	Rater − 0 +	Score − 0 +	Combined − 0 +	Total − 0 +
Therapist	0 0 0	0 1 0	0 2 0	0 2 0	0 0 0	0 5 0
Rater	0 1 1	0 1 1	1 4 3	1 2 3	0 2 2	2 10 10
Total	0 1 1	0 2 1	1 6 3	1 4 3	0 2 2	2 15 10

[a]+ = therapist's focusing on relationships and transference positively related to outcome; 0 = no significant association; − = focus negatively related to outcome.

[b]Patients in psychodynamic therapy whose therapists focused interpretations on core relationship themes had better outcomes.

[c]Therapists' focus on "reactions to parental figures linked to reactions to therapist" in time-limited psychodynamic therapy.

[d]Proportion of transference interpretations was inversely related to posttermination but not follow-up outcome.

[e]Interpretive focus on mother associated with better outcome at follow-up but not posttermination.

[f]Interpretive focus on therapist-parent and therapist-other linkages associated with better posttermination outcome, but not follow-up.

[g]Interpretive focus on family generally associated with poorer outcome at posttermination and follow-up.

[h]Therapists' focus on "reactions to parental figures linked to reactions to therapist" in time-limited psychodynamic therapy was unrelated to outcome in interaction with patients' level of self-concept development, except patients high in initial motivation for treatment had better outcomes when offered transference interpretations, whereas patients low in initial motivation for treatment had poorer outcomes when offered transference interpretations.

[i]Interpretive interventions focused on family of origin/transference patterns that elicited affective response were associated with better outcomes in brief dynamic psychotherapy.

N.B. For Tables 8.19 through 8.26: *Process* refers to the observational perspective from which process was assessed. P = patient ratings; T = therapist ratings; R = ratings by nonparticipant raters; I = objectively determined index of process, for example, assignment to a specified treatment condition. *Outcome* refers to the observational perspective from which outcome was evaluated. P = patient ratings; T = therapist ratings; R = ratings by independent raters; S = psychometric test score or objective index; CI = combined perspectives index. *ES* = effect size. na = data not available; a/c = data available but not computed.

TABLE 8.19 Change strategies (heuristics)

Reference	Process	Outcome	Finding[a]	ES
Ambühl (1991)/Ambühl & Grawe (1988)[b1]	R	CI	+	a/c
Ambühl (1991)/Ambühl & Grawe (1988)[b2]	R	CI	0	a/c
Ambühl (1991)/Ambühl & Grawe (1988)[b3]	R	CI	0	a/c
Ambühl (1991)/Ambühl & Grawe (1988)[b4]	R	CI	0	a/c
Hartung (1990)/Hartung & Schulte (1991)[c]	R	CI	+	na
Horowitz et al. (1984)[d]	T	R	0	na
Horowitz et al. (1984)[d]	R	R	0	na
Horowitz et al. (1984)[d]	T	S	0	na
Horowitz et al. (1984)[d]	R	S	0	na
INTERACTION EFFECTS				
Ambühl (1991)/Ambühl & Grawe (1988)[b5]	R	CI	+	a/c
Hill et al. (1988)[e]	I	CI	+	na
Horowitz et al. (1984)[f]	T	R	0	na
Horowitz et al. (1984)[f]	R	R	+	.07
Horowitz et al. (1984)[f]	T	S	0	na
Horowitz et al. (1984)[f]	R	S	0	na
Jones et al. (1988)[g]	R	S	+	.07
[postsession outcome]				
Orlinsky & Howard (1967, 1975)[h]	T	P	+	na
Orlinsky & Howard (1967, 1975)[h]	T	T	+	na
Orlinsky & Howard (1967, 1975)[i]	T	P	+	na
Orlinsky & Howard (1967, 1975)[i]	T	T	+	na
Orlinsky & Howard (1967, 1975)[j]	T	P	0	na
Orlinsky & Howard (1967, 1975)[j]	T	T	+	na

SUMMARY: TOTAL TO DATE   *OUTCOME*

	Patient			Therapist			Rater			Score			Combined			Total		
	−	0	+	−	0	+	−	0	+	−	0	+	−	0	+	−	0	+
Therapist	0	1	2	0	0	3	0	2	0	0	2	0	0	0	0	0	5	5
Rater	0	0	0	0	0	0	0	1	1	0	2	1	0	3	3	0	6	5
Index	0	0	0	0	0	0	0	0	0	0	0	0	0	0	1	0	0	1
Total	0	1	2	0	0	3	0	3	1	0	4	1	0	3	4	0	11	11

[a] + = change strategy positively related to outcome; 0 = no significant association; − = change strategy negatively related to outcome.

[b] The heuristic aim of (1) "furthering the therapeutic relationship" was positively associated with good outcome; the heuristic aims to (2) "further reflective abstraction," (3) "further emotional processing," and (4) "increase competence" in their patients were not associated with outcome directly, but (5) each was positively associated with outcome whenever patients showed a specific openness to it.

[c] Therapists of phobic patients who had good outcomes in cognitive-behavioral therapy more often encouraged an "action-oriented" intentional disposition, whereas therapists of unsuccessful patients more often reinforced "state-oriented" and neutral intentional dispositions.

[d] Therapist encouraging "reliving feelings of affect-laden ideas in treatment situation."

[e] Substantially more significant associations were found between therapist intentions and client reactions to therapist interventions for the two most versus the two least successful cases.

[f]Therapist encouraging "reliving feelings of affect-laden ideas in treatment situation" was unrelated to outcome in interaction with level of patients' initial motivation and self-concept development, except when both process and outcome were assessed by independent judges.

[g]For patients with low levels of pretreatment disturbance, good outcome was associated with therapists' emphasizing feelings in order to deepen patients' affective experiencing.

[h]The therapist's aim to increase patient's insight and understanding.

[i]The therapist's aim to support patient's self-esteem.

[j]The therapist's aim to move the patient closer to experiencing real feeling (further emotional processing).

TABLE 8.20 Paradoxical intention

Reference	Process	Outcome	Finding[a]	ES
Ascher (1981)	I	P	+	a/c
Ascher & Turner (1979)	I	S	+	.33
Beck & Strong (1982)	I	S	+	a/c
Conoley & Garber (1985)	I	S	+	a/c
Feldman et al. (1982)	I	S	+	a/c
Horvath & Goheen (1990)	I	CI	+	a/c
Kraft et al. (1985)	I	S	+	a/c
Lopez & Wambach (1982)	I	P	+	a/c
Mavissakalian et al. (1983)	I	P	+	a/c
Mavissakalian et al. (1983)	I	R	+	a/c
Mavissakalian et al. (1983)	I	S	+	a/c
Swoboda et al. (1990)	I	S	+	a/c
Wright & Strong (1982)	I	P	+	a/c
META-ANALYSIS [not tallied]				
Hill (1987)[b]	I	•	+	.56 – .99
Shoham-Salomon & Rosenthal (1987)[c]	I	•	+	.42

SUMMARY: TOTAL TO DATE				*OUTCOME*													
	Patient			Therapist			Rater			Score			Combined			Total	
	−	0	+	−	0	+	−	0	+	−	0	+	−	0	+	−	0	+
Index	0	0	4	0	0	0	0	0	1	0	0	7	0	0	1	0	0	13

[a]+ = paradoxical intention positively related to outcome; 0 = no significant association; − = paradoxical intention negatively related to outcome.

[b]Mean ES = .99 when paradoxical intervention was compared with no-treatment controls; mean ES = .56 when compared with placebo-control groups only.

[c]Use of paradoxical intervention with positive (but not negative) connotations was associated with good outcome (assessed from diverse perspectives), was equal to other comparative interventions at termination, and was superior to others one month posttermination.

•Various outcome perspectives.

TABLE 8.21   Experiential confrontation

Reference	Process	Outcome	Finding[a]	ES
Beutler et al. (1984)[b]	I	R	0	.00
Beutler et al. (1984)[b]	I	S	−	.12
Buckley et al. (1981)[c]	P	P	+	.10
Clarke & Greenberg (1986)	I	S	+	a/c
Hill, Helms, Tichenor, et al. (1988)	R	S	0	.01
Meyer (1981)/Meyer (1990)[d1]	R	S	0	.12
Meyer (1981)/Meyer (1990)[d2]	R	S	+	.38
Rabavilas et al. (1979)[e]	P	R	+	a/c
Tyson & Range (1987)[f]	I	S	0	a/c
Williams & Chambless (1990)[g]	P	R	0	.03
INTERACTION EFFECTS				
Jones et al. (1988)[h]	R	S	+	.07
Tscheulin (1983)[i]	I	P	+	a/c
Tscheulin (1988)[i]	I	P	+	a/c
[postsession outcome]				
Lietaer (1992)	P	P	0	na
Lietaer (1992)	T	T	+	na

SUMMARY A: TO 1985   *OUTCOME*

Process	Patient − 0 +	Therapist − 0 +	Rater − 0 +	Score − 0 +	Combined − 0 +	Total − 0 +
Patient	0 0 1	0 0 0	0 0 0	0 0 0	0 0 0	0 0 1
Therapist	0 0 0	0 0 1	0 0 0	0 0 0	0 0 0	0 0 1
Rater	0 0 2	0 0 0	0 0 0	0 0 3	0 0 0	0 0 5
Total	0 0 3	0 0 1	0 0 0	0 0 3	0 0 0	0 0 7

SUMMARY B: TOTAL TO DATE   *OUTCOME*

Process	Patient − 0 +	Therapist − 0 +	Rater − 0 +	Score − 0 +	Combined − 0 +	Total − 0 +
Patient	0 1 2	0 0 0	0 1 1	0 0 0	0 0 0	0 2 3
Therapist	0 0 0	0 0 2	0 0 0	0 0 0	0 0 0	0 0 2
Rater	0 0 2	0 0 0	0 0 0	0 2 5	0 0 0	0 2 7
Index	0 0 2	0 0 0	0 1 0	1 1 1	0 0 0	1 2 3
Total	0 1 6	0 0 2	0 2 1	1 3 6	0 0 0	1 6 15

[a] + = experiential confrontation positively related to outcome; 0 = no significant association; − = experiential confrontation negatively related to outcome.

[b] Participation in expressive-experiential group treatment during psychiatric hospitalization was associated with negative outcome.

[c] Abreaction.

[d] "Stimulating activity" by therapist (1) was unrelated to outcome in short-term individual client-centered therapy but (2) was associated with better outcome in short-term individual psychodynamic therapy.

[e] Therapist "challenging" during in-vivo desensitization (flooding).

[f] Mildly depressed subjects recruited for experimental 4-session Gestalt dialogue treatment.

[g] Therapist perceived by client as "challenging" in fourth session of in-vivo exposure behavior therapy.

[h] For patients with low levels of pretreatment disturbance, good outcome was associated with therapists' emphasizing feelings to deepen patients' affective experiencing.

[i] Use of experiential confrontation with "action-centered" clients was associated with better outcomes in client-centered therapy, whereas use of experiential confrontation with "self-centered" [self-reflective] clients was associated with poorer outcomes.

TABLE 8.22   Interpretation

Reference	Process	Outcome	Finding[a]	ES
Beck & Strong (1982)	I	S	+	a/c
Buckley et al. (1981)	P	P	+	.22
Cadbury et al. (1990)[b]	P	P	+	na
Coady (1991b)	R	CI	0	a/c
Hill, Helms, Tichenor, et al. (1988)	R	S	0	.14
Jones et al. (1992)	R	CI	+	.13
Meyer (1981)/Meyer (1990)[c]	R	R	+	.48
Meyer (1981)/Meyer (1990)[d]	R	R	+	.54
INTERACTION EFFECTS				
Claiborn & Dowd (1985)[e]	I	S	0	a/c
Coady (1991b)[f]	R	CI	+	a/c
Jones et al. (1988)[g]	R	S	+	.12
Jones et al. (1988)[h]	R	S	+	.07
Torhorst & Stitz (1988)[i]	R	P	+	.39
[postsession outcome]				
Hoyt (1980)	R	R	+	.09
Hoyt et al. (1983)	T	T	+	.04
Hoyt et al. (1983)	R	R	+	.11

SUMMARY A: TO 1985 — *OUTCOME*

Process	Patient −	0	+	Therapist −	0	+	Rater −	0	+	Score −	0	+	Combined −	0	+	Total −	0	+
Patient	0	0	3	0	1	0	0	0	0	0	0	0	0	0	0	0	1	3
Therapist	0	1	0	1	0	3	1	1	1	0	1	0	0	0	0	2	3	4
Rater	0	0	1	0	2	0	0	0	1	1	2	2	0	0	0	1	4	4
Total	0	1	4	1	3	3	1	1	2	1	3	2	0	0	0	3	8	11

SUMMARY B: TOTAL TO DATE — *OUTCOME*

Process	Patient −	0	+	Therapist −	0	+	Rater −	0	+	Score −	0	+	Combined −	0	+	Total −	0	+
Patient	0	0	5	0	1	0	0	0	0	0	0	0	0	0	0	0	1	5
Therapist	0	1	0	1	0	4	1	1	1	0	1	0	0	0	0	2	3	5
Rater	0	0	2	0	2	0	0	0	5	1	3	4	0	1	2	1	6	13
Index	0	0	0	0	0	0	0	0	0	0	1	1	0	0	0	0	1	1
Total	0	1	7	1	3	4	1	1	6	1	5	5	0	1	2	3	11	24

[a] + = interpretation positively related to outcome; 0 = no significant association; − = interpretation negatively related to outcome.
[b] Two-thirds of patients in a successful anxiety-management group indicated explanation of anxiety was the most salient therapist technique that "helped a lot."
[c] Short-term individual client-centered therapy.
[d] Short-term individual psychodynamic conflict-centered therapy.
[e] Match between patient attributional style and attributional style of interpretations was unrelated to outcome.
[f] Therapists of patients with poorer outcomes made interpretations that were rated as more disaffiliative and less focused on patient feelings or the therapeutic relationship.
[g] For patients with low levels of pretreatment disturbance, good outcome was associated with therapists' making genetic and transference interpretations.
[h] For patients with high levels of pretreatment disturbance, good outcome was associated with therapists' interpreting the behavior of others.
[i] Combination of interpretation and patient acceptance of interpretation was associated with outcome for patients who had made suicide attempts.

TABLE 8.23 Exploration

Reference	Process	Outcome	Finding[a]	ES
Bachelor (1991)	P	R	+	.30
Coady (1991b)	R	CI	0	a/c
Hill, Helms, Tichenor, et al. (1988)	R	S	0	.20
Hill et al. (1989)[b]	R	P	0	na
Hill et al. (1989)[b]	R	R	0	na
Hill et al. (1989)[b]	R	S	0	na
Rounsaville et al. (1987)	R	P	+	.25
Rounsaville et al. (1987)	R	T	+	.05
Rounsaville et al. (1987)	R	R	+	.15
Windholz & Silberschatz (1988)[c]	R	P	0	.01
Windholz & Silberschatz (1988)[c]	R	T	0	.04
Windholz & Silberschatz (1988)[c]	R	R	0	.00
Worthington (1986)[d]	T	R	+	a/c
[postsession outcome]				
Hill et al. (1989)[b]	R	P	0	na
Hill et al. (1989)[b]	R	R	0	na
Hill et al. (1989)[b]	R	S	0	na
Hoyt (1980)	R	R	0	.01
Hoyt et al. (1983)	T	T	−	.11
Hoyt et al. (1983)	R	R	+	.05

SUMMARY A: TO 1985 — OUTCOME

Process	Patient −	Patient 0	Patient +	Therapist −	Therapist 0	Therapist +	Rater −	Rater 0	Rater +	Score −	Score 0	Score +	Combined −	Combined 0	Combined +	Total −	Total 0	Total +
Patient	0	1	1	0	1	0	0	0	0	0	0	0	0	0	0	0	2	1
Therapist	0	1	0	0	1	0	0	0	0	0	0	2	0	0	0	0	2	2
Rater	0	3	0	0	1	3	0	2	1	0	2	3	0	0	0	0	8	7
Total	0	5	1	0	3	3	0	2	1	0	2	5	0	0	0	0	12	10

SUMMARY B: TOTAL TO DATE — OUTCOME

Process	Patient −	Patient 0	Patient +	Therapist −	Therapist 0	Therapist +	Rater −	Rater 0	Rater +	Score −	Score 0	Score +	Combined −	Combined 0	Combined +	Total −	Total 0	Total +
Patient	0	1	1	0	1	0	0	0	1	0	0	0	0	0	0	0	2	2
Therapist	0	1	0	1	1	0	0	0	1	0	0	2	0	0	0	1	2	3
Rater	0	6	1	0	2	4	0	6	3	0	5	3	0	1	0	0	20	11
Total	0	8	2	1	4	4	0	6	5	0	5	5	0	1	0	1	24	16

[a] + = exploration positively related to outcome; 0 = no significant association; − = exploration negatively related to outcome.
[b] 10-session course of focused Gestalt therapy involving six patients with active rheumatoid arthritis.
[c] "Exploratory processes" includes both therapist and patient exploration.
[d] Counselor directly inquiring about homework compliance, independent of compliance level.

TABLE 8.24 Support

Reference	Process	Outcome	Finding[a]	ES
Braswell et al. (1985)[b]	R	T	+	.45
Braswell et al. (1985)[b]	R	R	+	.18
Braswell et al. (1985)[b]	R	S	0	na
Buckley et al. (1984)[c]	T	T	+	.53
Coady (1991b)	R	CI	0	a/c
Hill, Helms, Tichenor, et al. (1988)	R	S	0	.12
Jones et al. (1992)	R	CI	+	.10
Rabavilas et al. (1979)	P	R	+	a/c
INTERACTION EFFECTS				
Jones et al. (1988)[d]	R	S	+	.12
Schindler (1991)[e]	R	S	+	na
[postsession outcome]				
Hoyt (1980)	R	R	0	.02
Hoyt et al. (1983)	T	T	0	.02
Hoyt et al. (1983)	R	R	0	.00

SUMMARY A: TO 1985 — OUTCOME

Process	Patient −	Patient 0	Patient +	Therapist −	Therapist 0	Therapist +	Rater −	Rater 0	Rater +	Score −	Score 0	Score +	Combined −	Combined 0	Combined +	Total −	Total 0	Total +
Patient	0	3	1	0	2	0	0	1	0	0	0	0	0	0	0	0	6	1
Therapist	0	1	1	0	4	0	0	1	1	0	1	1	0	0	0	0	7	3
Rater	0	1	1	0	2	0	0	1	0	0	2	1	0	0	0	0	6	2
Total	0	5	3	0	8	0	0	3	1	0	3	2	0	0	0	0	19	6

SUMMARY B: TOTAL TO DATE — OUTCOME

Process	Patient −	Patient 0	Patient +	Therapist −	Therapist 0	Therapist +	Rater −	Rater 0	Rater +	Score −	Score 0	Score +	Combined −	Combined 0	Combined +	Total −	Total 0	Total +
Patient	0	3	1	0	2	0	0	1	1	0	0	0	0	0	0	0	6	2
Therapist	0	1	1	0	5	1	0	1	1	0	1	1	0	0	0	0	8	4
Rater	0	1	1	0	2	1	0	3	1	0	4	3	0	1	1	0	11	7
Total	0	5	3	0	9	2	0	5	3	0	5	4	0	1	1	0	25	13

[a] + = support positively related to outcome; 0 = no significant association; − = support negatively related to outcome.
[b] Cognitive-behavioral treatment of classroom behavior problems.
[c] Therapist support versus interpretation.
[d] For patients with high levels of pretreatment disturbance, good outcome was associated with therapist giving direct assurance and strengthening defenses.
[e] Outcome was positively associated with therapist support when occurring during early and later (but not middle) sessions.

TABLE 8.25 Reflection/clarification

Reference	Process	Outcome	Finding[a]	ES
Coady (1991b)	R	CI	0	a/c
Hill, Helms, Tichenor, et al. (1988)	R	S	+	.25
McCullough et al. (1991)[b]	R	CI	0	.18
[cited but untabulated in 1986]				
Ashby et al. (1957)[c]	R	T	–	na
Ashby et al. (1957)[c]	R	S	0	na
Baker (1960)[c]	R	S	–	na
Rogers, M. (1973)[d]	R	S	0	na
Rounsaville et al. (1981)	T	R	0	.04
[postsession outcome]				
Greenberg & Dompierre (1981)[e]	I	P	–	a/c
Greenberg & Dompierre (1981)[e]	I	S	–	a/c
Greenberg & Rice (1981)[e]	I	P	–	a/c
Hoyt (1980)	R	R	0	.00
Hoyt et al. (1983)	T	T	0	.03
Hoyt et al. (1983)	R	R	0	.00

SUMMARY: TOTAL TO DATE   *OUTCOME*

Process	Patient − 0 +	Therapist − 0 +	Rater − 0 +	Score − 0 +	Combined − 0 +	Total − 0 +
Therapist	0 0 0	0 1 0	0 1 0	0 0 0	0 0 0	0 2 0
Rater	0 0 0	1 0 0	0 2 0	1 2 1	0 2 0	2 6 1
Index	2 0 0	0 0 0	0 0 0	1 0 0	0 0 0	3 0 0
Total	2 0 0	1 1 0	0 3 0	2 2 1	0 2 0	5 8 1

[a] + = reflection positively related to outcome; 0 = significant association; − = reflection negatively related to outcome.
[b] Discrepancy between Finding and ES due to sample size ($n = 16$).
[c] Therapist nondirective "reflection" was associated with poorer outcomes than was therapist "leading behavior" in individual therapy.
[d] Children in play therapy.
[e] Therapist "empathic reflection" was comparatively less effective than Gestalt two-chair technique in promoting short-term conflict resolution, behavior change, and reported progress.

strategies and heuristics, indicating that these are more consistently associated with positive session outcomes than with macro-outcomes. Of the four heuristics distinguished by Ambühl and Grawe (1988; Ambühl, 1991), only the aim of "furthering the therapeutic relationship" with the patient is directly linked with overall outcome. This heuristic includes the goals of helping patients feel more comfortable in therapy, develop trust in their therapists, and feel more positive about themselves. Therapist competence in this heuristic is also significantly associated with outcome (see Table 8.9), suggesting that the effect of the heuristic on outcome is probably mediated by the therapist's success in enhancing the therapeutic bond. The three other heuristics are not directly related to outcome, but therapists' efforts to "further reflective abstraction," "further emotional processing," and "increase competence" in their patients are positively associated with outcome whenever their patients show a specific openness to that type of impact (see Table 8.49).

The particular techniques or methods employed by therapists can be thought of as tactical interventions made to implement heuristic goals. These vary according to the treatment model being followed, the therapist's own technical skills and preferences, and, hopefully, the patient's needs and capacities. Techniques used in a varied psychosocial treatment models have been studied in relation to outcome.[10]

The most impressive record of effectiveness has been established for the technique of *paradoxical intention* in a number of simulated therapy experiments. Table 8.20 lists 11 studies in which all 13 findings showed significantly positive associations

[10] Techniques specific to behavioral, cognitive, and other therapies are addressed in other chapters in this volume.

TABLE 8.26 Therapist's self-disclosure

Reference	Process	Outcome	Finding[a]	ES
Barrett & Berman (1991)	I	S	+	a/c
Braswell et al. (1985)[b]	R	T	−	.28
Braswell et al. (1985)[b]	R	R	0	na
Braswell et al. (1985)[b]	R	S	0	na
Coady (1991b)	R	CI	0	a/c
Hill, Helms, Tichenor, et al. (1988)	R	S	0	.00
Williams & Chambless (1990)[c]	P	R	0	.00
[cited but untabulated in 1986]				
Alexander et al. (1976)	R	R	0	a/c
Beutler & Mitchell (1981)	R	CI	0	.05
Dickenson (1969)	R	S	0	na
Hayward (1974)	P	CI	0	na
Hayward (1974)	T	CI	0	na
Hayward (1974)	R	CI	0	na
INTERACTION EFFECTS				
Hayward (1974)[d]	P	CI	+	na

SUMMARY: TOTAL TO DATE

OUTCOME

Process	Patient			Therapist			Rater			Score			Combined			Total		
	−	0	+	−	0	+	−	0	+	−	0	+	−	0	+	−	0	+
Patient	0	0	0	0	0	0	0	1	0	0	0	0	0	1	1	0	2	1
Therapist	0	0	0	0	0	0	0	0	0	0	0	0	0	1	0	0	1	0
Rater	0	0	0	1	0	0	0	2	0	0	3	0	0	3	0	1	8	0
Index	0	0	0	0	0	0	0	0	0	0	0	1	0	0	0	0	0	1
Total	0	0	0	1	0	0	0	3	0	0	3	1	0	5	1	1	11	2

[a] +=therapist self-disclosure positively related to outcome; 0=no significant association; −=therapist self-disclosure negatively related to outcome.
[b] Cognitive-behavioral treatment of children with classroom behavior problems.
[c] Therapist perceived by client as "willing to be known" in fourth session of in-vivo exposure therapy.
[d] Positive association with outcome was found for clients expecting low (but not high) therapist self-disclosure.

with outcome, and 2 meta-analyses showing substantial effect sizes.

The technique of *experiential confrontation* (e.g., the Gestalt two-chair dialogue) is another consistently effective mode of intervention. Table 8.21 shows a significantly positive association with outcome in nearly 70% of 22 findings drawn from 11 studies, although one negative effect of this potent technique was observed in an inpatient setting.

Interpretation has also emerged as a rather effective mode of intervention in recent studies. Table 8.22 shows that 63% of 38 accumulated findings indicate a significant positive association with outcome (in contrast to 50% of 22 findings in the last edition). However, several interaction effects suggest that certain conditions may be necessary for this positive influence to occur, and 3 negative findings also indicate that there are circumstances in which interpretation should not be used.

Other techniques are less consistently effective.

Only 39% of 41 findings listed in Table 8.23 on the relation of outcome to *therapist exploration* (e.g., open-ended questioning) are significantly positive (although only one is negative). Similarly, only 34% of 38 findings listed in Table 8.24 on the relation of outcome to *therapist support* (e.g., encouragement) are significantly positive, although the consistent absence of negative findings indicate that it is a technique that can be used safely.

Less evidence of effectiveness can be marshaled for other therapist interventions. Table 8.25 indicates that *reflection and clarification* are not positively associated with outcome, although they are not harmful (the several negative findings in this case reflect unfavorable comparisons with alternative interventions rather than negative outcome). Table 8.26 shows that *therapist self-disclosure* is rarely associated with outcome, and when it is, the impact is negative nearly as often as positive. Finally, findings from 5 studies indicate that giving *advice* is more likely to be unhelpful or even harmful than beneficial (Coady, 1991b; Hill et al., 1988b; Hoyt, 1980; Rounsaville, Weissman, & Prusoff, 1981), except with patients having high levels of pretreatment disturbance who may be at risk with uncovering techniques (Jones, Cumming, & Horowitz, 1988).

Patient Cooperation

Therapeutic operations require the patient's cooperative participation, whatever the strategic aims and tactics of the therapist. This is amply demonstrated by the impressive series of recent studies (some with very high ES) listed in Table 8.27. Of nearly 50 findings, 69% show significant associations of *patient cooperation* with favorable outcomes and *patient resistance* with unfavorable outcomes.

Process–outcome findings also highlight the importance of the patient's affective reactions to therapy. Table 8.28 lists a few studies that show significant positive associations between outcome and the patient's *total affective response* (not differentiating between positive and negative affects) in 50% of 10 findings. Table 8.29 shows that, when *positive affective response* is considered, all 9 findings in 3 relevant studies show significant associations with favorable outcome. In other words, when patients respond with positive feelings during sessions (as perceived by themselves and their therapists) it may be taken as a sign that therapy is going well. However, it does not necessarily follow that therapy is going poorly when patients experience negative feelings during sessions, as indicated in Table 8.30. Of the 46 findings summarized there, 35% do show poorer outcomes are predicted by the patient's *negative affective response*. However, 39% of the findings showed no significant association with outcome, and arousal of negative affect is actually associated with *positive* outcomes in 26% of the findings. The latter may reflect circumstances in which an initially negative affective arousal is relieved or replaced by positive feeling. This is one area in which more research is urgently needed.

Patient self-exploration has often been viewed as a desirable response to therapist intervention, particularly in client-centered therapy, and this variable has received much attention. However, 67% of the 79 findings summarized in Table 8.31 show no significant association with outcome. Although only 30% of the findings show a significantly positive association with outcome, these cannot be easily dismissed because they do in fact represent a substantial number of cases.

Another form of response to therapist interventions that has been little studied but seems promising is the patient's *identification with or internalization of the therapist* (Buckley, Conte, Plutchik, Wild, & Karasu, 1984; Buckley, Karasu, & Charles, 1981; Geller, Cooley, & Hartley, 1982).

In sum, several features of therapeutic operations seem important for outcome. Patients' participation is vital both in respect to problem presentation, where the appropriateness of their cognitive and behavioral processes is even more important than the topics they discuss, and in respect to their active collaboration in therapeutic procedures, where their cooperativeness or resistance makes a decisive difference. Affective arousal, particularly but not only of positive affect in response to therapy, also seems to be quite important. Focus on problems of living and on core personal relationships by both patients and therapists seems to contribute positively to outcome more often than not, and paradoxical intention, experiential confrontation, and interpretation appear to be potent modes of therapist intervention. Thus, although comparative outcome studies may have revealed "no differential effectiveness of psychotherapies" between specific clinical schools or treatment models (Stiles, Shapiro, & Elliott, 1986), process–outcome research has in fact succeeded in documenting consistent differential effects related to therapeutic operations.

Therapeutic Bond

No aspect of process reviewed in the last edition had been studied as intensively as the therapeutic bond, and researchers have not slackened in their zeal. Theoretical interest in the therapeutic alliance (e.g., Horvath & Greenberg, in press) has continued the movement launched by Carl Rogers's (1957) conception of the therapeutic relationship as providing "necessary and sufficient conditions" of change. Process–outcome studies have focused both on particular aspects of the therapeutic bond and on its quality as a whole.

Table 8.32, for example, summarizes a total of 132 findings on the association of outcome with the global quality of the *therapeutic bond and group cohesion*, only 34 of which were presented in the last edition. The same large proportion of older and of more recent findings showed a significant positive association with outcome (overall 66%), and ES is .25 or more for at least one-fourth of recent positive findings (a figure consistent with Horvath's meta-analysis). In this vast total, only one negative finding was reported (in an earlier study).

Table 8.33 focuses on the overall quality of the *therapist's contribution to the bond*, and shows a significantly positive association with outcome for

Text continues on p. 321.

N.B. For Tables 8.27 through 8.31: *Process* refers to the observational perspective from which process was assessed. P = patient ratings; T = therapist ratings; R = ratings by nonparticipant raters; I = objectively determined index of process, for example, assignment to a specified treatment condition. *Outcome* refers to the observational perspective from which outcome was evaluated. P = patient ratings; T = therapist ratings; R = ratings by independent raters; S = psychometric test score or objective index; CI = combined perspectives index. *ES* = effect size. na = data not available; a/c = data available but not computed.

TABLE 8.27 Patient's cooperation versus resistance

Reference	Process	Outcome	Finding[a]	ES
Allen et al. (1988)	P	P	+	.07
Allen et al. (1988)	P	R	0	na
Buckley et al. (1984)[b]	T	T	+	.18
Bugge et al. (1985)	P	P	+	.12
Burns & Nolen-Hoeksema (1991)[c]	P	P	+	a/c
Burns & Nolen-Hoeksema (1991)[c]	T	P	+	a/c
Colson et al. (1991)[d]	R	R	+	.42
Dziewas (1980)/Dziewas et al. (1979)[e]	P	CI	0	.16
Gelso, Mills, & Spiegel (1983)[f,g]	T	P	0	.10
Gelso, Mills, & Spiegel (1983)[f,h]	T	P	+	.20
Gelso, Mills, & Spiegel (1983)[f,i]	T	P	0	.10
Gelso, Mills, & Spiegel (1983)[f,g]	T	T	+	.25
Gelso, Mills, & Spiegel (1983)[f,h]	T	T	+	.31
Gelso, Mills, & Spiegel (1983)[f,i]	T	T	0	.14
Henry et al. (1990)	R	S	+	na
Hoberman et al. (1988)[c,j]	T	S	0	na
Jones et al. (1992)	R	CI	+	.14
Kolb et al. (1985)	T	P	+	a/c
Kolb et al. (1985)	T	T	+	a/c
Kolb et al. (1985)[k]	T	S	+	a/c
Marmar, Weiss, & Gaston (1989)	R	S	0	na
Perri et al. (1989)[c]	P	S	+	.18
Persons et al. (1988)[c,l]	T	S	+	a/c
Piper et al. (1985)	P	P	+	.72
Piper et al. (1985)	P	T	0	na
Piper et al. (1985)	P	R	0	na
Piper et al. (1985)	P	S	+	.34
Rounsaville et al. (1987)	R	P	+	.12
Rounsaville et al. (1987)	R	T	+	.15
Rounsaville et al. (1987)	R	R	0	.00
Rudy et al. (1985)[m]	T	P	0	na
Rudy et al. (1985)[m]	T	T	0	na
Rudy et al. (1985)[m]	T	S	+	.10
Schindler (1991)	T	S	+	.22
Westerman et al. (1986)/Westerman et al. (1987)[n]	R	R	+	.61
Windholz & Silberschatz (1988)	R	P	0	.00
Windholz & Silberschatz (1988)	R	T	+	.18
Windholz & Silberschatz (1988)	R	R	0	.04
Worthington (1986)[c]	T	R	+	a/c
Worthington (1986)[o]	T	R	+	a/c
INTERACTION EFFECT				
Coady (1991a)[p]	I	R	+	a/c
Persons et al. (1988)[q]	T	S	+	a/c
Schindler (1991)[r]	R	S	+	na
Soldz et al. (1992)[s]	R	CI	+	a/c
Westerman et al. (1987)[t]	R	R	+	a/c

continued

TABLE 8.27   *continued*

Reference	Process	Outcome	Finding[a]	ES
[postsession outcome]				
Orlinsky & Howard (1967, 1975)	P	P	+	na
Orlinsky & Howard (1967, 1975)	P	T	0	na
Orlinsky & Howard (1967, 1975)	T	P	+	na
Orlinsky & Howard (1967, 1975)	T	T	+	na

SUMMARY: TOTAL TO DATE   *OUTCOME*

Process	Patient −	0	+	Therapist −	0	+	Rater −	0	+	Score −	0	+	Combined −	0	+	Total −	0	+
Patient	0	0	5	0	2	0	0	2	0	0	0	2	0	1	0	0	5	7
Therapist	0	3	4	0	2	5	0	0	2	0	1	5	0	0	0	0	6	16
Rater	0	0	1	0	0	2	0	2	3	0	2	2	0	0	2	0	4	10
Index	0	0	0	0	0	0	0	0	1	0	0	0	0	0	0	0	0	1
Total	0	3	10	0	4	7	0	4	6	0	3	9	0	1	2	0	15	34

[a] + = patient cooperation positively related to good outcome, or patient resistance negatively related to poor outcome; 0 = no significant association; − = patient cooperation negatively related to good outcome, or patient resistance positively related to poor outcome.

[b] Patient resistance negatively related to outcome.

[c] Homework assignment compliance.

[d] Staff ratings of "inaccessibility" of inpatients associated with poor patient progress.

[e] Patient "criticism of the therapeutic concept and procedure" in behavioral group therapy.

[f] Therapist rating of patient's "willingness to change" after first session.

[g] 8-session time-limited treatment.

[h] 16-session time-limited treatment.

[i] Time-unlimited treatment; outcome assessed at termination.

[j] Attendance at meetings of 12-session psychoeducational group treatment based on social learning view of depression.

[k] Positive outcome on "somatization" and "paranoia" but not other scales or global symptom index of SCL-90R.

[l] For patients who completed treatment.

[m] Patient "taking hostile autonomy" and "protesting and withdrawing."

[n] Resistant ("noncoordinating") patients in brief behavioral and paradoxical treatments had poorer outcomes than nonresistant patients.

[o] Client spontaneous report of homework compliance, independent of compliance level.

[p] Interpersonal behaviors of patients with poorer outcomes were rated higher on "wall off and avoid" early in treatment, and higher on "watch and manage" late in treatment.

[q] Interaction effect indicated that homework completion had a significantly greater positive effect on outcome for patients with higher initial levels of depression.

[r] Patient cooperation was associated with better outcomes for early but not later sessions.

[s] Better outcomes in group therapy were associated with less resistant behavior in patients who were often the "main actor," but with more resistant behavior in patients who were the "main actor" only a few times.

[t] Interaction of treatment type with patient cooperation/resistance indicated that resistant patients in brief behavioral treatment had significantly poorer outcomes than resistant patients in paradoxical treatment.

TABLE 8.28 Patient's total affective response

Reference	Process	Outcome	Finding[a]	ES
Jones et al. (1986)	P	P	+	.04
Jones et al. (1986)	P	T	0	na
Lietaer et al. (1985)[b]	P	P	0	na
Lietaer et al. (1985)[b]	T	T	+	na
McCullough et al. (1991)	R	CI	0	.04
Taurke et al. (1990)	R	CI	0	a/c
[postsession outcome]				
Orlinsky & Howard (1967, 1975)	P	P	+	na
Orlinsky & Howard (1967, 1975)	P	T	0	na
Orlinsky & Howard (1967, 1975)	T	P	+	na
Orlinsky & Howard (1967, 1975)	T	T	+	na

SUMMARY: TOTAL TO DATE — OUTCOME

Process	Patient −	Patient 0	Patient +	Therapist −	Therapist 0	Therapist +	Rater −	Rater 0	Rater +	Score −	Score 0	Score +	Combined −	Combined 0	Combined +	Total −	Total 0	Total +
Patient	0	1	2	0	2	0	0	0	0	0	0	0	0	0	0	0	3	2
Therapist	0	0	1	0	0	2	0	0	0	0	0	0	0	0	0	0	0	3
Rater	0	0	0	0	0	0	0	0	0	0	0	0	0	2	0	0	2	0
Total	0	1	3	0	2	2	0	0	0	0	0	0	0	2	0	0	5	5

[a]+ = total affective arousal positively related to outcome; 0 = no significant association; − = total affective arousal negatively related to outcome.
[b]Patients' focus on affective experiences in relation to session outcome.

TABLE 8.29 Patient's positive affective response

Reference	Process	Outcome	Finding[a]	ES
Andrews (1990)	P	P	+	.18
Bennun et al. (1986)[b]	T	P	+	.09
Bennun et al. (1986)[b]	T	T	+	.08
Bennun et al. (1986)[c]	T	P	+	.20
Bennun et al. (1986)[c]	T	T	+	.44
[postsession outcome]				
Orlinsky & Howard (1967, 1975)	P	P	+	na
Orlinsky & Howard (1967, 1975)	P	T	+	na
Orlinsky & Howard (1967, 1975)	T	P	+	na
Orlinsky & Howard (1967, 1975)	T	T	+	na

SUMMARY: TOTAL TO DATE — OUTCOME

Process	Patient −	Patient 0	Patient +	Therapist −	Therapist 0	Therapist +	Rater −	Rater 0	Rater +	Score −	Score 0	Score +	Combined −	Combined 0	Combined +	Total −	Total 0	Total +
Patient	0	0	2	0	0	1	0	0	0	0	0	0	0	0	0	0	0	3
Therapist	0	0	3	0	0	3	0	0	0	0	0	0	0	0	0	0	0	6
Total	0	0	5	0	0	4	0	0	0	0	0	0	0	0	0	0	0	9

[a]+ = positive affective arousal positively related to outcome; 0 = no significant association; − = positive affective arousal negatively related to outcome.
[b]German inpatient sample.
[c]U.K. outpatient sample.

TABLE 8.30 Patient's negative affective response

Reference	Process	Outcome	Finding[a]	ES
Buckley et al. (1981)	P	P	—	.16
Kozak et al. (1988)[b]	P	CI	0	.00
Kozak et al. (1988)[b]	I	CI	+	.11
Nergaard & Silberschatz (1989)	R	P	—	.11
Nergaard & Silberschatz (1989)	R	T	—	.10
Nergaard & Silberschatz (1989)	R	R	—	.16
Nergaard & Silberschatz (1989)	R	S	—	.13
Rounsaville et al. (1987)	R	P	0	.05
Rounsaville et al. (1987)	R	T	—	.11
Rounsaville et al. (1987)	R	R	0	.01
Soldz et al. (1992)[c]	R	P	0	.00
Soldz et al. (1992)[c]	R	T	—	.05
Soldz et al. (1992)[c]	R	R	0	.01
Soldz et al. (1992)[c]	R	S	—	.08
INTERACTION EFFECT				
Jones et al. (1988)[d]	R	S	+	.16
Soldz et al. (1992)	R	P	0	.00
Soldz et al. (1992)[e]	R	T	+	.05
Soldz et al. (1992)[e]	R	T	—	.05
Soldz et al. (1992)	R	R	0	.01
Soldz et al. (1992)[e]	R	S	+	.04
Soldz et al. (1992)[e]	R	S	—	.04
[postsession outcome]				
Orlinsky & Howard (1967, 1975)	P	P	—	na
Orlinsky & Howard (1967, 1975)	P	T	0	na
Orlinsky & Howard (1967, 1975)	T	P	—	na
Orlinsky & Howard (1967, 1975)	T	T	0	na

SUMMARY A: TO 1985   *OUTCOME*

Process	Patient −	Patient 0	Patient +	Therapist −	Therapist 0	Therapist +	Rater −	Rater 0	Rater +	Score −	Score 0	Score +	Combined −	Combined 0	Combined +	Total −	Total 0	Total +
Patient	0	2	0	0	1	1	0	0	0	0	0	1	0	0	0	0	3	2
Therapist	0	1	0	0	2	2	0	1	1	2	1	1	0	0	0	2	5	4
Rater	0	0	0	1	1	0	0	0	0	1	0	2	0	0	0	2	1	2
Total	0	3	0	1	4	3	0	1	1	3	1	4	0	0	0	4	9	8

SUMMARY B: TOTAL TO DATE   *OUTCOME*

Process	Patient −	Patient 0	Patient +	Therapist −	Therapist 0	Therapist +	Rater −	Rater 0	Rater +	Score −	Score 0	Score +	Combined −	Combined 0	Combined +	Total −	Total 0	Total +
Patient	2	2	0	0	2	1	0	0	0	0	0	1	0	1	0	2	5	2
Therapist	1	1	0	0	3	2	0	1	1	2	1	1	0	0	0	3	6	4
Rater	1	3	0	5	1	1	1	3	0	4	0	4	0	0	0	11	7	5
Index	0	0	0	0	0	0	0	0	0	0	0	0	0	0	1	0	0	1
Total	4	6	0	5	6	4	1	4	1	6	1	6	0	1	1	16	18	12

[a] + = negative affective arousal associated with positive outcome; 0 = no significant association; − = negative affective arousal associated with negative outcome.
[b] Greater physiological (but not subjective) reactivity to feared stimulus situation during exposure therapy of obsessive-compulsive patients was associated with better outcomes.
[c] "Negative reaction" in group therapy (negative reaction to comments by others and feeling hostile, frustrated, and impatient).
[d] For patients with high levels of pretreatment disturbance, good outcome was associated with patients' feeling "inadequate and inferior" and "sad or depressed."
[e] "Negative reaction" in group therapy (negative reaction to comments by others and feeling hostile, frustrated, and impatient) were associated with poorer outcomes in group therapy for patients who were often the "main actor," but with better outcomes for patients who were the "main actor" only a few times.

TABLE 8.31 Patient's self-exploration

Reference	Process	Outcome	Finding[a]	ES
Bommert et al. (1972)	R	P	0	.00
Bommert et al. (1972)	R	S	0	.05
Bruhn et al. (1980)	R	S	+	.09
Gaston et al. (1991)[b]	P	S	0	.00
Hill et al. (1989)[c]	R	P	0	na
Hill et al. (1989)[c]	R	R	0	na
Hill et al. (1989)[c]	R	S	0	na
Horowitz et al. (1984)[d]	T	R	0	na
Horowitz et al. (1984)[d]	R	R	0	na
Horowitz et al. (1984)[d]	T	S	0	na
Horowitz et al. (1984)[d]	R	S	0	na
Marmar, Weiss, & Gaston (1989)	R	S	+	.12
Minsel, Bommert, Bastine, et al. (1972)	R	P	0	.00
Minsel, Bommert, Bastine, et al. (1972)	R	S	−	.09
Rounsaville et al. (1987)	R	P	0	.10
Rounsaville et al. (1987)	R	T	+	.09
Rounsaville et al. (1987)	R	R	0	.00
Sachse (in press, b)[e]	R	P	+	.25
Sachse (in press, b)[e]	R	T	+	.33
Sachse (in press, b)[e]	R	S	+	.29
Safran & Wallner (1991)	P	S	+	.15
Sander et al. (1973)	R	S	+	.07
Torhorst & Stitz (1988)[f]	R	P	+	.51
Westermann et al. (1983)[g]	P	CI	+	na
Windholz & Silberschatz (1988)[h]	R	P	0	.01
Windholz & Silberschatz (1988)[h]	R	T	0	.04
Windholz & Silberschatz (1988)[h]	R	R	0	.00
INTERACTION EFFECTS				
Horowitz et al. (1984)[d]	T	R	0	na
Horowitz et al. (1984)[d]	R	R	0	na
Horowitz et al. (1984)[d]	T	S	0	na
Horowitz et al. (1984)[d]	R	S	0	na
Marmar, Gaston, et al. (1989)[i]	P	S	0	.06
[postsession outcome]				
Hill et al. (1989)[c]	R	P	0	na
Hill et al. (1989)[c]	R	R	0	na
Hill et al. (1989)[c]	R	S	0	na
Hoyt (1980)	R	R	+	.19
Lietaer et al. (1985)[j]	P	P	0	na
Lietaer et al. (1985)[j]	T	T	+	na
Orlinsky & Howard (1967, 1975)	P	P	0	na
Orlinsky & Howard (1967, 1975)	P	T	0	na
Orlinsky & Howard (1967, 1975)	T	P	+	na
Orlinsky & Howard (1967, 1975)	T	T	+	na

SUMMARY A: TO 1985   *OUTCOME*

Process	Patient −	Patient 0	Patient +	Therapist −	Therapist 0	Therapist +	Rater −	Rater 0	Rater +	Score −	Score 0	Score +	Combined −	Combined 0	Combined +	Total −	Total 0	Total +
Rater	0	6	0	0	5	6	0	5	0	1	10	4	0	0	0	1	26	10

continued

TABLE 8.31 *continued*

SUMMARY B: TOTAL TO DATE *OUTCOME*

Process	Patient			Therapist			Rater			Score			Combined			Total		
	−	*0*	+	−	*0*	+	−	*0*	+	−	*0*	+	−	*0*	+	−	*0*	+
Patient	0	2	0	0	1	0	0	0	0	0	2	1	0	0	1	0	5	2
Therapist	0	0	1	0	0	2	0	2	0	0	2	0	0	0	0	0	4	3
Rater	0	12	2	0	6	8	0	11	1	2	15	8	0	0	0	2	44	19
Total	0	14	3	0	7	10	0	13	1	2	19	9	0	0	1	2	53	24

[a] + = patient self-exploration positively related to outcome; 0 = no significant association; − = patient self-exploration negatively related to outcome.

[b] CALPAS scale of "patient working capacity."

[c] 10-session course of focused Gestalt therapy involving six patients with active rheumatoid arthritis.

[d] Patients' attempts to "change understanding of self in relationship to key person involved in stress" was unrelated to outcome as a main effect and in interaction with patient levels of initial motivation for treatment or self-concept development.

[e] Maximum processing mode of client in self-explication of experiential meanings.

[f] Patient use of focal interpretation in subsequent sessions was positively associated with outcome for patients who had made suicide attempts.

[g] Group psychotherapy.

[h] "Exploratory processes" include both patient and therapist exploration.

[i] Study of behavioral, cognitive, and brief dynamic treatments: negative nonsignificant association between alliance and outcome for behavioral, but positive nonsignificant association of alliance and outcome for cognitive and brief dynamic treatments.

[j] Patients' reflections on the meaning of patterns in their self-experience and relationships.

N.B. For Tables 8.32 through 8.34: *Process* refers to the observational perspective from which process was assessed. P = patient ratings; T = therapist ratings; R = ratings by nonparticipant raters; I = objectively determined index of process, for example, assignment to a specified treatment condition. *Outcome* refers to the observational perspective from which outcome was evaluated. P = patient ratings; T = therapist ratings; R = ratings by independent raters; S = psychometric test score or objective index; CI = combined perspectives index. *ES* = effect size. na = data not available; a/c = data available but not computed.

TABLE 8.32   Therapeutic bond/group cohesion

Reference	Process	Outcome	Finding[a]	ES
Bachelor 1991)	T	P	+	.27
Bachelor (1991)	T	R	+	.39
Barber et al. (1992)[b]	P	S	+	.11
Budman et al. (1987)[c]	R	P	+	.58
Budman et al. (1987)[c]	R	T	0	.00
Budman et al. (1989)[d]	R	P	0	.25
Budman et al. (1989)[d]	R	T	0	na
Budman et al. (1989)[d]	R	R	0	na
Budman et al. (1989)[d]	R	S	+	.58
Collins et al. (1985)[e]	R	P	+	.11
Collins et al. (1985)[e]	R	R	+	.09
Collins et al. (1985)[e]	R	S	+	.12
Colson et al. (1991)	R	R	+	.38
Crits-Christoph et al. (1988)	R	CI	+	.10
DeRubeis & Feeley (1990)[f]	R	S	0	.00
Dziewas (1980)/Dziewas et al. (1979)	P	CI	0	.12
Gaston et al. (1991)	T	S	0	.03
Gerstley et al. (1989)	P	R	+	.20
Gerstley et al. (1989)	T	R	+	.17
Goldstein et al. (1988)[g]	P	P	+	.18
Goldstein et al. (1988)[g]	T	T	0	.01
Grawe et al. (1978)[h]	P	S	+	.19
Grawe et al. (1978)[i]	P	S	+	.10
Grawe (1989a)/Grawe et al. (1990)[j1]	I	CI	0	.12
Grawe (1989a)/Grawe et al. (1990)[j2]	I	CI	0	.15
Grawe (1989a)/Grawe et al. (1990)[j3]	I	CI	+	.48
Henry et al. (1986)[k]	R	S	+	a/c
Hoberman et al. (1988)	P	S	+	.16
Hoge et al. (1988)[l]	P	P	+	na
Hoogduin et al. (1989)	P	P	+	.10
Hoogduin et al. (1989)	T	P	+	.22
Hoogduin et al. (1989)	P	P	+	.05
Hoogduin et al. (1989)	T	P	+	.18
Horvath (1981)	P	P	+	.18
Horvath (1981)	T	T	+	.27
Johnson (1988)	P	S	0	.03
Johnson (1988)	P	CI	+	.22
Johnson (1988)	R	S	0	.01
Johnson (1988)	R	CI	0	.00
Jones et al. (1986)	P	P	+	.13
Jones et al. (1986)	P	T	0	na
Kolden (1991)	P	R	0	.11
Lansford (1986)	R	R	+	.66
Luborsky et al. (1983)[m]	R	T	+	.35
Luborsky et al. (1983)[m]	R	S	+	.34
Luborsky et al. (1983)[m]	R	CI	+	.32
Luborsky et al. (1985)	P	CI	+	.40

continued

TABLE 8.32   *continued*

Reference	Process	Outcome	Finding[a]	ES
Mallinckrodt (1989)[n]	P	S	+	.03
Moseley (1983)	P	P	+	.20
Moseley (1983)	P	S	0	.00
Neimeyer et al. (1991)[o,q]	I	R	0	na
Neimeyer et al. (1991)[o,q]	I	S	0	na
Neimeyer et al. (1991)[o,r]	I	R	0	na
Neimeyer et al. (1991)[o,r]	I	S	+	.09
Neimeyer et al. (1991)[p,q]	I	R	0	na
Neimeyer et al. (1991)[p,q]	I	S	+	.10
Neimeyer et al. (1991)[p,r]	I	R	0	na
Neimeyer et al. (1991)[p,r]	I	S	0	na
Nergaard & Silberschatz (1989)[s]	R	P	+	.10
Nergaard & Silberschatz (1989)[s]	R	T	+	.04
Nergaard & Silberschatz (1989)[s]	R	R	+	.14
Nergaard & Silberschatz (1989)[s]	R	S	0	.02
Piper et al. (1991)	P	S	+	a/c
Piper et al. (1991)	P	CI	+	a/c
Piper et al. (1991)	T	S	+	a/c
Piper et al. (1991)	T	CI	+	a/c
Rudolf (1991)[t]	P	P	+	.09
Rudolf (1991)[t]	P	T	+	.07
Rudolf (1991)[t]	T	P	0	a/c
Rudolf (1991)[t]	T	T	+	.20
Rudolf (1991)[u]	P	P	+	.06
Rudolf (1991)[u]	P	T	+	.24
Rudolf (1991)[u]	T	P	0	a/c
Rudolf (1991)[u]	T	T	+	.09
Sachse (in press)	P	P	+	.73
Sachse (in press)	P	T	+	.24
Sachse (in press)	P	S	+	.36
Sachse (in press)	T	P	+	.27
Sachse (in press)	T	T	+	.77
Sachse (in press)	T	S	+	.26
Safran & Wallner (1991)	P	P	+	.50
Safran & Wallner (1991)	P	T	+	.28
Safran & Wallner (1991)	P	S	+	.14
Saunders et al. (1989)	P	R	+	.04
Svartberg & Stiles (1992)[v]	R	R	+	.27
Svartberg & Stiles (1992)[w]	R	R	0	.05
Westermann et. al. (1983)[x]	P	CI	+	na
INTERACTION EFFECTS				
Bourgeois et al. (1990)[y]	P	S	+	.08
Bourgeois et al. (1990)[y]	T	S	+	.10
Bourgeois et al. (1990)[z]	P	S	+	.05
Bourgeois et al. (1990)[z]	T	S	0	.00
Kolden (1991)[aa]	P	R	+	.06
Marmar, Gaston, et al. (1989)	T	S	0	.04
META-ANALYSIS [not tallied]				
Barker et al. (1988)[bb]	I	CI		.47
Barker et al. (1988)[cc]	I	CI		.73
Bowers & Clum (1988)	I	CI		.27
Horvath & Symonds (1991)	P	P		$.31 \pm .22$
Horvath & Symonds (1991)	P	T		$.22 \pm .40$
Horvath & Symonds (1991)	P	R		$.29 \pm .28$
Horvath & Symonds (1991)	T	P		$.13 \pm .23$
Horvath & Symonds (1991)	T	T		$-.04 \pm .53$
Horvath & Symonds (1991)	T	R		$-.17 \pm .49$
Horvath & Symonds (1991)	R	P		$.20 \pm .14$

Reference	Process	Outcome	Finding[a]	ES
Horvath & Symonds (1991)	R	T		.31 ± .27
Horvath & Symonds (1991)	R	R		.18 ± .17
[postsession outcome]				
Ambühl (1993)	R	CI	+	.81
Kolden (1991)	P	R	+	.14
Saunders et al. (1989)	P	P	+	.36
INTERACTION EFFECTS				
Kolden (1991)[dd]	P	R	+	.46
Kolden (1991)[ee]	P	R	0	.04

SUMMARY A: TO 1985   *OUTCOME PERSPECTIVE*

Process	Patient −	0	+	Therapist −	0	+	Rater −	0	+	Score −	0	+	Combined −	0	+	Total −	0	+
Patient	0	1	2	0	1	2	0	1	0	0	3	1	0	0	0	0	6	5
Therapist	0	1	2	0	0	5	0	1	0	0	3	0	0	0	0	0	5	7
Rater	0	0	2	0	1	1	0	0	1	1	2	3	0	0	0	1	3	7
Total	0	2	6	0	2	8	0	2	1	1	8	4	0	0	0	1	14	19

SUMMARY B: TOTAL TO DATE   *OUTCOME PERSPECTIVE*

Process	Patient −	0	+	Therapist −	0	+	Rater −	0	+	Score −	0	+	Combined −	0	+	Total −	0	+
Patient	0	1	14	0	2	6	0	3	5	0	5	11	0	1	4	0	12	40
Therapist	0	3	6	0	2	8	0	1	2	0	6	3	0	0	1	0	12	20
Rater	0	1	5	0	3	3	0	2	6	1	5	7	0	1	3	1	12	24
Index	0	0	0	0	0	0	0	4	0	0	2	2	0	2	1	0	8	3
Total	0	5	25	0	7	17	0	10	13	1	18	23	0	4	9	1	44	87

[a]+ = good therapeutic bond positively related to outcome, or poor bond positively related to outcome; 0 = no significant association; − = good therapeutic bond negatively related to outcome, or poor bond positively related to outcome.
[b]Alliance subscale of HAQ when assessed at session 3 (but not session 6) was associated with prior improvement in depression, but also predicted subsequent improvement in depression for patients in short-term dynamic psychotherapy.
[c]Cohesiveness in psychotherapy groups related to average outcome for group members.
[d]Cohesive alliance between members in therapy groups.
[e]Inpatients had better outcomes in psychiatric wards that were characterized by higher levels of social informality and cohesiveness (e.g., patients called staff by first name, dayroom furniture was arranged to encourage group interaction, fewer socially passive patients, etc.).
[f]Subsequent improvement in depressive symptomatology was not predicted by prior levels of helping alliance in cognitive-behavioral treatment.
[g]Cohesive support and involvement as experienced in partial hospital programs.
[h]Patient's perception of group cohesion.
[i]Patient's perception of relation with the therapist.
[j]Process variable constructed from patient and therapist perspectives jointly for (1) client-centered therapy, (2) broad-spectrum behavior therapy, and (3) interpersonal behavior therapy.
[k]High-change cases showed greater positive complementarity, lower negative complementarity in patient-therapist interactions rated on SASB scales.
[l]Interpersonal contact (including elements of acceptance, belonging, companionship, sharing, and support) was endorsed as an important therapeutic factor by 95% of participants in a partial hospitalization program.
[m]Positive signs of helping alliance (but not negative signs or index of positive-negative signs) in early sessions were associated with outcome; positive signs of helping alliance and index of positive-negative signs (but not negative signs) in later sessions were associated with outcome.
[n]Four aspects of perceived support from other group members were positively associated with outcome in group therapy (reassurance of worth, social integration, reliable alliance, and opportunity for nurturance); two aspects of support were not associated with outcome (attachment and guidance).
[o]Cohesion as identification with other patients in 10-session group treatment for incest survivors.
[p]Cohesion as identification with therapists in 10-session group treatment for incest survivors.
[q]Outcome at termination.
[r]Outcome at 6-month follow-up.

continued

Footnote continued from Table 8.32

[s]Patient-therapist interaction and global subscales of VNIS.
[t]155 inpatients.
[u]148 outpatients.
[v]Patient-therapist SASB complementarity in early session positively related to mid-term outcome.
[w]Patient-therapist SASB complementarity in early session unrelated to termination outcome.
[x]Perceived relationship atmosphere in group therapy.
[y]Male partners in marital couple group therapy.
[z]Female partners in marital couple group therapy.
[aa]Interaction of "therapeutic bond" and "patient self-relatedness" was predictive of posttreatment outcome by session 10.
[bb]Outcome at termination.
[cc]Outcome at follow-up.
[dd]Combined variance of 46% in postsession outcome predicted when "therapeutic bond" was entered jointly with "therapeutic realizations" as first term in multiple regression equation.
[ee]Interaction of "therapeutic bond" and "patient self-relatedness" not associated with postsession outcome in sessions 1, 3, 7 or 10.

TABLE 8.33   Therapist's contribution to the bond

Reference	Process	Outcome	Finding[a]	ES
Allen et al. (1988)	P	P	+	.31
Bachelor (1991)	P	P	+	.42
Bennun & Schindler (1988)	P	P	+	.56
Bennun & Schindler (1988)	P	T	+	.40
Bennun & Schindler (1988)	P	S	+	.45
Bruhn et al. (1980)	R	S	+	.16
Brykczynska (1990)[b1]	P	S	+	.12
Brykczynska (1990)[b2]	P	S	+	.08
Eaton et al. (1988)	R	P	0	na
Eaton et al. (1988)	R	T	0	na
Eaton et al. (1988)	R	S	0	na
Glass et al. (1989)[c]	R	CI	+	.20
Hill et al. (1989)[d]	R	P	0	na
Hill et al. (1989)[d]	R	R	0	na
Hill et al. (1989)[d]	R	S	0	na
Hoberman et al. (1988)	P	S	+	.15
Hoberman et al. (1988)	T	S	0	na
Horowitz et al. (1984)	P	R	0	na
Horowitz et al. (1984)	P	S	0	na
Kolb et al. (1985)	P	P	0	a/c
Kolb et al. (1985)	P	T	0	a/c
Kolb et al. (1985)	P	S	0	a/c
Marmar, Gaston, et al. (1989)	P	S	0	.00
Marmar, Weiss, & Gaston (1989)[e]	R	S	0	na
Marziali (1984)[e]	P	P	+	.07
Marziali (1984)[e]	T	P	+	.08
Marziali (1984)[e]	R	P	+	.03
Marziali (1984)[e]	P	T	+	.07
Marziali (1984)[e]	T	T	+	.10
Marziali (1984)[e]	R	T	0	.00
Marziali (1984)[e]	P	R	+	.10
Marziali (1984)[e]	T	R	0	.01
Marziali (1984)[e]	R	R	0	.01
Marziali (1984)[e]	P	S	+	.02
Marziali (1984)[e]	T	S	+	.02
Marziali (1984)[e]	R	S	0	.02
Safran & Wallner (1991)	P	S	0	.08
Sander et al. (1973)	P	S	+	.28

Reference	Process	Outcome	Finding[a]	ES
INTERACTION EFFECTS				
DeRubeis & Feeley (1990)[f]	R	S	−	.21
Eaton et al. (1988)	R	P	0	na
Eaton et al. (1988)[g1]	R	T	+	.36
Eaton et al. (1988)[h1]	R	S	−	na
Eaton et al. (1988)[h2]	R	S	−	na
Talley et al. (1990)[i]	P	P	+	.13
Talley et al. (1990)[i]	P	T	0	na
Talley et al. (1990)[i]	P	R	0	na
Talley et al. (1990)[i]	P	S	0	na
[postsession outcome]				
Hill et al. (1989)[d]	R	S	0	na
Lietaer (1992)/Lietaer & Neirinck (1987)	P	P	+	na
Lietaer (1992)/Lietaer & Neirinck (1987)	T	T	+	na
INTERACTION EFFECTS				
Hill et al. (1989)[d]	R	P	0	na
Hill et al. (1989)[d]	R	R	0	na

SUMMARY A: TO 1985 — *OUTCOME PERSPECTIVE*

Process	Patient −	Patient 0	Patient +	Therapist −	Therapist 0	Therapist +	Rater −	Rater 0	Rater +	Score −	Score 0	Score +	Combined −	Combined 0	Combined +	Total −	Total 0	Total +
Patient	0	0	6	0	1	2	0	0	0	0	4	5	0	0	0	0	5	13
Therapist	0	1	0	1	0	3	0	0	0	0	1	0	0	0	0	1	2	3
Rater	0	2	2	1	1	5	0	4	0	0	6	9	0	0	0	1	13	16
Total	0	3	8	2	2	10	0	4	0	0	11	14	0	0	0	2	20	32

SUMMARY B: TOTAL TO DATE — *OUTCOME PERSPECTIVE*

Process	Patient −	Patient 0	Patient +	Therapist −	Therapist 0	Therapist +	Rater −	Rater 0	Rater +	Score −	Score 0	Score +	Combined −	Combined 0	Combined +	Total −	Total 0	Total +
Patient	0	1	12	0	3	4	0	2	1	0	8	12	0	0	0	0	14	29
Therapist	0	1	1	1	0	5	0	1	0	0	2	1	0	0	0	1	4	7
Rater	0	6	3	1	3	6	0	7	0	3	11	10	0	0	1	4	27	20
Total	0	8	16	2	6	15	0	10	1	3	21	23	0	0	1	5	45	56

[a] + = therapist relational contribution positively related to outcome; 0 = nonsignificant association; − = therapist relational contribution negatively related to outcome.

[b] Increasingly positive perception of therapists (1) in individual therapy and (2) in group therapy.

[c] Schizophrenic patients in individual exploratory and supportive dynamic psychotherapy.

[d] 10-session focused Gestalt therapy involving six patients with active rheumatoid arthritis.

[e] Therapist's positive and negative contributions rated separately but reported together within each process-outcome cell since results were consistent.

[f] Improvement in depressive symptomatology was predicted by lower therapist facilitative conditions from early to middle of cognitive-behavioral treatment, but not from beginning to early in treatment or from middle to later in treatment.

[g] Negative therapist contribution to alliance was associated with poorer outcomes for long-term (>40 session) cases, but not for short- or medium-term cases.

[h] Improvement was (1) associated with negative therapist contribution to alliance on SCL somatization scale in long-term (>40 session) cases, but not in short-term (<29 session) cases, and (2) negatively associated with positive therapist contribution to alliance on SCL paranoia and psychoticism scales for medium-term (20–40 session) cases.

[i] Complementary relation between patient's prior self-concept and patient's view of therapist's contribution to the relationship (on dimensions of interpersonal affiliation and control).

TABLE 8.34 Patient's contribution to the bond

Reference	Process	Outcome	Finding[a]	ES
Bachelor (1991)	P	T	+	.26
Bennun & Schindler (1988)	T	P	+	.68
Bennun & Schindler (1988)	T	T	+	.33
Bennun & Schindler (1988)	T	S	+	.36
Buckley et al. (1981)[b]	P	P	+	.25
Eaton et al. (1988)	R	P	0	na
Eaton et al. (1988)	R	T	0	na
Eaton et al. (1988)	R	S	0	na
Horowitz et al. (1984)	R	R	0	na
Horowitz et al. (1984)[c]	R	S	+	.12
Johnson & Greenberg (1988)[d]	R	S	+	a/c
Klee et al. (1990)[e]	R	S	0	.12
Lansford (1986)[f]	R	R	+	a/c
Marziali (1984)[g]	P	P	+	.19
Marziali (1984)[g]	T	P	+	.19
Marziali (1984)[g]	R	P	+	.27
Marziali (1984)[g]	P	T	+	.12
Marziali (1984)[g]	T	T	+	.20
Marziali (1984)[g]	R	T	+	.23
Marziali (1984)[g]	P	R	+	.04
Marziali (1984)[g]	T	R	0	.02
Marziali (1984)[g]	R	R	+	.07
Marziali (1984)[g]	P	S	+	.03
Marziali (1984)[g]	T	S	+	.04
Marziali (1984)[g]	R	S	0	.01

INTERACTION EFFECTS

Reference	Process	Outcome	Finding[a]	ES
Eaton et al. (1988)	R	P	0	na
Eaton et al. (1988)[h]	R	T	+	na
Eaton et al. (1988)[h]	R	T	−	na
Eaton et al. (1988)[i]	R	S	+	na
Eaton et al. (1988)[i]	R	S	−	na
Frank & Gunderson (1990)[j]	T	CI	+	.15
Gerin et al. (1987)[k]	T	R	+	.35
Horowitz et al. (1984)	R	R	0	na
Horowitz et al. (1984)[l]	R	S	+	.29
Horowitz et al. (1984)[l]	R	S	−	.29
Talley et al. (1990)[m]	T	P	0	na
Talley et al. (1990)[m]	T	T	0	na
Talley et al. (1990)[m]	T	R	−	.15
Talley et al. (1990)[m]	T	S	−	.19

SUMMARY A: TO 1985   OUTCOME

Process	Patient − 0 +	Therapist − 0 +	Rater − 0 +	Score − 0 +	Combined − 0 +	Total − 0 +
Therapist	0 0 1	0 0 2	0 0 0	0 0 0	0 0 0	0 0 3
Rater	0 1 1	0 0 4	0 0 2	0 2 4	0 0 0	0 3 11
Total	0 1 2	0 0 6	0 0 2	0 2 4	0 0 0	0 3 14

SUMMARY B: TOTAL TO DATE   OUTCOME

Process	Patient − 0 +	Therapist − 0 +	Rater − 0 +	Score − 0 +	Combined − 0 +	Total − 0 +
Patient	0 0 2	0 0 2	0 0 1	0 0 1	0 0 0	0 0 6
Therapist	0 1 3	0 1 4	1 1 1	1 0 2	0 0 1	2 3 11
Rater	0 3 2	1 1 6	0 2 4	2 5 8	0 0 0	3 11 20
Total	0 4 7	1 2 12	1 3 6	3 5 11	0 0 1	5 14 37

ᵃ+ = patient relational contribution positively related to outcome; 0 = no significant association; − = patient relational contribution negatively related to outcome.

ᵇHarmful effects related to unresolved transferential attachment after termination (dreaming of, idealizing, missing, and "feeling the presence" of the therapist).

ᶜPatients' negative contributions to the alliance were associated with a slower rate of decline in symptoms, but patients' positive contributions were not associated with outcome.

ᵈGood outcome in "emotionally focused marital therapy" was associated with a shift toward "affiliative autonomy (disclose self, affirm other)" by the blaming partner.

ᵉPatients' contribution to alliance in the first session.

ᶠPatient's "ability to repair" weakened therapeutic alliance in short-term psychodynamic therapy.

ᵍPatient's positive and negative contributions rated separately but reported together within each process-outcome cell since results were consistent.

ʰPatient positive contribution to therapeutic alliance was associated with good outcome for medium-term (20–40 session) cases, but not for short-term (<20 session) cases; for long-term (>40 session) cases, there was an inverse relation of patient alliance contribution to outcome.

ⁱGood patient alliance was associated with improvement in SCL somatization and anxiety scales for long-term (>40 session) cases, but not for short-term (<20 session) cases; for medium-term (20–40 session) cases, patient negative contribution to alliance was associated with improvement in SCL depression, paranoia, and psychoticism scales.

ʲNonchronic schizophrenics who made positive alliances in individual psychotherapy between 3 and 6 months of beginning treatment had better outcomes after 2 years.

ᵏImprovement of psychotic (but not nonpsychotic) inpatients was associated with informal attachment to, and level of informal involvement with, members of the clinical team or other patients.

ˡFor patients initially judged to be poorly motivated for treatment, positive patient contribution to alliance was associated with better outcome, and negative contribution to alliance was associated with poorer outcome; but, for patients initially judged to be highly motivated for treatment, positive contribution to alliance was associated with poorer outcome, and negative patient contribution to alliance was associated with better outcome.

ᵐAnticomplementary relation between therapist's prior self-concept and therapist's view of patient contribution to the relationship (on dimensions of interpersonal affiliation and control).

53% of 106 findings, compared with only 4 negative findings. Moreover, the therapist's contribution is positively associated with outcome 67% of the time and is never negatively implicated when viewed from the *patient's* process perspective. Table 8.34 presents 55 findings on the association of outcome with the *patient's contribution to the bond*, of which 67% were significantly positive.

Specific aspects of the therapeutic bond have also been the subject of intense study. Personal role investment and interactive coordination jointly determine the task-instrumental side of the therapeutic bond; that is, the quality of patient-therapist teamwork. Communicative contact and mutual affect jointly determine the social-emotional side of the therapeutic bond; that is, the quality of personal rapport.

Personal Role Investment

Research on *patient role engagement* reflects the personal involvement of participants in the patient role. Table 8.35 summarizes 54 findings, 65% of which show a significant positive association with outcome, as do 92% of findings from the *therapist's* process perspective. Closely related are studies of *patient motivation*, which refers to the perceived

desire for therapeutic involvement by participants in the patient role. Table 8.36 summarizes 28 findings, 50% of which show a significant association with outcome; again, the percentage is higher when viewed from the participants' process perspective (80% for patients).

Therapist engagement versus detachment reflects the corresponding personal participants in the therapist role. Table 8.37 shows that, once more, the association with outcome is most salient from the patient's process perspective (78% compared with 22% from the therapist's perspective and 50% from the external rater's perspective). *Therapist credibility (sureness) versus unsureness* reflects the therapist's professional self-confidence and persuasiveness, perceived from various perspectives. Overall, Table 8.38 indicates that 59% of the 27 findings show a significant positive association with outcome, with nonparticipant perspectives showing a more favorable rate in this case.

Only three studies focused on *reciprocal role investment* in the therapeutic relationship, but 3 of the 4 findings they yielded are positively related to outcome (Halkides, 1958; Saunders, Howard, & Orlinsky, 1989; Waterhouse, 1982).

Text continues on p. 326.

N.B. For Tables 8.35 through 8.38: *Process* refers to the observational perspective from which process was assessed. P = patient ratings; T = therapist ratings; R = ratings by nonparticipant raters; I = objectively determined index of process, for example, assignment to a specified treatment condition. *Outcome* refers to the observational perspective from which outcome was evaluated. P = patient ratings; T = therapist ratings; R = ratings by independent raters; S = psychometric test score or objective index; CI = combined perspectives index. *ES* = effect size. na = data not available; a/c = data available but not computed.

TABLE 8.35 Patient's role engagement

Reference	Process	Outcome	Finding[a]	ES
Allen et al. (1988)	P	P	+	.16
Allen et al. (1988)	P	R	0	na
Bennun et al. (1986)[b]	T	P	+	.06
Bennun et al. (1986)[b]	T	T	+	.09
Bennun et al. (1986)[c]	T	P	+	.26
Bennun et al. (1986)[c]	T	T	+	.40
Braswell et al. (1985)[d]	R	T	+	.15
Braswell et al. (1985)[d]	R	R	−	.45
Braswell et al. (1985)[d]	R	S	0	na
Gaston et al. (1991)[e]	P	S	0	.06
Hill et al. (1989)[f]	R	P	0	na
Hill et al. (1989)[f]	R	R	0	na
Hill et al. (1989)[f]	R	S	0	na
Holtzworth-Munroe et al. (1989)[g]	P	P	+	.27
Holtzworth-Munroe et al. (1989)	T	P	+	.15
Martin et al. (1986)	P	P	+	.25
Martin et al. (1986)	P	T	+	.14
Meyer (1981)/Meyer (1990)[h1]	P	S	+	.36
Meyer (1981)/Meyer (1990)[h]	P	S	0	.07
Rounsaville et al. (1987)	R	P	0	.02
Rounsaville et al. (1987)	R	T	+	.17
Rounsaville et al. (1987)	R	R	0	.01
Soldz et al. (1992)[i]	R	P	+	.07
Soldz et al. (1992)[i]	R	T	+	.14
Soldz et al. (1992)[i]	R	R	+	.07
Soldz et al. (1992)[i]	R	S	0	.01
Westermann et al. (1983)[j]	P	CI	+	na
[postsession outcome]				
Hill et al. (1989)[f]	R	P	0	na
Hill et al. (1989)[f]	R	R	+	.12
Hill et al. (1989)[f]	R	S	−	.14
Martin et al. (1986)	P	P	+	.49
Martin et al. (1986)	P	T	0	.06
Orlinsky & Howard (1967, 1975)	P	P	+	na
Orlinsky & Howard (1967, 1975)	P	T	+	na
Orlinsky & Howard (1967, 1975)	T	P	+	na
Orlinsky & Howard (1967, 1975)	T	T	+	na

SUMMARY A: TO 1985   OUTCOME

Process	Patient −	Patient 0	Patient +	Therapist −	Therapist 0	Therapist +	Rater −	Rater 0	Rater +	Score −	Score 0	Score +	Combined −	Combined 0	Combined +	Total −	Total 0	Total +
Patient	0	1	3	0	0	1	0	0	0	0	1	0	0	0	0	0	2	4
Therapist	0	1	2	0	0	3	0	0	0	0	0	0	0	0	0	0	1	5
Rater	0	1	0	0	0	2	0	0	1	0	1	1	0	0	0	0	2	4
Total	0	3	5	0	0	6	0	0	1	0	2	1	0	0	0	0	5	13

SUMMARY B: TOTAL TO DATE   *OUTCOME*

Process	Patient −	Patient 0	Patient +	Therapist −	Therapist 0	Therapist +	Rater −	Rater 0	Rater +	Score −	Score 0	Score +	Combined −	Combined 0	Combined +	Total −	Total 0	Total +
Patient	0	1	8	0	1	3	0	1	0	0	3	1	0	0	1	0	6	13
Therapist	0	1	6	0	0	6	0	0	0	0	0	0	0	0	0	0	1	12
Rater	0	4	1	0	0	5	1	2	3	1	4	1	0	0	0	2	10	10
Total	0	6	15	0	1	14	1	3	3	1	7	2	0	0	1	2	17	35

[a]+ = patient engagement positively related to outcome; 0 = no significant association; − = patient engagement negatively related to outcome.
[b]German inpatient sample.
[c]U.K. outpatient sample.
[d]Cognitive-behavioral treatment of children with classroom behavior problems.
[e]CALPAS scale of patient commitment.
[f]10-session focused Gestalt therapy involving six patients with active rheumatoid arthritis.
[g]Husbands' and wives' ratings of process in behavioral marital therapy.
[h]"Patient engagement" was (1) associated with better outcome in short-term individual client-centered therapy, but (2) unrelated to outcome in short-term individual psychodynamic conflict-centered therapy.
[i]Patient's therapeutic participation (problem focus, initiative, etc.) versus passivity as "main actor" in group therapy was associated with better outcome if patient was often "main actor" but with poorer outcome if patient was "main actor" less frequently.
[j]Patient "engagement" in group psychotherapy.

TABLE 8.36 Patient's motivation

Reference	Process	Outcome	Finding[a]	ES
Dziewas (1980)/Dziewas et al. (1979)[b]	P	CI	+	.31
Dziewas (1980)/Dziewas et al. (1979)[b]	R	CI	0	.28
Gelso, Mills, & Spiegel (1983)[c1]	T	P	0	.11
Gelso, Mills, & Spiegel (1983)[c2]	T	P	+	.29
Gelso, Mills, & Spiegel (1983)[c3]	T	P	0	.16
Gelso, Mills, & Spiegel (1983)[c1]	T	T	+	.17
Gelso, Mills, & Spiegel (1983)[c2]	T	T	+	.53
Gelso, Mills, & Spiegel (1983)[c3]	T	T	+	.36
Lafferty et al. (1989)	T	S	−	a/c
Marmar, Gaston, et al. (1989)[d]	P	S	+	.19
Marmar, Weiss, & Gaston (1989)	R	S	0	na
Sachse (in press)[e]	R	P	0	na
Sachse (in press)[e]	R	T	0	na
Sachse (in press)[e]	R	S	0	na
Safran & Wallner (1991)	P	S	+	.14
[cited but untabulated in 1986]				
Baer et al. (1980)	T	T	+	a/c
Conrad (1952)	T	T	+	na
Hartley & Strupp (1983)	R	S	0	a/c
Malan (1976)	R	R	+	na
Prager (1971)	T	P	0	na
Prager (1971)	T	T	0	na
Prager (1971)	T	R	0	na
Prager (1971)	T	S	0	na
Strupp et al. (1963)	T	T	+	.21

continued

TABLE 8.36   *continued*

Reference	Process	Outcome	Finding[a]	ES
[postsession outcome]				
Orlinsky & Howard (1967, 1975)	P	P	+	na
Orlinsky & Howard (1967, 1975)	P	T	0	na
Orlinsky & Howard (1967, 1975)	T	P	+	na
Orlinsky & Howard (1967, 1975)	T	T	+	na

SUMMARY: TOTAL TO DATE   *OUTCOME*

Process	Patient −	Patient 0	Patient +	Therapist −	Therapist 0	Therapist +	Rater −	Rater 0	Rater +	Score −	Score 0	Score +	Combined −	Combined 0	Combined +	Total −	Total 0	Total +
Patient	0	0	1	0	1	0	0	0	0	0	0	2	0	0	1	0	1	4
Therapist	0	3	3	0	1	6	0	1	0	1	1	0	0	0	0	1	6	9
Rater	0	1	0	0	1	0	0	0	1	0	3	0	0	1	0	0	6	1
Total	0	4	4	0	3	6	0	1	1	1	4	2	0	1	1	1	13	14

[a]+ = patient motivation positively related to outcome; 0 = no significant association; − = patient motivation negatively related to outcome.
[b]Patient "motivation for cooperation" in behavioral group therapy.
[c]Patient's "motivation for counseling" after first session: (1) 8-session time-limited treatment; (2) 16-session time-limited treatment; (3) time-unlimited treatment, outcome rated at termination.
[d]Study of behavioral, cognitive, and brief dynamic treatments; significant positive association between patient motivation and outcome for cognitive, but nonsignificant association of motivation and outcome for behavioral and brief dynamic treatments (more stringent estimate of ES for all groups was 5% and for cognitive therapy was 12%).
[e]Client's "motivation to clarify (intensity of grappling with oneself)."

TABLE 8.37   Therapist's engagement versus detachment

Reference	Process	Outcome	Finding[a]	ES
Bennun et al. (1986)[b]	P	P	+	.10
Bennun et al. (1986)[b]	P	T	+	.04
Bennun et al. (1986)[c]	P	P	+	.18
Bennun et al. (1986)[c]	P	T	+	.37
Dziewas (1980)/Dziewas et al. (1979)[d]	P	CI	0	.09
Dziewas (1980)/Dziewas et al. (1979)[d]	R	CI	0	.06
Gaston et al. (1991)[e]	P	S	0	.00
Jones et al. (1986)	P	P	+	.06
Jones et al. (1986)	P	T	+	.08
[postsession outcome]				
Orlinsky & Howard (1967, 1975)	P	P	+	na
Orlinsky & Howard (1967, 1975)	P	T	+	na
Orlinsky & Howard (1967, 1975)	T	P	0	na
Orlinsky & Howard (1967, 1975)	T	T	+	na

SUMMARY A: TO 1985   *OUTCOME*

Process	Patient −	Patient 0	Patient +	Therapist −	Therapist 0	Therapist +	Rater −	Rater 0	Rater +	Score −	Score 0	Score +	Combined −	Combined 0	Combined +	Total −	Total 0	Total +
Patient	0	2	3	0	0	2	0	0	1	0	0	0	0	0	0	0	2	6
Therapist	0	1	0	0	2	1	0	0	0	0	3	0	0	0	0	0	6	1
Rater	0	0	1	0	0	1	0	0	0	0	4	3	0	0	0	0	4	5
Total	0	3	4	0	2	4	0	0	1	0	7	3	0	0	0	0	12	12

SUMMARY B: TOTAL TO DATE   *OUTCOME*

Process	Patient −	0	+	Therapist −	0	+	Rater −	0	+	Score −	0	+	Combined −	0	+	Total −	0	+
Patient	0	2	7	0	0	6	0	0	1	0	1	0	0	1	0	0	4	14
Therapist	0	2	0	0	2	2	0	0	0	0	3	0	0	0	0	0	7	2
Rater	0	0	1	0	0	1	0	0	0	0	4	3	0	1	0	0	5	5
Total	0	4	8	0	2	9	0	0	1	0	8	3	0	2	0	0	16	21

[a] + = engagement positively related to outcome, or detachment negatively related to outcome; 0 = no significant association; − = engagement negatively related to outcome, or detachment positively related to outcome.
[b] German inpatient sample.
[c] U.K. outpatient sample.
[d] Therapist "paying attention to the client" in behavioral group therapy.
[e] CALPAS scale of therapist understanding and involvement.

TABLE 8.38   Therapist's credibility (sureness) versus unsureness

Reference	Process	Outcome	Finding[a]	ES
Crane et al. (1986)[b]	P	P	0	na
Grimes & Murdock (1989)	P	S	+	.17
Hagborg (1991)[c]	P	P	0	.04
Hagborg (1991)[c]	P	S	0	.01
Horvath (1981)	P	P	0	.00
Lafferty et al. (1989)	P	S	0	na
McNeill et al. (1987)[c]	P	P	+	.12
Schulte (in press)[d]	I	CI	+	.11
Williams & Chambless (1990)	P	R	+	.15

SUMMARY A: TO 1985   *OUTCOME PERSPECTIVE*

Process	Patient −	0	+	Therapist −	0	+	Rater −	0	+	Score −	0	+	Combined −	0	+	Total −	0	+
Patient	0	0	2	0	1	1	0	0	2	0	1	0	0	0	0	0	2	5
Therapist	0	1	1	0	1	0	0	0	1	0	0	1	0	0	0	0	2	3
Rater	0	0	1	0	0	1	0	0	1	0	2	1	0	0	0	0	2	4
Total	0	1	4	0	2	2	0	0	4	0	3	2	0	0	0	0	6	12

SUMMARY B: TOTAL TO DATE   *OUTCOME*

Process	Patient −	0	+	Therapist −	0	+	Rater −	0	+	Score −	0	+	Combined −	0	+	Total −	0	+
Patient	0	3	3	0	1	1	0	0	3	0	3	1	0	0	0	0	7	8
Therapist	0	1	1	0	1	0	0	0	1	0	0	1	0	0	0	0	2	3
Rater	0	0	1	0	0	1	0	0	1	0	2	1	0	0	0	0	2	4
Index	0	0	0	0	0	0	0	0	0	0	0	0	0	0	1	0	0	1
Total	0	4	5	0	2	2	0	0	5	0	5	3	0	0	1	0	11	16

[a] + = credibility positively related to outcome, or unsureness negatively related to outcome; 0 = no significant association; − = credibility negatively related to outcome, or unsureness positively related to outcome.
[b] Patients' ratings of therapists (all inexperienced) as "experienced," "confident," and "seemed to know how to deal with client problems" was unrelated to outcome.
[c] Patients' perception of therapist "trustworthiness."
[d] Frequent change by therapists in level of "processing" (i.e., unsureness) was associated with poorer outcomes at termination in behavioral treatment of phobias.

Interactive Coordination

Leadership style and the orientation and management of collaborative effort constitute the main features of interactive coordination.[11] Table 8.39 presents 46 process–outcome findings on *therapist collaboration versus directiveness or permissiveness*. The results are unusually mixed, probably because the studies summarized involve different treatment models. Overall, 43% show a significant association of outcome with a collaborative therapeutic style (64% from the patient's process perspective) and 22% show a significant association of outcome with a directive therapeutic style (only 9% from the patient's process perspective). The findings are less complex with respect to the corresponding variable of *patient collaboration versus dependence or controlling*: 64% of 42 findings presented in Table 8.40 show outcome is positively associated with a collaborative style of relating by patients, whereas none favor either a dependent or controlling style of relating.

Communicative Contact

When there is good communicative contact, patient and therapist are on the same wavelength; when there is not, they simply talk past each other. The cycle of communicative contact consists of complementary phases of expressiveness and empathic understanding in each participant.

Findings on the relation of *patient expressiveness* to outcome are presented in Table 8.41. Of the 51 findings, 63% show a positive association with outcome (although the rate is only 55% from the patient's perspective). Table 8.42 summarizes 115 findings on the association between outcome and *therapist empathic understanding*. Only 5 studies (9 findings) were published since 1985, indicating a precipitous drop in research interest for this variable. Overall, 54% show a significant positive association with outcome, and none are negative. From the *patient's* process perspective, however, 72% of the 47 findings are positively related to outcome, indicating that the patient's perception of therapist empathy is an important factor. (The reader has probably observed by now that the patient's perspective is often the most discriminating with respect to therapist process variables, whereas the therapist's process perspective is most discriminating with respect to patient process variables. Researchers who have lost interest in this variable might also take note.)

Few studies have investigated the corresponding effects on outcome of therapist expressiveness and

patient empathic understanding. Table 8.43 lists 16 process–outcome findings on *therapist expressiveness*; of those, the most promising involve ratings of therapist voice quality (Rice, 1965). Table 8.44 lists a dozen findings on *patient empathic understanding*, which in the aggregate appear somewhat indeterminate, if not contradictory. More careful research on the communicative aspect of the therapeutic bond might shed a welcome light. Investigators should be encouraged by the 42 process–outcome findings in Table 8.45, which show a clear pattern linking *communicative attunement* to positive outcome (especially when process was assessed by patient ratings or objective indexes and outcome was evaluated by patients and therapists.)

Mutual Affect

The aspect of therapeutic bond that has been most extensively studied is *therapist affirmation*, that is, acceptance, nonpossessive warmth, or positive regard. Table 8.46 summarizes 154 process–outcome findings, of which 56% are positive (once again, the patient's process perspective a higher rate of 65%). Overall, nearly 90 findings indicate that therapist affirmation is a significant factor, but considerable variation in ES suggests that the contribution of this factor to outcome differs according to specific conditions. Thus the task of future research on this variable should not be simply to add more evidence, but to determine the circumstances in which it plays a major role in determining outcome.

Patient affirmation toward the therapist (typically, respect or liking) has been less often studied, but the 59 findings summarized in Table 8.47 show that it is more consistently associated with outcome than is therapist affirmation (69% vs. 56%). Of course, patient affirmation may be a result rather than a cause of therapeutic progress (see e.g., Barber, Crits-Christoph, & Luborsky, 1992; DeRubeis & Feeley, 1990; Gaston, Marmar, Gallagher, & Thompson, 1991). Even so, it can be used as a clinically important sign that therapy is going well, and, in fact, it may well function both as a sign of past progress and as a contributing factor to future progress.

The importance of the social-emotional side of the therapeutic bond is emphasized again by Table 8.48, which shows a very consistent relation of *reciprocal affirmation* between patient and therapist to outcome: 78% of 32 findings are significantly positive (mostly from the patient's or external rater's process perspectives.)

After a period of continued intensive study since the last edition of this *Handbook*, the therapeutic

Text continues on p. 339.

---

[11]Therapist and patient styles of coordination were reviewed in the last edition as an aspect of implementation of the therapeutic contract.

N.B. For Tables 8.39 and 8.40: *Process* refers to the observational perspective from which process was assessed. P = patient ratings; T = therapist ratings; R = ratings by nonparticipant raters; I = objectively determined index of process, for example, assignment to a specified treatment condition. *Outcome* refers to the observational perspective from which outcome was evaluated. P = patient ratings; T = therapist ratings; R = ratings by independent raters; S = psychometric test score or objective index; CI = combined perspectives index. *ES* = effect size. na = data not available; a/c = data available but not computed.

TABLE 8.39   Therapist's collaboration (Cb) versus directiveness (D) or permissiveness (P)

Reference	Process	Outcome	Finding[a]	ES
Bachelor (1991) (Cb)	T	T	+	.29
Glass et al. (1989) (D)[b]	R	CI	0	.09
Hartung (1990)/Hartung & Schulte (1991) (D)	R	CI	−	na
Holtzworth-Munroe et al. (1989) (D)[c]	T	P	+	.11
Kolb et al. (1985) (D)	T	P	0	a/c
Kolb et al. (1985) (D)	T	T	0	a/c
Kolb et al. (1985) (D)	T	S	0	a/c
Lafferty et al. (1989) (D)	T	S	−	a/c
Rabavilas et al. (1979) (D)[d]	P	R	−	a/c
Rabavilas et al. (1979) (P)[d]	P	R	+	a/c
Schindler (1991) (D)	P	S	0	.14
Schulte & Künzel (in press) (D)[e1]	R	CI	+	.15
INTERACTION EFFECT				
Jones et al. (1988) (D)[f]	R	S	−	.09
Kolb et al. (1985) (D)[g]	T	S	−	a/c
Schulte & Künzel (1991) (D)[h]	T	T	−	.44
Schulte & Künzel (in press) (D)[i]	T	CI	−	.13
Schulte & Künzel (in press) (D)[e2]	R	CI	+	.17
[postsession outcome]				
Orlinsky & Howard (1967, 1975)	P	P	+	na
Orlinsky & Howard (1967, 1975)	P	T	+	na
Orlinsky & Howard (1967, 1975)	T	P	0	na
Orlinsky & Howard (1967, 1975)	T	T	+	na

SUMMARY A: TO 1985   *OUTCOME*

Process	Patient −	Patient 0	Patient +	Therapist −	Therapist 0	Therapist +	Rater −	Rater 0	Rater +	Score −	Score 0	Score +	Combined −	Combined 0	Combined +	Total −	Total 0	Total +
Patient	0	1	2	0	1	1	0	0	0	0	0	1	0	0	0	0	2	4
Therapist	0	0	2	0	1	3	0	0	1	0	3	1	0	0	0	0	4	7
Rater	0	0	0	1	1	0	1	0	0	1	3	1	0	0	0	3	4	1
Total	0	1	4	1	3	4	1	0	1	1	6	3	0	0	0	3	10	12

SUMMARY B: TOTAL TO DATE   *OUTCOME*

Process	Patient −	Patient 0	Patient +	Therapist −	Therapist 0	Therapist +	Rater −	Rater 0	Rater +	Score −	Score 0	Score +	Combined −	Combined 0	Combined +	Total −	Total 0	Total +
Patient	0	1	3	0	1	2	1	0	1	0	1	1	0	0	0	1	3	7
Therapist	0	2	3	1	2	5	0	0	1	2	4	1	1	0	0	4	8	10
Rater	0	0	0	1	1	0	1	0	0	2	3	1	1	1	2	5	5	3
Total	0	3	6	2	4	7	2	0	2	4	8	3	2	1	2	10	16	20

[a] + = therapist collaboration positively related to outcome, or therapist directiveness or permissiveness negatively related to outcome; 0 = no significant association; − = therapist collaboration negatively related to outcome, or therapist directiveness or permissiveness positively related to outcome.

continued

Footnote continued from Table 8.39

[b]Schizophrenic patients in individual exploratory and supportive dynamic psychotherapy.

[c]Therapists' ratings of own "structuring" in behavioral marital therapy was negatively associated with outcome, and therapists' ratings of "inducing collaboration" was positively associated with outcome.

[d]Therapist "directiveness" was positively associated with outcome and therapist "permissiveness" was negatively associated with outcome during in-vivo exposure (flooding) treatment of phobic and obsessive-compulsive patients.

[e]Therapist "directive" behavior was (1) negatively related to outcome in behavioral treatment of phobic patients at follow-up but (2) negatively related to outcome at termination in late (but not early or middle) sessions.

[f]For patients with high levels of pretreatment disturbance, good outcome was associated with therapist behaving in a "teacherlike (didactic) manner."

[g]Outcome (only on SCL paranoia scale) was negatively associated with therapist "directive support" for patients who rated their therapists high in facilitative conditions.

[h]Positive outcome was associated with therapist sense of "control" strongly in early (but only moderately in middle, and not in late) sessions of behavioral treatment of phobic patients.

[i]Therapists' sense of "control" during middle (but not early or late) sessions was positively associated with good outcome at termination (but not at 2-year follow-up).

TABLE 8.40 Patient's collaboration (Cb) versus dependence (Dp) or controlling (Cn)

Reference	Process	Outcome	Finding[a]	ES
Bachelor (1991) (Cb)	T	T	+	.26
Bachelor (1991) (Cb)	T	R	+	.44
Coady (1991a)[b]	R	CI	+	a/c
Hill et al. (1989) (Dp)[c]	R	P	0	na
Hill et al. (1989) (Dp)[c]	R	R	0	na
Hill et al. (1989) (Dp)[c]	R	S	0	na
Jones et al. (1992) (Dp)	R	CI	+	.23
Jones et al. (1992) (Cn)	R	CI	+	.25
Rudy et al. (1985)[d]	T	P	0	na
Rudy et al. (1985)[d]	T	T	+	.10
Rudy et al. (1985)[d]	T	S	0	na
INTERACTION EFFECT				
Schulte & Künzel (1991) (Cb)[e]	P	P	+	.29
Schulte & Künzel (in press) (Cb)[f]	P	CI	+	.10
Schulte (in press)/Schulte & Künzel (in press) (Cn)[g]	R	CI	+	.21
[postsession outcome]				
Hill et al. (1989) (Dp)[c]	R	P	0	na
Hill et al. (1989) (Dp)[c]	R	R	0	na
Hill et al. (1989) (Dp)[c]	R	S	0	na
Hoyt (1980) (Dp)	R	R	+	.14
Orlinsky & Howard (1967, 1975)	P	P	+	na
Orlinsky & Howard (1967, 1975)	P	T	+	na
Orlinsky & Howard (1967, 1975)	T	P	+	na
Orlinsky & Howard (1967, 1975)	T	T	+	na

SUMMARY A: TO 1985   *OUTCOME*

Process	Patient − 0 +	Therapist − 0 +	Rater − 0 +	Score − 0 +	Combined − 0 +	Total − 0 +
Patient	0 1 3	0 1 1	0 0 1	0 1 0	0 0 0	0 3 5
Therapist	0 1 1	0 1 3	0 1 1	0 1 0	0 0 0	0 4 5
Rater	0 0 0	0 0 0	0 0 0	0 0 3	0 0 0	0 0 3
Total	0 2 4	0 2 4	0 1 2	0 2 3	0 0 0	0 7 13

SUMMARY B: TOTAL TO DATE

OUTCOME

Process	Patient			Therapist			Rater			Score			Combined			Total		
	−	0	+	−	0	+	−	0	+	−	0	+	−	0	+	−	0	+
Patient	0	1	5	0	1	2	0	0	1	0	1	0	0	0	1	0	3	9
Therapist	0	2	2	0	1	6	0	1	2	0	2	0	0	0	0	0	6	10
Rater	0	2	0	0	0	0	0	2	1	0	2	3	0	0	4	0	6	8
Total	0	5	7	0	2	8	0	3	4	0	5	3	0	0	5	0	15	27

[a] + = patient collaboration positively related to good outcome, or patient dependence/controlling negatively related to good outcome; 0 = no significant difference; − = patient collaboration negatively related to good outcome, or patient dependency positively related to good outcome.

[b] Interpersonal behaviors of patients with good outcomes were rated lower on "assert and separate" (but not on "defer and submit" or "sulk and appease") than patients with poorer outcomes.

[c] 10-session focused Gestalt therapy involving six patients with active rheumatoid arthritis.

[d] Patient "enjoy friendly autonomy" (collaboration); patient "defer and submit" or "sulk and appease" (dependence).

[e] Positive outcome was associated with patient sense of "autonomy" (collaboration—"having the opportunity to make his own contribution") strongly in late (but only moderately in middle, and not in early) sessions of behavioral treatment of phobic patients.

[f] Outcome was positively associated with patient sense of "autonomy" in late (but not early or middle) sessions.

[g] Outcome at termination and 2-year follow-up was negatively associated with patient "directive" behavior in late (but not early or middle) sessions.

N.B. For Tables 8.41 through 8.45: *Process* refers to the observational perspective from which process was assessed. P = patient ratings; T = therapist ratings; R = ratings by nonparticipant raters; I = objectively determined index of process, for example, assignment to a specified treatment condition. *Outcome* refers to the observational perspective from which outcome was evaluated. P = patient ratings; T = therapist ratings; R = ratings by independent raters; S = psychometric test score or objective index; CI = combined perspectives index. *ES* = effect size. na = data not available; a/c = data available but not computed.

TABLE 8.41 Patient's expressiveness

Reference	Process	Outcome	Finding[a]	ES
Allen et al. (1988)	P	P	+	.12
Allen et al. (1988)	P	R	0	na
Braswell et al. (1985)[b]	R	T	−	.27
Braswell et al. (1985)[b]	R	R	0	na
Braswell et al. (1985)[b]	R	S	0	na
Bugge et al. (1985)	P	P	+	.12
Henry et al. (1986)	R	S	+	na
Henry et al. (1990)	R	S	+	na
Jones et al. (1992)	R	CI	+	.14
Piper et al. (1985)	P	P	+	.42
Piper et al. (1985)	P	T	0	na
Piper et al. (1985)	P	R	0	na
Piper et al. (1985)	P	S	0	na
Rudy et al. (1985)[c]	T	P	0	na
Rudy et al. (1985)[c]	T	T	+	.07
Rudy et al. (1985)[c]	T	S	0	na
Soldz et al. (1992)	R	P	+	.09
Soldz et al. (1992)	R	T	0	.01
Soldz et al. (1992)	R	R	0	.04
Soldz et al. (1992)[d]	R	S	−	.05
INTERACTION EFFECT				
Coady (1991a)[e]	R	CI	+	a/c
Jones et al. (1988)[f]	R	S	+	.11
Schulte & Künzel (in press)[g]	P	CI	+	.10
[cited but untabulated in 1986]				
Amira (1982)	R	CI	0	na
Brown (1970)	T	T	+	a/c
Butler et al. (1962)	R	P	0	a/c
Butler et al. (1962)	R	T	+	a/c
Butler et al. (1962)	R	S	+	a/c
Church (1982)	R	S	+	na
Conrad (1952)	T	T	+	a/c
Gendlin et al. (1960)	T	T	+	.24
Landfield (1971)	T	R	+	a/c
Lerner (1972)	R	P	0	a/c
Lerner (1972)	R	T	0	a/c
Lerner (1972)	R	S	0	a/c
Rice (1973)	R	P	+	.07
Rice (1973)	R	T	+	.12
Rice (1973)	R	S	+	.03
Rice & Wagstaff (1967)	R	P	+	na
Rice & Wagstaff (1967)	R	T	+	na
Rice & Wagstaff (1967)	R	S	+	na
Roshal (1953)	I	CI	+	na
Truax & Wittmer (1971)	R	CI	+	a/c
Wogan (1970)	P	P	+	.07
Wogan (1970)	P	T	+	.06

Reference	Process	Outcome	Finding[a]	ES
INTERACTION EFFECTS				
Barrington (1961)[h]	I	T	+	.18
Barrington (1961)[h]	I	S	+	.15
[postsession outcome]				
Orlinsky & Howard (1967, 1975)	P	P	+	na
Orlinsky & Howard (1967, 1975)	P	T	0	na
Orlinsky & Howard (1967, 1975)	T	P	0	na
Orlinsky & Howard (1967, 1975)	T	T	+	na
INTERACTION EFFECTS				
Hoyt (1980)	R	R	+	.16

SUMMARY: TOTAL TO DATE   *OUTCOME*

Process	Patient			Therapist			Rater			Score			Combined			Total		
	−	0	+	−	0	+	−	0	+	−	0	+	−	0	+	−	0	+
Patient	0	0	4	0	2	1	0	2	0	0	1	0	0	0	1	0	5	6
Therapist	0	2	0	0	0	5	0	0	1	0	1	0	0	0	0	0	3	6
Rater	0	2	4	1	2	3	0	2	1	1	2	7	0	1	2	2	9	17
Index	0	0	0	0	0	1	0	0	0	0	0	1	0	0	1	0	0	3
Total	0	4	8	1	4	10	0	4	2	1	4	8	0	1	4	2	17	32

[a] + = patient expressiveness positively related to outcome; 0 = no significant association; − = patient expressiveness negatively related to outcome.

[b] Cognitive-behavioral treatment of children with classroom behavior problems.

[c] Patient "disclose and express."

[d] Patient's "ease of self-expression" (spontaneity, trust, focus on feelings versus intellectualizing, defensiveness) was associated with decrease on self-esteem scale but not on other psychometric measures.

[e] Interpersonal behaviors of patients with good outcome were rated higher on "disclose and express" late in therapy but not in early or middle sessions.

[f] For patients with low levels of pretreatment disturbance, good outcome was associated with patients being "clear and organized in self-expression."

[g] Patients' perceptions of their own freedom to express themselves during the last third (but not the first two-thirds) of treatment was positively associated with outcome at termination.

[h] "Combined client and counselor syllables per word score."

TABLE 8.42   Therapist's empathic understanding

Reference	Process	Outcome	Finding[a]	ES
Bommert et al. (1972)	R	P	0	.03
Bommert et al. (1972)	R	S	+	.10
Bommert et al. (1972)	P	P	0	.04
Bommert et al. (1972)	P	S	+	.14
Buckley et al. (1981)	P	P	+	.15
Bugge et al. (1985)	P	P	+	.33
Burns & Nolen-Hoeksema (1991)	P	P	+	.46
Dormaar et al. (1989)	I	P	0	na
Dormaar et al. (1989)	I	T	+	a/c
Dormaar et al. (1989)	I	S	+	a/c
Gabbard et al. (1986)	P	P	+	.14
Gabbard et al. (1986)	P	P	+	.14
Gabbard et al. (1986)	R	R	+	.22
Horvath (1981)	P	P	0	.02
Lafferty et al. (1989)	P	S	+	a/c
Minsel, Bommert, Bastine, et al. (1972)	P	P	+	.15
Minsel, Bommert, Bastine, et al. (1972)	P	S	0	.01
Minsel, Bommert, Bastine, et al. (1972)	R	P	0	.01
Minsel, Bommert, Bastine, et al. (1972)	R	S	+	.01
Rabavilas et al. (1979)	P	R	+	a/c
Westermann et al. (1983)[b1]	P	CI	+	na
Westermann et al. (1983)[b2]	P	CI	+	na
INTERACTION EFFECT				
Filak & Abeles (1984)[c]	I	P	+	.20
Filak & Abeles (1984)[c]	I	T	+	.32
Willutzki & Schulte (1991)[d]	I	CI	+	.27
[postsession outcome]				
Orlinsky & Howard (1967, 1975)	P	P	+	na
Orlinsky & Howard (1967, 1975)	P	T	0	na
Orlinsky & Howard (1967, 1975)	T	P	+	na
Orlinsky & Howard (1967, 1975)	T	T	+	na

SUMMARY A: TO 1985   OUTCOME

Process	Patient −	0	+	Therapist −	0	+	Rater −	0	+	Score −	0	+	Combined −	0	+	Total −	0	+
Patient	0	2	5	0	0	6	0	2	3	0	5	8	0	0	0	0	9	22
Therapist	0	4	0	0	3	2	0	3	0	0	5	0	0	0	0	0	15	2
Rater	0	5	1	0	6	2	0	2	1	0	8	13	0	0	0	0	21	17
Total	0	11	6	0	9	10	0	7	4	0	18	21	0	0	0	0	45	41

SUMMARY B: TOTAL TO DATE   OUTCOME

Process Perspective	Patient −	0	+	Therapist −	0	+	Rater −	0	+	Score −	0	+	Combined −	0	+	Total −	0	+
Patient	0	4	12	0	1	6	0	2	4	0	6	10	0	0	2	0	13	34
Therapist	0	4	1	0	3	3	0	3	0	0	5	0	0	0	0	0	15	4
Rater	0	7	1	0	6	2	0	3	1	0	8	15	0	0	0	0	24	19
Index	0	1	1	0	0	2	0	0	0	0	0	1	0	0	1	0	1	5
Total	0	16	15	0	10	13	0	8	5	0	19	26	0	0	3	0	53	62

[a] + = therapist attunement positively related to outcome; 0 = no significant association; − = therapist attunement negatively related to outcome.

[b] Outcome in group therapy was positively associated with "empathic understanding" of (1) senior therapist and (2) student cotherapist.

[c] Therapists' accurate perception of patients' symptomatic state at termination (but not at intake) was associated with good outcome.

[d] Therapists' accurate perception of phobic patients' adaptive experiences (but not phobic situations) was positively related to outcome (especially after the third session, the association still significant but markedly diminishing in strength toward the end of treatment).

TABLE 8.43   Therapist's expressiveness

Reference	Process	Outcome	Finding[a]	ES
Coady (1991a)[b]	R	CI	0	a/c
Jones et al. (1986)[c]	P	P	0	na
Jones et al. (1986)[c]	P	T	0	na
Meyer (1981)/Meyer (1990)[d1]	R	S	+	.44
Meyer (1981)/Meyer (1990)[d2]	R	S	0	.10
Minsel, Bommert, & Pieritz (1972)	I	S	0	.02
[cited but untabulated in 1986]				
Alexander et al. (1976)	R	R	0	na
Amira (1982)	R	CI	0	na
DiLoreto (1971)	R	S	0	.05
Rice (1965)	R	P	+	.25
Rice (1965)	R	T	+	.18
Rice (1965)	R	S	+	.21
Schauble & Pierce (1974)	R	S	+	a/c
Sloane et al. (1975)	P	CI	0	a/c
INTERACTION EFFECTS				
Barrington (1961)[e]	I	T	+	.18
Barrington (1961)[e]	I	S	+	.15

SUMMARY A: TOTAL TO DATE   *OUTCOME*

Process	Patient			Therapist			Rater			Score			Combined			Total		
Perspective	−	0	+	−	0	+	−	0	+	−	0	+	−	0	+	−	0	+
Patient	0	1	0	0	1	0	0	0	0	0	0	0	0	1	0	0	3	0
Rater	0	0	1	0	0	1	0	1	0	0	2	3	0	2	0	0	5	5
Index	0	0	0	0	0	1	0	0	0	0	1	1	0	0	0	0	1	2
Total	0	1	1	0	1	2	0	1	0	0	3	4	0	3	0	0	9	7

[a] + = therapist expressiveness positively related to outcome; 0 = no significant association; − = therapist expressiveness negatively related to outcome.
[b] Therapists' interpersonal behavior on "disclose and express."
[c] Therapist "neutrality" (talks little, does not structure, remains neutral).
[d] "Concreteness" of therapist was associated with better outcome in (1) short-term individual client-centered but (2) not in psychodynamic conflict-centered therapy.
[e] "Combined client and counselor syllables per word score."

TABLE 8.44   Patient's empathic understanding

Reference	Process	Outcome	Finding[a]	ES
Dormaar et al. (1989)	I	P	0	na
Dormaar et al. (1989)	I	T	0	na
Dormaar et al. (1989)	I	S	0	na
Hill, Helms, Spiegel, & Tichenor (1988)[b]	I	CI	+	na
Martin et al. (1987)	I	P	−	.42
Martin et al. (1987)	I	T	0	na
Westermann et al. (1983)[c]	P	CI	+	na
[cited but untabulated in 1986]				
Feitel (1968)	P	R	+	a/c
Jeske (1973)	P	S	+	.42
[postsession outcome]				
Martin et al. (1986)	I	P	0	na
Martin et al. (1986)	I	T	+	.22
Martin et al. (1986)	I	T	−	.19

continued

TABLE 8.44   *continued*

SUMMARY A: TOTAL TO DATE																	OUTCOME
	Patient			Therapist			Rater			Score			Combined			Total		
Process	−	*0*	+	−	*0*	+	−	*0*	+	−	*0*	+	−	*0*	+	−	*0*	+
Patient	0	0	0	0	0	0	0	0	1	0	0	1	0	0	1	0	0	3
Index	1	2	0	1	2	1	0	0	0	0	1	0	0	0	1	2	5	2
Total	1	2	0	1	2	1	0	0	1	0	1	1	0	0	2	2	5	5

[a]+ = patient attunement positively related to outcome; 0 = no significant association; − = patient attunement negatively related to outcome.
[b]Substantially more significant associations were found between "therapist intentions" and "client reactions to therapist interventions" for the two most successful versus the two least successful cases.
[c]"Patient empathic resonance" in group psychotherapy.

TABLE 8.45   Communicative attunement

Reference	*Process*	*Outcome*	*Finding*[a]	*ES*
Sachse (in press)[b]	R	P	+	.49
Sachse (in press)[b]	R	T	+	.56
Sachse (in press)[b]	R	S	+	.51
Saunders et al. (1989)[c]	P	R	0	.03
[postsession outcome]				
Saunders et al. (1989)[c]	P	P	+	.26

SUMMARY A: TO 1985																	OUTCOME
	Patient			Therapist			Rater			Score			Combined			Total		
Process	−	*0*	+	−	*0*	+	−	*0*	+	−	*0*	+	−	*0*	+	−	*0*	+
Patient	0	0	1	0	0	1	0	0	1	0	0	1	0	0	0	0	0	4
Therapist	0	1	0	0	1	1	0	1	1	0	1	0	0	0	0	0	4	2
Index	0	2	6	0	2	6	0	0	0	0	3	2	0	0	0	0	7	14
Total	0	3	7	0	3	8	0	1	2	0	4	3	0	0	0	0	11	20

SUMMARY B: TOTAL TO DATE																	OUTCOME
	Patient			Therapist			Rater			Score			Combined			Total		
Process	−	*0*	+	−	*0*	+	−	*0*	+	−	*0*	+	−	*0*	+	−	*0*	+
Patient	0	0	2	0	0	1	0	1	1	0	0	1	0	0	0	0	1	5
Therapist	0	1	0	0	1	1	0	1	1	0	1	0	0	0	0	0	4	2
Rater	0	1	1	0	1	2	0	1	1	0	1	1	0	0	0	0	4	5
Index	0	2	6	0	2	6	0	0	0	0	3	2	0	0	0	0	7	14
Total	0	4	9	0	4	10	0	3	3	0	5	4	0	0	0	0	16	26

[a]+ = reciprocal attunement positively related to outcome; 0 = no significant association; − = reciprocal attunement negatively related to outcome.
[b]Quality of explicating teamwork.
[c]"Empathic resonance" in third session.

N.B. For Tables 8.46 through 8.48: *Process* refers to the observational perspective from which process was assessed. P = patient ratings; T = therapist ratings; R = ratings by nonparticipant raters; I = objectively determined index of process, for example, assignment to a specified treatment condition. *Outcome* refers to the observational perspective from which outcome was evaluated. P = patient ratings; T = therapist ratings; R = ratings by independent raters; S = psychometric test score or objective index; CI = combined perspectives index. *ES* = effect size. na = data not available; a/c = data available but not computed.

TABLE 8.46 Therapist's affirmation of patient

Reference	Process	Outcome	Finding[a]	ES
Bachelor (1991)	P	R	+	.28
Bennun et al. (1986)[b]	P	P	+	.11
Bennun et al. (1986)[b]	P	T	+	.05
Bennun et al. (1986)[c]	P	P	+	.24
Bennun et al. (1986)[c]	P	T	+	.38
Bommert et al. (1972)	P	P	0	.15
Bommert et al. (1972)	P	S	0	.06
Buckley et al. (1981)	P	P	+	.35
Coady (1991a, 1991b)[d]	R	CI	+	a/c
Eckert et al. (1988)	P	P	+	.25
Eckert et al. (1988)	P	S	0	.02
Gaston et al. (1991)[e]	P	S	0	.00
Gelso, Mills, & Spiegel (1983)[f1]	T	P	+	.21
Gelso, Mills, & Spiegel (1983)[f2]	T	P	0	.10
Gelso, Mills, & Spiegel (1983)[f3]	T	P	0	.02
Gelso, Mills, & Spiegel (1983)[f1]	T	T	+	.45
Gelso, Mills, & Spiegel (1983)[f2]	T	T	0	.08
Gelso, Mills, & Spiegel (1983)[f3]	T	T	0	.14
Green & Herget (1991)[g]	R	P	+	.40
Green & Herget (1991)[g]	R	T	+	.40
Green & Herget (1991)[g]	R	R	+	.34
Green & Herget (1991)[h]	R	R	+	.62
Grimes & Murdock (1989)	P	S	+	.14
Grunebaum (1986)[i]	P	P	+	na
Henry et al. (1986)[j]	R	S	+	a/c
Henry et al. (1986)[k]	R	S	+	a/c
Henry et al. (1990)[k]	R	S	+	.28
Holtzworth-Munroe et al. (1989)[l]	P	P	+	.15
Holtzworth-Munroe et al. (1989)[m]	P	P	−	.17
Holtzworth-Munroe et al. (1989)	T	P	0	.04
Jones et al. (1986)	P	P	+	.06
Jones et al. (1986)	P	T	+	.06
Lafferty et al. (1989)	P	S	0	na
Meyer (1981)/Meyer (1990)[n1]	R	S	+	.43
Meyer (1981)/Meyer (1990)[n2]	R	S	0	.05
Quintana & Meara (1990)[o]	P	S	+	.96
Rabavilas et al. (1979)[p]	P	R	+	a/c
Rounsaville et al. (1987)	R	P	+	.36
Rounsaville et al. (1987)	R	T	+	.19
Rounsaville et al. (1987)	R	R	+	.16
Rudy et al. (1985)[q]	P	P	+	a/c
Rudy et al. (1985)[q]	P	T	+	a/c
Rudy et al. (1985)[q]	P	S	0	a/c
Rudy et al. (1985)[r]	P	P	0	a/c
Rudy et al. (1985)[r]	P	T	+	a/c
Rudy et al. (1985)[r]	P	S	0	a/c
Schindler (1991)	P	S	0	.12

continued

TABLE 8.46   *continued*

Reference	Process	Outcome	Finding[a]	ES
Westermann et al. (1983)[s1]	P	CI	+	na
Westermann et al. (1983)[s2]	P	CI	0	na
Williams & Chambless (1990)	P	R	+	.09
Windholz & Silberschatz (1988)	R	P	0	.03
Windholz & Silberschatz (1988)	R	T	+	.18
Windholz & Silberschatz (1988)	R	R	0	.00
INTERACTION EFFECTS				
Eckert et al. (1988)[f]	P	S	+	.11
[postsession outcome]				
Hoyt et al. (1983)	T	T	0	.00
Hoyt et al. (1983)	R	R	0	.02
Orlinsky & Howard (1967, 1975)	P	P	+	na
Orlinsky & Howard (1967, 1975)	P	T	−	na
Orlinsky & Howard (1967, 1975)	T	P	+	na
Orlinsky & Howard (1967, 1975)	T	T	0	na

SUMMARY A: TO 1985   OUTCOME

Process	Patient −	0	+	Therapist −	0	+	Rater −	0	+	Score −	0	+	Combined −	0	+	Total −	0	+
Patient	0	2	5	0	2	7	0	1	2	0	5	6	0	0	0	0	10	20
Therapist	0	3	3	0	0	11	0	4	1	1	5	1	0	0	0	1	12	16
Rater	1	3	0	0	4	1	0	5	4	0	8	9	0	0	0	1	20	14
Total	1	8	8	0	6	19	0	10	7	1	18	16	0	0	0	2	42	50

SUMMARY B: TOTAL TO DATE   OUTCOME

Process	Patient −	0	+	Therapist −	0	+	Rater −	0	+	Score −	0	+	Combined −	0	+	Total −	0	+
Patient	1	4	14	1	2	12	0	1	5	0	12	9	0	1	1	2	20	41
Therapist	0	6	5	0	4	12	0	4	1	1	5	1	0	0	0	1	19	19
Rater	1	4	2	0	4	4	0	7	7	0	9	13	0	0	1	1	24	27
Total	2	14	21	1	10	28	0	12	13	1	26	23	0	1	2	4	63	87

[a] + = therapist warmth/acceptance positively related to outcome, or therapist coldness/hostility negatively related to outcome; 0 = no significant association; − = therapist warmth/acceptance negatively related to outcome, or therapist coldness/hostility positively related to outcome.
[b] German inpatient sample.
[c] U.K. outpatient sample.
[d] Patients with good outcomes had therapists whose interpersonal behaviors were rated higher on "help and protect" and lower in "disaffiliative" quality.
[e] CALPAS scale of therapist negative contribution.
[f] Therapist's expected "enjoyment working with patient" rated after first session: (1) 8-session time-limited treatment; (2) 16-session time-limited treatment; (3) time-unlimited treatment, outcome at termination.
[g] 1-month outcome.
[h] 3-year outcome.
[i] Two-fifths of therapists who felt harmed in their own personal therapy described their therapists as having been cold, distant, rigid, and unable to respond in "ordinary human ways."
[j] SASB ratings of "affirming and understanding" and "helping and protecting" for therapist interpersonal behavior.
[k] SASB ratings of "belittling and blaming" for therapist interpersonal behavior.
[l] Husbands' ratings of process in behavioral marital therapy.
[m] Wives' ratings of process in behavioral marital therapy.
[n] "Emotional warmth" of therapist was associated with better outcome (1) in short-term individual client-centered therapy but (2) not in psychodynamic conflict-centered therapy.
[o] Patients who perceived their therapists as "affirming and understanding," "loving and approaching," and "nurturing and protecting" showed most positive changes in self-experience, whereas patients who perceived their therapists as "belittling and blaming," "attacking and rejecting," and "ignoring and neglecting" showed most negative changes in self-experience.
[p] Therapist qualities of warmth, acceptance, respect, interest, and liking.

[q]Therapist "encouraging friendly autonomy"; other SASB quadrants not related to outcome.

[r]Therapist "belittling and blaming" was associated with therapist-rated negative outcome; other SASB clusters not related to outcome.

[s]Outcome in group therapy was (1) positively associated with "warmth" of senior therapist, but (2) unrelated to "warmth" of student cotherapist.

[t]Therapist affirmation associated with better outcomes for patients with severe (but not mild) initial symptoms.

TABLE 8.47   Patient's affirmation of therapist

Reference	Process	Outcome	Finding[a]	ES
Bennun et al. (1986)[b]	T	P	+	.13
Bennun et al. (1986)[b]	T	T	+	.23
Bennun et al. (1986)[c]	T	P	+	.25
Bennun et al. (1986)[c]	T	T	+	.38
Buckley et al. (1981)	P	P	+	.26
Coady (1991a)[d]	R	CI	+	a/c
Grawe et al. (1978)	P	S	+	.10
Grawe (1989a)/Grawe et al. (1990)[e1]	I	CI	+	.23
Grawe (1989a)/Grawe et al. (1990)[e2]	I	CI	+	.48
Grawe (1989a)/Grawe et al. (1990)[e3]	I	CI	+	.52
Hagborg (1991)	P	P	+	.07
Hagborg (1991)	P	S	+	.12
Henry et al. (1986)	R	S	+	na
Henry et al. (1990)	R	S	+	na
Horvath (1981)	P	P	0	.00
McNeill et al. (1987)[f]	P	P	+	.04
Meyer (1981)/Meyer (1990)[g1]	P	S	0	.13
Meyer (1981)/Meyer (1990)[g2]	P	S	+	.40
Rudy et al. (1985)[h]	T	P	0	na
Rudy et al. (1985)[h]	T	T	+	.08
Rudy et al. (1985)[h]	T	S	0	na
Schindler (1991)	T	S	0	.11
INTERACTION EFFECT				
Jones et al. (1988)[i]	R	S	+	.13
Jones et al. (1988)[j]	R	S	+	.07
[postsession outcome]				
Orlinsky & Howard (1967, 1975)	P	P	+	na
Orlinsky & Howard (1967, 1975)	P	T	0	na
Orlinsky & Howard (1967, 1975)	T	P	+	na
Orlinsky & Howard (1967, 1975)	T	T	+	na

SUMMARY A: TO 1985   *OUTCOME*

Process	Patient −	Patient 0	Patient +	Therapist −	Therapist 0	Therapist +	Rater −	Rater 0	Rater +	Score −	Score 0	Score +	Combined −	Combined 0	Combined +	Total −	Total 0	Total +
Patient	0	2	2	1	1	5	0	0	2	0	2	0	0	0	0	1	5	9
Therapist	0	0	2	0	1	6	0	1	0	0	2	0	0	0	0	0	4	8
Rater	0	0	0	0	0	1	1	0	1	0	1	0	0	0	0	1	1	2
Total	0	2	4	1	2	12	1	1	3	0	5	0	0	0	0	2	10	19

continued

TABLE 8.47   *continued*

Process	Patient			Therapist			Rater			Score			Combined			Total		
	−	0	+	−	0	+	−	0	+	−	0	+	−	0	+	−	0	+
Patient	0	3	6	1	2	5	0	0	2	0	3	3	0	0	0	1	8	16
Therapist	0	1	5	0	1	10	0	1	0	0	4	0	0	0	0	0	7	15
Rater	0	0	0	0	0	1	1	0	1	0	1	4	0	0	1	1	1	7
Index	0	0	0	0	0	0	0	0	0	0	0	0	0	0	3	0	0	3
Total	0	4	11	1	3	16	1	1	3	0	8	7	0	0	4	2	16	41

SUMMARY B: TOTAL TO DATE — OUTCOME

[a] + = patient affirmation positively related to outcome, or patient hostility negatively related to outcome; 0 = no significant association; − = patient affirmation negatively related to outcome or patient hostility positively related to outcome.
[b] German inpatient sample.
[c] U.K. outpatient sample.
[d] Interpersonal behaviors of patients with good outcomes were rated as higher in "trust and rely" (but not different in "belittle and blame").
[e] Process variable constructed from patient and therapist perspectives jointly in (1) client-centered therapy, (2) broad-spectrum behavior therapy, and (3) interpersonal behavior therapy.
[f] Patient perception of therapist "attractiveness."
[g] Patients' "emotional closeness" to therapist was (1) unrelated to outcome in short-term client-centered therapy but (2) related to positive outcome in short-term psychodynamic conflict-centered therapy.
[h] Patient "friendly and accepting" and "approach and enjoy."
[i] For patients with low levels of pretreatment disturbance, good outcome was associated with "seeking greater intimacy with the therapist."
[j] For patients with high levels of pretreatment disturbance, good outcome was associated with "seeking therapist approval, affection or sympathy."

TABLE 8.48   Reciprocal affirmation

Reference	Process	Outcome	Finding[a]	ES
Buckley et al. (1981)[b]	P	P	+	.16
Collins et al. (1985)[c]	R	P	+	.08
Collins et al. (1985)[c]	R	R	+	.13
Collins et al. (1985)[c]	R	S	+	.08
Goldstein et al. (1988)[c]	P	P	0	.02
Goldstein et al. (1988)[c]	T	T	0	.00
Jones et al. (1992)[b]	R	CI	+	.25
Rudy et al. (1985)[d]	I	P	+	.16
Rudy et al. (1985)[d]	I	T	+	.14
Rudy et al. (1985)[d]	I	S	+	.10
Saunders et al. (1989)[e]	P	R	0	.03
INTERACTION EFFECT				
Jones et al. (1988)[f]	R	S	+	.14
[postsession outcome]				
Saunders et al. (1989)[e]	P	P	+	.25

Process	Patient			Therapist			Rater			Score			Combined			Total		
	−	0	+	−	0	+	−	0	+	−	0	+	−	0	+	−	0	+
Patient	0	0	5	0	1	1	0	1	2	0	0	1	0	0	0	0	2	9
Therapist	0	0	0	0	0	1	0	0	0	0	1	0	0	0	0	0	1	1
Rater	0	0	2	0	0	0	0	0	2	0	1	1	0	0	0	0	1	5
Total	0	0	7	0	1	2	0	1	4	0	2	2	0	0	0	0	4	15

SUMMARY A: TO 1985 — OUTCOME

SUMMARY B: TOTAL TO DATE   OUTCOME

Process	Patient −	0	+	Therapist −	0	+	Rater −	0	+	Score −	0	+	Combined −	0	+	Total −	0	+
Patient	0	1	7	0	1	1	0	2	2	0	0	1	0	0	0	0	4	11
Therapist	0	0	0	0	1	1	0	0	0	0	1	0	0	0	0	0	2	1
Rater	0	0	3	0	0	0	0	0	3	0	1	3	0	0	1	0	1	10
Index	0	0	1	0	0	1	0	0	0	0	0	1	0	0	0	0	0	3
Total	0	1	11	0	2	3	0	2	5	0	2	5	0	0	1	0	7	25

[a] + = mutual affirmation positively related to outcome; 0 = no significant association; − = mutual affirmation negatively related to outcome.
[b] Competitive relationship.
[c] Acceptability for expression of negative feelings by patients and staff on wards.
[d] Matching of client's rating of therapist and therapist's rating of client with respect to "encouraging and enjoying friendly autonomy," "offering and accepting friendly influence," and not "invoking and taking hostile autonomy."
[e] "Mutual affirmation" in third session.
[f] For patients with low levels of pretreatment disturbance, good outcome was associated with use of humor.

bond still looms large as an aspect of process consistently associated with outcome. As a whole and in its several parts, the bond of relatedness between patient and therapist seems to be a central factor both in individual and in group psychotherapies. Future research on this factor should aim to refine our understanding of the circumstances in which the bond is most and least influential. Researchers planning comparative outcome studies or process–outcome studies on other facets of process should be sure to control for differences induced by varying levels of the therapeutic bond.

SELF-RELATEDNESS

Self-relatedness refers to people's styles of responding to themselves. It concerns the ways they experience their internal ideational and affective arousal, formulate their self-awareness, evaluate themselves, and control their ideas, feelings, and urges. Individuals can be open-minded, receptive, and flexible in responding, or guarded, critically selective, and rigidly constrained. In the former case, they are regarded as open and centered; in the latter case, they are typically viewed as defensive. Presumably this varies with the level of threat or danger experienced by a person at different times and in different situations. Individuals in an open state can absorb what is offered or available to them in their surroundings, adapting to take advantage of what is useful. Individuals in a defensive state need to screen and filter their responses more strictly in order to maintain their self-control, self-esteem, or sense of safety, and they are only able to avail themselves of experiences that fit their self-imposed limitations. Questions about self-rela-

tedness in therapy tend to focus on a patient's ability to assimilate the interventions and relationship offered by the therapist.

Patient Self-Relatedness

Patients' openness vs. defensiveness has been dealt with focally or peripherally in a number of process–outcome studies. Table 8.49 summarizes 45 findings that show this factor to be consistently related to outcome, no matter which process or outcome perspectives are considered. Overall, 80% of the findings show a significant positive association between patient openness and outcome. The strength as well as consistency of the association is suggested by the large effect sizes of a number of findings.

Patient experiencing (articulation of felt meaning) is a related variable, reflecting the patient's personal construction of the meaning of events in therapy. Table 8.50 summarizes 39 findings, 51% of which show experiencing to be positively associated with outcome. (Most of these process assessments are based on ratings by external observers and show mixed results, but 83% of the few findings using patients' and therapists' ratings show a significant positive association with outcome.)

Therapist Self-Relatedness

Therapist self-congruence (genuineness) is the variable that comes closest to assessing the intrapersonal aspect of participation for therapists.[12] Although only 38% of the 60 process–outcome

[12] This process variable was reviewed as an aspect of therapeutic bond in the last edition, under therapist personal role investment.

Text continues on p. 343.

N.B. For Tables 8.49 through 8.52: *Process* refers to the observational perspective from which process was assessed. P = patient ratings; T = therapist ratings; R = ratings by nonparticipant raters; I = objectively determined index of process, for example, assignment to a specified treatment condition. *Outcome* refers to the observational perspective from which outcome was evaluated. P = patient ratings; T = therapist ratings; R = ratings by independent raters; S = psychometric test score or objective index; CI = combined perspectives index. *ES* = effect size. na = data not available; a/c = data available but not computed.

TABLE 8.49   Patient's openness versus defensiveness

Reference	Process	Outcome	Finding[a]	ES
Grawe et al. (1978)	P	S	+	.12
Grawe (1989a)/Grawe et al. (1990)[b]	I	CI	0	.05
Grawe (1989a)/Grawe et al. (1990)[c]	I	CI	+	.34
Grawe (1989a)/Grawe et al. (1990)[d]	I	CI	+	.34
Bruhn et al. (1980)	R	S	+	.16
Henry et al. (1986)	R	S	+	na
Henry et al. (1990)	R	S	+	na
Jones et al. (1992)	R	CI	+	.25
Kolden (1991)	P	R	0	.04
McCullough et al. (1991)[e]	R	CI	0	.00
Meyer (1981)/Meyer (1990)[f1]	P	S	0	.10
Meyer (1981)/Meyer (1990)[f2]	P	S	+	.40
Schindler (1991)	T	S	0	.17
Taurke et al. (1990)[e]	R	CI	+	.41
Westermann et al. (1983)[g]	P	CI	+	na
INTERACTION EFFECTS				
Ambühl & Grawe (1988)[h1]	R	CI	+	.49
Ambühl & Grawe (1988)[h2]	R	CI	0	.01
Ambühl & Grawe (1988)[h3]	R	CI	+	.43
Kolden (1991)[i]	P	R	+	.01
McCullough et al. (1991)[j]	R	CI	+	.25
Schindler (1991)[k]	R	S	+	na
[postsession outcome]				
Hoyt (1980)	R	R	+	.06
Kolden (1991)[l]	P	R	+	.04
Lietaer & Neirinck (1987)	T	T	+	na
Orlinsky & Howard (1967, 1975)	P	P	+	na
Orlinsky & Howard (1967, 1975)	P	T	+	na
Orlinsky & Howard (1967, 1975)	T	P	+	na
Orlinsky & Howard (1967, 1975)	T	T	+	na
INTERACTION EFFECTS				
Kolden (1991)[m]	P	R	0	.04

SUMMARY A: TO 1985															*OUTCOME*		
	Patient			Therapist			Rater			Score			Combined			Total		
Process	−	0	+	−	0	+	−	0	+	−	0	+	−	0	+	−	0	+
Therapist	0	0	1	0	0	4	0	0	1	0	0	0	0	0	0	0	0	6
Rater	0	1	1	0	0	2	0	0	0	0	1	5	0	0	0	0	2	8
Total	0	1	2	0	0	6	0	0	1	0	1	5	0	0	0	0	2	14

SUMMARY B: TOTAL TO DATE   *OUTCOME*

Process	Patient −	0	+	Therapist −	0	+	Rater −	0	+	Score −	0	+	Combined −	0	+	Total −	0	+
Patient	0	0	1	0	0	1	0	2	2	0	1	2	0	0	1	0	3	7
Therapist	0	0	2	0	0	6	0	0	1	0	1	0	0	0	0	0	1	9
Rater	0	1	1	0	0	2	0	0	1	0	1	9	0	2	5	0	4	18
Index	0	0	0	0	0	0	0	0	0	0	0	0	0	1	2	0	1	2
Total	0	1	4	0	0	9	0	2	4	0	3	11	0	3	8	0	9	36

[a]+ = patient inner openness positively related to outcome, or defensiveness negatively related to outcome; 0 = no significant association; − = patient openness negatively related to outcome, or defensiveness positively related to outcome.
[b]Client-centered therapy.
[c]Broad-spectrum behavior therapy.
[d]Interpersonal behavior therapy.
[e]Based on same data set, McCullough et al. reported frequency of defensive response while Taurke et al. reported total defense/activity proportion.
[f]Patients' "acceptance of own feelings" was (1) unrelated to outcome in short-term client-centered therapy but (2) related to better outcome in short-term psychodynamic conflict-centered therapy.
[g]Patient "openness" in group therapy.
[h]Interaction of therapist "reflective abstraction" with specific patient openness in (1) client-centered therapy, (2) broad-spectrum behavior therapy, and (3) interpersonal behavior therapy.
[i]Interaction of "therapeutic bond" and "patient self-relatedness" predicted positive posttreatment outcome by session 10.
[j]Reflective (and, to a lesser degree, interpretive) interventions that elicit defensive responses in brief dynamic psychotherapy.
[k]Patient "defensiveness" in later but not early sessions associated with poorer outcomes.
[l]Outcome positively associated with "patient self-relatedness" in sessions 7 and 10 (but not in sessions 1 or 3).
[m]Interaction of "therapeutic bond" and "patient self-relatedness" in sessions 1, 3, 7, and 10.

TABLE 8.50   Patient's experiencing (articulation of felt meaning)

Reference	Process	Outcome	Finding[a]	ES
Hill et al. (1989)[b]	R	P	0	na
Hill et al. (1989)[b]	R	R	0	na
Hill et al. (1989)[b]	R	S	0	na
Johnson & Greenberg (1988)[c]	R	S	+	a/c
Jones et al. (1992)[d]	R	CI	+	.20
Sachse (in press)	R	P	0	na
Sachse (in press)	R	T	0	na
Sachse (in press)	R	S	0	na
Westermann et al. (1983)[e]	P	CI	+	na
[postsession outcome]				
Hill et al. (1989)[b]	R	P	0	na
Hill et al. (1989)[b]	R	R	0	na
Hill et al. (1989)[b]	R	S	−	.08
Lietaer (1992)	P	P	+	na
Lietaer (1992)	T	T	+	na

SUMMARY A: TO 1985   *OUTCOME*

Process	Patient −	0	+	Therapist −	0	+	Rater −	0	+	Score −	0	+	Combined −	0	+	Total −	0	+
Therapist	0	0	0	0	0	2	0	0	0	0	1	0	0	0	0	0	1	2
Rater	0	1	1	0	2	5	0	0	0	0	6	7	0	0	0	0	9	13
Total	0	1	1	0	2	7	0	0	0	0	7	7	0	0	0	0	10	15

continued

TABLE 8.50   *continued*

SUMMARY B: TOTAL TO DATE   *OUTCOME*

Process	Patient − 0 +	Therapist − 0 +	Rater − 0 +	Score − 0 +	Combined − 0 +	Total − 0 +
Patient	0 0 1	0 0 0	0 0 0	0 0 0	0 0 1	0 0 2
Therapist	0 0 0	0 0 3	0 0 0	0 1 0	0 0 0	0 1 3
Rater	0 4 1	0 3 5	0 2 0	1 8 8	0 0 1	1 17 15
Total	0 4 2	0 3 8	0 2 0	1 9 8	0 0 2	1 18 20

[a] + = affective immediacy positively related to outcome; 0 = no significant association; − = affective immediacy negatively related to outcome.
[b] 10-session focused Gestalt therapy involving six patients with active rheumatoid arthritis.
[c] Good outcome in emotionally focused marital therapy was associated with higher levels of "experiencing" in the blaming spouse.
[d] Low affective immediacy negatively related to outcome.
[e] "Patient affective immediacy" in group psychotherapy.

TABLE 8.51   Therapist's self-congruence (genuineness)

Reference	Process	Outcome	Finding[a]	ES
Ascher & Turner (1980)	I	P	+	a/c
Lafferty et al. (1989)	P	S	0	—
Bommert et al. (1972)	P	P	0	.05
Bommert et al. (1972)	R	S	0	.10
Buckley et al. (1981)[b]	P	P	+	.10
Westermann et al. (1983)[c1]	P	CI	0	na
Westermann et al. (1983)[c2]	P	CI	+	na

SUMMARY A: TO 1985   *OUTCOME*

Process	Patient − 0 +	Therapist − 0 +	Rater − 0 +	Score − 0 +	Combined − 0 +	Total − 0 +
Patient	0 2 3	0 2 1	0 1 0	0 6 5	0 0 0	0 11 9
Therapist	0 3 0	0 0 4	0 1 0	0 3 0	0 0 0	0 7 4
Rater	0 2 0	0 2 1	0 1 0	1 9 6	0 0 0	1 14 7
Total	0 7 3	0 4 6	0 3 0	1 18 11	0 0 0	1 32 20

SUMMARY B: TOTAL TO DATE   *OUTCOME*

Process	Patient − 0 +	Therapist − 0 +	Rater − 0 +	Score − 0 +	Combined − 0 +	Total − 0 +
Patient	0 3 4	0 2 1	0 1 0	0 7 5	0 1 1	0 14 11
Therapist	0 3 0	0 0 4	0 1 0	0 3 0	0 0 0	0 7 4
Rater	0 2 0	0 2 1	0 1 0	1 10 6	0 0 0	1 15 7
Index	0 0 1	0 0 0	0 0 0	0 0 0	0 0 0	0 0 1
Total	0 8 5	0 4 6	0 3 0	1 20 11	0 1 1	1 36 23

[a] + = therapist genuineness positively related to outcome; 0 = no significant association; − = therapist genuineness negatively related to outcome.
[b] Honesty and genuineness.
[c] Outcome in group therapy was (1) not associated with "congruence" of senior therapist, but (2) positively associated with "congruence" of student cotherapist.

TABLE 8.52 Therapist's self-acceptance and assurance versus self-rejection and control

Reference	Process	Outcome	Finding[a]	ES
Grawe (1989)/Grawe et al. (1990)[b]	I	CI	+	.36
Grawe (1989)/Grawe et al. (1990)[c]	I	CI	0	.12
Grawe (1989)/Grawe et al. (1990)[d]	I	CI	+	.45
Rudy et al. (1985)[e]	T	P	0	.01
Rudy et al. (1985)[e]	T	T	−	.24
Rudy et al. (1985)[e]	T	S	0	.02
Rudy et al. (1985)[f]	T	P	0	.00
Rudy et al. (1985)[f]	T	T	+	.19
Rudy et al. (1985)[f]	T	S	0	.02
Rudy et al. (1985)[g]	T	P	+	.07
Rudy et al. (1985)[g]	T	T	0	.02
Rudy et al. (1985)[g]	T	S	+	.08

SUMMARY: TOTAL TO DATE   OUTCOME

Process	Patient −	Patient 0	Patient +	Therapist −	Therapist 0	Therapist +	Rater −	Rater 0	Rater +	Score −	Score 0	Score +	Combined −	Combined 0	Combined +	Total −	Total 0	Total +
Therapist	0	2	1	1	1	1	0	0	0	0	2	1	0	0	0	1	5	3
Index	0	0	0	0	0	0	0	0	0	0	0	0	0	1	2	0	1	2
Total	0	2	1	1	1	1	0	0	0	0	2	1	0	1	2	1	6	5

[a]+ = therapist self-acceptance associated with good outcome, or therapist self-rejection and control associated with poor outcome; 0 = no significant association; − = therapist self-rejection and control associated with good outcome, or therapist self-acceptance associated with poor outcome.
[b]Client-centered therapy.
[c]Broad-spectrum behavior therapy.
[d]Interpersonal behavior therapy.
[e]Therapist "spontaneous self."
[f]Therapist "self-accepting and exploring" and "self-nourishing and cherishing."
[g]Therapist "self-indicting and oppressing" and "self-rejecting and destroying."

findings summarized in Table 8.51 are significantly positive, these 23 findings (in contrast to one negative finding) nevertheless suggest that this factor may contribute to therapeutic success under some conditions. Table 8.52 also shows mixed results for the related variable of therapist *self-acceptance and assurance versus self-rejection and control.*

The self-relatedness of participants in therapy is a process factor that research to date has found associated with outcome—most notably the patient's self-relatedness. This resonates with related findings concerning the patient's suitability for treatment, style of participation in the therapeutic relationship, and modes of cognitive and behavioral processing during sessions. These reflect the patient's possession of positive characteristics that permit more constructive involvement in treatment. To those who have, much appears to be given.

IN-SESSION IMPACTS

Like outcomes, in-session impacts may be positive or negative in quality. *Therapeutic realizations* is

the phase we use to denote patients' positive in-session impacts, and Table 8.53 shows a consistent association of therapeutic realizations with outcome. Of the 79 findings, 67% show a positive association with outcome (the single negative finding reflects an interaction with session frequency in a treatment emphasizing emotional catharsis). However, that 32% of the findings are statistically nonsignificant suggests that in-session impacts are not identical with outcome; even with the 18 findings relating postsession outcome to therapeutic realizations, 24% are nonsignificant.

A few process–outcome findings concerning in-session impacts on therapists suggest that *therapist accruals* (e.g., feelings of efficacy and satisfaction vs. frustration and discouragement) are also positively associated with patient outcome (Orlinsky & Howard, 1967, 1975). Such therapist feelings are more likely the result rather than the cause of therapeutic outcome, but—if supported by further research—they may provide therapists with another clinically useful indicator of their patients' progress.

Text continues on p. 346.

N.B. For Table 8.53: *Process* refers to the observational perspective from which process was assessed. P = patient ratings; T = therapist ratings; R = ratings by nonparticipant raters; I = objectively determined index of process, for example, assignment to a specified treatment condition. *Outcome* refers to the observational perspective from which outcome was evaluated. P = patient ratings; T = therapist ratings; R = ratings by independent raters; S = psychometric test score or objective index; CI = combined perspectives index. *ES* = effect size. na = data not available; a/c = data available but not computed.

TABLE 8.53   Therapeutic realizations

Reference	Process	Outcome	Finding[a]	ES
Buckley et al. (1981)[b]	P	P	+	.21
Bugge et al. (1985)	P	P	+	.49
Cadbury et al. (1990)[c]	P	P	+	na
Dziewas (1980)/Dziewas et al. (1979)	P	CI	+	.39
Dziewas (1980)/Dziewas et al. (1979)	R	CI	+	.31
Eckert & Biermann-Ratjen (1985)[d]	P	T	+	na
Eckert et al. (1977)	P	S	+	.25
Grawe (1989)/Grawe et al. (1990)[e1]	I	CI	+	.24
Grawe (1989)/Grawe et al. (1990)[e2]	I	CI	+	.64
Grawe (1989)/Grawe et al. (1990)[e3]	I	CI	+	.31
Hill et al. (1989)[f]	P	P	0	na
Hill et al. (1989)[f]	P	R	0	na
Hill et al. (1989)[f]	P	S	0	na
Hill et al. (1989)[f]	T	P	0	na
Hill et al. (1989)[f]	T	R	0	na
Hill et al. (1989)[f]	T	S	0	na
Jones et al. (1988)	R	S	+	a/c
Jones et al. (1992)[g]	R	CI	+	.19
Jones et al. (1992)[b]	R	CI	+	.37
Jones et al. (1992)[h]	R	CI	+	.12
Kahn et al. (1986)[i]	P	CI	+	a/c
Kolden (1991)	P	R	0	.00
Llewelyn (1988)[j]	P	CI	+	a/c
Llewelyn (1988)[k]	T	CI	+	a/c
Llewelyn et al. (1988)	P	R	0	na
Llewelyn et al. (1988)	P	S	0	na
Sander et al. (1973)	P	S	+	.18
Stiles et al. (1990)/Shapiro et al. (1985)[l]	P	S	0	.02
Stiles et al. (1990)/Shapiro et al. (1985)[m]	P	S	0	.00
Stiles et al. (1990)/Shapiro et al. (1985)[l]	T	S	+	.15
Stiles et al. (1990)/Shapiro et al. (1985)[m]	T	S	+	.21
Stiles et al. (1990)/Shapiro et al. (1985)[l]	R	S	0	.05
Stiles et al. (1990)/Shapiro et al. (1985)[m]	R	S	+	.15
Westermann et al. (1983)[n]	P	CI	+	na
Willutzki (1991)	I	CI	+	.20
INTERACTION EFFECTS				
Kolden (1991)[o]	P	R	+	.06
Kozak et al. (1988)[p]	P	CI	0	.08
Kozak et al. (1988)[p]	I	CI	+	.18
Llewelyn (1988)[q]	I	CI	+	a/c
Llewelyn et al. (1988)[r]	P	R	+	.29
[cited but untabulated in 1986]				
Cabral et al. (1975)	R	P	0	a/c
Cabral et al. (1975)	R	R	0	a/c
Nichols (1974)	R	P	+	a/c
Nichols (1974)	R	S	0	a/c
Werman et al. (1976)	P	P	+	na

Reference	Process	Outcome	Finding[a]	ES
INTERACTION EFFECTS				
Bierenbaum et al. (1976)[e]	I	R	+	a/c
Bierenbaum et al. (1976)[e]	I	R	−	a/c
[postsession outcome]				
Ambühl (1993)[t]	R	CI	+	.28
Hill et al. (1989)[f]	P	P	+	.20
Hill et al. (1989)[f]	P	R	0	na
Hill et al. (1989)[f]	P	S	+	.13
Hill et al. (1989)[f]	T	P	0	na
Hill et al. (1989)[f]	T	R	+	.11
Hill et al. (1989)[f]	T	S	0	na
Kolden (1991)	P	R	+	.12
Lietaer (1992)/Lietaer & Neirinck (1987)	P	P	+	na
Orlinsky & Howard (1967, 1975)	P	P	+	na
Orlinsky & Howard (1967, 1975)	P	T	+	na
Orlinsky & Howard (1967, 1975)	T	P	+	na
Orlinsky & Howard (1967, 1975)	T	T	+	na
Stiles & Snow (1984)[l]	P	P	+	.13
Stiles & Snow (1984)[l]	T	P	0	.00
Stiles & Snow (1984)[m]	P	P	+	.52
Stiles & Snow (1984)[m]	T	P	+	.12
INTERACTION EFFECTS				
Kolden (1991)[u]	P	R	0	.04

SUMMARY A: TO 1985 — OUTCOME

Process	Patient −	Patient 0	Patient +	Therapist −	Therapist 0	Therapist +	Rater −	Rater 0	Rater +	Score −	Score 0	Score +	Combined −	Combined 0	Combined +	Total −	Total 0	Total +
Patient	0	1	0	0	0	1	0	0	1	0	0	0	0	0	0	0	1	2
Therapist	0	1	0	0	1	1	0	0	0	0	0	0	0	0	0	0	2	1
Rater	0	0	2	0	0	5	0	0	1	0	1	3	0	0	0	0	1	11
Total	0	2	2	0	1	7	0	0	2	0	1	3	0	0	0	0	4	14

SUMMARY B: TOTAL TO DATE — OUTCOME

Process	Patient −	Patient 0	Patient +	Therapist −	Therapist 0	Therapist +	Rater −	Rater 0	Rater +	Score −	Score 0	Score +	Combined −	Combined 0	Combined +	Total −	Total 0	Total +
Patient	0	2	8	0	0	2	0	5	4	0	4	3	0	1	4	0	12	21
Therapist	0	4	1	0	1	1	0	1	1	0	2	2	0	0	1	0	8	6
Rater	0	1	3	0	0	5	0	1	1	0	3	5	0	0	5	0	5	19
Index	0	0	0	0	0	0	1	0	1	0	0	0	0	0	6	1	0	7
Total	0	7	12	0	1	8	1	7	7	0	9	10	0	1	16	1	25	53

[a] + = positive session impact positively related to outcome, or negative session impact negatively related to outcome; 0 = no significant association; − = negative session impact positively related to outcome, or positive session impact negatively related to outcome.

[b] Insight.

[c] Three-fifths of patients in a successful anxiety management group indicated "universality" as the "most helpful" nonspecific therapeutic factor.

[d] Inpatient group therapy.

[e] Process variable constructed from patient and therapist perspectives jointly in (1) client-centered therapy, (2) broad-spectrum behavior therapy, and (3) interpersonal behavior therapy.

[f] 10-session focused Gestalt therapy involving six patients with active rheumatoid arthritis.

[g] Help from therapist.

[h] Catharsis.

[i] Inpatient group therapy.

[j] Clients' reports of problem solving (but not other positive or negative impacts).

continued

Footnote continued from Table 8.53

[k]Therapists' reports of client "reassurance/relief" (but not other positive or negative impacts).

[l]Rated "depth" (power, value) of session.

[m]Rated "smoothness" (comfort, safety) of session.

[n]Patient "learning" in group psychotherapy.

[o]"Therapeutic realizations" in sessions 1, 3, 7, and 10.

[p]Greater habituation across exposure sessions during exposure therapy of obsessive-compulsive patients was associated with better outcomes for physiological (but only marginally for subjective) process measures.

[q]Significant differences between clients and therapists in reported frequency of "insight," "clarification," and "reassurance/relief" found in low outcome cases.

[r]Retrospective (but not session by session) report of "negative thoughts" was associated with poorer outcome in prescriptive (but not exploratory) treatment.

[s]Better outcome associated with higher level of emotional catharsis (laughing, crying, anger) in brief emotive psychotherapy in weekly 1-hour sessions, but with lower level of emotional catharsis in biweekly half-hour sessions.

[t]Effect size excluding the strong influence of therapeutic bond.

[u]"Therapeutic realizations" in sessions 1, 3, and 7 (but not session 10).

SEQUENTIAL FLOW

The temporal aspect of process was represented in the last edition of this *Handbook* only by findings assessing the relation of outcome to the total amount of therapy received. Since that time, several factors have enabled process–outcome research to penetrate further into this area. The availability of powerful desktop computers and sophisticated statistical programs has made it easier for investigators to explore complex sequential contingencies among response units, both within sessions and across series of sessions.

Session Development

Table 8.54 lists a number of findings concerning the relation of outcome to patterns of *session development*. Since the nature of the sequentially connected units varies, the findings are simply code 0 or + to indicate whether an association with outcome was established, and the table footnotes are used to indicate the types of sequential dependencies that were studied. These ranged from relatively external factors that do not seem to have much inherent relation to outcome (e.g., topic of conversation) to others that are theoretically more interesting (e.g., cohesiveness in group therapy sessions and mode of cognitive processing). Although initial results are mixed, these studies represent a promising start. Future studies of session development in relation to outcome might find it profitable to focus particularly on postsession assessments of outcome.

Stage of Treatment

An increased interest in studying brief (e.g., 12–26 sessions) time-limited therapies has made it possible to standardize the duration of treatment and to subdivide the therapeutic course quantitatively, albeit somewhat arbitrarily, into stages or phases (e.g., by categorizing sessions 1–4, 5–15, and 16–20 as early, middle, and late stages). Findings on the differential effects of *stage of treatment* on outcome are listed in Table 8.55, coded 0 or + to indicate whether an association with outcome was established, with footnotes to provide an inkling as to what each of the findings involved. Overall, 74% of 54 findings show a significant association with outcome, indicating the general importance of time in treatment. It remains to be seen how much these findings, based on relatively brief time-limited treatment, apply to longer therapies of unlimited and typically quite variable duration, where it is impossible to define stages in purely quantitative terms. One problem that will have to be dealt with in less temporally constrained therapies is the highly idiosyncratic patterning that emerges in different dyads (Czogalik & Hettinger, 1987, 1988). A potentially useful method for analyzing stage effects in terms of qualitative changes in process, and in therapies of unlimited duration, is the state-sequential strategy described by Runyan (1982) for life-history studies.

Treatment Duration

The duration of therapy is usually measured by counting the number of sessions in a treatment episode. Although rarely the main focus of research, *treatment duration* has often been studied along with other variables because it seemed so easy to measure. Table 8.56 summarizes a grand total of 156 findings on the association of treatment duration and outcome, of which 100 (64%) are significantly positive (including some findings with a substantial ES). The handful of negative findings seem to be explained by special circumstances, for example, the fact that patients who

Text continues on p. 352.

N.B. For Tables 8.54 through 8.56: *Process* (in Table 8.54 only) refers to the observational perspective from which process was assessed. P = patient ratings; T = therapist ratings; R = ratings by nonparticipant raters; I = objectively determined index of process, for example, assignment to a specified treatment condition. *Outcome* refers to the observational perspective from which outcome was evaluated. P = patient ratings; T = therapist ratings; R = ratings by independent raters; S = psychometric test score or objective index; CI = combined perspectives index. *ES* = effect size. na = data not available; a/c = data available but not computed.

TABLE 8.54 Session development

Reference	Process	Outcome	Finding[a]	ES
Budman et al. (1989)[b]	I	P	+	.44
Budman et al. (1989)[b]	I	T	0	na
Budman et al. (1989)[b]	I	R	0	na
Budman et al. (1989)[b]	I	S	+	.64
Lansford (1986)[c]	I	R	+	.92
Schulte (in press)[d]	I	CI	+	.13
Tracey (1985)[e]	I	CI	+	a/c
Tracey (1987)[f]	R	CI	0	a/c
Tracey (1987)[g]	R	CI	+	a/c
INTERACTION EFFECTS				
Schulte (in press)[h]	I	CI	+	.12
Schulte (in press)[i]	I	CI	+	.11
Schulte (in press)[j]	I	CI	+	.12
[postsession outcome]				
Wampold & Kim (1989)[k]	I	P	+	.34
Wampold & Kim (1989)[k]	I	T	0	.10
Wampold & Kim (1989)[k]	I	R	0	.10
Wampold & Kim (1989)[l,g]	I	P	0	.13
Wampold & Kim (1989)[l,g]	I	T	0	.14
Wampold & Kim (1989)[l,g]	I	R	0	.06

SUMMARY: TOTAL TO DATE — OUTCOME

Process	Patient 0	+	Therapist 0	+	Rater 0	+	Score 0	+	Combined 0	+	Total 0	+
Rater	0	0	0	0	0	0	0	0	1	1	1	1
Index	1	2	3	0	3	1	0	1	0	5	7	9
Total	1	2	3	0	3	1	0	1	1	6	8	10

[a] + = sequential effect positively related to outcome; 0 = no significant association.

[b] Cohesiveness among members related to outcome especially in first third of 90-minute sessions.

[c] Discussion of focal issue (but not dynamic "quality of focus") in alliance weakening/repair sequences was associated with positive outcome in short-term psychodynamic therapy.

[d] Poorer outcome at termination and 2-year follow-up was associated with "processing control" by therapists (defined as proportion of patient following "processing" initiations by therapist) in all stages of behavior therapy of phobias.

[e] Topic initiation and topic following in patient-therapist statement sequences showed successful counselors were more consistently influential on patient responses (i.e., statistically "dominant") in successful cases of time-limited counseling, but clients and counselors were not differentially "dependent" in regard to topic initiation and following in successful and unsuccessful cases.

[f] Amount of topic initiating and topic following in client verbal responses successful were unrelated to outcome in time-limited counseling, as were sequential (intrachain) consistency and interactive (interchain) patterns.

[g] Therapist verbal responses more often followed patient-initiated topics in successful as compared with unsuccessful cases of time-limited counseling, but were not different with respect to sequential (intrachain) consistency or interactive (interchain) pattern.

[h] Outcome at termination was positively associated with "topic control" by therapists during early (but not middle or late) sessions, but outcome at follow-up was positively associated with "topic control" by therapists during late (but not early or middle) sessions.

[i] "Processing control" by patients in late (but not early or middle) sessions was negatively associated with outcome.

[j] "Topic control" by patients in late (but not early or middle) sessions was positively associated with outcome at follow-up.

[k] Sequence of "client experiencing" followed by "counselor minimal encourager" within sessions of a single case.

[l] Sequence of "client description" followed by "counselor minimal encourager" within sessions of a single case.

TABLE 8.55   Stage of treatment

Reference	Outcome	Finding[a]	ES
Beckham (1989)[b]	S	+	a/c
Budman et al. (1989)[c]	P	0	na
Budman et al. (1989)[c]	T	0	na
Budman et al. (1989)[c]	R	0	na
Budman et al. (1989)[c]	S	0	na
DeRubeis et al. (1990)[d]	S	+	.28
Fennell & Teasdale (1987)[e]	R	+	a/c
Fennell & Teasdale (1987)[e]	S	+	a/c
Howard et al. (1992)[f]	CI	+	na
Klee et al. (1990)[g]	S	+	a/c
Luborsky et al. (1983)[h]	CI	+	a/c
Martin et al. (1986)[i]	P	+	a/c
Martin et al. (1986)[i]	T	0	na
Miller et al. (1983)[j]	T	0	a/c
Schwartz & Bernard (1981)[b]	P	+	.29
Schwartz & Bernard (1981)[b]	T	0	.08
Schwartz & Bernard (1981)[k]	P	0	.00
Schwartz & Bernard (1981)[k]	T	0	.08
Schwartz & Bernard (1981)[l]	P	+	.40
Schwartz & Bernard (1981)[l]	T	+	.23
Taurke et al. (1990)[m]	CI	+	a/c
Tracey (1987)[n]	CI	+	a/c
Tracey (1989)[o]	CI	+	a/c
Tracey & Dundon (1988)[p]	CI	+	na
Tracey & Ray (1984)[q]	CI	+	na
Willutzki & Schulte (1991)[r]	CI	+	.27

INTERACTION EFFECT

Reference	Outcome	Finding[a]	ES
Coady (1991a)[s]	CI	+	a/c
DeRubeis & Feeley (1990)[t]	S	+	.28
DeRubeis & Feeley (1990)[u]	S	+	.21
Frank & Gunderson (1990)[v]	CI	+	.15
Horowitz et al. (1984)[w]	R	+	.10
Horvath & Symonds (1991)[x]	CI	0	.01
Kolden (1991)[y]	R	+	.06
Kozak et al. (1988)[z]	CI	0	.08
Kozak et al. (1988)[z]	CI	+	.18
Schindler (1991)[aa]	S	+	na
Schindler (1991)[bb]	S	+	na
Schindler (1991)[cc]	S	+	na
Schulte (in press)[dd]	CI	+	.15
Schulte (in press)[ee]	CI	+	.09
Schulte (in press)[ff]	CI	+	.11
Schulte & Künzel (1991)[gg]	T	+	.44
Schulte & Künzel (in press)[hh]	CI	+	.13
Schulte & Künzel (1991)[ii]	P	+	.29
Schulte (in press)/Schulte & Künzel (in press)[jj]	CI	+	.19
Schulte (in press)/Schulte & Künzel (in press)[kk]	CI	+	.17
Schulte (in press)/Schulte & Künzel (in press)[ll]	CI	+	.10
Wiseman et al. (in press)[mm]	CI	+	a/c
Wiseman et al. (in press)[nn]	CI	+	a/c

META-ANALYSIS [not tallied]

Reference	Outcome	Finding[a]	ES
Howard et al. (1986)[oo]	•	+	a/c

[cited but untabulated in 1986]

Reference	Outcome	Finding[a]	ES
Schauble & Pierce (1974)[pp]	R	+	a/c

[postsession outcome]

Reference	Outcome	Finding[a]	ES
Hill et al. (1989)	P	+	a/c

Reference	Outcome	Finding[a]	ES
Hill et al. (1989)	R	0	a/c
Hill et al. (1989)	S	0	a/c
INTERACTION EFFECT			
Kolden (1991)[qq]	R	0	.04

SUMMARY: TOTAL TO DATE   *OUTCOME*

	Patient		Therapist		Rater		Score		Combined		Total	
	0	+	0	+	0	+	0	+	0	+	0	+
Stage	2	5	5	2	3	4	2	9	2	20	14	40

[a]+ = stage associated with outcome; 0 = no significant association.

[b]Early session improvement.

[c]Cohesiveness in therapy groups in early versus late sessions (1–7 versus 8–15).

[d]Improvement in dysfunctional cognition from early to middle treatment predicted improvement in depressive symptoms from middle to end of treatment in short-term cognitive-behavioral therapy (but not pharmacotherapy).

[e]Rapid improvement in the early stage of cognitive-behavioral treatment was associated with better outcomes.

[f]Patients' reports of subjective well-being, symptomatic distress, and problematic life functioning after second, fourth, and seventeenth sessions of individual psychodynamic therapy indicated a progressive, stage-dependent quality of improvement across these outcome areas.

[g]Patients who improved showed a significant increase in positive contribution to therapeutic alliance from early to late in treatment.

[h]Quality of helping alliance improved from early to late sessions among most improved patients, but declined from early to late sessions among least improved patients in individual psychodynamic therapy.

[i]Middle and later sessions were rated more as effective than early sessions by clients (but not therapists).

[j]Time-limited individual therapy (12 sessions) divided into fourths.

[k]Improvement in middle sessions.

[l]Improvement in late sessions.

[m]Successful cases show an increasingly favorable balance of affect to defensiveness over the course of treatment in two dynamically oriented therapies, owing to an increasing differentiation between successful and unsuccessful cases in defensiveness during the last two quartiles of treatment.

[n]In successful cases of time-limited counseling, both clients and counselors initiated topics more often in the first and last thirds of treatment and less in the middle third of treatment, whereas clients and counselors in unsuccessful cases were more constant in initiating topics over the course of treatment; also, in successful cases, clients and counselors were more self-consistent in topic-initiating behavior during the last third of treatment, but not in the first or middle third of treatment.

[o]For successful as compared with unsuccessful cases, client session satisfaction over the course of treatment showed a curvilinear pattern (high-low-high) and therapist session satisfaction showed both linear and curvilinear (high-low-high) patterns.

[p]Successful cases in time-limited counseling showed a pattern of increasing, then stabilizing or declining, anticipation of and preference for "approval," "audience," and "collaborative relationship," over beginning, middle, and final thirds of treatment; whereas unsuccessful cases showed varied patterns over treatment.

[q]Successful cases in time-limited counseling showed a pattern of high-low-high patient-therapist complementarity, as assessed by topic following and topic initiation, over beginning, middle, and final thirds of treatment.

[r]Therapists' accurate perception of phobic patients' adaptive experiences (but not in phobic situations) was positively related to outcome, especially after the third session (the association still significant but markedly diminishing in strength toward the end of treatment).

[s]Interpersonal behaviors of patients with poorer outcomes were rated higher on "wall off and avoid" early in treatment, and higher on "watch and manage" late in treatment; they were also rated lower on "disclose and express" late in treatment and generally more "disaffiliative" late in treatment.

[t]Improvement in depressive symptoms predicted by adherence to concrete cognitive-behavioral methods (but not to abstract discussion of cognitive therapy rationale) early in treatment only.

[u]Improvement in depressive symptomatology was predicted by lower therapist "facilitative conditions" from early to middle of cognitive-behavioral treatment, but not from beginning to early in treatment or from middle to later in treatment.

[v]Nonchronic schizophrenics who made positive alliances in individual psychotherapy between 3 and 6 months of beginning treatment had better outcomes after 2 years.

[w]Therapist's "effort to clarify focus of treatment" early in treatment (but not at other times) was associated with better outcome.

[x]Relation of working alliance to outcome was not different when alliance was assessed in sessions 1–5 and at (or near) termination.

[y]Interaction of "therapeutic bond" and "patient self-relatedness" was predictive of positive outcome by session 10.

[z]Greater habituation across exposure sessions during exposure therapy of obsessive-compulsive patients was associated with better outcomes for physiological (but only marginally for subjective) process measures.

[aa]Patient "cooperation" in early but not later sessions was associated with better outcome.

[bb]Patient "defensiveness" in later but not early sessions was associated with poorer outcome.

continued

Footnote continued from Table 8.55

[cc]Therapist "support" in early and later (but not middle) sessions outcome was associated with better outcome.

[dd]Amount of "topic initiation" by patient in middle and late (but not early) sessions was positively associated with outcome at termination and 2-year follow-up.

[ee]Amount of "topic initiation" by therapist in early (but not middle or late) sessions was positively associated with outcome at termination (but not at 2-year follow-up).

[ff]Patient initiating/changing level of "processing" in early and middle (but not late) sessions was negatively associated with outcome at termination (but not at follow-up).

[gg]Positive outcome was strongly associated with therapists' sense of "control" in early (but only moderately in middle, and not in late) sessions.

[hh]Positive outcome at termination (but not at 2-year follow-up) was associated with therapists' sense of "control" in middle (but not early or late) sessions.

[ii]Positive outcome was strongly associated with patients' sense of "autonomy" in late (but only moderately in middle, and not in early) sessions.

[jj]Patients' sense of "autonomy" in late (but not early or middle) sessions was positively associated with outcome at termination.

[kk]Therapists' "controlling" behavior in late (but not early or middle) sessions was negatively related to outcome at termination.

[ll]Patients' "controlling" behavior in late (but not early or middle) sessions was negatively related to outcome at termination and follow-up.

[mm]Comparison of initial, middle, and termination phases in 12 session time-limited therapy of a successful and an unsuccessful case with the same therapist indicated (1) for patient behavior in the successful case, increasing level of VPPS "participation" and decreasing level of "psychic distress" and, in the unsuccessful case, decreasing level of "exploration" and increasing level of "dependency"; (2) for the therapist behavior in the successful case, increasing level of "warmth and friendliness" and increasing, then decreasing, level of "exploration."

[oo]Improvement was a negatively accelerated (log-linear) function of treatment duration.

[pp]Patients' internal (versus external) view of relationship problems in the last (but not the first) third of treatment was associated with better outcomes.

[qq]Interaction of "therapeutic bond" and "patient self-relatedness" in sessions 1, 3, 7, and 10.

[*]Varied outcome perspectives.

TABLE 8.56 Treatment duration

Reference	Outcome	Finding[a]	ES
Andrews (1990)[b]	P	0	na
Bennett (1986)	S	+	.35
Bugge et al. (1985)	P	+	.11
Bush et al. (1986)	CI	+	.12
Clementel-Jones et al. (1990)	R	+	.08
Erle (1979)	T	+	na
Friedman & West (1987)[c]	S	−	a/c
Gelso, Spiegel, & Mills (1983)[d1]	P	+	.18
Gelso, Spiegel, & Mills (1983)[d1]	T	+	.37
Gelso, Spiegel, & Mills (1983)[d2]	P	0	.04
Gelso, Spiegel, & Mills (1983)[d2]	T	+	.23
Gelso, Spiegel, & Mills (1983)[d3]	P	+	.24
Gelso, Spiegel, & Mills (1983)[d3]	T	0	.16
Goldstein et al. (1988)[e]	P	+	a/c
Harris (1986)	•	+	a/c
Hynan (1991)	P	+	a/c
Jones et al. (1986)[f]	P	+	.07
Jones et al. (1986)[f]	T	+	.12
Jones et al. (1986)[f]	P	+	.08
Jones et al. (1986)[f]	T	0	.03
Kang et al. (1991)[g]	CI	0	a/c
McNeill et al. (1987)[f]	P	+	.13
Perri et al. (1989)	S	+	a/c
Persons et al. (1988)[h]	S	0	a/c
Pilkonis et al. (1984)	T	0	a/c
Pilkonis et al. (1984)[i]	R	−	a/c
Pilkonis et al. (1984)[i]	S	−	a/c
Pilkonis et al. (1984)[j]	S	+	a/c

Reference	Outcome	Finding[a]	ES
Quintana & Holahan (1992)	T	0	a/c
Rudy et al. (1985)	P	0	na
Rudy et al. (1985)[k]	T	+	.25
Rudy et al. (1985)[k]	T	−	.14
Rudy et al. (1985)	S	0	na
Weber et al. (1985a)[l]	R	+	.22
Weber et al. (1985a)[m]	R	+	.09
Weber et al. (1985a)[l,n]	S	+	.19
Weber et al. (1985a)[m,n]	S	+	.05
Weber et al. (1985b)[l]	R	+	.16
Weber et al. (1985b)[m]	R	0	.07
Weber et al. (1985b)[l,n]	S	+	.53
Weber et al. (1985b)[m,n]	S	0	.00

INTERACTION EFFECTS

Gerin et al. (1987)[o]	R	+	.52

META-ANALYSIS [not tallied]

Bowers & Clum (1988)[p]	CI	+	.31
Casey & Berman (1985)[q]	CI	−	.08
Dobson (1989)	S	0	.08

SUMMARY A: TO 1985   *OUTCOME*

	Patient			Therapist			Rater			Score			Combined			Total		
	−	0	+	−	0	+	−	0	+	−	0	+	−	0	+	−	0	+
Long > Short	0	12	8	1	9	28	0	6	15	1	11	23	0	0	0	2	38	74

SUMMARY B: TOTAL TO DATE   *OUTCOME*

	Patient			Therapist			Rater			Score			Combined			Total		
	−	0	+	−	0	+	−	0	+	−	0	+	−	0	+	−	0	+
Long > Short	0	15	16	2	13	33	1	7	20	3	14	30	0	1	1	6	50	100

[a] + = treatment duration positively associated with outcome; 0 = no significant association; = treatment duration negatively associated with outcome.

[b] Limited range of 10–16 sessions for $n = 45$.

[c] Low users (1–2 sessions) in VA outpatient psychiatric clinics had better outcomes than high users (3+ sessions).

[d] Patients at 18-month follow-up, therapists at termination, for (1) 8-session time-limited treatment, (2) 16-session time-limited treatment, and (3) time-unlimited treatment.

[e] Longer attendance in partial hospital programs was associated with better outcomes.

[f] Computed for premature terminators only.

[g] Comparison of cocaine-abusers receiving once-weekly psychosocial treatment for fewer than 6 weeks versus 6 weeks.

[h] Treatment dropouts excluded.

[i] Longer treatment for patients assigned to individual, group, or conjoint therapies, according to their own preference, was associated with poorer outcomes as rated by patients' family members and by patients with regard to their family environment (but *not* by patients with regard to themselves); no association with treatment duration was found for patients randomly assigned to treatment modality.

[j] Longer treatment was associated with better outcomes on "private self-consciousness."

[k] Treatment duration positively associated with therapist-rated "change" but negatively associated with therapist-rated "success."

[l] Psychoanalyses.

[m] Psychoanalytically oriented psychotherapy.

[n] Outcome as measured by ego-strength scales.

[o] Improvement in nonpsychotic inpatients was associated with number of individual and group therapy sessions attended, whereas improvement in psychotic inpatients was associated with the number of family therapy sessions attended.

[p] ES related to duration in meta-analysis of 69 controlled studies of behavior therapy.

[q] Length of treatment negatively related to mean effect size for studies, explained by tendency of studies of shorter therapies to use outcome measures producing largest effect sizes.

require longer hospital treatment are usually more disturbed and more difficult to treat effectively. Three meta-analyses show mixed results, but these may also be explained by special circumstances. Overall, the findings indicate that patients tend to improve more the longer they stay in treatment, although the relationship between duration and outcome is clearly far from linear (Howard, Kopta, Krause, & Orlinsky, 1986).

CONCLUSION

An impressive amount of data on the relation of process to outcome has been amassed by psychotherapy researchers since 1950 — as witnessed by 2,354 separate findings summarized in Tables 8.57 and 8.58. The volume of process – outcome findings has more than doubled since the last edition of this *Handbook*, which reviewed approximately 1,100 findings. This increase is partly due to the inclusion of research previously published in German as well as some English language studies that were overlooked, but it mainly reflects an astonishing rate of growth in the number and activity of researchers since 1985. Newly reported findings were drawn from 192 papers published in 46 journals, 13 books, and a few conference papers, and the number would have been larger had we the time and resources to solicit conference papers systematically and to search for relevant material in *Dissertation Abstracts*.

This great accumulation of findings represents the emergence of a new stage of development in researched-based knowledge about psychotherapy. In the early years, every empirical study was preliminary and often yielded more insight about how to do better research than understanding of how to do better psychotherapy. For that reason many clinicians concluded that research on psychotherapy was of little interest or practical value and could be safely ignored in favor of reliance on traditional case reports and clinical theory. This situation has basically changed in just the last few years. The point has been reached where certain findings about comparative outcomes and the relation of various facets of process to outcome are so well replicated that they can be accorded the status of established facts. Clinicians and health care managers who choose to remain ignorant of the facts will increasingly put their professional competence at the risk. Researchers are not yet working within a single paradigm, but the pace of progress has quickened and the field has moved measurably closer to the state of "normal science" described by Kuhn (1970).

SUMMARY OF CONSISTENT FINDINGS

If *facts* are defined as consistently replicated empirical findings, what facts have been established by process – outcome research? Table 8.57 aggregates across outcome perspectives to show the percentages of significant positive process – outcome findings for process variables separately within each *observational perspective on process*. In other words, Table 8.57 indicates which process variables — assessed by patients, therapists, independent raters, or objective indexes — are responsive to outcome as evaluated from any combination of outcome perspectives. The table is designed to highlight process – outcome relations where the rate of significant positive findings is greater than 50% or, if there are only a few findings, where the rate of significant positive findings was substantially higher. It shows which process – outcome links are robust, in the sense that they have been observed from multiple process perspectives; which seem to be specialized, in the sense of having been observed from only one or two process perspectives; and, finally, which fail to show a significant process – outcome link from any process perspective or have not been sufficiently examined.

Therapeutic Contract

In and of themselves, the provisions of the *therapeutic contract* studied to date show no consistent relation to outcome. The cumulative record indicates that effective therapy can be conducted in different formats, under different schedules, and with varied term and fee arrangements. While the lack of consistent findings on some variables (group versus individual therapy or time-limited versus unlimited treatment) hold potential implications with regard to issues of cost-effectiveness, the available findings are far too sketchy to draw clinically responsible conclusions. Moreover, the relative lack of consistent differential relations between outcome and contractual provisions applies only to their study singly as main effects, and does not rule out the possibility of significant interaction effects when combinations of contractual provisions are studied (e.g., long-term once-weekly group therapy versus short-term twice-weekly individual therapy) or when the effects of contractual provisions on outcome are studied in conjunction with other variables (e.g., level of patient impairment).

The record shows a different situation with regard to aspects of *contractual implementation*. Several variables meet the criterion set for consistency of findings, including *goal consensus and expectational clarity*, *patient role preparation*, *patient verbal activity*, *patient suitability*, and *therapist skill*. Stabil-

Text continues on p. 359.

TABLE 8.57 Summary of consistent findings by process perspective

Table Number and Process Variable	TOTAL† %	n	Patient %	n	Therapist %	n	Rater %	n	Index %	n
I. THERAPEUTIC CONTRACT										
A. Contractual Provisions										
8.2 Collectivity: Dyad vs. group/family	20%	30	—	—	—	—	—	—	—	30
8.3 Schedule: Weekly vs. other	16%	25	—	—	—	—	—	—	—	25
8.4 Term: Time-limited vs. unlimited	33%	12	—	—	—	—	—	—	—	12
8.5 Fee: Normal vs. reduced	25%	12	—	—	—	—	—	—	—	12
*Use of co-therapist	0%	2	—	—	—	—	—	—	—	2
*Use of patient self-monitoring	67%	3	—	—	—	—	—	—	—	3
B. Contractual Implementation										
8.6 Goal consensus/clarity	51%	35	63%	8	—	7	—	8	67%	12
*Timeliness vs. delay	43%	14	—	—	—	—	—	—	—	14
8.7 Patient role preparation	57%	42	—	—	—	—	—	—	57%	42
8.8 Therapist verbal activity	37%	35	—	5	—	3	—	12	—	15
*Patient verbal activity	64%	14	—	—	—	—	—	2	67%	12
8.9 Therapist skill	67%	36	59%	17	—	2	71%	17	—	—
8.10 Patient suitability	68%	40	75%	4	67%	27	67%	9	—	—
8.11 Procedure for termination	32%	19	—	—	—	8	—	6	—	5
*Use of supervision	40%	5	—	—	—	1	—	—	—	4
*Stability of arrangements	83%	6	—	1	—	—	100%	3	—	2
*Adherence to therapeutic norms	100%	3	—	1	—	—	—	2	—	—
II. THERAPEUTIC OPERATIONS										
A. Problem Presentation										
8.12 Focusing on life problems	64%	11	—	3	—	2	67%	6	—	—
8.13 Focusing on here-now involvement	26%	19	—	2	—	8	—	9	—	—
*Focusing on core personal relations	75%	8	—	2	—	2	100%	4	—	—
8.14 Cognitive and behavioral processes	87%	15	100%	4	—	2	75%	4	80%	5
B. Expert Understanding										
8.15 Focusing on patient problems	53%	19	—	2	—	8	67%	9	—	—
8.16 Focusing on patient affect	50%	18	—	—	—	1	—	17	—	—
8.17 Focusing on here-now	9%	11	—	—	—	—	—	11	—	—
8.18 Focusing on core personal relations and transference	37%	27	—	—	—	5	—	22	—	—
*Focusing on patient self-understanding	27%	11	—	—	—	5	—	6	—	—
C. Therapist Intervention										
8.19 Change strategies (heuristics)	50%	22	—	—	—	10	—	11	—	1
8.20 Paradoxical intention	100%	13	—	—	—	—	—	—	100%	13
8.21 Experiential confrontation	68%	22	60%	5	—	2	78%	9	—	6
8.22 Interpretation	63%	38	83%	6	—	10	65%	20	—	2
8.23 Exploration	39%	41	—	4	—	6	—	31	—	—
8.24 Support	34%	38	—	8	—	12	—	18	—	—
8.25 Reflection/clarification	7%	14	—	—	—	2	—	9	—	3
8.26 Self-disclosure	14%	14	—	3	—	1	—	9	—	1
*Advice	20%	5	—	—	—	1	—	4	—	—
D. Patient Cooperation										
8.27 Cooperation vs. resistance	69%	49	58%	12	73%	22	71%	14	—	1

continued

TABLE 8.57 *continued*

Table Number and Process Variable	TOTAL† %	n	Patient %	n	Therapist %	n	Rater %	n	Index %	n
					PROCESS PERSPECTIVE					
8.28 Patient total affective response	50%	10	—	5	100%	3	—	2	—	—
8.29 Positive affective response	100%	9	100%	3	100%	6	—	—	—	—
8.30 Negative affective response	26%	46	—	9	—	13	—	23	—	1
8.31 Self-exploration	30%	79	—	7	—	7	—	65	—	—
*Internalization of therapist function	100%	3	—	2	—	1	—	—	—	—

III THERAPEUTIC BOND
A. Global Relational Quality

Table Number and Process Variable	TOTAL† %	n	Patient %	n	Therapist %	n	Rater %	n	Index %	n
8.32 Therapeutic bond/cohesion	66%	132	77%	52	63%	32	67%	36	—	11
8.33 Therapist contribution to bond	53%	106	67%	43	58%	12	—	51	—	—
8.34 Patient contribution to bond	67%	55	100%	6	69%	16	61%	33	—	—

B. Personal Role-Investment

Table Number and Process Variable	TOTAL† %	n	Patient %	n	Therapist %	n	Rater %	n	Index %	n
8.35 Patient engagement	65%	54	68%	19	92%	13	—	22	—	—
8.36 Patient motivation	50%	28	80%	5	56%	16	—	7	—	—
8.37 Therapist engaged vs. detached	57%	37	78%	18	—	9	—	10	—	—
8.38 Therapist credible vs. unsure	59%	27	53%	15	60%	5	67%	6	—	1
*Reciprocal investment	75%	4	—	2	—	—	—	2	—	—

C. Interactive Coordination

Table Number and Process Variable	TOTAL† %	n	Patient %	n	Therapist %	n	Rater %	n	Index %	n
8.39 Therapist collaborative vs. directive/permissive	43%	46	64%	11	—	22	—	13	—	—
8.40 Patient collaborative vs. dependent/controlling	64%	42	75%	12	63%	16	57%	14	—	—

D. Communicative Contact

Table Number and Process Variable	TOTAL† %	n	Patient %	n	Therapist %	n	Rater %	n	Index %	n
8.41 Patient expressiveness	63%	51	55%	11	67%	9	61%	28	100%	3
8.42 Therapist empathy	54%	115	72%	47	—	19	—	43	83%	6
8.43 Therapist expressiveness	44%	16	—	3	—	—	—	10	—	3
8.44 Patient empathy	42%	12	100%	3	—	—	—	—	—	9
8.45 Reciprocal attunement	62%	42	83%	6	—	6	56%	9	67%	21

E. Mutual Affect

Table Number and Process Variable	TOTAL† %	n	Patient %	n	Therapist %	n	Rater %	n	Index %	n
8.46 Therapist affirmation of patient	56%	154	65%	63	—	39	52%	52	—	—
8.47 Patient affirmation of therapist	69%	59	64%	25	68%	22	78%	9	100%	3
8.48 Reciprocal affirmation	78%	32	73%	15	—	3	91%	11	100%	3

IV. SELF-RELATEDNESS
A. Patient Self-Relatedness

Table Number and Process Variable	TOTAL† %	n	Patient %	n	Therapist %	n	Rater %	n	Index %	n
8.49 Patient openness vs. defensiveness	80%	45	70%	10	90%	10	82%	22	—	3
8.50 Patient experiencing	51%	39	—	2	75%	4	—	33	—	—

B. Therapist Self-Relatedness

Table Number and Process Variable	TOTAL† %	n	Patient %	n	Therapist %	n	Rater %	n	Index %	n
8.51 Therapist self-congruence	38%	60	—	25	—	11	—	23	—	1
8.52 Therapist self-acceptance	42%	12	—	—	—	9	—	—	—	3

V. IN-SESSION IMPACT
A. Patient Impacts

Table Number and Process Variable	TOTAL† %	n	Patient %	n	Therapist %	n	Rater %	n	Index %	n
8.53 Therapeutic realizations	67%	79	64%	33	—	14	79%	24	88%	8

B. Therapist Impacts

Table Number and Process Variable	TOTAL† %	n	Patient %	n	Therapist %	n	Rater %	n	Index %	n
*Therapist accruals	100%	4	—	2	—	2	—	—	—	—

Table Number and Process Variable	PROCESS PERSPECTIVE									
	TOTAL†		Patient		Therapist		Rater		Index	
	%	n	%	n	%	n	%	n	%	n
VI. SEQUENTIAL FLOW										
A. Session Development										
8.54 Sequential patterns	56%	18	—	—	—	—	—	2	56%	16
B. Therapeutic Course										
8.55 Stage of treatment	74%	54	—	—	—	—	—	—	74%	54
8.56 Treatment duration	64%	156	—	—	—	—	—	—	64%	156

†Percentages for process perspectives are cited when frequency of significant positive findings is substantial; i.e., 3 of 3, 3 of 4, 3 of 5, 4 of 6, and over 50% for 7 or more findings. 'Positive' finding indicates 'high' process level associated with 'better' outcome, or 'low' process level associated with 'poorer' outcome.

*Mentioned in text but not tabulated.

TABLE 8.58 Summary of consistent findings by outcome perspective

Table Number and Process Variable	OUTCOME PERSPECTIVE											
	TOTAL†		Patient		Therapist		Rater		Score		Combined	
	%	n	%	n	%	n	%	n	%	n	%	n
I. THERAPEUTIC CONTRACT												
A. Contractual Provisions												
8.2 Collectivity: Dyad vs. group/family	20%	30	—	4	—	5	—	6	—	15	—	0
8.3 Schedule: Weekly vs. other	16%	25	—	7	—	3	—	2	—	13	—	0
8.4 Term: Time-limited vs. unlimited	33%	12	—	3	—	1	—	0	—	8	—	0
8.5 Fee: Normal vs. reduced	25%	12	—	4	—	4	—	0	—	3	—	1
*Use of co-therapist	0%	2	—	1	—	—	—	—	—	1	—	—
*Use of patient self-monitoring	67%	3	—	1	—	—	—	—	—	2	—	—
B. Contractual Implementation												
8.6 Goal consensus/clarity	51%	35	—	8	67%	9	—	5		11	—	2
*Timeliness vs. delay	43%	14	—	2	—	3	—	4	—	4	—	1
8.7 Patient role preparation	57%	42	—	14	63%	8	80%	5	67%	15	—	—
8.8 Therapist verbal activity	37%	35	—	7	—	8	—	5	—	10	80%	5
*Patient verbal activity	64%	14	—	3	—	2	—	2	100%	5	—	2
8.9 Therapist skillfulness	67%	36	57%	14	100%	6	63%	8	—	4	75%	4

continued

TABLE 8.58 *continued*

Table Number and Process Variable	TOTAL† %	n	OUTCOME PERSPECTIVE Patient %	n	Therapist %	n	Rater %	n	Score %	n	Combined %	n
8.10 Patient suitability	68%	40	—	7	82%	11	80%	10	64%	11	—	1
8.11 Procedure for termination	32%	19	—	2	—	4	—	7	—	6	—	—
*Use of supervision	40%	5	—	—	—	2	—	3	—	—	—	—
*Stability of arrangements	83%	6	—	1	—	1	—	2	—	2	—	—
*Adherence to therapeutic norms	100%	3	—	1	—	—	—	—	—	1	—	1

II. THERAPEUTIC OPERATIONS

A. Problem Presentation

Table Number and Process Variable	TOTAL† %	n	Patient %	n	Therapist %	n	Rater %	n	Score %	n	Combined %	n
8.12 Focusing on life problems	64%	11	—	4	—	1	—	3	—	2	—	1
8.13 Focusing on here-now	26%	19	—	5	—	5	—	5	—	4	—	—
*Focusing on core personal relations	75%	8	—	2	—	2	—	1	100%	3	—	—
8.14 Cognitive and behavioral processing	87%	15	—	2	—	2	100%	3	100%	4	—	—

B. Expert Understanding

Table Number and Process Variable	TOTAL† %	n	Patient %	n	Therapist %	n	Rater %	n	Score %	n	Combined %	n
8.15 Focusing on patient problems	53%	19	—	2	—	2	—	7	71%	7	—	1
8.16 Focusing on patient affect	50%	18	—	1	—	4	80%	5	—	6	—	2
8.17 Focusing on here-now	9%	11	—	2	—	2	—	1	—	4	—	1
8.18 Focusing on core personal relations and transference	37%	27	—	2	—	3	—	10	—	8	—	4
*Focus on patient self-understanding	27%	11	—	—	—	1	—	6	—	4	—	—

C. Therapist Intervention

Table Number and Process Variable	TOTAL† %	n	Patient %	n	Therapist %	n	Rater %	n	Score %	n	Combined %	n
8.19 Change strategies (heuristics)	50%	22	—	3	100%	3	—	4	—	5	57%	7
8.20 Paradoxical intention	100%	13	100%	4	—	—	—	1	100%	7	—	1
8.21 Experiential confrontation	68%	22	86%	7	—	2	—	3	60%	10	—	—
8.22 Interpretation	63%	38	88%	8	—	8	75%	8	—	11	—	3

Table Number and Process Variable	OUTCOME PERSPECTIVE											
	TOTAL†		Patient		Therapist		Rater		Score		Combined	
	%	n	%	n	%	n	%	n	%	n	%	n
8.23 Exploration	39%	41	—	10	—	9	—	11	—	10	—	1
8.24 Support	34%	38	—	8	—	11	—	8	—	9	—	2
8.25 Reflection/clarification	7%	14	—	2	—	2	—	3	—	5	—	2
8.26 Self-disclosure	14%	14	—	—	—	1	—	3	—	4	—	6
*Advice	20%	5	—	—	—	—	—	1	—	3	—	1
D. Patient Cooperation												
8.27 Cooperation vs. resistance	69%	49	77%	13	64%	11	60%	10	75%	12	—	3
8.28 Patient total affective response	50%	10	75%	4	—	4	—	—	—	—	—	2
8.29 Positive affective response	100%	9	100%	5	100%	4	—	—	—	—	—	—
8.30 Negative affective response	26%	46	—	10	—	15	—	6	—	13	—	2
8.31 Self-exploration	30%	79	—	17	59%	17	—	14	—	30	—	1
*Internalization of therapist function	100%	3	—	2	—	1	—	—	—	—	—	—
III. THERAPEUTIC BOND												
A. Global Relational Quality												
8.32 Therapeutic bond/cohesion	66%	132	83%	30	71%	24	57%	23	55%	42	69%	13
8.33 Therapist contribution to bond	53%	106	67%	24	65%	23	—	11	—	47	—	1
8.34 Patient contribution to bond	67%	55	64%	11	80%	15	60%	10	61%	18	—	1
B. Personal Role-Investment												
8.35 Patient engagement	65%	54	71%	21	93%	15	—	7	—	10	—	1
8.36 Patient motivation	50%	28	—	8	67%	9	—	2	—	7	—	2
8.37 Therapist engaged vs. detached	57%	37	67%	12	82%	11	—	1	—	11	—	2
8.38 Therapist credible vs. unsure	59%	27	56%	9	—	4	100%	5	—	8	—	1
*Reciprocal investment	75%	4	—	1	—	—	—	1	—	2	—	—

continued

TABLE 8.58 *continued*

						OUTCOME PERSPECTIVE					
Table Number and Process Variable	TOTAL†		Patient		Therapist		Rater		Score		Combined	
	%	n	%	n	%	n	%	n	%	n	%	n
C. Interactive Coordination												
8.39 Therapist collaborative vs. directive/permissive	43%	46	67%	9	54%	13	—	4	—	15	—	5
8.40 Patient collaborative vs. dependent/controlling	64%	42	58%	12	80%	10	57%	7	—	8	100%	5
D. Communicative Contact												
8.41 Patient expressiveness	63%	51	67%	12	67%	15	—	6	62%	13	80%	5
8.42 Therapist empathy	54%	115	—	31	57%	23	—	13	58%	45	100%	3
8.43 Therapist expressiveness	44%	16	—	2	—	3	—	1	57%	7	—	3
8.44 Patient empathy	42%	12	—	3	—	4	—	1	—	2	—	2
8.45 Reciprocal attunement	62%	42	69%	13	71%	14	—	6	—	9	—	0
E. Mutual Affect												
8.46 Therapist affirmation of patient	56%	154	54%	37	72%	39	52%	25	—	50	—	3
8.47 Patient affirmation of therapist	69%	59	73%	15	80%	20	60%	5	—	15	100%	4
8.48 Reciprocal affirmation	78%	32	92%	12	60%	5	71%	7	71%	7	—	1
IV. SELF-RELATEDNESS												
A. Patient Self-Relatedness												
8.49 Patient openness vs. defensiveness	80%	45	80%	5	100%	9	67%	6	79%	14	73%	11
8.50 Patient experiencing	51%	39	—	6	73%	11	—	2	—	18	—	2
B. Therapist Self-Relatedness												
8.51 Therapist self-congruence	38%	60	—	13	60%	10	—	3	—	32	—	2
8.52 Therapist self-acceptance	42%	12	—	3	—	3	—	—	—	3	—	3
V. IN-SESSION IMPACT												
A. Patient Impacts												
8.53 Therapeutic realizations	67%	79	63%	19	88%	9	—	15	53%	19	94%	17

Table Number and Process Variable	TOTAL†		OUTCOME PERSPECTIVE									
			Patient		Therapist		Rater		Score		Combined	
	%	n	%	n	%	n	%	n	%	n	%	n
B. Therapist Impacts												
*Therapist accruals	100%	4	—	2	—	2	—	—	—	—	—	—
VI. SEQUENTIAL FLOW												
A. Session Development												
8.54 Sequential patterns	56%	18	—	3	100%	3	—	4	—	1	86%	7
B. Therapeutic Course												
8.55 Stage of treatment	74%	54	71%	7	—	7	57%	7	82%	11	91%	22
8.56 Treatment duration	64%	156	52%	31	69%	48	71%	28	64%	47	—	2

†Percentages for outcome perspectives are cited when frequency of significant positive findings is substantial; i.e., 3 of 3, 3 of 4, 3 of 5, 4 of 6, and over 50% for 7 or more findings. 'Positive' finding indicates 'high' process level associated with 'better' outcome, or 'low' process level associated with 'poorer' outcome.
*Mentioned in text but not tabulated.

ity of treatment arrangements and *therapist adherence to treatment model* show promise for future research. The relations of *patient suitability* and *therapist skill* to outcome stand out as particularly robust, considering the consistency of findings across the various process perspectives from which they have been studied. Taken together, these findings strongly imply that if an appropriately prepared patient who is viewed as suited to the form of treatment in question[13] becomes actively engaged in talking to a therapist who is seen as skillful,[14] the result of therapy will be viewed as beneficial.[15]

Therapeutic Operations

A larger number of findings is available with regard to the several facets of *therapeutic operations*. The *cognitive and behavioral processes* observable in the patient's *problem presentation* during sessions show a very high rate of significant positive association with outcome from every perspective that has been studied. These processes probably reflect factors that are also related to judgments of the patient's suitability for treatment. Although content does not seem as important as process in problem

[13]By the patient, the therapist, or an independent rater.
[14]By the patient or an independent rater.
[15]From some observational perspective.

presentation, the evidence to date suggests that patients might do well to focus their therapeutic conversations on *life problems* and *core personal relationships*.

Findings on the complementary aspects of expert understanding are less consistent, but at least suggest that therapists can be helpful by focusing their interventions on *patient problems* and, with sufficient tact and caution, on *patient's affective responses* during sessions.

By contrast, the evidence is more decisive concerning modes of therapist intervention. *Experiential confrontation* appears to be a potent form of intervention across several process perspectives. Viewed from the patient's and rater's (but *not* the therapist's) process perspectives, *interpretation* also appears to be a frequently beneficial intervention. The experimental evidence on *paradoxical intention* is remarkably consistent, demonstrating a very robust association with outcome in situations where it can be used appropriately. Other therapist interventions and response modes show a less consistent association with outcome.

Process – outcome findings amply document the importance of patient cooperation with therapist interventions. The evidence is especially strong with regard to *patient cooperation versus resistance* across three independent process perspectives but is also very consistent for *positive affective arousal*

Therapeutic Bond

The strongest evidence linking process to outcome concerns the *therapeutic bond* or alliance, reflecting more than 1,000 process–outcome findings. Table 8.57 shows high rates of significant positive association for large numbers of these findings across multiple process perspectives for the bond as a whole and for its various aspects—role investment, interactive coordination, communicative contact, and affective attitude. This is especially notable from the *patient's perspective* on the relationship, where 16 of the 18 variables studied (representing a total of more than 350 findings) exceed the 50% criterion for consistency of process–outcome linkage, usually by a substantial margin.

Self-Relatedness

Equally strong evidence links outcome to *patient openness versus defensiveness*. The four process perspectives on this variable provide convincing evidence about the salience of this factor, which probably should be seen in conjunction with other patient variables, such as *patient suitability for treatment*, *patient cooperation* with therapist interventions, and *patient contribution to the bond* (role *engagement* and interactive *collaboration* in terms of teamwork, *expressiveness* and *affirmation* in terms of rapport). Taken together, they document the critical importance of the patient's contribution to treatment—and, by implication, of the role that therapists can play in helping patients, who are distressed and dysfunctional in their personal lives, make a constructive contribution to their own treatment.

In-Session Impact

A consistent relation of *therapeutic realizations* (patients' positive in-session impacts) to outcome is evident from every process perspective except that of therapists. This lacuna in therapists' perceptiveness was particularly noticeable with respect to aspects of their own participation, such as the use of interpretive interventions and their own contributions of engagement, collaborativeness, empathy, and affirmation to the therapeutic bond. Perhaps because their role in treatment is psychologically involving, therapists seem not to discriminate the relatedness of certain process factors to outcome.

Sequential Flow

The study of temporal factors in relation to outcome is at an early but very promising stage of development, except with respect to overall length of therapy. A large body of findings already indicates that longer *treatment duration* is very generally (though not linearly) associated with better outcome. Although positive effects can be documented for relatively brief episodes of psychotherapy, process–outcome research as well as follow-up outcome data suggest that patients often seek and generally benefit from additional care. This fact contradicts the belief of many supporters of short-term treatment, whose enthusiastic advocacy of brief therapy may be based more on financial than on scientific considerations.

Outcome Perspectives

A complementary view of consistent process–outcome findings can be formed by aggregating percentages of significant positive associations across process perspectives and examining the rates for each variable within separate *outcome perspectives* (see Table 8.58). This analysis identifies areas of consensus and divergence in outcome assessments formulated by patients, therapists, external raters, and psychometric measures (e.g., Strupp et al., 1977).

It is especially interesting to ask which aspects of process are most salient when outcome is assessed from the *patient's perspective*. Table 8.58 indicates that, for patients, outcome is consistently related to 24 process variables, 13 of which reflect the importance of the therapeutic bond. *Mutual affirmation*, *communicative attunement*, and *global relational quality* reflect joint aspects of the bond. Significant patient relational variables include the *patient's contribution to the bond*, role *engagement*, interactive *collaboration*, *expressiveness* in communication, and *affirmation of the therapist*. From the patient's outcome perspective, important therapist relational variables include such parallel factors as the *therapist's contribution to the bond*, role *engagement*, *credibility versus unsureness*, interactive *collaboration*, and *affirmation of the patient*. With regard to other process aspects, outcome as assessed by patients is consistently associated with therapist interventions such as *interpretation*, *experiential confrontation*, and *paradoxical intention*, complemented by *patient cooperation* and (positive and total) *affective arousal*. *Therapist skillfulness* also makes a significant difference, as does *patient openness* and the experience of *therapeutic realizations* (positive in-session impacts). Among temporal factors, *stage of treatment* and *treatment duration* tends to be positively associated with outcome for patients.

Table 8.58 also indicates that 28 process variables were important from the *therapist's perspective* on outcome, of which 18 overlap with the list for patients and 10 do not. This indicates a theoretically interesting situation in which areas of convergence and divergence must both be explained. Patient and therapist outcome perspectives are convergent with regard to the global relational quality and numerous specific aspects of the *therapeutic bond*, as well as *therapist skillfulness*, *patient cooperation*, *patient positive affect*, *patient openness*, *therapeutic realizations*, and *treatment duration*. Areas of divergence that are readily identified include *goal consensus*, *role preparation*, *patient suitability*, *change strategies*, *patient self-exploration*, *patient motivation*, and therapist *empathy*, patient experiencing, and *therapist self-congruence*—all consistently significant in *therapists' but not patients' evaluations* of outcome. On the other hand, findings that were consistently significant from the *patient's but not the therapist's perspective* on outcome included the therapist interventions of *paradoxical intention*, *experiential confrontation*, and *interpretation*, as well as *patient total affective response*, *therapist credible versus unsure*, and *stage of treatment*. What therapists do, when they do it, and whether they are credible in doing it all clearly matter to patients, as does the level of the patient's emotional involvement in the process.

Reference to Tables 8.57 and 8.58 shows that 11 process–outcome variables are very robustly linked to outcome, in the sense that significant associations are found across *multiple* observational perspectives for *both* process and outcome assessments. These are *patient suitability*, *patient cooperativeness vs. resistance*, global *therapeutic bond/group cohesion*, *patient contribution to the bond*, *patient interactive collaboration*, *patient expressiveness*, *patient affirmation of the therapist*, *reciprocal affirmation*, *patient openness versus defensiveness*, *therapeutic realizations*, and *treatment duration*.[16]

The quality of the patient's participation in therapy stands out as the most important determinant of outcome. The therapeutic bond, especially as perceived by the patient, is importantly involved in mediating the process–outcome link. The therapist's contribution toward helping the patient achieve a favorable outcome is made mainly through empathic, affirmative, collaborative, and self-congruent engagement with the patient, and the skillful application of potent interventions such as experiential confrontation, interpretation, and paradoxical intention. These consistent process–outcome relations, based on literally hundreds of empirical findings, can be considered *facts* estab-

lished by 40-plus years of research on psychotherapy; but, scientific understanding requires more than facts. It requires theoretical analysis and interpretation of the facts, and further tests of these analyses and interpretations by well constructed studies.

THE GENERIC MODEL OF PSYCHOTHERAPY AS INTEGRATIVE THEORY

Thus far we have used our conceptual model simply as the means to organize a very large number of process variables into a limited set of plausible categories. However, the model also proposes a set of hypotheses concerning the functional relations among input, process, and outcome variables that can be used to interpret the most consistent findings of process–outcome research. Figure 8.1 presents these hypotheses in graphic form. They are discussed briefly here; more detailed presentations can be found in Orlinsky and Howard (1986a, 1987) and Orlinsky (1989), and some examples of research generated by these hypotheses can be found in Ambühl (1993) and Kolden (1991).

Figure 8.1 is divided into upper, middle, and lower thirds. The top section specifies a set of input variables, which reflect the state of affairs in the environment of the therapeutic system prior to the beginning of treatment (or, once treatment has begun, prior to any particular therapy session). The institutional and cultural patterns of the society constitute an overarching context for psychotherapy. They exert a direct influence on the therapeutic delivery system and an indirect influence on the therapeutic contract via cultural ideals and models for care-giving relationships. The treatment setting is located within the treatment delivery system and has a more direct influence on the therapeutic contract.

The characteristics of the patients, therapists, and other contracting parties are the most proximal determinants of the therapeutic contract. Professional characteristics, such as the therapist's orientation and experience and the patient's treatment history, influence what the participants expect their roles to be and how they understand their goals and tasks. At the same time, their personal characteristics—for example, their respective self-concepts, relationship histories, and preferred modes of interpersonal behavior—also influence their interpersonal contributions to the therapeutic bond and their intrapersonal states of self-relatedness.

The central section of the diagram depicts a set

---

[16]Only one process perspective on treatment duration has been used, i.e., an objective index.

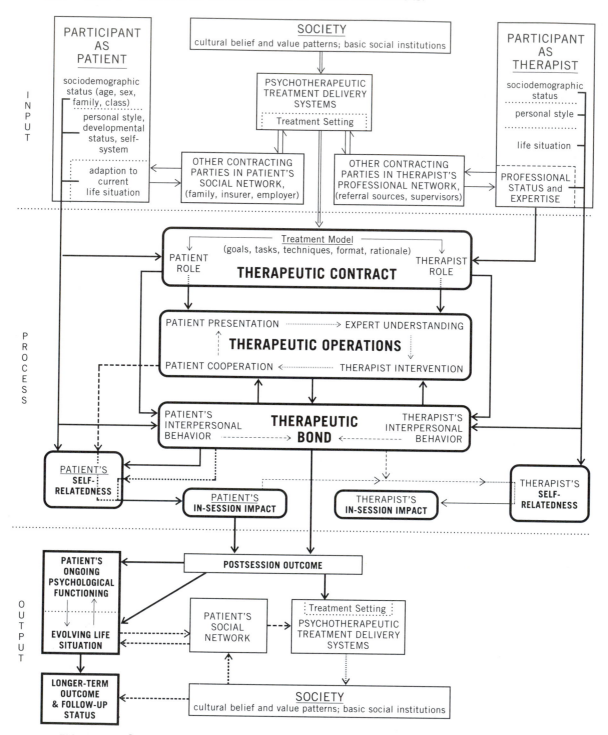

FIGURE 8.1   Generic model of psychotherapy: interrelation of input, process, and output components.

of hypotheses concerning the relationships among process variables, which provide possible explanations for the main findings of process–outcome research. For example, the influence of the therapeutic contract on therapeutic operations may be seen as mediated through implementation of the patient's role by such factors as the patient's suitability for the treatment and by role preparation. Suitability would be most importantly manifested in terms of cognitive and behavioral processes displayed in the patient's conversational activity. These factors reflect on the ability of patients to implement the patient role and to present themselves in ways that can be construed and influenced in terms of their therapists' treatment theories.

Therapists put their treatment models into action through performance of the therapist role. This involves construing selective aspects of patient presentation, formulating heuristic aims with regard to them, and attempting relevant technical interventions. With respect to outcome, the most influential therapist factors in contractual implementation are therapist skillfulness, maintaining stability in the therapeutic frame, and adherence to the treatment model.

The therapeutic contract is also depicted in Figure 8.1 as one determinant of the therapeutic bond. Patients' and therapists' contributions to the therapeutic bond are influenced by their normative conceptions of how they ought to relate to each other. The facets of the bond that are most sensitive to such normative influence are interactive coordination (e.g., should one person lead and the other follow, or should they collaborate equally in deciding how to proceed?) and mutual affect (e.g., how much of their feelings should they expect or permit themselves to show to each other?). The compatibility of the patient's and therapists's expectations about these matters determines the level of contractual consensus they achieve, and their expectations in turn influence how each contributes through interpersonal behavior to forming a therapeutic bond. This is a matter of some importance, since actual modes of interactive coordination and mutual affect in the therapeutic bond have been consistently linked with outcome.

Figure 8.1 proposes two routes by which process variables become linked to outcome. The main path leads from the patient's in-session impacts to immediate postsession outcome and constitutes the final link through which therapeutic operations and features of the therapeutic bond that affect the patient's self-concept become effective. In the long run, these represent the most important influences that therapy can have on the patient's life and personality. However, a second path leads directly from the therapeutic bond to immediate postsession outcome and reflects a direct short-term influence that the bond appears to have on the patient's morale. The association between outcome and in-session impact (therapeutic realization) is well supported by process–outcome research, especially in relation to session outcome. Years of research also confirm a consistent link between outcome and therapeutic bond. (Daily life events also affect the patient's immediate postsession outcome.)

However, the paths to in-session impact are more complex. The model proposes that the effectiveness of therapist interventions depends critically on the patient's cooperation and inner openness. This hypothesis explains two established process–outcome findings: first, the strong links observed between outcome and patient's positive cooperation and inner openness; second, the less consistent links observed between outcome and therapist interventions. Clinical experience makes it plausible to suppose that therapist interventions can be negated by patient resistance and discounted or deflected by patient defensiveness (although the consistent impact of paradoxical intention suggests that it has a potentiating effect on patient cooperation). Patients who are cooperative and open in this sense are more willing to participate, can more readily absorb the experiences generated by effective therapeutic operations, and thus are likely to benefit more from therapy. A parallel situation exists with respect to the control that the patient's self-relatedness exerts over indirect influence messages generated within the therapeutic bond by the therapist's contribution. If the patient is able to feel it, there is an implicit attribution of worth to the patient in the therapist's engagement, empathy, and affirmation, which in due time can enhance the patient's sense of self-worth. The patient's self-relatedness acts as a kind of psychological filter with respect to these interpersonal messages and with respect to the therapeutic operations that the patient accepts, which explains the consistent relation to outcome that this process aspect has in its own right.

Figure 8.1 also helps to explain the consistent finding of a link between the therapeutic bond and outcome. The diagram shows three ways in which such a link can be established. One was already traced directly to the patient's postsession outcome, relating the patient's morale to the overall quality of the bond and the state of mutual affect within it. A second path, traced through the patient's self-relatedness, involves implicit messages embodied in the therapist's interpersonal behavior that can have a powerful impact. Finally, the therapeutic bond is envisioned as having an influence on the patient's self-relatedness, so that over time the quality of the bond affects the level of patient openness versus defensiveness. To the extent that patients experience a positively stimulating and supportive bond, they should tend to become less defensive, and hence more likely to convert therapeutic operations and interpersonal messages from the therapist into positive in-session impacts. Thus, the therapeutic bond provides leverage from within the therapeutic system itself to influence the conditions under which therapy can be effective. (This may explain why building and maintaining a good therapeutic bond over a long period can be important in treating patients who, owing to personality types or pathology, have great difficulty engaging in interpersonal relationships.)

Given its centrality in the therapeutic system, it is interesting to note other factors that influence the quality of the therapeutic bond. Aside from the major input of patient and therapist personal characteristics, there is a positive feedback link between therapist's self-relatedness and the therapeutic bond, which explains how the ability to maintain an open or self-congruent state can function as an important part of the therapist's contribution to forming a good therapeutic bond.

The lower section of Figure 8.1 presents various output variables, reflecting the state of affairs in the environment of the therapeutic system following any particular therapy session and also subsequent to the termination of treatment. The complex connections here indicate a contingent path from immediate postsession outcomes to posttreatment outcome and beyond, to the impact of therapy on long-term patient characteristics. The finding of greatest relevance here is the relationship of treatment duration to outcome, since it implies that postsession outcomes must be recurrently experienced over a period of time if they are to be transformed into long-term outcomes. The findings indicate that this may not be so in every case, but it is probably most true when countervailing influences affect the patient's psychological functioning and life situation.

Much more can, should, and eventually will be said on all these points. Space here permits only a few final reflections.

L'ENVOI

We have examined the research literature diligently for empirical findings concerning the relation of process to outcome in psychotherapy. Although we undoubtedly missed some findings, we were able to gather a very large number — more than 2,300 overall from 1950 to 1992. More than half of these appeared in the last 7 years, indicating an astonishing rate of growth. The most remarkable example is research on the global quality of the therapeutic bond or alliance, which has added 100 new process–outcome findings in the period under review. This more than triples the number of previous findings, and it is not an isolated case. Five of the 55 primary data tables now summarize more than 100 findings apiece, and 15 other tables summarize between 40 and 100 findings.

We have added these many new findings to those already tabulated in the last edition in order to summarize the totality of process–outcome findings. We have tried to be as explicit as possible about the basis for decisions in matters requiring judgment, and as accurate as possible in matters of fact, but in the end ask readers to be sympathetically but critically vigilant. The findings have been organized according to the observational perspective from which process and outcome variables were assessed, and an attempt has been made to indicate effect sizes as well as levels of significance. Researchers and journal editors can help greatly by ensuring that in the future this information is clearly presented in research reports. Above all, null findings as well as statistically significant findings should be reported (and effect sizes for null as well as significant findings), since it is just as important to know what *isn't* as what *is* related to outcome.

We have analyzed the total cumulative record of process–outcome research to determine the major trends of scientific evidence. By searching for findings that have been well replicated across process and outcome perspectives, we have identified a modest but methodologically robust set of results that can be accorded the status of established facts. We hope to bring these facts to the attention of clinicians and theorists as well as researchers. In designing future studies, researchers in particular should remember to control for the effects of process variables that have been found consistently related to outcome. These include, *among others*, the overall quality of the therapeutic relationship, therapist skill, patient cooperation versus resistance, patient openness versus defensiveness, and treatment duration. Although little new knowledge will be gained by testing their main effects over and over again in relation to outcome, their interaction effects with other process and input variables in relation to outcome still need to be studied.

We have offered a conceptual model that attempts to integrate and explain the established facts of process–outcome research. In doing so, we have tried to clarify the basic concepts of process and outcome, showing how these terms have acquired various meanings over past decades that now need to be controlled with greater specificity. We have drawn these conceptual distinctions into our model and have used that model both as a framework for organizing the research literature and as a source of hypotheses to explain the most robust results in the literature. In both respects, the model has proved well able to assimilate large amounts of new data and accommodate a variety of new research variables through further elaboration of its original categories.

Finally, after offering a conceptual synthesis, questions about the quality of empirical data on which it is based must be raised. All the studies reviewed suffer from methodological flaws, some rather more than others; but all studies suffer from some flaws. Our safeguard was to rely not on individual studies but only on findings that have been replicated in a significant number of studies. The old adage rightly states that one cannot make a sow's ears into a silk purse, but one can at least try to stitch them together tightly enough to make a leather bucket that holds water.

REFERENCES

Alexander, J. F., Barton, C., Schiavo, R. S., & Parsons, B. V. (1976). Systems-behavioral intervention with families of delinquents: Therapist characteristics, family behavior, and outcome. *Journal of Consulting and Clinical Psychology, 44*, 656–664.

Allen, J. G., Deering, C. D., Buskirk, J. R., & Coyne, L. (1988). Assessment of therapeutic alliances in the psychiatric hospital milieu. *Psychiatry, 51*, 291–299.

Ambühl, H. (1989). *Patient self-relatedness as a crucial link between therapeutic interventions and outcome.* Paper presented at the 20th Annual Meeting of the Society for Psychotherapy Research, Toronto.

Ambühl, H. (1991). Die Aufnahmebereitschaft des Klienten als zentrales Bindeglied zwischen therapeutischer Tätigkeit und Therapieerfolg [Openness of clients as a central mediator between therapy intervention and therapeutic success.] In D. Schulte (Ed.), *Therapeutische Entscheidungen* (pp. 71–87). Göttingen: Hogrefe.

Ambühl, H. (1993). Was ist therapeutisch an Psychotherapie? Eine empirische Überprüfung der Annahmen im "Generic Model of Psychotherapy" [What is therapeutic about psychotherapy? An empirical test of the assumptions in the "Generic Model of Psychotherapy"]. *Zeitschrift für Klinische Psychologie, Psychopathologie, und Psychotherapie, 41*, 285–303.

Ambühl, H., & Grawe, K. (1988). Die Wirkungen von Psychotherapien als Ergebnis der Wechselwirkung zwischen therapeutischem Angebot und Aufnahmebereitschaft der Klient/inn/en [Therapy outcome as a result of the interaction between therapeutic offer and patient openness]. *Zeitschrift für Klinische Psychologie, Psychopathologie und Psychotherapie, 36*, 308–327.

Amira, S. A. (1982). Figurative language and metaphor in successful and unsuccessful psychotherapy. *Dissertation Abstracts International, 43*, 1244B.

Andrews, J. D. (1990). Interpersonal self-confirmation and challenge in psychotherapy. *Psychotherapy, 27*, 485–504.

Ascher, L. M. (1981). Employing paradoxical intention in the treatment of agoraphobia. *Behavioural Research and Therapy, 19*, 533–542.

Ascher, L. M., & Turner, R. M. (1979). Paradoxical intention and insomnia: An experimental investigation. *Behavioural Research and Therapy, 17*, 408–411.

Ashby, J. D., Ford, D. H., Guerney, B. G., & Guerney, L. F. (1957). Effects on clients of a reflective and a leading type of pscyhotherapy. *Psychological Monographs, 71* (24).

Bachelor, A. (1991). Comparison and relationship to outcome of diverse dimensions of the helping alliance as seen by client and therapist. *Psychotherapy, 28*, 534–549.

Baer, P. E., Dunbar, P. W., Hamilton, J. E. II, & Beutler, L. E. (1980). Therapists' perceptions of the psychotherapeutic process: Development of a psychotherapy process inventory. *Psychological Reports, 46*, 563–570.

Baker, E. (1960). The differential effects of two psychotherapeutic approaches on client perceptions. *Journal of Counseling Psychology, 7*, 46–50.

Bänninger-Huber, E. (1992). Prototypical affective microsequences in psychotherapeutic interaction. *Psychotherapy Research, 2*, 291–306.

Barber, J., Crits-Christoph, P., & Luborsky, L. (1992). *The helping alliance, early improvement, and the prediction of outcome in supportive expressive dynamic psychotherapy.* Paper presented at the 23rd Annual Meeting of the Society for Psychotherapy Research, Berkeley, CA.

Barker, S. L., Funk, S. D., & Houston, B. K. (1988). Psychological treatment versus nonspecific factors: A meta-analysis of conditions that engender comparable expectations for improvement. *Clinical Psychology Review, 78*, 579–594.

Barrett, M. S., & Berman, J. S. (1991). *Is psychotherapy more effective when therapists disclose information about themselves?* Paper presented at the first conference of the North American Society for Psychotherapy Research, Panama City, FL.

Barrington, B. L. (1961). Prediction from counselor behavior of client perception and of case outcome. *Journal of Counseling Psychology, 8*, 37–42.

Bastine, R., Fiedler, P., & Kommer, D. (1989). Was ist therapeutisch an der Psychotherapie? Versuch einer Bestandsaufnahme und Systematisierung der psychotherapeutischen Prozessforschung [What is therapeutic in psychotherapy? A review and systematization of psychotherapy process research]. *Zeitschrift für Klinische Psychologie, 18*, 3–22.

Beck, J. T., & Strong, S. R. (1982). Stimulating therapeutic change with interpretations: A comparison of positive and negative connotation. *Journal of Counseling Psychology, 29*, 551–559.

Beckham, E. E. (1989). Improvement after evaluation in psychotherapy of depression: Evidence of a placebo effect? *Journal of Clinical Psychology, 45*, 945–950.

Bellah, R. N., Madsen, R., Sullivan, W. M., Swidler, A., & Tipton, S. M. (1985). *Habits of the heart: Individualism and commitment in American life.* Berkeley: University of California Press.

Benjamin, L. S., Foster, S. W., & Estroff, S. E. (1986). Breaking the family code: Analyses of videotapes of family interactions by structural analysis of social behavior (SASB). In L. S. Greenberg & W. M. Pinsof (Eds.), *The psychotherapeutic process: A research handbook.* New York: Guilford.

Bennett, G. A. (1986). Behavior therapy for obesity: A

quantitative review of the effects of selected treatment characteristics on outcome. *Behavior Therapy, 17,* 554–562.

Bennun, I., Hahlweg, K., Schindler, L., & Langlotz, M. (1986). Therapists' and clients' perceptions in behavior therapy: The development and cross-cultural analysis of an assessment instrument. *British Journal of Clinical Psychology, 25,* 275–283.

Bennun, I., & Schindler, L. (1988). Therapist and patient factors in the behavioural treatment of phobic patients. *British Journal of Clinical Psychology, 27,* 145–150.

Beutler, L. E., & Clarkin, J. F. (1990). *Systematic treatment selection: Toward targeted therapeutic interventions.* New York: Brunner/Mazel.

Beutler, L. E., & Crago, M. (Eds.). (1991). *Psychotherapy research: An international review of programmatic studies.* Washington, DC: American Psychological Association.

Beutler, L. E., Frank, M., Scheiber, S. C., Calvert, S., & Gaines, J. (1984). Comparative effects of group psychotherapies in a short-term inpatient setting: An experience with deterioration effects. *Psychiatry, 47,* 66–76.

Beutler, L. E., & Mitchell, R. (1981). Differential psychotherapy outcome among depressed and impulsive patients as a function of analytic and experiential treatment procedures. *Psychiatry, 44,* 297–306.

Beutler, L. E., Mohr, D. C., Grawe, K., Engle, D., & MacDonald, R. (1991). Looking for differential treatment effects: Cross-cultural predictors of differential psychotherapy efficacy. *Journal of Psychotherapy Integration, 1,* 121–142.

Bierenbaum, H., Nichols, M. P., & Schwartz, A. J. (1976). Effects of varying session length and frequency in brief emotive psychotherapy. *Journal of Consulting and Clinical Psychology, 44,* 790–798.

Bommert, H., Minsel, W.-R., Fittkau, B., Langer, I., & Tausch, R. (1972). Empirische Kontrolle der Effekte und Prozesse klienten-zentrierter Gesprächspsychotherapie bei psychoneurotischen Klienten [Empirical analysis of process–outcome relations for client-centered therapy with neurotic clients.] *Zeitschrift für Klinische Psychologie, 1,* 48–63.

Bordin, E. S. (1948). Dimensions in the counseling process. *Journal of Clinical Psychology, 4,* 240–244.

Bordin, E. S. (1979). The generalizability of the psychoanalytic concept of the working alliance. *Psychotherapy: Theory, Research, and Practice, 16,* 252–260.

Bourgeois, L., Sabourin, S., & Wright, J. (1990). Predictive validity of therapeutic alliance in group marital therapy. *Journal of Consulting and Clinical Psychology, 58,* 608–613.

Bowers, T. G., & Clum, G. A. (1988). Relative contribution of specific and nonspecific treatment effects: Meta-analysis of placebo-controlled behavior therapy research. *Psychological Bulletin, 103,* 315–323.

Braaten, L. J. (1961). The movement from non-self to self in client-centered psychotherapy. *Journal of Counseling Psychology, 8,* 20–24.

Braswell, L., Kendall, P. C., Braith, J., Carey, M. P., & Vye, C. S. (1985). "Involvement" in cognitive-behavioral therapy with children: Process and its relationship to outcome. *Cognitive Therapy & Research, 9,* 611–630.

Brown, R. D. (1970). Experienced and inexperienced counselor's first impressions of clients and case outcomes: Are first impression lasting? *Journal of Counseling Psychology, 17,* 550–558.

Bruhn, M., Schwab, R., & Tausch, R. (1980). Die Auswirkung intensiver personenzentrierter Gesprächsgruppen bei Klienten mit seelischen Beeinträchtigungen [The effects of intensive person-centered group therapy (encounter groups) with psychologically disturbed clients]. *Zeitschrift für Klinische Psychologie, Forschung und Praxis, 9,* 266–280.

Brykczynska, C. (1990). Changes in the patient's perception of his therapist in the process of group and individual psychotherapy. *Psychotherapy and Psychosomatics, 53,* 179–184.

Buckley, P., Conte, H. R., Plutchik, R., Wild, K. V., & Karasu, T. B. (1984). Psychodynamic variables as predictors of psychotherapy outcome. *American Journal of Psychiatry, 141,* 742–748.

Buckley, P., Karasu, T. B., & Charles, E. (1981). Psychotherapists view their personal therapy. *Psychotherapy: Theory, Research, and Practice, 18,* 299–305.

Budman, S. H., Demby, A., Feldstein, M., Redondo, J., Scherz, B., Bennett, M. J., Koppenaal, G., Daley, B., Hunter, M., & Ellis, J. (1987). Preliminary findings on a new instrument to measure cohesion in group psychotherapy. *International Journal of Group Psychotherapy, 37,* 15–91.

Budman, S. H., Soldz, S., Demby, A., Feldstein, M., Springer, T., & Davis, M. S. (1989). Cohesion, alliance and outcome in group psychotherapy: An empirical examination. *Psychiatry, 52,* 339–350.

Budman, S. H., & Springer, T. (1987). Treatment delay, outcome, and satisfaction in time-limited group and individual psychotherapy. *Professional Psychology: Research & Practice, 18,* 647–649.

Bugge, I., Hendel, D. D., & Moen, R. (1985). Client evaluations of therapeutic processes and outcomes in a university mental health center. *Journal of American College Health, 33,* 141–146.

Burns, D. D., & Nolen-Hoeksema, S. (1991). Coping styles, homework compliance, and the effectiveness of cognitive-behavioral therapy. *Journal of Consulting and Clinical Psychology, 59,* 305–311.

Bush, R. M., Glenwick, D. S., & Stephens, M. P. (1986). Predictors of psychotherapy outcome for children at a community mental health center. *Journal of Clinical Psychology, 42,* 873–877.

Butler, J. M. (1948). On the role of directive and nondirective techniques in the counseling process. *Educational and Psychological Measurement, 8,* 201–207.

Butler, J. M., Rice, L. N., & Wagstaff, A. F. (1962). On the naturalistic definition of variables: An analogue of clinical analysis. In H. H. Strupp & L. L. Luborsky (Eds.), *Research in psychotherapy* (Vol. 2). Washington DC: American Psychological Association.

Cabral, R. J., Best, J., & Paton, A. (1975). Patients' and observers' assessments of process and outcome in group therapy: A follow-up study. *American Journal of Psychiatry, 132,* 1052–1054.

Cadbury, S., Childs-Clark, A., & Sandhu, S. (1990). Group anxiety management: Effectiveness, perceived helpfulness and follow-up. *British Journal of Clinical Psychology, 29,* 243–244.

Calvert, S. J., Beutler, L. E., & Crago, M. (1988). Psychotherapy outcome as a function of therapist-patient matching on selected variables. *Journal of Social and Clinical Psychology, 6,* 104–117.

Casey, R. J., & Berman, J. S. (1985). The outcome of psychotherapy with children. *Psychological Bulletin, 98,* 388–400.

Church, M. S. (1982). Sequential analysis of moment-by-moment psychotherapy interactions. *Dissertation Abstracts International, 42,* 4185B.

Claiborn, C. D., & Dowd, E. T. (1985). Attributional interpretations in counseling: Content versus discrepancy. *Journal of Counseling Psychology, 32,* 188–196.

Clarke, K. M., & Greenberg, L. S. (1986). Differential effects of the Gestalt two-chair intervention and problem solving in resolving decisional conflict. *Journal of Counseling Psychology, 33*, 11–15.

Clementel-Jones, C., Malan, D., & Trauer, T. (1990). A retrospective follow-up study of 84 patients treated with individual psychoanalytic psychotherapy: Outcome and predictive factors. *British Journal of Psychotherapy, 6*, 363–374.

Coady, N. F. (1991a). The association between client and therapist interpersonal processes and outcomes in psychodynamic psychotherapy. *Research on Social Work Practice, 1*, 122–138.

Coady, N. F. (1991b). The association between complex types of therapist interventions and outcomes in psychodynamic psychotherapy. *Research on Social Work Practice, 1*, 257–277.

Coleman, D. J., & Kaplan, M. S. (1990). Effects of pretherapy videotape preparation on child therapy outcomes. *Professional Psychology: Research & Practice, 21*, 199–203.

Collins, J. F., Ellsworth, R. B., Casey, N. A., Hyer, L., Hickey, R. H., Schoonover, R. A., Twemlow, S. W., & Nesselroade, J. R. (1985). Treatment characteristics of psychiatric programs that correlate with patient community adjustment. *Journal of Clinical Psychology, 41*, 299–308.

Colson, D. B., Allen, J. G., Coyne, L., Deering, D., Jehl, N., Kearns, W., & Spohn, H. (1985). Patterns of staff perception of difficult patients in a long-term psychiatric hospital. *Hospital and Community Psychiatry, 36*, 168–172.

Colson, D. B., Cornsweet, C., Murphy, T., O'Malley, F., Hyland, P. S., McParland, M., & Coyne, L. (1991). Perceived treatment difficulty and therapeutic alliance on an adolescent psychiatric hospital unit. *American Journal of Orthopsychiatry, 61*, 221–229.

Conoley, C. W., & Garber, R. A. (1985). Effects of reframing and self-control directives on loneliness, depression, and controllability. *Journal of Counseling Psychology, 32*, 139–142.

Conrad, D. C. (1952). An empirical study of the concept of psychotherapeutic success. *Journal of Consulting Psychology, 16*, 92–97.

Covner, B. J. (1942). Studies in phonographic recordings of verbal material: I. The use of phonographic recordings in counseling practice and research. *Journal of Consulting Psychology, 6*, 105–113.

Crane, D. R., Griffin, W., & Hill, R. D. (1986). Influence of therapist skills on client perceptions of marriage and family therapy outcome: Implications for supervision. *Journal of Marital and Family Therapy, 12*, 91–96.

Crits-Christoph, P., Cooper, A., & Luborsky, L. (1988). The accuracy of therapists' interpretations and the outcome of dynamic psychotherapy. *Journal of Consulting and Clinical Psychology, 56*, 490–495.

Czogalik, D. (1991). University of Ulm: Interactional processes in psychotherapy. In L. E. Beutler & M. Crago (Eds.), *Psychotherapy research: An international review of programmatic studies.* Washington, DC: American Psychological Association.

Czogalik, D., & Hettinger, R. (1987). The process of psychotherapeutic interaction: A single case study. In W. Huber (Ed.), *Progress in psychotherapy research.* Louvain-la-Neuve, Belgium: Presses Universitaires de Louvain.

Czogalik, D., & Hettinger, R. (1988). Mehrebenenanalyse der psychotherapeutischen Interaktion: Eine Verlaufsstudie am Einzelfall [Multilevel analysis of psychotherapeutic interaction: A process study of a single case]. *Zeitschrift für Klinische Psychologie, 17*, 31–45.

Dahl, H., Kächele, H., & Thomä, H. (Eds.). (1988). *Psychoanalytic process research strategies.* Berlin, Heidelberg, New York:Springer-Verlag.

Deane, F. P., Spicer, J., & Leathem, J. (1992). Effects of videotaped preparatory information on expectations, anxiety, and psychotherapy outcome. *Journal of Consulting and Clinical Psychology, 60*, 980–984.

De Carufel, F. L. & Piper, W. E. (1988). Group psychotherapy or individual psychotherapy: Patient characteristics as predictive factors. *International Journal of Group Psychotherapy, 38*, 169–188.

DeRubeis, R. J., Evans, M. D., Hollon, S. D., Garvey, M. J., Grove, W. M., & Tuason, V. B. (1990). How does cognitive therapy work? Cognitive change and symptom change in cognitive therapy and pharmacotherapy for depression. *Journal of Consulting and Clinical Psychology, 58*, 862–869.

DeRubeis, R. J., & Feeley, M. (1990). Determinants of change in cognitive therapy for depression. *Cognitive Therapy & Research, 14*, 469–482.

Dickenson, W. B. (1969). Therapist self-disclosure as a variable in pscyhotherapeutic process and outcome. *Dissertation Abstracts International, 30*, 2434B.

DiLoreto, A. O. (1971). *Comparative psychotherapy: An experimental analysis.* Chicago: Aldine-Atherton.

Dobson, K. S. (1989). A meta-analysis of the efficacy of cognitive therapy for depression. *Journal of Consulting and Clinical Psychology, 57*, 414–419.

Dormaar, J. M., Dijkman, C. I., & de Vries, M. W. (1989). Consensus in patient-therapist interactions: A measure of the therapeutic relationship related to outcome. *Psychotherapy and Psychosomatics, 51*, 69–76.

Dziewas, H. (1980). Das interaktionelle Problemlösungsvorgehen (IPV) in ambulanten und stationären Gruppen [Interactional problem solving therapy: A controlled comparison between inpatient and outpatient therapy]. Universität Hamburg: Unveroffentlichte Habilitationsschrift.

Dziewas, H., Grawe, K., Wedel, S., Singmann, J., Tönsing, M., & Wegner, J. (1979). Verhaltenstherapeutische Gruppentherapie unter stationären und ambulanten Bedingungen [Behavioral group therapy under inpatient and outpatient conditions]. *Sonderheft 1 der Mitteilungen der DGVT, 9* (35).

Eaton, T. T., Abeles, N., & Gutfreund, M. J. (1988). Therapeutic alliance and outcome: Impact of treatment length and pretreatment symptomatology. *Psychotherapy, 25*, 536–542.

Eckert, J., & Biermann-Ratjen, E.-M. (1985). *Stationäre Gruppenpsychotherapie: Prozesse-Effekte-Vergleiche* [Inpatient group therapy: Processes, effects, comparisons]. Berlin, Heidelberg: Springer-Verlag.

Eckert, J., Schwarz, H.-J., & Tausch, R. (1977). Klienten-Erfahrungen und Zusammenhang mit psychischen Änderungen in personenzentrierter Gesprächspsychotherapie [The relation of client experiences and outcome in client-centered therapy]. *Zeitschrift für Klinische Psychologie, 6*, 177–184.

Eckert, P. A., Abeles, N., & Graham, R. N. (1988). Symptom severity, psychotherapy process, and outcome. *Professional Psychology: Research and Practice, 19*, 560–564.

Eisenthal, S., Koopman, C., & Lazare, A. (1983). Process analysis of two dimensions of the negotiated approach in relation to satisfaction in the initial interview. *Journal of Nervous and Mental Disease, 171*, 49–54.

Elliott, R. (1984). A discovery-oriented approach to significant change events in psychotherapy: Interpersonal process recall and comprehensive process analysis. In L. N. Rice & L. S. Greenberg (Eds.), *Patterns of change: Inten-*

sive analysis of psychotherapy process. New York: Guilford.

Elliott, R. (1985). Helpful and nonhelpful events in brief counseling interviews: An empirical taxonomy. *Journal of Counseling Psychology, 32,* 307–322.

Elliott, R. (1986). Interpersonal process recall (IPR) as a psychotherapy process research method. In L. S. Greenberg & W. M. Pinsof (Eds.), *The psychotherapeutic process: A research handbook.* New York: Guilford.

Elliott, R. (1991). Five dimensions of therapy process. *Psychotherapy Research, 1,* 92–103.

Elliott, R., James, E., Reimschuessel, C., Cislo, D., & Sack, N. (1985). Significant events and the analysis of immediate therapeutic impacts. *Psychotherapy, 22,* 620–630.

Erle, J. B. (1979). An approach to the study of analyzability and analyses: The course of forty consecutive cases selected for supervised analysis. *Psychoanalytic Quarterly, 48,* 198–228.

Eysenck, H. J. (1952). The effects of psychotherapy: An evaluation. *Journal of Consulting Psychology, 16,* 319–324.

Farber, B. A. (1983). The effects of psychotherapeutic practice upon psychotherapists. *Psychotherapy: Theory, Research, and Practice, 20,* 174–182.

Farber, B. A., & Heifetz, L. J. (1981). The satisfactions and stresses of psychotherapeutic work: A factor analytic study. *Professional Psychology, 12,* 621–630.

Feifel, H., & Eells, J. (1963). Patients and therapists assess the same psychotherapy. *Journal of Consulting Psychology, 27,* 310–318.

Feitel, B. (1968). *Feeling understood as a function of a variety of therapist activities.* Unpublished doctoral dissertation, Teachers College, Columbia University, New York.

Feldman, D. A., Strong, S. R., & Danser, D. B. (1982). A comparison of paradoxical and nonparadoxical interpretations and directives. *Journal of Counseling Psychology, 29,* 572–579.

Fennell, M. J., & Teasdale, J. D. (1987). Cognitive therapy for depression: Individual differences and the process of change. *Cognitive Therapy & Research, 11,* 253–271.

Fiedler, F. E. (1950). A comparison of therapeutic relationships in psychoanalytic, nondirective, and Adlerian therapy. *Journal of Consulting Psychology, 14,* 239–245.

Filak, J., & Abeles, N. (1984). Posttherapy congruence on client symptoms and therapy outcome. *Professional Psychology: Research & Practice, 15,* 846–855.

Foppa-Drew, S. (1989). *The empirical validity of the Generic Model on a single case level: A longitudinal correlational analysis of 47 cases.* Paper presented at the 20th Annual Meeting of Society for Psychotherapy Research, Toronto.

Frank, A. F., & Gunderson, J. G. (1990). The role of the therapeutic alliance in the treatment of schizophrenia: Relationship to course and outcome. *Archives of General Psychiatry, 47,* 228–236.

Freud, S. (1957). Instincts and their vicissitudes. *The standard edition of the complete psychological works of Sigmund Freud* (Vol. 14). London: Hogarth Press. (Original work published 1915).

Freud, S. (1958). The dynamics of the transference. *The standard edition of the complete psychological works of Sigmund Freud* (Vol. 12). London: Hogarth Press. (Original work published 1912).

Friedman, M. J., & West, A. N. (1987). Current need versus treatment history as predictors of use of outpatient psychiatric care. *American Journal of Psychiatry, 144,* 355–357.

Frieswyk, S. H., Allen, J. G., Colson, D. B., Coyne, L.,

Gabbard, G. O., Horwitz, L., & Newsom, G. (1986). Therapeutic alliance: Its place as a process and outcome variable in dynamic psychotherapy research. *Journal of Consulting and Clinical Psychology, 54,* 32–38.

Frieswyk, S. H., Colson, D. B., & Allen, J. G. (1984). Conceptualizing the alliance from a psychoanalytic perspective. *Psychotherapy, 27,* 460–464.

Gabbard, C. E., Howard, G. S., & Dunfee, E. J. (1986). Reliability, sensitivity to measuring change, and construct validity of a measure of counselor adaptability. *Journal of Counseling Psychology, 33,* 377–386.

Gardner, C. S., Hurt, S. W., Maltman, G., Greenberg, R., & Holtzman, S. R. (1985). Clinical turmoil and staff transitions. *American Journal of Orthopsychiatry, 55,* 439–445.

Garfield, S. L. (1986). Research on client variables in psychotherapy. In S. L. Garfield & A. E. Bergin (Eds.), *Handbook of psychotherapy and behavior change* (3rd ed.) New York: Wiley.

Gasman, D. H. (1992). Double-exposure therapy: Videotape homework as a psychotherapeutic adjunct. *American Journal of Psychiatry, 46,* 91–101.

Gaston, L., Marmar, C. R., Gallagher, D., & Thompson, L. W. (1991). Alliance prediction of outcome beyond intreatment symptomatic change as psychotherapy processes. *Psychotherapy Research, 1,* 104–113.

Geller, J. D., Cooley, R. S., & Hartley, D. (1982). Images of the psychotherapist: A theoretical and methodological perspective. *Imagination, Cognition and Personality, 1,* 123–146.

Gelso, C. J., & Johnson, D. H. (1983). *Explorations in time-limited counseling and psychotherapy.* New York: Teachers College Press.

Gelso, C. J., Mills, D. H., & Spiegel, S. B. (1983). Client and therapist factors influencing the outcomes of time-limited counselilng one month and eighteen months after treatment. In C. J. Gelso & D. H. Johnson, *Explorations in time-limited counseling and psychotherapy.* New York: Teachers College Press.

Gelso, C. J., Spiegel, S. B., & Mills, D. H. (1983). Clients' and counselors' reactions to time-limited and time-unlimited counseling. In C. J. Gelso & D. H. Johnson, *Explorations in time-limited counseling and psychotherapy.* New York: Teachers College Press.

Gendlin, E. T., Jenney, R. H., & Shlien, J. M. (1960). Counselor ratings of process and outcome in client-centered therapy. *Journal of Clinical Psychology, 16,* 210–213.

Gerlin, P., Dazord, A., Sali, A., Guisti, P., & Marie-Cardine, M. (1987). Psychotherapeutic factors within psychiatric institutions: A comparison of effectiveness of treatments. In W. Huber (Ed.), *Progress in psychotherapy research.* Louvain-la-Neuve, Belgium, Presses Universitaires de Louvain.

Gerstley, L., McLellan, A. T., Alterman, A. I., Woody, G. E., Luborsky, L., & Prout, M. (1989). Ability to form an alliance with the therapist: A possible marker of prognosis for patients with antisocial personality disorder. *American Journal of Psychiatry, 146,* 508–512.

Glass, L. L., Katz, H. M., Schnitzer, R. D., Knapp, P. H., Frank, A. F., & Gunderson, J. G. (1989). Psychotherapy of schizophrenia: An empirical investigation of the relationship of process to outcome. *American Journal of Psychiatry, 146,* 603–608.

Goffman, E. (1956). The nature of deference and demeanor. *American Anthropologist, 58,* 473–502.

Goldfried, M. (1980). Toward the delineation of therapeutic change principles. *American Psychologist, 35,* 991–999.

Goldfried, M., Greenberg, L., & Marmar, C. (1990). Individual psychotherapy: Process and outcome. *Annual Review of Psychology, 41*, 659–688.

Goldstein, J. M., Cohen, P., Lewis, S. A., & Struening, E. L. (1988). Community treatment environments: Patient vs. staff evaluations. *Journal of Nervous and Mental Disease, 176*, 227–233.

Gomes-Schwartz, B. A. (1978). Effective ingredients in psychotherapy: Prediction of outcomes from process variables. *Journal of Consulting and Clinical Psychology, 46*, 1023–1035.

Gordon, T., & Cartwright, D. S. (1954). The effect of psychotherapy on certain attitudes toward others. In C. R. Rogers & R. F. Dymond (Eds.), *Psychotherapy and personality change*. Chicago: University of Chicago Press.

Grawe, K. (1989a). *A comparison of the intercorrelations between input, process, and outcome variables of the Generic Model for different forms of psychotherapy*. Paper presented at the 20th Annual Meeting of the Society for Psychotherapy Research, Toronto.

Grawe, K. (1989b). Von der psychotherapeutischen Outcomeforschung zur differentiellen Prozessanalyse [From psychotherapeutic outcome research to differential process analysis]. *Zeitschrift für Klinische Psychologie, 18*, 23–34.

Grawe, K. (1991). The Bernese Psychotherapy Research Program. In L. E. Beutler & M. Crago (Eds.), *Psychotherapy research: An international review of programmatic studies*. Washington, DC: American Psychological Association.

Grawe, K., Caspar, F., & Ambühl, H. (1990). Themenheft: Differentielle Psychotherapieforschung: Vier Therapieformen im Vergleich [Topical Issue: Differential psychotherapy research: Comparative evaluation of four forms of therapy]. *Zeitschrift für Klinische Psychologie, 19*, 292–376.

Grawe, K., Schütte, C., & Thiem, T. (1978). Der Therapieprozess in Assertiveness-Training-Gruppen aus der Sicht der Patienten: Eine Prozessanalyse mit Hilfe des Gruppenstundenbogens (GSB) [The therapy process in assertiveness training groups from the patients' point of view: A process analysis with the Group Session Questionnaire]. In R. Ullrich & R. Ullrich de Muynck (Eds.), *Soziale Kompetenz: Band 1. Experimentelle Ergebnisse zum Assertiveness-Training-Programm ATP: Messmittel und Grundlagen* (pp. 331–371). Munich: J. Pfeiffer.

Green, R. J., & Herget, M. (1989). Outcomes of systemic/strategic team consultation: II. Three-year follow-up and a theory of "emergent design." *Family Process, 28*, 419–437.

Green, R. J., & Herget, M. (1991). Outcomes of systemic/strategic team consultation: III. The importance of therapist warmth and active structuring. *Family Process, 30*, 321–336.

Greenberg, L. S. (1986). Research strategies. In L. S. Greenberg & W. M. Pinsof (Eds.), *The psychotherapeutic process: A research handbook*. New York: Guilford.

Greenberg, L. S. (1991). Research on the process of change. *Psychotherapy Research, 1*, 3–16.

Greenberg, L. S., & Dompierre, L. M. (1981). Specific effects of Gestalt two-chair dialogue on intrapsychic conflict in counseling. *Journal of Counseling Psychology, 28*, 288–294.

Greenberg, L. S., & Pinsof, W. M. (1986a). Process research: Current trends and perspectives. In L. S. Greenberg & W. M. Pinsof (Eds.), *The psychotherapeutic process: A research handbook*. New York: Guilford.

Greenberg, L. S., & Pinsof, W. M. (Eds.). (1986b). *The psychotherapeutic process: A research handbook*. New York: Guilford.

Greenberg, L. S., & Rice, L. N. (1981). The specific effects of a Gestalt intervention. *Psychotherapy: Theory, Research, and Practice, 18*, 31–37.

Grimes, W. R., & Murdock, N. L. (1989). Social influence, revisited: Effects of counselor influence on outcome variables. *Psychotherapy, 26*, 469–474.

Grunebaum, H. (1986). Harmful psychotherapy experience. *American Journal of Psychotherapy, 40*, 165–176.

Gully, K. J., & Harris, M. D. (1982). The impact of fee setting procedures in a mental health center setting. *Community Mental Health Journal, 18*, 210–219.

Gurman, A. S. (1977). The patient's perception of the therapeutic relationship. In A. S. Gurman & A. M. Razin (Eds.), *Effective psychotherapy: A handbook of research*. Oxford: Pergamon.

Hagborg, W. J. (1991). Adolescent clients and perceived counselor characteristics: A study of background characteristics, therapeutic progress, psychological distress, and social desirability. *Journal of Clinical Psychology, 47*, 107–113.

Hahlweg, K., & Jacobson, N. S. (Eds.). (1984). *Marital interaction: Analysis and modification*. New York: Guilford.

Halkides, G. (1958). *An experimental study of four conditions necessary for therapeutic change*. Unpublished doctoral dissertation, University of Chicago.

Harris, J. (1986). Counseling violent couples using Walker's model. *Psychotherapy, 23*, 613–621.

Hartley, D. E., & Strupp, H. H. (1983). The therapeutic alliance: Its relationship to outcome in brief psychotherapy. In J. Masling (Ed.), *Empirical studies of psychoanalytical theories* (Vol. 1). Hillsdale, NJ: The Analytic Press.

Hartung, J. (1990). *Psychotherapie phobischer Störungen. Handlungs und Lageorientierung im Therapieprozess* [Psychotherapy of phobic disorders: Action-orientation and state-orientation in the therapeutic process]. Wiesbaden: Deutscher Universitäts-Verlag.

Hartung, J., & Schulte, D. (1991). Anregung eines handlungsorienterten Kontrollmodus im Therapieprozess [Stimulation of an action-oriented mode of control in the therapeutic process]. In D. Schulte (Ed.), *Therapeutische Entscheidungen*. Göttingen: Hogrefe.

Hayward, R. H. (1974). Process and outcome consequences of therapist self-disclosure. *Dissertation Abstracts International, 34*, 6210–6211B.

Henry, W. P., Schacht, T. E., & Strupp, H. H. (1986). Structural analysis of social behavior: Application to a study of interpersonal process in differential psychotherapeutic outcome. *Journal of Consulting and Clinical Psychology, 54*, 27–31.

Henry, W. P., Schacht, T. E., & Strupp, H. H. (1990). Patient and therapist introject, interpersonal process, and differential psychotherapy outcome. *Journal of Consulting and Clinical Psychology, 58*, 768–774.

Herink, R. (Ed.). (1980). *The psychotherapy handbook: The A to Z guide to more than 250 different therapies in use today*. New York: New American Library.

Hill, C. E. (1986). An overview of the Hill counselor and client verbal response modes category systems. In L. S. Greenberg & W. M. Pinsof (Eds.), *The psychotherapeutic process: A research handbook*. New York: Guilford.

Hill, C. E. (1989). *Therapist techniques and client outcomes: Eight cases of brief psychotherapy*. Newbury Park, CA: Sage Publications.

Hill, C. E., Helms, J. E., Spiegel, S. B., & Tichenor, V. (1988). Development of a system for categorizing client reactions to therapist interventions. *Journal of Counseling Psychology, 35,* 27–36.

Hill, C. E., Helms, J. E., Tichenor, V., Spiegel, S. B., O'Grady, K. E., & Perry, E. (1988). Effects of therapist response modes in brief psychotherapy. *Journal of Counseling Psychology, 35,* 222–233.

Hill, D., Beutler, L. E., & Daldrup, R. (1989). The relationship of process to outcome in brief experiential psychotherapy for chronic pain. *Journal of Clinical Psychology, 45,* 951–957.

Hill, K. A. (1987). Meta-analysis of paradoxical interventions. *Psychotherapy, 24,* 266–270.

Hisli, N. (1987). Effect of patient's evaluation of group behavior on therapy outcome. *International Journal of Group Psychotherapy, 37,* 119–124.

Hoberman, H. M., Lewinsohn, P. M., & Tilson, M. (1988). Group treatment of depression: Individual predictors of outcome. *Journal of Consulting and Clinical Psychology, 56,* 393–398.

Hoffman, I. Z., & Gill, M. M. (1988). A scheme for coding the patient's experience of the relationship with the therapist (PERT): Some applications, extensions, and comparisons. In H. Dahl, H. Kächele, & H. Thomä (Eds.), *Psychoanalytic research process strategies.* Berlin, Heidelberg, New York, London, Paris, Tokyo: Springer-Verlag.

Hoge, M. A., Farrell, S. P., Munchel, M. E., & Strauss, J. S. (1988). Therapeutic factors in partial hospitalization. *Psychiatry, 51,* 199–210.

Holtzworth-Munroe, A., Jacobson, N. S., DeKlyen, M., & Whisman, M. A. (1989). Relationship between behavioral marital therapy outcome and process variables. *Journal of Consulting and Clinical Psychology, 57,* 658–662.

Hoogduin, C. A., de Haan, E., & Schaap, C. (1989). The significance of the patient-therapist relationship in the treatment of obsessive-compulsive neurosis. *British Journal of Clinical Psychology, 28,* 185–186.

Horowitz, M. J. (Ed.). (1991). *Person schemas and maladaptive interpersonal patterns.* Chicago: University of Chicago Press.

Horowitz, M. J., Marmar, C., Weiss, D., Dewitt, D., & Rosenbaum, R. (1984). Brief psychotherapy of bereavement reactions: The relationship of process to outcome. *Archives of General Psychiatry, 41,* 438–448.

Horvath, A. O. (1981). *An exploratory study of the concept of therapeutic alliance and its measurement.* Unpublished doctoral dissertation, University of British Columbia, Vancouver, Canada. Reported in Horvath, A. O., & Greenberg, L. S. (1989). Development and validation of the working alliance inventory. *Journal of Counseling Psychology, 36,* 223–233.

Horvath, A. O., & Goheen, M. D. (1990). Factors mediating the success of defiance- and compliance-based interventions. *Journal of Counseling Psychology, 37,* 363–371.

Horvath, A. O., & Greenberg, L. S. (Eds.). (in press). *The working alliance: Theory, research, and practice.* New York: Wiley.

Horvath, A. O., & Symonds, B. D. (1991). Relation between working alliance and outcome in psychotherapy: A meta-analysis. *Journal of Counseling Psychology, 38,* 139–149.

Howard, K., Kopta, M., Krause, M., & Orlinsky, D. (1986). The dose-effect relationship in psychotherapy. *American Psychologist, 41,* 149–164.

Howard, K. I., Lueger, R. J., Maling, M. S., & Martinovich, Z. (1992). *A phase model of psychotherapy outcome: Causal mediation of change.* Paper presented at the 23rd Annual Meeting of the Society for Psychotherapy Research, Berkeley, CA.

Hoyt, M. (1980). Therapist and patient actions in "good" psychotherapy sessions. *Archives of General Psychiatry, 37,* 159–161.

Hoyt, M., Xenakis, S., Marmar, C., & Horowitz, M. J. (1983). Therapists' actions that influence their perceptions of "good" psychotherapy sessions. *Journal of Nervous and Mental Disease, 171,* 400–404.

Huber, W. (Ed.) (1987). *Progress in psychotherapy research.* Louvain-la-Neuve, Belgium: Presses Universitaires de Louvain.

Hynan, D. J. (1991). Client reasons and experiences in treatment that influence termination of psychotherapy. *Journal of Clinical Psychology, 46,* 891–895.

Jeske, J. O. (1973). Identification and therapeutic effectiveness in group therapy. *Journal of Counseling Psychology, 20,* 528–530.

Johnson, M. E. (1988). *Construct validation of the therapeutic alliance.* Paper presented at the 19th Annual Meeting of the Society for Psychotherapy Research, Santa Fe, NM.

Johnson, S. M., & Greenberg, L. S. (1988). Relating process to outcome in marital therapy. *Journal of Marital and Family Therapy, 14,* 175–183.

Jones, E. E., Cumming, J. D., & Horowitz, M. J. (1988). Another look at the nonspecific hypothesis of therapeutic effectiveness. *Journal of Consulting and Clinical Psychology, 56,* 48–55.

Jones, E. E., Parke, L. A., & Pulos, S. M. (1992). How therapy is conducted in the private consultation room: A multidimensional description of brief psychodynamic treatments. *Psychotherapy Research, 2,* 16–30.

Jones, E. E., Wynne, M. F., & Watson, D. D. (1986). Client perception of treatment in crisis intervention and longer-term psychotherapies. *Psychotherapy, 23,* 120–132.

Kächele, H. (1992). Narration and observation in psychotherapy research: Reporting on a 20 year long journey from qualitative case reports to quantitative studies on the psychoanalytic process. *Psychotherapy Research, 2,* 1–15.

Kahn, E. M., Webster, P. B., & Storck, M. J. (1986). Curative factors in two types of inpatient psychotherapy groups. *International Journal of Group Psychotherapy, 36,* 579–585.

Kang, S.-Y., Kleinman, P. H., Woody, G. E., Millman, R. B., Todd, G. C., Kemp, J., & Lipton, D. S. (1991). Outcomes for cocaine abusers after once-a-week psychosocial therapy. *American Journal of Psychiatry, 148,* 630–635.

Kaschak, E. (1978). Therapist and client: Two views of the process and outcome of psychotherapy. *Professional Psychology,* 271–277.

Kaufman, I., Frank, T., Friend, J., Heims, L. W., & Weiss, R. (1962). Success and failure in the treatment of childhood schizophrenia. *American Journal of Psychiatry, 118,* 909–913.

Keilson, M. V., Dworkin, F. H., & Gelso, C. J. (1983). The effectiveness of time-limited therapy in a university counseling center. In C. J. Gelso & D. H. Johnson, *Explorations in time-limited counseling and psychotherapy.* New York: Teachers College Press.

Kernberg, O. F., Bernstein, C. S., Coyne, R., Appelbaum, D. A., Horwitz, H., & Voth, T. J. (1972). Psychotherapy and psychoanalysis: Final report of the Menninger Foundation's psychotherapy research project. *Bulletin of the Menninger Clinic, 36,* 1–276.

Kirk, A. K., Stanley, G. V., & Brown, D. F. (1988). Changes in patients' stress and arousal levels associated with therapists' perception of their requests during crisis intervention. *British Journal of Clinical Psychology, 27,* 363–369.

Klee, M., Abeles, N., & Muller, R. T. (1990). Therapeutic

alliance: Early indicators, course, and outcome. *Psychotherapy, 27,* 166–174.

Kleinman, A. (1988). *Rethinking psychiatry: From cultural category to personal experience.* New York: Free Press.

Knight, R. P. (1941). Evaluation of the results of psychoanalytic therapy. *American Journal of Psychiatry, 98,* 434–446.

Kolb, D. L., Beutler, L. E., Davis, C. S., Crago, M., & Shanfield, S. B. (1985). Patient and therapy process variables relating to dropout and change in psychotherapy. *Psychotherapy, 22,* 702–710.

Kolden, G. G. (1991). The Generic Model of Psychotherapy: An empirical investigation of process and outcome relationships. *Psychotherapy Research, 1,* 62–73.

Kozak, M. J., Foa, E. B., & Steketee, G. L. (1988). Process and outcome of exposure treatment with obsessive-compulsives: Psychophysiological indicators of emotional processing. *Behavior Therapy, 19,* 157–169.

Kraft, R. G., Claiborn, C. D., & Dowd, E. T. (1985). Effects of positive reframing and paradoxical directives in counseling for negative emotions. *Journal of Counseling Psychology, 32,* 617–621.

Kuhn, T. (1970). *The structure of scientific revolutions* (rev. ed.). Chicago: University of Chicago Press.

Labov, W., & Fanshel, D. (1977). *Therapeutic discourse: Psychotherapy as conversation.* New York: Academic Press.

Lafferty, P., Beutler, L. E., & Crago, M. (1989). Differences between more and less effective psychotherapists: A study of selected therapist variables. *Journal of Consulting and Clinical Psychology, 57,* 76–80.

Landfield, A. W. (1971). *Personal construct systems in psychotherapy.* Chicago: Rand McNally.

Lansford, E. (1986). Weakenings and repairs of the working alliance in short-term psychotherapy. *Professional Psychology: Research & Practice, 17,* 364–366.

Lerner, B. (1972). *Therapy in the ghetto.* Baltimore: The Johns Hopkins University Press.

Libman, E., Fichten, C. S., & Brender, W. (1985). The role of therapeutic format in the treatment of sexual dysfunction: A review. *Clinical Psychology Review, 5,* 103–117.

Lietaer, G. (1992). Helping and hindering processes in client-centered/experiential psychotherapy: A content analysis of client and therapist post-session perceptions. In S. G. Toukmanian & D. L. Rennie (Eds.), *Psychotherapy process research: Paradigmatic and narrative approaches.* Newbury Park, CA: Sage Publications.

Lietaer, G., Dierick, P., & Neirinck, M. (1985). Inhoud en proces in experiëntiële psychotherapie: Een emprirische exploratie [Content and process in experiential psychotherapy: An empirical exploration]. *Psychologica Belgica, 25,* 127–147.

Lietaer, G., & Neirinck, M. (1987). Non-helping and hindering processes in experiential psychotherapy: A content analysis of post-session comments. In W. Huber (Ed.), *Progress in psychotherapy research.* Louvain-la-Neuve, Belgium: Presses Universitaires de Louvain.

Lietaer, G., Rombauts, J., & Van Balen, R. (Eds.). (1990). *Client-centered and experiential psychotherapy in the nineties.* Leuven, Belgium: Leuven University Press.

Lipman, R. S., & Covi, L. (1976). Outpatient treatment of neurotic depression: Medication and group psychotherapy. In R. L. Spitzer & D. F. Klein (Eds.), *Evaluation of psychological therapies: Psychotherapies, behavior therapies, drug therapies, and their interactions.* Baltimore: The Johns Hopkins University Press.

Llewelyn, S. P. (1988). Psychological therapy as viewed by clients and therapists. *British Journal of Clinical Psychology, 27,* 223–237.

Llewelyn, S. P., Elliott, R., Shapiro, D. A., Hardy, G., & Firth-Cozens, J. (1988). Client perceptions of significant events in prescriptive and exploratory periods of individual therapy. *British Journal of Clinical Psychology, 27,* 105–114.

Lopez, F. G., & Wambach, C. A. (1982). Effects of paradoxical and self-control directive in counseling. *Journal of Counseling Psychology, 29,* 115–124.

LoPiccolo, J., Heiman, J. R., Hogan, D. R., & Roberts, C. W. (1985). Effectiveness of single therapists versus cotherapy teams in sex therapy. *Journal of Consulting and Clinical Psychology, 53,* 287–294.

Luborsky, L., & Crits-Christoph, P. (1988). The assessment of transference by the CCRT method. In H. Dahl, H. Kächele, & H. Thomä (Eds.), *Psychoanalytic research process strategies.* Berlin, Heidelberg, New York, London, Paris, Tokyo: Springer-Verlag.

Luborsky, L., & Crits-Christoph, P. (1990). *Understanding transference: The CCRT method.* New York: Basic Books.

Luborsky, L., Crits-Christoph, P., Alexander, L., Margolis, M., & Cohen, M. (1983). Two helping alliance methods for predicting outcomes of psychotherapy. *Journal of Nervous and Mental Disease, 171,* 480–491.

Luborsky, L., Crits-Christoph, P., & Mellon, J. (1986). Advent of objective measures of the transference concept. *Journal of Consulting and Clinical Psychology, 54,* 39–47.

Luborsky, L., Crits-Christoph, P., Mintz, J., & Auerbach, A. (1988). *Who will benefit from psychotherapy? Predicting therapeutic outcomes.* New York: Basic Books.

Luborsky, L., McLellan, T., Woody, G. E., O'Brien, C. P., & Auerbach, A. (1985). Therapist success and its determinants. *Archives of General Psychiatry, 42,* 602–611.

MacIntyre, A. (1981). *After virtue: A study in moral theory* (chap. 3). Notre Dame, IN: University of Notre Dame Press.

Malan, D. H. (1976). *Toward the validation of dynamic psychotherapy.* London: Plenum Medical Book Company.

Mallinckrodt, B. (1989). Social support and the effectiveness of group therapy. *Journal of Counseling Psychology, 36,* 170–175.

Marmar, C. R., Gaston, L., Gallagher, D., & Thompson, L. W. (1989). Alliance and outcome in late-life depression. *Journal of Nervous and Mental Disease, 177,* 464–472.

Marmar, C. R., Weiss, D. S., & Gaston, L. (1989). Toward the validation of the California Therapeutic Alliance Rating System. *Psychological Assessment, 1,* 46–52.

Martin, J., Martin, W., Meyer, M., & Slemon, A. G. (1986). Empirical investigation of the cognitive mediational paradigm for research on counseling. *Journal of Counseling Psychology, 33,* 115–123.

Martin, J., Martin, W., & Slemon, A. G. (1987). Cognitive mediation in person-centered and rational emotive therapy. *Journal of Counseling Psychology, 34,* 251–260.

Marziali, E. A. (1984). Three viewpoints on the therapeutic alliance: Similarities, differences, and associations with psychotherapy outcome. *Journal of Nervous and Mental Disease, 172,* 417–423.

Mavissakalian, M., Michelson, L., Greenwald, D., Kornblith, S., & Greenwald, M. (1983). Cognitive-behavioral treatment of agoraphobia: Paradoxical intention versus self-statement training. *Behaviour Research and Therapy, 21,* 75–86.

McCall, G. J. & Simmons, J. L. (1978). *Identities and interactions: An examination of human associations in everyday life* (rev. ed.). New York: Free Press.

McCullough, L., Winston, A., Farber, B. A., Porter, P.,

Pollack, J., Laikin, M., Vingiano, W., & Trujillo, M. (1991). The relationship of patient-therapist interaction to outcome in brief psychotherapy. *Psychotherapy, 28,* 525–533.

McNeill, B. W., May, R. J., & Lee, V. E. (1987). Perceptions of counselor source characteristics by premature and successful terminators. *Journal of Counseling Psychology, 34,* 86–89.

Meinberg, R. A., & Yager, G. G. (1985). Effects of a workshop fee on women's stress management skills and evaluations. *Journal of Counseling Psychology, 32,* 626–629.

Meyer, A.-E. (1981). The Hamburg Short Psychotherapy Comparison Experiment. *Psychotherapy and Psychosomatics, 35,* 77–270.

Meyer, A.-E. (1990). *Nonspecific and common factors in treatment outcome: Another myth?* Paper presented at the 21st Annual Meeting of the Society for Psychotherapy Research, Wintergreen, VA.

Miller, J. M., Courtois, C. A., Pelham, J. P., Riddle, P. E., Spiegel, S. B., Gelso, C. J., & Johnson, D. H. (1983). The process of time-limited therapy. In C. J. Gelso & D. H. Johnson, *Explorations in time-limited counseling and psychotherapy.* New York: Teachers College Press.

Minsel, W.-R., Bommert, H., Bastine, R., Langer, I., Nickel, H., & Tausch, R. (1972). Weitere Untersuchung der Auswirkung und Prozesse klienten-zentrierter Gesprächspsychotherapie [Further analyses of processes and effects of client-centered therapy]. *Zeitschrift für Klinische Psychologie, 3,* 232–250.

Minsel, W.-R., Bommert, H., & Pieritz, R. (1972). Beziehungen zwischen sprachformalen Psychotherapeuten-Merkmalen und dem Erfolg von klientenzentrierter Gesprächspsychotherapie [Relationship between formal speech characteristics of psychotherapists and the success of client-centered psychotherapy]. *Zeitschrift für Klinische Psychologie und Psychotherapie, 20,* 303–310.

Morokoff, P. J., & LoPiccolo, J. (1986). A comparative evaluation of minimal therapist contact and 15-session treatment for female orgasmic dysfunction. *Journal of Consulting and Clinical Psychology, 54,* 294–300.

Morrison, L. A., & Shapiro, D. A. (1987). Expectancy and outcome in prescriptive versus exploratory psychotherapy. *British Journal of Clinical Psychology, 26,* 59–60.

Moseley, D. C. (1983). *The therapeutic relationship and its association with outcome.* Unpublished master's thesis, University of British Columbia, Vancouver, Canada. Reported in Horvath, A. O., & Greenberg, L. S. (1989). Development and validation of the working alliance inventory. *Journal of Counseling Psychology, 36,* 223–233.

Mowrer, O. H. (1953). Introduction. In O. H. Mowrer (Ed.), *Psychotherapy: Theory and Research.* New York: Ronald Press.

Munton, A. G., & Antaki, C. (1988). Causal beliefs amongst families in therapy: Attributions at the group level. *British Journal of Clinical Psychology, 27,* 91–97.

Neimeyer, R. A., & Feixas, G. (1990). The role of homework and skill acquisition in the outcome of group cognitive therapy for depression. *Behavior Therapy, 21,* 281–292.

Neimeyer, R. A., Harter, S., & Alexander, P. C. (1991). Group perceptions as predictors of outcome in the treatment of incest survivors. *Psychotherapy Research, 1,* 149–157.

Neimeyer, R. A., Robinson, L. A., Berman, J. S., & Haykal, R. F. (1989). Clinical outcome of group therapies for depression. *Group Analysis, 22,* 73–86.

Nergaard, M. O., & Silberschatz, G. (1989). The effects of shame, guilt, and the negative reaction in brief dynamic psychotherapy. *Psychotherapy, 26,* 330–337.

Newman, F. L., & Howard, K. I. (1986). Therapeutic effort, treatment outcome, and national health policy. *American Psychologist, 41,* 181–187.

Nichols, M. P. (1974). Outcome of brief cathartic psychotherapy. *Journal of Consulting and Clinical Psychology, 42,* 403–410.

Nietzel, M. T., Russell, R. L., Hemmings, K. A., & Gretter, M. L. (1987). Clinical significance of psychotherapy for unipolar depression: A meta-analytic approach to social comparison. *Journal of Consulting and Clinical Psychology,* 155–161.

Oclatis, K. A. (1978). The effects of patient feedback on the process and outcome of brief psychotherapy. *Dissertation Abstracts International, U,* 1119B.

O'Malley, S. S., Foley, S. H., Rounsaville, B. J., Watkins, J. T., Sotsky, S. M., Imber, S. D., & Elkin, I. (1988). Therapist competence and patient outcome in interpersonal psychotherapy of depression. *Journal of Consulting and Clinical Psychology, 56,* 496–501.

Orlinsky, D. E. (1988). *From micro-outcome to mega-outcome: Observational timeframes in the measurement of outcome.* Paper presented at the 19th Annual Meeting of the Society for Psychotherapy Research, Santa Fe, NM.

Orlinsky, D. E. (1989). Researchers' images of psychotherapy: Their origins and influence on research. *Clinical Psychology Review, 9,* 413–441.

Orlinsky, D. E., & Howard, K. I. (1967). The good therapy hour: Experiential correlates of patients' and therapists' evaluations of therapy sessions. *Archives of General Psychiatry, 12,* 621–632.

Orlinsky, D. E., & Howard, K. I. (1975). *Varieties of psychotherapeutic experience: Multivariate analyses of patients' and therapists' reports.* New York: Teachers College Press.

Orlinsky, D. E., & Howard, K. I. (1978). The relation of process to outcome in psychotherapy. In S. L. Garfield & A. E. Bergin (Eds.), *Handbook of psychotherapy and behavior change* (2nd ed.). New York: Wiley.

Orlinsky, D. E., & Howard, K. I. (1980). The relation of gender to psychotherapeutic outcome. In A. Brodsky & R. Hare-Mustin (Eds.), *Women in psychotherapy: An assessment of research and practice.* New York: Guilford.

Orlinsky, D. E., & Howard, K. I. (1986a). Process and outcome in psychotherapy. In S. L. Garfield & A. E. Bergin (Eds.), *Handbook of psychotherapy and behavior change* (3rd ed.). New York: Wiley.

Orlinsky, D. E., & Howard, K. I. (1986b). The psychological interior of psychotherapy: Explorations with the Therapy Session Reports. In L. S. Greenberg & W. M. Pinsof (Eds.), *The psychotherapeutic process: A research handbook.* New York: Guilford.

Orlinsky, D. E., & Howard, K. I. (1987). A generic model of psychotherapy. *Journal of Integrative and Eclectic Psychotherapy, 6,* 6–27.

Parloff, M. B., London, P., & Wolfe, B. (1986). Individual psychotherapy and behavior change. *Annual Review of Psychology, 37,* 321–349.

Parsons, T. (1951). *The social system.* Glencoe, IL: Free Press.

Peiser, I. (1982). Similarity, liking and missed sessions in relation to psychotherapy outcome. *Dissertation Abstracts International, 42,* 4587B.

Perri, M. G., Nezu, A. M., Patti, E. T., & McKann, K. L. (1989). Effect of length of treatment on weight loss. *Journal of Consulting and Clinical Psychology, 57,* 450–452.

Persons, J. B., Burns, D. D., & Perloff, J. M. (1988). Predictors of dropout and outcome in cognitive therapy for depression in a private practice setting. *Cognitive Therapy & Research, 12,* 557–576.

Phillips, E. L. (1985). *Psychotherapy revised: New frontiers in research and practice.* Hillsdale, NJ: Lawrence Erlbaum.

Pilkonis, P. A., Imber, S. D., Lewis, P., & Rubinsky, P. (1984). A comparative outcome study of individual, group, and conjoint psychotherapy. *Archives of General Psychiatry, 41,* 431–437.

Piper, W. E., Azim, H. F., Joyce, A. S., & McCallum, M. (1991). Transference interpretations, therapeutic alliance, and outcome in short-term individual psychotherapy. *Archives of General Psychiatry, 48,* 946–953.

Piper, W. E., Debanne, E. G., Bienvenu, J. P., De Carufel, F., & Garant, J. (1986). Relationships between the object focus of therapist interpretations and outcome in short-term, individual psychotherapy. *British Journal of Medical Psychology, 59,* 1–11.

Piper, W. E., Debanne, E. G., Bienvenu, J. P., & Garant, J. (1984). A comparative study of four forms of psychotherapy. *Journal of Consulting and Clinical Psychology, 52,* 268–279.

Piper, W. E., De Carufel, F., & Szkrumelak, N. (1985). Patient predictors of process and outcome in short-term individual psychotherapy. *Journal of Nervous and Mental Disease, 173,* 726–733.

Piper, W. E., Doan, B. D., Edwards, E. M., & Jones, B. D. (1979). Cotherapy behavior, group therapy process, and treatment outcome. *Journal of Consulting and Clinical Psychology, 47,* 1081–1089.

Pittenger, R. E., Hockett C. F., & Danehy, J. H. (1960). *The first five minutes.* Ithaca, NY: Paul Martineau.

Pope, K. S., Geller, J. D., & Wilkinson, L. (1975). Fee assessment and outpatient psychotherapy. *Journal of Consulting and Clinical Psychology, 43,* 835–841.

Prager, R. A. (1971). The relationship of certain client characteristics to therapist-offered conditions and therapeutic outcome. *Dissertation Abstracts International, 31,* 5634B–5635B.

Quintana, S. M., & Holahan, W. (1992). Termination in short-term counseling: Comparison of successful and unsuccessful cases. *Journal of Counseling Psychology, 39,* 299–305.

Quintana, S. M., & Meara, N. M. (1990). Internalization of therapeutic relationships in short-term psychotherapy. *Journal of Counseling Psychology, 37,* 123–130.

Rabavilas, A. D., Boulougouris, J. C., & Perissaki, C. (1979). Therapist qualities related to outcome with exposure in vivo in neurotic patients. *Journal of Behaviour Therapy & Experimental Psychiatry, 410,* 293–294.

Raimy, V. (1948). Self-reference in counseling interviews. *Journal of Consulting Psychology, 12,* 153–163.

Rice, L. N. (1965). Therapist's style of participation and case outcome. *Journal of Consulting Psychology, 29,* 155–160.

Rice, L. N. (1973). Client behavior as a function of therapist style and client resources. *Journal of Counseling Psychology, 20,* 306–311.

Rice, L. N., & Greenberg, L. S. (Eds.), (1984). *Patterns of change: Intensive analysis of psychotherapy process.* New York: Guilford.

Rice, L. N., & Wagstaff, A. K. (1967). Client voice quality and expressive styles as indexes of productive psychotherapy. *Journal of Consulting Psychology, 31,* 557–563.

Rogers, C. R. (1957). The necessary and sufficient conditions of therapeutic personality change. *Journal of Consulting Psychology, 21,* 95–103.

Rogers, C. R. (1961). A process conception of psychotherapy. In C. R. Rogers, *On becoming a person* (ch. 7). Boston: Houghton Mifflin.

Rogers, M. B. M. (1973). Therapists' verbalization and outcome in monitored play therapy. *Dissertation Abstracts International, 34,* 424B.

Rosenbaum, M., Friedlander, J., & Kaplan, S. M. (1956). Evaluation of results of psychotherapy. *Psychosomatic Medicine, 18,* 113–132.

Rosenbaum, R. L., Horowitz, M. J., & Wilner, N. (1986). Clinician assessments of patient difficulty. *Psychotherapy, 23,* 417–425.

Roshal, J. G. (1953). The type-token ratio as a measure of changes in behavior variability during psychotherapy. In W. U. Snyder (Ed.), *Group report of a program of research in psychology.* State College, PA: Pennsylvania State College Press.

Roth, I., Rhudick, P. J., Shaskan, D. A., Slobin, M. S., Wilkinson, A. E., & Young, H. (1964). Long-term effects on psychotherapy of initial treatment conditions. *Journal of Psychiatric Research, 2,* 283–297.

Rounsaville, B. J., Chevron, E. S., Prusoff, B. A., Elkin, I., Imber, S., Sotsky, S., & Watkins, J. (1987). The relation between specific and general dimensions of the psychotherapy process in interpersonal psychotherapy of depression. *Journal of Consulting and Clinical Psychology, 55,* 379–384.

Rounsaville, B. J., Weissman, M. M., & Prusoff, B. A. (1981). Psychotherapy with depressed outpatients: Patient and process variables as predictors of outcome. *British Journal of Psychiatry, 138,* 67–74.

Rudolf, G. (1991). *Die therapeutische Arbeitsbeziehung: Untersuchung zum Zustandekommen, Verlauf und Ergebnis analytischer Psychotherapien* [The therapeutic working alliance: Investigations on the process and outcome of analytic psychotherapies]. Berlin, Heidelberg: Springer-Verlag.

Rudy, J. P., McLemore, C. W., & Gorsuch, R. L. (1985). Interpersonal behavior and therapeutic progress: Therapists and clients rate themselves and each other. *Psychiatry, 48,* 264–281.

Runyan, W. M. (1982). *Life histories and psychobiography: Explorations in theory and method.* New York: Oxford University Press.

Russell, R. L., Greenwald, S., & Shirk, S. (1991). Language change in child psychotherapy: A meta-analytic review. *Journal of Consulting and Clinical Psychology, 59,* 916–919.

Sachs, J. S. (1983). Negative factors in brief psychotherapy: An empirical assessment. *Journal of Consulting and Clinical Psychology, 51,* 557–564.

Sachse, R. (1992a). *Zielorientierte Gesprächspsychotherapie* [Goal-directed client-centered therapy]. Göttingen: Hogrefe.

Sachse, R. (1992b). Differential effects of processing proposals and content references on the explication process of clients with different starting conditions. *Psychotherapy Research, 2,* 235–251.

Sachse, R. (in press). Determinants of success in goal-oriented client-centered psychotherapy: There are no successful clients but only successful teams. *Psychotherapy Research.*

Safran, J. D., & Segal, Z. V. (1990). *Interpersonal process in cognitive therapy.* New York: Basic Books.

Safran, J. D., & Wallner, L. K. (1991). The relative predictive validity of two therapeutic alliance measures in cognitive therapy. *Psychological Assessment, 3,* 188–195.

Sandell, R. (1985). Influence of supervision, therapist's competence, and patient's ego level on the effects of time-limited psychotherapy. *Psychotherapy and Psychosomatics, 44,* 103–109.

Sander, K., Langer, I., Bastine, R., Tausch, A.-M., Tausch, R., & Wieczerkowski, W. (1973). Gesprächspsychotherapie bei 73 psychoneurotischen Klienten mit alternierenden Psychotherapeuten ohne Abwahlmöglichkeit [Client-centered therapy with 73 neurotic clients with alternating therapists]. *Zeitschrift für Klinische Psychologie und Psychotherapie, 21,* 218–229.

Sashin, J. I., Eldred, S. H., & Van Amerongen, S. T. (1975). A search for predictive factors in institute supervised cases: A retrospective study of 183 cases from 1959–1966 at the Boston Psychoanalytic Society and Institute. *International Journal of Psycho-Analysis, 56,* 343–359.

Saunders, S. M., Howard, K. I., & Orlinsky, D. E. (1989). The Therapeutic Bond Scales: Psychometric characteristics and relationship to treatment effectiveness. *Psychological Assessment, 1,* 323–330.

Schauble, P. G., & Pierce, R. M. (1974). Client in-therapy behavior: A therapist guide to progress. *Psychotherapy: Theory, Research and Practice, 11,* 229–234.

Scheflen, A. E. (1973). *Communicational structure: analysis of a psychotherapy transaction.* Bloomington, IN: University of Indiana Press.

Schindler, L. (1991). *Die empirische Analyse der therapeutischen Beziehung. Beiträge zur Prozessforschung in der Verhaltenstherapie* [The empirical analysis of the therapeutic relation: Contributions to process research in behavior therapy]. Berlin, Heidelberg: Springer-Verlag.

Schlesinger, H. J., Mumford, E., Glass, G. V., Patrick, C., & Sharfstein, S. (1983). Mental health treatment and medical care utilization in a fee-for-service system: Outpatient mental health treatment following the onset of a chronic disease. *American Journal of Public Health, 73,* 422–429.

Schulte, D. (in press). Directivity and control of therapeutic dialogue. *Journal of Clinical Psychology and Psychotherapy.*

Schulte, D., & Künzel, R. (1991). *Relevance and meaning of therapist's control.* Paper presented at the 22nd Annual Meeting of the Society for Psychotherapy Research, Lyon, France.

Schulte, D., & Künzel, R. (in press). Relevance and meaning of the therapist's control in the therapeutic process. *Psychotherapy Research.*

Schwartz, A. J., & Bernard, H. S. (1981). Comparison of patient and therapist evaluations of time-limited therapy. *Psychotherapy: Theory, Research, and Practice, 18,* 101–108.

Seeman, J. (1949). A study of the process of nondirective therapy. *Journal of Consulting Psychology, 13,* 157–168.

Seeman, J. (1954). Counselor judgments of therapeutic process and outcome. In C. R. Rogers & R. F. Dymond (Eds.), *Psychotherapy and personality change.* Chicago: University of Chicago Press.

Shapiro, D. A., Firth, J., Stiles, W. B., Elliott, R. K., & Llewelyn, S. P. (1985). Therapeutic outcome: Research strategies, cost-effectiveness, and meta-analysis. In W. Huber (Ed.), *Progress in psychotherapy research.* Louvain-la-Neuve, Belgium: Presses Universitaires de Louvain.

Shoham-Salomon, V., & Rosenthal, R. (1987). Paradoxical interventions: A meta-analysis. *Journal of Consulting and Clinical Psychology, 55,* 22–28.

Shyne, A. W., & Kogan, L. S. (1957). *A study of components of movement.* New York: Institute of Welfare Research, Community Service Society.

Silberschatz, G., Curtis, J. T., Fretter, P. B., & Kelly, T. J. (1988). Testing hypotheses of psychotherapeutic change processes. In H. Dahl, H. Kächele, & H. Thomä (Eds.), *Psychoanalytic research process strategies.* Berlin, Heidelberg, New York, London, Paris, Tokyo: Springer-Verlag.

Sloane, R. B., Staples, F. R., Cristol, A. H., Yorkston, N. J.,

& Whipple, K. (1975). *Psychotherapy versus behavior therapy.* Cambridge: Harvard University Press.

Snyder, W. U. (1945). An investigation of the nature of nondirective psychotherapy. *Journal of General Psychology, 33,* 193–223.

Snyder, W. U. (1946). Warmth in nondirective counseling. *Journal of Abnormal and Social Psychology, 41,* 491–495.

Soldz, S., Budman, S., & Demby, A. (1992). The relationship between main actor behaviors and treatment outcome in group psychotherapy. *Psychotherapy Research, 2,* 52–62.

Sorenson, R. L., Gorsuch, R. L., & Mintz, J. (1985). Moving targets: Patients' changing complaints during psychotherapy. *Journal of Consulting and Clinical Psychology, 53,* 49–54.

Stanton, H. E. (1976). Fee-paying and weight loss: Evidence for an interesting interaction. *American Journal of Clinical Hypnosis, 19,* 47–49.

Steinhelber, J., Patterson, V., Cliffe, K., & LeGoullon, M. (1984). An investigation of some relationships between psychotherapy supervision and patient change. *Journal of Clinical Psychology, 41,* 1346–1353.

Stiles, W. B. (1986). Development of a taxonomy of verbal response modes. In L. S. Greenberg & W. M. Pinsof (Eds.), *The psychotherapeutic process: A research handbook.* New York: Guilford.

Stiles, W. B., & Shapiro, D. A. (1989). Abuse of the drug metaphor in psychotherapy process–outcome research. *Clinical Psychology Review, 9,* 521–543.

Stiles, W. B., Shapiro, D. A., & Elliott, R. (1986). "Are all psychotherapies equivalent?" *American Psychologist, 41,* 165–180.

Stiles, W. B., Shapiro, D. A., & Firth-Cozens, J. A. (1990). Correlations of session evaluations with treatment outcome. *British Journal of Clinical Psychology, 29,* 13–21.

Stiles, W. B., & Snow, J. S. (1984a). Counseling session impact as viewed by novice counselors and their clients. *Journal of Counseling Psychology, 31,* 3–12.

Stiles, W. B., & Snow, J. S. (1984b). Dimensions of psychotherapy session impact across sessions and across clients. *British Journal of Clinical Psychology, 23,* 59–63.

Strupp, H. H., Hadley, S. W., & Gomes-Schwartz, B. (1977). *Psychotherapy for better or worse: The problem of negative effects.* New York: Jason Aronson.

Strupp, H. H., Wallach, M. S., Wogan, M., & Jenkins, J. W. (1963). Psychotherapists' assessments of former patients. *Journal of Nervous and Mental Disease, 137,* 222–230.

Subich, L. M., & Hardin, S. I. (1985). Counseling expectations as a function of fee for service. *Journal of Counseling Psychology, 32,* 323–328.

Svartberg, M., & Stiles, T. C. (1992). Predicting patient change from therapist competence and patient-therapist complementarity in short-term anxiety-provoking psychotherapy: A pilot study. *Journal of Consulting and Clinical Psychology, 60,* 304–307.

Swoboda, J. S., Dowd, E. T., & Wise, S. L. (1990). Reframing and restraining directives in the treatment of clinical depression. *Journal of Counseling Psychology, 37,* 254–260.

Szapocznik, J., Kurtines, W. M., Foote, F., Perez-Vidal, A., & Hervis, A. (1983). Conjoint versus one-person family therapy: Some evidence for the effectiveness of conducting family therapy through one person. *Journal of Consulting and Clinical Psychology, 51,* 889–899.

Szapocznik, J., Kurtines, W. M., Foote, F., Perez-Vidal, A., & Hervis, A. (1986). Conjoint versus one-person family therapy: Further evidence for the effectiveness of conducting family therapy through one person with drug-abusing adolescents. *Journal of Consulting and Clinical Psychology, 54*, 395–397.

Talley, P. F., Strupp, H. H., & Morey, L. C. (1990). Matchmaking in psychotherapy: Patient-therapist dimensions and their impact on outcome. *Journal of Consulting and Clinical Psychology, 58*, 182–188.

Taube, C. A., Mechanic, D., & Hohmann, A. A. (Eds.). (1989). *The future of mental health services research.* Washington, DC: U. S. Department of Health and Human Services.

Taurke, E. A., Flegenheimer, W., McCullough, L., Winston, A., Pollack, J., & Trujillo, M. (1990). Change in patient affect/defense ratio from early to late sessions in brief psychotherapy. *Journal of Clinical Psychology, 46*, 657–668.

Thommen, B., Ammann, R., & von Cranach, M. (1988). *Handlungsorganisation durch soziale Repräsentationen. Welchen Einfluss haben therapeutische Schule auf das Handeln ihrer Mitglieder?* Bern, Switzerland: Huber.

Torhorst, A., & Stitz, S. (1988). Therapieverlaufsstudie bei Patienten nach Suizidversuch unter Brücksichtigung linguistischer Untersuchungsergebnisse [Study of treatment course for patients after attempted suicide with consideration of linguistic findings]. *Suizidprophylaxe, 15*, 211–220.

Toukmanian, S. G., & Rennie, D. L. (Eds.). (1992). *Psychotherapy process research: Paradigmatic and narrative approaches.* Newbury Park, CA: Sage Publications.

Tracey, T. J. (1985). Dominance and outcome: A sequential examination. *Journal of Counseling Psychology, 32*, 119–122.

Tracey, T. J. (1987). Stage differences in the dependencies of topic initiation and topic following behavior. *Journal of Counseling Psychology, 34*, 121–131.

Tracey, T. J. (1988). Relationship of responsibility attribution congruence to psychotherapy outcome. *Journal of Social and Clinical Psychology, 7*, 131–142.

Tracey, T. J. (1989). Client and therapist session satisfaction over the course of psychotherapy. *Psychotherapy, 26*, 177–182.

Tracey, T. J., & Dundon, M. (1988). Role anticipations and preferences over the course of counseling. *Journal of Counseling Psychology, 35*, 3–14.

Tracey, T. J., & Ray, P. B. (1984). Stages of successful time-limited counseling: An interactional examination. *Journal of Counseling Psychology, 31*, 13–27.

Truax, C. B., & Wittmer, J. (1971). Patient non-personal reference during psychotherapy and therapeutic outcome. *Journal of Clinical Psychology, 27*, 300–302.

Tscheulin, D. (1983). Über differentielles therapeutisches Vorgehen in der klientenzentrierten Therapie. In D. Tscheulin (Ed.), *Beziehung und Technik in der klientenzentrierten Therapie.* Cited in D. Tscheulin, Confrontation and non-confrontation as differential techniques in differential client-centered therapy. In G. Lietaer, J. Rombauts, & R. Van Balen (Eds.), *Client-centered and experiential psychotherapy in the nineties.* Leuven, Belgium: Leuven University Press.

Tscheulin, D. (1988). *Wirkfaktoren psychotherapeutischer Intervention. Ein heuristisches Modell zur einheitlichen Betrachtung psychotherapeutischer Intervention aus klientenzentrierter Perspektive.* Cited in D. Tscheulin, Confrontation and non-confrontation as differential techniques in differential client-centered therapy. In G. Lietaer, J. Rombauts, & R. Van Balen (Eds.), *Client-centered and experiential psychotherapy in the nineties.* Leuven, Belgium: Leuven University Press.

Tscheulin, D. (1992). *Wirkfaktoren psychotherapeutischer Interaktion* [Working mechanism of psychotherapeutic interaction]. Göttingen: Hogrefe.

Turner, J. H. (1988). *A theory of social interaction.* Stanford, CA: Stanford University Press.

Tyson, G. M., & Range, L. M. (1987). Gestalt dialogues as a treatment for mild depression: Time works just as well. *Journal of Clinical Psychology, 43*, 227–231.

Uhlenhuth, E. H., & Duncan, D. B. (1968). Subjective change with medical student therapists: II. Some determinants of change in psychoneurotic outpatients. *Archives of General Psychiatry, 18*, 532–540.

Wallerstein, R. S. (1986). *Forty-two lives in treatment: A study of psychoanalysis and psychotherapy.* New York: Guilford.

Wampold, B. E., & Kim, K-H. (1989). Sequential analysis applied to counseling process and outcome: A case study revisited. *Journal of Counseling Psychology, 36*, 357–364.

Waterhouse, G. C. J. (1982). Countertransference in short-term psychotherapy: Interpersonal diagnosis and reciprocal response: *Dissertation Abstracts International, 42*, 4218B.

Weber, J. J., Bachrach, H. M., & Solomon, M. (1985a). Factors associated with the outcome of psychoanalysis: Report of the Columbia Psychoanalytic Center research project (II). *International Review of Psycho-Analysis, 12*, 127–141.

Weber, J. J., Bachrach, H. M., & Solomon, M. (1985b). Factors associated with the outcome of psychoanalysis: Report of the Columbia Psychoanalytic Center research project (III). *International Review of Psycho-Analysis, 12*, 251–262.

Werman, D. S., Agle, D., McDaniel, E., & Schoof, K. G. (1976). Survey of psychiatric treatment effectiveness in a medical student clinic. *American Journal of Psychotherapy, 30*, 294–302.

Westerman, M. A., Frankel, A. S., Tanaka, J. S., & Kahn, J. (1987). Client cooperative interview behavior and outcome in paradoxical and behavioral brief treatment approaches. *Journal of Counseling Psychology, 34*, 99–102.

Westerman, M. A., Tanaka, J. S., Frankel, A. S., & Kahn, J. (1986). The coordinating style construct: An approach to conceptualizing patient interpersonal behavior. *Psychotherapy, 23*, 540–547.

Westermann, B., Schwab, R., & Tausch, R. (1983). Auswirkungen und Prozesse personenzentrierter Gruppenpsychotherapie bei 164 Klienten einer Psychotherapeutischen Beratungsstelle [Effects and processes of person-centered group psychotherapy with 164 clients in a psychotherapeutic counseling center]. *Zeitschrift für Klinische Psychologie, 12*, 273–292.

Williams, K. E., & Chambless, D. L. (1990). The relationship between therapist characteristics and outcome of in vivo exposure treatment for agoraphobia. *Behavior Therapy, 21*, 111–116.

Willutzki, U. (1991). *Zur kognitiven Seite phobischer Ängste. Ein individuúm zentrierter Zugang.* Frankfurt: Lang.

Willutzki, U., & Schulte, D. (1991). Wissen Therapeuten und Therapeutinnen um die situationsbezogenen Kognitionen ihrer Klienten und Klientinnen? Eine Analyse mit dem Kelly-Gitter [Do therapists know about the situation-specific cognitions of their clients? An analysis with the Kelly grid]. In D. Schulte (Ed.), *Therapeutische Entscheidungen.* Göttingen: Hogrefe.

Windholz, M., & Silberschatz, G. (1988). Vanderbilt Psychotherapy Process Scale: A replication with adult outpatients. *Journal of Consulting and Clinical Psychology, 56,* 56–60.

Winnicott, D. W. (1965). *The maturational process and the facilitating environment.* New York: International Universities Press.

Wiseman, H., Shefler, G., Caneti, L., & Ronen, Y. (in press). A systematic comparison of two cases in Mann's time-limited psychotherapy: An events approach. *Psychotherapy Research.*

Wogan, M. (1970). Effect of therapist-patient personality variables on therapeutic outcome. *Journal of Consulting and Clinical Psychology, 35,* 356–361.

Wogan, M., Getter, H., Amdur, M. J., Nichols, M. F., & Okman, G. (1977). Influencing interaction and outcomes in group psychotherapy. *Small Group Behavior, 8,* 25–46.

Wood, W. D. (1982). Do fees help heal? *Journal of Clinical Psychology, 38,* 669–673.

Worthington, E. L. (1986). Client compliance with homework directive during counseling. *Journal of Counseling Psychology, 33,* 124–130.

Wright, R. M., & Strong, S. R. (1982). Stimulating therapeutic change with directives: An exploratory study. *Journal of Counseling Psychology, 29,* 199–202.

Yalom, I. D., Houts, P. S., Zimerberg, S. M., & Rand, K. H. (1967). Prediction of improvement in group therapy. *Archives of General Psychiatry, 17,* 159–168.

Yoken, C., & Berman, J. S. (1987). Third-party payment and the outcome of psychotherapy. *Journal of Consulting and Clinical Psychology, 55,* 571–576.

Zeiss, A. M., Lewinsohn, P. M., & Munoz, R. F. (1979). Nonspecific improvement effects in depression using interpersonal, cognitive and pleasant events focused treatments. *Journal of Consulting and Clinical Psychology, 47,* 427–439.

Zola, M. A., Howard, K. I., & Orlinsky, D. E. (1987). *The process of outcome: The individual remission patterns of self-reported psychiatric symptoms.* Paper presented at the 18th Annual Meeting of the Society for Psychotherapy Research, Ulm, Germany.

Zwick, R., & Attkisson, C. C. (1985). Effectiveness of a client pretherapy orientation videotape. *Journal of Counseling Psychology, 32,* 514–524.

PART
III

MAJOR APPROACHES

9

BEHAVIOR THERAPY
WITH ADULTS

- **PAUL M. G. EMMELKAMP**

  Academic Hospital
  Groningen, The Netherlands

viewed, the text may not make for exciting reading. It is hoped, however, that the chapter will provide a fair evaluation of the progress that has been achieved in behavior therapy.

This chapter provides an overview of the current status of behavior therapy with adult disorders. Emphasis throughout is on the application of behavioral procedures on clinical patients. Since separate chapters in this volume are devoted to behavior medicine and behavior therapy with children, these topics will not be dealt with in this chapter. Cognitive interventions are covered only insofar as they are contrasted with behavioral procedures or form an integral part of cognitive-behavioral procedures. For a more detailed discussion of cognitive therapy, the reader is referred to Chapter 10 by Hollon and Beck in this volume. As an aside, to separate procedures that are truly behavioral from procedures that are purely cognitive is rather artificial. Most cognitive procedures have clear behavioral techniques in them, and, although less obvious, most behavioral procedures also contain cognitive elements.

The research on behavior therapy with adults has proliferated to such an extent that it is impossible to provide a comprehensive review of the whole area in one chapter. In the last decade, significant progress has been made in a number of areas, although the development of effective behavioral treatments has advanced in an uneven fashion. Therefore, the scope of this chapter is limited to those disorders for which the behavioral approach has been most influential. This chapter reviews the state of the art of current behavior approaches to anxiety disorders, depression, alcoholism, sexual dysfunctions, paraphilias, marital distress, and schizophrenia. Recent comprehensive reviews of other areas can be found in Bellack, Hersen, and Kazdin (1990) and in two review series: *Progress in Behavior Modification* and *Annual Review of Behavior Therapy*.

Given the numerous studies that had to be re-

SIMPLE PHOBIAS

Systematic desensitization was developed by Wolpe (1958) and is presumably the most thoroughly investigated behavioral procedure with simple phobics, although much of this research is not clinically relevant, since mildly distressed subjects — often students — were used, rather than truly phobic patients.

In systematic desensitization, patients are first trained in muscular relaxation; then they move gradually up a hierarchy of anxiety-arousing situations, while remaining relaxed. Systematic desensitization may be applied either in imagination or in vivo, but most studies involved the imaginal variant. Although numerous studies have demonstrated the effectiveness of systematic desensitization in reducing circumscribed phobias in analogue populations, the theoretical underpinnings are still vague. Several theoretical explanations have been put forward, including reciprocal inhibition (Wolpe, 1958), counterconditioning (Davison, 1968), and cognitive processes (Emmelkamp, 1975). For an overview of research into the various theoretical explanations, the interested reader is referred to Emmelkamp (1982).

Flooding in imagination is a technique in which the patient has to imagine situations and experiences that she or he finds frightening for a prolonged period of time until anxiety declines. It has also been found effective with specific phobics. Systematic desensitization and flooding — both in imagination — were found to be equally effective with specific phobias (for review, see Emmelkamp, 1982).

A number of studies demonstrated the effectiveness of *prolonged exposure in vivo*. In most cases, treatment was completed in a few sessions lasting

for several hours. Öst (1989) treated 20 simple phobics by one single session of prolonged exposure to the phobic stimulus and found this treatment to be effective in 90 percent of the patients up to 4 years follow-up. The mean treatment time in this study was only 2.1 hours. Far more sessions are required to achieve similar improvement with systematic desensitization.

The element that most behavioral treatments have in common is exposure to distressing stimuli. Exposure can be carried out in two ways: (1) in imagination, in which patients must imagine themselves to be in phobic situations, or (2) in vivo, in which patients are really exposed to the situation. Exposure in vivo is usually more effective than exposure in imagination. Other important variables in exposure treatments are the degree of anxiety and the duration of exposure trials. The most successful exposure programs are those carried out in vivo, during a long uninterrupted period of time (prolonged), and in which escape and avoidance of the phobic situation are prevented. Too early termination of exposure sessions, when anxiety has not sufficiently been reduced, may lead to a worsening rather than a reduction of the phobia (Marshall, 1985, 1988). Although anxiety is a by-product of exposure treatment, deliberate anxiety provocation is unnecessary and may lead to early dropout of treatment. A number of problems remain in which it is difficult or impossible to realize exposure in vivo, and here imaginary methods may be of help.

According to Williams, Dooseman, and Kleifield (1984), the therapist should accelerate patients' performance attainments by providing performance induction aids and behavioral guidance during exposure in vivo in order to enhance patients' feelings of self-efficacy. In their study, height phobics and patients with driving phobia were treated by exposure in vivo or a mastery-oriented treatment. All subjects received exposure in vivo, but the treatments differed in the extent to which the therapist provided mastery-induction aids to the subjects. With the mastery-oriented treatment, the therapist provided a variety of performance-induction aids and behavioral guidance whenever subjects were having difficulty making progress. These guidance procedures included having the therapist accompany the subject, having the subject focus on an intermediate goal, eliminating avoidance rituals, and so on. The mastery-oriented treatment proved to be slightly superior to exposure alone.

Exposure treatment can be done through a self-help book or a computer (Ghosh Marks & Carr, 1987). However, there is some evidence that therapist-guided exposure is more effective than self-exposure with simple phobics. Öst, Salkovskis, and

Hellström (1991) compared one session of therapist-directed exposure with a two-week program of self-directed exposure using a manual. Self-exposure fared poor: Only 6 percent of the patients met stringent criteria for clinical improvement, whereas 71 percent of the therapist-directed patients met these criteria.

Individual Differences

Öst, Johansson, and Jerremalm (1982) investigated the interaction between treatment factors and individual characteristics. Claustrophobics were divided into two groups showing different response patterns: behavioral and physiological reactors. Within each group, half of the patients received a more psychophysiologically focused method (exposure in vivo plus relaxation—"applied relaxation") or a more behaviorally focused treatment (exposure in vivo). The results showed that for the behavioral reactors, exposure in vivo was superior to applied relaxation, whereas the reverse was true for the physiological reactors.

Two more studies have been reported that investigated whether tailoring the treatment to specific response patterns would be beneficial. In both studies, physiological reactors and cognitive reactors were treated with either exposure in vivo plus relaxation (applied relaxation) or exposure plus self-instructional training. With fear of flying, there was a slight superiority for the consonant method (Haug et al., 1987), while with dental phobics (Jerremalm, Jansson, & Öst, 1986), the results did not support the hypothesis that greater effects are achieved when the method used fits the patient's response pattern. Although the results are somewhat inconsistent, it might be important to consider individual differences in response patterns of simple phobics when planning the treatment.

The Process of Exposure

Several studies investigated whether habituation of subjective anxiety and physiological arousal occurred during exposure in vivo with specific phobics, and this was indeed the case (e.g., Emmelkamp & Felten, 1985). This process of anxiety reduction as a function of continuous exposure is usually explained in terms of habituation. Results of an analogue study on spider phobics suggest that habituation to phobic stimuli occurring in depressed mood may not be as enduring as habituation in elated mood (Mills & Salkovskis, 1988).

An interesting series of experiments (Rachman & Levitt, 1988) on claustrophobic subjects provide further information on the habituation process during exposure in vivo. In analyzing the differences between habituators and nonhabituators, Rachman and Levitt (1988) found that the best predictor of nonhabituation was the cognition "I am going to pass out." Their results also point to the role of bodily symptoms in retarding habituation. Shortness of breath was reported by all nonhabituators, while only 54 percent of the habituators endorsed this item on the first exposure trial. These results suggest that certain physical sensations and cognitions associated with them may impede the habituation of fear during exposure in vivo. Whether this is restricted to claustrophobics or is applicable to other simple phobics needs to be studied.

Cognitive Therapy

A number of studies with clinically revelant populations have studied the effectiveness of cognitive strategies in overcoming simple phobias. There is some evidence that simple phobics are characterized by negative thinking of catastrophic nature and that these catastrophizing thoughts may predict actual phobic behavior (Marshall, Bristoll, & Barbarree, 1992). Biran and Wilson (1981) found exposure in vivo clearly superior to cognitive therapy with phobics with fears of either heights, elevators, or darkness. Results of studies that investigated a combination of rehearsal of self-statements and exposure in vivo have produced conflicting results. Immediately after treatment, no positive results (Ladouceur, 1983; Marshall, 1985) or only a slight positive result (Emmelkamp & Felten, 1985) was found for adding coping rehearsal to exposure in vivo. At follow-up, however, one study (Ladouceur, 1983) found a negative effect of adding coping self-instructions whereas another study (Marshall, 1985) found positive effects. Only further studies can solve this discrepancy in results.

Specific Application with Blood Phobics

Although prolonged exposure in vivo seems to be the treatment of choice for most specific phobias, in blood phobics additional measures may be required. Blood phobic patients deserve special attention since an unusual pattern of physiological responses has been reported. Instead of an increase in heart rate (HR) and respiration as typically seen in phobics, blood phobics show bradycardia (Connolly, Hallam, & Marks, 1976) and a decrease in blood pressure (BP) which may result in fainting (Öst, Sterner, & Lindahl, 1984). Despite this different physiological reaction pattern, blood phobics can also be treated by real-life exposure. In the Thyrer, Hinsle, and Curtic (1985) study 15 blood phobics were gradually exposed to anxiety-evoking stimuli that included the viewing of horror and surgical movies and medical texts illustrated with pictures of trauma victims, receiving and administering repeated venipunctures and intramuscular injections, donating blood, or having the patient

wash his or her hands in a small amount of blood. When a vasovagal faint occurred, recovery was usually rapid when the patient was placed in a supine position. Graduated exposure was successful in most cases.

Three controlled studies have been conducted. Öst, Rindahl, Sterner, & Jerremalm, (1984) compared exposure in vivo with exposure in vivo plus relaxation (applied relaxation); both methods yielded good results. In a more recent study, Öst, Sterner, and Fellenius (1989) compared (1) applied relaxation, (2) applied tension, and (3) a combination of these two methods. With applied tension, patients are taught to tense their muscles when exposed to a series of slides of wound injuries and blood. In later sessions, patients have to donate blood and observe open-heart or lung surgery. Patients learn to recognize the earliest sign of a drop in blood pressure and to apply the tension technique to reverse it. Seventy-three percent of the patients were clinically improved at the end of treatment and 77 percent at follow-up. Although no significant differences among the three groups were found, there was a trend favoring applied tension. Finally, Öst, Fellenius, and Sterner (1991) found that acquiring the coping skills of recognizing the early sign of a drop in blood pressure and applying the applied tension technique to reverse the blood pressure fall were more effective than just exposure to blood stimuli.

Concluding Remarks

With simple phobics, the treatment of choice is usually exposure in vivo. There is hardly any evidence that cognitive therapy may enhance the effects of exposure in vivo. With blood phobics, it might be therapeutically wise to add applied tension to the exposure procedure.

PANIC DISORDER AND AGORAPHOBIA

Until recently, research did not focus specifically on the panic attacks of agoraphobics. Most of the research involved investigating effective parameters of exposure treatment, and it has been reviewed in the 1986 edition of this *Handbook*. Therefore, it will suffice to summarize the main conclusions.

Exposure in vivo is superior to imaginal exposure. Most studies that investigated this issue found exposure in vivo superior to imaginal exposure (Emmelkamp, 1974; Emmelkamp & Wessels, 1975; Stern & Marks, 1973; Watson, Mullett, & Pilley, 1973).

Prolonged exposure in vivo is superior to brief exposure. Stern and Marks (1973) compared short (four half-hour sessions) with long (two-hour) sessions. Prolonged exposure in vivo sessions were clearly superior to shorter ones.

Having the opportunity to escape during exposure in vivo does not have the detrimental effects as once thought (de Silva & Rachman, 1984; Rachman, Craske, Tallman, & Solyom, 1986).

Group exposure is about equally effective as individually conducted exposure programs. (For a review, see Emmelkamp & Kuipers, 1985.)

Treatment can be conducted as a self-help program (Emmelkamp, 1982; Mathews, Gelder, & Johnston, 1981) *and can be done through a self-help book or a computer* (Ghosh and Marks, 1987) *or telephone-guided* (McNamee, O'Sullivan, Lelliot, & Marks, 1989).

Therapist guidance enhances effects of exposure. Williams and Zane (1989) compared exposure in which the therapist was quite active in guiding agoraphobics in how to perform therapeutic tasks with an exposure condition with less therapist involvement. Guided mastery treatment was found to be superior.

Effects of exposure programs are long lasting. Follow-up reports ranging from four to nine years after treatment were published by Burns, Thorpe, and Cavallero (1986), Emmelkamp and Kuipers (1979), Lelliott, Marks, Monteiro, Tsakiris, and Noshirvani (1987), McPherson, Brougham, and McLaren (1980), and Munby and Johnston (1980). Generally, improvements brought about by the treatment were maintained or improved upon. However, results of the behavioral treatment were variable. Some patients were symptom free, some were moderately improved, and a few patients did not benefit at all.

Exposure in vivo is effective irrespective of individual response pattern. The importance of individual response patterns in agoraphobics was examined by Mackay and Liddell (1986) and Öst, Jerremalm, and Jansson (1984). Exposure in vivo was found to be equally effective for cognitive and noncognitive responders (Mackay & Liddell, 1986) and for behavioral and physiological reactors (Öst, Jerremalm, Jansson, 1984).

Cognitive Therapy Versus Exposure in Vivo
Cognitive therapy programs for agoraphobia have usually employed one or more of the following cognitive strategies: (1) self-instructional training, (2) rational-emotive therapy, and (3) paradoxical intention. With *self-instructional training* (SIT), patients are instructed to substitute positive coping self-statements for the anxiety-engendering self-statements. During treatment sessions, patients cognitively rehearse self-instructional ways of handling anxiety by means of an imagination procedure. The critical elements of *rational-emotive therapy* (RET) involve determining the irrational thoughts that mediate the anxiety and confronting and modifying them so that undue anxiety is no longer experienced. *Paradoxical intention* is used as a coping procedure to reverse the vicious circle of fearful responding. With this approach, patients are instructed to go to a very difficult phobic situation, to focus on the physiological experiences of anxiety and to try to increase the symptoms in an attempt to court the anticipated disastrous consequences. Thus, exposure in vivo forms an essential part of this so-called "cognitive" approach.

A number of studies with agoraphobics have shown that exposure in vivo is superior to cognitive therapy consisting of insight into irrational beliefs (RET) and training of incompatible positive self-statements (SIT) (Emmelkamp, Brilman, Kuipers, & Mersch, 1986; Emmelkamp, Kuipers, & Eggeraat, 1978; Emmelkamp & Mersch, 1982). Mavissakalian, Michelson, Greenwald, Kornblith, and Greenwald (1983) investigated the impact of self-instructional training and paradoxical intention on exposure in vivo. The results revealed equivalent long-term effectiveness of the two treatments. In a subsequent study by Michelson, Mavissakalian, and Marchione (1985), neither paradoxical intention nor relaxation enhanced the effects of exposure in vivo. Taken together, the results of cognitive therapy (rational-emotive therapy, self-instructional training, and paradoxical intention) with agoraphobics are negative.

Cognitive Therapy for Panic
The recent interest in panic has led to cognitively based treatments focusing more directly on the panic attacks of agoraphobics. A number of cognitively oriented researchers have stressed psychological factors in accounting for panic attacks (e.g., Clark, 1986; Ehlers & Margraf, 1989; Rapee, 1987). In these models, it is assumed that patients misinterpret bodily sensations as a sign of a serious physical danger (e.g., a heart attack) and may panic. Central to the cognitive conceptualization of panic is that bodily sensations are interpreted as dangerous. A positive feedback loop between physiological arousal and anxiety that leads to an ascending "spiral" ending in the full-blown panic attack is postulated (Margraf, Ehlers, & Roth, 1987).

A number of authors have proposed that the panic attack consists of a synergistic interaction between hyperventilation and fear (Bass & Lelliott, 1989; Ley, 1985; Rapee, 1987). The concept of the vicious circle effect may be helpful to understand the course of the hyperventilation. A hyperventilation attack results in a number of somatic symptoms that are caused by a drop in arterial CO_2 levels. The individual who is unaware of the connection between overbreathing and somatic symptoms may misinterpret these sensations as a sign of a serious disease, leading to increased anxiety, which by itself may provoke hyperventilation in the future.

Those formulations of panic have led to a renewed interest in the treatment of panic by cognitive and behavioral methods. Clark's treatment approach consists of explanation and discussion of the way hyperventilation induces panic, breathing exercises, interoceptive exposure, and relabeling of bodily symptoms. This package produced a substantial and rapid reduction in panic attack frequency in two studies with a small number of patients (Clark, Salkovskis, & Chalkley, 1985; Salkovskis, Jones, & Clark, 1986). However, both studies lacked a formal control group. In a controlled study by de Ruiter, Rijken, Garssen, and Kraaimaat (1989), this package was not found to lead to a reduction in frequency of panic attacks. Clark (1991) compared cognitive therapy for panic with applied relaxation and drug treatment (imipramine). All three treatments were found to be effective in reducing panic, anxiety, and avoidance. The cognitive therapy was found to be superior to the other two treatments on 12 out of 17 measures. Patients treated with imipramine relapsed significantly more than patients treated with cognitive therapy. At 15-month follow-up, 80 percent of cognitive therapy patients, 47 percent of applied relaxation, and 50 percent of imipramine patients were panic free.

A clear limitation of this approach is that this treatment can be applied only to patients who recognize a marked similarity between the effects of hyperventilation and their panic symptoms. Further, it is not yet established whether the improvements achieved are due to exposure to the physical sensations (interoceptive exposure), to the breathing exercises, or to the cognitive components of the treatment package. Bonn, Readhead, and Timmons (1984) studied the effectiveness of breathing retraining without cognitive interventions. Breathing exercises were not found to enhance the effects of exposure in vivo at the end of treatment. At six-month follow-up, however, breathing exercises plus exposure in vivo were found to be superior to exposure in vivo alone.

The aim of a recent study by Bouman and Emmelkamp (1993) was to dismantle the treatment package of Clark et al. (1985) into its essential ingredients with panic patients with moderate-to-

severe avoidance who all suffered from hyperventilation. Therefore four treatments were compared: (1) breathing exercises, (2) breathing exercises plus cognitive therapy, (3) breathing exercises, cognitive therapy, and exposure in vivo, and (4) exposure in vivo. All four treatment conditions led to significant clinical improvements on anxiety and avoidance. The only evidence for an additive effect of cognitive procedures comes from two highly correlated measures, the Agoraphobic Cognitions Questionnaire (ACQ) and the Bodily Sensation Questionnaire (BSQ). This finding indicates a greater decrease in catastrophic thoughts in the combined treatment (breathing exercises, cognitive therapy, and exposure in vivo) in comparison to the other conditions. On all other measures, the four treatment packages emerge as equally effective.

Exposure to Interoceptive Stimuli

Griez and van den Hout (1983) hypothesized that repeated exposure to an interoceptive cue by means of CO_2 inhalation would lead to anxiety reduction in panic patients. In two studies (Griez & van den Hout, 1986; van den Hout, van der Molen, Griez, Lousberg, & Nansen, 1987), CO_2-induced subjective anxiety in patients was found to decrease as the number of CO_2-induced exposures to interoceptive anxiety symptoms increased.

Barlow, Craske, Cerny, and Klosko (1989) evaluated the effects of a comprehensive package consisting of exposure to interoceptive stimuli, imaginal exposure, breathing retraining, and cognitive restructuring. This package was found to be more effective than applied relaxation and no-treatment. In a second study from the same group (Klosko, Barlow, Toussinari, & Cerny, 1990), this package was found to be more effective than alprazolam and placebo.

Applied Relaxation

Applied relaxation has also been evaluated with panic patients. The purpose of applied relaxation is to teach the patient to observe the very first signs of a panic attack (small bodily sensations) and to apply a relaxation technique to cope with these symptoms before they have developed into a full-blown panic attack. When patients have learned to relax, they have to apply this technique in vivo in anxiety/panic situations. In a study by Öst (1988), applied relaxation proved to be superior to progressive relaxation and led to clinically meaningful changes not only in reducing panic attacks but also on measures of general anxiety and depression. However, applied relaxation was found to be less effective than cognitive therapy (Clark 1991) and a package consisting of exposure to introceptive stimuli, imaginal exposure, and cognitive restructuring (Barlow et al., 1989).

Research into the cognitive-behavioral treatment of panic is just beginning, but the results of the few studies that have been conducted are promising. Common elements in these procedures are exposure to bodily sensations (e.g., by hyperventilation, CO_2 inhalation, or direct exposure to anxiety-arousing situations) and implicit or explicit attempts to restructure negative cognitions associated with these bodily sensations, either by information giving or cognitive restructuring.

Problem Solving and Assertiveness Training

It has been suggested (Emmelkamp, 1982; Goldstein & Chambless, 1978) that agoraphobics are inclined to respond to stressful experiences by misattributing physiological arousal associated with panic attacks to external situational factors and that they lack adequate problem-solving skills (Brodbeck & Michelson, 1987; Fisher & Wilson, 1985). Therefore, problem-solving and assertive training may be important techniques to prevent relapse.

Kleiner, Marshall, and Spevack (1987) developed a problem-solving skills program for agoraphobics. The main targets of this program are to increase the patient's awareness of ongoing interpersonal problems, to understand the effects of these problems on the phobia, and to learn basic skills in dealing with these problems, including assertiveness. Both the patients who had received exposure in vivo and patients who had received a combined treatment consisting of exposure in vivo and problem solving improved significantly after 12 treatment sessions. Subjects in the in vivo exposure alone condition either failed to show further gains at follow-up or relapsed, while the group receiving training in problem solving showed further improvement at follow-up. Interestingly, the latter patients also showed a significant change in locus of control. Two studies by the Oxford groups are also of interest. In the first study Jannoun, Munby, Catalan, and Gelder (1980) investigated the effectiveness of a problem-solving treatment involving couples' discussion of life stresses and problems. Exposure in vivo was superior to the problem-solving treatment, but one of the two therapists involved obtained unexpectedly good results with problem solving. However, in the second study (Cullington, Butler, Hibbert, & Gelder, 1984), the favorable results of problem solving were not replicated. Taking together the results of Kleiner et al. (1987) and the studies of the Oxford group, it does seem that problem solving has something to offer when added to exposure in vivo. When exposure in vivo is left out of the treatment program, problem

solving alone has not been an effective treatment for agoraphobia.

A number of panic patients and agoraphobics are also socially anxious (Arrindell & Emmelkamp, 1987). Although in some cases social anxiety improves as a result of improvement of the agoraphobia, in a number of cases the social anxiety has to be dealt with more directly. Two studies evaluated the effects of assertiveness training with agoraphobics. Emmelkamp, van der Hout, and de Vries (1983) contrasted (1) assertiveness training, (2) exposure in vivo, and (3) a combination of assertiveness training and exposure in vivo. Only unassertive agoraphobics participated in this study. Exposure in vivo was found to be more effective on phobic measures, whereas assertiveness training was found to be more effective on assertiveness measures. The results of this study indicate that both forms of treatment have something to offer to unassertive agoraphobics. Exposure in vivo leads to improvement of anxiety and avoidance. On the other hand, assertiveness training leads to more improvement than exposure in vivo with respect to assertiveness. Essentially similar results were found by Thorpe, Freedman, and Lazar (1985). Since assertive and unassertive agoraphobics benefited equally from exposure (Emmelkamp, 1980), the best therapeutic strategy seems to be to start with exposure in vivo and continue with assertiveness training if necessary.

Relational Problems

A number of therapists have suggested that interpersonal, particularly marital, difficulties play an important part in the development and maintenance of patients' phobic symptoms (Goldstein & Chambless, 1978; Hafner, 1982). The partners of phobics have been described as impeding or reversing the positive effects of treatment or as developing psychiatric symptoms themselves. Furthermore, it has been suggested that a change in phobic symptoms through treatment may have a negative impact upon the patient's marriage (e.g., Hafner, 1982). On the basis of such clinical observations, it has been claimed that a system-theoretic interactional approach is needed to understand the etiology and maintenance of agoraphobia (Hafner, 1982).

A number of different research groups have addressed the issue of the relationship between marital distress and agoraphobia. There appears to be little, if any, evidence that the relationships of agoraphobic couples are distressed (Arrindell & Emmelkamp, 1986; Emmelkamp, Van Dyck, Bitter, Heins, Onstein, & Eisen, 1992; Fisher & Wilson, 1985) or that the partner of the agoraphobic has problems himself (Arrindell & Emmelkamp, 1985).

However, there is some evidence that the quality of the marital relationship may affect the outcome of behavior therapy (i.e., exposure in vivo), but results are inconclusive. Previous studies in this area found a significant impact of relationship problems of agoraphobics on the outcome of behavioral treatment (e.g., Emmelkamp & van der Hout, 1983; Milton & Hafner, 1979; Monteiro, Marks, & Ramm, 1985; Bland & Hallam, 1981), while others found no relationship between initial marital ratings and improvement (Arrindell, Emmelkamp, & Sanderman, 1986; Cobb, Mathews, Child-Clarker, & Blowers, 1984; Emmelkamp, 1980; Emmelkamp, Van Dyck, Bitter, Heins, Onstein, & Eisen, 1992; Himadi, Cerny, Barlow, Cohen, & O'Brien, 1986).

A related issue is whether spouse-aided therapy is superior to treatment of the agoraphobic patient alone. In the Cobb et al. (1984) and Emmelkamp, Van Dyck, Bitter, Heins, Onstein, and Eisen (1992) studies, spouse-aided exposure therapy was found to be no more effective than treatment of the patient alone. In contrast, one study (Barlow, O'Brien, & Last, 1984; Cerny, Barlow, Craske, & Himadi, 1987) found a superiority for the spouse-aided exposure condition when compared to a nonspouse group on measures of agoraphobia. There are a number of important differences between the Cobb et al. study and the Emmelkamp, Van Dyck, Bittern, Heins, Onstein, and Eisen study on the one hand and the Barlow et al. study on the other. First of all, treatment in the Cobb et al. and Emmelkamp et al. studies was identical, consisting of individual treatment based on the manuals of Mathews et al. (1981). In contrast, treatment in the Barlow et al. study consisted of group therapy rather than individual therapy. In addition, treatment consisted not only of exposure in vivo, but cognitive therapy was also included in the package. Besides the differences between treatments among the various studies, it should also be noted that in the Barlow et al. study, a statistically significant difference between groups was not found on any of the many individual measures of anxiety, phobia, or frequency, duration, and intensity of panic and depression. Only on a composite score based on five of these measures was a significant difference between spouse-aided therapy and treatment of the patient alone found. Taken together, the results of studies that have been conducted so far indicate that there is no need to include the spouse in the exposure treatment of agoraphobics.

The effects of treatment focusing on the relationship rather than on the phobia were investigated by Cobb, McDonald, Marks, and Stern (1980). Subjects were both agoraphobics and obsessive-compulsives who also manifested marital discord. Exposure in vivo was contrasted with marital treatment and results indicated that exposure in vivo led to improvements with respect to both the phobic/obsessive-compulsive problems and the marital relationship, while marital therapy had an effect on only the marital relationship and did not improve the phobic/obsessive-compulsive complaints. More recently, Arnow, Taylor, Agras, and Telch (1985) investigated the effects of communication training with agoraphobics. Communication training enhanced the improvement in phobic symptoms resulting from exposure therapy but did not affect marital satisfaction. This is not surprising since the training focused on communications about the phobia rather than on other relationship problems. Further, only a limited number of agoraphobics were maritally distressed.

SOCIAL PHOBIA

Social anxiety or social phobia is clinically distinguished from the shyness and social anxiety many individuals experience by the intensity of the fears and the avoidance of situations involved. In contrast with the numerous analogue studies that deal with social anxiety, speech anxiety, dating anxiety, and unassertiveness, relatively few studies in the area of social anxiety have used actual patients.

Generally, three models are distinguished to explain the functioning of social phobia, each emphasizing different aspects of the disorder. Anxiety experienced in social situations may be the result of inadequate handling of these situations. The *skills-deficit model* asserts that social anxiety results from a lack of social skills within the patients' behavioral repertoire. A patient may lack the skills to initiate conversations or to handle himself or herself in groups. If it is assumed that such lack of social skills provokes anxiety, then anxiety may be overcome through social skill-training. If patients have adequate social skills but are inhibited in social situations by anxiety that has become conditioned to interpersonal settings and avoidance of social situations, the principal goal of therapy is the direct reduction of anxiety and avoidance (*conditioned-anxiety model*). Others have stressed that faulty evaluation of one's performance in social situations or that "irrational beliefs" mediate social anxiety. Thus, the *cognitive-inhibition model* suggests that maladaptive cognitions rather than conditioned anxiety or skills deficit are responsible for the impairments in social situations. The emphasis on various aspects of social anxiety has led to a number of different treatment strategies, such as systematic desensitization and exposure in vivo for conditioned anxiety, social skills training to deal with the lack of skills, and cognitive therapy to treat the presumed underlying cognitive distortions. Since the research in this area has recently been reviewed (Emmelkamp & Scholing, 1990) only the main findings will be summarized here:

Results of systematic desensitization are not impressive (Gelder et al., 1973; Hall & Goldberg, 1977; Marzillier, Lambert, & Kellett, 1976; Shaw, 1979; Trower, Yardley, Bryant, & Shaw, 1978; van Son, 1978).

Exposure in vivo is as effective as cognitive therapy (Emmelkamp, Mersch, Vissia, & van der Helm, 1985; Mattick, Peters, & Clarke, 1989; Scholing & Emmelkamp, 1993a, 1993b).

Self-instructional training was found to be as effective as RET (Emmelkamp et al., 1985).

Cognitive therapy may enhance the effects of exposure in vivo but results are inconclusive. Three studies found a combination of cognitive therapy and exposure in vivo slightly more effective than exposure alone (Butler, Cullington, Munby, Amies, & Gelder, 1984; Mattick, Peters, & Clarke, 1989; Mattick & Peters, 1988). Further, Heimberg et al. (1990) found such a combined cognitive-behavioral package more effective than an equally credible placebo therapy. More recently two studies (Scholing & Emmelkamp, 1992, 1993) found no evidence that a combination of cognitive therapy and exposure in vivo is more effective than exposure alone. Further studies are needed to solve these discrepant results.

There is some evidence that social skills training leads to more beneficial effects than systematic desensitization (Marzillier et al., 1976; van Son, 1978).

Social skills training is as effective as cognitive therapy (Mersch, Emmelkamp, Bögels, & van der Sleen, 1989; Scholing & Emmelkamp, 1989) *and exposure in vivo* (Scholing & Emmelkamp, 1989; Wlazlo, Schroeder-Hartwis, Hand, Kaiser, & Münchau, 1990).

The addition of cognitive techniques to social skills training does not enhance the effectiveness of social skills training (Frisch, Elliott, Atsaides, Salva, & Denney, 1982; Hatzenbühler & Schröder, 1982; Stravinsky, Marks, & Jule, 1982). However, it is questionable whether the subjects in these studies were truly phobic rather than socially inadequate.

Patients with skills deficits do profit less from treatment than social phobics with adequate social skills, especially at follow-up (Mersch, Emmelkamp, & Lips, 1991; Wlazlo et al., 1990).

Treatment taking into account individual response patterns has not consistently been found to be superior to treatment that was not matched to the individual response pattern. Three clinical studies with social phobics have been located to date that attempted to identify optimal matches between patient and treatment procedure. In these studies, it was hypothesized that patients who were treated with a method that matched their response pattern would achieve better results than patients treated with the other method. Only in the Öst, Jerremalm, and Johansson study (1981) was this hypothesis partly supported: Physiological reactors responded better to applied relaxation than to social skills training, whereas the reverse was found for behavioral reactors characterized by social skills deficits. Neither in the Jerremalm et al. (1986) study nor in the Mersch et al. (1989) and Mersch et al. (1991) studies was there evidence that matching of treatment (applied relaxation, cognitive therapy, and social skills training) to different reactor types (physiological reactors, cognitive reactors, and behavioral reactors) enhanced treatment effectiveness.

In sum, both cognitive therapy, exposure in vivo, and social skills training have shown promise as treatment procedures for social phobics. When social phobics do possess the necessary social skills, either exposure in vivo or cognitive therapy or a combination of these methods may result in beneficial effects. When social phobics lack the necessary social skills, treatment may focus first on the teaching of appropriate skills and add other procedures if necessary. On the theoretical side, it should be noted that exposure in vivo may account for part of the effects achieved with social skills training. Modeling may be superfluous and the effects may be entirely due to repeated behavior rehearsal in vivo (exposure) in the group and the structured homework practice involving real-life rehearsal of feared situations. Further studies are needed to solve this issue.

POST-TRAUMATIC STRESS DISORDER

Post-traumatic stress disorder (PTSD) may follow exposure to any psychological event that is "outside the usual range of experience." The learning theoretical model explains the development of post-traumatic stress disorder in terms of classical and operant conditioning. The traumatic event serves as an aversive unconditioned stimulus, leading to extreme tension. The process of conditioning transforms the neutral stimuli associated with the traumatic event to conditioned stimuli that in turn provoke anxiety reactions. This leads to the avoidance of these conditioned stimuli. The behavioral treatment of post-traumatic stress disorder generally consists of some form of exposure or stress management. Exposure can be in imagination, in which the patient imagines all kinds of aversive images until habituation takes place, or in vivo. In the latter form of the treatment, the patient is confronted with all kinds of real situations related to the trauma until habituation occurs and anxiety diminishes. The treatments may be conducted gradually in which increasingly difficult situations are presented, but in many cases it seems necessary to confront the patient with the worst possible situations from the beginning (flooding). This applies particularly to patients who are afraid of being overwhelmed with painful sensations and who avoid thinking of aspects of the traumatic situation. Most studies have involved rape victims and people suffering from war trauma.

War Trauma
Three controlled studies have been published on the behavioral treatment of war trauma. Treatment consisting of relaxation and imaginal exposure resulted in significant reduction of symptoms associated with post-traumatic stress disorder and was significantly more effective than no-treatment in a study by Keane, Fairbank, Caddell, and Zimering (1989). Both Cooper and Clum (1989) and Boudewyns, Hyer, Woods, Harrison, and McCronie (1990) found imaginal exposure (flooding) more effective than conventional therapy. Although research in this area is just beginning, these studies indicate that imaginal exposure procedures are of value in the treatment of war trauma.

Rape Trauma
Two behavioral and cognitive-behavioral treatments are now widely applied in the treatment of rape victims: stress management/stress inoculation training and exposure. Stress management was found to be effective in studies by Veronen and Kilpatrick (1983), Frank et al. (1988), Resick, Jordan, Girelli, Kotsis-Hutter, and Marhoefer-Dvorak (1988), and Foa, Rothbaum, Riggs, and Murdock (1991). In the latter study, exposure, stress inoculation training, and supportive counseling were compared. Exposure consisted of imaginal exposure in order to relive the rape scene in imagination. Homework involved in vivo exposure to "safe" feared and avoided situations. At the end of treatment, stress inoculation was found to be more effective than the other conditions on measures of PTSD symptoms. However, at follow-up 3.5

months later, exposure was found to be the most effective treatment.

In sum, (imaginal) exposure and stress management approaches have shown promise in the treatment of post-traumatic stress disorders. Further controlled studies are needed to come to a more balanced evaluation of the contribution of these approaches to alleviating distress and improving social functioning of PTSD sufferers. It should be noted that the effects of stress management have not yet been evaluated with individuals suffering from war traumas. One point of major concern is the high dropout rate in a number of the studies with rape victims reported so far. Whether the approaches found promising with PTSD patients suffering from war trauma and sexual assault are also effective with PTSD sufferers from other traumas is a matter for further study.

GENERALIZED ANXIETY

In recent years a number of studies have been conducted that investigated the effectiveness of behavioral and cognitive procedures on patients who suffered from generalized anxiety disorder (GAD). While exposure procedures are effective when anxiety is triggered by external stimuli, avoidance is less obvious in GAD. Therefore the emphasis is on reducing the excessive psychophysiological activation characteristic of GAD by means of relaxation or biofeedback procedures and on changing the worrying by cognitive techniques.

Results of treatment by progressive muscle relaxation and biofeedback for generalized anxiety have been recently reviewed (Emmelkamp, 1990) and can be summarized as follows:

When relaxation instruction is tape recorded, this procedure appears to be ineffective as a method for teaching relaxation as a skill that can be used across situations.

Most patients do not comply with instructions to perform relaxation daily.

Progressive relaxation is superior to meditation in studies that involved moderately to severely anxious subjects.

Biofeedback does not have a specific value, since other forms of relaxation training tend to yield comparable clinical effects.

In more recent studies, the importance of teaching relaxation as a coping skill has been stressed. Clients are trained to recognize the physiological cues of tension and to apply relaxation whenever tension is perceived. Anxiety management includes procedures for reducing anxiety symptoms, such as relaxation, distraction, controlling upsetting thoughts, and panic management. Anxiety management has been found successful in the treatment of generalized anxiety (e.g., Barlow et al., 1984; Butler, Cullington, Hibbert, Klines, & Gelder, 1987; Jannoun, Oppenheimer, & Gelder, 1982; Tarrier & Main, 1986). In the Powell (1987) and Eayrs, Rowan, and Harvey (1984) studies, anxiety management training was successfully applied in a group format.

Cognitive Therapy

The cognitive treatment for generalized anxiety is to a large extent based on research that demonstrates the association between generalized anxiety and cognitions (Rapee, 1991). This has led to the development of treatment approaches that directly challenge cognitions and beliefs associated with anxiety.

Woodward and Jones (1980) and Ramm, Marks, Yüksel, and Stern (1981) found meager results from self-instructional training with patients with anxiety states. The emphasis in the cognitive treatment in these studies was on changing self-statements. More recently, a number of studies have evaluated more comprehensive cognitive approaches based on Beck and Emery (1985) that emphasized insight into irrational beliefs. Cognitive therapy, conducted according to the guidelines given by Beck and Emery (1985), was found to be equally effective as anxiety management training (AMT) based on relaxation (Lindsay, Gramsu, Laughlin, Hood, & Espie, 1987) and more effective than diazepam and placebo (Power, Simpson, Swanson, & Wallace, 1990). Both Durham and Turvey (1987) and Butler, Fennell, Robson, and Gelder (1991) found some evidence that cognitive therapy was more effective than behavior therapy consisting of relaxation, exposure in vivo, and reengagement in pleasurable and rewarding activities. The cognitive therapy included behavioral techniques when appropriate in the context of the cognitive model of treatment. However, White, Keenan, and Brooks (1992) found behavior therapy, cognitive therapy, and a combined cognitive-behavioral therapy equally effective. Finally, Borkovec et al. (1987) found a combination of cognitive therapy and relaxation more effective than nondirective therapy plus placebo.

Thus, results of studies into cognitive therapy with GAD patients are promising. While earlier studies primarily focusing on changing self-statements led to meager results, more recent studies, using the more comprehensive cognitive-behavioral approach of Beck and Emery (1985), found some superiority of this approach over other therapeutic approaches.

On the theoretical side, terminology in this area is confusing to say the least. Pure cognitive therapy has not yet been tested with patients with generalized anxiety. Beck and Emery's cognitive therapy is an amalgam of cognitive and behavioral techniques. Behavioral procedures include graded task assignments, entering feared situations (exposure in vivo), and self-monitoring. These behavioral strategies are selected to help the client disconfirm previously held beliefs. Thus, behavioral change is viewed as essential in order to change cognitions. However, by confounding cognitive and behavioral procedures, it becomes impossible to substantiate the claim of proponents of the cognitive approach that the *cognitive* (in contrast to the behavioral) procedures are responsible for the improvements achieved (Emmelkamp, 1990).

OBSESSIVE-COMPULSIVE DISORDER

The effects of behavior therapy (i.e., exposure in vivo and response prevention) with obsessive-compulsive patients have been well established (Emmelkamp, 1982, 1992; Marks, 1987; Rachman & Hodgson, 1980; Steketee & Cleere, 1990). Both exposure to distressing stimuli and response prevention of the ritual are essential components (Foa, Steketee, & Milby, 1980). The most important research findings of the last two decades can be summarized as follows:

Gradual exposure in vivo is as effective as flooding in vivo (Boersma, den Hengst, Dekker, & Emmelkamp, 1976; Marks, Hodgson, & Rachman, 1975). This implies that it is not necessary to invoke maximal anxiety during exposure in vivo. Therefore this method is preferred over flooding, because gradual exposure invokes less tension and is easier for the patient to carry out.

Generally modeling by the therapist does not lead to greater treatment effect. Although empirical research on a limited number ($n = 5$) of patients (Hodgson, Rachman, & Marks, 1972) suggests that modeling enhances the effect of exposure in vivo, later studies suggest this is not the case (Boersma et al., 1976; Marks et al., 1975).

Treatment can be carried out by the patient in his or her natural environment without the therapist being present. Emmelkamp and Kraanen (1977) compared therapist-controlled exposure and self-controlled exposure. In the latter method, the patient carried out the exposure program on his or her own by means of homework assignments, without the therapist being present. Although no significant differences in effects were found between the two treatments, at the follow-up a month after completion of the treatment, self-controlled exposure in vivo was more effective than therapist-controlled exposure. In a study by Emmelkamp, van Linden, van den Heuvell, Rüphan & Sanderman, 1989), self-controlled exposure appeared to be as effective as exposure when the therapist was present. Combining the results of both studies, it can be concluded that treatment of obsessive-compulsive patients in their own home without the therapist being present is as effective and clearly more cost-effective than therapist-controlled treatment.

Engaging the partner in exposure is no more effective than treating the patient alone. From studies by Emmelkamp and de Lange (1983) and Emmelkamp, de Haan, and Hoogduin (1990), it appeared that engaging the partner in exposure in vivo did not enhance the treatment effect. In the study by Emmelkamp and de Lange, the partner condition appeared to be more effective at the end of treatment, but at the follow-up a month later this effect had disappeared. Metah (1990), however, found some evidence that involving a significant other (not necessarily the partner) enhanced treatment effects. Treatment consisted not only of exposure but also of relaxation.

Exposure sessions of long duration are more effective than those of short duration. Rabavilas, Boulougouris, and Stefanis (1976) investigated the optimal duration of exposure sessions in obsessive-compulsive patients. Exposure in vivo of long duration (two hours) appeared to be significantly more effective than a short duration exposure.

Both exposure to the anxiety-provoking stimuli as well as response prevention of the compulsive action are essential components. Several studies compared the effect of exposure alone and response prevention alone in obsessive-compulsive patients. Exposure generally led to more anxiety reduction than response prevention, whereas response prevention generally led to a greater decrease of compulsive rituals than exposure. The combination of both procedures proved to yield the most effect (Foa, Steketee & Milby, 1980; Foa, Steketee, Grayson, Turner, & Latimer, 1984). A remarkable number of patients appeared to relapse when treatment consisted of only one of both components. In summary, both exposure in vivo as well as response prevention are essential elements in the treatment of obsessive-compulsive disorder.

Exposure in vivo versus exposure in imagination. Although exposure in vivo has proven to be more effective in simple phobia and agoraphobia than exposure in imagination, the differential effect of both forms of exposure in obsessive-compulsive patients is less clear. There is little research re-

ported thus far and this renders no unequivocal results (Rabavilas, Boulougouris & Stefanis, 1976; Foa, Stekee, Turner & Fischer; 1980, Foa, Steketee, & Grayson, 1985). In general, however, exposure in vivo seems to be more effective than exposure in imagination. However, in patients with checking compulsions, imaginary exposure appears to be as effective as exposure in vivo. This could be explained by the fact that it is more difficult to expose patients with checking compulsions to situations that they fear. For example, in patients who have to carry out all kinds of checking rituals for fear of a disaster (for example, a war or something dreadful happening to their family), it is easier to have these scenes imagined than to apply exposure in vivo.

Frequent exposure is no more effective than spaced exposure. Emmelkamp, van Linden, van den Heuvell, Rüphan, and Sanderman (1989) studied the influence of frequency of exposure in vivo sessions on the treatment results. They compared 10 massed practice sessions with 10 spaced practice sessions. In the massed practice condition, 4 sessions each week were given and in the spaced practice condition there were only 2 sessions each week. The results indicated that massed practice was as effective as spaced practice. Although patients in the latter condition had the possibility of avoiding fearful situations between sessions, this did not hinder improvement. Theoretically, one could have expected that anxiety would increase in the spaced condition, but this was not found empirically. The results of this study have direct practical consequences. The fact that there was no difference between frequent and less frequent exposure sessions indicates that it is not necessary to carry out exposure every day. The results imply that it is possible to carry out exposure treatment with a limited frequency of 2 sessions a week.

Outpatient treatment is often equally effective as clinical treatment. For most obsessive-compulsive patients, hospital admission is no longer necessary because treatment in their own environment yields similar results. In a study by van den Hout, Emmelkamp, Kraaykamp, and Griez (1988), no difference was found between a gradual exposure program carried out by patients at their own homes and a behavior therapy program of long duration in a psychiatric hospital.

Treatment effects are lasting. Several follow-up studies indicate that the effects of exposure in vivo and response prevention are maintained up to two years (Kasvikis & Marks, 1988) and four years (Visser, Hoekstra, & Emmelkamp, 1992).

The amount of improvement varies among patients. The following factors appeared to relate to a less favorable treatment result: severity and duration of complaints (Basoglu, Lax, Kasvikis, & Marks, 1988; Hoogduin, Duivenvoorden, Schaap, & de Haan, 1989), nature of the obsessive-compulsive behaviors (checking compulsions have a less favorable prognosis than washing compulsions, Basoglu et al., 1988; Boulougouris, 1977), delusional obsessions (Basoglu et al., 1988; Foa, Stekelee, Grayson, & Doppelt, 1983), and negative rearing experiences (Visser et al., 1992).

Cognitive therapy is equally effective as exposure in vivo. Self-instructional training did not enhance the effects of exposure in vivo (Emmelkamp, Van der Helm, van Zanten, & Plochg, 1980). In two more recent studies (Emmelkamp, Visser, & Hoekstra, 1988; Emmelkamp & Beens, 1991), the effectiveness of self-controlled exposure in vivo was compared with cognitive therapy (RET). The results showed cognitive therapy to be equally effective as exposure in vivo. In addition, a combination of exposure in vivo and cognitive therapy proved to be no more effective than exposure in vivo alone. Although some (e.g., Kendall, 1983; Reed, 1985) have proposed that cognitive therapy may be inappropriate for treating obsessive-compulsives, since these patients already overemphasize their thoughts, the results of our studies indicate that this does not necessarily have to be the case. While self-instructional training was not found to enhance the effects of exposure in vivo, cognitive therapy was found to be as effective as exposure in vivo. Further studies are needed to examine for which type of obsessive-compulsive patients cognitive therapy is helpful and for which type of patients treatment can better focus on deemphasizing the thoughts and reducing the attention paid to them. Further, there is a clear need to establish the long-term effects of cognitive therapy with obsessive-compulsives.

In some cases the obsessive-compulsive disorder appears to serve a function other than anxiety reduction. According to our experience, many obsessive patients are socially anxious and nonassertive. In some of them, the obsessive-compulsive behaviors have the additional function of avoiding other people. In such cases, exposure in vivo and response prevention are only of limited use and should be supplemented by other interventions. Emmelkamp (1982) described the successful treatment of some obsessive-compulsive patients by means of assertiveness training. In some other cases, the function of obsessive-compulsive behaviors is the hiding of painful emotions. Frequently, obsessive-compulsive patients try to get rid of loneliness, depression and boredom by compulsive actions. It seems that in these patients anxiety reduction began to play a later role in the onset of the obsessive-compulsive disorder.

Drugs may enhance effects of exposure. There are still a number of obsessive-compulsives who cannot be treated or are inadequately treated by behavnioral methods only (Foa et al., 1983; Rachman, 1983). Although for some patients treatment effects of behavior therapy may be enhanced by adding drugs such as clomipramine or fluvoxamine, there is little evidence yet that the effects of a combined behavioral-drug treatment are superior to those of behavioral therapy on its own in the long run (Mawson, Marks, & Ramm, 1982; Kasvikis & Marks, 1988; Marshall & Segal, 1990).

Individual Differences

Emmelkamp, Bouman, and Blaauw (1993) studied whether treatment based on a functional analysis would be better than a standardized exposure/response prevention program. Obsessive-compulsive patients were randomly assigned to two conditions. In one condition, the patients were treated with the standardized behavioral program of exposure in vivo and response prevention. The other treatment program was individually tailored to the needs of the patient. Therefore *all* patients had four to five interviews with an experienced behavior therapist in order to make a functional analysis and a treatment plan based upon this analysis. Results were rather disappointing. Neither on obsessive-compulsive complaints nor on depression and general psychopathology were the treatments found to be differentially effective. Exposure in vivo plus response prevention was as effective as treatment that included other techniques and focused on other targets than just the obsessive-compulsive behavior. Thus, at least in the short term, results of an individually tailored treatment were comparable to the results of a standardized behavioral package. Of course, long-term follow-up results are needed in order to make more definite claims for either a standardized treatment package or a broader multimodal treatment approach for obsessive-compulsives.

DEPRESSION

A number of controlled outcome studies into the effectiveness of cognitive-behavioral interventions for depression have been reported in the last few years. Before embarking on the task of reviewing these studies, I will provide a brief discussion of the major theoretical models of depression that have led to various treatment approaches.

Models

Contemporary cognitive-behavioral formulations of depression fall into three major categories:

1. Cognitive approaches (e.g., Beck, Rush, Shaw, & Emery, 1979).

2. Behavioral approaches (e.g., Lewinsohn & Hoberman, 1982).

3. Self-control theory (e.g., Rehm, 1977).

Cognitive model.   Beck and his colleagues attribute a central role to cognitions in the etiology of depression. Certain cognitive patterns (schemas) become activated and prepotent in depression and structure the kinds of interpretations that are made by the patient. These negative interpretations lead to a deterioration of the patient's mood and activation. For a more detailed description of the cognitive theories of depression, the reader is referred to Chapter 10, this volume.

Behavioral model.   The behavioral approach is based on the assumption that depressive symptoms result from too low a rate of response-contingent reinforcement and that depression will be ameliorated when the rate of reinforcement for adaptive behavior is increased (Lewinsohn, 1975). Treatment approaches that are suggested by this formulation of depression include (1) reengagement of the depressed individual in constructive and rewarding activities and (2) training in social skills to enhance the individual's capacity to receive social reinforcements resulting from social interactions. It has been suggested (e.g., Lewinsohn & Hoberman, 1982) that lack of social skills could be one of the antecedent conditions producing a low rate of positive reinforcement. Indeed, a number of studies have shown depressed individuals to be less socially skillful than controls (e.g., Coyne, 1976; Lewinsohn, Mischel, Chaplin, & Barton, 1980; Youngren & Lewinsohn, 1980). It should be pointed out, however, that an association between depressed mood and (lack of) social skills does not necessarily imply a causal relationship. Depressed individuals may have been socially skillful before they became depressed, and then it is the depression that is responsible for the inadequate social performance. Only prospective studies can answer the question of the direction of causality between depression on the one hand and social skills on the other.

Although it has consistently been found that daily mood ratings correlate with rate of pleasant activities (e.g., Lewinsohn & Hoberman, 1982), this finding does not necessarily imply that increasing the pleasant-activity rate will improve mood. Biglan and Craker (1982) studied this issue and found that such increases in pleasant activities did not produce improvements in mood, thus challenging one of the basic assumptions of Lewinsohn's theory of depression. More recently, Hoevenaars and van Son (1990) studied the causal relationship between unpleasant events and depression in a longitudinal study. Results did not support Lewinsohn's theory.

Self-control model.   Rehm (1977) has proposed a self-control model of depression that provides a framework for integrating the cognitive and behavioral models previously discussed. Rehm acknowledges the importance of reinforcement in the development of depression, but he holds that the reinforcement can be self-generated rather than derived from environmental sources. In Rehm's view, the depressed mood and the low rate of behavioral characteristics for depressed individuals are the result of negative self-evaluations, lack of self-reinforcement, and high rates of self-punishment.

Several studies have been conducted to test Rehm's hypotheses about the role of self-reinforcement in depression, but results are inconclusive.

Cognitive-Behavioral Interventions

As we have seen, the major approaches differ with respect to the role that they ascribe to the various factors in the etiology and functioning of depression, which leads to different emphases in the various therapeutic procedures based on these models.

Cognitive therapies focus on changing patients' depressogenic cognitions and hence their depressed affect and behavior. Cognitive therapy aims to help patients identify the assumptions and schemas that support patterns of stereotypical negative thinking and to change specific errors in thinking (see Chapter 10, this volume). Behavioral approaches attempt to change the maladaptive behavior in order to increase positive reinforcement. Here cognitions are seen as the consequence of depression, and hence it is assumed that these faulty cognitions will change as a result of the behavioral treatment. Self-control therapy aims to change deficits in self-control behavior: self-monitoring, self-evaluation, and self-reinforcement.

Table 9.1 provides an overview of the major outcome studies of depression. Only controlled studies are included, and studies using analogue populations (e.g., volunteering students) have been excluded.

In order to enable cross-study comparisons, criteria for acceptance in the study are provided when available. Both Feigner's criteria and Research Diagnostic Criteria (RDC) indicate that the individual suffers from a depressive disorder.

Behavioral Approaches

Behavioral programs have included two behavioral strategies: (1) increasing pleasant activities and (2) social skills training either alone or in combination.

TABLE 9.1   Depression: Major Controlled Outcome Studies of Behavior Therapy

Study	Population	Criteria	N	Treatment	Sessions	Follow-up	Results
Boelens (1990)	Outpatients	RDC[a] BDI[b] ≥ 16	79	(1) Cognitive–behavioral (2) Behavioral–cognitive (3) Combined (4) Cognitive–cognitive (5) Routine treatment	16 × 2 hr	2.4 yrs	1 = 2 = 3 = 4 > 5[cd]
Brown & Lewinsohn (1984)	Outpatients Volunteers	RDC	63	(1) Behavior (group) (2) Behavior (individual) (3) Bibliotherapy (4) No treatment	12 × 2 hr 12 × 50 min.	6 months	1 = 2 = 3 4 < all others
Comas-Díaz (1981)	Low socioeconomic Puerto Rican women	—	26	(1) Cognitive (2) Behavioral (3) No treatment	5 × 1.5 hr	1 month	Posttest: 1 = 2; 1 & 2 > 3 Follow-up: 1 > 2 (Hamilton)
De Jong et al. (1981)	Inpatients	BDI ≥ 20	20	(1) Cognitive–behavioral (2) Behavioral–cognitive (3) Routine treatment	± 14 weeks		1 = 2 1 & 2 > 3
Fleming & Thornton (1980)	Volunteers	BDI ≥ 17	35	(1) Self-control (2) Cognitive (3) Nondirective	8 × 2 hr	1.5 months	Posttest: 1 > 2 & 3 on some measures Follow-up: 1 = 2 = 3
Fuchs & Rehm (1977)	Volunteers	MMPI-D ≥ 70[e]	36	(1) Self-control (2) Nonspecific (3) No treatment	6 × 2 hr	1.5 months	1 > 2 & 3 (posttest)
Gardner & Oei (1981)	Volunteers	BDI ≥?	16	(1) Cognitive (2) Task assignments	6 × ?	1 month	1 = 2
Harpin et al. (1982)	Outpatients	Hamilton > 20[f]	12	(1) Cognitive (2) No treatment	20 × ?	3 months	1 > 2 (not statistically significant)

Study	Population	Diagnosis	N	Treatment	Sessions	Follow-up	Results
Hersen et al. (1984)	Outpatients & volunteers	Feighner[a] Raskin[h] ≥ 7	120	(1) Social skill + placebo (2) Social skill + amitripyltine (3) Amitripyltine (4) Psychotherapy + placebo	12 × 1 hr ± 6–8 hr Maintenance	6 months	1 = 2 = 3 = 4
Jacobson et al. (1991)	Volunteers	DSM-III major depression BDI ≥ 20 Hamilton ≥ 14	60	(1) BMT (2) Cognitive–behavioral (3) Combined	20×	—	Distressed couples: 1 = 2 on depression; 1 > 2 on marital satisfaction Non-distressed couples: 1 < 2; 3 > 1 & 2 on marital satisfaction
Kornblith et al. (1983)	Volunteers	RDC BDI ≥ 20	39	(1) Self-control package (2) Self-monitoring + self-evaluation (3) Didactic principles (4) Psychodynamic group therapy	12 × 1.5 hr	3 months	1 = 2 = 3 = 4
McLean & Hakstian (1979) McLean & Hakstian (1990)	Volunteers	RDC BDI ≥ 23	178	(1) Psychotherapy (2) Relaxation (3) Behavior therapy (4) Amitriptyline	10 × 1 hr	2.2 yrs	Posttest: 3 > all others 2 = 4 1 < all others Follow-up: 3 > all others
McLean et al. (1973)	Outpatients	—	20	(1) Marital therapy (2) Support & drugs	8 × 1 hr	3 months	1 > 2
Miller et al. (1989)	Inpatients	BDI > 17 DSM-III Major depression		(1) Standard hospital treatment (2) Idem + cognitive therapy (3) Idem + social skills training			1 < 2 & 3 2 = 3

continued

TABLE 9.1 *continued*

Study	Population	Criteria	N	Treatment	Sessions	Follow-up	Results
Nezu & Perri (1989)	Volunteers	RDC BDI ≥ 20 Hamilton ≥ 18	43	(1) Problem-solving (2) Abbreviated problem-solving (3) No-treatment	10 × 1.5 hr (group)	6 months	1 & 2 > 3 1 > 2
O'Leary & Beach (1990)	Volunteers	DSM-III Major depression or dysthymia BDI ≥ 14	36	(1) Cognitive-behavior therapy (2) BMT (3) No-treatment	15 × ?	1 yr	depression: 1 & 2 > 3 marital distress: 2 > 1 & 3
Rehm et al. (1979)	Volunteers	MMPI-D ≥ 70	24	(1) Self-control (2) Assertiveness training	6 × 2 hr	1.5 months	1 > 2 (self-control) 2 > 1 (assertion) 1 > 2 (depression)
Rehm et al. (1981)	Volunteers	RDC MMPI-D ≥ 70	49	(1) Self-monitoring (2) Self-monitoring + self-evaluation (3) Self-monitoring + self-reinforcement (4) Self-control package (5) No-treatment	7 × 1.5 hr		1, 2, 3 & 4 > 5 1 = 2 = 3 = 4
Roth et al. (1982)	Volunteers	RDC BDI ≥ 18	26	(1) Self-control (2) Self-control + desimipramine	12 × 2 hr	3 months	1 = 2, more rapid improvement in (2) than in (1)
Sanchez et al. (1980)	Outpatients	MMPI-D ≥ 70	32	(1) Assertiveness training (2) Group psychotherapy	10 × 1.5 hr	1 month	1 = 2 at posttest 1 > 2 at follow-up
Schmidt & Miller (1983)	Volunteers	BDI ≥ 10	54	(1) Individual (2) Small group (3) Large group (4) Bibliotherapy (5) No-treatment	8 × 90 min.	2 months	1 = 2 = 3 = 4 1 & 2 & 3 & 4 > 5

Study	Population	Criteria	N	Treatments	Sessions	Follow-up	Results
Scogin et al. (1989)	Elders	Hamilton ≥ 10		(1) Cognitive bibliotherapy (2) Behavioral bibliotherapy (3) No-treatment	4 × 5 min. phone calls	6 months	1 = 2 / 1 & 2 > 3
Teri & Lewinsohn (1986)	Outpatients Volunteers	RDC major or minor depression	66	(1) Behavioral (group) (2) Behavioral (individual)	12 × 2 hr / 12 × 1 hr	6 months	1 = 2
Thompson et al. (1987) Gallagher-Thompson et al. (1990)	Elders	RDC BDI ≥ 17 Hamilton ≥ 14	100	(1) Cognitive (2) Behavioral (3) Psychodynamic (4) No-treatment	16–20 × ?	2 yrs	1 = 2 = 3 / 1 & 2 & 3 > 4
Wilson (1982)	Volunteers	BDI ≥ 20	64	(1) Tasks assignments[l] (2) Relaxation[l] (3) Minimal contact[l]	7 × 1 hr / 7 × 1 hr / 2 × 1 hr	6 months	1 = 2 = 3 / Amitriptyline > placebo
Wilson et al. (1983)	Volunteers	BDI ≥ 17	25	(1) Cognitive (2) Tasks assignments (3) No-treatment	8 × 1 hr	5 months	1 = 2 / 1 & 2 > 3
Zeiss et al. (1979)	Volunteers	MMPI-D ≥ 70	66	(1) Social skill (2) Cognitive (3) Tasks assignments	12 sessions	—	1 = 2 = 3

[a]RDC = research Diagnostic Criteria for major depression
[b]BDI = Beck Depression Inventory
[c]a = b Treatment a about as effective as treatment b
[d]a > b Treatment a is superior to treatment b; a < b Treatment a is inferior to treatment b
[e]MMPI-D = Depression subscale MMPI
[f]Hamilton = Hamilton Depression Scale
[g]Feighner = Feighner diagnostic criteria for primary depression
[h]Raskin = Raskin Depression Scale
[l]All conditions with either placebo or amitriptyline

Pleasant activities. Increasing pleasant activities by means of homework assignments has been suggested by Lewinsohn (1975) as one way of increasing positive reinforcement to the depressed person. Several studies have investigated whether this approach on its own would be successful in improving depression. Typically, activities that are rated as enjoyable but not engaged in during the last few weeks are given as homework assignments. Activities that appear to be relatively easy are chosen first, while more difficult tasks are assigned in later sessions. While all studies (Brown & Lewinsohn, 1984; Gardner & Oei, 1981; Terri & Lewinsohn, 1986; Wilson, 1982; Wilson, Goldin, & Charbonneau-Powis, 1983; Zeiss, Lewinsohn, & Munoz, 1979) found this behavioral approach to result in improvement of depression, the question is whether this is due to the increase in pleasant activities per se or to "nonspecific" variables. Wilson (1982) found that improvement of depression was not related to an increase of pleasant activities. Further, Zeiss et al. (1979) found that cognitive therapy and social skills training led to similar increases in pleasant activities. These findings cast doubt on the validity of Lewinsohn's behavioral theory of depression.

Social skills training. Assertiveness training was found to lead to improved social functioning and amelioration of mood in studies by Sanchez, Lewinsohn, and Larson (1980) and Rehm, Fuchs, Roth, Kornblith, and Ramono (1979). Zeiss et al. (1979) also included a social skills training condition in their comprehensive study and found this treatment equally effective as cognitive therapy and task assignments. On most measures of social skills, patients were found to have improved at the end of therapy. None of these effects could be directly attributed to the social skills training, since patients receiving social skills training did not show more improvement than patients receiving a different treatment modality. It should be noted that a relatively weak mode of assertiveness training — covert modeling — was used, which does not seem to be particularly suited for a clinical population.

The most intensive study to date was conducted by Hersen, Bellack, Himmelhoch, and Thase (1984). Experienced therapists versed in their respective therapies treated 120 depressed outpatients and volunteers. Four treatments were compared: (1) social skills training plus placebo, (2) social skills training plus amitriptyline, (3) amitriptyline, and (4) psychotherapy plus placebo. Social skills plus placebo yielded the best clinical results in depression but failed to reach acceptable levels of statistical significance. In general, all four treatment formats were about equally effective. Bellack, Her-

sen, and Himmelhoch (1983) analyzed behavioral measures of social skills of these patients and found that patients receiving social skills were, after treatment, more similar to normal controls on these measures than patients from the other two groups.

In sum, while a number of studies have shown social skills training to lead to increased assertiveness and improved social performance, the relationship between improved social performance and reduction in depressed mood remains unclear. The studies conducted so far do not show that social skills training per se was related to reduction of depression.

Cost-effective treatment. Given the fact that many depressed patients can profit from behavioral treatments and that resources are limited, two strategies have been evaluated that are more cost effective than long-term intensive individual treatment: group therapy and bibliotherapy. Brown and Lewinsohn (1984), Schmidt and Miller (1983), and Terri and Lewinsohn (1986) found no evidence that behavioral group therapy was inferior to individual behavior therapy. The effect of bibliotherapy was evaluated by Schmidt and Miller (1983), Scogin, Jamison, and Gochneaur (1989), and Brown and Lewinsohn (1984). In all three studies, bibliotherapy resulted in a significant improvement of depression and was found to be more effective than no-treatment. In the Schmidt and Miller (1983) and Brown and Lewinsohn (1984) studies, bibliotherapy was equally effective as individual and group behavior therapy. The results of these studies suggest that the behavioral approach can be applied to large numbers of depressed patients either in the form of group therapy or as bibliotherapy with minimal supervision of a therapist.

Self-Control Therapies

A number of studies by Rehm and his colleagues have evaluated the effectiveness of a self-control therapeutic package and its individual components.

The self-control program developed by Fuchs and Rehm (1977) consists of six weeks of training in self-monitoring, self-evaluation, and self-reinforcement. Subjects were given log forms on which to monitor each day's positive activities (self-monitoring). During the self-evaluation phase of the program, the importance of setting realistic goals in evaluating oneself accurately was stressed. Subjects had to choose subgoals that were concrete and attainable and to rate their accomplished behavior toward those goals. Finally, subjects were instructed to self-administer rewards contingent on accomplishment of a behavioral subgoal (self-reinforcement). Treatment was conducted in a group. This program was found to be slightly more effective than nonspecific group psychotherapy and no-treatment control (Fuchs & Rehm, 1977), cognitive therapy (Fleming & Thornton, 1980), and social skills training (Rehm et al., 1979) on some measures of depression, but most of these differences were not maintained at follow-up.

Taking the "self-control" studies together, there is some evidence that this program may be of help in dealing with mild to moderate depression, although the therapeutic processes are not yet well understood (Emmelkamp, 1986). It should be noted that most studies did not include clinically depressed patients.

Behavioral Therapy Versus Cognitive Therapy

A number of studies evaluated the relative efficacy of cognitive therapy with various forms of behavior therapy; these studies are summarized in Table 9.1. A number of studies (Boelens, 1990; Comas-Diaz, 1981; Scogin et al., 1989; Thompson, Gallagher, & Steinmetz Breckenridge, 1987; Wilson et al., 1983) found both forms of treatment more effective than no-treatment control or routine psychiatric treatment (Boelens, 1990; de Jong, Henrich, & Ferstl; 1981; Miller, Norman, Keitner, Bishop, & Dow, 1989). In none of these studies was one treatment (cognitive or behavioral) superior to the other. Similar results were reported by Gardner and Oei (1981) and Zeiss et al. (1979). Since a variety of depressed patients were involved in these studies (i.e., outpatients, inpatients, geriatric patients, and low-socioeconomic Puerto Rican women, and the results were quite consistent across these populations), the finding that both treatments were equally effective is quite robust. Boelens (1990) compared behavior therapy, cognitive therapy, and a combination of these methods and found no evidence that the combined procedure enhanced the effects of each of the treatments on its own.

Recently, a number of meta-analyses have been published on the relative efficacy of behavioral and cognitive treatments of depression. The results of these meta-analyses are inconclusive. In the meta-analyses by Dobson (1989), Nietzel, Russel, Hemmings, and Gretter (1987), and Robinson, Berman, and Neimeyer (1991), cognitive therapy was found to be equally effective as behavior therapy, but in the Dobson and Robinson et al. studies, there was a slight superiority for the combined cognitive-behavioral therapy condition. It should be noted, however, that in these meta-analyses nonclinical studies were also included. In addition, in both the Dobson and Nietzel et al. meta-analyses, only studies that used the Beck Depression Inventory (BDI) as outcome measure were included, and results were only analyzed in terms of improvement on the BDI. The

conclusions in the present review are based on the clinical studies only.

A question of some interest is whether cognitive therapy and behavior therapy have differential effects on cognitive and behavioral variables. Although a number of studies were designed to show that treatments have specific effects on relevant targets, results are rather negative. Generally, relevant behavioral and cognitive variables are changed as much by cognitive therapy as by behavior therapy (e.g., Boelens, 1990; de Jong et al., 1981; Thompson et al., 1987; Zeiss et al., 1979). Thus, there is no evidence that each treatment modality selectively influenced the specific target behaviors. Similarly, in the NIMH study comparing interpersonal psychotherapy, cognitive-behavioral therapy, and imipramine, hardly any mode-specific difference was found (Imber et al., 1990).

In sum, cognitive and behavioral programs have shown statistically and clinically significant results in reduction of depression, change of thinking patterns, and improvement in social performance. Most studies were unable to show, however, that the target behavior directly addressed in the treatment modality was selectively affected. Rather, effects of behavioral and cognitive programs were "nonspecific"—changing both behavioral and cognitive components—thus precluding conclusions with respect to the therapeutic processes responsible for the improvement.

One major problem in interpreting the results of cognitive therapy for depression concerns the behavioral components included in the "cognitive" package. Beck's cognitive therapy seeks to uncover dysfunctional depressogenic cognitions and to correct these cognitions by systematic "reality testing." Actually, this particular treatment approach is an amalgam of cognitive and behavioral interventions, including behavioral tasks assignments and assertiveness training. Very few studies used a "pure" cognitive condition (e.g., Boelens, 1990); thus, it is questionable whether the positive effects of cognitive therapy should be ascribed to the cognitive elements of treatment, to the behavioral elements of treatments, or to nonspecific variables.

Behavior Therapy Versus Drug Treatment

Various pharmacological interventions have long been established as the standard of treatment for major depression. Although a number of studies have compared the effects of drug treatment with cognitive therapy (reviewed by Hollon, Shelton, & Loosen, 1991), relatively few studies have compared behavioral procedures with drug treatment. Hersen et al. (1984) found social skills training as effective as amitriptyline, but no evidence that a combination of drug and social skills training was superior. McLean and Hakstian (1979, 1990) found behavior therapy more effective than amitriptilyne. Even with severely depressed patients, pharmacotherapy was found to be no more effective than behavior therapy (McLean & Taylor, 1992). Both Boelens (1990), de Jong et al. (1981), and Miller et al. (1989) found behavior therapy somewhat more effective than routine psychiatric treatment that included the prescription of drugs, usually tricyclic antidepressants.

It is generally assumed that treatment is only effective to the degree that it addresses a patient's specific problems and compensates for the deficit. Thus, social skills training is supposed to be most effective with patients lacking in social skills and cognitive therapy is supposed to be most effective with patients characterized by dysfunctional cognitions. However, a recent review by Rude and Rehm (1991) shows that this is often not the case. In fact, a number of studies show an advantage for high-functioning subjects. There is a trend that assertive and well-functioning depressed patients react better to behavioral procedures while patients with less maladaptive beliefs profit more from cognitive therapy.

Maintenance of Treatment Effects

Unfortunately, long-term follow-up studies are relatively rare. Given the episodic character of depressed mood and the chance of "spontaneous" improvement in the course of time, long-term outcome of behavioral interventions needs to be studied.

Only a few studies have addressed the issue of maintenance of treatment effects. McLean and Hakstian (1990) published the results of a follow-up 2.2 years after treatment. The effects of behavior therapy were maintained at follow-up. No details are provided with respect to the number of patients who were depressed at follow-up or had experienced a relapse. Boelens (1990) reported the results of a follow-up study 2.4 years after treatment with cognitive therapy, behavior therapy, and a combination of these methods. Generally, results were meager. Two-thirds of the patients reported a depressive episode, in between posttest and follow-up half of these were classified as an RDC depressive episode. With two-thirds of the patients improvement was maintained at follow-up: No differences were found between the various conditions. Finally, Gallagher-Thompson, Hanley-Peterson, and Thompson (1990) reported follow-up results on the effects of cognitive and behavior therapy with older patients two years after treatment. Most of the patients who were in remission at the end of therapy (77%) were still so at follow-

up, although some had experienced a period of depression between posttest and follow-up. Taken together, the studies of Boelens and Gallagher et al. indicate that the prognosis was not favorable for those who were still depressed at the end of treatment. However, if patients react favorably to treatment, response at follow-up was generally good. Although it is tempting to assume that additional booster sessions may act prophylactically in preventing relapse, a study by Baker and Wilson (1985) showed that this is not necessarily the case. According to Lewinsohn, patients who had been treated with a combination of cognitive therapy and behavior therapy were randomly assigned to either four booster sessions of cognitive-behavioral therapy, four sessions of nonspecific therapy, or no booster sessions at all. Booster sessions were not effective in reducing relapse.

Morbid Grief

When depression is caused by grief, alternative (behavioral) procedures other than the behavioral and cognitive methods discussed so far may be indicated. Ramsay (1979) treated patients with pathological grief with a kind of imaginal prolonged exposure to bereavement cues and found this treatment to be effective in an uncontrolled series of 23 cases. Two controlled studies that investigated the value of exposure in morbid grief have been reported. In the Mawson, Marks, Ramm, and Stern (1981) study, imaginal exposure (guided mourning) was found to be slightly superior to a treatment with antiexposure instructions, but this difference was no longer significant at two-months follow-up. More recently, this study was replicated in a larger series of patients (Sireling, Cohen, & Marks, 1988). Again, there was only a slight superiority for the guided mourning condition. Patients who had received antiexposure instructions and had been encouraged to undertake new activities and "not to think about the loss . . . and to think about the future rather than to dwell on the past" (p. 123) also improved markedly despite the continued avoidance of bereavement cues.

Problem-Solving Training

An interesting new development is problem-solving training for depression. Social problem-solving can be defined as a process by which individuals "discover, create, or identify effective means of coping with stressful events encountered in living" (Nezu & Perri, 1989, p. 408). There is now a large body of literature (reviewed by Nezu, 1987) that demonstrates a relation between depression and a deficit in problem solving. There is some evidence that training in problem solving leads to improved mood in depressed individuals. In this treatment, the following phases can be distinguished: problem orientation, problem definition and formulation, generation of alternative solutions, decision making, and solution implementation and verification. Nezu and Perri (1989), using a dismantling research methodology, found the total problem-solving package more effective than an abbreviated version. Although the results are encouraging, further comparative studies are needed before more definite statements can be made with respect to the clinical value of this treatment.

Marital Therapy

Marital discord results in a dramatic increase in the relative risk of major depression. About half of the women referred for treatment of depression have significant marital problems. Only a few studies have been reported that evaluated the effects of behavioral marital therapy (BMT) on depression. McLean, Ogston, and Grauer (1973) evaluated the effectiveness of BMT with depressed patients. Marital therapy led to improved communication between the couple and improved mood, whereas the control group did not improve. O'Leary and Beach (1990) compared individual cognitive-behavioral therapy and BMT with depressed patients who were also maritally distressed. Cognitive-behavioral therapy led to improved mood, but not to increased marital satisfaction, while BMT led to improvements in both areas. Jacobson, Dobson, Fruzetti, Schmaling, and Salusky (1991) compared cognitive-behavioral therapy, BMT, and a combination of these two procedures. Results were different for maritally distressed and nondistressed patients. With nondistressed patients, BMT was inferior to cognitive-behavioral therapy. With maritally distressed patients, however, BMT was as effective as the individual cognitive-behavioral therapy on measures of depression and slightly more effective in reducing marital distress. There was no clear superiority for the combined procedure. The results of these studies suggest that for depressed individuals whose marriages are discordant, BMT is to be preferred to individual (cognitive) behavior therapy. However, if both partners are not willing to change their relationship, individual therapy may be considered.

Concluding Remarks

There is now increasing evidence that cognitive and behavioral approaches are effective in alleviating depression in mildly to moderately depressed individuals, but no one approach has been found to be consistently superior. The self-control therapy of Rehm and his colleagues has not yet been tested on clinical samples, which precludes conclusions with respect to the clinical effectiveness of this particular approach.

The principal finding of the present review is that a variety of cognitive-behavioral procedures are successful in improving depression, but one cannot conclude that the specific components of treatment are responsible for improvement. This finding suggests that common elements in these treatments are responsible for the improvements achieved. Such common elements are a clear rationale, highly structured therapy, homework assignments, and the training of skills (either cognitive or behavioral) that the patient can utilize in handling his or her problems.

Recent developments such as grief therapy, behavioral marital therapy, and problem-solving training have already led to some encouraging results. However, further studies are needed to substantiate the available results and to determine those subgroups of depressed patients for whom these specific approaches are particularly suited.

ALCOHOLISM

This section provides a selective review of the steadily accumulating literature on the behavioral treatment of alcoholism. Evaluation of work in this area is clouded by the use of poorly defined patient characteristics in most of these studies. While there is consensus that alcoholism is characterized by excessive drinking, there is no agreement on how much drinking is excessive.

In DSM-III-R, "alcohol abuse" is differentiated from "alcohol dependence," the latter being more or less similar to alcoholism. Alcohol dependence is characterized by either tolerance (need for markedly increased amounts of alcohol to achieve the desired effect) or alcohol withdrawal symptoms after cessation or reduction in drinking. Jellinek (1960) recognized a number of different types of alcoholism. The essential feature of gamma alcoholism is the loss of control, that is, the inability to stop drinking once started. As Jellinek describes it, "Loss of control means that any drinking of alcohol starts a chain reaction which is felt by the drinker as a physical demand for alcohol" (p. 679).

After briefly discussing the current status of "conventional" behavioral procedures such as aversion therapy and covert sensitization, the bulk of this discussion is devoted to more recent developments in the behavioral treatment of problem drinking: social skills training, communication training, controlled-drinking approaches, multi-modal treatments, and cue exposure.

Aversive Methods

Aversive methods have long been used in the treatment of alcoholism, although interest has waned in the last decade. With aversive conditioning, a noxious stimulus (UCS) is paired with actual drinking (CS) or with visual or olfactory cues related to drinking. Aversive conditioning is intended to produce a conditioned aversion to drinking. A variety of aversive stimuli have been used, the most popular of which were electric shock and nausea- or apnea-inducing substances. Covert sensitization is a variant of aversive conditioning wherein images of drinking are paired with imaginal aversive stimuli.

Electrical and chemical aversion therapy. Although taste-aversion conditioning is one of the oldest aversive treatments (Voegtlin & Broz, 1949), interest in emetic aversion therapy declined in favor of electrical-shock aversion therapy. It was argued that shock was a more desirable UCS than drugs in a classical conditioning paradigm to allow for a more exact control of the UCS–CS relationship. Further, there are a number of practical disadvantages associated with chemical aversion therapy that have precluded its widespread use. Studies into the effects of electrical aversion therapy have shown this form of treatment generally to be ineffective, and there is now a consensus in the field that treatment by electrical aversion therapy should be discontinued, on both clinical (Nathan & Bridell, 1977) and theoretical (Hallam & Rachman, 1976) grounds.

More recently, some (e.g., Elkins, 1991) have concluded that nausea rather than electrical stimulation is the preferred noxious basis for the induction of therapeutic aversions to alcohol. To date, only one well-controlled study has been conducted. In this study (Cannon & Baker, 1981), psychophysiological, attitudinal, and behavioral responses to alcoholic and nonalcoholic flavors were assessed in alcoholics given either group therapy alone (controls), group therapy plus electrical aversion therapy, or group therapy plus emetic aversion therapy. The emetic therapy subjects showed evidence of a conditioned aversion to alcohol but not to nonalcoholic flavors. Subjects in the other two groups did not show evidence of conditioning.

Cannon, Baker, and Wehl (1981) reported one-year follow-up data for subjects in the Cannon and Baker (1981) study. The results of this follow-up suggest that emetic aversion therapy can enhance posttreatment abstinence rates and that this enhanced outcome is related to the effect of treatment on heart rate response to alcohol. In a related study, Cannon, Baker, Gino, and Nathan (1986) found evidence that conditioned aversion was indeed established and that this was related to the maintenance of improvement.

In sum, given the poor results, the use of electrical aversion conditioning as a treatment modality with alcoholics should be discontinued. Although research by Cannon and his colleagues suggests that techniques based on taste aversion conditioning might be more promising, further controlled clinical studies are necessary before any recommendations can be made. It should be noted that all patients in the Cannon and Baker (1981) study received standard inpatient alcoholism treatment in addition to any aversion therapy, which precludes the drawing of firm conclusions with respect to the clinical efficacy of emetic aversion therapy per se. Given the low acceptability of this treatment, the availability of less intrusive alternative methods, and its high costs, Wilson (1978, 1991) concluded that chemical aversion therapy cannot be recommended as a standard form of treatment for alcoholism.

Covert sensitization. Covert sensitization with alcoholics involves the induction of verbally produced nausea following the imagination of a drinking scene. After the patient has imagined himself or herself consuming an alcoholic beverage, disgusting nausea and vomiting scenes are described by the therapist, and the patient then imagines himself or herself running from the drinking setting. Results of most of the studies into covert sensitization with alcoholics are made uninterpretable by severe methodological limitations (Little & Curran, 1978).

Elkins (1980) provided some evidence that conditioned nausea could be produced in a number of alcoholics receiving covert sensitization treatment. Approximately 90 percent of patients who remained in treatment for at least six covert sensitization sessions reacted with genuine nausea responses as evidenced by swallowing, muscular tremor, facial grimacing, and occasionally by actual vomiting, but only two-thirds of these subjects developed some degree of *conditioned* nausea. Significant degrees of extended abstinence were observed for conditioned nausea subjects as opposed to other subjects. Since no control groups were used and subjects were inpatients in a traditional alcoholism rehabilitation program, conclusions with respect to covert sensitization as a primary form of treatment are not warranted.

Olson, Ganley, Devine, and Dorsey (1981) compared (1) milieu therapy (control group), (2) covert sensitization, (3) insight-oriented therapy, and (4) a combination of covert sensitization and insight-oriented therapy with 137 alcoholics. All patients participated in a milieu treatment program. At four-year follow-up 36.6 percent of all patients were abstinent, while 73.5 percent were abstinent six months after treatment. The behavioral treatment was significantly superior to the insight-oriented therapy. The insight-oriented group did worse than the routine milieu treatment. The results of this study suggest that adding covert sensitization to a hospital milieu program may be beneficial, whereas adding insight-oriented therapy is not. Telch, Hannon, and Telch (1984) found covert sensitization to be less effective than supportive group therapy. However, covert sensitization was not adapted to the individual patient but was group administered, which may explain the meager results.

Concluding remarks. Although chemical aversion therapy and covert sensitization appear to have some promise as adjunct techniques in preventing drinking immediately after treatment, their long-term effectiveness is far from proven. Given its safeness, relative pleasantness, acceptability to a large number of alcoholics, and cost effectiveness, covert sensitization is to be preferred to chemical aversion therapy. However, aversive therapy, if applied at all, should be part of a more comprehensive cognitive-behavioral program.

Social Skills Training

Based on cognitive-social learning theory, a number of cognitive-behavioral treatments have been devised, including self-management programs, social skills training, cognitive restructuring, and problem solving. A central feature of these various methods is the development of coping skills to enable the patient to stop or control his or her drinking. These approaches are at least partly based on the assumption that alcoholism or problem drinking are habitual, maladaptive ways of coping with stress. Although recent social learning approaches still stress psychosocial factors in the development and maintenance of addictive behavior, it is now acknowledged that there may be a genetic disposition for alcoholism. As Monti, Abrams, Kadden, and Cooney (1989) state: "it is possible that a genetic vulnerability interacts with psychosocial factors, resulting in coping skills deficits that require a skills training approach for remediation" (p. 4).

Ninety percent of people who receive treatment for alcoholism will experience some degree of relapse over a four-year period (Polich, Armor, & Braiker, 1980). A clear advantage of recent cognitive-behavioral programs is that they attempt to teach coping skills to deal with stressful events after the end of treatment.

Exposure to a heavy drinking model is likely to increase the risk of relapse and maintenance of heavy drinking. Marlat and Gordon (1980) reported that for alcoholics, 23 percent of relapses involved social pressure situations such as being offered a drink, and in another 29 percent of the cases, drinking behavior was preceded by frustrating situations in which the individual was unable to express anger. Further, some authors have suggested that alcoholics lack general assertiveness skills (O'Leary, O'Leary, & Donovan, 1976; Van

Hasselt, Hersen, & Milliones, 1978). Taken together, these findings suggest that social skills training may be a useful treatment procedure.

Previous controlled studies on the effects of social skills training with alcoholics were reviewed in the last edition of this *Handbook* (Emmelkamp, 1986). The controlled studies in this area clearly showed beneficial effects of social skills training with previous drinkers. There was some evidence that cognitive restructuring enhanced the effectiveness of the social skills training program. As to the addition of training in problem-solving skills to social skills training, results were inconclusive. It was concluded that social skills training may be an important ingredient in multimodal treatment programs for socially anxious alcoholics who lack the necessary social skills.

Two other studies are particularly interesting and deserve some attention. Eriksen, Björnstad, and Götestam (1986) evaluated the effects of social skills training (SST) with hospitalized alcoholics in Norway. They compared SST with a control group. Both groups received the traditional treatment program at the institute. Patients who had received social skills training drank on the average two-thirds of the amount of alcohol that the patients in the control group drank at one-year follow-up. In addition, the social skills patients had many more sober days and working days than the controls: 97 percent working days in the experimental group as compared to 45 percent in the control group. Given the severity of the alcohol problem, these results are highly encouraging.

Kadden, Cooney, Getter, and Litt (1989) randomly assigned alcoholics who had been treated as inpatients to either a coping skills training or interaction group therapy aftercare program. Coping skills training included problem solving, interpersonal skills, relaxation, and skills for coping with negative moods and urges to drink. Although both treatment formats were found to be equally effective, coping skills training was found to be more effective for subjects higher in sociopathy or psychopathology. Interactional therapy was more effective for subjects lower in sociopathy. Nearly identical results were found at two-year follow-up (Cooney, Kadden, Litt, & Getter, 1991). Results of this study are consistent with the view that treatment should be matched to the patient's needs, rather than providing uniform treatment to all alcoholics.

Communication Training

Following the earlier work of Azrin and his colleagues (e.g., Hunt & Azrin, 1973) in which behavioral family therapy was included in a broad-spectrum treatment program, Monti et al. (1990) evaluated the effects of communication training more directly. In addition to standard treatment, seventy-three male hospitalized alcoholics received either (1) cognitive-behavioral mood management training, (2) individual communication training, or (3) communication training with a family member or close friend participating.

The two communication skills group included training in effective communication skills in general and in alcohol-specific situations. Cognitive-behavioral mood management was designed to cope with negative emotions and desires to drink using cognitive restructuring, relaxation training, and stimulus control. Both communication training conditions were significantly more effective than the cognitive-behavioral mood management training. All three groups improved significantly in coping skills and showed reduced anxiety in both general and alcohol-specific situations.

In an additional analysis (Rohsenow, et al., 1991), the two communication conditions were combined. Results of this analysis revealed that the level of initial skills deficit did not predict benefit from skills training. Anxious patients benefited as much as did less anxious patients in communication training. The more cognitively oriented mood management training only benefited alcoholics with higher education who were less anxious. As Rohsenow et al. conclude:

> It appears that a more highly educated population of alcoholics with less anxiety or urge to drink would benefit equally well from cognitive-behavioral mood management training or communication skills training but that alcoholics who are less educated and have more anxiety and urge to drink will fail to benefit from cognitive-behavioral mood management training but will improve when provided communication skills training. (p. 68)

Controlled Drinking

While there was almost consensus several years ago that total abstinence was the only acceptable treatment goal, more recently the results of a number of studies have suggested that a substantial number of problem drinkers can learn and maintain a pattern of moderate and nonproblem drinking.

Proponents of the abstinence goal for alcoholics hold that alcoholism is more or less an irreversible disease, as illustrated by the Alcoholics Anonymous insistence that its members are but "one drink away from a drunk." There is now considerable evidence (reviewed by Miller, 1983) that a substantial number of problem drinkers can drink without problems, even when the treatment had focused on total abstinence.

Multimodal Treatments

Sobell and Sobell (1973) were the first to investigate the efficacy of a self-control program on severe alcoholics. Seventy subjects were assigned to either a traditional abstinence-oriented treatment program or to an experimental treatment program. The experimental subjects participated in 17 sessions of intensive broad-spectrum behavioral treatment. Half of the subjects had an objective of controlled drinking, the other half of abstinence. Treatment involved aversion conditioning for inappropriate drinking, problem solving, assertiveness training, education, rehearsal of coping responses, and videotapes of the patient's own drunken behavior. Follow-up measures were taken at 6 months, 1 year, 1.5 years, and 2 years. Experimental controlled-drinking subjects had fewer drunken days and fewer days in hospitals or jails, and they also had more abstinent and controlled-drinking days than the experimental abstinent group. However, follow-up data 11 years after discharge are rather negative (Sobell & Sobell, 1984). Of the 20 experimental subjects treated with a controlled-drinking objective, 4 were found to have died of alcohol-related problems. Six out of 20 of the traditionally treated subjects were found to have died, and the deaths of 4 of these were clearly alcohol related. Thus, in terms of mortality rate, the traditionally treated subjects did at least as badly as the controlled-drinking subjects. When placed in this perspective, it does seem that neither a controlled-drinking approach nor more traditional treatment was of lasting benefit to patients diagnosed as severe alcoholics.

Several investigators have evaluated multifaceted treatment programs for problem drinkers, using controlled drinking as the therapeutic goal. For example, Pomerleau, Pertchuk, Adkins, and Bradley (1978) conducted an outpatient program for largely socially intact problem drinkers. Treatment included (1) a functional analysis of the subjects' drinking, using daily drinking records; (2) strengthening of nondrinking activities; (3) training in self-management techniques to control drinking; and (4) the use of a prepaid commitment fee that was refunded for program compliance. At nine-month follow-up, 72 percent of behaviorally treated patients and 50 percent of traditionally treated participants in a control group that stressed abstinence were rated as improved (abstinent or reduced intake), but this difference was not statistically significant. Another finding was that fewer subjects dropped out of the behavioral program (2 of 18) than the traditional program (6 of 14). A few more studies are relevant since severe alcoholics were involved. Foy, Nunn, and Rychtarik (1984) also compared abstinence-oriented treatment with a behavioral program with moderation rather than abstinence as the treatment goal. Although the abstinence-oriented treatment was slightly superior six months after treatment, no differences were found at one-year and five-year follow-up (Rychtarik, Foy, Scott, Lokey & Prue, 1987). Further, Nordström and Berglund (1987) found that controlled drinking led to less relapse than abstinence, many years after treatment. This study, however, was uncontrolled.

The objective of the Sobell and Sobell (1973), the Pomerleau et al. (1978), and the Foy et al. (1984) studies was to test the hypothesis that a behavioral program with a controlled-drinking goal would prove superior to a traditional abstinence-oriented program. In these studies, the goals of abstinence and controlled drinking were embedded in very different treatment interventions; thus, it is unclear whether the difference in outcome should be ascribed to the nature of the interventions or to the drinking goal per se.

To prevent the pitfalls of the studies discussed here, Sanchez-Graig, Annis, Bornet, and MacDonald (1984) investigated the comparative efficacy of abstinence versus controlled drinking when all participants receive the same treatment program. "Early-stage" problem drinkers were randomly assigned to a goal of abstinence or controlled drinking. Treatments in both conditions were identical, except for training in controlled drinking that was introduced in the fourth treatment session. Treatment involved self-monitoring of drinking, training in problem solving, and cognitive coping (self-statements).

The results of this study did not support the hypothesis that assignment to a goal of controlled drinking would produce a better outcome than assignment to a goal of abstinence. Most controlled-drinking clients achieved moderation of alcohol use, and most abstinence-oriented clients failed to abstain but nonetheless moderated their drinking. Six months after treatment, drinking had been reduced from an average of about 51 drinks per week to 13, and this reduction was maintained throughout the second year. Most of the individuals assigned to abstinence rejected this goal from the outset.

Behavioral self-control training. Miller and his associates have developed a less intensive controlled-drinking treatment program than the multimodal programs just discussed. This approach, labeled "behavioral self-control training," includes self-monitoring, training in drinking rate control, self-reinforcement, functional analysis of drinking behavior, and instructions in alternatives to alcohol abuse (Miller & Muñoz, 1982). A series of studies

have evaluated this particular approach, and there is some evidence that this program is as effective as a more extensive multifaceted program (Miller & Hester, 1980). Miller and Baca (1983) reported follow-up data of 69 out of 82 problem drinkers treated by behavioral self-control training. Improvements on drinking were found to be maintained at two-year follow-up. Overall success rate was 72 percent at 6 months, 65 percent at 12 months, and 67 percent at two-year follow-up.

Although the results of controlled-drinking approaches with problem drinkers are impressive, clearly not every alcoholic is suited for such a program. To the extent that controlled drinking succeeds, it appears to succeed with individuals with less severe alcohol problems in terms of duration of illness and physical dependence. Successful controlled drinkers are generally found to be younger and less addicted and to have fewer life problems related to alcohol (Miller, 1983). In a recent long-term follow-up study, measures of severity of dependence and alcohol problems reliably separated successful abstainers from successful asymptomatic drinkers (Miller, Leckman, Delaney, & Tinchom, 1992). It should be noted, however, that two studies (Elal-Lawrence, Slade, & Dewey, 1986; Orford & Keddie, 1986) found no relationship between severity of drinking problem and type of drinking outcome, thus casting some doubt on the assertion that severe alcoholics cannot learn to control drinking.

The controversy over controlled drinking is a typically American one. In Europe and Australia, controlled drinking is widely accepted as a treatment goal for (some) alcoholics. It has been suggested that prominent behavior therapists in the United States who once advocated the moderation approach have shifted to an abstinence orientation for political rather than empirical reasons (Peele, 1992), but this view is controversial (Rankin, Miller, & Hersen, 1992). Ironically, a substantial number of alcoholics in abstinence-oriented treatment programs are quite successful in moderation rather than in abstinence at ten-year follow-up (Finney & Moos, 1991).

Prevention

Another recent development is the use of coping skills programs as preventive measures. Kivlaham, Marlatt, Fromme, Coppel, and Williams (1990) evaluated the effects of an alcohol skills training program with heavy social drinkers. The program consisted of the following elements: knowledge of blood alcohol levels, development of drinking moderation skills, setting moderate drinking limits, relaxation training, awareness of antecedents of heavy drinking, assertiveness training, and development of drink refusal skills. This program was found to be more effective in terms of drinking measures at one-year follow-up than lectures and films containing information on alcohol use.

Rohsenow, Smith, and Johnson (1985) evaluated the prevention effects of a less intensive and less comprehensive program with young adults at risk for alcoholism. Their program taught relaxation and cognitive restructuring as coping skills. Results with respect to drinking were less impressive. Although the men in the stress-management group showed a slight reduction in daily drinking rates at posttreatment, drinking returned to baseline levels at follow-up, half a year after the end of the program.

Finally, a study by Alden (1988) is of interest. He investigated the effectiveness of the "behavioral self-control training" of Miller and Muñoz (1982) that consisted of self-monitoring of drinking and training in drinking rate control. This program was compared with counseling and waiting-list control. Both programs were equally effective and more effective than no-treatment. Treatment improvements were generally maintained over a follow-up period of 24 months.

Although the studies of Alden (1988) and Kivlahan et al. (1990) indicate that alcohol skills training has long-lasting preventive effects for drinking behavior, these studies are not without limitations. At the start of treatment, subjects had a mean number of standard drinks per week of 38 (Alden) and 15 (Kivlahan et al.) respectively, which suggests that only subjects with minor problems were recruited. Whether or not these programs will also be effective with more severe social drinkers needs to be studied. Further, it is questionable if the results of these programs should be attributed to the behavioral components since an alternative treatment (counseling) was found to be equally effective in the Alden (1988) study.

Cue Exposure

One of the latest developments in the field of addiction concerns cue exposure. Siegel (1983) suggested that drug cues may serve as conditioned stimuli for a compensatory response (opposite in direction to the unconditioned drug effect) that compensates for the impending unconditioned drug response. In alcoholics, this compensatory response would probably be an aversive state and may be interpreted as craving. Over 40 years ago, Wikler (1948) asked whether drug craving should be considered a form of a classically conditioned response that results in urges to engage in drug-taking behavior. For example, the sight and smell of alcohol, or indeed a pub or bar in which alcohol

is usually drunk, may become conditioned stimuli and lead to a similar physical and emotional state (conditioned response) as induced by the alcohol itself. Wikler further postulated that withdrawal symptoms can be conditioned too. It has since been demonstrated that the abstinence syndrome can indeed be conditioned to specific environmental stimuli not only in animals but also in humans (reviewed by Powell et al., 1990). This theory has gained renewed interest by workers in the area of addiction, and cue exposure procedures have been developed. Most of this work is based on the assumption that repeated exposure to drug-taking cues (e.g., sight and smell of alcoholic beverages) will eventually lead to habituation or extinction of the craving response. Rankin, Hodgson, and Stockwell (1983) conducted a controlled study on 10 alcoholics. Although in vivo cue exposure resulted in reduction of craving responses, the clinical results of treatment were modest. Imaginal exposure was less effective. Since then, a number of studies have demonstrated that alcoholics show significantly greater psychological reactivity to the sight and smell of alcohol than do nonproblem drinkers, thus demonstrating a conditioned response (Laberg, 1990; Niaura et al., 1988). A study by Staiger and White (1991) showed that the sight plus smell of favorite drinks produced the largest heart rate responses and the largest increase in withdrawal symptoms and desire to drink. Seeing but not smelling a favorite drink resulted in lowered responses, thus indicating that the smell of a drink is an important component of the stimulus in a cue-exposure program. Eriksen and Gotestam (1984) demonstrated that relaxation reduced conditioned abstinence in alcoholics.

Laberg and Ellertsen (1987) found further support for cue exposure and response prevention in a study with 16 alcoholics. The results of their study showed that exposure to alcohol per se did not elicit craving. Increased autonomic arousal and craving were found only in subjects given alcohol and exposed to more available alcohol. Exposure and response prevention led to a significant reduction within and between exposure sessions.

Although the first results of cue-exposure programs look promising, some cautioning remarks have to be made. Hammerley (1992) argued on theoretical grounds that spontaneous recovery is to be expected after extinction trials, which will undoubtedly lead to relapse in a number of alcoholics after cue-exposure treatment unless additional measures are taken. He recommends that patients in cue-exposure programs be taught how to deal with craving when it occurs and how to cope with relapse. He further recommends booster exposure sessions to reduce the probability of spontaneous recovery.

SEXUAL DYSFUNCTIONS

In recent years, an increased number of clients have sought treatment for sexual dysfunctions, partly as a result of the development of brief sex therapies that are now widely available.

Of most importance has been the publication of Masters and Johnson's (1970) volume in which the brief sex treatment of a large number of males and females was evaluated. Although this study had a number of major methodological shortcomings, at that time it was revolutionary for a number of reasons. First, treatment was highly directive and behaviorally rather than psychoanalytically oriented—the approach that had been most influential up to that time. Second, sexual dysfunctions were conceptualized as relationship dysfunctions rather than as an individual pathological condition; this conceptualization resulted in the emphasis on treating the partners as a couple. Finally, the statistics provided by Masters and Johnson gave the impression of a very high success rate.

Before the publication of Masters and Johnson's (1970) book, behavior therapists had been treating sexual dysfunctions—most often with systematic desensitization (Wolpe, 1958)—but controlled studies were lacking. Sexual dysfunctions were considered to be the result of phobiclike anxiety and avoidance reactions.

With Masters and Johnson's approach, the couple is requested to carry out homework assignments. The assignments start with mutual touching that excludes genital areas and intercourse and gradually develops into full intercourse. When necessary, specific techniques dealing with premature ejaculation, vaginismus, or other specific dysfunctions are added to this process.

Masters and Johnson's program is essentially behavioral in nature and can be conceived of as graded exposure in vivo. Similarly, a number of behavioral procedures currently used in the treatment of sexual dysfunctions can be conceptualized as exposure procedures. Exposure to sexual situations and experiences can be accomplished along several lines: (1) imaginal (e.g., systematic desensitization), (2) in vivo (e.g., graded homework assignments along the lines of Masters and Johnson), and (3) vicarious (e.g., videotapes).

Although there is general agreement that there is a complex relationship among *desire, anxiety*, and *performance* in sexual dysfunctions, in most studies dysfunctions are defined as performance problems. Typically, criteria for success of treatment are frequency of orgasm during intercourse, restoration of erectile functioning, and so on. The relationship among desire, anxiety, and performance, however, makes assessment that is primarily based on performance difficult to interpret.

The following discussion involves a review of studies on treatment of sexual dysfunctions; controlled studies are discussed for male and female dysfunctions respectively.

According to Masters and Johnson (1970), orgasmic dysfunctions are usually classified as either primary or secondary. Primary orgasmic dysfunction is defined as the condition in which a female has never experienced orgasm. Secondary orgasmic dysfunction refers to women who achieve orgasm only in response to restricted types of stimulation, or women who in the past were orgasmic but are currently unable to experience orgasm. Other female sexual dysfunctions include vaginismus and dyspareunia.

Male sexual dysfunctions are classified by Masters and Johnson (1970) as primary and secondary impotence, premature ejaculation, and ejaculation impotence.

More recently, attention has been focused on problems of low sexual desire (Friedman, Weiler, LoPiccolo, & Hogan, 1982; Kaplan, 1977). Patients with an inhibition of sexual desire report a lack of desire for engaging in sexual activities or even aversion of sex. Friedman et al. (1982) report that 69 percent of the cases treated at their Sex Therapy Center included a complaint of low sexual desire. Problems of sexual desire are often not differentiated from other sexual complaints, which inhibits the generalizability of the findings.

Male Sexual Dysfunction

Exposure programs. Based on the notion that erectile failure is associated with performance anxiety, two controlled studies have investigated the effectiveness of systematic desensitization (SD). Results of SD were no better than standard advice, as far as performance was concerned (Kockott, Dittmar, & Nusselt, 1975), better than relaxation (Auerback & Killman, 1977), and as effective as a Masters and Johnson program (Everaerd & Dekker, 1985; Mathews, Bancroft et al., 1976).

Treatment conducted in groups. Research indicates that men's group sex therapy may offer an alternative for men without steady sexual partners or for men whose partner does not want to be involved in the therapy.

Price, Reynolds, Cohen, Anderson, and Schochet (1981) randomly assigned men with secondary erectile failure to either eight sessions of men's group therapy or to a waiting-list control group. Treatment involved sex education and self-stimulation exercises in which they learned that they could gain, lose, and then regain erections. Sexual intercourse was banned at the beginning of the treatment program. Group sex therapy was superior to the control group in terms of sexual satisfaction. However, the treated group did not differ from the control group in the reported frequency of erection difficulties following treatment.

In a following study of the same research group (Reynolds, Cohen, Schochet, Price, & Anderson, 1981), social skills training was added to the therapy program. Female guest therapists helped men role play difficult social/sexual situations. Treatment was further identical to that of Price et al. (1981). The men's group met for 10 weekly sessions. Results of treatment were compared with changes during a waiting period before treatment started. In addition to positive attitudinal changes, treatment resulted in a significant reduction of erection difficulties. The men also reported a significant reduction in social anxiety, whereas in the previous study, which did not include social skills training, there was no reduction in social anxiety.

Cognitive therapy. Since psychogenic erectile failure has been assumed to be caused by performance anxiety, some have argued that dealing with such cognitions is a necessary prerequisite for successful treatment. Munjack et al. (1984) found some evidence that rational-emotive therapy (RET) was effective in reducing sexual anxiety and improving sexual intercourse. However, at follow-up six to nine months after the end of treatment, most men had fallen back.

Everaerd and Dekker (1985) found RET equally effective as sex therapy at posttest; at follow-up the RET group was found to be superior. Dekker and colleagues investigated the effects of a comprehensive program focusing on irrational cognitions, sexual behavior, and social functioning. The treatment program consisted of RET, masturbation exercises (in the form of homework assignments), and social skills training. Treatment was conducted in groups. In two studies (Everaerd et al., 1982; Dekker, Dronkers, & Stafleu, 1985), this program led to improved sexual functioning of men with partners. In the Dekker et al. (1985) study, treatment was ineffective with men without a partner. If the primary problem was inhibited sexual desire, treatment was found to be ineffective.

Biofeedback. There have been some suggestions in the literature that men with erectile failure could profit from biofeedback training, but a well-controlled study has cast some doubt on the effectiveness of erectile biofeedback. Reynolds (1980) found no evidence that feedback of erection changes plus exposure to erotic film delivered contingent on erection increases was more effective than exposure to erotic film only. Thus, contrary to expectations, the addition of feedback did not enhance erectile change. The findings of Reynolds's study seriously question the clinical utility of biofeedback for the treatment of erectile dysfunction. Since it could be argued that focusing attention on erection as is done by biofeedback might actually increase performance anxiety, biofeedback cannot be recommended.

In summarizing the results of studies into erectile failure, a few conclusions can be drawn. Averaging across studies, sex therapy results in improvements in about two-thirds of dysfunctional males. Gradual exposure in vivo to sexual situations, as used in Masters and Johnson's approach, is an important element of treatment for male dysfunctions. Recent innovations, including masturbation exercises, social skills training, and cognitive restructuring, may also result in beneficial effects, but whether the addition of these techniques would enhance treatment of a "conventional" Masters and Johnson program has not yet been investigated.

Disorders in ejaculation. Patients hardly refer themselves to treatment for retarded ejaculation, so no controlled studies have been reported for this type of problem. Premature ejaculation, defined in DSM-III as "ejaculation occurring before the individual wishes it, because of persistent and recurrent absence of reasonable voluntary control of ejaculation and orgasm during sexual activity," is much more prevalent and a number of studies have reported successful outcome after behavior therapy (reviewed by Ruft & St. Lawrence, 1989). This treatment is based on the pause technique of Semans (1956). The patient is required to masturbate and ejaculation has to be prevented by stopping the stimulation by the partner (or the patient himself) as the male feels that ejaculation is imminent. This sequence has to be repeated several times and has to be practiced later during intercourse. This procedure can be expanded with the squeeze technique in which the partner squeezes the frenulum of the penis thus preventing ejaculation. Although a number of studies found these procedures to be highly effective, neither controlled comparative studies nor long-term follow-up studies have been reported.

Female Sexual Dysfunctions

Systematic desensitization. Many articles have reported the effects of systematic desensitization in the treatment of female sexual dysfunctions, and they were reviewed in the last edition of this *Handbook* (Emmelkamp, 1986).

Based on the results of studies that investigated the effects of systematic desensitization on female sexual dysfunctions, the following conclusions seem warranted: There is considerable evidence that systematic desensitization is more effective in reducing anxiety than other approaches such as sex education by means of a videotape, a Masters and Johnson program, or masturbation training. Unfortunately, a number of studies did not provide sufficient information to evaluate whether systematic desensitization leads to improved orgasmic functioning (e.g., Everaerd & Dekker, 1982; O'Gorman, 1978). When orgasmic functioning was evaluated, results of systematic desensitization were generally poor and less than those achieved with masturbation training.

Masters and Johnson program. A number of studies have evaluated the effects of a Masters and Johnson program with dysfunctional women (e.g., Emmelkamp, 1986). To summarize, the Masters and Johnson program has been found to be quite effective. There is no evidence that testosterone enhances improvement. Further, diazepam negatively influences the effects of this sex therapy program.

Masturbation training. Although the effects of the Masters and Johnson program are now well established, one of the questions addressed by researchers is whether or not treatment of the couple is a necessary prerequisite for success. Heiman, LoPiccolo, and LoPiccolo (1976) designed a treatment in which the involvement of the partner is not necessary. In contrast with Masters and Johnson, the idea behind this program is that the woman herself is primarily responsible for the dysfunction and can do something about it. In this treatment, a graded series of exercises are used to enhance acceptance of the body and feelings of pleasure, eventually resulting in an orgasm by means of self-stimulation. Two studies compared this program applied to the dysfunctional woman only with couples sex therapy (Libman et al., 1984; Whitehead, Mathews, & Ramage, 1987). There was some evidence in both studies that involvement of the partner enhanced treatment outcome.

A number of other controlled studies have been conducted investigating the value of self-stimulation exercises in dealing with female orgasmic dysfunctions. Although a number of authors claim superior results with masturbation training in "preorgasmic groups" without any involvement of the partner (Barbach, 1974; Ersner-Hershfield & Kopel, 1979), a closer scrutinizing of their data show that this superiority is merely a question of semantics. As noted by Wakefield (1987), the preorgasmic group concept of "partner orgasm" appears to be based on a different conception of what is important and meaningful in sex than is the current opinion among patients. Treatment in most preorgasmic groups results in learning to masturbate to orgasm in the presence of the partner, rather than having orgasms with the partner in any other way. As put by Wakefield: "The semantics of outcome here do not mesh well with what is clinically meaningful from most clients' point of view" (p. 9).

After reanalyzing the data of the Ersner-Hershfield and Kopel (1979) study, Wakefield (1987) concludes that at the end of treatment only one woman (7%) had achieved partner orgasm by manual stimulation and none had achieved coital orgasm, results that are clearly inferior to those achieved with conventional sex therapy along the lines of Masters and Johnson.

Cotton-Huston and Wheeler (1983) compared the effects of masturbation training on primary and secondary orgasmic failure with data of patients on a waiting list. Although the treatment group reported having orgasms more frequently through self-stimulation than the control group, this did not generalize to orgasms during intercourse. As noted by the authors, many women listed orgasm during intercourse as their only acceptable goal.

Assertiveness. There is some evidence that sexual dysfunctions are related to unassertiveness (Fahrner, 1983). In this context, assertive behavior might involve a variety of behaviors such as initiating a sexual encounter, requesting specific stimulation, or refusing requests (Delehanty, 1982; Fahrner, 1983). Delehanty (1982) investigated the impact of masturbation training groups on assertiveness of the participants and found a significant increase in assertiveness as measured by questionnaire.

Kuriansky, Sharpe, and O'Connor (1982) reported a two-year follow-up on 19 women who participated in a short-term group therapy using masturbation training and assertiveness training. At the end of treatment, 95 percent of the women were able to reach orgasm; at two-year follow-up, 84 percent could. While immediately after treatment 20 percent of the women were able to reach orgasm with a partner, by two years later, nearly half the sample could do so. It should be noted, however, that many of the women who transferred orgasm response to partner-related activities also participated in further marital and/or sex therapy.

Concluding comment. When anxiety reduction is the therapeutic target, both desensitization procedures and a Masters and Johnson program have been shown to be effective. However, anxiety reduction hardly affected orgasmic capacity. Other methods that focus more directly on reaching orgasm (e.g., masturbation training) seem to be more effective in dealing with this target, at least with primary orgasmic failure, but not all clients accept this treatment approach (e.g., Riley & Riley, 1978). Whether the partner should be involved in sex therapy should not be dependent on the attitude of the therapist but on the wishes of the patient. If the goal of therapy is to experience orgasm with the partner, the partner should be involved in the therapy in one way or another (e.g., at least minimally by means of homework assignments).

Unfortunately, most studies investigating the effects of masturbation training did not assess sexual anxiety, so that conclusions with respect to anxiety reduction are precluded. The only study that did assess sexual anxiety found changes in anxiety to be negligible (Andersen, 1981). Finally, there is some evidence that anxiety is more important in secondary than in primary cases. This suggests that with secondary anorgasmic women, treatment may need to be directed to anxiety reduction, while this may be less necessary with primary anorgasmic women. It has been suggested that sexual unassertiveness may change as a result of participation in a female group masturbation program (Delehanty, 1982). When sexual assertiveness is the only therapeutic target, however, assertiveness training directed to specific difficulties in social/sexual encounters seems to be more appropriate (Hammond & Oei, 1982).

Other Research Questions

Treatment format. Masters and Johnson used an intensive treatment format, involving daily therapy sessions by a male and female cotherapist team for an intensive two-week period. Crowe, Gillan, and Golombach (1981), Clement and Schmidt (1983), and Mathews, Bancroft et al. (1976) found that treatment was equally effective when conducted by one therapist as when conducted by two therapists of opposite sexes. Thus, the claim that dual sex teams are necessary has not been supported by research.

As to the intensive treatment format proposed by Masters and Johnson, there is no evidence that "massed" sessions are superior to "spaced" ses-

sions (e.g., once a week) (Clement & Schmidt, 1983; Ersner-Hershfield & Kopel, 1979; Heiman & LoPiccolo, 1983).

In sum, the short-term effectiveness of the Masters and Johnson program has been established in a series of studies, but there is no evidence that either a dual therapist team is essential or that treatment sessions should be held daily.

Behavioral marital therapy. A number of studies evaluated the differential effectiveness of a modified Masters and Johnson program and marital therapy. In the Crowe et al. study (1981), couples (n = 16) who had received marital therapy involving discussion of marital problems and relaxation and communication training improved as much as couples (n = 32) treated by sex therapy on variables associated with sexual and relationship satisfaction. Similarly, Killman et al. (1986, 1987) found communication training of the couple as effective as sex therapy; a combination of sex therapy and communication training was not more effective than either treatment alone. These results suggest that the programs directed at sexual technique are no more effective in the treatment of sexual dysfunctions than treatment focusing on the relationship.

In the Hartman and Dally (1983) study, sex therapy was compared with marital therapy. Marital therapy consisted of communication skills and problem-solving training. Sex therapy achieved a superior outcome on the measure of sexual satisfaction, whereas both treatments were equally effective in enhancing marital satisfaction.

Everaerd and Dekker (1981) compared a Masters and Johnson program with communication training. After 16 therapy sessions, sex therapy was more effective than communication training on sexual functioning. Thus, contrary to the findings of Crowe et al. (1981) and Killman et al. (1986, 1987), the results of Hartman and Dally (1983) and Everaerd and Dekker (1981) suggest that sex therapy helps both sexual and marital problems, whereas marital therapy helps marital problems only.

Finally, a study by Zimmer (1987) is of some importance. He found marital therapy to enhance the effects of sex therapy. Treatment directed at both the sexual problem and the relationship resulted in more pronounced and more consistent sexual improvement as well as in better marital adjustment.

Concluding Comment
A number of controlled studies have shown the short-term effectiveness of the behavioral sex therapies, but generally, results are less than originally claimed by Masters and Johnson. For example,

Mathews, Whitehead, and Kellett (1983) state that improvements after a modified form of the Masters and Johnson program are often less than complete. Everaerd (1983) found that with couples complaining of male sexual dysfunction the original complaints showed little improvement. Yet the majority of couples indicated improved satisfaction with their sexual functioning. On the other hand, Arentewicz and Schmidt (1980) found that in half of their patients, the improvement of the original symptoms did not lead to improved sexual functioning. In recent years, therapeutic goals have changed and orgasm through coition is no longer considered to be the only criterion for success by therapists, although a substantial number of patients still may find this the only acceptable goal (e.g., Cotton-Huston & Wheeler, 1983).

Few studies evaluated the long-term effectiveness of sex therapy. Masters and Johnson (1970) reported a follow-up of their patients up to five years after treatment and found results of treatment maintained. Other follow-up studies were less optimistic about the improvements achieved. In a follow-up study 2.5 to 4 years after treatment Arentewicz and Schmidt (1980) found a slight relapse. Only 50 percent of the patients completed questionnaires. Dekker and Everaerd (1983) reported a follow-up study 5 to 8 years after treatment. Of the original treated patients, 63 percent participated. A substantial number of couples were divorced or had received additional therapy. With the remaining patients ($n = 46$), results of treatment were maintained, although satisfaction with noncoital sex, time spent together, and affection showed a decline at follow-up.

Hawton, Catalan, Martin, and Fagg (1986) reported follow-up data one to six years after treatment. Generally, results were maintained. When a lapse occurred, effective coping strategies were accepting the relapse as a passing phase, talking to the partner, and practicing techniques learned in therapy.

Results of the follow-up studies are difficult to evaluate because of the limited participation of original treated patients in a number of studies. Assertions concerning the long-term efficacy of sex therapy are not yet warranted, given the dropouts during treatment, the divorce rate (14% in Arentewicz & Schmidt, and 21% in Dekker & Everaerd), the limited participation in the follow-up studies, and the number of patients receiving additional treatment.

PARAPHILIAS

In contrast with the increase in the number of controlled studies into sexual dysfunctions, pro-

gress in the area of deviant sexual preferences has still been limited.

Exhibitionism

While the prevalent opinion on exhibitionism is that it is a relatively harmless disorder, recent data indicate that a number of exhibitionists engage in more serious sexual offenses including rape (Abel & Rouleau, 1990).

Earlier work in this area was based on the assumption that sexual motivation was primary in the offense and was aimed at reducing deviant arousal to exhibitionistic themes. Both aversive therapy and covert sensitization have been given experimental support as effective in the treatment of exhibitionism (reviewed by Emmelkamp, 1986; Marshall & Barbaree, 1990). Maletzky (1980) reported the largest series ($n = 155$) so far, and follow-up ranged from one to nine years. Treatment was covert sensitization by means of the inhalation of noxious odors, but for about half of the subjects other procedures were added. This treatment was found to be surprisingly effective with a failure rate of only 13 percent.

Rooth and Marks (1974) compared (1) aversion therapy, (2) a self-regulation procedure, and (3) relaxation (control) with 12 exhibitionists. All patients received all three treatments in a counterbalanced order. Relaxation was ineffective, while the aversion therapy was slightly superior to self-regulation. The most effective treatment combination tended to be self-regulation preceded by aversion therapy. At follow-up 5 months after treatment, 7 out of 12 patients had exposed again. Thus, results were meager.

Shame aversion has also been used with exhibitionists. With this procedure, the exhibitionist has to undress for an audience, which provokes anxiety and shame. Wickramasekera (1980) found this procedure to be highly effective with 23 patients.

Two more studies were recently published by Marshall, Eccles, and Barbaree (1991). An interesting feature of these studies is that outcome data were derived from official and unofficial records. The unofficial local police files contained numerous reports of exhibiting that did not lead to charges and revealed rates that were 2.3 times higher than the rates revealed by the official data. Treatment was primarily directed at changing deviant sexual thoughts by means of electrical aversion therapy and orgasmic reconditioning. With this latter procedure, patients learn to switch their deviant fantasies during masturbation into fantasies thought to be more appropriate. In addition, patients were also required to take an inhalation of smelling salts whenever they felt an urge to expose. Among the treated men, 39 percent reoffended within a mean follow-up period of approximately nine years — a recidivism rate that is only slightly (but not significantly) better than the 57 percent recidivism rate in an untreated group. However, patients were not randomly assigned to both conditions.

Marshall and his colleagues reconceptualized exhibitionism in terms of a deficit in intimacy. According to more recent studies of this group, exhibitionists are characterized less by sexual motivation and more by poor attachment bonds in childhood and severe deficits in intimate relationships. Based on the notion of a deficit in intimacy, Marshall et al. (1991) developed a program to teach exhibitionists skills so that they can more effectively deal with stress. This program consisted of assertiveness training, stress management, cognitive restructuring, and training in relationship skills. In addition, patients received covert sensitization and had to use smelling salts as in the Marshall, Eccles, and Barbaree (1991) study. At 3.5 years follow-up, 23.6% of the treated men reoffended.

Given the lack of proper controlled studies with a large number of patients, the relative effectiveness of the various behavior therapy procedures is unknown. The attention is now shifting away from deviant sexual arousal toward a broader conceptualization of exhibitionism. Further controlled studies are needed to investigate whether a broad-spectrum therapy dealing with underlying problems is more effective than aversive programs directed at deviant sexuality.

Pedophilia

Previous reviews of the behavioral treatment of pedophiles and child molesters (Emmelkamp, 1986; Kelly, 1982) found some evidence that behavioral procedures such as electrical aversion therapy, covert sensitization, and orgasmic reconditioning could be effective, but this evidence was primarily based on case studies and uncontrolled studies. More recently, Johnston, Hudson, and Marshall (1992) reported the results of orgasmic reconditioning in a series of 10 nonfamilial child molesters. Although — as expected — deviant sexual arousal was reduced at the end of the treatment, appropriate sexual arousal was also reduced rather than increased, which poses both theoretical questions and questions with respect to the practical value of this method. Although such behavioral programs may be promising, a recent study by Rice, Quinsey, and Harris (1991) tempers optimism about the long-term effects with serious offenders. In their study, follow-up information was gathered on 136 child molesters from a maximum security psychiatric institution. The mean follow-up

period was 6.3 years. Forty-three percent committed a violent or sexual offense. Fifty of these patients had received aversive therapy to alter inappropriate sexual age preference. However, such behavioral treatment did not affect recidivism. Further, improvement in sexual arousal during treatment did not predict recidivism.

Marshall and Barbaree (1988) reported the results of a study in which a large group of child molesters were treated. The treatment program had two goals. The first was changing the sexual preference toward appropriate partners and the second was enhancement of social functioning, including dealing with social deficits that restrict access to appropriate partners. The treatment for modifying of sexual preferences was basically the same as that used in their study with exhibitionists (Marshall et al., 1991) and consisted of electrical aversion therapy, masturbatory reconditioning, and the self-administration of smelling-salts contingent upon sexual thoughts or urges. Treatment led to a reduction of deviant sexual arousal as measured by a penile plethysmograph. However, these changes were not related to subsequent recidivism. Further, treatment led to a substantial reduction in reoffenses in the treated group as compared to a comparable group that did apply for treatment but did not receive it at this agency for a variety of reasons. The recidivism rate (based on official and unofficial sources) in the treated group was 13.2 percent as compared to 34.5 percent in the untreated group. As the follow-up period increased in length, there was a dramatic increase in recidivism and number of reoffenses, in both the treated and control group. Two factors predicted treatment outcome: younger age of the child molester and genital–genital contact between the offender and the victim.

This study underscores that reduction in sexual arousal and official police records as outcome measures for child molesters are unreliable. The official recidivism figures are underestimates of actual reoffending.

Concluding Remarks

Occasionally, reports have been published on the treatment of voyeurism, transvestism, fetishism, transsexuality, and sadomasochism (reviewed by McConaghy, 1982), but to the best of this writer's knowledge, no controlled group studies have been reported.

The major impression obtained from reviewing the literature on sexual deviation is that a number of procedures may be effective in decreasing deviant sexual behavior, although methodological flaws in most of these studies preclude the drawing

CHAP 9 ■ BEHAVIOR THERAPY WITH ADULTS **411**

of firm conclusions. Theoretically, it is often unclear by which processes these procedures work (Barlow, 1982), and the contribution of placebo factors cannot be ruled out (Emmelkamp & Walta, 1978).

Because appropriate arousal patterns do not usually emerge when deviant arousal is eliminated (Abel & Rouleau 1990; Brownell & Barlow, 1977), researchers have become interested in techniques to increase appropriate arousal such as "orgasmic reconditioning" and "fantasy alternation." Although these methods have been found to be effective in enhancing arousal in a number of case studies, controlled laboratory studies found the improvements achieved variable results at best (Leonard & Hayes, 1983). Further, it is highly questionable whether reduction in deviant sexual arousal is predictive of recidivism. The recent emphasis by Marshall and his colleagues on broad-spectrum programs, not only focusing on changing deviant arousal and preferences but also directed at enhancing social functioning, is interesting. Further controlled studies along these lines are needed before more definite recommendations can be made. Another important area of research involves the abstinence violation effect in sex offenders. Hudson, Ward, and Marshall (1992) presented a heuristic model of relapse in sex offenders, emphasizing the abstinence violation effect. They formulated a number of attributional scenarios that may occur when a relapse occurs. Research into attributional processes may reveal important clues about why some sex offenders relapse while others do not.

HOMOSEXUALITY

Homosexuality per se is no longer considered to be a paraphilia. However, changes in attitudes toward homosexuality have not been reflected in the research literature on behavior therapy with homosexuals. It is now widely accepted that treatment focusing on changing a homosexual into a heterosexual may reinforce the idea that homosexuality is bad or "sick." Few behavior therapists will conduct such treatments and the goal of treatment in the last decades has changed from sexual reorientation to enhancing homosexual functioning. Russell and Winkler (1977) randomly assigned 27 homosexuals to either a behaviorally oriented assertiveness training group designed to facilitate homosexual functioning or a nondirective group run by a homosexual guidance service. Assertiveness training dealt both with assertive behavior in general and with discrimination. Both treatments led to significant improvements in social anxiety and assertiveness, although this was not reflected on the behavioral measure used. Both procedures were about equally effective.

A few studies have been reported on the treatment of homosexuals complaining of sexual dysfunctions. Everaerd et al. (1982) included homosexuals in male-only groups treated for sexual dysfunctions. Masters and Johnson (1979) applied their sex therapy program to homosexual couples and asserted that 90 percent of their patients were improved at the end of treatment. Unfortunately, neither of these studies was controlled.

Given the numerous controlled studies on aversive procedures designed to change a homosexual orientation into a heterosexual one (reviewed by McConaghy, 1982), the relative absence of controlled studies on behavioral procedures to enhance homosexual or bisexual functioning is remarkable.

The AIDS Crisis

Compulsive sexual behavior has received increased attention in the last few years due to an increased awareness of the risks of AIDS. Although the risks are well known, many homosexuals (Martin, 1990) and presumably many heterosexuals as well are unable to change their sexual behaviors. Quadland (1985) found a group treatment directed at changing sexual behavior quite effective in reducing the number of sexual contacts. Patients reduced the mean monthly number of different sexual partners from 11.5 at the start of treatment to 3.3 at 6-month follow-up. A cognitive-behavioral program directed at changing risky sexual activities was also found to be highly effective in a study by Kelly, St. Lawrence, Hood, and Brasfield (1989).

The developments of tests to identify the antibody to the human immunodeficiency virus (HIV) has made it possible to diagnose infection with the virus prior to the development of physical symptoms. Knowing that one is HIV-seropositive leads to increased stress and depression, which may have a negative effect on the immune system. Antoni et al. (1991) found a cognitive-behavioral stress-management program effective in reducing affective distress and immunologic impairments caused by learning HIV-1 antibody test results. Whether such immunologic changes will have an impact on the health status of such individuals has not yet been tested.

Both the stigma of being HIV-seropositive and the connection between sexual activity and HIV-transmission may threaten the self-esteem of gay men and lead to social isolation.

Mulder, Emmelkamp, Antoni, Sandfort, and de Vries (1993) compared the effects of a cognitive-behavioral stress-management program with those of experiential therapy with 32 HIV-seropositive homosexuals. Both treatments were applied in groups. Treatment led to a significant reduction in anxiety and mood and was more effective than a waiting-list control group. Stress management was found to be as effective as experiential therapy.

MARITAL DISTRESS

This section discusses cognitive and behavioral approaches to the treatment of marital distress. For a more general discussion of marital therapy, the reader is referred to Chapter 14, this volume.

Behavior therapy has shown promise in treating marital problems (Baucom & Hoffman, 1986; Emmelkamp, 1986), although there is some concern about the clinical significance of the effects achieved (Hahlweg & Markman, 1988).

It is assumed that reciprocity of reinforcement underlies successful marriages. Behavioral contracting or "reciprocity counseling" is designed to promote marital satisfaction by instigating positive changes in the natural environment. With this approach, each partner should provide reinforcement for the reinforcing behavior of his or her partner, according to the "give to get" principle. Several controlled outcome studies have demonstrated the effectiveness of this approach (reviewed by Baucom & Hoffman, 1986).

Many of the behavioral programs reported in the literature have combined elements from contingency contracting and communication skills training. As stated by Luber (1978), "These models seem to be largely subjective, random combinations apparently based on the assumption that since each method has accumulated some independent validation they should be effective in unison" (p. 86).

Some (e.g., Jacobson, 1978; Liberman, Levie, Wheeler, Sanders, and Wallace, 1976) have questioned the utility of contingency contracting as a treatment strategy. Liberman et al. suggest "that contingency contracting is worth just about the paper it's printed on without the family members having adequate interpersonal communication skills" (p. 32). Emmelkamp, Van der Helm, MacGillavry, and Van Zanten (1984), Jacobson (1984), and O'Leary and Turkewitz (1978) compared communication training and behavioral exchange directly. No significant differences between the two conditions were found. However, in the Jacobson study there was a trend for the couples who had not received communication training to relapse somewhat at six-month follow-up, while the other couples maintained their treatment gains.

Another question of some interest is whether different components of BMT are equally accept-

able to clients. In our experience, communication skills training and problem solving are more acceptable than quid pro quo contracting. In a recent survey (Lipton & Jensen, 1991), both forms of BMT were found to be differently acceptable to potential clients: Communication skills training and problem solving were favored over contracting procedures.

In the studies discussed so far, behavioral techniques were highly structured for research purposes and do not reflect actual clinical practice in which therapists are much more flexible in dealing with couples. Jacobson et al. (1989) compared a structured research-based version of BMT with a more flexible clinical version. In the flexible BMT, the therapist could choose which modules were particularly suited for each couple and the number of sessions could be tailored to the individual needs. At the posttest, both treatments were found to be equally effective; at six-month follow-up, however, the flexible treatment couples maintained their improvements, whereas a number of couples treated with the structured format were found to have deteriorated.

BMT Versus Alternative Approaches

To date, a number of controlled studies have been reported that compared behavioral marriage therapy with a nonbehavioral approach, using actual clinical patients as subjects. A system-theoretic approach was compared to BMT in two Dutch studies. In the first study of this series (Boelens, Emmelkamp, MacGillavry, & Markvoort, 1980), contingency contracting and system-theoretic counseling were contrasted. Both treatment groups improved on marital satisfaction and the target problems in contrast to couples from the waiting-list control group. The improvement was maintained six months after the posttest, although a relapse was found for some couples from the system-theoretic counseling group. Emmelkamp et al. (1984) compared communication skills training and system-theoretic counseling: Both treatments were found to be equally effective.

In the Liberman et al. (1976) study, behavioral group therapy was found to be more effective on behavioral measures only than an interaction–insight-oriented group treatment. One major limitation of the Liberman et al. (1976) study is the small number of couples used. Johnson and Greenberg (1985) compared BMT with an emotionally focused treatment. The latter approach was derived from client-centered and Gestalt therapy. Generally, both treatments were found to be equally effective. Finally, Snyder and Wills (1989) compared the effects of BMT with insight-oriented marital therapy.

Again, no significant differences between the treatment formats were found at the posttest and six-month follow-up.

Summarizing the studies discussed, the following conclusions seem warranted: Both contingency contracting and communication skills training appear to be at least equally effective as system-theoretic–oriented therapy. The effects of both behavioral procedures are broadly comparable. Generally, BMT appears to be equally effective as insight-oriented approaches. A disadvantage of between-group comparisons as presented here is that it is unclear whether the same couples profit from behavioral, system-theoretic, or insight-oriented procedures. Rather than continuing comparative studies, there is now a clear need for studies that address the issue of matching individual needs of patients to particular treatments. Who are the failures of BMT? Do patients who fail with behavioral approaches also fail with system-theoretic counseling or insight-oriented therapy and vice versa? Are specific patients' characteristics related to success or failure with the various approaches? A study by Holtzworth-Munroe, Jacobson, Deklyen, and Whisman (1989) provides some answers to the latter question. In their study, positive client behavior, defined as collaboration, active participation, and homework compliance, was positively associated with therapy outcome. Results suggest that success of BMT depends on the clients' involvement and compliance in therapy, which is consistent with data from other forms of individual therapy.

Cognitive Interventions

The evolution of behavioral marital therapy has been characterized by a broadened conceptualization of relationship dysfunction and an expanded range of intervention procedures. Of particular significance is the increased attention that behavioral marital therapists have paid to the assessment and modification of cognitive processes that may mediate spouses' behaviors toward one another. A substantial minority of couples have not responded to traditional behavioral marital therapy or have remained distressed after achieving successful behavior change. Based on clinical observations and research, behavioral researchers and therapists have stressed that the impact of behaviors exchanged by spouses is subjective and idiosyncratic and that the planning of behavior change must take into account the individuals' cognitive appraisals (Baucom & Epstein, 1990).

Such clinical observations have led to the inclusion of cognitive restructuring techniques in the repertoires of many behavioral marital therapists. The cognitive strategies generally used in cognitive therapy of marital distress focus on changing irrational beliefs, faulty attributional processes, and negative self-statements. Baucom and Lester (1986) compared behavioral marital therapy with a treatment including behavioral marital therapy plus cognitive restructuring. The combined treatment approach was no more effective than BMT on its own.

Emmelkamp, van Linden van den Heuvell, Rüphan, Sanderman, Scholing & Stroink (1988) compared the efficacy of cognitive restructuring alone versus behavioral marital therapy. Thirty-two clinically distressed couples were randomly assigned to two conditions: (1) cognitive restructuring and (2) communication skills training. Cognitive restructuring focused on (1) the causal attributions or explanations that maritally distressed couples give for events that took place in the marriage, (2) individual irrational beliefs that the married individual held for himself or herself or his or her partner, and (3) unrealistic expectations that couples held for the relationship. At the posttest, both groups showed significant improvement on most measures. On the target problems, cognitive restructuring proved to be slightly superior to communication skills training. Overall, the results of this clinical outcome study indicate that cognitive restructuring might be at least as effective as communication skills training, but there is little evidence that the effects of both treatments are mediated by changes in either communication patterns or cognitive processes. Rather, the results of this study suggest that changes in communication and irrational relationship beliefs occur irrespective of the particular treatment received.

Baucom, Sayers, and Sher (1990) studied whether supplementing BMT with cognitive therapy or emotional expression training would enhance the overall effectiveness of treatment. The results were disappointing from a clinical point of view. Neither supplementing cognitive therapy, supplementing emotional expressiveness training, nor supplementing a combination of these two approaches did increase the overall effectiveness of BMT alone.

Concluding Remarks

Behavioral marital therapy has been shown to be moderately effective with clinically distressed couples. There is, however, no evidence that it is more effective than alternative approaches. Cognitive therapies have also shown promise in dealing with marital distress. At present, however, there is no confirming evidence that the treatment procedures achieve their results through the presumed treatment mechanisms.

The overall impression of comparative studies evaluating different treatments is that no single approach or combination of treatments is superior. In none of the studies was an attempt made to match couples to treatment. Thus, at present it is unclear what couple parameters may interact with type of treatment to enhance treatment effectiveness. One of the most important research areas is to investigate which characteristics of couples might interact with type of treatment. It might be reasonable to hold that communication training is indicated when both partners lack the necessary communication skills and, on the other hand, that cognitive restructuring is indicated when both partners hold irrational (relationship) beliefs and expectations. However, the situation becomes more complex when only one of the partners lacks adequate communication skills while the other is highly irrational in his or her (relationship) beliefs —a pattern that might be quite common among clinically distressed couples. This indicates that studies are needed that take into account not only differences between couples but also individual differences within couples. Although such studies will be difficult to realize, it is likely that such efforts will produce more new knowledge than studies comparing different treatment procedures irrespective of couples' and individuals' characteristics.

Long-term follow-up studies are relatively rare. Jacobson, Schmaling, and Holtzworth-Munroe (1989) evaluated the effects of components of behavioral marital therapy two years after treatment and found approximately one-third of the couples to have deteriorated at follow-up. Other negative results were reported by Snyder, Wills, and Grady-Fletcher (1991). At follow-up four years after treatment, behavioral marital therapy was significantly less effective than insight-oriented marital therapy (IOMT). However, as noted by Jacobson (1991), the behavioral marital therapy used in this study was outmoded and the so-called insight-oriented treatment consisted primarily of behavioral techniques: "Of the 31 intervention strategies listed in the IOMT treatment manual, none are incompatible with BMT, and 26 would be considered integral to a behavioral approach" (p. 142). In any event, the results of the Snyder et al. (1991) follow-up study and of Jacobson et al. (1989) suggest that purely technique-oriented behavioral marital therapy is less effective than a much broader conceptualized treatment approach, which includes many behavioral techniques.

SCHIZOPHRENIA

In the early days of behavior therapy, many books focused on the application of behavior therapy with psychiatric inpatients (e.g., Ayllon & Azrin's, [1968] *The Token Economy* and Ullmann & Krasner's [1965] *Case Studies in Behavior Modification*). In the tradition of operant conditioning, token economies were devised for chronic psychiatric inpatients. In a token economy, tokens are provided for appropriate behavior, thus reinforcing it (e.g., teeth brushing, getting up on time in the morning, having a conversation, cleaning one's room) and withheld (according to the principle of extinction) for inappropriate behavior (e.g., crying, lying in bed all day, quarreling). Tokens can be exchanged for reinforcers such as money, preferred consumables, or a free walk through the city.

In the seventies, a number of studies evaluated the effectiveness of token economies with psychiatric patients. A landmark study was published by Paul and Lentz (1977) in which nearly a hundred patients were randomly assigned to a token economy ward, a milieu therapy ward, or a traditional ward. The token economy program was the most effective, resulting in a greater number of discharged patients, less time spent in the hospital, and less medication taken. Despite the successful outcome for the token economy in this and other studies, the interest in the token economy appears to have waned in more recent years (Glynn, 1990). This lack of interest in a potentially powerful treatment method is due to a variety of factors including (1) staff resistance and shortages, (2) a dramatic decrease in the length of hospitalization and a concomitant emphasis on community-based programs that are not particularly suited for a token economy approach, and (3) legal and ethical concerns (Glynn, 1990; Kazdin, 1983). There have been a number of court decisions in the United States that have had a profound impact on the functioning of token economy programs, such as the patient's right to have free access to food, storage space, and furniture, as well as freedom of movement. The implication of these court decisions is that a number of reinforcers that only could be earned in token economy programs now have to be provided noncontingently to the patients.

The increased evidence that biological factors are involved in schizophrenia led to a decreasing interest in this disorder by behavior therapists. More recently, however, it has been increasingly recognized that schizophrenia does not belong only to the domain of biological psychiatry. For example, Bellack (1986) noted that "simply identifying the specific neurochemical underlying a class of behaviors or documenting a genetic linkage does not ipso facto rule out any role for psychological factors or psychosocial treatment" (p. 202). Many schizophrenics do not take their medication after discharge or do not respond to it. Further, medication alone is inadequate in treating problems in social functioning. While such medication is important in managing the acute phase of the disorder, its main impact is on positive symptoms such as hallucinations and delusions rather than on interpersonal deficits and social functioning. Many schizophrenics on adequate dosage of neuroleptic medication still experience considerable problems in social functioning. Thus, there is a clear need for alternative approaches that may be effective in remedying the problems left untouched by medication.

Zubin and Spring (1977) formulated a diathesis stress model for understanding schizophrenia. In this model, it is assumed that some individuals are born with a biological vulnerability to develop schizophrenia. If an individual experiences more stress than his or her body can handle, the illness may develop or a relapse may occur. An inability to cope in the social environment is thought to be a significant source of stress and to contribute to an exacerbation of symptoms (e.g., a psychotic episode). If the model is correct, then coping skills training to deal more adequately with stressors could have something to offer to such patients.

Two types of interventions have been developed to teach the patient and his or her family to deal more adequately with stress: social skills training and family education. Both types of interventions have been empirically evaluated in a number of controlled studies.

Social Skills Training
Many schizophrenics are characterized by deficits in social functioning since childhood. Even when the positive psychotic symptoms react favorably to neuroleptic medication, most schizophrenics will still exhibit severe social skills deficits. In social skills training (SST), patients are trained in basic skills such as conversation and assertiveness in order to respond to stressors more adequately and thus reduce the stress. SST aims to improve the quality of life by increasing the individual's social competence. Improving the social competence is an important goal because social competence is a significant predictor of the course and outcome of schizophrenia (Strauss & Carpenter, 1977). Although the effects of SST with schizophrenics were studied at the end of the 1960s in Europe (Boerwinkel, Boink, & Emmelkamp, 1971), most later studies have been conducted in the United States.

SST with schizophrenics is usually conducted in small groups and consists of structured training of interpersonal competencies by means of instructions, modeling, behavior rehearsal, in vivo exercises in the community, and feedback. Of recent interest is the transfer of learned skills to a variety of situations in the natural environment. Another recent innovation in these programs involves training in social problem solving in addition to training in basic conversation skills and assertiveness. In social problem solving, patients practice dealing with difficult social situations by following a number of steps: problem identification, goal definition, evaluation of alternative solutions, and decision making (e.g., Hansen, St. Lawrence, & Cristo, 1985).

Studies evaluating the effects of SST training with inpatient schizophrenics have been reviewed by Donahoe and Driesenga (1989) and Halford and Hayes (1991). Generally, SST led to significant improvements in social skills on role-play tests, and there is some evidence that the effects achieved on social skills generalized to the ward. It is questionable, however, whether improvements achieved are maintained over a longer time span and generalize to settings outside the hospital. Although there is some evidence that SST, including social problem solving, was more effective than alternative approaches in reducing symptomatology and preventing rehospitalization (Hogarty et al., 1986; Liberman, Mueser, & Wallace, 1986), results are as yet inconclusive.

Family Intervention
Since schizophrenia usually develops in late adolescence or early adulthood, the family of origin is often the patient's most important social network. There is now increasing evidence that high expressed emotion (EE) by family members, including high criticism, hostility, and overinvolvement, is probably stressful for schizophrenics. As shown by Vaughn and Leff (1976), schizophrenics living with family members characterized by high levels of EE are five times as likely to relapse as are patients not living in high EE households. Tarrier and Barrowclough (1990) reviewed 12 subsequent studies and found that 53 percent of patients living with a high-EE relative relapsed, compared to 23 percent living with a low-EE relative. Given this state of affairs, it is not surprising that family intervention programs have been designed to change relatives from high to low EE.

In contrast to social skills training, which focuses on improving patients' coping efforts, behavioral family training programs are designed to improve the relatives' coping efforts and to reduce negative affect toward the patient. The best-known programs are that of Falloon et al. (1984), which consists of an educational program, communication training, and problem-solving training, and that of Tarrier and his colleagues, which also involves an educational program, coping skills training, and problem solving. Recently, the effects of these programs have been reviewed by Mueser and Glynn (1990) and Tarrier and Barrowclough (1990). The main conclusions of these reviews are

There is substantial evidence that behavioral family intervention combined with maintenance neuroleptic medication is effective in reducing relapse rate of schizophrenics in the first year of discharge.

Relapse can be forestalled, but not prevented — There is an increase in relapse in the second year of discharge.

Behavioral interventions are superior to routine care and the educational program alone.

Interventions need to be long term.

Reduction in relapse is associated with change in the relatives' EE levels from high to low.

These results are highly encouraging. One of the major tasks for further studies is to demonstrate that these programs can also be conducted effectively outside of a research context. When adequate training in behavior therapy and continuous supervision are provided, it might be possible that these programs can be conducted by nurse-therapists on a routine basis.

Concluding Remark

Since schizophrenics are characterized by attentional deficits and deficits in social perception, it has been argued that training that focuses on cognitive function deficits and social perception should be included in behavioral programs. In the studies on social skills training and behavioral family therapy, variations in the cognitive deficits of patients have been neglected. Presumably, behavioral approaches have to be modified for patients with severe cognitive deficits. Brenner (1987) designed a treatment program in which a cognitive function training was combined with social skills training and reported good results. Studies are now needed that investigate whether the addition of a cognitive function training enhances the effects of a social skills training program.

SUMMARY AND CONCLUDING REMARKS

Research on phobias is falling into place. The effects of exposure in vivo are now well established for agoraphobia, simple phobia, social phobia, and obsessive-compulsive disorders. Research into the cognitive-behavioral treatment of panic attacks is promising, but further studies are needed to unravel its specific components (breathing retraining, interoceptive exposure, exposure in vivo, and cognitive restructuring). In recent years, the interest in the behavioral treatment of post-traumatic stress disorders has increased. The studies that have been conducted suggest that both imaginal exposure procedures and cognitive coping strategies may alleviate the suffering, but only a few controlled studies have been conducted to date.

Studies of the behavioral and cognitive treatment of depression represent one of the more exciting areas of clinical research. The progression of research in this area has advanced our knowledge, but there are still a number of important issues that need to be studied. For example, we have no idea why both cognitive and behavioral interventions work with depressed patients, although various researchers provide various theoretical explanations. Unfortunately, to date there is no evidence that either cognitive, behavioral, or self-control theories explain the improvements achieved with these various treatment procedures.

In the area of alcoholism, the interest has moved away from aversive procedures into multifaceted self-control programs. The results of a series of studies that investigated coping skills programs to prevent relapse look promising. Relatively new is the interest in cue exposure. Further studies are needed before conclusions with respect to its clinical usefulness can be drawn.

In the area of sexual dysfunctions, progress was small. While the short-term effects of time-limited sex therapies have been well established, there is still some concern about the long-term effects of these approaches. An area that deserves further study is the treatment of paraphilias. A number of controlled studies have been published in recent years attesting to the effectiveness of behavioral procedures, but more recent follow-up studies suggest that relapse is common. The state of the art in the treatment of marital distress has advanced. One issue deserving a great deal of attention in future research on marital therapy is the integration of behavioral and cognitive interventions. Finally, significant progress has been made in the treatment of schizophrenia.

The predominant type of outcome research in behavior therapy involved between-groups studies comparing different procedures or treatment components. In the group designs, within-group variance is perceived as an unfortunate occurrence rather than as a major source of relevant information. While it is often acknowledged that effective clinical behavior therapy is only as good as its initial behavioral analysis, this issue has been totally neglected by researchers. Behavior therapy research has been more techniqe than problem oriented. Research remains to be done on the reliability and validity of functional analyses.

Although behavior therapists have been very productive in evaluating the efficacy of various techniques, relatively little attention has been devoted to the therapeutic process. It is, however, becoming increasingly clear that the quality of the therapeutic relationship may be influential in determining success or failure of behavioral therapies, although well-controlled studies in this area are rare (Emmelkamp, 1986).

REFERENCES

Abel, G. G., & Rouleau, J. L. (1990). The nature and extent of sexual assault. In W. L. Marshall, D. R. Laws, & H. E. Barbaree (Eds.), *Handbook of sexual assault: Issues, theories, and treatment of the offender* (pp. 9–21). New York: Plenum.

Alden, L. E. (1988). Behavioral self-management controlled-drinking strategies in a context of secondary prevention. *Journal of Consulting and Clinical Psychology, 56,* 280–286.

Andersen, B. L. A. (1981). A comparison of systematic desensitization and directed masturbation in the treatment of orgasmic dysfunction in females. *Journal of Consulting and Clinical Psychology, 49,* 568–570.

Antoni, M. H., Baggett, L., Ironson, G., La Perriere, A., August, S., Klimas, N., Schneiderman, N., & Fletcher, M. A. (1991). Cognitive-behavioral stress management intervention buffers distress responses and immunologic changes following notification of HIV-1 seropositivity. *Journal of Consulting and Clinical Psychology, 59,* 763–765.

Arentewicz, G., & Schmidt, G. (1980). *Sexuell gestörte Beziehungen.* Berlin: Springer Verlag.

Arnow, B. B., Taylor, C. B., Agras, W. S., & Telch, M. J. (1985). Enhancing agoraphobia treatment outcome by changing couple communication patterns. *Behaviour Research and Therapy, 16,* 452–467.

Arrindell, W. A., & Emmelkamp, P. M. G. (1985). Psychological profile of the spouse of the female agoraphobic patient: Personality and symptoms. *British Journal of Psychiatry, 146,* 405–414.

Arrindell, W. A., & Emmelkamp, P. M. G. (1986). Marital adjustment, intimacy and needs in female agoraphobics and their partners: A controlled study. *British Journal of Psychiatry, 149,* 592–602.

Arrindell, W. A., & Emmelkamp, P. M. G. (1987). Psychological states and traits in female agoraphobics: A controlled study. *Journal of Psychopathology and Behavioral Assessment, 9,* 237–253.

Arrindell, W. A., Emmelkamp, P. M. G., & Sanderman, R. (1986). Marital quality and general life adjustment in relation to treatment outcome in agoraphobia. *Advances in Behaviour Research and Therapy,* 139–185.

Ascher, L. M. (1981) Employing paradoxical intention in the treatment of agoraphobia. *Behaviour Research and Therapy, 19,* 533–542.

Ascher, L. M., Schotte, D. E., & Grayson, J. B. (1986) Enhancing effectiveness of paradoxical intention in treating travel restriction in agoraphobia. *Behavior Therapy, 17,* 124–130.

Auerbach, R., & Killman, P. R. (1977). The effects of group systematic desensitization on secondary erectile failure. *Behavior Therapy, 8,* 330–339.

Ayllon, T., & Azrin, N. S. (1968). *The token economy.* New York: Appleton-Century-Crofts.

Baker, A.L., & Wilson, P. H. (1985). Cognitive-behavior therapy for depression: The effects of booster sessions on relapse. *Behaviour Therapy, 16,* 335–344.

Banner, C. N., & Meadows, W. M. (1984). Examination of

the effectiveness of various treatment techniques for reducing tension. *British Journal of Clinical Psychology, 22,* 183–194.

Barbach, L. G. (1974). Group treatment of preorgasmic women. *Journal of Sex and Marital Therapy, 1,* 139–145.

Barlow, D. (1982). The context of learning in behaviour therapy. In J. C. Boulougouris (Ed.), *Learning theory approaches to psychiatry.* Chichester: Wiley. (pp. 75–85).

Barlow, D. H., Craske, M., Cerny, J., & Klosko, J. (1989). Behavioral treatment of panic disorder. *Behavior Therapy, 20,* 261–282.

Barlow, D. H., O'Brien, G. T., & Last, C. G. (1984). Couples treatment of agoraphobia. *Behavior Therapy, 15,* 41–58.

Barnett, P. A., & Gotlib, J. H. (1988). Psychological functioning and depression: Distinguishing among antecedents, concomitants, and consequences. *Psychological Bulletin, 104,* 97–126.

Basoglu, M., Lax, T., Kasvikis, Y., & Marks, I. M. (1988). Predictors of improvement in obsessive-compulsive disorder. *Journal of Anxiety Disorders, 2,* 299–317.

Bass, C., & Lelliott, P. (1989). Hyperventilation in the aetiology and treatment of anxiety disorders. In P. M. G. Emmelkamp, W. Everaerd, F. Kraaimaat, & M. van Son (Eds.), *Fresh perspectives on anxiety.* Amsterdam: Swets.

Baucom, D. H., & Hoffman, J. A. (1986). The effectiveness of marital therapy: Current status and application to the clinical setting. In N. S. Jacobson & A. S. Gurman (Eds.), *Clinical handbook of marital therapy* (pp. 597–620). New York: Guilford.

Baucom, D. H., & Epstein, N. (1990). The role of cognitive variables in the assessment and treatment of marital disorders. In M. Hersen, M. Eisler, & N. Miller (Eds.), *Progress in behavior modification,* pp. 223–251.

Baucom, D. H., & Lester, G. W. (1986). The usefulness of cognitive restructuring as an adjunct to behavioral marital therapy. *Behavior Therapy, 17,* 385–403.

Baucom, D. H., Sayers, S. L., & Sher, T. G. (1990). Supplementing behavioral marital therapy with cognitive restructuring and emotional expressiveness training: An outcome investigation. *Journal of Consulting and Clinical Psychology, 58,* 636–645.

Beach, S. R. H., Sandeen, E. E., & O'Leary, K. D. (1990). *Depression in marriage: A model for etiology and treatment.* New York: Guilford Press.

Beck, A. T., & Emery, G. (1985). *Anxiety disorders and phobias: A cognitive perspective.* New York: Basic Books.

Beck, A. T., Rush, A. J., Shaw, B. F., & Emery, G. (1979). *Cognitive therapy of depression.* New York: Guilford.

Bellack, A. S. (1986). Schizophrenia: Behavior therapy's forgotten child. *Behavior Therapy, 17,* 199–214.

Bellack, A. S., Hersen, M., & Himmelhoch, J. M. (1983). A comparison of social-skills training, pharmacotherapy and psychotherapy for depression. *Behavior Research and Therapy, 21,* 101–108.

Bellack, A. S., Hersen, M., & Kazdin, A. E. (Eds.). (1990). *International handbook of behavior modification and therapy.* New York: Plenum.

Biglan, A., & Craker, D. (1982). Effects of pleasant-activities manipulation on depression. *Journal of Consulting and Clinical Psychology, 50,* 436–438.

Biran, M., & Wilson, G. T. (1981). Treatment of phobic disorders using cognitive and exposure methods. *Journal of Consulting and Clinical Psychology, 49,* 886–899.

Bland, K., & Hallam, R. S. (1981). Relationship between response to graded exposure and marital satisfaction in agoraphobics. *Behaviour Research and Therapy, 19,* 335–338.

Blowers, C., Cobb, J., & Mathews, A. (1987). Generalised

anxiety: A controlled treatment study. *Behaviour Research and Therapy, 25,* 493–502.

Boelens, W. (1990). *Cognitieve en gedragstherapie bij depressie.* Dissertation, University of Groningen.

Boelens, W., Emmelkamp, P. M. G., MacGillavry, D., & Markvoort, M. (1980). A clinical evaluation of marital treatment: Reciprocity counseling vs. system-theoretic counseling. *Behavioral Analysis and Modification, 4,* 85–96.

Boersma, K., den Hengst, S., Dekker, J., & Emmelkamp, P. M. G. (1976). Exposure and response prevention in the natural environment: A comparison with obsessive-compulsive patients. *Behaviour Research and Therapy, 14,* 19–24.

Boerwinkel, A., Boink, R., & Emmelkamp, P. M. G. (1971). *Modeling and role playing with chronic mental patients to increase social interaction.* University of Utrecht, Department of Clinical Psychology, Utrecht.

Bonn, J. A., Readhead, C. P. A., & Timmons, B. H. (1984). Enhanced adaptive behavioural response in agoraphobic patients pretreated with breathing retraining. *The Lancet, 2,* 665–669.

Borkovec, T. D., Mathews, A. M., Chambers, A., Ebrahimi, S., Lytle, R., & Nelson, R. (1987). Effects of relaxation training with cognitive or nondirective therapy and the role of relaxation-induced anxiety in the treatment of generalized anxiety. *Journal of Consulting and Clinical Psychology, 55,* 883–888.

Boudewyns, P. A., Hyer, L., Woods, M. G., Harrison, W. R., & McCronie, E. (1990). PTSD among Vietnam veterans: An early look at treatment outcome using direct therapeutic exposure. *Journal of Traumatic Stress, 3,* 359–368.

Boulougouris, J. C. (1977). Variables affecting outcome in obsessive-compulsive patients treated by flooding. In J. C. Boulougouris & A. D. Rabavilas (Eds.), *Treatment of phobic and obsessive-compulsive disorders.* Oxford: Pergamon.

Bouman, T. K., & Emmelkamp, P. M. G. (1993). Panic disorder and severe agoraphobia: A comparative evaluation of exposure, breathing retraining and cognitive therapy. Unpublished manuscript, University of Groningen, Department of Clinical Psychology, Groningen.

Brenner, H. D. (1987). On the importance of cognitive disorders in treatment and rehabilitation. In J. S. Strauss, W. Boker, & H. D. Brenner (Eds.), *Psychosocial treatment of schizophrenia* (pp. 136–151). Toronto: Hans Huber.

Brodbeck, C., & Michelson, L. (1987) Problem-solving skills and attributional styles of agoraphobics. *Cognitive Therapy and Research, 11,* 593–610.

Brown, R., & Lewinsohn, P. M. (1984). A psychoeducational approach to the treatment of depression: Comparison of group, individual, and minimal contact procedures. *Journal of Consulting and Clinical Psychology, 52,* 774–783.

Brownell, K. D., & Barlow, D. H. (1977). Measurement and treatment of two sexual deviations in one person. *Journal of Behavior Therapy and Experimental Psychiatry, 7,* 349–354.

Burns, L. E., Thorpe, G. L., & Cavallero, A. (1986). Agoraphobia 8 years after behavioural treatment. *Behavior Therapy, 17,* 580–591.

Butler, G., Cullington, A., Hibbert, G., Klimes, I., & Gelder, M. (1987). Anxiety management for persistent generalised anxiety. *British Journal of Psychiatry, 151,* 535–542.

Butler, G., Cullington, A., Munby, M., Amies, P., & Gelder, M. (1984). Exposure and anxiety management in the treatment of social phobia. *Journal of Consulting and Clinical Psychology, 52,* 642–650.

Butler, G., Fennell, M., Robson, P., & Gelder, M. (1991). Comparison of behavior therapy and cognitive behavior therapy in the treatment of generalized anxiety disorder. *Journal of Consulting and Clinical Psychology, 59,* 167–175.

Butler, G., Gelder, M., Hibbert, G., Cullington, A., & Klimes, I. (1987). Anxiety management: Developing effective strategies. *Behaviour Research and Therapy, 25,* 517–522.

Cannon, D. S., & Baker, T. B. (1981). Emetic and electric shock alcohol aversion therapy: Assessment of conditioning. *Journal of Consulting and Clinical Psychology, 49,* 20–33.

Cannon, D. S., Baker, T. B., Gino, A., & Nathan, P. E. (1986). Alcohol-aversion therapy: Relation between strength of aversion and abstinence. *Journal of Consulting and Clinical Psychology, 54,* 825–830.

Cannon, D. S., Baker, T. B., & Wehl, W. K. (1981). Emetic and electric shock alcohol aversion therapy: Six and twelve-month follow-up. *Journal of Consulting and Clinical Psychology, 49,* 360–368.

Cerny, J. A., Barlow, D. M., Craske, M. G., & Himadi, W. G. (1987). Couples treatment of agoraphobia: A two-year follow-up. *Behavior Therapy, 18,* 401–415.

Chambless, D., & Goldstein, A. (1982). *Agoraphobia: Multiple perspectives on theory and treatment.* New York: Wiley.

Clark, D. M. (1986). A cognitive approach to panic. *Behaviour Research and Therapy, 24,* 461–470.

Clark, D. M., Salkovskis, P. M., & Chalkley, A. J. (1985). Respiratory control as a treatment for panic attacks. *Journal of Behavior Therapy and Experimental Psychiatry, 16,* 23–30.

Clark, D. M. (1991). *Cognitive therapy for panic disorder.* Paper presented at the NIH Consensus Development Conference on Treatment of Panic Disorder, September 1991, Washington.

Clement, U., & Schmidt, G. (1983). The outcome of couple therapy for sexual dysfunctions using three different formats. *Journal of Sex and Marital Therapy, 9,* 67–78.

Cobb, J. P., Mathews, A. A., Childs-Clarke, A., & Blowers, C. M. (1984). The spouse as co-therapist in the treatment of agoraphobia. *British Journal of Psychiatry, 144,* 282–287.

Cobb, J., McDonald, R., Marks, I., & Stern, R. (1980). Marital versus exposure therapy. Psychological treatments of co-existing marital and phobic-obsessive problems. *Behavioural Analysis and Modification, 4,* 4–16.

Comas-Diaz, L. (1981). Effects of cognitive and behavioral group treatment on the depressive symptomatology of Puerto Rican women. *Journal of Consulting and Clinical Psychology, 49,* 627–632.

Connolly, J., Hallam, R. S., & Marks, I. M. (1976). Selective association of fainting with blood-injury-illness fear. *Behavior Therapy, 7,* 8.

Cooney, N. L., Kadden, R. M., Litt, M.D., & Getter, H. (1991). Matching alcoholics to coping skills or interactional therapies. Two-year follow-up results. *Journal of Consulting and Clinical Psychology, 59,* 598–601.

Cooper, N. A., & Clum, G. A. (1989). Imaginal flooding as a supplementary treatment for PTSD in combat veterans: A controlled study. *Behaviour Therapy, 20,* 381–391.

Cotton-Huston, A. L., & Wheeler, K. A. (1983). Preorgasmic group treatment: Assertiveness, marital adjustment and sexual function in women. *Journal of Sex and Marital Therapy, 9,* 296–302.

Coyne, J. C. (1976). Depression and the response of others. *Journal of Abnormal Psychology, 85,* 186–193.

Crowe, M. J., Gillan, P., & Golombock, S. (1981). Form and content in the conjoint treatment of sexual dysfunction: A controlled study. *Behaviour Research and Therapy*, 19, 47–54.

Cullington, A., Butler, G., Hibbert, G., & Gelder, M. (1984). Problem-solving: Not a treatment for agoraphobia. *Behavior Therapy*, 15, 280–286.

Davison, G. C. (1968). Systematic desensitization as a counterconditioning process. *Journal of Abnormal Psychology*, 73, 91.

Delehanty, R. (1982). Changes in assertiveness and changes in orgasmic response occurring with sexual therapy for preorgasmic women. *Journal of Sex and Marital Therapy*, 8, 198–208.

Dekker, J., & Everaerd, W. (1983). A long-term follow-up study of couples treated for sexual dysfunctions. *Journal of Sex and Marital Therapy*, 9, 99–113.

Dekker, J., Dronkers, J., & Stafleu, J. (1985). Treatment of sexual dysfunctions in male-only groups: Predicting outcome. *Journal of Sex and Marital Therapy*, 11, 80–90.

Dobson, K. S. (1989). A meta-analysis of the efficacy of cognitive therapy for depression. *Journal of Consulting and Clinical Psychology*, 57, 414–419.

Donahoe, C. P., & Driesenga, S. A. (1989). A review of social skills training with chronic mental patients. In M. Hersen, R. M. Eisler, & P. M. Miller (Eds.), *Progress in behavior modification* (Vol. 21, pp. 131–164).

Durham, R. C., & Turvey, A. A. (1987). Cognitive therapy vs behaviour therapy in the treatment of chronic general anxiety. *Behavior Research and Therapy*, 25, 229–234.

Eayrs, C. B., Rowan, D., & Harvey, P. G. (1984). Behavioural group training for anxiety management. *Behavioural Psychotherapy*, 12, 117–129.

Ehlers, A., & Margraf, J. (1989). The psychophysiological model of panic attacks. In P. M. G. Emmelkamp, W. Everaerd, F. Kraaimaat, & M. van Son (Eds.), *Fresh perspectives on anxiety* (pp. 1–29). Amsterdam: Swets.

Ehlers, A., Margraf, J., Roth, W. T., Taylor, C. B., & Birbaumer, N. (1988). Anxiety induced by false heart rate feedback in patients with panic disorders. *Behaviour Research and Therapy*, 26, 1–12.

Elal-Lawrence, G., Slade, P. D., & Dewey, M. E. (1986). Predictors of outcome type in treated problem drinkers. *Journal of Studies on Alcohol*, 47, 41–47.

Elkins, R. L. (1980). Covert sensitization treatment of alcoholism: Contributions of successful conditioning to subsequent abstinence maintenance. *Addictive Behavior*, 5, 67–89.

Elkins, R. L. (1991). An appraisal of chemical aversion (emetic therapy) approaches to alcoholism treatment. *Behaviour Research and Therapy*, 29, 387–414.

Ellis, A. (1962). *Reason and emotion in psychotherapy*. New York: Lyle-Stuart.

Emmelkamp, P. M. G. (1974). Self-observation versus flooding in the treatment of agoraphobia. *Behaviour Research and Therapy*, 12, 229–237.

Emmelkamp, P. M. G. (1975). Effects of expectancy on systematic desensitization and flooding. *European Journal of Behavioural Analysis and Modifications*, 1, 1.

Emmelkamp, P. M. G. (1980). Agoraphobics' interpersonal problems: Their role in the effects of exposure in vivo therapy. *Archives of General Psychiatry*, 37, 1303–1306.

Emmelkamp, P. M. G. (1982). *Phobic and obsessive-compulsive disorders: Theory, research and practice*. New York: Plenum.

Emmelkamp, P. M. G. (1986). Behavior therapy. In S. Garfield & A. Bergin (Eds.), *Handbook of psychotherapy and behavior change* (3rd ed., pp. 385–442). New York: Wiley.

Emmelkamp, P. M. G. (1990). Anxiety and fear. In A. S. Bellack, M. Hersen, & A. E. Kazdin (Eds.), *International handbook of behavior modification and therapy* (2nd ed., pp. 283–306). New York: Plenum.

Emmelkamp, P. M. G. (1992). Obsessive-compulsive disorder: The contribution of an experimental clinical approach. In A. Ehlers, W. Fiegenbaum, J. Margraf, & I. Florin (Eds.), *Perspectives and promises of clinical psychology* pp. 149–156. New York: Plenum.

Emmelkamp, P. M. G., & Beens, H. (1991). Cognitive therapy with obsessive-compulsive disorder: A comparative evaluation. *Behaviour Research and Therapy*, 29, 293–300.

Emmelkamp, P. M. G., Bouman, T. K. & Blaauw, E. (1993). Individualized versus standardized therapy: A comparative evaluation in obsessive-compulsive disorder. *Clinical Psychology & Psychotherapy*.

Emmelkamp, P. M. G., Brillman, E., Kuipers, H., & Mersch, P. P. (1986). The treatment of agoraphobia: A comparison of self-instructional training, rational emotive therapy and exposure in vivo. *Behavior Modification*, 10, 37–53.

Emmelkamp, P. M. G., de Haan, E., & Hoogduin, C. A. L. (1990). Marital adjustment and obsessive-compulsive disorder. *British Journal of Psychiatry*, 156, 55–60.

Emmelkamp, P. M. G., & de Lange, I. (1983). Spouse involvement in the treatment of obsessive-compulsive patients. *Behaviour Research and Therapy*, 21, 341–346.

Emmelkamp, P. M. G., & Felten, M. (1985). The process of exposure in vivo: Cognitive and physiological changes during treatment of acrophobia. *Behaviour Research and Therapy*, 23, 219–223.

Emmelkamp, P. M. G., & Foa, E. B. (1983). The study of failures. In E. B. Foa & P. M. G. Emmelkamp (Eds.), *Failures in behavior therapy* (pp. 1–9). New York: Wiley.

Emmelkamp, P. M. G., Kloek, J, & Blaauw, E. (1992). Obsessive compulsive disorder. In P. H. Wilson (Ed.), *Principles and practice of relapse prevention*. New York: Guilford.

Emmelkamp, P. M. G., & Kraanen, J. (1977). Therapist controlled exposure in vivo versus self-controlled exposure in vivo: A comparison with obsessive-compulsive patients. *Behaviour Research and Therapy*, 15, 491–495.

Emmelkamp, P. M. G., & Kuipers, A. (1979). Agoraphobia: A follow-up study four years after treatment. *British Journal of Psychiatry*, 134, 352–355.

Emmelkamp, P. M. G., & Kuipers, A. C. M. (1985). Group therapy of anxiety disorders. In D. Upper & S. M. Ross (Eds.), *Handbook of behavioral group therapy*. New York: Plenum.

Emmelkamp, P. M. G., Kuipers, A., & Eggeraat, J. (1978). Cognitive modification versus prolonged exposure in vivo: A comparison with agoraphobics. *Behaviour Research and Therapy*, 16, 33–41.

Emmelkamp, P. M. G., & Mersch, P. P. (1982). Cognition and exposure in vivo in the treatment of agoraphobia: Short-term and delayed effects. *Cognitive Therapy and Research*, 6, 77–90.

Emmelkamp, P. M. G., Mersch, P. P., Vissia, E., & van der Helm, M. (1985). Social phobia: A comparative evaluation of cognitive and behavioral interventions. *Behaviour Research and Therapy*, 23, 365–369.

Emmelkamp, P. M. G., Van der Helm, M., MacGillavry, D., & Van Zanten, B. (1984). Marital therapy with clinical distressed couples: A comparative evaluation of system-theoretic, contingency contracting and communication skills approaches. In K. Hahlweg & N. Jacobson (Eds.), *Marital therapy and interaction* (pp. 36–52). New York: Guilford.

Emmelkamp, P. M. G., Van der Helm, M., van Zanten, B., & Plochg, I. (1980). Contributions of self-instructional training to the effectiveness of exposure in vivo: A comparison with obsessive-compulsive patients. *Behaviour Research and Therapy, 18*, 61–66.

Emmelkamp, P. M. G., & van der Hout, A. (1983). Failure in treating agoraphobia. In E. B. Foa & P. M. G. Emmelkamp (Eds.), *Failures in behaviour therapy.* New York: Wiley.

Emmelkamp, P. M. G., van der Hout, A., & de Vries, K. (1983) Assertive training for agoraphobics. *Behaviour Research and Therapy, 21*, 63–68.

Emmelkamp, P. M. G., Van Dyck, R., Bitter, M., Heins, R., Onstein, E. J., & Eisen, B. (1992). Spouse-aided therapy with agoraphobics. *British Journal of Psychiatry, 160*, 51–56.

Emmelkamp, P. M. G., van Linden van den Heuvell, G., Rüphan, M., & Sanderman, R. (1989). Home-based treatment of obsessive-compulsive patients: Intersession interval and therapist involvement. *Behaviour Research and Therapy, 27*, 89–93.

Emmelkamp, P. M. G., van Linden van den Heuvell, C., Rüphan, M., Sanderman, R., Scholing, A., & Stroink, F. (1988). Cognitive and behavioral interventions: A comparative evaluation with clinical distressed couples. *Journal of Family Psychology, 1*, 365–377.

Emmelkamp, P. M. G., & Scholing, A. (1990). Behavioral treatment for simple and social phobics. In G. D. Burrows, R. Noyes, & G. M. Roth (Eds.), *Handbook of anxiety* (Vol. 4, pp. 327–361). Amsterdam: Elsevier.

Emmelkamp, P. M. G., Visser, S., & Hoekstra, R. J. (1988). Cognitive therapy vs exposure in vivo in the treatment of obsessive-compulsives. *Cognitive Therapy and Research, 12*, 103–144.

Emmelkamp, P. M. G., & Walta, C. (1978). The effects of therapy-set on electrical aversion therapy and covert sensitization. *Behaviour Therapy, 9*, 185–188.

Emmelkamp, P. M. G., & Wessels, H. (1975). Flooding in imagination vs. flooding in vivo: A comparison with agoraphobics. *Behaviour Research and Therapy, 13*, 7–16.

Eriksen, L., Björnstad, S., & Götestam, K. G. (1986). Social skills training in groups for alcoholics: One-year treatment outcome for groups and individuals. *Addictive Behaviors, 11*, 309–329.

Eriksen, L. M., & Götestam, K. G. (1984). Conditioned abstinence in alcoholics. A controlled experiment. *International Journal of the Addictions, 19*, 287–294.

Ersner-Hershfield, R., & Kopel, S. (1979). Group treatment of pre-orgasmic women. *Journal of Consulting and Clinical Psychology, 47*, 750–759.

Esse, J. T., & Wilkins, W. (1978). Empathy and imagery in avoidance behavior reduction. *Journal of Consulting and Clinical Psychology, 46*, 202–203.

Everaerd, W. T. A. M. (1983). Failure in treating sexual dysfunction. In E. B. Foa & P. M. G. Emmelkamp (Eds.), *Failures in behavior therapy* (pp. 392–405). New York: Wiley.

Everaerd, W. T. A. M., & Dekker, J. (1981). A comparison of sex therapy and communication therapy: Couples complaining of orgasmic dysfunction. *Journal of Sex and Marital Therapy, 7*, 278–289.

Everaerd, W. T. A. M., & Dekker, J. (1982) Treatment of secondary orgasmic dysfunction: A comparison of systematic desensitization and sex therapy. *Behaviour Research and Therapy, 20*, 269–274.

Everaerd, W. T. A. M., & Dekker, J. (1985). Treatment of male sexual dysfunction: Sex therapy compared with systematic desensitization and rational emotive therapy. *Behaviour Research and Therapy, 23*, 13–24.

Everaerd, W. T. A. M., Dekker, J., Dronkers, J., Van der Rhee, K., Stafleu, J., & Wisselius, G. (1982). Treatment of homosexual and heterosexual dysfunction in male-only groups of mixed sexual orientation. *Archives of Sexual Behavior, 11*, 1–10.

Fahrner, E. M. (1983). Selbstunsicherheit-ein allgemeines Symptom bei funktionellen Sexualstörungen? *Zeitschrift für Klinische Psychologie, 12*, 1–11.

Fairbank, J. A., Gross, R. T., & Keane, T. M. (1983). Treatment of posttraumatic stress disorder: Evaluating outcome with a behavioral mode. *Behavior Modification, 7*, 557–568.

Fairbank, J. A., & Keane, T. M. (1982). Flooding for combat-related stress disorders: Assessment of anxiety reduction across traumatic memories. *Behavior Therapy, 13*, 499–510.

Falloon, I. R. H., Boyd, J. L., & McGill, C. (1984). *Family care of schizophrenia.* New York: Guilford.

Falloon, I. R. H., Lindley, P., McDonald, R., & Marks, I. M. (1977). Social skills training of out-patient groups. A controlled study of rehearsal and homework. *British Journal of Psychiatry, 131*, 599–609.

Finney, J. W., & Moos, R. M. (1991). The long-term course of treated alcoholism: I. Mortality, relapse and remission rates and comparisons with community controls. *Journal of Studies on Alcohol, 51*, 44–54.

Fisher, L. M., & Wilson, G. T. (1985). A study of the psychology of agoraphobia. *Behaviour Research and Therapy, 23*, 99–107.

Fleming, B. M., & Thornton, F. (1980). Coping skills training as a component in the short term treatment of depression. *Journal of Consulting and Clinical Psychology, 48*, 652–654.

Foa, E. B., Jameson, J. R., Turner, R. M., & Payne, L. L. (1980). Massed vs. spaced exposure sessions in the treatment of agoraphobia. *Behaviour Research and Therapy, 18*, 333–338.

Foa, E. B., Rothbaum, B. O., Riggs, D. S., & Murdock, T. B. (1991). Treatment of posttraumatic stress disorder in rape victims: A comparison between cognitive-behavioral procedures and counseling. *Journal of Consulting and Clinical Psychology, 59*, 715–723.

Foa, E. B., Steketee, G. S., Grayson, J. B., & Doppelt, H. (1983). Treatment of obsessive-compulsives: When do we fail? In E. B. Foa & P. M. G. Emmelkamp (Eds.), *Failures in behavior therapy.* New York: Wiley.

Foa, E. B., Steketee, G., & Grayson, J. B. (1985). Imaginal and in vivo exposure: A comparison with obsessive-compulsive checkers. *Behavior Therapy, 16*, 292–302.

Foa, E. B., Steketee, G. S., Grayson, J. B., Turner, R. M., & Latimer, P. R. (1984). Deliberate exposure and blocking of obsessive-compulsive rituals: Immediate and long term effects. *Behavior Therapy, 15*, 450–472.

Foa, E. B., Steketee, G., & Milby, J. B. (1980). Differential effects of exposure and response prevention in obsessive-compulsive washers. *Journal of Consulting and Clinical Psychology, 48*, 71–79.

Foa, E. B., Steketee, G., Turner, R. M., & Fischer, S. C. (1980). Effects of imaginal exposure to feared disasters in obsessive-compulsive checkers. *Behaviour Research and Therapy, 18*, 449–455.

Ford, J. D. (1978). Therapeutic relationship in behavior therapy: An empirical analysis. *Journal of Consulting and Clinical Psychology, 46*, 1302–1314.

Foy, D. W., Donahoe, C. P., Carroll, E. M., Gallers, J., & Reno, R. (1987). Posttraumatic stress disorder. In L. Michelson & L. M. Ascher (Eds.), *Anxiety and stress disorders* (pp. 361–378). New York: Guilford.

Foy, D. W., Nunn, L. B., & Rychtarik, R. G. (1984). Broad-spectrum behavioral treatment of chronic alcoholics: Effects of training controlled drinking skills. *Journal of Consulting and Clinical Psychology, 52*, 218–230.

Frank, E., Anderson, B., Stewart, B. D., Dancu, C., Hughes, C., & West, D. (1988). Efficacy of cognitive behavior therapy and systematic desensitization in the treatment of rape trauma. *Behavior Therapy, 19,* 403–420.

Freeman, A., & Davis, D. D. (1990). Cognitive therapy of depression. In A. S. Bellack, M. Hersen, & A. E. Kazdin (Eds.), *International handbook of behavior modification* (2nd ed., pp. 333–352). New York: Plenum.

Friedman, J. M., Weiler, S. J., LoPiccolo, J., & Hogan, D. R. (1982). Sexual dysfunctions and their treatment. In A. S. Bellack, M. Hersen, & A. E. Kazdin (Eds.), *International handbook of behavior modification and therapy.* New York: Plenum.

Frisch, M. B., Elliott, C. H., Atsaides, J. P., Salva, D. M., & Denney, D. R. (1982). Social skills and stress management training to enhance patients' interpersonal competencies. *Psychotherapy: Theory, Research, and Practice, 19,* 349–358.

Fuchs, C. Z., & Rehm, L. P. (1977). A self-control behavior therapy program for depression. *Journal of Consulting and Clinical Psychology, 45,* 206–215.

Gallagher-Thompson, D., Hanley-Peterson, P., & Thompson, L. W. (1990). Maintenance of gains versus relapse following brief psychotherapy for depression. *Journal of Consulting and Clinical Psychology, 58,* 371–374.

Gardner, P., & Oei, T. S. (1981). Depression of self-esteem: An investigation that used behavioral and cognitive approaches to the treatment of clinically depressed clients. *Journal of Clinical Psychology, 37,* 128–135.

Gelder, M. G., Bancroft, J. H. J., Gath, D. H., Johnston, D. W., Mathews, A. M., & Shaw, P. M. (1973). Specific and non-specific factors in behaviour therapy. *British Journal of Psychiatry, 123,* 445–462.

Ghosh, A., & Marks, I. M. (1987). Self-treatment of agoraphobia by exposure. *Behavior Therapy, 18,* 3–16.

Glynn, S. M. (1990). Token economy approaches for psychiatric patients. *Behavior Modification, 14,* 383–407.

Goldstein, A., & Chambless, D. (1978). A reanalysis of agoraphobia. *Behaviour Therapy, 9,* 47–59.

Gosh, A., Marks, I. M., & Carr, A. C. (1987). Therapist contact and outcome of self-exposure treatment for phobias. *British Journal of Psychiatry, 152,* 234.

Griez, E., & van den Hout, M. A. (1983). Treatment of phobophobia by exposure to CO_2-induced anxiety symptoms. *Journal of Nervous and Mental Disease, 171,* 506–508.

Griez, E., & van den Hout, M. A. (1986) CO_2 inhalation in the treatment of panic attacks. *Behaviour Research and Therapy, 24,* 145–150.

Hafner, R. J. (1982). The marital context of the agoraphobic syndrome. In D. L. Chambless & A. J. Goldstein (Eds.), *Agoraphobia: Multiple perspectives on theory and treatment.* New York: Wiley.

Hahlweg, K., & Markham, H. J. (1988). The effectiveness of behavioral marital therapy: Empirical status of behavioral techniques in preventing and alleviating marital distress. *Journal of Consulting and Clinical Psychology, 56,* 440–447.

Halford, W. K., & Haynes, R. (1991). Psychosocial rehabilitation of chronic schizophrenic patients: Recent findings on social skills training and family psychoeducation. *Clinical Psychology Review, 11,* 23–44.

Hall, R., & Goldberg, D. (1977). The role of social anxiety in social interaction difficulties. *British Journal of Psychiatry, 131,* 610–615.

Hallam, R. S., & Rachman, S. (1976). Current status and aversion therapy. In M. Hersen, R. M. Eisler, & P. M. Miller (Eds.), *Progress in behavior modification* (Vol. 2, pp. 179–222). New York: Academic Press.

Hammerley, R. (1992). Cue exposure and learning theory. *Addictive Behaviors, 17,* 297–300.

Hammond, P. D., & Oei, T. P. S. (1982). Social skills training and cognitive restructuring with sexual unassertiveness in women. *Journal of Sex and Marital Therapy, 8,* 297–304.

Hansen, D. J., St. Lawrence, J. S., & Cristoff, K. A. (1985). Effects of interpersonal problem-solving training with chronic aftercare patients on problem-solving component skills and effectiveness of solutions. *Journal of Consulting and Clinical Psychology, 53,* 167–174.

Hartman, L. M., & Dally, E. M. (1983). Relationship factors in the treatment of sexual dysfunction. *Behavior Research and Therapy, 21,* 153–160.

Hatzenbühler, L. C., & Schröder, H. E. (1982). Assertiveness training with outpatients: The effectiveness of skill and cognitive procedures. *Behavioral Psychotherapy, 10,* 234–252.

Haug, T., Brenne, L., Johnsen, B. H., Berntzen, D., Gostestam, K-G., Hugdahl, K. (1987). A three-systems analysis of fear of flying: A comparison of a consonant versus a non-consonant treatment method. *Behaviour Research and Therapy, 25,* 187–194.

Hawton, K., Catalan, J., Martin, P., & Fagg, J. (1986). Long-term outcome of sex therapy. *Behaviour Research and Therapy, 24,* 665–675.

Heiman, J. R., & LoPiccolo, J. (1983). Clinical outcome of sex therapy: Effects of daily vs. weekly treatment. *Archives of General Psychiatry, 40,* 443–449.

Heiman, J., LoPiccolo, L., & LoPiccolo, J. (1976). *Becoming orgasmic.* Englewood Cliffs, NJ: Prentice Hall.

Heimberg, R. G., Dodge, C. S., Hope, D. A., Kennedy, C. R., Zollo, L. J., & Becker, R. E. (1990). Cognitive behavioural group treatment for social phobias: A comparison with a credible placebo control. *Cognitive Therapy and Research, 14,* 1–23.

Hersen, M., Bellack, A. S., Himmelhoch, J. M., & Thase, M. E. (1984). Effects of social skill training, amitriptyline, and psychotherapy in unipolar depressed women. *Behavior Therapy, 15,* 21–40.

Himadi, W. G., Cerny, J. A., Barlow, D. H., Cohen, S., & O'Brien, G. T. (1986). The relationship of marital adjustment to agoraphobia treatment outcome. *Behaviour Research and Therapy, 24,* 107–115.

Hodgson, R., Rachman, S., & Marks, I. (1972). The treatment of chronic-obsessive-compulsive neurosis: Follow-up and further findings. *Behaviour Research and Therapy, 10,* 181–184.

Hoevenaar, J., & van Son, M. J. M. (1990). New chances for Lewinsohn's social reinforcement theory of depression. In H. G. Zapotoczky & T. Wenzel (Eds.), *The scientific dialogue: From basic research to clinical interventions.* Amsterdam: Swets.

Hogarty, G. E., Jorna, C. M., Reiss, D. J., Kornblith, S. J., Greenwald, D. P., Jorna, C. D., & Madonia, M. J. (1986). Family psychoeducation, social skills training and maintenance chemotherapy in the aftercare treatment of schizophrenia. *Archives of General Psychiatry, 43,* 633–642.

Hollon, S. D., Shelton, R. C., & Loosen, P. T. (1991). Cognitive therapy and pharmacotherapy for depression. *Journal of Consulting and Clinical Psychology, 59,* 88–99.

Holtzworth-Munroe, A., Jacobson, N. S., Deklyen, M., & Whisman, M. A. (1989). Relationship between behavioral marital therapy outcome and process variables. *Journal of Consulting and Clinical Psychology, 57,* 658–662.

Hoogduin, C. A. L., Duivenvoorden, H., Schaap, C., & de Haan, E. (1989). On the outpatient treatment of obsessive-compulsives: Outcome, prediction of outcome and follow-up. In P. M. G. Emmelkamp, W. T. A. M. Everaerd,

F. Kraaimaat, & M. van Son (Eds.), *Fresh perspectives on anxiety disorders*. Amsterdam: Swets.

Hout, M. A. van den, Emmelkamp, P. M. G., Kraaykamp, J., & Griez, E. (1988). Behavioural treatment of obsessive-compulsives: Inpatient versus outpatient. *Behaviour Research and Therapy, 26*, 331–332.

Hout, M. A. van den, Molen, M. van der, Griez, E., Lousberg H., & Nansen, A. (1987). Reduction of CO_2-induced anxiety in patients with panic attacks after repeated CO_2-exposure. *American Journal of Psychiatry, 144*, 788–791.

Hudson, S. M., Ward, T., & Marshall, W. L. (1992). The abstinence violation effect in sex offenders: A reformulation. *Behaviour Research and Therapy, 30*, 435–441.

Hunt, G. M., & Azrin, N. H. (1973). A community-reinforcement approach to alcoholism. *Behaviour Research and Therapy, 11*, 91–104.

Imber, S. D., Pilkonis, P. A., Sotsky, S. M., Elkin, I., Watkins, J. T., Collins, J. F., Shea, M. T., Leber, W. R., & Glass, D. R. (1990). Mode-specific effects among three treatments for depression. *Journal of Consulting and Clinical Psychology, 58*, 352–359.

Jacobson, N. S. (1977). Problem solving and contingency contracting in the treatment of marital discord. *Journal of Consulting and Clinical Psychology, 45*, 92–100.

Jacobson, N. S. (1978). Specific and non-specific factors in the effectiveness of a behavioral approach to the treatment of marital discord. *Journal of Consulting and Clinical Psychology, 46*, 442–452.

Jacobson, N. S. (1984). A component analysis of behavioral marital therapy: The relative effectiveness of behavior exchange and communication/problem solving training. *Journal of Consulting and Clinical Psychology, 52*, 295–305.

Jacobson, N. S. (1991). Behavioral versus insight-oriented marital therapy: Labels can be misleading. *Journal of Consulting and Clinical Psychology, 59*, 142–145.

Jacobson, N. S., Dobson, K., Fruzetti, A. E., Schmaling, K. B., & Salusky, S. (1991). Marital therapy as a treatment for depression. *Journal of Consulting and Clinical Psychology, 59*, 547–557.

Jacobson, N. S., Schmaling, K. B., & Holtzworth-Munroe, A. (1989). Component analysis of behavioral marital therapy: Two-year follow-up and prediction of relapse. *Journal of Marital and Family Therapy, 13*, 187–195.

Jacobson, N. S., Schmaling, K. B., Holzworth-Munroe, A., Katt, J. L., Wood, L. F., & Folette, V. M. (1980). Research-structured vs. clinically flexible versions of social learning-based marital therapy. *Behaviour Research and Therapy, 27*, 173–180.

Jannoun, L., Munby, M., Catalan, J., & Gelder, M. (1980). A home-based treatment program for agoraphobia: Replication and controlled evaluation. *Behavior Therapy, 11*, 294–305.

Jannoun, L., Oppenheimer, C., & Gelder, M. (1982). A self-help treatment program for anxiety state patients. *Behaviour Therapy, 13*, 103–111.

Jellinek, E. M. (1960). *The disease concept of alcoholism*. New Jersey: Hillhouse Press.

Jerremalm, A., Jansson, L., & Öst, L. G. (1986). Individual response patterns and the effects of different behavioral methods in the treatment of dental phobia. *Behaviour Research and Therapy, 24*, 587.

Johnson, S. M., & Greenberg, L. S. (1981). Differential effects of experiential and problem-solving interventions in resolving marital conflict. *Journal of Consulting and Clinical Psychology, 53*, 175–184.

Johnson, S. M., & Greenberg, L. S. (1985). Differential effects of experiential and problem-solving interventions in resolving marital conflict. *Journal of Consulting and Clinical Psychology, 53*, 175–184.

Johnston, P., Hudson, S. M., & Marshall, W. L. (1992). The effects of masturbatory reconditioning with nonfamilial child molesters. *Behaviour Research and Therapy, 30*, 559–561.

Jong, R., de, Henrich, G., & Ferstl, R. (1981). A behavioral treatment program for neurotic depression. *Behavioural Analysis and Modifications, 4*, 275–287.

Kadden, R. M., Cooney, N. L., Getter, H., & Litt, M. D. (1989). Matching alcoholics to coping skills or interactional therapies: Posttreatment results. *Journal of Consulting and Clinical Psychology, 57*, 698–704.

Kaplan, H. S. (1977). Hypoactive sexual desire. *Journal of Sex and Marital Therapy, 3*, 3–9.

Kappes, B. M. (1983). Sequence effects of relation training, EMG, and temperature biofeedback on anxiety symptom report, and self-concept. *Journal of Clinical Psychology, 39*, 203–208.

Kasviskis, Y., & Marks, I. M. (1988). Clomipramine, self-exposure, and therapist-accompanied exposure in obsessive-compulsive ritualizers: Two-year follow-up. *Journal of Anxiety Disorders, 2*, 291–298.

Kazdin, A. E. (1983). Failure of persons to respond to the token economy. In E. B. Foa & P. M. G. Emmelkamp (Eds.), *Failures in behavior therapy* (pp. 335–354). New York: Wiley.

Keane, T. M., Fairbank, J. A., Caddell, J. M., & Zimering, R. T. (1989). Implosive (flooding) therapy reduces symptoms of PTSD in Vietnam combat veterans. *Behavior Therapy, 20*, 245–260.

Kelly, R. J. (1982). Behavioral reorientation of pedophiliacs: Can it be done? *Clinical Psychology Review, 2*, 387–408.

Kelly, J. A., St. Lawrence, J. S., Hood, H. V., & Brasfield, T. Z. (1989). Behavioral intervention to reduce AIDS risk activities. *Journal of Consulting and Clinical Psychology, 57*, 60–67.

Kendall, P. C. (1983). Methodology and cognitive-behavioral assessment. *Behavioural Psychotherapy, 11*, 285–301.

Killman, P. R., Mills, K. H., Bella, B. S., Davidson, E. R., Caid, C. D., Drose, G. S., Milan, R. J., Boland, J., Follingstad, D. R., Montgomery, B., & Wanlass, R. L. (1986). The treatment of secondary orgasmic dysfunction: An outcome study. *Archives of Sexual Behavior, 15*, 211–229.

Killman, P. R., Milan, R. J., Boland, J. P., Nankin, H. R., Davidson, E., West, M. O., Sabalis, R. F., Caid, C., & Devine, J. M. (1987). Group treatment of secondary erectile dysfunction. *Journal of Sex and Marital Therapy, 13*, 186–182.

Kindness, K., & Newton, A. (1984). Patients and social skills groups: Is social skills training enough? *Behavioral Psychotherapy, 12*, 212–222.

Kleiner, L., & Marshall, W. L. (1985). Relationship difficulties and agoraphobia. *Clinical Psychology Review, 5*, 581–595.

Kleiner, L., Marshall, W. L., & Spevack, M. (1987). Training in problem-solving and exposure treatment for agoraphobics with panic attacks. *Journal of Anxiety Disorders, 1*, 219–238.

Kivlaham, D. R., Marlatt, G. A., Fromme, K., Coppel, D. B., & Williams, E. (1990). Secondary prevention with college drinkers: Evaluation of an alcohol skills training program. *Journal of Consulting and Clinical Psychology, 58*, 805–810.

Klosko, J. S., Barlow, D. H., Toussinari, R. B., & Cerny, J. A. (1990) A comparison of alprazolam and behavior therapy in the treatment of panic disorder. *Journal of Consulting and Clinical Psychology, 58*, 77–84.

Kockott, G., Dittmar, F., & Nusselt, L. (1975). Systematic desensitization and erectile impotence: A controlled study. *Archives of Sexual Behavior, 4*, 493–500.

Kuriansky, J. B., Sharpe, L., & O'Connor, D. (1982). The treatment of anorgasmia: Long-term effectiveness of a short-term behavioral group therapy. *Journal of Sex and Marital Therapy, 8,* 29–43.

Laberg, J. C. (1990). What is presented, and what prevented, in cue exposure and response prevention with alcohol dependent subjects? *Addictive Behavior, 15,* 367–386.

Laberg, J. C., & Ellertsen, B. (1987). Psychophysiological indicators of craving in alcoholics: Effects of cue exposure. *British Journal of Addiction, 82,* 1341–1348.

Ladouceur, R. L. (1983). Participant modeling with or without cognitive treatment for phobias. *Journal of Consulting and Clinical Psychology, 51,* 942–944.

Lelliott, P. T., Marks, I. M., Monteiro, W. O., Tsakiris, F., & Noshirvani, H. (1987). Agoraphobics 5 years after imipramine and exposure. *Journal of Nervous and Mental Disease, 175,* 599–605.

Leonard, S. R., & Hayes, S. C. (1983). Sexual fantasy alternation. *Journal of Behavior Therapy and Experimental Psychiatry, 14,* 241–249.

Lewinsohn, P. M. (1975). The behavioral study and treatment of depression. In M. Hersen, R. M. Eisler, & P. M. Miller (Eds.), *Progress in behavior modification* (Vol. 1, pp. 19–65). New York: Academic Press.

Lewinsohn, P. M., & Hoberman, H. M. (1982). Depression. In A. S. Bellack, M. Hersen, & A. E. Kazdin (Eds.), *International handbook of behavior modification and therapy,* (pp. 397–431). New York: Plenum.

Lewinsohn, P. M., Mischel, W., Chaplin, W., & Barton, R. (1980). Social competence and depression: The role of illusory self-perception? *Journal of Abnormal Psychology, 89,* 203–212.

Ley, R. (1985) Blood, breath and fears: A hyperventilation theory of panic attacks and agoraphobia. *Clinical Psychology Review, 5,* 271–285.

Liberman, R. P., Levie, J., Wheeler, E., Sanders, N., & Wallace, C. J. (1976). Marital therapy in groups: A comparative evaluation of behavioral and interactional formats. *Acta Psychiatrica Scandinavica, 266,* 3–34.

Liberman, R. P., Mueser, K. T., & Wallace, C. J. (1986). Social skills training for schizophrenic individuals at risk for relapse. *American Journal of Psychiatry, 143,* 523–526.

Libman, E., Fichten, C. S., Brender, W., Burstein, R., Cohen, J., & Binik, I. (1984). A comparison of three therapeutic formats in the treatment of secondary orgasmic dysfunctions. *Journal of Sex and Marital Therapy, 10,* 147–159.

Lindsay, W. R., Gramsu, C. V., McLaughlin, E., Hood, E. M., & Espie, C. A. (1987). A controlled trial of treatments for generalized anxiety. *British Journal of Clinical Psychology, 26,* 3–15.

Lipton, L. R., & Jensen, B. J. (1991). The acceptability of behavioral treatments for marital problems: A comparison of behavioral exchange and communication skill training procedures. *Behavior Modifications, 15,* 51–63.

Little, L. M., & Curran, J. P. (1978). Covert sensitization: A clinical procedure in need of some explanations. *Psychological Bulletin, 85,* 513–531.

Luber, R. F. (1978). Teaching models in marital therapy: A review and research issue. *Behavior Modification, 2,* 77–91.

Mackay, W., & Liddell, A. (1986). An investigation into the matching of specific agoraphobic anxiety response characteristics with specific types of treatment. *Behaviour Research and Therapy, 24,* 361–364.

Maletzky, B. M. (1980). Assisted covert sensitization. In D. J. Cox & R. J. Daitzman (Eds.), *Exhibitionism: Description, assessment and treatment.* New York: Garland.

Marchione, K. E., Michelson, L., Greenwald, M., & Dancu, C. (1987). Cognitive behavioral treatment of agoraphobia. *Behaviour Research and Therapy, 25,* 319–328.

Margraf, J., Ehlers, A., & Roth, W. T. (1987). Panic attack associated with perceived heart rate acceleration: A case report. *Behavior Therapy, 18,* 84–89.

Marks, I. M. (1987). *Fears, phobias and rituals.* Oxford: Oxford University Press.

Marks, I. M., Boulougouris, J., & Marset, P. (1971). Flooding versus desensitization in the treatment of phobic patients. *British Journal of Psychiatry, 119,* 353–375.

Marks, I. M., Hodgson, R., & Rachman, S. (1975). Treatment of chronic obsessive-compulsive neurosis by in vivo exposure. *British Journal of Psychiatry, 127,* 349–364.

Marlat, G. A., & Gordon, J. R. (1980). Determinants of relapse: Implications for the maintenance of behavior change. In P. Davidson (Ed.), *Behavioral medicine, changing health lifestyles.* New York: Brunner/Mazel.

Marshall, W. L. (1985). Variable exposure in flooding. *Behaviour Research and Therapy, 23,* 117.

Marshall, W. L. (1988). Behavioral indices of habituation and sensitization during exposure to phobic stimuli. *Behaviour Research and Therapy, 26,* 67.

Marshall, W. L., & Barbaree, H. E. (1988). The long term evaluation of a behavioral treatment program for child molesters. *Behaviour Research and Therapy, 26,* 499–511.

Marshall, W. L., & Barbaree, H. E. (1990). Outcome of comprehensive cognitive-behavioral treatment programs. In W. L. Marshall, D. R. Laws, & H. E. Barbaree (Eds.), *Handbook of sexual assault: Issues, theories, and treatment of the offender* (pp. 363–385). New York: Plenum.

Marshall, W. L., Bristol, D., & Barbaree, H. E. (1992). Cognitions and courage in the avoidance behavior of acrophobics. *Behaviour Research and Therapy, 30,* 463–470.

Marshall, W. L., Eccles, A., & Barbaree, H. E. (1991). The treatment of exhibitionists: A focus on sexual deviance versus cognitive and relationship features. *Behaviour Research and Therapy, 29,* 129–136.

Marshall, W. L., & Segal, Z. V. (1990). Drugs combined with behavioral psychotherapy. In A. S. Bellack, M. Hersen, & A. E. Kazdin (Eds.), *International handbook of behavior modification and therapy* (pp. 267–279). New York: Plenum.

Martin, J. L. (1990). Drug use and unprotected anal intercourse among gay men. *Health Psychology, 9,* 450–465.

Marzillier, J. S., Lambert, C., & Kellett, J. (1976). A controlled evaluation of systematic desensitization and social skills training for socially inadequate psychiatric patients. *Behavior Research and Therapy, 14,* 225–228.

Masters, W. H., & Johnson, V. E. (1970). *Human sexual inadequacy.* Boston: Little, Brown.

Masters, W. H., & Johnson, V. E. (1979). *Homosexuality in perspective.* Boston: Little, Brown.

Mathews, A., Whitehead, A., & Kellett, J. (1983). Psychological and hormonal factors in the treatment of female sexual dysfunction. *Psychological Medicine, 13,* 83–92.

Mathews, A. M., Bancroft, J., Whitehead, A., Hackman, A., Julier, D., Bancroft, J., Gath, D., & Show, P. (1976). The behavioural treatment of sexual inadequacy: A comparative study. *Behaviour Research and Therapy, 14,* 427–436.

Mathews, A. M., Gelder, M. G., & Johnston, D. W. (1981). *Agoraphobia: Nature and treatment.* New York: Guilford.

Mathews, A. M., Johnston, D. W., Lancashire, M., Munby, M., Shaw, P. M., & Gelder, M. G. (1976). Imaginal flooding and exposure to real phobic situations: Treatment outcome with agoraphobic patients. *British Journal of Psychiatry, 129,* 362–371.

Mattick, R. P., & Peters, L. (1988). Treatment of severe

social phobia: Effects of guided exposure with and without cognitive restructuring. *Journal of Consulting and Clinical Psychology, 56*, 251–260.

Mattick, R. P., Peters, L., & Clarke, J. D. (1989). Exposure and cognitive restructuring. *Behavior Therapy, 20*, 3–24.

Mavissakalian, M., Michelson, L., Greenwald, D., Kornblith, S., & Greenwald, M. (1983). Cognitive-behavioral treatment of agoraphobia: Paradoxical intention vs self-statement training. *Behaviour Research and Therapy, 21*, 75–86.

Mawson, D., Marks, I. M., & Ramm, E. (1982). Clomipramine and exposure for chronic OC rituals: III. Two year follow-up. *British Journal of Psychiatry, 140*, 11–18.

Mawson, D., Marks, I., Ramm, E., & Stern, R. S. (1981). Guided mourning for morbid grief: A controlled study. *British Journal of Psychiatry, 138*, 185–193.

McConaghy, N. (1982). Sexual deviation. In A. S. Bellack, M. Hersen, & A. E. Kazdin (Eds.), *International handbook of behavior modification and therapy* (pp. 683–716). New York: Plenum.

McLean, P. D., & Hakstian, A. R. (1979). Clinical depression: Comparative efficacy of out-patient treatment. *Journal of Consulting and Clinical Psychology, 47*, 818–836.

McLean, P. D., & Hakstian, A. R. (1990). Relative endurance of unipolar depression treatment effects: Longitudinal follow-up. *Journal of Consulting and Clinical Psychology, 58*, 482–488.

McLean, P. D., Ogston, K., & Grauer, L. (1973). A behavioral approach to the treatment of depression. *Journal of Behavior Therapy and Experimental Psychiatry, 4*, 323–330.

McLean, P. D., & Taylor, S. (1992). Severity of unipolar depression and choice of treatment. *Behavior Research and Therapy, 30*, 443–451.

McNamee, G., O'Sullivan, G., Lelliott, P., & Marks, I. (1989). Telephone-guided treatment for housebound agoraphobics with panic disorder: Exposure vs. relaxation. *Behavior Therapy, 20*, 491–497.

McPherson, F. M., Brougham, L., & McLaren, S. (1980). Maintenance of improvement in agoraphobic patients treated by behavioural methods — a four year follow-up. *Behaviour Research and Therapy, 18*, 150–152.

Mersch, P. P. A., Emmelkamp, P. M. G., Bögels, S. M., & van der Sleen, J. (1989). Social phobia: Individual response patterns and the effects of behavioral and cognitive interventions. *Behaviour Research and Therapy, 27*, 421–434.

Mersch, P. P. A., Emmelkamp, P. M. G., & Lips, C. (1991). Social phobia: Individual response patterns and the long-term effects of behavioral and cognitive interventions. A follow-up study. *Behaviour Research and Therapy, 29*, 357–362.

Metah, M. (1990). A comparative study of family-based and patient-based behavioural management in obsessive-compulsive disorder. *British Journal of Psychiatry, 157*, 133–135.

Michelson, L., Mavissakalian, M., & Marchione, K. (1985). Cognitive behavioral and psychophysiological treatments of agoraphobia: A comparative outcome investigation. *Behavior Therapy, 20*, 97–120.

Miller, W. R. (1983). Controlled drinking: A history and a critical review. *Journal of Studies on Alcohol, 44*, 68–83.

Miller, W. R., & Muñoz, R. F. (1982). *How to control your drinking* (rev. ed.). Albuquerque: University of New Mexico Press.

Miller, W. R., & Baca, L. M. (1983). Two-year follow-up bibliotherapy and therapist-directed controlled drinking training for problem drinkers. *Behavior Therapy, 14*, 441–448.

Miller, W. R., & Hester, R. K. (1980). Treating the problem drinker: Modern approaches. In W. R. Miller (Ed.), *The addictive behaviors.* Oxford: Pergamon.

Miller, W. R., Leckman, A. L., Delaney, H. D., & Tinchom, M. (1992). Long-term follow-up of behavioral self-control training. *Journal of Studies on Alcohol, 51*, 108–115.

Miller, I. W., Norman, W. H., Keitner, G. I., Bishop, S. B., & Dow, M. G. (1989). Cognitive-behavioral treatment of depressed inpatients. *Behavior Therapy, 20*, 25–47.

Mills, I., & Salkovskis, P. M. (1988). Mood and habituation to phobic stimuli. *Behaviour Research and Therapy, 26*, 435.

Milton, F., & Hafner, J. (1979). The outcome of behavior therapy for agoraphobia in relation to marital adjustment. *Archives of General Psychiatry, 361*, 807–811.

Monteiro, W., Marks, I. M., & Ramm, E. (1985). Marital adjustment and treatment outcome in agoraphobia. *British Journal of Psychiatry, 149*, 383–390.

Monti, P. M., Abrams, D. B., Binkoff, J. A., Zwick, W. R., Liepman, M. R., Nirenberg, T. D., & Rohsenow, D. J. (1990). Communication skills training, communication skills training with family and cognitive-behavioral mood management training for alcoholics. *Journal of Studies on Alcohol, 51*, 263–270.

Monti, P. M., Abrams, D. B., Kadden, R. M., & Cooney, N. L. (1989). *Treating alcohol dependence.* New York: Guilford.

Mueser, K. T., & Glynn, S. M. (1990). Behavioural family therapy for schizophrenia. In M. Hersen, M. Eisler, & N. Miller (Eds.), *Progress in behavior modification* (Vol. ????, pp. 122–149).

Mulder, C. L., Emmelkamp, P. M. G., Mulder, J. W., Antoni, M. H., & de Vries, M. J. (1993) Cognitive-behavioral compared to experiential group psychotherapy for HIV infected homosexual men. Submitted for publication.

Munby, M., & Johnston, D. W. (1980). Agoraphobia: The long-term follow-up of behavioral treatment. *British Journal of Psychiatry, 137*, 418–427.

Munjack, D. J., Schlaks, A., Sanchez, V. C., Usigli, R., Zulueta, A., & Leonard, M. (1984). Rational emotive therapy in the treatment of erectile failure: An initial study. *Journal of Sex and Marital Therapy, 10*, 170–175.

Nathan, P. E., & Bridell, D. W. (1977). Behavioral assessment and treatment of alcoholism. In B. Kissin & H. Begleiter (Eds.), *The biology of alcoholism* (Vol. 5). New York: Plenum.

Niaura, R. S., Rohsenow, D. M., Binkoff, J. D., Monti, P. M., Pedraza, M., & Abrams, D. B. (1988). Relevance of Cue Reactivity to understanding alcohol and smoking relapse. *Journal of Abnormal Psychology, 97*, 133–152.

Nezu, A. H. (1987). A problem-solving formulation of depression: A literature review and proposal of a pluralistic model. *Clinical Psychology Review, 7*, 121–144.

Nezu, A. H., & Perri, M. G. (1989). Social problem-solving therapy for unipolar depression: An initial dismantling investigation. *Journal of Consulting and Clinical Psychology, 57*, 408–413.

Nietzel, M. T., Russell, R. L., Hemmings, K. A., & Gretter, M. L. (1987). Clinical significance of psychotherapy for unipolar depression: A meta-analytic approach to social comparison. *Journal of Consulting and Clinical Psychology, 55*, 156–161.

Nordström, G., & Berglund, M. (1987). A prospective study of successful long-term adjustment in alcohol dependence. *Journal of Studies on Alcohol, 48*, 95–103.

O'Gorman, E. C. (1978). The treatment of frigidity: A comparative study of group and individual desensitization. *British Journal of Psychiatry, 132*, 580–584.

O'Leary, K. D., & Beach, S. R. H. (1990) Marital therapy: A

viable treatment for depression and marital discord. *American Journal of Psychiatry. 47*, 183–186.

O'Leary, D. E., O'Leary, M. E., & Donovan, B. M. (1976). Social skill acquisition and psychosocial development of alcoholics: A review. *Addictive Behavior, 1*, 110–120.

O'Leary, K. D., & Turkewitz, H. (1978). The treatment of marital disorder from a behavioral perspective. In T. J. Paolino & B. S. McGrady (Eds.), *Marriage and marital therapy.* New York: Bruner/Mazel.

Olson, R. P., Ganley, R., Devine, V. T., & Dorsey, G. C. (1981). Long-term effects of behavioral versus insight oriented therapy with inpatient alcoholics. *Journal of Consulting and Clinical Psychology, 49*, 866–877.

Orford, J., & Keddie, A. (1986). Abstinence or controlled drinking: A test of the dependence and persuasion hypotheses. *British Journal of Addictions, 81*, 495–504.

Öst, L. G. (1988). Applied relaxation vs progressive relaxation in the treatment of panic disorder. *Behaviour Research and Therapy, 26*, 13–22.

Öst, L. G. (1989). One-session treatment for specific phobias. *Behaviour Research and Therapy, 27*, 1.

Öst, L. G., Fellenius, J., & Sterner, K. (1991). Applied tension, exposure in vivo, and tension-only in the treatment of blood phobia. *Behavior Research and Therapy, 29*, 561–574.

Öst, L. G., Jerremalm, A., & Jansson, L. (1984). Individual response patterns and the effects of different behavioral methods in the treatment of agoraphobia. *Behaviour Research and Therapy, 22*, 697–707.

Öst, L. G., Jerremalm, A., & Johansson, J. (1981). Individual response patterns and the effect of different behavioral methods in the treatment of social phobia. *Behaviour Research and Therapy, 19*, 1–16.

Öst, L. G., Johansson, J., & Jerremalm, A. (1982). Individual response patterns and different behavioral treatments of claustrophobia. *Behaviour Research and Therapy, 20*, 445–460.

Öst, L. G., Lindahl, I. L., Sterner, U., & Jerremalm, A. (1984). Exposure in vivo versus applied relaxation in the treatment of blood phobia. *Behaviour Research and Therapy, 22*, 205.

Öst, L. G., Salkovskis, P. M., & Hellström, K. (1991). One-session therapist directed exposure vs. self-exposure in the treatment of spider phobia. *Behavior Therapy, 22*, 407–422.

Öst, L. G., Sterner, U., & Fellenius, J. (1989). Applied tension, applied relaxation in the treatment of blood phobia. *Behaviour Research and Therapy, 27*, 109.

Öst, L. G., Sterner, U., & Lindahl, I. L. (1984). Physiological responses in blood phobics. *Behaviour Research and Therapy, 22*, 109.

Paul, G. L., & Lentz, R. J. (1977). *Psychosocial treatment of chronic mental patients: Milieu versus social-learning programs.* Cambridge, MA: Harvard University Press.

Peele, S. (1992). Alcoholism, politics, and bureaucracy: The consensus against controlled-drinking therapy in America. *Addictive Behaviors, 17*, 49–62.

Polich, J. M., Armor, D. J., & Braiker, H. B. (1980). Patterns of alcoholism over four years. *Journal of Studies on Alcohol, 41*, 397–415.

Pomerleau, O., Pertchuk, M., Adkins, D., & Bradley, J. P. (1978). A comparison of behavioral and traditional treatment for middle-income problem drinkers. *Journal of Behavioral Medicine, 1*, 187–200.

Powell, T. J. (1987) Anxiety management groups in clinical practice: A preliminary report. *Behavioral Psychotherapy, 15*.

Powell, J., Gray, J. A., Bradley, B. P., Kasvikis, Y., Strang, J., Barratt, L., & Marks, I. (1990). The effects of exposure to drug-related cues in detoxified opiate addicts: A theoretical review and some new data. *Addictive Behavior, 15*, 339–355.

Power, K. G., Simpson, R. J., Swanson, V., & Wallace, L. A. (1990). A controlled comparison of cognitive-behavior therapy, diazepam, and placebo, alone and in combination, for the treatment of generalized anxiety disorder. *Journal of Anxiety Disorders, 4*, 267–292.

Price, S., Reynolds, B. S., Cohen, B. D., Anderson, A. J., & Schochet, B. V. (1981). Group treatment of erectile dysfunction for men without partners: A controlled evaluation. *Archives of Sexual Behavior, 10*, 253–268.

Quadland, M. C. (1985). Compulsive sexual behavior: Definition of a problem and an approach to treatment. *Journal of Sex and Marital Therapy, 11*, 121–132.

Rabavilas, A. D., Boulougouris, J. C., & Stefanis, C. (1976). Duration of flooding sessions in the treatment of obsessive-compulsive patients. *Behaviour Research and Therapy, 14*, 349–355.

Rachman, S. J. (1983). Obstacles to the successful treatment of obsessions. In E. B. Foa & P. M. G. Emmelkamp (Eds.), *Failures in behavior therapy* (pp. 35–57). New York: Wiley.

Rachman, S., Craske, M., Tallman, K., & Solyom, C. (1986). Does escape behavior strengthen agoraphobic avoidance? A replication. *Behavior Therapy, 17*, 366–384.

Rachman, S., & Hodgson, R. J. (1980). *Obsessions and compulsions.* Englewood Cliffs, NJ: Prentice Hall.

Rachman, S., & Levitt, K. (1988). Panic, fear reduction and habituation. *Behaviour Research and Therapy, 26*, 199.

Ramm, E., Marks, I. M., Yüksel, S., & Stern, R. S. (1981). Anxiety management training for anxiety states: Positive compared with negative self-statements. *British Journal of Psychiatry, 140*, 367–373.

Ramsay, R. (1979). Bereavement. In D. Sjödén et al. (Eds.), *Trends in behavior therapy.* New York: Academic Press.

Rankin, H., Hodgson, R., & Stockwell, T. (1983). Cue exposure and response prevention with alcoholics: A controlled trial. *Behaviour Research and Therapy, 21*, 435–446.

Rankin, H., Miller, P., & Hersen, M. (1992). Editorial: Controlled drinking revisited. *Addictive Behaviors, 17*, 47.

Rapee, R. M. (1987). The psychological treatment of panic attacks: Theoretical conceptualization and review of evidence. *Clinical Psychology Review, 7*, 427–438.

Rapee, R. M. (1991). Generalized anxiety disorder: A review of clinical features and theoretical concepts. *Clinical Psychology Review, 11*, 419–440.

Reed, G. F. (1985). *Obsessional experience and compulsive behavior: A cognitive structural approach.* Orlando, FL: Academic Press.

Rehm, L. P. (1977). A self-control model of depression. *Behavior Therapy, 8*, 787–804.

Rehm, L. P., Fuchs, C. Z., Roth, D. M., Kornblith, S. J., & Ramono, J. M. (1979). A comparison of self-control and assertion skills treatment of depression. *Behavior Therapy, 10*, 429–442.

Resick, P. A., Jordan, C. G., Girelli, S. A., Kotsis-Hutter, C., & Marhoefer-Dvorak, S. (1988). A comparative outcome study of behavioral group therapy for sexual assaults victims. *Behavior Therapy, 19*, 385–401.

Reynolds, B. S. (1980). Biofeedback and facilitation of erection in men with erectile dysfunction. *Archives of Sexual Behavior, 9*, 101–113.

Reynolds, B. S., Cohen, B. D., Schochet, B. V., Price, S. C., & Anderson, A. J. (1981). Dating skills training in the group treatment of erectile dysfunction for men without partners. *Journal of Sex and Marital Therapy, 7*, 184–194.

Rice, M. E., Quinsey, V. L., & Harris, G. T. (1991). Sexual

recidivism among child molesters released from a maximum security psychiatric institution. *Journal of Consulting and Clinical Psychology, 59*, 381–386.

Riley, A. J., & Riley, E. J. (1978). A controlled study to evaluate directed masturbation in the management of primary orgasmic failure in women. *British Journal of Psychiatry, 133*, 404–409.

Robinson, L., Berman, J., & Neimeyer, R. (1990). Psychotherapy for treatment of depression: A comprehensive review of controlled outcome research. *Psychological Bulletin, 108*, 30–49.

Rohsenow, D. J., Monti, P. M., Binkoff, J. A., Leipman, M. R., Nirenberg, T. D., & Abrams, D. B. (1991). Patient-treatment matching for alcoholic men in communication skills versus cognitive-behavioral mood management training. *Addictive Behaviors, 16*, 63–69.

Rohsenow, D. J., Smith, R. E., & Johnson, S. (1985). Stress management training as a prevention program for heavy social drinkers: Cognitions, affect, drinking, and individual differences. *Addictive Behaviors, 10*, 45–54.

Rooth, F. G. & Marks, I. M. (1979) Persistent exhibitionism. *Archives of Sexual Behavior, 3*, 227–248.

Rude, S. S., & Rehm, L. P. (1991). Response to treatments for depression: The role of initial status on targeted cognitive and behavioral skills. *Clinical Psychology Review, 11*, 493–514.

Ruft, G. A, & St. Lawrence, J. S. (1989). Premature ejaculation: Past research progress, future directions. *Clinical Psychology Review*, 627–639.

Ruiter, C. de, Rijken, H., Garssen, B., & Kraaimaat, F. (1989). Breathing retraining, exposure and a combination of both in the treatment of panic disorder with agoraphobia. *Behaviour Research and Therapy, 27*, 647–655.

Russell, A. R., & Winkler, R. (1977). Evaluation of assertive training and homosexual guidance service groups designed to improve homosexual functioning. *Journal of Consulting and Clinical Psychology, 45*, 1–13.

Rychtarik, R. G., Foy, D. W., Scott, T., Lokey, L., & Prue, D. M. (1987). Five-six-year follow up of broad-spectrum behavioral treatment for alcoholism: Effects of training controlled drinking skills. *Journal of Consulting and Clinical Psychology, 55*, 106–108.

Rychtarik, R. G., Silverman, W. K., Van Landingham, W. P., & Prue, D. M. (1984). Treatment of an incest victim with implosive therapy: A case study. *Behavior Therapy, 15*, 410–420.

Salkovskis, P. M., Jones, D. R. G., & Clark, D. M. (1986). Respiratory control in the treatment of panic attacks: Replication and extension with concurrent measurement of behaviour and pCO_2. *British Journal of Psychiatry, 148*, 526–532.

Salkovskis, P. M., Warwick, H. M. C., Clark, D. M., & Wessels, D. J. (1986). A demonstration of acute hyperventilation during naturally occurring panic attacks. *Behaviour Research and Therapy, 24*, 91–94.

Sanchez-Graig, M., Annis, H. M., Bornet, A. R., & MacDonald, K. R. (1984). Random assignment to abstinence and controlled drinking: Evaluation of a cognitive-behavioral program for problem drinkers. *Journal of Consulting and Clinical Psychology, 52*, 390–403.

Sanchez, V. C., Lewinsohn, P. M., & Larson, D. W. (1980). Assertion training: Effectiveness in the treatment of depression. *Journal of Clinical Psychology, 36*, 526–529.

Schmidt, M. M., & Miller, W. R. (1983). Amount of therapist contact and outcome in a multidimensional depression treatment program. *Acta Psychiatrica Scandinavica, 67*, 319–332.

Scholing, A., & Emmelkamp, P. M. G. (1989). Individualized treatment for social phobia. In P. M. G. Emmelkamp, W.

Everaerd, F. Kraaimaat, & M. van Son (Eds.), *Fresh perspectives on anxiety disorders* (pp. 213–228). Amsterdam: Swets.

Scholing, A., & Emmelkamp, P. M. G. (1993a). Cognitive and behavioral treatments of fear of blushing, sweating or trembling. *Behaviour Research and Therapy, 31*, 155–170.

Scholing, A., & Emmelkamp, P. M. G. (1993b). Exposure with and without cognitive therapy for generalized social phobia: Effects of individual and group treatment. *Behaviour Research & Therapy* (in press).

Scogin, F., Jamison, C., & Gochneaur, K. (1989). Comparative efficacy of cognitive and behavioral bibliotherapy for mildly and moderately depressed adults. *Journal of Consulting and Clinical Psychology, 57*, 403–407.

Semans, J. H. (1956). Premature ejaculation: A new approach. *Southern Medical Journal, 49*, 353–357.

Shaw, P. M. (1979). *A comparison of three behavior therapies in the treatment for social phobia.* Paper read at the British Association for Behavioral Psychotherapy, Exeter.

Sherman, A. R. (1972). Real-life exposure as a primary therapeutic factor in the desensitization treatment of fear. *Journal of Abnormal Psychology, 79*, 19–28.

Siegel, S. (1983). Classical conditioning, drug tolerance, and drug dependence. In R. G. Smart, F. B. Glaser, Y. Israel, H. Kalant, R. E. Popham, & W. Schmidt (Eds.), *Research advances in alcohol and drug problems.* (Vol. 7, pp. 207–246). New York: Plenum.

Silva, P. de, & Rachman, S. (1984). Does escape behaviour strengthen agoraphobic avoidance? A preliminary study. *Behaviour Research and Therapy, 22*, 87–91.

Sireling, L., Cohen, D., & Marks, I. (1988). Guided mourning for morbid grief: A controlled replication. *Behavior Therapy, 19*, 121–132.

Sloane, R. B., Staples, F. R., Cristol, A. H., Yorkston, N. J., & Whipple, K. (1975). *Psychotherapy versus behavior therapy.* Cambridge, MA: Harvard University Press.

Snyder, D. K., & Wills, R. M. (1989). Behavioral versus insight-oriented marital therapy: Effects on individual and interspousal functioning. *Journal of Consulting and Clinical Psychology, 57*, 39–46.

Snyder, D. K., Wills, R. M., & Grady-Fletcher, A. (1991). Long-term effectiveness of behavioral versus insight-oriented marital therapy: A 4-year follow-up study. *Journal of Consulting and Clinical Psychology, 59*, 138–141.

Sobell, M. B., & Sobell, L. C. (1973). Alcoholics treated by individualized behavior therapy: One year treatment outcome. *Behavior Research and Therapy, 11*, 599–618.

Sobell, M. B., & Sobell, L. C. (1984). The aftermath of heresy: A response to Pendery et al.'s (1982) critique of "individualized behavior therapy for alcoholics." *Behavior Research and Therapy, 22*, 413–440.

Son, M. J. M. van (1978). *Sociale vaardigheidstherapie.* Amsterdam: Swets & Zeitlinger.

Staiger, P. K., & White, J. M. (1991). Cue reactivity in alcohol abusers: Stimulus specificity and extinction of the responses. *Addictive Behaviors, 16*, 211–221.

Stampfl, T. G., & Levis, D. J. (1967). Essentials of implosive therapy. *Journal of Abnormal Psychology, 72*, 496–503.

Steketee, G., & Cleere, L. (1990). Obsessional-compulsive disorders. In A. S. Bellack, M. Hersen, & A. E. Kazdin (Eds.), *International handbook of behavior modification and therapy* (2nd ed.). New York: Plenum.

Stern, R., & Marks, I. M. (1973). Brief and prolonged flooding: A comparison in agoraphobic patients. *Archives of General Psychiatry, 28*, 270–276.

Strauss, J. S., & Carpenter, W. T. (1977). Prediction of outcome in schizophrenia. *Archives of General Psychiatry, 34*, 159–163.

Stravinsky, A., Marks, I. M., & Jule, W. (1982). Social skills problems in neurotic outpatients. *Archives of General Psychiatry, 39,* 1378–1385.

Tarrier, N., & Barrowclough, C. (1990). Family interventions for schizophrenia. *Behavior Modification, 14,* 408–440.

Tarrier, N., & Main, C. J. (1986). Applied relaxation training for generalised anxiety and panic attacks. *British Journal of Psychiatry, 149,* 330–336.

Telch, M. J., Hannon, R., & Telch, C. F. (1984). A comparison of cessation strategies for the outpatient alcoholic. *Addictive Behaviors, 9,* 103–109.

Terri, L., & Lewinsohn, P. M. (1986). Individual and group treatment of unipolar depression: Comparison of treatment outcome and identification of predictors of successful treatment outcome. *Behavior Therapy, 17,* 215–228.

Thompson, L. W., Gallagher, D., & Steinmetz Breckenridge, J. S. (1987). Comparative effectiveness of psychotherapies for depressed elders. *Journal of Consulting and Clinical Psychology, 55,* 385–390.

Thorpe, G. L., Freedman, E. G., & Lazar, J. D. (1985). Assertiveness training and exposure in vivo for agoraphobics. *Behavioural Psychotherapy, 13,* 132–141.

Thorpe, G. L., Hecker, J. E., Cavallaro, L. A., & Kulberg, G. E. (1987). Insight versus rehearsal in cognitive-behaviour therapy: A cross-over study with sixteen phobics. *Behavioural Psychotherapy, 15,* 319–336.

Thyrer, B. A., Hinsle, J., & Curtic, G. C. (1985). Blood-injury-illness phobia: A review. *Journal of Clinical Psychology, 41,* 451.

Trower, P., Yardley, K., Bryant, B. M., & Shaw, P. (1978). The treatment of social failure: A comparison of anxiety reduction and skills-acquisition procedures on two social problems. *Behavior Modification, 2,* 41–60.

Ullmann, L. P., & Krasner, L. (1965). *Case studies in behavior modification.* Englewood Cliffs, NJ: Prentice Hall.

Van Hasselt, V. B., Hersen, M., & Milliones, J. (1978). Social skill training for alcoholics and drug addicts: A review. *Addictive Behaviors, 3,* 221–223.

Vaughn, C. E., & Leff, J. P. (1976). The influence of family and social factors on the cause of psychiatric illness. *British Journal of Psychiatry, 129,* 125–137.

Veronen, L. J., & Kilpatrick, D. G. (1983). Stress management for rape victims. In D. Meichenbaum & M. E. Jaremko (Eds.), *Stress reduction and prevention.* New York: Plenum.

Visser, S., Hoekstra, R. J., & Emmelkamp, P. M. G. (1992). Follow-up study on behavioural treatment of obsessive-compulsive disorders. In A. Ehlers, W. Fiegenbaum, I. Florin, & J. Margraf (Eds.), *Perspectives and promises of clinical psychology* (pp. 157–170). New York: Plenum.

Voegtlin, W., & Broz, W. B. (1949). The conditioned reflex treatment of chronic alcoholism. An analysis of 3125 admissions over a period of ten and a half years. *Annals of Internal Medicine, 30,* 580–597.

Wakefield, J. C. (1987). The semantics of success: Do masturbation exercises lead to partner orgasm? *Journal of Sex and Marital Therapy, 13,* 3–14.

Watson, J. P., Mullett, G. E., & Pilley, H. (1973). The effects of prolonged exposure to phobic situations upon agoraphobic patients treated in groups. *Behaviour Research and Therapy, 11,* 531–546.

White, J., Keenan, M., & Brooks, N. (1992). Stress control: A controlled comparative investigation of large group therapy for generalized anxiety disorder. *Behavioural Psychotherapy, 20,* 97–114.

Whitehead, A., Mathews, A., & Ramage, M. R. (1987). The treatment of sexually unresponsive women. *Behaviour Research and Therapy, 25,* 195–205.

Wickramasekera, I. (1980). Aversive behavior rehearsal: A cognitive-behavioral procedure. In D. J. Cox & R. J. Daitzman (Eds.), *Exhibitionism: Description, assessment, and treatment* (pp. 123–149). New York: Garland STPM Press.

Wikler, A. (1948). Recent progress in research on the neurophysiologic basis of morphine addiction. *American Journal of Psychiatry, 105,* 329–338.

Williams, S. L., Dooseman, G., & Kleifield, E. (1984). Comparative effectiveness of guided mastery and exposure treatments for intractable phobias. *Journal of Consulting and Clinical Psychology, 52,* 505.

Williams, S. L., & Zane, G. (1989). Guided mastery and stimulus exposure treatments for severe performance anxiety in agoraphobics. *Behaviour Research and Therapy, 27,* 237–245.

Wilson, G. T. (1978). Alcoholism and aversion therapy: Issues, ethics and evidence. In G. A. Marlat & P. E. Nathan (Eds.), *Behavioral approaches to alcoholism.* New Brunswick, NJ: Rutgers Center of Alcohol Studies.

Wilson, G. T. (1984) Fear reduction methods and the treatment of anxiety disorders. In G. T. Wilson, C. M. Franks, K. D. Brownell, & P. C. Kendall (Eds.), *Annual Review of Behavior Therapy. Theory and Practice* (Vol. 9). Guilford Press, New York.

Wilson, G. T. (1987) Chemical aversion conditioning as a treatment for alcoholism: A re-analysis. *Behaviour Research and Therapy, 25,* 503–516.

Wilson, G. T. (1991). Chemical aversion conditioning in the treatment of alcoholism: Further comments. *Behaviour Research and Therapy, 29, 41,* 405–420.

Wilson, P. H. (1982). Combined pharmacological and behavioral treatment of depression. *Behaviour Research and Therapy, 20,* 173–184.

Wilson, P. H., Goldin, J. C., & Charbonneau-Powis, M. (1983). Comparative efficacy of behavioral and cognitive treatments of depression. *Cognitive Therapy and Research, 7,* 111–124.

Wlazlo, Z., Schroeder-Hartwig, K., Hand, I., Kaiser, G., & Münchau, N. (1990). Exposure in vivo vs. social skills training for social phobia: Long term outcome and differential effects. *Behaviour Research and Therapy, 28,* 181–193.

Wolpe, J. (1958). *Psychotherapy and reciprocal inhibition.* Stanford: Stanford University Press.

Woodward, R., & Jones, R. B. (1980). Cognitive restructuring treatment: A controlled trial with anxious patients. *Behavior Research and Therapy, 18,* 401–409.

Youngren, M. A., & Lewinsohn, P. M. (1980). The functional relationship between depression and problematic interpersonal behavior. *Journal of Abnormal Psychology, 89,* 333–341.

Yuksel, S., Marks, I., Ramm, E., & Ghosh, A. (1984). Slow versus rapid exposure *in vivo* of phobics. *Behavioural Psychotherapy, 12,* 249–256.

Zeiss, A. M., Lewinsohn, P. M., & Munoz, R. F. (1979). Nonspecific improvement effects in depression using interpersonal skills training, pleasant activity schedules, or cognitive training. *Journal of Consulting and Clinical Psychology, 47,* 427–439.

Zimmer, D. (1987). Does marital therapy enhance the effectiveness of treatment for sexual dysfunction. *Journal of Sex and Marital Therapy, 13,* 193–209.

Zubin, J., & Spring, B. (1977). Vulnerability: A new view of schizophrenia. *Journal of Abnormal Psychology, 86,* 103–126.

10

COGNITIVE AND COGNITIVE-BEHAVIORAL THERAPIES

- **STEVEN D. HOLLON**
  Vanderbilt University

- **AARON T. BECK**
  University of Pennsylvania

Few approaches have generated as much interest over the last two decades as the cognitive and cognitive-behavioral interventions. Based on the notion that thinking plays a role in the etiology and maintenance of at least some disorders, these interventions seek to reduce distress by changing maladaptive beliefs and providing new information-processing skills. Although widely accepted in the clinical community, enthusiasm for these approaches has sometimes outstripped their empirical support. In a previous review, we concluded that although these interventions held considerable promise, they were largely untested in clinical populations and often unimpressive in the few such studies that had been conducted (Hollon & Beck, 1986).

This is clearly no longer the case. There has been a virtual explosion of controlled clinical trials dealing with a diverse array of fully clinical populations (over 120 such trials have been added to the literature in the last 8 years alone). For the most part, the cognitive and cognitive-behavioral interventions have fared well in these trials, typically proving superior to minimal treatment and nonspecific controls and at least equal or superior to alternative psychosocial or pharmacological approaches. Particularly exciting are indications that these interventions may produce longer lasting change than some of those alternative approaches.

In this chapter, we review the conceptual underpinnings and empirical status of the cognitive and cognitive-behavioral interventions. Despite their common core, these approaches differ with respect to the processes presumed to mediate and the procedures used to produce change. We try to highlight this variability and to examine its relation to clinical efficacy. However, few direct comparisons exist between the respective interventions, forcing us to rely on extrapolations based on relative efficacy across studies and populations. We turn first to a definition of cognitive therapy and a delineation of the major types of cognitive and cognitive-behavioral interventions.

Definition of Cognitive Interventions

All cognitive interventions attempt to produce change by influencing thinking (Mahoney, 1977). A cognitive perspective does not ignore the contribution of innate propensities or prior experience, but it does suggest that the way in which an individual interprets an event plays a role in determining how he or she responds. According to this perspective, thinking plays a role in determining subsequent affect and behavior, but is itself influenced by existing moods and the consequences of prior actions (Bandura, 1986). Although it does not insist on exclusivity, cognitive theory suggests that thinking plays a causal role, in concert with other factors, in the etiology and maintenance of at least some disorders and can therefore serve to mediate therapeutic change.

We limit our definition to those approaches that explicitly seek to produce change in cognition as a means of influencing other phenomena of interest, such as affect or behavior, and that conceptualize this effort in terms of central mechanisms (Bandura, 1977). This definition excludes interventions, such as systematic desensitization, that may work through cognitive mediation but are neither intended nor perceived to do so. It also excludes interventions, such as covert control, that seek to produce cognitive change via the application of peripheral conditioning techniques.

Even within this definition, there is considerable room for variation with respect to both process and procedure. Some approaches emphasize the modification of distortions in existing beliefs, whereas others seek to compensate for perceived deficits in cognitive skills (Kendall & Braswell, 1985). Similarly, the approaches differ in the extent to which they incorporate behavioral components and in the extent to which they adhere to a central model of change as opposed to a peripheral one. Finally, some approaches are more closely tied to differentiated theories of psychopathology than are others, with the former more likely to develop specific subtheories to account for the different disorders and procedural modifications to deal with them.

Cognitive Versus Cognitive-Behavioral Approaches

Cognitive approaches to treatment have a long history in psychology (see Raimy, 1975). Although systems emphasizing the role of subjective meaning have a respected place in philosophy and science, early therapeutic efforts based on those principles were derided as simplistic and unduly semantic in nature. George Kelly's seminal work in the mid-1950s did much to renew interest in cognitive approaches to treatment and to bring such efforts into the mainstream of scientific inquiry (Kelly, 1955). Although Kelly's specific approach to treatment never received widespread clinical acceptance, it had a profound influence on the development of subsequent interventions.

The cognitive and cognitive-behavioral interventions differ with respect to their developmental histories. The cognitive interventions were typically developed by dynamically trained theorists and tend to emphasize the role of meaning. In these approaches, what a person thinks (or says) is not so important as what he or she believes. The cognitive-behavioral interventions were typically developed by theorists trained as behaviorists. In these approaches, thinking tends to be conceptualized in a more concrete fashion and is often regarded as a set of covert self-statements (private behaviors) that can be influenced by the same laws of conditioning that influence other overt behaviors. The cognitive theorists have led in developing strategies for examining the rationality or validity of existing beliefs, whereas the cognitive-behavioral theorists have focused on the development of strategies for teaching specific cognitive skills.

In fact, both approaches combine cognitive and behavioral elements, albeit in different ways and to different extents, and both legitimately belong to the larger family of cognitive-behavioral interventions. Moreover, each approach has borrowed from the other over the years, blurring the distinctions between them. Finally, there has been a growing interest among the cognitive-behavioral theorists in

a constructivist approach that suggests that reality is a product of the personal meanings that people create (Mahoney, 1993; Meichenbaum & Fitzpatrick, 1993). This has led them to eschew the emphasis on rationality or empiricism that is the hallmark of the original cognitive theorists. As a consequence, some of the cognitive-behavioral theorists have become even more cognitive in their perspectives than the original cognitive theorists, further blurring the distinctions between the approaches.

Specific Interventions

Ellis's rational-emotive therapy (RET; Ellis, 1962) was the first of the modern cognitive interventions to gain widespread clinical acceptance. In this approach, clients are taught to examine the rationality of their beliefs and are encouraged to adopt a more stoic philosophy (Ellis, 1980). Trained dynamically, Ellis retained an interest in exploring his clients' idiosyncratic meaning systems, and he pioneered the development of strategies designed to change existing beliefs. As an approach to treatment, RET tends to rely more on verbal persuasion than do the other cognitive and cognitive-behavioral approaches; the role of the therapist is to help the client identify and actively dispute his or her irrational beliefs. Behavioral components are often incorporated, but more to help clients practice living in accordance with their new philosophy and beliefs than as a means of changing those beliefs themselves. Closely related is systematic rational restructuring (SRR; Goldfried, DeCanteceo, & Weinberg, 1974), which was originally conceived as a way of operationalizing RET in a more structured fashion for use in controlled clinical trials. Both RET and SRR rely heavily on persuasion and reason and emphasize rationality as the primary mechanism of change.

Beck's cognitive therapy (CT) represents the other major cognitive intervention (Beck, 1976). Beck was also trained dynamically, and, like Ellis, was more concerned with exploring his clients' idiosyncratic meaning systems than were most of his contemporaries. However, Beck's therapy tends to emphasize the process of empiricism to a greater extent than does Ellis's RET; clients in CT are encouraged to treat their beliefs as hypotheses to be tested and are trained to use their own behaviors as experiments to examine the accuracy of those beliefs. Whereas Ellis strives for a philosophical conversion based on reason and logic, Beck encourages a reliance on scientific empiricism to change existing beliefs. Behavioral components are more likely to be incorporated in CT than in RET and are used largely in the service of gathering data to test hypotheses.

Meichenbaum's approach represents the prototype of the behaviorally oriented cognitive-behavioral interventions (Meichenbaum, 1977). Trained as a behaviorist, Meichenbaum initially conceptualized cognitions as covert self-statements, a form of private speech that could be modified via modeling and repetition. Over the years, he became increasingly interested in the exploration of idiosyncratic meaning systems and the role of metaphor in personal narratives, but, in its classic form, his approach emphasizes the acquisition of cognitive skills as much as the examination of existing beliefs. Meichenbaum is best known for his development of stress inoculation training (SIT), an approach to treatment designed to help clients cope with problematic life events (Meichenbaum, 1985). SIT combines efforts at cognitive restructuring with training in verbal self-instruction and behavioral self-management techniques; clients are encouraged to apply these skills to a series of increasingly stressful situations as therapy progresses. Self-instructional training is both a component of SIT and an intervention in its own right. It relies on a process of observation and repetition to introduce new cognitive skills, in much the same fashion in which complex motor skills are acquired. When used with children or adults with developmental disabilities, it is typically combined with contingency management techniques, such as response cost or positive reinforcement, in order to sustain attention on the therapeutic task.

Problem-solving training (PST; D'Zurilla & Goldfried, 1971) is designed to provide clients with a set of sequential procedures for dealing with problematic situations and interpersonal conflicts. The approach is typically considered cognitive in nature because it deals explicitly with decision-making skills. However, attention to existing beliefs is limited, and the approach often relies on more purely behavioral procedures, such as behavior rehearsal and role-play, to produce change. Closely related, but independently conceived, are procedures developed to facilitate the acquisition of problem-solving skills in children and adolescents (Spivak, Platt, & Shure, 1976).

Several other approaches combine cognitive and behavioral components for use with specific disorders. Rehm developed a self-control therapy (SCT) for the treatment of depression (Rehm, 1977). Barlow and colleagues developed a panic control treatment (PCT) that combines behavioral and cognitive components in the treatment of panic and agoraphobia (Barlow & Cerny, 1988).

Marlatt and colleagues developed an approach to relapse prevention (RP) in the treatment of addictions that emphasizes the acquisition of self-regulatory skills (Marlatt & Gordon, 1985). Finally, Linehan developed a cognitive-behavioral approach to the treatment of borderline personality disorder called dialectical behavior therapy (DBT; Linehan, 1993).

Summary

Although all these approaches incorporate both cognitive and behavioral elements, they differ with respect to just how these components are integrated and the processes believed to mediate change. RET and CT, the two more purely cognitive approaches, emphasize the exploration of idiosyncratic meaning systems and stress rationality and empiricism, respectively, as the primary processes for producing change in existing beliefs. Among the more behaviorally oriented cognitive-behavioral approaches, SIT combines both cognitive and behavioral strategies in a somewhat integrative fashion, whereas self-instructional training and PST incorporate cognitive elements into largely behavioral interventions. The remaining cognitive-behavioral interventions stand somewhere between SIT and PST in this respect. Although it is clear that differences in process and procedure do exist, it is still not known whether these variations have implications for efficacy. We next turn to a discussion of the consequences of applying these diverse interventions to specific disorders.

DEPRESSION AND THE PREVENTION OF RELAPSE

No disorder has received more attention from cognitive theorists than depression. Beginning with Beck's early observations regarding the role of cognition in depression (Beck, 1963), work in this area has played an integral role in the development of cognitive theory and has given rise to a number of discriminable interventions, CT chief among them. These approaches can be distinguished from behavioral or biological theories, which view depression, respectively, as a consequence of a deficit in positive reinforcement or of dysregulation in neurotransmitters or related biological systems (Shelton, Hollon, Purdon, & Loosen, 1991).

Cognitive Therapy

According to cognitive theory, people who are depressed hold unrealistically negative views of themselves and their futures and fall prey to systematic distortions in information processing that leave them unable to correct these maladaptive beliefs (Beck, 1976). Their minds are filled with negative automatic thoughts that seem to arise unbidden, and, even when not depressed, they ascribe to certain underlying dysfunctional attitudes that put them at risk for future depression. These maladaptive beliefs and information-processing proclivities are seen as parts of a larger depressive schema, an integrated knowledge structure that influences both what can be remembered and how judgments are formed. According to cognitive theory, these schemata are latent predispositions that can lie dormant for years before being activated, typically by some stressful life event (Kovacs & Beck, 1978).

In CT, patients are taught to systematically evaluate their beliefs and information-processing proclivities in the service of becoming less depressed and reducing subsequent risk (Beck, Rush, Shaw, & Emery, 1979). The approach relies heavily on the process of empirical disconfirmation; patients are taught to treat their beliefs as hypotheses that can be tested and to gather information and conduct behavioral experiments to test them. In essence, patients are encouraged to act like scientists, withholding judgment about the validity of their beliefs until those beliefs have been examined in a systematic fashion.

Is CT effective?   CT has typically fared well in comparisons with alternative interventions with respect to the reduction of acute distress. In a recent quantitative review of 27 studies involving unipolar outpatients, Dobson (1989) concluded that CT was more effective than either no treatment or nonspecific treatment and at least as effective as alternative psychosocial or pharmacological interventions. Other studies suggest that its efficacy may extend to inpatient samples as well (Bowers, 1990; Miller, Norman, Keitner, Bishop, & Dow, 1989; Thase, Bowler, & Harden, 1991), and work is currently under way to examine its applicability to bipolar disorder.

Nonetheless, it would be premature to conclude that the efficacy of CT has been established or that CT is superior to other interventions, particularly antidepressant medications (Hollon, Shelton, & Loosen, 1991). The problems are twofold. First, studies comparing CT with alternative psychosocial interventions have typically been conducted in less than fully clinical populations (e.g., Shaw, 1977) or have not operationalized those other approaches in a compelling way (e.g., Covi & Lipman, 1987). Moreover, most of the studies in the literature have

been conducted by adherents to CT. A recent quantitative review found that investigator allegiance largely accounted for the apparent advantage found for CT over other approaches (Robinson, Berman, & Neimeyer, 1990). Studies should sample truly clinical populations and should be overseen jointly by proponents of the respective interventions to ensure that each modality is competently executed.

Second, although CT has fared well in direct comparisons with pharmacotherapy in fully clinical samples, few of these trials have included pill-placebo controls (see Elkin et al., 1989, for an exception). In the absence of such controls, it is not possible to be certain that the samples studied were drug-responsive or that pharmacotherapy was adequately operationalized (Hollon et al., 1991). Pharmacotherapy has often been chosen as the standard for comparison precisely because it is presumed effective; failure to establish its specific efficacy in the samples studied undermines the interpretability of those trials. Moreover, the efficacy of pharmacotherapy has itself been challenged on the basis of meta-analyses suggesting that drug-placebo differences are most evident in studies that fail to assess the adequacy of the blind (Greenberg & Fisher, 1989).

CT was found superior to medications in two studies, but it is precisely those studies in which the operationalization of pharmacotherapy is most suspect. Rush and colleagues found CT superior to imipramine pharmacotherapy in the treatment of nonpsychotic, nonbipolar depressed outpatients, but began medication withdrawal 2 weeks prior to the posttreatment assessment (Rush, Beck, Kovacs, & Hollon, 1977). Similarly, Blackburn and colleagues found CT superior to tricyclic pharmacotherapy among depressed patients in a general practice setting, but did so in the context of such an uncharacteristically poor response to pharmacotherapy as to raise questions about the adequacy of its execution (Blackburn, Bishop, Glen, Whalley, & Christie, 1981).

Questions can also be raised about the adequacy with which CT was operationalized in the only trial that suggested an advantage for pharmacotherapy, the National Institute of Mental Health's Treatment of Depression Collaborative Research Program (Elkin et al., 1989; see also Chapter 4 in this *Handbook*). In that study, both imipramine pharmacotherapy and interpersonal psychotherapy (IPT), but not CT, were found superior to a pill-placebo control among more severely depressed outpatients; no differences were evident among less severely depressed patients. Differences fell short of significance among the active treatments in the more severely depressed subsample, but their magnitude was large enough to suggest that CT might be less effective than pharmacotherapy with such patients.

This finding was not robust across sites, however. Pharmacotherapy was superior to CT among the more severely depressed patients at only one site; cognitive therapy performed as well as pharmacotherapy at a second site; and there were too few severely depressed patients to support separate analyses at a third site (Elkin et al., 1989). The sites differed considerably in the extent of their prior involvement with cognitive therapy, with the Oklahoma site having the most extensive prior history. Although training appeared adequate, the monthly supervision provided during the study proper was less intensive than that provided in comparable trials and may not have been sufficient to maintain competent performance from newly trained cognitive therapists. CT thus may not have been adequately implemented at all sites. It should prove possible to address this concern, since competency ratings were conducted by expert cognitive therapists during both the pilot training phase and the actual study (Shaw & Dobson, 1988). However, until these data are reported and outcomes are reported by site, the findings from the NIMH study cannot be adequately interpreted.

The remaining studies comparing CT with pharmacotherapy have produced a series of tie scores, typically in the absence of any minimal-treatment or placebo controls (the psychiatric sample in Blackburn et al., 1981; Hollon, DeRubeis, Evans, et al., 1992; Murphy, Simons, Wetzel, & Lustman, 1984). Although null findings are open to multiple interpretations, it is likely that pharmacotherapy was adequately operationalized in these studies. All were conducted at sites known for their biological orientation by teams that included experienced research pharmacologists. Drug dosage levels were appropriate and, in the latter two studies, monitored with plasma medication checks. Moreover, there was no indication in any of these studies that CT was less effective than pharmacotherapy for more severely depressed outpatients (see, for example, Hollon, DeRubeis, Evans, et al., 1992). Thus, it seems reasonable to conclude that CT is about as effective as pharmacotherapy regardless of severity, at least among nonpsychotic patients. Nevertheless, additional placebo-controlled trials should directly address this issue.

There is also no indication that combined treatment does anything more to enhance CT than it does to enhance pharmacotherapy, as would be the case if pharmacotherapy were truly superior to CT

(Hollon et al., 1991). Combined treatment has typically been associated with an advantage over either single modality of about a quarter of a standard deviation. Such an effect is too small to meet conventional criteria for significance in the rather modest samples typically studied, but is large enough to be of interest clinically if it should prove to be robust. Additional trials using larger samples are needed to determine whether combined treatment provides any advantage over either modality alone.

Does CT prevent symptom return?   Depression tends to be an episodic disorder; even patients who have been successfully treated appear to be at considerable risk for future episodes. Although pharmacotherapy suppresses the reemergence of symptoms so long as it is continued, there is no indication that it does anything to reduce underlying risk (Hollon, Evans, & DeRubeis, 1990). Current pharmacological practice is moving in the direction of maintaining medications indefinitely for patients with a history of recurrence (Frank et al., 1990).

Naturalistic follow-ups of the major controlled trials suggest that CT may reduce risk following the termination of treatment (Blackburn, Eunson, & Bishop, 1986; Evans et al., 1992; Kovacs, Rush, Beck, & Hollon, 1981; Shea et al., 1992; Simons, Murphy, Levine, & Wetzel, 1986). These studies found that responders to CT were only half as likely to relapse or seek additional treatment following termination than responders to pharmacotherapy alone (Hollon et al., 1991). For example, as shown in Figure 10.1, Evans and colleagues found that patients treated to remission with CT (with or without medications) were less likely to relapse following termination of treatment than patients treated to remission pharmacologically, and no more likely to relapse than patients continued on medications for the first year of the 2-year follow-up (Evans et al., 1992).

These studies do have their problems. Samples were small, definitions of response and relapse diverse, and return to treatment only partially controlled. Most critically, only about half the patients initially randomized to treatment were actually included in the follow-ups, since rates of treatment completion and response among completers rarely exceeded 70 percent each. It is possible that acute treatment acted as a differential sieve, systematically unbalancing the treatment conditions with respect to the types of patients graduated into the follow-ups (Hollon et al., 1991). For example, if patients with greater underlying risk need medications to respond (or can better tolerate their side

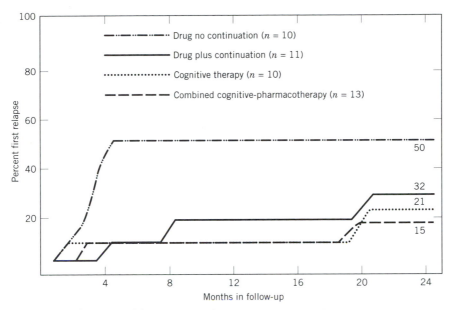

FIGURE 10.1 Relapse after successful treatment. Values represent time to first relapse after at least partial response to initial treatment. Relapse is defined as two consecutive scores of 16 or above on the Beck Depression Inventory. Only patients in the medication-continuation condition continued to receive treatment during this period, and for those patients, medications were discontinued after the 12th month of follow-up. *Note.* From "Differential Relapse Following Cognitive Therapy and Pharmacotherapy for Depression" by M.D. Evans et al., 1992, *Archives of General Psychology, 49,* p. 805. Copyright © 1992 by the American Medical Association. Reprinted by permission.

effects), then such patients would be overrepresented among the samples of responding completers to pharmacotherapy and could bias any subsequent comparison with prior CT. Although there is little evidence of any such artifact in our own work (and it is difficult to imagine how it could account for differences favoring prior combined treatment over prior pharmacotherapy alone), more severely dysfunctional patients were overrepresented in the sample of patients responding to prior pharmacotherapy in the NIMH study (Shea et al., 1992).

There is also a growing consensus in the field that relapse, the return of symptoms associated with the prior episode, needs to be distinguished from recurrence, the onset of a wholly new episode (Frank et al., 1991). Most episodes of depression run their course in 6 to 12 months, even if left untreated. Although pharmacological interventions accelerate the pace of remission, patients are at elevated risk for symptom return if medications are withdrawn prematurely (Prien & Kupfer, 1986). This may mean that drugs do little to alter the course of the underlying episode and that symptom return during this interval is more likely to reflect relapse than recurrence (Hollon et al., 1990). In the follow-up studies previously cited, the majority of

the instances of differential symptom return occurred during the first several months following the end of treatment. This situation suggests that the advantage enjoyed by prior CT probably had more to do with the prevention of relapse than of recurrence. Although any suggestion of a preventive effect is most welcome, the implications of these findings would be far greater if they proved to apply to recurrence as well. Studies are needed to determine whether CT's enduring effect can extend to the prevention of new episodes, either among patients with recurrent depression or among persons at risk with no prior history (Hollon, DeRubeis, & Seligman, 1992).

Who benefits from CT? There are no clear indications that specific types of patients do better or worse in CT than in other types of interventions, at least among patients with nonpsychotic depressions. The suggestion from the NIMH study that more severely depressed outpatients do less well in CT than in pharmacotherapy was not robust across sites (Elkin et al., 1989) and has not been replicated in other studies (e.g., Hollon, DeRubeis, Evans, et al., 1992). Similarly, neither endogenicity nor melancholia predicted differential response in any of the studies. In a recent review Rude and

Rehm (1991) found little evidence that degree of cognitive dysfunction predicted differential response, and McKnight and colleagues reported that dexamethasone nonsuppression did not predict differential response to CT versus pharmacotherapy in a controlled trial (McKnight, Nelson-Gray, & Barnhill, 1992).

Nonetheless, it would be premature to conclude that such prescriptive indexes do not exist. For a variety of reasons, it is simply more difficult to detect moderation than it is to detect a main effect for treatment (Smith & Sechrest, 1991). The appropriate designs are more complex; prescriptive indexes need to be carefully assessed; and larger samples are required to generate comparable power. As few of the existing studies were designed with such considerations in mind, it is possible that such indexes may be detected in more methodologically adequate trials.

What are CT's active ingredients? Cognitive theory assumes that change is brought about in CT by virtue of efforts to examine the accuracy of existing beliefs; nonspecific aspects of the therapeutic relationship are seen as playing a secondary role (Beck et al., 1979). Measures have been developed that can discriminate such theoretically specific therapist behaviors from nonspecific aspects of the therapeutic relationship (Hollon, Evans, Elkin, & Lowery, 1984; Shaw & Dobson, 1988). However, efforts to relate quality of execution to response in controlled trials have been disappointing, largely because the training and supervision provided in such studies reduce variability in therapist performance (Crits-Christoph et al., 1991).

Patterns of covariation have typically been more apparent in uncontrolled trials that include a wider range of therapist competence and experience. For example, in a sample that included both experienced and inexperienced cognitive therapists, DeRubeis and Feeley (1990) found that adherence to CT early in treatment predicted subsequent response, whereas rated quality of the therapeutic alliance appeared to be more a consequence than a cause of symptom change. Burns and Nolen-Hoeksema (1992) found that experienced therapists, who might be expected to be more proficient with the approach, produced superior clinical outcomes. They also found that patients' perceptions of therapist empathy did covary with response to CT, but they collected those ratings on a retrospective basis. Thus, the existing literature, sparse though it is, is consistent with the notion that CT works through processes specified by theory.

Does CT work by changing cognition? Similarly, theory suggests that change in beliefs is the primary mechanism of change in CT. However, comparative trials have suggested that pharmacotherapy or other interventions can produce as much change in cognition as does CT (e.g., DeRubeis et al., 1990; Imber et al., 1990; Simons, Garfield, & Murphy, 1984). Such findings are sometimes interpreted as indicating that cognition is merely epiphenomenal, but specificity of change is not informative with respect to mediational status (Hollon, DeRubeis, & Evans, 1987). However, differential covariation is informative; studies that have examined the relation between change in beliefs (particularly expectations) and subsequent change in depression have found stronger relations in CT than in pharmacotherapy (DeRubeis et al., 1990; Rush, Kovacs, Beck, Weissenburger, & Hollon, 1981). Such a pattern is consistent with the notion that cognitive change mediates change in depression in CT.

Several theorists have suggested that the modification of underlying propensities such as attributional styles should reduce subsequent risk (prevention), whereas the disconfirmation of negative expectations should mediate the resolution of existing distress (treatment) (Abramson, Metalsky, & Alloy, 1989; Hollon & Garber, 1980). Consistent with these predictions, Hollon et al. (1990) found that CT produced greater change in attributional styles than did pharmacotherapy and that change in attributional style appeared to mediate CT's relapse preventive effect, as determined by causal modeling based on recommendations by Baron and Kenny (1986). These findings, along with those just reported with respect to expectancy change, are consistent with the notion that different aspects of cognitive change mediate different aspects of response to CT.

Other Cognitive-Behavioral Approaches

Several approaches to the treatment of depression incorporate cognitive components into largely behavioral frameworks. SCT seeks to remedy perceived deficits in self-regulatory skills (Rehm, 1977). Early trials in adult populations were generally supportive, but typically involved recruited volunteers treated by graduate-student therapists (Rehm, 1984). Perhaps because of this lack of clinical realism, little has been done with adult populations since the previous edition of this *Handbook* (see Hollon & Beck, 1986). However, additional studies found the approach to be effective with both children (Stark, Reynolds, & Kaslow, 1987) and adolescents (Reynolds & Coats, 1986).

PST was found superior to nonspecific- and minimal-treatment controls in adult populations, but again, studies have lacked clinical realism (Nezu, 1986; Nezu & Perri, 1989). How the approach will fare in more clinically representative trials remains to be seen. PST was effective in the treatment of suicidal adolescents (Lerner & Clum, 1990) and reduced depression and hopelessness in patients with a history of repeated suicide attempts (Salkovskis, Atha, & Storer, 1990).

Finally, Lewinsohn and colleagues developed a psychoeducational approach for the prevention and treatment of depression that incorporates cognitive strategies into a more conventional behavioral framework. Initial trials in adult samples were somewhat supportive, although the magnitude of change was not always large and the approach did not always prove superior to minimal-treatment controls (e.g., Brown & Lewinsohn, 1984; Teri & Lewinsohn, 1986). However, a modified version of the approach was found superior to a wait-list control in the treatment of depressed adolescents, with some indication that the inclusion of parent training enhanced response even further (Lewinsohn, Clarke, Hops, & Andrews, 1990).

Summary

The cognitive and cognitive-behavioral interventions appear to be effective in the treatment of depression. CT, in particular, has been extensively tested in clinical populations. It appears to be no less effective than pharmacotherapy with respect to the reduction of acute distress and may be superior with respect to the reduction of subsequent risk. The other cognitive-behavioral interventions have fared well in more limited trials and have shown promise in the treatment of children and adolescents.

Nonetheless, more needs to be done. With respect to CT, additional placebo-controlled comparisons with antidepressant medications are warranted, particularly in light of the NIMH collaborative findings, and further studies are needed to determine whether CT's preventive effect extends to recurrence. With respect to the other cognitive-behavioral interventions, controlled trials in fully clinical populations are desired.

PANIC AND THE ANXIETY DISORDERS

Some of the most exciting work in the last decade has been in the treatment of panic and the anxiety disorders. The controlled trials available at the time of the previous *Handbook* tended to lack clinical realism; most involved studies in which subclinical volunteers were treated by inexperienced therapists for relatively minor disorders, such as assertion deficits or evaluation anxiety (Hollon & Beck, 1986). The few studies with truly clinical populations suggested that the cognitive and cognitive-

behavioral interventions were less effective than, or did little to enhance the efficacy of, more purely behavioral approaches. Subsequent and more methodologically adequate studies have indicated that that is not the case. For at least some of the anxiety disorders, the cognitive and cognitive-behavioral interventions appear to be at least as effective as, and possibly more enduring than, the best of the available alternatives.

Catastrophic Cognitions in Panic and Agoraphobia

The efficacy of the cognitive and cognitive-behavioral interventions is readily apparent in the treatment of panic disorder. Cognitive theory suggests that the tendency to interpret benign bodily sensations as signs of impending physical or mental catastrophe, such as a heart attack or psychotic decompensation, is central to the development of panic disorder (Beck & Emery, 1985; Clark, 1986). Once such a misinterpretation is made, the individual succumbs to a vicious cycle in which the panic reaction triggered by the misperception is taken as further confirmation that some type of physical or psychological catastrophe is imminent. Some individuals then begin to avoid situations in which they think such catastrophes are likely to occur or in which they think assistance would be difficult to obtain, hence the development of agoraphobia. In contrast, behavior theory views panic as a conditioned response to external cues that is preserved from extinction by negatively reinforced avoidance behaviors (Marks, 1987), and biological theory assumes that panic is the consequence of the spontaneous discharge of neural centers mediating response to stress (Klein, 1981).

PCT (Barlow & Cerny, 1988) and focused CT (Beck & Emery, 1985; Clark & Salkovskis, 1991) both focus specifically on catastrophic cognitions. The two overlap to a considerable extent, but also differ somewhat in their emphases. PCT incorporates a broad range of behavioral and coping techniques, including relaxation training, whereas focused CT relies more exclusively on the reinterpretation of bodily sensations. Both make use of interoceptive exposure (the induction of feared bodily sensations via hyperventilation or other means), but in different ways and for different reasons. PCT makes extensive use of interoceptive exposure because it assumes that classical extinction is a mediating mechanism and that repeated exposure is necessary to produce change. Interoceptive exposure is repeated less extensively in focused CT and is used largely to test beliefs about the implications of the experienced sensations.

Early studies with the cognitive and cognitive-behavioral interventions were largely unimpressive, but tested generic treatments that did not explicitly focus on catastrophic misinterpretations. Moreover, the cognitive treatments used in these studies were often superficial in nature and marginal in their quality of execution. For example, Emmelkamp and colleagues found cognitive restructuring, purportedly based on RET, less effective than exposure alone in a series of studies with agoraphobic samples (Emmelkamp, Brilman, Kuiper, & Mersch, 1986; Emmelkamp, Kuipers, & Eggeraat, 1978; Emmelkamp & Mersch, 1982). However, the cognitive intervention consisted of exhortations to adopt more positive beliefs provided by graduate-student therapists. Although some qualitative reviews have suggested that therapist competence is unrelated to clinical outcome (Berman & Norton, 1985; Robinson et al., 1990), this does not appear to be the case for the cognitive interventions (Burns & Nolen-Hoeksema, 1992; Lyons & Woods, 1991). Similarly, self-statement training was found to add little to in vivo exposure in three studies (Emmelkamp & Mersch, 1982; Mavissakalian, Michelson, Greenwald, Kornblith, & Greenwald, 1983; Williams & Rappoport, 1983), although, again, none of the cognitive interventions was explicitly targeted at catastrophic misinterpretations and the quality of execution was often quite limited.

Interventions that have focused explicitly on catastrophic cognitions have been more successful. Barlow and colleagues found a forerunner of PCT superior to a wait-list control in a sample of patients with either panic or generalized anxiety disorder (Barlow et al., 1984). In a subsequent study, Barlow and colleagues found PCT, with or without relaxation training, superior to a wait-list control and, on some measures, relaxation training as well (Barlow, Craske, Cerny, & Klosko, 1989). Patients treated with PCT alone were more likely to be panic free at a 2-year follow-up than patients treated with relaxation training alone, whereas patients treated with PCT plus relaxation training were not (Craske, Brown, & Barlow, 1991). Finally, this same group found PCT, but not alprazolam, superior to pill-placebo and a wait-list control in the treatment of panic disorder (Klosko, Barlow, Tassinari, & Cerny, 1990). Of the patients completing the trial, over 85 percent of the PCT patients were panic free at the end of treatment, compared with about 50 percent of the alprazolam patients and only about 35 percent of the patients in the placebo and wait-list controls. Moreover, patients had real difficulty withdrawing from alprazolam, a high-potency benzodiazepine that tends to provoke rebound panic attacks when discontinued.

Results with focused CT have also been impressive. Focused CT totally eliminated panic attacks in an open trial with 17 panic-disordered patients, all of whom remained panic free at a 1-year follow-up (Sokol, Beck, Greenberg, Wright, & Berchick, 1989). In a subsequent study, Beck and colleagues found CT superior to a nonspecific supportive therapy in a sample comprising mostly patients with panic disorder and a few with agoraphobia (Beck, Sokol, Clark, Berchick, & Wright, 1992). At the end of 8 weeks of treatment, over 70 percent of the patients treated with focused CT were panic free, compared with only about 25 percent of the patients treated with supportive therapy. Twelve months following treatment termination, nearly 90 percent of the patients originally treated with focused CT were panic free, as were over 75 percent of the patients crossed over to focused CT following treatment with supportive therapy.

In the most impressive study to date, Clark and colleagues found focused CT superior to both applied relaxation and imipramine pharmacotherapy in a sample of patients with panic disorder, with all three conditions superior to a wait-list control (Clark, Salkovskis, Hackmann, Middleton, & Gelder, 1992). As shown in Figure 10.2, nearly 90 percent of the patients treated with focused CT were panic free at the end of 3 months of intensive treatment versus only about 50 percent of the patients treated with either applied relaxation or imipramine pharmacotherapy and virtually none of the patients assigned to the wait-list control. Focused CT also produced greater change in catastrophic cognitions, as well as anxiety and avoidance, than did the other conditions. Medications were continued for 6 months and then withdrawn, with patients in the psychosocial conditions receiving only a limited number of booster sessions between Months 3 and 6. All patients were then followed across the next 9 months. During the follow-up period, only 5 percent of the patients previously treated with focused CT relapsed, compared with 40 percent of the pharmacotherapy patients. Consistent with theory, patients who reported fewer catastrophic cognitions at the end of treatment were at lower risk for subsequent relapse.

This study is important in that imipramine is at least as effective as and less difficult to withdraw than alternative pharmacological agents, such as alprazolam, for the treatment of panic (Michelson & Marchione, 1991). Similarly, applied relaxation training is an especially promising behavioral intervention. Finding focused CT superior to both, in a study in which all three appear to have been competently executed, suggests that the cognitive intervention may be particularly effective in the treatment of panic disorder.

Focused CT has also fared well in studies by

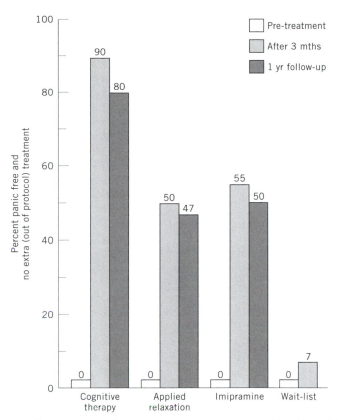

FIGURE 10.2 Percentage of patients panic free and not receiving treatment. *Note.* From "Cognitive Therapy for Panic Disorder" by D.M. Clark, in press, in B.E. Wolfe and J.D. Maser, Eds., *Treatment of Panic Disorder: A Consensus Development Conference,* Washington, DC, American Psychiatric Press. Copyright © 1994 by the American Psychiatric Press. Reprinted by permission.

investigators other than its originators, although there is less evidence for its specificity in those trials. Ost (1991) found focused CT at least as effective as his own applied relaxation training. Margraf and Schneider (1991) found no differences among cognitive restructuring, interoceptive exposure, and their combination, although all three were superior to a wait-list control. In both trials, the proportion of patients who became panic free was comparable to that observed in the studies already cited (Beck, Sokol, et al., 1992; Clark et al., 1992). Michelson and colleagues found that agoraphobic patients with panic disorder were nearly twice as likely to be panic free at the end of treatment as were patients treated with exposure alone; patients treated with relaxation training plus grade exposure were intermediate and not significantly different from either of the other two conditions (Michelson, Marchione, & Greenwald, 1989). This study is important because it suggests that focused CT can reduce panic frequency in patients with agoraphobia. More work is needed, in particular with respect to agoraphobic populations, but it

is hard to imagine a more promising set of initial findings.

Generalized Anxiety Disorder and the Competence of Implementation

The cognitive and cognitive-behavioral interventions also appear to be effective for the treatment of generalized anxiety disorder (GAD). According to cognitive theory, chronic and diffuse states of anxious overarousal are largely the product of a systematic tendency to overestimate the presence of danger across situations and to underestimate one's ability to cope with those risks (Beck & Emery, 1985). According to this theory, any intervention that reduces the unrealistic perception of danger or enhances the perception of one's ability to cope with threat should reduce distress. Exposure and systematic desensitization are of little use in GAD, because there are no apparent external stimuli to target; behavioral efforts have primarily centered on helping clients learn to use relaxation-based methods to manage their own internal states (Barlow, 1988). Pharmacological interventions, such as the benzodiazepines, provide some relief and are widely prescribed, but can induce dependence and appear to lose potency with prolonged use (Committee on the Review of Medicines, 1980).

Early studies of the cognitive interventions were unimpressive, but typically tested simplistic versions of the approach (e.g., Ramm, Marks, Yuksel, & Stern, 1981; Woodward & Jones, 1980). Subsequent studies that incorporated somewhat more sophisticated cognitive components into largely behavioral interventions produced more promising results (Barlow et al., 1984; Borkovec & Costello, in press; Borkovec et al., 1987; Butler, Cullington, Hibbert, Klimes, & Gelder, 1987). The specificity of these interventions is open to question, however, as they have not always proved superior to more purely behavioral or supportive interventions (Blowers, Cobb, & Mathews, 1987; Borkovec & Mathews, 1988).

Studies that have used even more sophisticated cognitive approaches have suggested still greater efficacy. Durham and Turvey (1987) found that CT produced more stable gains across a 6-month posttreatment follow-up than did the combination of relaxation plus graded exposure. CT also produced greater change in dysfunctional attitudes, although no test was made for mediation. In an elegantly crafted study, Butler and colleagues found cognitive-behavioral therapy modeled after CT superior to behavioral therapy alone (relaxation training plus graded exposure), with both superior to a wait-list control in a clinical outpatient sample (Butler, Fennell, Robson, & Gelder, 1991). As shown in Figure 10.3, the cognitive-behavioral intervention produced not only greater change in both symptoms and beliefs, but also greater stability of change across an extended posttreatment follow-up.

This study was particularly noteworthy for the care that went into ensuring that both treatments were well executed. The group that conducted the study has a long history of involvement in behavioral treatment research and can be considered expert with that approach. In addition, study therapists received intensive training in CT at the Center for Cognitive Therapy in Philadelphia prior to par-

ticipation. Supervision by senior research personnel expert in each modality was ongoing, and independent raters monitored the fidelity of treatment implementation. This study can be considered a model of how comparative research ought to be conducted.

The cognitive and cognitive-behavioral interventions have also fared well in direct comparisons with pharmacotherapy. Lindsay and colleagues found that although lorazepam (a benzodiazepine) produced more rapid initial response than did cognitive-behavioral therapy (based loosely on both CT and self-instructional training) or relaxation training, patients treated pharmacologically were reluctant to stop taking medications and were particularly likely to relapse if drugs were withdrawn (Lindsay, Gamsu, McLaughlin, Hood, & Espie, 1987). Power and colleagues found CT, supplemented with brief relaxation training, superior to pharmacotherapy in a pair of studies with general practice patients. In the first, cognitive-behavioral therapy was superior to both diazepam and a pill-placebo at both posttreatment and 12-month follow-up (Power, Jerrom, Simpson, Mitchell, & Swanson, 1989). In the second, cognitive-behavioral therapy both proved superior to pill-placebo and enhanced the efficacy of diazepam alone, and exhibited better maintenance of gains (and less frequent return to treatment), during a 6-month follow-up (Power et al., 1990). These findings suggest that cognitive interventions may be both more effective and longer lasting than pharmacotherapy in the treatment of GAD.

The cognitive and cognitive-behavioral interventions thus seem to be effective in the treatment of generalized anxiety disorder, especially those versions that use more sophisticated approaches to changing beliefs. They have generally been found superior to minimal- or nonspecific-treatment controls and to compare favorably with, and enhance the efficacy of, more purely behavioral or pharmacological interventions, particularly with respect to the stability of treatment gains. These findings are all the more striking because they were often produced by research groups with decidedly behavioral orientations. Although the studies are still too few to be conclusive, they suggest a possible speci-

---

FIGURE 10.3 The pattern of change in three domains: anxiety, depression, and cognition. (BAI = Beck Anxiety Inventory; CBT = cognitive-behavioral therapy; BT = behavioral therapy; WL = wait-list; STAI-T = State-Trait Anxiety Inventory — Trait; Hamilton = Hamilton Anxiety Scale; BDI = Beck Depression Inventory; DAS = Dysfunctional Attitude Scale.) *Note.* From "Comparison of Behavior Therapy and Cognitive Behavior Therapy in the Treatment of Generalized Anxiety Disorder" by G. Butler, M. Fennell, P. Robson, and M. Gelder, 1991, *Journal of Consulting and Clinical Psychology, 59,* p. 173. Copyright © 1991 by the American Psychological Association. Reprinted by permission.

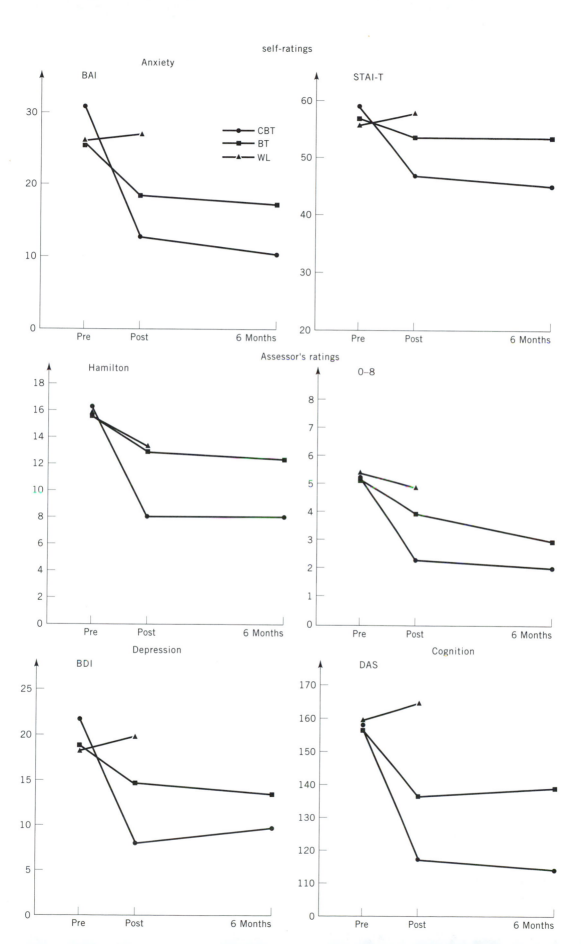

ficity of effect for the cognitive and cognitive-behavioral interventions that may transcend that found for other approaches.

Interpersonal Anxiety and Social Phobia

Social phobia involves an undue fear of evaluation by others and the accompanying desire to avoid situations in which such scrutiny is anticipated. According to cognitive theory, persons with social phobia have an underlying belief that they are defective or inadequate in some way that will be exposed in social situations, leading to ridicule or censure from others (Beck & Emery, 1985). Because the symptoms of the disorder appear to flow so clearly from these beliefs, it has long been suggested that cognitive interventions might prove to be particularly effective in its treatment. Behavior theory has focused on deficits in social skills or on the inhibiting effect of conditioned anxiety; both social skills training and anxiety-reduction methods, such as desensitization and exposure, have proved somewhat effective (Heimberg, 1989). Recent pharmacological trials have suggested good results with the monoamine oxidase inhibitors (MAOIs; see, for example, Liebowitz et al., 1992). However, little is known about the long-term effects of such drugs.

At the time of the prior review, the majority of the existing studies involved analogue populations selected on the basis of elevated evaluation anxiety or interpersonal concerns (Hollon & Beck, 1986). In those studies, any of several cognitive interventions (with or without behavioral components) typically proved superior to minimal-contact or nonspecific-treatment controls and at least equaled, or enhanced the efficacy of, more purely behavioral interventions. In general, the more competently executed the study, the more compelling the support for the cognitive intervention. Initial trials with fully clinical populations were not so encouraging, as cognitive interventions were either less effective than, or failed to enhance the efficacy of, more purely behavioral approaches (Biran, Augusto, & Wilson, 1981; Emmelkamp, Mersch, Vissia, & van der Helm, 1985; Stravynski, Marks, & Yule, 1982). However, these studies were conducted by groups better known for their expertise with behavioral therapy; the cognitive interventions again tended to be simplistic in nature and the therapists, usually graduate students, relatively inexperienced with the approach.

Subsequent studies that provided more adequate cognitive operationalizations were more supportive of the efficacy of the approach. Butler and colleagues found that the addition of a somewhat more sophisticated cognitive-restructuring component facilitated the maintenance of treatment gains

associated with guided exposure (Butler, Cullington, Munby, Amies, & Gelder, 1984), as did Mattick and colleagues in a pair of studies (Mattick & Peters, 1988; Mattick, Peters, & Clarke, 1989). Gelernter and colleagues found cognitive restructuring somewhat less effective than phenelzine and no more effective than either alprazolam or a pill-placebo control in an outpatient sample (all patients were encouraged to engage in guided exposure), but also found indications that treatment gains were better maintained following the cognitive-behavioral intervention than following pharmacotherapy (Gelernter et al., 1991).

Heimberg (in press) developed a sophisticated combination of cognitive restructuring and guided exposure for use in a group context that has performed well in empirical studies. An early trial with a multiple-baseline design found good response among seven patients with social phobia, with treatment gains for the most part maintained across a 6-month follow-up (Heimberg, Becker, Goldfinger, & Vermilyea, 1985). In a subsequent trial, cognitive-behavioral therapy proved superior to supportive therapy, again in a clinical sample (Heimberg et al., 1990). An extended follow-up suggested that differential gains were evident up to 5 years after treatment termination (Heimberg, Salzman, Holt, & Blendell, 1993). In a multisite comparison, cognitive-behavioral group therapy proved to be as effective as phenelzine pharmacotherapy, and both were superior to supportive group therapy or a pill-placebo control (Heimberg & Liebowitz, 1992). Although full details are not yet available and the posttreatment follow-up is ongoing, this study appears to be the most elegantly crafted treatment comparison in the social-phobia literature, with fully clinical samples receiving state-of-the-art interventions from experienced professional therapists under the supervision of recognized experts in the respective modalities.

The cognitive and cognitive-behavioral interventions thus appear to be effective in the treatment of social phobia and related interpersonal concerns. Although early studies in fully clinical samples were not particularly supportive, subsequent and more competently executed trials suggest that these interventions compare favorably with more purely behavioral or pharmacological interventions, most notably with respect to the stability of treatment gains.

Simple Phobias and the Perception of Danger

Simple phobias comprise an intense fear of certain objects or situations and a corresponding desire to avoid being in their presence. According to cognitive theory, individuals with simple phobias perceive greater risk of bodily harm or danger in the feared situation than do other people, although they may be able to recognize that their fears are unwarranted when not in the phobic situation (Beck & Emery, 1985). According to behavior theory, simple phobias are established via traumatic (classical) conditioning and maintained by avoidance behaviors that protect them from extinction (Marks, 1987). Behavioral interventions, such as systematic desensitization or exposure plus response prevention, are clearly effective and are considered the standard for treatment. Pharmacological interventions have proved largely unsatisfying, with the minor tranquilizers providing little more than temporary relief and carrying a considerable risk for dependence.

Only a handful of studies have examined the efficacy of the cognitive and cognitive-behavioral interventions in the treatment of simple phobias, all available at the time of the previous review (Hollon & Beck, 1986). Although cognitive interventions were typically found superior to minimal-treatment controls and no less effective than more purely behavioral interventions, few of these studies were especially compelling. Samples were generally small and subclinical; treatments brief and superficial; and the therapists often inexperienced graduate students. Cognitive restructuring fared poorly in the one study conducted in a clinical population (Biran & Wilson, 1981). In that trial, patients phobic with respect to heights, darkness, or elevators showed greater change if treated with guided exposure than if treated with cognitive restructuring. However, the cognitive intervention was again operationalized in a less than optimal fashion; treatment was brief and somewhat superficial (subjects were simply encouraged to replace problematic self-statements with more positive ones), and the therapists were relatively inexperienced graduate students.

Thus, although the existing empirical literature provides little support for the utility of the cognitive and cognitive-behavioral interventions in the treatment of simple phobias, it is not clear that these approaches have been adequately tested. Additional trials in clinical populations are needed that do justice to the theoretical models. Given the apparent success of the cognitive interventions with other types of anxiety disorders, such efforts are warranted.

Obsessive-Compulsive Disorder and Personal Responsibility

According to cognitive theory, obsessions involve the recurrent perception that one has placed oneself or others at risk through some action or failure to act; compulsions consist of attempts to undo this risk through some type of subsequent action (Beck,

1976). From a cognitive perspective, the issue of personal responsibility looms large; it is this theme that is believed to most distinguish obsessive-compulsive disorder (OCD) from the other anxiety disorders, which have more generic perceptions of danger. In a recent theoretical article, Salkovskis (1985) suggested that it is the propensity to assign blame or responsibility to oneself, rather than the occurrence of the threat-related intrusive thoughts, that is the critical feature in OCD.

Behavior theory views OCD as a product of traumatic conditioning and subsequent negative reinforcement, whereas biological theory views it as the consequence of dysregulation in central neurotransmitter systems. Although OCD was once considered largely intractable, it is now known that many patients respond to fairly brief interventions, notably behavioral exposure plus response prevention or the serotonin reuptake blockers (Christensen, Hadzi-Pavlovic, Andrews, & Mattick, 1987). However, although behavioral interventions reduce compulsive behaviors, they are less effective with ruminations and appear to be of little use with patients who are free of compulsions (Salkovskis & Westbrook, 1989). Similarly, there is little evidence that the therapeutic gains achieved with pharmacotherapy are maintained after treatment termination (Christensen et al., 1987).

Tests of the cognitive and cognitive-behavioral interventions in the treatment of OCD have been few and, with a single exception, all conducted by a single behaviorally oriented research group. In those studies, Emmelkamp and colleagues found no differences between exposure therapy and either self-statement training or RET (Emmelkamp & Beens, 1991; Emmelkamp, van der Helm, van Zanten, & Plochg, 1980; Emmelkamp, Visser, & Hoekstra, 1988). However, these studies were marginal in quality. The samples were small, the therapists relatively inexperienced graduate students, and the cognitive interventions somewhat unsophisticated (particularly in the earliest trial). Nonetheless, it is worth noting that these marginal cognitive interventions performed as well as they did. Salkovskis and Westbrook (1989) proposed that patients free of overt compulsions may engage in covert cognitive rituals that serve the same functions. They suggested that such patients be prevented from engaging in these cognitive rituals so as to heighten their exposure to the anxiety-inducing obsessive thoughts, and they described a series of clinical cases in which such cognitive exposure plus response prevention produced better results than did standard habituation training.

Despite the availability of sophisticated clinical theory, little is known about the efficacy of the cognitive and cognitive-behavioral interventions for

OCD. Controlled empirical trials have been few and, for the most part, marginal in nature. Nonetheless, the findings have not been wholly negative. Given that early studies with the other anxiety disorders appeared to underestimate the efficacy of the cognitive and cognitive-behavioral interventions, additional trials that do a more competent job of operationalizing those approaches are indicated.

Post-Traumatic Stress Disorder

Exposure to traumatic events outside the range of normal human experience can produce a clinical syndrome known as post-traumatic stress disorder (PTSD). Although it shares the symptoms of increased arousal and persistent avoidance with the phobic disorders, other symptoms, such as flashbacks and intrusive recollections or affective constriction and a sense of interpersonal detachment, are relatively distinct. Foa and colleagues argued that an adequate account of the disorder must consider the subjective meaning of the traumatic event and proposed that cognitive-behavioral interventions designed to identify and address those problematic beliefs can be of use in treating PTSD (Foa, Steketee, & Rothbaum, 1989).

The cognitive-behavioral interventions have been tested in two controlled studies, both involving women who were victims of sexual assault. Resick and colleagues found brief SIT comparable to assertion training or supportive psychotherapy, with all three active treatment conditions superior to a wait-list control (Resick, Jordan, Girelli, Hutter, & Marhoefer-Dvorak, 1988). Treatment gains were generally maintained through a 6-month follow-up. Foa and colleagues found a somewhat more extensive course of SIT superior to supportive counseling or a wait-list control; prolonged exposure was intermediate and did not differ from any of the other conditions (Foa, Rothbaum, Riggs, & Murdock, 1991). Patients treated with SIT showed some loss of gains after treatment termination, whereas patients treated with prolonged exposure continued to improve, although differences were not significant.

These initial studies suggest that SIT may have a role to play in the treatment of PTSD, although additional work needs to address the issues of specificity and stability. Neither of the existing studies operationalized treatment in an optimal fashion. Treatment provided by Resick and colleagues was brief and simplistic, whereas that provided by Foa and colleagues seemed overstructured and not well integrated. Although a more intensive, flexible, and integrated approach to treatment might produce even stronger effects, the initial findings are at least somewhat promising.

Summary

Recent studies suggest that the cognitive and cognitive-behavioral interventions may be particularly effective in the treatment of panic disorder, GAD, and social phobia. Recent trials have been more supportive than early ones, perhaps because of the increasing sophistication with which the interventions have been operationalized. Indications that these approaches may produce enduring effects not found with alternative interventions are particularly exciting. The cognitive and cognitive-behavioral interventions have not been as adequately tested in the treatment of OCD or PTSD, although initial studies have been somewhat supportive, and adequate tests have yet to be conducted in the treatment of simple phobias. Although more work is needed, it appears that the cognitive and cognitive-behavioral interventions may be particularly effective and long lasting in the treatment of at least some of the anxiety disorders.

EATING DISORDERS AND OBESITY

The eating disorders represent yet another diagnostic group in which the cognitive and cognitive-behavioral interventions have met with success. Aberrant beliefs about food and weight appear to play a particularly important role in these disorders (Vitousek & Hollon, 1990). Recent controlled clinical trials suggest that cognitive-behavioral therapy may be effective in the treatment of bulimia nervosa. Less has been done in the treatment of anorexia nervosa, although a sophisticated clinical approach has been proposed, which has not been done with respect to the treatment of obesity.

Bulimia Nervosa and the Mechanisms of Change

Bulimia nervosa is a disorder characterized by a chaotic eating pattern that consists of extreme dieting punctuated by episodes of binge eating and subsequent efforts to purge, typically via vomiting, laxative abuse, or fasting (Fairburn, Agras, & Wilson, 1992). Self-esteem is often poor and associated psychopathology, particularly affective distress and substance abuse, is common. Initially thought to be refractory to treatment, recent studies suggest that the disorder is quite responsive to a number of different interventions, including both cognitive-behavioral therapy and certain antidepressants (Craighead & Agras, 1991).

Cognitive theory states that overvalued ideas concerning body weight and shape and unrealistic beliefs about what should and should not be eaten, often driven by underlying doubts about self-worth and attractiveness to others, play a major role in the etiology and maintenance of bulimia nervosa (Fairburn, 1981). According to this view, these beliefs lead to excessive dietary restraint, which in turn increases risk for losing control and engaging in episodes of binge eating, particularly under stress. Once a binge has occurred, purge behaviors are used in an effort to avoid weight gain. This theory contrasts with a more purely behavioral model that views binge behaviors as negatively reinforced by the anxiety reduction produced by the subsequent purge (Rosen & Leitenberg, 1982), or a biological model that views bulimia nervosa as a consequence of an excessive craving for carbohydrates produced by a deficit in central serotonin regulation (Wurtman, 1987).

Therapies based on cognitive theory usually incorporate both behavioral and cognitive components, with the former emphasized in the early sessions and the latter coming increasingly into play as treatment proceeds (Fairburn, 1981). Behavioral components include self-monitoring food intake and binge–purge behaviors and using simple behavioral prescriptions to establish more regular eating patterns. Cognitive components typically involve efforts to identify and change beliefs regarding food, weight, and body image, particularly those that interfere with carrying out the behavioral prescriptions. Some versions of therapy incorporate adjunctive strategies, such as exposure plus response prevention, relaxation training, or assertion training. Still others deal explicitly with underlying concerns about the self and interpersonal relationships believed to contribute to the development and maintenance of the disorder. Whether such strategies are included appears to depend on the nature of the conceptual approach driving the particular program (Garner, Fairburn, & Davis, 1987).

There is little doubt that cognitive-behavioral therapy is effective in the treatment of bulimia nervosa (Wilson & Fairburn, 1993). It has been found superior to wait-list or minimal-treatment controls in numerous comparisons and has typically equaled or exceeded alternative interventions, including both behavioral therapy and pharmacotherapy, in direct comparisons. Across these studies, nearly 80 percent of all patients treated for bulimia nervosa have shown a reduction in binge and purge behaviors and nearly 60 percent have become abstinent with regard to those symptoms (Craighead & Agras, 1991). Treatment is generally well tolerated, and change appears to be well maintained following treatment termination.

A recent well-crafted study by Fairburn and colleagues is illustrative. In that study, cognitive-behavioral therapy produced greater change in dietary restraint and beliefs about shape and weight than did either behavioral therapy or IPT and greater change in purge behaviors than did IPT; all three interventions produced comparable reductions in binge behaviors and associated psychopathology (Fairburn et al., 1991). As shown in Figure 10.4, a posttreatment follow-up indicated that treatment gains were better maintained among patients who had received cognitive-behavioral therapy than among those who had received behavioral therapy alone (Fairburn, Jones, Peveler, Hope, & O'Connor, 1993). Moreover, residual level of attitudinal disturbance regarding shape and weight at posttreatment predicted subsequent relapse following treatment termination (Fairburn, Peveler, Jones, Hope, & Doll, in press). Patients treated with IPT continued to improve after the end of treatment, suggesting that attention to more generic beliefs about the self and interpersonal relationships can have a delayed effect on bulimic behaviors. This effect appears to be robust, as supportive-expressive psychotherapy also had a delayed effect on dietary restraint and attitudes about weight in a separate study (Garner, Rockert, et al., 1993).

The cognitive and cognitive-behavioral interventions have also fared well in comparisons with pharmacotherapy. Mitchell and colleagues found a structured group therapy containing both cognitive and behavioral components superior to imipramine alone in a placebo-controlled trial (Mitchell et al., 1990). The addition of medication added little to group therapy with respect to the reduction of bulimic behaviors, although it did facilitate change in depression. A subsequent 6-month follow-up indicated that patients who received group therapy were less likely to relapse following treatment termination than were patients who did not, whether medications were continued or not (Pyle et al., 1990). Similarly, Agras and colleagues found cognitive-behavioral therapy (with or without medications) superior to desipramine pharmacotherapy alone, with respect to acute response and the maintenance of treatment gains (Agras et al., 1992). These studies suggest that cognitive-behavioral therapy is both more effective and more enduring than drugs for bulimia nervosa.

Pharmacotherapy and cognitive-behavioral therapy may work through different mechanisms (Craighead & Agras, 1991). Antidepressant medications appear to be effective in the treatment of bulimia nervosa because they suppress appetite; that is, they make it easier for bulimic patients to restrict their food intake and thereby decrease the urge to binge. Cognitive-behavioral therapy, on the other hand, appears to decrease the need to diet, as shown by an increase in nonpurged calories not evident in pharmacotherapy (Rossiter, Agras, Losch, & Telch, 1988), possibly as a consequence

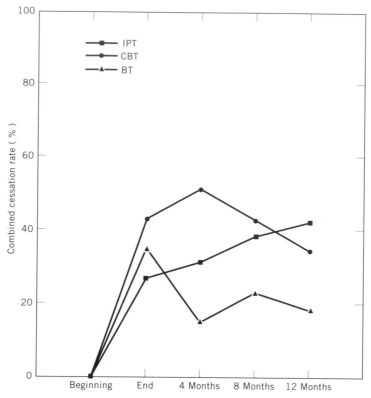

FIGURE 10.4 Proportions of patients ($N = 75$) receiving cognitive-behavioral therapy (CBT), behavioral therapy (BT), or interpersonal psychotherapy (IPT) who no longer purged or had bulimic episodes. *Note.* From C. G. Fairburn, R. Jones, et al. (1993). "Psychotherapy and Bulimia Nervosa: Longer-Term Effects of Interpersonal Psychotherapy, Behavior Therapy and Cognitive Behavior Therapy," by C.G. Fairburn, R. Jones, R.C. Peveler, R.A. Hope, and M. O'Connor, 1993, *Archives of General Psychiatry, 50,* p. 419. Copyright © 1993 by the American Medical Association. Reprinted by permission.

of changing aberrant beliefs about food and weight (see, for example, Fairburn et al., 1991). Pharmacotherapy may thus be effective because it facilitates acting on a pathological desire to diet, whereas cognitive-behavioral therapy may deal more directly with those problematic desires (Craighead & Agras, 1991).

One caveat is in order. Despite the apparent success of the cognitive and cognitive-behavioral approaches, it is still not clear that they have been operationalized in the most powerful manner possible. Attention has often been restricted to specific beliefs regarding weight and food, rather than extended to include more generic concerns about self-worth and the nature of interpersonal relationships. Moreover, little use is made of standard cognitive techniques, such as charting beliefs and using specific lines of inquiry to evaluate their accuracy (e.g., evidence, alternatives, and implications). It might be possible to produce even greater and more enduring change by enhancing the depth and power of the cognitive strategies.

Anorexia Nervosa and the Ascetics of Self-Denial

Anorexia nervosa involves a pervasive pattern of self-starvation, often to the point that weight loss becomes life threatening. Anorexia nervosa shares the same misguided beliefs about food and weight found in bulimia nervosa, but also involves the notion that exercising control over physiological desires is consistent with a higher ascetic ideal (Garner & Bemis, 1982). Treatment is complicated not only by the rigidity of the beliefs regarding the consequences of becoming fat, but also by the sense of accomplishment that accompanies the pursuit of thinness. Garner and Bemis argued that these beliefs are so entrenched that efforts to challenge their validity early in treatment are likely to fail. They recommended that patients first be encouraged to consider the functionality of their beliefs (i.e., whether it is really worth the time and effort required to so thoroughly deny their appetites), before gradually shifting the focus of therapy to a more conventional examination of the validity of the beliefs themselves and questioning the ascetic ideals that fuel the sense of accomplishment through self-denial. The importance of thinness is examined in relation to other life goals, and considerable attention is paid to underlying concerns about self-worth and interpersonal relationships.

This approach remains virtually untested. In an open trial with a small sample, Cooper and Fairburn (1984) found that cognitive-behavioral therapy was effective with bulimic anorexics but not those who only restrict. However, treatment was largely directed at specific beliefs about weight and food. In the only controlled trial in the literature, Channon and colleagues found little evidence that cognitive-behavioral therapy was superior to either standard behavioral therapy or a nonspecific control (Channon, de Silva, Hemsley, & Perkins, 1989). However, the sample was small and the quality of treatment suspect. Sessions were infrequent for such a severely disturbed population, and all treatment was provided by a single therapist of unknown competence. Most importantly, despite claiming to follow Garner and Bemis's recommendations, efforts at cognitive change were directed exclusively at specific beliefs about weight and shape, rather than also addressing the importance of thinness as a life goal and more generic concerns about the self.

Thus, although a coherent cognitive approach to the treatment of anorexia nervosa has been articulated, it has yet to be adequately tested. Whether this approach will improve on the limited success afforded by existing treatments remains to be determined, but careful tests of efficacy are clearly desired.

Obesity and Weight Regain

There is considerable controversy as to whether it is possible to produce lasting weight loss through purely psychosocial means in people who are obese (Garner & Wooley, 1991). It has become clear over the last two decades that basic behavioral therapy programs produce weight loss in most obese individuals (Foreyt, 1987). However, the majority of those individuals regain most of the weight lost within a few years of treatment termination (Brownell & Jeffery, 1987). Although extending the length of treatment appears to increase weight loss and building in posttreatment contacts appears to slow the process of weight regain, these strategies may simply forestall the inevitable. Given that the medical risks of obesity may be more closely tied to gaining weight than to being obese and given that an obsessive preoccupation with weight loss can lead to demoralization and the development of pathological eating habits, some investigators have

suggested that dieting be discouraged altogether (Garner & Wooley, 1991). Others are less pessimistic, calling instead for the adoption of more gradual weight loss strategies and more realistic goals regarding what can be accomplished (Brownell & Wadden, 1992).

There currently exists no specific cognitive theory of obesity. This may be a consequence of the absence of studies that simply characterize cognitive patterns in obese individuals. However, there continues to be a sense that beliefs and attitudes play a role in mediating behaviors relevant to weight regulation, particularly with respect to the maintenance of change following successful weight loss. Studies have shown that the addition of relapse-prevention or problem-solving training to more purely behavioral programs can slow the process of weight regain (see, for example, Perri et al., 1988), but these cognitive components are little more than minor adjuncts to more prominent behavioral techniques, and their independent contribution to change or its maintenance has only rarely been assessed.

Several studies have examined the efficacy of largely cognitive or cognitive-behavioral interventions in the treatment of obesity. Dunkel and Glaros (1978) found self-instructional training superior to either behavioral self-control or relaxation training in terms of sustained weight loss. However, the quality of the treatments was suspect (descriptions were sketchy and the therapists were inexperienced graduate students), and massive attrition rendered the findings largely uninterpretable. In a more methodologically adequate trial, Collins and colleagues found that a purely cognitive intervention was less effective than, and did not add to the efficacy of, behavioral therapy alone, but they also relied on graduate-student therapists (Collins, Rothblum, & Wilson, 1986). Self-instructional training proved no more effective than nonspecific controls and less effective than behavioral therapy in a pair of trials that used professional therapists but relied on a rather superficial version of cognitive-behavioral therapy (Bennett, 1986a, 1986b). Finally, Marcus and colleagues found that the addition of a rather simplistic version of self-statement training did little to enhance or maintain weight loss produced by a more purely behavioral intervention (Marcus, Wing, & Hopkins, 1988). Thus, the existing literature provides little support for the utility of cognitive components in the treatment of obesity, although it is not clear that these studies provided a particularly adequate test. At the same time, there are indications that the efficacy of the cognitive-behavioral interventions in the treatment of bulimia nervosa extends to nonpurging obese patients who

order. Three overlapping approaches have generated particular interest, including Novaco's (1975) modification of SIT for use in anger-provoking situations, adaptations of self-instructional and perspective-taking training (Kendall & Braswell, 1985), and approaches to PST suitable for children and adolescents (Spivak et al., 1976). Each of these approaches uses a combination of cognitive and behavioral components in a structured fashion to facilitate the acquisition of skills designed to foster a more thoughtful and deliberate approach to frustrating situations and interpersonal conflict. Novaco's modification of SIT was originally intended for use with adult populations and has shown some promise in that regard (Hollon & Beck, 1986). However, little work has been done with that approach with adults since publication of the previous *Handbook*.

Early studies with aggressive or conduct-disordered children largely emphasized the use of SIT or self-instructional training. In most instances, these programs proved superior to minimal-treatment controls and at least comparable to more purely behavioral interventions (e.g., Camp, Blom, Hebert, & van Doornick, 1977; Lochman, Burch, Curry, & Lampron, 1984; Schlichter & Horan, 1981). However, the most impressive work in the literature comes from a series of studies conducted by Kazdin and colleagues involving the application of PST to prepubertal children hospitalized for severe conduct disorder. In these studies, PST (including a self-instructional component) was consistently superior to relationship therapy or an attention placebo (Kazdin, Bass, Siegel, & Thomas, 1989; Kazdin, Esveldt-Dawson, French, & Unis, 1987a, 1987b) and comparable to parent management training (Kazdin et al., 1987a; Kazdin, Siegel, & Bass, 1992), with the combination of PST plus parent management training most effective of all (Kazdin et al., 1992). As shown in Figure 10.5, PST produced decrements in aggressive behaviors and increments in prosocial behaviors that were both generalized and sustained following termination of treatment.

These studies were quite clinically representative. The children were severely disturbed, the treatments differed in their underlying rationales but were all consistent with established clinical practice, and the therapists were trained professionals with considerable experience applying the respective interventions with disturbed children. In short, the studies dealt with a fully clinically population in a sophisticated fashion. Although it is not possible to determine the extent to which the cognitive components contributed to the efficacy of the full treatment package, it is clear that the cognitive-behavioral interventions produced impressive (and

engage in binge eating (Smith, Marcus, & Kaye, 1992; Telch, Agras, Rossiter, Wilfley, & Kenardy, 1990).

Summary

The efficacy of the cognitive and cognitive-behavioral interventions varies across the eating disorders and obesity. These interventions appear to be effective in the treatment of bulimia nervosa, with respect to both acute response and the maintenance of change, and might be made more effective still if even more powerful cognitive change strategies were adopted. Although a sophisticated approach to the treatment of anorexia nervosa has been articulated, it has yet to be adequately tested. The cognitive and cognitive-behavioral interventions have been largely relegated to adjunctive status in the treatment of obesity and, like other maintenance strategies, appear to be able to slow, but not prevent, the process of weight regain. There is some reason for optimism that the cognitive interventions will play a role in the treatment of anorexia nervosa given that a conceptual model has already been articulated, but it is important for work to go forward with respect to the treatment of obesity as well.

CHILD AND ADOLESCENT DISORDERS

Disorders of childhood and adolescence are often divided into undercontrolled (or externalizing) versus overcontrolled (or internalizing) disorders (Kazdin, 1991). Undercontrolled disorders typically involve behaviors that are problematic to others, such as aggression or hyperactivity, whereas overcontrolled disorders tend to involve more private distress. Most of the work in this area has focused on the undercontrolled disorders, which appear to involve deficits in cognitive mediation (Kendall & Braswell, 1985). Not surprisingly, skills-training approaches, such as PST and self-instructional training, have generally been preferred for these disorders. The overcontrolled disorders, which are presumed to involve existing distortions in beliefs, have only recently begun to attract attention from cognitive theorists (Kendall, 1993). The few studies that have addressed the treatment of depression in children and adolescents have already been reviewed, and those dealing with children's anxiety about medical procedures are discussed in a later section. The remainder of this section focuses on the treatment of the undercontrolled disorders.

Aggression and Conduct Disorder
Real strides have been made over the last decade in the treatment of aggression and conduct dis-

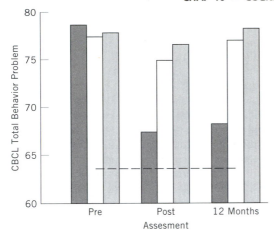

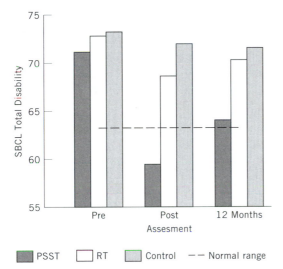

FIGURE 10.5 Behavior problems and school disability as a function of treatment for conduct disorder. Mean T scores for the problem-solving skills training (PSST), relationship therapy (RT), and control groups for the Total Behavior Problem scale of the Child Behavior Checklist (CBCL, upper panel) and the Total Disability scale of the School Behavior Checklist (SBCL, lower panel). The horizontal lines represent the upper limit of the normal range of children of the same gender and age. The T scores below these lines fall within the normal range. 12 Months indicates 12-month follow-up. *Note.* From "Problem-Solving Skills Training and Relationship Therapy in the Treatment of Antisocial Child Behavior" by A.E. Kazdin, K. Esveldt-Dawson, N.H. French, and A.S. Unis, 1987b, *Journal of Consulting and Clinical Psychology, 55,* p. 83. Copyright © 1987 by the American Psychological Association. Reprinted by permission.

sustained) change in a population that has traditionally been considered refractory to treatment. Although treatment did not produce full normalization, the fact that meaningful change was produced at all, and that it was both generalized and sustained, suggests that these interventions may have a role to play in the treatment of severe conduct disorders in children.

Impulsivity and Attention-Deficit Hyperactivity Disorder

Attention-deficit hyperactivity disorder (ADHD) is characterized by symptoms of inattentiveness and impulsivity and is often associated with poor school performance and inadequate interpersonal relationships. From a cognitive perspective, children with attention-deficit disorder lack the capacity to inhibit their own behavior such that they tend to respond too rapidly to external events and fail to anticipate consequences or engage in planful problem solving (Kendall & Braswell, 1985). The goal of cognitive training with such children is to help them develop skills that allow them to handle situations in a more reflective fashion; that is, to teach them to think before they act. Self-instructional training has been the most widely used cognitive-behavioral approach for dealing with impulsivity and ADHD. In this approach, modeling and faded rehearsal are used to teach children how to engage in more reflective problem solving and task performance. Observation and repetition are the primary processes of change, and contingency management techniques (especially response cost) are often used to sustain attention and enhance compliance.

Beginning with the landmark study by Meichenbaum and Goodman (1971), numerous studies have applied self-instructional training to the treatment of impulsivity, typically in nonclinical samples. These studies have suggested that such training facilitates subsequent performance on cognitive tasks, chiefly by inhibiting the tendency to make impulsive errors (see, for example, Kendall & Finch, 1978). However, gains have not always generalized beyond training tasks (e.g., to behavior in school or at home) or been stable over time (see Hollon & Beck, 1986, for a review).

It is even less clear that such training produces clinically meaningful change in children diagnosed with ADHD. Although some studies have found that cognitive-behavioral training enhances performance on specific training tasks, others have not, and generalization beyond those tasks is rare (see Abikoff, 1985, for a review of this literature). Further, direct comparisons have typically found that cognitive-behavioral training is less effective than, and does little to enhance the efficacy of, stimulant medications. For example, Abikoff and

Gittelman (1985) found that up to 16 weeks of twice-weekly sessions of cognitive training (designed to enhance control over impulsive behavior and instill problem-solving skills) did little to enhance the efficacy of pharmacotherapy alone in a sample of children with ADHD. Hinshaw and colleagues found that brief cognitive training could facilitate the acquisition of greater behavioral self-control in response to interpersonal provocation in a medicated sample of children with ADHD, but there was little indication that these gains generalized to other situations or were stable across time (Hinshaw, Henker, & Whalen, 1984a, 1984b).

Thus, despite early success with nonclinical samples, it remains unclear whether cognitive-behavioral training can produce clinically meaningful changes in children with ADHD. The approach has some promise, but there are still few compelling indications of generalized and sustained change in a fully clinical population. Moreover, work in the area appears to have stopped; we could find no empirical trials published in the last 5 years. Given that stimulant medications neither produce enduring change nor address ongoing deficits in problem solving or reasoning, this seems particularly unfortunate. Although there is little justification for claiming that the cognitive-behavioral interventions are effective in the treatment of ADHD, the results from studies with impulsive samples are sufficiently promising to warrant further clinical trials.

Developmental Disability and Life-Skills Training

There are indications that self-instructional training can be used to enhance independent functioning in people with developmental disabilities (Agran & Martella, 1991). Training in verbal self-instruction is sometimes used to introduce problem-solving skills and to facilitate less complex behavioral tasks, like recalling the sequence of steps in a task or associating a given task to a given site. Given the level of deficit involved, standard training procedures typically have to be simplified, but it is quite clear that such approaches are feasible with this population.

Numerous studies have demonstrated the efficacy of self-instructional training for purposes of behavior management, academic instruction, and prevocational training (see Agran & Martella, 1991, for a review). For example, controlled studies have found self-instructional training superior to either modeling or didactic instruction alone in enhancing academic skills (e.g., Leon & Pepe, 1983) and within subject designs have shown that self-instructional training can promote problem-solving skills and productivity in the workplace (e.g.,

Moore, Agran, & Fodor-Davis, 1989). Thus, it appears that self-instructional training can be useful in enhancing adaptive functioning in people with developmental disabilities.

Summary

The picture with respect to the efficacy of the cognitive-behavioral interventions in the treatment of disorders of childhood and adolescence is mixed. Skills-training approaches, especially PST, appear to have real promise in the treatment of aggression and conduct disorder, especially when used as part of a larger, multifaceted program. Self-instructional training appears to be somewhat effective in the treatment of impulsivity in nonclinical samples, but it has yet to be shown to be effective in the treatment of children with diagnosable ADHD. Training in verbal self-instruction can be used to enhance adaptive capacity in people with developmental disabilities, but the deficits involved are so profound that even successful cognitive training must be incorporated into larger, multifaceted treatment programs.

SUBSTANCE ABUSE AND THE PREVENTION OF RELAPSE

As with obesity, it is easier to produce change in the substance-abuse disorders than it is to maintain it. Theorists in the area thus emphasize the development of procedures designed to prevent relapse following successful treatment (Brownell, Marlatt, Lichtenstein, & Wilson, 1986). Marlatt and colleagues developed a skills-training approach to relapse prevention (RP) that has generated considerable interest (Marlatt & Gordon, 1985). It has not only been applied in the treatment of substance abuse, but it has also served as the basis for novel approaches to other disorders that can be conceptualized as habit problems, for example, in the treatment of sexual deviance (see, for example, Marshall, Hudson, & Ward, 1992). However, despite the widespread enthusiasm this approach has generated, empirical support remains modest.

Relapse Prevention and the Controlled-Drinking Controversy

Few areas of research have been as heavily politicized as the treatment of alcohol abuse. Strong competing models exist, and disputes over the proper interpretation of empirical trials have spilled into the popular press (Marlatt, 1983). A traditional disease model suggests that alcoholism is a progressive disorder that cannot be reversed. According to this model, once an individual develops an addiction, control over drinking behavior can never be reestablished and lifelong abstinence becomes the only option. A cognitive social-learning theory approach suggests that self-regulatory skills can be acquired at any time. According to this perspective, acceptance of the disease model can undermine efforts at behavioral self-control by creating the expectation that a minor lapse must invariably lead to a full-blown relapse.

The empirical evidence remains ambiguous. There are clear indications that expectations play a role in determining patterns of use and abuse, including the phenomenon of loss of control once drinking has begun (see Wilson, 1987, for a review). Cognitive-behavioral interventions, typically combining training in behavioral self-regulation with limited efforts at the modification of beliefs and attitudes, have been shown to be somewhat successful in the reduction of drinking behaviors (Chaney, O'Leary, & Marlatt, 1978; Sanchez-Craig, Annis, Bornet, & MacDonald, 1984). Nonetheless, there continues to be skepticism in the field regarding this approach and a sense that its applicability is limited to early-stage problem drinkers (Nathan & Skinstad, 1987).

Moreover, recent efforts by Marlatt's group to apply RP to precisely this population have been somewhat disappointing. In the first of two studies, RP was no more effective than either didactic information or an assessment-only control in the treatment of college students with moderate drinking problems (Kivlahan, Marlatt, Fromme, Coppel, & Williams, 1990). However, the sample was small and the nonsignificant differences that were evident consistently favored the RP condition. In a subsequent study with a larger sample, skills training was again no more effective than either a correspondence course or a single motivational interview in reducing alcohol consumption and high-risk behaviors (Baer et al., 1992). All three conditions were associated with a significant reduction in drinking behaviors that was largely maintained over a 2-year follow-up, but the absence of group differences precluded drawing any conclusions regarding treatment efficacy. Although the basic RP principles were provided in all three conditions, so little time was allotted to that training in the two control conditions that the full program should have produced greater change.

Recent studies suggest that naltrexone, an opioid antagonist, may be effective in the treatment of alcohol dependence (O'Malley et al., 1992; Volpicelli, Alterman, Hayashida, & O'Brien, 1992). In the study by O'Malley and colleagues, naltrexone (versus placebo) was crossed with coping skills training modeled after RP (versus supportive ther-

apy) in a factorial design. In that study, patients exposed to coping skills training (with or without medication) were less likely to remain abstinent than were patients treated with naltrexone plus supportive therapy. This result was not unexpected, since the basic philosophy underlying RP tends to deemphasize the importance of abstinence. However, patients who received coping skills training were no more likely to remain free of relapse than were patients who did not, regardless of medication status; nonmedicated patients showed consistently higher rates of relapse regardless of whether they received skills training or not. Among nonabstinent patients, however, those who received both coping skills training and naltrexone were less likely to relapse than were patients in the other conditions.

These findings suggest that RP may increase the capacity of medicated patients to engage in controlled drinking, but not the overall likelihood of maintaining sobriety among either medicated or nonmedicated patients. Thus, RP may have complex and offsetting effects; it may increase the capacity for behavioral self-regulation but simultaneously increase the likelihood that patients will put themselves at risk by choosing not to be abstinent.

More work is needed to sort out these complex and potentially contradictory relations. There is little justification for claiming that RP is effective in the treatment of alcoholism or that it can prevent relapse following successful treatment, but it does appear to have an effect. Whether that effect will prove to be clinically beneficial remains to be determined, but continued work is warranted.

Drug Abuse and Treatment-by-Severity Interactions

There are indications that RP may be effective in the treatment of drug abuse, at least among patients with more severe patterns of abuse. Carroll and colleagues adapted RP for the treatment of cocaine abuse, retaining much of the original approach, but with abstinence as an explicit goal of treatment (Carroll, Rounsaville, & Keller, 1991). In an initial study, they found RP superior to IPT, but only among patients with more severe patterns of cocaine abuse (Carroll, Rounsaville, & Gawin, 1991). In a subsequent trial, RP (versus clinical management) was crossed with desipramine (versus placebo) in a factorial design (Carroll et al., in press). In that trial, RP once again proved particularly effective among patients with more severe patterns of abuse, whereas desipramine had only a short-lived effect that dissipated before the end of treatment. These studies suggest that RP may be effective in the treatment of cocaine abuse, at least among patients with more severe patterns of abuse (and when abstinence is a treatment goal). Why its effect should be limited to more severe patients remains unclear, but these initial findings are somewhat encouraging with respect to the potential utility of RP in the treatment of drug abuse.

CT is the other major approach that has been applied to the treatment of drug abuse. In CT, an emphasis is placed on identifying and testing both those specific thoughts associated with actual drug-taking behaviors and the underlying beliefs presumed to increase risk (Beck, Wright, & Newman, 1992). Patients are taught to cope with cravings for the drug via empirical disconfirmation (like any other impulse, cravings will also pass if not acted on) and to identify and counter those specific beliefs that undermine adherence to abstinence.

An early study suggested that both a generic version of CT or supportive-expressive psychotherapy might contribute to the treatment of opiate addiction when added to standard drug counseling (Woody et al., 1983). However, a careful reading of that article suggests that those claims were somewhat overstated, at least with respect to CT. Patients treated with CT did require lower doses of methadone and adjunctive medications than did patients receiving counseling alone, but they also exhibited more opiate and sedative use than did patients in counseling alone or supportive-expressive psychotherapy and had less stable work performance and higher levels of residual psychopathology than did patients treated with supportive-expressive psychotherapy. Given that the version of CT used in this study was essentially unmodified for use with a substance-abuse population and that the results were equivocal at best, it would be premature to draw any conclusions regarding the utility of CT in the treatment of drug abuse.

Smoking Cessation and Subsequent Relapse

There is currently little evidence that RP is effective in the prevention of relapse following smoking cessation (Lichtenstein & Glasgow, 1992). Although multicomponent treatment programs incorporating RP techniques are typically successful in helping participants stop smoking, there is little indication that any of the components, including the cognitive ones, are integral to their success. Moreover, most participants resume smoking within several months of treatment termination.

Programs devoted more explicitly to RP have also not proved particularly successful in preventing relapse. For example, Curry and colleagues found coping skills training based on RP principles

no more effective than an approach emphasizing abstinence (Curry, Marlatt, Gordon, & Baer, 1988). Given that this study was conducted by the leading advocates of this approach, these findings are hard to dismiss. Other studies have produced mixed results, with RP sometimes superior to control conditions and sometimes not. However, even in the more positive trials, the magnitudes of the effects observed tended to be so small as to call into question their clinical relevance (see, for example, Stevens & Hollis, 1989). Studies combining RP with pharmacological treatments have also produced mixed results. For example, although one study found that RP enhanced relapse prevention among former smokers also receiving nicotine gum (Goldstein, Niaura, Follick, & Abrams, 1989), two other studies did not (Hall, Tunstall, Ginsberg, Benowitz, & Jones, 1987; Killen, Fortmann, Newman, & Varady, 1990). Thus, there is little robust evidence that RP is effective in preventing relapse following smoking cessation.

Nonetheless, there is reason to think that the picture may not be as bleak as it first seems (Mermelstein, Karnatz, & Reichmann, 1992). For example, Curry and colleagues found that although participants who received RP were more likely to lapse than were those encouraged to remain abstinent, they were also more likely to recover from that lapse and remain abstinent throughout the remainder of the follow-up (Curry et al., 1988). This is similar to the finding in the alcoholism literature that RP both reduced the likelihood of remaining abstinent and increased the likelihood of maintaining sobriety if drinking were resumed (O'Malley et al., 1992). Such findings suggest that RP may have a more complex effect on smoking behavior than is typically recognized. Although there is clearly little justification for claiming that RP is effective in the treatment of smoking, it would be premature to conclude that it is not.

Summary

It remains unclear whether RP is truly effective in the treatment of substance abuse. Evidence of its efficacy in the treatment of alcoholism is modest at best, although there are indications that it may facilitate controlled drinking in medicated former alcoholics. Evidence of its efficacy in the treatment of drug abuse is more compelling, although limited to more severe abusers. Evidence of its efficacy in the treatment of smoking is least impressive of all, although there are indications that, as for alcohol addiction, RP may facilitate recovery from lapses. Both the alcohol and the smoking literatures suggest that RP may have two somewhat offsetting effects. It does seem to reduce risk for relapse among these who choose not to remain abstinent (or cannot maintain it, even if they try), but it also appears to increase the likelihood that people will put themselves at risk by making that choice. It is of interest that RP fared best in the treatment of drug abuse, in which abstinence is adopted as a treatment goal.

Again, more work needs to be done. In particular, it is important for investigators to differentiate between abstinence and freedom from relapse; although the former may be a worthwhile means to a desirable end, it is the latter that is the critical outcome of interest. Studies that have assessed both have shown that relations between the two are sometimes quite complex. Whether it will prove possible to enhance the latter without promoting the former remains to be seen, but the impact of treatment on each and the relations between them should certainly be assessed in any study.

TREATMENT OF PERSONALITY DISORDERS

In the last decade there has been an increased interest in approaching personality disorders from a cognitive perspective. These disorders have long been assumed to be the consequence of constitutional and developmental factors and to be largely refractory to treatment. Purely prognostic studies have suggested that such patients, particularly those with borderline personality disorder, tend to respond less well than other patients to the cognitive and cognitive-behavioral interventions (e.g., Burns & Nolen-Hoeksema, 1992). Nonetheless, recent theoretical and empirical work suggests that the cognitive and cognitive-behavioral interventions may be helpful in the treatment of the personality disorders. For example, considerable effort has gone into adapting CT for use with such patients (Beck et al., 1990). Although controlled empirical trials have yet to be conducted, the approach now appears to be ready for inclusion in such studies.

Another approach that has already been subjected to empirical scrutiny is dialectical behavior therapy (DBT; Linehan, 1993). DBT is a cognitive-behavioral intervention designed for use with persons with borderline personality disorder. Such patients often engage in suicidal or other life-threatening behaviors (referred to as parasuicidal behaviors) and relate to others in an unpredictable, affectively driven fashion. According to Linehan, the inability to tolerate strong states of negative affect is central to the disorder. In DBT, the patient is encouraged to accept this negative affect without engaging in self-destructive or maladaptive behav-

iors. A variety of cognitive and behavioral techniques are used within a problem-oriented framework to accomplish this goal, including behavioral skills training, contingency management, cognitive modification, and exposure to emotional cues. Instances of parasuicidal behavior are exhaustively explored with an emphasis on identifying alternative strategies that could have been adopted to deal with the situations that triggered their occurrence, and an effort is made to help patients learn to accept and manage emotional distress.

As shown in Figure 10.6, Linehan and colleagues found that borderline patients treated with up to a year of DBT showed a greater reduction in parasuicidal behaviors than did patients receiving treatment as usual in the community (Linehan, Armstrong, Suarez, Allmon, & Heard, 1991). Patients treated with DBT were also more likely to complete therapy and to require fewer days of hospitalization. No differences were evident between the groups on self-reported levels of depression, hopelessness, or suicidal ideation, although scores decreased across treatment for both groups.

This study is particularly noteworthy for its high degree of clinical realism. The patients were drawn from a fully representative (and difficult) clinical population; treatment was both rich and extended in time (the experimental treatment consisted of 1 hour of individual treatment and 2.5 hours of group

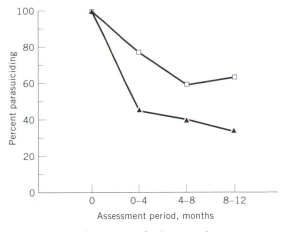

FIGURE 10.6 Proportion of subjects with parasuicide as a function of treatment. Months 0 to 4 ($z = 2.7$, $p < .05$) and months 8 to 12 ($z = 1.74$, $p < .05$) indicated significant difference between subjects (triangles) who received dialectical behavior therapy and control subjects (squares). *Note.* From "Cognitive-Behavioral Treatment of Chronically Parasuicidal Borderline Patients," by M.M. Linehan, H.E. Armstrong, A. Suarez, D. Allmon, and H.L. Heard, 1991, *Archives of General Psychiatry, 48,* p. 1062. Copyright © 1991 by the American Medical Association. Reprinted by permission.

treatment per week for a full year); and the therapists were experienced professionals. At the same time, only about three-quarters of the subjects in the control group actually received treatment (a sizable minority of the patients referred for treatment in the community failed to pursue those referrals). More work is needed before any firm conclusions can be drawn, but the findings from this initial trial appear to be promising.

SCHIZOPHRENIA AND DELUSIONAL THINKING

Delusions have traditionally been regarded as impervious to logic or empirical disconfirmation. Conventional wisdom has held that the cognitive and cognitive-behavioral interventions have little to offer with respect to the amelioration of the thought disorder itself, although they might play an adjunctive role in the reduction of distress. Nonetheless, a series of studies, few of them controlled, have suggested that the cognitive interventions might have a greater potential in the treatment of schizophrenia and the other psychotic disorders than has typically been assumed.

Over four decades ago, Beck (1952) described the resolution of a long-standing persecutory delusion in a chronic schizophrenic patient using a forerunner of CT. Treatment consisted of considering alternative explanations for the antecedent experiences that led to the formation of the delusion and helping the patient systematically test their accuracy and plausibility. A subsequent uncontrolled trial found that such an approach reduced the degree of conviction in delusional beliefs in four of eight medicated schizophrenic patients (Hole, Rush, & Beck, 1979).

Watts and colleagues similarly found that cognitive techniques resulted in a substantial reduction in the conviction with which three schizophrenic patients held their delusions (Watts, Powell, & Austin, 1973). The authors initially targeted less strongly held beliefs, asking only that the patients consider alternative explanations for their experiences. They next examined the evidence supporting the delusional beliefs and encouraged the patients to consider whether that evidence better supported the delusions or more plausible alternative interpretations. Following these guidelines, Chadwick and Lowe (1990), using a multiple-baseline design, were able to reduce the conviction with which delusional beliefs were held with six medicated schizophrenic patients. Kingdon and Turkington (1991) reported similar positive results in a consecutive series of medicated schizophrenic patients.

Implicit in these approaches is the notion that delusions represent an attempt to make sense out of troublesome or puzzling experiences and that the schizophrenic patient is not wholly impervious to reason or evidence. Milton and colleagues showed that, consistent with clinical lore, direct confrontation regarding the implausibility of the beliefs is relatively ineffective, whereas a more gradual and indirect approach, such as the one described here, has a greater effect (Milton, Patwa, & Hafner, 1978). Such strategies would clearly need to be embedded in a larger, multifaceted program of intervention. Although it would be premature to draw any conclusions regarding their utility and further clinical refinement is needed, the time may be approaching when these interventions will merit testing in more carefully controlled designs.

BEHAVIORAL MEDICINE

The cognitive and cognitive-behavioral interventions have been widely adopted in the field of behavioral medicine. Approaches that enhance the acquisition of cognitive skills have been most prominent in this domain, with SIT and self-instructional training serving as a model for many of the specific programs (Turk, Meichenbaum, & Genest, 1983). Unlike patients who have psychopathological disorders, the typical medical patient is not apt to have entrenched maladaptive beliefs or problematic information-processing styles that need to be changed. In most instances, the task in this literature has been to help people who are relatively well adjusted deal with negative life events that fall outside the range of everyday human experience.

Preparation for Noxious Medical Procedures
One of the classic applications of this approach has been to help people prepare for and cope with a variety of noxious medical procedures. For example, Kendall and colleagues found SIT superior to a variety of control conditions in terms of reducing anxiety and enhancing adjustment to surgery during cardiac catheterization (Kendall et al., 1979). Similarly, Peterson and Shigetomi (1981) found that self-statement training reduced surgical fears in young children, and Kaplan and colleagues found that self-instructional training reduced distress during sigmoidoscopy exams (Kaplan, Atkins, & Lenhard, 1982). Elliott and Olson (1983) found stress-management procedures helpful in managing children's distress during painful treatment for burns, and Jay and Elliot (1990) found that SIT reduced parents' distress when their children had to undergo painful medical procedures. Numerous studies have found that cognitive-behavioral stress-

management procedures help both adults and children cope with painful dental procedures (see, for example, Getka & Glass, 1992). These and other studies suggest that stress-management techniques modeled on SIT can help people cope with noxious medical procedures (see Ludwick-Rosenthal & Neufeld, 1988, for a review).

Coping With Cancer

Closely related to the applications just discussed are efforts to use the cognitive-behavioral interventions to mitigate the more negative aspects of cancer treatment. For example, Jay and colleagues found that SIT reduced distress in children undergoing painful bone marrow aspirations and lumbar punctures (e.g., Jay, Elliott, Katz, & Siegel, 1987). Dahlquist and colleagues found that a cognitive-behavioral treatment package modeled after SIT reduced conditioned nausea and corollary distress in patients undergoing chemotherapy (Dahlquist, Gil, Armstrong, Ginsberg, & Jones, 1985). Moreover, the cognitive-behavioral interventions have also been used to enhance adjustment to the disease itself. For example, in a well-executed study, Telch and Telch (1986) found that a program consisting of relaxation, activity scheduling, cognitive restructuring, problem solving, and assertion training improved adjustment and perceived self-efficacy relative to either supportive group therapy or a no-treatment control in a mixed sample of oncology patients. Such programs are important not only because of their potential to reduce distress and contribute to the overall quality of life, but also because they may have an indirect effect on the disease process itself by virtue of enhancing immune system functions (Kiecolt-Glaser & Glaser, 1992).

Prevention and Treatment of HIV Infection and AIDS

The cognitive and cognitive-behavioral interventions are beginning to be applied to the prevention and treatment of HIV infection and AIDS (Kelly & Murphy, 1992). Several studies have sought to reduce risk for HIV infection. For example, Kelly and colleagues found that a 12-session cognitive-behavioral package that included modeling, behavior rehearsal, and problem-solving training led to an increase in sexual assertion skills and a decrease in sexual risk behavior relative to a wait-list control among gay men, with those changes maintained across a 16-month follow-up (Kelly, St. Lawrence, Hood, & Brasfield, 1989). Rotheram-Borus and colleagues similarly found that a cognitive-behavioral skills-training program produced a greater reduction in high-risk sexual behavior among sexually

active runaway adolescents than did standard risk education (Rotheram-Borus, Koopman, & Haignere, 1991), and Jemmott and colleagues found that a cognitive-behavioral skills-training workshop produced similar behavior change among African-American male adolescents (Jemmott, Jemmott, & Fong, 1992).

Two studies have evaluated the impact of cognitive-behavioral programs on psychological distress following notification of HIV status. Perry and colleagues found a brief stress-prevention program based on a combination of SIT and CT superior to either an interactive video or standard counseling in preventing distress among persons who had learned that they were HIV positive (Perry, Fishman, Jacobsberg, Young, & Frances, 1991). Antoni and colleagues found that a similar but more extensive program not only protected participants against distress following notification, but, as shown in Figure 10.7, was also associated with better preservation of immune system functioning among those participants who proved to be infected (Antoni et al., 1991).

Although it would be premature to conclude that such effects are specific to these approaches, it does appear that they have a role to play, either in reducing high-risk behaviors or in enhancing adaptation following notification of HIV status. The suggestion that such treatment can influence immune system functioning is particularly exciting and warrants efforts at replication.

Chronic Pain

The cognitive and cognitive-behavioral interventions also appear to be effective in the treatment of chronic pain, although questions remain as to how they compare with more purely operant behavioral approaches (Keefe, Dunsmore, & Burnett, 1992). Unlike operant approaches, which focus exclusively on the modification of pain behaviors, the cognitive and cognitive-behavioral interventions also attend to the interpretative and affective aspects of the pain experience. Most of these programs are modeled after SIT and combine training in relaxation and behavioral coping skills with cognitive restructuring and self-statement modification.

Numerous studies have found such interventions superior to control conditions in the treatment of chronic pain associated with a number of diverse disorders (see, for example, Keefe et al., 1990, with respect to arthritis; Linton, Bradley, Jensen, Spangfort, & Sundell, 1989, with respect to back problems; and Sanders et al., 1989, with respect to recurrent abdominal pain in children). Several studies have compared the cognitive-behavioral interventions with more purely behavioral programs,

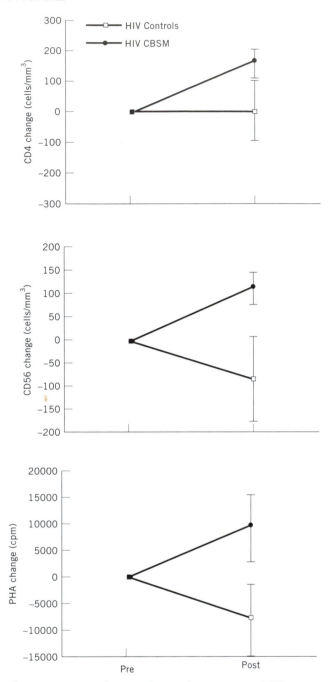

FIGURE 10.7 Immune system functioning pre- and postnotification for seropositive HIV status as a function of treatment: helper = inducer (CD4) and natural killer (CD56) cell counts and lymphocyte proliferative responses to phytohemagglutinin (PHA). CBSM = cognitive-behavioral stress management; HIV = human immunodeficiency virus. *Note.* From "Cognitive-Behavioral Stress Management Intervention Buffers Distress Responses and Immunologic Changes Following Notification of HIV-1 Seropositivity" by M.H. Antoni et al., 1991, *Journal of Consulting and Clinical Psychology, 59,* p. 911. Copyright © 1991 by the American Psychological Association. Reprinted by permission.

with mixed results. Turner (1982) found either cognitive-behavioral therapy or relaxation training superior to a wait-list control in the treatment of low back pain; although there were few differences between the two active treatments, those that were observed tended to favor the cognitive condition. Similarly, Kerns and colleagues found some indications that cognitive-behavioral therapy was superior to a purely operant approach in the treatment of chronic pain (Kerns, Turk, Holzman, & Rudy, 1986). On the other hand, two studies found a purely operant approach superior to more inclusive cognitive-behavioral programs in the treatment of low back pain (Nicholas, Wilson, & Grogen, 1991; Turner & Clancy, 1988). Thus, although the cognitive-behavioral interventions appear to be effective in the treatment of chronic pain, it is still not clear how they compare with more purely behavioral approaches.

Tension and Migraine Headaches

The cognitive-behavioral interventions seem to be effective in the treatment of tension headaches, although it is less clear that they are effective with regard to migraine headaches (Blanchard, 1992). As in the case of chronic pain, more purely behavioral interventions, including progressive muscle relaxation and both electromyographic and thermal biofeedback, are already well established. The cognitive-behavioral interventions are largely modeled after SIT and typically include training in attentional redeployment, cognitive restructuring, and verbal self-instruction, usually in combination with more purely behavioral techniques.

With respect to tension headaches, the cognitive-behavioral interventions have usually proved superior to minimal-treatment or nonspecific controls and at least as effective as (and likely to enhance the efficacy of) more purely behavioral interventions (see, for example, Blanchard, Applebaum, Radnitz, Michultka, et al., 1990). In the one study in which they have been compared, cognitive-behavioral therapy proved superior to amitriptyline pharmacotherapy (Holroyd, Nash, Pingel, Cordingley, & Jerome, 1991). Gains appear to be well maintained following cognitive-behavioral treatment, something that has not been the case for the pharmacological approaches (Blanchard, 1992).

The evidence is not so clear that the cognitive-behavioral interventions are effective in the treatment of migraine headaches. Early studies failed to find such interventions superior to even minimal-treatment controls (e.g., Lake, Rainey, & Papsdorf, 1979), and later studies tended to find that the addition of cognitive components did little to enhance the efficacy of more purely behavioral interventions (e.g., Blanchard, Appelbaum, Radnitz, Morrill, et al., 1990). Thus, although the cognitive-behavioral interventions appear to be effective in the treatment of tension headaches, their efficacy in the treatment of migraine headaches is far less certain.

Rehabilitation Training Following Traumatic Brain Injury

There are indications that the cognitive-behavioral interventions can be used to facilitate rehabilitation following traumatic brain injuries (see Meichenbaum, 1993, for a review). Such injuries often produce deficits in executive functions, such as metacognitive and self-regulatory skills, and undermine the capacity for emotional regulation. Recent efforts have focused on adapting skills-training approaches, such as SIT, PST, and self-instructional training, for use with such patients. Although controlled trials have yet to be conducted, findings from initial uncontrolled studies appear promising and the approaches appear ready for inclusion in more systematic evaluations.

Summary

The cognitive-behavioral interventions appear to be effective in the treatment of a variety of medical disorders, particularly the approaches, such as SIT, PST, and self-instructional training, that aid in the acquisition of cognitive skills. These approaches appear to facilitate coping with noxious medical procedures and may help enhance the quality of life for people with cancer. They appear to reduce risk for HIV infection and help preserve immune system functioning in those who are infected. They seem to ameliorate chronic pain and help prevent headache pain, at least with respect to tension headaches. Finally, there are suggestions, as yet unconfirmed by controlled research, that these interventions may facilitate rehabilitation following traumatic brain injury. Although questions of specificity remain, particularly with respect to more purely behavioral interventions, these approaches have been found superior to nonspecific- and minimal-treatment controls. Although the cognitive strategies incorporated in these approaches are not as sophisticated as those applied to some other disorders, they appear to be adequate to meet the pragmatic needs of patients in a medical setting.

MARITAL DISTRESS

A cognitive theory of marital distress suggests that the way in which partners interpret one another's behavior and the expectations they hold play an important role in determining how they behave toward one another and their satisfaction with the relationship (Baucom, Epstein, Sayers, & Sher, 1989). According to this theory, any intervention that systematically changes maladaptive beliefs regarding the partner's behaviors or the more general standards to which the partner is held should lead to a reduction in marital distress (Baucom & Epstein, 1990; Beck, 1988).

Cognitive components have often been superimposed on more purely behavioral strategies, such as contingency contracting and communication skills training. Although behavioral marital therapy has been shown to be consistently superior to non-specific- and minimal-treatment controls, there are limits to its effectiveness (Jacobson et al., 1984). Fewer than half of all treated couples can be said to be nondistressed by the end of therapy, and change is often short-lived. Part of the impetus for developing a cognitive approach was to improve on the magnitude and stability of change produced by behavioral marital therapy.

Studies have shown that the cognitive and cognitive-behavioral approaches are superior to minimal-treatment controls in the treatment of marital distress (Baucom et al., 1990; Huber & Milstein, 1985). What is not so clear is how these approaches compare with more purely behavioral interventions. Although early studies suggested that cognitive interventions might be superior to or enhance the efficacy of more purely behavioral approaches (Epstein, Pretzer, & Fleming, 1982; Margolin & Weiss, 1978), subsequent studies did not (Baucom & Lester, 1986; Baucom et al., 1990; Emmelkamp, van den Heuvel, et al., 1988). Findings with respect to the maintenance of treatment gains in these trials have been similarly mixed, and change in beliefs and attitudes has been largely nonspecific.

However, there are questions about the adequacy of the implementation of treatment in these trials. Many studies relied on graduate-student therapists or less than fully representative operationalizations of the respective treatments. In particular, several of the more recent studies presented the cognitive and behavioral components in a sequential fashion, rather than as a truly integrated approach. Such a strategy may not do justice to the complex interrelations between cognition, affect, and behavior that tend to underly issues encountered in therapy and does not appear to adequately represent the sophistication of current clinical practice (Epstein, 1992).

The most reasonable conclusion based on the existing studies is that the cognitive and cognitive-behavioral approaches are neither more nor less effective than more purely behavioral interventions in the treatment of marital distress (see also Chapters 9 and 14 of this *Handbook*). However, firm conclusions are premature. Subsequent trials should integrate the cognitive and behavioral components in a more clinically sophisticated fashion and use experienced professional therapists to provide treatment to ensure that the respective interventions have been adequately tested.

CONCLUSIONS AND RECOMMENDATIONS

The cognitive and cognitive-behavioral interventions appear to be effective in the treatment of a variety of clinical disorders. In the previous edition of this book, we concluded that these interventions had fulfilled some, but not all, of their initial promise (Hollon & Beck, 1986). We were particularly troubled by the dearth of studies involving truly clinical populations, with depression being the sole exception. Since that time, there has been a virtual explosion of carefully controlled, high-quality studies, most supporting the efficacy of these approaches. With regard to the specific areas of disorder, the following conclusions can be drawn:

1. CT appears to be at least as effective as alternative interventions in the treatment of depression and may reduce risk following treatment termination. However, additional placebo-controlled comparisons to medication in fully clinical populations and efforts to determine whether those enduring effects extend to the prevention of recurrence are needed. The suggestion from the recent NIMH study that more severely depressed outpatients may do less well in CT than in pharmacotherapy does not appear to be robust, but it does raise an important concern. There are indications that CT may also be effective in the treatment of inpatient populations and, perhaps, in bipolar disorder, although work with this latter population is still quite preliminary. Other cognitive-behavioral approaches have shown promise in the treatment of children and adolescents, but have not been extensively evaluated in adult clinical populations.

2. Perhaps the most dramatic breakthroughs in the last decade have come in the treatment of panic and the anxiety disorders. Recent studies have suggested that approaches that focus on the disconfirmation of catastrophic misinterpretations (PCT and focused CT) can produce rapid and lasting reductions in the frequency of panic symptoms. Whether these approaches will prove as effective with patients with agoraphobic avoidance remains to be seen, but initial studies are promising. Similarly,

recent work with GAD suggests that cognitive interventions based on CT may be particularly effective and stable over time. The cognitive-behavioral interventions appear to have real promise in the treatment of the social phobias, and initial studies suggest that SIT may have a role to play in the treatment of PTSD. Interesting conceptual models have been put forward with respect to both the simple phobias and OCD that merit empirical examination. Although more work is needed, the quality and clinical realism of the empirical support for these approaches in the treatment of the anxiety disorders is far stronger than it was at the time of our last review.

3. Cognitive-behavioral therapy has emerged as a leading intervention in the treatment of bulimia nervosa, and appears to be at least as effective as, and perhaps more enduring than, alternative interventions. There is reason to think that the cognitive components in these interventions could be made more powerful still and that greater attention to more generic concerns about the self might further facilitate the maintenance of change. On the other hand, despite the availability of a clear conceptual model, little quality work has been done in the treatment of anorexia nervosa. Similarly, the cognitive and cognitive-behavioral interventions have yet to be applied to the treatment of obesity in a powerful fashion; in most studies they have been relegated to a largely adjunctive role and appear to do little more than slow the process of weight regain following treatment termination.

4. Among the childhood disorders, recent studies with conduct-disordered children have suggested that training in problem solving and perspective taking may produce lasting change in a disorder that has typically been assumed to be refractory to treatment. On the other hand, although early trials with nonclinical impulsive samples suggested real promise for self-instructional training, subsequent studies with children diagnosed as having ADHD have not been particularly supportive. It remains unclear whether this lack of efficacy reflects an inherent limitation in the approach or a failure to operationalize it in an adequate fashion. Self-instructional training does appear to be effective in promoting adaptive life skills in people with developmental disabilities.

5. Although both theory and research suggest that cognitive processes are involved in the regulation of substance-use behaviors, efforts to enhance treatment efficacy or prevent relapse using cognitive social-learning principles have met with mixed success. In the treatment of alcoholism, it is not clear that RP has a direct effect on relapse, although it may facilitate controlled drinking in medicated patients. RP does appear to prevent relapse in drug abuse, but only among patients with more severe problems. There is little evidence that RP has any beneficial effect with respect to smoking, although there are some indications that it may facilitate recovery from relapse. Once again, it is questionable whether these mixed findings reflect inherent limitations in the approach or problems in its operationalization. Future studies should clearly differentiate between abstinence and freedom from relapse, with the latter the more important clinical outcome.

6. Sophisticated treatment models for the personality disorders are now available to be tested. Considerable effort has gone into adapting CT for use in the treatment of personality disorder, but it has yet to be evaluated empirically. DBT has already been shown to reduce parasuicidal behavior in a sample with borderline personality disorder. Additional empirical trials can be expected over the next several years.

7. There are also indications that patients with schizophrenia or other psychotic disorders may be more amenable to cognitive interventions than clinical lore would suggest. Although there is little reason to think that such interventions can control florid psychotic turmoil, they may help reduce delusional thinking in patients who are stabilized on medication or otherwise in remission. Clinical trials now appear warranted.

8. The cognitive and cognitive-behavioral interventions, particularly SIT and related skills-training strategies, appear to have much to offer in the area of behavioral medicine, although the applications are rarely as sophisticated as they need to be in the treatment of the psychopathological disorders. Such interventions help patients tolerate noxious medical procedures, cope with pain and distress, reduce high-risk behaviors, preserve immune system functions, and compensate for lost capacities.

9. Work in the area of marital discord has been disappointing, if only because misunderstandings and misperceptions appear to play such an important role in the maintenance of such distress. Although interesting theoretical models have been articulated, the existing empirical studies have tended to operationalize cognitive interventions in a mechanistic fashion and have typically failed to integrate them with more purely behavioral components. Thus it is not known whether these interventions truly do little to enhance the efficacy of more purely behavioral interventions or whether they have simply not been implemented in an adequate fashion.

The cognitive and cognitive-behavioral interventions appear to be effective for a broad range of clinical and medical disorders. Negative findings are few and may often be a consequence of a failure to operationalize the approach in an adequate manner. Early studies in clinical populations frequently relied on graduate-student therapists to deliver rather unsophisticated versions of these approaches; for the most part, these initial nonsupportive studies have been supplanted by more methodologically adequate trials that support the efficacy of the cognitive and cognitive-behavioral interventions. In most instances, these interventions have been found to be at least as effective as, and sometimes superior to, more purely behavioral or pharmacological interventions. Comparisons with dynamic or humanistic therapies have been few, but also generally supportive. Moreover, there are numerous indications that the cognitive and cognitive-behavioral interventions may produce more lasting change than do at least some of those other interventions, particularly the pharmacological approaches.

Important issues remain. Few of the existing studies used samples large enough to detect small-to-moderate-sized effects of the kind likely to exist among active interventions (Kazdin & Bass, 1989). Thus modest but clinically meaningful differences among the respective interventions may have simply escaped detection. Similarly, power limitations may have precluded the detection of patient-by-treatment interactions (Smith & Sechrest, 1991). Although few patient characteristics have been identified that predict differential response to different treatments (moderator variables), the fault may lie more with the inadequacy of the designs than with the absence of such interactions. Finally, it is not clear whether these interventions work, when they work, by virtue of changing beliefs or thinking, as specified by theory. Mediational theories are notoriously difficult to test, and the widespread tendency to assume that nonspecificity of change rules out causal status has retarded progress in this area (Hollon et al., 1987). The cognitive and cognitive-behavioral interventions typically produce cognitive change, but, in many instances, so do other effective interventions. There are sophisticated analytic strategies that can detect mediation under such circumstances, but they have rarely been applied (Baron & Kenny, 1986).

Some types of cognitive and cognitive-behavioral interventions have received more empirical attention than others. RET remains the least adequately tested of all the major approaches, although recent studies suggest that its proponents are making a real effort in this regard (see, for example, DiGiu-

seppe, McGowan, Simon, & Gardner, 1990; or Finn, DiGiuseppe, & Culver, 1991). Lack of adequate evaluation should not be confused with lack of efficacy. Although the problems with the existing studies have been amply documented (Haaga & Davison, 1989b), it does appear that RET has generally performed well in studies in which it was adequately operationalized (Haaga & Davison, 1989a; Lyons & Woods, 1991). CT appears to have fared well relative to alternative interventions in controlled trials in a number of different patient populations, including those with depression, panic disorder, and generalized anxiety disorder, and may well be ready for inclusion in trials with other disorders. SIT appears to be well established in the treatment of a variety of medical and stress-related disorders, whereas PST and self-instructional training appear to be of use in the treatment of children and adolescents with externalizing disorders. Whether any of these approaches will prove effective with disorders other than the ones with which they have been tested, or whether any one approach will prove superior to the others with any of these populations, remains open to speculation, but each appears to be effective in the treatment of at least some disorder.

Although important questions remain, it appears that the cognitive and cognitive-behavioral interventions may be effective in the treatment of a broad range of disorders. The growth in the quality and quantity of the empirical support for these approaches in just the few years since publication of the previous edition of the *Handbook* has been truly impressive. In most instances, those studies have suggested that these approaches are at least as effective as the best available alternatives for a number of disorders. Moreover, there are indications that they may produce enduring effects not always shared by other approaches. Although questions of specificity, moderation, and mediation need to be resolved, it appears that the cognitive and cognitive-behavioral interventions are no longer simply promising, but have come of age.

REFERENCES

Abikoff, H. (1985). Efficacy of cognitive training interventions in hyperactive children: A critical review. *Clinical Psychology Review, 5,* 479–512.

Abikoff, H., & Gittelman, R. (1985). Hyperactive children treated with stimulants: Is cognitive training a useful adjunct? *Archives of General Psychiatry, 42,* 953–961.

Abramson, L. Y., Metalsky, G. I., & Alloy. L. B. (1989). Hopelessness depression: A theory-based subtype of depression. *Psychological Review, 96,* 358–372.

Agran, M., & Martella, R. C. (1991). Teaching self-instructional skills to persons with mental retardation: A descriptive and experimental analysis. In M. Hersen, R. M. Eisler, & P. M. Miller (Eds.), *Progress in behavior modification* (pp. 108–149). Newbury Park, CA: Sage Publications.

Agras, W. S., Rossiter, E. M., Arnow, B., Schneider, J. A., Telch, C. F., Raeburn, S. D., Bruse, B., Perl, M., & Koran, L. M. (1992). Pharmacological and cognitive-behavioral treatment for bulimia nervosa: A controlled comparison. *American Journal of Psychiatry, 149,* 82–87.

Antoni, M. H., Baggett, L., Ironson, G., LaPerriere, A., August, S., Klimas, N., Schneiderman, N., & Fletcher, M. A. (1991). Cognitive-behavioral stress management intervention buffers distress responses and immunologic changes following notification of HIV-1 seropositivity. *Journal of Consulting and Clinical Psychology, 59,* 906–915.

Baer, J. S., Marlatt, G. A., Kivlahan, D. R., Fromme, K., Larimer, M., & Williams, E. (1992). An experimental test of three methods of alcohol risk-reduction with young adults. *Journal of Consulting and Clinical Psychology, 60,* 974–979.

Bandura, A. (1977). Self-efficacy: Toward a unifying theory of behavioral change. *Psychological Review, 84,* 191–215.

Bandura, A. (1986). *Social foundations of thought and action: A social cognitive theory.* Englewood Cliffs, NJ: Prentice Hall.

Barlow, D. H. (1988). *Anxiety and its disorders: The nature and treatment of anxiety and panic.* New York: Guilford.

Barlow, D. H., & Cerny, J. A. (1988). *Psychological treatment of panic.* New York: Guilford.

Barlow, D. H., Cohen, A. S., Waddell, M. T., Vermilyea, B. B., Klosko, J. S., Blanchard, E. B., & DiNardo, P. A. (1984). Panic and generalized anxiety disorder: Nature and treatment. *Behavior Therapy, 15,* 431–449.

Barlow, D. H., Craske, M. G., Cerny, J. A., & Klosko, J. S. (1989). Behavioral treatment of panic disorder. *Behavior Therapy, 20,* 261–282.

Baron, R. M., & Kenny, D. A. (1986). The moderator–mediator variable distinction in social psychological research: Conceptual, strategic, and statistical considerations. *Journal of Personality and Social Psychology, 51,* 1173–1182.

Baucom, D. H., & Epstein, N. (1990) *Cognitive-behavioral marital therapy.* New York: Brunner/Mazel.

Baucom, D. H., Epstein, N., Sayers, S., & Sher, T. G. (1989). The role of cognitions in marital relationships: Definitional, methodological, and conceptual issues. *Journal of Consulting and Clinical Psychology, 57,* 31–38.

Baucom, D. H., & Lester, G. W. (1986). The usefulness of cognitive restructuring as an adjunct to behavioral marital therapy. *Behavior Therapy, 17,* 385–403.

Baucom, D. H., Sayers, S. L., & Sher, T. G. (1990). Supplementing behavioral marital therapy with cognitive restructuring and emotional expressiveness training: An outcome investigation. *Journal of Consulting and Clinical Psychology, 58,* 636–645.

Beck, A. T. (1952). Successful outpatient psychotherapy of a chronic schizophrenic with a delusion based on borrowed guilt. *Psychiatry, 15,* 305–312.

Beck, A. T. (1963). Thinking and depression: I. Idiosyncratic content and cognitive distortions. *Archives of General Psychiatry, 9,* 324–333.

Beck, A. T. (1976). *Cognitive therapy and the emotional disorders.* New York: International Universities Press.

Beck, A. T. (1988). *Love is never enough.* New York: Harper & Row.

Beck, A. T., & Emery, G. (1985). *Anxiety disorders and phobias: A cognitive perspective.* New York: Basic Books.

Beck, A. T., Freeman, A., Pretzer, J., Davis, D. D., Fleming, B., Ottaviani, R., Beck, J., Simon, K. M., Padesky, C., Meyer, J., & Trexler, L. (1990). *Cognitive therapy of personality disorders.* New York: Guilford.

Beck, A. T., Rush, A. J., Shaw, B. F., & Emery, G. (1979). *Cognitive therapy of depression.* New York: Guilford.

Beck, A. T., Sokol, L., Clark, D. A., Berchick, R., & Wright, F. (1992). A crossover study of focused cognitive therapy for panic disorder. *American Journal of Psychiatry, 149,* 778–783.

Beck, A. T., Wright, F. D., & Newman, C. F. (1992). Cocaine abuse. In A. Freeman & F. M. Dattilio (Eds.), *Comprehensive casebook of cognitive therapy* (pp. 185–192). New York: Plenum.

Bennett, G. A. (1986a). Cognitive rehearsal in the treatment of obesity: A comparison against cue avoidance and social pressure. *Addictive Behaviors, 11,* 225–237.

Bennett, G. A. (1986b). An evaluation of self-instructional training in the treatment of obesity. *Addictive Behaviors, 11,* 125–134.

Berman, J. S., & Norton, N. C. (1985). Does professional training make a therapist more effective? *Psychological Bulletin, 98,* 401–407.

Biran, M., Augusto, F., & Wilson, G. T. (1981). In vivo exposure vs. cognitive restructuring in the treatment of scriptophobia. *Behaviour Research and Therapy, 19,* 525–532.

Biran, M., & Wilson, G. T. (1981). Treatment of phobic disorders using cognitive and exposure methods: A self-efficacy analysis. *Journal of Consulting and Clinical Psychology, 49,* 886–899.

Blackburn, I. M., Bishop, S., Glen, A. I. M., Whalley, L. J., & Christie, J. E. (1981). The efficacy of cognitive therapy in depression: A treatment trial using cognitive therapy and pharmacotherapy, each alone and in combination. *British Journal of Psychiatry, 139,* 181–189.

Blackburn, I. M., Eunson, K. M., & Bishop, S. (1986). A two-year naturalistic follow-up of depressed patients treated with cognitive therapy, pharmacotherapy and a combination of both. *Journal of Affective Disorders, 10,* 67–75.

Blanchard, E. B. (1992). Psychological treatment of benign headache disorders. *Journal of Consulting and Clinical Psychology, 60,* 537–551.

Blanchard, E. B., Appelbaum, K. A., Radnitz, C. L., Michultka, D., Morrill, B., Kirsch, C., Hillhouse, J., Evans, D. D., Guarnieri, P., Attanasio, V., Andrasik, F., Jaccard, J., & Dentinger, M. P. (1990). Placebo-controlled evaluation of abbreviated progressive muscle relaxation and of relaxation combined with cognitive therapy in the treatment of tension headache. *Journal of Consulting and Clinical Psychology, 58,* 210–215.

Blanchard, E. B., Appelbaum, K. A., Radnitz, C. L., Morrill, B., Michultka, D., Kirsch, C., Guarnieri, P., Hillhouse, J., Evans, D. D., Jaccard, J., & Barron, K. D. (1990). A controlled evaluation of thermal biofeedback and thermal biofeedback combined with cognitive therapy in the treatment of vascular headache. *Journal of Consulting and Clinical Psychology, 58,* 216–224.

Blowers, C., Cobb, J., & Mathews, A. (1987). Generalized anxiety: A controlled treatment study. *Behavior Research and Therapy, 25,* 493–507.

Borkovec, T. D., & Costello, E. (in press). Efficacy of applied relaxation and cognitive behavioral therapy in the treatment of generalized anxiety disorder. *Journal of Consulting and Clinical Psychology.*

Borkovec, T. D., & Mathews, A. M. (1988). Treatment of nonphobic anxiety disorders: A comparison of nondirective, cognitive, and coping desensitization therapy. *Journal of Consulting and Clinical Psychology, 56*, 877–884.

Borkovec, T. D., Mathews, A. M., Chambers, A., Ebrakimi, S., Lytle R., & Nelson, R. (1987). The effects of relaxation training with cognitive vs. nondirective therapy and the role of relaxation-induced anxiety in the treatment of generalized anxiety. *Journal of Consulting and Clinical Psychology, 55*, 883–888.

Bowers, W. A. (1990). Treatment of depressed inpatients: Cognitive therapy plus medication, relaxation plus medication, and medication alone. *British Journal of Psychiatry, 156*, 73–78.

Brown, R. A., & Lewinsohn, P. M. (1984). A psychoeducational approach to the treatment of depression: Comparison of group, individual, and minimal contact procedures. *Journal of Consulting and Clinical Psychology, 52*, 774–783.

Brownell, K. D., & Jeffery, R. W. (1987). Improving long-term weight loss: Pushing the limits of treatment. *Behavior Therapy, 18*, 353–374.

Brownell, K. D., Marlatt, G. A., Lichtenstein, E., & Wilson, G. T. (1986). Understanding and preventing relapse. *American Psychologist, 41*, 765–782.

Brownell, K. D., & Wadden, T. A. (1992). Etiology and treatment of obesity: Toward understanding a serious, prevalent, and refractory disorder. *Journal of Consulting and Clinical Psychology, 60*, 505–517.

Burns, D. D., & Nolen-Hoeksema, S. (1992). Therapeutic empathy and recovery from depression in cognitive-behavioral therapy: A structural equation model. *Journal of Consulting and Clinical Psychology, 60*, 441–449.

Butler, G., Cullington, A., Hibbert, G., Klimes, I., & Gelder, M. (1987). Anxiety management for persistent generalized anxiety. *British Journal of Psychiatry, 151*, 535–542.

Butler, G., Cullington, A., Munby, M., Amies, P., & Gelder, M. (1984). Exposure and anxiety management in the treatment of social phobia. *Journal of Consulting and Clinical Psychology, 52*, 642–650.

Butler, G., Fennell, M., Robson, P., & Gelder, M. (1991). Comparison of behavior therapy and cognitive behavior therapy in the treatment of generalized anxiety disorder. *Journal of Consulting and Clinical Psychology, 59*, 167–175.

Camp, B. W., Blom, G. E., Hebert, F., & van Doornick, W. J. (1977). "Think aloud": A program for developing self-control in young aggressive boys. *Journal of Abnormal Child Psychology, 5*, 157–169.

Carroll, K. M., Rounsaville, B. J., & Gawin, F. H. (1991). A comparative trial of psychotherapies for ambulatory cocaine abusers: Relapse prevention and interpersonal psychotherapy. *American Journal of Drug and Alcohol Abuse, 17*, 229–247.

Carroll, K. M., Rounsaville, B. J., Gordon, L. T., Nich, C., Jatlow, P., Bisighini, R. M., & Gawin, F. H. (in press). Psychotherapy and pharmacotherapy for ambulatory cocaine abusers. *Archives of General Psychiatry.*

Carroll, K. M., Rounsaville, B. J., & Keller, D. S. (1991). Relapse prevention strategies for the treatment of cocaine abuse. *American Journal of Drug and Alcohol Abuse, 17*, 249–265.

Chadwick, P. D. J., & Lowe, C. F. (1990). Measurement and modification of delusional beliefs. *Journal of Consulting and Clinical Psychology, 58*, 225–232.

Chaney, E. F., O'Leary, M. R., & Marlatt, G. A. (1978). Skill training with alcoholics. *Journal of Consulting and Clinical Psychology, 46*, 1092–1104.

Channon, S., de Silva, P., Hemsley, D., & Perkins, R. (1989). A controlled trial of cognitive-behavioural and behavioural treatment of anorexia nervosa. *Behaviour Research and Therapy, 27*, 529–535.

Christensen, H., Hadzi-Pavlovic, D., Andrews, G., & Mattick, R. (1987). Behavior therapy and tricyclic medication in the treatment of obsessive-compulsive disorder: A quantitative review. *Journal of Consulting and Clinical Psychology, 55*, 701–711.

Clark, D. M. (1986). A cognitive approach to panic. *Behavior Research and Therapy, 24*, 461–470.

Clark, D. M. (in press). Cognitive therapy for panic disorder. In B. E. Wolfe & J. D. Maser (Eds.), *Treatment of panic disorder: A consensus development conference.* Washington, DC: American Psychiatric Press.

Clark, D. M., & Salkovskis, P. M. (1991). *Cognitive therapy with panic and hypochondriasis.* New York: Pergamon.

Clark, D. M., Salkovskis, P. M., Hackmann, A., Middleton, H., & Gelder, M. (1992). *A comparison of cognitive therapy, applied relaxation and imipramine in the treatment of panic disorder.* Manuscript submitted for publication.

Collins, R. L., Rothblum, E. D., & Wilson, G. T. (1986). The comparative efficacy of cognitive and behavioral approaches to the treatment of obesity. *Cognitive Therapy and Research, 10*, 299–317.

Committee on the Review of Medicines. (1980). Systematic review of the benzodiazepines. *British Medical Journal, 280*, 910–912.

Cooper, P. J., & Fairburn, C. G. (1984). Cognitive behaviour therapy for anorexia nervosa: Some preliminary findings. *Journal of Psychosomatic Research, 28*, 493–499.

Covi, L., & Lipman, R. S. (1987). Cognitive-behavioral group psychotherapy combined with imipramine in major depression. *Psychopharmacological Bulletin, 23*, 173–176.

Craighead, L. W., & Agras, W. S. (1991). Mechanisms of action in cognitive-behavioral and pharmacological interventions for obesity and bulimia nervosa. *Journal of Consulting and Clinical Psychology, 59*, 115–125.

Craske, M. G., Brown, T. A., & Barlow, D. H. (1991). Behavioral treatment of panic disorder: A two-year follow-up. *Behavior Therapy, 22*, 289–304.

Crits-Christoph, P., Baranackie, K., Kurcias, J. S., Beck, A. T., Carroll, K., Perry, K., Luborsky, L., McLellan, A. T., Woody, G. E., Thompson, L., Gallagher, D., & Zitrin, C. (1991). Meta-analysis of therapist effects in psychotherapy outcome studies. *Psychotherapy Research, 1*, 81–91.

Curry, S. J., Marlatt, G. A., Gordon, J., & Baer, J. S. (1988). A comparison of alternative theoretical approaches to smoking cessation and relapse. *Health Psychology, 7*, 545–556.

Dahlquist, L. M., Gil, K. M., Armstrong, F. D., Ginsberg, A., & Jones, B. (1985). Behavioral management of children's distress during chemotherapy. *Journal of Behavior Therapy and Experimental Psychiatry, 16*, 325–329.

DeRubeis, R. J., Evans, M. D., Hollon, S. D., Garvey, M. J., Grove, W. M., & Tuason, V. B. (1990). How does cognitive therapy work? Cognitive change and symptom change in cognitive therapy and pharmacotherapy for depression. *Journal of Consulting and Clinical Psychology, 58*, 862–869.

DeRubeis, R. J., & Feeley, M. (1990). Determinants of change in cognitive therapy for depression. *Cognitive Therapy and Research, 14*, 469–482.

DiGiuseppe, R., McGowan, L., Simon, K. S., & Gardner, F. (1990). A comparative outcome study of four cognitive therapies in the treatment of social anxiety. *Journal of Rational-Emotive and Cognitive-Behavioral Therapy, 8*, 129–146.

Dobson, K. S. (1989). A meta-analysis of the efficacy of

cognitive therapy for depression. *Journal of Consulting and Clinical Psychology, 57,* 414–419.

Dunkel, L. D., & Glaros, A. G. (1978). Comparison of self-instructional and stimulus control treatments for obesity. *Cognitive Therapy and Research, 2,* 75–78.

Durham, R. C., & Turvey, A. A. (1987). Cognitive therapy vs. behaviour therapy in the treatment of chronic general anxiety: Outcome at discharge and at six-month follow-up. *Behaviour Research and Therapy, 25,* 229–234.

D'Zurilla, T. J., & Goldfried, M. R. (1971). Problem-solving and behavior modification. *Journal of Abnormal Psychology, 78,* 107–126.

Elkin, I., Shea, M. T., Watkins, J. T., Imber, S. D., Sotsky, S. M., Collins, J. F., Glass, D. R., Pilknios, P. A., Leber, W. R., Docherty, J. P., Fiester, S. J., & Parloff, M. B. (1989). NIMH Treatment of Depression Collaborative Research Program: I. General effectiveness of treatments. *Archives of General Psychiatry, 46,* 971–982.

Elliott, C. H., & Olson, R. A. (1983). The management of children's behavioral distress in response to painful medical treatment for burn injuries. *Behaviour Research and Therapy, 21,* 675–683.

Ellis, A. (1962). *Reason and emotion in psychotherapy.* New York: Lyle Stuart.

Ellis, A. (1980). Rational-emotive therapy and cognitive behavior therapy: Similarities and differences. *Cognitive Therapy and Research, 4,* 325–340.

Emmelkamp, P. M. G., & Beens, H. (1991). Cognitive therapy with obsessive-compulsive disorder: A comparative evaluation. *Behaviour Research and Therapy, 29,* 293–300.

Emmelkamp, P. M. G., Brilman, E., Kuiper, H., & Mersch, P. (1986). The treatment of agoraphobia: A comparison of self-instructional training, rational emotive therapy, and exposure in vivo. *Behavior Modification, 10,* 37–53.

Emmelkamp, P. M. G., Kuipers, A., & Eggeraat, J. (1978). Cognitive modification versus prolonged exposure in vivo: A comparison with agoraphobics. *Behaviour Research and Therapy, 16,* 33–41.

Emmelkamp, P. M. G., & Mersch, P. P. (1982). Cognition and exposure in vivo in the treatment of agoraphobia: Short-term and delayed effects. *Cognitive Research and Therapy, 16,* 77–90.

Emmelkamp, P. M. G., Mersch, P. P., Vissia, E., & van der Helm, M. (1985). A comparative evaluation of cognitive and behavioral interventions. *Behaviour Research and Therapy, 23,* 365–369.

Emmelkamp, P. M. G., van der Helm, M., van Zanten, B., & Plochg, I. (1980). Contributions of self-instructional training to the effectiveness of exposure in vivo. *Behaviour Research and Therapy, 18,* 61–66.

Emmelkamp, P. M. G., van den Heuvel, C. V. L., Ruphan, M., Sanderman, R., Scholing, A., & Stroink, F. (1988). Cognitive and behavioral interventions: A comparative evaluation with clinically distressed couples. *Journal of Family Psychology, 1,* 365–377.

Emmelkamp, P. M. G., Visser, S., & Hoekstra, R. J. (1988). Cognitive therapy vs. exposure in vivo in the treatment of obsessive-compulsives. *Cognitive Therapy and Research, 12,* 103–114.

Epstein, N. (1992, November). *Cognitive and behavioral marital therapy techniques: Complementary approaches to behavior change.* Paper presented at the meeting of the Association for the Advancement of Behavior Therapy, Boston.

Epstein, N., Pretzer, J. L., & Fleming, B. (1982, November). *Cognitive therapy and communication training: Comparisons of effects with distressed couples.* Paper presented at the meeting of the Association for the Advancement of Behavior Therapy, Los Angeles.

Evans, M. D, Hollon, S. D., DeRubeis, R. J., Piasecki, J. M., Grove, W. M., Garvey, M. J., & Tuason, V. B. (1992). Differential relapse following cognitive therapy and pharmacotherapy for depression. *Archives of General Psychiatry, 49,* 802–808.

Fairburn, C. G. (1981). A cognitive behavioral approach to the treatment of bulimia. *Psychological Medicine, 11,* 707–711.

Fairburn, C. G., Agras, W. S., & Wilson, G. T. (1992). The research on the treatment of bulimia nervosa: Practical and theoretical implications. In G. H. Anderson & S. H. Kennedy (Eds.), *The biology of feast and famine: Relevance to eating disorders* (pp. 318–340). New York: Academic Press.

Fairburn, C. G., Jones, R., Peveler, R. C., Carr, S. J., Solomon, R. A., O'Connor, M. E., Burton, J., & Hope, R. A. (1991). Three psychological treatments for bulimia nervosa: A comparative trial. *Archives of General Psychiatry, 48,* 463–469.

Fairburn, C. G., Jones, R., Peveler, R. C., Hope, R. A., & O'Connor, M. (1993). Psychotherapy and bulimia nervosa: Longer-term effects of interpersonal psychotherapy, behavior therapy and cognitive behavior therapy. *Archives of General Psychiatry, 50,* 419–428.

Fairburn, C. G., Peveler, R. C., Jones, R., Hope, R. A., & Doll, H. A. (in press). Predictors of twelve-month outcome in bulimia nervosa and the influence of attitudes to shape and weight. *Journal of Consulting and Clinical Psychology.*

Finn, T., DiGiuseppe, R., & Culver, C. (1991). The effectiveness of rational-emotive therapy in the reduction of muscle contraction headaches. *Journal of Cognitive Psychotherapy: An International Quarterly, 5,* 93–103.

Foa, E. B., Rothbaum, B. O., Riggs, D. S., & Murdock, T. B. (1991). Treatment of posttraumatic stress disorder in rape victims: A comparison between cognitive-behavioral procedures and counseling. *Journal of Consulting and Clinical Psychology, 59,* 715–723.

Foa, E. G., Steketee, G., & Rothbaum, B. O. (1989). Behavioral/cognitive conceptualizations of post-traumatic stress disorder. *Behavior Therapy, 20,* 155–176.

Foreyt, J. P. (1987). Issues in the assessment and treatment of obesity. *Journal of Consulting and Clinical Psychology, 55,* 677–684.

Frank, E., Kupfer, D. J., Perel, J. M., Cornes, C., Jarrett, D. B., Mallinger, A. G., Thase, M. E., McEachran, A. B., & Grochocinski, V. J. (1990). Three-year outcomes for maintenance therapies in recurrent depression. *Archives of General Psychiatry, 47,* 1093–1099.

Frank, E., Prien, R. F., Jarrett, R. B., Keller, M. B., Kupfer, D. J., Lavori, P. W., Rush, A. J., & Weissman, M. M. (1991). Conceptualization and rationale for consensus definitions of terms in major depressive disorder: Remission, recovery, relapse, and recurrence. *Archives of General Psychiatry, 48,* 851–855.

Garner, D. M., & Bemis, K. M. (1982). A cognitive-behavioral approach to anorexia nervosa. *Cognitive Therapy and Research, 6,* 123–150.

Garner, D. M., Fairburn, C. G., & Davis, R. (1987). Cognitive-behavioral treatment of bulimia nervosa. *Behavior Modification, 11,* 398–431.

Garner, D. M., Rockert, W., Davis, R., Garner, M. V., Olmstead, M. P., & Eagle, M. (1992). A comparison between cognitive-behavioral and supportive-expressive therapy for bulimia nervosa. *American Journal of Psychiatry, 150,* 37–46.

Garner, D. M., & Wooley, S. C. (1991). Confronting the failure of behavioral and dietary treatments for obesity. *Clinical Psychology Review, 11,* 729–780.

Gelernter, C. S., Uhde, T. W., Cimbolic, P., Arnkoff, D. B.,

Vittone, B. J., Tancer, M. E., & Bartko, J. J. (1991). Cognitive-behavioral and pharmacological treatments of social phobia: A controlled study. *Archives of General Psychiatry, 48,* 938–945.

Getka, E. J., & Glass, C. R. (1992). Behavioral and cognitive-behavioral approaches to the reduction of dental anxiety. *Behavior Therapy, 23,* 433–448.

Goldfried, M. R., DeCanteceo, E. T., & Weinberg, L. (1974). Systematic rational restructuring as a self-control technique. *Behavior Therapy, 5,* 247–254.

Goldstein, M. S., Niaura, R., Follick, M. J., & Abrams, D. B. (1989). Effects of behavioral skills training and schedule of nicotine gum administration on smoking cessation. *American Journal of Psychiatry, 146,* 56–60.

Greenberg, R. P., & Fisher, S. (1989). Examining antidepressant effectiveness: Findings, ambiguities, and some vexing puzzles. In S. Fisher & R. P. Greenberg (Eds.), *The limits of biological treatments for psychological distress: Comparisons with psychotherapy and placebo* (pp. 1–37). Hillsdale, NJ: Lawrence Erlbaum.

Haaga, D. A. F., & Davison, G. C. (1989a). Outcome studies of rational-emotive therapy. In M. E. Bernard & R. DiGiuseppe (Eds.), *Inside rational-emotive therapy: A critical appraisal of the theory and therapy of Albert Ellis* (pp. 155–197). San Diego: Academic Press.

Haaga, D. A. F., & Davison, G. C. (1989b). Slow progress in rational-emotive therapy outcome research: Etiology and treatment. *Cognitive Therapy and Research, 13,* 493–508.

Hall, S. M., Tunstall, C. D., Ginsberg, D., Benowitz, N. L., & Jones, R. T. (1987). Nicotine gum and behavioral treatment: A placebo controlled trial. *Journal of Consulting and Clinical Psychology, 55,* 603–605.

Heimberg, R. (1989). Cognitive and behavioral treatments for social phobia: A critical analysis. *Clinical Psychology Review, 9,* 107–128.

Heimberg, R. G. (in press). *Treatment of social fears and phobias.* New York: Guilford.

Heimberg, R. G., Becker, R. E., Goldfinger, K., & Vermilyea, J. A. (1985). Treatment of social phobia by exposure, cognitive restructuring, and homework assignments. *Journal of Nervous and Mental Disorders, 173,* 236–245.

Heimberg, R. G., Dodge, C. S., Hope, D. A., Kennedy, C. R., Zollo, L. J., & Becker, R. E. (1990) Cognitive behavior group treatment for social phobia: Comparison with a credible placebo control. *Cognitive Therapy and Research, 14,* 1–23.

Heimberg, R. G., & Liebowitz, M. R. (1992, April). *A multicenter comparison of the efficacy of phenelzine and cognitive-behavioral group treatment for social phobia.* Research presentation at the annual meeting of the Anxiety Disorders Association of America, Houston.

Heimberg, R. G., Salzman, D. G., Holt, C. S., & Blendell, K. A. (1993). Cognitive behavioral group treatment for social phobia: Effectiveness at five-year follow-up. *Cognitive Therapy and Research, 17,* 325–339.

Hinshaw, S. P., Henker, B., & Whalen, C. K. (1984a). Cognitive-behavioral and pharmacologic interventions for hyperactive boys: Comparative and combined effects. *Journal of Consulting and Clinical Psychology, 52,* 739–749.

Hinshaw, S. P., Henker, B., & Whalen, C. K. (1984b). Self-control in hyperactive boys in anger-inducing situations: Effects of cognitive-behavioral training and of methylphenidate. *Journal of Abnormal Child Psychology, 12,* 55–77.

Hole, R. W., Rush, A. J., & Beck, A. T. (1979). A cognitive investigation of schizophrenic delusions. *Psychiatry, 42,* 312–319.

Hollon, S. D., & Beck, A. T. (1986). Cognitive and cognitive-behavioral therapies. In S. L. Garfield & A. E. Bergin (Eds.), *Handbook of psychotherapy and behavior change* (3rd ed., pp. 443–482). New York: Wiley.

Hollon, S. D., DeRubeis, R. J., & Evans, M. D. (1987). Causal mediation of change in treatment for depression: Discriminating between nonspecificity and noncausality. *Psychological Bulletin, 102,* 139–149.

Hollon, S. D., DeRubeis, R. J., Evans, M. D., Wiemer, M. J., Garvey, M. J., Grove, W. M., & Tuason, V. B. (1992). Cognitive therapy and pharmacotherapy for depression: Singly and in combination. *Archives of General Psychiatry, 49,* 774–781.

Hollon, S. D., DeRubeis, R. J., & Seligman, M. E. P. (1992). Cognitive therapy and the prevention of depression. *Applied and Preventive Psychology, 1,* 89–95.

Hollon, S. D., Evans, M. D., & DeRubeis, R. J. (1990). Cognitive mediation of relapse prevention following treatment for depression: Implications of differential risk. In R. E. Ingram (Ed.), *Psychological aspects of depression* (pp. 117–136). New York: Plenum.

Hollon, S. D., Evans, M. D., Elkin, I., & Lowery, A. (1984, May). *System for rating therapies for depression.* Paper presented at the annual meeting of the American Psychiatric Association, Los Angeles.

Hollon, S. D., & Garber, J. (1980). A cognitive-expectancy theory of therapy for helplessness and depression. In J. Garber & M. E. P. Seligman (Eds.), *Human helplessness: Theory and applications* (pp. 173–195). New York: Academic Press.

Hollon, S. D., Shelton, R. C., & Loosen, P. T. (1991). Cognitive therapy and pharmacotherapy for depression. *Journal of Consulting and Clinical Psychology, 59,* 88–99.

Holroyd, K. A., Nash, J. M., Pingel, J. D., Cordingley, G. E., & Jerome, A. (1991). A comparison of pharmacological (amitriptyline HCl) and nonpharmacological (cognitive-behavioral) therapies for chronic tension headaches. *Journal of Consulting and Clinical Psychology, 59,* 387–393.

Huber, C. H., & Milstein, B. (1985). Cognitive restructuring and a collaborative set in couples' work. *American Journal of Family Therapy, 13,* 17–27.

Imber, S. D., Pilkonis, P. A., Sotsky, S. M., Elkin, I., Watkins, J. T., Collins, J. F., Shea, M. T., Leber, W. R., & Glass, D. R. (1990). Mode-specific effects among three treatments for depression. *Journal of Consulting and Clinical Psychology, 58,* 352–359.

Jacobson, N. S., Follette, W. C., Revenstorf, D., Baucom, D. H., Hahlweg, K., & Margolin, G. (1984). Variability in outcome and clinical significance of behavioral marital therapy: A reanalysis of outcome data. *Journal of Consulting and Clinical Psychology, 52,* 497–504.

Jay, S. M., & Elliott, C. H. (1990). A stress inoculation program for parents whose children are undergoing painful medical procedures. *Journal of Consulting and Clinical Psychology, 58,* 799–804.

Jay, S. M., Elliott, C. H., Katz, E., & Siegel, S. E. (1987). Cognitive behavioral and pharmacological interventions for childrens' distress during painful medical procedures. *Journal of Consulting and Clinical Psychology, 55,* 860–865.

Jemmott, J. B., Jemmott, L. S., & Fong, G. T. (1992). Reductions in HIV risk-associated sexual behaviors among black male adolescents: Effects of an AIDS prevention intervention. *American Journal of Public Health, 82,* 372–377.

Kaplan, R. M., Atkins, C. J., & Lenhard, L. (1982). Coping with a stressful sigmoidoscopy: Evaluation of cognitive and relaxation preparations. *Journal of Behavioral Medicine, 5,* 67–82.

Kazdin, A. E. (1991). Effectiveness of psychotherapy with children and adolescents. *Journal of Consulting and Clinical Psychology, 59,* 785–798.

Kazdin, A. E., & Bass, D. (1989). Power to detect differences between alternative treatments in comparative psychotherapy outcome research. *Journal of Consulting and Clinical Psychology, 57,* 138–147.

Kazdin, A. E., Bass, D., Siegel, T., & Thomas, C. (1989). Cognitive-behavioral therapy and relationship therapy in the treatment of children referred for antisocial behavior. *Journal of Consulting and Clinical Psychology, 57,* 522–535.

Kazdin, A. E., Esveldt-Dawson, K., French, N. H., & Unis, A. S. (1987a). Effects of parent management training and problem-solving skills training combined in the treatment of antisocial child behavior. *Journal of the American Academy of Child and Adolescent Psychiatry, 26,* 416–424.

Kazdin, A. E., Esveldt-Dawson, K., French, N. H., & Unis, A. S. (1987b). Problem-solving skills training and relationship therapy in the treatment of antisocial child behavior. *Journal of Consulting and Clinical Psychology, 55,* 76–85.

Kazdin, A. E., Siegel, T. C., & Bass, D. (1992). Cognitive problem-solving skills training and parent management training in the treatment of antisocial behavior in children. *Journal of Consulting and Clinical Psychology, 60,* 733–747.

Keefe, F. J., Caldwell, D. S., Williams, D. A., Gil, K. M., Mitchell, D., Robertson, C., Martinez, S., Nunley, J., Beckham, J. C., Crisson, J. E., & Helms, M. (1990). Pain coping skills training in the management of osteoarthritic knee pain: A comparative study. *Behavior Therapy, 21,* 49–62.

Keefe, F. J., Dunsmore, J., & Burnett, R. (1992). Behavioral and cognitive-behavioral approaches to chronic pain: Recent advances and future directions. *Journal of Consulting and Clinical Psychology, 60,* 528–536.

Kelly, G. A. (1955). *The psychology of personal constructs.* New York: W. W. Norton.

Kelly, J. A., & Murphy, D. A. (1992). Psychological interventions with AIDS and HIV: Prevention and treatment. *Journal of Consulting and Clinical Psychology, 60,* 576–585.

Kelly, J. A., St. Lawrence, J. S., Hood, H. V., & Brasfield, T. L. (1989). Behavioral intervention to reduce AIDS risk activities. *Journal of Consulting and Clinical Psychology, 57,* 60–67.

Kendall, P. C. (1993). Cognitive-behavioral therapies with youth: Guiding theory, current status, and emerging developments. *Journal of Consulting and Clinical Psychology, 61,* 235–247.

Kendall, P. C., & Braswell, L. B. (1985). *Cognitive-behavioral modification with impulsive children.* New York: Guilford.

Kendall, P. C., & Finch, A. J. (1978). A cognitive-behavioral treatment for impulsivity: A group comparison study. *Journal of Consulting and Clinical Psychology, 46,* 110–118.

Kendall, P. C., Williams, L., Pechacek, T. F., Graham, L. E., Shisslak, C., & Herzoff, N. (1979). Cognitive-behavioral and patient education interventions in cardiac catheterization procedures. *Journal of Consulting and Clinical Psychology, 47,* 49–58.

Kerns, R. D., Turk, D. C., Holzman, A. D., & Rudy, T. E. (1986). Comparison of cognitive-behavioral and behavioral approaches for the treatment of chronic pain. *Clinical Journal of Pain, 1,* 195–203.

Kiecolt-Glaser, J. K., & Glaser, R. (1992). Psychoneuroimmunology: Can psychological interventions modulate immunity? *Journal of Consulting and Clinical Psychology, 60,* 569–575.

Killen, J. D., Fortmann, S. P., Newman, B., & Varady, A. (1990). Evaluations of a treatment approach combining nicotine gum with self-guided behavioral treatments for smoking relapse prevention. *Journal of Consulting and Clinical Psychology, 58,* 85–92.

Kingdon, D. G., & Turkington, D. (1991). The use of cognitive behavior therapy with a normalizing rationale in schizophrenia: Preliminary report. *Journal of Nervous and Mental Disease, 179,* 207–211.

Kivlahan, D. R., Marlatt, G. A., Fromme, K., Coppel, D. B., & Williams, E. (1990). Secondary prevention with college drinkers: Evaluation of an alcohol skills training program. *Journal of Consulting and Clinical Psychology, 58,* 805–810.

Klein, D. F. (1981). Anxiety reconceptualized. In D. F. Klein & J. Rabkin (Eds.), *Anxiety: New research and changing concepts.* New York: Raven.

Klosko, J. S., Barlow, D. H., Tassinari, R., & Cerny, J. A. (1990). A comparison of alprazolam and behavior therapy in treatment of panic disorder. *Journal of Consulting and Clinical Psychology, 58,* 77–84.

Kovacs, M., & Beck, A. T. (1978). Maladaptive cognitive structures in depression. *American Journal of Psychiatry, 135,* 525–533.

Kovacs, M., Rush, A. J., Beck, A. T., & Hollon, S. D. (1981). Depressed outpatients treated with cognitive therapy or pharmacotherapy: A one-year follow-up. *Archives of General Psychiatry, 38,* 33–39.

Lake, A., Rainey, J., & Papsdorf, J. D. (1979). Biofeedback and rational emotive therapy in the management of migraine headache. *Journal of Applied Behavior Analysis, 12,* 127–140.

Leon, J. A., & Pepe, H. J. (1983). Self-instructional training: Cognitive behavior modification for remediating arithmetic deficits. *Exceptional Children, 50,* 54–60.

Lerner, M. S., & Clum, G. A. (1990). Treatment of suicide ideators: A problem-solving approach. *Behavior Therapy, 21,* 403–411.

Lewinsohn, P. M., Clarke, G. N., Hops, H., & Andrews, J. (1990). Cognitive-behavioral treatment for depressed adolescents. *Behavior Therapy, 21,* 385–401.

Lichtenstein, E., & Glasgow, R. E. (1992). Smoking cessation: What have we learned over the past decade? *Journal of Consulting and Clinical Psychology, 60,* 518–527.

Liebowitz, M. R., Schneier, F., Campeas, R., Hollander, E., Hatterer, J., Fyer, A., Gorman, J., Papp, L., Davies, S., Gully, R., & Klein, D. F. (1992). Phenelzine vs. atenolol in social phobia: A placebo-controlled comparison. *Archives of General Psychiatry, 49,* 290–300.

Lindsay, W. R., Gamsu, C. V., McLaughlin, E., Hood, E., & Espie, C. A. (1987). A controlled trial of treatment for generalized anxiety disorder. *British Journal of Clinical Psychology, 26,* 3–15.

Linehan, M. M. (1993). *Cognitive-behavioral treatment for borderline personality disorder.* New York: Guilford.

Linehan, M. M., Armstrong, H. E., Suarez, A., Allmon, D., & Heard, H. L. (1991). Cognitive-behavioral treatment of chronically parasuicidal borderline patients. *Archives of General Psychiatry, 48,* 1060–1064.

Linton, S. J., Bradley, L. A., Jensen, I., Spangfort, E., & Sundell, L. (1989). The secondary prevention of low back pain: A controlled study with follow-up. *Pain, 36,* 197–207.

Lochman, J. E., Burch, P. R., Curry, J. F., & Lampron, L. B. (1984). Treatment and generalized effects of cognitive-behavioral and goal-setting interventions with aggressive boys. *Journal of Consulting and Clinical Psychology, 52,* 915–916.

Ludwick-Rosenthal, R., & Neufeld, R. W. J. (1988). Stress

management during noxious medical procedures: An evaluative review of outcome studies. *Psychological Bulletin, 104,* 326–342.

Lyons, L. C., & Woods, P. J. (1991). The efficacy of rational-emotive therapy: A quantitative review of the outcome research. *Clinical Psychology Review, 11,* 357–369.

Mahoney, M. J. (1977). Reflections on the cognitive learning trend in psychotherapy. *American Psychologist, 32,* 5–13.

Mahoney, M. J. (1993). Theoretical developments in the cognitive psychotherapies. *Journal of Consulting and Clinical Psychology, 61,* 187–193.

Marcus, M. D., Wing, R. R., & Hopkins, J. (1988). Obese binge eaters: Affect, cognitions, and response to behavioral weight control. *Journal of Consulting and Clinical Psychology, 56,* 433–439.

Margolin, G., & Weiss, R. L. (1978). Comparative evaluation of therapeutic components associated with behavioral marital treatments. *Journal of Consulting and Clinical Psychology, 46,* 1476–1486.

Margraf, J., & Schneider, S. (1991, November). *Outcome and active ingredients of cognitive-behavioral treatments for panic disorder.* Paper presented at the annual meeting of the Association for the Advancement of Behavior Therapy, New York.

Marks, I. M. (1987). *Fears, phobias and rituals.* New York: Oxford University Press.

Marlatt, G. A. (1983). The controlled-drinking controversy: A commentary. *American psychologist, 38,* 1097–1110.

Marlatt, G. A., & Gordon, J. (1985). *Relapse prevention: Maintenance strategies in the treatment of addictive behaviors.* New York: Guilford.

Marshall, W. L., Hudson, S. M., & Ward, T. (1992). Sexual deviance. In P.H. Wilson (Ed.), *Principles and practice of relapse prevention* (pp. 235–254). New York: Guilford.

Mattick, R. P., & Peters, L. (1988) Treatment of severe social phobia: Effects of guided exposure with and without cognitive restructuring. *Journal of Consulting and Clinical Psychology, 56,* 251–260.

Mattick, R. P., Peters, L., & Clarke, J.C. (1989). Exposure and cognitive restructuring for social phobia: A controlled study. *Behavior Therapy, 20,* 3–23.

Mavissakalian, M., Michelson, L., Greenwald, D., Kornblith, S., & Greenwald, M. (1983). Cognitive-behavioral treatment of agoraphobia: Paradoxical intention vs. self-statement training. *Behavior Research and Therapy, 21,* 75–86.

McKnight, D. L., Nelson-Gray, R. O., & Barnhill, J. (1992). Dexamethasone suppression test and response to cognitive therapy and antidepressant medication. *Behavior Therapy, 23,* 99–111.

Meichenbaum, D. (1977). *Cognitive-behavior modification: An integrative approach.* New York: Plenum.

Meichenbaum, D. (1985). *Stress inoculation training.* New York: Pergamon.

Meichenbaum, D. (1993). The "potential" contributions of cognitive behavior modification to the rehabilitation of individuals with traumatic brain injury. In M. Ylvisaker (Ed.), *Seminars in speech and language* (pp. 18–30). New York: Thieme Medical Publishers.

Meichenbaum, D., & Fitzpatrick, D. (1993). A constructive narrative perspective of stress and coping: Stress inoculation applications. In L. Goldberger & S. Breznitz (Eds.), *Handbook of stress.* New York: Free Press.

Meichenbaum, D., & Goodman, J. (1971). Training impulsive children to talk to themselves: A means of developing self-control. *Journal of Abnormal Psychology, 77,* 115–126.

Mermelstein, R. J., Karnatz, T., & Reichmann, S. (1992). Smoking. In P. H. Wilson (Ed.), *Principles and practice of relapse prevention* (pp. 43–68). New York: Guilford.

Michelson, L. K., & Marchione, K. (1991). Behavioral, cognitive, and pharmacological treatments of panic disorder with agoraphobia: Critique and synthesis. *Journal of Consulting and Clinical Psychology, 59,* 100–114.

Michelson, L. K., Marchione, K., & Greenwald, M. (1989, November). *Cognitive-behavioral treatments of agoraphobia.* Paper presented at the annual meeting of the Association for the Advancement of Behavior Therapy, Washington, DC.

Miller, I. W., Norman, W. H., Keitner, G. I., Bishop, S. B., & Dow, M. G. (1989). Cognitive-behavioral treatment of depressed inpatients. *Behavior Therapy, 20,* 25–47.

Milton, F., Patwa, K., & Hafner, R. J. (1978). Confrontations vs. belief modification in persistently deluded patients. *British Journal of Medical Psychology, 51,* 127–130.

Mitchell, J. E., Pyle, R. L., Eckert, E. D., Hatsukami, D., Pomeroy, C., & Zimmerman, R. (1990). A comparison study of antidepressants and structured intensive group psychotherapy in the treatment of bulimia nervosa. *Archives of General Psychiatry, 47,* 149–157.

Moore, S. C., Agran, M., & Fodor-Davis, J. (1989). Using self-management strategies to increase the production rates of workers with severe handicaps. *Education and Training in Mental Retardation, 24,* 324–332.

Murphy, G. E., Simons, A. D., Wetzel, R. D., & Lustman, P. J. (1984). Cognitive therapy and pharmacotherapy, singly and together, in the treatment of depression. *Archives of General Psychiatry, 41,* 33–41.

Nathan, P. E., & Skinstad, A. (1987). Outcomes of treatment for alcohol problems: Current methods, problems, and results. *Journal of Consulting and Clinical Psychology, 55,* 332–340.

Nezu, A. M. (1986). Efficacy of a social problem-solving therapy approach for unipolar depression. *Journal of Consulting and Clinical Psychology, 54,* 196–202.

Nezu, A. M., & Perri, M. G. (1989). Social problem-solving therapy for unipolar depression: An initial dismantling investigation. *Journal of Consulting and Clinical Psychology, 57,* 408–413.

Nicholas, M., Wilson, P., & Grogen, J. (1991). Operant-behavioral and cognitive-behavioral treatment for chronic low back pain. *Behaviour Research and Therapy, 29,* 225–238.

Novaco, R. N. (1975). *Anger control: The development and evaluation of an experimental treatment.* Heath: Lexington, MA.

O'Malley, S. S., Jaffe, A. J., Chang, G., Schottenfeld, R. S., Meyer, R. E., & Rounsaville, B. (1992). Naltrexone and coping skills therapy for alcohol dependence: A controlled study. *Archives of General Psychiatry, 49,* 881–887.

Ost, L. G. (1991). *Cognitive therapy versus applied relaxation in the treatment of panic disorder.* Paper presented at the annual meeting of the European Association for Behavior Therapy, Oslo.

Perri, M. G., McAllister, D. A., Gange, J. J., Jordan, R. C., McAdoo, W. G., & Nezu, A. M. (1988). Effects of four maintenance programs on the long-term management of obesity. *Journal of Consulting and Clinical Psychology, 56,* 529–534.

Perry, S., Fishman, B., Jacobsberg, L., Young, J., & Frances, A. (1991). Effectiveness of psychoeducational interventions in reducing emotional distress after human immunodeficiency virus antibody testing. *Archives of General Psychiatry, 48,* 143–147.

Peterson, L., & Shigetomi, C. (1981). The use of coping

techniques in minimizing anxiety in hospitalized children. *Behavior Therapy, 12,* 1–14.

Power, K. G., Jerrom, D. W. A., Simpson, R. J., Mitchell, M. J., & Swanson, V. (1989). A controlled comparison of cognitive behaviour therapy, diazepam and placebo in the management of generalized anxiety. *Behavioural Psychotherapy, 17,* 1–14.

Power, K. G., Simpson, R. J., Swanson, V., Wallace, L. A., Feistner, A. T. C., & Sharp, D. (1990). A controlled comparison of cognitive-behavior therapy, diazepam, and placebo, alone and in combination, for the treatment of generalized anxiety disorder. *Journal of Anxiety Disorder, 4,* 267–292.

Prien, R. F., & Kupfer, D. J. (1986). Continuation drug therapy for major depressive episodes: How long should it be maintained? *American Journal of Psychiatry, 143,* 18–23.

Pyle, R. L., Mitchell, J. E., Eckert, E. D., Hatsukami, D., Pomeroy, C., & Zimmerman, R. (1990). Maintenance treatment and 6-month outcome for bulimic patients who respond to initial treatment. *American Journal of Psychiatry, 147,* 871–875.

Raimy, V. (1975). *Misunderstandings of the self.* San Francisco: Jossey-Bass.

Ramm, E., Marks, I. M., Yuksel, S., & Stern, R. S. (1981). Anxiety management training for anxiety states: Positive compared with negative self-statements. *British Journal of Psychiatry, 140,* 367–373.

Rehm, L. P. (1977). A self-control model of depression. *Behavior Therapy, 8,* 787–804.

Rehm, L. P. (1984). Self-management therapy for depression. *Advances in Behaviour Therapy and Research, 6,* 83–98.

Resick, P. A., Jordan, C. G., Girelli, S. A., Hutter, C. K., & Marhoefer-Dvorak, S. (1988). A comparative outcome study of behavioral group therapy for sexual assault victims. *Behavior Therapy, 19,* 385–401.

Reynolds, W. M., & Coats, K. I. (1986). A comparison of cognitive-behavioral therapy and relaxation training for the treatment of depression in adolescents. *Journal of Consulting and Clinical Psychology, 54,* 653–660.

Robinson, L. A., Berman, J. S., & Neimeyer, R. A. (1990). Psychotherapy for the treatment of depression: A comprehensive review of controlled outcome research. *Psychological Bulletin, 108,* 30–49.

Rosen, J. C., & Leitenberg, H. (1982). Bulimia nervosa: Treatment with exposure and response prevention. *Behavior Therapy, 13,* 117–124.

Rossiter, E. M., Agras, W. S., Losch, M., & Telch, C. F. (1988). Dietary restraint of bulimic subjects following cognitive-behavioral or pharmacological treatment. *Behaviour Research and Therapy, 26,* 495–498.

Rotheram-Borus, M. J., Koopman, C., & Haignere, C. (1991). Reducing HIV sexual risk behaviors among runaway adolescents. *Journal of the American Medical Association, 266,* 1237–1241.

Rude, S. S., & Rehm, L. P. (1991). Response to treatments for depression: The role of initial status on targeted cognitive and behavioral skills. *Clinical Psychology Review, 11,* 493–514.

Rush, A. J., Beck, A. T., Kovacs, M., & Hollon, S. D. (1977). Comparative efficacy of cognitive therapy and pharmacotherapy in the treatment of depressed outpatients. *Cognitive Therapy and Research, 1,* 17–38.

Rush, A. J., Kovacs, M., Beck, A. T., Weissenburger, J., & Hollon, S. D. (1981). Differential effects of cognitive therapy and pharmacotherapy in depressive symptoms. *Journal of Affective Disorders, 3,* 221–229.

Salkovskis, P. M. (1985). Obsessional-compulsive problems: A cognitive-behavioural analysis. *Behaviour Research and Therapy, 25,* 571–583.

Salkovskis, P. M., Atha, C., & Storer, D. (1990). Cognitive-behavioural problem solving in the treatment of patients who repeatedly attempt suicide: A controlled trial. *British Journal of Psychiatry, 157,* 871–876.

Salkovskis, P. M., & Westbrook, D. (1989). Behaviour therapy and obsessional ruminations: Can failure be turned into success? *Behaviour Research and Therapy, 27,* 149–160.

Sanchez-Craig, M., Annis, H. M., Bornet, A. R., & MacDonald, K. R. (1984). Random assignment to abstinence and controlled drinking: Evaluation of a cognitive-behavioral program for problem disorders. *Journal of Consulting and Clinical Psychology, 52,* 390–403.

Sanders, M. R., Rebgetz, M., Morrison, M., Bor, W., Gordon, A., Dadds, M., & Shepherd, R. (1989). Cognitive-behavioral treatment of recurrent nonspecific abdominal pain in children: An analysis of generalization, maintenance, and side effects. *Journal of Consulting and Clinical Psychology, 57,* 294–300.

Schlichter, K. J., & Horan, J. J. (1981). Effects of stress inoculation on the anger and aggression management skills of institutionalized juvenile delinquents. *Cognitive Therapy and Research, 5,* 359–366.

Shaw, B. F. (1977). Comparison of cognitive therapy and behavior therapy in the treatment of depression. *Journal of Consulting and Clinical Psychology, 45,* 543–551.

Shaw, B. F., & Dobson, K. S. (1988). Competency judgments in the training and evaluation of psychotherapists. *Journal of Consulting and Clinical Psychology, 56,* 666–672.

Shea, M. T., Elkin, I., Imber, S. D., Sotsky, S. M., Watkins, J. T., Collins, J. F., Pilkonis, P. A., Beckham, E., Glass, D. R., Dolan, R. T., & Parloff, M. B. (1992). Course of depressive symptoms over follow-up: Findings from the National Institute of Mental Health Treatment of Depression Collaborative Research Program. *Archives of General Psychiatry, 49,* 782–787.

Shelton, R. C., Hollon, S. D., Purdon, S. E., & Loosen, P. T. (1991). Biological and psychological aspects of depression. *Behavior Therapy, 22,* 201–228.

Simons, A. D., Garfield, S. L., & Murphy, G. E. (1984). The process of change in cognitive therapy and pharmacotherapy for depression. *Archives of General Psychiatry, 41,* 45–51.

Simons, A. D., Murphy, G. E., Levine, J. L., & Wetzel, R. D. (1986). Cognitive therapy and pharmacotherapy for depression: Sustained improvement over one year. *Archives of General Psychiatry, 43,* 43–48.

Smith, B., & Sechrest, L. (1991). Treatment of aptitude X treatment interactions. *Journal of Consulting and Clinical Psychology, 59,* 233–244.

Smith, D., Marcus, M. D., & Kaye, W. (1992). Cognitive-behavioral treatment of obese binge eaters. *International Journal of Eating Disorders, 12,* 257–262.

Sokol, L., Beck, A. T., Greenberg, R. L., Wright, F. D., & Berchick, R. J. (1989). Cognitive therapy of panic disorder: A nonpharmacological alternative. *Journal of Nervous and Mental Disease, 12,* 711–716.

Spivak, G., Platt, J. J., & Shure, M. B. (1976). *The problem-solving approach to adjustment.* San Francisco: Jossey-Bass.

Stark, K. D., Reynolds, W. M., & Kaslow, N. J. (1987). A comparison of the relative efficacy of self-control therapy and a behavioral problem-solving therapy for depression in children. *Journal of Abnormal Child Psychology, 15,* 91–113.

Stevens, V. J., & Hollis, J. F. (1989). Preventing smoking relapse, using an individually tailored skills-training technique. *Journal of Consulting and Clinical Psychology, 57,* 420–424.

Stravynski, A., Marks, I., & Yule, W. (1982). Social skills problems in neurotic outpatients: Social skills training with and without cognitive modification. *Archives of General Psychiatry, 39,* 1378–1385.

Telch, C. F., Agras, W. S., Rossiter, E. M., Wilfley, D., & Kenardy, J. (1990). Group cognitive-behavioral treatment for the nonpurging bulimic: An initial evaluation. *Journal of Consulting and Clinical Psychology, 58,* 629–635.

Telch, C. F., & Telch, M. J. (1986). Group coping skills instruction and supportive group therapy for cancer patients: A comparison of strategies. *Journal of Consulting and Clinical Psychology, 54,* 802–808.

Teri, L., & Lewinsohn, P. M. (1986). Individual and group treatment of unipolar depression: Comparison of treatment outcome and identification of predictors of successful treatment outcome. *Behavior Therapy, 17,* 215–228.

Thase, M. E., Bowler, K., & Harden, T. (1991). Cognitive behavior therapy of endogenous depression: Part 2. Preliminary findings in 16 unmedicated inpatients. *Behavior Therapy, 22,* 469–477.

Turk, D. C., Meichenbaum, D., & Genest, M. (1983). *Pain and behavioral medicine: A cognitive-behavioral perspective.* New York: Plenum.

Turner, J. A. (1982). Comparison of group progressive-relaxation training and cognitive-behavioral group therapy for chronic low back pain. *Journal of Consulting and Clinical Psychology, 50,* 757–765.

Turner, J. A., & Clancy, S. (1988). Comparison of operant behavioral and cognitive-behavioral group treatment for chronic low back pain. *Journal of Consulting and Clinical Psychology, 56,* 261–266.

Vitousek, K. B., & Hollon, S. D. (1990). The investigation of schematic content and processing in eating disorders. *Cognitive Therapy and Research, 14,* 191–214.

Volpicelli, J. R., Alterman, A. I., Hayashida, M., & O'Brien, C. P. (1992). Naltrexone in the treatment of alcohol dependence. *Archives of General Psychiatry, 49,* 876–880.

Watts, F. N., Powell, E. G., & Austin, S. V. (1973). The modification of abnormal beliefs. *British Journal of Medical Psychology, 46,* 359–363.

Williams, S. L., & Rappoport, A. (1983). Cognitive treatment in the natural environment for agoraphobics. *Behavior Therapy, 14,* 299–313.

Wilson, G. T. (1987). Cognitive studies in alcoholism. *Journal of Consulting and Clinical Psychology, 55,* 325–331.

Wilson, G. T., & Fairburn, C. G. (1993). Cognitive treatments for eating disorders. *Journal of Consulting and Clinical Psychology, 61,* 261–269.

Woodward, R., & Jones, R. B. (1980). Cognitive restructuring treatment: A controlled trial with anxious patients. *Behaviour Research and Therapy, 18,* 401–407.

Woody, G. E., Luborsky, L., McLellan, A. T., O'Brien, C. P., Beck, A. T., Blaine, J., Herman, I., & Hole, A. (1983). Psychotherapy for opiate addiction? Does it help? *Archives of General Psychiatry, 40,* 639–645.

Wurtman, R. J. (1987). Nutrients affecting brain composition and behavior. *Integrative Psychiatry, 5,* 226–257.

11

PSYCHODYNAMIC APPROACHES

- **WILLIAM P. HENRY**

  Vanderbilt University

- **HANS H. STRUPP**

  Vanderbilt University

- **THOMAS E. SCHACHT**

  James H. Quillen College of Medicine

- **LOUISE GASTON**

  McGill University

REEXAMINING PSYCHODYNAMIC PSYCHOTHERAPY

The first and second editions of this *Handbook* contained a chapter on psychoanalytic therapy, which dealt with "psychoanalytic treatment itself, not . . . psychoanalytically oriented psychotherapy" (p. 331). The authors, Luborsky and Spence, chose to confine their review to psychoanalytic treatment in the strict (or "classical") sense, omitting for the most part the most widely practiced forms of psychoanalytically oriented or psychodynamic psychotherapy (we use the terms interchangeably). In the third edition of the *Handbook* (1986), the editors decided to omit the chapter on the grounds that "there was insufficient *new* material to warrant [a complete chapter]" (p. ix, emphasis in original). They also noted that "Advances and research in psychodynamic therapy have been evident primarily in the briefer forms of therapy, and these findings were presented in a number of the chapters in the present volume" (p. x).

Admittedly, psychoanalytic practice is not guided by solid empirical research any more today than it was a decade and a half ago, when Luborsky and Spence (1978) concluded that "quantitative research . . . presents itself, so far, as an unreliable guide to clinical practice" (p. 358). Nonetheless, there are now several compelling reasons to reintroduce a chapter under the broadened heading of "psychodynamic approaches." First, empirical evidence is leading to a revision of the strict distinction between psychoanalysis and psychodynamic psychotherapy. Second, psychodynamic approaches continue to enjoy a preeminent role in theory and practice, and during the last decade a small, but growing body of research related to core psychodynamic constructs has emerged. This body of research has direct and indirect implications for the efficacy of psychodynamic therapy, a central concern of the psychotherapy research community. Unlike earlier research that simply aimed to establish the general benefit of psychodynamic approaches, however, recent research addresses more specifically the central processes inherent in psychodynamic therapy (e.g., the nature of the therapeutic alliance, the process of interpretation, and psychodynamic formulation). Indeed, we are much closer today to foreseeing the time when research will provide guidelines for practice. Thus, the continued growth of psychodynamic theory and practice, coupled with the emergence of promising new research, would amply seem to justify the reintroduction of a chapter based on the psychoanalytic tradition.

Psychoanalytic Versus Psychodynamic

The "proper" distinction between psychoanalysis and psychodynamic psychotherapy has been controversial since the time of Freud. In brief, the distinctions have most often involved the aim of treatment (personality reconstruction vs. symptom alleviation and the restoration of defenses) and the permissibility of techniques other than interpretation (support, advice, etc.). Debates have raged between those in favor of a sharp distinction (Bibring, 1954; Gill, 1954; Glover, 1931) and those who would blur the boundaries (or see none at all), placing psychoanalysis and psychodynamic psychotherapy on a continuum (Alexander, 1954; Fromm-Reichmann, 1954; Panel, 1955). Frosch (1990) provides an excellent summary of this controversy.

Historically, these distinctions have been the

product of intellectual polemics, but are they mirrored in actual psychoanalytic practice? The well-known Psychotherapy Research Project (PRP) of the Menninger Foundation, which started in the early 1950s, was designed to study, in a naturalistic setting, the differences between treatment outcomes in psychoanalysis proper and other modes of expressive and supportive psychoanalytic psychotherapy. The results of the PRP, summarized by Wallerstein (1989), cast considerable doubt on the previously assumed distinction between psychoanalysis and other forms of more "supportive" and less "expressive" forms of psychotherapy.[1] Wallerstein concluded:

> The therapeutic modalities of psychoanalysis, expressive psychotherapy, and supportive psychotherapy hardly exist in ideal or pure form in the real world of actual practice; real treatments in actual practice are intermingled blends of expressive-interpretive and supportive-stabilizing elements; almost all treatments (including even pure psychoanalyses [if such a treatment ever existed]) carry many more supportive components than they are usually credited with; the overall outcomes achieved by more analytic and more supportive treatments converge more than our usual expectations for those differing modalities would portend; and the kinds of changes achieved in treatment from the two ends of this spectrum are less different in nature and in permanence than is usually expected. (p. 205)

At this juncture, then, it would seem most appropriate to review contemporary research based on the analytic theoretical tradition under the expanded rubric of psychodynamic approaches. While the practice of "classical" psychoanalysis has declined in recent years, psychotherapy based on psychodynamic principles has shown a remarkable viability, perhaps even a renascence. In a recent survey of theoretical orientations (Sammons & Gravitz, 1990), the psychodynamic orientation was still the most dominant specific category among clinicians and educators, trailing only those who labeled themselves eclectic. Additionally, Jensen and Bergin (1988) found that 73 percent of those individuals embracing an eclectic approach reported the use of psychodynamic concepts, making

analytic theory the single greatest contributor to the eclectic mix.

For the purpose of this chapter, we shall define psychodynamic psychotherapy as "an approach to diagnosis and treatment characterized by a way of thinking about both patient and clinician that includes unconscious conflict, deficits and distortions of intrapsychic structures, and internal object relations" (Gabbard, 1990, p. 4). This definition clearly covers a wide range of historical and contemporary drive, ego, object, and self-psychologies (see Pine, 1990, for an excellent review of these four major strands of analytic thought).

Selection Criteria

Given our expanded definition of psychodynamic, a potentially enormous number of research studies might be included. Due to the nature of this volume, we first eliminated studies that were not directly relevant to psychotherapy per se. For example, studies slanted toward the confirmation of certain constellations of psychopathology as seen from a psychodynamic perspective (such as the link between early traumas brought about by child abuse and the developmental level of object relations) were not reviewed. Second, we sought research that was clearly psychodynamic in origin, that is, research that explored major time-honored and central tenets of dynamic theory. This eliminated a number of process–outcome studies that employed psychodynamic therapists but did not specifically address core psychodynamic principles. We also eliminated studies designed to test the efficacy (or comparative efficacy) of dynamic therapy per se because such studies were not designed to shed light on the central principles or processes of psychodynamic therapy. We also felt that the psychodynamic outcome research would be sufficiently covered elsewhere in this volume. We will, however, briefly mention two major recent meta-analyses of short-term dynamic psychotherapy, as we feel they have implications for future research in the areas we do review. Finally, we wished to focus on research that is representative of the major trends within the psychodynamic research community. Inclusion of a topic required that sufficient research by multiple researchers had been accumulated to permit some tentative conclusions. This may have unfortunately eliminated some excellent research by single investigators.[2] What has

---

[1]We do not mean to suggest that the distinction between more or less supportive or expressive approaches is spurious. Indeed, it is likely one of the fundamental parameters of therapeutic process and has been linked to differential outcomes dependent upon patient characteristics. However, like Wallerstein, we question the sharp division between psychoanalysis and "everything else."

[2]For example, Mardi Horowitz and colleagues at Langly Porter have developed an ambitious program to study unconscious processes, combining elements of cognitive science and psychodynamics. As of this writing, however, insufficient published empirical data are available to permit summary or tentative conclusions.

emerged should thus be seen as a selective review of major research themes, not an exhaustive review of all relevant psychodynamic research.

Overview of Selected Topics

Using these criteria and carefully considering the available empirical research, we were led to focus on three main topics. First, we review the emergent empirical literature on *interpretations,* specifically transference interpretations. The transference interpretation represents the central defining technique of psychodynamic psychotherapy, and for the first time, a body of quantitative research on the efficacy of interpretation is available. As we shall see, this research may challenge many long-held assumptions and has direct implications for therapeutic practice.

Next, we review research relevant to the therapeutic relationship or *alliance.* While adherents of most theoretical perspectives now recognize the importance of a positive therapeutic relationship, specific theoretical debates about the nature and function of the alliance have been central to psychodynamic theory. These debates can be traced back to Freud's earliest writings (Freud, 1912/1966) and continue in analytic circles today (Frieswyk et al., 1986). Thus, we give particular emphasis to a growing body of studies addressing the fundamental question of whether the alliance is a unidimensional or multidimensional theoretical construct, and we discuss the need for more theoretically precise research.

Finally, we review research in the area of psychodynamic *formulation.* The last decade has witnessed tremendous interest in the development of methods to standardize and operationalize the psychodynamic case formulation, that most basic of clinical activities. This topic is of central importance because formulation schemes attempt to operationalize more precisely *what* is being treated by dynamic psychotherapy. Although this general line of research does not specifically address psychotherapeutic process or outcome per se, it was included because we feel that such formulation procedures provide a potential methodological bedrock for more refined psychodynamic process–outcome research in the future. Therefore, in the section on systematic formulation, we summarize the major available procedures, but we focus on the research issues arising from the use of such methodology.

The three areas chosen for review embody the essence of psychodynamic therapy. We begin our review by summarizing the research on interpretations. We chose this topic as a point of departure, because, as L. Silverman and Wolitzky (1982, p. 328) state, "There is no disagreement among

[traditional] psychoanalytic clinicians that the chief role of the therapist is to offer interpretations and make whatever other interventions are necessary (e.g., clarifications, confrontations, and questioning) to pave the way for interpretations."

EMPIRICAL STUDIES OF TRANSFERENCE INTERPRETATION

Psychotherapy first began to achieve widespread public attention during a period in its development that was heavily dominated by psychoanalytic conceptions and procedures. For many—patient, therapist, and general public alike—the process of interpretation became almost synonymous with psychotherapy. In a seminal paper, Bibring (1954, p. 763) refers to insight through interpretation as the "supreme agent in the hierarchy of therapeutic principles." More specifically, focus on transference interpretations has become the hallmark of psychoanalytically oriented technique in psychotherapy. The widely held orthodox view posits that the "ultimate instrument" of therapeutic change is the "mutative interpretation" of the fully developed transference neurosis (Strachey, 1934). Historically, these beliefs were articles of faith, as the analytic community was slow to champion empirical tests of core tenets. In an earlier edition of this *Handbook,* Luborsky and Spence (1978) could uncover almost no quantitative research on the patient's transference response or the process of interpretation. If the psychoanalytic theory of therapeutic change is to move beyond the "belief" stage, an investigation of the processes related to transference interpretations is a first priority.

Fortunately, the last decade has witnessed an increasing emphasis on psychotherapy process research, coupled with a continued widespread interest in psychodynamic theory and a greater openness to research on the part of the analytic community. As a result, a fledgling empirical literature on transference interpretations has begun to appear, and it now seems possible to offer some very tentative, empirically based conclusions. Ironically, at the very time that quantitative research in this area has finally begun to emerge, a complicating factor has also arisen—the growth of short-term approaches to analytic therapy. Freud (1913/1958) recommended that transference should not be interpreted until it had clearly become a resistance, a process that might not have sufficient time to develop during time-limited therapy. Thus, some authors have argued that transference interpretations should be avoided altogether in brief therapy, while others continue to see them as indispensable (see Frances & Perry, 1983, for a review of this issue). Researchers are now faced not only with understanding the effects of transference interpretations, but also with questions of their differential efficacy in open-ended versus time-limited modalities. The studies currently available for review investigate therapies ranging from under 20 sessions to 150 sessions, with the majority considered to fall within a liberal definition of short-term therapy (under 50 sessions).[3] Therefore, the question of differential efficacy as a function of duration remains unaddressed.

In this section, we review empirical process studies of transference interpretations.[4] We also discuss methodological issues and problems encountered in trying to interpret the meaning of these studies. Finally, we offer some tentative conclusions and discuss directions for future research.

Before reviewing the empirical literature, it is important to note briefly that there are no universally agreed upon definitions of the terms *transference* and *interpretation*. Definitions of transference vary according to the breadth of relationships included in the concept (see Sandler, Holder, Kawenoka, Kennedy, & Neurath, 1969, for a review). A narrow definition restricts the term *transference* to the transferring of thoughts, feelings, and fantasies about early childhood figures onto the therapist, while a broader definition includes aspects of the patient's relationships that are similar across a number of people, including the therapist (also called *character transference:* Luborsky, Barber, & Crits-Christoph, 1990). The specificity of the term *interpretation* varies even more widely (see Piper, Debbane, de Carufel, & Bienvenu, 1987, for a review of concepts associated with interpretation). When the terms are combined, a number of possible definitions of *transference interpretation* exist. A complete discussion of the research implications of these definitional issues is beyond the scope of this review, but we touch on the problem later.

Research studies on transference interpretations have generally followed one of three basic designs. The first approach involves the study of the *frequency* and/or *concentration* of transference interpretations as they relate to the process and outcome of therapy. A second approach aims to study the *immediate effects* of transference interpretations compared to other therapist interventions on patient process in the minutes following the intervention. A third approach concerns itself with the relative *accuracy* of interpretations as a predictor of subsequent process and outcome. Each of these designs addresses fundamentally different questions, and we now examine each in turn.

Frequency of Interpretive Activity

The question of the optimal frequency of transference interpretations (and indeed, whether to employ them at all) has become a more compelling question with the advent of short-term dynamic therapies. Time limits force therapists to make interpretations earlier in therapy, often with less evidence and greater frequency. Even strong advocates of transference interpretations such as Gill (1982) have warned against their overuse. Nonetheless, most of the pioneers of short-term psychodynamic therapy have advocated their frequent use (Davanloo, 1978; Malan, 1976a; Mann, 1973; Sifneos, 1972). Malan (1976b) claimed support for the "more is better" position, citing a significant correlation between the frequency of transference/parent interpretations and positive outcome. However, serious methodological problems (such as the use of process notes instead of independent ratings, raters who were not blind to outcome status, etc.) have led most researchers to treat Malan's findings with skepticism (Frances & Perry, 1983). Marziali (1984a) attempted a more rigorous replication of Malan's study, using audiotaped recordings to replace session notes, and reported that Malan's results had been confirmed. Marziali's conclusions have also been questioned, however, both on methodological grounds and on the basis that only a small number of her results were supportive of Malan, while many findings were not (Piper, Debbane, Bienvenu, Carufel, & Garant, 1986).

More recent and more methodologically sound research has uniformly failed to confirm a link between frequency of transference interpretations and positive outcome. Piper et al. (1986) criticized earlier designs that relied on the raw frequency of interpretations, noting that frequency per se might simply reflect greater therapist activity or interest. They distinguished 10 therapist intervention categories, including 4 types of interpretation (depending upon the number of dynamic components addressed). Furthermore, they linked all interpretations to the object of the interpretation (parents, significant other, therapist, etc.). They hypothesized that the greater the *proportion* of interpretations that link the patient's parents to feelings

---

[3]Luborsky, Bachrach, Graff, Pulver, & Christoph's (1979) study of three patients in classical analysis is the lone exception.

[4]A number of studies involving the effects of differential "therapist response modes" include data relevant to patient response to interpretations (Elliott, James, Reimschuessel, Cislo, & Sacks, 1985). However, since they were not designed to study interpretation exclusively or necessarily from a psychodynamic perspective, they have not been included. Also omitted were case studies, or studies based on informal methodology and impressionistic conclusions.

toward the therapist, the better the outcome of therapy. Rating 8 sessions each from 21 cases of short-term dynamic therapy (average length = 23 sessions), they reported some interesting descriptive statistics. For instance, 14 percent of all interventions were considered interpretations, with an average of 10 per session, or 80 interpretations per entire therapy. Although interpretations comprised only 14 percent of all interventions, they consumed 44 percent of the therapists' "speaking time." Overall, however, they found no evidence to support their main hypothesis, as the proportion of transference interpretations was not related to outcome.

Piper's group later replicated and expanded this study, using a larger sample of patients (N = 64) seen for 20 sessions in a structured form of short-term, transference-oriented dynamic therapy modeled after Malan (1976a) and Strupp and Binder (1984) (Piper, Azim, Joyce, & McCallum, 1991). In addition to examining the relationship between transference interpretations and outcome, they examined the moderating roles of alliance and patients' quality of object relations. A total of 22,500 therapist interventions were rated, and therapists were observed to average over five transference interpretations per session. The results revealed an *inverse* relationship between the proportion of transference interpretations (out of total therapist interventions) and patient-reported alliance as well as outcome. This relationship was particularly pronounced in patients with a high quality of object relations and was also stronger when there was a high level of transference interpretations late in therapy. These findings were not general to all interpretations but were specific to transference interpretations. Piper, Azim, Joyce, and McCallum concluded:

> We believe that the evidence is sufficiently strong to warrant alerting clinicians to the possibilities of negative effects and the seeming ineffectiveness of trying to improve alliance or resolve resistance by providing high levels of transference interpretations during short-term psychotherapy. (1991, p. 952)

Using a different methodology, the Vanderbilt research group has also provided data that is consistent with the results reported by Piper, Azim, Joyce, and McCallum. In a five-year study of the effects of time-limited dynamic psychotherapy, experienced, dynamically oriented therapists were trained in a form of brief (25 sessions) focal therapy that emphasized the frequent exploration of the patient–therapist relationship (Henry, Strupp, Butler, Schacht, & Binder, 1993; Henry, Schacht,

Strupp, Butler, & Binder, 1993). Although the study was not designed to explore the effects of transference interpretations per se, the adherence measure used to rate an early and a late session (Sessions 3 and 16) did contain specific items (which were analyzed separately) measuring the frequency with which therapists addressed the patient–therapist relationship and linked it to recurrent interpersonal patterns. After training, therapists were significantly more active and engaged in significantly more interventions that could be described as transference interpretations.[5] The design permitted a comparison of relatively low versus relatively high levels of interpretations on a similar patient sample, using the same therapists to serve as their own controls.

Consistent with Piper, Azim, Joyce, and McCallum, some alliance measures deteriorated after training in the context of earlier and more frequent transference exploration and interpretation. Independent raters reported a significantly higher frequency of hostile interpersonal communication by the therapists as measured by the Structural Analysis of Social Behavior (SASB: Benjamin, 1974). Additionally, therapists were judged to be less supportive and optimistic, less approving, and more authoritarian and defensive as rated by the Vanderbilt Psychotherapy Process Scale (VPPS: O'Malley, Suh, & Strupp, 1983). Patients also reported that their therapists were more impatient with them.[6] After training, there was some evidence of a negative relationship between adherence to the protocol (and thus indirectly the level of transference interpretations) and outcome. As with Piper, Azim, Joyce, and McCallum, this relationship was most pronounced when therapist interpretive activity was measured later in therapy.[7]

One possible exception to this trend was reported by Gutfreund (1992), who sampled 4 ses-

---

[5]Since the Vanderbilt group employed a global rating method, the absolute frequency of interpretive activity cannot be directly compared to the descriptive results of Piper, Azim, Joyce, and McCallum (1991).

[6]The link between an increase in transference interpretations and a deterioration in interpersonal process variables may not seem immediately clear and may perhaps be counterintuitive. Indeed, the Vanderbilt research group had predicted the opposite effect. We do not believe that transference interpretation must inevitably be accompanied by such processes; however, they may be uniquely "dangerous" in this regard. This point is discussed more fully in the conclusion of this section.

[7]It should be noted that there was also some evidence that training had a positive impact on outcomes in certain cases (Henry, Strupp, Schacht, Binder, & Butler, 1992). However, the results relating *frequency* of transference exploration to poorer outcomes were in line with earlier research.

sions (2 early, a middle, and a late phase session) each from 46 cases seen by student therapists for a median of 29 sessions at a university counseling center. The frequency of transference interpretation was rated, using a global impression scale applied to 20-minute segments. These ratings were then compared to the patients' self-reported therapeutic alliance (California Psychotherapy Alliance Scales) and outcome (from patient and therapist perspectives). A path analytic strategy was used to test various models linking pretreatment symptom status, alliance, transference interpretations, and two types of outcome (dynamic and symptomatic).

Gutfreund reported several results of interest to the current discussion. Transference interpretations in the first session were positively correlated with third session alliance. However, due to the low absolute frequency of first session transference interpretations, this result may be based on a very limited subset of unique cases. When the ratings of transference interpretations were combined across sessions and related to outcome, mixed results were obtained. Transference interpretations were found to be positively associated with a measure of dynamic, therapist-rated outcome. This potentially countervailing finding is obscured somewhat by the nature of the outcome measure itself. Outcome was based on a comparison of pre- and posttherapy ratings on the same items. However, both sets of ratings were made retrospectively, a questionable procedure. The student therapists may also have been influenced by the fact that they made a large number of transference interpretations (i.e., overestimating their effect in line with their theoretical bias). On the other hand, transference interpretations were inversely related to patient-reported symptom change (in the presence of a positive alliance), a finding in keeping with the other studies. Finally, McCullough et al. (1991), in a study described more extensively in the next section, found no relationship between frequency of any class of interpretation and eventual outcome.

Immediate Effects of Transference Interpretations

Psychotherapy researchers in general have increasingly called for the study of variables in a context-sensitive manner, and they suggested that "outcomes" may also rightly be seen as the immediate process effects of an intervention (Greenberg, 1986). In this vein, several studies have attempted to explore patients' immediate reactions to transference interpretations. This type of design may be of particular theoretical importance for several reasons. First, one of the traditional reasons offered for the unique efficacy of transference interpreta-

tions is that greater "emotional urgency" is available, and hence, patients respond with greater affect (Strachey, 1934). While it is true that some empirical evidence exists to suggest that patients' affective response to interpretation is associated with positive outcome (Luborsky, Bachrach, Graff, Pulver, & Christoph, 1979), the unique ability of transference interpretations to *elicit* such responses has not been demonstrated. Second, given the fact that few overall differences in outcome have been found among various forms of psychotherapy, the burden of proof is upon proponents to demonstrate some form of differential efficacy for their preferred techniques (Frances & Perry, 1983). A demonstration that greater affective responding or depth of experiencing follows transference interpretations compared to other types of interventions would help to answer both of these questions.

Luborsky et al. (1979) provided the initial study of the immediate effects of transference interpretations. Three patients in long-term psychoanalysis were selected based on differential outcomes (poor, moderate, and very positive). Trained analysts rated the 250 words before and after 16 selected transference interpretations for each case on a number of process variables, including resistance, involvement, affect, understanding, and transference (positive and negative). The three patients show different, but self-consistent responses across the interpretations studied, with each patient's response style mirroring his or her outcome status (i.e., the poor outcome patient had the most negative and resistant reaction). Luborsky et al. concluded that the patient, not technical factors, was central to understanding the different responses to transference interpretations. They also observed that while theory would predict a decrease in transference following the interpretation, an increase in transference manifestations was actually observed for the two successful cases. To explain this, they speculated that the interpretations led to an increase in openness, and therefore the *recognizability* of the transference. In summary, this pioneering effort challenged the view that transference interpretations necessarily lead to certain patient processes. These results are enhanced by the fact that well-trained analysts were used as subjects and judges, and also by the fact that efforts were made to ensure that the interpretations studied were equally well timed by traditional analytic criteria.

McCullough et al. (1991) studied 4 sessions each from 16 dyads in brief dynamic therapy (27–53 sessions) designed to confront defenses and elicit affect. Three types of therapist interventions were isolated: interpretations involving the patient and therapist, interpretations involving the patient and a significant other, and clarifications (used as a control condition). Patient responses were measured in the 3 minutes following the therapist intervention and were classified as affective or defensive. When the data were collapsed and viewed nonsequentially, the frequency of each of the types of interventions failed to correlate significantly with outcome. When viewed sequentially and collapsed across intervention type, level of patient defensive responding was significantly negatively correlated with outcome ($r = -.50$), while affective responding was significantly positively correlated with improvement ($r = .51$). The only specific intervention–response sequence to reach significance when correlated with outcome was the patient–therapist interpretation followed by affect, which was related to good outcome ($r = .60$), as theory would predict.

Several caveats are in order, however. Nontransference interpretations when followed by affect were also positively correlated with outcome ($r = .44$), but the small sample size prevented this result from reaching statistical significance. Thus, the evidence for the unique positive benefits of transference interpretations is weak at best. Additionally, the difference in mean number of patient affective responses following each intervention type was quite small (ranging from an average of .12 affective responses per minute for clarifications to .17 for patient–therapist interpretations). However, interpretations in general were almost twice as likely to provoke defensive responses compared to clarification, with patient–therapist interpretations slightly more likely to be followed by defensive responses than were interpretations involving significant others.

Porter (1987) employed a design similar to that of McCullough et al., but he categorized patient responses into four dimensions—defensive, affective, static, and insightful. His results mirrored those of McCullough et al. Interpretations in general were more likely to evoke defensive responses, but no more likely to produce an affective response. Porter found no significant differences between transference and nontransference interventions with respect to any category of patient response. In keeping with these results, Strisik (1990) failed to confirm the hypothesis that the patient's depth of experiencing would increase following a shift to the discussion of the patient–therapist relationship.

Accuracy of Interpretation
The few studies in this category are based on the idea than *any* methodology used to explore the relationship between interpretation and outcome is

incomplete if the design fails to take into account the "goodness of fit" between the therapist's intervention and the individual patient's particular problems and treatment goals (Silberschatz, Fretter, & Curtis, 1986). In other words, not all interpretations are necessarily suitable or accurate, and to treat them as such perpetuates another uniformity myth (Kiesler, 1966). While this may seem intuitively obvious, the research procedures necessary to assess interpretive accuracy present a daunting conceptual and methodological challenge. It may be no accident that two of the three major studies of accuracy have followed from extensive initial efforts designed to reliably measure patients' central problems in a structured, standardized format.

The first of these studies grew out of the Mount Zion research group's work on "plan diagnosis" (Rosenberg, Silberschatz, Curtis, Sampson, & Weiss, 1986). According to their theory, psychopathology stems from unconscious pathogenic beliefs rooted in childhood experience, and each patient enters psychotherapy with a plan or strategy for disconfirming these beliefs by testing them in relationship to the therapist (J. Weiss, 1977). Therapists' interventions are thought to be most helpful when that are "plan-compatible," that is, when they accurately address the patient's conscious and unconscious goals and the false beliefs that prevent goal attainment. Silberschatz et al. (1986) used the plan diagnosis methodology to test the hypothesis that the suitability of therapists' interventions (the extent to which they were plan-compatible) would be more predictive of patient progress than the category of interpretation (transference vs. nontransference). Three patients with outcomes ranging from good to poor who received 16 sessions of brief dynamic therapy were studied. All transference and nontransference interpretations were located and rated for degree of plan-compatibility. Additionally, the patients' behavior in the three minutes before and after each intervention was rated for depth of experiencing.

The residual change in experiencing scores from pre- to postintervention did not differ significantly between transference and nontransference interpretations. This finding is consistent with the results cited in the previous section. When the data were collapsed, the proportion of transference interpretations was not significantly correlated with increases in experiencing in two cases and was negatively correlated in the third ($r = -.81$). However, positive and significant correlations were observed between plan-compatibility scores and changes in the level of experiencing. Depending on the individual case, these correlations ranged from .25 to .54 for individual interpretations, and from .54 to .78

for aggregated session scores. When only plan-compatible interventions were examined, there was still no significant difference in process effects between transference and nontransference interpretations. Additionally, the percentage of pro-plan interpretations was significantly higher in the two good outcome cases as compared to the poor outcome case. Silberschatz et al. concluded that the *suitability* of interpretation to the patient was important, while the category of interpretation was not.

Another major study of accuracy (Crits-Christoph, Cooper, & Luborsky, 1988) was based on Luborsky's Core Conflictual Relationship Theme (CCRT: Luborsky, 1977), a systematic methodology for arriving at a structured, dynamic case formulation.[8] Independent raters formulated the central CCRT for each of 43 patients seen for an average of 53 sessions (range 21 – 149) of weekly psychodynamic psychotherapy. Separate sets of judges rated therapists' interpretations (mean of 6.1 per patient) in 2 early sessions. Accuracy was assessed on a 1 – 4 scale for degree of congruence with the CCRT categories of wish, response from other, and response of self. The wish and response of other categories were later combined due to their high correlation and are said to represent the interpersonal aspects of the core theme. The response of self is described more as a patient feeling state. Additionally, the Errors in Technique subscale of the Vanderbilt Negative Indicators Scale (Strupp et al., 1981) and the Helping Alliance Scale (counting sign method: Luborsky, Crits-Christoph, Alexander, Margolin, & Cohen, 1983) were rated. Crits-Christoph, Cooper, and Luborsky (1988) were interested in determining whether accuracy would predict outcome, whether it would predict outcome only in the presence of a positive alliance, and the degree of overlap between accuracy and more general technical skill.

Multiple regression analysis indicated that the accuracy of wish plus response of other (but not response of self) and Helping Alliance scores (but not Errors in Technique) contributed significant, independent variance in predicting outcome. However, the interaction of accuracy and alliance scores was a nonsignificant predictor, disconfirming the

proposition that accuracy might predict outcome only in the presence of a positive alliance. Finally, accuracy was not significantly correlated with the more general skill measure, Errors in Technique. The authors concluded that a specific therapist skill had been shown to be related to outcome, and that this specific skill (accuracy of interpretation) was independent of general technical and relationship factors. They also concluded that "limiting the focus of interpretations to the patient's usual responses (typical feeling states) in interpersonal situations is not by itself a productive technique" (p. 494).

In a methodologically similar follow-up to this study, Crits-Christoph, Barber, and Kurcias (1993) examined the relationship of therapist accuracy in two early sessions to late phase (75% of therapy completed) alliance as independently rated using the Penn Helping Alliance Scale, counting sign method. They reported no significant relationships between early accuracy and early alliance, but they did find that early accuracy (of the wish plus response of other, not response of self) significantly predicted later alliance in the expected direction. These results did not change when the level of early alliance was partialed out. The interaction between early alliance and early accuracy was insignificant in a hierarchial regression, indicating that accuracy was positively related to later alliance regardless of the initial level of the alliance. The authors concluded that while accurate interpretations about patient feeling states (response of self) may be important in forming an early therapeutic bond, the repair of a poor alliance or maintenance of a positive alliance may be dependent on accurate interpretation of the interpersonal aspects of core conflictual themes.

Finally, a conceptually and methodologically different measure of therapist accuracy has been offered by Joyce (1992). A structured formulation of the patient's wishes and needs, anxieties and fears, defenses, maladaptive outcomes, and important object relationships was extracted from the therapist's own initial written case formulation made following the second session. Accuracy was then defined as the interpretation's *correspondence* to the therapist's own initial dynamic formulation and rated on a three-point scale (none, moderate, or strong correspondence). Using cases from Piper, Azim, Joyce, and McCallum's (1991) sample described earlier ($N = 64$), Joyce and his colleagues isolated 2,381 transference interpretations and examined the relationship among correspondence, immediate patient response, alliance, and outcome in patients with high and low quality of object relations.

Joyce's findings indicated that transference cor-

---

[8]Although the study was not specific to transference interpretations per se, transference interpretations did comprise a subset of the interpretations studied. This research was considered of sufficient relevance, merit, and methodological importance to warrant inclusion. As a caveat, the extent to which these results, based on interpretations in general, apply specifically to transference interpretations is an open question. However, there is little reason to believe that they do not.

respondence was a strong predictor of patients' immediate reactions to the interpretation. Highly correspondent interpretations led to more active patient engagement, openness, and disclosure and reduced the probability that the patient would respond with "hesitant acknowledgment." Consistent with Luborsky et al.'s (1979) finding suggesting an increase in transference response following an interpretation, Joyce noted that correspondence was also associated with increased oppositionality by the patient. Thus, the heightened involvement was not always positively toned.

When correspondence scores were aggregated, no significant correlations between correspondence and either alliance or outcome were obtained for the sample as a whole. In a finding of some potential importance, however, when patients were separated into high and low quality of object relations (QOR) groups, significant and opposite correlations were observed. For low QOR groups, inverse relationships between correspondence and patient-rated ($r = -.37$) and therapist-rated ($r = -.37$) alliance measures were found, as well as an inverse relationship with individualized outcome objectives measured at a six-month follow-up ($r = .49$). For high QOR patients, no significant relationships were obtained with alliance measures or outcome at termination, but correspondence was positively associated with general symptomatic improvement at follow-up ($r = .39$). Joyce speculated that low QOR patients may be in more need of forming a gratifying relationship with the therapist than engaging in historical exploration and interpretation. On the other hand, high QOR patients may continue to work through transferential projections after termination by incorporating the analytic functions of the therapist, accounting for the results obtained at follow-up.[9]

As a final step, Joyce conducted a series of stepwise multiple regressions to determine the relative effects of concentration (the percentage of transference interpretations compared to other interventions), correspondence, and the interaction of the two on alliance and outcome for the two QOR groups. The only significant findings involved general symptom improvement at follow-up for the high QOR group. Interestingly, as the level of concentration decreased, correspondence changed

---

[9]These results mirror those reported by Henry, Strupp, Schacht, Binder, and Butler (1992), who found that patients who were highly avoidant interpersonally had worse outcomes in a therapy condition that placed greater emphasis on early transference exploration and interpretation. Henry et al. also found positive effects of early transference exploration for the sample as a whole at follow-up, but not at termination.

from having a negative effect to having a positive effect on outcome, suggesting that for high QOR patients, the optimal conditions were low concentration and high correspondence.

Research Conclusions

Empirical studies of transference interpretations have only recently begun to appear, and any conclusions may be premature. The studies reviewed have many possible alternative implications or meanings, and we will discuss some of these possibilities shortly. Nonetheless, the handful of studies in each category seem unusually consistent, and they do paint an emergent picture that challenges some long-held assumptions. Taking this body of research at face value, the following tentative conclusions might be reached:

1. *More is not better and may even be damaging.* Disregarding the early, methodologically weak work by Malan, there is little sound evidence linking the frequency of interpretive activity to superior outcomes. In fact, several studies have linked greater frequency of transference interpretations to poorer outcomes. This conclusion challenges the proponents of several variants of short-term therapy, but it is in keeping with mainstream analytic thinkers, such as Gill, who warned against the overuse of transference interpretations.

2. *Transference interpretations do not necessarily repair poor alliances and may damage the existing alliance.* Piper, Azim, Joyce, and McCallum (1991) noted that frequent transference interpretations may cause patients to feel criticized and to withdraw. In our own experience, such interpretations are often pursued vigorously even when the patient has shown little response, leading to the disruption of more productive exploration. This is not to suggest that transference interpretations are never useful in repairing or maintaining the alliance (see Crits-Christoph et al., 1993), but they are clearly not a panacea.

3. *Transference interpretations do not elicit differentially greater affective response or necessarily increase depth of experiencing when compared to nontransference interpretations or other interventions.* This conclusion is perhaps the strongest, as it is based on four studies of sequential response patterns, all yielding similar results. Of course, to predict a differential response pattern, one has to assume that the *category* of the link per se is uniquely affect arousing, disregarding all other factors (timing, accuracy, patient variables, etc.). This appears not to be the case.

4. *Interpretations are more likely to elicit defensive responding than other types of interventions.* This

finding is not surprising clinically and does no necessary damage to analytic theory. However, the findings linking defensive responding in general to poor outcome do suggest that the greater preponderance of defensive responding to interpretation deserves careful study. While some defensiveness is clearly to be expected, some therapists may elicit undue and harmful resistance, as we discuss later. Additionally, as Luborsky et al. (1979) note, these results do challenge the assumption that transference interpretations *reduce* the immediate manifestation of transference reactions.

5. *The average level of therapist accuracy may be much lower than assumed.* The study of differential accuracy may obscure the levels of *absolute* accuracy reported in the research reviewed (taking the concept of accuracy at face value). The average level of therapist accuracy compared to either the independently generated CCRT or the therapist's own formulation was below the midpoint on the respective rating scales.

6. *Transference interpretations followed by affective patient responding do seem related to positive outcome.* This positive finding, however, is tempered by the fact that the transference interpretation–affect sequence was only marginally more highly correlated with outcome than the nontransference interpretation–affect sequence, which was also positively related to outcome. Thus, the uniquely mutative effect of the transference interpretation, even when followed by affective responding, remains to be convincingly demonstrated.

7. *Therapist skill may make a difference.* There are few researchers or clinicians who do not believe that therapists are variably skillful and that skill relates to outcome. Proving this empirically, however, has been surprisingly difficult. The studies exploring the link between accuracy of interpretation and outcome provide welcome evidence that the skill of the individual therapist does make a difference. Furthermore, there is some evidence that "accuracy" is not related to other technical skills or general relationship factors. Although this line of research is fraught with more than its share of possible alternative explanations and methodological difficulties, the early results are intriguing and potentially quite important.

8. *The effectiveness of transference interpretations is a function of numerous interacting factors.* Luborsky et al. (1979) reported the interesting observation that for a given patient, response to transference interpretations is highly predictable (although this was based on a small number of cases). Other studies (Joyce, 1992; Piper, Azim, Joyce, & McCallum, 1991) suggest that the patients' quality

of object relationships mediates the response to both frequency and accuracy of interpretation. From the available data, the optimum conditions for effective transference interpretation appear to be accurate interpretations (however defined) delivered with relatively low frequency to more highly functioning patients.

Methodological Problems

The tentative conclusions previously listed may be challenged on any number of grounds, and the authors of these studies have by and large acknowledged the limitations of their work. Most of the problems encountered in interpreting these results are common to psychotherapy research in general. The most immediate difficulty is establishing the direction of causality. Are poor alliances and lack of therapeutic progress the cause or the effect of a greater proportion of transference interpretations? Piper, Azim, Joyce, and McCallum (1991) attempted to investigate this question by examining instances of long pauses (greater than 30 seconds) in the therapeutic dialogue. They reasoned that if the pause preceded the interpretation, the elicitation of the interpretation might stem from a difficult alliance, rather than vice versa. They reported evidence to support both causal sequences, but two-thirds of the time the silence followed the interpretation, suggesting that the transference interpretation had hindered the process. In addition, Gutfreund (1992) found no relationship between the state of the alliance and type of therapist activity, indicating that therapists did not respond to poor alliances with an increase in transference interpretations.

All of the studies cited employed correlational methodology, which always opens the door for the possibility that unknown variables might account for some or all of the observed relationships. For instance, the tendency to respond affectively may simply be a prognostically positive patient characteristic unrelated to the nature of the intervention per se. The "third variable" problem is particularly germane to studies of accuracy. In the case of the CCRT research, operationally speaking, "accuracy" simply indicates that independent raters and the therapist have both listened to (or read) the same patient dialogue and interpreted it in the same way. Accuracy might thus be an epiphenomenon of the patient's ability to describe interpersonal relationships clearly, and with specificity. This ability has been linked to positive outcome, whereas a deficit in this capacity is differentially found in patients whose interpersonal style is hostile-dominant—an indicator of poor prognosis in short-term dynamic psychotherapy (L. Horowitz, Rosenberg, & Kalehzan, 1992). Additionally, the vaguer descriptions typical of patients high in hostile dominance have been shown to be harder to recall, creating a potential for greater therapist inaccuracy. Accuracy might also be a noncausal manifestation of other therapist skills or personality traits.

Accuracy measured as correspondence to the therapists' own initial formulation (Joyce, 1992) is also a measure of therapist consistency or focus. Obviously, a number of interpretations that may be accurate by different standards would be deemed inaccurate with this procedure (a problem for the other two accuracy procedures as well). The findings based on correspondence are quite intriguing, but at this stage, difficult to interpret. It may be that more skillful therapists arrive at more accurate formulations sooner and thus appear more consistent. Sustained focus on a given theme (which would result in correspondence) may be beneficial in its own right. It may also be that consistent therapists are more confident in their formulation, and that it is actually the therapist's conveyed confidence that is therapeutically beneficial. In short, this is considered a provocative area for research in need of more extensive follow-up. Of particular interest would be the possible existence of critical periods for correspondence.

A final problem involves the possible confound between accuracy and frequency. In the study by Crits-Christoph, Cooper, and Luborsky (1988), the range of interpretations per patient studied was from 1 to 16. It would be interesting to note the correlation between accuracy and frequency. It is quite possible that therapists who make frequent interpretations are less accurate, but that it is the frequency of the interpretations, not their relative accuracy, that accounts for the poor outcomes (in line with other research). Of course, a reverse argument could be made to question the frequency–outcome results.

Interpretation and Interpersonal Process

The subtle underlying interpersonal processes between patient and therapist, coded on the fundamental axes of affiliation and control, have been shown to be strongly related to differential outcome (Henry, Schacht, & Strupp, 1986, 1990). In particular, we have noted that therapists often offer interpretations with a complex process that involves simultaneous teaching (friendly control) and criticism (hostile dominance). Wile (1984, p. 353) commented on this phenomenon, stating:

> Certain interpretations commonly made in psychoanalysis and psychodynamic therapy are accusatory. Therapists appear to make them, not because they are hostile or insensitive, but because

> of the dictates of their theory. Clients are seen as gratifying infantile impulses, being defensive, having developmental defects, and resisting the therapy. Therapists who conceptualize people in these ways may have a hard time making interpretations that do not communicate at least some element of this pejorative view.

A number of the authors of the studies reviewed here also seemed to implicitly acknowledge this danger. For example, Piper, Azim, Joyce, and McCallum (1991) noted that high levels of interpretations may make patients feel criticized and cause them to "shut down." Silberschatz et al. (1986) speculated that with given patients, certain interpretations might be perceived as irrelevant or intrusive and traumatizing. It is our experience that therapists sometimes doggedly pursue their interpretive agenda in the face of a lack of patient response or understanding, and even outright disavowal. Furthermore, therapists have often not "socialized" their patients into the process of therapy sufficiently (particularly in short-term work), and explorations of the patient–therapist relationship are not perceived by the patient as pertinent to their difficulties.

Many of the current data on transference interpretations could be potentially understood through the lens of interpersonal process. For example, if the content of the interpretation is consistently inaccurate (and the therapist does not solicit "error-correcting feedback"), the interpersonal process may be perceived by the patient as hostile separation or neglect by the therapist. High levels of interpretations may be perceived as intrusive control, while embedded criticism is experienced as hostile dominance. The interpersonal complement of hostile dominance is hostile submission, which may account in part for the observed rates of defensive responding. Elliot et al. (1985), for instance, reported in a study of therapist intervention categories that patients often felt attacked by interpretations. Additionally, a skill variable, such as timing, may be conceptualized interpersonally when ill-timed interventions are perceived as controlling or neglectful. All of these interpersonal processes directed by the therapist toward the patient may serve only to entrench existing negative introject structures in the patient, leading to the poor outcomes reported (see Henry & Strupp, in press, for a discussion).

Traditionally, a patient's resistance or defensiveness in the face of transference interpretations has been viewed as a manifestation of the underlying pathology. However, it may be the case that transference interpretations, in practice, tend to be accompanied by a differentially higher rate of negative interpersonal process. The patient's defensive response to an interpretation may simply represent the natural process of interpersonal complementarily. If this is true a significant percentage of the time, the present studies may attest to the potential dangers of transference interpretations; but they may actually leave questions regarding efficacy and accuracy per se unanswered.

Future Directions

It seems safe to conclude that the available research provides no evidence of any categorically unique benefits of transference interpretations. Quite the contrary, the evidence suggests the possibility of unique dangers that call for caution. Nonetheless, most psychodynamic clinicians can recall moments in their therapies when transference interpretations were quite useful, perhaps even pivotal. Few would argue that transference interpretations should never be made or that they are *categorically* harmful in all cases. The negative results can almost certainly be attributed to some combination of patient characteristics, therapist interpersonal process, poor timing, inaccuracy, unsuitability of the intervention to the problem, and so on.

It has become something of a cliché to point out the need for further research. We do believe, however, that continued study of the effects of transference interpretations should be a main task of psychodynamic researchers. It is not only a topic of theoretical interest, but with the growing reality of short-term treatments as the norm, it is also a pragmatic necessity if we are to practice analytically oriented therapy efficaciously. Future studies in this area would do well to follow the current research *zeitgeist* in two ways. First, they should abandon the theoretical warfare that marked much early research, that is, attempts to "prove" one overacting metatheory superior to another. Although transference interpretations are the theoretical linchpin of psychodynamic technique, attempts to demonstrate their unique value seem doomed to failure and will contribute little new knowledge. However, a better understanding of how and when they are effective will add not only to improvements in psychodynamic technique, but to other integrative therapies as well. Second, researchers should abandon the search for simple, overriding main effects. There is no logical reason to believe that more of *any* intervention is superior in all cases. Accordingly, we offer the following guidelines:

1. *Achieve greater specificity and uniformity of operational constructs and research questions.* As noted earlier, a variety of subtly different definitions of transference interpretations exist. These differences may or may not color research results, but the differences do make it harder to perform comparisons across studies. Distinguishing transference from other interpretations is difficult even within the same research group using common definition, as the modest kappa (.56) reported by Crits-Christoph et al. (1993) will attest. In addition to differences in the *structure* of definitions (such as a narrow vs. a broad definition of transference), transference definitions may differ in terms of *function*, an as yet unexplored area. For example, transference manifestations may function as a resistance or distraction from conflictual issues or they may emerge as transference love, serving a different function. The level of *specificity* of transference expectations and transference interpretations is also an important variable to consider in process studies (see Weston, 1988). For instance, a patient's transference expectancy and/or a therapist's interpretation may involve a relatively specific phenomenon (e.g., older women in positions of authority) or an encompassing belief (e.g., "Anyone who really gets to know me will reject me"). More precise and specific definitions will lead to a greater ability to compare results of different studies and may guide the development of better, more interesting questions as well.[10]

2. *Study effective transference interpretations.* Transference interpretations do sometimes have the desired effect, leading to increased affect, deeper levels of experience, and new insights. The results of Silberschatz et al. (1986) suggest that plan-compatibility may be one variable that moderates the patient's response. What other variables may be associated with interpretive effectiveness or affective versus defensive responding at the level of the individual intervention? As another example, no study has addressed whether or not clear manifestations of transference enactments were evident at the time transference interpretations were made.

3. *Isolate relevant patient personality dimensions.* There has been much debate about whether or not transference interpretations should be used with

---

[10]Although it was considered to be an issue beyond the scope of the current review, it should also be noted that the nature of transference interpretations may vary markedly among different brands of short-term dynamic therapy. For instance, Davanloo's form of Short Term Dynamic Psychotherapy, STDP, offers interpretations in a much more confrontative context than Malan's approach. Thus, the meaning and impact of interpretation may differ as a function of the therapeutic model being followed. This too needs to be considered when making cross-study comparisons.

specific diagnostic groups (such as borderline personality disorder), but relatively little attention has been paid to the prognostic significance of basic personality dimensions applicable to a wide range of patients. For instance, in one of our recent studies (Henry, Schacht, et al., 1992), we observed that patients high in social avoidance or withdrawal do more poorly in short-term therapy when the focus on the therapeutic relationship is more frequent. The study of patient characteristic times process interactions as opposed to simple main effects may lead to more meaningful and useful research results. These interactions should be studied particularly in relation to early dropouts, a group that has not yet been studied.

4. *Measure accompanying interpersonal process.* As discussed earlier, the seeming negative effects of some transference interpretations may have more to do with the underlying interpersonal process than with the actual content of the interpretation. The utility of transference interpretations and the role of other moderating variables will be difficult to determine unless interpersonal process can be held constant.[11] For example, with benign interpersonal process, higher frequencies of transference interpretations might be advisable with some patients, even in brief therapy. The study of interpersonal process associated with interpretive activity would also provide valuable direction in the design of new approaches to therapist training.

5. *Aim to develop realistic clinical heuristic guidelines.* Research questions should be framed in such a way as to have maximum applicability to clinical practice. For instance, Frances and Perry (1983) offer a set of guidelines for the relative appropriateness or inappropriateness of transference interpretations in focal therapy. Transference interpretations are seen as appropriate when transference feelings have become major resistances to therapy, the patient can tolerate and understand the interpretation, and sufficient time remains in the therapy to explore the interpretation. They may be inappropriate if the patient does not develop strong and apparent transference distortions. Guidelines such as these might prove difficult to operationalize for research purposes, but the attempt is important if research is to have any significant impact on practice.

6. *Encourage cross-group replication.* Achieving in-

terrater reliability within a given research group on measures such a plan-compatibility or the CCRT is only half the battle. Since studies of accuracy rest on the formulation to which the therapist's intervention is compared, different research groups must be able to arrive at similar formulations based on the same clinical material to establish the external validity of the research. As Messer (1991, p. 1349) notes, "Viewed from an empirical perspective, establishing the accuracy of a dynamic formulation requires proving its validity." Messer goes on to provide empirical evidence that two different research groups, studying the same clinical material, may both achieve internal reliability, while differing substantially on the formulations generated. This is a difficult problem that will be discussed in greater depth in the section on dynamic formulation.

Conclusion

Determining the extent of progress achieved toward the empirical understanding of transference interpretations is clearly a value judgment. In the 14 years since the last review was undertaken, the "count" of such studies has risen from zero to 16. This amounts to slightly over one per year, and three of these studies were unpublished doctoral dissertations. Although some studies may have been inadvertently overlooked, this is still a rather meager output on so central a topic. When all of the published articles on transference are considered, the ratio of theoretical to empirical articles is roughly 500 to one.

On the other hand, most of the studies reviewed were considered to be of very good quality and for the most part the products of established research groups that will likely continue this general line of research. More importantly, Luborsky and Spence concluded in 1978 that quantitative research was not a reliable guide to clinical practice. Today, many of the studies of transference interpretations do suggest that we are on the threshold of developing empirically sound heuristics to guide the use of psychodynamic techniques. This possibility raises a final crucial question—will those who employ these techniques be influenced by the research? The available findings challenge some dearly held beliefs. In short, transference interpretations do not seem uniquely effective, may pose greater process risks, and may be countertherapeutic under certain conditions. If these findings continue to hold, will the message be heard or will the messenger be dismissed?

The probable answer is some of both. These studies certainly do not refute basic analytic theory,

---

[11]It should be noted that Crits-Christoph and colleagues have already begun to expand their research on accuracy by considering moderating variables such as supportiveness versus criticalness of the interpretation, clarity, conciseness, and so on.

although they do pose some challenge to carte blanche technical assumptions. The typical psychodynamic clinician employing transference interpretations as a therapeutic staple is likely to be unfazed by these results and to assume that they reflect poor technique, overuse, and so on (i.e., problems that apply to *other* therapists, not problems inherent to the intervention itself). To an extent they may be right. However, it has been our experience that even good therapists are often unaware of the effects of their interventions on momentary process. Old habits and ways of thinking die hard. While the present research has the *potential* to guide practice, it is unlikely to do so unless it first guides the training of therapists.

RESEARCH ON THE THERAPEUTIC ALLIANCE

Although interpretations are the chief technical focus of psychodynamic psychotherapy, they do not occur in a vacuum. Analytic thinkers have long accorded the patient–therapist relationship a central role in the process of therapy. The recognition of alliance phenomena can be traced back to Freud, who, in his early theoretical papers on transference, spoke of "the friendly and affectionate aspects of the transference which are admissible to consciousness and which are the vehicle of success" (Freud, 1912/1966, p. 105). Over the past decade or more, various measures of the therapeutic alliance have become a central process variable in psychotherapy research (Gaston, 1990).

The quality of the therapeutic alliance is now generally recognized to be an important predictor of outcome in many forms of psychotherapy (Bordin, 1979; Gelso & Carter, 1985; Pinsof & Catherall, 1986; Safran, Crocker, McMain, & Murray, 1990; Wolfe & Goldfried, 1989). However, important questions remain about the definition, structure, and function of the alliance. In this section, we briefly review various definitions and measures of the alliance and summarize the empirical literature relevant to the dimensional structure, its association with outcome, its relationship to patient and therapist variables, the variation of the alliance over time, and the interaction of relationship and technique. Finally we offer some guidelines for future alliance research.

The Definition and Structure of the Alliance

Although alliance research is a growing field of investigation, a single, clear definition of the concept still does not exist. Sterba (1934) used the term *ego alliance* to stress the importance of the

patient's capacity to work in analysis through an oscillation between experiencing and observing. He regarded this type of alliance, which was later labeled *working alliance* (Greenson, 1965), as stemming from the patient's mature ego functioning and partial identification with the working style of the analyst. The *working alliance* thus refers to the working aspects of the therapeutic relationship, with the focus on the patient's contribution (a definition later adopted by Frieswyk et al., 1986).[12] Greenson recommended that the analyst actively differentiate the patient's realistic reactions to the treatment situation, or alliance, from the internal misperceptions of the therapist, or transference. Referring to an aspect of positive transference, Zetzel (1956) introduced the term *therapeutic alliance*, which she viewed as the patient's attachment to and identification with the analyst, stemming from the good aspects of the mother–child relationship. The term *therapeutic alliance* thus refers to the affectionate aspects of the therapeutic relationship and is similar to Luborsky's (1976) Type 1 helping alliance, which reflects the patient's experience of being helped or nurtured. These definitions vary in their emphasis on the working or the affective aspects of the relationship, but all focus on the patient's contributions, capacity, or experience. Freud (1912/1966) and others have also recognized the importance of the therapist's attitudes, and most current conceptualizations of the alliance employed in psychotherapy process research include the contributions of both patient and therapist.

Bordin (1979) proposed a general definition that encompasses three main components of the alliance: (1) the bond between patient and therapist, (2) the patient–therapist agreement on goals, and (3) the patient–therapist agreement on tasks. While the bonding dimension reiterates the importance of the affective aspects of the alliance (i.e., Zetzel, 1956), the agreement on goals and tasks refers to more cognitive aspects by focusing on the congruence between the participants' beliefs about how people change.

Gaston (1990) attempted to reconcile various definitions of the alliance by proposing that it is a multidimensional construct composed of four relatively independent dimensions. Her model encompasses a number of earlier definitions and proposes that the alliance is composed of (1) the working

---

[12]Greenson introduced the term *working alliance,* but he employed it interchangeably with *therapeutic alliance,* which led to some theoretical confusion because these terms appear to refer to relatively different aspects of the therapeutic relationship (Dickes, 1975; Kanzer, 1975).

alliance or patient's capacity to purposefully work in therapy, (2) the therapeutic alliance or patient's affective bond to the therapist, (3) the therapist's emphatic understanding and involvement, and (4) the patient–therapist agreement on the treatment goals and tasks.

Measurement of the Alliance

Two general methods used by independent raters for assessing the alliance have emerged over the last 10 or 15 years—the counting sign method and the global rating method (e.g., Luborsky, Crits-Christoph, Alexander, Margolis, & Cohen, 1983). In the counting sign method, independent observers first locate patients' statements that reflect on the alliance. These statements are then rated for intensity on a Likert-type scale, and a mean score is computed for any given session. In the global rating method, either a segment or the whole of a therapy session is viewed first. Then a series of impressionistic ratings are made on items that reflect alliance behaviors. Due to large correlations between these methods and the tedious work involved in the counting sign method, the global rating method has become the predominant methodology.

More recently, the Vanderbilt research group has employed a somewhat different procedure (Henry et al., 1986, 1990). They have used Benjamin's (1974) Structural Analysis of Social Behavior (SASB) to code each thought unit of patient and therapist speech (roughly a sentence) on the fundamental interpersonal axes of affiliation and control. Henry argues pragmatically that this interpersonal process *is* the alliance, and that other definitions (such as affective bond or task agreement) of the alliance are actually higher order concepts that follow from the basic interpersonal transactions (Henry & Strupp, in press).

Original measures. The first alliance measures were designed to be used in individual psychotherapy for adults and were rated by independent observers or trained clinical judges. A number of such alliance scales have been developed, including the Vanderbilt Therapeutic Alliance Scale (VTAS: Hartley & Strupp, 1983), the Penn Helping Alliance Rating Scale (HA: Morgan, Luborsky, Crits-Christoph, Curtis, & Solomon, 1982), and the Therapeutic Alliance Rating System (TARS: Marmar, Weiss, & Gaston, 1989; Marziali, 1984b). These measures were constructed by developing clinically sound items aimed at reflecting aspects of the alliance described in theoretical papers. Underlying alliance dimensions were identified statistically through exploratory factor analysis. The analysis of the VTAS and the TARS suggested that the

alliance had a multidimensional structure, while the HA yielded only a single factor (Morgan et al., 1982).

These first empirical efforts were important steps because they confirmed the prognostic value of the alliance in predicting psychotherapy outcome. However, these instruments tended to be drawn from a diverse assortment of theoretical writings and were not designed to measure specific theoretical constructs. Recognizing that important theoretical considerations were left unaddressed, the more recent alliance measures have been primarily guided by theoretical conceptualization.

New advances. The more recent alliance measures emerged from specific theoretical perspectives and were designed to be rated by patients and therapists, as well as by independent observers, The Working Alliance Inventory (WAI: Horvath & Greenberg, 1989) was developed to assess the alliance as defined by Bordin's (1979) eclectic conceptualization and it yielded three scales corresponding to the therapeutic bond and agreement on goals and tasks. The California Psychotherapy Alliance Scale (CALPAS: Marmar, Gaston, Gallagher, & Thompson, 1989) was developed within an analytic perspective but also included Bordin's conceptualization. The CALPAS was developed in two stages, and the most recent version reflects the four alliance dimensions proposed by Gaston (1990). Finally, Saunders, Howard, and Orlinsky (1989) designed the Therapeutic Bond Scales (TBS) based on the generic model of psychotherapy proposed by Orlinsky and Howard (1986). The TBS taps the bonding and working dimensions of the alliance among other relational aspects such as empathic resonance and mutual affirmation.

Although most alliance measures continue to be applied to individual psychotherapy for adults, research on the alliance in more diverse contexts is emerging. The Couples Therapy Alliance Scale (CAS: Pinsof & Catherall, 1986) taps the alliance in marital therapy by assessing two dimensions: (1) the content as reflected by Bordin's (1979) categories of bond, goals, and tasks; and (2) the interpersonal system with respect to self, other, and group. The CAS was found to be somewhat predictive of outcome in group marital therapy (Bourgeois, Sabourin, & Wright, 1990). A version of the CALPAS for group psychotherapy has been developed, and it taps the collaborative aspects of the alliance between the group members and the two cotherapists. In a study of group therapy for patients presenting with bulimia nervosa, the CALPAS-G was found to be predictive of outcome, defined as the number of binging days (Gaston &

Schnieder, 1992). There are also measures specifically designed to assess the alliance in pharmacotherapy (Frank & Gunderson, 1990; Gaston, Wisebord, & Weiss, 1992), as well as in child psychotherapy (Shirk, Saiz, Green, Hanze, & Wanstrath, 1992).

Correspondence. The extent to which these scales tap overlapping versus unique phenomena is an important question. Accumulating evidence suggests that the association among these various measures varies widely: .65 to .89 (Hatcher et al., 1990); .34 to .84 (Tichenor & Hill, 1989); and .37 to .60 (Sabourin, Coallier, Cournoyer, & Gaston, 1990). Moreover, some alliance measures were found to be more predictive of outcome than others (Safran & Wallner, 1991).

The alliance concept may also overlap a previously recognized and important construct, that of "perceived therapist-offered relationship" as conceptualized in the client-centered tradition and measured by the Barrett-Lennard Relationship Inventory (RI: Barrett-Lennard, 1962). There are few empirical data that address this question, and the research that is available is contradictory. Salvio, Beutler, Wood, and Engle (1992) have examined the convergence between the WAI and the RI in three different types of psychotherapy and found high convergence among all subscales of these instruments. In another study (Johnson, 1988), no association was observed between either the HA or VTAS scales and the RI.

In conclusion, given the diversity and multiplicity of alliance measures already available, it may be time for a halt in the production of new alliance scales. Rather, the reliability, validity, and convergence of existing measures should be further examined. Future scale development could then be based on a more solid and coherent empirical base.

Empirical Verification of Alliance Dimensions

The structure of the alliance has been examined by various statistical methods: correlation, principal component factor analysis, and confirmatory factor analysis. A review of the findings associated with each method illustrates the complexity of the field.

Correlational findings. Correlational studies tend to provide little support for the existence of distinct or orthogonal alliance dimensions. For some alliance measures, large to very large correlation coefficients were observed between scales purporting to assess separate alliance dimensions. For example, a correlation of .91 between the two HA scales has been observed (Morgan et al., 1982). Correlations ranging from .59 to .88 among the

three WAI scales have been reported in one study (Horvath & Greenberg, 1989) and from .78 to .93 in another study (Salvio et al., 1992). With respect to the CALPAS, mixed findings have been reported. Hatcher et al. (1990) found associations varying from .22 to .76; Gaston (1991) observed correlations ranging from .37 to .66; and Sabourin et al. (1990) obtained associations varying from .28 to .75. These findings would seem to question multidimensional models of the alliance. It could be argued that the observed correlations do not necessarily invalidate the *conceptual* distinctiveness of different dimensions. Nonetheless, the research would seem to support the parsimony of an unidimensional model and shift the burden of proof to multidimensional theorists to validate the utility of their approach.

Defining the alliance as monolithic, however, may be premature. The studies reporting high subscale intercorrelations were conducted on samples derived from relatively homogeneous populations, which is likely to increase correlations (e.g., Horvath & Greenberg, 1989). Additionally, for most alliance measures, items were typically grouped on an a priori rational basis and subscale item content was not subsequently refined to achieve maximum interitem or item-total correlations. If such a procedure had been followed, less consistent or discriminating items might have been dropped, increasing the capacity of each subscale to reflect unique dimensions. Therefore, while the evidence from correlational studies to date seems to favor a unidimensional model of the alliance, we believe the question is still unresolved.

Exploratory factor analysis. Studies using principal component factor analysis are more supportive of multidimensional models, but results are still mixed (Gomes-Schwartz, 1978; Hartley & Strupp, 1983; Marmar, Gaston et al., 1989; Marmar, Weiss, & Gaston, 1989). For instance, Marmar, Gaston et al. (1989) reported only one significant intercorrelation among the five factor scale scores of the CALPAS-P, while Marmar, Weiss, and Gaston (1989) observed correlations ranging from .43 to .69 among CALTARS factor scale scores. Nonetheless, different research groups have found relatively separate factors representing the therapeutic and the working alliance when scales encompassed items measuring both the effective and working aspects of the patient's collaboration in psychotherapy (Gomes-Schwartz, 1978; Hartley & Strupp, 1983; Marmar, Gaston et al., 1989; Marmar, Weiss, & Gaston, 1989). When items reflecting aspects of the therapist's empathic understanding were included, a factor representing the therapist's positive contribution to the alliance was also repeatedly identified as a component distinct from that of the patient's contribution (Gomes-Schwartz, 1978; Hartley & Strupp, 1983; Marmar, Gaston et al., 1989; Marmar, Weiss, & Gaston, 1989). Finally, a relatively separate dimension of patient–therapist agreement on goals and tasks has been observed (Marmar, Gaston et al., 1989).

Factor analytic research has also supported the distinction between the transferential and "real" aspects of the therapeutic relationship. Items reflecting the patient's hostility toward the therapist have repeatedly been distinguished from those representing the therapeutic and working alliances (Gomes-Schwartz, 1978; Hartley & Strupp, 1983; Marmar, Gaston et al., 1989; Marmar, Weiss, & Gaston, 1989). That is, a patient may have a good working capacity and a positive affective bond with the therapist and still display hostile behaviors. Similarly, when items reflecting the therapist's hostility toward the patient were included in alliance scales, they were clearly distinguished from items representing the therapist's positive contribution to the alliance (Marmar, Gaston et al., 1989; Marmar, Weiss, & Gaston, 1989). This empirical distinction between collaboration and hostility may indicate that the alliance constitutes a phenomenon distinct from the negative aspects of the therapeutic relationship. These findings are in line with Greenson's (1965) comments suggesting that some patients are able to explore their own reactions while in the throes of intense transference feelings. Thus, a good-enough alliance allows the patient to work through intense negative reactions toward the therapist without dropping out of therapy.

Confirmatory factor analysis. Principal component factor analysis is limited with regard to testing theoretical models because of its exploratory nature. In contrast, confirmatory factor analysis, CFA, is aimed at the verification of theoretical models. Using CFA, Tracey and Kokotovic (1989) analyzed the data provided by 84 patients on the WAI and found support for Bordin's conceptualization (on which the WAI is based). They concluded that the data best fit a bilevel model with three alliance dimensions embedded within a larger alliance factor, rather than a simple one-factor model. Due to the relatively small size of their data set for the application of CFA, their finding is considered tentative.

When the structure of the patient self-report version of the CALPAS was tested using CFA, results also tended to support the bilevel model, that is, four relatively independent alliance dimensions embedded within a larger alliance construct. In a sample of 308 patients, satisfactory fit indices were obtained in addition to relatively large and discriminatory loadings on all items across the four scales (Gaston, Sabourin, Hatcher, & Hansell, 1992). However, in a study of the CAS applied to group marital therapy, Bourgeois, Sabourin, and Wright (in press) concluded that the CAS assessed a unidimensional phenomenon only.

It is of interest to note that the findings supportive of a multidimensional model were observed only for shortened forms of the alliance measures (WAI and CALPAS), emphasizing further the necessity of using item analysis methods in the construction of alliance measures. Item content and test development procedures clearly influence whether the alliance structure appears uni- or multidimensional. The ultimate test of the validity, or at least of the utility, of a multidimensional model of the alliance may reside in the examination of the differential associations of these alliance dimensions with outcome as well as with patient and therapist characteristics.

Construct validity. A central question about the construct validity of alliance measures per se remains. In analytic circles, there is a controversy regarding the distinctiveness of alliance and transference concepts, a question that has been left unaddressed by most researchers. Some analytic authors have asserted that the alliance concept is neither valid nor useful (e.g., Brenner, 1979), and others have simply proposed that it might be clinically misleading (Arlow, 1975; Curtis, 1979; Kanzser, 1975) and would lead to a shift away from interpretation as the main technique in analysis.

As noted earlier, factor analytic research would seem to lend support for the distinctiveness of alliance and transference phenomena, but these studies were not designed to directly address this problem. We know of only one direct test of this question. In a sample of 32 patients and 126 sessions of analytically oriented psychotherapy (Gaston, 1990), reliable ratings of positive transference were found to be unrelated to reliable ratings of both the therapeutic and working alliances (rs = .05 and .07, $p > .05$). While the validity of these transference ratings remains to be verified, the findings are consistent with the views that distinguish alliance and transference constructs (i.e., Bowlby, 1988; Greenson, 1965).

The Role of Alliance

A review of the literature (Gaston, 1990) has pointed to three major roles that could be played by the alliance in psychotherapy. Viewed as complementary, these hypotheses follow:

1. The alliance could have a *direct* therapeutic effect in and of itself. The establishment of an alliance would thus represent a type of corrective interpersonal experience (Balint, 1968; Bowlby, 1988; Henry & Strupp, in press; Rogers, 1957).

2. The alliance could have an *indirect* effect by acting to mediate the efficacy of interpretations. As conceptualized by most analytic authors, the establishment of an alliance is a prerequisite for successful interpretations (e.g., Greenson, 1965). Henry and Strupp (in press) theorize that the ongoing interpersonal process activates corresponding introject states that serve to facilitate or impede the therapeutic process.

3. The alliance might *interact* with at least two broad classes of interventions (supportive and exploratory or interpretive) in predicting outcome. For patients presenting with difficulties in establishing a good-enough alliance, supportive strategies might be more helpful in contrast to an exclusive focus on interpretation (Balint, 1968; Bowlby, 1988; Zetzel, 1956) and vice versa.

Alliance and outcome. The quantification of the alliance construct has paved the way for empirical research relating the alliance to outcome across a variety of psychotherapies. It has been examined in dynamic (e.g., Barber, Crits-Christoph, & Luborsky, 1990; Gomes-Schwartz, 1978), experiential (e.g., Gomes-Schwartz, 1978; Horvath & Greenberg, 1989), eclectic (e.g., Gaston, 1991; Horvath & Greenberg, 1989), behavioral and cognitive (e.g., Gaston, 1991; Gaston, Marmar, Gallagher, & Thompson, 1991; Krupnick, Sotsky, Simmens, & Moyer, 1992; Marmar, Gaston et al., 1989), and group psychotherapy (Bourgeois et al., 1990; Gaston & Schneider, 1992). More recently, the alliance–outcome association was tested in pharmacotherapy (Frank & Gunderson, 1990; Gaston, Wisebord, & Weiss, 1992; Krupnick et al., 1992; M. Weiss, Gaston, Wisebord, Propst, & Zicherman, 1992). The strength of the alliance–outcome association has also been examined across a variety of populations, from relatively well-functioning individuals (e.g., Marmar, Weiss, & Gaston, 1989) to elderly depressed patients (Marmar, Gaston et al., 1989), opiate addicts (Luborsky, McLellan, Woody, O'Brien, & Auerbach, 1985), and schizophrenics (Frank & Gunderson, 1990).

The quality as well as the quantity of alliance research has improved in recent years as researchers identify potential confounds. In alliance–outcome research, it is now standard to use residual change scores, that is, outcome measures that control for the pretherapy level of the outcome

variable. The importance of controlling for in-therapy symptomatic improvement up to the moment where the alliance was measured has been discussed (Gaston, Marmar et al., 1991), and Barber, Crits-Christoph, and Luborsky (1992) have raised the point that some "alliance" items on rating scales are actually early outcome measures. Typically, alliance scores are gathered early in therapy (e.g., Kokotovic & Tracey, 1990; Luborsky et al., 1985) or averaged across sessions (e.g., Eaton, Abeles, & Gutfreund, 1988; Marmar, Weiss, & Gaston, 1989). Other researchers have explored whether or not alliance–outcome relationships vary as a function of phase of therapy (e.g., Gaston, Marmar et al., 1991; Luborsky et al., 1983). Despite the increased methodological sophistication, alliance–outcome research has still been hampered by a relative lack of clear theoretical statements linking the alliance to outcome. Therefore, the available findings basically address only the three general classes of alliance–outcome relationship discussed earlier.

A direct association. In general, a direct association between alliance and outcome has been found in short-term individual psychotherapy. In a meta-analytic review of 24 studies, Horvath and Symonds (1991) found that the alliance accounted for moderate amounts of outcome variance, with an average effect size of .26. This estimate is conservative, however, because it was calculated on the assumption that all correlations computed but not reported by researchers or reported as not being significant equaled zero.

Similar results have been obtained involving long-term psychotherapy. With a sample treated in analytically oriented psychotherapy, Gaston et al. (in press) found that the alliance, as rated by independent observers, was predictive of outcome in long-term psychotherapy and that it interacted with exploratory and supportive techniques in predicting outcome. Eaton et al. (1988) also reported that alliance ratings were predictive of outcome in long-term psychotherapy, and Frank and Gunderson (1990) reported that the alliance predicted a two-year outcome for patients presenting with schizophrenia. While these findings are consistent with the hypothesis stating that the alliance could be therapeutic in and of itself, alternative "third variable" hypotheses cannot yet be ruled out.

Across outcome indices. The association between alliance and outcome does not seem limited to a specific type of outcome measure and has been consistently observed across a variety of outcome indices. When outcome is defined in terms of symptomatology, most studies have reported a moderate association; for example, Eaton et al. (1988)

reported a correlation of .59 between the therapist's contribution to the alliance and somatization at the end of treatment, and Marmar, Weiss, and Gaston (1989) observed that the working alliance was correlated .29 with symptomatic improvement. The alliance has also been found to be significantly correlated with indices of interpersonal functioning; for example, Marmar, Weiss, and Gaston (1989) reported that working alliance scores were related ($r = .39$) to a measure of interpersonal functioning at termination. Others have investigated the relationship of alliance to target complaints; for example, Gomes-Schwartz (1978) observed correlations ranging from −.14 to .54 between alliance ratings and the severity of target complaints after treatment as rated by patients, therapists, and observers. One study examined the association between alliance and patient satisfaction, yielding correlations ranging from .37 to .68 (Gaston, 1991). There is some evidence, however, that the alliance–outcome relationship may not hold for all types of therapeutic outcome. More equivocal findings have been observed with respect to patient self-concept (e.g., Horvath & Greenberg, 1989) and social functioning (e.g., Luborsky et al., 1985; Marziali, 1984b; Piper, Azim, Joyce, McCallum, Nixon, & Segal, 1991).

Across perspectives. The predictive validity of the alliance was first examined from the point of view of independent observers (e.g., M. Horowitz, Marmar, Weiss, DeWitt, & Rosenbaum, 1984; Luborsky et al., 1983; Hartley & Strupp, 1983). This line of investigation was then extended to other perspectives such as the viewpoints of patients and therapists (e.g., Marziali, 1984b). In their meta-analytic study, Horvath and Symonds (1991) found that patients and independent observers were better judges of the alliance than therapists in that their ratings correlated most highly with outcome. Whether or not therapists have a "blind spot" when judging the alliance is an interesting question for future research.

Across therapy modalities. It is also of interest to briefly examine whether or not the alliance correlates with outcome in nondynamic forms of psychotherapy. Using judges' ratings of alliance, mixed findings have been obtained. The alliance, as measured by the HA, was found to be unrelated to outcome in cognitive therapy (Crits-Christoph & Beebe, 1988; DeRubeis, Feeley, & Barber, 1988). In contrast, the alliance as assessed by the VTAS was found to explain 21 percent of the outcome variance across all therapy conditions (cognitive-behavioral, interpersonal, and pharmacological) in the NIMH Treatment of Depression Collaborative Research Program (Krupnick et al., 1992). When pa-

tients' ratings were employed, the alliance has been more uniformly and substantially correlated with outcome in a variety of psychotherapy approaches (Gaston, 1991; Gaston, Marmar et al., 1991; Gaston & Schneider, 1992; Gomes-Schwartz, 1978; Horvath & Greenberg, 1989; Luborsky et al., 1985). For example, in one study, alliance ratings were found to account for at least 35 percent of outcome variance in behavior therapy, cognitive therapy, and brief dynamic therapy (Gaston et al., 1991).

Empirical results also argue in favor of an alliance–outcome association in treatment modalities other than individual psychotherapy. The alliance was found to be related to marital adjustment in group marital psychotherapy, but only for men and correlations were small (about 5% of outcome variance) (Bourgeois et al., 1990). In group psychotherapy for bulimia nervosa (dynamic and cognitive-behavioral), the alliance was found to account for about 20 percent of the variance of patients' binging behaviors both at the end of treatment and at a six-month follow-up (Gaston & Schneider, 1992). In studies of the pharmacotherapy of depression, alliance ratings have been found to account for 21 percent (Krupnick et al., 1992) and 25% to 41% of the variance in depressive symptoms at termination (M. Weiss et al., 1992). Finally, in a study of the impact of the alliance on the placebo response, the alliance was found to be correlated with depressive symptoms after only one week of patients' taking inactive pills (Gaston, Wisebord, & Weiss, 1992).

A plausible alternative hypothesis. Taken together, these findings provide empirical support for the predictive validity of the alliance. However, a plausible alternative hypothesis could explain these associations. The alliance could simply be a consequence of in-treatment change rather than an active ingredient of psychotherapy; as patients get better, their collaboration and involvement in therapy could proportionally increase. Gaston et al. (1991) addressed this question in behavioral, cognitive, and brief dynamic therapy. When measured near termination, alliance scores were found to account for at least 35 percent of outcome variance, *over and above* initial symptomatology and in-treatment symptomatic change up to that point. If replicated, such findings would lend further support to the hypothesis that the alliance is a causal ingredient of change.

Interaction with technique. The previous section of this chapter pointed to the lack of evidence of the efficacy of transference interpretations per se, despite clinical reports of their pivotal usefulness. These findings suggest the importance of studying the context within which interpretations occur, and measures of the alliance may provide one such useful context. The role of the alliance has been explored in interaction with two broad types of therapist interventions, exploratory and supportive. M. Horowitz, Marmar, Weiss et al. (1984) reported that the patient's capacity for establishing an alliance during the intake evaluation interacted inversely with exploratory and supportive interventions in predicting outcome of brief dynamic therapy in a bereaved sample. Gaston, Piper, Debbane, Bienvenu, and Garant (1991) also observed that alliance ratings in analytically oriented psychotherapy inversely interacted with technique in predicting outcome. In both studies, the results suggest that patients who are able to quickly form a strong alliance are also able to make use of an interpretive approach (consistent with Marziali, 1984b), while those patients who find it difficult to initially establish such a working relationship or bond are better served by more supportive interventions (see Wallerstein, 1989). These findings have since been replicated (Gaston & Ring, 1992).

Although these hypotheses are important first steps in exploring the interaction between alliance and technique, the clinical reality is probably far more complex. For example, when the accuracy of interpretations was considered, the alliance did not interact with interpretations in promoting change (Crits-Christoph, Cooper, & Luborsky, 1988). Accurate interpretations may thus be effective under some conditions even when they are provided in the context of a poor alliance. Various dimensions of the alliance may also interact differentially with technique.

Variations over time.   The study of the variation in the alliance over time encompasses a number of distinct questions: (1) Does the "average level" of the alliance vary across therapy? (2) Are different patterns of variation differentially predictive of outcome or predictive of different outcomes? and (3) Is there a critical period for alliance formation? Although these questions are not theoretically driven per se, their answers might aid in the development of more specific theories about the role of the alliance in therapeutic process and outcome. Research addressed to these questions is still relatively sparse, and results are mixed.

Several studies have found alliance ratings to be relatively stable across individuals over the course of therapy (Eaton et al., 1988; Gomes-Schwartz, 1978; Marmar, Weiss et al., 1989; Marmar, Gaston et al., 1989; Morgan et al., 1982), but there

are exceptions (Gaston & Schneider, 1992; Hartley & Strupp, 1983; Klee, Abeles, & Muller, 1990). For example, Hartley and Strupp examined 5 sessions drawn from across 25 sessions of short-term therapy in 28 dyads. For patients completing therapy, alliance scores declined somewhat across therapy, but actually increased in the group of early terminators. The primary contributor to this increase in the alliance scores was the therapist subscale score, and the authors concluded that the therapists were somehow "trying harder" when they perceived that therapy was not going well. There was a significant drop in the Patient Motivation and Patient Resistance subscales of the VTAS in all patient groups from the first to the last sessions, perhaps suggesting a natural rhythm to therapy. Finally, the high- and low-outcome groups differed in their pattern, but not their overall mean across sessions. The high-outcome group peaked on the alliance scale at about Session 6, while the low-outcome group showed a drop at this point. Using a different instrument (VPPS: The Vanderbilt Psychotherapy Process Scale), O'Malley et al., (1983) found that the strength of association between the dimension of Patient Involvement and outcome increased linearly across the first three sessions but was not statistically significant until Session 3. These researchers later reported that poor outcome cases (regardless of initial prognosis) were typified by a pattern of deteriorating therapist-offered conditions across early sessions, while poor prognosis but good outcome cases showed the reverse (Suh, O'Malley, & Strupp, 1986).

Taken together, these findings suggest that simply examining group means of alliance measures across the whole course of therapy may lead to misleading findings. That is, group data may mask important identifiable subgroups of patients and therapists. Additionally, differences across time may appear on only select subscales of alliance measures, not summed scores. Although the data are certainly not conclusive, there is evidence for the importance of different *patterns* of change in the alliance. The question of differential correlation between the alliance and outcome as a function of phase of therapy remains open. Some researchers observed no differential association of alliance with outcome across the course of psychotherapy (Morgan et al., 1982), but others have reported various differences (O'Malley et al., 1983; Gaston, Marmar et al., 1991) Studies exploring alliance–outcome correlations over time cannot directly address questions about a crucial period for alliance development, but such a period is likely to occur quite early in therapy (Henry & Strupp, in press). As suggested by Safran et al. (1990), early detections of alliance ruptures by the therapist may be critical to successful therapy and resolution of ruptures in the alliance may be a potent change catalyst.

Factors Influencing the Alliance

We might divide the factors influencing the alliance or various alliance dimensions into three categories. First, each alliance dimension, although conceptually distinct, is seen as influencing and being influenced by the others. (These interrelations were previously addressed; therefore, they are omitted from the following discussion.) Second, the participant's characteristics are hypothesized to impact the status of the alliance. Third, technique may influence the collaboration between patient and therapist.

Participants' characteristics. Horvath and Symonds (1991) summarized 11 studies that explored the link between patients' pretherapy characteristics and the alliance, an area of research that seems to be growing. According to their classification, both interpersonal and intrapersonal characteristics of patients have similar and significant impact on the alliance; the average correlations (weighted by sample size) between these variables and the alliance were .30 and .32, respectively.

Some authors have suggested that alliance partially emerges from the patient's early positive experiences with parental figures (Bowlby, 1988; Zetzel, 1956), but only a few studies have explored this proposition empirically. Mallinckrodt (1991) observed that the alliance was associated with the quality of the bond patients had with their fathers. Christenson (1991) presented data drawn from the Structural Analysis of Social Behavior (SASB) IN-TREX questionnaire on two cases seen by the same therapist in short-term dynamic psychotherapy. In these case studies, each patient's perception of the same therapist differed markedly and coincided with the patient's view of his or her own parents.

It stands to reason that variables associated with a patient's interpersonal functioning would be correlated with the quality of the therapeutic alliance. A moderate association between alliance scales and pretherapy interpersonal measures has repeatedly been observed (e.g., Gaston, 1991; Kokotovic & Tracey, 1990; Moras & Strupp, 1982; Marmar, Weiss et al., 1989; Wallner, Muran, Segal, & Schumann, 1992), although there are exceptions (e.g., Gaston, Marmar, Thompson, & Gallagher, 1988). Patients with a lower level of object relations (Piper, Azim, Joyce, McCallum, Nixon, & Segal, 1991) and more rigid or inflexible interpersonal styles (Kiesler & Watkins, 1989) have been found to establish poorer alliances.

With respect to therapist characteristics influencing the alliance, qualities such as attractiveness, expertness, and trustworthiness were observed to be only modestly related to the alliance (Horvath & Greenberg, 1989) and to load on a factor distinct from one composed of the four CALPAS scales (Sabourin et al., 1990). Other variables that have been found to correlate positively with higher alliance scores include the amount of therapist training (Mallinckrodt & Nelson, 1991), patient–therapist interpersonal complementarity (Kiesler & Watkins, 1989), and patient–therapist sociodemographic similarity (Luborsky et al., 1985). Finally, Henry et al. (1990), who define the alliance in terms of momentary interpersonal process, reported that therapists who have a self-disaffiliative introject structure engage in significantly more hostile interpersonal interactions with their patients.

In attempting to define the nature of the alliance and how it develops, it may be equally important to detail factors that are *not* correlated with the alliance. Excluding the Luborsky et al. (1985) study, no associations have been found between measures of the patient's sociodemographic characteristics and the alliance, with two exceptions involving education (Marmar, Weiss et al., 1989) and yearly income (Gaston, 1991). Similarly, no significant relationship was observed between the alliance and estimates of social desirability (Gaston, 1991). Finally, as expected, only low-to-moderate correlations were observed between alliance scores and patients' pretherapy levels of symptomatology (e.g., Gaston et al., 1988; Sabourin et al., 1990) or psychological distress (e.g., Eaton et al., 1988; Moras & Strupp, 1982). In summary, the alliance, however specifically defined, is a measure of two people's ability to relate to each other, work together, and respond affectively to a human relationship. It should thus come as little surprise that interpersonal variables seem to relate to alliance formation while symptomatic or demographic variables fail to do so. It still remains to be shown more precisely how interpersonal variables aid or disrupt specific therapeutic processes.

Technique. Theoretical viewpoints differ greatly with respect to the technical handling of the alliance. Some authors argue that interpretations remain the only useful technique for either developing a good-enough alliance or repairing a difficult one (e.g., Freud, 1912/1966). Others recommend the use of more supportive and/or educational interventions, usually in combination with exploratory strategies (e.g., Bowlby, 1988; Greenson, 1965; Zetzel, 1956). There are few studies directly designed to study the influence of technique on the alliance, and the empirical data that do address this relationship are mixed.

In a preliminary and uncontrolled study, some support was found in favor of the role of interpretations in improving alliance levels (e.g., Foreman & Marmar, 1985). In another study, interpretations led to a decrease in meaningful work for patients presenting with marginal levels of object relations, while the reverse association was observed for patients presenting with more adequate levels of object development (Piper, Azim, Joyce, McCallum, Nixon, & Segal, 1991). Comparing the impact of interpretive, experiential, and directive interventions, Van Egeren (1992) observed that interventions had little impact upon the therapeutic alliance. Svartberg and Stiles (1992) explored the association between therapist adherence to technique and the alliance in brief dynamic psychotherapy, and they too found no association. As to the accuracy of interpretations, this variable does not seem to be related to the status of the alliance per se early in therapy (Crits-Christoph, Cooper, & Luborsky, 1988) but rather seems to be associated with changes in alliance levels over the course of treatment (Crits-Christoph et al., 1993). Early accuracy was correlated with better alliances in the late phase of therapy.

Future Directions

Although the alliance construct emerged from clinical observations, research findings are now starting to pay off by indicating that relational and collaborative components of psychotherapy might substantially contribute to helping patients overcome their difficulties. In fact, the alliance may be even more central to change than initially thought. Research is needed to clarify whether the various alliance dimensions influence outcome in a similar or differential fashion across the major psychotherapy approaches (Wolfe & Goldfried, 1989). At the moment, the field of psychotherapy research seems particularly open to considering common factors as "active ingredients" in their own right. In previous decades, proponents of different approaches to psychotherapy often took pains to distance themselves from analytic therapeutic traditions. Now, research on the alliance, which sprang from that analytic perspective, may contribute significantly to the understanding of the therapeutic process in all forms of therapy. Nonetheless, before alliance research may truly guide psychotherapy, many questions remain to be answered, and the following conditions need to be met:

1. *Development of clear theoretical models leading to specific hypotheses about the roles of the alliance.*

To yield meaningful results, empirical questions will have to be increasingly derived from more specific and coherent theoretical formulations. As previously mentioned, three general hypotheses were articulated with respect to the role played by the alliance in promoting positive outcomes—direct, indirect, and interactional. Although these divisions provide a heuristic framework, specific mechanisms need to be proposed and tested to explain more precisely how these direct and indirect alliance processes function to promote change. For example, Henry and Strupp (in press) propose that the alliance be defined as interpersonal process and measured along the fundamental interpersonal axes of affiliation and control. In this model, the interpersonal process is directly internalized, potentially leading to a more positive introject structure and secondary symptomatic change. This proposition has received empirical support (Henry et al., 1990; Quintana & Meara, 1990).

Future models need to address not only how the alliance promotes change, but also how alliance variables might explain therapeutic failure. To fulfill this mandate for greater specificity, new alliance models should articulate the following:

a. What is the alliance? Is it a type of relationship, a set of behaviors, an affective state, a working agreement, an interpersonal schema with certain role relationship properties, and so on.

b. Is the alliance unidimensional or multidimensional, and if the latter, how do the dimensions interact?

c. What are the relative contributions of the patient and the therapist?

d. How does the alliance develop over time?

e. Are different dimensions of the alliance or different alliance models necessary to account for the working of the alliance in different treatment modalities?

f. Does the importance or role of the alliance vary as a function of the phase of therapy?

g. How are technique and alliance related?

h. What are the implications for clinical practice and training?

2. *Clarification of the functions of the various alliance dimensions as they relate to different disorders and patient characteristics.* The various alliance dimensions may well play different roles across disorders or levels of patient functioning. Empirically, most alliance dimensions were found to relate to outcome in samples composed of relatively well-functioning individuals (Gaston, 1990) but, in a

sample of patients presenting with a borderline personality disorder, therapists' understanding and involvement represented the single alliance dimension that was predictive of outcome (Clarkin, 1991). It may well be the case that dimensions such as agreement on goals are of primary importance to reasonably intact patients, in order to get them quickly involved in the tasks of therapy (an indirect or mediating role of the alliance). On the other hand, dimensions such as the emotional bond may be more important to patients less advanced in object development, simply to keep them in therapy long enough to allow a direct or internalizing function of the alliance to facilitate a "corrective emotional experience."

3. *Bringing research questions closer to topics relevant to practitioners.* Not only is the alliance a topic of theoretical and empirical interest, but it may have a profound impact on the practice of dynamic psychotherapy (Bowlby, 1988). To influence practitioners, however, researchers need to spell out more clearly the clinical implications of their findings. Future research might benefit the practitioner by specifying more clearly which role of the alliance is being examined in a given study and how to handle patients' difficulties in developing a good-enough alliance. In short, insofar as possible, specific guidelines for action should be seen as an important product for research.

4. *Articulation of the alliance with respect to transference.* To fully integrate the alliance concept within the analytical framework, the concept of the alliance, the transference, and their interaction need to be more clearly articulated theoretically and justified empirically. This, of course, will prove difficult. Not only might a patient's alliance ratings be influenced by transference, but reactions labeled as transference might actually be the result of common negative interpersonal complementarity (such as the patient's reaction to subtly hostile interpretations). As a first step, it might be useful to determine whether patients' alliance ratings are influenced by transferential reactions as hypothesized by Freud (1912/1966), who viewed the alliance as a continuation into consciousness of positive transferential feelings, or unrelated as proposed by Bowlby (1988), who conceived the alliance as stemming from a totally distinct source, that is, the attachment need. Most of all, these two concepts should not be opposed, but rather viewed as complementary.

5. *Direct training of therapists in alliance recognition and management.* It is worrisome that alliance ratings made by therapists generally do not predict outcome (Horvath & Symonds, 1991). This surprising finding suggests that dynamic therapists,

among others, may not adequately judge the collaborative aspects of psychotherapy and that they need to be trained in assessing the alliance to further enhance their efficacy. This may require training methods outside the traditional supervisory framework. Although it has not been formally tested, anecdotal evidence suggests that therapists might benefit from training in the same alliance rating procedures normally used by independent observers.

6. *Use of methodologies appropriate to the question addressed.* Traditional group, cross-sectional research designs have been useful in establishing the important link between the alliance and outcome in a global manner. A more precise understanding of the development of the alliance, its role in other therapeutic processes (such as insight or depth of experiencing), and the effects of specific interventions on the alliance (both short-term and long-range) will likely require more intensive work, greater design creativity, and more complex statistical procedures (i.e., time-series analysis). More emphasis might be placed on single-case studies, but such research should be conducted in a manner that permits a priori hypothesis testing and meaningful aggregation of results across cases. If individual alliance patterns and alliance shifts can be pinpointed by these methods, then the successful identification of specific techniques capable of promoting the alliance may emerge. Single-case studies are important, both in the hypothesis generation and confirmation stages of research, and should be pursued with the same empirical rigor as traditional group experimental designs (see Hilliard, in press, for a discussion of single-case methodology).

SYSTEMATIC METHODS FOR PSYCHODYNAMIC DIAGNOSIS

Having reviewed the chief technical intervention of psychodynamic psychotherapy and the relational dimensions within which they occur, we now turn our attention to a final central focus of analytic theory and research—*what* is being treated with these therapeutic processes. Psychodynamically important aspects of psychopathology, such as interpersonal transference propensities, defensive configurations, information-processing operations, or shifts in states of mind, are poorly represented in the dominant diagnostic taxonomy (DSM-III-R). A psychodynamic axis was omitted from the DSM-III series because of the difficulty in establishing reliable and valid measures of psychodynamic constructs (DeWitt, Kaltreider, Weiss, & Horowitz,

1983; Messer, 1991; Mintz, 1981; Seitz, 1966; Spence, 1982). To compensate for this deficiency, psychodynamic researchers have begun to develop more operationalized procedures and measures of problems, treatments, and outcomes that are congruent with psychodynamic concepts (Strupp, Schacht, & Henry, 1988).

In this section, we examine research issues associated with efforts to establish reliable and valid methods for psychodynamic diagnosis or "formulation" as it is commonly known. A psychodynamic diagnosis aspires, in the ideal, to integrate three complementary levels of understanding: by linking (1) concrete conscious problems with (2) recurrent patterns of problems and (3) unconscious core-ordering processes (cf. Mahoney, 1991). This psychodynamic integration complicates research efforts because each level of understanding corresponds to a different set of diagnostic constructs, which in turn invite different measures of psychopathology and different treatment targets. For example, because concrete problems are discrepancies between a desired and actual state of affairs as perceived by the patient, the corresponding diagnostic measures and treatment targets focus on specific conscious experiences and behaviors (as found in typical DSM-III operational criteria). In contrast, recurrent, organized patterns of problems yield corresponding diagnostic measures and treatment targets directed at underlying dynamics (e.g., a recurrent wish–fear conflict or an interpersonal vicious cycle). Finally, core-ordering processes, the deep structures that organize experience and provide a substrate for the surface structure patterns of problems, point diagnosis and treatment toward unconscious aspects of the patient's psychological structure, such as the conceptual level or degree of differentiation of self- and object-representations associated with various disturbances of interpersonal attachment (e.g., Blatt, 1974).

At the time of the last chapter on psychoanalytic research in this *Handbook* (Luborsky & Spence, 1978), there were only two existing research methods for systematically arriving at a psychodynamic diagnosis. However, interest in developing procedures for systematic psychodynamic diagnosis has mushroomed over the past decade, resulting in a proliferation of methods that selectively emphasize one or more of the three levels of understanding previously mentioned. Some methods allow a diagnosis to be constructed on a highly idiographic basis (e.g., Consensual Response Method: L. Horowitz, Rosenberg, Ureno, Kalehzan, & O'Halloran, 1989), while others prescribe a relatively Procrustean format. Most research methods for psychodynamic diagnosis have fo-

cused on recurrent relationship patterns, with fewer methods giving systematic attention to cognitive and/or affective functioning. Several psychodynamic therapy manuals have incorporated methods of systematic psychodynamic diagnosis into their clinical prescriptions (Benjamin, in press; M. Horowitz, Marmar, Krupnick, et al., 1984; Luborsky, 1984; Strupp & Binder, 1984; Weiss & Sampson, 1986), and we expect that this trend will continue. At the time of this writing, at least 17 different diagnostic methods had been developed (see Table 11.1, drawn primarily from Dahl, Kachele, & Thomae 1988, and Luborsky, 1990a).

Most methods for psychodynamic diagnosis have been applied only to very limited samples, often to case studies. However, a subset of methods has been applied to moderate-sized samples. These include core conflictual relationship theme, plan diagnosis, idiographic conflict formulation method, and consensual response formulation. Because a complete comparative discussion of each available method is beyond the space limitations of this review, we will emphasize a selection of methods with relatively substantial empirical records as a focus for elucidating general research issues that we believe apply across many methods. The reader is cautioned that this is a rapidly growing area, and many studies were unpublished and/or in progress at the time of this writing.

The Core Conflictual Relationship Theme (CCRT)

THe CCRT is hypothesized to be a traitlike core interpersonal pattern that operationalizes the central tendency of a patient's interpersonal transference propensities. The CCRT method extracts and organizes interpersonal information from a patient's verbalizations into a prototypic interpersonal micronarrative. The original (1977) CCRT was based on a Freudian model of psychopathology in which emotional difficulties stem from wishes that are conflicted because of anxiety about negative responses from others. Thus, the original (1977) CCRT was constructed according to a standard format that consisted of two elements: (1) interpersonal wishes, needs, or intentions, and (2) consequences of those wishes, expressed in a 2×2 matrix of positive versus negative and internal versus external. These wishes and consequences were extracted from narratives of relationship episodes drawn from therapy sessions. Consistent with the assumption that there was a single core relationship theme, this standard structure was described as a single tree with branching subthemes, with the main trunk composed of a wish, need, or

TABLE 11.1 Methods of systematic psychodynamic formulation

Year	Author	Method
1977	Luborsky Theme (CCRT)	Core conflictual relationship
1977	Weiss, Sampson, Caston, & Silberschatz	Plan diagnosis
1979/1987	M. Horowitz	Configurational analysis
1981	Teller & Dahl	Frame method
	Carlson	Tomkins's script method
1982	Gill & Hoffman	Patient's experience of relationship with therapist
1982/1984	Schacht & Binder	Dynamic focus
1983	Slap & Slaykin	Clinical summaries of schemas
1984	Grawe & Caspar	Plan analysis
1985	Kiesler et al.	Impact message inventory
1986	Bond & Shevrin	Clinical evaluation team
1986/1989	Maxim	Seattle Psychotherapy Language Analysis Schema
1987a	Kiesler	Impact Message Inventory
1987b	Kiesler	Checklists of Interpersonal and Psychotherapy Transactions-Revised (CLOIT-R & CLOPT-R)
1989	Perry, Augusto, & Cooper	Idiographic conflict summary
	L. Horowitz, Rosenberg, Ureno, Kalehzan, & O'Halloran	Consensual response formulation
1991	Schacht & Henry	SASB-cyclic maladaptive pattern
1992	Crits-Christoph & Baranackie	Quantitative Assessment of Interpersonal Themes (QUAINT)

intention and the branches composed of consequences of the wish, need, or intention, as follows:

ORIGINAL (1977) CCRT FORMAT

Wish, Need, Intention	Consequences
I want (*general theme*)	1. Negative external response
from	
(*person*), but:	2. Negative internal response
	3. Positive external response
	4. Positive internal response

Current versions of the CCRT have expanded the two-element structure to three elements by dividing "consequences" into the categories of "responses from others" and "responses from self." The addition of "responses from self" allows the CCRT to capture internalized or introjected elements of interpersonal relationships. The current CCRT thus appears to expand the Freudian perspective of conflicting wishes to include elements of self-psychology. A generic CCRT diagnosis would be stated as: "I wish, need, or intend in relation to the other person that . . . (fill in with interpersonal wish). As a consequence, the other person becomes . . . (fill in with responses from others) and I become . . . (fill in with responses from self)."

Data base and judges. The CCRT is typically constructed from the content of interpersonal narratives (called "relationship episodes"). These narratives are extracted from therapy sessions (transcripts) or from a specialized Relationship Paradigms Interview (RAP: Luborsky, 1990b). A third potential source of data, empirically untested, involves including observations of interpersonal process enactments between patient and interviewer in the definition of "relationship episodes."

Scoring and extraction of CCRT. The process of constructing a CCRT is essentially a frequency count that includes four steps: (1) extracting relationship episodes (REs) from transcripts; (2) rating each RE on its "degree of completeness" (those judged insufficiently complete may be excluded); (3) inspecting the REs in sequence to determine thematic consistencies (judges may refer to a list of "standard categories" for describing interpersonal wishes and consequences); (4) composing a final CCRT from those wishes, responses of others, and responses of self that have the highest frequencies in the sample of relationship episodes.

Reliability. In a study of 35 cases, reliability of RE completeness judgments by pooled-judge intraclass correlation was .68 ($N = 111$, $p < .001$); the per-judge intraclass correlation was .51 (Crits-Christoph, Luborsky et al., 1988). Reliability of the overall CCRT diagnosis has been assessed with several small samples and one moderate sample ($N = 35$), with weighted kappas ranging from .61 to .70 (Crits-Christoph, Luborsky et al., 1988).

Validity. Validity of the CCRT has been examined in a series of studies, a number of which are programmatically related to the evaluation of 22 propositions about transference derived from Freud's classic treatises (Luborsky, 1990d). The CCRT has been used to compare diagnoses derived from dreams with diagnoses based on waking experiences (Popp, Luborsky, & Crits-Christoph, 1990) and to compare diagnoses based on the patients' experience with significant others with diagnoses based on the relationship that is established with the therapist (Fried, Crits-Christoph, & Luborsky, 1990). Patients' self-interpretation of RAP narratives has been compared with CCRTs derived by independent judges (Crits-Christoph & Luborsky, 1990). Pervasiveness of perceived rejection in the CCRT "response of others component" correlated moderately ($r = .32$) with severity of depression in a sample of 21 depressed patients. The CCRT has also demonstrated moderate correlations ($r = .31$ to .44, $N = 43$) between outcome and empathic accuracy of therapists' interventions, when accuracy was measured in terms of the independently rated CCRT and also against a self-report scale that allows patients to describe their own CCRT (Crits-Christoph, Cooper, & Luborsky, 1990; Crits-Christoph & Luborsky, 1990).

Plan Diagnosis

Plan diagnosis is based on control–mastery theory (Sampson, 1990; Silverman, 1990; J. Weiss, 1990), as developed empirically by J. Weiss, Sampson, and the Mount Zion Psychotherapy Research Group (1986). Control–mastery theory posits that psychopathology stems from grim, constricting beliefs that impede normal functioning by evoking negative internal reactions such as guilt, shame, fear, and helplessness. These grim ideas, labeled "pathogenic beliefs," are believed to reflect unfortunate traumatic experiences associated with otherwise normal early motives and developmental goals (such as attachment to important caretakers).

Control–mastery theory holds that patients test pathogenic beliefs in the therapeutic relationship, hoping to disconfirm them and thereby give them up. Plan diagnosis formulates a patient's pathogenic beliefs and the associated plan for testing those beliefs. The plan diagnosis contains four elements: (1) conscious and unconscious goals for therapy; (2) pathogenic beliefs that interfere with reaching goals; (3) specific plans (tests) employed by the patient in the therapeutic relationship to

disconfirm these pathogenic beliefs; and (4) insights presumed necessary for improvement (J. Weiss et al., 1986).

Data base and judges. A plan diagnosis is extracted from therapy transcripts, usually the first three sessions. Judges have been experienced clinicians familiar with the underlying principles of control–mastery theory. However, Messer, Tishby, and Spillman (1992) describe successful use of advanced graduate students.

Scoring and extraction of plan diagnosis. The procedure for extracting a plan diagnosis is as follows: First, judges independently develop a diagnosis that includes all four elements previously mentioned. As part of this task, they construct lists of items from the transcripts that are highly relevant and less relevant. Researchers then combine the judge's lists separately for each element and return these master lists to the judges, who are asked to rate the relevance of each item on a five-point Likert-type scale. Means are calculated for each item, and below-median items are dropped. Second, a separate group of judges reassesses the items to eliminate redundancies. The remaining items, plus a narrative description of the patient, his or her complaints, and life situation, constitute the plan diagnosis.

Reliability. Reliability data for two 2-person teams of trained judges have been reported by J. Curtis, Silberschatz, Sampson, Weiss, & Rosenberg (1988) and Rosenberg et al. (1986). Pooled interjudge agreement on items included in the master lists for all four components of the plan diagnosis ranged from .78 to .97 with the exception of "tests" for one patient, which was .39. Collins and Messer (1991), working at a different site, reported interjudge agreement ranging from .81 to .93. However, this level of agreement was reached with difficulty and required judges to specify a theoretical framework within which judgments would be made. Collins and Messer (1991) also assessed cross-site reliability, comparing same-case diagnoses by investigators at Mount Zion and Rutgers University. Both groups created items for the cases, and the combined list was then rated by both Mount Zion and Rutgers judges. Each group produced highly reliable ratings internally, but the correlations between the groups' plan items were negative. Collins and Messer attributed this difference to divergent underlying theoretical assumptions (i.e., whether the patient's problems were due to guilt over surpassing others versus fear of losing others). Messer et al. (1992) report an intraclass correlation of .83 for 4 judges rating compatibility of all therapist interventions with a plan diagnosis in 2 complete cases of 16 and 17 sessions.

Validity. Silberschatz et al. (1986) defined suitability of interventions in terms of compatibility with the plan diagnosis. Ratings of intervention "plan-compatibility" correlated positive ($r = .25$ to .54) with level of experiencing in three patients (Klein, Mathieu-Coughlan, & Kiesler, 1986), suggesting that compatible interventions resulted in an improved therapeutic process. Similar findings based on a single case were reported by J. Weiss et al. (1986). Messer et al. (1992) reported significant correlations (ranging from .51 to .82) between plan-compatibility of therapist interventions and patient progress, as judged by a psychodynamically oriented progress/stagnation scale.

Idiographic Conflict Formulation Method (ICF)
Idiographic conflict formulation (ICF: J. Perry, Augusto, & Cooper, 1989) organizes psychodynamic hypotheses around five themes: wishes, fears, symptomatic and avoidant resultants (of the wishes and fears), vulnerability to specific stressors, and best available level of adaptation to conflicts.

Data base and judges. An ICF is extracted from videotaped interviews that do not require any particular format, except that they cover major areas of present life functioning. Judges have been experienced psychodynamically oriented clinicians and graduate students, working in two 2-member teams. Each team arrives at a consensual diagnosis to be cross-validated against the consensual diagnosis of the other team.

Scoring and extraction of ICF. Data from the whole interview are used (not just relationship episodes as in the CCRT). No unitizing procedure is specified. Judges work in consensus teams and may attend to any cognitive, affective, or behavioral patterns; however, inferences must be documented by listing specific supporting evidence from the interview.

Reliability. J. Perry et al. (1989) report intraclass correlations for the ICF components ranging from .54 to .75 in a sample of 20 cases rated for degree of similarity across two teams of raters. These cases were selected from a diagnostically narrow sample drawn from a separate study of the diagnostic validity of borderline personality as compared to antisocial personality and bipolar type II affective disorder. No studies have compared ICFs from separate interviews on the same patient.

Validity. No data are available to support the validity of the ICF. A second-stage procedure, the Eriksonian-based Psychodynamic Conflict Rating Scales, is available for rating the ICF components for the presence of 14 predefined conflicts. This procedure is intended to supplement the highly idiographic ICF with a nomothetic measure that facilitates comparison across subjects. Research in progress at the time of this writing is applying this method to the evaluation of dynamic change.

Consensual Response Method (CRM)
In contrast to the previous methods, each of which has incorporated a particular psychodynamic theoretical framework, the consensual response method (CRM) is relatively theory-neutral (L. Horowitz et al., 1989). CRM addresses the problem of attaining reliability by averaging the diagnoses of a group of clinicians. This approach draws from cognate research in cognitive psychology on the measurement of "fuzzy concepts." A core assumption is that characteristics of a diagnosis that are mentioned most often (consensual responses) form a set that can be used to describe a theoretical ideal or prototype.

Data base and judges. The CRM has been applied to videotaped semistructured clinical interviews of approximately one hour's duration. Ratings have been made by experienced clinicians with a psychodynamic orientation, working individually in panels of eight members, assisted by students who unitize and reduce data.

Scoring and extraction of the diagnostic formulation. The CRM is a complex, multistep procedure. Clinician-judges independently spend 20 minutes generating a one-page dynamic diagnosis, similar to what is recommended elsewhere for clinical use (cf. Faulkner, Kinzie, Angell, U'ren, & Shore, 1985; Friedman & Lister, 1987; S. Perry, Cooper, & Michels, 1987). Judges then discuss the case for half an hour as a group, followed by a 15-minute rewrite of the diagnosis. Each postdiscussion diagnostic write-up is then reduced to "thought units" unitized by a separate group of student raters. Then another group of judges follows a standardized procedure to review the thought units to identify those with similar meanings, which are then tabulated across the diagnoses. The CRM diagnosis includes all thought units that were mentioned by three or more judges (out of eight on the panel) integrated into a narrative that also includes biographical data and description of symptoms.

Reliability. In a sample of 15 cases, reliability of the unitizing procedure (thought-unit extraction) was high, with mean values of alpha ranging from .84 to .96 (L. Horowitz et al., 1989). Stability of the formulation was evaluated by replication with a single case using a different panel of clinicians. Using a panel of five graduate students as judges, 81 percent of the thought units appearing in the first formulation were judged present in the replication. A second group of five judges was 100 percent accurate in matching the replicated formulation to the original, which was embedded in a set of formulations that included 14 mismatched formulations along with the correct original formulation.

Validity. Reasoning that a valid psychodynamic diagnosis should predict issues that are discussed in therapy, the Inventory of Interpersonal Problems (IIP: L. Horowitz, Rosenberg, Baer, Ureno, & Villasenor, 1988) was distributed at Sessions 10 and 20 to examine correspondence between the formulation and problems discussed in therapy. Item-by-item comparison of the IIP responses with interpersonal problems identified in diagnostic formulations revealed that issues mentioned in the formulations were highly predictive of topics reported on the IIP to have been discussed in treatment. A second validity assessment affirmed an earlier finding that interpersonal problems (as opposed to other types of problems) predict positive therapy outcome (L. Horowitz et al., 1988). Using a composite outcome measure applied to the 15 cases in L. Horowitz et al. (1989), it was found that patients whose formulations had high interpersonal content tended to have positive outcome scores (mean z score 0.61), while those with low interpersonal content had negative outcome scores (mean z score −0.48).

Configurational Analysis

Perhaps the most comprehensive and ambitious vision of systematic psychodynamic diagnosis is M. Horowitz's method of configurational analysis (M. Horowitz, 1979, 1987, 1991). Its primary development to date has been theoretical rather than empirical. However, it deserves mention because of its conceptual elegance and because it is the focus of a substantial empirical effort in conjunction with the Program on Conscious and Unconscious Mental Processes funded by the MacArthur Foundation at Langley Porter Neuropsychiatric Institute. A configurational analysis is composed of three fundamental units: (1) recurrent patterns of experience and behavior termed *states of mind* that are clustered into desired, dreaded, problematic compromise, and adaptive compromise states; (2) interpersonal role-relationship models; and (3) informa-

tion-processing patterns. The method embodies no preferences about the origin of data. Hence, raw data that apply to these three categories may be accepted from any available source including psychotherapy sessions, statements about the patient by significant others, clinical history, behavioral observations, psychological testing, and so on. Raw data are organized with the aid of explicit heuristics (cf. M. Horowitz, 1987, chaps. 1–4) into the categories of states of mind, role-relationship models, and information-processing patterns. The categorized data are then used to describe three phases of the treatment process (initial problem, prescription and analysis of treatment process, and outcome). The final diagnostic formulation focuses on understanding the stability, transitions, and recurrent patterns in an individual's repertoire of possible states of mind, encompassing the domains of interpersonal, cognitive, and affective functioning.

Research Issues in Psychodynamic Formulation Procedures

Paradigm development. As suggested by Table 11.1, the field is presently in the early stages of paradigm development, with a high ratio of numbers of methods to number of studies. Even pioneering methods such as the CCRT and plan diagnosis have only a handful of studies dealing with substantive phenomena as opposed to development of the method itself. We expect that research in this area will continue to focus on basic methodological issues such as unitizing data and reliability, with cross-site replications and validity studies of substantive therapeutic phenomena to follow.

Potential for integration with treatment manuals. Methods for psychodynamic diagnosis may be useful in both basic research on psychodynamics and psychopathology and treatment research. Because manuals have become essential in treatment research, diagnostic formulation methods must be adaptable to the constraints of a manualized therapy. For this reason, formulation methods that require teams of judges will be difficult to integrate into manualized treatments, whereas methods that can be used by individual clinicians may have a relative logistical advantage.

Comparative studies. Comparing different formulation methods on the same case is complicated by diversity in domain, format, and units of analysis. Even comparison of basic psychometric properties, such as reliability, is difficult because the limited size of samples may introduce bias due to case selection (e.g., choice of easy-to-formulate cases could inflate apparent reliability of a method). Despite such difficulties, several comparative studies have been attempted. Luborsky and Crits-Christoph (1990) review five such comparisons, most of which had not yet been completed or published. All the studies included the CCRT and at least one of the following other methods: PERT, frame analysis, cyclical maladaptive pattern, role-relationship model from configurational analysis, and idiographic conflict summary. Luborsky and Crits-Christoph conclude that there is substantial similarity among the measures, based on comparison of interpersonal themes extracted in these five studies. However, comparisons using a wider range of cases are necessary before this conclusion can be held with confidence.

Idiographic versus nomothetic. Some formulation methods permit raters free access to the entire natural language vocabulary, claiming that this increases specificity for unique aspects of individual cases. However, this increase in expected validity has tended to occur at the expense of reliability and reduced ability to aggregate across cases, which supports opposite arguments for restricting raters to a limited, nomothetic vocabulary. Both of these extremes are integrated in the CCRT, ICF, and CRM, which allow initial free choice of vocabulary and then provide instruments or standard categories for further data reduction.

No method for psychodynamic diagnosis has directly assessed content validity of its ad hoc category system. The validity issue can be perilous, as illustrated by a study of CCRTs in patients with major depression by Eckert, Luborsky, Barber, and Crits-Christoph (1990). This study sampled CCRTs from 21 patients enrolled in a project investigating brief dynamic therapy for depression. A main finding was that CCRT narratives revealed frequent wishes "to be close and accepted" and "to be loved and understood." These wishes were viewed as consistent with theories that depression is related to issues of attachment and loss, specifically "anaclitic" depression as described by Blatt (1974) and Blatt and Zuroff (1992). However, the CCRT did not capture wishes that might be expected with Blatt's other psychodynamic variant of depression, the "introjective" form, which is characterized by tendencies to self-criticism and self-destructiveness. One possible conclusion might be that introjective depression did not occur in this sample of patients. However, it is also possible that the CCRT method itself has a blind spot. Indeed, inspection of the list of standard categories suggests they may be insensitive to the introjective form of depression because the category list contains no items that reflect self-destructiveness or suicidal tendencies.

As one response to such difficulties with ad hoc category systems, researchers may incorporate already well-developed measurement systems into their psychodynamic formulation schemes. Schacht and Henry (SASB-cyclic maladaptive pattern (CMP), in press) have proposed a dynamic formulation model derived almost entirely from the categories of interpersonal actions made available by Benjamin's (1974) SASB. Likewise, Crits-Christoph, Demorest, and Connolly (1990) and Crits-Christoph and Baranackie (1992) have begun to explore possible application of SASB to modeling interpersonal events in the CCRT.

Content versus process. Some diagnostic methods focus primarily on verbal content from interviews, while others permit judges to consider both content and interpersonal process between patient and interviewer. As compared to discrete content variables, the continuous nature of process variables may greatly complicate decisions about where a unit of analysis, such as a relationship episode, begins and ends. There are not yet any studies comparing the reliability of demarcating units based on analysis of process as opposed to content.

A related consideration involves validity problems that may result when process observations are artificially restricted to the same units of analysis as content observations. The example of the CCRT, which uses the unit of "relationship episode" to represent both content and process, is instructive in this regard. The CCRT manual defines a process episode as "the patient engages during the session in a *delimited episode* of *conflictual* interaction with the therapist" (Luborsky, 1990c, p. 18, emphasis added). While such a restriction preserves the "relationship episode" as a basic unit of analysis, the resulting method may be insensitive to important aspects of interpersonal process that do not meet the criteria of being conflictual or occurring in a delimited episode. For an extreme counterexample, consider the case of an ongoing tendency to ingratiate oneself with the therapist by adopting an overall pleasant and submissive stance. Such a relationship pattern could be very important therapeutically but would not be captured by the CCRT definition of enactment because it is relatively pervasive (nonepisodic), nonhostile, and noninterpersonally conflictual.

Deep-structure assumptions. The concept of *deep structure* helps us recognize that observable phenomena may differ in surface form while retaining a similar organization in terms of underlying ("deep") structure. Assumptions about the nature and form of the deep structure of diagnoses vary across formulation methods. For example, Teller and Dahl's (1981) "frame" method assumes that the deep structure of core schemas is unique for each patient and cannot be specified in advance. In contrast, the plan diagnosis, the CCRT, and the ICF illustrate a priori general statements about what constitutes a "well-formed" deep structure for a complete relationship pattern.

A central deep-structure issue relates to assumptions about linearity of underlying phenomena. Most diagnostic methods have relied on simple frequency counts as the best index for selecting elements to be included in a formulation. However, frequency counts can be misleading if the underlying phenomena are not simple linear functions. Frequency assumptions may have significant theoretical implications related to the most basic ideas about what a formulation method measures. For example: (1) If frequency does mark importance, does it do so directly or indirectly? That is, could frequency mark a theme indirectly by measuring defenses against it, such as rigidity and defensiveness associated with a reaction formation against a warded-off or forbidden theme? In such a case, the high frequency of an apparent pattern could represent a defense against another, unexpressed but feared low-frequency pattern. The low-frequency pattern might be expected to increase in frequency if, in the course of therapy, the individual became able to forgo the defenses against it. Such a situation would be consistent with clinical literature that describes transference manifestations as "unfolding" over time, as well as empirical research on the identification of warded-off mental contents (cf. L. Horowitz, Sampson, Siegelman, Wolfson, & Weiss, 1975). (2) If a clinically significant relationship pattern is viewed as the long-term developmental result of gradually accumulated interpersonal learning in the family, then it makes theoretical sense to expect frequency to be related to clinical importance. On the other hand, if a particular relationship pattern has its roots in later traumatic events, so that the recurrence of the pattern represents traumatic reenactment, some theories would suggest that the frequency of the pattern may vary with the presence or absence of other events that trigger or activate the traumatic material (cf. Marmar & Horowitz, 1988). In this case, the underlying traumatic vulnerability might be under- or overestimated depending on the particular circumstances at the time of a given measurement. The question of frequency as a basis for measurement goes to the heart of fundamental theoretical assumptions that have not been subjected to empirical scrutiny.

Unity versus multiplicity.   While some formulation theories and methods, such as the CCRT, assume that each person is characterized by a single core pattern, other approaches propose that multiple patterns may be the norm (e.g., configurational analysis, M. Horowitz, 1987; Markus & Nurius, 1986; Singer & Salovey, 1991). Assumptions regarding unity versus multiplicity have largely escaped empirical attention. A single case reported by Crits-Christoph, Demorest, and Connolly (1990) indicated the presence of multiple themes. In contrast, a second line of evidence showing pervasiveness of the CCRT element of "wishes" in 33 patients is reported by Crits-Christoph and Luborsky (1990) as supportive of the "single pattern" hypothesis. However, equating individual CCRT components with the entire relationship pattern may have the effect of overstating apparent pervasiveness of the overall pattern. Furthermore, 21 percent of the sample of 33 patients carried the uncommon diagnosis of schizoid personality disorder. Because constriction of interpersonal relatedness is a characteristic feature of such patients, it is possible that they may evidence a relatively greater tendency to demonstrate a single, dominant relationship theme. Finally, an important research question relates to the possibility that the presence of a single pervasive interpersonal theme may represent a developmental accomplishment that not all patients have achieved to an equal degree. With the notable exception of idiographic conflict formulation, which incorporates Erikson's developmental theory, most formulation methods are silent with respect to measuring developmental aspects of relationship patterns, such as degree of differentiation and integration of representations of self and others. If less developed themes are expressed in a defensively fragmented or warded-off manner alternative, it seems possible that the apparent "unity" of a formulation may be an artifact of prior scoring decisions that limit a data base to relatively developmentally advanced units of analysis, such as "complete" relationship episodes.

Data base: therapy sessions, diagnostic interviews, or questionnaires?   Most formulation methods may be applied to events drawn from treatment sessions. Some researchers also employ specialized diagnostic interviews and/or questionnaires. Examples include the RAP interview for the CCRT, the Inventory of Interpersonal Problems-Circumplex for the CRF, or the SASB INTREX questionnaires for the SASB-CMP. However, systematic differences in formulations are a function of data source of collection method. Additionally, no psychodynamic formulation methods have employed specialized interviews designed to systematically evoke expressions of habitual interpersonal process (as opposed to self-reported content), although such process-evoking interviews have been described elsewhere in literature on assessment of personality disorders (Selzer, Kernberg, Fibel, Cherbuliez, & Mortati, 1987).

A related issue involves comparison of formulations across patients, therapists, and independent clinical judges. Studies systematically comparing formulations across those data sources are virtually nonexistent. One exception is a study by Crits-Christoph and Luborsky (1990), which compared the wishes portion of a self-report CCRT questionnaire with two other procedures in a study of 16 patients. The other procedures included (1) self-interpretation of RAP narratives that required patients to rate their own narratives on the degree to which a standard list of wishes was applicable, and (2) the standard clinician-judged CCRT derived from the same RAP narratives. Results indicated that self-rated RAP and self-report CCRT were generally poorly correlated. Comparison of self-rated RAP and self-report CCRT with clinician-rated CCRT indicated that patients tended to agree with independent clinicians on ratings of wishes, but disagreed on descriptions of main conflicts. Indeed, in only 25 percent of cases did the patients' descriptions of conflicts from either measure match the clinicians' descriptions.

Based on the foregoing, Luborsky and Crits-Christoph conclude that clinician-based measures are to be preferred to patient-generated measures. However, given the limited data on this question it may be premature to dismiss questionnaires as useful sources of data for psychodynamic formulation. Expense for the labor of raters can be a major factor in the cost of research, which could be reduced by development of reliable and valid questionnaire methods. Furthermore, discrepancies between data generated by patients and by clinicians may represent potentially important phenomena rather than simple psychometric nuisances.

A Research Framework for the Future

At a minimum, psychodynamic diagnostic formulations can fulfill all of the logical roles filled by descriptive diagnosis (S. Perry et al., 1987). Indeed, potential research applications span the entire realm of psychotherapy research, although studies beyond development of the methods themselves have been rather limited for all psychodynamic formulation approaches. Replication of studies or even duplication of methods across sites remains rare. There is a significant need for such research

and clearly there is much room for future development. The following outline summarizes potential functions of psychodynamic diagnoses as research variables.

1. As *method/instrument* variables, diagnoses may be studied for their psychometric properties such as reliability and validity, either individually or in comparison to alternative formulation methods (Collins & Messer, 1991; J. Curtis et al., 1988; Leeds & Bucci, 1986; Rosenberg et al., 1986). Studies may also be conducted of the effects of various procedures for unitizing or extracting raw data (e.g., natural therapy transcripts vs. specialized assessment interviews or psychometric instruments; relationship episodes vs. thought units). A psychodynamic diagnosis may also serve to target the selection of other measurement tools. This might occur when certain features of a case are highlighted as important by a formulation, but the formulation method itself is not necessarily the best measure of those features. This use of formulations may be especially relevant to the design of intensive single-case studies.

2. As a *therapist*, variable, a psychodynamic diagnosis can be studied as a cognitive activity and/or product of the therapist's thought process. Several formulation methods propose to serve as heuristics for practitioners (e.g., CCRT, SASB-CMP, configurational analysis, plan diagnosis), in which learning to generate a psychodynamic formulation can be viewed as a type of highly focused therapist training (Faulkner et al., 1985; M. Horowitz, 1987, chap. 11). Claims of heuristic usefulness are largely untested but might be empirically investigated by studies of therapist thinking and behavior before and after training. Results from the Vanderbilt II study (Henry, Schacht, Strupp, Butler, & Binder, 1993) indicate that therapists' response to such training may be complexly influenced by nontraining factors such as therapist personality, which may also be studied with psychodynamic formulation methods.

3. As a *patient* variable, psychodynamic diagnosis may complement DSM diagnosis in defining a patient sample structuring initial inclusion/exclusion criteria, or evaluating differential outcome or attrition from treatment. In short, a formulation may be used in research as is any other patient characteristic assessed at intake. Psychodynamic diagnoses may be studied for their value as guides to predicting therapeutic process on a continuum that ranges from choosing a momentary intervention to planning or selecting treatment strategies for an entire case.

4. As a *treatment or process variable*, formulation

may serve as the unit of analysis for comparative studies that ask whether psychodynamic diagnoses constructed along different theoretical lines are associated with differences in treatment process or outcome, or that evaluate the impact of more or less accurate therapist interventions. Alternately, to the extent that diagnostic formulation is seen as an *activity* of patient and/or therapist, as well as a *product*, it may be studied as a process variable in its own right, with both the formulation and the relationship within which it is jointly constructed contributing to the overall treatment (see Messer et al., 1992).

5. With respect to *outcome* evaluation, diagnostic formulations may help researchers be more explicit in their assumptions about where they elect to assess change (Crits-Christoph & Luborsky, 1990, chap. 9; Henry, 1990; M. Horowitz, Marmar, Weiss, Kaltreider, & Wilner, 1986; Silberschatz, Curtis, & Nathans, 1989). For example, in the case of M. Horowitz's (1987) method of configurational analysis, outcome may be assessed by measuring (1) changes in the frequency, intensity, and duration of states of mind; (2) changes in the events that trigger state transitions; (3) additions of new states or elements of states to a patient's repertoire; (4) changes in attitudes toward various states or processes, or sense of potential mastery or control over a particular state or transition process. Use of formulations in outcome assessment is complicated by the absence of studies that would provide preliminary base-rate data on the general frequency with which psychodynamic diagnoses may change (with or without treatment).

6. Finally, as a source of *alternative research designs*, some authors have argued that formulation, broadly construed, may serve as the basis for an entire general investigative approach, termed the *formulation hypothesis*. Persons (1991) and Persons, Curtis, and Silberschatz (1991) contrast this approach with traditional research approaches that purportedly suffer from self-defeating emphasis on a theoretical standardization at the expense of ecological validity. From this perspective, the repeated failure to find differences between therapies in controlled outcome studies is attributable to insufficient precision in specifying relevant patient and treatment variables, rather than true causal predominance of nonspecific or common factors. Arguments in favor of case formulation as a core organizing principle for research are controversial and have generated significant rebuttal and commentary, but little in the way of empirical data beyond simple case demonstrations (Garfield, 1991; Herbert & Mueser, 1991; Messer, 1991; Schacht, 1991; W. Silverman, 1991).

PSYCHODYNAMIC RESEARCH: CURRENT STATE AND FUTURE PROSPECTS

Contemporary Trends

The task of summarizing the contemporary body of psychodynamic research is daunting and one might reasonably question whether or not general conclusions are even possible at this juncture. Throughout the entire field of psychotherapy research, investigators have struggled with the problem of operationalizing and measuring exceedingly fluid constructs. By their very nature, psychodynamic constructs have been the most intractable to scientific scrutiny. Perhaps then, the most important observation that can be made about the current research is that it exists at all. Psychodynamic researchers have made a promising start to a most challenging endeavor — that of operationalizing complex constructs and developing replicable measurement procedures. This quest has already begun to pay off, as some old concepts have been empirically supported (e.g., Luborsky's work on the measurement of transference phenomena), while others have been challenged (e.g., the allegedly unique efficacy of transference interpretations). Research on the therapeutic alliance continues to demonstrate the fundamentally interpersonal nature of psychotherapy. Finally, the foundation is being laid for a uniquely psychodynamic diagnostic nosology, a development that could serve to anchor research and encourage accumulated empirical progress for many years to come.

It is clear that the analytic tradition remains a fresh and vital spawning ground for contemporary clinical theory and research. In brief, the past decade or so of empirical research suggests the following trends:

1. *A blurring of traditional boundaries.* The boundaries between psychoanalysis proper and psychodynamic psychotherapy have blurred, and the distinction no longer seems as defensible as evidence accumulates that, in practice, therapists' actual activities are quite similar in the two broadly defined approaches. Additionally, there is little evidence to support the distinction based on the assumed superior efficacy of classical analysis.

2. *The roles of technique and alliance.* The boundaries between technical and "relationship" factors in psychodynamic therapy have also begun to blur. Earlier conceptualizations of the therapeutic process tended to relegate the alliance (however defined) to a facilitative role, while interpretive interventions remained the active ingredient of change. Now, the balance may have shifted or even re-

versed, as more investigators recognize and demonstrate a direct role of the alliance in the change process. More importantly, however, technique and alliance are increasingly seen as inseparable components that *mutually* convey important *meanings* to the patient. A number of authors comment that the wording, tone, and timing of an interpretation may also carry unrecognized or unintentional meaning for the patient about the assumed nature of the dyadic relationship (Henry & Strupp, in press; Piper, Azim, Joyce, & McCallum, 1991; Silberschatz et al., 1986; Wile, 1984). At least one recent treatment manual has made the alliance itself the chief focus of technical intervention (Strupp & Binder, 1984).

3. *Absorption and mutual influence.* There has been increasing mutual influence between psychodynamic theory and therapy and other theoretical camps. The research reviewed here, with its emphasis on operational definitions and measurement, suggests the influence of other traditions (such as behavioral and cognitive-behavioral approaches) that have grown more out of experimental psychology than the observational or clinical methods of traditional psychoanalytic thought. On the other hand, the psychodynamic tradition has influenced the development (if not the inception) of other approaches to psychotherapy. For example, alliance factors are now considered important in behavior therapy, which has moved beyond a simple arsenal of techniques, and now, like psychodynamic therapy, concerns itself with underlying mechanisms and encompassing case-formulations (Turkat & Maisto, 1985). In an excellent book, Safran and Segal (1990) integrate much of the contemporary research on the therapeutic alliance into the understanding of cognitive therapy. Finally, influences from outside the clinical area are also being brought to bear. For example, the research of M. Horowitz and his colleagues on unconscious mental processes combines psychodynamic research and cognitive psychology.

4. *Specificity and contextual relevance.* In the two major empirical areas reviewed—research on the alliance and interpretation—research designs and questions are becoming more sophisticated and specific. The alliance construct has been recast as a multidimensional model, and it may be possible to posit specific functions for different dimensions with different patients at different points in therapy. Investigators are no longer content to show *that* the alliance contributes to outcome, but seek to show *how* it does so. Research on transference interpretations has moved beyond simple frequency counts and global correlations to the measurement of contextually sensitive intervention–response sequences. Additionally, the challenge of defining and measuring the accuracy or suitability of interpretations for specific patients has begun. All of these trends hold the promise of moving beyond the demonstration of efficacy to the more precise detailing of how the psychodynamic approach to therapy works for change when it works at its best.

5. *The emergence of the individual therapist.* In research, the individual therapist has often been considered an unimportant or at best a nuisance variable to be standardized, with technical operations being emphasized in a somewhat disembodied fashion. In a recent paper, Crits-Christoph and Mintz (1991) stressed the importance of statistically measuring and controlling for the variance attributable to individual therapists in psychotherapy studies. The importance of the individual therapist in the treatment–outcome equation can be seen in much of the research we have reviewed, although therapist variables are typically not the stated focus. Nonetheless, the ability to forge a positive working alliance, make accurate interpretations, and act in a plan-compatible fashion involves skills that reside in individuals, not in a body of theory. It is hoped that as research moves to more precisely pinpoint the characteristics of successful dynamic interventions, investigators will also work to specify the characteristics of those who deliver them.

The Ultimate Question

Underlying all psychotherapy research is the ultimate question of efficacy—how effective are our treatments, for whom, and how might we improve them? The present review has focused on questions of differential efficacy as a function of process variables and participant characteristics. What of the larger question—how effective is psychodynamic therapy in general when compared to other forms of treatment? Two recent meta-analyses of the short-term psychodynamic psychotherapy (STPP) treatment literature address this question. Since these reviews are summarized elsewhere in this volume, we will not describe them at length. However, the two reviews themselves raise issues important to dynamic therapy because they seem to reach opposing conclusions.

Svartberg and Stiles (1991) reviewed 19 comparative outcome studies published from 1978 to 1988 and examined the efficacy of STPP relative to no-treatment controls (NT) and alternative psychotherapies (AP). These alternative therapies included supportive, behavioral (systematic desensitization, social skills training, relaxation, etc.), cognitive, and cognitive-behavioral approaches.

Svartberg and Stiles employed an innovative (and possibly controversial) procedure — the summary effect size for each study (mean effect size across outcome measures) was weighted by an index of methodological quality, giving more weight to studies deemed to be of superior quality. Methodological rigor was assessed with a specially developed set of rating scales that measured internal validity, quality of therapists, quality of treatments, quality of outcome measures, and the validity of statistical conclusions (including an estimate of the adequacy of the sample size used).

Space limits preclude discussion of all of their findings, but we will mention the highlights. STPP was superior to NT but showed a small inferiority to AP at posttreatment (termination), and a large inferiority to AP at one-year follow-up. This finding argues against the popular "incubation theory" — that the effects of psychodynamic therapy continue to accrue long after termination. STPP was equally effective in treating groups of mixed neurotics, but inferior to AP in treating depression, particularly when compared to cognitive-behavioral therapy for depression. Improvements in the quality of research from 1978 to 1988 were noted, but with improving quality, STPP became less superior to NT. Despite a number of comparisons involving patient, therapist, and treatment characteristics, Svartberg and Stiles reported a dearth of findings that might suggest factors that increase the relative efficacy of STPP. Within psychodynamic variants, the combination of transference interpretation with fixed time limits seemed superior to a combination of directive and interpretive techniques with flexible time limits.

Doubtless, Svartberg and Stiles (themselves adherents of short-term psychodynamic approaches) were dismayed by these results. On the other hand, Crits-Christoph (1992) reviewed 11 studies and reached different conclusions about the relative efficacy of STPP. Crits-Christoph's method and questions differed in several important ways. He reasoned that one of the greatest problems with psychodynamic outcome research was the lack of control and specification of the treatment variable, resulting in a vulnerability to excessive therapist effects. Therefore he chose only those studies that employed a treatment manual as part of the research protocol, losing some ecological validity, but gaining a purer test of dynamic therapy's efficacy. Furthermore, he did not combine various outcome measures into a summed index, but rather examined the effectiveness of STPP with reference to different outcome types — specific target symptoms, general symptomatology, and social functioning. He compared STPP to waiting-list controls (WL), alternative nonpsychiatric treatments (ANP,

such as placebo and clinical management and self-help groups), and alternative psychotherapies (AP, including medication).

Using Cohen's d effect size, Crits-Christoph reported a large differential effect across all outcome types for STPP versus WL (.81 to 1.10 average effect size). These effects are considerably larger than those found in the Svartberg and Stiles review in their STPP versus NT condition. When compared to ANP, STPP still showed modest positive differential effect sizes (.20 to .32) across two of the outcome measures, but it did not differ on social adjustment. Despite this modest positive evidence, Crits-Christoph concluded that on balance, "the average effect sizes indicate little difference between the outcomes of brief dynamic therapy and the comparison conditions [alternate nonpsychiatric treatments]" (pp. 154–155). When comparing STPP to other forms of therapy (AP), average differential effect sizes were minimal, ranging from −.01 to −.05. He concluded: "The predominant trend is clear: only small differences between brief dynamic therapy and other treatments are generally apparent. No individual study effect size was greater than .30" (p. 155). While these data do not support the superior efficacy of dynamic therapy, they do suggest equivalence when compared to other approaches, in contrast to the Svartberg and Stiles review.[13]

In attempting to make sense of these two contrasting meta-analyses, it should first be recognized that there was little overlap in the studies reviewed (only 2 of the 11 studies reviewed by Crits-Christoph were also reviewed by Svartberg and Stiles), and the studies cited by Crits-Christoph tended to be more up-to-date. Procedural differences, such as the use of a single summed effect size versus calculating separate effect sizes for different outcome measures may also have had a strong impact. Average summed effect sizes may have obscured outcome measurements more favorable to STPP. The therapists in the studies reviewed by Crits-Christoph were probably more clearly psychodynamic because of the requirement for a treatment manual.[14] Additionally, the distinction among types of dynamic therapy made by Svartberg and Stiles may have been problematic in some cases. For instance, the Vanderbilt study cited as an exemplar of flexible time limits was actually time-limited from

---

[13]It should be noted that Crits-Christoph also presents evidence suggesting the relative equivalence of dynamic and cognitive-behavioral treatments for depression, again, a finding in direct opposition to the earlier meta-analysis.

[14]For example, in the Vanderbilt study cited by Svartberg and Stiles, two of the five therapists were clearly nonpsychodynamic in orientation.

the start of therapy. Finally, the quality weighting procedure employed by Svartberg and Stiles, although perhaps a good idea, may have been difficult in practice because they were working only from published summaries of studies.

In conclusion, we feel that although the negative findings of the innovative Svartberg and Stiles review should not be dismissed, there is sufficient reason for caution in accepting their findings as a definitive statement. The review by Crits-Christoph is likely a more accurate reflection of contemporary psychodynamic outcome research and indeed presents a more favorable view of the relative efficacy of dynamic therapy. It may be that the Svartberg and Stiles review has greater ecological validity (in terms of generalizability to actual practice), while the Crits-Christoph review has greater construct validity (in terms of testing purer forms of dynamic therapy). Nonetheless, even Crits-Christoph's review suggests that well-controlled brief dynamic therapy showed only a marginal superiority of effect size over nonpsychiatric alternative treatments and no superiority over other forms of therapy. Clearly, we still have some distance to go.

An important caveat concerning these outcome studies was offered by Crits-Christoph (1992). He noted that in the studies he reviewed, many of the patient groups were types that clinicians find difficult to treat by any means (such as opiate addicts, cocaine abusers, and people with serious personality disorders). Comparative studies have by and large not been performed on patient samples deemed ideally suitable for a short-term dynamic approach (such as some anxiety disorders, relationship conflicts, etc.).[15] Furthermore, typical outcome measures do not usually tap specific areas where dynamic therapy should theoretically be superior. To provide an adequate test of efficacy, future psychodynamic outcome research should further refine the construct "suitability for dynamic psychotherapy," select more appropriate patient samples, and measure treatment outcomes with more specific, theory-relevant measures.

The research areas reviewed in this chapter hold considerable promise for enhancing the efficacy of psychodynamic therapy, because the studies address specific dimensions, constructs, and intervention–response sequences identified with maximum effectiveness. Additionally, emergent formulation schemes may provide a methodology for theory-relevant outcome measurement. One logical end toward which the body of psychody-

namic research might aspire is to create the conditions for optimal tests of efficacy, both in general, and with specified patient populations.

The Future of Psychodynamic Psychotherapy: Training and the Vanderbilt Experience

The studies summarized in this chapter do hold the promise for making psychodynamic therapy more effective for more individuals. Ultimately, however, research is of practical benefit only to the extent it can be employed to guide actual therapies, and this involves therapist training—an area traditionally neglected by the research community (Alberts & Edelstein, 1990). We conclude this chapter by discussing our own experience in the recently completed Vanderbilt II project, a five-year study in the manual-guided training of dynamic therapists in a specialized form of time-limited dynamic psychotherapy. Our experience in the project touches on all three of the areas reviewed here, and it offers some practical lessons in the difficulty of translating research into practice.

The Vanderbilt II project (Strupp, 1993; Henry, Strupp, Butler, Schacht, & Binder, 1993; Henry, Schacht, Strupp, Butler, & Binder, 1993) stemmed from observations made during earlier Vanderbilt research (Strupp & Hadley, 1979) that suggested that the nature of the therapeutic relationship or alliance was established early in therapy, over the first three sessions. Furthermore, experienced psychodynamic therapists, well versed in the phenomena of countertransference, nonetheless showed a surprising vulnerability to such countertransference reactions when faced with a hostile or difficult patient. It was believed that specialized training in time-limited dynamic therapy (TLDP: Strupp & Binder, 1984), with emphasis on exploring and managing the therapeutic relationship as the *modus operandi* of therapy, might help ameliorate these difficulties and extend the range of patients suitable for short-term dynamic therapy. Additionally, the treatment manual called for the therapists to concentrate on one central interpersonal problem or cyclical maladaptive pattern (CMP, similar to the CCRT). The research design employed therapists as their own controls. The performance of 16 experienced therapists (psychologists and psychiatrists) was measured before and after a year's training in TLDP on a patient sample carefully selected for comparability and stratified as high or low in suitability for short-term work.

The Vanderbilt II study thus touched on all three major foci of this chapter. It was based on alliance research and aimed to improve the working relationship between patient and therapist by focusing on systematic transference exploration and interpretation within the context of a structured formu-

---

[15]Several studies by Sifneos, which do meet these criteria, are not included in meta-analyses because the data are not presented in a manner amenable to meta-analysis.

lation. In brief, the training program successfully changed therapists' interventions in line with technical prescriptions of the TLDP manual. However, other changes in their behavior was unexpected and ran counter to the aims of training. Some interpersonal and interactional process measures actually deteriorated after training, with *higher* levels of interpersonal hostility (as measured by SASB) noted as a group trend. The *percentage* of therapists' hostile communications did not change, but the absolute *frequency* increased as therapists became more active to meet the demands of a semistructured time-limited approach. Additionally, unforeseen variables such as the therapists' own introject structure and differences in the instructional style of the two different trainers mediated both technical adherence and changes in interpersonal process measures from pre- to posttraining.

In summary, the data did not suggest that, on balance, the therapeutic relationships were improved and in fact might have worsened in some cases. In terms of outcome, there were no clear-cut global improvements after training, although the balance of symptomatic versus interpersonal changes was altered. Some patient groups may have benefited more from the TLDP approach as compared to the therapists' usual therapy, but these tended to be the more well-functioning groups. One class of patients for whom TLDP was designed, socially avoidant individuals, may actually have done worse under conditions that stressed the early and systematic exploration of the therapeutic relationship. In short, the results were complex, often unexpected, and certainly revealed no straight-line function between the aims of training and the results of training.

What are the lessons of this study and how do they apply to the current chapter? It has been suggested by some that therapists in the project simply did not have experience with a sufficient number of patients during training to adequately master the skills required. Although this may be partially true, we believe that the explanations run deeper. Here then, are a few of our observations as they apply to the areas covered in this chapter:

1. *The alliance.* Therapists were sensitized to the importance of the alliance and to the subtle interpersonal meanings embodied in the ongoing process of therapy, as evidence by their comments while viewing videotapes during supervision. However, in *action,* they often seemed unaware of their own interpersonal process and its effect on their patients. A conceptual understanding does not necessarily transfer to the ability to act out of this awareness. Future training efforts might do well to provide training in fundamental interpersonal pro-

cess perception and the ability to communicate ideas without potentially countertherapeutic interpersonal process (see Henry & Strupp, in press, for examples drawn from actual therapy transcripts). Altering the alliance (insofar as the alliance is based on therapists' contributions) will likely be a major challenge because of the seemingly ingrained nature of individuals' subtle underlying communicative style as measured in interpersonal terms.

2. *Interpretation.* Two main factors seemed to have limited the effectiveness of therapists' transference exploration and interpretation. The first was therapists' failure to socialize the patient into the process of therapy, that is, to provide some simple, basic rationale to explain *why* it was important to explore the therapeutic relationship (see Strupp & Bloxom, 1973). Patients frequently seemed irritated by therapist-initiated inquiry into the patients' feelings toward the therapist, because they were not helped to see the relevance of these interventions. The other factor that seemed to limit the effectiveness of the interpretive approach was that therapists' interventions often seemed contextless or forced. This may be a particular problem for therapists faced with limited time and the dictates of a treatment manual that emphasizes such interventions. To overcome this difficulty, psychodynamic adherence scales might have to tap the "spirit" rather than the "letter of the law," giving therapists more flexibility. Of course, this would require expert judgments and may reduce the cross-group replicability of manual-guided adherence rating procedures.

3. *Formulation.* A structured formulation scheme may encourage clarity of thinking and consistency across time in therapists' interpretations and may provide a more concrete way to chart patient progress in a manner consistent with psychodynamic principles. However, our experience has also suggested several potential dangers in its use. Therapists may unconsciously begin to "fit" a patient's dialogue into an a priori structure in a forced manner that impedes the process and may damage the alliance. Once a formulation is arrived at, the therapist may also begin to focus exclusively on information that fits the formulation, ignoring other potentially important material, particularly material that runs counter to the formulation (or at least limits its scope). Most formulation schemes ideally enhance an awareness of *process,* that is, the interpersonal and intrapsychic processes that link one element (feeling, cognition, behavior, etc.) to another. However, at times it seems as if these process-based formulations are reduced to content-based "stories," and the activity of the therapist is to uncover "content-matched" stories. In short, for-

mulations may sometimes have the effect of limiting interpretive activity to "*X* is like *Y*," rather than fostering a deeper exploration of how *X* and *Y* came to be and the processes that link them.

Conclusions

Most psychotherapy research studies conclude with some statement about the potential relevance of the findings to clinical practice. "Relevance to clinical practice" is another way of saying relevance to improved efficacy. We are encouraged that the emerging psychodynamic research literature is not focused simply on "proving" old theoretical tenets, but rather seems to be exploring how the traditional elements of dynamic therapy actually work in practice, in a specific, context-relevant manner. As we have stated, we do believe these studies may finally lead to the long-promised goal of guiding clinical practice in a manner that enhances therapeutic outcomes. However, to conclude on this note seems incomplete.

Our own experience just discussed indicates how difficult it may actually be in reality to translate research into tangible benefits for our patients. We applied a body of programmatic empirical evidence directly to training and clinical practice in a well-controlled study that adhered to all of the contemporary guidelines for adequate research (e.g., the use of treatment manuals, adherence scales, relatively homogeneous patient populations). Although we succeeded in some measure, our results were also often unexpected and contradictory to our aims. Alliance, interpretation, and formulation are interactive, for better or for worse. While these lines of research have developed relatively independently, the areas of mutual influence have begun to be recognized, as the Penn group's work on accuracy of interpretation and the alliance (Crits-Christoph, et al., 1993) or the Vanderbilt group's work on technique and interpersonal process (Henry & Strupp, in press) will attest. However, understanding how these relational, technical, and theoretical parameters interact is still not the final step.

As our research clearly indicates, understanding and performance are different things. By nature of the variables studied, psychodynamic research tends to be more difficult than research on some of the other therapeutic approaches (such as behavioral or cognitive-behavioral) to translate directly into improved practice. If this promising body of psychodynamic research is truly to influence practice, another area of research must develop, must be seen as equally important, and must receive adequate research funding. In other words, learning how to translate these research findings into improved clinical training and practice should become an important empirical focus in its own right, as it may be the only way to realize the long-sought tie between psychotherapy research and practice.

REFERENCES

Alexander, F. (1954). Psychoanalysis and psychotherapy. *Journal of the American Psychoanalytic Association, 11,* 722–733.

Alberts, G., & Edelstein, B. (1990). Therapist training: A critical review of skill training studies. *Clinical Psychology Review, 10,* 497–512.

Arlow, J. A. (1975). Discussion of Kanzer's paper. *International Journal of Psychoanalytic Psychotherapy, 4,* 69–73.

Balint, M. (1968). *The basic fault.* London: Tavistock.

Barber, J. P., Crits-Christoph, P., & Luborsky, L. (1990). A guide to the CCRT standard categories and their classification. In L. Luborsky & P. Crits-Christoph (Eds.), *Understanding transference: The CCRT method* (pp. 37–50). New York: Basic Books.

Barber, J. P., Crits-Christoph, P., & Luborsky, L. (1992, June). *Purified helping alliance, early symptomatic improvement and outcome in dynamic psychotherapy for depression.* Paper presented at the annual convention of the Society for Psychotherapy Research, Berkeley, CA.

Barrett-Lennard, G. T. (1962). Dimension of therapist response as a causal factor in therapeutic change. *Psychological Monographs, 76,* 1–36.

Benjamin, L. S. (1974). Structural analysis of social behavior. *Psychological Review, 81,* 392–425.

Benjamin, L. S. (in press). *Interpersonal diagnosis and treatment: The SASB approach.* New York: Guilford.

Bibring, E. (1954). Psychoanalysis and the dynamic psychotherapies. *Journal of the American Psychoanalytic Association, 2,* 745–770.

Blatt, S. J. (1974). Levels of object representations in anaclitic and introjective depressions. *The Psychoanalytic Study of the Child, 29,* 107–157.

Blatt, S. J., & Zuroff, D. C. (1992). Interpersonal relatedness and self-definition: Two prototypes for depression. *Clinical Psychology Review, 12,* 527–562.

Bond, J., & Shevrin, H. (1986). *The clinical evaluation team method.* Unpublished manuscript, University of Michigan, Ann Arbor.

Bordin, E. S. (1979). The generalizability of the psychoanalytic concept of the working alliance. *Psychotherapy, 16,* 252–260.

Bourgeois, L., Sabourin, S., & Wright, J. (1990). Predictive validity of therapeutic alliance in group marital therapy. *Journal of Consulting and Clinical Psychology, 58,* 608–613.

Bourgeois, L., Sabourin, S., & Wright, J. (in press). Therapeutic alliance in marital therapy: A unidimensional phenomena? *Journal of Marital and Family Therapy.*

Bowlby, J. (1988). *A secure base: Clinical applications of attachment theory.* Routledge: London.

Christensen, J. (1991). *Understanding the patient–therapist interaction and therapeutic change in light of pre-therapy interpersonal relations.* Unpublished doctoral dissertation, Vanderbilt University, Nashville, TN.

Clarkin, J. (1991, July). *Borderline personality disorder: Review of studies in progress and future directions.* Paper presented at the annual meeting of the Society for Psychotherapy Research, Lyon, France.

Collins, W., & Messer, S. B. (1991). Extending the Plan Formulation Method to an object relations perspective: Reliability, stability, and adaptability. *Psychological As-*

sessment: A Journal of Consulting and Clinical Psychology, 3, 75–81.

Crits-Christoph, P. (1992). The efficacy of brief dynamic psychotherapy: A meta-analysis. The American Journal of Psychiatry, 149(2), 151–158.

Crits-Christoph, P., & Baranackie, K. (1992, June). The Quantitative Assessment of Relationship Themes method. Paper presented at the annual meeting of the Society for Psychotherapy Research, Berkeley, CA.

Crits-Christoph, P., Barber, J., & Kurcias J. S. (1993). The accuracy of therapists' interpretations and the development of the alliance. Psychotherapy Research, 3, 25–35.

Crits-Christoph, P., & Beebe, K. (1988, June). Quality of cognitive therapy, helping alliance, and the outcome of cognitive therapy with opiate addicts. Paper presented at the annual meeting of the Society for Psychotherapy Research, Santa Fe, NM.

Crits-Christoph, P., Cooper, A., & Luborsky, L. (1988). The accuracy of therapists' interpretations and the outcome of dynamic psychotherapy. Journal of Consulting and Clinical Psychology, 56, 490–495.

Crits-Christoph, P., Cooper, A., & Luborsky, L. (1990). The measurement of accuracy of interpretations. In L. Luborsky & P. Crits-Christoph (Eds.), Understanding transference: The CCRT method (pp. 173–188). New York: Basic Books.

Crits-Christoph, P., Demorest, A., & Connolly, M. B. (1990). Quantitative assessment of interpersonal themes over the course of psychotherapy. Psychotherapy, 27, 513–521.

Crits-Christoph, P., & Luborsky, L. (1990). The perspective of patients versus clinicians in the assessment of central relationship themes. In L. Luborsky & P. Crits-Christoph (Eds.), Understanding transference: The CCRT method (pp. 197–210). New York: Basic Books.

Crits-Christoph, P., Luborsky, L., Dahl, L., Popp, C., Mellon, J., & Mark, D. (1988). Clinicians can agree in assessing relationship patterns in psychotherapy: The Core Conflictual Relationship Theme Method. Archives of General Psychiatry, 45, 1001–1004.

Crits-Christoph, P., & Mintz, J. (1991). Implications of therapist effects for the design and analysis of comparative studies of psychotherapies. Journal of Consulting and Clinical Psychology, 59, 20–26.

Curtis, H. C. (1979). The concept of the therapeutic alliance: Implications for the "widening scope." Journal of the American Psychoanalytic Association, 27, 159–192.

Curtis, J. T., Silberschatz, G., Sampson, H., Weiss, J., & Rosenberg, S. E. (1988). Developing reliable psychodynamic case formulation: An illustration of the Plan Diagnosis Method. Psychotherapy, 25, 256–265.

Dahl, H., Kachele, H., & Thomae, H. (Eds.). (1988). Psychoanalytic process research strategies. New York: Springer-Verlag.

Davanloo, H. (1978). Basic principles and techniques in short-term dynamic psychotherapy. New York: Spectrum Publications.

DeRubeis, R. J., Feeley, M., & Barber, J. (1988, June). Facilitative, conditions, adherence, client cooperation and helping alliance in cognitive therapy. Paper presented at the annual meeting of the Society for Psychotherapy Research, Santa Fe, NM.

DeWitt, K. N., Kaltreider, N., Weiss, D. S., & Horowitz, M. J. (1983). Judging change in psychotherapy: Reliability of clinical formulations. Archives of General Psychiatry, 40, 1121–1128.

Dickes, R. (1975). The technical considerations of the therapeutic and working alliances. International Journal of Psychoanalytic Psychotherapy, 4, 1–24.

Eaton, T. T., Abeles, N., & Gutfreund, M. J. (1988). Therapeutic alliance and outcome: Impact of treatment length and pretreatment symptomatology. Psychotherapy, 25, 536–542.

Eckert, R., Luborsky, L., Barber, J., & Crits-Christoph, P. (1990). The narratives and CCRTs of patients with major depression. In L. Luborsky & P. Crits-Christoph (Eds.), Understanding transference: The CCRT method (pp. 222–234). New York: Basic Books.

Elliot, R., James, E., Reimschuessel, C., Cislo, D., & Sack, N. (1985). Significant events and the analysis of immediate therapeutic impacts. Psychotherapy, 22, 620–630.

Fassinger, R. E. (1987). Use of structural equation modeling in counseling psychology research. Journal of Counseling Psychology, 34, 425–436.

Faulkner, L. R., Kinzie, J. D., Angell, R., U'ren, R. C., & Shore, J. H. (1985). A comprehensive psychiatric formulation model. The Journal of Psychiatric Education, 9(3), 189–202.

Foreman, S., & Marmar, C. R. (1985). Therapist actions that address initially poor therapeutic alliances in psychotherapy. American Journal of Psychiatry, 142, 922–926.

Frances, A., & Perry, S. (1983). Transference interpretations in focal therapy. American Journal of Psychiatry, 140, 405–409.

Frank, A. F., & Gunderson, J. G. (1990). The role of the therapeutic alliance in the treatment of schizophrenia. Archives of General Psychiatry, 47, 228–236.

Freud, S. (1958). On beginning the treatment: Further recommendations on the technique of psychoanalysis. In J. Strachey (Ed. and Trans.), The standard edition of the complete psychological works of Sigmund Freud (Vol. 12). London: Hogarth Press, (Original work published 1913)

Freud, S. (1966). The dynamics of transference. In J. Strachey (Ed. and Trans.), The standard edition of the complete psychological works of Sigmund Freud (Vol. 12, pp. 99–108). London: Hogarth Press. (Original work published 1912)

Fried, D., Crits-Christoph, P., & Luborsky, L. (1990). The parallel of the CCRT for the therapist with the CCRT for other people. In L. Luborsky & P. Crits-Christoph (Eds.), Understanding transference: The CCRT method (pp. 147–157). New York: Basic Books.

Friedman, R. S., & Lister, P. (1987). The current status of psychodynamic formulation. Psychiatry, 50, 126–141.

Frieswyk, S. H., Allen, J. G., Colson, D. B., Coyne, L., Gabbard, G. O., Horwitz, L., & Newsom, G. E. (1986). Therapeutic alliance: Its place as a process and outcome variable in dynamic psychotherapy research. Journal of Consulting and Clinical Psychology, 54, 32–38.

Fromm-Reichmann, F. (1954). Psychoanalytic and general dynamic conception of theory and therapy. Differences and similarities. Journal of the American Psychoanalytic Association, 11, 711–721.

Frosch, J. (1990). Psychodynamic psychiatry: Theory and practice (Vol. II). Madison, CT: International Universities Press.

Gabbard, G. O. (1990). Psychodynamic psychiatry in clinical practice. Washington, DC: American Psychiatric Press.

Garfield, S. L. (1991). Psychotherapy models and outcome research. American Psychologist, 46(12), 1350–1351.

Gaston, L. (1990). The concept of the alliance and its role in psychotherapy: Theoretical and empirical considerations. Psychotherapy, 27, 143–153.

Gaston, L. (1991). Reliability and criterion-related validity of the California Psychotherapy Alliance Scales. Psychological Assessment, 3, 68–74.

Gaston, L., Marmar, C. R., Gallagher, D., & Thompson, L. W. (1991). Alliance prediction of outcome beyond in-treatment symptomatic change as psychotherapy processes. Psychotherapy Research, 1, 104–113.

Gaston, L., Marmar, C. R., Thompson, L. W., & Gallagher,

D. (1988). Relation of patient pretreatment characteristics to the therapeutic alliance in diverse psychotherapies. *Journal of Consulting and Clinical Psychology, 56,* 483–489.

Gaston, L., Piper, W. E., Debbane, E. G., Bienvenu, J. P., & Garant, J. (in press). Alliance and technique interaction in predicting outcome of short and long term dynamic psychotherapy. *Psychotherapy Research.*

Gaston, L., & Ring, J. M. (1992). Preliminary results on the Inventory of Therapeutic Strategies. *Journal of Psychotherapy Research and Practice, 1,* 1–13.

Gaston, L., Sabourin, S., Hatcher, R., & Hansell, J. (1992, June). *Confirmatory factor analysis of the patient version of the CALPAS.* Paper presented at the meeting of the Society for Psychotherapy Research, Berkeley, CA.

Gaston, L., & Schneider, J. (1992, August). *The alliance in group psychotherapy.* Paper presented at the meeting of the International Association of Group Psychotherapy, Montreal, Canada.

Gaston, L., Wisebord, S., & Weiss, M. (1992). *The alliance as predictor of placebo response in pharmacological treatment of depression.* Manuscript submitted for publication.

Gelso, C. J., & Carter, J. A. (1985). The relationship in counseling and psychotherapy: Components, consequences, and theoretical antecedents. *The Counseling Psychologist, 13,* 155–243.

Gill, M. M. (1954). Psychoanalysis and exploratory frames of psychotherapy. *Journal of the American Psychoanalytic Association, 2,* 771–797.

Gill, M. M. (1982). *Analysis of transference: Vol. I. Theory and technique.* New York: International Universities Press.

Gill, M., & Hoffman, I. Z. (1976). Paper delivered to the mid-winter meeting of the American Psychoanalytic Association, George Klein Forum, on definitions and scoring of latent transference in psychoanalytic sessions.

Gill, M., & Hoffman, I. Z. (1982). A method for studying the analysis of aspects of the patient's experience of the relationship in psychoanalysis and psychotherapy. *Journal of the American Psychoanalytic Association, 30,* 137–168.

Glover, E. (1931). The therapeutic effect of inexact interpretation: A contribution to the theory of suggestion. *International Journal of Psychoanalysis, 12,* 397–411.

Gomes-Schwartz, B. (1978). Effective ingredients in psychotherapy: Prediction of outcome from process variables. *Journal of Consulting and Clinical Psychology, 46,* 1023–1035.

Grawe, K., & Caspar, F. (1984). Die Plan Analyse als Konzept und Instrument fur die Psychotherapie Forschung. In U. Bauman (Ed.), *Psychotherapie: Makro und mikro perspectiven* (pp. 177–197). Cologne: Hogrete.

Greenberg, L. S. (1986). Change process research. *Journal of Consulting and Clinical Psychology, 54,* 4–9.

Greenson, R. R. (1965). The working alliance and the transference neuroses. *Psychoanalysis Quarterly, 34,* 155–181.

Gutfreund, M. J. (1992). *Therapist interventions: Their relation to therapeutic alliance and outcome in dynamic psychotherapy.* Unpublished doctoral dissertation, Michigan State University, East Lansing.

Hartley, D., & Strupp, H. (1983). The therapeutic alliance: Its relationship to outcome in brief psychotherapy. In J. Masling (Ed.), *Empirical studies of psychoanalytic theories* (Vol. 1, pp. 1–27). Hillsdale, NJ: Lawrence Erlbaum.

Hatcher, R., Hansell, J., Barends, A., Leary, K., Stuart, J., & White, K. (1990, June). *Comparison of several psychotherapy alliance measures.* Paper presented at the annual convention of the Society for Psychotherapy Research, Wintergreen, VA.

Henry, W. P. (1990, June). The use of the SASB INTREX questionnaire to measure change in cyclical maladaptive interpersonal patterns. Presented at the annual meeting of the Society for Psychotherapy Research, Wintergreen, VA.

Henry, W. P., Schacht, T. E., & Strupp, H. H. (1986). Structural Analysis of Social Behavior: Application to a study of interpersonal process in differential psychotherapeutic outcome. *Journal of Consulting and Clinical Psychology, 54,* 27–31.

Henry, W. P., Schacht, T. E., & Strupp, H. H. (1990). Patient and therapist introject, interpersonal process and differential psychotherapy outcome. *Journal of Consulting and Clinical Psychology, 58,* 768–774.

Henry, W. P., Schacht, T. E., Strupp, H. H., Butler, S. F. & Binder, J. L. (1993). Effects of training in time-limited dynamic psychotherapy: Mediators of therapists' responses to training. *Journal of Consulting and Clinical Psychology, 61,* 441–447.

Henry, W. P., & Strupp, H. H. (in press). The therapeutic alliance as interpersonal process. In A. Horvath & L. Greenberg (Eds.), *The working alliance: Theory, research and practice.* New York: Wiley.

Henry, W. P., Strupp, H. H., Butler, S. F., Schacht, T. E., & Binder, J. L. (1993). The effects of training in time-limited dynamic psychotherapy: Changes in therapist behavior. *Journal of Consulting and Clinical Psychology, 61,* 434–440.

Henry, W. P., Schacht, T. E., Strupp, H. H., Binder, J. L., & Butler, S. F. (1992). *The effects of training in time-limited dynamic psychotherapy: Changes in therapeutic outcome.* Unpublished manuscript, Vanderbilt University, Nashville, TN.

Herbert, J. D., & Mueser, K. T. (1991). The proof is in the pudding: A commentary on Persons. *American Psychologist, 46*(12), 1347–1348.

Horowitz, L., Rosenberg, S., Baer, B., Ureno, G., & Villasenor, V. (1988). The inventory of interpersonal problems: Psychometric properties and clinical applications. *Journal of Consulting and Clinical Psychology, 56,* 885–892.

Horowitz, L., Rosenberg, S. E., & Kalehzan, B. M. (1992). The capacity to describe other people clearly: A predictor of interpersonal problems in brief dynamic psychotherapy. *Psychotherapy Research, 2,* 37–51.

Horowitz, L., Rosenberg, S., Ureno, G., Kalehzan, B., & O'Halloran, P. (1989). Psychodynamic formulation, Consensual Response Method and interpersonal problems. *Journal of Consulting and Clinical Psychology, 57,* 599–606.

Horowitz, L., Sampson, H., Siegelman, E. Y., Wolfson, A. Q., & Weiss, J. (1975). On the identification of warded-off mental contents. *Journal of Abnormal Psychology, 84,* 545–558.

Horowitz, M. J. (1979). *States of mind: Analysis of change in psychotherapy.* New York: Plenum.

Horowitz, M. J. (1987). *States of mind: Analysis of change in psychotherapy* (2nd ed.). New York: Plenum.

Horowitz, M. J. (Ed.). (1991). *Person schemas and maladaptive interpersonal patterns.* Chicago: University of Chicago Press.

Horowitz, M., Marmar, C., Krupnick, J., Wilner, N., Kaltreider, N., & Wallerstein, R. (1984). *Personality styles and brief psychotherapy.* New York: Basic Books.

Horowitz, M. J., Marmar, C. R., Weiss, D., DeWitt, K. N., & Rosenbaum, R. (1984). Brief psychotherapy of bereavement reactions: The relationship of process to outcome. *Archives of General Psychiatry, 41,* 438–448.

Horowitz, M. J., Marmar, C., Weiss, D. D., Kaltreider, N., & Wilner, N. (1986). Comprehensive analysis of change after brief dynamic psychotherapy. *American Journal of Psychiatry, 143,* 582–589.

Horvath, A. O., & Greenberg, L. S. (1989). Development and validation of the Working Alliance Inventory. *Journal of Counseling Psychology, 36,* 223–233.

Horvath, A. O., & Symonds, D. B. (1991). Relationship between working alliance and outcome in psychotherapy: A meta-analysis. *Journal of Counseling Psychology, 38,* 139–149.

Jensen, J. P., & Bergin, A. E. (1988). Mental health values of professional therapists: A national interdisciplinary survey. *Professional Psychology: Research and Practice, 19*(3), 290–297.

Johnson, M. (1988, June). *Construct validation of the therapeutic alliance.* Paper presented at the annual meeting of the Society for Psychotherapy Research, Santa Fe, NM.

Joyce, A. S. (1992, June). *Assessing the correspondence of interpretation with the therapist's initial problem formulation.* Paper presented at the annual convention of the Society for Psychotherapy Research, Berkeley, CA.

Kanzer, M. (1975). The therapeutic and working alliances. *International Journal of Psychoanalytic Psychotherapy, 4,* 48–68.

Kiesler, D. J. (1966). Some myths of psychotherapy research and the search for a paradigm. *Psychological Bulletin, 65,* 110–136.

Kiesler, D. J. (1987a). *Research manual for the Impact Message Inventory.* Palo Alto, CA: Consulting Psychologists Press.

Kiesler, D. J. (1987b). *Check List of Psychotherapy Transactions-Revised (CLOPT-R) and Check List of Interpersonal Transactions-Revised (CLOIT-R).* Richmond: Virginia Commonwealth University Press.

Kiesler, D. J., Anchin, J. C., Perkins, M. J., Chirico, B. M., Kyle, E. M., & Federman, E. J. (1985). *The Impact Message Inventory: Form II.* Palo Alto, CA: Consulting Psychologists Press.

Kiesler, D. J., & Watkins, L. M. (1989). Interpersonal complementarity and the therapeutic alliance: A study of relationship in psychotherapy. *Psychotherapy, 26,* 183–194.

Klee, M. R., Abeles, N., & Muller, R. T. (1990). Therapeutic alliance: Early indicators, course, and outcome. *Psychotherapy, 27,* 166–174.

Klein, M., Mathieu-Coughlan, P., & Kiesler, D. (1986). The Experiencing Scale. In L. S. Greenberg & W. M. Pinsof (Eds.), *The psychotherapeutic process: A research handbook* (pp. 21–71). New York: Guilford.

Kokotovic, A. M., & Tracey, T. J. (1990). Working alliance in early phase of counseling. *Journal of Counseling Psychology, 37,* 16–21.

Krupnick, J., Sotsky, S., Simmens, S., & Moyer, J. (1992, June). *The role of the therapeutic alliance in psychotherapy and pharmacotherapy outcome: Findings from the NIMH Treatment of Depression Collaborative Research Program.* Paper presented at the annual meeting of the Society for Psychotherapy Research, Berkeley, CA.

Leeds, J., & Bucci, W. (1986, June). *A reliable method for the detection of repetitive structures in a transcript of an analytic session.* Presentation to the Society for Psychotherapy Research, Wellesley, MA.

Luborsky, L. (1976). Helping alliances in psychotherapy. In J. L. Claghorn (Ed.), *Successful psychotherapy* (pp. 92–116). New York: Brunner/Mazel.

Luborsky, L. (1977). Measuring a pervasive psychic structure in psychotherapy: The core conflictual relationship theme. In N. Freedman & S. Grand (Eds.), *Communication structures and psychic structures.* New York: Plenum.

Luborsky, L. (1984). *Principles of psychoanalytic psychotherapy: A manual for supportive-expressive treatment.* New York: Basic Books.

Luborsky, L. (1990a). Alternative measures of the central relationship pattern. In L. Luborsky & P. Crits-Christoph

(Eds.), *Understanding transference: The CCRT method* (pp. 235–247). New York: Basic Books.

Luborsky, L. (1990b). The relationship anecdotes paradigm (RAP) interview as a versatile source of narratives. In L. Luborsky & P. Crits-Christoph (Eds.), *Understanding transference: The CCRT method* (pp. 102–113). New York: Basic Books.

Luborsky, L. (1990c). A guide to the CCRT method. In L. Luborsky & P. Crits-Christoph (Eds.), *Understanding transference: The CCRT method* (pp. 15–36). New York: Basic Books.

Luborsky, L. (1990d). The convergence of Freud's observations about transference and the CCRT evidence. In L. Luborsky & P. Crits-Christoph (Eds.), *Understanding transference: The CCRT method* (pp. 251–266). New York: Basic Books.

Luborsky, L., Bachrach, H., Graff, H., Pulver, S., & Christoph, P. (1979). Preconditions and consequences of transference interpretations: A clinical quantitative investigation. *Journal of Nervous and Mental Disease, 167,* 391–401.

Luborsky, L., Barber, J., & Crits-Christoph, P. (1990). Theory based research for understanding the process of dynamic psychotherapy. *Journal of Consulting and Clinical Psychology, 58,* 281–287.

Luborsky, L., & Crits-Christoph, P. (Eds.). (1990). *Understanding transference: The CCRT method.* New York: Basic Books.

Luborsky, L., Crits-Christoph, P., Alexander, L., Margolis, M., & Cohen, M. (1983). Two helping alliance methods for predicting outcomes of psychotherapy: A counting sign vs. a global rating method. *Journal of Nervous and Mental Disease, 171,* 480–492.

Luborsky, L., McLellan, A. T., Woody, G. E., O'Brien, C. P., & Auerbach, A. (1985). Therapist success and its determinants. *Archives of General Psychiatry, 42,* 602–611.

Luborsky, L., & Spence, D. P. (1978). Quantitative research on psychoanalytic therapy. In S. L. Garfield & A. E. Bergin (Eds.), *Handbook of psychotherapy and behavior change: An empirical analysis* (2nd ed.). New York: Wiley.

Mahoney, M. (1991). *Human change processes.* New York: Basic Books.

Markus, H. & Nurius, P. (1986). Possible selves. *American Psychologist, 41*(9), 954–969.

Malan, D. H. (1976a). *The frontier of brief psychotherapy.* New York: Plenum.

Malan, D. H. (1976b). *Toward the validation of dynamic psychotherapy.* New York: Plenum.

Mallinckrodt, B. (1991). Clients' representations of childhood emotional bonds with parents, social support, and formation of the working alliance. *Journal of Counseling Psychology, 38,* 401–409.

Mallinckrodt, B., & Nelson, M. L. (1991). Counselor training level and the formation of the psychotherapeutic working alliance. *Journal of Counseling Psychology, 38,* 133–138.

Mann, J. (1973). *Time-limited psychotherapy.* Cambridge, MA: Harvard University Press.

Marmar, C. R. Gaston, L., Gallagher, D., & Thompson, L. W. (1989). Alliance and outcome in late-life depression. *Journal of Nervous and Mental Disease, 177,* 464–472.

Marmar, C., & Horowitz, M. J. (1988). Diagnosis and phase-oriented treatment of post-traumatic stress disorders. In J. Wilson (Ed.), *Human adaptation to extreme stress: From the Holocaust to Vietnam.* New York: Brunner/Mazel.

Marmar, C. R., Weiss, D. S., & Gaston, L. (1989). Towards the validation of the California Therapeutic Alliance Rating System. *Psychological Assessment, 1,* 46–52.

Marziali, E. A. (1984a). Prediction of outcome of brief psychotherapy from therapist interpretive interventions. *Archives of General Psychiatry, 41,* 301–304.

Marziali, E. A. (1984b). Three viewpoints on the therapeutic alliance: Similarities, differences, and associations with psychotherapy outcome. *Journal of Nervous and Mental Diseases, 172,* 417–423.

Maxim, P. (1986). *The Seattle Psychotherapy Language Analysis Schema.* Seattle: University of Washington Press.

Maxim, P., & Sprague, M. (1989). *Metacommunication of interactive sequences in therapy.* Seattle: University of Washington Press.

McCullough, L., Winston, A., Farber, B. A., Porter, F., Pollack, J., Laikin, M., Vingiano, W., & Trujillo, M. (1991). The relationship of patient–therapist interaction to outcome in brief psychotherapy. *Psychotherapy, 28,* 525–533.

Messer, S. B. (1991). The case formulation approach; Issues of reliability and validity. *American Psychologist, 46,* 1348–1350.

Messer, S. B., Tishby, O., & Spillman, A. (1992). Taking context seriously in psychotherapy research: The relation of therapist interventions to patient progress in brief psychodynamic therapy. *Journal of Consulting and Clinical Psychology, 60,* 678–688.

Mintz, J. (1981). Measuring outcome in dynamic psychotherapy. *Archives of General Psychiatry, 38,* 503–506.

Moras, K., & Strupp, H. H. (1982). Pretherapy interpersonal relations, patients' alliance, and outcome in brief therapy. *Archives of General Psychiatry, 39,* 405–409.

Morgan, R., Luborsky, L., Crits-Christoph, P., Curtis, H., & Solomon, J. (1982). Predicting the outcome of psychotherapy by the Penn Helping Alliance Rating method. *Archives of General Psychiatry, 39,* 397–402.

O'Malley, S. S., Suh, C. S., & Strupp, H. H. (1983). The Vanderbilt Psychotherapy Process Scale: A report on scale development and a process–outcome study. *Journal of Consulting and Clinical Psychology, 51,* 581–586.

Orlinsky, D. E., & Howard, K. I. (1986). Process and outcome in psychotherapy. In S. L. Garfield & A. E. Bergin (Eds.), *Handbook of psychotherapy and behavior change* (3rd ed., pp. 311–381). New York: Wiley.

Panel. (1955). Psychoanalysis and psychotherapy. Reporter: J. Chassell. *Journal of the American Psychoanalytic Association, 3,* 528–533.

Perry, J. C., Augusto, F., & Cooper, S. H. (1989). Assessing psychodynamic conflicts: I. Reliability of the Idiographic Conflict Formulation Method. *Psychiatry, 52,* 289–301.

Perry, S., Cooper, A. M., & Michels, R. (1987). The psychodynamic formulation: Its purpose, structure and clinical application. *American Journal of Psychiatry, 144*(5), 543–550.

Persons, J. B. (1991). Psychotherapy outcome studies do not accurately represent current models of psychotherapy: A proposed remedy. *American Psychologist, 46,* 99–106.

Persons, J. B., Curtis, J. T., & Silberschatz, G. (1991). Psychodynamic and behavioral formulations of a single case. *Psychotherapy, 28*(4), 608–617.

Pinsof, W. M., & Catherall, D. R. (1986). The integrative psychotherapy alliance: Family, couple, and individual therapy scales. *Journal of Marital and Family Therapy, 12,* 137–151.

Piper, W. E., Azim, F. A., Joyce, S. A., & McCallum, M. (1991). Transference interpretations, therapeutic alliance and outcome in short-term individual psychotherapy. *Archives of General Psychiatry, 48,* 946–953.

Piper, W. E., Azim, F. A., Joyce, S. A., McCallum, M., Nixon, G., & Segal, P. S. (1991). Quality of object relations vs. interpersonal functioning as predictors of alliance and outcome. *Journal of Nervous and Mental Disease, 179,* 432–438.

Piper. W. E., Debbane, E. G., Bienvenu, J., Carufel, F., &

Garant, J. (1986). Relationships between the object focus of therapist interpretations and outcome in short-term individual psychotherapy. *British Journal of Medical Psychology, 59,* 1–11.

Piper, W. E., Debbane, E. G., de Carufel, F., & Bienvenu, J. (1987). A system for differentiating therapist interpretations from other interventions. *Bulletin of the Menninger Clinic, 51,* 532–550.

Popp, C., Luborsky, L., & Crits-Christoph, P. (1990). The parallel of the CCRT from therapy narratives with the CCRT from dreams. In L. Luborsky & P. Crits-Christoph (Eds.), *Understanding transference: The CCRT method* (pp. 158–172). New York: Basic Books.

Porter, F. A. (1987). *The immediate effects of interpretation on patient response in short-term dynamic psychotherapy.* Doctoral dissertation, Columbia University, New York.

Quintana, S. M., & Meara, N. M. (1990). Internalization of therapeutic relationships in short-term psychotherapy. *Journal of Counseling Psychology, 37,* 123–130.

Rogers, C. R. (1957). The necessary and sufficient conditions of therapeutic personality change. *Journal of Consulting Psychology, 21,* 95–103.

Rosenberg, S. E., Silberschatz, G., Curtis, J. T., Sampson, H., & Weiss, J. (1986). A method for establishing reliability of statements from psychodynamic case formulations. *American Journal of Psychiatry, 143,* 1454–1456.

Sabourin, S., Coallier, J. C., Cournoyer, L. G., & Gaston, L. (1990, June). *Further aspects of the validity of the California Psychotherapy Alliance Scales.* Paper presented at the annual meeting of the Society for Psychotherapy, Wintergreen, VA.

Safran, J., Crocker, P., McMain, S., & Murray, P. (1990). Therapeutic alliance rupture as therapy event for empirical investigation. *Psychotherapy, 27,* 154–165.

Safran, J., & Segal, Z. (1990). *Interpersonal process in cognitive therapy,* (pp 11–33). New York: Basic Books.

Safran, J., & Wallner, L. (1991). The relative predictive validity of two therapeutic alliance measures in cognitive therapy. *Psychological Assessment, 3,* 188–195.

Salvio, M. A., Beutler, L. E., Wood, J. M., & Engle, D. (1992). The strength of the therapeutic alliance in three treatments for depression. *Psychotherapy Research, 2,* 31–36.

Sampson, H. (1990). How the patient's sense of danger and safety influence the analytic process. *Psychoanalytic Psychology, 7,* 115–124.

Sandler, J., Holder, A., Kawenoka, M., Kennedy, H., & Neurath, L. (1969). Notes on some theoretical and clinical aspects of transference. *International Journal of Psychoanalysis, 50,* 633–645.

Saunders, S. M., Howard, K. I., & Orlinsky, D. E. (1989). The Therapeutic Bond Scales: Psychometric characteristics and relationship to treatment effectiveness. *Psychological Assessment, 1,* 323–330.

Schacht, T. E. (1991). Formulation-based psychotherapy research: Some further considerations. *American Psychologist, 46*(12), 1346–1347.

Schacht, T. E., & Binder, J. (1982). *Focusing: A manual for identifying a circumscribed area of work for time-limited dynamic psychotherapy (TLDP).* Unpublished manuscript, Vanderbilt University, Nashville, TN.

Schacht, T. E., Binder, J., & Strupp, H. (1984). The dynamic focus. In H. Strupp & J. Binder (Eds.), *Psychotherapy in a new key: A guide to time-limited dynamic psychotherapy* (pp. 65–109). New York: Basic Books.

Schacht, T. E., & Henry, W. P. (in press). Modeling recurrent relationship patterns with Structural Analysis of Social Behavior: The SASB-CMP. *Psychotherapy Research.*

Seitz, P. (1966). The consensus problem in psychoanalytic research. In L. Gottschaclk & A. Auerbach (Eds.),

Methods of research in psychotherapy (pp. 209–225). New York: Appleton-Century-Crofts.

Selzer, M. A., Kernberg, P., Fibel, B., Cherbuliez, P., & Mortati, S. (1987). *The Personality Assessment Interview: Preliminary Report. Psychiatry, 50,* 142–153.

Shirk, S., Saiz, C., Green, B., Hanze, D., & Wanstrath, J. (1992, June). *Measuring the affective alliance in child therapy.* Paper presented at the annual meeting of the Society for Psychotherapy Research, Berkeley, CA.

Sifneos, P. E. (1972). *Short-term psychotherapy and emotional crisis.* Cambridge, MA: Harvard University Press.

Silberschatz, G., Curtis, J. T., & Nathans, S. (1989). Using the patient's plan to assess progress in psychotherapy. *Psychotherapy, 26,* 40–46.

Silberschatz, G., Fretter, P. B., & Curtis, J. T. (1986). How do interpretations influence the process of psychotherapy? *Journal of Consulting and Clinical Psychology, 54,* 646–652.

Silverman, D. K. (1990). Extenders or modifiers: A discussion of Weiss & Sampson's Control-Mastery Theory. *Psychoanalytic Psychology, 7,* 125–136.

Silverman, L. H., & Wolitzky, D. L. (1982). Toward the resolution of controversial issues in psychoanalytic treatment. In S. Slipp (Ed.), *Curative factors in dynamic psychotherapy.* New York: McGraw-Hill.

Silverman, W. K. (1991). Persons's description of psychotherapy outcome studies does not accurately represent psychotherapy outcome studies. *American Psychologist, 46*(12), 1351–1352.

Singer, J., & Salovey, P. (1991). Organized knowledge and personality. In M. J. Horowitz (Ed.), *Person schemas and maladaptive interpersonal patterns* (pp. 34–80). Chicago: University of Chicago Press.

Slap, J., & Slaykin, A. (1983). The schema: Basic concept in a nonmetapsychological model of the mind. *Psychoanalysis and Contemporary Thought, 6,* 305–325.

Spence, D. P. (1982). *Narrative truth and historical truth.* New York: Norton.

Sterba, R. (1934). The fate of the ego in analytic therapy. *International Journal of Psychoanalysis, 15,* 117–126.

Strachey, J. (1934). The nature of the therapeutic action of psychoanalysis. *International Journal of Psychoanalysis, 15,* 127–159.

Strisik, P. (1990). *In-session discussion about the therapist–client relationship as a facilitator of client experiencing (transference).* Doctoral dissertation, Georgia State University, Atlanta.

Strupp, H. H. (1993). The Vanderbilt psychotherapy studies: Synopsis. *Journal of Consulting and Clinical Psychology, 61,* 431–433.

Strupp, H. H., & Binder, J. L. (1984). *Psychotherapy in a new key: A guide to time-limited dynamic psychotherapy.* New York: Basic Books.

Strupp, H. H., & Bloxom, A. L. (1973). Preparing lower-class patients for group psychotherapy: Development and evaluation of a role induction film. *Journal of Consulting and Clinical Psychology, 41,* 373–384.

Strupp, H. H., Moras, K., Sandell, J., Waterhouse, G., O'Malley, S., Keithly, L., & Gomes-Schwartz, B. (1981). *Vanderbilt Negative Indicators Scale: An instrument for identification of deterrents to progress in time-limited dynamic psychotherapy.* Unpublished manuscript, Vanderbilt University, Nashville, TN.

Strupp, H. H. Schacht, T. E., & Henry, W. P. (1988). Problem–treatment–outcome congruence: A principle whose time has come. In H. Dahl & H. Kachele (Eds.), *Psychoanalytic process research strategies.* (pp. 1–14) New York: Springer.

Suh, C. S., O'Malley, S. S., & Strupp, H. H. (1986). The Vanderbilt Process Measures: The Psychotherapy Process Scale (VPPS) and the Negative Indicators Scale (VNIS). In L. S. Greenberg & W. M. Pinsolf (Eds.), *The psychotherapeutic process: A research handbook* (pp. 285–324). New York: Guilford.

Svartberg, M., & Stiles, T. C. (1991). Comparative effects of short-term psychodynamic psychotherapy: A meta-analysis. *Journal of Consulting and Clinical Psychology, 59*(5), 704–714.

Svartberg, M., & Stiles, T. C. (1992, June). *Therapeutic alliance and therapist competence: Their relations to patient change in short-term dynamic psychotherapy.* Paper presented at the annual meeting of the Society for Psychotherapy Research, Berkeley, CA.

Teller, V., & Dahl, H. (1981). The framework for a model of psychoanalytic inference. *Proceedings of the Seventh International Joint Conference on Artificial Intelligence, 1,* 394–400.

Tichenor, V., & Hill, C. E. (1989). A comparison of six measures of working alliance. *Psychotherapy: Research and Practice, 26,* 195–199.

Tracey, T. J., & Kokotovic, A. M. (1989). Factor structure of the Working Alliance Inventory. *Psychological Assessment, 1,* 207–210.

Turkat, I. D., & Maisto, S. A. (1985). Personality disorders: Application of the experimental method to the formulation and modification of personality disorders. In D. H. Barlow (Ed.), *Clinical handbook of psychological disorders.* New York: Guilford.

Van Egeren, L. (1992, June). *Therapeutic intervention styles related to therapeutic bond quality and duration.* Paper presented at the annual meeting of the Society for Psychotherapy Research, Berkeley, CA.

Wallerstein, R. S. (1989). The psychotherapy research project of the Menninger Foundation: An overview. *Journal of Consulting and Clinical Psychology, 57,* 195–205.

Wallner, L., Muran, J. C., Segal, Z. V., Schumann, C. (1992, June). *Patient pretreatment interpersonal problems and therapeutic alliance in short-term cognitive therapy.* Paper presented at the annual meeting of the Society for Psychotherapy Research, Berkeley, CA.

Weiss, J. (1977). Part I: Theory and clinical observation. In J. Weiss, H. Sampson, & the Mount Zion Psychotherapy Research Group (Eds.), *The psychoanalytic process: Theory, clinical observation, and empirical research.* New York: Guilford.

Weiss, J. (1990). The nature of the patient's problems and how in psychoanalysis the individual works to solve them. *Psychoanalytic Psychology, 7,* 105–113.

Weiss, J., Sampson, H., Caston, J., & Silberschatz, G. (Eds.). (1977). *Research on the psychoanalytic process.* San Francisco: Psychotherapy Research Group, Department of Psychiatry, Mount Zion Hospital and Medical Center.

Weiss, J., Sampson, H., & the Mount Zion Psychotherapy Research Group. (1986). *The psychoanalytic process: Theory, clinical observation, and empirical research.* New York: Guilford.

Weiss, M., Gaston, L., Wisebord, S., Propst, A., & Zicherman, V. (1992). *The role of the alliance in the treatment of depression.* Manuscript submitted for publication.

Weston, D. (1988). Transference and information processing. *Clinical Psychology Review, 8,* 161–179.

Wile, D. B. (1984). Kohut, Kernberg, and accusatory interpretations. *Psychotherapy, 21,* 353–364.

Wolfe, B. E., & Goldfried, M. R. (1989). Research on psychotherapy integration: Recommendations and conclusions from an NIMH workshop. *Journal of Consulting and Clinical Psychology, 56,* 448–451.

Zetzel, E. (1956). Current concepts of transference. *International Journal of Psychoanalysis, 37,* 369–375.

12

RESEARCH ON EXPERIENTIAL PSYCHOTHERAPIES

- **LESLIE GREENBERG**
  York University

- **ROBERT ELLIOTT**
  University of Toledo

- **GERMAIN LIETAER**
  University of Leuven

The approaches to psychotherapy generally referred to as experiential include client-centered therapy (Rogers, 1951) Gestalt therapy (Perls, Hefferline, & Goodman, 1951), the experiential approaches of Gendlin (1981) and Mahrer (1983), and a cluster of emotionally focused expressive approaches (Janov, 1970; Pierce, Nichols, & DuBrin, 1983). Existential approaches (e.g., Bugental, 1978; Yalom, 1980) and transpersonal approaches fall within the frame of this review, but coverage is limited by a lack of research. Although the experiential approaches vary in technique and conception, they nevertheless share a number of distinctive features (Rice & Greenberg, 1992).

First, all these approaches utilize the phenomenological method, taking the client's ongoing awareness of his or her own experience as the primary datum for therapy. They are thus discovery oriented. Second, they consider an egalitarian, person-centered, therapeutic relationship central to therapy and view the client as expert on his or her experience, thus giving emphasis to the relationship and value to the client's uniqueness. Third, these approaches all seek to foster the client's potential for growth, self-determination, and choice. Fourth, they hold that new awareness and the generation of new meaning are the basis of change in the client.

The writing of this chapter was supported by grants from SSHRC of Canada and NIMH to the first author and was completed while the second author was on sabbatical leave at York University.

Experiential therapies all define the facilitation of experiencing as the key therapeutic task, and almost all also view the therapeutic relationship as potentially curative. Experiential approaches dispute the psychoanalytic claim that the relationship between the client and the therapist can be reduced to an unconscious repetition of previous attachments. Rather, they generally share the view that a real relationship with the therapist provides the client with a new, emotionally validating experience and an opportunity to discriminate between past and present and to discover and own experience.

This chapter reviews the research literature from 1978 to 1992 on these therapies, succeeding several major reviews of research on empathy and the client-centered relationship conditions (Gurman, 1977; Lambert, DeJulio, & Stein, 1978; Mitchell, Bozarth, & Krauft, 1977; Parloff, Waskow, & Wolfe, 1978). Relevant research on experiential marital, family, and group therapy is included, although a thorough review of this literature is not attempted.

HISTORY AND RECENT DEVELOPMENTS

As Lietaer (1990) noted, programmatic empirical research on experiential therapy was virtually nonexistent in North America through the 1970s, owing in part to the antipositivist ideals of the humanists. It was only in the 1980s that research on specific experiential interventions began to emerge (e.g., Rice & Greenberg, 1984). Fortunately, research in Europe during this period was less subject to this disaffection and produced a number of interesting programs, particularly involving client-centered therapy (e.g., Eckert & Biermann-Ratjen, 1985; Grawe, Caspar, & Ambühl, 1990; Sachse & Maus, 1987; Tausch, 1990). Summaries of some of this research have recently become available in English (Lietaer, Rombauts, & Van Balen, 1990). We hope that the appearance of this review marks a return of interest in research on humanistic and experiential therapies.

Rogers founded client-centered therapy on empirical grounds and established a tradition of listening to audiotapes of therapy sessions in order to understand the process of change. Much of the recent interest in research on change processes has emerged from this tradition (Gendlin, 1986; Greenberg, 1986; Mahrer, 1988; Rice & Greenberg, 1984). Furthermore, a renewed interest in the role of empathy in both experiential and psychodynamic therapies (e.g., Bohart, 1988; 1991a; Kohut, 1982; Vanaerschot, 1990) suggests the possibility that researchers will again attempt the complex task of understanding how empathy and experiencing operate in the change process. Although results of past research on Rogers' necessary and sufficient conditions indicated that the conditions were not sufficient and possibly not even necessary in all approaches to treatment, results did suggest that client-perceived empathy was related to outcome, particularly in the client-centered approach (Gurman 1977; Orlinsky & Howard, 1986). However, the conclusions drawn from this body of research have also been criticized (Patterson, 1984, Cramer, 1990) suggesting that an adequate test of the Rogerian hypothesis has yet to be carried out.

Recent developments in the field have highlighted differences between two somewhat different strands of experiential therapy, namely, a purely nondirective, person-centered approach and a more process-directive, experiential approach (Brodley, 1990). Advocates of the person-centered approach, drawing on classical client-centered theory, regard the relationship conditions as necessary and sufficient for change.

Advocates of the experiential approaches emphasize the importance of active, process-directive intervention procedures oriented toward deepening experience within the context of a person-centered relationship. This implies that the relationship may not be sufficient for change. This distinction can be characterized as *being* with the client, in the client-centered view, or *doing* something with the client, in the experiential view. The adherents of the more active experiential approach, to differing degrees, regard the relationship as a crucial element, generally suggesting that the client-centered relationship conditions are essential to the success of the active interventions (e.g., Gendlin, 1990; Greenberg, Rice, & Elliott, 1993; Lietaer, 1990; Rice & Greenberg, 1990; Sachse, 1990a; but see Mahrer, 1986), yet they also see the therapist as directing the process. The development, articulation, and initiation of research on a set of new, more active experiential approaches represents one of the major developments in the humanistic area over the last decade (Lietaer, 1990).

This development is epitomized by the emergence of what we refer to in this review as the *process-experiential* approach, in which more active interventions, often from Gestalt therapy, are integrated into a broadly client-centered relationship (e.g., Greenberg et al., 1993; Greenberg & Johnson, 1987).

Two other developments are noteworthy: the development and evolution of *integrated* approaches, predominantly the supplementation of the client-centered approach with interventions from other orientations, particularly behavioral (e.g., Bohart, 1990; Tausch, 1990); and an emerging focus on *differential humanistic treatments for different types of clients*, including those with clinical disorders (e.g., anxiety, depression), personality disorders (e.g., borderline), and problems (e.g., recovery from cancer), and those with different coping styles (e.g., externalizing or action oriented). This development can be found in all the major streams of experiential-humanistic therapy, including client-centered therapy (e.g., Prouty, 1990; Speierer, 1990; Swildens, 1990), Gestalt therapy (Daldrup, Beutler, Greenberg, & Engle, 1988; Yontef, 1988, 1991), experiential focusing (Katonah, 1991), and the process-experiential approach (e.g., Greenberg, Elliott, & Foerster, 1990).

HOW EFFECTIVE ARE EXPERIENTIAL THERAPIES?

The first question about the experiential therapies concerns their general effectiveness. Compared with research on cognitive-behavioral treatments, there is relatively little systematic research on the outcomes of experiential treatments. This situation has several consequences. First, it has led adherents of cognitive-behavioral treatment (e.g., Giles, Niems, & Prial, in press) to dismiss the experiential therapies, arguing that lack of data should be taken as evidence for their *in*effectiveness.

Second, much of the existing literature involves the use of supportive or nondirective therapies as so-called placebo controls for cognitive-behavioral treatments (e.g., Borkovec & Mathews, 1988; Lerner & Clum, 1990); these treatments are not necessarily client-centered therapy while results obtained in these studies are probably subject to investigator-allegiance effects (cf. Elliott, Stiles, & Shapiro, in press; Robinson, Berman, & Neimeyer, 1990), including less than enthusiastic implementation of the alternate treatment by researchers and therapists whose true loyalties lie elsewhere.

Third, lack of research necessitates the use of alternative, meta-analytic methods for evaluating effects in order to recover as much information as possible. Thus the analysis presented here is based primarily on pre–post change effect sizes (cf. Jacobson, Follette, & Revenstorf, 1984; Lambert, Hatch, Kingston, & Edwards, 1986). Where possible, amount of change in experiential therapy treatment groups is also compared to change in control and comparative treatment groups.

Meta-Analysis of Pre–Post Change

In conducting the meta-analysis, we attempted to locate all outcome studies of experiential therapies from 1978 on. We included all studies for which it was possible to calculate a change effect size. We were able to locate and calculate pre–post change effect sizes on 136 measures from 37 studies involving 1,272 clients.

Effect sizes (ES) were calculated by finding the difference between pretreatment and posttreat-

ment (or follow-up) mean scores and dividing by the pretreatment standard deviation; these were calculated for all experiential therapy conditions as well as for control and comparative treatment conditions. Calculating effect sizes in this way made it possible to use data from uncontrolled one-group studies and still allow comparisons of experiential with control or comparative treatment conditions. Where means or standard deviations were not given, we used the standard procedures described by Smith, Glass, and Miller. For each assessment period, ESs were averaged first within measures (across subscales), then across measures. Mean ESs for each study are given in Table 12.1, which also provides summary information on the studies.

Evaluations of overall treatment effect. Immediately following treatment, the average change ef-

TABLE 12.1   Outcome research on experiential-humanistic therapies: Pre–post effect sizes

Study	Treatment (length)[a]	Population (n)	Type of Measure[b]	Mean Change ES[c]
		Client-Centered (mean ES = 1.15)		
Borkovec (1991)	Nondirective (12)	Generalized anxiety (14)	CSy, SSy	Post: 2.20
Braaten (1989)	CCT group (14)	Volunteer professionals (25)	SSy, Exp	Post (3): .36 FU10mo(2): .20
Dircks, Grimm, Tausch, & Wittern (1980)	CCT group (11)	Cancer (30)	Imp	Post: .91
Eckert & Biermann-Ratjen (1990)	CCT group in inpatient setting (50)	Mixed severe (nonpsychotic) (117)	PC, SIm Adj	Post: .18 +
Eymael (1987)	CCT (16)	Neurotic, psychosomatic (14)	Imp	FU7mo: 2.20
Grawe, Caspar, & Ambühl (1990)	CCT (M = 32)	Interpersonal problems (15)	Adj, CSy, Exp, PC, SIm SSy, TC	Post(9): .79 FU6mo(7): .83 FU12mo(7): .96
Lietaer (1989)	CCT (50)	Neurotic (33)	Imp	Post: 1.92
Meyer (1981)	CCT (M = 19)	Psychosomatic (immediate and delayed groups = 33)	CSy, PC, SIm	Post(3): .59 FU3mo(3): .66 FU9mo(3): .84 FU12yr(1): 1.22
Pomrehn, Tausch, & Tönnies (1986)	CCT group marathon (2.5 days)	Neurotic (87)	Imp, SIm Exp	FU1mo(3): .46 + FU12mo(1): 1.23
Rudolph, Langer, & Tausch (1980)	CCT (M = 11)	Neurotic (149)	Imp	Post: 1.15
Teusch (1990)	CCT inpatient program (12 weeks)	Schizophrenic (high-functioning) (73)	Imp	Post: 1.54

Continued

TABLE 12.1   *continued*

Study	Treatment (length)[a]	Population (n)	Type of Measure[b]	Mean Change ES[c]
Teusch & Boehme (1991)	CCT inpatient program (12 weeks)	Agoraphobia with panic (31)	CSy, PC	FU12mo: 1.32
Westermann, Schwab, & Tausch (1983)	CCT group marathon (2.5 days)	Neurotic (164)	Imp, Slm, PC	FU1mo(4): .47 + FU6mo(1): 1.32
Nondirective/Supportive Plus Minor Directive (mean ES = 1.15)				
Beutler (1991)	Supportive/self-directed (20)	Depressed (20)	CSy, SSy	Post: 1.22 FU3mo: 2.22 FU10mo: 1.19
Borkovec et al. (1987)	Nondirective with relaxation (12)	Generalized anxiety (14)	CSy, SSy	Post: .92
Borkovec & Mathews (1988)	Nondirective with relaxation (12)	Generalized anxiety and panic (10)	CSy, SSy	Post: 1.17 FU6mo: .93 FU12mo: 1.06
Lerner & Clum (1990)	Supportive (10)	Suicidal students (9)	Adj, SSy	Post: .68 FU3mo: .67
Propst, Ostrom, Watkins, Dean, & Mashburn (in press)	Pastoral counseling (18)	Depressed religious (10)	Adj, CSy, SSy	Post: 1.35 FU3mo: 1.57 FU2yr: 1.80
Focusing (mean ES = .65)				
Holstein (1990)	Focusing and cognitive-behavioral group (20)	Weight problems (7)	Weight change	Post: .38 FU3mo: .66
Katonah (1991)	Focusing (6)	Cancer (in remission) (12)	PC, SSy	Post: .50 FU6mo: 1.03
Process-Experiential (Marker Guided) (mean ES = 1.84)				
Clarke & Greenberg (1986)	Experiential 2-chair (2)	Decisional conflicts (16)	Adj	Post: 1.14
Dandeneau & Johnson (in press)	EFT couples (6)	Normal/mildly distressed (12)	Rel, TC	Post(5): 1.33 FU3mo(4): 2.29
Elliott et al. (1990)	Process-experiential (16)	Depressed (14)	Adj, CSy, Exp, Slm, SSy, TC	Mid(11): .73 Post(11): 1.52 FU6mo(8): 2.28
Goldman & Greenberg (1992)	EFT couples (10)	Marital distressed (14)	Rel, TC	Post(4): 2.51 FU4mo(4): 1.52
Gordon Walker, Manion, Johnson, & Cloutier (1992)	EFT couples (10)	Parents of chronically ill children (10)	Rel	Post(2): .64 FU3mo (2): 1.23
Greenberg & Webster (1982)	Experiential 2-chair (6 max)	Decisional conflicts (31)	Adj, SSy	Post: 1.32 FU1mo: 1.03
Johnson & Greenberg (1985a)	EFT couples (8)	Marital distress (15)	Rel, TC	Post(4): 2.97 FU2mo(2): 3.95
Johnson & Greenberg (1985b)	EFT couples (8)	Marital distress (14)	Rel, TC	Post(4): 2.81

TABLE 12.1   *continued*

Study	Treatment (length)[a]	Population (n)	Type of Measure[b]	Mean Change ES[c]
Lowenstein (1985)	CCT and evocative unfolding (5)	Interpersonal plus anxiety (12)	SIm, SSy, TC	Post: .97
Paivio & Greenberg (1992)	Process-experiential chair work (12)	Unresolved relationship issues (15)	SSy, Adj TC, Rel SIm	Post: 1.83
Toukmanian & Grech (1991)	Perceptual processing experiential (10)	Interpersonal problems (18)	SIm Exp	Post(4): 1.19
Gestalt Therapy (mean ES = 1.27)				
Beutler, Frank, Schieber, Calver, & Gaines (1984)	Gestalt group (3)	Mixed inpatients (39)	Adj, Ssy	Post(2): .78 FU13mo(1): 1.09
Beutler (1991)	Gestalt group (20)	Depressed (22)	CSy, SSy	Post: 1.18 FU3mo: 1.89 FU10mo: 1.87
Cross, Sheehan, & Khan (1982)	Gestalt/ transactional analysis (12)	Mixed (15)	Adj, Exp, TC	Post: 1.22 FU4mo: 1.23 FU1yr: 1.26
Cathartic-Emotive (mean ES = 1.27)				
Bierenbaum, Nichols, & Schwartz (1976)	Emotive ($M = 9$ hours)	Neurotic students (41)	Exp, SSy, TC	Post: 1.09
Dahl & Waal (1983)	Primal therapy (1 year)	Chronic neurotic (13)	CSy, TC	FU2yr: 1.10
Nichols (1974)	Emotive ($M = 9$)	Neurotic students (21)	Exp, SSy, TC	Post: 1.28 FU2mo(2): 1.73

[a]Individual treatment unless otherwise noted; number of sessions given in parentheses. CCT = client-centered therapy; EFT = emotionally focused therapy.
[b]Adj = social adjustment or interpersonal problems measures; CSy = clinicial ratings of symptoms; Exp = measures of experiential functioning; Imp = estimates based on improvement ratings or percentage recovered; PC = measures of personality and coping style; Rel = measures of relationship quality (e.g., marital); SIm = self-image measures; SSy = self-ratings of symptoms; TC = target complaint or individualized problem measures.
[c]Change ESs were calculated as the difference between pre and post means divided by the pretest standard deviation. ESs for multiple outcome measures were first averaged within instruments (e.g., eight scales of Freiberg Personality Inventory), then across instruments for each treatment group and each assessment period. If number of instruments at different assessments differed, these are given in parentheses. FU = follow-up (followed by time period; e.g., 3mo = 3 months); + = ES underestimated owing to calculation method (e.g., estimating ES from significance level).

fect size was 1.24 ($SD = .63$; $n = 33$). Effect sizes were found to be slightly larger at early follow-up (1–8 months posttreatment; ES = 1.51; $SD = .86$; $n = 20$) but were comparable at late follow-up (9–144 months; ES = 1.16; $SD = .43$; $n = 12$); thus, there was no general pattern of relapse or loss of posttreatment gains. Averaging across the three assessment periods provides a more stable estimate of treatment effects and makes it possible to combine data from all 37 treatment groups; the average combined treatment effect was 1.32 ($SD = .66$), which means that the average treated

client moved from the 50th to the 90th percentile in relation to the pretreatment population. Although change ESs cannot be compared directly with the more typical control-group ESs (e.g., Smith et al., 1980)—because they could be expected to run somewhat larger—these figures nevertheless can be considered to represent a large effect (cf. Cohen, 1988).

The best available point of comparison for these data is the Quality Assurance Project (1983), which reported pre–post change effect sizes for psychosocial treatments of nonendogenous depression.

Using client-rated and clinician-rated symptom measures, an average effect size of 1.72 was reported for predominantly cognitive-behavioral therapies. The comparable overall figure in our meta-analysis is 1.47 for five studies of treatments of depression (e.g., Beutler, Engle et al., 1991).

However, these effects do not address the question of whether the experiential therapies studied were better than no treatment. To address this question, we examined a subset of 15 studies in which experiential therapies were compared with wait-list or no-treatment controls. Pre–post change effects were calculated for control conditions, and differences between treatment and control effect sizes were computed (averaging across measures and assessment periods), yielding control-referenced ESs, which are given in Table 12.2. The mean control-referenced ES for these studies was also large, 1.30 ($SD = .77$), and of the same order as the pre–post change effect size of 1.32. Thus, when compared with controls, clients who received experiential therapy showed a much greater amount of pre–post change, whereas controls remained at pretreatment levels. Although untreated controls might be expected to improve, they did not, on the average, partly because of deterioration in some of the controls.

The next logical question raised is whether experiential therapies are as effective as nonexperiential treatments. Twenty-six of the studies also included other forms of psychosocial treatment, ranging from psychoeducational interventions or treatment-as-usual conditions to cognitive, behavioral, or psychodynamic therapies. Pre–post ESs were calculated for these comparative treatments as well and compared with the ESs for the experiential treatments in the same studies (see Table 12.3). Although the results were quite variable, the average difference between treatments was essentially zero ($M = +.04$; $SD = .74$). Echoing the oft-cited and controversial "dodo bird" verdict (e.g., Luborsky, Singer, & Luborsky, 1975; Stiles, Shapiro, & Elliott, 1986), these data are thus consistent with the conclusion that experiential and nonexperiential treatments appear to be equally effective, based on the available research.

TABLE 12.2 Controlled outcome research on experiential therapies

Study	Treatment	Control Condition	Mean Difference in ES
Braaten (1989)	CCT	No treatment	+ 1.19
Clarke & Greenberg (1986)	PrExp	Wait-list	+ .94
Dandeneau & Johnson (in press)	PrExp	Wait-list	+ 1.71
Dircks, Grimm, Tausch, & Wittern (1980)	CCT	No treatment	+ .27
Eymael (1987)	CCT	Wait-list	+ 2.20
Goldman & Greenberg (1992)	PrExp	Wait-list	+ 2.14
Gordon Walker, Manion, Johnson, & Cloutier (1992)	PrExp	Wait-list	+ 1.39
Johnson & Greenberg (1985a)	PrExp	Wait-list	+ 2.59
Johnson & Greenberg (1985b)	PrExp	Delay period	+ 2.51
Katonah (1991)	Focusing	Wait-list	+ 1.57
Meyer (1981)	CCT	Wait-list	+ .56
Meyer, Stuhr, Wirth, & Ruester (1988)	CCT	Treatment refusers (12 yr. f.u.)	+ .46
Pomrehn, Tausch, & Tönnies (1986)	CCT	Wait-list	+ .96
Propst, Ostrom, Watkins, Dean, & Mashburn (in press)	ND +	Wait-list	+ .55
Rudolph, Langer, & Tausch (1980)	CCT	Wait-list	+ .30
Westermann, Schwab, & Tausch (1983)	CCT	Wait-list	+ 1.07
M Control-referenced ES			+ 1.29

Note. Effect sizes are mean differences in change effect sizes (pre vs. post/follow-up) averaged across measures and assessment periods. Types of treatment. CCT = client-centered therapy; ND + = nondirective plus minor directive; PrExp = process-experiential therapy (a marker-guided synthesis of client-centered and Gestalt therapies).

TABLE 12.3   Comparative-outcome research on experiential therapies

Study	Experiential Treatment	Comparison Treatment	Mean Difference in ES
Beutler, Frank, Schieber, Calver, & Gaines (1984)	Gestalt	Inpatient treatment as usual (without group)	−.41
Beutler, Frank, Schieber, Calver, & Gaines (1984)	Gestalt	Process-supportive (psychodynamic) group	−.55
Beutler, Frank, Schieber, Calver, & Gaines (1984)	Gestalt	Behavioral therapy group	−.17
Beutler, Engle, Mohr, Daldrup, Bergan, Meredith, & Merry (1991)	Gestalt	Cognitive therapy group	+ .17
Beutler et al. (1991)	ND +	Cognitive therapy group	+ .06
Beutler & Mitchell (1981)	Unspec	Analytically oriented therapy	+ .82
Borkovec (1991)	CCT	Desensitization/cognitive therapy	−1.08
Borkovec (1991)	CCT	Relaxation	−.77
Borkovec et al. (1987)	ND +	Cognitive therapy/relaxation	−.68
Borkovec & Mathews (1988)	ND +	Cognitive therapy/relaxation	−.50
Borkovec & Mathews (1988)	ND +	Desensitization/relaxation	+ .02
Clarke & Greenberg (1986)	PrExp	Behavioral problem-solving treatment	+ .54
Cross, Sheehan, & Khan (1982)	Gestalt	Behavioral therapy	−.45
Dandeneau & Johnson (in press)	PrExp	Cognitive therapy	+ .78
Eckert & Biermann-Ratjen (1990)	CCT	Psychodynamic inpatient group	.00[a]
Eymael (1987)	CCT	Behavioral therapy	−.53
Goldman & Greenberg (1992)	PrExp	Structural-systemic therapy	−.02
Grawe, Caspar, & Ambühl (1990)	CCT	Behavioral therapy (broadband and individualized)	−.08
Grawe, Caspar, & Ambühl (1990)	CCT	Group behavioral therapy	−.22
Holstein (1990)	Focusing	Cognitive-behavioral weight-loss group	+ .14
Johnson & Greenberg (1985a)	PrExp	Marital problem-solving therapy	+ 1.77
Lerner & Clum (1990)	ND +	Behavioral problem-solving group	−1.42
Meyer (1981)	CCT	Short-term dynamic therapy	+ .44
Nichols (1974)	Cathartic	Dynamic therapy	+ 1.16
Paivio & Greenberg (1992)	PrExp	Psychoeducational group	+ 1.25
Propst (in press)	ND +	Cognitive therapy (nonreligious or religious)	+ .09
Toukmanian & Grech (1991)	PrExp	Self-help/psychoeducational groups	+ .60
M Comparative ES			+ .04

Note. Multiple treatments for a given study are listed separately. Effect sizes are mean differences in change effect sizes (pre vs. post/follow-up) averaged across measures and assessment periods; positive values indicate larger effect sizes for experiential therapies in relation to comparative treatments. Types of experiential treatment correspond to main headings in Table 12.1. CCT = client-centered therapy; ND + = nondirective plus minor directive; PrExp = process-experiential therapy; Unspec = unspecified experiential treatment.
[a]Based on reported equivalence.

When experiential therapies are compared with the cognitive and behavioral treatments ($n = 13$) there is an ES difference of .28 in favor of the latter. However when we look at the seven studies comparing directive experiential treatments (pro-cess-experiential and Gestalt) with cognitive or behavioral treatments, we find an ES difference of .4 in favor of the directive experiential treatments. Although these differences are not statistically significant (the samples are very small), the comparisons are intriguing and suggest the need for further research. This is especially important in light of the difference between these findings and the less favorable results reported in Smith et al. (1980) for experiential therapy for a small sample of older studies.

Correlates of effect size.   Using the combined assessments data, we next looked at a number of parameters in order to estimate the importance of various features of the treatments, clients, or studies. Change effect size was significantly related to treatment modality, apparently reflecting large effects found in five studies of experiential marital therapy (mean ES = 2.21; e.g., Johnson & Greenberg, 1985a). Similarly, ES also varied with type of client disorder or problem: The largest effects were found for relationship problems (ES = 2.03; e.g., Gordon Walker, Manion, Johnson, & Cloutier, 1992); large effects were found for depression and anxiety disorders (ES = 1.42; e.g., Elliott et al., 1990); and the smallest effects were found for chronic and severe problems, such as personality disorders and schizophrenia (ES = .92; e.g., Teusch, 1990), or physical problems, such as psychosocial adjustment in cancer (ES = .73; e.g., Dircks, Grimm, Tausch, & Wittern, 1980). There were no significant effects for researcher allegiance, setting, or length of treatment.

Finally, we classified the treatments included in our sample into a six-category framework organized along a directive–nondirective dimension (see Table 12.1). Overall, effect size did not significantly vary as a function of treatment type although this is probably the result of the relatively small number of studies within each type.

In considering the results of this meta-analysis, it should be kept in mind that they are based on a relatively small number of studies of diverse treatments with diverse clients and diverse therapists, studied with diverse methods. More sophisticated analyses and many more data points are needed to clarify the meaning of these data. Nevertheless, the results suggest that there is room for cautious optimism about the effectiveness of experiential therapies and their comparability to other treatments.

Summary of Selected Outcome Studies

Client-centered therapy.   Two thorough, modern investigations of client-centered therapy are the Hamburg Short Psychotherapy Comparison Experiment (Meyer, 1981) and the Berne Study (Grawe et al., 1990); both were carried out by proponents of other approaches.

In the Hamburg study (Meyer, 1981; Meyer,

Stuhr, Wirth, & Ruester, 1988; Stuhr & Meyer, 1991), clients at a German clinic for psychosomatic disorders were assigned to either immediate or delayed client-centered (*Gesprächstherapie*) or psychodynamic treatments and assessed on the Freiburg Personality Inventory, Saarbruecken Anxiety List, and Giessen Test (a measure of self-image). Clients in each treatment did better than wait-list controls. Clients in the client-centered condition did slightly better than clients in the psychodynamic condition, mostly on symptom measures (e.g., depression) and on the 9-month follow-up data; however, Meyer (1981) reported that clients in client-centered therapy showed less judge-rated insight than did psychodynamically treated clients. (This pattern of differential outcome between client-centered and psychodynamically treated clients was replicated by Eckert & Biermann-Ratjen, 1990.) Maintenance of change at 12-year follow-up has also been reported (Meyer et al., 1988).

The Berne Psychotherapy Project (Grawe et al., 1990) involved a comparison of individual client-centered therapy, broad-spectrum behavioral therapy, and interactional behavior therapy in both individual and group formats. The researchers employed a mixed sample of clients whose problems were primarily interpersonal in nature and assessed them on a broad range of measures, including SCL-90, the Goal Attainment Scale, the Giessen Test, Changes in Experiencing and Behavior (a measure of experiential functioning), and others. Overall, the four treatments were equivalent in effectiveness on a large battery of measures. However, the treatments manifested different patterns of response on outcome measures across assessment periods and different patterns of client and process predictors of outcome (reviewed later).

Several other important studies or programs of European research have focused on client-centered therapy (see Tables 12.1, 12.2, and 12.3): Eymael, 1987; Dircks et al., 1982; Pomrehn, Tausch, & Tönnies, 1986; Rudolph, Langer, & Tausch, 1980; Westermann, Schwab, & Tausch, 1983; Teusch, 1990; Teusch & Boehme, 1991; and Eckert & Biermann-Ratjen, 1990.

Gestalt therapy.   There has been very little outcome research on Gestalt therapy. Cross, Sheehan, and Khan (1982) compared an individual Gestalt–transactional analysis treatment with a behavioral treatment. They reported large pre–post effects for the Gestalt–transactional analysis therapy on measures including Target Complaints, Current Adjustment Rating Scale, and Personal Orientation Inventory. Although the two treatments did not differ statistically, outcome for the Gestalt treatment was slightly less than for behavioral therapy.

Using a treatment manual and highly skilled therapists to carry out group treatment of depressed outpatients, Beutler, Engle et al. (1991) found large effects on the Beck Depression Inventory, Hamilton Depression Rating Scale, and Brief Symptom Inventory, especially at 3- and 10-month follow-ups (see Table 12.1 and Beutler, Machado, & Engle, 1991—completer and follow-up data were averaged in this analysis). Gestalt therapy was found equally effective in comparison with cognitive and a nondirective-plus bibliotherapy treatment in this study, although the Gestalt treatment was slightly but not significantly superior at the last follow-up.

Process-experiential therapy. The term *process-experiential* applies to a set of treatments in which therapist interventions are guided by the various process markers presented by clients at different moments in therapy (Greenberg, Rice, & Elliott, 1993; Rice & Greenberg, 1984). In general, these treatments combine a client-centered relationship with more active interventions or tasks, including two-chair work for resolving conflicts (Greenberg, 1984), systematic unfolding for resolving problematic reactions (Rice & Saperia, 1984), or focusing for symbolizing an unclear felt sense (Gendlin, 1981). As Table 12.1 indicates, process-experiential therapy is currently an active area of process and outcome research. The three studies summarized here involved manual-guided treatments.

In a study of an experientially generated, emotionally focused couples therapy, Johnson and Greenberg (1985a, 1985b) reported evidence for treatment effectiveness in comparison with wait-list controls and couples in a behavioral problem-solving treatment. Large pre–post and control-referenced ESs were obtained in these studies (see Tables 12.1 and 12.2), and posttreatment (comparative ES = 1.41) superiority over the behavioral condition was maintained at 2-month follow-up (ES = 2.12). Two recent studies (Dandeaneau & Johnson, in press; Gordon Walker et al., 1992) replicated the effectiveness of this experiential marital therapy with different populations and designs.

Elliott et al. (1990; see also Jackson & Elliott, 1990) examined the use of an individual, integrated, process-experiential approach (Greenberg et al., in press) in the treatment of clinical depression. Using a broad range of measures, substantial pre–post change was observed, including significant clinical change between posttreatment and 6-month follow-up; overall change was equivalent to that reported in a parallel study of cognitive and dynamic treatments (Shapiro & Firth, 1987). Similar preliminary results have been reported recently

in a current study demonstrating the effects of both process-experiential and client-centered therapy on depression (Greenberg & Watson, 1993).

Paivio and Greenberg (1992) demonstrated the effectiveness of a process-experiential treatment featuring empty-chair dialogue for resolving unfinished emotional issues with significant others. In this study, clients showed substantial pre–post change on measures of general distress (SCL-90) and on the Unfinished Business Resolution Scale. This treatment also proved to be more effective than a psychoeducational comparison condition.

Considering these comparative treatment outcome studies, it appears that there is evidence for the comparability of the effects of experiential therapy with those of cognitive-behavioral and dynamic treatments. More studies of this type are needed to replicate these findings.

WHICH CLIENTS BENEFIT FROM EXPERIENTIAL-HUMANISTIC THERAPIES?

This section summarizes the results of 15 client-outcome predictor studies. The review generally takes a meta-analytic perspective, translating and reporting results as correlation coefficients (and averaging effects as mean rs within and between studies).

Grawe et al. (1990) found that clients with higher pretherapy levels of general social skills, assertiveness, and affiliation did best in client-centered therapy (mean $r = .50$). Along the same lines, Brinkerhoff (1991) found that higher levels of need for intimacy predicted treatment success in process-experiential treatment ($r = .44$).

Several studies point to the possibility that client reactance or resistance to influence may interact with the directiveness of different experiential treatments. This includes the finding that clients with high reactance (including high dominance, low submissiveness) appear to do better in client-centered or nondirective therapies (Beutler, Engle et al., 1991; Beutler, Machado, & Engle, 1991; Grawe et al., 1990; see also Beutler, Mohr, Grawe, Engle, & MacDonald, in press), whereas clients with low reactance do better in Gestalt therapy (Beutler et al., 1991). However, this finding is not uniform in these studies, involving only some change measures (overall mean $r = .25$). On the other hand, Meyer (1981) reported that clients with greater oral or dependency issues fared much better in client-centered therapy ($r = .63$).

Then, it seems that clients with good interpersonal interests and skills may do better in experiential therapies, whereas the hypothesis that high reactance predisposes clients to do better in nondirective therapies remains in need of further study.

There are also some tantalizing indications that one particular client dimension, internal versus external coping style, may interact with treatment type. Internally oriented clients may profit more than externally oriented clients in client-centered or nondirective therapy (mean $r = .19$; Beutler, Engle, et al., 1991; Beutler, Machado, & Engle, 1991; Grawe et al., 1990). The strongest support for this pattern comes from several studies that used different approaches to defining or measuring internalization. In an experimental matching study, Tscheulin (1990) reported that self-oriented (i.e., internalizing) clients did better with a nonconfrontational therapist approach ($r = .63$). In addition, in two separate studies Sachse (1991b, in press) reported substantial links between outcome in client-centered therapy and internalizing "clarifying motivation" measured early in therapy and viewed as a client individual difference variable (mean $r = .57$).

If internalizing clients do better in client-centered therapy, it would seem that externalizing clients should profit more from highly active, expressive, experiential treatments. However, research by Beutler, Engle et al. (1991), Nichols and Bierenbaum (1978), and Pierce et al. (1983) suggests that this is not the case (mean $r = .02$). On the other hand, data from Tscheulin's (1990, 1992) matching study suggest that action-oriented (externalizing) clients may be more successful in a client-centered therapy that incorporates therapist confrontation, that is, pointing out discrepant messages ($r = .63$).

It appears that a client's general openness and interest in inner experience (Dahl & Waal, 1983; Grawe et al., 1990) may be a useful predictor of success in experiential therapy. However, the issue of whether more active or confronting approaches are differentially effective for externally oriented clients requires additional investigation.

Because of the trend toward differential outcome research, it might be assumed that different forms of experiential-humanistic therapy might vary in their effectiveness across disorders. However, two studies we found (Nichols & Bierenbaum, 1978; Pierce et al., 1993) provided very little evidence to support this, showing only weak effects ($r = .06$ to .18), indicating that cathartic therapy may be slightly more successful with depression and obsessive-compulsive personality disorder.

Despite the belief currently prevalent among some psychotherapy researchers that experiential therapies are not effective or are contraindicated for certain disorders, there is as yet no clear evidence for selecting or deselecting experiential therapy in treating any specific disorder. The relationship between specific client disorders or problems

and outcome is likely to be a complex one involving moderator variables and more subtle fine-tuning adaptations of treatments to particular clients' needs.

WHAT ARE THE EFFECTIVE INGREDIENTS IN EXPERIENTIAL THERAPIES?

We review here two approaches to research on the in-therapy effective ingredients or processes that lead to treatment success: process–outcome research and helpful-factors studies.

Process–Outcome Research on Experiential Therapies

Studies correlating process to outcome have traditionally been promoted as an important means of studying the effective ingredients of therapy. They have, however, been criticized by Stiles (1988) and others (e.g., Rice & Greenberg, 1984) as suffering from a number of inherent conceptual flaws that militate against finding meaningful effects. These problems include circular causal effects, curvilinear relationships, and misleading sampling and aggregation techniques.

The alternatives to process–outcome designs (i.e., helpful factors and sequential analysis) have problems as well; thus, combining process–outcome with other approaches appears to be the best strategy. Despite drawbacks, relating process to outcome remains an important type of psychotherapy research, and some cumulative patterns have begun to appear in the process–outcome literature on experiential therapies.

The results of our examination of 19 process–outcome studies of experiential therapy are quite consistent with other reviews (e.g., Orlinsky & Howard, 1986) in pointing to the importance of four factors: alliance, client participation, therapist facilitativeness, and in-treatment positive impact or progress.

Therapeutic alliance. A number of studies point to the existence of a strong link between positive, productive therapeutic or working alliance and treatment outcome in experiential therapy, obtained using a variety of measures. Grawe et al. (1990), in a test of the generic model of therapy (Orlinsky & Howard, 1986) with a client-centered treatment, used client and therapist postsession ratings of alliance to predict outcome ($r = .35$). Sachs, in analyzing experiential therapists in the Vanderbilt study (1983), used raters' judgments on a measure of negative alliance, the Patient–Therapist Interaction Problems subscale of the Vanderbilt Negative Indicators Scale (VNIS) ($r =$

−.48), and Eckert and Biermann-Ratjen (1990) used expert judges' ratings of client "responsiveness to the therapeutic relationship being offered" (mean $r = .50$). In addition, Sachse (1991a, 1991b) used a measure of the task (or therapeutic work) aspect of the alliance: expert judges' ratings of "quality of explicating teamwork" (mean $r = .66$). Adler (1988) and Greenberg and Adler (1989), using a sample of broadly humanistic treatments, found that clients' perceptions of the working alliance correlated with outcome (mean $r = .39$). Overall, therapeutic alliance appears to be the best predictor of outcome examined in this set of studies (mean $r = .48$).

Client participation. The extent to which a client actively engages in the relevant tasks of treatment can be viewed as a component of therapeutic alliance or as a process variable in its own right. The client process variables that best predicted outcome in this literature could be grouped under the heading "depth or involvement in experiential work." Client Experiencing scale (Klein, Mathieu-Coughlan, & Kiesler, 1986) ratings predicted outcome in the client-centered treatment of generalized anxiety disorder ($r = .46$; Borkovec, 1991). Sachse (1991a, 1991b) found a strong relationship between maximum processing mode (defined in terms of his information-processing model) and outcome, also in client-centered therapy (mean $r = .49$). Brinkerhoff (1991) found more explication of interpersonal conflicts in successful cases in process-experiential therapy (mean $r = .35$). A somewhat lower association was found for amount of emotional discharge and outcome (controlling for treatment differences, mean $r = .16$; Nichols, 1974). Finally, Adler (1988) and Greenberg and Adler (1989) found client self-ratings on a newly devised measure of client involvement to be a promising predictor of outcome ($r = .39$). Across these five studies, client participation in the form of quality of experiential work was a substantial predictor of outcome (mean $r = .37$).

Client openness to therapy, based on Sachse's (1983) observer-rated negative attitude and Grawe et al.'s (1990) client-rated negative evaluation of therapy and client relatedness, was a second type of client participation that seems to bear a somewhat smaller relationship to outcome (mean $r = .22$). In addition, Dahl and Waal (1983) provide a useful demonstration of what might be called "discriminant predictor validity" by showing the absence of a relationship between judge-rated client transference feelings (which should be irrelevant) and outcome in primal therapy.

Therapist facilitativeness. Therapist facilitativeness in experiential therapies includes both the traditional client-centered warmth/prizing, accurate empathy, and genuineness/transparency as well as the facilitation of therapeutic tasks (process directiveness). The available research, though sparse, offers some support for the proposition that therapist facilitativeness fosters treatment success. Thus, improvement was found to correlate with therapist warmth, concreteness, and activeness (mean $r = .34$; Stuhr and Meyer, 1991), with facilitative interventions ($r = .25$; Horton and Elliott, 1991), and with at least two of the three client-centered facilitative conditions ($r = .31$; Rudolph, Langer and Tausch, 1980). However, by far the largest effect for therapist facilitativeness was reported by Grawe et al. (1991) for the generic model component, therapist self-relatedness (i.e., genuineness; $r = .61$). Overall, then, therapist facilitativeness (construed broadly) also appears to bear a fairly consistent, substantial relation to outcome in experiential therapy (mean $r = .43$).

Session impact/resolution. Early or in-process treatment impact is a commonsense indicator of eventual treatment success, although the linking of session impact and treatment outcome is fraught with difficulty (e.g., Stiles, 1988; Stiles, Shapiro & Firth-Cozens, 1990). Nevertheless, we noted a number of instances in which either general session impact or resolution of specific in-session tasks predicted outcome. Grawe et al. (1990) found a relationship between outcome and client and therapist ratings of therapeutic realizations (mean $r = .48$), Sachse (1983) with ratings on negative session subscale ($r = -.40$), and Lietaer (1989) with client and therapist session evaluations predicted outcome ($r = .38$). Greenberg and Webster (1982) and Lowenstein (1985) each obtained significantly better outcomes for clients who resolved in-session tasks (mean $r = .54$ and $.43$, respectively). Katonah (1991) reported positive associations between the degree of focusing achieved (conceived as an index of resolution) and psychosocial outcome for cancer patients ($r = .39$). Session impact and resolution also proved to be a substantial correlate of eventual outcome (mean $r = .42$).

The nonspecific nature of these cumulative findings may reflect the conservative or limiting effects of various methodological problems, such as those described by Stiles (1988). More sophisticated approaches (e.g., sequential or task analysis) will probably be needed to identify the role of specific interventions.

Helpful Factors in
Experiential-Humanistic Therapy

In addition to process–outcome research, another, more direct method for understanding what is effective or change producing in experiential-humanistic therapies is to ask the involved parties or clinical observers to identify aspects of incidents that are helpful or hindering. Although helpful-factors research also has limitations, including lack of specificity and possible biasing effects in memory and self-report, it is much more in keeping with the underlying philosophical assumptions of the experiential approach than is the process–outcome method.

We located 10 helpful-factors studies that employed samples mostly or entirely made up of experiential therapies (see Table 12.4). The most common helpful aspects in these studies were client understanding/insight and awareness/experiencing, followed by client involvement and self-disclosure. The therapeutic relationship apparently played a secondary role.

Although the data on hindering aspects are more sparse, the results of our thematic analysis of the most hindering aspects of experiential-humanistic therapy suggest that the most common problem may be therapist intrusiveness or pressure, not only in the more active experiential therapies but even in client-centered therapy (Lietaer, 1992). To

---

TABLE 12.4   Thematic analysis of helpful factors in experiential therapies

I. *Positive Relational Environment*

A. *Alliance*: Cohesion, closeness with therapist or group (Dierick & Lietaer, 1990;[a,b,c] Elliott et al., 1990[d])

B. *Empathy*: Feeling understood; experiencing therapist as an understanding person (Cross, Sheehan, & Khan, 1982;[d] Elliott et al., 1990[d,e])

C. *Support*: Client feels supported, reassured, validated, or safe with therapist (Elliott, James, Reimschuessel, Cislo, & Sack, 1985;[a] Elliott et al., 1990;[d,e] Greenberg, James, & Conry, 1988;[a] Mancinelli, 1992[a])

D. *Personality of therapist* (Cross et al., 1982[d])

II. *The Client's Therapeutic Work* (Mancinelli, 1992[a])

A. *Involvement*: Client feels more actively involved in therapy, including more cognitively stimulated (Boulet, Souliere, & Sterner, in press;[f] Dierick & Lietaer, 1990;[a,b,c] Elliott et al., 1985,[a] 1990[d,e])

B. *Self-disclosure*: Client is able or dares to talk about difficult or personal matters; authenticity, self-revelation; providing significant material about self, reporting expression of strong feelings (Cross et al., 1982;[d] Dierick & Lietaer, 1990;[a,b,c] Elliott, Clark, & Kemeny, 1991;[a] Lietaer & Neirinck, 1986;[b] Mahrer, Dessaulles, Nadler, Geruaize, & Sterner, 1987[f])

C. *Expression*: Client expresses feelings or needs in session (Boulet et al., in press;[f] Greenberg et al., 1988;[a] Mahrer, Dessaulles et al., 1987[f])

D. *Exploration*: Client explores personal and interpersonal experiences more deeply (Dierick & Lietaer, 1990;[c] Lietaer & Neirinck, 1986[a,b])

III. *Therapist Facilitation of the Client's Work*

A. *Therapist fostering of client exploration* (Cross et al., 1982;[d] Elliott et al., 1991;[a] Lietaer & Neirinck, 1986[b])

B. *Therapist confrontation/feedback*: Therapist gives client feedback regarding what is currently happening in the session (Dierick & Lietaer, 1990;[b,c] Lietaer & Neirinck, 1986[a,b])

IV. *Client Changes or Impacts*

A. *Awareness/experiencing*: Client becomes more fully aware of immediate experiences and feelings (Boulet et al., in press;[f] Elliott et al., 1985;[a] 1990,[d,e] 1991;[a] Greenberg et al., 1988;[a] Lietaer & Neirinck, 1986[a,b])

B. *Understanding/insight*: Client comes to better understanding of self, problems, others (Cross et al., 1982;[d] Dierick & Lietaer, 1990;[a,c] Elliott et al., 1985;[a] 1990,[e] 1991;[a] Greenberg et al., 1988;[a] Lietaer & Neirinck, 1986[a,b])

C. *Positive feelings*: Client experiences hope, progress, relief (Cross et al., 1982;[d] Dierick & Lietaer, 1990;[a,b] Lietaer & Neirinck, 1986[a])

D. *Expresses or experiences changed self*: Client manifests or undertakes new ways of being or acting, comes to own or value aspects of self (Greenberg et al., 1988;[a] Mahrer, Dessaulles et al., 1987[f])

E. *Other changes* (Dierick & Lietaer, 1990;[a] Elliott et al., 1991[a])

Note. Analysis based on 5 most strongly or frequently endorsed items or categories for each of 14 sets of data; some sources contained more than one set of rankings (e.g., by clients, therapists, and raters).
[a]Client descriptions of most helpful event/aspect of session or treatment.
[b]Therapist descriptions of most helpful event/aspect of session or treatment.
[c]Client descriptions of most helpful event for another group member.
[d]Client ratings of within-session significant events.
[e]Therapist ratings of within-session significant events.
[f]Raters' judgments of good moments in therapy sessions.

a lesser extent, client-centered and experiential therapies also appear to be vulnerable to problems, with confusion/distraction derailing the client's process when there is insufficient therapist direction.

Three of the ten studies examined clients' perceptions after the completion of some or all of their treatment (Cross et al., 1982; Greenberg, James, & Conry, 1988; Mancinelli, 1992) and identified the following as key helpful factors: having a safe, understanding environment; expressing feelings; organizing experience; and clarifying and solving problems.

In several studies, postsession questionnaires were administered to clients or therapists. Lietaer and Neirinck (1986; see also Lietaer, 1992) obtained postsession descriptions of most helpful and hindering aspects from 41 clients in client-centered therapy. They then developed a content analysis system for these data, consisting of 33 categories divided into three headings, relational climate, specific therapist interventions, and client process. "Insight into self" was the most common client-reported category, and "exploring personal experiences more deeply" was the most common therapist-reported category. Clients and therapists alike typically attributed hindering processes to themselves (e.g., clients — disappointment about lack of progress; therapists — focusing too little on the personal meaning of the client's message). Dierick and Lietaer (1990) carried out a similar study of a sample consisting primarily of client-centered groups with results similar to those obtained in the earlier study.

Elliott, Clark, and Kemeny (1991) conducted a content analysis study of clients' postsession descriptions of most helpful events in process-experiential therapy. The most common categories were self-awareness, client self-disclosure, and therapist basic experiential techniques (e.g., reflection). On the other hand, Elliott et al. (1991) found that when clients and therapists were given rating scales to evaluate the impact of significant events, both awarded the highest ratings to feeling understood (followed by awareness and either feeling closer to the therapist or feeling supported).

Mahrer and Nadler's (1986) list of 12 good moments in therapy provides a final approach to studying helpful aspects of experiential-humanistic therapy. Mahrer, Boulet, and Stalikas (1987) used clinical judges to rate the presence of these helpful aspects in client responses in three sessions of Mahrer's radical experiential therapy (Mahrer, 1989). More recently, Boulet, Souliere, and Sterner (in press) developed a version of this list for rating good moments in Gestalt therapy. In both studies, expression of feelings ranked among the most common good moments, followed by either

providing significant personal material (in experiential therapy) or awareness of ongoing experiencing (in Gestalt therapy).

WHAT OCCURS IN EXPERIENTIAL-HUMANISTIC THERAPIES?

Much of the substantial body of research on various aspects of client and therapist in-session performances has utilized the Gloria films (Shostrom, 1965), making generalizations to other therapists and to experiential therapy as a whole difficult. These films and their successors constitute a *de facto* therapy archive for calibrating and comparing new process rating systems, although their use needs to be supplemented by studies that sample more broadly from garden-variety humanistic and experiential therapies.

Therapist Performance

Client-centered therapy. The most frequent response mode in the 10 studies of speech act usage in client-centered therapy was therapist reflection (Bozarth, 1988; Brodley & Brody, 1990; Edwards, Boulet, Mahrer, Chagnon, & Mook, 1982; Elliott et al., 1987; Gustavson, Cundick, & Lambert, 1981; Hill, Thames, & Rardin, 1979; Lee & Uhlemann, 1984; Stiles, 1979; Stuhr & Meyer, 1991; Weinrach, 1990). Consistent with Rogers's theory and the popular view of client-centered therapy, an average of 72 percent of all therapist responses were reflections. Interpretations of some type were also found to occur (mean = 19%; Elliott et al., 1987; Hill et al., 1979).

With regard to content, the studies showed that client-centered therapists talked frequently about the client's feelings, roughly 42 percent of the time (e.g., Mercier & Johnson, 1984), and the verbalization of feelings received greater emphasis in client-centered therapy than in psychodynamic therapy (Stuhr & Meyer, 1991). However, actions and cognitions also received therapist attention in this therapy (Meara, Pepinsky, Shannon, & Murray, 1981; Tausch, 1988). Two other patterns in the literature are consistent with client-centered emphases: therapist responses were predominantly present focused (Edwards et al., 1982; Gustavson et al., 1981) and were more positive in content (O'Dell & Bahmer, 1981; Stuhr & Meyer, 1991) than were other therapies.

Communicated empathy. Empathy is the central process of client-centered therapy, and so deserves more detailed coverage here. Again, unfortunately, research on this key process was sparse in the eighties. Numerous reviews of research on therapist facilitating conditions or interpersonal skills, published toward the end of the seventies, concluded that this research area was plagued with severe methodological problems, only modestly supported the Rogerian hypothesis, and was unlikely to hold for all therapy approaches (Gurman, 1977; Lambert, DeJulio, & Stein, 1978; Mitchell, Bozarth, & Krauft, 1977; Parloff, Waskow, & Wolfe, 1978).

Although there seems to be a continuing belief among client-centered therapists (e.g., Bohart, 1990; Bozarth, 1990; Brodley, 1990; Rogers, 1975) that empathy is inherently curative, there have been few recent studies to support this belief. Researchers' discouragement regarding the investigation of empathy has resulted from a number of factors. On the one hand, previous definitional, conceptual, and methodological problems with the measurement of empathy have been recognized; more accurate, differentiated, and multidimensional definitions are required if empathy research is to flourish. On the other hand, researchers have been daunted by the complexity of the empathy construct. For example, Gladstein and associates (1987) defined 18 types of empathy based on existing measures and, after completing a number of analogue studies using these measures, concluded that empathy was very difficult and virtually too complex to study.

In spite of these problems, the development of psychodynamic self-psychology and its views on the importance of empathy has resulted in a renewed interest in this core variable by those in the clinical domain and in psychoanalytic circles (e.g., Basch, 1983; Bohart, 1990; Vanaerschot, 1990). The little research done in the past decade has shifted toward a more contextual approach. Empathy has been studied within the context of the bond in the therapeutic alliance (Horvath & Greenberg, 1989; Orlinsky & Howard, 1986) or within the broad range of therapeutic impacts (Elliott et al., 1985), and investigations have attempted to specify its components and its application in greater detail (Barrett-Lennard, 1981; Elliott et al., 1982). The question of whether empathy works no longer seems useful and is being replaced by questions about how and when particular aspects of empathy work (e.g., Lambert, DeJulio, & Stein, 1978; Lietaer, 1990; Rice & Greenberg, 1991).

Two other examples of the specification of empathy may point a way between oversimplification and overcomplication. Barrett-Lennard (1981, 1986) clarified the concept of empathy and its interactional nature by proposing a three-phase, cyclical model of the empathic process in which

first, a therapist resonates with the client (therapist experienced empathy); second, the therapist communicates empathy (expressed empathy); and third, the client perceives the therapist's understanding (client received empathy). Client received empathy was shown to have the strongest correlations with outcome (Gurman 1977) and is discussed later.

Elliott et al. (1982) developed a new approach to the measurement of the empathic quality of therapist behavior. They devised the Response Empathy Rating Scale, consisting of eight components: intention to enter client's frame of reference; accuracy; here and now; topic centrality; choice of words; voice quality; exploratory manner; and impact. Centrality was found to be the core component of this scale, and factor analysis suggested two underlying factors, depth expressiveness and empathic exploration. Evidence of the validity of the scale was found by correlating it with clients' feelings of being understood (received empathy).

Gestalt therapy. Researchers investigating response mode usage in Gestalt therapy found a much greater variety than in client-centered therapy (Bouchard, Lecomte, Carbonneau, & Lalonde, 1987; Brunink & Schroeder, 1979; Gustavson et al., 1981; Hill et al., 1979; Stiles, 1979). Consistent with the high value placed in the therapy on stimulating in-session experiences through therapeutic experiments or exercises, advisement was the single most prevalent mode, occurring on an average in 26 percent of therapist responses. Most therapist advisements in Gestalt therapy are, however, process (in-session) directives. Several other important experiential response modes were also found in studies on Gestalt therapy, including reflections, interpretations, disclosure, questions, and information (Brunink & Schroeder, 1979; Gustavson et al., 1981; Hill et al., 1979).

There is less research on what Gestalt therapists talk about than on what they do, but two clear themes are: (1) an almost exclusive focus on the here and now (at least 90% of responses; Gustavson et al., 1981); and (2) emphasis on experiences or feelings (40%; e.g., Meara et al., 1981). In addition, Meara et al. (1981) found that a majority (56%) of therapist responses used action verbs.

Process-experiential therapy. Three studies measured therapist response mode use in process-experiential therapy tasks (e.g., chair work and focusing; Benjamin, 1979; Goldman, 1991; Hirscheimer, 1991) and found in-session advisement or process directives the most common type of therapist response, occurring on average in 40 percent of all therapist responses. This mode also occurred in experiential focusing; Clark (1990) found process directives in almost all focusing events. Therapists gave moderate to high ratings to session intentions associated with process directives (e.g., channeling the discussion) in two studies (Horton & Elliott, 1991; Wexler & Elliott, 1988). As in client-centered therapy, reflections were used both to convey empathy and to foster exploration of feelings.

In an innovative program of research on a process-experiential approach, Martin and colleagues (Cummings, Martin, Hallberg, & Slemon, 1992; Martin, 1991, 1992; Martin, Paivio, & Labadie, 1990) found that client-identified important events were characterized by therapist verbal processing that was significantly deeper and more conclusion oriented than that in control events.

Manuals and Techniques

A few approaches have been manualized. Daldrup et al. (1988) created a manual and adherence measures for a form of Gestalt therapy (focused expressive psychotherapy) that promotes active expression of feelings. The adherence measures covered the basic tasks in the treatment, including the increasing of affective arousal and the development of plans and homework based on the in-session work. Therapists were shown to perform consistently and significantly higher on treatment-specific compliance measures at the end of training than they did before training and in comparison with cognitive therapists.

Hudgins and Kiesler (1987) developed a manual for a three-stage psychodramatic doubling intervention, including the order or sequence of stages, that is, the rules that guide the therapist's concrete operations. In an analogue study, they found that therapists' compliance was extremely high (83–100%) and that the doubling intervention was more effective in increasing experiential self-disclosure than was a control standard interview.

Manuals and adherence measures have also been constructed for three specific therapist process-experiential therapy task interventions. Adherence measures have been shown to discriminate evocative unfolding, two-chair, and empty-chair interventions from one another and from empathic reflection (Greenberg & Rice, 1991; Goldman, 1991). Two other general manuals of the process-experiential approach to treatment have also been developed (Greenberg & Goldman, 1988; Greenberg, Rice, & Elliott, 1993). In addition, Goldman (1991) showed that raters could discriminate between process-experiential and both brief dynamic and cognitive-behavioral approaches.

Mahrer (1983, 1986, 1989) has written extensively on his approach and has provided a manual of his experiential therapy, consisting of four steps that occur in each session. First, by attaining a level of strong feeling, the client accesses an inner, deeper experiencing and brings it closer to the surface. Second, the deeper experience is received and appreciated. Third, the client undergoes a qualitative transformation by becoming (i.e., enacting and owning) the deeper potential. Fourth, the client tries out this new way of being in the extra-therapy world.

Finally, the Therapist Experiencing Scale (Klein, Mathieu-Coughlan, & Kiesler, 1986) provides a judge-rated measure of the general adherence of therapist interventions to the manner and focus in client-centered and experiential approaches.

Client Performance

Client behavior. We found evidence for four types of client in-session action in the research: agreement, self-disclosure, emotional expression, and presentations of tasks (Brodley and Brody, 1990; Horton and Elliott, 1991; Mahrer, Dessaulles et al., 1987; Nichols, 1974; O'Dell and Bahmer, 1981; Pierce et al., 1983).

Client content. The most thorough examination of what clients talk about in sessions can be found in Lietaer, Dierick, and Neirinck's (1985) content analysis of client and therapist postsession descriptions of what clients discussed in client-centered therapy. They found that clients talked about three major topics (1) situational or external action, e.g., relationships with parent or spouses, or social and work contacts; (2) experiences and feelings especially anger, fear, dependency, and happiness; and (3) patterns and cognitions, especially patterns of experiencing, relating or behaving, in which clients reflected on an aspect or general pattern of the self (e.g., "I talked about my perfectionism"; 16% of client descriptions). This category is very close to Rennie's (1990, 1992) category of reflexivity and Corbishley's (in press) category of cognitions.

Client state. Several studies have documented a therapeutically desirable client state of inward involvement or depth, for example, as measured by the Client Experiencing Scale (Klein et al., 1986) or client focused voice on the Client Vocal Quality Scale (Rice & Kerr, 1986). Borkovec (1991) reported that clients in nondirective therapy had higher experiencing scale ratings than did clients in cognitive therapy. Shifts in level of client experiencing and occurrence of client focused voice were shown to be important in the resolution of splits (Greenberg, 1984) and problematic reactions (Wiseman & Rice, 1989). In addition, Toukmanian

(1986, 1990) and Sachse (1986, 1988) both developed measures of depth of client processing in client-centered therapy.

Client experience. In studies of client recollections on reviewing session tapes, a key component of clients' in-session experience was their sense of the *immediate impact*, or of what they or their therapist did (cf. Elliott et al., 1985; Hill, Helms, Spiegel, & Tichenor, 1988). In a study of clients' postsession ratings of therapeutic impact, Elliott and Wexler (1992) found that relationship impacts (e.g., feeling supported) received higher ratings than did task impacts (e.g., becoming aware) and that the highest rated relationship impact was feeling understood, that is, received empathy.

Empathy research has moved from global studies of its effect in outcome studies (Mitchell et al., 1977), through studies of specific therapist behaviors (Barkham & Shapiro, 1986; Elliott et al., 1982), to research on clients' subjective experiences of empathy (Bachelor, 1988). Barkham and Shapiro (1986) used interpersonal process recall to investigate therapist response modes associated with client received empathy. They found that exploratory responses, in which the therapist attempted to understand the client's experience within an emerging, shared frame of reference, led clients to feel more understood than did either reflection or interpretation.

Bachelor (1988) carried the trend further by examining how clients perceived empathy, utilizing a qualitative analysis of clients' phenomenological reports of their experience of empathy. Bachelor found that clients reported four different types of received empathy: cognitive, affective, shared, and nurturant. The cognitive and affective types followed the fundamental cognitive-affective dichotomy in the conceptualization of empathy. Perceived empathy also occurred through shared client and therapist self-disclosure and through the nurturant, supportive, or attentive presence of the therapist. This study suggests that even from the client's point of view, empathy is a complex, differentiated, and multimodal phenomenon.

A final form of therapeutic impact that has been studied is the degree of in-session resolution reached by clients on specific experiential tasks (Greenberg & Rice, 1991; Katonah, 1991).

Deep structures of client experience. Emerging new genres of phenomenological and interpretive psychotherapy research are more consistent with basic assumptions of experiential therapists than are the traditional positivistic research methods (see Toukmanian & Rennie, 1992). These studies have begun to reveal a deeper set of processes and dimensions underlying the more observable client actions, contents, and impacts reviewed here. Rennie (1990, 1992), Angus and Rennie (1988, 1989), and Clark (1990) have provided glimpses into the operation of some of these deep structures of experiential-humanistic therapy (and perhaps of other therapies as well).

Building on his elaborate analysis of clients' moment-by-moment experiences in therapy sessions, Rennie (1990, 1992) found that the center of client experience is *reflexivity*, or the turning of the client's awareness back on itself. According to Rennie, the central process of therapy consists in the client's alternation between immersion in action or experience and reflexive self-awareness.

Another deep structure is *inner/outer*; Rennie (Angus & Rennie, 1988; Rennie, 1985) has documented the existence of disjunctions between what clients say and their inner track of internal experience and dialogue. Minor disjunctions occur frequently, but they take on clinical importance when clients develop reservations or concerns about their therapist's approach. At these points, Rennie (1985, 1990) found, they rarely speak explicitly of their concerns, but instead engage in a process of deference in which they seek to protect themselves and the therapist by covering over their concerns and attempting to go along with the therapist. Angus and Rennie (1988) illustrated how this process unfolds in noncollaborative metaphor elaboration, with client and therapist developing discrepant understandings of the same image.

Many of these deep structures involve dialectical processes, or opposites that alternate and sometimes conflict with one another. Other such processes can be found in this line of research. *Pursuit versus avoidance* of personal meaning (Rennie, 1990, 1992) appears clearly in clients' use of narrative to either distance themselves from or to work through their inner disturbances (Rennie, 1991). A final dialectic is that of *self versus other*. Angus and Rennie (1989) illustrated how clients can use metaphor to symbolize either themselves or others, and Rennie (1990) described how clients' awareness alternates between being focused on themselves and being focused on the therapist.

A final deep structure apparent in these phenomenological studies is *contextualization*. Angus and Rennie's (1989) analysis of the role of metaphor in therapy revealed that a critical function of metaphor is to help the client access a contextual network of associated meanings and memories. In addition, interpretive research studies by Clark (1990) and Labott, Elliott, and Eason (1992) of significant events in experiential therapy illustrate the same point, that is, the elaborate role played by client background and other contextual factors in giving rise to clients' in-session change.

RESEARCH ON SPECIFIC THERAPEUTIC TASK INTERVENTIONS

Experiential therapy researchers have proposed a new approach for studying how change occurs in psychotherapy. The major forms of this approach, known as the task analytic and significant events paradigms, can be described as follows (Elliott, 1983; Gendlin, 1986; Greenberg, 1986; Greenberg & Pinsof, 1986; Mahrer, 1988; Rice & Greenberg, 1984; Stiles, Shapiro, & Elliott, 1986). The change process in therapy should be studied by focusing on specific types of therapy process (especially task interventions, e.g., empty-chair work with unfinished business) and then describing these, intensively and in context, in a discovery-oriented manner. Researchers should focus on key episodes in which actual therapeutic change or impact is occurring. The ultimate success of this research should be evaluated in terms of the development of clinically useful information (in the form of micro-theories) about how clients change and what the therapist should do in therapy to facilitate resolution of specific client change tasks.

In the period under review, the study of particular task interventions has been one of the strongest areas in experiential therapy. The following sections describe research on major methods.

Focusing for Unclear or Painful Felt Sense

In focusing (Gendlin, 1981, 1984), the therapist helps clients imagine an internal psychological space in which they experience, explore, and symbolize experiences that are either unclear or painful. The full focusing procedure consists of six steps, each with its own markers and involving a particular task-relevant microprocess (Leijssen, 1990). The most common initial marker is the immediate presence of an unclear internal feeling (felt sense).

There is a substantial body of Japanese psychotherapy analogue research on focusing. Tamura and associates (Tamura 1987, 1990; Tamura & Murayama, 1988) found that focusers experienced positive feelings of self-acceptance and of reduced internal disorganization after focusing and that the state of ease in maintaining continual reference to the felt sense predicted the degree of success in focusing. In investigating 130 focusing sessions, Tamura (1990) found two important therapist factors: a relationship, or safe field, factor, in which the listener and experiencer were in tune; and a task intervention factor, in which the therapist either passively helped the focuser to make a space for the problem or actively helped the focuser to dwell in the experience by referring to it.

Another study of the steps of focusing showed that the handle step of focusing (involving the label-ing of experience) was more effective than the asking step in deepening experience (Nakata & Murayama, 1986). Oishi and Murayama (1989) interviewed focusers and found that three conditions were important to enable the focuser to perform well: concentrating while being relaxed; dwelling in the body sense and putting this into words; and experiencing a comfortable psychological climate with the therapist. In addition to the aforementioned research on focusing, a Japanese version of the experiencing scale was developed and tested (Ikemi, Kira, Murayama, Tamura, & Yuba, 1986). This focusing research gives some insight into how people experience focusing. Further process and outcome research on the use of focusing in the ongoing treatment of clinical populations from this group of active Japanese researchers would be helpful in demonstrating when and with whom focusing is most effective.

North American focusing researchers have shown more interest in assessing outcome, as indicated by four studies demonstrating the effects of focusing (Holstein, 1990; Katonah, 1991; Sherman, 1990; Wagner et al., 1991). In a study of focusing as an adjunct treatment for adaptive recovery from cancer, Katonah (1991) found that cancer patients (currently in remission) treated with focusing were significantly less depressed and significantly more improved in body image than a wait-list control and that this change was maintained at 6-month follow-up. In addition, the degree of focusing correlated with change in body awareness but not in depression or hardiness. In another study related to health, Holstein (1990) compared a weight-loss treatment program incorporating focusing with one consisting entirely of cognitive-behavioral procedures; although there was no significant difference immediately after treatment, clients in the focusing treatment showed significantly more weight loss at 3-month follow-up.

Iberg (1990) studied the client's internal processing in focusing and found differential use of dominant and nondominant hemispheric class of cognitions in different phases of focusing with the direct-focusing phase involving more of the nondominant hemisphere class of cognition.

Clark (1990) used comprehensive process analysis (Elliott, 1989) in an intensive analysis of significant events involving focusing. She found the handle step of focusing most important in these events. The clients tended to be unassertive, self-critical, and to have problems in interpersonal relationships, but showed a general ability to contact their inner experiences spontaneously. In the course of the events, clients became more aware of the nature of their difficulties.

Schneider and Sachse (1991) investigated whether a repression–sensitization (R–S) measure predicted focusing performance. Clients with medium to high scores on the R–S dimension and high on a process variable called clarifying motivation were more successful in focusing. In addition, Leijssen (1991) reported four cases involving unsuccessful therapies of longer than 2 years' duration in which focusing was used to enhance client process. The results of four sessions of focusing training by a different therapist showed that the clients varied in response to the intervention, yielding no conclusive results for the effects of focusing.

Existing research on this procedure needs to be supplemented by larger-scale comparative studies of the effects of focusing, and more research needs to be done on clinical populations before this approach can claim established effects for clinical disorders.

Evocative Unfolding of Problematic Reactions

This task intervention, identified in the context of client-centered therapy (Rice, 1974, 1984), addresses a class of difficulties that involve interactions with other people and situations. The problematic reaction point (PRP) marker for this event consists of three identifiable features: a particular incident; a reaction on the part of the patient; and an indication that the patient views his or her reaction as puzzling, inappropriate, or otherwise problematic. In this perspective the fact that the patient is aware of a discrepancy between his or her expected reaction and the actual reaction indicates a current readiness to examine such interactions. These markers of problematic reaction points have been shown to be identifiable with high reliability (95% agreement between raters; Greenberg & Rice, 1991) and act as process diagnostic indicators that the client is in a particular problem state that is amenable to a type of intervention designed to deal with that type of problem.

Rice and colleagues developed a manual for an experiential intervention appropriate to this marker (Rice, 1986) and demonstrated empirically that when an incident is vividly reevoked and reprocessed more slowly and completely, clients recognize that their reactions were a direct response to their subjective construals of the eliciting stimulus. A model of the components of the resolution of problematic reactions was derived empirically (Rice & Saperia, 1984) and is central to the treatment manual.

Research on this task has provided evidence for its effectiveness. In an initial analogue study, Rice and Saperia (1984) compared the effects of purely empathic responding with evocative unfolding and found that clients' productivity ratings for the evocative sessions were significantly higher.

In a further study (Lowenstein, 1985), clients with anxiety and interpersonal problems were seen for brief, time-limited, client-centered therapy. Therapists used evocative unfolding to respond to a PRP marker in either the third or fourth session. The evocative session was rated by the clients as significantly deeper than the other two middle sessions on Stiles's (1980) Session Evaluation Questionnaire. Evocative unfolding sessions were also rated significantly higher on a scale assessing the degree of shift in the clients' own perspective, whereas productivity ratings were in the predicted direction but failed to reach significance (Lowenstein, 1985). On final outcome, the clients who had successfully resolved the PRP in the task-focused evocative interview had significantly greater reduction in state anxiety.

In a further study (Wiseman, 1986; Wiseman & Rice, 1989), a series of sequential analyses were conducted on two evocative unfolding sessions from each of five clients in client-centered therapy. In the sequential analyses, therapist interventions specific to the particular step of the PRP task had a highly significant effect on client experiencing level. Thus, differential manual-specified, moment-by-moment interventions had the expected differential impacts when appropriately applied at differentially diagnosed client process states on the path to resolution of the problematic reaction. This finding lent support to the utility of the manual and to the validity of the model of resolution. In addition, the evocative, task-focused sessions were rated as deeper and more valuable than the comparable nontask sessions in the treatment. Clients also rated the evocative sessions as producing significantly greater shifts in perspective, new self-understanding, and progress. This method appears promising, but more research on clinical populations is needed before it can claim demonstrated effects for clinical disorders.

Two-Chair Dialogue for Conflict Splits

This intervention addresses a class of processing difficulties in which two schemes or aspects of the self are in opposition and is most clearly manifested when clients present verbal statements of splits, indicating an experienced conflict between the two aspects of self (Greenberg, 1979). The marker of a split has been shown to have four features. The first two are statements of the two conflicting aspects of self; the third is a juxtaposition indicator, which places the two aspects in opposition; and the fourth is an indicator that the client is currently experiencing struggle. These markers have been shown to be identifiable with very high reliability (100% agreement between raters; Greenberg, 1984) and act as process diagnoses of clients' affective states that are amenable to two-chair dialogue.

To determine its effectiveness in resolving splits,

the Gestalt two-chair dialogue has been compared with a number of methods drawn from other therapeutic approaches. In several analogue and therapy studies, the two-chair method was compared with client-centered empathy, cognitive-behavioral problem solving, and experiential focusing.

The first studies compared the two-chair method with high-level empathy in helping clients at a university counseling center resolve conflict splits. An initial, multiple, single-case study showed that in three clients the two-chair method led repeatedly to greater depth of experiencing and greater change of awareness than did empathic reflection (Greenberg, 1975; Greenberg & Rice, 1981).

The next study sought to generalize the findings of an earlier analogue study (Greenberg & Clarke, 1979) in an investigation of clients in outpatient therapies of varied length (Greenberg & Dompierre, 1981). Two sessions were designated as experimental sessions. Half the clients received the two-chair intervention first and half received empathic reflection first. Depth of experiencing and shifts in awareness were higher following two-chair sessions. Reported conflict resolution immediately after the session and in a 1-week follow-up was also greater for the two-chair sessions. However, level of discomfort on a postsession target-complaint discomfort box scale was not significantly different for the two treatments. Level of therapist experience did not significantly influence the efficacy of the two-chair intervention.

The two-chair method was next compared with focusing plus empathic reflection (Greenberg & Higgins, 1980). Results of this analogue study showed that the two-chair work applied at a split produced significantly greater depth of experiencing than did focusing applied at a split. However, both treatments produced significantly more reported shifts in awareness and progress in target complaints than were found in a no-treatment control group.

The next step was to compare the two-chair method with an intervention drawn from cognitive-behavioral treatment (Clarke & Greenberg, 1986). Two-chair work was compared with behavioral problem solving (D'Zurilla & Goldfried, 1971) in the treatment of decisional conflicts. Clients were randomly assigned to three conditions: behavioral problem solving; two-chair work; or wait-list control. Therapists saw clients for two sessions, working on the same decision in each session. The two-chair method was more effective than behavioral problem solving or no treatment for reducing indecision. Both treatments were more effective than no treatment for facilitating movement through the stages of decision making.

Although the differential effects studies addressed the question of what specific treatments helped with resolving conflict, they did not identify how the change took place. To this end, Greenberg (1980, 1983, 1984) conducted a series of intensive analyses of client performances in successful episodes of conflict resolution and compared these with unsuccessful episodes. In the first study, the two sides of the conflict were found to function as independent systems, proceeding at different levels of experiencing. One side, the other chair, contained clients' criticisms and expectations and proceeded at lower levels of experiencing than did the second side, called the experiencing chair. At a certain point, the two sides converged, becoming indistinguishable in their experiencing level and moving to a higher level of experiencing. This pattern was revealed consistently throughout nine events in the three clients studied. Patterns of vocal quality (Rice, Koke, Greenberg, & Wagstaff, 1979) also corroborated the findings on depth of experiencing.

The pattern of performances in these episodes of split resolution led to the construction of a three-stage model of intrapsychic conflict resolution: opposition, merger, and integration (Greenberg, 1983). Greenberg (1984) then used additional process ratings to evaluate and elaborate this initial model into one containing six components necessary for conflict resolution. In this refined model, the critic, through role-playing, first identifies its harsh, critical evaluations of the experiencing part of the self. The experiencing part, in turn, expresses its affective reactions to the harsh criticism. The harsh critic then moves from general statements to more concrete and specific criticisms of the person or situation. Specific behaviors may be criticized and specific changes demanded. In response to these criticisms, the experiencing chair begins to react in a more differentiated fashion until a new aspect of its experience is expressed. A sense of direction then emerges for the experiencer, which is expressed to the critic as a want or a need. The critic next moves to a statement of standards and values. At this point in the dialogue, the critic softens. This step is followed by a negotiation, an integration, or both between the two parts.

Relating process to outcome.   To investigate the relationship between the observed resolution processes and outcome, Greenberg and Webster (1982) selected three essential components of resolution from the model: criticism in the other chair; expression of felt wants in the experiencing chair; and softening in the other chair.

To relate these processes to outcome, 31 clients completed a 6-week program using two-chair dialogue to work on an intrapsychic conflict related to a decision. The clients were classified as resolvers or nonresolvers based on the rated presence or absence over the course of treatment of the three specified components of conflict resolution. Resolvers were found to be significantly less undecided and less anxious after treatment than were nonresolvers. Resolvers also showed greater improvement on target complaints and behavioral change. After the particular session in which the critic softened, resolvers reported greater conflict resolution, less discomfort, greater mood change, and greater goal attainment than did nonresolvers.

These results support the validity and clinical utility of the proposed approach to internal conflict resolution. Although this method shows some promise, it needs to be applied to specified clinical populations to determine with whom and for what disorders it is most useful. Further research on individual differences that may mediate the process – outcome link would provide further differentiation on who benefits most from this process.

Empty-Chair Dialogue for Unfinished Business

This task intervention, also drawn from Gestalt therapy, addresses a class of emotional processing difficulties in which schematic emotion memories of significant others continue to trigger the reexperiencing of unresolved emotional reactions. Thus, when a person thinks of the other, bad feelings ensue. The intervention involves reexperiencing the unresolved feelings in the safety of the therapeutic environment, with the immediacy and intensity of the original situation, in order to allow the emotional expression to run its course and be restructured (Daldrup et al., 1988; Greenberg & Safran, 1987). In addition, the client's present resources and capacities promote schematic restructuring and the achievement of closure.

The marker of unfinished business (Greenberg & Safran, 1987) consists of the following: (1) There is a current live experience of a lingering bad feeling, such as hurt, resentment, loss, or regret; (2) the feeling is related to a significant other, such as a parent or spouse; (3) the experience is not being fully and directly expressed; and (4) the experience is unresolved for the client as evidenced by direct verbal statements of giving up or cynicism or nonverbal signs of restricted emotional expression, such as tightening of the jaw or fist. This marker has been shown to be identified with high reliability (90% agreement; Greenberg & Rice, 1991).

The purpose of the intervention is to allow the person to express feelings fully to the imagined significant other (such as an alcoholic parent) in an empty chair. This act helps remobilize the client's suppressed needs and the sense of entitlement to those needs, thereby empowering the client to separate appropriately from the other. Separation

occurs by either achieving a better understanding of the other or holding the other accountable for wronging the self (Greenberg, 1991).

The process of resolution has been modeled, and components that distinguish resolved from unresolved events have been established (Forester, 1991). Critical components of the resolution of unfinished business appear from this preliminary study to be the arousal of intense emotion, the declaration of a need, and a shift in view of the significant other.

An analogue study (King, 1988) comparing the effects of empty-chair dialogue and empathic responding with unfinished business showed that, although at the end of the session there was no significant difference between treatments, 1 week after the session the empty-chair work resulted in a greater increase in tolerance for the significant other and in self-confidence in relation to the significant other as measured by an affective reactions questionnaire. Results from a study of the in-session process revealed that empty-chair sessions were characterized by a significantly greater depth of experiencing than were empathic responding sessions (Maslove, 1989). A 12-to-14 session study, described earlier in this review, demonstrated significantly superior effects for an empty-chair dialogue treatment when compared with a psychoeducational treatment for resolving unfinished business with a significant other (Paivio & Greenberg, 1992). In this treatment, postsession change (in experience of the other), which endured over the week following the session, was found to correlate strongly with outcome, more so than session change alone (Singh & Greenberg, 1992). This result begins to demonstrate a complex process – outcome chain of intervention, in-session change, postsession change, intersession change, and final outcome (Greenberg, 1986; Orlinsky & Howard, 1986).

In addition to the aforementioned research on empty-chair dialogue, work by Beutler and his group (Beutler et al., 1987; Daldrup et al., 1988) showed that focused expressive therapy based on empty-chair work for the expression of constricted anger led to some improvement in depression and, for some patients, to a decrease in subjective pain. However, this treatment was not found to be more effective than an education group in reducing pain in a depressed, chronic pain group (Beutler et al., 1988). In an innovative set of six single-case studies on the effects of therapeutically induced affect arousal among rheumatoid arthritis patients, Beutler et al. (1987) found that focused expressive treatments activated the beta-endorphin system, particularly during the early and late phases of treatment, and reduced depressive symptoms. The beta-endorphin response was not, however, correlated with subjective pain or depression.

In a further study Mohr, Shoham-Salomon, Engle, and Beutler (in press) found that high levels of expressed anger in sessions were associated with session success, supporting the use of expressive methods. A comparative outcome study of the use of Focused Expressive Psychotherapy (FEP), demonstrating that it was equally effective as a cognitive-behavioral and a support plus bibliotherapy treatment, was described earlier in this review. Although further research is needed, the use of the expressive empty-chair method appears promising, at least for depression and resolution of lingering bad feelings toward a significant other.

Therapist Processing Proposals for the Explication of Meaning

Sachse and Maus (Sachse, 1988, 1990a, 1990b, 1991a, 1991b; Sachse & Maus, 1987, 1991) suggested that key events in client-centered therapy involve clients explicating relevant parts of their meaning structures by putting forward self-relevant questions that describe, define, and finally clarify a problem involving the client's feelings and felt meanings. They proposed eight different modes of client processing as well as the therapist interventions (processing proposals) to best facilitate each mode.

These modes, which involve the client raising different types of questions about internal experience and producing answers, constitute a model of the steps toward the explication of meaning. The process starts at step 1 with no relevant question and therefore no processing of relevant content and proceeds through questions and answers, which at step 2 are intellectualized; at step 3, report the content of a situation; at step 4, evaluate this content; at step 5, involve personally assessing the content; at step 6, result in generating personal meaning; at step 7, involve explicating and verbalizing relevant structures of meaning that are recognized as belonging to the self; and, finally, at step 8, result in an integration and the raising of connections with other aspects of meaning.

The assumption guiding this research program is that the client's processing can be directed by differential processing proposals, which affect not only the client's conscious verbalizations, but also the client's automatic memory processes. In an innovative research program, Sachse (1987) studied the effects of therapist processing proposals (PP) on the client's processing modes (PM) across different types of content references from the material of 60 clients in therapy.

Using sequential analysis, he showed that deepening proposals led to significantly deeper modes of processing, whereas constant level and flattening proposals led to constant and lowered processing modes. This finding demonstrated the overall directing effect of therapist processing proposals on the client's explication of meaning. In addition, Sachse (1991a) showed that when a therapist referred to a peripheral content or a content mentioned earlier by the client, the directing effect was still significant; when the therapist referred to core or important aspects of the client's message, the directing effect became more pronounced; but when the therapist misunderstood the client, there was only a weak directing effect. He also found that a deepening of the processing mode occurred significantly more often when the therapist offered deepening proposals.

This study thus indicates that therapist processing proposals have a significant effect on the client's explication process, that this effect depends on the quality of the therapist's empathic understanding, and that reference to what is central in the client's message is the best possible way to advance the process of explication. These results suggest that understanding at a purely interchangeable level is generally not enough for the explication of meaning.

In a further sequential analysis of how different characteristics of therapist statements affect the client's explication process, Sachse (1991a) studied 80 client-centered therapies. He found that if therapists express their statements clearly and succinctly, explicate what they mean, and utilize meaning constructions of medium complexity, there is a good chance that clients will utilize the therapist's processing proposals. This research also demonstrated that deepening the explication process becomes more difficult as clients go deeper in their processing and that deeper levels of processing are vulnerable to being reduced by inadequate therapist responses. The deeper the client works, the more the explication is affected by the therapist's proposals.

This research program has clearly demonstrated that therapists' moment-by-moment actions in therapy, and how they perform these actions, have decisive effects on the type of processing in which clients engage. Thus therapists' actions in client-centered therapy have a distinctly process-directive effect, and their specific actions, over and above their attitudes of empathy, unconditional positive regard, and genuineness, are decisive determiners of how clients process in therapy. The activities of client-centered therapists are not restricted to understanding alone but also exert an influence on clients' manner and type of processing. Thus, empathic understanding and responding are not sufficient to produce optimal effects on client processing; in addition, processing proposals are needed to explicate meaning. Sachse (1990b) argued that these results support a view of an action-oriented client-centered therapy in which processing aims are of great significance.

A similar approach was taken by Toukmanian (1986, 1990, 1992), who maintains that the central process of therapy involves clients learning to modify the manner with which they construe their experiences of self and self-relevant events in their environment in response to interventions that engage them in different kinds of information-processing operations. In her schematic developmental model of the client's perceptual functioning in psychotherapy, Toukmanian (1992) argued that this process entails the elaboration and development of the structural and operational components of the client's perceptual processing system. According to this perspective, a significant event in therapy is characterized by client construals that are formulated through a predominantly consciously controlled mode of processing wherein qualitatively different kinds of mental operations process information at a number of deeper or more complex semantic associative levels of analysis. According to Toukmanian, it is through this mode of processing that simple schemata develop into more complex networks of meaning structures, resulting in fundamental changes in the client's perception of a given experience.

The interaction between structure and mode of processing in this approach is operationalized by the levels of client perceptual processing (Toukmanian, 1986). This seven-part category system is used to code clients' statements and evaluate their level of perceptual functioning in a segment or session of therapy. Each category depicts a particular pattern of client processing (moving from shallow to deeper levels): undifferentiated statement; elaboration; externally focused differentiation; differentiation with analytic focus; internally focused differentiation; evaluation; and integration. Coding entails looking at configurations of factors including: (1) whether the mode of processing is automated or controlled, (2) what kind of mental operation is featured most prominently in the process, and (3) whether the source of information being dealt with is external or internal to the client. Studies using this measure have shown that in later therapy sessions clients process their experiences at a more complex, internally differentiating, reevaluating, and integrating level than they do in earlier sessions (Toukmanian, 1986; Zink, 1990). It has also been shown that clients who gain more from treatment are more likely to engage in these complex mental operations than those for whom ther-

apy is less successful (Toukmanian & Grech, 1991).

Creation of Meaning in Emotional Crises

Consistent with the interests of existential therapists, meaning-creation events occur when a patient seeks to understand the meaning of an emotional experience or crisis (Clarke, 1989, 1990). This task involves the linguistic symbolization of emotional experience when high emotional arousal is present. Following a task analytic procedure for studying change events, Clarke (1989) defined the marker for meaning-creation events as containing three indicators: the presence of strong emotional arousal (positive or negative emotion); an indication of a confronted or challenged cherished belief; and an indication of confusion, surprise, or lack of understanding. These often involve loss, disappointments, or other life crises.

The therapist intervention that facilitates construction of meaning at these points was empirically derived, yielding the following cluster of optimal meaning symbolization interventions: use of metaphor; condensation of feelings into words and symbols; synthesizing the relationship between thoughts and feelings; symbolizing the discrepancy between the cherished belief and the experience; and symbolizing the emotional reaction to this discrepancy.

An analogue study (Clarke, 1989) of this process contrasted the effects of the focused use of meaning symbolization interventions with ordinary empathic reflection in meaning crisis ("creation of meaning events"). As hypothesized, meaning symbolization led to deeper levels of experiencing, more focused voice, greater reduction in discomfort, and more positive inner feeling and clarity than did empathic reflection. However, the treatments did not produce significantly different results on the ratio of positive to negative thoughts.

Clark (1989) then used task analysis to construct a performance model of the path to resolution. This model consisted of three phases: first, *specification*, involving emotional arousal, statement of the discrepant experience, symbolization of the cherished belief, and the emotional reaction to the challenge; second, *exploration*, consisting of an explanatory proposition, a hypothesis as to the origin of the cherished belief, and the evaluation of the tenability of the belief; third, *revision*, involving the alteration of the belief and specifying the nature of the change and plans for new behavior.

Clarke (1991) evaluated some of the performance patterns in successful and unsuccessful meaning-creation events. Empirical validation confirmed that four specific component processes distinguish between successful and unsuccessful meaning-making events. These processes involve the exact symbolization of both the cherished belief and the client's emotional reaction, as well as the generation of a hypothesis about the origin of the belief and the evaluation of the present tenability of the cherished belief. These components were measured using client experiencing, client vocal quality, and referential activity (Bucci, 1985). Therapist referential activity was found to be significantly higher than client referential activity at the moment of meaning making in successful events and not so in unsuccessful events, supporting the idea that therapists help by providing symbols that link perceptual and verbal domains. Although in its early stages and based on therapy analogue studies, this task appears promising.

Confrontation in Client-Centered Therapy

Tscheulin (1990, 1992) investigated the optimal conditions for constructive confrontation in client-centered therapy. Confrontation is defined as an experience-activating technique in which the therapist picks up discrepant messages from the client. In this view, when a therapist confronts, he or she offers the client a perception that differs from the client's own perception. Confrontation offered in an empathic relational context is viewed as an extension of advanced accurate empathy.

Tscheulin (1983a) compared a set of 10 successful therapies with both extremely outer-directed, action-oriented clients and inner-directed, self-focused clients. He found that the therapies of the action-oriented clients lasted four times longer and that during sessions with these clients, therapists confronted them about four times as much. In an experimental design exploring the best conditions for confrontations (Tscheulin, 1983b), clients of each type (action oriented or self-focused) were assigned to confrontation or nonconfrontation treatment conditions. As predicted, the clients in the matched conditions (confrontation of action-oriented clients and nonconfrontation of self-focused clients) experienced significantly greater positive change and more helpful interactions with their therapists.

This study was later replicated (Tscheulin, 1988) and a six-category system of different types of discrepancies in client statements was constructed and found to discriminate different types of client statements used by therapists as markers for confrontation. These categories are: (1) client contradictions between communications (e.g., verbal vs. nonverbal; present vs. earlier statements); (2) limitations in client statements; (3) the search for reasons and explanations (i.e., intellectualizing); (4) description

of problems being beyond one's control; (5) generalizations; and (6) other statements.

RESEARCH AND TREATMENT RECOMMENDATIONS

Research Recommendations

1. *More research.* Our most important recommendation is a call for more research on experiential and related humanistic therapies in general and with clinical populations. Very little research on these treatments has been done in North America in the past decade, and what has been done has been carried out with virtually no external funding. This situation suggests that experiential methods are often used in treatment without sufficient research to fully understand their most effective application is urgently needed.

2. *Methodological pluralism.* We support the use of a wide range of types of research on experiential-humanistic treatments, including research on outcome, process (qualitative and quantitative), process–outcome associations, helpful factors, and task events (discovery oriented, sequential analysis, and verification oriented). A pluralistic approach to research methodology is essential for advancing our knowledge of these therapies.

We applaud the development of new, empirical research procedures more able to capture the meaning of what occurs in therapy and participants' complex views of their experience, particularly as these provide an opportunity for more phenomenologically oriented human-science researchers to contribute to the investigation of experiential therapies (e.g., Seeman, 1989; Toukmanian & Rennie, 1992).

3. *Improved quality of outcome research.* Researchers in the experiential tradition have generally concentrated on process research and on populations with general self-esteem or interpersonal problems, rather than on populations with specific disorders. For political and economic as well as for scientific reasons, it is now important to invest more energy in assessing treatment outcome for specific populations and disorders. Researchers should also develop more sensitive outcome measures for theoretically important change processes and forms of experience and action (e.g., changes in views of self and others; resolution of particular emotional problems). In addition to the study of treatment effects at termination and follow-up, we recommend the study of outcome effects throughout the course of treatment. The development and

study of postsession and intersession effects and the investigation of the relationship of these effects to outcome at termination and follow-up are particularly important. In addition researchers should not confuse nondirective control groups with client-centered therapy. It would be more productive, for example, for cognitive-behavioral and experiential researchers to collaborate in the design and conduct of comparative research on specific disorders.

4. *Continued study of change events.* The initial demonstrations of treatment efficacy documented here provide additional justification for further research on traditional topics, such as what active ingredients operate in the treatment and which clients change and which don't. Furthermore, continued research on particular task interventions seems likely to result in clinical payoffs. We advocate more research in which researchers first specify therapeutic tasks and their components, then identify episodes in which they are carried out, and finally describe them intensively using both observational and phenomenological methods. With the development of postsession measures as described, the in-session processes can then be related to postsession effects.

5. *Study of experiential change processes.* This review clearly suggests that the relational conditions or the facilitative working environment is only one factor in experiential therapy. Numerous other client and therapist processes facilitate change. Research on the relational conditions alone in the period prior to this review tended to restrict research on other important experiential change processes. More precise, fine-grained studies of the psychotherapeutic process, both of client in-session performance and client subjective experience, will greatly help illuminate how change occurs in experiential therapy (cf. Watson, 1992).

6. *Research on the role of empathy and emotion.* Investigators should reapply themselves to the investigation of empathy in a more complex and differentiated fashion, perhaps investigating the phenomena of empathy with central aspects of the client's message (e.g., Sachse, 1991a), process empathy or moment-by-moment following of client experiences (e.g., Goldman, 1991), empathic prizing (Rice & Greenberg, 1991), and the varieties of received empathy identified by Bachelor (1988). With evident advances in our understanding of behavior and cognition, there is a deficit in research on emotional processes in therapeutic change (Greenberg & Safran, 1987, 1989). Questions such as when and with whom is it helpful to stimulate, acknowledge, and regulate affect in treatment need to be addressed, as well as how each of these processes helps. Investigation of client experience

of empathy and emotion could shed light on these important aspects of experiential therapy.

7. *Research on individual differences.* (a) More research is needed to help understand the nature, strength, and generality of the apparent interaction between treatment directiveness, client high versus low reactance, and treatment focus and client internal–external coping style (cf. Beutler, Engle et al., 1991). (b) Research on other prognostic factors such as first session vocal quality or depth of experience would enhance client selection for experiential treatments. More research is needed on the integration or supplementation of experiential methods with nonexperiential methods, such as desensitization (cf. Tausch, 1990) and the use of homework and practice; with whom is this most helpful and what are the advantages, dangers, and optimal circumstances for such supplementation?

Treatment Recommendations

1. *Utility of experiential therapies.* Experiential therapies show some effects across a range of disorders and treatment varieties; as well as being effective for the "worried well," they should not be dismissed as possible treatments for disorders such as depression and anxiety, and, under certain circumstances, for more severe or chronic problems (e.g., personality disorders, schizophrenia).

2. *Hindering factors.* Therapists should be sensitive to the occurrence of client deference (Rennie, 1990) and the typical hindering factors noted in this review, including client concerns such as lack of perceived safety, confusion or distraction, therapist misattunement, insufficient therapist direction, and, most importantly, therapist intrusiveness or pressure. This list of factors may be useful for guiding training and supervision.

3. *Adaptation of treatments to clients.* Probably the most obvious trend that emerges from this review is the shift away from the practice of offering a uniform treatment to all clients and toward adapting experiential treatments to specific disorders or problems (e.g., depression, panic, decision making). Treatments can be adapted by varying parameters, such as therapist process directiveness, or applying different aspects or tasks of treatments to different clients and in different situations. For example, therapists should be sensitive to the possibility that clients high in autonomy or reactance may react negatively to the effects of the more process-directive experiential therapies (e.g., Gestalt), whereas more dependent or externally oriented clients may react negatively to nondirective therapies. One possibility is to provide a balance of

directive and nondirective elements individualized for each client.

4. *Task interventions*. Even more fundamental than adapting treatment is the use of particular task interventions at particular points in treatment (e.g., evocative unfolding). Research on task interventions suggests the need for a much more differentiated formulation of experiential therapy as a process in which client and therapist both engage in a variety of activities at different points. Processing proposals (cf. Sachse, 1992) are made by the therapist with differential effects on the client, who then engages in the optimal mode of processing for that particular moment. Therapists and clients can thus benefit from what is known about the specific task interventions reviewed here, including focusing, evocative unfolding, two-chair and empty-chair work, and the explication and creation of meaning. Each intervention provides a working microtheory of an important therapeutic process, including marker, client steps, and accompanying therapist interventions for helping clients reach resolution.

REFERENCES

Adler, J. (1988). *The client's perception of the working alliance*. Unpublished doctoral dissertation, University of British Columbia, Vancouver, Canada.

Angus, L. E., & Rennie, D. L. (1988). Therapist participation in metaphor generation: Collaboration and noncollaborative styles. *Psychotherapy, 26*, 552–560.

Angus, L. E., & Rennie, D. L. (1989). Envisioning the representational world: The client's experience of metaphoric expression in psychotherapy. *Psychotherapy, 26*, 372–379.

Bachelor, A. (1988). How clients perceive therapist empathy: A content analysis of "received" empathy. *Psychotherapy, 25*, 227–240.

Barkham, M., & Shapiro, D. A. (1986). Counselor verbal response modes and experienced empathy. *Journal of Counseling Psychology, 33*, 3–10.

Barrett-Lennard, G. T. (1981). The empathy cycle: Refinement of a nuclear concept. *Journal of Counseling Psychology, 28*, 91–100.

Barrett-Lennard, G. T. (1986). The Relationship Inventory now: Issues and advances in theory, method, and use. In L. Greenberg & W. Pinsof (Eds.), *The psychotherapeutic process* (pp. 439–476). New York: Guilford.

Basch, M. (1983). Empathic understanding: A review of the concept and some theoretical considerations. *Journal of the American Psychoanalytic Association, 31*, 101–126.

Beutler, L. E., Daldrup, R. J., Engle, D., Guest, P., Corbishley, A., & Meredith, K. (1988). Family dynamics and emotional expression among patients with chronic pain and depression. *Pain, 32*, 65–72.

Beutler, L. E., Daldrup, R. J., Engle, D., Oro'-Beutler, M. E., Meredith, K., & Boyer, J. T. (1987). Effects of therapeutically induced affect arousal on depressive symptoms, pain and beta-endorphins among rheumatoid arthritis patients. *Pain, 29*, 325–334.

Beutler, L. E., Engle, D., Mohr, D., Daldrup, R. J., Bergan, ential response to cognitive, experiential, and self-directed psychotherapeutic procedures. *Journal of Consulting and Clinical Psychology, 59*, 333–340.

Beutler, L. E., Frank, M., Schieber, S. C., Calver, S., & Gaines, J. (1984). Comparative effects of group psychotherapies in a short-term inpatient setting: An experience with deterioration effects. *Psychiatry, 47*, 66–76.

Beutler, L. E., Machado, P. P. P., & Engle, D. (1993). *Differential maintenance of treatment effects among cognitive, experiential, and self-directed psychotherapeutic procedures*. Unpublished manuscript, University of California, Santa Barbara.

Beutler, L. E., & Mitchell, R. (1981). Differential psychotherapy outcome among depressed and impulsive patients as a function of analytic and experiential treatment procedures. *Psychiatry, 44*, 297–306.

Beutler, L. E., Mohr, D. C., Grawe, K., Engle, D., & MacDonald, R. (in press). Looking for differential treatment effects: Cross-cultural predictors of differential psychotherapy efficacy. *Journal of Psychotherapy Integration*.

Bierenbaum, H., Nichols, M. P., & Schwartz, A. J. (1976). Effects of varying session length and frequency in brief emotive psychotherapy. *Journal of Consulting and Clinical Psychology, 44*, 790–798.

Bohart, A. C. (1988). Empathy: Client-centered and psychoanalytic. *American Psychologist, 43*, 667–668.

Bohart, A. C. (1990). Psychotherapy integration from a client-centered perspective. In G. Lietaer, J. Rombauts, & R. Van Balen (Eds.), *Client-centered and experiential psychotherapy in the nineties* (pp. 481–500). Leuven, Belgium: Leuven University Press.

Bohart, A. C. (1991a). Empathy in client-centered therapy. *Journal of Humanistic Psychology, 31*, 34–48.

Borkovec, T. D. (1991). *Progress report*. Unpublished grant proposal, Pennsylvania State University, University Park, PA.

Borkovec, T. D., & Mathews, A. (1988). Treatment of nonphobic anxiety disorders: A comparison of nondirective, cognitive, and coping desensitization therapy. *Journal of Consulting and Clinical Psychology, 56*, 877–884.

Borkovec, T. D., Mathews, A. M., Chambers, A., Ebrahimi, S., Lytle, R., & Nelson, R. (1987). The effects of relaxation training with cognitive or nondirective therapy and the role of relaxation-induced anxiety in the treatment of generalized anxiety. *Journal of Consulting and Clinical Psychology, 55*, 883–888.

Bouchard, M. -A., Lecomte, C., Carbonneau, H., & Lalonde, F. (1987). Inferential communications of expert psychoanalytically oriented, gestalt and behavior therapists. *Canadian Journal of Behavioral Sciences, 19*, 275–286.

Boulet, D. B., Souliere, M. D., & Sterner, I. (in press). Development of a category system of good moments in Gestalt therapy. *Psychotherapy*.

Bozarth, J. D. (1988, August). *The evolution of Carl Rogers as a therapist*. Paper presented at general meeting of the American Psychological Association, Atlanta.

Bozarth, J. D. (1990). The essence of client-centered therapy. In G. Lietaer, J. Rombauts, & R. Van Balen (Eds.), *Client-centered and experiential psychotherapy in the nineties* (pp. 59–64). Leuven, Belgium: Leuven University Press.

Braaten, L. J. (1989). The effects of person-centered group therapy. *Person-Centered Review, 4*, 183–209.

Brinkerhoff, L. J. (1991). *Application of the core conflictual relationship method to an analysis of significant events in an experiential therapy of depression*. Unpublished doctoral dissertation, University of Toledo, OH.

Brodley, B. T. (1990). Client-centered and experiential: Two different therapies. In G. Lietaer, J. Rombauts, & R. Van Balen (Eds.), *Client-centered and experiential psychother-*

apy in the nineties (pp. 87–107). Leuven, Belgium: Leuven University Press.

Brodley, B. T., & Brody, A. F. (1990, August). *Understanding client-centered therapy through interviews conducted by Carl Rogers.* Paper presented at the annual meeting of the American Psychological Association, Boston.

Brunink, S. A., & Schroeder, H. E. (1979). Verbal therapeutic behavior of expert psychoanalytically oriented, Gestalt, and behavior therapists. *Journal of Consulting and Clinical Psychology, 47,* 567–574.

Bucci, W. (1985). Dual coding: A cognitive model for psychoanalytic research. *Journal of the American Psychoanalytic Association, 33,* 571–607.

Bugental, J. F. T. (1978). *Psychotherapy and process: The fundamentals of an existential-humanistic approach.* New York: Random House.

Clark, C. A. (1990). *A comprehensive process analysis of focusing events in experiential therapy.* Unpublished doctoral dissertation, University of Toledo, OH.

Clarke, K. M. (1989). Creation of meaning: An emotional processing task in psychotherapy. *Psychotherapy, 26,* 139–148.

Clarke, K. M. (1990, June). *Task analysis of a meaning-making event.* Paper presented at the Society for Psychotherapy Research, Wintergreen, VA.

Clarke, K. M. (1991). A performance model of the creation of meaning event. *Psychotherapy, 28,* 395–401.

Clarke, K. M., & Greenberg, L. S. (1986). Differential effects of the Gestalt two-chair intervention and problem solving in resolving decisional conflict. *Journal of Counseling Psychology, 33,* 11–15.

Cohen, J. (1988). *Statistical power analysis for the behavioral sciences* (2nd ed). Hillsdale, NJ: Lawrence Erlbaum.

Corbishley, A. (in press). Behavior, affect and cognition among psychogenic pain patients in group expressive psychotherapy. *Journal of Pain Symptom Management.*

Cramer, D. (1990). The necessary conditions for evaluating client-centered therapy. In G. Lietaer, J. Rombauts, & R. Van Balen (Eds.), *Client-centered and experiential psychotherapy in the nineties* (pp. 415–428). Leuven, Belgium: Leuven University Press.

Cross, D. G., Sheehan, P. W., & Khan, J. A. (1982). Short- and long-term follow-up of clients receiving insight-oriented therapy and behavior therapy. *Journal of Consulting and Clinical Psychology, 50,* 103–112.

Cummings, A. L., Martin, J., Hallberg, E., & Slemon, A. (1992). Memory for therapeutic events, session effectiveness, and working alliance in short-term counseling. *Journal of Counseling Psychology, 39,* 306–312.

Dahl, A. A., & Waal, H. (1983). An outcome study of primal therapy. *Psychotherapy and Psychosomatics, 39,* 1554–1564.

Daldrup, R., Beutler, L., Greenberg, L., & Engle, D. (1988). *Focused expressive therapy: A treatment for constricted affect.* New York: Guilford.

Dandeneau, M., & Johnson, S. (in press). Facilitating intimacy: Interventions and effects. *Journal of Marital and Family Therapy.*

Dierick, P., & Lietaer, G. (1990). Member and therapist perceptions of therapeutic factors in therapy and growth groups: Comments on a category system. In G. Lietaer, J. Rombauts, & R. Van Balen (Eds.), *Client-centered and experiential psychotherapy in the nineties* (pp. 741–770). Leuven, Belgium: Leuven University Press.

Dircks, P., Grimm, F., Tausch, A., & Wittern, O. (1982). Förderung der seelischen Lebensqualität von Krebspatienten durch personenzentrierte Gruppengespräche. *Zeitschrift für Klinische Psychologie, 9,* 241–251.

D'Zurilla, T. J., & Goldfried, M. R. (1971). Problem solving and behavior modification. *Journal of Abnormal Psychology, 78,* 107–126.

Eckert, J., & Biermann-Ratjen, E. -M. (1985). *Stationäre Gruppenpsychotherapie: Prozesse, Effekte, Vergleiche.* Berlin: Springer.

Eckert, J., & Biermann-Ratjen, E. -M. (1990). Client-centered therapy versus psychoanalytic psychotherapy. Reflections following a comparative study. In G. Lietaer, J. Rombauts, & R. Van Balen (Eds.), *Client-centered and experiential psychotherapy in the nineties* (pp. 457–468). Leuven, Belgium: Leuven University Press.

Edwards, H. P., Boulet, D. B., Mahrer, A. R., Chagnon, G. J., & Mook, B. (1982). *Journal of Counseling Psychology, 29,* 14–18.

Elliott, R. (1983). Fitting process research to the practicing psychotherapist. *Psychotherapy: Theory, Research & Practice, 20,* 47–55.

Elliott, R. (1985). Helpful and nonhelpful events in brief counseling interviews: An empirical taxonomy. *Journal of Counseling Psychology, 32,* 307–322.

Elliott, R. (1989). Comprehensive Process Analysis: Understanding the change process in significant therapy events. In M. Packer & R. B. Addison (Eds.), *Entering the circle: Hermeneutic investigation in psychology* (pp. 165–184). Albany, NY: SUNY Press.

Elliott, R., Clark, C., & Kemeny, V. (1991, July). *Analyzing clients' postsession accounts of significant therapy events.* Paper presented at the Society for Psychotherapy Research, Lyon, France.

Elliott, R., Clark, C., Wexler, M., Kemeny, V., Brinkerhoff, J., & Mack, C. (1990). The impact of experiential therapy of depression: Initial results. In G. Lietaer, J. Rombauts, & R. Van Balen (Eds.), *Client-centered and experiential psychotherapy in the nineties* (pp. 549–577). Leuven, Belgium: Leuven University Press.

Elliott, R., Filipovich, H., Harrigan, L., Gaynor, J., Reimschuessel, C., & Zapadka, J. K. (1982). Measuring response empathy: The development of a multi-component rating scale. *Journal of Counseling Psychology, 29,* 379–387.

Elliott, R., Hill, C. E., Stiles, W. B., Friedlander, M. L., Mahrer, A., & Margison, F. (1987). Primary therapist response modes: A comparison of six rating systems. *Journal of Consulting and Clinical Psychology, 55,* 218–223.

Elliott, R., & James, E. (1989). Varieties of client experience in psychotherapy: An analysis of the literature. *Clinical Psychology Review, 9,* 443–467.

Elliott, R., James, E., Reimschuessel, C., Cislo, D., & Sack, N. (1985). Significant events and the analysis of immediate therapeutic impacts. *Psychotherapy, 22,* 620–630.

Elliott, R., Stiles, W. B., & Shapiro, D. A. (in press). Are some psychotherapies more equivalent than others? In T. R. Giles (Ed.), *Handbook of effective psychotherapy.* New York: Plenum.

Elliott, R., & Wexler, M. M. (1992, June). *Measuring the impact of therapy sessions: The Session Impacts Questionnaire.* Paper presented at the meeting of the Society for Psychotherapy Research, Berkeley, CA.

Eymael, J. (1987). *Gedragstherapie en client-centered therapie vergeleken* [Behavior therapy and client-centered therapy compared]. Leuven, Belgium: Acco.

Foerster, F. S. (1991). *Refinement and verification of a model of the resolution of unfinished business.* Unpublished master's thesis, York University, Toronto.

Gendlin, E. T. (1981). *Focusing* (2nd ed.). New York: Bantam Books.

Gendlin, E. T. (1984). The client's client: The edge of awareness. In F. R. Levant & J. M. Shlien (Eds.), *Client-centered therapy and the person-centered approach: New directions in theory, research and practice* (pp. 76–107). New York: Praeger.

Gendlin, E. T. (1986). What comes after traditional psychotherapy research? *American Psychologist, 41,* 131–136.

Gendlin, E. T. (1990). The small steps of the therapy process: How they come and how to help them come. In G. Lietaer, J. Rombauts, & R. Van Balen (Eds.), *Client-centered and experiential psychotherapy in the nineties* (pp. 205–224). Leuven, Belgium: Leuven University Press.

Giles, T. R., Neims, D. M., & Prial, E. M. (in press). The relative efficacy of prescriptive techniques. In T. R. Giles (Ed.), *Handbook of effective psychotherapy.* New York: Plenum.

Gladstein, G. A., & associates (1987). *Empathy and counseling.* New York: Springer-Verlag.

Goldman, A., & Greenberg, L. (1992). Comparison of integrated systemic and emotionally focused approaches to couples therapy. *Journal of Consulting & Clinical Psychology, 60,* 962–969.

Goldman, R. (1991). *The validation of the experiential therapy adherence measure.* Unpublished master's thesis, York University, Toronto.

Gordon Walker, J., Manion, R., Johnson, S., & Cloutier, P. (1992, April 26). *Marital intervention program for couples with chronically ill children.* Paper presented at the West Coast Regional Conference of the Society of Pediatric Psychology, San Francisco.

Grawe, K., Caspar, F., & Ambühl, H. (1990). Differentielle Psychotherapieforschung: Vier Therapieformen im Vergleich. *Zeitschrift für Klinische Psychologie, 19,* 287–376.

Greenberg, L. S. (1975). A task analytic approach to the study of psychotherapeutic events (Doctoral dissertation, York University). *Dissertation Abstracts International, 37,* 4647B.

Greenberg, L. S. (1979). Resolving splits: The two-chair technique. *Psychotherapy: Theory, Research & Practice, 16,* 310–318.

Greenberg, L. S. (1980). An intensive analysis of recurring events from the practice of Gestalt therapy. *Psychotherapy: Theory, Research and Practice, 17,* 143–152.

Greenberg, L. S. (1982). Toward a task analysis of conflict resolution in Gestalt therapy. *Psychotherapy: Theory, Research and Practice, 20,* 190–201.

Greenberg, L. S. (1984). A task analysis of intrapersonal conflict resolution. In L. Rice & L. Greenberg (Eds.), *Patterns of change.* New York: Guilford.

Greenberg, L. S. (1986). Change process research. *Journal of Consulting and Clinical Psychology, 54,* 4–9.

Greenberg, L. S. (1991). Research in the process of change. *Psychotherapy Research, 1,* 14–24.

Greenberg, L. S., & Adler, J. (1989, June). *Clients' perception of the working alliance.* Paper presented at the Society for Psychotherapy Research, Toronto.

Greenberg, L. S., Clarke, D. (1979). The differential effects of the two-chair experiment and empathic reflections at a conflict marker. *Journal of Counseling Psychology, 26,* 1–8.

Greenberg, L. S., & Dompierre, L. (1981). The specific effects of Gestalt two-chair dialogue on intrapsychic conflict in counseling. *Journal of Counseling Psychology, 28,* 288–296.

Greenberg, L. S., Elliott, R., & Foerster, F. (1990). Experiential processes in the psychotherapeutic treatment of depression. In N. Endler & D. C. McCann (Eds.), *Contemporary perspectives on emotion* (pp. 157–185). Toronto: Wall & Emerson.

Greenberg, L. S., & Goldman, R. (1988). Training in exper-

iential psychotherapy. *Journal of Consulting and Clinical Psychology, 56,* 696–702.

Greenberg, L. S., & Higgins, H. (1980). The differential effects of two-chair dialogue and focusing on conflict resolution. *Journal of Counseling Psychology, 27,* 221–225.

Greenberg, L. S., James, P. S., & Conry, R. F. (1988). Perceived change in couples therapy. *Journal of Family Psychology, 2,* 5–23.

Greenberg, L., & Johnson, S. (1987). *Emotionally focused therapy for couples.* New York. Guilford.

Greenberg, L. S., & Pinsof, W. M. (1986). *The psychotherapeutic process: A research handbook.* New York: Guilford.

Greenberg, L. S., & Rice, L. N. (1981). The specific effects of a Gestalt intervention. *Psychotherapy: Theory, Research and Practice, 18,* 31–37.

Greenberg, L. S., & Rice, L. N. (1991). *Change processes in experiential psychotherapy* (NIMH Grant No. 1RO1MH45040). York University.

Greenberg, L. S., Rice, L. N., & Elliott, R. (in press). *Process-experiential therapy: Facilitating emotional change.* New York: Guilford.

Greenberg, L. S., & Safran, J. D. (1987). *Emotion in psychotherapy: Affect, cognition, and the process of change.* New York: Guilford.

Greenberg, L. S., & Safran, J. D. (1989). Emotion in psychotherapy. *American Psychologist, 44,* 19–29.

Greenberg, L. S. & Watson, J. (1993). *The York experiential psychotherapy of depression: preliminary results.* Paper presented at the annual meeting of the Society for Psychotherapy Research, Pittsburgh, PA.

Greenberg, L. S., & Webster, M. (1982). Resolving decisional conflict by means of two-chair dialogue and empathic reflection at a split in counseling. *Journal of Counseling Psychology, 29,* 468–477.

Gurman, A. S. (1977). The patient's perception of the therapeutic relationship. In A. S. Gurman & A. M. Razin (Eds.), *Effective psychotherapy: A handbook of research* (pp. 503–543). New York: Pergamon.

Hill, C. E., Helms, J. E., Spiegel, S. B., & Tichenor, V. (1988). Development of a system for categorizing client reactions to therapist interventions. *Journal of Counseling Psychology, 35,* 27–36.

Hill, C. E., & O'Grady, K. E. (1985). List of therapist intentions illustrated in a case study and with therapists of varying theoretical orientations. *Journal of Counseling Psychology, 32,* 3–22.

Hill, C. E., Thames, T. B., & Rardin, D. K. (1979). Comparison of Rogers, Perls, and Ellis on the Hill Counselor Verbal Response Category System. *Journal of Counseling Psychology, 26,* 198–203.

Hirscheimer, K. (1991). *Integration in psychotherapy: An empirical investigation.* Unpublished thesis, York University, Toronto.

Holstein, B. E. (1990, August). *The use of focusing in combination with a cognitive-behavioral weight loss program.* Paper presented at the annual meeting of American Psychological Association, Boston.

Horton, C., & Elliott, R. (1991, November). *The experiential session form: Initial data.* Paper presented at the annual meeting for the Society for Psychotherapy Research, Panama City, FL.

Horvath, A., & Greenberg, L. S. (1989). Development and validation of the Working Alliance Inventory. *Journal of Counseling Psychology, 36,* 223–233.

Hudgins, M. K., & Kiesler, D. J. (1987). Individual experiential psychotherapy: An analogue validation of the intervention module of psychodramatic doubling. *Psychotherapy, 24,* 245–255.

Iberg, J. R. (1990). Ms. C's focusing and cognitive functions.

In G. Lietaer, J. Rombauts, & R. Van Balen (Eds.), *Client-centered and experiential psychotherapy in the nineties* (pp. 173–203). Leuven, Belgium: Leuven University Press.

Ikemi, A., Kira, Y., Murayama, S., Tamura, R., & Yuba, N. (1986). Rating the process of experiencing: The development of a Japanese version of the experiencing scale. *Japanese Journal of Humanistic Psychology, 4*, 50–64.

Jackson, L., & Elliott, R. (1990, June). *Is experiential therapy effective in treating depression? Initial outcome data.* Paper presented at the annual meeting of Society for Psychotherapy Research, Wintergreen, VA.

Jacobson, N. S., Follette, W. C., & Revenstorf, D. (1984). Psychotherapy outcome research: Methods for reporting variability and evaluating clinical significance. *Behavior Therapy, 15*, 336–352.

Janov, A. (1970). *The primal scream: Primal therapy, the cure for neurosis.* New York: Dell.

Johnson, S. M., & Greenberg, L. S. (1985a). The differential effects of experiential and problem-solving interventions in resolving marital conflict. *Journal of Consulting and Clinical Psychology, 53*, 175–184.

Johnson, S. M., & Greenberg, L. S. (1985b). Emotionally focused marital therapy: An outcome study. *Journal of Marital and Family Therapy, 11*, 313–317.

Katonah, D. G. (1991). *Focusing and cancer: A psychological tool as an adjunct treatment for adaptive recovery.* Unpublished dissertation, Illinois School of Professional Psychology, Chicago.

King, S. (1988). *The differential effects of empty-chair dialogue and empathic reflection for unfinished business.* Unpublished master's thesis, University of British Columbia, Vancouver, Canada.

Klein, M. H., Mathieu-Coughlan, P., & Kiesler, D. J. (1986). The Experiencing Scales. In L. Greenberg & W. Pinsof (Eds.), *The psychotherapeutic process* (pp. 21–71). New York: Guilford.

Kohut, H. (1982). Introspection, empathy, and the semi-circle of mental health. *International Journal of Psychoanalysis, 63*, 395–407.

Kurtz, R. R., & Grummon, D. L. (1972). Different approaches to the measurement of therapist empathy and their relationship to therapy outcome. *Journal of Consulting and Clinical Psychology, 39*, 106–115.

Labott, S., Elliott, R., & Eason, P. (1992). "If you love someone, you don't hurt them": A comprehensive process analysis of a weeping event in psychotherapy. *Psychiatry, 55*, 49–62.

Lambert, M. J., DeJulio, S. S., & Stein, D. M. (1978). Therapist interpersonal skills: Process, outcome, methodological considerations, and recommendations for future research. *Psychological Bulletin, 85*, 467–489.

Lambert, M. J., Hatch, D. R., Kingston, M. D., & Edwards, B. C. (1986). Zung, Beck, and Hamilton rating scales as measures of treatment outcome: A meta-analytic comparison. *Journal of Consulting and Clinical Psychology, 54*, 54–59.

Larson, D. (1980). Therapeutic schools, styles, and schoolism: A national survey. *Journal of Humanistic Psychology, 20*, 3–20.

Lee, D. Y., & Uhlemann, M. R. (1984). Comparison of verbal responses of Rogers, Shostrom, and Lazarus. *Journal of Counseling Psychology, 31*, 91–94.

Leijssen, M. (1990). On focusing and the necessary conditions of therapeutic personality change. In G. Lietaer, J. Rombauts, & R. Van Balen (Eds.), *Client-centered and experiential psychotherapy in the nineties* (pp. 225–250). Leuven, Belgium: Leuven University Press.

Leijssen, M. (1991, July). *Teaching focusing to "unsuccessful" clients. Research project in progress.* Paper presented

at the Second Conference on Client-Centered and Experiential Therapy, Stirling, Scotland.

Lerner, M. S., & Clum, G. A. (1990). Treatment of suicide ideators: A problem-solving approach. *Behavior Therapy, 21*, 403–411.

Lietaer, G. (1979). The relationship as experienced by client and therapist in client-centered and psychoanalytically oriented therapy: An empirical contribution. *Tijdschrift voor Psychotherapie, 3*, 141–160.

Lietaer, G. (1989). The working alliance in client-centered therapy. Reflections on findings with post-session questionnaires. In H. Vertommen, G. Cluckers, & G. Lietaer (Eds.), *De relatie in therapie* [The relationship in therapy] (pp. 207–235). Leuven, Belgium: Leuven University Press.

Lietaer, G. (1990). The client-centered approach after the Wisconsin Project: A personal view on its evolution. In G. Lietaer, J. Rombauts, & R. Van Balen (Eds.), *Client-centered and experiential psychotherapy in the nineties* (pp. 19–45). Leuven, Belgium: Leuven University Press.

Lietaer, G. (1992). Helping and hindering processes in client-centered/experiential psychotherapy: A content analysis of client and therapist post-session perceptions. In S. G. Toukmanian & D. L. Rennie (Eds.), *Psychotherapy process research: Theory-guided and phenomenological research strategies.* Beverly Hills, CA: Sage Publications.

Lietaer, G., Dierick, P., & Neirinck, M. (1985). Inhoud en proces in experiëntiële psychotherapie: Een empirische exploratie [Content and process in experiential psychotherapy: An empirical exploration]. *Psychologica Belgica, 25*, 127–147.

Lietaer, G., & Neirinck, M. (1986). Client and therapist perceptions of helping processes in client-centered/experiential psychotherapy. *Person-Centered Review, 1*, 436–455.

Lietaer, G., Rombauts, J., & Van Balen, R. (Eds.). (1990). *Client-centered and experiential psychotherapy in the nineties.* Leuven, Belgium: Leuven University Press.

Lowenstein, J. (1985). *A test of a performance model of problematic reactions: An examination of differential client performances in therapy.* Unpublished thesis, York University, Toronto.

Luborsky, L., Singer, B., & Luborsky, L. (1975). Comparative studies of psychotherapies: Is it true that "Everyone has won and all must have prizes"? *Archives of General Psychiatry, 32*, 995–1006.

Mahrer, A. R. (1983). *Experiential psychotherapy: Basic practices.* New York: Brunner/Mazel.

Mahrer, A. R. (1986). *Therapeutic experiencing: The process of change.* New York: W. W. Norton.

Mahrer, A. R. (1988). Discovery-oriented psychotherapy research. *American Psychologist, 43*, 694–702.

Mahrer, A. R. (1989). *How to do experiential psychotherapy: A manual for practitioners.* Ottawa, Canada: University of Ottawa Press.

Mahrer, A. R., Boulet, D. B., & Stalikas, A. (1987). Comparative analysis of the "good moments" in rational-emotive and experiential psychotherapies. *Psychological Reports, 61*, 284.

Mahrer, A. R., Dessaulles, A., Nadler, W. P., Gervaize, P. A., & Sterner, I. (1987). Good and very good moments in psychotherapy: Content, distribution, and facilitation. *Psychotherapy, 24*, 7–14.

Mahrer, A. R., & Nadler, W. P. (1986). Good moments in psychotherapy: A preliminary review, a list, and some promising research avenues. *Journal of Consulting and Clinical Psychology, 54*, 10–15.

Mancinelli, B. (1992). *A grounded theory analysis of helpful factors in experiential therapy of depression.* Unpublished master's thesis, University of Toledo, OH.

Martin, J. (1991). The social-cognitive construction of therapeutic change: A dual coding analysis. *Journal of Social and Clinical Psychology, 10,* 305–321.

Martin, J. (1992). Cognitive-mediational research on counseling and psychotherapy. In S. Toukmanian & D. Rennie (Eds.), *Psychotherapy process research: Paradigmatic and narrative approaches* (pp. 108–133). Newbury Park, CA: Sage Publications.

Martin, J., Paivio, S., & Labadie, D. (1990). Memory-enhancing characteristics of client-recalled important events in cognitive and experiential therapy: Integrating cognitive and experimental and therapeutic psychology. *Counseling Psychology Quarterly, 3,* 239–256.

Maslove, V. J. (1989). *The differential effects of empathic reflection and the Gestalt empty-chair dialogue on depth of experiencing when used with an issue of unfinished business.* Unpublished master's thesis, University of British Columbia, Vancouver, Canada.

Meara, N. M., Pepinsky, H. B., Shannon, J. W., & Murray, W. A. (1981). Semantic communication and expectations for counseling across three theoretical orientations. *Journal of Counseling Psychology, 28,* 110–118.

Meyer, A. E. (Ed.). (1981). The Hamburg Short Psychotherapy Comparison Experiment. *Psychotherapy and Psychosomatics, 35,* 81–207.

Meyer, A. E., Stuhr, U., Wirth, U., & Ruester, P. (1988). 12-year follow-up study of the Hamburg short psychotherapy experiment: An overview. *Psychotherapy and Psychosomatics, 50,* 192–200.

Mitchell, K. M., Bozarth, J. D., & Krauft, C. C. (1977). A reappraisal of the therapeutic effectiveness of accurate empathy, nonpossessive warmth, and genuineness. In A. S. Gurman & A. M. Razin (Eds.), *Effective psychotherapy: A handbook of research* (pp. 482–502). New York: Pergamon.

Mohr, D. C., Shoham-Salomon, V., Engle, D., & Beutler, L. E. (in press). The expression of anger in psychotherapy for depression: Its role and measurement. *Psychotherapy Research.*

Nakata, Y., & Murayama, S. (1986). Handle-giving technique to get a felt sense. *Research Bulletin of Educational Psychology, Faculty of Education, Kyushu University, 31,* 65–72.

Nichols, M. P. (1974). Outcome of brief cathartic psychotherapy. *Journal of Consulting and Clinical Psychology, 42,* 403–410.

Nichols, M. P., & Bierenbaum, H. (1978). Success of cathartic therapy as a function of patient variables. *Journal of Clinical Psychology, 34,* 726–728.

O'Dell, J. W., & Bahmer, A. J. (1981). Rogers, Lazarus, and Shostrom in content analysis. *Journal of Clinical Psychology, 37,* 507–510.

Oishi, E., & Murayama, S. (1989). A study on "experiential words" of the focuser: Discussions on what determines the meaning of focusing. *Research Bulletin of Educational Psychology, Faculty of Education, Kyushu University, 34,* 181–188.

Orlinsky, D. E., & Howard, K. I. (1986). The relation of process to outcome in psychotherapy. In S. L. Garfield & A. E. Bergin (Eds.), *Handbook of psychotherapy and behavior change* (3rd ed., pp. 311–381). New York: Wiley.

Paivio, S., & Greenberg, L. S. (1992). *Resolving unfinished business: A study of effects.* Paper presented at the annual meeting of the Society for Psychotherapy Research, Berkeley, CA.

Parloff, M., Waskow, I. E., & Wolfe, B. E. (1978). Research on therapist variables in relation to process and outcome. In S. L. Garfield & A. E. Bergin (Eds.), *Handbook of psychotherapy and behavior change* (2nd ed., pp. 233–282). New York: Wiley.

Patterson, C. H. (1984). Empathy, warmth, and genuineness: A review of reviews. *Psychotherapy, 21,* 431–438.

Perls, F. S., Hefferline, R. F., & Goodman, P. (1951). *Gestalt therapy.* New York: Julian Press.

Pierce, R. A., Nichols, M. P., & DuBrin, J. R. (1983). *Emotional expression in psychotherapy.* New York: Gardner Press.

Pomrehn, G., Tausch, R., & Tönnies, S. (1986). Personenzentrierte Gruppenpsychotherapie: Prozesse und Auswirkungen nach 1 Jahr bei 87 Klienten. *Zeitschrift für Personenzentrierte Psychologie und Psychotherapie, 5,* 19–31.

Propst, L. R., Ostrom, R., Watkins, P., Dean, T., & Mashburn, D. (in press). Comparative efficacy of religious and nonreligious cognitive-behavioral therapy for the treatment of clinical depression in religious individuals. *Journal of Consulting and Clinical Psychology.*

Prouty, G. F. (1990). Pre-therapy: A theoretical evolution in the person-centered/experiential psychotherapy of schizophrenia and retardation. In G. Lietaer, J. Rombauts, & R. Van Balen (Eds.), *Client-centered and experiential psychotherapy in the nineties* (pp. 645–658). Leuven, Belgium: Leuven University Press.

Quality Assurance Project. (1983). A treatment outline for depressive disorders. *Australian and New Zealand Journal of Psychiatry, 17,* 129–146.

Rennie, D. L. (1985, June). *Client deference in the psychotherapy relationship.* Paper presented at the Society for Psychotherapy Research, Evanston, IL.

Rennie, D. L. (1990). Toward a representation of the client's experience of the psychotherapy hour. In G. Lietaer, J. Rombauts, & R. Van Balen (Eds.), *Client-centered and experiential psychotherapy in the nineties* (pp. 155–172). Leuven, Belgium: Leuven University Press.

Rennie, D. L. (1991). *Functions of storytelling in psychotherapy: The client's subjective experience.* Unpublished manuscript, York University, Toronto.

Rennie, D. L. (1992). Qualitative analysis of the client's experience of psychotherapy: The unfolding of reflexivity. In S. Toukmanian & D. L. Rennie (Eds.), *Psychotherapy process research: Paradigmatic and narrative approaches.* Newbury Park, CA: Sage Publications.

Rice, L. N. (1974). The evocative function of the therapist. In L. N. Rice & D. A. Wexler (Eds.), *Innovations in client-centered therapy* (pp. 289–311). New York: Wiley.

Rice, L. N. (1984). *Manual for systematic evocative unfolding.* Unpublished manuscript, York University, Toronto.

Rice, L. N. (1986). *Therapist manual for unfolding problematic reactions.* Unpublished manuscript, York University, Toronto.

Rice, L. N., & Greenberg, L. (Eds.). (1984). *Patterns of change.* New York: Guilford.

Rice, L. N., & Greenberg, L. S. (1991). Two affective change events in client-centered therapy. In J. Safran & L. Greenberg (Eds.), *Emotion, psychotherapy, and change* (pp. 197–226). New York: Guilford.

Rice, L. N., & Greenberg, L. S. (1992). Humanistic approaches to psychotherapy. In D. Freedheim (Ed.), *History of psychotherapy: A century of change* (pp. 197–224). Washington, DC: American Psychological Association.

Rice, L. N., & Kerr, G. P. (1986). Measures of client and therapist vocal quality. In L. Greenberg & W. Pinsof (Eds.), *The psychotherapeutic process: A research handbook* (pp. 73–105). New York: Guilford.

Rice, L. N., Koke, C. J., Greenberg, L. S., & Wagstaff, A. K. (1979). *Manual for client vocal quality* (Vols. 1, 2). Toronto Counseling Development Centre, York University.

Rice, L. N., & Saperia, E. P. (1984). Task analysis and the resolution of problematic reactions. In L. N. Rice & L. S. Greenberg (Eds.), *Patterns of change.* New York: Guilford.

Robinson, L. A., Berman, J. S., & Neimeyer, R. A. (1990). Psychotherapy for the treatment of depression: A comprehensive review of controlled outcome research. *Psychological Bulletin, 108,* 30–49.

Rogers, C. R. (1951). *Client-centered therapy.* Boston: Houghton Mifflin.

Rogers, C. R. (1975). Empathic: An unappreciated way of being. *Counseling Psychologist, 5*(2), 2–10.

Rudolph, J., Langer, I., & Tausch, R. (1980). An investigation of the psychological affects and conditions of person-centered individual psychotherapy. *Zeitschrift für Klinische Psychologie: Forschung und Praxis, 9,* 23–33.

Sachs, J. S. (1983). Negative factors in brief psychotherapy: An empirical assessment. *Journal of Consulting and Clinical Psychology, 51,* 557–564.

Sachse, R. (1986). *Gesprächspsychotherapie.* Hagen: Fernuniversität Hagen.

Sachse, R. (1987). Wat Betekent "zelfexploratie" en hoe kan een therapeut het zelfexploratie-proces van de cliënt bevorderen? *Psychotherapeutisch Paspoort, 4,* 71–93.

Sachse, R. (1988). *From attitude to action: On the necessity of an action-oriented approach in client-centered therapy* (Berichte aus der Arbeitseinheit Klinische Psychologie, Fakultät für Psychologie, No. 64). Bochum, Germany: Ruhr Universität.

Sachse, R. (1990a). Acting purposefully in client-centered therapy. In P. J. D. Drenth, J. A. Sergeant, & R. J. Takens (Eds.), *European perspectives in psychology* (Vol. 2, pp. 65–79). New York: Wiley.

Sachse, R. (1990b). The influence of therapist processing proposals on the explication process of the client. *Person-Centered Review, 5,* 321–344.

Sachse, R. (1991a). *Clients must understand their therapists. The phrasing of interventions determines their effect.* Unpublished manuscript, University of Ruhr, Bochum, Germany.

Sachse, R. (1991b). *Determinants of success in goal-oriented client-centered therapy: There are no successful clients but only success teams.* Unpublished manuscript, University of Ruhr, Bochum, Germany.

Sachse, R. (1992). Differential effects of processing proposals and content references on the explication process of clients with different starting conditions. *Psychotherapy Research, 2,* 235–251.

Sachse, R., Maus, C. (1987). Einfluss differentieller Bearbeitungsangebote auf den Explizierungsprozess von Klienten in der Klientenzentrierten Psychotherapie. *Zeitschrift für Personenzentrierte Psychologie und Psychotherapie, 6,* 75–86.

Sachse, R., Maus, C. (1991). *Zielorientiertes Handeln in der Gesprachtspsychotherapie.* Stuttgart: Kohlhammer.

Schneider, R., & Sachse, R. (1991). Repression-sensitization: A personality dimension of prognostic value for the therapeutic process in focusing. Unpublished manuscript, University of Ruhr, Bochum, Germany.

Seeman, J. (1989). A reaction to "Psychodiagnosis: A person-centered perspective." *Person-Centered Review, 4,* 152–156.

Shapiro, D. A., & Firth, J. (1987). Prescriptive versus exploratory psychotherapy: Outcomes of the Sheffield psychotherapy project. *British Journal of Psychiatry, 151,* 790–799.

Sherman, E. (1990). Experiential reminiscence and life-review therapy with the elderly. In G. Lietaer, J. Rombauts, & R. Van Balen (Eds.), *Client-centered and experiential psychotherapy in the nineties* (pp. 709–732). Leuven, Belgium: Leuven University Press.

Shostrom, E. (Producer). (1965). *Three approaches to psychotherapy* [Film]. Santa Ana, CA: Psychological Films.

Singh, M., & Greenberg, L. S. (1992, June). *Development and validation of a measure of the resolution of unfinished business: Relating session change to outcome.* Paper presented at the annual meeting Society for Psychotherapy Research, Berkeley, CA.

Smith, M. L., Glass, G. V., & Miller, T. I. (1980). *The benefits of psychotherapy.* Baltimore: The Johns Hopkins University Press.

Speierer, G. -W. (1979). Ergebnisse der ambulanten Gesprächspsychotherapie. *Fortschritte der Medizin, 35,* 1527–1533.

Speierer, G. -W. (1990). Toward a specific illness concept of client-centered therapy. In G. Lietaer, J. Rombauts, & R. Van Balen (Eds.), *Client-centered and experiential psychotherapy in the nineties* (pp. 337–359). Leuven, Belgium: Leuven University Press.

Stiles, W. B. (1979). Verbal response modes and psychotherapeutic technique. *Psychiatry, 42,* 49–62.

Stiles, W. B. (1980). Measurement of the impact of psychotherapy sessions. *Journal of Consulting and Clinical Psychology, 48,* 176–185.

Stiles, W. B. (1988). Psychotherapy process–outcome correlations may be misleading. *Psychotherapy, 25,* 27–35.

Stiles, W. B., Shapiro, D. A., & Elliott, R. (1986). "Are all psychotherapies equivalent?" *American Psychologist, 41,* 165–180.

Stuhr, U., & Meyer, A. E. (1991). Hamburg Short Psychotherapy Comparison Experiment. In M. Crago & L. Beutler (Eds.), *Psychotherapy research: An international review of programmatic studies.* American Psychological Association.

Swildens, J. C. A. G. (1990). Client-centered psychotherapy for patients with borderline symptoms. In G. Lietaer, J. Rombauts, & R. Van Balen (Eds.), *Client-centered and experiential psychotherapy in the nineties* (pp. 623–635). Leuven, Belgium: Leuven University Press.

Tamura, R. (1987). Floatability: A focuser variable related to success in focusing. *Japanese Journal of Humanistic Psychology, 5,* 83–87.

Tamura, R. (1990). The interrelation between the focuser–listener relationship and the focuser's floatability during focusing. *Journal of Japanese Clinical Psychology, 8,* 16–25.

Tamura, R., & Murayama, S. (1988). Are symbolizations indispensable for the process of personality change? A consideration from focusing cases. *Research Bulletin of Educational Psychology, Faculty of Education, Kyushu University, 33,* 135–144.

Tausch, R. (1990). The supplementation of client-centered communication therapy with other valid therapeutic methods: A client-centered necessity. In G. Lietaer, J. Rombauts, & R. Van Balen (Eds.), *Client-centered and experiential psychotherapy in the nineties* (pp. 447–455). Leuven, Belgium: Leuven University Press.

Teusch, L. (1990). Positive effects and limitations of client-centered therapy with schizophrenic patients. In G. Lietaer, J. Rombauts, & R. Van Balen (Eds.), *Client-centered and experiential psychotherapy in the nineties* (pp. 637–644). Leuven, Belgium: Leuven University Press.

Teusch, L., & Boehme, H. (1991). Results of a one-year follow-up of patients with agoraphobia and/or panic disorder treated with an inpatient therapy program with client-centered basis. *Psychotherapie-Psychosomatik Medizinische Psychologie, 41,* 68–76.

Toukmanian, S. G. (1986). A measure of client perceptual processing. In L. Greenberg & W. Pinsof (Eds.), *The psychotherapeutic process* (pp. 107–130). New York: Guilford.

Toukmanian, S. G. (1990). A schema-based information processing perspective on client change in experiential psychotherapy. In G. Lietaer, J. Rombauts, & R. Van Balen (Eds.), *Client-centered and experiential psychotherapy in the nineties* (pp. 309–326). Leuven, Belgium: Leuven University Press.

Toukmanian, S. G. (1992). Studying the client's perceptual processes and their outcomes in psychotherapy. In S. G. Toukmanian & D. L. Rennie (Eds.), *Psychotherapy process research: Paradigmatic and narrative approaches.* Newbury Park, CA: Sage Publications

Toukmanian, S. G., & Grech, T. (1991). *Changes in cognitive complexity in the context of perceptual-processing experiential therapy* (Tech. Rep. No. 174). North York, Ontario, Canada: York University, Department of Psychology.

Toukmanian, S. G., & Rennie, D. L. (Eds.). (1992). *Psychotherapy process research: Paradigmatic and narrative approaches.* Newbury Park, CA: Sage Publications.

Tscheulin, D. (1983a). Differentielle Gesprächspsychotherapie. Kontradiktion oder Innovation? In G. Bittner (Ed.), *Personale Psychologie: Festschrift für L. J. Pongratz* (pp. 241–257). Göttingen: Hogrefe.

Tscheulin, D. (1983b). Über differentielles therapeutisches Vorgehen in der klientenzentrierten Therapie. Ein empirischer Beitrag zu einer differentiellen Gesprächspsychotherapie. In D. Tscheulin (Ed.), *Beziehung und Technik in der klientenzentrierten Therapie* (pp. 53–64). Weinheim: Beltz, Germany.

Tscheulin, D. (1988). *Wirkfaktoren psychotherapeutischer Intervention: Ein heuristisches Modell zur einheitlichen Betrachtung psychotherapeutischer Intervention aus klientenzentrierter Perspektive.* Unpublished habilitations thesis, Universität Würzburg, Germany.

Tscheulin, D. (1990). Confrontation and non-confrontation as differential techniques in differential client-centered therapy. In G. Lietaer, J. Rombauts, & R. Van Balen (Eds.), *Client-centered and experiential psychotherapy in the nineties* (pp. 327–336). Leuven, Belgium: Leuven University Press.

Tscheulin, D. (1992). *Wirkfaktoren psychotherapeutischer Intervention.* Göttingen: Hogrefe, Germany

Vanaerschot, G. (1990). The process of empathy: Holding and letting go. In G. Lietaer, J. Rombauts, & R. Van Balen (Eds.), *Client-centered and experiential psychotherapy in* the nineties (pp. 269–294). Leuven, Belgium: Leuven University Press.

Wagner, A. C., Berckhan, B., Krause, C., Röder, U., Schenk, B., & Schütze, U. (1991). Imperative-centered focusing as a method of psychotherapy and research. In L. Beutler & M. Crago (Eds.), *Psychotherapy research: An international review of programmatic studies* (pp. 309–311). Washington, DC: American Psychological Association.

Watson, J. (1992). *Exploring problematic reactions: An inquiry into self. A process study of change in therapy.* Unpublished doctoral dissertation, York University, Toronto.

Westermann, B., Schwab, R., & Tausch, R. (1983). Auswirkungen und Prozesse personenzentrierter Gruppenpsychotherapie bei 164 Klienten einer Psychotherapeutischen Beratungsstelle. *Zeitschrift für Klinische Psychologie, 9,* 241–252.

Wexler, M. M., & Elliott, R. (1988, June). *Experiential therapy of depression: Initial psychometric analyses of session data.* Paper presented at annual meeting of the Society for Psychotherapy Research, Santa Fe, NM.

Wiseman, H. (1986). *Single-case studies of the resolution of problematic reactions in short-term client-centered therapy: A task-focused approach.* Unpublished doctoral dissertation, York University, Toronto.

Wiseman, H., & Rice, L. N. (1989). Sequential analyses of therapist–client interaction during change events: A task-focused approach. *Journal of Consulting and Clinical Psychology, 57,* 281–286.

Yalom, I. D. (1980). *Existential psychotherapy.* New York: Basic Books.

Yontef, G. (1988). Assimilating diagnostic and psychoanalytic perspectives into Gestalt therapy. *The Gestalt Journal, 11,* 5–32.

Yontef, G. (1991). Recent trends in Gestalt therapy in the U.S. and what we need to learn from them. *British Gestalt Journal, 1,* 5–20.;

Zielke, M. (1979). *Indikation zur Gesprächspsychotherapie.* Stuttgart: Kohlhammer.

Zink, D. A. (1990). *Change in anxiety in the context of perceptual-processing in experiential therapy: Process and outcome research.* Unpublished master's thesis, York University, Toronto.

PART
IV

RESEARCH ON APPLICATIONS IN SPECIAL GROUPS AND SETTINGS

13

PSYCHOTHERAPY FOR CHILDREN AND ADOLESCENTS

- **ALAN E. KAZDIN**

  Yale University

Research in psychotherapy has advanced considerably in the last few decades. The progress can be attested to by a large corpus of empirical investigations on the effectiveness of alternative techniques; the nature and emergence of therapeutic processes; and the impact of patient, therapist, and other factors that moderate outcome (Goldfried, Greenberg, & Marmar, 1990; Kazdin, 1986; Smith, Glass, & Miller, 1980; VandenBos, 1986). Conceptualization of critical processes, efforts to integrate alternative approaches, and growth of process evaluation point to a few areas of major advances. Unfortunately, these conceptual and empirical developments in psychotherapy have focused primarily on the treatment of adults. Evaluation of treatments for children and adolescents has been less substantial.

With greater awareness of the scope of emotional and behavioral problems of children and adolescents, the paucity of treatment research has come into increasingly sharp focus (Institute of Medicine [IOM], 1989; U.S. Congress, 1986, 1991). Recent epidemiological studies indicate that between 17 and 22 percent of youth under 18 years of age suffer developmental, emotional, or behavioral problems (Costello, 1989; Zill & Schoenborn, 1990). In the United States alone, this means that 11–14 million of the 63 million children suffer significant impairment. Thus, a large segment of youth are in need of special attention in light of their emotional and behavioral functioning.

The costs in human suffering to children and their families are difficult to assess. An estimate has suggested that mental disorders in children under 14 years of age cost $1.5 billion in the United States in 1985, based on information from mental health services and service providers (IOM, 1989). The actual cost no doubt is greater as the age range is extended through adolescence and the costs of multiple care agencies (mental health, education, juvenile justice) and professionals (psychologists, psychiatrists, pediatricians, social workers) are considered (see National Center for Education on Maternal and Child Health, 1992).

The importance of developing effective treatment to reduce suffering in childhood and adolescence is obvious. The lifelong consequences of many forms of severe dysfunction such as mental retardation and autism are widely known. Many other dysfunctions identified in childhood and adolescence, such as attention deficit disorder, conduct disorder, and depression, also can have lifelong consequences (see Robins & Rutter, 1990; G. Weiss & Hechtman, 1986). The continuity of many dysfunctions across the life span, beginning in childhood, heightens the significance of early intervention, not only to reduce the suffering of children and adolescents, but also to prevent or attenuate impairment in adulthood.

Psychotherapy for children and adolescents is one of many interventions to address emotional and behavioral problems. Other interventions encompass a variety of social services—home, school, and community-based programs; residential and hospital treatment; and foster care arrangements (Rapoport, 1987; Wells & Biegel, 1991). Psychotherapy is of special interest for separate reasons. First, among treatments for children, outpatient psychotherapy can obviate the use of more

Completion of the present chapter was facilitated greatly by the support of a Research Scientist Award (MH00353) and by a grant (MH35408) from the National Institute of Mental Health. The support of these projects is gratefully acknowledged.

restrictive, costly, and disruptive interventions such as hospitalization and residential care. Maintenance of the child in the context of his or her everyday life, if possible, is much more desirable from the standpoint of child adjustment and family preservation. Second, models of psychotherapy and the specific treatment techniques themselves are used in diverse settings, including schools, day treatment and residential hospital services, and juvenile justice programs. Thus, even when restrictive treatment programs are used, psychotherapy in some form often bears the burden of producing the desired change. Consequently, research on psychotherapeutic treatments is critically important.

Although psychotherapy research for children and adolescents has been relatively neglected, important inroads have emerged recently not only in treatment studies but also in areas of research that provide the underpinnings for intervention research. The present chapter examines the current status of psychotherapy research with children and adolescents.[1] The purpose is to highlight empirical developments in the treatment of childhood and adolescent dysfunction, to convey substantive and methodological advances on which such research draws, to identify limitations of current research, and to derive from these limitations future research directions. Current lines of research are sampled to illustrate diverse conceptual views of treatment, intervention techniques, and clinical dysfunctions.

Psychotherapy, as usually defined, consists of interventions designed to decrease distress, symptoms, and maladaptive behavior and to improve adaptive and prosocial functioning. The type of interventions or means to accomplish these goals include various forms of counseling, structured or unstructured interactions, training procedures, or plans that utilize such psychosocial influences as discussion, learning, persuasion, and conflict resolution. The interventions usually focus on how clients feel (affect), think (cognition), and act (behavior) (see Garfield, 1980; Walrond-Skinner, 1986). The definition is sufficiently generic to encompass treatments for children, adolescents, and adults. At the same time, psychotherapy across the life span is not merely the application of similar strategies to people who differ in age. As evident throughout the chapter, fundamental differences emerge in the

delineation of dysfunction and application of treatments for children and adolescents.

The present chapter focuses on models and techniques of psychotherapy as applied to youth across a wide range of dysfunctions and domains of maladjustment. Excluded from the chapter are a number of interventions that also have an impact on child and adolescent mental health, such as various residential placements (e.g., psychiatric hospitalization, camp and wilderness programs, foster care), educational interventions (e.g., Head Start), and medication. Also, the focus of the chapter is on youth who are identified for or in need of treatment based on signs of dysfunction or maladjustment. Preventive interventions designed to avert the onset of disorders (primary prevention) are not covered in the chapter.[2]

THE EFFECTIVENESS OF PSYCHOTHERAPY FOR CHILDREN AND ADOLESCENTS

Historical Overview
Evaluation of the child and adolescent therapy research literature began with Levitt (1957), who evaluated 18 studies of psychotherapy that focused on youth whose problems could be classified generally as neuroses. The therapeutic approaches included a mixture of counseling, guidance, and psychoanalytic and other treatments that were not consistently well specified in the original reports. Levitt combined the studies for his analyses and concluded that the rates of improvement among children who received psychotherapy were approximately 67 and 78 percent at posttreatment and follow-up, respectively. Children who did not receive treatment improved at about the same rate (73%). Thus, the general conclusion was that the efficacy of traditional forms of psychotherapy for children had not been demonstrated.

The clarity of the general conclusion masked a number of problems. To begin with, the "children" encompassed by the studies were quite diverse in age (preschool to 21 years old) and clinical dysfunc-

[1]For present purposes, children and adolescents refer to youth up to age 18. The end of adolescence is often defined at 18 because of the legal age set for adult responsibility in almost all states (U.S. Congress, 1991).

[2]The areas of treatment and prevention overlap because in many cases prevention is applied to youth who show early or mild signs of dysfunction, and because some of the same interventions (e.g., problem-solving skills training) often are used. Yet there are significant conceptual and applied differences between treatment and prevention. The present chapter is devoted to psychotherapeutic approaches as applied to youth identified because of maladjustment or dysfunction.

tions. Second, baseline or improvement rates of nontreated youths were derived from two studies and from children who received treatment but terminated treatment early. Youth who fail to complete treatment may differ systematically from those who complete treatment and hence might not adequately reflect the base rate of improvement without treatment. Third, improvement rates were based on evaluation of children by the therapists at the end of treatment. Therapist ratings alone, especially by current methodological standards, certainly are limited as a measure of outcome.

As might be expected, Levitt's review generated rebuttals and reevaluations of the data (Eisenberg & Gruenberg, 1961; Heinicke & Goldman, 1960; Hood-Williams, 1960). Cogent points were raised that not only challenged Levitt's conclusions, but also drew attention to methodological issues in designing outcome studies such as the need to consider diagnoses of children and family factors as moderators of treatment and to use multiple measures to examine treatment outcome. Essentially, the rebuttals conveyed that the original method of analysis, criteria, and research reviewed by Levitt did not permit clear conclusions about the effectiveness of treatment.

Levitt's (1963) subsequent review evaluated 22 additional studies and addressed a number of criticisms including the consideration of different diagnoses. The conclusions essentially remained the same. Summing across diagnostic groups, Levitt's analyses showed improvement rate of treated youths to be approximately 65 percent, slightly below the rate of children who did not receive treatment (73%). Rebuttals and reevaluations of these later reviews continued (Barrett, Hampe, & Miller, 1978; Heinicke & Strassmann, 1975). From the interchanges, two conclusions seemed warranted: The research base was quite sparse and the effectiveness of treatment was not clearly established.

Levitt's reviews (1957, 1963) of child psychotherapy followed Eysenck's (1952) review that focused mainly on psychotherapy for adults. In the years following the initial Eysenck review and its revisions (1960, 1966), scores of controlled outcome studies emerged for treatments with adult patient samples (see Lambert, Shapiro, & Bergin, 1986; Meltzoff & Kornriech, 1970; Smith et al., 1980). The challenge to the effectiveness of psychotherapy for children was not followed by the same empirical effort. The number of studies of child and adolescent psychotherapy and the range of research questions they address have lagged greatly behind research with adults (see Barrett et al., 1978; Kazdin, 1990a).

Contemporary Reviews

In the last two decades, research on child and adolescent psychotherapy has increased as attested to in several reviews (e.g., Barrnett, Docherty, & Frommelt, 1991; Casey & Berman, 1985; Kazdin, 1990a; Kovacs & Paulauskas, 1986; Ollendick, 1986; Tuma & Sobotka, 1983; Weisz, Weiss, Alicke, & Klotz, 1987). The literature has been systematically canvassed in meta-analyses in an effort to derive conclusions about treatments for children and adolescents and the factors that contribute to therapeutic change. *Meta-analysis* refers to a set of quantitative procedures that can be used to evaluate multiple studies. Results within a given study are quantified in such a way as to permit their combination with data from other studies. The most common way of evaluating the literature through meta-analysis is to compute *effect size*, which provides a common metric across investigations. Effect size is calculated as the difference between means of a treatment and a no-treatment or an alternative treatment group divided by the standard deviation of the control group (or of the pooled sample of both groups). Effect size constitutes the dependent variable for the meta-analysis and is used as a summary statistic to examine the impact of other variables (e.g., types of treatment and clinical problem).

Meta-analytic reviews of psychotherapy completed by Smith and Glass (1977; Smith et al., 1980) initiated a wave of analyses of psychotherapy. The initial Smith and Glass reviews included treatment of children, but this was not the primary focus nor was it evaluated in depth. The initial meta-analysis for child and adolescent psychotherapy was completed by Casey and Berman (1985), who summarized 75 studies published between 1952 and 1983. In each study, psychotherapy was compared to a control group or another treatment. The studies assessed results with children ages 3–15 across a wide range of clinical problems and treatment approaches (e.g., psychodynamic, client-centered, behavioral, and cognitive-behavioral treatments). All treatment versus no-treatment comparisons were averaged across treatment techniques and yielded a mean effect size of .71. This number is based on standard deviation units and indicates that the average outcome for treated children is .71 of a standard deviation better than that of untreated control children. Based on the assumption of a normal distribution of outcome effects for treated and control subjects, effect sizes can be stated another way. With an effect size of .71, the average child who is treated is better off at the end of therapy than 76 percent of the persons who did not receive treatment. (The 76th percentile is obtained by identifying the point on the normal curve that reflects $+.71$ standard deviations above the mean.) Therapy was clearly shown to be effective on the average in improving children.

Behavior therapies, as a general class of procedures, led to greater effect sizes than nonbehavior therapies. However, the differences appeared to be restricted to certain types of outcome measures. When the possible bias produced by these measures was controlled, the superiority of behavioral techniques was no longer evident. Finer grained evaluations of specific treatment techniques revealed no significant differences in outcomes between play versus nonplay therapy, individual versus group therapy, or child versus parent-focused treatment.

Weisz et al. (1987; B. Weiss & Weisz, 1990) extended the evaluation by examining over 100 controlled studies that encompassed youth from ages 4 to 18. Only 29.6 percent of the studies overlapped with those reviewed by Casey and Berman (1985). The mean effect size across different treatments, clinical problems, and patient samples was .79. Effect sizes tended to be greater for behavioral than for nonbehavioral techniques. This difference was maintained across different types of measures, whether or not they might, on a priori grounds, be considered to favor behavior therapies. Evaluation of treatment at a more molecular level included comparisons among treatment "classes," such as behavioral techniques (e.g., modeling, desensitization) and nonbehavioral techniques (e.g., client-centered, psychodynamic treatments). No technique differences were evident within a treatment class.

In a meta-analysis of family therapies, Hazelrigg, Cooper, and Borduin (1987) identified 20 studies upon which to base an evaluation. The selection required at least one parent and child to be included. The results indicated generally that family therapies were effective when compared to no-treatment. Mean effect sizes were .45 and .50 as a function of different types of outcome measures (family interaction and measures of the child's behavior, respectively). More fine-grained conclusions among various types of family treatments were not possible given the paucity of studies.

The three meta-analyses highlighted here do not exhaust the quantitative evaluations of therapies for children and adolescents (e.g., Durlak, Fuhrman, & Lampman, 1991; Kazdin, Bass, Ayers, & Rodgers, 1990). Overall, the varied analyses are consistent in their conclusion that therapy in general is effective when compared to no-treatment. Of course, beyond the general question, we would like to know more about the effects of specific treatment techniques as applied to various clinical problems and youth of different ages. The paucity of studies of the same treatments as applied to youth with similar problems has limited the ability to derive specific conclusions.

In an effort to draw conclusions about the relative effectiveness of different treatments, meta-analytic reviews usually devise superordinate classes to group techniques (e.g., behavior therapy, family therapy). These classes reflect broad approaches to orientations to treatment and combine many different treatment techniques. Consequently, conceptual views and treatment techniques *within* a class often bear little resemblance to each other. For example, systematic desensitization and token reinforcement are recognized as techniques that belong to the general class of behavioral approaches. However, the techniques differ markedly in their theoretical origin, conceptual view of dysfunction, and concrete treatment procedures. Their combination into a general class is of unclear value. Similarly, multigenerational, structural, and behavioral family therapies are occasionally grouped to comprise an overarching approach of family therapy. Here again, at conceptual and technique levels, the differences among constituent treatments might argue against their meaningful combination. In short, meta-analytic reviews often look to broad classes of treatment as part of the evaluation. The move to less, rather than more, specific levels of analysis yields findings that are difficult to interpret or to extrapolate to clinical or research applications.

Reviews have also examined the question of whether treatment is more effective for different types of dysfunction. Studies of child psychotherapy infrequently use a formal diagnostic system or standardized method of delineating dysfunction (Kazdin, Bass et al., 1990), making evaluation of the literature difficult. From the standpoint of contemporary reviews, two broad categories are often used to delineate emotional and behavioral problems of children and adolescents, namely, overcontrolled and undercontrolled dysfunctions. *Overcontrolled* problems refer to inward-directed child disturbances such as anxiety, depression, and social withdrawal. *Internalizing behaviors* is another term used for this category. *Undercontrolled* problems refer to outward-directed child behaviors such as hyperactivity, tantrums, aggression, and antisocial behavior. *Acting out* and *externalizing behaviors* are other terms often used for this classification. Notably missing from these categories are more severe forms of dysfunction, including autism, severe forms of mental retardation, and schizophrenia, to mention a few. Psychotherapy is applied most often to undercontrolled disorders in both research and practice with children and adolescents

(Kazdin, Bass et al., 1990; Kazdin, Siegel, & Bass, 1990).

Integrative reviews that group dysfunctions into broad categories indicate that treatment is better than no-treatment for both over- and undercontrolled dysfunctions. Moreover, at the level of broad categorization, treatments have not consistently varied in effectiveness as a function of different types of problems. For example, Weisz et al. (1987) found that effect sizes were not significantly different for treatment studies that focused on over- versus undercontrolled behaviors. The absence of clear differences in the outcome obtained for these broad classes of dysfunction is difficult to evaluate. The lack of a consistent way to operationalize over- and undercontrolled disorders among studies, the frequent presence of both types of symptoms and disorders within a given individual, and variation in symptom constellations over the course of childhood and adolescence could readily obscure systematic outcome differences when multiple studies are combined.

From the meta-analyses of child and adolescent psychotherapy, the main general conclusions are noteworthy. First, *psychotherapy appears to be better than no-treatment*. This finding has been consistent across meta-analytic reviews that have sampled well over 300 studies. Second, *the magnitude of these effects closely parallels those obtained from outcome research with adults* (Brown, 1987). Effect sizes for treatment versus no-treatment tend to hover within the range of .7 – .8, although reviews of some treatments (e.g., cognitive therapies, family therapies) have shown different effect size estimates (higher and lower, respectively). Third, *treatment differences, when evident, tend to favor behavioral rather than nonbehavioral techniques*. Yet, this conclusion can be argued, given the different foci and measures confounded with alternative approaches. And, as noted previously, the meaningfulness of comparisons of broad classes itself is unclear, whatever the direction or pattern of results. Fourth, *individual treatment techniques (i.e., specific treatments within a broad class) have not been found to differ from each other*. The paucity of studies of a given technique and their variation with respect to clinical problems and populations may render such comparisons difficult to interpret from integrative reviews. Finally, *different classes of behavioral problems or clinical dysfunctions (over- versus undercontrolled) have not been found to respond differently to treatment*. Here, too, broad classes of problem domains, great differences in constituent problems within a class, and combining youth of different ages are quite plausible explanations for no-difference findings.

General Comments

Contemporary reviews of psychotherapy for children and adolescents have been useful in culling the available studies, identifying the strength of effects among alternative classes of treatment, and characterizing how treatment is conducted and evaluated. Reviews have yielded very general conclusions (e.g., psychotherapy is better than no-treatment, different techniques yield similar outcomes) and conclusions about general classes of treatment (e.g., behavioral treatments may have a slight edge over nonbehavioral treatments). Broad conclusions are important as a response to the initial question of whether psychotherapies for children and adolescents surpass in impact the changes that otherwise occur in time. The question is not trivial, given the marked maturational changes in symptoms and behavioral patterns for children and adolescents as a matter of developmental course.

RESEARCH ON SPECIFIC TREATMENT APPROACHES AND TECHNIQUES

General conclusions about the effectiveness of treatment have been important in light of the historical context highlighted earlier. Efforts to draw specific conclusions about the relative effectiveness of various techniques for different types of dysfunction have produced an unclear yield. Too few studies are usually available to compare individual treatments (e.g., play therapy, systematic desensitization) for a given clinical problem. Generating superordinate classes to analyze broad approaches or types of clinical dysfunction is not likely to yield statements about techniques as they are applied in practice or evaluated in research. The gains in contemporary work can be conveyed by examining individual studies of treatment as applied to specific domains of dysfunction.

Overview: Range of Treatments

One difficulty in examining treatments for children and adolescents might be the daunting range of interventions currently in use. A very conservative count has identified over 230 different therapy techniques in use for children and adolescents (Kazdin, 1988). In addition to the large number of treatments, application of a given approach or technique can vary widely as a function of the age of the child. For example, psychoanalytic and relationship-based therapies with adolescents are more likely to resemble analogous treatments with adults in terms of the medium of exchange (e.g., talk), processes (e.g., alliance), and themes (e.g., conflicts, feelings about oneself and others). In elementary school or preschool children, other techniques (e.g., play, storytelling) may be used to reflect the same overall approach. Thus, a conceptual approach may generate quite different techniques as a function of developmental abilities.

In a related way, treatments can differ in the person(s) to whom they are directed. The child may be brought to treatment, but therapy may be aimed at the child, parent(s), or family, either alone or in varying combinations. As a rule, in clinical work parents are directly involved in some way in the treatment process with children (Kazdin, Siegel, & Bass, 1990). Teachers are often involved as well. Thus, treatment routinely has multiple foci to involve potentially important adult influences in the therapeutic process.

The focus of treatment may be dictated in part by the age of the child. For example, parent training is often used as a treatment for young children. The focus is on child-rearing practices in the home and on contingencies related specifically to the problem domain of interest. However, the applicability of the procedure is likely to depend on the age of the child because parental influences on children vary over the course of development. The application of contingency-based programs for young children (e.g., 4–10 years old) is much more feasible than for adolescents (e.g., ages 16–18). Among adolescents, the greater influence of peers, greater mobility, and more time out of the home may make them less amenable to simple contingency manipulations within the home, as is the case with younger children.

With techniques for children and adolescents numbering well over 200, individual techniques generally defy comprehensive review in a single chapter. The task is lightened by the regrettable fact that most treatments have not been subjected to outcome research. For the remaining techniques, the evidence is scattered across different problem domains and youth of different ages (e.g., young children, older adolescents). The purpose of the present, as well as the next, section is to sample research on major approaches to treatment. The present section illustrates research on several different treatment approaches and techniques; the section that follows illustrates research progress for several different disorders and domains of clinical functioning. Across both sections, a broad range of treatments and outcomes are sampled.

In presenting research on various treatment approaches, it is important to bear in mind a number of considerations. To begin, there are many treatment models or approaches and techniques within a given approach. The purpose here is to illustrate, rather than to review exhaustively, different approaches and models. Second, the literatures for various approaches are uneven in quantity (by general consensus of prior reviews) and in quality (in my own opinion). The differences in quantity of studies within a given treatment approach are noteworthy. For example, behavioral and cognitive-behavioral treatments dominate therapy research with children and adolescents (Kazdin, Bass et al., 1990). More traditional techniques including psychoanalysis, psychoanalytically oriented therapy, nondirective therapy, and play therapy, for example, comprise a small fraction of contemporary research. *More* research is not invariably *better* research within an area. At the same time, more research often signals replicable findings beyond a single investigator or program of research, greater generality of findings across client populations and clinical problems as studies expand in the treatment focus, and more in-depth analyses of variables that contribute to therapeutic change as studies attempt to build on prior findings. In selecting illustrations of research, an effort was made to represent techniques from diverse literatures but the samples from which to draw vary considerably.

Finally, the treatments that are in frequent use in clinical practice vary from those that are studied in research. Traditional forms of therapy, as previously mentioned, are often used in clinical practice but are not well studied in research (Kazdin, Siegel, & Bass, 1990). Behavior modification, cognitive-behavioral modification, and family therapies are frequently used in practice and studied in contemporary psychotherapy research. Eclectic treatments are frequently subscribed to among practitioners but rarely studied in ways approximating practice in contemporary outcome research. The purpose of illustrating treatment approaches and treatments for various disorders is to sample the range and richness of psychotherapies used in research as well as practice.

Psychoanalysis and Psychodynamic Treatments

Psychoanalysis and psychodynamically oriented psychotherapy as applied to children and adolescents are widely subscribed to and employed in clinical practice (Kazdin, Siegel, & Bass, 1990; Koocher & Pedulla, 1977) and hence serve as a useful point of departure for illustrating treatment. Reviews of these treatments have lamented the paucity of empirical research (e.g., Barrnett et al., 1991; Kovacs & Paulauskas, 1986; Tuma & Sobotka, 1983). There are a few studies that have emerged recently that convey very promising lines of work.

Fonagy and Moran (1990), conducting research at the Anna Freud Centre (London), have focused on the impact of psychoanalysis with children and adolescents who suffer "brittle diabetes." Youth with brittle diabetes have severe difficulty in controlling their diabetes and in maintaining blood glucose levels that are close to those of nondiabetic youth. The authors posited that the mismanagement of the treatment regimen by the patients serves as a partial basis for the lack of diabetic control. Failure to adhere to the regimen is considered to reflect neurotic adaptation to anxiety and guilt aroused by unconscious conflict. For example, in one case diabetic mismanagement was traced to conflicts of a teenage girl in relation to her father (e.g., feeling unloved by him, angry with him for his unresponsiveness), her mother (e.g., ambivalence toward her based on the mother's psychiatric illness when the girl was a child, rivalry in relation to the father), and parents (e.g., anxiety and guilt in death wishes toward them), among others. Although conflict and ambivalence serve as central foci, their expression is individually determined and then operationalized to proceed with treatment. Psychoanalysis is used in each case to reveal and address intrapsychic and interpersonal conflicts considered to undermine treatment adherence.

In one study, inpatient children and adolescents (ages 6–18) received *psychoanalytic treatment and routine medical management* versus *routine medical management alone*. Analytic treatment lasted from 5–28 weeks, with 3–5 sessions per week. Subjects in the two groups were matched on severity of illness and were in the same hospital. They were not randomly assigned to conditions and did not necessarily receive equal amounts of professional time and attention. At the end of treatment, the primary outcome measure was obtained from blood assays that revealed average blood glucose level (glycosylated hemoglobin [HbA_1]). Immediately after treatment and at a one-year follow-up, youth who received psychoanalysis showed lower blood glucose than the comparison group. More than one-half of the psychoanalysis cases fell within acceptable ranges of glucose levels for diabetics; none of the comparison cases did.

Similar results were obtained in another study in the same report that evaluated diabetic control among three youths (ages 8–13) who suffered growth retardation. A single-case design was used to evaluate the impact of treatment on growth. Baseline data on height were obtained to assess growth and growth rate over a period of two to three years. Assessment was conducted every three months. After treatment (duration and frequency of sessions not noted), assessment contin-

ued up to a two-year follow-up. For each youth, individual *psychoanalysis* was associated with improvements in glucose control (HbA_1) and increases in height velocity (bone growth). The impact on youth continued to be evident at follow-up two years later. This study and the prior investigation are significant in their careful specification of outcome and evaluation of follow-up.

Other work on variants of psychoanalytic treatment has been reported as well. Heinicke and Ramsey-Klee (1986) evaluated psychoanalytic therapy to improve learning disturbances. The purpose of the investigation was to evaluate the frequency of treatment sessions over the course of two years. Children ages 7–10 participated in one of three treatment conditions. In the first condition, children received *psychoanalytically oriented individual therapy once per week for two years;* in the second condition, children received *therapy four times per week for two years;* in the final condition, children received *therapy once per week for year one and then four times per week for year two.* The first two conditions were presented in an initial study (Heinicke, 1969), which indicated that short- and long-term effects varied with the different treatment frequencies. In the 1986 study, a third group was matched to the two other groups previously reported and given the abbreviated treatment in the first year (1 × /week) and the extended treatment in the second year (4 × /week). Based on the prior study, this condition was expected to maximize short- and long-term changes.

Outcome measures included academic performance (reading level, grades) and a personality profile to assess psychodynamically relevant processes. During the first year of treatment, groups with treatment once per week showed greater gains in reading than the group with treatment four times per week. At the end of treatment, group differences were not evident; thus, there was no advantage to the more frequent version of treatment. At a one-year follow-up, the groups that had received treatment more frequently in the second year of treatment showed continued improvements in reading. Thus, how treatment was delivered in the second year had an impact on the amount of improvement at follow-up. The benefits of the more frequent treatment during the second year were not only evident in reading levels, but also on measures of personality processes, including the capacity for relationships, frustration tolerance, flexible adaptation, and others. The study is of interest because of the focus on a parameter (frequency of treatment contact) central to psychoanalytic treatment. Also, the study is noteworthy in the assessment of school performance as well as changes in psychodynamically relevant intrapersonal characteristics.

These studies illustrate important lines of research on psychoanalytic treatment. The careful documentation of outcome, the replication of treatment effects, and the assessment of follow-up are highlights of these examples. The studies focus on health care and reading levels, two obviously important domains. At the same time, the bulk of problems seen in clinical work relate to conduct problems, anxiety, and other disorders. Investigations of psychodynamic treatments in the areas to which the treatments are routinely applied and with the exemplary methodology of the previous examples are greatly needed.

Nondirective and Relationship-Based Therapy

Nondirective therapy refers to treatment based on a client-centered approach (Rogers, 1961). In current child and adolescent psychotherapy research, there are few efforts to test nondirective treatments as originally formulated. A more generic and integrative therapy is often used in practice and studied in research. This therapy adheres in principle to features of client-centered therapy in which emphasis is placed on the therapist–client relationship to provide a corrective emotional experience and encourage the expression of feeling and self-exploration. The relationship and efforts to work through problems as they emerge in affective experiences characterize nondirective and more generic relationship therapies. In general, relationship-based treatment is advocated for an extremely broad range of child clinical problems (C. Patterson, 1979). The treatment can be provided in different formats (individual or group therapy) and with different media of exchange between the client and the therapist (talk or play). Play therapy, of course, is typically reserved for younger children. (Because play therapy spans diverse conceptual approaches and is widely used in its own right, it is treated and illustrated separately.)

Nondirective and relationship-based treatments for children and adolescents received significant attention in the 1960s and 1970s. Several outcome studies were completed, particularly with delinquent youth (see Kazdin, 1985). For example, Truax, Wargo, and Silber (1966) evaluated the effectiveness of group psychotherapy with institutionalized delinquent females (ages 14–18). *Group therapy* youth received client-centered treatment (2 × /week for 3 months). *Control* youth received routine institutional care but no additional treatment. Two therapists who administered treatment were selected because of their ability to provide therapeutic conditions deemed critical for treat-

ment success (e.g., accurate empathy, warmth). Results indicated significantly greater improvement on several measures of personality for group therapy youth, including self-confidence, delinquency proneness, responsibility, attitude toward authority, adjustment, self-concept, and congruence between the self and the ideal self. The control group became worse on several measures over the course of pre- to posttreatment assessment. Interestingly, over the course of follow-up, approximately one year later, group therapy cases showed a greater number of days out of the institution than did control cases. Thus, the effects of treatment were reflected in community adjustment.

Individual and group relationship-based treatments were evaluated with delinquent adolescent males (ages 15–19) who were incarcerated for such crimes as theft and breaking and entering (Persons, 1966, 1967; Persons & Pepinsky, 1966). Youth were matched on several subject and demographic variables and assigned randomly to treatment or control groups. Treated youth received *individual psychotherapy* (1 × /week) and *group therapy* (2 × /week) for over 20 weeks. Treatment focused on the expression of past behaviors and development of an interpersonal relationship with the therapist and relationships with peers. The therapist was supportive, accepting, and nonthreatening. Over time, the therapist became more directive in helping the youth discriminate socially acceptable and unacceptable behaviors. Youth in the *control condition* received routine institutional care but no special therapy regimen.

At the end of treatment, treated subjects showed greater improvement than controls in measures of anxiety, delinquency, psychopathology, classroom performance (within the institution), and number of discipline reports. At a one-year follow-up assessment, and after youth were released to the community, treated youth showed a lower rate of reinstitutionalization in a penal institution, fewer parole violations, and greater employment than did control youth. Treated boys who were judged to have responded especially well at the end of treatment were shown at follow-up to be better able to remain in the community than those who were judged as previously unsuccessful. In fact, those in treatment who had not been judged as successes were, at follow-up, no different from control youth in remaining in the community. Interestingly, the extent to which youth became similar to their therapists was related to therapeutic improvements (Persons & Pepinsky, 1966).

This study is noteworthy for several features, including follow-up assessment and the evaluation of community adjustment; however, the precise nature of treatment makes it difficult to interpret the results. In addition to including client-centered conditions of treatment and group processes, other strategies and techniques were employed, including interpretation of behavior, efforts to induce "extreme amounts of anxiety and stress concerning antisocial behavior" (Persons, 1966, p. 338), role playing, and direct consequences for inappropriate behavior.

The results from these examples and others that might be cited convey extremely promising treatments that have not been pursued extensively in more contemporary research. In a number of more recent studies, variants of relationship and nondirective therapy have been included in comparative outcome studies. For example, studies of children identified because of maladjustment in the schools (Durlak, 1980) or referred for inpatient treatment based on their antisocial behavior (Kazdin, Esveldt-Dawson, French, & Unis, 1987) have indicated that relationship-based therapy leads to modest changes compared to no-treatment, but the changes are not as strong as those achieved with behavioral or cognitive-behavioral treatments. Even so, further tests of relationship-based treatments are warranted. Relationship-based treatment emphasizes treatment processes and the interchanges between therapist and client. Research on such processes may elaborate phenomena that have broad generality among diverse treatment approaches.

Play Therapy
Play therapy refers to a broad range of treatments. Psychoanalytic and client-centered views have dominated the conceptual underpinnings of play therapy (see Landreth, 1982). Hence it might be included under approaches covered previously. Play therapy is delineated separately here because it has extended beyond any one or two conceptual approaches and is widely subscribed to in clinical practice. The literature on play therapy is rich in terms of conceptualization of play, case illustrations, and descriptions of treatment (e.g., Schaefer, 1976; Schaefer & O'Connor, 1983). However, reviews of treatment have noted that controlled studies of play therapy are scant (e.g., Barrett et al., 1978; Kazdin, Bass et al., 1990). Nevertheless a number of demonstrations suggest that the use of play can produce change.

Critical to play therapy is the assumption that play can lead to change in clinically relevant domains of functioning among children. A test of that was reported in a study of young children (ages 2–6) who were selected on the basis of teacher ratings of separation anxiety (Milos & Reiss, 1982). The children were randomly assigned to one of four

conditions. Three experimental conditions provided play experiences relevant to separation themes, as reflected in play with a nursery school dollhouse. The control condition provided play experiences that were unrelated to separation. The three play conditions were used to represent different models of play therapy. The free-play condition permitted separation-relevant play as the child desired and was an analogue of *nondirective play therapy*. The directed-play condition provided instructions that focused the child's attention on separation-relevant play and served as an analogue of *structured play therapy*. The modeling-play condition provided the child with an opportunity to observe the experimenter play out separation themes and served as an analogue for *modeling* used in play therapy. Children received three sessions (10 minutes each with 2–3 days between sessions). The primary outcome measure was speech disturbances in response to separation-relevant and separation-irrelevant questions following completion of treatment. (Separate data reported within this study established the relation of the speech measure to anxiety.) Posttreatment teacher ratings were also obtained to measure separation anxiety (on a one-item global rating). The three play conditions were associated with reductions of anxiety on the speech measure but not on teacher ratings. No differences were evident among the three play therapies. The results were interpreted to support the notion that thematic play can lead to reductions in anxiety.

As the authors noted, this was not a treatment study per se given the objectives of the investigation, the duration of the interventions, and the absence of a multimeasure outcome assessment battery. The study is noteworthy for providing a test of a basic hypothesis about the therapeutic role of play. Within the study itself, interesting questions were raised about the precise role of play. Significant differences were found in the extent to which the three experimental play groups engaged in separation-relevant themes, even though no group differences in anxiety emerged at outcome.

In another study, teachers from several schools selected boys and girls from the third grade who exhibited disruptive behavior (Bleck & Bleck, 1982). Six youth in each of 13 schools were assigned to receive group play therapy or no-treatment. *Group play therapy* consisted of two meetings per week for a five-week period. The sessions included efforts to foster group interaction, awareness and understanding of self and others, exploration of feelings, and discussion of consequences of behavior. Play was used as the primary therapeutic agent in which youth alone and together made clay models of something important to them, drew animals, painted pictures related to a time they were disruptive or aggressive, worked on puzzles, used puppets to dramatize alternative responses and their consequences, and engaged in role play. The results indicated that treated youth showed greater gains in self-esteem and on teacher ratings of defiance–disrespect (a factor from a broader scale) at posttreatment. Follow-up data were not reported. The results indicate that play therapy can lead to systematic changes.

In general, play therapy is an area in need of accelerated research, especially given the widespread use of play for young children seen in clinical practice. Studies with well-specified play therapy procedures for carefully delineated clinical dysfunctions or domains of impairment are needed. In addition and as important, research is needed on the assumptive base about processes through which play operates. For example, the precise means through which play can controvert dysfunctions and maladjustment associated with sexual abuse, depression, or aggression in children need to be specified, operationalized, and tested.

Behavior Therapy

As noted previously, psychoanalytic, psychodynamic, nondirective, and play therapies are widely subscribed to and used in clinical work but are infrequently studied. In contrast, as an approach toward treatment, behavioral therapy is used frequently in clinical practice and is the dominant approach studied in outcome research (Kazdin, Bass et al., 1990). Behavioral treatments encompass multiple learning paradigms, models, and treatment techniques. Individually, the treatments vary across different disorders and types of child functioning. Two areas are illustrated here.

Parent management training is probably the most well-investigated technique in child psychotherapy research, based on the number of controlled outcome studies and range of populations encompassed by these studies. Hundreds of controlled studies of parent training have been reported, and they encompass diverse clinical populations, including youth with conduct problems, attention deficit disorder, pervasive developmental disorder, mental retardation, learning delays, eating disorders, enuresis and encopresis, and others (see Kazdin, 1987a; G. Miller & Prinz, 1990; Schaefer & Briesmeister, 1989). Parent training refers to social learning/behavioral procedures in which parents are trained to alter a child's behavior in the home. The parents meet with a therapist who teaches them to use behavior-change techniques to alter the behaviors that serve as the basis for clinical referral.

Although many variations of parent training exist, several common characteristics can be identified. First, treatment is conducted primarily with the parent(s) who directly implement several procedures in the home. Usually there is little or no direct intervention by the therapist with the child. Second, parents are trained to identify, define, and observe behavior in new ways. The careful specification of the behaviors of interest is essential for the delivery of reinforcing or punishing consequences and for evaluating if the program is achieving the desired goals. Third, the treatment sessions cover social learning principles and the procedures that follow from them, including positive reinforcement (e.g., the use of social praise and tokens or points for prosocial behavior), mild punishment (e.g., use of time out from reinforcement, loss of privileges), negotiation, and contingency contracting. Fourth, the sessions provide opportunities for parents to see how the techniques are implemented, to practice using the techniques, and to review the behavior change programs in the home. The immediate goal of the program is to develop specific skills in the parents, so they can implement procedures effectively at home.

The most frequent application of parent training has been with children who show disruptive behavior and conduct problems. As an illustration, Webster-Stratton, Kolpacoff, and Hollinsworth (1988) evaluated parent training with parents of children ages 3–8 referred for conduct problems including noncompliance, aggression, and oppositional behavior. Families were randomly assigned to one of four conditions that examined variations of the presentation and delivery of parent training. The three treatment conditions included *parenting materials, group discussion, and videotaped presentation of the parent training content, individually administered videotaped presentation without group discussion,* and *group discussion of parenting without the videotapes.* Each of these groups received parent training in a different form over a period of 10–12 weeks, in weekly 2-hour sessions. A *waiting-list control* group did not receive treatment during this period.

At posttreatment, all three treatment groups showed significant improvement in child functioning on rating scales and home observations. Among the three intervention groups, the outcomes were similar. However, the group discussion and videotaped presentation group tended to show greater improvements on outcome measures and significantly lower dropout rates, higher rates of attendance at the sessions, and greater satisfaction with treatment. Assessment of a one-year follow-up indicated that the effects were maintained (Webster-Stratton, Hollinsworth, & Kolpacoff, 1989). At follow-up, participants in the three treatments were significantly improved on several outcome measures relative to pretreatment. Overall, 67 and 78 percent of treated cases across the three groups achieved clinically significant change, as defined by returning to the normative range of functioning on mother- and father-completed standardized rating scales (e.g., Child Behavior Checklist).

Several other studies of parent training have demonstrated improvements in child behavior at home, at school, and in the community (see Kazdin, 1987a; McMahon & Wells, 1989; G. Miller & Prinz, 1990). Parent training has brought the problematic behaviors of treated children within the normative levels of their peers who are functioning adequately. Improvements often remain evident one-year after treatment; the continued benefits of treatment have been reported up to 10 years later (Forehand & Long, 1988).

Because parent training has been investigated more often than some other therapies for children, several characteristics of treatment have been studied. For example, parent and family characteristics that contribute to change have been documented. Families characterized by multiple risk factors associated with childhood dysfunction (e.g., marital discord, parent psychopathology, social isolation, and socioeconomic disadvantage) tend to show fewer gains in treatment and are less likely to maintain therapeutic gains (e.g., Dadds & McHugh, 1992; Dumas & Wahler, 1983; Strain, Young, & Horowitz, 1981; Webster-Stratton, 1985). Also, the beneficial effects of treatment have been shown on the behavior of siblings of the referred child as well as on measures of psychopathology (especially depression) of the parents (see Kazdin, 1985). Nevertheless, many fundamental issues regarding the effects of parent training remain to be addressed. The requirement of active participation on the part of a parent makes the treatment inapplicable to those cases in which parent dysfunction and unwillingness cannot be surmounted. In addition, different types of clinical dysfunction and youth of different ages may vary in the extent to which they are amenable to contingency management in the home. The applicability of the procedures to different problem domains, ages, and subtypes of youth with a given type of dysfunction is infrequently studied. Finally, the long-term effects of treatment (e.g., beyond one or two years) are rarely reported with clinically referred samples.

Social skills training provides another illustration of behavior therapy research. Social skills training is based on the view that deficiencies in prosocial behavior and interpersonal skills underlie diverse clinical problems and/or can be used to promote adjustment and improved functioning (see Strain,

Guralnick, & Walker, 1986). Training is designed to develop positive approach responses in interpersonal situations. Typically, clients are trained to engage in interactions by making requests of others, responding to comments from others, giving and receiving praise, and approaching others. The specific training techniques include instructions, modeling, role playing, feedback, and social reinforcement. Repeated rehearsal and reinforcement are used to shape, improve, and refine performance in verbal and nonverbal interpersonal behaviors.

As an illustration, social skills training was applied to elementary school children (grades 1–3, age range 6–10) who displayed high levels of peer rejection and negative peer interaction (Bierman, Miller, & Stabb, 1987). Youth were carefully selected based on sociometric ratings and direct observations of social interaction. Children were assigned randomly to one of four conditions: *instructions, prohibitions, instructions + prohibitions,* or *no-treatment.* In the instructions condition, discussion of the desired target behaviors (e.g., prosocial behavior related to addressing and interacting with others) was emphasized and trained using examples, direct reinforcement, and practice. In the prohibition condition, rules for not engaging in negative behaviors were emphasized—in other words, emphasis was placed on *not* breaking rules rather than on performing positive behaviors. The combined group received both conditions. Treatment was provided in 10 sessions (each $\frac{1}{2}$ hour) at school.

Each of the treatments led to significant improvements relative to no-treatment. The prohibition condition led to immediate and stable declines in negative social interaction; instructions promoted more sustained intervention effects as evident at a six-month follow-up assessment. Only the combined treatment led to changes in sociometric ratings (reduced negative ratings). At follow-up, ratings of aggression by teachers and peers and sociometric ratings did not show differences among groups. The authors note that changes in social behavior appear to be more easily achieved than changes in peer acceptance, an issue of significance perhaps in conceptualizing and evaluating treatment. The study is notable for the care taken in delineating and selecting impaired children, evaluating components of a broader social skills training package, and including multiple measures based on different perspectives (teachers, peers, direct observation).

Few studies have evaluated social skills training with clinically referred youth. As an exception, McKenna and Gaffney (1982) evaluated social skills training with youth ages 12–16 referred for a variety of problems (e.g., anxiety, shyness, aggressiveness) at child guidance clinics. Youth were randomly assigned to one of three conditions: *social skills training, nonspecific therapy control,* or *waiting-list control.* Social skills youth participated in groups where they received instructions, practice, role playing, and other procedures noted previously to develop interpersonal skills. Nonspecific control youth also participated in groups during sessions with therapists. They engaged in activities (e.g., games, exercises, viewing films) and discussed interpersonal problems and possible solutions. No specific training in social skills was provided. Waiting-list youth did not receive treatment in the 10-week period in which the other conditions were provided. At posttreatment, measures of social behavior and problem solving completed by youth and parents showed that social skills training led to significant changes and greater changes than the other conditions. Nonspecific therapy and waiting-list control conditions were no different from each other and did not show improvement. The outcome measures included a number of scales of social functioning. Changes in presenting problems or maintenance of therapeutic gains were not reported.

A significant application of social skills training beyond the scope of the present chapter is in the area of prevention. A salient goal of preventive interventions is to promote prosocial competence and coping as a means to increase resilience and to promote adjustment. Training in social skills often plays a significant role in applications to children and adolescents (see Weissberg, Caplan, & Harwood, 1991).

Cognitive-Behavioral Therapy

Cognitively based treatment for children and adolescents overlaps with behavioral treatment in conceptual heritage and methodological approach toward treatment. The special focus of cognitively based treatments has been on conceptualization of dysfunction on the basis of cognitive processes such as attributions, schemas, beliefs, and expectations, changes in this cognitive processes are considered to be central for therapeutic change. For many of the treatments, role playing, direct reinforcement, and assignment of concrete behavioral tasks outside of treatment are also used. Efforts to change behavior directly are seen as a means of modifying cognitions. Consequently, the hyphenated term *cognitive-behavioral* better captures the broad domain of the treatments. Cognitive-behavioral treatments have been examined in several controlled outcome studies with children and adolescents across a variety of clinical dysfunctions and

problem domains (Durlak et al., 1991; Kendall, 1991).

As an illustration, problem-solving skills training is a cognitively based technique that has been applied to the treatment of aggressive and antisocial behavior among children. Cognitive processes (perceptions, self-statements, attributions, and problem-solving skills) are frequently accorded a major role in conduct problems. A variety of processes have been identified, such as a predisposition to attribute hostile intent to others when confronted with ambiguous situations, as well as deficiencies in generating alternative solutions to interpersonal problems, in recognizing consequences of one's actions, and in taking the perspective of others (see Dodge, 1985; Rubin, Bream, & Rose-Krasnor, 1991; Shirk, 1988; Spivack & Shure, 1982). Problem-solving skills training consists of developing skills to address deficiencies and distortions in approaching interpersonal situations. Many variations of problem-solving skills training have been applied to conduct problem children. Generally, several characteristics are shared among different programs. First, the emphasis is on *how* children approach situations. Although it is obviously important that children ultimately select appropriate means of behaving in everyday life, the primary focus is on the thought *processes* rather than the *outcome* or specific behavioral acts that result. Second, children are taught to engage in a step-by-step approach to solve interpersonal problems. They make statements to themselves that direct attention to certain aspects of the problem or tasks and lead to effective solutions. Third, treatment utilizes structured tasks involving games, academic activities, and stories. Over the course of treatment, the cognitive problem-solving skills are increasingly applied to real-life situations. Fourth, therapists usually play an active role in treatment. They model the cognitive processes by making verbal self-statements, applying the sequence of statements to particular problems, providing cues to prompt use of the skills, and delivering feedback and praise to develop correct use of the skills. Finally, treatment usually combines several different procedures including modeling and practice, role playing, reinforcement, and mild punishment (loss of points or tokens).

In an example from our own research, we examined the effectiveness of *problem-solving skills training, nondirective relationship therapy,* and *minimal treatment contact* with hospitalized antisocial children ages 7–13 (Kazdin et al., 1987). In the problem-solving skills training condition, youth were seen individually and trained to apply the skills to interpersonal interactions in which they had engaged in aggressive and antisocial behavior.

Relationship therapy consisted of sessions that focused on developing a close therapeutic relationship; providing empathy, positive regard, and warmth; and helping the child to express feelings. Minimal-contact children met briefly in sessions with a therapist and played games or engaged in other activities that provided contact but no specific treatment regimen to alter antisocial behavior. The results showed significant improvements on antisocial behavior and other symptom areas for children who received problem-solving skills training, as reflected on parent and teacher checklists of child functioning at home and at school immediately after treatment (after discharge from the hospital) and up to one year later. Problem-solving skills training children were more improved than relationship therapy and minimal contact children who did not reliably improve. Similarly, in other controlled studies, cognitively based treatments have led to significant improvements in child and adolescent behavior at home, at school, and in the community. Follow-up has indicated that the gains in treatment often are maintained up to one year later (Arbuthnot & Gordon, 1986; Kendall & Braswell, 1982; Lochman, Burch, Curry, & Lampron, 1984), although loss of gains has been reported as well (Kendall, Ronan, & Epps, 1991). Also gains have been reflected on measures of parent functioning (e.g., depression) (Kazdin et al., 1992).

Another cognitive-behavioral treatment used with children and adolescents is *anger control training* (see Feindler, 1991; Novaco, 1975). Treatment is based on the view that anger arousal is mediated by a person's expectations and appraisals of interpersonal and environmental events. Cognitive processes (e.g., attributions) promote impulsive and aggressive reactions. Anger control training includes a set of procedures that are designed to restructure cognitive processes and develop self-control. The procedures are designed to train children to control anger by appraising (processing) potentially provocative events differently and by prompting their own behavior with self-instructions and coping responses. For example, self-instructions to relax, to slow down before responding, and to apply problem-solving strategies to generate responses are central components.

As an illustration, anger control training was applied to aggressive hospitalized adolescents in an inpatient psychiatric hospital (Feindler, Ecton, Kingsley, & Dubey, 1986). Male adolescents (13–18 yeas old) were assigned to *anger control training* or *waiting-list control* conditions. Youth within and from another unit in the hospital served as controls, since random assignment to conditions on an individual basis was not possible. Anger control training was provided in a group format in 12 sessions over an 8-week period. Training consisted of diverse cognitive and behavioral procedures including modeling, rehearsal, self-instructions to guide and control behavior, self-monitoring of conflict situations, and others. Training and control youth participated in a behavioral program in the wards. Posttreatment assessment within the hospital revealed that anger control training led to an increase in reflective (less impulsive) responding on a laboratory measure and improvements in self-control as rated by hospital staff, decreases in hostile reactions during conflict, and decreased aggressive behavior on the unit. Waiting-list control subjects showed some deterioration in aggressive behavior.

Anger control training has been examined in other studies showing that changes can be obtained in aggressive behavior (e.g., Saylor, Benson, & Einhaus, 1985). Current limitations include unclear evidence about the magnitude, clinical importance, and durability of the changes (see Feindler, 1991). Significantly, some of the key studies have been applied to aggressive, inpatient, adolescent youth. Generally this would be regarded as a particularly difficult population to treat given the severity, duration, and scope of dysfunction.

Cognitively based treatment for children and adolescents represents an active area of research. Applications extend to a number of clinical domains, as illustrated in the examples of treatment of various domains of functioning presented later in the chapter. Key issues remain to be addressed. Few applications have been provided for clinically impaired samples. Long-term follow-up remains to be studied. In addition, further work is needed to understand the bases for therapeutic change. Changes in cognitive processes do not invariably relate to therapeutic change. Consequently, the mechanisms of influence are unclear (Durlak et al., 1991).

Family Therapy

Family therapy refers to a broad class of interventions in which clinical dysfunction is viewed from the standpoint of the family as a system. Family therapy is used frequently in clinical work with children and adolescents (Kazdin, Siegel, & Bass, 1990). The child or adolescent referred for treatment is considered to be the "identified patient," that is, the person whom the family identifies as problematic but who actually is considered to reflect the dysfunction, conflict, and maladaptive processes within the family. There are multiple approaches to and techniques of family therapy based on different views about the structure, functions, roles, and sources of conflict that lead to dysfunction (see Schaefer, Briesmeister, & Fitton, 1984).

Until recently, the empirical literature on family therapies in which the child or adolescent, rather than adult, has served as the identified patient has been quite modest. For example, in their review in 1987, Hazelrigg et al. identified only 20 such studies spread across diverse "disorders" (identified patient problems) and family therapy approaches. Since that review, several well-controlled studies have emerged from programs of research on family therapy (e.g., Henggeler & Borduin, 1990; Szapocznik & Kurtines, 1989).

As an example, Szapocznik and his collegues (1990; Szapocznik & Kurtines, 1989) have evaluated treatment for drug-abusing Hispanic children and adolescents with behavioral problems. Based on their research with Hispanic families, the authors identified intergenerational conflicts mixed with cultural and value issues as critical to child and adolescent dysfunction. A structural family approach was selected as consistent with these characteristics, given the emphasis on such issues as leadership, system organization, communication flow, and conflict resolution.

In one of the studies, structural family therapy was compared to psychodynamic psychotherapy (Szapocznik et al., 1989). Hispanic children ages 6–12 referred for a variety of behavioral and emotional problems were assigned to either *structural family therapy, individual psychodynamic child therapy,* or a *recreation control condition.* This latter group was included to control for common (nonspecific) factors associated with attending treatment. Youth in the control condition received sessions in small groups where they engaged in recreational activities (arts, crafts). Youth in the treatment conditions received a maximum of six months of treatment (12–24 contact hours). The results (obtained from parent behavior checklist ratings) indicated that both active treatment conditions led to significant change in child dysfunction, psychodynamic functioning (e.g., psychosexual development, ego functioning), and family functioning (e.g., family flexibility, conflict resolution). In general, treatment did not differ systematically from each other at posttreatment. However, at a one-year follow-up, family functioning of cases who participated in family therapy improved greatly; during this same interval, family functioning of youth who received psychodynamic treatment deteriorated; controls remained unchanged. Thus, family functioning, but not child deviance, was differentially influenced by the treatments.

Additional studies from this research program have made important contributions to the theory and practice of family-based treatment for children and adolescents (see Szapocznik & Kurtines, 1989). The contributions include outcome research showing that family therapy can be completed with individuals rather than with the family as a whole. That is, the conceptual approach of family therapy does not necessarily require the active participation of all family members; individual family therapy can also be effective. Also, family-based interventions have been shown to engage patients in treatment and to reduce attrition from therapy.

Parent–child conflict is an area in which family-based treatment would seem to be essential because of the inherently interactional nature of the presenting problem. In a recent study, three models of family therapy were compared for adolescents with attention-deficit hyperactivity disorder (Barkley, Guevremont, Anastopoulos, & Fletcher, 1992). Apart from core or defining symptoms (impulsivity, inattention, motoric overactivity), such youth often show a variety of other disruptive behaviors including aggression, defiance, and noncompliance. Barkley et al. (1992) compared *parent management training, structural family therapy,* and *problem-solving and communication training.* The first two treatments have been illustrated in examples reviewed previously. The problem-solving communication therapy included elements of parent training (behavioral skills and contingency management) and structural family therapy (family system issues), and the added focus on cognitive processes (restructuring irrational beliefs). Youth ages 12–17 and their mothers were assigned to one of the three family therapies and received 8–10 weekly sessions of treatment.

The results indicated that all three treatments produced significant improvement in parent–youth communication, number of conflicts, and anger intensity during conflicts at home, as rated separately by adolescents and parents. Improvements in overall child symptoms and in functioning at school also occurred over the course of treatment. A three-month follow-up indicated that treatment gains continued. The clinical significance of therapeutic change was evaluated by examining the magnitude of change for individuals on a variety of outcome measures. The results revealed that 5–30 percent of the youth showed a clinically significant change, depending on the outcome measure. Groups were not reliably different in the extent to which they showed clinically significant changes. The results are interesting in comparing different models of treatment, showing significant changes over the course of treatment, and as well by documenting that only a minority of youth showed clinically significant change.

School- and Community-Based Interventions

Occasionally, treatment of children and adolescents is conducted in community settings. Community-based treatment attempts to take advantage of the resources in the everyday environment that can support prosocial behavior and help to integrate individuals into the network and influences of their prosocial peers. Two examples illustrate outcome research of community-based treatment.

Kolvin et al. (1981) conducted a large-scale outcome study in England between 1972 and 1979 to evaluate different interventions for maladjusted children in the schools. The objective was to examine the impact of different treatments on different types of clinical problems, with children at different stages of development and dysfunction. Two different types of child dysfunction were investigated, namely, neurotic disorder (e.g., overcontrolled problems such as depression and anxiety) and conduct disorder (e.g., undercontrolled problems such as disruptive behavior, bullying, and delinquency). Because of the potential significance of developmental stage on the nature of child dysfunction and response to treatment, two different age levels were selected: children ages 7–8 and 11–12. Screening of 4,300 children was undertaken to identify the final group (slightly less than 600) of children included in the study. Multiple measures involving parent, teacher, peer, and clinician evaluations were used to conduct screening and to evaluate treatment outcome.

Once identified, children were assigned randomly to one of four conditions. The conditions varied slightly for younger and older children; for each age group, there was a no-treatment condition that provided the basis for comparison over the course of treatment and follow-up. *Parent counseling plus teacher consultation* consisted of social work consultation with parents and teachers in an effort to coordinate school and home activities, casework with the family, and support for the teacher. *Nurture work* consisted of providing enrichment activities for the children, close interaction with the child, and behavioral shaping for individual child goals. *Group therapy* was based on client-centered principles and practices and consisted of play group therapy (for younger children) or discussion (more traditional) group therapy for older children. In each case, the focus was on the expression of feelings, acceptance of the child, warmth, and the therapeutic relationship. The *behavior modification* program (for older children) consisted of classroom reinforcement systems relying on social and token reinforcement to improve deportment and classroom performance.

Among the major findings for the younger children, play group therapy and nurture work led to significantly greater changes than the parent–teacher and no-treatment conditions. These effects were evident primarily for neurotic rather than conduct problem behavior. For the older children, group therapy and behavior modification led to greater changes than the parent–teacher condition or no-treatment. Among the different treatments, children with neurotic disorders, as defined earlier, responded better than children with conduct disorders. Also, females responded better to treatments than did males. There were no consistent interactions between the type of treatment and type of child disorder nor between treatment and child sex.

There are several excellent features of this study, including the use of multiple measures for screening, a comparison of separate treatments with a randomly comprised no-treatment control group, relatively large sample sizes (60–90) in each group, assessment of multiple domains of functioning (maladjustment, cognitive functioning, social relations with peers), and the evaluation of follow-up. Few studies have attempted to examine the effects of different treatments on alternative problems and with children of different ages.

Treatments for youth have been conducted and carefully evaluated outside of the school setting. As an example, Feldman, Caplinger, and Wodarski (1983) conducted a community-based treatment project for antisocial youths. The treatment program was integrated with activities of the Jewish Community Centers Association in St. Louis, Missouri. The study included youth (ages 8–17) who were referred for antisocial behavior (referred youths) or who normally attended the regular activities programs and were not identified as showing problem behavior (nonreferred youths). The project began with approximately 700 youths; this number declined to approximately 450 by the end of treatment.

The study evaluated the effects of three types of treatment, two levels of therapist experience, and three different ways to compose the groups. The three treatments were *traditional group social work* (focus on group processes, social organization, and norms within the group), *behavior modification* (use of reinforcement contingencies, focus on prosocial behavior), and *minimal treatment* (no explicit application of a structured treatment plan; spontaneous interactions of group members). Activity groups within the center were formed and assigned to one of these three interventions. The groups were led by trainers, some of whom were experienced (graduate students of social work with previous experience) and others who were inexperienced (undergraduate students). Finally, the groups were comprised in three ways: all members referred for antisocial behavior, all members nonreferred ("normal"), and a mixture of referred and nonreferred.

The objective was to evaluate changes in antisocial behavior of referred youths over the course of the intervention. Measures were obtained from parents, referral agents, group members, and group leaders as well as direct observations of the groups. The intervention was conducted over a period of a year in which the youths attended sessions and engaged in a broad range of activities (e.g., sports, arts and crafts, fund-raising). The specific treatments were superimposed on the usual activity structure of the community facility. Treatment sessions ranged from 8 to 29 sessions (mean = 22.2 sessions), each lasting about 2–3 hours.

The results indicated that youth with experienced, rather than inexperienced, leaders showed greater reductions in antisocial behavior. Referred (antisocial) youths in the mixed groups that included nonreferred children showed greater improvements than similar participants in groups comprised of only antisocial youths. Very modest outcome differences were noted as a function technique. Behavior modification tended to lead to greater reductions in antisocial behavior than did traditional group treatment. Traditional treatment led to some decrements in antisocial behavior relative to the minimal contact group. Evaluation of treatment integrity indicated that each of the active treatments was not executed as intended and that the activity (no-treatment) condition received some therapy. Thus, lack of clear differences in outcome among treatment conditions could be explained on methodological grounds. Overall, antisocial youths benefited from the program, especially those who received the most favorable intervention condition (i.e., behavior modification with an experienced leader in a mixed group of referred and nonreferred peers). Several features of the study are noteworthy, including evaluation of therapist characteristics and group composition in relation to outcome and the assessment of treatment integrity.

As evident by these examples, school- and community-based treatments do not necessarily involve different approaches from those highlighted previously. However, intervention in the community is not merely a change in locale from where a given treatment (e.g., play therapy, behavior modification) is applied. Schools and other settings provide special opportunities to intervene to reach larger numbers of youth than those seen in or referred for treatment. Also, such settings can mobilize resources and sources of influences that can contribute to therapeutic change. For example, in the Feldman et al. (1983) study, peers contributed in important ways to therapeutic change. These influences otherwise would be difficult to mobilize in more traditional mental health and private practice treatment settings. Other sources of influence such as parent groups and community volunteers raise similar potential advantages of community-based treatments.

General Comments

It is worth reiterating that the previous illustrations only sample the research from major treatment approaches. Even with a necessarily restrictive set of examples to illustrate outcome research, several points emerge and are worth highlighting. First, many treatment approaches are available for children and adolescents. Second, treatments are conducted in diverse settings. Programs at home, at school, and in the community complement the more traditional models of individual and group therapy in treatment settings. Third, parents, families, and teachers are often involved in treatment. These and other points are conveyed further in the illustrations of treatments for various child and adolescent dysfunctions.

RESEARCH ON SPECIFIC DISORDERS AND DOMAINS OF DYSFUNCTION

Overview: Range of Foci

In the prior section, illustrations sampled research from various treatment approaches. Another way to examine progress in treatment research is to focus on clinical dysfunction. From the standpoint of clinical work, primary interest is in the effectiveness of treatments for various clinical dysfunctions. In this context, one is less concerned with a single approach and more concerned with the status of any treatment(s) alone or in combination and their evidence in achieving clinically important changes in a given area of functioning.

There are many areas to which psychotherapy is applied for children and adolescents. To begin, a large number of clinical disorders are recognized in current diagnostic systems (e.g., *Diagnostic and Statistical Manual of Mental Disorders* [DSM-III-R], International Classification of Diseases [ICD-10]). As an illustration, Table 13.1 lists currently recognized disorders *arising in infancy, childhood, and adolescence* in the DSM-III-R (American Psychiatric Association, 1987). The table excludes a large number of disorders that are not considered to be unique to childhood (i.e., where similar or identical

TABLE 13.1   Disorders first evident in infancy, childhood, or adolescence

Mental Retardation

Pervasive Developmental Disorders

Autistic disorder

Pervasive developmental disorder not otherwise specified

Specific Developmental Disorders

Developmental arithmetic disorder

Developmental expressive writing disorder

Developmental reading disorder

Developmental articulation disorder

Developmental expressive language disorder

Developmental coordination disorder

Specific developmental disorder not otherwise specified

Disruptive Behavior Disorders

Attention-deficit hyperactivity disorder

Conduct disorder

Oppositional-defiant disorder

Anxiety Disorders of Childhood or Adolescence

Separation anxiety disorder

Avoidant disorder

Overanxious disorder

Eating Disorders

Anorexia nervosa

Bulumia nervosa

Pica

Rumination disorder of infancy

Eating disorder not otherwise specified

Gender Identity Disorders

Gender identity disorder of childhood

Transsexualism

Nontranssexual gender identity disorder

Gender identity disorder not otherwise specified

Tic Disorder

Tourette's disorder

Chronic motor or vocal tic disorder

Transient tic disorder

Tic disorder not otherwise specified

Elimination Disorders

Functional enuresis

Functional encopresis

Speech Disorders Not Elsewhere Classified

Cluttering

Stuttering

Other Disorders of Infancy, Childhood, or Adolescence

Elective mutism

Identity disorder

Reactive attachment disorder of infancy and early childhood

Stereotype/habit disorder

Undifferentiated attention deficit disorder

Note. These disorders are likely to *arise* in infancy, childhood, or adolescence as identified in the *Diagnostic and Statistical Manual of Mental Disorders* (DSM-III-R; American Psychiatric Association, 1987). There are several other disorders in which the essential features are considered to be the same in children and adults. Mood disorders and schizophrenia are primary examples. No special categories are provided for children because the criteria utilized with adults are considered to be applicable across the age spectrum.

criteria are used across the life span). Examples include mood, adjustment, obsessive-compulsive, post-traumatic stress, and substance abuse disorders. There are ongoing revisions of the DSM system and of other diagnostic schemes as well that vary in their delineation and classification of childhood and adolescent dysfunction (e.g., ICD-10; World Health Organization, 1988). Thus, the specific list provided in Table 13.1 is illustrative of the types and range of clinical disorders currently recognized, rather than an immutable statement of established symptom constellations. One need not

subscribe to a particular diagnostic system nor accept any particular disorder and its criteria to make the point, to wit, that there are many dysfunctions, however delineated, recognized in clinical work.

Psychotherapy is also applied to a variety of other conditions and circumstances that do not necessarily meet diagnostic criteria for "disorders." These include temporary perturbations of adjustment (e.g., in reaction to parental separation or divorce), effects of victimization (e.g., physical or sexual abuse, or neglect), and management of or adjustment to health-related domains (e.g., adherence to treatment for illness, pain or stress management with invasive tests or treatments). Clearly, the number of domains to which psychotherapy can be and has been applied with children and adolescents is vast. As with the prior section on treatment approaches, the present section illustrates treatment research for children and adolescents by sampling diverse domains.

Compendia on the effects of treatments for children and adolescents have organized the literature by problem domains such as anxiety, conduct problems, hyperactivity, depression, autism, and other areas (Bornstein & Kazdin, 1985; Kratochwill & Morris, 1991; Mash & Barkley, 1989). Although a large number of intervention studies can be identified, a small proportion rely on clinical samples and youth with clinically severe levels of dysfunction. In the present section, several areas are identified because they constitute frequent foci in clinical research or practice and illustrate contemporary progress. As in the discussion of research on treatment techniques, the scope of research can only be illustrated rather than reviewed exhaustively.

Conduct Disorder and Delinquency

Conduct problems refer generally to undercontrolled behaviors including aggressive and oppositional acts, theft, vandalism, fire setting, lying, truancy, running away, teasing, arguing, and so on. In contemporary diagnosis, *conduct disorder* is the term used to denote a pattern of antisocial behavior among children and adolescents (American Psychiatric Association, 1987). The significance of conduct disorder among children and adolescents stems from the relatively high prevalence rate (e.g., 2–6% in the United States), the stability of the problem and its poor long-term prognosis, and the continuation of the dysfunction in families across generations (IOM, 1989; Kazdin, 1987b). Moreover, for children and adolescents, the general class of conduct/oppositional problems constitutes the type of dysfunction seen most frequently in clinical practice and evaluated in treatment research (Kazdin, Bass et al., 1990; Kazdin, Seigel, & Bass, 1990). Such behaviors obviously can vary greatly in type and severity.

Apart from the diagnosis of conduct disorder, severe antisocial behavior also is designated by the juvenile justice system. Delinquent youth are defined as those who have committed illegal acts. Conduct disorder and delinquency overlap insofar as they both refer to rule violation, can involve similar acts (e.g., theft), and can be applied to the same youth. However, they are not identical because criteria for their designation in terms of patterns of defining characteristics are different. For example, delinquent youth may be caught for selling drugs or for a felonious crime but would not meet the criteria for conduct disorder because the symptoms required for the disorder are not based on illegal acts per se or contact with the courts. However, there is overlap in the population of interest and in the treatments that are applied (for reviews see Brandt & Zlotnick, 1988; Dumas, 1989; Kazdin, 1985).

Applications of treatment include a continuum of severity of dysfunction from youth who are noncompliant and primarily oppositional to those who are more chronically delinquent. Treatments, particularly cognitively based treatment, behavior modification, and family therapy, have shown considerable promise for treatment of clinically referred conduct problem youth (Kazdin, 1987a). Prior examples of research in the present chapter have included approaches with such youth. Examples with more severely delinquent youth are illustrated here to convey diverse interventions, progress in research, and dilemmas raised by treatment.

A *multifaceted behavioral program* has been used to rehabilitate predelinquent males who committed various offenses (e.g., thefts, fighting, school truancy, and academic failure) (Fixsen, Phillips, Phillips, & Wolf, 1976). The program was conducted at a home-style cottage setting, called Achievement Place, managed by two houseparents. A token economy served as the basis of the intervention in which points (tokens) were earned for a variety of adaptive and prosocial behaviors such as engaging in self-care behaviors, performing chores, and completing school work. Points could be lost for poor grades, aggressive talk (making threats), disobeying rules, lying, stealing, being late, fighting, and other disruptive behaviors. Points were used to purchase privileges such as staying up late, going downtown, watching TV, using tools, riding one's bicycle, and receiving an allowance. Interestingly, the youth participated actively in running the program by supervising each other's work, recording their own behavior, and developing and enforcing rules among their peers. The program has been shown to alter a variety of behaviors (e.g., social interaction, completion of homework, and chores) in the home setting. While involved in the program, participants committed fewer criminal offenses in the community and had fewer contacts with police and greater attendance at school compared to those who were on probation or participated in other settings where a behavioral program was not in effect (Kirigin, Braukmann, Atwater, & Wolf, 1982; Kirigin, Wolf, Braukmann, Fixsen, & Phillips, 1979). Yet rates of criminal offense and reinstitutionalization one to two years after treatment were not significantly better among Achievement Place youth compared with youth who participated in other types of programs.

In a recent study of chronically offending adolescent delinquents (≤ 16 years old), *parent management training* was compared to *court-provided family treatment* (including family therapy, group therapy, and drug counseling) (Bank, Marlowe, Reid, Patterson, & Weinrott, 1991). Parent training procedures, usually applied to less severely disturbed and younger children, were adapted to adolescents. Parents were trained to better monitor delinquent behavior and to use more age-appropriate incentives and punishment (e.g., work details, parent reporting of law violations to authorities). Outcome measures included official offense reports, direct observation of home behavior, and parent report of problem behaviors. The major results indicated that offense rates for both groups declined significantly after the onset of treatment. The decline was more rapid for the parent training group, as evident in lower offense rates during treatment and at the one-year follow-up assessment. By the second and third year follow-up assessments, rates for the two groups were no different. Parent training cases spent significantly fewer days of incarceration during the first two follow-up years (for which data were available), which the authors note represented a significant cost savings favoring parent training. For the five-year period of the project from initial assessment through the three-year follow-up, rate of nonstatus (more serious) offenses (e.g., misdemeanors, felonies) but not status (age-related) offenses (e.g., curfew violation, running away), were lower for the parent training condition.

Functional family therapy (Alexander & Parsons, 1982) has been used with marked effects with delinquent youth. Clinical problems are conceptualized from the standpoint of the functions they serve in the family as a system, as well as for individual family members. The assumption is made that problem behavior evident in the child is the only way some interpersonal functions (e.g., intimacy, distancing, support) can be met among family members. Treatment focuses on directly altering interaction and communication patterns in such a way as to foster more adaptive functioning. Behavior therapy (e.g., altering contingencies at home) and cognitive-behavioral therapy (e.g., identifying attributions, expectations) are integrated into a family focus of treatment. The main goals of treatment are to increase reciprocity and positive reinforcement among family members, to establish clear communication, to help specify behaviors that family members desire from each other, to negotiate constructively, and to help identify solutions to interpersonal problems.

The few available outcome studies of functional family therapy have produced relatively clear effects. The initial study included male and female delinquent adolescents referred to juvenile court for such behaviors as running away, truancy, theft, and unmanageability (Alexander & Parsons, 1973). In comparison to other treatments (e.g., client-centered or psychodynamically oriented family treatment) and control conditions (e.g., attention-placebo, no-treatment), family therapy has fared well. For example, family therapy, relative to other treatments, has shown greater improvement on family interaction measures and lower recidivism rates from juvenile court records up to 18 months after treatment (Alexander & Parsons, 1973). Follow-up data obtained two-and-one-half years later indicated that the siblings of those who received family therapy showed significantly lower rates of referral to juvenile courts (Klein, Alexander, & Parsons, 1977).

The available studies also provide information regarding factors that influence outcome. First, the effectiveness of treatment is influenced by the relationship (e.g., warmth, integration of affect and behavior) and structuring (e.g., directiveness) skills of the therapist (Alexander, Barton, Schiavo, & Parsons, 1976). Second, process measures of family interactions at posttreatment are related to subsequent recidivism (Alexander & Parsons, 1973). This finding lends credence to the model from which treatment was derived. Finally, in the outcome studies, client-centered and psychodynamically oriented forms of family-based therapies have not achieved the positive effects of functional family therapy; treatment of the clinical problem at the level of the family per se does not appear to be sufficient to alter conduct problems.

Attention-Deficit Hyperactivity Disorder

Attention-deficit hyperactivity disorder has as its central characteristics inattentiveness, impulsivity, and motoric overactivity. Hyperactivity and poor attention span are mentioned frequently as characteristics of such children. The disorder has been studied extensively and has a number of characteristics related to cognitive, interpersonal, and behavioral functioning (Barkley, 1988). As a clinical disorder, epidemiological studies estimate that between 2 and 10 percent of school-age children (4 – 16 years old) show the dysfunction (IOM, 1989). Attention deficit disorder and conduct disorder often occur together. Hence, youth with the diagnosis of attention deficit disorder may show a variety of oppositional, aggressive, and antisocial behaviors as well.

Unlike most clinical disorders for children, there is a "standard" treatment for attention-deficit hyperactivity disorder, namely, stimulant medication, primarily methylphenidate (Ritalin) and d-amphetamine (Dexedrine). Stimulant medication has an impact on multiple domains of functioning, including improved attention, impulse control, reduced off-task activity and disruptive behavior, and improved academic task performance (productivity and accuracy) (Barkley, 1989; Hinshaw, 1991). Although medication has become the standard treatment, there is broad consensus that this is not a sufficient treatment for the disorder nor one that necessarily promotes long-term clinical change (e.g., G. Weiss & Hechtman, 1986; Whalen & Henker, 1991). Indeed, the fast-acting nature of the drug is also associated with quickly dissipating treatment effects when the medication is stopped.

Diverse psychological treatments have been applied alone or in combination with medication (see Barkley, 1989; Rapport, 1992). The primary treatments that have been explored are behavior modification using contingency management in the home and at school to alter disruptive behavior and to sustain academic performance and cognitive-behavioral strategies to control impulsivity and inattention. The general view is that no single treatment approach is likely to controvert the range of problems attention deficit disorder youth present. Consequently, combined treatments are often studied.

As an illustration, the separate and combined use of *stimulant medication* (methylphenidate) and *behavior modification* were compared during a summer treatment program (Carlson, Pelham, Milich, & Dixon, 1992). Boys ages 6–12 received placebo, lower (0.3 mg/kg), and higher (0.6 mg/kg) doses of medication over the course of the study. A behavior modification program (e.g., reinforcement for compliance, appropriate behavior, and academic performance; response cost for noncompliance) during a classroom period as well as home-based reinforcement were also part of treatment. Performance was observed during periods in which the behavior modification program was and was not in effect over separate phases of the study in which medication and placebo conditions were prescribed. The results revealed that the separate effects of medication and behavior modification were positive. Both treatments alone improved classroom behavior. Only medication improved academic performance and children's self-ratings of their own performance. For the medication conditions, the higher dose tended to be associated with greater improvements. Behavior modification was

as effective as low-dose medication on on-task and disruptive behavior but did not affect academic work. Medication and behavior modification combined was not superior to higher dose medication alone. Interestingly, lower dose medication plus behavior modification generally was as effective as higher dose medication alone. The long-term impact of treatment was not evaluated.

The combination of one or two viable treatments in child and adolescent psychotherapy research is an approximation, and only an approximation, of what practitioners report in their delivery of treatment. More common is the use of several techniques based on clinician perceptions of what the individual child needs. Few studies approximate this approach in research. A notable exception is the work of Satterfield and his colleagues (e.g., Satterfield, Satterfield, & Cantwell, 1980, 1981; Satterfield, Satterfield, & Schell, 1987), who have evaluated the short- and long-term impact of treatment with hyperactive youth. In this treatment program, hyperactive and oppositional boys ages 6–12 were carefully selected, treated, and followed for several years to examine the impact of treatment on their delinquent behavior. Separate cohorts were run and received different treatments and hence were not randomly assigned. Two comparison groups were examined. The *medication only* group received stimulant medication with doses titrated to achieve clinical improvement. The *multimodality treatment* group received medication as well. However, this group also received intensive therapies involving cognitive, behavioral, and interpretive treatments. Each youth was assigned one educational and three social work therapists to provide these other treatments. The treatments included individual therapy, group therapy, parent and family therapy, educational therapy, and cognitive-behavioral modification in the home. The treatments varied for each individual based on an ongoing evaluation by the treatment team of what the case needed. Some families were in treatment 2 to 3 years. There have been several follow-up evaluations (e.g., one, two, and three years after treatment).

The results are illustrated by the extraordinary follow-up assessment obtained approximately nine years after treatment when the youth were into late adolescence and early adulthood. At follow-up, multimodality treatment cases showed a significantly lower rate of arrest for felony offenses and institutionalization than medication-only youth. Clearly, the multimodality treatment led to clear differences on measures of delinquency.

There are several noteworthy features of this study, including the selection of a clinically impaired sample, evaluation of viable treatments, unusually long-term follow-up, use of socially important outcome measures (arrest, institutionalization), and selection of sufficiently large samples ($N >$ 100) to provide a sensitive test of treatment. Separate cohorts were assigned to the different treatments and hence were not randomly assigned. However, given the assessment, matching, and evaluation at different points, selection is not very plausible as an explanation of the results. One point that at once is exemplary and problematic deserves mention. The study tested treatments as they are applied clinically, that is, with clinicians making decisions based on putative needs of the patient. There is no standard, operational, or replicable way to accomplish this initial evaluation of needs. The reliability of decisions regarding patient needs and whether such decisions enhance outcome are not known. In the present study, for example, no clear guidelines are provided as to the criteria for providing a particular treatment (e.g., parent therapy, group therapy) to any individual. Not everyone in the multimodality condition received all of the options or a given option for the same amount of time. The study is exemplary by including multiple treatments and at the same time raises central issues regarding replicability of the findings in research and extension in practice.

Anxiety Disorder

As noted previously (Table 13.1), a number of anxiety disorders emerge during childhood and adolescence. In addition, other anxiety disorders appear in children (e.g., obsessive-compulsive disorder, post-traumatic stress disorder) and can emerge in childhood, adolescence, or adulthood. Epidemiological studies tend to evaluate various disorders separately. For example, among school-age children, between 3 and 5 percent meet criteria for separation anxiety disorder (IOM, 1989). A similar percentage meet criteria for overanxious disorder. Anxiety disorders co-occur in many youth, so that these percentages include an overlapping population.

Anxiety disorders in children and adolescents have been delineated relatively recently in psychiatric diagnosis. The study of fears and anxiety in children has a much longer history of research (e.g., Jersild & Holmes, 1935; Lapouse & Monk, 1958). Well known are the findings that fears are likely to develop early in childhood and to evolve in focus over the course of development. Most fears and sources of anxiety that emerge during childhood seem to dissipate and to have no long-term implications for adolescent and adult adjustment.

There are more extreme variations that impair daily performance and are not likely to disappear over time. A dilemma for treatment is to decide whether anxiety evident in early development is of the type that warrants intervention (Barrios & O'Dell, 1989). The dilemma has had implications for identifying treatments for anxiety disorders. Reviews indicate a large number of studies that focus on fear and anxiety in children (see Barrios & O'Dell, 1989; Morris & Kratochwill, 1991). The majority of reports include fears that are not usually seen clinically, such as fear of dental treatment, medical procedures, test taking, small animals, darkness, and public speaking (see Barrios & O'Dell, 1989). To be sure, alleviation of anxiety in any domain is laudable insofar as stress is reduced and daily functioning is improved. However, the focus indicates that there is a great lacuna in controlled studies of treatment of those anxiety disorders usually seen clinically (see Last, 1988).

Two examples illustrate evaluation of treatments for anxiety disorders. In one of the few comparisons of alternative treatments for children referred for anxiety, psychotherapy, systematic desensitization, and waiting-list control conditions were compared in the treatment of children referred for phobias (L. Miller, Barrett, Hampe, & Noble, 1972). *Psychotherapy* consisted of having the child talk about his or her feelings and conflicts and efforts to foster awareness regarding factors related to fear. *Desensitization* consisted of a number of procedures including assertiveness training and parent involvement to develop alternative child responses. Children were randomly assigned to conditions; treated youth were seen three times per week for a period of eight weeks.

At the end of treatment, parent ratings showed that both treatments were significantly better in reducing child symptoms than the waiting-list control condition. Clinician ratings did not show treatment to be superior to the waiting-list condition. Age of the child contributed to the outcome and in fact accounted for more variance than treatment technique. Younger children (ages 6–10) showed greater improvement than older children (ages $\geq$ 11). Follow-up results one and two years later indicated that youth who had improved retained their gains (Hampe, Noble, Miller, & Barrett, 1973). Those who had not improved over the course of treatment generally showed marked improvements over the course of follow-up. Interestingly, among all cases, by the end of the second follow-up year, only 7 percent of the sample continued to have significant phobia. Several features of this study are notable, including the use of a clinically referred sample, extended follow-up, multiple measures of

treatment outcome, and evaluation of age in relation to outcome.

In another study, alternative interventions were
compared to treat school phobics (refusers), most
of whom were between 11 and 14 years of age
(lower range not stated) (Blagg & Yule, 1984).
Youth received one of three conditions: *behavior
modification, inpatient hospitalization,* and *home tutoring plus psychotherapy.* Cases were not assigned
randomly; rather, those from the hospital and
home tutoring group were selected from ongoing
treatment programs and matched on a variety of
subject and demographic variables so as to be similar to behavior modification cases. Behavioral
treatment included reinforcement (praise) for
school attendance, ignoring of somatic complaints
in the morning prior to school, in vivo flooding, and
contact with school personnel to facilitate student
reentry into school. Hospitalization consisted of
separating children from their families and engaging them in a therapeutic milieu and school placement planning, and pharmacology if warranted.
Home tutoring and therapy consisted of educa-
tional/academic tutoring and psychotherapy.

Assessment was conducted from one to slightly
less than two years after treatment to evaluate the
impact on school attendance. Rates of school attendance were 93, 38, and 10 percent for youth
who received behavioral treatment, hospitalization,
and tutoring plus therapy, respectively. Measures
of separation anxiety also showed greater improvement for the behavioral condition. The investigators highlighted the differential cost of the treatments in terms of therapist time. Behavioral
treatment was much shorter in duration and required less therapist time (mean 2.5 weeks) compared to hospitalization (mean = 45.3 weeks) and
tutoring and psychotherapy (mean = 72.1 weeks).
Although the cases were not randomly assigned,
subject differences are not particularly plausible as
an explanation for the very marked treatment differences. Among the hallmarks of this study was
the direct assessment of school attendance.

As previously mentioned, the treatment literature for anxiety disorders among children is quite
sparse. In the last 10 years, methods of delineating
and assessing anxiety disorders among children and
adolescents have increased greatly. Consequently,
it is likely that treatment trials will accelerate in this
area.

Depression

Depression is characterized by sad affect; loss of
interest and pleasure in activities; diminished activity; feelings of worthlessness; and changes in appetite, weight, and sleep. The persistence of several

symptoms for at least a week or two and their
impact on daily functioning serve to define the
disorder. Within the last 20 years, research on
adult depression has made major strides in understanding the nature of the disorder, alternative subtypes, family history, clinical course, treatment,
and prevention (e.g., Beckham & Leber, 1985;
McCann & Endler, 1990). However, depression in
children and adolescents has been neglected until
quite recently.

For years, the dominant conceptual position
maintained that children could not experience depression as a clinical syndrome; their insufficiently
developed personality structures prior to adolescence were considered to preclude appearance of
the disorder. Changes in approaches to diagnosis
(e.g., the focus on presenting symptoms and the
application of the same diagnostic criteria for depression to children, adolescents, and adults) fostered research that demonstrated that depression
can be reliably diagnosed in children and adolescents (Kazdin, 1990b). Within the last decade, a
great deal of research has elaborated the descriptive features; familial, interpersonal, and biological
correlates; and course of childhood dysfunction.
Depression is now recognized as a significant problem among children, with a course that can continue over childhood, adolescence, and adulthood.
In the United States, approximately 2 percent of
children ages 4–16 meet diagnostic criteria (DSM-
III or DSM-III-R) for major depression (IOM, 1989).
Current research suggests that among prepubertal
children, prevalence rates are similar for boys and
girls. However, postpubertal differences suggest
greater prevalence for girls than boys. Sex differences in rate and severity of depression appear to
begin early in adolescence and to increase into
adulthood (Kazdin, 1990b).

The treatment of depression in children and adolescents has only begun to emerge as an area of
research. For both psychopharmacological and psychotherapeutic approaches, treatments devised for
children and adolescents have been based largely
on direct extrapolations of treatments that have
been shown to be effective with adults. Consider a
few of the psychotherapeutic approaches to illustrate initial work in a young empirical literature.

Lewinsohn, Clark, Hops, and Andrews (1990)
evaluated a school-based program for adolescents
ages 14–18 who met diagnostic criteria (DSM-III
or Research Diagnostic Criteria) for a depressive
disorder. The intervention consisted of *a course
(Coping with Depression)* designed to address areas
central to depression (e.g., discomfort and anxiety,
irrational and negative thoughts, and low levels of
pleasant activities), as well as areas likely to be

relevant for adolescent adjustment (conflict with parents, the use of problem-solving skills). The program was conducted in a group format at night (rather than during the school day) and consisted of 14 two-hour sessions over a seven-week period. Two variations of treatment were provided based on whether parents participated in the treatment. For the condition in which parents participated, a separate group of parents met to learn the skills and techniques taught to the adolescents and to address family problems.

On measures completed by youth and parents, those who received treatment improved over the course of treatment and were significantly lower on measures of depression and internalizing symptoms than a waiting-list control condition. Both treatment groups reflected these gains and were not differentially effective. Follow-up assessment was conducted on different occasions up to two years after treatment had ended. Over the course of follow-up, the gains appeared to be maintained. Indeed, the proportion of youth meeting diagnostic criteria for depression continued to decline over the course of follow-up. The follow-up course could not be attributed to treatment specifically, given that the waiting-list group by this time had received the intervention and could not serve as a comparison group to control for changes without treatment.

A number of features of this study are notable. Prominent among these are the identification of cases through standardized diagnostic assessment and careful screening for clinical levels of dysfunction. Of interest as well was the intervention, which had been devised and carefully evaluated for depressed adults. The present study extended the intervention to adolescents with developmentally relevant modifications, including consideration of parent–youth conflict and parent involvement in treatment.

As another example, Stark, Reynolds, and Kaslow (1987) evaluated self-control and behavioral problem-solving approaches in the treatment of children ages 9–12 identified as moderately to severely depressed (on the Children's Depression Inventory). Treatments were administered in small groups (5 children each) for 12 sessions over a 5-week period. *Self-control therapy* focused on self-monitoring, self-evaluation, and self-reinforcement. *Behavioral problem-solving therapy* trained children in problem-solving skills and self-improvements in pleasant activities. The treatments overlapped in a number of features such as problem-solving, self-monitoring, and homework assignments. Self-control therapy tended to be more highly structured, and the problem-solving approach tended to focus more on social relations. Both treatments de-

creased depressive symptoms; they were superior to a *waiting-list control* group but were not consistently different from each other. An eight-week follow-up suggested that the gains were maintained.

Other studies of depression have been reported as well (e.g., Butler, Miezitis, Friedman, & Cole, 1980; Reynolds & Coats, 1986). To date, the primary focus has been on cognitive-behavioral treatment, self-control training, and relaxation. The results have shown that treatments tend to be more effective than waiting-list control conditions and to produce changes that are maintained for at least several weeks. In the few available studies, various treatments have not been consistently different in the outcomes they produce.

The outcome literature of psychological treatments of depression has begun quite recently and hence the research provides an opportunity to see the budding of an area of work. The focus reflects extension of treatments devised for adults. The extension is reasonable, given basic research showing that many features of depression in children, adolescents, and adults are similar (e.g., cognitive functioning, biological markers, recovery rates) (Kazdin, 1990b). Extensions to youth have included modifications to address contexts and influences associated with childhood and adolescence.

Autistic Disorder

Autistic disorder reflects impairment in diverse domains of functioning, including social interaction, communication skills, cognitive functioning, comprehension, and imaginative activity. A variety of other characteristics are likely to be present, including mental retardation, stereotyped and repetitive movements, and self-stimulatory and self-injurious behavior. The disorder is rare, with estimated prevalence in childhood of approximately 4 to 5 per 10,000. Treatment of the disorder usually consists of interventions designed to alter a specific area of functioning, such as rudimentary speech and language, self-injury, and social responsiveness (see Charlop, Schreibman, & Kurtz, 1991).

Among therapeutic studies, Lovaas's (1987) investigation has received considerable attention in light of its focus, intensity of the intervention, and outcome. In this study, young autistic children (< four years old) were assigned to an experimental group that provided an intensive treatment program or to one of two control conditions. The treatment condition was a *behavioral program* that was conducted in the child's home, school, and community for an average of 40 hours per week for two or more years. Several college student-therapists who worked on a part-time basis administered the treatment over this period. In addition, parents were trained extensively, so that treatment could take place at home for almost all of the child's waking hours, 365 days a year.

Treatment focused on eliminating maladaptive behavior (e.g., self-stimulation, aggression) and developing a variety of prosocial (e.g., play) and cognitive/academic skills (e.g., language, reading, writing, and other tasks). A major goal of treatment was to place children into a regular classroom where they would function largely as other children did. For children who entered a regular first-grade class, treatment was reduced from 40 hours per week to 10 hours or less per week and eventually was terminated with minimal contact. For treated children who did not enter regular first grade, the intervention continued at 40 hours per week for over 6 years (more than 14,000 hours of one-to-one treatment per child). Two separate control groups were included. In the *first control condition*, 10 hours per week of treatment were provided but not all of the behavioral contingencies were invoked. In the *second control condition*, children did not participate in treatment. Multiple measures were used to evaluate outcome but primary emphasis was on educational functioning at follow-up.

The results indicated that 47 percent of the treated group achieved normal intellectual and educational functioning, as reflected by scoring within the normal range on standardized intelligence tests and successfully completing first grade in the public schools. The two control groups did not differ from each other in educational functioning, and only 2 percent achieved normal educational functioning. The impact of treatment was dramatic; children gained an average of 30 points on standardized intelligence tests (WISC-R, Stanford Binet, or other measures) over control subjects who did not participate in the treatment.

Follow-up was conducted for both treatment and control groups (McEachin, Smith, & Lovaas, 1993). At the time of follow-up intervention, youth had been out of treatment for a mean of 5 years (range 0–12 years); control subjects were out of treatment for a mean of 3 years (range 0–9 years). The results indicated that the benefits of treatment were maintained. Significantly more youth in the intervention group remained in a regular class placement, mean IQ scores were higher, and adaptive behavior scores were superior to those of the control group. The original treatment and more recent follow-up results represent critically important findings. There have been discussions about the extent to which the children were autistic and were matched appropriately among treatment and control conditions, as well as other features (see McEachin et al., with commentaries, 1993). Never-

theless, the results stand as an important demonstration. Clearly, there is a need for replication of treatment effects because of the importance of the results and the impact of the treatment.

Child Physical Abuse: An Illustration of Children as Victims

As mentioned previously, the domains to which therapy is applied to children and adolescents are vast. Contributing to this is a range of problems, conditions, and circumstances to which children are exposed that produce or contribute to deleterious consequences. Among the problem areas are physical and sexual abuse and neglect, exposure to family violence (e.g., children of battered wives), exposure to parents experiencing significant dysfunction (e.g., ongoing substance abuse in the home, major depression), and homelessness (see U.S. Congress, 1986, 1991). The crisis that these problems represent has led to the development of many services and protective programs to manage difficult and dangerous situations. By and large, the empirical literature on intervention programs in controlled trails is scant.

Child abuse research illustrates applications of treatment as well as dilemmas that clinical research raises. In an early controlled study in this area, child management (parent) training was provided to families who had been identified by a local child welfare agency following investigation for or suspicion of child physical abuse (Wolfe, Sandler, & Kaufman, 1981). the first group of families was assigned to receive the *parent training* program; subsequent families were assigned to a *waiting-list control* group. Parent training was conducted in a weekly group (two-hour sessions for a period of eight weeks). Training included instructions in human development, child management, and problem solving and modeling of child management techniques and self-control strategies (e.g., relaxation training, use of self-statements). In addition, families were visited at home to help implement child management techniques (mean = eight home sessions). The waiting-list control group received standard services provided to abusive families, which included biweekly monitoring of child safety in the home and/or provision of community resources (homemaker services, welfare support).

At the end of treatment, child management families improved in child management skills in the home, as assessed through direct observation. Measures of child behavior problems and case worker ratings of treatment did not reflect differences. By the one-year follow-up, none of the treated families had been reported or been suspected of abuse. However, by this time the waiting-list group had received treatment and no comparison was possible to assess the longer term impact of treatment. Small sample size of the study, nonrandom assignment of cases and some pretest differences, and no comparison group at follow-up make evaluation difficult.

In a subsequent study, the program was expanded (Wolfe, Edwards, Manion, & Koverola, 1988). Parents and children under supervision from a child protective service agency and screened for problems in parenting and abuse potential participated and were randomly assigned to one of two conditions. All parents received the *agency-sponsored information condition*, which included several sessions. Some of the parents also received *parent training* to manage their children at home. In addition to the usual parenting practices of parent training (as discussed earlier in the chapter), coping responses and videotaped feedback of parent behavior were also provided. Treatment was provided in groups; families received a median of nine sessions (1½ hours). The information condition included meetings with social activities and informal discussion of topics related to health and family, the mother's personal growth, self-esteem, and social support. Posttreatment, three-month, and one-year follow-up data were obtained. The results indicated that the parent training was associated with reductions in mother report of child behavior problems that increase risk for physical abuse. Case worker evaluations one year after treatment also favored the group that had received parent training. A number of measures did not differentiate conditions including quality of child-rearing environment and observed child behavior at home.

Stress During Medical Treatment: An Illustration From Health Psychology

Therapeutic approaches are applied to a large number of domains related to physical health for both treatment and prevention. The broad area of health psychology encompasses a vast array of areas including dieting, exercise, eating disorders, and adherence to medical regimens, each with its own literature (Karoly, 1988; Routh, 1988). Applications of alternative therapies to help youth manage and cope with invasive and painful medical procedures illustrate some of the progress in this area of work.

As an illustration of applications, Jay and her colleagues have conducted several studies with children who experience distress during painful medical procedures. In one study, leukemia patients between the ages of 3½ and 13 were included (Jay, Elliott, Katz, & Siegel, 1987). As part of their treatment and care, the children were routinely required to complete three bone marrow aspirations, a traumatic and aversive medical procedure. The test requires insertion of a large needle into the child's hip bone to extract bone marrow. The information obtained from the procedure is critical to assess the presence or absence of cancer cells. Typically (in the United States), a local anesthetic is administered, but this does not alleviate the pain of the entire procedure.

Jay and her colleagues compared three procedures (*cognitive-behavioral therapy, Valium,* and *minimal treatment-attention control*). For the three bone marrow tests, the treatments were delivered to each child in a counterbalanced design. The cognitive-behavioral procedure included viewing a modeling film of children coping with the procedure, breathing exercises, emotive imagery and distraction techniques, and behavioral rehearsal (e.g., role-playing the doctor). Minimal treatment included routine hospital support for child and parent plus the addition of a film (cartoons) to control for a special intervention. The results were evaluated on direct observations of distress during the aspiration procedure, child self-report immediately after the procedure, and physiological measures (blood pressure, pulse rate). In general, the cognitive-behavioral procedure led to significantly less fear than the minimal treatment condition. The medication condition was not consistently different from the minimal treatment condition.

In a related study, interventions were evaluated in helping parents cope with the stress of seeing their child receive bone marrow aspirations or lumbar punctures (Jay & Elliott, 1990). Parents of pediatric leukemia or lymphoma patients (ages 3–12) received one of two conditions. In one condition, parents accompanied their child as he or she was given cognitive-behavioral therapy (alone or with Valium). These parents were in the *child-focused condition*. In the other condition, parents themselves received *stress inoculation training* to learn coping strategies. These parents viewed a modeling tape to illustrate coping responses and were trained to make coping self-statements and in relaxation techniques. Parents in the stress inoculation condition showed greater changes in self-reported anxiety than those who received the child-focused intervention, but there were no differences in other measures (observation of parent behavior and parent physiological data). The effects in this study were modest. However, self-report is not to be minimized here given the scope of distress and the importance of any change that might be systematically demonstrated.

A number of other studies have shown the effectiveness of various therapies to reduce stress among children undergoing medical procedures. For example, in one study children ages 4–10 were prepared for surgery by viewing a *modeling film and practicing coping responses* or by receiving *routine hospital procedures* that included information and seeing the equipment (Faust, Olson, & Rodriguez, 1991). Modeling led to significantly less stress during recovery from the operation. In another study, two interventions were compared to reduce stress among young children ages 3–9 undergoing venipuncture as part of their cancer treatment (Manne et al., 1990). A *behavioral intervention* (parent coaching, attentional distraction, and positive reinforcement) led to less observed child stress and lower parent ratings of child stress and parental ratings of their own distress than a *control procedure* (in which the parents tried to aid their children in any way they wished). Controlled trials of treatment techniques for children undergoing medical procedures have repeatedly shown the benefits of diverse procedures over the routine, standardized care that patients are provided.

General Comments

The previously discussed studies sample interventions across several disorders and domains of functioning. There are multiple treatment foci that were not addressed, including various disorders (e.g., eating disorders, tic disorders), domains of dysfunction that arise in families (e.g., parent–child conflict), and sources of distress for youth (e.g., parental divorce, homelessness). Also, adults may experience a variety of dysfunctions (e.g., psychiatric impairment, loss of job, drastic change in socioeconomic status, drug use) that have an impact on their offspring.

Illustrations of research by various disorders is useful as a way of delineating the literature. A focus on disorders or response domains conveys greater use of combined and multiple component interventions (e.g., Satterfield et al., 1987) and intensive, long-term treatment spanning several years (e.g., Lovaas, 1987) to maximize the likelihood of impact. Issues related to type, combination, and intensity of treatment are discussed later because of their broad implications for therapy research with children and adolescents.

UNDERPINNINGS OF CONTEMPORARY PROGRESS

The treatment techniques and areas of clinical dysfunction illustrated previously merely sample the literature. The number of controlled outcome studies is increasing; the areas to which they are extended are expanding as well. Part of the progress stems from the increased attention to childhood and adolescent dysfunction generally, improved specification of criteria to identify dysfunction, and the development of assessment techniques. Progress in the development of effective interventions depends on much more than the accumulation of treatment trials where plausible interventions are contrasted against each other and the de rigueur control conditions. Progress requires understanding the emergence of specific clinical dysfunctions, risk factors, and mechanisms that contribute to the dysfunctions as well as models that identify paths that might be interrupted with interventions.

Understanding Childhood and Adolescent Dysfunction

Progress in treatment has depended on research on the characteristics, diagnosis, and clinical course of disorders of children and adolescents. *Developmental psychopathology,* the area of study in which these topics are addressed, has grown remarkably within the last decade (see Lewis & Miller, 1990; Walker & Roberts, 1992). The area consists of the study of dysfunction from a developmental perspective. In principle, developmental psychopathology covers the entire life span because affect, cognition, and behavior and psychopathology can vary from the beginning to the end of life. However, the area has focused on infancy, childhood, and adolescence and serves as an umbrella for several fields (e.g., clinical psychology, child and adolescent psychiatry, social work, epidemiology, pediatrics, and others) in which dysfunction in youth is studied. Advances in elaborating the nature of clinical dysfunction and features of development that contribute to dysfunction are particularly relevant to developing effective treatment.

As an example, consider research on aggressive and antisocial child behavior to illustrate the type of work that can serve as critical conceptual and empirical underpinnings of treatment. Processes that may underlie aggressive behavior represent a foundation on which treatments can draw. For example, Dodge and his colleagues have identified a significant *attributional bias* among aggressive children and adolescents (e.g., Dodge, Price, Bachorowski, & Newman, 1990; Dodge & Somberg, 1987). Aggressive youth tend to view ambiguous situations (those in which intention of others is unclear) as hostile. The attribution of hostility to others helps to precipitate aggressive acts that are merely retaliatory from the standpoint of the aggressive child. These acts, however, do not seem justified in the views of the child's peers. Peer rejection appears to follow aggressive behavior. The reactions of the peers and their dislike of and isolation from the aggressive child provide additional cues to the aggressive child that the environment is hostile. Thus, a vicious circle of aggressive behavior and untoward peer reactions can be sustained. Research such as the work on attributional bias serves to identify potential points of intervention to interrupt aggressive behavior. Further research that would elaborate the development of attributional biases and related maladaptive cognitions might have potential implications for developing interventions to prevent aggression.

Antisocial behavior encompasses a variety of acts and youth. Efforts to describe youth and their families have focused on possible ways of identifying subgroups who may vary in amenability to treatment and prognosis. Studies have proposed and tested alternative ways of dividing antisocial youth. Different subtypes of conduct disorders have been proposed, including those who engage in aggression rather than theft (e.g., G Patterson, 1982); those whose aggression seems to be reactive (in response to others) rather than proactive (as an initial way of goal attainment) (Dodge, 1991); and those whose antisocial behavior is primarily overt (fighting) rather than covert (lying, truancy) (Loeber & Schmalling, 1985), to mention a few. Different subtypes are designed to draw attention to possible developmental paths leading to antisocial behavior. It is likely that identification of varied paths will have implications for early identification, prevention, and treatment. For example, for some time it has been known that coercive parent–child interactions are more likely in the homes of children whose antisocial behavior involves primarily acts of aggression rather than theft (G. Patterson, 1982). The implication is that parent training that focuses on the restructuring of these interactions is likely to be more appropriate with aggressive children. To date, few studies have attempted to match youth who vary on patterns for antisocial behavior and various treatments or to test predictions showing child characteristics × treatment interactions. However, the underpinnings for more specific types of predictions about the impact of treatment for varied types of dysfunctions and youth continue to develop.

Longitudinal studies of youth and identification of factors that place youth at risk for dysfunction also have critical implications for intervention. To be "at risk," of course, refers to the increased likelihood, above base rates in the population, that persons will show the condition or dysfunction. For example, the factors that predispose children and adolescents to antisocial behavior have been studied extensively in the context of community samples, clinical referrals, and adjudicated delinquents

(see Pepler & Rubin, 1991; Robins & Rutter, 1990). Diverse factors have been identified related to the child (e.g., temperament, early onset of unmanageable behavior), parents (e.g., criminal behavior, harsh child-rearing practices), family (e.g., large family size, marital discord), school (e.g., poor work ethos, physical disarray), and other domains (Kazdin, 1987b).

Obviously, not all individuals at risk will show later dysfunction. This can be deduced as a matter of imperfections of assessment of risk (the predictors) and disorder (the criterion) as well as changes in risk status on a particular factor over time. A conceptually interesting and potentially critical set of influences that may affect onset are referred to as protective factors. These factors refer to influences that may cancel or attenuate the influence of known risk factors. Researchers have identified protective factors by studying groups of individuals known to be at risk because of the presence of several risk factors and by identifying a subgroup that does not later evince the disorder.

For example, in a longitudinal study from birth through young adulthood, youth were identified as at risk for delinquency based on a number of risk factors (Werner, 1987; Werner & Smith, 1992). Those at-risk youth who did not evince delinquency by adolescence were more likely to be first born, to be perceived by their mothers as affectionate, to show higher self-esteem and locus of control, to have caretakers in the family other than the parents, and to have a supportive same-sex model who provided structure. Such factors are important to help suggest why many individuals who are at risk do not develop antisocial behavior.

In the study of more general clinical dysfunction, several related factors have been identified that increase resilience to risk and foster competence and adaptive outcomes. Factors that increase resilience are less well studied than those that increase risk. Salient factors that promote resilience of youth at risk include stable care from a competent adult, good learning and problem-solving abilities, social responsiveness to others, and competence and perceived self-efficacy (see Masten, Best, & Garmezy, 1990). In general, the study of risk and protective factors is important not only for describing the characteristics of dysfunction but also for providing the building blocks for theories about mechanisms of dysfunction and for the design of prevention efforts.

Research has focused on how factors might interrelate and lead to dysfunction. For example, family influences on the development of antisocial behavior have been elaborated by G. Patterson and his colleagues (e.g., Patterson, 1986; Patterson, Capaldi, & Bank, 1991). Separate models have been developed to explain how parents train antisocial behavior in the home; the impact of the child's coercive interactions and noncompliance on self-esteem, peer relations, and academic performance; and the impact of stressors on maternal discipline practices. Evaluation of one of the models, for example, has suggested that inept discipline practices and coercive parent–child interaction escalate and foster increasingly aggressive child behavior. Parent training, illustrated previously, has been used to alter coercive processes in the home to reduce aggressive child behavior.

Other researchers have evaluated models to identify factors that contribute to maladaptive behavior. For example, to identify critical paths toward deviance, Newcomb and Bentler (1988) examined the consequences of drug use during adolescence on young adulthood. Several domains of functioning (latent variables) were assessed (e.g., drug use, social conformity, criminal activity, deviant peer networks). During adolescence, teen drug use was related to lower social conformity and greater criminal activity and to having a deviant friendship network. Early drug use was related years later to reduction in academic pursuits (less involvement in college), job instability (unemployment, being fired), and increased psychoticism (e.g., disorganized thought processes). Evaluating the relations among various domains and paths leading to deviance has implications for designing interventions. For example, for many youth an intervention devoted to drug use alone might not be optimally effective because drug use often reflects a broader lifestyle involving deviant attitudes and behavior in other areas.

As a final example of paths toward deviance, Elliott, Huizinga, and Ageton (1985) conducted a longitudinal study of delinquency and drug use in the United States (national Youth Survey). The sample included youth ages 11–17 who were evaluated annually. A variety of constructs were measured, including the youths' family and school aspirations and involvement; exposure to delinquent peers; and personal characteristics such as isolation, educational goals, and attitudes toward deviance. These variables were used to predict self-reported delinquency and drug use three years later. One of the salient findings was that bonding (or attachment) to deviant peers was directly related to delinquency and later drug use. This finding held for males and females and for a number of different measures of delinquency and drug use. An additional finding indicated that weak conventional bonding (i.e., poor connections with family and school) was a factor that led to increases in deviant bonding. Thus, early in the path toward delinquency is a breakdown in connections to home, school, and family. The model suggests that interventions need to focus on these connections to effect change or prevent delinquency.

In general, the previously discussed research samples a small portion of the literature in developmental psychopathology. Research that examines clinical dysfunction not only generates and tests theory about the nature of dysfunction, but also has implications for intervention research. The specific predictions about what interventions to apply, for whom, and when during their development are guided by basic research.

Improved Methods of Evaluation

Along with improved understanding of child and adolescent dysfunction, there have been advances in research practices, procedures, and methods of evaluation. Methodological developments that have contributed directly to progress in child therapy research can be illustrated with several examples. To begin, development of measures of childhood dysfunction has accelerated greatly (e.g., Ollendick & Hersen, 1993; Rutter, Tuma, & Lann, 1988). For example, the development of diagnostic interviews has aided research on childhood disorders. The assessment of disorders with standardized measures has permitted diverse lines of research, including the study of prevalence and incidence of dysfunction, developmental course, family studies, and the presence of multiple disorders. In general, development of standardized measures has broad implications for better description and identification of clinical populations, evaluation of a broad range of theoretical constructs to evaluate youth, and finer grained evaluation of treatment outcomes.

A second methodological development in research has been the assessment on psychological measures of nonreferred youth of different ages (e.g., Achenbach & Edelbrock, 1981). The assessment of normative levels of functioning at different age levels charts the patterns of individual behaviors as well as constellations of behavior that wax and wane over the course of development. Description of normative levels of functioning serves as a basis to help understand the course of development and provides baseline information for evaluating the functioning of clinically referred youth before and after treatment.

A third methodological advance in research has been improved operationalization of treatment. The codification of treatment in the form of therapy manuals and guidebooks has proliferated in the last decade (Lambert & Ogles, 1988; Luborsky & DeRubeis, 1984). A large number of manuals have appeared for a variety of treatments for children and adolescents. For examples, manuals, guidebooks, and texts are available to conduct:

Psychoanalytically and psychodynamically oriented treatments (e.g., Kernberg & Chazan, 1991; Lord, 1985).

Diverse cognitively based treatments (e.g., Camp & Bash, 1985; Feindler & Ecton, 1986; Horne & Sayger, 1990; Kendell & Braswell, 1985; Santostefano, 1985.)

Parent training (e.g., Forehand & McMahon, 1981; Kozloff, 1979; G. Patterson, Rud, Jones, & Conger, 1975).

Behavioral social skills training (e.g., King & Kirschenbaum, 1992; Michelson, Sugai, Wood, & Kazdin, 1983).

Experiential psychotherapy (e.g., L. Wright, Everett, & Roisman, 1986).

Community-based treatment (e.g., Steen & Monnette, 1989).

The manuals specify in varying degrees of detail critical events and practices and serve to guide the therapist through the treatment regimen. By providing concrete guidelines for carrying out particular techniques, one can better assess treatment integrity, that is, the extent to which those persons delivering the treatment have actually adhered to the treatment prescriptions. Specification of treatment in manual form can also facilitate replication studies among researchers and dissemination of empirically developed treatments to clinical practice.

A fourth development has been the use of methods to study small numbers of patients in experimental and quasi-experimental designs (see Kazdin, 1992). Most treatment research involves group designs in which various intervention (treatment) and control groups are compared. However, single-case designs have been used to investigate the impact of treatment with one or a few cases. These designs permit inferences to be drawn about the effects of treatment as well as evaluation of alternative versions of treatment. Although the designs have been used frequently in behavior modification, they have been extended to evaluate a broader range of treatments for children, including, for example, the effects of child psychoanalysis (Fonagy & Moran, 1990) and paradoxical intervention (Kolko & Milan, 1983). The development of designs to evaluate the individual case serves separate functions for improving treatment. Treatment innovations that emerge in practice can be carefully evaluated on a small scale; those that show promise can then be extended in larger scale group studies. In this way, single-case research helps to generate promising techniques in a systematic fashion. Conversely, the findings obtained from group

studies can be extended on a small scale to clinical work by using single-case methodology.

A final illustration of methodological advances that have enhanced treatment research includes expansion of the range of statistical models and data analytic methods. As one example, the description and evaluation of models of dysfunction, already mentioned, have profited from such methods as structural equation modeling (e.g., Newcomb & Bentler, 1988). Structural equation modeling provides a way of examining the relations among domains of interest (e.g., use of drugs and dropping out of school in adolescence) and subsequent outcomes (e.g., adult adjustment, criminal activity). The method allows the investigator to test various models or theoretical views about the likely paths that lead to a particular outcome. The paths refer to influences that increase the likelihood of a particular outcome and how several influences may relate to each other as well as to the final outcome of interest. The procedure utilizes several measures of a given domain of interest or construct. The ability to evaluate multiple measures of a given construct (latent variable), to examine relations among variables at a given point in time and over time, and to identify possible paths of influence and direct and indirect influences on a particular outcome can clarify possible points of intervention.

Meta-analysis is another analytic method that has contributed to treatment research. Although meta-analyses are driven by substantive questions (e.g., the effectiveness of treatment), their use has helped identify weaknesses and areas of neglect in both the focus and reporting of treatment research with children and adolescents (Kazdin, Bass et al., 1990; B. Weiss & Weisz, 1990).

General Comments

The substantive and methodological examples highlighted here by no means exhaust the range of developments that contribute to identifying effective interventions. The full scope of research on "normal" development is relevant beyond studies of clinical dysfunction mentioned previously. For example, theory and research on prenatal development, child temperament, attachment, and parent child-rearing practices relate to affective, cognitive, and behavioral development and to patterns of adjustment. From the standpoint of methodological advances, here too more might be mentioned. For example, improved assessment of child characteristics permits elaboration of possible child $\times$ treatment interactions in treatment outcome and hence finer grained analyses of treatment. Overall, the methodological advances place the field in a position to evaluate treatments more analytically than ever before.

CHALLENGES OF THERAPY WITH CHILDREN AND ADOLESCENTS

Application and investigation of psychotherapy with children and adolescents raise special challenges in relation to the focus of treatment and the means of evaluating processes and outcome. As a general statement, the challenges result from the implications of child development on all facets of the treatment process. The challenges are central to research on therapy both in understanding current progress and as background for the future research agenda.

Identifying and Treating Dysfunction

The initial task of identifying problems worthy of treatment raises special issues. Extreme and pervasive departures in functioning of affect, cognition, and behavior by definition are readily identifiable early in life. Examples include pervasive developmental disorders (e.g., autism) and more severe forms of mental retardation. Less severe dysfunctions usually are the focus of psychotherapy. However, several emotional and behavioral problems that characterize maladjustment and are candidates for therapy are relatively common in childhood (see Lewis & Miller, 1990). For example, fears, lying, destructiveness, and signs of sadness are symptoms of currently recognized disorders. They are also relatively common at different points in early development. For most youth, these characteristics attenuate greatly as part of normal growth and development and do not portend dysfunction. Often the significance of the behavior is clinically derived from the age at which it occurs. For example, a given behavioral pattern (e.g., fighting and bedwetting) is viewed quite differently and has different prognoses based on child age (e.g., 2 vs. 10 years old). Identification of dysfunction among children is not always the appearance of a symptom or symptom constellation but rather the relation of that characteristic to expected development.

Related is the fact that children are undergoing rapid changes. Problem behaviors wax and wane at different ages. Whether and when to intervene raise special challenges because many of the seemingly problematic behaviors may pass with maturation and socialization. Although one can identify points when behaviors are likely to be problematic and to impair functioning, individual variation is sufficiently great as to preclude sharp guidelines. Other characteristics (e.g., impairment in daily functioning, threshold of referring for treatment on the part of parents) may dictate whether therapy is sought.

In general, the evolving nature of affect, cognition, and behavior raises unique issues for child treatment. The nature and interaction of different psychological systems are incompletely understood in their own right and in relation to the emergence of clinical dysfunction and its treatment. Patterns of dysfunction change over the course of development and the course is only beginning to be charted. For example, clinical depression among children appears to increase with age. Also, both sexes show similar prevalence rates prior to adolescence but then the balance shifts markedly; at puberty adolescent females begin to show higher rates of depression (Kazdin, 1990b). How to adapt treatment developmentally to different patterns is not well understood. The task poses a significant challenge for treating children and adolescents.

In general, the challenge of identifying and treating dysfunction in children is encompassed by a developmental perspective. This perspective, stated broadly, acknowledges that the processes of growth and development, the emergence of psychological and biological processes, and the interaction of the child with the environment serve as a basis for conceptualizing treatment. The child passes through a variety of periods, stages, or levels in which experience with the environment and affective, cognitive, and behavioral repertoires are evolving and mingling in a dynamic way (see Achenbach, 1986; Petersen, 1988). The rapidity of changes in childhood and adolescence and the dynamic development and interconnectedness of multiple domains are somewhat unique in childhood and pose challenges for treatment.

Motivation for Seeking Treatment

In the majority of cases, youth do not refer themselves for treatment nor identify themselves as experiencing stress, symptoms, or problems. Young children may not have the cognitive development or perspective to identify their own psychological impairment, and its impact on daily functioning, nor to consider the possibility that therapy is a viable means of intervention. Also, problems commonly referred for treatment involve disruptive behavior (e.g., aggression, hyperactivity) (Kazdin, Bass et al., 1990). In such cases, it is likely that adults experience the child as disturbing. Adults (parents, teachers) serve as the impetus for treatment, so the focus may in part be someone else's stress rather than the child's. Youth themselves are less likely to report dysfunction or a problem in relation to their own experience. The absence of a felt problem on the part of the child or adolescent affects the motivation for seeking treatment and for engaging in much of the "work" required in psychotherapy. The challenge to the clinician and researcher is to engage the child in treatment.

Not perceiving the need for treatment or participating in treatment based on parent or school referral is a special challenge. In some conceptual views of treatment and in clinical lore, insight into one's problems is often viewed as a prerequisite to therapeutic change. Leaving aside the empirical status of this assumption and the techniques, problem domains, and samples to which it might apply, insight into one's problems can be very different in relation to children. Limited cognitive development alone could greatly limit the perspective of conceptualizing dysfunction, problems, and the loci of these problems.

The motivation for seeking treatment also affects remaining in treatment. The number of youth who drop out of treatment is high. Among youth who are referred for treatment, 50–75 percent either do not initiate treatment or terminate early if they do begin (e.g., Armbruster & Kazdin, in press; Pekarik & Stephenson, 1988). Attrition has been less well studied in relation to child and adolescent therapy, compared to research with adults. An array of parent, family, as well as child factors may predict attrition. For example, our own work has focused on premature termination from outpatient therapy in a clinic for oppositional and conduct disorder youth (Kazdin, 1990c; Kazdin, Mazurick, & Bass, 1993). Premature termination from treatment is greater for younger mothers, single parents, and minority group families; for families with socioeconomic disadvantage, high stress and frequent or salient life events, and adverse (e.g., harsh) family child-rearing practices; and for children with greater severity, breadth, and history of antisocial behavior, greater academic and educational dysfunction, and multiple (comorbid) diagnoses. The range of factors that contribute to attrition and the processes through which a given factor mediates attendance and participation in treatment are by no means well understood. The challenge for psychotherapy research and practice is to attend to a variety of domains that might place youth at risk for dropping out.

Contextual Factors

Mention of the importance of parent and family factors in attrition raises a broader issue that is central to therapy for children. The dependence of children on adults makes them particularly vulnerable to influences over which they have little control. For example, poor prenatal care and nutrition, prenatal substance abuse by the mother, physical and sexual abuse, and neglect are some of the early influences that can affect functioning of the children and have direct implications for childhood adjustment and psychopathology. Parent mental health and marital and family functioning, living circumstances, and socioeconomic disadvantage are a few of the factors that can influence both child adjustment and parent and child participation in the treatment process. Attrition was mentioned earlier, but this is only one area shown to be influenced by broader contextual factors. Research has shown as well that parent and family adversity (e.g., socioeconomic disadvantage, level of stress and disruptive life events, parent psychopathology) can influence the degree of therapeutic change at posttreatment and the extent to which changes are maintained at follow-up (e.g., Dadds & McHugh, 1992; Dumas & Wahler, 1983; Strain et al., 1981; Webster-Stratton, 1985).

In clinical work, treatment of child dysfunction frequently incorporates the parent and family in some way. A few studies have evaluated the impact of addressing parent and family issues in treatment outcome. As an illustration, in one study for youth with conduct disorder, a parent training program was evaluated for altering child functioning (Dadds, Schwartz, & Sanders, 1987). Parents were classified as experiencing marital discord or not experiencing discord at the beginning of treatment. All families received parent training to alter their child's behavior. Families were randomly assigned to receive an additional treatment component (partner support) designed to address marital conflict, communication, and problem solving. This additional component did not yield differences in therapeutic change among the children at posttreatment assessment. However, at a six-month follow-up, families with marital discord who had received partner support maintained the gains in treatment to a greater extent than did those who did not receive partner support. Thus, addressing parent and family issues among families with marital discord had an impact on the child's therapeutic change.

In general, the importance of parent and family influences is widely acknowledged in clinical applications of treatment for children and adolescents (Kazdin, Siegel, & Bass, 1990). However, the impact of interventions that address these influences is infrequently studied. There are reasons for the minor attention accorded these issues in research. Parent and family influences on dysfunction vary by type of childhood disorder. For example, parent and family characteristics associated with conduct disorder and depression are likely to vary. Thus, the task is not merely one of addressing a particular source of stress (e.g., marital conflict) across all child disorders. Rather, it is important to conceptualize how the influence may relate to clinical dysfunction or treatment delivery.

Methodological Issues

Research on psychotherapy presents many methodological challenges that are quite similar in studies with children, adolescents, and adults. The desirability and difficulty of recruiting homogeneous subjects; randomly assigning subjects to conditions, including a sufficiently large sample to provide a sensitive (powerful) test; monitoring and evaluating treatment integrity; retaining subjects within the study; using multiple measures to evaluate outcome; and evaluating follow-up are a few of the features upon which valid inferences can depend (see Hersen, Michelson, & Bellack, 1984; Kazdin, 1992). There are special methodological challenges related to treatment research on children and adolescents that warrant comment.

Assessment issues. As noted previously, assessment for children and adolescents has advanced considerably in terms of developing measures of specific domains of dysfunction. In the process of measurement development and treatment evaluation, a number of assessment issues that influence interpretation of treatment research have come to light.

Parents are usually the primary source of information because they are readily available as informants, are knowledgeable about the child's behavior across time and situations, and usually play a central role in the referral of children for treatment. Parent evaluations usually are obtained on standardized rating scales (e.g., Behavior Problem Checklist, Child Behavior Checklist) that assess several domains of child functioning (e.g., aggression, hyperactivity, anxiety, depression). The information parents provide about their child's functioning raises its own interpretive problems. Several studies have shown that maternal perceptions of child adjustment and functioning are related to maternal psychopathology (especially anxiety and depression), marital discord, stressors, and social support outside of the home (e.g., Forehand, Lautenschlager, Faust, & Graziano, 1986; Mash & Johnston, 1983; Moretti, Fine, Haley, & Marriage, 1985). Thus, parents' reports of child dysfunction depend on their own subjective states and functioning. Consequently, use of multiple informants is essential to provide convergent information regarding changes in the child.

Children and adolescents are often asked to report on their own dysfunction (LaGreca, 1990). An initial issue is the extent to which children are capable of, or willing to, report on their symptoms. This concern does not merely derive from the possibility that children might deny symptoms. Rather, measures often ask subtle questions about specific symptoms including their basis, onset, duration, and intensity. Research has suggested that children are likely to be better reporters of symptoms related to private or subjective experience (e.g., hopelessness, low self-esteem, depression, anxiety), whereas significant others such as parents and teachers are better informants in relation to the children's overt behaviors (e.g., sleep and eating patterns, aggression, hyperactivity) (see Kazdin, in press, for a review). The research has focused on whether the child and other raters, usually parents, report greater frequency or severity of a given symptom domain. Even though children and parents often provide different information about the child's symptoms, both perspectives have been validated based on the study of various concurrent and predictive correlates.

The relations among measures from different informants about child and adolescent dysfunction have raised critical assessment issues. Child therapy research often relies on ratings completed by parents, teachers, and children themselves. There is now a rather extensive body of research showing that parent, teacher, and child ratings of dysfunction show relatively little agreement (Achenbach, McConaughy, & Howell, 1987; Kazdin, in press). For example, in the Achenbach et al. (1987) review, agreement among informants in assessing emotional and behavioral problems was examined across a large number of studies. The findings indicated that parent and child evaluations of child problems showed reliable but relatively low agreement (mean $r = .25$). Correspondence between child and teacher and child and mental health worker evaluations was also low ($rs = .20$ and $.27$, respectively).

The imperfect correlations among measures are not unique in the assessment of children and adolescents (see Lambert, Christensen, & DeJulio, 1983). The noteworthy feature in relation to child and adolescent therapy is the relatively low correlations that are often obtained and the implications these correlations have for research and treatment outcome. Identification of dysfunction for selecting cases for treatment can yield different findings depending on the source of information. For example, for a given population from which to draw, different samples of youth will be identified as depressed based on whether parent, child, or some combination of ratings is used as the basis for selection (Kazdin, 1989). Similarly, at outcome, conclusions about the effectiveness of treatment (e.g., Kazdin,

Bass, Siegel, & Thomas, 1989) and the factors that predict outcome (e.g., Clarke et al., 1992) might be quite different in a given study depending on the measure or source of information. A current area of research in developmental psychopathology is evaluation of the integration of information from separate informants and the validity and utility of the combined information (Angold, Weissman, John, Wickramaratne, & Prusoff, 1991; Bird, Gould, & Staghezza, 1992).

A final challenge for treatment research pertains to interpretation of assessment in treatment trials. Interpretation of scores on a given measure may vary depending on the age, sex, and stage of development of the child. It is possible that the "same numerical score" on a given measure would have different meaning normatively as a function of age of the child and that different scores would have a similar meaning at different ages, given developmental change. The dynamic nature of development means that interpretation of test scores must be based on charting the developmental course of youth on the measure. There has been little standardization of measures and evaluation of normative data that vary as a function of age and sex.

As an exception, the Child Behavior Checklist (CBCL; Achenbach & Edelbrock, 1983) is a rating scale that is used frequently in child and adolescent research. The measure has separate versions completed by parents, teachers, and adolescents. The parent version has been factor analyzed to provide scales that vary as a function of child age and sex. The age groupings (e.g., 6–11, 12–16) reflect one of the more refined divisions for obtaining normative data, even though they are difficult to defend developmentally. For example, within the 6–11 age range, some portion of youth will have entered puberty, a time when significant changes may occur in emotional and behavioral characteristics. Nevertheless, the CBCL is one of the better measures for providing normative data for age and sex groupings. The normative data have facilitated evaluation of treatment outcome because same-sex and same-age youth can be used as a comparison standard for evaluating posttreatment standing of a treated sample. For most measures used to evaluate treatment, normative data are unavailable for age and sex groupings. Evaluation of treatment can identify whether there has been change (pre- to posttreatment) and whether groups differ. Yet, the extent to which performance of youth represents an important change or places them within a normative range is difficult to determine.

Heterogeneous samples. Treatment evaluation is facilitated by the selection of homogeneous samples in research. Homogeneity of the sample minimizes within-group variability and hence increases the sensitivity of statistical tests comparing different groups. However, there are important exceptions. When one predicts that treatment will vary by sample characteristics, heterogeneous samples may be selected intentionally. In such cases, sample characteristics are included as a factor in the design and data analysis. However, when such characteristics are not part of the design, generally it is advisable to select relatively homogeneous samples.

In studies of child and adolescent therapy, samples often are heterogeneous. One area that has emerged is the appearance of multiple or comorbid diagnoses. Examples of common comorbid conditions include attention-deficit hyperactivity disorder and conduct disorder, anxiety disorder and depression, Tourette's syndrome and attention-deficit hyperactivity disorder, and autism and mental retardation (see IOM, 1989). Epidemiological studies have found that among children and adolescents who meet criteria for one psychiatric disorder, approximately half also meet criteria for at least one other disorder as well (Anderson, Williams, McGee, & Silva, 1987; Bird et al., 1988). For clinically referred youth, comorbid disorders are likely to be more prevalent. For example, in our own outpatient clinic for conduct disordered youth, approximately 70 percent of youth ages 7–13 meet criteria for more than one disorder (DSM-III-R) (Kazdin, Seigel, & Bass, 1992). The mean number of diagnoses of cases is slightly over two disorders.

The comorbidity of conditions raises fundamental questions about the diagnosis and delineation of disorders. For example, conduct disorder and attention-deficit hyperactivity disorder in children are often comorbid, sometimes in as many as 70 percent of the cases (e.g., Fergusson, Horwood, & Lloyd, 1991). The extent to which the disorders are separate in onset, course, prognosis, and treatment reflects important substantive questions. Yet comorbidity raises important methodological challenges as well. In a given treatment study, cases are likely to be selected on the basis of meeting criteria on a rating scale or diagnostic instrument so that all youth show the problem(s) on which the intervention will focus. It is possible that youth will be heterogeneous in terms of the type and number of other comorbid diagnoses. The diversity of comorbid diagnoses can greatly increase the heterogeneity of the sample and make identification of intervention effects more difficult.

Within a given study, it is possible that sample sizes would be insufficient to analyze the data by alternative patterns of comorbidity. For example, in a study of depressed youth, the sample might be too small to provide a statistically sensitive test of the effects of treatment on depressed youth with and without a comorbid anxiety disorder. The reason is that patterns of comorbidity can be quite varied. In this example alone, the comorbid anxiety disorder could include any of a number of disorders.

In some cases, patterns of comorbidity may be evaluated in the analyses, and this would provide important information about the impact of treatment. Also, the presence of comorbid diagnoses, rather than the specific pattern, may be significant in its own right. For example, in outpatient treatment, the occurrence of two or more comorbid diagnoses among children is a factor that places youth at risk for premature termination of treatment (Kazdin, Mazurick, & Bass, in press). Comorbid diagnoses raise a challenge for treatment research because of the heterogeneity introduced into a sample of youth with similar referral problems. As an initial strategy for research, it would be useful to assess the full range of diagnoses within the sample so that the extent and type of comorbidity is documented. Assessment may permit opportunities for analyses within a study and for evaluation in secondary analyses (e.g., meta-analyses) in which data are culled from several studies.

General comments. Assessment and sampling issues are two salient methodological challenges that emerge in the evaluation of treatment with children and adolescents. Another issue that has broad significance pertains to the consideration of age, sex, and developmental differences in the samples selected for a given study. Studies unwittingly combine youth of different ages and stages of development who might be expected to respond quite differently to treatment. Consequently, problems associated with heterogeneous samples, discussed in relation to comorbidity, are relevant here as well. However, age, sex, and stage of development raise special substantive issues for identifying treatments for children and adolescents. Hence, these issues are discussed later in relation to future research directions.

CURRENT LIMITATIONS AND FUTURE RESEARCH DIRECTIONS

The characteristics highlighted previously are salient features related to childhood and adolescence that render the conceptualization, application, and evaluation of treatment different for children and adolescents when compared to adults. The characteristics are challenges because they require further research to understand the context in which treatment is provided, determinants of dysfunction, and

factors that influence responsiveness to treatment. In addition, fundamental issues such as how treatments achieve their effects and the persons for whom treatments are effective remain to be elaborated. Characteristics of current research and the mental health needs of children and adolescents are described next to identify several priority areas for research.

Expanding the Range of Research Questions

Developing and identifying effective treatments requires evaluation of the impact of alternative techniques as well as the conditions that influence their outcomes. Among the salient issues, for a given intervention we wish to know the:

Impact of treatment relative to no-treatment.

Components of the treatment that contribute to change.

Parameters of treatment (e.g., duration) that influence outcome.

Relative effectiveness of alternative treatments.

Treatment combinations that can improve outcome.

Role of various treatment processes (e.g., therapeutic alliance) in therapy.

Impact of patient, family, or therapist characteristics alone and in combination with alternative treatments.

Role of developmental considerations in delivery and effectiveness of treatment.

The different questions are addressed by alternative treatment evaluation strategies that denote the question and treatment and control groups required by the experimental design (see Kazdin, 1992a). The adult psychotherapy literature has a rich tradition of research that addresses the range of questions previously noted. In contrast, the child and adolescent psychotherapy literature has a much more narrow focus. For example, in a report referred to previously, we examined published psychotherapy studies involving children and adolescents (Kazdin, Bass et al., 1990). Studies ($N =$ 223) spanning a 19-year period (1970–1988) were coded to examine if the focus was on evaluating the effect of a single treatment versus a control condition (treatment package strategy); dissecting a treatment by varying the components across groups (dismantling strategy); varying a parameter (e.g., duration) of the treatment and comparing these variations (parametric strategy); comparing conceptually different treatments (comparative outcome strategy); developing more effective treatments by adding components or combining different treatments (constructive strategy); evaluating treatment processes (process strategy); and examining if patient, family, or therapist characteristics influence treatment outcome (client–therapist variation strategy).

Table 13.2 presents the percentage of studies in which these different strategies were addressed. Dominant among the studies was the treatment package strategy (58.3%) in which treatment was compared to one or more control conditions. Efforts to understand more about a given technique and to improve its efficacy are reflected in dismantling, constructive, and parametric strategies; each addressed between approximately 20 and 25 percent of the studies. Comparative outcome research accounted for 26.0 percent of the studies.

Each of the previous strategies focuses on treatment technique and hence on only a small segment of the questions to guide research. Client–therapist variation strategy research examines treatment in relation to subject (e.g., patient, family) and therapist classification variables alone or in conjunction with treatment. This strategy encompasses diverse factors that may moderate treatment outcome. As evident in the table, the results also indicated that only a small segment (7.2%) of the studies examined patient, family, and therapist variables in relation to outcome. An even smaller percent included the process strategy (2.2%), in which intratherapy processes were examined.

In general, the bulk of the child and adolescent therapy literature has focused on evaluating some facet of the treatment approach or technique. Scant attention is accorded evaluation of nontechnique variables (e.g., classification variables to divide the groups) that may moderate treatment outcome. The oft-cited research question of what types of therapy work, with whom, and under what conditions draws attention to a host of conditions other than treatment technique that might influence change. Researchers have consistently encouraged such a focus to avoid the implicit view that a given treatment is likely to operate in a uniform fashion across all conditions (e.g., Kiesler, 1971). The published research generally focuses heavily on treatment technique alone. A major research priority for the field is to expand the range of questions asked of psychotherapies for children and adolescents.

Among the questions that warrant attention, special emphasis might be accorded efforts to match children and treatment. A given treatment is likely to vary in effectiveness as a function of child, parent, and family characteristics. Only rarely have studies examined factors that may moderate treatment outcome for children and adolescents. For example, occasionally studies have examined treat-

TABLE 13.2   Types of research questions and comparisons

Research Questions	Percentage of Studies (N = 223)
Treatment Evaluation Strategies	
Treatment package strategy	58.3
Dismantling strategy	26.0
Parametric strategy	20.2
Comparative outcome strategy	26.0
Constructive strategy	19.3
Process strategy	2.2
Client–therapist variation strategy	7.2
Research Focus	
Compare treatment vs. no-treatment	51.6
Compare treatment vs. active control	39.5
Examine characteristics of treatment	38.6
Compare two or more treatments	60.1
Examine treatment process in relation to outcome	2.7
Examine child/adolescent characteristics	9.0
Examine parent or family characteristics	2.2
Examine therapist characteristics	2.7
Examine characteristics of dysfunction	0.0
Match child/adolescent characteristics and treatment	0.4
Match family characteristics to treatment	0.0

Note. Treatment evaluation strategy (evaluating the effect of a single treatment vs. a control condition); dismantling strategy (dissecting a treatment by varying the components across groups); parametric strategy (varying a parameter of the treatment and comparing these variations); comparative outcome strategy (comparing conceptually different treatments); constructive strategy (developing more effective treatments by adding components or combining different treatments); process strategy (evaluating treatment processes); client–therapist variation strategy (examining if patient, family, or therapist characteristics influenced treatment outcome). Within the treatment evaluation strategies and research focus categories, a study could be classified into more than one alternative in the table, depending on the range of conditions included in the study. (Adapted from Kazdin, Bass, Ayers, & Rodgers, 1990.)

ment in relation to chronological age (e.g., L. Miller et al., 1972), sex (Kolvin et al., 1981), influence of peers (Feldman et al., 1983), frequency of treatment delivery (Heinicke & Ramsey-Klee, 1986), and parent involvement in treatment (Lewinsohn et al., 1990). By and large, these are isolated studies across diverse problem domains. Sufficient evidence has not emerged to permit conclusions within a domain. In general, a high priority for research is to relate domains of child, parent, and family functioning or characteristics to treatment. Such research would increase our understanding of disorders as well as hold the potential for improving treatment outcome.

Testing a Broader Range of Treatments and Treatment Combinations

Psychotherapy research for children and adolescents has focused on a relatively narrow range of treatment techniques. Specifically, behavior modification and cognitive-behavioral techniques dominate research, as noted previously (Kazdin, Bass et al., 1990). Other "more traditional" techniques, such as psychoanalysis, psychodynamic therapy, client-centered therapy, family therapy, play and art therapies, and combinations as part of eclectic approaches, are infrequently studied (each less than 5% of the studies). Surveys have consistently found that psychodynamic, family, and eclectic treatments are commonly used in clinical practice with children and adolescents (Kazdin, Siegel, & Bass, 1990; Koocher & Pedulla, 1977; Silver & Silver, 1983). A critical research priority is to expand the range of treatment approaches that are investigated. As illustrated previously, a small number of studies have examined the impact of variations of psychoanalysis and psychoanalytically oriented treatment in controlled clinical trials (e.g., Fonagy & Moran, 1990; Heinecke & Ramsey-Klee, 1986). Such work is exemplary in expanding the empirical base of treatment. At the same time, psychoanalytic and psychoanalytically oriented treatments are applied to a wide range of dysfunctions in clinical practice. A small set of studies does not begin to address the research needs.

Greater research attention is also needed on the impact of alternative combinations of treatment. In many ways, advocating research on treatment combinations may seem premature. If additional work is needed to understand individual treatment techniques, research that combines alternative techniques may serve only to obscure the knowledge base. However, there are different types of treatment combinations that warrant comment. Initially, in clinical practice, multiple interventions and approaches are used under the guise of eclectic treatment. Treatments are likely to be therapeutically combined based on multiple problems that children, parents, and families present. For example, individual psychotherapy for an adolescent may focus on identity and independence issues. At the same time, family therapy may be used to supple-

ment individual psychotherapy with the youth in light of parent–child conflict. As yet, precisely how treatments are combined in clinical practice and the decision-making processes involved in combining treatments are unclear. A research priority is to identify how treatments are combined in practice and to begin to examine their outcomes.

A second area for research on combined treatments pertains to the combination of psychosocial and psychopharmacological treatments. Although these separate treatments occasionally are viewed as reflecting clashing paradigms, there has been reason for one paradigm to look to the other for assistance. In some cases, both alternative psychotherapies and medications represent viable treatment approaches. For example, an emerging albeit sparse treatment literature for childhood depression has outcome studies suggesting that cognitively based treatment and medication lead to a remission of symptoms (see Kazdin, 1990b; Reynolds, 1992). The different models these treatments reflect raise the prospect that combined modalities may provide a broader level of attack.

Combined treatments may also be viable when the impact of an available treatment does not achieve the desired short- or long-term effect. For example, stimulant medication is frequently used for attention-deficit hyperactivity disorder. As mentioned previously, the evidence has suggested reliable improvements in core features of the dysfunction, such as in level of activity, impulsiveness, inattentiveness, and aggressive behavior. Although important gains are evident, questions about the magnitude of the changes and long-term impact have been raised (e.g., G. Weiss & Hechtman, 1986; Whalen & Henker, 1991). Combinations of treatment that take advantage of the gains achieved with medication but make an effort to achieve greater and more protracted benefits represent a viable alternative to augment impact (e.g., Satterfield et al., 1987).

A final consideration lobbying for research on combined treatments derives from current findings that children often show more than one disorder (comorbidity). One reason practitioners may combine treatments is to address the range of dysfunctions a given child brings to treatment. As yet, there is little research to guide clinical work in selecting combinations of treatment when children evince multiple problems.

Evaluating the Long-Term Effects of Treatment

Treatment outcome usually is evaluated by administering measures immediately after treatment (posttreatment assessment); occasionally outcome is evaluated at a later point in time (follow-up assessment). Many of the gains demonstrated in psychotherapy with children and adolescents have been tested over a relatively brief time frame. In our evaluation of the child therapy research, we found that the majority of studies (59%) did not include follow-up assessment. Among studies that included follow-up, assessment typically took place five to six months after treatment ended (Kazdin, Bass et al., 1990; Weisz et al., 1987).

Follow-up studies are critically important because the effects evident immediately after treatment are not always the same as those evident over time. For example, in one study of several school-based treatments, mentioned earlier, outcome results for some of the constituent treatments varied markedly over time (Kolvin et al., 1981). Specifically, two of the interventions (group therapy and behavior modification) provided to the children yielded relatively few improvements on measures of neuroticism, antisocial behavior, and total symptom scores. These domains improved markedly over the course of follow-up approximately 18 months after treatment and altered the conclusions about the impact of these interventions relative to other treatment and no-treatment control conditions. In other studies involving child and adult samples, the treatment that appeared more or most effective at posttreatment did not retain this status at follow-up (for reviews see Kazdin, 1988; D. Wright, Moelis, & Pollack, 1976). Thus, the conclusions about the efficacy of a given treatment in any particular study might well depend on when the assessment is conducted.

An unspoken ideal in treatment research is to report long-term follow-up data to evaluate client functioning years after treatment. The importance of follow-up assessment of treatment may be heightened in the evaluation of therapy for children and adolescents. Given the developmental perspective in which problematic behavior must be viewed and evaluated, marked changes in deviant and prosocial behavior are a matter of course independent of intervention efforts. Quite possibly, treatments that appear effective or differentially effective in the short run may not suppress the impact of developmental changes. The difficulties and costs of following subjects over time, the inevitable increases in attrition, and the ambiguities that can result from selective losses of cases over time are among the salient disincentives for conducting follow-up (Kazdin, 1992a). Nevertheless, such assessment is critically important to evaluate the impact of the intervention on developmental course.

If we are to understand fully the extent to which treatments are effective, further research is needed to evaluate the long-term impact of interventions for alternative therapies and clinical problems. Different time periods reflect different questions, each of which is important in its own right. For example, we wish to know if therapy can produce change, whether gains are maintained, and whether long-term adjustment (e.g., in adulthood) is affected. Knowledge about the short- and long-term impact of treatment may help guide both the type of interventions that are selected and when and how they are to be deployed during the course of development.

Bridging Research and Clinical Practice

One of the goals of treatment research is to provide a firm empirical footing for clinical practice. Ideally, basic processes examined in research as well as process and outcome research can inform clinical application. There is a widely recognized hiatus between research and practice (see Stricker & Keisner, 1985). Part of the hiatus can be attributed to the discrepancy between how treatment is implemented in practice and studied in psychotherapy research. In clinical practice, the therapist focuses on intensive evaluation of the individual case with an effort to provide any and all treatment that might be needed to ameliorate the situation. The flexibility and fluidity of treatment and its administration stand in contrast to the situation facing the researcher. In the case of psychotherapy research, the investigator usually is interested in the recruitment of a large number of subjects with well-specified problems or dysfunction, the use of control conditions (e.g., no-treatment, "attention-placebo"), experimental control over the intervention and its delivery, and other features. Understandably, research on psychotherapy for children and adolescents is often conducted under conditions that depart from those in clinical work. An issue for all research is the extent to which the results can be generalized from the circumstances of the investigation (e.g., subjects, setting) to those in which the variables might ordinarily operate. Generality of findings warrants special mention in the context of evaluation of treatment for children and adolescents.

Studies have examined characteristics of psychotherapy for children and adolescents as conducted in *research* (Casey & Berman, 1985; Kazdin, Bass et al., 1990; Weisz et al., 1987) and in *clinical practice* (Kazdin, Siegel, & Bass, 1990; Koocher & Pedulla, 1977; Silver & Silver, 1983; Tuma & Pratt, 1982). Table 13.3 summarizes salient differences between psychotherapy as conducted in research and in clinical practice. The differences deserve elaboration given the significance of the

TABLE 13.3   Comparison of selected features of psychotherapy with children and adolescents as conducted in research and clinical practice

In Research . . .	In Clinical Practice . . .
Cases usually recruited for treatment	Cases usually referred for treatment
Cases usually seen in the schools	Cases usually seen in clinics or private practice settings
Treatment duration averages 8–10 weeks	Treatment duration averages 6–12 months
Treatment usually provided in groups	Treatment usually provided individually
Parents infrequently involved in treatment	Parents usually involved in treatment
Family infrequently seen in treatment	Family often seen as a unit
Psychodynamic, psychoanalytically oriented, family, and eclectic approaches are rarely studied	Psychodynamic, psychoanalytically oriented, family, and eclectic approaches are often used

Note. The present table summarizes information obtained from evaluations of clinical practice (Kazdin, Siegel, & Bass, 1990; Koocher & Pedulla, 1977; Silver & Silver, 1983; Tuma & Pratt, 1982) and clinical research (Casey & Berman, 1985; Kazdin, Bass, Ayers, & Rodgers, 1990; Weisz, Weiss, Alicke, & Klotz, 1987). For precise estimates of specific practices, the original sources should be consulted directly.

issues they may reflect in relation to current research and practice.

Major differences are evident in research and clinical practice. To begin, consider the *types of cases seen in treatment.* The majority of cases in clinical practice are clinically referred, that is, they come to treatment through direct referral (e.g., parents, school, courts). In therapy research, the majority of children (over 75%) are solicited as volunteers. The motivation for treatment as well as the type of problems might be expected to vary as a result of these different methods of recruitment. Indeed, some problems that are commonly seen in clinical practice (e.g., adjustment disorder) are rarely reported in research on treatments for children.

The *methods of treatment delivery* convey further discrepancies between clinical practice and research. The majority of treatment studies focus on behavior modification and cognitive-behavioral techniques. These are often used in clinical practice. However, in practice greater attention is accorded psychodynamically oriented psychotherapy, relationship-based therapy, family therapy, and eclectic treatment than is evident in psychotherapy research.

The duration of treatment too varies markedly across clinical work and research. When studied in research, treatment is relatively brief (means from separate evaluations span 8–10 weeks) (Casey & Berman, 1983; Weisz et al., 1987). In clinical practice, treatment is much longer (means from separate evaluations span 27–55 weeks) (Kazdin, Siegel, & Bass, 1990; Silver & Silver, 1983). These differences remain evident even when the evaluation is restricted to the same dysfunctions (e.g., conduct disorder, attention deficit disorder, and anxiety disorder) seen in both research and practice.

Other features of child and adolescent therapy as conducted in clinical practice and research are discrepant. For example, in clinical practice, most cases are seen in private practice or mental health facilities (e.g., clinics, hospitals), whereas in therapy research, treatment is usually conducted in the schools. In clinical practice, parents and teachers often are actively involved in the treatment process; this is rarely true of treatments examined in the context of research. The family is often seen as a unit in clinical work, although this is rare in investigations of treatment for children. Also, in clinical work, treatment is usually provided individually whereas in research group administration is more common.

Not all characteristics distinguish clinical research and practice. In both child therapy research and practice, there is a tendency to focus on youth within the 6–11 age group, to pay slightly greater attention to boys than girls, and to attend to dysfunctions that approximate conduct/oppositional disorder, attention-deficit/hyperactivity, and anxiety disorders. However, these similarities are relatively minor when compared with the differences.

In general, several conditions that characterize clinical research depart from the conditions of clinical practice. The discrepancies do not necessarily mean that the results from the restricted conditions of research do not apply to the conditions of clinical practice. At the same time, the discrepancies alert us to the prospect that manifold conditions of clinical practice are not addressed in contemporary research. The danger pertains to the generality of findings from research to the conditions of clinical practice.

The effectiveness of treatment in clinical practice is not well investigated. In an effort to examine the impact of treatment in practice, Weisz and Weiss (1989) evaluated youth ages 6–17 who attended treatment at one of nine clinics. Youth who never began treatment were compared with those who completed five or more treatment sessions. The rationale for the comparison was that if therapy is effective, those who receive treatment would be expected to show greater change six months and one year later (after intake). The results indicated no consistent differences on parent and teacher checklist measures between those who never began treatment relative to those who received some treatment. The results were interpreted to suggest that treatment in clinical practice may not be effective. The heterogeneity of the youth, treatment techniques, therapists, and clinical problems and the inclusion of youth who did not complete treatment (in the completer group) obscure evaluation of the impact of treatment. Nevertheless, the focus of the study raises important questions about the extent to which treatment conducted in clinic settings achieves the effects often found in research.

A critical research issue for the field is to address the chasm between research and practice on treatments for children and adolescents. The chasm can be bridged in different ways. To begin, characteristics of clinical work can be integrated into research studies. Investigation of clients who are referred for treatment and examination of treatments commonly used in clinical practice would by themselves increase the clinical relevance of therapy research. Second, the gulf between research and practice could be narrowed by using single-case research designs more often in clinical work. The designs would permit utilization of clinical situations as a setting for developing and testing directly hypotheses about interventions and their effects. Third, many interventions for children and adolescents can be evaluated in clinical practice in quasi-experimental designs that permit inferences to be drawn about treatment (e.g., Weisz & Weisz, 1989). Evaluations of applications in practice serve important service functions of value in their own right. In relation to a broader research agenda, such evaluations can also raise critical research questions and foster the reciprocal exchange between research and practice.

Extending Treatments Among Underserved and Understudied Populations

A critical priority for treatment research is greater attention to the treatment and mental health needs of the underserved. Reports already attest to the notion that children and adolescents constitute underserved populations (IOM, 1989; U.S. Congress, 1990). Within these populations, subsamples can be readily identified. To begin, minority groups within the United States are comprised primarily of blacks, Hispanics, Asians, and Native Americans.[3] Currently 20 percent of youth under 18 years of age belong to a minority group. By the year 2000, the figure is projected at 30 percent for school-age children (Gibbs & Huang, 1991). For many youth, minority status is also associated with low socioeconomic status, higher incidence of clinical dysfunction, and poor access to health and mental health services (U.S. Congress, 1986, 1990, 1991).

Minority youth are underrepresented in clinical practice as well as in treatment research, and the available data are sparse (Kazdin, Bass et al., 1990; Kazdin, Siegel, & Bass, 1990). Indeed, in the last 20 years the majority of treatment studies with children and adolescents have not reported race and ethnicity in descriptions of the participants. Providing and evaluating treatment for minorities are multifaceted tasks because ethnic and racial status have an impact on when and how youth are identified for treatment, manifestations of symptoms, help-seeking patterns, and treatment utilization (Tharp, 1991). Research designed to address the mental health of minorities requires scrutiny of each step of case identification and treatment delivery.

From the narrow perspective of the interventions themselves, an important challenge is to identify culturally sensitive, relevant, and acceptable treatments (see Chapter 19, this volume). Promising developments have emerged in recent treatment studies. For example, Malgady, Rogler, and Costantino (1990; Costantino, Malgady, & Rogler, 1986) have developed and empirically evaluated treatments for Puerto Rican children and adolescents. The treatments are designed to integrate cultural values in the context of modeling (social learning) therapy. For young children, prosocial models are presented in the context of folktales (*cuentos*); for adolescents, stories involving adult role models are based on biographies of heroic Puerto Ricans. The treatments are designed to develop prosocial behavior in ways that are culturally relevant, to foster ethnic pride, and to provide methods of coping with stresses common to the Puerto Rican community. As another example, mentioned previously, Szapocznik and his colleagues (1989, 1990) have examined family therapy with Cuban youth. A family-based treatment approach was selected to focus on ethnically relevant family structure and values, to improve entry

[3]Although these groups are discussed as such, each can be divided into other subgroups to which the points of this discussion apply. For example, Hispanic youth in the United States are composed primarily of Mexican-American and mainland Puerto Rican youth; Asian youth are primarily Japanese and Chinese American but other groups are included as well (see Gibbs & Huang, 1991).

into treatment, to reduce attrition, and to augment therapeutic change.

A number of child and adolescent samples are underrepresented in treatment research. For many groups, identification of their need for treatment is relatively recent. Among these are children of adults who have severe disorders (e.g., depression, alcohol abuse), children with physical handicaps and chronic diseases, children exposed to physical or sexual abuse and neglect, persons with mental retardation, and homeless youth, to mention a few examples (see Dryfoos, 1990; IOM, 1989; Kazdin, 1992b; U.S. Congress, 1991). Youth in these groups have higher rates of clinical dysfunction and represent a high priority for intervention for both treatment and preventive purposes.

A research priority is to extend treatment and treatment research to underserved populations. The task obviously involves more than recruiting a broader range of subjects. Theoretical and empirical work is required to identify the extent to which special treatment and alternative service models are needed; what facets of existing treatments can be modified to extend the benefits to special groups; and what novel measures, modalities, and procedures are required. The diverse ethnic identities and the co-occurrence of factors that can affect the treatment process (e.g., ethnic status and socioeconomic standing) could call for an indefinite number of models and adaptations of treatment because of the large groups and subgroups that can be identified. For example, among Native Americans over 500 recognized national entities can be identified; currently over 200 distinct tribal languages are spoken (see LaFromboise & Low, 1991). An effort to develop separate models, interventions, and approaches suited to each tribal entity is not only overwhelming but may also be unnecessary. Research that follows from conceptualizing treatment and the factors that affect its cultural relevance, use, and adoption may be helpful to derive culturally relevant principles to guide treatment development and modification.

CONCEPTUALIZATION OF TREATMENT RESEARCH

The previous discussion identifies specific questions and areas in need of further research. Although research on child and adolescent psychotherapy has proliferated in recent years, the area is still at a relatively preliminary stage. This conclusion is based on the current status of accumulated findings. At present, there are few disorders for which demonstrably effective treatments exist, few long-term evaluations of the impact of treatment on well-defined or delineated dysfunctions, and few

treatment studies that have identified the factors that predict responsiveness to treatment. Also, as mentioned previously, treatment approaches (e.g., psychodynamic treatment, relationship therapy) and their eclectic combinations are rarely studied in research.

At this relatively early stage of research in child and adolescent psychotherapy, there may be special value in considering broader issues to conceptualize the research process. The goal of therapy is to identify effective interventions and the conditions that influence their effectiveness and to understand the mechanisms of therapeutic change. In the case of children and adolescents, this task is particularly challenging because of the marked impact of development on child and adolescent functioning. Future research directions can address the specific domains highlighted in the previous section. At the same time, it is useful to consider broader issues that can help chart the course for identifying effective treatments and understanding how they operate.

A Plan for Treatment Development

Although one can easily point to forward movement in research, the progression of treatment research may be haphazard. Perhaps treatment research will reach the promised land, to wit, identification of a set of effective interventions for youth of different ages and different types and severity of dysfunction. While there may be no likely shortcut, perhaps there is a way to reduce wandering a bit by mapping the various stages or steps needed to develop and identify an effective intervention. The utility would derive from being better able to match the extent to which years of research are moving toward the goal and as a guide to researchers to add in an incremental way to prior studies.

There are many steps that might be identified to move toward the end goal of developing effective interventions. Table 13.4 identifies the steps from conceptualization of the problem to development and evaluation of treatment. The steps elaborate some of the criteria used to identify promising treatments, mentioned previously. In Table 13.4, they are included as part of the sequence of steps that evaluates a broad range of research questions to understand treatment, its basis, and optimal application.

The steps emphasize theoretical development of treatment, so that there is some connection to processes that can be investigated and established in their own right. Demonstration that particular processes are in fact relevant and play a pivotal role in dysfunction greatly enhances the prospect of developing effective treatment. Conceptualization of treatment follows to ensure that the process and

TABLE 13.4   Steps in developing effective treatments

1. **Conceptualization of the Dysfunction**

   Conceptualization of key areas that relate to the development, onset, and escalation of dysfunction, proposal of key processes that are antecedents to some facet of conduct disorder and the mechanisms by which these processes emerge or operate.

2. **Research on Processes Related to Dysfunction**

   Research that examines the relation of processes proposed to be critical to the dysfunction (conduct disorder) to test the model.

3. **Conceptualization of Treatment**

   Conceptualization of the treatment focus, how specific procedures relate to other processes implicated in the dysfunction and to desired treatment outcomes.

4. **Specification of Treatment**

   Concrete operationalization of the treatment, preferably in manual form, so that the integrity of treatment can be evaluated, the material learned from treatment trials can be codified, and the treatment procedures can be replicated.

5. **Tests of Treatment Process**

   Studies to identify whether the intervention techniques, methods, and procedures within treatment actually affect those processes that are critical to the model.

6. **Tests of Treatment Outcome**

   Treatment studies to evaluate the impact of treatment. A wide range of treatment tests (e.g., open [uncontrolled] studies, single-case designs, full-fledged clinical trials) can provide evidence that change is produced. Several types of studies (e.g., dismantling, parametric, and comparative outcome studies) are relevant.

7. **Tests of the Boundary Conditions and Moderators**

   Examination of the child, parent, family, and contextual factors with which treatment interacts. The boundary conditions or limits of application are identified through interactions of treatment $\times$ diverse attributes within empirical tests.

foci of the intervention relate to development of the problem. Specification of treatment processes, tests of treatment effects, and examination of process and outcome relations are familiar steps in therapy research in large measure because of their precedence in studies of adult psychotherapy. The steps and their progression need not be viewed as a rigid formula to apply to treatment. Advances, breakthroughs, and innovations can readily emerge free from a broad overarching framework. On the other hand, there may be value to tracking treatment approaches in terms of their progress in moving toward establishing their effectiveness.

Expanding the Models to Develop and Evaluate Treatment

Psychotherapy outcome research usually consists of a specific intervention that is applied to a clinically identified group for a specific, time-limited duration and is evaluated after treatment is terminated. Consider these characteristics as representing a *conventional model* of evaluating treatment. There are other models that may be particularly useful in relation to clinical dysfunctions that are difficult to treat or pervasive in the domains of dysfunction they impact (Kazdin, 1988).

High-strength intervention model. In the conventional model, treatment obviously is intended to have an impact but rarely is it explicitly designed to provide a particularly potent test. Considerations about the dose, strength, duration, and other parameters of treatment are not explicitly based on an effort to maximize clinical impact. The high-strength intervention model begins with an effort to maximize therapeutic change. For severe clinical problems in particular, it may be valuable to address the question, "What is the likely impact on the problem with the maximum or seemingly most potent treatment(s) available?" One should aim for the *strongest feasible version* of treatment to see if the problem can be altered. The high-strength model is not only an effort to maximize clinical change, but also a test of where the field is at a given point. Given the best available treatment(s), what can we expect from the maximum dose, regimen, or variation?

For psychosocial treatments, strength and intensity of treatment are difficult to define. The problem stems in part from nebulous or poor conceptualizations of treatment. To vary or increase the strength of treatment, one must have some idea regarding the procedures or processes that account for therapeutic change. To convey the possible change that the high-strength model of treatment reflects, relative to the conventional model, consider one parameter of treatment, namely, duration of therapy. As mentioned previously, in contemporary child and adolescent therapy research, the mean duration of treatment is 8–10 weeks. For many problems (e.g., clinical depression, conduct disorder, attention deficit disorder, bulimia), this duration is relatively brief considering the likely long-term consequences. More (treatment) is not invariably better. At the same time, current tests by and large seem weak. Much longer treatments, perhaps even spanning years, might seem more promising to maximize impact. Again, duration is a single parameter of treatment merely to illustrate the model rather than one of the salient dimensions or characteristics on which high-strength treatments necessarily depend.

Mentioned previously were the studies by Lovaas (1987) and McEachin et al. (1993) that provided extensive treatment for autistic children. Some of the children received treatment for 40 hours per week for more than 6 years (more than 14,000 hours of one-to-one treatment per child). Most would agree that this is a high-strength test of treatment. The findings are extremely interesting on conceptual and applied grounds. Increases in IQ, placement of youth into regular classrooms, and sustained gains years later among treated cases provide an important test and status report of what can be accomplished for seriously impaired youth.

High-strength interventions may be expensive, as reflected in the costs of therapists, therapist training, number of sessions, and patient contact hours. Yet, even if such a test were very expensive in terms of professional resources and patient care, the resulting knowledge might obviate the need for multiple other tests with weaker versions of treatment. If the strongest version of treatment produces change, then it is reasonable to study whether less protracted, less costly, and less difficult-to-implement procedures can achieve similar outcomes and whether any loss in treatment gains is worth the savings in cost or ease of administration. However, knowledge of what can be accomplished is important for both a test of current knowledge and clinical care.

Amenability-to-treatment model. Implicit in much of treatment research is the view that the specific technique, at the exclusion of other factors, accounts for most of the change (variance) that is achieved. This view can be inferred by the almost exclusive focus on treatment and treatment variations as the basis for treatment outcome

studies, as mentioned earlier. The amenability-to-treatment model considers child, parent, and family factors that might moderate the effects of treatment.

The model is designed to identify where interventions are likely to be successful (viz., with those children who are most *amenable to treatment*). Youth with a given type of dysfunction often are quite heterogeneous in terms of symptoms of the dysfunction, adaptive skills, and resources (e.g., family support). There are remarkable leads from research on risk and protective factors related to child, parent, family, and other conditions that might be used to identify youth likely to vary in their amenability to change (see Rutter & Giller, 1983; Werner & Smith, 1992). For example, in the case of conduct disorder youth, children with early onset of antisocial behavior who engage in diverse behaviors across multiple settings (e.g., home and school) are more likely to continue antisocial behavior into adolescence and adulthood (Kazdin, 1987b). These and several other child, parent, and family variables can be distinguished among youths who are referred clinically for conduct disorder and may influence amenability or responsiveness to treatment.

The amenability model considers the population of youth with a particular dysfunction (e.g., depression) as varying in degrees of amenability to treatment. The place to begin is not necessarily fixed in the model. One obvious point would be to evaluate in a systematic way the impact of treatment with youth who would be the most amenable to treatment. Is there any group of youth with a particular type of dysfunction for whom we can reliably produce potent and durable treatment effects? Progress in treatment might be accelerated by trying to select subgroups that can be effectively treated. Treatment of amenable cases does not mean neglect of the more recalcitrant cases. However, in the accumulation of knowledge, ways of dividing the population to treat any subgroup effectively would be a major accomplishment. Also, once subgroups of youth who can be effectively treated are identified, a more concentrated focus can be provided to those less amenable and for whom effective treatments are unavailable.

The approach of identifying youth more or less amenable to treatment can be integrated into existing controlled outcome research. Within a given study, youth can be identified as more or less amenable to the intervention based on characteristics of the sample and hypotheses about the interface of treatment and these characteristics. Analyses of outcome effects are then based on comparisons of subgroups within the investigation to assess responsiveness to treatment as a function of hypothesized amenability to treatment.

Broad-based interventions. This model begins with the fact that many dysfunctions of childhood and adolescence are multifaceted and include a broad range of symptoms, areas of dysfunction, and parent and family problems. Attention-deficit hyperactivity disorder, for example, may include a variety of symptoms beyond attention problems, hyperactivity, and impulsiveness that are its defining features. Academic dysfunction, poor peer relations, and aggressive behavior are likely to be present as well. In conventional applications of treatment, a particular intervention is implemented to alter an important facet (e.g., psychic conflict, self-esteem, family processes) of the child and/or the system in which the child functions. The domain that is targeted is considered, on theoretical or clinical grounds, to be central to the child's problem. For many dysfunctions, central or associated features of the disorder or consequences resulting from the symptoms (e.g., peer rejection from aggressive attacks) may require a broader range of treatment foci than any one technique can reasonably reflect.

The broad-based intervention model is an effort to expand the comprehensiveness or scope of interventions to address a large set of domains relevant to the individual youth's dysfunction. Treatments can be conceived in a *modular fashion* in which separate components (modules) are woven into an overall treatment regimen. Implementation of the model requires separate steps. The model requires evaluation of child functioning in diverse domains (e.g., home, school, community; deviance, interpersonal behavior, academic functioning). The model focuses on providing multiple treatments or components of treatment designed to address the domains of functioning identified as problematic. Plausible treatment combinations might include individual psychotherapy or cognitively based treatment, school-based reinforcement, family therapy, and parent training.

The idea of broad-based and multifaceted treatments is not an endorsement for eclecticism in treatment in which multiple interventions are used to meet the putative "individual needs of the client." Rarely are the putative needs known, systematically assessed, or used as a basis for selecting among the very diverse psychotherapies and medications available for treatment. Also, the agglomeration of techniques is often haphazard; multiple procedures are selected for their intuitive appeal and face validity. In the broad-based model, the combination is justified on the basis of the assessment of specific domains prior to treatment and an effort to match dysfunction in these domains to alternative interventions based on conceptualization or evidence in behalf of these interventions.

Future research might move toward a more comprehensive approach with multiple treatment components. The approach should be guided by initial evidence that the constituent techniques produce some change and that the domain of the focus is relevant to the problem. The danger of multifaceted treatments is that at the end of the investigation one cannot identify what component(s) accounted for change. Yet, once such a multifaceted treatment was shown to produce change, it might be quite worthwhile then to begin to analyze the contributions of individual components.

A chronic care model. For a number of disorders or a number of youth with a particular disorder, the course of maladjustment may be lifelong. Obviously, the more pervasive developmental disorders and more severe forms of mental retardation are in this class. In addition, less pervasive and more commonly referred dysfunctions have a lifelong course for many youth. Long-term follow-up studies of conduct disorder and attention-deficit hyperactivity disorder, for example, suggest that as adults a significant proportion (e.g., one-third to one-half) continue the dysfunction identified in childhood (e.g., Robins, 1978; G. Weiss & Hechtman, 1986). Those who do not may show other types of disorders or significant social maladjustment as well.

The conventional model of treatment is to apply time-limited and brief treatment. Perhaps treatment ought to be evaluated in terms of a need for chronic care or at least chronic monitoring. Many mental and physical health problems (e.g., depression, diabetes) require more than a time-limited, short-term intervention. For many types of dysfunction (e.g., conduct disorder, attention-deficit hyperactivity disorder, major depression), it may be useful to conceive of treatment as a routine and ongoing part of everyday life. Perhaps after the child is referred, treatment would be provided, possibly in the usual way (conventional model) or based on other models (high-strength, broad-based), noted previously. After improvement is achieved, treatment would be suspended rather than terminated. At that point, the child and his or her functioning would be monitored systematically (with standardized measures) and regularly (e.g., every three months). Treatment could be provided *pro re nata* based on the assessment data or emergent issues raised by the family, teachers, or others. The approach might be likened to the more familiar model of dental care in which individuals are checked every six months; an intervention is provided if, and as, needed based on these periodic checks.

Obviously, the use of a chronic care model is not advocated in cases where there is evidence that short-term treatment is effective. Indeed, short-term treatment is not incompatible with a chronic care model. The model requires monitoring of youth who are likely to continue the dysfunction so that treatment can be reintroduced as needed. However, a very different conceptualization of clinical dysfunction, treatment, and treatment research is required to address more recalcitrant clinical problems.

General comments. Typically, research on treatment of child and adolescent disorders is conducted in ways opposite from what might be needed to develop and identify effective interventions. For example, in treatment research, the amount and duration of treatment is relatively brief (e.g., one-hour sessions, 8–10 sessions total), probably not a test of a high-strength treatment. Child, parent, family, and other characteristics are rarely examined to identify case × treatment interactions. Thus, few efforts are made to identify who is more or less amenable or responsive to treatment. Individual techniques are usually contrasted with one another, rather than combined in an effort to augment therapeutic change. Thus, broad-based treatments are not usually tested. Finally, treatment is usually terminated after the brief regimen is provided, so that chronic care is not evaluated. These characteristics of therapy research would not be problematic if effective treatments were identified with the conventional model of treatment evaluation. However, the yield from research and the very severe and pervasive impairment of many disorders serve as impetus to reconsider the focus, design, and model of treatment trials.

Research From a Developmental Perspective

Many of the inroads psychotherapy research has made in the treatment of adults can serve to guide child and adolescent psychotherapy research. The range of variables, types of treatment processes, and assessment of both process and outcome established in research with adults may have heuristic value in developing treatments for children and adolescents. At the same time, a developmental perspective is required that considers changes over time in child functioning and the interface of these changes with the interpersonal environment. The perspective requires integration of the child's varying interdependence on others such as parents,

teachers, and peers whose influence is related to adjustment, treatment application, and outcome.

Age, stage, and level of development. The delineation of childhood and adolescence in research and the analysis of differences as a function of age and developmental level are critical for future work. The impact of development on clinical dysfunction and how this information can be integrated into treatment may have important implications for conclusions about the effectiveness of treatment. Outcome research rarely considers features of development that may affect treatment. A small number of outcome studies have evaluated "age" in an initial effort to integrate developmental differences into treatment research and have shown differences in outcome (e.g., Kolvin et al., 1981; L. Miller et al., 1972). Similarly, reviews have examined child age as a variable across studies in relation to treatment outcomes (effect sizes) (Durlak et al., 1991; G. Patterson, Dishion, & Chamberlain, in press; Weisz et al., 1987). Chronological age represents an empirical beginning to evaluate whether treatment effects vary among samples. However, age, as a construct for research, is conceptually weak because it does not identify specific processes nor does it sort cases by these processes in an analytic fashion. A task for research is to consider and then to go beyond age as a mediator of treatment outcome by considering developmental levels and processes (e.g., attachment, moral development).

The gross neglect of developmental differences even at the level of age is long standing in child and adolescent psychotherapy research. For example, in the earliest review of psychotherapy research with "children," preschoolers to 21-years-olds were included (Levitt, 1957). Obviously, it is likely to be critically important to make the division between children and adolescents more sharply in research. The age range, usually delineated as 4–18 years of age, represents a period of remarkable diversity. Even within a fairly narrow age range, many differences can be identified. For example, with preteens, markedly different patterns of depression are evident for boys and girls as a function of pubertal status (Rutter, 1986). Of course, pubertal status is only one of many relevant variables that might be addressed and developmentally relevant for youth.

Sex differences over the course of development raise important issues relevant to dysfunction and intervention. Males and females differ in normal development as well in psychopathology in multiple ways of potential relevance for treatment. For example, entry into puberty for females often is associated with low self-esteem, poor body image, and concern with being overweight. Maturing early or late in relation to one's peers exacerbates these reactions. Females who mature early or late are more likely to show high levels of depression and a propensity toward self-harm (see Richards & Petersen, 1987). Entry into puberty for males, on the other hand, is associated with increases in self-esteem and feelings of attractiveness. Early maturation is not associated with negative views but merely brings on an earlier onset of positive reactions. Similarly, transitions to new schools (elementary to junior high, junior to senior high) often are associated with decreases in self-esteem for females but not for males. Sex differences in adolescence go well beyond reactions to transitions (e.g., maturation, school change). The prevalence rates for disorders, the types of disorders experienced, and stability of disorders over time differ for female and male adolescents (e.g., McGee, Feehan, Williams, & Anderson, 1992).

Factors that predict onset and course of disorders can vary considerably by sex. For example, Tremblay et al. (1992) evaluated childhood predictors of delinquent acts in adolescents to isolate the contribution of early disruptive behavior and poor school accomplishment. For boys, early signs of disruptive behavior (at age 7) predicted later delinquency (at age 14); poor school accomplishment did not predict to delinquent acts once disruptive behavior was taken into account. For girls, neither early disruptive behavior nor poor school achievement was especially useful in predicting delinquent acts. If the factors that influence onset of antisocial behavior vary for male and female youth, effective preventive and treatment interventions may vary as well. In general, the task in relation to treatment is to identify developmentally meaningful ways to delineate youth so that interventions can be optimally applied. Differences in normal development at different ages, stages, and sexes point to domains that will need to be integrated into intervention research.

Developmentally relevant opportunities for intervention. Providing treatment to youth often has focused on downward extensions of treatments provided to adults. The approach can be evaluated on its own merit in light of outcome evidence. At the same time, a developmental perspective begins with recognition of the changing nature of youth, their contexts, and the influences on their functioning. Special opportunities for intervention might be identified from a developmental perspective that would not derive from extrapolation of advances in adult psychotherapy research. Opportunities for in-

tervention encompass special periods of development in which specific stage-appropriate influences can be harnessed.

As an example, research on antisocial behavior in adolescence has pointed to the strong role that peer relations and bonding may play in deviant behavior (e.g., Elliott et al., 1985; Newcomb & Bentler, 1988; Swaim, Oetting, Edwards, & Beauvais, 1989). Drawing on the influence of peers may provide special opportunities for treatment. As a case in point, Feldman et al. (1983) found that the type of peers included in group therapies affected outcome among antisocial youth. Youth in treatment groups with nonantisocial peers profited more from treatment than youth in groups composed of all antisocial youth. The possibility of bonding to other antisocial youth during treatment could even serve to produce detrimental effects (see Fo & O'Donnell, 1975). The more active use of peers in the treatment process (e.g., as therapeutic agents or adjunctive roles to assist in treatment) would follow from current research. Peer influences and their changing role over development represent only one type of influence prompted by developmentally based research. Also, youth undergo a variety of transition periods when change and varying influences operate. The transition that occurs when youth progress from one level of school to the next represents potential stress but at the same time an opportunity for intervention (e.g., Felner & Adan, 1988). Changes in cognitive development, peer influences, and transition periods (e.g., in schools) in adolescence may provide special intervention opportunities. Also, the transitional nature and normal disequilibrium of adolescence (e.g., dependence to autonomy, parent to peer influence) may represent an especially sensitive period for intervention and influence.

In discussions of interventions (treatment and prevention), an assumption is often made that earlier intervention is better than later intervention and that the earlier the better in terms of long-term impact. A strong case can be made for early intervention, as is evident, for example, from early maternal care and long-term outcome in offspring. More than one demonstration has shown that early intervention with mothers and children can have significant impact on later deviance of the children (see Schweinhart & Weikart, 1989; Seitz, Rosenbaum, & Apfel, 1985). However, it is rarely the case that the "earlier the better" assumption is tested empirically or derived from theoretically coherent and specific views about treatment or developmental change. The challenge for theory, research, and practice is to identify intervention windows of opportunity in which processes critically related to dysfunction can be interrupted and redirected. The range and degree of opportunity are not necessarily an inverse linear function of age. Different ages, stages, and developmental periods may provide different opportunities for intervention on conceptual and empirical grounds.

CONCLUSIONS

Research on child and adolescent psychotherapy has made significant progress. Large-scale integrative evaluations of the outcome literature have indicated that treatments produce beneficial effects. This broad conclusion is important in light of historical challenges to the effectiveness of psychotherapy. In addition, changes in affect, cognition, and behavior are often marked during childhood and adolescence. Hence, treatment effects often have maturational processes as strong competitors in demonstrating change.

In the present chapter, progress in therapy research was illustrated by examining contemporary reviews of research as well as by sampling research from several treatment approaches including psychoanalysis and psychodynamically oriented psychotherapy, nondirective and relationship-based treatment, play therapy, behavior therapy, cognitive-behavioral therapy, family therapy, and school- and community-based treatment. Also, progress in the treatment of several child and adolescent disorders and domains of functioning was illustrated by studies that focused on conduct disorder, attention-deficit hyperactivity disorder, anxiety disorder, depression, autistic disorder, child abuse, and stress. These illustrations convey progress in several areas of treatment. Nevertheless, many techniques in widespread use remain neglected in research. Also noted was the restricted set of questions that are addressed in research. Empirical efforts are needed to elaborate the moderators of treatment outcome and mechanisms of therapeutic change.

For children and adolescents, research is at a critical, challenging, and promising stage. Problems of childhood and adolescence currently are receiving greater attention in research than they have in the past. This means that conceptual and empirical underpinnings of treatment research are actively developing. Also, methods of treatment research and development of assessments for children and adolescents are at an excellent stage as well. The means to define and assess child dysfunction and to specify and codify treatment techniques are at a high point. What remains is systematic progress to build the empirical base. Based on current research progress, several research priorities were identi-

fied, including expanding the range of research questions about treatment, testing a broader range of treatments and treatment combinations, evaluating long-term treatment effects, bridging research and practice, extending treatments further to underserved and understudied populations, and integrating developmental theory and research into treatment research. A plan for developing and identifying effective treatments was also discussed to provide a framework to guide research. The plan incorporates a series of steps from conceptualization of treatment and processes to evaluation in clinical trials.

REFERENCES

Achenbach, T. M. (1986). Developmental perspectives on psychotherapy and behavior change. In S. L. Garfield & A. E. Bergin (Eds.), *Handbook of psychotherapy and behavior change* (3rd ed., pp. 117–154). New York: Wiley.

Achenbach, T. M., & Edelbrock, C. S. (1981). Behavioral problems and competencies reported by parents of normal and disturbed children aged four through sixteen. *Monographs of the Society for Research in Child Development, 46,* 188.

Achenbach, T. M., & Edelbrock, C. S. (1983). *Manual for the Child Behavior Checklist and Revised Child Behavior Profile.* Burlington, VT: University Associates in Psychiatry.

Achenbach, T. M., McConaughy, S. H., & Howell, C. T. (1987). Child/adolescent behavioral and emotional problems: Implications of cross-informant correlations for situational specificity. *Psychological Bulletin, 101,* 213–232.

Alexander, J. F., Barton, C., Schiavo, R. S., & Parsons, B. V. (1976). Systems-behavioral intervention with families of delinquents: Therapist characteristics, family behavior, and outcome. *Journal of Consulting and Clinical Psychology, 44,* 656–664.

Alexander, J. F., & Parsons, B. V. (1973). Short-term behavioral intervention with delinquent families: Impact on family process and recidivism. *Journal of Abnormal Psychology, 81,* 219–225.

Alexander, J. F., & Parsons, B. V. (1982). *Functional family therapy.* Monterey, CA: Brooks/Cole.

American Psychiatric Association. (1987). *Diagnostic and statistical manual of mental disorders* (3rd ed., rev.). Washington, DC: Author.

Anderson, J. C., Williams, S., McGee, R., & Silva, P. A. (1987). The prevalence of DSM III disorders in pre-adolescent children: Prevalence in a large sample from the general population. *Archives of General Psychiatry, 44,* 69–76.

Angold, A., Weissman, W., John, K., Wickramaratne, P., & Prusoff, B. (1991). The effects of age and sex on depression ratings in children and adolescents. *Journal of the American Academy of Child and Adolescent Psychiatry, 30,* 67–74.

Arbuthnot, J., & Gordon, D. A. (1986). Behavioral and cognitive effects of a moral reasoning development intervention for high-risk behavior-disordered adolescents. *Journal of Consulting and Clinical Psychology, 54,* 208–216.

Armbruster, P., & Kazdin, A. E. (in press). Attrition in child psychotherapy. In T. Ollendick & R. Prinz (Eds.), *Advances in clinical child psychology* (Vol. 16).

Bank, L., Marlowe, J. H., Reid, J. B., Patterson, G. R., &

Weinrott, M. R. (1991). A comparative evaluation of parent-training interventions for families of chronic delinquents. *Journal of Abnormal Child Psychology, 19,* 15–33.

Barkley, R. A. (1988). Attention deficit disorder with hyperactivity. In E. J. Mash & L. G. Terdal (Eds.), *Behavioral assessment of childhood disorders* (2nd ed., pp. 69–104). New York: Guilford.

Barkley, R. A. (1989). Attention-deficit hyperactivity disorder. In E. J. Mash & R. A. Barkley (Eds.), *Treatment of childhood disorders* (pp. 39–72). New York: Guilford.

Barkley, R. A., Guevremont, D. C., Anastopoulos, A. D., & Fletcher, K. E. (1992). A comparison of three family therapy programs for treating family conflicts in adolescents with attention-deficit hyperactivity disorder. *Journal of Consulting and Clinical Psychology, 60,* 450–462.

Barrett, C. L., Hampe, I. E., & Miller, L. C. (1978). Research on child psychotherapy. In S. L. Garfield & A. E. Bergin (Eds.), *Handbook of psychotherapy and behavior change: An empirical analysis* (2nd ed., pp. 411–435). New York: Wiley.

Barrios, B. A., & O'Dell, S. L. (1989). Fears and anxieties. In E. J. Mash & R. A. Barkley (Eds.), *Treatment of childhood disorders* (pp. 167–221). New York: Guilford.

Barrnett, R. J., Docherty, J. P., & Frommelt, G. M. (1991). A review of psychotherapy research since 1963. *Journal of the American Academy of Child and Adolescent Psychiatry, 30,* 1–14.

Beckham, E. E., & Leber, W. R. (Eds). (1985). *Handbook of depression: Treatment, assessment, and research.* Homewood, IL: Dorsey.

Bierman, K. L., Miller, C. L., & Stabb, S. D. (1987). Improving the social behavior and peer acceptance of rejected boys: Effects of social skill training with instructions and prohibitions. *Journal of Consulting and Clinical Psychology, 55,* 194–200.

Bird, H. R., Canino, G., Rubio-Stipec, M., Gould, M. S., Ribera, J., Sesman, M., Woodbury, M., Huertas-Goldman, S., Pagan, A., Sanchez-Lacay, A., & Moscoso, M. (1988). Estimates of the prevalence of childhood maladjustment in a community survey of Puerto Rico: The use of combined measures. *Archives of General Psychiatry, 45,* 1120–1126.

Bird, H. R., Gould, M. S., & Staghezza, B. (1992). Aggregating data from multiple informants in child psychiatry epidemiological research. *Journal of the American Academy of Child and Adolescent Psychiatry, 31,* 78–85.

Blagg, N. R., & Yule, W. (1984). The behavioral treatment of school refusal: A comparative study. *Behavior Research and Therapy, 22,* 119–127.

Bleck, R. T., & Bleck, B. L. (1982). The disruptive child's play group. *Elementary School Guidance and Counseling, 16,* 137–140.

Bornstein, P. H., & Kazdin, A. E. (Eds.). (1985). *Handbook of clinical behavior therapy with children.* Homewood, IL: Dorsey.

Brandt, D. E., & Zlotnick, S. J. (1988). *The psychology and treatment of the youthful offender.* Springfield, IL: Charles C. Thomas.

Brown, J. (1987). A review of meta-analyses conducted on psychotherapy outcome research. *Clinical Psychology Review, 7,* 1–23.

Butler, L., Miezitis, S., Friedman, R., & Cole, E. (1980). The effect of two school-based intervention programs on depressive symptoms in preadolescents. *American Educational Research Journal, 17,* 111–119.

Camp, B. W., & Bash, M. A. S. (1985). *Think aloud: Increasing social and cognitive skills—a problem solving program for children.* Champaign, IL: Research Press.

Carlson, C. L., Pelham, W. E., Milich, R., & Dixon, J. (1992). Single and combined effects of methylphenidate and behavior therapy on the classroom performance of children with attention-deficit hyperactivity disorder. *Journal of Abnormal Child Psychology, 20,* 213–232.

Casey, R. J., & Berman, J. S. (1985). The outcome of psychotherapy with children. *Psychological Bulletin, 98,* 388–400.

Charlop, M. H., Schreibman, L., & Kurtz, P. F. (1991). Childhood autism. In T. R. Kratochwill & R. J. Morris (Eds.), *The practice of child therapy* (2nd ed., pp 257–297). Elmsford, NY: Pergamon.

Clarke, G., Hops, H., Lewinsohn, P. M., Andrews, J., Seeley, J. R., & Williams, J. (1992). Cognitive-behavioral group treatment of adolescent depression: Prediction of outcome. *Behavior Therapy, 23,* 341–354.

Costantino, G., Malgady, R. G., & Rogler, L. H. (1986). Cuento therapy: A culturally sensitive modality for Puerto Rican children. *Journal of Consulting and Clinical Psychology, 54,* 639–645.

Costello, E. J. (1989). Developments in child psychiatric epidemiology. *Journal of the American Academy of Child and Adolescent Psychiatry, 28,* 836–841.

Dadds, M. R., & McHugh, T. A. (1992). Social support and treatment outcome in behavioral family therapy for child conduct problems. *Journal of Consulting and Clinical Psychology, 60,* 252–259.

Dadds, M. R., Schwartz, S., Sanders, M. R. (1987). Marital discord and treatment outcome in behavioral treatment of child conduct disorders. *Journal of Consulting and Clinical Psychology, 55,* 396–403.

Dodge, K. A. (1985). Attributional bias in aggressive children. In P. C. Kendall (Ed.), *Advances in cognitive-behavioral research and therapy* (Vol. 4, pp. 73–110). Orlando, FL: Academic Press.

Dodge, K. A. (1991). The structure and function of reactive and proactive aggression. In D. J. Pepler & K. H. Rubin (Eds.), *The development and treatment of childhood aggression* (pp. 201–218). Hillsdale, NJ: Lawrence Erlbaum.

Dodge, K. A., Price, J. M., Bachorowski, J., & Newman, J. P. (1990). Hostile attributional biases in severely aggressive adolescents. *Journal of Abnormal Psychology, 99,* 385–392.

Dodge, K. A., & Somberg, D. R. (1987). Hostile attributional biases among aggressive boys are exacerbated under conditions of threats to the self. *Child Development, 58,* 213–224.

Dryfoos, J. G. (1990). *Adolescents at risk: Prevalence and prevention.* New York: Oxford University Press.

Dumas, J. E. (1989). Treating antisocial behavior in children: Child and family approaches. *Clinical Psychology Review, 9,* 197–222.

Dumas, J. E., & Wahler, R. G. (1983). Predictors of treatment outcome in parent training: Mother insularity and socioeconomic disadvantage. *Behavioral Assessment, 5,* 301–313.

Durlak, J. A. (1980). Comparative effectiveness of behavioral and relationship group treatment in the secondary prevention of maladjustment. *American Journal of Community Psychology, 8,* 327–339.

Durlak, J. A., Fuhrman, T., & Lampman, C. (1991). Effectiveness of cognitive-behavioral therapy for maladapting children: A meta-analysis. *Psychological Bulletin, 110,* 204–214.

Eisenberg, L., & Gruenberg, E. M. (1961). The current status of secondary prevention in child psychiatry. *American Journal of Orthopsychiatry, 31,* 355–367.

Elliott, D. S., Huizinga, D., & Ageton, S. S. (1985). *Explain-

ing delinquency and drug use. Beverly Hills, CA: Sage Publications.

Eysenck, H. J. (1952). The effects of psychotherapy: An evaluation. *Journal of Consulting Psychology, 16,* 319–324.

Eysenck, H. J. (1960). The effects of psychotherapy. In H. J. Eysenck (Ed.), *Handbook of abnormal psychology: An experimental approach.* London: Pitman Medical Publishing.

Eysenck, H. J. (1966). *The effects of psychotherapy* (with commentary). New York: International Science Press.

Faust, J., Olson, R., & Rodriguez, H. (1991). Same-day surgery preparation: Reduction of pediatric patient arousal and distress through participant modeling. *Journal of Consulting and Clinical Psychology, 59,* 475–478.

Feindler, E. L. (1991). Cognitive strategies in anger control interventions for children and adolescents. In P. C. Kendall (Ed.), *Child and adolescent therapy: Cognitive-behavioral procedures* (pp. 66–97). New York: Guilford.

Feindler, E. L., & Ecton, R. B. (1986). *Adolescent anger control: Cognitive-behavioral techniques.* Elmsford, NY: Pergamon.

Feindler, E. L., Ecton, R. B., Kingsley, D., & Dubey, D. R. (1986). Group anger-control training for institutionalized psychiatric male adolescents. *Behavior Therapy, 17,* 109–123.

Feldman, R. A., Caplinger, T. E., & Wodarski, J. S. (1983). *The St. Louis conundrum: The effective treatment of antisocial youths.* Englewood Cliffs, NJ: Prentice Hall.

Felner, R. D., & Adan, A. M. (1988). The school transitional environment project: An ecological intervention and evaluation. In R. H. Price, E. L. Cowen, R. P. Lorion, & J. Ramos-McKay (Eds.), *14 ounces of prevention: A casebook for practitioners* (pp. 111–122). Washington, DC: American Psychological Association.

Fergusson, D. M., Horwood, L. J., & Lloyd, M. (1991). Confirmatory factor models of attention deficit and conduct disorder. *Journal of Child Psychology and Psychiatry, 32,* 257–274.

Fixsen, D. L., Phillips, E. L., Phillips, E. A., & Wolf, M. M. (1976). The teaching-family model of group home treatment. In W. E. Craighead, A. E. Kazdin, & M. J. Mahoney (Eds.), *Behavior modification: Principles, issues, and applications.* Boston: Houghton Mifflin.

Fo, W. S. O., & O'Donnell, C. R. (1975). The buddy system: Effect of community intervention on delinquent offenses. *Behavior Therapy, 6,* 522–524.

Fonagy, P., & Moran, G. S. (1990). Studies on the efficacy of child psychoanalysis. *Journal of Consulting and Clinical Psychology, 58,* 684–695.

Forehand, R., Lautenschlager, G. J., Faust, J., & Graziano, W. G. (1986). Parent perceptions and parent–child interactions in clinic-referred children: A preliminary investigation of the effects of maternal depressive moods. *Behaviour Research and Therapy, 24,* 73–75.

Forehand, R., & Long, N. (1988). Outpatient treatment of the acting out child: Procedures, long-term follow-up data, and clinical problems. *Advances in Behaviour Research and Therapy, 10,* 129–177.

Forehand, R., & McMahon, R. J. (1981). *Helping the noncompliant child: A clinician's guide to parent training.* New York: Guilford.

Garfield, S. L. (1980). *Psychotherapy: An eclectic approach.* New York: Wiley.

Gibbs, J. T., & Huang, L. N. (Eds.). (1991). *Children of color: Psychological interventions with minority youth.* San Francisco, CA: Jossey-Bass.

Goldfried, M. R., Greenberg, L. S., & Marmar, C. (1990). Individual psychotherapy: Process and outcome. *Annual Review of Psychology, 41,* 659–688.

Hampe, E., Noble, H., Miller, L. C., & Barrett, C. L. (1973). Phobic children one and two years posttreatment. *Journal of Abnormal Psychology, 82,* 446–453.

Hazelrigg, M. D., Cooper, H. M., & Borduin, C. M. (1987). Evaluating the effectiveness of family therapies: An integrative review and analysis. *Psychological Bulletin, 101,* 428–442.

Heinicke, C. M. (1969). Frequency of psychotherapeutic session as a factor affecting outcome: Analysis of clinical ratings and test results. *Journal of Abnormal Psychology, 74,* 553–560.

Heinicke, C. M., & Goldman, A. (1960). Research on psychotherapy with children: A review and suggestions for further study. *American Journal of Orthopsychiatry, 30,* 483–494.

Heinicke, C. M., & Ramsey-Klee, D. M. (1986). Outcome of child psychotherapy as a function of frequency of session. *Journal of the American Academy of Child Psychiatry, 25,* 247–253.

Heinicke, C. M., & Strassman, L. H. (1975). Toward more effective research on child psychotherapy. *Journal of the American Academy of Child Psychiatry, 3,* 561–588.

Henggeler, S. W., & Borduin, C. M. (1990). *Family therapy and beyond: A multisystemic approach to treating the behavior problems of children and adolescents.* Pacific Grove, CA: Brooks/Cole.

Hersen, M., Michelson, L., & Bellack, A. S. (Eds.). (1984). *Issues in psychotherapy research.* New York: Plenum.

Hinshaw, S. P. (1991). Stimulant medication and the treatment of aggression in children with attentional deficits. *Journal of Clinical Child Psychology, 20,* 301–312.

Hood-Williams, J. (1960). The results of psychotherapy with children: A reevaluation. *Journal of Consulting Psychology, 24,* 84–88.

Horne, A. M., & Sayger, T. V. (1990). *Treating conduct and oppositional disorders in children.* Elmsford, NY: Pergamon.

Institute of Medicine [IOM]. (1989). *Research on children and adolescents with mental, behavioral, and developmental disorders.* Washington, DC: National Academy Press.

Jay, S. M., & Elliott, C. H. (1990). A stress inoculation program for parents whose children are undergoing painful medical procedures. *Journal of Consulting and Clinical Psychology, 58,* 799–804.

Jay, S. M., Elliott, C. H., Katz, E., & Siegel, S. E. (1987). Cognitive-behavioral and pharmacologic interventions for children's distress during painful medical procedures. *Journal of Consulting and Clinical Psychology, 55,* 860–865.

Jersild, A. T., & Holmes, F. B. (1935). *Children's fears* (Child Development Monograph-20). New York: Columbia University.

Karoly, P. (Ed.), (1988). *Handbook of child health assessment.* New York: Wiley.

Kazdin, A. E. (1985). *Treatment of antisocial behavior in children and adolescents.* Homewood, IL: Dorsey Press.

Kazdin, A. E. (Ed.). (1986). Psychotherapy research [Special issue]. *Journal of Consulting and Clinical Psychology, 54.*

Kazdin, A. E. (1987a). Treatment of antisocial behavior in children: Current status and future directions. *Psychological Bulletin, 102,* 187–203.

Kazdin, A. E. (1987b). *Conduct disorder in childhood and adolescence.* Newbury Park, CA: Sage Publications.

Kazdin, A. E. (1988). *Child psychotherapy: Developing and identifying effective treatments.* Elmsford, NY: Pergamon.

Kazdin, A. E. (1989). Identifying depression in children: A

comparison of alternative selection criteria. *Journal of Abnormal Child Psychology, 17,* 437–454.

Kazdin, A. E. (1990a). Psychotherapy for children and adolescents. *Annual Review of Psychology, 41,* 21–54.

Kazdin, A. E. (1990b). Childhood depression. *Journal of Child Psychology and Psychiatry, 31,* 121–160.

Kazdin, A. E. (1990c). Premature termination from treatment among children referred for antisocial behavior. *Journal of Child Psychology and Psychiatry, 31,* 415–425.

Kazdin, A. E. (1992a). *Research design in clinical psychology* (2nd ed.). Needham Heights, MA: Allyn & Bacon.

Kazdin, A. E. (1992b). Child and adolescent dysfunction and paths toward maladjustment: Targets for intervention. *Clinical Psychology Review, 12,* 795–817.

Kazdin, A. E. (1993). Adolescent mental health: Prevention and treatment. *American Psychologist, 48,* 127–141.

Kazdin, A. E. (in press). Informant variability in the assessment of childhood depression. In W. M. Reynolds & H. Johnston (Eds.), *Handbook of depression in children and adolescents.* New York: Plenum.

Kazdin, A. E., Bass, D., Ayers, W. A., & Rodgers, A. (1990). Empirical and clinical focus of child and adolescent psychotherapy research. *Journal of Consulting and Clinical psychology, 58,* 729–740.

Kazdin, A. E., Bass, D., Siegel, T., & Thomas, C. (1989). Cognitive-behavioral therapy and relationship therapy in the treatment of children referred for antisocial behavior. *Journal of Consulting and Clinical Psychology, 57,* 522–535.

Kazdin, A. E., Esveldt-Dawson, K., French, N. H., & Unis, A. S. (1987). Problem-solving skills training and relationship therapy in the treatment of antisocial child behavior. *Journal of Consulting and Clinical Psychology, 55,* 76–85.

Kazdin, A. E., Mazurick, J. L., & Bass, D. (1993). Risk for attrition in treatment of antisocial children and families. *Journal of Clinical Child Psychology, 22,* 2–16.

Kazdin, A. E., Seigel, T. C., & Bass, D. (1990). Drawing upon clinical practice to inform research on child and adolescent psychotherapy: A survey of practitioners. *Professional Psychology: Research and Practice, 21,* 189–198.

Kazdin, A. E., Siegel, T., & Bass, D. (1992). Cognitive problem-solving skills training and parent management training in the treatment of antisocial behavior in children. *Journal of Consulting and Clinical Psychology, 60,* 733–747.

Kendall, P. C. (Ed.). (1991). *Child and adolescent therapy: Cognitive-behavioral procedures.* New York: Guilford.

Kendall, P. C., & Braswell, L. (1982). Cognitive-behavioral self-control therapy for children: A components analysis. *Journal of Consulting and Clinical Psychology, 50,* 672–689.

Kendall, P. C., & Braswell, L. (1985). *Cognitive-behavioral therapy for impulsive children.* New York: Guilford.

Kendall, P. C., Ronan, K. R., & Epps, J. (1991). Aggression in children/adolescents: Cognitive-behavioral treatment perspectives. In D. J. Pepler & K. H. Rubin (Eds.), *The development and treatment of childhood aggression* (pp. 341–360). Hillsdale, NJ: Lawrence Erlbaum.

Kernberg, P. F., & Chazan, S. E. (1991). *Children with conduct disorders: A psychotherapy manual.* New York: Basic Books.

Kiesler, D. J. (1971). Experimental designs in psychotherapy research. In A. E. Bergin & S. L. Garfield (Eds.), *Handbook of psychotherapy and behavior change: An empirical analysis* (pp. 36–74). New York: Wiley.

King, C. A., & Kirschenbaum, D. S. (1992). *Helping young children develop social skills.* Pacific Grove, CA: Brooks/Cole.

Kirigin, K. A., Braukmann, C. J., Atwater, J. D., & Wolf, M. M. (1982). An evaluation of teaching-family (Achievement Place) group homes for juvenile offenders. *Journal of Applied Behavior Analysis, 15,* 1–16.

Kirigin, K. A., Wolf, M. M., Braukmann, C. J., Fixsen, D. L., & Phillips, E. L. (1979). Achievement Place: A preliminary outcome evaluation. In J. S. Stumphauzer (Ed.), *Progress in behavior therapy with delinquents.* Springfield, IL: Charles C. Thomas.

Klein, N. C., Alexander, J. F., & Parsons, B. V. (1977). Impact of family systems intervention on recidivism and sibling delinquency: A model of primary prevention and program evaluation. *Journal of Consulting and Clinical Psychology, 45,* 469–474.

Kolko, D. J., & Milan, M. A. (1983). Reframing and paradoxical instruction to overcome "resistance" in the treatment of delinquent youths: A multiple-baseline analysis. *Journal of Consulting and Clinical Psychology, 51,* 655–660.

Kolvin, I., Garside, R. F., Nicol, A. R., MacMillan, A., Wolstenholme, F., & Leitch, I. M. (1981). *Help starts here: The maladjusted child in the ordinary school.* London: Tavistock.

Koocher, G. P., & Pedulla, B. M. (1977). Current practices in child psychotherapy. *Professional Psychology, 8,* 275–287.

Kovacs, M., & Paulauskas, S. (1986). The traditional psychotherapies. In H. D. Quay & J. S. Werry (Eds.), *Psychopathological disorders of childhood* (3rd ed., pp. 496–522). New York: Wiley.

Kozloff, M. A. (1979). *A program for families of children with learning and behavior problems.* New York: Wiley.

Kratochwill, T. R., & Morris, R. J. (Eds.). (1991). *The practice of child therapy* (2nd ed.). Elmsford, NY: Pergamon.

LaFromboise, T. D., & Low, K. G. (1991). American Indian children and adolescents. In J. T. Gibbs & L. N. Huang (Eds.), *Children of color: Psychological interventions with minority youth* (pp. 114–147). San Francisco, CA: Jossey-Bass.

LaGreca, A. M. (1990). *Through the eyes of the child: Obtaining self-reports from children and adolescents.* Needham Heights, MA: Allyn & Bacon.

Lambert, M. J., Christensen, E. R., & DeJulio, S. S. (Eds.). (1983). *The assessment of psychotherapy outcome.* New York: Wiley.

Lambert, M. J., & Ogles, B. M. (1988). Treatment manuals: Problems and promise. *Journal of Integrative and Eclectic Psychotherapy, 7,* 187–204.

Lambert, M. J., Shapiro, D. A., & Bergin, A. E. (1986). The effectiveness of psychotherapy. In S. L. Garfield & A. E. Bergin (Eds.), *Handbook of psychotherapy and behavior change* (3rd ed., pp. 157–211). New York: Wiley.

Landreth, G. L. (Ed.). (1982). *Play therapy: Dynamics of the process of counseling with children.* Springfield, IL: Charles C Thomas.

Lapouse, R., & Monk, M. A. (1958). An epidemiologic study of behavior characteristics in children. *American Journal of Public Health, 48,* 1134–1144.

Last, C. G. (ed.). (1988). Behavioral assessment and treatment of childhood anxiety disorders [Special series]. *Behavior Modification, 12.*

Levitt, E. E. (1957). The results of psychotherapy with children: An evaluation. *Journal of Consulting Psychology, 21,* 189–196.

Levitt, E. E. (1963). Psychotherapy with children: A further evaluation. *Behaviour Research and Therapy, 60,* 326–329.

Lewinsohn, P. M., Clarke, G. N., Hops, H., & Andrews, J. (1990). Cognitive-behavioral treatment for depressed adolescents. *Behavior Therapy, 21,* 385–401.

Lewis, M., & Miller, S. M. (Eds.). (1990). *Handbook of developmental psychopathology.* New York: Plenum

Lochman, J. E., Burch, P. R., Curry, J. F., & Lampron, L. B. (1984). Treatment and generalization effects of cognitive-behavioral and goal-setting interventions with aggressive boys. *Journal of Consulting and Clinical Psychology, 52,* 915–916.

Loeber, R., & Schmalling, K. B. (1985). Empirical evidence for overt and covert patterns of antisocial conduct problems: A meta-analysis. *Journal of Abnormal Child Psychology, 13,* 337–352.

Lord, J. P. (1985). *A guide to individual psychotherapy with school-age children and adolescents.* Springfield, IL: Charles C. Thomas.

Lovaas, O. I. (1987). Behavioral treatment and normal educational/intellectual functioning in young autistic children. *Journal of Consulting and Clinical Psychology, 55,* 3–9.

Luborsky, L., & DeRubeis, R. J. (1984). The use of psychotherapy treatment manuals: A small revolution in psychotherapy research style. *Clinical Psychology Review, 4,* 5–14.

Malgady, R. G., Rogler, L. H., & Costantino, G. (1990). Culturally sensitive psychotherapy for Puerto Rican children and adolescents: A program of treatment. *Journal of Consulting and Clinical Psychology, 58,* 704–712.

Manne, S. L., Redd, W. H., Jacobsen, P. B., Gorfinkle, K., Schorr, O., & Rapkin, B. (1990). Behavioral intervention to reduce child and parent distress during venipuncture. *Journal of Consulting and Clinical Psychology, 58,* 565–572.

Mash, E. J., & Barkley, R. A. (Eds.). (1989). *Treatment of childhood disorders.* New York: Guilford.

Mash, E. J., & Johnston, C. (1983). Parental perceptions of child behavior problems, parenting self-esteem, and mothers' reported stress in younger and older hyperactive and normal children. *Journal of Consulting and Clinical Psychology, 51,* 86–99.

Masten, A. S., Best, K. M., & Garmezy, N. (1991). Resilience and development: Contributions from the study of children who overcome adversity. *Development and Psychopathology, 2,* 425–444.

McCann, C. D., & Endler, N. S. (Eds.). (1990). *Depression: New directions in theory, research, and practice.* Toronto, Ontario: Wall & Emerson.

McEachin, J. J., Smith, T., & Lovaas, O. I. (1993). Long-term outcome for children with autism who received early intensive behavioral treatment. *American Journal of Mental Retardation, 97,* 359–372.

McGee, R., Feehan, M., Williams, S., & Anderson, J. (1992). DSM-III disorders from age 11–15 years. *Journal of the American Academy of Child and Adolescent Psychiatry, 31,* 50–59.

McKenna, J. G., & Gaffney, L. R. (1982). An evaluation of group therapy for adolescents using social skills training. *Current Psychological Research, 2,* 151–160.

McMahon, R. J., & Wells, K. C. (1989). Conduct disorders. In E. J. Mash & R. A. Barkley (Eds.), *Treatment of childhood disorders* (pp. 73–132). New York: Guilford.

Meltzoff, J., & Kornreich, M. (1970). *Research in psychotherapy.* New York: Atherton.

Michelson, L., Sugai, D. P., Wood, R. P., & Kazdin, A. E. (1983). *Social skills assessment and training with children.* New York: Plenum.

Miller, G. E., & Prinz, R. J. (1990). Enhancement of social

learning family interventions for child conduct disorder. *Psychological Bulletin, 108,* 291–307.

Miller, L. C., Barrett, C. L., Hampe, E., & Noble, H. (1972). Comparison of reciprocal inhibition, psychotherapy, and waiting list control for phobic children. *Journal of Abnormal Psychology, 79,* 269–279.

Milos, M. E., & Reiss, S. (1982). Effects of three play conditions on separation anxiety in young children. *Journal of Consulting and Clinical Psychology, 500,* 389–395.

Moretti, M. M., Fine, S., Haley, G., & Marriage, K. (1985). Childhood and adolescent depression: Child-report versus parent-report information. *Journal of the American Academy of Child Psychiatry, 24,* 298–302.

Morris, R. J., & Kratochwill, T. R. (1991). In T. R. Kratochwill & R. J. Morris (Eds.), *The practice of child therapy* (2nd ed., pp. 76–114). Elmsford, NY: Pergamon.

National Center for Education in Maternal and Child Health. (1992). *The financing of mental health services for children and adolescents.* Washington, DC: Author.

Newcomb, M. D., & Bentler, P. M. (1988). *Consequences of adolescent drug use: Impact on the lives of young adults.* Newbury Park, CA: Sage Publications.

Novaco, R. W. (1975). *Anger control: The development and evaluation of an experimental treatment.* Lexington, MA: D. C. Heath.

Ollendick, T. H. (1986). Behavior therapy with children and adolescents. In S. L. Garfield & A. E. Bergin (Eds.), *Handbook of psychotherapy and behavior change* (3rd ed., pp. 525–564). New York: Wiley.

Ollendick, T. H., & Hersen, M. (Eds.). (1993). *Handbook of child and adolescent assessment.* Needham Heights, MA: Allyn & Bacon.

Patterson, C. H. (1979). Rogerian counseling. In S. H. Harrison (Ed.), *Basic handbook of child psychiatry: Therapeutic interventions* (Vol. 3, pp 203–215). New York: Basic Books.

Patterson, G. R. (1982). *Coercive family process.* Eugene, OR: Castalia.

Patterson, G. R. (1986). Performance models for antisocial boys. *American Psychologist, 41,* 432–444.

Patterson, G. R., Capaldi, D., & Bank, L. (1991). An early starter model for predicting delinquency. In D. J. Pepler & K. H. Rubin (Eds.), *The development and treatment of childhood aggression* (pp. 139–168). Hillsdale, NJ: Lawrence Erlbaum.

Patterson, G. R., Dishion, T. J., & Chamberlain, P. (in press). Outcomes and methodological issues relating to treatment of antisocial children. In T. R. Giles (Ed.), *Effective psychotherapy: A handbook of comparative research.* New York: Plenum.

Patterson, G. R., Reid, J. B., Jones, R. R., & Conger, R. E. (1975). *A social learning approach to family interaction* (Vol. 1). Eugene, OR: Castalia.

Pekarik, G., & Stephenson, L. A. (1988). Adult and child client differences in therapy dropout research. *Journal of Clinical Child Psychology, 17,* 316–321.

Pepler, D. J., & Rubin, K. H. (Eds.). (1991). *The development and treatment of childhood aggression.* Hillsdale, NJ: Lawrence Erlbaum.

Persons, R. W. (1966). Psychological and behavioral change in delinquents following psychotherapy. *Journal of Clinical Psychology, 22,* 337–340.

Persons, R. W. (1967). Relationship between psychotherapy with institutionalized boys and subsequent community adjustment. *Journal of Consulting Psychology, 31,* 137–141.

Persons, R. W., & Pepinsky, H. B. (1966). Convergence in psychotherapy with delinquent boys. *Journal of Counseling Psychology, 13,* 329–334.

Petersen, A. C. (1988). Adolescent development. *Annual Review of Psychology, 39,* 583–607.

Rapport, M. D. (Ed.). (1992). Treatment of children with attention-deficit hyperactivity disorder (ADHD) [Special series]. *Behavior Modification, 16.*

Rapoport, R. N. (1987). *New interventions for children and youth: Action-research approaches.* Cambridge: Cambridge University Press.

Reynolds, W. M. (1992). Depression in children and adolescents. In W. M. Reynolds (Ed.), *Internalizing disorders in children and adolescents* (pp. 149–253). New York: Wiley.

Reynolds, W. M., & Coats, K. I. (1986). A comparison of cognitive-behavioral therapy and relaxation training for the treatment of depression in adolescents. *Journal of Consulting and Clinical Psychology, 54,* 653–660.

Richards, M., & Petersen, A. C. (1987). Biological theoretical models of adolescent development. In V. B. Van Hasselt & M. Hersen (Eds.), *Handbook of adolescent psychology* (pp. 34–52). Elmsford, NY: Pergamon.

Robins, L. N. (1978). Sturdy childhood predictors of adult antisocial behavior: Replications from longitudinal studies. *Psychological Medicine, 8,* 611–622.

Robins, L., & Rutter, M. (Eds.). (1990). *Straight and devious pathways from childhood to adulthood.* Cambridge: Cambridge University Press.

Rogers, C. (1961). *On becoming a person.* Boston: Houghton Mifflin.

Routh, D. K. (Ed.). (1988). *Handbook of pediatric psychology.* New York: Guilford.

Rubin, K. H., Bream, L. A., Rose-Krasnor, L. (1991). Social problem solving and aggression in childhood. In D. J. Pepler & K. H. Rubin (Eds.), *The development and treatment of childhood aggression* (pp. 219–248). Hillsdale, NJ: Lawrence Erlbaum.

Rutter, M. (1986). The developmental psychopathology of depression: Issues and perspectives. In M. Rutter, C. E. Izard, & P. B. Read (Eds.), *Depression in young people: Developmental and clinical perspectives* (pp. 3–30). New York: Guilford.

Rutter, M., & Giller, H. (1983). *Juvenile delinquency: Trends and perspectives.* New York: Penguin Books.

Rutter, M., Tuma, A. H., & Lann, I. S. (Eds.). (1988). *Assessment and diagnosis of child psychopathology.* New York: Guilford.

Santostefano, S. (1985). *Cognitive control therapy with children and adolescents.* Elmsford, NY: Pergamon.

Satterfield, J. H., Satterfield, B. T., & Cantwell, D. P. (1980). A two-year evaluation of 61 hyperactive boys. *Archives of General Psychiatry, 37,* 915.

Satterfield, J. H., Satterfield, B. T., & Cantwell, D. P. (1981). Three-year multimodality treatment study of 100 hyperactive boys. *Journal of Pediatrics, 98,* 650–655.

Satterfield, J. H., Satterfield, B. T., & Schell, A. M. (1987). Therapeutic interventions to prevent delinquency in hyperactive boys. *Journal of the American Academy of Child and Adolescent Psychiatry, 26,* 56–64.

Saylor, D. G., Benson, B., & Einhaus, L. (1985). Effects of stress inoculation on the anger and aggression management skills of institutionalized juvenile delinquents. *Journal of Child and Adolescent Psychotherapy, 2,* 5–15.

Schaefer, C. (Ed.). (1976). *The therapeutic use of child's play.* New York: Jason Aronson.

Schaefer, C. E., & Briesmeister, J. M. (Eds.). (1989). *Handbook of parent training: Parents as co-therapists for children's behavior problems.* New York: Wiley.

Schaefer, C. E., Briesmeister, J. M., & Fitton, M. E. (Eds.). (1984). *Family therapy techniques for problem behaviors of children and teenagers.* San Francisco: Jossey-Bass.

Schaefer, C. E., & O'Connor, K. J. (Eds.). (1983). *Handbook of play therapy.* New York: Wiley.

Schweinhart, L. J., & Weikart, D. P. (1989). The High/Scope Perry preschool study. Implications for early childhood care and education. *Prevention in Human Services, 7,* 109–132.

Seitz, V., Rosenbaum, L. K., & Apfel, N. H. (1985). Effects of family support intervention: A ten-year follow-up. *Child Development, 56,* 376–391.

Shirk, S. R. (Ed.). (1988). *Cognitive development and child psychotherapy.* New York: Plenum.

Silver, L. B., & Silver, B. J. (1983). Clinical practice of child psychiatry: A survey. *Journal of the American Academy of Child Psychiatry, 22,* 573–579.

Smith, M. L., & Glass G. V. (1977). Meta-analysis of psychotherapy outcome studies. *American Psychologist, 32,* 752–760.

Smith, M. L., Glass, G. V., & Miller, T. I. (1980). *The benefits of psychotherapy.* Baltimore: The Johns Hopkins University Press.

Spivack, G., & Shure, M. B. (1982). The cognition of social adjustment: Interpersonal cognitive problem solving thinking. In B. B. Lahey & A. E. Kazdin (Eds.), *Advances in clinical child psychology* (Vol. 5, pp. 323–372). New York: Plenum.

Stark, K. D., Reynolds, W. M., & Kaslow, N. (1987). A comparison of the relative efficacy of self-control therapy and a behavioral problem-solving therapy for depression in children. *Journal of Abnormal Child Psychology, 15,* 91–113.

Steen, C., & Monnette, B. (1989). *Treating adolescent sex offenders in the community.* Springfield, IL: Charles C. Thomas.

Strain, P. S., Guralnick, M. J., & Walker, H. M. (Eds.). (1986). *Children's social behavior: Development, assessment, and modification.* Orlando, FL: Academic Press.

Strain, P. S., Young, C. C., & Horowitz, J. (1981). Generalized behavior change during oppositional child training: An examination of child and family demographic variables. *Behavior Modification, 5,* 15–26.

Stricker, G., & Keisner, R. H. (Eds.). (1985). *From research to clinical practice: The implications of social and developmental research for psychotherapy.* New York: Plenum.

Swaim, R. C., Oetting, E. R., Edwards, R. W., & Beauvais, F. (1989). Links from emotional distress to adolescent drug use: A path model. *Journal of Consulting and Clinical Psychology, 57,* 227–231.

Szapocznik, J., & Kurtines, W. M. (1989). *Breakthroughs in family therapy with drug-abusing and problem youth.* New York: Springer.

Szapocznik, J., Kurtines, W., Santisteban, D. A., & Rio, A. (1990). Interplay of advances between theory, research, and application in treatment interventions aimed at behavior problem children and adolescents. *Journal of Consulting and Clinical Psychology, 58,* 696–703.

Szapocznik, J., Rio, A., Murray, E., Cohen, R., Scopetta, M., Rivas-Vasquez, A., Hervis, O., Posada, V., & Kurtines, W. (1989). Structural family versus psychodynamic child therapy for problematic Hispanic boys. *Journal of Consulting and Clinical Psychology, 57,* 571–578.

Tharp, R. G. (1991). Cultural diversity and treatment of children. *Journal of Consulting and Clinical Psychology, 59,* 799–812.

Tremblay, R. E., Masse, B., Perron, D., Leblanc, M., Schwartzman, E., & Ledingham, J. E. (1992). Early disruptive behavior, poor school achievement, delinquent behavior, and delinquent personality: Longitudinal analyses. *Journal of Consulting and Clinical Psychology, 60,* 64–72.

Truax, C. B., Wargo, D. G., & Silber, L. D. (1966). Effects of group psychotherapy with high accurate empathy and nonpossessive warmth upon female institutionalized delinquents. *Journal of Abnormal Psychology, 71,* 267–274.

Tuma, J. M., & Pratt, J. M. (1982). Clinical child psychology practice and training: A survey. *Journal of Clinical Child Psychology, 11,* 27–34.

Tuma, J. M., & Sobotka, K. R. (1983). Traditional therapies with children. In T. H. Ollendick & M. Hersen (Eds.), *Handbook of child psychopathology* (pp. 391–426). New York: Plenum.

U.S. Congress, Office of Technology Assessment. (1986). *Children's mental health: Problems and services — A background paper* (OTA-BP-H-33). Washington, DC: U.S. Government Printing Office.

U.S. Congress, Office of Technology Assessment. (1990). *Indian adolescent mental health* (OTA-H-446). Washington, DC: U.S. Government Printing Office.

U.S. Congress, Office of Technology Assessment. (1991). *Adolescent health* (Vols. I–III) (OTA-H-468). Washington, DC: U.S. Government Printing Office.

VandenBos, G. R. (Ed.). (1986). Psychotherapy research [Special issue]. *American Psychologist, 41,* 111–214.

Walker, C. E., & Roberts, M. C. (Eds.). (1992). *Handbook of clinical child psychology* (2nd ed.). New York: Wiley.

Walrond-Skinner, S. (1986). *Dictionary of psychotherapy.* London: Routledge & Kegan Paul.

Webster-Stratton, C. (1985). Predictors of treatment outcome in parent training for conduct disordered children. *Behavior Therapy, 16,* 223–243.

Webster-Stratton, C., Hollinsworth, T., & Kolpacoff, M. (1989). The long-term effectiveness of treatment and clinical significance of three cost-effective training programs for families with conduct problem children. *Journal of Consulting and Clinical Psychology, 57,* 550–553.

Webster-Stratton, C., Kolpacoff, M., & Hollinsworth, T. (1988). Self-administered videotape therapy for families with conduct problem children: Comparison with two cost-effective treatments and a control group. *Journal of Consulting and Clinical Psychology, 56,* 558–566.

Weiss, B., & Weisz, J. R. (1990). The impact of methodological factors on child psychotherapy outcome research: A meta-analysis for researchers. *Journal of Abnormal Child Psychology, 18,* 639–670.

Weiss, G., & Hechtman, L. T. (1986). *Hyperactive children grown up.* New York: Guilford.

Weissberg, R. P., Caplan, M., & Harwood, R. L. (1991). Promoting competent young people in competence-enhancing environments: A systems-based perspective on primary prevention. *Journal of Consulting and Clinical Psychology, 59,* 830–841.

Weisz, J. R. & Weiss, B. (1989). Assessing the effects of clinic-based psychotherapy with children and adolescents. *Journal of Consulting and Clinical Psychology, 57,* 741–746.

Weisz, J. R., Weiss, B., Alicke, M. D., & Klotz, M. L. (1987). Effectiveness of psychotherapy with children and adolescents: Meta-analytic findings for clinicians. *Journal of Consulting and Clinical Psychology, 55,* 542–549.

Wells, K., & Biegel, D. E. (Eds.). (1991). *Family preservation services: Research and evaluation.* Newbury Park, CA: Sage Publications.

Werner, E. E. (1987). Vulnerability and resiliency in children at risk for delinquency: A longitudinal study from birth to young adulthood. In J. D. Burchard & S. N. Burchard (Eds.), *Prevention of delinquent behavior* (pp. 16–43). Newbury Park, CA: Sage Publications.

Werner, E. E., & Smith, R. S. (1992). *Overcoming the odds: High risk children from birth to adulthood.* Ithaca, NY: Cornell University Press.

Whalen, C. K., & Henker, B. (1991). Therapies for hyperactive children: Comparisons, combinations, and compromises. *Journal of Consulting and Clinical Psychology, 59,* 126–137.

Wolfe, D. A., Edwards, B., Manion, I., & Koverola, C. (1988). Early intervention for parents at risk of child abuse and neglect: A preliminary investigation. *Journal of Consulting and Clinical Psychology, 56,* 40–47.

Wolfe, D. A., Sandler, J., & Kaufman, K. (1981). A competency-based parent training program for child abusers. *Journal of Consulting and Clinical Psychology, 49,* 633–640.

World Health Organization. (1988). *International classification of diseases* (ICD-10 Draft). Geneva: Author.

Wright, D. M., Moelis, I., & Pollack, L. J. (1976). The outcome of individual child psychotherapy: Increments at follow-up. *Journal of Child Psychology and Psychiatry, 17,* 275–285.

Wright, L., Everett, F., & Roisman, L. (1986). *Experiential psychotherapy with children.* Baltimore: The Johns Hopkins University Press.

Zill, N., & Schoenborn, C. A. (1990, November). Developmental, learning, and emotional problems: Health of our nation's children, United States 1988. *Advance Data: National Center for Health Statistics,* Number 190.

14

THE PROCESS AND OUTCOME OF MARITAL AND FAMILY THERAPY: RESEARCH REVIEW AND EVALUATION

- **JAMES F. ALEXANDER**
  University of Utah

- **AMY HOLTZWORTH-MUNROE**
  Indiana University

- **PENNY JAMESON**
  University of Utah

The chapter dealing with research on marital and family therapy in past editions of this *Handbook* has been seen as a definitive, encyclopedic benchmark defining the underlying coherence of the field and as providing a signpost for the future. One of the accomplishments of the authors of previous chapters (Alan Gurman and David Kniskern in 1978, joined by William Pinsof in 1986) was their presentation of a broad and diverse field in a relatively integrated and coherent manner. Some 7 years later we found this to be a difficult task, for the underlying coherence is elusive at best.

To begin, in the published literature the overlap between research in marital therapy and research in family therapy is small; researchers and clinical model builders generally restrict themselves to one or the other domain. Recent meta-analytic contributions (Hahlweg & Markman, 1988; Hazelrigg, Cooper, & Borduin, 1987) describe marital and family therapy research independently in ways that seem to reflect different treatment techniques, different populations, different clinical syndromes, and different indexes of effectiveness. In a like manner, the most recent comparative meta-analysis (i.e., Shadish et al., 1993) emphasizes the differences, not the similarities, of marital therapy and family therapy.

Thus, other than titular traditions (e.g., of associations like the American Association for Marital and Family Therapy [AAMFT] and licensing designations such as marital and family therapist [MFT] that have integrated the two domains), the only *operational* justification for evaluating the two together is that they both involve treatment units of more than one person who consider themselves as having some sort of relationship outside the therapeutic context. However, even this numerical criterion no longer uniquely characterizes the two domains. Whereas marital therapy almost inevitably involves a therapist and the marital dyad, such uniformity does not characterize family therapy operationally or conceptually. The treatment unit in face-to-face contact with a family therapist can be a single individual, a dyad, a larger nontraditional family group (with myriad configurations), or a traditional family, with or without extended family members (e.g., Bowen, 1978; Szapocznik, Kurtines, Foote, Perez-Vidal, & Hervis, 1983). In fact, direct face-to-face treatment may even not include the individual or individuals who are overtly performing the problematic behaviors that are usually the impetus for intervention (i.e., the so-called identified patient)!

To deal with this last issue, Gurman et al. (1986) proposed a presumably consistent set of systemic theoretical underpinnings to which all family and marital therapies adhere. These systemic theoretical underpinnings are not tied together in any concrete operational sense, but rather with respect to the "goals and conceptual framework of family therapy" (Pinsof, 1989). Unfortunately, the uniformity of goals across various approaches to marital and family therapy can no longer be taken for granted. An examination of the field as a whole suggests considerable definitional ambiguity and controversy with respect to epistemology, issues of sensitivity (to culture, ethnicity, gender, sexual preference), and the methodologies that accrue from them (e.g., Hare-Mustin, 1991).

An additional problem we face is the schism that is often apparent between clinicians and researchers. Quantitative (i.e., "traditional" as it has been represented in previous editions of this chapter) research doesn't represent a basis, in the eyes of many practitioners, for choosing among the many options for treatment philosophies and techniques. Indeed, articles in a recent research-focused publication of a major family therapy association severely challenged research as it is currently practiced (e.g., *AFTA Newsletter*, 1992; Keeney & Ray, 1992). Some researchers (e.g., Reiss, 1991) have pointed out that with the requirements of adherence to protocol and the homogeneity of client characteristics, well-researched clinical trials can only provide a model for clinical practice and do not reflect the actual *process* of family therapy as it is practiced in the great majority of clinical settings (see also Persons, 1991).

Such attitudes create powerful images and considerable concern for us as authors. We are concerned that a chapter based primarily on the facts and figures of traditional research will have no utility for clinicians. Many of the issues raised by clinicians, feminists, new epistemologists, and others in the field are incompatible with, or still too emergent to be evaluated by, traditional research methodologies. Newer qualitative research strategies have emerged in the marital and family therapy literatures (e.g., Atkinson, Heath, & Chenail, 1991; Moon, Dillon, & Sprenkle, 1990) as popular discovery-oriented alternatives to understanding clinical activity; these reports are preferred sources of information for many family clinicians.

However, we agree with such authors as Gurman et al. (1986), Liddle (1991a), and McFall (1991), who argue that to abandon or even minimize traditional process – outcome research as a basis for clinical decision making jeopardizes the integrity and accountability of the field. Clinicians must responsibly demonstrate the viability of treatment modalities in the eyes of consumers, funding agencies, insurance companies, and colleagues. Thus it is important to remain sensitive to demands for rigor and accountability. However, this review includes important challenges from scholars representing feminist, ecosystemic, and other nontraditional perspectives; while these perspectives as yet have limited empirical support, they are included as a means of opening discussion about the limitations in traditional research. In doing so we are reflecting and advocating the stance of Gurman et al. (1986), who in their earlier review asserted that

the "family therapy research field, like the field of family therapy generally, is now a good deal more mature developmentally, and is, thus, more open to self-criticism and thoughtful self-reflection (p. 570)." Indeed, this flexible position with respect to research perspectives may also be pertinent to the other areas of research reviewed in this *Handbook* (see, for example, discussions in Chapter 1 and 20).

We begin our undertaking by reviewing marital therapy outcome research. In doing so we face one more set of conceptual issues. Specifically, many reasons exist to avoid basing marital and family therapy and therapy research on individual diagnoses or individual symptom expressions, all of which reflect nonsystemic, linear thinking (Gurman et al., 1986). At the same time, most published journal articles still relate certain patterns of marital or family interactions with specific individual syndromes. Although this apparent disregard of a true systemic perspective may represent our inability to operationalize ecosystemic issues and develop appropriate methodologies, it may also be that researchers are attending as much (if not more) to pragmatic as to conceptual and methodological considerations. Specifically, the pragmatics of funding are that the great majority of funding sources (e.g., foundations, federal agencies, legislatures, corporations) seem tied to behavior patterns of *individuals* that are seen as symptoms, or to diagnostic categories (examples include requests for proposals that target such behaviors as physical abuse, teen pregnancy, rape, agoraphobia, conduct disorder, depression, "at-risk" behaviors for HIV infection, and substance abuse). However, we do not have to be stymied by the reality of this individualistic focus and give up on new systemic epistemology. Nor do we have to abandon completely our hypothetical-deductive approach to methodology. Instead we must pay attention to context and recognize the conceptual limitations of nonsystemic research as well as integrate new research paradigms and data as they are developed. Rather than decrying category-based and so-called linear efficacy research, we must do a better job of it so that our conclusions can be methodologically clear and appropriate.

To that end, we first examine the impact of various forms of marital therapy on certain (often individually based) diagnostic categories, as well as on marital satisfaction in general, much in the style of the earlier (Gurman et al., 1986) edition of this chapter. We then introduce some of the issues, often unstated, that are embedded in that research and expand our focus to the even murkier and controversial domain of family therapy and some reconciling research approaches. We attempt to complement rather than repeat the incisive, prescriptive, and direction-setting content of the earlier chapter. The principles raised therein have not changed essentially — especially those pertaining to process research and the questions that need to be addressed in that research. We attempt instead to write more to the clinician's concerns, emphasizing the directions that future research must take to be useful to (1) the clinician's decision-making and clinical intervention needs; (2) the researcher's need for rigor and generalizability; and (3) the clinician's, the policy maker's, and funding source's need for accountability.

BEHAVIORAL MARITAL THERAPY

Three recent reviews (Baucom & Hoffman, 1986; Gurman et al., 1986; Jacobson & Addis, 1993) and a meta-analysis (Hahlweg & Markman, 1988) of behavioral marital therapy (BMT) outcome studies are available; all draw similar conclusions about the effectiveness of BMT. As seen in Table 14.1, the majority of BMT outcome studies have been reviewed in one or more of these publications. We summarize and build on findings from these reviews.

BMT Versus Wait List and Placebo Control Groups

In their meta-analysis, Hahlweg and Markman (1988) included 17 studies of BMT, involving 613 couples, 50 therapists, and 81 effect-size outcome measures. The average effect size of BMT versus control or placebo control groups was 0.95. In other words, "the average person who had received BMT was better off at the end of treatment than 83% of the people who had received either no treatment or a placebo treatment," and "the chance of improving for control couples was 28%, whereas the chance of improving for experimental couples was 72%" (p. 443). Self-report and observational measures yielded very similar effect sizes. However, BMT versus placebo control groups (.55) had a smaller effect size than did BMT versus no-treatment control groups (1.02), although this difference was not statistically significant. The authors concluded that "it no longer seems necessary to conduct more of this type of outcome research (comparing BMT with a control group) because the efficacy of BMT seems to be clearly established" (p. 446).

Baucom and Hoffman (1986) and Gurman et al. (1986) similarly concluded that BMT is effective relative to wait-list control groups, with BMT leading to significant increases in marital satisfaction,

decreases in reported problem areas and requests for behavior change, and decreases in negative communication behaviors. However, BMT has rarely been found to lead to significant increases in positive communication behavior. Both sets of reviewers (Baucom & Hoffman, 1986; Gurman et al., 1986) were more conservative in their conclusions regarding the efficacy of BMT versus attention or nonspecific control groups, stating that "the superiority of BMT over nonspecific and attention control groups is equivocal" (Baucom & Hoffman, 1986, p. 601).

In summary, BMT has been investigated in a large number of published studies. BMT has repeatedly been demonstrated superior to wait-list control groups, and the effects of BMT cannot simply be attributed to nonspecific or placebo therapy factors. Basically, BMT "is the closest thing that couple therapy has to an established treatment" (Jacobson & Addis, 1993, p. 4).

Clinical Significance of BMT

A relatively recent development in the field of marital therapy is the inclusion of data regarding the clinical significance of therapy outcome, including the proportion of couples who have improved (i.e., demonstrated reliable change on outcome measures) and the proportion of couples who have moved into the nondistressed range on outcome measures at the end of therapy. Criteria for reliable change and clinically significant change were originally set forth in Jacobson, Follette, and Revenstorf (1984) and have been adapted by Christensen and Mendoza (1986).

Jacobson, Follette, Revenstorf, Baucom et al. (1984) applied these criteria in a reanalysis of data from four previous BMT outcome studies (i.e., Baucom, 1982; Hahlweg, Revenstorf, & Schindler, 1982; Jacobson, 1984; Margolin & Weiss, 1978). Fifty-five percent of the couples manifested statistically reliable improvement. However, a more stringent criteria of clinically significant improvement (i.e., how many couples made a statistically reliable move from the maritally distressed to the nondistressed range on self-reported marital adjustment) revealed that "65% of couples treated by BMT either remained somewhat distressed or failed to change during the course of therapy" (Jacobson, Follette, Revenstorf, Baucom et al., 1984, pp. 500–501). In addition, although the most likely status at 6-month posttherapy assessments was maintenance of treatment gains, the relapse rate among couples receiving BMT was a disappointing 28 percent.

Two more comprehensive reviews of previous BMT studies have also examined the clinical signifi-

TABLE 14.1   Behavioral marital therapy (BMT) outcome studies

Reference	Focus of Study	Previous Review
Azrin et al. (1980)	BMT vs. attention/nonspecific group	G,K,P; B&H; H&M
Baucom (1982)	BMT components [communication training (CT) vs. contracting vs. CT + contracting] vs. WL	G,K,P; B&H; H&M
Baucom & Lester (1986)	BMT vs. cognitive therapy + BMT vs. WL	G,K,P; B&H; H&M
Baucom, Sayers, & Sher (1990)	BMT vs. cognitive restructuring (CR) + BMT vs. emotional expressiveness training (EET) + BMT vs. CR + EET + BMT vs. WL	Not previously reviewed
Boelens, Emmelkamp, MacGillavry, & Markvoort (1980)	Behavioral contingency contracting vs. strategic/systems therapy vs. WL	G,K,P; B&H; H&M
Crowe (1978)	BMT vs. group-analytic approach vs. attention/nonspecific	G,K,P; B&H; H&M
Emmelkamp et al. (1984)	BMT vs. strategic/systems	G,K,P; B&H; H&M
Emmelkamp et al. (1988)	BMT components: contracting followed by communication training vs. communication training followed by contracting	G,K,P; B&H; H&M
Epstein & Jackson (1978)	Communication training (emphasizing assertion training) vs. insight interaction vs. WL	G,K,P
Ewart (1978)	BMT components (goal setting, communication training, good-faith contracts, quid pro quo contracts) vs. WL	G,K,P; B&H
Gebris, Schroetter, & Hautzinger (1980)		H&M
Girodo, Stein, & Dotzenroth (1980)	Communication training vs. emotional expression and listening training vs. WL	G,K,P; B&H
Halweg, Revenstorf, & Schindler (1982); Hahlweg, Schindler, Revenstorf, & Brengelmann (1984)	BMT vs. communication training in expression/listening vs. WL; therapy offered in conjoint or group format	G,K,P; B&H
Jacobson (1977)	BMT vs. control	G,K,P; B&H; H&M
Jacobson (1978a, 1978b)	BMT components (communication training — contracting vs. communication training — quid pro quo contracts) vs. attention/ nonspecific control	G,K,P; B&H; H&M
Jacobson (1984)	BMT components (behavior exchange vs. communication training vs. combination) vs. WL	G,K,P; B&H; H&M
Johnson & Greenberg (1985a)	BMT (problem-solving training) vs. emotionally focused therapy vs. WL	G,K,P; B&H
Liberman, Levine, Wheeler, Sanders, & Wallace (1976)	BMT vs. attention/nonspecific (group interaction) control	G,K,P; B&H
Margolin & Weiss (1978)	Communication training (CT) vs. CT + cognitive therapy vs. WL	H&M
Mehlman, Baucom, & Anderson (1983)	BMT (single therapist vs. cotherapists; immediate vs. delayed) vs. WL	G,K,P; B&H; H&M

TABLE 14.1   *continued*

Reference	Focus of Study	Previous Review
O'Farrell, Cutter, & Floyd (1983,1985)	BMT vs. interactional group vs. control group (for alcoholics)	G,K,P; B&H
Snyder & Wills (1989); Snyder, Wills, & Grady-Fletcher (1991a)	BMT vs. insight-oriented marital therapy vs. WL	Not previously reviewed
Tsoi-Hoshmand (1976)	BMT vs. WL	H&M
Turkewitz & O'Leary (1981); O'Leary & Turkewitz (1978)	BMT vs. communication training vs. WL	G,K,P; B&H; H&M
Van Steenwegen (1982)		H&M
Wilson, Bornstein, & Wilson (1988)	BMT in conjoint vs. group format	Not previously reviewed
Zimmer et al. (1977)		H&M

Note. WL = wait-list control group.
References to articles where study has been previously reviewed. G,K,P = Gurman, Kniskern, & Pinsof (1986) review; B&H = Baucom & Hoffman (1986) review; H&M = Hahlweg & Markman (1988) meta-analysis.

cance of the outcome data. Examining how many couples were nondistressed on measures of marital satisfaction at the end of BMT, Hahlweg and Markman's (1988) meta-analysis found an effect size of .15, indicating that many couples were still distressed. Similarly, Baucom and Hoffman (1986), reviewing nine studies using standardized measures of marital satisfaction, found that BMT had produced mean posttherapy marital satisfaction scores in the nondistressed range in only four of the studies.

All these authors have expressed concern about the significant proportion of couples who are treated with BMT but are not happily married at the end of therapy. Awareness of such statistics has led to recent interest in expanding or modifying BMT (e.g., adding cognitive components to BMT) in hopes of improving its effectiveness for a broader range of couples.

Long-Term Effects of BMT

Less is known about the long-term impact of BMT, since the majority of studies have failed to include lengthy follow-up assessment periods. In their meta-analysis, Hahlweg and Markman (1988) found that among studies that did include a follow-up assessment, the effect size of BMT was 1.17 at 3–6 months, 1.07 at 9-month, and 1.16 at 12-month follow-ups. One 2-year follow-up study found that approximately 30 percent of couples who had recovered during therapy had relapsed at follow-up (Jacobson, Schmaling, & Holtzworth-Munroe, 1987). Another recent study (Snyder, Wills, & Grady-Fletcher, 1991a; reviewed later) revealed a 38 percent divorce rate among BMT couples at a 4-year follow-up. These findings suggest that the initially positive effects of BMT may be difficult to maintain over time. Interviews conducted with couples in the Jacobson et al. (1987) study suggested that stressful life events were related to decreases in marital satisfaction during the follow-up period, leading the authors to recommend the routine inclusion of therapy booster sessions to help couples cope with new stressors as they arise.

Generalizability of BMT Treatment Effects

An issue recently raised in the literature is the question of how well marital therapy effects generalize to the home environment. For example, Behrens, Sanders, and Halford (1990) had four couples tape-record their discussions at home in low- or high-risk settings (i.e., high-risk settings involved discussion of "hot" topics in a setting with distractions) to see whether gains made in therapy would generalize to discussions in such settings. Similarly, Krokoff's (1991) data suggest that the conflict resolution tasks used in marital laboratories may have low ecological validity for couples who are conflict avoidant; therapists may need to examine how new communication skills gained in the therapy setting are used at home by such couples. Future researchers should systematically examine these issues.

Components of BMT

Baucom and Hoffman (1986) and Gurman et al. (1986) concluded that in general studies have not demonstrated significant differences in outcome when various BMT treatment components or different sequencing of BMT components have been compared. In contrast, Hahlweg and Markman (1988) found that behavior exchange techniques (i.e., procedures oriented toward creating immediate change in the home environment by decreasing negative behaviors and increasing positive behaviors) had a smaller effect size (.78) than did communication and problem-solving training (1.00; procedures aimed at long-term change and designed to teach couples to solve their problems with new communication skills), although this difference was not statistically significant. Jacobson and colleagues found that at 1-year (Jacobson et al., 1985) and 2-year (Jacobson et al., 1987) follow-ups, couples who had received a combination of behavior exchange and communication/problem-solving training were the most likely to be happily married and the least likely to be separated or divorced relative to couples receiving only one of these treatment components. Jacobson and Addis (1993) concluded that "both BE (behavior exchange) and CPT (communication/problem-solving treatment) are necessary components for the treatment effect to last beyond a one-year follow-up" (p. 13).

Manipulating Treatment Parameters of BMT

In general, research has suggested that manipulating treatment parameters does not affect the outcome of BMT (Baucom & Hoffman, 1986). Mehlman, Baucom, and Anderson (1983) found no differences in therapy outcomes between BMT administered by single therapists or cotherapists or between immediate versus delayed BMT. Two research groups have compared BMT offered in a group versus a conjoint format. Hahlweg et al. (1982) found that BMT was effective in either a conjoint or group therapy format, although conjoint BMT was superior to group BMT in improving couples' self-reports of marital happiness. Wilson, Bornstein, and Wilson (1988) found no differences between BMT offered in a conjoint format or in a group format at either posttherapy or a 6-month follow-up; both groups had improved significantly relative to a wait-list control group.

BMT Versus Other Approaches

Hahlweg and Markman (1988) examined four studies in which BMT was compared with other approaches. The effect sizes of treatment were .88 for BMT and .83 for other approaches. Baucom and Hoffman (1986) similarly concluded that "with certain exceptions, few significant differences have been found between BMT and these other approaches" (p. 606).

OTHER (NONBEHAVIORAL) MARITAL THERAPY APPROACHES

Reviewing a series of studies on communication training approaches (Ely, Guerney, & Stover, 1973; Epstein & Jackson, 1978; Girodo, Stein, & Dotzenroth, 1980; Hahlweg, Schindler, Revenstorf, & Brengelmann, 1984; Jessee & Guerney, 1981; Turkewitz & O'Leary, 1981), Baucom and Hoffman (1986) concluded that communication training results in improved communication, but not in overall changes in marital adjustment, relative to no treatment. Given the limited number of studies regarding other theoretical approaches (i.e., Boelens, Emmelkamp, MacGillavry, & Markvoort, 1980; Crowe, 1978; Epstein & Jackson, 1978; Johnson & Greenberg, 1985a; O'Farrell, Cutter, & Floyd, 1983), earlier reviewers (Baucom & Hoffman, 1986; Gurman et al., 1986) decided that conclusions about the effectiveness of other approaches would be premature. However, more empirical data regarding the efficacy of other marital therapy approaches have become available since and are reviewed here.

Cognitive and Cognitive-Behavioral Marital Therapy

The relationship between cognitive processes and marital distress has been well documented. Maritally distressed and nondistressed spouses offer different types of causal attributions for relationship events (Bradbury & Fincham, 1990, review this literature), and distressed spouses are more likely than happily married partners to hold unrealistic beliefs and irrational expectations about marriage (e.g., Epstein & Eidelson, 1981). Research examining other types of marital cognitions is under way (e.g., Baucom, Epstein, Sayers, & Sher, 1989; Fincham, Bradbury, & Scott, 1990).

Given the association between marital distress and various cognitive processes, cognitive therapists have begun to apply their interventions to marital problems, introducing cognitive marital therapy to the public (e.g., Beck, 1988) and to clinicians (e.g., Dattilio & Padesky, 1990). Despite this enthusiasm, to date there have been few well-controlled outcome studies of cognitive marital therapy. In addition, each of the studies that has been conducted has examined a different variant of cognitive marital therapy.

Two studies have compared cognitive marital

therapies with wait-list control groups. Huber and Milstein (1985) randomly assigned 17 couples to either a wait-list control group or to six sessions of cognitive restructuring therapy (CRT). CRT focused on modifying unrealistic beliefs spouses might hold about themselves (i.e., Ellis, 1981) and about their relationship (i.e., Epstein & Eidelson, 1981); couples were taught Ellis's ABC method for identifying the relationship between cognitions and reactions to situations. Relative to control group couples, spouses receiving CRT demonstrated significant changes in relationship beliefs but not in individual beliefs. At posttest, CRT couples were significantly more likely than control couples to believe that there was a chance for their relationship to improve with therapy, to express a preference for improving their relationship, and to report less marital distress. The authors concluded that cognitive restructuring may help create a positive collaborative set for marital therapy. However, since the average marital adjustment score of the treatment couples at the end of therapy was still in the distressed range, six sessions of CRT may not be an effective intervention by itself.

Waring (1988) developed cognitive marital therapy (CMT) to enhance marital intimacy by helping spouses self-disclose their personal constructs (Kelly, 1955) to one another. Waring and colleagues (Waring, Stalker, Carver, & Gitta, 1991) randomly assigned 41 severely distressed couples to either CMT or a wait-list control group. At posttest, couples in both conditions reported improvements in personal distress and symptomatology. However, the CMT couples did not improve relative to the control couples on measures of marital satisfaction or intimacy. The authors concluded that "10 sessions of CMT is not the treatment of choice for severe marital discord" (Waring et al., 1991, p. 254).

Another study has compared cognitive marital therapy with an established therapy. Emmelkamp et al. (1988) randomly assigned 32 couples to nine sessions of either cognitive marital therapy (CMT) or behavioral communication skills training (CST). CMT focused on faulty attributions, irrational beliefs, and unrealistic expectations about relationships. Regarding reductions in target complaints, both treatments led to equal and significant reductions at posttest; at a 1-month follow-up, CMT led to greater improvement than CST for women only. Women in both treatments showed equivalent changes on cognitive measures, whereas men receiving CST improved significantly on cognitive measures and men receiving CMT did not; the authors concluded that "changes in irrational relationship beliefs occur irrespective of the particular treatment received" (Emmelkamp et al., 1988, p. 374). In contrast, only CST led to significant observed changes in communication during marital interactions.

In summary, these three studies of cognitive marital therapies have not demonstrated the effectiveness of CMT relative to wait-list control groups or a standard behavioral treatment. The data from these studies are inconsistent regarding whether or not CMT is associated with changes in cognitions.

Other researchers have examined the efficacy of adding cognitive interventions to behavioral marital therapy. In an early analogue study (four therapy sessions administered by paraprofessionals), Margolin and Weiss (1978) randomly assigned 27 couples to a behavioral communication treatment, a behavioral-attitudinal treatment, or a nonspecific control treatment. Couples receiving the behavioral-attitudinal therapy, designed to change attributions about marital problems, had the most positive outcome. They demonstrated significantly more improvement than either of the other groups in marital satisfaction and significantly greater increases than the behavioral therapy group in positive behavior during marital interactions.

Behrens et al. (1990) conducted an intrasubject replication design with multiple baselines across couples to examine the impact of BMT followed by cognitive-behavioral marital therapy (CBMT) on four couples. CBMT combined traditional cognitive interventions, such as exploring dysfunctional relationship beliefs, with training in the identification and management of high-risk conflict situations. The results suggested that the initial BMT intervention was associated with strong effects on observational measures of communication (i.e., decreases in verbal negativity); the addition of the CBMT phase was associated with the maintenance of these treatment effects. In contrast, although the initial BMT phase had minimal impact on the cognitions of spouses during marital interactions, the addition of CBMT was associated with increases in spouses' positive thoughts about their partners.

Baucom and colleagues conducted two studies examining the effects of adding a focus on cognitions to behavioral marital therapy. Baucom and Lester (1986) randomly assigned 24 couples to a wait-list control group, a BMT-alone condition, or BMT and cognitive treatment (CBT+BMT; 6 weeks of CBT, focusing on attributions and expectations, followed by 6 weeks of BMT). Both BMT and CBT+BMT couples showed improvements in marital satisfaction and behavioral indexes of change; only couples receiving CBT+BMT showed consistent changes on cognitive measures. Both BMT and CBT+BMT resulted in approximately 50 percent of spouses reporting marital satisfaction scores in the nondistressed range at the end of therapy. Direct comparisons of BMT and CBT+BMT failed to demonstrate the superiority of CBT+BMT. These findings were maintained at a 6-month follow-up assessment.

Baucom, Sayers, and Sher (1990) randomly assigned 60 couples to a wait-list control group or to one of four 12-session therapies: BMT alone, CR (cognitive restructuring) followed by BMT (CR+BMT), and BMT followed by emotional expressiveness training (EET, based on the relationship enhancement work of Guerney, 1977; BMT+EET), or a combination treatment (CR+BMT+EET). The treatments appeared effective in producing changes in measures specific to their focus of intervention (i.e., CR+BMT produced changes on cognitive measures, whereas BMT+EET produced changes in emotion-related measures). Across all four treatment conditions, approximately 50 percent of couples became nondistressed by the end of therapy. However, although all the treatments increased marital adjustment relative to the control group, there were few significant differences among the treatments. Thus, the addition of CR and/or EET did not increase the overall effectiveness of BMT.

In summary, only one study has indicated that adding a cognitive component to BMT may increase the efficacy of BMT, and this investigation is generally viewed as an analogue study (Margolin & Weiss, 1978). In contrast, more recent work (e.g., Baucom & Lester, 1986; Baucom, Sayers, & Sher, 1990) suggests that the addition of cognitive interventions does not increase the efficacy of BMT. However, the data (i.e., the Baucom studies and the Behrens et al., 1990, study) consistently indicate that the addition of CMT to BMT does lead to changes in cognitions.

Discussing the lack of demonstrated effects of CMT, Jacobson (1991c) has suggested that the

> finding that cognitions changed more in the cognitive than in the behavioral condition actually creates problems for their model: If the cognitive condition improved cognitive appraisals but did not facilitate marital satisfaction any more than did the behavioral condition, does this not imply that altering cognitive processes is not necessary for enhancing marital satisfaction? (p. 437)

Similarly, Coyne (1990) has argued that a focus on cognitions in marital therapy will not prove fruitful. Drawing parallels to depression treatment, he has suggested that cognitive therapy is actually an action-oriented approach involving behavioral inter-

ventions and that such behavioral interventions are the active therapeutic ingredient. In contrast, cognitive marital therapists have focused exclusively on changing cognitions, relying on verbal persuasion and discussion rather than behavior change.

Fincham, Bradbury, and Beach (1990), along with Baucom, Sayers, and Sher (1990), are more optimistic about the potential of cognitive marital therapy. They have noted that the relatively unimpressive outcomes obtained thus far might be due to a variety of factors, including limited statistical power (i.e., small sample sizes), the artificial separation and sequencing of cogntive and behavioral interventions, the lack of matching between treatment approach and client needs (i.e., the random assignment of clients to treatments), and the limitations of currently available cognitive measures that restrict a researcher's ability to demonstrate changes resulting from cognitive therapy. Fincham, Bradbury, and Beach (1990) have also suggested that current research on the role of cognitive processes in marriage, and resulting cognitive interventions in marital therapy, may be overly simplistic. This research has generally focused on a few types of cognitive contents (i.e., attributions, irrational beliefs), rather than on cognitive processes or structures. Although final answers regarding the usefulness of cognitive interventions for marital problems must await further research, it is clear at this point that claims about the potential of cognitive marital therapy are currently unsubstantiated and should be made cautiously.

Emotionally Focused Marital Therapy

A recent development has been the specification and empirical investigation of emotionally focused (EFT) marital therapy (e.g., Greenberg & Johnson, 1988). EFT represents an integrated affective-systemic approach; it emphasizes the role of affective experience in change and the role of negative interactional cycles in the maintenance of a couple's problems. The goal of EFT is to repair the intimate emotional bond between spouses so that they may become more responsive to one another's legitimate attachment needs. EFT focuses on spouses' expression and acceptance of feelings and wants.

Greenberg, Johnson, and their colleagues have conducted studies examining the effectiveness of EFT. Their studies have generally involved the specification of treatments in manuals, checks of adherence to the treatment manuals, random assignment of couples to treatments, wait-list control groups, standardized self-report measures, and follow-up assessments.

In an initial study, Johnson and Greenberg

(1985a) randomly assigned 45 couples to eight sessions of EFT, problem-solving (PS) training derived from BMT, or a wait-list control group. At posttherapy, husbands who had received EFT reported higher marital satisfaction than either PS or control-group husbands, whereas wives in both treatment groups reported greater marital satisfaction than wives in the control group. Couples in both treatments had improved relative to the control couples on measures of consensus, intellectual intimacy, reduction in target complaints, and goal attainment. However, EFT couples reported greater cohesion, intellectual intimacy, conventionality, and reductions in target complaints than did couples in PS; wives in the EFT condition also reported more emotional intimacy and affectional expression. At a 2-month follow-up assessment, the EFT couples reported greater marital satisfaction and cohesion than did the PS couples.

Johnson and Greenberg (1985b) later studied the 14 couples who had been assigned to the wait-list control group in the original study but were treated with EFT after the termination of the waiting period. These couples reported no changes in marital satisfaction, intimacy, target complaint reduction, or goal attainment during the waiting period, but they demonstrated significant improvement on all these measures after therapy. A 2-month follow-up indicated that couples maintained their treatment gains.

James (1991) attempted to enhance the long-term benefits of EFT by adding a communication training (CT) treatment component derived from relationship enhancement training (RE; Guerney, 1977). Forty-two couples were randomly assigned to 12 sessions of EFT, 8 sessions of EFT and 4 sessions of CT (EFT+CT), or a wait-list control group. Couples in both treatments attained greater marital satisfaction and reductions in target complaints than did control-group couples. Across both treatments, approximately 75 percent of the couples were no longer distressed at the end of therapy and over 50 percent were still nondistressed at the 4-month follow-up. However, very few differences between the two treatment groups emerged. Although only the EFT+CT couples were superior to control couples on a self-report measure of communication, at the 4-month follow-up assessment, EFT couples were superior to EFT+CT couples in reduction in target complaints. James concluded that CT failed to enhance the effectiveness of EFT and speculated that this may have been due to the limited dose (i.e., four sessions) of CT or to insufficient statistical power to detect group differences.

Goldman and Greenberg (1991) compared EFT with integrated systemic marital therapy (IST). The integrated systemic approach views negative interaction patterns as attempted solutions to problems; it is designed to change these interactional patterns, resulting in second-order change. A team of therapists served as consultants, sending suggestions to the therapists from behind a one-way observational mirror. Interventions included reframing, positive connotation, prescribing the symptom, and prescribing a relapse. Forty-two couples were randomly assigned to EFT, IST, or a wait-list control group; couples received 10 sessions of therapy. At posttherapy, couples in both therapy conditions were significantly better than control couples on the self-report outcome variables, including marital satisfaction, conflict resolution, reductions in target complaints, and goal attainment; 67 percent of all couples ended therapy with scores in the nondistressed range. There were no differences between the EFT and IST couples. In contrast, whereas the IST couples had maintained their gains at a 4-month follow-up assessment, the EFT couples showed reductions in marital satisfaction, goal attainment, and, less conclusively, in reductions in target complaints. The authors speculated that the persuasiveness of the team approach in IST may have been more effective than the approach of individual therapists in EFT. In addition, the authors noted that more severely maritally distressed couples were included in this study than in previous EFT studies, suggesting that time-limited EFT may not lead to maintenance of change among severely distressed couples.

One of the major limitations of these EFT outcome studies is their exclusion of severely distressed couples. Couples scoring below a certain criterion (below 65 in Johnson & Greenberg, 1985a; below 70 in James, 1991; and below 60 in Goldman & Greenberg, 1991) on the Dyadic Adjustment Scale (DAS; Spanier, 1976) have been screened out. In addition, all these studies involved rather brief follow-up assessment periods (2–4 months), making it difficult to assess the long-term effectiveness of EFT. None of the EFT studies has included observational outcome measures, thus providing little information regarding the behavioral changes in marital interactions that EFT may produce. Despite these limitations, at this time, with the exception of BMT, EFT is the most thoroughly researched marital therapy.

Insight-Oriented Marital Therapy

Snyder and Wills conducted a study comparing behavioral marital therapy (BMT), insight-oriented marital therapy (IOMT), and a wait-list control group. This study included random assignment to treatment condition, documentation of therapist adherence to treatment manuals, a multimethod assessment package, and the longest follow-up (4 years) ever conducted in marital therapy research. Relative to the control group, both BMT and IOMT produced positive changes in individual and marital functioning at termination. These effects were maintained at a 6-month follow-up. Examining clinical significance data, both treatments resulted in approximately 50 percent of the couples becoming nondistressed by the end of therapy and just less than 50 percent being in the nondistressed range at the follow-up. At termination and the 6-month follow-up, there were essentially no differences between BMT and IOMT (Snyder & Wills, 1989). In contrast, at the 4-year follow-up (Snyder et al., 1991a), a significantly higher percentage of BMT couples had divorced (38% of 26 BMT couples; only 3% of 29 IOMT couples), and BMT couples showed significantly higher rates of deterioration than did IOMT couples. These findings sparked a lively debate in the literature (e.g., Jacobson, 1991a; Snyder, Wills, & Grady-Fletcher, 1991b) and a series of articles in the *Journal of Family Psychology* (*JFP*) (Baucom & Epstein, 1991; Gurman, 1991; Jacobson, 1991b, 1991c; Johnson & Greenberg, 1991; Markman, 1991a; Snyder & Wills, 1991).

In particular, although the interventions used in the BMT and IOMT sessions were reliably distinguishable (Wills, Faitler, & Snyder, 1987), Jacobson (1991a, 1991b, 1991c) argued that the IOMT condition was more representative of clinically sensitive BMT and recent expansions of BMT (i.e., new wave BMT) than was the BMT condition. Jacobson (1991a) and Markman (1991b), prominent behavioral marital therapists, both noted that the IOMT treatment manual was consistent with their own practice of BMT (e.g., it included therapist skills and nonspecific interventions advocated in the BMT literature, along with communication training and newer behavioral techniques). Thus, Jacobson asserted that the Snyder et al. (1991a) results simply demonstrated the superiority of clinically sensitive BMT (labeled IOMT) over rigidly structured, outdated BMT (labeled BMT). Jacobson's assertions elicited a debate regarding what constitutes BMT, a discussion of how the context, timing, and sequencing of identical interventions may distinguish various theoretical approaches (i.e., BMT vs. IOMT), and a call for more detailed treatment manuals to prevent such confusion in future research.

In addition, Jacobson (1991a, 1991c) and others (e.g., Baucom & Epstein, 1991; Johnson & Greenberg, 1991) expressed concern that a psychodynamically trained therapist (i.e., Wills) conducted the training and supervision in both conditions (IOMT and BMT) in the Snyder et al. (Snyder & Wills, 1989; Snyder et al., 1991a) study. However, Snyder and colleagues (Snyder et al., 1991b; Snyder & Wills, 1991) argued that assessment of the therapists' expectations showed that any potential bias actually favored the BMT conditions and that, despite therapist differences in exposure to BMT or IOMT prior to the study, no therapist main effects or therapist-by-treatment interactions were significant on any outcome measure. In response to Jacobson's concerns about therapist competency (Jacobson, 1991c), Snyder and Wills (1991) noted that the therapists were all experienced; unfortunately, assessment of therapist competence from tapes of the sessions could not be completed, since the tapes were not preserved.

Based on the Snyder et al. (1991a) study, it appears that IOMT, which may or may not have been representative of newer versions of BMT, produced better long-term outcomes than a traditional and highly structured version of BMT. Such findings must be replicated before definitive conclusions can be drawn. Rather than continuing the debate, several authors have suggested that it is more important to examine how IOMT led to such impressive long-term outcomes. What therapy interventions contained in the IOMT condition led couples to maintain the positive gains they made during treatment over such a long follow-up period? Many of these authors have hypothesized that affective changes (i.e., changes accompanied by strong affect; Gurman, 1991) were the key ingredients in IOMT; they have labeled these insights into emotional conflicts (Snyder et al., 1991b), acceptance of unresolvable conflicts (Jacobson, 1991b, 1991c), cognitive-emotional shifts and sharing of thoughts and feelings (Baucom & Epstein, 1991), increased emotional engagement between spouses (Johnson & Greenberg, 1991), and an increased ability to manage and handle negative affect (Markman, 1991b). Several authors have suggested that problem-solving/communication skills per se may not be as important to long-term maintenance of marital satisfaction as the ability of couples to engage around conflict and to handle expressions of negative affect; these notions are related to recent longitudinal research predicting marital satisfaction (Gottman & Krokoff, 1989; studies cited in Markman, 1991a, 1991b). Future research, examining the usefulness of interventions resulting in affective changes, insight, and engagement in conflict, is needed to empirically validate these speculations.

SOME CONCLUSIONS REGARDING THE EFFICACY OF MARITAL THERAPY FOR THE TREATMENT OF MARITAL DISTRESS

This summary draws heavily on a recent review by Jacobson and Addis (1993).

Which Marital Therapy Approaches Work Relative to Control Groups?

As can be seen in Table 14.1, virtually all marital therapy approaches investigated to date (i.e., BMT, EFT, IOMT, and IST) are effective relative to no-treatment control groups. However, as noted by Jacobson and Addis (1993), this statement may not be as impressive as it first appears — even small changes among therapy couples are likely to be statistically significant relative to wait-list control groups, since untreated couples generally remain unchanged or deteriorate during the waiting period.

How Effective Are Various Treatment Approaches?

Improvement rates are relatively consistent across a variety of studies and theoretical approaches, with data indicating that only approximately 50 percent of treated couples are happily married at the end of therapy. Thus, "all treatments are leaving substantial numbers of couples unchanged or still distressed by the end of therapy; all treatments appear to have about the same success rate" (Jacobson & Addis, 1993, pp. 6–7).

What Are the Long-Term Effects of Marital Therapy?

Few researchers have consistently examined the long-term effects of marital therapy. However, it appears that a fair proportion of couples treated with BMT are likely to experience relapse or divorce over the course of 2–4 years following therapy. In contrast, the one study of IOMT demonstrated a remarkable long-term success rate (only 3% of the couples had divorced at the 4-year follow-up). Such findings, although exciting, must be replicated before it can be concluded that IOMT leads to better long-term outcome than other marital therapy approaches. The general paucity of follow-up data points out the need for researchers to routinely include long-term follow-up assessments in outcome studies.

Are Some Approaches More Effective than Others?

As noted, most studies contrasting BMT with other approaches have failed to demonstrate differences. The same general conclusion can be reached regarding comparisons of other treatment approaches with one another. In addition, both Baucom and Hoffman (1986) and Jacobson and Addis (1993) note that when differences are demonstrated they consistently favor the theoretical orientation and expertise of the investigators. Jacobson and Addis (1993) label this consistent pattern of findings the allegiance effect and conclude that "we have learned very little from these studies, especially given the time and expense that has gone into them" (p. 15).

PREDICTING DROPOUT FROM MARITAL THERAPY

Very few studies have been conducted comparing marital therapy dropouts and completers, although marital cases have been included in more general studies of treatment dropout (e.g., Fiester, Mahrer, Giambra, & Ormiston, 1974). In addition, findings from early studies are often not generalizable to conjoint marital therapy. For example, Hollis (1968) coded intake interviews with clients presenting with marital problems; however, these clients were then treated in individual therapy.

In a more recent study, Anderson and colleagues (Anderson, Atilano, Bergen, Russell, & Jurich, 1985) examined 52 marital and family therapy cases. Based on therapists' ratings of interventions, they found that families or couples who received more problem-solving training and probing and fewer interventions designed to emphasize structural changes and help families maintain a high level of intensity during sessions (e.g., firming up boundaries, conflict escalation, and advice giving) were the most likely to drop out of treatment. In addition, relative to couples who completed treatment, both partners in couples who dropped out had reported less marital and life satisfaction at pretherapy.

In a study of marital therapy dropouts, Allgood and Crane (1991) found that treatment dropouts (N = 72) were more likely than completers (N = 72) to have had a male intake clinician, to have fewer children, and to have presenting problems relating to an individual or family problem. However, these variables accounted for less than 20 percent of the variance in predicting who would drop out of treatment. In addition, it may be difficult to generalize from this sample, since 95 percent of the couples were members of The Church of Jesus Christ of the Latter Day Saints.

Very little information is currently available regarding the characteristics of treatment dropouts versus completers in marital therapy. Future research elucidating such characteristics should be of interest to clinicians, given relatively high dropout rates in these studies (e.g., in Allgood & Crane, 15% of couples did not return for therapy after the first session).

PREDICTORS OF MARITAL THERAPY OUTCOME

Recent reviews (Baucom & Hoffman, 1986; Gurman et al., 1986; Jacobson & Addis, 1993) have included the following studies of BMT outcome predictors: Baucom (1984), Baucom and Aiken (1984), Baucom and Mehlman (1984), Beach and Broderick (1983), Crowe (1978), Ewart (1978), Hahlweg et al. (1984), Turkewitz and O'Leary (1981). Additional studies have been conducted more recently, including Crane, Newfield, and Armstrong (1984), Jacobson, Follette, and Pagel (1986), and Whisman and Jacobson (1990). The available data suggest that the couples who are *least* likely to benefit from BMT include older couples, couples who have given more thought and taken more steps toward divorce, couples who are severely distressed, and couples who have a low "quality of emotional affection" (Baucom & Hoffman, 1986) or a high level of "emotional disengagement" (Jacobson & Addis, 1993) (i.e., less frequent sex and less tenderness, togetherness, and communication; Hahlweg et al., 1984).

The findings regarding the relationship between gender roles and power and marital therapy outcome are conflicting. Couples with a highly affiliative wife and highly independent husband were less likely to benefit from BMT (Jacobson et al., 1986), leading Jacobson and Addis (1993) to suggest that "couples whose relationships are rigidly organized according to traditional gender roles are relatively poor risks for BCT (behavioral couples therapy)" (p. 12). However, other studies have demonstrated that wives with higher self-reported femininity (Baucom & Aiken, 1984) and couples demonstrating greater power inequality during pretherapy marital interactions (Whisman & Jacobson, 1990) benefited more from BMT than did other couples, suggesting that BMT may promote egalitarianism through the procedures it employs (Margolin, Talovic, Fernandez, & Onorato, 1983; Whisman & Jacobson, 1990). Further study of this issue is needed before definitive conclusions can be reached.

No data are currently available regarding which couples will have the best outcome when treated with various therapeutic approaches. It would seem time for researchers to examine how to match clients to treatments, although, as noted by Jacobson and Addis (1993), this may be premature, since "there is little empirical basis at present for predicting what kinds of couple characteristics should interact with type of treatment" (p. 26).

MARITAL THERAPY PROCESS RESEARCH

Research examining the process of marital therapy and its relationship with treatment outcome is still in its infancy. Each researcher has used his or her own exploratory methods and measures.

In a study of BMT, Holtzworth-Munroe, Jacobson, DeKlyen, and Whisman (1989) had 13 therapists and the 32 couples they treated rate therapist and client behaviors after each therapy session. Averaged ratings were computed across all therapy sessions and composite rating scales were formed. Examining therapists' ratings, marital satisfaction at termination was primarily predicted by ratings of couples' facilitative behavior. Couples who responded positively to BMT had therapists who viewed the couple as collaborating and participating in therapy and who viewed themselves as able to induce collaboration between the spouses; after controlling for pretherapy marital satisfaction, therapist ratings accounted for 34 percent of the variance in therapy outcome. Couples who rated themselves as collaborating and actively participating in sessions and as complying with homework assignments reported the greatest marital satisfaction at therapy termination; after controlling for pretherapy marital satisfaction, husband and wife ratings accounted for 26 percent (wives) or 29 percent (husbands) of the variance in therapy outcome. The results clearly suggest that in BMT success depends on clients' involvement in sessions and compliance with homework assignments.

In a study of group marital therapy using a behavioral-humanistic approach, Bourgeois, Sabourin, and Wright (1990) had therapists and clients complete measures of therapeutic alliance after the third therapy session; they used the only available standardized measure of marital therapy alliance, the Couples Therapeutic Alliance Scale (CTAS; Pinsof & Catherall, 1986). After adjusting for pretherapy marital satisfaction scores, therapeutic alliance had little relationship to therapy outcome for wives. Therapeutic alliance was significantly related to husbands' posttherapy marital satisfaction; however, after controlling for pretherapy marital satisfaction, the percentage of variance in therapy outcome accounted for by therapeutic alliance ratings was very modest, ranging from 3 percent to 10 percent across measures. The authors noted that low variability in the alliance scores (i.e., everyone reported a good therapeutic alliance) may have reduced the predictive power of this variable.

In another study using the CTAS, Heatherington and Friedlander (1990) had spouses complete the CTAS and the Session Evaluation Questionnaire (SEQ), a measure of clients' immediate perceptions of a therapy session's depth/value and smoothness/ease (Stiles & Snow, 1984), after each session, from the third to the sixth session. Among 16 couples in marital therapy, the alliance measure did not correlate significantly with clients' perceptions of the smoothness of therapy sessions. Only one of the three subscales of the CTAS (i.e., Tasks, a measure of the clients' belief in the therapist's power and methods, along with the therapist's ability to understand the client and be helpful) was correlated significantly with clients' perceptions that the sessions had been valuable. Thus there were few significant relationships between ratings of therapeutic alliance and clients' perceptions of therapy sessions.

Greenberg and colleagues have completed two studies of therapy process in EFT using very different methodologies. In one study of couples treated with EFT, Johnson and Greenberg (1988) coded the best therapy session, identified by therapist and client, for six extreme couples; three of the couples had the least change in marital satisfaction following therapy and three had the most change. Coding indicated that in these sessions, successful couples were more accepting and affiliative, had attained a deeper level of emotional experiencing and integration, and had more softening experiences (i.e., shifts from negative interaction cycles to increased accessibility and responsiveness between spouses).

In a study using task analysis methodology, Greenberg, James, and Conry (1988) conducted interviews with 21 couples 4 months after EFT termination. They asked spouses to describe critical change incidents that had been helpful during therapy. Sorting the descriptions of 52 incidents led to the identification of five categories of change: expressing underlying feelings leading to changes in interpersonal perception; expressing feelings and needs; acquiring understanding; taking responsibility (as opposed to blaming the spouse) for experiences; and receiving validation (from the therapist). Although Wile (1988) suggested that the common ingredient in these change categories was the fact that spouses became less accusing of one another, Greenberg and Johnson (1988) replied that diminishing accusation, although an essential first step in marital therapy, is not the crucial common factor

needed for therapeutic change. Instead, they proposed that, for change to occur, couples must experience, not merely understand, the self and others as different and must fundamentally redefine their relationship in terms of experienced accessibility and responsiveness to one another.

While most studies in this area have used different methodologies, exceptions are found in the two studies that employed the Couples Therapeutic Alliance Scale (Bourgeois et al., 1990; Heatherington & Friedlander, 1990). The results of these two studies were disappointing, however; measures of therapeutic alliance were unable to explain much variance in either clients' immediate perceptions of therapy sessions or overall therapy outcome. As noted by the developers of the CTAS (Pinsof & Catherall, 1986), it may be difficult to directly apply notions of therapeutic alliance derived from individual psychotherapy research to the study of marital and family therapy. Similarly, the CTAS is a relatively new measure and may require further refining. With such theoretical and methodological developments, the notion of therapeutic alliance in marital therapy may still prove useful in future research, but, as noted by Bourgeois et al. (1990), change is a multidimensional process, and it may be "simplistic to expect one factor to account for a large part of outcome" (p. 612).

More encouraging are the findings from studies of EFT (Greenberg et al., 1988; Johnson & Greenberg, 1988) and the study of process in BMT (Holtzworth-Munroe et al., 1989). Although the EFT study methodologies have not reported the percentage of variance in outcome accounted for by therapy processes, the findings are intriguing and should lead to further interesting research. In investigating the process of BMT, Holtzworth-Munroe et al. (1989) were able to account for a moderate proportion of variance in therapy outcome by examining ratings of client involvement in therapy. Unfortunately, their study did not examine the determinants of client involvement; that is, which therapy processes, if any, help to shape client collaboration and participation.

Research in this area could be improved by implementing recent suggestions (e.g., Pinsof, 1989). Marital therapists need to devote attention to theoretical issues, developing their ideas regarding how the process of therapy should be related to treatment outcome. Ideas from individual therapy process research may or may not be generalizable to marital therapy process. In addition, time must be devoted to measurement development; reliable and valid measures of therapy process are a prerequisite for progress in this area. A combination of standardized measures, used across laboratories, and individualized measures, developed by individual researchers to examine particular theoretical questions, may prove most useful.

RESEARCH ON MARITAL THERAPY FOR SPECIFIC DISORDERS

Researchers recently have become interested in the application of marital therapy to the treatment of individual problems (e.g., depression and alcoholism). This interest is due, in part, to theoretical developments emphasizing the role of interpersonal processes in individual psychopathology (e.g., Coyne's interpersonal theories of depression). Similarly, in a relatively new body of literature, researchers have directly examined the interpersonal interactions of couples in which one spouse is diagnosed with a psychological disorder (e.g., coding the discussions of couples in which one spouse is depressed or alcoholic). Descriptions of the problematic interaction patterns of such couples have led to the conclusion that marital therapy may be of use in treating individual disorders. This section reviews the empirical research conducted to test the efficacy of marital therapy in treating three psychological disorders, depression, agoraphobia, and alcoholism; these disorders were chosen because the majority of the research has been conducted in these areas.

Depression

Two controlled studies comparing marital therapy and individual therapy for depression have been conducted. Both involved depressed married women whose husbands were willing to participate. Both used random assignment and standardized measures of depression and marital satisfaction.

O'Leary and Beach (1990) assigned depressed women in maritally distressed relationships to conjoint behavioral marital therapy, individual cognitive therapy, or a wait-list control group. Based on wives' self-reports, depression was reduced significantly and equivalently in both treatment groups relative to the control group. However, marital therapy also led to significant improvements in the wives' marital satisfaction relative to both the individual cognitive therapy and control groups. These differences were maintained at a 1-year follow-up assessment.

Jacobson, Dobson, Fruzzetti, Schmaling, and Salusky (1991) compared the efficacy of conjoint behavioral marital therapy, individual cognitive-behavioral therapy, and a combination therapy for depression among married women. They selected clients solely on the basis of depression; maritally

distressed and nondistressed couples were included. In addition, Jacobson et al. used a more stringent severity criterion for depression than did O'Leary and Beach (1990).

All groups reported statistically significant reductions in depression. However, for nondistressed couples, marital therapy was not as effective as were the other conditions at reducing depression. In contrast, marital therapy was a viable treatment for depression among maritally distressed couples. The combination treatment did not offer a clear advantage over either of the component treatments with regard to changes in depression.

With regard to marital satisfaction, statistically significant changes were observed only among maritally distressed couples treated with marital therapy and among nondistressed couples treated with the combination therapy; similar levels of change were found among distressed couples in the combination therapy but these changes were not statistically significant. No between-group comparisons reached statistical significance. In addition, the combination treatment led to positive changes in marital interactions (i.e., decreases in wife and husband aversive behavior and increases in wife's facilitative behavior), although between-group comparisons were not statistically significant.

Taken together, these two studies (Jacobson et al., 1991; O'Leary & Beach, 1990) suggest that BMT can be an effective treatment for depression among maritally distressed couples. Both groups of researchers hypothesized that marital therapy changes depression among depressed, maritally distressed women by increasing marital satisfaction.

Two other studies have examined the interaction of marital therapy and drug therapy for depression. Friedman (1975) randomly assigned 150 depressed patients and their spouses to one of four conditions; drug–marital therapy, drug–minimal contact, placebo–marital therapy, or placebo–minimal contact. In the drug treatment, amitriptyline was administered for 10 weeks; in the marital therapy condition, 12 sessions of marital therapy were provided, but the orientation of this therapy was not clearly described. Both drug and marital therapy led to greater improvements than their control conditions. Although drug therapy was faster and generally superior in symptom relief and clinical improvement, marital therapy led to superior outcomes on measures of family role task performance, perceptions of the marital relationship, and reductions in hostility. No follow-up data were provided.

Waring et al. (1988) assigned female patients with dysthymia to either pharmacotherapy (i.e., doxepin) or placebo and to either 10 weeks of Waring's cognitive marital therapy (CMT; 1988) or minimal contact therapy. All the woman showed statistically significant improvements on depression and marital intimacy measures, but the treatment groups did not differ significantly from one another. However, at the time of the report, only 12 patients had been treated and assessed, making interpretation of these findings difficult. In general, very little information is available regarding the relative efficacy of marital therapy, pharmacotherapy, and their interaction in the treatment of depression.

As part of a larger study of marital therapy, Sher, Baucom, and Larus (1990) compared the responses of depressed and nondepressed couples to behavioral marital therapy. Couples were seeking marital therapy; they were not necessarily complaining of depression and did not have to be diagnosed as having a major depressive episode to be included in the study. Based on MMPI scores, couples were grouped into those in which one spouse (i.e., the target spouse) had elevated scores on the depression scale, those in which one spouse showed psychopathology other than depression (i.e., another MMPI scale was elevated), and those in which neither spouse showed symptoms of individual psychopathology (i.e., no elevated MMPI scores.).

Relative to a wait-list control group, marital therapy led to increased marital satisfaction for all groups and there were no significant group differences in response to treatment for either the target or nontarget spouse. However, the depressed target group had the lowest percentage of spouses who were nondistressed at the end of therapy. Treatment led to significant decreases in the frequency of negative communication during marital interactions for all three groups. Among the depressed spouses, level of depression, as measured with the MMPI, decreased significantly in response to therapy and 64 percent of the spouses who were depressed at pretest were nondepressed at posttest. Sher et al. (1990) concluded that distressed/depressed couples seeking marital therapy do respond to behavioral marital therapy, but that some marital distress and depression will remain at the end of a short-term (12-week) treatment program.

In summary, the findings regarding the efficacy of marital therapy for depression occurring in the context of marital distress are encouraging. Marital therapy appears to decrease depression. In addition, it may lead to increases in marital satisfaction and decreases in negative marital communication, thereby decreasing the probability of relapse among depressives (e.g., Hooley & Teasdale, 1989). However, further research is needed to clar-ify certain issues (e.g., the usefulness of marital therapy as an adjunct to drug therapy and the usefulness of marital therapy for patients with relatively low levels of depression).

Agoraphobia

Data regarding the relationship between marital quality and agoraphobia are inconsistent. Some researchers have found a relationship between pretreatment marital satisfaction level and therapy outcome among agoraphobics; others have not (see reviews of this literature in Brown & Barlow, in press; Craske, Burton, & Barlow, 1989; Hafner, 1988). Despite the mixed data, a recent development has been the inclusion of the agoraphobic patient's spouse in therapy sessions.

Several researchers have directly examined the effects of involving the agoraphobic's spouse in therapy. Cobb, Mathews, Childs-Clarke, and Blowers (1984) failed to find any differences between spouse-involved and non–spouse-involved groups at either posttest or at a 6-month follow-up. However, both groups involved a home-based treatment and involved the spouse in assessment sessions. The authors noted that spouses in the nonspouse group showed interest in the therapy; thus, they may have become involved in the treatment (Brown & Barlow, in press). In addition, the patients in this study were generally not maritally distressed, making it difficult to generalize these findings to maritally distressed agoraphobics (i.e., complex agoraphobia; Hafner, 1988).

Barlow and colleagues compared clinic-based spouse-involved and non–spouse-involved treatments for agoraphobics (Barlow, O'Brien, & Last, 1984; Barlow, O'Brien, Last, & Holden, 1983). To be included in this study, spouses had to agree to participate in treatment; half the patients were then randomly assigned to a condition in which spouses attended all treatment sessions. A significantly greater number of agoraphobics in the spouse-involved group were classified as responders at posttest, and on a variety of measures patients in the spouse-involved group showed an advantage over patients in the non–spouse-involved group. A follow-up study indicated that these group differences were maintained at 1- and 2-year follow-ups (Cerny, Barlow, Craske, & Himadi, 1987).

Arnow, Taylor, Agras, and Telch (1985) initially treated 24 agoraphobic patients in a spouse-assisted exposure program. The patients were then divided into two matched groups according to their change scores on behavioral measures of agoraphobia. One group received couples communication training, and the other received couples relaxation training. Both at posttest and at an 8-month follow-up, the group receiving the communication training showed a significantly greater response to treatment.

The data support the efficacy of spouse involvement in the treatment for agoraphobia. However, the mechanism by which spouse involvement leads to increased treatment response is unknown. Brown and Barlow (in press) noted that spouse involvement consistently results in lower dropout rates, suggesting that continued participation in therapy may lead to greater improvements in agoraphobic symptoms. They also suggested that spouse involvement may facilitate a patient's practice of new skills, as the spouse may facilitate, or at least not interfere with, such practice. Consistent with this notion are two studies demonstrating the importance of social support to treatment outcome. Oatley and Hodgson (1987) demonstrated that a treatment including friends and a treatment including spouses were equally effective; Sinnott, Jones, Scott-Fordham, and Woodward (1981) demonstrated that agoraphobics selected from the same neighborhood and treated together had better outcomes than a group of agoraphobics selected from different neighborhoods.

Alternatively, it has been suggested that spouse involvement in therapy may lead to decreases in marital tension, which would result in less vulnerability to panic among agoraphobics. In fact, the Arnow et al. (1985) study suggests that marital therapy focusing directly on marital issues and communication, when given as an adjunct to spouse-involved standard treatments, may be beneficial to at least some couples (Jacobson, Holtzworth-Munroe, & Schmaling, 1989). Given the mixed data regarding changes in marital satisfaction following therapy for agoraphobia, it is possible that the reduction in marital tensions may be important for only a subset of agoraphobic patients — those who experience marital distress prior to treatment.

Alcoholism
Early studies suggested that involving spouses of alcoholics in treatment for the alcoholic might increase therapy efficacy (e.g., Azrin, Sisson, Meyers, & Godley, 1982; Burton & Kaplan, 1968; Corder, Corder, & Laidlaw, 1972). Recently, a series of more methodologically sound studies of spouse involvement in the treatment of alcoholism have been conducted. All these studies have required that the spouses of alcoholics be willing to participate and have involved the random assignment of patients to various treatment conditions.

Three studies have examined the efficacy of adding marital therapy to more traditional, individual

alcohol treatment programs. In the first of these studies, following discharge from an inpatient treatment program, Cadogan (1973) assigned alcoholics and their spouses to either a conjoint marital therapy group, focusing on alcohol-related issues and problem solving, or to a no-treatment group. Follow-up data were collected 6 months after hospital discharge. Although the group comparison was confounded because the marital therapy group couples were being treated during the follow-up period, questionnaire responses indicated that more of the marital therapy group were abstinent at follow-up than were control group patients. Self-reports regarding marital communication, gathered from a subset of the couples, did not demonstrate group differences.

In the second study, O'Farrell, Cutter, and Floyd (1985) assigned alcoholics who were beginning outpatient clinic treatment, usually following inpatient treatment, to a behavioral marital therapy (BMT) group, an interactional couples therapy group, or a no-marital-therapy control group. At posttest, the couples treated in BMT were more satisfied with their marriages than were the control or interactional group couples, and the BMT group reported having taken fewer steps toward marital separation than the control couples. Few significant differences emerged on observational measures of marital communication. The BMT group reported fewer alcohol-involved days during treatment than did the interactional therapy group, although neither treatment group was significantly better than the control group on this measure; patients in all groups showed improvement in drinking.

O'Farrell, Cutter, Choquette, and Floyd (1992) recently reported the follow-up data, gathered five times over a 2-year period, from this sample. Husbands treated with BMT were not more satisfied with their marriages than were husbands in the other two groups at any posttest assessment. In contrast, BMT wives were the only group of wives to report significant improvement in marital satisfaction throughout follow-up; BMT wives were more satisfied with their marriages than were the control group wives at several of the follow-up assessments. BMT couples also spent fewer days separated during the follow-up period than did the control couples, although the BMT and interactional therapy group couples did not differ in number of days separated. Thus, during follow-up, the BMT couples' marital adjustment outcome was superior only to the no-marital-therapy group and mostly on measures of wives' adjustment. The three groups did not differ on number of days abstinent or alcohol dependence symptoms during the 2-year follow-up period. Although a nonsignificant trend suggested that BMT husbands had fewer negative consequences from drinking than the control couples during the follow-up period, BMT did not produce better drinking outcomes than the interactional couples therapy.

Given this evidence that the initially positive effects of BMT decrease over time, O'Farrell and colleagues conducted a second study to examine the potential effectiveness of relapse prevention sessions (O'Farrell, Choquette, & Cutter, 1992). Fifty-nine couples of which the husband was entering outpatient alcohol treatment received approximately 17 weeks of BMT. Half the couples were then randomly assigned to receive 15 additional relapse prevention sessions over the course of a year; these sessions focused on marital issues and alcohol relapse prevention. Throughout the year, the relapse prevention group reported significantly more days abstinent than the BMT only group. Although marital adjustment results were less consistent, they generally indicated that couples in the relapse prevention group were more maritally satisfied during the year following BMT than were couples in the BMT-only group. Couples in the relapse prevention group tended to be more likely to use treatment-targeted behaviors, such as Antabuse contracts and behaviors learned in marital therapy (e.g., communication skills), than were couples in the BMT-only group; the use of such targeted behaviors was correlated with better outcomes.

Three studies have examined the effectiveness of marital therapy relative to other possible therapies as the sole treatment for alcoholism. In an early study, Hedberg and Campbell (1974) assigned patients to one of four behavioral treatments: systematic desensitization, covert sensitization, electric shock, or behavioral family counseling focusing on communication skills. At a 6-month follow-up assessment, patients from the family counseling group reported the highest rates of goal attainment (i.e., either abstinence or controlled drinking) and improvement in drinking.

McCrady and colleagues assigned couples to one of three possible treatments: minimal spouse involvement, alcohol-focused spouse involvement, or behavioral marital therapy. At posttherapy and 6-month follow-up assessment periods (McCrady et al., 1986), couples assigned to BMT had reduced their drinking more quickly and were more compliant with homework than were couples in the alcohol-focused spouse-involvement treatment; relative to patients in the minimal spouse involvement condition, the BMT couples were more likely to remain in treatment. In addition, relative to the other two groups, couples receiving BMT were more likely to maintain higher levels of marital satisfaction following treatment, although there were no posttherapy differences in marital satisfaction. No posttherapy group differences were demonstrated on observational measures of marital communication.

Data gathered at an 18-month follow-up assessment (McCrady, Stout, Noel, Abrams, & Nelson, in press) indicated that all groups had decreased abstinence during the first 9 months following treatment termination. However, during the second 9 months of follow-up, while patients in the minimal spouse involvement and alcohol-focused spouse-involvement treatments continued to deteriorate, patients who had received BMT gradually increased their proportion of abstinent and abstinent-plus-light-drinking days. In addition, patients in the BMT condition reported fewer marital separations and greater improvement in marital satisfaction and subjective well-being. Finally, it was demonstrated that assignment to BMT resulted in less attrition compared with that of patients assigned to the other treatment conditions (Noel, McCrady, Stout, & Fisher-Nelson, 1987).

In contrast to the positive impact of BMT in the Hedberg and Campbell (1974) and McCrady et al. (1986, in press) studies, a more recent study conducted by Zweben, Pearlman, and Li (1988) did not find differences between couples assigned to an 8-week systems-based marital therapy group and those assigned to a single session of advice counseling that included the spouse. An 18-month follow-up assessment was conducted, and there were no group differences in percentage of heavy drinking days, consequences of drinking, or marital satisfaction; patients in both groups improved on these measures.

It is difficult to draw definitive conclusions from these data, given the variety of data across studies. However, some tentative conclusions can be made. First, data from studies examining the addition of marital therapy to more traditional alcohol treatments (Cadogan, 1973; O'Farrell et al., 1985) suggest that couples receiving marital therapy do better, on both marital and drinking measures, than their counterparts who do not receive marital therapy. Although the initial superiority of marital treatment diminishes as time after treatment increases (O'Farrell, Cutter et al., 1992), relapse prevention sessions can help maintain the effectiveness of BMT treatment (O'Farrell, Choquette, & Cutter, 1992). Second, data from studies examining BMT as the sole treatment for alcoholism (Hedberg & Campbell, 1974; McCrady et al., 1986, in press) suggest that this treatment approach leads to less drinking and greater marital satisfaction than other therapeutic approaches. However, marital therapy derived from systems theory does not appear to have the same beneficial effects (Zweben et al., 1988).

Examining the studies that presented pretherapy marital satisfaction scores, an interesting trend emerges. O'Farrell et al. (1985) found that, among maritally distressed couples, BMT led to the greatest improvement in marital satisfaction at treatment termination; during follow-up, BMT wives reported better marital adjustment than did wives in the no-marital-therapy condition (O'Farrell, Cutter et al., 1992). In contrast, in studies that examined nondistressed couples (McCrady et al., 1986; Zweben et al., 1988), there were no posttherapy group differences in marital satisfaction. This lack of group differences continued across the follow-up period in the Zweben et al. (1988) study of systems-based therapy; however, in the McCrady et al. (in press) study, the BMT couples maintained their marital satisfaction levels over the course of the follow-up period better than couples in the other treatment groups. The findings suggest that BMT helps to improve the marital satisfaction of distressed couples and to prevent deterioration of marital satisfaction among nondistressed couples. Group differences have not been demonstrated on observational measures of communication skills (McCrady et al., 1986; O'Farrell et al., 1985), making it difficult to attribute changes in marital satisfaction to changes in observable behavior. However, couples participating in couples relapse prevention sessions did report continued use of Antabuse contracts and learned marital behaviors (O'Farrell, Choquette, & Cutter, 1992), suggesting that the use of behaviors targeted by BMT is related to the positive outcomes among these couples. Further research is needed to examine which patients benefit most from marital therapy and to elucidate the mechanisms of change leading to improvement from marital interventions among alcoholics.

MARITAL PREVENTION AND ENRICHMENT PROGRAMS

Giblin and colleagues (Giblin, 1986; Giblin, Sprenkle, & Sheehan, 1985) conducted a meta-analysis of 85 studies of premarital, marital, and family enrichment programs. Their findings were reviewed by Gurman et al. (1986), Guerney and Maxson (1990), and Bradbury and Fincham (1990) and are reviewed only briefly here. Average effect sizes were .53 for premarital, .42 for marital, and .55 for family programs. In other words, across these types of programs, the average person who participated in an enrichment program was better off than 67 percent of the people in the no-treatment control groups. Follow-up effect sizes (.34) were smaller than posttest effect sizes (.44), indicating that the effects of such programs decrease over time, although follow-up scores were still above pretest averages. However, many of the studies did not include a follow-up assessment and, among those that did, the average follow-up period was only 12 weeks. Among marital programs, Guerney's relationship enhancement (RE) program (Guerney, 1977) had the largest effect size (.96). Behavioral measures had greater effect sizes (.76) than did self-report measures (.35). Although enrichment programs are generally not designed for distressed couples, the average effect size for programs that included more than 35 percent distressed couples was .51, whereas the average effect size for programs with fewer distressed couples was only .27. This difference may indicate that enrichment effects are effective for distressed couples; however, it might also be attributed to the lack of a ceiling effect or regression to the mean among distressed couples. The meta-analysis indicated that increasing program length and structure was associated with increasing the effect size of the program, although these relationships were weak.

More recently, Hahlweg and Markman (1988) completed a meta-analysis of seven marital distress prevention programs. The programs were delivered to an average of 4 or 5 couples seen together, as a group; the mean length of the programs was six sessions, each 2.5 to 3 hours in duration. Across a total of 38 effect sizes, the average effect size was .79. In other words, the average person who participated in a prevention program was better off than 79 percent of the people who had not participated; the chance of improving was 33 percent for control subjects and 67 percent for couples participating in a prevention program. Thus, even though prevention programs target couples who are nondistressed and are aimed at preventing long-term deterioration in marital satisfaction, they still have a positive short-term effect on relationships. The effect size was .55 in three studies that included a no-treatment control and 1.12 in four studies with a placebo control, indicating that effects are not due to placebo factors. A larger effect size (1.51) was demonstrated for observational outcome measures than for self-report measures (.52). Relationship enhancement (RE) programs had the largest effect size (1.14) relative to other program types (effect sizes of .71 and .57). Only four studies included a follow-up assessment; for the three studies with a 6–18-month follow-up, the follow-up effect size was 1.01; for the one study with a 3-year follow-up, the effect size was .65.

The findings are relatively consistent across these two meta-analyses. First, enrichment and prevention programs have positive effects on relationships that do not seem to be attributable to placebo factors. Second, greater effects are demonstrated with observational measures than on self-report measures. This finding suggests that these programs are successful in teaching couples new skills that are observed during marital interactions. However, this finding may also be due to a ceiling effect, since couples are usually happily married, based upon self-report, when they begin the programs. Third, Guerney's relationship enhancement program consistently has the largest immediate, posttherapy effect. This finding is not unexpected, since RE focuses on enhancing current relationship functioning whereas other programs (e.g., Markman's PREP; Markman, Floyd, Stanley, & Lewis, 1986) focus on the long-term prevention of future problems. However, the relative effectiveness of RE enrichment programs suggests that it would be fruitful to examine which ingredients of this program facilitate change among couples (Guerney & Maxson, 1990). Fourth, relatively few data regarding the long-term effects of prevention and enrichment programs are available; this lack of data is of particular concern in the prevention literature, since the efficacy of prevention programs by definition can be evaluated only over a long period of time (Bradbury & Fincham, 1990). The follow-up data available indicate that, although the programs help prevent deterioration in marital satisfaction, their effectiveness decreases over time.

In a recent review of marital and family enrichment based upon the Giblin et al. (1985) meta-analysis, Guerney and Maxson (1990) suggested that "there is no doubt that, on the whole, enrichment programs work and the field is an entirely legitimate one. No more research or interpretive energy needs to be devoted to that basic concern" (p. 1133). They suggested that future researchers should focus on increasing our understanding of the process of enrichment and prevention therapy, and they suggested the expansion of prevention and enrichment programs to new populations (e.g., couples in which a spouse has individual psychopathology) and new settings (e.g., the workplace).

Jacobson and Addis (1993) are similarly optimistic; they concluded: "given the impressive findings from the enrichment and prevention literatures, it seems clear that such efforts should be encouraged" (p. 29).

Bradbury and Fincham (1990) drew more conservative conclusions: "(1) there is a slight tendency for prevention programs to improve relationships relative to no-treatment and attention-only control groups, and (2) prevention programs have

not yet been shown to produce lasting changes in relationships" (p. 397). They cited a need for "research of a higher caliber that attends to essential aspects of research design and analysis (e.g., appropriate control groups, random assignment of subjects to groups, use of reliable and valid measures)" (p. 386). They also pointed out that "attention must shift to a new phase of examining whether these programs are capable of producing a durable and beneficial impact on marriages" (p. 387); Hahlweg and Markman (1988) similarly concluded that "the most important implication of these findings is the need for more well-controlled, long-term outcome studies" (p. 445).

In addition, Bradbury and Fincham recommended research designed to increase our understanding of the causes of marital distress as a basis for designing prevention programs. They noted that marital prevention researchers have generally focused solely on intrapersonal and interpersonal variables, rather than looking at the context in which marriages occur. Drawing ideas from preventive and community psychology, they suggested that it might be fruitful to design interventions that eliminate factors that are external to the couple but contribute to marital distress (e.g., legislation to permit parental leave following the birth of a child).

LIMITATIONS TO OUR CURRENT RESEARCH

As noted earlier, it would not be inappropriate to conclude that, in general, marital therapy approaches are relatively equivalent in their effectiveness; none consistently results in more than half the couples reliably moving from marital distress to marital satisfaction by the end of therapy. These figures suggest that we have reached the limit of our ability to help couples with interventions derived from our current understanding of marital relationships and processes. This section suggests that improving this situation requires expanding clinical theories and the research that bears on them in terms of three perspectives: longitudinal, developmental, and contextual.

Longitudinal Issues

Longitudinal research points to the necessity of enlarging the temporal context within which we view marital relationships. For example, researchers have demonstrated that the cross-sectional correlates and longitudinal predictors of marital satisfaction are not necessarily the same. Although the expression of negative affect is related to concurrent marital distress, longitudinal work has suggested that it is more functional in the long term than are patterns of withdrawal, disengagement, and avoidance of marital conflict (e.g., Gottman & Krokoff, 1989; review of the literature by Smith, Vivian, & O'Leary, 1991).

Such findings have sparked a lively discussion about the usefulness of the construct of *negative communication*, and the necessity of differentiating constructive versus destructive communication processes (e.g., Haefner, Notarius, & Pellegrini, 1991; Krokoff, 1991; Markman, 1991b; Sayers, Baucom, Sher, Weiss, & Heyman, 1991; Sher & Weiss, 1991; Smith et al., 1991). In addition, several relevant variables have been identified for inclusion in these studies of marital conflict, most notably gender differences in physiological reactions, in desire for affiliation versus independence, and in communication patterns (e.g., Bell, Daly, & Gonzalez, 1987; Christensen & Heavey, 1990; Christensen & Shenk, 1991; Gottman, 1991, in press; Markman, 1991a).

Developmental Issues

Enlarging our understanding of the *variability* in longitudinal patterns of normal marital and family development is a related avenue through which research can address problems faced by clinicians. Developmental family systems theory and research articulate normal processes of change in structures and patterns across time (e.g., Ford & Lerner, 1992). For example, building on the work of mainstream marital and family systems researchers, Olson and Lavee (1989) propose a circumplex model defined by dimensions of adaptability (structure vs. flexibility) and cohesion (separation vs. connection) that describe various family styles. Consideration of these dimensions demonstrates curvilinear relationships in which behavioral, affective, and communication problems occur when there is either *too little* or *too much* cohesion, *too little* or *too much* adaptability. However, it is not yet clear whether extreme positioning on one or the other variable is the cause or the result of the problems. Further, longitudinal studies indicate that family style descriptions often change across the family life cycle, adding more structure and cohesion when there are relatively high caregiving requirements such as young children, aging parents, or chronic illness. When there are no children or older children the "normal" system may be characterized by more flexibility and separateness (e.g., Hinde, 1989).

Marital and family researchers must take into account the developmental variations in individuals, in dyads, and in larger family systems. Researchers must also remember that subsystem and family developmental processes often differ in nontraditional family forms (Alexander & Parsons,

1982), such as in blended and single-parent families as well as in cultural variations. In light of such normative variation, researchers evaluating a "one size fits all" intervention model and using developmentally insensitive measures of marital or family therapy process and outcome could add troublesome error variance or could draw inappropriate conclusions. Developmental models should have relevance for determining goals and selecting measures in marital, and even more so in family, therapy.

Contextual Issues

Contextual issues are extensions of the potentially problematic "one size fits all" approach to application of intervention models. Feminists and representatives of ethnic groups have for some time been pointing out the politics inherent in existing methods and measures. Many of the issues raised here were anticipated by Gurman et al. (1986), yet they have not been rendered less salient since the previous edition of this *Handbook*. Thus we have chosen to highlight them in the belief that to sidestep them would continue the impetus toward confrontation and fragmentation in the field. For example, as noted earlier, some researchers have begun to incorporate gender role variables in their analyses of marital relationships. Other writers, however, suggest that there has been only superficial acknowledgment with no substantial change in methods (e.g., Rampage, 1989; Witkin, 1989a, 1989b) and critique current research with respect to issues of context and method.

The central theme running through the work of those previously considered outsiders is that many of the existing models and methods of measurement take for granted traditional marital and family models and fail to acknowledge potential problems in these models as well as reasonable alternatives to them. Essentially, these groups ask who should define the cultural context within which behavior is understood. These critics assert that context gives meaning to behavior and behavior must be understood in the particularity of its context, not generalized beyond that context.

With respect to marital therapy, contextual variables, such as marital ideals, roles, values, and power relationships in and out of marriage, strongly affect the meaning of any behavior or communication. Further, marriage is normally a leaky system, vulnerable to numerous effects from the community and the institutional context in which it exists (Witkin, 1989b). Researchers may be aware of these contextual variables but, bound by methodological insistence on parsimony and generalizable conclusions, continue to focus on therapeutic technique, preferably as put forth in manuals, and evaluate its adequacy with respect to narrowly defined clinical criteria. These researchers may acknowledge the existence of anomalous findings that suggest the necessity of considering context (Beach & Broderick, 1983; Whisman & Jacobson, 1990), but generally have not yet been able to include it in their research designs or evaluation methods.

Some specific examples point to the need for contextual consideration. Cultural values make some techniques that are a central focus in marital therapy research (e.g., conflict resolution) inappropriate. For example, for many Latinos a traditional cultural value dominating civil exchanges is that of "saving face" and the communication of respect ("respecto"). Confronting another person requires doing it in a way that is sensitive to these issues, and traditional communication training focusing on "*I* statements" or assertiveness training can easily violate those traditions (see Chapter 19, this volume).

Feminists assert that power relationships constitute a fundamental contextual variable omitted from many analyses of marital patterns, which can be particularly problematic in situations of violence. They argue that typical couples therapy techniques and language, and the traditional research approaches that accompany them, obscure both violence and the responsibility for perpetrating violence by defining marital problems in purely relational terms that presume shared responsibility and power equality. Further, the presence of an abusive pattern puts a couples therapist in an impossible situation; either the truth will not be told or, if it is, the wife (most often) is placed at risk (Avis, 1992; Bograd, 1992; Holtzworth-Munroe, Beatty, & Anglin, in press; Jacobson & Margolin, 1979; Kaufman, 1992).

Failure to deal overtly with a couple's disagreements about power issues may also explain both the temporary nature of many of the successes as well as the reason for many failures. More often than not the wife is more interested in therapy and change than is her husband (Jacobson, 1983, 1989, 1990). Thus the methods of most couples therapies may implicitly shift the power imbalance in favor of the wife, but only temporarily, and only in those cases where the imbalance is moderate. The improvement that occurs may be primarily related to the power shift introduced by therapy and maintained only as long as the therapist is part of the marital system. If power issues are not addressed, they may be responsible for the relapse that occurs in half the couples who show improvement. Unfortunately, this speculation represents a conceptual-analytic explanation only; such important issues await and require more direct empirical evidence. Further, marital problems involving power may center not on behavior per se, but on who determines the rules pertaining to a couple's structure and process (Haley, 1963).

The list of potentially significant contextual variables could be extended. The moral is that parsimony and a clearly limited and defined focus may be a value for the scientific clinical researcher, but raises other problems; context is significant, whether it is the researcher's paradigmatic context or the couple's social and personal context. Not considering context makes it difficult for therapists to translate the generalized conclusions of the researcher into the particularity of the couples and families with whom they work. Little is known about the extent to which the data presented in this chapter generalize to other ethnic and socioeconomic groups and to other forms of committed, long-term relationships. Although research involving these groups is increasing, it is often from a sociological, rather than a psychological, perspective (e.g., Taylor, Chatters, Tucker & Lewis, 1990; Vega, 1990). A few marital researchers have included blue collar couples in their samples (e.g., Krokoff, 1987; Krokoff, Gottman, & Roy, 1988), but virtually no research has specifically examined the effectiveness of marital therapy for couples from various ethnic groups or varying socioeconomic backgrounds. Only the work of Szapocznik and colleagues (1988) with Latino families represents a long-term and programmatic exception in the family field.

Methodological and Measurement Issues

Related to the issues of context and developmental processes are those of measurement and methodology. With respect to marriage therapy, for example, most of the outcome research summarized earlier combines the evaluation of specific domains presumed central to a healthy relationship with self-report measures of the couple's overall marital adjustment or satisfaction. However, these measures also define, by their choice of questions, an implicit view of what marriage ought to be. Although there is some debate in the field about what constitutes successful marital therapy and appropriate outcome measures, the content of the most commonly used measures, the Dyadic Adjustment Scale (DAS; Spanier, 1976) and the Marital Adjustment Test (MAT; Locke & Wallace, 1959), suggest that what might be called blissful enmeshment or codependency is the ultimate outcome goal; high levels of agreement and satisfaction with such an arrangement on matters such as sexual relations, relations with in-laws, and finances lead to the highest adjustment scores. The *process* by which the consensus is reached (intimidation, negotiation, or a basic sharing of values), however, is not addressed, nor is the couple's willingness/ability to tolerate disagreement. This is seen as a conceptual weakness by some feminists and is the basis of the view that such measures support traditional, patriarchal, or even pathological relationship forms (Rampage, 1989; Witkin, 1989a, 1989b). Developmental changes such as those referred to earlier predict increasing differentiation of spouses over time, yet such normative changes are not included in methods of therapy or of measurement of outcome.

Other researchers criticize these measures and question whether only global, summary measures or specific subscale scores on available measures should be used (note the exchange between Kazak, Jarmas, & Snitzer, 1988, and Spanier, 1988, and Thompson, 1988; note also commentaries by Fincham & Bradbury, 1987, and Sabatelli, 1988). As the models of the developmental system theorists suggest, it may be inappropriate to assume any single model or measure of healthy relationships. Despite feminist and other critiques, however, most studies continue to use such measures. It must once again be remembered that the continued use of such measures stems in part from the fact that those critiquing traditional measures have failed to provide new measures and new data that demonstrate a scientifically acceptable alternative for process and outcome research. We cannot merely critique; we must offer rigorous and ethical alternative that still allow for accountability.

Another unresolved question is how to conceptualize and measure *dyadic* satisfaction (Whisman, Jacobson, Fruzzetti, & Waltz, 1989). The normal method yields two scores, one for each partner, which can be averaged to create a composite measure of dyadic satisfaction, subtracted to create a difference score, or kept separate. Combining scores has rather obvious pitfalls; since there are a variety of ways to obtain the same individual score, the number of ways a couple could get a dyad score is multiplied by the same magnitude! Further, analyses of men's and women's responses to evaluation of marital satisfaction reflect apparently quite different dimensions; men tend to emphasize the degree of consensus in evaluating satisfaction, while women reflect a more global evaluation of satisfaction with the relationship (Kazak, 1989). Certainly the issue of constructive conflict needs to be incorporated, if only to recognize that extremely high scores on the DAS and MAT may reflect an absence of any conflict, which could indicate a poor long-term prognosis (a suggestion made by Kazak, Jarmas, & Snitzer, 1989, but rebuffed by Spanier, 1990).

Other measurement concerns pertain to the relative advantages of observational versus self-report measures of marital therapy outcome (e.g., Bradbury & Fincham, 1987; Gottman, 1985; Jacobson, 1985a, 1985b); many researchers use the former measures alone or as a supplement to self-reports. However, observational measures have a number of problems ranging from a poor correspondence between couples' observational ratings of their taped interactions and trained observers' ratings of the same tapes (Beach & Broderick, 1983) to findings that arguments are poor predictors of marital satisfaction 5 years later (Gottman & Krokoff, 1989). Also, behavioral competence apparently does not ensure performance (Jacobson, 1990), suggesting that some other variable drives the negative interchanges and escalations. Such findings seem to point back to the necessity of considering the couple's as well as the researcher's definition of context.

Matching to Sample Philosophy, Qualitative Research, and Context

A fundamental plea in this discussion is for us to become self-conscious about our epistemology. Statistics and research methodology provide a mechanism for epistemological accountability. Although there are limitations in that mechanism, accountability is an ethical necessity. But there are alternative mechanisms as well as ways of using existing methods to deal with some of the issues.

The marital and family therapy literature contains a long debate about the virtues of linear versus systemic epistemologies (Allman, 1982; Andolfi & Angelo, 1988; Auerswald, 1985; Bogdan, 1987; Colapinto, 1979; Dell, 1982; de Shazer, 1988; Falzer, 1984; Keeney & Sprenkle, 1982; Wilder, 1982) that threatens to be repeated in the qualitative versus quantitative domain (Atkinson et al., 1991; Cavell & Snyder, 1991; Moon, Dillon, & Sprenkle, 1990, 1991). Rather than pit one against the other, we would like to suggest alternative ways of approaching quantitative research and a way of thinking about qualitative research as complementary to quantitative.

The concept of "matching-to-sample" represents a contextually sensitive clinical and research philosophy and is thus relevant to clinicians as well as researchers. Matching-to-sample refers to the process of determining the goals and targets of intervention in as context-sensitive a way as possible (Alexander & Parsons, 1982). In adopting this concept, therapists (researchers, policy makers, etc.) must first be aware of their own values with respect to what couples ideally should be.

Using a matching-to-sample approach, researchers and therapists rely on *contextualized* goals which are derived from an appreciation of what *this type* of couple, from *this subculture* with *this system of values and beliefs* looks (acts, feels) like in its normal state; *normal* is defined as the absence of pathology and a sense of general satisfaction for a couple in this particular context. Therapist's choice of intervention models (e.g., behavioral, humanistic, feminist, functional, psychodynamic, structural) depends on the kinds of changes needed to move the family to this contextualized norm; techniques are selected to modify the couple so they approximate the sample of normal, adaptive couples *in their own subculture.* Such a shift forces the therapist and researcher to recognize the limitations (i.e., lack of ecological or external validity) of most traditional research projects, which constitute the bulk of this review and on which most of the conclusions about marital therapy process and outcome efficacy have been based. This more intimate, transactional, and flexible approach to research (e.g., Moon & Sprenkle, 1992; Wark, 1992) requires clinicians and researchers to attend to context, including the biases introduced by all participants (also see Chapter 1, this volume).

The American Psychological Association's Ethical Principles for Psychologists (1992) cautions against the imposition of therapist's values on clients. This caution ought to apply equally to research findings. A discussion of the merits of one or more alternatives regarding what should be therapists' or researchers' resolution of the ethical dilemmas inherent in any situation in which behavior is being described and/or changed is beyond the scope of this chapter. Nonetheless, the insistence that context represent a central aspect of our consideration at least forces therapists and researchers to articulate (at least to themselves) when and why they choose to pursue research definitions or clinical goals that are inconsistent with those of the couples they treat and the cultures in which those couples live. It also forces integration of the perspectives of many disciplines (e.g., anthropology), ways of knowing (e.g., qualitative research, literature), and intervention strategies (multilevel, multisystemic, integrative) at a time when all kinds of research are essential for the field (Moon & Sprenkle, 1992) and a combination of methods provides the most sensitive and productive understanding of process and outcome (Liddle, 1991a).

FAMILY THERAPY

The complexities that exist in marital therapy and marital therapy research are magnified in family therapy for several reasons. As previously discussed, the treatment unit is often much more variable. Issues of gender, ethnicity, and the like are expanded and intensified in the realm of family therapy as, for example, male–female role transactions are expanded into traditional mother–father roles. In addition, the range of syndromes treated in family therapy and the number of therapy models used to treat them are greater, reflecting differences in evolution. Marital therapy was able to evolve along generic lines in addressing relational issues such as marital dysfunction, marital distress, and marital conflict. Family therapy, in contrast, evolved as an alternative to more traditional (especially individually based) ways of thinking about and treating specific syndromes, often of children and adolescents, such as schizophrenia (e.g., Haley, 1963), childhood brittle diabetes and eating disorders (e.g., Minuchin, 1974), and juvenile delinquency (Alexander & Parsons, 1973; Stuart, 1971). This resulted in a proliferation of model variations and treatment foci considerably greater than those of marital therapy (Shadish et al., 1993).

To add to the complexity of the situation, funding agencies are enamored with manualized treatments, yet such an a priori or linear philosophy is inconsistent with the current clinical *zeitgeist* in family therapy. Many current, presumably state-of-the-art, family therapies emphasize decision-making processes that lead to wide variations in therapist behavior. These variations are influenced, driven, or cocreated by client variables and interactive processes that often cannot be ascertained prior to and independently of the actual transaction. For example, Pinsof (in press) detailed a sequential decision-making process that could lead two therapists, using the same generic integrative model with the same presenting complaint, to apply very different techniques with very different foci (e.g., relational here and now as opposed to individual and historical) and with different members of the therapy system. Liddle (1991a), in a similar vein, described a multidimensional family therapy model (MDFT) in which a second session could involve an adolescent (identified patient) alone, the adolescent with parent(s) and/or other family members, or other variations.

Such integrative approaches are very much in keeping with a systemic perspective in that decisions are a function of the transactional process between therapist and family member(s). Unfortunately, this perspective makes a priori operational definitions almost impossible. Thus the traditional approach to research is more consistent with the behavioral marital therapies reviewed here and is much more conceptually appropriate for component analyses (dismantling strategies), the search for common effective ingredients (Gurman et al., 1986), and the orderly search for process measures and traditional end-point outcome measures. In contrast, understanding the processes involved in the interactive, multilevel, and often multisystemic new wave family therapies seems, to many clinicians and theorists, to be much more suited to clinically oriented formats, such as workshops, case-study narratives, and qualitative research.

Methodological and statistical complexities also make family therapy research more difficult than marital therapy research to design and to understand. Data-analytic strategies and interpretations become considerably more complex when the unit of analysis moves from an interacting dyad to a larger unit. For example, many of the lag-sequential analyses that have the potential to capture the interdependency (reciprocal influence vs. auto-correlations) of marital interactions lose much of their meaning when the interacting unit increases from two to three or more, and when the meaning units that are coded become more molecular (i.e., coding thought units rather than speeches, and using complex or multiple codes). Many of these same issues obviously also pertain to group therapy research (see Chapter 15, this volume).

Finally, as awkward as it is to deal with the relationship between couple members' perceptions of their relationship (see the earlier discussion of marital satisfaction inventories), the interpretive problems escalate dramatically when researchers try to relate the perceptions of three or more family members, especially when the perceptions of most children are heavily influenced by developmental differences in cognitive processes.

We have raised and reiterated issues of increased complexity and controversy regarding family therapy (and accompanying research) in order to put this review in context, not to negate it. Stated bluntly, we agree with Beavers's (1991) statement that "We hurt people when we are too certain of our theories and when we continue to teach absolutes *without supportive data and without outcome studies to guide us* [italics added]" (p. 20). Unfortunately, we can also hurt people when we base decisions solely on outcome studies (even well-designed and scientifically sophisticated ones) that demonstrate treatment effectiveness using variables that are insensitive to, or perhaps even reflect, unacceptably configured power relationships and are insensitive to issues of gender, race, culture, sexual preference, and the like. We cannot take too much comfort in preferring a scientifically supported approach over one without empirical support one way or another when the supported one still fails in a significant proportion of cases and

has not been applied to many of the populations we hope to treat. Perhaps we need to focus more attention on developing acceptable methodologies that might be more likely to make research clinically relevant, *and* clinical practice accountable.

Since qualitative research has its limitations (e.g., see Liddle, 1991b) and has provided more criticism of existing process–outcome research than constructive alternatives (unfortunately, the conclusions made by Gurman et al., 1986, still seem appropriate), there are no clear solutions. However, we hope that eventually various approaches to research can interactively advance our knowledge base. Qualitative research may generate a rich source of contextualized information which can be used to generate hypotheses and refine methods. Another approach, introduced but not discussed extensively in earlier sections, is meta-analysis; this method allows us to evaluate general effectiveness using traditional research methodologies, but it disembeds the conclusions from the contextual issues particular to individual studies. A final exciting approach integrates process and outcome research with clinical model building and technique adapted to demonstrated relevant contextual variables. We discuss these two approaches in sequence.

Qualitative Research and Meta-Analysis: Into or Beyond Context

Proponents of both qualitative research (a microanalytic and recursive research philosophy) and meta-analysis (a macroanalytic data strategy in which the researcher can be far removed from actual subjects or clients) have criticized traditional single-study outcome designs. Both have argued that traditional data-analytic methods derive from an excessive emphasis on logical positivism and have thereby slowed the progress of knowledge (e.g., see Schmidt, 1992). As a more appropriate alternative to developing theory, qualitative researchers have argued for the utility of a contextualized and intensive narrative focus with as little as a single subject. In stark contrast, proponents of meta-analysis have argued that the only way to provide the appropriate empirical building blocks for theory development is to employ statistical analyses that can clean up large data sets collected across various studies, even those mixed with respect to randomization versus quasi-experimental design (Schmidt, 1992). They have argued that meta-analysis provides an appropriate solution to the problem of Type II error and the excessive reliance on data derived from single studies that generally suffer from sampling and measurement errors to some extent.

Of course, meta-analysis, like every other approach to understanding data, has its limitations; the conclusions of meta-analysis can only be as solid as the accumulated quality of the individual studies that provide the constituent data sets. And although meta-analysis researchers in family therapy have weighted studies according to their sample size, as yet none have weighted the studies according to methodological quality. Instead, the two major meta-analytic studies of family therapy effectiveness have attempted to ensure the quality of constituent studies by including only a subset of available studies based on such criteria as published studies with at least one control group (Hazelrigg et al., 1987) or studies that represent randomized trials (Shadish, in press).

Despite what may be seen as limitations, meta-analysis represents a new conceptual and statistical tool for researchers and reviewers in determining the general efficacy of family therapy (Kazdin, 1993). As argued by Hazelrigg et al. (1987), the traditional narrative method of summary and integration (e.g., used by Gurman et al., 1986, as well as the 22 previous reviews identified therein) may fail to provide efficient mechanisms for synthesizing data from different studies. We therefore review here the general conclusions of the two major meta-analyses of family therapy efficacy.

At the most general level the conclusions of the Hazelrigg et al. (1987) and the Shadish et al. (1993) meta-analytic studies of family therapy outcome are remarkably similar to those of the Gurman et al. (1986) and numerous other reviews; namely, family therapy has positive effects compared with no-treatment and alternative-treatment controls. However, in some studies the alternative treatments were only attention or placebo treatments such as bibliotherapy (Hazelrigg et al., 1987). Hazelrigg and colleagues also found a trend toward decreasing differences between family therapy and alternative treatments as follow-up periods lengthened. Thus, conclusions regarding the superiority of family therapy must be tempered somewhat. Proponents of meta-analysis have reasserted the need for more research that meets the familiar (but still rarely attained) methodological standards identified in earlier reviews (e.g., Gurman et al., 1986) such as inclusion of control or comparison groups, especially those that represent realistic alternative treatments; multilevel (individual, marital, family system, and even larger system based) indexes of change derived from multiple vantage points; clear identification of procedures (independent variables or treatments, measurement instruments, and statistical operations) at all levels; better integration of process and outcome measures (e.g., pre-, during, post-, and multiple follow-up period

assessments to provide more fluid and more complete indexes of the change process); and more internally consistent, theory-related measures applied across studies to facilitate generalization across studies and populations.

Not surprisingly, meta-analytic researchers have also echoed Gurman and colleagues' (Gurman, 1983; Gurman et al., 1986) assertions that "standard research methods are the only ethically responsible means currently available for evaluating family therapy outcomes" (Hazelrigg et al., 1987, p. 440).

Based on approximations of these standards, existing research suggests that, as a general intervention strategy, family therapy is a viable and perhaps even preferred vehicle for positive change, with no indications that it represents an undesirable alternative to no treatment or alternative treatments.

Beyond the most general conclusion of effectiveness, it appears that certain family-based models are more effective than others. Hazelrigg et al. (1987) found support for the efficacy of the pragmatic family therapies (primarily structural, strategic, and behavioral) and concluded that "family therapies do work, in their general form, and seem to work better than some alternative treatments" (p. 440). The more recent meta-analysis by Shadish et al. (1993) included many more studies and found a similar pattern of support for some approaches and little to no support for others. In particular, outcome studies involving psychodynamic approaches were still almost nonexistent, and the humanistic approaches failed to produce any significant effect sizes. The other generic approaches demonstrated overall efficacy, although Shadish et al. found that behaviorally oriented family therapies outperformed humanistic, eclectic, and other therapies, but not systemic therapies, when compared directly with one another.

This conclusion by Shadish et al. (1993) represents a challenge to the so-called aesthetic family therapies, therapies that were not even included in the Hazelrigg et al. (1987) review because there were no outcome studies reflecting that general perspective! Based on the new epistemologies (Hoffman, 1981), these "aesthetic" family therapies are derived from phenomenological, psychodynamic, existential, and systems perspectives and argue that an immediate focus on symptoms with the goal of rapid alleviation is inappropriate and perhaps even unethical (Keeney & Sprenkle, 1982). As previously mentioned, although proponents of these aesthetic family therapies have raised valid criticisms of current research, they have to date not offered acceptable alternative avenues to accountability.

Shadish et al. thus reiterated previously expressed concerns about the future of some forms of family therapy based on their lack of representation or empirical support in the outcome literature. However, they also provided an interesting alternative to the conclusion that some therapies work better than others. Specifically, they concluded that when comparative analyses include adjustments for covariates, the differences between models disappear! The unadjusted differences found between clinical models are, according to mediational analyses proposed by Shadish et al., perhaps a function of choices made by researchers of different theoretical orientations in designing and conducting the outcome research. This reframes the assertion of therapist allegiance made by Jacobsen and Addis (1993) about similar findings in marital therapy outcome research. Shadish et al., however, refined the assertion by arguing that behavioral researchers (the most consistently effective approach) paid careful attention to standardizing and implementing treatment (which increases effect size) and chose dependent measures (in particular behavioral vs. nonbehavioral measures; ratings by others vs. self-reports; more reactive measures; measures specifically tailored to the behavioral targets of treatment rather than general well-being) that seem to result in higher effect sizes. Shadish et al. (1993) further concluded that if all treatments were similarly designed, implemented, measured, and reported, significant differences between orientations might not be found.

At the same time, Shadish (in press) pointed out that in some analyses "behavioral orientations (and some other within-orientation comparisons) outperform non-behavioral orientations" when one component is pitted against another. According to Shadish then, global orientation may not represent the distinguishing characteristic between effective versus noneffective interventions. Instead, effectiveness may be a function of one technique or a combination of certain techniques within a general orientation. This hypothesis remains to be tested and is dependent on clinician-researchers being able and willing to develop high-quality research projects that undertake component analyses. To date most clinical researchers in the family therapy field have not been willing to do so.

In light of the issues already discussed, the conclusions of meta-analytic approaches present an interesting dilemma. Specifically, approaches that involve concrete a priori prescribed (i.e., manualized) treatment operations and dependent measures are those that demonstrate clinical effectiveness. At the same time, those very same approaches (and their underlying philosophy) have

been the object of criticism by the many outsider groups described in earlier sections. If those critical groups can help responsive clinician-researchers develop more appropriate (but still rigorous and independently accountable) designs and measures, family therapy can reestablish the clinical research base that characterized its beginnings and facilitated its tremendous growth as an intervention approach (Gurman et al., 1986). If, however, the majority of family therapy clinicians reject or otherwise become estranged from research as *one* of the essential sources of input to clinical practice, the field will lose one of its major sources of legitimacy, corrective feedback, and accountability. Like some others (e.g., Liddle, 1991b; McFall, 1991), we find this a dreadful option for the future.

The question thus becomes: Why should (or how can) research represent a major credible source of expertise for clinicians that is at least as compelling as a persuasive case example or a workshop presented by a charismatic leader? Researchers cannot simply berate clinicians into relying on the research literature, or subtly (and not so subtly) imply that a lack of a research base places the clinician at the edge of irresponsibility. Instead, research programs have to be able to answer the "What do I do now" question based on meaningful process and outcome research data. To do so, programs must satisfy several general criteria:

1. Does the program target a clinically meaningful syndrome or situation?

2. Is there a coherent conceptual framework underlying the clinical interventions?

3. Are the specific interventions, and the therapist qualities necessary to carry them out, described somewhere with sufficient detail and clinical meaningfulness that other clinicians can attempt them without too much guesswork? Further, do these descriptions cover most of what *actually occurs* in the intervention process? Because the traditional research journal format does not allow for this level of dissemination, in addition to presenting the research data per se, clinical researchers are going to have to ensure the availability of clinically compelling treatment manuals, books, workshops, and videotaped examples in order to address the needs of clinicians.

4. Does the process research, whether qualitative or quantitative in nature, demonstrate *how* the process works?

5. Does the process and outcome research demonstrate *that* it works (this might be called the internal validity issue)?

6. Are questions being raised about, and perhaps even attempts made to demonstrate, generalizability to other populations (i.e., external validity)?

One final problem facing evaluators of family therapy techniques and models has already been mentioned, the fact that many current models are less undimensional and doctrinaire than in the past. As pointed out by Shadish et al. (1993), since theoretical orientation is no longer easily coded in this "age of eclecticism and integration," the multiple studies included in some of the major categories (e.g., behavioral, humanistic, strategic, etc.) often differ from one another in important ways that are not considered in the meta-analysis. Thus the general picture derived from meta-analyses is at best only a fuzzy approximation, with considerable within-cell variability, of any particular variant of a generic model. In addition, as models continue to evolve along integrative lines, meta-analyses will become increasingly removed from what actually occurs in therapy. At this point, we can only identify, as Gurman et al. (1986) did, examples of promising clinical models based on their developing research base. The clinical-research programs briefly described here are beginning to show promise as sources of credible knowledge for clinicians, as well as for other clinician-researchers who are attempting to develop new clinical models and/or a more rigorous context for already developed ones.

Some Exemplary Integrative Programs
The most promising programs integrate process and outcome research with clinical model building and technique development. Information from successes and failures is integrated into refinements of both the model and its related techniques; thus the research is not only evaluating program outcome, but it also refines clinical technique. The information from these programs is thus richer and potentially more useful than that provided by single studies.

One of the most (if not the most) consistent, long-term, and respected clinical research programs is that of Gerald Patterson and his colleagues at the Oregon Social Learning Center (OSLC). This program was represented in the Shadish et al. (1993), Gurman et al. (1986), and Kazdin (1993) reviews and is notable for its continuing contributions in four major domains: (1) outcome research, (2) process research, (3) model building with respect to both of those activities as well as basic research into dysfunctional family process (e.g., Patterson, 1985), and (4) absolute insistence on rigor and conservatism when conducting and evaluating research.

The outcome research, particularly with aggressive children and more recently with preadolescents, continues to demonstrate the absolute and comparative efficacy of social learning–based parent training interventions (Dishion, Patterson, & Kavanaugh, in press; Patterson, Reid, & Dishion, in press). The preadolescent clinical population demands increasingly creative intervention techniques (Reid & Patterson, 1992) that push the limits of what can now be called a traditional, social learning–based parent training model. The work of the OSLC group has been augmented by other groups, some working independently and others trained directly in the OSLC model, all adhering to the same general principles. An example is time-limited social learning therapy with second through sixth grade boys, which in contrast to randomly assigned wait-list controls produced posttreatment and follow-up positive changes in child behavior at home and school (Sayger, Horne, Walker, & Passmore, 1988). Process measures involving independent observer coding and parent reports also demonstrated improvement in various aspects of family relationships. McMahon and Wells (1989) and Patterson, Dishion, and Chamberlain (1992) have provided excellent summaries of the history of and recent developments in parent training with oppositional and aggressive children.

By focusing on therapy process, Patterson and Chamberlain (1992) have isolated significant contextual influences on outcome; in response, they have developed a model of parent resistance that identifies both parent-centered (e.g., depression) and bidirectional (e.g., therapist behaviors differentially produce resistant behaviors and parent resistance influences therapist behavior) influences. Using a combination of various theoretical and empirical sources (e.g., Domjan & Burkhard, 1986; Forgatch, Ray, & Patterson, 1992), their own clinical experience, and a variety of sophisticated data analytic techniques, these authors have evolved a sophisticated (and parent-gender sensitive) model of clinical process that promises to meet researchers' needs for rigor and replicability, clinicians' needs for clinical sensitivity and utility, and funding agencies' needs for accountability.

A second program with a long history of research rigor, theoretical development, and successful clinical application has focused on Latino behavior-problem youth and their families (Szapocznik, Kurtines, Santisteban, & Rio, 1990). This program, like that of the OSLC, has retained a singular theoretical orientation — in this case structural family therapy. Also like the OSLC group, Szapocznik et al. (1988) have gone far beyond traditional practices to increase clinical sensitivity and effectiveness; like the Oregon group they have paid attention to contextual variables affecting client response to their methods. For example, with Latino drug abusing adolescents and their families, Szapocznik et al., (1988) developed and empirically evaluated different cultural engagement strategies prior to any traditional structural family therapy. Blending culturally sensitive clinical experience with a theoretical model of resistance, these authors more than doubled the rate of client engagement in therapy (to over 92%) and significantly increased their impact on therapy outcome measures as well. Further, Szapocznik et al. (1990) demonstrated the superiority of their family therapy condition over individual child psychodynamic therapy but found that the relationship between process and outcome was not entirely consistent with a traditional structural family therapy model. In addition to such quantitative-research–based findings, these authors identified four clinically based, theoretically coherent, and qualitatively derived types of resistant families and developed intervention strategies for each.

A third clinical research program, functional family therapy (FFT) (Alexander & Parsons, 1982; Barton & Alexander, 1981), was also represented in the Shadish et al. (1993) and Gurman et al. (1986) reviews. Previously limited by the population characteristics in their early process–outcome research (i.e., status offender adolescents in Caucasian families, 60% of whom were Mormon; Alexander & Parsons), 1973; Parsons & Alexander, 1973, this model underwent several replications with more diverse and much more seriously disturbed populations. For example, Barton and colleagues (Barton, Alexander, Waldron, Turner, & Warburton, 1985) included a sample of multiply offending (over 20 prior adjudicated offenses) hardcore delinquents, all of whom were in maximum security prison wards prior to intervention. Gordon, Arbuthnot, Gustofson, and McGreen (1988) applied the principles of the earlier FFT work to a rural Ohio population. Both these studies demonstrated significant superiority of family-based intervention over alternative treatments, treatments that in both studies were actual (not artificially created), ongoing programs in the respective communities.

As with the OSLC and Szapocznik et al. (1988) programs, evaluation of outcome efficacy of the functional family therapy (FFT) program is giving way to evaluation of the process variables influencing outcome. Process research (e.g., Newberry, Alexander, & Turner, 1991) has begun to identify in-session therapist behaviors such as structuring and supportiveness that influence family members'

responsiveness. More importantly, this research has begun to identify interactions between therapist gender, family member gender, and therapist behavior. These interactions (e.g., female therapist supportive behaviors elicit significantly higher conditional probabilities of family supportive responses than do supportive responses of male therapists, whereas therapist structuring behaviors do not demonstrate this gender-based difference; fathers respond positively to therapist structuring behaviors whereas mothers do not) suggest that writing treatment manuals without considering the effects of such therapist characteristics as gender ignores important, and perhaps critical, components of treatment delivery. However, few treatment manuals include systematic attention to such variables. In another study, Newberry, Alexander, and Liddle (1988) demonstrated that, in first family therapy sessions with a delinquent sample, warm statements alone did not increase client acceptance, whereas warm humor (a form of reframing) did. This possibly counterintuitive pattern represents an example of how process research can actually inform clinicians about processes that are not always clearly identified in the clinical literature.

The FFT group has also used an alternative method for hypothesis testing and model building, namely, analogue research. For example, Morris, Alexander, and Turner (1991) compared the effect of positive reframes versus no information and an attention placebo condition on a college sample in whom a negative set about members of a family had been induced. Results indicated that reframes indeed significantly reduce blaming attributions, not only about the target of the reframe, but about other family members as well. Although not an in vivo demonstration, this carefully controlled study provides strong support for a clinical technique that is quite popular but has received little research attention.

The OSLC, Szapocznik et al. (1988), and FFT programs have been highlighted for several reasons, including the fact that each represents one of the pragmatic types of successful therapy identified by Shadish et al. (1993) and Hazelrigg et al. (1987). Each has a long history of demonstrating a blend of scientific rigor, clinical and contextual sensitivity, and continuous evolution of process and outcome data, all of which reciprocally influence each other. At the same time that all three programs have shown openness to input from clinical *and* scientific sources, they have also retained a theoretical center of gravity that has forced them to keep their assumptions, techniques, and results internally consistent. All three programs have developed treatment manuals but have emphasized the importance of therapists' sensitivity to client characteristics and reciprocal client–therapist influences, with flexibility within the constraints of the therapy manuals. In fact, the FFT model (Alexander, Barton, Waldron, & Mas, 1983) specifically articulates different phases of intervention, the first major phase (induction, or therapy) being characterized by contingent directiveness, which in turn is determined by the matching-to-sample philosophy discussed earlier. This concept requires that the therapist base all his or her behaviors on understanding and showing respect for the family reality, which includes the value system, cultural context, and experiential nature of all family members. Only after creating a positive climate based on this understanding and respect (not unlike the hypothesized effects of empathy and joining), and thereby changing the emotional and perceptual bases that family members use to experience themselves and each other, can therapists begin to focus on changing family members' long-term maladaptive behaviors and interaction patterns (Alexander, 1992).

Although all three programs described here have manuals, are evaluation oriented, and have demonstrated rigorously evaluated comparative treatment efficacy, they nonetheless reflect a commitment to clinical sensitivity consistent with the needs of practitioners. At the level of research, these programs reflect a constructive alternative to the debate between box score (see Gurman et al., 1986) outcome research approaches versus the anti-empirical approaches that sometimes seem to underlie the clinician-researcher splits already discussed. Greenberg (1991) has offered a similar alternative, proposing that in order to understand clinical intervention we should engage in *process analytic research* to attempt to identify processes that discriminate between positive and negative outcomes *within* a given intervention model. This type of research is process centered: it focuses on context (that is, clinically defined therapeutic episodes); it is discovery oriented (in identifying patterns and regularities); and it leads to model building. Greenberg argues it must also satisfy more traditional scientific criteria by being deducible from theory, by demonstrating control, and by being able to survive hypothetico-deductive challenge (Greenberg, 1991). Approaches such as these respect *all* sources of knowledge and force us to rely singularly on none. Further, they create a higher level of meaning by integrating information from all sources, by articulating the context in which the information is developed, and by developing formal conceptual relationships among the various types and levels of information. Such a philosophy, informed by clinical experience *and* good theory *and* rigorous re-

search, must guide future activities in family therapy.

CONCLUSIONS

As implied at the beginning of this chapter, we have consciously taken a different approach from that of our predecessors. Particularly with respect to family therapy, discussion has been less comparative and evaluative at the level of specific studies using different intervention models with particular clinical syndromes. This is in part due to the fact that the intervening years between the preceding and the current edition of this chapter have not produced a dramatically different pattern than existed in 1986; the same generic family-based programs emerge as empirically supported in 1993. At the same time, the approach we chose emphasizes that those programs are more promising at the comparative rather than at the absolute level, since many failures still occur. Thus we have chosen to shift our focus to contextual issues possibly related to the failures, and to research programs that attempt to systematically identify and address these issues in process modification.

This chapter has been more evaluative and even confrontational with respect to the role of research in the field of family therapy. The majority of research to date suffers from many limitations and has the potential to be dangerously misleading. At the same time, abandoning research-based accountability as a central theme in the field would be devastating. As a result, the emphasis has been on understanding the limits of current research practices, while suggesting that certain avenues to family therapy practice appear much more promising than others. There are examples of enduring research-based clinical intervention models that at least begin to bridge the gap between scientific demands for rigor and clinical demands for responsiveness and immediacy. Careful attention to developmental issues, to context and process, and to longitudinal patterns, particularly in those instances where our models fail, may identify the variables that can create that bridge.

This emphasis has resulted in giving less attention to some very good recent work which is worth noting. For example, although the difficulties in categorizing some of the newer hybrid models has been mentioned, such promising work as that represented in Joanning, Quinn, Thomas, and Mullen (1992) has not been described in detail. Their family systems therapy represents an integration of structural and strategic family therapy models and appears to have the potential to emerge as an effective intervention with families of drug-abusing youth. The work of Henggeler, Melton, and Smith (1992) represents another structural/strategic integration, with a social ecology (i.e., Bronfenbrenner, 1979) framework guiding their multisystemic therapy (MST). Like the integrative multidimensional family therapy (MDFT) of Liddle (1991a), which emphasizes cultural sensitivity, Henggeler et al.'s work shows tremendous promise with substance-abusing youth. These models represent a new wave of theoretically and technically integrative approaches that engage very difficult treatment populations and have the potential to advance our understanding of the multilevel nature of therapeutic change.

Three additional major concerns remain. First, although females have provided leading roles in the projects just described, the programs are generally linked to males, usually white. Why does this pattern exist alongside the fact that many of the creative, competent, and articulate women in the field have represented the nontraditional research views discussed? What factors contribute to the paucity of process–outcome research programs from these perspectives?

A second concern is the general lack of attention to developmental issues (see Kazdin, 1993) in both marital and family therapy research. Developmental theory and research provide potentially significant sources of information that could be used to refine both technique and measurement.

The third concern is that the research programs and studies that have been reviewed here and elsewhere have consistently ignored issues of comorbidity—a problem that "clean" research projects usually avoid but that frequently (if not usually) faces the clinician (Kazdin, 1993). Readers are urged to review the recent special issue of the *Journal of Consulting and Clinical Psychology* (1992) on comorbidity. This review identifies many issues that must be addressed by family-based intervention models, but that to date have not been well represented in the traditional family therapy literature.

Finally, we have not provided a tabular summary evaluating more or less effective programs as has been done in the past (Gurman et al., 1986) to avoid creating an inappropriately static flavor in a review that has focused on the dynamic, evolutionary, and controversial nature of family therapy as it now exists. As mentioned at the outset, we wanted to avoid creating a sense of coherence when one, in fact, doesn't exist. What does exist is considerable promise based on both long-standing and more recently developed programs, standing side by side with considerable criticism and lack of utilization of

research findings. We hope this chapter, with this approach, might provide the impetus for accelerated growth, especially in the development of research findings that reflect both rigor and clinical utility.

REFERENCES

AFTA Newsletter (1992, Spring), 47.

Alexander, J. F. (1992, October). *Conflicted families with acting-out adolescents.* "Learning Edge" presentation at the annual convention of the American Association for Marital and Family Therapy, Miami Beach, FL.

Alexander, J. F., Barton, C., Waldron, H., & Mas, C. H. (1983). Beyond the technology of family therapy: The anatomy of intervention model. In K. D. Craig & R. J. McMahon (Eds.), *Advances in clinical behavior therapy.* New York: Brunner/Mazel.

Alexander, J. F., & Parsons, B. V. (1973). Short-term behavioral intervention with delinquent families: Impact on family process and recidivism. *Journal of Abnormal Psychology, 81*(3), 219–225.

Alexander, J. F., & Parsons, B. V. (1982). *Functional family therapy: Principles and procedures.* Carmel, CA: Brooks/Cole.

Allgood, S. M., & Crane, D. R. (1991). Predicting marital therapy dropouts. *Journal of Marital and Family Therapy, 17*(1), 73–79.

Allman, L. R. (1982). The poetic mind: Further thoughts on an "aesthetic preference." *Family Process, 21*, 415–428.

Anderson, S. A., Atilano, R. B., Bergen, L. P., Russell, C. S., & Jurich, A. P. (1985). Dropping out of marriage and family therapy: Intervention strategies and spouses' perceptions. *American Journal of Family Therapy, 13*(1), 39–54.

Andolfi, M., & Angelo, C. (1988). Toward constructing the therapeutic system. *Journal of Marital and Family Therapy, 14*(3), 237–247.

Arnow, B. A., Taylor, C. B., Agras, W. S., & Telch, M. J. (1985). Enhancing agoraphobia treatment outcome by changing couple communication patterns. *Behavior Therapy, 16*, 452–467.

Atkinson, B. J., Heath, A. W., & Chenail, R. (1991). Qualitative research and the legitimization of knowledge. *Journal of Marital and Family Therapy, 17*, 161–166.

Auerswald, E. H. (1985). Thinking about thinking in family therapy. *Family Process, 24*, 1–12.

Avis, J. M. (1992). Where are all the family therapists? Abuse and violence within families and family therapy's response. *Journal of Marital and Family Therapy, 18*, 223–230.

Azrin, N. H., Besalel, V. A., Bechtel, R., Michalicek, A., Mancera, M., Carroll, D., Shuford, D., & Cox, J. (1980). Comparison of reciprocity and discussion-type counseling for marital problems. *American Journal of Family Therapy, 8*, 31–38.

Azrin, N. H., Sisson, R. W., Meyers, R., & Godley, M. (1982). Alcoholism treatment by disulfiram and community reinforcement therapy. *Journal of Behavior Therapy and Experimental Psychiatry, 13*(2), 105–112.

Barlow, D. H., O'Brien, G. T., & Last, C. G. (1984). Couples treatment of agoraphobia. *Behavior Therapy, 15*, 41–58.

Barlow, D. H., O'Brien, G. T., Last, C. G., & Holden, A. E.

(1983). Couples treatment of agoraphobia: Initial outcome. In K. D. Craig & R. J. McMahon (Eds.), *Advances in clinical behavior therapy*. New York: Brunner/Mazel.

Barton, C., & Alexander, J. F. (1981). Functional family therapy. In A. S. Gurman & D. P. Kniskern (Eds.), *Handbook of family therapy*. New York: Brunner/Mazel.

Barton, C., Alexander, J. F., Waldron, H., Turner, C. W., & Warburton, J. (1985). Generalizing treatment effects of functional family therapy: Three replications. *American Journal of Family Therapy* 13(3), 16–26.

Baucom, D. H. (1982). A comparison of behavioral contracting and problem solving/communications training in behavioral marital therapy. *Behavior Therapy, 13*, 162–174.

Baucom, D. H. (1984). The active ingredients of behavioral marital therapy: The effectiveness of problem-solving/communication training, contingency contracting, and their combination. In K. Hahlweg & N. S. Jacobson (Eds.), *Marital interaction: Analysis and modification*. New York: Guilford.

Baucom, D. H., & Aiken, P. A. (1984). Sex role identity, marital satisfaction, and response to behavioral marital therapy. *Journal of Consulting and Clinical Psychology, 52*, 438–444.

Baucom, D. H., & Epstein, N. (1990). *Cognitive-behavioral marital therapy*. New York: Brunner/Mazel.

Baucom, D. H., & Epstein, N. (1991). Will the real cognitive-behavioral marital therapy please stand up? *Journal of Family Psychology, 4*(4), 394–401.

Baucom, D. H., Epstein, N., Sayers, S., & Sher, T. G. (1989). The role of cognitions in marital relationships: Definitional, methodological and conceptual issues. *Journal of Consulting and Clinical Psychology, 57*, 31–38.

Baucom, D. H., & Hoffman, J. A. (1986). The effectiveness of marital therapy: Current status and application to the clinical setting. In N. S. Jacobson & A. Gurman (Eds.), *Clinical handbook of marital therapy* (pp. 597–620). New York: Guilford.

Baucom, D. H., & Lester, G. W. (1986). The usefulness of cognitive restructuring as an adjunct to behavioral marital therapy. *Behavior Therapy, 17*, 385–403.

Baucom, D. H., & Mehlman, S. K. (1984). Predicting marital status following behavioral marital therapy: A comparison of models of marital relationships. In K. Hahlweg & N. S. Jacobson (Eds.), *Marital interaction: Analysis and modification*. New York: Guilford.

Baucom, D. H., Sayers, S. L., & Sher, T. G. (1990). Supplementing behavioral marital therapy with cognitive restructuring and emotional expressiveness training: An outcome investigation. *Journal of Consulting and Clinical Psychology, 58*(5), 636–645.

Beach, S. R., & Broderick, J. E. (1983). Commitment: A variable in women's response to marital therapy. *American Journal of Family Therapy, 11*, 16–24.

Beavers, R. (1991, Spring). A personal view of science and family therapy. *AFTA Newsletter, 43*, 19–20.

Beck, A. (1988). *Love is never enough*. New York: Harper & Row.

Behrens, B. C., Sanders, M. R., & Halford, W. K. (1990). Behavioral marital therapy: An evaluation of treatment effects across high and low risk settings. *Behavior Therapy, 21*, 423–433.

Bell, R. A., Daly, J. A., & Gonzalez, M. C. (1987). Affinity-maintenance in marriage and its relationship to women's marital satisfaction. *Journal of Marriage and the Family, 49*, 445–454.

Boelens, W., Emmelkamp, P., MacGillavry, D., & Markvoort, M. (1980). A clinical evaluation of marital treatment: Reciprocity counseling versus system-theoretic counseling. *Behavioral Analysis and Modification, 4*, 85–96.

Bogdan, J. (1987). "Epistemology" as a semantic pollutant. *Journal of Marital and Family Therapy, 13*, 27–35.

Bograd, M. (1992). Values in conflict: Challenges to family therapist's thinking. *Journal of Marital and Family Therapy, 18*, 243–253.

Bourgeois, L., Sabourin, S., & Wright, J. (1990). Predictive validity of therapeutic alliance in group marital therapy. *Journal of Consulting and Clinical Psychology, 58*(5), 608–613.

Bowen, M. (1978). *Family therapy in clinical practice*. New York: Jason Aronson.

Bradbury, T. N., & Fincham, F. D. (1987). Assessing the effects of behavioral marital therapy: Assumptions and measurement strategies. *Clinical Psychology Review, 7*, 525–538.

Bradbury, T. N., & Fincham, F. D. (1990). Attributions in marriage: Review and critique. *Psychological Bulletin, 107*, 3–33.

Bronfenbrenner, U. (1977). Toward an experimental ecology of human development. *American Psychologist, 32*(7), 513–531.

Brown, T. A., & Barlow, D. H. (in press). Long-term outcome following cognitive-behavioral treatment of panic disorder and panic disorder with agoraphobia. In P. H. Wilson (Ed.), *Relapse prevention in cognitive and behavior therapy*. New York: Garland Press.

Burton, G., & Kaplan, H. M. (1968). Group counseling in conflicted marriages where alcoholism is present: Client's evaluation of effectiveness. *Journal of Marriage and the Family, 30*, 74–79.

Cadogan, D. A. (1973). Marital group therapy in the treatment of alcoholism. *Quarterly Journal of Studies on Alcohol, 34*, 1187–1194.

Cavell, T. A., & Snyder, D. K. (1991). Iconoclasm versus innovation: Building a science of family therapy. *Journal of Marital and Family Therapy, 17*, 167–171.

Cerny, J. A., Barlow, D. H., Craske, M. G., & Himadi, W. G. (1987). Couples treatment of agoraphobia: A two-year follow-up. *Behavior Therapy, 18*, 401–415.

Christensen, A., & Heavey, C. L. (1990). Gender and social structure in the demand/withdraw pattern of marital conflict. *Journal of Personality and Social Psychology, 59*(1), 73–81.

Christensen, A., & Shenk, J. L. (1991). Communication, conflict, and psychological distance in nondistressed, clinic, and divorcing couples. *Journal of Consulting and Clinical Psychology, 59*(3), 458–463.

Christensen, L., & Mendoza, J. L. (1986). A method of assessing change in a single subject: An alteration of the RC index. *Behavior Therapy, 17*, 305–308.

Cobb, J. P., Mathews, A. M., Childs-Clarke, M. G., & Blowers, C. M. (1984). The spouse as co-therapist in the treatment of agoraphobia. *British Journal of Psychiatry, 144*, 282–287.

Colapinto, J. (1979). The relative value of empirical evidence. *Family Process, 18*, 427–441.

Corder, B. F., Corder, R. F., & Laidlaw, N. D. (1972). An intensive treatment program for alcoholics and their wives. *Quarterly Journal of Studies on Alcohol, 33*, 1144–1146.

Coyne, J. C. (1990). Concepts for understanding marriage and developing techniques of marital therapy: Cognition uber alles? *Journal of Family Psychology, 4*(2), 185–194.

Crane, D. R., Newfield, N., & Armstrong, D. (1984). Predicting divorce at marital therapy intake: Wives' distress and the marital status inventory. *Journal of Marital and Family Therapy, 10*(3), 305–312.

Craske, M. G., Burton, T., & Barlow, D. H. (1989). Relationships among measures of communication, marital satisfaction and exposure during couples treatment of agoraphobia. *Behavior Research Therapy, 27*(2), 131–140.

Crowe, M. J. (1978). Conjoint marital therapy: A controlled outcome study. *Psychological Medicine, 8*, 623–636.

Dattilio, F. M., & Padesky, C. A. (1990). *Cognitive therapy with couples.* Saratoga, FL: Professional Resource Exchange.

Dell, P. F. (1982). Beyond homeostasis: Toward a concept of coherence. *Family Process, 21*(1), 21–42.

de Shazer, S. (1988). *Clues: Investigating solutions in brief therapy.* New York: W. W. Norton.

Dishion, T. J., Patterson, G. R., & Kavanagh, K. (in press). An experimental test of the coercion model: Linking theory, measurement, and intervention. In J. McCord & R. Tremblay (Eds.). *The interaction of theory and practice: Experimental studies of intervention.* New York: Guilford.

Domjan, M., & Burkhard, B. (1986). *The principles of learning and behavior* (2nd ed.). Monterey, CA: Brooks/Cole.

Ellis, A. (1977). The nature of disturbed marital interactions. In A. Ellis & R. Grieger (Eds.), *Handbook of rational emotive therapy.* New York: Springer.

Ellis, A. (1981). *Ideas to make you disturbed.* New York: Institute for Rational-Emotive Therapy.

Ely, A. L., Guerney, B. G., & Stover, L. (1973). Efficacy of the training phase of conjugal therapy. *Psychotherapy: Theory, Research and Practice, 10*, 201–207.

Emmelkamp, P. M., van Linden, G., van den Heuvell, C., Ruphan, M., Sanderman, R., Scholing, A., & Stroink, F. (1988). Cognitive and behavioral interventions: A comparative evaluation with clinically distressed couples. *Journal of Family Psychology, 1*(4), 365–377.

Emmelkamp, P., Von der Helm, M., MacGillavry, D., van Zanten, B. (1984). Marital therapy with clinically distressed couples: A comparative evaluation of system theoretic, contingency contracting, and communication skills approaches. In K. Hahlweg & N. S. Jacobson (Eds.), *Marital interaction: Analysis and modification* (pp. 36–52). New York: Guilford Press.

Epstein, N., & Eidelson, R. J. (1981). Unrealistic beliefs of clinical couples: Their relationship to expectations, goals and satisfaction. *American Journal of Family Therapy, 9*(4), 13–22.

Epstein, N., & Jackson, E. (1978). An outcome study of short-term communication training with married couples. *Journal of Consulting and Clinical Psychology, 46*, 207–212.

Ewart, C. K. (1978). *Behavioral marriage therapy with older couples: Effects of training measured by the Marital Adjustment Scale.* Paper presented at the annual meeting of the Association for the Advancement of Behavior Therapy, Chicago.

Falzer, P. R. (1984). The cybernetic metaphor: A critical examination of ecosystemic epistemology as a foundation of family therapy. *Family Process, 25*, 353–364.

Fiester, A. R., Mahrer, A. R., Giambra, L. M., & Ormiston, D. W. (1974). Shaping a clinic population: The dropout problem reconsidered. *Community Mental Health Journal, 10*, 173–179.

Fincham, F. D., & Bradbury, T. N. (1987). The assessment of marital quality: A reevaluation. *Journal of Marriage and the Family, 49*, 797–809.

Fincham, F. D., Bradbury, T. N., & Beach, S. R. H. (1990). To arrive where we began: A reappraisal of cognition in marriage and in marital therapy. *Journal of Family Psychology, 4*(2), 167–184.

Fincham, F. D., Bradbury, T. N., & Scott, C. (1990). Cognition in marriage. In F. D. Fincham & T. N. Bradbury (Eds.), *The psychology of marriage: Basic issues and applications* (pp. 118–149). New York: Guilford.

Ford, D., & Lerner, R. (1992). *Developmental systems theory: An integrative approach.* New York: Sage Publications.

Forgatch, M. S., Ray, J., & Patterson, G. R. (1992). Observed emotional reactions during family problem solving for two samples. Unpublished manuscript.

Friedman, A. S. (1975). Interaction of drug therapy with marital therapy in depressive patients. *Archives of General Psychiatry, 32*, 619–637.

Gerbis, K. E., Schroetter, R., & Hautzinger, M. (1980). Reciprocity counseling: Eine Replikationsstudie zu einem verhalten therapeutischen Programm [A replication of a behavior therapy program]. In M. Hautzinger & W. Schulz (Eds.), *Klinische Psychologiund Psychotherapie* (pp. 151–162). Tubingen, Federal Republic of Germany: DGVT-Kongressbericht.

Giblin, P. (1986). Research and assessment in marriage and family enrichment: A meta-analysis study. *Journal of Psychotherapy and the Family, 2*, 79–96.

Giblin, P., Sprenkle, D. H., & Sheehan, R. (1985). Enrichment outcome research: A meta-analysis of premarital, marital, and family interventions. *Journal of Marital and Family Therapy, 11*(3), 257–271.

Girodo, M., Stein, S. J., & Dotzenroth, S. E. (1980). The effects of communication skills training and contracting on marital relations. *Behavioral Engineering, 6*(2), 61–76.

Goldman, A., & Greenberg, L. (1991). Comparison of integrated systemic and emotionally focused approaches to couples therapy. *Journal of Consulting and Clinical Psychology, 60*(6), 1–8.

Gordon, D. A., Arbuthnot, J., Gustafson, K. E., & McGreen, P. (1988). Home-based behavioral-systems family therapy with disadvantaged juvenile delinquents. *The American Journal of Family Therapy, 16*(3), 243–255.

Gottman, J. M. (1985). Observational measures of behavior therapy outcome: A reply to Jacobson. *Behavioral Assessment, 7*, 317–321.

Gottman, J. M. (1991). Predicting the longitudinal course of marriages. *Journal of Marital and Family Therapy, 17*(1), 3–7.

Gottman, J. M. (in press). An agenda for marital therapy. In S. M. Johnson & L. S. Greenberg (Eds.), *Emotion in marriage and marital therapy.* New York: Brunner/Mazel.

Gottman, J. M., & Krokoff, L. J. (1989). Marital interaction and satisfaction: A longitudinal view. *Journal of Consulting and Clinical Psychology, 57*(1), 47–52.

Greenberg, L. S. (1991). Research on the process of change. *Psychotherapy Research, 1*(1), 3–16.

Greenberg, L. S., James, P. S., & Conry, R. F. (1988). Perceived change processes in emotionally focused couples therapy. *Journal of Family Psychology, 2*(1), 5–23.

Greenberg, L. S., & Johnson, S. M. (1988). *Emotionally focused couples therapy.* New York: Guilford.

Grotevant, H. D. (1989). Current issues in the assessment of marital and family systems. *Journal of Family Psychology, 3*, 101–103.

Guerney, B. G. (1977). *Relationship enhancement: Skill training programs for therapy, problem formation and enrichment.* San Francisco: Jossey-Bass.

Guerney, B., Jr., & Maxson, P. (1990). Marital and family enrichment research: A decade review and look ahead. *Journal of Marriage and the Family, 52*, 1127–1135.

Gurman, A. S. (1983). Family therapy research and the "New Epistemology." *Journal of Marital and Family Therapy, 9*, 227–234.

Gurman, A. S. (1991). Back to the future, ahead of the past: Is marital therapy going in circles? *Journal of Family Psychology, 4*(4), 402–406.

Gurman, A. S., & Kniskern, D. P. (1978). Research on marital and family therapy: Progress, perspective, and prospect. In S. L. Garfield & A. E. Bergin (Eds.), *Handbook of psychotherapy and behavior change: An empirical analysis* (2nd ed., pp. 817–901). New York: Wiley.

Gurman, A. S., Kniskern, D. P., & Pinsof, W. M. (1986). Research on the process and outcome of marital and family therapy. In S. L. Garfield & A. E. Bergin (Eds.), *Handbook of psychotherapy and behavior change* (3rd ed., pp. 565–624). New York: Wiley.

Haefner, P. T., Notarius, C. I., & Pellegrini, D. S. (1991). Determinants of satisfaction with marital discussions: An exploration of husband–wife differences. *Behavioral Assessment, 13*, 67–82.

Hafner, R. J. (1988). Marital and family therapy. In C. G. Last & M. Hersen (Eds.), *Handbook of anxiety disorders*. New York: Pergamon.

Hahlweg, K., & Markman, H. J. (1988). Effectiveness of behavioral marital therapy: Empirical status of behavioral techniques in preventing and alleviating marital distress. *Journal of Consulting and Clinical Psychology, 56*(3), 440–447.

Hahlweg, K., Revenstorf, D., & Schindler, L. (1982). Treatment of marital distress: Comparing formats and modalities. *Advances in Behaviour Research and Therapy, 4*, 57–74.

Hahlweg, K., Schindler, L., Revenstorf, D., & Brengelmann, J. C. (1984). The Munich marital therapy study. In K. Hahlweg & N. S. Jacobson (Eds.), *Marital interaction: Analysis and modification* (pp. 3–26). New York: Guilford.

Haley, J. (1963). *Strategies of psychotherapy*. New York: Grune & Stratton.

Hare-Mustin, R. T. (1991). Sex, lies, and headaches: The problem is power. In T. J. Goodrich (Ed.), *Women and power: Perspectives for therapy* (pp. 63–85). New York: W. W. Norton.

Hazelrigg, M. D., Cooper, H. M., & Borduin, C. M. (1987). Evaluating the effectiveness of family therapies: An integrative review and analysis. *Psychological Bulletin, 101*, 428–442.

Heatherington, L., & Friedlander, M. L. (1990). Couple and family therapy alliance scales: Empirical considerations. *Journal of Marital and Family Therapy, 16*(3), 299–306.

Hedberg, A. G., & Campbell, L., III. (1974). A comparison of four behavioral treatments of alcoholism. *Journal of Behavior Therapy and Experimental Psychiatry, 5*, 251–256.

Henggeler, S. W., Melton, G. B., & Smith, L. A. (1992). Family preservation using multisystemic therapy: An effective alternative to incarcerating serious juvenile offenders. *Journal of Consulting and Clinical Psychology, 60*(6), 953–961.

Hinde, R. A. (1989). Reconciling the family systems and the relationships approaches to child development. In K. Kreppner & R. M. Lerner (Eds.), *Family systems and life-span development* (pp. 149–164). Hillsdale, NJ: Lawrence Erlbaum.

Hoffman, L. (1981). *Foundations of family therapy*. New York: Basic Books.

Hollis, F. (1968). Continuance and discontinuance in marital counseling and some observations on joint interviews. *Social Casework, 49*, 167–174.

Holtzworth-Munroe, A., Beatty, S. B., & Anglin, K. (in press). The assessment and treatment of marital violence: An introduction for the marital therapist. In N. S. Jacob-

son & A. S. Gurman (Eds.), *Clinical handbook of marital therapy* (2nd ed.). New York: Guilford.

Holtzworth-Munroe, A., Jacobson, N. S., DeKlyen, M., & Whisman, M. A. (1989). Relationship between behavioral marital therapy outcome and process variables. *Journal of Consulting and Clinical Psychology, 57*(5), 658–662.

Hooley, J. M., & Teasdale, J. D. (1989). Predictors of relapse in unipolar depressives: Expressed emotion, marital distress, and perceived criticism. *Journal of Abnormal Psychology, 98*(3), 229–235.

Huber, C. H., & Milstein, B. (1985). Cognitive restructuring and a collaborative set in couples' work. *American Journal of Family Therapy, 13*(2), 17–27.

Jacobson, N. S. (1977). Problem solving and contingency contracting in the treatment of marital discord. *Journal of Consulting and Clinical Psychology, 45*, 92–100.

Jacobson, N. S. (1978a). Specific and nonspecific factors in the effectiveness of a behavioral approach to the treatment of marital discord. *Journal of Consulting and Clinical Psychology, 46*, 442–452.

Jacobson, N. S. (1978b). A stimulus control model of change in behavioral couples therapy: Implications for contingency contracting. *Journal of Marriage and Family Counseling, 4*, 29–35.

Jacobson, N. S. (1983). Beyond empiricism: The politics of marital therapy. *American Journal of Family Therapy, 11*, 11–24.

Jacobson, N. S. (1984). A component analysis of behavioral marital therapy: The relative effectiveness of behavior exchange and communication/problem-solving training. *Journal of Consulting and Clinical Psychology, 52*(2), 295–305.

Jacobson, N. S. (1985a). The role of observational measures in behavior therapy outcome research. *Behavioral Assessment, 7*, 297–308.

Jacobson, N. S. (1985b). Uses versus abuses of observational measures. *Behavioral Assessment, 7*, 323–330.

Jacobson, N. S. (1989). The politics of intimacy. *Behavior Therapist, 12*, 29–32.

Jacobson, N. S. (1990). Contributions from psychology to an understanding of marriage. In F. D. Fincham & T. N. Bradbury (Eds.), *The psychology of marriage* (pp. 258–275). New York: Guilford.

Jacobson, N. S. (1991a). Behavioral versus insight-oriented marital therapy: Labels can be misleading. *Journal of Consulting and Clinical Psychology, 59*(1), 142–145.

Jacobson, N. S. (1991b). To be or not to be behavioral when working with couples: What does it mean? *Journal of Family Psychology, 4*(4), 436–445.

Jacobson, N. S. (1991c). Toward enhancing the efficacy of marital therapy and marital therapy research. *Journal of Family Psychology, 4*(4), 373–393.

Jacobson, N. S., & Addis, M. E. (1993). *Research on couple therapy: What do we know? Where are we going?* Submitted for publication.

Jacobson, N. S., Dobson, K., Fruzzetti, A. E., Schmaling, K. B., & Salusky, S. (1991). Marital therapy as a treatment for depression. *Journal of Consulting and Clinical Psychology, 59*(4), 547–557.

Jacobson, N. S., Follette, V. M., Follette, W. C., Holtzworth-Munroe, A., Katt, J. L., & Schmaling, K. B. (1985). A component analysis of behavioral marital therapy: 1-year follow-up. *Behavior Research Therapy, 23*(5), 549–555.

Jacobson, N. S., Follette, W. C., & Pagel, M. (1986). Predicting who will benefit from behavioral marital therapy. *Journal of Consulting and Clinical Psychology, 54*(4), 518–522.

Jacobson, N. S., Follette, W. C., & Revenstorf, D. (1984). Psychotherapy outcome research: Methods for reporting variability and evaluating clinical significance. *Behavior Therapy, 15,* 336–352.

Jacobson, N. S., Follette, W. C., Revenstorf, D., Baucom, D. H., Hahlweg, K., & Margolin, G. (1984). Variability in outcome and clinical significance of behavioral marital therapy: A reanalysis of outcome data. *Journal of Consulting and Clinical Psychology, 52*(4), 497–504.

Jacobson, N. S., Holtzworth-Munroe, A., & Schmaling, K. B. (1989). Marital therapy and spouse involvement in the treatment of depression, agoraphobia, and alcoholism. *Journal of Consulting and Clinical Psychology, 57*(1), 5–10.

Jacobson, N. S., & Margolin, G. (1979). *Marital therapy: Strategies based on social learning and behavior exchange principles.* New York: Brunner/Mazel.

Jacobson, N. S., Schmaling, K. B., & Holtzworth-Munroe, A. (1987). Component analysis of behavioral marital therapy: 2-year follow-up and prediction of relapse. *Journal of Marital and Family Therapy, 13*(2), 187–195.

James, P. S. (1991). Effects of a communication training component added to an emotionally focused couples therapy. *Journal of Marital and Family Therapy, 17*(3), 263–275.

Jessee, R. E., & Guerney, B. G. (1981). A comparison of Gestalt and relationship enhancement treatment with married couples. *American Journal of Family Therapy, 9,* 31–41.

Joanning, H., Quinn, W., Thomas, F., & Mullen, R. (1992). Treating adolescent drug abuse: A comparison of family systems therapy, group therapy, and family drug education. *Journal of Marital and Family Therapy, 18*(4), 346–356.

Johnson, S. M., & Greenberg, L. S. (1985a). Differential effects of experiential and problem-solving interventions in resolving marital conflict. *Journal of Consulting and Clinical Psychology, 53,* 175–184.

Johnson, S. M., & Greenberg, L. S. (1985b). Emotionally focused couples therapy: An outcome study. *Journal of Marital and Family Therapy, 11*(3), 313–317.

Johnson, S. M., & Greenberg, L. S. (1988). Relating process to outcome in marital therapy. *Journal of Marital and Family Therapy, 14*(2), 175–183.

Johnson, S. M., & Greenberg, L. A. (1991). There are more things in heaven and earth than dreamed of in BMT: A response to Jacobson. *Journal of Family Psychology, 4*(4), 407–415.

Kaufman, G. (1992). The mysterious disappearance of battered women from family therapists' offices. *Journal of Marital and Family Therapy, 18,* 231–241.

Kazak, A. E. (1989). Families with disabled children: Stress and social networks in three samples. *Journal of Abnormal Child Psychology, 15,* 137–146.

Kazak, A. E., Jarmas, A., & Snitzer, L. (1988). The assessment of marital satisfaction: An evaluation of the Dyadic Adjustment Scale. *Journal of Family Psychology, 2,* 82–91.

Kazdin, A. E. (1993). Psychotherapy for children and adolescents: Current progress and future research directions. *American Psychologist, 48,* 644–657.

Keeney, B. P., & Ray, W. A. (1992, Spring). Kicking research in the ass: Provocations for reform. *AFTA Newsletter, 47,* 67–68.

Keeney, B. P., & Sprenkle, D. H. (1982). Ecosystemic epistemology: Critical implications for the aesthetics and pragmatics of family therapy. *Family Process, 21*(1), 1–20.

Kelley, G. A. (1955). *The psychology of personal constructs.* New York: W. W. Norton.

Kendall, P. C. (Ed). (1992). Comorbidity and treatment implications [Special section]. *Journal of Consulting and Clinical Psychology, 60.*

Krokoff, L. J. (1987). Recruiting representative samples for marital interaction research. *Journal of Social and Personal Relationships, 4,* 317–328.

Krokoff, L. J. (1991). Communication orientation as a moderator between strong negative affect and marital satisfaction. *Behavioral Assessment, 13,* 51–65.

Krokoff, L. J., Gottman, J. M., & Roy, A. K. (1988). Blue-collar and white-collar marital interaction and communication orientation. *Journal of Social and Personal Relationships, 5,* 201–221.

Liberman, R., Levine, J., Wheeler, E., Sanders, N., & Wallace, C. J. (1976). Marital therapy in groups: A comparative evaluation of behavioral and interaction formats. *Acta Psychiatrica Scandinavica, 266,* 1–34.

Liddle, H. A. (1991a). A multidimensional model for treating the adolescent drug abuser. In W. Snyder & T. Ooms (Eds.). *Empowerment families: Family centered treatment of adolescents with mental health and substance abuse problems* (ADAMHA Monograph), Washington, DC: U.S. Government Printing Office.

Liddle, H. A. (1991b, Spring). Empirical values and the culture of family therapy. *AFTA Newsletter, 43,* 16–18.

Locke, H. J., & Wallace, K. M. (1959). Short marital-adjustment and prediction tests: Their reliability and validity. *Marriage and Family Living, 21,* 251–255.

Margolin, G., Talovic, S., Fernandez, V., & Onorato, R. (1983). Sex role considerations and behavioral marital therapy: Equal does not mean identical. *Journal of Marital and Family Therapy, 9,* 131–145.

Margolin, G., & Weiss, R. L. (1978). Comparative evaluation of therapeutic components associated with behavioral marital treatments. *Journal of Consulting and Clinical Psychology, 46*(6), 1476–1486.

Markman, H. J. (1991a). Backwards into the future of couples therapy and couples therapy research: A comment on Jacobson. *Journal of Family Psychology, 4*(4), 416–425.

Markman, H. J. (1991b). Constructive marital conflict is not an oxymoron. *Behavioral Assessment, 13,* 83–96.

Markman, H. J., Floyd, F. J., Stanley, S. M., & Lewis, H. C. (1986). Prevention. In N. S. Jacobson & A. S. Gurman (Eds.), *Clinical handbook of marital therapy* (pp. 173–195). New York: Guilford.

McCrady, B. S., Noel, N. E., Abrams, D. B., Stout, R. L., Nelson, H. F., & Hay, W. M. (1986). Comparative effectiveness of three types of spouse involvement in outpatient behavioral alcoholism treatment. *Journal of Studies on Alcohol, 47*(6), 459–467.

McCrady, B. S., Stout, R., Noel, N., Abrams, D., & Nelson, H. F. (in press). Comparative effectiveness of three types of spouse involved behavioral alcoholism treatment: Outcomes 18 months after treatment. *British Journal of Addictions.*

McFall, R. M. (1991). Manifesto for a science of clinical psychology. *The Clinical Psychologist, 44*(6), 75–88.

McMahon, R. J., & Wells, K. C. (1989). Conduct disorders. In E. J. Mash & R. A. Barkley (Eds.), *Treatment of childhood disorders* (pp. 73–132). New York: Guilford.

Mehlman, S. K., Baucom, D. H., & Anderson, D. (1983). Effectiveness of cotherapists versus single therapists and immediate versus delayed treatment in behavioral marital therapy. *Journal of Consulting and Clinical Psychology, 51,* 258–266.

Minuchin, S. (1974). *Families and family therapy.* Cambridge, MA: Harvard University Press.

Moon, S. M., Dillon, D. R., & Sprenkle, D. H. (1990). Family therapy and qualitative research. *Journal of Marital and Family Therapy, 16,* 357–373.

Moon, S. M., Dillon, D. R., & Sprenkle, D. H. (1991). On balance and synergy: Family therapy and qualitative research revisited. *Journal of Marital and Family Therapy, 17,* 173–178.

Moon, S. M., & Sprenkle, D. H. (1992, Spring). Multi-methodological family therapy research. *AFTA Newsletter, 47,* 29–30.

Morris, S. M., Alexander, J. F., & Turner, C. W. (1991). Do reattributions reduce blame? *Journal of Family Psychology, 5*(2), 192–203.

Newberry, A. M., Alexander, J. F., & Liddle, N. (1988, August). The effects of therapist gender on family therapy process. In *Female and male clients and counselors: Do their differences matter?* Symposium conducted at the annual convention of the American Psychological Association, Atlanta.

Newberry, A. M., Alexander, J. F., & Turner, C. W. (1991). Gender as a process variable in family therapy. *Journal of Family Psychology, 5*(2), 158–175.

Noel, N. E., McCrady, B. S., Stout, R. L., & Fisher-Nelson, F. (1987). Predictors of attrition from an outpatient alcoholism treatment program for couples. *Journal of Studies on Alcohol, 48*(3), 229–235.

Oatley, K., & Hodgson, D. (1987). Influence of husbands on the outcome of their agoraphobic wives' therapy. *British Journal of Psychiatry, 150,* 380–386.

O'Farrell, T. J., Choquette, K. A., & Cutter, H. S. G. (1992). *Behavioral marital therapy with and without additional relapse prevention sessions for alcoholics and their wives.* Manuscript submitted for publication.

O'Farrell, T. J., Cutter, H. S. G., Choquette, K. A., & Floyd, F. J. (1992). *Behavioral marital therapy for male alcoholics: Marital and drinking adjustment during the two years after treatment.* Manuscript submitted for publication.

O'Farrell, T. J., Cutter, H. S. G., & Floyd, F. J. (1983). *The class on alcoholism and marriage (CALM) project: Results on marital adjustment and communication from before to after therapy* (Tech. Rep. No. 4-1). Brockton, MA: Brockton/West Roxbury Veterans Administration Medical Center.

O'Farrell, T. J., Cutter, H. S. G., & Floyd, F. J. (1985). Evaluating behavioral marital therapy for male alcoholics: Effects on marital adjustment and communication from before to after treatment. *Behavior Therapy, 16,* 147–167.

O'Leary, K. D., & Beach, R. H. (1990). Marital therapy: A viable treatment for depression and marital discord. *American Journal of Psychiatry, 147*(2), 183–186.

O'Leary, K. D., & Turkewitz, H. (1978). Marital therapy from a behavioral perspective. In T. J. Paolino & B. S. McCrady (Eds.), *Marriage and marital therapy: Psychoanalytic, behavioral, and systems theory perspectives* (pp. 240–297). New York: Brunner/Mazel.

Olson, D., & Lavee, Y. (1989). Family systems and family stress: A family life cycle perspective. In K. Kreppner & R. Lerner (Eds.) *Family systems and life span development* (pp. 165–195) Hillsdale, NJ: Lawrence Erlbaum.

Parsons, B. V., Jr., & Alexander, J. F. (1973). Short-term family intervention: A therapy outcome study. *Journal of Consulting and Clinical Psychology, 41,* 195–201.

Patterson, G. R. (1985). Beyond technology: The next stage in developing an empirical base for training. In L. L'Abate (Ed.), *The handbook of family psychology and therapy* (Vol. 2, pp. 1344–1379). Homewood, IL: Dorsey.

Patterson, G. R., & Chamberlain, P. (1992). A functional analysis of resistance (a neobehavioral perspective). In H. Arkowitz (Ed.), *Why don't people change? New perspectives on resistance and noncompliance.* New York: Guilford.

Patterson, G. R., Dishion, T. J., & Chamberlain, P. (1992). Outcomes and methodological issues relating to treatment of antisocial children. In T. R. Giles (Ed.), *Effective psychotherapy: A handbook of comparative research.* New York: Plenum.

Patterson, G. R., Reid, J. B., & Dishion, T. J. (in press). *A social learning approach: IV. Antisocial boys.* Eugene, OR: Castalia Press.

Persons, J. B. (1991). Psychotherapy outcome studies do not accurately represent current models of psychotherapy. *American Psychologist, 46*(2), 99–106.

Pinsof, W. M. (1989). A conceptual framework and methodological criteria for family therapy process research. *Journal of Consulting and Clinical Psychology, 57*(1), 53–59.

Pinsof, W. (in press). *Integrative problem centered therapy: The synthesis of family and individual therapies.* New York: Basic Books.

Pinsof, W. M., & Catherall, D. R. (1986). The integrative psychotherapy alliance: Family, couple and individual therapy scales. *Journal of Marital and Family Therapy, 12*(2), 137–151.

Rampage, C. R. (1989). Revolution and resistance: A comment on Witkin. *Journal of Family Psychology, 2*(4), 447–450.

Reid, J. B., & Patterson, G. R. (1992). *Clinical case studies: Problems and tactics for parent training with families of antisocial boys.* Unpublished manuscript.

Reiss, D. (1991, Spring). Voyeurism: The link between good family therapy and good family research. *AFTA Newsletter, 43,* 34–36.

Sabatelli, R. M. (1988). Measurement issues in marital research: A review and critique of contemporary survey instruments. *Journal of Marriage and the Family, 50,* 891–915.

Sayers, S. L., Baucom, D. H., Sher, T. G., Weiss, R. L., & Heyman, R. E. (1991). Constructive engagement, behavioral marital therapy, and changes in marital satisfaction. *Behavioral Assessment, 13,* 25–49.

Sayger, T. V., Horne, A. M., Walker, J. M., & Passmore, J. L. (1988). Social learning family therapy with aggressive children: Treatment outcome and maintenance. *Journal of Family Psychology, 1*(3), 261–285.

Schmidt, F. L. (1992). What do data really mean? Research findings, meta-analysis, and cumulative knowledge in psychology. *American Psychologist, 47*(10), 1173–1181.

Shadish, W. R. (in press). Do family and marital psychotherapies change what people do? A meta-analysis of behavioral outcomes. In T. D. Cook, H. M. Cooper, D. S. Cordray, H. Hortmann, L. V. Hedges, R. J. Light, T. A. Louis, & F. Mosteller (Eds.), *Meta-analysis for explanation: A casebook.* New York: Russell Sage Foundation.

Shadish, W. R., Montgomery, L. M., Wilson, P., Wilson, M. R., Bright, I., & Okwumabua, T. (1993). *The effects of family and marital psychotherapies: A meta-analysis.* Manuscript submitted for publication.

Sher, T. G., Baucom, D. H., & Larus, J. M. (1990). Communication patterns and response to treatment among depressed and nondepressed maritally distressed couples. *Journal of Family Psychology, 4*(1), 63–79.

Sher, T. G., & Weiss, R. L. (1991). Negativity in marital communication: Where's the beef? *Behavioral Assessment, 13,* 1–5.

Sinnott, A., Jones, R. B., Scott-Fordham, A., & Woodward, R. (1981). Augmentation of in vivo exposure treatment for agoraphobia by the formation of neighborhood self-help groups. *Behavior Research and Therapy, 19,* 339–347.

Smith, D. A., Vivian, D., & O'Leary, K. D. (1990). Longitudinal prediction of marital discord from premarital expressions of affect. *Journal of Consulting and Clinical Psychology, 58*(6), 790–798.

Snyder, D. K., & Wills, R. M. (1989). Behavioral versus insight-oriented marital therapy: Effects on individual and interspousal functioning. *Journal of Consulting and Clinical Psychology, 57*(1), 39–46.

Snyder, D. K., & Wills, R. M. (1991). Facilitating change in marital therapy and research. *Journal of Family Psychology, 4*(4), 426–435.

Snyder, D. K., Wills, R. M., & Grady-Fletcher, A. (1991a). Long-term effectiveness of behavioral versus insight-oriented marital therapy: A 4-year follow-up study. *Journal of Consulting and Clinical Psychology, 59*(1), 138–141.

Snyder, D. K., Wills, R. M., & Grady-Fletcher, A. (1991b). Risks and challenges of long-term psychotherapy outcome research: Reply to Jacobson. *Journal of Consulting and Clinical Psychology, 59*(1), 146–149.

Spanier, G. (1976). Measuring dyadic adjustment. *Journal of Marriage and the Family, 38,* 15–28.

Spanier, G. B. (1988). Assessing the strengths of the Dyadic Adjustment Scale. *Journal of Family Psychology, 2,* 92–94.

Stiles, W. B., & Snow, J. S. (1984). Counseling session impact as viewed by novice counselors and their clients. *Journal of Counseling Psychology, 31,* 3–12.

Stuart, R. B. (1971). Behavioral contracting within the families of delinquents. *Journal of Behavior Therapy and Experimental Psychiatry, 2,* 1–11.

Szapocznik, J., Kurtines, W., Foote, F., Perez-Vidal, A., and Hervis, O. (1986). Conjoint versus one-person family therapy: Further evidence for the effectiveness of conducting family therapy through one person. *Journal of Consulting and Clinical Psychology, 51,* 889–899.

Szapocznik, J., Kurtines, W., Santisteban, D. A., & Rio, A. T. (1990). Interplay of advances between theory, research, and applications in treatment interventions aimed at behavior problem children and adolescents. *Journal of Consulting and Clinical Psychology, 58,* 696–703.

Szapocznik, J., Perez-Vidal, A., Brickman, A. L., Foote, F. H., Santisteban, D., Hervis, O., & Kurtines, W. M. (1988). Engaging adolescent drug abusers and their families in treatment: A strategic structural systems approach. *Journal of Consulting and Clinical Psychology, 56*(4), 552–557.

Taylor, R. J., Chatters, L. M., Tucker, M. B., & Lewis, E. (1990). Developments in research on black families: A decade review. *Journal of Marriage and the Family, 52,* 993–1014.

Thompson, L. (1988). Women, men, and marital quality. *Journal of Family Psychology, 2,* 95–100.

Tsoi-Hoshmand, L. (1976). Marital therapy: An integrated behavioral-learning approach. *Journal of Marriage and Family Counseling, 2,* 179–191.

Turkewitz, H., & O'Leary, K. D. (1981). A comparative outcome study of behavioral marital therapy and communication therapy. *Journal of Marital and Family Therapy, 7,* 159–169.

Van Steenwegen, A. (1982). Intensive psycho-education couple therapy. *Cahiers des Sciences Familial et Sexologiques, 5,* 25–36.

Vega, W. A. (1990). Hispanic families in the 1980s: A decade of research. *Journal of Marriage and the Family, 52,* 1015–1024.

Waring, E. M. (1988). *Enhancing marital intimacy through cognitive self-disclosure.* New York: Brunner/Mazel.

Waring, E. M., Chamberlaine, C. H., McCrank, E. W., Stalker, C. A., Carver, C., Fry, R., & Barnes, S. (1988). Dysthymia: A randomized study of cognitive marital therapy and antidepressants. *Canadian Journal of Psychiatry, 33,* 96–99.

Waring, E. M., Stalker, C. A., Carver, C. M., & Gitta, M. Z. (1991). Waiting list controlled trial of cognitive marital therapy in severe marital discord. *Journal of Marital and Family Therapy, 17*(3), 243–256.

Wark, L. (1992, Spring). Characteristics of qualitative approaches to research. *AFTA Newsletter, 47,* 61–62.

Whisman, M. A., & Jacobson, N. S. (1990). Power, marital satisfaction, and response to marital therapy. *Journal of Family Psychology, 4*(2), 202–212.

Whisman, M. A., Jacobson, N. S., Fruzzetti, A. E., & Waltz, J. A. (1989). Methodological issues in marital therapy. *Advances in Behavioral Research and Therapy, 11,* 175–189.

Wilder, C. (1982). Muddles and metaphors: A response to Keeney and Sprenkle. *Family Process, 21,* 397–400.

Wile, D. B. (1988). In search of the curative principle in couples therapy. *Journal of Family Psychology, 2*(1), 24–27.

Wills, R. M., Faitler, S. L., & Snyder, D. K. (1987). Distinctiveness of behavioral versus insight-oriented marital therapy: An empirical analysis. *Journal of Consulting and Clinical Psychology, 55*(5), 685–690.

Wilson, G. L., Bornstein, P. H., & Wilson, L. J. (1988). Treatment of relationship dysfunction: An empirical evaluation of group and conjoint behavioral marital therapy. *Journal of Consulting and Clinical Psychology, 56*(6), 929–931.

Witkin, S. L. (1989a). Responding to sexism in marital research and therapy: Is awareness enough? *Journal of Family Psychology, 3*(1), 82–85.

Witkin, S. L., (1989b). Scientific ideology and women: Implications for marital research and therapy. *Journal of Family Psychology, 2*(4), 430–446.

Zimmer, D., Anneken, R., Echelmayer, L., Kaluza, K., Klein, H., & Klockgeter-Kelle, A. (1977). Beschreibung und erster empirische eberpruefung eines Kommunikationstrainings fuer Paare [Description and first empirical evaluation of communication skills training for couples]. *DGVT-Mitteilungen, 4,* 566–577.

Zweben, A., Pearlman, S., & Li, S. (1988). A comparison of brief advice and conjoint therapy in the treatment of alcohol abuse: The results of the marital systems study. *British Journal of Addiction, 83,* 899–916.

15

EXPERIENTIAL GROUP RESEARCH: CAN THE CANON FIRE?

- **RICHARD L. BEDNAR**
Brigham Young University

- **THEODORE J. KAUL**
Ohio State University

In 1986, we concluded our review of experiential group research in this prominent volume with mention of a cartoon from *The American Scientist*. It read:

> There are two bewhiskered men wearing lab coats. They are standing in front of a blackboard, one of them holding a piece of chalk. On the board, literally covering it, is a truly monumental equation. It contains a few Arabic numerals, but consists mostly of exponents, logs, radicals, and nearly the entire Greek alphabet. In the middle of this amazing composition there are three dots, a box, and another three dots. In the box are written the words, "Then a miracle occurs." One man is saying to the other, who is holding the piece of chalk, "I think you need to be more specific in step two." (Kaul & Bednar, 1986, p. 710)

We suggested that only one essential change would be required for this cartoon to reflect the underlying dilemma facing most of the experiential small group research. The caption would have to be changed to read: "I think you need to be more specific in step one." Step one in science is always careful observation and clear description.

Because of the centrality of astute observation and careful description in all scientific work, we use them as a focal point for our review and analysis of contemporary group research. Our chapter is, therefore, divided into three sections.

The first section discusses the most generic conclusions suggested by the collective body of group research over the past 40 or 50 years. Our intent is to identify the thematic thrust and scholarly advances of the group disciplines during this time.

The second section illustrates and explains the crucial role that observation and description have played in shaping the form and substance of the current body of research. Even though our analysis of this topic is uncommon, we suggest that it leads to some guidelines and recommendations that warrant the careful consideration of group researchers.

The third section is a substantive review of recent developments in the field. This is where we can not only identify emerging trends and developments, but also ponder such crucial questions as, "Are we asking the right questions?" and "Are we using the right methods?"

GROUP RESEARCH: TWO MAJOR CONCLUSIONS

There has been a gradual, but orderly evolution of knowledge in the group disciplines, particularly during the past 30 or 40 years. The most obvious improvements have been in the area of research design and data analysis. Case studies and testimonials have gradually been replaced by more quantitative studies in which sophisticated design and data analyses are more the rule than the exception. As a result, both the quality and quantity of group research have been substantially improved over recent decades.

This observation led us to believe that it would be interesting and useful to identify the major conclusions that could be supported with research evidence from the last 30 or 40 years of group research. Naturally, this would be a difficult and controversial task. Nevertheless, it is a task worth pursuing.

After reviewing and synthesizing the major reviews of group research, we suggest that there are two major conclusions that can be supported. Even though these conclusions may seem unduly modest to some, they are the only ones that seem robust enough to be useful, as well as scientifically supportable. Certainly, additional conclusions could be suggested, some of which could prove to be rather provocative. But none is as revealing or supportable as those we are about to suggest. The first conclusion is about the effectiveness of group treatments; the second is about central group processes.

TREATMENT EFFECTIVENESS

Treatment efficacy is important to any applied discipline. Bednar and Kaul (1978) as well as many others have pointed out that it is only through a careful and dispassionate evaluation of the consequences of its accepted treatment techniques that a profession can make legitimate claims for social responsibility. And nowhere is it more important to demonstrate treatment efficacy than in psychological services. Please remember that a mere 50 years ago we administered treatments such as cold water immersions and even imprisonment in the name of improved mental health. Each of these treatments had a loyal following at the time and reported positive effects in the literature of its day. And today we continue to have some systems of psychological help giving that are notorious for fads, movements of near missionary zeal, and an abundance of unsubstantiated claims. It is only through carefully controlled outcome studies that treatment techniques will eventually find their rightful place in our museums of therapeutic history (Bergin & Lambert, 1978; Lambert, Shapiro, & Bergin, 1986).

Conclusion 1: Treatment Effects
In 1978, Bednar and Kaul ended their review of group outcome research with the following conclusion. It is as applicable today as when it was first formulated.

> Accumulated evidence indicates that group treatments have been more effective than no treatment, than placebo or nonspecific treatments, or than other recognized psychological treatments, at least under some circumstances. This evidence has been gathered under a variety of conditions, from a wide range of individuals, and in many different ways. Although it may not be the best question to ask, there is a large body of research that indicates that group treatments "work." This conclusion must be qualified, however, since it is

> empirically and intuitively obvious that not all groups have had uniformly beneficial results. We have seen nonrejections of the null hypothesis in the research, and evidence of casualties as well. (p. 792)

GROUP PROCESSES

If outcome studies tell us when our treatments work, then carefully constructed process studies can tell us why. Kaul and Bednar (1986, 1978) suggested that quality process studies are our most essential defense against the fatal error of scientific misattribution. Misattribution is of particular concern to the scientist because it misinforms in a way that is dangerously similar to simple superstitions. If we define superstition as the misattribution of cause-and-effect relationships, it becomes clear why it is scientifically awkward to maintain that group treatments work without specifying the curative factors that account for this success. In principle, claiming success in the absence of understanding how it occurs is perilously similar to the conditions that allowed some to prescribe bear fat for baldness or hawk blood for myopia because they may have worked some time in the past. Good process research asks us to clearly account for the specific treatment elements that are operative in effective forms of group treatment.

Conclusion 2: Curative Factors
In 1978, Bednar and Kaul formulated the following conclusion after reviewing the group processes literature:

> Statements about why these treatments [group treatments] elicit therapeutic benefits from some participants seem premature. Causal statements about the curative forces operating in the group context, the circumstances under which they may be brought to bear, or the form in which they may be expressed cannot be supported on the basis of the available literature. (p. 793)

In a more positive vein, however, it should be noted that a small number of group process variables have established their potential value in group theory and practice during the last several decades. These variables include such well-recognized treatment elements as (1) group cohesion, (2) interpersonal feedback, (3) leadership styles and characteristics, (4) group structure and/or ambiguity, (5) group composition, (6) massed versus distributed learning, (7) therapist and client self-disclosure, and (8) personal risk and responsibility. Even though these variables are generally accepted as crucial elements in small group treatments because of the existing research, the determination of their actual effects on client improvement is only in the exploratory stage.

The full spectrum of implications embedded in these conclusions raises two questions for our consideration. These questions are so basic to the discipline that orderly advances in group research and practice may not be possible until they are addressed and accommodated by group practitioners and researchers alike.

1. Controlled outcome studies have been regularly reporting successful treatment effects for small group treatments for several decades now. Even though we do not know which types of clients, client problems, or groups will be effective in advance, the fact that some groups are effective under some circumstances and not others has been demonstrated by hundreds of researchers representing different geographic regions, populations, treatment orientations, and measurement methods (Bednar & Kaul, 1978; Bednar & Lawlis, 1971; Kaul & Bednar, 1986).

We must now ask why the group disciplines have persisted with the same generic research question (Are group treatments effective?) decades after this question has essentially been answered; and equally important, why we have not yet been very successful with the next logical step of trying to isolate some of the more specific treatment elements that account for the variable success in group treatment results. In brief, why is it that we know so little about the most potent curative factors in group treatments and the conditions under which they are, and are not, effective?

2. What can be done differently so that the next decade of group research will continue the gradual, but orderly evolution of knowledge about small group treatments?

Obviously, these questions are basic. To answer them, we must carefully consider the most fundamental steps in advancing knowledge as well as the developmental status of group theory research and practice. This approach requires a discussion of the most substantive issues in the group disciplines, and the way in which these issues have been addressed in a scientific context in the past. Although it may seem paradoxical to some, we are about to suggest that much of the group research has been done with considerable care and rigor, but unfortunately, the benefits of these efforts have been compromised because this work has not been done in a way that is consistent with the developmental sequence "cumulative science" usually requires. We will explain this point more fully.

GROUP RESEARCH: THE HIDDEN PROBLEM

Understanding the developmental level of any scientific discipline is important for two reasons.

First, it prescribes the type of research products that are needed for a discipline to advance from one developmental stage to another. Although this observation is both reasonable and innocent, it is seldom accorded the procedural respect it deserves in group research. But developmental sequences are important in all research. Bakers, for example, never bake a box of cake mix; they always mix it first. Always. They simply do not expect a cake to turn out without mixing before baking. And group researchers must come to understand that research projects will not be meaningful just because they are guided by interesting questions. There are always technical considerations that influence how significant or successful a research project can be. If you understand science, you also understand why it cannot be any other way. Careful observation, accurate description, and precise measurement always precede good experimentation. But to a great extent, group researchers seem to focus on experimentation in the absence of these cardinal qualities. And experimentation in the absence of these qualities just will not work very well.

Second, a clear understanding of the maturation level of a discipline provides a guiding framework within which diverse and multiple research efforts can be organized. This may be the only way in which a discipline can coordinate its research efforts and products so they can help satisfy the developmental demands of a maturing discipline. Among the most basic developmental needs of young disciplines are (1) the identification and description of its most central conceptual variables, such as the curative factors in group treatment; (2) the development of descriptive taxonomies for classifying the central phenomena of the discipline, such as the invariant elements of a therapeutic group; and (3) the development of measurement methods for quantifying basic concepts. As these developmental steps are satisfied, a discipline becomes equipped for more advanced investigations involving manipulation of treatment variables and research that can be cumulative and perhaps lead to theory development.

When we apply these considerations to the group literature, we find a curious thing. In spite of the fact that the conceptual and measurement refinement in the field is in its infancy, most of the published reports in the better group journals are experimental in nature! As will be shown in the following section, many of these reports include few conceptual variables that are indigenous to group treatments. Attempts to measure the conceptual variables that are studied are even more scarce. On the whole, most group research variables are rather generic and nonspecific in nature. Because of this, we thought it would be instructive to identify and describe the types of variables that are being studied in the group literature.

CHARACTERISTICS OF THE GROUP LITERATURE

To approach this question, we decided to identify the specific independent variables in the methodologically superior studies that have been published in peer-reviewed journals since the early 1950s. Table 15.1 summarizes these results. It should be noted that some of these studies are methodologically quite sophisticated and include such impressive design considerations as multiple control groups, multiple outcome measures, long- and short-term follow-up evaluations, authentic clinical populations, appropriate data analyses, and experienced therapists. Space limitations prevent us from reviewing all of the better studies, but citations are provided for all the potentially suitable studies we found. Table 15.1 summarizes 26 outcome and 24 process studies. These 50 studies are reasonably representative of the larger pool of better investigations.

We were particularly interested in the theoretical relevance, conceptual clarity, and measurement precision involved in these studies. Table 15.1 contains our ratings of the (1) conceptual clarity, (2) theoretical relevance, and (3) measurement precision of this literature.

Conceptual Clarity
Regardless of the oblique origins of much of the theoretical underpinnings of group research, it is nevertheless important to discuss the clarity and precision with which group research variables are defined, both conceptually and operationally. Our guiding concern is determining if research reports generally provide sufficient information to allow replication of treatment conditions in future experiments — a cardinal requirement in any conception of good science.

Clear and precise definitions of crucial variables are generally accepted to have two basic properties. First, the definition is sufficiently clear to tell us what the variable is and what its most central components are. With these conceptual tools in hand, we are then prepared to recognize the presence of a concept's major components with at least an acceptable level of reliability.

Second, and as important, a good conceptual definition also helps us determine what the variable is not. In other words, clear conceptual definitions will provide both inclusion and exclusion criteria. Both are equally important. For example, consider the following definition: Group psychotherapy takes place when a small group of individuals meets with a leader for the purpose of discussing and resolving problems. Even though this definition may initially sound reasonable, it is unacceptable because it could include as group psychotherapy such diverse events as corporate board meetings, family discussions over dinner, most faculty meetings, and almost all meetings of Weight Watchers on Tuesday evenings. Although it is true that many of these meetings may be therapeutic, it is equally clear they are not group psychotherapy in the traditional sense of the word, or the phenomena we study when we are trying to increase our knowledge of group psychotherapy. Clearly, then, good conceptual definitions must tell what a variable is, as well as what it is not. Failure to satisfy these two criteria, at least to some degree, makes it virtually impossible to operationally capture the essence of important variables in a research context.

But there is more to definitional adequacy than just its conceptual substance. Even when we have clear and precise conceptual meaning, we still have the problem of accurately operationalizing these conceptual elements in experimental procedures. In other words, there must be a clear and generally stable level of correspondence between concepts and operational procedures in our research efforts. Although it is not uncommon for researchers to try to establish logical links between conceptual elements and operational procedures, they often are unable to capitalize on the efforts of their experimental ancestors and, hence, often repeat mistakes.

For example, if a therapy group is called "Rogerian," it is usually because the therapist had Rogerian training some time in the past or simply intended to take a more nondirective approach. Obviously, such semantic labeling is not an acceptable basis for defining a group approach as nondirective or Rogerian in even the most impoverished research environment. Neither of these considerations is sufficient to provide the necessary documentation that the treatment practices in the group were an accurate reflection of the basic conceptual elements that guide Rogerian therapy. Researchers, and practitioners for that matter, need more specification if they are to take from the research what can be taken. We are regularly exposed to conclusions about concepts and procedures in group treatments that have not met even the most modest criteria for conceptual or operational adequacy.

TABLE 15.1 Ratings of the clarity, relevance, and measurement of group research variables

Authors	Experimental Conditions	Clarity	Relevance	Measurement
Outcome Studies				
Jones & Peters (1953)	Short-term therapy: pretest vs. posttest	3	3	1
Baehr (1954)	Group therapy	2	2	1
	Individual therapy	2	2	1
	Group and individual therapy	2	2	1
Barron & Leary (1955)	Group therapy	3	2	1
	Individual therapy	3	2	1
	Control group	—	—	—
Semon & Goldstein (1957)	Group therapy	3	2	1
	Control group	—	—	—
Ends & Page (1959)	Alcoholics Anonymous	3	2	1
	Alcoholics Anonymous and group therapy	3	2	1
Luria (1959)	Group therapy	2	2	1
	Control group	—	—	—
Fairweather & Simon (1960)	Group therapy	3	2	1
	Individual therapy	3	2	1
	Group living	3	2	1
	Control	—	—	—
McDavid (1964)	Posttherapy attitudes	2	3	3
	Pretherapy control	—	—	—
Novick (1965)	Group vs. individual therapy	3	2	1
	High vs. low ego strength	2	1	3
Persons (1966)	Group therapy	3	2	1
	Control group	—	—	—
Wilson, Wilson, Sakata, & Frumkin (1967)	Short-term therapy	1	1	1
	Control group	—	—	—
Vernallis, Shipper, Butler, & Tomlinson (1970)	Saturation group therapy	2	2	2
	No-therapy control group	—	—	—
Meichenbaum, Gilmore, & Fedoravicius (1971)	Insight-oriented group therapy	3	3	2
	Group desensitization therapy	4	4	2
	Insight and desensitization group therapy	4	4	2
J. Shapiro & Diamond (1972)	Encounter group therapy	3	2	1
	No-therapy control group	—	—	—
Lieberman, Yalom, & Miles (1973)	Various group approaches	2	2	1
	Leader's leadership style	4	2	1
	No-treatment control group	—	—	—
Levin & Kurtz (1974)	Structured group therapy with exercises	3	3	1
	Unstructured group therapy with interaction	3	3	1
Jesness (1975)	Group transactional analysis	4	3	2
	Individual behavior modification	4	3	2
	Comparison/control groups	—	—	—
Foulds & Hannigan (1976)	Marathon group therapy	3	3	1
	No contact control group	—	—	—
Lundgren & Knight (1977)	Leader and trainer behavior traits, including			
	low vs. high control	2	3	3
	low vs. high affection	2	3	3

continued

TABLE 15.1   *continued*

Authors	Experimental Conditions	Clarity	Relevance	Measurement
Anderson (1978)	Rogerian encounter group	3	2	2
	Gestalt sensory-awareness group	3	2	2
	Leaderless group	3	2	2
	No-treatment control group	—	—	—
LaPointe & Rimm (1980)	Insight-oriented group	3	3	1
	Cognitive group	3	3	1
	Assertiveness training group	3	3	1
Comas-Diaz (1981)	Cognitive therapy group	4	3	1
	Behavioral treatment group	4	3	1
	Waiting-list control group	—	—	—
Steinmetz, Lewinsohn, & Antonuc-cio (1983)	Client characteristics, including			
	adjustment	1	1	1
	locus of control	1	1	1
	life-stress events	1	1	1
Piper, Debbane, Bienvenu, & Garant (1984)	Short-term individual therapy	3	2	2
	Short-term group therapy	3	2	2
	Long-term individual therapy	3	2	2
	Long-term group therapy	3	2	2
Harvey, Scharamski, Feldman, Brooks, & Barbara (1987)	Short-term eclectic group therapy	2	2	1
	Minimal treatment control group	—	—	—
Fueher & Keys (1988)	High-structure self-help group	1	3	1
	Low-structure self-help group	1	3	1

Process Studies

Authors	Experimental Conditions	Clarity	Relevance	Measurement
Zimet & Fine (1955)	Group lecture	3	2	1
	Group-centered therapy	3	2	1
Cabeen (1961)	Effects of group therapy	2	2	1
Kapp et al. (1964)	Perceived group unity	2	2	3
	Feelings of personal inducement	2	2	3
Traux, Carkhuff, & Kedman (1965)	Levels of group vs. therapist:			
	Empathy	2	2	2
	Warmth	2	2	2
	Genuineness	2	2	2
Yalom & Rand (1966)	Popularity within group	2	2	3
	Group cohesiveness	2	3	3
Zimpfer (1967)	Expressions of feelings:			
	Warmth	3	3	3
	Hostility	3	3	3
	Flight	3	3	3
Whalen (1969)	Factorial (2 × 2) arrangement of pretreatment training:			
	With and without filmed models	2	3	—
	Detailed or minimal instructions	2	3	1
Anchor, Vojtisek, & Berger (1972)	Social desirability of member	3	2	3
	Frequency of member self-disclosure	2	2	3
Jacobs, Jacobs, Feldman, & Cavior (1973)	Type and valence of feedback:			
	Positive vs. negative vs. mixed	3	2	3
	Emotional vs. behavioral	3	2	3
Strassburg, Roback, Anchor, & Abramowitz (1975)	Perceived quality of therapeutic relationship	3	2	3
	Frequency of self-disclosure	2	3	3
Bednar & Battersby (1976)	Factorial arrangement (2 × 2 × 2) of treatments:			

TABLE 15.1 *continued*

Author	Experimental Conditions	Clarity	Relevance	Measurement
	Behavioral instructions	4	3	4
	Goal instructions	4	3	4
	Persuasive explanation	4	3	4
Wogan, Getter, Amdur, Nichols, & Okman (1977)	Taped pretraining with cognitive-experiential instructions	3	2	2
	Structured T-group pretraining	3	2	2
	No-pretraining control group	—	—	—
	Placebo control group	—	—	—
Ware & Barr (1977)	Structured group experience	2	2	1
	Unstructured group experience	2	2	1
	Control group	—	—	—
Lockwood, Salzberg, & Heckel (1978)	Videotaped feedback	2	2	—
	Videotaped feedback with guided discussion	2	2	—
	Verbal feedback from group participants	2	2	—
	No-feedback control group	—	—	—
Hurst, Stein, Korchin, & Saskin (1978)	Leadership style, including			
	Caring	3	2	2
	Controlling	3	2	2
	Meaning attribution	3	2	2
	Self-expressive	3	2	2
Garrison (1978)	Preparatory interview	3	3	1
	Written introduction	3	3	1
	Attention placebo interview	—	—	—
Rose & Bednar (1980)	Positive vs. negative feedback	2	2	1
	Positive vs. negative self-disclosure	2	2	1
Jensen (1982)	Directive leader style	2	2	1
	Nondirective leader style	2	2	1
Butler & Fuhriman (1983)	Client's level of functioning	3	2	3
	Length of time in treatment	—	—	—
Piper, Debbane, Bienvenu, & Garant (1984)	Previous participant interaction with			
	Group leader	3	2	1
	Other group participants	3	2	1
	Research associate	3	2	1
Friedlander, Thiabodeau, Nichols, Tucker, & Snyder (1985)	Self-disclosing leadership style	3	2	3
	Nondisclosing leadership style	3	2	3
McGuire, Taylor, Broome, Blau, & Abbott (1986)	Pre- and early structured group	3	2	2
	Nonstructured group	—	—	—
Robison, Stockton, Morran, & Uhl-Wagner (1988)	Corrective behavioral feedback	1	2	2
Braaten (1989)	Factors of early group climate:			
	Cohesion/relationship	2	2	3
	Conformity	2	2	3
	System maintenance	2	2	3

Scale Summary

Clarity
1. No or little effort at clear definition. Meaning of terms is either ignored or merely implied.
2. Some effort at clear definition. Meaning of terms is specified, although not clearly described.

Relevance
1. Little or no effort to tie work or terms used to viable theories or a recognized body of literature.
2. Ties to viable theories or a recognized body of literature are made by implication or mere mention.

Measurement
1. Little or no effort at measurement.
2. Some effort at measurement, although not empirical and only relative to other concepts.
3. Empirical measurement is attempted. Although only ordinal

continued

TABLE 15.1 *continued*

3. Terms are defined with sufficient clarity to allow at least minimal or approximate replication of study.
4. Terms are defined clearly and completely, making replication possible. Replication is encouraged and instructions are available.
5. Same as 4, except the theoretical and empirical context is made precise.

3. Some adequate and specific ties to viable theories or bodies of literature are suggested.
4. Specific and meaningful ties are explicitly made to viable theories or a recognized body of literature.
5. Same as 4, except the theoretical and empirical context is made precise.

data are given. Reliability and validity are not mentioned.
4. Empirical measurement is attempted and interval or ratio data are offered. Reliability and validity of measures are not established.
5. Same as number 4, except reliability and validity are established and adequate.

Other References

Abramowitz & Abramowitz (1974); Abramowitz et al. (1974); Anchor (1979); Anchor et al. (1972); Anker (1961); Antonuccio et al. (1982); Bassin (1962); Berberich et al. (1979): Beutler et al. (1974); Blumer & McNamara (1985); Boe (1966); Bonney et al., (1986); Bramlett & Tucker (1981); Brown (1983); Budman et al. (1987); Cadman (1954); Caine et al. (1973); Caple & Cox (1989); Coché, Cooper, & Petermann (1984); Coons (1957); Cooper (1972); Corder et al. (1981); Cowden (1956); Crews & Melnick (1976); D'Augelli & Chinsky (1974); DeJulio et al. (1976); Diamond & Shapiro (1973); Dies (1973); Elder-Jucker (1979): Epperson (1979); Evans & Jarvis (1986): Evensen & Bednar (1976); Exener (1966); Fairweather (1963); Feder (1962); Feifel (1953); Fenton & Kaczkowski (1987); Flowers et al. (1981); Foulds & Guinan (1973); Foulds & Hannigan (1974); France & Dugo (1985); Fuchs & Rehm (1977); Fuhriman et al. (1986); Grotjan (1972); Hanson & Sander (1973); Haven & Wood (1970); Hewitt & Kraft (1973); Hilkey et al. (1982); Hodgson (1981); Hogg & Deffenbacher (1988); Imber (1957); Jacobs (1977); Jacobs et al. (1973a); Jacobs et al. (1973b); Jacobson & Smith (1972); Jeske (1973); Jew et al. (1971); Johnson (1964); Johnson et al. (1984); Jones & Medvene (1975); Kadden, Cooney, Getter, & Litt (1989); Kane et al. (1971); Kaplan (1982); Kilmann et al. (1975); Kimball & Gelso (1974); Kirshner et al. (1978); Kivlighan & Mullison (1988); Kivlighan, McGovern, & Corazzini (1984); Kivlighan, Johnsen, & Fretz (1987); Koch (1983); Koran & Costell (1973); Kraus (1959); LaTorre (1977); Lee & Bednar (1976); Lieberman (1990); Lieberman & Videka-Sherman (1986); Lundgren (1977); Martin & Jocobs (1980); May & Thompson (1973); McGinnis (1963); Mintz (1969); Mitchell & Ng (1973); Mordock et al. (1969); Morran & Stockton (1980); Morran et al. (1985); Muller & Scott (1984); Palmo, Rex, & Newman (1989); Peretz (1974); Piper et al. (1977); Piper et al. (1982); Piper et al. (1983); Piper & Marrache (1981); Pollack (1971); Posthuma & Posthuma (1973); Rashkis (1946); Reddy (1970); Redfering (1973); Reiser (1961); Ribner (1974); Roach (1976); Roark & Sharah (1989); Roback (1972); Robison et al. (1982); Rosenzweig & Folman (1974); Ross et al. (1971); Rush & Watkins (1981); Sacks (1954); Schaible & Jacobs (1974); Scott (1976); Sechrest (1961); Semon (1957b); Sethna & Harrington (1971); Shaffer et al. (1981); Shoemaker (1987); Slocum (1987); Smith (1975); Smith (1987); Smith & Evans (1971); Snyder (1959); Soeken et al. (1981); Somers (1966); Stern, Plionis, & Kaslow (1984); Stockton & Morran (1981); Stockton, Robison, & Morran (1983); Stokes et al. (1983); Strupp & Bloxom (1973); Tavormina (1975); Teahan (1966): Thoma (1964); Tinsley, Roth, & Lease (1989); Treppa & Fricke (1972); Truax (1961); Truax (1968); Tucker (1956); Warren & Rice (1972); Weber (1980); Weigel et al. (1972); Weissman et al. (1972); Wilcox (1957); Williams (1962); Wright & Duncan (1986); Zarle & Willis (1975).

Note. Because of space limitations, not all of these citations are listed in the current reference section. Those not listed here can be found in Bednar & Lawlis (1971); Bednar & Kaul (1978); or Kaul & Bednar (1986).

Conclusion. Inspection of Table 15.1 suggests that virtually all studies contain at least some attempt by the authors to define their experimental variables. More often than not, however, these definitions lack treatment specificity both conceptually and operationally. Replication of the actual treatments would be virtually impossible because of inadequate information that describes the style of group leadership, the frequency and intensity of critical group events, the composition of the group, the modal styles of group interactions, and group norms about such basic considerations as confidentiality, outside social contacts between group members, or length of group meetings. We suggest that the underlying problem in the area of definitional adequacy is not a lack of effort by most well-trained group researchers. Rather it is a lack of descriptive data based on truly astute observations about group events that add order, detail, and

information about the central events in group treatments.

Theoretical Relevance

Theoretical relevance was a primary consideration because it reflects the degree to which research variables represent the primary and unique dimensions of small group treatments. Although it is clear that determining what constitutes the primary and unique dimensions of group treatments is a topic that still generates considerable dispute, there can be little doubt that there are treatment processes that are more indigenous to group forms of treatment than to other forms. These are the nuclear elements of the group literature. Generally speaking, these staple ingredients would include (1) group interaction styles, (2) the use of multiple and diverse sources of interpersonal feedback, (3) group atmosphere, (4) leadership styles, (5) interpersonal risk taking, (6) the effects of group composition, (7) consensual validation, and (8) emphasis on roles played by group members within a developing social microcosm.

High ratings on theoretical relevance would indicate the presence of research variables that we view as highly relevant to group theory and practice. Low ratings would indicate the opposite, even when these variables are highly relevant to the practice of psychotherapy in general.

Many research reports made at least some reference to an established psychological theory. More often than not, however, these theoretical foundations have little to do with group theory, group dynamics, or group development. For example, a number of studies refer to Rogers's client-centered theory of psychotherapy as an experimental treatment condition. It is usually called "client centered" or "Rogerian group psychotherapy." While client-centered philosophy and treatment conditions may well play an important role in effective group psychotherapy, it should also be noted that this orientation is based on a system of psychological thought that defines individual psychopathology and the ingredients for its cure on an individual basis. The theoretical relevance of these concepts for group-level treatments may seem obvious to some, but they are far from explicit or systematically formulated.

Theorizing about group phenomena with concepts borrowed from systems of individual psychotherapy can be hazardous. Such a practice is based on the assumption that principles of individual psychotherapy capture the essence of group-oriented treatments. This is at best a questionable paradigm for group research. Nevertheless, this point of view is largely the basis for such group treatments as psychoanalytic groups, rationale-emotive groups, and Adlerian groups, to name but a few.

Although this approach to conceptual development can have much to recommend it, we must not lose sight of the fact that borrowing the theoretical basis for group research from individual psychotherapy has a number of potentially devastating consequences. These include (1) not developing or clarifying the primary, potent, and unique dimensions of group-level treatments, (2) limiting our understanding of group dynamics and treatment conditions to much more individualized and intrapsychic processes and dynamics, and (3) using units of analysis and observations that were not designed or derived from individuals interacting in a group format.

Conclusion. A review of the studies presented in Table 15.1 suggests that the theoretical relevance of much of the group research is not primarily based on relevant elements of group theory and practice. Most outcome studies are generic in nature, with group treatment being defined both conceptually and operationally as whatever a particular group therapist did during a session. The process literature is more promising, however. Here we see the beginning of serious attempts to identify and clarify some of the more indigenous variables that are assumed to be involved in effective group treatments.

Measurement Precision

The problem of measurement in the group literature has two major components. The first is the availability of technically acceptable methods of measurement for events that are central to group treatments. The second is the appropriateness with which these measures are used in the group literature. Our primary focus is on determining the frequence with which independent variables are quantified for empirical purposes. Obviously, independent variables that can be measured and quantified provide the best support for clear statements about how other group events may vary or covary with some specified amount of a particular treatment condition. High ratings in Table 15.1 refer to better levels of quantification; low ratings refer to the opposite.

Conclusion. Review of Table 15.1 suggests that only on rare occasions have group researchers even attempted precise measurement of independent variables as a means of documenting the type and intensity of treatment conditions that were actually operative in an experimental setting. This finding is not surprising, given the definitional and theoretical problems that we have just discussed. Good measurement technology usually evolves from well-developed and fertile conceptual soil. It is these conceptual and theoretical elements that tell us what phenomena need to be measured. Certainly the measurement problems in the group disciplines are compounded by the lack of agreement regarding the empirical measurement of such variables as "cognitiveness," "Rogerian-ness," "gestaltness," "confrontiveness," or "interactiveness." But these issues are merely expressions of the definitional problems we have already discussed.

Summary

Our review of the conceptual clarity, theoretical relevance, and measurement precision of group research variables has led us to some rather awkward realities that should not be ignored. For the most part, group research has a history of being guided by theoretical considerations that tend to be borrowed and fail to capture some of the most basic elements of group forms of psychological treatment. Additionally, few research variables have been defined with sufficient clarity to allow them to be quantified for empirical investigations. Fortunately, there are some exceptions to this description of the group research, but the modal investigation seems to be an attempt to establish empirical relationships between events that are barely described, defined, and measured. This is not a happy picture, but neither is it immutable. Our scientific interests seem to have settled on experimentation when the developmental status of our discipline also calls for astute observation; precise description of central events; and the development, measurement, and classification of crucial variables within descriptive taxonomies (i.e., leadership styles, types of improvement, precise treatment techniques).

UNDERSTANDING A PROBLEM IS ESSENTIAL TO ITS SOLUTION

The level of conceptual clarity, theoretical relevance, and measurement precision in the field is central to the two questions we raised earlier about the lack of cumulativeness in group research over the last few decades. These questions are reviewed and discussed here.

Question 1. Why have the group disciplines persisted in addressing the same generic research question (Are group treatments effective?) for well over two decades after this question has been essentially answered? Equally important, why have we not yet been very successful with the next logical step of trying to isolate some of the more specific treatment elements that account for this relatively reliable outcome?

We suggest that we have repeatedly asked the same generic outcome question because we have not completed the requisite conceptual and measurement materials required to ask more specific and penetrating questions! The underlying reason we know little about the most central group process variables is that we devote so little time to clarifying their essential nature and meaning with astute observation and careful description. For example, group cohesion is almost universally accepted as a vital consideration in group treatment. Yet we are unsure what cohesion is or how to measure it (Drescher, Burlingame, & Fuhriman, 1985; Lieberman, 1990; Mudrack, 1989). The conceptual definitions of the concept are simply legion. And in most studies, the model method of

measurement is a 10- to 15-item Likert scale in which the items show a relatively high level of internal consistency. Our point is simply that virtually every practicing clinician understands that cohesion is central to effective group treatment, that the concept is complex and multidimensional, and that levels of cohesion vary from session to session and from one stage of group development to another. Research on group cohesion that continues to be based on definitions and methods of measurement so impoverished as we commonly find can only produce a noncohesive body of literature.

In recent years, however, noticeable improvements have started to appear. The research on feedback is beginning to clarify its multidimensional characteristics (Morran & Hulse, 1984). The same is true of such important elements as initiating group treatments (Braaten, 1989; Crews & Melnick, 1976; Kaul & Bednar, 1986), multidimensional aspects of cohesion (Stokes, Fuehrer, & Childs, 1983), and leadership styles (Stinchfield & Burlingame, 1991). Research efforts like these may be important trendsetters because they are attempting to address the true complexity of human behavior in small groups with patience and diligence.

The group discipline has made tremendous improvements in its methodological sophistication in the last two decades. Now it is time to attempt equivalent improvement in the conceptual and measurement foundations of our research. The time is simply past when it can be considered acceptable to publish generic outcome studies that do not help clarify the more specific elements involved in effective and ineffective group treatments. The first, and probably most important, step in this process is observing, defining, and classifying central treatment elements so their comparative treatment efficacy can be examined. It may take decades of research to satisfy this requirement, but it is one of the most important developments facing the group disciplines.

Question 2. What can be done differently so the next decade of group research will contribute to the gradual, but orderly evolution of knowledge about small group treatments?

Obviously this is a complex question that cannot be addressed in its entirety here. But the direction of several major changes can be noted.

The first and most obvious change is a shift in emphasis. The modal research project needs to shift from experimentation to description, classification, and development of measurement techniques. With empirical tools such as factor analyses, cluster analyses, item analyses, and multidimensional scaling already available, we have never been in a better position to clearly describe, classify, and measure the central phenomena of the discipline.

Examples of some of the topics that are crucial in this process would include (1) leadership styles, (2) personality and cognitive characteristics of effective group leaders, (3) styles and patterns of group interaction, (4) crucial roles filled by group participants at various stages of group development in high-functioning groups, (5) types and levels of emotional expression and involvement in productive group processes, (6) styles and patterns of effective interpersonal communication, (7) major obstacles and sources of resistance to group development, (8) group composition, (9) major treatment techniques, and (10) types and levels of client improvement or deterioration.

In the absence of basic advances in areas like these, any attempts at future experimentation will be fundamentally compromised. These topics are among the bedrock foundation of the discipline; and until substantial progress has been made in our ability to describe, classify, and measure them, attempts at more advanced experimental manipulations will remain questionable.

Because of the importance of this undertaking, we would like to see national organizations committed to the development of group theory and practice regularly sponsor small working conferences in which recognized experts discuss the most cardinal elements of group theory and practice. Such meetings could be held annually with different participants and perspectives represented. The proceedings of these working groups should be published in national journals. The objective of these meetings would be to start developing a unified framework containing descriptions of the most cardinal concepts and elements of group treatments.

We continue to suggest that methods of scientific inquiry must be carefully matched with the developmental progress of research in the group disciplines. When a maturing discipline manages this fidelity properly, the quality and significance of its professional knowledge tend to improve more systematically as it moves from one developmental level of scientific maturation to another. In other words, good science is a developmental process, and the quality of technical work at each stage of development affects the quality of all subsequent stages of development. The most obvious and relevant scientific projects that will benefit the group discipline are not so much experimental ones as they are descriptive and clarifying. The group disciplines are in desperate need of work that helps

clarify, classify, and measure its most central phenomena. The tools for these efforts are already at hand to transform the collective experience of skilled practitioners into intersubjectively applicable measurement schemes.

SUMMARY

We have attempted to outline in broad strokes the developmental status of scientific progress in the area of small group treatments. Several trends seem noteworthy. First, and probably most important, is the observation that as a discipline we seem inclined to continue asking the same basic research questions long after they have, for all practical purposes, been answered by years of research. This observation tends to be true of both process and outcome studies. We suggested that this unsatisfactory state of affairs is a reflection of our limited conceptual and measurement capacity to ask more penetrating and informative questions. A review of some of the better research efforts in the group literature seems to confirm this observation. On the whole, the level of conceptual clarity, theoretical relevance, and measurement sophistication tends to be marginal at best.

Because of this, we reviewed the stages of development that characterize most scientific disciplines. When we applied this developmental framework to the group disciplines, we found that there is a strong tendency for group research to favor experimentation even though the conceptual and measurement prerequisites for this type of scientific work are still in their infancy. We proposed that the group disciplines shift their research emphasis to clarifying, describing, and measuring the central phenomena of the discipline instead of "causal" experimental manipulations. Failing that, we propose that at least a parallel track of descriptive research be ascribed similar prestige as experimentation. Experimentation in the absence of clear and measurable concepts is not the path of successful scientific development.

CONTEMPORARY GROUP LITERATURE

With our assessment of the developmental status of the group disciplines completed, we now turn to the research trends of the last decade or so. We have two purposes in mind. One is to resist the natural temptation to divide this literature into "process" and "outcome" studies as we have in the past. The other is to focus on the most recent developments in the most productive areas of research.

Our topical review has three primary objectives. The first is to summarize the most recent developments in the field. The second is to illustrate some of the conceptual and measurement problems we have already discussed as well as some possible solutions. And the third is to discuss the theoretical and clinical implications of the most recent research.

THE LITERATURE SEARCH

Two advanced graduate students were hired to search the literature. They used a CD-ROM system for their PsychLit search of the group literature from January 1983 to September 1990. Using the keywords "group therapy, group counseling, group treatment, group process, group outcome, and group leader," *Silverplatter 1.6* produced a daunting four inches of printout and 3,826 articles for our consideration.

Some were dropped because they were untranslated from a foreign language. Some were in media not held by the Ohio State University library system (among the largest in the nation). Some, of course, were lost, missing, or at the bindery. Still, the volume of publications was prohibitive. When we eliminated all nonresearch articles from consideration, however, the light at the end of the tunnel began to glow invitingly. Finally, we decided to narrow our primary consideration to those research articles that involved comparisons of group treatment with something, especially with other treatments or control groups but also with itself, including variants of time-series designs.

Our students plunged into the literature and emerged with 208 articles that met these rather generous conditions. Two judges were set to the task of determining the research design employed in the 208 studies, using Cook and Campbell (1979) as their guide. Despite the clarity of this guide, there were a number of discrepant judgments. Differences in classification were resolved through discussion and consultation even though that decision precluded any meaningful estimate of our judges' agreement. Orlinsky and Howard (1978), in their critique of process–outcome studies, commented that "One of the persistent problems that we encountered in reading the report of a . . . study was the feeling that we never knew enough about what was being investigated. We really didn't know much about what was done or what happened" (p. 318). We found that we had to

add, "nor how it was done." We believed that the primary source of ambiguity in the system came from the manuscripts themselves and not from the judges, so we instructed the judges to resolve their differences through discussion and consultation, where possible, and to favor the author's label in the absence of compelling evidence to the contrary.

The results of the judges' efforts are summarized in Table 15.2. Given the difficulty of determining with certainty the design of some studies, the contents probably are better taken as reasonable estimates rather than exact data points.

We reviewed other material, of course. We looked at some case studies that seemed unique and interesting, some reviews, position papers, pretheoretical speculations, and the like. Some of them will work their way into our discussion, but we will devote the bulk of our attention to the empirical work previously summarized.

GENERAL CURATIVE FACTORS

The range of phenomena considered curative in small group treatments is as broad as it is diverse. It includes highly specific and easily recognized elements such as interpersonal feedback, social learning, catharsis, cohesion, and behavioral practice to name but a few examples. Other more global attributes that are relatively unique to group treatments are also considered potent elements in the curative process. Prime examples would include the opportunity for group members to participate in an evolving social microcosm that is the object of continual review and self-examination, or the relatively unique opportunity to function in an open social system that values authenticity, candor, and the open expression of feelings. The rationales offered in support of the curative power of these various techniques are as diverse and novel as the techniques themselves. The search for the primary and unique curative factors in a group treatment

TABLE 15.2 Design characteristics of group research

Design	Number of Studies
Pretest-posttest with control	102
Pretest-posttest, no control	39
Pretest-posttest, nonequivalent control	19
Posttest only, with control	19
Time-series variations	15
Other/irreconcilable	14

format is as interesting and important as it is urgent.

Historically speaking, one of the most striking observations about general curative factors is the consistency with which some factors seem to be more universally acknowledged than others. Most of this work is based on Yalom's (1975) description of 12 curative factors in small group treatments: (1) catharsis, (2) cohesion, (3) self-understanding, (4) universality, (5) altruism, (6) interpersonal learning (input), (7) interpersonal learning (output), (8) installation of hope, (9) identification, (10) recapitulation of the primary family, (11) guidance, and (12) existential factors.

We do not mean to imply, however, that these are the only important curative processes. That clearly is not the case. But Yalom has provided one of the few conceptual entry points into this important area of research that is based on prolonged and perspicacious observations of contemporary therapy groups with real clients. Yalom's ideas about the origin and substance of curative processes in small groups has probably been so influential because his formulations are more indigenous to group psychotherapy as well as comprehensive and insightful.

Over the years, a series of investigations has been reported that seems to indicate that catharsis, insight, interpersonal learning, and cohesion may be particularly useful concepts in understanding central curative process in group treatments (Butler & Fuhriman, 1980, 1983; Lieberman, Yalom, & Miles, 1973; Marcovitz & Smith, 1983). There is also some evidence to suggest that the most influential curative factors may vary from group to group depending on the type of group and clients being studied (Yalom, 1985). This body of evidence is important because it is based on multiple samples, treatment methods, and geographical locations. Our review of general curative factors focuses on the more recent developments in this fertile area of investigation.

Yalom (1985) has suggested that the values of curative factors do not remain constant at all stages of group development. Instead, he proposed that the value of therapeutic factors shifts as a function of group development. Kivlighan and Mullison (1988) attempted to test this proposition by using critical incident reports obtained from 18 group participants in three 11-session counseling groups. Judges were used to identify the curative factors that seemed to be operating in these critical incidents. The results provided partial support for Yalom's original suggestion that the perceived value of curative factors shifts as a function of

group development. Universality was perceived as more important in early group sessions and interpersonal learning was perceived as more important in later group sessions.

Interestingly, additional data in this study provided some support for the idea that client change may occur in stages. These data were consistent with the general view that client improvement may be best understood as a sequential process. The first step may be coming to clearly understand one's maladaptive behavior, and the second may be trying out new and more adaptive behaviors. Using Yalom's curative factors as a conceptual framework, Fuhriman, Drescher, Hanson, Henrie, and Rybicki (1986) completed a sophisticated factor analytic study of curative factors. Their sample consisted of 161 group participants from four different mental health settings. These participants were asked to complete a modified version of a five-point Likert scale designed to reveal client perceptions of the value of various curative factors. The results indicated that cohesion and catharsis were consistently valued more than insight, but the setting also seemed to influence the absolute magnitude of the ratings.

Several studies have been reported that involve special populations. For example, Bonney, Randall, and Cleveland (1986) examined the factors considered the most and least helpful in group treatments for women who had experienced childhood incest. These group participants valued self-understanding and family reenactment more than did nonincest victims. But bulimia clients and their group therapists seemed to place the highest therapeutic value on self-understanding, acceptance, instillation of hope, vicarious learning, and universality (Hobbs, Birtchnell, Harte, & Lacey, 1989). Finally, members of career counseling groups most highly valued the expression of feelings, universality, cohesion, and taking responsibility for oneself (Kivlighan, Johnsen, & Fretz, 1987).

The substantative merit of these findings is not limited to the individual reports. In fact, each of the reports is seriously flawed in one way or another as are most reports in this difficult field. Knowing the limits of generalizability, therefore, borders on the impossible. But collectively, these reports can be instructive if we look at patterns of results across them. The most obvious pattern suggests the general relevance of Yalom's characterization of basic curative factors. Although the individual reports vary in the specific curative factors that are seen as most therapeutic as a function of type of group, type of client, and stage of group development, some of these curative factors have an undeniable tendency to be consistently more valued than others. Cohesion, interpersonal learning, catharsis, and self-understanding all seem to represent potent curative elements for at least some groups or types of clients.

Second, the collective body of research again illustrates the complexity of group phenomena. In virtually every report, we see markings of the same trend. In spite of the fact that some curative factors seem to be more valued than others, the most potent curative factors for any particular group can vary as a function of the group being studied, the stages of group development being sampled, or the type of clients participating in the group. This observation suggests the likely possibility that the most potent curative factors between groups will seldom be identical, and the most potent curative factors for individuals within the same group may be no more similar.

To the degree that this tentative observation is valid, it suggests a basic point for our consideration—the value of working diligently to develop a variety of conceptual schemes for identifying, describing, classifying, and understanding curative process from a variety of conceptual perspectives. Yalom has made an incisive step in this direction both substantively and methodologically by initially emphasizing careful observation and description of central group phenomena. His observations are outstanding candidates for the conceptual and measurement refinement needed to develop the conceptual tools and technology required for the next developmental step in group research and clinical practice. We simply must establish more consistency and depth in multidimensional conceptions and measurement of central curative factors before their effects can be tested and compared.

It is important to remember that keen observation and description are not unitary phenomena. They have many levels of specificity and rigor that can range from the informal methods that often precede creative hunches (Bondi, 1975) to structured case study methods (Yin, 1984), to the observational techniques of qualitative inquiry (Miles & Huberman, 1984), to the rigorous quantification of theoretical constructs (Nunally, 1978). In spite of the diversity and varying levels of rigor in these methods, they all represent potentially appropriate and valuable attempts to carefully match research methods with the developmental needs of research in the discipline. A decade or two of rigorous research at this level of inquiry could have a profound impact on the conceptual adequacy of the discipline, in measurement technology, research products, and clinical practice.

PREGROUP TRAINING AND GROUP STRUCTURE

Is it therapeutically advantageous to train clients in the skills of group membership? Are there attitudes that predispose some clients to positive change and are they amenable to training? Should we indoctrinate members in the roles that they may be called upon to play in successful groups? There is a long and consistent history of fairly impressive research that suggests affirmative answers to each of these questions (Friedlauder & Kaul, 1983; Kaul & Bednar, 1986; LaTorre, 1977). In fact, pregroup training may be one of the more potent factors involved in creating successful treatment groups. In spite of the consistency of this evidence, however, we are still struggling with the problem of knowing precisely what type of training to offer and how and when to offer it. We will review some of the most recent studies in this fertile field of research.

Design Considerations

Almost all of these questions are susceptible to experimental attack with the research tools at hand. The first step, of course, would be to decide exactly what questions we wanted to answer. We would then specify them both conceptually and operationally. We probably would use a factorial arrangement of the independent variables. The experimental design surely would include at least one control group, maybe more. Random assignment of treatment conditions to a modest number of relatively homogeneous participants would be necessary. The dependent variables would need to be related to the constructs of interest and assessed in several ways. Multivariate analysis would probably be the most appropriate form of data analysis. These considerations are nothing out of the ordinary.

There is one additional consideration that needs more attention than it usually receives in the existing literature. We would want to be sure that we assessed what our participants had learned before they participated in their groups. At a minimum, we would want to know how much or how well they mastered their assignments. We surely would not be interested in the effects of unlearned lessons on group performance. If our measures suggested that the participants were unaffected by our experimental treatments, there would be no reason to continue with the study. So, demonstrating in some unequivocal way that our participants actually possessed, at least to some degree, the attitudes, skills, or roles that we had in mind would be absolutely crucial in this type of study.

Results

The five most recent investigations on pregroup training, summarized in Table 15.3, generally meet most of these criteria. All employed control groups, random assignment of treatments, relatively homogeneous participants, and multiple dependent variables. Several employed sophisticated multivariate analyses.

The pregroup training varied in the way it was presented, at the very least. And the studies probably differed in terms of what was emphasized in the training or screening. There is no way of knowing from the manuscripts just what knowledge, attitudes, or skills were being presented to the participants. The outcomes, although somewhat mixed, seem generally to favor the training groups over the control conditions. This is a continuation of a pattern of results that was established some time ago (Kaul & Bednar, 1986; A. Shapiro & Morris, 1978). Pregroup training of various sorts has continually been shown to affect group development favorably under a variety of conditions.

To illustrate the general methods and findings of this body of research, we will discuss two studies in more detail. The first was reported by France and Dugo (1985). It has a number of clinical and methodological virtues to recommend it. In this study, 20 psychiatric outpatients who received a pregroup therapy orientation program were compared with 20 non–pretreatment control group subjects. The orientation program lasted one hour and consisted of an instructional lecture-discussion and a videotape of a simulated group session with client participation solicited throughout the presentation. Dependent measures included dropout and attendance rates, a self-report symptom inventory, and a therapist rating scale. The results indicated that over the first 10 group therapy session, the Ss receiving the pregroup training had more favorable rates of attendance. The results of this study are far from spectacular, but the use of a real clinical population, experienced group leaders working in a professional setting, and the nature of the pregroup training presented add a sampling reality to this study that should not be ignored.

The second study, reported by Muller and Scott (1984), compared the effects of five pregroup training procedures on college students before they participated in a personal growth group experience. Volunteer students were randomly assigned to one of the following five treatment or control conditions: (1) a 17-minute film presentation designed to clarify the group counseling process; (2) a reading group that was given written material equivalent in content to the film presentation; (3) a film plus written material group; (4) a minimal no-treatment control condition in which students read general material not specifically related to their concerns or expectations about group counseling; and (5) a no-treatment control condition.

Ss from these pretreatment conditions were randomly assigned to personal growth groups such that every group included participants from all of the pretreatment conditions. The results of this study are consistent with a reasonably consistent pattern of results demonstrating that pregroup training can have important and beneficial effects on group processes and outcomes. In this particular study, it was demonstrated by analysis of covariance procedures that those who received the written pregroup training reduced their number of concerns about the group experience; showed tendencies to make appropriate use of their time; and moved toward increased feelings of self-acceptance and independence, accompanied by a reduction in hostile comments. It was also found that the film presentation had similar, but less consistent beneficial effects.

These two studies are not atypical representatives of the large body of research on pregroup training. They represent the flaws and benefits of this research rather well. We will comment on both.

First, a methodological comment: If we consider pretraining to occur prior to group therapy, the two will always be hopelessly confounded unless their effects are assessed sequentially and separately. If we consider pretraining as a way of initiating therapy, the effects of the training still are confounded. In the current research, there were no cases in which the effects of the training condition were assessed immediately following pretraining. In the absence of these procedural checks to determine if the pregroup training was effective, we cannot know if the training improved the competence of the participants as members of a therapeutic group. We cannot determine whether it worked, except as it interacts with the group therapy.

In this light, the generally favorable, though mixed, pattern of results raises a squadron of new questions. If the pretreatments effectively train members in therapeutic participation, does the subsequent group therapy dilute their effects? Given that the pretraining generally is completed in an hour or two, would additional training time make the effects more sustainable? If an hour or two is enough time to learn what we are teaching, are we training people to perform what they already can do? But if the pretraining treatments are ineffective, is the pattern of results attributable to experimenter effects, Hawthorne effects, or some other artifactual circumstance? If the pretraining is ineffective, does that account for the mixed nature of

TABLE 15.3 *Pregroup training research*

Authors	Design	Treatment	Clients/Ss	Group	Leader	Dependent Variables	Results
France & Dugo (1985)	Posttest only with control	1 structured interview + videotape	Outpatient neurotics	Open-ended	6 M.A.s, 1 Ph.D., 1 M.D. Experienced	Attendance Therapist rating SCL-90 dropouts	Higher attendance rates
Budman, Demby, Feldstein, & Gold (1984)	Pretest-posttest with control	90-minute screening workshop	Outpatient neurotics	Here-and-now directive	1 Ph.D., 15 years; 2 M.A.s, 7 years each	7 measures, including SCL-90	Increased positive attitude toward group treatment; greater change in targeted problem areas
Steuer et al. (1984)	Pretest-posttest with control	1 individual session with leader	Depressed geriatric	Psychodynamic, cognitive-behavioral	Experienced	Observer ratings depression, anxiety BDI	Significant decrease in depression
O'Farrell, Cutter, & Floyd (1985)	Pretest-posttest with control	2 individual sessions of psychotherapy, 1-hour pregroup training	Married couples, alcoholic husband	Behavioral, interactional, no marital Rx	Ph.D. and internal "similar in commitment to treatment"	Marital Adjustment Test; Marital Status Inventory; Communication	Improvement in Marital Adjustment and communication positiveness
Muller & Scott (1984)	Pretest-posttest with control	Film, written, film + written, control	College students	Growth groups	"Several years of experience"	Personal Orientation Inventory; Pregroup Experience Checklist; Reaction to Group Test	7 of 18 tests, generally favoring pregroup training

the outcomes? Does the training impede the effectivenss of the therapy? All of these questions are legitimate, important, and appropriate. And answering them does not pose a monumental methodological nightmare; most of the design qualities needed are already at hand. What is missing and needed in our problem solving is more conceptual guidance regarding the crucial elements in this process that will produce measurable constructs for empirical consideration.

On the other hand, just because we cannot answer all of the questions about pregroup training and how it works does not mean we do not know anything at all. Consider, for example, the fact that this literature has now advanced to the stage wherein it is looking at specific elements and practices of pregroup training and their differential effectiveness. The most common elements are various types and levels of behavioral practice, film-mediated role models, and cognitive instructions. Furthermore, it is not uncommon for researchers to test the interaction effects of these pretraining procedures with different types of clients and personality styles, a most promising line of inquiry. The clinical implications of the entire body of pregroup training research (Bednar & Kaul, 1978; Kaul & Bednar, 1986), although not as secure and specific as we might hope, are nonetheless significant. We have substantial evidence from a variety of sources that indicates that pregroup training can have significant effects on both group processes and client outcomes. We do not really know why this process seems so important, which variables are the most potent in this process, or what type of clients may benefit the most. But the available evidence suggests that preparing clients for participation in group therapy by role induction interviews, cognitive instructions, behavioral rehearsal, or watching models may well prove to be one of the most important single considerations in effective group treatment.

The next developmental step in this line of investigation calls for the development of a taxonomy of relevant and measurable conceptual variables that would systematically guide our search for the most relevant variables in this important pretraining process.

COHESION

It seems that everyone involved with groups recognizes the importance of cohesion. When it occurs, individual clients participate more freely and more fully in the group; they attend more consistently; and they are more susceptible to therapeutic interventions from the leader or the group. Cohesion is not the only therapeutic factor in group treatment, of course, but it seems to be an exceptionally important one. More than a therapeutic equal, cohesion seems to have been ascribed a role greater than other sources of gain in group treatment. Almost by default, cohesion has come to rule the pantheon of group treatment.

In earlier reviews (Bednar & Kaul, 1978; Bednar & Lawlis, 1971; Kaul & Bednar, 1986), we did not treat cohesion research very kindly. We suggested that the emperor was wearing no clothes. And we were not convinced that there even was an emperor. We argued that the construct (or constructs) central to cohesion had not been clarified, that we could not tell in any scientifically useful way how it had been operationalized, and that induction from the body of research on cohesion was unjustifiable because of these problems. We pointed out that this was not a mandated state of affairs. The problems were known and not insurmountable. The methodological technology was at hand. Models of successful solutions existed in cognate areas. The successful explication of group cohesion seemed largely a matter of direction, diligence, and persistence. If group theory were to leave its preadolescent stage, if it were to begin establishing its own identity as a separate and maturing entity, the complexion of cohesion would begin to clear.

Nine recent investigations of cohesion are summarized in Table 15.4. Reading the studies themselves reveals that cohesion still is seen as cause and effect, as process and outcome, as necessary and sufficient.

In six studies, cohesion was an independent or predictor variable (Blumer & McNamara, 1985; Braaten, 1989; Budman et al., 1987; Hurley, 1989; Jeffrey, Snell, & Forster, 1985; Wright & Duncan, 1986).

In three of the six studies using cohesion as an independent variable, group cohesion was assessed through self-report questionnaires and its effects on outcome were noted. Braaten (1989) used the Group Atmosphere Scale (GAS; Silbergeld, Koenig, Manderscheid, Meeder, & Hornung, 1975), which includes five subscales that appear under the general heading of "cohesion and relationship." Correlations between these scores and one subjective outcome measure suggested that graduate students and mental health professionals in "semitherapeutic" Rogerian training groups who reported greater affiliation, involvement, and support also reported greater benefit from the group. The autonomy and spontaneity subscales were not significantly correlated with either outcome measure. Only the affiliation subscale was correlated

TABLE 15.4 Cohesion studies

Authors	Group	Members	Independent Variables	Dependent Variables	Results
Blumer & McNamara (1985)	Human relations training	55 college students	1. Didactic lectures 2. Group problem solving 3. Cohesion enhancement (disclosure and physical contact)	1. Videotaped social interaction 2. Self/others ratings of social anxiety and skill	1. Group and videotaped feedback improved social skills 2. Cohesion treatment (self-disclosure and physical contact) not significant
Braaten (1989)	Rogerian training and therapy	110 college students and health professionals	1. Group Atmosphere Scale (GAS) 2. Group Climate Questionnaire	1. Mental health growth tasks 2. Symptom Check List-90 (SCL-90)	1. GAS affiliative best predictor of both dependent variables 2. GAS involvement and support predicts task success, not SCL-90 3. GAS autonomy and spontaneity not significant
Budman et al. (1988)	Short-term groups	Outpatient young adults	Harvard Community Health Plan Group Cohesiveness Scale	Patient rating of benefit	1. Cohesion subscales predict benet 2. Observers and patients agree on cohesion, not therapists 3. Cohesion ratings closer to end predict benefit best
Caple & Cox (1989)	Growth groups	64 college students	1. Structured discussion of Meyers-Briggs (first, second meetings) 2. No discussion	1. Group Attitude Scale (GATTS) 2. Personal Anticipations Questionnaire 3. Group Satisfaction Scale	No differences in early sessions; structured groups showed greater attraction to group at later sessions
Hurley (1989)	Experiential small group	393 college small group students	Group Climate Questionnaire (affiliativeness subscale)	1. Member's rating of session/group outcome 2. Leader's rating of session/group outcome	1. Affiliativeness significantly associated with outcome 2. Members' ratings more positive than leaders' on affiliativeness and outcome

Study	Type of group	Sample	Independent variables	Dependent measure	Results
Jeffrey, Snell, & Forster (1985)	Weight-loss groups	139 obese clients	Heterogeneity or homogeneity of group (gender and degree of overweight)	Weight loss	Composition not significant
Roark & Sharah (1989)	1. Personal growth 2. Driving under influence (DUI) 3. Psychotherapy	1. 30 students 2. 20 DUI 3. 15 patients	Self-report of (1) empathy, (2) self-disclosure, (3) acceptance, (4) trust	Cohesion	1. All independent and dependent variables significantly correlated 2. Growth groups had higher cohesion 3. Trust may be a core factor in cohesion
Stokes, Fuehrer, & Childs (1983)	Videotaped analogue group sessions	273 college students	1. High/low topic intimacy 2. High/low topic immediacy	Gross Cohesion Questionnaire	1. High-intimacy topics associated with higher cohesion 2. Low-immediacy topics associated with higher cohesion (risk–cohesion relationship unclear)
Wright & Duncan (1986)	Experiential group training	27 college students	1. Questionnaire on cohesiveness Yalom et al. (1966) 2. 2 attraction items from cohesiveness questionnaire. Yalom et al. (1966)	Self-reported outcome	Attraction to group and cohesiveness associated with positive outcome, especially attraction

significantly with a more objective outcome measure (Symptom Check List-90; Derogatis, Rickels, & Rock, 1976).

Wright and Duncan (1986) employed a different self-report questionnaire (Yalom, Hout, Zimerberg, & Rand, 1966) in assessing cohesion in experiential groups. College student participants who reported greater cohesion, especially attraction to group, also were more likely to report greater success in the group. Finally, Hurley (1989) and Braaten (1989) apparently used two similar versions of the Group Climate Questionnaire (GCQ; MacKenzie, 1981, 1983) in designs parallel to those just mentioned. Braaten reported that GCQ engagement and Hurley that GCQ affiliation were associated with outcome. Braaten did not mention affiliation and Hurley did not mention engagement. In none of these studies was cohesion manipulated.

If there is a generalization in these studies, it is that the descriptions of group climate or atmosphere (seemingly cognate constructs) are correlated with descriptions of group outcome, at least when given by well-educated persons interested in groups. This may yet prove heuristic.

Three investigations manipulated cohesion through differential treatments. Blumer and McNamara (1985) provided college students with specific activities designed to enhance cohesion in groups: group experiences of self-disclosure and physical contact. The cohesion enhancement treatment showed no superiority to didactic lectures or group problem solving, although all were successful in increasing participants' social skills. Jeffrey et al. (1985) attempted to manipulate cohesion by controlling for homogeneity in their weight-loss groups. Here as well, no significant impact of cohesion was detected.

Two investigations did combine manipulation of cohesion and its measurement. Caple and Cox (1989) manipulated cohesion by having some groups discuss their Meyers-Briggs Type Indicator results in early group sessions, on the assumption that this structuring activity would enhance cohesion. They included a measure of attraction to group in their study, the Group Attitude Scale (N. Evans & Jarvis, 1986). Caple and Cox's results are puzzling, however. They reported that the structured (cohesive) groups were indistinguishable from the nonstructured groups in early readings of the dependent measures. Near the end of the 13-week group experience, the structured-group participants' ratings of attraction to group diverged significantly and positively from those of the nonstructured participants. Whether this is a true "sleeper effect," an anomaly, the consequence of some confound, or something else cannot be determined

from the available data. Finally, Stokes et al. (1983) manipulated interpersonal risk through topic intimacy and immediacy as a means of influencing cohesiveness and put to the test some of the notions of Bednar, Melnick, and Kaul (1974). As predicted, high-intimacy (high-risk) topics were associated with higher levels of self-reported cohesion. Contrary to prediction, however, high immediacy was not, and Stokes et al. speculated about the roles of intimacy and immediacy in the development and maintenance of group cohesion. This study warrants replication and refinement.

Collectively, the conceptual and measurement problems of cohesion are rather well known and need not be repeated in their entirety here (Bednar & Kaul, 1976; Kaul & Bednar, 1986). One example will be used, however, to demonstrate the impact of these problems on the cohesion literature; and another will be used to illustrate one of the more promising studies that attempted to amend these problems. We will use only these two illustrations because of space limitations. Accordingly, one example is more representative of what we typically do, and the other of what we could be doing.

Roark and Sharah (1989) investigated the relationship of group cohesion to empathy, self-disclosure, acceptance, and trust. To approach this problem, they compared three different groups (personal growth, DUI, and psychotherapy) on measures of cohesion. Conceptually, cohesion was considered to be the group members' attraction to the group. The authors reported that the levels of cohesion in the growth groups were higher than the DUI or psychotherapy groups, as they expected. The results of this study, however, are not what commands our attention. It is the methods of measurement that were used to assess its central conceptual elements. The authors developed a questionnaire with the aid of members of a doctoral seminar in group work. The questionnaire included 20 questions: four on empathy, four on self-disclosure, four on acceptance, four on trust, and four on group cohesion. Respondents had five choices in responding to the questions: never, seldom, sometimes, often, and always. Now the problem becomes clear.

Logic and experience have taught most experienced group practitioners that cohesion is a complex developmental process involving the expression and resolution of varying levels of anger and intimacy within groups, that it is often an unstable attribute subject to situational fluctuations, and that it is multidimensional. Yet this report measured this complex phenomenon with four items; most likely constructed on the basis of the face validity of the items. In spite of the lack of correspondence between the most essential conceptual elements of cohesion and the way it was measured, and the absence of the accepted psychometric qualities present in most good measures, the results of this study will be cited with some regularity regarding the importance of cohesion in group theory and practice until we define and measure the concept more precisely. The irony, of course, is that this study teaches us very little about what cohesion is or the role it plays in group theory and practice.

In sharp contrast to this approach is one of the more impressive attempts to conceptually understand and psychometrically assess cohesion. The Group Atmosphere Scale (Silbergeld et al., 1975) was designed to measure the psychosocial environment in outpatient therapy groups. The original scale was developed on the basis of self-reports from 149 participants in 17 different therapy groups. The researchers found that group cohesion seemed to be a function of the following six subscales: (1) spontaniety, (2) support, (3) affiliation, (4) involvement, (5) insight, and (6) clarity. In addition to this, it was reported that long-term therapy groups showed more cohesion than either long-term counseling or short-term intervention groups, that more cohesive groups showed lower scores on the submission subscale, and the stable difference between more and less cohesive groups could be found on the HIM (Hill Interaction Matrix) and on self-reports of communication and anxiety in the group. Even though replications and extensions of this type of work are necessary before the limits and utility of these findings become clear, this work is a good example of a research contribution that is matched in the developmental needs of the field.

Looking over the studies as a whole, the field is about where it was in 1985. There is no consensus about the definition or composition of the cohesion construct. It is like the concept of *dignity*, in that everyone can recognize it but no one apparently can describe it, much less measure it. A plurality in favor of a multidimensional construct may be developing, but it probably is due as much to the intractability of the measurement problem as to anything else. Interesting work is reported, but seldom systematically developed through follow-up studies, and never directly replicated. Again, it combines at best into a series of uncontrolled single observations, some of which we emphasize, may be sound. But uncontrolled single observations do not permit ready estimates of error. Try as we might, we cannot be sanguine about building a discipline upon a foundation of uncontrolled single observations of unknown accuracy.

GROUP LEADERSHIP

In many ways, the functions of the therapist do not change from the individual consulting room to the group therapy arena. In either case, we anticipate that special training and experience will have led to an understanding beyond that of the novice. There should then be some therapeutic actions following from that understanding. And the therapist should be able to monitor the clients' progress in an expert fashion. To be overly abrupt, perhaps, we expect therapists to understand what is happening, do something appropriate about it, and adjust the treatment as necessary. It does not matter whether there is a single client or a platoon of clients sitting there.

In light of the similarities in the two situations, we could expect commonalities in reviews of therapist effects—and there have been. No one seems to doubt any more that the therapist needs to be a decent human being, no matter the level of technical skill and no matter what theory guides that technique. Much beyond this, however, into the domain of specific techniques and specific theory, our vision begins to fade. Progress toward answering the better question of "What kind of treatment, by whom, and so on" has been less rapid than some had expected and all had hoped.

Nearly all the questions remaining unanswered in individual therapy remain unanswered in the area of experiential group therapy as well. But, in addition, there remain issues unique to therapist understandings and actions in the group situation.

Inspection of Table 15.5 suggests that researchers have investigated group leaders' cognitive activity, specific behavior, and style of leadership. Their effects on group members' perceptions and evaluations have been noted. In all candor, probably nothing in the literature will change the ways in which therapists approach their groups, but some characteristics seem heuristically fecund.

Two analogue studies (Curran & Loganbill, 1983; Morran & Hulse, 1984) addressed the ways in which members and leaders perceive and interpret the data of groups. Taken together, they begin to suggest how leader and member reciprocally affect one another. We want to know more, of course. Do leaders and members perceive the same phenomena when they make their responses? Is the effect of leader self-disclosure on members' attributions of attractiveness a long-term effect or a fleeting one? Do the differences in judgments about the helpfulness or appropriateness of interpretation or process observations translate into interesting process or outcome effects? Can any of these relationships withstand replication? All of these, and

TABLE 15.5 Group leadership studies

Authors	Group	Members	Leader	Independent Variables	Dependent Variables	Results
Morran & Hulse (1984)	None — analogue	32 "experienced group leaders"; 32 members	None — analogue	1. Interpretive, process, or feedback statements 2. Delivered by leader or member 3. 2nd or 10th session	1. Self-report of statement's appropriateness, helpfulness, effect on group	1. Leaders see interpretation more appropriate, helpful, positive at 10th session; members see interpretation more appropriate, helpful, positive at 2nd session 2. Leaders see process statements more appropriate and helpful than do members 3. No differences in feedback ratings
McWhirter & Frey (1987)	Career awareness and self-awareness	273 college students	24 graduate students	1. Group Embedded Figure Test (leader and member cognitive style) 2. State-Trait Anxiety Inventory (leader and member anxiety)	1. Session reactions 2. Final group evaluation 3. Final evaluation of leader	1. Leaders with higher field independence, higher state anxiety rated more favorably 2. Members' cognitive style influences evaluation of 1st group session only (higher field independence — higher evaluation of group)
Curran & Loganbill (1983)	None — analogue	40 college students	None — analogue	1. Leader self-disclosure (high or low) 2. Leader nonverbal behavior (affiliative or nonaffiliative)	Counselor Rating Form (expertness, attractiveness, trustworthiness)	1. High self-disclosure leads to high attractiveness 2. No effects for nonverbal behaviors

Study						Results
Shoemaker (1987)	5 human relations training groups	College and extension students	Interns and center staff (2 + years experience)	Post hoc division into 2 interpersonal groups; 2 intrapersonal groups; 1 in-between group	1. Member perceptions of self, ideal-self; self as seen by others; as they act to others 2. Members' rating of leader on above	1. Interpersonal interventions, feedback lead to interpersonal gains 2. Intrapersonal inverventions, low feedback lead to more gains in self-esteem
Fenton & Kaczkowski (1987)	10 weeks, 3 types	86 graduate students	Senior author for all groups	Post hoc division into group type/leader style 1. Structured T-group 2. Rotating leadership 3. Rogerian 4. Control	1. Edwards Personal Preference Schedule 2. Rotter Incomplete Sentences Blank 3. Mooney Problem Check List 4. Reaction to Group (group process)	1. 18 Edwards PPS comparisons, 7 significant 2. 6 Rotter ISB comparisons, 1 significant 3. 6 Reaction to Group comparisons, 3 significant. 4. Sleeper effect (6–8 weeks postgroup, members learn more about group process)
Stinchfield & Burlingame (1991)	15 weeks therapy	40 adults; personal problems	4 "experts"	1. Session 3, 8, or 14 2. Leader directives – imperative, requesting, or advisory 3. Directed in or out of group	Analysis of transcripts	1. In-group target, leader used imperatives 2. Out-of-group target, leader used advisories 3. Fewer in-group directives over time

more, would be interesting to theory, research, and practice.

Stinchfield and Burlingame (1991) studied experienced, expert group leaders' verbal behavior over time. The fact that leaders were more directive when they had more direct influence, and less directive when they had less, suggests their good sense. More interesting to theory, perhaps, are the results suggesting how leaders alter their use of directives as the group progresses. Stinchfield and Burlingame's results may represent a partial description of how expert leaders structure their groups and how they modify their influence attempts as the group progresses.

Even more important, however, is the implicit recognition of how leaders and members influence one another throughout the group's life. Only the most obtuse leader would ignore the unique qualities brought by each member. And only the most obtuse would ignore the uniqueness of each group. The rest would recognize and respond to these characteristics of members and groups. Sometimes unknowingly, they would choose from their nearly infinite repertoire of behavior a way to function in the essential interdependence of leadership and followership. Acknowledgment of this complex relationship among leadership roles and follower roles, and persons designated as leaders and persons designated as followers (members), should lead to more informative group research.

Demonstration Projects

Even a brief glimpse of the group literature is sufficient to reveal the prominence of one of its most charming, irritating, and frustrating attributes. It is the predominance of demonstration projects in the literature. Because they are so common, we decided to comment on them.

Demonstrations are reports of the application of group techniques. To be classified as a demonstration, a report had to include a number of characteristics. Among the positive attributes was that it had to purport, explicitly or implicitly, some unique components of group treatment. These could include unusual group leaders, leadership technique, intervention style, conditions of treatment, and the like. Oftentimes, demonstrations included novel clientele, which could be demonstrated in client diagnoses or other personal characteristics. Demonstration projects are simply reports that say "I did thus-and-so with these people, and this is what happened." The potential utility of such reports seems self-evident.

Demonstrations are also characterized by what they do not include. Generally they do not provide procedural checks or clear descriptions of the treat-

ment intervention. The treatment is described in greater or lesser detail, but usually no attempt is made to determine if it is presented or received as intended. And the dependent variables of the studies generally do not include the assessment of dimensions that are specifically and logically related to the intervention. The implicit assumption seems to be that if the clients change following treatment, the treatment must have "worked." Interestingly, if the clients do not change significantly, the treatment almost never is called into question. Instead, common speculations include the need for more time, better support, increased understanding, more precise measurement, and so on. This is not unique to the group literature, but it may be more common. The potential limitations of such reports seem self-evident, as well. As an illustration of the "scientifically better" demonstration projects in the area, we will review the application of group techniques to the treatment of bulimia. Our search uncovered a substantial number of such reports but only a small number of them included comparisons in their design. The eight comparative studies we found are summarized in Table 15.6.

Inspection of Table 15.6 is informative. A total of 481 women, 477 of whom were diagnosed bulimic, participated in the eight studies. The research was done in seven different locations and two different countries. Leaders ranged from inexperienced to experienced, and their training ranged from almost none to M.S.W., M.D., and Ph.D. levels. The group treatments were compared pre to post, with individual therapy, and with other versions of group treatment. One (Mitchell et al., 1990) even included a placebo condition. All reported significant results. One might be tempted to conclude that bulimia is ready prey for group treatment. Some authors did, and that is understandable. But were their conclusions warranted? And, if so, to what degree? If not, why not?

One place to begin looking for answers to these questions is under the "Treatment" heading in Table 15.6. All treatments salient to this question were labeled group treatments. All included 4–12 participants, it appears, and lasted 6 to 15 sessions. Treatments were "highly structured," "semistructured," and "nondirective." One (Freeman, Sinclair, Turnbull, & Annandale, 1985) employed "occasional" videotapes to make procedural checks of the group, and another (Kirkley, Schneider, Agras, & Bachman, 1985) asked participants to rate the credibility of the treatment. Other than that, we noticed nothing that would serve as a manipulation check on the treatment dimension. Although several suggested that a treatment manual was available, the material in the table is a fair summary of the information given specific to the group treatment — not exhaustive, but more than representative. If the studies were about group treatment, one would expect to find some procedural or manipulation checks relevant to the independent variable.

A second place to look for inferential power in this research is in the "Dependent Variables" column. There are behavioral and self-report indicators of bulimia, and there are indicators of syndromes, symptoms, or traits believed salient to bulimia. Of course, one would expect to find bulimia-related indicators there; after all, that is what the studies are about. But if the studies are about the effects of group treatments as well, one would expect to find at least some indicators of client change that are logically related to the form of treatment they received. There are none.

As a group, these are commendable studies. There are some sophisticated designs and statistical analyses here. And there are knowledgeable experimenters and state-of-the-art measures. So what inferential warrant is there in these eight studies? Unfortunately, not very much. There may be some reason to posit limited tentative inferences about bulimia. The psychoeducational components of the treatments and the specific dependent variables employed might be conceptually combined to provide a basis for some speculation about the nature and course of bulimia.

But we suggest that there is very little justification for any statements about the value of group treatments. Assertions of causality become somewhat vacuous without a well-defined and carefully implemented independent variable. Given the shorthand description of any actual or specific group intervention, the reader can only look to manipulation checks and group-related dependent variables for inferential power. If the manipulation checks suggest that any group phenomena actually took place, we could feel more confident that some important group process might be related to the client improvement. Similarly, if the dependent variables include those believed to be uniquely influenced by group therapy, any appropriate patterns of results could be used to persuade readers that group therapy took place, *cetaris paribus*.

However, in the absence of any of these considerations, all that can be said is that 477 women, diagnosed and screened for bulimia, were offered treatments designed to help them, some on a delayed schedule. The treatments were conducted in the presence of several other participants. We cannot determine if the presence of these participants was central to the treatment, or simply a matter of economics or convenience. Additionally, we do not

know (1) if these participants got to know one another, (2) if participants tried to help each other, (3) the level of group development that was achieved, and (4) the nature and quality of communications between the participants and leader. Without manipulation checks or group-specific dependent variables, it requires an act of faith to presume that group psychotherapy even occurred. Put another way, given the effect, we presume the cause. That is a logical error and mistaken science.

So when we find significant results on the dependent measures, what can we conclude? Perhaps tentatively that the treatment seems to have "worked" for bulimic women in several countries. What kind of treatment, given by whom, under what circumstances, we cannot say.

Innovative Interventions. In our previous reviews (Bednar & Kaul, 1978; Bednar & Lawlis, 1971; Kaul & Bednar, 1986), we ignored demonstrations, thus forfeiting their potential contributions and escaping their limitations. If nothing else, an acquaintance with the demonstrations can give a flavor of the variety of work being reported in the group literature. For example, Berry and Abramowitz (1989) reported that subliminal psychodynamic activation ("Mommy and I are two") seemed to act independently of an education/support group experience. They correctly concluded that their design did not enable "isolation of specific curative factors" (p. 84). Clients made masks that represented unintegrated parts of their personas in another demonstration (Fryrear & Stephens, 1988). Then, the masked (private) part of the persona engaged in a dialogue with the unmasked (public) part through videotape. Fryrear and Stephens suggested that the technique had promise but appropriately would "draw no conclusions about the relative merits of the program compared with other psychotherapy methods" (p. 234).

Reminiscing among the elderly was highlighted in an interesting study by Fielden (1990). Two groups were contrasted, one of which involved slides and discussion of current health and well-being issues of the elderly (the "here-and-now" group). The "reminiscence" group received pictures, slides, and sound tracks covering the period from 1900 to 1980, reflecting the life span of an 80-year-old. The goal, it must be stressed, was not to encourage participants to withdraw into the past, but just the opposite. Reminiscences were intended to enhance current relationships. Participants discussed their reminiscences and brought personal mementoes to subsequent meetings. Self-report questionnaires of health and morale were taken pre–post, as was a sociometric rating of

TABLE 15.6   Demonstration projects on bulimia

Authors	Treatment	Leaders	Comparison	Members	Dependent Variables	Primary Results
Freeman, Barry, Dunkeld-Turnbull, & Henderson (1988)	Supportive and educational semistructured (leader presents, then is nondirective), 15 sessions	2 female	Cognitive–behavioral Behavior Rx Wait-list	92 women DSM criteria Bulimic 6 years Great Britain	bulimia self-esteem, anxiety, depression	All groups improved over control on bulimia behavior and self-report
Freeman, Sinclair, Turnbull, & Annandale (1985)	Semi-structured, educational and supportive, explorative, 15 sessions	2 "relatively inexperienced"	Individual behavior Rx Individual Cognitive-behavioral Wait-list	60 women DSM criteria Bulimic 6 months Great Britain	bulimia self-esteem, anxiety, depression, locus of control	1. All treatments significant pre-post on bulimia behavior 2. Individual superior to group on self-ratings
Huon & Brown (1985)	Semi-structured; review control issues, alternatives, relaxation; food preparation, 12 sessions	Not given	Wait-list	45 women DSM criteria Bulimic 2 years Great Britain	bulimia	Group superior to wait-list on binging, body cathexis
Kirkley, Schneider, Agras, & Bachman (1985)	Nondirective, emphasized self-discovery, cognitive-behavioral, gave specific change recommendations	2 Ph.D. clinical psychologists	Group A vs. Group B Pre–post	28 women DSM criteria Bulimic 1 year USA	bulimia depression, anxiety, assertion	1. Both groups credible 2. Cognitive-behavioral superior on bulimia behaviors 3. Both significant on self-reports

Study	Treatment	Therapist	Control	Sample	Measures	Results
Laessle, Waadt, & Pirke (1987)	Behavioral and cognitive to improve coping and problem solving, 16 weeks	2 years' experience	Wait-list	17 women DSM criteria Bulimic M = 6.8 years Great Britain	bulimia depression	Significant improvement on binging
Lee & Rush (1986)	Cognitive-behavioral, supportive, 6 weeks	Ph.D. candidate, 4 years' experience	Wait-list	30 women DSM criteria USA	bulimia depression	Significant improvement on bulimia and depression
Mitchell et al. (1990)	Highly structured, intensive, cognitive-behavioral, 12 weeks	M.D.s	Drug Rx Drug + group Placebo Placebo + group	171 women DSM criteria USA	bulima depression anxiety	1. Group superior to no group on all measures 2. Group superior to drug on bulimia measures 3. Group superior to drug on anxiety, depression
Scheuble, Dixon, Levy, & Kagan-Moore (1987)	Focus primarily on personal and interpersonal issues, concurrent individual psychotherapy	Experienced M.S.W.s	Individual Rx	38 women 34 bulimic 4 anorexic USA	Premature termination	Group leader more instrumental than individual therapist

relationships. Behavioral measures included observations of visits to the communal lounge and number of interactions in the group. Fielden (1990) concluded that those in the "reminiscence intervention showed a marked improvement in all measures, whereas people from the . . . here-and-now intervention showed no significant change in measures" (p. 28). We may be less persuaded about the technique's efficacy than Fielden seems to be, but it is interesting. Perhaps here-and-now use of then-and-there is a therapeutic lubricant, at least under some circumstances.

Another demonstration demands mentioning. Denga (1983) employed "mobile group counseling" to encourage nomadic Fulani parents to send their children to Nigerian government-sponsored schools. The counseled group was composed of 184 parents who attended "rallies" once every two weeks for nine months. Counseling information was played over loudspeakers, following which three trained counselors would work with individuals in groups of four to six. The control group was composed of 166 Fulani parents living in another state. Both groups were given a measure of educational acceptance pre and post. The counseled group showed significantly more favorable educational acceptance, but the t test had 348 degrees of freedom and neither the absolute differences between the two groups nor the differential pre–post change was very dramatic. Although we cannot be absolutely sure, Denga's study may represent the *only* instance of sampling from an actual population that we have ever seen in the group literature.

Finally, two demonstration studies suggest the unrealized heuristic potential of this genre. R. Evans, Kleinman, Halar, & Herzer (1984) held group sessions via telephone conference calls with physically disabled participants on a largely unsuccessful attempt to improve their life satisfaction. Another study (Decker & Evans, 1989) employed a "minimal contact by mail version consisting of weekly mailings of program materials" (p. 487) as a comparison for smoking-cessation groups led by first-year graduate students; the null hypothesis was not rejected. What a tremendous control group for a study of some curative factors in group therapy! It would be most interesting to know what effects these delivery systems had on group cohesion, participants' feelings of universality, or the roles that participants took, to name but a few dimensions. Can you have a nonproximal therapy group held together by common problems, common beliefs, or common values or hopes? Why not? But, if you do, what is curative? Because neither of these studies employed manipulation

checks or dependent variables specific to group treatment, we can only speculate.

What is particularly interesting about demonstrations is the breadth of techniques and applications that are sheltered under the umbrella of group counseling. A great number of creative and earnest investigators are hard at work in this field. But they seem largely to be planting seeds and moving on, and the cultivation and harvesting are being left to chance.

What is particularly troubling about demonstrations is that they are similar to single observations. Their nature is such that replication is exceptionally difficult, except by the original investigator, who apparently has little interest in replication. So we have a mass of individual observations of perhaps unique phenomena under conditions of practically unknown control — hardly the stuff for confident scientific assertions. We cannot tell whether we have observed a true effect or error if we cannot replicate our observation. We cannot generalize one observation. These demonstrations, wonderful and mundane, superficial and arcane, are thereby excluded from "the corpus on the basis of which we act, and relative to which the probabilities of the various possible outcomes of our actions are defined, . . . the corpus of practical certainties" (Kyberg, 1990, p. 164).

SUMMARY

We have surveyed a small sample of the better group process and outcome studies. We have noted that many of these studies have attained a relatively sophisticated level of research methodology and data analysis. Our hope was that the data from these studies would help power professional development by shaping and refining the course and direction of theory development and shaping and refining effective treatment practices and innovations. However, these reasonable expectations cannot be fulfilled with the data at hand. Generally speaking, it seems that group research has not yet achieved a level of semantic and measurement precision sufficient to allow for the clear specification of the primary treatment variables it is investigating. This trend is a continuation of a recent pattern in which our methodological and design sophistication outstrips our conceptual clarity and measurement precision. It seems clear that the next several decades of research will need to demonstrate improvements in conceptual and measurement development just as the last several decades have demonstrated radical improvements in methodology and data analyses. We seem to have learned a good deal about the methods of good research; now we need to develop the conceptual input necessary to use these methods more productively.

CONCLUDING COMMENTS

We have emphasized the importance of the early stages of scientific development to help create a more favorable foundation for the next decade of group research. Even the most casual reading of the history and philosophy of science leaves little doubt that the quality and relevance with which we describe and measure the central phenomena of our discipline will determine in large measure the quality and relevance of our later experimental efforts. Developmentally, astute observations must precede conceptual relevance, and conceptual clarity must precede measurement precision. Meaningful experimentation then follows naturally. This developmental sequence has been so universally accepted because its utility has been so consistently and powerfully demonstrated across time and disciplines. Although our science is young and clearly struggling with the problem of conceptual and measurement clarity, it already seems obvious that our most instructive research products tend to appear in the areas where this developmental sequence has been followed most faithfully.

There can be no doubt that technically sound research may enhance our understanding of group treatments. But our plea is not for more methodological rigor, although that can hardly ever be harmful. Instead, we are emphasizing the need for more penetrating observations about the most central phenomena of small group treatments. What we want is a more complete menu of relevant conceptual propositions that are both clear and measurable. The most glaring deficiencies in group research are more conceptual than methodological, and a reflection of our improvised measurement technology more than our capacity to analyze data thoroughly and rigorously. Experimental control and manipulation, essential for determining causation, are difficult, if not impossible, to achieve in group research right now. The complex nature of group processes makes the following statement by John Steinbeck particularly relevant to the study of this subject matter.

The Mexican Sierra has "XVII-15-IX" spines in the dorsal fin. These can easily be counted. But if the sierra strikes hard on the line so that our hands are burned, if the fish sounds and nearly

escapes and finally comes in over the rail, his colors pulsing and his tail beating the air, a whole new relational externality has come into being — an entity which is more than the sum of the fish plus the fisherman. The only way to count the spines of the sierra unaffected by this second relational reality is to sit in a laboratory, open an evil-smelling jar, remove a stiff colorless fish from the formalin solution, count the spines and write the truth "D.XVII-15-IX." There you have recorded a reality which cannot be assailed — probably the least important reality concerning either the fish or yourself.

It is good to know what you are doing. The man with his pickled fish has set down one truth and recorded in his experience many lies. The fish is not that color, that texture, that dead, nor does he smell that way. (Steinbeck, 1951, p. 2)

We started this chapter by noting that careful observation and description are the first steps in good science — the steps that first identify and then conceptually preserve the quintessential qualities of the phenomena we hope to understand. Meehl (1978) understood the importance of this process. He noted that

careful observation and description seem to be more valued and better understood in the more well-developed physical sciences than the social sciences. The meetings and publications of the hard sciences accommodate the reports emphasizing careful observations and description with as much respect as the results of experiments. They understand, it appears, that while the power to explain is the crown jewel of science, description is its base. (p. 711)

REFERENCES

Abrams, D., & Follock, M. (1983). Behavioral weight-loss intervention at the worksite: Feasibility and maintenance. *Journal of Consulting and Clinical Psychology, 51,* 226–233.

Alexander, P. C., Neimeyer, R. A., Follette, V. M., Moore, M. K., & Harter, S. (1989). A comparison of group treatments of women sexually abused as children. *Journal of Consulting and Clinical Psychology, 57,* 479–483.

Anchor, K. N., Vojtisek, J. E., & Berger, S. E. (1972). Social desirability as a predictor of self-disclosure in groups. *Psychotherapy: Theory, Research, and Practice, 9,* 261–264.

Anderson, J. D. (1978). Growth groups and alienation: A comparative study of Rogerian encounter, self-directed encounter, and Gestalt. *Group and Organization Studies, 3,* 85–107.

Baehr, B. O. (1954). The comparative effectiveness of individual psychotherapy, group psychotherapy, and a combination of these methods. *Journal of Consulting Psychology, 13,* 179–183.

Barron, F., & Leary, T. F. (1955). Changes in psychometric patients with and without psychotherapy. *Journal of Consulting Psychology, 19,* 239–245.

Bednar, R. L., & Battersby, C. (1976). The effects of specific cognitive structure on early group development. *Journal of Applied Behavioral Sciences, 12,* 513–522.

Bednar, R. L., Burlingame, G. M., & Masters, K. S. (1988). Systems of family treatment: Substance or semantics? *Annual Review of Psychology, 39,* 401–434.

Bednar, R. L., & Kaul, T. J. (1978). Experiential group research: Current perspectives. In S. L. Garfield & A. E. Bergin (Eds.), *Handbook of psychotherapy and behavior change: An empirical analysis* (2nd ed., pp. 769–815). New York: Wiley.

Bednar, R. L., & Lawlis, G. F. (1971). Empirical research in group psychotherapy. In A. E. Bergin & S. L. Garfield (Eds.), *Handbook of psychotherapy and behavior change: An empirical analysis* (pp. 812–838). New York: Wiley.

Bednar, R. L., Melnick, J., & Kaul, T. (1974). Risk, responsibility, and structure: Ingredients of a conceptual framework for initiating group counseling and psychotherapy. *Journal of Counseling Psychology, 21,* 31–37.

Bergin, A. E., & Lambert, M. J. (1978). The evaluation of therapeutic outcomes. In S. L. Garfield & A. E. Bergin (Eds.), *Handbook of psychotherapy and behavior change: An empirical analysis* (2nd ed., pp. 139–190). New York: Wiley.

Berry, D. M., & Abramowitz, S. I. (1989). Educative/support groups and subliminal psychodynamic activation for bulimic college women. *International Journal of Eating Disorders, 8,* 75–85.

Beutler, L. E., Scogin, F., Kirkish, P., Schretlen, D., Corbishley, A., Hamblin, D., Meredith, K., Potter, R., Bamford, C. R., & Levenson, A. I. (1987). Group cognitive therapy and Alprazolam in treatment of depression in older adults. *Journal of Consulting and Clinical Psychology, 55,* 550–556.

Blumer, C. H., & McNamara, R. J. (1985). Preparatory procedures for videotaped feedback to improve social skills. *Psychological Reports, 57,* 549–550.

Bondi, H. (1975). What is progress in science? In R. Harve (Ed.), *Problems of scientific revolution.* Oxford: Clarendon.

Bonney, W. C., Randall, D. A., Jr., & Cleveland, J. D. (1986). An analysis of client-perceived curative factors in a therapy group of former incest victims. *Small Group Behavior, 17,* 303–321.

Braaten, L. J. (1989). Predicting positive goal attainment and symptom reduction from early group climate dimensions. *International Journal of Group Psychotherapy, 39,* 377–387.

Brown, S. D. (1983). Coping skills training: Attitude toward mental illness, depression, and quality of life 1 year later. *Journal of Counseling Psychology, 30,* 117–120.

Budman, S. H., Demby, A., Feldstein, M., & Gold, M. (1984). The effects of time-limited group psychotherapy: A controlled study. *International Journal of Group Psychotherapy, 34,* 587–603.

Budman, S. H., Demby, A., Feldstein, M., Redondo, J., Scherz, B., Bennett, M. J., Koppenaal, G., Daley, B. S., Hunter, J., & Ellis, J. (1987). Preliminary findings on a new instrument to measure cohesion in group psychotherapy. *International Journal of Group Psychotherapy, 37,* 75–94.

Budman, S. H., Demby, A., Redondo, J. P., Hannan, M., Feldstein, M., Ring, J., & Springer, T. (1988). Comparative outcome in time-limited individual and group psy-

chotherapy. *International Journal of Group Psychotherapy, 38,* 63–86.

Butler, T., & Fuhriman, A. (1980). Patient perspective on the curative process: A comparison of day treatment and outpatient psychotherapy groups. *Small Group Behavior, 11,* 371–388.

Butler, T., & Fuhriman, A. (1983). Level of functioning and length of time in treatment: Variables influencing patients' therapeutic experience in group psychotherapy. *International Journal of Group Psychotherapy, 33,* 489–505.

Cabeen, C. W. (1961). Group therapy with sex offenders: Description and evaluation of group therapy program in an institutional setting. *Journal of Clinical Psychology, 17,* 122–129.

Caple, R. B., & Cox, P. L. (1989). Relationships among group structure, member expectations, attraction to group, and satisfaction with the group experience. *The Journal for Specialists in Group Work, 14,* 16–24.

Coché, E., Cooper, J. B., & Petermann, K. J. (1984). Differential outcomes of cognitive and interactional group therapies. *Small Group Behavior, 15,* 497–509.

Comas-Diaz, L. (1981). Effects of cognitive and behavioral group treatment on the depressive symptomatology of Puerto Rican women. *Journal of Consulting and Clinical Psychology, 49,* 627–632.

Cook, T. D., & Campbell, D. T. (1979). *Quasi-experimentation: Design and analysis issues for field settings.* Chicago: Rand McNally.

Crews, C., & Melnick, J. (1976). The initial use of initial and delayed structure in facilitating group development. *Journal of Counseling Psychology, 23,* 92–98.

Curran, J., & Loganbill, C. R. (1983). Factors affecting the attractiveness of a group leader. *Journal of College Student Personnel, 24,* 350–355.

Decker, B. D., & Evans, R. G. (1989). Efficacy of a minimal contact version of a multimodal smoking cessation program. *Addictive Behaviors, 14,* 487–491.

Denga, D. I. (1983). The effect of mobile group counseling on nomadic Fulani's attitudes toward formal education. *Journal of Negro Education, 52,* 170–175.

Derogatis, L. R., Rickels, K., & Rock, A. F. (1976). The SCL-90 and the MMPI: A step in the validation of a new self-report scale. *British Journal of Psychiatry, 128,* 280–289.

Drescher, S., Burlingame, G. & Fuhriman, A. (1985). Cohesion: An odyssey in empirical understanding. *Small Group Behavior, 16,* 3–30.

Ends, E. J., & Page, C. W. (1959). Group psychotherapy and concomitant psychological change. *Psychological Monographs: General and Applied, 73,* 1–31.

Evans, N. J., & Jarvis, P. A. (1986). The group attitude scale: A measure of attraction to group. *Small Group Behavior, 17,* 203–216.

Evans, R. L., Kleinman, L., Halar, E. M., & Herzer, K. (1984). Predicting change in life satisfaction as a function of group counseling. *Psychological Reports, 55,* 199–204.

Fairweather, G. W., & Simon, R. (1960). A further follow-up comparison of psychotherapeutic programs. *Journal of Consulting Psychology, 27,* 186.

Fenton, M. O., & Kaczkowski, H. (1987). The effects of group leadership style on counselor trainees' personal functioning. *Small Group Behavior, 18,* 498–512.

Feynman, R. P. (1963). *The Feynman lectures on physics* (Vol. 1). Reading, MA: Addison-Wesley.

Fielden, M. A. (1990). Reminiscence as a therapeutic intervention with sheltered housing residents: A comparative study. *British Journal of Social Work, 20,* 21–44.

Foulds, M. L., & Hannigan, P. S. (1976). Effects of gestalt marathon workshops on measured self-actualization: A replication and follow-up study. *Journal of Counseling Psychology, 23,* 60–65.

France, D. G., & Dugo, J. M. (1985). Pretherapy orientation as preparation for open psychotherapy groups. *Psychotherapy, 22,* 256–261.

Freeman, C. P. L., Barry, F., Dunkeld-Turnbull, J., & Henderson, A. (1988). Controlled trial of psychotherapy for bulimia nervosa. *British Medical Journal, 296,* 521–525.

Freeman, C., Sinclair, F., Turnbull, J., & Annandale, A. (1985). Psychotherapy for bulimia: A controlled study. *Journal of Psychiatric Research, 19,* 473–478.

Friedlander, M. L., Thiabodeau, J. R., Nichols, M. P., Tucker, C., & Snyder, J. (1985). Introducing semantic cohesion analysis: A study of group talk. *Small Group Behavior, 16,* 285–302.

Friedlander, M. L., & Kaul, T. J. (1983). Preparing clients for counseling: Effects of role induction on counseling process and outcome. *Journal of College Student Personnel, 24,* 207–214.

Fryrear, J. L., & Stephens, B. C. (1988). Group psychotherapy using masks and video to facilitate intrapersonal communication. *The Arts in Psychotherapy, 15,* 227–234.

Fuehrer, A., & Keys, C. (1988). Group development in self-help groups for college students. *Small Group Behavior, 19,* 325–341.

Fuhriman, A., Drescher, S., Hanson, E., Henrie, R., & Rybicki, W. (1986). Refining the measurement of curativeness: An empirical approach. *Small Group Behavior, 17,* 186–201.

Garrison, J. E. (1978). Written vs. verbal preparation of patients for group psychotherapy. *Psychotherapy: Theory, Research, and Practice, 15,* 130–134.

Harvey, D. R., Scharamski, T. G., Feldman, C. M., Brooks, R. J., & Barbara, J. B. (1987). Contract counseling: An evaluation of short-term group counseling in a community release corrections program. *Small Group Behavior, 18,* 513–532.

Hobbs, M., Birtchnell, S., Harte, A., & Lacey, H. (1989). Therapeutic factors in short-term group therapy for women with bulimia. *International Journal of Eating Disorders, 8,* 623–633.

Hogg, J. A., & Deffenbacher, J. L. (1988). A comparison of cognitive and interpersonal-process group therapies in the treatment of depression among college students. *Journal of Counseling Psychology, 35,* 304–310.

Huon, G. F., & Brown, L. B. (1985). Evaluating a group treatment for bulimia. *Journal of Psychiatric Research, 19,* 479–483.

Hurley, J. R. (1989). Affiliativeness and outcome in interpersonal groups: Member and leader perspectives. *Psychotherapy, 26,* 520–523.

Hurst, A. G., Stein, K. B., Korchin, S. J., & Soskin, W. F. (1978). Leadership style determinants of cohesiveness in adolescent groups. *International Journal of Group Psychotherapy, 28,* 263–277.

Jacobs, M., Jacobs, A., Feldman, G., & Cavior, N. (1973). Feedback II — The credibility gap: Delivery of positive and negative emotional and behavioral feedback in groups. *Journal of Consulting and Clinical Psychology, 41,* 215–223.

Jeffery, R. W., Snell, M. K., & Forster, J. L. (1985). Group composition in the treatment of obesity: Does increasing group homogeneity improve treatment results? *Behavioral Research Therapy, 23,* 371–373.

Jensen, J. L. (1982). The relationship of leadership technique and anxiety level in group therapy with chronic schizophrenics. *Psychotherapy: Theory, Research, and Practice, 19,* 237–248.

Jessness, C. G. (1975). Comparative effectiveness of behavior modification and transactional analysis programs for delinquents. *Journal of Consulting and Clinical Psychology, 43,* 758–779.

Jones, F. D., & Peters, H. H. (1953). An experimental evaluation of group psychotherapy. *Journal of Abnormal Social Psychology, 47,* 345–353.

Kadden, R. M., Cooney, N. L., Getter, H., & Litt, M. D. (1989). Matching alcoholics to coping skills or interactional therapies: Posttreatment results. *Journal of Consulting and Clinical Psychology, 57,* 698–704.

Kapp, F., Gleser, G., Brissenden, A., Emerson, R., Wingt, J., & Kashdan, B. (1964). Group participation and self-perceived personality change. *Journal of Nervous and Mental Disease, 139,* 255–265.

Kaul, T. J., & Bednar, R. L. (1986). Experiential group research: Results, questions, and suggestions. In S. L. Garfield & A. E. Bergin (Eds.), *Handbook of psychotherapy and behavior change: An empirical analysis* (pp. 671–714). New York: Wiley.

Kirkley, B. G., Schneider, J. A., Agras, W. S., & Bachman, J. A. (1985). Comparison of two group treatments for bulimia. *Journal of Consulting and Clinical Psychology, 53,* 43–48.

Kivlighan, D. M., & Mullison, D. (1988). Participants' perception of therapeutic factors in group counseling: The role of interpersonal style and stage of group development. *Small Group Behavior, 19,* 452–468.

Kivlighan, D. M., McGovern, T. V., & Corazzini, J. G. (1984). Effects of content and timing of structuring interventions on group therapy process and outcome. *Journal of Counseling Psychology, 31,* 363–370.

Kivlighan, D. M., Johnsen, B., & Fretz, B. (1987). Participant's perception of change mechanisms in career counseling groups: The role of emotional components in career problem solving. *Journal of Career Development, 14,* 35–44.

Koch, H. C. H. (1983). Changes in personal construing in three psychotherapy groups and a control. *British Journal of Medical Psychology, 56,* 245–254.

Kofoed, P. L., Tolson, R. L., Atkinson, R. M., Toth, R. L., & Turner, J. A. (1987). Treatment compliance of older alcoholics: An elder-specific approach is superior to "mainstreaming." *Journal of Studies on Alcohol, 48,* 47–51.

Kyburg, H. E. Jr. (1990). Theories as mere conventions. In C. W. Savage (Ed.), *Minnesota studies in the philosophy of science: Vol. XIV. Scientific theories.* Minneapolis: University of Minnesota Press.

Laessle, R. G., Waadt, S., & Pirke, K. M. (1987). A structured behaviorally oriented group treatment for bulimia nervosa. *Psychotherapy and Psychosomatics, 48,* 141–145.

Lambert, M. J., Shapiro, D. A., & Bergin, A. E. (1986). The effectiveness of psychotherapy. In S. L. Garfield & A. E. Bergin (Eds.), *Handbook of psychotherapy and behavior change* (3rd ed., pp. 157–212). New York: Wiley.

LaPointe, K. A., & Rimm, D. C. (1980). Cognitive, assertive, and insight-oriented group therapies in the treatment of reactive depression in women. *Psychotherapy: Theory, Research, and Practice, 17,* 312–321.

Latorre, R. A. (1977). Pretherapy role induction procedures. *Canadian Psychological Review, 18,* 308–321.

Lee, N. F., & Rush, A. J. (1986). Cognitive-behavioral group therapy for bulimia. *International Journal of Eating Disorders, 5,* 599–615.

Levin, E. M., & Kurtz, R. R. (1974). Structured and nonstructured human relations training. *Journal of Counseling Psychology, 21,* 526–531.

Levine, M. (1974). Scientific method and the adversary model. *American Psychologist, 29,* 661–667.

Lieberman, M. A. (1990). Understanding how groups work: A study of homogeneous peer group failures. *International Journal of Psychotherapy, 40,* 31–52.

Lieberman, M. A., & Videka-Sherman, L. (1986). The impact of self-help groups on the mental health of widows and widowers. *American Journal of Orthopsychiatry, 56,* 435–449.

Lieberman, M. A., Yalom, I. D., & Miles, M. B. (1973). *Encounter groups: First facts.* New York: Basic Books.

Lockwood, G., Salzberg, H. C., & Heckel, R. V. (1978). The effects of videotape feedback on self-concept, role-playing ability, and growth in a leaderless therapy group. *Journal of Clinical Psychology, 34,* 718–720.

Lundgren, D. C., & Knight, D. J. (1977). Trainer style and member attitudes toward trainer and group in t-groups. *Small Group Behavior, 8,* 47–63.

Luria, Z. (1959). A semantic analysis of a normal and neurotic therapy group. *Journal of Abnormal Social Psychology, 58,* 216–220.

MacKenzie, K. R. (1981). Measurement of group climate. *International Journal of Group Psychotherapy, 31,* 287–296.

MacKenzie, K. R. (1983). The clinical application of a group climate measure. In R. R. Dies & K. R. MacKenzie (Eds.), *Advances in group psychotherapy: Integrating research and practice.* New York: International Universities Press.

Marcovitz, R. J., & Smith, J. E. (1983). Patient's perceptions of curative factors in short-term group psychotherapy. *International Journal of Group Psychotherapy, 33,* 21–39.

McDavid, J. W. (1964). Immediate effects of group therapy upon response to social reinforcement among juvenile delinquents. *Journal of Consulting Psychology, 28,* 409–412.

McGuire, J. M., Taylor, D. R., Broome, D. H., Blau, B. I., & Abbott, D. W. (1986). Group structuring techniques and their influence on process involvement in a group counseling training group. *Journal of Counseling Psychology, 33,* 270–275.

McWhirter, J. J., & Frey, R. (1987). Group leader and member characteristics and attraction to initial and final group sessions and to the group and group leader. *Small Group Behavior, 18,* 533–547.

Meehl, P. E. (1978). Theoretical risks and tabular asterisks: Sir Karl and Sir Ronald and the slow progress of soft psychology. *Journal of Consulting and Clinical Psychology, 46,* 806–834.

Meichenbaum, D. H., Gilmore, J. B., & Fedoravicius, A. (1971). Group insight versus group desensitization in treating speech anxiety. *Journal of Consulting and Clinical Psychology, 36,* 410–421.

Miles, M. B., & Huberman, A. M. (1984). *Qualitative data analysis: A sourcebook of new methods.* Beverly Hills: Sage Publications.

Mitchell, J., Pyle, R., Eckert, E., Hatsukami, D., Pomeroy, C., & Zimmerman, R. (1990). A comparison study of antidepressants and structured intensive group psychotherapy in the treatment of bulimia nervosa. *Archives of General Psychiatry, 47,* 149–157.

Morran, D. K., & Hulse, D. (1984). Group leader and member reactions to selected intervention statements: A comparison. *Small Group Behavior, 15,* 278–288.

Mudrack, P. E. (1989). Defining group cohesiveness: A legacy of confusion? *Small Group Behavior, 20,* 37–49.

Muller, E. J., & Scott, T. B. (1984). A comparison of film

and written presentations used for pregroup training experiences. *Journal for Specialists in Group Work, 9,* 122–126.

Novick, J. I. (1965). Comparison between short-term group and individual psychotherapy in effecting change in nondesirable behavior in children. *International Journal of Group Psychotherapy, 15,* 366–373.

Nunnally, J. C. (1978). *Psychometric theory* (2nd ed.). New York: McGraw-Hill.

O'Farrell, T. J., Cutter, H., & Floyd, F. J. (1985). Evaluating behavioral marital therapy for male alcoholics: Effects on marital adjustment and communication from before to after treatment. *Behavior Therapy, 16,* 147–167.

Orlinsky, D., & Howard, K. (1978). The relation of process to outcome in psychotherapy. In S. L. Garfield & A. E. Bergin, (eds.), *Handbook of psychotherapy and behavior change* (2nd ed., pp. 283–329). New York: Wiley.

Palmo, A. J., Rex, T., & Newman, W. (1989). Effects of a structured learning time interval in growth groups with college students. *The Journal for Specialists in Group Work, 14,* 84–92.

Persons, R. W. (1966). Psychological and behavioral change in delinquents following psychotherapy. *Journal of Clinical Psychology, 22,* 337–340.

Piper, W. E., Debbane, E. G., Bienvenu, J. P., & Garant, J. (1984). A comparative study of four forms of psychotherapy. *Journal of Consulting and Clinical Psychology, 2,* 268–279.

Ravetz, J. R. (1975). ". . . Et Augebitur Scientia." See Bondi (1975).

Roark, A. E., & Sharah, H. S. (1989). Factors related to group cohesiveness. *Small Group Behavior, 20,* 62–69.

Robison, F. F., Stockton, R. A., Morran, D. K., & Uhl-Wagner, A. N. (1988). Anticipated consequences of communicating corrective feedback during early counseling group development. *Small Group Behavior, 19,* 469–484.

Rose, G. S., & Bednar, R. L. (1980). Effects of positive and negative self-disclosure and feedback on early group development. *Journal of Counseling Psychology, 27,* 63–70.

Scheuble, K. J., Dixon, K., Levy, A. B., & Kagan-Moore, L. (1987). Premature termination: A risk in eating disorder groups. *Group, 11,* 85–93.

Semon, R. G., & Goldstein, W. (1957). The effectiveness of group psychotherapy with chronic schizophrenics and an evaluation of different therapeutic methods. *Journal of Consulting Psychology, 21,* 317–322.

Shapiro, A., & Morris, L. (1978). Placebo effects in medical and psychological therapies. In S. L. Garfield & A. E. Bergin (Eds.), *Handbook of psychotherapy and behavior change: An empirical analysis* (2nd ed., pp. 369–410). New York: Wiley.

Shapiro, J. L., & Diamond, M. J. (1972). Increases in hypnotizability as a function of encounter group training: Some confirming evidence. *Journal of Consulting and Clinical Psychology, 43,* 460–469.

Shoemaker, G. (1987). A study of human relations training groups: Leadership style and outcome. *Small Group Behavior, 18,* 356–367.

Silbergeld, S., Koenig, G., Manderscheid, R., Meeder, B., & Hornung, C. (1975). Assessment of environment-therapy systems: The group atmosphere scale. *Journal of Consulting and Clinical Psychology, 43,* 460–469.

Smith, P. B. (1987). Laboratory design and group process as determinants of the outcome of sensitivity training. *Small Group Behavior, 18,* 291–308.

Steinbeck, J. (1951). *Log from the Sea of Cortez.* New York: Penguin Books.

Steinmetz, J. L., Lewinsohn, P. M., & Antonuccio, D. O. (1983). Prediction of individual outcome in a group intervention for depression. *Journal of Consulting and Clinical Psychology, 51,* 331–337.

Stern, M. J., Plionis, E., & Kaslow, L. (1984). Group process expectations and outcome with post-myocardial infarction patients. *General Hospital Psychiatry, 6,* 101–108.

Steuer, J., Mintz, J., Hammen, C., Hill, M., Jarvik, L., McCarley, T., Motoike, P., & Rosen, R. (1984). Cognitive-behavioral and psychodynamic group psychotherapy in treatment of geriatric depression. *Journal of Consulting and Clinical Psychology, 52,* 180–189.

Stinchfield, R. D., & Burlingame, G. M. (1991). Development and use of the directives rating system in group therapy. *Journal of Counseling Psychology, 38,* 251–257.

Stockton, R., Robison, F. F., & Morran, D. K. (1983). A comparison of the HIM-B with the Hill Interaction Matrix Model of Group Interaction Styles: A factor analytic study. *Journal of Group Psychotherapy, Psychodrama, and Sociometry, 34,* 102–113.

Stokes, J., Fuehrer, A., & Childs, L. (1983). Group members' self-disclosures: Relation to perceived cohesion. *Small Group Behavior, 14,* 63–76.

Strassberg, D. S., Roback, H. B., Anchor, K. N., & Abramowitz, S. I. (1975). Self-disclosure in group therapy with schizophrenics. *Archives of General Psychiatry, 32,* 1259–1261.

Tinsley, H. E. A., Roth, J. A., & Lease, S. H. (1989). Dimensions of leadership and leadership style among group intervention specialists. *Journal of Counseling Psychology, 36,* 48–53.

Traux, C. B., Carkhuff, R. R., & Kodman, F., Jr. (1965). Relationships between therapist-offered conditions and patient change in group psychotherapy. *Journal of Clinical Psychology, 21,* 327–329.

Vernallis, F. F., Shipper, J. C., Butler, D. C., & Tomlinson,

T. M. (1970). Saturation group psychotherapy in a weekend clinic: An outcome study. *Psychotherapy: Theory, Research, and Practice, 7,* 144–152.

Ware, J. R., & Barr, J. E. (1977). Effects of a nine-week structured and unstructured group experience on measures of self-concept and self-actualization. *Small Group Behavior, 8,* 93–99.

Whalen, C. (1969). Effects of a model and instructions of group verbal behaviors. *Journal of Consulting and Clinical Psychology, 33,* 509–521.

Wilson, D. L., Wilson, M. E., Jr., Sakata, R., & Frumkin, R. M. (1967). Effects of short-term group interaction on social adjustment on a group of mentally retarded clients. *Psychological Reports, 21,* 7–16.

Wogan, M., Getter, H., Amdur, M. J., Nichols, M. F., & Okman, G. (1977). Influencing interaction and outcomes in group psychotherapy. *Small Group Behavior, 8,* 25–45.

Wright, T. L., & Duncan, D. (1986). Attraction to group, group cohesiveness, and individual outcome: A study of training groups. *Small Group Behavior, 17,* 487–492.

Yalom, I. D. (1975). *The theory and practice of group psychotherapy* (2nd ed.). New York: Basic Books.

Yalom, I. D. (1985). *The theory and practice of group psychotherapy* (3rd ed.). New York: Basic Books.

Yalom, I.D., & Rand, K. (1966). Compatibility and cohesiveness in therapy groups. *Archives of General Psychiatry, 15,* 267–277.

Yin, R. K. (1984). *Case study research: Design and methods.* Beverly Hills: Sage Publications.

Zimet, C. N., & Fine, H. J. (1955). Personality changes with a group therapeutic experience in human relations seminar. *Journal of Abnormal Social Psychology, 51,* 68–73.

Zimpfer, D. G. (1967). Expression of feelings in group counseling. *Personnel and Guidance Journal, 45,* 703–708.

16

RESEARCH ON BRIEF PSYCHOTHERAPY

- **MARY P. KOSS**
  University of Arizona

- **JULIA SHIANG**
  Stanford University

Over the last decade of psychotherapy research, a major effort has been made to evaluate brief psychotherapy. Both the quality and quantity of empirical research on short-term therapy have increased. In a recent compilation of North American and European research (Beutler & Crago, 1991), 12 programs were identified as specifically investigating aspects of brief psychotherapy. Once viewed as a superficial and expedient treatment to be used only in "emergency" situations until long-term therapy could begin, brief psychotherapy is now considered to be a treatment of choice for most patients (Wells & Phelps, 1990). Mental health care providers find that an increasing percentage of their time is spent providing care within a time-limited framework. Furthermore, brief therapy is now seen as an entity in its own right and not merely as an analogue to understanding long-term therapy. In this light, research on brief therapy has made significant contributions to the enhancement of general and scientific theory about the ways in which people change and adapt to contextual differences. Several factors account for the contemporary emphasis on brief therapy treatment methods in clinical practice:

1. It is now generally recognized that when patients enter psychological treatment, they do not anticipate that their therapy will be prolonged but believe that their problems will require a few sessions at most (Garfield, 1978). Indeed, patients

J. S. would like to acknowledge helpful discussion with Dr. Hanna Levenson, especially on the section regarding research in training.

typically come to psychological treatment seeking specific and focal problem resolution, rather than general personality "overhauls" as assumed in the past. The duration of therapeutic contact, regardless of the therapeutic orientation of the therapist, is a median number of six to eight sessions (Garfield, 1986). Furthermore, research has found that 75 percent of those clients who benefit from therapy do so in the first six months of contact (Lambert, Shapiro, & Bergin, 1986).

2. Brief therapy methods, once thought to be appropriate only for less severe problems, have actually been shown to be effective in treating a wide range of psychological and health-related problems, including severe and chronic problems, if treatment goals are kept reasonable. Outpatient psychotherapy in organized health care settings has been shown to reduce the subsequent utilization of medical care (Sharfstein, Muszynski, & Myers, 1984).

3. Brief treatment methods have generally reported the same success rates as longer treatment programs. But it has also been found that not everyone benefits to the same degree and that the benefits of psychotherapy are not always stable. The relatively recent use of manualized therapies has contributed to greater clarification of the therapy actually provided and the components of the interaction between the therapist–patient dyad, as well as to the ability to make more meaningful comparisons across therapies.

4. Brief therapy is seen as a means to treat specific emotional difficulties effectively at a relatively reasonable cost. Thus, the recent pressures to limit the liability of payment for psychotherapy to a predetermined number of sessions has resulted in most insurance programs' advocating therapy modalities that are, in fact, brief treatment approaches. Budman and Gurman (1983) observe that institutional supports (e.g., limits on therapy duration, staff training in brief methods) are important in determining whether planned brief psychotherapy becomes a dominant practice in a given setting: "If

such supports do not exist, therapy will probably be either unplanned and brief (because so many patients drop out or unilaterally terminate) or, for a smaller number of patients, continuous and open-ended" (p. 282).

This chapter provides an overview of the contemporary practice of brief psychotherapy and examines the existing empirical evidence on its effectiveness. We present brief therapy as it is practiced clinically by examining (1) the historical antecedents, (2) the types of brief therapy offered, and (3) the characteristics common to brief as opposed to long-term psychotherapy. We then consider empirical research on the variables that relate to process and outcome of brief therapy.

THE CLINICAL PRACTICE OF BRIEF PSYCHOTHERAPY

HISTORICAL ANTECEDENTS OF BRIEF PSYCHOTHERAPY

During the early days of psychoanalysis, the treatment period was often quite brief. As analytic treatment became more involved with transference interpretation and less involved with focal symptom relief, however, the course of treatment concomitantly became more prolonged (Malan, 1963). Some early efforts were made by a few psychoanalytic theorists to reverse the trend and shorten psychoanalysis. For example, Ferenczi (1920/1960) attempted to keep analysis short by assigning a more active, directive role to the analyst. Alexander and French (1946) became concerned that neurotic adjustment had become a problem for a larger proportion of the population than could be treated by traditional psychoanalysis. They adapted techniques from psychoanalysis that would "give rational aid to all those who show early signs of maladjustment" (p. 341). They pointed out that psychodynamic principles could be used for therapeutic effect, regardless of the length of treatment.

Much of the impetus for brief treatment came as a result of psychological emergencies. In periods of great stress in which many individuals experience psychological difficulties and "breakdowns," available treatment resources and traditional therapeutic techniques have not been sufficient to handle the problems. During World War II, when a large number of soldiers developed stress-related symptoms, short-term treatment programs were de-

signed to provide help as soon as possible after the initial trauma had occurred. This early form of crisis intervention was aimed at stress reduction, symptom relief, and prevention of greater breakdown by restoring self-esteem and avoiding further retreat into maladjustment (Grinker & Speigel, 1944; Kardiner, 1941). Other important contributions were made by Lindemann (1944) as a result of his work with families of victims of the Coconut Grove nightclub fire in 1943. He delineated phases of grief work through which people must pass in order to free themselves from the deceased and readjust to a changed environment.

Another antecedent of brief therapy was the free clinic movement of the 1960s (Glasscote, Raybin, Reifler, & Kane, 1975). During this period, there was a great deal of social upheaval created by political "counterculture" activities, widely accessible drugs, and changing moral standards. As a result, many individuals experienced both situational and personal turmoil that often led to a need for psychological help. At the same time, there was widespread mistrust of "traditional" institutions, leaving many people in need of psychological help without acceptable treatment resources. The rapid development of counterculture "rap" centers, drop-in clinics, and other alternative agencies was a response to this mistrust. These free clinics provided a nonestablishment staff who shared the values and spoke the language of the "disenfranchised." Although many of these clinics provided limited services such as chemical dependency, abortion, and draft counseling by nonprofessional volunteers, there were also numerous clinics operated by volunteer professionals who provided more or less "traditional" counseling in a nontraditional setting (Butcher, Stelmachers, & Maudal, 1984).

Another important historical development in brief treatment has been the use of cognitive-behavioral techniques in the modification of behavior. The brief treatment of behavioral problems using learning-based principles has a long history beginning with the demonstration of "unlearning" by Watson and Rayner (1920). Considering cognitive-behavioral therapy as a brief therapy may be questioned by some clinicians, because it may be fairly long term and may not fit well in the *psycho*therapy category. However, sufficient numbers of these techniques are integral parts of effective brief therapy as to require their presentation in a historical context. The directive nature of brief psychotherapy that is discussed later entails the use of some cognitive-behavioral procedures, language, and "habits," such as checking up on the effectiveness of outside-therapy assignments.

The most recent source of pressure for clinicians

to practice brief therapy has been cost–benefit considerations. The need to curtail the rising costs of health care has promoted greater use of managed health care organizations. Studies have shown that patients in managed health care settings who participate in brief therapy reduce their overall direct health care costs (Sharfstein et al., 1984).

APPROACHES TO BRIEF PSYCHOTHERAPY

The clinical literature on brief psychotherapy is quite consistent in considering a 25-session contact as the upper limit of a brief treatment. The theoretical rationale governing the setting of time limits in brief therapy is discussed more fully later. Orientations to brief psychotherapy can be classified as (1) psychodynamic; (2) behavioral, cognitive, and cognitive-behavioral; (3) eclectic; (4) crisis-oriented; and (5) other verbal approaches. The following discussion includes therapeutic approaches designed for the one-to-one outpatient psychotherapy of nonpsychotic adults with any type of behavioral problem. We have excluded from consideration group treatment, family therapy, marital counseling, telephone approaches to psychotherapy, preventive interventions, and inpatient programs. Because the focus of this volume is on empirical research findings, our presentation of clinical methods is brief.

Psychodynamically Oriented Techniques
There are many psychodynamic approaches to brief psychotherapy. The goals of these systems include developing at least limited psychogenetic understanding of the focal problem. Interpretations are still the major therapeutic technique, but they are usually slightly modified for the brief format. Interpretations are designed to be integrative instead of regressive. They focus on present circumstances, not on childhood experiences (Sarvis, Dewees, & Johnston, 1958). Positive transference is generally thought to be essential to the success of brief therapy. Interpretations of negative transference may be made, but allowing a transference neurosis to develop is considered undesirable. Psychodynamically oriented techniques include psychoanalytic therapy (Alexander & French, 1946), Adlerian psychotherapy (Ansbacher, 1972), focal psychotherapy (Balint, Ornstein, & Balint, 1972), emergency and brief psychotherapy (Bellak & Small, 1978), brief psychotherapy (Burdon, 1963), dynamic psychotherapy (Davanloo, 1979, 1980), applied psychoanalysis (Deutsch, 1949), active psychoanalytic technique (Ferenczi, 1920), brief psychotherapy (Gillman, 1965), psychoanalysis and

brief psychotherapy (Gutheil, 1944), short-term psychotherapy (Hoch, 1965), brief dynamic psychotherapy focusing on stress responses (M. Horowitz, Marmar, Krupnick, et al., 1984), interpersonal psychotherapy (Klerman, Weissman, Rounsaville, & Chevron, 1984), time-limited psychotherapy (K. A. Lewis, 1966; Malan, 1963, 1976a, 1976b; Mann, 1984), brief confrontative therapy (K. K. Lewin, 1970), supportive-expressive therapy (Luborsky, 1984), short-term insight psychotherapy (McGuire, 1965a, 1965b), anxiety-provoking psychotherapy (Merrill & Cary, 1975; Semrad, Binstock, & White, 1966; Sifneos, 1987), time-limited dynamic psychotherapy (Strupp & Binder, 1984), flexible short-term psychotherapy (Wolberg, 1980), and briefer psychotherapy (Gustafson, 1986).

Two recent approaches that focus on the first contact with the patient are those of Bloom (1981), who has advocated focused single-session psychotherapy, and Talmon (1990), who also describes single-session therapy. The two-plus-one-model, developed in England, advocates once-a-week sessions for two consecutive weeks followed by a single session three months later (Barkham, 1989; Shapiro, Barkham, Hardy, & Morrison, 1990).

Brief Behavioral, Cognitive, and Cognitive-Behavioral Therapies
Although treatment length is not a primary consideration, most behavioral and cognitive-behavioral therapies can be completed within the time limits of brief psychotherapy. There has been an explosion of interest in the behavioral, cognitive, and especially the cognitive-behavioral therapies during the last decade — particularly for those patients diagnosed with agoraphobia, social anxiety, obsessive-compulsive disorders, weight problems, and somatic disorders. However, it is not always possible to separate clearly the techniques of a behavioral approach from a cognitive approach or from a cognitive-behavioral approach, and so on. For example, when a patient presents with a phobia about cats, all three approaches focus on delineating the patient's present circumstances and associated variables that maintain both the inappropriate behavior(s) and cognition(s). As two behavioral researchers note, "We still are looking for the perfect textbook case but have not yet found it . . . there are no simple cases" (Bellack & Hersen, 1985, p. 9). In our review, we often found that an author would identify his or her research as behavioral, for example, and yet the methods used in the provision of therapy were clearly cognitive as well. However, these approaches do differ from the other general orientations in that they are more specifically fo-

cused on diagnoses and the discrete behaviors that maintain the disorders.

Brief modifications of traditional behavioral techniques include implosive therapy (Hogan, 1966, 1967; Levis & Carrera, 1967), massed desensitization (Gelder, Marks, & Wolff, 1967; Mitchell & Orr, 1974), structured behavior change (Phillips & Weiner, 1966), and accelerated massed desensitization (Suinn, Edie, & Spinelli, 1970). These modified approaches to desensitization include fewer but longer sessions. Several cognitive and cognitive-behavioral therapies that use verbal or cognitive mediation to bring about behavior change also fit into a brief treatment mode. These approaches, such as rational-emotive therapy (Ellis & Grieger, 1977), provocative therapy (Farrelly & Brandsma, 1974), brief strategic psychotherapy or ordeal therapy (Haley, 1976, 1984, 1987), self-instructional therapy (Meichenbaum, 1977) or cognitive restructuring therapy (Beck, 1976; Beck, Rush, Shaw, & Emery, 1984; Lehman & Salovey, 1990; Moretti, Feldman, & Shaw, 1990) assume an active role on the part of the therapist and employ techniques to encourage cognitive mediation and early therapeutic change.

Eclectic Psychotherapy

The basic assumption of eclectic psychotherapy is that complex patient problems must be addressed using a variety of approaches and techniques (de Shazer, 1988; Garfield, 1989; Lazarus & Fay, 1990; Weakland, 1990). This process of rapprochement and integration of theoretical approaches has produced a number of new approaches that are called eclectic. However, Norcross (1986) states in the *Handbook of Eclectic Psychotherapy,* "Not all clinicians sympathetic to eclecticism label themselves eclectics. Conversely, many self-proclaimed eclectics do not adhere to similar principles. At best, eclectics are a loosely formed, self-designated group who are united in their interest in pursuing effective procedures without restricting themselves to a single theory" (p. 6). Eclecticism involves "selecting concepts, methods, and strategies from a variety of current theories which work" (Brammer & Shostrom, 1982, p. 35).

Eclectic approaches can include behavioral techniques, focused problem solution, problem-solving methods, and family techniques. One eclectic approach that is specifically time limited is called eclectic time-limited therapy. It was developed in a university counseling center by Fuhriman, Paul, and Burlingame (1986). Other approaches that use a time limitation include systematic eclectic psychotherapy (Beutler, 1983); eclectic psychotherapy (Garfield, 1980); functional orientation to counsel-

ing and psychotherapy (Hart, 1983); multimodel therapy (Lazarus, 1981); transtheoretical approach (Goldfried, 1980; Prochaska & DiClemente, 1984; Thorne, 1973); interpersonal-developmental-existential approach, which integrates family and systems approaches (Budman & Gurman, 1988); and the structural-phenomenological approach (Apter, 1982; Murgatroyd & Apter, 1982). A critique of these approaches with an emphasis on therapeutic decision making in each is provided by Dryden (1986).

Crisis-Oriented Therapies

Crisis intervention is generally provided when the patient has experienced an extreme stressor such as rape, an earthquake, or the death of a significant other. Clinical experience has shown that these can be times when patients are willing and able to address issues concerning the crisis and their abilities to cope, as well as fundamental personality changes. It is the patient's perception of the situation that can create "a turning point in the person's life" (Bard & Ellison, 1974, p. 68). Kolotkin and Johnson (1983) note that the rapid expansion of crisis intervention services has contributed to confusion about the meaning of the term *crisis intervention* and that there are unique measurement difficulties associated with research in this area.

G. Jacobson, Strickler, and Morley (1968) describe four levels of crisis intervention, all of which are effective with certain types of clients. The first level is environmental manipulation, where the helper serves as a referral source. The second level, general support, involves active listening without threatening or challenging the basic personality structure. Approaches to supportive crisis therapy include dynamically oriented supportive psychotherapy (Coleman, 1960; Coleman & Zwerling, 1959). In the third level, the generic approach, a particular crisis is believed to have a similar meaning to most affected individuals, regardless of their personality dynamics. Generic crisis intervention requires that the therapist have techniques that are particularly helpful in resolving specific crises. This approach is exemplified by Caplan (1964) and Klein and Lindemann (1961). The fourth level is the individual approach; it stresses understanding the personality dynamics of patients and helping them to develop insight into why the present situation developed into a "crisis." Characteristic of individual approaches to crisis intervention are crisis therapy (Butcher et al., 1984), precipitating stress approach (Harris, Kalis, & Freeman, 1963), early access brief treatment (Jacobson, 1965, 1979), crisis-oriented psychotherapy (Levy, 1966), and crisis support therapy

(Sifneos, 1972), Recent reviews of crisis-oriented therapy are available (Ewing, 1990; Roberts, 1990).

Miscellaneous Brief Verbal Therapies

Several clinicians (Frankel, 1973; London, 1947; Stein, 1972, 1975; Wolberg, 1965, 1980) have discussed the value of hypnosis, hypnoanalysis, and narcoanalysis as techniques of brief therapy. Hypnosis is usually used as a treatment for a "target symptom" (Wolberg, 1980) in conjunction with other techniques, but occasionally recovery can be effected solely through the use of hypnosis. Wolberg (1965) cautions, however, that symptoms serving an important purpose in the psychological economy may resist influence.

Brief cathartic psychotherapy emphasizes emotional catharsis (Bierenbaum, Nichols, & Schwartz, 1976; Nichols, 1974; Nichols & Reifler, 1973). Techniques include role playing, repetition of affect-laden phrases, and expressive movements such as striking the couch. These procedures are designed to intensify the emotional tone of the sessions and to promote affective discharge. The confrontation problem-solving technique (Garner, 1970) is a short-session psychotherapy designed for use by nonpsychiatrically trained physicians.

COMMON CHARACTERISTICS OF BRIEF APPROACHES

A survey of brief approaches to psychotherapy reveals a core set of principles that are reinforced by technical aspects considered essential to the practice of short-term treatment. The core set of principles follows:

1. Therapeutic goals are based on the view that patients are capable of making changes throughout their life span.

2. The time required to achieve these goals is limited.

3. The development of a working alliance between therapist and patient is required to achieve the goals in a stated period of time.

The technical aspects that support these principles include the following:

1. The careful selection and exclusion of patients.

2. Rapid and early assessment of the patient.

3. Therapist actions that serve to promote the preceding principles.

A number of organizational systems have been proposed by clinicians and researchers in the field (e.g., Garfield, 1989; Koss, Butcher, & Strupp, 1986; Ursano & Hales, 1986; Wells & Phelps, 1990). In this review, we have organized the presentation as follows: First, we discuss the core principles of brief therapy. Second, we delineate the technical aspects of brief therapy that support these principles. Both principles and techniques are essential; without clearly defined techniques and adherence to them, the realization of core principles is impossible. No attempt will be made to summarize in detail all the studies or issues in each of these areas, since entire books have been devoted to these topics.

PRINCIPLES

Life Span Changes

Therapeutic goals are based on the view that patients are capable of making changes throughout their life span. The belief system that guides the practice of brief therapy is that people continue to grow throughout their life span and that carefully honed interventions, based on the environmental context, can contribute to growth and adaptive functioning (Ursano & Hales, 1986). All orientations — ranging from crisis-oriented models to more psychodynamically oriented models — generally agree on this premise. This stance toward therapy calls upon therapists to take an active role in assisting their patients toward defined goals (Wells & Phelps, 1990). Budman and Gurman (1988) suggest that brief therapy can be understood as focusing on the patient's interpersonal, developmental, and existential domains. In their own work, this orientation "is an attempt to capture and understand the core interpersonal life issues that are leading the patient to seek psychotherapy at a given moment in time, and to relate these issues to the patient's stage of life development and to his or her existential concerns" (p. 27).

Most brief psychotherapists strive to accomplish one or more of the following goals: removal or amelioration of the patient's most disabling symptoms as rapidly as possible; prompt reestablishment of the patient's previous emotional equilibrium; and development of the patient's understanding of the current disturbance and increased coping ability in the future. The patient frequently brings to therapy his or her knowledge of the symptoms he or she would most like to alleviate. Most clinicians suggest that the patient have major input in choosing the goals of limited therapy. The time limitations of brief psychotherapy make impossible many of the goals of traditional psychotherapy, such as extensive personality reconstruction or dynamic insight into psychogenetic origins of behavior. Brief psychotherapy requires abandonment of "therapeutic perfectionism" (Malan, 1963) and "prejudices of depth" (Wolberg, 1965).

Many psychotherapists have inadvertently (through training or mentoring) adopted an infectious disease model of psychotherapy (Sarvis et al., 1958). In this view, disturbing behaviors are seen as diseases and psychotherapeutic techniques are seen as the specific and permanent cure (like antibiotics) that will transform the patient into a healthy individual for the rest of his or her life. In contrast, the conceptual basis of the brief model is that adaptive coping is a lifelong process; psychotherapy can only facilitate growth by increasing a patient's coping skills in the present — which may or may not lead to psychogenetic change. There has recently been a broader acceptance of therapy based on limited goals.

There are people who want relief from a specific symptom, help with a particular area of their personality functioning, improvements of their relationships with a certain person, and so forth, and there has been an increasing acceptance within the mental health provider community that such restriction of goals is consistent with a legitimate and important therapeutic enterprise. (Pardes & Pincus, 1981, pp. 12–13)

Limited Time

Brief therapy is time oriented, in contrast to long-term psychoanalytically oriented therapy, which is based on the assumption of timelessness or unlimited time. The concept of time, in and of itself, varies. Time can be viewed as the overall duration of the contact between patient and therapist or it can be viewed as the duration of each therapy session (Hoyt, 1990). For example, overall duration can refer to once a week for six months or once a month for two years (equal number of contact "hours"). The duration of each session can refer to the "50-minute hour" or the two-hour single-session employed by Bloom (1981). The importance of this issue becomes more apparent when researchers attempt to determine what "dose" is most effective for a patient, depending on his or her presenting problems (Howard, Kopta, Krause, & Orlinsky, 1986). Bloom (1992) suggests that researchers distinguish among the concepts of *threshold* (the lowest dose of therapy to produce a discernible effect), *potency* (the absolute amount of treatment needed to produce a specified effect), and *efficacy* (the maximum effect of a treatment when provided in its optimum dosage).

Most brief therapists have been careful to define the maximum number of therapeutic interviews they consider "brief" and to discuss the meaning and effect of the short time limit on the progress of therapy. Alexander and French (1946) suggested that brief therapy should be limited to 40 sessions, but they often concluded their own cases in as few as three sessions. Today, most practitioners agree that 25 sessions is the upper limit of "brief" therapy. However, there is a wide range in the number of sessions considered necessary. Recently, Talmon (1990) and Bloom (1992) have made the case for the effectiveness of single-session therapy. Shapiro and colleagues (1990) have advocated a model in which a patient receives three contacts: once a week for two consecutive weeks and then the last contact three months later. The duration in time for most crisis-oriented psychotherapy is at the short duration end of the range. Crisis-oriented therapists follow Lindemann's (1944) conceptualization of crisis as a time-limited phenomenon that is resolved one way or another in six weeks. Slightly longer therapy durations may occur in focal psychotherapy (Balint et al., 1972; Malan, 1963, 1976a, 1976b), which usually averages 10 to 40 sessions, and anxiety-provoking psychotherapy (Sifneos, 1972), which lasts 2 to 12 months.

Many therapists recommend telling the patient during the first session that the therapy will be brief and time limited, with either a fixed limit on number of sessions or a calendar date when therapy will end. Informing patients of the time limits accomplishes three therapeutic goals. It confronts the patient with the reality of work, encourages optimism through the therapist's confidence that improvement is possible in a relatively short time, and provides a set of shared goals that define the benefits and limitations of therapy. Additionally, time limits give the therapy the added structure of a definite beginning, middle, and end. Budman and Gurman (1983) observe, "Whatever else is focused on during treatment, the brief therapist must maintain a constant ancillary focus on the time issue" (p. 284).

Although most practitioners adhere to the standard 45-to-60–minute hour and the 1-week interval, there is variability in both length and spacing of sessions. Short sessions are used most frequently when service demands are great, such as in the military, or where supportive goals are the object of the therapy. Crisis-oriented approaches, particularly, may use variable session lengths (R. A. Levy, 1966). The initial session may be long in order to obtain all necessary information and allow for the emotional ventilation that may occur at this stage of crisis. Later sessions might then be shorter.

Close spacing of initial sessions with gradually increasing inter-session intervals and a planned follow-up or booster session have also been advocated by some clinicians (e.g., Budman & Gurman, 1983; Wolberg, 1980). Thus, while brief therapy always involves a relatively small number of sessions, they may be spaced out over a number of months. The use of multiple courses of brief therapy over many years as opposed to a single course of unlimited long-term therapy also has been recommended by a number of writers (e.g., Bloom, 1981; Budman & Gurman, 1983; Cummings & Vandenbos, 1979; Rabkin, 1977). Intermittent brief therapy is being provided in many health maintenance organizations (HMO) where patients engage in therapy for short periods of time, terminate as problems are resolved, and then reenter treatment again when problems recur (Cummings & Vandenbos, 1979; Siddall, Haffey, & Feinman, 1988). This pattern of involvement with patients has been reported to comprise a significant proportion of a therapist's caseload in HMO settings. After noting the range of options in the length, spacing, and session duration of brief therapies, Budman and Gurman (1983) conclude, "(to paraphrase Thurber) 'There is no length in number.' What is, in fact, being examined in any discussion of brief treatment is therapy in which the time allotted to treatment is rationed" (p. 277).

Development of a Working Alliance

The therapeutic relationship is emphasized as a primary change strategy across almost all schools of psychotherapy (Goldfried, 1980). Freud originally described the therapeutic alliance as the understanding shared by both the patient and therapist that the purpose of their work was the improvement of the patient. The cognitive-behavioral approaches have recently placed greater emphasis on the development of the therapeutic relationship (Moretti et al., 1990). Burns and Nolen-Hoeksema (1992) found that therapeutic empathy had a moderate-to-large causal effect on patients who were treated for depression with cognitive-behavioral therapy. They were able to show that empathy was robustly associated with clinical improvement and that empathy was not associated with the facilitation of homework compliance. A number of writers in the psychodynamic orientation (e.g., Bordin, 1979; Gomes-Schwartz, 1978; Hartley & Strupp, 1983; Marziali, Marmar, & Krupnick, 1981) retain the term *working alliance* to emphasize the interactional nature of the therapeutic relationship.

Psychoanalytically oriented therapists often discuss the importance of positive transference to the success of brief psychotherapy. While strong feelings of warmth, liking for the therapist, trust, admiration, and confidence are often considered unrealistic in long-term therapy and are interpreted as such, they are considered necessary for success in the time-limited situation. Most brief therapists recommend developing a confident attitude and communicating this hope and expectation of change to the patient. Malan (1963, 1976b) believes that the therapist's enthusiasm has a critical effect on therapeutic outcome. He notes that many young therapists experience several brief, dramatic "cures" early in their careers that they are unable to duplicate in later years. Waning enthusiasm for one's therapeutic techniques may account for this phenomenon.

TECHNICAL ASPECTS

Selection and Exclusion Criteria

In general, brief therapy is offered in outpatient settings to patients who are capable of some adaptive functioning in at least one sphere of their lives. The "acceptance rate" of various therapies ranges from about 20 percent of the population (Sifneos, 1987) to over 50 percent (Donovan, 1987). The least restrictive approach is that of Bellack (Bellack & Siegal, 1983a). Here the selection process is waived and even psychotic individuals are accepted. Some clinicians advise that any patient thought suitable for psychotherapy should first be tried in brief treatment (Budman & Gurman, 1983; Wolberg, 1965). If no gains are made, transfer to a different therapist is recommended. This second trial should also involve brief therapy but possibly with different techniques than the first trial. Regressive long-term therapy is viewed by some as a disservice to any patient who perceives his or her functioning prior to the current problem as satisfactory (Gillman, 1965).

Brief treatment is a highly desirable treatment option for patients who do not readily turn to the mental health system because of the prohibitive cost of long-term treatment. Brief treatment methods are both more affordable and effective for a range of patients and problems. The techniques followed by brief therapists (directiveness, concrete goal orientation, etc.) may be the mode of helping that is expected and preferred by patients of certain ethnic backgrounds. Their cultural belief systems may contribute to a readiness for therapy that is time limited and goal focused (Bellak & Siegel, 1983a, 1983b; Hoehn-Saric et al., 1964; G. Jacobson, 1965; Lorion, 1973; Roberts, 1990; Shiang, 1993; Sue & Morishima, 1982).

The criteria that determine whether a patient is

selected for or excluded from brief treatment vary widely, depending on the therapeutic approach being offered and the setting in which therapy is to take place. Cognitive-behavioral approaches generally serve those patients who present with circumscribed behavioral symptoms and exclude those patients who exhibit impaired cognitive functioning. The patient must be able to recognize and record symptoms as well as cognitions. Without this ability and organization, interventions cannot be made in a meaningful way. In these approaches, less emphasis has been placed on the actual selection of patients than on the assessment of behaviors and cognitions of patients once they have entered therapy.

Patients who are considered unsuitable for brief therapy are those who desire personality reconstruction, are deeply dependent, act out persistently, are unrestrainably anxious, have less than a fifth-grade education, have an organic or toxic illness, or are mentally deficient or psychotic (J. Frank, 1974; Wolberg, 1965). Brief treatment also will not be effective if the patient is outspokenly self-centered, passive-dependent, masochistic, negativistic, rigid, or self-destructive (Castelnuovo-Tedesco, 1966; Gomes-Schwartz, 1978; Reich & Neenan, 1986; Strupp & Hadley, 1979).

The psychodynamic brief therapies have provided the most elaborate and detailed patient selection criteria. Not all the criteria have been tested empirically to establish their contribution to overall therapy outcome; however, in the opinion of many clinicians, the patients best suited for brief psychodynamic techniques include

1. *Those patients in whom the behavioral problem is of acute onset.* A number of therapists have pointed to recent onset as an important selection criterion for brief therapy (Bellack & Small, 1978; Wolberg, 1965, 1980). However, some therapists consider recency of onset irrelevant (e.g., Davanloo, 1979; Strupp & Binder, 1984). Correlated with recent onset is an expressed preference for focal as opposed to diffuse problems.

2. *Those patients whose previous adjustment has been satisfactory.* Many brief psychotherapies are recommended primarily for patients with a history of relatively good psychological and social functioning. However, several brief therapists have turned their attention to work with "difficult" patients who present severe symptoms often in the context of characterological disturbances. Recent work by Winston et al. (1991) with patients diagnosed with personality disorders showed that two forms of brief psychotherapy produced improvement on patients' target symptoms and that the specific techniques of each approach produced changes in specific personality traits.

3. *Those patients with good ability to relate.* The quality of the patient's human relationships is considered of prime importance in determining suitability to treatment (Piper, Azim, McCallum, & Joyce, 1990). Often, the outcome of brief therapy can be maximized by selection of patients who relate well with the therapist during the first session and demonstrate the capacity to experience feelings and develop insight (Marmor, 1979). Davanloo (1979) evaluates the patients' prognosis by their ability to respond to trial interpretations.

4. *Those patients with high initial motivation.* Many therapists have emphasized the importance of high initial motivation for successful therapy. However, Garfield (1986) points out that the empirical evidence for this view is not convincing. Problems of random selection, nonuniform assessments of motivation, varying conceptualizations of motivation, and biased ratings suggest that motivation is difficult to operationalize. However, researchers have used the concept and related it to outcome. For example, Malan (1976b) believes that initial motivation was the most important patient characteristic included in his studies. Contrasting results were found in a more recent study by Clementel-Jones, Malan, and Trauer (1990). In a retrospective study of 84 patients who had been treated for three to nine years with individual psychoanalytic psychotherapy, they found that the patient's level of motivation and quality of childhood experiences were unrelated to good outcome. Results suggest that motivation is not a useful predictor, but this finding may be due to the fact that this was a study of long-term therapy in which the effects of motivation may be ameliorated after a long period of treatment. The differential effect of motivational factors might be more apparent if researchers compared those patients who stay in therapy with those who drop out after a few sessions. Sifneos (1979) considers motivation to be of such prognostic significance that he has developed seven criteria to operationalize what he views as its components, including the ability to recognize problems as psychological; the tendency to be introspective and to be given an honest account of emotional difficulties; willingness to participate actively in treatment; curiosity and willingness to understand oneself; willingness to change, explore, and experiment; and willingness to make reasonable sacrifices. It is important to note that a high percentage of patients entering a mental health setting would fail to meet these criteria.

Rapid and Early Assessment in the Initial Interviews

Virtually all the literature is in agreement that the selection of patients for brief psychotherapy requires rapid initial assessment, the exploration of current problems, and a focus on information gathering during the first session. The focus of assessment differs among therapists. Many crisis-oriented therapists strive for an understanding of the precipitating event of the crisis and the dynamic meaning of the crisis situation in the history of the patient (Harris et al., 1963; Roberts, 1990; Sifneos, 1972). A comprehensive review of the issues involved in assessing clients for crisis intervention and a survey of assessment methods are provided by Butcher and Herzog (1982). Behavioral, cognitive, and cognitive-behavioral therapists engage the patient in a detailed account of the behaviors and cognitions that are associated with the area of dysfunction (Kendall, Vitousek, & Kane, 1991). With this information in hand, it is then possible for the therapist to determine which areas will provide the greatest leverage for change. The rapid proliferation of cognitive and behavioral questionnaires has led to the availability of several alternatives for every common diagnostic category (Kendall et al., 1991). There are more than a dozen available for depression; in recent years, the Beck Depression Inventory and the Hamilton Rating Scale have become standard parts of most research projects on depression.

Garfield (1989) discusses the importance of the initial interview in brief therapy from an eclectic orientation. He is critical of the use of psychometric instruments with reference to psychotherapy, but he believes in the importance of an orientation to the process of psychotherapy as well as clinical assessment. Assessment should address the patient's strengths, weaknesses, and personal style; expectations of therapy; and suitability for brief therapy. Wolberg (1980) uses clinical assessment to develop a working understanding of the patient's psychodynamics and neurotic patterns. The therapist attempts to gauge the degree of homeostatic imbalance as indicated by anxiety and its equivalents, the mechanisms of defense that are being used, the amount of self-esteem, dependence–independence, the character of interpersonal relationships, and the potential for disintegration. Rosenberg, Silberschatz, Curtis, Sampson, and Weiss (1986) identify pathogenic belief systems that prohibit adaptive functioning.

An alternative form of psychodynamic assessment involves articulating a "dynamic formulation" that describes the nature and etiology of a patient's psychological problems (Perry, Cooper, & Michels, 1987; Strupp & Binder, 1984). The formulation serves as a basis for choosing the focus of therapy, as a reference for the choice of therapist interventions, and as a baseline against which to evaluate the outcome of the therapy. L. Horowitz, Rosenberg, Ureno, Kalehzan, and O'Halloran (1989) describe a new method of aggregating psychodynamic formulations made independently by a number of clinicians to generate a single standardized, reliable, and valid guide for therapy.

Therapist Actions

To bring about change in the most efficacious manner, several technical behaviors are required of the brief therapist: the maintenance of focus, high therapist activity, therapist flexibility, promptness of intervention, and addressing the termination. Each of the different orientations suggests therapist actions that are consistent with its view of human change and the helping process.

Maintenance of focus. The goals of brief therapy can be accomplished most effectively if therapeutic attention is carefully focused on thorough exploration of a primary problem area. Small (1971) believes that "achievement and maintenance of a focus can be regarded as the single most important technical aspect of brief psychotherapy" (p. 121). Whether the focus is interpersonal, behavioral, cognitive, centered largely on the patients' dynamic relations in the past, or some combination of these factors is determined by the orientation of the therapy. Some clinicians suggest that the focus be determined in the first interview and communicated to the patient as part of the description of the terms and structure of the therapy. Other clinicians believe it might be harmful to explicitly share the focus of therapy with the patient. In general, however, the patient's verbalizations are kept centered on the focal problem through skillful use of "selected attention" (Malan, 1963) and "benign neglect" (Pumpian-Mindlin, 1953). The major technical error related to negative outcomes in brief therapy is the failure of the therapist to structure or focus the sessions (Budman & Gurman, 1983). In psychodynamic approaches, the exploration of childhood memories, dreams, or transference interpretations may all have a place in brief therapy, but only if they are directly related to the focus (Wolberg, 1965).

High therapist activity. Maintaining a focus requires that the therapist participate more actively in the therapeutic process than is characteristic of many long-term approaches. Generally, being "active" means directing the conversation when necessary, actively exploring areas of interest, offering support and guidance, formulating plans of action for the patient to follow, assigning homework, teaching problem solving, and encouraging a constructive life philosophy. Brief therapists often actively foster behavior change through the use of homework assignments, involvement of significant others in treatment, and the use of adjunctive aids to therapy such as self-help organizations. Persons (1989) elaborates on the function of homework in an approach called formulation-based cognitive-behavioral therapy. She states, "No matter how many insights and changes occur during the session, patients will not solve the problems on their problem list or make significant changes in their underlying irrational beliefs unless they make behavioral and cognitive changes outside the session" (p. 141). Role plays are also commonly used in some brief therapy approaches as they can serve to bring the complexity of the problem to life right in the session. According to Wolberg (1980), passivity is "anathema" in brief therapy. The well-trained therapist can guide clients toward new behavior and interactions different from their customary modes and lead them to more satisfactory and productive lives (Gelb & Ullman, 1967). A more active therapeutic style may meet certain patients' expectations of the therapist, especially if they are from a cultural background that emphasizes the authority of the therapist (Shiang, 1984, 1986; Sue & Zane, 1987). Other clinicians emphasize the importance of a patient's real-life, outside-therapy behavior over the importance of behavior in the consulting room (Budman & Gurman, 1983).

Therapist flexibility. Brief and crisis-oriented psychotherapies serve a wide range of patients, including those who are anxious, depressed, suicidal, excited, panicky, delirious, assaultive, or antisocial. Treating diverse problems requires a variety of techniques. Although school identifications exist in brief psychotherapy, most approaches are considerably more eclectic in the choice of interventions than is true of long-term therapy (e.g., Beutler & Clarkin, 1990; Budman & Gurman, 1988; Horowitz, Marmar, Krupnick, et al., 1984). The techniques used in brief psychotherapy may come from psychiatry, psychoanalysis, psychology, or sociology (Wolberg, 1980). Hill and colleagues (Hill, Carter, & O'Farrell, 1983) have shown that the therapist changes his or her behaviors over the course of therapy. Using a single-case study design, Hill compared the first third to the final two-thirds of therapy. Although there were increases in activity level, silence, and interpretations, there were also decreases in minimal encouragers. The flexibility of the therapist in adapting interventions to meet the requirements of the individual is the primary mode of shortening psychotherapy (Alexander & French, 1946).

Promptness of intervention. Much of the impetus for providing brief forms of therapy stems from the desire to be responsive to a greater range of patients and reduce the waiting list at clinics. In addition, the emphasis in brief therapy on current life problems suggests the necessity of offering the therapy when a patient has problems and is motivated to work on them. Brief therapists strive to provide treatment to a patient as early as possible after the initial request, and they discourage the use of intake interviewers different from the future therapist or lengthy psychometric assessment before therapy has been started. Most formulations of crisis situations (Caplan, 1964; Lindemann, 1944) stress the time-limited nature of these disequilibriums and the heightened susceptibility to intervention during the crisis period. Crisis intervention centers try to offer an appointment within 24 hours, and many are open 24 hours a day. Bellak and Small (1965) report attempts to reach out immediately to people involved in a disaster through the use of mobile counseling units. Wolkon (1972) found that better outcome occurred in a group of patients who were given immediate crisis therapy than in a group asked to wait several days for an appointment.

Addressing the termination. As brief therapy is inherently defined as time dependent, the issue of termination is viewed as a part of the therapy from the very first meeting, whether explicitly stated or not (Reid, 1990). Strupp and Binder (1984) believe that "termination represents one of the most critical challenges to the therapist. Depending on the management of the issue, therapy may turn out to be a success or a failure" (p. 259). In reality, clinicians vary in the amount of time they advocate for a "successful" termination. Relatively little attention is paid to the process of termination in those approaches based on stringent selection criteria, avoidance of patient regression, dependence on the therapist, and dyadic conflicts that stem from issues of childhood dependency (Davanloo, 1980; Sifneos, 1979). In contrast, the significance of termination is explicitly stated in Mann's (1973) time-limited psychotherapy by setting a termination date in the first session. Based on a developmental model of separation–individuation, the patient is expected to move through predictable stages that reactivate prior issues with separation and loss. Flegenheimer (1978) suggests that powerful termination effects can be felt even by the patient in crisis intervention based on the strength of the relationship developed at a time of crisis. The planning of termination will vary considerably from patient to patient (Garfield, 1989). There are at least three sets of variables and their interactions that may affect the termination process: (1) client variables, such as issues of dependency and attachment; (2) therapist variables, such as overinvolvement with the patient and a desire to "cure" the patient; and (3) the length of therapy itself (Garfield, 1989).

Summary

Can a unitary view of the basic elements or main themes of what constitutes brief psychotherapy be gleaned from this material? It is clear from examining the literature that there are many brief therapy approaches with different foci, structures, goals, tactics, and probably outcomes.

However, several common elements characterize most brief therapies and these features have remained fairly constant over the past decade.

Most brief therapeutic approaches are aimed at prompt and early intervention at the onset of symptoms or during an experienced crisis. Such intervention can aid in resolving immediate problems and preventing more serious or chronic pathology that may require more lengthy treatment at a later date.

Regardless of symptom severity, patients who have a good ability to relate are considered to be better candidates for brief therapy than those who have difficulty forming relationships.

Most therapists inform the patient in advance of the time limitations and expect that the focused and limited goals will be achieved in that period.

Most therapists limit therapeutic goals to those that are attainable. Goals such as amelioration of the most disabling symptoms, reestablishment of a previous level of functioning, and development of some understanding of the current disturbance and increasing coping ability are adopted.

Most brief therapy sessions are centered on concrete content and are focused on the "here and now" instead of early life events.

Most therapists tend to be both active and directive in relating to the patient in order to maintain the focus and organization of sessions. With the constraints imposed by the time limitation, the brief therapist is often caught between antagonistic roles: "relating-understanding" and "directive-confronting." The success of directive intervention generally depends on the patient's acceptance of the competence, authority, and benevolence of the therapist.

Most therapists believe that effective brief therapy requires an experienced therapist who can keep therapeutic goals in sight and not get bogged down in content that is irrelevant to the agreed-on goals. The necessity of early, rapid assessment in brief therapy underscores the importance of having an experienced therapist. It is important for the therapist to be able to gather relevant information and develop a working formulation during the early sessions. This assessment must provide an understanding of the extent of the patient's problem, the critical nature of the present situation, and the personal resources the patient might have that could be called into play to increase his or her coping skills.

Most brief therapeutic approaches consider flexibility in the therapist's role to be an essential element in abbreviating therapy.

RESEARCH ON ISSUES OF TRAINING IN BRIEF THERAPY

The importance of effective and reliable training in brief therapy has become increasingly recognized as relevant to psychotherapy research. Recent research studies are placing greater emphasis on therapy manuals in order to check therapists' adherence to the model of therapy under examination. There has also been an increasing interest in determining how theoretical orientations are actually manifested in behavior during therapy sessions. Furthermore, prescriptive therapy has emphasized the need to "match" the needs of the patient to the various ways in which the therapist provides the therapy.

In prior research, the therapists participating in the study were often expected to provide therapy without systematic training in the form of brief therapy under study. Most were actively engaged in practicing long-term therapy; the researchers expected that "good" therapists could modify their therapy using a shorter time frame without training. Budman (1981) has suggested that these therapists, well trained in the practice of long-term psychotherapy, lack the specific competencies to practice brief psychotherapy and possess habits that interfere in time-limited therapy. In these instances, it is possible that the therapy offered under time-limited conditions does not reflect well-conceptualized, planned brief psychotherapy but consists of truncated techniques borrowed from long-term psychotherapy. Improvements in future research hinge on assuring technical competence by practitioners of brief psychotherapy.

EMPIRICAL RESEARCH ON BRIEF PSYCHOTHERAPY TRAINING

Formal Training for Therapists

How many psychologists practice brief therapy and have they been formally trained? Levenson, Speed, and Budman (1992) surveyed 701 licensed psychologists in California and Massachusetts and found that over 80 percent were conducting some type of brief therapy, averaging 9.5 hours of brief therapy per week (40% of their time). A comparison of the number of brief therapy hours conducted by therapists with specific orientations showed that psychodynamically oriented therapists (40% of the sample) were responsible for 22 percent, whereas cognitive-behavioral therapists (17% of the sample) were responsible for 29 percent of the total. Most therapists stated that they had some training, but more than one-third stated that they had received little or no training. This finding has serious ramifications for what type of therapy is actually being practiced, by whom, and whether or not patients are receiving competent care.

A comparison of therapists who received different levels of training in brief methods was carried out by Burlingame, Fuhriman, Paul, and Ogles (1989). Twelve therapists (who ranged from interns to experienced therapists) were randomly assigned to treat 57 preselected clients. Therapists who had participated in a 12-hour training program on time-limited therapy were compared with nontrained and self-trained therapists. The study showed that increased levels of training were associated with lower rates of attrition and recidivism and clinically significant positive change for patients. The authors concluded that more experienced therapists did not necessarily suffer from skill deficits. Once the more experienced therapists were attitudinally "accepting" of short-term therapy, their effectiveness increased. Levenson and Bolter (1988) showed that beginning therapists had more positive attitudes toward brief therapy after participation in a planned brief therapy training program.

Values and Attitudes

The importance of attitudes and values is underscored by the research of Bolter, Levenson, and Alvarez (1990), who surveyed 222 randomly selected licensed psychologists using a self-report measure. Two factors differentiated the short-term and long-term therapists: orientation toward time and assumptions regarding the nature of psychological change. Short-term therapists valued an awareness of limited time whereas long-term therapists valued a "timeless" quality in therapy. Short-term therapists took a more developmental perspective

with their patients; they saw growth and change possible even over a short period of time. In contrast, long-term therapists placed more emphasis on the static aspects of personality. Interestingly enough, the two groups did not differ on a number of issues, including the importance of defining the major goals of therapy, a focus on the weakness or strength of the patient, their perception of change during or after therapy, economic issues, the negative consequences of therapy, and the importance of therapy.

Integrating changed self-concepts into behavior is often a lengthy process (Wolberg, 1980). The long-term therapist observes these changes during the "working through" period. The brief therapist, who must discharge a patient before the changes are complete, may consequently be vulnerable to occasional feelings of dissatisfaction with the results of therapy. Due to the amount of energy required to terminate patients and the high activity level required, brief therapy has been considered more emotionally demanding of the therapist than longer term therapy (Budman & Gurman, 1983). In fact, Hoyt (1985) suggests the therapist may experience considerable stress and discomfort as he or she continually "loses" patients.

Adherence to Therapy Form

The use of training manuals and manuals for conducting therapy has recently gained greater credibility. A number of research projects are now making use of these manuals (Beck et al., 1984; Klerman et al., 1984; Luborsky & Crits-Christoph, 1990; Strupp & Binder, 1984). While it is foolish to expect that all moment-to-moment decisions in a therapy session can be based on a manual, it is reasonable to expect that the decision-making process can be guided through the use of an organized, explicit overview of the therapeutic tenets of the approach. Research based on the training model used in the Vanderbilt study has demonstrated that trainees were able to adhere to the technical principles of the treatment model (Binder, 1991). Those therapists who were better in adhering to the technique tended to be more characterologically self-critical. They were also found to be more susceptible to negative interactions with patients. Further analysis showed that technical adherence and competence are very different constructs, with competence being the more difficult to measure (Henry, Strupp, & Binder, 1992). The therapists' interpersonal behavior tended to deteriorate from pre- to posttraining in part because of their susceptibility to traps posed by negative transference and their own countertransference reactions.

Summary

Unfortunately, many clinicians have not had formal training in brief therapy, yet they spend approximately 40 percent of their time providing some form of brief therapy (Levenson et al., 1992). The systematic training of clinicians is a requirement for any outcome research that attempts to draw conclusions about the effectiveness of therapy. Training, supervision, and the use of manuals provide guidelines for the practice of brief therapy. No matter what theoretical orientation is espoused, systematic training begins to address the issues of reliable measurement—a key component of quality psychotherapy research. Generally, it has been found that

Increased levels of systematic training on the part of the therapist enhance patient outcome, lower rates of attrition, and decrease recidivism.

Attitudes and values are important markers that affect the therapists' approach to providing therapy.

Programmatic training has been shown to change therapists' attitudes concerning the provision of brief therapy.

Adherence to the technical aspects of brief therapy is not always stable over time and requires continual supervision.

EMPIRICAL STUDIES OF THE ESSENTIAL COMPONENTS OF BRIEF PSYCHOTHERAPY

OVERALL EFFECTIVENESS OF BRIEF PSYCHOTHERAPY

Many researchers now believe that the question "Is psychotherapy effective?" has been addressed adequately by existing research (e.g., Smith & Glass, 1977; Smith, Glass, & Miller, 1980). There is now considerable empirical evidence showing that brief therapy, practiced in various forms, is efficacious with specific patient populations. The people who benefit from brief therapy are those in the mental health system whose lives are problematic in some specific areas but who are functioning without impairment in other areas. For example, the different approaches to brief therapy have been shown to be effective for the treatment of job-related stress (Barkham & Shapiro, 1990), maladaptive patterns of interpersonal functioning (Strupp & Binder, 1984), anxiety disorders (Klosko, Barlow, Tassinari, & Cerny, 1990; Michelson, Marchione, Green-

wald, & Glantz, 1990), depression (Dobson, 1989; Elkin et al., 1989), panic disorders (Beck, Sokol, Clark, Berohick, & Wright, 1992; Michelson et al., 1990), post-traumatic stress disorder (Brom, Kleber, & Defares, 1989; Foa, Rothbaum, Riggs, & Murdock, 1991), methadone-maintained opiate addicts (Rounsaville, Glazer, Wilber, Weissman, & Kleber, 1983), and to some degree, personality disorders (Alden, 1989; Winston et al., 1991). Promising research is also being conducted in the areas of brief treatment with group therapy as well as marital and family therapy (see Chapters 14 and 15 in this volume).

Brief psychotherapy has been described as "a unique proving ground for testing the efficacy and utility of techniques, something that is difficult to accomplish in open-ended approaches" (Strupp, 1981, p. 227). There are a number of reasons researchers choose brief psychotherapy for the evaluation of therapy in general:

1. Most of the variables and processes are similar or identical to those in long-term therapy. Consequently, variables important to long-term psychotherapeutic change are studied more easily in the context of a brief therapy contact.

2. Brief therapy provides a greater possibility of control of extraneous influences in a research design.

3. The logistics of arranging and monitoring numbers of patients, therapists, assistants, and significant others are more manageable over a short period of time than over longer periods.

4. The operational criteria of improvement that are required for sound outcome and process research are easier to define since brief treatment is generally more focused and goal oriented.

5. Important questions that can be answered only by adequate follow-up can be studied more readily in the context of a brief therapeutic contact.

Literature reviews have traditionally been divided into process sections and outcome sections. This approach was based on the historical fact that many researchers focused solely on process or on outcome. In the past decade, improved methodology has led to an increased sophistication in how psychotherapy has been studied. Many process researchers have found that clinically meaningful statements about the mechanisms of psychotherapy depend on how process variables relate to overall outcome. The purpose of process research, in current terms, is to "describe and explain the actions, interactions, and states of mind that are deliberately produced or emerge during psychotherapy and affect intermediate and final therapeutic outcomes" (Shoham-Salomon, 1990, p. 295). Outcome researchers have realized that consideration of in-session variables and their relation to outcome makes their results more clinically relevant. This parallel development may help bridge the gulf between clinicians and researchers (Cohen, Sargent, & Sechrest, 1986; Newman & Howard, 1991). New paradigms are being suggested for the study of brief psychotherapy. Greenberg (1986) calls for research to account for the specific context of the event by focusing on the change process. For example, the same therapeutic episode may have quite different results depending upon when it occurs in the therapy, in what context, and how the patient perceives the episode. He suggests a focus on three types of outcome: immediate, intermediate, and final. In the following section we have chosen to review the literature without separating process and outcome in the traditional manner. The review is limited to a consideration of those variables that have been subjected to empirical investigation within a brief therapy context.

Conducting psychotherapy research is not easy, as Garfield (1990) has cogently argued. The problems that researchers face are varied and extremely complicated, including "selecting therapies, therapists, and patients for research investigation; preparing training manuals; training the therapists; selecting appropriate and sufficient criteria of outcome; deciding on control groups; satisfying human subject requirements; getting sufficient subjects; conducting a follow-up evaluation; and securing adequate funding" (Garfield, 1990, p. 273). The reader is referred to Chapter 2 on research design and methodology in this volume as well as the chapters on client variables, therapist variables, and process and outcome studies of psychotherapy for discussions of the complexity of the issues. Investigators must also concern themselves with measuring clinically significant change (Jacobson & Truax, 1991). Meta-analytic approaches may contribute to the assessment of clinical significance through comparison with normative populations (Nietzel, Russell, Hemmings, & Gretter, 1987).

THE OUTCOME OF BRIEF PSYCHOTHERAPY

Comparative Studies of Brief Psychotherapy

The relationship between length of therapy and amount of change has serious implications for third-party financial support for psychotherapy. Howard and colleagues (1986) summarized the relationship between length of treatment and patient benefit on the basis of available literature. The data included information on 2,400 patients covering a

period of 30 years of research. Meta-analytic pooling provided estimates of the expected benefits of specific "doses" of psychotherapy. The authors reported that (1) 15 percent of patients felt and showed measurable improvement before attending the first session of therapy; (2) 50 percent of patients were measurably improved after the first six to eight sessions; and (3) 75 percent were improved by 26 sessions. While their analysis did not address whether nontreated comparison groups would follow the same trajectory over the same time frame, their analysis begins to establish empirical guidelines that can be used for peer review and third-party financial support of psychotherapy. A number of questions related to length of treatment are relevant to the comparative research on brief therapy: Does brief therapy provide better outcomes than time-unlimited therapy? Within the general framework of providing approximately 25 sessions in brief therapy, are positive outcomes related to the number of sessions? Are there interaction effects that result from the duration of therapy and the type of therapy with specific populations?

Time-limited versus time unlimited therapy. Time-limited treatment has been contrasted with time-unlimited treatment, for which no set limit on the length of treatment is expressed by the therapist, although the patient may be informed that the therapy course is expected to be a long one. It is useful to review a group of earlier studies for the purpose of clarifying the ways in which interpretations about the effectiveness of brief therapy have been made in the past. Luborsky, Chandler, Auerbach, Cohen, and Bachrach (1971) reviewed these studies and found that in "20 of the 22 studies of essentially time unlimited treatment, the length of treatment was positively related to outcome; the longer the duration of treatment or the more sessions, the better the outcome! It is tempting to conclude . . . that if psychotherapy is a good thing, the more the better. Other interpretations, however, may fit" (p. 154). Luborsky, Singer, and Luborsky (1975) later reviewed a small group of more tightly controlled comparative studies of time-limited versus time-unlimited approaches. They concluded, "Since Otto Rank, treatments that are structured at the outset as time-limited have been thought by some practitioners to be as good as the more usual time-unlimited treatment. The eight available controlled comparative studies are mostly (five out of eight) consistent with this view in that there is no significant difference between the two" (p. 1001). Johnson and Gelso (1980), discussing Luborsky et al.'s

(1975) review, note that when all studies of therapy duration are considered together, 67 percent suggest that the more the treatment the greater the improvement.

However, more definitive analysis reveals the ways in which outcomes were dependent on the source of measurement, time of measurement, and criteria for improvement. For example, limiting consideration to the studies that employed therapist-rated outcome raises the figure to 89 percent of the studies in favor of longer duration therapy. Including only studies that utilized behavioral measures or psychological tests lowers the number to 25 percent. These figures suggest bias on the part of therapist-raters, who may tend to feel more invested in long-term therapy and may be more likely to observe changes in patients who have remained longer in therapy (Johnson & Gelso, 1980). Likewise, bias can exist in the criteria for improvement and the outcome measures chosen for use. Studies that focus on personality reorganization, measured by rating scales designed to reflect dynamic change, are more likely to favor long-term psychotherapy; studies that focus on concrete behavior changes favor short-term psychotherapy.

Time of measurement can also have an impact on the results of therapy-duration studies, which often confound time per se with time in therapy. Lorr, McNair, Michaux, and Raskin (1964) designed a study that allowed examination of both time and number of sessions. They randomly assigned patients to therapy twice weekly, weekly, or biweekly. Improvement was related to length of treatment but not to the number of treatment sessions. Comparisons should be made at equivalent points (i.e., after a specified number of sessions and at termination) as well as after equal periods of follow-up. Comparison of time-limited to time-unlimited therapy at follow-up allows consideration of whether time per se fostered further behavior change as effectively as extended time in unlimited treatment. For example, Shlien, Mosak, and Dreikurs (1962) compared time-limited (18 sessions) to time-unlimited therapy (averaging 39 sessions). Comparison of outcome data at the 39-week point demonstrated no group differences. Thus, "[t]he curative powers of time may be set in motion by counseling but apparently need not be prodded constantly by continuous therapy" (Johnson & Gelso, 1980, p. 79).

There is little contemporary interest in research that compares time-unlimited therapy to time-limited therapy. Instead, investigators focus on the effects of various lengths of therapy all within the brief model and on the interaction between type and length of therapy.

Length of therapy within the brief model. Is there a unique contribution to the therapeutic process that lies in the time constraints inherent in brief psychotherapy? Many clinicians believe that the therapeutic process is speeded up by a patient's awareness that therapeutic time is limited. For example, J. Frank (1959) reported that patients responded more promptly to treatment when they knew in advance that the therapy was to be limited. He hypothesized that improvement in treatment is produced by a "nonspecific expectancy of relief," which alleviates discomfort early in therapy independent of the duration of treatment, and by relearning, which is related to time but not necessarily to time spent in treatment. A number of comparative studies of various brief psychotherapy approaches have failed to establish a relationship between the duration of the treatment and the effectiveness of the therapy (Robinson, Berman, & Neimeyer, 1990 [used 1–46 sessions]; Shapiro & Shapiro, 1982). It is generally accepted that the major impact of psychological treatment occurs in the first 6 to 8 sessions (Smith et al., 1980). After this, there is a reduction in impact that lasts for the next 10 sessions. In a meta-analysis of 19 clinically relevant comparative outcome studies, Svartberg and Stiles (1991) found that both short-term psychodynamically oriented therapies and cognitive-behavioral therapies were more effective (when compared to patients receiving no-treatment) as the duration in treatment increased, but they were differentially effective depending on the nature of the presenting problem of the patient (e.g., neurotic problems, depression, or personality disorders). Therapy that focused on personality change was clinically more effective than event-centered therapy, and fixed time-limit therapies were found to be more effective than therapies with a flexible time limit.

Interaction between the length of therapy and type of therapy. Evidence that the length (short and long) and the type (individual versus group) of therapy interact is provided by Piper, Debbane, Bienvenu, and Garant (1984), who studied 106 outpatients with mild neurotic and characterological problems. Brief treatments averaged 22 sessions while long treatments averaged 76 sessions. Minimal evidence was found for main effects based on either form of therapy or duration of therapy, but considerable evidence was found for an interaction whereby the impact of time limitation was modified by the format of therapy. Therapist and patient comments on the therapy process highlighted this finding. Regarding brief individual psychotherapy, both therapists and patients noted a "facilitative atmosphere of time pressure." While the range of problems that were explored was narrow, those problems that were explored were treated in depth. Satisfaction was also expressed with long-term individual therapy by patients but not by therapists. Therapists believed that one session a week for 76 weeks seemed to favor increased resistance and decreased working through. The therapists encountered a number of problems with long-term treatment: Patients tended to defend against affective involvement, to control regression, and to restrict expression of transference, which made these processes more difficult to clarify and interpret. Time limitation was not viewed favorably by therapists and patients assigned to group therapy—both perceived an atmosphere of deprivation. The long-term group, on the other hand, was viewed quite favorably. Both patients and therapists felt a high degree of involvement and attentiveness.

Relative Effectiveness of Alternative Brief Psychotherapy Approaches

The prevalent view is that the outcomes of different psychotherapies are equivalent (Stiles, Shapiro, & Elliott, 1986). However, the field may be too young to adequately answer this question because the measurement of variables across types of therapies may not be equivalent. For example, if a cognitive-behavioral approach attempts to change a person's schema in a certain domain, the use of a measurement tool that indicates symptom change may not necessarily tap the desired change. Nevertheless, the question of which brief therapy approach is most efficacious, and for what population, is still asked. Recent studies have examined the comparative outcome of different approaches to brief psychotherapy, including behavior therapy, cathartic therapy, client-centered therapy, cognitive therapy, dynamic psychotherapy, Gestalt therapy, rational therapy, and alternate psychotherapy as practiced by humane but untrained college professors (e.g., Bolz & Meyer, 1981; Cross, Sheehan, & Khan, 1982; Levene, Breger, & Patterson, 1972; Nichols, 1974; Nichols & Reifler, 1973; Patterson, Levene, & Breger, 1971; Paul, 1966, 1967b; Sloane, Staples, Cristol, Yorkston, & Whipple, 1975, 1976; Strupp & Hadley, 1979).

Svartberg and Stiles (1991) provided a meta-analysis of 19 studies that compared short-term psychodynamic psychotherapies with alternative therapies such as cognitive-supportive therapies, cognitive-behavioral therapies, experiential therapies, and attendance at self-help groups, and with no-treatment (NT) controls. They concluded that dynamic therapies were (1) inferior to alternative treatments both at posttreatment and at one-year follow-up although they were superior to no-treatment at posttreatment; and (2) less successful for treating depression, especially major depression, but equally successful for mixed neurotic patients. Crits-Christoph (1992) also conducted a meta-analytic review of recent well-controlled studies of therapies with a brief dynamic orientation. The criteria employed for inclusion in the review were (1) use of a specific short-term dynamic psychotherapy, of at least 12 sessions, guided by a treatment manual or manual-like guide; (2) use of experienced therapists who had specific training in the modality being offered; (3) use of a patient group (rather than analogue study); (4) focus on the effectiveness of a comparative group, an alternative psychotherapy, or pharmacotherapy; and (5) reported data that allowed for the calculation of effect sizes based on Cohen's d statistic (1977). Eleven studies met the criteria for inclusion. Results indicate that brief dynamic therapy demonstrated large effects relative to waiting-list conditions but was only slightly superior to nonpsychiatric treatments. What is noteworthy is that in studies that employed manuals, all treatments and medications were found to be equally effective. The largest effect size was for target symptoms, indicating that the average dynamic therapy patient was better off than 62 percent of the comparison group patients. However, Crits-Christoph warns against generalizing the findings to all patient populations, outcome measures, and treatment types.

The NIMH collaborative study of depression (Elkin et al., 1989) compared four treatment modalities: (1) interpersonal psychotherapy (IPT) described by Klerman and colleagues (1984), (2) cognitive-behavioral therapy (CBT) described by Beck and colleagues (Beck et al., 1984), (3) imipramine hydrochloride plus clinical management, and (4) placebo plus clinical management. This study included a number of methodological improvements over most comparative studies. Training in one therapeutic modality was supported by the use of training manuals that outlined the theoretical foundation of the treatment approach, recommended specific treatment techniques, and provided guidance in the handling of various critical incidents consistent with the philosophy of the approach. Therapists met competence criteria; assessments were conducted at several points during the treatment; and measures of depressive symptoms, overall symptoms, and general functioning were gathered. Two hundred and fifty patients were randomly assigned to one of the four groups for a 16-week course of treatment. Over the 16-week period, patients in all treatments showed significant reduction in their depressive symptoms and general improvement in their functioning. In general, there was consistent ordering of the effectiveness of treatments at termination: imipramine hydrochloride plus clinical management was most effective and placebo plus clinical management was least effective, with the two brief therapies in between but falling closer to the more effective side of the spectrum. Andrews (1991) expressed the outcome differences between the therapies in terms of effect size (ES). For the more severe cases, the greatest effect was achieved with imipramine at 1.40 ES; next, IPT at 0.72 ES; and then cognitive-behavioral therapy at 0.46 ES.

However, one serious limitation in the study concerned the assumption of homogeneity of the patients. Even though all met the criteria for a diagnosis of depression, the specific constellation of symptoms presented by the patients may have been more or less amenable to change by certain interventions. In other words, patients may react to the same therapeutic procedures in different ways. A further limitation involves the restriction in generalizability to ambulatory patients.

E. Frank (1991) evaluated patients suffering from recurrent unipolar depression who were treated with a modified form of interpersonal psychotherapy (IPT-M) over the course of three years or for approximately 36 sessions. Although this study utilized a time frame that is somewhat longer than the typical time-limited brief therapy, it represents a prototype of intermittent therapy that may prove to be important to the maintenance of everyday functioning for certain types of patients. Prior to the commencement of the research, patients were first treated for acute depression with imipramine and IPT. Those who were in stable remission for 20 weeks were then randomly assigned to one of five maintenance treatment cells: interpersonal therapy alone, interpersonal therapy with active imipramine, interpersonal therapy with placebo, medication clinic with imipramine, or medication clinic with placebo. Patients were seen for three years on a monthly basis. A primary focus of the therapy was to identify interpersonal, cognitive, and somatic issues that were related to the onset of a depressive episode. Patients who received interpersonal therapy either alone or with placebo were in remission for an average of 10 months longer than the patients receiving medication clinic plus placebo (61 weeks versus 21 weeks).

Thompson, Gallagher, and Breckenridge (1987) conducted a comparative study of 91 depressed elderly who were randomly assigned to one of four conditions: the cognitive therapy of Beck and colleagues (Beck et al., 1984); the behavioral therapy of Gallagher and Thompson (1981); and brief psychodynamic therapy with an emphasis on responses to stress (M. Horowitz & Kaltreider, 1979). The control condition was a delayed treatment of six weeks' duration. All elderly patients met the criteria of major depressive disorder using Research Diagnostic Criteria (Spitzer, Endicott, & Robins, 1978) and were assigned to one of the four conditions after being matched on age, sex, level of severity of depression, and presence of symptoms related to depression. Manualized treatments were used in the cognitive and behavioral approaches and a prescribed outline was used in the brief psychodynamic therapy approach. Therapists were trained and monitored as they provided therapy. Clinically significant change was indexed through the use of methods outlined by Jacobson, Follette, and Revenstorf (1984). After 16–20 weeks of therapy, 52 percent of the patients in all three therapeutic conditions showed improvement and 18 percent showed significant improvement. The remaining 30 percent showed no remission of their depression. There was no significant difference found in the efficacy of any one of the therapies. Positive response rates (those patients who were in remission or significantly improved) were 80 percent for behavior therapy, 62 percent for cognitive therapy, and 70 percent for brief psychodynamic therapy. These general rates of improvement and failure were found to be in agreement with research findings on younger patients. However, the spontaneous remission rates were lower than previously found by Lambert (1976) in a younger, untreated outpatient sample, suggesting that elderly depressed patients are less likely to improve without intervention in some form. In a follow-up study with the same population, Gallagher-Thompson, Hanley-Peterson, and Thompson (1990) found that a large percentage of the patients in each of the therapies maintained their gain in functioning two years later with no significant differences in response rate by therapy modality.

Behaviorally oriented therapy may be better received as a brief therapeutic contact than more dynamic approaches. Sloane et al.'s (1975) follow-up study of patients who had been treated in either brief analytic or behavior therapy found that none of the behavior therapy patients complained of the brevity of treatment. However, four out of the nine patients who failed to improve in psychotherapy complained about the length of treatment. The researchers concluded that behavioral methods are probably better suited to the very brief durations of therapy; even if treatment does not succeed, patients feel as if they have received a fair trial.

The impact of the scheduling of sessions on outcome has also been examined. A comparative study of two forms of brief therapy presented in two time frames was conducted by Shapiro and colleagues in England (Shapiro et al., 1990). Participants were adults with a major depressive disorder. As part of a larger study, patients were treated with either 8 or 16 sessions of prescriptive (cognitive-behavioral) or exploratory (relationship-oriented) therapy using a 2×2 design. The results suggested that regardless of duration of treatment both forms of therapy provided substantial clinical improvement for patients. There was some evidence that exploratory therapy was more effective than prescriptive therapy for addressing interpersonal difficulties. The same two therapies were also examined in a time frame in which the patient was seen once for two consecutive weeks, followed by a third session three months later, called the two-plus-one model (Barkham & Shapiro, 1990). Twelve patients who met the criteria for mild depression related to job distress were treated with either the prescriptive or exploratory approach using the two-plus-one time frame. Twenty percent of the patients showed improvement prior to the first session; between 42–67 percent showed improvement after two sessions; and 55–73 percent showed improvement after the third session.

Regular sessions of at least one hour in duration may be important for enhancing intense emotional experience. Bierenbaum et al. (1976) studied the relationship of length and frequency of brief psychotherapy sessions and emotional catharsis. They found that patients seen for weekly one-hour sessions experienced more catharsis than patients seen for half-hour sessions twice weekly or patients seen for two hours every two weeks. However, patients who received the most frequent sessions (half an hour twice weekly) improved most on personality tests, regardless of the amount of emotional catharsis produced.

Summary

In the past, many of the studies of therapy that attempted to relate improvement to therapy duration did not actually employ planned brief psychotherapy. The subjects in the short-therapy group were often those who unilaterally terminated what was intended by the therapist to be long-term therapy. It is inappropriate to conclude that a patient has received brief therapy when actually he or she received three history-taking sessions preliminary to long-term therapy and then dropped out. Many studies that purport to correlate therapy duration to outcome have methodological problems (e.g., confounding of time with time in treatment, biased raters of outcome criteria, failure to utilize planned brief-therapy techniques) that render them irrelevant to the efficacy of brief methods.

Recent research has become much more sophisticated in the areas of conceptualization of terms, design, and methods. During the past decade, there has been considerable progress in clarifying both the concepts and the methodology required to ask more specific research questions. Contemporary comparative studies of brief psychotherapy offer little empirical evidence of differences in overall effectiveness between time-limited and time-unlimited therapy or between alternate approaches to brief therapy. There is now compelling empirical evidence that brief psychotherapy is effective with specific populations (Smith, Glass, & Miller, 1980) including:

1. patients with less severe problems, such as job-related stress, anxiety disorders, mild depression, and grief reactions.
2. patients who have experienced unusual stress situations, such as those with PTSD, earthquake experience, and rape.

On the other hand, brief therapy has been found to be less effective for patients with more severe disorders such as those of personality, substance abuse, and psychosis.

Among the issues requiring attention in future outcome studies is the systematic control of the areas where bias is likely, such as in therapist-rated outcome, allegiance to a particular orientation, and tools used to measure outcome. In some cases, measurement tools do not actually capture the change in the relevant areas that a specific form of short-term therapy purports to change. For example, when the therapy focuses on cognitions, a measurement tool that assesses cognitive change is required. The same is true for changes in interpersonal skills. Most studies use outcome assessments that focus largely on symptomatic change, where the effect size has generally been the greatest. While this is clearly important because it is the patient characteristic that is most amenable to change, the measurement of change in specific goal areas must also be directly assessed.

Research efforts are still needed in the clarification and study of time, time in therapy, factors associated with continuation in therapy, outcome, and maintenance of gain over time. Most comparative studies have chosen to study only one time frame in a number of therapy approaches; the study of patients exposed to therapies in multiple time frames can provide rich data as to the differential impact of therapy over time. Beyond effectiveness, other considerations in the choice of technical approach are cost-effectiveness, teachability, and acceptability to patients and therapists. Brief psychotherapy has been demonstrated to be equally effective and more cost-effective than unlimited psychotherapy with specific populations. Furthermore, mandatory limits on psychotherapy are now commonplace in most clinics and university settings. Yet, Strupp (1981) noted little evidence of technical flexibility among established practitioners. Consequently, future research must evaluate retraining formats that address issues of attitude, improve the image, and teach the techniques of brief therapy to experienced clinicians.

VARIABLES AFFECTING OUTCOME

To predict whether one treatment will be better than another for a specific patient, it is necessary to define and understand the salient patient and therapist variables, as well as their interactions, that contribute to outcome.

THE INTERACTIONAL FIELD OF PATIENT AND THERAPIST

Many early studies of brief dynamic psychotherapy examined transference, which by definition limited consideration to the patient's relationship to the therapist. Recently there has been a "resurgence of interest in the 'therapeutic alliance' or 'working alliance' . . . (i.e., the interactive patient–therapist relationship)" (Strupp, 1981, p. 228). Much of the past research on patient–therapist interaction has been guided by psychodynamic and client-centered traditions. The interactional process is now also being recognized as relevant for study by other approaches, such as cognitive, behavioral, and cognitive-behavioral therapies, as well as pharmacotherapy (Docherty & Feister, 1985; Moretti et al., 1990; Rush, 1985). Therapists generally appear to agree that the development of a working relationship between patient and therapist is necessary for some positive change. In our review, we first address the research that focuses on the discrete units that contribute to understanding the nature of the alliance within the brief therapy model. Second, we review a relatively new line of research that focuses on the reciprocal interactional patterns between the patient and therapist.

The Therapeutic Alliance

At a 1991 meeting of the North American Society for Psychotherapy Research, authorities in the field gathered in a "working" session to determine the active ingredients of the relationship between patient and therapist, known in general terms as the "therapeutic relationship" (Garfield, 1989), but also referred to as the "therapeutic alliance" (Zetzel, 1956), the "bond, tasks, and goals" (Bordin, 1979), the "working alliance" (Greenson, 1965), and the "helping alliance" (Luborsky, 1976). As prominent researchers discussed and elaborated upon theoretical frameworks, concepts, definitions, techniques, and methodologies, it became clear that a consensus for the definition of working alliance has not yet been achieved. Frieswyk and colleagues (1986) suggest that the alliance should be defined as the "patient's collaboration in tasks of psychotherapy" in order to "distinguish the alliance from various aspects of the patient's experience of the relationship and to separate the alliance from issues of technique" (p. 32). Thus, the therapeutic alliance refers to the emotional bond and reciprocal involvement that develop between patient and therapist during the course of therapy. Studies of this bond often consider its dynamics separate from the concretized tasks or actions of the therapy; they are seen respectively as the "nonspecific" as opposed to the "specific" contributions to therapy.

Over the past 10 years, the empirical evidence has favored a direct association between the therapeutic alliance and positive therapeutic outcome. In a theoretical and empirical review of the therapeutic alliance, Gaston (1990) differentiated four independent aspects of the alliance: (1) the therapeutic alliance, or the patient's affective relationship to the therapist; (2) the working alliance, or the patient's capacity to purposefully work in therapy; (3) the therapist's empathic understanding and involvement; and (4) the patient–therapist agreement on the goals and tasks of treatment. Although different definitions of the overall construct have been used in the past, these four categories have been repeatedly identified in empirical studies (Gomes-Schwartz, 1978; Hartley & Strupp, 1983; Marmar, Weiss, & Gaston, 1989). A number of research instruments are now being used to study the therapeutic alliance. These instruments can be categorized as either nonparticipant observation systems or participant observation systems. Both approaches have been applied to examining the contribution of the patient and/or the therapist to the "working alliance." Examples of nonparticipant observation systems that have been used to study brief therapy are the Vanderbilt Therapeutic Alliance Scale (Hartley & Strupp, 1983) and the California Alliance Scales (Marmar, Gaston, Gallager, & Thompson, 1989). Participant observation ratings used in brief therapy research include the Session Evaluation Questionnaire (Stiles, 1980) and the Session Intentions Questionnaire (Elliott, 1986). The same tools can be used to study both long- and short-term therapy, but the differences between the two forms must be carefully considered.

Kolden's (1991) empirical research on aspects of the therapeutic bond, based on the theoretical work of Orlinsky and Howard (1987), showed that patient self-relatedness and therapeutic bond are associated with therapeutic realizations early in the treatment. Studies that attend to patient collaboration point to its importance in the study of therapeutic alliance (Allen, Gabbard, Newsom, & Coyne, 1990; Colson et al., 1988). Further research using therapeutic alliance scales has shown that type of therapist intervention (Gaston, Ring, & Marmar, 1989) has an impact on symptomatic change (Eaton, Abeles, & Gutfreund, 1988), as well as on interpersonal functioning (Marmar et al., 1989). In one study of the relation between therapeutic alliance and outcome in three different modalities of brief therapy with a population of older depressed patients, no substantial association was found between alliance and outcome (5 to 18%) over and above initial symptomatology and in-treatment symptomatic change (Gaston, Marmar, Gallagher, & Thompson, 1991). However, consideration of the within-treatment condition showed that the alliance uniquely, although nonsignificantly, contributed to outcome as the therapy progressed, particularly for behavioral and cognitive therapy. Brief dynamic therapy was found to have the weakest alliance–outcome associations. This result was surprising; it was suggested that dynamic therapists may place greater emphasis on the alliance early in the therapy thereby reducing the impact across sessions. Also, the three different psychotherapy approaches appeared to place emphasis on different dimensions of the alliance.

Interactional Research

Greenberg and Pinsof (1986) suggest that the therapeutic process can be studied most effectively by actively framing research questions in a systems, rather than an individual, perspective. Task analysis has been fruitfully applied to the study of complex interactions (Rice & Greenberg, 1984). Treatment decisions are described by Horvath and Greenberg (1989) as interactive, contextual, and cumulative. This avenue of research is grappling with questions such as how to decide which interactions between patient and therapist are the most significant. Relatively few studies have examined the interactional process itself rather than the components that make up the process. One example is based on contemporary interpersonal theory (Anchin & Kiesler, 1982; Kiesler, 1986). The assumption underlying theory is that the interactions of people in a dyad are based on the continual negotiation of two key relationship dimensions: affiliation (how friendly or hostile they will be with each other) and control (how much one will be in charge of the other or yield to the other). The interpersonal behaviors of the dyad in 127 sessions from 8 cases of brief psychotherapy were coded by Thompson, Hill, and Mahalik (1991) using Kiesler's (1987) Checklist of Interpersonal Transactions. Patients were being treated for anxiety and depression. Their results suggest that therapist and clients were most often complementary in initial sessions when the clients were seen as friendly on the affiliative dimension and dominant on the control dimension. No systematic patterns of complementarity were found across treatment, but therapists and patients were complementary in about one-half of their initial sessions. Thus, the findings failed to confirm Kiesler and Watkins's (1989) study and suggest that success in therapeutic outcome did not require the therapist to act in ways complementary to the patient's behaviors. However, the researchers cautioned that the Checklist of Interpersonal Transactions may fail to measure adequately the complexity of complementarity.

Sequential analyses are exemplified by the work of McCullough et al., (1991). Two forms of brief therapy were provided: short-term dynamic psychotherapy and brief adaptation-oriented psychotherapy. The interaction sequences of 16 patient–therapist dyads were reviewed using a process coding system developed by one of the authors. Their results indicated that the frequency of patients' affective and defensive responses to a therapist's intervention accounted for 66 percent of the outcome variance. An interpretation by the therapist followed within three minutes by an affective response on the part of the patient was related to improvement at termination, whereas a therapist interpretation followed by a defensive response by the patient was linked to negative outcome. These findings are based on a small sample and there are inherent problems with the use of self-reports as measures of outcome. Nevertheless, sequential analysis holds promise for understanding the interactional process that contributes to successful outcome.

Stiles et al., (1991) have used an assimilation

model to understand the systematic sequence of changes that describe a patient's experience during psychotherapy. They examined the interactional patterns that involved change in case studies. These cognitive-affective changes of assimilation are both process and outcome; the researchers point out that this approach highlights how arbitrary it has been to make the traditional distinction between process and outcome research. Significant therapy events, or critical events, have been studied with the Therapeutic Impacts Content Analysis System (Elliott, James, Reimschuessel, Cislo, & Sack, 1985) and its shorter version, Brief Structured Recall (Elliot & Shapiro, 1988), which measures the immediate impact on patients of therapist interventions. Results indicate that patients typically identified significant events in the therapy that occurred in the last half of the session and were approximately 5 to 10 minutes in duration. Significant events were generally interchanges between the dyad but were attributed mainly to the therapist. Patients reported that the most helpful interventions were those related to specific tasks as opposed to interpersonal issues. The main drawback of the study was that there was a small sample size, which is a direct trade-off in a study involving this type of depth of knowledge. Rennie (1990) employed a participant observation method to extend Elliott's (1986) work on the Interpersonal Process Recall. Utilizing a grounded theory (Glaser & Strauss, 1967) type of qualitative analysis, he studied how the client experiences the psychotherapy hour (it was not clear whether the patients were engaged in time-limited therapy). Patients were presented with an audiotape or videotape of the therapy session that was just completed. The client was free to stop the replay of the tape at points that were recalled as meaningful in some way. The interviewer inquired about these points and the resulting "meaning units" were analyzed. Rennie highlighted the active ways in which patients monitor themselves during the session. He concluded that patients devise plans that guide their therapy. They also use strategies to carry out their plans. If patients have plans and are cognizant of the therapy's time limitation, will their plans change? To our knowledge this empirical work has not been conducted.

The Structural Analysis of Social Behavior or SASB (Benjamin, 1982) has been found effective for categorizing therapist behaviors as helpful or harmful and determining how they relate to successful or poor outcomes (Henry, Schacht, & Strupp, 1986). The SASB provides a fine-grained, highly specific analysis of interpersonal events and also allows for the coding of utterances into a num-

ber of categories. Henry et al. (1986) compared four therapists, each of whom saw a good and a poor outcome case ($N = 8$). The good therapeutic outcomes could be differentiated from poor outcomes on interpersonal process variables such as helping and protecting, and affirming and understanding, as well as blaming and belittling. Negative complementarity between therapist and patient was greater in cases with poor outcome. In the poor outcome studies, 22 percent of the therapist responses and 17 percent of the patient responses were coded as complex communications compared to the successful outcomes for which the respective figures were 0 and 2 percent. The stages of brief psychotherapy have also been addressed from a systems perspective (Tracey, 1985; Tracey & Ray, 1984). Here the change process is seen as a movement out of an initial state of homeostasis into a state of flux with a termination in a new point of homeostasis. These stages have been explored by comparing the sequence of patient–therapist topic initiation and topic continuation among successful and unsuccessful therapy dyads. Successful therapy cases reveal a pattern in topic initiation/topic following of initial high complementarity, followed by low complementarity in the middle phase of therapy, returning to high complementarity at termination. Therapists in successful dyads were found to initiate more topics during the middle or "conflict" stage of therapy. This finding suggests that in cases with successful outcomes, the middle phase of therapy consisted of the therapist's directing attention to issues the patient did not necessarily want to address. Agreement over the focus then gradually emerged in the final stage of therapy. When outcome was unsuccessful, these changes were not seen.

PATIENT CHARACTERISTICS

We now turn to a review of a number of the patient variables that contribute to the change process and outcomes in brief psychotherapy. For a comprehensive review of patient characteristics that pertain to therapy in general, the reader is referred to Chapter 6 in this volume. Elliott and James (1989) identify nine domains of patient experience. The first five pertain to the patients' experience of their own psychological processes during therapy, including their style of self-relatedness, style of relating to the therapist, intentions, in-session expression of feelings, and central concerns (e.g., salient issues patients bring to therapy). The next two domains relate to patient experiences of their therapist and include patient perceptions of the therapist's actions and perceptions of the therapist's characteristics. The final two domains involve patient satisfaction with therapeutic outcome and patient perception of helpful aspects of therapy. Elliot and James suggest that further elaboration of the various ways in which patients experience therapy is essential to understanding the relationship between process and outcome. Based on a comprehensive review of the research in the area, three dimensions were found to underlie much of the research: (1) evaluation/affiliation or the positive versus negative evaluation toward a certain aspect of the therapy; (2) interpersonal control/independence or the degree to which the patient was active in the therapy; and (3) interpersonal/task factors, which are an "updated version of the 'specific versus nonspecific' distinction" (Elliott & James, 1989, p. 459). Research related to these three dimensions is discussed in the material that follows.

Levels of Expectation and Motivation to Change

The patient's expectation that therapy will create change and that he or she will receive help is an important consideration for any type of psychotherapy, but perhaps especially so for brief therapy, since the time constraints require that treatment sessions be fast moving and goal oriented. The influence of patient expectations on positive therapeutic outcome has become recognized as an important factor to control for in any psychotherapy-outcome study. Patients who believe they are receiving some form of help even though contact is minimal generally show greater improvement than comparison patients who receive no contact (e.g., Cross et al., 1982; Frank, 1974; Sloane et al., 1975). Frank (1974) has asserted that early psychotherapeutic gains and placebo effects are both due to mobilization of hope. Later in therapy, symptomatic changes due to relearning appear.

The underutilization of psychotherapy by ethnic groups in the United States has been noted by researchers (Shiang, 1993; Sue & Zane, 1987). They suggest that it is essential to address the issues of credibility and giving in order to establish an alliance with people from culturally diverse groups. *Credibility* is the client's perception of the therapist and *giving* is the client's perception that something was received from the therapeutic encounter. Gim, Atkinson, and Kim (1991) studied Asian-American students and found that those counselors who were rated as more culturally competent and credible were those who had been introduced as culturally sensitive and of the same ethnic

background. These studies suggest that providing treatment for members of ethnic groups requires an assessment of the client's perception of the therapist and the culture-specific ways in which a therapeutic alliance can be formed.

Patient readiness to change has been studied in therapies with limited goals, such as relieving problems related to medical illnesses or job-related distress. The assumption underlying this work is that patients enter therapy in different states of readiness and that specific techniques that correspond to these states of readiness will provide patients with more successful outcomes. For example, DiClemente and Prochaska (1982) studied smokers in two settings: those engaged in therapy and those attempting to quit on their own. They examined patients' level of readiness to change and found that they could differentiate four levels: precontemplation, contemplation, action, and maintenance. They recommended therapeutic techniques depending on the stage of readiness. For example, behavioral techniques such as counterconditioning and contingency control are best suited for patients who are in the action stage (Prochaska, 1991). The match of technique to stage of readiness was found to facilitate the greatest gains in alleviating the patient's presenting problem. A recent review of the area by Levenson and Hales (in press) shows that brief therapy can be an effective, efficient, and economical treatment modality for the medically ill. Patients who have recently experienced medical illnesses and hospitalization are more psychologically available than others to engage in brief therapeutic interventions (Stein, Murdaugh, & McLeod, 1969).

Another approach to the question of patient expectation of therapy and motivation to change has been used in the study of brief dynamic therapy for bereavement reactions (M. Horowitz, Marmar, Weiss, DeWitt, & Rosenbaum, 1984; Marmar, Mardi, Weiss, Wilner, & Kaltreider, 1988). They found that patient demographics and dispositional variables did not predict outcome. Process measures of therapeutic alliance and actions by the therapist also did not predict outcome. However, when these latter two variables were considered in interaction with two dispositional variables (level of motivation to engage in dynamic therapy and the developmental level of the self-concept), they found significant predictions of outcome. Their results suggest that therapist interventions emphasizing more exploratory actions are better suited to patients who are highly motivated or have more coherent self-concepts, whereas supportive interventions are more suited for patients who are less motivated and whose self-concepts are less stable.

Horowitz and colleagues have also used short-term, dynamic psychotherapy to address the specific problems of stress response syndromes (M. Horowitz, 1988; M. Horowitz, Marmar, Krupnick et al., 1984). They identified a number of factors such as the patient's state of mind and his or her schema of relationship between self and other that are related to positive therapeutic outcome as well as improved physical health. In addition, their analysis also showed that two variables (motivation for dynamic therapy and developmental level of the self-concept) in combination with select process variables could significantly predict outcome.

Not all patient expectations improve the likelihood of therapeutic success, however. Hornstra, Lubin, Lewis, and Willis (1972) surveyed 611 consecutive applicants (and 443 relatives) to a community mental health center. They found unrealistic expectations of services in this predominantly lower socioeconomic class population. Only 16.7 percent of the sample felt that regularly scheduled appointments to talk about their problems would be helpful. Several studies have been reported in which patients were prepared for psychotherapy by films or special interviews to reduce unrealistic ideas and enhance positive expectations (e.g., Hoehn-Saric et al., 1964; Sloane, Cristol, Pepernik, & Staples, 1970; Warren & Rice, 1972). Patients who received preparations showed more appropriate behavior, remained in therapy longer, and had better outcomes than patients who failed to receive preparation. Heitler (1976) summarizes.

> While further research is needed, it is clear that a variety of preparatory techniques hold promise for facilitating a therapeutic alliance in expressive psychotherapy with unsophisticated patients from any social class, and that these techniques may be particularly useful with lower class patient populations, in which unsophisticated and potentially counterproductive role expectations seem to be more prevalent. (p. 350)

Patient Actions and Experiences in Therapy

Patient involvement has consistently been the best predictor of outcome (Gomes-Schwartz, 1978). It accounted for 30 percent of the variance as opposed to 18 percent for "exploratory processes" and 38 percent of the variance as opposed to 24 percent for "therapist offered relationship." Gomes-Schwartz concluded,

> Patients who were not hostile or mistrustful and who actively contributed to the therapy interactions achieved greater changes than those who were withdrawn, defensive, or otherwise unwilling

> to engage in the therapy process. . . . The variables that best predicted change were not related to therapeutic techniques but to the positiveness of the patient's attitude toward his therapist and his commitment to work at changing. (1978, p. 1032)

Use of patient action scales, such as the Experiencing Scale (Klein, Mathieu-Couglan, & Kiesler, 1986), has shown that patient characteristics of neuroticism, introspectiveness, and cognitive complexity were related to high levels of experiencing in therapy. The presence of high levels of experiencing during the last phases of therapy was associated with positive outcome. In other words, the more invested the patient was in the therapy, the more likely that a positive outcome would result.

Stiles and colleagues (1991) have used an assimilation and schema model to attempt to understand the systematic sequence of changes that characterize the patient's experience during psychotherapy. Using case studies, they are able to follow the course of change and to examine the role of various process components. They find that the rates of assimilation of new cognitive-affective experiences vary from patient to patient, with some stages in the process being more or less difficult and time consuming. In addition, different therapeutic approaches (exploratory vs. psychodynamic), guided by therapists with specific training in each approach, focus energies on the assimilation of different material in the therapy.

Pretherapy Interpersonal Relationships

The role of the quality of a patient's pretherapy interpersonal relationships on the prediction of outcome has been extensively studied. For example, Moras and Strupp (1982) used independent clinicians' ratings of the quality of patient's interpersonal relationships, including the presence of meaningful relationships and absence of mistrust or hostility: "The results . . . suggest that an appreciable portion of the variance (up to 25%) in a patient's collaborative participation in therapy can be linked to . . . assessments of interpersonal relations" (p. 408). However, they also reported that the quality of a patient's pretherapy interpersonal relationships — while a potent predictor of the therapeutic alliance — generally had very low correlation with outcome measures. Research by Piper et al. (1990) used an object relations perspective to assess interpersonal relationships and outcome. Using an approach based on prior evidence from two independent studies (M. Horowitz, Marmar, Weiss et al., 1984; Piper, de Carfel, & Szkrumelak, 1985), they examined the relationship to outcome in short-term psychodynamic therapy of differing qualities of object relations. A randomized, controlled, clinical trial design with 144 patients was used with a standardized form of therapy, an experienced team of therapists, and a comprehensive set of measures of outcome and process. Results provided support for a strong treatment effect expressed in terms of statistical significance, effect size, and clinical significance. There was also some evidence for an additive effect of treatment and preexisting qualities of object relationships. Another recent study assessed the patient's developmental level of object representation (Alpher, Perfetto, Henry, & Strupp, 1990). These researchers found that the variables that predicted a higher level of patient change were the measures of object relatedness such as "differentiation" and "articulation" (using the Rorschach) and not the clinical interpersonal interview. They did show some evidence of a relationship between the Rorschach and the capacity to engage in short-term dynamic psychotherapy as assessed through an interview.

Gaston, Marmar, Thompson, and Gallagher (1988) studied pretreatment interpersonal functioning and avoidance of problems in an elderly outpatient population seeking therapy for depression. The subjects were assigned to one of three short-term treatments: behavioral, cognitive, or psychodynamic. The findings failed to establish that the pretreatment quality of interpersonal relationships predicted the patient contribution to the alliance in any of the three therapies. However, environmental support contributed to the patient's commitment to therapy across treatments. The authors note potential confounding problems in that the patients were seeking treatment for depression, not interpersonal or characterological problems, and the assessment of pretreatment interpersonal functioning was based on archival self-report data.

Studies of Dispositional Characteristics

These studies look to enduring "traits" rather than present "states" as a guide for understanding how patients will react in brief therapy. A comprehensive review of the field by Orlinsky and Howard (1986) found that the most consistent correlate of therapeutic outcome was patients' self-relatedness (the relative degree of patient openness as opposed to patient defensiveness). They reported that 88 percent of the research findings related to self-relatedness were statistically significant. Efforts to achieve optimal matching between patient and treatment are also being carried out along a number of different lines. Beutler and colleagues (Beutler, 1989, 1991; Beutler & Clarkin, 1990) have proposed a model of dispositional assessment

that emphasizes the interactional nature of patient, setting, relationship, and treatment variables in order to capture the complexity of clinical practice. Treatment decisions exert compounding influences on outcome and therefore a true estimate of treatment effectiveness must necessarily take into account the combined influences of multiple decisions. Patient predisposing variables that include the traditional diagnoses of DSM-III-R as well as interpersonal variables (e.g., coping style, capacity to form a relationship, etc.), environmental enabling factors (social supports, work roles, etc.), and expectations of therapy (degree of directiveness, task orientation, etc.) must be taken into account.

A recent example of this work is the attempt to optimally match patients with therapy according to variations in patient's defensiveness and coping styles (Beutler et al., 1991). Patients with externalizing coping styles reacted most positively to behavioral/symptom-focused procedures of cognitive therapy. Some evidence also suggested that patients who were self-punitive and depressed benefited from an internally focused and reflective treatment. Those therapy approaches that emphasize more authority-directed interventions were found to yield poor results among individuals who were prone to be resistant to therapy.

Pilkonis, Heape, and Proietti (1991) also considered dispositional characteristics. They hypothesized that the dropout rate from psychotherapy is related to therapists' and patients' levels of attachment and personality style. Using the theoretical framework of Bowlby (1979), and measures such as the Checklist of Interpersonal Transactions (Kiesler, 1987), the study examined differences in the attachment, security, and personality styles of patients and therapists. The pairing of insecurely attached patients with less securely attached therapists was associated with a high dropout rate as was pairing dependent patients with autonomous therapists.

Diagnosis as a Salient Variable

In the search for salient variables that relate to positive outcome, researchers have begun to focus on diagnosis as a variable. In some studies, only patients who meet the DSM-III-R criteria for a certain diagnosis were admitted to the study (e.g., Elkin et al., 1989; E. Frank, 1991). In other research, a model of dispositional assessment employs a sequential formulation based on a number of patient parameters, of which diagnosis is a part, to determine which treatment will be most efficacious (e.g., Beutler, 1989). An example of the use of DSM-III-R diagnostic criteria for inclusion in a research protocol was the NIMH multisite study of depression (Elkin et al., 1989). The researchers recognized that the assignment of a diagnosis of major depressive disorder did not guarantee a homogeneous population. Further analyses have helped tease apart the effects related to specific patient characteristics. Differences in effectiveness of treatments were found when the patients were ranked according to the severity of their illness; more severely depressed patients were more effectively treated by use of imipramine plus clinical management. The same group was also found to be somewhat effectively treated by the interpersonal psychotherapy. For those patients who exhibited less severe depression, there was no evidence of effectiveness for any of the treatments in comparison to the placebo plus clinical management condition. Klerman and Weissman (1991) have warned against interpreting the results of the collaborative study to mean that all forms of psychotherapy are efficacious for all forms of depression: "Just as there are specific forms of medication, there are specific forms of psychotherapy" (p. 39).

THERAPIST CHARACTERISTICS

Therapist characteristics such as age, SES, personality, attitudes/values, theoretical orientation, and level of training/experience have been empirically studied and found to be related to outcome. In addition, process variables such as therapeutic style (verbal response modes), therapist techniques (interpretation, interventions), and relationship attitudes (level of object relations) have also been found to be important to therapeutic outcome (see Chapters 7 and 8 in this volume for a more detailed discussion of these factors). In short-term therapy, the contribution of the therapist is particularly important because therapeutic change must be accomplished within a shortened time frame.

Therapist Actions
A therapist action is a "specific meaningful act that the therapist might do" (Hoyt, Marmar, Horowitz, & Alvarez, 1981). It has also been called a task or a basis for action, specifically as it applies to brief therapy (Levy & Shelton, 1990). There has been a long-standing debate concerning the action of specific versus nonspecific factors in psychotherapy. Strupp and Hadley (1979) noted that a central research question is, "To what extent are therapeutic effects the result of specific techniques . . . as opposed to so-called nonspecific factors inherent in any benign human relationship that affects the patient's expectations and hope?" (p. 1125).

Therapist action scales have been used to investigate whether therapists from different schools of psychotherapy actually talk and behave differently and, if so, whether these differences translate into differential outcomes. An example of this approach is the work of Stiles (1986). Verbal response modes are taxonomized into eight categories: disclosure, edification (statements of objective information), confirmation, question, acknowledgment, interpretation, reflection, and advisement. Based on this taxonomy, Stiles compared different theoretical orientations. A fourfold typology of therapies was suggested: (1) nondirective therapies, in which the therapist mainly uses the patient's frame of reference and response modes such as confirmation, acknowledgment, and reflection (e.g., client-centered therapy); (2) directive therapies in which the therapist mainly uses his or her own frame of reference and response modes such as disclosure, advisement, and question (e.g., Gestalt therapy); (3) analytic therapies, in which the therapist mainly uses the client's experience as the frame of reference and response modes such as question, interpretation, and reflection; and (4) hortatory therapies, in which the therapist uses his or her own experiences and response modes such as disclosure, advisement, and confirmation (e.g., use of lectures, sermons). Another group of scales addresses process more globally and results in ratings of entire segments of a session. Representative of these scales is the Vanderbilt Psychotherapy Process Scale (e.g., Gomes-Schwartz, 1978), which is composed of seven factor scales (four represent therapist actions and three represent patient actions). Using this scale, Gomes-Schwartz (1978) compared analytic therapists, experiential therapists, and nonprofessional alternate therapists. Although there were differences in therapists' behaviors, no differences in therapeutic outcome were found among the three groups of therapists. Likewise, Staples, Sloane, Whipple, Cristol, and Yorkston (1976) reported no major differences in the outcomes achieved through the diverse techniques.

Several studies have explored alterations in therapist behavior both within a single session of psychotherapy and across an entire treatment course (e.g., Hawton, Reibstein, Fieldsend, & Whalley, 1982; Hill et al., 1983; Luborsky et al., 1986). For example, Hill and coworkers use a single-case study design to describe the changes in counselor behavior that occurred over the course of a 12-session brief therapy. Statistical comparison of the first third to the final two-thirds of the treatment course suggested increases in activity level, silence, and interpretations and decreases in minimal encouragers. Comparison of counselor intentions during the first third to the last two-thirds of the sessions demonstrated increases in direct change attempts and analysis of the relationship and decreases in clarification. While these comparisons are a necessary starting point, this line of process research will be most valuable when it is extended to differences between successful and unsuccessful therapy. A step in this direction is demonstrated by the study of the therapist actions characteristic of "good" and "bad" hours of psychotherapy (e.g., Hoyt, Xenakis, Marmar, & Horowitz, 1983; O'Farrell, Hill, & Patton, 1992). For example, Hoyt et al. compared the therapist actions in 46 brief dynamic psychotherapy sessions rated for goodness of quality by expert raters. Good sessions were positively correlated with therapists' emphasis on patient expression and discussion of the patient–therapist relationship, the meaning of the patient's reactions, and the links or patterns between the patient's past and present life.

Negative Actions

Deterioration or negative effects from psychotherapy have also received attention (e.g., Bergin, 1963, 1971; Hadley & Strupp, 1976; Henry et al., 1986; Strupp, Hadley, & Gomes-Schwartz, 1977). There are a number of reasons why brief psychotherapy might be vulnerable to negative change: The important area of patient and situational assessment may not receive adequate attention under the imposed time pressures; more direct involvement on the part of the therapist might allow greater opportunity for negative impact; the relatively fast pace and the need for prompt therapist intervention may result in premature or incorrect therapeutic action; and finally, the brevity of the intervention and the difficulty or lack of follow-up may not provide the therapist with sufficient time to observe the effects (either positive or negative) of the interventions and take corrective action. There have been two studies that examine crisis intervention (Gottschalk, Mayerson, & Gottlieb, 1967; Green, Gleser, Stone, & Siefert, 1975) and indicate that there may be deterioration after an intervention. However, no evidence exists to suggest that brief psychotherapy produces any greater negative effects than long-term psychotherapy.

Sachs (1983) studied negative factors in brief psychotherapy, which she defines as variables that "impede therapeutic progress or are believed to result in negative outcomes (i.e., ineffective therapy and harmful therapy)" (p. 557). She employed the Vanderbilt Negative Indicators Scale (Strupp et al., 1981), which consists of five subscales that reflect patient negative attitudes, therapist exploitative tendencies, errors in technique, problems in

the therapeutic relationship, and ineffectiveness. Trained clinical raters listened to audiotaped segments from the first three therapy sessions of 18 male participants in the Vanderbilt Psychotherapy Project (Strupp & Hadley, 1979). In none of the cases were patients judged to have deteriorated in therapy, but in several instances therapy was felt to have been ineffective in inducing change. A statistically significant partial correlation was obtained between errors in technique and outcome. The association was stronger for psychodynamic therapy than for experiential therapy. Thus, while type of technique was not related to outcome, quality of technique was. There is some evidence to suggest that the instrument may be more appropriate for the evaluation of psychodynamically oriented therapies than other therapies (Suh, Strupp, & O'Malley, 1986). Henry et al. (1986) found that hostile and controlling therapist behavior, as measured by the use of the SASB, was related to outcome. In the positive outcomes cases, only 1 percent of the therapists' verbalizations and none of the patients' communications were judged to be hostile, whereas in low-outcome cases, 20 and 19 percent of the patients' and therapists' verbalizations, respectively, were judged to be hostile.

Individual Differences Among Therapists

Lambert (1989) calls for the field to consider the therapist's contribution to process and outcome. To tease apart some of the factors that contribute to these differences, Lambert conducted a retabulation of work by Orlinsky and Howard (1980). He found that some therapists are better at working with difficult cases and other therapists do better with less severely disturbed patients. A similar conclusion was found in a study of nine therapists seeing substance-abusing patients (Luborsky, McLellan, Woody, O'Brien, & Auerbach, 1985). Despite the use of manualized treatments and continual supervision and monitoring, therapists providing the same treatment had varying degrees of success with their patients. Substantial differences between therapists were evident, both within and between the various treatment modalities. Lambert suggests that the individual therapist might be treated as an independent variable in factorial research. Studies of dispositional qualities of therapist and patient attempt to measure the quality of each person's object relations and its contribution to the therapeutic relationship as well as outcome (Alpher et al., 1990; Pilkonis et al., 1991; see previous discussion).

Formulation and Maintenance of Focus

There are few empirical studies that actually test the contribution of the therapeutic focus to process and outcome even though there is uniform agreement that the therapist must take responsibility for determining a focus in brief therapy. Lambert (1983) attributed the lack of positive outcome subsequent to brief psychotherapy in a case study (Hill et al., 1983) to lack of focus. There are, however, varying positions on what the focus of the therapy should be, on whether to share the focus with the patient, and on its supposed contribution to therapy outcome.

The behavioral, cognitive, and cognitive-behavioral approaches generally build on detailed behavioral and cognitive assessments to determine the focus. Adherence to the focus is monitored by both therapist and patient as they review tasks such as homework, role play, and so on. A narrow range of variables is then earmarked for change. In recent years, some of these approaches have also advocated the consideration of the impact of affective factors on dysfunctional behaviors, as in the work of Margolin and Fernandez (1985) on marital discord. Persons (1989) suggests the use of a case formulation model that focuses on behaviors and cognitions in both overt difficulties and underlying psychological mechanisms. The model is based on the interdependence hypothesis; interventions in one system produce change in other systems. Zeiss, Lewinsohn, and Muñoz (1979) showed that depressed patients exhibited change in many systems even though they were provided treatment in only one modality (cognition, behavior, or social skills). Persons, Burns, and Perloff (1989) studied depressed patients treated in private practice and found that those patients who completed homework outside the sessions showed a greater level of improvement than those who did not complete homework. Furthermore, the improvement was greater for the more severely depressed at the beginning of treatment.

The focus of crisis intervention is determined by the nature of the crisis or trauma. Generally the emphasis is on the here and now, on a systems perspective, and on rallying various resources to help the patient through the immediate future. The eclectic model determines a focus based on the problems of the patient and then draws on a wide range of approaches and techniques to work with the patient. For example, Beutler and Clarkin (1990) determine the focus for therapy through a process of matching factors such as patient characteristics (coping ability, expectations, and personality patterns) and type of therapy approach. The therapist who has been trained in the specific approach that best suits the patient then takes responsibility for determining the focus of therapy.

The "dynamic focus" forms the basis for successful interventions in a number of psychodynamically oriented short-term approaches. If any depth in the context of a brief treatment process is to occur, some limits must be exerted on the number of different topics that are considered. The interpretations the therapist uses revolve around this focus both in content as well as in building a relationship with the particular patient. In other words, the dynamic focus guides both the limits that are set on the content of the sessions as well as the types of interpersonal reactions that the therapist tries to foster in the sessions. The Penn Psychotherapy Research Project (Luborsky, Crits-Christoph, & Barber, 1991) formulates the patient's central relationship pattern as the dynamic focus. The relationship pattern is made up of wishes toward others, the responses of others, and the responses of the self. These are derived from the spontaneous narratives that occur within the therapy session about the patient's relations with others and the therapist. The Mount Zion Psychotherapy Group (Silberschatz, Curtis, Sampson, & Weiss, 1991) suggests that the patient's psychopathology is based on unconscious pathogenic beliefs that impede the patient's adaptive functioning. A study of 16 cases in short-term dynamic psychotherapy (Silberschatz & Curtis, 1986) addressed these pathogenic beliefs during the course of therapy. The researchers were interested in determining whether therapist adherence to a plan derived from the patient's pathogenic belief system was related to outcome. They found a strong relationship between the patient's progress in therapy and the compatibility of the therapist interventions with the dynamic plan. L. Horowitz and colleagues (1989) describe a new method for finding consensus among clinicians regarding patient's dynamic focus. Their attempt is to develop procedures for generating a dynamic formulation for a patient that is standardized, reliable, and valid. With a consensual definition of the dynamic formulation, further research concerning interventions and interpretations can more clearly address their exact impact.

Summary

In this section we have reviewed research studies that focus on the variables that affect the outcome of brief therapy. Many processes in brief therapy are so similar to those in long-term therapy (e.g., therapeutic alliance, interpretation, and expectancy effects) that they can be studied more easily in research utilizing brief therapy. At the same time, it has become increasingly clear that brief therapy has "essential" ingredients of its own, some that overlap with long-term therapy and others that are specific to the brief context. From the studies reviewed, we arrived at several tentative conclusions that might serve as guides to further empirical research.

The major importance of the working alliance or therapeutic alliance was highlighted. Researchers have made headway in determining both the components and the interactional sequences that affect process and outcome, although there is no clear consensus on the definition of the alliance. Measurement tools based on a common conceptual understanding are not yet available. The use of the SASB and other measures of interactional sequences promises to provide rich information on therapist interventions, the reaction of the patient to these interventions, and the relation of interventions to outcome. Common sense tells us that some people get along better with certain people and not others, but it is not clear how this is actually studied in the research setting. A promising avenue of research is to relate variables and outcome to enduring patient and therapist personality traits, as well as to specific presenting problems such as bereavement or job-related distress. This will begin to allow research to address the issues of "what treatment, by whom, is more effective" (Paul, 1967a, p. 111).

- There is considerable evidence of a direct association between therapeutic alliance and outcome, although this result has not been found in every study.

- There is evidence of a strong relationship between therapeutic alliance, type of therapist interventions, symptomatic change, and interpersonal functioning.

- The therapeutic alliance varies across sessions regardless of orientation. Different therapies appear to emphasize different aspects of the alliance.

- The study of interactional sequences between therapist and patient suggests that complementary behaviors between the dyad are related to improved alliance, that patterns of affective response to interventions can be related to positive outcome, and that certain therapist variables such as "helping and protecting" can be related to positive outcome.

- Patient characteristics such as coping ability and personality variables provide a rationale for prescriptive therapies or selective matching to heighten change within a shortened time frame.

- The study of critical events helps to isolate those variables perceived by the patients as being essential to the therapeutic process and outcome.

- Therapist qualities, actions, interventions, and degree of collaboration have been found to be related to outcome. Therapists differ along specific dimensions (e.g., use of confirmation, acknowledgment) depending upon training and theoretical orientation.

- Increasing numbers of studies focus on patient and therapist dispositional qualities, such as quality of object relations, personality styles, predominant cognitive styles, and defensiveness, as ways to understand the contribution of the patient both to the interactional process as well as to outcome.

CONCLUSIONS AND FUTURE DIRECTIONS

Empirical research in the area of brief therapy has dramatically changed during the past decade. New methodologies, concern for clinical significance, and the matching of specific approaches to people that present their problems in a certain way have all contributed to the development of more precise scientific theories of change and adaptation. The traditional distinction between process and outcome research is being replaced by research attempts to understand discrete events in the therapy and interactional sequences, as well as the characteristics of the patient and therapist, and how these variables relate to outcome. The next decade promises a much better understanding of the specific components of the process of therapy; how they interact with the characteristics of patient, therapist, and setting; and what types of outcomes they produce.

Many psychotherapeutic contacts, by virtue of premature termination, are brief, lasting less than eight sessions. However, brief psychotherapy is now more firmly established as a treatment of choice and has been found to be effective for specific populations. In general, these populations come to therapy to address circumscribed problems such as poor interpersonal relations, grief and loss, depression, and job-related stress. The outcome research literature on brief therapies suggests that these techniques produce positive change. Behavioral techniques seem to produce the most rapid change in symptomatology with specific populations, but they are not superior to other brief approaches in overall results. Patients followed up over very long time periods tend to show gradual improvement for several years after treatment. The chief value of brief psychotherapy may be that it helps to accelerate positive change in the patient.

Comparative studies of brief and time-unlimited therapies show essentially no differences in results. Consequently, brief therapy results in a great saving of available clinical time and can reach more people in need of treatment. It is quite likely that brief therapies will be more widely utilized in the future as government health plans and insurance programs increasingly govern the practice of psychotherapy.

We examined a number of brief therapeutic approaches and noted that they could be classified into five broad orientations: (1) psychoanalytic; (2) behavioral, cognitive, and cognitive-behavioral; (3) eclectic; (4) crisis intervention therapy; and (5) other verbal psychotherapies. We have delineated three core principles that guide brief therapy orientations (see p. 668).

The search for salient variables—patient characteristics as well as therapist characteristics—that contribute to specific processes and treatment outcomes has been highly productive in the last 10 years. The importance of the therapeutic alliance in brief treatment was highlighted. Even in behaviorally oriented approaches that minimize the relationship, patient–therapist interaction is thought to be an important variable. Although the quality of the therapeutic relationship is considered by many to be the major determinant in therapeutic change, the complexity of the components and operations that bring about patient change are only slowly beginning to be reliably operationalized. This has become increasingly viewed as an interactional field with both patient and therapist characteristics affecting both process and outcome. It appears that the important issue is not whether it is *only* the nonspecific or the specific factors that create positive outcome, but which aspects of the relationship itself must be present for a working collaboration to occur and what specific techniques must be maintained by the therapist within the context of the relationship. Studies of critical events are beginning to place more emphasis on the salience of micro-events in studying process variables and their relation to outcomes. Most brief therapies entail interpretation, directiveness, and a high therapist activity level. Brief psychotherapies depend on these therapeutic techniques to keep the sessions moving at a productive pace. Further research is needed to provide clearer delineation of the effective range of techniques and processes, as well as guidelines for handling patients who are failing to respond.

Time limitation and techniques of temporal awareness are thought to be important for keeping the patient tuned in to the need for rapid goal attainment. While the effectiveness of time-limited approaches has been established, behavior change does require time. Howard et al.'s (1986) "dose-effect" relationship is one way to understand this relationship. The evidence suggests that, depending on the problem, particular solutions do not require continuous long-term psychotherapy. Indeed, it is increasingly becoming common for patients to enter therapy on an intermittent basis—seeking help when they are in greatest need.

Previous reviews concluded that many empirical studies failed to employ planned brief therapy with trained therapists and were characterized by methodological problems such as confounding of time with time in treatment, biased raters of criteria, and absence of multiple outcome measures, which rendered them unable to clarify our understanding of efficacy. Today the field has matured. Well-organized and highly productive research projects are now found in both the Unites States and Europe. These large-scale research projects benefit by being able to look at complex issues using a number of different research paradigms. Research at the level of examining specific variables and their relation to outcome as well as the development of detailed descriptive bases are both necessary for advancement in the field. Many new and exciting studies are attempting to find solutions to the difficulties of objective measurement of the processes and outcomes that take place in the therapeutic setting. The instrumentation in brief psychotherapy process research has also grown dramatically. However, difficulties for both researchers and clinicians arise when the constructs of one theoretical base are not viewed in relation to other, already existing, theoretical orientations. Are the components of the working alliance of one research project similar to those components described in another research project?

The major outcome studies in brief psychotherapy completed in recent years have been well designed and have adequately addressed the overall and comparative effectiveness of brief techniques for heterogeneous groups of complex neurotics. The use of training manuals has been an important step in improving the rigor of research. At the same time, it is foolish to believe that the use of manuals alone will "standardize" a therapy. The actual delivery of therapy is dependent on the contributions and interactions that take place between the two people. Some authors have suggested that the competence to carry out brief psychotherapy does not flow directly from the experience of working in settings where brief psychotherapy is generally provided. Greater emphasis needs to be placed on training in brief psychotherapy techniques. Studies of brief psychotherapy process must consider not only whether the therapists under examination are trained in the specific form, but also the degree to which they adhere to the planned brief psychotherapy.

Increased specificity is called for in future research so that issues of patient–therapist and patient–treatment interactions can be described. In the outcome field, some of the variables to be investigated will require collaborative studies or at minimum the adoption of some elements of a standard assessment battery. Prescriptive matching entails the study of large patient populations so that the effects of treatment in various subgroups can be examined with acceptable levels of power. Few individual sites can offer the variety and number of clients needed to examine the prescriptive understanding of treatment, particularly as we enter an era where an extension of our interventions to diverse cultural groups will be critically needed. At the same time, the need for a detailed descriptive data base demands that methodologies such as the case study approach be accepted as a necessary component of the overall research endeavor. In addition, research needs to be directed toward a greater understanding of the relationship between time, time in therapy, and outcome. It was noted that in spite of evidence of cost-effectiveness, brief psychotherapy has a negative image among many clinicians. If the general trend toward cost containment in health care continues, long-term psychotherapy is likely to become less prevalent in the future.

We may be coming to the end of the era in which brief psychotherapy must be reviewed separately from psychotherapy. In addition to being a clearly viable clinical treatment option, brief psychotherapy is now routinely utilized in research studies examining "psychotherapy." However, this successful evolution into the prototype therapy for research should not deter adherents of the brief approaches from continuing to press for greater understanding of those unique elements that define the format in order to contribute to scientific theory about the ways people change.

REFERENCES

Alden, L. (1989). Short-term structured treatment for avoidant personality disorder. *Journal of Consulting and Clinical Psychology, 57*, 756–764.

Allen, J. G., Gabbard, G. O., Newsom, G. W., & Coyne, L. (1990). Detecting patterns of change in patient's collaboration within individual psychotherapy sessions. *Psychotherapy, 27*, 522–530.

Alpher, V. S., Perfetto, X. X., Henry, W. P., & Strupp, H. H. (1990). Dynamic factors in patient assessment and prediction of change in short-term dynamic psychotherapy. *Psychotherapy, 27*, 350–361.

Alexander, F., & French, T. M. (1946). *Psychoanalytic therapy: Principles and applications.* New York: Ronald Press.

Anchin, J. C., & Kiesler, D. J. (Eds.). (1982). *Handbook of interpersonal psychotherapy.* Elmsford, NY: Pergamon.

Andrews, G. (1991). The evaluation of psychotherapy. *Current Opinion in Psychiatry, 4*, 379–383.

Ansbacher, H. L. (1972). Adlerian psychology: The tradition of brief psychotherapy. *Journal of Individual Psychology, 28*, 137–151.

Apter, M. J. (1982). *The experience of motivation: A theory of psychological reversals.* London: Academic Press.

Bard, M., & Ellison, K. (1974). Crisis intervention and investigation of forcible rape. *The Police Chief, 41*, 68–73.

Balint, M., Orstein, P., & Balint, E. (1972). *Focal psychotherapy.* London: Tavistock.

Barkham, M. (1989). Exploratory therapy in two-plus-one sessions: I. Rationale for a brief psychotherapy model. *British Journal of Psychotherapy, 6*, 79–86.

Barkham, M., & Shapiro, D. A. (1990). Brief psychotherapeutic interventions for job-related distress: A pilot study of prescriptive and exploratory therapy. *Counseling Psychology Quarterly, 3*, 133–147.

Beck, A. T., Rush, A. J., Shaw, B. F., & Emery, G. (1984). *Cognitive therapy of depression. A treatment manual.* New York: Guilford.

Beck, A. T., Sokol, L., Clark, D. A., Berchick, R., & Wright, F. (1992). A crossover study of focused cognitive therapy for panic disorder. *American Journal of Psychiatry, 149*, 778–783.

Bellack, A. S., & Hersen, M. (1985). General considerations. In M. Hersen & A. S. Bellack (Eds.), *Handbook of clinical behavior therapy with adults.* New York: Plenum.

Bellak, L., & Siegel, H. (1983a). *Brief and emergency psychotherapy.* Larchmont, NY: C.P.S.

Bellak, L., & Siegel, H. (1983b). *Handbook of intensive brief and emergency psychotherapy.* Larchmont, NY: C.P.S.

Bellak, L., & Small, L. (1965). *Emergency psychotherapy and brief psychotherapy.* New York: Grune & Stratton.

Bellak, L., & Small, L. (1978). *Emergency psychotherapy and brief psychotherapy* (2nd ed.). New York: Grune & Stratton.

Benjamin, L. S. (1982). Use of structural analysis of social behavior (SASB) to guide intervention in psychotherapy. In J. C. Anchin & D. J. Kiesler (Eds.), *Handbook of interpersonal psychotherapy* (pp. 190–212). Elmsford, NY: Pergamon.

Bergin, A. E. (1963). The effects of psychotherapy: Negative results revisited. *Journal of Counseling Psychology, 10*, 244–250.

Bergin, A. E. (1971). The evaluation of therapeutic outcomes. In A. E. Bergin & S. L. Garfield (Eds.), *Handbook of psychotherapy and behavior change* (pp. 217–270). New York: Wiley.

Beutler, L. E. (1983). *Eclectic psychotherapy: A systematic approach.* Elmsford, NY: Pergamon.

Beutler, L. E. (1989). Differential treatment selection: The role of diagnosis in psychotherapy. *Psychotherapy, 26*, 271–281.

Beutler, L. E. (1991). Selective treatment matching: Systematic eclectic psychotherapy. *Psychotherapy, 28*, 457–462.

Beutler, L. E., & Clarkin, J. F. (1990). *Systematic treatment selection toward targeted therapeutic interventions.* New York: Brunner/Mazel.

Beutler, L. E., & Crago, M. (Eds.). (1991). *Psychotherapy research.* Washington, DC: American Psychological Association.

Beutler, L. E., Engle, D., Mohr, D., Daldrup, R. J., Meredith,

K., & Merry, W. (1991). Predictors of differential response to cognitive, experiential, and self-directed psychotherapeutic procedures. *Journal of Consulting and Clinical Psychology, 59,* 333–340.

Bierenbaum, H., Nichols, M. P., & Schwartz, A. J. (1976). Effects of varying length and frequency in brief emotive psychotherapy. *Journal of Consulting and Clinical Psychology, 44,* 790–798.

Binder, J. L. (1991, August). *Observations on the training of therapists in time-limited dynamic psychotherapy: Critical issues in the teaching and learning of brief therapy.* Symposium conducted at the annual meeting of the American Psychological Association, San Francisco, CA.

Bloom, B. L. (1981). Focused single session therapy: Initial development and evaluation. In S. L. Budman (Ed.), *Forms of brief therapy* (pp. 167–218). New York: Guilford.

Bloom, B. L. (1992). *Planned short-term psychotherapy.* Boston: Allyn & Bacon.

Bolter, K., Levenson, H., & Alvarez, W. (1990). Differences in values between short-term and long-term therapists. *Professional Psychology: Research and Practice, 21,* 285–290.

Bolz, W., & Meyer, A. E. (1981). The general setting (of the Hamburg Short Psychotherapy Comparison Project). *Psychotherapy and Psychosomatics, 35,* 85–95.

Bordin, E. S. (1979). The generalizability of the psychoanalytic concept of the working alliance. *Psychotherapy: Theory, Research, and Practice, 16,* 252–260.

Bowlby, J. (1979). Psychoanalysis as art and science. *International Review of Psychoanalysis, 6,* 3–14.

Brammer, L. M., & Shostrom, E. L. (1982). *Therapeutic psychology: Fundamentals of counseling and psychotherapy* (4th ed.). Englewood Cliffs, NJ: Prentice Hall.

Brom, D., Kleber, R. J., & Defares, P. B. (1989). Brief psychotherapy for posttraumatic stress disorders. *Journal of Consulting and Clinical Psychology, 57,* 607–612.

Budman, S. H. (1981). Introduction. In S. H. Budman (Ed.), *Forms of brief therapy* (pp. 1–5). New York: Guilford.

Budman, S. H., & Gurman, A. S. (1983). The practice of brief therapy. *Professional Psychology: Research and Practice, 14,* 277–292.

Budman, S. H., & Gurman, A. S. (1988). *Theory and practice of brief therapy.* New York: Guilford.

Burdon, A. F. (1963). Principles of brief psychotherapy. *Journal of the Louisiana Medical Society, 115,* 374–378.

Burlingame, G., Fuhriman, A., Paul, S., & Ogles, B. M. (1989). Implementing a time-limited therapy program: Differential effects of training and experience. *Psychotherapy, 26,* 303–313.

Burns, D. D., & Nolen-Hoeksema, S. (1992). Therapeutic empathy and recovery from depression in cognitive-behavioral therapy: A structural equation model. *Journal of Consulting and Clinical Psychology, 60,* 441–449.

Butcher, J. N., & Herzog, J. (1982). Individual assessment in crisis intervention: Observation, life history, and personality. In C. Spielberger & J. N. Butcher (Eds.), *Advances in personality assessment* (Vol. 1, pp. 115–168). Hillsdale, NJ: Lawrence Erlbaum.

Butcher, J. N., Stelmachers, Z., & Maudal, G. R. (1984). Crisis intervention. In E. B. Weiner (Ed.), *Clinical methods in psychology* (2nd ed., pp. 572–633). New York: Wiley.

Caplan, G. (1964). *Principles of preventive psychiatry.* New York: Basic Books.

Castelnuovo-Tedesco, P. (1966). Brief psychotherapeutic treatment of depressive reactions. In G. J. Wayne and R. R. Koegler (Eds.), *Emergency psychiatry and brief therapy.* Boston: Little, Brown.

Clementel-Jones, C., Malan, D., & Trauer, T. (1990). A retrospective study of 84 patients treated with individual psychoanalytic psychotherapy: Outcome and predictive factors. *British Journal of Psychotherapy, 6,* 363–374.

Cohen, J. (1977). *Statistical power analysis for the behavioral sciences.* New York: Academic Press.

Cohen, L. H., Sargent, M. M., & Sechrest, L. B. (1986). Use of psychotherapy research by professional psychologists. *American Psychologist, 41,* 198–206.

Coleman, M. D. (1960). Methods of psychotherapy: Emergency psychotherapy. In J. H. Masserman & J. L. Moreno (Eds.), *Progress in psychotherapy.* New York: Grune & Stratton.

Coleman, M. D., & Zwerling, I. (1959). The psychiatric emergency clinic: A flexible way of meeting community mental health needs. *American Journal of Psychiatry, 115,* 980–984.

Colson, D. B., Horowitz, L., Allen, J. G., Frieswyk, S. H. (1988). Patient collaboration as a criterion for the therapeutic alliance. *Psychoanalytic Psychology, 5,* 259–268.

Crits-Christoph, P. (1992). The efficacy of brief dynamic psychotherapy: A meta-analysis. *American Journal of Psychiatry, 149,* 151–158.

Cross, D. G., Sheehan, P. W., & Khan, J. A. (1982). Short and long term follow-up of clients receiving insight-oriented therapy and behavior therapy. *Journal of Consulting and Clinical Psychology, 50,* 103–112.

Cummings, N. A., & Vandenbos, C. (1979). The general practice of psychology. *Professional Psychology: Research and Practice, 10,* 439–440.

Davanloo, H. (1979). Techniques of short-term dynamic psychotherapy. *Psychiatric Clinics of North America, 2,* 11–22.

Davanloo, H. (1980). A method of short-term dynamic psychotherapy. In H. Davanloo (Ed.), *Short-term dynamic psychotherapy* (pp. 43–71). New York: Jason Aronson.

de Shazer, S. (1988). *Clues: Investigating solutions in brief therapy.* New York: W. W. Norton.

Deutsch, F. (1949). *Applied psychoanalysis: Selected lectures on psychotherapy.* New York: Grune & Stratton.

DiClemente, C. C., & Prochaska, J. (1982). Self-change and therapy change of smoking behavior: A comparison of processes of change in cessation and maintenance. *Addictive Behaviors, 7,* 133–142.

Dobson, K. (1989). A meta analysis of the efficacy of cognitive therapy for depression. *Journal of Consulting and Clinical Psychology, 57,* 414–419.

Docherty, J. P., & Feister, S. J. (1985). The therapeutic alliance and compliance with psychopharmacology. In R. E. Hales & A. J. Frances (Eds.), *Psychiatry Update, 4,* 607–632. Washington, DC: American Psychiatric Press.

Donovan, J. M. (1987). Brief dynamic psychotherapy: Toward a more comprehensive model. *Psychiatry, 50,* 167–183.

Dryden, W. (1986). Eclectic psychotherapies: A critique of leading approaches. In J. C. Norcross (Ed.), *Handbook of eclectic psychotherapy* (pp. 353–375). New York: Brunner/Mazel.

Eaton, T. T., Abeles, N., & Gutfreund, M. J. (1988). Therapeutic alliance and outcome: Impact of treatment length and pretreatment symptomatology. *Psychotherapy, 25,* 536–542.

Elkin, I., Shea, M. T., Watkins, J. T., Imber, S. D., Sotsky, S. M., Collins, J. F., Glass, D. R., Pilkonis, P. A., Leber, W. R., Docherty, J. P., Fiester, S. J., & Parloff, M. B. (1989). National Institute of Mental Health Treatment of Depression Collaborative Research Study. *Archives of General Psychiatry, 46,* 971–982.

Elliott, R. (1986). Interpersonal process recall (IPR) as a psychotherapy process recall method. In L. S. Greenberg & W. M. Pinsof (Eds.), *The psychotherapeutic process: A research handbook* (pp. 503–528). New York: Guilford.

Elliott, R., & James, E. (1989). Varieties of client experience in psychotherapy: An analysis of the literature. *Clinical Psychology Review, 9,* 443–467.

Elliott, R., James, E., Reimschuessel, C., Cislo, D., & Sack, N. (1985). Significant events and the analysis of immediate therapeutic impacts. *Psychotherapy, 22,* 620–630.

Elliott, R., & Shapiro, D. A. (1988). Brief structured recall: A more efficient method for studying significant therapy events. *British Journal of Medical Psychology, 61,* 141–153.

Ellis, A., & Grieger, R. (1977). *Handbook of rational-emotive therapy.* New York: Springer.

Ewing, C. P. (1990). Crisis intervention as brief psychotherapy. In R. A. Wells & V. J. Giannetti (Eds.), *Handbook of the brief psychotherapies* (pp. 277–294). New York: Plenum.

Farrelly, F., & Brandsma, J. (1974). *Provocative therapy.* Cupertino, CA: Meta Publications.

Ferenczi, S. (1960). The further development of an active therapy in psychoanalysis. In J. Richman (Ed.), *Further contributions to the theory and techniques of psychoanalysis* (pp. 198–216). London: Hogarth. (Original work published 1920)

Flegenheimer, W. V. (1978). The patient–therapist relationship in crisis intervention. *Journal of Clinical Psychiatry, 39,* 348–350.

Foa, E. B., Rothbaum, B. O., Riggs, D. S., & Murdock, T. B. (1991). Treatment of posttraumatic stress disorder in rape victims: A comparison between cognitive-behavioral procedures and counseling. *Journal of Consulting and Clinical Psychology, 59,* 715–723.

Frank, E. (1991). Interpersonal psychotherapy as a maintenance treatment for patients with recurrent depression. *Psychotherapy, 28,* 259–266.

Frank, J. D. (1959). The dynamics of the psychotherapeutic relationship. *Psychiatry, 22,* 17–39.

Frank, J. D. (1974). Therapeutic components of psychotherapy: A 25-year progress report of research. *Journal of Nervous and Mental Disease, 159,* 325–342.

Frankel, F. H. (1973). The effects of brief hypnotherapy in a series of psychosomatic problems. *Psychotherapy and Psychosomatics, 22,* 269–275.

Frieswyk, S. H., Allen, J. G., Colson, D. B., Coyne, L., Gabbard, G. O., Horowitz, L., & Newsom, G. (1986). Therapeutic alliance: Its place as a process and outcome variable in dynamic psychotherapy research. *Journal of Consulting and Clinical Psychology, 54,* 32–38.

Fuhriman, A., Paul, S. C., & Burlingame, G. M. (1986). Eclectic time-limited therapy. In J. C. Norcross (Ed.), *Handbook of eclectic psychotherapy* (pp. 226–259). New York: Brunner/Mazel.

Gallagher, D., & Thompson, L. (1981). *Depression in the elderly: A behavioral treatment manual.* Los Angeles: University of Southern California Press.

Gallagher-Thompson, D., Hanley-Peterson, P., & Thompson, L. W. (1990). Maintenance of gains versus relapse following brief psychotherapy for depression. *Journal of Consulting and Clinical Psychology, 58,* 371–374.

Garfield, S. L. (1978). Research on client variables in psychotherapy. In S. L. Garfield & A. E. Bergin (Eds.), *Handbook of psychotherapy and behavior change* (2nd ed., pp. 191–232). New York: Wiley.

Garfield, S. L. (1980). *Psychotherapy: An eclectic approach.* New York: Wiley.

Garfield, S. L. (1986). Research on client variables in psychotherapy. In S. L. Garfield & A. E. Bergin (Eds.), *Handbook of psychotherapy and behavior change* (3rd ed., pp. 213–256). New York: Wiley.

Garfield, S. L. (1989). *The practice of brief psychotherapy.* Elmsford, NY: Pergamon.

Garfield, S. L. (1990). Issues and methods in psychotherapy process research. *Journal of Consulting and Clinical Psychology, 58,* 273–280.

Garner, H. H. (1970). *Psychotherapy: Confrontation problem solving techniques.* St. Louis, MO: W. H. Green.

Gaston, L. (1990). The concept of the alliance and its role in psychotherapy: Theoretical and empirical considerations. *Psychotherapy, 27,* 143–153.

Gaston, L., Marmar, C. R., Gallager, D., & Thompson, L. W. (1991). Alliance prediction of outcome beyond intreatment symptomatic change as psychotherapy processes. *Psychotherapy Research, 1,* 104–113.

Gaston, L., Marmar, C. R., Thompson, L. W., & Gallagher, D. (1988). Relation of patient pretreatment characteristics to the therapeutic alliance in diverse psychotherapies. *Journal of Consulting and Clinical Psychology, 56,* 483–489.

Gaston, L., Ring, J. M., & Marmar, C. R. (1989). *Development of the Inventory of Therapeutic Strategies (ITS): Preliminary results for cognitive and brief dynamic psychotherapy.* Paper presented at the annual meeting of the Society for Psychotherapy Research, Toronto, Canada.

Gelb, L. A., & Ullman, A. (1967). As reported anon. in Instant psychotherapy offered at an outpatient psychiatric clinic. *Frontiers of Hospital Psychiatry, 4,* 14.

Gelder, M. G., Marks, I. M., & Wolff, H. H. (1967). Desensitization and psychotherapy in the treatment of phobic states: A controlled inquiry. *British Journal of Psychiatry, 13,* 53–73.

Gillman, R. D. (1965). Brief psychotherapy: A psychoanalytic view. *American Journal of Psychiatry, 122,* 601–611.

Gim, R., Atkinson, D., & Kim, S. (1991). Asian-American acculturation, counselor ethnicity and cultural sensitivity, and ratings of counselors. *Journal of Counseling Psychology, 38,* 57–62.

Glaser, B. G., & Strauss, A. (1967). *The discovery of grounded theory: Strategies for qualitative research.* Chicago: Aldine.

Glasscote, R. M., Raybin, J. B., Reifler, C. B., & Kane, A. W. (1975). *The alternate services: Their role in mental health.* Washington DC: American Psychiatric Service.

Goldfried, M. R. (1980). Toward the delineation of therapeutic change principles. *American Psychologist, 35,* 991–999.

Gomes-Schwartz, B. (1978). Effective ingredients in psychotherapy; Prediction of outcome from process variables. *Journal of Consulting and Clinical Psychology, 46,* 1023–1035.

Gottschalk, L. A., Mayerson, P., & Gottlieb, A. A. (1967). Prediction and evaluation of outcome in an emergency brief psychotherapy clinic. *Journal of Nervous and Mental Disease, 144,* 77–96.

Green, B. L., Gleser, G. C., Stone, W. N., & Seifert, R. F. (1975). Relationships among diverse measures of psychotherapy outcome. *Journal of Consulting and Clinical Psychology, 43,* 689–699.

Greenberg, L. S. (1986). Research strategies. In L. S. Greenberg & W. M. Pinsof (Eds.), *The psychotherapeutic process: A research handbook* (pp. 707–734). New York: Guilford.

Greenberg, L. S., & Pinsof, W. M. (1986). Process research:

Current trends and future perspectives. In L. S. Greenberg & W. M. Pinsof (Eds.), *The psychotherapeutic process: A research handbook* (pp. 3–20). New York: Guilford.

Greenson, R. R. (1965). The working alliance and the transference neurosis. *Psychoanalytic Quarterly, 34,* 155–181.

Grinker, R. R., & Spiegel, J. P. (1944). *Management of neuropsychiatric casualties in the zone of combat. Manual of military neuropsychiatry.* Philadelphia: W. B. Saunders.

Gustafson, J. P. (1986). *The complex secret of psychotherapy.* New York: W. W. Norton.

Gutheil, E. A. (1944). Psychoanalysis and brief psychotherapy. *Journal of Clinical Psychopathology, 6,* 207–230.

Hadley, S. W., & Strupp, H. H. (1976). Contemporary views of negative effects in psychotherapy. *Archives of General Psychiatry, 33,* 1291–1302.

Haley, J. (1976). *Problem-solving therapy: New strategies for effective family therapy.* San Francisco: Jossey-Bass.

Haley, J. (1984). *Ordeal therapy.* San Francisco: Jossey-Bass.

Haley, J. (1987). *Problem-solving therapy* (2nd ed.). San Francisco: Jossey-Bass.

Harris, M. R., Kalis, B. L., & Freeman, E. H. (1963). Precipitating stress: An approach to brief therapy. *American Journal of Psychotherapy, 17,* 465–471.

Hart, J. (1983). *Modern eclectic therapy: A functional orientation to counseling and psychotherapy.* New York: Plenum.

Hartley, D. E., & Strupp, H. H. (1983). The therapeutic alliance: Its relationship to outcome in brief psychotherapy. In J. Masling (Ed.), *Empirical studies of psychoanalytic theories* (Vol. 1, pp. 1–38). Hillsdale, NJ: Analytical Press.

Hawton, K., Reibstein, J., Fieldsend, R., & Whalley, M. (1982). Content analysis of brief psychotherapy sessions. *British Journal of Medical Psychology, 55,* 167–176.

Henry, W. P., Schacht, T. E., & Strupp, H. E. (1986). Structural analysis of social behavior: Application to a study of interpersonal process in differential psychotherapeutic outcome. *Journal of Consulting and Clinical Psychology, 54,* 27–31.

Henry, W., Strupp, H., & Binder, J. (1992). *Treatment manuals — what they can and cannot do: Lessons from the Vanderbilt-II study.* Paper presented at the annual meeting of Society for Psychotherapy Research, Berkeley, CA.

Heitler, J. B. (1976). Preparatory techniques in initiating expressive psychotherapy in lower-class unsophisticated patients. *Psychological Bulletin, 83,* 339–352.

Hill, C. E., Carter, J. A., & O'Farrell, M. K. (1983). A case study of the process and outcome of time-limited counseling. *Journal of Counseling Psychology, 30,* 3–18.

Hoch, P. H. (1965). Short-term versus long-term therapy. In L. R. Wolberg (Ed.), *Short-term psychotherapy* (pp. 51–66). New York: Grune & Stratton.

Hoehn-Saric, R., Frank, J. D., Imber, S. D., Nash, E. H., Stone, A. R., & Battle, C. C. (1964). Systematic preparation of patients for psychotherapy: Effects of therapy behavior and outcome. *Journal of Psychiatric Research, 2,* 267–281.

Hogan, R. A. (1966). Implosive therapy in the short-term treatment of psychotics. *Psychotherapy, 3,* 25–32.

Hogan, R. A. (1967). Preliminary report of the extinction of learned fears via short-term implosive therapy. *Journal of Abnormal Psychology, 72,* 106–109.

Hornstra, R., Lubin, B., Lewis, R., & Willis, B. (1972). Worlds apart: Patients and professionals. *Archives of General Psychiatry, 27,* 553–557.

Horowitz, L., Allen, J. G., Colson, D. B., Frieswyk, S. H., Gabbard, G. O., Coyne, L., & Newsom, G. E. (1991). Psychotherapy of borderline patients at the Menninger Foundation: Expressive compared with supportive interventions and the therapeutic alliance. In L. E. Beutler & M. Crago (Eds.), *Psychotherapy research* (pp. 48–55). Washington, DC: American Psychological Association.

Horowitz, M. J. (1988). *Introduction to psychodynamics: A new synthesis.* New York: Basic Books.

Horowitz, L. M., Rosenberg, S. E., Ureno, G., Kalehzan, B. M., & O'Halloran, P. (1989) Psychodynamic formulation, consensual response method, and interpersonal problems. *Journal of Consulting and Clinical Psychology, 57,* 599–606.

Horowitz, M., & Kaltreider, N. (1979). Brief therapy of the stress response syndrome. *Psychiatric Clinics of North America, 2,* 365–377.

Horowitz, M. J., Marmar, C. Krupnick, J., Wilner, J., Kaltreider, N., & Wallerstein, R. (1984). *Personality styles and brief psychotherapy.* New York: Guilford.

Horowitz, M. J., Marmar, C., Weiss, D. S., DeWitt, K. N., & Rosenbaum, R. (1984). Brief psychotherapy of bereavement reactions. *Archives of General Psychiatry, 41,* 438–448.

Horvath, A. O., & Greenberg, L. (1989). Development and validation of the Working Alliance Inventory. *Journal of Counseling Psychology, 36,* 223–233.

Howard, K. I., Kopta, S. M., Krause, M. S., & Orlinsky, D. E. (1986). The dose-effect relationship in psychotherapy. *American Psychologist, 41,* 159–164.

Hoyt, M. F. (1985). Therapist resistances to short-term dynamic psychotherapy. *Journal of the American Academy of Psychoanalysis, 13,* 93–112.

Hoyt, M. F. (1990). On time in brief therapy. In R. A. Wells & V. J. Giannetti (Eds.), *Handbook of the brief psychotherapies* (pp. 115–143). New York: Plenum.

Hoyt, M. F., Marmar, C. R., Horowitz, M. J., & Alvarez, W. F. (1981). The therapist action scale and the patient action scale: Instruments of the assessment of activities during dynamic psychotherapy. *Psychotherapy: Theory, Research, and Practice, 18,* 109–116.

Hoyt, M. F., Xenakis, S. N., Marmar, C. R., & Horowitz, M. J. (1983). Therapists' actions that influence their perceptions of "good" psychotherapy sessions. *Journal of Nervous and Mental Disease, 171,* 400–404.

Jacobson, G. F. (1965). Crisis theory and treatment strategy: Some sociocultural and psychodynamic considerations. *Journal of Nervous and Mental Disease, 141,* 209–218.

Jacobson, G. F. (1979). Crisis-oriented therapy. *Psychiatric Clinics of North America, 2,* 39–54.

Jacobson, G. F., Strickler, M., & Morley, W. E. (1968). Generic and individual approaches to crisis intervention. *American Journal of Public Health, 58,* 339–343.

Jacobson, N., Follette, W., & Ravenstorf, D. (1984). Psychotherapy outcome research: Methods for reporting variability and evaluating clinical significance. *Behavior Therapy, 15,* 336–352.

Jacobson, N. S., & Truax, P. (1991). Clinical significance: A statistical approach to defining meaningful change in psychotherapy research. *Journal of Consulting and Clinical Psychology, 59,* 12–19.

Johnson, D. H., & Gelso, C. J. (1980). The effectiveness of time limits in counseling and psychotherapy: A critical review. *The Counseling Psychologist, 9,* 70–83.

Kardiner, A. (1941). *The traumatic neurosis of war.* New York: Hoeber.

Kendall, P. C., Vitousek, K. B., & Kane, M. (1991). Thought and action in psychotherapy: Cognitive behavioral approaches. In M. Hersen, A. E. Kazdin, & A. S. Bellack

(Eds.), *The clinical psychology handbook* (pp. 596–626). Elmsford, NY: Pergamon.

Keisler, D. J. (1986). Interpersonal methods of diagnosis and treatment. In J. O. Cavenar (Ed.), *Psychiatry* (Vol. 1, pp. 1–23). Philadelphia: Lippincott.

Kiesler, D. J. (1987). *Revised version of the Checklist of Interpersonal Transactions.* Richmond: Virginia Commonwealth University.

Keisler, D. J., & Watkins, L. M. (1989). Interpersonal complementarity and the therapeutic alliance: A study of relationship in psychotherapy. *Psychotherapy, 26,* 183–194.

Klein, D., & Lindemann, E. (1961). Preventive intervention in individual and family crisis situations. In G. Caplan (Ed.), *Prevention of mental disorders in children. Initial exploration* (pp. 283–306). New York: Basic Books.

Klein, M. J., Mathieu-Coughlan, P., & Kiesler, D. J. (1986). The experiencing scales. In L. S. Greenberg & W. M. Pinsof (Eds.), *The psychotherapeutic process: A research handbook* (pp. 21–72). New York: Guilford.

Klerman, G. L., & Weissman, M. M. (1991). Interpersonal psychotherapy: Research program and future prospects. In L. E. Beutler & M. Crago (Eds.), *Psychotherapy research* (pp. 33–40). Washington, DC: American Psychological Association.

Klerman, G. L., Weissman, M. M., Rounsaville, B. J., & Chevron, E. S. (1984). *Interpersonal psychotherapy of depression.* New York: Basic Books.

Klosko, J. S., Barlow, D. H., Tassinari, R., & Cerny, J. A. (1990). A comparison of alprazolam and behavior therapy in treatment of panic disorder. *Journal of Consulting and Clinical Psychology, 58,* 77–84.

Kolden, G. G. (1991). The generic model of psychotherapy: An empirical investigation of patterns of process and outcome relationships. *Psychotherapy Research, 1,* 62–73.

Kolotkin, R. L., & Johnson, M. (1983). Crisis intervention and measurement of treatment outcome. In M. J. Lambert, E. R. Christensen, & S. S. DeJulio (Eds.), *The assessment of psychotherapy outcome.* New York: Wiley.

Koss, M. P., Butcher, J. N., & Strupp, H. H. (1986). Psychotherapy methods in clinical research. *Journal of Consulting and Clinical Psychology, 54,* 60–67.

Lambert, M. J. (1976). Spontaneous remission in adult neurotic disorders: A revision and summary. *Psychological Bulletin, 83,* 107–119.

Lambert, M. J. (1983). Comments on "A case study of the process and outcome of time-limited counseling." *Journal of Counseling Psychology, 30,* 22–25.

Lambert, M. J. (1989). The individual therapist's contribution to psychotherapy process and outcome. *Clinical Psychology Review, 9,* 469–485.

Lambert, M. J., Shapiro, D. A., & Bergin, A. E. (1986). The effectiveness of psychotherapy. In S. L. Garfield & A. E. Bergin (Eds.), *Handbook of psychotherapy and behavior change* (3rd ed., pp. 157–212). New York: Wiley.

Lazarus, A. A. (1981). *The practice of multimodal therapy.* New York: McGraw-Hill.

Lazarus, A. A., & Fay, A. (1990). Brief psychotherapy: Tautology or oxymoron? In J. K. Zeig & S. C. Gilligan (Eds.), *Brief therapy: Myths, methods, and metaphors* (pp. 36–54). New York: Brunner/Mazel.

Lehman, A. K., & Salovey, P. (1990). An introduction to cognitive-behavior therapy. In R. A. Wells & V. J. Giannetti (Eds.), *Handbook of the brief psychotherapies* (pp. 239–259). New York: Plenum.

Levene, H., Breger, L., & Patterson, V. (1972). A training and research program in brief psychotherapy. *American Journal of Psychotherapy, 26,* 90–100.

Levenson, H., & Bolter, K. (1988, August). *Short-term psychotherapy values and attitudes: Changes with training.* Paper presented at the annual meeting of the American Psychological Association, Atlanta, GA.

Levenson, H., & Hales, R. E. (in press). Brief psychodynamically-informed therapy: Relevance for the medically ill. In A. Stoudemire & B. S. Fogel (Eds.), *Medical psychiatric practice.* Washington, DC: American Psychiatric Press.

Levenson, H., Speed, J. L., & Budman, S. H. (1992, June). *Therapists' training and skill in brief therapy: A survey of Massachusetts and California psychologists.* Paper presented to the Society for Psychotherapy Research, Berkeley, CA.

Levis, D. J., & Carrera, R. N. (1967). Effects of ten hours of implosive therapy in the treatment of outpatients: A preliminary report. *Journal of Abnormal Psychology, 72,* 504–508.

Levy, R. A. (1966). How to conduct 6 session crisis oriented psychotherapy. *Hospital and Community Psychiatry, 17,* 340–343.

Levy, R. L., & Shelton, J. L. (1990). Tasks in brief therapy. In R. A. Wells & V. J. Giannetti (Eds.), *Handbook of the brief psychotherapies* (pp. 145–164). New York: Plenum.

Lewin, K. K. (1970). *Brief encounters: Brief psychotherapy.* St. Louis, MO: Green.

Lewis, K. A. (1966). A method of brief psychotherapy. *Psychiatric Quarterly, 40,* 482–489.

Lindemann, E. (1944). Symptomatology and management of acute grief. *American Journal of Psychiatry, 101,* 141–148.

London, L. S. (1947). Hypnosis, hypno-analysis and narco-analysis. *American Journal of Psychotherapy, 1,* 443–447.

Lorion, R. P. (1973). Socioeconomic status and traditional treatment approaches reconsidered. *Psychological Bulletin, 79,* 263–270.

Lorr, M., McNair, D. M., Michaux, W. W., & Raskin, A. (1964). Frequency of treatment and change in psychotherapy. *Journal of Abnormal and Social Psychology, 64,* 281–292.

Luborsky, L. (1976). Helping alliances in psychotherapy. In J. L. Claghorn (Ed.), *Successful psychotherapy* (pp. 92–116). New York: Brunner/Mazel.

Luborsky, L. (1984). *Principles of psychoanalytic psychotherapy: A manual for supportive-expressive treatment.* New York: Basic Books.

Luborsky, L., Chandler, M., Auerbach, A. H., Cohen, J., & Bachrach, H. M. (1971). Factors influencing the outcome of psychotherapy: A review of quantitative research. *Psychological Bulletin, 75,* 145–185.

Luborsky, L., & Crits-Christoph, P. (1990). *Understanding transference: The core conflictual relationship theme method.* New York: Basic Books.

Luborsky, L., Crits-Christoph, P., & Barber, J. (1991). University of Pennsylvania: The Penn psychotherapy research projects. In L. E. Beutler & M. Crago (Eds.) *Psychotherapy research* (pp. 133–141). Washington, DC: American Psychological Association.

Luborsky, L., Crits-Christoph, P., McLellan, A. T., Woody, G., Piper, W., Liberman, B., Imber, S., & Pilkonis, P. (1986). Do therapists vary much in their success? Findings from four outcome studies. *American Journal of Orthopsychiatry, 56,* 501–512.

Luborsky, L., McLellan, A. T., Woody, G. E., O'Brien, C. P., & Auerbach, A. (1985). Therapist success and its determinants. *Archives of General Psychiatry, 42,* 602–611.

Luborsky, L., Singer, B., & Luborsky, L. (1975). Comparative studies of psychotherapies. *Archives of General Psychiatry, 32,* 995–1008.

Malan, D. H. (1963). *A study of brief psychotherapy*. London: Tavistock.

Malan, D. H. (1976a). *The frontier of brief psychotherapy*. New York: Plenum.

Malan, D. H. (1976b). *Toward the validation of dynamic psychotherapy: A replication*. New York: Plenum.

Mann, J. (1973). *Time-limited psychotherapy*. Cambridge, MA: Harvard University Press.

Mann, J. (1984). Time-limited psychotherapy. In L. Grinspoon (Ed.), *Psychiatry update: The American Psychiatric Association Annual Review, III* (pp. 35–44). Washington, DC: American Psychiatric Press.

Marmar, C. R., Gaston, L., Gallagher, D., & Thompson, L. (1989). Alliance and outcome in late-life depression. *Journal of Nervous and Mental Disease, 177*, 464–472.

Marmar, C. R., Mardi, J. H., Weiss, D. S., Wilner, N. R., & Kaltreider, N. B. (1988). A controlled trial of brief psychotherapy and mutual-help group treatment of conjugal bereavement. *American Journal of Psychiatry, 145*, 203–209.

Marmar, C. R., Weiss, D. S., & Gaston, L. (1989). Toward the validation of the California Therapeutic Alliance Rating System. *Psychological Assessment, 1*, 46–52.

Marmor, J. (1979). Short-term dynamic psychotherapy. *American Journal of Psychiatry, 136*, 149–155.

Margolin, G., & Fernanadez, V. (1985). Marital dysfunction. In M. Hersen & A. S. Bellack (Eds.), *Handbook of clinical behavior therapy with adults* (pp. 693–728). New York: Plenum.

Marziali, E., Marmar, C., & Krupnick, J. (1981). Therapeutic alliance scales: Development and relationship to psychotherapy outcome. *American Journal of Psychiatry, 138*, 361–364.

McCullough, L., Winston, A., Farber, B. A., Porter, F., Pollack, J., Laikin, M., Vingiano, W., & Trujillo, M. (1991). The relationship of patient–therapist interaction to outcome in brief psychotherapy. *Psychotherapy, 28*, 525–533.

McGuire, M. T. (1965a). The process of short-term insight psychotherapy: I. *Journal of Nervous and Mental Disease, 141*, 89–94.

McGuire, M. T. (1965b). The process of short-term insight psychotherapy: II. Content, expectations, and structure. *Journal of Nervous and Mental Disease, 141*, 219–230.

Meichenbaum, D. (1977). *Cognitive behavioral modification*. New York: Plenum.

Merrill, S., & Cary, G. L. (1975). Dream analysis in brief psychotherapy. *American Journal of Psychotherapy, 29*, 185–193.

Michelson, L., Marchione, K., Greenwald, M., & Glanz, L. (1990). Panic disorder: Cognitive-behavioral treatment. *Behavior Research and Therapy, 28*, 141–151.

Mitchell, K. R., & Orr, F. E. (1974). Note on treatment of heterosexual anxiety using short-term massed desensitization. *Psychological Reports, 35*, 1093–1094.

Moras, K., & Strupp, H. H. (1982). Pretherapy interpersonal relations, patients' alliance and outcome in brief therapy. *Archives of General Psychiatry, 39*, 405–409.

Moretti, M. M., Feldman, L. A., & Shaw, B. F. (1990). Cognitive therapy: Current issues in theory and practice. In R. A. Wells & V. J. Giannetti (Eds.), *Handbook of the brief psychotherapies* (pp. 217–237). New York: Plenum.

Murgatroyd, S., & Apter, M. J. (1986). A structural-phenomenological approach to eclectic psychotherapy. In J. C. Norcross (Ed.), *Handbook of eclectic psychotherapy* (pp. 260–281). New York: Brunner/Mazel.

Newman, F. L., & Howard, K. I. (1991). Introduction to the special section on seeking new clinical research methods. *Journal of Consulting and Clinical Psychology, 59*, 8–11.

Nichols, M. P. (1974). Outcome of brief cathartic psychotherapy. *Journal of Consulting and Clinical Psychology, 42*, 403–410.

Nichols, M. P. (1974). Outcome of brief cathartic psychotherapy. *Journal of Consulting and Clinical Psychology, 42*, 403–410.

Nichols, M. P., & Reifler, C. B. (1973). The study of brief psychotherapy in a college health setting. *Journal of the American College Health Association, 22*, 128–133.

Nietzel, M. T., Russell, R. L., Hemmings, K. A., & Gretter, M. L. (1987). Clinical significance of psychotherapy for unipolar depression: A meta-analytic approach to social comparison. *Journal of Consulting and Clinical Psychology, 55*, 156–161.

Norcross, J. C. (1986). Eclectic psychotherapy: An introduction and overview. In J. C. Norcross (Ed.), *Handbook of eclectic psychotherapy* (pp. 3–24). New York: Brunner/Mazel.

O'Farrell, M. K., Hill, C. E., & Patton, S. (1992). *A case study of the process and outcome of time-limited psychotherapy: A methodological replication*. Manuscript submitted for publication.

Orlinsky, D. E., & Howard, K. L. (1980) Gender and psychotherapeutic outcome. In A. M. Brodsky & R. T. Hare-Mustin (Eds.), *Women and psychotherapy* (pp. 3–34). New York: Guilford.

Orlinsky, D. E., & Howard, K. L. (1986). The psychological interior of psychotherapy: Explorations with therapy session reports. In L. S. Greenberg & W. M. Pinsof (Eds.), *The psychotherapeutic process: A research handbook*. New York: Guilford.

Orlinsky, D. E., & Howard, K. L. (1987). A generic model of psychotherapy. *Journal of Integrative and Eclectic Psychotherapy, 6*, 6–27.

Pardes, H., & Pincus, A. (1981). Brief therapy in the context of national mental health issues. In S. H. Budman (Ed.), *Forms of brief therapy* (pp. 7–21). New York: Guilford.

Patterson, V., Levene, H., & Breger, L. (1971). Treatment and training outcomes with two time-limited therapies. *Archives of General Psychiatry, 25*, 161–167.

Paul, G. L. (1966). *Insight versus desensitization in psychotherapy*. Stanford, CA.: Stanford University Press.

Paul, G. L. (1967a). Strategy of outcome research in psychotherapy. *Journal of Consulting Psychology, 31*, 109–118.

Paul, G. L. (1967b). Insight versus desensitization in psychotherapy two years after termination. *Journal of Consulting Psychology, 31*, 333–348.

Perry, J. C., Cooper, A. M., & Michels, R. (1987). The psychodynamic formulations: Its purpose, structure, and clinical application. *American Journal of Psychiatry, 144*, 543–550.

Persons, J. (1989). *Cognitive therapy in practice*. New York: W. W. Norton.

Persons, J., Burns, D. D., & Perloff, J. M. (1989). Predictors of dropout and outcome in cognitive therapy for depression in a private practice setting. *Cognitive Therapy and Research, 12*, 557–575.

Phillips, E. L., & Weiner, D. N. (1966). *Short-term psychotherapy and structured behavior change*. New York: McGraw-Hill.

Pilkonis, P., Heape, C. L., & Proietti, J. M. (1991, November). *Adult attachment styles, personality disorder, and treatment outcome in depression*. Paper presented at the annual meeting of the North American Society for Psychotherapy Research, Panama City, FL.

Piper, W. E., Azim, H. F. A., McCallum, M., & Joyce, A. S.

(1990). Patient suitability and outcome in short-term individual psychotherapy. *Journal of Consulting and Clinical Psychology, 58,* 475–481.

Piper, W. E., Debbane, E. G., Bienvenu, J. P., & Garant, J. (1984). A comparative study of four forms of psychotherapy. *Journal of Consulting and Clinical Psychology, 52,* 268–279.

Piper, W. E., de Carufel, F. L., & Szkrumelak, N. (1985). Patient predictors of process and outcome in short-term individual psychotherapy. *Journal of Nervous and Mental Disease, 173,* 726–733.

Prochaska, J. O. (1991). Prescribing to the stage and level of phobic patients. *Psychotherapy, 28,* 463–468.

Prochaska, J. O., & DiClemente, C. C. (1984). *The transtheoretical approach: Crossing the traditional boundaries of therapy.* Homewood, IL: Dow Jones-Irvin.

Pumpian-Mindlin, E. (1953). Consideration in the selection of patients for short-term therapy. *American Journal of Psychotherapy, 7,* 641–652.

Rabkin, R. (1977). *Strategic psychotherapy: Brief and symptomatic treatment.* New York: Basic Books.

Reich, J., & Neenan, P. (1986). Principles common to different short-term psychotherapies. *American Journal of Psychotherapy, 40,* 62–69.

Reid, W. J. (1990). An integrative model for short-term treatment. In R. A. Wells & V. J. Gianetti (Eds.), *Handbook of the brief psychotherapies* (pp. 55–78). New York: Plenum.

Rennie, D. L. (1990). Toward a representation of the client's experience of the psychotherapy hour. In G. Lietaer, J. Rombauts, & R. Van Balen (Eds.), *Client-centered and experiential psychotherapy in the nineties.* Leuren, Belgium: Leuren University Press.

Rice, L., & Greenberg, L. S. (1984). *Patterns of change: Intensive analysis of psychotherapy process.* New York: Guilford.

Roberts, A. R. (Ed.). (1990). *Crisis intervention handbook: Assessment, treatment, and research.* Belmont, CA: Wadsworth.

Robinson, L. A., Berman, J. S., & Neimeyer, R. A. (1990). Psychotherapy for the treatment of depression: A comprehensive review of controlled outcome research. *Psychological Bulletin, 108,* 30–49.

Rosenberg, S. E., Silberschatz, G., Curtis, J. T., Sampson, H., & Weiss, J. (1986). A method for establishing reliability of statements from psychodynamic case formulations. *American Journal of Psychiatry, 143,* 1454–1456.

Rounsaville, B. J., Glazer, W., Wilber, C. H., Weismann, M. M., & Kleber, H. D. (1983). Short-term interpersonal psychotherapy in methadone-maintained opiate addicts. *Archives of General Psychiatry, 40,* 629–636.

Rush, A. J. (1985). The therapeutic alliance in short-term directive psychotherapies. In R. E. Hales & A. J. Frances (Eds.), *Psychiatry Update, 4,* 562–572.

Sachs, J. S. (1983). Negative factors in brief psychotherapy: An empirical assessment. *Journal of Consulting and Clinical Psychology, 51,* 557–564.

Sarvis, M. A., Dewees, M. S., & Johnston, R. F. (1958). A concept of ego-oriented psychotherapy. *Psychiatry, 22,* 277–287.

Semrad, E. V., Binstock, W. A., & White, B. (1966). Brief psychotherapy. *American Journal of Psychotherapy, 20,* 576–596.

Shapiro, D. A., Barkham, M., Hardy, G., & Morrison, L. (1990). The second Sheffield psychotherapy project: Rationale, design, and preliminary outcome data. *British Journal of Medical Psychology, 63,* 97–108.

Shapiro, D. A., & Shapiro, D. (1982). Meta-analysis of comparative therapy outcome studies: A replication and refinement. *Psychological Bulletin, 92,* 581–604.

Sharfstein, S. S., Muszynski, S., & Myers, E. S. (1984). *Health insurance and psychiatric care: Update and appraisal.* Washington, DC: American Psychiatric Press.

Shiang, J. (1984). *The significance of transactions: Reciprocity between Chinese elderly and their adult children living in Boston and its suburbs.* Unpublished Dissertation. Harvard University.

Shiang, J. (1986). 'Heart' and self in old age: A Chinese model. In M. White & S. Pollack (Eds.), *The cultural transition: human experience and social transformation in the third world and Japan* (pp. 211–239). Boston: Routledge and Kegan Paul.

Shiang, J. (August, 1993). *Transactions, behavior, and emotions in Chinese American families.* Paper presented to the American Psychological Association, Toronto, Canada.

Shlien, J. M., Mosak, H. H., & Dreikurs, R. (1962). Effects of time limits: A comparison of two psychotherapies. *Journal of Counseling Psychology, 2,* 31–34.

Shoham-Salomon, V. (1990). Interrelating research processes of process research. *Journal of Consulting and Clinical Psychology, 58,* 295–303.

Siddall, L. B., Haffey, N. A., & Feinman, J. A. (1988). Intermittent brief psychotherapy in an HMO setting. *American Journal of Psychotherapy, 62,* 96–106.

Sifneos, P. E. (1972). *Short-term psychotherapy and emotional crisis.* Cambridge, MA: Harvard University Press.

Sifneos, P. E. (1979). *Short-term dynamic psychotherapy: Evaluation and technique.* New York: Plenum.

Sifneos, P. E. (1987). *Short-term dynamic psychotherapy: Evaluation and technique* (2nd ed.). New York: Plenum.

Silberschatz, G., & Curtis, J. T. (1986). Clinical implications of research on brief dynamic psychotherapy: II. How the therapist helps or hinders the therapeutic process. *Psychoanalytic Psychology, 3,* 27–37.

Silberschatz, G., Curtis, J. T., Sampson, H., & Weiss, J. (1991). Mount Zion Hospital and Medical Center: Research on the process of change in psychotherapy. In L. E. Beutler & M. Crago (Eds.), *Psychotherapy research* (pp. 56–64). Washington, DC: American Psychological Association.

Sloane, R. B., Cristol, A. H., Pepernik, M. C., & Staples, F. R. (1970). Role preparation and expectation of improvement in psychotherapy. *Journal of Nervous and Mental Disease, 150,* 18–26.

Sloane, R. B., Staples, F. R., Cristol, A. H., Yorkston, N. J., & Whipple, K. (1975). Short-term analytically oriented psychotherapy versus behavior therapy. *American Journal of Psychiatry, 132,* 373–377.

Sloane, R. B., Staples, F. R., Cristol, A. H., Yorkston, N. J., & Whipple, K. (1976). Patient characteristics and outcome in psychotherapy and behavior therapy. *Journal of Consulting and Clinical Psychology, 44,* 330–339.

Small, L. (1971). *The briefer psychotherapies.* New York: Brunner/Mazel.

Smith, M. L., & Glass, G. V. (1977). Meta-analysis of psychotherapy outcome studies. *American Psychologist, 32,* 752–760.

Smith, M. L., Glass, G. V., & Miller, T. I. (1980). *The benefits of psychotherapy.* Baltimore: The Johns Hopkins University Press.

Spitzer, R., Endicott, J., & Robins, E. (1978). Research diagnostic criteria: Rationale and reliability. *Archives of General Psychiatry, 35,* 773–782.

Staples, F. R., Sloane, R. D., Whipple, K., Cristol, A. H., & Yorkston, N. (1976). Process and outcome in psychotherapy and behavior therapy. *Journal of Consulting and Clinical Psychology, 44,* 340–350.

Stein, C. (1972). Hypnotic projection in brief psychotherapy. *American Journal of Clinical Hypnosis, 14,* 143–155.

Stein, C. (1975). Brief hypnotherapy for conversion cephalgia (repression headache). *American Journal of Clinical Hypnosis, 17,* 198–201.

Stein, E. H., Murdaugh, J., & MacLeod, J. A. (1969). Brief psychotherapy of psychiatric reactions to hysterical illness. *American Journal of Psychiatry, 125,* 76–83.

Stiles, W. B. (1980). Measurement of the impact of psychotherapy sessions. *Journal of Consulting and Clinical Psychology, 48,* 176–185.

Stiles, W. B. (1986). Development of a taxonomy of verbal response modes. In L. S. Greenberg & M. W. Pinsof (Eds.), *The psychotherapeutic process: A research handbook* (pp. 161–200). New York: Guilford.

Stiles, W. B., Morrison, L. A. Haw, S. K., Harper, D. A., Shapiro, A. A., & Firth-Cozens, J. (1991). Longitudinal study of assimilation in exploratory psychotherapy. *Psychotherapy, 28,* 195–206.

Stiles, W. B., Shapiro, D. A., & Elliott, R. (1986). Are all psychotherapies equivalent? *American Psychologist, 41,* 165–180.

Strupp, H. H. (1981). Toward the refinement of time-limited dynamic psychotherapy. In S. L. Budman (Ed.), *Forms of brief therapy* (pp. 219–240). New York: Guilford.

Strupp, H. H., & Binder, J. L. (1984). *Psychotherapy in a new key: A guide to time-limited dynamic psychotherapy.* New York: Basic Books.

Strupp, H. H., & Hadley, S. W. (1979). Specific versus nonspecific factors in psychotherapy: A controlled study of outcome. *Archives of General Psychiatry, 36,* 1125–1136.

Strupp, H. H., Hadley, S. W., & Gomes-Schwartz, B. (1977). *Psychotherapy for better or worse: An analysis of the problem of negative effects.* New York: Jason Aronson.

Strupp, H. H., Moras, K., Sandell, J., Waterhouse, G., O'Malley, S., Keithly, L., & Gomes-Schwartz, B. (1981). *Vanderbilt Negative Indicators Scale: An instrument for the identification of deterrents to progress in time-limited dynamic psychotherapy.* Unpublished manuscript, Vanderbilt University, Nashville, TN.

Sue, S., & Morishima, J. K. (1982). *The mental health of Asian Americans.* San Francisco: Jossey-Bass.

Sue, S., & Zane, N. (1987). The role of culture and cultural techniques in psychotherapy. *American Psychologist, 42,* 37–45.

Suh, C., Strupp, H. H., & O'Malley, S. S. (1986). The Vanderbilt process measures: The Psychotherapy Process Scale (VPPS) and the Negative Indicators Scale (VNIS). In L. S. Greenberg & W. M. Pinsof (Eds.), *The psychotherapeutic process: A research handbook* (pp. 285–324). New York: Guilford.

Suinn, R. M., Edie, C. A., & Spinelli, P. R. (1970). Accelerated massed desensitization: Innovation in short-term treatment. *Behavior Therapy, 1,* 303–311.

Svartberg, M., & Stiles, T. C. (1991). Comparative effects of short-term psychodynamic psychotherapy: A meta-analysis. *Journal of Consulting and Clinical Psychology, 59,* 704–714.

Talmon, M. (1990). *Single session therapy: Maximizing the effect of the first (and often only) therapeutic encounter.* San Francisco: Jossey-Bass.

Thompson, B. J., Hill, C. E., & Mahalik, J. R. (1991). A test of the complementarity hypotheses in the interpersonal theory of psychotherapy: Multiple case comparisons. *Psychotherapy, 28,* 572–579.

Thompson, L., Gallagher, D., & Breckenridge, J. (1987). Comparative effectiveness of psychotherapies for depressed elders. *Journal of Consulting and Clinical Psychology, 55,* 385–390.

Thorne, F. C. (1973). Eclectic psychotherapy. In R. Corsini (Ed.), *Current psychotherapies.* Itasca, IL: F. E. Peacock.

Tracey, T. J. (1985). Dominance and outcome: A sequential examination. *Journal of Counseling Psychology, 32,* 119–122.

Tracey, T. J., & Ray, P. B. (1984). Stages of successful time-limited counseling: An interactional examination. *Journal of Counseling Psychology, 31,* 13–27.

Ursano, R. J., & Hales, R. E. (1986). A review of brief individual psychotherapies. *American Journal of Psychiatry, 143,* 1507–1517.

Warren, N. C., & Rice, L. N. (1972). Structuring and stabilizing of psychotherapy for low prognosis clients. *Journal of Consulting and Clinical Psychology, 39,* 173–181.

Watson, J. B., & Rayner, P. (1920). Conditioned emotional reactions. *Journal of Experimental Psychology, 3,* 1–14.

Weakland, J. (1990). Myths about brief therapy; Myths of brief therapy. In J. K. Zeig & S. C. Gilligan (Eds.), *Brief therapy: Myths, methods, and metaphors* (pp. 100–110). New York: Brunner/Mazel.

Wells, R. A., & Phelps, P. A. (1990). The brief psychotherapies: A selective overview. In R. A. Wells & V. J. Giannetti (Eds.), *Handbook of the brief psychotherapies* (pp. 3–26). New York: Plenum.

Winston, A., Pollack, J., McCullough, L., Flegenheimer, W., Kentenbaum, R., & Trujillo, M. (1991). Brief psychotherapy of personality disorders. *Journal of Nervous and Mental Disease, 179,* 188–193.

Wolberg, L. R. (Ed.). (1965). *Short-term psychotherapy.* New York: Grune & Stratton.

Wolberg, L. R. (1980). *Handbook of short-term psychotherapy.* New York: Thieme-Stratton.

Wolkon, G. H. (1972). Crisis theory, the application for treatment and dependency. *Comprehensive Psychiatry, 13,* 459–464.

Zeiss, A. M., Lewinsohn, P. M. & Muñoz, R. F. (1979). Nonspecific improvements effects in depression using interpersonal skills training, pleasant activity schedules, or cognitive training. *Journal of Consulting and Clinical Psychology, 47,* 427–439.

Zetzel. E. (1958). Current concepts of transference. *International Journal of Psychoanalysis, 37,* 369–375.

17

BEHAVIORAL MEDICINE AND HEALTH PSYCHOLOGY

■ **EDWARD B. BLANCHARD**

University at Albany—SUNY

The previous version of this chapter (Pomerleau & Rodin, 1986) took a broad focus on the fields of behavioral medicine and health psychology and illustrated each with in-depth coverage of a few selected topics. Faced with the formidable task of revising this chapter for the current edition, I have chosen to omit most of the research on what would be considered health psychology and instead to focus on a limited aspect of behavioral medicine, namely, intervention or treatment research, especially empirical research from the last 10 years.

While preparing this chapter, I was fortunate enough to have served as the guest editor for a special issue on behavioral medicine of the *Journal of Consulting and Clinical Psychology*, which appeared in the summer of 1992. In that issue, several authors reviewed the research on primary areas of behavioral medicine with two special emphases: one on updating an earlier (Blanchard, 1982) issue of the journal and another on intervention research. This present chapter draws heavily on the expert opinions of the contributing authors to that volume and addresses the following areas: obesity, smoking, hypertension, chronic pain, and headache—topics that have long been a part of behavioral medicine. In addition, I discuss cancer, GI disorders, insomnia, rheumatoid arthritis, and Type A behavior, as well as the emerging field of psychoneuroimmunology.

For a succinct summary of the history of this field, see the earlier chapter by Pomerleau and Rodin (1986).

OBESITY

Obesity is one of the oldest areas of study in behavioral medicine, dating back to Stuart's (1967) pioneering uncontrolled study on the successful behav-

ioral treatment of obesity in eight women. In some ways, it is also one of the most successful areas: Many of its ideas and principles, and much of its technology, have been incorporated into commercial weight-loss programs, demonstrating that the technology passed the test of the marketplace.

Obesity continues to represent a significant public health problem because it is associated with increased risk for hypertension, diabetes, and other cardiovascular disease (Bray, 1986). In like fashion, loss of weight in the hypertensive obese individual can lead to a substantial, almost linear, decrease in blood pressure (Kaplan, 1986). Moreover, Wing et al. (1987) have shown that modest weight losses can have substantial benefits for obese patients with Type II diabetes.

As pointed out in an excellent, wide-ranging review of the topic by Brownell and Wadden (1992), there is both good news and bad news in the obesity area. On the "good news" front is the fact that the average weight loss in most behavioral treatment studies is now about 20+ pounds, rather than the 8 to 10 pounds found in the 1970s. The primary reason for this improvement seems to be that treatment programs have been extended from 8 to 10 weeks out to 20 weeks. In fact, comprehensive reviews of the effect of length of treatment (e.g., Brownell & Kramer, 1989) show a strong positive relation, and experimental studies (e.g., Perri, Nezu, Patti, & McCann, 1989) have confirmed this. Moreover, retention of subjects in studies is generally good and one-year follow-up data are encouraging in that 60 to 70 percent of initial weight loss is likely to be maintained.

One treatment innovation that has seemed to make a difference in the short term is the use of very low-calorie diets. According to Brownell and Wadden (1992), average weight losses of 30 to 45 pounds can be achieved in 12-week programs, more than double those found in standard behavioral programs. Although maintenance is fairly good at one year (Wadden & Stunkard, 1986), longer term follow-ups show substantial loss of benefits (Wadden, Sternberg, Letizia, Stunkard, & Foster, 1989).

The "bad news" is that there is a growing prevalence of obesity in the United States (Flegal, Harlan, & Landix, 1988) and an ever-increasing number of dieters. The reasons for this growing prevalence seem linked to a higher proportion of total caloric intake in the diet coming from fats and to a reduced level of exercise.

It seems clear that an increased level of exercise is an important part of a comprehensive weight-loss program (Dubbert, 1992), and a critical feature of maintenance programs. Stuart's (1967) early work included an exercise component, but it then disappeared from major emphasis for the next dozen years. Emphasis needs to be placed again on increasing activity levels in everyday activities as well as beginning a program of supplementary, regular aerobic exercise. Although long-term compliance is a major problem in the area of exercise (Dubbert, 1992), research continues to find ways to make exercise more effective and continues to show the benefits of its systematic inclusion in obesity treatment (Craighead & Blum, 1989; Foreyt & Goodrick, 1991).

Additional bad news is that it is now clear that there is a substantial genetic contribution to obesity (Stunkard, Harris, Pedersen, & McClearn, 1990; Stunkard et al., 1986). Moreover, there is good evidence that among the extremely obese, those 100 percent or more over ideal body weight, the number of fat cells may be more than double those found in the normal weight or mildly obese individual. These additional fat cells may be laid down early in life, leading to the need for early intervention (by ages two or three). These facts point to the biological barriers that prevent some individuals from ever achieving a so-called ideal body weight.

Brownell and Wadden (1992) make the point that our culture has dictated a lean and fit body as the ideal and that many individuals, who seek to sculpt their body to meet this ideal, are doomed to failure and frustration. They thus advocate strongly that clinicians who treat obesity try to get their clients to shift the goal of treatment from *ideal weight* as determined by national norms and cultural expectations to what they (Brownell & Wadden) term *reasonable weight*. They also advise some attention be paid in treatment to potential body image distortion.

The last piece of bad news is that the long-term results (those from follow-ups beyond one year) are not as positive as the one-year results. There is apparently a continuing erosion of benefits (i.e., regain of lost weight) out to five years (Brownell & Jeffrey, 1987). Thus, one of the key issues for continuing research is to understand and help prevent relapse (Brownell, Marlatt, Lichtenstein, & Wilson, 1986).

Ideas that Brownell and Wadden (1992) believe have some merit in this search include the previously mentioned extension of length of formal treatment and the introduction of exercise into the program. Other factors are the introduction of cognitive and behavioral coping skills to deal with potential relapse (as shown by Grilo, Shiffman, & Wing, 1989) and an attempt to recruit and make use of social support (Kayman, Bruvold, & Stern, 1990).

Finally, Brownell and Wadden (1992) call attention to two other factors. One is a long-term tendency of the obese to continue to gain weight, rather than to remain stable (Shah, Hannan, & Jeffrey, 1991). This means that very long-term results that show a return to 90 or 95 percent of initial baseline weight do, in fact, show some benefit over what the situation would likely have been if the individual were untreated. Second, they join others in calling attention to binge eating among the obese. The binging is not followed by purging as in bulimia, but merely results in added weight (Marcus, Wing, & Hopkins, 1988). Focusing attention on this problem in part of the obese population appears to help overall outcome (Marcus et al., 1990).

This last point helps illustrate Brownell and Wadden's second major thesis — treatment needs to be individualized, taking into account various factors in the patient's obesity history. This call for individualized treatment complements the idea of setting treatment goals for a reasonable weight.

Conclusion

It seems clear that substantial weight loss (20 pounds or more) is achievable at one-year follow-ups. Longer term maintenance is much less impressive and remains the focus of research. Attention has also returned to including regular aerobic exercise in any long-term weight-control program. Echoing Brownell and Wadden (1992), the goals for future research, and especially clinical practice, in obesity should probably be to strive for a goal of "reasonable weight" (rather than norm-based "ideal weight") and to individualize treatment rather than relying on a fixed regimen.

SMOKING

Smoking continues to represent the largest potentially modifiable public health problem in the United States. It is a known risk factor for heart disease, lung cancer, stroke, and chronic obstructive pulmonary disease (COPD, emphysema) and is estimated to account for over 400,000 premature deaths each year (Lichtenstein & Glasgow, 1992). Smoking cessation thus seems a worthwhile target for clinical and counseling psychologists in terms of the size of the potential population to be served and its overall health impact.

After examining recent reviews of the smoking cessation literature (e.g., Lichtenstein & Glasgow, 1992), several points seem clear: First of all, most smokers quit on their own or with minimal professional assistance (Fiore et al., 1990). This fact, along with the size of the smoking population, over 50 million Americans, has led experts such as Lichtenstein and Glasgow to call for a public health perspective that moves beyond the individual clinical perspective.

A second important point is the acceptance of smoking cessation as a process, involving "stages-of-change" in DiClemente et al.'s (1991) terminology. Much clinical research has targeted the so-called *action stage*, from the time the individual is considering quitting within the next 30 days through the time just after quitting, with additional emphasis on the *maintenance stage*.

As Lichtenstein and Glasgow (1992) summarize, two decades of comparing one set of behavioral techniques or a "multicomponent treatment package" with another set of techniques have led to a large literature filled with no reliable differences among treatment regimens, even when the regimens were well designed from a theoretical point of view. It does seem that longer periods of contact are better (Baille, Mattick, & Webster, 1990), echoing the point made earlier about obesity (Brownell & Wadden, 1992), but that additional treatment components have not seemed to matter over the long term.

Lichtenstein and Glasgow (1992) note two other conclusions: First, Lando (e.g., Lando, 1977; Lando & McGovern, 1985; Lando, McGovern, & Sipfle, 1989) has developed a reasonably effective, consistent, clinical approach (with confirmed one-year quit rates of 30–35%). Its components include setting a definite "quit date," an aversive element such as oversmoking (since replaced with nicotine fading [Lando & McGovern, 1985]), group support and contingency contracts during early phases of abstinence, and then a gradual fading of formal group contact. Second, formal incorporation of relapse prevention strategies into treatment programs (Marlatt & Gordon, 1985) has had generally disappointing results, even when performed by the originators of the idea (Curry, Marlatt, Gordon, &

Baer, 1988). As Lichtenstein and Glasgow (1992) conclude, "Intensive programming aimed at relapse prevention is probably not worth the effort; it may be more efficient to encourage those who relapse to 'recycle' and make another quit attempt" (p. 521).

Another recent factor in smoking cessation research and practice has been the formal recognition of nicotine addiction as a key barrier to smoking cessation efforts (U.S. Department of Health and Human Services, 1988). Lichtenstein and Glasgow (1992) speculate that this recognition may make third-party payment for smoking cessation treatment more readily available.

Another key related factor in intervention research has been the use of nicotine replacement strategies (primarily nicotine chewing gum) as part of treatment. A recent meta-analysis (Baille et al., 1990) seems to indicate that nicotine gum increase the effectiveness of smoking cessation treatments. Another careful review by one of the leaders in this area, John Hughes (Hughes, 1991), concludes that nicotine gum and behavioral treatments combined are consistently superior in short-term quit rates and longer term maintenance than either approach separately.

A new development is the potential availability of a more efficient way to deliver an adequate dose of nicotine through the use of skin (technically, transdermal) patches. The patch has several advantages over nicotine gum (e.g., better dosing, easier movement of nicotine into the bloodstream) and may well supplant it (Tonnesen, Norregaard, Simonsen, & Sawe, 1991; Transdermal Nicotine Study Group, in press). Since nicotine replacement delivery systems (gum, patch) must be prescribed by a physician, it may well be that psychologists involved in smoking cessation will need to work closely with physicians to provide optimal care.

An approach to smoking cessation that has conceptual appeal is the idea of "stepped care" — the application of minimal interventions (physician advice, pamphlets) as an initial stage to be followed with more expensive and intensive treatments in groups if the earlier intervention fails. Intensive individual treatment would be the final step.

Related to this concept is interest in the physician as smoking cessation agent. Research has shown that even brief advice to quit by the physician to the smoker can have some beneficial impact (Ockene, 1987a). It is probably not practical to have the physician become the primary counselor or agent of change, but he or she can have an impact or can be trained to do brief counseling (Ockene, 1987b). As Lichtenstein and Glasgow

(1992) point out, it may be possible to organize the health care team to lead smoking cessation efforts, with intensive follow-up available from a member of the team. In addition to potentially being that primary counselor, the psychologist may also serve as a consultant to the physician to make his or her brief contacts with smokers more potent.

Research and clinical practice opportunities in the near future are likely to center around understudied populations, such as minorities and high-risk smokers. Blacks and other minorities have not tended to be part of most clinical research on smoking cessation, yet they have smoking rates greater than well-educated Caucasians who have been the targets (Lichtenstein & Glasgow, 1992). Whether or not there need to be culturally specific modifications remains to be learned.

Research and treatment attention need to be targeted toward the high-risk smoker (such as the postmyocardial infarction patient who continues to smoke). Such individuals may well warrant intensive group or individual treatment. Others are the heavy, seriously addicted smokers (more than two packs per day) who have been unsuccessful with other efforts. Although research on these special populations may be difficult because of their relative scarcity, the challenge and benefits to the patients are clearly evident.

A last point to be made about smoking cessation research is the confusing role of social support. As Lichtenstein and Glasgow (1992) point out, numerous studies show significant positive correlations between parameters of social support and smoking cessation and maintenance and between social support and abstinence (see also Lichtenstein, Glasgow, & Abrams, 1986). However, interventions that have attempted to enhance quit rates and maintenance through manipulating social support by such methods as forming special support groups during maintenance have uniformly failed. This probably means that manipulating the whole social context is difficult.

The federal government has apparently embraced the public health approach to smoking cessation through its commitment to community-based programs by means of educational and media interventions. A major research trial (Lichtenstein, Wallack, & Pechacek, 1990–91) in 11 communities (Community Intervention Trial for Smoking Cessation [acronym COMMIT]) is under way, based on some of the success of Farquhar et al.'s (1990) Stanford Five City Project, which found a reduction in smoking rate within the community of 13 percent. The Government has apparently "decreed" the success of COMMIT (rather than waiting for the results) and moved toward a major policy intervention with the American Stop Smoking Intervention Study (ASSIST) involving statewide agencies in 17 states.

Conclusion

The federal government and leading behavioral researchers (e.g., Lichtenstein & Glasgow, 1992) seem to have moved to a public health model in dealing with smoking cessation, taking the approach that community-based programs involving education and media interventions are the most cost-effective way to deal with the problem. While this may well be true, echoing Lichtenstein and Glasgow's call, research continues to be needed across the whole spectrum of interventions, including nicotine replacement, so as to provide guidance for the practicing clinician faced with the needy, but refractory client. A stepped-care approach, relying initially on mass communication and education but backed up by physician advice and nicotine replacement at the individual level, and finally by intensive, group behavioral interventions, seems the wisest overall approach to this problem.

HYPERTENSION

Despite improvements over the last 20 years, hypertension (elevated blood pressure [BP]) continues to be a major public health problem in the United States, affecting perhaps 60 million Americans. Primarily through an aggressive public education program, 85 percent of those affected are aware of their elevated BP status (up from about 50%), and the percentage of those affected whose BP is under control has increased from 16 to 57 percent, as noted by Kaufmann, Chesney, and Weiss (1991). Thus, while there has been some success, much remains to be done to control this well-documented risk factor for cardiovascular disease and stroke, respectively, the nation's number one and number three causes of death.

Almost 10 years ago, the assistant secretary for health for the Department of Health and Human Services (DHHS) recommended an initial trial of nondrug therapy for newly discovered cases of mild hypertension (Brandt, 1983). Three broad categories (or approaches) of nondrug treatments have been described: stress management, aerobic exercise, and dietary alterations (primarily weight loss or sodium restriction) (Blanchard, Martin, & Dubert, 1988). (A fourth category in which psychologists can certainly play a role is increasing compliance with drug regimens.) While the medical community, as represented by the Joint National Committee on Detection, Evaluation and Treatment of High Blood Pressure, has been enthusiastic in its endorsement of dietary strategies (1980, 1984, 1988), its initial lukewarm appraisal of stress management (see following definition) approaches (1984) has tended to cool (1988), as noted in a recent review Jacob, Chesney, Williams, Ding, and Shapiro (1991).

Stress Management Approaches

Stress management refers to various arousal reduction techniques such as relaxation training in its several varieties, biofeedback training, and more cognitive procedures that emphasize changes in strategies used to cope with environmental events and with personal reactions (such as anger) to such events. Recent reviews of this literature (Blanchard, Martin, & Dubbert, 1988; Jacob et al., 1991; McCaffrey & Blanchard, 1985) draw markedly different conclusions. Jacob et al., relying upon meta-analytic and regression techniques, conclude that "we have become increasingly concerned that what we see as being the result of relaxation therapy is an epiphenomenon . . . and that this variability cannot be harnessed as persistent BP reductions," and that "both the HIPP (Hypertension Intervention Pooling Project) and our present meta-analysis indicated that patients with significant BP elevations might benefit from relaxation treatments. However, it is unlikely that these patients could serve as a population in which the efficacy of relaxation in the absence of medication could be shown" (p. 14).

In essence, relying upon their regression analysis, and upon the results of HIPP, Jacob et al. (1991) seem skeptical of any meaningful role for stress management in the treatment of hypertension; they attribute much of the reported BP effects to inadequate baselines, use of "new" patients, and possible habituation of the patients' BP pressor responses to repeated measurement and contact with the treatment team and setting.

A consistent finding from Jacob and colleagues (Jacob, Kraemer, & Agras, 1977; Jacob et al., 1991) has been that the decrease in BP from stress management approaches is a strong function of pretreatment BP. Thus, in the 1991 review, they report for treated subjects average decreases in systolic BP (SBP) of 6.8 mm mercury (Hg) (for baseline SBP = 140) and 16.7 mm Hg (for baseline SBP = 160) and of 4.5 mm Hg (for baseline diastolic BP [DBP] = 90) and 11.0 mm Hg (for baseline DBP = 105). The meta-analysis revealed effect

sizes when treated groups were compared with controls in the range 0.5 to 0.6, meaning that almost two-thirds of treated patients had greater reductions in BP than patients in control conditions.

While Jacob et al.'s (1991) methodological recommendations should certainly be heeded, in my view they are overly pessimistic in their assessment of the potential role of stress management in the treatment of hypertension. Part of this pessimism stems undoubtedly from the results of the HIPP.

The HIPP (Kaufmann et al., 1988) was an aggregation, sponsored by the National Heart, Lung and Blood Institute (NHLBI), of the individual subject data from 12 different randomized controlled trials of the stress management treatment of hypertension. Data from 1,100 patients were potentially available. However, because of various decisions by the primary authors, full advantage was not taken of this very large sample size; instead mean values from each group in each study were entered into the analyses, markedly reducing the degrees of freedom.

The conclusions drawn by HIPP were that there was no effect on SBP for groups treated with relaxation, various forms of biofeedback, and the two in combination in comparison with patients in control groups at posttreatment or one-year follow-up, while there was a small (about 2 mm Hg) advantage in DBP for treatment over control. These very disappointing results have weighed heavily on the field, despite the lack of a full analysis of all of the ways to view these data.

McCaffrey and Blanchard (1985), in an earlier qualitative review, were much more positive about potential benefits of the various stress management procedures. In reviewing several recent individual publications from our laboratory and elsewhere, I tend to share this continuing enthusiasm. Additional research will be needed to determine where the truth actually lies.

We (Blanchard et al., 1986) had also found that our thermal biofeedback treatment was helpful in ing (a meditative form of relaxation) and a BP monitoring control condition in 30 unmedicated male hypertensives at each of two sites, Albany, New York, and Moscow, Russia. At end of the 16 treatment sessions, an average decrease in DBP of 8.5 mm Hg was found for the treated patients, as compared to 3.7 mm Hg for controls, with a corresponding decrease of 8.7 mm Hg in SBP, as compared to 2.9 mm Hg in controls. Both differences were statistically and clinically significant.

The results held up well at six-month posttreatment for the Russian patients, with BPs continuing to decrease, while much poorer results were found for the American patients (over half had relapsed by this point). The differences between sites were probably attributable to higher levels of regular home practice in the Russian sample than in the American sample.

Interestingly, in the American sample, those few patients (all males) who had borderline left ventricular hypertrophy as a result of elevated BPs showed reductions in left ventricular mass to within the normal range (McCoy, et al., 1988). This change in an end organ as a result of this behavioral treatment is very encouraging.

We (Blanchard et al., 1986) had also found that our thermal biofeedback treatment was helpful in allowing medicated patients to reduce their levels of medication. Thirty-six percent remained off a previously needed sympathetically active antihypertensive agent at a 13-month follow-up. A similar successful use of stress management techniques to reduce medication in patients whose BPs were controlled with one or more medications was reported by Glasgow, Engel, and D'Lugoff (1989). Their 51 "behavioral stepped-care" patients received a systematic program of relaxation and BP biofeedback. Nineteen of their patients were medication free at a 12-month follow-up (vs. 2 out of 51 controls).

Lee et al. (1988) compared relaxation plus health education with health education alone and with a beta blocker (atenolol). Significantly greater reductions were found in BP for the relaxation and education group versus the education alone group. However, the drug led to BP decreases that were approximately twice as large as those in the relaxation and education group. Interestingly, decreases in left ventricular mass, comparable to those of McCoy et al. (1988), were found in the relaxation group.

Most direct comparisons of stress management approaches with antihypertensive medication have shown the medication both to work more rapidly and to have a greater antihypertensive effect. For example, Goldstein, Shapiro, Thananopavaren, and Sambi (1982) compared patients on medications (seven on diuretics, one on propranolol, one on clonidine) with those treated with blood pressure biofeedback and with relaxation using the Relaxation Response (a brief meditative form of relaxation); drugs were significantly better for lowering SBP (decreases of 14.8 mm Hg, compared with 4.1 mm Hg for biofeedback, and 2.1 mm Hg for relaxation); however, for DBP the drugs and biofeedback were effective but not different (decreases of 5.6 mm Hg, compared with 4.4 mm Hg for biofeedback, and 3.5 mm Hg for relaxation) and both surpassed the comparison conditions.

Jacob et al. (1986) compared relaxation (abbre-viated progressive muscle relaxation) to a diuretic and a beta blocker in a complex design in which patients received either placebo, diuretic, or beta blocker alone in differing phases and then had relaxation training added to the drug. (It is not at all clear that one can "remove relaxation" after it has been taught initially.) There was a statistically significant effect of relaxation across all drug conditions for SBP (average incremental effect of 2.4 mm Hg) and for DBP measured in the therapist's office (average incremental effect of 2.1 mm Hg).

There were no direct comparisons of drugs with relaxation. The indirect comparisons indicated the beta blocker was superior to relaxation, but this conclusion must be tempered because of the unusual manner of the comparison.

Richter-Heinrich et al. (1981), in a comparison of relaxation training with beta blockers (talinolol) done in Germany showed equivalent results in the short term and good maintenance at one year.

In terms of long-term results, Patel et al. (1985) reported a four-year prospective follow-up on patients who received either stress management plus health education or regular medical care. Overall, cardiological morbidity was much reduced in the treated group. SBPs were 7 mm Hg lower at four years than at baseline and DBPs were 2.7 mm Hg lower. Both had increased above baseline levels in the controls. The acute effects present at eight months posttreatment (SBP = 16.2 mm Hg, DBP = 6.8 mm Hg) had dissipated somewhat but were still present to some degree.

A final criticism leveled at the stress management literature by Jacob et al. (1991) has been that the lowered BP results are specific to the treatment situation but do not generalize (see also Jacob et al., 1992). This criticism is supported by Jacob's own data (Jacob et al., 1986), in which he found no effects of relaxation on 24-hour ambulatory BP (ABP) measurements. In our work, however, we have found significant effects on 24-hour ABPs from thermal biofeedback in uncontrolled trials with medicated and unmedicated patients, respectively (Musso, Blanchard, & McCoy, 1991; Wittrock & Blanchard, 1992). Thus, the final word is not in on this important topic either.

Further details of stress management treatment procedures can be found in Blanchard, Martin, and Dubbert (1988).

Dietary Approaches

While the efficacy of stress management approaches to hypertension remains controversial within the medical community, there is reasonably strong agreement that various dietary interventions have marked utility (Joint National Committee,

1988). In fact, one review of this literature (Jeffery, 1991) concludes "that weight loss is the single most effective nonpharmacological approach to the management and prevention of hypertension" (p. 18). Other reviews on this topic (Blanchard, Martin, & Dubbert, 1988; Hovell, 1982; Schlundt & Langford, 1985) tend to agree with Jeffery.

A regression analysis by the author of the data on this topic in Kaplan's (1986) book shows that there is about a one-millimeter decrease in BP for each kilogram of weight loss. Thus, a 10 kg loss of weight (a reasonable goal for a 20-week obesity program) should result in about a 9 mm Hg decrease in SBP and an 8 mm Hg decrease in DBP.

A second, and possible complementary, dietary approach is through sodium restriction, and possibly an increase in potassium. Severe sodium restriction has long been known to be a viable nondrug approach to treating hypertension, yet the compliance problems associated with it were great.

In one of the major prospective studies in this area, Langford et al. (1985) tried dietary interventions as a substitute for medication in 496 hypertensives whose BPs had been stabilized and well-controlled on medication. All patients were initially withdrawn from their medication. Those who were overweight were assigned to weight reduction, sodium restriction, or no-treatment, while those who were not overweight were assigned to sodium restriction or no-treatment. Patients were followed up in their respective conditions for one year. The major dependent variable was whether patients experienced sufficient rise in BP to warrant their being remedicated.

Both interventions worked reasonably well in that the weight-loss subjects lost about 10 pounds and kept them off while the sodium restriction subjects reduced sodium excretion by about one-third (rather than the approximately one-half [to 70 milli-equivalents per day] that had been the goal). Among no-treatment (medication removal only) patients, only 35 percent still had BP controlled at one year as compared to 60 percent of the weight-loss subjects. The overweight sodium restriction group was in between at 45 percent with BP still controlled. Among normal-weight subjects in the sodium restriction condition, 53 percent still were off medication with BP controlled.

Working prospectively with unmedicated mild hypertensives, Wing et al. (1984) randomly assigned 52 patients to either weight reduction or low-sodium/high-potassium diets. The weight-loss group averaged a 10-pound loss and showed a reduction in BP of 14/8 (SBP/DBP) mm Hg; the sodium restriction group reduced sodium by about one-third and changed the sodium/potassium ratio

from 2.50 to 1.52 while losing only 3 pounds. Their BPs were reduced by 6/4 mm Hg.

In a study combining both approaches, Jeffery et al. (1983) showed good results with about a 13-pound weight loss and a sodium reduction of about 30 percent. The average change in BP was about 8/5 mm Hg.

Problems. As noted in an earlier section of this chapter, short-term weight reduction among overweight patients seems readily obtainable (with total weight loss determined in part by the length of treatment program); a more crucial issue is the maintenance of this weight loss over long periods. All indications are that over three to five years, most patients regain much of the weight. Thus, the key to successful treatment of hypertension through weight loss is long-term maintenance.

Sodium restriction (with or without potassium supplementation) seems to work in reducing BP but not as well as weight loss. Reduction of sodium by about one-third seems readily obtainable with good dietary interventions. However, most studies have sought to reduce sodium by about 50 percent or greater and have not been successful, on a group basis, in achieving this goal. As a result, the BP effects have been more modest. It could also be that not all hypertensives are sodium-sensitive; thus, only a portion of a sample assigned to sodium restriction will show pronounced effects.

Aerobic Exercise

Aerobic exercise, the third nonpharmacological approach to the treatment of hypertension, is the least researched. Recent reviews can be found in W. Siegel and Blumenthal (1991) and J. Martin and Dubbert (1985) as well as in Blanchard, Martin, and Dubbert (1988). In the latest review, Siegel and Blumenthal note that evidence from controlled studies is mixed as to the antihypertensive effects of regular aerobic exercise. Of the four studies they summarized, three showed significant advantages for aerobic exercise over a sedentary control (two studies) or a nonaerobic exercise control, while a fourth study found similar decreases in BP for both aerobic exercise or repeated measurement of BP.

A difficulty in many studies of aerobic exercise as a treatment for hypertension is that the exercise group frequently loses weight. We have already noted the strong antihypertensive effect of weight loss, so that a potential confound is present that must be controlled statistically.

In one of the best studies, J. Martin, Dubbert, and Cushman (1990) randomly assigned 27 sedentary unmedicated males with mild hypertension to either a program of supervised aerobic exercise

(30-minute sessions 4 times per week for 10 weeks with heart rate accelerated to above 65 percent of maximal heart rate) versus comparable time periods of stretching and light calisthenics (nonaerobic). The control group was virtually unchanged in BP while the exercise group had significant reductions for SBP/DBP of 6/9 mm Hg; moreover, resting heart rate, as a measure of fitness, also decreased for the exercise group. A later crossover of 9 of 14 controls showed comparable decreases (9/6) in BP once they completed the aerobic training. Long-term follow-up was not available. Thus, this study controlled for expectancy and therapist attention effects as well as for potential individual differences with the crossover of the controls to the experimental condition. Details of implementing the exercise program can be found in Blanchard, Martin, and Dubbert (1988).

Potential problems for the exercise treatment area are the well-known difficulties with even moderate term compliance (see Dubbert, 1992, for a partial review) and for potential self-selection biases (only a very limited portion of the population will enter and exercise trial.)

Given the potential synergistic effects on BP of increased fitness with weight loss, one would certainly recommend aerobic exercise. It might be better, however, to incorporate it into a weight-loss program as the nondrug approach to treating hypertension, rather than relying upon exercise alone.

One potential strategy, which has great clinical appeal, would be to combine all three nonpharmacological strategies so as to maximize the likelihood of having a clinically significant antihypertensive effect. Kostis, et al. (1992) have evaluated such a combined nonpharmacological approach in controlled comparison with a beta blocker (propranolol) and drug placebo. The nonpharmacological therapy included weight loss, mild sodium restriction, graduated exercise, and relaxation training.

Both active treatments, propranolol and multicomponent nonpharmacological therapy, decreased BP more than placebo: Decreases in DBP were 9.5, 8.0, and 0.1 mm Hg, respectively; while decreases in SBP were 12.2, 12.4, and 4.9 mm Hg, respectively. The nondrug group lost 14 pounds on average and improved in fitness as well as showing significantly greater improvements in cholesterol levels than the drug group.

Conclusions

Whether psychologists have a role in the long-term treatment of hypertension is unclear. Despite 20-plus years of research history, primarily psychological treatments, lumped under the title of "stress management," continue to be controversial. Strong

positive results continue to emerge, but so do failures to replicate. The lack of consistency in outcome, while an intriguing research question in itself, dampens enthusiasm for these approaches.

It certainly seems clear, however, that the dietician may have a role in treating newly discovered cases of mild hypertension because of the reliability of the beneficial effects of weight loss (and to a lesser degree, sodium restriction) on BP. Thus the psychologist, as expert in the treatment of obesity, may also clearly have a role.

An issue for future systematic research, which should eventually guide clinical practice, is whether comprehensive, multimodal nondrug approaches are a viable long-term alternative, or adjunct, to drug therapy in the management of hypertension.

TYPE A (CORONARY PRONE) BEHAVIOR PATTERN

The leading cause of death in the United States is heart disease. In a large-scale, prospective study (Western Collaborative Group Study, Rosenman et al., 1975), two cardiologists (see also M. Friedman & Rosenman, 1974) showed that a certain cluster, or pattern, of behaviors elicited during a structured interview was an independent risk factor for the development of coronary heart disease (CHD) among white males. That is, if one statistically controlled for all other known risk factors (elevated blood pressure, elevated cholesterol levels, etc.), the presence of this pattern of behaviors, which they termed *Type A*, was associated with twice as many eventual incidents of CHD as were found in those who were not positive for this behavior pattern (Type Bs). The behaviors in this cluster included time urgency, hostility, unrewarded striving, and certain facial and motor behaviors as well as speech styles.

Given the relative uniqueness of the finding, a set of behaviors predicting a major cause of morbidity and mortality, a great deal of research was spawned (for reviews see Booth-Kewley & Friedman, 1987; Matthews, 1988; Thoresen & Powell, 1992). Although confirmation of Type A's status as a risk factor (especially when assessed by interview) was found in most studies, other correlational studies failed to confirm the finding. The latter has led to much reexamination of the idea, with some (e.g., Williams, 1989) claiming that essentially all of the pathogenic load in Type A was carried by *hostility*, while others (Thoresen & Powell, 1992) have called for a closer examination of the theory and psychological processes underlying Type A (particularly from a contextual point of view [i.e., person–environment interaction], rather than as a stable personality trait), and for improved, theory-based, measurement operations. Thoresen and Powell also call attention to the need for additional research on women and minority populations.

While Type A behavior pattern continues to be the subject of much debate and research among psychologists, cardiologists, and epidemiologists, the key question for this writer, a clinician interested in health outcomes, has always been, Can one change Type A behavior? And if so, does it make a difference in morbidity or mortality?

There are several reviews of the intervention literature that provide more detailed analysis than is found in this chapter (Levenkron & Moore, 1988; Nunes, Frank, & Kornfeld, 1987; Price, 1988; Thoresen & Powell, 1992). In particular, the Nunes et al. (1987) meta-analysis showed a standardized effect size of 0.61 (±0.20, for the 95% confidence interval), indicating that the average change in Type A behavior, from the specific treatment conditions, compared with control conditions, was more than one-half of a standard deviation. From that review, it was also concluded that interventions involving multiple procedures were relatively more effective.

Thoresen and Powell (1992) call attention to three intervention studies that sought to alter Type A behavior among males (overwhelmingly Caucasian) (Gill et al., 1985; Levenkron, Cohen, Mueller, & Fisher, 1983; Roskies et al., 1986). Common to all of the studies were the positive findings from the use of a multicomponent treatment with a strong dose of cognitive therapy procedures.

Roskies et al. (1986), in the Montreal Type A Intervention Project, randomly assigned 107 Caucasian male managers who had been screened to be free of CHD to one of three conditions: a multicomponent stress management condition that included relaxation, instruction in communications skills, and cognitive therapy (cognitive restructuring and problem solving) to improve stress coping techniques. In one comparison condition, subjects engaged in regular aerobic exercise (usually jogging), while in the other subjects engaged in isometric exercises using Nautilus equipment. All subjects were seen in small groups, but treatment were still individually tailored. The stress management group reduced Type A behaviors, as assessed by structured interview, significantly more than either the aerobic exercise or isometric exercise groups, which generally did not differ. Interestingly, there were no differential effects on cardiovascular reactivity to stressors.

In a much briefer cognitive-behavioral treatment program (6 sessions vs. about 20 in Roskies et al.),

Levenkron et al. (1983), also working with male managerial workers, found significant changes for the intervention condition in Type A behavior (as measured by self-report questionnaire) in comparison with group social support and brief information treatments.

Gill et al. (1985), working with military officers, found large changes in Type A behaviors in a group receiving a multicomponent cognitive-behavioral treatment in comparison to a measurement-only control group. The changes in Type A behavior were verified by spousal report. This treatment program was spread over 21 sessions across 9 months. Interestingly, confidential peer ratings of participants revealed no diminution of leadership skills or other performance of duties in the intervention group members. In summary, all three studies have shown it is possible to change Type A behaviors in adult males who are young to middle-aged managers.

By far, the most important study in this area is the Recurrent Coronary Prevention Project (M. Friedman et al., 1986) in which 862 postmyocardial infarction (MI) patients were randomized to receive either group cardiologic counseling ($n = 270$) or group cardiologic counseling plus group Type A behavior counseling ($n = 592$). All patients continued under the medical care of their own physician. The cardiologic counseling was designed to enhance compliance to dietary, exercise, and drug regimens prescribed by their personal physicians. In addition, there was a visit every three months to a psychologist or psychiatrist to deal with possible anxiety, depression, and so on. Patients attended, on average, approximately twenty 90-minute group sessions over three years.

In the main experimental condition, patients were scheduled to attend forty-four 90-minute group sessions over 3 years, but they actually averaged 29 sessions. The Type A behavior counseling was comprised of relaxation training, training in detailed self-observation and self-monitoring to detect exaggerated emotional reactions to events, and cognitive affective learning ("modification of some earlier held beliefs, assumptions, and attributes, establishment of new and realistically internally constructed values and goals, and self-instruction and self-management" [M. Friedman et al., 1986, p. 239]). In other words, this represented a direct attack on the core schema of the Type A behavior pattern.

At three years, the Type A behavior counseling group had decreased self-rated and observer-rated (from videotaped interviews) Type A behavior by approximately one standard deviation (significantly more than the control group). Of all those enrolled in the treatment, 43.8 percent exhibited noticeable reductions in Type A behavior at three years, and 79.8 percent of those who stayed continuously in treatment ($n = 328$) showed similar reductions when compared to 25.2 percent of those in cardiological counseling. Thus, the study did show a marked effect of behavior counseling on Type A behavior.

Most important, at the three-year point, there were significantly fewer nonfatal recurrences (of myocardial infarctions) and cardiac deaths in the treated group (7.2% of those randomized to the condition) than in the cardiological counseling group (13.2%; $p < .005$). For the patients in each condition who attended the bulk of their respective treatment sessions, the effects were even greater (8.9% vs. 18.9%; $p < .001$). An interesting internal analysis showed a significantly ($p = .01$) lower year two and three recurrence rate of 1.7 percent ($n = 181$) in treated patients who significantly reduced Type A behavior versus 8.6 percent ($n = 326$) of those who were randomized to treatment. This does–response relation between reduced recurrence and reduced Type A behavior highlights the study. Significant advantages for the treated group have continued through an eight-year follow-up (Thoresen, 1990).

Conclusions

It thus seems clear that, at least for males, Type A behavior can be changed through intensive (and extensive — up to three years of intervention) cognitive-behavioral treatment. Whether comparable results can be obtained for women and minorities remains to be seen. There has yet to be a primary prevention trial with Type A behavior, analogous to the multiple risk factor intervention trial, to see if changing Type A behavior can reduce the incidence of initial morbidity from CHD.

However, there has been a large-scale secondary prevention trial (M. Friedman et al., 1986) that showed that Type A behavior among male MI victims could be changed and that such a change led to reduced nonfatal recurrences and cardiac deaths. It would thus seem prudent to add an appropriate intervention for Type A behavior into routine rehabilitation programs for cardiac patients. While counseling on exercise, dietary management, and smoking cessation is a routine part of such rehabilitation programs, wholesale inclusion of an "anti–Type A" component has yet to occur.

A final point to keep in mind is the controversy surrounding the relative contributions of hostility versus the entire Type A behavior pattern. Treatment research is clearly needed to determine if targeting hostility alone will have the same beneficial effects one can show from targeting the entire Type A behavior pattern.

These topics discussed so far; obesity — smoking, hypertension, and Type A behavior — are all related to cardiovascular disease, the number one (heart disease) and number three (stroke) killers in the United States. It seems clear that there is a role for psychological interventions in many of the risk factors for cardiovascular disease at the prevention level and also as part of a comprehensive cardiac rehabilitation program. In sections to follow, we leave the cardiovascular system for other body systems for which behavioral medicine has a contribution to make.

CANCER

In addition to being the second leading cause of death in the United States, cancer is one of the most dreaded diseases because its victims face the possibility of a prolonged period of progressive physical deterioration and loss of function as well as the potential for unrelenting pain. Moreover, the side effects of some treatments (e.g., radiation therapy and chemotherapy) are often themselves serious sources of stress and discomfort. These problems are sometimes discussed as "quality of life" issues.

However, despite the magnitude of human distress caused by cancer, surprisingly little research on psychological treatment has been done. The existing research can be roughly divided into (1) studies aimed at palliating or ameliorating symptoms, such as pain, or the side effects of medical treatments, such as anticipatory nausea and vomiting associated with some chemotherapy and (2) studies aimed at improving the overall quality of life of the cancer patient. For a review of research on psychological interventions with chemotherapy-related nausea and vomiting, see Carey and Burish (1988). Suffice it to say that procedures such as systematic desensitization (Morrow & Morrell, 1982), relaxation training (Burish, Carey, Krozely, & Greco, 1987; Carey & Burish, 1987) and hypnosis (Zeltzer, LeBaron, & Zeltzer, 1984), specifically adapted to the chemotherapy setting, have been shown to be beneficial in controlled studies. Turk and Fernandez (1990) have noted that the pain of cancer is different from that of many other chronic pain problems and could perhaps best be characterized as chronic, acute pain, a point made earlier by Ahles, Ruckdeschel, and Blanchard (1984). Turk and Fernandez (1990) review research on behavioral strategies to help with this dreaded and serious problem.

An excellent critical review of the literature on

psychosocial interventions to improve quality of life of the cancer patient has been provided by Andersen (1992). The following summary draws heavily on her review and her conceptual framework for examining studies. In particular, given the heterogeneity of the diseases known as cancer, with the attendant varying prognoses and treatment regimens associated with different stages of a particular cancer site, one is potentially faced with markedly different expectations of morbidity and mortality risk across a sample of cancer patients. Andersen has consequently suggested organizing studies based upon patients' morbidity risk. It has been shown that the overall degree of psychological distress and the degree of spontaneous recovery (that is, not specifically aided by a professional) from this distress is also associated with degree of morbidity risk.

For *low morbidity risk* (localized Stage I or Stage II disease, usually treated by a single modality, with 70–95% five-year survival), Andersen (1992) concludes that most studies show little advantage for treatment over control conditions at short-term follow-ups of three to six months and speculates that this is probably because "longitudinal data suggest that when localized disease is controlled and recovery proceeds unimpaired, the severe distress of diagnosis dissipates and emotions stabilize by one-year post-treatment" (p. 556).

Thus, for example, Capone, Good, Westie, and Jacobson (1980), working with women newly diagnosed with gynecological cancer, found no differential effects of their brief, crisis-oriented intervention of structured counseling to help patients express feelings and fears and information on treatment sequelae and education on sexual information (for those who were sexually active) on level of personal distress across one-year follow-ups but did find an advantage in that treated women returned to work and resumed sexual activity more quickly.

Davis (1986) worked with women with localized breast cancer and assigned them to a brief stress management condition (relaxation and biofeedback), a cognitive therapy condition, and no-treatment. No differential effects on anxiety levels were found (perhaps also due to small sample sizes) but urinary cortisol measures (an indirect indication of distress level) were lower at follow-up for treated subjects.

By far the largest, and best controlled, studies of low morbidity risk cancer patients were large-scaled studies by Fawzy, Cousins et al. (1990) and Fawzy, Kemeny et al. (1990) with newly diagnosed melanoma patients. Important aspects of this report were the elaborate immune system measures taken and the good follow-up. Although equal numbers ($n = 40$) of Stage I or Stage II melanoma

patients were assigned to psychosocial treatment versus control conditions (no psychosocial treatment but routine university-hospital–based medical care), significantly more (25%) of the controls dropped out than those in the experimental condition. The brief (six-week) intervention consisted of 1½-hour group sessions emphasizing (1) basic health education about the disease and health care promotion; (2) stress management (primarily forms of relaxation); (3) instruction and practice in problem solving and coping skills; and (4) group support.

Results showed only minor differences between the two groups at posttreatment. However, at a six-month follow-up, Profile of Mood States (POMS) scores showed significantly less depression, fatigue, inertia, and overall mood disturbance in the treated group versus the controls. Moreover, the treatment group, at this follow-up point, also reported more use of specific coping skills.

It is very interesting that there were significant differences in a number of immune function parameters between the two groups at the six-month follow-up point (Fawzy, Kemeny et al. 1990). Significant differences were not present at posttreatment. The change in immune function for treated subjects was generally in the moderate-to-large increase range and was present for a majority of patients. Correlational analyses point to relations between improved immune function and improved affective state, thus providing a possible pathway by which the psychological intervention helped patients (see later section in this chapter on psychoneuroimmunology).

For *moderate morbidity risk* (regional disease, Stage III, or first recurrence from Stage I disease, usually treated with combination therapy, with 40–60% five-year survival), Andersen (1992) concluded that "a wider variety of outcome measures detected improvement. Intervention effects were found reliably with self-reports of emotional distress" (p. 559).

One of the more interesting of these studies was done by Telch and Telch (1986), who studied 41 psychologically depressed patients with various types of regional disease (breast, Hodgkin's lymphoma, etc.). Two treatment conditions, (1) group instruction in coping skills and (2) a standard support group, each lasting 1½ hours once a week for 6 weeks, were compared with a no-treatment control condition. The instruction in coping skills emphasized behavioral, cognitive, and affective coping with much attention paid to homework assignments. Relaxation and stress management as well as pleasant activity scheduling were included.

Results showed a significant advantage for both treated groups versus the no-treatment controls on most scales of the POMS. Moreover, the coping skills group was significantly better than the support group on all scales but anger. The coping skills group also showed better incorporation and use of coping skills than the other two groups and reported coping better with many aspects of the disease. There was no systematic follow-up due to subject loss (at three months, seven patients had died and five were too ill to be reassessed).

For *high morbidity risk* (extensive metastatic disease, Stage IV, usually treated systemically or for palliation [pain control] with only 15–40% survival at *one* year), Andersen (1992) notes that treatment is usually superior to no-treatment in terms of alleviating distress, even in the short term, and even in the face of a potential rapid decline of overall status. Long-term follow-ups (even three months) are difficult because of subject loss due to death or physical incapacitation.

One of the most important studies in this area is that of Spiegel, Bloom and associates (Spiegel, Bloom, & Yalom, 1981; Spiegel, Bloom, Kraemer, & Gottheil, 1989), who randomized women with metastatic breast cancer to either weekly participation in a structured, professionally led (social worker or psychiatrist) support group or no psychosocial treatment. All patients continued to receive medical care. In the support group, which met weekly for one year, attention was paid to expression of feelings and discussion of problem solving, improving communication with family, and fears of death, as well as to social support from the group. An autohypnotic technique was taught for pain control. Fifteen of the 50 experimental subjects died within the first year as did 8 of the 36 controls.

The major findings appeared at a 10-year follow-up. The experimental subjects *survived* on average 18 months longer than the controls (36.6 months vs. 18.9 months) with the major divergence apparent at about 20 months (8 months posttreatment) after starting the project. Thus, while most of the earlier research emphasized alleviation of distress (hence quality of life), in this study the chief dependent variable on which there is a difference is *quantity of life* itself.

Prevention

As medical "cures" for many forms of cancer continue to prove elusive, national attention has begun to focus on prevention and early detection. Psychologists, as experts in behavior change, have much to offer to these efforts. In the area of early detection, the work on promoting and maintaining regular breast self-examination in women and testicular self-examination in men has the potential to be of great benefit. Work by Mayer and others (e.g., Mayer & Frederiksen, 1986) has shown that regular breast self-examination can be initiated and maintained, at least to some extent.

In terms of prevention, as noted earlier, *smoking cessation* is the single greatest behavioral disease prevention step available in the United States. While progress has been made in reducing the death rate from some kinds of cancer through treatment innovations and/or early detection efforts, lung cancer mortality rates have been little affected despite intensive medical research efforts. Given this situation, psychosocial interventions to assist and promote smoking cessation are seen as highly important since the risk for lung cancer seems to bear a dose–response relation to number of "pack-years" in the patient's smoking history (the term *pack-years* summarizes a smoker's history in terms of number of packs (of 20) cigarettes smoked per day summed over the number of years of smoking).

Although there continues to be some research on developing techniques to merely reduce the tar and nicotine dosage smokers receive, the best method of preventing lung cancer continues to be abstinence (Blanchard & Schwarz, 1988). Very encouraging recent research (LaCroix et al., 1991) indicates that prolonged abstinence (10 to 20 years) may lead to a reduction of the risk of lung cancer to that of a comparably aged nonsmoker.

Conclusions

As the material previously summarized indicates, given the magnitude of the problem cancer represents (in terms of number of patients and severity of its impact on quality of life), there has been surprisingly little controlled intervention research. It seems clear that there is a role for psychosocial treatments to improve the quality of life of the cancer patient.

From this limited data base and echoing Andersen (1992), in an almost dose–response manner, it appears that the strongest effects can be found in the "sickest" patients. This points to the need for development of brief but intensive interventions for the more advanced patients. Two other areas in which psychologists may play an important role are the design and implementation of prevention and early detection programs and possibly during the potential emotional crisis of initial diagnosis and treatment.

CHRONIC PAIN

One of the areas of behavioral medicine in which psychological treatment has found the greatest acceptance is the multidisciplinary pain clinic. Beginning with the pioneering work of Fordyce (summarized in his 1976 book) on a behavioral, primarily operant, approach, psychological assessment and treatment have won general acceptance. For a good review of recent advances in psychological assessment and treatment of chronic pain, see Keefe, Dunsmore, and Burnett (1992).

In addition to Fordyce's (1976) more strictly behavioral approach to chronic pain, another approach, best represented by the thinking and work of Turk, Meichenbaum, and Genest (1983), is characterized as "cognitive-behavioral" because of its joint focus on the cognitive and affective components of pain as well as its behavioral aspects.

Later in this chapter, I review the literature on the treatment of two specific categories of pain problems, chronic headache and rheumatoid arthritis. This present section focuses on other forms of chronic pain, primarily back pain.

There are many uncontrolled reports about the benefits of behavioral treatment for chronic pain. As with other areas, however, one tends to put greater credence in the reports of randomized controlled trials. An important study by Heinrich, Cohen, Naliboff, Collins, and Bonebakker (1985) compared treatment with behavior therapy ($n = 18$) with treatment with physical therapy ($n = 15$) in a randomized trial with chronic low back pain (CLBP) patients who were followed up prospectively for six months. The physical therapy (PT) was standard state-of-the-art treatment and included education, exercise, and relaxation. The behavioral program, likewise, stressed education, self-responsibility, communication skills, pain control through relaxation and breathing, and goal setting and activity management.

Patients in PT were superior to those in the behavioral condition at end of treatment and at follow-up in physical abilities related to the back as well as in knowledge of back protection maneuvers. On measures of psychological distress (such as depression), the behavior therapy group was more improved than the PT group. Both groups reported significantly less pain at posttreatment and follow-up.

Comparisons of a multifaceted cognitive-behavioral program with a waiting-list control (H. Phillips, 1987) or placebo-medication (Engstrom, 1983) have shown significantly greater improvement in chronic pain patients with mixed sites of pain across an array of measures from different domains such as self-report of pain and distress and in activity levels for the cognitive-behavioral conditions. Good maintenance of gains was shown at follow-up.

Turner (1982), working with CLBP patients, compared a multicomponent cognitive-behavioral treatment program with progressive muscle relaxation and with a waiting-list control. While both treated groups improved on functional measures as well as self-reports of pain, the control condition did not. At short-term (about one-month) follow-up, the cognitive-behavioral group continued to improve (decrease) on pain measures and then surpassed the relaxation condition. This same pattern also appeared on functional measures.

Three studies have provided direct, randomized comparisons of cognitive-behavioral approaches with more strictly behavioral approaches to the treatment of chronic pain. Kerns, Turk, Holzman, and Rudy (1986), working with chronic pain patients from the Veterans Administration who had a variety of pain problems, randomly assigned patients to (1) a cognitive-behavioral program emphasizing education about and reconceptualization of pain, acquisition of cognitive and behavioral coping skills (including relaxation), and regular practice ($n = 10$); (2) a more strictly behavioral program based on operant principles with relaxation, goal setting, and contracting for increased nonpain behaviors ($n = 10$); and (3) a waiting-list control condition ($n = 8$). The cognitive-behavioral group improved more than the other two conditions on pain reports at end of treatment and at follow-up. Similar trends were present for improvements in behavior (goal attainment, reduction of health care use).

In an outstanding effort, Turner and Clancy (1988), working with CLBP on an outpatient basis, compared a cognitive-behavioral treatment program ($n = 24$) with an operant (behavioral) approach that included a graded exercise component and spouse involvement ($n = 29$) and with a waiting-list control ($n = 21$). Both treatment groups improved significantly on a range of measures, including self-reports of pain and increased physical activity and performance, and were superior to the waiting-list controls at posttreatment. Improvements were generally maintained at 12 months. An overall trend in the data was for the behaviorally treated patients to improve more rapidly and then maintain their gains whereas those in the cognitive-behavioral condition showed less initial improvement but continued to improve throughout the follow-up period until there were no significant differences between the two.

In a follow-up study, Turner, Clancy, McQuade, and Cardenas (1990) examined the contribution of the exercise program to the operant behavioral treatment program. Spouses were involved in all three conditions: behavioral alone ($n = 18$), exercise alone ($n = 21$), or behavioral plus exercise ($n = 18$). The three treated groups improved more than the waiting-list controls across an array of measures.

The group receiving the combined intervention improved more on pain and distress measures than the exercise alone group but was not superior to the purely behavioral treatment. The combined condition was also superior to both single components in spousal ratings. At 6-month and 12-month follow-ups, although improvement was maintained, there were no differences among the three conditions despite high retention (82%) of the sample.

Conclusions

Overall, it appears that there are no consistent advantages for a strictly behavioral (operant) approach to the treatment of chronic back pain over those obtainable with a cognitive-behavioral approach emphasizing cognitive change and coping skills. Clinically, one would probably want to incorporate both in order to have the best chance of helping the patient. It does seem clear that cognitive and behavioral treatments are important adjuncts to the comprehensive care of the chronic pain patient.

CHRONIC HEADACHE

Although headache is a relatively minor health problem in comparison to cardiovascular disease and cancer, it is a widespread and costly disorder in our society. Estimates from 1986 reveal that almost 200 million workdays were lost in the United States due to headaches. Because of both my own long-standing interest in this problem and the extensive literature on psychological treatments, the coverage on this topic is more detailed than that for other topics.

The first reports on the direct behavioral treatment of chronic headache appeared slightly over 20 years ago. Direct psychological treatment of chronic headache is thus one of the more mature, well-developed areas of behavioral medicine. In fact, these procedures have gained general acceptance from the medical community specializing in headache; biofeedback and other behavioral forms of treatment are routinely available as part of the total armamentarium in comprehensive headache treatment centers.

Three general classes of treatment for chronic headache have received relatively widespread controlled evaluation: biofeedback,[1] relaxation train-

ing, and specific forms of cognitive therapy. Comprehensive reviews of the literature on the biofeedback treatment of vascular headache (Blanchard & Andrasik, 1987) and tension headache (Andrasik & Blanchard, 1987) are available. Blanchard (1992) summarized the literature on various cognitive therapy approaches to chronic headache. Although all three of these summaries also address the literature on the use of relaxation with chronic headache, a recent review specific to relaxation is not available.

Biofeedback for Headache

The "standard" biofeedback treatment for tension headache has been electromyographic (EMG) biofeedback from a forehead (or frontal or frontalis) placement (Budzynski, 1978). Controlled evaluations, dating back to 1973 (Budzynski, Stoyva, Adler, & Mullaney, 1973), have shown its efficacy. Several controlled evaluations of frontal EMG biofeedback have shown it superior to attention-placebo control conditions (Budzynski et al., 1973; Cox, Freundlich, & Meyer, 1975; Holroyd, Andrasik, & Noble, 1980).

The putative mechanism by which this form of biofeedback leads to headache relief is through relaxation of the muscles of the face and scalp. Sustained contractions of these muscles, along with those of the neck and upper back, are the assumed etiological agent in this form of headache. (This etiological mechanism has been seriously questioned, however; see reviews by Haber, Kuczmierczky, & Adams, 1985; Haynes, Cuevas, & Gannon, 1982; Philips, 1978).

Given this putative mechanism, two additional lines of research are not surprising. There have been at least six controlled comparisons of frontal EMG biofeedback and various forms of relaxation training (usually variants of Jacobson's [1938] progressive muscle relaxation [PMR]) in the treatment of tension headache: One favored biofeedback, one favored relaxation training, while the other four were "ties" (i.e., no significant difference between the two). Thus, direct comparisons seem to show no differential effectiveness of these two approaches. However, a sequential comparison (Blanchard, Andrasik, Neff, Arena, et al. 1982), in which a cohort of tension headache sufferers was initially given PMR with the relaxation nonresponders subsequently given frontal EMG biofeedback (in a stepped-care fashion), revealed that almost 50 percent of the relaxation nonresponders had a clinically significant reduction (at least 50% [Blanchard & Schwarz, 1988]) in headache activity from the biofeedback treatment.

Another line of research has challenged the frontal electrode placement (Hudzynski & Lawrence,

[1]*Biofeedback* refers to the process of (1) monitoring biological responses electronically, (2) converting the response measure to an easy to process form, such as an audio or visual signal (again electronically), and (3) *feeding* this easy to process signal *back* to the individual on a relatively immediate basis. Within such a feedback loop, individuals learn to gain control of normally involuntary responses (Blanchard & Epstein, 1978).

1988), contending that biofeedback from electrodes on the upper trapezius (upper back or rear of neck) was more logical and such treatment more efficacious. Despite the logical appeal, the empirical comparisons of these two placements reveal no difference in headache reduction (P. Martin & Mathews, 1978).

Whereas the "standard" biofeedback treatment for tension headache is fairly logical, the "standard" biofeedback treatment for migraine headache, so-called thermal biofeedback in which the patient is taught to regularly "warm the hands," that is, engage in peripheral vasodilation, is much less so. Initially described by a group at the Menninger Clinic (Sargent, Green, & Walters, 1973), thermal biofeedback for migraine headache has received many controlled evaluations. Although it is clearly superior to headache monitoring (e.g., Blanchard, Theobald, Williamson, Silver, & Brown, 1978), it has not been shown in a controlled trial to be superior to an attention-placebo condition. In one large-scale controlled study, thermal biofeedback for hand warming (combined with brief autogenic training [a form of meditative relaxation]) was superior to three comparison groups given frontal EMG biofeedback, autogenic training, and headache monitoring alone, respectively. Inclusion of the headache monitoring control confounds these results, of course. No comparisons of the primary treatment with the separate control groups were reported (Sargent, Solbach, Coyne, Spohn, & Ferguson, 1986).

The mechanisms by which thermal biofeedback has its beneficial effects on migraine headache remain unclear and are the subject of continuing investigation. Sargent et al. (1973) propose that the regular elicitation of hand-warming response leads to reduced peripheral sympathetic nervous system activity. Dalessio, Kunzel, Sternbach, and Sovak (1979), on the other hand, proposed that "hand warming" leads to the development of a "conditioned adaptive relaxation response." (Data from Morrill & Blanchard [1989] are consistent with this later interpretation.) Finally, Gauthier, Bois, Allaire, and Drolet (1981) have speculated that it is the potential stabilization of an unstable peripheral vascular system that leads to the beneficial effects.

Most research studies have excluded the patients with so-called mixed, or combined, migraine and tension headache. However, since they represent about 25 to 35 percent of the chronic, benign headache population, they certainly seem worthy of consideration. My colleagues and I (Blanchard, Andrasik, Neff, Arena et al., 1982; Blanchard, Andrasik, Appelbaum et al., 1985; Blanchard, Appelbaum, Radnitz, Morrill et al., 1990) have treated

patients with mixed headache in the same manner as those with pure migraine and repeatedly found similar results for the two groups of vascular headache patients.

An alternate form of biofeedback treatment for migraine has been direct feedback of cephalic vasomotor activity (CVM) in which patients are taught to voluntarily constrict and dilate cerebral arteries, most typically the external temporal artery. There has been a small but steady flow of studies of this general procedure (e.g., Bild & Adams, 1980; Friar & Beatty, 1976; Gauthier, Doyn, LaCroix, & Drolet, 1983). In general, CVM biofeedback has been superior to control conditions. However, a direct comparison with thermal biofeedback (Gauthier et al., 1983) showed no difference between the two. The rationale for this treatment is certainly more straightforward than that for thermal biofeedback. However, the complexity of the feedback system may have limited its widespread adoption.

Relaxation for Headache

Although various forms of relaxation training have been applied to the treatment of chronic headache, the most widely studied have been adaptations of progressive muscle relaxation (PMR). For tension headache, relaxation has been generally superior to headache monitoring in controlled trials. When compared to attention-placebo conditions, however, the record is mixed. Cox, Freundlich, and Meyer (1975) found relaxation significantly superior, whereas Blanchard, Appelbaum, Radnitz, Michultka et al. 1990 did not. Relaxation training for migraine headache provides an even more confusing picture. At least one moderate-sized study (Blanchard et al., 1978) found PMR superior to headache monitoring with migraine sufferers whereas a later study (Blanchard, Andrasik, Neff, Arena et al., 1982) found fairly poor results, especially for mixed headache patients.

Given the results of their stepped-care evaluations,[2] Blanchard and Andrasik (1985) have consistently recommended the combination of thermal biofeedback and relaxation for vascular headache. This combination was found to be superior to headache monitoring and showed a strong tendency to be superior to a placebo condition (Blanchard, Appelbaum, Radnitz, Morrill et al., 1990).

---

[2]Blanchard, Andrasik, Neff, Arena et al. (1982) initially treated all headache patients with relaxation training; those patients who failed to respond well to this first "step" were then given biofeedback as a second "step," analogous to medication stepped care previously recommended (Kaplan, 1986) for hypertensives.

Cognitive Therapy

As noted by Blanchard (1992), as in much of be-havioral treatment, there has been a growing inter-est in applying cognitive therapy to chronic head-ache. Holroyd and his associates have been the leaders in this area (for a detailed description of the procedures, see Holroyd & Andrasik, 1982). Through a series of studies, they have shown that for tension headache cognitive therapy (their term is *cognitive stress coping therapy*) is superior to frontal EMG biofeedback (Holroyd, Andrasik, & Westbrook, 1977) and can be delivered in a group format (Holroyd & Andrasik, 1978) or in a minimal–therapist-contact, home-based format (Tobin, Holroyd, Baker, Reynolds, & Holm, 1988). They have also shown that cognitive therapy com-bined with relaxation is superior to relaxation alone for tension headache (a finding replicated by Murphy, Lehrer, & Jurish, 1990, and by Blan-chard, Applebaum, Radnitz, Michultka, et al., 1990; however, Applebaum et al., [1990] did not replicate the finding in a comparison of minimal contact treatments). Blanchard, Applebaum, Rad-nitz, Michultka et al. (1990) showed the combina-tion of cognitive therapy plus PMR was superior to a placebo treatment. Holroyd, Nash, Pinsel, Cor-dingley, and Jerome (1991) found it superior to a standard drug treatment for tension headache, ami-triptyline. Thus, on balance, cognitive therapy seems a highly viable treatment by itself for tension headache and often adds a significant increment of headache relief when combined with other therapies.

There have also been several reports of the ap-plication of cognitive therapy to vascular headache (Blanchard, Appelbaum, Radnitz, Morrill et al., 1990; Lake, Raney, & Papsdorf, 1979; Sorbi & Tellegen, 1984). Although it appears to be as ef-fective as biofeedback or relaxation, in no instance was it superior to these other therapies. Moreover, in a relatively large-scale study (*n* = approx. 30 per cell), Blanchard, Appelbaum, Radnitz, Morrill et al. (1990) showed that cognitive therapy added noth-ing to the combination of relaxation and thermal biofeedback. Treated patients showed a trend to do better than patients in a placebo condition. Thus, it is not clear that adding cognitive therapy to more psychophysiological treatment leads to any improvement in outcome in the treatment of vascu-lar headache.

Maintenance and Follow-up

While Blanchard and Andrasik (1982), in a well-received review of the headache literature, could identify only 4 headache treatment studies with prospective follow-ups of at least 12 months, in a more recent review, Blanchard (1992) noted at least 5 prospective follow-ups of at least 3-years duration and 3 studies with prospective follow-ups, including daily headache diary data, of at least 5 years (Blanchard, Applebaum, Guarnieri, Morrill, & Dentinger, 1987; Gauthier & Carrier, 1991; Lisspers & Ost, 1990). In the latter two studies, retention rates were 93 and 79 percent, respec-tively. All of the previously described treatments were involved. In all cases, good maintenance has been reported, despite the apparent lack of regular continued practice of the treatment procedures by patients.

Given that the basic efficacy issues in the behav-ioral treatment of chronic headache have been re-solved, more recent research attention has begun to focus on four related areas: treatment of under-served (nonadult) populations, treatment of appar-ently refractory headache populations, direct com-parisons of psychological treatments to standard drug treatments; and studies of the mechanisms involved in the standard treatments (review of this last topic is beyond the scope of this chapter).

Pediatric Headache

Whereas there were no controlled evaluations of psychological treatments for headaches in a pediat-ric population (children and adolescents up through about age 16) noted in the 1982 review by Blan-chard and Andrasik, Blanchard (1992) summarized 7 controlled evaluations involving pediatric mi-graine, several with follow-ups of at least 12 months. The primary conclusions to be drawn are that thermal biofeeedback, usually with adjunctive autogenic training, was consistently more effective than headache monitoring and led to clinical im-provement in an average of 67 percent of the participants (at least a 50% reduction in headache activity as documented by daily headache diary [Blanchard & Schwarz, 1988]). For the most part, the results held up well at follow-ups of 12 months. Relaxation training (versions of PMR) has not been as effective as thermal biofeedback (summarized in Blanchard & Andrasik, 1985). In a large-scale study, McGrath et al. (1988) found relaxation no more effective than brief psychotherapy. Minimal–therapist-contact regimens of thermal biofeedback have also been shown to be as effective as individu-alized treatment (Guarnieri & Blanchard, 1990). Blanchard (1992), noting the high degree of suc-cess with thermal biofeedback among pediatric mi-graine sufferers, has suggested it may be the treat-ment of choice, superior even to medication. Additional research is clearly needed on this point.

Geriatric Headache

Headaches tend to be a disorder of the young and middle-aged adult. However, over 9 percent of adults over the age of 65 complain of frequent and severe headache (Hale, May, Marks, Moore, & Stewart, 1987). Early uncontrolled studies (Blanchard, Andrasik, Evans, & Hillhouse, 1985; Diamond & Montrose, 1984) indicated that older headache patients were relatively refractory to standard behavioral treatments such as relaxation and biofeedback. Arena, Hightower, and Chong (1988) challenged this idea and found very good success with a relaxation treatment of tension headache (70% clinically improved) when the treatments were specifically tailored to the information-processing capacities of the elderly. In other uncontrolled trials, similar improved success rates in elderly headache patients have been reported by Arena, Hannah, Bruno, and Meador (1991) with frontal EMG biofeedback in tension headache and by Kabela, Blanchard, Appelbaum, and Nicholson (1989) using combinations of cognitive therapy and other procedures across all varieties of benign headache. Nicholson and Blanchard (1993) have replicated Kabela et al. (1989) findings in a small-scale controlled trial. It appears that the headaches of the elderly are amenable to behavioral treatments tailored to this rapidly growing population. Moreover, substantial reductions in headache medications have also been found.

Refractory Headache Populations

At lest three subpopulations of headache sufferers have been identified who are relatively refractory to standard behavioral treatments: those with cluster headaches, those with chronic daily high-intensity headaches, and those who chronically consume high levels of headache medication (so called Hi Med HA). Cluster headache is a vascular headache with a distinctive temporal pattern (Kudrow, 1980) highlighted by relatively brief, but excruciating headaches. In the only moderate-sized study of this problem, Blanchard, Andrasik, Jurish, and Teders (1982) found only limited headache relief effects in 2 of 11 patients.

For chronic daily high-intensity headache (moderate to severe headache ratings almost every day), in a case-control comparison, Blanchard, Applebaum, Radnitz, Jaccard, and Dentinger (1989) found only 13 percent of patients responded to standard behavioral treatments as compared with approximately 50 percent of a comparison group matched on age, sex, and headache diagnosis who received the same treatments. This subpopulation, accounting for about 6 percent of headache clinic attenders, warrants further study.

In a similar case-control study, Michultka et al. (1989) found that patients with chronic headache who regularly consume sizable quantities of analgesics (at least six aspirin, or three Fiorinal, etc., daily) respond significantly worse (approximately 29% improved) than similarly treated patients with the same headache disorder who do not take that level of medication (55% improved). Mathew, Kurman, and Perez (1990) have similarly reported relatively poor results from a combined behavioral treatment administered to a comparable Hi Med HA population. They also reported almost a 50 percent dropout rate. Kudrow (1982) has provided data showing very poor response to regular drug therapy (amitriptyline) in this population with a much improved response rate once the analgesic medication was discontinued.

In one uncontrolled treatment series of these Hi Med HA patients, Blanchard, Taylor, and Dentinger (1992) have shown that a majority (70–80%) can be weaned from the medication with the assistance of relaxation training and frequent contacts for psychological support during the "rebound headache" phase of withdrawal. Once detoxified, 75 percent responded well to various additional behavioral treatment. The successful reductions were maintained for up to one year; those who failed to withdraw from drugs (despite repeated attempts) continued to have chronic headache and to use large quantities of analgesics at follow-ups.

Direct Comparisons of Drug and Behavioral Treatments

Although many of the treatment studies previously summarized have been indirect comparisons of drug and nondrug treatments, since most patients enter treatment on regular doses of medication and decrease them significantly with successful treatment, there have been relatively few direct controlled comparisons of drug and nondrug therapy. Two early studies compared propranolol, a beta adrenergic blocking agent, to thermal biofeedback in the treatment of migraine. While Sovak, Kunzel, Sternbach, and Dalessio (1981) found comparable headache relief and more psychological symptom improvement in the biofeedback treated group, Mathew (1981) found a clear advantage for propranolol over biofeedback. He also found a clear advantage of amitriptyline over combined behavioral treatment for mixed headache patients.

Holroyd and his colleagues (Holroyd et al., 1988, 1991) have conducted controlled comparisons of drug and nondrug therapy. In the first (Holroyd et al., 1988), they found that a minimal-contact biofeedback and relaxation treatment, modeled after that of Blanchard, Andrasik, Appelbaum et al. (1985), was superior to standard abortive drug therapy (ergotamine) in migraine headache. In the second study (Holroyd et al., 1991) the minimal-contact treatment combining relaxation and cognitive therapy was superior to amitriptyline in treating tension headache.

Conclusions

Behavioral treatments have "won" a place in the standard armamentarium of centers treating chronic headache through reported controlled demonstrations of efficacy and long-term follow-ups showing good maintenance of headache relief. Moreover, the treatments seem effective across the entire life span. Research attention has recently been focused on two issues of great clinical relevance: identification of the refractory headache patient and development of treatments for these subgroups and direct comparisons of behavioral and drug treatments.

It appears that behavioral treatments compare favorably to standard pharmacotherapy in headache. This might lead to recommending them over drug treatments because of potentially lessened side effects and good durability of treatment effects without continuing therapy.

RHEUMATOID ARTHRITIS

The last pain problem discussed is rheumatoid arthritis (RA). Although it is much less prevalent than headache, it is a serious, often debilitating condition.

As noted by L. Young (1992) in his recent review, rheumatoid arthritis is a chronic, systemic inflammatory disorder characterized by joint pain and stiffness of varying intensity usually accompanied by an unpredictable fluctuating, but progressively deteriorating course. Its prevalence is approximately 1 percent, with females outnumbering males by three to one. The vast majority of RA patients eventually experience marked impairment in ability to work and perform the activities of daily living (ADL), *despite* appropriate medical therapy.

Although early psychological research tended to focus on potential "arthritic personality" factors in etiology and possibly treatment, such research is now generally discredited and has been more or less abandoned (see review by Anderson, Bradley, Young, McDaniel, & Wise [1985] for more on this). Recent attention has focused more on the pain, mood disturbances, and difficulties in coping with ADLs (L. Young, 1992) and has led to several controlled trials of various behavioral and cognitive approaches to treatment. These are reviewed in detail by both L. Young (1992) and McCracken (1991). In most instances, the assessments have been across a wide array of dependent variable domains (pain, mood, ADL, coping strategies, range of motion measures), including some disease parameters (erthrocyte sedimentation rate [ESR]).

Several early studies of the behavioral treatment of RA featured thermal biofeedback of the most affected joints and relaxation training as the key components of treatment (Achterberg, McGraw, & Lawlis, 1981; Mitchell, 1986). Decreased reports of pain and stiffness were found.

Four more recent studies (Applebaum, Blanchard, Hickling, & Alfonson 1988; Bradley et al., 1987; O'Leary, Shoor, Lorig, & Holman, 1988; Parker et al., 1988) have all emphasized a combination of cognitive and behavioral treatment procedures, including relaxation training and use of imagery; pain management including an explanation of pain theory as well as changes in attributions and self-talk (all borrowing heavily from the work of Turk et al. [1983]); and a heavy dose of education about RA and practical advice. In fact, the similarities of the regimens are striking. Two of these studies also provided thermal biofeedback (Applebaum et al., 1988; Bradley et al., 1987).

In all four studies, significant reductions in pain report and pain-related behaviors were found in the short term. Other improvements were noted in morning stiffness and joint impairment or range of motion. In most cases, the degree of improvement (reduction) in pain, the most debilitating symptom of RA, was greater in the cognitive-behavioral treated group than in the various controls (Applebaum et al., 1988 — symptom monitoring; Bradley et al., 1987 — social support group and no-treatment; O'Leary et al., 1988 — bibliotherapy utilizing a validated arthritis self-help manual; Parker et al., 1988 — arthritis education and no-treatment), despite sample sizes ranging from 9 per condition (Applebaum et al.) to 29 per condition (Parker et al.).

While Applebaum et al. delivered treatment individually, in the three other studies, treatments were delivered in small groups. No decrements were found with the group treatment format; in fact, the additional social support may be a benefit.

Gender made no apparent difference in the short term: O'Leary et al.'s sample was entirely female and Bradley et al.'s was over 80 percent female, while Appelbaum et al. and Parker et al. had 90 percent or greater male (VA populations). There might be a difference in longer term outcome associated with gender, however. Bradley et al. reported good results at a 12-month follow-up, while O'Leary et al. had good results at a 4-month follow-up (but the treated group was no longer superior to the controls). By way of contrast, in the studies on male RA patients, at an 18-month follow-up, Appelbaum et al. showed no advantage of treatment in their male veteran population. Parker et al., also working with a primarily male veteran population, had little long-term improvement over pretreatment except in use of cognitive coping strategies. In this latter study, Parker et al. were able to document that there was significant disease progression in their sample and that the patients in the control groups had deteriorated in the year across all spheres assessed while the patients receiving the cognitive-behavioral treatments had not deteriorated.

Conclusions

Unlike headache, for which behavioral treatments may represent a clear-cut alternative to standard pharmacotherapy, with RA it seems clear that cognitive-behavioral treatment regimens are most likely to be useful adjuncts in its total management. The uniformly positive results across diverse subsamples of RA patients achieved with cognitive-behavioral programs bodes well for the routine inclusion of psychological services in the management of RA.

INSOMNIA

As Lacks and Morin (1992) noted in their recent review, "insomnia is a widespread and persistent health problem that profoundly affects mood, efficiency and relationships" (p. 58). The prevalence of notable sleep difficulties (at least a two-week duration within the past six months) has been estimated to be 10 percent (D. Ford & Kamerow, 1989). Although there are at least 88 distinct sleep/wake disorders (American Sleep Disorders Association, 1990), the 12 insomnia subtypes, classified under the heading of disorders of initiating and maintaining sleep (DIMS), are the problems most likely to be treated by psychologists and the ones most likely to involve psychological and behavioral factors (Lacks & Morin, 1992).

Although many insomniacs and their physicians may turn to medication for the treatment of their DIMS, it seems clear that there are no satisfactory long-term pharmacological treatments of insomnia. (However, most benzodiazepines can be helpful for improving sleep in the *short term* [Morin & Kwentus, 1988].) Thus, the long-term answers to insomnia, to some degree by default, are psychological treatments.

In their review, and in an additional meta-analysis (Morin, Culbert, Kowatch, & Walton, 1989), Lacks and Morin (1992) identified three broad cate-

gories of primarily behavioral procedures that had been shown in controlled studies to be efficacious in the treatment of insomnia: relaxation techniques, cognitive procedures to correct cognitive distortions, and training to correct learned maladaptive sleep habits. In addition to being used alone as a monotherapy, many investigators have used combinations of these procedures in multicomponent programs. For detailed description of treatment techniques, see Lacks (1987) or Hauri (1991).

Relaxation

Various forms of relaxation training have been used to reduce tension and anxiety often associated with insomnia. Although the most widely used techniques have been variations on Jacobson's (1938) progressive muscle relaxation (e.g., Espie, Lindsay, Brooks et al., 1989; Lacks, Bertelson, Gans, & Kunkel, 1983; Woolfolk & McNulty, 1983), other relaxation-based procedures such as autogenic training (Lichstein, Johnson, Womack, Dean, & Childers, 1990), meditation (Schoicket, Bertelson, & Lacks, 1988), and imagery training (Morin & Azrin, 1987; Woolfolk & McNulty, 1983) have been used. Interestingly, according to Lacks and Morin's (1992) analysis (see their Table 1), pure relaxation treatments, although clearly better than symptom monitoring and wait-list controls, tend to yield the weakest results of the various behavioral procedures. Progressive muscle relaxation, the most widely studied relaxation technique, has the poorest outcome, averaging only 28 percent improvement at posttreatment and 37 percent improvement at long-term follow-up.

Cognitive Procedures

The results with the most widely used cognitive procedures, paradoxical instructions (Espie, Lindsay, Brooks et al., 1989; Lacks, Bertelson, Gans, & Kunkel, 1983) have shown mixed results after some early enthusiastic reports. Combinations of cognitive procedures, reported in a single study by Sanavio (1988), have been promising. Lacks and Morin (1992) rightfully note that this is an area in need of further research.

Correction of Learned Maladaptive Sleep Habits

By far the most widely used behavioral technique is the stimulus control procedure first described by Bootzin (1972; for a recent description, see Bootzin, Epstein, & Wood [1991]). In this approach, patients are instructed to eliminate all sleep-incompatible behaviors and cues (such as watching TV, eating, etc.), as well as tossing and turning while trying to fall asleep) from the bed and bedroom and instead to associate a relatively rapid falling asleep with going to bed. Most important, if the patient does not fall asleep within a prescribed brief interval (usually 10 to 20 minutes), he or she is to get out of bed and continue any other activity until he or she is again drowsy.

Lacks and Morin (1992) report that this simple technique has consistently shown improvement rates of 50 to 70 percent (with an average in their meta-analysis of 55% at posttreatment and 52% at one-year follow-up). Moreover, direct comparisons of the stimulus control procedure with other techniques usually find it superior (Epsie, Brooks, & Lindsay, 1989; Lacks, Bertelson, Sugerman, & Kenkel, 1983; Morin & Azrin, 1987).

A variant on this technique is sleep restriction therapy, in which clients are prescribed an individualized sleep-wake schedule and allowed to spend only a minimum amount of time in bed (consistent with their mean time asleep per night). Although it leads to some initial daytime drowsiness (Glovinsky & Spielman, 1991), it does seem effective.

Another set of instructional procedures, termed by Hauri (1982, 1991) *sleep hygiene rules*, should be included under this heading. This procedure incorporates all of the "practical" advice (such as avoiding stimulants [such as caffeine] or stimulating activity at bedtime) that has typically been incorporated in most treatments. Schoicket et al. (1988) evaluated this component by itself and found it to yield 26 percent improvement at posttreatment and 33 percent at long-term follow-up. It could be that this condition should serve as the baseline condition, rather than symptom monitoring with a sleep diary, against which to compare any other techniques.

Multiple component therapies typically incorporate stimulus control and other techniques such as varieties of relaxation. Lacks and Morin (1992) note that on average multicomponent regimens have performed about as well as stimulus control alone (Morawetz, 1989; Morin, Jones, Stone, & Mercer, 1991). The average improvement rate at posttreatment was 55 percent, and at long-term follow-up it was 50 percent.

At this point, no single technique or combination of procedures has consistently outperformed the stimulus control procedure (usually supplemented with instruction in sleep hygiene). Future research might well consider using stimulus control as the "standard" behavioral therapy against which to evaluate any treatment innovations.

An approach to treating insomnia that is much discussed, especially by clinicians, is tailoring the treatment to the insomniac's idiosyncratic problems (Hauri, 1991; Lacks, 1987; Lacks & Morin, 1992). The attempts to bring this notion into the research arena (Espie, Brooks, & Lindsay, 1989; Sanavio, 1988), however, have not had great success in showing dramatic increments in improvement for the population treated.

Follow-up. Lacks and Morin (1992) note a large number of studies in the experimental literature with 6-to-12-month follow-up assessments (see their Table 1). What is especially encouraging is that one-year results are typically as good as, and sometimes better than, immediate posttreatment results. The improvements from the behavioral treatments of insomnia thus seem durable with good maintenance of results being documented out to three years posttreatment (Sanavio, Vidotto, Bettinardi, Roletto, & Zorzi, 1990).

Insomnia in the Elderly and Children

As with the research in other areas of behavioral medicine, much of the body of research on insomnia has focused on young and middle-aged adults, deliberately excluding the pediatric and geriatric populations. More recently, attention has turned to these two populations, with special attention to the elderly. For a long time, sleep difficulties were seen as a natural consequence of aging (Miles & Dement, 1980; NIH, 1991). It has come to be recognized, however, that insomnia in the elderly, although potentially more complicated because of the presence of other disorders and their pharmacological treatment, is amenable to the same treatments as the general adult population (Bootzin, Engle, Friedman, & Hazelwood, 1983).

More recent studies targeting the elderly population (L. Friedman, Bliwise, Yesavage, & Salom, 1991; Hoelscher & Edinger, 1988; Lichstein et al., 1990; Morin & Azrin, 1988) have generally shown levels of improvement with stimulus control, sleep hygiene, and relaxation comparable to those found with younger adults. Given the ever-increasing size of our older population, this area of research will undoubtedly grow.

Research on sleep problems in the very young has tended to emphasize in-home treatments that focus on extinction of parental attention to sleep-incompatible behaviors and positive reinforcement (Durand & Mindell, 1990; Richman, Douglas, Hunt, Lansdown, & Levere, 1985) and has had good success.

Prediction of outcome. In an interesting reanalysis of several studies from the same laboratory, Lacks and Powlishta (1988) were able to identify a few factors that were associated with good outcome: younger age, earlier onset, longer duration, and less psychopathology. Morin and Azrin (1988) would add that subjects who do not take sleep medication are also better candidates.

Conclusions

From the existing research record, it seems clear that multicomponent psychological therapies are probably the treatment of choice for long-term benefit among many chronic insomniacs. However, there is also a clear need for the careful multidisciplinary assessment of insomniacs so as to parse out those for whom biomedical treatments are more appropriate (e.g., those with sleep apnea). Thus, the psychologist has a clear role in treating this class of disorders.

LOWER GASTROINTESTINAL TRACT DISORDERS

A class of disorders that are fairly widespread, in terms of the number of actual and potential patients, but are relatively understudied in terms of psychological treatment are disorders of the lower gastrointestinal (GI) tract. Whitehead (1992) has provided a succinct overview of research on psychosocial treatment of the disorders of the entire GI tract with special emphasis on those of the lower GI tract. Thus, we are concerned primarily with irritable bowel syndrome (IBS), inflammatory bowel disease (IBD), and a relatively new disorder, pelvic floor dyssynergia (Whitehead, Chaussade, Corazziari, Kumar, 1991).

Irritable Bowel Syndrome

IBS represents by far the greatest potential target of opportunity for psychologists and other mental health professionals. This functional disorder of the lower GI tract, characterized by chronic (at least three to six months) abdominal pain or tenderness and altered bowel habits (either diarrhea, constipation, or alternating diarrhea and constipation) in the absence of other demonstrable causes for such symptoms (such as IBD, lactose intolerance, parasites) has a prevalence in the general population of 7 to 17 percent (Whitehead, Winget, Fedoravicius, Wooley, & Blackwell, 1982; Drossman, Sandler, McKee, & Lovitz, 1982, respectively) and may account for up to 50 percent of new referrals to gastroenterologists (Ferguson, Sircus, & Eastwood, 1977). More recent studies (Drossman et al., 1988; Whitehead, Bosmajian, Zonderman, Costa, & Schusteur, 1988) call into question the earlier epidemiologic data: Among community samples who met the symptomatic inclusion criteria, most (70 – 80%) had not consulted a physician. Moreover,

although symptomatically indistinguishable from IBS patients who had sought medical attention, those with IBS symptoms who had not sought help were relatively normal on psychological tests while those who sought help showed tests results typical of a so-called "neurotic" or "chronic illness" population.

This replicated finding is consistent with another well-established finding (Blanchard, Scharff, Schwarz et al., 1990; M. Ford et al., 1987; Lydiard, Laraia, Howell, & Ballenger, 1986; Wender & Kalm, 1983; S. Young, Alpers, Norland, & Woodruff, 1976) that among a treatment-seeking IBS population, there are a sizable majority who will meet the diagnostic criteria for one or more anxiety disorders (usually generalized anxiety disorder or social phobia) or mood disorders (dysthymia or major depressive disorder).

As Whitehead (1992) notes, when he (Whitehead & Bosmajian, 1982) reviewed this literature 10 years ago, they found no controlled trials for psychological treatment of IBS; however, there have been a number of controlled evaluations of psychological treatments for IBS over the past 9 years (for another somewhat older review, see Blanchard, Schwarz, & Radnitz [1987]. Whitehead (1992) has subcategorized the treatment approaches in these studies as "insight-oriented psychotherapy," "hypnotherapy," and "stress management." A closer examination of the treatment conditions, however, finds considerable overlap among all of the treatment packages that have been tested.

In one of the earliest, and best, controlled trials, Svedlund, Sjodin, Ottosson, and Dotevall (1983) randomly assigned 101 IBS patients to receive standard medical therapy alone (bulk laxatives, anticholinergics [antispasmodics], and minor tranquilizers) or to receive the medical therapy plus 10 one-hour sessions (spread over three months) of psychotherapy. The therapy was described as "dynamically oriented short-term individual psychotherapy" but was focused on teaching new coping strategies for stressful problems as well as on an educational behavioral analysis in which patients were taught to identify connections between stressful life events and GI symptoms. Thus, the therapy is very much akin to the cognitive stress coping techniques of Holroyd and Andrasik (1982), which are very effective with chronic tension headache.

Outcome was evaluated by physician ratings (based on structured interviews) of mental and GI symptoms at pretreatment, posttreatment, and one-year follow-up. Treated patients were more improved in all areas than controls but only the ratings for abdominal pain and total somatic complaints reached significance. At the 12-month follow-up, ratings of abdominal pain, overall bowel dysfunction, and total somatic complaints all showed significant improvement relative to the control group. The mental (or psychological) symptom ratings were not significantly different.

Whorwell, Prior, and Faragher (1984) compared hypnotherapy with supportive psychotherapy plus placebo medication in 30 IBS patients. The hypnotherapy, 7 one-half – hour sessions over three months, was aimed at general relaxation and relaxation and control of the intestinal smooth muscle plus compatible visual imagery. All patients were to practice autohypnotic relaxation daily with the assistance of a tape. Results showed greater improvement in the hypnotherapy group than the control group in reduction of abdominal pain and distention as well as on "bowel habits," all assessed by daily symptom diary, and general well-being as assessed by weekly rating. Informal follow-up and clinical replication have been reported by Whorwell (1989). Harvey, Hinton, Gunary, and Barry (1989) have reported a replication of these results using a group form of treatment.

A partial replication of these results was reported by Guthrie, Creed, Dawson, and Tonenson (1991), who compared psychotherapy plus regular practice of relaxation in addition to standard medical therapy with standard medical therapy. In the psychotherapy (the actual number of contacts or sessions is unclear), there was an exploration of the patients' feelings about their IBS and any other emotional problems. At end of the three months of treatment, the psychotherapy group was more improved on abdominal pain and diarrhea than the controls, based on patient symptom diaries and physician global ratings.

In the stress management area, Blanchard and colleagues (Blanchard & Schwarz, 1987, Blanchard, Schwarz, Suls, et al., 1992; Neff & Blanchard, 1987) have reported on several trials of a multicomponent treatment that combined relaxation, thermal biofeedback, and cognitive stress coping therapy in a 12-session, 8-week treatment program. All results were evaluated by daily GI symptom diary completed by the patient.

In the Neff and Blanchard study, (1987), treated subjects surpassed controls on a composite symptom score derived from the diary. A replication (Blanchard & Schwarz, 1987), using a group format and within-subject design, again showed treatment superior to symptom monitoring. Interestingly, prospective follow-ups of these patients for up to four years, using the daily GI symptom diary (Schwarz, Taylor, Scharff, & Blanchard, 1990),

have shown good maintenance of reduced GI symptoms.

In their latest effort (Blanchard et al., 1992), this group reported on two controlled evaluations of this cognitive-behavioral treatment combination in comparison with (1) an attention-placebo condition (whose members received pseudomeditation and biofeedback to suppress alpha in the EEG) and (2) a symptom-monitoring control. All evaluations were by daily GI symptom diary. In the first study (n = 10 per condition), there were nonsignificant trends for the cognitive-behavioral treatment to improve more than the attention-placebo condition. The treated patients did better than symptom-monitoring controls. In the larger scale replication trial (n = 30 per condition), there were no differences between the two treatments but both improved more than the symptom-monitoring control. Blanchard, Schwarz, Suls et al. (1992) interpret the findings as showing that the patients in the attention-placebo condition converted it into an active treatment involving relaxation and distraction. Process data are consistent with this interpretation. Results from the cognitive-behavioral treatment held up at a six-month follow-up.

Interestingly, treated subjects, especially those in the cognitive-behavioral condition, showed significant reductions in anxiety and depression to within the normal range on standard measures by posttreatment (Beck Depression Inventory, State-Trait Anxiety Inventory).

Similar results (cognitive-behavioral treatment vs. symptom monitoring) have been reported by Lynch and Zamble (1989). Bennett and Wilkinson (1985) found a similar combination of cognitive-behavioral procedures statistically superior to the best available medical treatment.

Overall, it appears that IBS is imminently treatable by a variety of psychological packages. Commonalities appear to be teaching some form of relaxation (and how to use it as a coping strategy) and some form of cognitive coping strategies. As long as the treatment is highly involving and credible and contains these elements, it seems to help and the results are durable. One should note, however, that there are no studies that have demonstrated the superiority of some from of psychotherapy or behavior therapy to a credible attention-placebo control condition.

There are contradictory data on prediction of outcome. Blanchard, Scharff et al. (1992) found that IBS patients who had a diagnosable DSM-III-R (American Psychiatric Association, 1987) Axis I disorder responded significantly poorer than patients who did not meet diagnostic criteria. Similar results have been reported by Harvey et al. (1989). Contradictory results emerged from the study by Guthrie et al. (1991): Those patients who were relatively higher on anxiety and depression and whose symptoms seemed more likely to be exacerbated by stressful events responded more favorably. Given the differences in treatment regimens and assessment strategies, these results may be reconcilable.

Inflammatory Bowel Disease

IBD shares many of the symptoms of IBS (pain, diarrhea, perhaps lethargy) but is an entirely different disorder. Two different diseases—Crohn's disease (CD) and ulcerative colitis (UC)—make up IBD. They are histologically distinct and have different natural histories. For the most part, CD affects the small intestine (but can affect the large bowel), while UC is confined to the colon. IBD's prevalence is about 1 per 1,000 in the United States. (For a recent review of psychological factors in IBD and its treatment, see Schwarz & Blanchard [1990].)

Although early research seemed to indicate that there was a high prevalence of psychopathology among IBD patients, these studies focused on hospitalized patients. More recent studies find slightly higher levels of psychologic distress in IBD patients versus healthy controls (with trends for more distress in CD than in UC patients), but considerably less than is found in IBS patients (for example, see Blanchard, Scharff, Schwarz et al., 1990).

There has been only limited recent research on psychological treatment for IBD, although it was earlier seen as a classical psychosomatic disorder (Alexander, 1950). Milne, Joachin, and Niedhardt (1986) randomized 80 IBD patients to receive either a six-session stress management program emphasizing relaxation and interpersonal communication techniques or no additional treatment. Periodic assessments over one year showed significant improvement in the treated subjects on the Crohn's Disease Activity Index and Inflammatory Bowel Disease Stress Index with no change in the controls. Unfortunately, despite random assignment and a large sample, the treated group was noticeably higher on the measures at pretreatment and reduced to the same level as the controls at posttreatment. Thus, although they "improved" significantly, one cannot rule out a regression-to-the-mean effect.

Shaw and Ehrlich (1987) compared a six-session relaxation regimen to no-treatment to assist in pain control among 40 IBD patients. The treated pa-

tients were significantly improved on a number of pain measures, including the McGill Pain Questionnaire.

Schwarz and Blanchard (1991) attempted to apply their cognitive-behavioral treatment regimen (developed and tested on IBS patients [see previous discussion and Blanchard, Schwarz, Suls et al., 1992]) to IBD patients. Eleven patients were initially treated while 10 monitored symptoms; 8 of the latter group were subsequently treated. While there was some symptomatic improvement across both conditions, the symptom-monitoring group improved more than the treated group. During subsequent treatment, most of the treated controls returned to pretreatment symptom levels.

Thus, these data show an apparent detrimental effect of treatment. This unusual result seemed partially explained by differences between the two subcategories of IBD: CD patients generally responded favorably (with reduced symptoms) to cognitive-behavioral treatment while UC patients tended to deteriorate. This interesting apparent partial failure is in need of replication. It may also be that treatment should focus primarily on the pain and secondary psychological distress rather than the whole array of GI symptoms.

Pelvic Floor Dyssynergia

This disorder is an apparent functional disorder of the muscles involved in evacuation of the colon and rectum and could account for up to 50 percent of cases of chronic constipation (Whitehead, 1992). Preliminary reports of biofeedback treatment in this disorder (Wald, Chandra, Gabel, & Chiponis, 1987), in a controlled comparison with mineral oil therapy, showed no immediate difference at end of treatment but an advantage at 6- and 12-month follow-ups.

Conclusions

It seems clear that psychosocial interventions have a potential major role to play in the management of IBS. Controlled trials are needed to compare the various multicomponent treatment packages with standard medical regimens, including the preferred drug regimens. There is probably less of a role for direct psychological treatment of IBD, but there may be an adjunctive role as with rheumatoid arthritis.

There are a limited number of psychologists conducting research on lower GI tract disorders or practicing in gastroenterology clinics. Given the widespread prevalence of these disorders, and a growing body of literature, this area seems to represent a field "ripe" for psychological interventions.

PSYCHONEUROIMMUNOLOGY

Psychoneuroimmunology (PNI) is a rapidly developing area of behavioral medicine and may become one of the *most* important areas for psychological and behavioral interventions into medical disorders.

The present section does not pretend to do justice to this rapidly developing field; instead, the focus, as in *every* other section, is on *intervention*. A recent review of this developing field by two of its acknowledged leaders, Kiecolt-Glaser and Glaser (1992), makes three important points: (1) It seems clear that various stressors can adversely affect immune function (see also, Ader, Felten, & Cohen, 1991). This finding has naturally led researchers and clinicians to wonder if the reciprocal relation also held, that is, could psychological interventions enhance immune function? (2) The tentative answer to this question advanced by the Glasers (1992) is that, "If an individual's immune system is functioning satisfactorily, it may not be possible to 'enhance' immune function above normal levels; in fact, it is possible that it would be undesirable to do so" (p. 569). (3) Thus, they believe the appropriate populations for clinical research are those in whom immune functioning is somewhat compromised. A final point they make is that given the complexity of the functioning of the immune system and of the links between immune function and disease end point, and the array of tests available, it may be difficult to demonstrate changes in disease end points from PNI manipulations.

With these caveats firmly in place, one can then view the limited controlled experimental literature on PNI interventions. Perhaps the strongest study to date is the one by Fawzy et al. (1990) described earlier in the section on cancer. Subjects included those with Stage I or II malignant melanoma who received either an intensive group treatment program emphasizing health education; stress management, including relaxation; and cognitive coping skills training or routine medical care. Although there were significant advantages for the intervention condition in measures of psychological distress at end of treatment, the immune function parameters were not significantly different. At the six-month follow-up point, however, the immune function of the intervention group was significantly improved relative to the controls.

Kiecolt-Glaser et al. (1985), working with older adults (average age 74, range 60 to 88) in sheltered living facilities, compared relaxation with guided imagery with a control condition with equivalent social contact and a measurement-only control over a one-month intensive-contact period and then at a one-month follow-up. Psychological distress measures (Hopkins Symptom Checklist) improved in the relaxation group at end of treatment but returned to essentially baseline levels at followup. More importantly, several of the immune function measures improved in the relaxation group at the end of active training.

Another important set of PNI intervention studies has come from the University of Miami. In both studies, the basic population was homosexual males who were being tested for the presence of HIV. In one part of the project (LaPerriere et al., 1990, 1991), a program of regular aerobic exercise was evaluated. After an initial assessment for psychological state and immune system functioning, subjects were randomized to an aerobic exercise condition or a control condition for five weeks. At the conclusion of this intervention, the psychological measures were repeated and blood was again drawn for immune measures. Part of this blood sample was used to determine HIV status. Patients were notified as to their status 72 hours later. Thus, the posttreatment measures were taken prior to notification. This design produced four groups: subjects who were seropositive and were in either the exercise program or the control condition; and subjects who were seronegative and also in the exercise or control condition.

Those subjects who were found to be seropositive who had participated in the five-week exercise condition resembled those who were seronegative (regardless of condition) in psychological distress and immune function measures whereas the seropositive controls deteriorated significantly in both dependent variable spheres.

In a parallel study of the same design, Antoni et al. (1991) compared a cognitive-behavioral stress management program to a no-intervention control condition, again in both seropositive and seronegative gay males. Similar results were found: The seropositive controls tended to deteriorate in psychological status and immune competence while the treated seropositive subjects either improved on some immune measures or did not deteriorate. The seronegative subjects either stayed stable or improved.

A related study by Coates, McKusick, Kuno, and Stites (1989), however, failed to find any advantage for an 8-week stress management program (relaxation, coping skills, education) versus controls on either psychological distress measures or immune functioning measures. A major difference between the studies was that in the Coates et al. study, all participants were homosexual males who already knew they were HIV positive at the time of their participation and thus presumably had been infected for a longer length of time. The Glasers (1992) speculate that the immune systems of subjects in this latter population were already too compromised to benefit from the intervention.

Some clinicians claim that imagery is the key to manipulating the immune system. While there has been much publicity for the role of specific guided imagery and the adoption of positive attitude in fighting cancer, presumably through PNI linkages (Acterberg, 1985; B. Siegel, 1986), little empirical data have yet emerged on these topics.

Conclusions

As noted earlier, the area of PNI interventions is in its beginning stages and tentative guidelines for this research are just emerging (Kiecolt-Glaser & Glaser, 1992). It may prove to be one of the most important parts of behavioral medicine, but only future research will determine that. For now, it remains an exciting area of research without a strong empirical base to guide clinical practice.

CONCLUDING REMARKS

The 11 areas reviewed in this chapter represent only a portion of the disorders and diseases for which psychological treatments have been shown to be useful. In surveying the content summarized on these 11 disorders, two things stand out: First, most of the treatments are multicomponent, combining specific techniques and procedures from behavior therapy, such as relaxation training or biofeedback, and from the cognitive therapies of Meichenbaum, Beck, and Ellis. In this way, they are fairly explicit and lend themselves to being described in treatment manuals (e.g., Blanchard & Andrasik, 1985). Second, the treatments tend to be very focused and relatively brief (6 to 20 sessions). There are exceptions to this, such as the three-year program of M. Friedman et al. (1986) for Type A behavior and E. Spiegel et al.'s (1989) year-long support group program for women with recurrent breast cancer.

A convenient way of conceptualizing the vast array of research in behavioral medicine is in terms of the maturity of the subfields and the extent to which the ideas and procedures from behavioral medicine have penetrated (or even come to dominate) routine medical care for these problems. For example, principles and practices from behavioral medicine tend to dominate work in obesity and smoking cessation. They are so well-accepted that they are regularly "sold" to the public as part of franchised weight-loss and smoking cessation clinics. Pharmacological and other medical interventions still play a role, but the psychological ones seem dominant. As these areas have matured, long-term follow-up has become important as have interventions at the public health level rather than the individual level.

In the areas of insomnia, chronic pain, and headache, behavioral approaches are well accepted. In most comprehensive sleep disorder clinics, pain clinics, or headache clinics, psychological assessment and intervention are typically an integral part of the total treatment armamentarium. They may be the exclusive approach in some instances, whereas in others they are adjuncts. Controlled trials comparing pharmacological with behavioral treatments have begun to emerge.

While there are few, if any, clinical facilities that specialize in Type A behavior, it is a concern in some cardiac rehabilitation programs. Psychosocial interventions for possible Type A behavior have yet to win full acceptance as a necessary part of cardiac rehabilitation or primary prevention efforts for individuals at risk for CHD.

Even though dietary interventions have begun to be a regular component in the work of hypertension clinics, the exercise and stress management approaches continue to be controversial. Given the long-standing (20 years) and widespread research on stress management and BP, this status seems somewhat surprising. It may be that most of the direct comparisons of drug with nondrug therapy have tended to favor pharmacological approaches and that the stress management approaches are less reliable in producing uniformly positive results.

For the other topics, rheumatoid arthritis, lower GI tract disorders, and cancer, behavioral medicine approaches are still widely regarded as experimental and, at best, adjunctive to standard medical care. Much more research will be needed to establish the full role of psychological interventions with these problems. Finally, psychological intervention at the immune system level (PNI) must clearly be seen as experimental.

It thus seems clear that much interesting research remains to be done as psychological treatment continues to earn its place in the health care arena.

REFERENCES

Achterberg, J. (1985). *Immagery in healing: Shamanism and modern medicine*. Boston: New Science Library/Random House.

Achterberg, J., McGraw, P., & Lawlis, G. F. (1981). Rheumatoid arthritis: A study of the relaxation and temperature biofeedback training as an adjunctive therapy. *Biofeedback and Self-Regulation*, 6, 207–233.

Ader, R., Felten, D. L., & Cohen, N. (Eds). (1991). *Psychoneuroimmunology*. New York: Academic Press.

Ahles, C. A., Ruckdeschel, J. C., & Blanchard, E. B. (1984). Cancer-related pain: II. Assessment with visual analog scales. *Journal of Psychosomatic Research, 28*, 121–124.

Alexander, F. (1950). *Psychosomatic medicine: Its principles and applications*. New York: Norton.

American Psychiatric Association. (1987). *Diagnostic and statistical manual of mental disorders* (3rd ed., revised). American Psychiatric Association: Washington.

American Sleep Disorders Association. (1990). *International classification of sleep disorders (ICSD): Diagnostic and coding manual*. Rochester, MN: Author.

Andersen, B. L. (1992). A review of psychological interventions for cancer patients: Predicting risk and enhancing the quality of life. *Journal of Consulting and Clinical Psychology, 60*, 552–568.

Anderson, K. O., Bradley, L. A., Young, L. D., McDaniel, L. K., & Wise, C. M. (1985). Rheumatoid arthritis: Review of psychological factors related to etiology, effects, and treatment. *Psychological Bulletin, 98*, 358–387.

Andrasik, F., & Blanchard, E. B. (1987). Task Force report on the biofeedback treatment of tension headache. In J. P. Hatch, J. D. Rugh, & J. G. Fisher (Eds), *Biofeedback studies in clinical efficacy* (pp. 281–321). New York: Plenum.

Antoni, M. H., Baggett, L., Ironson, G., August, S., LaPerriere, A., Klimas, N., Schneiderman, N., & Fletcher, M. A. (1991). Cognitive behavioral stress management intervention buffers distress responses and elevates immunologic markers following notification of HIV-1 seropositivity. *Journal of Consulting and Clinical Psychology, 59*, 906–915.

Applebaum, K. A., Blanchard, E. B., Hickling, E. J., & Alfonso, M. (1988). Cognitive behavioral treatment of a veteran population with moderate to severe rheumatoid arthritis. *Behavior Theory, 19*, 489–502.

Applebaum, K. A., Blanchard, E. B., Nicholson, N. L., Radnitz, C. L., Kirsch, C., Michultka, D., Attanasio, V., Andrasik, F., & Dentinger, M. P. (1990). Controlled evaluation of the addition of cognitive strategies to a home-based relaxation protocol for tension headache. *Behavior Therapy, 21*, 293–303.

Arena, J. G., Hannah, S. L., Bruno, G. M., & Meador, K. J. (1991). Electromyographic biofeedback training for tension headache in the elderly: A prospective study. *Biofeedback and Self-Regulation, 16*, 379–390.

Arena, J. G., Hightower, N. E., & Chong, G. C. (1988). Relaxation therapy for tension headache in the elderly: A prospective study. *Psychology and Aging, 1*, 96–98.

Baille, A., Mattick, R. P., & Webster, P. (1990). *Review of published treatment outcome literature on smoking cessation: Preparatory readings for the Quality Assurance Project Smoking Cessation Expert Committee*. National Campaign Against Drug Abuse, National Drug and Alcohol Research Center, Working Paper No. 1, University of New South Wales.

Beck, A. T., Rush, J. A., Shaw, B. F., & Emery, G. (1980). *Cognitive Therapy of Depression*. NY: Guilford Press.

Bennett, P., & Wilkinson, S. (1985). Comparison of psychological and medical treatment of the irritable bowel syndrome. *British Journal of Clinical Psychology, 24*, 215–216.

Bild, R., & Adams, H. E. (1980). Modification of migraine headaches by cephalic blood volume pulse and EMG biofeedback. *Journal of Consulting and Clinical Psychology, 48*, 51–57.

Blanchard, E. B. (1982). Behavioral medicine: Past, present, and future. *Journal of Consulting and Clinical Psychology, 50*, 795–796.

Blanchard, E. B. (1992). Psychological treatment of benign headache disorders. *Journal of Consulting and Clinical Psychology, 60*, 537–551.

Blanchard, E. B., & Andrasik, F. (1982). Psychological assessment and treatment of headache: Recent developments and emerging issues. *Journal of Consulting and Clinical Psychology, 50*, 859–879.

Blanchard, E. B., & Andrasik, F. (1985). *Management of chronic headache: A psychological approach*. Elmsford, NY: Pergamon.

Blanchard, E. B., & Andrasik, F. (1987). Biofeedback treatment of vascular headache. In J. P. Hatch, J. D. Rugh, & J. G. Fisher (Eds.), *Biofeedback studies in clinical efficacy* (pp. 1–79). New York: Plenum.

Blanchard, E. B., Andrasik, F., Appelbaum, K. A., Evans, D. D., Jurish, S. E., Teders, S. J., Rodichok, L. D., & Barron, K. D. (1985). The efficacy and cost-effectiveness of minimal–therapist-contact, non-drug treatments of chronic migraine and tension headache. *Headache, 25*, 214–220.

Blanchard, E. B., Andrasik, F., Evans, D. D., & Hillhouse, J. (1985). Biofeedback and relaxation treatments for headache in the elderly: A caution and a challenge. *Biofeedback and Self-Regulation, 10*, 69–73.

Blanchard, E. B., Andrasik, F., Jurish, S. E., & Teders, S. J. (1982). The treatment of cluster headache with relaxation and thermal biofeedback. *Biofeedback and Self-Regulation, 7*, 185–191.

Blanchard, E. B., Andrasik, F., Neff, D. F., Arena, J. G., Ahles, T. A., Jurish, S. E., Pallmeyer, T. P., Saunders, N. L., Teders, S. J., Barron, K. D., & Rodichok, L. D. (1982). Biofeedback and relaxation training with three kinds of headache: Treatment effects and their prediction. *Journal of Consulting and Clinical Psychology, 50*, 562–575.

Blanchard, E. B., Andrasik, F., Neff, D. F., Teders, S. J., Pallmeyer, T. P., Arena, J. G., Jurish, S. E., Saunders, N. L., & Rodichok, L. D. (1982). Sequential comparisons of relaxation training and biofeedback in the treatment of three kinds of chronic headache or, the machines may be necessary some of the time. *Behaviour Research and Therapy, 20*, 469–481.

Blanchard, E. B., Appelbaum, K. A., Guarnieri, P., Morrill, B., & Dentinger, M. P. (1987). Five year prospective follow-up on the treatment of chronic headache with biofeedback and/or relaxation. *Headache, 27*, 580–583.

Blanchard, E. B., Appelbaum, K. A., Radnitz, C. L., Jaccard, J., & Dentinger, M. P. (1989). The refractory headache patient: I. Chronic, daily, high intensity headache. *Behaviour Research and Therapy, 27*, 403–410.

Blanchard, E. B., Appelbaum, K. A., Radnitz, C. L., Michultka, D. M., Morrill, B., Kirsch, C., Hillhouse, J., Evans, D. D., Guarnieri, P., Attanasio, V., Andrasik, F., Jaccard, J., & Dentinger, M. P. (1990). A placebo-controlled evaluation of abbreviated progressive muscle relaxation and relaxation combined with cognitive therapy in the treatment of tension headache. *Journal of Consulting and Clinical Psychology, 58*, 210–215.

Blanchard, E. B., Appelbaum, K. A., Radnitz, C. L., Morrill,

B., Michultka, D., Kirsch, C., Guarnieri, P., Hillhouse, J., Evans, D. D., Jaccard, J., & Barron, K. D. (1990). A controlled evaluation of thermal biofeedback and thermal biofeedback combined with cognitive therapy in the treatment of vascular headache. *Journal of Consulting and Clinical Psychology, 58,* 216–224.

Blanchard, E. B., & Epstein, L. H. (1978). *A biofeedback primer.* Reading, MA: Addison-Wesley.

Blanchard, E. B., Martin, D. J., & Dubbert, P. M. (1988). *Non-drug treatments for essential hypertension.* Elmsford, NY: Pergamon.

Blanchard, E. B., McCoy, G. C., McCaffrey, R. J., Musso, A., Wittrock, D. A., Berger, M., Gerardi, M. A., Pangburn, L., Khramelashvili, V. V., Aivasyan, T. A., & Salenko, B. B. (1988). The USSR–USA collaborative cross-cultural comparison of autogenic training and thermal biofeedback in the treatment of mild hypertension. *Health Psychology, 7,* 19–33.

Blanchard, E. B., McCoy, G. C., Musso, A., Gerardi, M. A., Pallmeyer, T. P., Gerardi, R. J., Cotch, P. A., Siracusa, K., & Andrasik, F. (1986). A controlled comparison of thermal biofeedback and relaxation training in the treatment of essential hypertension: I. Short-term and long-term outcome. *Behavior Therapy, 17,* 563–579.

Blanchard, E. B., Scharff, L., Payne, A., Schwarz, S. P., Suls, J. M., & Malamood, H. S. (1992). Prediction of outcome from cognitive-behavioral treatment of irritable bowel syndrome. *Behaviour Research and Therapy, 30,* 647–650.

Blanchard, E. B., Scharff, L., Schwarz, S. P., Suls, J. M., & Barlow, D. H. (1990). The role of anxiety and depression in the irritable bowel syndrome. *Behaviour Research and Therapy, 28,* 401–405.

Blanchard, E. B., & Schwartz, S. P. (1987). Adaptation of a multi-component treatment program for irritable bowel syndrome to a small group format. *Biofeedback and Self-Regulation, 12,* 63–69.

Blanchard, E. B., & Schwarz, S. P. (1988). Clinically significant changes in behavioral medicine. *Behavioral Assessment, 10,* 171–188.

Blanchard, E. B., Schwarz, S. P., & Radnitz, C. L. (1987). Psychological assessment and treatment of irritable bowel syndrome. *Behavior Modification, 12,* 31–38.

Blanchard, E. B., Schwarz, S. P., Suls, J. M., Gerardi, M. A., Scharff, L., Greene, B., Taylor, A. E., Berreman, C., & Malamood, H. S. (1992). Two controlled evaluations of multicomponent psychological treatment of irritable bowel syndrome. *Behaviour Research and Therapy, 30,* 175–189.

Blanchard, E. B., Taylor, A. E., & Dentinger, M. P. (1992). Preliminary results from the self-regulatory treatment of high medication consumption headache. *Biofeedback and Self-Regulation, 17,* 179–202.

Blanchard, E. B., Theobald, D. E., Williamson, D. A., Silver, B. V., & Brown, D. A. (1978). Temperature biofeedback in the treatment of migraine headaches. *Archives of General Psychiatry, 35,* 581–588.

Booth-Kewley, S., & Friedman, H. (1987). Psychological predictors of heart disease: A quantitative review. *Psychological Bulletin, 101,* 342–362.

Bootzin, R. R. (1972). Stimulus control treatment for insomnia [Summary]. *Proceedings of the 80th Annual Convention of the American Psychological Association, 7,* 395–396.

Bootzin, R. R., Engle-Friedman, M., & Hazelwood, L. (1983). Insomnia. In P. M. Lewinsohn & L. Teri (Eds), *Clinical geropsychology: New directions in assessment and treatment* (pp. 81–115). Elmsford, NY: Pergamon.

Bootzin, R. R., Epstein, D., & Wood, J. M. (1991). Stimulus control instructions. In P. Hauri (Ed.), *Case studies in insomnia* (pp. 19–28). New York: Plenum.

Bradley, L. A., Young, L. D., Anderson, K. O., Turner, R. A., Agudelo, C. A., McDaniel, L. K., Pisko, E. J., Semble, E. L., & Morgan, T. M. (1987). Effects of psychological therapy on pain behavior of rheumatoid arthritis patients: Treatment outcome and six-month follow-up. *Arthritis and Rheumatism, 30,* 1105–1114.

Brandt, E. N. (1983). Assistant Secretary for Health's advisory on treatment of mild hypertension. *FDA Drug Bulletin, 13,* 24–25.

Bray, G. A. (1986). Effects of obesity on health and happiness. In K. D. Brownell & J. P. Foreyt (Eds.), *Handbook of eating disorders: Physiology, psychology and treatment of obesity, anorexia, and bulimia* (pp. 3–44). New York: Basic Books.

Brownell, K. D., & Jeffrey, R. W. (1987). Improving long-term weight loss: Pushing the limits of treatment. *Behavior Therapy, 18,* 353–374.

Brownell, K. D., & Kramer, F. M. (1989). Behavioral management of obesity. *Medical Clinics of North America, 73,* 185–201.

Brownell, K. D., Marlatt, G. A., Lichtenstein, E., & Wilson, G. T. (1986). Understanding and preventing relapse. *American Psychologist, 41,* 765–782.

Brownell, K. D., & Wadden, T. A. (1992). Etiology and treatment of obesity: Toward understanding a serious, prevalent, and refractory disorder. *Journal of Consulting and Clinical Psychology, 60,* 505–517.

Budzynski, T. H. (1978). Biofeedback in the treatment of muscle-contraction (tension) headache. *Biofeedback and Self-Regulation, 3,* 409–434.

Budzynski, T. H., Stoyva, J. M., Adler, C. S., & Mullaney, D. J. (1973). EMG biofeedback and tension headache: A controlled outcome study. *Psychosomatic Medicine, 6,* 509–514.

Burish, T. G., Carey, M. P., Krozely, M. G., & Greco, F. A. (1987). Conditions and side effects induced by cancer chemotherapy: Prevention through behavioral treatment. *Journal of Consulting and Clinical Psychology, 55,* 42–48.

Capone, M. A., Good, R. S., Westie, K. S., & Jacobson, A. F. (1980). Psychosocial rehabilitation of gynecologic oncology patients. *Archives of Physical Medicine and Rehabilitation, 61,* 128–132.

Carey, M. P., & Burish, T. G. (1987). Providing relaxation training to cancer chemotherapy patients: Comparison of three delivery techniques. *Journal of Consulting and Clinical Psychology, 55,* 732–737.

Carey, M. P., & Burish, T. G. (1988). Etiology and treatment of the psychological side effects associated with cancer chemotherapy. *Psychological Bulletin, 104,* 307–325.

Coates, T. J., McKusick, L., Kuno, R., & Stites, D. P. (1989). Stress reduction training changed number of sexual partners but not immune function in men with HIV. *American Journal of Public Health, 79,* 885–887.

Cox, D. J., Freundlich, A., & Meyer, R. G. (1975). Differential effectiveness of electromyographic feedback, verbal relaxation instructions, and medication placebo with tension headaches. *Journal of Consulting and Clinical Psychology, 43,* 892–898.

Craighead, L. W., & Blum, M. D. (1989). Supervised exercise in behavioral treatment of obesity. *Behavior Therapy, 20,* 49–59.

Curry, S. J., Marlatt, G. A., Gordon, J., & Baer, J. S. (1988). A comparison of alternative theoretical approaches to smoking cessation and relapse. *Health Psychology, 7,* 545–556.

Dalessio, D. J., Kunzel, M., Sternbach, R., & Sovak, M. (1979). Conditioned adaptation-relaxation reflex in migraine therapy. *Journal of the American Medical Association, 242*, 2102–2104.

Davis, H. (1986). Effects of biofeedback and cognitive therapy on stress in patients with breast cancer. *Psychological Reports, 59*, 967–974.

Diamond, S., & Montrose, D. (1984). The value of biofeedback in the treatment of chronic headache: A four-year retrospective study. *Headache, 24*, 5–18.

DiClemente, C. C., Prochaska, J. O., Fairhurst, S. K., Velicer, W. F., Velasquez, M. M., & Rossi, J. S. (1991). The process of smoking cessation: An analysis of precontemplation, contemplations, and preparation stages of change. *Journal of Consulting and Clinical Psychology, 59*, 295–304.

Drossman, D. A., McKee, D. C., Sandler, R. S., Mitchell, C. M., Cramer, E. M., Lowman, B. C., & Burger, A. L. (1988). Psychological factors in the irritable bowel syndrome: A multivariate study of patients and non-patients with irritable bowel syndrome. *Gastroenterology, 95*, 701–708.

Drossman, D. A., Sandler, R. S., McKee, D. C., & Lovitz, A. J. (1982). Bowel patterns among subjects not seeking health care: Use of a questionnaire to identify a population with bowel dysfunction. *Gastroenterology, 83*, 529–534.

Dubbert, P. (1992). Exercise in behavioral medicine. *Journal of Consulting and Clinical Psychology, 60*, 613–618.

Durand, V. M., & Mindell, J. A. (1990). Behavioral treatment of multiple childhood sleep disorders. *Behavior Modification, 14*, 37–49.

Ellis, A. (1962). *Reason and emotion in psychotherapy*. New York: Lyle Stuart.

Engstrom, D. (1983). Cognitive behavioral therapy methods in chronic pain treatment. In J. J. Bonica (Ed.), *Advances in pain research and therapy* (Vol. 5, pp. 829–838). New York: Raven Press.

Espie, C. A., Brooks, D. N., & Lindsay, W. R. (1989). An evaluation of tailored psychological treatment of insomnia. *Journal of Behavior Therapy and Experimental Psychiatry, 20*, 143–153a.

Espie, C. A., Lindsay, W. R., Brooks, D. N., Hood, E. H., & Turvey, T. (1989). A controlled comparative investigation of psychological treatments of chronic sleep-onset insomnia. *Behaviour Research and Therapy, 27*, 79–88b.

Farquhar, J. W., Fortmann, S. P., Flora, J. A., Taylor, D. B., Haskell, W. L., Williams, P. T., Maccoby, N. & Woods, P. D. (1990). Effects of community-wide education on cardiovascular disease risk factors. *Journal of the American Medical Association, 264*, 359–365.

Fawzy, F. I., Cousins, N., Fawzy, N., Kemeny, M. E., Elashoff, R., & Morton, D. (1990). A structured psychiatric intervention for cancer patients: I. Changes over time in methods of coping and affective disturbance. *Archives of General Psychiatry, 47*, 720–725.

Fawzy, F. I., Kemeny, M. E., Fawzy, N., Elashoff, R., Morton, D., Cousins, N., & Fahey, J. L. (1990). A structured psychiatric intervention for cancer patients: I. Changes over time in immunological measures. *Archives of General Psychiatry, 47*, 729–735.

Ferguson, A., Sircus, W., & Eastwood, N. A. (1977). Frequency of "functional" gastrointestinal disorders. *Lancet, 2*, 613–614.

Fiore, M. C., Novotny, T. F., Pierce, J. P., Giovino, G. A., Hatziandreau, E. J., Newcomb, P. A., Surawicz, T. S., & Davis, R. M. (1990). Methods used to quit smoking in the United States: Do cessation programs help? *Journal of the American Medical Association, 263*, 2760–2765.

Flegal, K. M., Harlan, W. R., & Landix, J. R. (1988). Secular trends in body mass index and skinfold thickness with socioeconomic factors in young adult women. *American Journal of Clinical Nutrition, 48*, 535–543.

Ford, D. E., & Kamerow, D. B. (1989). Epidemiologic study of sleep disturbances and psychiatric disorders. *Journal of the American Medical Association, 262*, 1479–1484.

Ford, M. J., Miller, P. M., Eastwood, J., & Eastwood, M. A. (1987). Life events, psychiatric illness and the irritable bowel syndrome. *Gut, 28*, 160–165.

Fordyce, W. E. (1976). *Behavioral methods for chronic pain and illness*. St. Louis, MO: C.V. Mosby.

Foreyt, J. P., & Goodrick, G. K. (1991). Factors common to successful therapy for the obese patient. *Medicine and Science in Sports and Exercise, 23*, 292–297.

Friar, L. R., & Beatty, J. (1976). Migraine: Management by trained control of vasoconstriction. *Journal of Consulting and Clinical Psychology, 44*, 46–53.

Friedman, L., Bliwise, D. L., Yesavage, J. A., & Salom, S. R. (1991). A preliminary study comparing sleep restriction and relaxation treatments for insomnia in older adults. *Journal of Gerontology, 46*, 1–8.

Friedman, M., & Rosenman, R. H. (1974). *Type A behavior and your heart*. New York: Knopf.

Friedman, M., Thoresen, C. E., Gill, J., Ulmer, D., Powell, L. H., Price, V. A., Brown, B., Thompson, L., Rabin, D. D., Breall, W. S., Bourg, W., Levy, R., & Dixon T. (1986). Alteration of Type A behavior and its effect on cardiac recurrences in post-myocardial infarction patients: Summary results of the Recurrent Coronary Prevention Project. *American Heart Journal, 112*, 653–665.

Gauthier, J., Bois, R., Allaire, D., & Drolet, M. (1981). Evaluation of skin temperature biofeedback training at two different sites for migraine. *Journal of Behavioral Medicine, 4*, 407–419.

Gauthier, J .G., & Carrier, S. (1991). Long-term effects of biofeedback on migraine headache: A prospective follow-up study. *Headache, 31*, 605–612.

Gauthier, J., Doyn, J., LaCroix, R., & Drolet, M. (1983). Blood volume pulse biofeedback in the treatment of migraine headache: A controlled evaluation. *Biofeedback and Self-Regulation, 8*, 427–442.

Gill, J. S., Price, V. A., Friedman, M., Thoresen, E. E., Powell, L. H., Ulmer, D., Brown, B., & Drews, F. R. (1985). Reduction in Type A behavior in healthy, middle-aged American military officers. *American Heart Journal, 110*, 503–514.

Glasgow, M. S., Engel, B. T., & D'Lugoff, B. C. (1989). Control study of a standardized behavioral stepped treatment for hypertension. *Psychosomatic Medicine 51*, 10–26.

Glovinsky, P. B., & Spielman, A. J. (1991). Sleep restriction therapy. In P. Hauri (Ed.), *Case studies in insomnia* (pp. 49–63). New York: Plenum.

Goldstein, I. B., Shapiro, D., Thananopavaren, C., & Sambi, M. P. (1982). Comparison of drug and behavioral treatments of essential hypertension. *Health Psychology, 1*, 7–26.

Gordon, W. A., Freidenbergs, I., Diller, L., Hibberd, M., Wold, C., Levine, L., Lipkins, R., Ezrachi, O., & Lucido, D. (1980). Efficacy of psychosocial intervention with cancer patients. *Journal of Consulting and Clinical Psychology, 48*, 743–759.

Grilo, C. M., Shiffman, S., & Wing, R. R. (1989). Relapse crises and coping among dieters. *Journal of Consulting and Clinical Psychology, 57*, 488–495.

Guarnieri, P., & Blanchard, E. B. (1990). Evaluation of home-based thermal biofeedback treatment of pediatric migraine headache. *Biofeedback and Self-Regulation, 15*, 179–184.

Guthrie, E., Creed, F., Dawson, D., & Tonenson, B. (1991). A controlled trial of psychological treatment for the irritable bowel syndrome. *Gastroenterology, 100*, 450–457.

Haber, J. D., Kuczmierczyk, A. R., & Adams, H. E. (1985).

Tension headaches: Muscle overactivity or psychogenic pain. *Headache, 25,* 23–29.

Hale, W. E., May, F. E., Marks, R. G., Moore, M. P., & Stewart, R. B. (1987). Headache in the elderly: An evaluation of risk factors. *Headache, 27,* 272–276.

Harvey, R. F., Hinton, R. A., Gunary, R. M., & Barry, R. E. (1989). Individual and group hypnotherapy in treatment of refractory irritable bowel syndrome. *Lancet, i,* 424–425.

Hauri, P. (1982). *The sleep disorders.* Kalamazoo, MI: Upjohn.

Hauri, P. (1991). *Case studies in insomnia.* New York: Plenum.

Haynes, S. N., Cuevas, J., & Gannon, L. R. (1982). The psychophysiological etiology of muscle-contraction headache. *Headache, 22,* 122–132.

Heinrich, R. L., Cohen, M. J., Naliboff, B. D., Collins, G. A., & Bonebakker, A. D. (1985). Comparing physical and behavior therapy for chronic low back pain on physical abilities, psychological distress, and patients' perceptions. *Journal of Behavioral Medicine, 8,* 61–78.

Hoelscher, T. J., & Edinger, J. D. (1988). Treatment of sleep-maintenance insomnia in older adults: Sleep period reduction, sleep education, and modified stimulus control. *Psychology and Aging, 3,* 258–263.

Holroyd, K. A., & Andrasik, F. (1978). Coping and the self-control of chronic tension headache. *Journal of Consulting and Clinical Psychology, 5,* 1036–1045.

Holroyd, K. A., & Andrasik, F. (1982). A cognitive-behavioral approach to recurrent tension and migraine headache. In P. E. Kendall (Ed.), *Advances in cognitive-behavioral research and therapy* (Vol. 1, pp. 275–320). New York: Academic.

Holroyd, K. A., Andrasik, F., & Noble, J. (1980). Comparison of EMG biofeedback and a credible pseudotherapy in treating tension headache. *Journal of Behavioral Medicine, 3,* 29–39.

Holroyd, K. A., Andrasik, F., & Westbrook, T. (1977). Cognitive control of tension headache. *Cognitive Therapy and Research, 1,* 121–133.

Holroyd, K. A., Holm, J. E., Hursey, K. G., Penzien, D. B., Cordingley, G. E., Theofanous, A. G., Richardson, S. C., & Tobin, D. L. (1988). Recurrent vascular headache: Home-based behavioral treatment versus abortive pharmacological treatment. *Journal of Consulting and Clinical Psychology, 56,* 218–223.

Holroyd, K. A., Nash, J. M., Pingel, J. D., Cordingley, G. E., & Jerome, A. (1991). A comparison of pharmacological (Amitriptyline HCL) and nonpharmacological (Cognitive-Behavioral) therapies for chronic tension headaches. *Journal of Consulting and Clinical Psychology, 59,* 387–393.

Hovell, M. F. (1982). The experimental evidence for weight-loss treatment of essential hypertension: A critical review. *American Journal of Public Health, 72,* 359–362.

Hudzinski, L. G., & Lawrence, G. S. (1988). Significance of EMG surface electrode placement models and headache findings. *Headache, 28,* 30–35.

Hughes, J. R. (1991). Combined psychological and pharmacological treatment of smoking: A critical review. *Journal of Substance Abuse, 3,* 337–350.

Hypertension Prevention Trial Research Group: The Hypertension Prevention Trial (HPT). (1990). Three-year effects of dietary changes on blood pressure. *Archives of Internal Medicine, 150,* 153–162.

Jacob, R. G., Chesney, M. A., Williams, D. M., Ding, Y., & Shapiro, A. P. (1991). Relaxation therapy for hypertension: Design effects and treatment effects. *Annals of Behavioral Medicine, 13,* 5–17.

Jacob, R. G., Kraemer, H. C., & Agras, W. S. (1977). Relaxation therapy in the treatment of hypertension: A review. *Archives of General Psychiatry, 34,* 1417–1427.

Jacob, R. G., Shapiro, A. P., O'Hara, P., Portser, S., Kruger, A., Gatsonis, C., & Ding, Y. (1992). Relaxation therapy for hypertension: Setting-specific effects. *Psychosomatic Medicine, 54,* 87–101.

Jacob, R. G., Shapiro, A. P., Reeves, R. A., Johnsen, A. M., McDonald, R. H., & Coburn, P. C. (1986). Relaxation therapy for hypertension: Comparison of effects with concomitant placebo, diuretic and B-blocker. *Archives of Internal Medicine, 146,* 2335–2340.

Jacobson, E. (1938). *Progressive relaxation.* Chicago: University of Chicago Press.

Jeffery, R. W. (1991). Weight management and hypertension. *Annals of Behavioral Medicine, 13,* 18–22.

Jeffery, R. W., Gillum, R., Gerber, W. B., Jacobs, D., Elmer, P. J., & Prineas, R. J. (1983). Weight and sodium reduction for the prevention of hypertension: A comparison of group treatment and individual counseling. *American Public Health Journal, 73,* 691–693.

Joint National Committee on Detection, Evaluation, and Treatment of High Blood Pressure. (1980). The 1980 Report of the Joint National Committee on Detection, Evaluation and Treatment of High Blood Pressure. *Archives of Internal Medicine, 140,* 1280–1285.

Joint National Committee on Detection, Evaluation, and Treatment of High Blood Pressure. (1984). The 1984 Report of the Joint National Committee on Detection, Evaluation and Treatment of High Blood Pressure. *Archives of Internal Medicine, 144,* 1045–1057.

Joint National Committee on Detection, Evaluation, and Treatment of High Blood Pressure. (1988). The 1988 Report of the Joint National Committee on Detection, Evaluation and Treatment of High Blood Pressure. *Archives of Internal Medicine, 148,* 1023–1038.

Kabela, E., Blanchard, E. B., Appelbaum, K. A., & Nicholson, N. (1989). Self-regulatory treatment of headache in the elderly. *Biofeedback and Self-Regulation, 14,* 219–228.

Kaplan, N. M. (1986). *Clinical Hypertension* (4th ed.). Baltimore: Williams & Wilkins.

Kaufmann, P. G., Chesney, M. A., & Weiss, S. M. (1991). Behavioral medicine in hypertension: Time for new frontiers? *Annals of Behavioral Medicine, 13,* 3–4.

Kaufmann, P. G., Jacob, R. G., Ewart, C. K., Chesney, M. A., Muenz, L. R., Doub, N., Mercer, W., & HIPP Investigators. (1988). Hypertension intervention pooling project. *Health Psychology, 7,* (Suppl.), 209–224.

Kayman, S., Bruvold, W., & Stern, J. S. (1990). Maintenance and relapse after weight loss in women: Behavioral aspects. *American Journal of Clinical Nutrition, 52,* 800–807.

Keefe, F. J., Dunsmore, J., & Burnett, R. (1992). Behavioral and cognitive-behavioral approaches to chronic pain: Recent advances and future directions. *Journal of Consulting and Clinical Psychology, 60,* 528–536.

Kiecolt-Glaser, J. K., & Glaser, R. (1992). Psychoneuroimmunology: Can psychological interventions modulate immunity? *Journal of Consulting and Clinical Psychology, 60,* 569–575.

Kiecolt-Glaser, J. K., Glaser, R., Willinger, D., Stout, J., Messick, G., Sheppard, S., Ricker, D., Romisher, S. C., Briner, W., Bonnel, G., & Donnerberg, R. (1985). Psychosocial enhancement of immunocompetence in a geriatric population. *Health Psychology, 4,* 25–41.

Kostis, J. B., Rosen, R. C., Brondolo, E., Taska, L., Smith, D. E., & Wilson, A. C. (1992). Superiority of nonpharmacological therapy compared to propranolol and placebo in men with mild hypertension: A randomized, prospective trial. *American Heart Journal, 123,* 466–474.

Kudrow, L. (1980). *Cluster headache: Mechanisms and management.* New York: Oxford University Press.

Kudrow, L. (1982). Paradoxical effects of frequent analgesic use. In M. Critchley et al. (Eds.), *Advances in neurology, 33*, 335–341. New York: Raven Press.

Lacks, P. (1987). *Behavioral treatment for persistent insomnia.* Elmsford, NY: Pergamon.

Lacks, P., Bertelson, A. D., Gans, L., & Kunkel, J. (1983). The effectiveness of three behavioral treatments for different degrees of sleep onset insomnia. *Behavior Therapy, 14*, 593–605a.

Lacks, P., Bertelson, A. D., Sugerman, J. L., & Kunkel, J. (1983). The treatment of sleep maintenance insomnia with stimulus control techniques. *Behaviour Research and Therapy, 21*, 291–295b.

Lacks, P., & Powlishta, K. (1989). Improvement following behavioral treatment for insomnia: Clinical significance, long-term maintenance, and predictors of outcome. *Behavior Therapy, 20*, 117–134.

Lacks, P., & Morin, C. M. (1992). Recent advances in the assessment and treatment of insomnia. *Journal of Consulting and Clinical Psychology, 60*, 586–594.

LaCroix, A. Z., Lang, J., Scherr, P., Wallace, R. B., Cornoni-Huntley, J., Berkman, L., Curb, D. J., Evans, D., & Hennekens, C. H. (1991). Smoking and mortality among older men and women in three communities. *New England Journal of Medicine, 324*, 1619–1625.

Lake, A., Raney, J., & Papsdorf, J. D. (1979). Biofeedback and rational-emotive therapy in the management of migraine headache. *Journal of Applied Behavior Analysis, 12*, 127–140.

Lando, H. A. (1977). Successful treatment of smokers with a broad-spectrum behavioral approach. *Journal of Consulting and Clinical Psychology, 45*, 361–366.

Lando, H. A., & McGovern, P. G. (1985). Nicotine fading as a nonaversive alternative in a broad-spectrum treatment for eliminating smoking. *Addictive Behaviors, 10*, 153–161.

Lando, H. A., McGovern, P. G., & Sipfle, C. (1989). Public service application of an effective clinic approach to smoking cessation. *Health Education Research, 4*, 103–109.

Langford, H. G., Blaufox, D., Oberman, A., Hawkins, M., Curb, J. D., Cutter, G. R., Wassertheil-Smoller, S., Pressel, S., Babock, C., Abernethy, J. D., Hotchkiss, J., & Taylor, M. (1985). Dietary therapy slows the return of hypertension after stopping prolonged medication. *Journal of the American Medical Association, 253*, 657–664.

LaPerriere, A. R., Antoni, M. H., Schneiderman, N., Ironson, G., Klimas, N., Caralis, P., & Fletcher, M. A. (1990). Exercise intervention attenuates emotional distress and natural killer cell decrements following notification of positive serologic status for HIB-1. *Biofeedback and Self-Regulation, 15*, 229–242.

LaPerriere, A., Fletcher, M. A., Antoni, M. H., Ironson, G., Klimas, N., & Schneiderman, N. (1991). Aerobic exercise training in an AIDS risk group. *International Journal of Sports Medicine, 12*, S53–S57.

Lee, D. D., DeQuattro, V., Allen, J., Kimura, S., Aleman, E., Konugres, G., & Davison, G. (1988). Behavioral vs. B-blocker therapy in patients with primary hypertension: Effects on blood pressure, left ventricular function and mass, and the pressor surge of social stress anger. *American Heart Journal, 116*, 637–644.

Levenkron, J. C., Cohen, J. D., Mueller, H. S., & Fisher, E. B. (1983). Modifying the Type A coronary-prone behavior pattern. *Journal of Consulting and Clinical Psychology, 51*, 192–204.

Levenkron, J. C., & Moore, G. L. (1988). Type A behavior pattern: Issues for intervention research. *Annals of Behavior Medicine, 10*, 78–83.

Lichtenstein, E., & Glasgow, R. E. (1992). Smoking cessation: What have we learned over the past decade? *Journal of Consulting and Clinical Psychology, 60*, 518–527.

Lichtenstein, E., Glasgow, R. E., & Abrams, D. B. (1986). Social support in smoking cessation: In search of effective interventions. *Behavior Therapy, 17*, 607–619.

Lichtenstein, E., Wallack, L., & Pechacek, T. F. (1990–1991). Introduction to the Community Intervention Trial for Smoking Cessation (COMMIT). *International Quarterly of Community Health Education, 11*, 173–185.

Lichstein, K. L., Johnson, R. S., Womack, T. D., Dean, J. E., & Childers, C. K. (1990, June). Relaxation therapy for polypharmacy use in elderly insomniacs and noninsomniacs. In T. L. Rosenthal (Chair), *Reducing medication in geriatric populations.* Symposium conducted at the meeting of the First International Congress of Behavioral Medicine, Uppsala, Sweden.

Liss, J. L., Alpers, D. H., & Woodruff, R. A. (1973). The irritable colon syndrome and psychiatric illness. *Diseases of the Nervous System, 34*, 151–157.

Lisspers, J., & Ost, L. G. (1990). Long-term follow-up with migraine treatment: Do the effects remain up to six years? *Behaviour Research and Therapy, 28*, 313–322.

Lydiard, R. D., Laraia, M. T., Howell, E. F., & Ballenger, J. C. (1986). Can panic disorder present as irritable bowel syndrome? *Journal of Clinical Psychiatry, 47*, 470–473.

Lynch, P. N., & Zamble, E. (1989). A controlled behavioral treatment study of irritable bowel syndrome. *Behavior Therapy, 20*, 509–523.

Marcus, M. D., Wing, R. R., Ewing, L., Kern, E., McDermott, M., & Gooding, W. (1990). A double-blind placebo-controlled trial of fluoxetine plus behavior modification in the treatment of obese binge eaters. *American Journal of Psychiatry, 147*, 876–881.

Marcus, M. D., Wing, R. R., & Hopkins, J. (1988). Obese binge eaters: Affect, cognitions, and response to behavioral weight control. *Journal of Consulting and Clinical Psychology, 56*, 433–439.

Marlatt, G. A., & Gordon, J. R. (1985). *Relapse prevention: Maintenance strategies in the treatment of addictive behaviors.* New York: Guilford.

Martin, J. E., & Dubbert, P. M. (1985). Exercise in hypertension. *Annals of Behavioral Medicine, 7*, 13–18.

Martin, J. E., Dubbert, P. M., & Cushman, W. C. (1990). Controlled trial of aerobic exercise in hypertension. *Circulation, 81*, 1560–1567.

Martin, P. R., & Mathews, A. M. (1978). Tension headaches: Psychophysiological investigation and treatment. *Journal of Psychosomatic Research, 22*, 389–399.

Mathew, N. T. (1981). Prophylaxis of migraine and mixed headache. A randomized controlled study. *Headache, 21*, 105–109.

Mathew, N. T., Kurman, R., & Perez, F. (1990). Drug induced refractory headache—Clinical features and management. *Headache, 30*, 634–638.

Matthews, K. A. (1988). CHD and Type A behaviors: Update on an alternative to the Booth-Kewley and Friedman quantitative review. *Psychological Bulletin, 104*, 373–380.

Mayer, J. A., & Frederiksen, L. W. (1986). Encouraging long-term compliance with breast self-examination: The evaluation of prompting strategies. *Journal of Behavioral Medicine, 9*, 179–189.

McCaffrey, R. J., & Blanchard, E. B. (1985). Stress management approaches to the treatment of essential hypertension. *Annals of Behavioral Medicine, 7*, 5–12.

McCoy, G. C., Fein, S., Blanchard, E. B., Wittrock, D. A., McCaffrey, R. J., & Pangburn, L. (1988). End organ changes associated with the self-regulatory treatment of mild essential hypertension. *Biofeedback and Self-Regulation*, *13*, 39–46.

McCracken, L. M., (1991). Cognitive-behavioral treatment of rheumatoid arthritis: A preliminary review of efficacy and methodology. *Annals of Behavioral Medicine*, *13*, 57–65.

McGrath, P. J., Humphreys, P., Goodman, J. T., & Keene, D., Firestone, P., Jacob, P., & Cunningham, S. J. (1988). Relaxation prophylaxis for childhood migraine: A randomized placebo-controlled trial. *Developmental Medicine and Child Neurology*, *30*, 626–631.

Michultka, D. M., Blanchard, E. B., Appelbaum, K. A., Jaccard, J., & Dentinger, M. P. (1989). The refractory headache patient: II. High medication consumption (analgesic rebound) headache. *Behaviour Research and Therapy*, *27*, 411–420.

Miles, L. E., & Dement, W. C. (1980). Sleep and aging. *Sleep*, *3*, 119–220.

Milne, B., Joachim, G., & Niedhardt, J. (1986). A stress management programme for inflammatory bowel disease patients. *Journal of Advanced Nursing*, *11*(5), 561–567.

Mitchell, K. R. (1986). Peripheral temperature autoregulation and its effect on the symptoms of rheumatoid arthritis. *Scandinavian Journal of Behavioral Therapy*, *15*, 55–64.

Morawetz, D. (1989). Behavioral self-help treatment for insomnia: A controlled evaluation. *Behavior Therapy*, *20*, 365–379.

Morin, C. M., & Azrin, N. H. (1987). Stimulus control and imagery training in treating sleep maintenance insomnia. *Journal of Consulting and Clinical Psychology*, *55*, 260–262.

Morin, C. M., & Azrin, N. H. (1988). Behavioral and cognitive treatments of geriatric insomnia. *Journal of Consulting and Clinical Psychology*, *45*, 748–753.

Morin, C. M., Culbert, J. P., Kowatch, R. A., & Walton, E. (1989). Efficacy of cognitive-behavioral treatments for insomnia: A meta-analytic review. *Sleep Research*, *18*, 272a.

Morin, C. M., Jones, S., Stone, J., & Mercer, J. (1991, June). *Cognitive-behavioral treatment of persistent insomnia: Preliminary data from a clinical replication series.* Paper presented at the annual meeting of the Association of Professional Sleep Societies, Toronto, Canada.

Morin, C. M., & Kwentus, J. A. (1988). Behavioral and pharmacological treatments for insomnia. *Annals of Behavioral Medicine*, *10*, 91–100.

Morrill, B., & Blanchard, E. B. (1989). Two studies of the potential mechanisms of action in the thermal biofeedback treatment of vascular headache. *Headache*, *29*, 169–176.

Morrow, G. R., & Morrell, C. (1982). Behavioral treatment for the anticipatory nausea induced by cancer chemotherapy. *New England Journal of Medicine*, *307*, 1476–1480.

Murphy, A. I., Lehrer, P. M., & Jurish, S. (1990). Cognitive coping skills training and relaxation training as treatments for tension headaches. *Behavior Therapy*, *21*, 89–98.

Musso, A., Blanchard, E. B., & McCoy, G. C. (1991). Evaluation of thermal biofeedback treatment of hypertension using 24-hour ambulatory blood pressure monitoring. *Behaviour Research and Therapy*, *29*, 469–478.

National Institute of Health. (1991). Consensus development conference statement: The treatment of sleep disorders of older people. *Sleep*, *14*, 169–177.

Neff, D. F., & Blanchard, E. B. (1987). A multicomponent treatment for irritable bowel syndrome. *Behavior Therapy*, *18*, 70–83.

Nicholson, N. L., & Blanchard, E. B. (1993). A controlled evaluation of behavioral treatment of chronic headache in the elderly. *Behavior Therapy*.

Nunes, E. V., Frank, K. A., & Kornfeld, D. S. (1987). Psychologic treatment for Type A behavior pattern and for coronary heart disease: A meta-analysis of the literature. *Psychosomatic Medicine*, *48*, 159–173.

Ockene, J. K. (1987a). Smoking intervention: The expanding role of the physician. *American Journal of Public Health*, *77*, 782–783.

Ockene, J. K. (1987b). Physician delivered interventions for smoking cessation: Strategies for increasing effectiveness. *Preventive Medicine*, *7*, 723–737.

O'Leary, A., Shoor, S., Lorig, K., & Holman, H. R. (1988). A cognitive-behavioral treatment for rheumatoid arthritis. *Health Psychology*, *7*, 527–544.

Parker, J. C., Frank, R. G., Beck, N. C., Smarr, K. L., Buescher, K. L., Phillips, L. R., Smith, E. L., Anderson, S. K., & Walker, S. E. (1988). Pain management in rheumatoid arthritis patients: A cognitive-behavioral approach. *Arthritis and Rheumatism*, *31*, 593–601.

Patel, C., Marmot, M. G., Terry, D. J., Carruthers, M., Hunt, B., & Patel, M. (1985). Trial of relaxation and reducing coronary risk: Four-year follow-up. *British Medical Journal*, *286*, 1103–1106.

Perri, M. G., Nezu, A. M., Patti, E. T., & McCann, K. L. (1989). Effect of length of treatment on weight loss. *Journal of Consulting and Clinical Psychology*, *57*, 450–452.

Philips, C. (1978). Tension headache: Theoretical problems. *Behaviour Research and Therapy*, *16*, 249–261.

Philips, C. (1987). The effects of behavioural treatment on chronic pain. *Behaviour Research and Therapy*, *25*, 365–377.

Pomerleau, O. F., & Roden, J. (1986). Behavioral medicine and health psychology. In A. E. Bergin & S. L. Garfield (Eds.), *Handbook of psychotherapy and behavior change* (3rd ed., pp. 483–522). New York: Wiley.

Price, V. A. (1988). Research and clinical issues in treatment of Type A behavior. In B. K. Houston & C. R. Snyder (Eds.), *Type A behavior pattern: Research, theory and intervention* (pp. 275–311). New York: Wiley.

Richman, N., Douglas, J., Hunt, H., Lansdown, R., & Levere, R. (1985). Behavioural methods in the treatment of sleep disorders: A pilot study. *Journal of Child Psychology and Psychiatry*, *26*, 581–590.

Richter-Heinrich, E., Homuth, V., Heinrich, B., Schmidt, K. H., Wiedemann, R., & Gohlke, H. R. (1981). Long term application of behavioral treatments in essential hypertension. *Psychology and Behavior*, *26*, 915–920.

Rosenman, R. H., Brand, R. J., Jenkins, D., Friedman, M., Straus, R., & Wurm, M. (1975). Coronary heart disease in the Western Collaborative Group Study: Final follow-up experience of 8½ years. *Journal of the American Medical Association*, *233*, 872–877.

Roskies, E., Seraganian, P., Oseasohn, R., Hanley, J. A., Collee, R., Martin, N., & Smilga, C. (1986). The Montreal Type A Intervention Project: Major findings. *Health Psychology*, *5*, 45–69.

Sanavio, E. (1988). Pre-sleep cognitive intrusions and treatment of onset-insomnia. *Behaviour Research and Therapy*, *26*, 451–459.

Sanavio, E., Vidotto, G., Bettinardi, O., Roletto, T., & Zorzi, M. (1990). Behavior therapy for DIMS: Comparison of three treatment procedures with follow-up. *Behavioural Psychotherapy*, *18*, 151–167.

Sargent, J. D., Green, E. E., & Walter, E. D. (1973). Preliminary report on the use of autogenic feedback training in the treatment of migraine and tension headaches. *Psychosomatic Medicine*, *35*, 129–135.

Sargent, J., Solbach, P., Coyne, L., Spohn, H., & Fegerson, J. (1986). Results of a controlled, experimental, outcome study of non-drug treatments for the control of migraine headaches. *Journal of Behavioral Medicine, 9,* 291–323.

Schlundt, D. G., & Langford, H. G. (1985). Dietary approaches to the treatment of hypertension. *Annals of Behavioral Medicine, 7,* 19–24.

Schoicket, S. L., Bertelson, A. D., & Lacks, P. (1988). Is sleep hygiene a sufficient treatment for sleep maintenance insomnia? *Behavior Therapy, 19,* 183–190.

Schwarz, S. P., & Blanchard, E. B. (1990). Inflammatory bowel disease: A review of the psychological assessment and treatment literature. *Annals of Behavioral Medicine, 12,* 95–105.

Schwarz, S. P., & Blanchard, E. B. (1991). Evaluation of a psychological treatment for inflammatory bowel disease. *Behaviour Research and Therapy, 29,* 167–177.

Schwarz, S. P., Taylor, A. E., Scharff, L., & Blanchard, E. B. (1990). A four-year follow-up of behaviorally treated irritable bowel syndrome patients. *Behaviour Research and Therapy, 28,* 331–335.

Shah, M., Hannan, P. J., & Jeffery, R. W. (1991). Secular trend in body mass index in the adult population of three communities in the upper mid-western part of the USA: The Minnesota Heart Health Program. *International Journal of Obesity, 15,* 499–503.

Shaw, L., & Ehrlich, A. (1987). Relaxation training as a treatment for chronic pain caused by ulcerative colitis. *Pain, 29,* 287–293.

Siegel, B. S. (1986). *Love, medicine and miracles.* New York: Harper & Row.

Siegel, W. C., & Blumenthal, J. A. (1991). The role of exercise in the prevention and treatment of hypertension. *Annals of Behavioral Medicine, 13,* 23–30.

Sorbi, M., & Tellegen, B. (1984). Multimodal migraine treatment: Does thermal feedback add to the outcome? *Headache, 24,* 249–255.

Sovak, M., Kunzel, M., Sternbach, R. A., & Dalessio, D. J. (1981). Mechanism of the biofeedback therapy of migraine: Volitional manipulation of the psychophysiological background. *Headache, 21,* 89–92.

Spiegel, D., Bloom, J. R., Kraemer, H. C., & Gottheil, E. (1989). Effect of psychosocial treatment on survival of patients with metastatic breast cancer. *Lancet,* 888–891.

Spiegel, D., Bloom, J. R., & Yalom, I. (1981). Group support for patients with metastatic cancer: A randomized outcome study. *Archives of General Psychiatry, 38,* 527–533.

Stuart, R. B. (1967) Behavioral control of overeating. *Behaviour Research Therapy, 5,* 357–365.

Stunkard, A. J., Harris, J. R., Pedersen, N. L., & McClean, G. E. (1990). A separated twin study of the body mass index. *New England Journal of Medicine, 322,* 1483–1487.

Stunkard, A. J., Sorenson, T. I. A., Hanis, C., Teasdale, T. W., Chakraborty, R., Schull, W. J., & Schlusinger, F. (1986). An adoption study of human obesity. *New England Journal of Medicine, 314,* 193–198.

Svedlund, J., Sjodin, I., Ottosson, J.-O., & Dotevall, G. (1983). Controlled study of psychotherapy in irritable bowel syndrome. *Lancet, ii,* 589–592.

Telch, C. F., & Telch, M. J. (1986). Group coping skills instruction and supportive group therapy for cancer patients: A comparison of strategies. *Journal of Consulting and Clinical Psychology, 54,* 802–808.

Thoresen, C. E. (1990, June). *The Recurrent Coronary Prevention Project: Findings at 8½ years.* Invited paper, First International Congress of Behavioral Medicine, Uppsala, Sweden.

Thoresen, C. E., & Powell, L. H. (1992). Type A behavior pattern: New perspectives on theory, assessment and intervention. *Journal of Consulting and Clinical Psychology, 60,* 595–604.

Tobin, D. L., Holroyd, K. A., Baker, A., Reynolds, R. V. C., & Holm, J. E. (1988). Development in clinical trial of a minimal contact, cognitive-behavioral treatment for tension headache. *Cognitive Therapy and Research, 12,* 325–339.

Tonnesen, P., Norregaard, J., Simonsen, K., & Sawe, U. (1991). A double-blind trial of a 16-hour transdermal nicotine patch in smoking cessation. *New England Journal of Medicine, 325,* 311–315.

Transdermal Nicotine Research Group. (1991). Transdermal nicotine for smoking cessation: Six-month results from two multicenter, controlled clinical trials. *Journal of the American Medical Association, 266,* 3133–3138.

Turk, D. C., & Fernandez, E. (1990). On the putative uniqueness of cancer pain: Do psychological principles apply? *Behaviour Research and Therapy, 28,* 1–13.

Turk, D., Meichenbaum, D., & Genest, M. (1983). *Pain and behavioral medicine: A cognitive-behavioral perspective.* New York: Guilford.

Turner, J. A. (1982). Comparison of group progressive-relaxation training and cognitive-behavioral group therapy for chronic low back pain. *Journal of Consulting and Clinical Psychology, 50,* 757–765.

Turner, J. A., & Clancy, S. (1988). Comparison of operant-behavioral and cognitive-behavioral group treatment for chronic low back pain. *Journal of Consulting and Clinical Psychology, 56,* 261–266.

Turner, J. A., Clancy, S., McQuade, K. J., & Cardenas, D. D. (1990). Effectiveness of behavioral therapy for chronic low back pain: A component analysis. *Journal of Consulting and Clinical Psychology, 58,* 573–579.

U.S. Department of Health and Human Services. (1988). *The health consequences of smoking: Nicotine addiction —A report of the Surgeon General* (DHHS Publication No. 88–8306). Washington, DC: U.S. Government Printing Office.

Wadden, T. A., Sternberg, J. A., Letizia, J. A., Stunkard, A. J., & Foster, G. D. (1989). Treatment of obesity by very low calorie diet, behavior therapy, and their combination: A five-year perspective. *International Journal of Obesity, 13,* 39–46.

Wadden, T. A., & Stunkard, A. J. (1986). Controlled trial of very-low-calorie diet, behavior therapy, and their combination in the treatment of obesity. *Journal of Consulting and Clinical Psychology, 54,* 482–488.

Wald, A., Chandra, R., Gabel, S., & Chiponis, D. (1987). Evaluation of biofeedback in childhood encopresis. *Journal of Pediatric Gastroenterology and Nutrition, 6,* 554–558.

Wender, P. H., & Kalm, M. (1983). Prevalence of attention deficit disorder, residual type, and other psychiatric disorders in patients with irritable colon syndrome. *American Journal of Psychiatry, 140,* 1579–1582.

Whitehead, W. E. (1992). Behavioral medicine approaches to gastrointestinal disorders. *Journal of Consulting and Clinical Psychology, 60,* 605–612.

Whitehead, W. E., & Bosmajian, L. S. (1982). Behavioral medicine approaches to gastrointestinal disorders. *Journal of Consulting and Clinical Psychology, 50,* 972–983.

Whitehead, W. E., Bosmajian, L., Zonderman, A. B., Costa, P. T., & Schuster, M. M. (1988). Symptoms of psychologic distress associated with irritable bowel syndrome: Comparison of community and medical clinic samples. *Gastroenterology, 95,* 709–714.

Whitehead, W. E., Chaussade, S., Corazziari, E., & Kumar, D. (1991). Report of an international workshop on management of constipation. *Gastroenterology International*, *4*, 99–113.

Whitehead, W. E., Winget, C., Fedoravicius, A. S., Wooley, S., & Blackwell, B. (1982). Learned illness behavior in patients with irritable bowel syndrome and peptic ulcer. *Digestive Diseases and Sciences, 27*, 202–208.

Whorwell, P. J. (1989). Hypnotherapy in irritable bowel syndrome. *Lancet, i*, 622.

Whorwell, P. J., Prior, A., & Faragher, E. B. (1984). Controlled trial of hypnotherapy in the treatment of severe refractory irritable bowel syndrome. *Lancet, ii*, 1232–1234.

Williams, R. B. (1989). *The trusting heart: Great news about Type A behavior.* New York: Times Books.

Wing, R. R., Caggiula, A. W., Nowalk, M. P., Koeske, R., Lee, S., & Langford, H. (1984). Dietary approaches to the reduction of blood pressure: The independence of weight and sodium/potassium interventions. *Preventive Medicine, 13*, 233–244.

Wing, R. R., Koeske, R., Epstein, L. H., Nowalk, M. P., Gooding, W., & Becker, D. (1987). Long-term effects of modest weight loss in Type II diabetic patients. *Archives of Internal Medicine, 147*, 1749–1753.

Wittrock, D. A., & Blanchard, E. B. (1992). Thermal feedback treatment of mild hypertension: A comparison of effects on conventional and ambulatory blood pressure measures. *Behavior Modification, 16*, 283–304.

Woolfolk, R. L., & McNulty, T. F. (1983). Relaxation treatment for insomnia: A component analysis. *Journal of Consulting and Clinical Psychology, 51*, 495–503.

Young, L. D. (1992). Psychological factors in rheumatoid arthritis. *Journal of Consulting and Clinical Psychology, 60*, 619–643.

Young, S. J., Alpers, D. H., Norland, C. C., & Woodruff, R. A. (1976). Psychiatric illness and the irritable bowel syndrome: Practical implications for the primary physician. *Gastroenterology, 20*, 162–166.

Zeltzer, L. K., LeBaron, S., & Zeltzer, P. (1984). The effectiveness of behavioral intervention over inducing nausea and vomiting in children receiving chemotherapy. *Journal of Clinical Oncology, 2*, 683–690.

18

MEDICATION AND PSYCHOTHERAPY[1&2]

- **GERALD L. KLERMAN***
  Cornell University

- **MYRNA M. WEISSMAN**
  Columbia University
  New York State Psychiatric Institute

- **JOHN MARKOWITZ**
  Cornell University

- **IRA GLICK**
  Stanford University

- **PHILIP J. WILNER**
  Cornell University

- **BARBARA MASON**
  University of Miami

- **M. KATHERINE SHEAR**
  University of Pittsburgh

INTRODUCTION

Purpose of This Chapter

This chapter reviews the state of knowledge regarding medication and psychotherapy pertinent to mental health in general and to the treatment of mental disorders in particular. The title of the chapter has been changed for this edition: The term *medication* has been substituted for *drugs*. Recent U.S. and international concerns over illicit drugs, especially opiates, amphetamines, cocaine, and marijuana and other cannabis derivatives, have blurred the denotation and connotation of the term *drug*. For the general public and many patients or clients *drug* now signifies illicit substances, such as cocaine and heroin. For this reason, we employ the term *medication* to refer to compounds used for treatments of emotional distress, psychiatric symptoms, and mental disorders.

Relevance to Mental Health

The topic of medication and psychotherapy remains timely. For a number of reasons, it is important that psychiatrists, psychologists, and other professionals in the mental health field be familiar with advances in psychopharmacology and the relationship between medications and psychotherapy.

For mental health professionals. All mental health professionals should be aware that large numbers of individuals use psychoactive drugs. In some instances, this use may be for recreational (nontherapeutic) purposes, as with the use of cocaine or marijuana. In most instances, however, medications are taken for treatment purposes. Use of medication for the relief of emotional symptoms and distress is increasingly part of modern culture. Surveys in the United States and other urban, industrial societies find that about 10 percent of the

---

Editor's footnote. We note with regret the death of Dr. Gerald L. Klerman on April 3, 1992, at the age of 63. He was a distinguished contributor to research in this field and a former director of the Alcohol, Drug Abuse, and Mental Health Administration. A significant portion of the first draft of this chapter was completed prior to his passing. His wife and colleague, Myrna Weissman, and Dr. John Markowitz finalized the chapter for publication, for which we are most grateful. We acknowledge this chapter as a contribution in his memory.

[1]Supported in part by Grant No. U-01-MH-43077 from the National Institute of Mental Health, Alcohol, Drug Abuse, and Mental Health Administration, Public Health Service, Rockville, MD.

[2]Address correspondence to Myrna M. Weissman, Ph.D., College of Physicians and Surgeons, Columbia University, Department of Clinical and Genetic Epidemiology, New York State Psychiatric Institute, 722 West 168th Street, Unit 14, New York, NY 10032. Telephone: (212) 960-5880; Fax (212) 568-3534

population receive a prescribed psychoactive medication in any given year (Balter, Levine, & Manheimer, 1974).

For psychotherapists, behavioral therapists, counselors, and other clinicians. In treatment planning for individual patients, decisions should be made based on knowledge of the possible value of medication in comparison to, or in combination with, psychotherapy. Patients often enter treatment with specific expectations, either requesting medications or opposed to them. A significant proportion of patients in mental health treatment receive a combination of medication and psychotherapy. This situation may be the result of an intentional decision by their psychotherapists, or it may be inadvertent, since many patients take tranquilizers, sleeping pills, or other medications without their psychotherapists' knowledge.

For researchers. Experimental and clinical psychologists and other mental health researchers need to be aware that medications and recreational drugs have a profound impact on brain processes and psychological and neurological functions related to sensation, perception, memory, cognition, psychomotor activity, speech and language, information processing, sleep and biological rhythms, central and peripheral autonomic nervous system regulation and functioning, memory, and other psychological and psychophysiologic processes. Knowledge of actions of medications is important to researchers involved in investigations of psychopathology and treatment studies, including psychotherapy and behavioral therapy.

For research methodologists, biostatisticians, and psychometricians interested in design and data-analysis assessment. These researchers need knowledge of this area to address the problems attendant on the design and conduct of experiments, statistical analysis, and the interpretation of results in pharmacotherapy research and to combining and comparing psychotherapy and pharmacotherapy.

For theorists

1. The actions of drugs on mental processes and behavior have generated new knowledge concerning long-standing questions about the relationships of brain and behavior and of mind and biology. The fact that defined chemical substances can influence aggression, anxiety, guilt, performance, and so on creates opportunities for research on the neurobiological substrate of mental functioning and behavior.

2. The comparative and interactive effects of medication and psychotherapy have implications for theories of treatment.

3. Understanding the nature of the comparative and interactive effects of pharmacotherapy and psychotherapy in the treatment of individual disorders, such as schizophrenia, panic disorder, and phobias, can elucidate aspects of the disorder.

Several publications review selected aspects of this topic (Beitman & Klerman, 1984; Greenhill & Gralnich, 1983; Group for the Advancement of Psychiatry, 1975). Beitman and Klerman recently revised their volume (1991). In addition, edited collections, proceedings of symposia, and monographs discuss the role of medication and psychotherapy and behavioral therapy for individual conditions and disorders. These publications are reviewed in sections of this chapter devoted to specific disorders.

General Approach: The Disease or Medical Model

It is useful to make explicit the theoretical approach taken here to psychopathology. This is the only chapter in the *Handbook* written from the point of view of a biological treatment, in this case psychopharmacology. Readers of this *Handbook* are likely to have only a limited awareness of the scope of psychopharmacologic research and practice.

A number of premises are usually implicit in clinical psychopharmacologic research.

1. There is no one condition of mental illness, but rather multiple mental disorders and symptom states that require diagnostic assessment for their differentiation.

2. The major mode of assessment for patient assignment to strata or groups within medication trials is the categorical approach (making a diagnosis). Since 1980, the *Diagnostic and Statistical Manual of Mental Disorders* (DSM-III) system developed by the American Psychiatric Association has become the major, but not exclusive, basis for diagnosing patients for assignment to medication trials. Although dimensional approaches are often used to characterize the severity and diversity of psychopathology and associated social functioning, they are not the major mode of patient selection and assignment to strata.

3. Treatments, including medications and psychotherapies, are tailored to specified symptoms, conditions, syndromes, or disorders.

4. Medication and psychotherapy are regarded as treatment modalities in the context of illness. Claims for the efficacy and safety of any individual treatment, such as a psychotropic medication or a form of psychotherapy, are evaluated in the same manner as are claims for other treatment modalities, such as medication for hypertension or surgery for breast cancer.

5. Findings from outcome studies take precedence over those from process studies. Process studies have clinical utility and scientific value only to the extent that they demonstrate the *efficacy* of the particular therapy.

6. Efficacy is best established by randomized, controlled clinical trial design. Use of naturalistic designs or comparisons without a control group provide only limited information regarding the efficacy of a treatment.

This approach embodies what is commonly, but vaguely, referred to as the *medical model*. Aspects of the medical model are controversial, and resolution of these controversies is complicated by interprofessional rivalries, particularly between psychiatrists and psychologists. Perhaps this approach would better be regarded as constituting a disease model, or illness model, rather than a medical model (Beitman & Klerman, 1991; Klerman, 1977, 1990, 1991).

The Role of Ideology in Intraprofessional and Interprofessional Relations

Discussion of the relative efficacy of pharmacotherapy and psychotherapy, in comparison and in combination with one another, often evokes feelings, beliefs, and convictions related to ideology and to interprofessional tensions in the mental health field. Numerous observers of the field have documented splits within psychiatry, psychology, and other mental health disciplines (Hollingshead & Redlich, 1958). Mental health professionals tend to identify with biological, psychodynamic, behavioral, interpersonal, social, and existential groups or schools. Often the intensity of their beliefs and group commitments has the quality of ideology (Armor & Klerman, 1968; Klerman, 1984; Strauss, Schatzman, Bucher, Ehrlich, & Sabshin, 1964).

These ideological and theoretical differences within professional groups contribute to intraprofessional and interprofessional tensions (Klerman, cited in Beitman & Klerman, 1991). The mental health professions involved in psychotherapy and pharmacotherapy are currently rivals in the marketplace for patients or clients as well as in the intellectual and scientific marketplace. Evaluation of the data on efficacy and safety of medication alone, as well as in comparison and in combination

with psychotherapy, is complicated by the fact that psychiatrists, as physicians, are the only mental health professionals legally authorized to prescribe medications and usually the only mental health professionals whose training has involved significant exposure to neuroscience and pharmacology. Thus, there may be a tendency for some psychiatrists, as physicians, to overvalue psychopharmacologic evidence. On the other hand, many nonpsychiatric mental health professionals, including psychologists, counselors, and social workers, are skeptical about the value of medications and emphasize their adverse effects rather than their possible therapeutic value.

Nevertheless, psychiatry is not of a single mind on these matters: There are tensions within psychiatry, often related to psychodynamic versus biological approaches and group loyalties.

These attitudes are evident in the research literature, especially in review articles and meta-analytic reports. For example, reviews of psychopharmacologic treatments often ignore the demonstrated efficacy of behavioral techniques for the treatment of phobias or of short-term psychotherapies for depressed patients. Similarly, reviews of psychotherapy often ignore the demonstrated value of medications for psychoses, certain forms of depression, and panic states.

These interprofessional tensions are manifested in clinical practice, where many patients seek consultation with expectations and preferences regarding their treatment. Similarly, clinicians approach therapeutic decision making with individual patients heavily influenced by their professional loyalties and ideological positions. Hopefully, as controlled trials yield greater scientific evidence, a more balanced approach to the relative value of medications and psychotherapy for specific disorders, alone and in combination, will emerge.

Organization

This chapter reviews several aspects of pharmacotherapy and psychotherapy. Following this introduction, general aspects of psychopharmacology, including the scientific status of the field, issues of research design, methodology, and public policy, are reviewed and the various classes of medications used in the treatment of emotional symptoms and mental disorders are briefly presented.

Selected issues of research design and methodology are then discussed in detail, with particular attention to the problems of comparative and combined studies, especially the value of factorial designs in elucidating interactions as well as main effects. The possible outcomes of comparative and constructive designs are defined.

The next section reviews the status of research and clinical practice for selected disorders: schizophrenia, mood disorders, agoraphobia and other anxiety disorders, and alcoholism.

GENERAL ISSUES

THE SCOPE OF PSYCHOPHARMACOLOGY

Introduction

Modern psychopharmacology has grown and evolved in the decades since its inception in the early 1950s. This growth is evident in several dimensions. First, there has been a proliferation of the classes and types of compounds, mostly synthetics with psychotropic action, many of which have application in the treatment of mental disorders. Second, the number of scientists and investigators involved in psychopharmacology has grown at a rapid rate. This phenomenon is evidenced in the increased applications for membership and numbers of members and fellows in the American College of Neuropsychopharmacology (ACNP) and in the growth in participation and attendance at the two major U.S. meetings: the annual meetings of the ACNP and of the New Clinical Drug Evaluation Unit Program (NCDEU), a major forum for discussion of clinical psychopharmacology research convened and organized by NIMH. Journals devoted to psychopharmacology have appeared in the United States and elsewhere as have a large number of publications, particularly edited volumes, proceedings of symposia, workshops, and conferences, and textbooks. The public has shown increasing interest in psychopharmacologic agents, including drugs used for abuse or recreational purposes as well as medications used for therapies. The range of psychiatric and mental conditions for which psychopharmacologic agents have demonstrated efficacy has greatly expanded and now includes schizophrenia, mood disorders, anxiety states, phobias, obsessive-compulsive disorders, and, increasingly, personality disorders.

Terminology

It is useful to review and define the terms used regarding drugs and medications relevant to mental processes, psychotherapy, and behavior change (see Table 18.1).

An *agent* may be chemical or nonchemical, as with radiation or electrical stimulation. *Agent* is usually used interchangeably with *drug*, *compound*, and *substance*. The terms *substances* and *com-*

TABLE 18.1   Terms used in psychopharmacology

Term	Definition
Agent	Biologically active, i.e., chemical, light, electricity, radiation
Substance	Organic or synthetic
Compound	Chemical structures
Drug	Any substance, natural or synthetic, that alters bodily functions, including mental processes and behavior

pounds refer to both naturally occurring chemicals, such as coffee, tea, and opium, as well as to synthetic compounds. A compound is a drug with a known chemical structure.

Drug refers to any substance, natural or synthetic, that alters bodily functions, including mental processes and behavior. *Medication* usually connotes a drug intentionally used for health purposes—for the treatment of symptoms and illnesses, including emotional and psychological disorders. By this definition, tobacco, coffee, tea, and alcoholic beverages are drugs, but not medications. Similarly, marijuana and other cannabis derivatives, opiates, cocaine, and amphetamines are drugs, but usually not medications. Under certain circumstances, such as when opiates are used for pain or analgesics or amphetamines are used to treat depression, these drugs are considered medications.

Various terms are used interchangeably to refer to drugs that influence brain and behavior, including *psychotropic*, *psychoactive*, *psychopharmacologic*, and *psychopharmaceutic*. When used for treatment purposes, these substances are sometimes called *psychopharmacotherapeutic* agents, compounds, drugs, or medications.

Not all psychoactive drugs are intended for therapeutic use. There is no agreement about terminology for nontherapeutic uses, although nontherapeutic drug use is sometimes called recreational, as in the case of marijuana and alcohol.

Drugs that induce altered mental states of cognition, perception, and memory may be called *psychedelic*, a term popular in the 1960s. Psychedelic drugs include hallucinogenic compounds as a subclass. Hallucinogenic drugs induce hallucinations, usually visual. Hallucinogenics include mescaline, LSD, and psilocybin. Tetrahydrocannabinol, the active component of marijuana and other substances derived from cannabis plants, may have hallucinogenic properties, particularly in purified form and in high doses.

Other terms describe relevant scientific fields. *Psychopharmacology* refers to the scientific discipline concerned with psychoactive drugs and their effects on behavioral, psychological, and brain processes. It can also refer to an emerging subspecialty within psychiatry in which psychiatrists devote their practice to treating mental disorders with medication. The use of psychopharmacologic treatment has so far been restricted to licensed physicians, especially psychiatrists. However, recent proposals developed in the U.S. armed forces would allow psychologists and other mental health professionals to prescribe psychopharmacologic agents under special circumstances. It is not known whether these proposals will reach fruition and result in granting legal authority to nonmedical mental health professionals to prescribe psychopharmacologic medication. *Neuropharmacology* is the branch of pharmacology concerned with the action of drugs on the nervous system, particularly the brain. Neuropharmacologic research focuses on the ways in which drugs affect electrophysiologic or neurochemical processes within the brain and the nervous system in normal and clinical states. *Behavioral pharmacology* refers to a branch of pharmacology concerned with understanding the actions of drugs that influence behavior in animals and humans. Many members of this subdiscipline have a background in psychology, usually learning theory and most often Skinnerian theory.

Historical Background

The emergence of psychopharmacology in the early 1950s. Anthropologists report that almost every known society uses some ferment, brew, potion, or plant derivative intended to influence behavior for health purposes, recreational use, or religious ritual. In western civilization, interest in drugs that influence behavior and psychological functioning is as old as recorded history. In the mid-nineteenth century, there was great interest in drugs that today would be called psychopharmacologic agents; for example, nitrous oxide in New England and opiates and marijuana among poets and writers in France and Great Britain. The introduction of cocaine into clinical ophthalmology in Vienna in the late nineteenth century was attended by drama around Freud's role and its impact on his personal and professional life (Byck, 1974). Aldous Huxley (1954) described his personal hallucinogenic experiences with mescaline in the 1920s. These experiences remained isolated from mainstream medicine, biology, and psychology and seemed to influence writers and philosophers more than physicians and scientists. It is conventional to date the onset of modern psychopharmacology by

the introduction of reserpine and the phenothiazines in the 1950s. However, Cade reported on the value of lithium for manic states in 1949 (Cade, 1949). As so often happens in the history of science, Cade's observations were overlooked and did not attract clinical or research interest until the 1960s.

Psychopharmacology emerged as a scientific field in the mid-1950s following the development of new classes of medications and the impressive response of psychiatric patients to them, particularly the responses of hospitalized psychotic patients to the "tranquilizers" reserpine and the phenothiazines. Other classes of medications were rapidly developed in the late 1950s and 1960s, when many new research compounds were synthesized and introduced into clinical practice. Many of these compounds were initially called tranquilizers. The first tranquilizers included reserpine, the phenothiazines, and meprobamate. In the late 1950s, the larger group of tranquilizers was divided into major tranquilizers and minor tranquilizers.

The original major tranquilizers, later called antipsychotics or neuroleptics, included rauwolfia derivatives and the phenothiazines. Members of both groups were shown to have efficacy in treating psychotic states, including mania and schizophrenia. Subsequently, other classes of medications, such as thioxanthenes and butyrophenones, proved effective against psychotic symptoms and behavior. Meprobamate was introduced at about the same time that reserpine and chlorpromazine appeared. Grouping these drugs together as tranquilizers followed theories that ascribed the central role in the genesis of psychopathology to anxiety. Influenced by psychoanalytic theory, most psychopathological manifestations of neuroses and psychoses were understood to be defenses against underlying anxiety. The tranquilizers were thought to reduce anxiety, and subsequently psychotic and other symptoms. It soon became apparent, however, that tranquilizers had not only quantitative differences, but important qualitative differences as well. Major tranquilizers were effective against psychotic states, produced extrapyramidal side effects, and presumably acted on central nervous system (CNS) dopamine. In contrast, meprobamate and other minor tranquilizers were not effective in treating psychotic states and had no neuropharmacologic action on dopamine or other catecholamines. Meprobamate, and later the benzodiazepines, showed pharmacologic and therapeutic similarities to older sedative/hypnotic drugs, such as barbiturates. Consequently, meprobamate and the benzodiazepines were grouped as minor tranquilizers.

The minor tranquilizers are also called anxiolytics and antianxiety medications. The introduction of the benzodiazepines, particularly diazepam (Valium) and chlordiazepoxide (Librium), led to a rapid expansion in the 1960s and 1970s in the number of such compounds and in their prescription use. Nonbenzodiazepine anxiolytics, such as buspirone, have been developed to treat anxiety. Two classes of antidepressant medications became available in the late 1950s, the tricyclic antidepressants, of which imipramine was the prototype, and the monoamine oxidase (MAO) inhibitors. Atypical antidepressants with structures different from tricyclics have since become available, and selective serotonin reuptake inhibitors (SSRI) have demonstrated efficacy in treating depression. For treatment of psychoses, including schizophrenia and delusional states, various atypical neuroleptics have been developed. The prototypical and most important member of this new class is clozapine (Clozaril), which has marked antipsychotic effects, particularly in chronic patient with defect states unresponsive to other antipsychotic medications, and minimal extrapyramidal side effects. However, because of the potential for agranulocytosis, a possibly fatal bone-marrow suppression, treatment with clozapine requires special blood monitoring and surveillance.

In the 1980s, medications effective against manic states (antimanic drugs), panic states and phobia (antipanic drugs), and obsessive-compulsive symptoms and behaviors were introduced. The combination of scientific controversy and legal requirements following the 1962 Kefauver-Harris amendments to the federal food and drug statutes resulted in numerous controlled clinical trials to evaluate the claims for efficacy and the safety of various psychotropic drugs. These historical forces produced intense interest among researchers of different professions (psychiatry, neurology, clinical psychology), an scientific disciplines (neurosciences, experimental psychology, pharmacology, medicinal chemistry, biostatics) in the new field of psychopharmacology.

Emergence of neurosciences. The introduction of psychopharmacologic agents with demonstrated efficacy in the 1950s coincided with the emergence of the neurosciences as a coherent field of scientific investigation. The growth of neuroanatomy, neurophysiology, neuropharmacology, and neurochemistry and the development of new technologies for brain imaging have since led to an explosion of knowledge about brain functioning in normal and clinical conditions, including in neurological and psychiatric disorders. Conventional boundaries between disciplines have been eroded by the overlap in theory and technology. Many graduate and medical schools have developed departments of neurobiology or neuroscience to provide an academic and institutional framework for research in this area and to train new investigators.

One major impetus to the development of neuroscience has been the desire to understand brain mechanisms and CNS processes that explain the modes of action of therapeutic compounds. The fortuitous discovery of classes of most medications has stimulated extensive research and theoretical activity to understand their mode of action on the brain and their effects on psychopathology and clinical symptomatology.

Classes of Medications Used in the Treatment of Mental Disorders

There is no single best way to classify these medications. Sometimes they are classified by their chemical structure (e.g., phenothiazines, tricyclics, benzodiazepines), at other times according to their mode of neurochemical actions (i.e., monoamine oxidase inhibitors, neuroleptics), and in other instances according to their mode of psychological action (e.g., psychomotor stimulants, hallucinogens). Because our main interest in this chapter is in the use of medications alone or in combinations with methods of psychotherapy or behavior change in the treatment of mental disorders, we shall classify medications according to their intended clinical use (Table 18.2). The main classes include antipsychotic, antidepressant, antianxiety, sedative/hypnotic, and antimanic medications.

This usage does not necessarily imply any specific causation for the disorder or even a common mechanism for therapeutic effects in a given disorder. For example, the etiology of hypertension is not known and there is probably more than one form of hypertension. Nevertheless, several different classes of compounds that have demonstrated efficacy in reducing blood pressure and have contributed to decreased mortality and improved social and personal functioning are conventionally called antihypertensives. Not only do these medications have different chemical structures, but they act via different pharmacologic mechanisms. Diuretics induce the excretion of fluid and reduce sodium in the body; other antihypertensive medications act by blocking autonomic neurotransmitters. There is a parallel between treatments for hypertension and for depression. It is possible to treat depression with various classes of medications and also by various forms of psychotherapy — some of which influence cognitive mechanisms, others interpersonal processes, and still others behavioral reinforcement.

TABLE 18.2   Medications used for treatment of mental disorders

Therapeutic Use	Chemical Structure or Psychopharmacologic Action	Generic Name	Trade Name
Antipsychotics (also called major tranquilizers or neuroleptics)	Phenothiazines		
	Aliphatic	Chlorpromazine	Thorazine
	Piperidine	Thioridazine	Mellaril
	Piperazine	Trifluoperazine	Stelazine
	Thioxanthenes		
	Aliphatic	Chlorprothixene	Taractan
	Piperazine	Thiothixene	Navane
	Butyrophenones	Haloperidol	Haldol
	Dibenzoxazepines	Loxapine	Loxitane
	Dihydroindolines	Molindone	Moban
	Rauwolfia alkaloids	Reserpine	Sandril
	Benzoquinolines	Tetrabenazine	
	Atypical neuroleptics	Clozapine	Clozaril
Antidepressants	Tricyclic antidepressants (TCAs)		
	Tertiary amines	Amitriptyline	Elavil
		Imipramine	Tofranil
		Doxepin	Sinequan
	Secondary amines	Desipramine	Norpramin
		Nortriptyline	Pamelor
		Protriptyline	Vivactil
	Monoamine oxidase inhibitors (MAOIs)	Phenelzine	Nardil
		Tranylcypromine	Parnate
		Pargyline	Eutonyl
		Isocarboxazid	Marplan
	Atypical antidepressants	Trazodone	Desyrel
		Amoxapine	Asendin
	Selective Serotonin Reuptake Inhibitor	Bupropion	Wellbutrin
		Fluoxetine	Prozac
Psychomotor stimulants	Amphetamines	Amphetamine	Benzedrine
		Dextroamphetamine	Dexedrine
	Other	Methylphenidate	Ritalin
		Pemoline	Cylert
Antimanic		Lithium	Eskalith
		Carbamazepine	Tegretol
		Valproic acid	Depakene
Anxiolytic (also called antianxiety or minor tranquilizers)	Benzodiazepines	Chlordiazepoxide	Librium
		Diazepam	Valium
		Chlorazepate	Tranxene
		Oxazepam	Serax
		Lorazepam	Ativan
	Triazolobenzodiazepine	Alprazolam	Xanax
	Propanediol carbamates	Meprobamate	Miltown
Sedative hypnotic	Barbiturates	Phenobarbital	
	Benzodiazepines	Triazolam	Halcion
Antipanic	Benzodiazepines	Alprazolam	Xanax
	MAOIs	Phenelzine	Nardil
	TCAs	Imipramine	Tofranil
Antiobsessional	TCA	Chlorimipramine	Anafranil
	SSRI	Fluoxetine	Prozac

In the ideal of scientific medicine, knowledge of etiology and pathogenesis provides the most powerful explanation of illness and a rational guide to design of treatments. In fact, many of the most effective treatments in modern medicine are not etiologic but symptomatic. Steroids are used for the treatment of allergic reactions and anticonvulsants and antihypertensives have demonstrated efficacy despite our lack of knowledge of the etiology of cardiovascular disease or epilepsy.

The therapeutic efficacy of most of these compounds was discovered through clinical observation and serendipity, rather than by rational knowledge of pathophysiology or the neuropharmacologic mode of actions. Efforts to understand the neuropharmacologic and behavioral basis of a therapeutic mode of action have usually followed the demonstration of therapeutic efficacy.

Stages of Medication Development

The process of development of medications has become increasingly complex in its scientific and professional aspects (see Table 18.3) and increasingly regulated, particularly by the Food and Drug Administration (FDA). The FDA's extensive powers over the development and clinical evaluation of medications derive from several statutes, particularly the 1908 Federal Food, Drug, and Cosmetic Act, which established the FDA and mandated disclosure of chemical composition and purity of composition. The 1938 amendment, prompted by toxicity associated with the newly introduced antibacterial sulfa compounds, mandated safety prior to approval of a drug for prescription use. Standards for preclinical testing of toxicity evolved rapidly. The most far-reaching amendments were the 1962 Kefauver-Harris amendments, which established efficacy as a re-

quirement for new drugs. The statutory requirement for efficacy prompted regulations defining other criteria for efficacy, particularly the importance of controlled studies with appropriate design and statistical consideration. Subsequent FDA regulations and guidelines have created well-defined standards for the field, regulating the activities of pharmaceutical firms in particular, but recently and increasingly governing the activities of clinical investigators, whether sponsored by pharmaceutical firms or not.

The guidelines, which translate statutes and regulations into operational criteria and procedures for classes of medications defined by therapeutic purposes, have become increasingly diverse and complex and are now applied to all classes of compounds (analgesics, antibiotics, antihypertensives, anticompulsives, etc.) including psychopharmacologic agents used in the treatment of mental disorders and emotional symptoms. Two important projects have assisted the FDA in these guidelines. The 1971 report *Principles and Practices in Evaluating Psychoactive Drugs* was developed by the NIMH and ACNP, with a first edition in 1971 (Levine, Schiele, & Bouthilet, 1971) and an updated edition in 1992 (Klerman et al., 1993). The FDA has made a great effort to emphasize that its statutory power and the intent of its regulations is to govern pharmaceutical companies and clinical investigators involved in the evaluation of drugs. It disclaims any attempt to determine or regulate the use of medications in the clinical practice of medicine, leaving that responsibility to the judgment of individual physicians and professional societies. However, boundary problems exist, particularly concerning the use of drugs not yet approved by the FDA and the use of approved medications for clinical indications other than those specified by the FDA in issuing the New Drug Application (NDA).

The following discussion of the state of development of medications indicates the immense influence of the FDA on clinical trials in psychopharmacology. Yet the scope of psychopharmacology extends beyond those studies initiated by the pharmaceutical industry to comply with FDA regulations. A large volume of preclinical psychopharmacology related to basic neuropharmacology and behavioral pharmacology is driven not by the desire to obtain FDA approval for new compounds, but rather by scientific endeavor seeking basic understanding of mechanisms and processes.

Scientific Issues

Establishing efficacy and safety. The introduction of effective therapeutic psychotropic compounds in the 1950s generated intense controversy

---

TABLE 18.3 Phases of drug development

1. Preclinical studies: animal models for depression
2. Issue of IND by FDA
3. Phase I: Clinical pharmacology
4. Phase II: Early clinical trials
5. Phase III
   - (a) Placebo-controlled trials
   - (b) Comparative trials
   - (c) Multisite collaborative trials
6. Issue of NDA by FDA
7. Phase IV: Postmarketing studies (post–NDA)
   - (a) Refinement of clinical use
   - (b) Use in other indications
   - (c) Surveillance for detection of adverse effects with low frequency
   - (d) Long-term treatment studies

as to whether the claims made for their efficacy in psychosis, depression, and anxiety were real, or due to bias, therapeutic zeal, and placebo effect. In response to this criticism, the quality of scientific research on the safety and efficacy of drugs improved rapidly, and the randomized placebo-controlled trial gained acceptance as the standard design for assessment of psychopharmacologic agents.

Establishing modes of action

Pharmacologic. The emergence of psychopharmacology in the 1950s occurred simultaneously with the development of modern neurosciences (neurobiology). The neurosciences are among the most exciting areas of scientific investigation, and developments in neuropharmacology have been powerful stimuli to help clarify the role of neurotransmitters and neuropeptides in brain functioning.

Psychopathological, psychological, and behavioral. Interest in mode of action is not limited to anatomical, chemical, and physiologic functioning of the brain. There is active concern for behavioral modes of action, particularly as these compounds influence perception, sensation, motor and affective regulation, and patterns of reward and performance.

RESEARCH DESIGNS AND METHODOLOGY

This section discusses selected issues of design and methodology in comparing medication with psychotherapy and evaluating the combination of medication and psychotherapy. Other chapters in this *Handbook* discuss general issues of research design and assessment. Again, ideally, the flow of medical information derives from knowledge of etiology and pathogenesis; it proceeds through pathophysiology, diagnosis, and ultimately pharmacology and therapeutics; specific treatments for a disorder are deduced from knowledge of etiology and pathogenesis and result in specific and rational therapeutic interventions. A rare manifestation of this approach in psychopharmacology was the development of L-dopa as treatment for Parkinson's disease, which was based on autopsy evidence of a deficit in dopaminergic neurons in the basal ganglia of patients with parkinsonism combined with knowledge of the neuropharmacology of dopamine from neuroleptics and other medications.

Scientific strategies for evaluating that a treatment works are different from those for determining how a treatment works. The therapeutic value of treatments can often be established even though

the etiology or pathophysiology of the disorder is uncertain or the underlying mechanism of action has not been identified (Group for the Advancement of Psychiatry, 1975). For example, the efficacy of vaccination for the prevention of smallpox was established long before the invention of the electron microscope or knowledge of viruses.

Research Designs

Controlled clinical trials. There are important parallels in thinking about the nature of evidence for demonstrating the efficacy of medications and that for demonstrating the efficacy of psychotherapies. The most powerful evidence for the efficacy and safety of any health intervention, including pharmacologic, surgical, radiation, and psychological treatments, comes from the randomized controlled trial (RCT). This design has been most widely used for evaluating medications but is increasingly being used with other forms of treatment, including psychotherapies. Although the theoretical basis for the controlled trial goes back to seventeenth-century writings on scientific investigation, its first applications in medical therapeutics did not appear until the twentieth century, when placebo-controlled trials were used in evaluating medication for angina.

In the late 1950s, there was considerable debate in the young field of psychopharmacology about the feasibility, desirability, and necessity of clinical trials. This debate centered on the necessity for double-blind design and on the magnitude and significance of the placebo effect. Scientific consensus emerged in the early 1960s through a series of conferences and publications sponsored by the NIMH Psychopharmacology Service Center (Levine, 1978, 1979; Levine et al., 1971). The Kefauver-Harris Amendment resulted in FDA regulations that operationalized these criteria. As part of this process, the FDA contracted with the ACNP for scientific guidance in developing guidelines for the evaluation of antipsychotic, antidepressant, and antianxiety classes of medications (Wittenborn et al., 1977).

At the same time, Eysenck's (1952) famous article raised controversies about the efficacy of psychotherapy and led to intense discussions that culminated in guidelines developed by the NIMH Psychotherapy Research Review Committee, published by Fiske et al. (1970). By the mid-1970s, most of these controversies had subsided. There is currently widespread agreement on the necessity for controlled clinical trials for both drugs and psychotherapy (Eysenck, 1965; Fiske et al., 1970; Luborsky, Singer, & Luborsky, 1975). Comparative and constructive strategies are used only if the respective medication and psychotherapy treatments have demonstrated safety and efficacy.

Comparative strategies for assessing medications and psychotherapies. A number of different designs are employed for comparing medications and psychotherapy. In the two-group design, a psychotherapy is compared to a medication. For example, Rush, Beck, Kovacs, and Hollon (1977) compared cognitive therapy to amitriptyline. This design is scientifically inadequate, because without a control group it cannot be concluded that differences within the two treatments are greater than might be expected given time. Even though the pharmacotherapy or psychotherapy may have demonstrated efficacy in prior studies, the question remains whether the research group has the capacity to detect such change in this treatment sample. The researchers may have insufficient training, assessment methods may be inadequate, or the patient group may be unresponsive to either treatment. There may be ethical reasons for avoiding a nontreatment control group; however, scientifically, a control group is always necessary.

Another comparative design is the three-group design, in which the psychotherapy is compared to a medication and to a control group. This is the minimum adequate design for comparative assessment. An interesting and important extension of this three-group design is the four-group design employed in the NIMH Collaborative Study of the Treatment of Depression (Elkin, Parloff, Hadley, & Autry, 1985). Two brief psychotherapies, cognitive-behavioral therapy (Beck, Rush, Shaw, & Emery, 1979) and interpersonal psychotherapy (Klerman, Weissman, Rounsaville, & Chevron, 1984), were evaluated for efficacy in depression and compared to a standard antidepressant medication treatment, imipramine, and a control group that received psychological clinical management

plus placebo. As shown in Figure 18.1 this four-group design represents an extension of the three-group comparative design. The data from the study allow evaluation of the efficacy of the two psychological treatments against one another, in comparison to a pharmacologic standard, and relative to a minimal treatment condition (Elkin et al., 1989). Since it does not employ a combined treatment group, however, the four-group design does not permit study of the interaction of medication and psychotherapy, that is, of the value of combined treatment.

Constructive strategies. Constructive strategies, employing various designs, are useful for studying combination treatment and elucidating possible interactions. Combined treatments are represented clinically in alternate packages. To establish the value of combined treatments, some form of constructive strategy is needed.

The four-group factorial design. To evaluate a combined treatment, such as the combination of two medications (a tricyclic and a benzodiazepine) or of a medication plus psychotherapy (amitriptyline plus interpersonal therapy), the minimum adequate design is the four-group factorial design. Both treatments are evaluated singly against one another, against a control group, and against their combination. The factorial allows for statistical tests of interactions (see Figure 18.2).

The placebo effect, selection of control group, and the need for complex design. Until recently, the nature of the control group has not been specified. In most psychopharmacologic research, the standard control is a placebo treatment group. In psychotherapy research, however, there is no agreement as to what constitutes a standard control group. In psychopharmacologic research, the placebo group provides a control for a package of factors: the tendency toward improvement inherent in many disorders; the attention subjects receive as

Experimental treatment 1	Experimental treatment 2	Standard treatment	Control group
Cognitive-behavioral therapy	Interpersonal therapy	Imipramine plus psychological management	Placebo plus psychological management

FIGURE 18.1 Comparative strategies — the expanded three-group design. *Note.* From "NIMH Treatment of Depression Collaborative Research Project" by I. Elkin, M. B. Parloff, S. W. Hadley, and J. H. Autry, 1985, *Archives of General Psychiatry, 42,* 305–316.

		Psychotherapy	
		Experimental treatment	Control treatment
Pharmacotherapy	Experimental treatment	Combined treatment group	Psychotherapy treatment group
	Control treatment	Drug treatment group	Control group

FIGURE 18.2 Constructive strategies — four-group factorial design for evaluating combined treatment.

part of a research project; and the possible benefit of repeated assessment. In the psychopharmacologic literature, these factors are often called nonspecific effects. Possible placebo effects also include the social-psychological expectation attendant to prescription of a drug by a physician and the act of pill taking. Often, the placebo effect is used in a general sense to refer to the combination of these nonpharmacologic effects, including expectations, time, and interpersonal transactions.

Discussions of the placebo effect may have distorted the selection of research designs for establishing the efficacy of psychotherapy (Wilkins, 1984). In psychopharmacologic research, the placebo control group attempts to simultaneously control a number of nonspecific "specific" pharmacologic features. In psychotherapy research, however, it is exactly these nonspecific social psychological processes (patient expectation, personal features of treatment relationships) that are believed to be components of effective psychotherapy. Beyond these general problems regarding the selection of controls lies a specific problem of possible limitations of placebo controls in studies of medications and psychotherapy. The usual setting for conducting psychotherapy does not involve the use of a placebo. Use of a placebo group may alter the sociopsychological context of the psychotherapy, especially by generating changes in the expectations of the therapist and the patient. Therefore, a more powerful design for evaluating combined treatment is a six-group design, employing a no-pill control group. This design was used in a trial of medication and psychotherapy in the maintenance treatment of acute depressions reported by Klerman, DeMascio, Weissman, Prusoff, and Paykel (1974).

By employing a no-pill group, the six-group design tests whether the placebo effect produces an increment over and above the nonspecific conditions of numerous rating scales and of the illness itself (see Figure 18.3). There seems to be an assumption implicit in much of the placebo literature that the placebo effect is positive in all conditions and in all circumstances. Most of the literature on placebos deals with expectations about pill taking: its magical quality, dependency expectations, the sick role it implies, and the additional attention resulting from the subject being in a research project. The Boston–New Haven study (Klerman et al., 1974) found no placebo effect over the no-pill condition in a long-term (8 month) treatment study of depressed patients. Medication versus no-pill and medication versus placebo differences were found, but no placebo effect was detected over and above the no-pill condition. Moreover, no negative inter-

		Psychotherapy	
		Present	Absent
Pharmacotherapy	Drug	Psychotherapy and amitriptyline	Amitriptyline
	Placebo	Psychotherapy and placebo	Placebo
	No pill	Psychotherapy and no pill	No pill No psychotherapy

FIGURE 18.3 Constructive strategies—six-group design for evaluating placebo effect in combined treatment. *Note.* From "Treatment of depression by drugs and psychotherapy" by G. L. Klerman, A. DiMascio, M. M. Weissman, B. Prusoff, and E. Paykel, 1974, *American Journal of Psychiatry, 131*, 186–191.

actions between medication and psychotherapy were observed (Rounsaville, Klerman, & Weissman, 1981). However, others have reanalyzed these data and interpreted them as showing an interaction between ingestion of pill, placebo, and psychotherapy (Hollon & DeRubeis, 1981).

Standard therapy as the control with psychotherapy or medication as additional treatment. Although the factorial design is the scientific ideal, there may be valid reasons to preclude its execution. In the presence of overwhelming evidence for the efficacy of a standard treatment, it may be unethical to withhold standard treatment from patients by assigning them to a no-treatment control group. This seems to be the case for studies of acutely psychotic hospitalized patients with schizophrenia, a group for which antipsychotic pharmacotherapy is now considered standard.

An alternative justification for avoiding a no-treatment control group is the desire to simulate clinical practice. Where a standard treatment exists, the clinician wants to know how much supplemental improvement may be gained by adding another treatment to the standard therapy. For example, in the maintenance treatment of bipolar patients, what is the value of adding group or family therapy to lithium treatment? In these designs, which are variants of the constructive strategy, the standard treatment is given to all patients, and certain patients are assigned to the experimental treatment. Of course, assignment to standard or experimental treatment should be determined by randomized matching or some similar nonbiased method. The standard treatment may be pharmacologic, as in the studies of family therapy of schizophrenics in which all patients receive fluphenazine, an antipsychotic medication (Goldstein, 1984); psychological, as in the use of exposure treatment in anxiety disorders (Mavissakalian, 1984); or a combination of medication and psychotherapy, as in the Philadelphia studies of opiate addicts in which all patients received methadone maintenance plus peer counseling as the standard treatment (Woody et al., 1983).

The simplest version of this design is a two-group design, in which one group receives the standard treatment alone and the other group receives the standard treatment plus an experimental treatment. Jamison employed this design in an unpublished comparison of lithium alone versus lithium plus group treatment for outpatients with bipolar disorder. A more complex design is the three-group design employed in the Philadelphia studies of drug addiction (see Figure 18.4). In this design, the standard treatment was methadone maintenance plus peer counseling by ex-addicts. Two experimental forms of psychotherapy were evaluated, cognitive-behavioral therapy, as developed by Beck et al. (1979), and supportive-expressive psychodynamic psychotherapy, developed by Luborsky (1984).

A similar design was employed by Schooler and Keith in the NIMH Treatment Strategies in Schizophrenia Study (1984). In this study, the medication dosage varied and a form of family management developed by Falloon and associates (1982) was evaluated for possible interaction with three levels of neuroleptic dosage. In such a design, if a standard treatment exists, the timing and sequence of additional experimental treatments may vary. For example, it is common for all patients to first receive the standard treatment; then only those patients who have a stable response are assigned by matching or randomization to experimental conditions involving standard treatment alone or standard treatment plus experimental treatment. This sequencing is closer to clinical practice in which the timing of packages is often determined by the clinician based on the degree of response to the standard treatment.

Other research designs. Other research designs have been employed in medication–psychotherapy comparisons. Retrospective analyses of naturalistic clinical data are often used to support the value of the various treatment programs. For example, Feinsilver and Yates (1984) reported a retrospective study documenting a particular sequence for the combined use of psychotherapy and medication in chronic, treatment-resistant schizophrenic patients. They used naturalistic observation to test the hypothesis that treatment-resistant schizophrenic patients would experience a prolonged regressive phase when withdrawn from medications and that, when subsequently remedicated, patients treated with adjunctive psychotherapy would respond better than patients treated by medication alone.

Selection of Subjects and the Role of DSM-III Diagnosis

The criteria for selection of subjects constitute a key difference between psychopharmacologic and psychotherapeutic research. Most psychopharmacologic research selects patients on the basis of a level of diagnosis. Three levels of diagnosis have been used: symptom, syndrome, and disorder. Diagnostic criteria can be an individual symptom, such as insomnia, anxiety, or weight gain. Some studies have used syndromal diagnoses to evaluate medication for psychotic states, panic attacks, or endogenous depression.

Early in the history of psychopharmacology, the concept of a target symptom was widely employed in guiding the selection of subjects. Patients were selected on the basis of salient symptoms for which the drug was targeted. This concept contributed to the terminology of drug classes in psychopharmacology, such as major tranquilizers or psychomotor stimulants. In recent years, there has been a trend toward standardization of selection criteria and procedures, with increasing use of structured interviews to assess symptom patterns and of diagnostic algorithms to assign patients to appropriate groups. Since many psychotherapies are not oriented toward reduction of symptoms or the treatment of a disorder, there have often been disputes over selection criteria when research designs have attempted to combine medication and psychotherapy. A major characteristic of the new wave of

Group 1	Group 2	Group 3
No supplemental treatment	Cognitive-behavioral psychotherapy	Supportive-expressive psychotherapy
Standard treatment: Methadone plus peer counseling		

FIGURE 18.4 Constructive strategies — standard treatment as control and experimental treatments as supplements. *Note.* From "Psychotherapy for opiate addicts: Dies it help?" by G. E. Woody, L. Luborsky, T. McLellan, C. P. O'Brien, A. T. Beck, J. Blaine, I. Herman, and A. Hole, 1983, *Archives of General Psychiatry, 40,* 639–645.

psychotherapy research is the growing acceptance of the concept of mental disorders as targets for psychotherapy effect, with increasing attention to diagnosis in patient selection. This trend is evident in the development of psychotherapies for specific disorders: for example, cognitive-behavioral and interpersonal psychotherapies for depression, desensitization and exposure in vivo for agoraphobia, and family therapy directed at reducing expressed emotion (EE) in families of patients with schizophrenia. Research on these psychotherapies targeted for a disorder now employs structured interviews to obtain information about history, and symptoms and research criteria, usually defined by research diagnostic criteria (RDC; Spitzer, Endicott, & Robins, 1978) or DSM-III-R (American Psychiatric Association, 1987), to make diagnoses.

These trends represent a departure from the past, when classification and diagnosis were deemphasized and patients were selected for psychotherapy on the basis of personality characteristics, such as ego strength, defensive structure, or MMPI profile. The use of categorical diagnosis in the design and conduct of psychotherapy research increasingly places psychotherapy research in a health care context. Viewing psychotherapy as a treatment modality legitimizes reimbursement by health insurance companies and other third-party payers, whether or not psychotherapy is delivered by a medical practitioner and biological factors are considered etiologic for the disorder. For example, biofeedback, relaxation, exercise, and dietary control are behavioral and psychotherapeutic interventions valuable for the treatment of hypertension.

There are potential adverse consequences attendant upon regarding psychotherapy as a mental health procedure. In the short term, the "sick role" may enhance the patient's dependency and passivity, promoting compliance and facilitating symptom reduction. In psychodynamic theory, the patient's acceptance of the sick role is often regarded as an attempt to manipulate the transference and to view the therapist as authoritarian and paternalistic. In behavioral terms, there is concern that taking the sick role encourages maladaptive behaviors, particularly those aspects of the sick role that excuse the individual from social responsibility and reinforce avoidant behavior. These considerations, however, only emphasize the need for research to assess the efficacy and safety of all aspects of therapeutic interventions, including clinical context and sick-role expectations. Moreover, some of these theoretical concerns may prove exaggerated—comparable to the overconcern about treating surgical patients with potentially addicting opiate medications—or may in any case be outweighed

by the efficacy of psychotherapies in treating mental disorders.

Integrity of Treatments
Psychopharmacologic research usually assures that the chemical composition of the medication used in treatment is uniform. Standards of medicinal chemistry ensure clinical purity. Methods of quality control in the pharmaceutical industry generally maintain high standards. In such research there are concerns over whether and in what concentration the medication prescribed reaches the part of the CNS presumed to produce change. One concern focuses on differences in compliance and patient adherence. Another concern is the biological variation in pharmacokinetics and metabolism of the medication. For these reasons, psychopharmacologic research increasingly employs blood level determinations to measure patient compliance and to control for patient differences in medication absorption and metabolism.

Parallel problems arise in psychotherapy research. Ensuring the comparability, purity, and integrity of the psychotherapy across therapists is a serious problem in psychotherapy research, but it is not insurmountable. Several methodological advances have been made within this area in recent years.

Treatment manuals. These manuals identify characteristics of the psychotherapy, including its goals, tasks, and the recommended sequence from the stage of initiation through termination (Luborsky, 1984). They specify methods for assessment of these tasks and operationalize the therapy through definitions and case examples. Manuals have been used in comparative constructive evaluations of medication and psychotherapy for depression (see Chapter 4, this volume) and also in studies of psychotherapy and methadone treatment for opiate drug addicts. Treatment manuals also have been developed for the psychological management associated with medication delivery to ensure that pharmacotherapists limit their psychotherapeutic interventions (Fawcett & Epstein, 1980).

Training of psychotherapists and psychopharmacologists for research. Another important development in psychotherapy and psychopharmacology research is the standardization of training programs based on protocols and formalized procedures. Most of these training programs have been designed not to teach inexperienced students to become psychotherapists but rather to help experienced therapists learn the particular methods and skills required for the research treatments. Certification criteria for psychotherapists have been developed for research participation, and videotape review has allowed independent assessment (Chevron & Rounsaville, 1983; Chevron, Rounsaville, Rothblum, & Weissman, 1983; Hollon, 1984; Weissman, Rounsaville, & Chevron, 1982).

Monitoring the quality of the conduct and process of the therapy. The availability of manuals and training in their use does not guarantee that the treatment actually delivered in the research project is the psychotherapy specified in the protocol; quality control is required. In psychopharmacology research, drug plasma levels are useful to evaluate compliance. Various techniques for monitoring psychotherapy adherence and competence through videotapes and supervision of the therapist based on videotaped sessions have been developed by Luborsky, Woody, McLellan, and O'Brien (1982), Hollon and associates (DeRubeis, Hollon, Evans, & Bemis, 1982; Hollon, Evans, Elkin, & Lowery, 1984), and in the NIMH Collaborative Study of the Treatment of Depression (Hill, O'Grady, & Elkin, 1992).

Assessment of Change and Outcome

Designing research on medications and psychotherapy requires decisions about the assessment of change. Which variables should be assessed? Who should rate improvement: the therapist, an independent evaluator, a relative, or the patient? How should assessments be timed? Almost all investigators accept that assessment of outcome is multidimensional, and almost all research projects use a battery of assessment measures, which may include therapist global assessment, patient global assessment, symptom assessment by clinical interview and by self-report, measures of social adjustment, and measures of personality functioning.

Psychopharmacologic research tends to emphasize assessment of symptomatic variables, usually by means of standardized rating scales. There has been a trend toward assessing social functioning and quality of life. Comparisons of clinician ratings with patient ratings indicate greater sensitivity to medication effects on clinicians' assessments. Lesser patient sensitivity may reflect distorted cognitions related to affect states, particularly anxiety and depression (Lambert, 1983). A major issue in the assessment of medication and psychotherapy research concerns the interaction between the timing of effects and the differential effects of these treatments. Medication effects are often evident within the first weeks of treatment, particularly effects on psychobiological functions, such as sleep, appetite, and psychomotor activity. Psychotherapy effects often take longer to appear and alter different variables, such as social functioning, interpersonal relations, and self-esteem. It is essential that studies of pharmacotherapy and psychotherapy include outcome measures appropriate to both types of treatment and at appropriate time intervals.

Process Research

Once safety and efficacy have been demonstrated for a particular treatment, the question then arises, How does this treatment work? Investigation of modes of therapeutic action is standard in both pharmacology and psychotherapy. For example, in the pharmacotherapy of depression, there are hypotheses that the efficacy of antidepressant drugs is mediated through their modulation of catecholamine or serotonin neurotransmitters. In the cognitive-behavioral psychotherapy of depression, it is hypothesized that improvement occurs through changes in dysfunctional attitudes. If so, change in dysfunctional attitude should precede reduction in depressive mood symptoms. Similarly, the interpersonal psychotherapy of depression presumes that a decrease in role conflict mediates reduction of depressive symptoms. Analyses of process, particularly of the sequence of change, can indirectly test the rationale for a psychotherapy. Thus process research in psychotherapy is analogous to research on the mechanism of action in pharmacology.

Process research may also identify subgroups of those within the clinical population who are most responsive to the treatment. Thus, process research on cognitive-behavioral therapy may yield techniques to identify subgroups of depressed patients whose cognitive style makes them most responsive to this therapy. Findings from one large study suggest that depressed patients with significant cognitive impairment do least well in cognitive therapy (Sotsky et al., 1991). Similarly, it would be hypothesized that patients with agoraphobia without panic disorder who have significant degrees of avoidance behavior would be most responsive to behavioral therapy, whereas patients with panic disorder without agoraphobia would be most responsive to pharmacotherapy. The interplay between pharmacotherapy and behavioral therapy for agoraphobia has sparked a debate on the relative frequency, importance, and temporal sequencing of panic attacks and avoidance behavior. Pharmacologic theories presume that panic attacks precede the onset of avoidant behavior and that the avoidant behavior results from aversive distress associated with panic attacks. Process research on the sequence of change in response to drugs and behavioral therapy could help resolve these issues.

Follow-Up Studies

Follow-up studies test whether the effects of the psychotherapy or pharmacotherapy endure. Although many psychotherapies claim to have enduring effects based on social learning and the undoing of maladaptive patterns of cognition and interpersonal relations, few attempts have been made to test these hypotheses. Notable are the 1-year follow-up studies of cognitive therapy (Kovacs, Rush, Beck, & Hollon, 1981) and the 1-year and 4-year follow-ups of depressed patients treated with medication and IPT (Klerman, 1980; Weissman, Klerman, Prusoff, Sholomskas, & Padian, 1981).

In the treatment of panic disorder and agoraphobia, there is a major controversy over possible enduring effects of pharamacologic and psychotherapeutic treatments. Marks (1976) asserts that patients treated with behavioral therapy make enduring gains, and points out that patients treated with medication have a high relapse rate when therapy is discontinued. Marks interprets this as a form of state-dependent learning and as evidence for the superiority of behavioral therapy over pharmacotherapy. Nevertheless, this is an area of continuing dispute. Marks (1985b) is completing a factorial design study comparing alprazolam with exposure therapy and including follow-up.

Long-Term Treatments

Many psychotherapies, particularly those based on psychoanalysis and psychodynamic theory, make claims for the value of long-term treatment. Empirical support of these claims in very limited. For certain disorders, long-term treatment with psychopharmacologic agents has been demonstrated to have some efficacy: neuroleptics for schizophrenia, particularly long-acting injectable compounds, such as fluphenazine decanoate; and lithium for bipolar disorder to prevent relapse and recurrence. There is significant diagnosis by medication interaction: tricyclic antidepressants may be deleterious to bipolar patients by inducing manic states. For nonbipolar (unipolar) depressions, both lithium and tricyclics have demonstrated efficacy. For opiate dependence, methadone maintenance treatment is now standard. Research projects using constructive designs have attempted to assess the value of psychotherapy for patients being treated with long-term maintenance pharmacotherapies. These are discussed in the specific diagnostic sections. Most designs based on constructive strategies in such research presume the facilitative interaction described earlier, namely, that the psychotherapy is unlikely to be effective by itself, but becomes effective in the presence of ongoing medication. This conclusion generally seems to be accepted in long-term studies of outpatients with schizophrenia, opiate addiction, and bipolar disorder.

Cost–Benefit and Cost-Effectiveness Assessments

The conventional focus of treatment research in psychopharmacology and psychotherapy has been on measures of safety, efficacy, and related outcomes. More recently, with growing concern about the economic costs of health care, cost–benefit analysis and cost-effectiveness analysis have been advocated for psychotherapy research (Fein, 1980). Future studies are expected to apply these methods, particularly to assess whether treatments with equal clinical efficacy differ in cost-effectiveness.

POSSIBLE OUTCOMES OF RESEARCH ON COMPARATIVE AND COMBINED PSYCHOTHERAPY TREATMENTS

Having reviewed some of the possible research designs, we now analyze the possible outcomes for studies of pharmacotherapy and psychotherapy, focusing on comparative and constructive strategies for evaluating combination therapy. Most of the discussion uses results from the four-group design shown in Figure 18.2. The advantage of a factorial design is that is allows a simultaneous comparison of pharmacotherapy against psychotherapy and against a control group, as well as a constructive strategy to assess the possible advantage of combining medication and psychotherapy.

In Figures 18.5 through 18.7, the height of the bars representing treatment outcome is equal for the psychotherapy and the pharmacotherapy groups. This reflects an attempt to equalize the efficacies of the two forms of treatment. For example, in studies of depression, Rush and Beck (1980) published evidence from a two-group design that cognitive therapy is equal in treatment efficacy to a tricyclic antidepressant. Similar findings were reported with interpersonal therapy (Prusoff, Weissman, Klerman, & Rounsaville, 1980). These findings challenged conventional wisdom within the depression field, which assumed that medication would have more impact than any behavioral or psychotherapeutic intervention. On the other hand, Elkin et al. (1989), in an ambitious, multicenter, randomized antidepressant treatment trial, found that pharmacotherapy tended to outperform two psychotherapies, at least with sicker outpatients.

Outcomes of Constructive Designs for Assessing Combined Drugs and Psychotherapy

Figure 18.5 catalogues the possible outcomes of the combined treatment groups in relationship to

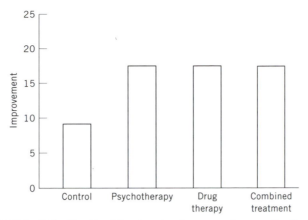

FIGURE 18.5 Combined treatment outcome: no therapeutic effect.

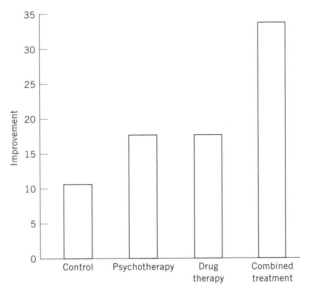

FIGURE 18.6 Combined treatment outcome: positive effect—additive.

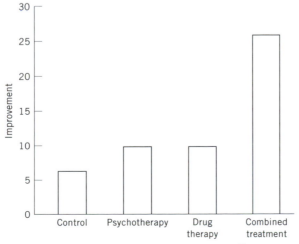

FIGURE 18.7 Combined treatment outcome: positive effect—synergistic.

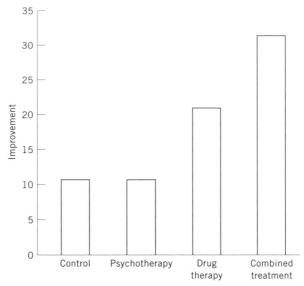

FIGURE 18.8 Combined treatment outcome: positive effect — facilitative.

the two individual treatments. In Figures 18.6 through 18.8, the left bar refers to the control group, the middle bar refers to the two active therapies of pharmacotherapy, and the bar on the right refers to the combined treatment.

At least three groups of outcome are reported in the literature.

1. No therapeutic effect (Figure 18.5): Combined treatment provides the same improvement as the individual treatments.

2. Positive effects (Figures 18.6 – 18.8): Combined treatment provides improvement over the individual treatments.

3. Negative effects: Combined treatment shows less improvement than either treatment alone.

No therapeutic effect of combined therapy. No therapeutic effect of combination is depicted in Figure 18.5. The effects of combined treatment offer no greater benefit than the single treatments, each of which is better than outcome for the control group. This outcome has been reported for the combination of medication and cognitive therapy for depression, in which combined treatment did not offer any advantage over either amitriptyline or cognitive therapy alone (Klerman, 1984; Rush & Watkins, 1981).

Positive effects of combined therapies. In constructed combination treatments, the researcher hopes for additive effects (Figure 18.6) in which the sum is greater than its parts so that the combined

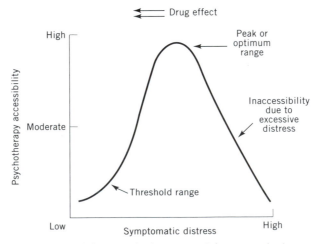

FIGURE 18.9 Medications facilitate acessibility to psychotherapy.

treatment will produce a magnitude of effect greater than that of the two individual treatments.

Additive and synergistic effects. The ideal effects would be synergistic, with the effect of combined treatment greater than the sum of the two competent treatments. This result has been reported from some outcomes in the Boston–New Haven project on the treatment of acutely depressed outpatients. In this study, the Hamilton Depression Scale showed a synergistic effect (Hamilton, 1967). This effect can also be called a cocktail or martini effect: The assumption in a cocktail is that the combination of gin plus vermouth produces greater psychopharmacologic punch than equal amounts of gin and vermouth taken separately (Figure 18.7).

Facilitative interaction. A more complex effect is facilitation, an interaction in which one treatment is effective only when combined with the other. For example, as shown in Figure 18.8, one of the treatments (psychotherapy) is ineffective alone, but the combination is most effective. This is the outcome reported in most studies of hospitalized schizophrenics. Individual psychotherapy alone is ineffective, but has an additive effect when combined with pharmacotherapy (Figure 18.9). This facilitative effect is implicit in current clinical practice in the treatment of patients with bipolar disorder, psychotic depression, and melancholic (or endogenous) depression. Psychotherapy alone is ineffective for these diagnoses as well; they require medication, and combined treatment is presumed to offer an advantage. The converse possibility exists, that is, where pharmacotherapy alone is ineffective, psychotherapy alone is effective, and the medication gains efficacy only in combination with psychotherapy. This possibility has not been documented. Yet theoretically, encouragement of compliance and patient adherence by psychotherapy facilitates the action of medication, which in the absence of some form of psychotherapy might be ineffective.

Negative effects of combined treatment. Ideological concerns have been raised that one form of therapy might undercut another, as noted later. Some patients may not only not benefit from combined therapy, but might experience a negative synergy. Despite this theoretical possibility, there have been no reports of such negative effects of combined treatment.

Indeed, it generally has been difficult to demonstrate significant benefits for combined treatments in comparison with single modalities. This difficulty arises in part because single therapies are often highly effective, particularly in the treatment of mood and anxiety disorders, and their high efficacy

leaves little room at the top for added benefit. Another obstacle to proving the benefits of combined treatment has been the small sample size of most combined treatment research. Thus inadequate power raises the possibility of a type II error; that is, of not finding a difference where one may truly exist (Manning, Markowitz, & Frances, 1992). Although combined treatment outcome is usually no worse than monotherapy, it is certainly more expensive, and the challenge remains to demonstrate which subgroups of patients with a given disorder do best with which treatment or combination of treatments.

CLINICAL MECHANISMS OF ACTION OF COMBINED TREATMENTS

The clinical literature has suggested a variety of mechanisms responsible for the efficacy of combined treatments that produce either additive or synergistic effects.

Medications Facilitate Psychotherapeutic Accessibility

This hypothesis embodies the most commonly stated rationale for the use of combined therapies and supports prevailing clinical practice in psychiatry. Advertisements and promotional materials of many pharmaceutical firms propose that their medications facilitate psychotherapy by making the patient more accessible. The mechanism for this effect is readily specified: Pharmacologic action ameliorates the presumed CNS dysfunction underlying symptom formation, reducing the patient's symptomatology, psychopathology, and/or affective discomfort. Reduction in discomfort by medication renders the patient better able to communicate and benefit from psychotherapy. This hypothesis presumes that whereas some level of anxiety, dysphoria, or symptomatology is necessary to provide drive or motivation for participation in psychotherapy, excessive levels of tension, anxiety, or symptom intensity decrease the patient's capacity to participate effectively in psychotherapy.

Medications Influence the Ego Psychological Functions Required for Participation in Psychotherapy

It is widely accepted that adequate ego functioning is a prerequisite for psychotherapeutic participation. Another hypothesis predicts that medications may improve verbal skills or cognitive functioning, reducing distractibility or promoting attention, concentration, and memory. Pharmacologic enhancement of these psychological components of the large domain of ego function increases the patient's benefit from participation in psychotherapy. Although many psychoanalysts are skeptical of, if not hostile toward, pharmacotherapy, some have attempted to integrate psychoanalytic thinking with medication therapy (Cooper, 1985; Ostow, 1962; Reiser, 1984).

Drugs Promote Psychotherapeutic Abreaction

Abreaction is a basic psychotherapeutic technique. Several medications, especially intravenous barbiturates and amphetamines, have been used to promote this effect in what Wikler (1957) referred to as "psychoexploratory" techniques. These medications help uncover memory, break down defenses, and bring into consciousness material against which the person otherwise defends. A variant of this practice was the use of LSD, mescaline, and psilocybin to promote peak experiences; the heightened sense of self-awareness and emotional, affective, and bodily experiences that occur with these psychedelic drugs was advocated as facilitating the psychotherapeutic process.

There is a long history of the use of medication to assist interviewing, primarily with Amytal (Kwentus, 1984). In the 1940s, use of intravenous Amytal was extended to the development of a reactive treatment, sometimes called narcoanalysis. During World War II, this technique was widely used in military psychiatry (Grinker & Spiegel, 1945). During the 1950s, psychedelic drugs were also used to facilitate abreaction (Abramson, 1967) as described earlier. However, controlled studies failed to sustain the early claims for this action of drugs. Abreactive therapies currently are not popular, either in clinical practice or in research.

Positive Effects of Pharmacotherapy on Patients' Expectations, Attitudes, and Stigmata

In addition to the short-term symptomatic relief of pharmacotherapy, a positive placebo effect may often contribute to a patient's optimism and confidence. Advocates of biological methods, such as the purported megavitamin treatment of schizophrenia, are often successful in decreasing the stigma of psychiatric illness and making it easier for the patients and their families to accept the diagnosis of mental illness. Thus, a patient's request for medication may in fact represent an indirect attempt to seek psychotherapeutic counseling. In this context, the skillful psychopharmacologist often uses the patient's initial request for pharmacotherapy as a starting point for initiating psychotherapy.

Having discussed mechanisms by which medication may have positive effects on psychotherapy, we now turn to mechanisms by which psychotherapy may produce positive effects on pharmacotherapy.

Psychotherapy Facilitates Medication Compliance and Adherence

Psychotherapeutic input in psychopharmacology employing such techniques as reassurance, psychoeducation, and clear instructions, enhance the patient's positive attitude and cooperation. May (1968a) and others have distinguished between psychological management and psychotherapy. Psychological management refers to extension of general aspects of doctor–patient relationships to enhance patient medication compliance, cooperation, and general therapeutic alliance. Psychotherapy, in this view, refers to efforts to influence the patient's symptoms and psychological functions by verbal and behavioral techniques.

Psychotherapy as Rehabilitation Effort

Many pharmacotherapists hypothesize value for psychotherapy as a secondary, ameliorative treatment. They propose that psychotherapy does not operate on etiologic mechanisms or the core of the psychological process, but rather corrects secondary difficulties in interpersonal relations, self-esteem, and psychological functions that result from affective symptoms. In this view, psychotherapy is rehabilitative rather than therapeutic, an elective rather than a required treatment. Many advocates of this approach employ a sequence in which the medication is administered first and psychotherapy introduced after the appearance of symptom reduction, stabilization of affective states, and early improvement in social adjustment.

Negative Effects of Combined Pharmacotherapy and Psychotherapy

Much attention was once given to the possible negative effects of introducing medications into psychotherapy. Although relatively little empirical research has been done to test these hypotheses, it is possible to identify possible interactions.

Negative effects of medication on psychotherapy

Negative placebo effect of medication in the presence of psychotherapy. Much of the criticism of medication enunciated by psychotherapists in the 1950s implied a negative placebo effect — that pill taking had harmful effects in the presence of psychotherapy. It was hypothesized that the prescription of any medication adversely affected the psychotherapeutic relationship and the attitudes and behavior of both patient and therapist—

effects independent of the specific pharmacologic actions of the pill. Moreover, the prescribing of medication was felt to promote an authoritarian attitude on the part of the psychiatrist, making the patient more dependent, more reliant on magical thinking, and more passive and compliant, as in the conventional doctor–patient relationship in medical specialties other than psychiatry.

Medication-induced reduction of symptoms as patient's motives for discontinuing psychotherapy. The negative placebo effect hypothesis assumes only a symbolic and psychological meaning to the administration of medication. If the pharmacologic activity and therapeutic efficacy of the drug are assumed, however, then a resultant decrease of the patient's symptoms, anxiety, and tension might reduce the patient's motivation for psychotherapy. The hypothesis predicts that too effective a drug will shift patient attitudes and behaviors counter to psychotherapy; patients will no longer seek psychotherapy because they will be satisfied with mere symptom reduction. Thus, if a psychoactive medication, such as a phenothiazine or MAO inhibitor, obliterates psychotic turmoil, depression, anxiety, or other symptoms, the patient's motivation for reflection, insight, and psychotherapeutic work will be lessened.

Pharmacotherapy undermines defenses, providing symptom substitutes. This hypothesis predicts that if the pharmacologic effect prematurely undercuts some important defenses, symptom substitution or other compensatory mechanisms of symptom formation will ensue. For example, in psychotherapeutic practice, Seitz (1953) reported instances of new symptom formation following hypnosis, and Weiss (1965) cautioned against an overly rapid relief of the anxiety of agoraphobic patients, arguing that if such anxiety were reduced too rapidly, before new defenses could develop, other symptoms would arise to maintain a psychic balance between conflict and defenses. Systematic research data and replications germane to this specific hypothesis are few and inconclusive.

Possible negative effects of psychotherapy on medication. Most of the discussion in the literature has focused on the possible effects of pharmacotherapy on psychotherapy. Relatively little attention has been paid to the obverse of the process, namely, the impact of psychotherapy on the patient receiving pharmacotherapy. It is interesting to note how seldom this problem is discussed or even mentioned in clinical settings. Considering the efficacy of antidepressant medications in the treatment of mood disorders and the less extensive body of

evidence for the efficacy of psychotherapy, the question perhaps should be stated, What negative effects or benefits, if any, accrue to the patient if psychotherapy is added to medication? During the discussions in the 1950s and 1960s, psychotherapists were the assertive members of the dialogue, with pharmacotherapists on the defensive. There was a subsequent shift in the 1970s and 1980s in response to evidence from controlled studies regarding the efficacy of medications. In the 1990s, we are approaching a more sophisticated synthesis of the views of the formerly warring camps.

Pharmacotherapy alone is necessary and sufficient. Some pharmacotherapists make simplistic analogies for psychotropic treatment, especially to endocrine agents such as insulin for diabetes. For those who hold this view, the rectification of the presumed neurophysiologic dysfunction or deficiency is the critical treatment factor, and psychotherapy is considered unnecessary, irrelevant, or, at best, neutral. Television and news reports have widely diffused the concept of a chemical imbalance into public thinking as an explanation for depression and bipolar disorder. Thus, patients may regard medication treatment as a simple correction of their chemical imbalance. A variation of this view is expressed by some proponents of the lithium treatment of mania.

Psychotherapy may be symptomatically disruptive. Some pharmacotherapies further hypothesize that psychotherapy may be deleterious to pharmacologic treatment, since symptoms may be aggravated by excessive probing and uncovering of defenses. Some psychiatrists who work with depressed and schizophrenic patients feel that psychotherapeutic intervention may be harmful, particularly during the acute state, and that during the early recovery process patients are best left alone to seal over and to reconstitute their defenses. They advocate pharmacologic symptom reduction alone and dispute psychotherapists who advocate working through underlying conflicts even if it involves sealing over by promoting denial, repression, and other defenses. Many pharmacotherapists are concerned that psychotherapy, by focusing on patient conflicts, increases the patient's level of emotional tension.

Psychotherapy may undercut compliance. The fear is that psychotherapists with overtly or indirectly negative attitudes toward pharmacotherapy may communicate these attitudes to the patient in psychotherapy and thus may discourage medication compliance on the part of the patient, obviating any possible value of pharmacotherapy.

STATUS OF KNOWLEDGE CONCERNING SPECIFIC DISORDERS

SCHIZOPHRENIA

The introduction of the tranquilizers in the middle 1950s had its greatest impact on hospitalized patients with schizophrenia. Claims for the antipsychotic and behavioral efficacy of these new medications came at a time of controversy about the nature of schizophrenia as a disorder and about the efficacy and safety of the interventions advocated for its treatment. Numerous biological treatments for schizophrenia had been utilized through the first half of the twentieth century, including dental extraction, colonic resection, tonsillectomy, and adrenalectomy. Their use was based on unsubstantiated presumptions as to the cause of schizophrenia. Therapeutic claims were seldom accompanied by any evidence for efficacy from systematic evaluations and follow-up, let alone controlled trials. By the 1930s, biological treatments of schizophrenia were regarded as unscientific and inhuman (Klerman, 1981).

In the late 1930s three new biological treatments were introduced: electroconvulsive therapy, insulin coma treatment, and prefrontal lobotomy. Because of the drastic nature of these interventions and the strong claims made for their efficacy, considerable debate attended their introduction. These controversies set the stage for the reactions to the phenothiazines and reserpine derivatives introduced in the 1950s. By the 1950s, however, randomized controlled trials were being increasingly adopted in medicine, particularly in studies on the treatment of tuberculosis and angina. Pressure from scientific quarters and from Congress led to the utilization of controlled trial designs in the new field of psychopharmacology. U.S. government agencies as well as the British Medical Research Council mounted large, multicenter studies. These studies demonstrated the feasibility of conducting randomized trials in assessing treatments for mental illness and the importance of multicenter collaborative trials to generate sample size sufficient to ensure that findings could be generalized beyond a single setting. By the mid-1960s, the value of pharmacotherapy for symptom reduction of hospitalized schizophrenic patients had been conclusively established.

In comparison with the biological treatments of schizophrenia, psychotherapeutic treatments of schizophrenia developed slowly. Interest in the psychopathology of the psychoses, particularly schizophrenia and paranoia, characterized early psychoanalytic writings. Freud's papers established the general principles for the separation of psychotic and neurotic disorders based on the criterion of failure of reality testing by the ego. This psychoanalytic criterion is almost identical to the descriptive psychopathological criteria of impairment of higher mental functions, memory, orientation, language, and cognition derived from nineteenth-century psychology.

After World War I, psychoanalytic interest in the psychoses diminished greatly because of Freud's doctrine that the narcissistic neuroses (i.e., psychoses) were not amenable to psychoanalysis. Despite this, a number of psychoanalytic writers maintained interest in the psychoses. These efforts cumulated in the theories of the neo-Freudians and of the emerging interpersonal school, particularly in the writing of Frieda Fromm-Reichmann and also Harry Stack Sullivan (1953). The modification of classic psychoanalytic techniques by Fromm-Reichmann and her associates at Chestnut Lodge led to the widespread application of intensive individual psychotherapy for hospitalized schizophrenic patients. Although the efficacy of this treatment was never supported by systematic studies, the writings of this group profoundly influenced a generation of American psychotherapists and contributed to theories of the developmental and intrafamily origin of schizophrenia (Bowen, 1960; Lidz, Fleck, & Cornelison, 1965) and to new forms of family therapy.

Efficacy of Medication and Psychotherapy for Acute Schizophrenic Inpatients

Several scholarly reviews have evaluated treatments of hospitalized schizophrenics (Hollon & Beck, 1978). Many studies have documented the efficacy of neuroleptic medications for the symptomatic treatment of schizophrenic inpatients. These have been reviewed extensively (Cole, Klerman, & Jones, 1960; Davis, 1965; Gilligan, 1965; Klein, Gittleman, Quitkin, Rifkin, 1980). The Quality Assurance Project of the Royal Australian and New Zealand College of Psychiatrists applied meta-analysis to data from 600 controlled trials of schizophrenia (Andrews et al., in press). They calculated effect size for 200 studies of medication and 26 studies of psychotherapy or social intervention and found no effect for psychotherapy, but a very strong effect for pharmacotherapies.

The most controversial issues are those relating to the efficacy of psychotherapy, milieu therapy, and other psychosocial interventions (Mosher & Keith, 1980). Among the studies on psychosocial treatments, five have attempted to assess the efficacy of individual psychotherapy for acute schizophrenic inpatients. These have been reviewed by

Hollon and Beck (1978). With the exception of the study in Michigan reported by Karon and VandenBos (1981), the results are negative. Without concomitant medication, individual psychotherapy based on the intensive psychodynamic model has relatively little to offer hospitalized schizophrenics (Klein, 1976; Schooler, 1978).

Comparative studies of the relative efficacy of pharmacotherapy and psychotherapy are few in number, but generally indicate the greater value of medication over psychotherapy for reducing symptoms and improving social functioning within the hospital setting. Major studies conducted at the Massachusetts Mental Health Center (Grinspoon, Ewalt, & Shader, 1972) and at the Camarillo State Hospital in California (May, 1968b) reported little or no therapeutic efficacy for individual psychotherapy alone. The May study provided evidence for a modest additive effect of psychotherapy when combined with pharmacotherapy. The Grinspoon, Ewalt, and Shader study indicated that psychotherapy was effective only in the presence of medication treatment. This pattern of results follows the type of outcome called facilitative interaction in the previous section on combined treatments.

An important research effort to evaluate intensive, psychodynamically oriented individual psychotherapy of schizophrenia undertaken by Stanton et al. in Boston was reported in a special issue of the *Schizophrenia Bulletin* (1984). Their study employed a constructive design and evaluated two forms of psychotherapy, one based on psychodynamic exploration and the other a practical approach. These therapies differed in theoretical focus and in the intensity of contact between therapist and patient. The investigators designed the study with the expectation of demonstrating the efficacy of psychotherapy based on psychodynamic theory. This study attempted to assess whether or not psychotherapy offers anything above standard antipsychotic neuroleptic medication. All patients in both psychotherapy treatment groups received antipsychotic medication. The study's design precluded evaluation of the efficacy of psychotherapy against a placebo or psychotherapy control condition. Another feature of this study was its assessment of a wide range of outcome variables. Treatment studies in the psychopharmacology of schizophrenia have been criticized by psychotherapists as relying exclusively on measures of symptom reduction. The Stanton project investigators developed comprehensive assessment batteries of cognitive functioning, ego activity, social adjustment, and interpersonal relations.

Duration of treatment was 2 years, and the study employed experienced therapists in both treatment groups. Nevertheless, the attrition rate was very high, such that only about one-third of the patients initially allocated to the two treatment groups completed the projected 2 years of treatment. An evaluation of this study concludes that the assessment of intensive individual psychotherapy failed to produce evidence for its claims of efficacy. Even in the presence of medication, this treatment failed to achieve any of the goals of the proponents who designed the experiment.

The Nature of the Hospital Milieu

At about the same time that interest in psychotherapy and psychopharmacology of schizophrenia was emerging after World War II, a strong interest in social psychiatry also developed, with the psychiatric hospital and the creation of community treatment programs as its main agenda. Much of this reform centered on countering the adverse effects of the social structure of large mental hospitals on the clinical course of mental disorders, particularly schizophrenia. Significant innovations were introduced: open-door policies, restrictions on the use of restraints and seclusion, lessening of the authoritarian social structure, upgrade of the status and training of nurses and other ward personnel, and, most notably, the concept of the therapeutic community. Unfortunately for historical analyses, these innovations coincided with the introduction of chlorpromazine and reserpine. It is difficult, in retrospect, to disentangle the relative contributions of these two innovations to the resultant decrease in the length of stay of schizophrenic inpatients and the dramatic decrease in the overall number of hospitalized patients. In the United Kingdom, reduction in the length of stay and in hospital census antedated the introduction of the medications, a situation that social psychiatry advocates offer as evidence of the power of institutional change. It is likely that the two innovations had an additive effect and that the introduction of the medications served to accelerate trends already evident. Attempts have been made to assess the efficacy of milieu therapy alone, without concomitant pharmacotherapy (May & Simpson, 1980a, 1980b). They have concluded that active inpatient milieu programs have defined but circumscribed effects, mostly on social adjustment and duration of stay.

An interesting controversy around complex medication–milieu interactions occurred during this period. Social psychiatric observers pointed out that the most enthusiastic reports of the efficacy of the new tranquilizers came from public mental hospitals, particularly state, county, and VA hospitals, which were overcrowded, understaffed, and had limited milieu programs. In contrast, better staffed programs at university hospitals and small institutions did not report dramatic drug effects. It was postulated that the degree of success of the new pharmacotherapies was inversely related to the intensity of preexisting treatment programs. A partial test of this hypothesis by Goldberg, Cole, and Klerman (1966) found significant differences among institutions participating in a nine-hospital study; medication–placebo differences were less striking in small, intensive treatment centers, such as the Payne Whitney Clinic at Cornell Medical Center, than in large public hospitals. However, when adjustment was made for the social background and clinical prognostic characteristics of admitted patients, many of the milieu differences disappeared, suggesting that differences in outcome across institutions depended more on the better prognosis of patients admitted to smaller institutions than on milieu influence per se.

Controlled studies have documented the value of brief hospitalization using medication (Burhan, 1967; Caton, 1982; Glick & Hargreaves, 1979). Whereas prior to 1950 the average length of stay for schizophrenic inpatients was over 6 months, by the 1970s it had dropped to less than 2 weeks. Controlled studies showed no advantage to lengths of hospitalization beyond 60 days, compared with a shorter duration of stay with more intensive treatment (Caffey, Galbrecht, & Klett, 1971; Herz, Endicott, & Spitzer, 1977). Patients treated with brief hospitalizations did not have higher rates of subsequent readmission. Thus, prolonged hospitalization does not seem to have an enduring effect. The main functions of hospitalization seem to be symptom reduction, promotion of social adjustment, and a transition to aftercare treatment. Brief hospitalization has become standard clinical practice reinforced by the fiscal restraints of reimbursement policies.

Still unresolved, is the optimal nature of the hospital milieu. The concept of the therapeutic community, developed in the United Kingdom for the treatment of patients with personality disorder, in the United States has been widely advocated for acute schizophrenic inpatients. These programs emphasize intensive social interaction, verbal expression of feelings and attitudes, and the blurring of social status boundaries between staff and patients. These practices have been challenged, however. Critics suggest that the therapeutic community is conceptually unsound and clinically ineffective for psychotic patients. Relying on psychophysiologic studies of arousal level in schizophrenic patients, they advocate decreased social interaction, increased structure, standard patient–staff relations, clear expectations of role performance, and

use of medications (Herz et al., 1977; May & Simpson, 1980b; VanPutten, 1973). No controlled studies have been reported that test the differential effects of alternative types of milieu (VanPutten, 1973).

Community Alternatives to Hospital Treatment of Acute Schizophrenic Patients

Because of dissatisfaction with the adverse effects of hospitalization, a variety of community alternatives have been proposed. These include day hospital, home treatment and family involvement, and community residences. An impressive body of controlled studies has demonstrated the value of these community treatment alternatives to hospitalization for acutely psychotic individuals. Day hospitals, first developed in Moscow and modified in London by Bierer (1951), emerged in the United States at the Massachusetts Mental Health Center and the Yale Psychiatric Institute. A number of controlled studies, notably the study reported by Zwerling and Wilder (1964), demonstrated that approximately 80 percent of acutely ill patients who might otherwise require hospitalization could be treated effectively by a day treatment program. Almost all of these patients were treated with medication.

Another important innovation was the home treatment of schizophrenia by public health nurses. Pasamanick, Scarpitti, and Dinitz (1967) conducted a well-controlled study in Louisville, Kentucky, that demonstrated the value of home treatment using medication and social psychotherapeutic techniques.

Mosher reported the utility of the community residence in the social rehabilitation of schizophrenic patients (Mosher & Menn, 1978). Using as a control group patients routinely hospitalized at a nearby county hospital, Mosher claimed the superiority of an innovative program based on community residential treatment over standard hospitalization and medication.

Pharmacotherapy and Psychotherapy for Formerly Hospitalized Patients in Aftercare

There is a small but growing body of sophisticated research on the value of pharmacotherapy and psychotherapy alone, and in combination, in the aftercare of discharged outpatients with schizophrenia. Inpatient findings have been reported by the collaboration among Schooler et al. (1980), Goldberg, Schooler, Hogarty, and Roper (1977) at NIMH, and Hogarty, Schooler, and Ulrich (1979) at Pittsburgh. They reported research from two sets of studies, one using oral medication, the other emphasizing injectable long-acting medication combined with a version of psychotherapy called major role training (MRT). The results of this complex study indicate a high efficacy of maintenance medication therapy in reducing relapse rates, particularly in the first year following discharge. In the placebo-treated group, over 70 percent of the patients relapsed and were rehospitalized within 1 year. This rate was considerably reduced by the maintenance treatment with fluphenazine. Relatively little difference was noted whether the fluphenazine was administered orally or by injection. By itself, the social treatment of major role therapy was relatively ineffective in influencing the relapse rate; in fact, for certain patients it seemed to have a deleterious effect. However, the combination did offer some added benefits.

Complementing these studies (Goldberg et al., 1977; Hogarty et al., 1979; Schooler et al., 1980) are the important findings from the United Kingdom on expressed emotions (EE). Early studies by Brown, Birley, and Wing (1972) indicated that families of schizophrenic patients who were high in EE, characterized by critical comments, hostility, censure, and overinvolvement, were associated with higher relapse rate. The adverse impact of the high EE environment could be reduced either through the reduction of the amount of time the patient spent with the family or through the use of medication. The inference was that medication increased the patient's ability to cope with the stressful impact of interfamilial tension. Based on these findings, family intervention strategies have been developed, most notably by Falloon et al. (1982) in southern California. Four controlled trials reported the value of family therapy over individual therapy for newly discharged patients (Goldstein, 1984).

These findings of the efficacy of family therapy for patients in aftercare were sufficiently interesting to prompt the NIMH to design and initiate a multicenter collaborative project on treatment strategies in schizophrenia (Schooler et al., 1980). The design of the study is an experimental model with two factors, pharmacotherapy (targeted medication vs. continuous low dose vs. continuous standard dose) and family management (applied vs. supportive) in a 3 × 2 factorial design. The study is being conducted at five sites. Patients are identified when acutely symptomatic, randomized to one of the two family treatment strategies, and treated with the assigned family treatment and a standard dosage of fluphenazine decanoate for up to 6 months. If successfully stabilized, they are further randomized into the double-blind dosage study for a 2-year trial in the full 3 × 2 factorial design.

This study attempts to test an important issue for the long-term treatment of schizophrenia, namely, whether care can reduce medication exposure (and consequent risk of tardive dyskinesia) in combination with psychoeducational family treatment. Although prior studies have provided substantial evidence of the effectiveness of individual components of the treatments being investigated, they have left two major gaps that this study is designed to fill. First, there has been no direct comparison of the two reduced dosage strategies: targeted medication on an as-needed basis when symptoms arise; and continuous low dosage. This comparison is of particular interest because the strategies are based on different principles of medication management, clinical indication versus prophylaxis. Second, there are no long-term controlled studies of the relationship between reduced medication dosage strategies and family treatment. As clinicians attempt to integrate pharmacologic and psychosocial treatments for shizophrenia into treatment programs, understanding the additive or interactive effects of these treatment modalities gains increasing importance.

Chronic Hospitalized Patients

Studies of chronically hospitalized schizophrenic patients have markedly decreased in the past decade. In large part, this reflects the impact of the public policy of deinstitutionalization, which has resulted in a dramatic decrease in the resident population in large mental hospitals. In 1955, almost 600,000 patients were hospitalized in public mental hospitals, half of whom carried a diagnosis of schizophrenia. By 1980, the number was less than 100,000. Many of the early studies on pharmacotherapy in schizophrenic patients focused on these inpatients. The focus of clinical care and public policy debate has shifted to the needs of patients in the community, particularly to the emergence of large numbers of homeless patients. Almost all studies support the value of long-term medication treatment and involve comparative strategies to assess the value of group psychotherapy and social rehabilitative efforts (Schooler, 1978).

A notable exception to this trend is provided by the reports by Paul, Tobias, and Holly (1972), who studied inpatient populations with the diagnosis of schizophrenia and found many functioning at low social levels. Some of the patients were maintained on medication, whereas others were withdrawn to placebo conditions. Contrary to expectations, there was no difference between the group that was continued on medication and those transferred to placebo. There were no interactions with social therapy. Schooler interpreted the Paul study as supporting the possibility that withdrawal of medication from very chronic unresponsive patients does not necessarily lead to increased psychopathology and called for an attempt to test these hypotheses again. Recent studies of the psychopathology of schizophrenia have highlighted the value of separating patients with positive versus negative symptoms, have correlated negative symptoms with enlarged brain ventricles on CAT scans, and have reported unresponsiveness to neuroleptic drugs. Positive symptoms refer to delusions, hallucinations, and overactivity, whereas negative symptoms refer to apathy, withdrawal, absence of affect, and social inactivity. Paul's sample may have included such patients. However, systematic studies using the positive–negative symptom separation are required to test these hypotheses fully.

Prospects for the Future

Although it is widely accepted that antipsychotic medications are highly effective, particularly in the short term, and over time will prevent relapse, there are troubling aspects of the pharmacotherapy of schizophrenia that prompt continued research on combined therapy. A substantial percentage of patients relapse and a moderate percentage of patients slowly become chronic and more socially disabled. It is hoped that combining pharmacotherapy and various psychosocial interventions, such as community residences, day programs, and family involvement, will augment the efficacy of treatment programs. Neuroleptic medications have contributed to patients becoming "better but not well" (Klerman, 1977), and the deinstitutionalized population exhibits high degrees of social deviance and social dependence. It is apparent that findings from research studies, particularly about the value of day programs and family programs and the limited value of individual psychotherapy, have not fully diffused into clinical practice: There is a wide gap between current practice and knowledge from research. The most important problem, however, involves the adverse effects of neuroleptic antipsychotic medication. The most serious is the tardive dyskinesia syndrome, whose risk increases with cumulative dose and duration of treatment. This serious and at times disabling side effect has prompted various experimental regimens, such as medication holidays, intermittent medication, and low-dose strategies, often combined with psychosocial interventions.

The development of novel antipsychotic medications that produce relatively few extrapyramidal side effects has offered a new approach. Clozapine, an atypical antipsychotic medication, is being used with increasing frequency around the world and has recently been commercially marketed in the United States. Although clozapine has proved to be effective in some treatment-refractory schizophrenic patients and to produce relatively few extrapyramidal side effects in comparison with classical neuroleptics, several issues require further investigation, including the definition of neuroleptic intolerance, the optimal dose range, and the appropriate duration of a clozapine treatment trial (Safferman et al., 1991). Agranulocytosis remains a significant, but manageable, risk with this medication. Finally, a number of studies have found that lower doses of neuroleptics — in the range of 10–20 mg/day of haloperidol medication equivalents — are equally as effective as, and better tolerated than, higher doses. For both medication-refractory and low-dose-responsive patients, the addition of a supportive or educational psychotherapeutic intervention for both patient and family seems necessary.

MOOD DISORDERS

Mood disorders refer to a group of clinical conditions whose common feature is the patient's mood, either depression or elation. This definition does not imply a common etiology. Mood disorders are probably biologically heterogeneous, with a syndrome comparable to those of mental retardation or jaundice. The major distinction in mood disorders is between bipolar and depressive disorders and, within the depressive disorders, between major depression and dysthymia. The concept of a mood disorder (sometimes called affective disorder) itself is noteworthy. This chapter could not have been written 2 decades ago. The conditions that today are grouped together as mood disorders were treated separately in the American Psychiatric Association's *Diagnostic and Statistical Manual of Mental Disorders*, second edition (DSM-II), as part of either psychosis or neurosis, the two predominant psychiatric categories in the 1960s.

Bipolar Disorder

The presence of mania defines bipolar disorder. Mania is a distinct period during which the predominant mood is either elevated, expansive, or irritable, and there are associated symptoms, including hyperactivity, pressure of speech, racing thoughts, inflated self-esteem, decreased need for sleep, distractibility, and excessive involvement in activities that have high potential for painful consequences. Mania without major depression, sometimes called unipolar mania, is uncommon, but does occur. Bipolar disorder can present as either a manic or a depressive state. Cyclothymia, which is a chronic form of mild mood swings, is interesting because of its aggregation in the biological relatives of patients with bipolar disorder. For this reason, cyclothymia is considered part of the spectrum of bipolar disorder. However, it is often difficult to differentiate the boundaries between cyclothymia and normal moods.

Treatment of acute manic episodes. The value of pharmacotherapy for treatment of acute manic episodes has been well established by numerous controlled trials (Klerman, 1978a); lithium and neuroleptics have demonstrated efficacy. More recently, two anticonvulsant drugs, carbamazepine and valproic acid, have been used for lithium-refractory patients. The psychodynamics of the acute manic episode have been described, but few psychotherapists advocate the use of psychotherapy alone in the treatment of the acute mania. In clinical practice, most patients with acute manic episodes receive pharmacotherapy plus various kinds of psychological management directed at containing the disruptive behavior and laying the groundwork for a treatment alliance for possible psychotherapy in the posthospital phase.

Observations of the interpersonal behavior of manic patients, particularly the work of Janowsky, El-Yousef, and Davis (1974), have contributed to structuring the milieu for the hospital treatment of manic patients. Practical recommendations are that the milieu should reduce stimuli, provide structure, and set limits, particularly on the expression of anger and hostility and other aspects of interpersonal behavior. The psychotherapeutic approach, with frequent staff and group meetings and a high level of social participation, is usually considered countertherapeutic for the psychological management of hospitalized acute manic patients.

Far more common than manic episodes in clinical practice are episodes of depression in patients with a history of manic episodes, who thus meet diagnostic criteria for bipolar disorder. Although the symptomatology of these patients as they present for treatment is similar in many respects to acute episodes of unipolar major depression, the propensity of these patients to switch into mania is an important therapeutic issue. Many psychiatrists believe that the tricyclics are particularly prone to induce this switch, and that tricyclics or antidepressants alone should not be used in the treatment of acute episodes of depression for bipolar patients but that lithium and other antidepressants, such as monoamine oxidase inhibitors, should be combined. Controlled trials on this issue are still not conclusive. For bipolar patients, psychotherapy in combination with the medication continues to play an important rehabilitative role, and the guidelines put forth by Goodwin and Jamison (1990) are of

particular value. The full details of treatment of bipolar disorder, as well as our scientific understanding of it, have been recently summarized (Goodwin & Jamison, 1990). Because of its reliance on and gleanings from empirical evidence, this book itself is an achievement of this past decade.

Long-term treatment. For maintenance therapy, lithium has demonstrated efficacy in preventing recurrences of both depressive and manic episodes (Davis, 1976; Klerman, 1978b; Prien, Caffey, & Klett, 1973). Several reports, albeit not from controlled clinical trials, have assessed the effects of combining psychotherapy with lithium treatment for long-term treatment of patients with bipolar disorder. Three types of psychotherapeutic treatment have been described: individual psychotherapy based on the psychodynamic model, group therapy, and family and marital therapy.

As regards individual psychotherapy, a few reports have appeared on the feasibility of conducting psychoanalytically oriented treatment in the presence of lithium (Cooper, 1985; Ostow, 1962). Traditionally, patients with bipolar disorder have been considered poor candidates for group psychotherapy; however, Shakir, Volkmar, Bacon, and Pfefferbaum (1979) reported a positive experience with a long-term ongoing psychotherapy group composed exclusively of patients with bipolar disorder who were receiving maintenance lithium therapy. They found enhanced lithium compliance, although it was difficult to determine whether the relatively high rate of adherence to the medication regimen reflected the effect of group therapy per se or the close supervision patients received each week. Powell, Othmer, and Sinkhorn (1977) reported similar findings from uncontrolled trials.

Davenport, Ebert, Adland, and Goodwin (1976) described the use of couples therapy groups in conjunction with lithium. Married bipolar patients on lithium in couples group therapy reportedly had more stable posthospital courses than those given only minimal support beyond medication. Jamison and Goodwin (1983) described psychotherapeutic techniques for bipolar patients on lithium and their families and reported preliminary results of a trial comparing bipolar patients on lithium alone with those receiving lithium plus family group theraoy. Patients receiving group therapy had better compliance, better social adjustment, and less frequent hospitalization.

Clarkin, Glick, Spencer, and Haas (1990) completed a controlled clinical trial of a psychoeducationally oriented family intervention combined with a standard medication regimen for hospitalized bipolar disorder patients. Results demonstrated efficacy for bipolar but not unipolar patients who received the family interventions. The data suggested that previous hospitalization, a high level of familial rejection of the patient, and poor treatment compliance after discharge were each associated with a markedly higher rate of rehospitalization at 18 months. For each of these variables assignment to family intervention was associated with a dramatic reduction in the rate of rehospitalization for the high risk groups. Similarly, Miklowitz et al. (1988), using a behavioral family treatment plus lithium versus lithium alone, showed that combined treatment decreased relapse.

Like psychoeducational techniques and family methods, psychotherapy also enhances the efficacy of medication, as detailed by Goodwin and Jamison (1990) in their volume on manic-depressive illness. Goodwin and Jamison also emphasize the value of local patient self-support groups; the National Depressive and Manic Depressive Association has recently gained national attention, based in large part on a coalition of local self-supported groups.

Cyclothymic disorder. There are no controlled or uncontrolled studies of the efficacy of psychotherapy with cyclothymic patients. In clinical practice, these patients are treated with psychotherapy alone or in combination with lithium.

Depressive Disorders

Major depression. The essential feature of major depression is a dysphoric mood or a loss of interest or pleasure in all or almost all usual activities and pastimes for at least 2 weeks. The disturbance is prominent, relatively persistent, and associated with other symptoms, including disturbance of appetite, weight, and sleep; psychomotor agitation or retardation; decreased energy; feelings of worthlessness or guilt; difficulty concentrating or thinking; and thoughts of death or suicide or suicidal attempts. Major depression is only diagnosed in the absence of current or past manic symptoms. Although there is general agreement that major depression is a heterogeneous disorder, there is no consensus and little empirical basis for most of the subtypes used clinically, such as endogenous, seasonal, and melancholic depression.

Treatment of acute depressive episodes. The clinical treatment of depressive disorders was revolutionized in the late 1950s by the introduction of the antidepressant medications — tricyclics and monoamine oxidase inhibitors. Their effectiveness has been documented in a large number of well-controlled clinical trials (Klein, 1980). The Royal

Australian and New Zealand College of Psychiatrists applied meta-analysis to the controlled trials of medications used in depression as part of their Quality Assurance Program. They found psychotherapy effective for treating neurotic depression and medications effective for endogenous depression (Andrews et al., 1983).

Brief psychotherapies for depression have been developed and evaluated (Rush, 1982). Weissman identified 25 controlled studies in the period 1974–1984; over half these involved some study of pharmacotherapy–psychotherapy comparison or combination. Among these therapies, the most widely studied is cognitive-behavioral therapy, developed by Beck et al. (1979); (see Chapter 10, this volume). Interpersonal psychotherapy (Klerman et al., 1984) has also been evaluated in studies of acute treatment and maintenance treatment. A group of behavioral techniques are widely used, including relaxation techniques, social skills techniques, and techniques aimed at promoting behavior mastery (Bellack, Hersen, & Himmelhoch, 1980; Kovacs, 1980; Lewinsohn, Sullivan, & Grosscup, 1982; Rehm & Kornblith, 1979; Thase, 1983). Several reviews have summarized the efficacy of these treatments for acute depression (Thase, 1983; Weissman, 1984; Weissman, Jarrett, & Rush, 1987).

Pharmacotherapy–psychotherapy comparison. Data have been reported comparing cognitive-behavioral therapy and interpersonal psychotherapy with antidepressant medications. The majority of the studies find equivalence or superiority of the psychotherapy compared to an antidepressant medication, usually a tricyclic (Bellack, Hersen, & Himmelhoch, 1981; Blackburn, Bishop, Glen, Whalley, & Christie, 1981; McLean & Hakstian, 1979). In the Blackburn study, cognitive therapy was superior to tricyclics among depressed patients in general practice, but not in patients attending psychiatric specialty clinics (Rush, 1982). The data comparing social skills therapy and medication indicate no significant difference (M. Hersen, personal communication, March 1, 1983). Interpersonal therapy was evaluated in comparison with medication and also found to be relatively equal in effectiveness (Weissman et al., 1981).

Combination of pharmacotherapy and psychotherapy. The data on the possible additive or synergistic effects of combined drugs and psychotherapy are inconsistent. Interpersonal therapy is reported to be more effective for endogenous depression in combination with medication than is either treatment alone (Klerman et al., 1984). Blackburn et al. (1981) found that cognitive therapy in combination with tricyclics was superior to either treatment alone, but only among psychiatric outpatients, not among patients attending a general practice. However, this finding was not replicated with social skills therapy (Bellack et al., 1980).

Possible interactions with subtypes of depression. There is long-standing controversy over the utility and validity of subtypes of depressive disorders. Many diagnostic proposals have been debated: endogenous versus reactive depression, psychotic versus neurotic, agitated versus retarded, and so on. In the pharmacotherapy–psychotherapy arena, attention has focused on endogenous subtypes of depression because of the widely held conviction among psychopharmacotherapists that this type of depression responds specifically to tricyclics and to electroconvulsive therapy. Reports of psychotherapeutic efficacy for endogenous patients have challenged conventional wisdom and strongly held theoretical positions. A few studies have reported medication–psychotherapy effects on endogenous depression, usually diagnosed by RDC (Spitzer et al., 1978) or by DSM-III melancholia. Prusoff et al. (1980) reported that endogenous depression responded best to the combination of pharmacotherapy and psychotherapy, and poorly to IPT alone. Patients with situational, also called neurotic or reactive, depressions did equally well with medication, IPT, or the combination; all active treatments did better than the control. In contrast, Blackburn et al. (1981) did not find a difference in response between endogenous and nonendogenous patients treated with cognitive-behavioral therapy. Kovacs (1980) found no significant correlation between endogenous depression and poor response to cognitive psychotherapy.

Elkin et al. (1989) reported that the NIMH Collaborative Study of Outpatient Treatment of Depression did not find that RDC endogenous features were strong predictors of response to imipramine. They reported that RDC endogenous patients treated with IPT also did well, and they questioned the specificity of this depressive subtype for tricyclic medication. The endogenous–neurotic distinction nonetheless remains in use in treatment research, and the Australian Quality Assurance Project endorsed the selective value of psychotherapy, both psychodynamic and behavioral, for neurotic depressions and emphasized the value of medication and ECT for endogenous depressions; they also endorsed the value of combined treatment.

Specificity and duration of effects. Two studies, by Weissman et al. (1981) and Kovacs et al. (1981), reported that acutely depressed patients who had received psychotherapy without medication functioned better than pharmacotherapy patients at 1-year follow-up.

The specificity of the psychotherapies has been investigated by studies of content (DeRubeis et al., 1982; Luborsky et al., 1982). These studies found that independent judges were able to distinguish the forms of psychotherapy being used. Although treatment procedures can be differentiated, they appear to have comparable efficacy (DeRubeis et al., 1982; Zeiss, Lewinsohn, & Munoz, 1979). Attempts to study differential outcome have had only limited success (Jarvik, Mintz, Steuer, & Gerner, 1982; Sotsky et al., 1991; Zeiss et al., 1979). Kovacs (1983) attempted to integrate the findings across studies to identify common features of brief psychotherapy for depression that may account for their apparently equivalent efficacy. She identified features such as clinical diagnosis, time-limited contract, therapeutic activity, and focused nature of the psychotherapy.

Long-term continuation and maintenance treatment. Although most depressive episodes are self-limited, a substantial percentage of patients experience recurrent or chronic episodes. Both lithium and tricyclics have demonstrated efficacy in prevention of relapse and recurrence (Davis, 1976; Klerman, 1978a). Four controlled studies have evaluated pharmacotherapy and psychotherapy for the long-term treatment of depression. The maintenance studies were similar in several respects. All employed a factorial design to test psychotherapy in comparison and in combination with medication in ambulatory settings. Patients consisted primarily of neurotic depressives, who were followed regularly and received multiple outcome assessments of symptoms and social functioning gathered from patient self-reports and clinician evaluations. These studies differed primarily in the type of psychotherapy and length of treatment offered.

Klerman et al. (1974) examined 8 months of maintenance treatment on amitriptyline placebo, and no pill, with and without individual interpersonal psychotherapy, in 150 partially recovered depressed women. In Baltimore, Covi, Lipman, Derogatis, Smith, and Pattison (1974) compared 16 months of treatment on imipramine, diazepam, or placebo, with or without 4 months of group therapy, in 149 partially recovered depressed women. Friedman (1975), in Philadelphia, compared 3 months of amitriptyline and placebo, with or without marital therapy, in 196 married depressed men and women. Findings from these three studies were remarkably similar. They indicated that antidepressants, as compared with placebo or psychotherapy, were most efficacious in symptom reduction and relapse prevention. Although some recovery of social performance occurred as a result of symptom reduction, medications had only a limited impact on problems in living. Compared with a low contact, control intervention or medication, all three studies also showed a positive effect for psychotherapy, which was strongest in areas related to problems in living, social functioning, and interpersonal relationships, but less strong than medication for depression per se.

These studies allow us to answer partially some of the hypotheses about interactive effects of combined treatments. The Boston–New Haven study (Klerman et al., 1974), which found a psychotherapeutic effect only in patients who remained symptom free, best supported the hypothesis that medications have a positive effect on psychotherapy in that symptom relief, more readily produced by pharmacotherapy, rendered the patient more accessible to psychotherapy. There was no evidence in any of the studies for a negative interaction between pharmacotherapy and psychotherapy. Therefore, there was no evidence for the hypothesis that medication has a negative effect on the psychotherapy of patients who experience early symptom relief. Medication did not decrease patients' interest in psychotherapy and did not lead to early termination or poor psychotherapeutic response nor was there any evidence for a negative effect of psychotherapy on medication response. Patients receiving psychotherapy were not symptomatically disrupted.

New developments in the psychotherapy of depression. Over the last 10 years there has been considerable improvement in the quality and quantity of information on the efficacy of psychotherapy in comparison and in combination with pharmacotherapy for adults with major depression. Similar data on the efficacy of psychotherapy are not available for bipolar disorder or dysthymia or for adolescents with major depression, although several clinical trials are now in the planning phase (Moreau, Mufson, Weissman, & Klerman, 1992). Two recently published, large-scale treatment studies deserve attention: the NIMH Collaborative Treatment Study (Elkin et al., 1989) and the Maintenance Treatment Study of Recurrent Depression (Frank et al., 1990).

NIMH collaborative treatment study. In 1980, the encouraging results of several small clinical trials led the NIMH to initiate the first multisite collaborative study of antidepressant treatment to include psychotherapy. Based on the models used to test the efficacy of new psychotropic medications in the 1960s, this study was designed to test two psychotherapies, IPT and CBT. Two hundred fifty depressed patients were studied at three university centers. Findings showed that all active treatments were superior to a placebo in reducing symptoms over a 16-week period. The overall degree of improvement was highly clinically significant. Over two-thirds of the patients were symptom free at the end of treatment. More patients in the placebo–clinical management condition dropped out or were withdrawn, twice as many as for IPT, which had the lowest attrition rate. After 12 weeks of treatment, the two psychotherapies and imipramine were equivalent in the reduction of depressive symptoms and in overall functioning. Imipramine had the most rapid onset of action and the most consistent positive effect on the various symptom measures. Although less severely depressed patients improved with all treatment conditions, including placebo–clinical management, the more severely depressed patients in the placebo condition did poorly. For the less severely depressed group there were no differences among the treatments. Severely ill patients in the imipramine and IPT groups had significantly better response (fewer depressive symptoms) than the placebo group (Elkin et al., 1989). There has been controversy about the data analytic approach used in this study; reanalysis is forthcoming.

Maintenance treatment study of recurrent major depression. Also in the early 1980s, the University of Pittsburgh group undertook a long-term clinical trial to determine the efficacy of antidepressant medication (imipramine) and/or IPT for the prevention of relapse in severe recurrent depression (Frank, Kupfer, Wagner, McEachran, & Cornes, 1991; Frank et al., 1990). The impetus for this study was the finding that many patients with multiple recurrent episodes were difficult to treat, had a high relapse rate, and were high utilizers of medical and social services. In this study patients with recurrent depression who had responded to imipramine plus interpersonal psychotherapy were randomly assigned to one of five treatments for 3 years of maintenance treatment: (1) IPT alone; (2) IPT and placebo; (3) IPT and imipramine; (4) clinical management and imipramine; or (5) clinical management and placebo. Contrary to previous studies, imipramine was chronically maintained at high doses (over 200 mg), rather than being tapered from acute treatment levels; IPT was administered monthly, the lowest dose ever used in the clinical trials. There were four major findings: a high rate of recurrence in 1 year for untreated control groups; clinically meaningful and statistically significant prevention of relapse and recurrence by both imipramine and IPT; no significant trend toward value of combined treatment over either treatment alone; and the value of high maintenance doses of imipramine (over 200 mg/day). This long-term study, along with several others using antidepressant medications with and without psychotherapy, clearly established the value of maintenance treatment in the prevention of relapse and recurrence in unipolar depression. Alternatives to medication as a treatment for depression are enormously important since, for various reasons, many patients will not or cannot take medication: for example, pregnant women and elderly patients with concomitant medical problems (Klerman, 1990).

The NIMH depression awareness, recognition, and treatment program (DART). Numerous studies have indicated that only half the patients diagnosed with depressive and other psychiatric conditions are so diagnosed by general and family practitioners. In 1989, the NIMH initiated DART, a program of secondary prevention of depression. This program is comparable to the one initiated by National Institute of Health to educate the public about the treatment of hypertension. Initial efforts have focused on educating the public and professionals about the availability of effective treatments for severe disorders, particularly bipolar and recurrent unipolar depression. In early policy discussions on the focus of DART, relatively low priority was given to patients with milder depressions, including those with depressive symptoms seen in general medical health settings. It is still too early to know whether the program will help improve detection and treatment of depression; it lacks a strong evaluation component.

Dysthymia

Dysthymia has been a topic of diagnostic and therapeutic controversy (Kocsis & Frances, 1987). For much of the twentieth century chronic depression was considered a form of character disorder for which the treatment of choice was psychotherapy. The third edition of the *Diagnostic and Statistical Manual of Mental Disorders* (APA, 1980) reconceptualized chronic depression under the rubric of dysthymic disorder, an affective disorder defined by a duration of at least 2 years and by depressive symptom criteria.

This distinction, persisting in the DSM-III-R (1987) concept of dysthymia, encouraged psychiatric use of antidepressant medications. Several studies have now found antidepressant medication effective in treating the depressive symptoms and impaired social functioning seen in this condition (Harrison et al., 1986, Kocsis et al., 1988), which has shifted the burden of proof for efficacy to the psychotherapies. About 3 percent of American adults suffer from dysthymia. Many chronically depressed individuals eventually suffer a period of worsening mood symptoms and thus qualify for both major depression and dysthymia (double depression). Dysthymic patients rarely require psychiatric hospitalization unless they develop a double depression, but the unrelenting chronicity of their disorder saps energy, inhibits sociability, and dampens pleasure. Dysthymic patients often have comorbid anxiety or other disorders that may contribute to misdiagnosis and mistreatment.

The primary distinction between dysthymia and major depression is that dysthymia is chronic, but symptomatically less severe, and must persist for at least 2 years (1 year in children and adolescents). A 1987 consensus conference of the National Institute of Mental Health suggested that dysthymia, because of its chronicity and low placebo response rate, would be an ideal disorder to use in studying combined treatment with pharmacotherapy and psychotherapy. Manuals have been written for the treatment of dysthymia with variants of IPT (Markowitz & Klerman, 1991) and cognitive therapy (McCullough, 1992). To date, however, there have been few standardized comparative or combined trials of medication and psychotherapy for dysthymic patients.

Comparative trials. Mason and colleagues (Mason, Markowitz, & Klerman, in press) treated nine dysthymic patients with interpersonal therapy and, in a quasi-experimental design, compared them to randomly chosen matched dysthymic patients receiving a trial of desipramine, a tricyclic antidepressant medication. Improvement was comparable in the two groups. Of the IPT cases, five had previously failed to respond to desipramine; four were treated with IPT because they refused medication. Most reported lifelong dysthymia. Subjects received a mean 12.0 ± 4.9 sessions of IPT. Initial Hamilton Depression Rating Scale (Ham-D; Hamilton, 1967) scores for the IPT subjects averaged 19.4 ± 5.0. Ham-D scores fell for all subjects, and at termination averaged 7.4 ± 3.8.

Combined trials. Becker, Heimberg, and Bellach (1987) reported preliminary results on 36 dysthymic subjects randomly assigned to social skills training or crisis-supportive psychotherapy and to nortriptyline or placebo. Self-report and clinician ratings showed equally significant improvement for all four treatment conditions. Waring et al. (1988) described preliminary data on 12 women meeting RDC criteria for chronic depression who were randomized to a 10-week cognitive marital or supportive therapy and to doxepin (maximum 150 mg/day) or atropine placebo. All patients improved (mean Ham-D before = 14.5, after = 7.1; t = 4.01, p = .003), although final results have not been reported for either study. The prevalence of dysthymia, the growing research interest in psychotherapy of this disorder (McCullough, 1991; Weissman & Akiskal, 1984), and its suitability as a testing ground for combined treatment outcome studies suggest that this short list of studies will grow.

Mood Disorder Associated with Human Immunodeficiency Virus (HIV) Infection

Depression is one of the most common psychiatric disorders associated with HIV infection, although only a minority of HIV-seropositive individuals become depressed. HIV-related depression deserves attention because of the poignant and pressing social needs of infected individuals. These individuals, usually young and previously healthy, must come to terms with the likelihood of shortened longevity and a chronic patient role. They face stigma and discrimination because of HIV and often must struggle to alter the chronic social risk behaviors that led to infection. There has long been research interest in the depression of the medically ill. HIV infection can cause a variety of neuropsychiatric disorders, adding to the importance of psychiatric research in this area. Numerous case reports and a few small, open treatment trials describe the favorable response of this depression to psychotherapeutic (Markowitz, Klerman, & Perry, 1992) or various psychopharmacologic (Fernandez & Levy, 1990; Manning, Jacobsberg, Erhart, Perry, & Francies, 1990; Rabkin & Harrison, 1990); interventions. We are aware of only one, as yet unfinished, comparative treatment trial.

A team at Cornell University Medical College headed by Samuel Perry, M.D., is undertaking a randomized comparative treatment study of HIV-positive patients who meet the criteria for major depression or dysthymia. Subjects are randomized to treatment with either IPT, CBT, or supportive psychotherapy alone or supportive therapy plus pharmacotherapy with desipramine. Some depressed patients appear wary of the potential immunosuppressive effects of antidepressant medica-

tion (Rabkin & Harrison, 1990) but are highly motivated for psychotherapy. A review of the treatment literature suggests that most depressed HIV-positive individuals respond to either psychotherapy or pharmacotherapy, hence combined treatment may rarely be necessary.

Adjustment Disorder with Depressed Mood

Many patients have depressive symptoms but do not meet diagnostic criteria for either dysthymia or major depression and do not have manic episodes. These patients often appear in primary care and medical clinics. They are important from a public health viewpoint because of their high prevalence and disability. Depressive symptoms that fail to meet syndromal criteria do not appear in the official DSM-III-R nomenclature but may be classified as an adjustment disorder secondary to the major identifiable psychosocial stresses. The overlap between this diagnosis and posttraumatic stress disorder has not been clearly established. Although there have been no controlled studies, these patients often receive psychotropic medications, particularly anxiolytics or antidepressants. Various forms of psychotherapy and counseling are widely employed, although, again, there have been few controlled studies. Klerman et al. (1987) reported the efficacy of a brief psychosocial intervention for patients with distress seen in a primary care, general medical facility. There was also some evidence for the efficacy of a brief, modified form of IPT, called interpersonal counseling (IPC), administered by psychiatric nurses, under psychiatric supervision. See Klerman and Weissman (1993) for adaptations of IPT including IPC.

ANXIETY DISORDERS

The past few decades have witnessed a major shift in thinking about symptomatic anxiety states. Previously, symptoms such as phobias, obsessions, and free-floating anxiety were thought to be related to each other and to occur as a manifestation of poorly resolved intrapsychic conflict and associated maladaptive defense mechanisms. Treatment focused on psychotherapy, with antianxiety medications such as barbiturates, or later benzodiazepines, used as temporary adjunctive interventions. However, since the development of the research diagnostic criteria in the mid-1970s and the publication of DSM-III in 1980, research and clinical thinking about anxiety states have changed dramatically. Considerable research now indicates that several distinct disorders exist, each characterized by persistent high levels of anxiety. These include simple (specific) and social phobic disorders, agoraphobia, panic disorder, generalized anxiety disorder, and obsessive-compulsive disorder. Posttraumatic stress disorder is also categorized as an anxiety disorder.

There is now good evidence for distinct neurobiological underpinnings or specific cognitive-behavioral mechanisms for each of these conditions. Moreover, categorical discrimination of the different disorders has led to the identification of specific, effective treatment interventions. The availability of focused, short-term medication and cognitive-behavioral treatment interventions for anxiety disorders has been a major advance in psychotherapeutics. However, problems remain. Although short-term efficacy has been clearly documented for treatments such as imipramine or alprazolam for panic disorder and clomipramine or fluoxetine for obsessive-compulsive disorder, long-term amelioration of the full range of symptoms associated with these disorders has not yet been accomplished. In addition, some patients fail to respond to medication. The success of cognitive-behavioral interventions has also been documented, with similar caveats about the degree and duration of effectiveness.

Moreover, etiologic heterogeneity within each anxiety disorder is likely, and syndromal and symptom comorbidity among the disorders is common. Comorbidity with depressive disorders (Barlow, DiNardo, Vermilyea, Vermilyea, & Blanchard, 1986), substance abuse (Leckman et al., 1983), and personality disorders (Reich, 1988) is also common. It is not yet known whether the presence of multiple disorders should be approached using an additive strategy or whether patients who meet the criteria for several diagnoses should be considered to have a different disorder, responsive to different treatment techniques. It is also not yet known whether and when psychological treatments should be combined with medication, or whether and when nondirective psychotherapy might be used instead of, or in addition to, directive, cognitive-behavioral interventions. With these caveats in mind, we review here current data documenting the efficacy of medication and/or psychological (usually cognitive-behavioral) treatment of each of the anxiety disorders.

Agoraphobia and Panic Disorder

Models of etiology and pathogenesis. There are currently two prominent models of panic pathogenesis, each formulated in recent years and associated with one of the major treatment approaches. A third, integrated model can be constructed using principles of each of the others. Most experts in the field now favor some form of integrated model, although the emphasis varies. The neurobiological model postulates a defect in brain function, possibly related to the part of the brain that orchestrates infant separation responses. The defect is thought to be best described by characterizing physiologic processes, such as neurotransmitter abnormalities and hormonal or metabolic imbalance. According to this model, panic occurs because a brain separation center, usually inhibited in adult life, fires sporadically. There may or may not be a trigger stimulus. Anticipatory anxiety and phobic avoidance, as well as other psychological disturbances, are seen as secondary to the experience of panic. Treatment is targeted at blocking panic, and medication is considered the treatment of choice. Neurobiological studies suggest that a variety of neurotransmitters (noradrenaline, GABA, serotonin) may have a role in panic vulnerability. Imaging studies point to the involvement of the parahippocampal and temporal (Reiman et al., 1986) areas in anticipatory anxiety and panic, respectively.

The cognitive-behavioral model takes a different perspective. Panic occurs because of a psychological mechanism in which conditioned reactivity to bodily sensations occurs, mediated by a conditioned fear response or cognitive misinterpretation of interoceptive cues. Prospective controlled studies have documented the efficacy of brief, cognitive-behavioral treatment in blocking panic (Clark, 1986; Craske, 1988; Craske, Brown, & Barlow, 1991; Craske, Cerny, & Klosko, 1989). This treatment focuses on the correction of cognitive misinterpretations of bodily sensations and exposure to interoceptive cues. In this model, physiologic disturbance is seen as secondary to behavioral disturbances, such as hyperventilation. As with the neurobiological model, anticipatory anxiety and agoraphobic fear and avoidance are seen as secondary to panic. Studies of memory and attentional processes in panic disorder support the interoceptive sensitivity model.

Psychological treatment. Cognitive-behavioral treatments for panic disorder have been well studied and have documented efficacy. The treatment approach (Barlow & Craske, 1989) includes cognitive restructuring, interoceptive exposure, and breathing retraining. Treatment of agoraphobia centers on exposure to phobic situations. CBT for panic is explicitly based on the interoceptive sensitivity model and includes a role for hyperventilation in producing panic symptoms. Anxiety-management strategies, such as progressive muscle relaxation techniques and breathing retraining, are usually included, but studies indicate that correction of cognitive misinterpretation and exposure to interoceptive cues are the more crucial treatment components. Results of studies using these techniques show a high response rate. The single existing study comparing these techniques with medication in panic disorder shows comparable efficacy (Klosko, Barlow, Tassinari, & Cerny, 1990). Several studies of agoraphobia show comparable efficacy of imipramine and behavioral therapy focused on exposure to agoraphobic situations. A multicenter trial is under way to further elucidate comparative effects of medication and cognitive-behavioral treatment in panic disorder, as are studies comparing different parts of the cognitive-behavioral treatment with each other.

Studies assessing the efficacy of psychodynamic techniques for panic have not yet been conducted. In general, development of reproducible operational criteria for psychodynamic assessment and intervention strategies have lagged behind. However, there is some hope that the next decade will see publication of some prospective trials of psychodynamic treatment. There is anecdotal evidence that psychodynamic interventions may prove useful in ameliorating vulnerability to panic as well as in treating acute symptoms. The fact that many patients seen at anxiety disorders treatment centers report previous unsuccessful experience with psychotherapy is often cited as evidence against this possibility. However, the situation may be analogous to the early view that benzodiazepines were not useful. We have learned that these medications are effective antipanic agents if used in appropriate dosages in conjunction with standardized tracking of panic episodes. Psychodynamic treatment is well suited to address the interpersonal problems and pervasive anxiety states that disturb many panic disorder patients. Such a treatment, if accompanied by regular monitoring of panic episodes, may prove useful to at least some panic patients, either alone or in combination with other modalities.

Pharmacologic treatment. There is substantial evidence for the efficacy of a range of medications in blocking panic. Most research data is available for tricyclic antidepressants, and they are considered by many clinicians the treatment of choice. The large-scale double-blind studies cited as evidence for tricyclic efficacy were conducted with patients meeting DSM-III criteria for agoraphobia with panic attacks (Ballenger et al., 1988; Sheehan, Ballenger, & Jacobsen, 1980; Zitrin, Klein, & Woerner, 1980), rather than panic disorder with more limited phobic avoidance. Nevertheless, these studies demonstrate the clearly antipanic effects of imipramine. Open trials of imipramine (Rifkin et al.,

1981), desipramine (Liebowitz et al., 1985), nortriptyline (Munjack et al., 1988), and chlomipramine (Gloger, Grunhaus, Birmacher, & Troudart, 1981) have provided further support for the usefulness of tricyclics. Moreover, since noradrenergic and serotonergic mechanisms may be involved in the pathogenesis of panic, any of the currently marketed tricyclics are likely to be effective antipanic agents in at least some patients.

Most experts recommended starting treatment with low doses (10–25 mg/day) and increasing gradually. Even so, the literature indicates a 20–40 percent incidence of an amphetamine-like reaction characterized by jitteriness, tachycardia, insomnia, irritability, and increased energy. About half the patients who develop this syndrome are unable to continue to take the medication. One study found that jitteriness led to lower dosing and poorer outcome. The possibility that tricyclics with fewer anticholinergic side effects may be better tolerated has not been confirmed. Doses of tricyclics adequate to achieve panic blockade are often in the range of 250–300 mg, or occasionally even higher.

The duration of treatment needed to produce lasting remission has not been well studied. Relapse rates vary, based in part on the definition of relapse (Noyes, Garvey, & Cook, 1989; Zitrin, Klein, Woerner, & Ross, 1983). However, it seems that chronic symptomatology, in the form of various anxiety symptoms and persistent functional impairment, remains the rule. A panic relapse rate of about 25 percent within 2 years of discontinuation of medication is likely.

Monoamine oxidase inhibitors and other nontricyclic antidepressant medications also show documented efficacy for panic. In one study (Sheehan et al., 1980) phenelzine produced slightly better results than imipramine in a group of agoraphobic patients. In addition, there is some evidence of efficacy for trazadone (Mavissakalian et al., 1987), fluoxetine (Gorman et al., 1987), maprotiline (Lydiard, 1987), fluvoxamine (Servant, Bailly, & Parquet, 1988), and zimelidine (Koczkas, Guirguis, & Wedin, 1981). Benzodiazepines have been extensively studied in the treatment of panic disorder. The inferences from reported clinical treatment of their ineffectiveness appears to be erroneous, and possibly related to inadequate dosing. A large multinational trial documented the treatment efficacy of alprazolam (Ballenger et al., 1988). Studies indicate similar efficacy of other benzodiazepines (Charney & Woods, 1989; Tesar et al., 1987). Benzodiazepines have the advantage of rapid onset of action and a relatively low side-effect profile, but discontinuation often leads to relapse, withdrawal, or rebound symptoms (Fyer et al., 1987;

Roy Byrne, Dager, Cowley, Vitiliano, & Dunner, 1989).

Noyes and Perry (1990) suggest that all medications used in the treatment of panic have problems. There is a need for continued research in this area. Recently, calcium channel blockers have shown some promise (Klein & Uhde, 1988), and the antiseizure medication carbamazepine (Uhde et al., 1988) has been studied with mixed results. The latter medication may have a specific usefulness in managing benzodiazepine discontinuation in panic patients (Klein, Uhde, & Post, 1986) and in treating patients who have cocaine-induced panic disorder (Louie, Lannon, & Ketter, 1989). A multicenter study is currently under way to assess the usefulness of carbamazepine in alprazolam discontinuation. One study using the serotonin precursor 5-hydroxytryptophan along with carbidopa suggested efficacy (Kahn & Westenberg, 1985).

Combination medication treatment is a strategy for handling problem patients. The addition of benzodiazepines may be useful for the subgroup of patients who experience the jitteriness syndrome with tricyclics alone. Carbamazepine may be useful in managing symptom recurrence during a benzodiazepine taper. Virtually any combination of medications may be useful in refractory patients. In general, combination medication treatment has not been well studied, although combined cognitive-behavioral and medication treatment has been studied in agoraphobics. These studies document a potentiating effect of imipramine on behavioral treatment alone, and of behavioral treatment on imipramine alone (Mavissakalian, 1991). The cognitive-behavioral treatment provided in these studies was a behavioral exposure treatment. It did not include antipanic strategies, such as breathing retraining, interoceptive exposure, or correction of cognitive misinterpretation of bodily sensations. The effectiveness of combined medication and cognitive-behavioral treatment in panic disorder with no or mild agoraphobia has not yet been determined.

Summary and future directions. There have been substantial gains in the treatment of panic and agoraphobia in the last few decades. About 60 percent of patients presenting for treatment are effectively managed by current methods. Dropout rates are comparable to those of medication and cognitive-behavioral techniques and tend to be around 20 percent. Thus, although there is reason for optimism, there is still considerable work to be done in developing new psychological and pharmacologic interventions, exploring the usefulness of various combinations, both concurrently and serially, and developing effective maintenance strate-

gies for patients with panic disorder and agoraphobia.

Obsessive-Compulsive Disorder

Models of etiology and pathogenesis. Obsessive-compulsive disorder (OCD) has traditionally been considered a rare and refractory disorder. This poorly understood disorder was conceptualized by some as a psychotic disorder and by others as a personality disorder. More recently biological and family studies of OCD have provided data supporting a neurobiological model. There is now clear evidence for a dysfunction in the serotonin system in OCD, although the nature of the dysfunction and its role in symptom generation have not yet been fully elucidated. Imaging studies implicate frontal cortex and basal ganglia as sites of a CNS defect (Baxter et al., 1988; Khanna, 1988). The high rates of cormorbidity with motor tics and Gilles de la Tourette syndrome (Pauls et al., 1986) further support a possible disturbance in these brain areas.

Learning theorists have focused on processes involved in the maintenance of OCD symptomatology, leaving the question of etiology unanswered. These researchers suggest that obsessions are evoked anxiety responses and that compulsions are apparently conditioned reinforcing behaviors. In other words, obsessions (and some compulsions) are thought of as anxiety-increasing reactions to an anxiety-provoking stimulus. Compulsions are anxiety-reducing responses to the obsession. Foa (Foa & Kozak, 1985) proposed a slightly different model in which symptoms result from an impairment in interpretive rules for making inferences about harm.

Psychological treatment. The most effective psychological treatment of OCD is a cognitive-behavioral treatment consisting of exposure and response prevention. Several studies have documented the efficacy of this approach (Baer & Minichiello, 1990; Foa, Steketee, & Ozarow, 1985). In these short-term studies, improvement was seen in 60–70 percent of subjects, but full symptom remission was rarely achieved. The most effective of these therapies use home treatment to solidify gains. There have been some efforts to include cognitive techniques, but to date these have not been shown to add substantially to effectiveness. Patients who are depressed who have schizotypal personality disorder may respond more poorly to behavioral treatment. There is also a suggestion that patients with checking compulsions respond more poorly to behavioral treatment than those with cleaning compulsions.

Pharmacologic treatment. Pharmacologic treatment of OCD has made great strides in the past decade. A large multicenter trial confirmed unequivocally the efficacy of clomipramine, and a second large study documenting the efficacy of fluoxetine is scheduled for publication shortly (Wheadon, personal communication). It is now well documented that medication with serotonergic effects effectively treats OCD, although agents may vary in potency. An initial report of a small number of patients treated in a crossover design with clomipramine and fluoxetine indicated the efficacy of both agents. Several studies comparing serotonergic compounds, such as clomipramine or fluvoxamine, with the noradrenergic compound desipramine have shown clear advantages for the former.

Enthusiasm for newly identified serotonergic compounds in the treatment of OCD must be tempered by the recognition that the relief these medications offer is usually partial at best. Statistically and clinically significant changes in OCD symptomatology rarely reflect full remission of the syndrome. Moreover, in a substantial minority of cases, there is little or no response to these medications. Some work has been done to identify subgroups responsive to adjunctive medication. For example, there is now evidence that patients with comorbid tic or Tourette symptoms and those with motor tics in their family members may respond well to adjunctive neuroleptic treatment. Similarly, adjunctive neuroleptics may be useful in OCD patients with psychotic symptomatology. On the other hand, the promise of lithium as an adjunctive treatment has not been realized.

Summary and directions for future research. Recent gains in the identification and treatment of OCD and related symptomatology (e.g., motor tic syndromes) have been impressive. Good treatment now available to OCD patients includes either medication, cognitive-behavioral treatment, or a combination of the two. A multicenter study is under way that compares these two approaches. Yet much work remains to be done in characterizing and treating residual symptoms, developing optimal combinations of medication and psychotherapy, and identifying subgroups of patients who are candidates for treatments such as neuroleptic augmentation or psychosurgery.

Social Phobia

Diagnostic issues and illness models. Social phobia was identified as a specific disorder for the first time in DSM-III. The disorder is characterized by fear and avoidance of situations in which the person is exposed to possible scrutiny by others. The fear is of humiliation or embarrassment. DSM-III-R criteria further subdivide social phobics into those who suffer from a specific phobia (e.g., fear of public speaking, fear of writing, or fear of urinating in public facilities) and those who are better characterized as general social phobics, with a fear of being embarrassed or humiliated in almost any social situation. Social phobia has a lifetime prevalence of 1–2 percent (Myers et al., 1984), affecting approximately equal numbers of males and females. The disorder is associated with substance abuse, depression, and possibly with suicidality. Differential diagnosis includes panic disorder and avoidant personality disorder.

Psychological treatment. Studies of the psychological treatment of social phobia have primarily used cognitive-behavioral approaches and have been based on different models of the psychopathology of the disorder. One model postulates that social phobia occurs because of skills deficits; other models hypothesize conditioned fear or faulty cognitive processing as the basis for the symptoms. Treatment using social skills training, behavioral exposure strategies, and cognitive techniques (Alstrom et al., 1984; Wlazlo, Schroeder-Hartwig, Hand, Kaiser, & Munchau, 1990; Falloon, Lloyd, & Harpin 1981; Heimberg, 1989; Stravynski, Marks, & Yule, 1982) have been undertaken, all with moderate success. Studies attempting to combine these approaches have not generally shown greater benefit from the combination treatments. Currently, use of cognitive and behavioral techniques in a group setting is the most widely accepted treatment.

Pharmacologic treatment. It appears that beta-adrenergic blockers are useful in specific social phobia (Gorman et al., 1985), but of limited value in the generalized form of the disorder. Monoamine oxidase inhibitors appear to be the pharmacologic treatment of choice for generalized social phobia (Liebowitz et al., 1988). Recent studies also suggest that clonazepam (Davidson, Ford, Smith, & Potts, 1991) or fluoxetine (Sternbeck, 1990) may be beneficial in this disorder.

Summary and directions for future research. Although great progress has been made in the diagnosis and treatment of individuals with social anxiety, much remains to be done. Existing treatments, both pharmacologic and cognitive-behavioral, have been demonstrated to be effective, but are not likely to produce full remission for most patients. New psychotherapeutic and pharmacologic interventions are needed as well as combination interventions.

Generalized Anxiety Disorder

Diagnostic issues and illness models. Generalized anxiety disorder (GAD) is a residual category of anxious individuals, thought by many to comprise a heterogeneous group of patients. Generalized anxiety is a common concomitant of other anxiety disorders and depression; it may occur as a consequence of alcohol or sedative abuse or as a variant of a normal anxiety state (Cowley & Roy Bryne, 1991). Although anxiety neurosis and a tendency to chronic nervousness appear to run in families, the only family study reported to date fails to document a familial pattern (Noyes, Clarkson, Crowe, Yates, & McChesney, 1987). Diagnostic criteria for GAD include two or more spheres of persistent worry, accompanied by prominent somatic symptomatology in the area(s) of autonomic arousal, muscle tension, easy startle, or hypervigilance.

Psychological treatment. Psychological studies of GAD suggest that overperception of threat and underestimation of controllability may both contribute to the underlying mechanism of symptom generation (Rapee, 1991). Empirical studies document a consistent attentional bias toward threat stimuli in GAD subjects. Treatments of GAD focus on the central psychopathological features, worry and physiologic arousal. Cognitive-behavioral techniques (Borkovec et al., 1987; Butler, Cullington, Hibbert, Klimes, & Gelder, 1987; Dunham & Turvey, 1987) have been used, including relaxation strategies and cognitive techniques to identify and test hypotheses about overestimating the probability and consequences of negative events or worrisome situations.

Pharmacologic treatment. Pharmacologic treatment of GAD has focused on the relief of tension and physiologic arousal as well as the accompanying worry. Medications that have demonstrated efficacy include benzodiazepines (Downing & Rickels, 1985), azapirones (Rickels et al., 1990), and tricyclic antidepressants (Kahn et al., 1986). Benzodiazepines, active at GABA receptors in the brain, were the earliest compounds identified as effective against generalized anxiety. These medications take effect quickly and have relatively few side effects, although memory impairment and disinhibition are possible consequences that are sometimes ignored (Schweitzer, Rickels, Case, & Greenblatt, 1990).

Alcoholism

Drugs and psychotherapy. Alcohol is a common, legal drug in the United States to which most citizens are repeatedly exposed without incident. Approximately 14 percent of Americans, however, meet criteria for an alcohol use disorder at some point in their lifetime (Robins et al., 1984). Explanations for this high incidence are complex and interactive, ranging from biological predispositions, which may include a family history of alcoholism and variations in neurochemistry, to environmental factors as diverse as cultural acceptance of excessive drinking, the price and availability of alcohol, and the severity of psychosocial stressors. Additionally, certain psychiatric disorders are associated with an increased risk of alcoholism, particularly antisocial personality disorder, other substance use disorders, and mania (Helzer & Pryzbeck, 1988).

Although DSM-III-R does not specify cutoffs for pathological levels of consumption, a recent cross-sectional study of hospital patients found that regular intake of more than three drinks (40 g) per day by males and two drinks (25 g) per day by females was associated with an increased risk of alcohol-related medical and psychosocial problems. Similarly, frequent consumption of six or more drinks significantly increased the risk of alcohol-related problems for both males and females (Kranzler, Babor, & Laverman, 1990). Such criteria, although not constituting a syndrome, may alert clinicians to the potential need for preventive measures or early intervention (Frances & Franklin, 1989).

Alcoholism treatment considerations. Excessive use of alcohol is associated with the deterioration of health, careers, families, and relationships. In 1990 alone, alcohol use cost the United States more than 65,000 lives, including 22,000 lost in highway accidents, and an estimated $136 billion, primarily for lost wages and medical treatment (National Institute of Alcohol Abuse and Alcoholism [NIAAA], 1990). Excessive drinking during pregnancy is the leading cause of mental retardation in this country (NIAAA, 1990). These massive costs associated with alcoholism make its treatment a major public health goal. However, the diversity of factors influencing its development and course suggest that no single treatment approach will be effective for all alcoholics. Rather, the strategy encouraged by the National Institute of Alcohol Abuse and Alcoholism (NIAAA) in its program of treatment research is the identification of subgroups of alcoholics who are likely to benefit from specific treatment approaches.

The standard components of alcoholism treatment are management of withdrawal followed by long-term management of dependence and prevention of relapse. Withdrawal has typically been the domain of pharmacotherapy, with the latter treatment phases dominated by psychological treatments. Recent treatment research has expanded treatment options and identified potential roles for nonpharmacologic management of mild withdrawals as well as for pharmacotherapy in the management of dependence and prevention of relapse. Long-term studies are needed to determine the relative contributions of these therapies, alone and in combination, on alcoholism outcome.

Alcohol withdrawal

Pharmacologic management of alcohol withdrawal. Abrupt cessation of sustained, heavy use of alcohol-dependent individuals may result in a withdrawal syndrome. Prescription of benzodiazepines, especially diazepam or chlordiazepoxide, in decreasing doses over the period of withdrawal remains the most used pharmacologic strategy because of its safety and efficacy in relieving symptoms and in inhibiting hyperactivity of neuronal systems. Liabilities of benzodiazepine treatment of withdrawal include exposure to another abusable substance that is cross-tolerant and synergistic with alcohol; oversedation; respiratory depression; memory impairment; and drowsiness. Two modifications of standard benzodiazepine treatment have been developed to reduce these liabilities. Sellers et al. (1983) have suggested loading doses of diazepam every 1 to 2 hours until withdrawal symptoms subside. Because the long half-lives of diazepam (33 hours) and its active metabolite, desmethyldiazepam (90 hours), eliminate repetitive seeking of another addictive drug for relief of symptoms, there is usually no need for further medication. A different strategy is to use short-acting benzodiazepines, such as oxazepam or lorazepam, which have elimination half-lives of less than 20 hours. This approach is advantageous in the patient with serious respiratory or liver disease for whom slower drug metabolism and longer half-lives could lead to dangerous accumulation. Shorter acting benzodiazepines may also be indicated when daytime lethargy is to be avoided or for acute treatment of withdrawal-related insomnia (Peachey & Naranjo, 1984). A potential disadvantage of the shorter acting benzodiazepines is their fluctuation in blood levels, resulting in an increase in the risk of seizures or drug-seeking behavior.

Other classes of medications currently under investigation for the management of withdrawal include beta-adrenergic blockers (e.g., atenolol and propranolol), alpha-2 adrenergic agonists (e.g., clonidine and lofexidine), calcium channel blockers (e.g., caroverine), and anticonvulsants (e.g., carbamazepine, phenytoin, and valproic acid) (Litten & Allen, 1991). Unlike the benzodiazepines, these medications have not been found to treat the full syndrome of withdrawal and therefore must be combined with other medications that complement their mode of action. Additionally, some have specific medical contraindications, but their low likelihood of abuse or dependence and relative safety for patients with respiratory disorders may offer an advantage for some alcoholics. A randomized, double-blind trial of atenolol in alcoholic outpatients found reduced subjective craving for alcohol during the withdrawal period in atenolol-treated patients relative to placebo (Horwitz, Gottlieb, & Kraus, 1989), suggesting the medication's utility during withdrawal.

Nonpharmacologic management of alcohol withdrawal. Reports of the relatively low frequency of serious withdrawal symptoms suggest that routine prescription of psychotropic medications may not be indicated for all alcoholics (Shaw, Kolesar, & Sellers, 1981; Whitfield, 1980). Whitfield (1980) reported seizures occurred in 1 percent, hallucinations in 3.7 percent, and delirium tremens in less than 1 percent of 1,114 detoxifying patients. Similarly, Naranjo and colleagues (Naranjo, Sellers, & Chator, 1983) demonstrated that patients randomly assigned to placebo did nearly as well as patients receiving oral lorazepam on a standardized alcohol withdrawal scale. A score less than 20 on a modified version of the Clinical Institute Withdrawal Assessment Scale (CIWA; Foy, March, & Drinkwater, 1988) is associated with mild alcohol withdrawal that can usually be managed with psychological supportive treatment (Adinoff, Bone, & Linnoila, 1988). Psychological treatment for withdrawal is necessarily supportive due to the psychological and physiologic stresses of this period.

The *Seventh Special Report to the U.S. Congress on Alcohol and Health* (NIAAA, 1990) reported that 45 to 70 percent of patients entering alcoholism treatment have deficits in problem solving, abstract thinking, concept shifting, psychomotor performance, or difficult memory tasks. Thus, cognitive processing and retention of treatment concepts in this initial phase of intervention may be limited, especially in patients taking benzodiazepines. A benefit of nonpharmacologic management of mild withdrawal is the avoidance of drug substitution. Relaxation or other behavioral techniques might be taught that could be constructively applied to stressful life events outside the treatment setting. A possible liability of nonpharmacologic treatment of withdrawal, noted by Litten and Allen (1991) in their review of animal and preliminary clinical data, is the potential for kindling, that is, an increased predisposition to alcohol withdrawal seizures with repeated unmedicated withdrawals.

Comparative trials of nonpharmacologic medications and placebo treatments of mild withdrawal have yet to be developed. Studies by Whitfield (1980) and Naranjo et al. (1983) suggest that a substantial potential subject pool exists for such trials. Long-term follow-up may clarify differential effects on outcome and test the kindling hypothesis of Litten and Allen (1991) and others. The CIWA, or other instruments that assess the severity of withdrawal, may identify alcoholics with milder syptomatology as potential subjects for such comparative studies. Factorial studies may identify benefits of combined medication and nonpharmacologic treatments for defined subgroups of alcoholics. Gordis and Sereny (1981) noted that withdrawal is the first step toward rehabilitation and that research is needed to clarify the impact of the withdrawal experience on retention in treatment and outcome of rehabilitation.

Alcohol rehabilitation

General treatment considerations. Alcoholism is a disorder with a very high rate of relapse following withdrawal. Protracted abstinence symptoms or a strong subjective experience of craving may prompt resumption of drinking, as may untreated psychiatric disorders, such as depression (Hatsukami & Pickens, 1982). The alcoholic entering rehabilitation may lack the skills needed to develop relationships that do not revolve around drinking. Self-esteem and neuropsychological functioning may be impaired. Additionally, a confluence of medical, professional, economic, and legal difficulties may have accrued from years of alcoholism. Assessment of such risks may suggest appropriate components and intensity of rehabilitation treatment and whether it should begin on an inpatient or outpatient basis. Instruments that assess functioning in a variety of areas associated with alcoholism, for example, the Addiction Severity Index (ASI; McLellan, Luborsky, Woody, & O'Brien, 1980), may be used at the beginning of treatment to determine the therapeutic regime and to periodically assess outcome across these areas. It is widely acknowledged that complete abstinence is the preferred outcome for alcoholics, given the rapid return of tolerance and withdrawal that commonly occurs when drinking is resumed. However, the associations between quantity and pattern of alcohol intake and negative medical and psychosocial consequences (Kranzler et al., 1990) suggest that interventions aimed at reducing consumption may prove beneficial for early-stage problem drinkers and for alcoholics who recognize that they have a problem with drinking but are unwilling or unable to commit to abstinence. Agents to decrease craving and consumption may ultimately serve to make this resistant group accessible to traditional rehabilitation treatments.

Pharmacologic approaches to alcoholism rehabilitation.

General considerations. Advances in the basic sciences are expanding our understanding of alcohol's effect on neurotransmitters, receptors, second messenger compounds, and other neuroproteins. These findings have stimulated new pharmacologic approaches to alcoholism rehabilitation. General considerations when prescribing medication for alcoholics include providing information about the relative risks and benefits of pharmacotherapy, including potential adverse effects and whether the medication has mood-altering or habit-forming properties. Patients should be advised, on initial prescription and during subsequent visits, of possible medication interactions with alcohol or other drugs and of the necessity for taking the medication as directed. Providing this information in both oral and written forms is often helpful. Pharmacotherapy for alcoholics with impaired hepatic functioning requires careful monitoring, as this condition can affect drug metabolism and result in accumulation and side effects disproportionate to the prescribed dose (Weller & Preskorn, 1984). Alcohol-related cerebral damage may also modify the metabolism and action of medications (Saunders & Williams, 1984).

Aversive agents to foster sobriety. For decades disulfiram (Antabuse) was regarded as the primary pharmacologic agent for fostering sobriety. The disulfiram–alcohol interaction involves inhibition of aldehyde dehydrogenase, the enzyme associated with the catabolism of acetaldehyde. Acetaldehyde, a product of alcohol oxidation, has toxic effects when its blood levels increase. When an alcoholic with adequate blood levels of disulfiram drinks, the level of acetaldehyde rises, causing toxic symptoms of increasing severity as alcohol consumption continues. However, a recent, well-designed, multicenter VA study with biological markers to assess compliance (Fuller et al., 1986) found that only 20 percent of subjects were compliant with double-blind medication and that compliance to disulfiram or placebo was the most important determinant of abstinence. Although the frequency of drinking was reduced in males who relapsed, the rate and duration of abstinence and measures of social stability and employment did not differ between disulfiram and placebo groups. Other investigators have reported more successful outcomes with disulfiram when given in a supervised setting (Brewer & Smith, 1983; Sereny, Sharma, Holt, & Gordis, 1986), or in the presence of a spouse or significant other (Azrin, Sisson, Meyers, & Godley, 1982; 1984; Keane, Foy,

Nunn, & Rychtarik, 1984; O'Farrell & Bayog, 1986), suggesting that disulfiram may help some alcoholics abstain if compliance can be assured. Disulfiram may be especially useful as a maintenance aversive drug for alcoholics who are unable to recognize situations with a high-risk potential for drinking.

Agents to reduce craving and consumption. The opiate antagonist naltrexone was shown to significantly reduce craving in recently abstinent alcohol-dependent patients relative to placebo in two independent, double-blind, 12-week trials (O'Malley et al., 1992, Volpicelli, O'Brien, Alterman, & Hayashida, 1990). Better patient retention in treatment, lower levels of alcohol consumption, reduced rates of relapse, and fewer mean drinking days were also associated with naltrexone treatment. Naltrexone seemed especially effective in patients who had at least one relapse to drinking, in attenuating their loss of control over drinking. Explanations for these findings include the notion that alcohol is reinforcing because of its effects on opioidergic systems and that when opioceptors are blocked, alcohol loses its reinforcing properties George, Roldan, Lue, & Naranjo, 1991; Ho & Rossi, 1982; Volpicelli, Davis, & Olgin, 1986). Sinclair (1990) proposed a learning theory model of extinction to account for the reduction in alcohol consumption associated with opiate antagonist treatment: If the reward is no longer paired with a behavior, the behavior diminishes. Alternatively, naltrexone may affect the desire to consume alcohol as part of a general effect on consummatory behavior. Patients in both studies were enrolled in standard concomitant nonpharmacologic treatments: weekly individual coping skills therapy in the O'Malley et al. (1992) study, and intensive outpatient rehabilitation in the Volpicelli et al. (1990) study.

The effect of serotonin selective reuptake inhibitors (SSRIs), including fluoxetine, citalopram, and zimelidine, on alcohol consumption has been studied in a series of double-blind experiments, with random assignment to treatment (Amit et al., 1985; Gorelick, 1986, 1989; Naranjo et al., 1984, 1987, 1988, 1989). Results of these studies indicate a modest decrease in the number of drinks consumed in samples of social drinkers, early problem drinkers, and chronic alcoholics. Early-stage problem drinkers also showed an increase in abstinent days (Naranjo et al., 1989; Naranjo, Kadlec, Sanhueza, Woodley-Remus, & Sellers, 1990). SSRIs are effective within a few days of administration, and side effects are relatively mild and transient for most patients for these drugs, with the exception of zimelidine, which has been withdrawn from the market because of toxicity. Antidepres-

sant action may resolve depressive symptoms that could precipitate relapse (Pottenger et al., 1978), and SSRIs have also been found to reduce alcohol-induced memory and cognitive impairment (Linnoila, Eckardt, Durcan, Lister, & Martin, 1987; Weingartner, Buchsbaum, & Linnoila, 1983), further increasing their potential utility in the rehabilitation phase of alcoholism treatment. Bromocriptine, a dopamine agonist, has also been associated with reduced craving and consumption relative to placebo in a study of alcohol-dependent patients (Borg, 1983; NIAAA, 1990).

Treatment of cormorbid psychiatric disorders. Psychiatric syndromes, depression among the most common, reduce the likelihood of abstinence in recovering alcoholics (NIAAA, 1987). Concurrent depression significantly increases the morbidity and mortality associated with alcoholism, particularly in terms of suicide (Berglund, 1984; Mayfield & Montgomery, 1972). These features make clinical management of depression in recovering alcoholics important. The relationship between alcoholism and depression is complex and controversial, in part because of confusion in definitions, for example, the distinction between drinking and alcoholism, or sadness and major depressive disorder (Schuckit, 1983). Similarly, depression-like symptoms of withdrawal commonly clear within a week of sobriety (Liskow, Mayfield, & Thiele, 1982; Sedlacek & Miller, 1982), which may create a bias that depression in alcoholism is not real and therefore does not merit treatment. A double-blind comparison of desipramine (DMI) and placebo in alcoholics with less than 3 months of sobriety found that DSM-III-R major depression in alcoholism is diagnosable with standardized interviews and is responsive to DMI treatment (Mason & Kocsis, 1991). Posttreatment depression ratings were unchanged from pretreatment measures in placebo-treated depressives; this group also displayed a greater relapse rate to drinking, despite the concomitant group therapy and referral to Alcoholics Anonymous (AA) offered to all study participants. Work by Ciraulo, Barnhill, and Jaffe (1988), Sandoz et al. (1983), and others indicates that the interaction between such medications as DMI and a recent history of heavy alcohol abuse is relevant for clinical management of alcohol-related depressions, in terms of both efficacy and toxicity.

Lithium treatment has been studied extensively, producing no conclusive support for efficacy in treatment alcoholism (Dorus et al., 1989; Fawcett et al., 1984, 1987). The most recent large-scale study concluded that lithium does not affect the course of alcoholism in either depressed or nondepressed subjects (Dorus et al., 1989). The narrow safety range plasma levels and potential side effects of lithium suggest that lithium may be best reserved for alcoholics with concurrent psychiatric disorders for which lithium is the indicated treatment. The rates of noncompliance reported in lithium treatment studies of alcoholism also suggest that lithium plasma levels should be carefully monitored (Dorus et al., 1989; Fawcett et al., 1984, 1987).

Buspirone, a nonbenzodiazepine anxiolytic agent, has a number of advantages over the benzodiazepines for the treatment of anxiety disorders in recovering alcoholics. It is not an abused or addictive medication; it is not synergistic with alcohol; it is less sedating; and it does not impair cognitive or motor functioning. One open trial reported reduced anxiety and craving in highly anxious alcoholics treated with buspirone (Kranzler & Meyer, 1989). An 8-week, double-blind trial of alcohol-abusing patients similarly found less craving, anxiety, and global psychopathology and better retention in treatment for buspirone patients (Bruno, 1989), thus lending support to the potential utility of buspirone treatment of anxiety disorders in alcoholism.

Psychological approaches to alcoholism rehabilitation. Psychotherapy, counseling, group therapy, behavioral therapy, family intervention, and referral to AA are frequently utilized psychological approaches to alcoholism rehabilitation. Until recently, few of these modalities were systemically evaluated for efficacy in controlled studies. An ongoing, multisite clinical trial sponsored by the NIAAA seeks to test the matching hypothesis, that is, that certain patient characteristics interact with treatment parameters in a way that reliably affects outcome. Three treatment approaches are being studied in this project: (1) a 12-step approach that involves AA participation and teachings; (2) CBT focused on the communication and assertiveness skills needed to develop a supportive social network and to resist peer pressure and other high-risk situations that commonly precipitate relapse; and (3) motivational enhancement therapy, which uses motivational techniques to mobilize the alcoholic's personal resources. It is anticipated that results from the matching study, available in 1994, will determine whether patient–treatment matching improves treatment effectiveness and reduced treatment costs.

Matching principles have also been applied to group therapy. Based on prognostic significance, Kadden and colleagues (Kadden, Cooney, Getter, & Litt, 1989) specified patient matching variables of sociopathy, global psychopathology, and neuropsychological impairment. Treatment was either coping skills training based on cognitive-behavioral

principles or interactional group therapy aimed at fostering insight and healthier interpersonal functioning. Coping skills training was more effective for alcoholics with more severe sociopathy or psychopathology. Interactional therapy was more effective for patients lower in sociopathy or with more neuropsychological impairment. In addition to decreased cost, potential advantages of group treatment of alcoholism include the power of a peer group to provide support, decrease alienation, offer role modeling, counter cultural pressures to drink, and confront denial and resistance.

Therapist characteristics and training have been studied less often than patient or treatment variables but are also believed to influence outcome. In developing their interactive group therapy approach to chemical dependency, Matano and Yalom (1991) emphasized the importance of therapist familiarity with AA language, steps, and traditions and with common themes arising in the treatment of the alcoholic patient, including idealization and devaluation, externalization, defiance and grandiosity, conning, and avoidance. Zweben (1989) addressed training and competency issues for the individual psychotherapist, including the ability to take a drug history and to assess the role of substance abuse in the patient's presenting complaints without colluding with the patient's denial and minimalization. She suggested viewing resistance to giving up symptoms as a subject of therapeutic work with alcoholics instead of as an obstacle to treatment, and recommended that the therapist have a broad repertoire of skills, including behavior-shaping techniques, and group and family skills, as well as educational information about alcoholism. Zweben also pointed out that cognitive impairment is sometimes mistaken for denial or decreased motivation and that the therapist should be attentive to the possibility of neuropsychological impairment, particularly in alcoholics in early recovery. Various cognitive remediative (Goldman, 1986) and computer-assisted retraining techniques (Gordon, Kennedy, & McPeake, 1988) have been developed to improve neuropsychological functioning impaired by chronic alcohol abuse.

Behavioral marital therapy has been associated with improved outcome in terms of both drinking and marital satisfaction in comparative trials with other forms of marital therapy and minimal-treatment control groups (McCrady et al., 1986; NIAAA, 1990; O'Farrell, Cutter, & Floyd, 1985). Unmotivated alcoholics have been found to reduce drinking and initiate treatment when family members were trained in the use of techniques to reinforce reduced drinking (NIAAA, 1990; Sisson & Azrin, 1986).

Combined pharmacologic and psychological approaches to alcoholism rehabilitation. There have been no factorial studies evaluating medication and psychological approaches to alcohol rehabilitation against one another, a control group, and a group receiving both pharmacotherapy and psychotherapy. Nevertheless, it is commonly believed that treatment outcome may be significantly enhanced if pharmacotherapy is integrated with psychosocial interventions and abstinence support groups. However, pharmacologic treatments for alcoholism are often resisted by both treatment providers and patients, many of whom are influenced by the drug-free philosophy of AA. When administering pharmacologic treatment an effort should be made to deter any shift in responsibility for sobriety to the medication or the physician prescribing it and to locate and refer patients to AA groups that are open to the idea of such treatment. Compliance with medication is a critical predictor of outcome in many pharmacologic studies. Another way in which nonpharmacologic strategies are integrated with medication treatments involves development of behavioral techniques to enhance medication compliance, for example, by encouraging the patient to take medication at a set time of day, preferably in the presence of a reliable significant other (Azrin, 1976; Azrin et al., 1982).

Future Directions. Alcoholism treatment research is rapidly expanding. Increasing knowledge of brain mechanisms and the actions of alcohol on neurotransmitters, receptors, and second messenger systems, combined with the emergence of new medications, offers a number of areas in which pharmacologic treatments of alcoholism may evolve. Of potential interest are agents to relieve mechanisms responsible for craving; attenuate alcohol consumption; block the reinforcing effects of alcohol; prevent the neuroadaption to alcohol that forms the basis for tolerance, withdrawal, and protracted abstinence; and improve the recovery rate of cognitive functioning.

Matching studies promise to enhance the efficacy and reduce the costs of psychological treatments by identifying patient, treatment, and therapist characteristics that reliably interact with outcome. Diagnosis and treatment of alcohol-related problems, such as marital disruption, neuropsychological impairment, and comorbid psychiatric disorders, also constitute important research topics. A challenge in applying alcoholism research findings to clinical situations is the stringent limitation on third-party payment for alcoholism treatment, despite the high medical costs of alcoholism. A second challenge lies in overcoming the bias that many traditional alcoholism therapists exhibit toward pharmacologic treatments for alcoholism. Conversely, pharmacologists may require education regarding behavioral methods to increase medication compliance and in determining the need for psychological treatments of alcohol-related problems. The complexity of the biochemical and psychosocial variations that contribute to and maintain alcohol dependence suggests that an integrative approach to treatment may provide the strongest insurance against relapse.

SUMMARY

This era of exploring psychiatric research is yielding increasing knowledge of mental illnesses and their treatments. The combined advent of a new diagnostic system, new medications, and newly standardized and testable psychotherapies has contributed to the evolving knowledge base. Most psychiatric disorders can now be effectively treated with psychological or pharmacologic therapies or their combination. Despite these advances, much work remains to clarify the etiologies and mechanisms of psychiatric disorders and to determine their optimal forms of treatment.

Psychotherapists have historically resisted categorical diagnostic classifications and pharmacotherapeutic approaches. It is no longer reasonable for them to do so. Patients should receive treatments that have been validated by clinical research and are appropriately fitted to their disorders, rather than submit to a given practitioner's procrustean approach. As this chapter demonstrates, appropriate treatment frequently involves a combination of pharmacologic and psychotherapeutic interventions.

REFERENCES

Abramson, H. A. (Ed.). (1967). *The use of LSD in psychotherapy and alcoholism.* New York: Bobbs-Merrill.

Adinoff, B., Bone, G. H. A., & Linnoila, M. (1988). Acute ethanol poisoning and the ethanol withdrawal syndrome. *Medical Toxicology and Adverse Drug Experiences 3,* 172–196.

Alstrom, J. E., Nordlund, C. L., Persson, G., Hardin, M., & Ljungqvist, C. (1984). Effects of four treatment methods on social phobic patients not suitable for insight-oriented psychotherapy. *Acta Psychiatrica Scandinavica, 70,* 97–110.

American Psychiatric Association. (1980). *Diagnostic and Statistical Manual of Mental Disorders III.* Washington, DC: American Psychiatric Association.

American Psychiatric Association. (1987). *Diagnostic and*

statistical manual of mental disorders (3rd ed., rev.). Washington, DC: American Psychiatric Association.

Amit, Z., Brown, Z., Sutherland, A. Rockman, G., Gill, K. & Selvaggi, N. (1985). Reduction in alcohol intake in humans as a function of treatment with zimelidine: Implications for treatment. In C. A. Naranjo, & E. M. Sellers (Eds.), *Research advances in new psychopharmacological treatments for alcoholism* (pp. 189–198). Amsterdam: Excerpta Medica.

Andrews, G., Armstrong, M. S., Brodaty, H., Hadzi-Pavlovic, D., Hall, W., Harvey, P. R., Sansom, D. J., Tennant, C. C., Weeks, P., Grigor, J., Hughson, B. J., Johnson, G., & Kiloh, L. G. (1983). A treatment outline for depressive disorder: The Quality Assurance Project. *Australian and New Zealand Journal of Psychiatry, 17*, 129–146.

Andrews, G., Brodaty, H., Hadzi-Pavlovic, D., Harvey, P. R., Holt, P., Tennant, C., & Vaughan, K. (in press). Treatment outlines for the management of schizophrenia: The Quality Assurance Project. *Australian and New Zealand Journal of Psychiatry.*

Armor, D., & Klerman, G. L. (1968). Psychiatric treatment orientations and professional ideology. *Journal of Health and Social Behavior, 9*, 243–255.

Azrin, N. H. (1976). Improvements in the community-reinforcement approach to alcoholism. *Behavioral Research and Therapy, 14*, 339–348.

Azrin, N. H., Sisson, R. W., Meyers, R., & Godley, M. (1982). Alcoholism treatment by disulfiram and community reinforcement therapy. *Journal of Behavior Therapy and Experimental Psychiatry, 13*, 105–112.

Baer, L., & Minichiello, W. E. (1990). Behavioral treatment for obsessive-compulsive disorder. In R. Noyes, M. Roth, & G. D. Burrows (Eds.), *Handbook of anxiety*. New York: Elsevier.

Ballenger, J. C., Burrows, G. D., DuPont, R. L., Lesser, I. M., Noyes, R., Pecknold, J. C., Rifkin, A., & Swinson, R. P. (1988). Alprazolam in panic disorder and agoraphobia: Results from a multicenter trial: I. Efficacy in short-term treatment. *Archives of General Psychiatry, 45*, 413–422.

Balter, M. B., Levine, J., Manheimer, D. I. (1974). Cross-national study of the extent of anti-anxiety sedative drug use. *New England Journal of Medicine, 290*, 769–774.

Barlow, D. H., & Craske, M. (1989). *Mastery of your anxiety and panic.* Center for Stress and Anxiety Disorders, State University of New York, Albany.

Barlow, D. H., DiNardo, P. A., Vermilyea, B. B., Vermilyea, J., & Blanchard, E. (1986). Comorbidity and depression among anxiety disorders: Issues in diagnosis and classification. *Journal Nervous and Mental Disorders, 174*, 63–72.

Baxter, L. R., Schwartz, J. M., Mazziotta, J. C., Phelphs, M. E., Pahl, J. J., Guze, B. H., & Fairbanks, L. (1988). Cerebral glucose metabolic rates in nondepressed patients with obsessive-compulsive disorder. *American Journal of Psychiatry, 145*, 1560–1563.

Beck, A. T., Rush, J., Shaw, B., & Emery, G. (1979). *Cognitive therapy of depression: A treatment manual.* New York: Guilford.

Becker, R. E., Heimberg, R. G., & Bellack, A. S. (1987). *Social skills training treatment for depression.* New York: Pergamon.

Beitman, B. D., & Klerman, G. L. (Eds.). (1984). *Combining pharmacotherapy and psychotherapy in clinical practice.* New York: Spectrum.

Beitman, B., & Klerman, G. L. (Eds.). (1991). *Integrating pharmacotherapy and psychotherapy.* Washington, DC: American Psychiatric Association.

Bellack, A. S., Hersen, M., & Himmelhoch, J. M. (1980). Social skills training for depression: A treatment manual. *JSAS Catalog of Selected Documents in Psychology 10*, 21–56.

Bellack, A. S., Hersen, M., & Himmelhoch, J. M. (1981). Social skills training compared with pharmacotherapy in the treatment of unipolar depression. *American Journal of Psychiatry, 138*, 1562–1567.

Berglund, M. (1984). Suicide in alcoholism. A prospective study of 88 suicides: I. The multidimensional diagnosis at first admission. *Archives of General Psychiatry, 41*(9), 888–894.

Blackburn, I. N., Bishop, S., Glen, A. I. M., Whalley, L. J., & Christie, J. E. (1981). The efficacy of cognitive therapy in depression: A treatment trial using cognitive therapy and pharmacotherapy, each alone and in combination. *British Journal of Psychiatry, 139*, 181–189.

Borg, V. (1983). Bromocriptine in the prevention of alcohol abuse. *Acta Psychiatrica Scandinavica, 68*, 100–110.

Borkovec, T. D., Mathews, A. M., Chambers, A., Ebrahimi, S., Lytle, R., & Nelson, R. (1987). The effects of relaxation training with cognitive therapy or nondirective therapy and the role of relaxation-induced anxiety in the treatment of generalized anxiety. *Journal of Consulting and Clinical Psychology, 55*, 883–888.

Bowen, J. (1960). A family concept of schizophrenia. In D. D. Jackson (Ed.), *The etiology of schizophrenia.* New York: Basic Books.

Brewer, C., & Smith, J. (1983). Probation linked supervised disulfiram in the treatment for habitual drunken offenders: Result of a pilot study. *British Medical Journal of Clinical Research, 287*, 1282–1283.

Brown, G. W. Birley, J. L. T., & Wing, J. K. (1972). Influence of family life on the course of schizophrenic disorders: A replication. *British Journal of Psychiatry, 121*, 241–258.

Bruno, F. (1989). Buspirone in the treatment of alcoholic patients. *Psychopathology, 22*, 49–59.

Burhan, A. S. (1967). Short-term hospital treatment: A study. *Hospital and Community Psychiatry, 20*, 369–370.

Butler, G. Cullington, A., Hibbert, G., Klimes, I., & Gelder, M. (1987). Anxiety management for persistent generalized anxiety. *British Journal of Psychiatry, 151*, 524–535.

Butler, G., Cullington, A., Munby, M., (1990). Exposure in vivo versus social skills training for social phobia: Long-term outcome and differential effects. *Behaviour Research Therapy, 28*, 181–193.

Byck, R. (Ed.). (1974). *Cocaine papers by Sigmund Freud.* New York: Stonehill.

Cade, J. F. J. (1949). Lithium salts in the treatment of psychiatric excitement. *Medical Journal of Australia, 36*, 349–357.

Caffey, E. M., Galbrecht, C. R., & Klett, C. J. (1971). Brief hospitalization and aftercare in the treatment of schizophrenia. *Archives of General Psychiatry, 24*, 81–86.

Caton, C. L. M. (1982). Effect of length of inpatient treatment for chronic schizophrenia. *American Journal of Psychiatry, 139*, 856–861.

Charney, D. S., & Woods, S. W. (1989). Benzodiazepine treatment of panic disorder: A comparison of alprazolam and lorazepam. *Journal of Clinical Psychiatry, 50*(11), 418–423.

Chevron, E. S., & Rounsaville, B. J. (1983). Evaluating the clinical skill of psychotherapists. *Archives of General Psychiatry, 40*, 1129–1132.

Chevron, E. S. Rounsaville, B. J., Rothblum, E. D., & Weissman, M. M. (1983). Selecting psychotherapists to participate in psychotherapy outcome studies. *Journal of Nervous and Mental Disease, 171*, 348–353.

Ciraulo, D. A., Barnhill, J. G., Jaffe, J. H. (1988). Clinical pharmacokinetics of imipramine and desipramine in alcoholics and normal volunteers. *Clinical Pharmacology and Therapeutics, 43,* 509–512.

Clark, D. M. A. (1986). Cognitive approach to panic. *Behavior Research Therapy 24,* 461–470.

Clarkin, J. F., Glick, I. D. Haas, G. L. Spencer, J. H., Lewis, A. B., Peyser, J. DeMane, N., Good-Ellis, M., Harris, E., & Lestelle, V. (1990). A randomized clinical trial of inpatient family intervention: V. Results for affective disorders. *Journal of Affective Disorders, 18,* 17–28.

Cochran, W. G. (1954). Some methods of strengthening the common chi-square tests. *Biometrics, 10,* 417–451.

Cole, J. O., Klerman, G. L., & Jones, R. T. (1960). Drug therapy. In E. J. Spiegel (Ed.), *Progress in neurology and psychiatry* (Vol. 15, pp. 540–576). New York: Grune & Stratton.

Cooper, A. M. (1985). Will neurobiology influence psychoanalysis? *American Journal of Psychiatry, 142,* 1395–1402.

Covi, L., Lipman, R. S., Derogatis, L. R., Smith, J. E., & Pattison, J. H. (1974). Drugs and group psychotherapy in neurotic depression. *American Journal of Psychiatry, 131,* 191–198.

Cowley, D., & Roy Byrne, P. (1991). The biology of generalized anxiety disorder and chronic anxiety. In R. Rapee & D. Barlow (Eds.), *Chronic anxiety: Generalized anxiety disorder and mixed anxiety-depression.* New York: Guilford.

Craske, M. G. (1988). Cognitive behavioral treatment of panic. In A. Frances & R. Hale (Eds.), *Annual review of psychiatry* (Vol. 7, pp. 121–137) Washington, DC: American Psychiatric Press.

Craske, M. G., Brown, T. A., & Barlow, D. H. (1991). Behavioral treatment of panic: A two-year follow-up. *Behavior Therapy 22,* 129–136.

Craske, M. G., Cerny, J. A., & Klosko, J. S. (1989). Behavioral treatment of panic disorder. *Behavior Therapy 20,* 261–282.

Davenport, Y. B., Ebert, M. H., Adland, M. L., & Goodwin, F. K. (1976). Couples group therapy as an adjunct to lithium maintenance of the manic patient. *American Journal of Orthopsychiatry, 47,* 496–502.

Davidson, J. R. T., Ford, S. M., Smith, R. D., & Potts, N. L. S. (1991). Long-term treatment of social phobia with clonazepam. *Journal of Clinical Psychiatry, 52,* 16–20.

Davis, J. J. (1965). Efficacy of tranquilizing and antidepressant drugs. *Archives of General Psychiatry, 13,* 552–572.

Davis, J. M. (1976). Overview: Maintenance therapy in psychiatry: II. Affective disorders. *American Journal of Psychiatry, 133,* 1–13.

DeRubeis, R. J. Hollon, S. D., Evans, M. D., & Bemis, K. M. (1982). Can psychotherapies for depression be discriminated? A systematic investigation of cognitive therapy and interpersonal therapy. *Journal of Consulting and Clinical Psychology, 5,* 744–756.

Dorus, W., Ostrow, D. G. Anton, R., Cushman, P., Collins, J. F., Schaefer, M., Charles, H. L., Desai, P., Hayashida, M., Malkerneker, U., Willenbring, M., Fiscella, R., & Sather, M. R. (1989). Lithium treatment of depressed and nondepressed alcoholics. *Journal of the American Medical Association, 262,* 1646–1652.

Downing, R. W., & Rickels, K. (1985). Early treatment response in anxious outpatients treated with diazepam. *Acta Psychiatrica Scandinavica, 72,* 522–528.

Durham, R. C., & Turvey, A. A. (1987). Cognitive therapy versus behavior therapy in the treatment of chronic general anxiety: Outcome at discharge and at six month follow-up. *Behaviour Research Therapy, 25,* 229–234.

Elkin, I., Parloff, M. B., Hadley, S. W., & Autry, J. H. (1985). NIMH Treatment of Depression Collaborative Research Program. *Archives of General Psychiatry, 42,* 305–316.

Elkin, I., Shea, M. T., Watkins, T., Imber, S. D., Sotsky, S. M., Collins, J. F., Glass, D. R., Pilkonis, P. A., Leber, W. R., Docherty, J. P., Fiester, S. J., & Parloff, M. B. (1989). National Institute of Mental Health Treatment of Depression Collaborative Research Program: General effectiveness of treatment. *Archives of General Psychiatry, 46,* 971–983.

Eysenck, H. J. (1975). The effects of psychotherapy. *International Journal of Psychiatry 1,* 99–178.

Falloon, I. R. H., Boyd, J. L., McGill, C. W., Ratani, J., Moss, H. B., & Gilderman, A. M. (1982). Family management in the prevention of exacerbations of schizophrenia. *New England Journal of Medicine, 306,* 1437–1440.

Falloon, I. R. H., Lloyd, G. G., & Harpin, R. E. (1981). Real-life rehearsal with nonprofessional therapists. *Journal of Nervous and Mental Disease, 169,* 180–184.

Fawcett, J., Clark, D. C., Aagesen, D. O., Pisani, V. D., Tilkin, J. M., Sellers, D., McGuire, M., & Gibbons, R. D. (1987). A double-blind, placebo-controlled trial of lithium carbonate therapy for alcoholism. *Archives of General Psychiatry, 44,* 248–256.

Fawcett, J., Clark, D. C., Gibbons, R. D., Aagesen, C. A., Pisani, V. D., Tilkin, J. M., Sellers, D., & Stutzman, D. (1984). Evaluation of lithium therapy for alcoholism. *Journal of Clinical Psychiatry, 45,* 494–499.

Fawcett, J., & Epstein, P. (1980). Clinical management — imipramine–placebo administration manual. Rush–Presbyterian–St. Luke's Medical Center, Pharmacotherapy Training Center, Chicago.

Fein, L. (1980). *The efficacy and cost-effectiveness of psychotherapy: The implications of cost-effectiveness analysis of medical technology* (Office of Technology Assessment Background Paper No. 3). Washington, DC: U.S. Government Printing Office.

Feinsilver, D. B., Yates, B. T. (1984). Combined use of psychotherapy and drugs in chronic treatment-resistant schizophrenic patients: A retrospective study. *Journal of Nervous and Mental Disease, 172,* 133–139.

Fernandez, F., & Levy, J. K. (1990). Psychiatric diagnosis and pharmacotherapy of patients with HIV infection. In A. Tasman, S. M. Goldfinger, & C. A. Kaufmann (Eds.), *Review of psychiatry* (Vol. 9). Washington, DC: American Psychiatric Press.

Fiske, D. W., Hunt, H. F., Luborsky, L., Orne, M. T., Parloff, M. B., Reiser, M. F., & Tuma, A. H. (1970). Banning of research on effectiveness of psychotherapy. *Archives of General Psychiatry, 22,* 22–32.

Foa, E. G., & Kozak, M. J. (1985). Treatment of anxiety disorders: Implications for psychopathology. In A. H. Tuma & J. D. Maser (Eds.), *Anxiety and the anxiety disorders:* (pp. 421–452). Hillsdale, NJ: Lawrence Erlbaum.

Foa, E. B., Steketee, G. S., & Ozarow, B. J. (1985). Behavior therapy with obsessive-compulsives: From theory to treatment. In M. Mavissakalian (Ed.), *Obsessive-compulsive disorders: Psychological and pharmacological treatments* (pp. 49–129). New York: Plenum.

Foy, A., March, S., & Drinkwater, V. (1988). Use of an objective clinical scale in the assessment and management of alcohol withdrawal in a large general hospital. *Alcoholism: Clinical and Experimental Research, 12,* 360–364.

Frances, R. J., & Franklin, J. E. (1989). *Concise guide to treatment of alcoholism and addictions*. Washington, DC: American Psychiatric Press.

Frank, E., Kupfer, D. J., Perel, J. M., Cornes, C., Jarrett, D. B., Mallinger, A. G., Thase, M. E., McEachran, A. B., & Grochocinski, V. J. (1990). Three-year outcomes for maintenance therapies in recurrent depression. *Archives of General Psychiatry, 47*(12), 1093–1099.

Frank, E., Kupfer, D. J., Wagner, E. F., McEachran, A. B., & Cornes, C. (1991). Efficacy of interpersonal therapy as a maintenance treatment of recurrent depression: Contributing factors. *Archives of General Psychiatry, 48*, 1053–1059.

Friedman, A. S. (1975). Interaction of drug therapy with marital therapy in depressed patients. *Archives of General Psychiatry, 32*, 619–637.

Fuller, R. K., Branchey, L., Brightwell, D. R., Derman, R. M., Emrick, C. D., Iber, F. L., James, K. E., Lacoursiere, R. B., Lee, K. K., Lowenstam, I., Maany, I., Neiderhiser, D., Nocks, J. J., & Shaw, S. (1986). Disulfiram treatment of alcoholism: A Veterans Administration Cooperative Study. *Journal of the American Medical Association, 256*, 1449–1455.

Fryer, A. J., Liebowitz, M. R., Gorman, J. M., Campeas, R., Levin, A., Davies, S. O., Goetz, D., & Klein, D. F. (1987). Withdrawal syndrome with gradual tapering of alprazolam in panic patients. *American Journal of Psychiatry, 144*, 303–308.

George, S. R., Roldan, L., Lue, A., & Naranjo, C. A. (1991). Endogenous opioids are involved in the genetically determined high preference for ethanol consumption. *Alcoholism: Clinical and Experimental Research, 15*, 668–672.

Gilligan, J. (1965). Review of literature. In M. Greenblatt, M. H. Solomon, A. S. Evans, & G. W. Brooks (Eds.), *Drug and social therapy in chronic schizophrenia* (pp. 24–76). Springfield, IL: Charles C. Thomas.

Glick, I. D., & Hargreaves, W. A. (1979). Hospitals in the 1980s: Service, training, and research. *Hospital and Community Psychiatry, 30*(2), 125–128.

Gloger, S., Grunhaus, L., Birmacher, B., & Troudart, T. (1981). Treatment of spontaneous panic attacks with chlomipramine. *American Journal of Psychiatry 138*, 1215–1217.

Goldberg, S. C., Cole, J. O., Klerman, G. L. (1966). Differential prediction of improvement under three phenothiazines. In J. R. Wittenborn (Ed.), *Prediction of response to pharmacotherapy* (pp. 69–84). Springfield, IL: Charles C. Thomas.

Goldberg, S. C., Schooler, N. R., Hogarty, G. E., & Roper, M. (1977). Prediction of relapse in schizophrenic outpatients treated by drug and sociotherapy. *Archives of General Psychiatry, 34*(2), 171–184.

Goldman, M. S. (1986). Neuropsychological recovery in alcoholics: Endogenous and exogenous processes. *Alcoholism, 10*, 136–144.

Goldstein, N. J. (1984). Schizophrenia: The interaction of family and neuroleptic therapy. In B. D. Beitman & G. L. Klerman (Eds.), *Combining pharmacotherapy and psychotherapy in clinical practice* (pp. 167–186). New York: Spectrum.

Goodwin, F. K., & Jamison, K . R. (1990). *Manic depressive illness*. New York: Oxford University Press.

Gordis, E., & Sereny, G. (1981). Controversy in approaches to alcoholism. In V. M. Rosender, & M. A. Rothschild (Eds.), *Controversies in clinical care* (pp. 37–55). New York: SP Medical and Scientific Books.

Gordon, S., Kennedy, B., & McPeake, J. D. (1988). Neuropsychologically impaired alcoholics: Assessment, treat-ment considerations, and rehabilitation. *Journal of Substance Abuse Treatment, 5*, 99–104.

Gorelick, D. A. (1986). Effect of fluoxetine on alcohol consumption in male alcoholics. *Alcoholism: Experimental and Clinical Research, 10*, 113.

Gorelick, D. A. (1989). Serotonin-uptake blockers and the treatment of alcoholism. In M. Galanter (Ed.), *Recent developments in alcoholism: Treatment research* (Vol. 7, pp. 267–281). New York: Plenum.

Gorman, J. M., Liebowitz, M. R., Fyer, A. J., Goetz, D. Campeas, R. B., Fyer, M. R., Davies, S. D., & Klein, D. F. (1987). An open trial of fluoxetine in the treatment of panic attacks. *Journal of Clinical Psychopharmacology, 7*, 329–332.

Gorman, J. M., Liebowitz, M. R., Fyer, A. J., Campeas, R., & Klein, D. F. (1985). Treatment of social phobia with atenolol. *Journal of Clinical Psychopharmacology, 5*, 298–301.

Greenhill, M. H., & Gralnich, A. (Eds.). (1983). *Psychopharmacology and psychotherapy*. New York: Free Press.

Grinker, R., & Spiegel, J. B. (1945). *War neurosis*. Philadelphia, Blakiston.

Grinspoon, L., Ewalt, J. R., & Shader, R. I. (1972). *Schizophrenia: Pharmacotherapy and psychotherapy*. Baltimore: Williams & Wilkins.

Group for the Advancement of Psychiatry. (1975). *Pharmacotherapy and psychotherapy: Paradoxes and progress* (Vol. 9, Report 93). New York: Mental Health Materials Center.

Hamilton, M. (1967). *The Hamilton Rating Scale for Depression*. Unpublished manuscript.

Harrison, W., Rabkin, J., Stewart, J. W., McGrath, B. J., Tricamo, E., & Quitkin, F. (1986). Phenelzine for chronic depression: A study of continuation treatment. *Journal of Clinical Psychiatry, 47*(7), 346–349.

Hatsukami, D., & Pickens, R. W. (1982). Posttreatment depression in an alcohol and drug abuse population. *American Journal of Psychiatry, 139*, 1563–1566.

Heimberg, R. G. (1989). Cognitive and behavioral treatments for social phobia: A critical analysis. *Clinical Psychology Review, 9*, 107–128.

Helzer, J. E., & Pryzbeck, T. R. (1988). The co-occurrence of alcoholism with other psychiatric disorders in the general population and its impact on treatment. *Journal of Studies on Alcohol, 49*, 2219–2224.

Herz, M. I. Endicott, J., & Spitzer, R. L. (1977). Brief hospitalization: A two-year follow-up. *American Journal of Psychiatry, 734*, 502–507.

Hill, C. E., O'Grady, K. E., & Elkin, E. (1992). Applying the collaborative study psychotherapy rating scale to rate therapist adherence in cognitive-behavior therapy, interpersonal therapy, and clinical management. *Journal of Consulting and Clinical Psychology, 60*, 73–79.

Ho, A., & Rossi, N. (1982). Suppression of ethanol consumption by MET-enkephalin in rats. *Journal of Pharmacy and Pharmacology, 34*, 118–119.

Hogarty, G. E., Schooler, N. R., & Ulrich, R. (1979). Fluphenazine and social therapy in the aftercare of schizophrenic patients. *Archives of General Psychiatry, 36*, 1283–1294.

Hollingshead, A., & Redlich, F. (1958). *Social class and mental illness*. New York: Wiley.

Hollon, S. D. (1984). *Final report: System for rating psychotherapy audiotapes*. (Contract No. 278-81-0031). Bethesda, Maryland: National Institute of Mental Health.

Hollon, S. D., & Beck, A. T. (1978). Psychotherapy and drug therapy: Comparison and combinations. In S. L.

Garfield & A. E. Bergin (Eds.), *Handbook of psychotherapy and behavior change: An empirical analysis* (pp. 437–485). New York: Wiley.

Hollon, S. D., & DeRubeis, R. J. (1981). Placebo-psychotherapy combinations: Inappropriate representations of psychotherapy in drug–psychotherapy comparative trials. *Psychological Bulletin, 90,* 467–477.

Hollon, S. D., Evans, M., Elkin, I., & Lowery, H. A. (1984). *System for rating therapies for depression.* Paper presented at the annual meeting of the American Psychiatric Association, Los Angeles.

Horwitz, R. I., Gottlieb, L. D., & Kraus, M. L. (1989). The efficacy of atenolol in the outpatient management of the alcohol withdrawal syndrome. *Archives of Internal Medicine, 149,* 1089–1093.

Huxley, A. (1954). *The doors of perception.* New York: Harper & Row.

Jamison, K. R., Goodwin, F. K. (1983). Psychotherapeutic treatment of manic-depressive patients on lithium. In M. H. Greenhill & A. Gralnick (Eds.), *Psychopharmacology and psychotherapy.* New York: Free Press.

Janowsky, D. S., El-Yousef, M. K., & Davis, J. M. (1974). Interpersonal maneuvers of manic patients. *American Journal of Psychiatry, 131*(3), 250–255.

Jarvik, L. F., Mintz, J., Steuer, J., & Gerner, R. (1982). Treating geriatric depression: A 26-week interim analysis. *Journal of the American Geriatrics Society, 30,* 713–717.

Kadden, R. M., Cooney, N. L., Getter, H., & Litt, M. D. (1989). Matching alcoholics to coping skills or interactional therapies: Posttreatment results. *Journal of Consulting and Clinical Psychology, 57*(6), 698–704.

Kahn, R. J., McNair, D. M., Lipman, R. S., Covi, L., Rickels, K., Downing, R., Risher, S., & Frankenthaler, L. M. (1986). Imipramine and chlordiazepoxide in depressive and anxiety disorders: II. Efficacy in anxious outpatients. *Archives of General Psychiatry, 43,* 79–85.

Kahn, R. S., & Westenberg, G. M. (1985). L-5-hydroxytryptophan in the treatment of anxiety disorders. *Journal of Affective Disorders, 8,* 197–200.

Karon, B. P., & VandenBos, G. R. (1981). *Psychotherapy of schizophrenia: The treatment of choice.* New York: Jason Aronson.

Keane, T. M., Foy, D. W., Nunn, B., & Rychtarik, R. G. (1984). Spouse contracting to increase Antabuse compliance in alcoholic veterans. *Journal of Clinical Psychology, 40,* 340–344.

Khanna, S. (1988). Obsessive compulsive disorder: Is there a frontal lobe dysfunction? *Biological Psychiatry, 24,* 602–613.

Klein, D. F. (1976). Psychosocial treatment of schizophrenia, or psychosocial help for people with schizophrenia. *Schizophrenia Bulletin, 6,* 122–130.

Klein, D. F. (1980). Anxiety reconceptualized. *Comprehensive Psychiatry, 21,* 411–427.

Klein, D. F., Gittleman, R., Quitkin, F., & Rifkin, A. (1980). *A diagnosis on drug treatment of psychiatric disorders.* Baltimore: Williams & Wilkins.

Klein, E., & Uhde, T. W. (1988). Controlled study of verapamil for treatment of panic disorder. *Journal of American Psychiatry, 145,* 431–434.

Klein, E., Uhde, T. W., Post, R. M. (1986). Preliminary evidence for the role of carbamazepine in alprazolam withdrawal. *American Journal of Psychiatry, 143,* 235–236.

Klerman, G. L. (1977). Better but not well. Social and ethical issues in the deinstitutionalization of the mentally ill. *Schizophrenia Bulletin, 3,* 617–631.

Klerman, G. L. (1978a). Combining drugs and psychotherapy in the treatment of depression. In J. O. Cole, A. F.

Schatzberg, & S. H. Frazier (Eds.), *Depression: Biology, psychodynamics, and treatment* (pp. 213–227). New York: Plenum.

Klerman, G. L. (1978b). Long-term treatment of affective disorders. In M. A. Lipton, A. DiMascio, & K. F. Killam (Eds.), *Psychopharmacology: A generation of progress* (pp. 1303–1311). New York: Raven.

Klerman, G. L. (1980). Long-term outcomes of neurotic depressions. In S. B. Sells, R. Crandall, M. Roff, J. Strauss, & W. Pollin (Eds.), *Human functioning in longitudinal perspective: Studies of normal and psychopathic populations* (pp. 58–73). Baltimore: Williams & Wilkins.

Klerman, G. L. (1981). Biological psychiatry research. A paradigm for the relationship between basic investigations and clinical applications. In S. Matthysse (Ed.), *Psychiatry and the biology of the human brain: A symposium dedicated to Seymour S. Kety* (pp. 287–296). North Holland: Elsevier.

Klerman, G. L. (1984). Ideologic conflicts in combined treatments. In B. Beitman & G. L. Klerman (Eds.), *Combining pharmacotherapy and psychotherapy in clinical practice* (pp. 17–34). New York: Guilford.

Klerman, G. L. (1990). Treatment of recurrent unipolar major depressive disorder: Commentary on the Pittsburgh study. *Archives of General Psychiatry, 47,* 1158–1162.

Klerman, G. L. (1991). An American perspective on the conceptual approaches to psychopathology. In A. Kerr & H. McClelland (Eds.), *Concepts of mental disorder: A continuing debate* (pp. 74–83). Gaskell, England: Royal College of Psychiatrists.

Klerman, G. L., Budman, S., Berwick, D. Weissman, M. M. Damico-White, J., Demby, A., & Felstein, M. (1987). Efficacy of a brief psychosocial intervention for symptoms of stress and distress among patients in primary care. *Medical Care, 25,* 1978–1088.

Klerman, G. L., DiMascio, A., Weissman, M. M., Prusoff, B., & Paykel, E. (1974). Treatment of depression by drugs and psychotherapy. *American Journal of Psychiatry, 131,* 186–191.

Klerman, G. L., Frank, E., Kocsis, J., Markowitz, J., Montgomery, S., & Weissman, M. M. (1993). Evaluating drug treatment of depressive disorders. In R. F. Prien & D. S. Robinson (Eds.), *Clinical evaluation of psychotropic drugs: Principles and guidelines.* New York: Raven Press.

Klerman, G. L., & Weissman, M. M. (Eds.). (1993). *New applications of interpersonal psychotherapy.* Washington, DC: American Psychiatric Association.

Klerman, G. L., Weissman, M. M., Rounsaville, B., & Chevron, E. (1984). *Interpersonal psychotherapy of depression (IPT).* New York: Basic Books.

Klosko, J. S., Barlow, D. G., Tassinari, R., & Cerny, J. A. (1990). A comparison of alprazolam and behavior therapy in treatment of panic disorder. *Journal of Clinical and Consulting Psychology, 58,* 77–84.

Kocsis, J. H., & Frances, A. J. (1987). A critical discussion of DSM-III dysthymic disorder. *American Journal of Psychiatry, 144*(12), 1534–1542.

Kocsis, J. H., Frances, A. J., Voss, C., Mann, J. J., Mason, B. J., and Sweeney, J. (1988). Imipramine treatment for chronic depression. *Archives of General Psychiatry, 45*(3), 253–257.

Koczkas, D., Guirguis, F., & Wedin, L. A. (1981). A pilot study of the effect of the 5-HT uptake inhibitor zimelidine on phobic anxiety. *Acta Psychiatrica Scandinavica, 63*(Suppl. 290), 329–341.

Kovacs, M. (1980). The efficacy of cognitive and behavior therapies for depression. *American Journal of Psychiatry, 137,* 1495–1501.

Kovacs, M. (1983). Psychotherapies for depression. In L. I. Grinspoon (Ed.), *Psychiatry update* (Vol. 2, pp. 511–528). Washington, DC: American Psychiatric Press.

Kovacs, M., Rush, J., Beck, A. T., & Hollon, S. D. (1981). Depressed outpatients treated with cognitive therapy or pharmacotherapy. *Archives of General Psychiatry, 38,* 33–39.

Kranzler, H. R., Babor, T. F., & Lauerman, R. J. (1990). Problems associated with average alcohol consumption and frequency of intoxication in a medical population. *Alcoholism, 14*(1), 119–126.

Kranzler, H. R., & Meyer, R. E. (1989). An open trial of buspirone in alcoholics. *Journal of Clinical Psychopharmacology, 9,* 379–380.

Kwentus, J. A. (1984). The drug-assisted interview. In F. G. Guggenheim & M. F. Weiner (Eds.), *The manual of psychiatric consultation and emergency care* (pp. 329–338). New York: Jason Aronson.

Lambert, M. J. (1983). Introduction to assessment of psychotherapy outcome: Historical perspective and current issues. In M. J. Lambert, E. R. Christensen, & S. S. DeJulio (Eds.), *The assessment of psychotherapy outcome* (pp. 3–22). New York: Wiley.

Leckman, J. F., Weissman, M. M., Merikangas, K. R., Pauls, D. L., & Prusoff, B. A. (1983). Panic disorder and major depression. *Archives of General Psychiatry, 40,* 1055–1060.

Levine, J. (Ed.). (1978). *Contemporary standards for the pharmacotherapy of mental disease.* New York: Futura Publishing.

Levine, J. (1979). Coordinating clinical trials in psychopharmacology: Planning, documentation, and analysis. Washington, D.C. Government Printing Office.

Levine, J., Schiele, B. C., & Bouthilet, L. (Eds.). (1971). Principles and problems in establishing the efficacy of psychotropic agents. Washington, DC: U.S. Government Printing Office.

Lewinsohn, P. M. Sullivan, J. M., & Grosscup, S. J. (1982). Behavioral therapy: Clinical applications. In A. J. Rush (Ed.), *Short-term psychotherapies for depression.* New York: Guilford.

Lidz, T., Fleck, S., & Cornelison, A. (1965). *Schizophrenia and the family.* New York: International Universities Press.

Liebowitz, M. R., Gorman, J. M. Fyer, A. J., Colmpeas, R., Levin, A. P., Sandberg, D., Hollander, E., Papp, L., & Goezt, D. (1988). Pharmacotherapy of social phobia: An interim report of a placebo-controlled comparison of phenelzine and atenolol. *Journal of Clinical Psychiatry, 49,* 252–257.

Liebowitz, M. R., Gorman, J. M., Fyer, A. J., Levitt, M., Dillon, D., Levy, G., Appleby, I. L., Anderson, S., Palij, M., Davies, S. O., & Klein, D. F. (1985). Lactate provocation of panic attacks: II. Biochemical and physiologic findings. *Archives of General Psychiatry, 42,* 709–718.

Linnoila, M., Eckardt, M., Durcan, M., Lister, F. R., & Martin, P. (1987). Interactions of serotonin with ethanol: Clinical and animal studies. *Psychopharmacology Bulletin, 23,* 452–457.

Liskow, B., Mayfield, D., & Thele, J. (1982). Alcohol and affective disorder: Assessment and treatment. *Journal of Clinical Psychiatry, 43,* 44–147.

Litten, R. Z., & Allen, J. P. (1991). Pharmacotherapies for alcoholism: Promising agents and clinical issues. *Alcoholism, 15*(4), 620–633.

Louie, A. K., Lannon, R. A., & Ketter, T. A. (1989). Treatment of cocaine induced panic disorder. *American Journal of Psychiatry, 146,* 40–44.

Luborsky, L. (1984). *Principles of psychoanalytic psychotherapy: A manual for supportive-expressive treatment.* New York: Basic Books.

Luborsky, L., Singer, B., & Luborsky, L. (1975). Comparative studies of psychotherapies. Is it true that "everyone has won and all must have prizes"? *Archives of General Psychiatry, 32,* 995–1108.

Luborsky, L., Woody, G., McLellan, A. T., & O'Brien, C. P. (1982). Can independent judges recognize different psychotherapies? An experience with manual-guided therapies. *Journal of Consulting and Clinical Psychology, 50,* 49–62.

Lydiard, B. R. (1987). Successful utilization of maprotiline in a panic disorder patient intolerant of tricyclics. *Journal of Clinical Psychopharmacology, 7,* 113.

Manning, D., Jacobsberg, L., Erhart, S., Perry, S., & Frances, A. (1990). The efficacy of imipramine in the treatment of HIV-related depression. Abstracts of the World Health Organization Sixth International Conference on AIDS. San Francisco, 1990, Abstract Th.B.32, p. 141.

Manning, D. W., Markowitz, J. C., & Frances, A. J. (1992). A review of combined psychotherapy and pharmacotherapy in the treatment of depression. *Journal of Psychotherapy Practice and Research, 1,* 103–116.

Markowitz, J. C., & Klerman, G. L. (1991). *Manual for interpersonal therapy of dysthymia.* Unpublished manuscript. Cornell University Medical College, New York.

Markowitz, J. C., Klerman, G. L., & Perry, S. (1992). Interpersonal psychotherapy of depressed HIV-seropositive outpatients. *Hospital and Community Psychiatry, 43,* 885–890.

Marks, I. (1976). The current status of behavioral psychotherapy: Theory and practice. *American Journal of Psychiatry, 133,* 253–261.

Marks I. (1985a). *The agoraphobic syndrome.* Paper presented at the International Symposium at the Academy of Medicine, Paris.

Marks, I. (1985b). *Fears, phobias, rituals.* New York: Oxford University Press.

Mason, B. J., & Kocsis, J. H. (1991). Desipramine treatment of alcoholism. *Psychopharmacology Bulletin, 27*(2), 155–161.

Mason B. J., Markowitz, J. C, & Klerman, G. L. (in press). Interpersonal psychotherapy for dysthymic disorders. In G. L. Klerman & M. M. Weissman (Eds.), *New applications of interpersonal psychotherapy.* Washington, DC: American Psychiatric Association.

Matano, R. A., & Yalom, I. D. (1991). Approaches to chemical dependency: Chemical dependency and interactive group therapy—a synthesis. *International Journal of Group Psychotherapy, 41*(3), 269–293.

Mavissakalian, M. R. (1984). Agoraphobia: Behavioral therapy and pharmacotherapy. In B. D. Beitman & G. L. Klerman (Eds.), *Combining pharmacotherapy and psychotherapy in clinical practice* (pp. 187–212). New York: Spectrum.

Mavissakalian, M. (1991). Agoraphobia. In B. Beitman & G. Klerman (Eds.), *Integrating pharmacotherapy and psychotherapy.* Washington, DC: American Psychiatric Association.

Mavissakalian, M., Perel, J., Bowler, K., & Degly, R. (1987). Trazadone in the treatment of panic disorder and agoraphobia with panic attacks. *American Journal of Psychiatry, 144,* 785–787.

May, P. R. A. (1968a). Anti-psychotic drugs and other forms of therapy. In D. H. Efron, J. O. Cole, J. Levine, & J. R. Wittenborn (Eds.), *Psychopharmcology: A review of progress. 1957–1967* (pp. 1155–1176). Washington, DC: National Institute of Mental Health, Public Health Service.

May, P. R. A. (1968b). *Treatment of schizophrenia: A comparative study of five treatments.* New York: Science House.

May, P. R. A., & Simpson, G. M. (1980a). Schizophrenia: Evaluation of treatment methods. In H. I. Kaplan, A. M. Freedman, & B. J. Sadock (Eds.), *Comprehensive textbook of psychiatry* (Vol. 3, pp. 1240–1275). Baltimore: Williams & Wilkins.

May, P. R. A., & Simpson, G. M. (1980b). Schizophrenia: Overview of treatment methods. In H. I. Kaplan, A. M. Freedman, & B. J. Sadock (Eds.), *Comprehensive textbook of psychiatry* (Vol. 3, pp. 1192–1240). Baltimore: Williams & Wilkins.

Mayfield, D. G., & Montgomery, D. (1972). Alcoholism, alcohol intoxication, and suicide attempts. *Archives of General Psychiatry, 27,* 349–353.

McCrady, B. S., Noel, N. E., Abrams, D. B., Stout, R. L., Nelson, H. F., & Hay, W. M. (1986). Comparative effectiveness of three types of spouse involvement in outpatient behavioral alcoholism treatment. *Journal of Studies on Alcohol, 47,* 459–467.

McCullough, J. P. (1991). Psychotherapy for dysthymia: A naturalistic study of ten patients. *Journal of Nervous and Mental Disease, 179,* 734–740.

McCullough, J. P. (1992). *The manual for therapists treating the chronic depressions and using the cognitive-behavioral analysis system of psychotherapy.* Unpublished manuscript. Virginia Commonwealth University, Richmond, VA.

McLean, P. D., & Hakstian, A. R. (1979). Clinical depression: Comparative efficacy of outpatient treatments. *Journal of Consulting and Clinical Psychology, 47,* 818–836.

McLellan, A. T., Luborsky, L., Woody, G. E., & O'Brien, C. P. (1980). An improved diagnostic evaluation instrument for substance abuse patients: The addiction severity index. *Journal of Nervous and Mental Disease, 68,* 26–33.

Miklowitz, D. H., Goldstein, M. J., Neuchterlein, K. H., Snyder, K. S., & Mintz, J. (1988). Family factors and the course of bipolar affective disorder. *Archives of General Psychiatry, 45,* 225–231.

Moreau, D., Mufson, L., Weissman, M. M., & Klerman, G. L. (1991). Interpersonal psychotherapy for adolescent depression: Description of modification and preliminary application. *Journal of the American Academy of Child and Adolescent Psychiatry, 30*(4), 642–651.

Mosher, L. R., & Keith, S. J. (1980). Psychosocial treatment: Individual, group, family, and community support approaches. *Schizophrenia Bulletin, 6,* 10–41.

Mosher, L. R., & Menn, A. Z. (1978). Community rsidential treatment for schizophrenia: Two-year follow-up. *Hospital and Community Psychiatry, 29,* 715–723.

Munjack, D. J., Usigli, R., Zulueta, A., Crocker, B., Adatia, N., Buckwalter, J. G., Baltazar, P., Kurvink, W., Inglove, H., Kelly, R., & Leonard, M. (1988). Nortriptyline in the treatment of panic disorder and agoraphobia with panic attacks. *Journal of Clinical Psychopharmacology, 8,* 204–207.

Myers, J. K., Weissman, M. M., Tischler, G. L., Holzer, C. E., III, Leaf, P. J., Orvaschel, H., Anthony, J. C., Boyd, J. H., Burke, J. D., Jr., Kramer, M., & Stoltzman, R. (1984). Six-month prevalence of psychiatric disorders in three communities. *Archives of General Psychiatry, 41,* 959–967.

Naranjo, C. A., Kadlec, K. E., Sanhueza, P., Woodley-Remus, D. V., & Sellers, E. M. (1990). Fluoxetine differentially alters alcohol intake and other consummatory behaviors in problem drinkers. *Clinical Pharmacology and Therapeutics, 47,* 490–498.

Naranjo, C. A., Sellers, E. M., & Chator, K. (1983). Nonpharmacological intervention in acute alcohol withdrawal. *Clinical Pharmacology and Therapeutics, 34,* 214–219.

Naranjo, C. A., Sellers, E. M., Roach, C. A., Woodley, D. V., Sanchez-Craig, M., & Sykora, K. (1984). Zimelidine-induced variations in alcohol intake by nondepressed heavy drinkers. *Clinical Pharmacology and Therapeutics, 35,* 374–381.

Naranjo, C. A., Sellers, E. M., Sanhueza, P., Valencia, H., Woodley-Remus, D. V., & Kadlec, K. E. (1988). The serotonin uptake inhibitor, fluoxetine, reduces alcohol consumption in problem drinkers. *Psychopharmacology, 96*(Suppl.), 311.

Naranjo, C. A., Sellers, E. M., Sullivan, J. T., Woodley, D. V., Kadlec, K., & Sykora, K. (1987). The serotonin uptake inhibitor citalopram attenuates ethanol intake. *Clinical Pharmacology and Therapeutics, 41,* 266–274.

Naranjo, C. A., Sullivan, J. T., Kadlec, K. E., Woodley-Remus, D. V., Kennedy, R. N., & Sellers, E. M. (1989). Differential effects of viqualine on alcohol intake and other consummatory behaviors. *Clinical Pharmacology and Therapeutics, 46,* 301–309.

National Institute of Alcohol Abuse and Alcoholism (1987). *Sixth Special Report to the U.S. Congress on Alcohol and Health.* Rockville, MD: U.S. Department of Health and Human Services.

National Institute of Alcohol Abuse and Alcoholism (1990). *Seventh Special Report to the U.S. Congress on Alcohol and Health.* Rockville, MD: U.S. Department of Health and Human Services.

Noyes, R., Clarkson, C., Crowe, R. R., Yates, W. R., & McChesney, C. M. (1987). A family study of generalized anxiety disorder. *American Journal of Psychiatry, 144,* 1019–1024.

Noyes, R., Garvey, M. J., & Cook, B. L. (1989). Follow-up study of patients with panic disorder and agoraphobia with panic attacks treated with tricyclic antidepressants. *Journal of Affective Disorders, 16,* 249–257.

Noyes, R., & Perry, P. (1990). Maintenance treatment with antidepressants in panic disorder. *Journal of Clinical Psychiatry,* Suppl. A, 24–30.

O'Farrell, R. J., & Bayog, R. D. (1986). Antabuse contracts for married alcoholics and their spouses: A method to maintain Antabuse ingestion and decrease conflict about drinking. *Journal of Substance Abuse Treatment, 3,* 1–8.

O'Farrell, T. J., Cutter, H. S., & Floyd, F. J. (1985). Evaluating behavioral marital therapy for male alcoholics: Effects of marital adjustment and communication from before to after treatment. *Behavior Therapy, 16,* 147–167.

O'Malley, S. S., Jaffe, A., Change, G., Witte, G., Schottenfeld, R. S., & Rounsaville, B. J. (1992). Naltrexone in the treatment of alcohol dependence: Preliminary findings. In C. A. Naranjo & E. M. Sellers (Eds.). *Novel pharmacological interventions for alcoholism* (pp. 148–160). New York: Springer-Verlag.

Ostow, M. (1962). *Drugs in psychoanalysis and psychotherapy.* New York: Basic Books.

Pasamanick, B., Scarpitti, F. R., & Dinitz, S. L. (1967). *Schizophrenia in the community: An experimental study in the prevention of hospitalization.* New York: Appleton-Century-Crofts.

Paul, G. L., Tobias, L. L., & Holly, B. L. (1972). Maintenance psychotropic drugs in the presence of active treatment programs. *Archives of General Psychiatry,* 106–115.

Pauls, D. L., Towbin, K. E., Leckman, J. F., Zahner, G. E. P., & Cohen, D. J. (1986). Gilles de la Tourette's syndrome and obsessive compulsive disorder: Evidence supporting genetic relationship. *Archives of General Psychiatry, 43,* 1180–1182.

Peachey, J. E., & Naranjo, C. A. (1984). The role of drugs in the treatment of alcoholism. *Drugs, 27,* 171–182.

Pottenger, M., McDernon, M. S., Patrie, L. E., Weissman, M. M., Ruben, H. L., & Newberry, P. (1978). The frequency and persistence of depressive symptoms in alcohol abuse. *Journal of Nervous and Mental Disease, 166,* 562–570.

Powell, B. J., Othmer, E., & Sinkhorn, C. (1977). Pharmacological aftercare for homogeneous groups of patients. *Hospital and Community Psychiatry, 26,* 125–127.

Prien, R. F., Caffey, E. M., Jr., & Klett, C. J. (1973). Prophylactic efficacy of lithium carbonate in manic-depressive illness. *Archives of General Psychiatry, 28,* 337–341.

Prusoff, B. A., Weissman, M. M., Klerman, G. L., & Rounsaville, S. J. (1980). Research diagnostic criteria subtypes of depression: Their role as predictors of differential response to psychotherapy and drug treatment. *Archives of General Psychiatry, 37,* 796–801.

Rabkin, J. G., & Harrison, W. M. (1990). Effect of imipramine on depression and immune status in a sample of men with HIV infection. *American Journal of Psychiatry, 147*(4), 495–497.

Rapee, R. M. (1991). Psychological factors involved in general anxiety. In R. Rapee & D. Barlow (Eds.), *Chronic anxiety: Generalized anxiety disorder and mixed anxiety-depression.* New York: Guilford.

Rehm, L. P., & Kornblith, S. J. (1979). Behavior therapy for depression: A review of recent developments. *Progressive Behavior Modification, 7,* 277–318.

Reich, J. (1988). DSM-III personality disorders and outcome of treated panic disorder. *American Journal of Psychiatry, 145,* 1149–1152.

Reiman, E. M., Raichle, M. E., Robins, E., Butler, F. K., Herscovitch, P., Fox, P., & Perlmutter, J. (1986). The application of positron emission tomography to the study of panic disorder. *American Journal of Psychiatry, 143*(4), 469–477.

Reiser, M. F. (1984). *Mind, brain, body: Toward a convergence of psychoanalysis and neurobiology.* New York: Basic Books.

Rickels, K., Amsterdam, J., Clary, C., Hassman, J., London, J., Puzzuoli, G., & Schweizer, E. (1990). Buspirone in depressed outpatients: A controlled study.

Rifkin, A., Klein, D. F., Dillon, D., & Levitt, M. (1981). Blockade by imipramine or desipramine of panic induced by sodium lactate. *American Journal of Psychiatry, 138,* 676–677.

Robins, L. N., Helzer, J. E., Weissman, M. M., Orvaschel, H. Gruenberg, E., Brude, J. D., Jr., & Reiger, D. A. (1984). Lifetime prevalence of specific psychiatric disorders in three sites. *Archives of General Psychiatry, 41,* 949–958.

Rounsaville, B. J., Klerman, G. L., & Weissman, M. M. (1981). Do psychotherapy and pharmacotherapy for depression conflict? Empirical evidence from a clinical trial. *Archives of General Psychiatry, 38,* 24–29.

Roy Byrne, P. P., Dager, S. R., Cowley, D. S., Vitiliano, P., & Dunner, D. L. (1989). Relapse and rebound following discontinuation of benzodiazepine treatment of panic attacks: Alprazolam versus diazepam. *American Journal of Psychiatry, 146,* 860–865.

Rush, A. J. (1982). Cognitive therapy of depression. In H. Akiskal (Ed.), *Psychiatric clinics of North America* (pp. 105–128). Philadelphia: Saunders.

Rush, A. J., & Beck, A. T. (1980). Behavior therapy in adults with affective disorders. In M. Hersen & A. C.

Bellack (Eds.), *Behavior therapy in the psychiatric setting* (pp. 69–93). Baltimore: Williams & Wilkins.

Rush, A. J., Beck, A. T., Kovacs, M., & Hollon, S. (1977). Comparative efficacy of cognitive therapy and pharmacotherapy in the treatment of depressed outpatients. *Cognitive Therapy and Research, 1,* 17–23.

Rush, A. J., & Watkins, J. T. (1981). Group versus individual cognitive therapy. A pilot study. *Cognitive Therapy Research, 5,* 95–103.

Safferman, A., Lieberman, J. A., Kane, J. M., Syzmanski, S., & Kinon, B. (1991). Update on the clinical efficacy and side effects of clozapine. *Schizophrenia Bulletin, 17,* 247–261.

Sandoz, M. Vandel, S., Vandel, B., Bonin, B., Allers, G., & Volmot, R. (1983). Biotransformation of amitriptyline in alcoholic depressive patients. *European Journal of Clinical Pharmacology, 24*(5), 615–621.

Saunders, J. B., & Williams, R. (1984). Drug–alcohol interactions and the effects of tissue damage on response to therapy. In G. Edwards & J. Littleton (Eds.), *Pharmacological treatments for alcoholism* (pp. 273–318). New York: Methuen.

Schooler, N. R. (1978). Antipsychotic drugs and psychological treatment in schizophrenia. In M. A. Lipton, A. DiMascio, & K. F. Killam (Eds.), *Psychopharmacology: A generation of progress* (pp. 1155–1168). New York: Raven.

Schooler, N. R., & Keith, S. J. (1984). NIMH protocol for treatment study. Strategies in schizophrenia study. Unpublished manuscript.

Schooler, N. R., Levine, J., Severe, J. B., Brauzer, B., DiMascio, A., Klerman, G. L., & Tuason, V. B. (1980). Prevention of relapse in schizophrenia: An evaluation of fluphenazine decanoate. *Archives of General Psychiatry, 37,* 16–24.

Schuckit, M. A. (1983). Extroversion and neuroticism in young men at higher risk or lower risk for alcoholism. *American Journal of Psychiatry, 140*(9), 711–714.

Schweitzer, E., Rickels, K., Case, W. G., & Greenblatt, D. J. (1990). Long-term therapeutic use of benzodiazepines. *Archives of General Psychiatry, 47,* 908–915.

Sedlacek, D. A., & Miller, S. I. (1982). A framework for relating alcoholism and depression. *Journal of Family Practice, 14*(1), 41–44.

Seitz, P. F. (1953). Experiments in the substitution of symptoms by hypnosis. *Psychosomatic Medicine, 15,* 405–411.

Sellers, E. M., Naranjo, C. A., Harrison, M., Devenyl, P., Roach, C., & Sykora, K. (1983). Diazepam loading: Simplified treatment of alcohol withdrawal. *Clinical Pharmacology and Therapeutics, 34,* 822–826.

Sereny, G. Sharma, V., Holt, J., & Gordis, E. (1986). Mandatory supervised Antabuse therapy in an outpatient alcoholism program: A pilot study. *Alcoholism: Clinical and Experimental Research, 10,* 290–292.

Servant, D., Bailly, D., & Parquet, P. H. J. (1988). Fluvoxamine in the treatment of panic disorder with obsessive compulsive symptoms. *American Journal of Psychiatry 145,* 1174.

Shakir, S. A., Volkmar, F. R., Bacon, S., & Pfefferbaum, H. (1979). Group psychotherapy as an adjunct to lithium maintenance. *American Journal of Psychiatry, 136,* 455–456.

Shaw, J. M., Kolesar, G. S., & Sellers, E. M. (1981). Development of optimal treatment tactics for alcohol withdrawal. *Journal of Clinical Pharmacology, 1,* 382–389.

Sheehan, D. V., Ballenger, J., & Jacobsen, G. (1980). Treatment of endogenous anxiety with phobic, hysterical and hypochondriacal symptoms. *Archives of General Psychiatry, 37,* 48–51.

Sinclair, J. D. (1990). Drugs to decrease alcohol drinking. *Annals of Medicine, 22*, 357–362.

Sisson, R. W., & Azrin, N. H. (1986). Family member involvement to initiate and promote treatment of problem drinkers. *Journal of Behavior Therapy and Experimental Psychiatry, 17*, 15–21.

Sotsky, S. M., Glass, D., R., Shea, M. T., Pilkonis, P. A., Collins, J. F., Elkin, I., Watkins, J. T., Imber, S. D., Leber, W. R., Moyer, J., & Oliveri, M. E. (1991). Patient predictors of response to psychotherapy and pharmacotherapy: Findings in the NIMH Treatment of Depression Collaborative Research Program. *American Journal of Psychiatry, 148*, 997–1008.

Spitzer, R. L., Endicott, J., & Robins, E. (1978). Research diagnostic criteria: Rationale and reliability. *Archives of General Psychiatry, 35*, 773–782.

Stanton, A. H., Gunderson, J. G., Knapp, P. H., Frank, A. F., Vannicelli, M. L., Schnitzer, R., & Rosenthal, R. (1984). Effects of psychotherapy in schizophrenia: I. Design and implementation of a controlled study. *Schizophrenia Bulletin, 10*, 520–551.

Sternbeck, H. (1990). Fluoxetine treatment of social phobia [letter]. *Journal of Clinical Psychopharmacology, 10*, 230.

Strauss, A., Schatzman, I. L., Bucher, R., Ehrlich, D., & Sabshin, M. (Eds.). (1964). *Psychiatric ideologies and institutions*. New York: Free Press.

Stravynski, A., Marks, I., & Yule, W. (1982). Social skills problems in neurotic outpatients: Social skills training with and without cognitive modification. *Archives of General Psychiatry, 39*, 1378–1385.

Sullivan, H. S. (1953). *The interpersonal theory of psychiatry*. New York; Norton.

Tesar, G. E., Rosenbaum, J. F., Pollack, M. H., Herman, J. B., Sachs, G. S., Mahoney, E. M., Cohen, L. S., McNamara, M., & Goldstein, S. (1987). Clonazepam versus alprazolam in the treatment of panic disorder: Interim analysis of data from a prospective double-blind placebo-controlled trial. *Journal of Clinical Psychiatry, 48*(10) (Suppl.), 16–19.

Thase, M. E. (1983). Cognitive and behavioral treatments for depression: A review of recent developments. In F. J. Ayd, I. J. Taylor, & B. T. Taylor (Eds.), *Affective disorders reassessed: 1983* (pp. 234–243). Baltimore: Ayd Medical Communications.

Uhde, T. W., Stein, M. B., & Post, R. M. (1988). Efficacy of carbamazepine in the treatment of panic disorder. *American Journal of Psychiatry, 145*, 1104–1109.

VanPuten, T. (1973). Milieu therapy: Contraindications? *Archives of General Psychiatry, 29*, 640–651.

Volpicelli, J., Davis, M., & Olgin, J. (1986). Naltrexone blocks the post-shock increase of ethanol consumption. *Life Science, 38*, 841–847.

Volpicelli, J., O'Brien, C. P., Alterman, A. I., & Hayashida, M. (1990). Naltrexone and the treatment of alcohol dependence: Initial observations. In L. Reid (Ed.), *Opioids, bulimia, and alcohol abuse and alcoholism* (pp. 195–214). New York: Springer-Verlag.

Waring, E. M., Chamberlaine, C. H., McCrank, E. W., Stalker, C. A., Carver, C., Fry, R., & Barnes, S. (1988). Dysthymia: A randomized study of cognitive marital therapy and antidepressants. *Canadian Journal of Psychiatry, 33*(2), 96–99.

Weingartner, H. Buchsbaum, M. S., & Linnoila, M. (1983). Zimelidine effects on memory impairments produced by ethanol. *Life Science, 33*:2159–2163.

Weiss, E. (1965). *Agoraphobia in the light of ego psychology*. New York: Grune & Stratton.

Weissman, M. M. (1984). The psychological treatment of depression: An update of clinical trials. In R. L. Spitzer & J. Williams (Eds.), *Psychotherapy research: Where are we and where should we go?* (pp. 89–105). New York: Guilford.

Weissman, M. M., & Akiskal, H. A. (1984). The role of psychotherapy in chronic depressions: A proposal. *Comprehensive Psychiatry, 25*, 23–31.

Weissman, M. M., Jarrett, R. B., & Rush, J. A. (1987). Psychotherapy and its relevance to the pharmacotherapy of major depression: A decade later (1976–1985). In H. Y. Meltzer (Ed.), *Psychopharmcology: The third generation of progress* (pp. 1059–1069). New York: Raven.

Weissman, M. M., Klerman, G. L., Prusoff, B. A., Sholomskas, D., & Padian, N. (1981). Depressed outpatients one year after treatment with drugs and/or interpersonal psychotherapy (IPT). *Archives of General Psychiatry, 38*, 51–55.

Weissman, M., M., Rounsaville, B. J., & Chevron, E. (1982). Training psychotherapists to participate in psychotherapy outcome studies: Identifying and dealing with the research requirements. *American Journal of Psychiatry, 139*, 1442–1446.

Weller, R. A., & Preskorn, S. H. (1984). Psychotropic drugs and alcohol: Pharmacokinetic and pharmacodynamic interactions. *Psychosomatics, 25*, 301–309.

Whitfield, C. L. (1980). Non-drug detoxification. In C. Whitfield (Ed.), *Phenomenology and treatment of alcoholism*. New York: Spectrum.

Wikler, A. (1957). *The relation of psychiatry to pharmacology*. Baltimore: Williams & Wilkins.

Wilkins, W. (1984). Psychotherapy: The powerful placebo. *Journal of Consulting and Clinical Psychology, 2*, 318–322.

Wittenborn, J. R., Klerman, G. L., Uhlenhuth, E. H. Scoville, B., Gardner, E. A., & Graft, S. C. (1977). *Testing drugs in anxiety and depression, ACNP-FDA guideline material for the clinical investigation of anxiolytic and antidepressant substances (FDAI BD-77-167)*. Washington, DC: Food and Drug Administration, Bureau of Drugs.

Wlazlo, Z., Schroeder-Hartwig, K., Hand, I., Kaiser, G., & Munchau, N. (1990). Exposure in vivo versus social skills training for social phobia: Long-term outcome and differential effects. *Behavior Research Therapy, 28*, 181–193.

Woody, G. E., Luborsky, L., McLellan, T., O'Brien, C. P., Beck, A. T., Blaine, J., Herman, I., & Hole, A. (1983). Psychotherapy for opiate addicts: Does it help? *Archives of General Psychiatry, 40*, 639–645.

Zeiss, A. M., Lewinsohn, P. M., & Munoz, R. F. (1979). Nonspecific improvement effects in depression using interpersonal skills training, pleasant activity schedules, or cognitive training. *Journal of Consulting and Clinical Psychology, 47*(3), 427–439.

Zitrin, C. M., Klein, D. F., & Woerner, M. G. (1980). Treatment of agoraphobia with group exposure in vivo and imipramine. *Archives of General Psychiatry, 37*, 63–72.

Zitrin, C. M., Klein, D. F., Woerner, M. G., & Ross, D. C. (1983). Treatment of phobias: I. Comparison of imipramine hydrochloride and placebo. *Archives of General Psychiatry, 40*, 125–138.

Zweben, J. E. (1989). Recovery-oriented psychotherapy: Patient resistances and therapist dilemmas. *Journal of Substance Abuse Treatment, 6*, 123–132.

Zwerling, I., & Wilder, J. F. (1964). An evaluation of the applicability of the day hospital in treatment of acutely disturbed patients. *Israel Annual Psychiatry, 2*, 162–166.

19

RESEARCH ON PSYCHOTHERAPY WITH CULTURALLY DIVERSE POPULATIONS

- **STANLEY SUE**

  University of California, Los Angeles

- **NOLAN ZANE**

  University of California, Santa Barbara

- **KATHLEEN YOUNG**

  University of California, Los Angeles

The analysis of research on psychotherapy with ethnic minority clients (i.e., African-Americans, American Indians, Asian-Americans, and Latino-Americans) is important. If we can identify those psychotherapeutic treatments that have universal applicability, then they should prove to be effective with different populations. If, however, current treatment practices work well only with certain populations, we need to know about these limitations and devise strategies to address the mental health needs of culturally diverse groups. Such tasks are not only theoretically meaningful (i.e., knowing the generality and limitations of theories and practices), but also consistent with psychology's goal to promote human welfare.

There are other reasons why psychotherapy research on ethnic minorities is important to consider. First, about 25 percent of the population in the United States in 1990 was composed of ethnic minorities, and in California, the figure was about 43 percent! Given the rapidly changing population, we are increasingly likely to encounter individuals from a variety of ethnic groups as clients and col-

The writing of this chapter was supported by NIMH Grant No. R01 MH44331

leagues. Intercultural skills in our roles as researchers and psychotherapists are needed; yet systematic investigations into these skills have not been conducted, and training programs in clinical psychology have not fully utilized what is known about them (Bernal & Padilla, 1982). Second, there is evidence that ethnic minority groups are experiencing significant mental health problems. Although it is beyond the scope of our review to analyze the prevalence of psychopathology, available data suggest that prevalence rates for these groups are at least as high as those in general population (Vega & Rumbaut, 1991). Immigrant/refugee background, encounters with prejudice and discrimination, cultural differences, and other experiences associated with minority group status may act as stressors that influence mental health. Third, considerable controversy has existed for the past three decades over the effectiveness of traditional psychotherapeutic approaches for members of ethnic minority clients. What evidence is there for the efficacy of psychotherapy? What are the conditions that promote effectiveness? These two questions are addressed in this chapter. Finally, psychotherapy research on ethnic minority groups is important because it is relevant to, and carries implications for, all of psychology (L. Clark, 1987).

We engage in a critical analysis of ethnic research, pointing to methodological and conceptual problems and to the need for more knowledge, as indeed any review of the literature should. Nevertheless, one cannot help but be impressed by the pioneering work of scholars in this area who continue to define and debate issues. These pioneering efforts to study relatively small populations and to grapple with issues of theoretical bias and methodological problems in the field can only help to strengthen what psychology is about — namely, the study of human beings, and not just a particular cultural group or population. In the process, the lessons learned from ethnic research are critical in helping to advance the field of psychology in general and psychotherapy in particular.

Ethnic Minority Groups

Our discussion has relevance especially for groups who have traditionally been considered ethnic minorities. They are defined by cultural characteristics, ethnic identity, and minority group status. Although other groups may indeed be included as ethnics or minorities, we focus on four groups in addition to whites (whom we define as non–Latino whites). Thus, although we recognize cultural differences among other groups, such as white ethnics, people who live in urban and rural areas, Christians and Jews, men and women, it is beyond the scope of the present chapter to include these and other groups.

It should be noted that the very terms used to refer to groups have varied — *blacks* versus *African-American*; *Native American* versus *American Indian*; *Asian* versus *Oriental*; *Hispanic* versus *Latino*; *Caucasian* versus *white*. While recognizing the variations, we have decided to use the terms *African-American*, *American Indian*, *Asian-American*, *Latino-American*, and white to refer to the groups. Furthermore, *ethnic minority* refers collectively to the four nonwhite groups because the phrase conveys culture and identity (ethnic) as well as race and social status (minority status).

Knowing the cultural values of each group is only one critical facet in understanding that group. What must also be acquired is knowledge of the history of racial/ethnic relations in this country. Thus, problems in mental health service delivery may occur not only because ethnic minority groups have different cultural values, but also because certain relationships have developed between majority and minority group individuals. Another point is that all of the groups exhibit heterogeneity (J. Jones, 1991; Lorion & Parron, 1985; Vontress, 1988). Given this heterogeneity, discussions concerning individual minority groups and whites often have a stereotypic quality. The different levels of discourse — whether the intent is to discuss cultural differences or within-group characteristics — are important to distinguish (S. Sue, 1991). At one level, when between-group comparisons are made, generalizations about group characteristics may be needed. In this case, for ethnicity and culture to have meaning, between-group differences in values and traits have to be highlighted in an abstract manner.

Inkeles and Levinson (1969) introduced the notion of *modal personality* to describe average characteristics of different ethnic groups. While members of a particular group may exhibit heterogeneity, the modal (i.e., average) characteristics of groups may show meaningful differences when between-group comparisons are made. For example, Asians and whites may exhibit differences on certain measures of individualism and collectivism. These differences provide the context for understanding ethnic groups. However, the context or modal patterns must not be confounded with the characteristics of individual members of a group who may or may not possess the modal patterns associated with the group. Otherwise, individuals are stereotyped according to their culture. At another level of communication, we may wish to emphasize within-group heterogeneity. Not all white Americans are individualistic, even though they may as a group be higher on individualism than members of other groups. By understanding the purpose of communication and by recognizing these levels of discourse, we can discuss both between– and within–ethnic group differences with more clarity and precision.

As mentioned previously, ethnic minority groups are quite heterogeneous. For example, Latinos include individuals who come from or whose family of origin comes from Mexico, the Caribbean, and Central or South America. American Indians come from hundreds of different tribes, and discussions of American Indians often include Alaska Natives. Asian-Americans can include Chinese, Japanese, Koreans, Pilipinos, Southeast Asians, and so on, as well as Pacific Islanders. Given this diversity, there are restrictions in our ability to generalize findings from a study of one subgroup even to other subgroups within the same ethnic minority. In addition, research on a group (e.g., Latino-Americans) may be based largely on one particular group (e.g., Mexican-Americans). What this means is that for some groups within a designated ethnic group, little research may be available (e.g., among the Asian and Pacific Islander American group, not much research has been conducted on Samoans). We do not deal here with issues regarding the definition of race or ethnicity or attempt to make fine distinctions about the groups who should or should not be included in one of the four major ethnic minority categories. Although important, such issues require elaborate and extensive discussion, which is beyond the scope of this chapter.

Finally, the designation of *ethnic minority* has also been challenged in that some feel the term conveys a sense of inferiority. We acknowledge that this designation is arbitrary. "Minority" status is relative (i.e., whites are not in the majority relative to the world population) and should not be interpreted to imply the sense of inferiority, separateness, or "minor" status sometimes associated with the term in the public mind. Thus, we need to clarify our intentions because we use a term that, by custom, is subject to misinterpretation.

Issues Discussed

We deal with several key issues. First, is there evidence that psychotherapy is effective with ethnic minority clients? In the previous reviews in the *Handbook of Psychotherapy and Behavior Change*, Lorion (1978) and Lorion and Felner (1986) noted that research on the disadvantaged, including ethnic minority groups, needs to proceed at all levels from the simple to the complex. The overall lack of research in this area was also acknowledged. Although much more research has been conducted in the years since those reviews, there continues to be a paucity of critical research on treatment outcomes for members of minority groups. There are virtually no studies comparing the outcomes of treated and untreated groups of ethnic minority clients. Moreover, most researchers and practitioners have reformulated the question of effectiveness into specifics: What type of treatment by which therapist is effective for which client with what specific problem under what conditions? Because we simply do not have much research into the specifics of psychotherapy with ethnic minorities, we can only provide glimpses into the answers to these questions. For heuristic purposes, we address three questions:

1. Do ethnic minority clients improve (show positive pre- and posttreatment changes) after undergoing psychotherapy?

2. Do they fare as well as other clients (e.g., when compared with whites or when ethnic groups are compared with each other) after treatment?

3. What client, therapist, and situational circumstances are associated with positive treatment outcomes and with the progress of psychotherapy?

The first two questions deal directly with the treatment outcome issue. We include a discussion not only of direct measures of outcome and treatment improvement but also indirect indexes such as utilization of services and dropout rates. The third question largely involves process research. Research findings pertinent to client characteristics such as acculturation and preferences, to therapist characteristics such as ethnicity and therapeutic style, and to situational variables such as treatment setting are included. Finally, a critique of research methodology and conceptual schemes is presented.

Much has been written about the problems faced by ethnic minorities in finding adequate psychotherapeutic services. The skepticism over the value of psychotherapy is based largely on conceptual models and anecdotal/experiential reports. Conceptual models derived from research on cross-cultural or ethnic/racial issues suggest that culture plays a critical role in the assessment, etiology, symptom expression, and treatment of mental disorders (Ivey, Ivey, & Simek-Morgan, 1993; Jackson, Neighbors, & Gurin, 1986; Jenkins, 1985; E. Jones & Thorne, 1987; Kleinman, 1979; Lin, 1986; Moore, Nagata, & Whatley, 1984; Munoz, 1982; Padilla & Salgadao De Snyder, 1985; Rogler, Malgady, & Rodriguez, 1989; Snowden, 1982; D. W. Sue & Sue, 1990; Suinn, Richard-Figuerod, Lew, & Vigil, 1985; Trimble & LaFromboise, 1985; Vraniak & Pickett, 1992; Zane, Sue, Castro, & George, 1982). Because the majority of ethnic minority clients are likely to see white therapists, and because many of these therapists are unfamiliar with the cultural values and lifestyles of various ethnic clients, performing valid clinical assessments and conducting effective psychotherapy logically seem to be problematic. Furthermore, there is little question that ethnic and race relations in the United States, often occurring in a context of prejudice and discrimination, may be reflected in the mental health profession. Therapist biases, stereotypes, discomfort, and so on may exist when working with clients who are dissimilar in ethnicity, race, or culture (K. Clark, 1972; Ibraham, 1985).

In the discussion of indirect and direct measures of outcome, we analyze the four ethnic groups together because much of the research offers comparisons of the outcomes for the different groups. However, in presenting the research on treatment process, each group is discussed separately. The reason for this is that process research on each group has proceeded more or less separately, with some issues being more salient for some groups than others. Indeed, it is difficult to compare ethnic groups on most variables because the extent of research varies from group to group and not all of the same variables have been studied for each group. Discussing the process research separately for each group also allows one to see the level of work conducted on each group.

INDIRECT MEASURES OF OUTCOMES FOR ETHNIC MINORITY GROUPS

We use utilization rates, dropout from treatment rates, and length of treatment as "indirect" indexes of outcomes. *Utilization* is defined as a help-seeking behavior in which the services of the mental health system are used. *Dropout* occurs when the client terminates treatment, presumably before receiving substantial psychotherapeutic benefits; and *length of treatment* is defined by number of treatment sessions. It should be noted that most studies have defined utilization by comparing the proportion of a population using services with the proportion of that population comprising the area being served. Thus, references to under- or overutilization of services are based on population comparisons and not on actual psychiatric need for services. Also, the view that premature termination (whether defined by the therapist or by failure to attend a certain minimum number of sessions) results in unfavorable outcomes is only an assumption. In most ethnic comparisons, the white population has been used as the comparison group because it is the majority group. While the wisdom of these assumptions and comparative procedures is debatable, ethnic differences on these indirect indexes of outcome are important to investigate per se.

Utilization of Services

In general, most studies reveal that African-Americans and American Indians overutilize services, and Asian-Americans and Latino-Americans underutilize them. Snowden and Cheung (1990) provided some information on the overall rates per 100,000 of the civilian population of admissions to inpatient psychiatric services (including state and county mental hospitals, nonfederal general hospitals, VA medical centers, and private psychiatric hospitals) in the United States during 1980. The rates were African-American, 932; American Indian/Alaska Native, 819; white, 550; Hispanic origin, 451; and Asian and Pacific American, 268. Differences in the kinds of services were apparent. Among African-Americans and whites, hospitalization rates were similar in private psychiatric hospitals but markedly different in all other inpatient services, with African-Americans having far higher rates. American Indians were admitted at higher rates than all other ethnic groups except African-Americans to state and county mental hospitals, nonfederal general hospitals, and VA medical centers. However, American Indian and Alaska Natives were admitted to private psychiatric hospitals at a lower rate than whites or African-Americans. Snowden and Cheung also found that overall, La-

tino-Americans had a lower admission rate than did whites at inpatient psychiatric services. In only one category of services, state and county mental hospitals, were Latino-Americans admitted at a higher rate than whites. In the case of Asian-Americans, underrepresentation was evident in all facilities. Two other studies, one involving 17 community mental health facilities in Seattle (S. Sue, 1977) and the other of outpatient services in the entire Los Angeles County Mental Health System (S. Sue, Fujino, Hu, Takeuchi, & Zane, 1991), found a similar pattern in which African-Americans and American Indians (only the first study reported on American Indians) overutilized and Asian-Americans and Latinos underutilized services. In a follow-up to the S. Sue (1977) study, O'Sullivan, Peterson, Cox, and Kirkeby (1989) also found overutilization by African-Americans and American Indians but no underutilization by Asian-Americans and Latino-Americans.

Other investigators have generally supported the observation of overutilization by African-Americans (Scheffler & Miller, 1989) and American Indians (Beiser & Attneave, 1982) and underutilization by Asian-Americans (T. Brown, Stein, Huang, & Harris, 1973) and Latino-Americans (Lopez, 1981).

Hu, Snowden, Jerrell, and Nguyen (1991) examined utilization patterns of a different nature. Rather than comparing the proportion of users with nonusers or with residents in a given community, the investigators confined their analysis to those who were clients within a mental health system. Based on data from San Francisco and Santa Clara counties in California, the investigators wanted to find out if there were ethnic differences in four types of mental health services used by clients seeking help. African-Americans had a relatively high probability of using emergency services, a low probability of using case management services and individual outpatient services, and an equal probability of using inpatient services compared with whites. Asian- and Latino-American clients used less emergency and inpatient but more outpatient care than did whites. Thus major ethnic differences do exist in the types of services used by clients.

Why do utilization differences exist? In Snowden and Cheung's (1990) analysis of hospitalization, the following possible explanations were discussed but none was considered sufficient to explain the results: racial differences in socioeconomic background, rates of psychopathology, help-seeking tendencies, diagnostic bias, and involuntary hospitalization. Utilization of inpatient and outpatient services may involve these factors and many others, such as knowledge of and accessibility to facilities, attitudes and values (e.g., feelings of shame or stigma), familiarity with Western forms of treatment, and presence of bilingual-bicultural staff (Wu & Windle, 1980). Indeed, with respect to the last factor, it is interesting to note that Asian-Americans and Latino-Americans, who show underutilization, are predominantly foreign born and speak English as a second language. Furthermore, there is evidence that minority group utilization is directly related to the number of minority group staff available at mental health facilities. The most appropriate conclusion at this time is that ethnic differences exist in utilization patterns and that not enough research has been conducted to explain the reason for these differences.

Some caveats are needed. In a national survey of adult African-Americans, Neighbors (1985) found that only a small proportion of respondents used traditional mental health services for serious personal problems. Thus, there is an apparent inconsistency between utilization rates when comparing treated cases with the survey results in the case of African-Americans. One study (Wood & Sherrets, 1984) has found that African-American and white clients may seek different services or programs at mental health clinics. In that study, clients were interviewed regarding their service requests. Compared with whites, African-Americans were more likely to seek help for administrative matters (problems with the law, social service agencies, school, or other agencies), medication, questions concerning reality contact, and directions as to where to get help in the community. Information concerning the rates of psychopathology, cultural expressions of symptoms, help-seeking behaviors, availability of alternative resources, perceptions of services, and barriers to utilization for ethnic minority groups is needed before conclusions can be drawn. The other caveat is that within-group differences may make a difference. Although most studies have revealed an underutilization of services among Latino-Americans, Rogler et al. (1983) concluded from their review of research that Puerto Ricans in New York had significantly higher rates of psychiatric admissions and use of outpatient psychiatric services and community mental health facilities than did non–Latino whites. It has only been more recently that Puerto Ricans have shown relatively low rates of admissions.

Dropout Rates and Length of Treatment

Length of treatment can be considered an indirect indicator of treatment outcome as it has been consistently associated with treatment change (Luborsky, Chandler, Auerbach, Cohen, & Bachrach, 1971; Pekarik, 1986). In the Seattle study of 17

community mental health facilities, S. Sue (1977) found that African-Americans, American Indians, Asian-Americans, and Latino-Americans terminated treatment after one session at a higher rate than white Americans. Whereas about half of the ethnic minority clients failed to return after the first session, fewer than 30 percent of the white clients did so. The difference in dropout rates was evident even after controlling for the possible influences of social class, age, marital status, referral source, diagnosis, and type of treatment. Not surprisingly, white clients were found to average more treatment sessions. Findings from other studies are mixed. In the follow-up of the S. Sue study in Seattle, O'Sullivan and his colleagues (1989) did not find any consistent differences in dropout rates between ethnics and whites. In the Los Angeles County study, S. Sue et al. (1991) found that African-Americans had a higher proportion, and Asian-Americans a lower proportion, of dropouts after one session that did whites. The results indicated that in outpatient treatment sessions, Asians had a higher, and African-Americans a lower, average number of sessions than did whites. Latino-Americans did not differ from whites. Length of treatment at various inpatient facilities did not show consistent differences between ethnic groups and whites (Snowden & Cheung, 1990). Thus, while some differences have emerged in number of sessions, they have not been consistent. The results perhaps reflect the influence of specific and local factors (e.g., regional, community, and service system differences), or time period differences (e.g., between 1977 and 1991, culturally responsive community programs were developed).

In the next sections, we review outcome and process research on the four ethnic minority groups: African-Americans, American Indians, Asian-Americans, and Latino-Americans.

RESEARCH ON AFRICAN-AMERICANS

African-Americans, with a 1990 population of 29,986,060, are currently the largest ethnic minority group in the United States. It is unfortunate that the general public's exposure to income, unemployment, crime, health, and educational statistics regarding African-Americans has reinforced popular stereotypes. Actually, in contrast to the stereotypes, about half of all African-Americans are members of the middle or upper class. A great deal of within-group heterogeneity exists in terms of family structure, socioeconomic status, educational background, cultural identity, and reactions to racism (B. Jones & Gray, 1983). Although African-Americans as a group hold certain values, such as the importance of the collective, sensitivity to interpersonal matters, and cooperation among peers (Nobles, 1980), these values have been influenced by culture, social class, and exposure to racism. Given these influences, it is not surprising that African-Americans are quite diverse. The diversity has implications for our analysis of treatment outcomes and client, therapist, and situational/treatment variables that affect psychotherapeutic processes.

Treatment Outcome

Reviews of the literature on the effectiveness of psychotherapy with African-Americans have yielded different conclusions. Sattler (1977) largely concluded that African-Americans did not differ from whites in treatment outcomes. On the other hand, Griffith and Jones (1978) found that the client's race did have an effect on psychotherapy outcomes. Others took a more moderate position. Parloff, Waskow, and Wolfe (1978) believed that the paucity of treatment outcome studies on African-Americans did not permit conclusions to be drawn, a point supported in a review by Abramowitz and Murray (1983). Past treatment studies using outcome measures have failed to show differential outcomes on the basis of the race or ethnicity of clients. One of the first major studies of treatment outcomes for African-American clients was conducted by Lerner (1972), who investigated the effects of treatment on severely disturbed and predominantly lower-class African-American and white clients seen by white therapists. All clients, regardless of ethnicity, tended to improve after treatment. E. Jones (1978) studied the effects of therapist and client race (African-American and white) on the outcome of psychotherapy. Although some process differences were found (e.g., African-American clients were more concerned about racial issues than were white clients), client outcomes were similar regardless of the race of the client or the therapist. Finally, E. Jones (1982) studied therapist ratings of treatment outcome among African-American and white clients seen by African-American or white therapists. All clients benefited equally, and no differences were found between racially matched or mismatched therapist–client combinations. The studies by Lerner (1972) and E. Jones (1978, 1982) demonstrate not only a lack of ethnic differences in outcomes but also improvement from pre- to posttreatment. Outcomes for African-Americans were found to be similar to those for whites.

Two studies have demonstrated poorer outcomes among African-Americans. B. Brown, Joe, and Thompson (1985) examined the outcomes of African-American, Mexican-American, and white American clients seen in different drug treatment programs — resident programs, methadone programs, and drug-free outpatient programs. Particularly in outpatient programs, ethnic clients had more unfavorable outcomes at discharge and were retained in treatment longer than whites. In a study of thousands of ethnic minority clients (African-Americans, Asian-Americans, and Mexican-Americans) seen in the Los Angeles County Mental Health System, S. Sue et al. (1991) analyzed the pre- and posttreatment Global Assessment Scale (GAS) scores of clients. The GAS is a rating given by therapists to clients in order to indicate clients' overall functioning; it is highly similar to the Global Assessment of Functioning scale used on Axis V of the *Diagnostic and Statistical Manual of Mental Disorders-III-R* (American Psychiatric Association, 1987). After covarying initial GAS scores, the investigators found that African-Americans had significantly lower positive treatment outcomes than did Asian-, Mexican-, and white Americans. Thus, while all groups showed positive changes, African-Americans had the lowest improvement scores.

Obviously, it is difficult to truly compare the studies because of the differences in outcome measures used as well as possible differences in the demographic characteristics of African-Americans, type of client seen, treatment received, and other factors. Furthermore, few investigators have examined the effects of treatment for African-Americans. As a general conclusion, one can state that in no studies have African-Americans been found to exceed white Americans in terms of favorable treatment outcomes, some investigations have revealed no ethnic differences, and some studies have supported the notion that outcomes are less beneficial for African-Americans.

Treatment Process

Client variables include expectancies, preferences, attitudes, and characteristics that are pertinent to the progress of psychotherapy. Research on client characteristics points to important differences within the African-American population and the influence of these characteristics on treatment. Also affecting the psychotherapeutic process are therapist variables such as ethnicity, style, and background. Finally, situational or treatment variables are also important to consider.

Client variables

Preferences for ethnicity of therapist. The most commonly addressed question in research on culturally specific counseling or therapy has been whether African-Americans prefer same-race or same–ethnic group therapists, whether within-group characteristics are associated with this preference, and whether ethnic preferences are a part of larger desires to find therapists who are similar in background characteristics (Helms & Carter, 1991). Some investigators have concluded that many clients prefer ethnically similar therapists (Atkinson, 1983; Harrison, 1975; Sattler, 1977), particularly in the case of African-American clients. For example, Tien and Johnson (1985) interviewed African-American clients utilizing a community mental health center in Los Angeles and found that 60 percent preferred working with an African-American therapist. While supporting an ethnic similarity position, this and other studies reveal that the preference is not unanimous among African-Americans. Therefore, some investigators have attempted to identify those within-group factors that are associated with the preference. The most widely studied factor has been African-American identity. Several investigators have tested the relationship between preferences for African-American therapists and the self-identity of African-American clients or students. In an early study, G. Jackson and Kirschner (1973) found that subjects who had a strong African-American identity (i.e., they identified themselves as black or Afro-American rather than Negro) tended to prefer an African-American counselor. However, Gordon and Grantham (1979) found racial self-designation to be unrelated to same-race preferences among African-American students. Other researchers have used measures of stages of racial identity development and then have tried to determine if preferences for African-American therapists are associated with a particular stage of identity development (Atkinson, Morten, & Sue, 1993). Based on Cross's (1971) model of racial identity, Helms has been in the forefront of developing identity measures and of stimulating research on stages of racial identity (e.g., see Helms, 1984). Parham and Helms (1981) and Morten and Atkinson (1983) found some evidence of a stage effect on preferences, with African-Americans who accept an African-American identity and are skeptical of white values being most likely to want a therapist of the same race. More complex findings were reported by Ponterotto, Anderson, and Grieger (1986), whose study revealed that the interaction between gender and stage of identity had a significant effect on preferences.

Given the array of possible variables besides race that may influence preferences for a particular therapist (attitude similarity, attractiveness of therapist, social class, etc.), perhaps race of therapist is a relatively weak predictor of preference. Preference

for therapists of the same social class rather than of the same ethnicity among African-Americans was found by Gordon and Grantham (1979), and physical attractiveness rather than ethnicity of therapist has been found to influence the favorability of attitudes toward therapists (Green, Cunningham, & Yanico, 1986). Atkinson, Furlong, and Poston (1986) asked African-American subjects to express their preferences for certain characteristics among counselors, such as ethnicity; gender; educational level; age; and similarity in attitudes, religion, and personality. The preferred characteristics, in descending order were: more education, similarity in attitudes and values, older, similar personality, and same ethnicity. Thus, ethnic preference was important but relatively less so than several other therapist characteristics. Furthermore, when subjects were divided into two groups on the basis of their self-reported commitment (strong or weak) to African-American culture, the two did not differ in preferences for characteristics among therapists. In a partial replication of the Atkinson et al. (1986) study, Ponterotto, Alexander, and Hinkston (1988) reported similar results in terms of the preferences of the African-American subjects for therapists who were similar to themselves in a number of characteristics. However, preference for a same-race therapist was ranked higher in the study by Ponterotto and his colleagues than in Atkinson et al.'s (1986) investigation. Ponterotto et al. also found that African-Americans who were strongly committed to Afro-American culture ranked a racially similar therapist higher in preference than those who were weakly committed. The investigators speculate that sample differences (e.g., differences in the type of universities or racial composition of the faculty, counseling staff, and students) in the two studies may have accounted for the discrepant findings.

Rather than simply examining preferences for African-American or white therapists, Helms and Carter (1991) wanted to find out how racial identity and demographic variables of African-Americans and whites predicted preferences for therapists who differed according to race and gender (African-American male and female and white male and female therapists). Because of the large number of variables and analyses, only a brief presentation of the results pertinent to our discussion is given. For white subjects, racial identity and gender (but not social class) were important in predicting preferences for a white therapist. However, predicting preferences for an African-American therapist was not possible from the variables examined. Among African-American subjects, predictors of preference for an African-American therapist failed to reach significance, although racial identity attitudes did predict their preferences for white male therapists. The overall findings suggest that predictors of preferences may be quite complex and interact according to the ethnicity and gender of subjects and therapists.

It is apparent that research on ethnic preferences has become increasingly systematized and specific. Several conclusions seem appropriate:

1. Research has evolved from simply ascertaining ethnic preferences to identifying the individual differences that are associated with ethnic, as well as other, preferences among African-Americans.

2. Ethnicity of the therapist is but one of many characteristics preferred by African-Americans.

3. In general, African-Americans prefer therapists who are similar in a wide range of characteristics.

4. Research has not yielded consistent findings regarding the role of identity and values in influencing preferences for the ethnicity of the therapist.

Perhaps the most obvious and yet the most unappreciated fact is that African-Americans represent a very heterogeneous group.

Other research on client variables. Although the issue of preference for the ethnicity of the therapist has dominated the literature, other client variables among African-Americans have also been discussed. Cultural differences between African-Americans and whites on values such as individualism and the importance of the collective have been found (Nobles, 1980) — values that may affect the attitudes, expectations, and behavioral patterns of clients and therapists. Furthermore, the relationship between clients and therapists may also be influenced by the minority group status of African-Americans and the accompanying prejudice and discrimination often experienced in society. Gibbs (1980; Gibbs & Huang, 1989) has noted the difficulties in establishing a therapeutic alliance among many ethnic minority clients. African-Americans often work from an interpersonal orientation. Individuals, such as psychotherapists, are evaluated by their ability to evoke positive attitudes and to obtain favorable reactions. The client sizes up the therapist and behaves in a "cool" manner in order to observe the therapist and to minimize expressions of distrust that may be present. If the therapist has evoked favorable responses from the client, the client becomes personally as well as professionally involved in the relationship, with increasing commitment and engagement. On the other hand, white therapists frequently have an instrumental orientation in which value is placed on the goal or task-related aspects in the relationship

between two people. The two different orientations may cause misunderstandings and problems in communication during psychotherapy because the therapist and client are each seeking different goals, evaluating the relationship in discrepant ways, and failing to understand each other.

A few studies have attempted to investigate some of the issues raised by others. Based on earlier work by the Terrells (Terrell & Terrell, 1981, 1984), Watkins and his colleagues conducted some studies on trust/mistrust and attitudes toward therapists among African-American students. In an analogue study, Watkins and Terrell (1988) assigned male and female African-Americans, who reported on their degree of trust for whites, to African-American or white therapists. Mistrust was related to negative expectations of the therapist. Not surprisingly, level of trust interacted with race of therapist in predicting expectations about the therapists' trustworthiness, acceptance, and expertise. African-Americans who were assigned to a white instead of an African-American therapist and who expressed a high degree of mistrust rated the therapist unfavorably. In an extension of that study, Watkins, Terrell, Miller, and Terrell (1989) examined the effects of subject's gender, mistrust, and therapist race on evaluations of the credibility and competence of therapists. Again, an interaction was found such that highly mistrustful African-Americans gave unfavorable ratings to the white therapist. The two studies suggest that racially relevant mistrust on the part of African-Americans may have considerable consequences in the treatment process.

Therapist variables. Research on therapist variables studies the characteristics, attitudes, values, knowledge, experience, and behaviors of therapists that influence the treatment outcomes or processes of African-American clients. One of the most salient controversies in this area has been the importance of therapists' ethnicity: Is it better for African-American clients to see an ethnically similar therapist?

Ethnic match between client and therapist. Most treatment studies have failed to show differential outcomes on the basis of the race or ethnicity of clients. As mentioned earlier, Lerner (1972) found that African-Americans did not demonstrate less favorable outcomes than whites when working with white therapists. The vast majority of clients improved after treatment, and no evidence of a racial difference in outcome was found. This was also true in E. Jones's (1978) study of the effects of therapist and client race (African-American and white) on the outcome of psychotherapy.

Results from the study indicated that race of therapist and race of client had no effect on outcome and that African-American and white clients improved equally. However, some process differences emerged when therapist–client interactions were tape-recorded and analyzed using a modified Q-sort. Regardless of whether African-American clients were seen by African-American or white therapists, they were more likely than white clients to express concerns involving racial issues.

In addition, no ethnic match effects on outcomes were found by E. Jones (1982), who compared therapist ratings of treatment outcome with African-American and white clients seen by African-American or white therapists. African-American and white clients benefit equally. Finally, S. Sue et al. (1991) reported on a large-scale study of the effects of ethnic match on the length of treatment and on outcomes of African-American outpatients seen in the Los Angeles County Mental Health System. African-American clients who were matched with therapists in ethnicity were compared with clients not matched in ethnicity (i.e., clients seeing a non–African-American therapist). Results revealed that African-Americans who saw an African-American rather than a non–African-American therapist attended a greater number of therapy sessions. However, on the Global Assessment Scale (GAS), no differences in treatment outcome were found as a function of match. Therefore, ethnic match appeared to affect the number of treatment sessions but not the one outcome measure that was used. The investigators speculated that perhaps the GAS is not a very sensitive measure or that ethnic match may influence interpersonal attraction and result in greater number of sessions but may fail to affect outcomes. In any event, there is no clear evidence from studies of actual clients that ethnic match enhances outcomes among African-Americans.

Clinical analogue studies in which individuals from different ethnic or racial groups are asked to play the role of therapist or client in a simulated therapy session have also been conducted. In some cases, actual counselors or therapists worked with students who presented "clinical" problems. The "clients" or "therapists" can be asked to evaluate the effectiveness (satisfaction, rapport, significance of the interaction, client preferences for ethnic therapists, etc.) of the treatment session, or the session can be rated by observers.

Evidence for a race effect has been found more often in clinical analogue studies than in actual treatment studies (Griffith & Jones, 1978). Banks (1972) as well as Carkhuff and Pierce (1967) found that self-exploration was higher in same, rather than different, race pairs involving therapists and clients. However, ethnic differences were not found in other studies, or the differences were minimal compared to those of other therapist variables (Atkinson, 1986; Porche & Banikiotes, 1982; Sattler, 1977). In addition to limitations posed by analogue designs, these studies have often used measures such as client self-exploration, preference, and ratings of therapist's level of understanding that do not directly assess client adjustment or outcomes. Also, the validity of the measures for diverse cultural groups is unknown.

Several researchers who have reviewed the literature have been unable to draw strong conclusions. As noted earlier, there is a lack of actual treatment studies. As late as 1978, Parloff et al., in a review of psychotherapy research, found that almost no reported studies of "real" therapy could be found in which African-American and white therapists were compared. In his 1986 review, Atkinson concluded that it was not possible to answer the question of the effects of client and therapist ethnicity, given the conflicting and contradictory findings. Studies that have focused on the question have also had methodological and conceptual limitations, to be discussed later.

Assessment bias among therapists. Clinical psychologists as well as researchers have become increasingly aware of limitations in the assessment tools used to evaluate the psychological status of culturally diverse groups. Many assessment tools and instruments have not been standardized, normed, or validated on these groups (Brislin, Lonner, & Thorndike, 1973). Despite these problems, assessment is essential. The clinician working with an ethnic minority client must somehow evaluate the client in order to provide treatment; researchers conducting cross-cultural investigations must often use psychological tests in order to compare different populations; and mental health planners or administrators need to evaluate treatment processes and outcomes of all clients.

Is there evidence that clinicians are biased in their assessment of African-American clients? This question has been addressed in analogue studies of clinical judgment and in archival and field studies. Many analogue studies were designed so that clinicians were given comparable case descriptions that differed in the designation of the race of the client. For example, Strickland, Jenkins, Myers, and Adams (1988) presented videotaped interviews of clients to graduate students in clinical psychology and manipulated client's race and level of psychopathology. There was some evidence that race of clinician and race of client interacted to affect clinical assessment. Archival or field studies were those investigations that reported on the symptoms or diagnosis of actual clients in hospitals or clinical settings. For example, Bishop and Richards (1987) compared counselors' intake judgments about African-American and white clients seen at a counseling center. The evaluations were highly similar for the two groups of clients. Sattler (1977) reviewed literature on racial bias in clinical assessment and concluded that clinical judgments were not systematically biased in favor of or against African-American clients. Although some race differences were found in the evaluations, there was not a consistent pattern to the differences. However, in another review, Abramowitz and Murray (1983) disagreed. They believed that Sattler's conclusion was supported largely by analogue studies and not by archival investigations and that the possibility of bias in diagnosis is still an open issue.

Significantly, some of the studies reviewed by Sattler did reveal racial differences. However, the conclusion that bias does not exist because of a failure to find consistency (systematic bias) has been questioned. Neighbors, Jackson, Campbell, and Williams (1989) suggest that diagnosticians or clinicians may make two kinds of errors. The first involves the incorrect assumption that blacks and whites are naturally different, so that similar symptoms exhibited by both groups are judged to be nonequivalent. That is, ethnic differences in the manifestations of psychopathology are believed to exist when this is not the case. The second error is the opposite of the first in that ethnic minorities may not actually exhibit the same symptoms for a particular disorder and yet the diagnostician assumes that all individuals must show the same symptoms for the disorder. Underlying the error is the belief that there are universal criteria for disorders and that groups can be evaluated in a similar fashion. This second error has been criticized more often in the literature.

In an insightful analysis of clinical judgment, Lopez (1989) also concluded that bias can occur in opposite directions. Underpathologizing is apparent when clinicians minimize the psychopathology among ethnic minority groups. For example, when symptoms of persecution seen in a black client are automatically assumed to be caused by prejudice and discrimination, the clinician may be underpathologizing (Ridley, 1984). On the other hand, overpathologizing can occur when symptoms of persecution are judged to be signs of a paranoid delusion rather than a reality-based response to a hostile environment. By using a broadened definition of bias, which includes over- and underpathologizing, and by reexamining past studies of clinical judg-

ments, Lopez (1989) found that more studies did than did not show bias.

Research on assessment, therefore, can fail to yield consistent results of a particular bias (i.e., over- or underpathologizing) and still demonstrate bias. The interesting research question that needs further investigation is the conditions under which clinicians show an over- or underpathologizing bias.

Other therapist variables. Although ethnic match (or therapist ethnicity) has dominated the pertinent literature, other therapist variables have also been studied, including therapist cultural sensitivity training, attitudes and behaviors, and physical characteristics.

In the past, cross-cultural mental health scholars and practitioners have devised strategies and programs to help train therapists to work with culturally different clients (see Barbarin, 1984; Myers, Wohlford, Guzman, & Echemendia, 1991). For example, Pedersen (1986) developed the DISC (Developing Interculturally Skilled Counselors) training program at the University of Hawaii. The Cross-Cultural Training Institute for Mental Health Professionals, developed by Lefley (1985), was a three-year, NIMH-funded project designed to enhance the diagnostic, therapeutic, and administrative skills of mental health professionals in providing culturally responsive services to African-American and Latino communities. The intensive eight-day training program empirically evaluated changes in trainees' abilities and changes in the agency's functioning. The program was favorably evaluated—without a control group—and found to be effective in enhancing therapeutic skills and in affecting positive changes in mental health agencies.

The effects of therapist cultural sensitivity training on African-American clients were investigated by Wade and Bernstein (1991). They assigned experienced African-American or white therapists to either a cultural sensitivity training program or a control group (no additional training). Therapists then saw as clients African-American women from the community who needed counseling. A main effect for training (but not therapist race) was found in that clients who saw culturally trained therapists rated the therapists as having greater expertise, trustworthiness, attractiveness, empathy, and unconditional positive regard than the clients whose therapists were not exposed to this training. In terms of the number of treatment sessions, main effects for training and therapist race were found. Clients of trained therapists and of therapists who were African-American attended more sessions than those with nontrained or white therapists. The effects of training appear to be dramatic, particularly because the training program took only *four* hours. If the results are replicated, the implications for programs and policies may be immense.

What aspects of cultural sensitivity training affect therapeutic processes and outcomes? Not enough research is available to address this question. However, several studies have investigated therapist characteristics that may influence the psychotherapeutic process. There is some evidence to suggest that the degree of intimate self-disclosure and interest in a client's culture or race have favorable effects. Interviewers who self-disclose in an intimate rather than a nonintimate fashion to African-American clients have been found to be better liked, to have more positive evaluations, and to elicit more intimate self-disclosures from the client (Berg & Wright-Buckley, 1988). Pomales, Claiborn, and La-Fromboise (1986) also demonstrated that therapists who acknowledge and deal with the cultural issues raised by African-American clients are judged to be more culturally competent than are therapists who avoid such issues. Significant interactions among several variables were also found, revealing the complexities in determining the effects of therapist factors.

In summary, the research literature on therapist variables has yielded mixed findings. There is no consistent evidence that ethnic matching of clients with therapists in the case of African-Americans results in more favorable outcomes. However, the research examining this question has been sparse and has suffered from methodological limitations. Furthermore, there is the possibility that match may show effects only with certain, and not all, African-American clients, and research on the interaction between match and other characteristics is warranted. Similarly, on the issue of assessment bias, where research seems to demonstrate the real possibility of some bias occurring, it needs to be targeted to more specific questions. Asking what factors are associated with over- and underpathologizing African-American clients is, perhaps, more meaningful than asking if bias occurs. Finally, there are a few studies that demonstrate the importance of training therapists to be culturally sensitive, open, and willing to self-disclose and to deal with cultural issues in working with African-American clients.

Situational or treatment variables. Are there certain situations or types of programs or therapies that have been found to be especially effective with African-Americans? The literature on this question is actually quite extensive. Many scholars have discussed the kinds of mental health services that may be culturally appropriate for African-Americans. Sometimes the discussions have focused on treatment modifications for particular African-American clients such as families (Boyd, 1982), women, adolescents (Franklin, 1982), and male adolescents in particular (Paster, 1985). Others have suggested modifications to traditional treatment approaches (Ramirez, 1991). For example, Lefley and Bestman (1984) have established a comprehensive mental health program with a staff that includes people indigenous to the community and is headed by a cultural broker or go-between. The investigators report that dropout rates have been low and that consumer satisfaction and treatment outcomes have been positive. Still others have recommended that ethnic-specific services (i.e., those that are specifically designed for African-Americans) or indigenous healers be more fully incorporated into the mental health system (S. Sue, 1977; White, 1984). While most of the scholars have offered suggestions regarding psychotherapy with African-Americans, few have empirically tested the effects of such suggestions.

One important modification that appears to be very helpful in the provision of services is pretherapy intervention. Ethnic minority clients may not know what psychotherapy is, how it can help, what to do, or what to expect. Acosta, Yamamoto, and Evans (1982) have devised client orientation programs aimed at familiarizing clients to psychotherapy. By using slides, audiotapes, or videotapes, the investigators try to show clients the process of seeing a therapist, and means by which to express problems, self-disclose, and communicate needs. Acosta, Yamamoto, Evans, and Skilbeck (1983) conducted an evaluation of the effectiveness of the orientation program. Prior to the first treatment session, they presented low-income African-American, Latino-American, and white outpatients with either the orientation program or a program that was neutral with regard to psychotherapy. Knowledge of and attitudes toward psychotherapy were assessed prior to and immediately after the programs. Results indicated that exposure to the orientation program increased knowledge and favorable attitudes toward psychotherapy. Therapist orientation programs have also been devised to familiarize therapists who are working with ethnic minority clients. Reviews of client and therapist preparation programs have been favorable (see E. Jones & Matsumoto, 1982).

In general, many scholars have made suggestions concerning treatment or situational variables that are important in working with African-Americans. However, few empirical studies are available that point to effective treatment strategies. The impact of ethnic-specific services has not yet been tested. Perhaps the most encouraging programs that have been evaluated are the pretherapy orientation programs involving clients and therapists.

RESEARCH ON AMERICAN INDIANS

American Indians and Alaska Natives are a culturally heterogeneous population, consisting of over 510 federally recognized tribes, including more than 200 Alaska Native villages (Bureau of Indian Affairs, 1991). Furthermore, about half of American Indians and Alaska Natives live in urban areas, and half in rural areas or areas on or adjacent to Indian reservations (Bureau of Indian Affairs, 1991; Manson, Walker, & Kivlahan, 1987), although many move back and forth (Yates, 1987).

Between 1970 and 1980, the American Indian and Alaska Native population nearly doubled to 1.5 million, and between 1980 and 1990, the population grew 37.9 percent to almost 1.96 million. This has resulted in a young population with a median age in 1980 that was significantly younger than the median age for the U.S. population in general: 20.4 and 17.9 respectively for American Indians and Alaska Natives, 30.3 for the U.S. population (Manson et al., 1987; U.S. Bureau of the Census, 1991b). At the time of the 1980 census, over half of the American Indian population was under 23 years old (McShane, 1988).

When compared to the U.S. population at large, as a group, American Indians and Alaska Natives are economically impoverished and educationally disadvantaged. The American Indian and Alaska Native mean family income in 1980 was $6,857, less than half the mean income of whites; unemployment ranged from 20 to 70 percent, depending on the community; their 9.6 mean years of formal education represented the lowest level of any ethnic group in the United States. Social and psychological problems with the American Indian and Alaska Native population include the highest arrest rates in the United States (10 times the arrest rate of whites), high rates of alcohol abuse and alcohol-related deaths, and high rates of serious psychiatric problems (Manson et al., 1987).

However, tribes vary in terms of familial and social organizations, religious practices, economic resources, and rates of social and psychological problems. There are 200 American Indian and Alaska Native languages still used by tribal members (LaFromboise, 1988). Besides linguistic and cultural differences between tribes, individuals affiliated with particular tribes differ in their acculturation to tribal or Anglo-American values. Further, significant within-tribe differences include whether individuals live on or off a reservation. Thus, generalizations about the population need to be qualified.

Although their diversity makes generalizing about American Indians and Alaska Natives difficult, it has been generally agreed that American Indians and Alaska Natives differ from whites in worldviews or value orientations. Such value differences have included American Indians' and Alaska Natives' sharing and redistribution instead of acquisition, cooperation instead of competition, noninterference instead of intervention, harmony with nature instead of control of nature, present time orientation instead of future planning, and promoting an extended family network instead of a nuclear family network (Guilmet & Whited, 1987; D. W. Sue & Sue, 1990; Trimble & LaFromboise, 1985). Other differences that have been suggested as relevant in psychotherapy with American Indians and Alaska Natives are culturally based faith in tribal rituals, ceremonial practices, Indian medicine and traditional healing practices; different beliefs in the cause of mental health problems and the ways such problems should be solved; and culturally specific mental disorders or culturally specific manifestations of mental disorders (Manson, Shore, & Bloom, 1985; Neligh, 1988; Trimble & LaFromboise, 1985).

Treatment Outcome

There have been very few empirical studies on the effectiveness of psychotherapy in the treatment of American Indians and Alaska Natives, and no research has investigated the relative effectiveness of different therapeutic modalities (Manson et al., 1987; Neligh, 1988). The need for outcome research is apparent, given the proliferation and funding of a wide variety of treatment and prevention programs that have arisen to target the serious mental health needs of many American Indians and Alaska Natives.

The most researched American Indian mental health problem has been drug and alcohol use and abuse, although treatment evaluation studies of this problem have not been conducted very often. Query (1985), in a comparative study of white and American Indian youth in an inpatient chemical dependency treatment program at a North Dakota state hospital, did find that American Indian youth were disproportionately represented in the unit as would be expected by their percentage in the population. The youths received reality therapy and were followed up six months after discharge. Upon follow-up, whites were found to be functioning much better than Indian youths on various outcome measures. Further, among the American Indian youth, 42 percent had thought of suicide and 25 percent had actually attempted suicide, compared to 21 and 16 percent of the white youth. From these and other outcome measures, Query suggests that the treatment program had produced more positive change in white than in American Indian youth.

More recently, prevention programs for American Indians have been advocated (see Manson, 1982, for a review). Although prevention programs are not normally discussed in terms of treatment outcome, due to the dearth of treatment outcome research with American Indians and Alaska Natives, since prevention approaches appear to be the trend in American Indian research, they are discussed here. Bobo, Gilchrist, Cvetkovich, Trimble, and Schinke (1988) developed a culturally tailored drug prevention program targeting American Indian youth that included extensive collaboration within the American Indian community. The program was found to be successful in that the researchers were able to deliver the program to six groups of American Indian youth, even highly traditional parents consented to their children's participation in the program, and the youth themselves evaluated the program favorably. However, of the six outcome variables, only one, "alcohol use identity," was found to have changed significantly after the prevention program. Bobo et al. attributed this lack of statistically significant change to their small sample size and the resulting insufficient power to detect change and also speculated that American Indian culture in general has a resistance to outside influences.

Skills training for bicultural competence is another recently suggested prevention approach, and social skills training may also have potential for intervention purposes (LaFromboise, Trimble, & Mohatt, 1990). LaFromboise and Rowe (1983) outlined the process of culturally adapting an assertion social skills training program for American Indians, with the rationale that skills training as an approach is less culturally biased than other approaches because it is less prescriptive than other approaches in its conceptualization of appropriate behaviors and thus is less culturally imposing on American Indian culture. In addition, skills training is flexible, allowing for the selection of target behaviors to be changed. This facilitates culturally appropriate modifications of the program.

Schinke et al. (1988) compared a bicultural competence skills training approach with a no-treatment control condition for preventing substance abuse in American Indian adolescents. They found

that there were greater posttest and follow-up improvements with the bicultural skills program than with no-treatment on measures of knowledge about the health and social effects of substance use, self-control, assertion, and substance use rates.

It is apparent that research on interventions (i.e., treatment and prevention) has proceeded very slowly, and it would be premature to try to address the question of the efficacy of mental health interventions with American Indians at this time.

Treatment Process

Client variables. In terms of expectancy and preferences, it has often been stated that American Indians distrust non-Indian therapists (LaFromboise, 1988). The empirical investigation of such a claim, especially as it relates to American Indian expectancy and preferences for an ethnically similar therapist, has yielded mixed results (see Atkinson, 1983, for a review). LaFromboise, Dauphinais, and Rowe (1980), in a study of American Indian high school students who were attending boarding, urban, and rural schools in Oklahoma, had the students rate their preferences for qualities in a helpful person. The ethnicity of a person, specifically being an American Indian, was found to be relatively less important than other qualities, such as trustworthiness, and no differences in ratings were found among students from boarding, urban, or rural schools.

In another study, LaFromboise and Dixon (1981) had American Indian reservation high school students in Nebraska observe and rate videotaped segments of one of four counseling conditions, within which the interviewer's ethnicity was crossed with the interviewer's performance. The interviewer's ethnicity was either American Indian or non-Indian, and the interviewer acted according to a trustworthy or nontrustworthy model of counseling. Ratings of trustworthiness, expertness, or attractiveness were found to be unrelated to the interviewer's ethnicity.

By contrast, Dauphinais, Dauphinais, and Rowe (1981) studied American Indian high school students from two federal boarding schools in Oklahoma and one tribally controlled boarding school in South Dakota (40 tribal affiliations were represented in the sample). Students were randomly assigned to listen to one of three tape-recorded conditions, which differed only in that counselor responses reflected either a directive, nondirective, or American Indian culturally oriented counseling style. For each condition, half of the students were told that the counselor was American Indian, and half were told that the counselor was non-Indian. Dauphinais et al. found that students gave more positive ratings on the Counselor Effectiveness Scale to counselors who were introduced as American Indian. Further, the culturally oriented counseling style was rated as more credible than the nondirective approach.

Havilland, Horswill, O'Connell, and Dynneson (1983) studied American Indian college students in Montana who represented 11 American Indian tribes, with a range of 3 to 100 percent American Indian blood quantum, with nearly 70 percent of the sample having lived on a reservation for some time in their lives. The researchers found that American Indian students had a strong preference for an ethnically similar counselor, and that students' willingness to use a counseling center that had an American Indian on staff was directly related to students' preferences for an ethnically similar counselor. Further, Havilland et al. found that American Indian students tended to report a preference for an American Indian counselor for personal, educational, and vocational problems. Blood quantum and percentage of life spent on a reservation were not found to affect students' preferences.

Bennett and BigFoot-Sipes (1991) utilized the methodology developed by Atkinson et al. (1986) for the study of African-American preferences. They found that although ethnicity was more important to American Indian college students than to white students, especially to those American Indian students who were more involved in American Indian culture, what tended to be more important to both American Indians and whites was having a counselor who shared similar attitudes and values.

Thus, there have been mixed results in the findings on American Indian expectancies and preferences. However, inconsistent results may be caused by the method used to study preferences. Thus, it will be useful for future preference research to take into account the type of problem a client presents and other counselor characteristics in addition to ethnicity (such as attitudes, personality, education, and especially American Indian ethnic identity or cultural commitment) (Bennett & BigFoot-Sipes, 1991). Finally, a pragmatic factor to consider is that ethnic preference studies may not reflect what is actually available to the American Indian and Alaska Native population. For example, many American Indians and Alaska Natives simply have few choices available to them, despite the preferences they may have. As noted by Mays and Albee (1992), the number of American Indian and Alaska Native therapists is quite small—in 1989, only six received doctorates in clinical or counseling psychology throughout the nation. While preference studies may provide additional justification for funding the education of American Indian and

Alaska Native researchers and therapists, further research clarifying the issues is needed.

Therapist variables. The paucity of empirical research is also evident with respect to the impact of therapist variables, and what has been done has yielded mixed results (Atkinson, 1983). Dauphinais, LaFromboise, and Rowe (1980) surveyed American Indian 11th- and 12th-grade students of a variety of tribal affiliations, such as Choctaw, Creek, Kiowa, Chicksaw, Comanche, Cherokee, Sioux, Cheyenne/Arapahoe, attending Bureau of Indian Affairs boarding schools and urban and rural schools in Oklahoma and found that the students' satisfaction with previous counseling was not related to whether the counselor's race was American Indian or non-Indian.

However, as mentioned previously, in the Dauphinais et al. (1981) study with American Indian high school students, counselors were rated as more credible on the Counselor Effectiveness Rating Scale when the counselor used a culturally relevant counseling style. In addition, independent of counseling style, the counselor who was introduced as American Indian received more positive ratings. This suggests that the ethnicity of the counselor may be an important factor in the counseling of American Indians. Littrell and Littrell (1982), in a study examining high schools students' preferences for counselors, found that the preferences of American Indian students from a North Dakota reservation varied with the sex and dress of the counselor and type of the client problem.

Situational or treatment variables. There is little empirical evidence about the effectiveness of specific modes of psychotherapy with the American Indian or Alaska Native population, and no information comparing the efficacy of different psychotherapeutic approaches. However, this has not impeded the proliferation of program development, most particularly, prevention interventions (see Manson, 1982) and the group modality. The majority of these programs target the most salient mental and social problem in many American Indian communities: alcohol and drug abuse and dependence.

In addition, family-network therapy, traditional healing practices, and bicultural skills training programs have been described in the literature as possible culturally appropriate modalities to be considered in working with American Indians. For instance, Manson et al. (1987), in their review of psychiatric assessment and treatment of American Indians and Alaska Natives, propose that family-network therapy may be culturally appropriate for some American Indians and Alaska Natives, given the cultural context of an extended family social organization. LaFromboise (1988) notes that American Indian communities have traditionally used extended families as sources of care and psychological support and describes work utilizing the extended family in a therapeutic setting.

While discussing tribally based mental health care programs, LaFromboise (1988) characterized the recent use of traditional healers and traditional approaches as "a renaissance and revitalization of traditional healing practices" (p. 391). It was feared that such practices were being extinguished in favor of Western forms of treatment. Examples of traditional practices that have been incorporated into the treatment of American Indian clients include the four circles (visualizing relationships in terms of concentric circles), the talking circle (a form of group therapy focused on the circle as a symbol of physical and psychological connectedness among individuals), and the sweatlodge (a ritual in which participants are exposed to hot rocks sprinkled with water, sweat, and experience a feeling of kinship with all living things and the universe). (See Manson et al., 1987, or Vraniak & Pickett, 1992, for a detailed description of these therapeutic strategies.)

LaFromboise and Rowe (1983) have argued that skills training for bicultural competence may meet the needs of American Indians without the imposition of more traditional forms of therapy, which they suggest may have a "culturally corrosive effect." They described the process of culturally adapting the skills training model, and as described previously, Schinke et al. (1988) have provided a preliminary investigation into the efficacy of such an approach.

Obviously, basic knowledge of psychotherapy processes and outcomes for American Indians and Alaska Natives is being established very slowly. The population is a particularly difficult one to study, given not only its cultural and linguistic heterogeneity, but also its geographical range across the United States and in cities, rural areas, and reservations. Another problem, which is by no means unique to American Indian research, is the tendency for researchers to use nonclinical populations, a methodology that limits the generalizability of findings. Additionally, there have been so few empirical studies on American Indians, and none on Alaska Natives, that those that have been done do not allow for broad generalizations. The literature on psychotherapy with American Indians and Alaska Natives consists predominantly of descriptive reports and program suggestions. However, the recent trend in American Indian research that utilizes and extends the methodologies developed to study other ethnic groups appears to have great potential to further the field in that comparisons can now be made across ethnic groups, and methodological and theoretical advances can be shared.

RESEARCH ON ASIAN-AMERICANS

Asian-American groups are the fastest growing ethnic minority populations in the United States. From 1980 to 1990, the population grew by 108 percent to 7.3 million. This increase can be attributed largely to immigration to the United States from China, the Philippines, India, Korea, Southeast Asia, and other countries, and secondarily to natural increases (births minus deaths). More than 20 Asian-American groups have been identified by the U.S. Bureau of the Census. The three largest in descending order are Chinese, Filipino, and Japanese. Most Asian-Americans (70%) live in just five States — California, Hawaii, New York, Illinois, and Texas. Comparisons of the Asian-American population with the white population have found substantial differences on characteristics such as college graduates aged 25 years and older (40 to 23%); average family size (62 to 46% living in households with children under 15); per capita income ($14,000 to $14,900), home ownership (54 to 76%), Social Security support (64 to 92%), and poverty levels (14 to 8%) (O'Hare & Felt, 1991).

An important characteristic of the population is the diversity among different Asian-American groups. For example, the vast majority of Vietnamese, Koreans, Asian Indians, Filipinos, and Chinese in the United States were born overseas. However, Samoans, Japanese, Guamanians, and Hawaiians were largely born in the United States (O'Hare & Felt, 1991). Japanese and Asian Indians had median ages that exceeded the national average, but other Asian groups had median ages lower than the national average. The median family income of Japanese-Americans ($27,400) was strikingly higher than that of Vietnamese-Americans ($12,800). Great variations also exist among Asian groups in educational attainment and achievement. The school dropout rate for Filipinos is substantially higher compared with other Asian groups and white Americans. There is also a great deal of within-group variability. For example, a majority of the Chinese are foreign born, but over one-third (37%) are American born. Moreover, foreign-born Chinese come from different parts of the world (e.g., mainland China, Taiwan, Hong Kong) and speak different Chinese dialects, adding to the within-group diversity.

Both the diversity between and within Asian-

American groups must be considered in the interpretation and generalizability of treatment process and outcome findings. Most of these studies have focused on the larger and more acculturated Asian-American groups, such as the Chinese and Japanese, and have primarily used student samples who tend to be more acculturated and homogeneous than those drawn from Asian communities. Some investigations have included different groups within the rubric of "Asian-Americans" so that differences among the groups are masked or it is unclear which Asian-American groups are being studied.

Treatment Outcome

Few studies have directly examined psychotherapy outcomes for Asian-American clients. Zane (1983) assessed outpatients at a community mental health center after the first and fourth sessions and found that Asian clients evinced significant improvement on both client self-report (Symptom Checklist) and therapist-rated (Brief Psychiatric Rating Scale) outcome measures. Most outcome studies have aggregated across different Asian groups with the exception of research on Southeast Asians. Mollica et al. (1990) reported improvement in depression among Cambodian clients following six months of psychotherapy, whereas no significant improvements in depression or anxiety were found for Vietnamese or Hmong/Laotian clients. In a pilot study of nine patients, Kinzie and Leung (1989) successfully decreased depression in Cambodians suffering from post-traumatic stress disorder, but the intervention primarily relied on drug therapy (using clonidine and imipramine) supplemented by group socialization therapy.

In terms of differential outcome, two studies have examined clinical outcome among Asian outpatients using the Global Assessment Scale (GAS), a therapist measure of general psychosocial functioning. Zane and Hatanaka (1988) found no differences between Asians and whites on posttreatment GAS adjusting for pretreatment GAS. S. Sue et al. (1991) obtained similar results as Asian outpatients showed similar improvement compared with white clients. Other studies have found some evidence of differential outcome. Zane (1983) found that by the fourth session, there were no differences in therapist-rated outcome and in self-reported symptoms of depression and anxiety. However, Asians reported greater anger than whites and were less satisfied with services and with their progress in treatment. The analyses controlled for both pretreatment level of severity and demographics that could have been confounded with ethnicity. W. Lee and Mixson (1985) had clients at a university counseling center rate the effectiveness of counseling

and their therapists and indicate the reasons why they sought treatment. Despite presenting a similar number of concerns prior to treatment, Asians rated both their counseling experience and therapists as less effective than did whites.

Any conclusions about the effectiveness of treatment for Asians would be premature given the limited data (four outcome studies), but several empirical trends should be noted. First, some evidence suggests that certain Asian groups improve with psychotherapy and/or adjunct treatments. Second, with respect to differential outcome, divergent trends are found, and these are associated with the type of outcome measure used. Studies reporting no differential outcome between Asians and whites relied on a measure of general psychological functioning (e.g., GAS), whereas differential outcomes were found in studies that used client satisfaction measures and/or specific symptom scales. It is possible that the null results may reflect the unreliability and insensitivity of the global outcome measure used. The GAS essentially constitutes a one-item measure. The GAS is highly reliable if raters are extensively trained in its use, but there appeared to be no such training conducted with therapists in either study. In sum, Asian clients appear to be deriving less positive experiences from therapy than whites, but it is unclear if this difference in client satisfaction actually reflects ethnic differences in actual treatment outcomes (e.g., symptom reduction).

Process Research

Much of the empirical work in Asian-American mental health has examined ethnic differences across a wide range of variables such as personality, values, ethnic identity, acculturation and adaptation, and family attitudes and relationships (e.g., Fukuyama & Greenfield, 1983). Extensive reviews of this empirical work have been presented elsewhere (e.g., Leong, 1986). Implications for the treatment of Asians are often drawn from this research. However, relatively few studies have directly investigated how these variables are related to or affect actual processes in treatment. The empirical work that has addressed psychotherapy issues has primarily focused on variables such as client preferences and mental health beliefs, treatment and therapist credibility, and ethnic match.

Client variables. In view of the great heterogeneity that exists between and within Asian-American groups, client variables would be an important area of focus for process research with these groups. The major empirical efforts have addressed acculturation influences and client preferences and expectancies. At times, these variables have been examined concurrently.

Client preferences and expectancies. A number of studies have examined the preferences of Asian-Americans for ethnicity of the therapist and type of counseling approach used. This research has primarily relied on nonclinical samples of Asian-American or foreign Asian students. One study (Atkinson, Maruyama, & Matsui, 1978) varied therapist ethnicity (white vs. Japanese-American) and counseling style (directive vs. nondirective). Japanese-American participants heard an audiotape on which the therapist counsels a client identified as Japanese-American. The two styles presented were based on scripts in which the directive therapist responded in a rational, problem-solving way and asked for specific information and the nondirective therapist restated and summarized the client's feelings and experience. The study used a sample of Japanese-American university students and a community sample of Japanese-American high school and college youth. In both samples, the directive therapist was rated as more credible and approachable while only the university sample indicated a preference for the Japanese-American therapist. Gim, Atkinson, and Kim (1991) used a similar design but varied therapist cultural sensitivity (culture-sensitive vs. culture-blind) instead of counseling style. In the culture-sensitive condition, therapists discussed and acknowledged cultural difference, whereas in the culture-blind condition therapists did not attend to such differences and emphasized commonalities among individuals. Asian-American students preferred Asian-American counselors over white American counselors and rated the culturally sensitive therapists as more credible and culturally competent than culturally blind therapists. These studies clearly show an Asian preference for a directive therapeutic style, but without a white comparison group, it is unclear if this effect is a preference of clients in general or an ethnic-specific preference. There also seems to be a preference for ethnically similar therapists among Asians, although ethnic match may not be the most important type of similarity that clients seek in their therapists (Atkinson, Poston, Furlong, & Mercado, 1989).

Studies that have made direct ethnic comparisons have also found a preference for or expectation of a more directive problem-solving approach in therapy on the part of Asian foreign students. Both Tan (1967) and Yuen and Tinsley (1981) found that Asian students expected therapists to have more experience and be more directive than did white students. Arkoff, Thaver, and Elkind

(1966) reported that Asians expected therapists to provide more advice and direct suggestions for solving problems than did whites. Using a causal modeling approach, Akutsu, Lin, and Zane (1990) found no relationship between directive style and therapist credibility for either Chinese or white students. As suggested by the investigators, one possible reason for the difference in findings is that the directive style presented included some elements of confrontation that were absent from the directive approaches used in the other studies.

Acculturation influences. Important variations in the way Asians seek, respond to, or experience psychotherapy may depend on the individual's level of acculturation. Acculturation refers to the extent to which members of an ethnic minority group have learned or adopted the cultural patterns of the majority group (S. Sue & Morishima, 1982). Atkinson and Gim (1989) compared the attitudes toward seeking and using psychological services of Chinese-, Japanese-, and Korean-American students. No intergroup differences were found, but more acculturated Asians were more cognizant of the need for psychological help and more open to using services. Gim, Atkinson, and Whiteley (1990) also found that the more acculturated students were more willing to use therapy. In one of the few studies of Asian clients, Tracey, Leong, and Glidden (1986) examined the presenting problems of whites and seven Asian-American groups (Chinese, Filipino, Hawaiian, Korean, Japanese, Asian-white, and Asian-Asian) at a university counseling center. The most acculturated groups, Asian-whites and Filipinos, were more likely to perceive their major presenting problem as involving emotional/interpersonal issues (e.g., "feel lonely and alienated from others," "have difficulty with close personal relationship") as opposed to academic/vocational concerns (e.g., "don't know how to study," "don't know what my interests are").

Other variables. There is some evidence that Asians define and think about mental health and emotional problems somewhat differently from members of other cultures. Clinicians have noted that Asians tend not to make a strong distinction between emotional and physical problems and attribute both to bodily imbalances (Flaskerud & Soldevilla, 1986). This holistic tendency was reflected in findings in which Asians believed that emotional problems were more influenced by organic and somatic factors than did whites (Arkoff et al., 1966). On the other hand, Asians were more likely to believe that mental health is enhanced by the avoidance of negative thinking and/or self-discipline (Lum, 1982). Given that the practice of psychotherapy often requires clients to focus on painful or negative thoughts, relies on emotional catharsis, and tends to deemphasize somatic interventions, it has been hypothesized that many Asian-American clients may find the initial conceptualization stage of psychotherapy inconsistent with their beliefs (E. Lee, 1982; Zane & Sue, 1991).

Symptom patterns of Asian clients in treatment have been examined. There is a tendency for Asians (particularly those with depressive disorders) to present with more somatic complaints that other clients, and this has been interpreted as evidence of somatization in which physical symptoms are expressed in place of psychological symptoms (Kleinman, 1977; Marsella, Kinzie, & Gordon, 1973). Tanaka-Matsumi and Marsella (1976) suggested that the experience of depression may, indeed, be somewhat different for Asians. In a word association study, Japanese Nationals (i.e., citizens) associated more external referent and somatic terms to the word *depression*, whereas white Americans associated terms that referred to internal mood states. The associations of a seemingly highly acculturated Japanese-American sample were similar to the white responses. Some research suggests that these somatic tendencies have resulted more from different help-seeking practices in which Asians have tended to use medical services for psychological disorders (Cheung & Lau, 1982). Regardless of the causal pathway, the process by which basic psychological problems are presented and/or experienced appears to be somewhat different for Asians.

Western psychotherapy relies on verbal expressiveness and open self-disclosure as primary means for resolving psychological problems. These aspects can conflict with the tendency on the part of Asians to be less verbal and to refrain from the public expression of feelings (B. Kim, 1973). In many East Asian cultures, the "language of emotion" for Asians is somewhat different in that affection is conveyed by the use of gestures, often involving the exchange of material goods and services that enhance the person's well-being (Chang, 1985). Also, metaphors are frequently used to communicate feelings. Thus, it is possible that differences in the communication styles of Asian-Americans may influence the therapeutic relationship and the development of rapport in psychotherapy. However, more research is needed to clarify the roles such differences may have.

Therapist variables

Match between the client and therapist. The match between a client and therapist has been considered to be an important factor in psychotherapy. One of the most salient aspects of match with

ethnic clients in general, and with Asian-American clients in particular, is ethnic match. For those Asian-American clients who are non–English speaking, language match would also appear to be crucial.

S. Sue et al. (1991), in the previously described study of Los Angeles County mental health services, found that ethnic match between the client and therapist was associated with an increase in the use of mental health services and a lowered likelihood of dropout for Asian-American clients. In addition, for those Asian-Americans for whom English was not a primary language, ethnic match, language match, and gender match were associated with a decrease in the likelihood of premature termination and an increase in the number of sessions. Thus, at least in terms of indirect indexes of treatment efficacy, ethnic match exerted a significant influence for Asian-American clients. Moreover, in terms of outcome, non–English-speaking Asian-Americans were found to have better outcomes, as measured by GAS change, when matched with a therapist of similar ethnicity and language.

Considering that the growth of the Asian-American population in the United States is due, in a large part, to immigration, and that those immigrants tend to be non–English speaking, the availability of therapists who are of the same ethnicity and/or who speak the same language of the Asian-American client is important for service utilization and to some extent, treatment outcome. However, further research is needed to replicate S. Sue et al.'s findings and to investigate potential differences in the significance of match between Asian-American groups.

Assessment bias. There is evidence that therapist and client ethnicity may affect diagnoses and evaluations of clients. Tseng and McDermott (1981) had Japanese and white psychiatrists evaluate the characteristics exhibited by white clients. The Japanese psychiatrists were more likely than white psychiatrists to rate the clients as emotionally labile. This is especially interesting since Asian-American clients have often been characterized as passive and unemotional. Li-Repac (1980) had five white and five Chinese-American therapists rate Chinese and white clients during a videotaped interview. White clinicians rated Chinese clients as "anxious," "awkward," "confused," "nervous," "quiet," and "reserved," in contrast to the Chinese clinicians who used adjectives including "adaptable," "alert," "dependable," "friendly," and "practical." In the ratings of white clients, the white clinicians used terms such as "affectionate," "adventurous," and "capable." Chinese clinicians described the white clients as "active," "aggressive," and "rebellious." The differences in the ratings were significant. White raters saw Chinese clients as more depressed and inhibited and less socially poised and as having less capacity for interpersonal relationships than did Chinese-American clinicians. Interestingly, Chinese-American clinicians rated white clients as more seriously disturbed than did white clinicians. The striking differences in evaluations point to possible problems in making valid assessments for culturally diverse groups.

Treatment variables.   It often has been hypothesized that modifications in the approach to psychotherapy are needed to adequately treat Asian-American clients (Chung & Okazaki, 1991; Ho, 1976; S. Kim, 1985; Kitano, 1981; E. Lee, 1982; J. Lee & Cynn, 1991; Murase, 1977; Nishio & Bilmes, 1987; Root, 1985; Shon & Ja, 1982; D. Sue & Sue, 1991; S. Sue & Morishima, 1982; Tomine, 1991; Toupin, 1980). For example, E. Lee (1982) and others have noted important differences in family structure, value orientation, and beliefs about mental health and illness between Asian-American and white cultures. Compared with Western culture, which focuses on the nuclear family with somewhat egalitarian relationships and emphasizes values of individualism, competition, self-worth, and direct expression of emotions, many Asians have strong ties to nonegalitarian societies that center on extended family arrangements based on structured, hierarchical role relationships and stress values of collectivism, group achievement, "face," and emotional restraint. Murase (1977) has recommended that treatment approaches for Asians should recognize the family as an integral part of treatment, establish an active, highly personalized therapeutic relationship, focus on survival-related tasks to facilitate the engagement process, address the possible conflict between the cultural dynamic of "loss of face" and the confessional character of psychotherapy, differentiate between cultural behavioral propensities and pathology, reevaluate the self-determination construct, permit flexibility in session scheduling and duration, and recognize the ameliorative effect of a familiar and predictable cultural milieu.

However, despite the extensive number of published recommendations for the modification of Western psychotherapeutic approaches, there have been no empirical comparisons of efficacy between mainstream Western modalities and culturally modified modalities in the treatment of Asian-Americans, nor have there been empirical studies of the effectiveness of the culturally specific treatments or culturally modified treatments themselves. Most research has focused on aspects of "culturally sensitive services" for Asian-Americans, such as the ethnic and language match discussed in the previous section.

Nevertheless, ethnic and language match are only part of "culturally sensitive services." S. Sue (1977) suggested parallel services, which would entail not only ethnic and language match, but a systemic change of integration into the community, altering the situation in which services are rendered. That is, parallel services should be based in the community, staffed by bilingual and bicultural staff, and designed in a way that would be culturally more responsive to the Asian-American clientele serviced.

Such parallel services appear to have increased utilization by Asian-American clients. In a study of community mental health care centers in Southern California, Flaskerud (1986) found that culturally compatible factors, such as ethnic and language match and location within the community, contributed to increased utilization of mental health services by Asian-Americans. In Oakland, True (1975) found that an Asian-American community-based agency served significantly more Chinese-Americans than the county outpatient emergency mental health facility. Wong (1977) found that in San Francisco, a community mental health center served more Asian-American clients in its first few months of operation than the total number of Asian-Americans who had been served in that area for the previous five years. More recently, Zane and Hatanaka (1988), in a study of an Asian community mental health center in Los Angeles, found that except for Southeast Asians, Asian-Americans received equitable services and did not differ in dropout rate and length of treatment when compared to whites.

Although these studies are limited in that treatment outcome was not often measured, the impact of parallel services on indirect indexes for Asian-Americans is apparent. Preliminary studies strongly suggest that parallel services have increased the utilization and efficacy of mental health services with most Asian-American groups, yet there remains the direct investigation of the effect of parallel services on treatment outcomes.

RESEARCH ON LATINO-AMERICANS

With a population of 22.4 million, Latinos are the second largest ethnic minority group in the United States. The population has grown at least 53 percent between 1980 and 1990, increasing from 6.4 percent of the total U.S. population in 1980 to 9 percent in 1990, not including undocumented Latino immigrants (U.S. Bureau of the Census, 1990). The tremendous growth in the Latino population has been due to the high levels of Latino immigration into the United States. Mexican-Americans comprise the largest group of Latinos with 58 percent of the Latino population, followed by Puerto Ricans, 13 percent; Cubans, 7 percent, and other Latinos originally from South and Central American countries, 23 percent (U.S. Bureau of the Census, 1991b). The majority of the Latino-American population lives in California and Texas, followed by New York and Florida. Most Mexican-Americans live in the southwestern states and the Midwest; Puerto Ricans tend to be located in New York City; and most Cubans live in Florida and New Jersey (Malgady, Rogler, & Costantino, 1990b; Rogler et al., 1989).

Compared to the non–Latino white population of the United States, Latinos have lower levels of income, education, and occupational status, although their disadvantage varies greatly by Latino group. For example, the median family income of Cuban-Americans was 89 percent of the income of non-Hispanic families, whereas the median family income of Puerto Ricans was 57 percent and of Mexican-Americans 63 percent of the incomes of non-Hispanic families (U.S. Bureau of the Census, 1991). In New York, Cubans were found to have relatively high levels of education and higher status jobs, whereas Puerto Ricans and Dominicans had less education and lower status jobs (Gurak & Rogler, 1983). Part of the reason for these differences is the educational and economic status of immigrants prior to their arrival in the United States. Cubans, for example, tend to be from the middle or upper class, while some other Latino groups come from impoverished economic backgrounds (Gurak & Rogler, 1983).

In an evaluation of over 2,000 publications on the mental health of Latinos, the Report to the President's Commission on Mental Health (Special Regulations Subtask Panel on the Mental Health of Hispanic Americans, 1987) concluded that the field of Latino mental health research lacked a programmatic plan, and that the methodological and analytic quality of research needed to be improved. Since this report, the research on Latino mental health has continued to grow in a more conceptually consistent manner, no doubt aided by Federal funding of research and research centers devoted to Latino mental health. Although the general question remains of whether psychotherapy is effective with Latinos, research in this area has attempted to clarify the question itself. That is, what kinds of psychotherapy are most effective with Latinos? What are the client, therapist, and

situational factors that influence psychotherapy with Latinos? How do within-group differences affect client preferences, leading to differential outcomes? And finally, given what is known, how can treatment programs be modified or developed to encourage service utilization and treatment effectiveness?

Treatment Outcome

It is generally assumed that mainstream mental health therapies are less effective with Latinos. This assumption, although not always tested directly, has been supported by indirect measures of treatment outcome such as treatment utilization, termination, and duration by Latinos in the mental health care system. Accordingly, there has been a movement toward "culturally sensitive" mental health services that consist of various strategies such as increasing the accessibility of treatment, selecting available treatments deemed most appropriate for Latino values or cultural orientation, modifying current therapies for Latinos, and developing therapies utilizing elements of Latino culture (Rogler, Malgady, Costantino, & Blumenthal, 1987).

Much emphasis has been given to investigating the efficacy of therapies that have been modified to fit Latino culture, and these studies will be discussed later in the section detailing the influence of treatment variables on the outcomes of psychotherapy. However, research focusing on the treatment outcome of Latinos given current Western modes of treatment has received less attention. One major large-scale study in Los Angeles County (described earlier) measured treatment outcome using pre- and posttreatment scores on the GAS; Mexican-Americans were found most likely to improve after treatment when compared to whites, blacks, and Asian-Americans (S. Sue et al., 1991). Thus, at least in this study based on data from a large metropolitan area, Mexican-Americans do appear to improve in their GAS scores. However, as discussed earlier, Mexican-Americans tend to underutilize services, so at this time it is unclear what the effect of underutilization may have been on the sample, and conclusions drawn from this study must be necessarily limited.

Treatment Process

Client variables. Client preference studies among Latino Americans have explored the relationship between client ethnicity and acculturation, and ratings of therapists of similar and different ethnicities and therapeutic styles. Acosta and Sheehan (1976) and Furlong, Atkinson, and Casas

(1979) found little evidence of an ethnic effect when subjects were asked to rate characteristics of therapists who were similar in all respects except ethnicity (or had a slight Spanish accent in the former study). Atkinson et al., (1989) found that Mexican-American students ranked similarity in therapist ethnicity sixth in order of preference for therapist characteristics, but three-fourths of the students preferred an ethnically similar therapist over an ethnically dissimilar therapist when given a choice. Atkinson (1983), in a review of the research on the role of ethnic similarity in psychotherapy, concluded that for Latinos, there did not appear to be a preference for therapist race or a race effect on therapy process variables such as perceived therapist credibility, perceived therapist effectiveness, and client verbal behavior.

In contrast, Lopez, Lopez, and Fong (1991), in a study of Mexican-American college students' preferences for ethnically similar therapists, argue that the results of previous studies that found no preferences for ethnically similar therapists may be attributable to the method by which preferences were measured. Lopez et al. contrasted the outcome of therapist preference studies by methodological approach. They propose that using a judgment method, by which subjects are asked to evaluate or rate therapists who are similar in all characteristics except ethnicity, the majority of past studies found no preference for an ethnically similar therapist. However, when a choice method was used, requiring subjects to select a therapist from several who differ in ethnicity, preferences were found for an ethnically similar therapist. Lopez et al. suggest that the choice method is a more ecologically valid means of assessing client preferences for the ethnicity of their therapist than the judgment method. They believe that the choice method more closely approximates the client's decision making at the time of the initial visit.

While investigating the main effects of client ethnicity, researchers began investigating other factors that may be related to rating differences, such as acculturation (Pomales & Williams, 1989; Ponce & Atkinson, 1989), attitudes toward acculturation (Atkinson, Ponce, & Martinez, 1984; Furlong et al., 1979), and cultural commitment to Mexican culture (Sanchez & Atkinson, 1983). Generally, researchers have found that factors such as acculturation and cultural commitment of the Latino rater, attitudinal match between the rater and therapist, and therapist style are more relevant factors in the therapeutic process than ethnic similarity alone.

Therapist variables

Match between client and therapist. In a previously discussed study of clients in Los Angeles County, S. Sue et al. (1991) found that ethnic match predicted a greater number of sessions for Mexican-American clients. When the Mexican-American clients were divided into two groups based on whether English was or was not their primary language, for those whose primary language was not English, ethnic match was found to significantly predict a decrease in premature termination, an increase in the number of sessions, and positive treatment outcomes. Thus, it appears that ethnic and language match is an important factor in the psychotherapeutic process, especially for Mexican-Americans whose primary language is not English. In an earlier described study of culturally compatible mental health services in Los Angeles, Flaskerud (1986) found that language match, ethnic-racial match, and community location made the largest contribution in discriminating between dropout and nondropout status.

In an analogue study, LeVine and Franco (1981) found different effects of ethnic match on self-disclosure. As a group, Anglo-American students were found to report more self-disclosures when compared with Latino students. The sex and ethnicity of the questionnaire administrator affected Latino student response rates in that Latino females made the most disclosures when the administrator was a female, and Latino males made the most disclosures when the administrator was a Latino female.

In addition to ethnic match, language match is a particularly important factor in the treatment of monolingual Spanish-speaking Latino clients. The Bilingual Interpreter Program in Los Angeles trained bilingual-bicultural community aides to become interpreters for English-speaking therapists (Acosta & Cristo, 1981). Spanish-speaking clients who used an interpreter believed they received more help and were understood better than bilingual Mexican-American clients who spoke to the therapist in English (Kline, Acosta, Austin, & Johnson, 1980). While more research needs to be conducted in this area, available evidence suggests that ethnic and language match are important variables in understanding psychotherapy and its outcomes among Latinos.

Assessment bias among therapists. The assessment of a client is clearly important to the treatment process, especially in regard to ethnic populations. In an overview of sources of ethnic and linguistic bias in the evaluation of Latino clients, Malgady, Rogler, and Costantino (1987) suggest that the psychodiagnosis of Latinos has been biased, due to clinician and instrument limitations. Some have suggested that the language used during the evaluation of Spanish-speaking Hispanic patients may lead to misdiagnosis. It was found that even if patients are bilingual, they appear more disturbed when asked to speak only in English (Marcos, Urcuyo, Kesselman, & Alpert, 1973). Analogue studies have generally supported the claim of therapist bias in the assessment of Latinos.

Stevens (1981) had school psychologists, teachers, and parents rate films of Anglo-American, African-American, and Mexican-American eight-year-old boys for hyperactivity. Ethnic minority boys and those of lower socioeconomic status tended to be rated as more hyperactive than Anglo or middle SES boys. Wampold, Casas, and Atkinson (1981) tested an information-processing model of stereotyping using an illusory correlation paradigm. Anglo and ethnic (including Asian-, Chicano-, and African-American) graduate counseling trainees were given information, such as ethnicity and stereotypic characteristics, on 54 hypothetical students. Information was varied such that ethnicity (Anglo-, Asian-, or Chicano-American) and stereotypic characteristics combined into descriptions that would be considered congruent, neutral, and incongruent with racial stereotypes. Subjects were then asked to complete a questionnaire on the relationship between ethnicity and student characteristics based on the information they had been given. An error was scored if judgments made were not based upon the information presented. Upon error analysis, Anglo-American trainees were found to make fewer errors than ethnic minority trainees when the correct answer reinforced a racial stereotype, which suggests that the Anglo-American students differentially processed information regarding ethnicity and were more susceptible to racial stereotyping than ethnic students.

Therapist style.   The effect of therapist style is a more recently investigated area in Latino psychotherapy research. Preliminary evidence supports the claim that Latinos prefer a directive counseling style over a nondirective style. Ponce and Atkinson (1989), as described previously, found that Mexican-American students gave more positive ratings to a directive counseling style than a nondirective style. In Pomales and Williams's (1989) study, described in a previous section, Puerto Rican and Mexican-American students were found to have an overall preference for a directive counseling style. This preference was found to exert a stronger influence than acculturation on the ratings of counselor characteristics.

However, the specific response modes associated with a directive style have not always been consistent across studies. For example, open questions have been considered directive in some studies and nondirective in others (Folensbee, Draguns, & Danish, 1986). Thus, a systematic investigation that clarifies what constitutes a directive style is

important because clients may be reacting to a particular response mode rather than a particular therapeutic style. Borrego, Chavez, and Titley (1982) examined the effects of particular therapist interviewing techniques on the willingness to self-disclose and the perception of a therapist among Anglo- and Mexican-American college students. Subjects listened to an audiotape of a session in which either probing, disclosing, or reflecting statements were made by the interviewer. Subjects were then asked to imagine themselves in the role of the client and complete a questionnaire based on their reactions to the interviewer. No differences were found in subjects' willingness to disclose to or perception of the therapist based upon subject ethnicity, therapist technique, or subject gender. However, in another analogue study, Folensbee et al. (1986) had Puerto Rican community college students participate in actual interviews in which a counselor used either affective responses or closed questions. Students rated counselors higher on a counselor rating form when affective responses rather than closed questions were employed. In addition, Puerto Rican students were found to use significantly more self-referent pronouns, present tense verbs, and affect words in the affective response condition than in the closed question condition.

Clinical sensitivity training.   As mentioned earlier, development of cultural sensitivity training for therapists has been an important trend toward providing effective services to minority populations (Acosta, 1984; Acosta et al., 1982; De La Cancela & Guzman, 1991; Lefley, 1985; Lopez et al., 1989). In an article reviewing clinical and empirical findings on psychotherapy with Mexican-Americans, Acosta (1984) described a research project investigating the orientation of therapists to low-income and minority patients at the Los Angeles County–University of Southern California Medical Center's Adult Psychiatric Outpatient Clinic. The orientation program consisted of a series of seminars whose topics were drawn from the book *Effective Psychotherapy for Low-Income and Minority Patients* (Acosta et al., 1982). Postprogram evaluations showed that therapists had significantly increased their knowledge and sensitivity in dealing with low-income and minority patients, and patient follow-up data suggested that therapists may have been more effective as a result of the orientation program (Evans, Acosta, Yamamoto, & Skilbeck, 1984; Yamamoto, Acosta, Evans, & Skilbeck, 1984). Another program mentioned earlier, Cross-Cultural Training for Mental Health Professionals, has also been evaluated positively for increasing the effectiveness of therapists in treating Latinos

(Lefley, 1985). Thus, preliminary research supports the efficacy of cultural sensitivity training; however, further empirical research needs to be done to replicate the findings of these studies.

Situational or treatment variables.   While the need for culturally sensitive treatments for minority populations has been argued, there has been limited research into the effectiveness of services for Latinos other than by indirect indexes such as treatment utilization, premature termination, and treatment duration. There have been no comparisons between the effectiveness of mainstream and culturally sensitive services. Thus, research has tended to focus on either mainstream treatments or culturally sensitive treatments, although recent studies on cultural modification of treatments have begun to bridge the gap. A burgeoning literature on the effectiveness of culturally sensitive treatments has dominated the treatment outcome literature and, in general, has shown positive results in terms of effectiveness with particular Latino groups.

Family therapy.   A number of scholars believe that the family plays an essential role for Latinos as a source of help and support (Acosta, 1984; Rogler et al., 1983; Rogler et al., 1989). Utilizing the family within treatment intervention has been advocated as potentially useful for Latino-Americans (Padilla & De Snyder, 1985). In a study comparing structural family therapy, individual psychodynamic child therapy, and a recreational control condition for Latino boys with behavioral and emotional problems, Szapocnik et al. (1989) found that both structural family therapy and individual psychodynamic child therapy were more effective than the control condition in limiting dropout and retaining cases. There were no significant differences found in the reduction of emotional and behavioral problems between the treatment conditions. However, upon follow-up, families whose child had been in individual psychodynamic child therapy were found to have deteriorated with regard to functioning, in direct contrast to those in the structured family therapy condition, where family functioning continued to improve, and the control condition, in which family functioning remained the same. Given this marked difference between conditions at follow-up, the long-term impact of intervention on family functioning appears to be an important consideration in the choice of particular therapies for Latino children.

Group therapy.   The group therapy format has been advocated as useful with Latinos in certain contexts (Acosta & Yamamoto, 1984). An empirical study by Comas-Diaz (1981) compared the effects of cognitive and behavioral group therapy for depressed Puerto Rican women. Both treatment groups were found to have improved significantly more than a control condition. More recent studies with Puerto Rican children and adolescents that did compare different types of group interventions have demonstrated the efficacy of a group format (Costantino, Malgady, & Rogler, 1986; Malgady et al., 1990b). These studies are described later.

Acosta (1982) has suggested that group psychotherapy with Spanish-speaking Latino patients might be an important treatment option to consider given the scarcity of Spanish-speaking therapists. While experiential reports have tended to support the group approach as a viable form of treatment with Latinos, other factors, which remain to be empirically investigated, should be taken into consideration. Acosta (1982) recounts that Spanish-speaking patients were initially more likely to accept individual therapy over group therapy. Language fluency also is important. Philipus (1971) reported that Mexican-Americans with various English language capacities had higher dropout rates when the group was conducted in English.

Patient orientation programs.   Clients of low socioeconomic backgrounds have been found to be more likely to drop out of treatment, and Rogler et al. (1983) propose that this factor may be of relevance for many Latinos. Acosta, Evans, Yamamoto, and Wilcox (1980) developed a brief audiovisual orientation program for low-income clients to enable them to understand the process of psychotherapy and act upon that understanding in therapy (e.g., be able to openly express problems and needs). As noted earlier, in an evaluation of this orientation program, low-income, Latino- and African-American and white patients who participated in the orientation program were found to be more knowledgeable and positive in their attitudes toward psychotherapy than those who participated in a control condition (Acosta et al., 1983).

Culturally specific treatments.   One of the most dynamic and innovative areas of psychotherapy research with Latinos has been the development of culturally sensitive treatment modalities. Examples of developed or currently developing treatments include Szapocznik's Life Enhancement Therapy for Cuban Elders and Bicultural Effectiveness Training; Maldonado-Sierra and Trent's group therapy for Puerto Rican schizophrenics; LeVine and Padilla's pluralistic counseling, hero/heroine modeling for Puerto Rican adolescents; the Unitas Therapeutic Community in New York for children; and cuento (folktale) therapy for Puerto Rican children (Costantino et al., 1986; Malgady, Rogler, & Costantino, 1990a; Padilla & De Snyder, 1985; Rogler et al., 1983). While the effectiveness of many of these treatments remains to be determined, those that have been subject to empirical study have been shown to be useful.

Cuento therapy utilizes *cuentos*, or folktales, to convey morals and models of adaptive behavior to children. The effectiveness of two types of cuento therapy, art/play therapy, and no intervention for high-risk kindergarten through third-grade Puerto Rican children was studied by Costantino et al. (1986). They found that there was a significant effect due to treatment, and a significant interaction between treatment and grade level, with differences between treatments only at the first-grade level. First-grade children who had received cuento therapy showed significantly less trait anxiety than those in the other groups after 20 weeks of treatment. Cuento therapy was more effective than no intervention in reducing trait anxiety, but it did not significantly differ from art/play therapy. In addition, cuento therapies significantly increased scores on the WISC-R comprehension subtest compared to art/play therapy and no intervention. In studies supporting the effectiveness of cuento therapy for Puerto Rican children, Malgady et al. (1990a, 1990b) found that cuento therapy had significant effects on anxiety, social judgment, and aggression.

Because cuento therapy seemed most effective with younger children and was perhaps age-inappropriate for older children, Malgady et al. (1990a) developed hero/heroine modeling for high-risk Puerto Rican adolescents. This social learning–based intervention used biographies of famous Puerto Rican historical individuals to convey appropriate adult role models. While there was no significant treatment effect on symptom distress, treatment did significantly affect ethnic identity. Interestingly, the effect of treatment on adolescents' self-concept varied as a function of sex and the presence or absence of the adolescent's father living in his or her household. In households where the father was absent, self-concept was enhanced by treatment; however, for those adolescents whose father was present, treatment did not affect the males' self-concept and adversely affected the females' self-concept. Malgady et al. speculate that the presentation of heroic figures may have resulted in negative outcomes because those who did have parental role models may have compared their parents to the heroic figures with resulting feelings of personal inadequacy.

It does appear that the development of culturally specific treatment for Latinos has yielded hopeful findings. However, as in the development of any treatment modality, care must be taken so that the negative effects of treatment are explored adequately.

EVALUATION OF RESEARCH METHODS AND THEORIES

Numerous methodological difficulties complicate any empirical inquiry into the process and efficacy of psychotherapy, and they have been well documented elsewhere (e.g., Kazdin, 1986). These problems include inadequate sample selection (Wolpe, 1977); inappropriate outcome criteria (Paul, 1967); ambiguity over the types of therapists and treatments used (Paul, 1967; Strupp, 1970); nonconvergence among outcome criteria (Garfield, Prager, & Bergin, 1971; Mintz, Luborsky, & Christoph, 1979); observational biases (Kent, O'Leary, Diament, & Dietz, 1974); incorrect statistical analysis of change (Manning & Du Bois, 1962); inappropriate designs for the outcome question being addressed (Kazdin, 1979; Paul, 1967); inadequate control groups (Jacobson & Baucom, 1977); uncertainty over the clinical and social value of the magnitude of change produced by treatment (Kazdin, 1977); and inadequate power in terms of design sensitivity (Kazdin & Bass, 1989). The purpose here is to examine the specific methodological and conceptual problems that have limited or complicated efforts to examine the influence of ethnicity and culture on psychotherapy processes and outcomes. These issues include types of research questions asked, reliance on analogue studies, types of samples used, selection of appropriate measures, interethnic versus intraethnic comparison designs, and controlling for potential confounds with ethnicity/culture.

Research Strategies and Issues

Research questions. Too often the research question posed has not directly addressed specific processes or outcomes of psychotherapy. Studies tend to be descriptive in nature, focusing on ethnic comparisons in values, personality styles, role relationships, and so on. A number of important implications for psychotherapy have been identified, but the actual functional relationship between these ethnic differences in values or other variables and psychotherapy process or outcome has not been ascertained. For example, Fukuyama and Greenfield (1983) found that Asians were less assertive in a number of behaviors, suggesting that Asians placed greater value on maintaining harmony in relationships. Although these findings would suggest that assertion therapy may not be as effective with Asians or that assertiveness on the part of Asians would vary depending on the target person selected in the intervention (e.g., stranger vs. family member), no outcome study has followed up on this study and empirically tested these possible hypotheses.

Selection of a certain research strategy is partially guided by the initial conceptualization of culturally related variables in the study. Studies have varied greatly in the manner by which they have operationalized cultural variables. It often has been assumed that ethnic affiliation is an adequate representation of cultural variation. However, ethnic differences and cultural differences are not equivalent and a distinction must be made between the two. Ethnic differences involve differences in group membership (i.e., a type of social identity) that *implies* differences in culture. Cultural differences refer to variations in attitudes, values, and perceptual constructs that result from different cultural experiences. As Zane and Sue (1991) have noted,

Whereas the former [ethnic differences] simply involves group membership, the latter [cultural differences] constitutes a host of cognitive variables which are linked to different cultural lifestyles and perspectives. These cognitive variables, and not ethnic membership, have been the ones implicated in culture-related problems for psychotherapists. . . . Ethnic match research, while important, has not directly tested the cultural difference hypothesis of treatment. (p. 52)

Ethnic differences are only indirect indexes of the more important cultural differences that tend to be more proximal to psychotherapy processes and outcomes. The question usually asked is: Does a certain ethnic group (compared to other ethnic groups) benefit more or less from treatment? It would be far more informative to address this question: Do differences between ethnic groups on culturally relevant variables (e.g., values, role relationships) affect a certain process or outcome in treatment? Essentially, the study of cultural influences is the study of individual difference variables that are associated with ethnic group experiences.

Use of analogue studies. In analogue studies, specific problems exist that result from the examination of cultural influences. First, it is questionable if the brevity and simulated nature of the treatment sessions in most analogue designs allow for the sensitive testing of cultural or ethnic effects. For example, studies on Latinos have found little ethnic effects in therapist credibility (e.g., Furlong et al., 1979; Hess & Street, 1991). However, Acosta et al. (1980) have noted how many ethnic minority and low-income clients have little familiarity with the process of psychotherapy. With little understanding, rating the credibility of one's therapist

may have little functional meaning for many ethnic minority clients at the initial stages of treatment. Second, the reliance of analogues on student samples may restrict variation in acculturation and ethnic identity. Both of these variables have been identified as important predictors of process in treatment. Most student samples tend to be more acculturated, but also more ethnically conscious. The restriction of range on acculturation and ethnic identity limits generalizability but, more importantly, limits the design's sensitivity in testing for cultural effects as operationalized by these two variables. Finally, analogues may curtail the range of clinical problems that are typically presented by ethnic clients having real problems. Issues such as racism, cultural adjustment, ethnic identity conflicts, and intergenerational difficulties are more frequently presented by ethnic clients.

Samples selected. The heterogeneity within each ethnic minority group has often been noted by researchers (e.g., K. Clark, 1972; Leong, 1986). For each group, there are important variations in sociodemographics and psychosocial characteristics that include country of origin, immigration history (length of stay in refugee camps, immigrant vs. refugee status), place of residence (urban vs. rural, urban vs. reservation), education level (in both the United States and country of origin), motivation for leaving country of origin, acculturation level, socioeconomic level, English proficiency, ethnic identification, and preferred language, among others. Despite this documented diversity, only recently have studies articulated the specific samples used in the research. When efforts are made to examine this within-group diversity, important relationships are frequently found. For example, Pomales and Williams (1989) assessed the acculturation level of Puerto Rican and Mexican college students in both Latino- and Anglo-American culture. In responding to a directive or nondirective style, Latino-acculturated students rated the nondirective therapist as more credible than did bicultural students. On the other hand, Anglo-acculturated students found the therapist more trustworthy than did bicultural or Latino-acculturated students regardless of therapist style. By not identifying subgroup characteristics (e.g., level of acculturation, tribal affiliation, different Asian groups, and different Latino groups), it is difficult to determine to what extent the findings can truly be generalized to the various subpopulations within a particular ethnic group. Moreover, the systematic investigation of critical treatment processes is difficult because it is unclear if studies of a particular ethnic group are comparable.

One of the most significant reasons for sampling difficulties is the relatively small populations of ethnic minority groups. Small population size creates problems in trying to find not only representative samples for study but also adequate numbers of subjects. For example, finding a sufficient sample of American Indians who are using mental health services is extremely difficult.

Selection of appropriate measures. Ethnic and cultural differences can be obscured by the use of unreliable, invalid, or insensitive measures. Many investigators have pointed to methodological and conceptual problems in the assessment of ethnic minority group individuals. These problems include clinical assessments that overpathologize or underpathologize the symptoms of ethnic clients (Helms, 1992; Levine & Padilla, 1980; Lopez, 1989; Marcos et al., 1973; Neighbors et al., 1989); evaluations based on norms developed on white populations (LaFromboise, 1988; Rogler et al., 1989); conceptual and scalar nonequivalence of measures across different cultural groups (Helms, 1992; Hui & Triandis, 1985); difficulties in administering instruments to limited–English-speaking clients or in making adequate translations (Brislin et al., 1973); and cultural differences in approaching assessment tasks (Manson & Trimble, 1982; D. Sue & Sue, 1987). Despite widespread concern over the cross-cultural validity of assessment measures, the nature of cultural bias has not been empirically examined to any great extent, and solutions for cultural bias have been difficult to find. In the past, clinical and personality assessments of ethnic minorities have proceeded without the benefit of validation studies, and diagnosticians and clinicians have simply been admonished to take into account cultural differences and to avoid making strong conclusions on the basis of the assessment results. Often when a popularly used instrument is finally tested on ethnic minority populations, the instrument is not widely used among these groups because another, more recent, and sophisticated measure is developed for the rest of the country. This results in the situation in which the assessment of ethnic minority populations frequently lags behind, and ethnic minorities are given assessment instruments of unknown validity for their particular ethnic group.

Inter- and intraethnic comparison designs. Two general strategies have dominated the examination of cultural influences in psychotherapy. Studies have used either interethnic designs involving comparisons between ethnic groups (usually ethnic minority with whites) or intraethnic designs in which comparisons are made within a group with respect to different levels of acculturation or ethnic identity. Some studies have used a combination of these two approaches. Interpretations of the research have implicitly assumed that interethnic comparisons are an extension for the intraethnic approach in that the white comparison group represents the most acculturated level of the culture variable. Usually it is assumed that whites are a homogeneous, highly acculturated group, but no study has assessed if this is actually the case. As indicated earlier, ethnic affiliation appears to be a more distal variable than acculturation with respect to treatment process and outcome. Therefore, it is unclear if the two approaches are functionally related.

Potential confounds. Many studies have failed to control for variables that may be confounded with ethnicity or culture. Research has consistently found that variables such as socioeconomic status, education level, place of residence, and English proficiency covary with ethnicity or culture. By not assessing these variables, questions of internal validity can be raised about much of the previous research. Moreover, these studies have missed opportunities for increasing design sensitivity (by covarying out their effects) because some of these variables have been identified as correlates of treatment outcome (Luborsky et al., 1971).

Role of Culture

Probably the most challenging issue for ethnic mental health researchers has been the development of viable strategies for specifically examining the role of culture in psychotherapy process and outcome. In other words, it has often been difficult to incorporate variables directly related to cultural experiences into psychotherapy research designs. Three conceptual issues have complicated this task; the distal nature of ethnicity, limitations of traditional outcome designs, and the lack of conceptual or theoretical approaches to guide the research.

Distal nature of ethnic variables. Earlier it was noted that ethnicity implies certain cultural differences, and it is these differences that should serve as the focus of process and outcome studies. The focus on the broad concept of ethnicity often has obscured important variations within both the ethnic minority *and* white groups that could be related to treatment outcome. In other words, cultural differences involve important intervening variables between the ethnicity of the client and clinical outcomes. The cultural-difference approach facilitates the integration of cultural findings with other psychotherapy research because many of these variables (e.g., coping styles) have also been the focus of previous studies on process and outcome.

Limitations of outcome research. Lack of specific guidelines as to what constitutes culturally responsive treatment for ethnic minorities cannot be solely attributed to problems in ethnic minority mental health research. Progress in this area is also constrained by limitations in clinical outcome research, in general. Often it is unclear what actually happens to the client in mental health interventions. Treatments may not be well articulated in terms of their rationale, the underlying theory on which they are based, the specific methods employed, or the specific outcomes expected from therapy.

Even when treatment procedures have been clearly delineated, the extent to which therapists and clients have complied with or carried out the therapeutic tasks is often unclear. This source of treatment ambiguity involves problems in procedural reliability, which refers to the degree to which the treatment has been implemented in accordance with the experimental plan. This problem is a critical one because it appears that procedural slippage can occur for both clients (Taylor, Agras, Schneider, & Allen, 1983) and therapists (Billingsley, White, & Munson, 1980).

Another source of treatment ambiguity centers on problems in defining the end points of therapy tasks, namely, the types of learning experiences that a client should have upon completion of the treatment procedures. What are the insights, emotional catharses, or skills that clients are supposed to experience or gain during the course of psychotherapy? Often this is not clear.

Lack of conceptual/theoretical models. Within the context of program evaluation, Weiss (1972) has distinguished between a program failure as opposed to a theory failure. Programs attempt to activate a "causal process" that then leads to some desired effect. Program failure occurs when the intervention has not been successfully implemented. Theory failure occurs when the program is successful in producing the intended impact but the resultant causal process does not lead to the desired end goals. In a similar manner, treatment failure with ethnic minorities can involve either procedure or theory failure. The treatment may be ineffective because its procedures did not have the expected impact; the targeted learning experiences did not occur because the treatment as implemented may have clashed with certain cultural values held by the client or adversely affected certain peer or family relations supporting the client's

adaptive behavior. On the other hand, the theory on which the treatment is based may not be sufficiently applicable to ethnic minority individuals, families, or communities. In this case, achievement of the desired changes in treatment would not be related to the mental health problem, and little improvement would result.

Few conceptual or theoretical models or approaches have been proposed to guide process and outcome research with ethnic minorities. Most conceptual schemes have focused on specific concrete recommendations for treating ethnic minorities with few ties to current theories of psychotherapy (Cervantes & Castro, 1985). What is needed are approaches that propose specific hypotheses as to how the psychosocial experiences of ethnic minorities affect certain important processes in psychotherapy.

CONCLUDING COMMENTS

We have attempted to indicate some of the major research findings on treatment outcomes and processes and to point to methodological and conceptual problems in the study of ethnic minority groups. In closing, we would like to highlight several points.

First, there is limited research on ethnic minority groups and the research is not highly programmatic. Because of the paucity of knowledge and baseline information, many studies have been descriptive and problem oriented rather than theoretical in nature. The following questions have been posed by researchers: Is psychotherapy effective for ethnic minority clients? What are the utilization and dropout rates? Which individual differences affect treatment, and how can therapy be modified and improved? Addressing these basic questions is important because they lay the foundation for other, more specific research issues that have not been adequately researched even now, and they have implications for programs and policies. Nevertheless, there is also a need for programmatic research that focuses on more theoretical issues: Why do we see underutilization of services by some ethnic groups? Why are culturally responsive or culturally congruent forms of treatment effective? A more theoretical focus is occurring in some areas, such as preferences for the ethnicity of the therapist and client's stage of ethnic identity. The field is in need of this kind of programmatic research, which helps to improve ideas, theories, and methodologies and to stimulate other research.

Second, although many researchers and practitioners believe that psychotherapy is ineffective with members of ethnic minority groups, providing a definitive answer based on research findings is not possible. The reason is that there are only a few available empirical studies and the question of the effectiveness of psychotherapy is complex, requiring more than an affirmative or negative response. If we put aside the subtleties and complexity involved in the question of overall effectiveness, we have some reason to believe that certain conditions are related to effectiveness: ethnic similarity for clients and therapists of some ethnic minority groups; the use of some culturally responsive forms of treatment; pretherapy intervention with ethnic clients; and the training of therapists to work with members of culturally diverse groups. The most meaningful research, therefore, deals with conditions of effectiveness rather than with attempts to answer the effectiveness question in general.

Third, research on ethnic minority groups is difficult to conduct. Throughout this chapter, we have noted the problems in conducting research — for example, difficulties in finding adequate samples, achieving representativeness in sampling, devising cross-culturally valid measures, applying existing theories, and so on. Ethnic researchers must often confront additional methodological and conceptual problems that are not encountered to the same extent by other researchers. These problems mean that for ethnic research to be more programmatic, rigorous, and sophisticated, greater resources are needed (e.g., personnel training, and research funding).

Fourth, and related to the second point, the heterogeneity of ethnic minority groups is an increasingly salient characteristic to consider. The research is going beyond the evaluation of treatment issues for African-Americans, American Indians, and others as ethnic groups. Rather, the focus is now on individual differences within a particular group.

These four points as well as our analysis of conceptual and methodological problems have been well recognized by ethnic researchers. As mentioned in the introductory comments, this critical review should be placed in proper perspective. Major advances in ethnic minority research have been made, knowledge has substantially improved because of the pioneering work of many scholars, and the viewpoints of "insiders" to the groups (i.e., ethnic minority researchers) have increasingly been expressed. In closing, we would like to offer some personal comments and observations about ethnic minority research.

Ethnic minority research in general, and ethnic psychotherapy research in particular, was largely initiated on African-Americans because of the long oppressive history of black–white relations in this country and the need to address these relations. The research established the major parameters for investigation: differences in cultural values and lifestyles between African-Americans and white Americans and the effects of racism. Indeed, these parameters are pertinent to the study of American Indians, Asian-Americans, and Latino-Americans, and much work on these groups has been patterned after the research and theories developed on African-Americans.

More recent literature on the different ethnic groups demonstrates a more ethnic-specific focus. That is, each group is beginning to more clearly define its own concerns and needs and to focus research efforts on these needs. For example, the responsiveness of mental health services for African-Americans is of concern, as it is for the other groups. However, additional issues such as the underutilization of services among Asian-Americans and Latino-Americans are also salient. Unlike African-Americans and American Indians, Asian-Americans and Latino-Americans are largely voluntary immigrants to this country. Language differences, separation from other kin who reside in the "old country," and adjustment to a new culture are important. American Indians who live on reservations are more isolated from mainstream American culture than are, say, Latino-Americans living in urban ethnic communities. Many American Indians have experienced cultural genocide — the destruction of traditional folkways. Using culturally based psychotherapy approaches serves not only to increase treatment effectiveness, but also to reaffirm those cultural folkways. As indicated previously, much research has been conducted by Helms and her colleagues (e.g., Carter & Helms, 1992) on the role of ethnic identity in psychotherapy among African-Americans. For Latino-Americans, ethnic identity is also important but it is part of larger issues — acculturation and assimilation (Padilla, 1980). With the continuing immigration of Latinos to this country, there is a constant source of cultural values coming from Latino "homelands." Also, many first-generation individuals, born and raised in another country, do not seem to have the identity issues faced by American-born ethnics who grow up as members of a minority group. Issues of undocumented aliens are also pertinent to Asian-Americans and Latino-Americans. The point is that in trying to understand ethnic populations, ethnicity, culture, and minority group status are important variables that are being redefined for each group.

REFERENCES

Abramowitz, S. I., & Murray, J. (1983). Race effects in psychotherapy. In J. Murray & P. Abramson (Eds.), *Bias in psychotherapy* (pp. 215–255). New York: Praeger.

Acosta, F. X. (1982). Group psychotherapy with Spanish-speaking patients. In R. M. Becerra, M. Karno, & J. I. Escobar (Eds.), *Mental health and Hispanic Americans* (pp. 183–197). New York: Grune & Stratton.

Acosta, F. X. (1984). Psychotherapy with Mexican Americans: Clinical and empirical gains. In J. L. Martinez, Jr., & Richard H. Mendoza (Eds.), *Chicano psychology* (pp. 163–189). Orlando, FL: Academic Press.

Acosta, F. X., & Cristo, M. H. (1981). Development of a bilingual interpreter program: An alternative model for Spanish-speaking services. *Professional Psychology, 12*, 474–482.

Acosta, F. X., Evans, L. A., Yamamoto, J., & Wilcox, S. A. (1980). Helping minority and low-income psychotherapy patients "Tell it like it is." *The Journal of Biocommunication, 7*, 13–19.

Acosta, F. X., & Sheehan, J. G. (1976). Preferences toward Mexican American and Anglo American psychotherapists. *Journal of Consulting and Clinical Psychology, 44*, 272–279.

Acosta, F. X., & Yamamoto, J. (1984). The utility of group work practice for Hispanic Americans. *Social Work with Groups, 7*, 63–73.

Acosta, F. X., Yamamoto, J., & Evans, L. A. (1982). *Effective psychotherapy for low-income and minority patients.* New York: Plenum.

Acosta, F. X., Yamamoto, J., Evans, L. A., & Skilbeck, W. M. (1983). Preparing low-income Hispanic, Black, and White patients for psychotherapy: Evaluation of a new orientation program. *Journal of Clinical Psychology, 39*, 872–877.

Akutsu, P. D., Lin, C. H., & Zane, N. W. S. (1990). Predictors of utilization intent of counseling among Chinese and White students: A test of the proximal–distal model. *Journal of Counseling Psychology, 37*, 445–452.

American Psychiatric Association. (1987). *Diagnostic and statistical manual of mental disorders* (3rd ed., rev.). Washington, DC: Author.

Arkoff, A., Thaver, F., & Elkind, L. (1966). Mental health and counseling ideas of Asian and American students. *Journal of Counseling Psychology, 13*, 219–223.

Atkinson, D. R. (1983). Ethnic similarity in counseling psychology: A review of research. *The Counseling Psychologist, 11*, 79–92.

Atkinson, D. R. (1986). Similarity in counseling. *The Counseling Psychologist, 14*, 319–354.

Atkinson, D. R., Furlong, M. J., & Poston, W. C. (1986). Afro-American preferences for counselors characteristics. *Journal of Counseling Psychology, 33*, 326–330.

Atkinson, D. R., & Gim, R. H. (1989). Asian-American cultural identity and attitudes toward mental health services. *Journal of Counseling Psychology, 36*, 209–212.

Atkinson, D. R., Maruyama, M., & Matsui, S. (1978). Effects of counselor race and counseling approach on Asian Americans' perceptions of counselor credibility and utility. *Journal of Counseling Psychology, 25*, 76–85.

Atkinson, D. R., Morten, G., & Sue, D. W. (1993). *Counseling American minorities: A cross-cultural perspective.* Dubuque, IA: Wm. C. Brown.

Atkinson, D. R., Ponce, F. Q., & Martinez, F. M. (1984). Effects of ethnic, sex, and attitude similarity on counselor credibility. *Journal of Counseling Psychology, 31*, 588–590.

Atkinson, D. R., Poston, W. C., Furlong, M. J., & Mercado, P. (1989). Ethnic group preferences of counselor characteristics. *Journal of Counseling Psychology, 36*, 68–72.

Banks, W. M. (1972). The differential effects of race and social class in helping. *Journal of Clinical Psychology, 28*, 90–92.

Barbarin, O. A. (1984). Racial themes in psychotherapy with Blacks: Effects of training on the attitudes of Black and White psychiatrists. *American Journal of Social Psychology, 4*, 13–20.

Beiser, M., & Attneave, C. L. (1982). Mental disorders among Native American children: Rates and risk periods for entering treatment. *American Journal of Psychiatry, 139*, 193–198.

Bennett, S. K. & BigFoot-Sipes, D. S. (1991). American Indian and white college student preferences for counselor characteristics. *Journal of Counseling Psychology, 38*, 440–445.

Berg, J. H., & Wright-Buckley, C. (1988). Effects of racial similarity and interviewer intimacy in a peer counseling analogue. *Journal of Counseling Psychology, 35*, 377–384.

Bernal, M. E., & Padilla, A. M. (1982). Status of minority curricula and training in clinical psychology. *American Psychologist, 37*, 780–787.

Billingsley, F., White, O. R., & Munson, R. (1980). Procedural reliability: A rationale and an example. *Behavioral Assessment, 3*, 229–241.

Bishop, J. B., & Richards, T. F. (1987). Counselor intake judgments about White and Black clients in a university counseling center. *Journal of Counseling Psychology, 34*, 96–98.

Bobo, J. K., Gilchrist, L. D., Cvetkovich, G. T., Trimble, J. E., & Schinke, S. P. (1988). Cross-cultural service delivery to minority communities. *Journal of Community Psychology, 16*, 263–272.

Borrego, R. L., Chavez, E. L., & Titley, R. W. (1982). Effect of counselor technique on Mexican-American and Anglo-American self-disclosure and counselor perception. *Journal of Counseling Psychology, 29*, 538–541.

Boyd, N. (1982). Family therapy with Black families. In E. E. Jones & S. J. Korchin (Eds.), *Minority mental health* (pp. 227–249). New York: Praeger.

Brislin, R. W., Lonner, W. J., & Thorndike, R. W. (1973). *Cross-cultural research methods.* New York: Wiley.

Brown, B. S., Joe, G. W., & Thompson, P. (1985). Minority group status and treatment retention. *International Journal of the Addictions, 20*, 319–335.

Brown, T. R., Stein, K. M., Huang, K., & Harris, D. E. (1973). Mental illness and the role of mental health facilities in China town. In S. Sue & N. Wagner (Eds.), *Asian-Americans: Psychological perspectives* (pp. 212–231). Palo Alto, CA: Science & Behavior Books.

Bureau of Indian Affairs. (1991). *American Indians today* (3rd ed.). Washington, DC: U.S. Department of the Interior.

Carkhuff, R. R., & Pierce, R. (1967). Differential effects of therapist race and social class upon patient depth of self-exploration in the initial clinical interview. *Journal of Consulting Psychology, 31*, 632–634.

Carter, R. T., & Helms, J. E. (1992). The counseling process as defined by relationship types: A test of Helms' interaction model. *Journal of Multicultural Counseling and Development, 20*, 181–201.

Cervantes, R. C., & Castro, F. G. (1985). Stress, coping, and

Mexican American mental health: A systematic review. *Hispanic Journal of Behavioral Sciences, 7*, 1–74.

Chang, W. (1985). A cross-cultural study of depressive symptomatology. *Culture, Medicine, and Psychiatry, 9*, 295–317.

Cheung, F. M., & Lau, B. W. K. (1982). Situational variations of help-seeking behavior among Chinese patients. *Comprehensive Psychiatry, 23*, 252–262.

Chung, R. C. Y., & Okazaki, S. (1991). Counseling Americans of Southeast Asian descent: The impact of the refugee experience. In E. E. Lee & B. L. Richardson (Eds.), *Multicultural issues in counseling: New approaches to diversity* (pp. 107–126). Alexandria, VA: American Association for Counseling and Development.

Clark, K. B. (1972). Foreword. In A. Thomas & S. Sillen (Eds.), *Racism and psychiatry*. New York: Brunner/Mazel.

Clark, L. A. (1987). Mutual relevance of mainstream and cross-cultural psychology. *Journal of Consulting and Clinical Psychology, 55*, 461–470.

Comas-Diaz, L. (1981). Effects of cognitive and behavioral group treatment on the depressive symptomatology of Puerto Rican women. *Journal of Consulting and Clinical Psychology, 49*, 627–632.

Costantino, G., Malgady, R. G., & Rogler, L. H. (1986). Cuento therapy: A culturally sensitive modality for Puerto Rican children. *Journal of Counseling and Clinical Psychology, 54*, 639–645.

Cross, W. E., Jr. (1971). The Negro-to-black conversion experience: Toward a psychology of black liberation. *Black World, 20*, 13–27.

Dauphinais, P., Dauphinais, L., & Rowe, W. (1981). Effects of race and communication style on Indian perceptions of counselor effectiveness. *Counselor Education and Supervision, 21*, 72–80.

Dauphinais, P., LaFromboise, T., & Rowe, W. (1980). Perceived problems and sources of help for American Indian students. *Counselor Education and Supervision, 20*, 37–46.

De La Cancela, V., & Guzman, L. P. (1991). Latino mental health service needs: Implications for training psychologists. In H. Myers, P. Wohlford, P. Guzman, & R. Echemendia (Eds.), *Ethnic minority perspectives on clinical training and services in psychology* (pp. 59–64). Washington, DC: American Psychological Association.

Evans, L. A., Acosta, F. X., Yamamoto, J., & Skilbeck, W. M. (1984). Orienting psychotherapists to better serve low income and minority patients. *Journal of Clinical Psychology, 40*, 90–96.

Flaskerud, J. H. (1986). The effects of culture-compatible intervention on the utilization of mental health services by minority clients. *Community Mental Health Journal, 22*, 127–141.

Flaskerud, J. H., & Soldevilla, E. Q. (1986). Pilipino and Vietnamese clients: Utilizing an Asian mental health center. *Journal of Psychosocial Nursing, 24*, 32–36.

Folensbee, R. W., Draguns, J. G., Jr., & Danish, S. J. (1986). Impact of two types of counselor intervention on Black American, Puerto Rican, and Anglo-American analogue clients. *Journal of Counseling Psychology, 33*, 446–453.

Franklin, A. J. (1982). Therapeutic interventions with urban Black adolescents. In E. E. Jones & S. J. Korchin (Eds.), *Minority mental health* (pp. 267–295). New York: Praeger.

Fukuyama, M. A., & Greenfield, T. K. (1983). Dimensions of assertiveness in an Asian-American student population. *Journal of Counseling Psychology, 30*, 429–432.

Furlong, M. J., Atkinson, D. R., & Casas, J. M. (1979).

Effects of counselor ethnicity and attitudinal similarity on Chicano students' perceptions of counselor credibility and attractiveness. *Hispanic Journal of Behavioral Science, 1*, 41–53.

Garfield, S. L., Prager, R. A., & Bergin, A. E. (1971). Evaluation of outcome in psychotherapy. *Journal of Consulting and Clinical Psychology, 37*, 307–313.

Gibbs, J. T. (1980). The interpersonal orientation in mental health consultation: Toward a model of ethnic variations in consultation. *Journal of Community Psychology, 8*, 195–207.

Gibbs, J. T., & Huang, L. N. (1989). *Children of color: Psychological interventions with minority youths*. San Francisco: Jossey-Bass.

Gim, R. H., Atkinson, D. R., & Kim, S. J. (1991). Asian-American acculturation, counselor ethnicity and cultural sensitivity, and ratings of counselors. *Journal of Counseling Psychology, 38*, 57–62.

Gim, R. H., Atkinson, D. R., & Whiteley, S. (1990). Asian-American acculturation, severity of concerns, and willingness to see a counselor. *Journal of Counseling Psychology, 37*, 281–285.

Gordon, M., & Grantham, R. J. (1979). Helper preferences in disadvantaged students. *Journal of Counseling Psychology, 26*, 337–343.

Green, C. F., Cunningham, J., & Yanico, B. J. (1986). Effects of counselor and subject race and counselor physical attractiveness on impressions and expectations of a female counselor. *Journal of Counseling Psychology, 33*, 349–352.

Griffith, M. S., & Jones, E. E. (1978). Race and psychotherapy: Changing perspectives. In J. H. Masserman (Ed.), *Current psychiatric therapies* (Vol. 18, pp. 225–235). New York: Grune & Stratton.

Guilmet, G. M., & Whited, D. L. (1987). Cultural lessons for clinical mental health practice for the Puyallup tribal community. *American Indian and Alaska Native Mental Health Research, 1*, 32–49.

Gurak, D. T., & Rogler, L. H. (1983). Hispanic diversity in New York City. In L. H. Rogler, R. C. Santana, G. Costantino, B. F. Earley, B. Grossman, D. T. Gurak, R. Malgady, & O. Rodriguez (Eds.), *A conceptual framework for mental health research on Hispanic populations* (pp. 59–65). Bronx, NY: Fordham University, Hispanic Research Center.

Harrison, D. K. (1975). Race as a counselor–client variable in counseling and psychotherapy: A review of the research. *The Counseling Psychologist, 5*, 124–133.

Havilland, M. G., Horswill, R. K., O'Connell, J. J., & Dynneson, V. V. (1983). Native American college students' preference for counselor race and sex and the likelihood of their use of a counseling center. *Journal of Counseling Psychology, 30*, 267–270.

Helms, J. E. (1984). Toward a theoretical explanation of the effects of race on counseling: A Black and White model. *Counseling Psychologist, 12*, 153–164.

Helms, J. E. (1992). Why is there no study of cultural equivalence in standardized cognitive ability testing? *American Psychologist, 47*, 1083–1101.

Helms, J. R., & Carter, R. T. (1991). Relationships of White and Black racial identity attitudes and demographic similarity to counselor preferences. *Journal of Counseling Psychology, 38*, 446–457.

Hess, R. S., & Street, E. M. (1991). The effect of acculturation on the relationship of counselor ethnicity and client ratings. *Journal of Counseling Psychology, 38*, 71–75.

Ho, M. K. (1976). Social work with Asian-Americans. *Social Casework, 57*, 195–201.

Hu, T. W., Snowden, L. R., Jerrell, J. M., & Nguyen, T. D. (1991). Ethnic populations in public mental health: Services choice and level of use. *American Journal of Public Health, 81,* 1429–1434.

Hui, C. H., & Triandis, H. C. (1985). Measurement in cross-cultural counseling: A review and comparison of strategies. *Journal of Cross-Cultural Psychology, 16,* 131–152.

Ibrahim, F. A. (1985). Effectiveness in cross-cultural counseling and psychotherapy: A framework. *Psychotherapy, 22,* 321–323.

Inkeles, A., & Levinson, S. J. (1969). National character: The study of modal personality and sociocultural systems. In G. Lindzey & E. Aronson (Eds.), *The handbook of social psychology.* Reading, MA: Addison-Wesley.

Ivey, A. E., Ivey, M. B., & Simek-Morgan, L. (1993). *Counseling and psychotherapy: A multicultural perspective.* Needham Heights, MA: Allyn & Bacon.

Jacobson, N. S., & Baucom, D. H. (1977). Design and assessment of nonspecific control groups in behavior modification research. *Behavior Therapy, 8,* 709–719.

Jackson, G. G., & Kirschner, S. A. (1973). Racial self-designation and preference for counselor race. *Journal of Counseling Psychology, 20,* 560–564.

Jackson, J. S., Neighbors, H. W., & Gurin, G. (1986). Findings from a national survey of Black mental health: Implications for practice and training. In M. R. Miranda & H. H. L. Kitano (Eds.), *Mental health research and practice in minority communities: Development of culturally sensitive training programs* (pp. 91–116). Washington, DC: U.S. Government Printing Office.

Jenkins, A. H. (1985). Attending to self-activity in the Afro-American client. *Psychotherapy, 22,* 335–341.

Jones, B. E., & Gray, B. A. (1983). Black males and psychotherapy: Theoretical issues. *American Journal of Psychotherapy, 37,* 77–85.

Jones, E. E. (1978). Effects of race on psychotherapy process and outcome: An exploratory investigation. *Psychotherapy: Theory, Research, and Practice, 15,* 226–236.

Jones, E. E. (1982). Psychotherapists' impressions of treatment outcome as a function of race. *Journal of Clinical Psychology, 38,* 722–731.

Jones, E. E., & Matsumoto, D. R. (1982). Psychotherapy with the underserved. In L. Snowden (Ed.), *Services to the underserved* (pp. 207–228). Beverly Hills, CA: Sage Publications.

Jones, E. E., & Thorne, A. (1987). Rediscovery of the subject: Intercultural approaches to clinical assessment. *Journal of Consulting and Clinical Psychology, 55,* 488–496.

Jones, J. M. (1991). Psychological models of race: What have they been and what should they be? In J. D. Goodchilds (Ed.), *Psychological perspectives on human diversity in America* (pp. 3–46). Washington, DC: American Psychological Association.

Kazdin, A. E. (1977). Assessing the clinical or applied importance of behavior change through social validation. *Behavior Modification, 1,* 427–451.

Kazdin, A. E. (1979). Therapy outcome questions requiring control of credibility and treatment-generated expectancies. *Behavior Therapy, 10,* 81–93.

Kazdin, A. E. (1986). Comparative outcome studies of psychotherapy: Methodological issues and strategies. *Journal of Consulting and Clinical Psychology, 54,* 95–105.

Kazdin, A. E., & Bass, D. (1989). Power to detect differences between alternative treatments in comparative psychotherapy outcome research. *Journal of Consulting and Clinical Psychology, 57,* 138–147.

Kent, R. N., O'Leary, K. D., Diament, C., & Dietz, A. (1974). Expectation biases in observational evaluation of therapeutic change. *Journal of Consulting and Clinical Psychology, 42,* 774–780.

Kim, B. L. C. (1973). Asian-Americans: No model minority. *Social Work, 18,* 44–54.

Kim, S. C. (1985). Family therapy for Asian Americans: A strategic-structural framework. *Psychotherapy, 22,* 342–348.

Kinzie, J. D., & Leung, P. (1989). Clonidine in Cambodian patients with post-traumatic stress disorder. *Journal of Nervous and Mental Disease, 177,* 546–550.

Kitano, H. H. L. (1981). Counseling and psychotherapy with Japanese-Americans. In A. J. Marsella & P. B. Pedersen (Eds.), *Cross-cultural counseling and psychology* (pp. 228–242). Elmsford, NY: Pergamon.

Kleinman, A. M. (1977). Depression, somatization and the new cross-cultural psychiatry. *Social Science and Medicine, 11,* 3–10.

Kleinman, A. M. (1979). *Patients and healers in the context of culture.* Berkeley: University of California Press.

Kline, F., Acosta, F. X., Austin, W., & Johnson, R. G. (1980). The misunderstood Spanish-speaking patient. *American Journal of Psychiatry, 137,* 1530–1533.

LaFromboise, T. D. (1988). American Indian mental health policy. *American Psychologist, 43,* 388–397.

LaFromboise, T. D., Dauphinais, P., & Rowe, W. (1980). Indian students' perceptions of positive helper attributes. *Journal of American Indian Education, 19,* 11–16.

LaFromboise, T. D., & Dixon, D. N. (1981). American Indian perception of trustworthiness in a counseling interview. *Journal of Counseling Psychology, 28,* 135–139.

LaFromboise, T. D., & Rowe, W. (1983). Skills training for bicultural competence: Rationale and application. *Journal of Counseling Psychology, 30,* 589–595.

LaFromboise, T. D., Trimble, J. E., & Mohatt, G. V. (1990). Counseling intervention and American Indian tradition: An integrative approach. *The Counseling Psychologist, 18,* 628–654.

Lee, E. (1982). A social systems approach to assessment and treatment for Chinese American families. In M. McGoldrick, J. K. Pearce, & J. Giordano (Eds.), *Ethnicity and family therapy* (pp. 527–551). New York: Guilford.

Lee, J. C., & Cynn, V. E. H. (1991). Issues in counseling 1.5 generation Korean Americans. In E. E. Lee & B. L. Richardson (Eds.), *Multicultural issues in counseling: New approaches to diversity* (pp. 127–142). Alexandria, VA: American Association for Counseling and Development.

Lee, W. M. L., & Mixson, R. J. (1985). *An evaluation of counseling services by college students of Asian and Caucasian ethnicity.* Unpublished manuscript.

Lefley, H. P. (1985). Mental health training across cultures. In P. Pedersen (Ed.), *Handbook of cross-cultural counseling and therapy* (pp. 259–266). Westport, CT: Greenwood Press.

Lefley, H. P., & Bestman, E. W. (1984). Community mental health and minorities: A multiethnic approach. In S. Sue & T. Moore (Eds.), *The pluralistic society: A community mental health perspective* (pp. 116–148). New York: Human Sciences Press.

Leong, F. T. L. (1986). Counseling and psychotherapy with Asian-Americans: Review of the literature. *Journal of Counseling Psychology, 33,* 196–206.

Lerner, B. (1972). *Therapy in the ghetto: Political impotence and personal disintegration.* Baltimore: The Johns Hopkins University Press.

Levine, E., & Franco, J. N. (1981). A reassessment of self-disclosure patterns among Anglo Americans and Hispanics. *Journal of Counseling Psychology, 28,* 522–524.

Levine, E. S., & Padilla, A. M. (1980). *Crossing cultures in therapy: Pluralistic counseling for the Hispanic.* Monterey, CA: Brooks/Cole.

Lin, K. M. (1986). Psychopathology and social disruption in refugees. In C. L. Williams & J. Westermeyer (Eds.), *Refugees and mental health.* Washington, DC: Hemisphere Publishing Corporation.

Li-Repac, D. (1980). Cultural influences on clinical perception: A comparison between Caucasian and Chinese-American therapists. *Journal of Cross-Cultural Psychology, 11,* 327–342.

Littrell, J., & Littrell, M. (1982). American Indian and Caucasian students' preferences for counselors: Effects of counselor dress and sex. *Journal of Counseling Psychology, 29,* 48–57.

Lopez, S. (1981). Mexican-American usage of mental health facilities: Underutilization reconsidered. In A. Baron, Jr. (Ed.), *Explorations in Chicano psychology* (pp. 139–164). New York: Praeger.

Lopez, S. R. (1989). Patient variable biases in clinical judgement: Conceptual overview and methodological considerations. *Psychological Bulletin, 106,* 184–203.

Lopez, S. R., Grover, K. P., Holland, D., Johnson, M. J., Kain, C. D., Kanel, K., Mellins, C. A., & Rhyne, M. C. (1989). Development of culturally sensitive psychotherapists. *Professional Psychology: Research and Practice, 20,* 369–376.

Lopez, S. R., Lopez, A. A., & Fong, K. T. (1991). Mexican Americans' initial preferences for counselors: The role of ethnic factors. *Journal of Counseling Psychology, 38,* 487–496.

Lorion, R. P. (1978). Research on psychotherapy and behavior change with the disadvantaged. In A. E. Bergin & S. L. Garfield (Eds.), *Handbook of psychotherapy and behavior change* (pp. 903–938). New York: Wiley.

Lorion, R. P., & Felner, R. D. (1986). Research on psychotherapy and behavior change with the disadvantaged. In A. E. Bergin & S. L. Garfield (Eds.), *Handbook of psychotherapy and behavior change* (3rd ed., pp. 739–776). New York: Wiley.

Lorion, R. P., & Parron, D. L. (1985). Countering the countertransference: A strategy for treating the untreatable. In P. Pedersen (Ed.), *Handbook of cross-cultural counseling and therapy* (pp. 79–86). Westport, CT: Greenwood Press.

Luborsky, L., Chandler, M., Auerbach, A. H., Cohen, J., & Bachrach, H. M. (1971). Factors influencing the outcome of psychotherapy: A review of quantitative research. *Psychological Bulletin, 75,* 145–185.

Lum, R. G. (1982). Mental health attitudes and opinions of Chinese. In E. E. Jones & S. J. Korchin (Eds.), *Minority mental health* (pp. 165–189). New York: Praeger.

Malgady, R. G., Rogler, L. H., & Costantino, G. (1987). Ethnocultural and linguistic bias in mental health evaluation of Hispanics. *American Psychologist, 42,* 228–234.

Malgady, R. G., Rogler, L. H., & Costantino, G. (1990a). Hero/heroine modeling for Puerto Rican adolescents: A preventive mental health intervention. *Journal of Counseling and Clinical Psychology, 58,* 469–474.

Malgady, R. G., Rogler, L. H., & Costantino, G. (1990b). Culturally sensitive psychotherapy for Puerto Rican children and adolescents: A program of treatment outcome research. *Journal of Counseling and Clinical Psychology, 58,* 704–712.

Manning, W. H., & Du Bois, P. H. (1962). Correlational methods in research on human learning. *Perceptual and Motor Skills, 15,* 287–321.

Manson, S. M. (1982). *New directions in prevention among American Indian and Alaska Native communities.* Portland, OR: Oregon Health Sciences University.

Manson, S. M., Shore, J. H., & Bloom, J. D. (1985). The depressive experience in American Indian communities: A challenge for psychiatric theory and diagnoses. In A. Kleinman & B. Good (Eds.), *Culture and depression* (pp. 331–368). Berkeley: University of California Press.

Manson, S. M., & Trimble, J. E. (1982). American Indian and Alaska Native communities: Past efforts, future inquiries. In L. R. Snowden (Ed.), *Reaching the underserved: Mental health needs of neglected populations* (pp. 143–164). Beverly Hills, CA: Sage.

Manson, S. M., Walker, R. D., & Kivlahan, D. R. (1987). Psychiatric assessment and treatment of American Indians and Alaska Natives. *Hospital and Community Psychiatry, 38,* 165–173.

Marcos, L. R., Urcuyo, L., Kesselman, M., & Alpert, M. (1973). The language barrier in evaluating Spanish-American patients. *Archives of General Psychiatry, 29,* 655–659.

Marsella, A. J., Kinzie, D., & Gordon, P. (1973). Ethnic variations in the expression of depression. *Journal of Cross-Cultural Psychology, 4,* 435–458.

Mays, V. M., & Albee, G. W. (1992). Psychotherapy and ethnic minorities. In D. K. Friedman (Ed.), *History of psychotherapy: A century of change* (pp. 552–570). Washington, DC: American Psychological Association.

McShane, D. (1988). An analysis of mental health research with American Indian youth. *Journal of Adolescence, 11,* 87–116.

Mintz, J., Luborsky, L., & Christoph, P. (1979). Measuring the outcomes of psychotherapy: Findings of the Penn Psychotherapy Project. *Journal of Consulting and Clinical Psychology, 47,* 319–334.

Mollica, R. F., Wyshak, G., Lavelle, J., Truong, T., Tor, S., & Yang, T. (1990). Assessment symptom change in Southeast Asian refugee survivors of mass violence and torture. *American Journal of Psychiatry, 147,* 83–88.

Moore, T., Nagata, D., & Whatley, R. (1984). Training community psychologists and other social interventionists: A cultural pluralistic perspective. In S. Sue & T. Moore (Eds.), *The pluralistic society: A community mental health perspective* (pp. 237–253). New York: Human Sciences Press.

Morten, G., & Atkinson, D. R. (1983). Minority identity development and preference for counselor race. *Journal of Negro Education, 52,* 156–161.

Muñoz, R. F. (1982). The Spanish-speaking consumer and the community mental health center. In E. E. Jones & S. J. Korchin (Eds.), *Minority mental health* (pp. 362–398). New York: Praeger.

Murase, K. (1977). Minorities: Asian-Americans. *Encyclopedia of Social Work, 2,* 953–960.

Myers, H. F., Wohlford, P., Guzman, L. P., & Echemendia, R. J. (1991). *Ethnic minority perspectives on clinical training and services in psychology.* Washington, DC: American Psychological Association.

Neighbors, H. W. (1985). Seeking professional help for personal problems: Black Americans' use of health and mental health services. *Community Mental Health Journal, 21,* 156–166.

Neighbors, H. W., Jackson, J. S., Campbell, L., & Williams, D. (1989). The influence of racial factors on psychiatric diagnosis: A review and suggestions for research. *Community Mental Health Journal, 25,* 301–311.

Neligh, G. (1988). Major mental disorders and behavior among American Indians and Alaska Natives [Monograph]. In *Behavioral health issues among American Indians and Alaska Natives: Explorations on the frontiers of the biobehavioral sciences. American Indian and Alaska Native Mental Health Research, 1,* 116–159.

Nishio, K., & Bilmes, M. (1987). Psychotherapy with Southeast Asian American clients. *Professional Psychology: Research and Practice, 18,* 342–346.

Nobles, W. W. (1980). African philosophy: Foundations for Black psychology. In R. Jones (Ed.), *Black psychology* (pp. 99–105). New York: Harper & Row.

O'Hare, W. P., & Felt, J. C. (1991). *Asian Americans: America's fastest growing minority group.* Washington, DC: Population Reference Bureau.

O'Sullivan, M. J., Peterson, P. D., Cox, G. B., & Kirkeby, J. (1989). Ethnic populations: Community mental health services ten years later. *American Journal of Community Psychology, 17,* 17–30.

Padilla, A. M. (1980). *Acculturation: Theory, models, and some new findings.* Boulder, CO: Westview Press.

Padilla, A. M., & Salgado De Snyder, N. (1985). Counseling Hispanics: Strategies for effective intervention. In P. Pedersen (Ed.), *Handbook of cross-cultural counseling and therapy* (pp. 157–164). Westport, CT: Greenwood Press.

Parham, T. A., & Helms, J. E. (1981). The influence of Black students' racial identity attitudes on preferences for counselor's race. *Journal of Counseling Psychology, 28,* 250–257.

Parloff, M. B., Waskow, I. E., & Wolfe, B. E. (1978). Research on therapist variables in relation to process and outcome. In S. L. Garfield & A. E. Bergin (Eds.), *Handbook of psychotherapy and behavior change: An empirical analysis* (2nd ed., pp. 233–282). New York: Wiley.

Paster, V. S. (1985). Adapting psychotherapy for the depressed, unacculturated, acting-out, Black male adolescent. *Psychotherapy, 22,* 408–417.

Paul, G. L. (1967). Strategy of outcome research in psychotherapy. *Journal of Consulting Psychology, 31,* 109–118.

Pedersen, P. B. (1986). Developing interculturally skilled counselors: A prototype for training. In H. P. Lefley & P. B. Pedersen (Eds.), *Cross-cultural training for mental health professionals* (pp. 73–89). Springfield, IL: Charles C Thomas.

Pekarik, G. (1986). The use of termination status and treatment duration patterns as an indicator of clinical improvement. *Evaluation and Program Planning, 9,* 25–30.

Philipus, M. J. (1971). Successful and unsuccessful approaches to mental health services for an urban Hispanic American population. *American Journal of Public Health, 61,* 820–830.

Pomales, J., Claiborn, C. D., & LaFromboise, T. D. (1986). Effects of Black students' racial identity on perceptions of White counselors varying in cultural sensitivity. *Journal of Counseling Psychology, 33,* 57–61.

Pomales, J., & Williams, V. (1989). Effects of level of acculturation and counseling style on Hispanic students' perceptions of counselor. *Journal of Counseling Psychology, 36,* 79–83.

Ponce, F. Q., & Atkinson, D. R. (1989). Mexican-American acculturation, counselor ethnicity, counseling style, and perceived counselor credibility. *Journal of Counseling Psychology, 36,* 203–208.

Ponterotto, J. G., Alexander, C. M., & Hinkston, J. A. (1988). Afro-American preferences for counselor characteristics: A replication and extension. *Journal of Counseling Psychology, 35,* 175–182.

Ponterotto, J. G., Anderson, W. H., & Grieger, I. Z. (1986). Black students' attitudes toward counseling as a function of racial identity. *Journal of Multicultural Counseling and Development, 14,* 50–59.

Porche, L. M., & Banikiotes, P. G. (1982). Racial and attitudinal factors affecting the perceptions of counselors by Black adolescents. *Journal of Counseling Psychology, 29,* 169–174.

Query, J. M. N. (1985). Comparative admission and follow-up study of American Indians and Whites in a youth chemical dependency unit on the North Central Plains. *The International Journal of the Addictions, 20,* 489–502.

Ramirez, M. (1991). *Psychotherapy and counseling with minorities. A cognitive approach to individual and cultural differences.* Elmsford, NY: Pergamon.

Ridley, C. R. (1984). Clinical treatment of the nondisclosing Black client: A therapeutic paradox. *American Psychologist, 39,* 1234–1244.

Rogler, L. H., Cooney, R. S., Costantino, G., Earley, B. F., Grossman, B., Gurak, D. T., Malgady, R., & Rodriguez, O. (1983). *A conceptual framework for mental health research on Hispanic populations.* Bronx, NY: Fordham University, Hispanic Research Center.

Rogler, L. H., Malgady, R. G., Costantino, G., & Blumenthal, R. (1987). What do culturally sensitive mental health services mean?: The case of Hispanics. *American Psychologist, 42,* 565–570.

Rogler, L. H., Malgady, R. G., & Rodriguez, O. (1989). *Hispanics and mental health: A framework for research.* Malabar, FL: Krieger Publishing Company.

Root, M. P. P. (1985). Guidelines for facilitating therapy with Asian American clients. *Psychotherapy, 22,* 349–356.

Sanchez, A. R., & Atkinson, D. R. (1983). Mexican-American cultural commitment, preference for counselor ethnicity, and willingness to use counseling. *Journal of Counseling Psychology, 30,* 215–220.

Sattler, J. M. (1977). The effects of therapist–client racial similarity. In A. S. Gurman & A. M. Razin (Eds.), *Effective psychotherapy: A handbook of research* (pp. 252–290). Elmsford, NY: Pergamon.

Scheffler, R. M., & Miller, A. B. (1989). Demand analysis of mental health service use among ethnic subpopulations. *Inquiry, 26,* 202–215.

Schinke, S. P., Orlandi, M. A., Botvin, G. J., Gilchrist, L. D., Trimble, J. E., & Locklear, V. B. (1988). Preventing substance abuse among American-Indian adolescents: A bicultural competence skills approach. *Journal of Counseling Psychology, 35,* 87–90.

Shon, S. P., & Ja, D. Y. (1982). Asian families. In M. McGoldrick, J. K. Pearce, & J. Giordano (Eds.), *Ethnicity and family therapy* (pp. 208–228). New York: Guilford.

Snowden, L. R. (1982). *Reaching the underserved: Mental health needs of neglected populations.* Beverly Hills, CA: Sage.

Snowden, L. R., & Cheung, F. K. (1990). Use of inpatient mental health services by members of ethnic minority groups. *American Psychologist, 45,* 347–355.

Special Populations Subtask Panel on the Mental Health of Hispanic Americans. (1978). *Report to the President's Commission on Mental Health.* Los Angeles: University of California, Spanish Speaking Mental Health Research Center.

Stevens, G. (1981). Bias in the attribution of hyperkinetic behavior as a function of ethnic identification and socioeconomic status. *Psychology in the Schools, 18,* 99–106.

Strickland, T. L., Jenkins, J. O., Myers, H. F., & Adams, H. E. (1988). Diagnostic judgements as a function of client and therapist race. *Journal of Psychopathology and Behavioral Assessment, 10,* 141–151.

Strupp, H. H. (1970). Specific vs. nonspecific factors in psychotherapy and the problem of control. *Archives of General Psychiatry, 23,* 393–401.

Sue, D., & Sue, D. W. (1991). Counseling strategies for Chinese Americans. In C. C. Lee & B. L. Richardson (Eds.), *Multicultural issues in counseling: New approaches to diversity* (pp. 79–90). Alexandria, VA: American Association for Counseling and Development.

Sue, D., & Sue, S. (1987). Cultural factors in the clinical assessment of Asian Americans. *Journal of Counseling and Social Psychology, 55,* 479–487.

Sue, D. W., & Sue, D. (1990). *Counseling the culturally different: Theory and practice.* New York: Wiley.

Sue, S. (1977). Community mental health services to minority groups: Some optimism, some pessimism. *American Psychologist, 32,* 616–624.

Sue, S. (1988). Psychotherapeutic services for ethnic minorities: Two decades of research findings. *American Psychologist, 43,* 301–308.

Sue, S. (1991). Ethnicity and culture in psychological research and practice. In J. D. Goodchilds (Ed.), *Psychological perspectives on human diversity in America* (pp. 47–85). Washington, DC: American Psychological Association.

Sue, S., Fujino, D. C., Hu, L. T., Takeuchi, D. T., & Zane, N. W. S. (1991). Community mental health services for ethnic minority groups: A test of the cultural responsiveness hypothesis. *Journal of Counseling Psychology, 59,* 533–540.

Sue, S., & Morishima, J. K. (1982). *The mental health of Asian-Americans.* San Francisco: Jossey-Bass.

Suinn, R. M., Richard-Figuerod, K., Lew, S., & Vigil, P. (1985). Career decisions and an Asian acculturation scale. *Journal of the Asian American Psychological Association, 10,* 20–28.

Szapocznik, J., Rio, A., Murray, E., Cohen, R., Scopetta, M., Rivas-Vazquez, A., Hervis, O., Posada, V., & Kurtines, W. (1989). Structural family versus psychodynamic child therapy for problematic Hispanic boys. *Journal of Counseling and Clinical Psychology, 57,* 571–578.

Tan, H. (1967). Intercultural study of counseling expectancies. *Journal of Counseling Psychology, 41,* 122–130.

Tanaka-Matsumi, J., & Marsella, A. J. (1976). Cross-cultural variations in the phenomenological experience of depression: I. Word association studies. *Journal of Cross-Cultural Psychology, 7,* 379–396.

Taylor, C. B., Agras, W. S., Schneider, J. A., & Allen, R. A. (1983). Adherence to instructions to practice relaxation. *Journal of Consulting and Clinical Psychology, 51,* 952–953.

Terrell, F., & Terrell, S. L. (1981). An inventory to measure cultural mistrust among blacks. *Western Journal of Black Studies, 5,* 180–184.

Terrell, F., & Terrell, S. L. (1984). Race of counselor, client sex, cultural mistrust level, and premature termination from counseling among black clients. *Journal of Counseling Psychology, 31,* 371–375.

Tien, J. L., & Johnson, H. L. (1985). Black mental health client's preference for therapists: A new look at an old issue. *International Journal of Social Psychiatry, 31,* 258–266.

Tomine, S. I. (1991). Counseling Japanese Americans: From internment to reparation. In C. C. Lee & B. L. Richardson (Eds.), *Multicultural issues in counseling: New approaches to diversity* (pp. 91–106). Alexandria, VA: American Association for Counseling and Development.

Toupin, E. (1980). Counseling Asians: Psychotherapy in the context of racism and Asian-American history. *American Journal of Orthopsychiatry, 50,* 76–86.

Tracey, T. J., Leong, F. T. L., & Glidden, C. (1986). Help seeking and problem perception among Asian Americans. *Journal of Counseling Psychology, 33,* 331–336.

Trimble, J. E., & LaFromboise, T. (1985). American Indians

and the counseling process: Culture, adaption, and style. In P. Pedersen (Ed.), *Handbook of cross-cultural counseling and therapy* (pp. 127–134). Westport, CT: Greenwood Press.

True, R. (1975). Mental health services in a Chinese American community. In W. Ishikawa & N. Hayashi (Eds.), *Service delivery in Pan Asian communities.* San Diego: Pacific Asian Coalition.

Tseng, W. S., & McDermott, J. F. (1981). *Culture, mind, and therapy: An introduction to cultural psychiatry.* New York: Brunner/Mazel.

Tyler, F. B., Brome, D. R., & Williams, J. E. (1991). *Ethnic validity, ecology, and psychotherapy: A psychosocial competence model.* New York: Plenum.

U.S. Bureau of the Census (1990). *The Hispanic population in the United States: March 1989* (Series P-20, No.444). Washington, DC: U.S. Government Printing Office.

U.S. Bureau of the Census (1991a). Published population census results for 1970 and 1980 and preliminary census figures for 1990. *Population Bulletin, 46,* Washington, DC: U.S. Government Printing Office.

U.S. Bureau of the Census (1991b). *The Hispanic population in the United States: March 1990* (Series P-20, No.449). Washington, DC: U.S. Government Printing Office.

Vega, W. A., & Rumbaut, R. G. (1991). Ethnic minorities and mental health. *Annual Review of Sociology, 17,* 351–383.

Vontress, C. E. (1988). An existential approach to cross-cultural counseling. *Journal of Multicultural Counseling and Development, 16,* 73–83.

Vraniak, D. A., & Pickett, S. A. (1992). Improving interventions with American ethnic minority children: Recurrent and recalcitrant challenges. In T. Kratchowill & R. Morris (Eds.), *The handbook of psychotherapy with children.* New York: Macmillan.

Wade, P., & Bernstein, B. (1991). Culture sensitivity training and counselor's race: Effects on Black female clients' perceptions and attrition. *Journal of Counseling Psychology, 38,* 9–15.

Wampold, E. E., Casas, J. M., & Atkinson, D. R. (1981). Ethnic bias in counseling: An information processing approach. *Journal of Counseling Psychology, 28,* 498–503.

Watkins, C. E., Jr., & Terrell, F. (1988). Mistrust level and its effects on counseling expectations in Black client–White counselor relationships: An analogue study. *Journal of Counseling Psychology, 35,* 194–197.

Watkins, C. E., Jr., Terrell, F., Miller, F.S., & Terrell, S. L. (1989). Cultural mistrust and its effects of expectational variables in Black client–White counselor relationships. *Journal of Counseling Psychology, 36,* 447–450.

Weiss, C. H. (1972). *Evaluation research.* Englewood Cliffs, NJ: Prentice Hall.

White, J. L. (1984). *The psychology of blacks: An Afro-American perspective.* Englewood Cliffs, NJ: Prentice Hall.

Wolpe, J. (1977). Inadequate behavior analysis: The Achilles' heel of outcome research in behavior therapy. *Journal of Behavior Therapy and Experimental Psychiatry, 8,* 1–3.

Wong, H. (1977, June). *Community mental health services and manpower and training concerns of Asian Americans.* Paper presented to the President's Commission on Mental Health, San Francisco.

Wood, W. D., & Sherrets, S. D. (1984). Requests for outpatient mental health services: A comparison of Whites and Blacks. *Comprehensive Psychiatry, 25,* 329–334.

Wu, I. H., & Windle, C. (1980). Ethnic specificity in the

relationship of minority use and staffing of community mental health centers. *Community Mental Health Journal, 16,* 156–169.

Yamamoto, J., Acosta, F. X., Evans, L. A., & Skilbeck, W. M. (1984). Orienting therapists about patients' needs to increase patient satisfaction. *American Journal of Psychiatry, 141,* 274–277.

Yates, A. (1987). Current status and future directions of research on the American Indian child. *American Journal of Psychiatry, 144,* 1135–1142.

Yuen, R. K. W., & Tinsley, H. E. A. (1981). International and American students' expectations about counseling. *Journal of Counseling Psychology, 28,* 66–69.

Zane, N. (1983, August). *Evaluation of outpatient psychotherapy for Asian and non–Asian American clients.* Paper presented at the American Psychological Association Conference, Anaheim, CA.

Zane, N., & Hatanaka, H. (1988, October). *Utilization and evaluation of a parallel service delivery model for ethnic minority clients.* Paper presented at the Professional Symposium: Recent Trends and New Approaches to the Treatment of Mental Illness and Substance Abuse, Oklahoma Mental Health Research Institute, Tulsa.

Zane, N., & Sue, S. (1991). Culturally-respective mental health services for Asian Americans: Treatment and training issues. In H. Myers, P. Wohlford, P. Guzman, & R. Echemendia (Eds.), *Ethnic minority perpsectives on clinical training and services in psychology* (pp. 49–58). Washington, DC: American Psychological Association.

Zane, N., Sue, S., Castro, F., & George, W. (1982). Service system models for ethnic minorities. In L. R. Snowden (Ed.), *Reaching the underserved: Mental health needs of neglected populations* (pp. 229–258). Beverly Hills, CA: Sage.

PART
V

SUMMATION

20

OVERVIEW, TRENDS, AND FUTURE ISSUES

- **ALLEN E. BERGIN**

  Brigham Young University

- **SOL L. GARFIELD**

  Washington University

A QUARTER-CENTURY PERSPECTIVE

We approach this overview and assessment of trends from the perspective of this fourth edition of the *Handbook* as well as the previous three editions, which we began working on in 1967. This chapter thus provides a quarter-century perspective. Coincidentally, this time span also includes the organization and development of the Society for Psychotherapy Research (SPR), an international, multidisciplinary scientific organization that was founded in 1968, held its first formal annual meeting in 1970, and established its international journal, *Psychotherapy Research*, in 1990.

AN AGE OF ECLECTICISM AND EMPIRICISM

This book gained its reputation and influence as a standard reference because it took an eclectic position of openness to diverse perspectives and insisted on an empirical appraisal of them. This view was not entirely popular at the time, though there were notable exceptions (Lazarus, 1967).

Today, this viewpoint appears to dominate the field. The empirical analysis and merging of behavioral and cognitive perspectives are the most notable examples—and trends that we forecast in 1970 (Bergin, 1970). Other examples are too numerous to mention, but they are prominently reflected in the *Handbook of Psychotherapy Integration* (Norcross & Goldfried, 1992) and in the activity of the Society for the Exploration of Psychotherapy Integration (SEPI), which was founded in 1983 and began publishing its *Journal of Psycho-*

therapy Integration in 1991. Leaders of this movement have come from a diversity of schools of thought. They prefer the term *integration* over *eclecticism* because the former implies a systematic use of concepts and techniques from different approaches as opposed to a hodgepodge of clinical techniques that might otherwise be applied in a simplistic and impromptu pragmatism. Although this movement is relatively new, it includes many outstanding psychologists and psychiatrists.

Surveys suggest that some form of eclecticism is preferred by most professionals in North America (Jensen, Bergin, & Greaves, 1990; Smith, 1982); and the chapters in this volume reflect this trend. For instance, Greenberg, Elliott, and Lietear (Chapter 12) show how the nondirective approach of Carl Rogers and others can be enhanced by its integration with more directive and expressive techniques, while Beutler, Machado, and Neufeldt (Chapter 7) suggest that nondirectiveness itself has special value with some cases and is counterproductive with others.

Such flexible approaches, undergirded by careful empirical evaluation, mark the maturation of this field. Nevertheless, there are still some who adhere, at least formally, to a single orientation or perspective, such as the relatively few remaining classical analysts, strict behaviorists, or biomedical reductionists. It is ironic that some of those individuals who claim to be the most scientific in their approaches have become the most rigid.

AN ATHEORETICAL ERA

Commensurate with the foregoing trends has been a steady decline in strict adherence to traditionally dominant theories of personality and therapeutic change, such as the behavioral, psychoanalytic, humanistic, and other major approaches.

Questions today are being asked at the micro level: What works with this type of case?, rather than at the macro level: What is the nature of human personality? This trend has been dictated partly by consumer, government, and insurance company pressures for evidence of prompt efficacy and partly by the failure of macro theories to yield definable practices that are clinically and empirically tenable.

Empirical research has speeded up this process, because many assumptions of the macro theories simply have not held up to scrutiny or have not been translatable into operations that will bear scrutiny.

Efforts today are more pragmatic and are guided by minitheories, such as "the therapeutic alliance should have certain characteristics in order to facilitate outcome" (Chapter 11), or "cognitive retraining adds to the effect of relaxation in reducing panic responses" (Chapter 9).

The absence of good theory is a problem. There is not much of the kind of conceptual coherence one would expect from an advancing scientific discipline. We seem to be in a pre–paradigm-shift phase where the old scaffoldings have fallen but new ones have not yet arisen. One of the inhibiting factors in theoretical advancement is the incredible complexity of the phenomena being addressed. It is not clear what will happen next, but there are certain to be ingenious efforts at filling the theory vacuum. Some efforts, like the renewed versions of phenomenological, hermeneutic, social constructionist, and qualitative approaches or the new "chaos theory," are on the horizon; but the promise of such developments, coming as they do from outside the clinical setting, may have limited value.

Future theory development will be watched with interest. In the meanwhile, much can be done at the level of the minitheories that guide immediate questions of technique effects. Lorna Benjamin's work is a good example of an effort to integrate personality assessment and the evaluation of change with innovative theory (Benjamin, 1993).

THE EQUAL OUTCOMES PHENOMENON

One of the most difficult findings to conceptualize theoretically or to use practically is the continuing and frequent lack of difference in the outcomes of various techniques. With some exceptions, which we will consider, there is massive evidence that psychotherapeutic techniques do not have specific effects; yet there is tremendous resistance to accepting this finding as a legitimate one. Numerous interpretations of the data have been given in order to preserve the idea that technical factors have substantial, unique, and specific effects. The reasons for this are not difficult to surmise. Such pro-

nouncements essentially appear to be rationalizations that attempt to preserve the role of special theories, the status of leaders of such approaches, the technical training programs for therapists, the professional legitimacy of psychotherapy, and the rewards that come to those having supposedly curative powers. What is the answer?

First, we have to face the fact that in a majority of studies, different approaches to the same symptoms, (e.g., depression) show little difference in efficacy (see Chapters 4 and 5). Group and family treatment methods show few differences in results as compared with individual methods. Cognitive-behavioral approaches show little advantage over others in many instances. Within the same system, different subtechniques often manifest few differences (see Chapter 9).

It is important to emphasize that none of this means that therapy is ineffective. We know that it generally is or can be, but we do not know precisely why. The issue is whether we can isolate and identify the ingredients of change and then enhance their influence. Some theoretical guidelines would help in deciding what to look for. The main theoretical interpretations assume that common factors exist in all or most therapies, that these account for a considerable amount of the change that occurs, and that this is why no differences occur.

Three main traditional views have been advocated as explanations of this phenomenon. One derives from learning theories. It argues that mental disorders are generally acquired via learning processes and that positive change consists of "unlearning" old response patterns and acquiring new ones. Two of the main mechanisms used in this view are desensitization or extinction of anxiety-associated responses and learning of mastery behaviors via rehearsal, positive reinforcement, or self-enactment of adaptive actions. It is said that all of these occur either wittingly or unwittingly in all therapies.

The second view, the humanistic, phenomenological perspective, suggests that the common factor is a caring relationship characterized by warmth, support, attention, understanding, and acceptance. These ingredients are said to have direct healing properties somewhat like the effects of good nutrition or solar radiation, which strengthen the organism and stimulate growth. The therapeutic relationship is thus seen as a "condition" that makes growth or the healthful blossoming of self possible.

A third major perspective has argued that all therapies provide a cathartic release of turbulent affect; a rationale or belief system for understanding and explaining one's troubles; a set of rituals or procedures for enacting an alternative, healthier lifestyle; and faith in the wisdom of the sanctioned healer. This view embraces the social psychology of persuasion and culturally defined social role behavior. Psychotherapies are all thus viewed as merely special cases of more general cultural phenomena having to do with religious beliefs and practices and cultural roles and norms.

All three of these views have merit and all three may apply to some degree, but none has held up as a complete explanation of the findings of psychotherapy research. Therapeutic change has been found to be far more cognitively guided than simple "reconditioning" via learning implies. Therapeutic healing conditions have not been sufficient in causing or explaining change. The dramatic effects of "faith," alternate beliefs, and newfound role conformity appear limited to certain kinds of people and may not be lasting.

Contemporary views amalgamate and refine these viewpoints in attempts to more precisely identify the common ingredients that, together, may add up to an optimal change process. Once again, there are three major ways of looking at the situation that are gaining contemporary prominence. Much of this work is discussed in Chapter 5 of this volume. Table 5.8 (p. 164) summarizes one perspective. There, the common ingredients are seen to be a combination of affective experiencing, cognitive mastery, and behavioral regulation. Techniques deriving from the different schools are subsumed under these categories. This table, and the thinking it represents, provides a template for pursuing the ingredients that may be the key factors in change; but there is, as yet, no precise description of these factors and no empirical tests of the effectiveness of combinations or integrations of the ingredients.

A second perspective is provided in Chapter 8 where a "generic model" of therapy is proposed as an overarching conceptual system. All therapies thus construed involve a formal aspect (therapeutic contract), a technical aspect (therapeutic operations), an interpersonal aspect (therapeutic bond), an intrapersonal aspect (self-relatedness), a clinical aspect (in-session impacts and therapeutic realizations), and a temporal aspect (sequential processes). A massive amount of data is summarized in Chapter 8 using this system and showing the statistical relations among its different aspects under the overall heading of "process and outcomes."

A third and very influential approach is Bandura's social cognitive theory (Bandura, 1986). Although this position is too complex to summarize adequately here, it is perhaps the most sophisticated descendant of the behavioral *cum* cognitive tradition, and it includes considerable substance from social psychology as well. Its main theses include the following:

1. Change takes place in a social context and is primarily cognitive.

2. Behavior is not controlled by its consequences so much as it is by forethought and by personal constructions of its meaning or value in relation to internal cognitive assessments, self-reflections, and controls.

3. Behavior is generally self-regulated by the person as an agent within a context of reciprocal causality.

4. One's self-estimated sense of self-efficacy is one of the best predictors of behavior.

According to this view, all therapies engage in cognitive reconstruction in the context of core relationships. This is what happens in the therapeutic relationship and in generalizations from therapy to the rest of life, and therapies vary somewhat in how efficiently they effect this process.

COMMON FACTORS VERSUS SPECIFIC EFFECTS

There are certain anomalies, however, that the common factors approach does not address. Although there are many instances in which no differences occur between therapeutic approaches or in comparisons of specific techniques with attention-placebo conditions, there are also a number of results showing such differences. How do we account for these? What are the mechanisms or processes involved?

It appears that certain kinds of cases respond well to the factors that are common to all conditions. Such cases were once described by the common term *neuroses* but are now subsumed under a number of other diagnostic categories having to do with depressive, anxiety, and bodily symptoms. When these symptoms are not too severe, they seem to respond to the influence of whatever the common factors are that facilitate change. Greater severity may, however, test the limits of the common factors. When more severe cases of depression, anxiety, and so on are considered, important technique differences emerge. The NIMH study discussed in Chapter 4 and the Sheffield project reported in Chapter 5 show this phenomenon, although such differences may diminish over time as indicated in the follow-up results secured in the NIMH study.

There also appear to be specific and superior effects of behavioral and cognitive methods with some otherwise difficult problems, such as severe phobias (e.g., agoraphobia and panic), compulsions, tension headaches, insomnia, and other health-related dysfunctions. Active and specifically targeted interventions have clearly added something unique to the therapeutic repertoire that should not be lost in arguments over "no differences" in some studies or in global meta-analyses.

Finally, as Beutler and colleagues have pointed out in Chapter 7, certain client personality traits may interact with therapy *modality* or therapist characteristics to produce specific interaction effects in relation to outcome. For instance, depressed clients who are resistance prone appear to do better with a nondirective technique than a directive one. If replicated and extended, such findings could prove to be of great importance.

DRAMATIC CHANGES IN THE NATURE OF THE MAJOR ORIENTATIONS

It appears that psychotherapy research has had a profound effect on how the major traditional orientations to therapy are being construed. Research evidence of the efficacy of cognitive interventions has had a dramatic influence on the way in which the behavioral movement is conceptualized, and the new redefinition of the behavioral approach as "cognitive-behavioral" represents a major shift in thought and practice. Most of the people who used to consider themselves behavioral therapists now identify themselves as cognitive-behavioral. Also, most people who once considered themselves strictly cognitive practitioners now are willing to take on the cognitive-behavioral label as well. Although many influences have produced these changes, it is pleasing to note that the effect of research has been substantial.

The client-centered or nondirective orientation has also been greatly influenced by research. Even though Beutler and colleagues have suggested that a nondirective technique may be a good match for certain resistant clients, overall the trend has been away from the nondirective orientation. This has largely been due to evidence indicating that therapy oriented entirely by the traditional client-centered, nondirective notion of treatment has not produced very large effect sizes. Despite making significant contributions in demonstrating the importance of empathy, warmth, and other therapist characteristics, this orientation has significantly de-

clined so far as its technical comparative efficacy is concerned. The *Person-Centered Review*, one of the major journals in this area, has recently stopped publication. How does this trend fit with the surprisingly large effect sizes summarized in Chapter 12 where research on the various experiential therapies is summarized?

The review by Greenberg, Elliott, and Lietaer shows rather dramatic new evidence supporting the efficacy of the humanistic experiential therapies; and this is important because it may become an influential force in resurrecting the credibility of this orientation. However, the evidence presented in Chapter 12 shows clearly that it is not the traditional nondirective, client-centered aspect of experiential therapy that is producing the large effect sizes. These effect sizes are being produced by more "directive" interventions. These include the process-experiential, the Gestalt, and so forth. So, it may be the action-oriented and specific targeting aspects of this orientation that are coming to the fore and ultimately changing the way many do therapy. According to major surveys or therapist orientations, there are few classical nondirectivists still practicing.

At the same time, we need to view some of the large effect sizes noted in Chapter 12 with a note of caution because many of them were produced by innovative therapists, like Greenberg, whose allegiance to the viewpoint is strong. We know from previous research that strong allegiances produce larger effect sizes in research studies. There is essentially nothing wrong with this. This phenomenon has been noted with respect to each of the major orientations, but we do find that over time the size of these large effects tends to decline somewhat and become more like the effects of other approaches. Indeed, the overall result of the Greenberg, Elliott, and Lietaer meta-analysis showed no differences in the outcomes of experiential and other major approaches. In any case, a major shift seems to have occurred in the way that experiential therapy is construed and implemented.

There has also been a dramatic change in the way that psychodynamic psychotherapy is practiced today. It has become much more eclectic, abbreviated, and specifically targeted. The therapy has become short term and focused. Research evidence has also significantly undermined the notion that interpretation in general, and transference interpretation in particular, is the key to efficacy in this approach. It is difficult to underestimate the significance of this shift in thought, which has been brought about largely by careful therapy research.

On the other hand, the innovative work on the therapeutic alliance has shown considerable promise and significant correlations with psychotherapy outcome. The therapeutic alliance is also a step forward beyond the notion of the therapeutic relationship posited by the client-centered or person-centered approach. The concept of the alliance requires much more active problem solving on the part of the client in collaboration with the therapist. The client is not seen so much as the object of the therapist's empathy but as a collaborator, and the therapist elicits this collaboration in a fairly direct way. So, the old directivism that used to be attributed to the psychodynamic approach, with interpretation as the magic key, has shifted to a new kind of directivism that is closer to a cognitive-behavioral orientation, but retains an important focus on the depth of the therapeutic relationship and resolution of defenses as clinical tools. (See Chapter 11 for documentation of these trends.)

It should also be mentioned that psychodynamic therapy is a broad designation that can be used to cover a variety of different emphases. Not only do the new changes described here apply mainly to recent developments featuring certain types of manual-guided brief therapies, but within this group there is also a fair amount of diversity (Garfield, 1990). These developments, however, are quite distinct from classical long-term psychoanalysis and psychoanalytically oriented psychotherapy. In these latter categories, very little systematic empirical research has been conducted.

Overall, however, the changes described in this section show a growth in the precision, discipline, and focusing of the major orientations, and all of these have been substantially influenced by research. They also have laid the basis for the new eclectic and integrative movements because similarities are emerging from each of the main viewpoints, and it is becoming empirically visible that these changes are important in helping clients to improve.

THE THERAPIST

In addition to changes in techniques, the evidence that therapist differences produce differences in outcome has increased substantially (see Chapter 7). Clearly, variations in therapists' adjustment and skill are correlated with variations in outcome. In addition, the use of therapy manuals has greatly assisted the refinement of therapist interventions and it appears to be the case that when manuals are used outcomes improve. When the therapist variable is allowed to vary uncontrollably, the influence of therapist factors becomes more dramatic.

Identification of the therapist as an important

variable mediating change, semi-independent of technique and orientation, has been an important research contribution. Until recently, the research focus has tended to be on the form of psychotherapy, thus minimizing the importance of therapist variability. At the same time, the use of therapy manuals to ensure that a specific type of therapy is actually being conducted does raise the issue of external validity — that is, are the results obtained in the research study applicable to everyday practice in the clinical setting? This is an issue that has arisen only lately and requires further study and thought. However, there is little question that research on the efficacy of psychotherapy should use competent therapists.

Although there is a great deal of variability within the medical profession, as a whole it embraces a standard of performance and quality control that the psychotherapy professions should aspire to achieve and maintain. Older research studies examined the efficacy of therapy "as practiced" in a variety of clinical agencies where quality control was minimal. In more recent studies that control for quality, efficacy is clearly better. The value of therapeutic techniques should be judged on the basis of these carefully controlled studies and not on evaluations of ordinary practices in varied agencies that may include mediocre work. Such is not a fair test, but rather a reflection of the failure of training and quality control.

THE CLIENT

As Chapter 6 clearly shows, client characteristics do make a difference with respect to outcomes, and Chapter 7 points out that interactions among therapists, techniques, and clients also lead to different types of results. When these possible interactions are not taken into account, the overall outcome data may gloss over rather divergent results.

Another important observation regarding the client variable is that it is the client more than the therapist who implements the change process. If the client does not absorb, utilize, and follow through on the facilitative efforts of the therapist, then nothing happens. Rather than argue over whether or not "therapy works," we could address ourselves to the question of whether or not "the client works"! In this regard, there needs to be a reform in our thinking about the efficacy of psychotherapy. Clients are not inert objects upon whom techniques are administered. They are not dependent variables upon whom independent variables operate. As Bandura (1986) has so clearly shown, people are agentive beings who are effective forces in the complex of causal events. It is important to rethink the terminology that assumes that "effects" are like Aristotelian impetus causality. As therapists have depended more upon the client's resources, more change seems to occur (see Chapter 11).

Relapse prevention also assumes a significant role on the part of the client in implementing the change procedures. This is not meant to attribute all poor results to a failure of the client to follow through. Certainly, much in the way of poor outcome can be attributed to poor technique or therapist problems, but clearly more emphasis needs to be put on the client's role, which is just what the concept of the therapeutic alliance suggests.

Indeed, the outcomes of brief therapies, including changes in one or two sessions, indicate that people can take hold of therapeutic ideas and run with them.

BRIEF THERAPY

It appears from the trends in psychotherapy research that almost all psychotherapy is now brief. This has been dictated in part by economic factors, but it is also influenced by the fact that a good deal of change can be stimulated in a much shorter time than previously thought. The dosage–response work done by Howard and others (Howard, Kopta, Krause, & Orlinsky, 1986) indicates that about half of the patients who undergo psychotherapy show significant improvement by the eighth session; that most cases obtain optimal results within about 26 sessions or 6 months at once a week; and that the more difficult cases can be significantly helped within a year. Thus, much of the change for many cases occurs in a relatively brief time. This needs to be clearly recognized, and it supports the trend initiated by the behavior therapy movement several decades ago.

We also need to acknowledge, however, that there are intractable cases, such as certain kinds of personality disorders, that may require more than a year of treatment or that may not respond to therapy. Despite such complications, it is important to recognize that empirical evidence shows major improvements being achieved by means of psychotherapy in far less than the two years that were once hypothesized as a norm. This, of course, does not mean that all change occurs in a few months but, rather, that a process of change has been effected that can be maintained and even improved upon by continued independent actions of the client and, in some cases, by occasional booster sessions with the therapist. This latter point is important to

emphasize for psychotherapy is no longer viewed as a long-term process that, once completed, implies a lifetime period of mental health and adjustment.

CLINICAL SIGNIFICANCE

One of the most important innovations in the field has been the renewed emphasis on clinical significance as opposed to statistical significance of results (see Chapters 2, 3, and 5). Clinical significance can be determined by using effect sizes or establishing a normative reference criterion based on the absence of symptoms or the status of a "normal" group. Clinical significance is important to practitioners and to agencies that may be paying the fees for treatment. Of course, it is ultimately most significant to the client, who must live whatever results occur. As criteria for clinical significance become more stringent, the effect sizes and proportions of patients who are judged improved decrease significantly. Whereas 70 to 80 percent may be judged improved by traditional statistical measures, far lower percentages are improved by the more stringent standards of clinical significance.

It is interesting that the more stringent standards are comparable to the results identified by simple rating scales that were used in clinical agencies and by therapists in the 1920s in the earliest attempts to evaluate clinical outcomes (Bergin 1971). These scales used categories such as cured, much improved, slightly improved, or unimproved. The cured and much improved groups were usually combined to obtain an overall improvement rate. What the more modern stringent clinical significant criteria do is establish a cutoff for improvement that is essentially equivalent to the criteria for "cured" that were used decades ago. Under these criteria, about one-fourth to one-third of outpatient cases were and are considered cured. Today's methods are more sophisticated, but the bottom line is about the same. If psychotherapy efficacy, regardless of the particular school or technique being studied, were to be judged solely on the criterion of cure, then much would be lost because the larger group who improve significantly (those who were "much improved" under the former system) constitute evidence of efficacy as well. It is helpful, however, to use the more stringent criterion of clinical significance because it is informative and gives us a goal to aspire to. On the other hand, we should not be discouraged by this criterion because of its severity, and it should not be applied to every situation. As in medicine, substantial improvement is valuable even though it does not result in cure.

Generally, the modern efforts at evaluating clinical significance constitute another rather important advance in psychotherapy research and one that can affect practical decisions. In this sense, the practitioner can benefit from the results of research, as we have found to be the case in other situations.

NEGATIVE EFFECTS

Readers will note that the topic of negative effects arises in various chapters in this book, and there seems to be no doubt on the part of researchers that deterioration or negative outcomes can and do occur. The seriousness of the problem has diminished somewhat as a result of new and stricter controls, manual-guided therapies, and training and selection of therapists for research studies. Negative effects are much less evident in such carefully designed and executed projects. On the other hand, when such controls do not exist, negative effects persist as a significant problem (see Chapter 5). There is probably no system of intervention in any profession that cannot be misused or does not, by inept application, produce useless or negative outcomes. The problem is not unique to the psychotherapies or to the mental health profession in general. There is evidence that not only researchers have been influenced by such problems, but also that training programs more assiduously take into account the potential for damage that can occur as a result of poor therapy. In many training programs, inexperienced therapists are more carefully initiated into client contacts and this is often preceded by a period of skills training. In addition, the videotaping and supervision processes are more rigorous; and accrediting agencies are more demanding of quality control on the part of supervising faculties. Still, where there is less rigorous management of quality in agencies, training programs, or research studies, there is more evidence of negative outcomes.

So, although the problem persists, it is encouraging to see the degree to which this liability has been recognized and actions taken. On the other hand, it is a matter of concern that so many new therapies that have no empirical support are invented and introduced by licensed practitioners, but even more so by entrepreneurial unlicensed persons. Numerous treatments are also applied by people who have merely attended a workshop or two in a procedure and then consider themselves to be experts. It is also unfortunate that fads continue to

dot the landscape of the mental health professions and that a fair amount of magical thinking regarding the power to change people is associated with such movements. The surge in the uses and abuses of hypnosis in North America is but one of many such therapeutic crazes that has flared in the last decade or so.

MEASUREMENT

It seems to be a fact that scientific advancements are frequently dependent on the invention of measuring devices that consolidate certain insights regarding nature, in our case human nature. In the physical sciences, Nobel prizes have been won by people who have developed ingenious ways of measuring or monitoring phenomena. Precise measurement of clinical phenomena continues to be a problem in evaluating psychotherapy processes and outcomes. Chapter 3 is new to this edition of the *Handbook* and is devoted to this issue and represents the importance of the topic.

Measurement innovations continue; however, as pointed out in Chapters 3 and 5, many of the new measures are essentially homemade devices that are used once or only a few times. The number of devices has also exploded into the hundreds. Some of these, such as some of the new alliance scales and some of the careful work on depression measurement, reflect significant progress, while many of the efforts lack the rigor and precision that would ordinarily be expected of people who understand the psychological and methodological requirements of good measurement. It is conceivable that better innovation in the measurement area awaits better theoretical insights concerning the phenomena at issue. Such insights might be followed by ingenious new constructions for estimating the effects of techniques or describing the phenomenological processes. In any case, we wish to identify clearly the measurement area as a problem area that presents special challenges. For the vigorous and rigorous researcher who can produce creative innovations in this area, great rewards are likely to follow.

THE NEW EMPHASIS ON PROCESS RESEARCH

Along with the concerns about clinical significance and measurement of outcomes, there has been a burst of energy devoted to process studies. There is a new level of sophistication that is way beyond the earlier focus on rudimentary aspects of therapy processes. The new developments, which are documented in many chapters in this book (e.g., Chapters 3, 8, 11, and 12), indicate a good deal of original thought. With a number of the outstanding issues regarding outcome settled to some degree, there has been much more focus on the "mechanisms" of change. Greenberg, Elliott, and Lietaer's section in Chapter 12 on "Specific Therapeutic Task Interventions" illustrates the point.

It is conceivable that as processes are more clearly defined in relation to outcome in the therapies that currently exist, we will be able to refine techniques based on such research in order to center them on those aspects that are most clearly correlated with positive change. This is the quest and, as indicated in many places in the book, there is significant progress being made.

METHODOLOGICAL PLURALISM

In Chapter 2, Kazdin refers to the term *methodological pluralism* in a positive way. We certainly endorse his view and it seems to be supported by more and more people who are studying clinical phenomena. Alexander, Holtzworth-Munroe, and Jameson, in Chapter 14, echo these sentiments. It seems that traditional experimental and multivariate methodologies have not consistently or adequately addressed the phenomenon of therapeutic change. Numerous writings have been intensely critical of the standard methodologies, but granting agencies, journal editors, and promotions committees still seem to focus primarily on them. As noted in Chapter 1, however, there has been a significant change in the thinking of researchers and theorists on this subject.

The growing endorsement of narrative, descriptive, and qualitative approaches represents a rather significant shift in attitude that is likely to become more and more manifest in the conduct and reporting of inquiries. We find ourselves endorsing a kind of pluralism that does not throw out the virtues of the traditional approaches to research, but complements those with a variety of more flexible techniques for getting at the complexity of the phenomena we deal with. We anticipate seeing much more along this line in the future. At the same time, we are not advocating a reversion to nineteenth-century phenomenology and hermeneutics, but, rather, an objective approach to subjective phenomena that can be addressed qualitatively and descriptively using rigor and, in many cases, quantification. The tremendous surge of single-case studies that occurred within the behavioral movement in the 1960s and 1970s is one form of inten-

sive design in the right direction, but the contemporary movements address much more complex phenomena than singly specified target responses. While this movement, and it has become a movement, does hold promise, it is a promise that has to be demonstrated by showing fruitful additions to research findings.

CONCLUSION

A longer list of trends and achievements could be developed here. However, an entire book, sponsored by the American Psychological Association for its centennial (Freedheim, 1992), was recently devoted to summarizing the history of psychotherapy practice and research. The editors of the present volume contributed to that analysis of a "century of change" with contributed chapters devoted to psychotherapy research in a subsection of the book edited by Hans Strupp (Strupp & Howard, 1992). Issues and achievements in psychotherapy research were outlined by Garfield (1992) and by Lambert and Bergin (1992). There is some overlap between the chapters in that volume and this chapter as well as Chapter 1 and other chapters in this edition of the *Handbook*. Among the many interesting items included in the 1992 volume is Michael Lambert's list of psychotherapy research achievements (Lambert & Bergin, 1992, p. 384).

1. Demonstrating that the general effects of therapy exceeded spontaneous remission.

2. Demonstrating that therapy effects were generally positive.

3. Providing evidence that therapy effects exceeded the effect of placebo controls.

4. Helping to change the definition of placebo controls in psychological studies so that we have a precise and appropriate definition.

5. Demonstrating that outcomes varied even in homogeneous samples, due to therapist factors rather than technique factors.

6. Demonstrating the relative equivalence in outcome for a large number of therapies, therapeutic modalities, and temporal arrangements.

7. Demonstrating the unique effectiveness of a few therapies with specific disorders.

8. Demonstrating the interactive and synergistic role of medication in psychotherapy.

9. Demonstrating the central importance of the therapist/patient relationship in predicting and possibly causing positive personality change.

10. Documenting negative effects in treatment and studying processes that lead to patient deterioration.

The progress made in the past leads naturally to a consideration of the future. Any comments about what the future may hold for the field have to be suggested with some tentativeness; however, certain trends have clearly occurred over the past quarter-century that seem likely to continue into the future. One of these is the trend toward an eclectic and integrative viewpoint along with the decline of school affiliations and doctrinaire allegiances. Another is the anchoring of professional therapeutic work in empirical research, whatever form that research may take within a pluralistic view of methodology. Indeed, the future is likely to include a variety of new contributions from diverse methodological perspectives. At the same time, we do not foresee any major new theoretical developments along the line of global, comprehensive theories that attempt to explain all aspects of personality, psychopathology, and psychotherapy, as we have had in the past. It is more likely that the trend toward minitheories centered on specific problem domains and empirical evaluations will continue.

It also seems clear that the effort to be more precise and to have clear and valid measurement of therapy effects, both within sessions and as estimates of outcome, will continue. Both external pressures from government and insurance agencies as well as the natural trend of scientific advancement are likely to continue to improve both precision and comprehension with regard to the phenomenon of therapeutic change.

In addition, the complexity of the phenomenon will likely be addressed in new and interesting ways. Efforts to reduce complexity, such as in the history of the cognitive and behavioral movements, and in the earlier microanalyses of content, did help us understand complexity to some degree; but this approach soon reached its limits and has now given way to addressing more directly the complexity of the whole person in the midst of the change process from a variety of perspectives. For example, behaviorists have not only accepted the importance of cognition but are now including affect and altered versions of the idea of unconscious processes in their treatment. Although it is true that complex processes must be isolated, divided, and comprehended, there is increasing awareness that the process of simplification alters the phenomenon and does an injustice to it that may ultimately reduce efficacy of treatment.

We would also expect the trend toward manual-guided therapy to continue, with the kinds of refinements referred to in Chapter 5 and other places in this book. This will include greater care in the design of manuals, inclusion of a rigorously defined flexibility to accommodate therapist differences in style, and more attempts to address the complexity of therapeutic transactions.

We would also hope that both federal and state agencies as well as professional organizations will become more concerned with psychotherapy research as they determine funding for treatments, accredit training programs, and license practitioners.

Before closing, we also wish to express a serious and deep concern regarding the underfunding of the evaluation of mental health treatment procedures. Although mental disorders are enormously costly to our society and are pervasive throughout it, the funding allotted for research is quite minor compared with the enormous sums devoted to the natural and biological sciences. We consider this to be a sad or even scandalous state of affairs. In the history of psychotherapy research, we have only one study, the NIMH collaborative study of the treatment of depression, that cost millions of dollars. Even then, the funds were distributed over many years. Although there is now a second collaborative program on the treatment of anxiety disorders, more could be done. Currently, the number of researchers is far too few, it takes far too long to complete projects, and the accumulation of information is dreadfully slow with respect to the factors that assist in altering mental disorders. A new report suggests a number of important conclusions and priorities that might guide future research efforts (Docherty, Herz, & Gunderson, 1993).

We believe that it is important for us, in this fourth edition of the *Handbook*, to go on record as strongly advocating a significant increase in funding for research in psychotherapy. This is a critical need, and a positive response to it could dramatically accelerate our ability to assist persons in mental distress. The chapters in this volume and the preceding editions clearly document significant progress in this area despite the fact that psychotherapy research has been primarily a cottage industry. The general disregard of this issue by public and private agencies and by state and federal legislatures is a tragic state of affairs. It is our hope that in the coming years, a new edition of this or a similar volume will include reference to scores of new major inquiries involving large numbers of new researchers that will show significant progress due to concerted effort and adequate financial support.

Despite the great need that we see for improvement with respect to future research support, we are pleased to acknowledge that over the past quarter-century substantial progress has been made. The burden of that progress has been carried by a relatively small number of dedicated researchers who have been idealistic, hard working, open to change, and unusually free from vain ambition. We commend them and we hope for many more like them in a future blessed by greater recognition of the significant contribution that psychotherapy research can make to human welfare.

REFERENCES

Bandura, A. (1986). *Social foundations of thought and action: A social cognitive theory.* Englewood Cliffs, NJ: Prentice Hall.

Benjamin, L. S. (1993). Every psychopathology is a gift of love. *Psychotherapy Research, 3*, 1–24.

Bergin, A. E. (1970). Cognitive therapy and behavior therapy: Foci for a multidimensional approach to treatment. *Behavior Therapy, 1*, 205–212.

Bergin, A. E. (1971). The evaluation of therapeutic outcomes. In A. E. Bergin & S. L. Garfield (Eds.), *Handbook of psychotherapy and behavior change* (1st ed., pp. 217–270). New York: Wiley.

Docherty, J., Herz, M. I., & Gunderson, J. (1993). *Psychosocial treatment research in psychiatry: A Task Force report of the American Psychiatric Association.* Washington, D.C.: American Psychiatric Association.

Freedheim, D. K. (Ed.). (1992). *History of psychotherapy: A century of change.* Washington, DC: American Psychological Association.

Garfield, S. L. (1990). Issues and methods in psychotherapy research. *Journal of Consulting and Clinical Psychology, 58*, 273–280.

Garfield, S. L. (1992). Major issues in psychotherapy research. In D. K. Freedheim (Ed.), *History of psychotherapy: A century of change* (pp. 335–359). Washington, DC: American Psychological Association.

Howard, K. I., Kopta, S. M., Krause, M. S., & Orlinsky, D. E. (1986). The dose–effect relationship in psychotherapy. *American Psychologist, 41*, 159–164.

Jensen, J. P., Bergin, A. E., & Greaves, D. W. (1990). The meaning of eclecticism: New survey and analysis of components. *Professional Psychology: Research and Practice, 21*, 124–130.

Lambert, M. J., & Bergin, A. E. (1992). Achievements and limitations of psychotherapy research. In D. K. Freedheim (Ed.), *History of psychotherapy: A century of change* (pp. 360–390). Washington, DC: American Psychological Association.

Lazarus, A. A. (1967). In support of technical eclecticism. *Psychological Reports, 21*, 415–416.

Norcross, J. D., & Goldfried, M. R. (Eds.). (1992). *Handbook of psychotherapy integration.* New York: Basic Books.

Smith, D. (1982). Trends in counseling and psychotherapy. *American Psychologist, 37*, 802–809.

Strupp, H. H., & Howard, K. I. (1992). A brief history of psychotherapy research. In D. K. Freedheim (Ed.), *History of psychotherapy: A century of change* (pp. 309–334). Washington, DC: American Psychological Association.

NAME INDEX

SUBJECT INDEX